THE NEW
ENGLISH

Favorite Hymns

"How Great Thou Art"
       sung by Waldo Hewitt
           Kirkwood Baptist Church

"Surely the Presence of the Lord
       is in this Place"

"Allelulia"

"Just a Closer Walk With Thee"

"It is no Secret what God
           can do"

"Here is My Life"

"In the Garden"

"Ivory Palaces"

THE BIBLE
A NEW ENGLISH TRANSLATION

Directed by Representatives of

THE BAPTIST UNION OF GREAT BRITAIN AND IRELAND

THE CHURCH OF ENGLAND

THE CHURCH OF SCOTLAND

THE CONGREGATIONAL CHURCH IN ENGLAND AND WALES

THE COUNCIL OF CHURCHES FOR WALES

THE IRISH COUNCIL OF CHURCHES

THE LONDON YEARLY MEETING OF
THE SOCIETY OF FRIENDS

THE METHODIST CHURCH OF GREAT BRITAIN

THE PRESBYTERIAN CHURCH OF ENGLAND

THE ROMAN CATHOLIC CHURCH IN ENGLAND AND WALES

THE ROMAN CATHOLIC CHURCH IN SCOTLAND

THE BRITISH AND FOREIGN BIBLE SOCIETY

THE NATIONAL BIBLE SOCIETY OF SCOTLAND

THE NEW
ENGLISH BIBLE

CAMBRIDGE

AT THE UNIVERSITY PRESS

PREFACE

TO THE NEW ENGLISH BIBLE

IN May 1946 the General Assembly of the Church of Scotland received an overture from the Presbytery of Stirling and Dunblane, where it had been initiated by the Reverend G. S. Hendry, recommending that a translation of the Bible be made in the language of the present day, inasmuch as the language of the Authorized Version, already archaic when it was made, had now become even more definitely archaic and less generally understood. The General Assembly resolved to make an approach to other Churches, and, as a result, delegates of the Church of England, the Church of Scotland, and the Methodist, Baptist, and Congregational Churches met in conference in October. They recommended that the work should be undertaken; that a completely new translation should be made, rather than a revision, such as had earlier been contemplated by the University Presses of Oxford and Cambridge; and that the translators should be free to employ a contemporary idiom rather than reproduce the traditional 'biblical' English.

In January 1947 a second conference, held like the first in the Central Hall, Westminster, included representatives of the University Presses. At the request of this conference, the Churches named above appointed representatives to form the Joint Committee on the New Translation of the Bible. This Committee met for the first time in July of the same year. By January 1948, when its third meeting was held, invitations to be represented had been sent to the Presbyterian Church of England, the Society of Friends, the Churches in Wales, the Churches in Ireland, the British and Foreign Bible Society, and the National Bible Society of Scotland: these invitations were accepted. At a much later stage the hierarchies of the Roman Catholic Church in England and Scotland accepted an invitation to appoint representatives, and these attended as observers.

The Joint Committee provided for the actual work of translation from the original tongues by appointing three panels, to deal, respectively, with the Old Testament, the Apocrypha, and the New Testament. Their members were scholars drawn from various British universities, whom the Committee believed to be representative of competent biblical scholarship at the present time. Apprehending, however, that sound scholarship does not necessarily carry with it a delicate sense of English style, the Committee appointed a fourth panel, of trusted literary advisers, to whom all the work of the translating panels was to be submitted for scrutiny. It should be said that denominational considerations played no part in the appointment of the panels.

The Joint Committee issued general directions to the panels, in pursuance of the aims which the enterprise had in view. The translating panels adopted the following procedure. An individual was invited to submit a draft translation of a particular book, or group of books. Normally he would be a member of the panel concerned. Very occasionally a draft translation was invited from a scholar outside the panel, who was known to have worked specially on the book in question. The draft was circulated in typescript to members of the panel for their consideration. They then met together and discussed the draft round a table, verse by verse, sentence by sentence.

Each member brought his view about the meaning of the original to the judgement of his fellows, and discussion went on until they reached a common mind. There are passages where, in the present state of our knowledge, no one could say with certainty which of two (or even more) possible meanings is intended. In such cases, after careful discussion, alternative meanings have been recorded in footnotes, but only where they seemed of sufficient importance. There is probably no member of a panel who has not found himself obliged to give up, perhaps with lingering regret, a cherished view about the meaning of this or that difficult passage, but in the end the panel accepted corporate responsibility for the interpretation set forth in the translation adopted.

The resultant draft was now remitted to the panel of literary advisers. They scrutinized it, once again, verse by verse, sentence by sentence, and took pains to secure, as best they could, the tone and level of language appropriate to the different kinds of writing to be found in the Bible, whether narrative, familiar discourse, argument, law, rhetoric or poetry. The translation thus amended was returned to the translating panel, who examined it to make sure that the meaning intended had not been in any way misunderstood. Passages of peculiar difficulty might on occasion pass repeatedly between the panels. The final form of the version was reached by agreement between the translators concerned and the literary advisers. It was then ready for submission to the Joint Committee.

Since January 1948 the Joint Committee has met regularly twice a year in the Jerusalem Chamber, Westminster Abbey, with four exceptions during 1954–5 when the Langham Room in the precincts of the Abbey was kindly made available. At these meetings the Committee has received reports on the progress of the work from the Conveners of the four panels,

and its members have had in their hands typescripts of the books so far translated and revised. They have made such comments and given such advice or decisions as they judged to be necessary, and from time to time they have met members of the panels in conference.

Of the original members of the panels most have happily been able to stay with the work all through, though some have been lost, through death or otherwise, and their places have been filled by fresh appointments.

The Committee has warmly appreciated the courteous hospitality of the Dean of Westminster and of the Trustees of the Central Hall. We owe a great debt to the support and the experienced counsel of the University Presses of Oxford and Cambridge. We recognize gratefully the service rendered to the enterprise by the Reverend Dr G. S. Hendry and the Reverend Professor J. K. S. Reid, who have successively held the office of Secretary to the Committee. To those who have borne special responsibility, as Chairmen of the Joint Committee, we owe more than could readily be told. Dr J. W. Hunkin, Bishop of Truro, our first Chairman, brought to the work an exuberant vigour and initiative without which the formidable project might hardly have got off the ground at all. On his lamented death in 1950 he was succeeded by Dr A. T. P. Williams, then Bishop of Durham and subsequently Bishop of Winchester, who for eighteen years guided our enterprise with judicious wisdom, tact, and benign firmness, but who to our sorrow died when the end of the task was in sight. To both of these we would put on record the gratitude of the Committee and of all engaged in the enterprise.

If we embarked on mentioning the names of those who have served on the various committees and panels, the list would be a long one; and if we mentioned some and not others, the selection would be an invidious one.

PREFACE

There are, nevertheless, three names the omission of which would be utterly wrong. As Vice-Chairman and Director, Dr C. H. Dodd has from start to finish given outstanding leadership and guidance to the project, bringing to the work scholarship, sensitivity, and an ever watchful eye. Professor Sir Godfrey Driver, Joint Director since 1965, has also brought to the work a wealth of knowledge and wisdom; to his enthusiasm, tenacity of purpose, and unflagging devotion the whole enterprise is greatly indebted. Professor W. D. McHardy, Deputy Director since 1968, has made an invaluable contribution particularly, but by no means exclusively, in the sphere of the Apocrypha. It is right that the names of these three scholars should always be associated with The New English Bible. Our debt to them is incalculably great.

DONALD EBOR:
Chairman of the Joint Committee

CONTENTS

Preface to The New English Bible   *page* v

THE OLD TESTAMENT

Introduction to the Old Testament   xv

Guide to the Notes   xix

Marginal Numbers   xx

Genesis   1
Exodus   55
Leviticus   99
Numbers   132
Deuteronomy   178
The Book of Joshua   219
The Book of Judges   245
Ruth   272
The First Book of Samuel   275
The Second Book of Samuel   310
The First Book of Kings   340
The Second Book of Kings   374
The First Book of the Chronicles   407
The Second Book of the Chronicles   438
The Book of Ezra   478
The Book of Nehemiah   490
Esther   507
The Book of Job   515
Psalms   554
Proverbs   645
Ecclesiastes   676
The Song of Songs   684
The Book of the Prophet Isaiah   691
The Book of the Prophet Jeremiah   762

CONTENTS

Lamentations	*page* 832
The Book of the Prophet Ezekiel	839
The Book of Daniel	896

THE TWELVE PROPHETS

Hosea	914
Joel	924
Amos	928
Obadiah	937
Jonah	938
Micah	940
Nahum	947
Habakkuk	950
Zephaniah	953
Haggai	956
Zechariah	958
Malachi	968
Appendix	971

THE NEW TESTAMENT

Introduction to the New Testament	v
Marginal Numbers	viii

THE GOSPEL

According to Matthew	3
According to Mark	39
According to Luke	62
According to John	101

ACTS OF THE APOSTLES | 135

LETTERS

The Letter of Paul to the Romans	177
The First Letter of Paul to the Corinthians	194
The Second Letter of Paul to the Corinthians	210
The Letter of Paul to the Galatians	221

CONTENTS

The Letter of Paul to the Ephesians   *page* 227

The Letter of Paul to the Philippians   232

The Letter of Paul to the Colossians   237

The First Letter of Paul to the Thessalonians   241

The Second Letter of Paul to the Thessalonians   244

The First Letter of Paul to Timothy   246

The Second Letter of Paul to Timothy   251

The Letter of Paul to Titus   254

The Letter of Paul to Philemon   257

A Letter to Hebrews   258

A Letter of James   270

The First Letter of Peter   274

The Second Letter of Peter   279

The First Letter of John   282

The Second Letter of John   286

The Third Letter of John   287

A Letter of Jude   288

THE REVELATION OF JOHN   293

THE
OLD TESTAMENT

INTRODUCTION

TO THE OLD TESTAMENT

THE Old Testament as here translated consists of a body of literature spread over a period extending from the twelfth to the second century B.C.; this literature is written in classical Hebrew, except some brief portions which are in Aramaic, a cognate or sister language (Ezra 4. 8 – 6. 18 and 7. 12–26, Jeremiah 10. 11, Daniel 2. 4 – 7. 28). No manuscripts of the Old Testament from the earlier part of this period have been preserved; indeed much of it must have been handed down by oral tradition from generation to generation. The impetus to collect, edit and make copies of the national literature may well have come from the disaster of 587/6 B.C., when the Babylonians captured and burnt Jerusalem and carried off many of its inhabitants into exile.

The earliest known Hebrew manuscripts containing any parts of the Old Testament are among the Scrolls (commonly called the Dead Sea Scrolls) found in caves at Qumran near the north-western end of the Dead Sea; they may be dated in the last two centuries B.C., though some may be a little earlier and others somewhat later. They include two copies of Isaiah, one complete and another badly damaged, a commentary containing most of the text of the first two chapters of Habakkuk, and fragments of every other Old Testament book, except Esther. The text which they present is to a large extent identical with that in our Hebrew Bibles.

In the second century A.D. or even earlier the Rabbis, the Jewish religious leaders, compiled a text from such manuscripts as had survived the destruction of Jerusalem in A.D. 70,

and on this basis was established the traditional or Massoretic text, so called from the Hebrew word *massorah* 'tradition'. This text incorporated the mistakes of generations of copyists, and, in spite of the care bestowed on it, many errors of later copyists also found their way into it. The earliest surviving manuscripts of this text date from the ninth to eleventh centuries A.D.; and it is this text, as printed in R. Kittel's *Biblia Hebraica* (3rd edition, 1937), which has been used for the present translation.

The traditional text was originally written only in consonants, but in order to preserve what they regarded as the correct pronunciation of the words the Rabbis added vowel-signs to the text. Of the various systems of vowel-signs which were devised, that developed at Tiberias in the fifth to sixth centuries A.D. ultimately prevailed and is still used in our printed Bibles. The vowels are here represented by means of strokes and dots added to the consonantal text, and this method of vocalization made it possible for the Rabbis to indicate variant readings which they preferred, without meddling with the consonants: they put in the margin of their manuscript the consonants of the reading which they wished to adopt and added the vowel-signs of this reading to the consonants in the text which they were rejecting. The reader knew that he was to pronounce the consonants in the margin with the vowels in the text.

One variation of this convention is of special importance, inasmuch as it affects the divine name. This personal proper name, written with the consonants YHWH, was considered too sacred to be uttered; so the vowels for the words 'my Lord' or 'God' were added to the consonants YHWH, and the reader was warned by these vowels that he must substitute other consonants. This change having to be made so frequently, the Rabbis did not consider it necessary to put the consonants of the new reading in the margin. In course of time the true pronunciation of the divine name, probably *Yahweh*, passed into oblivion, and YHWH was read with the intruded vowels, the vowels of an entirely different word, namely 'my Lord' or 'God'. In late medieval times this mispronunciation became current as *Jehova*, and it was taken over as *Jehovah* by the Reformers in Protestant Bibles. The present translators have retained this incorrect but customary form in the text of passages where the name is explained with a note on its pronunciation (e.g. Exodus 3. 15) and in four place-names of which it forms a constituent element; elsewhere they have followed ancient translators in substituting 'Lord' or 'God', printed as here in capital letters, for the Hebrew name.

So much for the text of the Hebrew Old Testament as it lies before us; but it is certain that this does not always represent what was originally written. The translator must often go behind the traditional text to discover the writer's meaning. For this purpose he may have recourse first to the Scrolls; but these cover only a very small part of the Old Testament writings. Secondly he may have recourse to the Samaritan Pentateuch, which, though extant only in late manuscripts, the earliest being dated about the eleventh century A.D., may be somewhat earlier than the Scrolls and represents the text of the five books of the Law (Genesis to Deuteronomy) which the Samaritans took with them when they seceded from Judaism. It differs from the traditional Hebrew text in a considerable number of small and mostly unimportant points.

For further help the translator may turn to the ancient versions. Of these the earliest is the Old Testament in Greek, designed to meet the needs of Greek-speaking Jews in Egypt in the third and second centuries B.C. According to tradition the Pentateuch was translated by seventy-two elders, six from each of the twelve tribes of Israel, and so the Greek version of the Old Testament came to be called the Septuagint, from the Latin *septuaginta* 'seventy'. Clearly it is the work of a number of translators of unequal skill; their rendering is now literal, now paraphrastic, and now interpretative. Not infrequently it contains absurd mistranslations. Yet it is valuable for the recovery of the original Hebrew, because it is based on an underlying Hebrew text older than the Massoretic, and it often preserves the correct reading in passages where our Hebrew manuscripts are manifestly in error, or the true interpretation where this has been obscured in the traditional text. Its defects, however, were patent, and early in the Christian era several scholars, Aquila, Symmachus and Theodotion, tried to improve on it; other scholars produced fresh recensions of it, among which the text associated with the name of Lucian is commonly included.

The Greek-speaking Christians adopted the Septuagint as their Scriptures, but with the spread of Christianity across the Mediterranean world there arose in time the need for a Latin translation. This, the Old Latin version, made from the Septuagint by unknown translators, was so unsatisfactory that towards the end of the fourth century Jerome produced a new translation. In the books with which we are here concerned he worked directly from the Hebrew text, and he had the help of Jewish scholars. His translation is idiomatic and forceful, and is specially helpful in recovering the form and sense of the Hebrew text. Jerome's new version is commonly called the Vulgate; it may be noted, however, that the Vulgate Psalter is not his translation from the

Hebrew but an earlier revision he had made of the Old Latin Psalms.

As the knowledge of Hebrew died out among the Jews, the reading of the Scriptures in the synagogue had to be followed by a translation of the passages into Aramaic, the language which had supplanted Hebrew. Such renderings, known as Targums (Aramaic *targum*, 'translation'), tended to become traditional and stereotyped and finally were written down. Some of them contain pre-Christian material. There are Targums to every book of the Old Testament except Daniel, Ezra, and Nehemiah, but only one, on the Pentateuch, is a straightforward translation.

Between the first and third centuries A.D. a Syriac translation, known as the Peshitta (i.e. 'simple') Version, was made; some parts of it are more literal than others, and, though it agrees in the main with the Hebrew text, it bears traces of the influence of the Septuagint. Other versions in various languages appeared between the third and thirteenth centuries A.D., but they are of little value for the recovery and interpretation of the Hebrew text.

In spite of this wealth of ancient versions, and even when the earliest known form of the text has been established, many obscurities still remain in the Hebrew Scriptures. The classical Hebrew vocabulary as known today is small, with the consequence that the meaning of an unusually large number of words is uncertain or unknown. In such cases recourse may be had to the cognate languages. Already medieval scholars had begun to use the Arabic language for this purpose, and in later centuries Syriac and Ethiopic also were used. In more recent times scholars have had access to the vast literature in Babylonian, Assyrian, and kindred dialects which has been preserved on cuneiform tablets. Archaeology, too, has at times been helpful in clearing up an obscurity in the Hebrew text. But in the last resort, the translator may have to arrive at the sense of a word from the context alone, or he may even have to emend what is demonstrably faulty; such corrections of the text, except when only the vowels are affected, are recorded in the notes of the present translation.

The paragraphs in this translation are a modified form of those in the Authorized and Revised Versions, and the present translators have added headings to the main sections into which the text falls. Sometimes, for what seemed sufficient reasons, the order of the verses has been changed, as will be seen from the verse-numbering. Occasionally passages have been brought together if a common refrain or other evidence shows that they have been wrongly separated; such changes are recorded in the notes.

The headings of the Psalms, consisting partly of musical instructions, of which the meanings have mostly been lost, and partly of historical notices, deduced (sometimes incorrectly) from the individual Psalms, have been omitted; they are almost certainly not original. On the other hand, the designations of the speakers in the Song of Songs, though absent from the Hebrew text, have been introduced, with occasional corrections, from two manuscripts of the Septuagint.

A major difficulty in translating the Old Testament lies in the difference of time and place. Palestine differs greatly from the Western world in its physical aspects, in its plants, birds and beasts, its arts and crafts, as it did also in its social, administrative and religious, institutions, so that no English words exist to represent much about which the Old Testament speaks. The modern translator then must be content to use paraphrase or even to transliterate certain Hebrew words. The present translators have transliterated the Hebrew words for technical terms, where verbal exactness has seemed essential, while in other passages they have allowed themselves a paraphrase to bring out the general sense, where no technical problem requiring particularization is involved; but they have adopted such devices as rarely as possible.

Finally, the translators have endeavoured to avoid anachronisms and expressions reminiscent of foreign idioms. They have tried to keep their language as close to current usage as possible, while avoiding words and phrases likely soon to become obsolete. They have made every effort not only to make sense but also to offer renderings that will meet the needs of readers with no special knowledge of the background of the Old Testament.

G. R. D.

GUIDE TO THE NOTES

The footnotes in this edition of the Old Testament serve (*a*) to give cross-references to parallel passages, chiefly in the historical books, (*b*) to indicate where verses or parts of verses have been transposed, (*c*) to give the meaning of proper names where it appears to be reflected in the context, (*d*) to give an alternative interpretation where the Hebrew is capable of such, and (*e*) to indicate places where the translators have adopted what seemed to them the most probable correction of the text where the Hebrew and the ancient versions cannot be convincingly translated as they stand.

Unless otherwise indicated by its wording, a note refers to the single word against which the reference is placed.

ABBREVIATIONS, ETC.

I. GENERAL

Aram.	Aramaic (text or word)	*prob.*	probable
ch(s).	chapter(s)	*rdg.*	reading
cp.	compare	*Sept.*	Septuagint (Greek version of the Old Testament)
Heb.	Hebrew (text or word)		
mng.	meaning		
MS(S).	manuscript(s)	[. . .]	In the text itself square brackets are used to indicate words that are probably late additions to the Hebrew text.
om.	omit(s)		
or	indicating an alternative interpretation		
poss.	possible		

II. BOOKS OF THE OLD TESTAMENT

Gen.	Genesis	*Eccles.*	Ecclesiastes
Exod.	Exodus	*S. of S.*	Song of Songs
Lev.	Leviticus	*Isa.*	Isaiah
Num.	Numbers	*Jer.*	Jeremiah
Deut.	Deuteronomy	*Lam.*	Lamentations
Josh.	Joshua	*Ezek.*	Ezekiel
Judg.	Judges	*Dan.*	Daniel
Ruth	Ruth	*Hos.*	Hosea
1 Sam.	1 Samuel	*Joel*	Joel
2 Sam.	2 Samuel	*Amos*	Amos
1 Kgs.	1 Kings	*Obad.*	Obadiah
2 Kgs.	2 Kings	*Jonah*	Jonah
1 Chr.	1 Chronicles	*Mic.*	Micah
2 Chr.	2 Chronicles	*Nahum*	Nahum
Ezra	Ezra	*Hab.*	Habakkuk
Neh.	Nehemiah	*Zeph.*	Zephaniah
Esther	Esther	*Hag.*	Haggai
Job	Job	*Zech.*	Zechariah
Ps(s).	Psalm(s)	*Mal.*	Malachi
Prov.	Proverbs		

MARGINAL NUMBERS

THE conventional verse divisions in the Old Testament are based on those in Hebrew manuscripts. Nevertheless any system of division into numbered verses is foreign to the spirit of this translation, which is intended to convey the meaning in natural English – the prose in paragraphs, the poetic passages in lines corresponding to the structure of the Hebrew.

For purposes of reference, and of comparison with other translations, verse numbers are placed in the margin opposite the line in which the first word belonging to the verse in question appears. Sometimes, however, successive verses are combined in a continuous translation, so that the precise point where a new verse begins cannot be fixed; in these cases the verse numbers, joined by a hyphen, are placed at the point where the passage begins.

GENESIS

The creation of the world

1 IN the beginning of creation,
when God made heaven and
2 earth,[a] the earth was without
form and void, with darkness over
the face of the abyss, and a mighty
wind that swept[b] over the surface of
3 the waters. God said, 'Let there be
4 light', and there was light; and God
saw that the light was good, and
he separated light from darkness.
5 He called the light day, and the
darkness night. So evening came,
and morning came, the first day.
6 God said, 'Let there be a vault
between the waters, to separate
7 water from water.' So God made
the vault, and separated the water
under the vault from the water
8 above it, and so it was; and God
called the vault heaven. Evening
came, and morning came, a second
day.
9 God said, 'Let the waters under
heaven be gathered into one place,
so that dry land may appear'; and
10 so it was. God called the dry land
earth, and the gathering of the waters he called seas; and God saw that
11 it was good. Then God said, 'Let
the earth produce fresh growth,
let there be on the earth plants
bearing seed, fruit-trees bearing
fruit each with seed according to its
12 kind.' So it was; the earth yielded
fresh growth, plants bearing seed
according to their kind and trees
bearing fruit each with seed according to its kind; and God saw that
13 it was good. Evening came, and
morning came, a third day.
14 God said, 'Let there be lights in
the vault of heaven to separate day
from night, and let them serve as
signs both for festivals and for seasons and years. Let them also shine 15
in the vault of heaven to give light
on earth.' So it was; God made the 16
two great lights, the greater to
govern the day and the lesser to
govern the night; and with them he
made the stars. God put these lights 17
in the vault of heaven to give light
on earth, to govern day and night, 18
and to separate light from darkness; and God saw that it was
good. Evening came, and morning 19
came, a fourth day.
God said, 'Let the waters teem 20
with countless living creatures, and
let birds fly above the earth across
the vault of heaven.' God then 21
created the great sea-monsters and
all living creatures that move and
swarm in the waters, according to
their kind, and every kind of bird;
and God saw that it was good. So 22
he blessed them and said, 'Be fruitful and increase, fill the waters of
the seas; and let the birds increase
on land.' Evening came, and morn- 23
ing came, a fifth day.
God said, 'Let the earth bring 24
forth living creatures, according to
their kind: cattle, reptiles, and
wild animals, all according to their
kind.' So it was; God made wild ani- 25
mals, cattle, and all reptiles, each
according to its kind; and he saw
that it was good. Then God said, 26
'Let us make man in our image and
likeness to rule the fish in the sea,
the birds of heaven, the cattle, all
wild animals on earth, and all reptiles that crawl upon the earth.' So 27
God created man in his own image;
in the image of God he created him;
male and female he created them.
God blessed them and said to them, 28

---

[a] Or In the beginning God created heaven and earth.
[b] Or and the spirit of God hovering.

'Be fruitful and increase, fill the earth and subdue it, rule over the fish in the sea, the birds of heaven, and every living thing that moves 29 upon the earth.' God also said, 'I give you all plants that bear seed everywhere on earth, and every tree bearing fruit which yields seed: 30 they shall be yours for food. All green plants I give for food to the wild animals, to all the birds of heaven, and to all reptiles on earth, every living creature.' So it was; 31 and God saw all that he had made, and it was very good. Evening came, and morning came, a sixth day.

2 Thus heaven and earth were completed with all their mighty throng. 2 On the sixth day God completed all the work he had been doing, and on the seventh day he ceased from all 3 his work. God blessed the seventh day and made it holy, because on that day he ceased from all the work he had set himself to do.

4 This is the story of the making of heaven and earth when they were created.

The beginnings of history

WHEN the LORD God made earth 5 and heaven, there was neither shrub nor plant growing wild upon the earth, because the LORD God had sent no rain on the earth; nor was there any man to till the ground. 6 A flood[a] used to rise out of the earth and water all the surface of 7 the ground. Then the LORD God formed a man[b] from the dust of the ground[c] and breathed into his nostrils the breath of life. Thus the 8 man became a living creature. Then the LORD God planted a garden in Eden away to the east, and there he put the man whom he had 9 formed. The LORD God made trees spring from the ground, all trees pleasant to look at and good for food; and in the middle of the gar-

den he set the tree of life and the tree of the knowledge of good and evil.

There was a river flowing from 10 Eden to water the garden, and when it left the garden it branched into four streams. The name of the 11 first is Pishon; that is the river which encircles all the land of Havilah, where the gold[d] is. The gold[d] of 12 that land is good; bdellium[e] and cornelians are also to be found there. The name of the second river 13 is Gihon; this is the one which encircles all the land of Cush. The 14 name of the third is Tigris; this is the river which runs east of Asshur. The fourth river is the Euphrates.

The LORD God took the man and 15 put him in the garden of Eden to till it and care for it. He told the 16 man, 'You may eat from every tree in the garden, but not from the tree 17 of the knowledge of good and evil; for on the day that you eat from it, you will certainly die.' Then the 18 LORD God said, 'It is not good for the man to be alone. I will provide a partner for him.' So God formed 19 out of the ground all the wild animals and all the birds of heaven. He brought them to the man to see what he would call them, and whatever the man called each living creature, that was its name. Thus 20 the man gave names to all cattle, to the birds of heaven, and to every wild animal; but for the man himself no partner had yet been found. And so the LORD God put the man 21 into a trance, and while he slept, he took one of his ribs and closed the flesh over the place. The LORD 22 God then built up the rib, which he had taken out of the man, into a woman. He brought her to the man, and the man said: 23

'Now this, at last –
bone from my bones,
flesh from my flesh! –
this shall be called woman,[f]
for from man[g] was this taken.'

---

[a] Or mist.   [b] Heb. adam.   [c] Heb. adamah.   [d] Or frankincense.
[e] Or gum resin.   [f] Heb. ishshah.   [g] Heb. ish.

24 That is why a man leaves his father and mother and is united to his wife, and the two become one flesh. 25 Now they were both naked, the man and his wife, but they had no feeling of shame towards one another.

3 THE serpent was more crafty than any wild creature that the LORD God had made. He said to the woman, 'Is it true that God has forbidden you to eat from any tree 2 in the garden?' The woman answered the serpent, 'We may eat the fruit of any tree in the garden, 3 except for the tree in the middle of the garden; God has forbidden us either to eat or to touch the fruit of 4 that; if we do, we shall die.' The serpent said, 'Of course you will 5 not die. God knows that as soon as you eat it, your eyes will be opened and you will be like gods[a] knowing 6 both good and evil.' When the woman saw that the fruit of the tree was good to eat, and that it was pleasing to the eye and tempting to contemplate, she took some and ate it. She also gave her husband 7 some and he ate it. Then the eyes of both of them were opened and they discovered that they were naked; so they stitched fig-leaves together and made themselves loincloths. 8 The man and his wife heard the sound of the LORD God walking in the garden at the time of the evening breeze and hid from the LORD God among the trees of the garden. 9 But the LORD God called to the man and said to him, 'Where are 10 you?' He replied, 'I heard the sound as you were walking in the garden, and I was afraid because I was naked, and I hid myself.' 11 God answered, 'Who told you that you were naked? Have you eaten from the tree which I forbade you?' 12 The man said, 'The woman you gave me for a companion, she gave me fruit from the tree and I ate 13 it.' Then the LORD God said to the

woman, 'What is this that you have done?' The woman said, 'The serpent tricked me, and I ate.' Then 14 the LORD God said to the serpent:

'Because you have done this you are accursed
more than all cattle and all wild creatures.
On your belly you shall crawl, and dust you shall eat
all the days of your life.
I will put enmity between you and 15 the woman,
between your brood and hers.
They shall strike at your head,
and you shall strike at their heel.'

To the woman he said: 16

'I will increase your labour and your groaning,
and in labour you shall bear children.
You shall be eager[b] for your husband,
and he shall be your master.'

And to the man he said: 17

'Because you have listened to your wife
and have eaten from the tree which I forbade you,
accursed shall be the ground on your account.
With labour you shall win your food from it
all the days of your life.
It will grow thorns and thistles for 18 you,
none but wild plants for you to eat.
You shall gain your bread by the 19 sweat of your brow
until you return to the ground;
for from it you were taken.
Dust you are, to dust you shall return.'

The man called his wife Eve[c] be- 20 cause she was the mother of all who live. The LORD God made tunics of 21 skins for Adam and his wife and clothed them. He said, 'The man 22 has become like one of us, knowing good and evil; what if he now

---

[a] Or God.　　　　[b] Or feel an urge.　　　　[c] That is Life.

3

reaches out his hand and takes fruit from the tree of life also, eats 23 it and lives for ever?' So the LORD God drove him out of the garden of Eden to till the ground from which 24 he had been taken. He cast him out, and to the east of the garden of Eden he stationed the cherubim and a sword whirling and flashing to guard the way to the tree of life.

4 The man lay with his wife Eve, and she conceived and gave birth to Cain. She said, 'With the help of the LORD I have brought a man 2 into being.' Afterwards she had another child, his brother Abel. Abel was a shepherd and Cain a 3 tiller of the soil. The day came when Cain brought some of the produce of the soil as a gift to the 4 LORD; and Abel brought some of the first-born of his flock, the fat portions of them.[a] The LORD re-5 ceived Abel and his gift with fav-our; but Cain and his gift he did 6 not receive. Cain was very angry and his face fell. Then the LORD said to Cain, 'Why are you so angry and cast down?

7 If you do well, you are accepted;[b] if not, sin is a demon crouching at the door.
It shall be eager for you, and you will be mastered by it.'[c]

8 Cain said to his brother Abel, 'Let us go into the open country.' While they were there, Cain attack-ed his brother Abel and murdered 9 him. Then the LORD said to Cain, 'Where is your brother Abel?' Cain answered, 'I do not know. Am I my 10 brother's keeper?' The LORD said, 'What have you done? Hark! your brother's blood that has been shed is crying out to me from the ground. 11 Now you are accursed, and banish-ed from[d] the ground which has opened its mouth wide to receive

your brother's blood, which you have shed. When you till the ground, 12 it will no longer yield you its wealth. You shall be a vagrant and a wan-derer on earth.' Cain said to the 13 LORD, 'My punishment is heavier than I can bear; thou hast driven 14 me today from the ground, and I must hide myself from thy pre-sence. I shall be a vagrant and a wanderer on earth, and anyone who meets me can kill me.' The 15 LORD answered him, 'No: if any-one kills Cain, Cain shall be avenged sevenfold.' So the LORD put a mark on Cain, in order that anyone meet-ing him should not kill him. Then 16 Cain went out from the LORD's presence and settled in the land of Nod[ef] to the east of Eden.

Then Cain lay with his wife; and 17 she conceived and bore Enoch. Cain was then building a city, which he named Enoch after his son. Enoch 18 begot Irad; Irad begot Mehujael; Mehujael begot Methushael; Meth-ushael begot Lamech.

Lamech married two wives, one 19 named Adah and the other Zillah. Adah bore Jabal who was the an-20 cestor of herdsmen who live in tents; and his brother's name was 21 Jubal; he was the ancestor of those who play the harp and pipe. Zillah, 22 the other wife, bore Tubal-cain, the master of all coppersmiths and blacksmiths, and Tubal-cain's sis-ter was Naamah. Lamech said to 23 his wives:

'Adah and Zillah, listen to me;
wives of Lamech, mark what I say:
I kill a man for wounding me,
a young man for a blow.
Cain may be avenged seven times, 24
but Lamech seventy-seven.'

Adam lay with his wife again. 25 She bore a son, and named him Seth,[g] 'for', she said, 'God has

---

[a] *Or some of the first-born, that is the sucklings, of his flock.*
[b] *Or you hold your head up.*   [c] *Or but you must master it.*
[d] *and banished from: or more than (cp. 3. 17).*   [e] *That is Wandering.*
[f] *and settled...Nod: or and he lived as a wanderer in the land.*
[g] *That is Granted.*

granted me another son in place of Abel, because Cain killed him.' 26 Seth too had a son, whom he named Enosh. At that time men began to invoke the LORD[a] by name.

5 THIS is the record of the descendants of Adam. On the day when God created man he made him in 2 the likeness of God. He created them male and female, and on the day when he created them, he blessed them and called them man.

3 Adam was one hundred and thirty years old when he begot a son in his likeness and image, and 4 named him Seth. After the birth of Seth he lived eight hundred years, and had other sons and daughters. 5 He lived nine hundred and thirty years, and then he died.

6 Seth was one hundred and five years old when he begot Enosh. 7 After the birth of Enosh he lived eight hundred and seven years, and 8 had other sons and daughters. He lived nine hundred and twelve years, and then he died.

9[b] Enosh was ninety years old when 10 he begot Kenan. After the birth of Kenan he lived eight hundred and fifteen years, and had other sons 11 and daughters. He lived nine hundred and five years, and then he died.

12 Kenan was seventy years old 13 when he begot Mahalalel. After the birth of Mahalalel he lived eight hundred and forty years, and had 14 other sons and daughters. He lived nine hundred and ten years, and then he died.

15 Mahalalel was sixty-five years 16 old when he begot Jared. After the birth of Jared he lived eight hundred and thirty years, and had 17 other sons and daughters. He lived eight hundred and ninety-five years, and then he died.

18 Jared was one hundred and sixty-two years old when he begot Enoch. 19 After the birth of Enoch he lived eight hundred years, and had other 20 sons and daughters. He lived nine hundred and sixty-two years, and then he died.

21 Enoch was sixty-five years old 22 when he begot Methuselah. After the birth of Methuselah, Enoch walked with God for three hundred years, and had other sons and 23 daughters. He lived three hundred 24 and sixty-five years. Having walked with God, Enoch was seen no more, because God had taken him away.

25 Methuselah was one hundred and eighty-seven years old when 26 he begot Lamech. After the birth of Lamech he lived for seven hundred and eighty-two years, and 27 had other sons and daughters. He lived nine hundred and sixty-nine years, and then he died.

28 Lamech was one hundred and eighty-two years old when he begot a son. He named him Noah, 29 saying, 'This boy will bring us relief from our work, and from the hard labour that has come upon us because of the LORD's curse upon the ground.' After the birth of 30 Noah, he lived for five hundred and ninety-five years, and had other sons and daughters. Lamech lived 31 seven hundred and seventy-seven years, and then he died. Noah was 32 five hundred years old when he begot Shem, Ham and Japheth.

The flood and the tower of Babel

6 WHEN mankind began to increase and to spread all over the earth and daughters were born to them, the sons of the gods saw that the 2 daughters of men were beautiful; so they took for themselves such women as they chose. But the 3 LORD said, 'My life-giving spirit shall not remain in man for ever; he for his part is mortal flesh: he shall live for a hundred and twenty years.'

---

[a] *This represents the Hebrew consonants* YHWH, *probably pronounced* Yahweh, *but traditionally read as* Jehovah.   [b] *Verses 9–32: cp. 1 Chr. 1. 2–4.*

4 In those days,[a] when the sons of the gods had intercourse with the daughters of men and got children by them, the Nephilim[b] were on earth. They were the heroes of old, men of renown.

5 When the LORD saw that man had done much evil on earth and that his thoughts and inclinations 6 were always evil, he was sorry that he had made man on earth, and he 7 was grieved at heart. He said, 'This race of men whom I have created, I will wipe them off the face of the earth – man and beast, reptiles and birds. I am sorry that I ever made 8 them.' But Noah had won the LORD's favour.

9 This is the story of Noah. Noah was a righteous man, the one blameless man of his time; he walked 10 with God. He had three sons, Shem, 11 Ham and Japheth. Now God saw that the whole world was corrupt[c] 12 and full of violence. In his sight the world had become corrupted, for all men had lived corrupt lives 13 on earth. God said to Noah, 'The loathsomeness[d] of all mankind has become plain to me, for through them the earth is full of violence. I intend to destroy them, and the 14 earth with them. Make yourself an ark with ribs of cypress; cover it with reeds and coat it inside and 15 out with pitch. This is to be its plan: the length of the ark shall be three hundred cubits, its breadth fifty cubits, and its height thirty 16 cubits. You shall make a roof for the ark, giving it a fall of one cubit when complete; and put a door in the side of the ark, and build three decks, upper, middle, and lower. 17 I intend to bring the waters of the flood over the earth to destroy every human being under heaven that has the spirit of life; everything on 18 earth shall perish. But with you I will make a covenant, and you shall go into the ark, you and your sons, your wife and your sons' wives

with you. And you shall bring living 19 creatures of every kind into the ark to keep them alive with you, two of each kind, a male and a fe-male; two of every kind of bird, 20 beast, and reptile, shall come to you to be kept alive. See that you take 21 and store every kind of food that can be eaten; this shall be food for you and for them.' Exactly as God 22 had commanded him, so Noah did.

The LORD said to Noah, 'Go into 7 the ark, you and all your house-hold; for I have seen that you alone are righteous before me in this gen-eration. Take with you seven pairs, 2 male and female, of all beasts that are ritually clean, and one pair, male and female, of all beasts that are not clean; also seven pairs, 3 male and female, of every bird – to ensure that life continues on earth. In seven days' time I will 4 send rain over the earth for forty days and forty nights, and I will wipe off the face of the earth every living thing that I have made.' Noah did all that the LORD had 5 commanded him. He was six hun- 6 dred years old when the waters of the flood came upon the earth.

And so, to escape the waters of 7 the flood, Noah went into the ark with his sons, his wife, and his sons' wives. And into the ark with Noah 8–9 went one pair, male and female, of all beasts, clean and unclean, of birds and of everything that crawls on the ground, two by two, as God had commanded. Towards the end 10 of seven days the waters of the flood came upon the earth. In the 11 year when Noah was six hundred years old, on the seventeenth day of the second month, on that very day, all the springs of the great abyss broke through, the windows of the sky were opened, and rain 12 fell on the earth for forty days and forty nights. On that very day 13 Noah entered the ark with his sons, Shem, Ham and Japeth, his own

---

[a] *Prob. rdg.; Heb. adds* and also afterwards (*cp. Num.* 13. 33).
[b] *Or* giants.   [c] *Or* ripe for destruction.   [d] *Or* end.

wife, and his three sons' wives.
14 Wild animals of every kind, cattle
of every kind, reptiles of every kind
that move upon the ground, and
15 birds of every kind – all came to
Noah in the ark, two by two of all
creatures that had life in them.
16 Those which came were one male
and one female of all living things;
they came in as God had commanded Noah, and the LORD closed the
17 door on him. The flood continued
upon the earth for forty days, and
the waters swelled and lifted up
the ark so that it rose high above
18 the ground. They swelled and increased over the earth, and the ark
floated on the surface of the waters.
19 More and more the waters increased
over the earth until they covered
all the high mountains everywhere
20 under heaven. The waters increased
and the mountains were covered to
21 a depth of fifteen cubits. Every
living creature that moves on earth
perished, birds, cattle, wild animals, all reptiles, and all mankind.
22 Everything died that had the
breath of life in its nostrils, every-
23 thing on dry land. God wiped out
every living thing that existed on
earth, man and beast, reptile and
bird; they were all wiped out over
the whole earth, and only Noah
and his company in the ark survived.
24 When the waters had increased
over the earth for a hundred and
8 fifty days, God thought of Noah
and all the wild animals and the
cattle with him in the ark, and he
made a wind pass over the earth,
and the waters began to subside.
2 The springs of the abyss were stopped up, and so were the windows of
the sky; the downpour from the
3 skies was checked. The water gradually receded from the earth, and
by the end of a hundred and fifty
4 days it had disappeared. On the
seventeenth day of the seventh
month the ark grounded on a
5 mountain in Ararat. The water

continued to recede until the tenth
month, and on the first day of the
tenth month the tops of the mountains could be seen.

After forty days Noah opened 6
the trap-door that he had made in
the ark, and released a raven to see 7
whether the water had subsided,
but the bird continued flying to
and fro until the water on the earth
had dried up. Noah waited for 8
seven days,[a] and then he released a
dove from the ark to see whether
the water on the earth had subsided further. But the dove found 9
no place where she could settle, and
so she came back to him in the ark,
because there was water over the
whole surface of the earth. Noah
stretched out his hand, caught
her and took her into the ark. He 10
waited another seven days and
again released the dove from the
ark. She came back to him towards 11
evening with a newly plucked olive
leaf in her beak. Then Noah knew
for certain that the water on the
earth had subsided still further.
He waited yet another seven days 12
and released the dove, but she
never came back. And so it came 13
about that, on the first day of the
first month of his six hundred and
first year, the water had dried up
on the earth, and Noah removed
the hatch and looked out of the ark.
The surface of the ground was dry.

By the twenty-seventh day of 14
the second month the whole earth
was dry. And God said to Noah, 15
'Come out of the ark, you and your 16
wife, your sons and their wives.
Bring out every living creature that 17
is with you, live things of every
kind, bird and beast and every reptile that moves on the ground, and
let them swarm over the earth and
be fruitful and increase there.' So 18
Noah came out with his sons, his
wife, and his sons' wives. Every 19
wild animal, all cattle, every bird,
and every reptile that moves on
the ground, came out of the ark by

---

[a] Noah...days: *prob. rdg., cp. verse 10; Heb. om.*

20 families. Then Noah built an altar to the LORD. He took ritually clean beasts and birds of every kind, and offered whole-offerings on the altar. 21 When the LORD smelt the soothing odour, he said within himself, 'Never again will I curse the ground because of man, however evil his inclinations may be from his youth upwards. I will never again kill every living creature, as I have just done.

22 While the earth lasts
seedtime and harvest, cold and heat,
summer and winter, day and night,
shall never cease.'

9 GOD blessed Noah and his sons and said to them, 'Be fruitful and 2 increase, and fill the earth. The fear and dread of you shall fall upon all wild animals on earth, on all birds of heaven, on everything that moves upon the ground and all fish in the sea; they are given 3 into your hands. Every creature that lives and moves shall be food for you; I give you them all, as once I gave you all green plants. 4 But you must not eat the flesh with the life, which is the blood, still 5 in it. And further, for your life-blood I will demand satisfaction; from every animal I will require it, and from a man also I will require satisfaction for the death of his fellow-man.

6 He that sheds the blood of a man,
for that man his blood shall be shed;
for in the image of God
has God made man.

7 But you must be fruitful and increase, swarm throughout the earth and rule*a* over it.'
8 God spoke to Noah and to his 9 sons with him: 'I now make my covenant with you and with your 10 descendants after you, and with every living creature that is with you, all birds and cattle, all the wild animals with you on earth, all that have come out of the ark. I 11 will make my covenant with you: never again shall all living creatures be destroyed by the waters of the flood, never again shall there be a flood to lay waste the earth.'

God said, 'This is the sign of the 12 covenant which I establish between myself and you and every living creature with you, to endless generations:

My bow I set in the cloud,   13
sign of the covenant
between myself and earth.
When I cloud the sky over the 14
earth,
the bow shall be seen in the cloud.

Then will I remember the covenant 15 which I have made between myself and you and living things of every kind. Never again shall the waters become a flood to destroy all living creatures. The bow shall be in the 16 cloud; when I see it, it will remind me of the everlasting covenant between God and living things on earth of every kind.' God said to 17 Noah, 'This is the sign of the covenant which I make between myself and all that lives on earth.'

The sons of Noah who came out 18 of the ark were Shem, Ham and Japheth; Ham was the father of Canaan. These three were the sons 19 of Noah, and their descendants spread over the whole earth.

Noah, a man of the soil, began 20 the planting of vineyards. He drank 21 some of the wine, became drunk and lay naked inside his tent. When Ham, father of Canaan, saw 22 his father naked, he told his two brothers outside. So Shem and Ja- 23 pheth took a cloak, put it on their shoulders and walked backwards, and so covered their father's naked body; their faces were turned the other way, so that they did not see their father naked. When Noah 24 woke from his drunken sleep, he

a Prob. rdg., cp. 1. 28; Heb. increase.

8

learnt what his youngest son had
25 done to him, and said:

'Cursed be Canaan,
slave of slaves
shall he be to his brothers.'

26 And he continued:

'Bless, O LORD,
the tents of Shem;[a]
may Canaan be his slave.
27 May God extend[b] Japheth's
bounds,
let him dwell in the tents of
Shem,
may Canaan be their slave.'

28 After the flood Noah lived for three
29 hundred and fifty years, and he
was nine hundred and fifty years
old when he died.

10 These are the descendants of the
sons of Noah, Shem, Ham and Japheth, the sons born to them after
the flood.

2[c] The sons of Japheth: Gomer,
Magog, Madai, Javan,[d] Tubal, Me-
3 shech and Tiras. The sons of Gomer: Ashkenaz, Riphath and Tog-
4 armah. The sons of Javan: Elishah,
Tarshish, Kittim[e] and Rodanim.
5 From these the peoples of the
coasts and islands separated into
their own countries, each with their
own language, family by family,
nation by nation.

6[f] The sons of Ham: Cush, Miz-
7 raim,[g] Put and Canaan. The sons
of Cush: Seba, Havilah, Sabtah,
Raamah and Sabtecha. The sons
of Raamah: Sheba and Dedan.
8 Cush was the father of Nimrod,
who began to show himself a man
9 of might on earth; and he was a
mighty hunter before the LORD, as
the saying goes, 'Like Nimrod, a
mighty hunter before the LORD.'
10 His kingdom in the beginning consisted of Babel, Erech, and Accad,
all of them in the land of Shinar.

From that land he migrated to As- 11
shur and built Nineveh, Rehoboth-
Ir, Calah, and Resen, a great city 12
between Nineveh and Calah. From 13[h]
Mizraim sprang the Lydians, Anamites, Lehabites, Naphtuhites, Pa- 14
thrusites, Casluhites, and the Caphtorites, from whom the Philistines
were descended.
Canaan was the father of Sidon, 15
who was his eldest son, and Heth,[i]
the Jebusites, the Amorites, the 16
Girgashites, the Hivites, the Ark- 17
ites, the Sinites, the Arvadites, the 18
Zemarites, and the Hamathites.
Later the Canaanites spread, and 19
then the Canaanite border ran from
Sidon towards Gerar all the way to
Gaza; then all the way to Sodom
and Gomorrah, Admah and Zeboyim as far as Lasha. These were 20
the sons of Ham, by families and
languages with their countries and
nations.
Sons were born also to Shem, 21
elder brother of Japheth, the ancestor of all the sons of Eber. The 22
sons of Shem: Elam, Asshur, Arphaxad, Lud[k] and Aram. The sons of 23
Aram: Uz, Hul, Gether and Mash.
Arphaxad was the father of Shelah, 24
and Shelah the father of Eber.
Eber had two sons: one was named 25
Peleg,[l] because in his time the
earth was divided; and his brother's name was Joktan. Joktan 26
was the father of Almodad, Sheleph, Hazarmoth, Jerah, Hadoram, 27
Uzal, Diklah, Obal, Abimael, She- 28
ba, Ophir, Havilah and Jobab. All 29
these were sons of Joktan. They 30
lived in the eastern hill-country,
from Mesha all the way to Sephar.
These were the sons of Shem, by 31
families and languages with their
countries and nations.
These were the families of the 32
sons of Noah according to their
genealogies, nation by nation; and

---

[a] Bless...Shem: *prob. rdg.*; *Heb.* Blessed is the LORD the God of Shem.
[b] *Heb.* japht.　　　[c] *Verses 2–4: cp.* 1 Chr. 1. 5–7.　　　[d] *Or* Greece.
[e] *Or* Tarshish of the Kittians.　　[f] *Verses 6–8: cp.* 1 Chr. 1. 8–10.　　[g] *Or* Egypt.
[h] *Verses 13–18: cp.* 1 Chr. 1. 11–16.　　　[i] *Or* the Hittites.
[j] *Verses 22–29: cp.* 1 Chr. 1. 17–23.　　[k] *Or* the Lydians.　　[l] *That is* Division.

from them came the separate nations on earth after the flood.

11 ONCE upon a time all the world spoke a single language and used 2 the same[a] words. As men journeyed in the east, they came upon a plain in the land of Shinar and settled 3 there. They said to one another, 'Come, let us make bricks and bake them hard'; they used bricks for stone and bitumen for mortar. 4 'Come,' they said, 'let us build ourselves a city and a tower with its top in the heavens, and make a name for ourselves; or we shall be 5 dispersed all over the earth.' Then the LORD came down to see the city and tower which mortal men had 6 built, and he said, 'Here they are, one people with a single language, and now they have started to do this; henceforward nothing they have a mind to do will be beyond 7 their reach. Come, let us go down there and confuse their speech, so that they will not understand what 8 they say to one another.' So the LORD dispersed them from there all over the earth, and they left off 9 building the city. That is why it is called Babel,[b] because the LORD there made a babble of the language of all the world; from that place the LORD scattered men all over the face of the earth.

10[c]   This is the table of the descendants of Shem. Shem was a hundred years old when he begot Arphaxad, two years after the 11 flood. After the birth of Arphaxad he lived five hundred years, and 12 had other sons and daughters. Arphaxad was thirty-five years old 13 when he begot Shelah. After the birth of Shelah he lived four hundred and three years, and had other sons and daughters.

14   Shelah was thirty years old when 15 he begot Eber. After the birth of Eber he lived four hundred and three years, and had other sons and daughters.

Eber was thirty-four years old 16 when he begot Peleg. After the 17 birth of Peleg he lived four hundred and thirty years, and had other sons and daughters.

Peleg was thirty years old when 18 he begot Reu. After the birth of 19 Reu he lived two hundred and nine years, and had other sons and daughters.

Reu was thirty-two years old 20 when he begot Serug. After the 21 birth of Serug he lived two hundred and seven years, and had other sons and daughters.

Serug was thirty years old when 22 he begot Nahor. After the birth of 23 Nahor he lived two hundred years, and had other sons and daughters.

Nahor was twenty-nine years 24 old when he begot Terah. After the 25 birth of Terah he lived a hundred and nineteen years, and had other sons and daughters.

Terah was seventy years old 26 when he begot Abram, Nahor and Haran.

This is the table of the descen- 27 dants of Terah. Terah was the father of Abram, Nahor and Haran. Haran was the father of Lot. Haran died in the presence of his 28 father in the land of his birth, Ur of the Chaldees. Abram and Nahor 29 married wives; Abram's wife was called Sarai, and Nahor's Milcah. She was Haran's daughter; and he was also the father of Milcah and of Iscah. Sarai was barren; she had 30 no child. Terah took his son Abram, 31 his grandson Lot the son of Haran, and his daughter-in-law Sarai Abram's wife, and they set out from Ur of the Chaldees for the land of Canaan. But when they reached Harran, they settled there. Terah 32 was two hundred and five years old when he died in Harran.

Abraham and Isaac

THE LORD said to Abram, 'Leave 12 your own country, your kinsmen,

---

[a] *Or used few.*   [b] *That is Babylon.*   [c] *Verses 10–26: cp. 1 Chr. 1. 24–27.*

and your father's house, and go to a country that I will show you.

2 I will make you into a great nation, I will bless you and make your name so great that it shall be used in blessings:

3 Those that bless you I will bless, those that curse you, I will execrate.
All the families on earth
will pray to be blessed as you are blessed.'

4 And so Abram set out as the LORD had bidden him, and Lot went with him. Abram was seventy-five years old when he left Harran.

5 He took his wife Sarai, his nephew Lot, all the property they had collected, and all the dependants they had acquired in Harran, and they started on their journey to Canaan.

6 When they arrived, Abram passed through the country to the sanctuary at Shechem, the terebinth-tree of Moreh. At that time the Canaanites lived in this land.

7 There the LORD appeared to Abram and said, 'I give this land to your descendants.' So Abram built an altar there to the LORD who had appeared to him.

8 Thence he went on to the hill-country east of Bethel and pitched his tent between Bethel on the west and Ai on the east. There he built an altar to the LORD and invoked the LORD by name.

9 Thus Abram journeyed by stages towards the Negeb.

10 There came a famine in the land, so severe that Abram went down to Egypt to live there for a while.

11 When he was approaching Egypt, he said to his wife Sarai, 'I know very well that you are a beautiful

12 woman, and that when the Egyptians see you, they will say, "She is his wife"; then they will kill me but

13 let you live. Tell them that you are my sister, so that all may go well with me because of you and my life may be spared on your account.'

14 When Abram arrived in Egypt, the Egyptians saw that she was

15 indeed very beautiful. Pharaoh's courtiers saw her and praised her to Pharaoh, and she was taken into Pharaoh's household.

16 He treated Abram well because of her, and Abram came to possess sheep and cattle and asses, male and female slaves, she-asses, and camels.

17 But the LORD struck Pharaoh and his household with grave diseases on account of Abram's wife Sarai.

18 Pharaoh summoned Abram and said to him, 'Why have you treated me like this? Why did you not tell

19 me that she is your wife? Why did you say that she was your sister, so that I took her as a wife? Here she is: take her and be gone.'

20 Then Pharaoh gave his men orders, and they sent Abram away with his wife and all that he had.

13 Abram went up from Egypt into the Negeb, he and his wife and all that he had, and Lot went with him. Abram was now very rich in

2 cattle and in silver and gold. From

3 the Negeb he journeyed by stages to Bethel, to the place between Bethel and Ai where he had pitched his tent in the beginning, where he

4 had set up an altar on the first occasion and had invoked the LORD by name. Now Lot was travelling

5 with Abram, and he too possessed sheep and cattle and tents. The

6 land could not support them both together; for their livestock were so numerous that they could not settle in the same district, and

7 there were quarrels between A-bram's herdsmen and Lot's. The Canaanites and the Perizzites were then living in the land. So Abram

8 said to Lot, 'Let there be no quarrelling between us, between my herdsmen and yours; for we are close kinsmen. The whole country

9 is there in front of you; let us part company. If you go left, I will go right; if you go right, I will go left.'

10 Lot looked up and saw how well-watered the whole Plain of the Jordan was; all the way to Zoar it was like the Garden of the LORD, like

the land of Egypt. This was before the LORD had destroyed Sodom 11 and Gomorrah. So Lot chose all the Plain of the Jordan and took the road on the east side. Thus they 12 parted company. Abram settled in the land of Canaan; but Lot settled among the cities of the Plain and 13 pitched his tents near Sodom. Now the men of Sodom were wicked, great sinners against the LORD.

14 After Lot and Abram had parted, the LORD said to Abram, 'Raise your eyes and look into the distance from the place where you are, north and south, east and 15 west. All the land you can see I will give to you and to your descen- 16 dants for ever. I will make your descendants countless as the dust of the earth; if anyone could count the dust upon the ground, then he 17 could count your descendants. Now go through the length and breadth 18 of the land, for I give it to you.' So Abram moved his tent and settled by the terebinths of Mamre at Hebron; and there he built an altar to the LORD.

14 IT was in the time of Amraphel king of Shinar, Arioch king of Ellasar, Kedorlaomer king of Elam, 2 and Tidal king of Goyim. They went to war against Bera king of Sodom, Birsha king of Gomorrah, Shinab king of Admah, Shemeber king of Zeboyim, and the king of 3 Bela, that is Zoar. These kings joined forces in the valley of Siddim, which is now the Dead Sea. 4 They had been subject to Kedorlaomer for twelve years, but in the 5 thirteenth year they rebelled. Then in the fourteenth year Kedorlaomer and his confederate kings came and defeated the Rephaim in Ashteroth-karnaim, the Zuzim in Ham, the Emim in Shaveh-kiria- 6 thaim, and the Horites in the hill-country from Seir[a] as far as El-paran on the edge of the wilderness. 7 On their way back they came to En-mishpat, which is now Kadesh, and laid waste all the country of the Amalekites and also that of the Amorites who lived in Hazazon-tamar. Then the kings of Sodom, 8 Gomorrah, Admah, Zeboyim, and Bela, which is now Zoar, marched out and drew up their forces against them in the valley of Siddim, against Kedorlaomer king of 9 Elam, Tidal king of Goyim, Amraphel king of Shinar, and Arioch king of Ellasar, four kings against five. Now the valley of Siddim was 10 full of bitumen pits; and when the kings of Sodom and Gomorrah fled, they fell into them, but the rest escaped to the hill-country. The 11 four kings captured all the flocks and herds of Sodom and Gomorrah and all their provisions, and went away. They also carried off Lot, 12 Abram's nephew, who was living in Sodom, and with him his flocks and herds. But a fugitive came and 13 told Abram the Hebrew, who at that time was dwelling by the terebinths of Mamre the Amorite. This Mamre was the brother of Eshcol and Aner, who were allies of Abram. When Abram heard that his 14 kinsman had been taken prisoner, he mustered his retainers, men born in his household, three hundred and eighteen of them, and pursued as far as Dan. Abram and 15 his followers surrounded the enemy by night, attacked them and pursued them as far as Hobah, north of Damascus; he then brought 16 back all the flocks and herds and also his kinsman Lot with his flocks and herds, together with the women and the other captives. On 17 his return from this defeat of Kedorlaomer and his confederate kings, the king of Sodom came out to meet him in the valley of Shaveh, which is now the King's Valley.

Then Melchizedek king of Salem 18 brought food and wine. He was priest of God Most High, and he 19

---

[a] *Prob. rdg.*; *Heb.* in their hill-country, Seir.

pronounced this blessing on A-bram:

'Blessed be Abram
by God Most High,
creator[a] of heaven and earth.
20 And blessed be God Most High,
who has delivered your enemies
into your power.'

Abram gave him a tithe of all the booty.
21 The king of Sodom said to A-bram, 'Give me the people, and
22 you can take the property'; but Abram said to the king of Sodom, 'I lift my hand and swear by the LORD, God Most High, creator of
23 heaven and earth: not a thread or a shoe-string will I accept of anything that is yours. You shall never
24 say, "I made Abram rich." I will accept nothing but what the young men have eaten and the share of the men who went with me. Aner, Eshcol, and Mamre shall have their share.'

15 AFTER this the word of the LORD came to Abram in a vision. He said, 'Do not be afraid, Abram, I am giving you a very great re-
2 ward.'[b] Abram replied, 'Lord GOD, what canst thou give me? I have no standing among men, for the heir to my household is Eliezer of Dam-
3 ascus.' Abram continued, 'Thou hast given me no children, and so my heir must be a slave born in my
4 house.' Then came the word of the LORD to him: 'This man shall not be your heir; your heir shall be a
5 child of your own body.' He took Abram outside and said, 'Look up into the sky, and count the stars if you can. So many', he said, 'shall your descendants be.'
6 Abram put his faith in the LORD, and the LORD counted that faith to
7 him as righteousness; he said to him, 'I am the LORD who brought you out from Ur of the Chaldees to
8 give you this land to occupy.' A-

bram said, 'O Lord GOD, how can I be sure that I shall occupy it?'
The LORD answered, 'Bring me a 9 heifer three years old, a she-goat three years old, a ram three years old, a turtle-dove, and a fledgling.'
He brought him all these, halved 10 the animals down the middle and placed each piece opposite its corresponding piece, but he did not halve the birds. When the birds of 11 prey swooped down on the carcasses, Abram scared them away. Then, as the sun was going down, a 12 trance came over Abram and great fear came upon him. The LORD 13 said to Abram, 'Know this for certain, that your descendants will be aliens living in a land that is not theirs; they will be slaves, and will be held in oppression there for four hundred years. But I will punish 14 that nation whose slaves they are, and after that they shall come out with great possessions. You your- 15 self shall join your fathers in peace and be buried in a good old age; and the fourth generation shall re- 16 turn here, for the Amorites will not be ripe for punishment till then.'
The sun went down and it was 17 dusk, and there appeared a smoking brazier and a flaming torch passing between the divided pieces. That very day the LORD made a 18 covenant with Abram, and he said, 'To your descendants I give this land from the River of Egypt to the Great River, the river Euph- rates, the territory of the Kenites, 19 Kenizzites, Kadmonites, Hittites, 20 Perizzites, Rephaim, Amorites, Ca- 21 naanites, Girgashites, Hivites, and Jebusites.'
Abram's wife Sarai had borne 16 him no children. Now she had an Egyptian slave-girl whose name was Hagar, and she said to Abram, 2 'You see that the LORD has not allowed me to bear a child. Take my slave-girl; perhaps I shall found a family through her.' Abram

[a] *Or* owner.
[b] I am giving...reward: *or* I am your shield, your very great reward.

3 agreed to what his wife said; so Sarai, Abram's wife, brought her slave-girl, Hagar the Egyptian, and gave her to her husband A-bram as a wife.[a] When this happened Abram had been in Canaan 4 for ten years. He lay with Hagar and she conceived; and when she knew that she was with child, she 5 despised her mistress. Sarai said to Abram, 'I have been wronged and you must answer for it. It was I who gave my slave-girl into your arms, but since she has known that she is with child, she has despised me. May the LORD see justice done 6 between you and me.' Abram replied to Sarai, 'Your slave-girl is in your hands; deal with her as you will.' So Sarai ill-treated her and she ran away.

7 The angel of the LORD found her by a spring of water in the wilder-8 ness on the way to Shur, and he said, 'Hagar, Sarai's slave-girl, where have you come from and where are you going?' She answered, 'I am running away from Sarai 9 my mistress.' The angel of the LORD said to her, 'Go back to your mistress and submit to her ill-10 treatment.' The angel also said, 'I will make your descendants too 11 many to be counted.' And the angel of the LORD said to her:

'You are with child and will bear a son.
You shall name him Ishmael,[b] because the LORD has heard of your ill-treatment.
12 He shall be a man like the wild ass, his hand against every man and every man's hand against him; and he shall live at odds with[c] all his kinsmen.'

13 She called the LORD who was speaking to her by the name El-Roi,[d] for she said, 'Have I indeed seen God and still live[e] after that vision?'

That is why men call the well Beer-14 lahai-roi;[f] it lies between Kadesh and Bered. Hagar bore Abram a 15 son, and he named the child she bore him Ishmael. Abram was 16 eighty-six years old when Hagar bore Ishmael.

When Abram was ninety-nine 17 years old, the LORD appeared to him and said, 'I am God Almighty. Live always in my presence and be perfect, so that I may set my cov-2 enant between myself and you and multiply your descendants.' A-3 bram threw himself down on his face, and God spoke with him and said, 'I make this covenant, and I 4 make it with you: you shall be the father of a host of nations. Your 5 name shall no longer be Abram,[g] your name shall be Abraham,[h] for I make you father of a host of nations. I will make you exceed-6 ingly fruitful; I will make nations out of you, and kings shall spring from you. I will fulfil my covenant 7 between myself and you and your descendants after you, generation after generation, an everlasting co-venant, to be your God, yours and your descendants' after you. As an 8 everlasting possession I will give you and your descendants after you the land in which you now are aliens, all the land of Canaan, and I will be God to your descendants.'

God said to Abraham, 'For your 9 part, you must keep my covenant, you and your descendants after you, generation by generation. This is how you shall keep my 10 covenant between myself and you and your descendants after you: circumcise yourselves, every male among you. You shall circumcise 11 the flesh of your foreskin, and it shall be the sign of the covenant between us. Every male among 12 you in every generation shall be circumcised on the eighth day,

---

[a] *Or* concubine.   [b] *That is* God heard.   [c] *Or* live to the east of . . .
[d] *That is* God of a vision.   [e] God and still live: *prob. rdg.*; *Heb.* hither.
[f] *That is* the Well of the Living One of Vision.   [g] *That is* High Father.
[h] *That is* Father of a Multitude.

both those born in your house and any foreigner, not of your blood 13 but bought with your money. Circumcise both those born in your house and those bought with your money; thus shall my covenant be marked in your flesh as an ever-14 lasting covenant. Every uncircumcised male, everyone who has not had the flesh of his foreskin circumcised, shall be cut off from the kin of his father. He has broken my covenant.'

15 God said to Abraham, 'As for Sarai your wife; you shall call her 16 not Sarai,[a] but Sarah.[b] I will bless her and give you a son by her. I will bless her and she shall be the mother of nations; the kings of many people shall spring from her.'
17 Abraham threw himself down on his face; he laughed and said to himself, 'Can a son be born to a man who is a hundred years old? Can Sarah bear a son when she is 18 ninety?' He said to God, 'If only Ishmael might live under thy 19 special care!' But God replied, 'No. Your wife Sarah shall bear you a son, and you shall call him Isaac.[c] With him I will fulfil my covenant, an everlasting covenant with his 20 descendants after him. I have heard your prayer for Ishmael. I have blessed him and will make him fruitful. I will multiply his descendants; he shall be father of twelve princes, and I will raise a 21 great nation from him. But my covenant I will fulfil with Isaac, whom Sarah will bear to you at this 22 season next year.' When he had finished talking with Abraham, God ascended and left him.

23 Then Abraham took Ishmael his son, everyone who had been born in his household and everyone bought with money, every male in his household, and he circumcised them that very same day in the flesh of their foreskins as God had 24 told him to do. Abraham was ninety-nine years old when he cir-

cumcised the flesh of his foreskin. Ishmael was thirteen years old 25 when he was circumcised in the flesh of his foreskin. Both Abraham 26 and Ishmael were circumcised on the same day, and all the men of 27 his household, born in the house or bought with money from foreigners, were circumcised with him.

THE LORD appeared to Abraham 18 by the terebinths of Mamre. As Abraham was sitting at the opening of his tent in the heat of the day, he looked up and saw three men 2 standing in front of him. When he saw them, he ran from the opening of his tent to meet them and bowed low to the ground. 'Sirs,' he said, 3 'if I have deserved your favour, do not pass by my humble self without a visit. Let me send for some water 4 so that you may wash your feet and rest under a tree; and let me 5 fetch a little food so that you may refresh yourselves. Afterwards you may continue the journey which has brought you my way.' They said, 'Do by all means as you say.' So Abraham hurried into the tent 6 to Sarah and said, 'Take three measures of flour quickly, knead it and make some cakes.' Then Abraham 7 ran to the cattle, chose a fine tender calf and gave it to a servant, who hurriedly prepared it. He took 8 curds and milk and the calf he had prepared, set it before them, and waited on them himself under the tree while they ate. They asked 9 him where Sarah his wife was, and he said, 'There, in the tent.' The 10 stranger said, 'About this time next year I will be sure to come back to you, and Sarah your wife shall have a son.' Now Sarah was listening at the opening of the tent, and he was close beside it. Both A- 11 braham and Sarah had grown very old, and Sarah was past the age of child-bearing. So Sarah laughed to 12 herself and said, 'I am past bearing children now that I am out of my

---

[a] *That is* Mockery. [b] *That is* Princess. [c] *That is* He laughed.

13 time, and my husband is old.' The
Lord said to Abraham, 'Why did
Sarah laugh and say, "Shall I indeed bear a child when I am old?"
14 Is anything impossible for the
Lord? In due season I will come
back to you, about this time next
year, and Sarah shall have a son.'
15 Sarah lied because she was frightened, and denied that she had laughed; but he said, 'Yes, you did
laugh.'
16   The men set out and looked down
towards Sodom, and Abraham went
with them to start them on their
17 way. The Lord thought to himself, 'Shall I conceal from Abra-
18 ham what I intend to do? He will
become a great and powerful nation, and all nations on earth
will pray to be blessed as he is
19 blessed. I have taken care of him
on purpose that he may charge his
sons and family after him to conform to the way of the Lord and to
do what is right and just; thus I
shall fulfil all that I have promised
20 for him.' So the Lord said, 'There
is a great outcry over Sodom and
Gomorrah; their sin is very grave.
21 I must go down and see whether
their deeds warrant the outcry
which has reached me. I am re-
22 solved to know the truth.' When
the men turned and went towards
Sodom, Abraham remained stand-
23 ing before the Lord. Abraham
drew near him and said. 'Wilt thou
really sweep away good and bad
24 together? Suppose there are fifty
good men in the city; wilt thou
really sweep it away, and not pardon the place because of the fifty
25 good men? Far be it from thee to
do this – to kill good and bad together; for then the good would
suffer with the bad. Far be it from
thee. Shall not the judge of all the
26 earth do what is just?' The Lord
said, 'If I find in the city of Sodom
fifty good men, I will pardon the
27 whole place for their sake.' Abraham replied, 'May I presume to
speak to the Lord, dust and ashes

that I am: suppose there are five 28
short of the fifty good men? Wilt
thou destroy the whole city for a
mere five men?' He said, 'If I find
forty-five there I will not destroy
it.' Abraham spoke again, 'Sup- 29
pose forty can be found there?';
and he said, 'For the sake of the
forty I will not do it.' Then Abra- 30
ham said, 'Please do not be angry,
O Lord, if I speak again: suppose
thirty can be found there?' He answered, 'If I find thirty there I will
not do it.' Abraham continued, 31
'May I presume to speak to the
Lord: suppose twenty can be found
there?' He replied, 'For the sake of
the twenty I will not destroy it.'
Abraham said, 'I pray thee not to 32
be angry, O Lord, if I speak just
once more: suppose ten can be
found there?' He said, 'For the
sake of the ten I will not destroy it.'
When the Lord had finished talk- 33
ing with Abraham, he left him, and
Abraham returned home.
    The two angels came to Sodom 19
in the evening, and Lot was sitting
in the gateway of the city. When
he saw them he rose to meet them
and bowed low with his face to the
ground. He said, 'I pray you, sirs, 2
turn aside to my humble home,
spend the night there and wash
your feet; you can rise early and
continue your journey.' 'No,' they
answered, 'we will spend the night
in the street.' But Lot was so 3
insistent that they did turn aside
and enter his house. He prepared a
meal for them, baking unleavened
cakes, and they ate them. Before 4
they lay down to sleep, the men
of Sodom, both young and old,
surrounded the house – everyone
without exception. They called to 5
Lot and asked him where the men
were who had entered his house
that night. 'Bring them out', they
shouted, 'so that we can have intercourse with them.'
    Lot went out into the doorway 6
to them, closed the door behind
him and said, 'No, my friends, do 7

8 not be so wicked. Look, I have two daughters, both virgins; let me bring them out to you, and you can do what you like with them; but do not touch these men, because they have come under the shelter of my roof.' 9 They said, 'Out of our way! This man has come and settled here as an alien, and does he now take it upon himself to judge us? We will treat you worse than them.' They crowded in on the man Lot and pressed close to smash in the 10 door. But the two men inside reached out, pulled Lot in, and 11 closed the door. Then they struck the men in the doorway with blindness, both small and great, so that they could not find the door.

12 The two men said to Lot, 'Have you anyone else here, sons-in-law, sons, or daughters, or any who belong to you in the city? Get them 13 out of this place, because we are going to destroy it. The outcry against it has been so great that the 14 LORD has sent us to destroy it.' So Lot went out and spoke to his intended sons-in-law.[a] He said, 'Be quick and leave this place; the LORD is going to destroy the city.' But they did not take him seriously. 15 As soon as it was dawn, the angels urged Lot to go, saying, 'Be quick, take your wife and your two daughters who are here, or you will be 16 swept away when the city is punished.' When he lingered, they took him by the hand, with his wife and his daughters, and, because the LORD had spared him, led him on until he was outside the 17 city. When they had brought them out, they said, 'Flee for your lives; do not look back and do not stop anywhere in the Plain. Flee to the 18 hills or you will be swept away.' Lot 19 replied, 'No, sirs. You have shown your servant favour and you have added to your unfailing care for me by saving my life, but I cannot escape to the hills; I shall be overtaken by the disaster, and die.

Look, here is a town, only a small 20 place, near enough for me to reach quickly. Let me escape to it – it is very small – and save my life.' He 21 said to him, 'I grant your request: I will not overthrow this town you speak of. But flee there quickly, 22 because I can do nothing until you are there.' That is why the place was called Zoar.[b] The sun had risen 23 over the land as Lot entered Zoar; and then the LORD rained down 24 fire and brimstone from the skies on Sodom and Gomorrah. He over- 25 threw these cities and destroyed all the Plain, with everyone living there and everything growing in the ground. But Lot's wife, behind 26 him, looked back, and she turned into a pillar of salt.

Next morning Abraham rose 27 early and went to the place where he had stood in the presence of the LORD. He looked down towards 28 Sodom and Gomorrah and all the wide extent of the Plain, and there he saw thick smoke rising high from the earth like the smoke of a lime-kiln. Thus, when God des- 29 troyed the cities of the Plain, he thought of Abraham and rescued Lot from the disaster, the overthrow of the cities where he had been living.

Lot went up from Zoar and set- 30 tled in the hill-country with his two daughters, because he was afraid to stay in Zoar; he lived with his two daughters in a cave. The 31 elder daughter said to the younger, 'Our father is old and there is not a man in the country to come to us in the usual way. Come now, let us 32 make our father drink wine and then lie with him and in this way keep the family alive through our father.' So that night they gave 33 him wine to drink, and the elder daughter came and lay with him, and he did not know when she lay down and when she got up. Next 34 day the elder said to the younger, 'Last night I lay with my father.

---

[a] Or his sons-in-law, who had married his daughters.   [b] *That is* Small.

17

Let us give him wine to drink again tonight; then you go in and lie with him. So we shall keep the family alive through our father.' 35 So they gave their father wine to drink again that night, and the younger daughter went and lay with him, and he did not know when she lay down and when she 36 got up. In this way both Lot's daughters came to be with child by 37 their father. The elder daughter bore a son and called him Moab; he was the ancestor of the present 38 Moabites. The younger also bore a son, whom she called Ben-ammi; he was the ancestor of the present Ammonites.

20 ABRAHAM journeyed by stages from there into the Negeb, and settled between Kadesh and Shur, 2 living as an alien in Gerar. He said that Sarah his wife was his sister, and Abimelech king of Gerar sent 3 and took her. But God came to Abimelech in a dream by night and said, 'You shall die because of this woman whom you have taken. She 4 is a married woman.' Now Abimelech had not gone near her; and he said, 'Lord, wilt thou destroy 5 an innocent people? Did he not tell me himself that she was his sister, and she herself said that he was her brother. It was with a clear conscience and in all innocence that I 6 did this.' God said to him in the dream, 'Yes: I know that you acted with a clear conscience. Moreover, it was I who held you back from committing a sin against me: that is why I did not let you touch her. 7 Send back the man's wife now; he is a prophet, and he will intercede on your behalf, and you shall live. But if you do not send her back, I tell you that you and all that is yours are doomed to 8 die, you and all that is yours.' So Abimelech rose early in the morning, summoned all his servants and told them the whole story; the 9 men were terrified. Abimelech then summoned Abraham and said to him, 'Why have you treated us like this? What harm have I done to you that you should bring this great sin on me and my kingdom? You have done a thing that ought not to be done.' And he asked A- 10 braham, 'What was your purpose in doing this?' Abraham answered, 11 'I said to myself, There can be no fear of God in this place, and they will kill me for the sake of my wife. She is in fact my sister, she is my 12 father's daughter though not by the same mother; and she became my wife. When God set me wan- 13 dering from my father's house, I said to her, "There is a duty towards me which you must loyally fulfil: wherever we go, you must say that I am your brother."' Then 14 Abimelech took sheep and cattle, and male and female slaves, gave them to Abraham, and returned his wife Sarah to him. Abimelech 15 said, 'My country lies before you; settle wherever you please.' To 16 Sarah he said, 'I have given your brother a thousand pieces of silver, so that your own people may turn a blind eye on it all, and you will be completely vindicated.' Then A- 17 braham interceded with God, and God healed Abimelech, his wife, and his slave-girls, and they bore children; for the LORD had made 18 every woman in Abimelech's household barren on account of Abraham's wife Sarah.

The LORD showed favour to 21 Sarah as he had promised, and made good what he had said about her. She conceived and bore a son 2 to Abraham for his old age, at the time which God had appointed. The son whom Sarah bore to him, 3 Abraham named Isaac.[a] When 4 Isaac was eight days old Abraham circumcised him, as God had commanded. Abraham was a hundred 5 years old when his son Isaac was born. Sarah said, 'God has given 6 me good reason to laugh, and every-

[a] *That is* He laughed.

body who hears will laugh with me.'
7 She said, 'Whoever would have told Abraham that Sarah would suckle children? Yet I have borne him a
8 son for his old age.' The boy grew and was weaned, and on the day of his weaning Abraham gave a feast.
9 Sarah saw the son whom Hagar the Egyptian had borne to Abraham
10 laughing at him, and she said to Abraham, 'Drive out this slave-girl and her son; I will not have this slave-girl's son sharing the in-
11 heritance with my son Isaac.' Abraham was vexed at this on his
12 son Ishmael's account, but God said to him, 'Do not be vexed on account of the boy and the slave-girl. Do what Sarah says, because you shall have descendants through
13 Isaac. I will make a great nation of the slave-girl's son too, because he is your own child.'
14 Abraham rose early in the morning, took some food and a waterskin full of water and gave it to Hagar; he set the child on her shoulder and sent her away, and she went and wandered in the wild-
15 erness of Beersheba. When the water in the skin was finished, she
16 thrust the child under a bush, and went and sat down some way off, about two bowshots away, for she said, 'How can I watch the child die?' So she sat some way off,
17 weeping bitterly. God heard the child crying, and the[a] angel of God called from heaven to Hagar, 'What is the matter, Hagar? Do not be afraid: God has heard the child crying where you laid him.
18 Get to your feet, lift the child up and hold him in your arms, because I will make of him a great nation.'
19 Then God opened her eyes and she saw a well full of water; she went to it, filled her waterskin and gave
20–21 the child a drink. God was with the child, and he grew up and lived in the wilderness of Paran. He became an archer, and his mother found him a wife from Egypt.

22 Now about that time Abimelech, with Phicol the commander of his army, addressed Abraham in these terms: 'God is with you in all that you do. Now swear an oath to me
23 in the name of God, that you will not break faith with me, my offspring, or my descendants. As I have kept faith with you, so shall you keep faith with me and with the country where you have come to live as an alien.' Abraham said,
24 'I swear.' It happened that A-
25 braham had a complaint against Abimelech about a well which Abimelech's men had seized. Abi-
26 melech said, 'I do not know who did this. You never told me, and I have heard nothing about it till now.' So Abraham took sheep and
27 cattle and gave them to Abimelech; and the two of them made a pact. Abraham set seven ewe-
28 lambs apart, and when Abimelech
29 asked him why he had set these lambs apart, he said, 'Accept these
30 from me in token that I dug this well.' Therefore that place was call-
31 ed Beersheba,[b] because there the two of them swore an oath. When
32 they had made the pact at Beersheba, Abimelech and Phicol the commander of his army returned at once to the country of the Philistines, and Abraham planted a strip
33 of ground[c] at Beersheba. There he invoked the LORD, the everlasting God, by name, and he lived as an
34 alien in the country of the Philistines for many a year.

THE time came when God put 22 Abraham to the test. 'Abraham', he called, and Abraham replied, 'Here I am.' God said, 'Take your 2 son Isaac, your only son, whom you love, and go to the land of Moriah. There you shall offer him as a sacrifice on one of the hills which I will show you.' So Abra- 3 ham rose early in the morning and saddled his ass, and he took with him two of his men and his son

[a] *Or* an. [b] *That is* Well of Seven *and* Well of an Oath. [c] *Or* planted a tamarisk.

Isaac; and he split the firewood for the sacrifice, and set out for the 4 place of which God had spoken. On the third day Abraham looked up and saw the place in the distance. 5 He said to his men, 'Stay here with the ass while I and the boy go over there; and when we have worship- 6 ped we will come back to you.' So Abraham took the wood for the sacrifice and laid it on his son Isaac's shoulder; he himself carried the fire and the knife, and the two 7 of them went on together. Isaac said to Abraham, 'Father', and he answered, 'What is it, my son?' Isaac said, 'Here are the fire and the wood, but where is the young 8 beast for the sacrifice?' Abraham answered, 'God will provide himself with a young beast for a sacrifice, my son.' And the two of them 9 went on together and came to the place of which God had spoken. There Abraham built an altar and arranged the wood. He bound his son Isaac and laid him on the altar 10 on top of the wood. Then he stretched out his hand and took 11 the knife to kill his son; but the angel of the LORD called to him from heaven, 'Abraham, Abraham.' He answered, 'Here I am.' 12 The angel of the LORD said, 'Do not raise your hand against the boy; do not touch him. Now I know that you are a God-fearing man. You have not withheld from 13 me your son, your only son.' Abraham looked up, and there he saw a ram caught by its horns in a thicket. So he went and took the ram and offered it as a sacrifice instead 14 of his son. Abraham named that place Jehovah-jireh;[a] and to this day the saying is: 'In the mountain 15 of the LORD it was provided.' Then the angel of the LORD called from heaven a second time to Abraham, 16 'This is the word of the LORD: By my own self I swear: inasmuch as you have done this and have not withheld your son, your only son,

I will bless you abundantly and 17 greatly multiply your descendants until they are as numerous as the stars in the sky and the grains of sand on the sea-shore. Your descendants shall possess the cities of their enemies. All nations on earth shall 18 pray to be blessed as your descendants are blessed, and this because you have obeyed me.'

Abraham went back to his men, 19 and together they returned to Beersheba; and there Abraham remained.

After this Abraham was told, 20 'Milcah has borne sons to your brother Nahor: Uz his first-born, then 21 his brother Buz, and Kemuel father of Aram, and Kesed, Hazo, Pildash, 22 Jidlaph and Bethuel; and a daugh- 23 ter, Rebecca, has been born to Bethuel.' These eight Milcah bore to Abraham's brother Nahor. His 24 concubine, whose name was Reumah, also bore him sons: Tebah, Gaham, Tahash and Maacah.

Sarah lived for a hundred and 23 twenty-seven years, and died in 2 Kiriath-arba, which is Hebron, in Canaan. Abraham went in to mourn over Sarah and to weep for her. At last he rose and left the 3 presence of the dead. He said to the Hittites, 'I am an alien and a 4 settler among you. Give me land enough for a burial-place, so that I can give my dead proper burial.' The Hittites answered Abraham, 5 'Do, pray, listen to what we have 6 to say, sir. You are a mighty prince among us. Bury your dead in the best grave we have. There is not one of us who will deny you his grave or hinder you from burying your dead.' Abraham stood up and 7 then bowed low to the Hittites, the people of that country. He said to 8 them, 'If you are willing to let me give my dead proper burial, then listen to me and speak for me to Ephron son of Zohar, asking him 9 to give me the cave that belongs to him at Machpelah, at the far end of

[a] *That is* the LORD will provide.

his land. Let him give it to me for the full price, so that I may take possession of it as a burial-place 10 within your territory.' Ephron the Hittite was sitting with the others, and he gave Abraham this answer in the hearing of everyone as they 11 came into the city gate: 'No, sir; hear what I have to say. I will make you a gift of the land and I will also give you the cave which is on it. In the presence of all my kinsmen I give it to you; so bury 12 your dead.' Abraham bowed low before the people of the country 13 and said to Ephron in their hearing, 'If you really mean it – but do listen to me! I give you the price of the land: take it and I will bury my 14 dead there.' And Ephron answer- 15 ed, 'Do listen to me, sir: the land is worth four hundred shekels of silver. But what is that between you and me? There you may bury your 16 dead.' Abraham came to an agreement with him and weighed out the amount that Ephron had named in the hearing of the Hittites, four hundred shekels of the standard recognized by merchants. 17 Thus the plot of land belonging to Ephron at Machpelah to the east of Mamre, the plot, the cave that is on it, every tree on the plot, within 18 the whole area, became the legal possession of Abraham, in the presence of all the Hittites as they 19 came into the city gate. After this Abraham buried his wife Sarah in the cave on the plot of land at Machpelah to the east of Mamre, 20 which is Hebron, in Canaan. Thus the plot and the cave on it became Abraham's possession as a burial-place, by purchase from the Hittites.

24 By this time Abraham had become a very old man, and the LORD had blessed him in all that he 2 did. Abraham said to his servant, who had been long in his service and was in charge of all his posses-

sions, 'Put your hand under my thigh: I want you to swear by the 3 LORD, the God of heaven and earth, that you will not take a wife for my son from the women of the Canaanites in whose land I dwell; you must go to my own country 4 and to my own kindred to find a wife for my son Isaac.' The ser- 5 vant said to him, 'What if the woman is unwilling to come with me to this country? Must I in that event take your son back to the land from which you came?' Abra- 6 ham said to him, 'On no account are you to take my son back there. The LORD the God of heaven who 7 took me from my father's house and the land of my birth, the LORD who swore to me that he would give this land to my descendants – he will send his angel before you, and from there you shall take a wife for my son. If the woman is unwilling 8 to come with you, then you will be released from your oath to me; but you must not take my son back there.' So the servant put his 9 hand under his master Abraham's thigh and swore an oath in those terms.

The servant took ten camels 10 from his master's herds, and also all kinds of gifts from his master; he set out for Aram-naharaim[a] and arrived at the city where Nahor lived. Towards evening, the time 11 when the women come out to draw water, he made the camels kneel down by the well outside the city. He said, 'O LORD God of my mast- 12 er Abraham, give me good fortune this day; keep faith with my master Abraham. Here I stand by the 13 spring, and the women of the city are coming out to draw water. Let 14 it be like this: I shall say to a girl, "Please lower your jar so that I may drink"; and if she answers, "Drink, and I will water your camels also", that will be the girl whom thou dost intend for thy servant Isaac. In this way I shall know

[a] *That is* Aram of Two Rivers.

21

that thou hast kept faith with my master.'

15 Before he had finished praying silently, he saw Rebecca coming out with her water-jug on her shoulder. She was the daughter of Bethuel son of Milcah, the wife of 16 Abraham's brother Nahor. The girl was very beautiful, a virgin, who had had no intercourse with a man. She went down to the spring, filled her jar and came up again. 17 Abraham's servant hurried to meet her and said, 'Give me a sip of 18 water from your jar.' 'Drink, sir', she answered, and at once lowered her jar on to her hand to let him 19 drink. When she had finished giving him a drink, she said, 'Now I will draw water for your camels 20 until they have had enough.' So she quickly emptied her jar into the water-trough, hurried again to the well to draw water and watered 21 all the camels. The man was watching quietly to see whether or not the LORD had made his journey 22 successful. When the camels had finished drinking, the man took a gold nose-ring weighing half a shekel, and two bracelets for her wrists weighing ten shekels, also of gold, 23 and said, 'Tell me, please, whose daughter you are. Is there room in your father's house for us to spend 24 the night?' She answered, 'I am the daughter of Bethuel, the son of 25 Nahor and Milcah; and we have plenty of straw and fodder and also room for you to spend the night.' 26 So the man bowed down and pro-27 strated himself to the LORD. He said, 'Blessed be the LORD the God of my master Abraham, who has not failed to keep faith and truth with my master; for I have been guided by the LORD to the house of my master's kinsman.'

28 The girl ran to her mother's house and told them what had hap-29-30 pened. Now Rebecca had a brother named Laban; and, when he saw the nose-ring, and also the bracelets on his sister's wrists, and heard his sister Rebecca tell what the man had said to her, he ran out to the man at the spring. When he came to him and found him still standing there by the camels, he 31 said, 'Come in, sir, whom the LORD has blessed. Why stay outside? I have prepared the house, and there is room for the camels.' So he 32 brought the man into the house, unloaded the camels and provided straw and fodder for them, and water for him and all his men to wash their feet. Food was set be- 33 fore him, but he said, 'I will not eat until I have delivered my message.' Laban said, 'Let us hear it.' He 34 answered, 'I am the servant of A-braham. The LORD has greatly 35 blessed my master, and he has be-come a man of power. The LORD has given him flocks and herds, sil-ver and gold, male and female slaves, camels and asses. My mas- 36 ter's wife Sarah in her old age bore him a son, to whom he has given all that he has. So my master made 37 me swear an oath, saying, "You shall not take a wife for my son from the women of the Canaanites in whose land I dwell; but you shall 38 go to my father's house and to my family to find a wife for him." So 39 I said to my master, "What if the woman will not come with me?" He answered, "The LORD, in whose 40 presence I have lived, will send his angel with you and will make your journey successful. You shall take a wife for my son from my family and from my father's house; then 41 you shall be released from the charge I have laid upon you. But if, when you come to my family, they will not give her to you, you shall still be released from the charge." So I came to the spring 42 today, and I said, "O LORD God of my master Abraham, if thou wilt make my journey successful, let 43 it be like this. Here I stand by the spring. When a young woman comes out to draw water, I shall say to her, 'Give me a little water

44 to drink from your jar.' If she answers, 'Yes, do drink, and I will draw water for your camels as well', she is the woman whom the LORD intends for my master's 45 son." Before I had finished praying silently, I saw Rebecca coming out with her water-jar on her shoulder. She went down to the spring and drew some water, and I said to her, 46 "Please give me a drink." She quickly lowered her jar from her shoulder and said, "Drink; and I will water your camels as well." So I drank, and she also gave my cam- 47 els water. I asked her whose daughter she was, and she said, "I am the daughter of Bethuel, the son of Nahor and Milcah." Then I put the ring in her nose and the brace- 48 lets on her wrists, and I bowed low and prostrated myself before the LORD. I blessed the LORD the God of my master Abraham, who had led me by the right road to take my 49 master's niece for his son. Now tell me if you will keep faith and truth with my master. If not, say so, and I will turn elsewhere.'

50 Laban and Bethuel answered, 'This is from the LORD; we can say 51 nothing for or against. Here is Rebecca herself; take her and go. She shall be the wife of your master's son, as the LORD has decreed.' 52 When Abraham's servant heard what they said, he prostrated himself on the ground before the LORD. 53 Then he brought out gold and silver ornaments, and robes, and gave them to Rebecca, and he gave costly gifts to her brother and her 54 mother. He and his men then ate and drank and spent the night there. When they rose in the morning, he said, 'Give me leave to go 55 back to my master.' Her brother and her mother said, 'Let the girl stay with us for a few days, say ten 56 days, and then she shall go.' But he said to them, 'Do not detain me, for the LORD has granted me suc-

cess. Give me leave to return to my master.' They said, 'Let us call the 57 girl and see what she says.' They 58 called Rebecca and asked her if she would go with the man, and she said, 'Yes, I will go.' So they let 59 their sister Rebecca and her nurse go with Abraham's servant and his men. They blessed Rebecca and 60 said to her:

'You are our sister, may you be the mother of myriads; may your sons possess the cities of their enemies.'

Then Rebecca and her companions 61 mounted their camels at once and followed the man. So the servant took Rebecca and went his way.

Isaac meanwhile had moved on 62 as far as Beer-lahai-roi and was living in the Negeb. One evening 63 when he had gone out into the open country hoping to meet them,[a] he looked up and saw camels approaching. When Rebecca raised 64 her eyes and saw Isaac, she slipped hastily from her camel, saying to 65 the servant, 'Who is that man walking across the open towards us?' The servant answered, 'It is my master.' So she took her veil and covered herself. The servant 66 related to Isaac all that had happened. Isaac conducted her into 67 the tent[b] and took her as his wife. So she became his wife, and he loved her and was consoled for the death of his mother.

ABRAHAM married another wife, 25 1[c] whose name was Keturah. She 2 bore him Zimran, Jokshan, Medan, Midian, Ishbak and Shuah. Jokshan 3 became the father of Sheba and Dedan. The sons of Dedan were Asshurim, Letushim and Leummim, and the sons of Midian were Ephah, 4 Epher, Enoch, Abida and Eldaah. All these were descendants of Keturah.

Abraham had given all that he 5

---

[a] hoping . . . them: *or* to relieve himself.
[b] *Prob. rdg.* ; *Heb. adds* Sarah his mother.
[c] *Verses 1–4: cp.* 1 *Chr.* 1. 32, 33.

6 had to Isaac; and he had already in his lifetime given presents to the sons of his concubines, and had sent them away eastwards, to a land of the east, out of his son 7 Isaac's way. Abraham had lived for a hundred and seventy-five 8 years when he breathed his last. He died at a good old age, after a very long life, and was gathered to 9 his father's kin. His sons, Isaac and Ishmael, buried him in the cave at Machpelah, on the land of Ephron son of Zohar the Hittite, east of 10 Mamre, the plot which Abraham had bought from the Hittites. There Abraham was buried with 11 his wife Sarah. After the death of Abraham, God blessed his son Isaac, who settled close by Beer-lahai-roi.

12   This is the table of the descendants of Abraham's son Ishmael, whom Hagar the Egyptian, Sarah's 13[a] slave-girl, bore to him. These are the names of the sons of Ishmael named in order of their birth: Nebaioth, Ishmael's eldest son, then 14 Kedar, Adbeel, Mibsam, Mishma, 15 Dumah, Massa, Hadad, Teman, Jetur, Naphish and Kedemah. 16 These are the sons of Ishmael, after whom their hamlets and encampments were named, twelve princes according to their tribal groups. 17 Ishmael had lived for a hundred and thirty-seven years when he breathed his last. So he died and was gathered to his father's kin. 18 Ishmael's sons inhabited the land from Havilah to Shur, which is east of Egypt on the way to Asshur, having settled to the east of his brothers.

19 THIS is the table of the descendants of Abraham's son Isaac. 20 Isaac's father was Abraham. When Isaac was forty years old he married Rebecca the daughter of Bethuel the Aramaean from Paddan-aram and the sister of Laban the Aramaean. Isaac appealed to the 21 LORD on behalf of his wife because she was barren; the LORD yielded to his entreaty, and Rebecca conceived. The children pressed hard 22 on each other in her womb, and she said, 'If this is how it is with me, what does it mean?' So she went to seek guidance of the LORD. The 23 LORD said to her:

'Two nations in your womb,
two peoples, going their own ways
   from birth!
One shall be stronger than the
   other;
the older shall be servant to the
   younger.'

When her time had come, there 24 were indeed twins in her womb. The first came out red, hairy all 25 over like a hair-cloak, and they named him Esau.[b] Immediately 26 afterwards his brother was born with his hand grasping Esau's heel, and they called him Jacob.[c] Isaac was sixty years old when they were born. The boys grew up; 27 and Esau became skilful in hunting, a man of the open plains, but Jacob led a settled life and stayed among the tents. Isaac favoured 28 Esau because he kept him supplied with venison, but Rebecca favoured Jacob. One day Jacob prepared 29 a broth and when Esau came in from the country, exhausted, he 30 said to Jacob, 'I am exhausted; let me swallow some of that red broth': this is why he was called Edom.[d] Jacob said, 'Not till you sell me 31 your rights as the first-born.' Esau 32 replied, 'I am at death's door; what use is my birthright to me?' Jacob 33 said, 'Not till you swear!'; so he swore an oath and sold his birthright to Jacob. Then Jacob gave 34 Esau bread and the lentil broth, and he ate and drank and went away without more ado. Thus Esau showed how little he valued his birthright.

---

[a] Verses 13–16: cp. 1 Chr. 1. 29–31.　　[b] That is Covering.
[c] That is He caught by the heel.　　[d] That is Red.

26 There came a famine in the land – not the earlier famine in Abraham's time – and Isaac went to Abimelech the Philistine king at ² Gerar. The LORD appeared to Isaac and said, 'Do not go down to Egypt, but stay in this country as ³ I bid you. Stay in this country and I will be with you and bless you, for to you and to your descendants I will give all these lands. Thus shall I fulfil the oath which I swore ⁴ to your father Abraham. I will make your descendants as many as the stars in the sky; I will give them all these lands, and all the nations of the earth will pray to be ⁵ blessed as they are blessed – all because Abraham obeyed me and kept my charge, my commandments, my statutes, and my laws.' ⁶ So Isaac lived in Gerar.

⁷ When the men of the place asked him about his wife, he told them that she was his sister; he was afraid to say that Rebecca was his wife, in case they killed him because of her; for she was very ⁸ beautiful. When they had been there for some considerable time, Abimelech the Philistine king looked down from his window and saw Isaac and his wife Rebecca laugh-⁹ ing together. He summoned Isaac and said, 'So she is your wife, is she? What made you say she was your sister?' Isaac answered, 'I ¹⁰ thought I should be killed because of her.' Abimelech said, 'Why have you treated us like this? One of the people might easily have gone to bed with your wife, and then you would have made us liable to retri-¹¹ bution.' So Abimelech warned all the people, threatening that whoever touched this man or his wife would be put to death.

¹² Isaac sowed seed in that land, and that year he reaped a hundred-¹³ fold, and the LORD blessed him. He became more and more powerful, until he was very powerful indeed.

He had flocks and herds and many ¹⁴ slaves, so that the Philistines were envious of him. They had stopped ¹⁵ up all the wells dug by the slaves in the days of Isaac's father Abraham, and filled them with earth. Isaac dug them again, all those ¹⁸ wells dug in his father Abraham's time, and stopped up by the Philistines after his death, and he called them by the names which his father had given them.

Then Abimelech said to him, ¹⁶ 'Go away from here; you are too strong for us.' So Isaac left that ¹⁷ place and encamped in the valley of Gerar, and stayed there. Then ¹⁹ᵃ Isaac's slaves dug in the valley and found a spring of running water, but the shepherds of Gerar quarrel-²⁰ led with Isaac's shepherds, claiming the water as theirs. He called the well Esek,ᵇ because they made difficulties for him. His men then ²¹ dug another well, but the others quarrelled with him over that also, so he called it Sitnah.ᶜ He ²² moved on from there and dug another well, but there was no quarrel over that one, so he called it Rehoboth,ᵈ saying, 'Now the LORD has given us plenty of room and we shall be fruitful in the land.'

Isaac went up country from there ²³ to Beersheba. That same night the ²⁴ LORD appeared to him there and said, 'I am the God of your father Abraham. Fear nothing, for I am with you. I will bless you and give you many descendants for the sake of Abraham my servant.' So Isaac ²⁵ built an altar there and invoked the LORD by name. Then he pitched his tent there, and there also his slaves dug a well. Abimelech came ²⁶ to him from Gerar with Ahuzzath his friend and Phicol the commander of his army. Isaac said to them, ²⁷ 'Why have you come here? You hate me and you sent me away.' They answered, 'We have seen ²⁸ plainly that the LORD is with you,

---

ᵃ *Verse 18 transposed to follow 15.*
ᶜ *That is Enmity.*

ᵇ *That is Difficulty.*
ᵈ *That is Plenty of room.*

so we thought, "Let the two of us put each other to the oath and make a treaty that will bind us."
29 We have not attacked you, we have done you nothing but good, and we let you go away peaceably. Swear that you will do us no harm, now that the LORD has blessed
30 you.' So Isaac gave a feast and
31 they ate and drank. They rose early in the morning and exchanged oaths. Then Isaac bade them farewell, and they parted from him in
32 peace. The same day Isaac's slaves came and told him about a well that they had dug: 'We have found
33 water', they said. He named the well Shibah.*a* This is why the city is called Beersheba*b* to this day.
34 When Esau was forty years old he married Judith daughter of Beeri the Hittite, and Basemath
35 daughter of Elon the Hittite; this was a bitter grief to Isaac and Rebecca.

Jacob and Esau

27 WHEN Isaac grew old and his eyes became so dim that he could not see, he called his elder son Esau and said to him, 'My son', and he
2 answered, 'Here I am.' Isaac said, 'Listen now: I am old and I do not
3 know when I may die. Take your hunting gear, your quiver and your bow, and go out into the country and get me some venison.
4 Then make me a savoury dish of the kind I like, and bring it to me to eat so that I may give you my
5 blessing before I die.' Now Rebecca was listening as Isaac talked to his son Esau. When Esau went off into the country to find some veni-
6 son and bring it home, she said to her son Jacob, 'I heard your father talking to your brother Esau, and
7 he said, "Bring me some venison and make it into a savoury dish so that I may eat it and bless you in the presence of the LORD before I
8 die." Listen to me, my son, and do

what I tell you. Go to the flock and 9 pick me out two fine young kids, and I will make them into a savoury dish for your father, of the kind he likes. Then take them in to 10 your father, and he will eat them so that he may bless you before he dies.' Jacob said to his mother Re- 11 becca, 'But my brother Esau is a hairy man, and my skin is smooth. Suppose my father feels me, he will 12 know I am tricking him and I shall bring a curse upon myself instead of a blessing.' His mother answered 13 him, 'Let the curse fall on me, my son, but do as I say; go and bring me the kids.' So Jacob fetched 14 them and brought them to his mother, who made them into a savoury dish of the kind that his father liked. Then Rebecca took her elder 15 son's clothes, Esau's best clothes which she kept by her in the house, and put them on her younger son Jacob. She put the goatskins on 16 his hands and on the smooth nape of his neck; and she handed her son 17 Jacob the savoury dish and the bread she had made. He came to 18 his father and said, 'Father.' He answered, 'Yes, my son; who are you?' Jacob answered his father, 19 'I am Esau, your elder son. I have done as you told me. Come, sit up and eat some of my venison, so that you may give me your blessing.' Isaac said to his son, 'What is this 20 that you found so quickly?', and Jacob answered, 'It is what the LORD your God put in my way.' Isaac then said to Jacob, 'Come 21 close and let me feel you, my son, to see whether you are really my son Esau.' When Jacob came close 22 to his father, Isaac felt him and said, 'The voice is Jacob's voice, but the hands are the hands of Esau.' He did not recognize him 23 because his hands were hairy like Esau's, and that is why he blessed him. He said, 'Are you really my 24 son Esau?', and he answered, 'Yes.' Then Isaac said, 'Bring me some of 25

a That is Oath.   *b That is Well of an Oath.*

your venison to eat, my son, so that I may give you my blessing.' Then Jacob brought it to him, and he ate it; he brought wine also, and he
26 drank it. Then his father Isaac said to him, 'Come near, my son, and
27 kiss me.' So he came near and kissed him, and when Isaac smelt the smell of his clothes, he blessed him and said:

'Ah! The smell of my son is like the smell of open country
blessed by the LORD.
28 God give you dew from heaven and the richness of the earth, corn and new wine in plenty!
29 Peoples shall serve you, nations bow down to you.
Be lord over your brothers; may your mother's sons bow down to you.
A curse upon those who curse you; a blessing on those who bless you!'

30 Isaac finished blessing Jacob; and Jacob had scarcely left his father Isaac's presence, when his brother Esau came in from his
31 hunting. He too made a savoury dish and brought it to his father. He said, 'Come, father, and eat some of my venison, so that you
32 may give me your blessing.' His father Isaac said, 'Who are you?' He said, 'I am Esau, your elder
33 son.' Then Isaac became greatly agitated[a] and said, 'Then who was it that hunted and brought me venison? I ate it all before you came in and I blessed him, and the
34 blessing will stand.' When Esau heard what his father said, he gave a loud and bitter cry and said,
35 'Bless me too, father.' But Isaac said, 'Your brother came treacherously and took away your blessing.'
36 Esau said, 'He is rightly called Jacob.[b] This is the second time he has supplanted me. He took away my right as the first-born and now he has taken away my blessing. Have you kept back any blessing for me?'
37 Isaac answered, 'I have made him

lord over you, and I have given him all his brothers as slaves. I have bestowed upon him corn and new wine for his sustenance. What is there left that I can do for you,
38 my son?' Esau asked his father, 'Had you then only one blessing, father? Bless me too, my father.'
39 And Esau cried bitterly. Then his father Isaac answered:

'Your dwelling shall be far from the richness of the earth,
far from the dew of heaven above.
40 By your sword shall you live, and you shall serve your brother; but the time will come when you grow restive
and break off his yoke from your neck.'

41 Esau bore a grudge against Jacob because of the blessing which his father had given him, and he said to himself, 'The time of mourning for my father will soon be here; then I will kill my brother Jacob.'
42 When Rebecca was told what her elder son Esau was saying, she called her younger son Jacob, and she said to him, 'Esau your brother is
43 threatening to kill you. Now, my son, listen to me. Slip away at once to my brother Laban in Harran.
44 Stay with him for a while until your brother's anger cools. When
45 it has subsided and he forgets what you have done to him, I will send and fetch you back. Why should I lose you both in one day?'

46 Rebecca said to Isaac, 'I am weary to death of Hittite women! If Jacob marries a Hittite woman like those who live here, my life will
28 not be worth living.' Isaac called Jacob, blessed him and gave him instructions. He said, 'You must not marry one of these women of
2 Canaan. Go at once to the house of Bethuel, your mother's father, in Paddan-aram, and there find a wife, one of the daughters of Laban, your mother's brother. God Almighty
3 bless you, make you fruitful and

---

[a] *Or* incensed.   [b] *That is* He supplanted.

increase your descendants until they become a host of nations.

4 May he bestow on you and your offspring the blessing of Abraham, and may you thus possess the country where you are now living, the land which God gave to Abra-

5 ham!' So Isaac sent Jacob away, and he went to Paddan-aram to Laban, son of Bethuel the Aramaean, and brother to Rebecca the mother of Jacob and Esau.

6 Esau discovered that Isaac had given Jacob his blessing and had sent him away to Paddan-aram to find a wife there; and that when he blessed him he had forbidden him

7 to marry a woman of Canaan, and that Jacob had obeyed his father and mother and gone to Paddan-

8 aram. Then Esau, seeing that his father disliked the women of Can-

9 aan, went to Ishmael, and, in addition to his other wives, he married Mahalath sister of Nebaioth and daughter of Abraham's son Ishmael.

10 Jacob set out from Beersheba and went on his way towards Har-

11 ran. He came to a certain place and stopped there for the night, because the sun had set; and, taking one of the stones there, he made it a pillow for his head and lay down

12 to sleep. He dreamt that he saw a ladder, which rested on the ground with its top reaching to heaven, and angels of God were going up

13 and down upon it. The LORD was standing beside him[a] and said, 'I am the LORD, the God of your father Abraham and the God of Isaac. This land on which you are lying I will give to you and your

14 descendants. They shall be countless as the dust upon the earth, and you shall spread far and wide, to north and south, to east and west. All the families of the earth shall pray to be blessed as you and your

15 descendants are blessed. I will be with you, and I will protect you wherever you go and will bring you

back to this land; for I will not leave you until I have done all that I have promised.' Jacob woke from 16 his sleep and said, 'Truly the LORD is in this place, and I did not know it.' Then he was afraid and said, 17 'How fearsome is this place! This is no other than the house of God, this is the gate of heaven.' Jacob 18 rose early in the morning, took the stone on which he had laid his head, set it up as a sacred pillar and poured oil on the top of it. He 19 named that place Beth-El;[b] but the earlier name of the city was Luz.

Thereupon Jacob made this vow: 20 'If God will be with me, if he will protect me on my journey and give me food to eat and clothes to wear, and I come back safely to my fa- 21 ther's house, then the LORD shall be my God, and this stone which I 22 have set up as a sacred pillar shall be a house of God. And of all that thou givest me, I will without fail allot a tenth part to thee.'

JACOB continued his journey and 29 came to the land of the eastern tribes. There he saw a well in the 2 open country and three flocks of sheep lying beside it, because the flocks were watered from that well. Over its mouth was a huge stone, and all the herdsmen used to ga- 3 ther there and roll it off the mouth of the well and water the flocks; then they would put it back in its place over the well. Jacob said to 4 them, 'Where are you from, my friends?' 'We are from Harran', they replied. He asked them if they 5 knew Laban the grandson of Nahor. They answered, 'Yes, we do.' 'Is he well?' Jacob asked; and they 6 answered, 'Yes, he is well, and here is his daughter Rachel coming with the flock.' Jacob said, 'The sun is 7 still high, and the time for folding the sheep has not yet come. Water the flocks and then go and graze them.' But they replied, 'We can- 8 not, until all the herdsmen have

---

[a] *Or* on it *or* by it.   [b] *That is* House of God.

gathered together and the stone is rolled away from the mouth of the well; then we can water our flocks.' 9 While he was talking to them, Rachel came up with her father's flock, for she was a shepherdess. 10 When Jacob saw Rachel, the daughter of Laban his mother's brother, with Laban's flock, he stepped forward, rolled the stone off the mouth of the well and wa- 11 tered Laban's sheep. He kissed Ra- 12 chel, and was moved to tears. He told her that he was her father's kinsman and Rebecca's son; so she 13 ran and told her father. When Laban heard the news of his sister's son Jacob, he ran to meet him, embraced him, kissed him warmly and welcomed him to his home. 14 Jacob told Laban everything, and Laban said, 'Yes, you are my own flesh and blood.' So Jacob stayed with him for a whole month.

15 Laban said to Jacob, 'Why should you work for me for nothing simply because you are my kinsman? Tell me what your wages 16 ought to be.' Now Laban had two daughters: the elder was called Leah, and the younger Rachel. 17 Leah was dull-eyed, but Rachel 18 was graceful and beautiful. Jacob had fallen in love with Rachel and he said, 'I will work seven years for your younger daughter Rachel.' 19 Laban replied, 'It is better that I should give her to you than to any- 20 one else; stay with me.' So Jacob worked seven years for Rachel, and they seemed like a few days 21 because he loved her. Then Jacob said to Laban, 'I have served my time. Give me my wife so that we 22 may sleep together.' So Laban gathered all the men of the place to- 23 gether and gave a feast. In the evening he took his daughter Leah and brought her to Jacob, and Ja- 24 cob slept with her. At the same time Laban gave his slave-girl Zil- 25 pah to his daughter Leah. But when morning came, Jacob saw that it was Leah and said to Laban, 'What have you done to me? Did I not work for Rachel? Why have you deceived me?' Laban answer- 26 ed, 'In our country it is not right to give the younger sister in marriage before the elder. Go through with 27 the seven days' feast for the elder, and the younger shall be given you in return for a further seven years' work.' Jacob agreed, and com- 28 pleted the seven days for Leah.

Then Laban gave Jacob his daughter Rachel as wife; and he 29 gave his slave-girl Bilhah to serve his daughter Rachel. Jacob slept 30 with Rachel also; he loved her rather than Leah, and he worked for Laban for a further seven years. When the LORD saw that Leah was 31 not loved, he granted her a child; but Rachel was childless. Leah 32 conceived and bore a son; and she called him Reuben,[a] for she said, 'The LORD has seen my humiliation; now my husband will love me.' Again she conceived and bore 33 a son and said, 'The LORD, hearing that I am not loved, has given me this child also'; and she called him Simeon.[b] She conceived again and 34 bore a son; and she said, 'Now that I have borne him three sons my husband and I will surely be united.' So she called him Levi.[c] Once 35 more she conceived and bore a son; and she said, 'Now I will praise the LORD'; therefore she named him Judah.[d] Then for a while she bore no more children.

When Rachel found that she 30 bore Jacob no children, she became jealous of her sister and said to Jacob, 'Give me sons, or I shall die.' Jacob said angrily to Rachel, 2 'Can I take the place of God, who has denied you children?' She said, 3 'Here is my slave-girl Bilhah. Lie with her, so that she may bear sons to be laid upon my knees, and through her I too may build up a family.' So she gave him her slave- 4 girl Bilhah as a wife, and Jacob lay

---

[a] *That is* See, a son. [b] *That is* Hearing. [c] *That is* Union. [d] *That is* Praise.

5 with her. Bilhah conceived and
6 bore Jacob a son. Then Rachel
said, 'God has given judgement for
me; he has indeed heard me and
given me a son', so she named him
7 Dan.^a Rachel's slave-girl Bilhah a-
gain conceived and bore Jacob
8 another son. Rachel said, 'I have
played a fine trick on my sister,
and it has succeeded'; so she
9 named him Naphtali.^b When Leah
found that she was bearing no
more children, she took her slave-
girl Zilpah and gave her to Jacob
10 as a wife, and Zilpah bore Jacob a
11 son. Leah said, 'Good fortune has
come', and she named him Gad.^c
12 Zilpah, Leah's slave-girl, bore Ja-
13 cob another son, and Leah said,
'Happiness has come, for young
women will call me happy.' So she
named him Asher.^d
14 In the time of wheat-harvest
Reuben went out and found some
mandrakes in the open country
and brought them to his mother
Leah. Then Rachel asked Leah for
15 some of her son's mandrakes, but
Leah said, 'Is it so small a thing to
have taken away my husband, that
you should take my son's mandrakes as well?' But Rachel said,
'Very well, let him sleep with you
tonight in exchange for your son's
16 mandrakes.' So when Jacob came
in from the country in the evening,
Leah went out to meet him and
said, 'You are to sleep with me tonight; I have hired you with my
son's mandrakes.' That night he
17 slept with her, and God heard
Leah's prayer, and she conceived
18 and bore a fifth son. Leah said,
'God has rewarded me, because I
gave my slave-girl to my husband.'
19 So she named him Issachar.^e Leah
again conceived and bore a sixth
20 son. She said, 'God has endowed
me with a noble dowry. Now my
husband will treat me in princely

style, because I have borne him six
sons.' So she named him Zebulun.^f
21 Later she bore a daughter and
22 named her Dinah. Then God
thought of Rachel; he heard her
23 prayer and gave her a child; so she
conceived and bore a son and said,
'God has taken away my humilia-
24 tion.' She named him Joseph,^g saying, 'May the LORD add another
son!'
25 When Rachel had given birth to
Joseph, Jacob said to Laban, 'Let
me go, for I wish to return to my
26 own home and country. Give me
my wives and my children for
whom I have served you, and I
will go; for you know what service
27 I have done for you.' Laban said to
him, 'Let me have my say, if you
please. I have become prosperous
and the LORD has blessed me for
28 your sake. So now tell me what I
owe you in wages, and I will give it
29 you.' Jacob answered, 'You must
know how I have served you, and
how your herds have prospered
30 under my care. You had only a few
when I came, but now they have
increased beyond measure, and
the LORD brought blessings to you
wherever I went. But is it not time
for me to provide for my family?'
31 Laban said, 'Then what shall I give
you?', but Jacob answered, 'Give
me nothing; I will mind your
flocks^h as before, if you will do what
32 I suggest. Today I will go over
your flocks and pick out from them
every black lamb, and all the
brindled and the spotted goats,
33 and they shall be my wages. This is
a fair offer, and it will be to my own
disadvantage later on, when we
come to settling my wages: every
goat amongst mine that is not spotted or brindled and every lamb
that is not black will have been
34 stolen.' Laban said, 'Agreed; let it
35 be as you have said.' But that day

---

^a *That is* He has given judgement.   ^b *That is* Trickery.
^c *That is* Good Fortune.   ^d *That is* Happy.   ^e *That is* Reward.
^f *That is* Prince.   ^g *The name may mean either* He takes away *or* May he add.
^h *Prob. rdg.; Heb. adds* I will watch.

he removed the he-goats that were striped and brindled and all the spotted and brindled she-goats, all that had any white on them, and every ram that was black, and he handed them over to his own sons.

36 Then he put a distance of three days' journey between himself and Jacob, while Jacob was left tending those of Laban's flocks that 37 remained. Thereupon Jacob took fresh rods of white poplar, almond, and plane tree, and peeled off strips of bark, exposing the white of the 38 rods. Then he fixed the peeled rods upright in the troughs at the watering-places where the flocks came to drink; they faced the she-goats that were on heat when they 39 came to drink. They felt a longing for the rods and they gave birth to young that were striped and spot- 40 ted and brindled. As for the rams, Jacob divided them, and let the ewes run only with such of the rams in Laban's flock as were striped and black; and thus he bred separate flocks for himself, which he did not add to Laban's sheep. 41 As for the goats, whenever the more vigorous were on heat, he put the rods in front of them at the troughs so that they would long 42 for the rods; he did not put them there for the weaker goats. Thus the weaker came to be Laban's and 43 the stronger Jacob's. So Jacob increased in wealth more and more until he possessed great flocks, male and female slaves, camels, and asses.

31 JACOB learnt that Laban's sons were saying, 'Jacob has taken everything that was our father's, and all his wealth has come from 2 our father's property.' He also noticed that Laban was not so well disposed to him as he had once 3 been. Then the LORD said to Jacob, 'Go back to the land of your fathers and to your kindred. I will be 4 with you.' So Jacob sent to fetch Rachel and Leah to his flocks out

in the country and said to them, 'I 5 see that your father is not as well disposed to me as once he was; yet the God of my father has been with me. You know how I have served 6 your father to the best of my power, but he has cheated me and 7 changed my wages ten times over. Yet God did not let him do me any harm. If Laban said, "The spotted 8 ones shall be your wages", then all the flock bore spotted young; and if he said, "The striped ones shall be your wages", then all the flock bore striped young. God has taken 9 away your father's property and has given it to me. In the season 10 when the flocks were on heat, I had a dream: I looked up and saw that the he-goats mounting the flock were striped and spotted and dappled. The angel of God said to me 11 in my dream, "Jacob", and I replied, "Here I am", and he said, 12 "Look up and see: all the he-goats mounting the flock are striped and spotted and dappled. I have seen all that Laban is doing to you. I am 13 the God who appeared to you at Bethel where you anointed a sacred pillar and where you made your vow. Now leave this country at once and return to the land of your birth."' Rachel and Leah answered 14 him, 'We no longer have any part or lot in our father's house. Does he 15 not look on us as foreigners, now that he has sold us and spent on himself the whole of the money paid for us? But all the wealth which God 16 has saved from our father's clutches is ours and our children's. Now do everything that God has said.' Ja- 17 cob at once set his sons and his wives on camels, and drove off all 18 the herds and livestock which he had acquired in Paddan-aram, to go to his father Isaac in Canaan.

When Laban the Aramaean had 19 gone to shear his sheep, Rachel stole her father's household gods, and Jacob deceived Laban, keep- 20 ing his departure secret. So Jacob 21 ran away with all that he had,

crossed the River and made for the
22 hill-country of Gilead. Three days
later, when Laban heard that Ja-
23 cob had run away, he took his
kinsmen with him, pursued Jacob
for seven days and caught up with
him in the hill-country of Gilead.
24 But God came to Laban in a dream
by night and said to him, 'Be careful to say nothing to Jacob, either
good or bad.'
25 When Laban overtook him, Jacob had pitched his tent in the hill-
country of Gilead, and Laban pitched his in the company of his kinsmen in the same hill-country.
26 Laban said to Jacob, 'What have
you done? You have deceived me
and carried off my daughters as
though they were captives taken
27 in war. Why did you slip away
secretly without telling me? I
would have set you on your way
with songs and the music of tam-
28 bourines and harps. You did not
even let me kiss my daughters and
their children. In this you were at
29 fault. It is in my power to do you
an injury, but yesterday the God
of your father spoke to me; he told
me to be careful to say nothing to
30 you, either good or bad. I know
that you went away because you
were homesick and pining for
your father's house, but why did
you steal my gods?'
31 Jacob answered, 'I was afraid;
I thought you would take your
32 daughters from me by force. Whoever is found in possession of your
gods shall die for it. Let our kinsmen here be witnesses: point out
anything I have that is yours, and
take it back.' Jacob did not know
that Rachel had stolen the gods.
33 So Laban went into Jacob's tent
and Leah's tent and that of the two
slave-girls, but he found nothing.
When he came out of Leah's tent
34 he went into Rachel's. Now she
had taken the household gods and
put them in the camel-bag and
was sitting on them. Laban went
through everything in the tent and

found nothing. Rachel said to her 35
father, 'Do not take it amiss, sir,
that I cannot rise in your presence:
the common lot of woman is upon
me.' So for all his search Laban did
not find his household gods.

Jacob was angry, and he expos- 36
tulated with Laban, exclaiming,
'What have I done wrong? What
is my offence, that you have come
after me in hot pursuit and gone 37
through all my possessions? Have
you found anything belonging to
your household? If so, set it here in
front of my kinsmen and yours,
and let them judge between the
two of us. In all the twenty years 38
I have been with you, your ewes
and she-goats have never mis-
carried; I have not eaten the rams
of your flocks; I have never brought 39
to you the body of any animal
mangled by wild beasts, but I bore
the loss myself; you claimed compensation from me for anything
stolen by day or by night. This was 40
the way of it: by day the heat consumed me and the frost by night,
and sleep deserted me. For twenty 41
years I have been in your household. I worked for you fourteen
years to win your two daughters
and six years for your flocks, and
you changed my wages ten times
over. If the God of my father, the 42
God of Abraham and the Fear of
Isaac, had not been with me, you
would have sent me away empty-
handed. But God saw my labour
and my hardships, and last night
he rebuked you.'

Laban answered Jacob, 'The 43
daughters are my daughters, the
children are my children, the flocks
are my flocks; all that you see is
mine. But as for my daughters,
what can I do today about them
and the children they have borne?
Come now, we will make an agree- 44
ment, you and I, and let it stand
as a witness between us.' So Jacob 45
chose a great stone and set it upright as a sacred pillar. Then he 46
told his kinsmen to gather stones,

and they took them and built a cairn, and there beside the cairn
47 they ate together. Laban called it Jegar-sahadutha,[a] and Jacob cal-
48 led it Gal-ed.[b] Laban said, 'This cairn is witness today between you and me.' For this reason it was
49 named Gal-ed; it was also named Mizpah,[c] for Laban said, 'May the LORD watch between you and me, when we are parted from each
50 other's sight. If you ill-treat my daughters or take other wives beside them when no one is there to see, then God be witness between
51 us.' Laban said further to Jacob, 'Here is this cairn, and here the pillar which I have set up between
52 us. This cairn is witness and the pillar is witness: I for my part will not pass beyond this cairn to your side, and you for your part shall not pass beyond this cairn and this pillar to my side to do an
53 injury, otherwise the God of Abraham and the God of Nahor will judge between us.' And Jacob swore this oath in the name of the
54 Fear of Isaac his father. He slaughtered an animal for sacrifice, there in the hill-country, and summoned his kinsmen to the feast. So they ate together and spent the night there.
55   Laban rose early in the morning, kissed his daughters and their children, blessed them and went home
32 again. Then Jacob continued his journey and was met by angels of
2 God. When he saw them, Jacob said, 'This is the company of God', and he called that place Mahanaim.[d]
3   Jacob sent messengers on ahead to his brother Esau to the district of Seir in the Edomite country,
4 and this is what he told them to say to Esau, 'My lord, your servant Jacob says, I have been living with Laban and have stayed there till
5 now. I have oxen, asses, and sheep, and male and female slaves, and I

have sent to tell you this, my lord, so that I may win your favour.'
6 The messengers returned to Jacob and said, 'We met your brother Esau already on the way to meet you with four hundred men.' Ja-
7 cob, much afraid and distressed, divided the people with him, as well as the sheep, cattle, and camels, into two companies, thinking
8 that, if Esau should come upon one company and destroy it, the other company would survive. Jacob
9 said, 'O God of my father Abraham, God of my father Isaac, O LORD at whose bidding I came back to my own country and to my kindred, and who didst promise me prosperity, I am not worthy of all
10 the true and steadfast love which thou hast shown to me thy servant. When I crossed the Jordan, I had nothing but the staff in my hand; now I have two companies. Save
11 me, I pray, from my brother Esau, for I am afraid that he may come and destroy me, sparing neither mother nor child. But thou didst
12 say, I will prosper you and will make your descendants like the sand of the sea, which is beyond all counting.'
13   Jacob spent that night there; and as a present for his brother Esau he chose from the herds he had with him two hundred she-
14 goats, twenty he-goats, two hundred ewes and twenty rams, thirty
15 milch-camels with their young, forty cows and ten young bulls, twenty she-asses and ten he-asses.
16 He put each herd separately into the care of a servant and said to each, 'Go on ahead of me, and leave gaps between the herds.' Then he
17 gave these instructions to the first: 'When my brother Esau meets you and asks you to whom you belong and where you are going and who owns these beasts you are driving, you are to say, "They belong to
18 your servant Jacob; he sends them

---

[a] *Aramaic for* Cairn of Witness.
[c] *That is* Watch-tower.

[b] *Hebrew for* Cairn of Witness.
[d] *That is* Two Companies.

19 as a present to my lord Esau, and he is behind us."' He gave the same instructions to the second, to the third, and all the drovers, telling them to say the same thing to 20 Esau when they met him. And they were to add, 'Your servant Jacob is behind us'; for he thought, 'I will appease him with the present that I have sent on ahead, and afterwards, when I come into his presence, he will perhaps receive 21 me kindly.' So Jacob's present went on ahead of him, but he himself spent that night at Mahaneh.

22 During the night Jacob rose, took his two wives, his two slave-girls, and his eleven sons, and 23 crossed the ford of Jabbok. He took them and sent them across 24 the gorge with all that he had. So Jacob was left alone, and a man wrestled with him there till[a] day-25 break. When the man saw that he could not throw Jacob, he struck him in the hollow of his thigh, so that Jacob's hip was dislocated 26 as they wrestled. The man said, 'Let me go, for day is breaking', but Jacob replied, 'I will not let 27 you go unless you bless me.' He said to Jacob, 'What is your name?', and he answered, 'Jacob.' 28 The man said, 'Your name shall no longer be Jacob, but Israel,[b] because you strove with God and 29 with men, and prevailed.' Jacob said, 'Tell me, I pray, your name.' He replied, 'Why do you ask my name?', but he gave him his bless-30 ing there. Jacob called the place Peniel,[c] 'because', he said, 'I have seen God face to face and my life is 31 spared.' The sun rose as Jacob passed through Penuel, limping 32 because of his hip. This is why the Israelites to this day do not eat the sinew of the nerve that runs in the hollow of the thigh; for the man had struck Jacob on that nerve in the hollow of the thigh.

33 Jacob raised his eyes and saw Esau coming towards him with four hundred men; so he divided the children between Leah and Ra-2 chel and the two slave-girls. He put the slave-girls with their children in front, Leah with her children next, and Rachel with Joseph 3 last. He then went on ahead of them, bowing low to the ground seven times as he approached his 4 brother. Esau ran to meet him and embraced him; he threw his arms round him and kissed him, and 5 they wept. When Esau looked up and saw the women and children, he said, 'Who are these with you?' Jacob replied, 'The children whom God has graciously given to your 6 servant.' The slave-girls came near, each with her children, and they 7 bowed low. Then Leah with her children came near and bowed low, and afterwards Joseph and Rachel came near and bowed low also. 8 Esau said, 'What was all that company of yours that I met?' And he answered, 'It was meant to 9 win favour with you, my lord.' Esau answered, 'I have more than enough. Keep what is yours, my 10 brother.' But Jacob said, 'On no account: if I have won your favour, then, I pray, accept this gift from me; for, you see, I come into your presence as into that of a god, and 11 you receive me favourably. Accept this gift which I bring you; for God has been gracious to me, and I have all I want.' So he urged him, and he accepted it.

12 Then Esau said, 'Let us set out, 13 and I will go at your pace.' But Jacob answered him, 'You must know, my lord, that the children are small; the flocks and herds are suckling their young and I am concerned for them, and if the men overdrive them for a single day, all 14 my beasts will die. I beg you, my lord, to go on ahead, and I will go by easy stages at the pace of the children and of the livestock that I am driving, until I come to my 15 lord in Seir.' Esau said, 'Let me

---

[a] Or at.   [b] That is God strove.   [c] That is Face of God (elsewhere Penuel).

detail some of my own men to escort you', but he replied, 'Why should my lord be so kind to me?'
16 That day Esau turned back towards Seir, but Jacob set out for
17 Succoth; and there he built himself a house and made shelters for his cattle. Therefore he named that place Succoth.[a]
18 On his journey from Paddanaram, Jacob came safely to the city of Shechem in Canaan and pitched his tent to the east of it.
19 The strip of country where he had pitched his tent he bought from the sons of Hamor father of She-
20 chem for a hundred sheep.[b] There he set up an altar and called it El-Elohey-Israel.[c]

34 DINAH, the daughter whom Leah had borne to Jacob, went out to visit the women of the country,
2 and Shechem, son of Hamor the Hivite the local prince, saw her; he took her, lay with her and dis-
3 honoured her. But he remained true to Jacob's daughter Dinah; he loved the girl and comforted
4 her. So Shechem said to his father Hamor, 'Get me this girl for a
5 wife.' When Jacob heard that Shechem had violated his daughter Dinah, his sons were with the herds in the open country, so he said nothing until they came home.
6 Meanwhile Shechem's father Hamor came out to Jacob to discuss it
7 with him. When Jacob's sons came in from the country and heard, they were grieved and angry, because in lying with Jacob's daughter he had done what the Israelites held to be an outrage, an intoler-
8 able thing. Hamor appealed to them in these terms: 'My son Shechem is in love with this girl; I beg you to let him have her as his wife.
9 Let us ally ourselves in marriage; you shall give us your daughters, and you shall take ours in exchange.
10 You must settle among us. The

country is open to you; make your home in it, move about freely and acquire land of your own.' And 11 Shechem said to the girl's father and brothers, 'I am eager to win your favour and I will give whatever you ask. Fix the bride-price 12 and the gift as high as you like, and I will give whatever you ask; but you must give me the girl in marriage.'

Jacob's sons gave a dishonest 13 reply to Shechem and his father Hamor, laying a trap for them because Shechem had violated their sister Dinah: 'We cannot do this,' 14 they said; 'we cannot give our sister to a man who is uncircumcised; for we look on that as a disgrace. There is one condition on which we 15 will consent: if you will follow our example and have every male among you circumcised, we will give 16 you our daughters and take yours for ourselves. Then we can live among you, and we shall all become one people. But if you refuse 17 to listen to us and be circumcised, we will take the girl and go away.' Their proposal pleased Hamor and 18 his son Shechem; and the young 19 man, who was held in respect above anyone in his father's house, did not hesitate to do what they had said, because his heart was taken by Jacob's daughter.

So Hamor and Shechem went 20 back to the city gate and addressed their fellow-citizens: 'These men 21 are friendly to us; let them live in our country and move freely in it. The land has room enough for them. Let us marry their daughters and give them ours. But these 22 men will agree to live with us and become one people on this one condition only: every male among us must be circumcised as they have been. Will not their herds, their 23 livestock, and all their chattels then be ours? We need only consent to their condition, and then

---

[a] *That is* Shelters.   [b] Or pieces of money (*cp. Josh.* 24. 32; *Job* 42. 11).
[c] *That is* God the God of Israel.

24 they are free to live with us.' All the able-bodied men agreed with Hamor and Shechem, and every single one of them was circumcised, 25 every able-bodied male. Then two days later, while they were still in great pain, Jacob's two sons Simeon and Levi, full brothers to Dinah, armed themselves with swords, boldly entered the city and 26 killed every male. They cut down Hamor and his son Shechem and took Dinah from Shechem's house 27 and went off with her. Then Jacob's other sons came in over the dead bodies and plundered the city, to avenge their sister's dishonour. 28 They seized flocks, cattle, asses, and everything, both inside the city and outside in the open coun- 29 try; they also carried off all their possessions, their dependants, and their women, and plundered everything in the houses. 30   Jacob said to Simeon and Levi, 'You have brought trouble on me, you have made my name stink among the people of the country, the Canaanites and the Perizzites. My numbers are few; if they muster against me and attack me, I shall be destroyed, I and my 31 household with me.' They answered, 'Is our sister to be treated as a common whore?'

35 GOD said to Jacob, 'Go up to Bethel and settle there; build an altar there to the God who appeared to you when you were running 2 away from your brother Esau.' So Jacob said to his household and to all who were with him, 'Rid yourselves of the foreign gods which you have among you, purify yourselves, and see your clothes are 3 mended.[a] We are going to Bethel, so that I can set up an altar there to the God who answered me in the day of my distress, and who has been with me all the way that I 4 have come.' So they handed over to Jacob all the foreign gods in

their possession and the rings from their ears, and he buried them under the terebinth-tree near Shechem. Then they set out, and the 5 cities round about were panic-stricken, and the inhabitants dared not pursue the sons of Jacob. Ja- 6 cob and all the people with him came to Luz, that is Bethel, in Canaan. There he built an altar, 7 and he called the place El-bethel, because it was there that God had revealed himself to him when he was running away from his brother. Rebecca's nurse Deborah 8 died and was buried under the oak below Bethel, and he named it Allon-bakuth.[b]

God appeared again to Jacob 9 when he came back from Paddan-aram and blessed him. God said to 10 him:

'Jacob is your name,
but your name shall no longer be Jacob:
Israel shall be your name.'

So he named him Israel. And God 11 said to him:

'I am God Almighty.
Be fruitful and increase as a nation;
a host of nations shall come from you,
and kings shall spring from your body.
The land which I gave to Abraham 12 and Isaac I give to you;
and to your descendants after you I give this land.'

God then left him, and Jacob 13, 14 erected a sacred pillar in the place where God had spoken with him, a pillar of stone, and he offered a drink-offering over it and poured oil on it. Jacob called the place 15 where God had spoken with him Bethel.

They set out from Bethel, and 16 when there was still some distance to go to Ephrathah, Rachel was in labour and her pains were severe. While her pains were upon her, the 17

---

[a] *Or* change your clothes.   [b] *That is* Oak of Weeping.

36

midwife said, 'Do not be afraid,
18 this is another son for you.' Then
with her last breath, as she was
dying, she named him Ben-oni,[a]
but his father called him Benja-
19 min.[b] So Rachel died and was
buried by the side of the road to
20 Ephrathah, that is Bethlehem. Jacob set up a sacred pillar over her
grave; it is known to this day as
21 the Pillar of Rachel's Grave. Then
Israel journeyed on and pitched
his tent on the other side of Migdal-
22 eder. While Israel was living in that
district, Reuben went and lay with
his father's concubine Bilhah, and
Israel came to hear of it.

The sons of Jacob were twelve.
23 The sons of Leah: Jacob's first-
born Reuben, then Simeon, Levi,
24 Judah, Issachar and Zebulun. The
sons of Rachel: Joseph and Benja-
25 min. The sons of Rachel's slave-
girl Bilhah: Dan and Naphtali.
26 The sons of Leah's slave-girl Zilpah: Gad and Asher. These were
Jacob's sons, born to him in Pad-
27 dan-aram. Jacob came to his father
Isaac at Mamre by Kiriath-arba,
that is Hebron, where Abraham
28 and Isaac had dwelt. Isaac had
lived for a hundred and eighty
years when he breathed his last.
29 He died and was gathered to his
father's kin at a very great age,
and his sons Esau and Jacob
buried him.

36 THIS is the table of the descen-
2 dants of Esau: that is Edom. Esau
took Canaanite women in marriage,
Adah daughter of Elon the Hittite
and Oholibamah daughter of Anah
3 son of Zibeon the Horite,[c] and
Basemath, Ishmael's daughter, sister of Nebaioth.
4[d] Adah bore Eliphaz to Esau; Ba-
5 semath bore Reuel, and Oholibamah bore Jeush, Jalam and Korah.
These were Esau's sons, born to
6 him in Canaan. Esau took his
wives, his sons and daughters and

everyone in his household, his
herds, his cattle, and all the chattels that he had acquired in Canaan,
and went to the district of Seir out
of the way of his brother Jacob, be- 7
cause they had so much stock that
they could not live together; the
land where they were staying could
not support them because of their
herds. So Esau lived in the hill- 8
country of Seir. Esau is Edom.

This is the table of the descen- 9
dants of Esau father of the Edomites in the hill-country of Seir.

These are the names of the sons 10
of Esau: Eliphaz was the son of
Esau's wife Adah. Reuel was the
son of Esau's wife Basemath. The 11
sons of Eliphaz were Teman, Omar,
Zepho, Gatam and Kenaz. Timna 12
was concubine to Esau's son Eliphaz, and she bore Amalek to him.
These are the descendants of Esau's
wife Adah. These are the sons of 13
Reuel: Nahath, Zerah, Shammah
and Mizzah. These were the descendants of Esau's wife Basemath.
These were the sons of Esau's wife 14
Oholibamah daughter of Anah son
of Zibeon. She bore him Jeush,
Jalam and Korah.

These are the chiefs descended 15
from Esau. The sons of Esau's eldest son Eliphaz: chief Teman, chief
Omar, chief Zepho, chief Kenaz,
chief Korah, chief Gatam, chief 16
Amalek. These are the chiefs descended from Eliphaz in Edom.
These are the descendants of Adah.

These are the sons of Esau's son 17
Reuel: chief Nahath, chief Zerah,
chief Shammah, chief Mizzah.
These are the chiefs descended from
Reuel in Edom. These are the des-
cendants of Esau's wife Basemath.

These are the sons of Esau's wife 18
Oholibamah: chief Jeush, chief Jalam, chief Korah. These are the
chiefs born to Oholibamah daughter of Anah wife of Esau.

These are the sons of Esau, that 19
is Edom, and these are their chiefs.

---

[a] *That is* Son of my ill luck.   [b] *That is* Son of good luck *or* Son of the right hand.
[c] *Prob. rdg. (cp. verses 20, 21)*; *Heb.* Hivite.   [d] *Verses 4, 5, 9–13: cp.* 1 Chr. 1. 35–37.

20ᵃ These are the sons of Seir the Horite, the original inhabitants of the land: Lotan, Shobal, Zibeon,
21 Anah, Dishon, Ezer and Dishan. These are the chiefs of the Horites,
22 the sons of Seir in Edom. The sons of Lotan were Hori and Hemam, and Lotan had a sister named Timna.
23 These are the sons of Shobal: Alvan, Manahath, Ebal, Shepho and Onam.
24 These are the sons of Zibeon: Aiah and Anah. This is the Anah who found some mules in the wilderness while he was tending the
25 asses of his father Zibeon. These are the children of Anah: Dishon and Oholibamah daughter of Anah.
26 These are the children of Dishon: Hemdan, Eshban, Ithran and Che-
27 ran. These are the sons of Ezer:
28 Bilhan, Zavan and Akan. These are the sons of Dishan: Uz and Aran.
29 These are the chiefs descended from the Horites: chief Lotan, chief Shobal, chief Zibeon, chief Anah,
30 chief Dishon, chief Ezer, chief Dishan. These are the chiefs that were descended from the Horites according to their clans in the district of Seir.
31ᵇ These are the kings who ruled over Edom before there were kings
32 in Israel: Bela son of Beor became king in Edom, and his city was
33 named Dinhabah; when he died, he was succeeded by Jobab son of
34 Zerah of Bozrah. When Jobab died, he was succeeded by Husham of
35 Teman. When Husham died, he was succeeded by Hadad son of Bedad, who defeated Midian in Moabite country. His city was
36 named Avith. When Hadad died, he was succeeded by Samlah of
37 Masrekah. When Samlah died, he was succeeded by Saul of Reho-
38 both on the River. When Saul died, he was succeeded by Baal-hanan
39 son of Akbor. When Baal-hanan died, he was succeeded by Hadar.ᶜ His city was named Pau; his wife's

name was Mehetabel daughter of Matred a woman of Me-zahab.ᵈ
40 These are the names of the chiefs descended from Esau, according to their families, their places, by name: chief Timna, chief Alvah,
41 chief Jetheth, chief Oholibamah,
42 chief Elah, chief Pinon, chief Kenaz, chief Teman, chief Mibzar,
43 chief Magdiel, and chief Iram: all chiefs of Edom according to their settlements in the land which they possessed. (Esau is the father of the Edomites.)

Joseph in Egypt

37 So Jacob lived in Canaan, the country in which his father had
2 settled. And this is the story of the descendants of Jacob.

When Joseph was a boy of seventeen, he used to accompany his brothers, the sons of Bilhah and Zilpah, his father's wives, when they were in charge of the flock; and he brought their father a bad report
3 of them. Now Israel loved Joseph more than any other of his sons, because he was a child of his old age, and he made him a long, sleeved
4 robe. When his brothers saw that their father loved him more than any of them, they hated him and could not say a kind word to him.
5 Joseph had a dream; and when he told it to his brothers, they
6 hated him still more. He said to them, 'Listen to this dream I have had. We were in the field binding
7 sheaves, and my sheaf rose on end and stood upright, and your sheaves gathered round and bowed
8 low before my sheaf.' His brothers answered him, 'Do you think you will one day be a king and lord it over us?' and they hated him still more because of his dreams and
9 what he said. He had another dream, which he told to his father and his brothers. He said, 'Listen: I have had another dream. The sun

---

ᵃ *Verses 20–28: cp. 1 Chr. 1. 38–42.*
ᶜ *Or Hadad; cp. 1 Chr. 1. 50.*

ᵇ *Verses 31–43: cp. 1 Chr. 1. 43–54.*
ᵈ *Or daughter of Mezahab.*

and moon and eleven stars were
10 bowing down to me.' When he told
it to his father and his brothers, his
father took him to task: 'What is
this dream of yours?' he said.
'Must we come and bow low to
the ground before you, I and your
11 mother and your brothers?' His
brothers were jealous of him, but
his father did not forget.

12 Joseph's brothers went to mind
their father's flocks in Shechem.
13 Israel said to him, 'Your brothers
are minding the flocks in Shechem;
come, I will send you to them', and
14 he said, 'I am ready.' He said to
him, 'Go and see if all is well with
your brothers and the sheep, and
bring me back word.' So he sent off
Joseph from the vale of Hebron
15 and he came to Shechem. A man
met him wandering in the open
country and asked him what he
16 was looking for. He replied, 'I am
looking for my brothers. Tell me,
please, where they are minding the
17 flocks.' The man said, 'They have
gone away from here; I heard them
speak of going to Dothan.' So Joseph followed his brothers and he
18 found them in Dothan. They saw
him in the distance, and before he
reached them, they plotted to kill
19 him. They said to each other,
20 'Here comes that dreamer. Now is
our chance; let us kill him and
throw him into one of these pits
and say that a wild beast has devoured him. Then we shall see what
21 will come of his dreams.' When
Reuben heard, he came to his rescue, urging them not to take his
22 life. 'Let us have no bloodshed', he
said. 'Throw him into this pit in
the wilderness, but do him no bodily harm.' He meant to save him
from them so as to restore him to
23 his father. When Joseph came up
to his brothers, they stripped him
of the long, sleeved robe which he
24 was wearing, took him and threw
him into the pit. The pit was empty
and had no water in it.

Then they sat down to eat some 25
food and, looking up, they saw an
Ishmaelite caravan coming in from
Gilead on the way down to Egypt,
with camels carrying gum tragacanth and balm and myrrh. Judah 26
said to his brothers, 'What shall we
gain by killing our brother and
concealing his death? Why not sell 27
him to the Ishmaelites? Let us do
him no harm, for he is our brother,
our own flesh and blood'; and his
brothers agreed with him. Mean- 28
while some Midianite merchants
passed by and drew Joseph up out
of the pit. They sold him for
twenty pieces of silver to the Ishmaelites, and they brought Joseph
to Egypt. When Reuben went 29
back to the pit, Joseph was not
there. He rent his clothes and went 30
back to his brothers and said, 'The
boy is not there. Where can I go?'

Joseph's brothers took his robe, 31
killed a goat and dipped it in
the goat's blood. Then they tore 32
the robe, the long, sleeved robe,
brought it to their father and said,
'Look what we have found. Do you
recognize it? Is this your son's robe
or not?' Jacob did recognize it, and 33
he replied, 'It is my son's robe. A
wild beast has devoured him. Joseph has been torn to pieces.' Ja- 34
cob rent his clothes, put on sackcloth and mourned his son for a
long time. His sons and daughters 35
all tried to comfort him, but he
refused to be comforted. He said,
'I will go to my grave mourning
for my son.' Thus Joseph's father
wept for him. Meanwhile the Mid- 36
ianites had sold Joseph in Egypt to
Potiphar, one of Pharaoh's eunuchs, the captain of the guard.[a]

ABOUT that time Judah left his 38
brothers and went south and pitched his tent in company with an
Adullamite named Hirah. There 2
he saw Bathshua the daughter of a
Canaanite and married her. He
slept with her, and she conceived 3

[a] Or executioner.

and bore a son, whom she called Er.
4 She conceived again and bore a son
5 whom she called Onan. Once more
she conceived and bore a son whom
she called Shelah, and she ceased to
bear children[a] when she had given
6 birth to him. Judah found a wife
for his eldest son Er; her name was
7 Tamar. But Judah's eldest son Er
was wicked in the LORD's sight,
8 and the LORD took his life. Then
Judah told Onan to sleep with his
brother's wife, to do his duty as
the husband's brother and raise up
9 issue for his brother. But Onan
knew that the issue would not be
his; so whenever he slept with his
brother's wife, he spilled his seed
on the ground so as not to raise up
10 issue for his brother. What he did
was wicked in the LORD's sight,
11 and the LORD took his life. Judah
said to his daughter-in-law Tamar,
'Remain as a widow in your father's house until my son Shelah
grows up'; for he was afraid that he
too would die like his brothers. So
Tamar went and stayed in her father's house.
12 Time passed, and Judah's wife
Bathshua died. When he had finished mourning, he and his friend
Hirah the Adullamite went up to
13 Timnath at sheep-shearing. When
Tamar was told that her father-in-
law was on his way to shear his
14 sheep at Timnath, she took off her
widow's weeds, veiled her face,
perfumed herself and sat where the
road forks in two directions on the
way to Timnath. She did this because she knew that Shelah had
grown up and she had not been
15 given to him as a wife. When Judah saw her, he thought she was a
prostitute, although she had veiled
16 her face. He turned to her where
she sat by the roadside and said,
'Let me lie with you', not knowing
that she was his daughter-in-law.
She said, 'What will you give me to
17 lie with me?' He answered, 'I will
send you a kid from my flock', but

she said, 'Will you give me a pledge
until you send it?' He asked what 18
pledge he should give her, and she
replied, 'Your seal and its cord,
and the staff which you hold in
your hand.' So he gave them to her
and lay with her, and she conceived. She then rose and went home, 19
took off her veil and resumed her
widow's weeds. Judah sent the kid 20
by his friend the Adullamite in
order to recover the pledge from
the woman, but he could not find
her. He asked the men of that 21
place, 'Where is that temple-
prostitute, the one who was sitting
where the road forks?', but they
answered, 'There is no temple-
prostitute here.' So he went back 22
to Judah and told him that he had
not found her and that the men of
the place had said there was no
such prostitute there. Judah said, 23
'Let her keep my pledge, or we
shall get a bad name. I did send a
kid, but you could not find her.'
About three months later Judah 24
was told that his daughter-in-law
Tamar had behaved like a common prostitute and through her
wanton conduct was with child.
Judah said, 'Bring her out so that
she may be burnt.' But when she 25
was brought out, she sent to her
father-in-law and said, 'The father
of my child is the man to whom
these things belong. See if you recognize whose they are, the engraving on the seal, the pattern of
the cord, and the staff.' Judah 26
recognized them and said, 'She is
more in the right than I am, because I did not give her to my son
Shelah.' He did not have intercourse with her again. When her 27
time was come, there were twins in
her womb, and while she was in 28
labour one of them put out a hand.
The midwife took a scarlet thread
and fastened it round the wrist,
saying, 'This one appeared first.'
No sooner had he drawn back his 29
hand, than his brother came out

---

[a] *ceased . . . children: or* was at Kezib.

and the midwife said, 'What! you have broken out first!' So he was named Perez.[a] Soon afterwards his brother was born with the scarlet thread on his wrist, and he was named Zerah.[b]

30

39 WHEN Joseph was taken down to Egypt, he was bought by Potiphar, one of Pharaoh's eunuchs, the captain of the guard, an Egyptian. Potiphar bought him from the Ishmaelites who had brought him there. The LORD was with Joseph and he prospered. He lived in the house of his Egyptian master, who saw that the LORD was with him and was giving him success in all that he undertook. Thus Joseph found favour with his master, and he became his personal servant. Indeed, his master put him in charge of his household and entrusted him with all that he had. From the time that he put him in charge of his household and all his property, the LORD blessed the Egyptian's household for Joseph's sake. The blessing of the LORD was on all that was his in house and field. He left everything he possessed in Joseph's care, and concerned himself with nothing but the food he ate.

2

3

4

5

6

Now Joseph was handsome and good-looking, and a time came when his master's wife took notice of him and said, 'Come and lie with me.' But he refused and said to her, 'Think of my master. He does not know as much as I do about his own house, and he has entrusted me with all he has. He has given me authority in this house second only to his own, and has withheld nothing from me except you, because you are his wife. How can I do anything so wicked, and sin against God?' She kept asking Joseph day after day, but he refused to lie with her and be in her company. One day he came into the house as usual to do his work, when none of the men of the household were

7

8

9

10

11

there indoors. She caught him by his cloak, saying, 'Come and lie with me', but he left the cloak in her hands and ran out of the house. When she saw that he had left his cloak in her hands and had run out of the house, she called out to the men of the household, 'Look at this! My husband has brought in a Hebrew to make a mockery of us. He came in here to lie with me, but I gave a loud scream. When he heard me scream and call out, he left his cloak in my hand and ran off.' She kept his cloak with her until his master came home, and then she repeated her tale. She said, 'That Hebrew slave whom you brought in to make a mockery of me, has been here with me. But when I screamed for help and called out, he left his cloak in my hands and ran off.' When Joseph's master heard his wife's story of what his slave had done to her, he was furious. He took Joseph and put him in the Round Tower, where the king's prisoners were kept; and there he stayed in the Round Tower. But the LORD was with Joseph and kept faith with him, so that he won the favour of the governor of the Round Tower. He put Joseph in charge of all the prisoners in the tower and of all their work. He ceased to concern himself with anything entrusted to Joseph, because the LORD was with Joseph and gave him success in everything.

12

13

14

15

16

17

18

19

20

21

22

23

It happened later that the king's butler and his baker offended their master the king of Egypt. Pharaoh was angry with these two eunuchs, the chief butler and the chief baker, and he put them in custody in the house of the captain of the guard, in the Round Tower where Joseph was imprisoned. The captain of the guard appointed Joseph as their attendant, and he waited on them. One night, when they had been in prison for some time, they both

40

2

3

4

5

---

[a] *That is* Breaking out.   [b] *That is* Redness.

had dreams, each needing its own interpretation – the king of Egypt's butler and his baker who were imprisoned in the Round
6 Tower. When Joseph came to them in the morning, he saw that they
7 looked dejected. So he asked these eunuchs, who were in custody with him in his master's house, why they were so downcast that day.
8 They replied, 'We have each had a dream and there is no one to interpret it for us.' Joseph said to them, 'Does not interpretation belong to
9 God? Tell me your dreams.' So the chief butler told Joseph his dream: 'In my dream', he said, 'there was
10 a vine in front of me. On the vine there were three branches, and as soon as it budded, it blossomed and its clusters ripened into grapes.
11 Now I had Pharaoh's cup in my hand, and I plucked the grapes, crushed them into Pharaoh's cup and put the cup into Pharaoh's
12 hand.' Joseph said to him, 'This is the interpretation. The three bran-
13 ches are three days: within three days Pharaoh will raise you and restore you to your post, and then you will put the cup into Pharaoh's hand as you used to do when you
14 were his butler. But when things go well with you, if you think of me, keep faith with me and bring my case to Pharaoh's notice and help me to get out of this house.
15 By force I was carried off[a] from the land of the Hebrews, and I have done nothing here to deserve being put in this dungeon.'
16   When the chief baker saw that Joseph had given a favourable interpretation, he said to him, 'I too had a dream, and in my dream there were three baskets of white
17 bread on my head. In the top basket there was every kind of food which the baker prepares for Pharaoh, and the birds were eating out
18 of the top basket on my head.' Joseph answered, 'This is the interpretation. The three baskets are

three days: within three days Pha- 19 raoh will raise you and hang you up on a tree, and the birds of the air will eat your flesh.'
    The third day was Pharaoh's 20 birthday and he gave a feast for all his servants. He raised the chief butler and the chief baker in the presence of his court. He restored 21 the chief butler to his post, and the butler put the cup into Pharaoh's hand; but he hanged the chief 22 baker. All went as Joseph had said in interpreting the dreams for them. Even so the chief butler did 23 not remember Joseph, but forgot him.

    Nearly two years later Pharaoh 41 had a dream: he was standing by the Nile, and there came up from 2 the river seven cows, sleek and fat, and they grazed on the reeds. After 3 them seven other cows came up from the river, gaunt and lean, and stood on the river-bank beside the first cows. The cows that were 4 gaunt and lean devoured the cows that were sleek and fat. Then Pharaoh woke up. He fell asleep again 5 and had a second dream: he saw seven ears of corn, full and ripe, growing on one stalk. Growing up 6 after them were seven other ears, thin and shrivelled by the east wind. The thin ears swallowed up 7 the ears that were full and ripe. Then Pharaoh woke up and knew that it was a dream. When morn- 8 ing came, Pharaoh was troubled in mind; so he summoned all the magicians and sages of Egypt. He told them his dreams, but there was no one who could interpret them for him. Then Pharaoh's chief butler 9 spoke up and said, 'It is time for me to recall my faults. Once Pharaoh 10 was angry with his servants, and he imprisoned me and the chief baker in the house of the captain of the guard. One night we both 11 had dreams, each needing its own interpretation. We had with us a 12 young Hebrew, a slave of the cap-

---

[a] *Or* stolen.

tain of the guard, and we told him our dreams and he interpreted them for us, giving each man's 13 dream its own interpretation. Each dream came true as it had been interpreted to us: I was restored to my position, and he was hanged.'

14 Pharaoh thereupon sent for Joseph, and they hurriedly brought him out of the dungeon. He shaved and changed his clothes, and came 15 in to Pharaoh. Pharaoh said to him, 'I have had a dream, and no one can interpret it to me. I have heard it said that you can under- 16 stand and interpret dreams.' Joseph answered, 'Not I, but God, will answer for Pharaoh's welfare.'

17 Then Pharaoh said to Joseph, 'In my dream I was standing on the 18 bank of the Nile, and there came up from the river seven cows, fat and sleek, and they grazed on the 19 reeds. After them seven other cows came up that were poor, very gaunt and lean; I have never seen such gaunt creatures in all Egypt. 20 These lean, gaunt cows devoured 21 the first cows, the fat ones. They were swallowed up, but no one could have guessed that they were in the bellies of the others, which looked as gaunt as before. Then I 22 woke up. After I had fallen asleep again, I saw in a dream seven ears of corn, full and ripe, growing on 23 one stalk. Growing up after them were seven other ears, shrivelled, thin, and blighted by the east wind. 24 The thin ears swallowed up the seven ripe ears. When I told all this to the magicians, no one could explain it to me.'

25 Joseph said to Pharaoh, 'Pharaoh's dreams are one dream. God has told Pharaoh what he is going 26 to do. The seven good cows are seven years, and the seven good ears of corn are seven years. It is 27 all one dream. The seven lean and gaunt cows that came up after them are seven years, and the empty ears of corn blighted by the east wind will be seven years of 28 famine. It is as I have said to Pharaoh: God has let Pharaoh see what 29 he is going to do. There are to be seven years of great plenty through- 30 out the land. After them will come seven years of famine; all the years of plenty in Egypt will be forgotten, and the famine will ruin the country. The good years will not 31 be remembered in the land because of the famine that follows; for it will be very severe. The doubling 32 of Pharaoh's dream means that God is already resolved to do this, and he will very soon put it into effect. Pharaoh should now look 33 for a shrewd and intelligent man, and put him in charge of the country. This is what Pharaoh should 34 do: appoint controllers over the land, and take one fifth of the produce of Egypt during the seven years of plenty. They should col- 35 lect all this food produced in the good years that are coming and put the corn under Pharaoh's control in store in the cities, and keep it under guard. This food will be 36 a reserve for the country against the seven years of famine which will come upon Egypt. Thus the country will not be devastated by the famine.'

37 The plan pleased Pharaoh and 38 all his courtiers, and he said to them, 'Can we find a man like this man, one who has the spirit of a god[a] in him?' He said to Joseph, 39 'Since a god[b] has made all this known to you, there is no one so shrewd and intelligent as you. You 40 shall be in charge of my household, and all my people will depend on your every word. Only my royal throne shall make me greater than you.' Pharaoh said to Joseph, 'I 41 hereby give you authority over the whole land of Egypt.' He took off 42 his signet-ring and put it on Joseph's finger, he had him dressed in fine linen, and hung a gold chain round his neck. He mounted him 43

[a] Or of God.   [b] Or God.

in his viceroy's chariot and men cried 'Make way!' before him. Thus Pharaoh made him ruler over all
44 Egypt and said to him, 'I am the Pharaoh. Without your consent no man shall lift hand or foot through-
45 out Egypt.' Pharaoh named him Zaphenath-paneah, and he gave him as wife Asenath the daughter of Potiphera priest of On. And Joseph's authority extended over the whole of Egypt.
46 Joseph was thirty years old when he entered the service of Pharaoh king of Egypt. When he took his leave of the king, he made a tour of inspection through the country.
47 During the seven years of plenty
48 there were abundant harvests, and Joseph gathered all the food produced in Egypt during those years and stored it in the cities, putting in each the food from the surround-
49 ing country. He stored the grain in huge quantities; it was like the sand of the sea, so much that he stopped measuring: it was beyond all measure.
50 Before the years of famine came, two sons were born to Joseph by Asenath the daughter of Potiphera
51 priest of On. He named the elder Manasseh,[a] 'for', he said, 'God has caused me to forget all my troubles and my father's family.'
52 He named the second Ephraim,[b] 'for', he said, 'God has made me fruitful in the land of my hard-
53 ships.' When the seven years of plenty in Egypt came to an end,
54 seven years of famine began, as Joseph had foretold. There was famine in every country, but throughout Egypt there was bread.
55 So when the famine spread through all Egypt, the people appealed to Pharaoh for bread, and he ordered them to go to Joseph and do as he
56 told them. In every region there was famine, and Joseph opened all the granaries and sold corn to the Egyptians, for the famine was
57 severe. The whole world came to Egypt to buy corn from Joseph, so severe was the famine everywhere.

WHEN Jacob saw that there was 42 corn in Egypt, he said to his sons, 'Why do you stand staring at each other? I have heard that there is 2 corn in Egypt. Go down and buy some so that we may keep ourselves alive and not starve.' So Joseph's 3 brothers, ten of them, went down to buy grain from Egypt, but 4 Jacob did not let Joseph's brother Benjamin go with them, for fear that he might come to harm.

So the sons of Israel came down 5 with everyone else to buy corn, because of the famine in Canaan. Now 6 Joseph was governor of all Egypt, and it was he who sold the corn to all the people of the land. Joseph's brothers came and bowed to the ground before him, and when he 7 saw his brothers, he recognized them but pretended not to know them and spoke harshly to them. 'Where do you come from?' he asked. 'From Canaan,' they answered, 'to buy food.' Although Joseph 8 had recognized his brothers, they did not recognize him. He remem- 9 bered also the dreams he had had about them; so he said to them, 'You are spies; you have come to spy out the weak points in our defences.' They answered, 'No, sir: 10 your servants have come to buy food. We are all sons of one man. 11 Your humble servants are honest men, we are not spies.' 'No,' he 12 insisted, 'it is to spy out our weaknesses that you have come.' They 13 answered him, 'Sir, there are twelve of us, all brothers, sons of one man in Canaan. The youngest is still with our father, and one has disappeared.' But Joseph said again 14 to them, 'No, as I said before, you are spies. This is how you shall be 15 put to the proof: unless your youngest brother comes here, by the life of Pharaoh, you shall not leave this place. Send one of your number to 16

---

[a] *That is* Causing to forget.   [b] *That is* Fruit.

bring your brother; the rest will be kept in prison. Thus your story will be tested, and we shall see whether you are telling the truth. If not, then, by the life of Pharaoh, 17 you must be spies.' So he kept them in prison for three days.

18 On the third day Joseph said to the brothers, 'Do what I say and your lives will be spared; for I am a 19 God-fearing man: if you are honest men, your brother there shall be kept in prison, and the rest of you shall take corn for your hungry 20 households and bring your youngest brother to me; thus your words will be proved true, and you will not die.'[a]

21 They said to one another, 'No doubt we deserve to be punished because of our brother, whose suffering we saw; for when he pleaded with us we refused to listen. That is why these sufferings have come 22 upon us.' But Reuben said, 'Did I not tell you not to do the boy a wrong? But you would not listen, and his blood is on our heads, and 23 we must pay.' They did not know that Joseph understood, because 24 he had used an interpreter. Joseph turned away from them and wept. Then, turning back, he played a trick on them. First he took Simeon and bound him before their 25 eyes; then he gave orders to fill their bags with grain, to return each man's silver, putting it in his sack, and to give them supplies for the journey. All this was 26 done; and they loaded the corn on to their asses and went away.

27 When they stopped for the night, one of them opened his sack to give fodder to his ass, and there he saw 28 his silver at the top of the pack. He said to his brothers, 'My silver has been returned to me, and here it is in my pack.' Bewildered and trembling, they said to each other, 'What is this that God has done to us?'

29 When they came to their father Jacob in Canaan, they told him all that had happened to them. They said, 'The man who is lord of the 30 country spoke harshly to us and made out that we were spies. We 31 said to him, "We are honest men, we are not spies. There are twelve 32 of us, all brothers, sons of one father. One has disappeared, and the youngest is with our father in Canaan." This man, the lord of the 33 country, said to us, "This is how I shall find out if you are honest men. Leave one of your brothers with me, take food for your hungry households and go. Bring your 34 youngest brother to me, and I shall know that you are not spies, but honest men. Then I will restore your brother to you, and you can move about the country freely."'

But on emptying their sacks, each 35 of them found his silver inside, and when they and their father saw the bundles of silver, they were afraid. Their father Jacob said to them, 36 'You have robbed me of my children. Joseph has disappeared; Simeon has disappeared; and now you are taking Benjamin. Everything is against me.' Reuben said to his 37 father, 'You may kill both my sons if I do not bring him back to you. Put him in my charge, and I shall bring him back.' But Jacob said, 38 'My son shall not go with you, for his brother is dead and he alone is left. If he comes to any harm on the journey, you will bring down my grey hairs in sorrow to the grave.'

The famine was still severe in 43 the country. When they had used 2 up the corn they had brought from Egypt, their father said to them, 'Go back and buy a little more corn for us to eat.' But Judah replied, 3 'The man plainly warned us that we must not go into his presence unless our brother was with us. If 4 you let our brother go with us, we will go down and buy food for you. But if you will not let him, we will 5

---

[a] *Prob. rdg.; Heb. adds* and they did so.

not go; for the man said to us, "You shall not come into my presence, unless your brother is with
6 you."' Israel said, 'Why have you treated me so badly? Why did you tell the man that you had yet ano-
7 ther brother?' They answered, 'He questioned us closely about ourselves and our family: "Is your father still alive?" he asked, "Have you a brother?", and we answered his questions. How could we possibly know that he would tell us to
8 bring our brother to Egypt?' Judah said to his father Israel, 'Send the boy with me; then we can start at once. By doing this we shall save our lives, ours, yours, and our dependants', and none of us will
9 starve. I will go surety for him and you may hold me responsible. If I do not bring him back and restore him to you, you shall hold me
10 guilty all my life. If we had not wasted all this time, by now we could have gone back twice over.'
11   Their father Israel said to them, 'If it must be so, then do this: take in your baggage, as a gift for the man, some of the produce for which our country is famous: a little balsam, a little honey, gum tragacanth, myrrh, pistachio nuts,
12 and almonds. Take double the amount of silver and restore what was returned to you in your packs;
13 perhaps it was a mistake. Take your brother with you and go
14 straight back to the man. May God Almighty make him kindly disposed to you, and may he send back the one whom you left behind, and Benjamin too. As for me, if I am bereaved, then I am be-
15 reaved.' So they took the gift and double the amount of silver, and with Benjamin they started at once for Egypt, where they presented themselves to Joseph.
16   When Joseph saw Benjamin with them, he said to his steward, 'Bring these men indoors, kill a beast and make dinner ready, for they will
17 eat with me at noon.' He did as Joseph told him and brought the
18 men into the house. When they came in they were afraid, for they thought, 'We have been brought in here because of that affair of the silver which was replaced in our packs the first time. He means to trump up some charge against us and victimize us, seize our asses and make us his slaves.' So they
19 approached Joseph's steward and spoke to him at the door of the
20 house. They said, 'Please listen, my lord. After our first visit to buy
21 food, when we reached the place where we were to spend the night, we opened our packs and each of us found his silver in full weight at the top of his pack. We have brought
22 it back with us, and have added other silver to buy food. We do not know who put the silver in our
23 packs.' He answered, 'Set your minds at rest; do not be afraid. It was your God, the God of your father, who hid treasure for you in your packs. I did receive the silver.' Then he brought Simeon out to them.
24   The steward brought them into Joseph's house and gave them water to wash their feet, and provided
25 fodder for their asses. They had their gifts ready when Joseph arrived at noon, for they had heard
26 that they were to eat there. When Joseph came into the house, they presented him with the gifts which they had brought, bowing to the ground before him. He asked them
27 how they were and said, 'Is your father well, the old man of whom
28 you spoke? Is he still alive?' They answered, 'Yes, my lord, our father is still alive and well.' And they bowed low and prostrated them-
29 selves. Joseph looked and saw his own mother's son, his brother Benjamin, and asked, 'Is this your youngest brother, of whom you told me?', and to Benjamin he said, 'May God be gracious to you, my son!' Joseph was overcome; his
30 feelings for his brother mastered

him, and he was near to tears. So he went into the inner room and
31 wept. Then he washed his face and came out; and, holding back his feelings, he ordered the meal to be
32 served. They served him by himself, and the brothers by themselves, and the Egyptians who were at dinner were also served separately; for Egyptians hold it an abo-
33 mination to eat with Hebrews. The brothers were seated in his presence, the eldest first according to his age and so on down to the youngest: they looked at one another in
34 astonishment. Joseph sent them each a portion from what was before him, but Benjamin's was five times larger than any of the other portions. Thus they drank with him and all grew merry.

44 Joseph gave his steward this order: 'Fill the men's packs with as much food as they can carry and put each man's silver at the top of
2 his pack. And put my goblet, my silver goblet, at the top of the youngest brother's pack with the silver for the corn.' He did as Jo-
3 seph said. At daybreak the brothers were allowed to take their
4 asses and go on their journey; but before they had gone very far from the city, Joseph said to his steward, 'Go after those men at once, and when you catch up with them, say, "Why have you repaid good
5 with evil? Why have you stolen the silver goblet? It is the one from which my lord drinks, and which he uses for divination. You have done
6 a wicked thing."' When he caught up with them, he repeated all this
7 to them, but they replied, 'My lord, how can you say such things? No, sir, God forbid that we should do
8 any such thing! You remember the silver we found at the top of our packs? We brought it back to you from Canaan. Why should we steal silver or gold from your master's
9 house? If any one of us is found with the goblet, he shall die; and, what is more, my lord, we will all

become your slaves.' He said, 'Very 10 well, then; I accept what you say. The man in whose possession it is found shall be my slave, but the rest of you shall go free.' Each man 11 quickly lowered his pack to the ground and opened it. The steward 12 searched them, beginning with the eldest and finishing with the youngest, and the goblet was found in Benjamin's pack.

At this they rent their clothes; 13 then each man loaded his ass and they returned to the city. Joseph 14 was still in the house when Judah and his brothers came in. They threw themselves on the ground before him, and Joseph said, 'What 15 have you done? You might have known that a man like myself would practise divination.' Judah 16 said, 'What shall we say, my lord? What can we say to prove our innocence? God has found out our sin. Here we are, my lord, ready to be made your slaves, we ourselves as well as the one who was found with the goblet.' Joseph answered, 'God 17 forbid that I should do such a thing! The one who was found with the goblet shall become my slave, but the rest of you can go home to your father in peace.'

Then Judah went up to him and 18 said, 'Please listen, my lord. Let me say a word to your lordship, I beg. Do not be angry with me, for you are as great as Pharaoh. You, my 19 lord, asked us whether we had a father or a brother. We answered, 20 "We have an aged father, and he has a young son born in his old age; this boy's full brother is dead and he alone is left of his mother's children, he alone, and his father loves him." Your lordship answered, 21 "Bring him down to me so that I may set eyes on him." We told you, 22 my lord, that the boy could not leave his father, and that his father would die if he left him. But you 23 answered, "Unless your youngest brother comes here with you, you shall not enter my presence again."

24 We went back to your servant our father, and told him what your 25 lordship had said. When our father 26 told us to go and buy food, we answered, "We cannot go down; for without our youngest brother we cannot enter the man's presence; but if our brother is with us, we will 27 go." Our father, my lord, then said to us, "You know that my wife 28 bore me two sons. One left me, and I said, 'He must have been torn to pieces.' I have not seen him to this 29 day. If you take this one from me as well, and he comes to any harm, 30 then you will bring down my grey hairs in trouble to the grave." Now, my lord, when I return to my father without the boy – and re- member, his life is bound up with 31 the boy's – what will happen is this: he will see that the boy is not with us and will die, and your ser- vants will have brought down our father's grey hairs in sorrow to the 32 grave. Indeed, my lord, it was I who went surety for the boy to my father. I said, "If I do not bring him back to you, then you shall 33 hold me guilty all my life." Now, my lord, let me remain in place of the boy as your lordship's slave, and let him go with his brothers. 34 How can I return to my father without the boy? I could not bear to see the misery which my father would suffer.'

45 Joseph could no longer control his feelings in front of his atten- dants, and he called out, 'Let every- one leave my presence.' So there was nobody present when Joseph made himself known to his bro- 2 thers, but so loudly did he weep that the Egyptians and Pharaoh's 3 household heard him. Joseph said to his brothers, 'I am Joseph; can my father be still alive?' His bro- thers were so dumbfounded at find- ing themselves face to face with Joseph that they could not an- 4 swer. Then Joseph said to his bro- thers, 'Come closer', and so they came close. He said, 'I am your brother Joseph whom you sold in- to Egypt. Now do not be distressed 5 or take it amiss that you sold me into slavery here; it was God who sent me ahead of you to save men's lives. For there have now been two 6 years of famine in the country, and there will be another five years with neither ploughing nor har- vest. God sent me ahead of you to 7 ensure that you will have descen- dants on earth, and to preserve you all, a great band of survivors. So it 8 was not you who sent me here, but God, and he has made me a father*a* to Pharaoh, and lord over all his household and ruler of all Egypt. Make haste and go back to my fa- 9 ther and give him this message from his son Joseph: "God has made me lord of all Egypt. Come down to me; do not delay. You shall live in 10 the land of Goshen and be near me, you, your sons and your grand- sons, your flocks and herds and all that you have. I will take care of 11 you there, you and your household and all that you have, and see that you are not reduced to poverty; there are still five years of famine to come." You can see for your- 12 selves, and so can my brother Ben- jamin, that it is Joseph himself who is speaking to you. Tell my father 13 of all the honour which I enjoy in Egypt, tell him all you have seen, and make haste to bring him down here.' Then he threw his arms 14 round his brother Benjamin and wept, and Benjamin too embraced him weeping. He kissed all his bro- 15 thers and wept over them, and afterwards his brothers talked with him.

When the report that Joseph's 16 brothers had come reached Pha- raoh's house, he and all his cour- tiers were pleased. Pharaoh said to 17 Joseph, 'Say to your brothers: "This is what you are to do. Load your beasts and go to Canaan. Fetch your father and your house- 18

a Or counsellor.

holds and bring them to me. I will give you the best that there is in Egypt, and you shall enjoy the fat 19 of the land." You shall also tell them: "Take wagons from Egypt for your dependants and your wives and fetch your father and 20 come. Have no regrets at leaving your possessions, for all the best that there is in Egypt is yours."'

21 The sons of Israel did as they were told, and Joseph gave them wagons, according to Pharaoh's or-22 ders, and food for the journey. He provided each of them with a change of clothing, but to Benjamin he gave three hundred pieces of silver and five changes of clo-23 thing. Moreover he sent his father ten asses carrying the best that there was in Egypt, and ten she-asses loaded with grain, bread, and 24 provisions for his journey. So he dismissed his brothers, telling them not to quarrel among themselves on 25 the road, and they set out. Thus they went up from Egypt and came to their father Jacob in Canaan.

26 There they gave him the news that Joseph was still alive and that he was ruler of all Egypt. He was stunned and could not believe it, 27 but they told him all that Joseph had said; and when he saw the wagons which Joseph had sent to take 28 him away, his spirit revived. Israel said, 'It is enough. Joseph my son is still alive; I will go and see him before I die.'

46 So Israel set out with all that he had and came to Beersheba where he offered sacrifices to the God of 2 his father Isaac. God said to Israel in a vision by night, 'Jacob, Jacob', 3 and he answered, 'I am here.' God said, 'I am God, the God of your father. Do not be afraid to go down to Egypt, for there I will make you 4 a great nation. I will go down with you to Egypt, and I myself will bring you back again without fail;

and Joseph shall close your eyes.' So Jacob set out from Beersheba. 5 Israel's sons conveyed their father Jacob, their dependants, and their wives in the wagons which Pharaoh had sent to carry them. They 6 took the herds and the stock which they had acquired in Canaan and came to Egypt, Jacob and all his descendants with him, his sons and 7 their sons, his daughters and his sons' daughters: he brought all his descendants to Egypt.

These are the names of the Israel-8*a* ites who entered Egypt: Jacob and his sons, as follows: Reuben, Jacob's eldest son. The sons of Reu-9 ben: Enoch, Pallu, Hezron and Carmi. The sons of Simeon: Jemuel, 10 Jamin, Ohad, Jachin, Zohar, and Saul, who was the son of a Canaanite woman. The sons of Levi: 11 Gershon, Kohath and Merari. The 12 sons of Judah: Er, Onan, Shelah, Perez and Zerah; of these Er and Onan died in Canaan. The sons of Perez were Hezron and Hamul. The 13 sons of Issachar: Tola, Pua, Iob and Shimron. The sons of Zebulun: 14 Sered, Elon and Jahleel. These are 15 the sons of Leah whom she bore to Jacob in Paddan-aram, and there was also his daughter Dinah. His sons and daughters numbered thirty-three in all.

The sons of Gad: Ziphion, Hag-16 gi, Shuni, Ezbon, Eri, Arodi and Areli. The sons of Asher: Imnah, 17 Ishvah, Ishvi, Beriah, and their sister Serah. The sons of Beriah: Heber and Malchiel. These are the 18 descendants of Zilpah whom Laban gave to his daughter Leah; sixteen in all, born to Jacob.

The sons of Jacob's wife Rachel: 19 Joseph and Benjamin. Manasseh 20 and Ephraim were born to Joseph in Egypt. Asenath daughter of Potiphera priest of On bore them to him. The sons of Benjamin: Be-21 la, Becher and Ashbel; and the sons of Bela: Gera, Naaman, Ehi, Rosh,

a Verses 8–25: cp. Exod. 6. 14–16; Num. 26. 5–50; 1 Chr. 4. 1, 24; 5. 3; 6. 1; 7. 1, 6, 13, 30; 8. 1–5.

22 Muppim, Huppim and Ard. These are the descendants of Rachel; fourteen in all, born to Jacob.

23, 24 The son*a* of Dan: Hushim. The sons of Naphtali: Jahzeel, Guni,

25 Jezer and Shillem. These are the descendants of Bilhah whom Laban gave to his daughter Rachel; seven in all, born to Jacob.

26 The persons belonging to Jacob who came to Egypt, all his direct descendants, not counting the wives of his sons, were sixty-six in

27 all. Two sons were born to Joseph in Egypt. Thus the house of Jacob numbered seventy when it entered Egypt.

28 Judah was sent ahead that he might appear before Joseph in Goshen, and so they entered Goshen.

29 Joseph had his chariot made ready and went up to meet his father Israel in Goshen. When they met, he threw his arms round him and wept, and embraced him for a long

30 time, weeping. Israel said to Joseph, 'I have seen your face again, and you are still alive. Now I am

31 ready to die.' Joseph said to his brothers and to his father's household, 'I will go and tell Pharaoh; I will say to him, "My brothers and my father's household who were in

32 Canaan have come to me."' Now his brothers were shepherds, men with their own flocks and herds, and they had brought them with them, their flocks and herds and all

33 that they possessed. So Joseph said, 'When Pharaoh summons you and asks you what your occupa-

34 tion is, you must say, "My lord, we have been herdsmen all our lives, as our fathers were before us." You must say this if you are to settle in the land of Goshen, because all shepherds are an abomination to the Egyptians.'

47 Joseph came and told Pharaoh, 'My father and my brothers have arrived from Canaan, with their flocks and their cattle and all that they have, and they are now in Goshen.' Then he chose five of his 2 brothers and presented them to Pharaoh, who asked them what 3 their occupation was, and they answered, 'My lord, we are shepherds, we and our fathers before us, and 4 we have come to stay in this land; for there is no pasture in Canaan for our sheep, because the famine there is so severe. We beg you, my lord, to let us settle now in Goshen.' Pharaoh said to Joseph, 'So your 5 father and your brothers have come to you. The land of Egypt is yours; 6 settle them in the best part of it. Let them live in Goshen, and if you know of any capable men among them, make them chief herdsmen over my cattle.'

Then Joseph brought his father 7 in and presented him to Pharaoh, and Jacob gave Pharaoh his blessing. Pharaoh asked Jacob his age, 8 and he answered, 'The years of my 9 earthly sojourn are one hundred and thirty; hard years they have been and few, not equal to the years that my fathers lived in their time.' Jacob then blessed Pharaoh and 10 went out from his presence. So Jo- 11 seph settled his father and his brothers, and gave them lands in Egypt, in the best part of the country, in the district of Rameses, as Pharaoh had ordered. He sup- 12 ported his father, his brothers, and all his father's household with all the food they needed.

There was no bread in the whole 13 country, so very severe was the famine, and Egypt and Canaan were laid low by it. Joseph collected all 14 the silver in Egypt and Canaan in return for the corn which the people bought, and deposited it in Pharaoh's treasury. When all the 15 silver in Egypt and Canaan had been used up, the Egyptians came to Joseph and said, 'Give us bread, or we shall die before your eyes. Our silver is all spent.' Joseph said, 16 'If your silver is spent, give me your herds and I will give you

---

a Prob. rdg.; Heb. sons.

17 bread in return.' So they brought their herds to Joseph, who gave them bread in exchange for their horses, their flocks of sheep and herds of cattle, and their asses. He maintained them that year with bread in exchange for their herds.

18 The year came to an end, and the following year they came to him again and said, 'My lord, we cannot conceal it from you: our silver is all gone and our herds of cattle are yours. Nothing is left for your lordship but our bodies and our lands.

19 Why should we perish before your eyes, we and our land as well? Take us and our land in payment for bread, and we and our land alike will be in bondage to Pharaoh. Give us seed-corn to keep us alive, or we shall die and our land will become desert.'

20 So Joseph bought all the land in Egypt for Pharaoh, because the Egyptians sold all their fields, so severe was the famine; the

21 land became Pharaoh's. As for the people, Pharaoh set them to work as slaves from one end of the terri-

22 tory of Egypt to the other. But Joseph did not buy the land which belonged to the priests; they had a fixed allowance from Pharaoh and lived on this, so that they had no need to sell their land.

23 Joseph said to the people, 'Listen; I have today bought you and your land for Pharaoh. Here is seed-corn for you. Sow the land,

24 and give one fifth of the crop to Pharaoh. Four fifths shall be yours to provide seed for your fields and food for yourselves, your house-

25 holds, and your dependants.' The people said, 'You have saved our lives. If it please your lordship, we

26 will be Pharaoh's slaves.' Joseph established it as a law in Egypt that one fifth should belong to Pharaoh, and this is still in force. It was only the priests' land that did not pass into Pharaoh's hands.

27 Thus Israel settled in Egypt, in Goshen; there they acquired land, and were fruitful and increased

greatly. Jacob stayed in Egypt for 28 seventeen years and lived to be a hundred and forty-seven years old. When the time of his death drew 29 near, he summoned his son Joseph and said to him, 'If I may now claim this favour from you, put your hand under my thigh and swear by the LORD that you will deal loyally and truly with me and not bury me in Egypt. When I die 30 like my forefathers, you shall carry me from Egypt and bury me in their grave.' He answered, 'I will do as you say'; but Jacob said, 31 'Swear it.' So he swore the oath, and Israel sank down over the end of the bed.

The time came when Joseph was 48 told that his father was ill, so he took with him his two sons, Manasseh and Ephraim. Jacob heard that 2 his son Joseph was coming to him, and he summoned his strength and sat up on the bed. Jacob said to Jo- 3 seph, 'God Almighty appeared to me at Luz in Canaan and blessed me. He said to me, "I will make you 4 fruitful and increase your descendants until they become a host of nations. I will give this land to your descendants after you as a perpetual possession." Now, your two 5 sons, who were born to you in Egypt before I came here, shall be counted as my sons; Ephraim and Manasseh shall be mine as Reuben and Simeon are. Any children born 6 to you after them shall be counted as yours, but in respect of their tribal territory they shall be reckoned under their elder brothers' names. As I was coming from Paddan- 7 aram I was bereaved of Rachel your mother on the way, in Canaan, whilst there was still some distance to go to Ephrath, and I buried her there by the road to Ephrath, that is Bethlehem.'

When Israel saw Joseph's sons, 8 he said, 'Who are these?' Joseph re- 9 plied to his father, 'They are my sons whom God has given me here.' Israel said, 'Bring them to me, I

beg you, so that I may take them
10 on my knees.'ᵃ Now Israel's eyes
were dim with age, and he could
not see; so Joseph brought the boys
close to his father, and he kissed
11 them and embraced them. He said
to Joseph, 'I had not expected to
see your face again, and now God
has granted me to see your sons
12 also.' Joseph took them from his
father's knees and bowed to the
13 ground. Then he took the two of
them, Ephraim on his right at
Israel's left and Manasseh on his
left at Israel's right, and brought
14 them close to him. Israel stretched
out his right hand and laid it on
Ephraim's head, although he was
the younger, and, crossing his
hands, laid his left hand on Manasseh's head; but Manasseh was
15 the elder. He blessed Joseph and
said:

'The God in whose presence my
  forefathers lived,
my forefathers Abraham and Isaac,
the God who has been my shepherd all my life until this day,
16 the angel who ransomed me from
  all misfortune,
may he bless these boys;
they shall be called by my name,
and by that of my forefathers,
  Abraham and Isaac;
may they grow into a great people
  on earth.'

17 When Joseph saw that his father
was laying his right hand on Ephraim's head, he was displeased; so
he took hold of his father's hand to
move it from Ephraim's head to
18 Manasseh's. He said, 'That is not
right, my father. This is the elder;
lay your right hand on his head.'
19 But his father refused; he said, 'I
know, my son, I know. He too shall
become a people; he too shall become great, but his younger brother shall be greater than he, and
his descendants shall be a whole
20 nation in themselves.' That day he
blessed them and said:

'When a blessing is pronounced in
  Israel,
men shall use your names and
  say,
God make you like Ephraim and
  Manasseh',

thus setting Ephraim before Manasseh. Then Israel said to Joseph, 'I 21
am dying. God will be with you and
will bring you back to the land of
your fathers. I give you one ridge of 22
land more than your brothers: I
took it from the Amorites with my
sword and my bow.'

JACOB summoned his sons and 49
said, 'Come near, and I will tell you
what will happen to you in days to
come.

Gather round me and listen, you 2
  sons of Jacob;
listen to Israel your father.
Reuben, you are my first-born,   3
my strength and the first fruit of
  my vigour,
excelling in pride, excelling in
  might,
turbulent as a flood, you shall not 4
  excel;
because you climbed into your father's bed;
then you defiled his concubine's
  couch.
Simeon and Levi are brothers,   5
their spades became weapons of
  violence.
My soul shall not enter their 6
  council,
my heart shall not join their company;
for in their anger they killed men,
wantonly they hamstrung oxen.
A curse be on their anger because it 7
  was fierce;
a curse on their wrath because it
  was ruthless!
I will scatter them in Jacob,
I will disperse them in Israel.
Judah, your brothers shall praise 8
  you,
your hand is on the neck of your
  enemies.

ᵃ Or *may bless them.*

Your father's sons shall do you
homage.

9 Judah, you lion's whelp,
you have returned from the kill,
my son,
and crouch and stretch like a lion;
and, like a lion,[a] who dare rouse
you?

10 The sceptre shall not pass from
Judah,
nor the staff from his descendants,
so long as tribute is brought to him
and the obedience of the nations is
his.

11 To the vine he tethers his ass,
and the colt of his ass to the red vine;
he washes his cloak in wine,
his robes in the blood of grapes.

12 Darker than wine are his eyes,
his teeth whiter than milk.

13 Zebulun dwells by the sea-shore,
his shore is a haven for ships,
and his frontier rests on Sidon.

14 Issachar, a gelded ass
lying down in the cattle-pens,

15 saw that a settled home was good
and that the land was pleasant,
so he bent his back to the burden
and submitted to perpetual forced
labour.

16 Dan – how insignificant his people,
lowly as any tribe in Israel![b]

17 Let Dan be a viper on the road,
a horned snake on the path,
who bites the horse's fetlock
so that the rider tumbles backwards.

18 For thy salvation I wait in hope,
O LORD.

19 Gad is raided by raiders,
and he raids them from the rear.

20 Asher shall have rich food as daily
fare,
and provide dishes fit for a king.

21 Naphtali is a spreading terebinth
putting forth lovely boughs.

22 Joseph is a fruitful tree[c] by a spring
with branches climbing over the
wall.

23 The archers savagely attacked him,
they shot at him and pressed him
hard,
but their bow was splintered by the 24
Eternal
and the sinews of their arms were
torn apart
by the power of the Strong One of
Jacob,
by the name of the Shepherd[d] of
Israel,
by the God of your father – so 25
may he help you,
by God Almighty – so may he
bless you
with the blessings of heaven above,
the blessings of the deep that lurks
below.
The blessings of breast and womb
and the blessings of your father are 26
stronger
than the blessings of the everlasting pools[e]
and the bounty of the eternal hills.
They shall be on the head of Joseph,
on the brow of the prince among[f]
his brothers.

Benjamin is a ravening wolf: 27
in the morning he devours the prey,
in the evening he snatches a share
of the spoil.'

These, then, are the twelve tribes 28
of Israel, and this is what their father Jacob said to them, when he
blessed them each in turn. He gave 29
them his last charge and said, 'I
shall soon be gathered to my father's kin; bury me with my forefathers in the cave on the plot of
land which belonged to Ephron the
Hittite, that is the cave on the plot 30
of land at Machpelah east of Mamre
in Canaan, the field which Abraham bought from Ephron the Hittite for a burial-place. There Abra- 31
ham was buried with his wife Sarah;
there Isaac and his wife Rebecca
were buried; and there I buried
Leah. The land and the cave on it 32
were bought from the Hittites.'
When Jacob had finished giving 33

---

[a] *Or* lioness.   [b] *Or* Dan shall judge his people as one of the tribes of Israel.
[c] *Or* a fruitful ben-tree.   [d] *Prob. rdg.*; *Heb. adds* stone.   [e] *Or* hills.
[f] the prince among: *or* the one cursed by.

his last charge to his sons, he drew his feet up on to the bed, breathed his last, and was gathered to his father's kin.

50 Then Joseph threw himself upon his father, weeping and kissing his 2 face. He ordered the physicians in his service to embalm his father 3 Israel, and they did so, finishing the task in forty days, which was the usual time for embalming. The Egyptians mourned him for seven- 4 ty days; and then, when the days of mourning for Israel were over, Joseph approached members of Pharaoh's household and said, 'If I can count on your goodwill, then speak for me to Pharaoh; tell him 5 that my father made me take an oath, saying, "I am dying. Bury me in the grave that I bought*a* for myself in Canaan." Ask him to let me go up and bury my father, and 6 afterwards I will return.' Pharaoh answered, 'Go and bury your father, as he has made you swear to 7 do.' So Joseph went to bury his father, accompanied by all Pharaoh's courtiers, the elders of his household, and all the elders of 8 Egypt, together with all Joseph's own household, his brothers, and his father's household; only their dependants, with the flocks and 9 herds, were left in Goshen. He took with him chariots and horsemen; they were a very great company. 10 When they came to the threshing-floor of Atad beside the river Jordan, they raised a loud and bitter lament; and there Joseph observed seven days' mourning for his father. 11 When the Canaanites who lived there saw this mourning at the threshing-floor of Atad, they said, 'How bitterly the Egyptians are mourning!'; accordingly they named the place beside the Jordan Abel-mizraim.*b*

12 Thus Jacob's sons did what he 13 had told them to do. They took him to Canaan and buried him in the cave on the plot of land at Machpelah, the land which Abraham had bought as a burial-place from Ephron the Hittite, to the east of Mamre. Then, after he had 14 buried his father, Joseph returned to Egypt with his brothers and all who had gone up with him.

When their father was dead Jo- 15 seph's brothers were afraid and said, 'What if Joseph should bear a grudge against us and pay us out for all the harm that we did to him?' They therefore approached 16 Joseph with these words: 'In his last words to us before he died, your father gave us this message for you: 17 "I ask you to forgive your brothers' crime and wickedness; I know they did you harm." So now forgive our crime, we beg; for we are servants of your father's God.' When they said this to him, Joseph wept. His bro- 18 thers also wept*c* and prostrated themselves before him; they said, 'You see, we are your slaves.' But 19 Joseph said to them, 'Do not be afraid. Am I in the place of God? You meant to do me harm; but 20 God meant to bring good out of it by preserving the lives of many people, as we see today. Do not be 21 afraid. I will provide for you and your dependants.' Thus he comforted them and set their minds at rest.

Joseph remained in Egypt, he 22 and his father's household. He lived there to be a hundred and ten years old and saw Ephraim's children to 23 the third generation; he also recognized as his the children of Manasseh's son Machir. He said to his 24 brothers, 'I am dying; but God will not fail to come to your aid and take you from here to the land which he promised on oath to Abraham, Isaac and Jacob.' He made 25 the sons of Israel take an oath, saying, 'When God thus comes to your aid, you must take my bones with you from here.' So Joseph died at 26 the age of a hundred and ten. He was embalmed and laid in a coffin in Egypt.

---

a Or dug.   *b* That is Mourning (or Meadow) of Egypt.   *c* Prob. rdg.; Heb. came.

EXODUS

Israel enslaved in Egypt

1 THESE are the names of the
Israelites who entered Egypt
with Jacob, each with his
2 household: Reuben, Simeon, Levi
3 and Judah; Issachar, Zebulun and
4 Benjamin; Dan and Naphtali, Gad
5 and Asher. There were seventy of
them all told, all direct descendants of Jacob. Joseph was already
in Egypt.

6 In course of time Joseph died, he
and all his brothers and that whole
7 generation. Now the Israelites were
fruitful and prolific; they increased
in numbers and became very powerful,[a] so that the country was over-
8 run by them. Then a new king ascended the throne of Egypt, one
9 who knew nothing of Joseph. He
said to his people, 'These Israelites
have become too many and too
10 strong for us. We must take pre-
cautions to see that they do not
increase any further; or we shall
find that, if war breaks out, they
will join the enemy and fight a-
gainst us, and they will become
11 masters of the country.' So they
were made to work in gangs with
officers set over them, to break their
spirit with heavy labour. This is
how Pharaoh's store-cities, Pithom
12 and Rameses, were built. But the
more harshly they were treated,
the more their numbers increased
beyond all bounds, until the Egyptians came to loathe the sight of
13 them. So they treated their Israelite
14 slaves with ruthless severity, and
made life bitter for them with cruel
servitude, setting them to work on
clay and brick-making, and all
sorts of work in the fields. In short
they made ruthless use of them

as slaves in every kind of hard
labour.

Then the king of Egypt spoke to 15
the Hebrew midwives, whose names
were Shiphrah and Puah. 'When 16
you are attending the Hebrew women in childbirth,' he told them,
'watch as the child is delivered and
if it is a boy, kill him; if it is a girl,
let her live.' But they were God- 17
fearing women. They did not do
what the king of Egypt had told
them to do, but let the boys live.
So he summoned those Hebrew 18
midwives and asked them why
they had done this and let the boys
live. They told Pharaoh that He- 19
brew women were not like Egyptian women. When they were in labour they gave birth before the
midwife could get to them. So God 20
made the midwives prosper, and
the people increased in numbers
and in strength. God gave the mid- 21
wives homes and families of their
own, because they feared him.
Pharaoh then ordered all his peo- 22
ple to throw every new-born Hebrew boy into the Nile, but to let
the girls live.

A descendant of Levi married a 2
Levite woman who conceived and 2
bore a son. When she saw what a
fine child he was, she hid him for
three months, but she could not con- 3
ceal him no longer. So she got a
rush basket for him, made it water-
tight with clay and tar, laid him in
it, and put it among the reeds by
the bank of the Nile. The child's 4
sister took her stand at a distance
to see what would happen to him.
Pharaoh's daughter came down to 5
bathe in the river, while her ladies-
in-waiting walked along the bank.
She noticed the basket among the

[a] Or numerous.

reeds and sent her slave-girl for it.
6 She took it from her and when she opened it, she saw the child. It was crying, and she was filled with pity for it. 'Why,' she said, 'it is a little
7 Hebrew boy.' Thereupon the sister said to Pharaoh's daughter, 'Shall I go and fetch one of the Hebrew women as a wet-nurse to suckle the
8 child for you?' Pharaoh's daughter told her to go; so the girl went and
9 called the baby's mother. Then Pharaoh's daughter said to her, 'Here is the child, suckle him for me, and I will pay you for it myself.' So the woman took the child and
10 suckled him. When the child was old enough, she brought him to Pharaoh's daughter, who adopted him and called him Moses,[a] 'because', she said, 'I drew[b] him out of the water.'

11 ONE day when Moses was grown up, he went out to his own kinsmen and saw them at their heavy labour. He saw an Egyptian strike
12 one of his fellow-Hebrews. He looked this way and that, and, seeing there was no one about, he struck the Egyptian down and hid
13 his body in the sand. When he went out next day, two Hebrews were fighting together. He asked the man who was in the wrong, 'Why
14 are you striking him?' 'Who set you up as an officer and judge over us?' the man replied. 'Do you mean to murder me as you murdered the Egyptian?' Moses was alarmed. 'The thing must have become
15 known', he said to himself. When Pharaoh heard of it, he tried to put Moses to death, but Moses made good his escape and settled in the land of Midian.
16 Now the priest of Midian had seven daughters. One day as Moses sat by a well, they came to draw water and filled the troughs to wa-
17 ter their father's sheep. Some shepherds came and drove them away; but Moses got up, took the girls'

part and watered their sheep himself. When the girls came back to 18 their father Reuel, he asked, 'How is it that you are back so quickly today?' 'An Egyptian rescued us 19 from the shepherds,' they answered; 'and he even drew the water for us and watered the sheep.' 'But 20 where is he then?' he said to his daughters. 'Why did you leave him behind? Go and invite him to eat with us.' So it came about that 21 Moses agreed to live with the man, and he gave Moses his daughter Zipporah in marriage. She bore him 22 a son, and Moses called him Gershom, 'because', he said, 'I have become an alien[c] living in a foreign land.'

YEARS passed, and the king of 23 Egypt died, but the Israelites still groaned in slavery. They cried out, and their appeal for rescue from their slavery rose up to God. He 24 heard their groaning, and remembered his covenant with Abraham, Isaac and Jacob; he saw the 25 plight of Israel, and he took heed of it.

Moses was minding the flock of 3 his father-in-law Jethro, priest of Midian. He led the flock along the side of the wilderness and came to Horeb, the mountain of God. There 2 the angel of the LORD appeared to him in the flame of a burning bush. Moses noticed that, although the bush was on fire, it was not being burnt up; so he said to himself, 'I 3 must go across to see this wonderful sight. Why does not the bush burn away?' When the LORD saw that 4 Moses had turned aside to look, he called to him out of the bush, 'Moses, Moses.' And Moses answered, 'Yes, I am here.' God said, 5 'Come no nearer; take off your sandals; the place where you are standing is holy ground.' Then he said, 'I 6 am the God of your forefathers, the God of Abraham, the God of Isaac, the God of Jacob.' Moses covered

---

[a] *Heb.* Mosheh.   [b] *Heb. verb* mashah.   [c] *Heb.* ger.

his face, for he was afraid to gaze on God.

7 The LORD said, 'I have indeed seen the misery of my people in Egypt. I have heard their outcry against their slave-masters. I have 8 taken heed of their sufferings, and have come down to rescue them from the power of Egypt, and to bring them up out of that country into a fine, broad land; it is a land flowing with milk and honey, the home of Canaanites, Hittites, Amorites, Perizzites, Hivites, and 9 Jebusites. The outcry of the Israelites has now reached me; yes, I have seen the brutality of the 10 Egyptians towards them. Come now; I will send you to Pharaoh and you shall bring my people 11 Israel out of Egypt.' 'But who am I,' Moses said to God, 'that I should go to Pharaoh, and that I should bring the Israelites out of Egypt?' 12 God answered, 'I am*a* with you. This shall be the proof that it is I who have sent you: when you have brought the people out of Egypt, you shall all worship God here on this mountain.'

13 Then Moses said to God, 'If I go to the Israelites and tell them that the God of their forefathers has sent me to them, and they ask me 14 his name, what shall I say?' God answered, 'I AM; that is who I am.*b* Tell them that I AM has sent you to 15 them.' And God said further, 'You must tell the Israelites this, that it is JEHOVAH*c* the God of their forefathers, the God of Abraham, the God of Isaac, the God of Jacob, who has sent you to them. This is my name for ever; this is my title 16 in every generation. Go and assemble the elders of Israel and tell them that JEHOVAH the God of their forefathers, the God of Abraham, Isaac and Jacob, has appeared to you and has said, "I have indeed turned my eyes towards you;

I have marked all that has been done to you in Egypt, and I am re- 17 solved to bring you up out of your misery in Egypt, into the country of the Canaanites, Hittites, Amorites, Perizzites, Hivites, and Jebusites, a land flowing with milk and honey." They will listen to you, 18 and then you and the elders of Israel must go to the king of Egypt. Tell him, "It has happened that the LORD the God of the Hebrews met us. So now give us leave to go a three days' journey into the wilderness to offer sacrifice to the LORD our God." I know well that the 19 king of Egypt will not give you leave unless he is compelled. I shall 20 then stretch out my hand and assail the Egyptians with all the miracles I shall work among them. After that he will send you away. Further, I 21 will bring this people into such favour with the Egyptians that, when you go, you will not go empty-handed. Every woman shall ask 22 her neighbour or any woman who lives in her house for jewellery of silver and gold and for clothing. Load your sons and daughters with them, and plunder Egypt.'

Moses answered, 'But they will 4 never believe me or listen to me; they will say, "The LORD did not appear to you."' The LORD said, 2 'What have you there in your hand?' 'A staff', Moses answered. The LORD said, 'Throw it on the 3 ground.' Moses threw it down and it turned into a snake. He ran away from it, but the LORD said, 'Put 4 your hand out and seize it by the tail.' He did so and gripped it firmly, and it turned back into a staff in his hand. 'This is to convince the 5 people that the LORD the God of their forefathers, the God of Abraham, the God of Isaac, the God of Jacob, has appeared to you.' Then 6 the LORD said, 'Put your hand inside the fold of your cloak.' He did

---

a Or I will be; *Heb.* ehyeh.　　　　*b* I AM...I am: *or* I will be what I will be.
c The Hebrew consonants are YHWH, *probably pronounced* Yahweh, *but traditionally read* Jehovah.

7 so, and when he drew it out the skin was diseased, white as snow. The LORD said, 'Put it back again', and he did so. When he drew it out this time it was as healthy as the rest of 8 his body. 'Now,' said the LORD, 'if they do not believe you and do not accept the evidence of the first sign, they may accept the evidence of 9 the second. But if they are not convinced even by these two signs, and will not accept what you say, then fetch some water from the Nile and pour it out on the dry ground, and the water you take from the Nile will turn to blood on the ground.'

10 But Moses said, 'O LORD, I have never been a man of ready speech, never in my life, not even now that thou hast spoken to me; I am slow 11 and hesitant of speech.' The LORD said to him, 'Who is it that gives man speech? Who makes him dumb or deaf? Who makes him clear-sighted or blind? Is it not I, the 12 LORD? Go now; I will help your speech and tell you what to say.' 13 But Moses still protested, 'No, 14 Lord, send whom thou wilt.' At this the LORD grew angry with Moses and said, 'Have you not a brother, Aaron the Levite? He, I know, will do all the speaking. He is already on his way out to meet you, and he will be glad indeed to 15 see you. You shall speak to him and put the words in his mouth; I will help both of you to speak and 16 tell you both what to do. He will do all the speaking to the people for you, he will be the mouthpiece, and you will be the god he speaks for. 17 But take this staff, for with it you are to work the signs.'

18 At length Moses went back to Jethro his father-in-law and said, 'Let me return to my kinsfolk in Egypt and see if they are still a-live.' Jethro told him to go and wished him well.

19 THE LORD spoke to Moses in Midian and said to him, 'Go back to Egypt, for all those who wished to kill you are dead.' So Moses took 20 his wife and children, mounted them on an ass and set out for Egypt with the staff of God in his hand. The LORD said to Moses, 21 'While you are on your way back to Egypt, keep in mind all the portents I have given you power to show. You shall display these before Pharaoh, but I will make him obstinate and he will not let the people go. Then tell Pharaoh that 22 these are the words of the LORD: "Israel is my first-born son. I have 23 told you to let my son go, so that he may worship me. You have refused to let him go, so I will kill your first-born son."'

During the journey, while they 24 were encamped for the night, the LORD met Moses, meaning to kill him, but Zipporah picked up a 25 sharp flint, cut off her son's foreskin, and touched him with it, saying, 'You are my blood-bridegroom.' So the LORD let Moses 26 alone. Then she said,[a] 'Blood-bridegroom by circumcision.'

Meanwhile the LORD had order- 27 ed Aaron to go and meet Moses in the wilderness. Aaron went and met him at the mountain of God, and he kissed him. Then Moses told 28 Aaron everything, the words the LORD had sent him to say and the signs he had commanded him to perform. Moses and Aaron went 29 and assembled all the elders of Israel. Aaron told them everything 30 that the LORD had said to Moses; he performed the signs before the people, and they were convinced. 31 They heard that the LORD had shown his concern for the Israelites and seen their misery; and they bowed themselves to the ground in worship.

After this, Moses and Aaron 5 came to Pharaoh and said, 'These are the words of the LORD the God of Israel: "Let my people go so that they may keep my pilgrim-

[a] *Or* Therefore women say.

2 feast in the wilderness."' 'Who is the LORD,' asked Pharaoh, 'that I should obey him and let Israel go? I care nothing for the LORD: and I tell you I will not let Israel go.'
3 They replied, 'It has happened that the God of the Hebrews met us. So let us go three days' journey into the wilderness to offer sacrifice to the LORD our God, or else he will attack us with pestilence or sword.'
4 But the king of Egypt said, 'Moses and Aaron, what do you mean by distracting the people from their
5 work? Back to your labours! Your people already outnumber the native Egyptians; yet you would have them stop working!'
6 That very day Pharaoh ordered the people's overseers and their
7 foremen not to supply the people with the straw used in making bricks, as they had done hitherto. 'Let them go and collect their own
8 straw, but see that they produce the same tally of bricks as before. On no account reduce it. They are a lazy people, and that is why they are clamouring to go and offer sac-
9 rifice to their god. Keep the men hard at work; let them attend to that and take no notice of a pack of
10 lies.' The overseers and foremen went out and said to the people, 'Pharaoh's orders are that no more
11 straw is to be supplied. Go and get it for yourselves wherever you can find it; but there will be no reduc-
12 tion in your daily task.' So the people scattered all over Egypt to
13 gather stubble for straw, while the overseers kept urging them on, bidding them complete, day after day, the same quantity as when straw
14 was supplied. Then the Israelite foremen were flogged because they were held responsible by Pharaoh's overseers, who asked them, 'Why did you not complete the usual number of bricks yesterday or to-
15 day?' So the foremen came and appealed to Pharaoh: 'Why do you treat your servants like this?' they

16 said. 'We are given no straw, yet they keep on telling us to make bricks. Here are we being flogged, but it is your people's fault.' But
17 Pharaoh replied, 'You are lazy, you are lazy. That is why you talk about going to offer sacrifice to the LORD. Now go; get on with your
18 work. You will be given no straw, but you must produce the tally of bricks.' When they were told that
19 they must not let the daily tally of bricks fall short, the Israelite foremen saw that they were in trouble.
20 As they came out from Pharaoh's presence they found Moses and Aaron waiting to meet them, and
21 said, 'May this bring the LORD's judgement down upon you: you have made us stink in the nostrils of Pharaoh and his subjects; you have put a sword in their hands to kill us.'

22 Moses went back to the LORD, and said, 'Why, O Lord, hast thou brought misfortune on this people? And why didst thou ever send me?
23 Since I first went to Pharaoh to speak in thy name he has heaped misfortune on thy people, and thou hast done nothing at all to rescue them.' The LORD answered, 'Now 6 you shall see what I will do to Pharaoh. In the end Pharaoh will let them go with a strong hand, nay, will drive them from his country with an outstretched arm.'

2 God spoke to Moses and said, 'I am the LORD. I appeared to Abra-
3 ham, Isaac, and Jacob as God Almighty. But I did not let myself be known to them by my name JEHO-
VAH.[a] Moreover, I made a covenant 4 with them to give them Canaan, the land where they settled for a time as foreigners. And now I have 5 heard the groaning of the Israelites, enslaved by the Egyptians, and I have called my covenant to mind. Say therefore to the Israelites, "I 6 am the LORD. I will release you from your labours in Egypt. I will rescue you from slavery there. I

[a] *See note on 3. 15.*

will redeem you with arm outstretched and with mighty acts of
7 judgement. I will adopt you as my people, and I will become your God. You shall know that I, the LORD, am your God, the God who releases you from your labours in Egypt.
8 I will lead you to the land which I swore with uplifted hand to give to Abraham, to Isaac and to Jacob. I will give it you for your possession. I am the LORD."'
9 Moses repeated these words to the Israelites, but they did not listen to him; they had become impatient because of their cruel slavery.
10 Then the LORD spoke to Moses
11 and said, 'Go and tell Pharaoh king of Egypt to set the Israelites free to
12 leave his country.' Moses made answer in the presence of the LORD, 'If the Israelites do not listen to me, how will Pharaoh listen to such a halting speaker as I am?'
13 Thus the LORD spoke to Moses and Aaron and gave them their commission to the Israelites and to Pharaoh, namely that they should bring the Israelites out of Egypt.

14[a] THESE were the heads of fathers' families:
Sons of Reuben, Israel's eldest son: Enoch, Pallu, Hezron and Carmi; these were the families of Reuben.
15 Sons of Simeon: Jemuel, Jamin, Ohad, Jachin, Zohar, and Saul, who was the son of a Canaanite woman; these were the families of Simeon.
16 These were the names of the sons of Levi in order of seniority: Gershon, Kohath and Merari. Levi lived to be a hundred and thirty-seven.
17 Sons of Gershon, family by family: Libni and Shimei.
18 Sons of Kohath: Amram, Izhar, Hebron and Uzziel. Kohath lived to be a hundred and thirty-three.

19 Sons of Merari: Mahli and Mushi. These were the families of Levi
20 in order of seniority. Amram married his father's sister Jochebed, and she bore him Aaron and Moses. Amram lived to be a hundred and thirty-seven.
21 Sons of Izhar: Korah, Nepheg and Zichri.
22 Sons of Uzziel: Mishael, Elzaphan and Sithri.
23 Aaron married Elisheba, who was the daughter of Amminadab and the sister of Nahshon, and she bore him Nadab, Abihu, Eleazar and Ithamar.
24 Sons of Korah: Assir, Elkanah and Abiasaph; these were the Korahite families.
25 Eleazar son of Aaron married one of the daughters of Putiel, and she bore him Phinehas. These were the heads of the Levite families, family by family.
26 It was this Aaron, together with Moses, to whom the LORD said, 'Bring the Israelites out of Egypt, mustered in their tribal hosts.'
27 These were the men who told Pharaoh king of Egypt to let the Israelites leave Egypt. It was this same Moses and Aaron.

28 WHEN the LORD spoke to Moses in Egypt he said, 'I am the LORD.
29 Tell Pharaoh king of Egypt all that I say to you.' Moses made an-
30 swer in the presence of the LORD, 'I am a halting speaker; how will Pharaoh listen to me?' The LORD
7 answered Moses, 'See now, I have made you like a god for Pharaoh, with your brother Aaron as your
2 spokesman. You must tell your brother Aaron all I bid you say, and he will tell Pharaoh, and Pharaoh will let the Israelites go out of
3 his country; but I will make him stubborn. Then will I show sign after sign and portent after portent in the land of Egypt. But Pharaoh
4 will not listen to you, so I will assert my power in Egypt, and with

[a] *Verses 14–16: cp. Gen. 46. 8–11; Num. 26. 5, 6, 12, 13.*

mighty acts of judgement I will bring my people, the Israelites, out 5 of Egypt in their tribal hosts. When I put forth my power against the Egyptians and bring the Israelites out from them, then Egypt will 6 know that I am the LORD.' So Moses and Aaron did exactly as the 7 LORD had commanded. At the time when they spoke to Pharaoh, Moses was eighty years old and Aaron eighty-three.

8 The LORD said to Moses and 9 Aaron, 'If Pharaoh demands some portent from you, then you, Moses, must say to Aaron, "Take your staff and throw it down in front of Pharaoh, and it will turn into a ser- 10 pent."' When Moses and Aaron came to Pharaoh, they did as the LORD had told them. Aaron threw down his staff in front of Pharaoh and his courtiers, and it turned into 11 a serpent. At this, Pharaoh summoned the wise men and the sorcerers, and the Egyptian magicians too did the same thing by their 12 spells. Every man threw his staff down, and each staff turned into a serpent; but Aaron's staff swal- 13 lowed up theirs. Pharaoh, however, was obstinate; as the LORD had foretold, he would not listen to Moses and Aaron.

14 Then the LORD said to Moses, 'Pharaoh is obdurate: he has re- 15 fused to set the people free. Go to him in the morning on his way out to the river. Stand and wait on the bank of the Nile to meet him, and take with you the staff that turned 16 into a snake. Say this to him: "The LORD the God of the Hebrews sent me to bid you let his people go in order to worship him in the wilderness. So far you have not listened 17 to his words; so now the LORD says, 'By this you shall know that I am the LORD.' With this rod that I have in my hand, I shall now strike the water in the Nile and it will be 18 changed into blood. The fish will die and the river will stink, and the Egyptians will be unable to drink

water from the Nile."' The LORD 19 then told Moses to say to Aaron, 'Take your staff and stretch your hand out over the waters of Egypt, its rivers and its streams, and over every pool and cistern, to turn them into blood. There shall be blood throughout the whole of Egypt, blood even in their wooden bowls and jars of stone.' So Moses and 20 Aaron did as the LORD had commanded. He lifted up his staff and struck the water of the Nile in the sight of Pharaoh and his courtiers, and all the water was changed into blood. The fish died and the river 21 stank, and the Egyptians could not drink water from the Nile. There was blood everywhere in Egypt. But the Egyptian magicians did 22 the same thing by their spells; and still Pharaoh remained obstinate, as the LORD had foretold, and did not listen to Moses and Aaron. He 23 turned away, went into his house and dismissed the matter from his mind. Then the Egyptians all dug 24 for drinking water round about the river, because they could not drink from the waters of the Nile itself. This lasted for seven days from the 25 time when the LORD struck the Nile.

The LORD then told Moses to go 8 into Pharaoh's presence and say to him, 'These are the words of the LORD: "Let my people go in order to worship me. If you refuse to let 2 them go, I will plague the whole of your territory with frogs. The Nile 3 shall swarm with them. They shall come up from the river into your house, into your bedroom and on to your bed, into the houses of your courtiers and your people, into your ovens and your kneading-troughs. The frogs shall clamber 4 over you, your people, and your courtiers."' Then the LORD told 5 Moses to say to Aaron, 'Take your staff in your hand and stretch it out over the rivers, streams, and pools, to bring up frogs upon the land of Egypt.' So Aaron stretched 6 out his hand over the waters of Egypt, and the frogs came up and 7 covered all the land. The magicians did the same thing by their spells: they too brought up frogs upon the 8 land of Egypt. Then Pharaoh summoned Moses and Aaron. 'Pray to the LORD', he said, 'to take the frogs away from me and my people, and I will let the people go to sacrifice to the LORD.' 9 Moses said, 'Of your royal favour, appoint a time when I may intercede for you and your courtiers and people, so that you and your houses may be rid of the frogs, and none be left except 10 in the Nile.' 'Tomorrow', Pharaoh said. 'It shall be as you say,' replied Moses, 'so that you may know there is no one like our God, the 11 LORD. The frogs shall depart from you, from your houses, your courtiers, and your people: none shall 12 be left except in the Nile.' Moses and Aaron left Pharaoh's presence, and Moses appealed to the LORD to remove the frogs which he had 13 brought on Pharaoh. The LORD did as Moses had asked, and in house and courtyard and in the open the 14 frogs all perished. They piled them into countless heaps and the land 15 stank; but when Pharaoh found that he was given relief he became obdurate; as the LORD had foretold, he did not listen to Moses and Aaron.

16　　The LORD then told Moses to say to Aaron, 'Stretch out your staff and strike the dust on the ground, and it will turn into maggots 17 throughout the land of Egypt', and they obeyed. Aaron stretched out his staff and struck the dust, and it turned into maggots on man and beast. All the dust turned into maggots throughout the land of 18 Egypt. The magicians tried to produce maggots in the same way by their spells, but they failed. The maggots were everywhere, on man 19 and beast. 'It is the finger of God', said the magicians to Pharaoh, but Pharaoh remained obstinate; as

the LORD had foretold, he did not listen to them.

The LORD told Moses to rise 20 early in the morning and stand in Pharaoh's path as he went out to the river and to say to him, 'These are the words of the LORD: "Let my people go in order to worship me. If 21 you do not let my people go, I will send swarms of flies upon you, your courtiers, your people, and your houses. The houses of the Egyptians shall be filled with the swarms and so shall all the land they live in, but on that day I will make an 22 exception of Goshen, the land where my people live: there shall be no swarms there. Thus you shall know that I, the LORD, am here in the land. I will make a distinction 23 between my people and yours. Tomorrow this sign shall appear."' The LORD did this; dense swarms 24 of flies infested Pharaoh's house and those of his courtiers; throughout Egypt the land was threatened with ruin by the swarms. Pharaoh 25 summoned Moses and Aaron and said to them, 'Go and sacrifice to your God, but in this country.' 'That we cannot do,' replied Moses, 26 'because the victim we shall sacrifice to the LORD our God is an abomination to the Egyptians. If the Egyptians see us offer such an animal, will they not stone us to death? We must go a three days' 27 journey into the wilderness to sacrifice to the LORD our God, as he commands us.' 'I will let you 28 go,' said Pharaoh, 'and you shall sacrifice to your God in the wilderness; only do not go far. Now intercede for me.' Moses answered, 'As 29 soon as I leave you I will intercede with the LORD. Tomorrow the swarms will depart from Pharaoh, his courtiers, and his people. Only let not Pharaoh trifle any more with the people by preventing them from going to sacrifice to the LORD.' Then Moses left Pharaoh 30 and interceded with the LORD. The 31 LORD did as Moses had said; he removed the swarms from Pharaoh, his courtiers, and his people; not 32 one was left. But once again Pharaoh became obdurate and did not let the people go.

9 The LORD said to Moses, 'Go into Pharaoh's presence and say to him, "These are the words of the LORD the God of the Hebrews: 'Let my people go in order to worship 2 me.' If you refuse to let them go and still keep your hold on them, 3 the LORD will strike your grazing herds, your horses and asses, your camels, cattle, and sheep with a 4 terrible pestilence. But the LORD will make a distinction between Israel's herds and those of the Egyptians. Of all that belong to Israel not a single one shall die."'

5 The LORD fixed a time and said, 'Tomorrow I will do this through-6 out the land.' The next day the LORD struck. All the herds of Egypt died, but from the herds of the Israelites not one single beast 7 died. Pharaoh inquired and was told that not a beast from the herds of Israel had died; and yet he remained obdurate and did not let the people go.

8 The LORD said to Moses and Aaron, 'Take handfuls of soot from a kiln. Moses shall toss it into the 9 air in Pharaoh's sight, and it will turn into a fine dust over the whole of Egypt. All over Egypt it will become festering boils on man and 10 beast.' They took the soot from the kiln and stood before Pharaoh. Moses tossed it into the air and it produced festering boils on man 11 and beast. The magicians were no match for Moses because of the boils, which attacked them and all 12 the Egyptians. But the LORD made Pharaoh obstinate; as the LORD had foretold to Moses, he did not listen to Moses and Aaron.

13 The LORD then told Moses to rise early in the morning, present himself before Pharaoh, and say to him, 'These are the words of the LORD the God of the Hebrews:

"Let my people go in order to worship me. This time I will strike 14 home with all my plagues against you, your courtiers, and your people, so that you may know that there is none like me in all the earth. By now I could have stretch-15 ed out my hand, and struck you and your people with pestilence, and you would have vanished from the earth. I have let you live only to 16 show you my power and to spread my fame throughout the land. Since you still obstruct my people 17 and will not let them go, tomorrow 18 at this time I will send a violent hailstorm, such as has never been in Egypt from its first beginnings until now. Send now and bring 19 your herds under cover, and everything you have out in the open field. If anything, whether man or beast, which happens to be in the open, is not brought in, the hail will fall on it, and it will die."' Those of Pharaoh's subjects who 20 feared the word of the LORD hurried their slaves and cattle into their houses. But those who did not 21 take to heart the word of the LORD left their slaves and cattle in the open.

The LORD said to Moses, 'Stretch 22 out your hand towards the sky to bring down hail on the whole land of Egypt, on man and beast and every growing thing throughout the land.' Moses stretched out his 23 staff towards the sky, and the LORD sent thunder and hail, with fire flashing down to the ground. The LORD rained down hail on the land of Egypt, hail and fiery flashes 24 through the hail, so heavy that there had been nothing like it in all Egypt from the time that Egypt became a nation. Throughout 25 Egypt the hail struck everything in the fields, both man and beast; it beat down every growing thing and shattered every tree. Only in 26 the land of Goshen, where the Israelites lived, was there no hail.

Pharaoh sent and summoned 27

Moses and Aaron. 'This time I have sinned,' he said; 'the LORD is in the right; I and my people are in the

28 wrong. Intercede with the LORD, for we can bear no more of this thunder and hail. I will let you go

29 you need wait no longer.' Moses said, 'When I leave the city I will spread out my hands in prayer to the LORD. The thunder shall cease, and there shall be no more hail, so that you may know that the earth

30 is the LORD's. But you and your subjects – I know that you do not

31 yet fear the LORD God.' (The flax and barley were destroyed because the barley was in the ear and the

32 flax in bud, but the wheat and spelt were not destroyed because

33 they come later.) Moses left Pharaoh's presence, went out of the city and lifted up his hands to the LORD in prayer: the thunder and hail ceased, and no more rain fell.

34 When Pharaoh saw that the downpour, the hail, and the thunder had ceased, he sinned again, he and his

35 courtiers, and became obdurate. So Pharaoh remained obstinate; as the LORD had foretold through Moses, he did not let the people go.

10 Then the LORD said to Moses, 'Go into Pharaoh's presence. I have made him and his courtiers obdurate, so that I may show these my

2 signs among them, and so that you can tell your children and grandchildren the story: how I made sport of the Egyptians, and what signs I showed among them. Thus you will know that I am the LORD.'

3 Moses and Aaron went in to Pharaoh and said to him, 'These are the words of the LORD the God of the Hebrews: "How long will you refuse to humble yourself before me? Let my people go in order to

4 worship me. If you refuse to let my people go, tomorrow I will bring

5 locusts into your country. They shall cover the face of the land so that it cannot be seen. They shall eat up the last remnant left you by the hail. They shall devour every

tree that grows in your country- side. Your houses and your cour- 6 tiers' houses, every house in Egypt, shall be full of them; your fathers never saw the like nor their fathers before them; such a thing has not happened from their time until now."' He turned and left Pharaoh's presence. Pharaoh's cour- 7 tiers said to him, 'How long must we be caught in this man's toils? Let their menfolk go and wor- ship the LORD their God. Do you not know by now that Egypt is ruined?' So Moses and Aaron were 8 brought back to Pharaoh, and he said to them, 'You may go and wor- ship the LORD your God; but who exactly is to go?' 'All,' said Moses, 9 'young and old, boys and girls, sheep and cattle; for we have to keep the LORD's pilgrim-feast.' Pharaoh replied, 'Very well then; 10 take your dependants with you when you go; and the LORD be with you. But beware, there is trouble in store for you. No, your menfolk 11 may go and worship the LORD, for that is all you asked.' So they were driven out from Pharaoh's pre- sence.

Then the LORD said to Moses, 12 'Stretch out your hand over Egypt so that the locusts may come and invade the land and devour all the vegetation in it, everything the hail has left.' Moses stretched out 13 his staff over the land of Egypt, and the LORD sent a wind roaring in from the east all that day and all that night. When morning came, the east wind had brought the lo- custs. They invaded the whole land 14 of Egypt, and settled on all its ter- ritory in swarms so dense that the like of them had never been seen before, nor ever will be again. They 15 covered the surface of the whole land till it was black with them. They devoured all the vegetation and all the fruit of the trees that the hail had spared. There was no green left on tree or plant through- out all Egypt. Pharaoh hastily 16

summoned Moses and Aaron. 'I
have sinned against the LORD your
17 God and against you', he said. 'Forgive my sin, I pray, just this once.
Intercede with the LORD your God
and beg him only to remove this
18 deadly plague from me.' Moses left
Pharaoh and interceded with the
19 LORD. The LORD changed the wind
into a westerly gale, which carried
the locusts away and swept them
into the Red Sea.*a* There was not a
single locust left in all the territory
20 of Egypt. But the LORD made Pharaoh obstinate, and he did not let
the Israelites go.

21   Then the LORD said to Moses,
'Stretch out your hand towards the
sky so that there may be darkness
over the land of Egypt, darkness
22 that can be felt.' Moses stretched
out his hand towards the sky, and
it became pitch dark throughout
the land of Egypt for three days.
23 Men could not see one another; for
three days no one stirred from where
he was. But there was no darkness
24 wherever the Israelites lived. Pharaoh summoned Moses. 'Go,' he
said, 'and worship the LORD. Your
dependants may go with you; but
your flocks and herds must be left
25 with us.' But Moses said, 'No, you
must yourself supply us with animals for sacrifice and whole-offer-
26 ing to the LORD our God; and our
own flocks must go with us too –
not a hoof must be left behind. We
may need animals from our own
flocks to worship the LORD our
God; we ourselves cannot tell until
we are there how we are to worship
27 the LORD.' The LORD made Pharaoh obstinate, and he refused to
28 let them go. 'Out! Pester me no
more!' he said to Moses. 'Take care
you do not see my face again, for on
29 the day you do, you die.' 'You are
right,' said Moses; 'I shall never see
your face again.'

11   Then the LORD said to Moses,
'One last plague I will bring upon
Pharaoh and Egypt. After that he

will let you go; he will send you
packing, as a man dismisses a rejected bride. Let the people be told 2
that men and women alike should
ask their neighbours for jewellery
of silver and gold.' The LORD made 3
the Egyptians well-disposed towards them, and, moreover, Moses
was a very great man in Egypt in
the eyes of Pharaoh's courtiers and
of the people.

Moses then said, 'These are the 4
words of the LORD: "At midnight
I will go out among the Egyptians.
Every first-born creature in the 5
land of Egypt shall die: the first-
born of Pharaoh who sits on his
throne, the first-born of the slave-
girl at the handmill, and all the
first-born of the cattle. All Egypt 6
will send up a great cry of anguish,
a cry the like of which has never
been heard before, nor ever will be
again. But among all Israel not a 7
dog's tongue shall be so much as
scratched, no man or beast be
hurt." Thus you shall know that
the LORD does make a distinction
between Egypt and Israel. Then 8
all these courtiers of yours will
come down to me, prostrate themselves and cry, "Go away, you and
all the people who follow at your
heels." After that I will go away.'
Then Moses left Pharaoh's presence hot with anger.

The LORD said to Moses, 'Pha- 9
raoh will not listen to you; I will
therefore show still more portents
in the land of Egypt.' All these 10
portents had Moses and Aaron
shown in the presence of Pharaoh,
and yet the LORD made him obstinate, and he did not let the Israelites leave the country.

The institution of the Passover

THE LORD said to Moses and 12
Aaron in Egypt: This month is for 2
you the first of months; you shall
make it the first month of the year.
Speak to the whole community of 3

a Or the Sea of Reeds.

Israel and say to them: On the tenth day of this month let each man take a lamb or a kid for his 4 family, one for each household, but if a household is too small for one lamb or one kid, then the man and his nearest neighbour may take one between them. They shall share the cost, taking into account both the number of persons and the a- 5 mount each of them eats. Your lamb or kid must be without blemish, a yearling male. You may 6 take equally a sheep or a goat. You must have it in safe keeping until the fourteenth day of this month, and then all the assembled community of Israel shall slaughter the victim between dusk and dark. 7 They must take some of the blood and smear it on the two door-posts and on the lintel of every house in 8 which they eat the lamb. On that night they shall eat the flesh roast on the fire; they shall eat it with unleavened cakes and bitter herbs. 9 You are not to eat any of it raw or even boiled in water, but roasted, 10 head, shins, and entrails. You shall not leave any of it till morning; if anything is left over until morning, it must be destroyed by fire.

11   This is the way in which you must eat it: you shall have your belt fastened, your sandals on your feet and your staff in your hand, and you must eat it in urgent haste. 12 It is the LORD's Passover. On that night I shall pass through the land of Egypt and kill every first-born of man and beast. Thus will I execute judgement, I the LORD, a- 13 gainst all the gods of Egypt. And as for you, the blood will be a sign on the houses in which you are: when I see the blood I will pass over*a* you; the mortal blow shall not touch you, when I strike the land of Egypt.

14   You shall keep this day as a day of remembrance, and make it a pilgrim-feast, a festival of the LORD; you shall keep it generation after generation as a rule for all time. For seven days you shall eat 15 unleavened cakes. On the very first day you shall rid your houses of leaven; from the first day to the seventh anyone who eats leavened bread shall be outlawed from Israel. On the first day there shall be 16 a sacred assembly and on the seventh day there shall be a sacred assembly: on these days no work shall be done, except what must be done to provide food for everyone; and that will be allowed. You shall 17 observe these commandments because this was the very day on which I brought you out of Egypt in your tribal hosts. You shall observe this day from generation to generation as a rule for all time.

You shall eat unleavened cakes 18 in the first month from the evening which begins the fourteenth day until the evening which begins the twenty-first day. For seven 19 days no leaven may be found in your houses, for anyone who eats anything fermented shall be outlawed from the community of Israel, be he foreigner or native. You must eat nothing fermented. 20 Wherever you live you must eat your cakes unleavened.

Moses summoned all the elders 21 of Israel and said to them, 'Go at once and get sheep for your families and slaughter the Passover. Then take a bunch of marjoram,*b* 22 dip it in the blood in the basin*c* and smear some blood from the basin*d* on the lintel and the two door-posts. Nobody may go out through the door of his house till morning. The 23 LORD will go through Egypt and strike it, but when he sees the blood on the lintel and the two door-posts, he will pass over that door and will not let the destroyer enter your houses to strike you. You shall keep this as a rule for you 24 and your children for all time.

a Or stand guard over.
c Or on the threshold.

b Or hyssop.
d Or from the threshold.

25 When you enter the land which the
LORD will give you as he promised,
26 you shall observe this rite. Then,
when your children ask you, "What
27 is the meaning of this rite?" you
shall say, "It is the LORD's Passover, for he passed over the houses
of the Israelites in Egypt when he
struck the Egyptians but spared
our houses." ' The people bowed
down and prostrated themselves.
28 The Israelites went and did all
that the LORD had commanded
29 Moses and Aaron; and by midnight the LORD had struck down
every first-born in Egypt, from
the first-born of Pharaoh on his
throne to the first-born of the captive in the dungeon, and the first-
30 born of cattle. Before night was
over Pharaoh rose, he and all his
courtiers and all the Egyptians,
and a great cry of anguish went up,
because not a house in Egypt was
31 without its dead. Pharaoh summoned Moses and Aaron while it
was still night and said, 'Up with
you! Be off, and leave my people,
you and your Israelites. Go and
32 worship the LORD, as you ask; take
your sheep and cattle, and go; and
33 ask God's blessing on me also.' The
Egyptians urged on the people and
hurried them out of the country,
'or else', they said, 'we shall all be
34 dead.' The people picked up their
dough before it was leavened,
wrapped their kneading-troughs in
their cloaks, and slung them on
35 their shoulders. Meanwhile the Israelites had done as Moses had
told them, asking the Egyptians
for jewellery of silver and gold and
36 for clothing. As the LORD had made
the Egyptians well-disposed towards them, they let them have
what they asked; in this way they
plundered the Egyptians.

The exodus from Egypt

37 THE Israelites set out from Rameses on the way to Succoth, about
six hundred thousand men on foot,

not counting dependants. And 38
with them too went a large company of every kind, and cattle in
great numbers, both flocks and
herds. The dough they had brought 39
from Egypt they baked into unleavened cakes, because there was
no leaven; for they had been driven
out of Egypt and allowed no time
even to get food ready for themselves.

The Israelites had been settled 40
in Egypt for four hundred and
thirty years. At the end of four 41
hundred and thirty years, on this
very day, all the tribes of the LORD
came out of Egypt. This was a 42
night of vigil as the LORD waited
to bring them out of Egypt. It is
the LORD's night; all Israelites
keep their vigil generation after
generation.

The LORD said to Moses and 43
Aaron: These are the rules for the
Passover. No foreigner may partake of it; any bought slave may 44
eat it if you have circumcised him;
no stranger or hired man may eat 45
it. Each lamb must be eaten inside 46
the one house, and you must not
take any of the flesh outside the
house. You must not break a single
bone of it. The whole community of 47
Israel shall keep this feast. If there 48
are aliens living with you and they
are to keep the Passover to the
LORD, every male of them must be
circumcised, and then he can take
part; he shall rank as native-born.
No one who is uncircumcised may
eat of it. The same law shall apply 49
both to the native-born and to the
alien who is living among you.

The Israelites did all that the 50
LORD had commanded Moses and
Aaron; and on this very day the 51
LORD brought the Israelites out of
Egypt mustered in their tribal
hosts.

The LORD spoke to Moses and 13
said, 'Every first-born, the first 2
birth of every womb among the
Israelites, you must dedicate to me,
both man and beast; it is mine.'

3 Then Moses said to the people, 'Remember this day, the day on which you have come out of Egypt, the land of slavery, because the LORD by the strength of his hand has brought you out. No leaven 4 may be eaten this day, for today, in the month of Abib, is the day of 5 your exodus; and when the LORD has brought you into the country of the Canaanites, Hittites, Amorites, Hivites, and Jebusites, the land which he swore to your forefathers to give you, a land flowing with milk and honey, then you must observe this rite in this same 6 month. For seven days you shall eat unleavened cakes, and on the seventh day there shall be a pil-7 grim-feast of the LORD. Only unleavened cakes shall be eaten during the seven days; nothing fermented and no leaven shall be seen 8 throughout your territory. On that day you shall tell your son, "This commemorates what the LORD did for me when I came out of Egypt." 9 You shall have the record of it as a sign upon your hand, and upon your forehead as a reminder, to make sure that the law of the LORD is always on your lips, because the LORD with a strong hand brought 10 you out of Egypt. This is a rule, and you shall keep it at the appointed time from year to year.

11 'When the LORD has brought you into the land of the Canaanites as he swore to you and to your fore-12 fathers, and given it to you, you shall surrender to the LORD the first birth of every womb; and of all first-born offspring of your cattle the males belong to the LORD. 13 Every first-born male ass you may redeem with a kid or lamb, but if you do not redeem it, you must break its neck. Every first-born among your sons you must redeem. 14 When in time to come your son asks you what this means, you shall say to him, "By the strength of his hand the LORD brought us out of Egypt, out of the land of slavery. When Pharaoh proved stubborn 15 and refused to let us go, the LORD killed all the first-born in Egypt both man and beast. That is why I sacrifice to the LORD the first birth of every womb if it is a male and redeem every first-born of my sons. You shall have the record of it as 16 a sign upon your hand, and upon your forehead as a phylactery, because by the strength of his hand the LORD brought us out of Egypt."'

N o w when Pharaoh let the people 17 go, God did not guide them by the road towards the Philistines, although that was the shortest; for he said, 'The people may change their minds when they see war before them, and turn back to Egypt.' So God made them go 18 round by way of the wilderness towards the Red Sea; and the fifth generation of Israelites departed from Egypt.

Moses took the bones of Joseph 19 with him, because Joseph had exacted an oath from the Israelites: 'Some day', he said, 'God will show his care for you, and then, as you go, you must take my bones with you.'

They set out from Succoth and 20 encamped at Etham on the edge of the wilderness. And all the time 21 the LORD went before them, by day a pillar of cloud to guide them on their journey, by night a pillar of fire to give them light, so that they could travel night and day. The 22 pillar of cloud never left its place in front of the people by day, nor the pillar of fire by night.

The LORD spoke to Moses and 14 said, 'Speak to the Israelites: they 2 are to turn back and encamp before Pi-hahiroth,*a* between Migdol and the sea to the east of Baal-zephon; your camp shall be opposite, by the sea. Pharaoh will then think 3 that the Israelites are finding them-

a Or where the desert tracks begin.

selves in difficult country, and are
4 hemmed in by the wilderness. I will
make Pharaoh obstinate, and he
will pursue them, so that I may
win glory for myself at the expense
of Pharaoh and all his army; and
the Egyptians shall know that I am
the LORD.' The Israelites did as
they were bidden.

5 When the king of Egypt was told
that the Israelites had slipped a-
way, he and his courtiers changed
their minds completely, and said,
'What have we done? We have let
6 our Israelite slaves go free!' So
Pharaoh put horses to his chariot,
7 and took his troops with him. He
took six hundred picked chariots
and all the other chariots of Egypt,
8 with a commander in each. Then
Pharaoh king of Egypt, made obstinate by the LORD, pursued the
Israelites as they marched defiant-
9 ly away. The Egyptians, all Pharaoh's chariots and horses, cavalry
and infantry, pursued them and
overtook them encamped beside
the sea by Pi-hahiroth to the east
10 of Baal-zephon. Pharaoh was almost upon them when the Israelites looked up and saw the Egyptians close behind. In their terror
they clamoured to the LORD for
11 help and said to Moses, 'Were
there no graves in Egypt, that you
should have brought us here to die
in the wilderness? See what you
have done to us by bringing us out
12 of Egypt! Is not this just what we
meant when we said in Egypt,
"Leave us alone; let us be slaves to
the Egyptians"? We would rather
be slaves to the Egyptians than die
13 here in the wilderness.' 'Have no
fear,' Moses answered; 'stand firm
and see the deliverance that the
LORD will bring you this day; for as
sure as you see the Egyptians now,
14 you will never see them again. The
LORD will fight for you; so hold
your peace.'
15 The LORD said to Moses, 'What
is the meaning of this clamour?
Tell the Israelites to strike camp.

And you shall raise high your staff, 16
stretch out your hand over the sea
and cleave it in two, so that the Israelites can pass through the sea on
dry ground. For my part I will make 17
the Egyptians obstinate and they
will come after you; thus will I win
glory for myself at the expense of
Pharaoh and his army, chariots and
cavalry all together. The Egyp- 18
tians will know that I am the LORD
when I win glory for myself at the
expense of their Pharaoh, his
chariots and cavalry.'
The angel of God, who had kept 19
in front of the Israelites, moved a-
way to the rear. The pillar of cloud
moved from the front and took its
place behind them and so came be- 20
tween the Egyptians and the Israelites. And the cloud brought on
darkness and early nightfall, so
that contact was lost throughout
the night.
Then Moses stretched out his 21
hand over the sea, and the LORD
drove the sea away all night with
a strong east wind and turned the
sea-bed into dry land. The waters
were torn apart, and the Israelites 22
went through the sea on the dry
ground, while the waters made a
wall for them to right and to left.
The Egyptians went in pursuit of 23
them far into the sea, all Pharaoh's
horse, his chariots, and his cavalry.
In the morning watch the LORD 24
looked down on the Egyptian army
through the pillar of fire and cloud,
and he threw them into a panic. He 25
clogged their chariot wheels and
made them lumber along heavily,
so that the Egyptians said, 'It is
the LORD fighting for Israel against
Egypt; let us flee.' Then the LORD 26
said to Moses, 'Stretch out your
hand over the sea, and let the water flow back over the Egyptians,
their chariots and their cavalry.' So 27
Moses stretched out his hand over
the sea, and at daybreak the water
returned to its accustomed place;
but the Egyptians were in flight as
it advanced, and the LORD swept

28 them out into the sea. The water flowed back and covered all Pharaoh's army, the chariots and the cavalry, which had pressed the pursuit into the sea. Not one man 29 was left alive. Meanwhile the Israelites had passed along the dry ground through the sea, with the water making a wall for them to 30 right and to left. That day the LORD saved Israel from the power of Egypt, and the Israelites saw the Egyptians lying dead on the 31 sea-shore. When Israel saw the great power which the LORD had put forth against Egypt, all the people feared the LORD, and they put their faith in him and in Moses his servant.

15   Then Moses and the Israelites sang this song to the LORD:

I will sing to the LORD, for he has risen up in triumph;
   the horse and his rider he has hurled into the sea.
2 The LORD is my refuge and my defence,
   he has shown himself my deliverer.
He is my God, and I will glorify him;
   he is my father's God, and I will exalt him.
3 The LORD is a warrior: the LORD is his name.
4 The chariots of Pharaoh and his army
   he has cast into the sea;
   the flower of his officers
   are engulfed in the Red Sea.
5 The watery abyss has covered them,
   they sank into the depths like a stone.
6 Thy right hand, O LORD, is majestic in strength:
   thy right hand, O LORD, shattered the enemy.
7 In the fullness of thy triumph
   thou didst cast the rebels down:
   thou didst let loose thy fury;
   it consumed them like chaff.
8 At the blast of thy anger the sea piled up:

the waters stood up like a bank:
out at sea the great deep congealed.
The enemy said, 'I will pursue, I 9 will overtake;
I will divide the spoil,
I will glut my appetite upon them;
I will draw my sword,
I will rid myself of them.'
Thou didst blow with thy blast; 10 the sea covered them.
They sank like lead in the swelling waves.
Who is like thee, O LORD, among 11 the gods*a*?
Who is like thee, majestic in holiness,
worthy of awe and praise, who workest wonders?
Thou didst stretch out thy right 12 hand,
earth engulfed them.
In thy constant love thou hast led 13 the people
whom thou didst ransom:
thou hast guided them by thy strength
to thy holy dwelling-place.
Nations heard and trembled;   14
agony seized the dwellers in Philistia.
Then the chieftains of Edom were 15 dismayed,
trembling seized the leaders of Moab,
all the inhabitants of Canaan were in turmoil;
terror and dread fell upon them: 16
through the might of thy arm they stayed stone-still,
while thy people passed, O LORD,
while the people whom thou madest thy own*b* passed by.
Thou broughtest them in and didst 17 plant them
in the mount that is thy possession,
the dwelling-place, O LORD, of thy own making,
the sanctuary, O LORD, which thy own hands prepared.
The LORD shall reign for ever and 18 for ever.

---

a Or in might.   *b* madest thy own: or didst create.

19 For Pharaoh's horse, both chariots and cavalry, went into the
sea, and the LORD brought back
the waters over them, but Israel
had passed through the sea on dry
20 ground. And Miriam the prophetess, Aaron's sister, took up her
tambourine, and all the women followed her, dancing to the sound of
21 tambourines; and Miriam sang
them this refrain:

Sing to the LORD, for he has risen
    up in triumph;
the horse and his rider he has
    hurled into the sea.

22 MOSES led Israel from the Red Sea
out into the wilderness of Shur. For
three days they travelled through
the wilderness without finding wa-
23 ter. They came to Marah, but could
not drink the Marah water because
it was bitter; that is why the place
24 was called Marah. The people complained to Moses and asked, 'What
25 are we to drink?' Moses cried to the
LORD, and the LORD showed him a
log which he threw into the water,
and then the water became sweet.
    It was there that the LORD laid
down a precept and rule of life;
26 there he put them to the test. He
said, 'If only you will obey the
LORD your God, if you will do what
is right in his eyes, if you will listen
to his commands and keep all his
statutes, then I will never bring
upon you any of the sufferings
which I brought on the Egyptians;
for I the LORD am your healer.'
27 They came to Elim, where there
were twelve springs and seventy
palm-trees, and there they encamped beside the water.

16 The whole community of the Israelites set out from Elim and came
into the wilderness of Sin, which
lies between Elim and Sinai. This
was on the fifteenth day of the
second month after they had left
Egypt.
2 The Israelites complained to
Moses and Aaron in the wilderness
and said, 'If only we had died at 3
the LORD's hand in Egypt, where
we sat round the fleshpots and had
plenty of bread to eat! But you
have brought us out into this wilderness to let this whole assembly
starve to death.' The LORD said to 4
Moses, 'I will rain down bread from
heaven for you. Each day the people
shall go out and gather a day's supply, so that I can put them to the
test and see whether they will follow
my instructions or not. But on the 5
sixth day, when they prepare what
they bring in, it shall be twice as
much as they have gathered on
other days.' Moses and Aaron then 6
said to all the Israelites, 'In the
evening you will know that it was
the LORD who brought you out of
Egypt, and in the morning you will 7
see the glory of the LORD, because
he has heeded your complaints a-
gainst him; it is not against us that
you bring your complaints; we are
nothing.' 'You shall know this', 8
Moses said, 'when the LORD, in answer to your complaints, gives you
flesh to eat in the evening, and in
the morning bread in plenty. What
are we? It is against the LORD that
you bring your complaints, and
not against us.'
    Moses told Aaron to say to the 9
whole community of Israel, 'Come
into the presence of the LORD, for
he has heeded your complaints.'
While Aaron was speaking to the 10
community of the Israelites, they
looked towards the wilderness, and
there was the glory of the LORD appearing in the cloud. The LORD 11
spoke to Moses and said, 'I have 12
heard the complaints of the Israelites. Say to them, "Between dusk
and dark you will have flesh to eat
and in the morning bread in plenty.
You shall know that I the LORD am
your God."'
    That evening a flock of quails 13
flew in and settled all over the
camp, and in the morning a fall of
dew lay all around it. When the 14
dew was gone, there in the wilder-

ness, fine flakes appeared, fine as
15 hoar-frost on the ground. When
the Israelites saw it, they said to
one another, 'What is that?',[a] because they did not know what it
was. Moses said to them, 'That is
the bread which the LORD has gi-
16 ven you to eat. This is the command the LORD has given: "Each
of you is to gather as much as he
can eat: let every man take an
omer a head for every person in his
17 tent."' The Israelites did this, and
they gathered, some more, some
18 less, but when they measured it by
the omer, those who had gathered
more had not too much, and those
who had gathered less had not too
little. Each had just as much as he
19 could eat. Moses said, 'No one may
20 keep any of it till morning.' Some,
however, did not listen to Moses;
they kept part of it till morning,
and it became full of maggots and
stank, and Moses was angry with
21 them. Each morning every man
gathered as much as he could eat,
and when the sun grew hot, it
22 melted away. On the sixth day they
gathered twice as much food, two
omers each. All the chiefs of the
community came and told Moses.
23 'This', he answered, 'is what the
LORD has said: "Tomorrow is a day
of sacred rest, a sabbath holy to the
LORD." So bake what you want to
bake now, and boil what you want
to boil; put aside what remains
over and keep it safe till morning.'
24 So they put it aside till morning as
Moses had commanded, and it did
not stink, nor did maggots appear
25 in it. 'Eat it today,' said Moses,
'because today is a sabbath of
the LORD. Today you will find
26 none outside. For six days you may
gather it, but on the seventh day,
the sabbath, there will be none.'
27 Some of the people did go out to
gather it on the seventh day, but
28 they found none. The LORD said to
Moses, 'How long will you refuse to
obey my commands and instruc-

tions? The LORD has given you the 29
sabbath, and so he gives you two
days' food every sixth day. Let
each man stay where he is; no one
may stir from his home on the
seventh day.' And the people kept 30
the sabbath on the seventh day.

Israel called the food manna; it 31
was white, like coriander seed, and
it tasted like a wafer made with
honey.

'This', said Moses, 'is the com- 32
mand which the LORD has given:
"Take a full omer of it to be kept
for future generations, so that they
may see the bread with which I fed
you in the wilderness when I
brought you out of Egypt."' So 33
Moses said to Aaron, 'Take a jar and
fill it with an omer of manna and
store it in the presence of the LORD
to be kept for future generations.'
Aaron did as the LORD had com- 34
manded Moses, and stored it before
the Testimony for safe keeping. The 35
Israelites ate the manna for forty
years until they came to a land
where they could settle; they ate it
until they came to the border of
Canaan. (An omer is one tenth of an 36
ephah.)

The whole community of Israel 17
set out from the wilderness of Sin
and travelled by stages as the LORD
told them. They encamped at Rephidim, where there was no water
for the people to drink, and a dis- 2
pute arose between them and
Moses. When they said, 'Give us
water to drink', Moses said, 'Why
do you dispute with me? Why do
you challenge the LORD?' There 3
the people became so thirsty that
they raised an outcry against
Moses: 'Why have you brought us
out of Egypt with our children and
our herds to let us all die of thirst?'
Moses cried to the LORD, 'What 4
shall I do with these people? In a
moment they will be stoning me.'
The LORD answered, 'Go forward 5
ahead of the people; take with you
some of the elders of Israel and the

[a] *Heb.* man-hu (*cp. verse* 31).

staff with which you struck the
6 Nile, and go. You will find me waiting for you there, by a rock in Horeb. Strike the rock; water will pour out of it, and the people shall drink.' Moses did this in the sight
7 of the elders of Israel. He named the place Massah[a] and Meribah,[b] because the Israelites had disputed with him and challenged the LORD with their question, 'Is the LORD in our midst or not?'

8 The Amalekites came and at-
9 tacked Israel at Rephidim. Moses said to Joshua, 'Pick your men, and march out tomorrow to fight for us against Amalek; and I will take my stand on the hill-top with
10 the staff of God in my hand.' Joshua carried out his orders and fought against Amalek while Moses, Aaron and Hur climbed to the top
11 of the hill. Whenever Moses raised his hands Israel had the advantage, and when he lowered his hands
12 Amalek had the advantage. But when his arms grew heavy they took a stone and put it under him and, as he sat, Aaron and Hur held up his hands, one on each side, so that his hands remained steady till
13 sunset. Thus Joshua defeated Amalek and put its people to the sword.
14 The LORD said to Moses, 'Record this in writing, and tell it to Joshua in these words: "I am resolved to blot out all memory of Amalek from under heaven."'
15 Moses built an altar, and named it
16 Jehovah-nissi and said, 'My oath upon it: the LORD is at war with Amalek generation after generation.'

18 JETHRO priest of Midian, father-in-law of Moses, heard all that God had done for Moses and Israel his people, and how the LORD had
2 brought Israel out of Egypt. When Moses had dismissed his wife Zipporah, Jethro his father-in-law had
3 received her and her two sons. The name of the one was Gershom,

'for', said Moses, 'I have become an alien[c] living in a foreign land'; the other's name was Eliezer,[d] 'for', 4 he said, 'the God of my father was my help and saved me from Pharaoh's sword.'

Jethro, Moses' father-in-law, 5 now came to him with his sons and his wife, to the wilderness where he was encamped at the mountain of God. Moses was told, 'Here is Je- 6 thro, your father-in-law, coming to you with your wife and her two sons.' Moses went out to meet his 7 father-in-law, bowed low to him and kissed him, and they greeted one another. When they came into the tent Moses told him all that the 8 LORD had done to Pharaoh and to Egypt for Israel's sake, and about all their hardships on the journey, and how the LORD had saved them. Jethro rejoiced at all the good the 9 LORD had done for Israel in saving them from the power of Egypt. He said, 'Blessed be the LORD who 10–11 has saved you from the power of Egypt and of Pharaoh. Now I know that the LORD is the greatest of all gods, because he has delivered the people from the power of the Egyptians who dealt so arrogantly with them.' Jethro, Moses' father-in- 12 law, brought a whole-offering and sacrifices for God; and Aaron and all the elders of Israel came and shared the meal with Jethro in the presence of God.

The next day Moses took his seat 13 to settle disputes among the people, and they were standing round him from morning till evening. When 14 Jethro saw all that he was doing for the people, he said, 'What are you doing for all these people? Why do you sit alone with all of them standing round you from morning till evening?' 'The people come to 15 me', Moses answered, 'to seek God's guidance. Whenever there 16 is a dispute among them, they come to me, and I decide between man and man. I declare the statutes

---

[a] That is Challenge.   [b] That is Dispute.   [c] Cp. 2. 22.   [d] That is God my help.

17 and laws of God.' But his father-in-law said to Moses, 'This is not the 18 best way to do it. You will only wear yourself out and wear out all the people who are here. The task is too heavy for you; you cannot do 19 it by yourself. Now listen to me: take my advice, and God be with you. It is for you to be the people's representative before God, and 20 bring their disputes to him. You must instruct them in the statutes and laws, and teach them how they must behave and what they must 21 do. But you must yourself search for capable, God-fearing men a-mong all the people, honest and in-corruptible men, and appoint them over the people as officers over units of a thousand, of a hundred, 22 of fifty or of ten. They shall sit as a permanent court for the people; they must refer difficult cases to you but decide simple cases them-selves. In this way your burden will be lightened, and they will 23 share it with you. If you do this, God will give you strength, and you will be able to go on. And, more-over, this whole people will here and now regain peace and har-24 mony.' Moses listened to his father-in-law and did all he had suggested. 25 He chose capable men from all Is-rael and appointed them leaders of the people, officers over units of a thousand, of a hundred, of fifty or 26 of ten. They sat as a permanent court, bringing the difficult cases to Moses but deciding simple cases 27 themselves. Moses set his father-in-law on his way, and he went back to his own country.

Israel at Mount Sinai

19 IN the third month after Israel had left Egypt,[a] they came to the wil-2 derness of Sinai. They set out from Rephidim and entered the wilder-ness of Sinai, where they encamp-ed, pitching their tents opposite 3 the mountain. Moses went up the mountain of God, and the LORD called to him from the mountain and said, 'Speak thus to the house of Jacob, and tell this to the sons of Israel: You have seen with your 4 own eyes what I did to Egypt, and how I have carried you on eagles' wings and brought you here to me. If only you will now listen to me and 5 keep my covenant, then out of all peoples you shall become my spe-cial possession; for the whole earth is mine. You shall be my kingdom 6 of priests, my holy nation. These are the words you shall speak to the Israelites.'

Moses came and summoned the 7 elders of the people and set before them all these commands which the LORD had laid upon him. The peo-8 ple all answered together, 'What-ever the LORD has said we will do.' Moses brought this answer back to the LORD. The LORD said to Moses, 9 'I am now coming to you in a thick cloud, so that I may speak to you in the hearing of the people, and their faith in you may never fail.' Moses told the LORD what the peo-ple had said, and the LORD said to 10 him, 'Go to the people and hallow them today and tomorrow and make them wash their clothes. They must be ready by the third 11 day, because on the third day the LORD will descend upon Mount Sinai in the sight of all the people. You must put barriers round the 12 mountain and say, "Take care not to go up the mountain or even to touch the edge of it." Any man who touches the mountain must be put to death. No hand shall touch 13 him;[b] he shall be stoned or shot dead:[c] neither man nor beast may live. But when the ram's horn sounds, they may go up the moun-tain.' Moses came down from the 14 mountain to the people. He hal-lowed them and they washed their clothes. He said to the people, 'Be 15 ready by the third day; do not go near a woman.' On the third day, 16

---

[a] *Prob. rdg.; Heb. adds* on this day.   [b] *Or it.*   [c] *Or hurled to his death.*

when morning came, there were peals of thunder and flashes of lightning, dense cloud on the mountain and a loud trumpet blast; the people in the camp were all terrified.

17 Moses brought the people out from the camp to meet God, and they took their stand at the foot of

18 the mountain. Mount Sinai was all smoking because the LORD had come down upon it in fire; the smoke went up like the smoke of a kiln; all the people were terrified,

19 and the sound of the trumpet grew ever louder. Whenever Moses spoke, God answered him in a peal

20 of thunder.ᵃ The LORD came down upon the top of Mount Sinai and summoned Moses to the mountain-

21 top, and Moses went up. The LORD said to Moses, 'Go down; warn the people solemnly that they must not force their way through to the LORD to see him, or many of them

22 will perish. Even the priests, who have access to the LORD, must hallow themselves, for fear that the LORD may break out against them.'

23 Moses answered the LORD, 'The people cannot come up Mount Sinai, because thou thyself didst solemnly warn us to set a barrier to the mountain and so to keep it

24 holy.' The LORD therefore said to him, 'Go down; then come up and bring Aaron with you, but let neither priests nor people force their way up to the LORD, for fear that he may break out against

25 them.' So Moses went down to the people and spoke to them.

20 God spoke, and these were his words:

2 I am the LORD your God who brought you out of Egypt, out of the land of slavery.

3 You shall have no other godᵇ to set against me.

4 You shall not make a carved image for yourself nor the likeness of anything in the heavens above, or

on the earth below, or in the waters under the earth.

5 You shall not bow down to them or worshipᶜ them; for I, the LORD your God, am a jealous god. I punish the children for the sins of the fathers to the third and fourth generations of those who hate me.

6 But I keep faith with thousands, withᵈ those who love me and keep my commandments.

7 You shall not make wrong use of the name of the LORD your God; the LORD will not leave unpunished the man who misuses his name.

8 Remember to keep the sabbath day holy. 9 You have six days to la-

10 bour and do all your work. But the seventh day is a sabbath of the LORD your God; that day you shall not do any work, you, your son or your daughter, your slave or your slave-girl, your cattle or the alien

11 within your gates; for in six days the LORD made heaven and earth, the sea, and all that is in them, and on the seventh day he rested. Therefore the LORD blessed the sabbath day and declared it holy.

12 Honour your father and your mother, that you may live long in the land which the LORD your God is giving you.

13 You shall not commit murder.

14 You shall not commit adultery.

15 You shall not steal.

16 You shall not give false evidence against your neighbour.

17 You shall not covet your neighbour's house; you shall not covet your neighbour's wife, his slave, his slave-girl, his ox, his ass, or anything that belongs to him.

18 When all the people saw how it thundered and the lightning flashed, when they heard the trumpet sound and saw the mountain smoking, they trembled and stood at a

19 distance. 'Speak to us yourself,' they said to Moses, 'and we will listen; but if God speaks to us we

20 shall die.' Moses answered, 'Do not

ᵃ in...thunder: *or* by voice.   ᵇ *Or* gods.   ᶜ *Or* or be led to worship.
ᵈ with...with: *or* for a thousand generations with...

be afraid. God has come only to test you, so that the fear of him may remain with you and keep you 21 from sin.' So the people stood at a distance, while Moses approached the dark cloud where God was.

22 THE LORD said to Moses, Say this to the Israelites: You know now that I have spoken to you from 23 heaven. You shall not make gods of silver to be worshipped as well as me, nor shall you make yourselves 24 gods of gold. You shall make an altar of earth for me, and you shall sacrifice on it both your whole-offerings and your shared-offerings, your sheep and your cattle. Wherever I cause my name to be invoked, I will come to you and 25 bless you. If you make an altar of stones for me, you must not build it of hewn stones, for if you use a chisel on it, you will profane it. 26 You must not mount up to my altar by steps, in case your private parts be exposed on it.

21 These are the laws you shall set before them:

2 When you buy a Hebrew slave, he shall be your slave for six years, but in the seventh year he shall go free and pay nothing.

3 If he comes to you alone, he shall go away alone; but if he is married, his wife shall go away with him.

4 If his master gives him a wife, and she bears him sons or daughters, the woman and her children shall belong to her master, and the 5 man shall go away alone. But if the slave should say, 'I love my master, my wife, and my children; I will 6 not go free', then his master shall bring him to God: he shall bring him to the door or the door-post, and his master shall pierce his ear with an awl, and the man shall be his slave for life.

7 When a man sells his daughter into slavery, she shall not go free as 8 a male slave may. If her master has not had intercourse with her and

she does not please him, he shall let her be ransomed. He has treated her unfairly and therefore has no right to sell her to strangers. If he 9 assigns her to his son, he shall allow her the rights of a daughter. If he 10 takes another woman, he shall not deprive the first of meat, clothes, and conjugal rights. If he does 11 not provide her with these three things, she shall go free without any payment.

Whoever strikes another man 12 and kills him shall be put to death. But if he did not act with intent, 13 but they met by act of God, the slayer may flee to a place which I will appoint for you. But if a man 14 has the presumption to kill another by treachery, you shall take him even from my altar to be put to death.

Whoever strikes his father or 15 mother shall be put to death.

Whoever kidnaps a man shall be 16 put to death, whether he has sold him, or the man is found in his possession.

Whoever reviles his father or 17 mother shall be put to death.

When men quarrel and one hits 18 another with a stone or with a spade,[a] and the man is not killed but takes to his bed; if he recovers 19 so as to walk about outside with a stick, then the one who struck him has no liability, except that he shall pay for loss of time and shall see that he is cured.

When a man strikes his slave or 20 his slave-girl with a stick and the slave dies on the spot, he must be punished. But he shall not be pun- 21 ished if the slave survives for one day or two, because he is worth money to his master.

When, in the course of a brawl, 22 a man knocks against a pregnant woman so that she has a miscarriage but suffers no further hurt, then the offender must pay whatever fine the woman's husband demands after assessment.

---

[a] *Or* fist.

23 Wherever hurt is done, you shall
24 give life for life, eye for eye, tooth
for tooth, hand for hand, foot for
25 foot, burn for burn, bruise for
bruise, wound for wound.

26 When a man strikes his slave or
slave-girl in the eye and destroys
it, he shall let the slave go free in
27 compensation for the eye. When he
knocks out the tooth of a slave or
a slave-girl, he shall let the slave go
free in compensation for the tooth.

28 When an ox gores a man or a woman to death, the ox shall be stoned, and its flesh may not be eaten;
the owner of the ox shall be free
29 from liability. If, however, the ox
has for some time past been a
vicious animal, and the owner has
been duly warned but has not kept
it under control, and the ox kills a
man or a woman, then the ox shall
be stoned, and the owner shall be
30 put to death as well. If, however,
the penalty is commuted for a
money payment, he shall pay in
redemption of his life whatever is
31 imposed upon him. If the ox gores a
son or a daughter, the same rule
32 shall apply. If the ox gores a slave
or slave-girl, its owner shall pay
thirty shekels of silver to their
master, and the ox shall be stoned.

33 When a man removes the cover
of a well[a] or digs a well[a] and leaves
it uncovered, then if an ox or an ass
34 falls into it, the owner of the well
shall make good the loss. He shall
repay the owner of the beast in
silver, and the dead beast shall be
his.

35 When one man's ox butts another's and kills it, they shall sell
the live ox, share the price and also
36 share the dead beast. But if it is
known that the ox has for some
time past been vicious and the
owner has not kept it under control,
he shall make good the loss, ox for
ox, but the dead beast is his.

22 When a man steals an ox or a
sheep and slaughters or sells it, he
shall repay five beasts for the ox and
four sheep for the sheep. He shall 2–4[b]
pay in full; if he has no means, he
shall be sold to pay for the theft.
But if the animal is found alive in
his possession, be it ox, ass, or
sheep, he shall repay two.

If a burglar is caught in the act
and is fatally injured, it is not murder; but if he breaks in after sunrise and is fatally injured, then it
is murder.

When a man burns off a field or 5
a vineyard and lets the fire spread
so that it burns another man's
field,[c] he shall make restitution
from his own field according to the
yield expected; and if the whole
field is laid waste, he shall make
restitution from the best part of
his own field or vineyard.

When a fire starts and spreads 6
to a heap of brushwood, so that
sheaves, or standing corn, or a
whole field is destroyed, he who
started the fire shall make full
restitution.

When one man gives another sil- 7
ver or chattels for safe keeping, and
they are stolen from that man's
house, the thief, if he is found, shall
restore twofold. But if the thief is 8
not found, the owner of the house
shall appear before God, to make a
declaration that he has not touched his neighbour's property. In 9
every case of law-breaking involv-
ing an ox, an ass, or a sheep, a
cloak, or any lost property which
may be claimed, each party shall
bring his case before God; he whom
God declares to be in the wrong
shall restore twofold to his neighbour.

When a man gives an ass, an ox, 10
a sheep or any beast into his neighbour's keeping, and it dies or is injured or is carried off, there being
no witness, the neighbour shall 11
swear by the LORD that he has not

---

[a] Or cistern.　　　　[b] Verses 2–4 rearranged thus: 3b, 4, 2, 3a.
[c] Or When a man uses his field or vineyard for grazing, and lets his beast loose,
and it feeds in another man's field.

Israel at Mount Sinai

touched the man's property. The owner shall accept this, and no resti-
12 tution shall be made. If it has been stolen from him, he shall make res-
13 titution to the owner. If it has been mauled by a wild beast, he shall bring it in as evidence; he shall not make restitution for what has been mauled.

14 When a man borrows a beast from his neighbour and it is injured or dies while its owner is not with it, the borrower shall make
15 full restitution; but if the owner is with it, the borrower shall not make restitution. If it was hired, only the hire shall be due.

16 When a man seduces a virgin who is not yet betrothed, he shall pay the bride-price for her to be his
17 wife. If her father refuses to give her to him, the seducer shall pay in silver a sum equal to the bride-price for virgins.

18 You shall not allow a witch to live.

19 Whoever has unnatural connection with a beast shall be put to death.

20 Whoever sacrifices to any god but the LORD shall be put to death under solemn ban.

21 You shall not wrong an alien, or be hard upon him; you were your-
22 selves aliens in Egypt. You shall not ill-treat any widow or father-
23 less child. If you do, be sure that I
24 will listen if they appeal to me; my anger will be roused and I will kill you with the sword; your own wives shall become widows and your children fatherless.

25 If you advance money to any poor man amongst my people, you shall not act like a money-lender: you must not exact interest in advance from him.

26 If you take your neighbour's cloak in pawn, you shall return it to
27 him by sunset, because it is his only covering. It is the cloak in which he wraps his body; in what else can he sleep? If he appeals to me, I will listen, for I am full of compassion.

You shall not revile God, nor 28 curse a chief of your own people.

You shall not hold back the first 29 of your harvest, whether corn or wine. You shall give me your first-born sons. You shall do the same 30 with your oxen and your sheep. They shall stay with the mother for seven days; on the eighth day you shall give them to me.

You shall be holy to me: you 31 shall not eat the flesh of anything in the open country killed by beasts, but you shall throw it to the dogs.

You shall not spread a baseless 23 rumour. You shall not make common cause with a wicked man by giving malicious evidence.

You shall not be led into wrong- 2 doing by the majority, nor, when you give evidence in a lawsuit, shall you side with the majority to pervert justice; nor shall you favour 3 the poor man in his suit.

When you come upon your ene- 4 my's ox or ass straying, you shall take it back to him. When you see 5 the ass of someone who hates you lying helpless under its load, however unwilling you may be to help it, you must give him a hand with it.

You shall not deprive the poor 6 man of justice in his suit. Avoid all 7 lies, and do not cause the death of the innocent and the guiltless; for I the LORD will never acquit the guilty. You shall not accept a bribe, 8 for bribery makes the discerning man blind and the just man give a crooked answer.

You shall not oppress the alien, 9 for you know how it feels to be an alien; you were aliens yourselves in Egypt.

For six years you may sow your 10 land and gather its produce; but in 11 the seventh year you shall let it lie fallow and leave it alone. It shall provide food for the poor of your people, and what they leave the wild animals may eat. You shall do likewise with your vineyard and your olive-grove.

12 For six days you may do your work, but on the seventh day you shall abstain from work, so that your ox and your ass may rest, and your home-born slave and the alien may refresh themselves.

13 Be attentive to every word of mine. You shall not invoke other gods: your lips shall not speak their names.

14 Three times a year you shall keep
15 a pilgrim-feast to me. You shall celebrate the pilgrim-feast of Unleavened Bread for seven days; you shall eat unleavened cakes as I have commanded you, at the appointed time in the month of Abib, for in that month you came out of Egypt.

16 No one shall come into my presence empty-handed. You shall celebrate the pilgrim-feast of Harvest, with the firstfruits of your work in sowing the land, and the pilgrim-feast of Ingathering at the end[a] of the year, when you bring in the fruits of all your work on the
17 land. These three times a year shall all your males come into the presence of the Lord GOD.

18 You shall not offer the blood of my sacrifice at the same time as anything leavened.

The fat of my festal offering shall not remain overnight till morning.

19 You shall bring the choicest firstfruits of your soil to the house of the LORD your God.

You shall not boil a kid in its mother's milk.

20 And now I send an angel before you to guard you on your way and to bring you to the place I have
21 prepared. Take heed of him and listen to his voice. Do not defy him; he will not pardon your rebelliousness, for my authority rests in him.
22 If you will only listen to his voice and do all I tell you, then I will be an enemy to your enemies, and I will harass those who harass you.
23 My angel will go before you and bring you to the Amorites, the Hittites, the Perizzites, the Canaanites, the Hivites, and the Jebusites, and I will make an end of
them. You are not to bow down to 24 their gods, nor worship them, nor observe their rites, but you shall tear down all their images and smash their sacred pillars. Worship the LORD your God, and he will bless your bread and your water. I will take away all sickness out of your midst. None shall miscarry or be barren in your land. 26 I will grant you a full span of life.

I will send my terror before you 27 and throw into confusion all the peoples whom you find in your path. I will make all your enemies turn their backs. I will spread 28 panic before you to drive out in front of you the Hivites, the Canaanites and the Hittites. I will 29 not drive them out all in one year, or the land would become waste and the wild beasts too many for you. I will drive them out little by 30 little until your numbers have grown enough to take possession of the whole country. I will establish 31 your frontiers from the Red Sea to the sea of the Philistines, and from the wilderness to the River. I will give the inhabitants of the country into your power, and you shall drive them out before you. You 32 shall make no covenant with them and their gods. They shall not stay 33 in your land for fear they make you sin against me; for then you would worship their gods, and in this way you would be ensnared.

THEN he said to Moses, 'Come up 24 to the LORD, you and Aaron, Nadab and Abihu, and seventy of the elders of Israel. While you are still at a distance, you are to bow down; and then Moses shall approach the 2 LORD by himself, but not the others. The people may not go up with him at all.'

Moses came and told the people 3 all the words of the LORD, all his

[a] *Or beginning.*

laws. The whole people answered with one voice and said, 'We will do all that the LORD has told us.'

4 Moses wrote down all the words of the LORD. He rose early in the morning and built an altar at the foot of the mountain, and put up twelve sacred pillars, one for each

5 of the twelve tribes of Israel. He then sent the young men of Israel and they sacrificed bulls to the LORD as whole-offerings and shar-

6 ed-offerings. Moses took half the blood and put it in basins and the other half he flung against*ᵃ* the

7 altar. Then he took the book of the covenant and read it aloud for all the people to hear. They said, 'We will obey, and do all that the LORD

8 has said.' Moses then took the blood and flung it over the people, saying, 'This is the blood of the covenant which the LORD has made with you on the terms of this book.'

9 Moses went up with Aaron, Na-dab and Abihu, and seventy of the

10 elders of Israel, and they saw*ᵇ* the God of Israel. Under his feet there was, as it were, a pavement of sap-phire,*ᶜ* clear blue as the very hea-

11 vens; but the LORD did not stretch out his hand towards the leaders of Israel. They stayed there before God;*ᵈ* they ate and they drank.

12 The LORD said to Moses, 'Come up to me on the mountain, stay there and let me give you the tablets of stone, the law and the command-ment, which I have written down

13 that you may teach them.' Moses arose with Joshua his assistant and

14 went up the mountain of God; he said to the elders, 'Wait for us here until we come back to you. You have Aaron and Hur; if anyone has

15 a dispute, let him go to them.' So Moses went up the mountain and a

16 cloud covered it. The glory of the LORD rested upon Mount Sinai, and the cloud covered the moun-tain for six days; on the seventh

day he called to Moses out of the cloud. The glory of the LORD looked 17 to the Israelites like a devouring fire on the mountain-top. Moses 18 entered the cloud and went up the mountain; there he stayed forty days and forty nights.

THE LORD spoke to Moses and 25 said: Tell the Israelites to set aside 2 a contribution for me; you shall accept whatever contribution each man shall freely offer. This is what 3 you shall accept: gold, silver, copper; violet, purple, and scarlet 4 yarn; fine linen and goats' hair; tanned rams' skins, porpoise*ᵉ*- 5 hides, and acacia-wood; oil for the 6 lamp, balsam for the anointing oil and for the fragrant incense; cor- 7 nelian and other stones ready for setting in the ephod and the breast-piece.*ᶠ* Make me a sanctuary, and 8 I will dwell among them. Make it 9 exactly according to the design I show you, the design for the Taber-nacle and for all its furniture. This is how you must make it:

Make an Ark, a chest of acacia- 10 wood, two and a half cubits long, one cubit and a half wide, and one cubit and a half high. Overlay it 11 with pure gold both inside and out, and put a band of gold all round it. Cast four gold rings for it, and 12 fasten them to its four feet, two rings on each side. Make poles of 13 acacia-wood and plate them with gold, and insert the poles in the 14 rings at the sides of the Ark to lift it. The poles shall remain in the 15 rings of the Ark and never be re-moved. Put into the Ark the To- 16 kens of the Covenant,*ᵍ* which I shall give you. Make a cover of 17 pure gold, two and a half cubits long and one cubit and a half wide. Make two gold cherubim of beaten 18 work at the ends of the cover, one 19 at each end; make each cherub of

---

ᵃ Or upon. *ᵇ* Or they were afraid of... *ᶜ* Or lapis lazuli.
ᵈ Or They saw God; and... *ᵉ* Strictly sea-cow. *ᶠ* Or pouch.
ᵍ Tokens of the Covenant: or Testimony.

20 one piece with the cover. They shall be made with wings outspread and pointing upwards, and shall screen the cover with their wings. They shall be face to face, looking in-
21 wards over the cover. Put the cover above the Ark, and put into the Ark the Tokens that I shall
22 give you. It is there that I shall meet you, and from above the cover, between the two cherubim over the Ark of the Tokens, I shall deliver to you all my commands for the Israelites.

23 Make a table of acacia-wood, two cubits long, one cubit wide, and
24 one cubit and a half high. Overlay it with pure gold, and put a band of
25 gold all round it. Make a rim round it a hand's breadth wide, and a gold
26 band round the rim. Make four gold rings for the table, and put the rings at the four corners by the
27 legs. The rings, which are to receive the poles for carrying the table, must be adjacent to the rim.
28 Make the poles of acacia-wood and plate them with gold; they are to be used for carrying the table.
29 Make its dishes and saucers, and its flagons and bowls from which drink-offerings may be poured:
30 make them of pure gold. Put the Bread of the Presence*a* on the table, to be always before me.
31 Make a lamp-stand of pure gold. The lamp-stand, stem and branches, shall be of beaten work, its cups, both calyxes and petals, shall be of
32 one piece with it. There are to be six branches springing from its sides; three branches of the lamp-stand shall spring from the one side and three branches from the other
33 side. There shall be three cups shaped like almond blossoms, with calyx and petals, on the first branch, three cups shaped like almond blossoms, with calyx and petals, on the next branch, and similarly for all six branches
34 springing from the lamp-stand. On the main stem of the lamp-stand there are to be four cups shaped like almond blossoms, with calyx and petals, and there shall be 35 calyxes of one piece with it under the six branches which spring from the lamp-stand, a single calyx under each pair of branches. The 36 calyxes and the branches are to be of one piece with it, all a single piece of beaten work of pure gold. Make seven lamps for this and 37 mount them to shed light over the space in front of it. Its tongs and 38 firepans shall be of pure gold. The 39 lamp-stand and all these fittings shall be made from one talent of pure gold. See that you work to the 40 design which you were shown on the mountain.

Make the Tabernacle of ten hang- 26 ings of finely woven linen, and violet, purple, and scarlet yarn, with cherubim worked on them, all made by a seamster. The length of 2 each hanging shall be twenty-eight cubits and the breadth four cubits; all are to be of the same size. Five 3 of the hangings shall be joined together, and similarly the other five. Make violet loops along the edge of 4 the last hanging in each set, fifty 5 for each set; they must be opposite one another. Make fifty gold fast- 6 eners, join the hangings one to another with them, and the Tabernacle will be a single whole.

Make hangings of goats' hair, 7 eleven in all, to form a tent over the Tabernacle; each hanging is to 8 be thirty cubits long and four wide; all eleven are to be of the same size. Join five of the hangings together, 9 and similarly the other six; then fold the sixth hanging double at the front of the tent. Make fifty 10 loops on the edge of the last hanging in the first set and make fifty loops on the joining edge of the second set. Make fifty bronze*b* fas- 11 teners, insert them into the loops and join up the tent to make it a

---

a Or Shewbread.
b Or copper *and so throughout the description of the Tabernacle.*

12 single whole. The additional length of the tent hanging[a] is to fall over 13 the back of the Tabernacle. On each side there will be an additional cubit in the length of the tent hangings; this shall fall over the two sides of the Tabernacle to 14 cover it. Make for the tent a cover of tanned rams' skins and an outer covering of porpoise-hides.

15 Make for the Tabernacle planks 16 of acacia-wood as uprights, each plank ten cubits long and a cubit 17 and a half wide, and two tenons for each plank joined to each other. You shall do the same for all the 18 planks of the Tabernacle. Arrange the planks thus: twenty planks for the south side, facing southwards, 19 with forty silver sockets under them, two sockets under each 20 plank for its two tenons; and for the second or northern side of the 21 Tabernacle, twenty planks, with forty silver sockets, two under 22 each plank. Make six planks for the far end of the Tabernacle on the 23 west. Make two planks for the corners of the Tabernacle at the far 24 end; at the bottom they shall be alike, and at the top, both alike, they shall fit into a single ring. Do the same for both of them; they 25 shall be for the two corners. There shall be eight planks with their silver sockets, sixteen sockets in all, two sockets under each plank severally.

26 Make bars of acacia-wood: five for the planks on the one side of the 27 Tabernacle, five for the planks on the other side and five for the planks on the far end of the Taber- 28 nacle on the west. The middle bar is to run along from end to end 29 half-way up the planks. Overlay the planks with gold, make rings of gold on them to hold the bars, and 30 plate the bars with gold. Set up the Tabernacle according to the design you were shown on the mountain. 31 Make a Veil of finely woven linen and violet, purple, and scarlet

yarn, with cherubim worked on it, all made by a seamster. Fasten it 32 with hooks of gold to four posts of acacia-wood overlaid with gold, standing in four silver sockets. Hang the Veil below the fasteners 33 and bring the Ark of the Tokens inside the Veil. Thus the Veil will make a clear separation for you between the Holy Place and the Holy of Holies. Place the cover over the 34 Ark of the Tokens in the Holy of Holies. Put the table outside the 35 Veil and the lamp-stand at the south side of the Tabernacle, opposite the table which you shall put at the north side. For the entrance 36 of the tent make a screen of finely woven linen, embroidered with violet, purple, and scarlet. Make five 37 posts of acacia-wood for the screen and overlay them with gold; make golden hooks for them and cast five bronze sockets for them.

Make the altar of acacia-wood; it 27 shall be square, five cubits long by five cubits broad and three cubits high. Let its horns at the four cor- 2 ners be of one piece with it, and overlay it with bronze. Make for it 3 pots to take away the fat and the ashes, with shovels, tossing bowls, forks, and firepans, all of bronze. Make a grating for it of bronze net- 4 work, and fit four bronze rings on the network at its four corners. Put 5 it below the ledge of the altar, so that the network comes half-way up the altar. Make poles of acacia- 6 wood for the altar and overlay them with bronze. They shall be in- 7 serted in the rings at both sides of the altar to carry it. Leave the al- 8 tar a hollow shell. As you were shown on the mountain, so shall it be made.

Make the court of the Taber- 9 nacle. For the one side, the south side facing southwards, the court shall have hangings of finely woven linen a hundred cubits long, with 10 twenty posts and twenty sockets of bronze; the hooks and bands on

---

[a] *Prob. rdg.; Heb. adds* half the hanging which remains over.

11 the posts shall be of silver. Similarly all along the north side there shall be hangings a hundred cubits long, with twenty posts and twenty sockets of bronze; the hooks and bands on the posts shall be of sil-

12 ver. For the breadth of the court, on the west side, there shall be hangings fifty cubits long, with ten

13 posts and ten sockets. On the east side, towards the sunrise, which

14 was fifty cubits, hangings shall extend fifteen cubits from one corner, with three posts and three sockets,

15 and hangings shall extend fifteen cubits from the other corner, with

16 three posts and three sockets. At the gateway of the court, there shall be a screen twenty cubits long of finely woven linen embroidered with violet, purple, and scarlet, with four posts and four

17 sockets. The posts all round the court shall have bands of silver, with hooks of silver, and sockets of

18 bronze. The length of the court shall be a hundred cubits, and the breadth fifty, and the height five cubits, with finely woven linen and

19 bronze sockets throughout. All the equipment needed for serving the Tabernacle, all its pegs and those of the court, shall be of bronze.

20 You yourself are to command the Israelites to bring you pure oil of pounded olives ready for the

21 regular mounting of the lamp. In the Tent of the Presence*a* outside the Veil that hides the Tokens, Aaron and his sons shall keep the lamp in trim from dusk to dawn before the LORD. This is a rule binding on their descendants among the Israelites for all time.

28 You yourself are to summon to your presence your brother Aaron and his sons out of all the Israelites to serve as my priests: Aaron and his sons Nadab and Abihu, Elea-

2 zar and Ithamar. For your brother Aaron make sacred vestments, to

3 give him dignity and grandeur. Tell all the craftsmen whom I have en-

dowed with skill to make the vestments for the consecration of Aaron as my priest. These are the 4 vestments they shall make: a breast-piece, an ephod, a mantle, a chequered tunic, a turban, and a sash. They shall make sacred vestments for Aaron your brother and his sons to wear when they serve as my priests, using gold; violet, pur- 5 ple, and scarlet yarn; and fine linen.

The ephod shall be made of gold, 6 and with violet, purple, and scarlet yarn, and with finely woven linen worked by a seamster. It shall have 7 two shoulder-pieces joined back and front. The waist-band on it 8 shall be of the same workmanship and material as the fabric of the ephod, and shall be of gold, with violet, purple, and scarlet yarn, and finely woven linen. You shall 9 take two cornelians and engrave on them the names of the sons of Israel: six of their names on the 10 one stone, and the six other names on the second, all in order of seniority. With the skill of a craftsman, a 11 seal-cutter, you shall engrave the two stones with the names of the sons of Israel; you shall set them in gold rosettes, and fasten them on 12 the shoulders of the ephod, as reminders of the sons of Israel. Aaron shall bear their names on his two shoulders as a reminder before the LORD.

Make gold rosettes and two 13, 14 chains of pure gold worked into the form of ropes, and fix them on the rosettes. Make the breast-piece 15 of judgement; it shall be made, like the ephod, by a seamster in gold, with violet, purple, and scarlet yarn, and finely woven linen. It 16 shall be a square folded, a span long and a span wide. Set in it four 17 rows of precious stones: the first row, sardin, chrysolite and green felspar; the second row, purple 18 garnet, lapis lazuli and jade; the 19 third row, turquoise, agate and

---

a Or Tent of Meeting.

20 jasper; the fourth row, topaz, cornelian and green jasper, all set in
21 gold rosettes. The stones shall correspond to the twelve sons of Israel name by name; each stone shall bear the name of one of the twelve tribes engraved as on a seal.
22 Make for the breast-piece chains of pure gold worked into a rope.
23 Make two gold rings, and fix them on the two upper corners of the
24 breast-piece. Fasten the two gold ropes to the two rings at those
25 corners of the breast-piece, and the other ends of the ropes to the two rosettes, thus binding the breast-piece to the shoulder-pieces on the
26 front of the ephod. Make two gold rings and put them at the two lower corners of the breast-piece on the inner side next to the ephod.
27 Make two gold rings and fix them on the two shoulder-pieces of the ephod, low down in front, along its seam above the waist-band of the
28 ephod. Then the breast-piece shall be bound by its rings to the rings of the ephod with violet braid, just above the waist-band of the ephod, so that the breast-piece will not be
29 detached from the ephod. Thus, when Aaron enters the Holy Place, he shall carry over his heart in the breast-piece of judgement the names of the sons of Israel, as a constant reminder before the LORD.
30 Finally, put the Urim and the Thummim into the breast-piece of judgement, and they will be over Aaron's heart when he enters the presence of the LORD. So shall Aaron bear these symbols of judgement upon the sons of Israel over his heart constantly before the LORD.
31 Make the mantle of the ephod a
32 single piece of violet stuff. There shall be a hole for the head in the middle of it. All round the hole there shall be a hem of woven work, with an oversewn edge, so that it
33 cannot be torn. All round its skirts make pomegranates of violet, pur-

ple, and scarlet stuff, with golden bells between them, a golden bell 34 and a pomegranate alternately the whole way round the skirts of the mantle. Aaron shall wear it when 35 he ministers, and the sound of it shall be heard when he enters the Holy Place before the LORD and when he comes out; and so he shall not die.

Make a rosette of pure gold and 36 engrave on it as on a seal, 'Holy to the LORD'.ᵃ Fasten it on a violet 37 braid and set it on the very front of the turban. It shall be on Aaron's 38 forehead; he has to bear the blame for shortcomings in the rites with which the Israelites offer their sacred gifts, and the rosette shall be always on his forehead so that they may be acceptable to the LORD.

Make the chequered tunic and 39 the turban of fine linen, but the sash of embroidered work. For 40 Aaron's sons make tunics and sashes; and make tall head-dresses to give them dignity and grandeur. With these invest your brother 41 Aaron and his sons, anoint them, install them and consecrate them; so shall they serve me as priests. Make for them linen drawers reach- 42 ing to the thighs to cover their private parts; and Aaron and his sons 43 shall wear them when they enter the Tent of the Presence or approach the altar to minister in the Holy Place. Thus they will not incur guilt and die. This is a rule binding on him and his descendants for all time.

In consecrating them to be my 29 priests this is the rite to be observed. Take a young bull and two rams without blemish. Take un- 2 leavened loaves, unleavened cakes mixed with oil, and unleavened wafers smeared with oil, all made of wheaten flour; put them in a 3 single basket and bring them in it. Bring also the bull and the two rams. Bring Aaron and his sons to 4 the entrance of the Tent of the

---

ᵃ as...LORD: *or* 'JEHOVAH' *as on a seal in sacred characters.*

Presence, and wash them with water. 5 Take the vestments and invest Aaron with the tunic, the mantle of the ephod, the ephod itself and the breast-piece, and fasten the ephod 6 to him with its waist-band. Set the turban on his head, and the symbol of holy dedication on the turban. 7 Take the anointing oil, pour it on 8 his head and anoint him. Then bring his sons forward, invest them 9 with tunics, gird them with the sashes and tie their tall headdresses on them. They shall hold the priesthood by a rule binding for all time.

Next you shall install Aaron and 10 his sons. Bring the bull to the front of the Tent of the Presence, and they shall lay their hands on its 11 head. Slaughter the bull before the LORD at the entrance to the Tent 12 of the Presence. Take some of its blood, and put it with your finger on the horns of the altar. Pour all the rest of it at the base of the altar. 13 Then take the fat covering the entrails, the long lobe of the liver, and the two kidneys with the fat upon 14 them, and burn it on the altar; but the flesh of the bull, and its skin and offal, you shall destroy by fire outside the camp. It is a sin-offering.

15 Take one of the rams, and Aaron and his sons shall lay their hands on 16 its head. Then slaughter it, take its blood and fling it against the sides 17 of the altar. Cut the ram up; wash its entrails and its shins, lay them 18 with the pieces and the head, and burn the whole ram on the altar: it is a whole-offering to the LORD; it is a soothing odour, a food-offering to the LORD.

19 Take the second ram, and let Aaron and his sons lay their hands 20 on its head. Then slaughter it, take some of its blood, and put it on the lobes of the right ears of Aaron and his sons, and on their right thumbs and big toes. Fling the rest of the blood against the sides of the altar.

Take some of the blood which is on 21 the altar and some of the anointing oil, and sprinkle it on Aaron and his vestments, and on his sons and their vestments. So shall he and his vestments, and his sons and their vestments become holy. Take the 22 fat from the ram, the fat-tail, the fat covering the entrails, the long lobe of the liver, the two kidneys with the fat upon them, and the right leg: for it is a ram of installation. Take also one round loaf of 23 bread, one cake cooked with oil, and one wafer from the basket of unleavened bread that is before the LORD. Set all these on the hands of 24 Aaron and of his sons and present them as a special gift before the LORD. Then take them out of their 25 hands, and burn them on the altar with the whole-offering for a soothing odour to the LORD: it is a food-offering to the LORD. Take 26 the breast of Aaron's ram of installation, present it as a special gift before the LORD, and it shall be your perquisite.

Hallow the breast of the special 27 gift and the leg of the contribution, that which is presented and that which is set aside from the ram of installation, that which is for Aaron and that which is for his sons; and 28 they shall belong to Aaron and his sons, by a rule binding for all time, as a gift from the Israelites, for it is a contribution, set aside from their shared-offerings, their contribution to the LORD.

Aaron's sacred vestments shall 29 be kept for the anointing and installation of his sons after him. The 30 priest appointed in his stead from among his sons, the one who enters*a* the Tent of the Presence to minister in the Holy Place, shall wear them for seven days.

Take the ram of installation, and 31 boil its flesh in a sacred place; Aaron and his sons shall eat the 32 ram's flesh and the bread left in the basket, at the entrance to the Tent

a Or when he enters.

85

33 of the Presence. They shall eat the things with which expiation was made at their installation and their consecration. No unqualified person may eat them, for they are
34 holy. If any of the flesh of the installation, or any of the bread, is left over till morning, you shall destroy it by fire; it shall not be eaten, for it is holy.

35 Do this with Aaron and his sons as I have commanded you, spending seven days over their installation.

36 Offer a bull daily, a sin-offering as expiation for sin; offer the sin-offering on the altar when you make expiation for it, and consecrate it
37 by anointing. For seven days you shall make expiation for the altar, and consecrate it, and it shall be most holy. Whatever touches the altar shall be forfeit as sacred.

38 This is what you shall offer on the altar: two yearling rams regularly
39 every day. You shall offer the one ram at dawn, and the second be-
40 tween dusk and dark, a tenth of an ephah of flour mixed with a quarter of a hin of pure oil of pounded olives, and a drink-offering of a quarter of a hin of wine for the first
41 ram. You shall offer the second ram between dusk and dark, and with it the same grain-offering and drink-offering as at dawn, for a soothing odour: it is a food-offering
42 to the LORD, a regular whole-offering in every generation; you shall make the offering at the entrance to the Tent of the Presence before the LORD, where I meet you and
43 speak to you. I shall meet the Israelites there, and the place will be
44 hallowed by my glory. I shall hallow the Tent of the Presence and the altar; and Aaron and his sons I shall consecrate to serve me as
45 priests. I shall dwell in the midst of the Israelites, I shall become their
46 God, and by my dwelling among them they will know that I am the LORD their God who brought them

out of Egypt. I am the LORD their God.

Make an altar on which to burn 30 incense; make it of acacia-wood. It shall be square, a cubit long by a 2 cubit broad and two cubits high; the horns of one piece with it. Over- 3 lay it with pure gold, the top, the sides all round, and the horns; and put round it a band of gold. Make 4 pairs of gold rings for it; put them under the band at the two corners on both sides to receive the poles by which it is to be carried. Make 5 the poles of acacia-wood and overlay them with gold. Put it before 6 the Veil in front of the Ark of the Tokens where I will meet you. On it 7 Aaron shall burn fragrant incense; every morning when he tends the lamps he shall burn the incense, and when he mounts the lamps be- 8 tween dusk and dark, he shall burn the incense; so there shall be a regular burning of incense before the LORD for all time. You shall not 9 offer on it any unauthorized incense, nor any whole-offering or grain-offering; and you shall not pour a drink-offering over it. Aaron 10 shall make expiation with blood on its horns once a year; with blood from the sin-offering of the yearly Expiation[a] he shall do this for all time. It is most holy to the LORD.

The LORD spoke to Moses and 11 said: When you number the Is- 12 raelites for the purpose of registration, each man shall give a ransom for his life to the LORD, to avert plague among them during the registration. As each man crosses 13 over to those already counted he shall give half a shekel by the sacred standard (twenty gerahs to the shekel) as a contribution to the LORD. Everyone from twenty years 14 old and upwards who has crossed over to those already counted shall give a contribution to the LORD. The rich man shall give no more 15 than the half-shekel, and the poor man shall give no less, when you

[a] Or Atonement.

give the contribution to the LORD to make expiation for your lives. 16 The money received from the Israelites for expiation you shall apply to the service of the Tent of the Presence. The expiation for your lives shall be a reminder of the Israelites to the LORD.

17 The LORD spoke to Moses and 18 said: Make a bronze basin for ablution with its stand of bronze; put it between the Tent of the Presence and the altar, and fill it with water 19 with which Aaron and his sons shall 20 wash their hands and feet. When they enter the Tent of the Presence they shall wash with water, lest they die. So also when they approach the altar to minister, to burn a food-offering to the LORD, 21 they shall wash their hands and feet, lest they die. It shall be a rule for all time binding on him and his descendants in every generation.

22 The LORD spoke to Moses and 23 said: You yourself shall take spices as follows: five hundred shekels of sticks of myrrh, half that amount (two hundred and fifty shekels) of fragrant cinnamon, two hundred and fifty shekels of aromatic cane, 24 five hundred shekels of cassia by the sacred standard, and a hin of 25 olive oil. From these prepare sacred anointing oil, a perfume compounded by the perfumer's art. This shall be the sacred anointing 26 oil. Anoint with it the Tent of the Presence and the Ark of the Tokens, 27 the table and all its vessels, the lamp-stand and its fittings, the 28 altar of incense, the altar of whole-offering and all its vessels, the 29 basin and its stand. You shall consecrate them, and they shall be most holy; whatever touches them 30 shall be forfeit as sacred. Anoint Aaron and his sons, and consecrate 31 them to be my priests. Speak to the Israelites and say: This shall be the holy anointing oil for my service in 32 every generation. It shall not be used for anointing the human body,

and you must not prepare any oil like it after the same prescription. It is holy, and you shall treat it as holy. The man who compounds 33 perfume like it, or who puts any of it on any unqualified person, shall be cut off from his father's kin.

The LORD said to Moses, Take 34 fragrant spices: gum resin,[a] aromatic shell, galbanum; add pure frankincense to the spices in equal proportions. Make it into incense, 35 perfume made by the perfumer's craft, salted and pure, a holy thing. Pound some of it into fine 36 powder, and put it in front of the Tokens in the Tent of the Presence, where I shall meet you; you shall treat it as most holy. The incense 37 prepared according to this prescription you shall not make for your own use. You shall treat it as holy to the LORD. The man 38 who makes any like it for his own pleasure shall be cut off from his father's kin.

THE LORD spoke to Moses and 31 said, Mark this: I have specially 2 chosen Bezalel son of Uri, son of Hur, of the tribe of Judah. I have 3 filled him with divine spirit, making him skilful and ingenious, expert in every craft, and a master of 4 design, whether in gold, silver, copper, or cutting stones to be set, 5 or carving wood, for workmanship of every kind. Further, I have appointed Aholiab[b] son of Ahisamach of the tribe of Dan to help him, and I have endowed every skilled craftsman with the skill which he has. They shall make everything that I have commanded you: the 7 Tent of the Presence, the Ark for the Tokens, the cover over it, and all the furnishings of the tent; the 8 table and its vessels, the pure lamp-stand and all its fittings, the altar of incense, the altar of whole-offer- 9 ing and all its vessels, the basin and its stand; the stitched vestments, 10

---

[a] *Or* mastic.   [b] *Or* Oholiab.

that is the sacred vestments for Aaron the priest and the vestments for his sons when they minister as 11 priests, the anointing oil and the fragrant incense for the Holy Place. They shall carry out all I have commanded you.

12 The LORD spoke to Moses and 13 said, Speak to the Israelites, you yourself, and say to them: Above all you shall observe my sabbaths, for the sabbath is a sign between me and you in every generation that you may know that I am the 14 LORD who hallows you. You shall keep the sabbath, because it is a holy day for you. If anyone profanes it he must be put to death. Anyone who does work on it shall be cut off from his father's kin. 15 Work may be done on six days, but on the seventh day there is a sabbath of sacred rest, holy to the LORD. Whoever does work on the sabbath day must be put to death. 16 The Israelites shall keep the sabbath, they shall keep it in every generation as a covenant for ever. 17 It is a sign for ever between me and the Israelites, for in six days the LORD made the heavens and the earth, but on the seventh day he ceased work and refreshed himself.

18 When he had finished speaking with Moses on Mount Sinai, the LORD gave him the two tablets of the Tokens, tablets of stone written with the finger of God.

32 WHEN the people saw that Moses was so long in coming down from the mountain, they confronted Aaron and said to him, 'Come, make us gods to go ahead of us. As for this fellow Moses, who brought us up from Egypt, we do not know 2 what has become of him.' Aaron answered them, 'Strip the gold rings from the ears of your wives and daughters, and bring them to 3 me.' So all the people stripped themselves of their gold earrings 4 and brought them to Aaron. He took them out of their hands, cast the metal in a mould, and made it into the image of a bull-calf. 'These', he said, 'are your gods, O Israel, that brought you up from Egypt.' Then Aaron was afraid and 5 built an altar in front of it and issued this proclamation, 'Tomorrow there is to be a pilgrimfeast to the LORD.' Next day the 6 people rose early, offered wholeofferings, and brought sharedofferings. After this they sat down to eat and drink and then gave themselves up to revelry. But the 7 LORD said to Moses, 'Go down at once, for your people, the people you brought up from Egypt, have done a disgraceful thing; so quick- 8 ly have they turned aside from the way I commanded them. They have made themselves an image of a bull-calf, they have prostrated themselves before it, sacrificed to it and said, "These are your gods, O Israel, that brought you up from Egypt."' So the LORD said 9 to Moses, 'I have considered this people, and I see that they are a stubborn people. Now, let me 10 alone to vent my anger upon them, so that I may put an end to them and make a great nation spring from you.' But Moses set himself 11 to placate the LORD his God: 'O LORD,' he said, 'why shouldst thou vent thy anger upon thy people, whom thou didst bring out of Egypt with great power and a strong hand? Why let the Egyp- 12 tians say, "So he meant evil when he took them out, to kill them in the mountains and wipe them off the face of the earth"? Turn from thy anger, and think better of the evil thou dost intend against thy people. Remember Abraham, Isaac 13 and Israel, thy servants, to whom thou didst swear by thy own self: "I will make your posterity countless as the stars in the sky, and all this land, of which I have spoken, I will give to them, and they shall possess it for ever."' So the LORD 14

relented, and spared his people the evil with which he had threatened them.

15 Moses turned and went down the mountain with the two tablets of the Tokens in his hands, inscribed on both sides; on the front and on the back they were in-

16 scribed. The tablets were the handiwork of God, and the writing was God's writing, engraved on the

17 tablets. Joshua, hearing the uproar the people were making, said to Moses, 'Listen! There is fighting

18 in the camp.' Moses replied,

'This is not the clamour of warriors,
    nor the clamour of a defeated
    people;
it is the sound of singing that I
    hear.'

19 As he approached the camp, Moses saw the bull-calf and the dancing, and he was angry; he flung the tablets down, and they were shattered to pieces at the foot of the

20 mountain. Then he took the calf they had made and burnt it; he ground it to powder, sprinkled it on water, and made the Israelites

21 drink it. He demanded of Aaron, 'What did this people do to you that you should have brought such

22 great guilt upon them?' Aaron replied, 'Do not be angry, sir. The people were deeply troubled; that

23 you well know. And they said to me, "Make us gods to go ahead of us, because, as for this fellow Moses, who brought us up from Egypt, we do not know what has become of

24 him." So I said to them, "Those of you who have any gold, strip it off." They gave it me, I threw it in the fire, and out came this bull-

25 calf.' Moses saw that the people were out of control and that Aaron had laid them open to the secret

26 malice of their enemies. He took his place at the gate of the camp and said, 'Who is on the LORD's side? Come here to me'; and the

27 Levites all rallied to him. He said to them, 'These are the words of

the LORD the God of Israel: "Arm yourselves, each of you, with his sword. Go through the camp from gate to gate and back again. Each of you kill his brother, his friend,

28 his neighbour."' The Levites obeyed, and about three thousand of

29 the people died that day. Moses then said, 'Today you have consecrated yourselves to the LORD completely, because you have turned each against his own son and his own brother and so have this day brought a blessing upon yourselves.'

30 The next day Moses said to the people, 'You have committed a great sin. I shall now go up to the LORD; perhaps I may be able to

31 secure pardon for your sin.' So Moses returned to the LORD and said, 'O hear me! This people has committed a great sin: they have

32 made themselves gods of gold. If thou wilt forgive them, forgive. But if not, blot out my name, I pray, from thy book which thou hast

33 written.' The LORD answered Moses, 'It is the man who has sinned against me that I will blot

34 out from my book. But go now, lead the people to the place which I have told you of. My angel shall go ahead of you, but a day will come when I shall punish them for

35 their sin.' And the LORD smote the people for worshipping the bull-calf which Aaron had made.

33 THE LORD spoke to Moses: 'Come, go up from here, you and the people you have brought up from Egypt, to the land which I swore to Abraham, Isaac, and Jacob that I

2 would give to their posterity. I will send an angel ahead of you, and will drive out the Canaanites, the Amorites and the Hittites and the Perizzites, the Hivites and the

3 Jebusites. I will bring you to a land flowing with milk and honey, but I will not journey in your company, for fear that I annihilate you on the way; for you are a stubborn

4 people.' When the people heard this harsh sentence they went about like mourners, and no man 5 put on his ornaments. The LORD said to Moses, 'Tell the Israelites, "You are a stubborn people: at any moment, if I journey in your company, I may annihilate you. Put away your ornaments now, and I will determine what to do to you."'

6 And so the Israelites stripped off their ornaments, and wore them no more from Mount Horeb onwards.

7 Moses used to take a*ᵃ* tent and pitch it at a distance outside the camp. He called it the Tent of the Presence, and everyone who sought the LORD would go out to the Tent of the Presence outside the camp. 8 Whenever Moses went out to the tent, all the people would rise and stand, each at the entrance to his tent, and follow Moses with their eyes until he entered the tent. 9 When Moses entered it, the pillar of cloud came down, and stayed at the entrance to the tent while the 10 LORD spoke with Moses. As soon as the people saw the pillar of cloud standing at the entrance to the tent, they would all prostrate themselves, every man at the en-11 trance to his tent. The LORD would speak with Moses face to face, as one man speaks to another. Then Moses would return to the camp, but his young assistant, Joshua son of Nun, never moved from inside the tent.

12 Moses said to the LORD, 'Thou bidst me lead this people up, but thou hast not told me whom thou wilt send with me. Thou hast said to me, "I know you by name, and, further, you have found favour 13 with me." If I have indeed won thy favour, then teach me to know thy way, so that I can know thee and continue in favour with thee, for 14 this nation is thy own people.' The LORD answered, 'I will go with you in person and set your mind at 15 rest.' Moses said to him, 'Indeed if

thou dost not go in person, do not send us up from here; for how can it 16 ever be known that I and thy people have found favour with thee, except by thy going with us? So shall we be distinct, I and thy people, from all the peoples on earth.' The LORD said to Moses, 'I 17 will do this thing that you have asked, because you have found favour with me, and I know you by name.'

And Moses prayed, 'Show me thy 18 glory.' The LORD answered, 'I will 19 make all my goodness*ᵇ* pass before you, and I will pronounce in your hearing the Name JEHOVAH.*ᶜ* I will be gracious to whom I will be gracious, and I will have compassion on whom I will have compassion.' But he added, 'My face 20 you cannot see, for no mortal man may see me and live.' The LORD 21 said, 'Here is a place beside me. Take your stand on the rock and 22 when my glory passes by, I will put you in a crevice of the rock and cover you with my hand until I have passed by. Then I will take 23 away my hand, and you shall see my back, but my face shall not be seen.'

The LORD said to Moses, 'Cut 34 two stone tablets like the first, and I will write on the tablets the words which were on the first tablets, which you broke in pieces. Be ready 2 by morning. Then in the morning go up Mount Sinai; stand and wait for me there on the top. No man 3 shall go up with you, no man shall even be seen anywhere on the mountain, nor shall flocks or herds graze within sight of that mountain.' So Moses cut two stone tablets 4 like the first, and he rose early in the morning and went up Mount Sinai as the LORD had commanded him, taking the two stone tablets in his hands. And the LORD came 5 down in the cloud and took his place beside him and pronounced the Name JEHOVAH. Then the 6

ᵃ Or the.　　　*ᵇ Or character.*　　　*ᶜ See note on 3. 15.*

LORD passed in front of him and called aloud, 'JEHOVAH, the LORD, a god compassionate and gracious, long-suffering, ever constant and 7 true, maintaining constancy to thousands, forgiving iniquity, rebellion, and sin, and not sweeping the guilty clean away; but one who punishes sons and grandsons to the third and fourth generation for the 8 iniquity of their fathers!' Moses made haste, bowed to the ground 9 and prostrated himself. He said, 'If I have indeed won thy favour, O Lord, then may the Lord go in our company. However stubborn a people they are, forgive our iniquity and our sin and take us as thy own possession.'

10 The LORD said, Here and now I make a covenant. In full view of all your people I will do such miracles as have never been performed in all the world or in any nation. All the surrounding peoples shall see the work of the LORD, for fearful is 11 that which I will do for you.[a] Observe all I command you this day; and I for my part will drive out before you the Amorites and the Canaanites and the Hittites and the Perizzites and the Hivites and the 12 Jebusites. Be careful not to make a covenant with the natives of the land against which you are going, or they will prove a snare in your 13 midst. No: you shall demolish their altars, smash their sacred pillars and cut down their sacred poles. 14 You shall not prostrate yourselves to any other god. For the LORD's name is the Jealous God, and a 15 jealous god he is. Be careful not to make a covenant with the natives of the land, or, when they go wantonly after their gods and sacrifice to them, you may be invited, any one of you, to partake of their sacri-16 fices, and marry your sons to their daughters, and when their daughters go wantonly after their gods, they may lead your sons astray too.

You shall not make yourselves 17 gods of cast metal.

You shall observe the pilgrim-18 feast of Unleavened Bread: for seven days, as I have commanded you, you shall eat unleavened cakes at the appointed time, in the month of Abib, because in the month of Abib you went out from Egypt.

Every first birth of the womb 19 belongs to me, and the males of all your herds, both cattle and sheep. You may buy back the first birth 20 of an ass by giving a sheep instead, but if you do not buy it, you must break its neck. You shall buy back all the first-born of your sons, and no one shall come into my presence empty-handed.

For six days you shall work, but 21 on the seventh day you shall cease work; even at ploughing time and harvest you shall cease work.

You shall observe the pilgrim-22 feast of Weeks, the firstfruits of the wheat harvest, and the pilgrim-feast of Ingathering at the turn of the year. Three times a year all 23 your males shall come into the presence of the Lord, the LORD the God of Israel; for after I have 24 driven out the nations before you and extended your frontiers, there will be no danger from covetous neighbours when you go up these three times to enter the presence of the LORD your God.

You shall not offer the blood of 25 my sacrifice at the same time as anything leavened, nor shall any portion of the victim of the pilgrim-feast of Passover remain overnight till morning.

You shall bring the choicest first-26 fruits of your soil to the house of the LORD your God.

You shall not boil a kid in its mother's milk.

The LORD said to Moses, 'Write 27 these words down, because the covenant I make with you and with Israel is in these words.' So 28

---

[a] for fearful...for you: *or* (for he is to be feared) which I will do for you.

Moses stayed there with the LORD forty days and forty nights, neither eating nor drinking, and wrote down the words of the covenant,
29 the Ten Words,[a] on the tablets. At length Moses came down from Mount Sinai with the two stone tablets of the Tokens in his hands, and when he descended, he did not know that the skin of his face shone because he had been speak-
30 ing with the LORD. When Aaron and the Israelites saw how the skin of Moses' face shone, they were
31 afraid to approach him. He called out to them, and Aaron and all the chiefs in the congregation turned towards him. Moses spoke to them,
32 and afterwards all the Israelites drew near. He gave them all the commands with which the LORD had charged him on Mount Sinai,
33 and finished what he had to say.

Then Moses put a veil over his
34 face, and whenever he went in before the LORD to speak with him, he removed the veil until he came out. Then he would go out and tell the Israelites all the commands he
35 had received. Whenever the skin of Moses' face shone in the sight of the Israelites, he would put the veil back over his face until he went in again to speak with the LORD.

35 MOSES called the whole community of Israelites together and thus addressed them: These are the
2 LORD's commands to you: On six days you may work, but the seventh you are to keep as a sabbath of sacred rest, holy to the LORD. Whoever works on that day
3 shall be put to death. You are not even to light your fire at home on the sabbath day.
4 These words Moses spoke to all the community of Israelites: This is the command the LORD has
5 given: Each of you set aside a contribution to the LORD. Let all who wish, bring a contribution to the LORD: gold, silver, copper;
6 violet, purple, and scarlet yarn; fine linen and goats' hair; tanned
7 rams' skins, porpoise-hides, and acacia-wood; oil for the lamp,
8 perfume for the anointing oil and for the fragrant incense; cornel-
9 ians and other stones ready for setting in the ephod and the breastpiece. Let every craftsman among
10 you come and make everything the LORD has commanded. The Taber-
11 nacle, its tent and covering, fasteners, planks, bars, posts, and sock-
12 ets, the Ark and its poles, the cover and the Veil of the screen,
13 the table, its poles, and all its vessels, and the Bread of the Presence,
14 the lamp-stand for the light, its fit-
15 tings, lamps and the lamp oil; the altar of incense and its poles, the anointing oil, the fragrant incense, and the screen for the entrance of
16 the Tabernacle, the altar of wholeoffering, its bronze grating, poles, and all appurtenances, the basin
17 and its stand; the hangings of the court, its posts and sockets, and the screen for the gateway of the
18 court; the pegs of the Tabernacle
19 and court and their cords, the stitched vestments for ministering in the Holy Place, that is the sacred vestments for Aaron the priest and the vestments for his sons when they minister as priests.

20 The whole community of the Israelites went out from Moses' pre-
21 sence, and everyone who was so minded brought of his own free will a contribution to the LORD for the making of the Tent of the Presence and all its service, and for the
22 sacred vestments. Men and women alike came and freely brought clasps, earrings, finger-rings, and pendants, gold ornaments of every kind, every one of them presenting a special gift of gold to the LORD.
23 And every man brought what he possessed of violet, purple, and scarlet yarn, fine linen and goats' hair, tanned rams' skins and por-

[a] *Or* Ten Commandments.

24 poise-hides. Every man, setting a-
side a contribution of silver or
copper, brought it as a contribution
to the LORD, and all who had acacia-
wood suitable for any part of the
25 work brought it. Every woman
with the skill spun and brought the
violet, purple, and scarlet yarn,
26 and fine linen. All the women whose
skill moved them spun the goats'
27 hair. The chiefs brought cornelians
and other stones ready for setting
in the ephod and the breast-piece,
28 the perfume and oil for the light,
for the anointing oil, and for the
29 fragrant incense. Every Israelite
man and woman who was minded
to bring offerings to the LORD for all
the work which he had commanded
through Moses did so freely.

30   Moses said to the Israelites,
'Mark this: the LORD has specially
chosen Bezalel son of Uri, son of
31 Hur, of the tribe of Judah. He has
filled him with divine spirit, making
him skilful and ingenious, expert
32 in every craft, and a master of
design, whether in gold, silver, and
33 copper, or cutting precious stones
for setting, or carving wood, in
34 every kind of design. He has inspired both him and Aholiab son
of Ahisamach of the tribe of Dan
35 to instruct workers and designers
of every kind, engravers, seamsters,
embroiderers in violet, purple, and
scarlet yarn and fine linen, and
weavers, fully endowing them with
skill to execute all kinds of work.
36 Bezalel and Aholiab shall work exactly as the LORD has commanded,
and so also shall every craftsman
whom the LORD has made skilful
and ingenious in these matters, to
know how to execute every kind
of work for the service of the
sanctuary.'

2   Moses summoned Bezalel, Aholiab, and every craftsman to whom
the LORD had given skill and who
was willing, to come forward and
3 set to work. They received from
Moses every contribution which
the Israelites had brought for the

work of the service of the sanctuary,
but the people still brought freewill
offerings morning after morning,
so that the craftsmen at work on 4
the sanctuary left what they were
doing, every one of them, and came
to Moses and said, 'The people are 5
bringing much more than we need
for doing the work which the LORD
has commanded.' So Moses sent 6
word round the camp that no man
or woman should prepare anything
more as a contribution for the
sanctuary. So the people stopped
bringing gifts; what was there al- 7
ready was more than enough for
all the work they had to do.

    Then all the craftsmen among 8
the workers made the Tabernacle
of ten hangings of finely woven
linen, and violet, purple, and scarlet
yarn, with cherubim worked on
them, all made by a seamster. The 9
length of each hanging was twenty-
eight cubits and the breadth four
cubits, all of the same size. They 10
joined five of the hangings together,
and similarly the other five. They 11
made violet loops on the outer edge
of the one set of hangings and they
did the same for the outer edge of
the other set of hangings. They 12
made fifty loops for each hanging;
they made also fifty loops for the
end hanging in the second set, the
loops being opposite each other.
They made fifty gold fasteners, 13
with which they joined the hangings one to another, and the Tabernacle became a single whole.

    They made hangings of goats' 14
hair, eleven in all, to form a tent
over the Tabernacle; each hanging 15
was thirty cubits long and four
cubits wide, all eleven of the same
size. They joined five of the hang- 16
ings together, and similarly the
other six. They made fifty loops 17
on the edge of the outer hanging
in the first set and fifty loops on
the joining edge of the second set,
and fifty bronze fasteners to join 18
up the tent and make it a single
whole. They made for the tent a 19

cover of tanned rams' skins and an outer covering of porpoise-hides.

20 They made for the Tabernacle planks of acacia-wood as uprights,
21 each plank ten cubits long and a
22 cubit and a half wide, and two tenons for each plank joined to each other. They did the same for all the planks of the Tabernacle.
23 They arranged the planks thus: twenty planks for the south side,
24 facing southwards, with forty silver sockets under them, two sockets under each plank for its two tenons;
25 and for the second or northern side of the Tabernacle twenty planks
26 with forty silver sockets, two under
27 each plank. They made six planks for the far end of the Tabernacle on
28 the west. They made two planks for the corners of the Tabernacle
29 at the far end; at the bottom they were alike, and at the top, both alike, they fitted into a single ring. They did the same for both of them
30 at the two corners. There were eight planks with their silver sockets, sixteen sockets in all, two sockets under each plank.
31 They made bars of acacia-wood: five for the planks on the one side
32 of the Tabernacle, five bars for the planks on the second side of the Tabernacle, and five bars for the planks on the far end of the Taber-
33 nacle on the west. They made the middle bar to run along from end to
34 end half-way up the frames. They overlaid the frames with gold, made rings of gold on them to hold the bars and plated the bars with gold.
35 They made the Veil of finely woven linen and violet, purple, and scarlet yarn, with cherubim worked on it, all made by a seamster.
36 And they made for it four posts of acacia-wood overlaid with gold, with gold hooks, and cast four
37 silver sockets for them. For the entrance of the tent a screen of finely woven linen was made, embroidered with violet, purple, and scarlet,
38 and five posts of acacia-wood with their hooks. They overlaid the tops

of the posts and the bands round them with gold; the five sockets for them were of bronze.

Bezalel then made the Ark, a 37 chest of acacia-wood, two and a half cubits long, one cubit and a half wide, and one cubit and a half high. He overlaid it with pure gold, 2 both inside and out, and put a band of gold all round it. He cast four 3 gold rings to be on its four feet, two rings on each side of it. He made 4 poles of acacia-wood and plated them with gold, and inserted the 5 poles in the rings at the sides of the Ark to lift it. He made a cover 6 of pure gold, two and a half cubits long and one cubit and a half wide. He made two gold cherubim of 7 beaten work at the ends of the cover, one at each end; he made 8 each cherub of one piece with the cover. They had wings outspread 9 and pointing upwards, screening the cover with their wings; they stood face to face, looking inwards over the cover.

He made the table of acacia- 10 wood, two cubits long, one cubit wide, and one cubit and a half high. He overlaid it with pure gold and 11 put a band of gold all round it. He 12 made a rim round it a hand's breadth wide, and a gold band round the rim. He cast four gold 13 rings for it, and put the rings at the four corners by the four legs. The 14 rings, which were to receive the poles for carrying the table, were close to the rim. These carrying- 15 poles he made of acacia-wood and plated them with gold. He made 16 the vessels for the table, its dishes and saucers, and its flagons and bowls from which drink-offerings were to be poured; he made them of pure gold.

He made the lamp-stand of pure 17 gold. The lamp-stand, stem, and branches, were of beaten work, its cups, both calyxes and petals, were of one piece with it. There 18 were six branches springing from its sides; three branches of the lamp-stand sprang from one side and three branches from the other 19 side. There were three cups shaped like almond blossoms, with calyx and petals, on the first branch, three cups shaped like almond blossoms, with calyx and petals, on the next branch, and similarly for all six branches springing from the 20 lamp-stand. On the main stem of the lamp-stand there were four cups shaped like almond blossoms, 21 with calyx and petals, and there were calyxes of one piece with it under the six branches which sprang from the lamp-stand, a single calyx under each pair of 22 branches. The calyxes and the branches were of one piece with it, all a single piece of beaten work 23 of pure gold. He made its seven lamps, its tongs and firepans of 24 pure gold. The lamp-stand and all these fittings were made from one talent of pure gold.

25   He made the altar of incense of acacia-wood, square, a cubit long by a cubit broad and two cubits high, the horns of one piece with 26 it. He overlaid it with pure gold, the top, the sides all round, and the horns, and he put round it a 27 band of gold. He made pairs of gold rings for it; he put them under the band at the two corners on both sides to receive the poles by 28 which it was to be carried. He made the poles of acacia-wood and overlaid them with gold.

29   He prepared the sacred anointing oil and the fragrant incense, pure, compounded by the perfumer's art.

38   He made the altar of whole-offering of acacia-wood, square, five cubits long by five cubits broad 2 and three cubits high. Its horns at the four corners were of one piece with it, and he overlaid it with 3 bronze. He made all the vessels for the altar, its pots, shovels, tossing bowls, forks, and firepans, all of 4 bronze. He made for the altar a grating of bronze network under

the ledge, coming half-way up. He 5 cast four rings for the four corners of the bronze grating to receive the poles, and he made the poles 6 of acacia-wood and overlaid them with bronze. He inserted the poles 7 in the rings at the sides of the altar to carry it. He left the altar a hollow shell.

The basin and its stand of bronze 8 he made out of the bronze mirrors of the women who were on duty at the entrance to the Tent of the Presence.

He made the court. For the 9 south side facing southwards the hangings of the court were of finely woven linen a hundred cubits long, with twenty posts and twenty sock- 10 ets of bronze; the hooks and bands on the posts were of silver. Along 11 the north side there were hangings of a hundred cubits, with twenty posts and twenty sockets of bronze; the hooks and bands on the posts were of silver. On the west side 12 there were hangings fifty cubits long, with ten posts and ten sockets; the hooks and bands on the posts were of silver. On the east 13 side, towards the sunrise, fifty cubits, there were hangings on either 14–15 side of the gateway of the court; they extended fifteen cubits to one corner, with their three posts and their three sockets, and fifteen cubits to the second corner, with their three posts and their three sockets. The hangings of the court 16 all round were of finely woven linen. The sockets for the posts were of 17 bronze, the hooks and bands on the posts of silver, the tops of them overlaid with silver, and all the posts of the court were bound with silver. The screen at the gateway 18 of the court was of finely woven linen, embroidered with violet, purple, and scarlet, twenty cubits long and five cubits high to correspond to the hangings of the court, with four posts and four sockets 19 of bronze, their hooks of silver, and the tops of them and their bands

20 overlaid with silver. All the pegs for the Tabernacle and those for the court were of bronze.

21 These were the appointments of the Tabernacle, that is the Tabernacle of the Tokens which was assigned by Moses to the charge of the Levites under Ithamar son of

22 Aaron the priest. Bezalel son of Uri, son of Hur, of the tribe of Judah made everything the LORD

23 had commanded Moses. He was assisted by Aholiab son of Ahisamach of the tribe of Dan, an engraver, a seamster, and an embroiderer in fine linen with violet, purple, and scarlet yarn.

24 The gold of the special gift used for the work of the sanctuary amounted in all to twenty-nine tal-

25 ents seven hundred and thirty shekels, by the sacred standard. The silver contributed by the community when registered was one hundred talents one thousand seven hundred and seventy-five shekels, by the sacred standard.

26 This amounted to a beka a head, that is half a shekel by the sacred standard, for every man from twenty years old and upwards, who had been registered, a total of six hundred and three thousand five

27 hundred and fifty men. The hundred talents of silver were for casting the sockets for the sanctuary and for the Veil, a hundred sockets to a hundred talents, a talent to

28 a socket. With the one thousand seven hundred and seventy-five shekels he made hooks for the posts, overlaid the tops of the posts and

29 put bands round them. The bronze of the special gift came to seventy talents two thousand four hundred

30 shekels; with this he made sockets for the entrance to the Tent of the Presence, the bronze altar and its bronze grating, all the vessels for

31 the altar, the sockets all round the court, the sockets for the posts at the gateway of the court, all the pegs for the Tabernacle, and the pegs all round the court.

They used violet, purple, and 39 scarlet yarn in making the stitched vestments for ministering in the sanctuary and in making the sacred vestments for Aaron, as the LORD had commanded Moses.

They made the ephod of gold, 2 with violet, purple, and scarlet yarn, and finely woven linen. The 3 gold was beaten into thin plates, cut and twisted into braid to be worked in by a seamster with the violet, purple, and scarlet yarn, and fine linen. They made shoulder- 4 pieces for it, joined back and front. The waist-band on it was of the 5 same workmanship and material as the fabric of the ephod; it was gold, with violet, purple, and scarlet yarn, and finely woven linen, as the LORD commanded Moses.

They prepared the cornelians, 6 fixed in gold rosettes, engraved by the art of a seal-cutter with the names of the sons of Israel, and 7 fastened them on the shoulders of the ephod as reminders of the sons of Israel, as the LORD had commanded Moses.

They made the breast-piece; it 8 was worked like the ephod by a seamster, in gold, with violet, purple, and scarlet yarn, and finely woven linen. They made the breast- 9 piece square, folded, a span long and a span wide. They set in it 10 four rows of precious stones: the first row, sardin, chrysolite and green felspar; the second row, pur- 11 ple garnet, lapis lazuli and jade; the third row, turquoise, agate and 12 jasper; the fourth row, topaz, cor- 13 nelian and green jasper, all set in gold rosettes. The stones corre- 14 sponded to the twelve sons of Israel, name by name, each bearing the name of one of the twelve tribes engraved as on a seal. They 15 made for the breast-piece twisted cords of pure gold worked into a rope. They made two gold rosettes 16 and two gold rings, and they fixed the two rings on the two corners of the breast-piece. They fastened 17 the two gold ropes to the two rings at those corners of the breast-piece,

18 and the other ends of the two ropes to the two rosettes, thus binding them to the shoulder-pieces on the

19 front of the ephod. They made two gold rings and put them at the two corners of the breast-piece on the

20 inner side next to the ephod. They made two gold rings and fixed them on the two shoulder-pieces of the ephod, low down and in front, close to its seam above the waist-band

21 on the ephod. They bound the breast-piece by its rings to the rings of the ephod with a violet braid, just above the waist-band on the ephod, so that the breast-piece would not become detached from the ephod; so the LORD had

22 commanded Moses. They made the mantle of the ephod a single piece

23 of woven violet stuff, with a hole in the middle of it which had a hem round it, with an oversewn edge

24 so that it could not be torn. All round its skirts they made pomegranates of violet, purple, and scarlet stuff, and finely woven linen.

25 They made bells of pure gold and put them all round the skirts of the mantle between the pomegra-

26 nates, a bell and a pomegranate alternately the whole way round the skirts of the mantle, to be worn when ministering, as the LORD commanded Moses.

27 They made the tunics of fine linen, woven work, for Aaron and

28 his sons, the turban of fine linen, the tall head-dresses and their bands all of fine linen, the drawers

29 of finely woven linen, and the sash of finely woven linen, embroidered in violet, purple, and scarlet, as the LORD had commanded Moses.

30 They made a rosette of pure gold as the symbol of their holy dedication and inscribed on it as the engraving on a seal, 'Holy to the

31 LORD',[a] and they fastened on it a violet braid to fix it on the turban

at the top, as the LORD had commanded Moses.

32 Thus all the work of the Tabernacle of the Tent of the Presence was completed, and the Israelites did everything exactly as the LORD

33 had commanded Moses. They brought the Tabernacle to Moses, the tent and all its furnishings, its fasteners, planks, bars, posts and

34 sockets, the covering of tanned rams' skins and the outer covering of porpoise-hides, the Veil of the

35 screen, the Ark of the Tokens and

36 its poles, the cover, the table and its vessels, and the Bread of the Pre-

37 sence, the pure lamp-stand with its lamps in a row and all its fittings,

38 and the lamp oil, the gold altar, the anointing oil, the fragrant incense, and the screen at the entrance of the

39 tent, the bronze altar, the bronze grating attached to it, its poles and all its furnishings, the basin and its

40 stand, the hangings of the court, its posts and sockets, the screen for the gateway of the court, its cords and pegs, and all the equipment for the service of the Tabernacle

41 for the Tent of the Presence, the stitched vestments for ministering in the sanctuary, that is the sacred vestments for Aaron the priest and the vestments for his sons when

42 they minister as priests. As the LORD had commanded Moses, so the Israelites carried out the whole

43 work. Moses inspected all the work, and saw that they had carried it out according to the command of the LORD; and he blessed them.

40 THE LORD spoke to Moses and

2 said: On the first day of the first month you shall set up the Tabernacle, the Tent of the Presence.

3 You shall put the Ark of the Tokens in it and screen the Ark with the

4 Veil. You shall bring in the table and lay it; then you shall bring in the lamp-stand and mount its

5 lamps. You shall then set the gold altar of incense in front of the Ark

---

[a] on it...LORD: *or* 'JEHOVAH' on it in sacred characters as engraved on a seal.

of the Tokens and put the screen of the entrance of the Tabernacle 6 in place. You shall put the altar of whole-offering in front of the entrance of the Tabernacle, the Tent 7 of the Presence. You shall put the basin between the Tent of the Presence and the altar and put 8 water in it. You shall set up the court all round and put in place the screen of the gateway of the 9 court. You shall take the anointing oil and anoint the Tabernacle and everything in it; thus you shall consecrate it and all its furnishings, 10 and it shall be holy. You shall anoint the altar of whole-offering and all its vessels; thus shall you consecrate it, and it shall be most 11 holy. You shall anoint the basin and its stand and consecrate it. 12 You shall bring Aaron and his sons to the entrance of the Tent of the Presence and wash them with the 13 water. Then you shall clothe Aaron with the sacred vestments, anoint him and consecrate him; so shall 14 he be my priest. You shall then bring forward his sons, clothe them 15 in tunics, anoint them as you anointed their father, and they shall be my priests. Their anointing shall inaugurate a hereditary priesthood for all time.

16 Exactly as the LORD had com-
17 manded him, so Moses did. In the first month of the second year, on the first day of that month, the Tabernacle was set up.

18 Moses set up the Tabernacle. He put the sockets in place, inserted the planks, fixed the crossbars and 19 set up the posts. He spread the tent over the Tabernacle and fixed the covering of the tent above it, as the LORD had commanded him. 20 He took the Tokens and put them in the Ark, inserted the poles in the Ark, and put the cover over the 21 top of the Ark. He brought the Ark into the Tabernacle, set up the Veil of the screen and so screened the Ark of the Tokens, as the LORD had commanded him. He put the table 22 in the Tent of the Presence on the north side of the Tabernacle outside the Veil and arranged bread 23 on it before the LORD, as the LORD had commanded him. He set the 24 lamp-stand in the Tent of the Presence opposite the table at the south side of the Tabernacle and 25 mounted the lamps before the LORD, as the LORD had commanded him. He set up the gold altar in 26 the Tent of the Presence in front of the Veil and burnt fragrant in- 27 cense on it, as the LORD had commanded him. He set up the screen 28 at the entrance of the Tabernacle, fixed the altar of whole-offering at 29 the entrance of the Tabernacle, the Tent of the Presence, and offered on it whole-offerings and grain-offerings, as the LORD had commanded him. He set up the basin 30 between the Tent of the Presence and the altar and put water there for washing, and Moses and Aaron 31 and his sons used to wash their hands and feet when they entered 32 the Tent of the Presence or approached the altar, as the LORD had commanded Moses. He set up 33 the court all round the Tabernacle and the altar, and put a screen at the gateway of the court.

Thus Moses completed the work, and the cloud covered the Tent of 34 the Presence, and the glory of the LORD filled the Tabernacle. Moses 35 was unable to enter the Tent of the Presence, because the cloud had settled on it and the glory of the LORD filled the Tabernacle. At every 36 stage of their journey, when the cloud lifted from the Tabernacle, the Israelites broke camp; but if 37 the cloud did not lift from the Tabernacle, they did not break camp until the day it lifted. For 38 the cloud of the LORD hovered over the Tabernacle by day, and there was fire in the cloud by night, and the Israelites could see it at every stage of their journey.

LEVITICUS

Laws concerning offerings and sacrifices

1 THE LORD summoned Moses and spoke to him from the Tent of the Presence, and
2 said, Say this to the Israelites: When any man among you presents an animal as an offering to the LORD, the offering may be presented either from the herd or from the flock.
3 If his offering is a whole-offering from the cattle, he shall present a male without blemish; he shall present it at the entrance to the Tent of the Presence before the LORD so as to secure acceptance for
4 himself. He shall lay his hand on the head of the victim and it will be accepted on his behalf[a] to make
5 expiation for him. He shall slaughter the bull before the LORD, and the Aaronite priests shall present the blood and fling it against the altar all round at the entrance of
6 the Tent of the Presence. He shall then flay the victim and cut it up.
7 The sons of Aaron the priest shall kindle a fire on the altar and ar-
8 range wood on the fire. The Aaronite priests shall arrange the pieces, including the head and the suet, on
9 the wood on the altar-fire, the entrails and shins shall be washed in water, and the priest shall burn it all on the altar as a whole-offering, a food-offering of soothing odour to the LORD.
10 If the man's whole-offering is from the flock, either from the rams or from the goats, he shall present
11 a male without blemish. He shall slaughter it before the LORD at the north side of the altar, and the Aaronite priests shall fling the blood against the altar all round.
He shall cut it up, and the priest 12 shall arrange the pieces, together with the head and the suet, on the wood on the altar-fire, the entrails 13 and shins shall be washed in water, and the priest shall present and burn it all on the altar: it is a whole-offering, a food-offering of soothing odour to the LORD.

If a man's offering to the LORD 14 is a whole-offering of birds, he shall present turtle-doves or young pigeons as his offering. The priest 15 shall present it at the altar, and shall wrench off the head and burn it on the altar; and the blood shall be drained out against the side of the altar. He shall take away the 16 crop and its contents in one piece, and throw it to the east side of the altar where the ashes are. He shall 17 tear it by its wings without severing them completely, and shall burn it on the altar, on top of the wood of the altar-fire: it is a whole-offering, a food-offering of soothing odour to the LORD.

When any person presents a 2 grain-offering to the LORD, his offering shall be of flour. He shall pour oil on it and add frankincense to it. He shall bring it to the Aaron- 2 ite priests, one of whom shall scoop up a handful of the flour and oil with all the frankincense. The priest shall burn this as a token on the altar, a food-offering of soothing odour to the LORD. The remain- 3 der of the grain-offering belongs to Aaron and his sons: it is most sacred, it is taken from the food-offerings of the LORD.

When you present as a grain- 4 offering something baked in an oven, it shall consist of unleavened

---

[a] Or by him (the LORD).

cakes of flour mixed with oil and unleavened wafers smeared with oil. 5 If your offering is a grain-offering cooked on a griddle, it shall be an unleavened cake of flour mixed 6 with oil. Crumble it in pieces and pour oil on it. This is a grain-offering.

7 If your offering is a grain-offering cooked in a pan, it shall be made of 8 flour with oil. Bring an offering made up in this way to the LORD and present it to the priest, who 9 shall bring it to the altar; then he shall set aside part of the grain-offering as a token and burn it on the altar, a food-offering of sooth-10 ing odour to the LORD. The remainder of the grain-offering belongs to Aaron and his sons: it is most sacred, it is taken from the food-offerings of the LORD.

11 No grain-offering which you present to the LORD shall be made of anything that ferments; you shall not burn any leaven or any honey 12 as a food-offering to the LORD. As for your offering of firstfruits, you shall present them to the LORD, but they shall not be offered up at 13 the altar as a soothing odour. Every offering of yours which is a grain-offering shall be salted; you shall not fail to put the salt of your covenant with God on your grain-offering. Salt shall accompany all offerings.

14 If you present to the LORD a grain-offering of first-ripe grain, you must present fresh corn roasted, crushed meal from fully ripen-15 ed corn. You shall add oil to it and put frankincense upon it. This is 16 a grain-offering. The priest shall burn as its token some of the crushed meal, some of the oil, and all the frankincense as a food-offering to the LORD.

3 If a man's offering is a shared-offering from the cattle, male or female, he shall present it without 2 blemish before the LORD. He shall lay his hand on the head of the victim and slaughter it at the en-trance to the Tent of the Presence. The Aaronite priests shall fling the blood against the altar all round. One of them shall present part of 3 the shared-offering as a food-offering to the LORD: he shall remove the fat covering the entrails and all the fat upon the entrails, the 4 two kidneys with the fat on them beside the haunches, and the long lobe of the liver with the kidneys. The Aaronites shall burn it on the 5 altar on top of the whole-offering which is upon the wood on the fire, a food-offering of soothing odour to the LORD.

If a man's offering as a shared-6 offering to the LORD is from the flock, male or female, he shall present it without blemish. If he is 7 presenting a ram as his offering, he shall present it before the LORD, lay his hand on the head of the 8 victim and slaughter it in front of the Tent of the Presence. The Aaronites shall then fling its blood against the altar all round. He shall 9 present part of the shared-offering as a food-offering to the LORD; he shall remove its fat, the entire fat-tail cut off close by the spine, the fat covering the entrails and all the fat upon the entrails, the two kid-10 neys with the fat on them beside the haunches, and the long lobe of the liver with the kidneys. The 11 priest shall burn it at the altar, as food offered to the LORD.

If the man's offering is a goat, he 12 shall present it before the LORD, lay his hand on its head and slaugh-13 ter it in front of the Tent of the Presence. The Aaronites shall then fling its blood against the altar all round. He shall present part of the 14 victim as a food-offering to the LORD; he shall remove the fat covering the entrails and all the fat upon the entrails, the two kidneys 15 with the fat on them beside the haunches, and the long lobe of the liver with the kidneys. The priest 16 shall burn this at the altar, as a food-offering of soothing odour. All

17 fat belongs to the LORD. This is a rule for all time from generation to generation wherever you live: you shall not eat any fat or any blood.

4 THE LORD spoke to Moses and 2 said, Say this to the Israelites: These are the rules for any man who inadvertently transgresses any of the commandments of the LORD and does anything prohibited by them:

3 If the anointed priest sins so as to bring guilt on the people, for the sin he has committed he shall present to the LORD a young bull without blemish as a sin-offering.

4 He shall bring the bull to the entrance of the Tent of the Presence before the LORD, lay his hand on its head and slaughter it before the 5 LORD. The anointed priest shall then take some of its blood and bring it to the Tent of the Presence.

6 He shall dip his finger in the blood and sprinkle some of the blood in front of the sacred Veil seven times 7 before the LORD. The priest shall then put some of the blood before the LORD in the Tent of the Presence on the horns of the altar where fragrant incense is burnt, and he shall pour the rest of the bull's blood at the base of the altar of whole-offering at the entrance 8 of the Tent of the Presence. He shall set aside all the fat from the bull of the sin-offering; he shall set aside the fat covering the entrails and all the fat upon the entrails, 9 the two kidneys with the fat on them beside the haunches, and the long lobe of the liver with the kid-10 neys. It shall be set aside as the fat from the ox at the shared-offering is set aside. The priest shall burn the pieces of fat on the 11 altar of whole-offering. But the skin of the bull and all its flesh, including head and shins, its entrails and 12 offal, the whole of it, he shall take away outside the camp to a place ritually clean, where the ash-heap is, and destroy it on a wood-fire on top of the ash-heap.

If the whole community of Israel 13 sins inadvertently and the matter is not known to the assembly, if they do what is forbidden in any commandment of the LORD and so incur guilt, then, when the sin 14 they have committed is notified to them, the assembly shall present a young bull as a sin-offering and shall bring it in front of the Tent of the Presence. The elders of the 15 community shall lay their hands on the victim's head before the LORD, and it shall be slaughtered before the LORD. The anointed 16 priest shall then bring some of the blood to the Tent of the Presence, dip his finger in it and sprinkle it 17 in front of the Veil seven times before the LORD. He shall put some 18 of the blood on the horns of the altar before the LORD in the Tent of the Presence and pour all the rest at the base of the altar of whole-offering at the entrance of the Tent of the Presence. He shall 19 then set aside all the fat from the bull and burn it on the altar. He 20 shall deal with this bull as he deals with the bull of the sin-offering, and in this way the priest shall make expiation for their guilt and they shall be forgiven. He shall 21 take the bull outside the camp and burn it as the other bull was burnt. This is a sin-offering for the assembly.

When a man of standing sins by 22 doing inadvertently what is forbidden in any commandment of the LORD his God, thereby incurring guilt, and the sin he has com-23 mitted is made known to him, he shall bring as his offering a he-goat without blemish. He shall lay his 24 hand on the goat's head and shall slaughter it before the LORD in the place where the whole-offering is slaughtered. It is a sin-offering. The priest shall then take some of 25 the blood of the victim with his finger and put it on the horns of the altar of whole-offering. He shall pour out the rest of the blood at the base of the altar of whole-offering.

26 He shall burn all the fat at the altar in the same way as the fat of the shared-offering. Thus the priest shall make expiation for that man's sin, and it shall be forgiven him.

27 If any person among the common people sins inadvertently and does what is forbidden in any commandment of the LORD, thereby

28 incurring guilt, and the sin he has committed is made known to him, he shall bring as his offering for the sin which he has committed a she-

29 goat without blemish. He shall lay his hand on the head of the victim and slaughter it in the place where the whole-offering is slaughtered.

30 The priest shall then take some of its blood with his finger and put it on the horns of the altar of whole-offering. All the rest of the blood he shall pour at the base of the

31 altar. He shall remove all its fat as the fat of the shared-offering is removed, and the priest shall burn it on the altar as a soothing odour to the LORD. So the priest shall make expiation for that person's guilt, and it shall be forgiven him.

32 If the man brings a sheep as his offering for sin, it shall be a ewe

33 without blemish. He shall lay his hand on the head of the victim and slaughter it as a sin-offering in the place where the whole-offering is

34 slaughtered. The priest shall then take some of the blood of the victim with his finger and put it on the horns of the altar of whole-offering. All the rest of the blood he shall pour out at the base of the altar.

35 He shall remove all the fat, as the fat of the sheep is removed from the shared-offering. The priest shall burn the pieces of fat at the altar on top of the food-offerings to the LORD, and shall make expiation for the sin that the man has committed, and it shall be forgiven him.

5 IF a person hears a solemn adjuration to give evidence as a witness to something he has seen or heard and does not declare what he knows, he commits a sin and must accept responsibility.

2 If a person touches anything unclean, such as the dead body of an unclean animal, whether wild or domestic, or of an unclean reptile,

3 or if he touches anything unclean in a man, whatever that uncleanness may be, and it is concealed by him although he is aware of it, he shall incur guilt. Or if a person

4 rashly utters an oath to do something evil or good, in any matter in which such a man may swear a rash oath, and it is concealed by him although he is aware of it, he shall in either case incur guilt.

5 Whenever a man incurs guilt in any of these cases and confesses how he has sinned therein, he shall

6 bring to the LORD, as his penalty for the sin that he has committed, a female of the flock, either a ewe or a she-goat, as a sin-offering, and the priest shall make expiation for him on account of his sin which he has committed, and he shall be pardoned.

7 But if he cannot afford as much as a young animal, he shall bring to the LORD for the sin he has committed two turtle-doves or two young pigeons, one for a sin-offering and the other for a whole-

8 offering. He shall bring them to the priest, and present first the one intended for the sin-offering. He shall wrench its head back without

9 severing it. He shall sprinkle some of the blood of the victim against the side of the altar, and what is left of the blood shall be drained out at the base of the altar: it is

10 a sin-offering. He shall deal with the second bird as a whole-offering according to custom, and the priest shall make expiation for the sin the man has committed, and it shall be forgiven him.

11 If the man cannot afford two

turtle-doves or two young pigeons, for his sin he shall bring as his offering a tenth of an ephah of flour, as a sin-offering. He shall add no oil to it nor put frankincense on 12 it, because it is a sin-offering. He shall bring it to the priest, who shall scoop up a handful from it as a token and burn it on the altar on the food-offerings to the LORD: it 13 is a sin-offering. The priest shall make expiation for the sin the man has committed in any one of these cases, and it shall be forgiven him. The remainder belongs to the priest, as with the grain-offering.

14 The LORD spoke to Moses and 15 said: When any person commits an offence by inadvertently defaulting in dues sacred to the LORD, he shall bring as his guilt-offering to the LORD a ram without blemish from the flock, the value to be de-termined by you in silver shekels according to the sacred standard, 16 for a guilt-offering; he shall make good his default in sacred dues, adding one fifth. He shall give it to the priest, who shall make ex-piation for his sin with the ram of the guilt-offering, and it shall be forgiven him.

17 If and when any person sins un-wittingly and does what is forbid-den by any commandment of the LORD, thereby incurring guilt, he 18 must accept responsibility. He shall bring to the priest as a guilt-offering a ram without blemish from the flock, valued by you, and the priest shall make expiation for the error into which he has un-wittingly fallen, and it shall be for-19 given him. It is a guilt-offering; he has been guilty of an offence against the LORD.

6 The LORD spoke to Moses and 2 said: When any person sins and commits a grievous fault against the LORD, whether he lies to a fel-low-countryman about a deposit or contract, or a theft, or wrongs 3 him by extortion, or finds lost pro-perty and then lies about it, and swears a false oath; if a man sins and does any of these things, in any one of them, and does this, incurring 4 guilt, he shall restore what he has stolen or gained by extortion, or the deposit left with him or the lost 5 property which he found, or any-thing at all concerning which he swore a false oath. He shall make full restitution, adding one fifth to it, and give it back to the aggrieved party on the day when he offers his 6 guilt-offering. He shall bring to the LORD as his guilt-offering a ram without blemish from the flock, valued by you, as a guilt-offering. 7 The priest shall make expiation for his guilt before the LORD, and he shall be forgiven for any act which has brought guilt upon him.

8 THE LORD spoke to Moses and 9 said, Give this command to Aaron and his sons: This is the law of the whole-offering. The whole-offering shall remain on the altar-hearth all night till morning, and the altar-fire shall be kept burning there. 10 Then the priest, having donned his linen robe and put on linen draw-ers to cover himself, shall remove the ashes to which the fire reduces the whole-offering on the altar and 11 put them beside the altar. He shall then change into other garments and take the ashes outside the 12 camp to a ritually clean place. The fire shall be kept burning on the altar; it shall never go out. Every morning the priest shall have fresh wood burning thereon, arrange the whole-offering on it, and on top burn the fat from the shared-offer-13 ings. Fire shall always be kept burning on the altar; it shall not go out.

14 This is the law of the grain-offer-ing. The Aaronites shall present it before the LORD in front of the 15 altar. The priest shall set aside a handful of the flour from it, with the oil of the grain-offering, and all the frankincense on it. He shall burn this token of it on the altar

LEVI̶ ...our to the LORD. ̶er Aaron and his sons
16 as eat. It shall be eaten in the form of unleavened cakes and in a holy place. They shall eat it in the court of the Tent of the Pre-
17 sence. It shall not be baked with leaven. I have allotted this to them as their share of my food-offerings. Like the sin-offering and the guilt-
18 offering, it is most sacred. Any male descendant of Aaron may eat it, as a due from the food-offerings to the LORD, for generation after generation for all time. Whatever touches them is to be forfeit as sacred.

19 The LORD spoke to Moses and
20 said: This is the offering which Aaron and his sons shall present to the LORD:*a* one tenth of an ephah of flour, the usual grain-offering, half of it in the morning and half in
21 the evening. It shall be cooked with oil on a griddle; you shall bring it well-mixed, and so present it crumbled in small pieces as a grain-offering, a soothing odour to the
22 LORD. The anointed priest in the line of Aaron shall offer it. This is a rule binding for all time. It shall be burnt in sacrifice to the LORD as a
23 complete offering. Every grain-offering of a priest shall be a complete offering; it shall not be eaten.
24 The LORD spoke to Moses and
25 said, Speak to Aaron and his sons in these words: This is the law of the sin-offering. The sin-offering shall be slaughtered before the LORD in the place where the whole-offering is slaughtered; it is most
26 sacred. The priest who officiates shall eat of the flesh; it shall be eaten in a sacred place, in the court
27 of the Tent of the Presence. Whatever touches its flesh is to be forfeit as sacred. If any of the blood is splashed on a garment, that shall
28 be washed in a sacred place. An earthenware vessel in which the sin-offering is boiled shall be smashed. If it has been boiled in a copper vessel, that shall be scoured

and rinsed with water. Any male 29 of priestly family may eat of this offering; it is most sacred. If, how- 30 ever, part of the blood is brought to the Tent of the Presence to make expiation in the holy place, the sin-offering shall not be eaten; it shall be destroyed by fire.

This is the law of the guilt- 7 offering: it is most sacred. The 2 guilt-offering shall be slaughtered in the place where the whole-offering is slaughtered, and its blood shall be flung against the altar all round. The priest shall set aside 3 and present all the fat from it: the fat-tail and the fat covering the entrails, the two kidneys with the 4 fat on them beside the haunches, and the long lobe of the liver with the kidneys. The priest shall burn 5 these pieces on the altar as a food-offering to the LORD; it is a guilt-offering. Any male of priestly fami- 6 ly may eat it. It shall be eaten in a sacred place; it is most sacred. There is one law for both sin-offer- 7 ing and guilt-offering: they shall belong to the priest who performs the rite of expiation. The skin of 8 any man's whole-offering shall belong to the priest who presents it. Every grain-offering baked in an 9 oven and everything that is cooked in a pan or on a griddle shall belong to the priest who presents it. Every 10 grain-offering, whether mixed with oil or dry, shall be shared equally among all the Aaronites.

This is the law of the shared- 11 offering presented to the LORD. If 12 a man presents it as a thank-offering, then, in addition to the thank-offering, he shall present unleavened cakes mixed with oil, wafers of unleavened flour smeared with oil, and well-mixed flour and flat cakes mixed with oil. He shall present 13 flat cakes of leavened bread in addition to his shared thank-offering. One part of every offering he shall 14 present as a contribution for the LORD: it shall belong to the priest

---

a Prob. rdg.; Heb. adds on the day when he is anointed.

15 who flings the blood of the shared-offering against the altar. The flesh shall be eaten on the day of its presentation; none of it shall be put aside till morning.

16 If a man's sacrifice is a votive offering or a freewill offering, it may be eaten on the day it is pre-

17 sented or on the next day. Any flesh left over on the third day shall

18 be destroyed by fire. If any flesh of his shared-offering is eaten on the third day, the man who has presented it shall not be accepted. It will not be counted to his credit, it shall be reckoned as tainted and the person who eats any of it shall

19 accept responsibility. No flesh which comes into contact with anything unclean shall be eaten; it shall be destroyed by fire.

The flesh may be eaten by any-

20 one who is clean, but the person who, while unclean, eats flesh from a shared-offering presented to the LORD shall be cut off from his

21 father's kin. When any person is contaminated by contact with anything unclean, be it man, beast, or reptile, and then eats any of the flesh from the shared-offerings presented to the LORD, that person shall be cut off from his father's kin.

22 The LORD spoke to Moses and

23 said, Speak to the Israelites in these words: You shall not eat the fat of

24 any ox, sheep, or goat. The fat of an animal that has died a natural death or has been mauled by wild beasts may be put to any other use,

25 but you shall not eat it. Every man who eats fat from a beast of which he has presented any part as a food-offering to the LORD shall be cut off from his father's kin.

26 You shall eat none of the blood, whether of bird or of beast, wher-

27 ever you may live. Every person who eats any of the blood shall be cut off from his father's kin.

28 The LORD spoke to Moses and

29 said, Speak to the Israelites in these words: Whoever comes to present a shared-offering shall set aside

part of it as an offering to the LORD.

30 With his own hands he shall bring the food-offerings to the LORD. He shall also bring the fat together with the breast which is to be presented as a special gift before the

31 LORD; the priest shall burn the fat on the altar, but the breast shall belong to Aaron and his descen-

32 dants. You shall give the right hind-leg of your shared-offerings as a contribution for the priest;

33 it shall be the perquisite of the Aaronite who presents the blood and the fat of the shared-offering.

34 I have taken from the Israelites the breast of the special gift and the leg of the contribution made out of the shared-offerings, and have given them as a due from the Israelites to Aaron the priest and his descen-

35 dants for all time. This is the portion prescribed for Aaron and his descendants out of the LORD's food-offerings, appointed on the day when they were presented as priests

36 to the LORD; and on the day when they were anointed, the LORD commanded that these prescribed portions should be given to them by the Israelites. This is a rule binding on their descendants for all time.

37 This, then, is the law of the whole-offering, the grain-offering, the sin-offering, the guilt-offering, the installation-offerings, and the

38 shared-offerings, with which the LORD charged Moses on Mount Sinai on the day when he commanded the Israelites to present their offerings to the LORD in the wilderness of Sinai.

The hallowing and installation of the priests

8 THE LORD spoke to Moses and

2 said, 'Take Aaron and his sons with him, the vestments, the anointing oil, the ox for a sin-offering, the two rams, and the basket of un-

3 leavened cakes, and assemble all the community at the entrance to

4 the Tent of the Presence.' Moses

did as the LORD had commanded him, and the community assembled at the entrance to the Tent of 5 the Presence. He told the community that this was what the LORD 6 had commanded. He presented Aaron and his sons and washed 7 them in water. He invested Aaron with the tunic, girded him with the sash, robed him with the mantle, put the ephod on him, tied it with its waist-band and fastened the 8 ephod to him with the band. He put the breast-piece*a* on him and set the 9 Urim and Thummim in it. He then put the turban upon his head and set the gold rosette as a symbol of holy dedication on the front of the turban, as the LORD had command-10 ed him. Moses then took the anointing oil, anointed the Tabernacle and all that was within it and con-11 secrated them. He sprinkled some of the oil seven times on the altar, anointing the altar, all its vessels, the basin and its stand, to conse-12 crate them. He poured some of the anointing oil on Aaron's head and 13 so consecrated him. Moses then brought the sons of Aaron forward, invested them with tunics, girded them with sashes and tied their tall head-dresses on them, as the LORD had commanded him.

14 He then brought up the ox for the sin-offering; Aaron and his sons 15 laid their hands on its head, and he slaughtered it. Moses took some of the blood and put it with his finger on the horns round the altar. Thus he purified the altar, and when he had poured out the rest of the blood at the base of the altar, he consecrated it by making ex-16 piation for it. He took all the fat upon the entrails, the long lobe of the liver, and the two kidneys with their fat, and burnt them on the 17 altar, but the ox, its skin, its flesh, and its offal, he destroyed by fire outside the camp, as the LORD had commanded him.

18 Moses then brought forward the ram of the whole-offering; Aaron and his sons laid their hands on the ram's head, and he slaughtered 19 it. Moses flung its blood against 20 the altar all round. He cut the ram up and burnt the head, the pieces, and the suet. He washed the entrails 21 and the shins in water and burnt the whole on the altar. This was a whole-offering, a food-offering of soothing odour to the LORD, as the LORD had commanded Moses.

Moses then brought forward the 22 second ram, the ram for the installation of priests. Aaron and his sons laid their hands upon its head, and 23 he slaughtered it. Moses took some of its blood and put it on the lobe of Aaron's right ear, on his right thumb, and on the big toe of his right foot. He then brought for-24 ward the sons of Aaron, put some of the blood on the lobes of their right ears, on their right thumbs, and on the big toes of their right feet. He flung the rest of the blood against the altar all round; he took 25 the fat, the fat-tail, the fat covering the entrails, the long lobe of the liver, the two kidneys with their fat, and the right leg. Then from 26 the basket of unleavened cakes before the LORD he took one unleavened cake, one cake of bread made with oil, and one wafer, and laid them on the fatty parts and the right leg. He put the whole on 27 the hands of Aaron and of his sons, and he presented it as a special gift before the LORD. He took it from 28 their hands and burnt it on the altar on top of the whole-offering. This was an installation-offering, it was a food-offering of soothing odour to the LORD.

Moses then took the breast and 29 presented it as a special gift before the LORD; it was his portion of the ram of installation, as the LORD had commanded him. He took 30 some of the anointing oil and some of the blood on the altar and sprinkled it on Aaron and his vest-

a Or pouch.

ments, and on his sons and their vestments with him. Thus he consecrated Aaron and his vestments, and with him his sons and their vestments.

31 Moses said to Aaron and his sons, 'Boil the flesh of the ram at the entrance to the Tent of the Presence, and eat it there, together with the bread in the installation-basket, in accordance with the command: "Aaron and his sons 32 shall eat it." The remainder of the flesh and bread you shall destroy 33 by fire. You shall not leave the entrance to the Tent of the Presence for seven days, until the day which completes the period of your installation, for it lasts seven days. 34 What was done this day followed the LORD's command to make ex- 35 piation for you. You shall stay at the entrance to the Tent of the Presence day and night for seven days, keeping vigil to the LORD, so that you do not die, for so I was commanded.'

36 Aaron and his sons did everything that the LORD had commanded through Moses.

9 On the eighth day Moses summoned Aaron and his sons and the 2 Israelite elders. He said to Aaron, 'Take for yourself a bull-calf for a sin-offering and a ram for a whole-offering, both without blemish, and present them before the LORD. 3 Then bid the Israelites take a he-goat for a sin-offering, a calf and a lamb, both yearlings without 4 blemish, for a whole-offering, and a bull and a ram for shared-offerings to be sacrificed before the LORD, together with a grain-offering mixed with oil. This day the LORD will appear to you.'

5 They brought what Moses had commanded to the front of the Tent of the Presence, and all the community approached and stood 6 before the LORD. Moses said, 'This is what the LORD has commanded you to do, so that the glory of the 7 LORD may appear to you. Come

near to the altar,' he said to Aaron; 'prepare your sin-offering and your whole-offering and make expiation for yourself and for your household. Then prepare the offering of the people and make expiation for them, as the LORD has commanded.'

So Aaron came near to the altar 8 and slaughtered the calf, which was his sin-offering. The sons of 9 Aaron presented the blood to him, and he dipped his finger in the blood and put it on the horns of the altar. The rest of the blood he poured out at the base of the altar. Part of the sin-offering, the fat, the 10 kidneys, and the long lobe of the liver, he burnt on the altar as the LORD had commanded Moses, but 11 the flesh and the skin he destroyed by fire outside the camp. Then he 12 slaughtered the whole-offering; his sons handed him the blood, and he flung it against the altar all round. They handed him the pieces of the 13 whole-offering and the head, and he burnt them on the altar. He 14 washed the entrails and the shins and burnt them on the altar, on top of the whole-offering.

He then brought forward the 15 offering of the people. He took the he-goat, the people's sin-offering, slaughtered it and performed the rite of the sin-offering as he had previously done for himself. He 16 presented the whole-offering and prepared it in the manner prescribed. He brought forward the 17 grain-offering, took a handful of it and burnt it on the altar, in addition to the morning whole-offering. He slaughtered the bull and the 18 ram, the shared-offerings of the people. His sons handed him the blood, and he flung it against the altar all round. But the fatty parts 19 of the bull, the fat-tail of the ram, the fat covering the entrails, and the two kidneys with the fat upon them, and the long lobe of the liver, all this fat they first put on the 20 breasts of the animals and then

21 burnt it on the altar. Aaron presented the breasts and the right leg as a special gift before the LORD, as Moses had commanded.

22   Then Aaron lifted up his hands towards the people and pronounced the blessing over them. He came down from performing the rites of the sin-offering, the whole-offering, 23 and the shared-offerings. Moses and Aaron entered the Tent of the Presence, and when they came out, they blessed the people, and the glory of the LORD appeared to all 24 the people. Fire came out from before the LORD and consumed the whole-offering and the fatty parts on the altar. All the people saw, and they shouted and fell on their faces.

10 NOW Nadab and Abihu, sons of Aaron, took their firepans, put fire in them, threw incense on the fire and presented before the LORD illicit fire which he had not com-2 manded. Fire came out from before the LORD and destroyed them; and so they died in the presence of the 3 LORD. Then Moses said to Aaron, 'This is what the LORD meant when he said: Among those who approach me, I must be treated as holy; in the presence of all the people I must be given honour.' 4 Aaron was dumbfounded. Moses sent for Mishael and Elzaphan, the sons of Aaron's uncle Uzziel, and said to them, 'Come and carry your cousins outside the camp away 5 from the holy place.' They came and carried them away in their tunics outside the camp, as Moses 6 had told them. Moses then said to Aaron and to his sons Eleazar and Ithamar, 'You shall not leave your hair dishevelled or tear your clothes in mourning, lest you die and the LORD be angry with the whole community. Your kinsmen, all the house of Israel, shall weep for the destruction by fire which the LORD 7 has kindled. You shall not leave the entrance to the Tent of the

Presence lest you die, because the LORD's anointing oil is on you.' They did as Moses had said.

THE LORD spoke to Aaron and 8 said: You and your sons with you 9 shall not drink wine or strong drink when you are to enter the Tent of the Presence, lest you die. This is a rule binding on your descendants for all time, to make a distinction 10 between sacred and profane, between clean and unclean, and to 11 teach the Israelites all the decrees which the LORD has spoken to them through Moses.

Moses said to Aaron and his 12 surviving sons Eleazar and Ithamar, 'Take what is left over of the grain-offering out of the food-offerings of the LORD, and eat it without leaven beside the altar; it is most sacred. You shall eat it in a sacred 13 place; it is your due and that of your sons out of the LORD's food-offerings, for so I was commanded. You shall eat the breast of the 14 special gift and the leg of the contribution in a clean place, you and your sons and daughters; for they have been given to you and your children as your due out of the shared-offerings of the Israelites. The leg of the contribution and 15 the breast of the special gift shall be brought, along with the food-offerings of fat, to be presented as a special gift before the LORD, and it shall belong to you and your children together, a due for all time; for so the LORD has commanded.'

Moses made searching inquiry 16 about the goat of the sin-offering and found that it had been burnt. He was angry with Eleazar and Ithamar, Aaron's surviving sons, and said, 'Why did you not eat 17 the sin-offering in the sacred place? It is most sacred. It was given to you to take away the guilt of the community by making expiation for them before the LORD. If the 18 blood is not brought within the sacred precincts, you shall eat the

19 sin-offering there as I was commanded.' But Aaron replied to
Moses, 'See, they have today presented their sin-offering and their
whole-offering before the LORD,
and this is what has befallen me;
if I eat a sin-offering today, will it
be right in the eyes of the LORD?'
20 When Moses heard this, he deemed
it right.

Laws of purification and atonement

11 THE LORD spoke to Moses and
2 Aaron and said, Speak to the Israelites in these words: Of all animals on land these are the creatures
3 you may eat: you may eat any
animal which has a parted foot or
a cloven hoof and also chews the
4 cud; those which have only a cloven
hoof or only chew the cud you may
not eat. These are: the camel, because it chews the cud but has not
a cloven hoof; you shall regard it as
5 unclean; the rock-badger,*a* because
it chews the cud but has not a
parted foot; you shall regard it as
6 unclean; the hare, because it chews
the cud but has not a parted foot;
7 you shall regard it as unclean; the
pig, because it has a parted foot
and a cloven hoof but does not
8 chew the cud; you shall regard it
as unclean. You shall not eat their
flesh or even touch their dead
bodies; you shall regard them as
unclean.
9 Of creatures that live in water
these you may eat: all those that
have fins and scales, whether in
10 salt water or fresh; but all that
have neither fins nor scales, whether in salt or fresh water, including both small creatures in shoals
and larger creatures, you shall re-
11 gard as vermin. They shall be vermin to you; you shall not eat their
flesh, and their dead bodies you
shall treat as those of vermin.
12 Every creature in the water that

has neither fins nor scales shall be
vermin to you.
13 These are the birds you shall
regard as vermin, and for this
reason they shall not be eaten: the
griffon-vulture,*b* the black vulture,
14 and the bearded vulture;*c* the kite
15 and every kind of falcon; every
16 kind of crow,*d* the desert-owl, the
short-eared owl, the long-eared
17 owl, and every kind of hawk; the
tawny owl, the fisher-owl, and the
18 screech-owl; the little owl, the
19 horned owl, the osprey, the stork,*e*
every kind of cormorant, the hoopoe, and the bat.
20 All teeming winged creatures
that go on four legs shall be vermin
21 to you, except those which have
legs jointed above their feet for
22 leaping on the ground. Of these
you may eat every kind of great locust, every kind of long-headed
locust, every kind of green locust,
and every kind of desert locust.
23 Every other teeming winged creature that has four legs you shall re-
24 gard as vermin; you would make
yourselves unclean with them:
whoever*f* touches their dead bodies
25 shall be unclean till evening. Whoever picks up their dead bodies
shall wash his clothes but remain
unclean till evening.
26 You shall regard as unclean
every animal which has a parted
foot but has not a cloven hoof and
does not chew the cud: whoever*f*
touches them shall be unclean.
27 You shall regard as unclean all
four-footed wild animals that go
on flat paws; whoever*f* touches
their dead bodies shall be unclean
28 till evening. Whoever takes up their
dead bodies shall wash his clothes
but remain unclean till evening.
You shall regard them as unclean.
29 You shall regard these as unclean
among creatures that teem on the
ground: the mole-rat,*g* the jerboa,
and every kind of thorn-tailed liz-
30 ard; the gecko, the sand-gecko, the

a Or rock-rabbit.   *b* Or eagle.   *c* Or ossifrage.   *d* Or raven.
e Or heron.   *f* Or whatever.   *g* Or weasel.

31 wall-gecko, the great lizard, and the chameleon. You shall regard these as unclean among teeming creatures; whoever[a] touches them when they are dead shall be unclean 32 till evening. Anything on which any of them falls when they are dead shall be unclean, any article of wood or garment or skin or sacking, any article in regular use; it shall be plunged into water but shall remain unclean till evening, 33 when it shall be clean. If any of these falls into an earthenware vessel, its contents shall be unclean 34 and it shall be smashed. Any food on which water from such a vessel is poured shall be unclean, and any drink in such a vessel shall be un-35 clean. Anything on which the dead body of such a creature falls shall be unclean; an oven or a stove shall be broken, for they are unclean and you shall treat them as such; 36 but a spring or a cistern where water collects shall remain clean, though whatever[b] touches the dead 37 body shall be unclean. When any of their dead bodies falls on seed intended for sowing, it remains clean; 38 but if the seed has been soaked in water and any dead body falls on it, you shall treat it as unclean.

39 When any animal allowed as food dies, all that touch the carcass 40 shall be unclean till evening. Whoever eats any of the carcass shall wash his clothes but remain unclean till evening; whoever takes up the carcass shall wash his clothes 41 and be unclean till evening. All creatures that teem on the ground are vermin; they shall not be eaten. 42 All creatures that teem on the ground, crawl on their bellies, go on all fours or have many legs, you shall not eat, because they are 43 vermin which contaminate. You shall not contaminate yourselves through any teeming creature. You shall not defile yourselves with them and make yourselves unclean 44 by them. For I am the LORD your God; you shall make yourselves holy and keep yourselves holy, because I am holy. You shall not defile yourselves with any teeming creature that creeps on the ground. I am the LORD who brought you up 45 from Egypt to become your God. You shall keep yourselves holy, because I am holy.

This, then, is the law concerning 46 beast and bird, every living creature that swims in the water and every living creature that teems on the land. It is to make a distinction 47 between the unclean and the clean, between living creatures that may be eaten and living creatures that may not be eaten.

The LORD spoke to Moses and 12 said, Speak to the Israelites in 2 these words: When a woman conceives and bears a male child, she shall be unclean for seven days, as in the period of her impurity through menstruation. On the 3 eighth day, the child shall have the flesh of his foreskin circumcised. The woman shall wait for 4 thirty-three days because her blood requires purification; she shall touch nothing that is holy, and shall not enter the sanctuary till her days of purification are completed. If she bears a female child, she 5 shall be unclean for fourteen days as for her menstruation and shall wait for sixty-six days because her blood requires purification. When 6 her days of purification are completed for a son or a daughter, she shall bring a yearling ram for a whole-offering and a young pigeon or a turtle-dove for a sin-offering to the priest at the entrance to the Tent of the Presence. He shall 7 present it before the LORD and make expiation for her, and she shall be clean from the issue of her blood. This is the law for the woman who bears a child, whether male or female. If she cannot afford a ram, 8 she shall bring two turtle-doves or two young pigeons, one for a whole-

---

[a] *Or whatever.*   [b] *Or whoever.*

offering and the other for a sin-offering. The priest shall make expiation for her and she shall be clean.

13 The LORD spoke to Moses and 2 Aaron and said: When any man has a discoloration on the skin of his body, a pustule or inflammation, and it may develop into the sores of a malignant skin-disease, he shall be brought to the priest, either to Aaron or to one of his sons.

3 The priest shall examine the sore on the skin; if the hairs on the sore have turned white and it appears to be deeper than the skin, it shall be considered the sore of a malignant skin-disease, and the priest, after examination, shall pronounce him ritually unclean.

4 But if the inflammation on his skin is white and seems no deeper than the skin, and the hairs have not turned white, the priest shall isolate the affected person for seven 5 days. If, when he examines him on the seventh day, the sore remains as it was and has not spread in the skin, he shall keep him in isolation 6 for another seven days. When the priest examines him again on the seventh day, if the sore has faded and has not spread in the skin, the priest shall pronounce him ritually clean. It is only a scab; the man shall wash his clothes and so be 7 clean. But if the scab spreads on the skin after he has been to the priest to be pronounced ritually clean, the man shall show himself 8 a second time to the priest. The priest shall examine him again, and if it continues to spread, he shall pronounce him ritually unclean; it is a malignant skin-disease.

9 When anyone has the sores of a malignant skin-disease, he shall 10 be brought to the priest, and the priest shall examine him. If there is a white mark on the skin, turning the hairs white, and an ulceration 11 appears in the mark, it is a chronic skin-disease on the body, and the priest shall pronounce him ritually unclean; there is no need for isolation because he is unclean already. If the skin-disease breaks 12 out and covers the affected person from head to foot as far as the priest can see, the priest shall examine 13 him, and if he finds the condition spread all over the body, he shall pronounce him ritually clean. It has all gone white; he is clean. But 14 from the moment when raw flesh appears, the man shall be considered unclean. When the priest sees it, 15 he shall pronounce him unclean. Raw flesh is to be considered unclean; it is a malignant skin-disease. On the other hand, when 16 the raw flesh heals and turns white, the man shall go to the priest, who 17 shall examine him, and if the sores have gone white, he shall pronounce him clean. He is ritually clean.

When a fester appears on the 18 skin and heals up, but is followed 19 by a white mark or reddish-white inflammation on the site of the fester, the man shall show himself to the priest. The priest shall examine 20 him; if it seems to be beneath the skin and the hairs have turned white, the priest shall pronounce him ritually unclean. It is a malignant skin-disease which has broken out on the site of the fester. But if 21 the priest on examination finds that it has no white hairs, is not beneath the skin and has faded, he shall isolate him for seven days. If the affection has spread at all 22 in the skin, then the priest shall pronounce him unclean; for it is a malignant skin-disease. But if the 23 inflammation is no worse and has not spread, it is only the scar of the fester, and the priest shall pronounce him ritually clean.

Again, in the case of a burn on 24 the skin, if the raw spot left by the burn becomes a reddish-white or white inflammation, the priest 25 shall examine it. If the hairs on the inflammation have turned white and it is deeper than the skin, it is a malignant skin-disease which has broken out at the site of the burn. The priest shall pronounce the man ritually unclean; it is a malignant 26 skin-disease. But if the priest on examination finds that there is no white hair on the inflammation and it is not beneath the skin and has faded, he shall keep him in isolation 27 for seven days. When the priest examines him on the seventh day, if the inflammation has spread at all in the skin, the priest shall pronounce him unclean; it is a 28 malignant skin-disease. But if the inflammation is no worse, has not spread and has faded, it is only a mark from the burn. The priest shall pronounce him ritually clean because it is the scar of the burn.

29 When a man, or woman, has a 30 sore on the head or chin, the priest shall examine it; and if it seems deeper than the skin and the hair is yellow and sparse, the priest shall pronounce him ritually unclean; it is a scurf, a malignant skin-disease 31 of the head or chin. But when the priest sees the sore, if it appears to be no deeper than the skin and yet there is no yellow hair on the place, the priest shall isolate the affected 32 person for seven days. He shall examine the sore on the seventh day: if the scurf has not spread and there are no yellow hairs on it and it seems no deeper than the skin, 33 the man shall get himself shaved except for the scurfy part, and the priest shall keep him in isolation 34 for seven days. The priest shall examine it again on the seventh day, and if the scurf has not spread on the skin and appears to be no deeper than the skin, the priest shall pronounce him clean. The man shall wash his clothes and 35 so be ritually clean. But if the scurf spreads at all in the skin after the man has been pronounced clean, 36 the priest shall examine him again. If it has spread in the skin, the priest need not even look for yellow 37 hair; the man is unclean. If, however, the scurf remains as it was

but black hair has begun to grow on it, it has healed. The man is ritually clean and the priest shall pronounce him so.

When a man, or woman, has in- 38 flamed patches on the skin and they are white, the priest shall examine 39 them. If they are white and fading, it is dull-white leprosy that has broken out on the skin. The man is ritually clean.

When a man's hair falls out from 40 his head, he is bald behind but not ritually unclean. If the hair falls 41 out from the front of the scalp, he is bald on the forehead but clean. But if on the bald patch behind or 42 on the forehead there is a reddish-white sore, it is a malignant skin-disease breaking out on those parts. The priest shall examine him, and 43 if the discoloured sore on the bald patch behind or on the forehead is reddish-white, similar in appearance to a malignant skin-disease on the body, the man is suffering 44 from such a disease; he is ritually unclean and the priest must not fail to pronounce him so. The symptoms are in this case on his head.

One who suffers from a malig- 45 nant skin-disease shall wear his clothes torn, leave his hair dishevelled, conceal his upper lip, and cry, 'Unclean, unclean.' So long as 46 the sore persists, he shall be considered ritually unclean. The man is unclean: he shall live apart and must stay outside the settlement.

When there is a stain of mould, 47 whether in a garment of wool or linen, or in the warp or weft of 48 linen or wool, or in a skin or anything made of skin; if the stain is 49 greenish or reddish in the garment or skin, or in the warp or weft, or in anything made of skin, it is a stain of mould which must be shown to the priest. The priest 50 shall examine it and put the stained material aside for seven days. On 51 the seventh day he shall examine it again. If the stain has spread in the garment, warp, weft, or skin,

whatever the use of the skin, the stain is a rotting mould: it is ritual-
52 ly unclean. He shall burn the garment or the warp or weft, whether wool or linen, or anything of skin which is stained; because it is a rotting mould, it must be destroyed by
53 fire. But if the priest sees that the stain has not spread in the garment, warp or weft, or anything made of
54 skin, he shall give orders for the stained material to be washed, and then he shall put it aside for an-
55 other seven days. After it has been washed the priest shall examine the stain; if it has not changed its appearance, although it has not spread, it is unclean and you shall destroy it by fire, whether the rot is on the right side or the wrong.
56 If the priest examines it and finds the stain faded after being washed, he shall tear it out of the garment,
57 skin, warp, or weft. If, however, the stain reappears in the garment, warp or weft, or in anything of skin, it is breaking out afresh and you shall destroy by fire whatever
58 is stained. If you wash the garment, warp, weft, or anything of skin and the stain disappears, it shall be washed a second time and then it shall be ritually clean.
59 This is the law concerning stain of mould in a garment of wool or linen, in warp or weft, or in anything made of skin; by it they shall be pronounced clean or unclean.

14 THE LORD spoke to Moses and
2 said: This is the law concerning a man suffering from a malignant skin-disease. On the day when he is to be cleansed he shall be brought
3 to the priest. The priest shall go outside the camp and examine him. If the man is healed of his disease,
4 then the priest shall order two clean small birds to be brought alive for the man who is to be cleansed, together with cedar-wood, scarlet
5 thread, and marjoram.*a* He shall order one of the birds to be killed over an earthenware bowl containing fresh water. He shall then take 6 the living bird and the cedar-wood, scarlet thread, and marjoram and dip them and the living bird in the blood of the bird that has been killed over the fresh water. He shall 7 sprinkle the blood seven times on the man who is to be cleansed from his skin-disease and so cleanse him; the living bird he shall release to fly away over the open country. The man to be cleansed shall wash 8 his clothes, shave off all his hair, bathe in water and so be ritually clean. He may then enter the camp but must stay outside his tent for seven days. On the seventh day he 9 shall shave off all the hair on his head, his beard, and his eyebrows, and then shave the rest of his hair, wash his clothes and bathe in water; then he shall be ritually clean.

On the eighth day he shall bring 10 two yearling rams and one yearling ewe, all three without blemish, a grain-offering of three tenths of an ephah of flour mixed with oil, and one log of oil. The officiating priest 11 shall place the man to be cleansed and his offerings before the LORD at the entrance to the Tent of the Presence. He shall then take one 12 of the rams and offer it with the log of oil as a guilt-offering, presenting them as a special gift before the LORD. The ram shall be slaught- 13 ered where the sin-offerings and the whole-offerings are slaughtered, within the sacred precincts, because the guilt-offering, like the sin-offering, belongs to the priest. It is most sacred. The priest shall then 14 take some of the blood of the guilt-offering and put it on the lobe of the right ear of the man to be cleansed, and on his right thumb and the big toe of his right foot. He shall next take the log of oil and 15 pour some of it on the palm of his own left hand, dip his right fore- 16 finger into the oil on his left palm and sprinkle some of it with his

a Or hyssop.

finger seven times before the LORD.
17 He shall then put some of the oil remaining on his palm on the lobe of the right ear of the man to be cleansed, on his right thumb and on the big toe of his right foot, on top of the blood of the guilt-offer-
18 ing. The remainder of the oil on the priest's palm shall be put upon the head of the man to be cleansed, and thus the priest shall make expiation
19 for him before the LORD. The priest shall then perform the sin-offering and make expiation for the uncleanness of the man who is to be cleansed. After this he shall slaugh-
20 ter the whole-offering and offer it and the grain-offering on the altar. Thus the priest shall make expiation for him, and then he shall be clean.
21 If the man is poor and cannot afford these offerings, he shall bring one young ram as a guilt-offering to be a special gift making expiation for him, and a grain-offering of a tenth of an ephah of flour
22 mixed with oil, and a log of oil, also two turtle-doves or two young pigeons, whichever he can afford, one for a sin-offering and the other
23 for a whole-offering. He shall bring them to the priest for his cleansing on the eighth day, at the entrance to the Tent of the Presence before
24 the LORD. The priest shall take the ram for the guilt-offering and the log of oil, and shall present them as a special gift before the LORD.
25 The ram for the guilt-offering shall then be slaughtered, and the priest shall take some of the blood of the guilt-offering, and put it on the lobe of the right ear of the man to be cleansed and on his right thumb and on the big toe of his right foot.
26 He shall pour some of the oil on the
27 palm of his own left hand and sprinkle some of it with his right forefinger seven times before the
28 LORD. He shall then put some of the oil remaining on his palm on the lobe of the right ear of the man

to be cleansed, and on his right thumb and on the big toe of his right foot exactly where the blood of the guilt-offering was put. The 29 remainder of the oil on the priest's palm shall be put upon the head of the man to be cleansed to make expiation for him before the LORD. Of the birds which the man has 30 been able to afford, turtle-doves or young pigeons, whichever it may be, the priest shall deal with one 31 as a sin-offering and with the other as a whole-offering and shall make the grain-offering with them. Thus the priest shall make expiation before the LORD for the man who is to be cleansed. This is the law for 32 the man with a malignant skin-disease who cannot afford the regular offering for his cleansing.

The LORD spoke to Moses and 33 Aaron and said: When you have 34 entered the land of Canaan which I give you to occupy, if I inflict a fungous infection upon a house in the land you have occupied, its 35 owner shall come and report to the priest that there appears to him to be a patch of infection in his house. The priest shall order the house to 36 be cleared before he goes in to examine the infection, or everything in it will become unclean. After this the priest shall go in to inspect the house. If on inspection he finds 37 the patch on the walls consists of greenish or reddish depressions, apparently going deeper than the surface, he shall go out of the 38 house and, standing at the entrance, shall put it in quarantine for seven days. On the seventh day 39 he shall come back and inspect the house, and if the patch has spread in the walls, he shall order the in- 40 fected stones to be pulled out and thrown away outside the city in an unclean place. He shall then have 41 the house scraped inside throughout, and all the daub[a] they have scraped off shall be tipped outside the city in an unclean place. They 42

---

[a] *Or* mud.

shall take fresh stones to replace the others and replaster the house with fresh daub.

43 If the infection reappears in the house and spreads after the stones have been pulled out and the house 44 scraped and redaubed, the priest shall come and inspect it. If the infection has spread in the house, it is a corrosive growth; the house is 45 unclean. The house shall be demolished, stones, timber, and daub, and it shall all be taken away outside the city to an unclean place. 46 Anyone who has entered the house during the time it has been in quarantine shall be unclean till 47 evening. Anyone who has slept or eaten a meal in the house shall 48 wash his clothes. But if, when the priest goes into the house and inspects it, he finds that the infection has not spread after the redaubing, then he shall pronounce the house ritually clean, because the infection has been cured.

49 In order to rid the house of impurity, he shall take two small birds, cedar-wood, scarlet thread, 50 and marjoram. He shall kill one of the birds over an earthenware bowl 51 containing fresh water. He shall then take the cedar-wood, marjoram, and scarlet thread, together with the living bird, dip them in the blood of the bird that has been killed and in the fresh water, and sprinkle the house seven times. 52 Thus he shall purify the house, using the blood of the bird, the fresh water, the living bird, the cedar-wood, the marjoram, and 53 the scarlet thread. He shall set the living bird free outside the city to fly away over the open country, and make expiation for the house; and then it shall be clean.

54 This is the law for all malignant 55 skin-diseases, and for scurf, for mould in clothes and fungus in 56 houses, for a discoloration of the 57 skin, scab, and inflammation, to declare when these are pronounced unclean and when clean. This is the

law for skin-disease, mould, and fungus.

THE LORD spoke to Moses and 15 Aaron and said, Speak to the Is- 2 raelites and say to them: When any man has a discharge from his body, the discharge is ritually unclean. This is the law concerning the un- 3 cleanness due to his discharge whether it continues or has been stopped; in either case he is unclean.

Every bed on which the man 4 with a discharge lies down shall be ritually unclean, and everything on which he sits shall be unclean. Any man who touches the bed shall 5 wash his clothes, bathe in water and remain unclean till evening. Whoever sits on anything on which 6 the man with a discharge has sat shall wash his clothes, bathe in water and remain unclean till evening. Whoever touches the body of 7 the man with a discharge shall wash his clothes, bathe in water and remain unclean till evening. If the man spits on one who is 8 ritually clean, the latter shall wash his clothes, bathe in water and remain unclean till evening. Every- 9 thing on which the man sits when riding shall be unclean. Whoever 10 touches anything that has been under him shall be unclean till evening, and whoever handles such things shall wash his clothes, bathe in water and remain unclean till evening. Anyone whom the man 11 with a discharge touches without having rinsed his hands in water shall wash his clothes, bathe in water and remain unclean till evening. Any earthenware bowl touch- 12 ed by the man shall be smashed, and every wooden bowl shall be rinsed with water.

When the man is cleansed from 13 his discharge, he shall reckon seven days to his cleansing, wash his clothes, bathe his body in fresh water and be ritually clean. On the 14 eighth day he shall obtain two turtle-doves or two young pigeons

and, coming before the LORD at the entrance to the Tent of the Presence, shall give them to the priest.
15 The priest shall deal with one as a sin-offering and the other as a whole-offering, and shall make for him before the LORD the expiation required by the discharge.

16 When a man has emitted semen, he shall bathe his whole body in water and be unclean till evening.
17 Every piece of clothing or skin on which there is any semen shall be washed and remain unclean till
18 evening. This applies also to the woman with whom a man has had intercourse; they shall both bathe themselves in water and remain unclean till evening.

19 When a woman has a discharge of blood, her impurity shall last for seven days; anyone who touches her shall be unclean till evening.
20 Everything on which she lies or sits during her impurity shall be
21 unclean. Anyone who touches her bed shall wash his clothes, bathe in water and remain unclean till
22 evening. Whoever touches anything on which she sits shall wash his clothes, bathe in water and re-
23 main unclean till evening. If he is on the bed or seat where she is sitting, by touching it he shall become
24 unclean till evening. If a man goes so far as to have intercourse with her and any of her discharge gets on to him, then he shall be unclean for seven days, and every bed on which he lies down shall be unclean.
25 When a woman has a prolonged discharge of blood not at the time of her menstruation, or when her discharge continues beyond the period of menstruation, her impurity shall last all the time of her discharge; she shall be unclean as during the period of her menstru-
26 ation. Any bed on which she lies during the time of her discharge shall be like that which she used during menstruation, and everything on which she sits shall be unclean as in her menstrual unclean-

ness. Every person who touches 27 them shall be unclean; he shall wash his clothes, bathe in water and remain unclean till evening. If she is cleansed from her dis- 28 charge, she shall reckon seven days and after that she shall be ritually clean. On the eighth day she shall 29 obtain two turtle-doves or two young pigeons and bring them to the priest at the entrance to the Tent of the Presence. The priest 30 shall deal with one as a sin-offering and with the other as a whole-offering, and make for her before the LORD the expiation required by her unclean discharge.

In this way you shall warn the 31 Israelites against uncleanness, in order that they may not bring uncleanness upon the Tabernacle where I dwell among them, and so die.

This is the law for the man who 32 has a discharge, or who has an emission of semen and is thereby unclean, and for the woman who 33 is suffering her menstruation – for everyone, male or female, who has a discharge, and for the man who has intercourse with a woman who is unclean.

THE LORD spoke to Moses after 16 the death of Aaron's two sons, who died when they offered illicit fire before the LORD. He said to him: 2 Tell your brother Aaron that he must not enter the sanctuary within the Veil, in front of the cover over the Ark, except at the appointed time, on pain of death; for I appear in the cloud above the cover. When Aaron enters the 3 sanctuary, this is what he shall do. He shall bring a young bull for a sin-offering and a ram for a whole-offering. He shall wear a 4 sacred linen tunic and linen drawers to cover himself, and he shall put a linen sash round his waist and wind a linen turban round his head; all these are sacred vestments, and he shall bathe in water

5 before putting them on. He shall take from the community of the Israelites two he-goats for a sin-offering and a ram for a whole-
6 offering. He shall present the bull as a sin-offering and make expiation for himself and his household.
7 Then he shall take the two he-goats and set them before the LORD at the entrance to the Tent of the
8 Presence. He shall cast lots over the two goats, one to be for the LORD and the other for the Preci-
9 pice.[a] He shall present the goat on which the lot for the LORD has fallen and deal with it as a sin-offer-
10 ing; but the goat on which the lot for the Precipice has fallen shall be made to stand alive before the LORD, for expiation to be made over it before it is driven away into the wilderness to the Precipice.
11 Aaron shall present his bull as a sin-offering, making expiation for himself and his household, and then slaughter the bull as a sin-
12 offering. He shall take a firepan full of glowing embers from the altar before the LORD, and two handfuls of powdered fragrant incense, and bring them within the
13 Veil. He shall put the incense on the fire before the LORD, and the cloud of incense will hide the cover over the Tokens so that he shall
14 not die. He shall take some of the bull's blood and sprinkle it with his finger both on the surface of the cover, eastwards, and seven times in front of the cover.
15 He shall then slaughter the people's goat as a sin-offering, bring its blood within the Veil and do with its blood as he did with the bull's blood, sprinkling it on the
16 cover and in front of it. He shall make for the sanctuary the expiation required by the ritual uncleanness of the Israelites and their acts of rebellion, that is by all their sins; and he shall do the same for the Tent of the Presence, which dwells among them in the midst

of all their uncleanness. No other 17 man shall be within the Tent of the Presence from the time when he enters the sanctuary to make expiation until he comes out, and he shall make expiation for himself, his household, and the whole assembly of Israel.

He shall then come out to the 18 altar which is before the LORD and make expiation for it. He shall take some of the bull's blood and some of the goat's blood and put it all over the horns of the altar; he shall sprinkle some of the blood 19 on the altar with his finger seven times. So he shall purify it from all the uncleanness of the Israelites and hallow it.

When Aaron has finished making 20 expiation for the sanctuary, for the Tent of the Presence, and for the altar, he shall bring forward the live goat. He shall lay both his 21 hands on its head and confess over it all the iniquities of the Israelites and all their acts of rebellion, that is all their sins; he shall lay them on the head of the goat and send it away into the wilderness in charge of a man who is waiting ready. The goat shall carry all their 22 iniquities upon itself into some barren waste and the man shall let it go, there in the wilderness.

Aaron shall then enter the Tent 23 of the Presence, take off the linen clothes which he had put on when he entered the sanctuary, and leave them there. He shall bathe in water 24 in a consecrated place and put on his vestments; then he shall go out and perform his own whole-offering and that of the people, thus making expiation for himself and for the people. He shall burn the fat of the 25 sin-offering upon the altar. The 26 man who drove the goat away to the Precipice shall wash his clothes and bathe in water, and not till then may he enter the camp. The 27 two sin-offerings, the bull and the goat, the blood of which was

[a] *Or for Azazel.*

117

brought within the Veil to make expiation in the sanctuary, shall be taken outside the camp and destroyed by fire – skin, flesh, and 28 offal. The man who burns them shall wash his clothes and bathe in water, and not till then may he enter the camp.

29 This shall become a rule binding on you for all time. On the tenth day of the seventh month you shall mortify yourselves; you shall do no work, whether native Israelite 30 or alien settler, because on this day expiation shall be made on your behalf to cleanse you, and so make you clean before the LORD from 31 all your sins. This is a sabbath of sacred rest for you, and you shall mortify yourselves; it is a rule 32 binding for all time. Expiation shall be made by the priest duly anointed and installed to serve in succession to his father; he shall put on 33 the sacred linen clothes and shall make expiation for the holy sanctuary, the Tent of the Presence, and the altar, on behalf of the priests and the whole assembly of the 34 people. This shall become a rule binding on you for all time, to make for the Israelites once a year the expiation required by all their sins.

And Moses carried out the LORD's commands.

The law of holiness

17 THE LORD spoke to Moses and said, 2 Speak to Aaron, his sons, and all the Israelites in these words: This is what the LORD has commanded. 3 Any Israelite who slaughters an ox, a sheep, or a goat, either inside 4 or outside the camp, and does not bring it to the entrance of the Tent of the Presence to present it as an offering to the LORD before the Tabernacle of the LORD shall be held guilty of bloodshed: that man has shed blood and shall be cut off 5 from his people. The purpose is that the Israelites should bring to the LORD the animals which they slaughter in the open country; they shall bring them to the priest at the entrance to the Tent of the Presence and sacrifice them as shared-offerings to the LORD. The priest shall 6 fling the blood against the altar of the LORD at the entrance to the Tent of the Presence, and burn the fat as a soothing odour to the LORD. They shall no longer sacrifice their 7 slaughtered beasts to the demons[a] whom they wantonly follow. This shall be a rule binding on them and their descendants for all time.

You shall say to them: Any Is- 8 raelite or alien settled in Israel who offers a whole-offering or a sacrifice and does not bring it to the en- 9 trance of the Tent of the Presence to sacrifice it to the LORD shall be cut off from his father's kin.

If any Israelite or alien settled 10 in Israel eats any blood, I will set my face against the eater and cut 11 him off from his people, because the life of a creature is the blood, and I appoint it to make expiation on the altar for yourselves: it is the blood, that is the life, that makes expiation. Therefore I have told 12 the Israelites that neither you, nor any alien settled among you, shall eat blood.

Any Israelite or alien settled in 13 Israel who hunts beasts or birds that may lawfully be eaten shall drain out the blood and cover it with earth, because the life of every 14 living creature is the blood, and I have forbidden the Israelites to eat the blood of any creature, because the life of every creature is its blood: every man who eats it shall be cut off.

Every person, native or alien, 15 who eats that which has died a natural death or has been mauled by wild beasts shall wash his clothes and bathe in water, and remain ritually unclean till evening; then he shall be clean. If he does not 16

a Or satyrs.

wash his clothes and bathe his body, he must accept responsibility.

18 THE LORD spoke to Moses and 2 said, Speak to the Israelites in these words: I am the LORD your God. 3 You shall not do as they do in Egypt where you once dwelt, nor shall you do as they do in the land of Canaan to which I am bringing you; you shall not conform to their 4 institutions. You must keep my laws and conform to my institutions without fail: I am the LORD 5 your God. You shall observe my institutions and my laws: the man who keeps them shall have life through them. I am the LORD. 6 No man shall approach a blood-relation for intercourse. I am the 7 LORD. You shall not bring shame on your father by intercourse with your mother: she is your mother; you shall not bring shame upon 8 her. You shall not have intercourse with your father's wife: that is to 9 bring shame upon your father. You shall not have intercourse with your sister, your father's daughter, or your mother's daughter, whether brought up in the family or in another home; you shall not bring 10 shame upon them. You shall not have intercourse with your son's daughter or your daughter's daughter: that is to bring shame upon 11 yourself. You shall not have intercourse with a daughter of your father's wife, begotten by your father: she is your sister, and you shall not bring shame upon her. 12 You shall not have intercourse with your father's sister: she is a blood-13 relation of your father. You shall not have intercourse with your mother's sister: she is a blood-14 relation of your mother. You shall not bring shame upon your father's brother by approaching his wife: 15 she is your aunt. You shall not have intercourse with your daughter-in-law: she is your son's wife; you shall not bring shame upon her. 16 You shall not have intercourse with

your brother's wife: that is to bring shame upon him. You shall not 17 have intercourse with both a woman and her daughter, nor shall you take her son's daughter or her daughter's daughter to have intercourse with them: they are her blood-relations, and such conduct is lewdness. You shall not take a 18 woman who is your wife's sister to make her a rival-wife, and to have intercourse with her during her sister's lifetime.

You shall not approach a woman 19 to have intercourse with her during her period of menstruation. You 20 shall not have sexual intercourse with the wife of your fellow-countryman and so make yourself unclean with her. You shall not 21 surrender any of your children to Molech and thus profane the name of your God: I am the LORD. You 22 shall not lie with a man as with a woman: that is an abomination. You shall not have sexual inter- 23 course with any beast to make yourself unclean with it, nor shall a woman submit herself to intercourse with a beast: that is a violation of nature. You shall not 24 make yourselves unclean in any of these ways; for in these ways the heathen, whom I am driving out before you, made themselves unclean. This is how the land be- 25 came unclean, and I punished it for its iniquity so that it spewed out its inhabitants. You, unlike 26 them, shall keep my laws and my rules: none of you, whether natives or aliens settled among you, shall do any of these abominable things. The people who were there before 27 you did these abominable things and the land became unclean. So 28 the land will not spew you out for making it unclean as it spewed them out; for anyone who does any 29 of these abominable things shall be cut off from his people. Observe 30 my charge, therefore, and follow none of the abominable institutions customary before your time; do not make yourselves unclean with them. I am the LORD your God.

19 THE LORD spoke to Moses and 2 said, Speak to all the community of the Israelites in these words: You shall be holy, because I, the 3 LORD your God, am holy. You shall revere, every man of you, his mother and his father. You shall keep my sabbaths. I am the LORD 4 your God. Do not resort to idols; you shall not make gods of cast metal for yourselves. I am the LORD your God.

5 When you sacrifice a shared-offering to the LORD, you shall slaughter it so as to win acceptance 6 for yourselves. It must be eaten on the day of your sacrifice or the next day. Whatever is left over till the third day shall be destroyed 7 by fire; it is tainted, and if any of it is eaten on the third day, it will 8 not be acceptable. He who eats it must accept responsibility, because he has profaned the holy-gift to the LORD: that person shall be cut off from his father's kin.

9 When you reap the harvest of your land, you shall not reap right into the edges of your field; neither shall you glean the loose ears of 10 your crop; you shall not completely strip your vineyard nor glean the fallen grapes. You shall leave them for the poor and the alien. I am the LORD your God.

11 You shall not steal; you shall not cheat or deceive a fellow-country-12 man. You shall not swear in my name with intent to deceive and thus profane the name of your God. 13 I am the LORD. You shall not oppress your neighbour, nor rob him. You shall not keep back a hired man's wages till next morning. 14 You shall not treat the deaf with contempt, nor put an obstruction in the way of the blind. You shall fear your God. I am the LORD.

15 You shall not pervert justice, either by favouring the poor or by subservience to the great. You shall judge your fellow-country-man with strict justice. You shall 16 not go about spreading slander among your father's kin, nor take sides against your neighbour on a capital charge. I am the LORD. You shall not nurse hatred against 17 your brother. You shall reprove your fellow-countryman frankly and so you will have no share in his guilt.[a] You shall not seek re-18 venge, or cherish anger towards your kinsfolk; you shall love your neighbour as a man like yourself. I am the LORD.

You shall keep my rules. You 19 shall not allow two different kinds of beast to mate together. You shall not plant your field with two kinds of seed. You shall not put on a garment woven with two kinds of yarn.

When a man has intercourse with 20 a slave-girl who has been assigned to another man and neither ran-somed nor given her freedom, in-quiry shall be made. They shall not be put to death, because she has not been freed. The man shall 21 bring his guilt-offering, a ram, to the LORD to the entrance of the Tent of the Presence, and with it 22 the priest shall make expiation for him before the LORD for his sin, and he shall be forgiven the sin he has committed.

When you enter the land, and 23 plant any kind of tree for food, you shall treat it as bearing forbidden fruit. For three years it shall be forbidden and may not be eaten. In the fourth year all its fruit shall 24 be a holy-gift to the LORD, and this releases it for use. In the fifth year 25 you may eat its fruit, and thus the yield it gives you shall be increased. I am the LORD your God.

You shall not eat meat with the 26 blood in it. You shall not practise divination or soothsaying. You 27 shall not round off your hair from side to side, and you shall not shave

---

[a] *Or* and for that you will incur no blame.

28 the edge of your beards. You shall not gash yourselves in mourning for the dead; you shall not tattoo yourselves. I am the LORD.

29 Do not prostitute your daughter and so make her a whore; thus the land shall not play the prostitute

30 and be full of lewdness. You shall keep my sabbaths, and revere my sanctuary. I am the LORD.

31 Do not resort to ghosts and spirits, nor make yourselves unclean by seeking them out. I am the LORD your God.

32 You shall rise in the presence of grey hairs, give honour to the aged, and fear your God. I am the LORD.

33 When an alien settles with you in your land, you shall not oppress

34 him. He shall be treated as a native born among you, and you shall love him as a man like yourself, because you were aliens in Egypt. I am the LORD your God.

35 You shall not pervert justice in measurement of length, weight, or

36 quantity. You shall have true scales, true weights, true measures dry and liquid. I am the LORD your God who brought you out of

37 Egypt. You shall observe all my rules and laws and carry them out. I am the LORD.

20 The LORD spoke to Moses and

2 said, Say to the Israelites: Any Israelite or alien settled in Israel who gives any of his children to Molech shall be put to death: the common people shall stone him.

3 I, for my part, set my face against that man and cut him off from his people, because he has given a child of his to Molech, thus making my sanctuary unclean and profaning

4 my holy name. If the common people connive at it when a man has given a child of his to Molech and

5 do not put him to death, I will set my face against man and family, and both him and all who follow him in his wanton following after Molech,*a* I will cut off from their people.

6 I will set my face against the man who wantonly resorts to ghosts and spirits, and I will cut that person off from his people. Hallow 7 yourselves and be holy, because I the LORD your God am holy. You 8 shall keep my rules and obey them: I am the LORD who hallows you.

9 When any man reviles his father and his mother, he shall be put to death. He has reviled his father and his mother; his blood shall be on his own head. If a man commits 10 adultery with his neighbour's wife, both adulterer and adulteress shall be put to death. The man who has 11 intercourse with his father's wife has brought shame on his father. They shall both be put to death; their blood shall be on their own heads. If a man has intercourse 12 with his daughter-in-law, they shall both be put to death. Their deed is a violation of nature; their blood shall be on their own heads. If a 13 man has intercourse with a man as with a woman, they both commit an abomination. They shall be put to death; their blood shall be on their own heads. If a man takes 14 both a woman and her mother, that is lewdness. Both he and they shall be burnt; thus there shall be no lewdness in your midst. A man who 15 has sexual intercourse with any beast shall be put to death, and you shall kill the beast. If a woman 16 approaches any animal to have intercourse with it, you shall kill both woman and beast. They shall be put to death; their blood shall be on their own heads. If a man 17 takes his sister, his father's daughter or his mother's daughter, and they see one another naked, it is a scandalous disgrace. They shall be cut off in the presence of their people. The man has had intercourse with his sister and he shall accept responsibility. If a man lies 18 with a woman during her monthly period and brings shame upon her, he has exposed her discharge and

---

a Or in his lusting after human sacrifice.

she has uncovered the source of her discharge; they shall both be 19 cut off from their people. You shall not have intercourse with your mother's sister or your father's sister: it is the exposure of a blood-relation. They shall accept respon- 20 sibility. A man who has intercourse with his uncle's wife has brought shame upon his uncle. They shall accept responsibility for their sin and shall be proscribed and put to 21 death. If a man takes his brother's wife, it is impurity. He has brought shame upon his brother; they shall be proscribed.

22 You shall keep all my rules and my laws and carry them out, that the land into which I am bringing you to live may not spew you out. 23 You shall not conform to the institutions of the nations whom I am driving out before you: they did all these things and I abhorred 24 them, and I told you that you should occupy their land, and I would give you possession of it, a land flowing with milk and honey. I am the LORD your God: I have made a clear separation between 25 you and the nations, and you shall make a clear separation between clean beasts and unclean beasts and between unclean and clean birds. You shall not make yourselves vile through beast or bird or anything that creeps on the ground, for I have made a clear separation between them and you, declaring 26 them unclean. You shall be holy to me, because I the LORD am holy. I have made a clear separation between you and the heathen, that 27 you may belong to me. Any man or woman among you who calls up ghosts or spirits shall be put to death. The people shall stone them; their blood shall be on their own heads.

21 THE LORD said to Moses, Say to the priests, the sons of Aaron: A priest shall not render himself un-clean for the death of any of his kin except for a near blood-relation, 2 that is for mother, father, son, daughter, brother, or full sister who 3 is unmarried and a virgin; nor shall 4 he make himself unclean for any married woman^a among his father's kin, and so profane himself.

Priests shall not make bald 5 patches on their heads as a sign of mourning, nor cut the edges of their beards, nor gash their bodies. They 6 shall be holy to their God, and they shall not profane the name of their God, because they present the food-offerings of the LORD, the food of their God, and they shall be holy. A priest shall not marry a prostitute 7 or a girl who has lost her virginity, nor shall he marry a woman divorced from her husband; for he is holy to his God. You shall keep 8 him holy because he presents the food of your God; you shall regard him as holy because I the LORD, I who hallow them, am holy. When 9 a priest's daughter profanes herself by becoming a prostitute, she profanes her father. She shall be burnt to death.

The high priest, the one among 10 his fellows who has had the anointing oil poured on his head and has been consecrated to wear the vestments, shall neither leave his hair dishevelled nor tear his clothes. He 11 shall not enter the place where any man's dead body lies; not even for his father or his mother shall he render himself unclean. He shall 12 not go out of the sanctuary for fear that he dishonour the sanctuary of his God, because the consecration of the anointing oil of his God is upon him. I am the LORD. He shall 13 marry a woman who is still a virgin. He shall not marry a widow, a di- 14 vorced woman, a woman who has lost her virginity, or a prostitute, but only a virgin from his father's kin; he shall not dishonour his des- 15 cendants among his father's kin, for I am the LORD who hallows him.

---

^a for any married woman: *prob. rdg.*; *Heb.* husband.

16 The LORD spoke to Moses and
17 said, Speak to Aaron in these words:
No man among your descendants
for all time who has any physical
defect shall come and present the
18 food of his God. No man with a
defect shall come, whether a blind
man, a lame man, a man stunted
19 or overgrown, a man deformed in
20 foot or hand, or with mis-shapen
brows or a film over his eye or a
discharge from it, a man who has
a scab or eruption or has had a
21 testicle ruptured. No descendant
of Aaron the priest who has any
defect in his body shall approach
to present the food-offerings of the
LORD; because he has a defect he
shall not approach to present the
22 food of his God. He may eat the
bread of God both from the holy-
gifts and from the holiest of holy-
23 gifts, but he shall not come up to the
Veil nor approach the altar, because
he has a defect in his body. Thus he
shall not profane my sanctuaries,
because I am the LORD who hallows
them.
24 Thus did Moses speak to Aaron
and his sons and to all the Israelites.

22 The LORD spoke to Moses and
2 said, Tell Aaron and his sons that
they must be careful in the handling of the holy-gifts of the Israelites
which they hallow to me, lest they
profane my holy name. I am the
3 LORD. Say to them: Any man of
your descent for all time who while
unclean approaches the holy-gifts
which the Israelites hallow to the
LORD shall be cut off from my
4 presence. I am the LORD. No man
descended from Aaron who suffers
from a malignant skin-disease, or
has a discharge, shall eat of the
holy-gifts until he is cleansed. A
man who touches anything which
makes him unclean or who has an
5 emission of semen, a man who
touches any vermin which makes
him unclean or any human being
6 who makes him unclean: any person who touches such a thing shall
be unclean till sunset and unless

he washes his body shall not eat
of the holy-gifts. When the sun 7
goes down, he shall be clean, and
after that he may eat from the holy-
gifts, because they are his food. He 8
shall not eat an animal that has
died a natural death or has been
mauled by wild beasts, thereby
making himself unclean. I am the
LORD. The priests shall observe my 9
charge, lest they make themselves
guilty and die for profaning my
name. I am the LORD who hallows
them. No unqualified person may 10
eat any holy-gift; nor may a stranger lodging with a priest or a hired
man eat a holy-gift. A slave bought 11
by a priest with his own money
may do so, and slaves born in his
household may also share his food.
When a priest's daughter marries 12
an unqualified person, she shall not
eat any of the contributions of holy-
gifts; but if she is widowed or di- 13
vorced and is childless and comes
back to her father's house as in her
childhood, she shall share her father's food. No unqualified person
may eat any of it.
When a man inadvertently eats 14
a holy-gift, he shall make good the
holy-gift to the priest, adding a
fifth to its value. The priests shall 15
not profane the holy-gifts of the
Israelites which they set aside for
the LORD; they shall not let men 16
eat their holy-gifts and so incur
guilt and its penalty, because I am
the LORD who hallows them.
The LORD spoke to Moses and 17
said, Speak to Aaron and his sons 18
and to all the Israelites in these
words: When any man of the house
of Israel or any alien in Israel
presents, whether in fulfilment of
a vow or for a freewill offering, such
an offering as is presented to the
LORD for a whole-offering so as to 19
win acceptance for yourselves, it
shall be a male without defect, of
cattle, sheep, or goats. You shall 20
not present anything which is defective, because it will not be acceptable on your behalf. When a 21

man presents a shared-offering to the LORD, whether cattle or sheep, to fulfil a special[a] vow or as a free-will offering, if it is to be acceptable it must be perfect; there shall be 22 no defect in it. You shall present to the LORD nothing blind, disabled, mutilated, with running sore, scab, or eruption, nor set any such creature on the altar as a food-23 offering to the LORD. If a bull or a sheep is overgrown or stunted, you may make of it a freewill offering, but it will not be acceptable in ful-24 filment of a vow. If its testicles have been crushed or bruised, torn or cut, you shall not present it to the LORD; this is forbidden in your land.

25 You shall not procure any such creature from a foreigner and present it as food for your God. Their deformity is inherent in them, a permanent defect, and they will not be acceptable on your behalf.

26 The LORD spoke to Moses and 27 said: When a calf, a lamb, or a kid is born, it must not be taken from its mother for seven days. From the eighth day onwards it will be acceptable when offered as a food-28 offering to the LORD. You shall not slaughter a cow or sheep at the 29 same time as its young. When you make a thank-offering to the LORD, you shall sacrifice it so as to win 30 acceptance for yourselves; it shall be eaten that same day, and none be left till morning. I am the LORD.

31 You shall observe my commandments and perform them. I am the 32 LORD. You shall not profane my holy name; I will be hallowed among the Israelites. I am the LORD who 33 hallows you, who brought you out of Egypt to become your God. I am the LORD.

23 THE LORD spoke to Moses and 2 said, Speak to the Israelites in these words: These are the appointed seasons of the LORD, and you shall proclaim them as sacred assemblies; these are my appointed seasons. On six days work may be 3 done, but every seventh day is a sabbath of sacred rest, a day of sacred assembly, on which you shall do no work. Wherever you live, it is the LORD's sabbath.

These are the appointed seasons 4 of the LORD, the sacred assemblies which you shall proclaim in their appointed order. In the first month 5 on the fourteenth day between dusk and dark is the LORD's Passover. On the fifteenth day of this 6 month begins the LORD's pilgrim-feast of Unleavened Bread; for seven days you shall eat unleavened cakes. On the first day there 7 shall be a sacred assembly; you shall not do your daily work. For 8 seven days you shall present your food-offerings to the LORD. On the seventh day also there shall be a sacred assembly; you shall not do your daily work.

The LORD spoke to Moses and 9 said, Speak to the Israelites in these 10 words: When you enter the land which I give you, and you reap its harvest, you shall bring the first sheaf of your harvest to the priest. He shall present the sheaf as a 11 special gift before the LORD on[b] the day after the sabbath, so as to gain acceptance for yourselves. On 12 the day you present the sheaf, you shall prepare a perfect yearling ram for a whole-offering to the LORD, with the proper grain-offer-13 ing, two tenths of an ephah of flour mixed with oil, as a food-offering to the LORD, of soothing odour, and also with the proper drink-offering, a quarter of a hin of wine. You shall eat neither 14 bread, nor grain, parched or fully ripened, during that day, the day on which you bring your God an offering; this is a rule binding on your descendants for all time wherever you live.

From the day after the sabbath, 15

---

[a] fulfil a special: *or* discharge a...   [b] *Or* from.

the day on which you bring your sheaf as a special gift, you shall 16 count seven full weeks. The day after the seventh sabbath will make fifty days, and then you shall present to the LORD a grain-offering 17 from the new crop. You shall bring from your homes two loaves as a special gift; they shall contain two tenths of an ephah of flour and shall be baked with leaven. They 18 are the LORD's firstfruits. In addition to the bread you shall present seven perfect yearling sheep, one young bull, and two rams. They shall be a whole-offering to the LORD with the proper grain-offering and the proper drink-offering, a food-offering of soothing 19 odour to the LORD. You shall also prepare one he-goat for a sin-offering and two yearling sheep for a 20 shared-offering, and the priest shall present them in addition to the bread of the firstfruits as a special gift before the LORD. They shall be a holy-gift to the LORD for 21 the priest. On that same day you shall proclaim a sacred assembly for yourselves; you shall not do your daily work. This is a rule binding on your descendants for all time wherever you live.

22　When you reap the harvest in your land, you shall not reap right into the edges of your field, neither shall you glean the fallen ears. You shall leave them for the poor and for the alien. I am the LORD your God.

23　The LORD spoke to Moses and 24 said, Speak to the Israelites in these words: In the seventh month you shall keep the first day as a sacred rest, a day of remembrance and acclamation, a day of sacred as- 25 sembly. You shall not do your daily work; you shall present a food-offering to the LORD.

26　The LORD spoke to Moses and 27 said: Further, the tenth day of this seventh month is the Day of Atonement. There shall be a sacred as-

sembly; you shall mortify yourselves and present a food-offering to the LORD. On that same day you 28 shall do no work because it is a day of expiation, to make expiation for you before the LORD your God. Therefore every person who does 29 not mortify himself on that day shall be cut off from his father's kin. I will extirpate any person 30 who does any work on that day. You shall do no work; it is a rule 31 binding on your descendants for all time wherever you live. It is 32 for you a sabbath of sacred rest, and you shall mortify yourselves. From the evening of the ninth day to the following evening you shall keep your sabbath-rest.

The LORD spoke to Moses and 33 said, Speak to the Israelites in these 34 words: On the fifteenth day of this seventh month the LORD's pilgrim-feast of Tabernacles*ᵃ* begins, and it lasts for seven days. On the first 35 day there shall be a sacred assembly; you shall not do your daily work. For seven days you shall 36 present a food-offering to the LORD; and on the eighth day there shall be a sacred assembly, and you shall present a food-offering to the LORD. It is the closing ceremony; you shall not do your daily work.

These are the appointed seasons 37 of the LORD which you shall proclaim as sacred assemblies for presenting food-offerings to the LORD, whole-offerings and grain-offerings, shared-offerings and drink-offerings, each on its day, besides the LORD's sabbaths and 38 all your gifts, your vows, and your freewill offerings to the LORD.

Further, from the fifteenth day 39 of the seventh month, when the harvest has been gathered, you shall keep the LORD's pilgrim-feast for seven days. The first day is a sacred rest and so is the eighth day. On the first day you shall take the 40 fruit of citrus-trees, palm fronds, and leafy branches, and willows*ᵇ*

ᵃ Or Booths *or* Arbours.　　　　*ᵇ* Or poplars.

from the riverside, and you shall rejoice before the LORD your God
41 for seven days. You shall keep this as a pilgrim-feast in the LORD's honour for seven days every year. It is a rule binding for all time on your descendants; in the seventh month you shall hold this pilgrim-
42 feast. You shall live in arbours for seven days, all who are native Is-
43 raelites, so that your descendants may be reminded how I made the Israelites live in arbours when I brought them out of Egypt. I am the LORD your God.
44 Thus Moses announced to the Israelites the appointed seasons of the LORD.

24 THE LORD spoke to Moses and
2 said: Command the Israelites to take pure oil of pounded olives ready for the regular mounting of
3 the lamp outside the Veil of the Tokens in the Tent of the Presence. Aaron shall keep the lamp in trim regularly from dusk to dawn before the LORD: this is a rule binding on
4 your descendants for all time. The lamps on the lamp-stand, ritually clean, shall be regularly kept in trim by him before the LORD.
5 You shall take flour and bake it into twelve loaves, two tenths
6 of an ephah to each. You shall arrange them in two rows, six to a row on the table, ritually clean,
7 before the LORD. You shall sprinkle pure frankincense on the rows, and this shall be a token of the bread, offered to the LORD as a
8 food-offering. Sabbath after sabbath he shall arrange it regularly before the LORD as a gift from the Israelites. This is a covenant for
9 ever; it is the privilege of Aaron and his sons, and they shall eat the bread in a holy place, because it is the holiest of holy-gifts. It is his due out of the food-offerings of the LORD for all time.
10–11 Now there was in the Israelite camp a man whose mother was an Israelite and his father an Egyptian; his mother's name was Shelomith daughter of Dibri of the tribe of Dan; and he went out and became involved in a brawl with an Israelite of pure descent. He utter- ed the Holy Name in blasphemy, so they brought him to Moses; and 12 they kept him in custody until the LORD's will should be clearly made known to them.

The LORD spoke to Moses and 13 said, Take the man who blasphem- 14 ed out of the camp. Everyone who heard him shall put a hand*a* on his head, and then all the community shall stone him to death. You shall 15 say to the Israelites: When any man whatever blasphemes his God, he shall accept responsibility for his sin. Whoever utters the Name 16 of the LORD shall be put to death: all the community shall stone him; alien or native, if he utters the Name, he shall be put to death.

When one man strikes another 17 and kills him, he shall be put to death. Whoever strikes a beast 18 and kills it shall make restitution, life for life. When one man injures 19 and disfigures his fellow-country- man, it shall be done to him as he has done; fracture for fracture, eye 20 for eye, tooth for tooth; the injury and disfigurement that he has in- flicted upon another shall in turn be inflicted upon him.

Whoever strikes a beast and kills 21 it shall make restitution, but who- ever strikes a man and kills him shall be put to death. You shall 22 have one penalty for alien and native alike. For I am the LORD your God.

Thus did Moses speak to the 23 Israelites, and they took the man who blasphemed out of the camp and stoned him to death. The Is- raelites did as the LORD had com- manded Moses.

THE LORD spoke to Moses on 25 Mount Sinai and said, Speak to 2

a Or *their hands.*

the Israelites in these words: When you enter the land which I give you, the land shall keep sabbaths
3 to the LORD. For six years you may sow your fields and for six years prune your vineyards and gather
4 the harvest, but in the seventh year the land shall keep a sabbath of sacred rest, a sabbath to the LORD. You shall not sow your field
5 nor prune your vineyard. You shall not harvest the crop that grows from fallen grain, nor gather in the grapes from the unpruned vines. It shall be a year of sacred rest for
6 the land. Yet what the land itself produces in the sabbath year shall be food for you, for your male and female slaves, for your hired man, and for the stranger lodging under
7 your roof, for your cattle and for the wild animals in your country. Everything it produces may be used for food.
8   You shall count seven sabbaths of years, that is seven times seven
9 years, forty-nine years, and in the seventh month on the tenth day of the month, on the Day of Atonement, you shall send the ram's horn round. You shall send it through
10 all your land to sound a blast, and so you shall hallow the fiftieth year and proclaim liberation in the land for all its inhabitants. You shall make this your year of jubilee. Every man of you shall return to his patrimony, every man to his
11 family. The fiftieth year shall be your jubilee. You shall not sow, and you shall not harvest the self-sown crop, nor shall you gather in the grapes from the unpruned
12 vines, because it is a jubilee, to be kept holy by you. You shall eat the produce direct from the land.
13   In this year of jubilee you shall return, every one of you, to his
14 patrimony. When you sell or buy land amongst yourselves, neither party shall drive a hard bargain.
15 You shall pay your fellow-countryman according to the number of years since the jubilee, and he shall

sell to you according to the number of annual crops. The more years 16 there are to run, the higher the price, the fewer the years, the lower, because he is selling you a series of crops. You must not victimize 17 one another, but you shall fear your God, because I am the LORD your God. Observe my statutes, keep 18 my judgements and carry them out; and you shall live in the land in security. The land shall yield its 19 harvest; you shall eat your fill and live there secure. If you ask what 20 you are to eat during the seventh year, seeing that you will neither sow nor gather the harvest, I will 21 ordain my blessing for you in the sixth year and the land shall produce a crop to carry over three years. When you sow in the eighth 22 year, you will still be eating from the earlier crop; you shall eat the old until the new crop is gathered in the ninth year.

No land shall be sold outright, 23 because the land is mine, and you are coming into it as aliens and settlers. Throughout the whole 24 land of your patrimony, you shall allow land which has been sold to be redeemed.

When one of you is reduced to 25 poverty and sells part of his patrimony, his next-of-kin who has the duty of redemption shall come and redeem what his kinsman has sold. When a man has no such next-of- 26 kin and himself becomes able to afford its redemption, he shall take 27 into account the years since the sale and pay the purchaser the balance up to the jubilee. Then he may return to his patrimony. But if the man cannot afford to 28 buy back the property, it shall remain in the hands of the purchaser till the year of jubilee. It shall then revert to the original owner, and he shall return to his patrimony.

When a man sells a dwelling- 29 house in a walled town, he shall retain the right of redemption till the end of the year of the sale; for

a time he shall have the right of
30 redemption. If it is not redeemed
before a full year is out, the house
in the walled town shall vest in
perpetuity in the buyer and his
descendants; it shall not revert at
31 the jubilee. Houses in unwalled
hamlets shall be treated as property in the open country: the right
of redemption shall hold good, and
in any case the house shall revert
32 at the jubilee. Levites shall have
the perpetual right to redeem
houses of their own patrimony in
33 towns belonging to them. If one of
the Levites does not redeem his
house in such a town, then it shall
still revert to him at the jubilee,
because the houses in Levite towns
34 are their patrimony in Israel. The
common land surrounding their
towns shall not be sold, because it
is their property in perpetuity.

35 When your brother-Israelite is
reduced to poverty and cannot
support himself in the community,
you shall assist him as you would
an alien or a stranger, and he shall
36 live with you. You shall not charge
him interest on a loan, either by
deducting it in advance from the
capital sum, or by adding it on
repayment. You shall fear your
God, and your brother shall live
37 with you; you shall not deduct interest when advancing him money
nor add interest to the payment
due for food supplied on credit.
38 I am the LORD your God who
brought you out of Egypt to give
you the land of Canaan and to
become your God.

39 When your brother is reduced
to poverty and sells himself to you,
you shall not use him to work for
40 you as a slave. His status shall be
that of a hired man or a stranger
lodging with you; he shall work
for you until the year of jubilee.
41 He shall then leave your service,
with his children, and go back to
his family and to his ancestral pro-
42 perty: because they are my slaves
whom I brought out of Egypt, they

shall not be sold as slaves are sold.
You shall not drive him with ruth- 43
less severity, but you shall fear
your God. Such slaves as you have, 44
male or female, shall come from the
nations round about you; from
them you may buy slaves. You may 45
also buy the children of those who
have settled and lodge with you and
such of their family as are born in
the land. These may become your
property, and you may leave them 46
to your sons after you; you may use
them as slaves permanently. But
your fellow-Israelites you shall not
drive with ruthless severity.

When an alien or a stranger living 47
with you becomes rich, and your
brother becomes poor and sells
himself to the alien or stranger or
to a member of some alien family,
he shall have the right of redemp- 48
tion after he has sold himself. One
of his brothers may redeem him, or 49
his uncle, his cousin, or any blood-
relation of his family, or, if he can
afford it, he may redeem himself.
He and his purchaser together shall 50
reckon from the year when he sold
himself to the year of jubilee, and
the price shall be adjusted to the
number of years. His period of
service with his owner shall be
reckoned at the rate of a hired man.
If there are still many years to run 51
to the year of jubilee, he must repay
for his redemption a proportionate
amount of the sum for which he
sold himself; if there are few, he 52
shall reckon and repay accordingly.
He shall have the status of a labour- 53
er hired from year to year, and you
shall not let him be driven with
ruthless severity by his owner. If 54
the man is not redeemed in the
intervening years, he and his children shall be released in the year of
jubilee; for it is to me that the 55
Israelites are slaves, my slaves
whom I brought out of Egypt. I am
the LORD your God.

YOU shall not make idols for your- 26
selves; you shall not erect a carved

image or a sacred pillar; you shall not put a figured stone on your land to prostrate yourselves upon, because I am the LORD your God.

2 You shall keep my sabbaths and revere my sanctuary. I am the LORD.

3 If you conform to my statutes, if you observe my commandments 4 and carry them out, I will give you rain at the proper time; the land shall yield its produce and the trees of the country-side their fruit. 5 Threshing shall last till vintage and vintage till sowing; you shall eat your fill and live secure in your 6 land. I will give peace in the land, and you shall lie down to sleep with no one to terrify you. I will rid your land of dangerous beasts and it 7 shall not be ravaged by war. You shall put your enemies to flight and they shall fall in battle before you. 8 Five of you shall pursue a hundred and a hundred of you ten thousand; so shall your enemies fall in battle 9 before you. I will look upon you with favour, I will make you fruitful and increase your numbers: I will give my covenant with you its 10 full effect. Your old harvest shall last you in store until you have to clear out the old to make room for 11 the new. I will establish my Tabernacle among you and will not spurn 12 you. I will walk to and fro among you; I will become your God and 13 you shall become my people. I am the LORD your God who brought you out of Egypt and let you be their slaves no longer; I broke the bars of your yoke and enabled you to walk upright.

14 But if you do not listen to me, if you fail to keep all these com- 15 mandments of mine, if you reject my statutes, if you spurn my judgements, and do not obey all my commandments, but break my 16 covenant, then be sure that this is what I will do: I will bring upon you sudden terror, wasting disease, recurrent fever, and plagues that dim the sight and cause the appetite to fail. You shall sow your seed to no purpose, for your enemies shall eat the crop. I will set my face 17 against you, and you shall be routed by your enemies. Those that hate you shall hound you on until you run when there is no pursuit.

18 If after all this you do not listen to me, I will go on to punish you seven times over for your sins. I will 19 break down your stubborn pride. I will make the sky above you like iron and the earth beneath you like bronze. Your strength shall 20 be spent in vain; your land shall not yield its produce nor the trees of the land their fruit.

21 If you still defy me and refuse to listen, I will multiply your calamities seven times, as your sins deserve. I will send wild beasts 22 among you; they shall tear your children from you, destroy your cattle and bring your numbers low; and your roads shall be deserted. If after all this you have not learnt 23 discipline but still defy me, I in 24 turn will defy you and scourge you seven times over for your sins. I 25 will bring war in vengeance upon you, vengeance irrevocable under covenant; you shall be herded into your cities, I will send pestilence among you, and you shall be given over to the enemy. I will cut short 26 your daily bread until ten women can bake your bread in a single oven; they shall dole it out by weight, and though you eat, you shall not be satisfied.

27 If in spite of this you do not 27 listen to me and still defy me, I will 28 defy you in anger, and I myself will punish you seven times over for your sins. Instead of meat you 29 shall eat your sons and your daughters. I will destroy your hill- 30 shrines and demolish your incense-altars. I will pile your rotting carcasses on the rotting logs[a] that were your idols, and I will spurn you. I will make your cities desolate and 31

---

destroy your sanctuaries; the soothing odour of your offerings I will 32 not accept. I will destroy your land, and the enemies who occupy it 33 shall be appalled. I will scatter you among the heathen, and I will pursue you with the naked sword; your land shall be desolate and 34 your cities heaps of rubble. Then, all the time that it lies desolate, while you are in exile in the land of your enemies, your land shall 35 enjoy its sabbaths to the full. All the time of its desolation it shall have the sabbath rest which it did not have when you lived there. 36 And I will make those of you who are left in the land of your enemies so ridden with fear that, when a leaf flutters behind them in the wind, they shall run as if it were the sword behind them; they shall 37 fall with no one in pursuit. Though no one pursues them they shall stumble over one another, as if the sword were behind them, and there shall be no stand made against the 38 enemy. You shall meet your end among the heathen, and your enemies' land shall swallow you up. 39 Those who are left shall pine away in an enemy land under their own iniquities; and with their fathers' iniquities upon them too, they shall pine away as they did.

40 But though they confess their iniquity, their own and their fathers', their treachery, and even 41 their defiance of me, I will defy them in my turn and carry them off into their enemies' land. Yet if then their stubborn spirit is broken and they accept their punishment 42 in full, I will remember my covenant with Jacob and my covenant with Isaac, yes, and my covenant with Abraham, and I will remem- 43 ber the land. The land shall be rid of its people and enjoy in full its sabbaths while it lies desolate, and they shall pay in full the penalty because they rejected my judgements and spurned my statutes.

Yet even then, in their enemies' 44 land, I shall not have rejected nor spurned them, bringing them to an end and so breaking my covenant with them, because I am the LORD their God. I will remember 45 on their behalf the covenant with the men of former times whom I brought out of Egypt in full sight of all the nations, that I might be their God. I am the LORD.

These are the statutes, the judge- 46 ments, and the laws which the LORD established between himself and the Israelites on Mount Sinai through Moses.

THE LORD spoke to Moses and 27 said, Speak to the Israelites in these 2 words: When a man makes a special[a] vow to the LORD which requires your valuation of living persons, a male between twenty 3 and sixty years old shall be valued at fifty silver shekels, that is shekels by the sacred standard. If it is 4 a female, she shall be valued at thirty shekels. If the person is be- 5 tween five years old and twenty, the valuation shall be twenty shekels for a male and ten for a female. If the person is between a month 6 and five years old, the valuation shall be five shekels for a male and three for a female. If the person is 7 over sixty and a male, the valuation shall be fifteen shekels, but if a female, ten shekels. If the man is 8 too poor to pay the amount of your valuation, the person shall be set before the priest, and the priest shall value him according to the sum which the man who makes the vow can afford: the priest shall make the valuation.

If the vow concerns a beast such 9 as may be offered as an offering to the LORD, then every gift shall be holy to the LORD. He shall not 10 change it for another, or substitute good for bad or bad for good. But if a substitution is in fact made of one beast for another, then both the

_____
[a] makes a special: *or* discharges a...

11 original beast and its substitute shall be holy to the LORD. If the vow concerns any unclean beast such as may not be offered as an offering to the LORD, then the animal shall be brought before the 12 priest, and he shall value it whether good or bad. The priest's valuation 13 shall be decisive; in case of redemption the payment shall be increased by one fifth.

14 When a man dedicates his house as holy to the LORD, the priest shall value it whether good or bad, and the priest's valuation shall be de- 15 cisive. If the donor redeems his house, he shall pay the amount of the valuation increased by one fifth, and the house shall be his.

16 If a man dedicates to the LORD part of his ancestral land, you shall value it according to the amount of seed-corn it can carry, at the rate of fifty shekels of silver for a 17 homer of barley seed. If he dedicates his land from the year of jubilee, it 18 shall stand at your valuation; but if he dedicates it after the year of jubilee, the priest shall estimate the price in silver according to the number of years remaining till the next year of jubilee, and this shall be deducted from your valuation. 19 If the man who dedicates his field should redeem it, he shall pay the amount of your valuation in silver, increased by one fifth, and it shall 20 be his. If he does not redeem it but sells the land to another man, it shall no longer be redeemable; 21 when the land reverts at the year of jubilee, it shall be like land that has been devoted, holy to the LORD. It shall belong to the priest as his patrimony.

22 If a man dedicates to the LORD land which he has bought, land which is not part of his ancestral 23 land, the priest shall estimate the amount of the value for the period until the year of jubilee, and the man shall give the amount fixed as at that day; it is holy to the LORD. At the year of jubilee the 24 land shall revert to the man from whom he bought it, whose patrimony it is. Every valuation you 25 make shall be made by the sacred standard (twenty gerahs to the shekel).

Notwithstanding, no man may 26 dedicate to the LORD the first-born of a beast which in any case has to be offered as a first-born, whether an ox or a sheep. It is the LORD's. If it is any unclean beast, he may 27 redeem it at your valuation and shall add one fifth; but if it is not redeemed, it shall be sold at your valuation. Notwithstanding, noth- 28 ing which a man devotes to the LORD irredeemably from his own property, whether man or beast or ancestral land, may be sold or redeemed. Everything so devoted is most holy to the LORD. No human 29 being thus devoted may be redeemed, but he shall be put to death.

Every tithe on land, whether 30 from grain or from the fruit of a tree, belongs to the LORD; it is holy to the LORD. If a man wishes 31 to redeem any of his tithe, he shall pay its value increased by one fifth. Every tenth creature that passes 32 under the counting rod shall be holy to the LORD; this applies to all tithes of cattle and sheep. There 33 shall be no inquiry whether it is good or bad, and no substitution. If any substitution is made, then both the tithe-animal and its substitute shall be forfeit as holy; it shall not be redeemed.

These are the commandments 34 which the LORD gave Moses for the Israelites on Mount Sinai.

NUMBERS

Israel in the wilderness of Sinai

1 ON the first day of the second month in the second year after the Israelites came out of Egypt, the LORD spoke to Moses at the Tent of the Presence in the wilderness of Sinai in these words: 2 'Number the whole community of Israel by families in the father's line, recording the name of every 3 male person aged twenty years and upwards fit for military service. You and Aaron are to make a detailed list of them by their tribal 4 hosts, and you shall have to assist you one head of family from each 5 tribe. These are their names:

of Reuben, Elizur son of Shedeur;
6 of Simeon, Shelumiel son of Zurishaddai;
7 of Judah, Nahshon son of Amminadab;
8 of Issachar, Nethaneel son of Zuar;
9 of Zebulun, Eliab son of Helon;
10 of Joseph: of Ephraim, Elishama son of Ammihud;
of Manasseh, Gamaliel son of Pedahzur;
11 of Benjamin, Abidan son of Gideoni;
12 of Dan, Ahiezer son of Ammishaddai;
13 of Asher, Pagiel son of Ocran;
14 of Gad, Eliasaph son of Reuel;
15 of Naphtali, Ahira son of Enan.'

16 These were the conveners of the whole community, chiefs of their fathers' tribes and heads of Israelite 17 clans. So Moses and Aaron took these men who had been indicated 18 by name. They summoned the whole community on the first day of the second month, and they registered their descent by families in the father's line, recording every male person aged twenty years and upwards, as the LORD had told 19 Moses to do. Thus it was that he drew up the detailed lists in the wilderness of Sinai:

The tribal list of Reuben, Israel's 20 eldest son, by families in the father's line, with the name of every male person aged twenty years and upwards fit for service, the number 21 in the list of the tribe of Reuben being forty-six thousand five hundred.

The tribal list of Simeon, by 22 families in the father's line, with the name of every male person aged twenty years and upwards fit for service, the number in the list 23 of the tribe of Simeon being fifty-nine thousand three hundred.

The tribal list of Gad, by families 24 in the father's line, with the names of all men aged twenty years and upwards fit for service, the number 25 in the list of the tribe of Gad being forty-five thousand six hundred and fifty.

The tribal list of Judah, by families in the father's line, with the 26 names of all men aged twenty years and upwards fit for service, the 27 number in the list of the tribe of Judah being seventy-four thousand six hundred.

The tribal list of Issachar, by 28 families in the father's line, with the names of all men aged twenty years and upwards fit for service, the number in the list of the tribe 29 of Issachar being fifty-four thousand four hundred.

The tribal list of Zebulun, by 30 families in the father's line, with the names of all men aged twenty years and upwards fit for service, the number in the list of the tribe 31 of Zebulun being fifty-seven thousand four hundred.

32 The tribal lists of Joseph: that of Ephraim, by families in the father's line, with the names of all men aged twenty years and up-
33 wards fit for service, the number in the list of the tribe of Ephraim being forty thousand five hundred;
34 that of Manasseh, by families in the father's line, with the names of all men aged twenty years and
35 upwards fit for service, the number in the list of the tribe of Manasseh being thirty-two thousand two hundred.

36 The tribal list of Benjamin, by families in the father's line, with the names of all men aged twenty years and upwards fit for service,
37 the number in the list of the tribe of Benjamin being thirty-five thousand four hundred.

38 The tribal list of Dan, by families in the father's line, with the names of all men aged twenty years and
39 upwards fit for service, the number in the list of the tribe of Dan being sixty-two thousand seven hundred.

40 The tribal list of Asher, by families in the father's line, with the names of all men aged twenty years
41 and upwards fit for service, the number in the list of the tribe of Asher being forty-one thousand five hundred.

42 The tribal list of Naphtali, by families in the father's line, with the names of all men aged twenty years
43 and upwards fit for service, the number in the list of the tribe of Naphtali being fifty-three thousand four hundred.

44 These were the numbers recorded in the detailed lists by Moses and Aaron and the twelve chiefs of Israel, each representing one tribe and being the head of a family.
45 The total number of Israelites aged twenty years and upwards fit for service, recorded in the lists of
46 fathers' families, was six hundred and three thousand five hundred

and fifty. A list of the Levites by 47 their fathers' families was not made.

The LORD spoke to Moses and 48 said, 'You shall not record the total 49 number of the Levites or make a detailed list of them among the Israelites. You shall put the Levites 50 in charge of the Tabernacle of the Tokens, with its equipment and everything in it. They shall carry the Tabernacle and all its equipment; they alone shall be its attendants and shall pitch their tents round it. The Levites shall take the 51 Tabernacle down when it is due to move and shall put it up when it halts; any unqualified person who comes near it shall be put to death. All other Israelites shall pitch their 52 tents, each tribal host in its proper camp and under its own standard. But the Levites shall encamp 53 round the Tabernacle of the Tokens, so that divine wrath may not follow the whole community of Israel; the Tabernacle of the Tokens shall be in their keeping.'

The Israelites did exactly as the 54 LORD had told Moses to do.

The LORD spoke to Moses and 2 Aaron and said, 'The Israelites 2 shall encamp each under his own standard by the emblems of his father's family; they shall pitch their tents round the Tent of the Presence, facing it.

'In front of it, on the east, the 3 division of Judah shall be stationed under the standard of its camp by tribal hosts. The chief of Judah shall be Nahshon son of Amminadab. His host, with its members as 4 detailed, numbers seventy-four thousand six hundred men. Next 5 to Judah the tribe of Issachar shall be stationed. Its chief shall be Nethaneel son of Zuar; his host, 6 with its members as detailed, numbers fifty-four thousand four hundred. Then the tribe of Zebulun: 7 its chief shall be Eliab son of Helon; his host, with its members as detail-8 ed, numbers fifty-seven thousand

9 four hundred. The number listed in the camp of Judah, by hosts, is one hundred and eighty-six thousand four hundred. They shall be the first to march.

10 'To the south the division of Reuben shall be stationed under the standard of its camp by tribal hosts. The chief of Reuben shall 11 be Elizur son of Shedeur; his host, with its members as detailed, numbers forty-six thousand five hun- 12 dred. Next to him the tribe of Simeon shall be stationed. Its chief shall be Shelumiel son of Zurishad- 13 dai; his host, with its members as detailed, numbers fifty-nine thou- 14 sand three hundred. Then the tribe of Gad: its chief shall be Eliasaph 15 son of Reuel; his host, with its members as detailed, numbers forty-five thousand six hundred and fifty. 16 The number listed in the camp of Reuben, by hosts, is one hundred and fifty-one thousand four hundred and fifty. They shall be the second to march.

17 'When the Tent of the Presence moves, the camp of the Levites shall keep its station in the centre of the other camps; they shall all move in the order of their encamping, each man in his proper place under his standard.

18 'To the west the division of Ephraim shall be stationed under the standard of its camp by tribal hosts. The chief of Ephraim shall 19 be Elishama son of Ammihud; his host, with its members as detailed, numbers forty thousand five hun- 20 dred. Next to him the tribe of Manasseh shall be stationed. Its chief shall be Gamaliel son of 21 Pedahzur; his host, with its members as detailed, numbers thirty- 22 two thousand two hundred. Then the tribe of Benjamin: its chief shall 23 be Abidan son of Gideoni; his host, with its members as detailed, numbers thirty-five thousand four hun- 24 dred. The number listed in the camp of Ephraim, by hosts, is one hundred and eight thousand one

hundred. They shall be the third to march.

25 'To the north the division of Dan shall be stationed under the standard of its camp by tribal hosts. The chief of Dan shall be Ahiezer 26 son of Ammishaddai; his host, with its members as detailed, numbers sixty-two thousand seven hundred. 27 Next to him the tribe of Asher shall be stationed. Its chief shall be 28 Pagiel son of Ocran; his host, with its members as detailed, numbers forty-one thousand five hundred. 29 Then the tribe of Naphtali: its chief shall be Ahira son of Enan; 30 his host, with its members as detailed, numbers fifty-three thou- 31 sand four hundred. The number listed in the camp of Dan is a hundred and fifty-seven thousand six hundred. They shall march, under their standards, last.'

32 These were the Israelites listed by their fathers' families. The total number in the camp, recorded by tribal hosts, was six hundred and three thousand five hundred and fifty.

33 The Levites were not included in the detailed lists with their fellow-Israelites, for so the LORD had commanded Moses. 34 The Israelites did exactly as the LORD had commanded Moses, pitching and breaking camp standard by standard, each man according to his family in his father's line.

3 THESE were the descendants of Aaron and Moses at the time when the LORD spoke to Moses on Mount Sinai. 2 The names of the sons of Aaron were Nadab the eldest, Abihu, Eleazar and Ithamar. 3 These were the names of Aaron's sons, the anointed priests who had been installed in the priestly office. 4 Nadab and Abihu fell dead before the LORD because they had presented illicit fire before the LORD in the wilderness of Sinai. They left no sons; Eleazar and Ithamar continued to perform

the priestly office in their father's presence.

5 The LORD spoke to Moses and 6 said, 'Bring forward the tribe of Levi and appoint them to serve Aaron the priest and to minister to 7 him. They shall be in attendance on him and on the whole community before the Tent of the Presence, undertaking the service of the 8 Tabernacle. They shall be in charge of all the equipment in the Tent of the Presence, and be in attendance on the Israelites, undertaking the 9 service of the Tabernacle. You shall assign the Levites to Aaron and his sons as especially dedicated 10 to him out of all the Israelites. To Aaron and his line you shall commit the priestly office and they shall perform its duties; any unqualified person who intrudes upon it shall be put to death.'

11 The LORD spoke to Moses and 12 said, 'I take the Levites for myself out of all the Israelites as a substitute for the eldest male child of every woman; the Levites shall be 13 mine. For every eldest child, if a boy, became mine when I destroyed all the eldest sons in Egypt. So I have consecrated to myself all the first-born in Israel, both man and beast. They shall be mine. I am the LORD.'

14 The LORD spoke to Moses in the 15 wilderness of Sinai and said, 'Make a detailed list of all the Levites by their families in the father's line, every male from the age of one month and upwards.'

16 Moses made a detailed list of them in accordance with the command 17 given him by the LORD. Now these were the names of the sons of Levi:

Gershon, Kohath and Merari.

18 Descendants of Gershon, by families: Libni and Shimei.

19 Descendants of Kohath, by families: Amram, Izhar, Hebron and Uzziel.

20 Descendants of Merari, by families: Mahli and Mushi.

These were the families of Levi, by fathers' families:

21 Gershon: the family of Libni and the family of Shimei. These were 22 the families of Gershon, and the number of males in their list as detailed, from the age of one month and upwards, was seven thousand five hundred. The families of Ger- 23 shon were stationed on the west, behind the Tabernacle. Their chief 24 was Eliasaph son of Lael, and in 25 the service of the Tent of the Presence they were in charge of the Tabernacle and its coverings, of the screen at the entrance to the Tent of the Presence, the hangings 26 of the court, the screen at the entrance to the court all round the Tabernacle and the altar, and of all else needed for its maintenance.

27 Kohath: the family of Amram, the family of Izhar, the family of Hebron, the family of Uzziel. These 28 were the families of Kohath, and the number of males, from the age of one month and upwards, was eight thousand six hundred. They were the guardians of the holy things. The families of Kohath were 29 stationed on the south, at the side of the Tabernacle. Their chief was 30 Elizaphan son of Uzziel; they were 31 in charge of the Ark, the table, the lamp-stands and the altars, together with the sacred vessels used in their service, and the screen with everything needed for its maintenance. The chief over all the chiefs 32 of the Levites was Eleazar son of Aaron the priest, who was appointed overseer of those in charge of the sanctuary.

33 Merari: the family of Mahli, the family of Mushi. These were the families of Merari, and the number 34 of males in their list as detailed from the age of one month and upwards was six thousand two hundred. Their chief was Zuriel 35 son of Abihail; they were stationed on the north, at the side of the Tabernacle. The Merarites were in 36 charge of the planks, bars, posts,

Israel in the wilderness of Sinai

and sockets of the Tabernacle, together with its vessels and all the equipment needed for its mainten-37 ance, the posts, sockets, pegs, and cords of the surrounding court.

38 In front of the Tabernacle on the east, Moses was stationed, with Aaron and his sons, in front of the Tent of the Presence eastwards. They were in charge of the sanctuary on behalf of the Israelites; any unqualified person who came near would be put to death.

39 The number of Levites recorded by Moses on the detailed list by families at the command of the LORD was twenty-two thousand males aged one month and upwards.

40 The LORD said to Moses, 'Make a detailed list of all the male first-born in Israel aged one month and upwards, and count the number of 41 persons. You shall reserve the Levites for me – I am the LORD – in substitution for the eldest sons of the Israelites, and in the same way the Levites' cattle in substitution for the first-born cattle of the Is-42 raelites.' As the LORD had told him to do, Moses made a list of all the 43 eldest sons of the Israelites, and the total number of first-born males recorded by name in the register, aged one month and upwards, was twenty-two thousand two hundred and seventy-three.

44 The LORD spoke to Moses and 45 said, 'Take the Levites as a substitute for all the eldest sons in Israel and the cattle of the Levites as a substitute for their cattle. The Levites shall be mine. I am the 46 LORD. The eldest sons in Israel will outnumber the Levites by two 47 hundred and seventy-three. This remainder must be ransomed, and you shall accept five shekels for each of them, taking the sacred shekel and reckoning twenty gerahs 48 to the shekel; you shall give the money with which they are ransomed to Aaron and his sons.'

49 Moses took the money paid as ransom for those who remained over when the substitution of Levites was complete. The amount 50 received was one thousand three hundred and sixty-five shekels of silver by the sacred standard. In 51 accordance with what the LORD had said, he gave the money to Aaron and his sons, doing what the LORD had told him to do.

The LORD spoke to Moses and 4 Aaron and said, 'Among the 2 Levites, make a count of the descendants of Kohath between the 3 ages of thirty and fifty, by families in the father's line, comprising everyone who comes to take duty in the service of the Tent of the Presence.

'This is the service to be rendered 4 by the Kohathites in the Tent of the Presence; it is most sacred. When the camp is due to move, 5 Aaron and his sons shall come and take down the Veil of the screen and cover the Ark of the Tokens with it; over this they shall put 6 a covering of porpoise-hide[a] and over that again a violet cloth all of one piece; they shall then put its poles in place. Over the Table of 7 the Presence they shall spread a violet cloth and lay on it the dishes, saucers, and flagons, and the bowls for drink-offerings; the Bread regularly presented shall also lie upon it; then they shall spread over them 8 a scarlet cloth and over that a covering of porpoise-hide, and put the poles in place. They shall take 9 a violet cloth and cover the lampstand, its lamps, tongs, firepans, and all the containers for the oil used in its service; they shall put 10 it with all its equipment in a sheet of porpoise-hide slung from a pole. Over the gold altar they shall 11 spread a violet cloth, cover it with a porpoise-hide covering, and put its poles in place. They shall take 12 all the articles used for the service of the sanctuary, put them on a

---

[a] *Strictly* hide of sea-cow.

violet cloth, cover them with a porpoise-hide covering, and sling 13 them from a pole. They shall clear the altar of the fat and ashes, 14 spread a purple cloth over it, and then lay on it all the equipment used in its service, the firepans, forks, shovels, tossing-bowls, and all the equipment of the altar, spread a covering of porpoise-hide over it and put the poles in place. 15 Once Aaron and his sons have finished covering the sanctuary and all the sacred equipment, when the camp is due to move, the Kohathites shall come to carry it; they must not touch it on pain of death. All these things are the load to be carried by the Kohathites, the things connected with the Tent of 16 the Presence. Eleazar son of Aaron the priest shall have charge of the lamp-oil, the fragrant incense, the regular grain-offering, and the anointing oil, with the general oversight of the whole Tabernacle and its contents, the sanctuary and its equipment.'

17 The LORD spoke to Moses and 18 Aaron and said, 'You must not let the families of Kohath be extirpated, and lost to the tribe of Levi. 19 If they are to live and not die when they approach the most holy things, this is what you must do: Aaron and his sons shall come and set each man to his appointed task 20 and to his load, and the Kohathites themselves shall not enter to cast even a passing glance on the sanctuary, on pain of death.'

21 The LORD spoke to Moses and 22 said, 'Number the Gershonites by 23 families in the father's line. Make a detailed list of all those between the ages of thirty and fifty who come on duty to perform service in the Tent of the Presence. 24 'This is the service to be rendered by the Gershonite families, comprising their general duty and their 25 loads. They shall carry the hangings of the Tabernacle, the Tent of the Presence, its covering, that is the

covering of porpoise-hide which is over it, the screen at the entrance to the Tent of the Presence, the 26 hangings of the court, the screen at the entrance to the court surrounding the Tabernacle and the altar, their cords and all the equipment for their service; and they shall perform all the tasks connected with them. These are the acts of service they shall render. All the service of the Gershonites, 27 their loads and their other duties, shall be directed by Aaron and his sons; you shall assign them the loads for which they shall be responsible. This is the service as- 28 signed to the Gershonite families in connection with the Tent of the Presence; Ithamar son of Aaron shall be in charge of them.

'You shall make a detailed list 29 of the Merarites by families in the father's line, all those between the 30 ages of thirty and fifty, who come on duty to perform service in the Tent of the Presence.

'These are the loads for which 31 they shall be responsible in virtue of their service in the Tent of the Presence: the planks of the Tabernacle with its bars, posts, and sockets, the posts of the surround- 32 ing court with their sockets, pegs, and cords, and all that is needed for the maintenance of them; you shall assign to each man by name the load for which he is responsible. These are the duties of the Merarite 33 families in virtue of their service in the Tent of the Presence. Ithamar son of Aaron the priest shall be in charge of them.'

Moses and Aaron and the chiefs 34 of the community made a detailed list of the Kohathites by families in the father's line, taking all be- 35 tween the ages of thirty and fifty who came on duty to perform service in the Tent of the Presence. The number recorded by families in 36 the detailed lists was two thousand seven hundred and fifty. This was 37 the total number in the detailed lists of the Kohathite families who did duty in the Tent of the Presence; they were recorded by Moses and Aaron as the LORD had told them to do through Moses.

38-39 The Gershonites between the ages of thirty and fifty, who came on duty for service in the Tent of the Presence, were recorded in detailed lists by families in the father's 40 line. Their number, by families in the father's line, was two thousand 41 six hundred and thirty. This was the total recorded in the lists of the Gershonite families who came on duty in the Tent of the Presence, and were recorded by Moses and Aaron as the LORD had told them to do.

42-43 The families of Merari, between the ages of thirty and fifty, who came on duty to perform service in the Tent of the Presence, were recorded in detailed lists by families 44 in the father's line. Their number by families was three thousand two 45 hundred. These were recorded in the Merarite families by Moses and Aaron as the LORD had told them to do through Moses.

46 Thus Moses and Aaron and the chiefs of Israel made a detailed list of all the Levites by families in 47 the father's line, between the ages of thirty and fifty years; these were all who came to perform their various duties and carry their loads in the service of the Tent of the 48 Presence. Their number was eight thousand five hundred and eighty. 49 They were recorded one by one by Moses at the command of the LORD, according to their general duty and the loads they carried.[a] For so the LORD had told Moses to do.

5 THE LORD spoke to Moses and said: 2 Command the Israelites to expel from the camp everyone who suffers from a malignant skin-disease or a discharge, and everyone ritually unclean from contact with a 3 corpse. You shall put them outside the camp, both male and female, so that they will not defile your camps in which I dwell among you. 4 The Israelites did this: they put them outside the camp. As the LORD had said when he spoke to Moses, so the Israelites did.

5 The LORD spoke to Moses and 6 said, Say to the Israelites: When anyone, man or woman, wrongs another and thereby breaks faith with the LORD, that person has incurred guilt which demands reparation. He shall confess the sin 7 he has committed, make restitution in full with the addition of one fifth, and give it to the man to whom compensation is due. If 8 there is no next-of-kin to whom compensation can be paid, the compensation payable in that case shall be the LORD'S, for the use of the priest, in addition to the ram of expiation with which the priest makes expiation for him.

9 Every contribution made by way of holy-gift which the Israelites bring to the priest shall be the 10 priest's. The priest shall have the holy-gifts which a man gives; whatever is given to him shall be his.

11 The LORD spoke to Moses and 12 said, Speak to the Israelites in these words: When a married woman goes astray, is unfaithful to her husband, and has sexual inter- 13 course with another man, and this happens without the husband's knowledge, and the crime is undetected, because, though she has been defiled, there is no direct evidence against her and she was not caught in the act, but when in such 14 a case a fit of jealousy comes over the husband which causes him to suspect his wife, she being in fact defiled; or when, on the other hand, a fit of jealousy comes over a husband which causes him to suspect his wife, when she is not in fact defiled; then in either case, the 15 husband shall bring his wife to the

---

[a] *Prob. rdg.; Heb. adds* and his registered ones.

priest together with the prescribed offering for her, a tenth of an ephah of barley meal. He shall not pour oil on it nor put frankincense on it, because it is a grain-offering for jealousy, a grain-offering of pro-testation conveying an imputation
16 of guilt. The priest shall bring her forward and set her before the
17 LORD. He shall take clean*a* water in an earthenware vessel, and shall take dust from the floor of the Tab-
18 ernacle and add it to the water. He shall set the woman before the LORD, uncover her head, and place the grain-offering of protestation in her hands; it is a grain-offering for jealousy. The priest shall hold in his own hand the water of con-tention which brings out the truth.
19 He shall then put the woman on oath and say to her, 'If no man has had intercourse with you, if you have not gone astray and let your-self become defiled while owing obedience to your husband, then may your innocence be established by the water of contention which
20 brings out the truth. But if, while owing him obedience, you have gone astray and let yourself be-come defiled, if any man other than your husband has had intercourse
21 with you' (the priest shall here put the woman on oath with an adjur-ation, and shall continue), 'may the LORD make an example of you among your people in adjurations and in swearing of oaths by bring-ing upon you miscarriage and un-
22 timely birth; and this water that brings out the truth shall enter your body, bringing upon you miscarriage and untimely birth.' The woman shall respond, 'Amen,
23 Amen.' The priest shall write these curses on a scroll and wash them off into the water of contention;
24 he shall make the woman drink the water that brings out the truth, and the water shall enter her body.
25 The priest shall take the grain-

offering for jealousy from the wo-man's hand, present it as a special gift before the LORD, and offer it at the altar. He shall take a handful 26 from the grain-offering by way of token, and burn it at the altar; after this he shall make the woman drink the water. If she has let her- 27 self become defiled and has been unfaithful to her husband, then when the priest makes her drink the water that brings out the truth and the water has entered her body, she will suffer a miscarriage or un-timely birth, and her name will become an example in adjuration among her kin. But if the woman 28 has not let herself become defiled and is pure, then her innocence is established and she will bear her child.

Such is the law for cases of jea- 29 lousy, where a woman, owing obe-dience to her husband, goes astray and lets herself become defiled, or 30 where a fit of jealousy comes over a man which causes him to suspect his wife. He shall set her before the LORD, and the priest shall deal with her as this law prescribes. No 31 guilt will attach to the husband, but the woman shall bear the pen-alty of her guilt.

The LORD spoke to Moses and 6 said, Speak to the Israelites in these 2 words: When anyone, man or wo-man, makes a special*b* vow dedi-cating himself to the LORD as a Nazirite,*c* he shall abstain from 3 wine and strong drink. These he shall not drink, nor anything made from the juice of grapes; nor shall he eat grapes, fresh or dried. Dur- 4 ing the whole term of his vow he shall eat nothing that comes from the vine, nothing whatever, shoot or berry. During the whole term of 5 his vow no razor shall touch his head; he shall let his hair grow long and plait it until he has completed the term of his dedication: he shall keep himself holy to the LORD.

a Or holy.　　　*b* makes a special: *or* performs a...
c *That is* separated one *or* dedicated one.

6 During the whole term of his vow
7 he shall not go near a corpse, not
even when his father or mother,
brother or sister, dies; he shall not
make himself ritually unclean for
them, because the Nazirite vow to
8 his God is on his head. He shall
keep himself holy to the Lord
during the whole term of his Nazirite vow.

9 If someone suddenly falls dead
by his side touching him and thereby making his hair, which has been
dedicated, ritually unclean, he shall
shave his head seven days later, on
the day appointed for his ritual
10 cleansing. On the eighth day he
shall bring two turtle-doves or two
young pigeons to the priest at the
entrance to the Tent of the Pre-
11 sence. The priest shall offer one as
a sin-offering and the other as a
whole-offering and shall make expiation for him for the sin he has
incurred through contact with the
dead body; and he shall consecrate
12 his head afresh on that day. The
man shall re-dedicate himself to the
Lord for the term of his vow and
bring a yearling ram as a guilt-
offering. The previous period shall
not be reckoned, because the hair
which he dedicated became unclean.

13 The law for the Nazirite, when
the term of his dedication is completed, shall be this. He shall be
brought to the entrance to the
14 Tent of the Presence and shall present his offering to the Lord: one
yearling ram without blemish as
a whole-offering, one yearling ewe
without blemish as a sin-offering,
one ram without blemish as a
15 shared-offering, and a basket of
cakes made of flour mixed with oil,
and of wafers smeared with oil,
both unleavened, together with the
proper grain-offerings and drink-
16 offerings. The priest shall present
all these before the Lord and offer
the man's sin-offering and whole-
17 offering; the ram he shall offer as

a shared-offering to the Lord, together with the basket of unleavened cakes and the proper grain-
offering and drink-offering. The 18
Nazirite shall shave his head at the
entrance to the Tent of the Presence, take the hair which had been
dedicated and put it on the fire
where the shared-offering is burning. The priest shall take the shoul- 19
der of the ram, after boiling it, and
take also one unleavened cake from
the basket and one unleavened
wafer, and put them on the palms
of the Nazirite's hands, his hair
which had been dedicated having
been shaved. The priest shall then 20
present them as a special gift before the Lord; these, together
with the breast of the special gift
and the leg of the contribution, are
holy and belong to the priest. When
this has been done, the Nazirite is
again free to drink wine.

Such is the law for the Nazirite 21
who has made his vow. Such is the
offering he must make to the Lord
for his dedication, apart from anything else that he can afford. He
must carry out his vow in full according to the law governing his
dedication.

The Lord spoke to Moses and 22
said, Speak to Aaron and his sons 23
in these words: These are the words
with which you shall bless the
Israelites:

The Lord bless you and watch 24
over you;
the Lord make his face shine 25
upon*a* you
and be gracious to you;
the Lord look kindly on you and 26
give you peace.

They shall pronounce my name 27
over the Israelites, and I will bless
them.

On the day that Moses completed 7
the setting up of the Tabernacle,
he anointed and consecrated it; he
also anointed and consecrated its

a Or to.

equipment, and the altar and its
2 vessels. The chief men of Israel,
heads of families – that is the chiefs
of the tribes, who had assisted in
preparing the detailed lists – came
3 forward and brought their offering
before the LORD, six covered wagons
and twelve oxen, one wagon
from every two chiefs and from
each one an ox.ᵃ These they brought
forward before the Tabernacle;
4 and the LORD spoke to Moses and
5 said, 'Accept these from them: they
shall be used for the service of the
Tent of the Presence. Assign them
to the Levites as their several duties
require.'
6 So Moses accepted the wagons
and oxen and assigned them to the
7 Levites. He gave two wagons and
four oxen to the Gershonites as re-
8 quired for their service; four wagons
and eight oxen to the Merarites
as required for their service, in
charge of Ithamar the son of Aaron
9 the priest. He gave none to the
Kohathites because the service
laid upon them was that of the
holy things: these they had to carry
themselves on their shoulders.
10 When the altar was anointed,
the chiefs brought their gift for its
dedication and presented their of-
11 fering before it. The LORD said to
Moses, 'Let the chiefs present their
offering for the dedication of the
altar one by one, on consecutive
days.'
12 The chief who presented his offering on the first day was Nahshon son of Amminadab of the
13 tribe of Judah. His offering was
one silver dish weighing a hundred
and thirty shekels ˌby the sacred
standard and one silver tossing-
bowl weighing seventy, both full
of flour mixed with oil as a grain-
14 offering; one saucer weighing ten
15 gold shekels, full of incense; one
young bull, one full-grown ram,
and one yearling ram, as a whole-
16 offering; one he-goat as a sin-
17 offering; and two bulls, five full-

grown rams, five he-goats, and five
yearling rams, as a shared-offering.
This was the offering of Nahshon
son of Amminadab.
18 On the second day Nethaneel
son of Zuar, chief of Issachar,
19 brought his offering. He brought
one silver dish weighing a hundred
and thirty shekels by the sacred
standard and one silver tossing-
bowl weighing seventy, both full
of flour mixed with oil as a grain-
offering; one saucer weighing ten 20
gold shekels, full of incense; one 21
young bull, one full-grown ram,
and one yearling ram, as a whole-
offering; one he-goat as a sin- 22
offering; and two bulls, five full- 23
grown rams, five he-goats, and five
yearling rams, as a shared-offering.
This was the offering of Nethaneel
son of Zuar.
On the third day the chief of the 24
Zebulunites, Eliab son of Helon,
came. His offering was one silver 25
dish weighing a hundred and thirty
shekels by the sacred standard and
one silver tossing-bowl weighing
seventy, both full of flour mixed
with oil as a grain-offering; one 26
saucer weighing ten gold shekels,
full of incense; one young bull, one 27
full-grown ram, and one yearling
ram, as a whole-offering; one he- 28
goat as a sin-offering; and two bulls, 29
five full-grown rams, five he-goats,
and five yearling rams, as a shared-
offering. This was the offering of
Eliab son of Helon.
On the fourth day the chief of 30
the Reubenites, Elizur son of Shedeur, came. His offering was one 31
silver dish weighing a hundred and
thirty shekels by the sacred standard and one silver tossing-bowl
weighing seventy, both full of flour
mixed with oil as a grain-offering;
one saucer weighing ten gold shek- 32
els, full of incense; one young bull, 33
one full-grown ram, and one yearling ram, as a whole-offering; one 34
he-goat as a sin-offering; and two 35
bulls, five full-grown rams, five he-

Or a bull.

goats, and five yearling rams, as a shared-offering. This was the offering of Elizur son of Shedeur.

36 On the fifth day the chief of the Simeonites, Shelumiel son of Zuri- 37 shaddai, came. His offering was one silver dish weighing a hundred and thirty shekels by the sacred standard and one silver tossing-bowl weighing seventy, both full of flour mixed with oil as a grain- 38 offering; one saucer weighing ten 39 gold shekels, full of incense; one young bull, one full-grown ram, and one yearling ram, as a whole- 40 offering; one he-goat as a sin- 41 offering; and two bulls, five full-grown rams, five he-goats, and five yearling rams, as a shared-offering. This was the offering of Shelumiel son of Zurishaddai.

42 On the sixth day the chief of the Gadites, Eliasaph son of Reuel, 43 came. His offering was one silver dish weighing a hundred and thirty shekels by the sacred standard and one silver tossing-bowl weighing seventy, both full of flour mixed 44 with oil as a grain-offering; one 45 saucer weighing ten gold shekels, full of incense; one young bull, one full-grown ram, and one yearling 46 ram, as a whole-offering; one he- 47 goat as a sin-offering; and two bulls, five full-grown rams, five he-goats, and five yearling rams, as a shared-offering. This was the offering of Eliasaph son of Reuel.

48 On the seventh day the chief of the Ephraimites, Elishama son of 49 Ammihud, came. His offering was one silver dish weighing a hundred and thirty shekels by the sacred standard and one silver tossing-bowl weighing seventy, both full of flour mixed with oil as a grain- 50 offering; one saucer weighing ten 51 gold shekels, full of incense; one young bull, one full-grown ram, and one yearling ram, as a whole- 52 offering; one he-goat as a sin-offer- 53 ing; and two bulls, five full-grown rams, five he-goats, and five yearling rams, as a shared-offering.

This was the offering of Elishama son of Ammihud.

On the eighth day the chief of 54 the Manassites, Gamaliel son of Pedahzur, came. His offering was 55 one silver dish weighing a hundred and thirty shekels by the sacred standard and one silver tossing-bowl weighing seventy, both full of flour mixed with oil as a grain-offering; one saucer weighing ten 56 gold shekels, full of incense; one 57 young bull, one full-grown ram, and one yearling ram, as a whole-offering; one he-goat as a sin-offer- 58 ing; and two bulls, five full-grown 59 rams, five he-goats, and five yearling rams, as a shared-offering. This was the offering of Gamaliel son of Pedahzur.

On the ninth day the chief of the 60 Benjamites, Abidan son of Gid-eoni, came. His offering was one 61 silver dish weighing a hundred and thirty shekels by the sacred standard and one silver tossing-bowl weighing seventy, both full of flour mixed with oil as a grain-offering; one saucer weighing ten gold shek- 62 els, full of incense; one young bull, 63 one full-grown ram, and one yearling ram, as a whole-offering; one 64 he-goat as a sin-offering; and two 65 bulls, five full-grown rams, five he-goats, and five yearling rams, as a shared-offering. This was the offering of Abidan son of Gideoni.

On the tenth day the chief of the 66 Danites, Ahiezer son of Ammi-shaddai, came. His offering was 67 one silver dish weighing a hundred and thirty shekels by the sacred standard and one silver tossing-bowl weighing seventy, both full of flour mixed with oil as a grain-offering; one saucer weighing ten 68 gold shekels, full of incense; one 69 young bull, one full-grown ram, and one yearling ram, as a whole-offering; one he-goat as a sin-offer- 70 ing; and two bulls, five full-grown 71 rams, five he-goats, and five yearling rams, as a shared-offering.

This was the offering of Ahiezer son of Ammishaddai.

72 On the eleventh day the chief of the Asherites, Pagiel son of Ocran,
73 came. His offering was one silver dish weighing a hundred and thirty shekels by the sacred standard and one silver tossing-bowl weighing seventy, both full of flour mixed
74 with oil as a grain-offering; one saucer weighing ten gold shekels,
75 full of incense; one young bull, one full-grown ram, and one yearling
76 ram, as a whole-offering; one he-
77 goat as a sin-offering; and two bulls, five full-grown rams, five he-goats, and five yearling rams, as a shared-offering. This was the offering of Pagiel son of Ocran.

78 On the twelfth day the chief of the Naphtalites, Ahira son of En-
79 an, came. His offering was one silver dish weighing a hundred and thirty shekels by the sacred standard and one silver tossing-bowl weighing seventy, both full of flour mixed with oil as a grain-offering;
80 one saucer weighing ten gold shek-
81 els, full of incense; one young bull, one full-grown ram, and one year-
82 ling ram, as a whole-offering; one
83 he-goat as a sin-offering; and two bulls, five full-grown rams, five he-goats, and five yearling rams, as a shared-offering. This was the offering of Ahira son of Enan.

84 This was the gift from the chiefs of Israel for the dedication of the altar when it was anointed: twelve silver dishes, twelve silver tossing-bowls, and twelve golden saucers;
85 each silver dish weighed a hundred and thirty shekels, each silver tossing-bowl seventy shekels. The total weight of the silver vessels was two thousand four hundred shekels by the sacred standard.
86 There were twelve golden saucers full of incense, ten shekels each by the sacred standard: the total weight of the gold of the saucers was a hundred and twenty shekels.
87 The number of beasts for the whole-offering was twelve bulls, twelve full-grown rams, and twelve yearling rams, with the prescribed grain-offerings, and twelve he-goats for the sin-offering. The
88 number of beasts for the shared-offering was twenty-four bulls, sixty full-grown rams, sixty he-goats, and sixty yearling rams. This was the gift for the dedication of the altar when it was anointed. And when Moses entered the Tent
89 of the Presence to speak with God, he heard the Voice speaking from above the cover over the Ark of the Tokens from between the two cherubim: the Voice spoke to him.

The LORD spoke to Moses and 8
said, 'Speak to Aaron in these 2
words: "When you mount the seven lamps, see that they shed their light forwards in front of the lampstand." ' Aaron did this: he moun- 3
ted the lamps, so as to shed light forwards in front of the lampstand, as the LORD had instructed Moses. The lamp-stand was made 4
of beaten-work in gold, as well as the stem and the petals. Moses made it to match the pattern which the LORD had shown him.

The LORD spoke to Moses and 5
said: Take the Levites apart from 6
the rest of the Israelites and cleanse them ritually. This is what 7
you shall do to cleanse them. Sprinkle lustral water over them; they shall then shave their whole bodies, wash their clothes, and so be cleansed. Next, they shall take 8
a young bull as a whole-offering[a] with its prescribed grain-offering, flour mixed with oil; and you shall take a second young bull as a sin-offering. Bring the Levites before 9
the Tent of the Presence and call the whole community of Israelites together. Bring the Levites before 10
the LORD, and let the Israelites lay their hands on their heads. Aaron 11
shall present the Levites before the LORD as a special gift from the Israelites, and they shall be

---

[a] as a whole-offering: *prob. rdg.*; *Heb. om.*

dedicated to the service of the
12 LORD. The Levites shall lay their
hands on the heads of the bulls; one
bull shall be offered as a sin-offering
and the other as a whole-offering
to the LORD, to make expiation for
13 the Levites. Then you shall set the
Levites before Aaron and his sons,
presenting them to the LORD as a
14 special gift. You shall thus separate
the Levites from the rest of the
Israelites, and they shall be mine.

15 After this, the Levites shall enter the Tent of the Presence to
serve in it, ritually cleansed and
16 presented as a special gift; for they
are given and dedicated to me, out
of all the Israelites. I have accepted them as mine in place of all
that comes first from the womb,
every first child among the Israel-
17 ites; for every first-born male creature, man or beast, among the Israelites is mine. On the day when I
struck down every first-born creature in Egypt, I hallowed all the
first-born of the Israelites to my-
18 self, and I have accepted the Lev-
19 ites in their place. I have given the
Levites to Aaron and his sons,
dedicated among the Israelites to
perform the service of the Israelites in the Tent of the Presence and
to make expiation for them, and
then no calamity will befall them
when they come close to the sanctuary.

20 Moses and Aaron and the whole
community of Israelites carried
out all the commands the LORD
had given to Moses for the dedica-
21 tion of the Levites. The Levites
purified themselves of sin and
washed their clothes, and Aaron
presented them as a special gift before the LORD and made expiation
22 for them, to cleanse them. Then at
last they went in to perform their
service in the Tent of the Presence,
before Aaron and his sons. Thus
the commands the LORD had given
to Moses concerning the Levites
were all carried out.

23 The LORD spoke to Moses and
said: Touching the Levites: they 24
shall begin their active work in the
service of the Tent of the Presence
at the age of twenty-five. At the 25
age of fifty a Levite shall retire
from regular service and shall
serve no longer. He may continue 26
to assist his colleagues in attendance in the Tent of the Presence
but shall perform no regular service. This is how you shall arrange
the attendance of the Levites.

In the first month of the second 9
year after they came out of Egypt,
the LORD spoke to Moses in the
wilderness of Sinai and said, 'Let 2
the Israelites prepare the Passover
at the time appointed for it. This 3
shall be between dusk and dark on
the fourteenth day of this month,
and you shall keep it at this appointed time, observing every rule
and custom proper to it.' So Moses 4
told the Israelites to prepare the
Passover, and they prepared it on 5
the fourteenth day of the first
month, between dusk and dark, in
the wilderness of Sinai. The Israelites did exactly as the LORD had
instructed Moses.

It happened that some men were 6
ritually unclean through contact
with a corpse and so could not keep
the Passover on the right day. They
came before Moses and Aaron that
same day and said, 'We are unclean 7
through contact with a corpse.
Must we therefore be debarred from
presenting the LORD's offering at
its appointed time with the rest of
the Israelites?' Moses answered, 8
'Wait, and let me hear what commands the LORD has for you.'

The LORD spoke to Moses and 9
said, Tell the Israelites: If any one 10
of you or of your descendants is
ritually unclean through contact
with a corpse, or if he is away on a
long journey, he shall keep a Passover to the LORD none the less.
But in that case he shall prepare 11
the victim in the second month,
between dusk and dark on the
fourteenth day. It shall be eaten

with unleavened cakes and bitter
12 herbs; nothing shall be left over
till morning, and no bone of it shall
be broken. The Passover shall be
kept exactly as the law prescribes.
13 The man who, being ritually clean
and not absent on a journey, neg-
lects to keep the Passover, shall be
cut off from his father's kin, because he has not presented the
LORD's offering at its appointed
time. That man shall accept responsibility for his sin.
14 When an alien is settled among
you, he also shall keep the Passover to the LORD, observing every
rule and custom proper to it. The
same law is binding on you all,
alien and native alike.

The journey from Sinai to Edom

15 ON the day when they set up the
Tabernacle, that is the Tent of the
Tokens, cloud covered it, and in
the evening a brightness like fire
16 appeared over it till morning. So it
continued: the cloud covered it by
day and a brightness like fire by
17 night. Whenever the cloud lifted
from the tent, the Israelites struck
camp, and at the place where the
cloud settled, there they pitched
18 their camp. At the command of
the LORD they struck camp, and at
the command of the LORD they
encamped again, and continued in
camp as long as the cloud rested
19 over the Tabernacle. When the
cloud stayed long over the Tabernacle, the Israelites remained in
attendance on the LORD and did
20 not move on; and it was the same
when the cloud continued over the
Tabernacle only a few days: at the
command of the LORD they remained in camp, and at the command of the LORD they struck
21 camp. There were also times when
the cloud continued only from
evening till morning, and in the
morning, when the cloud lifted,
they moved on. Whether by day or
by night, they moved as soon as

the cloud lifted. Whether it was 22
for a day or two, for a month or a
year, whenever the cloud stayed
long over the Tabernacle, the Israelites remained where they were
and did not move on; they did so
only when the cloud lifted. At the 23
command of the LORD they encamped, and at his command they
struck camp. At the LORD's command, given through Moses, they
remained in attendance on the
LORD.

The LORD spoke to Moses and 10
said: Make two trumpets of beaten 2
silver and use them for summoning
the community and for breaking
camp. When both are sounded, the 3
whole community shall muster before you at the entrance to the Tent
of the Presence. If a single trumpet 4
is sounded, the chiefs who are
heads of the Israelite clans shall
muster. When you give the signal 5
for a shout, those encamped on the
east side are to move off. When the 6
signal is given for a second shout
those encamped to the south are to
move off. A signal to shout is the
signal to move off. When you con- 7
vene the assembly, you shall sound
a trumpet but not raise a shout.
This sounding of the trumpets is 8
the duty of the Aaronite priests
and shall be a rule binding for all
time on your descendants.

When you go into battle against 9
an invader and you are hard pressed by him, you shall raise a cheer
when the trumpets sound, and this
will serve as a reminder of you before the LORD your God and you
will be delivered from your enemies. On your festal days and at 10
your appointed seasons and on the
first day of every month, you shall
sound the trumpets over your
whole-offerings and your shared-
offerings, and the trumpets shall
be a reminder on your behalf before the LORD your God. I am the
LORD your God.

In the second year, on the twen- 11
tieth day of the second month, the

cloud lifted from the Tabernacle of
12 the Tokens, and the Israelites
moved by stages from the wilderness of Sinai, until the cloud came
to rest in the wilderness of Paran.
13 The first time that they broke
camp at the command of the LORD
14 given through Moses, the standard
of the division of Judah moved off
first with its tribal hosts: the host
of Judah under Nahshon son of
15 Amminadab, the host of Issachar
16 under Nethaneel son of Zuar, and
the host of Zebulun under Eliab
17 son of Helon. Then the Tabernacle
was taken down, and its bearers,
the sons of Gershon and Merari,
moved off.
18 Secondly, the standard of the
division of Reuben moved off with
its tribal hosts: the host of Reuben
19 under Elizur son of Shedeur, the
host of Simeon under Shelumiel
20 son of Zurishaddai, and the host of
Gad under Eliasaph son of Reuel.
21 The Kohathites, the bearers of the
holy things, moved off next, and
on their arrival found the Tabernacle set up.
22 Thirdly, the standard of the division of Ephraim moved off with its
tribal hosts: the host of Ephraim
under Elishama son of Ammihud,
23 the host of Manasseh under Gama-
24 liel son of Pedahzur, and the host
of Benjamin under Abidan son of
Gideoni.
25 Lastly, the standard of the division of Dan, the rearguard of all
the divisions, moved off with its
tribal hosts: the host of Dan under
26 Ahiezer son of Ammishaddai, the
host of Asher under Pagiel son of
27 Ocran, and the host of Naphtali
under Ahira son of Enan.
28 This was the order of march for
the Israelites, mustered in their
hosts, and in this order they broke
camp.
29 And Moses said to Hobab son of
Reuel the Midianite, his brother-
in-law, 'We are setting out for the
place which the LORD promised to
give us. Come with us, and we will
deal generously with you, for the
LORD has given an assurance of
good fortune for Israel.' But he 30
replied, 'No, I will not; I would
rather go to my own country and
my own people.' Moses said, 'Do not 31
desert us, I beg you; for you know
where we ought to camp in the
wilderness, and you will be our
guide. If you will go with us, then 32
all the good fortune with which the
LORD favours us we will share with
you.'

Then they moved off from the 33
mountain of the LORD and journeyed for three days, and the Ark
of the Covenant of the LORD kept a
day's journey ahead of them to find
them a place to rest. The cloud of 34
the LORD hung over them by day
when they moved camp. When- 35
ever the Ark began to move, Moses
said,

'Up, LORD, and may thy enemies
be scattered
and those that hate thee flee
before thee.'

When it halted, he said,   36

'Rest, LORD of the countless
thousands of Israel.'

There came a time when the 11
people complained to the LORD of
their hardships. When he heard, he
became angry and fire from the
LORD broke out among them, and
was raging at one end of the camp,
when the people appealed to Mo- 2
ses. He interceded with the LORD,
and the fire died down. Then they 3
named that place Taberah,[a] because the fire of the LORD had
burned among them there.

Now there was a mixed com- 4
pany of strangers who had joined
the Israelites. These people began
to be greedy for better things, and
the Israelites themselves wept
once again and cried, 'Will no 5
one give us meat? Think of it! In
Egypt we had fish for the asking,

a That is Burning.

cucumbers and water-melons, leeks
6 and onions and garlic. Now our
throats are parched; there is nothing wherever we look except this
7 manna.' (The manna looked like
coriander seed, the colour of gum
8 resin. The people went about collecting it, ground it up in hand-
mills or pounded it in mortars,
then boiled it in the pot and made
it into cakes. It tasted like butter-
9 cakes. When dew fell on the camp
at night, the manna fell with it.)
10 Moses heard the people wailing, all
of them in their families at the
opening of their tents. Then the
LORD became very angry, and Mo-
11 ses was troubled. He said to the
LORD, 'Why hast thou brought
trouble on thy servant? How have
I displeased the LORD that I am
burdened with the care of this
12 whole people? Am I their mother?
Have I brought them into the
world, and am I called upon to
carry them in my bosom, like a
nurse with her babies, to the land
promised by thee on oath to their
13 fathers? Where am I to find meat
to give them all? They pester me
with their wailing and their "Give
14 us meat to eat." This whole people
is a burden too heavy for me; I
15 cannot carry it alone. If that is
thy purpose for me, then kill me
outright. But if I have won thy
favour, let me suffer this trouble
at thy hands*a* no longer.'
16 The LORD answered Moses, 'Assemble seventy elders from Israel,
men known to you as elders and
officers in the community; bring
them to me at the Tent of the Presence, and there let them take
17 their stand with you. I will come
down and speak with you there. I
will take back part of that same
spirit which has been conferred on
you and confer it on them, and
they will share with you the burden of taking care for the people;
then you will not have to bear it
18 alone. And to the people you shall

say this: "Hallow yourselves in
readiness for tomorrow; you shall
have meat to eat. You wailed in
the LORD's hearing; you said, 'Will
no one give us meat? In Egypt we
lived well.' The LORD will give you
meat and you shall eat it. Not for 19
one day only, nor for two days, nor
five, nor ten, nor twenty, but for a 20
whole month you shall eat it until
it comes out at your nostrils and
makes you sick; because you have
rejected the LORD who dwells in
your midst, wailing in his presence
and saying, 'Why did we ever come
out of Egypt?'"'

Moses replied, 'Here am I with 21
six hundred thousand men on the
march around me, and thou dost
promise them meat to eat for a
whole month. How can the sheep 22
and oxen be slaughtered that
would be enough for them? If all
the fish in the sea could be caught,
would they be enough?' The LORD 23
said to Moses, 'Is there a limit to
the power of the LORD? You will
see this very day whether or not
my words come true.'

Moses came out and told the 24
people what the LORD had said. He
assembled seventy men from the
elders of the people and stationed
them round the Tent. Then the 25
LORD descended in the cloud and
spoke to him. He took back part of
that same spirit which he had conferred on Moses and conferred it on
the seventy elders; as the spirit
alighted on them, they fell into a
prophetic ecstasy, for the first and
only time.

Now two men named Eldad and 26
Medad, who had been enrolled
with the seventy, were left behind
in the camp. But, though they had
not gone out to the Tent, the spirit
alighted on them none the less, and
they fell into an ecstasy there in
the camp. A young man ran and 27
told Moses that Eldad and Medad
were in an ecstasy in the camp,
whereupon Joshua son of Nun, 28

a this trouble...hands: *prob. original rdg., altered in Heb.* to my trouble.

who had served with Moses since he was a boy, broke in, 'My lord 29 Moses, stop them!' But Moses said to him, 'Are you jealous on my account? I wish that all the LORD's people were prophets and that the LORD would confer his 30 spirit on them all!' And Moses rejoined the camp with the elders of Israel.

31 Then a wind from the LORD sprang up; it drove quails in from the west, and they were flying all round the camp for the distance of a day's journey, three feet above 32 the ground. The people were busy gathering quails all that day, all night, and all next day, and even the man who got least gathered ten homers. They spread them out 33 to dry all about the camp. But the meat was scarcely between their teeth, and they had not so much as bitten it, when the LORD's anger broke out against the people and he struck them with a deadly 34 plague. That place was called Kibroth-hattaavah[a] because there they buried the people who had been greedy for meat.

35 From Kibroth-hattaavah the Israelites went on to Hazeroth, and 12 while they were at Hazeroth, Miriam and Aaron began to speak against Moses. They blamed him for his Cushite wife (for he had 2 married a Cushite woman), and they said, 'Is Moses the only one with[b] whom the LORD has spoken? Has he not spoken with[b] us as 3 well?' Moses was in fact a man of great humility, the most humble man on earth. But the LORD heard 4 them and suddenly he said to Moses, Aaron and Miriam, 'Go out all three of you to the Tent of the Presence.' So the three went out, 5 and the LORD descended in a pillar of cloud; he stood at the entrance to the tent and summoned Aaron and Miriam. The two of them went 6 forward, and he said,

'Listen to my words.
If he[c] were your prophet and nothing more,
I would make myself known to him in a vision,
I would speak with him in a dream.
But my servant Moses is not such a 7 prophet;
he alone is faithful[d] of all my household.
With him I speak face to face, 8 openly and not in riddles.
He shall see the very form of the LORD.
How do you dare speak against my servant Moses?'

Thus the anger of the LORD was 9 roused against them, and he left them; and as the cloud moved 10 from the tent, there was Miriam, her skin diseased and white as snow. Aaron turned towards her and saw her skin diseased. Then he 11 said to Moses, 'Pray, my lord, do not make us pay the penalty of sin, foolish and wicked though we have been. Let her not be like something 12 still-born, whose flesh is half eaten away when it comes from the womb.' So Moses cried, 'Not this, 13 O LORD! Heal her, I pray.' The 14 LORD replied, 'Suppose her father had spat in her face, would she not have to remain in disgrace for seven days? Let her be kept for seven days in confinement outside the camp and then be brought back.' So Miriam was kept outside 15 for seven days, and the people did not strike camp until she was brought back. After this they set 16 out from Hazeroth and pitched camp in the wilderness of Paran.

THE LORD spoke to Moses and 13 said, 'Send men out to explore the 2 land of Canaan which I am giving to the Israelites; from each of their fathers' tribes send one man, and let him be a man of high rank.' So 3 Moses sent them from the wilder-

---

[a] *That is* the Graves of Greed.
[c] *Prob. rdg.; Heb.* the LORD.
[b] *Or by.*
[d] *Or* to be trusted.

ness of Paran at the command of the LORD, all of them leading men 4 among the Israelites. These were their names:

from the tribe of Reuben, Shammua son of Zaccur;

5 from the tribe of Simeon, Shaphat son of Hori;

6 from the tribe of Judah, Caleb son of Jephunneh;

7 from the tribe of Issachar, Igal son of Joseph;

8 from the tribe of Ephraim, Hoshea son of Nun;

9 from the tribe of Benjamin, Palti son of Raphu;

10 from the tribe of Zebulun, Gaddiel son of Sodi;

11 from the tribe of Joseph (that is from the tribe of Manasseh), Gaddi son of Susi;

12 from the tribe of Dan, Ammiel son of Gemalli;

13 from the tribe of Asher, Sethur son of Michael;

14 from the tribe of Naphtali, Nahbi son of Vophsi;

15 from the tribe of Gad, Geuel son of Machi.

16 These are the names of the men whom Moses sent to explore the land. But Moses called the son of Nun Joshua, not Hoshea.

17 When Moses sent them to explore the land of Canaan, he said to them, 'Make your way up by the Negeb, and go on into the hill-
18 country. See what the land is like, and whether the people who live there are strong or weak, few or
19 many. See whether it is easy or difficult country in which they live, and whether the cities in which they live are weakly defended or
20 well fortified; is the land fertile or barren, and does it grow trees or not? Go boldly in and take some of its fruit.' It was the season when the first grapes were ripe.

21 They went up and explored the country from the wilderness of Zin as far as Rehob by Lebo-hamath.
22 They went up by the Negeb and came to Hebron, where Ahiman, Sheshai and Talmai, the descendants of Anak,[a] were living. (Hebron was built seven years before Zoan in Egypt.) They came to the 23 gorge of Eshcol,[b] and there they cut a branch with a single bunch of grapes, and they carried it on a pole two at a time; they also picked pomegranates and figs. It was from 24 the bunch of grapes which the Israelites cut there that that place was named the gorge of Eshcol. After forty days they returned 25 from exploring the country, and 26 came back to Moses and Aaron and the whole community of Israelites at Kadesh in the wilderness of Paran. They made their report to them and to the whole community, and showed them the fruit of the country. And this was the story 27 they told Moses: 'We made our way into the land to which you sent us. It is flowing with milk and honey, and here is the fruit it grows; but its inhabitants are 28 sturdy, and the cities are very strongly fortified; indeed, we saw there the descendants of Anak. We also saw the Amalekites who 29 live in the Negeb, Hittites, Jebusites, and Amorites who live in the hill-country, and the Canaanites who live by the sea and along the Jordan.'

Then Caleb called for silence be- 30 fore Moses and said, 'Let us go up at once and occupy the country; we are well able to conquer it.' But 31 the men who had gone with him said, 'No, we cannot attack these people; they are stronger than we are.' Thus their report to the Is- 32 raelites about the land which they had explored was discouraging: 'The country we explored', they said, 'will swallow up any who go to live in it. All the people we saw there are men of gigantic size.

---

[a] descendants of Anak: *or* tall men.
[b] Eshcol: *that is* Bunch of Grapes.

33 When we set eyes on the Nephilim[a] (the sons of Anak[b] belong to
the Nephilim) we felt no bigger
than grasshoppers; and that is how
we looked to them.'

14 Then the whole Israelite community cried out in dismay; all
2 night long they wept. One and all
they made complaints against Moses and Aaron: 'If only we had died
in Egypt or in the wilderness!' they
3 said. 'Far happier if we had! Why
should the LORD bring us to this
land, to die in battle and leave our
wives and our dependants to become the spoils of war? To go back
to Egypt would be better than
4 this.' And they began to talk of
choosing someone to lead them
back.

5 Then Moses and Aaron flung
themselves on the ground before
the assembled community of the
6 Israelites, and two of those who
had explored the land, Joshua son
of Nun and Caleb son of Jephun-
7 neh, rent their clothes and addressed the whole community: 'The
country we penetrated and explored', they said, 'is very good
8 land indeed. If the LORD is pleased
with us, he will bring us into this
land which flows with milk and
9 honey, and give it to us. But you
must not rebel against the LORD.
You need not fear the people of the
land; for there we shall find food.
They have lost the protection that
they had: the LORD is with us. You
have nothing to fear from them.'
10 But by way of answer the assembled Israelites threatened to stone
them, when suddenly the glory of
the LORD appeared to them all in
the Tent of the Presence.

11 Then the LORD said to Moses,
'How much longer will this people
treat me with contempt? How
much longer will they refuse to
trust me in spite of all the signs I
12 have shown among them? I will
strike them with pestilence. I will
deny them their heritage, and you

and your descendants I will make
into a nation greater and more
numerous than they.' But Moses 13
answered the LORD, 'What if the
Egyptians hear of it? It was thou
who didst bring this people out of
Egypt by thy strength. What if 14
they tell the inhabitants of this
land? They too have heard of thee,
LORD, that thou art with this
people, and art seen face to face,
that thy cloud stays over them,
and thou goest before them in a
pillar of cloud by day and in a pillar of fire by night. If then thou 15
dost put them all to death at one
blow, the nations who have heard
these tales of thee will say, "The 16
LORD could not bring this people
into the land which he promised
them by oath; and so he destroyed
them in the wilderness."

'Now let the LORD's might be 17
shown in its greatness, true to
thy proclamation of thyself – "The 18
LORD, long-suffering, ever constant, who forgives iniquity and
rebellion, and punishes sons to the
third and fourth generation for the
iniquity of their fathers, though he
does not sweep them clean away."
Thou hast borne with this people 19
from Egypt all the way here; forgive their iniquity, I beseech thee,
as befits thy great and constant
love.'

The LORD said, 'Your prayer is 20
answered; I pardon them. But as I 21
live, in very truth the glory of the
LORD shall fill the earth. Not one 22–23
of all those who have seen my glory
and the signs which I wrought in
Egypt and in the wilderness shall
see the country which I promised
on oath to their fathers. Ten times
they have challenged me and not
obeyed my voice. None of those
who have flouted me shall see this
land. But my servant Caleb show- 24–25
ed a different spirit: he followed
me with his whole heart. Because
of this, I will bring him into the
land in which he has already set

---

[a] Or giants.   [b] sons of Anak: or tall men.

foot, the territory of the Amalekites and the Canaanites who dwell
in the Vale, and put his descendants in possession of it. Tomorrow
you must turn back and set out for
the wilderness by way of the Red
Sea.'ᵃ

26 The LORD spoke to Moses and
27 Aaron and said, 'How long must I
tolerateᵇ the complaints of this
wicked community? I have heard
the Israelites making complaints
28 against me. Tell them that this is
the very word of the LORD: As I
live, I will bring home to you the
words I have heard you utter.
29 Here in this wilderness your bones
shall lie, every man of you on the
register from twenty years old and
upwards, because you have made
30 these complaints against me. Not
one of you shall enter the land
which I swore with uplifted hand
should be your home, except only
Caleb son of Jephunneh and Jo-
31 shua son of Nun. As for your dependants, those dependants who,
you said, would become the spoils
of war, I will bring them in to the
land you have rejected, and they
32 shall enjoy it. But as for the rest of
you, your bones shall lie in this
33 wilderness; your sons shall be wanderers in the wilderness forty years,
paying the penalty of your wanton
disloyalty till the last man of you
34 dies there. Forty days you spent
exploring the country, and forty
years you shall spend – a year for
each day – paying the penalty of
your iniquities. You shall know
what it means to have me against
35 you.ᶜ I, the LORD, have spoken.
This I swear to do to all this wicked
community who have combined
against me. There shall be an end of
them here in this wilderness; here
36 they shall die.' But the men whom
Moses had sent to explore the land,
and who came back and by their
report set all the community com-
37 plaining against him, died of the

plague before the LORD; they died
of the plague because they had
made a bad report. Of those who 38
went to explore the land, Joshua
son of Nun and Caleb son of
Jephunneh alone remained alive.

When Moses reported the LORD's 39
words to all the Israelites, the
people were plunged in grief. They 40
set out early next morning and
made for the heights of the hill-
country, saying, 'Look, we are on
our way up to the place the LORD
spoke of. We admit that we have
been wrong.' But Moses replied, 41
'Must you persist in disobeying the
LORD's command? No good will
come of this. Go no further; you 42
will not have the LORD with you,
and your enemies will defeat you.
For in front of you are the Amal- 43
ekites and Canaanites, and you
will die by the sword, because you
have ceased to follow the LORD,
and he will no longer be with you.'
But they went recklessly on their 44
way towards the heights of the
hill-country, though neither the
Ark of the Covenant of the LORD
nor Moses moved with them out of
the camp; and the Amalekites and 45
Canaanites from those hills came
down and fell upon them, and
crushed them at Hormah.

THE LORD spoke to Moses and 15
said, Speak to the Israelites in these 2
words: When you enter the land
where you are to live, the land I am
giving you, you will make food- 3
offerings to the LORD; they may be
whole-offerings or any sacrifice
made in fulfilment of a specialᵈ
vow or by way of freewill offering
or at one of the appointed seasons.
When you thus make an offering
of soothing odour from herd or
flock to the LORD, the man who 4
offers, in presenting it, shall add a
grain-offering of a tenth of an ephah of flour mixed with a quarter of
a hin of oil. You shall also add to 5

ᵃ *Or* the Sea of Reeds.   ᵇ must I tolerate: *prob. rdg.*; *Heb.* for.
ᶜ *Or* to thwart me.   ᵈ in fulfilment of a special: *or* to discharge a...

the whole-offering or shared-offering a quarter of a hin of wine as a drink-offering with each lamb sacrificed.

6 If the animal is a ram, the grain-offering shall be two tenths of an ephah of flour mixed with a third 7 of a hin of oil, and the wine for the drink-offering shall be a third of a hin; in this way you will make an offering of soothing odour to the LORD.

8 When you offer to the LORD a young bull, whether as a whole-offering or as a sacrifice to fulfil a special[a] vow, or as a shared-offer-9 ing, you shall add a grain-offering of three tenths of an ephah of flour 10 mixed with half a hin of oil, and for the drink-offering, half a hin of wine; the whole will thus be a food-offering of soothing odour to the 11 LORD. This is what must be done in each case, for every bull or ram, 12 lamb or kid, whatever the number 13 of each that you offer. Every native Israelite shall observe these rules in each case when he offers a food-offering of soothing odour to the LORD.

14 When an alien residing with you or permanently settled among you offers a food-offering of soothing odour to the LORD, he shall do as 15 you do. There is one and the same rule for you and for the resident alien, a rule binding for all time on your descendants; you and the alien are alike before the LORD. 16 There shall be one law and one custom for you and for the alien residing with you.

17 The LORD spoke to Moses and 18 said, Speak to the Israelites in these words: After you have entered the land into which I am bring-19 ing you, whenever you eat the bread of the country, you shall set aside a contribution for the LORD. 20 You shall set aside a cake made of your first kneading of dough, as you set aside the contribution 21 from the threshing-floor. You must

give a contribution to the LORD from your first kneading of dough; this rule is binding on your descendants.

When through inadvertence you 22 omit to carry out any of these commands which the LORD gave to Moses – any command whatever 23 that the LORD gave you through Moses on that first day and thereafter and made binding on your descendants – if it be done inad- 24 vertently, unnoticed by the community, then the whole community shall offer one young bull as a whole-offering, a soothing odour to the LORD, with its proper grain-offering and drink-offering according to custom; and they shall add one he-goat as a sin-offering. The 25 priest shall make expiation for the whole community of Israelites, and they shall be forgiven. The omission was inadvertent; and they have brought their offering, a food-offering to the LORD; they have made their sin-offering before the LORD for their inadvertence; the 26 whole community of Israelites and the aliens residing among you shall be forgiven. The inadvertence was shared by the whole people.

If any individual sins inadvert- 27 ently, he shall present a yearling she-goat as a sin-offering, and the 28 priest shall make expiation before the LORD for the said individual, and he shall be forgiven. For any- 29 one who sins inadvertently, there shall be one law for all, whether native Israelite or resident alien. But the person who sins presump- 30 tuously, native or alien, insults the LORD. He shall be cut off from his people, because he has brought the 31 word of the LORD into contempt and violated his command. That person shall be wholly cut off; the guilt shall be on his head alone.

During the time that the Israel- 32 ites were in the wilderness, a man was found gathering sticks on the sabbath day. Those who had caught 33

[a] fulfil a special: *or* discharge a...

him in the act brought him to Moses and Aaron and all the community, and they kept him in custody, because it was not clearly known what was to be done with him. The LORD said to Moses, 'The man must be put to death; he must be stoned by all the community outside the camp.' So they took him outside the camp and all stoned him to death, as the LORD had commanded Moses.

The LORD spoke to Moses and said, Speak to the Israelites in these words: You must make tassels like flowers on the corners of your garments, you and your children's children. Into this tassel you shall work a violet thread, and whenever you see this in the tassel, you shall remember all the LORD's commands and obey them, and not go your own wanton ways, led astray by your own eyes and hearts. This token is to ensure that you remember all my commands and obey them, and keep yourselves holy, consecrated to your God.

I am the LORD your God who brought you out of Egypt to become your God. I am the LORD your God.

16 Now Korah son of Izhar, son of Kohath, son of Levi, with the Reubenites Dathan and Abiram sons of Eliab and On son of Peleth, challenged the authority of Moses. With them in their revolt were two hundred and fifty Israelites, all men of rank in the community, conveners of assembly and men of good standing. They confronted Moses and Aaron and said to them, 'You take too much upon yourselves. Every member of the community is holy and the LORD is among them all. Why do you set yourselves up above the assembly of the LORD?' When Moses heard this, he prostrated himself, and he said to Korah and all his company, 'Tomorrow morning the LORD shall declare who is his, who is holy and may present offerings to him. The man whom the LORD chooses shall present them. This is what you must do, you, Korah, and all your company: you must take censers and put fire in them, and then place incense on them before the LORD tomorrow. The man whom the LORD then chooses is the man who is holy. You take too much upon yourselves, you sons of Levi.'

Moses said to Korah, 'Now listen, you sons of Levi. Is it not enough for you that the God of Israel has set you apart from the community of Israel, bringing you near him to maintain the service of the Tabernacle of the LORD and to stand before the community as their ministers? He has brought you near him and your brother Levites with you; now you seek the priesthood as well. That is why you and all your company have combined together against the LORD. What is Aaron that you should make these complaints against him?'

Moses sent to fetch Dathan and Abiram sons of Eliab, but they answered, 'We are not coming. Is it a small thing that you have brought us away from a land flowing with milk and honey to let us die in the wilderness? Must you also set yourself up as prince over us? What is more, you have not brought us into a land flowing with milk and honey, nor have you given us fields and vineyards to inherit. Do you think you can hoodwink men like us? We are not coming.' This answer made Moses very angry, and he said to the LORD, 'Take no notice of their murmuring. I have not taken from them so much as a single ass; I have done no wrong to any of them.'

Moses said to Korah, 'Present yourselves before the LORD tomorrow, you and all your company, you and they and Aaron. Each man of you is to take his censer and put incense on it. Then you shall present them before the LORD with their two hundred and fifty censers, and you and Aaron 18 shall also bring your censers.' So each man took his censer and put fire in it and placed incense on it; Moses and Aaron took their stand at the entrance to the Tent of the 19 Presence, and Korah gathered his whole company together and faced them at the entrance to the Tent of the Presence.

Then the glory of the LORD appeared to the whole community. 20 And the LORD spoke to Moses and 21 Aaron and said, 'Stand apart from this company, so that I may make an end of them in a single instant.' 22 But they prostrated themselves and said, 'O God, God of the spirits of all mankind, if one man sins, wilt thou be angry with the whole 23 community?' But the LORD said to 24 Moses, 'Tell them to stand back from the dwellings of Korah, Dathan and Abiram.'

25 So Moses rose and went to Dathan and Abiram, and the elders of 26 Israel followed him. He said to the whole community, 'Stand well away from the tents of these wicked men; touch nothing of theirs, or you will be swept away because of 27 all their sins.' So they moved away from the places occupied by Korah, Dathan and Abiram. Now Dathan and Abiram, holding themselves erect, had come out to the entrance of their tents with their wives, their sons, and their depen-28 dants. Then Moses said, 'This shall prove to you that it is the LORD who sent me to do all these things, and it was not my own heart that 29 prompted me. If these men die a natural death and share the common fate of man, then the LORD 30 has not sent me; but if the LORD makes a great chasm, and the ground opens its mouth and swallows them and all that is theirs, and they go down alive to Sheol, then you will know that these

men have held the LORD in contempt.'

Hardly had Moses spoken when 31 the ground beneath them split; the earth opened its mouth and 32 swallowed them and their homes – all the followers of Korah and all their property. They went down 33 alive into Sheol with all that they had; the earth closed over them, and they vanished from the assembly. At their cries all the Israelites 34 round them fled, shouting, 'Look to yourselves! the earth will swallow us up.' Meanwhile fire had 35 come out from the LORD and burnt up the two hundred and fifty men who were presenting the incense.

Then the LORD spoke to Moses 36 and said, 'Bid Eleazar son of 37 Aaron the priest set aside the censers from the burnt remains, and scatter the fire from them far and wide, because they are holy. And 38 the censers of these men who sinned at the cost of their lives you shall make into beaten plates to cover the altar; they are holy, because they have presented before the LORD. Let them be a sign to the Israelites.' So Eleazar the 39 priest took the bronze[a] censers which the victims of the fire had presented, and they were beaten into plates to make a covering for the altar, as a reminder to the Is-40 raelites that no person unqualified, not descended from Aaron, should come forward to burn incense before the LORD, or his fate would be that of Korah and his company. All this was done as the LORD commanded Eleazar through Moses.

Next day all the community of 41 the Israelites raised complaints against Moses and Aaron and taxed them with causing the death of some of the LORD's people. As they 42 gathered against Moses and Aaron, they turned towards the Tent of the Presence and saw that the cloud covered it, and the glory of

[a] Or copper.

154

43 the LORD appeared. Moses and Aaron came to the front of the
44 Tent of the Presence, and the LORD spoke to Moses and Aaron
45 and said, 'Stand well clear of this community, so that in a single instant I may make an end of them.' Then they prostrated themselves,
46 and Moses said to Aaron, 'Take your censer, put fire from the altar in it, set incense on it, and go with it quickly to the assembled community to make expiation for them. Wrath has gone forth already from the presence of the
47 LORD. The plague has begun.' So Aaron took his censer, as Moses had said, ran into the midst of the assembly and found that the plague had begun among the people. He put incense on the censer and made
48 expiation for the people, standing between the dead and the living,
49 and the plague stopped. Fourteen thousand seven hundred died of it, in addition to those who had died
50 for the offence of Korah. When Aaron came back to Moses at the entrance to the Tent of the Presence, the plague had stopped.

17 The LORD spoke to Moses and
2 said, 'Speak to the Israelites and tell them to give you a staff for each tribe, one from every tribal chief, twelve in all, and write
3 each man's name on his staff. On Levi's staff write the name of Aaron, for there shall be one staff
4 for each head of a tribe. You shall put them all in the Tent of the Presence before the Tokens, where
5 I meet you, and the staff of the man I choose shall sprout. I will rid myself of the complaints of these Israelites, who keep on complaining against you.'
6 Moses thereupon spoke to the Israelites, and each of their chiefs handed him a staff, each of them one for his tribe, twelve in all, and
7 Aaron's staff among them. Moses put them before the LORD in the
8 Tent of the Tokens, and next day when he entered the tent, he found

that Aaron's staff, the staff for the tribe of Levi, had sprouted. Indeed, it had sprouted, blossomed, and produced ripe almonds. Moses 9 then brought out the staffs from before the LORD and showed them to all the Israelites; they saw for themselves, and each man took his own staff. The LORD said to Moses, 10 'Put back Aaron's staff in front of the Tokens to be kept as a warning to all rebels, so that you may rid me once and for all of their complaints, and then they shall not die.' Moses did this; as the LORD 11 had commanded him, so he did.

The Israelites said to Moses, 12 'This is the end of us! We perish, one and all! Every single person 13 who goes near the Tabernacle of the LORD dies. Is this to be our final end?'

THE LORD said to Aaron: You and 18 your sons, together with the members of your father's tribe, shall be fully answerable for the sanctuary. You and your sons alone shall be answerable for your priestly office; but you shall admit your kinsmen 2 of Levi, your father's tribe, to be attached to you and assist you while you and your sons are before the Tent of the Tokens. They shall be 3 in attendance on you and fulfil all the duties of the Tent, but shall not go near the holy vessels and the altar, or they will die and you with them. They shall be attached to 4 you and be responsible for the maintenance of the Tent of the Presence in every detail; no unqualified person shall come near you. You yourselves shall be re- 5 sponsible for the sanctuary and the altar, so that wrath may no more fall on the Israelites. I have 6 myself taken the Levites your kinsmen out of all the Israelites as a gift for you, given to the LORD for the maintenance of the Tent of the Presence. But only you and your 7 sons may fulfil the duties of your priestly office that concern the altar or lie within the Veil. This duty is yours; I bestow on you this gift of priestly service. The unqualified person who intrudes on it shall be put to death.

8 The LORD said to Aaron: I, the LORD, commit to your control the contributions made to me, that is all the holy-gifts of the Israelites. I give them to you and to your sons for your allotted portion due to 9 you in perpetuity. Out of the most holy gifts kept back from the altar-fire this part shall belong to you: every offering, whether grain-offering, sin-offering, or guilt-offering, rendered to me as a most holy gift, belongs to you and to your sons. 10 You shall eat it as befits most holy gifts; every male may eat it. You shall regard it as holy.

11 This also is yours: the contribution from all such of their gifts as are presented as special gifts by the Israelites. I give them to you and to your sons and daughters with you as a due in perpetuity. Every person in your household who is ritually clean may eat them. 12 I give you all the choicest of the oil, the choicest of the new wine and the corn, the firstfruits which 13 are given to the LORD. The first-ripe fruits of all produce in the land which are brought to the LORD shall be yours. Everyone in your household who is clean may eat them.

14 Everything in Israel which has been devoted to God shall be yours. 15 All the first-born of man or beast which are brought to the LORD shall be yours. Notwithstanding, you must accept payment in redemption of any first-born of man 16 and of unclean beasts: at the end of one month you shall redeem it at the fixed price of five shekels of silver by the sacred standard (twenty 17 gerahs to the shekel). You must not, however, allow the redemption of the first-born of a cow, sheep, or goat; they are holy. You shall fling their blood against the altar and burn their fat in sacrifice as a food-offering of soothing odour to the LORD; their flesh shall be yours, as 18 are the breast of the special gift and the right leg.

All the contributions from holy-19 gifts, which the Israelites set aside for the LORD, I give to you and to your sons and daughters with you as a due in perpetuity. This is a perpetual covenant of salt before the LORD with you and your descendants also.

The LORD said to Aaron: You 20 shall have no patrimony in the land of Israel, no holding among them; I am your holding in Israel, I am your patrimony.

To the Levites I give every tithe 21 in Israel to be their patrimony, in return for the service they render in maintaining the Tent of the Presence. In order that the Israelites 22 may not henceforth approach the Tent and thus incur the penalty of death, the Levites alone shall per-23 form the service of the Tent, and they shall accept the full responsibility for it. This rule is binding on your descendants for all time. They shall have no patrimony among the Israelites, because I give them 24 as their patrimony the tithe which the Israelites set aside as a contribution to the LORD. Therefore I say to them: You shall have no patrimony among the Israelites.

The LORD spoke to Moses and 25 said, Speak to the Levites in these 26 words: When you receive from the Israelites the tithe which I give you from them as your patrimony, you shall set aside from it the contribution to the LORD, a tithe of the tithe. Your contribution shall 27 count for you as if it were corn from the threshing-floor and juice from the vat. In this way you too 28 shall set aside the contribution due to the LORD out of all tithes which you receive from the Israelites and shall give the LORD's contribution to Aaron the priest. Out of all the 29 gifts you receive you shall set aside the contribution due to the LORD; and the gift which you hallow[a] must be taken from the choicest of them.

30 You shall say to the Levites: When you have set aside the choicest part of your portion, the remainder shall count for you as the produce of the threshing-floor and
31 the winepress, and you may eat it anywhere, you and your households. It is your payment for service in the Tent of the Presence.
32 When you have set aside its choicest part, you will incur no penalty in respect of it, and you will not be profaning the holy-gifts of the Israelites; so you will not die.

19 THE LORD spoke to Moses and
2 Aaron and said: This is a law and a statute which the LORD has ordained. Tell the Israelites to bring you a red cow without blemish or defect, which has never borne the
3 yoke. You shall give it to Eleazar the priest, and it shall be taken outside the camp and slaughtered[b]
4 to the east of it. Eleazar the priest shall take some of the blood on his finger and sprinkle it seven times towards the front of the Tent of the
5 Presence. The cow shall be burnt in his sight, skin, flesh, and blood, to-
6 gether with the offal. The priest shall then take cedar-wood, marjoram, and scarlet thread, and throw them into the heart of the fire in which the cow is burning.
7 He shall wash his clothes and bathe his body in water; after which he may enter the camp, but he remains ritually unclean till sunset.
8 The man who burnt the cow shall wash his clothes and bathe his body in water, but he also remains un-
9 clean till sunset. Then a man who is clean shall collect the ashes of the cow and deposit them outside the camp in a clean place. They shall be reserved for use by the Israelite community in the water of ritual

purification; for the cow is a sin-offering. The man who collected 10 the ashes of the cow shall wash his clothes, but he remains unclean till sunset. This rule shall be binding for all time on the Israelites and on the alien who is living with them.

Whoever touches a corpse shall 11 be ritually unclean for seven days. He shall get himself purified with 12 the water of ritual purification on the third day and on the seventh day, and then he shall be clean. If he is not purified both on the third day and on the seventh, he shall not be clean. Everyone who touches a 13 corpse, that is the body of a man who has died, and does not purify himself, defiles the Tabernacle of the LORD. That person shall be cut off from Israel. The water of purification has not been flung over him; he remains unclean, and his impurity is still upon him.

When a man dies in a tent, this 14 is the law: everyone who goes into the tent and everyone who was inside the tent shall be ritually unclean for seven days, and every 15 open vessel which has no covering tied over it shall also be unclean. In the open, anyone who touches 16 a man killed with a weapon or one who has died naturally, or who touches a human bone or a grave, shall be unclean for seven days. For such uncleanness, they shall 17 take some of the ash from the burnt mass of the sin-offering and add fresh water to it in a vessel. Then a 18 man who is clean shall take marjoram, dip it in the water, and sprinkle the tent with all the vessels in it and all the people who were there, or the man who has touched a human bone, a corpse (whether the man was killed or died naturally), or a grave. The 19 man who is clean shall sprinkle the unclean man on the third day and on the seventh; on the seventh day

[a] you hallow: *prob. rdg.*; Heb. *obscure.*
[b] *Or* he shall take it outside the camp and slaughter it...

he shall purify him; then the man shall wash his clothes and bathe in water, and at sunset he shall be 20 clean. If a man who is unclean does not get himself purified, that person shall be cut off from the assembly, because he has defiled the sanctuary of the LORD. The water of purification has not been flung 21 over him: he is unclean. This rule shall be binding on you for all time. The man who sprinkles the water of purification shall also wash his clothes, and whoever touches the water shall be unclean till sunset. 22 Whatever the unclean man touches shall be unclean, and any person who touches that shall be unclean till sunset.

20 IN the first month the whole community of Israel reached the wilderness of Zin and stayed some time at Kadesh; there Miriam died and was buried.
2   There was no water for the community; so they gathered against 3 Moses and Aaron. The people disputed with Moses and said, 'If only we had perished when our brothers perished in the presence of the 4 LORD! Why have you brought the assembly of the LORD into this wilderness for us and our beasts to die 5 here? Why did you fetch us up from Egypt to bring us to this vile place, where nothing will grow, neither corn nor figs, vines nor pomegranates? There is not even 6 any water to drink.' Moses and Aaron came forward in front of the assembly to the entrance of the Tent of the Presence. There they fell prostrate, and the glory of the LORD appeared to them.
7   The LORD spoke to Moses and 8 said, 'Take a*[a]* staff, and then with Aaron your brother assemble all the community, and, in front of them all, speak to the rock and it will yield its water. Thus you will produce water for the community out of the rock, for them and their beasts to drink.' Moses left the 9 presence of the LORD with the staff, as he had commanded him. Then he and Aaron gathered the 10 assembly together in front of the rock, and he said to them, 'Listen to me, you rebels. Must we get water out of this rock for you?' Mo- 11 ses raised his hand and struck the rock twice with his staff. Water gushed out in abundance and they all drank, men and beasts. But the 12 LORD said to Moses and Aaron, 'You did not trust me so far as to uphold my holiness in the sight of the Israelites; therefore you shall not lead this assembly into the land which I promised to give them.' Such were the waters of Meribah,*[b]* 13 where the people disputed with the LORD and through which his holiness was upheld.

The approach to the promised land

FROM Kadesh Moses sent envoys 14 to the king of Edom: 'This is a message from your brother Israel. You know all the hardships we have encountered, how our fathers 15 went down to Egypt, and we lived there for many years. The Egyptians ill-treated us and our fathers before us, and we cried to the 16 LORD for help. He listened to us and sent an angel, and he brought us out of Egypt; and now we are here at Kadesh, a town on your frontier. Grant us passage through 17 your country. We will not trespass on field or vineyard, or drink from your wells. We will keep to the king's highway; we will not turn off to right or left until we have crossed your territory.' But the 18 Edomites answered, 'You shall not cross our land. If you do, we will march out and attack you in force.' The Israelites said, 'But we will 19 keep to the main road. If we and our flocks drink your water, we will pay you for it; we will simply cross your land on foot.' But the 20

---

[a] Or the.   *[b]* That is Dispute.

Edomites said, 'No, you shall not', and took the field against them with a large army in full strength. 21 Thus the Edomites refused to allow Israel to cross their frontier, and Israel went a different way to avoid a conflict.

22 The whole community of Israel set out from Kadesh and came to 23 Mount Hor. At Mount Hor, near the frontier of Edom, the LORD 24 said to Moses and Aaron, 'Aaron shall be gathered to his father's kin. He shall not enter the land which I promised to give the Israelites, because over the waters of Meribah you rebelled against my 25 command. Take Aaron and his son Eleazar, and go up Mount Hor. 26 Strip Aaron of his robes and invest Eleazar his son with them, for Aaron shall be taken from you: he 27 shall die there.' Moses did as the LORD had commanded him: they went up Mount Hor in sight of the 28 whole community, and Moses stripped Aaron of his robes and invested his son Eleazar with them. There Aaron died on the mountain-top, and Moses and Eleazar came down 29 from the mountain. So the whole community saw that Aaron had died, and all Israel mourned him for thirty days.

21 When the Canaanite king of Arad who lived in the Negeb heard that the Israelites were coming by way of Atharim, he attacked them and took some of them prisoners. 2 Israel thereupon made a vow to the LORD and said, 'If thou wilt deliver this people into my power, 3 I will destroy their cities.' The LORD listened to Israel and delivered the Canaanites into their power. Israel destroyed them and their cities and called the place Hormah.[a]

4 Then they left Mount Hor by way of the Red Sea to march round the flank of Edom. But on 5 the way they grew impatient, and spoke against God and Moses. 'Why have you brought us up from Egypt', they said, 'to die in the desert where there is neither food nor water? We are heartily sick of this miserable fare.' Then the 6 LORD sent poisonous snakes among the people, and they bit the Israelites so that many of them died. The people came to Moses and 7 said, 'We sinned when we spoke against the LORD and you. Plead with the LORD to rid us of the snakes.' Moses therefore pleaded with the LORD for the people; and 8 the LORD told Moses to make a serpent[b] of bronze and erect it as a standard, so that anyone who had been bitten could look at it and recover. So Moses made a bronze 9 serpent and erected it as a standard, so that when a snake had bitten a man, he could look at the bronze serpent and recover.

The Israelites went on and en- 10 camped at Oboth. They moved on 11 from Oboth and encamped at Iye-abarim in the wilderness on the eastern frontier of Moab. From 12 there they moved and encamped by the gorge of the Zared. They 13 moved on from the Zared and encamped by the farther side of the Arnon in the wilderness which extends into Amorite territory, for the Arnon was the Moabite frontier; it lies between Moab and the Amorites. That is why the Book 14 of the Wars of the LORD speaks of Vaheb[c] in Suphah and the gorges:

Arnon and the watershed of the 15 gorges
that falls away towards the dwellings at Ar
and slopes towards the frontier of Moab.

From there they moved on to 16 Beer:[d] this is the water-hole where the LORD said to Moses, 'Gather the people together and I will give

---

[a] That is Destruction.
[c] Name meaning Watershed.
[b] Or snake.
[d] Name meaning Water-hole.

17 them water.' It was then that Israel sang this song:

Well up, spring water! Greet it with song,
18 the spring unearthed by the princes,
laid open by the leaders of the people
with sceptre and with mace,
a gift from the wilderness.

19 And they proceeded from Beer[a] to Nahaliel, and from Nahaliel to
20 Bamoth; then from Bamoth to the valley in the Moabite country below the summit of Pisgah overlooking the desert.
21 Then Israel sent envoys to the Amorite king Sihon and said,
22 'Grant us passage through your country. We will not trespass on field or vineyard, nor will we drink from your wells. We will travel by the king's highway till we have
23 crossed your territory.' But Sihon would not grant Israel passage through his territory; he mustered all his people and came out against Israel in the wilderness. He advanced as far as Jahaz and attack-
24 ed Israel, but Israel put them to the sword, giving no quarter, and occupied their land from the Arnon to the Jabbok, the territory of the Ammonites, where the country be-
25 came difficult. So Israel took all these Amorite cities and settled in them, that is in Heshbon and all its
26 dependent villages. Heshbon was the capital of the Amorite king Sihon, who had fought against the former king of Moab and taken from him all his territory as far as
27 the Arnon. Therefore the bards say:

Come to Heshbon, come!
Let us see the city of Sihon rebuilt and restored!
28 For fire blazed out from Heshbon, and flames from Sihon's city.
It devoured Ar of Moab,
and swept the high ground at Arnon head.

Woe to you, Moab; 29
it is the end of you, you people of Kemosh.
He has made his sons fugitives
and his daughters the prisoners of Sihon the Amorite king.
From Heshbon to Dibon their very 30
embers are burnt out
and they are extinct,
while the fire spreads onward to Medeba.

Thus Israel occupied the territory 31
of the Amorites.
Moses then sent men to explore 32
Jazer; the Israelites captured it together with its dependent villages and drove out the Amorites living there. Then they turned and ad- 33
vanced along the road to Bashan. Og king of Bashan, with all his people, took the field against them at Edrei. The LORD said to Moses, 34
'Do not be afraid of him. I have delivered him into your hands, with all his people and his land. Deal with him as you dealt with Sihon the Amorite king who lived in Heshbon.' So they put him to 35
the sword with his sons and all his people, until there was no survivor left, and they occupied his land.

Israel in the plains of Moab

THE Israelites went forward and 22
encamped in the lowlands of Moab on the farther side of the Jordan from Jericho.
Balak son of Zippor saw what 2
Israel had done to the Amorites, and Moab was in terror of the 3
people because there were so many of them. The Moabites were sick with fear at the sight of them; and they said to the 4
elders of Midian, 'This horde will soon lick up everything round us as a bull crops the spring grass.' Balak son of Zippor was at that time king of Moab. He sent a depu- 5
tation to summon Balaam son of Beor, who was at Pethor by the Euphrates in the land of the Ama-

[a] *Prob. rdg.; Heb. from a gift.*

vites, with this message, 'Look, an entire nation has come out of Egypt; they cover the face of the country and are settling at my 6 very door. Come at once and lay a curse on them, because they are too many for me; then I may be able to defeat them and drive them from the country. I know that those whom you bless are blessed, and those whom you curse are cursed.'

7 The elders of Moab and Midian took the fees for augury with them, and they came to Balaam and told 8 him what Balak had said. 'Spend this night here,' he said, 'and I will give you whatever answer the LORD gives to me.' So the Moabite 9 chiefs stayed with Balaam. God came to Balaam and asked him, 10 'Who are these men with you?' Balaam replied, 'Balak son of Zippor king of Moab has sent them to me 11 and he says, "Look, a people newly come out of Egypt is covering the face of the country. Come at once and denounce them for me; then I may be able to fight them and 12 drive them away."' God said to Balaam, 'You are not to go with them or curse the people, because 13 they are to be blessed.'[a] So Balaam rose in the morning and said to Balak's chiefs, 'Go back to your own country; the LORD has refused 14 to let me go with you.' Then the Moabite chiefs took their leave and went back to Balak, and told him that Balaam had refused to come 15 with them; whereupon Balak sent a second and larger embassy of 16 higher rank than the first. They came to Balaam and told him, 'This is the message from Balak son of Zippor: "Let nothing stand in the 17 way of your coming. I will confer great honour upon you; I will do whatever you ask me. But you must come and denounce this 18 people for me."' Balaam gave this answer to Balak's messengers: 'Even if Balak were to give me all the silver and gold in his house, I could not disobey the command of the LORD my God in anything, small or great. But stay here for 19 this night, as the others did, that I may learn what more the LORD has to say to me.' During the night 20 God came to Balaam and said to him, 'If these men have come to summon you, then rise and go with them, but do only what I tell you.' So in the morning Balaam rose, 21 saddled his ass and went with the Moabite chiefs.

But God was angry because Ba- 22 laam was going, and as he came riding on his ass, accompanied by his two servants, the angel of the LORD took his stand in the road to bar his way. When the ass saw the 23 angel standing in the road with his sword drawn, she turned off the road into the fields, and Balaam beat the ass to bring her back on to the road. Then the angel of the 24 LORD stood where the road ran through a hollow, with fenced vineyards on either side. The ass 25 saw the angel and, crushing herself against the wall, crushed Balaam's foot against it, and he beat her again. The angel of the LORD moved 26 on further and stood in a narrow place where there was no room to turn either to right or left. When 27 the ass saw the angel, she lay down under Balaam. At that Balaam lost his temper and beat the ass with his stick. The LORD then made 28 the ass speak, and she said to Balaam, 'What have I done? This is the third time you have beaten me.' Balaam answered the ass, 29 'You have been making a fool of me. If I had had a sword here, I should have killed you on the spot.' But the ass answered, 'Am I not 30 still the ass which you have ridden all your life? Have I ever taken such a liberty with you before?' He said, 'No.' Then the LORD open- 31 ed Balaam's eyes: he saw the angel of the LORD standing in the road with his sword drawn, and he

[a] *Or* are blessed.

bowed down and fell flat on his
32 face before him. The angel said to
him, 'What do you mean by beating your ass three times like this? I
came out to bar your way but you
33 made straight for me, and three
times your ass saw me and turned
aside. If she had not turned aside, I
should by now have killed you and
34 spared her.' Balaam replied to the
angel of the LORD, 'I have done
wrong. I did not know that you
stood in the road confronting me.
But now, if my journey displeases
35 you, I am ready to go back.' The
angel of the LORD said to Balaam,
'Go on with these men; but say
only what I tell you.' So Balaam
went on with Balak's chiefs.
36   When Balak heard that Balaam
was coming, he came out to meet
him as far as Ar of Moab by the
37 Arnon on his frontier. Balak said
to Balaam, 'Did I not send time and
again to summon you? Why did you
not come? Did you think that Ɩ
38 could not do you honour?' Balaam
replied, 'I have come, as you see.
But now that I am here, what power
have I of myself to say anything?
Whatever the word God puts into
my mouth, that is what I will say.'
39 So Balaam went with Balak till
40 they came to Kiriath-huzoth, and
Balak slaughtered cattle and sheep
and sent them to Balaam and to
the chiefs who were with him.
41   In the morning Balak took Balaam and led him up to the Heights
of Baal, from where he could see the
full extent of the Israelite host.
23 Then Balaam said to Balak, 'Build
me here seven altars and prepare
for me seven bulls and seven rams.'
2 Balak did as he asked and offered a
3-4 bull and a ram on each altar. Then
he said to him, 'I have prepared
the seven altars, and I have offered
the bull and the ram on each altar.'
Balaam said to Balak, 'Take your
stand beside your sacrifice, and let
me go off by myself. It may happen that the LORD will meet me.

Whatever he reveals to me, I will
tell you.' So he went forthwith, and
God met him. The LORD put words 5
into Balaam's mouth and said, 'Go
back to Balak, and speak as I tell
you.' So he went back, and found 6
Balak standing by his sacrifice, and
with him all the Moabite chiefs.
And Balaam uttered his oracle: 7

From Aram,*a* from the mountains
    of the east,
Balak king of Moab has brought me:
'Come, lay a curse for me on Jacob,
come, execrate Israel.'
How can I denounce whom God 8
    has not denounced?
How can I execrate whom the
    LORD has not execrated?
From the rocky heights I see them, 9
I watch them from the rounded
    hills.
I see a people that dwells alone,
that has not made itself one with
    the nations.
Who can count the host*b* of Jacob 10
or number the hordes*c* of Israel?
Let me die as men die who are
    righteous,
grant that my end may be as theirs!

Then Balak said to Balaam, 'What 11
is this you have done? I sent for you
to denounce my enemies, and what
you have done is to bless them.'
But he replied, 'Must I not keep to 12
the words that the LORD puts into
my mouth?'
  Balak then said to him, 'Come 13
with me now to another place
from which you will see them,
though not the full extent of them;
you will not see them all. Denounce
them for me from there.' So he 14
took him to the Field of the Watchers*d* on the summit of Pisgah,
where he built seven altars and
offered a bull and a ram on each
altar. Balaam said to Balak, 'Take 15
your stand beside your sacrifice,
and I will meet God over there.'
The LORD met Balaam and put 16
words into his mouth, and said, 'Go
back to Balak, and speak as I tell

a Or Syria.   *b* Or dust.   *c* Or quarter *or* sands.   *d* Or Field of Zophim.

17 you.' So he went back, and found him standing beside his sacrifice, with the Moabite chiefs. Balak ask-
18 ed what the LORD had said, and Balaam uttered his oracle:

Up, Balak, and listen:
hear what I am charged to say, son of Zippor.
19 God is not a mortal that he should lie,
not a man that he should change his mind.*a*
Has he not spoken, and will he not make it good?
What he has proclaimed, he will surely fulfil.
20 I have received command to bless; I will bless and I cannot gainsay it.
21 He has discovered no iniquity in Jacob
and has seen no mischief in Israel.*b*
The LORD their God is with them, acclaimed among them as king.*c*
22 What its curving horns are to the wild ox,
God is to them, who brought them out of Egypt.
23 Surely there is no divination in*d* Jacob,
and no augury in*d* Israel;
now is the time to say of Jacob and of Israel, 'See what God has wrought!'
24 Behold a people rearing up like a lioness,
rampant like a lion;
he will not couch till he devours the prey
and drinks the blood of the slain.

25 Then Balak said to Balaam, 'You will not denounce them; then at
26 least do not bless them'; and he answered, 'Did I not warn you that I must do all the LORD tells me?'
27 Balak replied, 'Come, let me take you to another place; perhaps God will be pleased to let you denounce
28 them for me from there.' So he took Balaam to the summit of Peor over-
29 looking Jeshimon, and Balaam told him to build seven altars for him

there and prepare seven bulls and seven rams. Balak did as Balaam 30 had said, and he offered a bull and a ram on each altar.

But now that Balaam knew that 24 the LORD wished him to bless Is-rael, he did not go and resort to divination as before. He turned to-wards the desert; and as he looked, 2 he saw Israel encamped tribe by tribe. The spirit of God came upon him, and he uttered his oracle: 3

The very word of Balaam son of Beor,
the very word of the man whose sight is clear,
the very word of him who hears the 4 words of God,
who with staring eyes sees in a trance
the vision from the Almighty:
how goodly are your tents, O 5 Jacob,
your dwelling-places, Israel,
like long rows of palms, 6
like gardens by a river,
like lign-aloes planted by the LORD,
like cedars beside the water!
The water in his vessels shall 7 overflow,
and his seed shall be like great waters
so that his king may be taller than Agag,
and his kingdom lifted high.
What its curving horns are to the 8 wild ox,
God is to him, who brought him out of Egypt;
he shall devour his adversaries the nations,
crunch their bones, and smash their limbs in pieces.
When he reclines he couches like a 9 lion,
like a lioness, and no one dares rouse him.
Blessed be they that bless you,
and they that curse you be accursed!

a Or feel regret.   *b Or* None can discover calamity in Jacob nor see trouble in Israel.   *c Or* royal care is bestowed on them.   *d Or* against.

10 At that Balak was very angry with Balaam, beat his hands together and said, 'I summoned you to denounce my enemies, and three times you have persisted in bless-
11 ing them. Off with you to your own place! I promised to confer great honour upon you, but now the LORD has kept this honour from
12 you.' Balaam answered, 'But I told your own messengers whom you
13 sent: "If Balak gives me all the silver and gold in his house, I cannot disobey the command of the LORD by doing anything of my own will, good or bad. What the LORD speaks to me, that is what
14 I will say." Now I am going to my own people; but first, I will warn you what this people will do
15 to yours in the days to come.' So he uttered his oracle:

The very word of Balaam son of Beor,
the very word of the man whose sight is clear,
16 the very word of him who hears the words of God,
who shares the knowledge of the Most High,
who with staring eyes sees in a trance
the vision from the Almighty:
17 I see him, but not now;
I behold him, but not near:
a star shall come forth out of Jacob,
a comet arise from Israel.
He shall smite the squadrons[a] of Moab,
and beat down all the sons of strife.
18 Edom shall be his by conquest and Seir, his enemy, shall be his.
Israel shall do valiant deeds;
19 Jacob shall trample them down,
the last survivor from Ar shall he destroy.

20 He saw Amalek and uttered his oracle:

First of all the nations was Amalek,
but his end shall be utter destruction.

21 He saw the Kenites and uttered his oracle:

Your refuge, though it seems secure,
your nest, though set on the mountain crag,
is doomed to burning, O Cain. 22
How long must you dwell there in my sight?

23 He uttered his oracle:

Ah, who are these assembling in the north,
invaders from the region of 24 Kittim?
They will lay waste Assyria; they will lay Eber waste:
he too shall perish utterly.

25 Then Balaam arose and returned home, and Balak also went on his way.

WHEN the Israelites were in 25 Shittim, the people began to have intercourse with Moabite women, who invited them to the sacrifices 2 offered to their gods; and they ate the sacrificial food and prostrated themselves before the gods of Moab. The Israelites joined in the 3 worship of the Baal of Peor, and the LORD was angry with them. He 4 said to Moses, 'Take all the leaders of the people and hurl them down to their death before the LORD in the full light of day, that the fury of his anger may turn away from Israel.' So Moses said to the judges 5 of Israel, 'Put to death, each one of you, those of his tribe who have joined in the worship of the Baal of Peor.'

One of the Israelites brought a 6 Midianite woman into his family in open defiance of Moses and all the community of Israel, while they were weeping by the entrance of the Tent of the Presence. Phine-7 has son of Eleazar, son of Aaron

[a] *Or* heads.

the priest, saw him. He stepped out from the crowd and took up a 8 spear, and he went into the inner room after the Israelite and transfixed the two of them, the Israelite and the woman, pinning them together. Thus the plague which had attacked the Israelites was brought 9 to a stop; but twenty-four thousand had already died.

10 The LORD spoke to Moses and 11 said, 'Phinehas son of Eleazar, son of Aaron the priest, has turned my wrath away from the Israelites; he displayed among them the same jealous anger that moved me, and therefore in my jealousy I did not 12 exterminate the Israelites. Tell him that I hereby grant him my 13 covenant of security of tenure. He and his descendants after him shall enjoy the priesthood under a covenant for all time, because he showed his zeal for his God and made 14 expiation for the Israelites.' The name of the Israelite struck down with the Midianite woman was Zimri son of Salu, a chief in a 15 Simeonite family, and the Midianite woman's name was Cozbi daughter of Zur, who was the head of a group of fathers' families in Midian.

16 The LORD spoke to Moses and 17–18 said, 'Make the Midianites suffer as they made you suffer with their crafty tricks, and strike them down; their craftiness was your undoing at Peor and in the affair of Cozbi their sister, the daughter of a Midianite chief, who was struck down at the time of the plague that followed Peor.'

19; 26 AFTER the plague the LORD said to Moses and Eleazar the priest, 2 son of Aaron, 'Number the whole community of Israel by fathers' families, recording everyone in Israel aged twenty years and up- 3 wards fit for military service.' Moses and Eleazar collected them in

the lowlands of Moab by the Jordan near Jericho,[a] all who were 4 twenty years of age and upwards, as the LORD had commanded Moses.

These were the Israelites who came out of Egypt:

Reubenites (Reuben was Israel's 5[b] eldest son): Enoch, the Enochite family; Pallu, the Palluite family; Hezron, the Hezronite family; Car- 6 mi, the Carmite family. These 7 were the Reubenite families; the number in their detailed list was forty-three thousand seven hundred and thirty. Son of Pallu: 8 Eliab. Sons of Eliab: Nemuel, Da- 9 than and Abiram. These were the same Dathan and Abiram, conveners of the community, who defied Moses and Aaron and joined the company of Korah in defying the LORD. Then the earth opened 10 its mouth and swallowed them up with Korah, and so their company died, while fire burnt up the two hundred and fifty men, and they became a warning sign. The Kora- 11 hites, however, did not die.

Simeonites, by their families: 12 Nemuel, the Nemuelite family; Jamin, the Jaminite family; Jachin, the Jachinite family; Zerah, the 13 Zarhite family; Saul, the Saulite family. These were the Simeonite 14 families; the number in their detailed list was twenty-two thousand two hundred.

Gadites, by their families: Zeph- 15 on, the Zephonite family; Haggi, the Haggite family; Shuni, the Shunite family; Ozni, the Oznite 16 family; Eri, the Erite family; Arod, 17 the Arodite family; Areli, the Arelite family. These were the Gadite 18 families; the number in their detailed list was forty thousand five hundred.

The sons of Judah were Er, Onan, 19 Shelah, Perez and Zerah; Er and Onan died in Canaan. Judahites, 20 by their families: Shelah, the

---

[a] *Prob. rdg.; Heb. adds* saying.
[b] *Verses* 5–50: *cp.* Gen. 46. 8–25; Exod. 6. 14, 15; 1 Chr. chs. 4–8.

Shelanite family; Perez, the Perezite family; Zerah, the Zarhite
21 family. Perezites: Hezron, the Hezronite family; Hamul, the Hamul-
22 ite family. These were the families of Judah; the number in their detailed list was seventy-six thousand five hundred.

23 Issacharites, by their families: Tola, the Tolaite family; Pua, the
24 Puite family; Jashub, the Jashubite family; Shimron, the Shimron-
25 ite family. These were the families of Issachar; the number in their detailed list was sixty-four thousand three hundred.

26 Zebulunites, by their families: Sered, the Sardite family; Elon, the Elonite family; Jahleel, the
27 Jahleelite family. These were the Zebulunite families; the number in their detailed list was sixty thousand five hundred.

28 Josephites, by their families:
29 Manasseh and Ephraim. Manassites: Machir, the Machirite family. Machir was the father of Gilead:
30 Gilead, the Gileadite family. Gileadites: Jeezer, the Jeezerite fami-
31 ly; Helek, the Helekite family; Asriel, the Asrielite family; Shechem,
32 the Shechemite family; Shemida, the Shemidaite family; Hepher,
33 the Hepherite family. Zelophehad son of Hepher had no sons, only daughters; their names were Mahlah, Noah, Hoglah, Milcah and
34 Tirzah. These were the families of Manasseh; the number in their detailed list was fifty-two thousand seven hundred.

35 Ephraimites, by their families: Shuthelah, the Shuthalhite family; Becher, the Bachrite family; Ta-
36 han, the Tahanite family. Shuthalhites: Eran, the Eranite family.
37 These were the Ephraimite families; the number in their detailed list was thirty-two thousand five hundred. These were the Josephites, by families.

38 Benjamites, by their families: Bela, the Belaite family; Ashbel, the Ashbelite family; Ahiram, the

Ahiramite family; Shupham, the 39 Shuphamite family; Hupham, the Huphamite family. Belaites: Ard 40 and Naaman. Ard, the Ardite family; Naaman, the Naamite family. These were the Benjamite fami- 41 lies; the number in their detailed list was forty-five thousand six hundred.

Danites, by their families: Shu- 42 ham, the Shuhamite family. These were the families of Dan by their families; the number in their detail- 43 ed list of the Shuhamite family was sixty-four thousand four hundred.

Asherites, by their families: Im- 44 na, the Imnite family; Ishvi, the Ishvite family; Beriah, the Beriite family. Beriite families: Heber, the 45 Heberite family; Malchiel, the Malchielite family. The daughter 46 of Asher was named Serah. These 47 were the Asherite families; the number in their detailed list was fifty-three thousand four hundred.

Naphtalites, by their families: 48 Jahzeel, the Jahzeelite family; Guni, the Gunite family; Jezer, 49 the Jezerite family; Shillem, the Shillemite family. These were the 50 Naphtalite families by their families; the number in their detailed list was forty-five thousand four hundred.

The total in the Israelite lists 51 was six hundred and one thousand seven hundred and thirty.

The LORD spoke to Moses and 52 said, 'The land shall be apportion- 53 ed among these tribes according to the number of names recorded. To 54 the larger group you shall give a larger property and to the smaller a smaller; a property shall be given to each in proportion to its size as shown in the detailed lists. The 55 land, however, shall be apportioned by lot; the lots shall be cast for the properties by families in the father's line. Properties shall be 56 apportioned by lot between the larger families and the smaller.'

The detailed lists of Levi, by 57 families: Gershon, the Gershonite family; Kohath, the Kohathite family; Merari, the Merarite family.

58 These were the families of Levi: the Libnite, Hebronite, Mahlite, Mushite, and Korahite families.

59 Kohath was the father of Amram: Amram's wife was named Jochebed daughter of Levi, born to him in Egypt. She bore to Amram Aaron, Moses, and their sister

60 Miriam. Aaron's sons were Nadab,

61 Abihu, Eleazar and Ithamar. Nadab and Abihu died because they presented illicit fire before the LORD.

62 In the detailed lists of Levi the number of males, aged one month and upwards, was twenty-three thousand. They were recorded separately from the other Israelites because no property was allotted to them among the Israelites.

63 These were the detailed lists prepared by Moses and Eleazar the priest when they numbered the Israelites in the lowlands of Moab by

64 the Jordan near Jericho. Among them there was not a single one of the Israelites whom Moses and Aaron the priest had recorded in

65 the wilderness of Sinai; for the LORD had said they should all die in the wilderness. None of them was still living except Caleb son of Jephunneh and Joshua son of Nun.

27 A claim was presented by the daughters of Zelophehad son of Hepher, son of Gilead, son of Machir, son of Manasseh, son of Joseph. Their names were Mahlah, Noah, Hoglah, Milcah and Tirzah.

2 They appeared at the entrance of the Tent of the Presence before Moses, Eleazar the priest, the chiefs, and all the community, and

3 spoke as follows: 'Our father died in the wilderness. He was not among the company of Korah which combined together against the LORD; he died for his own sin and

4 left no sons. Is it right that, because he had no son, our father's name should disappear from his

family? Give us our property on the same footing as our father's brothers.'

5 So Moses brought their case be-
6 fore the LORD, and the LORD spoke
7 to Moses and said, 'The claim of the daughters of Zelophehad is good. You must allow them to inherit on the same footing as their father's brothers. Let their father's patrimony pass to them.
8 Then say this to the Israelites: "When a man dies leaving no son, his patrimony shall pass to his
9 daughter. If he has no daughter, you shall give it to his brothers. If
10 he has no brothers, you shall give it to his father's brothers. If his
11 father had no brothers, then you shall give possession to the nearest survivor in his family, and he shall inherit. This shall be a legal precedent for the Israelites, as the LORD has commanded Moses."'

12 The LORD said to Moses, 'Go up this mountain, Mount Abarim, and look out over the land which I have
13 given to the Israelites. Then, when you have looked out over it, you shall be gathered to your father's
14 kin like your brother Aaron; for you and Aaron disobeyed my command when the community disputed with me in the wilderness of Zin: you did not uphold my holiness before them at the waters.' These were the waters of Meribah-by-Kadesh in the wilderness of Zin.

15, 16 Then Moses said, 'Let the LORD, the God of the spirits of all mankind, appoint a man over the com-
17 munity to go out and come in at their head, to lead them out and bring them home, so that the community of the LORD may not be like sheep without a shepherd.'
18 The LORD answered Moses, 'Take Joshua son of Nun, a man endowed with spirit; lay your hand on him
19 and set him before Eleazar the priest and all the community. Give him his commission in their pre-
20 sence, and delegate some of your

authority to him, so that all the community of the Israelites may 21 obey him. He must appear before Eleazar the priest, who will obtain a decision for him by consulting the Urim before the LORD; at his word they shall go out and shall come home, both Joshua and the whole community of the Israelites.'

22 Moses did as the LORD had commanded him. He took Joshua, presented him to Eleazar the priest 23 and the whole community, laid his hands on him and gave him his commission, as the LORD had instructed him.

28 THE LORD spoke to Moses and 2 said, Give this command to the Israelites: See that you present my offerings, the food for the food-offering of soothing odour, to me at the appointed time.

3 Tell them: This is the food-offering which you shall present to the LORD: the regular daily whole-offering of two yearling rams with- 4 out blemish. One you shall sacrifice in the morning and the second be- 5 tween dusk and dark. The grain-offering shall be a tenth of an ephah of flour mixed with a quarter of a hin of oil of pounded 6 olives. (This was the regular whole-offering made at Mount Sinai, a soothing odour, a food-offering to 7 the LORD.) The wine for the proper drink-offering shall be a quarter of a hin to each ram; you are to pour out this strong drink in the holy place as an offering to the LORD. 8 You shall sacrifice the second ram between dusk and dark, with the same grain-offering as at the morning sacrifice and with the proper drink-offering; it is a food-offering of soothing odour to the LORD.

9 For the sabbath day: two yearling rams without blemish, a grain-offering of two tenths of an ephah of flour mixed with oil, and the 10 proper drink-offering. This whole-offering, presented every sabbath, is in addition to the regular whole-offering and the proper drink-offering.

11 On the first day of every month you shall present a whole-offering to the LORD, consisting of two young bulls, one ram and seven yearling rams without blemish. 12 The grain-offering shall be three tenths of flour mixed with oil for each bull, two tenths of flour mixed with oil for the full-grown ram, and 13 one tenth of flour mixed with oil for each young ram. This is a whole-offering, a food-offering of soothing odour to the LORD. The proper 14 drink-offering shall be half a hin of wine for each bull, a third for the full-grown ram and a quarter for each young ram. This is the whole-offering to be made, month by month, throughout the year. Fur- 15 ther, one he-goat shall be sacrificed as a sin-offering to the LORD, in addition to the regular whole-offering and the proper drink-offering.

16 The Passover of the LORD shall be held on the fourteenth day of the first month, and on the fif- 17 teenth day there shall be a pilgrim-feast; for seven days you must eat only unleavened cakes. On the first 18 day there shall be a sacred assembly; you shall not do your daily work. As a food-offering, a whole- 19 offering to the LORD, you shall present two young bulls, one ram, and seven yearling rams, all without blemish. You shall offer the proper 20 grain-offerings of flour mixed with oil, three tenths for each bull, two tenths for the ram, and one tenth 21 for each of the seven young rams; and as a sin-offering, one he-goat to 22 make expiation for you. All these 23 you shall offer in addition to the morning whole-offering, which is the regular sacrifice. You shall re- 24 peat this daily till the seventh day, presenting food as a food-offering of soothing odour to the LORD, in addition to the regular whole-offering and the proper drink-

25 offering. On the seventh day there shall be a sacred assembly; you shall not do your daily work.

26 On the day of Firstfruits, when you bring to the LORD your grain-offering from the new crop at your Feast of Weeks, there shall be a sacred assembly; you shall not do

27 your daily work. You shall bring a whole-offering as a soothing odour to the LORD: two young bulls, one full-grown ram, and seven yearling

28 rams. The proper grain-offering shall be of flour mixed with oil, three tenths for each bull, two

29 tenths for the one ram, and a tenth for each of the seven young rams,

30 and there shall be one he-goat as a sin-offering to make expiation for

31 you; they shall all be without blemish. All these you shall offer in addition to the regular whole-offering with the proper grain-offering and drink-offering.

29 On the first day of the seventh month there shall be a sacred assembly; you shall not do your daily work. It shall be a day of acclama-

2 tion. You shall sacrifice a whole-offering as a soothing odour to the LORD: one young bull, one full-grown ram, and seven yearling

3 rams, without blemish. Their proper grain-offering shall be of flour mixed with oil, three tenths for the bull, two tenths for the one ram,

4 and one tenth for each of the seven

5 young rams, and there shall be one he-goat as a sin-offering to make

6 expiation for you. This is in addition to the monthly whole-offering and the regular whole-offering with their proper grain-offerings and drink-offerings according to custom; it is a food-offering of soothing odour to the LORD.

7 On the tenth day of this seventh month there shall be a sacred assembly, and you shall mortify yourselves; you shall not do any

8 work. You shall bring a whole-offering to the LORD as a soothing odour: one young bull, one full-grown ram, and seven yearling

rams; they shall all be without blemish. The proper grain-offering 9 shall be of flour mixed with oil, three tenths for the bull, two tenths for the one ram, and one 10 tenth for each of the seven young rams, and there shall be one he-goat 11 as a sin-offering, in addition to the expiatory sin-offering and the regular whole-offering, with the proper grain-offering and drink-offering.

On the fifteenth day of the sev- 12 enth month there shall be a sacred assembly. You shall not do your daily work, but shall keep a pil-grim-feast to the LORD for seven days. As a whole-offering, a food- 13 offering of soothing odour to the LORD, you shall bring thirteen young bulls, two full-grown rams, and fourteen yearling rams; they shall all be without blemish. The 14 proper grain-offering shall be of flour mixed with oil, three tenths for each of the thirteen bulls, two tenths for each of the two rams, and one tenth for each of the four- 15 teen young rams, and there shall 16 be one he-goat as a sin-offering, in addition to the regular whole-offering with the proper grain-offering and drink-offering.

On the second day: twelve young 17 bulls, two full-grown rams, and fourteen yearling rams, without blemish, together with the proper 18 grain-offerings and drink-offerings for bulls, full-grown rams, and young rams, as prescribed according to their number, and there 19 shall be one he-goat as a sin-offering, in addition to the regular whole-offering with the proper grain-offering and drink-offering.

On the third day: eleven bulls, 20 two full-grown rams, and fourteen yearling rams, without blemish, to- 21 gether with the proper grain-offerings and drink-offerings for bulls, full-grown rams, and young rams, as prescribed according to their number, and there shall be one 22 he-goat as a sin-offering, in addition to the regular whole-offering, with the proper grain-offering and drink-offering.

23 On the fourth day: ten bulls, two full-grown rams, and fourteen 24 yearling rams, without blemish, together with the proper grain-offerings and drink-offerings for bulls, full-grown rams, and young rams, as prescribed according to their 25 number, and there shall be one he-goat as a sin-offering, in addition to the regular whole-offering with the proper grain-offering and drink-offering.

26 On the fifth day: nine bulls, two full-grown rams, and fourteen yearling rams, without blemish, 27 together with the proper grain-offerings and drink-offerings for bulls, full-grown rams, and young rams, as prescribed according to 28 their number, and there shall be one he-goat as a sin-offering, in addition to the regular whole-offering with the proper grain-offering and drink-offering.

29 On the sixth day: eight bulls, two full-grown rams, and fourteen 30 yearling rams, without blemish, together with the proper grain-offerings and drink-offerings for bulls, full-grown rams, and young rams, as prescribed according to their 31 number, and there shall be one he-goat as a sin-offering, in addition to the regular whole-offering with the proper grain-offering and drink-offering.

32 On the seventh day: seven bulls, two full-grown rams, and fourteen 33 yearling rams, without blemish, together with the proper grain-offerings and drink-offerings for bulls, full-grown rams, and young rams, as prescribed according to their 34 number, and there shall be one he-goat as a sin-offering, in addition to the regular whole-offering with the proper grain-offering and drink-offering.

35 The eighth day you shall keep as a closing ceremony; you shall not 36 do your daily work. As a whole-offering, a food-offering of soothing odour to the LORD, you shall bring one bull, one full-grown ram, and seven yearling rams, without blemish, together with the proper 37 grain-offerings and drink-offerings for bulls, full-grown rams, and young rams, as prescribed according to their number, and there 38 shall be one he-goat as a sin-offering, in addition to the regular whole-offering with the proper grain-offering and drink-offering.

39 These are the sacrifices which you shall offer to the LORD at the appointed seasons, in addition to the votive offerings, the freewill offerings, the whole-offerings, the grain-offerings, the drink-offerings, and the shared-offerings.

40 Moses told the Israelites exactly what the LORD had commanded him.

30 THEN Moses spoke to the heads of the Israelite tribes and said, This is the LORD's command: When a man 2 makes a vow to the LORD or swears an oath and so puts himself under a binding obligation, he must not break his word. Every word he has spoken, he must make good. When 3 a woman, still young and living in her father's house, makes a vow to the LORD or puts herself under a binding obligation, if her father 4 hears of it and keeps silence, then any such vow or obligation shall be valid. But if her father disallows it 5 when he hears of it, none of her vows or obligations shall be valid; the LORD will absolve her, because her father has disallowed it. If the 6 woman is married when she is under a vow or a binding obligation rashly uttered, then if her hus- 7 band hears of it and keeps silence when he hears, her vow or obligation by which she has bound herself shall be valid. If, however, her 8 husband disallows it when he hears of it and repudiates the vow which she has taken upon herself or the rash utterance with which she has bound herself, then the LORD will

9 absolve her. Every vow by which a widow or a divorced woman has
10 bound herself shall be valid. But if it is in her husband's house that a woman makes a vow or puts herself under a binding obligation by
11 an oath, and her husband, hearing of it, keeps silence and does not disallow it, then every vow and obligation under which she has put
12 herself shall be valid; but if her husband clearly repudiates them when he hears of them, then nothing that she has uttered, whether vow or obligation, shall be valid. Her husband has repudiated them, and the LORD will absolve her.
13 The husband can confirm or repudiate any vow or oath by which a woman binds herself to mortifi-
14 cation. If he maintains silence day after day, he thereby confirms every vow or obligation under which she has put herself: he confirms them, because he kept silence
15 at the time when he heard them. If he repudiates them some time after he has heard them, he shall be responsible for her default.
16 Such are the decrees which the LORD gave to Moses concerning a husband and his wife and a father and his daughter, still young and living in her father's house.

31 THE LORD spoke to Moses and
2 said, 'You are to exact vengeance for Israel on the Midianites and then you will be gathered to your father's kin.'
3 Then Moses spoke to the people in these words: 'Let some men among you be drafted for active service. They shall fall upon Midian and exact vengeance in the
4 LORD's name. You shall send out a thousand men from each of the
5 tribes of Israel.' So the men were called up from the clans of Israel, a thousand from each tribe, twelve thousand in all, drafted for active
6 service. Moses sent out this force, a thousand from each tribe, with Phinehas son of Eleazar the priest,

who was in charge of the holy vessels and of the trumpets to give the signal for the battle-cry. They 7 made war on Midian as the LORD had commanded Moses, and slew all the men. In addition to those 8 slain in battle they killed the kings of Midian – Evi, Rekem, Zur, Hur, and Reba, the five kings of Midian – and they put to death also Balaam son of Beor. The Israelites 9 took captive the Midianite women and their dependants, and carried off all their beasts, their flocks, and their property. They burnt all 10 their cities, in which they had settled, and all their encampments. They took all the spoil and plun- 11 der, both man and beast, and 12 brought them – captives, plunder, and spoil – to Moses and Eleazar the priest and to all the community of the Israelites, to the camp in the lowlands of Moab by the Jordan at Jericho.

Moses and Eleazar the priest and 13 all the leaders of the community went to meet them outside the camp. Moses spoke angrily to the 14 officers of the army, the commanders of units of a thousand and of a hundred, who were returning from the campaign: 'Have you spared 15 all the women?' he said. 'Remem- 16 ber, it was they who, on Balaam's departure, set about seducing the Israelites into disloyalty to the LORD that day at Peor, so that the plague struck the community of the LORD. Now kill every male de- 17 pendant, and kill every woman who has had intercourse with a man, but spare for yourselves 18 every woman among them who has not had intercourse. You 19 yourselves, every one of you who has taken life and every one who has touched the dead, must remain outside the camp for seven days. Purify yourselves and your captives on the third day and on the seventh day, and purify also every 20 piece of clothing, every article made of skin, everything woven of goat's hair, and everything made of wood.'

21 Eleazar the priest said to the soldiers returning from battle, 'This is a law and statute which the LORD has ordained through
2–23 Moses. Anything which will stand fire, whether gold, silver, copper, iron, tin, or lead, you shall pass through fire and then it will be clean. Other things shall be purified by the water of ritual purification; whatever cannot stand fire shall be passed through the water.
24 On the seventh day you shall wash your clothes, and then be clean; after this you may re-enter the camp.'

25 The LORD spoke to Moses and
26 said, 'Count all that has been captured, man or beast, you and Eleazar the priest and the heads of fam-
27 ilies in the community, and divide it equally between the fighting men who went on the campaign
28 and the whole community. You shall levy a tax for the LORD: from the combatants it shall be one out of every five hundred, whether
29 men, cattle, asses, or sheep, to be taken out of their share and given to Eleazar the priest as a contribu-
30 tion for the LORD. Out of the share of the Israelites it shall be one out of every fifty taken, whether man or beast, cattle, asses, or sheep, to be given to the Levites who are in charge of the LORD's Tabernacle.'

31 Moses and Eleazar the priest did as the LORD had commanded Mo-
32 ses. These were the spoils, over and above the plunder taken by the fighting men: six hundred and
33 seventy-five thousand sheep, sev-
34 enty-two thousand cattle, sixty-
35 one thousand asses; and of persons, thirty-two thousand girls who had had no intercourse with a man.

36 The half-share of those who took part in the campaign was thus three hundred and thirty-seven
37 thousand five hundred sheep, the tax for the LORD from these being six hundred and seventy-five;

38 thirty-six thousand cattle, the tax
39 being seventy-two; thirty thousand five hundred asses, the tax
40 being sixty-one; and sixteen thousand persons, the tax being thirty-
41 two. Moses gave Eleazar the priest the tax levied for the LORD, as the LORD had commanded him.

42–43 The share of the community, being the half-share for the Israelites which Moses divided off from that of the combatants, was three hundred and thirty-seven thou-
44 sand five hundred sheep, thirty-six
45 thousand cattle, thirty thousand
46 five hundred asses, and sixteen
47 thousand persons. Moses took one out of every fifty, whether man or beast, from the half-share of the Israelites, and gave it to the Levites who were in charge of the LORD's Tabernacle, as the LORD had commanded him.

48 Then the officers who had commanded the forces on the campaign, the commanders of units of a thousand and of a hundred, came
49 to Moses and said to him, 'Sir, we have checked the roll of the fighting men who were under our command, and not one of them is miss-
50 ing. So we have brought the gold ornaments, the armlets, bracelets, finger-rings, earrings, and pendants that each man has found, to offer them before the LORD as a ransom for our lives.'

51 Moses and Eleazar the priest received this gold from the commanders of units of a thousand and of a hundred, all of it craftsman's
52 work, and the gold thus levied as a contribution to the LORD weighed sixteen thousand seven hundred
53 and fifty shekels; for every man in the army had taken plunder. So
54 Moses and Eleazar the priest received the gold from the commanders of units of a thousand and of a hundred, and brought it to the Tent of the Presence that the LORD might remember Israel.

32 Now the Reubenites and the Gadites had large and very numer-

ous flocks, and when they saw that the land of Jazer and Gilead was 2 good grazing country, they came and said to Moses and Eleazar the priest and to the leaders of the 3 community, 'Ataroth, Dibon, Jazer, Nimrah, Heshbon, Elealeh, 4 Sebam, Nebo, and Beon, the region which the LORD has subdued before the advance of the Israelite community, is grazing country, and our flocks are our livelihood. 5 If', they said, 'we have found favour with you, sir, then let this country be given to us as our possession, and do not make us cross 6 the Jordan.' Moses replied to the Gadites and the Reubenites, 'Are your kinsmen to go into battle 7 while you stay here? How dare you discourage the Israelites from crossing over to the land which the 8 LORD has given them? This is what your fathers did when I sent them out from Kadesh-barnea to view 9 the land. They went up as far as the gorge of Eshcol and viewed the land, and on their return so discouraged the Israelites that they would not enter the land which the 10 LORD had given them. The LORD became angry that day, and he 11 solemnly swore: "Because they have not followed me with their whole heart, none of the men who came out of Egypt, from twenty years old and upwards, shall see the land which I promised on oath to 12 Abraham, Isaac and Jacob." This meant all except Caleb son of Jephunneh the Kenizzite and Joshua son of Nun, who followed the 13 LORD with their whole heart. The LORD became angry with Israel, and he made them wander in the wilderness for forty years until that whole generation was dead which had done what was wrong in 14 his eyes. And now you are following in your fathers' footsteps, a fresh brood of sinful men to fire the LORD's anger once more against 15 Israel; for if you refuse to follow him, he will again abandon this whole people in the wilderness and you will be the cause of their destruction.'

Presently they came forward 16 with this offer: 'We will build folds for our sheep here and towns for our dependants. Then we can be 17 drafted as a fighting force to go at the head of the Israelites until we have brought them to the lands that will be theirs. Meanwhile our dependants can live in the walled towns, safe from the people of the country. We will not return until 18 every Israelite is settled in possession of his patrimony; we will 19 claim no share of the land with them over the Jordan and beyond, because our patrimony has already been allotted to us east of the Jordan.' Moses answered, 'If you 20 stand by your promise, if in the presence of the LORD you are drafted for battle, and the whole 21 draft crosses the Jordan in front of the LORD and remains there until the LORD has driven out his enemies, and the land falls before him, 22 then you may come back and be quit of your obligation to the LORD and to Israel; and this land shall be your possession in the sight of the LORD. But I warn you, 23 if you fail to do all this, you will have sinned against the LORD, and your sin will find you out. So build 24 towns for your dependants and folds for your sheep; but carry out your promise.'

The Gadites and Reubenites 25 answered Moses, 'Sir, we are your servants and will do as you command. Our dependants and wives, 26 our flocks and all our beasts shall remain here in the cities of Gilead; but we, all who have been drafted 27 for active service with the LORD, will cross the river and fight, according to your command.'

Accordingly Moses gave these 28 instructions to Eleazar the priest and Joshua son of Nun and to the heads of the families in the Israelite tribes: 'If the Gadites and 29

Reubenites, all who have been drafted for battle before the LORD, cross the Jordan with you, and if the land falls into your hands, then you shall give them Gilead for 30 their possession. But if, thus drafted, they fail to cross with you, then they shall acquire land alongside 31 you in Canaan.' The Gadites and Reubenites said in response, 'Sir, the LORD has spoken, and we will 32 obey. Once we have been drafted, we will cross over before the LORD into Canaan; then we shall have our patrimony here beyond the Jordan.'

33   So to the Gadites, the Reubenites, and half the tribe of Manasseh son of Joseph, Moses gave the kingdoms of Sihon king of the Amorites and Og king of Bashan, the whole land with its towns and 34 the country round them. The Gadites built Dibon, Ataroth, Aroer, 35 Atroth-shophan, Jazer, Jogbehah, 36 Beth-nimrah, and Beth-haran, all of them walled towns with folds 37 for their sheep. The Reubenites built Heshbon, Elealeh, Kiriath- 38 aim, Nebo, Baal-meon (whose name was changed), and Sibmah; these were the names they gave to 39 the towns they built. The sons of Machir son of Manasseh invaded Gilead, took it and drove out the 40 Amorite inhabitants; Moses then assigned Gilead to Machir son of Manasseh, and he made his home 41 there. Jair son of Manasseh attacked and took the tent-villages of Ham[a] and called them Havvoth- 42 jair.[b] Nobah attacked and took Kenath and its villages and gave it his own name, Nobah.

33 THESE are the stages in the journey of the Israelites, when they were led by Moses and Aaron in their tribal hosts out of Egypt. 2 Moses recorded their starting-points stage by stage as the LORD commanded him. These are their stages from one starting-point to the next:

The Israelites left Rameses on 3 the fifteenth day of the first month, the day after the Passover; they marched out defiantly in full view of all the Egyptians, while the 4 Egyptians were burying all the first-born struck down by the LORD as a judgement on their gods.

The Israelites left Rameses and 5 encamped at Succoth.

They left Succoth and encamped 6 at Etham on the edge of the wilderness.

They left Etham, turned back 7 near Pi-hahiroth[c] on the east of Baal-zephon, and encamped before Migdol.

They left Pi-hahiroth, passed 8 through the Sea into the wilderness, marched for three days through the wilderness of Etham, and encamped at Marah.

They left Marah and came to 9 Elim, where there were twelve springs of water and seventy palm-trees, and encamped there.

They left Elim and encamped by 10 the Red Sea.

They left the Red Sea and en- 11 camped in the wilderness of Sin.

They left the wilderness of Sin 12 and encamped at Dophkah.

They left Dophkah and encamp- 13 ed at Alush.

They left Alush and encamped 14 at Rephidim, where there was no water for the people to drink.

They left Rephidim and en- 15 camped in the wilderness of Sinai.

They left the wilderness of Sinai 16 and encamped at Kibroth-hattaavah.

They left Kibroth-hattaavah 17 and encamped at Hazeroth.

They left Hazeroth and en- 18 camped at Rithmah.

They left Rithmah and encamp- 19 ed at Rimmon-parez.

They left Rimmon-parez and en- 20 camped at Libnah.

[a] *Prob. rdg.; Heb.* their tent-villages.
[c] *See Exod.* 14. 2.

[b] *That is* Tent-villages of Jair.

21 They left Libnah and encamped at Rissah.

22 They left Rissah and encamped at Kehelathah.

23 They left Kehelathah and encamped at Mount Shapher.

24 They left Mount Shapher and encamped at Haradah.

25 They left Haradah and encamped at Makheloth.

26 They left Makheloth and encamped at Tahath.

27 They left Tahath and encamped at Tarah.

28 They left Tarah and encamped at Mithcah.

29 They left Mithcah and encamped at Hashmonah.

30 They left Hashmonah and encamped at Moseroth.

31 They left Moseroth and encamped at Bene-jaakan.

32 They left Bene-jaakan and encamped at Hor-haggidgad.

33 They left Hor-haggidgad and encamped at Jotbathah.

34 They left Jotbathah and encamped at Ebronah.[a]

35 They left Ebronah and encamped at Ezion-geber.

36 They left Ezion-geber and encamped in the wilderness of Zin, that is of Kadesh.

37 They left Kadesh and encamped on Mount Hor on the frontier of Edom.

38 Aaron the priest went up Mount Hor at the command of the LORD and there he died, on the first day of the fifth month in the fortieth year after the Israelites came out of Egypt; he was a hundred and twenty-three years old when he died there.

40 The Canaanite king of Arad, who lived in the Canaanite Negeb, heard that the Israelites were coming.

41 They left Mount Hor and encamped at Zalmonah.

42 They left Zalmonah and encamped at Punon.

43 They left Punon and encamped at Oboth.

44 They left Oboth and encamped at Iye-abarim on the frontier of Moab.

45 They left Iyim and encamped at Dibon-gad.

46 They left Dibon-gad and encamped at Almon-diblath-aim.

47 They left Almon-diblathaim and encamped in the mountains of A-barim east of Nebo.

48 They left the mountains of A-barim and encamped in the lowlands of Moab by the Jordan near Jericho. 49 Their camp beside the Jordan extended from Beth-jeshimoth to Abel-shittim in the lowlands of Moab. 50 In the lowlands of Moab by the Jordan near Jericho the LORD spoke to Moses and said, 51 Speak to the Israelites in these words: You will soon be crossing the Jordan to enter Canaan. 52 You must drive out all its inhabitants as you advance, destroy all their carved figures and their images of cast metal, and lay their hill-shrines in ruins. 53 You must take possession of the land and settle there, for to you I have given the land to occupy. 54 You must divide it by lot among your families, each taking its own territory, the large family a large territory and the small family a small. It shall be assigned to them according to the fall of the lot, each tribe and family taking its own territory. 55 If you do not drive out the inhabitants of the land as you advance, any whom you leave in possession will become like a barbed hook in your eye and a thorn in your side. They shall continually dispute your possession of the land, and what I meant to do to 56 them I will do to you.

34 The LORD spoke to Moses and 2 said, Give these instructions to the Israelites: Soon you will be entering Canaan. This is the land assigned to you as a perpetual patrimony, the land of Canaan thus defined by its frontiers. Your southern border 3

---

[a] Or Abronah.

shall start from the wilderness of Zin, where it marches with Edom, and run southwards from the end of the Dead Sea on its eastern side.
4 It shall then turn from the south up the ascent of Akrabbim and pass by Zin, and its southern limit shall be Kadesh-barnea. It shall proceed
5 by Hazar-addar to Azmon and from Azmon turn towards the Torrent of Egypt, and its limit shall be
6 the sea. Your western frontier shall be the Great Sea and the seaboard; this shall be your frontier to the
7 west. This shall be your northern frontier: you shall draw a line from
8 the Great Sea to Mount Hor and from Mount Hor to Lebo-hamath, and the limit of the frontier shall
9 be Zedad. From there it shall run to Ziphron, and its limit shall be Hazar-enan; this shall be your
10 frontier to the north. To the east you shall draw a line from Hazar-
11 enan to Shepham; it shall run down from Shepham to Riblah east of Ain, continuing until it strikes the ridge east of the sea of Kinnereth.
12 The frontier shall then run down to the Jordan and its limit shall be the Dead Sea. The land defined by these frontiers shall be your land.
13 Moses gave these instructions to the Israelites: This is the land which you shall assign by lot, each taking your own territory; it is the land which the LORD has ordered to be given to nine tribes and a half
14 tribe. For the Reubenites, the Gadites, and the half tribe of Manasseh have already occupied their terri-
15 tories, family by family. These two and a half tribes have received their territory here beyond the Jordan, east of Jericho, towards the sunrise.
16 The LORD spoke to Moses and
17 said, These are the men who shall assign the land for you: Eleazar the priest and Joshua son of Nun.
18 You shall also take one chief from each tribe to assign the land.
19 These are their names:

from the tribe of Judah: Caleb son of Jephunneh;
from the tribe of Simeon: Samuel 20 son of Ammihud;
from the tribe of Benjamin: Elidad 21 son of Kislon;
from the tribe of Dan: the chief 22 Bukki son of Jogli;
from the Josephites: from Manas- 23 seh, the chief Hanniel son of Ephod; and from Ephraim, the 24 chief Kemuel son of Shiphtan;
from Zebulun: the chief Elizaphan 25 son of Parnach;
from Issachar: the chief Paltiel son 26 of Azzan;
from Asher: the chief Ahihud son 27 of Shelomi;
from Naphtali: the chief Pedahel 28 son of Ammihud.

These were the men whom the 29 LORD appointed to assign the territories in the land of Canaan.

THE LORD spoke to Moses in the 35 lowlands of Moab by the Jordan near Jericho and said: Tell the Israelites to set aside towns in their patrimony as homes for the Levites, and give them also the common land surrounding the towns. They shall live in the towns, and 3 keep their beasts, their herds, and all their livestock on the common land. The land of the towns which 4 you give the Levites shall extend from the centre of the town outwards for a thousand cubits in each direction. Starting from the town 5 the eastern boundary shall measure two thousand cubits, the southern two thousand, the western two thousand, and the northern two thousand, with the town in the centre. They shall have this as the common land adjoining their towns.

When you give the Levites their 6 towns, six of them shall be cities of refuge, in which the homicide may take sanctuary; and you shall give them forty-two other towns. The 7 total number of towns to be given

to the Levites, each with its com-
8 mon land, is forty-eight. When you
set aside these towns out of the
territory of the Israelites, you shall
allot more from the larger tribe and
less from the smaller; each tribe
shall give towns to the Levites in
proportion to the patrimony assigned to it.

9 The LORD spoke to Moses and
10 said, Speak to the Israelites in
these words: You are crossing the
11 Jordan to the land of Canaan. You
shall designate certain cities to be
places of refuge, in which the homicide who has killed a man by acci-
12 dent may take sanctuary. These
cities shall be places of refuge from
the vengeance of the dead man's
next-of-kin, so that the homicide
shall not be put to death without
standing his trial before the com-
13 munity. The cities appointed as
places of refuge shall be six in
14 number, three east of the Jordan
15 and three in Canaan. These six
cities shall be places of refuge, so
that any man who has taken life
inadvertently, whether he be Israelite, resident alien, or temporary settler, may take sanctuary in
one of them.

16 If the man strikes his victim
with anything made of iron and he
dies, then he is a murderer: the
17 murderer must be put to death. If
a man has a stone in his hand capable of causing death and strikes
another man and he dies, he is a
murderer: the murderer must be
18 put to death. If a man has a wood-
en thing in his hand capable of
causing death, and strikes another
man and he dies, he is a murderer:
the murderer must be put to death.
19 The dead man's next-of-kin shall
put the murderer to death; he shall
put him to death because he had
20 attacked his victim. If the homicide sets upon a man openly of
malice aforethought or aims a missile at him of set purpose and he
21 dies, or if in enmity he falls upon
him with his bare hands and he

dies, then the assailant must be
put to death; he is a murderer. His
next-of-kin shall put the murderer
to death because he had attacked
his victim.

If he attacks a man on the spur 22
of the moment, not being his enemy, or hurls a missile at him not of
set purpose, or if without looking 23
he throws a stone capable of causing death and it hits a man, then if
the man dies, provided he was not
the man's enemy and was not
harming him of set purpose, the 24
community shall judge between
the striker and the next-of-kin according to these rules. The com- 25
munity shall protect the homicide
from the vengeance of the kinsman
and take him back to the city of
refuge where he had taken sanctuary. He must stay there till the
death of the duly anointed high
priest. If the homicide ever goes 26
beyond the boundaries of the city
where he has taken sanctuary, and 27
the next-of-kin finds him outside
and kills him, then the next-of-kin
shall not be guilty of murder. The 28
homicide must remain in the city
of refuge till the death of the high
priest; after the death of the high
priest he may go back to his property. These shall be legal prece- 29
dents for you for all time wherever
you live.

The homicide shall be put to 30
death as a murderer only on the
testimony of witnesses; the testimony of a single witness shall not
be enough to bring him to his
death. You shall not accept pay- 31
ment for the life of a homicide
guilty of a capital offence; he must
be put to death. You shall not 32
accept a payment from a man who
has taken sanctuary in a city of
refuge, allowing him to go back before the death of the high priest
and live at large. You shall not de- 33
file your land by bloodshed. Blood
defiles the land, and expiation cannot be made on behalf of the land
for blood shed on it except by the

34 blood of the man that shed it. You shall not make the land which you inhabit unclean, the land in which I dwell; for I, the LORD, dwell among the Israelites.

36 THE heads of the fathers' families of Gilead son of Machir, son of Manasseh, one of the families of the sons of Joseph, approached Moses and the chiefs, heads of families in Israel, and addressed them.
2 'Sir,' they said, 'the LORD commanded you to distribute the land by lot to the Israelites, and you were also commanded to give the patrimony of our brother Zelophe-
3 had to his daughters. Now if any of them shall be married to a husband from another Israelite tribe, her patrimony will be lost to the patrimony of our fathers and be added to that of the tribe into which she is married, and so part of our allot-
4 ted patrimony will be lost. Then, when the jubilee year comes round in Israel, her patrimony would be added to the patrimony of the tribe into which she is married, and it would be permanently lost to the patrimony of our fathers' tribe.'
5 So Moses, instructed by the LORD, gave the Israelites this ruling: 'The tribe of the sons of

Joseph is right. This is the LORD's 6 command for the daughters of Zelophehad: They may marry whom they please, but only within a family of their father's tribe. No patri- 7 mony in Israel shall pass from tribe to tribe, but every Israelite shall retain his father's patrimony. Any woman of an Israelite tribe 8 who is an heiress may marry a man from any family in her father's tribe. Thus the Israelites shall retain each one the patrimony of his forefathers. No patrimony shall 9 pass from one tribe to another, but every tribe in Israel shall retain its own patrimony.'

The daughters of Zelophehad ac- 10 ted in accordance with the LORD's command to Moses; Mahlah, Tir- 11 zah, Hoglah, Milcah and Noah, the daughters of Zelophehad, married sons of their father's brothers. They 12 married within the families of the sons of Manasseh son of Joseph, and their patrimony remained with the tribe of their father's family.

These are the commandments 13 and the decrees which the LORD issued to the Israelites through Moses in the lowlands of Moab by the Jordan near Jericho.

DEUTERONOMY

Primary charge of Moses to the people

1 THESE are the words that Moses spoke to all Israel in Transjordan, in the wilderness, that is to say in the Arabah opposite Suph, between Paran on the one side and Tophel, Laban, Hazeroth, and Dizahab on the
2 other. (The journey from Horeb through the hill-country of Seir

to Kadesh-barnea takes eleven days.)

On the first day of the eleventh 3–4 month of the fortieth year, after the defeat of Sihon king of the Amorites who ruled in Heshbon, and the defeat at Edrei of Og king of Bashan who ruled in Ashtaroth, Moses repeated to the Israelites all the commands that the LORD had given him for them. It was in 5 Transjordan, in Moab, that Moses

resolved to promulgate this law.
6 These were his words: The LORD
our God spoke to us at Horeb and
said, 'You have stayed on this
7 mountain long enough; go now,
make for the hill-country of the
Amorites, and pass on to all their
neighbours in the Arabah, in the
hill-country, in the Shephelah, in
the Negeb, and on the coast, in
short, all Canaan and the Lebanon
as far as the great river, the Eu-
8 phrates. I have laid the land open
before you; go in and occupy it, the
land which the LORD swore to give
to your forefathers Abraham, Isaac
and Jacob, and to their descendants after them.'

9 At that time I said to you, 'You
are a burden too heavy for me to
10 carry unaided. The LORD your God
has increased you so that today
you are as numerous as the stars in
11 the sky. May the LORD the God of
your fathers increase your number
a thousand times and may he bless
12 you as he promised. How can I
bear unaided the heavy burden
you are to me, and put up with
13 your complaints? Choose men of
wisdom, understanding, and repute for each of your tribes, and I
will set them in authority over
14 you.' Your answer was, 'What you
15 have told us to do is right.' So I
took men of wisdom and repute
and set them in authority over
you, some as commanders over
units of a thousand, of a hundred,
of fifty or of ten, and others as
officers, for each of your tribes.
16 And at that time I gave your judges
this command: 'You are to hear
the cases that arise among your
kinsmen and judge fairly between
man and man, whether fellow-
17 countryman or resident alien. You
must be impartial and listen to
high and low alike: have no fear of
man, for judgement belongs to
God. If any case is too difficult
for you, bring it before me and
18 I will hear it.' At the same time

I instructed you in all these
duties.

Then we set out from Horeb, in 19
obedience to the orders of the LORD
our God, and marched through that
vast and terrible wilderness, as you
found it to be, on the way to the
hill-country of the Amorites; and
so we came to Kadesh-barnea.
Then I said to you, 'You have 20
reached the hill-country of the A-
morites which the LORD our God is
giving us. The LORD your God has 21
indeed now laid the land open before you. Go forward and occupy it
in fulfilment of the promise which
the LORD the God of your fathers
made you; do not be discouraged
or afraid.' But you all came to me 22
and said, 'Let us send men ahead
to spy out the country and report
back to us about the route we
should take and the cities we shall
find.' I approved this plan and 23
picked twelve of you, one from
each tribe. They set out and made 24
their way up into the hill-country
as far as the gorge of Eshcol, which
they explored. They took samples 25
of the fruit of the country and
brought them back to us, and made
their report: 'It is a rich land that
the LORD our God is giving us.'

But you refused to go up and re- 26
belled against the command of the
LORD your God. You muttered 27
treason in your tents and said, 'It
was because the LORD hated us
that he brought us out of Egypt to
hand us over to the Amorites to be
wiped out. What shall we find up 28
there? Our kinsmen have discouraged us by their report of a
people bigger and taller than we
are, and of great cities with fortifications towering to the sky. And
they told us they saw there the
descendants of the Anakim.'[a]
Then I said to you, 'You must 29
not dread them nor be afraid of
them. The LORD your God who 30
goes at your head will fight for you
and he will do again what you saw

[a] the descendants... Anakim: *or* the tall men.

Moses' primary charge

31 him do for you in Egypt and in the wilderness. You saw there how the LORD your God carried you all the way to this place, as a father car- 32 ries his son.' In spite of this you did 33 not trust the LORD your God, who went ahead on the journey to find a place for your camp. He went in fire by night to show you the way you should take, and in a cloud by day.

34 When the LORD heard your complaints, he was indignant and 35 solemnly swore: 'Not one of these men, this wicked generation, shall see the rich land which I swore to 36 give your forefathers, except Caleb son of Jephunneh. He shall see it, and to him and his descendants I will give the land on which he has set foot, because he followed the 37 LORD with his whole heart.' On your account the LORD was angry with me also and said, 'You your- 38 self shall never enter it, but Joshua son of Nun, who is in attendance on you, shall enter it. Encourage him, for he shall put Israel in pos- 39 session of that land. Your dependants who, you thought, would become spoils of war, and your children who do not yet know good and evil, they shall enter; I will give it to them, and they shall 40 occupy it. You must turn back and set out for the wilderness by way of the Red Sea.'*a*

41 You answered me, 'We have sinned against the LORD; we will now go up and attack just as the LORD our God commanded us.' And each of you fastened on his weapons, thinking it an easy thing 42 to invade the hill-country. But the LORD said to me, 'Tell them not to go up and not to fight; for I will not be with them, and their enemies 43 will defeat them.' And I told you this, but you did not listen; you rebelled against the LORD's command and defiantly went up to the 44 hill-country. The Amorites living in the hills came out against you

and like bees they chased you; they crushed you at Hormah in Seir. Then you came back and wept be- 45 fore the LORD, but he would not hear you or listen to you. That is 46 why you remained in Kadesh as long as you did.

So we turned and set out for the 2 wilderness by way of the Red Sea as the LORD had told me we must do, and we spent many days marching round the hill-country of Seir. Then the LORD said to me, 2 'You have been long enough march- 3 ing round these hills; turn towards the north. And give the people this 4 charge: "You are about to go through the territory of your kinsmen the descendants of Esau who live in Seir. Although they are afraid of you, be on your guard and 5 do not provoke them; for I shall not give you any of their land, not so much as a foot's-breadth: I have given the hill-country of Seir to Esau as a possession. You may 6 purchase food from them for silver, and eat it, and you may buy*b* water to drink."' The LORD your 7 God has blessed you in everything you have undertaken; he has watched your journey through this great wilderness; these forty years the LORD your God has been with you and you have gone short of nothing. So we went on past our 8 kinsmen, the descendants of Esau who live in Seir, and along the road of the Arabah which comes from Elath and Ezion-geber, and we turned and followed the road to the wilderness of Moab. There the 9 LORD said to me, 'Do not harass the Moabites nor provoke them to battle, for I will not give you any of their land as a possession. I have given Ar to the descendants of Lot as a possession.' (The Emim once 10 lived there – a great and numerous people, as tall as the Anakim. The 11 Rephaim also were reckoned as Anakim; but the Moabites called them Emim. The Horites lived in 12

a Or the Sea of Reeds. *b* Or dig for.

Seir at one time, but the descendants of Esau occupied their territory: they destroyed them as they advanced and then settled in the land instead of them, just as Israel did in their own territory which 13 the LORD gave them.) 'Come now, cross the gorge of the Zared.' So we 14 went across. The journey from Kadesh-barnea to the crossing of the Zared took us thirty-eight years, until the whole generation of fighting men had passed away as the LORD had sworn that they 15 would. The LORD's hand was raised against them, and he rooted them out of the camp to the last man.

16 When the last of the fighting men among the people had died, 17, 18 the LORD spoke to me, 'Today', he said, 'you are to cross by Ar*a* which 19 lies on the frontier of Moab, and when you reach the territory of the Ammonites, you must not harass them or provoke them to battle, for I will not give you any Ammonite land as a possession; I have assigned 20 it to the descendants of Lot.' (This also is reckoned as the territory of the Rephaim, who lived there at one time; but the Ammonites call-21 ed them Zamzummim. They were a great and numerous people, as tall as the Anakim, but the LORD destroyed them as the Ammonites advanced and occupied their terri-22 tory instead of them, just as he had done for the descendants of Esau who lived in Seir. As they advanced, he destroyed the Horites so that they occupied their territory and took possession instead of 23 them: so it is to this day. It was Caphtorites from Caphtor who destroyed the Avvim who lived in the hamlets near Gaza, and settled in 24 the land instead of them.) 'Come, set out on your journey and cross the gorge of the Arnon, for I have put Sihon the Amorite, king of Heshbon, and his territory into your hands. Begin to occupy it and

provoke him to battle. Today I 25 will begin to put the fear and dread of you upon all the peoples under heaven; if they so much as hear a rumour of you, they will quake and tremble before you.'

Then I sent messengers from the 26 wilderness of Kedemoth to Sihon king of Heshbon with these peaceful overtures: 'Grant us passage 27 through your country by the highway: we will keep to the highway, trespassing neither to right nor to left, and we will pay you the full 28 price for the food we eat and the water we drink. The descendants 29 of Esau who live in Seir granted us passage, and so did the Moabites who live in Ar. We will simply pass through your land on foot, until we cross the Jordan to the land which the LORD our God is giving us.' But 30 Sihon king of Heshbon refused to grant us passage; for the LORD your God had made him stubborn and obstinate, in order that he and his land might become subject to you, as it still is. So the LORD said 31 to me, 'Come, I have begun to deliver Sihon and his territory into your hands. Begin now to occupy his land.' Then Sihon with all his 32 people came out to meet us in battle at Jahaz, and the LORD our 33 God delivered him into our hands; we killed him with his sons and all his people. We captured all 34 his cities at that time and put to death everyone in the cities, men, women, and dependants; we left no survivor. We took the cattle as 35 booty and plundered the cities we captured. From Aroer on the edge 36 of the gorge of the Arnon and the level land of the gorge, as far as Gilead, no city walls were too lofty for us; the LORD our God laid them all open to us. But you avoided the 37 territory of the Ammonites, both the parts along the gorge of the Jabbok and their cities in the hills, thus fulfilling all that the LORD our God had commanded.

a by Ar: *or* the gully.

3 Next we turned and advanced along the road to Bashan. Og king of Bashan, with all his people, **2** came out against us at Edrei. The LORD said to me, 'Do not be afraid of him, for I have delivered him into your hands, with all his people and his land. Deal with him as you dealt with Sihon the king of the Amorites who lived in Hesh- **3** bon.' So the LORD our God also delivered Og king of Bashan into our hands, with all his people. We slaughtered them and left no sur- **4** vivor, and at the same time we captured all his cities; there was not a single town that we did not take from them. In all we took sixty cities, the whole region of Ar- gob, the kingdom of Og in Bashan; **5** all these were fortified cities with high walls, gates, and bars, apart from a great many open settle- **6** ments. Thus we put to death all the men, women, and dependants in every city, as we did to Sihon king **7** of Heshbon. All the cattle and the spoil from the cities we took as booty for ourselves.

8 At that time we took from these two Amorite kings in Transjordan the territory that runs from the gorge of the Arnon to Mount Her- **9** mon (the mountain that the Sidon- ians call Sirion and the Amorites **10** Senir), all the cities of the table- land, and the whole of Gilead and Bashan as far as Salcah and Edrei, cities in the kingdom of Og in Ba- **11** shan. (Only Og king of Bashan remained as the sole survivor of the Rephaim. His sarcophagus of basalt[a] was nearly fourteen feet long and six feet wide, and it may still be seen in the Ammonite city of Rabbah.)

12 At that time, when we occupied this territory, I assigned to the Reubenites and Gadites the land beyond Aroer on the gorge of the Arnon and half the hill-country of Gilead with its towns. The rest of **13** Gilead and the whole of Bashan the kingdom of Og, all the region of Argob, I assigned to half the tribe of Manasseh. (All Bashan used to be called the land of the Rephaim. Jair son of Manasseh **14** took all the region of Argob as far as the Geshurite and Maacathite border. There are tent-villages in Bashan still called by his name, Havvoth-jair.[b]) To Machir I as- **15** signed Gilead, and to the Reuben- **16** ites and the Gadites I assigned land from Gilead to the gorge of the Arnon, that is to the middle of the gorge; and its territory ran[c d] to the gorge of the Jabbok, the Am- monite frontier, and included the **17** Arabah, with the Jordan and adja- cent land, from Kinnereth to the Sea of the Arabah, that is the Dead Sea, below the watershed of Pisgah on the east. At that time I **18** gave you this command: 'The LORD your God has given you this land to occupy; let all your fighting men be drafted and cross at the head of their fellow-Israelites. Only **19** your wives and dependants and your livestock – I know you have much livestock – shall stay in the towns I have given you. This you **20** shall do until the LORD gives your kinsmen security as he has given it to you, and until they too occupy the land which the LORD your God is giving them on the other side of the Jordan; then you may return to the possession which I have given you, every man to his own.'

At that time also I gave Joshua **21** this charge: 'You have seen with your own eyes all that the LORD your God has done to these two kings; he will do the same to all the kingdoms into which you will cross over. Do not be afraid of them, for **22** the LORD your God himself will fight for you.'

---

[a] *Or* iron.   [b] *That is* Tent-villages of Jair.
[c] that is...ran: *or* including the bed of the gorge and the adjacent strip of land...
[d] and its territory ran: *prob. rdg.*; *Heb.* and territory and...

23 At that same time I pleaded
24 with the LORD, 'O Lord GOD, thou
hast begun to show to thy servant
thy greatness and thy strong hand:
what god is there in heaven or on
earth who can match thy works
25 and mighty deeds? Let me cross
over and see that rich land which
lies beyond the Jordan, and the
fine hill-country and the Lebanon.'
26 But because of you the LORD
brushed me aside and would not
listen. 'Enough!' he answered. 'Say
27 no more about this. Go to the top
of Pisgah and look west and north,
south and east; look well at what
you see, for you shall not cross this
28 river Jordan. Give Joshua his commission, encourage him and strengthen him; for he will lead this people
across, and he will put them in possession of the land you see before
you.'
29 So we remained in the valley
opposite Beth-peor.

4 N o w, Israel, listen to the statutes
and laws which I am teaching you,
and obey them; then you will live,
and go in and occupy the land
which the LORD the God of your
2 fathers is giving you. You must not
add anything to my charge, nor
take anything away from it. You
must carry out all the commandments of the LORD your God which
I lay upon you.
3 You saw with your own eyes
what the LORD did at Baal-peor;
the LORD your God destroyed a-
mong you every man who went
4 over to the Baal of Peor, but you
who held fast to the LORD your
5 God are all alive today. I have
taught you statutes and laws, as
the LORD my God commanded me;
these you must duly keep when
you enter the land and occupy it.
6 You must observe them carefully,
and thereby you will display your
wisdom and understanding to other
peoples. When they hear about
these statutes, they will say, 'What

a wise and understanding people
this great nation is!' What great 7
nation has a god*a* close at hand as
the LORD our God is close to us
whenever we call to him? What 8
great nation is there whose statutes and laws are just, as is all this
law which I am setting before you
today? But take good care: be on 9
the watch not to forget the things
that you have seen with your own
eyes, and do not let them pass from
your minds as long as you live, but
teach them to your sons and to
your sons' sons. You must never 10
forget that day when you stood
before the LORD your God at Horeb, and the LORD said to me, 'Assemble the people before me; I will
make them hear my words and
they shall learn to fear me all their
lives on earth, and they shall teach
their sons to do so.' Then you came 11
near and stood at the foot of the
mountain. The mountain was a-
blaze with fire to the very skies:
there was darkness, cloud, and
thick mist. When the LORD spoke 12
to you from the fire you heard a
voice speaking, but you saw no
figure; there was only a voice. He 13
announced the terms of his covenant to you, bidding you observe
the Ten Words,*b* and he wrote
them on two tablets of stone. At 14
that time the LORD charged me to
teach you statutes and laws which
you should observe in the land into
which you are passing to occupy it.
On the day when the LORD spoke 15
to you out of the fire on Horeb, you
saw no figure of any kind; so take
good care not to fall into the de- 16
grading practice of making figures
carved in relief, in the form of a
man or a woman, or of any animal 17
on earth or bird that flies in the
air, or of any reptile on the ground 18
or fish in the waters under the
earth. Nor must you raise your 19
eyes to the heavens and look up to
the sun, the moon, and the stars,
all the host of heaven, and be led

---

a Or gods.   *b* Or Ten Commandments.

on to bow down to them and worship them; the LORD your God assigned these for the worship of[a] the various peoples under heaven. But
20 you are the people whom the LORD brought out of Egypt, from the smelting-furnace, and took for his own possession, as you are to this
21 day. The LORD was angry with me on your account and swore that I should not cross the Jordan nor enter the rich land which the LORD your God is giving you for your
22 possession. I shall die in this country; I shall not cross the Jordan, but you are about to cross and
23 occupy that rich land. Be careful not to forget the covenant which the LORD your God made with you, and do not make yourselves a carved figure of anything which the LORD your God has forbidden.
24 For the LORD your God is a devouring fire, a jealous god.
25 When you have children and grandchildren and grow old in the land, if you then fall into the degrading practice of making any kind of carved figure, doing what is wrong in the eyes of the LORD your
26 God and provoking him to anger, I summon heaven and earth to witness against you this day: you will soon vanish from the land which you are to occupy after crossing the Jordan. You will not live long
27 in it; you will be swept away. The LORD will disperse you among the peoples, and you will be left few in number among the nations to which the LORD will lead you.
28 There you will worship gods made by human hands out of wood and stone, gods that can neither see nor
29 hear, neither eat nor smell. But if from there you seek the LORD your God, you will find him, if indeed you search with all your heart and
30 soul. When you are in distress and all these things come upon you, you will in days to come turn back to the LORD your God and obey
31 him. The LORD your God is a merciful god; he will never fail you nor destroy you, nor will he forget the covenant guaranteed by oath with your forefathers.

Search into days gone by, long 32 before your time, beginning at the day when God created man on earth; search from one end of heaven to the other, and ask if any deed as mighty as this has been seen or heard. Did any people ever 33 hear the voice of God speaking out of the fire, as you heard it, and remain alive? Or did ever a god at- 34 tempt to come and take a nation for himself away from another nation, with a challenge, and with signs, portents, and wars, with a strong hand and an outstretched arm, and with great deeds of terror, as the LORD your God did for you in Egypt in the sight of you all? You have had sure proof that 35 the LORD is God; there is no other. From heaven he let you hear his 36 voice for your instruction, and on earth he let you see his great fire, and out of the fire you heard his words. Because he loved your fa- 37 thers and chose their children after them, he in his own person brought you out of Egypt by his great strength, so that he might drive 38 out before you nations greater and more powerful than you and bring you in to give you their land in possession as it is today. This day, 39 then, be sure and take to heart that the LORD is God in heaven above and on earth below; there is no other. You shall keep his statutes 40 and his commandments which I give you today; then all will be well with you and with your children after you, and you will live long in the land which the LORD your God is giving you for all time.

Then Moses set apart three cities 41 in the east, in Transjordan, to be 42 places of refuge for the homicide who kills a man without intent, with no previous enmity between them. If he takes sanctuary in one

---

[a] assigned . . . worship of: *or* created these for.

of these cities his life shall be safe.
43 The cities were: Bezer-in-the-Wilderness on the tableland for the
Reubenites, Ramoth in Gilead for
the Gadites, and Golan in Bashan
for the Manassites.
44 This is the law which Moses laid
45 down for the Israelites. These are
the precepts, the statutes, and the
laws which Moses proclaimed to
the Israelites, when they came out
46 of Egypt and were in Transjordan
in the valley opposite Beth-peor in
the land of Sihon king of the Amorites who lived in Heshbon. Moses
and the Israelites had defeated him
47 when they came out of Egypt and
had occupied his territory and the
territory of Og king of Bashan, the
two Amorite kings in the east, in
48 Transjordan. The territory ran
from Aroer on the gorge of the
Arnon to Mount Sirion, that is
49 Hermon; and all the Arabah on the
east, in Transjordan, as far as the
Sea of the Arabah below the watershed of Pisgah.

5 Moses summoned all Israel and
said to them: Listen, O Israel, to
the statutes and the laws which I
proclaim in your hearing today.
Learn them and be careful to ob-
2 serve them. The LORD our God
made a covenant with us at Horeb.
3 It was not with our forefathers
that the LORD made this covenant,
but with us, all of us who are alive
4 and are here this day. The LORD
spoke with you face to face on the
5 mountain out of the fire. I stood
between the LORD and you at that
time to report the words of the
LORD; for you were afraid of the
fire and did not go up the mountain. And the LORD said:
6 I am the LORD your God who
brought you out of Egypt, out of
the land of slavery.
7 You shall have no other god[a] to
set against me.
8 You shall not make a carved image for yourself nor the likeness of

anything in the heavens above, or
on the earth below, or in the waters
under the earth.
9 You shall not bow down to them
or worship[b] them; for I, the LORD
your God, am a jealous god. I punish the children for the sins of the
fathers to the third and fourth
generations of those who hate me.
10 But I keep faith with thousands,
with[c] those who love me and keep
my commandments.
11 You shall not make wrong use of
the name of the LORD your God;
the LORD will not leave unpunished the man who misuses his name.
12 Keep the sabbath day holy as
the LORD your God commanded
13 you. You have six days to labour
14 and do all your work. But the
seventh day is a sabbath of the
LORD your God; that day you shall
not do any work, neither you, your
son or your daughter, your slave or
your slave-girl, your ox, your ass,
or any of your cattle, nor the alien
within your gates, so that your
slaves and slave-girls may rest as
15 you do. Remember that you were
slaves in Egypt and the LORD your
God brought you out with a strong
hand and an outstretched arm, and
for that reason the LORD your God
commanded you to keep the sabbath day.
16 Honour your father and your
mother, as the LORD your God
commanded you, so that you may
live long, and that it may be well
with you in the land which the
LORD your God is giving you.
17 You shall not commit murder.
18 You shall not commit adultery.
19 You shall not steal.
20 You shall not give false evidence
against your neighbour.
21 You shall not covet your neighbour's wife; you shall not set your
heart on your neighbour's house,
his land, his slave, his slave-girl, his
ox, his ass, or on anything that belongs to him.

[a] Or gods.   [b] Or or be led to worship...
[c] with...with: or for a thousand generations with...

22 These Commandments the Lord spoke in a great voice to your whole assembly on the mountain out of the fire, the cloud, and the thick mist; then he said no more. He wrote them on two tablets of stone 23 and gave them to me. When you heard the voice out of the darkness, while the mountain was ablaze with fire, all the heads of your tribes and the elders came to me 24 and said, 'The Lord our God has shown us his glory and his greatness, and we have heard his voice out of the fire: today we have seen that God may speak with men and 25 they may still live. Why should we now risk death? for this great fire will devour us. If we hear the voice of the Lord our God again, we shall 26 die. Is there any mortal man who has heard the voice of the living God speaking out of the fire, as we 27 have, and has lived? You shall go near and listen to all that the Lord our God says, and report to us all that the Lord our God has said to you; we will listen and obey.' 28 When the Lord heard these words which you spoke to me, he said, 'I have heard what this people has said to you; every word 29 they have spoken is right. Would that they always had such a heart to fear me and to observe all my commandments, so that all might be well with them and their chil- 30 dren for ever! Go, and tell them to 31 return to their tents, but you yourself stand here beside me, and I will set forth to you all the commandments, the statutes and laws which you shall teach them to observe in the land which I am giving them to occupy.'

32 You shall be careful to do as the Lord your God has commanded you; do not turn from it to right 33 or to left. You must conform to all the Lord your God commands you, if you would live and prosper and remain long in the land you are to occupy.

These are the commandments, 6 statutes, and laws which the Lord your God commanded me to teach you to observe in the land into which you are passing to occupy it, a land flowing with milk and honey, so that you may fear the 2 Lord your God and keep all his statutes and commandments which I am giving you, both you, your sons, and your descendants all your lives, and so that you may live long. If you listen, O Israel, and 3 are careful to observe them, you will prosper and increase greatly as the Lord the God of your fathers promised you.

Hear, O Israel, the Lord[a] is our 4 God, one Lord, and you must love 5 the Lord your God with all your heart and soul and strength. These 6 commandments which I give you this day are to be kept in your heart; you shall repeat them to 7 your sons, and speak of them indoors and out of doors, when you lie down and when you rise. Bind 8 them as a sign on the hand and wear them as a phylactery on the forehead; write them up on the 9 door-posts of your houses and on your gates.

The Lord your God will bring 10 you into the land which he swore to your forefathers Abraham, Isaac and Jacob that he would give you, a land of great and fine cities which you did not build, houses full of 11 good things which you did not provide, rock-hewn cisterns which you did not hew, and vineyards and olive-groves which you did not plant. When you eat your fill there, be careful not to forget the Lord 12 who brought you out of Egypt, out of the land of slavery. You shall 13 fear the Lord your God, serve him alone and take your oaths in his name. You must not follow other 14 gods, gods of the nations that are around you; if you do, the Lord 15 your God who is in your midst will be angry with you, and he will

a See note on Exod. 3. 15.

sweep you away off the face of the earth, for the LORD your God is a jealous god.

16 You must not challenge the LORD your God as you challenged

17 him at Massah.[a] You must diligently keep the commandments of the LORD your God as well as the precepts and statutes which he

18 gave you. You must do what is right and good in the LORD's eyes so that all may go well with you, and you may enter and occupy the rich land which the LORD promised

19 by oath to your forefathers; then you shall drive out all your enemies before you, as the LORD promised.

20 When your son asks you in time to come, 'What is the meaning of the precepts, statutes, and laws which the LORD our God gave

21 you?', you shall say to him, 'We were Pharaoh's slaves in Egypt, and the LORD brought us out of

22 Egypt with his strong hand, sending great disasters, signs, and portents against the Egyptians and against Pharaoh and all his family,

23 as we saw for ourselves. But he led us out from there to bring us into the land and give it to us as he had

24 promised to our forefathers. The LORD commanded us to observe all these statutes and to fear the LORD our God; it will be for our own good at all times, and he will continue to

25 preserve our lives. It will be counted to our credit if we keep all these commandments in the sight of the LORD our God, as he has bidden us.'

7 WHEN the LORD your God brings you into the land which you are entering to occupy and drives out many nations before you – Hittites, Girgashites, Amorites, Canaanites, Perizzites, Hivites, and Jebusites, seven nations more numerous and powerful than you –

2 when the LORD your God delivers them into your power and you de-

feat them, you must put them to death. You must not make a treaty with them or spare them. You must 3 not intermarry with them, neither giving your daughters to their sons nor taking their daughters for your sons; if you do, they will draw your 4 sons away from the LORD[b] and make them worship other gods. Then the LORD will be angry with you and will quickly destroy you. But this is what you must do to 5 them: pull down their altars, break their sacred pillars, hack down their sacred poles and destroy their idols by fire, for you are a people 6 holy to the LORD your God; the LORD your God chose you out of all nations on earth to be his special possession.

It was not because you were more 7 numerous than any other nation that the LORD cared for you and chose you, for you were the smallest of all nations; it was because the 8 LORD loved you and stood by his oath to your forefathers, that he brought you out with his strong hand and redeemed you from the land of slavery, from the power of Pharaoh king of Egypt. Know 9 then that the LORD your God is God, the faithful God; with those who love him and keep his commandments he keeps covenant and faith for a thousand generations, but those who defy him and show 10 their hatred for him he repays with destruction; he will not be slow to requite any who so hate him.

You are to observe these com- 11 mandments, statutes, and laws which I give you this day, and keep them.

If you listen to these laws and 12 are careful to observe them, then the LORD your God will observe the sworn covenant he made with your forefathers and will keep faith with you. He will love you, 13 bless you and cause you to increase. He will bless the fruit of your body and the fruit of your land, your

---

[a] *That is* Challenge.   [b] *Prob. rdg.; Heb.* me.

corn and new wine and oil, the off-spring of your herds, and of your lambing flocks, in the land which he swore to your forefathers to give

14 you. You shall be blessed above every other nation; neither among your people nor among your cattle shall there be impotent male or

15 barren female. The LORD will take away all sickness from you; he will not bring upon you any of the foul diseases of Egypt which you know so well, but will bring them upon all

16 your enemies. You shall devour all the nations which the LORD your God is giving over to you. Spare none of them, and do not worship their gods; that is the snare which awaits you.

17 You may say to yourselves, 'These nations outnumber us, how

18 can we drive them out?' But you need have no fear of them; only remember what the LORD your God did to Pharaoh and to the whole of

19 Egypt, the great challenge which you yourselves witnessed, the signs and portents, the strong hand and the outstretched arm by which the LORD your God brought you out. He will deal thus with all the na-

20 tions of whom you are afraid. He will also spread panic among them until all who are left or have gone

21 into hiding perish before you. Be in no dread of them, for the LORD your God is in your midst, a great

22 and terrible god. He will drive out these nations before you little by little. You will not be able to exterminate them quickly, for fear the wild beasts become too nu-

23 merous for you. The LORD your God will deliver these nations over to you and will throw them into great panic in the hour of their des-

24 truction. He will put their kings into your hands, and you shall wipe out their name from under heaven. When you destroy them, no man will be able to withstand you.

25 Their idols you shall destroy by fire; you must not covet the silver and gold on them and take it for yourselves, or you will be ensnared by it; for these things are abominable to the LORD your God. You 26 must not introduce any abominable idol into your houses and thus bring yourselves under solemn ban along with it. You shall hold it loathsome and abominable, for it is forbidden under the ban.

You must carefully observe 8 everything that I command you this day so that you may live and increase and may enter and occupy the land which the LORD promised to your forefathers upon oath. You 2 must remember all that road by which the LORD your God has led you these forty years in the wilderness to humble you, to test you and to discover whether or no it was in your heart to keep his commandments. He humbled you and made 3 you hungry; then he fed you on manna which neither you nor your fathers had known before, to teach you that man cannot live on bread alone but lives by every word that comes from the mouth of the LORD. The clothes on your backs did not 4 wear out nor did your feet swell all these forty years. Take this lesson 5 to heart: that the LORD your God was disciplining you as a father disciplines his son; and keep the 6 commandments of the LORD your God, conforming to his ways and fearing him. For the LORD your 7 God is bringing you to a rich land, a land of streams, of springs and underground waters gushing out in hill and valley, a land of wheat and 8 barley, of vines, fig-trees, and pomegranates, a land of olives, oil, and honey. It is a land where you 9 will never live in poverty nor want for anything, a land whose stones are iron-ore and from whose hills you will dig copper. You will have 10 plenty to eat and will bless the LORD your God for the rich land that he has given you.

Take care not to forget the LORD 11 your God and do not fail to keep his commandments, laws, and sta-

tutes which I give you this day.
12 When you have plenty to eat and live in fine houses of your own
13 building, when your herds and flocks increase, and your silver and gold and all your possessions in-
14 crease too, do not become proud and forget the LORD your God who brought you out of Egypt, out of the
15 land of slavery; he led you through the vast and terrible wilderness infested with poisonous snakes and scorpions, a thirsty, waterless land, where he caused water to flow from
16 the hard rock; he fed you in the wilderness on manna which your fathers did not know, to humble you and test you, and in the end to
17 make you prosper. Nor must you say to yourselves, 'My own strength and energy have gained me this
18 wealth', but remember the LORD your God; it is he that gives you strength to become prosperous, so fulfilling the covenant guaranteed by oath with your forefathers, as he is doing now.
19 If you forget the LORD your God and adhere to other gods, worshipping them and bowing down to them, I give you a solemn warning this day that you will certainly be
20 destroyed. You will be destroyed because of your disobedience to the LORD your God, as surely as were the nations whom the LORD destroyed at your coming.

9 Listen, O Israel; this day you will cross the Jordan to occupy the territory of nations greater and more powerful than you, and great cities with walls towering to the
2 sky. They are great and tall people, the descendants of the Anakim, of whom you know, for you have heard it said, 'Who can with-
3 stand the sons of Anak?' Know then this day that it is the LORD your God himself who goes at your head as a devouring fire; he will subdue them and destroy them at your approach; you shall drive them out and overwhelm them, as he promised you.

When the LORD your God drives 4 them out before you, do not say to yourselves, 'It is because of my own merit that the LORD has brought me in to occupy this land.'
It is not because of your merit or 5 your integrity that you are entering their land to occupy it; it is because of the wickedness of these nations that the LORD your God is driving them out before you, and to fulfil the promise which the LORD made to your forefathers, Abraham, Isaac and Jacob.

Know then that it is not because 6 of any merit of yours that the LORD your God is giving you this rich land to occupy; indeed, you are a stubborn people. Remember and 7 never forget, how you angered the LORD your God in the wilderness: from the day when you left Egypt until you came to this place you have defied the LORD. In Horeb you 8 roused the LORD's anger, and the LORD in his wrath was on the point of destroying you. When I went up 9 the mountain to receive the tablets of stone, the tablets of the covenant which the LORD made with you, I remained on the mountain forty days and forty nights without food or drink. Then the 10 LORD gave me the two tablets of stone written with the finger of God, and upon them were all the words the LORD spoke to you out of the fire, upon the mountain on the day of the assembly. At the end 11 of forty days and forty nights the LORD gave me the two tablets of stone, the tablets of the covenant, and said to me, 'Make haste down 12 from the mountain because your people whom you brought out of Egypt have done a disgraceful thing. They have already turned aside from the way which I told them to follow and have cast for themselves an image of metal.'

Then the LORD said to me, 'I 13 have considered this people and I find them a stubborn people. Let 14 me be, and I will destroy them and blot out their name from under heaven; and of you alone I will make a nation more powerful and 15 numerous than they.' So I turned and went down the mountain, and it was ablaze; and I had the two tablets of the covenant in my 16 hands. When I saw that you had sinned against the LORD your God and had cast for yourselves an image of a bull-calf, and had already turned aside from the way the 17 LORD had told you to follow, I took the two tablets and flung them down and shattered them in 18 the sight of you all. Then once again I lay prostrate before the LORD, forty days and forty nights without food or drink, on account of all the sins that you had committed, and because you had done what was wrong in the eyes of the LORD and provoked him to anger. 19 I dreaded the LORD's anger and his wrath which threatened to destroy you; and once again the LORD lis-20 tened to me. The LORD was greatly incensed with Aaron also and would have killed him; so I prayed for him as well at that same time. 21 I took the calf, that sinful thing that you had made, and burnt it and pounded it, grinding it until it was as fine as dust; then I flung its dust into the torrent that flowed down 22 the mountain. You also roused the LORD's anger at Taberah, and at Massah, and at Kibroth-hattaavah. 23 Again, when the LORD sent you from Kadesh-barnea with orders to advance and occupy the land which he was giving you, you defied the LORD your God and did not trust 24 him or obey him. You were defiant from the day that the LORD first 25 knew you. Forty days and forty nights I lay prostrate before the LORD because he had threatened 26 to destroy you, and I prayed to the LORD and said, 'O Lord GOD, do not destroy thy people, thy own possession, whom thou didst redeem by thy great power and bring out of Egypt by thy strong hand. Remember thy servants, Abra-27 ham, Isaac and Jacob, and overlook the stubbornness of this people, their wickedness and their sin; otherwise the people in the land 28 out of which thou didst lead us will say, "It is because the LORD was not able to bring them into the land which he promised them and because he hated them, that he has led them out to kill them in the wilderness." But they are thy 29 people, thy own possession, whom thou didst bring out by thy great strength and by thy outstretched arm.'

AT that time the LORD said to me, 10 'Cut two tablets of stone like the first, and make also a wooden chest, an Ark. Come to me on the mountain, and I will write on the tablets 2 the words that were on the first tablets which you broke in pieces, and you shall put them into the Ark.' So I made the Ark of acacia-3 wood and cut two tablets of stone like the first, and went up the mountain taking the tablets with me. Then in the same writing as 4 before, the LORD wrote down the Ten Words[a] which he had spoken to you out of the fire, upon the mountain on the day of the assembly, and the LORD gave them to me. I turned and came down the 5 mountain, and I put the tablets in the Ark that I had made, as the LORD had commanded me, and there they have remained ever since.

(The Israelites journeyed by 6[b] stages from Beeroth-bene-jaakan to Moserah. There Aaron died and was buried; and his son Eleazar succeeded him in the priesthood. From there they came to Gudgo-7 dah and from Gudgodah to Jotbathah, a land of many ravines. At 8 that time the LORD set apart the tribe of Levi to carry the Ark of the Covenant of the LORD, to attend

---

[a] Or Ten Commandments.

[b] Verses 6, 7: cp. Num. 33. 31, 32.

on the LORD and minister to him, and to give the blessing in his name, as they have done to this 9 day. That is why the Levites have no holding or patrimony with their kinsmen; the LORD is their patrimony, as he promised them.)

10 I stayed on the mountain forty days and forty nights, as I did before, and once again the LORD listened to me; he consented not to 11 destroy you. The LORD said to me, 'Set out now at the head of the people so that they may enter and occupy the land which I swore to give to their forefathers.'

12 What then, O Israel, does the LORD your God ask of you? Only to fear the LORD your God, to conform to all his ways, to love him and to serve him with all your 13 heart and soul. This you will do by keeping the commandments of the LORD and his statutes which I give 14 you this day for your good. To the LORD your God belong heaven itself, the highest heaven, the earth 15 and everything in it; yet the LORD cared for your forefathers in his love for them and chose their descendants after them. Out of all nations you were his chosen people 16 as you are this day. So now you must circumcise the foreskin of your hearts and not be stubborn 17 any more, for the LORD your God is God of gods and Lord of lords, the great, mighty, and terrible God. He is no respecter of persons 18 and is not to be bribed; he secures justice for widows and orphans, and loves the alien who lives among you, giving him food and 19 clothing. You too must love the alien, for you once lived as aliens in 20 Egypt. You must fear the LORD your God, serve him, hold fast to him and take your oaths in his 21 name. He is your praise, your God who has done for you these great and terrible things which you have 22 seen with your own eyes. When your forefathers went down into

Egypt they were only seventy strong, but now the LORD your God has made you countless as the stars in the sky.

You shall love the LORD your 11 God and keep for all time the charge he laid upon you, the statutes, the laws, and the command- ments. This day you know the 2 discipline of the LORD, though your children who have neither known nor experienced it do not; you know his greatness, his strong hand and outstretched arm, the 3 signs he worked and his acts in Egypt against Pharaoh the king and his country, and all that he did 4 to the Egyptian army, its horses and chariots, when he caused the waters of the Red Sea to flow over them as they pursued you. In this way the LORD destroyed them, and so things remain to this day. You 5 know what he did for you in the wilderness as you journeyed to this place, and what he did to Dathan 6 and Abiram sons of Eliab, son of Reuben, when the earth opened its mouth and swallowed them in the sight of all Israel, together with their households and their tents and every living thing in their company. With your own eyes you have seen 7 the mighty work that the LORD did.

You shall observe all that I com- 8 mand you this day, so that you may have strength to enter and occupy the land into which you are crossing, and so that you may 9 live long in the land which the LORD swore to your forefathers to give them and their descendants, a land flowing with milk and honey. The land which you are entering to 10 occupy is not like the land of Egypt from which you have come, where, after sowing your seed, you irri- gated it by foot like a vegetable garden. But the land into which 11 you are crossing to occupy is a land of mountains and valleys watered by the rain of heaven. It is a land 12 which the LORD your God tends*a*

a which...tends: *or* whose soil the LORD your God has made firm.

and on which his eye rests from year's end to year's end. If you pay heed to the commandments which I give you this day, and love the LORD your God and serve him with all your heart and soul, then I will send rain for your land in season, both autumn and spring rains, and you will gather your corn and new wine and oil, and I will provide pasture in the fields for your cattle: you shall eat your fill. Take good care not to be led astray in your hearts nor to turn aside and serve other gods and prostrate yourselves to them, or the LORD will become angry with you: he will shut up the skies and there will be no rain, your ground will not yield its harvest, and you will soon vanish from the rich land which the LORD is giving you. You shall take these words of mine to heart and keep them in mind; you shall bind them as a sign on the hand and wear them as a phylactery on the forehead. Teach them to your children, and speak of them indoors and out of doors, when you lie down and when you rise. Write them up on the door-posts of your houses and on your gates. Then you will live long, you and your children, in the land which the LORD swore to your fore-fathers to give them, for as long as the heavens are above the earth.

If you diligently keep all these commandments that I now charge you to observe, by loving the LORD your God, by conforming to his ways and by holding fast to him, the LORD will drive out all these nations before you and you shall oc-cupy the territory of nations greater and more powerful than you. Every place where you set the soles of your feet shall be yours. Your bor-ders shall run from the wilderness to*a* the Lebanon and from the River, the river Euphrates, to the western sea. No man will be able to withstand you; the LORD your God will put the fear and dread of

you upon the whole land on which you set foot, as he promised you. Understand that this day I offer you the choice of a blessing and a curse. The blessing will come if you listen to the commandments of the LORD your God which I give you this day, and the curse if you do not listen to the commandments of the LORD your God but turn aside from the way that I command you this day and follow other gods whom you do not know.

When the LORD your God brings you into the land which you are entering to occupy, there on Mount Gerizim you shall pronounce the blessing and on Mount Ebal the curse. (These mountains are on the other side of the Jordan, close to Gilgal beside the terebinth of Moreh, beyond the road to the west which lies in the territory of the Canaanites of the Arabah.) You are about to cross the Jordan to enter and occupy the land which the LORD your God is giving you; you shall occupy it and settle in it, and you shall be careful to observe all the statutes and laws which I set before you this day.

God's laws delivered by Moses

THESE are the statutes and laws that you shall be careful to observe in the land which the LORD the God of your fathers is giving you to occupy as long as you live on earth. You shall demolish all the sanctuaries where the nations whose place you are taking wor-ship their gods, on mountain-tops and hills and under every spreading tree. You shall pull down their al-tars and break their sacred pillars, burn their sacred poles and hack down the idols of their gods and thus blot out the name of them from that place.

You shall not follow such prac-tices in the worship of the LORD your God, but you shall resort to

---

a Prob. rdg., Heb. and.

the place which the LORD your God will choose out of all your tribes to receive his Name that it may dwell there. 6 There you shall come and bring your whole-offerings and sacrifices, your tithes and contributions, your vows and freewill offerings, and the first-born of your 7 herds and flocks. There you shall eat before the LORD your God; so you shall find joy in whatever you undertake, you and your families, because the LORD your God has blessed you.

8 You shall not act as we act here today, each of us doing what he 9 pleases, for till now you have not reached the place of rest, the patrimony which the LORD your God is 10 giving you. You shall cross the Jordan and settle in the land which the LORD your God allots you as your patrimony; he will grant you peace from all your enemies on every side, and you will live in security. 11 Then you shall bring everything that I command you to the place which the LORD your God will choose as a dwelling for his Name – your whole-offerings and sacrifices, your tithes and contributions, and all the choice gifts that you have 12 vowed to the LORD. You shall rejoice before the LORD your God with your sons and daughters, your male and female slaves, and the Levites who live in your settlements because they have no holding or patrimony among you.

13 See that you do not offer your whole-offerings in any place at ran-14 dom, but offer them only at the place which the LORD will choose in one of your tribes, and there you 15 must do all I command you. On the other hand, you may freely kill for food in all your settlements, as the LORD your God blesses you. Clean and unclean alike may eat it, as they would eat the meat of 16 gazelle or buck. But on no account must you eat the blood; pour it out 17 on the ground like water. In all your settlements you may not eat

any of the tithe of your corn and new wine and oil, or any of the first-born of your cattle and sheep, or any of the gifts that you vow, or any of your freewill offerings and contributions; but you shall eat it 18 before the LORD your God in the place that the LORD your God will choose – you, your sons and daughters, your male and female slaves, and the Levites in your settlements; so you shall find joy before the LORD your God in all that you undertake. Be careful not 19 to neglect the Levites in your land as long as you live.

When the LORD your God ex- 20 tends your boundaries, as he has promised you, and you say to yourselves, 'I would like to eat meat', because you have a craving for it, then you may freely eat it. If the 21 place that the LORD your God will choose to receive his Name is far away, then you may slaughter a beast from the herds or flocks which the LORD has given you and freely eat it in your own settlements as I command you. You may eat it as 22 you would the meat of gazelle or buck; both clean and unclean alike may eat it. But you must strictly 23 refrain from eating the blood, because the blood is the life; you must not eat the life with the flesh. You 24 must not eat it, you must pour it out on the ground like water. If you 25 do not eat it, all will be well with you and your children after you; for you will be doing what is right in the eyes of the LORD. But such 26 holy-gifts as you may have and the gifts you have vowed, you must bring to the place which the LORD will choose. You must present your 27 whole-offerings, both the flesh and the blood, on the altar of the LORD your God; but of your shared-offerings you shall eat the flesh, while the blood is to be poured on the altar of the LORD your God. See that you listen and do all that 28 I command you, and then it will go well with you and your children after you for ever; for you will be doing what is good and right in the eyes of the LORD your God.

29 When the LORD your God exterminates, as you advance, the nations whose country you are entering to occupy, you shall take their place and settle in their land.

30 After they have been destroyed, take care that you are not ensnared into their ways. Do not inquire about their gods and say, 'How do these nations worship their gods? I too will do the same.'

31 You must not do for the LORD your God what they do, for all that they do for their gods is hateful and abominable to the LORD. As sacrifices for their gods they even burn their sons and their daughters.

32 See that you observe everything I command you: you must not add anything to it, nor take anything away from it.

13 When a prophet or dreamer appears among you and offers you a

2 sign or a portent and calls on you to follow other gods whom you have not known and worship them, even if the sign or portent should come

3 true, do not listen to the words of that prophet or that dreamer. God is testing you through him to discover whether you love the LORD your God with all your heart and

4 soul. You must follow the LORD your God and fear him; you must keep his commandments and obey him, serve him and hold fast to

5 him. That prophet or that dreamer shall be put to death, for he has preached rebellion against the LORD your God who brought you out of Egypt and redeemed you from that land of slavery; he has tried to lead you astray from the path which the LORD your God commanded you to take. You must rid yourselves of this wickedness.

6 If your brother, your father's son or your mother's son, or your son or daughter, or the wife of your bosom or your dearest friend should entice you secretly to go and worship other gods – gods whom neither you nor your fathers have known, gods of the people round 7 about you, near or far, at one end of the land or the other – then you 8 shall not consent or listen. You shall have no pity on him, you shall not spare him nor shield him, you 9 shall put him to death; your own hand shall be the first to be raised against him and then all the people shall follow. You shall stone him 10 to death, because he tried to lead you astray from the LORD your God who brought you out of Egypt, out of the land of slavery. All Israel shall hear of it and be 11 afraid; never again will anything as wicked as this be done among you.

When you hear that miscreants 12–13 have appeared in any of the cities which the LORD your God is giving you to occupy, and have led its inhabitants astray by calling on them to serve other gods whom you have not known, then you shall 14 investigate the matter carefully. If, after diligent examination, the report proves to be true and it is shown that this abominable thing has been done among you, you 15 shall put the inhabitants of that city to the sword; you shall lay the city under solemn ban together with everything in it. You shall 16 gather all its goods into the square and burn both city and goods as a complete offering to the LORD your God; and it shall remain a mound of ruins, never to be rebuilt. Let 17 nothing out of all that has been laid under the ban be found in your possession, so that the LORD may turn from his anger and show you compassion; and in his compassion he will increase you as he swore to your forefathers, provided that 18 you obey the LORD your God and keep all his commandments which I give you this day, doing only what is right in the eyes of the LORD your God.

14 You are the sons of the LORD your God: you shall not gash yourselves nor shave your forelocks in mourn-
2 ing for the dead. You are a people holy to the LORD your God, and the LORD has chosen you out of all peoples on earth to be his special possession.

3 You shall not eat any abomin-
4 able thing. These are the animals
5 you may eat: ox, sheep, goat, buck, gazelle, roebuck, wild-goat, white-rumped deer, long-horned ante-
6 lope, and rock-goat. You may eat any animal which has a parted foot or a cloven hoof and also chews
7 the cud; those which only chew the cud or only have a parted or cloven hoof you may not eat. These are: the camel, the hare, and the rock-badger,[a] because they chew the cud but do not have cloven hoofs; you shall regard them as unclean;
8 and the pig, because it has a cloven hoof but does not chew the cud, you shall regard as unclean. You shall not eat their flesh or even
9 touch their dead carcasses. Of creatures that live in water you may eat all those that have fins and
10 scales, but you may not eat any that have neither fins nor scales; you shall regard them as unclean.
11, 12 You may eat all clean birds. These are the birds you may not eat: the griffon-vulture,[b] the black vulture,
13 the bearded vulture,[c] the kite,
14 every kind of falcon, every kind of
15 crow,[d] the desert-owl, the short-eared owl, the long-eared owl,
16 every kind of hawk, the tawny owl, the screech-owl, the little owl,
17 the horned owl, the osprey, the
18 fisher-owl, the stork,[e] every kind of cormorant, the hoopoe, and the bat.
19 All teeming winged creatures you shall regard as unclean; they
20 may not be eaten. You may eat every clean insect.
21 You shall not eat anything that has died a natural death. You shall give it to the aliens who live in your settlements, and they may eat it, or you may sell it to a foreigner; for you are a people holy to the LORD your God.

You shall not boil a kid in its mother's milk.

Year by year you shall set aside 22 a tithe of all the produce of your seed, of everything that grows on the land. You shall eat it in the 23 presence of the LORD your God in the place which he will choose as a dwelling for his Name – the tithe of your corn and new wine and oil, and the first-born of your cattle and sheep, so that for all time you may learn to fear the LORD your God. When the LORD your God has 24 blessed you with prosperity, and the place which he will choose to receive his Name is far from you and the journey too great for you to be able to carry your tithe, then 25 you may exchange it for silver. You shall tie up the silver and take it with you to the place which the LORD your God will choose. There 26 you shall spend it as you will on cattle or sheep, wine or strong drink, or whatever you desire; you shall consume it there with rejoicing, both you and your family, in the presence of the LORD your God. You must not neglect the 27 Levites who live in your settlements; for they have no holding or patrimony among you.

At the end of every third year 28 you shall bring out all the tithe of your produce for that year and leave it in your settlements so that 29 the Levites, who have no holding or patrimony among you, and the aliens, orphans, and widows in your settlements may come and eat their fill. If you do this the LORD your God will bless you in everything to which you set your hand.

At the end of every seventh year 15 you shall make a remission of

---

[a] Or rock-rabbit.   [b] Or eagle.   [c] Or ossifrage.
[d] Or raven.   [e] Or heron.

2 debts. This is how the remission shall be made: everyone who holds a pledge shall remit the pledge of anyone indebted to him. He shall not press a fellow-countryman for repayment, for the Lord's year of

3 remission has been declared.[a] You may press foreigners; but if it is a fellow-countryman that holds anything of yours, you must remit all

4-5 claim upon it. There will never be any poor among you if only you obey the Lord your God by carefully keeping these commandments which I lay upon you this day; for the Lord your God will bless you with great prosperity in the land which he is giving you to

6 occupy as your patrimony. When the Lord your God blesses you, as he promised, you will lend to men of many nations, but you yourselves will not borrow; you will rule many nations, but they will not rule you.

7 When one of your fellow-countrymen in any of your settlements in the land which the Lord your God is giving you becomes poor, do not be hard-hearted or close-fisted with your countryman in his need.

8 Be open-handed towards him and lend him on pledge as much as he

9 needs. See that you do not harbour iniquitous thoughts when you find that the seventh year, the year of remission, is near, and look askance at your needy countryman and give him nothing. If you do, he will appeal to the Lord against you, and you will be found guilty of sin.

10 Give freely to him and do not begrudge him your bounty, because it is for this very bounty that the Lord your God will bless you in everything that you do or under-

11 take. The poor will always be with you in the land, and for that reason I command you to be open-handed with your countrymen, both poor and distressed, in your own land.

12 When a fellow-Hebrew, man or

woman, sells himself to you as a slave, he shall serve you for six years and in the seventh year you

13 shall set him free. But when you

14 set him free, do not let him go empty-handed. Give to him lavishly from your flock, from your threshing-floor and your winepress. Be generous to him, because the Lord your God has blessed you.

18 Do not take it amiss when you have to set him free, for his six years' service[b] to you has been worth twice[b] the wage of a hired man.

15 Then the Lord your God will bless you in everything you do. Remember that you were slaves in Egypt and the Lord your God redeemed you; that is why I am giving you this command today.

16 If, however, a slave is content to be with you and says, 'I will not leave you, I love you and your

17 family', then you shall take an awl and pierce through his ear to the door, and he will be your slave for life. You shall treat a slave-girl in the same way.

19[c] You shall dedicate to the Lord your God every male first-born of your herds and flocks. You shall not plough with the first-born of your cattle, nor shall you shear the first-born of your sheep. Year by

20 year you and your family shall eat them in the presence of the Lord your God, in the place which the Lord will choose. If any animal is

21 defective, if it is lame or blind, or has any other serious defect, you must not sacrifice it to the Lord

22 your God. Eat it in your settlements; both clean and unclean alike may eat it as they would the meat of gazelle or buck. But you

23 must not eat the blood; pour it out on the ground like water.

16 OBSERVE the month of Abib and keep the Passover to the Lord your God, for it was in that month that the Lord your God brought you

---

[a] *Or* has come.   [b] worth twice: *or* equivalent to.
[c] *Verse 18 transposed to follow verse 14.*

2 out of Egypt by night. You shall slaughter a lamb, a kid, or a calf as a Passover victim to the LORD your God in the place which he will choose as a dwelling for his Name. 3 You shall eat nothing leavened with it. For seven days you shall eat unleavened cakes, the bread of affliction. In urgent haste you came out of Egypt, and thus as long as you live you shall commemorate the day of your coming out of Egypt. 4 No leaven shall be seen in all your territory for seven days, nor shall any of the flesh which you have slaughtered in the evening of the first day remain overnight till 5 morning. You may not slaughter the Passover victim in any of the settlements which the LORD your 6 God is giving you, but only in the place which he will choose as a dwelling for his Name; you shall slaughter the Passover victim in the evening as the sun goes down, the time of your coming out of 7 Egypt. You shall boil it and eat it in the place which the LORD your God will choose, and then next morning you shall turn and go to 8 your tents. For six days you shall eat unleavened cakes, and on the seventh day there shall be a closing ceremony in honour of the LORD your God; you shall do no work. 9 Seven weeks shall be counted: start counting the seven weeks from the time when the sickle is 10 put to the standing corn; then you shall keep the pilgrim-feast of Weeks to the LORD your God and offer a freewill offering in proportion to the blessing that the LORD 11 your God has given you. You shall rejoice before the LORD your God, with your sons and daughters, your male and female slaves, the Levites who live in your settlements, and the aliens, orphans, and widows among you. You shall rejoice in the place which the LORD your God will choose as a dwelling 12 for his Name and remember that

you were slaves in Egypt. You shall keep and observe all these statutes.

You shall keep the pilgrim-feast 13 of Tabernacles[a] for seven days, when you bring in the produce from your threshing-floor and winepress. You shall rejoice in 14 your feast, with your sons and daughters, your male and female slaves, the Levites, aliens, orphans, and widows who live in your settlements. For seven days you 15 shall keep this feast to the LORD your God in the place which he will choose, when the LORD your God gives you his blessing in all your harvest and in all your work; you shall keep the feast with joy.

Three times a year all your 16 males shall come into the presence of the LORD your God in the place which he will choose: at the pilgrim-feasts of Unleavened Bread, of Weeks, and of Tabernacles. No one shall come into the presence of the LORD empty-handed. Each of 17 you shall bring such a gift as he can in proportion to the blessing which the LORD your God has given you.

You shall appoint for yourselves 18 judges and officers, tribe by tribe, in every settlement which the LORD your God is giving you, and they shall dispense true justice to the people. You shall not pervert the 19 course of justice or show favour, nor shall you accept a bribe; for bribery makes the wise man blind and the just man give a crooked answer. Justice, and justice alone, 20 you shall pursue, so that you may live and occupy the land which the LORD your God is giving you.

You shall not plant any kind of 21 tree as a sacred pole beside the altar of the LORD your God which you shall build. You shall not set 22 up a sacred pillar, for the LORD your God hates them.

You shall not sacrifice to the 17 LORD your God a bull or sheep that has any defect or serious blemish,

---

[a] Or Booths or Arbours.

for that would be abominable to the LORD your God.

2 If so be that, in any one of the settlements which the LORD your God is giving you, a man or woman is found among you who does what is wrong in the eyes of the LORD your God, by breaking his cove-
3 nant and going to worship other gods and prostrating himself before them or before the sun and moon and all the host of heaven – a
4 thing that I have forbidden – then, if it is reported to you or you hear of it, make thorough inquiry. If the report proves to be true, and it is shown that this abominable thing
5 has been done in Israel, then bring the man or woman who has done this wicked deed to the city gate
6 and stone him to death. Sentence of death shall be carried out on the testimony of two or of three witnesses: no one shall be put to death on the testimony of a single witness.
7 The first stones shall be thrown by the witnesses and then all the people shall follow; thus you shall rid yourselves of this wickedness.
8 When the issue in any lawsuit is beyond your competence, whether it be a case of blood against blood, plea against plea, or blow against blow, that is disputed in your courts, then go up without delay to the place which the LORD your
9 God will choose. There you must go to the levitical priests or to the judge then in office; seek their guidance, and they will pronounce the
10 sentence. You shall act on the pronouncement which they make from the place which the LORD will choose. See that you carry out all
11 their instructions. Act on the instruction which they give you, or on the precedent that they cite; do not swerve from what they tell you,
12 either to right or to left. Anyone who presumes to reject the decision either of the priest who ministers there to the LORD your God, or of the judge, shall die; thus you will
13 rid Israel of wickedness. Then all the people will hear of it and be afraid, and will never again show such presumption.

14 When you come into the land which the LORD your God is giving you, and occupy it and settle in it, and you then say, 'Let us appoint over us a king, as all the surrounding nations do', you shall
15 appoint as king the man whom the LORD your God will choose. You shall appoint over you a man of your own race; you must not appoint a foreigner, one who is not of your own race. He shall not acquire
16 many horses, nor, to add to his horses, shall he cause the people to go back to Egypt, for this is what the LORD said to you, 'You shall never go back that way.' He shall
17 not acquire many wives and so be led astray; nor shall he acquire great quantities of silver and gold for himself. When he has ascended
18 the throne of the kingdom, he shall make a copy of this law in a book at the dictation of the levitical priests. He shall keep it by him and
19 read from it all his life, so that he may learn to fear the LORD his God and keep all the words of this law and observe these statutes. In this
20 way he shall not become prouder than his fellow-countrymen, nor shall he turn from these commandments to right or to left; then he and his sons will reign long over his kingdom in Israel.

The levitical priests, the whole 18 tribe of Levi, shall have no holding or patrimony in Israel; they shall eat the food-offerings of the LORD, their patrimony. They shall have 2 no patrimony among their fellow-countrymen; the LORD is their patrimony, as he promised them.

This shall be the customary due 3 of the priests from those of the people who offer sacrifice, whether a bull or a sheep: the shoulders, the cheeks, and the stomach shall be given to the priest. You shall give 4 him also the firstfruits of your corn and new wine and oil, and the first

fleeces at the shearing of your
5 flocks. For it was he whom the
LORD your God chose from all your
tribes to attend on the LORD and
to minister in the name of the
LORD, both he and his sons for all
time.

6 When a Levite comes from any
settlement in Israel where he may
be lodging to the place which the
LORD will choose, if he comes in the
7 eagerness of his heart and ministers
in the name of the LORD his God,
like all his fellow-Levites who at-
8 tend on the LORD there, he shall
have an equal share of food with
them, besides what he may inherit from his father's family.

9 When you come into the land
which the LORD your God is giving
you, do not learn to imitate the
abominable customs of those other
10 nations. Let no one be found a-
mong you who makes his son or
daughter pass through fire, no
augur or soothsayer or diviner or
11 sorcerer, no one who casts spells or
traffics with ghosts and spirits, and
12 no necromancer. Those who do
these things are abominable to the
LORD, and it is because of these abominable practices that the LORD
your God is driving them out be-
13 fore you. You shall be whole-hearted in your service of the LORD your
God.

14 These nations whose place you
are taking listen to soothsayers and
augurs, but the LORD your God
does not permit you to do this.
15 The LORD your God will raise up a
prophet from among you like myself, and you shall listen to him.
16 All this follows from your request
to the LORD your God on Horeb on
the day of the assembly. There you
said, 'Let us not hear again the
voice of the LORD our God, nor see
this great fire again, or we shall
17 die.' Then the LORD said to me,
18 'What they have said is right. I will
raise up for them a prophet like
you, one of their own race, and I

will put my words into his mouth.
He shall convey all my commands
to them, and if anyone does not 19
listen to the words which he will
speak in my name I will require
satisfaction from him. But the pro- 20
phet who presumes to utter in my
name what I have not commanded
him or who speaks in the name of
other gods – that prophet shall
die.' If you ask yourselves, 'How 21
shall we recognize a word that
the LORD has not uttered?', this is 22
the answer: When the word spoken
by the prophet in the name of the
LORD is not fulfilled and does not
come true, it is not a word spoken
by the LORD. The prophet has spoken presumptuously; do not hold
him[a] in awe.

WHEN the LORD your God ex- 19
terminates the nations whose land
he is giving you, and you take their
place and settle in their cities and
houses, you shall set apart three 2
cities in the land which he is giving
you to occupy. Divide into three 3
districts the territory which the
LORD your God is giving you as
patrimony, and determine where
each city shall lie. These shall be
places in which homicides may
take sanctuary.

This is the kind of homicide who 4
may take sanctuary there and save
his life: the man who strikes another without intent and with no
previous enmity between them;
for instance, the man who goes 5
into a wood with his mate to fell
trees, and, when cutting a tree, he
relaxes his grip on the axe,[b] the
head glances off the tree, hits the
other man and kills him. The homicide may take sanctuary in any
one of these cities, and his life shall
be safe. Otherwise, when the dead 6
man's next-of-kin who had the
duty of vengeance pursued him in
the heat of passion, he might overtake him if the distance were great,
and take his life, although the

---

[a] Or it.   [b] when...axe: or as he swings the axe to cut a tree.

homicide was not liable to the death-penalty because there had been no previous enmity on his 7 part. That is why I command you to set apart three cities.

8 If the LORD your God extends your boundaries, as he swore to your forefathers, and gives you the whole land which he promised to 9 them, because you keep all the commandments that I am laying down today and carry them out by loving the LORD your God and by conforming to his ways for all time, then you shall add three more cities 10 of refuge to these three. Let no innocent blood be shed in the land which the LORD your God is giving you as your patrimony, or bloodguilt will fall on you.

11 When one man is the enemy of another, and he lies in wait for him, attacks him and strikes him a blow so that he dies, and then takes 12 sanctuary in one of these cities, the elders of his own city shall send to fetch him; they shall hand him over to the next-of-kin, and he 13 shall die. You shall show him no mercy, but shall rid Israel of the guilt of innocent blood; then all will be well with you.

14 Do not move your neighbour's boundary stone, fixed by the men of former times in the patrimony which you shall occupy in the land the LORD your God gives you for your possession.

15 A single witness may not give evidence against a man in the matter of any crime or sin which he commits: a charge must be established on the evidence of two or of three witnesses.

16 When a malicious witness comes forward to give false evidence a-17 gainst a man, and the two disputants stand before the LORD, before the priests and the judges then 18 in office, if, after careful examination by the judges, he be proved to be a false witness giving false evi-19 dence against his fellow, you shall treat him as he intended to treat

his fellow, and thus rid yourselves of this wickedness. The rest of the 20 people when they hear of it will be afraid: never again will anything as wicked as this be done among you. You shall show no mercy: life 21 for life, eye for eye, tooth for tooth, hand for hand, foot for foot.

WHEN you take the field against 20 an enemy and are faced by horses and chariots and an army greater than yours, do not be afraid of them; for the LORD your God, who brought you out of Egypt, will be with you. When you are about to 2 join battle, the priest shall come forward and address the army in 3 these words: 'Hear, O Israel, this day you are joining battle with the enemy; do not lose heart, or be afraid, or give way to panic in face of them; for the LORD your God 4 will go with you to fight your enemy for you and give you the victory.' Then the officers shall ad-5 dress the army in these words: 'Any man who has built a new house and has not dedicated it shall go back to his house; or he may die in battle and another man dedicate it. Any man who has planted a 6 vineyard and has not begun to use it shall go back home; or he may die in battle and another man use it. Any man who has pledged him-7 self to take a woman in marriage and has not taken her shall go back home; or he may die in battle and another man take her.' The officers 8 shall further address the army: 'Any man who is afraid and has lost heart shall go back home; or his comrades will be discouraged as he is.' When these officers have 9 finished addressing the army, commanders shall be appointed to lead it.

When you advance on a city to 10 attack it, make an offer of peace. If the city accepts the offer and 11 opens its gates to you, then all the people in it shall be put to forced labour and shall serve you. If it 12 does not make peace with you but offers battle, you shall besiege it, 13 and the LORD your God will deliver it into your hands. You shall 14 put all its males to the sword, but you may take the women, the dependants, and the cattle for yourselves, and plunder everything else in the city. You may enjoy the use of the spoil of your enemies which 15 the LORD your God gives you. That is what you shall do to cities at a great distance, as opposed to those which belong to nations near at 16 hand. In the cities of these nations whose land the LORD your God is giving you as a patrimony, you shall not leave any creature alive. 17 You shall annihilate them – Hittites, Amorites, Canaanites, Perizzites, Hivites, Jebusites – as the LORD your God commanded you, 18 so that they may not teach you to imitate all the abominable things that they have done for their gods and so cause you to sin against the LORD your God.

19 When you are at war, and lay siege to a city for a long time in order to take it, do not destroy its trees by taking the axe to them, for they provide you with food; you shall not cut them down. The trees of the field are not men that you 20 should besiege them. But you may destroy or cut down any trees that you know do not yield food, and use them in siege-works against the city that is at war with you, until it falls.

21 When a dead body is found lying in open country, in the land which the LORD your God is giving you to occupy, and it is not known who 2 struck the blow, your elders and your judges shall come out and measure the distance to the surrounding towns to find which is 3 nearest. The elders of that town shall take a heifer that has never 4 been mated*a* or worn a yoke, and bring it down to a ravine where there is a stream that never runs dry and the ground is never tilled or sown, and there in the ravine they shall break its neck. The 5 priests, the sons of Levi, shall then come forward; for the LORD your God has chosen them to minister to him and to bless in the name of the LORD, and their voice shall be decisive in all cases of dispute and assault. Then all the elders of the 6 town nearest to the dead body shall wash their hands over the heifer whose neck has been broken in the ravine. They shall solemnly de- 7 clare: 'Our hands did not shed this blood, nor did we witness the bloodshed. Accept expiation, O 8 LORD, for thy people Israel whom thou hast redeemed, and do not let the guilt of innocent blood rest upon thy people Israel: let this bloodshed be expiated on their behalf.' Thus, by doing what is right in the 9 eyes of the LORD, you shall rid yourselves of the guilt of innocent blood.

When you wage war against your 10 enemy and the LORD your God delivers them into your hands and you take some of them captive, then if you see a comely woman 11 among the captives and take a liking to her, you may marry her. You shall bring her into your 12 house, where she shall shave her head, pare her nails, and discard 13 the clothes which she had when captured. Then she shall stay in your house and mourn for her father and mother for a full month. After that you may have intercourse with her; you shall be her husband and she your wife. But if 14 you no longer find her pleasing, let her go free. You must not sell her, nor treat her harshly, since you have had your will with her.

When a man has two wives, one 15 loved and the other unloved, if they both bear him sons, and the son of the unloved wife is the elder, then, when the day comes for him 16 to divide his property among his

a Prob. rdg.; Heb. put to work.

sons, he shall not treat the son of the loved wife as his first-born in contempt of his true first-born, the
17 son of the unloved wife. He shall recognize the rights of his first-born, the son of the unloved wife, and give him a double share of all that he possesses; for he was the firstfruits of his manhood, and the right of the first-born is his.

18 When a man has a son who is disobedient and out of control, and will not obey his father or his mother, or pay attention when they
19 punish him, then his father and mother shall take hold of him and bring him out to the elders of the
20 town, at the town gate. They shall say to the elders of the town, 'This son of ours is disobedient and out of control; he will not obey us, he
21 is a wastrel and a drunkard.' Then all the men of the town shall stone him to death, and you will thereby rid yourselves of this wickedness. All Israel will hear of it and be afraid.

22 When a man is convicted of a capital offence and is put to death, you shall hang him on a gibbet;
23 but his body shall not remain on the gibbet overnight; you shall bury it on the same day, for a hanged man is offensive[a] in the sight of God. You shall not pollute the land which the LORD your God is giving you as your patrimony.

22 WHEN you see a fellow-countryman's ox or sheep straying, do not ignore it but take it back to him.
2 If the owner is not a near neighbour and you do not know who he is, take the animal into your own house and keep it with you until he claims it, and then give it back to
3 him. Do the same with his ass or his cloak or anything else that your fellow-countryman has lost, if you find it. You may not ignore it.
4 When you see your fellow-countryman's ass or ox lying on the road, do not ignore it; you

must help him to lift it to its feet again.

5 No woman shall wear an article of man's clothing, nor shall a man put on woman's dress; for those who do these things are abominable to the LORD your God.

6 When you come across a bird's nest by the road, in a tree or on the ground, with fledglings or eggs in it and the mother-bird on the nest, do not take both mother and
7 young. Let the mother-bird go free, and take only the young; then you will prosper and live long.

8 When you build a new house, put a parapet along the roof, or you will bring the guilt of bloodshed on your house if anyone should fall from it.

9 You shall not sow your vineyard with a second crop, or the full yield will be forfeit, both the yield of the seed you sow and the fruit of the vineyard.

10 You shall not plough with an ox and an ass yoked together.

11 You shall not wear clothes woven with two kinds of yarn, wool and flax together.

12 You shall make twisted tassels on the four corners of your cloaks which you wrap round you.

13 When a man takes a wife and after having intercourse with her
14 turns against her and brings trumped-up charges against her, giving her a bad name and saying, 'I took this woman and slept with her and did not find proof of vir-
15 ginity in her', then the girl's father and mother shall take the proof of her virginity to the elders of the
16 town, at the town gate. The girl's father shall say to the elders, 'I gave my daughter in marriage to this man, and he has turned against
17 her. He has trumped up a charge and said, "I have not found proofs of virginity in your daughter." Here are the proofs.' They shall then spread the garment before the
18 elders of the town. The elders shall

---

[a] Or accursed.

19 take the man and punish him: they shall fine him a hundred pieces of silver because he has given a bad name to a virgin of Israel, and hand them to the girl's father. She shall be his wife: he is not free to divorce 20 her all his life long. If, on the other hand, the accusation is true and no proof of the girl's virginity is found, 21 then they shall bring her out to the door of her father's house and the men of her town shall stone her to death. She has committed an outrage in Israel by playing the prostitute in her father's house: you shall rid yourselves of this wickedness.

22 When a man is discovered lying with a married woman, they shall both die, the woman as well as the man who lay with her: you shall rid Israel of this wickedness.

23 When a virgin is pledged in marriage to a man and another man comes upon her in the town and 24 lies with her, you shall bring both of them out to the gate of that town and stone them to death; the girl because, although in the town, she did not cry for help, and the man because he dishonoured another man's wife: you shall rid your- 25 selves of this wickedness. If the man comes upon such a girl in the country and rapes her, then the man alone shall die because he lay 26 with her. You shall do nothing to the girl, she has done nothing worthy of death: this deed is like that of a man who attacks another 27 and murders him, for the man came upon her in the country and, though the girl cried for help, there was no one to rescue her.

28 When a man comes upon a virgin who is not pledged in marriage and forces her to lie with him, and 29 they are discovered, then the man who lies with her shall give the girl's father fifty pieces of silver, and she shall be his wife because he has dishonoured her. He is not free to divorce her all his life long.

A man shall not take his father's 30 wife: he shall not bring shame on his father.

No man whose testicles have 23 been crushed or whose organ has been severed shall become a member of the assembly of the LORD.

No descendant of an irregular 2 union, even down to the tenth generation, shall become a member of the assembly of the LORD.

No Ammonite or Moabite, even 3 down to the tenth generation, shall become a member of the assembly of the LORD. They shall never become members of the assembly of the LORD, because they did not 4 meet you with food and water on your way out of Egypt, and because they hired Balaam son of Beor from Pethor in Aram-naharaim^a to revile you. The LORD your 5 God refused to listen to Balaam and turned his denunciation into a blessing, because the LORD your God loved you. You shall never 6 seek their welfare or their good all your life long.

You shall not regard an Edomite 7 as an abomination, for he is your own kin; nor an Egyptian, for you were aliens in his land. The third 8 generation of children born to them may become members of the assembly of the LORD.

When you are encamped against 9 an enemy, you shall be careful to avoid any foulness. When one of 10 your number is unclean because of an emission of seed ´at night, he must go outside the camp; he may not come within it. Towards even- 11 ing he shall wash himself in water, and at sunset he may come back into the camp. You shall have a sign 12 outside the camp showing where you can withdraw. With your 13 equipment you will have a trowel, and when you squat outside, you shall scrape a hole with it and then turn and cover your excrement. For the LORD your God goes about 14 in your camp, to keep you safe and

---

^a That is Aram of Two Rivers.

to hand over your enemies as you advance, and your camp must be kept holy for fear that he should see something indecent and go with you no further.

15 You shall not surrender to his master a slave who has taken re-
16 fuge with you. Let him stay with you anywhere he chooses in any one of your settlements, wherever suits him best; you shall not force him.

17 No Israelite woman shall become a temple-prostitute, and no Israelite man shall prostitute himself in this way.

18 You shall not allow a common prostitute's fee, cr the pay of a male prostitute, to be brought into the house of the LORD your God in fulfilment of any vow, for both of them are abominable to the LORD your God.

19 You shall not charge interest on anything you lend to a fellow-countryman, money or food or anything else on which interest can
20 be charged. You may charge interest on a loan to a foreigner but not on a loan to a fellow-country-man, for then the LORD your God will bless you in all you undertake in the land which you are entering to occupy.

21 When you make a vow to the LORD your God, do not put off its fulfilment; otherwise the LORD your God will require satisfaction of you and you will be guilty of sin.
22 If you choose not to make a vow,
23 you will not be guilty of sin; but if you voluntarily make a vow to the LORD your God, mind what you say and do what you have promised.

24 When you go into another man's vineyard, you may eat as many grapes as you wish to satisfy your hunger, but you may not put any into your basket.

25 When you go into another man's standing corn, you may pluck ears to rub in your hands, but you may not put a sickle to his standing corn.

When a man has married a wife, 24 but she does not win his favour because he finds something shameful in her, and he writes her a note of divorce, gives it to her and dismisses her; and suppose after leaving his 2 house she goes off to become the wife of another man, and this next 3 husband turns against her and writes her a note of divorce which he gives her and dismisses her, or dies after making her his wife – then in 4 that case her first husband who dismissed her is not free to take her back to be his wife again after she has become for him unclean. This is abominable to the LORD; you must not bring sin upon the land which the LORD your God is giving you as your patrimony.

When a man is newly married, 5 he shall not be liable for military service or any other public duty. He shall remain at home exempt from service for one year and enjoy the wife he has taken.

No man shall take millstones, or 6 even the upper one alone, in pledge; that would be taking a life in pledge.

When a man is found to have 7 kidnapped a fellow-countryman, an Israelite, and to have treated him harshly and sold him, he shall die: you shall rid yourselves of this wickedness.

Be careful how you act in all 8 cases of malignant skin-disease; be careful to observe all that the levitical priests tell you; I gave them my commands which you must obey. Remember what the LORD 9 your God did to Miriam, on your way out of Egypt.

When you make a loan to an- 10 other man, do not enter his house to take a pledge from him. Wait 11 outside, and the man whose creditor you are shall bring the pledge out to you. If he is a poor man, you 12 shall not sleep in the cloak he has pledged. Give it back to him at sunset so that he may sleep in it and 13 bless you; then it will be counted to your credit in the sight of the LORD your God.

14 You shall not keep back the wages of a man who is poor and needy, whether a fellow-countryman or an alien living in your country in one of your settlements.

15 Pay him his wages on the same day before sunset, for he is poor and his heart is set on them: he may appeal to the LORD against you, and you will be guilty of sin.

16 Fathers shall not be put to death for their children, nor children for their fathers; a man shall be put to death only for his own sin.

17 You shall not deprive aliens and orphans of justice nor take a

18 widow's cloak in pledge. Remember that you were slaves in Egypt and the LORD your God redeemed you from there; that is why I command you to do this.

19 When you reap the harvest in your field and forget a swathe, do not go back to pick it up; it shall be left for the alien, the orphan, and the widow, in order that the LORD your God may bless you in all that you undertake.

20 When you beat your olive-trees, do not strip them afterwards; what is left shall be for the alien, the orphan, and the widow.

21 When you gather the grapes from your vineyard, do not glean afterwards; what is left shall be for the alien, the orphan, and the

22 widow. Remember that you were slaves in Egypt; that is why I command you to do this.

25 When two men go to law and present themselves for judgement, the judges shall try the case; they shall acquit the innocent and con-

2 demn the guilty. If the guilty man is sentenced to be flogged, the judge shall cause him to lie down and be beaten in his presence; the number of strokes shall correspond

3 to the gravity of the offence. They may give him forty strokes, but not more; otherwise, if they go further and exceed this number,

your fellow-countryman will have been publicly degraded.

4 You shall not muzzle an ox while it is treading out the corn.

5 When brothers live together and one of them dies without leaving a son, his widow shall not marry outside the family. Her husband's brother shall have intercourse with her; he shall take her in marriage and do his duty by her as her husband's brother. The first son she

6 bears shall perpetuate the dead brother's name so that it may not be blotted out from Israel. But if

7 the man is unwilling to take his brother's wife, she shall go to the elders at the town gate and say, 'My husband's brother refuses to perpetuate his brother's name in Israel; he will not do his duty by me.' At this the elders of the town

8 shall summon him and reason with him. If he still stands his ground and says, 'I will not take her', his

9 brother's widow shall go up to him in the presence of the elders; she shall pull his sandal off his foot and spit in his face and declare: 'Thus we requite the man who will not build up his brother's family.'

10 His family shall be known in Israel as the House of the Unsandalled Man.

11 When two men are fighting and the wife of one of them comes near to drag her husband clear of his opponent, if she puts out her hand and catches hold of the man's

12 genitals, you shall cut off her hand and show her no mercy.

13 You shall not have unequal weights in your bag, one heavy, the

14 other light. You shall not have unequal measures in your house, one

15 large, the other small. You shall have true and correct weights and true and correct measures, so that you may live long in the land which the LORD your God is giving you.

16 All who commit these offences, all who deal dishonestly, are abominable to the LORD.

17 Remember what the Amalekites

did to you on your way out of
18 Egypt, how they met you on the
road when you were faint and
weary and cut off your rear, which
was lagging behind exhausted:
19 they showed no fear of God. When
the LORD your God gives you peace
from your enemies on every side,
in the land which he is giving you
to occupy as your patrimony, you
shall not fail to blot out the memory of the Amalekites from under
heaven.

26 WHEN you come into the land
which the LORD your God is giving
you to occupy as your patrimony
2 and settle in it, you shall take the
firstfruits of all the produce of the
soil, which you gather in from the
land which the LORD your God is
giving you, and put them in a basket. Then you shall go to the place
which the LORD your God will
choose as a dwelling for his Name
3 and come to the priest, whoever he
shall be in those days. You shall
say to him, 'I declare this day to
the LORD your God that I have
entered the land which the LORD
swore to our forefathers to give us.'
4 The priest shall take the basket
from your hand and set it down before the altar of the LORD your
5 God. Then you shall solemnly recite before the LORD your God:
'My father was a homeless*a* Aramaean who went down to Egypt
with a small company and lived
there until they became a great,
powerful, and numerous nation.
6 But the Egyptians ill-treated us,
humiliated us and imposed cruel
7 slavery upon us. Then we cried to
the LORD the God of our fathers for
help, and he listened to us and saw
our humiliation, our hardship and
8 distress; and so the LORD brought
us out of Egypt with a strong hand
and outstretched arm, with terrifying deeds, and with signs and
9 portents. He brought us to this
place and gave us this land, a land

flowing with milk and honey. And 10
now I have brought the firstfruits
of the soil which thou, O LORD,
hast given me.' You shall then set
the basket before the LORD your
God and bow down in worship before him. You shall all rejoice, you 11
and the Levites and the aliens
living among you, for all the good
things which the LORD your God
has given to you and to your
family.

When you have finished taking a 12
tithe of your produce in the third
year, the tithe-year, you shall give
it to the Levites and to the aliens,
the orphans, and the widows. They
shall eat it in your settlements and
be well fed. Then you shall declare 13
before the LORD your God: 'I have
rid my house of the tithe that was
holy to thee and given it to the Levites, to the aliens, the orphans,
and the widows, according to all
the commandments which thou
didst lay upon me. I have not
broken or forgotten any of thy
commandments. I have not eaten 14
any of the tithe while in mourning,
nor have I rid myself of it for unclean purposes, nor offered any of it
to*b* the dead. I have obeyed the
LORD my God: I have done all that
thou didst command me. Look 15
down from heaven, thy holy
dwelling-place, and bless thy people Israel and the ground which
thou hast given to us as thou didst
swear to our forefathers, a land
flowing with milk and honey.'

This day the LORD your God 16
commands you to keep these statutes and laws: be careful to observe them with all your heart and
soul. You have recognized the 17
LORD this day as your God; you
are to conform to his ways, to keep
his statutes, his commandments,
and his laws, and to obey him. The 18
LORD has recognized you this day
as his special possession, as he promised you, and to keep his commandments; he will raise you high 19

a Or wandering.   *b* Or for.

above all the nations which he has made, to bring him praise and fame and glory, and to be a people holy to the LORD your God, according to his promise.

Concluding charge of Moses to the people

27 MOSES, with the elders of Israel, gave the people this charge: 'Keep all the commandments that I lay 2 upon you this day. On the day that you cross the Jordan to the land which the LORD your God is giving you, you shall set up great 3 stones and plaster them over. You shall inscribe on them all the words of this law, when you have crossed over to enter the land which the LORD your God is giving you, a land flowing with milk and honey, as the LORD the God of your fathers 4 promised you. When you have crossed the Jordan you shall set up these stones on Mount Ebal, as I command you this day, and cover 5 them with plaster. You shall build an altar there to the LORD your God: it shall be an altar of stones on which you shall use no tool of 6 iron. You shall build the altar of the LORD your God with blocks of undressed stone, and you shall offer whole-offerings upon it to the 7 LORD your God. You shall slaughter shared-offerings and eat them there, and rejoice before the LORD your 8 God. You shall inscribe on the stones all the words of this law, engraving them with care.'

9 Moses and the levitical priests spoke to all Israel, 'Be silent, Israel, and listen; this day you have become a people belonging to the 10 LORD your God. Obey the LORD your God, and observe his commandments and statutes which I lay upon you this day.'

11 That day Moses gave the people 12 this command: 'Those who shall stand for the blessing of the people on Mount Gerizim when you have crossed the Jordan are these:

Simeon, Levi, Judah, Issachar, Jo-13 seph, and Benjamin. Those who shall stand on Mount Ebal for the curse are these: Reuben, Gad, Asher, Zebulun, Dan, and Naphtali.'

14 The Levites, in the hearing of all Israel, shall intone these words:

15 'A curse upon the man who carves an idol or casts an image, anything abominable to the LORD that craftsmen make, and sets it up in secret': the people shall all respond and say, 'Amen.'

16 'A curse upon him who slights his father or his mother': the people shall all say, 'Amen.'

17 'A curse upon him who moves his neighbour's boundary stone': the people shall all say, 'Amen.'

18 'A curse upon him who misdirects a blind man': the people shall all say, 'Amen.'

19 'A curse upon him who withholds justice from the alien, the orphan, and the widow': the people shall all say, 'Amen.'

20 'A curse upon him who lies with his father's wife, for he brings shame upon his father': the people shall all say, 'Amen.'

21 'A curse upon him who lies with any animal': the people shall all say, 'Amen.'

22 'A curse upon him who lies with his sister, his father's daughter or his mother's daughter': the people shall all say, 'Amen.'

23 'A curse upon him who lies with his wife's mother': the people shall all say, 'Amen.'

24 'A curse upon him who strikes another man in secret': the people shall all say, 'Amen.'

25 'A curse upon him who takes reward to kill a man with whom he has no feud': the people shall all say, 'Amen.'

26 'A curse upon any man who does not fulfil this law by doing all that it prescribes': the people shall all say, 'Amen.'

28 IF you will obey the LORD your God by diligently observing all his

commandments which I lay upon you this day, then the LORD your God will raise you high above all nations of the earth, and all these blessings shall come to you and light upon you, because you obey the LORD your God:

3 A blessing on you in the city; a blessing on you in the country.

4 A blessing on the fruit of your body, the fruit of your land and of your cattle, the offspring of your herds and of your lambing flocks.

5 A blessing on your basket and your kneading-trough.

6 A blessing on you as you come in; and a blessing on you as you go out.

7 May the LORD deliver up the enemies who attack you and let them be put to rout before you. Though they come out against you by one way, they shall flee before you by seven ways.

8 May the LORD grant you a blessing in your granaries and in all your labours; may the LORD your God bless you in the land which he is giving you.

9 The LORD will set you up as his own holy people, as he swore to you, if you keep the commandments of the LORD your God and 10 conform to his ways. Then all people on earth shall see that the LORD has named you as his very own, 11 and they shall go in fear of you. The LORD will make you prosper greatly in the fruit of your body and of your cattle, and in the fruit of the ground in the land which he swore to your forefathers to give you. 12 May the LORD open the heavens for you, his rich treasure house, to give rain upon your land at the proper time and bless everything to which you turn your hand. You shall lend to many nations, but you 13 shall not borrow; the LORD will make you the head and not the tail: you shall be always at the top and never at the bottom, when you listen to the commandments of the

LORD your God, which I give you this day to keep and to fulfil. You 14 shall turn neither to the right nor to the left from all the things which I command you this day nor shall you follow after and worship other gods.

BUT if you do not obey the LORD 15 your God by diligently observing all his commandments and statutes which I lay upon you this day, then all these maledictions shall come to you and light upon you:

A curse upon you in the city; a 16 curse upon you in the country.

A curse upon your basket and 17 your kneading-trough.

A curse upon the fruit of your 18 body, the fruit of your land, the offspring of your herds and of your lambing flocks.

A curse upon you as you come 19 in; and a curse upon you as you go out.

May the LORD send upon you 20 starvation, burning thirst, and dysentery,[a] whatever you are about, until you are destroyed and quickly perish for your evil doings, because you have forsaken me.

May the LORD cause pestilence 21 to haunt you until he has exterminated you out of the land which you are entering to occupy; may 22 the LORD afflict you with wasting disease and recurrent fever, ague and eruptions; with drought, black blight and red; and may these plague you until you perish. May 23 the skies above you be bronze, and the earth beneath you iron. May 24 the LORD turn the rain upon your country into fine sand, and may dust come down upon you from the sky until you are blotted out.

May the LORD put you to rout 25 before the enemy. Though you go out against them by one way, you shall flee before them by seven ways. May you be repugnant to all the kingdoms on earth. May your 26 bodies become food for the birds of

[a] Or cursing, confusion, and rebuke.

the air and the wild beasts, with no man to scare them away.

27 May the LORD strike you with Egyptian boils and with tumours, scabs, and itches, for which you 28 will find no cure. May the LORD strike you with madness, blind-29 ness, and bewilderment; so that you will grope about in broad day-light, just as a blind man gropes in darkness, and you will fail to find your way. You will also be oppressed and robbed, day in, day 30 out, with no one to save you. A wo-man will be pledged to you, but another shall ravish her; you will build a house but not live in it; you will plant a vineyard but not enjoy 31 its fruit. Your ox will be slaughter-ed before your eyes, but you will not eat any of it; and before your eyes your ass will be stolen and will not come back to you; your sheep will be given to the enemy, and there will be no one to recover 32 them. Your sons and daughters will be given to another people while you look on; your eyes will strain after them all day long, and 33 you will be powerless. A nation whom you do not know shall eat the fruit of your land and all your toil, and your lot will be nothing 34 but brutal oppression. The sights 35 you see will drive you mad. May the LORD strike you on knee and leg with malignant boils for which you will find no cure; they will spread from the sole of your foot to 36 the crown of your head. May the LORD give you up, you and the king whom you have appointed, to a nation whom neither you nor your fathers have known, and there you will worship other gods, 37 gods of wood and stone. You will become a horror, a byword, and an object-lesson to all the peoples amongst whom the LORD disperses you.

38 You will carry out seed for your fields in plenty, but you will har-vest little; for the locusts will de-39 vour it. You will plant vineyards and cultivate them, but you will not drink the wine or gather the grapes; for the grub will eat them. You will have olive-trees all over 40 your territory, but you will not a-noint yourselves with their oil; for your olives will drop off. You will 41 bear sons and daughters, but they will not remain yours because they will be taken into captivity. All 42 your trees and the fruit of the ground will be infested with the mole-cricket. The alien who lives 43 with you will raise himself higher and higher, and you will sink lower and lower. He will lend to 44 you but you will not lend to him: he will be the head and you the tail.

All these maledictions will come 45 upon you; they will pursue you and overtake you until you are destroy-ed because you did not obey the LORD your God by keeping the commandments and statutes which he gave you. They shall be a sign 46 and a portent to you and your descendants for ever, because you 47 did not serve the LORD your God with joy and with a glad heart for all your blessings. Then in hunger 48 and thirst, in nakedness and ex-treme want, you shall serve your enemies whom the LORD will send against you, and they will put a yoke of iron on your neck when they have subdued you. May the 49 LORD raise against you a nation from afar, from the other end of the earth, who will swoop upon you like a vulture, a nation whose lan-guage you will not understand, a 50 nation of grim aspect with no reverence for age and no pity for the young. They will devour the 51 young of your cattle and the fruit of your land, when you have been subdued. They will leave you neither corn, nor new wine nor oil, neither the offspring of your herds nor of your lambing flocks, until you are annihilated. They will be-52 siege you in all your cities until they bring down your lofty im-pregnable walls, those city walls throughout your land in which you trust. They will besiege you within all your cities, throughout the land which the LORD your God has 53 given you. Then you will eat your own children, the flesh of your sons and daughters whom the LORD your God has given you, because of the dire straits to which you will be reduced when your enemy be-54 sieges you. The pampered, delicate man will not share with his brother, or the wife of his bosom, or his 55 own remaining children, any of the meat which he is eating, the flesh of his own children. He is left with nothing else because of the dire straits to which you will be reduced when your enemy besieges you within 56 your cities. The pampered, delicate woman, the woman who has never even tried to put a foot to the ground, so delicate and pampered she is, will not share with her own husband or her son or her daughter 57 the afterbirth which she expels, or any boy or girl that she may bear. She will herself eat them secretly in her extreme want, because of the dire straits to which you will be reduced when your enemy besieges you within your cities.

58   If you do not observe and fulfil all the law written down in this book, if you do not revere this honoured and dreaded name, this 59 name 'the LORD*a* your God', then the LORD will strike you and your descendants with unimaginable plagues, malignant and persistent, and with sickness, persistent and 60 severe. He will bring upon you once again all the diseases of Egypt which you dread, and they will 61 cling to you. The LORD will bring upon you sickness and plague of every kind not written down in this book of the law, until you are 62 destroyed. Then you who were countless as the stars in the sky will be left few in number, because you did not obey the LORD your 63 God. Just as the LORD took de-

light in you, prospering and increasing you, so now it will be his delight to destroy and exterminate you, and you will be uprooted from the land which you are entering to occupy. The LORD will 64 scatter you among all peoples from one end of the earth to the other, and there you will worship other gods whom neither you have known nor your forefathers, gods of wood and stone. Among those 65 nations you will find no peace, no rest for the sole of your foot. Then the LORD will give you an unquiet mind, dim eyes, and failing appetite. Your life will hang continu-66 ally in suspense, fear will beset you night and day, and you will find no security all your life long. Every 67 morning you will say, 'Would God it were evening!', and every evening, 'Would God it were morning!', for the fear that lives in your heart and the sights that you see. The 68 LORD will bring you sorrowing back to Egypt by that very road of which I said to you, 'You shall not see that road again'; and there you will offer to sell yourselves to your enemies as slaves and slave-girls, but there will be no buyer.

These are the words of the cove-29 nant which the LORD commanded Moses to make with the Israelites in Moab, in addition to the covenant which he made with them on Horeb.

MOSES summoned all the Israel-2 ites and said to them: 'You have seen with your own eyes all that the LORD did in Egypt to Pharaoh, to all his servants, and to the whole land, the great challenge which you 3 yourselves witnessed, those great signs and portents, but to this day 4 the LORD has not given you a mind to learn, or eyes to see, or ears to hear. I led you for forty years in 5 the wilderness; your clothes did not wear out on you, nor did your sandals wear out and fall off your

a See note on Exod. 3. 15.

6 feet; you ate no bread and drank no wine or strong drink, in order that you might learn that I am the 7 LORD your God. You came to this place where Sihon king of Heshbon and Og king of Bashan came to at- 8 tack us, and we defeated them. We took their land and gave it as patrimony to the Reubenites, the Gadites, and half the tribe of Manasseh. 9 You shall observe the provisions of this covenant and keep them so that you may be successful in all you do.

10 'You all stand here today before the LORD your God, tribal chiefs, elders, and officers, all the men of 11 Israel, with your dependants, your wives, the aliens who live in your camp – all of them, from those who chop wood to those who draw wa- 12 ter – and you are ready to accept the oath and enter into the covenant which the LORD your God is 13 making with you today. The covenant is to constitute you his people this day, and he will be your God, as he promised you and as he swore to your forefathers, Abra- 14 ham, Isaac and Jacob. It is not with you alone that I am making 15 this covenant and this oath, but with all those who stand here with us today before the LORD our God and also with those who are not 16 here with us today. For you know how we lived in Egypt and how we and you, as we passed through the 17 nations, saw their loathsome idols and the false gods they had, the gods of wood and stone, of silver 18 and gold. If there should be among you a man or woman, family or tribe, who is moved today to turn from the LORD our God and to go worshipping the gods of those nations – if there is among you such a root from which springs gall and 19 wormwood, then when he hears the terms of this oath, he may inwardly flatter himself and think, "All will be well with me even if I follow the promptings of my stubborn heart"; but this will bring

everything to ruin. The LORD will 20 not be willing to forgive him; for then his anger and resentment will overwhelm this man, and the denunciations prescribed in this book will fall heavily on him, and the LORD will blot out his name from under heaven. The LORD 21 will single him out from all the tribes of Israel for disaster to fall upon him, according to the oath required by the covenant and prescribed in this book of the law.

'The next generation, your sons 22 who follow you and the foreigners who come from distant countries, will see the plagues of this land and the ulcers which the LORD has brought upon its people, the whole 23 land burnt up with brimstone and salt, so that it cannot be sown, or yield herb or green plant. It will be as desolate as were Sodom and Gomorrah, Admah and Zeboyim, when the LORD overthrew them in his anger and rage. Then they, and 24 all the nations with them, will ask, "Why has the LORD so afflicted this land? Why has there been this great outburst of wrath?" The an- 25 swer will be: "Because they forsook the covenant of the LORD the God of their fathers which he made with them when he brought them out of Egypt. They began to wor- 26 ship other gods and to bow down to them, gods whom they had not known and whom the LORD had not assigned to them. The anger of 27 the LORD was roused against that land, so that he brought upon it all the maledictions written in this book. The LORD uprooted them 28 from their soil in anger, in wrath and great fury, and banished them to another land, where they are to this day."

'There are things hidden, and 29 they belong to the LORD our God, but what is revealed belongs to us and our children for ever; it is for us to observe all that is prescribed in this law.

30 'When these things have befallen you, the blessing and the curse of which I have offered you the choice, if you and your sons take them to heart there in all the countries to which the LORD your 2 God has banished you, if you turn back to him and obey him heart and soul in all that I command you 3 this day, then the LORD your God will show you compassion and restore your fortunes. He will gather you again from all the countries to 4 which he has scattered you. Even though he were to banish you to the four corners of the world, the LORD your God will gather you from there, from there he will fetch 5 you home. The LORD your God will bring you into the land which your forefathers occupied, and you will occupy it again; then he will bring you prosperity and make you more numerous than your forefathers 6 were. The LORD your God will circumcise[a] your hearts and the hearts of your descendants, so that you will love him with all your heart 7 and soul and you will live. Then the LORD your God will turn all these denunciations against your enemies and the foes who persecute 8 you. You will then again obey the LORD and keep all his commandments which I give you this day. 9-10 The LORD your God will make you more than prosperous in all that you do, in the fruit of your body and of your cattle and in the fruits of the earth; for, when you obey the LORD your God by keeping his commandments and statutes, as they are written in this book of the law, and when you turn back to the LORD your God with all your heart and soul, he will again rejoice over you and be good to you, as he rejoiced over your forefathers.

11 'The commandment that I lay on you this day is not too difficult 12 for you, it is not too remote. It is not in heaven, that you should say, "Who will go up to heaven for us to fetch it and tell it to us, so that we can keep it?" Nor is it beyond the 13 sea, that you should say, "Who will cross the sea for us to fetch it and tell it to us, so that we can keep it?" It is a thing very near to 14 you, upon your lips and in your heart ready to be kept.

'Today I offer you the choice of 15 life and good, or death and evil. If you obey the commandments of 16 the LORD your God which I give you this day, by loving the LORD your God, by conforming to his ways and by keeping his commandments, statutes, and laws, then you will live and increase, and the LORD your God will bless you in the land which you are entering to occupy. But if your heart turns 17 away and you do not listen and you are led on to bow down to other gods and worship them, I tell you 18 this day that you will perish; you will not live long in the land which you will enter to occupy after crossing the Jordan. I summon 19 heaven and earth to witness against you this day: I offer you the choice of life or death, blessing or curse. Choose life and then you and your descendants will live; love 20 the LORD your God, obey him and hold fast to him: that is life for you and length of days in the land which the LORD swore to give to your forefathers, Abraham, Isaac and Jacob.'

Moses finished speaking these 31 words to all Israel, and then he 2 said, 'I am now a hundred and twenty years old, and I can no longer move about as I please; and the LORD has told me that I may not cross the Jordan. The LORD 3 your God will cross over at your head and destroy these nations before your advance, and you shall occupy their lands; and, as he directed, Joshua will lead you across. The LORD will do to these 4 nations as he did to Sihon and Og, kings of the Amorites, and to their

[a] *Or* incline.

5 lands; he will destroy them. The LORD will deliver them into your power, and you shall do to them as 6 I commanded you. Be strong, be resolute; you must not dread them or be afraid, for the LORD your God himself goes with you; he will not fail you or forsake you.'

7 Moses summoned Joshua and said to him in the presence of all Israel, 'Be strong, be resolute; for it is you who are to lead this people into the land which the LORD swore to give their forefathers, and you are to bring them into posses- 8 sion of it. The LORD himself goes at your head; he will be with you; he will not fail you or forsake you. Do not be discouraged or afraid.'

9 Moses wrote down this law and gave it to the priests, the sons of Levi, who carried the Ark of the Covenant of the LORD, and to all 10 the elders of Israel. Moses gave them this command: 'At the end of every seven years, at the appointed time for the year of remission, at the pilgrim-feast of Tabernacles, 11 when all Israel comes to enter the presence of the LORD your God in the place which he will choose, you shall read this law publicly in the 12 hearing of all Israel. Assemble the people, men, women, and depen- dants, together with the aliens who live in your settlements, so that they may listen, and learn to fear the LORD your God and observe 13 all these laws with care. Their chil- dren, too, who do not know them, shall hear them, and learn to fear the LORD your God all their lives in the land which you will occupy after crossing the Jordan.'

Joshua appointed successor to Moses

14 THE LORD said to Moses, 'The time of your death is drawing near; call Joshua, and then come and stand in the Tent of the Presence so that I may give him his com-

mission.' So Moses and Joshua went and took their stand in the Tent of the Presence; and the LORD 15 appeared in the tent in a pillar of cloud, and the pillar of cloud stood at the entrance of the tent.

The LORD said to Moses, 'You 16 are about to die like your fore- fathers, and this people, when they come into the land and live among foreigners, will go wantonly after their gods; they will abandon me and break the covenant which I have made with them. Then my 17 anger will be roused against them, and I will abandon them and hide my face from them. They will be an easy prey, and many terrible disas- ters will come upon them. They will say on that day, "These disas- ters have come because our God is not among us." On that day I will 18 hide my face because of all the evil they have done in turning to other gods.

'Now write down this rule of 19 life[a] and teach it to the Israelites; make them repeat it, so that it may be on record against them. When I 20 have brought them into the land which I swore to give to their fore- fathers, a land flowing with milk and honey, and they have plenty to eat and grow fat, they will turn to other gods and worship them, they will spurn me and break my covenant; and many calamities 21 and disasters will follow. Then this rule of life will confront them as a record, for it will not be forgotten by their descendants. For even be- fore I bring them into the land which I swore to give them, I know which way their thoughts incline already.'

That day Moses wrote down this 22 rule of life and taught it to the Israelites. The LORD[b] gave Joshua 23 son of Nun his commission in these words: 'Be strong, be resolute; for you shall bring the Israelites into the land which I swore to give them, and I will be with you.'

---

[a] rule of life: *or* song.   *Prob. rdg.; Heb.* He.

24 When Moses had finished writing down these laws in a book,
25 from beginning to end, he gave this command to the Levites who carried the Ark of the Covenant of the
26 LORD: 'Take this book of the law and put it beside the Ark of the Covenant of the LORD your God to
27 be a witness against you. For I know how defiant and stubborn you are; even during my lifetime you have defied the LORD; how much more, then, will you do so
28 when I am dead? Assemble all the elders of your tribes and your officers; I will say all these things in their hearing and will summon heaven and earth to witness against
29 them. For I know that after my death you will take to degrading practices and turn aside from the way which I told you to follow, and in days to come disaster will come upon you, because you are doing what is wrong in the eyes of the LORD and so provoking him to anger.'

Two historical poems

30 MOSES recited this song from beginning to end in the hearing of the whole assembly of Israel:

32 Give ear to what I say, O heavens, earth, listen to my words;
2 my teaching shall fall like drops of rain,
my words shall distil like dew,
like fine rain upon the grass
and like the showers on young plants.

3 When I call aloud the name of the LORD,[a]
you shall respond, 'Great is our God,
4 the creator[b] whose work is perfect, and all his ways are just,
a faithful god, who does no wrong,
righteous and true is He!'

Perverse and crooked generation 5
whose faults have proved you no children of his,
is this how you repay the LORD, 6
you brutish and stupid people?
Is he not your father who formed you?
Did he not make you and establish you?
Remember the days of old, 7
think of the generations long ago;
ask your father to recount it
and your elders to tell you the tale.

When the Most High parcelled out 8
the nations,
when he dispersed all mankind,
he laid down the boundaries of every people
according to the number of the sons of God;
but the LORD's share was his own 9
people,
Jacob was his allotted portion.
He found him in a desert land, 10
in a waste and howling void.
He protected and trained him,
he guarded him as the apple of his eye,
as an eagle watches over its nest, 11
hovers above its young,
spreads its pinions and takes them up,
and carries them upon its wings.
The LORD alone led him, 12
no alien god at his side.
He made him ride on the heights of 13
the earth
and fed him on the harvest of the fields;
he satisfied him with honey from the crags
and oil from the flinty rock,
curds from the cattle, milk from 14
the ewes,
the fat of lambs' kidneys,
of rams, the breed of Bashan, and of goats,
with the finest flour of wheat;
and he drank wine from the blood of the grape.
Jacob ate and was well fed, 15
Jeshurun grew fat and unruly,[c]

[a] Or the name JEHOVAH.   [b] Or rock.   [c] Or and kicked.

214

he grew fat, he grew bloated and
  sleek.
He forsook God who made him
and dishonoured the Rock of his
  salvation.
16 They roused his jealousy with
  foreign gods
and provoked him with abominable practices.
17 They sacrificed to foreign demons
  that are no gods,
gods who were strangers to them;
they took up with new gods from
  their neighbours,
gods whom your fathers did not
  acknowledge.
18 You forsook the creator*ᵃ* who begot you
and cared nothing for God who
  brought you to birth.
19 The LORD saw and spurned them;
his own sons and daughters provoked him.
20 'I will hide my face from them,' he
  said;
'let me see what their end will be,
for they are a mutinous generation,
sons who are not to be trusted.
21 They roused my jealousy with a
  god of no account,
with their false gods they provoked
  me;
so I will rouse their jealousy with a
  people of no account,
with a brutish nation I will provoke
  them.
22 For fire is kindled by my anger,
it burns to the depths of Sheol;
it devours earth and its harvest
and sets fire to the very roots of
  the mountains.
23 I will heap on them one disaster
  after another,
I will use up all my arrows on them:
24 pangs of hunger, ravages of plague,
  and bitter pestilence.
I will harry them with the fangs of
  wild beasts
and the poison of creatures that
  crawl in the dust.
25 The sword will make orphans in
  the streets
and widows in their own homes;

it will take toll of young man and
  maid,
of babes in arms and old men.
26 I had resolved to strike them down
and to destroy all memory of them,
27 but I feared that I should be provoked by their foes,
that their enemies would take the
  credit
and say, "It was not the LORD,
it was we who raised the hand that
  did this."'

28 They are a nation that lacks good
  counsel,
devoid of understanding.
29 If only they had the wisdom to
  understand this
and give thought to their end!
30 How could one man pursue a thousand of them,
how could two put ten thousand to
  flight,
if their Rock had not sold them to
  their enemies,
if the LORD had not handed them
  over?
31 For the enemy have no Rock like
  ours,
in themselves they are mere fools.
32 Their vines are vines of Sodom,
grown on the terraces of Gomorrah;
their grapes are poisonous,
the clusters bitter to the taste.
33 Their wine is the venom of serpents,
the cruel poison of asps;
34 all this I have in reserve,
sealed up in my storehouses
35 till the day of punishment and vengeance,
till the moment when they slip and
  fall;
for the day of their downfall is
  near,
their doom is fast approaching.
36 The LORD will give his people justice
and have compassion on his servants;
for he will see that their strength is
  gone:
alone, or defended by his clan, no
  one is left.

ᵃ Or rock.

37 He will say, 'Where are your gods,
   the rock in which you sought shelter,
38 the gods who ate the fat of your
   sacrifices
   and drank the wine of your drink-
   offerings?
   Let them rise to help you!
   Let them give you shelter!
39 See now that I, I am He,
   and there is no god beside me:
   I put to death and I keep alive,
   I wound and I heal;
   there is no rescue from my grasp.
40 I lift my hand to heaven
   and swear: As I live for ever,
41 when I have whetted my flashing
   sword,
   when I have set my hand to judgement,
   then I will punish my adversaries
   and take vengeance on my enemies.
42 I will make my arrows drunk with
   blood,
   my sword shall devour flesh,
   blood of slain and captives,
   the heads of the enemy princes.'
43 Rejoice with him, you heavens,
   bow down, all you gods, before him;
   for he will avenge the blood of his
   sons
   and take vengeance on his adversaries;
   he will punish those who hate him
   and make expiation for his people's
   land.

44   This is the song that Moses came
   and recited in the hearing of the
   people, he and Joshua son of Nun.
45   Moses finished speaking to all
46 Israel, and then he said, 'Take to
   heart all these warnings which I
   solemnly give you this day: command your children to be careful to
   observe all the words of this law.
47 For you they are no empty words;
   they are your very life, and by
   them you shall live long in the land
   which you are to occupy after
   crossing the Jordan.'

That same day the LORD spoke 48
to Moses and said, 'Go up this 49
mount Abarim, Mount Nebo in
Moab, to the east of Jericho, and
look out over the land of Canaan
that I am giving to the Israelites
for their possession. On this moun- 50
tain you shall die and be gathered
to your father's kin, just as Aaron
your brother died on Mount Hor
and was gathered to his father's
kin. This is because both of you 51
were unfaithful to me at the waters
of Meribah-by-Kadesh in the wilderness of Zin, where you did not
uphold my holiness among the
Israelites. You shall see the land 52
from a distance but you may not
enter the land I am giving to the
Israelites.'

THIS is the blessing that Moses the 33
man of God pronounced upon the
Israelites before his death:

The LORD came from Sinai   2
and shone forth from Seir.
He showed himself from Mount
   Paran,
and with him were myriads of holy
   ones[a]
streaming along at his right hand.
Truly he loves his people   3
and blesses his saints.[b]
They sit at his feet
and receive his instruction,
the law which Moses laid upon   4
   us,
as a possession for the assembly of
   Jacob.
Then a king arose[c] in Jeshurun, 5
when the chiefs of the people were
   assembled
together with all the tribes of Israel.

Of Reuben he said:[d]   6

May Reuben live and not die out,
but may he be few in number.

---

[a] and with...holy ones: *prob. rdg.*; *Heb.* and he came from myriads of holiness.
[b] Or holy ones.   [c] Or Then there was a king...
[d] Of Reuben he said: *prob. rdg.*; *Heb. om.*

7 And of Judah he said this:

Hear, O LORD, the cry of Judah
and join him to his people,
thou whose hands fight for him,
who art his helper against his foes.

8 Of Levi he said:

Thou didst give thy Thummim to
Levi,
thy Urim to thy loyal servant
whom thou didst prove at Massah,
for whom thou didst plead at the
waters of Meribah,
9 who said of his parents, I do not
know them,
who did not acknowledge his brothers,
nor recognize his children.
They observe thy word
and keep thy covenant;
10 they teach thy precepts to Jacob,
thy law to Israel.
They offer thee the smoke of sacrifice
and offerings on thy altar.
11 Bless all his powers,*a* O LORD,
and accept the work of his hands.
Strike his adversaries hip and
thigh,
and may his enemies rise no more.

12 Of Benjamin he said:

The LORD's beloved dwells in security,
the High God*b* shields him all the
day long,
and he dwells under his protection.

13 Of Joseph he said:

The LORD's blessing is on his land
with precious fruit watered from
heaven above
and from the deep that lurks below,
14 with precious fruit ripened by the
sun,
precious fruit, the produce of the
months,
with all good things from the 15
ancient mountains,
the precious fruit of the everlasting
hills,
the precious fruits of earth and all 16
its store,
by the favour of him who dwells in
the burning bush.
This shall rest*c* upon the head of
Joseph,
on the brow of him who was prince
among*d* his brothers.
In majesty he shall be like a first- 17
born ox,
his horns those of a wild ox
with which he will gore nations
and drive*e* them to the ends of
earth.
Such will be the myriads of
Ephraim,
and such the thousands of Manasseh.

Of Zebulun he said: 18

Rejoice, Zebulun, when you sally
forth,
rejoice in your tents, Issachar.
They shall summon nations to the 19
mountain,
there they will offer true sacrifices,
for they shall suck the abundance
of the seas
and draw out*f* the hidden wealth of
the sand.

Of Gad he said: 20

Blessed be Gad, in his wide domain;
he couches like a lion
tearing an arm or a scalp.
He chose the best for himself,   21
for to him was allotted a ruler's
portion,
when the chiefs of the people were
assembled together.
He did what the LORD deemed
right,
observing his ordinances for Israel.

---

a Or skill.   *b* the High God: *prob. rdg.*; *Heb.* upon him.   *c* *Prob. rdg., cp. Gen.*
49. 26; *Heb. has an unintelligible form.*   *d* him . . . among: *or* the one cursed by.
e and drive: *prob. rdg.*; *Heb.* together.   *f* draw out: *prob. rdg.*; *Heb. obscure.*

22 Of Dan he said:

> Dan is a lion's cub
> springing out from Bashan.

23 Of Naphtali he said:

> Naphtali is richly favoured
> and full of the blessings of the
>   LORD;
> his patrimony stretches to the sea
> and southward.

24 Of Asher he said:

> Asher is most blest of sons,
> may he be the favourite among[a]
>   his brothers
> and bathe his feet in oil.
> 25 May your bolts be of iron and
>   bronze,
> and your strength last as long as
>   you live.

26 There is none like the God of Je-
>   shurun
> who rides the heavens to your help,
> riding the clouds in his glory,
> 27 who humbled the gods of old
> and subdued[b] the ancient powers;
> who drove out the enemy before
>   you
> and gave the word to destroy.
> 28 Israel lives in security,
> the tribes of Jacob by them-
>   selves,
> in a land of corn and wine[c]
> where the skies drip with dew.
> 29 Happy are you, people of Israel,
>   peerless, set free;
> the LORD is the shield that guards
>   you,
> the Blessed One is your glorious
>   sword.
> Your enemies come cringing to you,
> and you shall trample their bodies
>   under foot.

The death of Moses

THEN Moses went up from the 34 lowlands of Moab to Mount Nebo, to the top of Pisgah, eastwards from Jericho, and the LORD showed him the whole land: Gilead as far as Dan; the whole of Naphtali; 2 the territory of Ephraim and Manasseh, and all Judah as far as the western sea; the Negeb and the 3 Plain; the valley of Jericho, the Vale of Palm Trees, as far as Zoar. The LORD said to him, 'This is the 4 land which I swore to Abraham, Isaac and Jacob that I would give to their descendants. I have let you see it with your own eyes, but you shall not cross over into it.'

There in the land of Moab Moses 5 the servant of the LORD died, as the LORD had said. He was buried 6 in a valley in Moab opposite Bethpeor, but to this day no one knows his burial-place. Moses was a 7 hundred and twenty years old when he died; his sight was not dimmed nor had his vigour failed. The Israelites wept for Moses in 8 the lowlands of Moab for thirty days; then the time of mourning for Moses was ended. And Joshua 9 son of Nun was filled with the spirit of wisdom, for Moses had laid his hands on him, and the Israelites listened to him and did what the LORD had commanded Moses.

There has never yet risen in Is- 10 rael a prophet like Moses, whom the LORD knew face to face: re- 11 member all the signs and portents which the LORD sent him to show in Egypt to Pharaoh and all his servants and the whole land; re- 12 member the strong hand of Moses and the terrible deeds which he did in the sight of all Israel.

---

[a] *Or* of.   [b] *Prob. rdg.; Heb.* under.   [c] *Or* new wine.

THE BOOK OF

JOSHUA

Israel's entry into the promised land

1 AFTER the death of Moses the servant of the LORD, the LORD said to Joshua son of 2 Nun, his assistant, 'My servant Moses is dead; now it is for you to cross the Jordan, you and this whole people of Israel, to the land 3 which I am giving them. Every place where you set foot is yours: I have given it to you, as I promised 4 Moses. From the desert and the Lebanon to the great river, the river Euphrates, and across all the Hittite country westwards to the Great Sea,ᵃ all this shall be our 5 land. No one will ever be able to stand against you: as I was with Moses, so will I be with you; I will 6 not fail you or forsake you. Be strong, be resolute; it is you who are to put this people in possession of the land which I swore to give to 7 their fathers. Only be strong and resolute; observe diligently all the law which my servant Moses has given you. You must not turn from it to right or left, if you would pros- 8 per wherever you go. This book of the law must ever be on your lips; you must keep it in mind day and night so that you may diligently observe all that is written in it. Then you will prosper and be suc- 9 cessful in all that you do. This is my command: be strong, be reso- lute; do not be fearful or dismayed, for the LORD your God is with you 10 wherever you go.' Then Joshua 11 told the officers to pass through the camp and give this order to the people: 'Get food ready to take with you; for within three days you will be crossing the Jordan to oc-

cupy the country which the LORD your God is giving you to possess.' To the Reubenites, the Gadites, 12 and the half tribe of Manasseh, Joshua said, 'Remember the com- 13 mand which Moses the servant of the LORD gave you when he said, "The LORD your God will grant you security here and will give you this territory." Your wives and de- 14 pendants and your herds may stay east of the Jordan in the territory which Moses has given you, but for yourselves, all the warriors among you must cross over as a fighting force at the head of your kinsmen. You must help them, until the 15 LORD grants them security like you and they too take possession of the land which the LORD your God is giving them. You may then return to the land which is your own pos- session, the territory which Moses the servant of the LORD has given you east of the Jordan.' They an- 16 swered Joshua, 'Whatever you tell us, we will do; wherever you send us, we will go. As we obeyed Moses, 17 so will we obey you; and may the LORD your God be with you as he was with Moses! Whoever rebels 18 against your authority, and fails to carry out all your orders, shall be put to death. Only be strong and resolute.'

Joshua son of Nun sent two spies 2 out from Shittim secretly with or- ders to reconnoitre the country. The two men came to Jericho and went to the house of a prostitute named Rahab, and spent the night there. It was reported to the king 2 of Jericho that some Israelites had arrived that night to explore the country. So the king sent to Rahab 3 and said, 'Bring out the men who

---

ᵃ *Or the Mediterranean Sea.*

have come to you and are now in your house; they are here to ex-
4 plore the whole country.' The woman, who had taken the two men and hidden them,[a] replied, 'Yes, the men did come to me, but I did not know where they came from;
5 and when it was time to shut the gate at nightfall, they had gone. I do not know where they were going, but if you hurry after them,
6 you will catch them up.' In fact, she had taken them up on to the roof and concealed them among the stalks of flax which she had
7 laid out there in rows. The messengers went in pursuit of them down the road to the fords of the Jordan, and the gate was closed as
8 soon as they had gone out. The men had not yet settled down, when Rahab came up to them on the roof
9 and said to them, 'I know that the LORD has given this land to you, that terror of you has descended upon us all, and that because of you the whole country is panic-strick-
10 en. For we have heard how the LORD dried up the water of the Red Sea[b] before you when you came out of Egypt, and what you did to Sihon and Og, the two Amorite kings beyond the Jordan,
11 whom you put to death. When we heard this, our courage failed us; your coming has left no spirit in any of us; for the LORD your God is God in heaven above and on earth
12 below. Swear to me now by the LORD that you will keep faith with my family, as I have kept faith with you. Give me a token of good
13 faith; promise that you will spare the lives of my father and mother, my brothers and sisters and all who belong to them, and save us from
14 death.' The men replied, 'Our lives for yours, so long as you do not betray our business. When the LORD gives us the country, we will deal honestly and faithfully by you.'

15 She then let them down through an opening by a rope; for the house where she lived was on an angle of the wall. 'Take to the hills,' she
16 said, 'or the pursuers will come upon you. Hide yourselves there for three days until they come back, and then go on your way.' The men
17 warned her that they would be released from the oath she had made them take unless she did what they
18 told her. 'When we enter the land,' they said, 'you must fasten this strand of scarlet cord in the opening through which you have lowered us, and get everybody together here in the house, your father and mother, your brothers and all your
19 family. If anybody goes out of doors into the street, his blood shall be on his own head; we shall be quit of the oath. But if a hand is laid on anyone who stays indoors with you, his blood shall be on our heads. Remember too that, if you
20 betray our business, then we shall be quit of the oath you have made
21 us take.' She replied, 'It shall be as you say', and sent them away.
22 They set off, and she fastened the strand of scarlet cord in the opening. The men made their way into the hills and stayed there three days until the pursuers returned. They had searched all along the road, but had not found them.[c]
23 The two men then turned and came down from the hills, crossed the river and returned to Joshua son of Nun. They told him all that had happened to them and said to him,
24 'The LORD has put the whole country into our hands, and now all its people are panic-stricken at our approach.'

3 Joshua rose early in the morning, and he and all the Israelites set out from Shittim and came to the Jordan, where they encamped
2 before crossing the river. At the end of three days the officers passed

---

[a] *Prob. rdg.; Heb.* him.   [b] *Or* the Sea of Reeds.
[c] three days...found them: *or* three days while the pursuers scoured the land and searched all along the road, but did not find them.

3 through the camp, and gave this order to the people: 'When you see the Ark of the Covenant of the LORD your God being carried forward by the levitical priests, then you too shall leave your positions 4 and set out. Follow it, but do not go close to it; keep some distance behind, about a thousand yards. This will show you the way you are to go, for you have not travelled 5 this way before.' Joshua then said to the people, 'Hallow yourselves, for tomorrow the LORD will do a 6 great miracle among you.' To the priests he said, 'Lift up the Ark of the Covenant and pass in front of the people.' So they lifted up the Ark of the Covenant and went in 7 front of the people. Then the LORD said to Joshua, 'Today I will begin to make you stand high in the eyes of all Israel, and they shall know that I will be with you as I was with 8 Moses. Give orders to the priests who carry the Ark of the Covenant, and tell them that when they come to the edge of the waters of the Jordan, they are to take their stand in the river.'

9 Then Joshua said to the Israelites, 'Come here and listen to the 10 words of the LORD your God. By this you shall know that the living God is among you and that he will drive out before you the Canaanites, the Hittites, the Hivites, the Perizzites, the Girgashites, the 11 Amorites, and the Jebusites; the Ark of the Covenant of the LORD,[a] the lord of all the earth, is to cross 12 the Jordan at your head. Choose twelve men from the tribes of Israel, one man from each tribe. 13 When the priests carrying the Ark of the LORD, the lord of all the earth, set foot in the waters of the Jordan, then the waters of the Jordan will be cut off; the water coming down from upstream will stand 14 piled up like a bank.' So the people set out from their tents to cross the Jordan, with the priests in front of them carrying the Ark of the Covenant. Now the Jordan is in full 15 flood in all its reaches throughout the time of harvest. When the priests reached the Jordan and dipped their feet in the water at the edge, the water coming down 16 from upstream was brought to a standstill; it piled up like a bank for a long way back, as far as Adam, a town near Zarethan. The waters coming down to the Sea of the Arabah, the Dead Sea, were completely cut off, and the people crossed over opposite Jericho. The 17 priests carrying the Ark of the Covenant of the LORD stood firm on the dry bed in the middle of the Jordan; and all Israel passed over on dry ground until the whole nation had crossed the river.

WHEN the whole nation had finish- 4 ed crossing the Jordan, the LORD said to Joshua, 'Take twelve men 2 from the people, one from each tribe, and order them to lift up 3 twelve stones from this place, out of the middle of the Jordan, where the feet of the priests stood firm. They are to carry them across and set them down in the camp where you spend the night.' Joshua sum- 4 moned the twelve men whom he had chosen out of the Israelites, one man from each tribe, and said 5 to them, 'Cross over in front of the Ark of the LORD your God as far as the middle of the Jordan, and let each of you take a stone and hoist it on his shoulder, one for each of the tribes of Israel. These stones 6 are to stand as a memorial among you; and in days to come, when your children ask you what these stones mean, you shall tell them 7 how the waters of the Jordan were cut off before the Ark of the Covenant of the LORD when it crossed the Jordan. Thus these stones will always be a reminder to the Israelites.' The Israelites did as Joshua 8 had commanded: they lifted up

---

[a] of the LORD: *prob. rdg., cp. verse 17*; Heb. *om.*

twelve stones from the middle of the Jordan, as the LORD had instructed Joshua, one for each of the tribes of Israel, carried them across to the camp and set them down there.

9 Joshua set up twelve stones in the middle of the Jordan at the place where the priests stood who carried the Ark of the Covenant,
10 and there they are to this day. The priests carrying the Ark remained standing in the middle of the Jordan until every command which the LORD had told Joshua to give to the people was fulfilled, and the people had made good speed across.
11 When all the people had finished crossing, then the Ark of the LORD crossed, and the priests with it.[a]
12 At the head of the Israelites, there crossed over the Reubenites, the Gadites, and the half tribe of Manasseh, as a fighting force, as
13 Moses had told them to do; about forty thousand strong, drafted for active service, they crossed over to the lowlands of Jericho in the presence of the LORD to do battle.
14 That day the LORD made Joshua stand very high in the eyes of all Israel, and the people revered him, as they had revered Moses all his life.
15, 16 The LORD said to Joshua, 'Command the priests carrying the Ark of the Tokens to come up from the
17 Jordan.' So Joshua commanded the priests to come up from the
18 Jordan; and when the priests carrying the Ark of the Covenant of the LORD came up from the riverbed, they had no sooner set foot on dry land than the waters of the Jordan came back to their place and filled up all its reaches as be-
19 fore. On the tenth day of the first month the people came up out of the Jordan and camped in Gilgal
20 in the district east of Jericho, and there Joshua set up the twelve stones which they had taken from
21 the Jordan. He said to the Israel-

ites, 'In days to come, when your descendants ask their fathers what these stones mean, you shall ex- 22 plain that the Jordan was dry when Israel crossed over, and that the 23 LORD your God dried up the waters of the Jordan in front of you until you had gone across, just as the LORD your God did at the Red Sea when he dried it up for us until we had crossed. Thus all people on 24 earth will know how strong is the hand of the LORD; and thus they will stand in awe of the LORD your God for ever.'

When all the Amorite kings to 5 the west of the Jordan and all the Canaanite kings by the sea-coast heard that the LORD had dried up the waters before the advance of the Israelites until they had crossed, their courage melted away and there was no more spirit left in them for fear of the Israelites.

At that time the LORD said to 2 Joshua, 'Make knives of flint, seat yourself, and make Israel a circumcised people again.' Joshua 3 thereupon made knives of flint and circumcised the Israelites at Gibeath-haaraloth.[b] This is why Jo- 4 shua circumcised them: all the males who came out of Egypt, all the fighting men, had died in the wilderness on the journey from Egypt. The people who came out 5 of Egypt had all been circumcised, but not those who had been born in the wilderness during the journey. For the Israelites travelled in 6 the wilderness for forty years, until the whole nation, all the fighting men among them, had passed away, all who came out of Egypt and had disobeyed the voice of the LORD. The LORD swore that he would not allow any of these to see the land which he had sworn to their fathers to give us, a land flowing with milk and honey. So it 7 was their sons, whom he had raised up in their place, that Joshua circumcised; they were uncircum-

---

[a] *Prob. rdg.; Heb. adds* before the people.   [b] *That is* the Hill of Foreskins.

cised because they had not been
8 circumcised on the journey. When
the circumcision of the whole nation was complete, they stayed
where they were in camp until they
9 had recovered. The LORD then said
to Joshua, 'Today I have rolled
away from you the reproaches of
the Egyptians.' Therefore the
place is called Gilgal*a* to this very
day.

10　The Israelites encamped in Gilgal, and at sunset on the fourteenth
day of the month they kept the
Passover in the lowlands of Jericho.
11 On the day after the Passover,
they ate their unleavened cakes
and parched grain, and that day it
12 was the produce of the country. It
was from that day, when they first
ate the produce of the country,
that the manna ceased. The Israelites received no more manna; and
that year they ate what had grown
in the land of Canaan.

13　When Joshua came near Jericho
he looked up and saw a man standing in front of him with a drawn
sword in his hand. Joshua went up
to him and said, 'Are you for us or
14 for our enemies?' And the man said
to him, 'I am here as captain of the
army of the LORD.' Joshua fell
down before him, face to the
ground, and said, 'What have you
to say to your servant, my lord?'
15 The captain of the LORD's army
said to him, 'Take off your sandals;
the place where you are standing is
holy'; and Joshua did so.

6 JERICHO was bolted and barred
against the Israelites; no one went
2 out, no one came in. The LORD said
to Joshua, 'Look, I have delivered
Jericho and her king*b* into your
3 hands. You shall march round the
city with all your fighting men,
making the circuit of it once, for
4 six days running. Seven priests
shall go in front of the Ark carrying
seven trumpets made from rams'
horns. On the seventh day you shall

march round the city seven times
and the priests shall blow their
trumpets. At the blast of the rams' 5
horns, when you hear the trumpet
sound, the whole army shall raise a
great shout; the wall of the city
will collapse and the army shall advance, every man straight ahead.'
So Joshua son of Nun summoned 6
the priests and gave them their
orders: 'Take up the Ark of the
Covenant; let seven priests with
seven trumpets of ram's horn go in
front of the Ark of the LORD.' Then 7
he said to the army, 'March on and
make the circuit of the city, and
let the men drafted from the two
and a half tribes go in front of the
Ark of the LORD.' When Joshua 8
had spoken to the army, the seven
priests carrying the seven trumpets of ram's horn before the LORD
passed on and blew the trumpets,
with the Ark of the Covenant of
the LORD following them. The 9
drafted men marched in front of
the priests who blew the trumpets,
and the rearguard followed the
Ark, the trumpets sounding as
they marched. But Joshua ordered 10
the army not to shout, or to raise
their voices or utter a word, till the
day came when he would tell them
to shout; then they were to give a
loud shout. Thus he caused the 11
Ark of the LORD to go round the
city, making the circuit of it once,
and then they went back to the
camp and spent the night there.
Joshua rose early in the morning 12
and the priests took up the Ark of
the LORD. The seven priests carry- 13
ing the seven trumpets of ram's
horn went marching in front of the
Ark of the LORD, blowing the
trumpets as they went, with the
drafted men in front of them and
the rearguard following the Ark of
the LORD, the trumpets sounding
as they marched. They marched 14
round the city once on the second
day and returned to the camp; this
they did for six days. But on 15

---

a *That is* Rolling Stones.　　*b* *Prob. rdg.; Heb. adds* the fighting men.

the seventh day they rose at dawn and marched seven times round the city in the same way; that was the only day on which they march-
16 ed round seven times. The seventh time the priests blew the trumpets and Joshua said to the army, 'Shout! The LORD has given you
17 the city. The city shall be under solemn ban: everything in it belongs to the LORD. No one is to be spared except the prostitute Rahab and everyone who is with her in the house, because she hid the
18 men whom we sent. And you must beware of coveting anything that is forbidden under the ban; you must take none of it for yourselves; this would put the Israelite camp itself under the ban and bring
19 trouble on it. All the silver and gold, all the vessels of copper and iron, shall be holy; they belong to the LORD and they must go into
20 the LORD's treasury.' So they blew the trumpets, and when the army heard the trumpet sound, they raised a great shout, and down fell the walls. The army advanced on the city, every man straight ahead,
21 and took it. Under the ban they destroyed everything in the city; they put everyone to the sword, men and women, young and old, and also cattle, sheep, and asses.
22 But the two men who had been sent out as spies were told by Joshua to go into the prostitute's house and bring out her and all who belonged to her, as they had sworn
23 to do. So the young men went and brought out Rahab, her father and mother, her brothers and all who belonged to her. They brought out the whole family and left them out-
24 side the Israelite camp. They then set fire to the city and everything in it, except that they deposited the silver and gold and the vessels of copper and iron in the treasury
25 of the LORD's house. Thus Joshua spared the lives of Rahab the prostitute, her household and all who

belonged to her, because she had hidden the men whom Joshua had sent to Jericho as spies; she and her family settled permanently among the Israelites. It was then that 26 Joshua laid this curse on Jericho:

May the LORD's curse light on the
  man who comes forward
to rebuild this city of Jericho:
the laying of its foundations shall
  cost him his eldest son,
the setting up of its gates shall cost
  him his youngest.

Thus the LORD was with Joshua, 27 and his fame spread throughout the country.

But the Israelites defied the ban: 7 Achan son of Carmi, son of Zabdi, son of Zerah, of the tribe of Judah, took some of the forbidden things, and the LORD was angry with the Israelites.

Joshua sent men from Jericho 2 with orders to go up to Ai, near Beth-aven, east of Bethel, and see how the land lay; so the men went up and explored Ai. They returned 3 to Joshua and reported that there was no need for the whole army to move: 'Let some two or three thousand men go forward to attack Ai. Do not make the whole army toil up there; the population is small.' And so about three thousand men 4 went up, but they turned tail before the men of Ai, who killed some 5 thirty-six of them; they chased them all the way from the gate to the Quarries[a] and killed them on the pass. At this the courage of the people melted and flowed away like water. Joshua and the elders of 6 Israel rent their clothes and flung themselves face downwards to the ground; they lay before the Ark of the LORD till evening and threw dust on their heads. Joshua said, 7 'Alas, O Lord GOD, why didst thou bring this people across the Jordan only to hand us over to the Amorites to be destroyed? If only we had been content to settle on the other

[a] Or to Shebarim.

8 side of the Jordan! I beseech thee, O Lord; what can I say, now that Israel has been routed by the ene- 9 my? When the Canaanites and all the natives of the country hear of this, they will come swarming a- round us and wipe us off the face of the earth. What wilt thou do then for the honour of thy great name?'

10 The LORD said to Joshua, 'Stand up; why lie prostrate on your face? 11 Israel has sinned: they have broken the covenant which I laid upon them, by taking forbidden things for themselves. They have stolen them, and concealed it by mingling them with their own possessions. 12 That is why the Israelites cannot stand against their enemies: they are put to flight because they have brought themselves under the ban. Unless they destroy every single thing among them that is forbid- den under the ban, I will be with 13 them no longer. Stand up; you must hallow the people; tell them they must hallow themselves before tomorrow. Tell them, These are the words of the LORD the God of Israel: You have forbidden things among you, Israel; you cannot stand against your enemies until you have rid yourselves of them. 14 In the morning come forward tribe by tribe, and the tribe which the LORD chooses shall come forward clan by clan; the clan which the LORD chooses shall come forward family by family; and the family which the LORD chooses shall come 15 forward man by man. The man who is chosen as the harbourer of for- bidden things shall be burnt, he and all that is his, because he has broken the covenant of the LORD and committed outrage in Israel.' 16 Early in the morning Joshua rose and brought Israel forward tribe by tribe, and the tribe of Judah 17 was chosen. He brought forward the clans of Judah, and the clan of Zerah was chosen; then the clan of Zerah family by family, and the

family of Zabdi was chosen. He 18 brought that family forward man by man, and Achan son of Carmi, son of Zabdi, son of Zerah, of the tribe of Judah, was chosen. Then 19 Joshua said to Achan, 'My son, give honour to the LORD the God of Israel and make your confession to him: tell me what you have done, hide nothing from me.' Achan an- 20 swered Joshua, 'I confess, I have sinned against the LORD the God of Israel. This is what I did: among 21 the booty I caught sight of a fine mantle from Shinar, two hundred shekels of silver, and a bar of gold weighing fifty shekels. I coveted them and I took them. You will find them hidden in the ground in- side my tent, with the silver under- neath.' So Joshua sent messengers, 22 who ran to the tent, and there was the stuff*a* hidden in the tent with the silver underneath. They took 23 the things from the tent, brought them to Joshua and all the Israel- ites, and spread them out before the LORD. Then Joshua took Ach- 24 an son of Zerah, with the silver, the mantle, and the bar of gold, to- gether with his sons and daughters, his oxen, his asses, and his sheep, his tent, and everything he had, and he and all Israel brought them up to the Vale of Achor.*b* Joshua 25 said, 'What trouble you have brought on us! Now the LORD will bring trouble on you.' Then all the Israelites stoned him to death; and 26 they raised a great pile of stones over him, which remains to this day. So the LORD's anger was a- bated. That is why to this day that place is called the Vale of Achor.

THE LORD said to Joshua, 'Do not 8 be fearful or dismayed; take the whole army and attack Ai. I de- liver the king of Ai into your hands, him and his people, his city and his country. Deal with Ai and her king 2 as you dealt with Jericho and her king; but you may keep for your-

a Or the mantle.   *b* *That is* Trouble.

selves the cattle and any other spoil that you may take. Set an ambush for the city to the west of
3 it.' So Joshua and all the army prepared for the assault on Ai. He chose thirty thousand fighting men and dispatched them by night,
4 with these orders: 'Lie in ambush to the west of the city, not far from it, and all of you hold yourselves in
5 readiness. I myself will approach the city with the rest of the army, and when the enemy come out to meet us as they did last time, we shall take to flight before them.
6 Then they will come out and pursue us until we have drawn them away from the city, thinking that we have taken to flight as we did last
7 time. While we are in flight, come out from your ambush and occupy the city; the LORD your God will
8 deliver it into your hands. When you have taken it, set it on fire. Thus you will do what the LORD commands. These are your orders.'
9 So Joshua sent them off, and they went to the place of ambush and waited between Bethel and Ai to the west of Ai, while Joshua spent the night with the army.
10 Early in the morning Joshua rose, mustered the army and marched against Ai, he himself and
11 the elders of Israel at its head. All the armed forces with him marched on until they came within sight of the city. They encamped north of Ai, with the valley between them
12 and the city; but Joshua took some five thousand men and set them in ambush between Bethel and Ai to
14 the west of the city.[a] When the king of Ai saw them, he and the citizens rose with all speed that morning and marched out to do battle against Israel; he did not know that there was an ambush set for him to the west of the city.
15 Joshua and all the Israelites made as if they were routed by them and
16 fled towards the wilderness, and

all the people in the city were called out in pursuit. So they pursued Joshua and were drawn away from the city. Not a man was left in Ai; 17 they had all gone out in pursuit of the Israelites and during the pursuit had left the city undefended.

Then the LORD said to Joshua, 18 'Point towards Ai with the dagger you are holding, for I will deliver the city into your hands.' So Joshua pointed with his dagger towards Ai. At his signal, the men 19 in ambush rose quickly from their places and, entering the city at a run, took it and promptly set fire to it. The men of Ai looked back 20 and saw the smoke from the city already going up to the sky; they were powerless to make their escape in any direction, and the Israelites who had feigned flight towards the wilderness turned on their pursuers. For when Joshua 21 and all the Israelites saw that the ambush had seized the city and that smoke was already going up from it, they turned and fell upon the men of Ai. Those who had come 22 out to meet the Israelites were now hemmed in with Israelites on both sides of them, and the Israelites cut them down until there was not a single survivor, nor had any escaped. The king of Ai was taken 23 alive and brought to Joshua. When 24 the Israelites had cut down to the last man all the citizens of Ai who were in the open country or in the wilderness to which they had pursued them, and the massacre was complete, they all turned back to Ai and put it to the sword. The number who were killed that day, men and women, was twelve thousand, the whole population of Ai. Joshua 26 held out his dagger and did not draw back his hand until he had put to death all who lived in Ai; but the Israelites kept for them- 27 selves the cattle and any other spoil that they took, following the

---

[a] *So Sept.; Heb. adds* (13) So the army pitched camp to the north of the city, and the rearguard to the west, while Joshua went that night into the valley.

word of the LORD spoken to Joshua.
28 So Joshua burnt Ai to the ground, and left it the desolate ruined
29 mound it remains to this day. He hanged the king of Ai on a tree and left him there till sunset; and when the sun had set, he gave the order and they cut him down and flung down his body at the entrance of the city gate. Over the body they raised a great pile of stones, which is there to this day.
30 At that time Joshua built an al-
31 tar to the LORD the God of Israel on Mount Ebal. The altar was of blocks of undressed stone on which no tool of iron had been used, following the commands given to the Israelites by Moses the servant of the LORD, as is described in the book of the law of Moses. At the altar they offered whole-offerings to the LORD, and slaughtered shared-
32 offerings. There in the presence of the Israelites he engraved on blocks[a] of stone a copy of the law
33 of Moses. And all Israel, elders, officers, and judges, took their stand on either side of the Ark, facing the levitical priests who carried the Ark of the Covenant of the LORD – all Israel, native and alien alike. Half of them stood facing Mount Gerizim and half facing Mount Ebal, to fulfil the command of Moses the servant of the LORD that the blessing should be pro-
34 nounced first. Then Joshua recited the whole of the blessing and the cursing word by word, as they are written in the book of the law.
35 There was not a single word of all that Moses had commanded which he did not read aloud before the whole congregation of Israel, including the women and dependants and the aliens resident in their company.

9 When the news of these happenings reached all the kings west of the Jordan, in the hill-country, the Shephelah, and all the coast of the Great Sea running up to the Lebanon, the kings of the Hittites, Amorites, Canaanites, Perizzites, Hivites, and Jebusites agreed to 2 join forces and fight against Joshua and Israel.

When the inhabitants of Gibeon 3 heard how Joshua had dealt with Jericho and Ai, they adopted a 4 ruse of their own. They went and disguised themselves, with old sacking for their asses, old wine-skins split and mended, old and 5 patched sandals for their feet, old clothing to wear, and by way of provisions nothing but dry and mouldy bread. They came to Jo- 6 shua in the camp at Gilgal and said to him and the Israelites, 'We have come from a distant country to ask you now to grant us a treaty.' The 7 Israelites said to the Hivites, 'But maybe you live in our neighbour-hood: if so, how can we grant you a treaty?' They said to Joshua, 'We 8 are your slaves.' Joshua asked them who they were and where they came from. 'Sir,' they replied, 'our coun- 9 try is very far away, and we have come because of the renown of the LORD your God. We have heard of his fame, of all that he did to Egypt, and to the two Amorite 10 kings east of the Jordan, Sihon king of Heshbon and Og king of Bashan who lived at Ashtaroth. Our elders and all the people of our 11 country told us to take provisions for the journey and come to meet you, and say, "We are your slaves; please grant us a treaty." Look at 12 our bread; it was hot from the oven when we packed it at home on the day we came away. Now it is dry and mouldy. Look at the wine- 13 skins; they were new when we filled them, and now they are all split; look at our clothes and our sandals, worn out by the long journey.' The 14 chief men of the community accepted some of their provisions, and did not at first seek guidance from the LORD. So Joshua received 15 them peaceably and granted them

[a] *Or on the blocks.*

a treaty, promising to spare their lives, and the chiefs pledged their faith to them on oath.

16 Within three days of granting them the treaty, the Israelites learnt that they were in fact neigh-

17 bours and lived near by. So the Israelites set out and on the third day they reached their cities; these were Gibeon, Kephirah, Beeroth,

18 and Kiriath-jearim. The Israelites did not slaughter them, because of the oath which the chief men of the community had sworn to them by the LORD the God of Israel, but the people were all indignant with their

19 chiefs. The chiefs all replied to the assembled people, 'But we swore an oath to them by the LORD the God of Israel; we cannot touch

20 them now. What we will do is this: we will spare their lives so that the oath which we swore to them may

21 bring no harm upon us. But though their lives must be spared, they shall be set to chop wood and draw water for the community.' The people agreed to do as their chiefs

22 had said. Joshua summoned the Gibeonites and said, 'Why did you play this trick on us? You told us that you live a long way off, when

23 you are near neighbours. There is a curse upon you for this: for all time you shall provide us with slaves, to chop wood and draw water for the

24 house of my God.' They answered Joshua, 'We were told, sir, that the LORD your God had commanded Moses his servant to give you the whole country and to exterminate all its inhabitants; so because of you we were in terror of our lives,

25 and that is why we did this. We are in your power: do with us whatever

26 you think right and proper.' What he did was this: he saved them from death at the hands of the Israelites,

27 and they did not kill them; but thenceforward he set them to chop wood and draw water for the community and for the altar of the LORD. And to this day they do it at the place which the LORD chose.

When Adoni-zedek king of Jeru- 10 salem heard that Joshua had captured Ai and destroyed it (for Joshua had dealt with Ai and her king as he had dealt with Jericho and her king), and that the inhabitants of Gibeon had made their peace with Israel and were living among them, he was greatly alarm- 2 ed; for Gibeon was a large place, like a royal city: it was larger than Ai, and its men were all good fighters. So Adoni-zedek king of 3 Jerusalem sent to Hoham king of Hebron, Piram king of Jarmuth, Japhia king of Lachish, and Debir king of Eglon, and said, 'Come up 4 and help me, and we will attack the Gibeonites, because they have made their peace with Joshua and the Israelites.' So the five Amorite 5 kings, the kings of Jerusalem, Hebron, Jarmuth, Lachish, and Eglon, joined forces and advanced to take up their positions for the attack on Gibeon. But the men of 6 Gibeon sent this message to Joshua in the camp at Gilgal: 'We are your slaves, do not abandon us, come quickly to our relief. All the Amorite kings in the hill-country have joined forces against us; come and help us.' So Joshua went up from 7 Gilgal with all his forces and all his fighting men. The LORD said to 8 Joshua, 'Do not be afraid of them; I have delivered them into your hands, and not a man will be able to stand against you.' Joshua came 9 upon them suddenly, after marching all night from Gilgal. The LORD 10 threw them into confusion before the Israelites, and Joshua defeated them utterly in Gibeon; he pursued them down the pass of Beth-horon and kept up the slaughter as far as Azekah and Makkedah. As they 11 were fleeing from Israel down the pass, the LORD hurled great hailstones at them out of the sky all the way to Azekah: more died from the hailstones than the Israelites slew by the sword.

On that day when the LORD 12

delivered the Amorites into the hands of Israel, Joshua spoke with the LORD, and he said in the presence of Israel:

Stand still, O Sun, in Gibeon; stand, Moon, in the Vale of Aijalon.

13 So the sun stood still and the moon halted until a nation had taken vengeance on its enemies, as indeed is written in the Book of Jashar.[a] The sun stayed in mid heaven and made no haste to set 14 for almost a whole day. Never before or since has there been such a day as this day on which the LORD listened to the voice of a man; for 15 the LORD fought for Israel. So Joshua and all the Israelites returned to the camp at Gilgal.

16 The five kings fled and hid them-17 selves in a cave at Makkedah, and Joshua was told that they had been found hidden in this cave. 18 Joshua replied, 'Roll some great stones to the mouth of the cave and post men there to keep watch over 19 the kings. But you must not stay; keep up the pursuit, attack your enemies from the rear and do not let them reach their cities; the LORD your God has delivered them 20 into your hands.' When Joshua and the Israelites had finished the work of slaughter and all had been put to the sword – except a few survivors who escaped and enter-21 ed the fortified cities – the whole army rejoined Joshua at Makkedah in peace; not a man of the Israelites suffered so much as a 22 scratch on his tongue. Then Joshua said, 'Open the mouth of the cave, and bring me out those five kings.' 23 They did so; they brought the five kings out of the cave, the kings of Jerusalem, Hebron, Jarmuth, La-24 chish, and Eglon. When they had brought them to Joshua, he summoned all the Israelites and said to the commanders of the troops who had served with him, 'Come for-

ward and put your feet on the necks of these kings.' So they came forward and put their feet on their necks. Joshua said to them, 'Do not 25 be fearful or dismayed; be strong and resolute; for the LORD will do this to every enemy you fight against.' And he struck down the 26 kings and slew them; then he hung their bodies on five trees, where they remained hanging till evening. At sunset, on Joshua's orders 27 they took them down from the trees and threw them into the cave in which they had hidden; they piled great stones against its mouth, and there the stones are to this day.[b]

On that same day, Joshua cap-28 tured Makkedah and put both king and people to the sword, destroying both them and every living thing in the city. He left no survivor, and he dealt with the king of Makkedah as he had dealt with the king of Jericho. Then Joshua and 29 all the Israelites marched on from Makkedah to Libnah and attacked it. The LORD delivered the city and 30 its king to the Israelites, and they put its people and every living thing in it to the sword; they left no survivor there, and dealt with its king as they had dealt with the king of Jericho. From Libnah 31 Joshua and all the Israelites marched on to Lachish, took up their positions and attacked it. The 32 LORD delivered Lachish into their hands; they took it on the second day and put every living thing in it to the sword, as they had done at Libnah.

Meanwhile Horam king of Gezer 33 had advanced to the relief of Lachish; but Joshua struck them down, both king and people, and not a man of them survived. Then 34 Joshua and all the Israelites marched on from Lachish to Eglon, took up their positions and attacked it; that same day they 35 captured it and put its inhabitants

---

[a] Or the Book of the Upright.   [b] and there...day: or on this very day.

to the sword, destroying every living thing in it as they had done
36 at Lachish. From Eglon Joshua and all the Israelites advanced to
37 Hebron and attacked it. They captured it and put its king to the sword together with every living thing in it and in all its villages; as at Eglon, he left no survivor, destroying it and every living thing in
38 it. Then Joshua and all the Israelites wheeled round towards Debir
39 and attacked it. They captured the city with its king, and all its villages, put them to the sword and destroyed every living thing; they left no survivor. They dealt with Debir and its king as they had dealt with Hebron and with Libnah and its king.
40 So Joshua massacred the population of the whole region – the hill-country, the Negeb, the Shephelah, the watersheds – and all their kings. He left no survivor, destroying everything that drew breath, as the LORD the God of
41 Israel had commanded. Joshua carried the slaughter from Kadeshbarnea to Gaza, over the whole land of Goshen and as far as Gi-
42 beon. All these kings he captured at the same time, and their country with them, for the LORD the God of Israel fought for Israel.
43 And Joshua returned with all the Israelites to the camp at Gilgal.
11 When Jabin king of Hazor heard of all this, he sent to Jobab king of Madon, to the kings of Shimron and
2 Akshaph, to the northern kings in the hill-country, in the Arabah opposite Kinnereth, in the Shephelah, and in the district of Dor on
3 the west, the Canaanites to the east and the west, the Amorites, Hittites, Perizzites, and Jebusites in the hill-country, and the Hivites below Hermon in the land of Miz-
4 pah. They took the field with all their forces, a great horde countless as the grains of sand on the seashore, among them a great number
5 of horses and chariots. All these

kings made common cause, and came and encamped at the waters of Merom to fight against Israel.
The LORD said to Joshua, 'Do not 6 be afraid of them, for at this time tomorrow I shall deliver them to Israel all dead men; you shall hamstring their horses and burn their chariots.' So Joshua and his army 7 surprised them by the waters of Merom and fell upon them. The 8 LORD delivered them into the hands of Israel; they struck them down and pursued them as far as Greater Sidon, Misrephoth on the west, and the Vale of Mizpah on the east. They struck them down until not a man was left alive. Joshua 9 dealt with them as the LORD had commanded: he hamstrung their horses and burnt their chariots.
At this point Joshua turned his 10 forces against Hazor, formerly the head of all these kingdoms. He captured the city and put its king to death with the sword. They killed 11 every living thing in it and wiped them all out; they spared nothing that drew breath, and Hazor itself they destroyed by fire. So Joshua 12 captured these kings and their cities and put them to the sword, destroying them all, as Moses the servant of the LORD had commanded. The cities whose ruined 13 mounds are still standing were not burnt by the Israelites; it was Hazor alone that Joshua burnt. The 14 Israelites plundered all these cities and kept for themselves the cattle and any other spoil they took; but they put every living soul to the sword until they had destroyed every one; they did not leave alive any one that drew breath. The 15 LORD laid his commands on his servant Moses, and Moses laid these same commands on Joshua, and Joshua carried them out. Not one of the commands laid on Moses by the LORD did he leave unfulfilled.
And so Joshua took the whole 16 country, the hill-country, all the

Negeb, all the land of Goshen, the Shephelah, the Arabah, and the Israelite hill-country with the ad-
17 joining lowlands. His conquests extended from the bare mountain which leads up to Seir as far as Baal-gad in the Vale of Lebanon under Mount Hermon. He took prisoner all their kings, struck them down and put them to death.
18 It was a long war that he fought
19 against all these kingdoms. Except for the Hivites who lived in Gibeon, not one of their cities came to terms with the Israelites; all
20 were taken by storm. It was the LORD's purpose that they should offer an obstinate resistance to the Israelites in battle, and that thus they should be annihilated without mercy and utterly destroyed,[a] as the LORD had commanded Moses.
21 It was then that Joshua proceeded to wipe out the Anakim from the hill-country, from Hebron, Debir, Anab, all the hill-country of Judah and all the hill-country of Israel, destroying both
22 them and their cities. No Anakim were left in the land taken by the Israelites; they survived only in Gaza, Gath, and Ashdod.
23 Thus Joshua took the whole country, fulfilling all the commands that the LORD had laid on Moses; he assigned it as Israel's patrimony, allotting to each tribe its share; and the land was at peace.

12 These are the names of the kings of the land whom the Israelites slew, and whose territory they occupied beyond the Jordan towards the sunrise from the gorge of the Arnon as far as Mount Hermon and
2 all the Arabah on the east. Sihon the Amorite king who lived in Heshbon: his rule extended from Aroer, which is on the edge of the gorge of the Arnon, along the middle of the gorge and over half Gilead as far as the gorge of the

Jabbok, the Ammonite frontier;
along the Arabah as far as the 3 eastern side of the Sea of Kinnereth and as far as the eastern side of the Sea of the Arabah, the Dead Sea, by the road to Beth-jeshimoth and from Teman under the watershed of Pisgah. Og king of Bashan, one 4 of the survivors of the Rephaim, who lived in Ashtaroth and Edrei: he ruled over Mount Hermon, Sal- 5 cah, all Bashan as far as the Geshurite and Maacathite borders, and half Gilead as far as the boundary of Sihon king of Heshbon. Moses the servant of the LORD 6 put them to death, he and the Israelites, and he gave their land to the Reubenites, the Gadites, and half the tribe of Manasseh, as their possession.

These are the names of the kings 7 whom Joshua and the Israelites put to death beyond the Jordan to the west, from Baal-gad in the Vale of Lebanon as far as the bare mountain that leads up to Seir. Joshua gave their land to the Israelite tribes to be their possession according to their allotted shares, in the hill-country, the Shephelah, 8 the Arabah, the watersheds, the wilderness, and the Negeb; lands of the Hittites, Amorites, Canaanites, Perizzites, Hivites, and Jebusites. The king of Jericho; the King of Ai 9 which is beside Bethel; the king of 10 Jerusalem; the king of Hebron; the king of Jarmuth; the king of 11 Lachish; the king of Eglon; the 12 king of Gezer; the king of Debir; 13 the king of Geder; the king of Hor- 14 mah; the king of Arad; the king of 15 Libnah; the king of Adullam; the 16 king of Makkedah; the king of Bethel; the king of Tappuah; the 17 king of Hepher; the king of Aphek; 18 the king of Aphek[b]-in-Sharon; the 19 king of Madon; the king of Hazor; the king of Shimron-meron; the 20 king of Akshaph; the king of 21

---

[a] offer...destroyed: *or* obstinately engage the Israelites in battle so that they should annihilate them without mercy, only that he might destroy them...
[b] of Aphek: *prob. rdg.; Heb. om.*

22 Taanach; the king of Megiddo; the
   king of Kedesh; the king of Jok-
23 neam-in-Carmel; the king of Dor
   in the district of Dor; the king of
24 Gaiam-in-Galilee; the king of Tirzah: thirty-one kings in all, one of
   each town.

The division of the land among the tribes

13 BY this time Joshua had become
   very old, and the LORD said to him,
   'You are now a very old man, and
   much of the country remains to be
2 occupied. The country which remains is this: all the districts of the
   Philistines and all the Geshurite
3 country (this is reckoned as Canaanite territory from Shihor to
   the east of Egypt as far north as
   Ekron; and it belongs to the five
   lords of the Philistines, those of
   Gaza, Ashdod, Ashkelon, Gath,
   and Ekron); all the districts of the
4 Avvim on the south; all the Canaanite country from the low-
   lying land which belongs to the
   Sidonians as far as Aphek, the
5 Amorite frontier; the land of the
   Gebalites and all the Lebanon to
   the east from Baal-gad under
   Mount Hermon as far as Lebo-
6 hamath. I will drive out in favour of
   the Israelites all the inhabitants of
   the hill-country from the Lebanon
   as far as Misrephoth on the west,
   and all the Sidonians. In the mean
   time you are to allot all this to the
   Israelites for their patrimony, as I
7 have commanded you. Distribute
   this land now to the nine tribes and
   half the tribe of Manasseh for their
8 patrimony.' For half the tribe of
   Manasseh and[a] with them the Reubenites and the Gadites had each
   taken their patrimony which Moses
   gave them east of the Jordan, as
   Moses the servant of the LORD had
9 ordained. It started from Aroer
   which is by the edge of the gorge of
   the Arnon, and the level land half-
   way along the gorge, and included

all the tableland from Medeba as
far as Dibon; all the cities of Sihon, 10
the Amorite king who ruled in
Heshbon, as far as the Ammonite
frontier; and it also included Gilead 11
and the Geshurite and Maacathite
territory, and all Mount Hermon
and the whole of Bashan as far as
Salcah, all the kingdom of Og 12
which he ruled from both Ashtaroth and Edrei in Bashan. He was a
survivor of the remnant of the Rephaim, but Moses put them both to
death and occupied their lands. But 13
the Israelites did not drive out the
Geshurites and the Maacathites;
the Geshurites and the Maacathites
live among the Israelites to this
day. The tribe of Levi, however, 14
received no patrimony; the LORD
the God of Israel is their patrimony, as he promised them.
   So Moses allotted territory to 15
the tribe of the Reubenites family
by family. Their territory started 16
from Aroer which is by the edge of
the gorge of the Arnon, and the
level land half-way along the gorge,
and included all the tableland as
far as Medeba; Heshbon and all 17
its cities on the tableland, Dibon,
Bamoth-baal, Beth-baal-meon, Ja- 18
haz, Kedemoth, Mephaath, Kiria- 19
thaim, Sibmah, Zereth-shahar on
the hill in the Vale, Beth-peor, the 20
watershed of Pisgah, and Beth-
jeshimoth, all the cities of the 21
tableland, all the kingdom of Sihon
the Amorite king who ruled in
Heshbon, whom Moses put to
death together with the princes of
Midian, Evi, Rekem, Zur, Hur,
and Reba, the vassals of Sihon who
dwelt in the country. Balaam son 22
of Beor, who practised augury, was
among those whom the Israelites
put to the sword. The boundary of 23
the Reubenites was the Jordan and
the adjacent land: this is the patrimony of the Reubenites family by
family, both the cities and their
hamlets.
   Moses allotted territory to the 24

---

[a] For half . . . Manasseh and: *prob. rdg.*; *Heb. om.*

25 Gadites family by family. Their territory was Jazer, all the cities of Gilead and half the Ammonite country as far as Aroer which is 26 east of Rabbah. It reached from Heshbon as far as Ramoth-mizpeh and Betonim, and from Mahanaim as far as the boundary of Lo-debar; 27 it included in the valley Beth-haram, Beth-nimrah, Succoth, and Zaphon, the rest of the kingdom of Sihon king of Heshbon. The boundary was the Jordan and the adjacent land as far as the end of the Sea of Kinnereth east of the Jor- 28 dan. This is the patrimony of the Gadites family by family, both the cities and their hamlets.

29 Moses allotted territory to the half tribe of Manasseh: it was for half the tribe of the Manassites 30 family by family. Their territory ran from Mahanaim and included all Bashan, all the kingdom of Og king of Bashan and all Havvoth- 31 jair in Bashan – sixty cities. Half Gilead, and Ashtaroth and Edrei the royal cities of Og in Bashan, belong to the sons of Machir son of Manasseh on behalf of half the Machirites family by family.

32 These are the territories which Moses allotted to the tribes as their patrimonies in the lowlands of 33 Moab east of the Jordan. But to the tribe of Levi he gave no patrimony: the LORD the God of Israel is their patrimony, as he promised them.

14 Now follow the possessions which the Israelites acquired in the land of Canaan, as Eleazar the priest, Joshua son of Nun, and the heads of the families of the Israelite tribes 2 allotted them. They were assigned by lot, following the LORD's command given through Moses, to the 3 nine and a half tribes. To two and a half tribes Moses had given patrimonies beyond the Jordan; but he gave none to the Levites as he did 4 to the others. The tribe of Joseph formed the two tribes of Manasseh and Ephraim. The Levites were given no share in the land, only cities to dwell in, with their common land for flocks and herds. So 5 the Israelites, following the LORD's command given to Moses, assigned the land.

Now the tribe of Judah had come 6 to Joshua in Gilgal, and Caleb son of Jephunneh the Kenizzite said to him, 'You remember what the LORD said to Moses the man of God concerning you and me at Kadesh-barnea. I was forty years old when 7 Moses the servant of the LORD sent me from there to explore the land, and I brought back an honest report. The others who went with me 8 discouraged the people, but I loyally carried out the purpose of the LORD my God. Moses swore an 9 oath that day and said, "The land on which you have set foot shall be your patrimony and your sons' after you as a possession for ever; for you have loyally carried out the purpose of the LORD my God." Well, the LORD has spared my life 10 as he promised; it is now forty-five years since he made this promise to Moses, at the time when Israel was journeying in the wilderness. To-day I am eighty-five years old. I 11 am still as strong as I was on the day when Moses sent me out; I am as fit now for war as I was then and am ready to take the field again. Give me today this hill-country 12 which the LORD then promised me. You heard on that day that the Anakim were there and their cities were large and well fortified. Perhaps the LORD will be with me and I shall dispossess them as he promised.' Joshua blessed Caleb and 13 gave him Hebron for his patrimony, and that is why Hebron re- 14 mains to this day in the patrimony of Caleb son of Jephunneh the Kenizzite. It is because he loyally carried out the purpose of the LORD the God of Israel. Formerly 15 the name of Hebron was Kiriath-arba. This Arba was the chief man of the Anakim. And the land was at peace.

15 This is the territory allotted to the tribe of the sons of Judah family by family. It started from the Edomite frontier at the wilderness of Zin and ran as far as the Negeb 2 at its southern end, and it had a common border with the Negeb at the end of the Dead Sea, where an inlet of water bends towards the 3 Negeb. It continued from the south by the ascent of Akrabbim, passed by Zin, went up from the south of Kadesh-barnea, passed by Hezron, went on to Addar and turned round 4 to Karka. It then passed along to Azmon, reached the Torrent of Egypt, and its limit was the sea. This was their southern boundary. 5 The eastern boundary is the Dead Sea as far as the mouth of the Jordan and the adjacent land northwards from the inlet of the sea, at the mouth of the Jordan. 6 The boundary goes up to Beth-hoglah; it passes north of Beth-arabah and thence to the stone of Bohan 7 son of Reuben, thence to Debir from the Vale of Achor, and then turns north to the districts*a* in front of the ascent of Adummim south of the gorge. The boundary then passes the waters of En-shemesh and the limit there is En-8 rogel. It then goes up by the Valley of Ben-hinnom to the southern slope of the Jebusites (that is Jerusalem). Thence it goes up to the top of the hill which faces the Valley of Hinnom on the west; this is at the northern end of the Vale of 9 Rephaim. The boundary then bends round from the top of the hill to the spring of the waters of Nephtoah, runs round to the cities of Mount Ephron and round to 10 Baalah, that is Kiriath-jearim. It then continues westwards from Baalah to Mount Seir, passes on to the north side of the slope of Mount Jearim, that is Kesalon, down to Beth-shemesh and on to Timnah. 11 The boundary then goes north to the slope of Ekron, bends round to Shikkeron, crosses to Mount Baalah and reaches Jabneel; its limit is the sea. The western boundary is 12 the Great Sea and the land adjacent. This is the whole circuit of the boundary of the tribe of Judah family by family.

Caleb son of Jephunneh received 13 his share of the land within the tribe of Judah as the Lord had said to Joshua. It was Kiriath-arba, that is Hebron. This Arba was the ancestor of the Anakim. Caleb 14 drove out the three Anakim: these were Sheshai, Ahiman and Talmai, descendants of Anak. From there 15 he attacked the inhabitants of Debir; the name of Debir was formerly Kiriath-sepher. Caleb announc- 16 ed that whoever should attack Kiriath-sepher and capture it would receive his daughter Achsah in marriage. Othniel, son of Caleb's 17 brother Kenaz, captured it, and Caleb gave him his daughter Achsah. When she came to him, he 18 incited her to ask her father for a piece of land. As she sat on the ass, she broke wind, and Caleb asked her, 'What did you mean by that?' She replied, 'I want a favour from 19 you. You have put me in this dry Negeb; you must give me pools of water as well.' So Caleb gave her the upper pool and the lower pool.

This is the patrimony of the 20 tribe of the sons of Judah family by family. These are the cities be- 21 longing to the tribe of Judah, the full count. By the Edomite frontier in the Negeb: Kabzeel, Eder, Jagur, Kinah, Dimonah, Ararah,*b* Ke- 22, 23 desh, Hazor, Ithnan, Ziph, Telem, 24 Bealoth, Hazor-hadattah, Keri- 25 oth-hezron, Amam, Shema, Mola- 26 dah, Hazar-gaddah, Heshmon, 27 Beth-pelet, Hazar-shual, Beershe- 28 ba and its villages, Baalah, Iyim, 29 Ezem, Eltolad, Kesil, Hormah, 30 Ziklag, Madmannah, Sansannah, 31 Lebaoth, Shilhim, Ain, and Rim- 32 mon: in all, twenty-nine cities with their hamlets.

---

a Prob. rdg., cp. 18. 17; Heb. to Gilgal.　　　*b* Prob. rdg.; Heb. Adadah.

33 In the Shephelah: Eshtaol, Zo-
34 rah, Ashnah, Zanoah, En-gannim,
35 Tappuah, Enam, Jarmuth, Adul-
36 lam, Socoh, Azekah, Shaaraim,
Adithaim, Gederah, namely both
parts of Gederah: fourteen cities
37 with their hamlets. Zenan, Hada-
38 shah, Migdal-gad, Dilan, Mizpeh,
39 Joktheel, Lachish, Bozkath, Eg-
40 lon, Cabbon, Lahmas, Kithlish,
41 Gederoth, Beth-dagon, Naamah,
and Makkedah: sixteen cities with
42 their hamlets. Libnah, Ether,
43 Ashan, Jiphtah, Ashnah, Nezib,
44 Keilah, Achzib, and Mareshah:
45 nine cities with their hamlets. Ekron, with its villages and hamlets,
46 and from Ekron westwards, all the
cities near Ashdod and their ham-
47 lets. Ashdod with its villages and
hamlets, Gaza with its villages and
hamlets as far as the Torrent of
Egypt and the Great Sea and the
land adjacent.
48 In the hill-country: Shamir, Jat-
49 tir, Socoh, Dannah, Kiriath-san-
50 nah, that is Debir, Anab, Eshte-
51 moh, Anim, Goshen, Holon, and
Giloh: eleven cities in all with their
52 hamlets. Arab, Dumah, Eshan,
53 Janim, Beth-tappuah, Aphek,[a]
54 Humtah, Kiriath-arba, that is
Hebron, and Zior: nine cities in all
55 with their hamlets. Maon, Carmel,
56 Ziph, Juttah, Jezreel, Jokdeam,
57 Zanoah, Cain, Gibeah, and Timnah: ten cities in all with their
58 hamlets. Halhul, Beth-zur, Gedor,
59 Maarath, Beth-anoth, and Elte-
kon: six cities in all with their hamlets. Tekoa, Ephrathah, that is
Bethlehem, Peor, Etam, Culom,
Tatam, Sores, Carem, Gallim, Bai-
ther, and Manach: eleven cities in
60 all with their hamlets. Kiriath-
baal, that is Kiriath-jearim, and
Rabbah: two cities with their
hamlets.
61 In the wilderness: Beth-arabah,
62 Middin, Secacah, Nibshan, Ir-me-
lach, and En-gedi: six cities with
their hamlets.
63 At Jerusalem, the men of Judah
were unable to drive out the Jebusites who lived there, and to this
day Jebusites and men of Judah
live together in Jerusalem.

This is the lot that fell to the sons 16
of Joseph: the boundary runs from
the Jordan at Jericho, east of the
waters of Jericho by the wilderness, and goes up from Jericho into
the hill-country to Bethel. It runs 2
on from Bethel to Luz and crosses
the Archite border at Ataroth.[b]
Westwards it descends to the 3
boundary of the Japhletites as far
as the boundary of Lower Beth-
horon and Gezer; its limit is the sea.
Here Manasseh and Ephraim the 4
sons of Joseph received their patrimony.

This was the boundary of the 5
Ephraimites family by family:
their eastern boundary ran from
Ataroth-addar up to Upper Beth-
horon. It continued westwards to 6
Michmethath on the north, going
round by the east of Taanath-
shiloh and passing by it on the east
of Janoah. It descends from Ja- 7
noah to Ataroth and Naarath,
touches Jericho and continues to
the Jordan, and from Tappuah it 8
goes westwards by the gorge of
Kanah; and its limit is the sea. This
is the patrimony of the tribe of
Ephraim family by family. There 9
were also cities reserved for the
Ephraimites within the patrimony
of the Manassites, each of these
cities with its hamlets. They did 10
not however drive out the Canaanites who dwelt in Gezer; the Canaanites have lived among the
Ephraimites to the present day but
have been subject to forced labour
in perpetuity.

This is the territory allotted to 17
the tribe of Manasseh, Joseph's
eldest son. Machir was Manasseh's
eldest son and father of Gilead, a
fighting man; Gilead and Bashan
were allotted to him.
The rest of the Manassites family 2
by family were the sons of Abiezer,

---

[a] Or Aphekah.   [b] Ataroth-addar *in* 16. 5; 18. 13.

the sons of Helek, the sons of Asriel, the sons of Shechem, the sons of Hepher, and the sons of Shemida; these were the male offspring of Manasseh son of Joseph family by family.

3 Zelophehad son of Hepher, son of Gilead, son of Machir, son of Manasseh, had no sons but only daughters: their names were Mahlah, Noah, Hoglah, Milcah and

4 Tirzah. They presented themselves before Eleazar the priest and Joshua son of Nun, and before the chiefs, and they said, 'The LORD commanded Moses to allow us to inherit on the same footing as our kinsmen.' They were therefore given a patrimony on the same footing as their father's brothers according to the commandment of the LORD.

5 There fell to Manasseh's lot ten shares, apart from the country of Gilead and Bashan beyond the Jor-

6 dan, because Manasseh's daughters had received a patrimony on the same footing as his sons. The country of Gilead belonged to the

7 rest of Manasseh's sons. The boundary of Manasseh reached from Asher as far as Michmethath, which is to the east of Shechem, and thence southwards towards

8 Jashub by[a] En-tappuah. The territory of Tappuah belonged to Manasseh, but Tappuah itself was on the border of Manasseh and be-

9 longed to Ephraim. The boundary then followed the gorge of Kanah to the south of the gorge (these cities[b] belong to Ephraim, although they lie among the cities of Manasseh), the boundary of Manasseh being on the north of the

10 gorge; its limit was the sea. The southern side belonged to Ephraim and the northern to Manasseh, and their boundary was the sea. They marched with Asher on the north

11 and Issachar on the east. But in Issachar and Asher, Manasseh possessed Beth-shean and its villages, Ibleam and its villages, the inhabitants of Dor and its villages, the inhabitants of En-dor and its villages, the inhabitants of Taanach and its villages, and the inhabitants of Megiddo and its villages. (The third is the district of Dor.[c])

12 The Manassites were unable to occupy these cities; the Canaanites maintained their hold on that part

13 of the country. When the Israelites grew stronger, they put the Canaanites to forced labour, but they did not drive them out.

14 The sons of Joseph appealed to Joshua and said, 'Why have you given us only one lot and one share as our patrimony? We are a numerous people; so far the LORD has blessed us.' Joshua replied, 'If you

15 are so numerous, go up into the forest in the territory of the Perizzites and the Rephaim and clear it for yourselves. You are their near neighbours[d] in the hill-country of

16 Ephraim.' The sons of Joseph said, 'The hill-country is not enough for us; besides, all the Canaanites have chariots of iron, those who inhabit the valley beside Beth-shean and its villages and also those in the

17 Vale of Jezreel.' Joshua replied to the tribes of Joseph, that is Ephraim and Manasseh: 'You are a numerous people with great resources. You shall not have one lot

18 only. The hill-country is yours. It is forest land; clear it and it shall be yours to its furthest limits. The Canaanites may be powerful and equipped with chariots of iron, but you will be able to drive them out.'

18 THE whole community of the Israelites met together at Shiloh and established the Tent of the Presence there. The country now

2 lay subdued at their feet, but there remained seven tribes among the

---

[a] Jashub by: *prob. rdg.*; *Heb.* the inhabitants of. [b] these cities: *prob. rdg.*; *Heb. obscure.* [c] The third . . . Dor: *prob. rdg.*; *Heb.* The three districts. [d] You are . . . neighbours: *prob. rdg.*; *Heb. obscure.*

Israelites who had not yet taken possession of the patrimonies which 3 would fall to them. Joshua therefore said to them, 'How much longer will you neglect to take possession of the land which the LORD the God of your fathers has given 4 you? Appoint three men from each tribe whom I may send out to travel through the whole country. They shall make a register showing the patrimony suitable for each tribe, and come back to me, 5 and then it can be shared out among you in seven portions. Judah shall retain his boundary in the south, and the house of Joseph 6 their boundary in the north. You shall register the land in seven portions, bring the lists here, and I will cast lots for you in the pre- 7 sence of the LORD our God. Levi has no share among you, because his share is the priesthood of the LORD; and Gad, Reuben, and the half tribe of Manasseh have each taken possession of their patrimony east of the Jordan, which Moses the servant of the LORD gave 8 them.' So the men set out on their journeys. Joshua ordered the emissaries to survey the country: 'Go through the whole country,' he said, 'survey it and return to me, and I will cast lots for you here be- 9 fore the LORD in Shiloh.' So the men went and passed through the country; they registered it on a scroll, city by city, in seven portions, and came to Joshua in the 10 camp at Shiloh. Joshua cast lots for them in Shiloh before the LORD, and distributed the land there to the Israelites in their proper shares. 11 This is the lot which fell to the tribe of the Benjamites family by family. The territory allotted to them lay between the territory of 12 Judah and Joseph. Their boundary at its northern corner starts from the Jordan; it goes up the slope on the north side of Jericho, continuing westwards into the hill-country, and its limit there is the wilderness of Beth-aven. From 13 there it runs on to Luz, to the southern slope of Luz, that is Bethel, and down to Ataroth-addar over the hill-country south of Lower Beth-horon. The bound- 14 ary then bends round at the west corner southwards from the hill-country above Beth-horon, and its limit is Kiriath-baal, that is Kiriath-jearim, a city of Judah. This is the western side. The southern 15 side starts from the edge of Kiriath-jearim and ends*a* at the spring of the waters of Nephtoah. It goes 16 down to the edge of the hill to the east of the Valley of Ben-hinnom, north of the Vale of Rephaim, down the Valley of Hinnom, to the southern slope of the Jebusites and so to En-rogel. It then bends round 17 north and comes out at En-shemesh, goes on to the districts in front of the ascent of Adummim and thence down to the Stone of Bohan son of Reuben. It passes to 18 the northern side of the slope facing the Arabah and goes down to the Arabah, passing the north- 19 ern slope of Beth-hoglah, and its limit is the northern inlet of the Dead Sea, at the southern mouth of the Jordan. This forms the southern boundary. The Jordan 20 is the boundary on the east side. This is the patrimony of the Benjamites, the complete circuit of their boundaries family by family.

The cities belonging to the tribe 21 of the Benjamites family by family are: Jericho, Beth-hoglah, Emek-keziz, Beth-arabah, Zemaraim, 22 Bethel, Avvim, Parah, Ophrah, 23 Kephar-ammoni, Ophni, and Geba: 24 twelve cities in all with their hamlets. Gibeon, Ramah, Beer- 25 oth, Mizpah, Kephirah, Mozah, 26 Rekem, Irpeel, Taralah, Zela, 27, 28 Eleph, Jebus, that is Jerusalem, Gibeah, and Kiriath-jearim: fourteen cities in all with their hamlets.

---

a *Prob. rdg.; Heb. adds* westwards and ends...

This is the patrimony of the Benjamites family by family.

19 The second lot cast was for Simeon, the tribe of the Simeonites family by family. Their patrimony 2 was included in that of Judah. For their patrimony they had Beer-3 sheba,*a* Moladah, Hazar-shual, Ba-4 lah, Ezem, Eltolad, Bethul, Hor-5 mah, Ziklag, Beth-marcaboth, Ha-6 zar-susah, Beth-lebaoth, and Sharuhen: in all, thirteen cities and 7 their hamlets. They had Ain, Rimmon, Ether, and Ashan: four cities 8 and their hamlets, all the hamlets round these cities as far as Baalathbeer, Ramath-negeb. This was the patrimony of the tribe of Simeon 9 family by family. The patrimony of the Simeonites was part of the land allotted to the men of Judah, because their share was larger than they needed. The Simeonites therefore had their patrimony within the territory of Judah.

10 The third lot fell to the Zebulunites family by family. The boundary of their patrimony extended to 11 Shadud.*b* Their boundary went up westwards as far as Maralah and touched Dabbesheth and the gorge 12 east of Jokneam. It turned back from Shadud eastwards towards the sunrise up to the border of Kisloth-tabor, on to Daberath and 13 up to Japhia. From there it crossed eastwards towards the sunrise to Gath-hepher, to Ittah-kazin, out to Rimmon, and bent round*c* to 14 Neah. The northern boundary went round to Hannathon, and its limits were the Valley of Jiphtah-el, 15 Kattath, Nahalal, Shimron, Idalah, and Bethlehem: twelve cities 16 in all with their hamlets. These cities and their hamlets were the patrimony of Zebulun family by family.

17 The fourth lot cast was for the sons of Issachar family by family. 18 Their boundary included Jezreel, Kesulloth, Shunem, Hapharaim, 19 Shion, Anaharath, Rabbith, Ki-20 shion, Ebez, Remeth, En-gannim, 21 En-haddah, and Beth-pazzez. The 22 boundary touched Tabor, Shahazumah, and Beth-shemesh, and its limit was the Jordan: sixteen cities with their hamlets. This was the 23 patrimony of the tribe of the sons of Issachar family by family, both cities and hamlets.

The fifth lot cast was for the 24 tribe of the Asherites family by family. Their boundary included 25 Helkath, Hali, Beten, Akshaph, Alammelech, Amad, and Mishal; 26 it touched Carmel on the west and the swamp of Libnath. It then 27 turned back towards the east to Beth-dagon, touched Zebulun and the Valley of Jiphtah-el on the north at Beth-emek and Neiel, and reached Cabul on its northern side, and Abdon, Rehob, Hammon, and 28 Kanah as far as Greater Sidon. The 29 boundary turned at Ramah, going as far as the fortress city of Tyre, and then back again to Hosah, and its limits to the west were Mehalbeh, Achzib, Acco,*d* Aphek, and 30 Rehob: twenty-two cities in all with their hamlets. This was the 31 patrimony of the tribe of Asher family by family, these cities and their hamlets.

The sixth lot cast was for the 32 sons of Naphtali family by family. Their boundary started from He-33 leph and from Elon-bezaanannim and ran past Adami-nekeb and Jabneel as far as Lakkum, and its limit was the Jordan. The bound-34 ary turned back westwards to Aznoth-tabor and from there on to Hukok. It touched Zebulun on the south, Asher on the west, and the low-lying land by the Jordan on the east. Their fortified cities were 35 Ziddim, Zer, Hammath, Rakkath, Kinnereth, Adamah, Ramah, Ha-36 zor, Kedesh, Edrei, En-hazor, 37

---

a Prob. rdg., cp. 1 Chr. 4. 28; *Heb. adds* and Sheba.   *b* Prob. rdg.; Heb. Sarid (*similarly in verse 12*).   *c* and bent round: *prob. rdg.; Heb.* which stretched.
d Mehalbeh...Acco: *prob. rdg.; Heb.* from the district of Achzib and Ummah.

38 Iron, Migdal-el, Horem, Beth-
39 anath, and Beth-shemesh: nineteen cities with their hamlets. This
was the patrimony of the tribe of
Naphtali family by family, both
cities and hamlets.

40   The seventh lot cast was for the
tribe of the sons of Dan family by
41 family. The boundary of their
patrimony was Zorah, Eshtaol,
42 Irshemesh, Shaalabbin, Aijalon,
43, 44 Jithlah, Elon, Timnah, Ekron, El-
45 tekeh, Gibbethon, Baalath, Jehud,
46 Bene-berak, Gath-rimmon; and on
the west Jarkon was the boundary
47 opposite Joppa. But the Danites,
when they lost this territory,
marched against Leshem, attacked
it and captured it. They put its people to the sword, occupied it and
settled in it; and they renamed the
place Dan after their ancestor Dan.
48 This was the patrimony of the
tribe of the sons of Dan family by
family, these cities and their
hamlets.

49   So the Israelites finished allocating the land and marking out
its frontiers; and they gave Joshua
son of Nun a patrimony within
50 their territory. They followed the
commands of the LORD and gave
him the city for which he asked,
Timnath-serah in the hill-country
of Ephraim, and he rebuilt the city
and settled in it.

51   These are the patrimonies which
Eleazar the priest and Joshua son
of Nun and the heads of families
assigned by lot to the Israelite
tribes at Shiloh before the LORD at
the entrance of the Tent of the
Presence. Thus they completed
the distribution of the land.

20 THE LORD spoke to Joshua and
2 commanded him to say this to the
Israelites: 'You must now appoint
your cities of refuge, of which I
3 spoke to you through Moses. They
are to be places where the homicide,
the man who kills another inadvertently without intent, may take
sanctuary. You shall single them

out as cities of refuge from the vengeance of the dead man's next-of-
kin. When a man takes sanctuary 4
in one of these cities, he shall halt
at the entrance of the city gate and
state his case in the hearing of the
elders of that city; if they admit
him into the city, they shall grant
him a place where he may live as
one of themselves. When the next- 5
of-kin comes in pursuit, they shall
not surrender him: he struck down
his fellow without intent and had
not previously been at enmity with
him. The homicide may stay in 6
that city until he stands trial before the community. On the death
of the ruling high priest, he may
return to the city and home from
which he has fled.' They dedicated 7
Kedesh in Galilee in the hill-country of Naphtali, Shechem in the
hill-country of Ephraim, and Kiriath-arba, that is Hebron, in the
hill-country of Judah. Across the 8
Jordan eastwards from Jericho
they appointed these cities: from
the tribe of Reuben, Bezer-in-the-
wilderness on the tableland, from
the tribe of Gad, Ramoth in Gilead, and from the tribe of Manasseh, Golan in Bashan. These were 9
the appointed cities where any
Israelite or any alien residing a-
mong them might take sanctuary.
They were intended for any man
who killed another inadvertently,
to ensure that no one should die at
the hand of the next-of-kin until
he had stood his trial before the
community.

    The heads of the Levite families 21
approached Eleazar the priest and
Joshua son of Nun and the heads of
the families of the tribes of Israel.
They came before them at Shiloh 2
in the land of Canaan and said,
'The LORD gave his command
through Moses that we were to receive cities to live in, together with
the common land belonging to
them for our cattle.' The Israelites 3
therefore gave part of their patrimony to the Levites, the following

cities with their common land, according to the command of the LORD.

4 This is the territory allotted to the Kohathite family: those Levites who were descended from Aaron the priest received thirteen cities chosen by lot from the tribes of Judah, Simeon, and Benjamin;

5 the rest of the Kohathites were allotted family by family[a] ten cities from the tribes of Ephraim, Dan, and half Manasseh.

6 The Gershonites were allotted family by family thirteen cities from the tribes of Issachar, Asher, Naphtali, and the half tribe of Manasseh in Bashan.

7 The Merarites were allotted family by family twelve cities from the tribes of Reuben, Gad, and Zebulun.

8 So the Israelites gave the Levites these cities with their common land, allocating them by lot as the LORD had commanded through Moses.

9 The Israelites designated the following cities out of the tribes of

10 Judah and Simeon for those sons of Aaron who were of the Kohathite families of the Levites, be-

11 cause their lot came out first. They gave them Kiriath-arba (Arba was the father of Anak), that is Hebron, in the hill-country of Judah, and

12 the common land round it, but they gave the open country near the city, and its hamlets, to Caleb son of Jephunneh as his patrimony.

13[b] To the sons of Aaron the priest they gave Hebron, a city of refuge

14 for the homicide, Libnah, Jattir,

15, 16 Eshtemoa, Holon, Debir, Ashan,[c] Juttah, and Beth-shemesh, each with its common land: nine cities

17 from these two tribes. They also gave cities from the tribe of Ben-

18 jamin, Gibeon, Geba, Anathoth,

and Almon, each with its common land: four cities. The number of 19 the cities with their common land given to the sons of Aaron the priest was thirteen.

The cities which the rest of the 20 Kohathite families of the Levites received by lot were from the tribe of Ephraim. They gave them She- 21 chem, a city of refuge for the homicide, in the hill-country of Eph- raim, Gezer, Kibzaim, and Beth- 22 horon, each with its common land: four cities. From the tribe of Dan, 23 they gave them Eltekeh, Gibbe- thon, Aijalon, and Gath-rimmon, 24 each with its common land: four cities. From the half tribe of Manas- 25 seh, they gave them Taanach and Gath-rimmon, each with its com- mon land: two cities. The number 26 of the cities belonging to the rest of the Kohathite families with their common land was ten.

The Gershonite families of the 27 Levites received, out of the share of the half tribe of Manasseh, Go- lan in Bashan, a city of refuge for the homicide, and Be-ashtaroth,[d] each with its common land: two cities. From the tribe of Issachar 28 they received Kishon, Daberah, Jarmuth, and En-gannim, each 29 with its common land: four cities. From the tribe of Asher they re- 30 ceived Mishal, Abdon, Helkath, 31 and Rehob, each with its common land: four cities. From the tribe of 32 Naphtali they received Kedesh in Galilee, a city of refuge for the homicide, Hammoth-dor, and Kar- tan, each with its common land: three cities. The number of the 33 cities of the Gershonite families with their common land was thirteen.

From the tribe of Zebulun the 34 rest of the Merarite families of the Levites received Jokneam, Kar- tah, Rimmon,[e] and Nahalal, each 35

---

[a] family by family: *prob. rdg.*; *Heb.* from the families (*similarly in verse 6*).
[b] Verses 13–39: cp. 1 Chr. 6. 57–81.   [c] *Prob. rdg., cp.* 1 Chr. 6. 59; *Heb.* Ain.
[d] *Prob. rdg.*; *Heb.* Be-ashtarah.
[e] *Prob. rdg., cp.* 19. 13; 1 Chr. 6. 77; *Heb.* Dimnah.

with its common land: four cities.

36 East of the Jordan at Jericho, from the tribe of Reuben they were given Bezer-in-the-wilderness on the tableland, a city of refuge for

37 the homicide, Jahaz, Kedemoth, and Mephaath, each with its common land: four cities. From the

38 tribe of Gad they received Ramoth in Gilead, a city of refuge for the

39 homicide, Mahanaim, Heshbon, and Jazer, each with its common

40 land: four cities in all. Twelve cities in all fell by lot to the rest of the Merarite families of the Levites.

41 The cities of the Levites within the Israelite patrimonies numbered forty-eight in all, with their

42 common land. Each city had its common land round it, and it was the same for all of them.

43 Thus the LORD gave Israel all the land which he had sworn to give to their forefathers; they oc-

44 cupied it and settled in it. The LORD gave them security on every side as he had sworn to their forefathers. Of all their enemies not a man could withstand them; the LORD delivered all their enemies

45 into their hands. Not a word of the LORD's promises to the house of Israel went unfulfilled; they all came true.

22 AT that time Joshua summoned the Reubenites, the Gadites, and

2 the half tribe of Manasseh, and said to them, 'You have observed all the commands of Moses the servant of the LORD, and you have obeyed me in all the commands that I too

3 have laid upon you. All this time you have not deserted your brothers; up to this day you have diligently observed the charge laid on

4 you by the LORD your God. And now that the LORD your God has given your brothers security as he promised them, you may turn now and go to your homes in your own land, the land which Moses the servant of the LORD gave you east of

the Jordan. But take good care to 5 keep the commands and the law which Moses the servant of the LORD gave you: to love the LORD your God; to conform to his ways; to observe his commandments; to hold fast to him; to serve him with your whole heart and soul.' Jo- 6 shua blessed them and dismissed them; and they went to their homes. He sent them home with 7-8 his blessing, and with these words: 'Go to your homes richly laden, with great herds, with silver and gold, copper and iron, and with large stores of clothing. See that you share with your kinsmen the spoil you have taken from your enemies.'

Moses had given territory to one half of the tribe of Manasseh in Bashan, and Joshua gave territory to the other half west of the Jordan among their kinsmen.

So the Reubenites, the Gadites, 9 and the half tribe of Manasseh left the rest of the Israelites and went from Shiloh in Canaan on their way into Gilead, the land which belonged to them according to the decree of the LORD given through Moses. When these tribes came to Geliloth 10 by the Jordan,[a] they built a great altar there by the river for all to see. The Israelites heard that the 11 Reubenites, the Gadites, and the half tribe of Manasseh had built the altar facing the land of Canaan, at Geliloth by the Jordan opposite the Israelite side. When the news 12 reached them, all the community of the Israelites assembled at Shiloh to advance against them with a display of force. At the same time 13 the Israelites sent Phinehas son of Eleazar the priest into the land of Gilead, to the Reubenites, the Gadites, and the half tribe of Manasseh, and ten leading men with him, 14 one from each of the tribes of Israel, each of them the head of a household among the clans of Israel. They came to the Reubenites, the 15

---

[a] *Prob. rdg.; Heb. adds* which was in Canaan.

241

Gadites, and the half tribe of Manasseh in the land of Gilead, and remonstrated with them in these
16 words: 'We speak for the whole community of the LORD. What is this treachery you have committed against the God of Israel? Are you ceasing to follow the LORD and building your own altar this day in
17 defiance of the LORD? Remember our offence at Peor, for which a plague fell upon the community of the LORD; to this day we have not been purified from it. Was that
18 offence so slight that you dare cease to follow the LORD today? If you defy the LORD today, then tomorrow he will be angry with the
19 whole community of Israel. If the land you have taken is unclean, then cross over to the LORD's own land, where the Tabernacle of the LORD now rests, and take a share of it with us; but do not defy the LORD and involve us in your defiance by building an altar of your own apart from the altar of the
20 LORD our God. Remember the treachery of Achan son of Zerah, who defied the ban and the whole community of Israel suffered for it. He was not the only one who paid for that sin with his life.'
21   Then the Reubenites, the Gadites, and the half tribe of Manasseh remonstrated with the heads of
22 the clans of Israel: 'The LORD the God of gods, the LORD the God of gods, he knows, and Israel must know: if this had been an act of defiance or treachery against the LORD, you could not save us today.
23 If we had built ourselves an altar meaning to forsake the LORD, or had offered whole-offerings or grain-offerings upon it, or had presented shared-offerings, the LORD himself would exact punishment.
24 The truth is that we have done this for fear that the day may come when your sons will say to ours, "What have you to do with the
25 LORD, the God of Israel? The LORD put the Jordan as a boundary be-

tween our sons and your sons. You have no share in the LORD, you men of Reuben and Gad." Thus your sons will prevent our sons from going in awe of the LORD. So 26 we resolved to set ourselves to build an altar, not for whole-offerings and sacrifices, but as a 27 witness between us and you, and between our descendants after us. Thus we shall be able to do service before the LORD, as we do now, with our whole-offerings, our sacrifices, and our shared-offerings; and your sons will never be able to say to our sons that they have no share in the LORD. And we thought, if 28 ever they do say this to us and our descendants, we will point to this copy of the altar of the LORD which we have made, not for whole-offerings and not for sacrifices, but as a witness between us and you. God forbid that we should 29 defy the LORD and forsake him this day by building another altar for whole-offerings, grain-offerings, and sacrifices, in addition to the altar of the LORD our God which stands in front of his Tabernacle.'

When Phinehas the priest and 30 the leaders of the community, the heads of the Israelite clans, who were with him, heard what the Reubenites, the Gadites, and the Manassites said, they were satisfied. Phinehas son of Eleazar the 31 priest said to the Reubenites, Gadites, and Manassites, 'We know now that the LORD is in our midst today; you have not acted treacherously against the LORD, and thus you have preserved all Israel from punishment at his hand.' Then Phinehas son of Eleazar the 32 priest and the leaders left the Reubenites and the Gadites in Gilead and reported to the Israelites in Canaan. The Israelites were 33 satisfied, and they blessed God and thought no more of attacking Reuben and Gad and ravaging their land. The Reubenites and 34

Gadites said, 'The altar is a witness between us that the LORD is God', and they named it 'Witness'.

Joshua's farewell and death

23 A LONG time had passed since the LORD had given Israel security from all the enemies who surrounded them, and Joshua was now 2 a very old man. He summoned all Israel, their elders and heads of families, their judges and officers, and said to them, 'I have become a 3 very old man. You have seen for yourselves all that the LORD our God has done to these peoples for your sake; it was the LORD God 4 himself who fought for you. I have allotted you your patrimony tribe by tribe, the land of all the peoples that I have wiped out and of all these that remain between the Jordan and the Great Sea which lies 5 towards the setting sun. The LORD your God himself drove them out for your sake; he drove them out to make room for you, and you occupied their land, as the LORD your 6 God had promised you. Be resolute therefore: observe and perform everything written in the book of the law of Moses, without swerving 7 to right or to left. You must not associate with the peoples that are left among you; you must not call upon their gods by name, nor[a] swear by them nor prostrate yourselves in worship before them. 8 You must hold fast to the LORD your God as you have done down 9 to this day. For your sake the LORD has driven out great and mighty nations; to this day not a man of them has withstood you. 10 One of you can put to flight a thousand, because the LORD your God fights for you, as he promised. 11 Be on your guard then, love the 12 LORD your God, for[b] if you do turn away and attach yourselves to the

peoples that still remain among you, and intermarry with them and associate with them and they with you, then be sure that the 13 LORD will not continue to drive those peoples out to make room for you. They will be snares to entrap you, whips for your backs and barbed hooks in your eyes, until you vanish from the good land which the LORD your God has given you. And now I am going the 14 way of all mankind. You know in your heart of hearts that nothing that the LORD your God has promised you has failed to come true, every word of it. But the same 15 LORD God who has kept his word to you to such good effect can equally bring every kind of evil on you, until he has rooted you out from this good land which he has given you. If you break the covenant 16 which the LORD your God has prescribed and prostrate yourselves in worship before other gods, then the LORD will be angry with you and you will quickly vanish from the good land he has given you.'

Joshua assembled all the tribes 24 of Israel at Shechem. He summoned the elders of Israel, the heads of families, the judges and officers; and they presented themselves before God. Joshua then said this to 2 all the people: 'This is the word of the LORD the God of Israel: "Long ago your forefathers, Terah and his sons Abraham and Nahor, lived beside the Euphrates, and they worshipped other gods. I took your 3 father Abraham from beside the Euphrates and led him through the length and breadth of Canaan. I gave him many descendants: I gave him Isaac, and to Isaac I gave 4 Jacob and Esau. I put Esau in possession of the hill-country of Seir, but Jacob and his sons went down to Egypt. I sent Moses and Aaron, 5 and I struck the Egyptians with

---

[a] you must not call...nor: *or* the name of their gods shall not be your boast, nor must you...
[b] Be on...for: *or* Take very good care to love the LORD your God, but...

plagues – you know well what I did among them – and after that I brought you out; I brought your 6 fathers out of Egypt and you came to the Red Sea. The Egyptians sent their chariots and cavalry to 7 pursue your fathers to the sea. But when they appealed to the LORD, he put a screen of darkness between you and the Egyptians, and brought the sea down on them and it covered them; you saw for yourselves what I did to Egypt. For a long time you lived in the wilder-8 ness. Then I brought you into the land of the Amorites who lived east of the Jordan; they fought against you, but I delivered them into your hands; you took possession of their country and I destroyed them for 9 your sake. The king of Moab, Balak son of Zippor, took the field against Israel. He sent for Balaam son of Beor to lay a curse on you, 10 but I would not listen to him. Instead of that he blessed you; and so I saved you from the power of 11 Balak. Then you crossed the Jordan and came to Jericho. The citizens of Jericho fought against you,[a] but I delivered them into your 12 hands. I spread panic before you, and it was this, not your sword or your bow, that drove out the two 13 kings of the Amorites. I gave you land on which you had not laboured, cities which you had never built; you have lived in those cities and you eat the produce of vineyards and olive-groves which you did not plant."

14　'Hold the LORD in awe then, and worship him in loyalty and truth. Banish the gods whom your fathers worshipped beside the Euphrates and in Egypt, and worship the 15 LORD. But if it does not please you to worship the LORD, choose here and now whom you will worship: the gods whom your forefathers worshipped beside the Euphrates, or the gods of the Amorites in whose land you are living. But I and my family, we will worship the LORD.' The people answered, 'God 16 forbid that we should forsake the LORD to worship other gods, for it 17 was the LORD our God who brought us and our fathers up from Egypt, that land of slavery; it was he who displayed those great signs before our eyes and guarded us on all our wanderings among the many peoples through whose lands we passed. The LORD drove out before us the 18 Amorites and all the peoples who lived in that country. We too will worship the LORD; he is our God.' Joshua answered the people, 'You 19 cannot worship the LORD. He is a holy god, a jealous god, and he will not forgive your rebellion and your sins. If you forsake the LORD and 20 worship foreign gods, he will turn and bring adversity upon you and, although he once brought you prosperity, he will make an end of you.' The people said to Joshua, 21 'No; we will worship the LORD.' He said to them, 'You are witnesses 22 against yourselves that you have chosen the LORD and will worship him.' 'Yes,' they answered, 'we are witnesses.' He said to them, 'Then 23 here and now banish the foreign gods that are among you, and turn your hearts to the LORD the God of Israel.' The people said to Joshua, 24 'The LORD our God we will worship and his voice we will obey.' So Jo-25 shua made a covenant that day with[b] the people; he drew up a statute and an ordinance for them in Shechem and wrote its terms in the 26 book of the law of God. He took a great stone and set it up there under the terebinth[c] in the sanctuary of the LORD, and said to all the 27 people, 'This stone is a witness against us; for it has heard all the words which the LORD has spoken to us. If you renounce your

---

[a] *Prob. rdg.; Heb. adds* Amorites, Perizzites, Canaanites, Hittites, Girgashites, Hivites, and Jebusites.
[b] *Or* for.　　　　　　　　　　　[c] *Or* pole.

God, it shall be a witness against
28 you.' Then Joshua dismissed the
people, each man to his patrimony.

29 After these things, Joshua son of
Nun the servant of the LORD died;
he was a hundred and ten years old.

30 They buried him within the border
of his own patrimony in Timnath-
serah in the hill-country of Ephraim to the north of Mount Gaash.

31 Israel served the LORD during the
lifetime of Joshua and of the elders
who outlived him and who well
knew all that the LORD had done
for Israel.

The bones of Joseph, which the 32
Israelites had brought up from
Egypt, were buried in Shechem, in
the plot of land which Jacob had
bought from the sons of Hamor
father of Shechem for a hundred
sheep;[a] and they passed into the
patrimony of the house of Joseph.
Eleazar son of Aaron died and was 33
buried in the hill which had been
given to Phinehas his son in the
hill-country of Ephraim.

THE BOOK OF

JUDGES

The conquest of Canaan completed

1 AFTER the death of Joshua
the Israelites inquired of the
LORD which tribe should at-
2 tack the Canaanites first. The LORD
answered, 'Judah shall attack. I
hereby deliver the country into his
3 power.' Judah said to his brother
Simeon, 'Go forward with me into
my allotted territory, and let us do
battle with the Canaanites; then I
in turn will go with you into your
territory.' So Simeon went with
4 him; then Judah advanced to the
attack, and the LORD delivered
the Canaanites and Perizzites into
their hands. They slaughtered ten
5 thousand of them at Bezek. There
they came upon Adoni-bezek, engaged him in battle and defeated
6 the Canaanites and Perizzites. A-
doni-bezek fled, but they pursued
him, took him prisoner and cut
7 off his thumbs and his great toes.
Adoni-bezek said, 'I once had
seventy kings whose thumbs and
great toes were cut off picking up
the scraps from under my table.
What I have done God has done to
me.' He was brought to Jerusalem
and died there.

The men of Judah made an as- 8
sault on Jerusalem and captured
it, put its people to the sword and
set fire to the city. Then they 9
turned south to fight the Canaanites of the hill-country, the Negeb,
and the Shephelah. Judah attack- 10
ed the Canaanites in Hebron, formerly called Kiriath-arba, and
defeated Sheshai, Ahiman and
Talmai. From there they marched 11
against the inhabitants of Debir,
formerly called Kiriath-sepher. Ca- 12
leb said, 'Whoever attacks Kiriath-
sepher and captures it, to him I
will give my daughter Achsah in
marriage.' Othniel, son of Caleb's 13
younger brother Kenaz, captured
it, and Caleb gave him his daughter
Achsah. When she came to him, he 14
incited her to ask her father for a
piece of land. As she sat on the ass,
she broke wind, and Caleb said,
'What did you mean by that?' She 15

[a] Or pieces of money (cp. Gen. 33. 19; Job 42. 11).

replied, 'I want to ask a favour of you. You have put me in this dry Negeb; you must give me pools of water as well.' So Caleb gave her the upper pool and the lower pool.

16 The descendants of Moses' father-in-law, the Kenite, went up with the men of Judah from the Vale of Palm Trees to the wilderness of Judah which is in the Negeb of Arad and settled among the Amalekites. 17 Judah then accompanied his brother Simeon, attacked the Canaanites in Zephath and destroyed it; hence the city 18 was called Hormah.[a] Judah took Gaza, Ashkelon, and Ekron, and 19 the territory of each. The LORD was with Judah and they occupied the hill-country, but they could not drive out the inhabitants of the Vale because they had chariots of 20 iron. Hebron was given to Caleb as Moses had directed, and he drove out the three sons of Anak. 21 But the Benjamites did not drive out the Jebusites of Jerusalem; and the Jebusites have lived on in Jerusalem with the Benjamites till the present day.

22 The tribes of Joseph attacked Bethel, and the LORD was with 23 them. They sent spies to Bethel, 24 formerly called Luz. These spies saw a man coming out of the city and said to him, 'Show us how to enter the city, and we will see that 25 you come to no harm.' So he showed them how to enter, and they put the city to the sword, but let the man and his family go free. 26 He went into Hittite country, built a city and named it Luz, which is still its name today.

27 Manasseh did not drive out the inhabitants of Beth-shean with its villages, nor of Taanach, Dor, Ibleam, and Megiddo, with the villages of each of them; the Canaanites held their ground in that 28 region. Later, when Israel became strong, they put them to forced labour, but they never completely drove them out.

29 Ephraim did not drive out the Canaanites who lived in Gezer, but the Canaanites lived among them there.

30 Zebulun did not drive out the inhabitants of Kitron and Nahalol, but the Canaanites lived among them and were put to forced labour.

31 Asher did not drive out the inhabitants of Acco and Sidon, of Ahlab, Achzib, Helbah, Aphik and Rehob. 32 Thus the Asherites lived among the Canaanite inhabitants and did not drive them out.

33 Naphtali did not drive out the inhabitants of Beth-shemesh and of Beth-anath, but lived among the Canaanite inhabitants and put the inhabitants of Beth-shemesh and Beth-anath to forced labour.

34 The Amorites pressed the Danites back into the hill-country and did not allow them to come down into the Vale. 35 The Amorites held their ground in Mount Heres and in Aijalon and Shaalbim, but the tribes of Joseph increased their pressure on them until they reduced them to forced labour.

36 The boundary of the Edomites ran from the ascent of Akrabbim, upwards from Sela.

2 The angel of the LORD came up from Gilgal to Bokim, and said, 'I brought[b] you up out of Egypt and into the country which I vowed I would give to your forefathers. I said, I will never break my cove2 nant with you, and you in turn must make no covenant with the inhabitants of the country; you must pull down their altars. But you did not obey me, and look what you have done! 3 So I said, I will not drive them out before you; they will decoy you, and their gods will shut you fast in the trap.' 4 When the angel of the LORD said this to the Israelites, they all wept and 5 wailed, and so the place was called

---

[a] *That is* Destruction.
[b] *Prob. rdg.; Heb.* I will bring.

Bokim;[a] and they offered sacrifices there to the LORD.

Israel under the judges

6 JOSHUA dismissed the people, and the Israelites went off to occupy the country, each man to his allott-
7 ed portion. As long as Joshua was alive and the elders who survived him – everyone, that is, who had witnessed the whole great work which the LORD had done for Is-
8 rael – the people worshipped the LORD. At the age of a hundred and ten Joshua son of Nun, the servant
9 of the LORD, died, and they buried him within the border of his own property in Timnath-heres north of Mount Gaash in the hill-country
10 of Ephraim. Of that whole genera-tion, all were gathered to their fore-fathers, and another generation followed who did not acknowledge the LORD and did not know what
11 he had done for Israel. Then the Israelites did what was wrong in the eyes of the LORD, and wor-
12 shipped the Baalim.[b] They forsook the LORD, their fathers' God who had brought them out of Egypt, and went after other gods, gods of the races among whom they lived; they bowed down before them and
13 provoked the LORD to anger; they forsook the LORD and worshipped
14 the Baal and the Ashtaroth.[c] The LORD in his anger made them the prey of bands of raiders and plunderers; he sold them to their enemies all around them, and they could no longer make a stand.
15 Every time they went out to battle the LORD brought disaster upon them, as he had said when he gave them his solemn warning, and they were in dire straits.
16 The LORD set judges over them, who rescued them from the ma-
17 rauding bands. Yet they did not listen even to these judges, but turned wantonly to worship other gods and bowed down before them; all too soon they abandoned the path of obedience to the LORD's commands which their forefathers had followed. They did not obey
18 the LORD. Whenever the LORD set up a judge over them, he was with that judge, and kept them safe from their enemies so long as he lived. The LORD would relent as often as he heard them groaning under oppression and ill-treatment.
19 But as soon as the judge was dead, they would relapse into deeper cor-ruption than their forefathers and give their allegiance to other gods, worshipping them and bowing down before them. They gave up none of their evil practices and their wilful ways. And the LORD
20 was angry with Israel and said, 'This nation has broken the cove-nant which I laid upon their fore-fathers and has not obeyed me,
21 and now, of all the nations which Joshua left at his death, I will not drive out to make room for them
22 one single man. By their means I will test Israel, to see whether or not they will keep strictly to the way of the LORD as their fore-
23 fathers did.' So the LORD left those nations alone and made no haste to drive them out or give them into Joshua's hands.

3 These are the nations which the LORD left as a means of testing all the Israelites who had not taken part in the battles for Canaan, his
2 purpose being to teach succeeding generations of Israel, or those at least who had not learnt in former
3 times, how to make war. These were: the five lords of the Philis-tines, all the Canaanites, the Si-donians, and the Hivites who lived in Mount Lebanon from Mount Baal-hermon as far as Lebo-hamath. His purpose also was to
4 test whether the Israelites would obey the commands which the LORD had given to their forefathers

---

[a] *That is* Weepers.   [b] The Baalim *were Canaanite deities.*
[c] The Ashtaroth *were Canaanite deities.*

5 through Moses. Thus the Israelites lived among the Canaanites, the Hittites, the Amorites, the Perizzites, the Hivites, and the Jebu-
6 sites. They took their daughters in marriage and gave their own daughters to their sons; and they worshipped their gods.

7   The Israelites did what was wrong in the eyes of the LORD; they forgot the LORD their God and worshipped the Baalim and the
8 Asheroth.[a] The LORD was angry with Israel and he sold them to Cushan-rishathaim, king of Aram-naharaim,[b] who kept them in sub-
9 jection for eight years. Then the Israelites cried to the LORD for help and he raised up a man to deliver them, Othniel son of Caleb's younger brother Kenaz, and
10 he set them free. The spirit of the LORD came upon him and he became judge over Israel. He took the field, and the LORD delivered Cushan-rishathaim king of Aram into his hands; Othniel was too
11 strong for him. Thus the land was at peace for forty years until Othniel son of Kenaz died.
12   Once again the Israelites did what was wrong in the eyes of the LORD, and because of this he roused Eglon king of Moab against
13 Israel. Eglon mustered the Ammonites and the Amalekites, advanced to attack Israel and took possession of the Vale of Palm
14 Trees. The Israelites were subject to Eglon king of Moab for eighteen
15 years. When they cried to the LORD for help, he raised up a man to deliver them, Ehud son of Gera the Benjamite, who was left-handed. The Israelites sent him to pay their tribute to Eglon king of
16 Moab. Ehud made himself a two-edged sword, only fifteen inches long, which he fastened on his
17 right side under his clothes, and he brought the tribute to Eglon king of Moab. Eglon was a very fat man.
18 When Ehud had finished present-

ing the tribute, he sent on the men who had carried it, and he himself 19 turned back from the Carved Stones at Gilgal. 'My lord king,' he said, 'I have a word for you in private.' Eglon called for silence and dismissed all his attendants. Ehud 20 then came up to him as he sat in the roof-chamber of his summer palace and said, 'I have a word from God for you.' So Eglon rose from his seat, and Ehud reached 21 with his left hand, drew the sword from his right side and drove it into his belly. The hilt went in after 22 the blade and the fat closed over the blade; he did not draw the sword out but left it protruding behind. Ehud went out to the 23 porch, shut the doors on him and fastened them. When he had gone 24 away, Eglon's servants came and, finding the doors fastened, they said, 'He must be relieving himself in the closet of his summer palace.' They waited until they were 25 ashamed to delay any longer, and still he did not open the doors of the roof-chamber. So they took the key and opened the doors; and there was their master lying on the floor dead. While they had been 26 waiting, Ehud made his escape; he passed the Carved Stones and escaped to Seirah. When he arrived 27 there, he sounded the trumpet in the hill-country of Ephraim, and the Israelites came down from the hills with him at their head. He 28 said to them, 'Follow me, for the LORD has delivered your enemy the Moabites into your hands.' Down they came after him, and they seized the fords of the Jordan against the Moabites and allowed no man to cross. They killed that 29 day some ten thousand Moabites, all of them men of substance and all fighting men; not one escaped. Thus Moab on that day became 30 subject to Israel, and the land was at peace for eighty years.
    After Ehud there was Shamgar 31

---

[a] *Plural of* Asherah, *the name of a Canaanite goddess.*   [b] *That is* Aram of Two Rivers.

of Beth-anath.[a] He killed six hundred Philistines with an ox-goad, and he too delivered Israel.

4 After Ehud's death the Israelites once again did what was wrong in the eyes of the LORD, so he sold them to Jabin the Canaanite king, who ruled in Hazor. The commander of his forces was Sisera, who lived in Harosheth-of-the-Gentiles. 3 The Israelites cried to the LORD for help, because Sisera had nine hundred chariots of iron and had oppressed Israel harshly for twenty 4 years. At that time Deborah wife of Lappidoth,[b] a prophetess, was 5 judge in Israel. It was her custom to sit beneath the Palm-tree of Deborah between Ramah and Bethel in the hill-country of Ephraim, and the Israelites went up to 6 her for justice. She sent for Barak son of Abinoam from Kedesh in Naphtali and said to him, 'These are the commands of the LORD the God of Israel: "Go and draw ten thousand men from Naphtali and Zebulun and bring them with you 7 to Mount Tabor, and I will draw Sisera, Jabin's commander, to the Torrent of Kishon with his chariots and all his rabble, and there I will deliver them into your hands."' 8 Barak answered her, 'If you go with me, I will go; but if you will 9 not go, neither will I.' 'Certainly I will go with you,' she said, 'but this venture will bring you no glory, because the LORD will leave Sisera to fall into the hands of a woman.' So Deborah rose and went with 10 Barak to Kedesh. Barak summoned Zebulun and Naphtali to Kedesh and marched up with ten thousand men, and Deborah went with him.

11 Now Heber the Kenite had parted company with the Kenites, the descendants of Hobab, Moses' brother-in-law, and he had pitched his tent at Elon-bezaanannim near Kedesh.

12 Word was brought to Sisera that Barak son of Abinoam had gone up to Mount Tabor; so he summoned 13 all his chariots, nine hundred chariots of iron, and his troops, from Harosheth-of-the-Gentiles to the Torrent of Kishon. Then De- 14 borah said to Barak, 'Up! This day the LORD gives Sisera into your hands. Already the LORD has gone out to battle before you.' So Barak came charging down from Mount Tabor with ten thousand men at his back. The LORD put Sisera to rout 15 with all his chariots and his army before Barak's onslaught; but Sisera himself dismounted from his chariot and fled on foot. Barak 16 pursued the chariots and the army as far as Harosheth, and the whole army was put to the sword and perished; not a man was left alive. Meanwhile Sisera fled on foot to 17 the tent of Jael wife of Heber the Kenite, because Jabin king of Hazor and the household of Heber the Kenite were at peace. Jael 18 came out to meet Sisera and said to him, 'Come in here, my lord, come in; do not be afraid.' So he went into the tent, and she covered him with a rug. He said to her, 'Give me 19 some water to drink; I am thirsty.' She opened a skin full of milk, gave him a drink and covered him up again. He said to her, 'Stand at the 20 tent door, and if anybody comes and asks if someone is here, say No.' But Jael, Heber's wife, took a 21 tent-peg, picked up a hammer, crept up to him, and drove the peg into his skull as he lay sound asleep. His brains oozed out on the ground, his limbs twitched, and he died. When Barak came up in pursuit of 22 Sisera, Jael went out to meet him and said to him, 'Come, I will show you the man you are looking for.' He went in with her, and there was Sisera lying dead with the tent-peg in his skull. That day God gave 23 victory to the Israelites over Jabin king of Canaan, and they pressed 24 home their attacks upon that king

---

[a] of Beth-anath: *or* son of Anath.   [b] wife of Lappidoth: *or* a spirited woman.

of Canaan until they had made an end of him.

5 That day Deborah and Barak son of Abinoam sang this song:

2 For the leaders, the leaders[a] in Israel,
for the people who answered the call,
bless ye the LORD.

3 Hear me, you kings; princes, give ear;
I will sing, I will sing to the LORD.
I will raise a psalm to the LORD the God of Israel.

4 O LORD, at thy setting forth from Seir,
when thou camest marching out of the plains of Edom,
earth trembled; heaven quaked;
the clouds streamed down in torrents.

5 Mountains shook in fear before the LORD, the lord of Sinai,
before the LORD, the God of Israel.

6 In the days of Shamgar of Beth-anath,[b]
in the days of Jael, caravans plied no longer;
men who had followed the high roads
went round by devious paths.

7 Champions there were none,
none left in Israel,
until I,[c] Deborah, arose,
arose, a mother in Israel.

8 They chose new gods,
they consorted with demons.[d]
Not a shield, not a lance was to be seen
in the forty thousand of Israel.

9 Be proud at heart, you marshals of Israel;
you among the people that answered the call,
bless ye the LORD.

10 You that ride your tawny she-asses,
that sit on saddle-cloths,
and you that take the road afoot,
ponder this well.

Hark, the sound of the players 11
striking up
in the places where the women draw water!
It is the victories of the LORD that they commemorate there,
his triumphs as the champion of Israel.

Down to the gates came the LORD's people:
'Rouse, rouse yourself, Deborah, 12
rouse yourself, lead out the host.
Up, Barak! Take prisoners in plenty,
son of Abinoam.'
Then down marched the column[e] 13
and its chieftains,
the people of the LORD marched down[f] like warriors.
The men of Ephraim showed a 14
brave front in the vale,
crying, 'With you, Benjamin!
Your clansmen are here!'
From Machir down came the marshals,
from Zebulun the bearers of the musterer's staff.
Issachar joined with Deborah in 15
the uprising,[g]
Issachar stood by Barak;
down into the valley they rushed.
But Reuben, he was split into factions,
great were their heart-searchings.
What made you linger by the 16
cattle-pens
to listen to the shrill calling of the shepherds?[h]
Gilead stayed beyond Jordan; 17
and Dan, why did he tarry by the ships?
Asher lingered by the sea-shore,
by its creeks he stayed.
The people of Zebulun risked their 18
very lives,
so did Naphtali on the heights of the battlefield.

---

a Or For those who had flowing locks.   *b* of Beth-anath: *or* son of Anath.
c Or you.   *d* Or satyrs.   *e* Prob. rdg.; Heb. survivor.
f Prob. rdg.; Heb. adds to me.   *g* in the uprising: prob. rdg.; Heb. my officers.
h Prob. rdg.; Heb. adds Reuben was split into factions, great were their heart-searchings.

19 Kings came, they fought;
   then fought the kings of Canaan
   at Taanach by the waters of Megid-
      do;
   no plunder of silver did they take.
20 The stars fought from heaven,
   the stars in their courses fought
      against Sisera.
21 The Torrent of Kishon swept him
      away,
   the Torrent barred his flight, the
      Torrent of Kishon;
   march on in might, my soul!
22 Then hammered the hooves of his
      horses,
   his chargers galloped, galloped
      away.
23 A curse on Meroz, said the angel of
      the LORD;
   a curse, a curse on its inhabitants,
   because they brought no help to
      the LORD,
   no help to the LORD and the fight-
      ing men.
24 Blest above women be Jael,
   the wife of Heber the Kenite;
   blest above all women in the tents.
25 He asked for water: she gave him
      milk,
   she offered him curds in a bowl fit
      for a chieftain.
26 She stretched out her hand for the
      tent-peg,
   her right hand to hammer the
      weary.
   With the hammer she struck Sisera,
      she crushed his head;
   she struck and his brains ebbed
      out.
27 At her feet he sank down, he fell,
      he lay;
   at her feet he sank down and fell.
   Where he sank down, there he fell,
      done to death.

28 The mother of Sisera peered
      through the lattice,
   through the window she peered
      and shrilly cried,
   'Why are his chariots so long
      coming?
   Why is the clatter of his chariots so
      long delayed?'

29 The wisest of her princesses an-
      swered her,
   yes, she found her own answer:
30 'They must be finding spoil, taking
      their shares,
   a wench to each man, two wenches,
   booty of dyed stuffs for Sisera,
   booty of dyed stuffs,
   dyed stuff, and striped, two
      lengths of striped stuff –
   to grace the victor's neck.'

31 So perish all thine enemies, O
      LORD;
   but let all who love thee be like the
      sun rising in strength.

The land was at peace for forty
years.

6 THE Israelites did what was
wrong in the eyes of the LORD and
he delivered them into the hands
of Midian for seven years. 2 The Midianites were too strong for Israel,
and the Israelites were forced to
find themselves hollow places in
the mountains, and caves and
strongholds. 3 If the Israelites had
sown their seed, the Midianites and
the Amalekites and other eastern
tribes would come up and attack
Israel. 4 They then pitched their
camps in the country and destroyed
the crops as far as the outskirts of
Gaza, leaving nothing to support
life in Israel, sheep or ox or ass.
5 They came up with their herds and
their tents, like a swarm of locusts;
they and their camels were past
counting. They had come into the
land for its growing crop,[a] and so 6
the Israelites were brought to desti-
tution by the Midianites, and they
cried to the LORD for help. 7 When
the Israelites cried to the LORD because of what they had suffered
from the Midianites, he sent them 8
a prophet who said to them, 'These
are the words of the LORD the God
of Israel: I brought you up from
Egypt, that land of slavery. 9 I delivered you from the Egyptians
and from all your oppressors. I

[a] *for its growing crop:* or *and laid it waste.*

drove them out before you and
10 gave you their lands. I said to you,
"I am the LORD your God: do not
stand in awe of the gods of the
Amorites in whose country you are
settling." But you did not listen to
me.'

11   Now the angel of the LORD came
and sat under the terebinth at
Ophrah which belonged to Joash
the Abiezrite. His son Gideon was
threshing wheat in the winepress,
so that ne might get it away quick-
12 ly from the Midianites. The angel
of the LORD showed himself to
Gideon and said, 'You are a brave
man, and the LORD is with you.'
13 Gideon said, 'But pray, my lord, if
the LORD really is with us, why has
all this happened to us? What has
become of all those wonderful
deeds of his, of which we have
heard from our fathers, when they
told us how the LORD brought us
out of Egypt? But now the LORD
has cast us off and delivered us into
14 the power of the Midianites.' The
LORD turned to him and said, 'Go
and use this strength of yours to
free Israel from the power of the
Midianites. It is I that send you.'
15 Gideon said, 'Pray, my lord, how
can I save Israel? Look at my clan:
it is the weakest in Manasseh, and
I am the least in my father's fami-
16 ly.' The LORD answered, 'I will be
with you, and you shall lay low all
17 Midian as one man.' He replied, 'If
I stand so well with you, give me a
sign that it is you who speak to me.
18 Please do not leave this place until
I come with my gift and lay it before you.' He answered, 'I will stay
19 until you come back.' So Gideon
went in, prepared a kid and made
an ephah of flour into unleavened
cakes. He put the meat in a basket,
poured the broth into a pot and
brought it out to him under the tere-
20 binth. As he approached, the angel
of God said to him, 'Take the meat

and the cakes, and put them here
on the rock and pour out the
broth', and he did so. Then the 21
angel of the LORD reached out
the staff in his hand and touched
the meat and the cakes with the tip
of it. Fire sprang up from the rock
and consumed the meat and the
cakes; and the angel of the LORD
was no more to be seen. Then 22
Gideon knew that it was the angel
of the LORD and said, 'Alas, Lord
GOD! Then it is true: I have seen
the angel of the LORD face to face.'
But the LORD said to him, 'Peace 23
be with you; do not be afraid, you
shall not die.' So Gideon built an 24
altar there to the LORD and named
it Jehovah-shalom.[a] It stands to
this day at Ophrah-of-the-Abiezrites.

   That night the LORD said to 25
Gideon, 'Take a young bull of your
father's, the yearling bull,[b] tear
down the altar of Baal which belongs to your father and cut down
the sacred pole which stands beside[c]
it. Then build an altar of the proper 26
pattern[d] to the LORD your God on
the top of this earthwork;[e] take the
yearling bull and offer it as a
whole-offering with the wood of
the sacred pole that you cut down.'
So Gideon took ten of his servants 27
and did as the LORD had told him.
He was afraid of his father's family
and his fellow-citizens, and so he
did it by night, and not by day.
When the citizens rose early in the 28
morning, they found the altar of
Baal overturned and the sacred
pole which had stood beside it cut
down and the yearling bull offered
up as a whole-offering on the altar
which he had built. They asked 29
each other who had done it, and,
after searching inquiries, were told
that it was Gideon son of Joash.
So the citizens said to Joash, 'Bring 30
out your son. He has overturned
the altar of Baal and cut down the

---

[a] *That is* the LORD is peace.
[b] the yearling bull: *prob. rdg.*; *Heb.* the second bull, seven years old.   [c] *Or* on.
[d] of...pattern: *or* with the stones in rows.   [e] *Or* stronghold *or* refuge.

sacred pole beside it, and he must
31 die.' But as they crowded round
him Joash retorted, 'Are you
pleading Baal's cause then? Do you
think that it is for you to save him?
Whoever pleads his cause shall be
put to death at dawn. If Baal is a
god, and someone has torn down
his altar, let him take up his own
32 cause.' That day Joash named
Gideon Jerubbaal,*a* saying, 'Let
Baal plead his cause against this
man, for he has torn down his altar.'

33 All the Midianites, the Amalekites, and the eastern tribes joined
forces, crossed the river and camp-
34 ed in the Vale of Jezreel. Then the
spirit of the LORD took possession
of Gideon; he sounded the trumpet
and the Abiezrites were called out
35 to follow him. He sent messengers
all through Manasseh; and they
too were called out. He sent messengers to Asher, Zebulun, and
Naphtali, and they came up to
36 meet the others. Gideon said to
God, 'If thou wilt deliver Israel
through me as thou hast promised –
37 now, look, I am putting a fleece of
wool on the threshing-floor. If
there is dew only on the fleece and
all the ground is dry, then I shall
be sure that thou wilt deliver Israel
through me, as thou hast pro-
38 mised.' And that is what happened.
He rose early next day and wrung
out the fleece, and he squeezed
enough dew from it to fill a bowl
39 with water. Gideon then said to
God, 'Do not be angry with me,
but give me leave to speak once
again. Let me, I pray thee, make
one more test with the fleece. This
time let the fleece alone be dry, and
all the ground be covered with
40 dew.' God let it be so that night:
the fleece alone was dry, and on all
the ground there was dew.

7 Jerubbaal, that is Gideon, and all
the people with him rose early and
pitched camp at En-harod;*b* the
Midianite camp was in the vale to
the north of the hill of Moreh. The 2
LORD said to Gideon, 'The people
with you are more than I need to
deliver Midian into their hands:
Israel will claim the glory for themselves and say that it is their own
strength that has given them the
victory. Now make a proclamation 3
for all the people to hear, that anyone who is scared or frightened is
to leave Mount Galud*c* at once and
go back home.' Twenty-two thousand of them went, and ten thousand were left. The LORD then said 4
to Gideon, 'There are still too many.
Bring them down to the water, and
I will separate them for you there.
When I say to you, "This man shall
go with you", he shall go; and if I
say, "This man shall not go with
you", he shall not go.' So Gideon 5
brought the people down to the
water and the LORD said to him,
'Make every man who laps the water with his tongue like a dog stand
on one side, and on the other every
man who goes down on his knees
and drinks.' The number of those 6
who lapped was three hundred,
and all the rest went down on their
knees to drink, putting their hands
to their mouths. The LORD said to 7
Gideon, 'With the three hundred
men who lapped I will save you
and deliver Midian into your hands,
and all the rest may go home.' So 8
Gideon sent all these Israelites
home, but he kept the three hundred, and they took with them the
jars*d* and the trumpets which the
people had. The Midianite camp
was below him in the vale.

That night the LORD said to him, 9
'Go down at once and attack the
camp, for I have delivered it into
your hands. If you are afraid to do 10
so, then go down first with your
servant Purah and listen to what 11
they are saying. That will give you
courage to go down and attack the
camp.' So he and his servant Purah
went down to the part of the camp

---

a *That is* Let Baal plead.
c *Prob. rdg.; Heb.* Mount Gilead.

b *That is* Spring of Fright.
d *Prob. rdg.; Heb.* provisions.

12 where the fighting men lay. Now the Midianites, the Amalekites, and the eastern tribes were so many that they lay there in the valley like a swarm of locusts; there was no counting their camels; in number they were like grains of sand on 13 the sea-shore. When Gideon came close, there was a man telling his companion a dream. He said, 'I dreamt that I saw a hard, stale barley-cake rolling over and over through the Midianite camp; it came to a tent, hit it*a* and turned it upside down, and the tent col- 14 lapsed.' The other answered, 'Depend upon it, this is the sword of Gideon son of Joash the Israelite. God has delivered Midian and the 15 whole army into his hands.' When Gideon heard the story of the dream and its interpretation, he prostrated himself. Then he went back to the Israelite camp and said, 'Up! The LORD has delivered the camp of the Midianites into 16 your hands.' He divided the three hundred men into three companies, and gave every man a trumpet and an empty jar with a torch inside it. 17 Then he said to them, 'Watch me: when I come to the edge of the 18 camp, do exactly as I do. When I and my men blow our trumpets, you too all round the camp will blow your trumpets, and shout, "For the LORD and for Gideon!"' 19 Gideon and the hundred men who were with him reached the outskirts of the camp at the beginning of the middle watch; the sentries had just been posted. They blew their trumpets and smashed 20 their jars. The three companies all blew their trumpets and smashed their jars, then grasped the torches in their left hands and the trumpets in their right, and shouted, 'A sword for the LORD and for Gi- 21 deon!' Every man stood where he was, all round the camp, and the whole camp leapt up in a panic and 22 fled. The three hundred blew their

trumpets, and throughout the camp the LORD set every man against his neighbour. The army fled as far as Beth-shittah in Zererah, as far as the ridge of Abel- 23 meholah by Tabbath. The Israelites from Naphtali and Asher and all Manasseh were called out and they pursued the Midianites. Gi- 24 deon sent men through all the hill-country of Ephraim with this message: 'Come down and cut off the Midianites. Hold the fords of the Jordan against them as far as Beth-barah.' So all the Ephraimites were called out and they held the fords of the Jordan as far as Beth-barah. They captured the 25 two Midianite princes, Oreb and Zeeb. Oreb they killed at the Rock of Oreb, and Zeeb by the Winepress of Zeeb, and they kept up the pursuit of the Midianites; afterwards they brought the heads of Oreb and Zeeb across the Jordan to Gideon.

The men of Ephraim said to 8 Gideon, 'Why have you treated us like this? Why did you not summon us when you went to fight Midian?'; and they reproached him violently. But he said to them, 'What have I 2 done compared with you? Are not Ephraim's gleanings better than the whole vintage of Abiezer? God 3 has delivered Oreb and Zeeb, the princes of Midian, into your hands. What have I done compared with you?' At these words of his, their anger died down.

Gideon came to the Jordan, and 4 he and his three hundred men crossed over to continue the pursuit, weary though they were. He 5 said to the men of Succoth, 'Will you give these men of mine some bread, for they are weary, and I am pursuing Zebah and Zalmunna, the kings of Midian?' But the chief 6 men of Succoth replied, 'Are Zebah and Zalmunna already in your hands, that we should give your army bread?' Gideon said, 'For 7

a Prob. rdg.; Heb. adds and it fell.

that, when the LORD delivers Zebah and Zalmunna into my hands, I will thresh your bodies with desert thorns and briars.'

8 He went on from there to Penuel and made the same request; the men of Penuel answered like the 9 men of Succoth. He said to the men of Penuel, 'When I return safely, I will pull down your castle.'

10 Zebah and Zalmunna were in Karkor with their army of fifteen thousand men. These were all that remained of the whole host of the eastern tribes; a hundred and twenty thousand armed men had fallen 11 in battle. Gideon advanced along the track used by the tent-dwellers east of Nobah and Jogbehah, and his attack caught the army when 12 they were off their guard. Zebah and Zalmunna fled; but he went in pursuit of these Midianite kings and captured them both; and their whole army melted away.

13 As Gideon son of Joash was returning from the battle by the 14 Ascent of Heres, he caught a young man from Succoth. He questioned him, and one by one he numbered off the names of the rulers of Succoth and its elders, seventy-seven 15 in all. Gideon then came to the men of Succoth and said, 'Here are Zebah and Zalmunna, about whom you taunted me. "Are Zebah and Zalmunna", you said, "already in your hands, that we should give 16 your weary men bread?"' Then he took the elders of the city and he disciplined those men of Succoth 17 with desert thorns and briars. He also pulled down the castle of Penuel and put the men of the city 18 to death. Then he said to Zebah and Zalmunna, 'What of the men you killed in Tabor?' They answered, 'They were like you, every one had the look of a king's son.' 19 'They were my brothers,' he said, 'my mother's sons. I swear by the LORD, if you had let them live I 20 would not have killed you'; and he said to his eldest son Jether, 'Up

with you, and kill them.' But he was still only a lad, and did not draw his sword, because he was afraid. So Zebah and Zalmunna 21 said, 'Rise up yourself and dispatch us, for you have a man's strength.' So Gideon rose and killed them both, and he took the crescents from the necks of their camels.

After this the Israelites said to 22 Gideon, 'You have saved us from the Midianites; now you be our ruler, you and your son and your grandson.' Gideon replied, 'I will 23 not rule over you, nor shall my son; the LORD will rule over you.' Then he said, 'I have a request to 24 make: will every one of you give me the earrings from his booty?' — for the enemy wore golden earrings, being Ishmaelites. They said, 'Of 25 course, we will give them.' So a cloak was spread out and every man threw on to it the golden earrings from his booty. The earrings 26 for which he asked weighed seventeen hundred shekels of gold; this was in addition to the crescents and pendants and the purple cloaks worn by the Midianite kings, not counting the chains on the necks of their camels. Gideon made 27 it into an ephod and he set it up in his own city of Ophrah. All the Israelites turned wantonly to its worship, and it became a trap to catch Gideon and his household.

Thus the Midianites were sub- 28 dued by the Israelites; they could no longer hold up their heads. For forty years the land was at peace, all the lifetime of Gideon, that is 29 Jerubbaal son of Joash; and he retired to his own home. Gideon had 30 seventy sons, his own offspring, for he had many wives. He had a 31 concubine who lived in Shechem, and she also bore him a son, whom he named Abimelech. Gideon son 32 of Joash died at a ripe old age and was buried in his father's grave at Ophrah-of-the-Abiezrites. After 33 his death, the Israelites again went wantonly to the worship of the

Baalim and made Baal-berith their 34 god. They forgot the LORD their God who had delivered them from 35 their enemies on every side, and did not show to the family of Jerubbaal, that is Gideon, the loyalty that was due to them for all the good he had done for Israel.

9 ABIMELECH son of Jerubbaal went to Shechem to his mother's brothers, and spoke with them and with all the clan of his mother's fa-2 mily. 'I beg you,' he said, 'whisper a word in the ears of the chief citizens of Shechem. Ask them which is better for them: that seventy men, all the sons of Jerubbaal, should rule over them, or one man. Tell them to remember that I am their 3 own flesh and blood.' So his mother's brothers repeated all this to each of them on his behalf; and they were moved to come over to Abimelech's side, because, as they 4 said, he was their brother. They gave him seventy pieces of silver from the temple of Baal-berith, and with these he hired idle and reckless men, who followed him. 5 He came to his father's house in Ophrah and butchered his seventy brothers, the sons of Jerubbaal, on a single stone block, all but Jotham the youngest, who survived be-6 cause he had hidden himself. Then all the citizens of Shechem and all Beth-millo came together and made Abimelech king beside the old propped-up terebinth at Shechem.
7 When this was reported to Jotham, he went and stood on the summit of Mount Gerizim. He cried at the top of his voice: 'Listen to me, you citizens of Shechem, and may God listen to you: 8 'Once upon a time the trees came to anoint a king, and they said to 9 the olive-tree: Be king over us. But the olive-tree answered: What, leave my rich oil by which gods and men are honoured, to come and hold sway over the trees?

'So the trees said to the fig-tree: 10 Then will you come and be king over us? But the fig-tree answered: 11 What, leave my good fruit and all its sweetness, to come and hold sway over the trees?
'So the trees said to the vine: 12 Then will you come and be king over us? But the vine answered: 13 What, leave my new wine which gladdens gods and men, to come and hold sway over the trees?
'Then all the trees said to the 14 thorn-bush: Will you then be king over us? And the thorn said to the 15 trees: If you really mean to anoint me as your king, then come under the protection of my shadow; if not, fire shall come out of the thorn and burn up the cedars of Lebanon.'
Then Jotham said, 'Now, have 16 you acted fairly and honestly in making Abimelech king? Have you done the right thing by Jerubbaal and his household? Have you given my father his due – who fought for 17 you, and threw himself into the forefront of the battle and delivered you from the Midianites? Today you have risen against my 18 father's family, butchered his seventy sons on a single stone block, and made Abimelech, the son of his slave-girl, king over the citizens of Shechem because he is your brother. In this day's work 19 have you acted fairly and honestly by Jerubbaal and his family? If so, I wish you joy in Abimelech and wish him joy in you! If not, may 20 fire come out of Abimelech and burn up the citizens of Shechem and all Beth-millo; may fire also come out from the citizens of Shechem and Beth-millo and burn up Abimelech.' After which Jotham 21 slipped away and made his escape; he came to Beer, and there he settled out of reach of his brother Abimelech.
After Abimelech had been prince 22 over Israel for three years, God 23 sent an evil spirit to make a breach

between Abimelech and the citizens of Shechem, and they played 24 him false. This was done on purpose, so that the violent murder of the seventy sons of Jerubbaal might recoil on their brother Abimelech who did the murder and on the citizens of Shechem who encouraged him to do it. 25 The citizens of Shechem set men to lie in wait for him on the hill-tops, but they robbed all who passed that way, and so the news reached Abimelech.

26 Now Gaal son of Ebed came with his kinsmen to Shechem, and the citizens of Shechem transferred their allegiance to him. 27 They went out into the country-side, picked the early grapes in their vineyards, trod them in the wine-press and held festival. They went into the temple of their god, where they ate and drank and reviled Abimelech. 28 'Who is Abimelech,' said Gaal son of Ebed, 'and who are the Shechemites, that we should be his subjects? Have not this son of Jerubbaal and his lieutenant Zebul been subjects of the men of Hamor the father of Shechem? Why indeed should we be subject 29 to him? If only this people were in my charge I should know how to get rid of Abimelech! I would say to him, "Get your men together, 30 and come out and fight."' When Zebul the governor of the city heard what Gaal son of Ebed said, 31 he was very angry. He resorted to a ruse and sent messengers to Abimelech to say, 'Gaal son of Ebed and his kinsmen have come to Shechem and are turning the city 32 against you. Get up now in the night, you and the people with you, and lie in wait in the open country. 33 Then be up in the morning at sunrise, and advance rapidly against the city. When he and his people come out, do to him what the situation 34 ation demands.' So Abimelech and his people rose in the night, and

lay in wait to attack Shechem, in four companies. 35 Gaal son of Ebed came out and stood in the entrance of the city gate, and Abimelech and his people rose from their hiding-place. 36 Gaal saw them and said to Zebul, 'There are people coming down from the tops of the hills', but Zebul replied, 'What you see is the shadow of the hills, looking like men.' 37 Once more Gaal said, 'There are people coming down from the central ridge of the hills, and one company is coming along the road of the Soothsayers' Terebinth.' 38 Then Zebul said to him, 'Where are your brave words now? You said, "Who is Abimelech that we should be subject to him?" Are not these the people you despised? Go out and fight him.' 39 Gaal led the citizens of Shechem out and attacked Abimelech, but Abimelech 40 routed him and he fled. The ground was strewn with corpses all the way to the entrance of the gate. 41 Abimelech established himself in Arumah, and Zebul drove away Gaal and his kinsmen and allowed them no place in Shechem.

42 Next day the people came out into the open, and this was reported to Abimelech. 43 He on his side took his supporters, divided them into three companies and lay in wait in the open country; and when he saw the people coming out of the city, he rose and attacked them. 44 Abimelech and the company with him advanced rapidly and took up position at the entrance of the city gate, while the other two companies advanced against all those who were in the open and struck them down. 45 Abimelech kept up the attack on the city all that day and captured it; he killed the people in it, pulled the city down and sowed the site with salt. 46 When the occupants of the castle of Shechem heard of this, they went into the great hall*a* of the temple of El-berith. It was reported to Abi- 47

---

a Or vault.

257

melech that all the occupants of the castle of Shechem had collected

48 together. So he and his people went up Mount Zalmon carrying axes; there he cut brushwood, and took it and hoisted it on his shoulder. He said to his men, 'You see what I am doing; be quick and do the same.'

49 So each man cut brushwood; then they followed Abimelech and laid the brushwood against the hall, and burnt it over their heads. Thus all the occupants of the castle of Shechem died, about a thousand men and women.

50 Abimelech then went to Thebez,

51 besieged it and took it. There was a strong castle in the middle of the city, and all the citizens, men and women, took refuge there. They shut themselves in and went on to

52 the roof. Abimelech came up to the castle and attacked it. As he approached the entrance to the castle

53 to set fire to it, a woman threw a millstone down on his head and

54 fractured his skull. He called hurriedly to his young armour-bearer and said, 'Draw your sword and dispatch me, or men will say of me: A woman killed him.' So the young man ran him through and he

55 died. When the Israelites saw that Abimelech was dead, they all went

56 back to their homes. It was thus that God requited the crime which Abimelech had committed against his father by the murder of his

57 seventy brothers, and brought all the wickedness of the men of Shechem on their own heads. The curse of Jotham son of Jerubbaal came home to them.

10 After Abimelech, Tola son of Pua, son of Dodo, a man of Issachar who lived in Shamir in the hill-country of Ephraim, came in

2 his turn to deliver Israel. He was judge over Israel for twenty-three years, and when he died he was buried in Shamir.

3 After him came Jair the Gileadite; he was judge over Israel for twenty-two years. He had thirty 4 sons, who rode thirty asses; they had thirty towns in the land of Gilead, which to this day are called Havvoth-jair.[a] When Jair 5 died, he was buried in Kamon.

Once more the Israelites did 6 what was wrong in the eyes of the LORD, worshipping the Baalim and the Ashtaroth, the deities of Aram and of Sidon and of Moab, of the Ammonites and of the Philistines. They forsook the LORD and did not worship him. The LORD was angry 7 with Israel, and he sold them to the Philistines and the Ammonites, who[b] for eighteen years harassed 8 and oppressed the Israelites who lived beyond the Jordan in the Amorite country in Gilead. Then 9 the Ammonites crossed the Jordan to attack Judah, Benjamin, and Ephraim, so that Israel was in great distress. The Israelites cried to the 10 LORD for help and said, 'We have sinned against thee; we have forsaken our God and worshipped the Baalim.' And the LORD said to 11 the Israelites, 'The Egyptians, the Amorites, the Ammonites, the Philistines; the Sidonians too and 12 the Amalekites and the Midianites – all these oppressed you and you cried to me for help; and did not I deliver you? But you forsook 13 me and worshipped other gods; therefore I will deliver you no more. Go and cry for help to the 14 gods you have chosen, and let them save you in the day of your distress.' But the Israelites said to the 15 LORD, 'We have sinned. Deal with us as thou wilt; only save us this day, we implore thee.' They ban- 16 ished the foreign gods and worshipped the LORD; and he could endure no longer to see the plight of Israel.

Then the Ammonites were called 17 to arms, and they encamped in Gilead, while the Israelites assembled and encamped in Mizpah. The people of Gilead and their chief 18

---

[a] *That is* Tent-villages of Jair.

[b] *Prob. rdg.*; *Heb. adds* in that year.

men said to one another, 'If any man will strike the first blow at the Ammonites, he shall be lord over the inhabitants of Gilead.'

11 Jephthah the Gileadite was a great warrior; he was the son of
2 Gilead by a prostitute. But Gilead had a wife who bore him several sons, and when they grew up they drove Jephthah away; they said to him, 'You have no inheritance in our father's house; you are another
3 woman's son.' So Jephthah, to escape his brothers, went away and settled in the land of Tob, and swept up a number of idle men who followed him.

4 The time came when the Am-
5 monites made war on Israel, and when the fighting began, the elders of Gilead went to fetch Jephthah
6 from the land of Tob. They said to him, 'Come and be our commander so that we can fight the Ammon-
7 ites.' But Jephthah said to the elders of Gilead, 'You drove me from my father's house in hatred. Why come to me now when you
8 are in trouble?' 'It is because of that', they replied, 'that we have turned to you now. Come with us and fight the Ammonites, and become lord over all the inhabitants
9 of Gilead.' Jephthah said to them, 'If you ask me back to fight the Ammonites, and if the LORD delivers them into my hands, then I
10 will be your lord.' The elders of Gilead said again to Jephthah, 'We swear by the LORD, who shall be witness between us, that we will do
11 what you say.' Jephthah then went with the elders of Gilead, and the people made him their lord and commander. And at Mizpah, in the presence of the LORD, Jephthah repeated all that he had said.

12 Jephthah sent a mission to the king of Ammon to ask what quarrel he had with them that made him
13 invade their country. The king gave Jephthah's men this answer: 'When the Israelites came up from

Egypt, they took our land from the Arnon as far as the Jabbok and the Jordan. Give us back these lands in peace.' Jephthah sent a 14 second mission to the king of Am-mon, and they said, 'This is Jeph- 15 thah's answer: Israel did not take either the Moabite country or the Ammonite country. When they 16 came up from Egypt, the Israelites passed through the wilderness to the Red Sea[a] and came to Kadesh. They then sent envoys to the king 17 of Edom asking him to grant them passage through his country, but the king of Edom would not hear of it. They sent also to the king of Moab, but he was not willing; so Israel remained in Kadesh. They 18 then passed through the wilder-ness, skirting Edom and Moab, and kept to the east of Moab. They en-camped beside the Arnon, but they did not enter Moabite territory, because the Arnon is the frontier of Moab. Israel then sent envoys to 19 the king of the Amorites, Sihon king of Heshbon, asking him to give them free passage through his country to their destination. But 20 Sihon would not grant Israel free passage through his territory; he mustered all his people, encamped in Jahaz and fought Israel. But the 21 LORD the God of Israel delivered Sihon and all his people into the hands of Israel; they defeated them and occupied all the territory of the Amorites in that region. They 22 took all the Amorite territory from the Arnon to the Jabbok and from the wilderness to the Jordan. The 23 LORD the God of Israel drove out the Amorites for the benefit of his people Israel. And do you now pro-pose to take their place? It is for 24 you to possess whatever Kemosh your god gives you; and all that the LORD our God gave us as we advanced is ours. For that matter, 25 are you any better than Balak son of Zippor, king of Moab? Did he ever quarrel with Israel or attack

[a] Or the Sea of Reeds.

26 them? For three hundred years Israelites have lived in Heshbon and its dependent villages, in Aroer and its villages, and in all the towns by the Arnon. Why did you not oust[a] them during all 27 that time? We have done you no wrong; it is you who are doing us wrong by attacking us. The LORD who is judge will judge this day between the Israelites and the Am-28 monites.' But the king of the Ammonites would not listen to the message which Jephthah had sent him.

29   Then the spirit of the LORD came upon Jephthah and he passed through Gilead and Manasseh, by Mizpeh of Gilead, and from Mizpeh 30 over to the Ammonites. Jephthah made this vow to the LORD: 'If thou wilt deliver the Ammonites 31 into my hands, then the first creature that comes out of the door of my house to meet me when I return from them in peace shall be the LORD's; I will offer that as a whole-32 offering.' So Jephthah crossed over to attack the Ammonites, and the LORD delivered them into his 33 hands. He routed them with great slaughter all the way from Aroer to Minnith, taking twenty towns, and as far as Abel-keramim. Thus Israel 34 crushed Ammon. But when Jephthah came to his house in Mizpah, who should come out to meet him with tambourines and dances but his daughter, and she his only child; he had no other, neither son 35 nor daughter. When he saw her, he rent his clothes and said, 'Alas, my daughter, you have broken my heart, such trouble you have brought upon me. I have made a vow to the LORD and I cannot go 36 back.' She replied, 'Father, you have made a vow to the LORD; do to me what you have solemnly vowed, since the LORD has avenged you on the Ammonites, your ene-

mies. But, father, grant me this one 37 favour. For two months let me be, that I may roam[b] the hills with my companions and mourn that I must die a virgin.' 'Go', he said, 38 and he let her depart for two months. She went with her companions and mourned her virginity on the hills. At the end of two 39 months she came back to her father, and he fulfilled the vow he had made; she died a virgin. It became a tradition that the 40 daughters of Israel should go year by year and commemorate the fate of Jephthah's daughter, four days in every year.

The Ephraimites mustered their 12 forces and crossed over to Zaphon. They said to Jephthah, 'Why did you march against the Ammonites and not summon us to go with you? We will burn your house over your head.' Jephthah answered, 'I and 2 my people had a feud with the Ammonites, and had I appealed to you for help, you would not have saved us[c] from them. When I saw that we 3 were not to look for help from you, I took my life in my hands and marched against the Ammonites, and the LORD delivered them into my power. Why then do you attack me today?' Jephthah then 4 mustered all the men of Gilead and fought Ephraim, and the Gileadites defeated them. The Gileadites 5 seized the fords of the Jordan and held them against Ephraim. When any Ephraimite who had escaped begged leave to cross, the men of Gilead asked him, 'Are you an Ephraimite?', and if he said, 'No', they would retort, 'Say Shibbo- 6 leth.' He would say 'Sibboleth', and because he could not pronounce the word properly, they seized him and killed him at the fords of the Jordan. At that time forty-two thousand men of Ephraim lost their lives.

[a] Or recover.   [b] Or that I may go down country to...
[c] and had I...saved us: or I did appeal to you for help, but you would not save us...

7 　　Jephthah was judge over Israel for six years; when he died he was buried in his own city in Gilead.

8 After him Ibzan of Bethlehem was 9 judge over Israel. He had thirty sons and thirty daughters. He gave away the thirty daughters in marriage and brought in thirty girls for his sons. He was judge over Israel 10 for seven years, and when he died he was buried in Bethlehem.

11 　　After him Elon the Zebulunite was judge over Israel for ten years. 12 When he died, he was buried in Ai- 13 jalon in the land of Zebulun. Next Abdon son of Hillel the Pirathonite 14 was judge over Israel. He had forty sons and thirty grandsons, who rode each on his own ass. He was judge over Israel for eight 15 years; and when he died he was buried in Pirathon in the land of Ephraim on the hill of the Amalekite.

Israel oppressed by the Philistines

13 ONCE more the Israelites did what was wrong in the eyes of the LORD, and he delivered them into the hands of the Philistines for forty years.

2 　　There was a man from Zorah of the tribe of Dan whose name was Manoah and whose wife was barren 3 and childless. The angel of the LORD appeared to her and said, 'You are barren and have no child, 4 but you shall conceive and give birth to a son. Now you must do as I say: be careful to drink no wine or strong drink, and to eat no for- 5 bidden food; you will conceive and give birth to a son, and no razor shall touch his head, for the boy is to be a Nazirite consecrated to God from the day of his birth. He will strike the first blow to deliver Israel from the power of the Philistines.' 6 The woman went and told her husband; she said to him, 'A man of God came to me; his appearance was that of an*ᵃ* angel of God, most

terrible to see. I did not ask him where he came from nor did he tell me his name. He said to me, "You 7 shall conceive and give birth to a son. From this time onwards drink no wine or strong drink and eat no forbidden food, for the boy is to be a Nazirite consecrated to God from his birth to the day of his death."' Manoah prayed to the LORD, 'If it 8 please thee, O LORD, let the man of God whom thou didst send come again to tell us what we are to do with the boy who is to be born.' God heard Manoah's prayer, and 9 the angel of God came again to the woman, who was sitting in the fields; her husband was not with her. The woman ran quickly and 10 said to him, 'The man who came to me the other day has appeared to me again.' Manoah went with her 11 at once and approached the man and said, 'Was it you who talked with my wife?' He said, 'Yes, it was I.' 'Now when your words come 12 true,' Manoah said, 'what kind of boy will he be and what will he do?' The angel of the LORD answered 13 him, 'Your wife must be careful to do all that I told her: she must not 14 taste anything that comes from the vine. She must drink no wine or strong drink, and she must eat no forbidden food. She must do what I say.' Manoah said to the angel of 15 the LORD, 'May we urge you to stay? Let us prepare a kid for you.' The angel of the LORD replied, 16 'Though you urge me to stay, I will not eat your food; but prepare a whole-offering if you will, and offer that to the LORD.' Manoah did not perceive that he was the angel of the LORD and said to him, 'What 17 is your name? For we shall want to honour you when your words come true.' The angel of the LORD said to 18 him, 'How can you ask my name? It is a name of wonder.' Manoah 19 took a kid with the proper grain-offering, and offered it on the rock to the LORD, to him whose works

ᵃ Or the.

are full of wonder. And while Manoah and his wife were watching,
20 the flame went up from the altar towards heaven, and the angel of the LORD went up in the flame; and seeing this, Manoah and his wife
21 fell on their faces. The angel of the LORD did not appear again to Manoah and his wife; and Manoah knew that he was the angel of the LORD.
22 He said to his wife, 'We are doomed
23 to die, we have seen God',[a] but she replied, 'If the LORD had wanted to kill us, he would not have accepted a whole-offering and a grain-offering at our hands; he would not now have let us see and hear all this.'
24-25 The woman gave birth to a son and named him Samson. The boy grew up in Mahaneh-dan between Zorah and Eshtaol, and the LORD blessed him, and the spirit of the LORD began to drive him hard.

14 Samson went down to Timnath, and there he saw a woman, one of
2 the Philistines. When he came back, he told his father and mother that he had seen a Philistine woman in Timnath and asked them
3 to get her for him as his wife. His father and mother said to him, 'Is there no woman among your cousins or in all our own people? Must you go and marry one of the uncircumcised Philistines?' But Samson said to his father, 'Get her
4 for me, because she pleases me.' His father and mother did not know that the LORD was at work in this, seeking an opportunity against the Philistines, who at that time were masters of Israel.

5 Samson[b] went down to Timnath and, when he reached the vineyards there, a young lion came at
6 him growling. The spirit of the LORD suddenly seized him and, having no weapon in his hand, he tore the lion in pieces as if it were a kid. He did not tell his parents
7 what he had done. Then he went down and spoke to the woman, and
8 she pleased him. After a time he went down again to take her to wife; he turned aside to look at the carcass of the lion, and he saw a swarm of bees in it, and honey. He 9 scraped the honey into his hands and went on, eating as he went. When he came to his father and mother, he gave them some and they ate it; but he did not tell them that he had scraped the honey out of the lion's carcass. His father 10 went down to see the woman, and Samson gave a feast there as the custom of young men was. When 11 the people saw him, they brought thirty young men to be his escort. Samson said to them, 'Let me ask 12 you a riddle. If you can guess it during the seven days of the feast, I will give you thirty lengths of linen and thirty changes of clothing; but if you cannot guess the 13 answer, then you shall give me thirty lengths of linen and thirty changes of clothing.' 'Tell us your riddle,' they said; 'let us hear it.' So he said to them: 14

Out of the eater came something to eat;
out of the strong came something sweet.

At the end of three days they had failed to guess the riddle. On the 15 fourth day they said to Samson's wife, 'Coax your husband and make him tell you the riddle, or we shall burn you and your father's house. Did you invite us here to beggar us?' So Samson's wife wept 16 over him and said, 'You do not love me, you only hate me. You have asked my kinsfolk a riddle and you have not told it to me.' He said to her, 'I have not told it even to my father and mother; and am I to tell you?' But she wept over 17 him every day until the seven feast days were ended, and on the seventh day, because she pestered him, he told her, and she told the riddle to her kinsfolk. So that same 18 day the men of the city said to

---

[a] Or a god.   [b] *Prob. rdg.*; *Heb. adds* and his father and mother.

Samson before he entered the bridal chamber:[a]

What is sweeter than honey?
What is stronger than a lion?

and he replied, 'If you had not ploughed with my heifer, you would not have found out my 19 riddle.' Then the spirit of the LORD suddenly seized him. He went down to Ashkelon and there he killed thirty men, took their belts and gave their clothes to the men who had answered his riddle; but he was very angry and went off to his 20 father's house. And Samson's wife was given in marriage to the friend who had been his groomsman.

15 After a while, during the time of wheat harvest, Samson went to visit his wife, taking a kid as a present for her. He said, 'I am going to my wife in our bridal chamber', but her father would not let him in. 2 He said, 'I was sure that you hated her, so I gave her in marriage to your groomsman. Her young sister is better than she – take her in- 3 stead.' But Samson said, 'This time I will settle my score with the Philistines; I will do them some 4 real harm.' So he went and caught three hundred jackals and got some torches; he tied the jackals tail to tail and fastened a torch between 5 each pair of tails. He then set the torches alight and turned the jackals loose in the standing corn of the Philistines. He burnt up standing corn and stooks as well, 6 vineyards and olive groves. The Philistines said, 'Who has done this?' They were told that it was Samson, because the Timnite, his father-in-law, had taken his wife and given her to his groomsman. So the Philistines came and burnt 7 her and her father. Samson said, 'If you do things like this, I swear I will be revenged upon you before I

have done.' He smote them hip and 8 thigh with great slaughter; and after that he went down to live in a cave in the Rock of Etam.

The Philistines came up and 9 pitched camp in Judah, and overran Lehi. The men of Judah said, 10 'Why have you attacked us?' They answered, 'We have come to take Samson prisoner and serve him as he served us.' So three thousand 11 men from Judah went down to the cave in the Rock of Etam. They said to Samson, 'Surely you know that the Philistines are our masters? Now see what you have brought upon us.' He answered, 'I only served them as they had served me.' They said to him, 'We 12 have come down to bind you and hand you over to the Philistines.' 'Then you must swear to me', he said, 'that you will not set upon me yourselves.' They answered, 'No; 13 we will only bind you and hand you over to them, we will not kill you.' So they bound him with two new ropes and brought him up from the cave in the Rock. He came 14 to Lehi, and when they met him, the Philistines shouted in triumph; but the spirit of the LORD suddenly seized him, the ropes on his arms became like burnt tow and his bonds melted away. He found the 15 jaw-bone of an ass, all raw, and picked it up and slew a thousand men. He made this saying: 16

With the jaw-bone of an ass[b] I have
　flayed them like asses;[c]
with the jaw-bone of an ass I have
　slain a thousand men.

When he had said his say, he threw 17 away the jaw-bone; and he called that place Ramath-lehi.[d] He began 18 to feel very thirsty and cried aloud to the LORD, 'Thou hast let me, thy servant, win this great victory, and must I now die of thirst and fall

---

[a] he entered...chamber: *prob. rdg.*; *Heb.* the sun went down.
[b] ass: *Heb.* hamor.
[c] I have...asses: *or* I have reddened them blood-red, *or* I have heaped them in heaps; *Heb.* hamor himmartim.　　[d] *That is* Jaw-bone Hill.

into the hands of the uncircum-
19 cised?' God split open the Hollow
of Lehi and water came out of it.
Samson drank, his strength returned and he revived. This is why
the spring in Lehi is called En-
hakkore[a] to this day.

20   Samson was judge over Israel
for twenty years in the days of the
Philistines.

16   Samson went to Gaza, and there
he saw a prostitute and went in to
2 spend the night with her. The people of Gaza heard that Samson had
come, and they surrounded him
and lay in wait for him all that
night at the city gate. During the
night, however, they took no action, saying to themselves, 'When
3 day breaks we shall kill him.' Samson lay in bed till midnight; and
when midnight came he rose,
seized hold of the doors of the city
gate and the two posts, pulled
them out, bar and all, hoisted them
on to his shoulders and carried
them to the top of the hill east of
Hebron.

4   After this Samson fell in love
with a woman named Delilah, who
5 lived in the valley of Sorek. The
lords of the Philistines went up
country to see her and said, 'Coax
him and find out what gives him
his great strength, and how we can
master him, bind him and so hold
him captive; then we will each give
you eleven hundred pieces of silver.'
6 So Delilah said to Samson, 'Tell me
what gives you your great strength,
and how you can be bound and
7 held captive.' Samson replied, 'If
they bind me with seven fresh bow-
strings not yet dry, then I shall be-
8 come as weak as any other man.' So
the lords of the Philistines brought
her seven fresh bowstrings not yet
dry, and she bound him with them.
9 She had men already hidden in the
inner room, and she cried, 'The
Philistines are upon you, Samson!'
But he snapped the bowstrings as

a strand of tow snaps when it feels
the fire, and his strength was not
tamed. Delilah said to Samson, 'I 10
see you have made a fool of me and
told me lies. Tell me this time how
you can be bound.' He said to her, 11
'If you bind me tightly with new
ropes that have never been used,
then I shall become as weak as any
other man.' So Delilah took new 12
ropes and bound him with them.
Then she cried, 'The Philistines are
upon you, Samson!', while the men
waited hidden in the inner room.
He snapped the ropes off his arms
like pack-thread. Delilah said to 13
him, 'You are still making a fool of
me and have told me lies. Tell me:
how can you be bound?' He said,
'Take the seven loose locks of my
hair and weave them into the warp,
and then drive them tight with the
beater; and I shall become as weak
as any other man.' So she lulled
him to sleep, wove the seven loose
locks of his hair into the warp, and 14
drove them tight with the beater,
and cried, 'The Philistines are upon you, Samson!' He woke from
sleep and pulled away the warp
and the loom with it.[b] She said to 15
him, 'How can you say you love
me when you do not confide in me?
This is the third time you have
made a fool of me and have not
told me what gives you your great
strength.' She so pestered him with 16
these words day after day, pressing
him hard and wearying him to
death, that he told her his secret. 17
'No razor has touched my head,' he
said, 'because I am a Nazirite, consecrated to God from the day of my
birth. If my head were shaved,
then my strength would leave me,
and I should become as weak as any
other man.' Delilah saw that he 18
had told her his secret; so she sent
to the lords of the Philistines and
said, 'Come up at once, he has told
me his secret.' So the lords of the
Philistines came up and brought

---

[a] *That is* the Crier's Spring.
[b] the warp . . . with it: *prob. rdg.; Heb. adds an unintelligible word.*

19 the money with them. She lulled him to sleep on her knees, summoned a man and he shaved the seven locks of his hair for her. She began to take him captive and his 20 strength left him. Then she cried, 'The Philistines are upon you, Samson!' He woke from his sleep and said, 'I will go out as usual and shake myself'; he did not know that 21 the LORD had left him. The Philistines seized him, gouged out his eyes and brought him down to Gaza. There they bound him with fetters of bronze, and he was set to 22 grinding corn in the prison. But his hair, after it had been shaved, began to grow again.

23 The lords of the Philistines assembled together to offer a great sacrifice to their god Dagon and to rejoice before him. They said, 'Our god has delivered Samson our ene- 24 my into our hands.' The people, when they saw him, praised their god, chanting:

Our god has delivered our enemy
  into our hands,
the scourge of our land who piled it
  with our dead.

25 When they grew merry, they said, 'Call Samson, and let him fight to make sport for us.' So they summoned Samson from prison and he made sport before them all. They 26 stood him between the pillars, and Samson said to the boy who held his hand, 'Put me where I can feel the pillars which support the temple, so that I may lean against 27 them.' The temple was full of men and women, and all the lords of the Philistines were there, and there were about three thousand men and women on the roof watching 28 Samson as he fought. Samson called on the LORD and said, 'Remember me, O Lord GOD, remember me: give me strength only this once, O God, and let me at one stroke be avenged on the Philistines for my

two eyes.' He put his arms round 29 the two central pillars which supported the temple, his right arm round one and his left round the other, and braced himself and said, 30 'Let me die with the Philistines.' Then Samson leaned forward with all his might, and the temple fell on the lords and on all the people who were in it. So the dead whom he killed at his death were more than those he had killed in his life. His 31 brothers and all his father's family came down, carried him up to the grave of his father Manoah between Zorah and Eshtaol and buried him there. He had been judge over Israel for twenty years.

Years of lawlessness

THERE was once a man named 17 Micah from the hill-country of Ephraim. He said to his mother, 2 'You remember the eleven hundred pieces of silver which were taken from you, and how you called down a curse on the thief in my hearing? I have the money; I took it and now I will give it back to you.'[a] His mother said, 'May the LORD bless you, my son.' So he gave the eleven 3 hundred pieces of silver back to his mother, and she said, 'I now solemnly dedicate this money of mine to the LORD for the benefit of my son, to make a carved idol and a cast image.' He returned the money 4 to his mother, and she took two hundred pieces of silver and handed them to a silversmith, who made them into an idol and an image, which stood in Micah's house.

This man Micah had a shrine, 5 and he made an ephod and teraphim[b] and installed one of his sons to be his priest. In those days there 6 was no king in Israel and every man did what was right in his own eyes. Now there was a young man 7 from Bethlehem in Judah, from the clan of Judah, a Levite named

_____
[a] and now...you: *transposed from verse 3.*
[b] Or household gods.

8 Ben-gershom.[a] He had left the city of Bethlehem to go and find somewhere to live. On his way he came to Micah's house in the hill-country 9 of Ephraim. Micah said to him, 'Where have you come from?' He replied, 'I am a Levite from Bethlehem in Judah, and I am looking for 10 somewhere to live.' Micah said to him, 'Stay with me and be priest and father to me. I will give you ten pieces of silver a year, and provide you with food and clothes.' 11 The Levite agreed to stay with the man and was treated as one of his 12 own sons. Micah installed the Levite, and the young man became his priest and a member of his 13 household. Micah said, 'Now I know that the LORD will make me prosper, because I have a Levite for my priest.'

18 In those days there was no king in Israel and the tribe of the Danites was looking for territory to occupy, because they had not so far come into possession of the territory allotted to them among 2 the tribes of Israel. The Danites therefore sent out five fighting men of their clan from Zorah and Eshtaol to prospect, with instructions to go and explore the land. They came to Micah's house in the hill-country of Ephraim and spent the 3 night there. While they were there, they recognized the speech of the young Levite; they turned there and then and said to him, 'Who brought you here? What are you doing? What is your business here?' 4 He said, 'This is all Micah's doing: he has hired me and I have become 5 his priest.' They said to him, 'Then inquire of God on our behalf whether our mission will be successful.' 6 The priest replied, 'Go in peace. Your mission is in the LORD's 7 hands.' The five men went on their way and came to Laish. There they

found the inhabitants living a carefree life, in the same way as the Sidonians, a quiet, carefree folk, with no hereditary king to keep the country under his thumb.[b] They were a long way from the Sidonians, and had no contact with the Aramaeans. So the five men went back 8 to Zorah and Eshtaol, and when their kinsmen asked their news, they said, 'Come and attack them. 9 It is an excellent country that we have seen. Will you hang back and do nothing about it? Start off now and take possession of the land. When you get there, you will find a 10 people living a carefree life in a wide expanse of open country. God has delivered it into your hands, a place where there is no lack of anything on earth.'

And so six hundred armed men 11 from the clan of the Danites set out from Zorah and Eshtaol. They 12 went up country and encamped in Kiriath-jearim in Judah: this is why that place to this day is called Mahaneh-dan;[c] it lies west of Kiriath-jearim. From there they 13 passed on to the hill-country of Ephraim and came to Micah's house. The five men who had been 14 to explore the country round Laish spoke up and said to their kinsmen, 'Do you know that in one of these houses there are now an ephod and teraphim, an idol and an image? Now consider what you had best do.' So they turned aside 15 to Micah's house and greeted him. The six hundred armed Danites 16 took their stand at the entrance of the gate, and the five men who had 17 gone to explore the country went indoors to take the idol and the image, ephod and teraphim, while the priest was standing at the entrance with the six hundred armed men. The five men entered Micah's 18 house and took the idol and the

---

[a] named Ben-gershom: *prob. rdg.*, *cp. 18. 30*; *Heb.* he lodged there.
[b] with no...thumb: *prob. rdg.*; *Heb.* and none humiliating anything in the land with inherited authority.
[c] *That is* the Camp of Dan.

image, ephod and teraphim.[a] The priest asked them what they were 19 doing, but they said to him, 'Be quiet; not a word. Come with us and be our priest and father. Which is better, to be priest in the household of one man or to be priest to a 20 whole tribe and clan in Israel?' This pleased the priest; so he took the ephod and teraphim, the idol and the image, and joined the com- 21 pany. They turned and went off, putting the dependants, the herds, 22 and the valuables in front. The Danites had gone some distance from Micah's house, when his neighbours were called out in pursuit and caught up with them. 23 They shouted after them, and the Danites turned round and said to Micah, 'What is the matter with you? Why have you come after 24 us?' He said, 'You have taken my gods which I made for myself, you have taken the priest, and you have gone off and left me nothing. How dare you say, "What is the matter 25 with you?"' The Danites said to him, 'Do not shout at us. We are desperate men and if we fall upon you it will be the death of yourself 26 and your family.' With that the Danites went on their way and Micah, seeing that they were too strong for him, turned and went home.

27 Thus they carried off the priest and the things Micah had made for himself, and attacked Laish, whose people were quiet and carefree. They put them to the sword and set 28 fire to their city. There was no one to save them, for the city was a long way from Sidon and they had no contact with the Aramaeans,[b] although the city was in the vale near Beth-rehob. They rebuilt the 29 city and settled in it, naming it Dan after the name of their forefather Dan, a son of Israel; but its 30 original name was Laish. The Danites set up the idol, and Jonathan

son of Gershom, son of Moses, and his sons were priests to the tribe of Dan until the people went into exile. (They set up for themselves 31 the idol which Micah had made, and it was there as long as the house of God was at Shiloh.)

IN those days when no king ruled 19 in Israel, a Levite was living in the heart of the hill-country of Ephraim. He had taken himself a concubine from Bethlehem in Judah. In a fit of anger she had left him 2 and had gone to her father's house in Bethlehem in Judah. When she had been there four months, her 3 husband set out after her with his servant and two asses to appeal to her and bring her back. She brought him in to the house of her father, who welcomed him when he saw him. His father-in-law, the girl's 4 father, pressed him and he stayed with him three days, and they were well entertained during their visit. On the fourth day, they rose early 5 in the morning, and he prepared to leave, but the girl's father said to his son-in-law, 'Have something to eat first, before you go.' So the two 6 of them sat down and ate and drank together. The girl's father said to the man, 'Why not spend the night and enjoy yourself?' When he rose 7 to go, his father-in-law urged him to stay, and again he stayed for the night. He rose early in the morning 8 on the fifth day to depart, but the girl's father said, 'Have something to eat first.' So they lingered till late afternoon, eating and drinking together. Then the man stood 9 up to go with his concubine and servant, but his father-in-law said, 'See how the day wears on towards sunset. Spend the night here and enjoy yourself, and then rise early tomorrow and set out for home.' But the man would not stay the 10 night; he rose and left. He had reached a point opposite Jebus,

---

[a] *Prob. rdg.; Heb.* the idol of the ephod, and teraphim and image.
[b] *Prob. rdg., cp. verse 7; Heb.* men.

that is Jerusalem, with his two
11 laden asses and his concubine, and
when they were close to Jebus, the
weather grew wild and stormy, and
the young man said to his master,
'Come now, let us turn into this
Jebusite town and spend the night
12 there.' But his master said to him,
'No, not into a strange town where
the people are not Israelites; let us
13 go on to Gibeah. Come, we will go
and find some other place, and
spend the night in Gibeah or Ra-
14 mah.' So they went on until sunset
overtook them; they were then
near Gibeah which belongs to Ben-
15 jamin. They turned in to spend the
night there, and went and sat down
in the open street of the town; but
nobody took them into his house
for the night.

16   Meanwhile an old man was coming home in the evening from his
work in the fields. He was from the
hill-country of Ephraim, but he
lived in Gibeah, where the people
17 were Benjamites. He looked up,
saw the traveller in the open street
of the town, and asked him where
he was going and where he came
18 from. He answered, 'We are travelling from Bethlehem in Judah to
the heart of the hill-country of
Ephraim. I come from there; I
have been to Bethlehem in Judah
and I am going home, but nobody
19 has taken me into his house. I have
straw and provender for the asses,
food and wine for myself, the girl,
and the young man; we have all we
20 need, sir.' The old man said, 'You
are welcome, I will supply all your
wants; you must not spend the
21 night in the street.' So he took him
inside and provided fodder for the
asses; they washed their feet, and
22 ate and drank. While they were enjoying themselves, some of the
worst scoundrels in the town surrounded the house, hurling themselves against the door and shouting to the old man who owned the
house, 'Bring out the man who has

gone into your house, for us to have
intercourse with him.' The owner 23
of the house went outside to them
and said, 'No, my friends, do nothing so wicked. This man is my
guest; do not commit this outrage.
Here is my daughter, a virgin;*a* let 24
me bring her*b* out to you. Rape her*b*
and do to her*b* what you please; but
you shall not commit such an outrage against this man.' But the 25
men refused to listen to him, so the
Levite took hold of his concubine
and thrust her outside for them.
They assaulted her and abused her
all night till the morning, and when
dawn broke, they let her go. The 26
girl came at daybreak and fell down
at the entrance of the man's house
where her master was, and lay
there until it was light. Her master 27
rose in the morning and opened the
door of the house to set out on his
journey, and there was his concubine lying at the door with her
hands on the threshold. He said to 28
her, 'Get up and let us be off'; but
there was no answer. So he lifted
her on to his ass and set off for
home. When he arrived there, he 29
picked up a knife, and he took hold
of his concubine and cut her up
limb by limb into twelve pieces;
and he sent them through the
length and breadth of Israel. He 30
told the men he sent with them to
say to every Israelite, 'Has the like
of this happened or been seen from
the time the Israelites came up
from Egypt till today? Consider
this among yourselves and speak
your minds.' So everyone who saw
them said, 'No such thing has ever
happened or been seen before.'

All the Israelites, the whole com- 20
munity from Dan to Beersheba
and out of Gilead also, left their
homes as one man and assembled
before the LORD at Mizpah. The 2
leaders of the people and all the
tribes of Israel presented themselves in the general assembly of
the people of God, four hundred

---

a Prob. rdg.; Heb. adds and his concubine.   *b* Prob. rdg.; Heb. them.

thousand foot-soldiers armed with
3 swords; and the Benjamites heard
that the Israelites had gone up to
Mizpah. The Israelites asked how
this wicked thing had come about,
4 and the Levite, to whom the murdered woman belonged, answered,
'I and my concubine came to Gibeah in Benjamin to spend the
5 night there. The citizens of Gibeah
rose against me that night and surrounded the house where I was,
intending to kill me; and they
raped my concubine and she died.
6 I took her and cut her in pieces,
and sent them through the length
and breadth of Israel, because of
the filthy outrage they had commit-
7 ted in Israel. Now it is for you, the
whole of Israel, to say here and now
what you think ought to be done.'
8 All the people rose to their feet
as one man and said, 'Not one of us
shall go back to his tent, not one
9 shall return home. This is what we
will now do to Gibeah. We will draw
10 lots for the attack: and we will take
ten men out of every hundred in all
the tribes of Israel, a hundred out
of every thousand, and a thousand
out of every ten thousand, to collect provisions from the people for
those who have taken the field
against Gibeah in Benjamin to
avenge the outrage committed in
11 Israel.' Thus all the Israelites to a
man were massed against the town.
12 The tribes of Israel sent men all
through the tribe of Benjamin saying, 'What is this wicked thing
which has happened in your midst?
13 Hand over to us those scoundrels
in Gibeah, and we will put them to
death and purge Israel of this
wickedness.' But the Benjamites
refused to listen to their fellow-
14 Israelites. They flocked from their
cities to Gibeah to go to war with
15 the Israelites, and that day they
mustered out of their cities twenty-
six thousand men armed with
swords. There were also seven

hundred picked men from Gibeah,
left-handed men, who could sling 16
a stone and not miss by a hair's
breadth. The Israelites, without 17
Benjamin, numbered four hundred thousand men armed with
swords, every one a fighting man.
The Israelites at once moved on to 18
Bethel, and there they sought an
oracle from God, asking, 'Which of
us shall attack Benjamin first?',
and the LORD's answer was, 'Judah
shall attack first.' So the Israelites 19
set out at dawn and encamped opposite Gibeah. They advanced to 20
do battle with Benjamin and drew
up their forces before the town.
The Benjamites made a sally from 21
Gibeah and left twenty-two thousand of Israel dead on the field that
day. The Israelites went up to 23[a]
Bethel,[b] lamented before the LORD
until evening and inquired whether
they should again attack their brother Benjamin. The LORD said,
'Yes, attack him.' Then the Israel- 22
ites took fresh courage and again
formed up on the same ground as
the first day. So the second day they 24
advanced against the Benjamites,
who sallied out from Gibeah to 25
meet them and laid another
eighteen thousand armed men low.
The Israelites, the whole people, 26
went back to Bethel, where they
sat before the LORD lamenting and
fasting until evening, and they
offered whole-offerings and shared-
offerings before the LORD. In those 27
days the Ark of the Covenant of
God was there, and Phinehas son 28
of Eleazar, son of Aaron, served
before the LORD.[c] The Israelites inquired of the LORD and said, 'Shall
we again march out to battle
against Benjamin our brother or
shall we desist?' The LORD answered, 'Attack him: tomorrow I
will deliver him into your hands.'
Israel then posted men in ambush 29
all round Gibeah.
On the third day the Israelites 30

---

[a] Verses 22 and 23 transposed.
[b] to Bethel: *prob. rdg., cp. verses 18, 26; Heb. om.*   [c] Or before the Ark.

advanced against the Benjamites and drew up their forces at Gibeah 31 as they had before; and the Benjamites sallied out to meet the army. They were drawn away from the town and began the attack as before by killing a few Israelites, about thirty,[a] on the highways which led across open country, one to Bethel and the other to Gibeah. 32 They thought they were defeating them once again, but the Israelites had planned a retreat to draw them away from the town out on to the 33 highways. Meanwhile the main body of Israelites left their positions and re-formed in Baal-tamar, while those in ambush, ten thousand picked men all told, burst out from their position in the neigh- 34 bourhood of Gibeah and came in on the east of the town. There was soon heavy fighting; yet the Benjamites did not suspect the disaster 35 that was threatening them. So the Lord put Benjamin to flight before Israel, and on that day the Israelites killed twenty-five thousand one hundred Benjamites, all armed men.

36 The men of Benjamin now saw that they had been defeated, for all that the Israelites, trusting in the ambush which they had set by Gibeah, had given way before 37 them. The men in ambush made a sudden dash on Gibeah, fell on the town from all sides and put all the 38 inhabitants to the sword. The agreed signal between the Israelites and those in ambush[b] was to be a column of smoke sent up from 39 the town. The Israelites then faced about in the battle; and Benjamin began to cut down the Israelites, killing about thirty of them,[c] in the belief that they were defeating them as they had done in the first 40 encounter. As the column of smoke began to go up from the town, the Benjamites looked back and

thought the whole town was going up in flames. When the Israelites 41 faced about, the Benjamites saw that disaster had overtaken them and were seized with panic. They 42 turned and fled before the Israelites in the direction of the wilderness, but the fighting caught up with them and soon those from the town were among them, cutting them down. They hemmed in the 43 Benjamites, pursuing them without respite,[d] and overtook them at a point to the east of Gibeah. Eighteen thousand of the Benja- 44 mites fell, all of them fighting men. The survivors turned and fled into 45 the wilderness towards the Rock of Rimmon. The Israelites picked off the stragglers on the roads, five thousand of them, and chased them until they had cut down and killed two thousand more. Twenty- 46 five thousand armed men of Benjamin fell in battle that day, all fighting men. The six hundred who 47 survived turned and fled into the wilderness as far as the Rock of Rimmon, and there they remained for four months. The Israelites 48 then turned back to deal with the Benjamites, and put to the sword the people in the towns and the cattle, every creature that they found; they also set fire to every town within their reach.

In Mizpah the Israelites had 21 bound themselves by oath that none of them would marry his daughter to a Benjamite. The peo- 2 ple now came to Bethel and remained there in God's presence till sunset, raising their voices in loud lamentation. They said, 'O Lord 3 God of Israel, why has it happened in Israel that one tribe should this day be lost to Israel?' Next day the 4 people rose early, built an altar there and offered whole-offerings and shared-offerings. At that the 5 Israelites asked themselves whether

---

[a] Or about thirty wounded men.　　[b] *Prob. rdg.; Heb. adds an unintelligible word.*
[c] to cut...them: *or* to kill about thirty wounded men among the Israelites.
[d] without respite: *or* from Nohah.

among all the tribes of Israel there was anyone who did not go up to the assembly before the LORD; for under the terms of the great oath anyone who had not gone up to the LORD at Mizpah was 6 to be put to death. And the Israelites felt remorse over their brother Benjamin, because, as they said, 'This day Israel has lost one whole 7 tribe.' So they asked, 'What shall we do for wives for those who are left? We have sworn to the LORD not to give any of our daughters to 8 them in marriage. Is there anyone in all the tribes of Israel who did not go up to the LORD at Mizpah?' Now it happened that no one from Jabesh-gilead had come to the 9 camp for the assembly; so when they held a roll-call of the people, they found that no inhabitant of 10 Jabesh-gilead was present. Thereupon the community sent off twelve thousand fighting men with orders to go and put the inhabitants of Jabesh-gilead to the sword, men, women, and dependants. 11 'This is what you shall do,' they said: 'put to death every male person, and every woman who has had intercourse with a man, but spare any who are virgins.' This they 12 did. Among the inhabitants of Jabesh-gilead they found four hundred young women who were virgins and had not had intercourse with a man, and they brought them to the camp at Shi-13 loh in Canaan. Then the whole community sent messengers to the Benjamites at the Rock of Rimmon to parley with them, and 14 peace was proclaimed. At this the Benjamites came back, and were given those of the women of Jabesh-gilead who had been spared; but these were not enough.

15 The people were still full of re-morse over Benjamin because the LORD had made this gap in the tribes of Israel, and the elders of the 16 community said, 'What shall we do for wives for the rest? All the women in Benjamin have been massacred.' They said, 'Heirs there 17 must be for the remnant of Benjamin who have escaped! Then Israel will not see one of its tribes blotted out. We cannot give them our own 18 daughters in marriage because we have sworn that there shall be a curse on the man who gives a wife to a Benjamite.' Then they be-19 thought themselves of the pilgrimage in honour of the LORD, made every year to Shiloh, the place which lies to the north of Bethel, on the east side of the highway from Bethel to Shechem and to the south of Lebonah. They said to the 20 Benjamites, 'Go and hide in the vineyards and keep watch. When 21 the girls of Shiloh come out to dance, sally out of the vineyards, and each of you seize one of them for his wife; then make your way home to the land of Benjamin. Then, if their fathers or brothers 22 come and complain to you, say to them, "Let us keep them with your approval, for none of us has captured a wife in battle. Had you offered them to us, the guilt would be yours."'

All this the Benjamites did. They 23 carried off as many wives as they needed, snatching them as they danced; then they went their way and returned to their patrimony, rebuilt their cities and settled in them. The Israelites also dispersed 24 by tribes and families, and every man went back to his own patrimony.

In those days there was no king 25 in Israel and every man did what was right in his own eyes.

RUTH

Naomi and Ruth

1 LONG ago, in the time of the judges, there was a famine in the land, and a man from Bethlehem in Judah went to live in the Moabite country with his wife
2 and his two sons. The man's name was Elimelech, his wife's name was Naomi, and the names of his two sons Mahlon and Chilion. They were Ephrathites from Bethlehem in Judah. They arrived in the Moabite country and there they stayed.
3 Elimelech Naomi's husband died, so that she was left with her two
4 sons. These sons married Moabite women, one of whom was called Orpah and the other Ruth. They had lived there about ten years,
5 when both Mahlon and Chilion died, so that the woman was bereaved of her two sons as well as of
6 her husband. Thereupon she set out with her two daughters-in-law to return home, because she had heard while still in the Moabite country that the LORD had cared for his people and given them food.
7 So with her two daughters-in-law she left the place where she had been living, and took the road home
8 to Judah. Then Naomi said to her two daughters-in-law, 'Go back, both of you, to your mothers' homes. May the LORD keep faith with you, as you have kept faith
9 with the dead and with me; and may he grant each of you security in the home of a new husband.' She kissed them and they wept aloud.
10 Then they said to her, 'We will return with you to your own people.'
11 But Naomi said, 'Go back, my daughters. Why should you go with me? Am I likely to bear any more sons to be husbands for you?
12 Go back, my daughters, go. I am too old to marry again. But even if I could say that I had hope of a child, if I were to marry this night
13 and if I were to bear sons, would you then wait until they grew up? Would you then refrain from marrying? No, no, my daughters, my lot is more bitter than yours, because the LORD has been against
14 me.' At this they wept again. Then Orpah kissed her mother-in-law and returned to her people, but Ruth clung to her.
15 'You see,' said Naomi, 'your sister-in-law has gone back to her people and her gods;[a] go back with
16 her.' 'Do not urge me to go back and desert you', Ruth answered. 'Where you go, I will go, and where you stay, I will stay. Your people shall be my people, and your God
17 my God. Where you die, I will die, and there I will be buried. I swear a solemn oath before the LORD your God: nothing but[b] death shall
18 divide us.' When Naomi saw that Ruth was determined to go with her, she said no more, and the two
19 of them went on until they came to Bethlehem. When they arrived in Bethlehem, the whole town was in great excitement about them, and the women said, 'Can this be
20 Naomi?' 'Do not call me Naomi,'[c] she said, 'call me Mara,[d] for it is a bitter lot that the Almighty has
21 sent me. I went away full, and the LORD has brought me back empty. Why do you call me Naomi? The LORD has pronounced against me;

---

[a] Or god.
[b] I swear...nothing but: or The LORD your God do so to me and more if...
[c] That is Pleasure.   [d] That is Bitter.

the Almighty has brought disaster
22 on me.' This is how Naomi's daughter-in-law, Ruth the Moabitess, returned with her from the Moabite country. The barley harvest was beginning when they arrived in Bethlehem.

Ruth and Boaz

2 N o w Naomi had a kinsman on her husband's side, a well-to-do man of the family of Elimelech; his
2 name was Boaz. Ruth the Moabitess said to Naomi, 'May I go out to the cornfields and glean behind anyone who will grant me that favour?' 'Yes, go, my daughter',
3 she replied. So Ruth went gleaning in the fields behind the reapers. As it happened, she was in that strip of the fields which belonged to
4 Boaz of Elimelech's family, and there was Boaz coming out from Bethlehem. He greeted the reapers, saying, 'The LORD be with you'; and they replied, 'The LORD bless
5 you.' Then he asked his servant in charge of the reapers, 'Whose girl
6 is this?' 'She is a Moabite girl', the servant answered, 'who has just come back with Naomi from the
7 Moabite country. She asked if she might glean and gather among the swathes behind the reapers. She came and has been on her feet with hardly a moment's rest[a] from day-
8 break till now.' Then Boaz said to Ruth, 'Listen to me, my daughter: do not go and glean in any other field, and do not look any further,
9 but keep close to my girls. Watch where the men reap, and follow the gleaners; I have given them orders not to molest you. If you are thirsty, go and drink from the jars the men
10 have filled.' She fell prostrate before him and said, 'Why are you so kind as to take notice of me when
11 I am only a foreigner?' Boaz answered, 'They have told me all that you have done for your mother-in-

law since your husband's death, how you left your father and mother and the land of your birth, and came to a people you did not know before. The LORD reward your 12 deed; may the LORD the God of Israel, under whose wings you have come to take refuge, give you all that you deserve.' 'Indeed, sir,' she 13 said, 'you have eased my mind and spoken kindly to me; may I ask you as a favour not to treat me only as one of your slave-girls?'[b] When 14 meal-time came round, Boaz said to her, 'Come here and have something to eat, and dip your bread into the sour wine.' So she sat beside the reapers, and he passed her some roasted grain. She ate all she wanted and still had some left over. When she got up to glean, Boaz 15 gave the men orders. 'She', he said, 'may glean even among the sheaves; do not scold her. Or you 16 may even pull out some corn from the bundles and leave it for her to glean, without reproving her.'

So Ruth gleaned in the field till 17 evening, and when she beat out what she had gleaned, it came to about a bushel of barley. She took 18 it up and went into the town, and her mother-in-law saw how much she had gleaned. Then Ruth brought out what she had saved from her meal and gave it to her. Her mother-in-law asked her, 19 'Where did you glean today? Which way did you go? Blessings on the man who kindly took notice of you.' So she told her mother-in-law whom she had been working with. 'The man with whom I worked today', she said, 'is called Boaz.' 'Blessings on him from the 20 LORD', said Naomi. 'The LORD has kept faith with the living and the dead. For this man is related to us and is our next-of-kin.' 'And what 21 is more,' said Ruth the Moabitess, 'he told me to stay close to his men until they had finished all his

---

[a] Prob. rdg.; Heb. adds in the house.
[b] may I . . . slave-girls?: or if you please, treat me as one of your slave-girls.

22 harvest.' 'It is best for you, my daughter,' Naomi answered, 'to go out with his girls; let no one catch 23 you in another field.' So she kept close to his girls, gleaning with them till the end of both barley and wheat harvests; but she lived with her mother-in-law.

3 One day Ruth's mother-in-law Naomi said to her, 'My daughter, I want to see you happily settled. 2 Now there is our kinsman Boaz; you were with his girls. Tonight he is winnowing barley at his thresh- 3 ing-floor. Wash and anoint your- self, put on your cloak and go down to the threshing-floor, but do not make yourself known to the man until he has finished eating and 4 drinking. But when he lies down, take note of the place where he lies. Then go in, turn back the covering at his feet and lie down. He will tell 5 you what to do.' 'I will do what- ever you tell me', Ruth answered. 6 So she went down to the threshing- floor and did exactly as her mo- 7 ther-in-law had told her. When Boaz had eaten and drunk, he felt at peace with the world and went to lie down at the far end of the heap of grain. She came in quietly, turned back the covering at his 8 feet and lay down. About midnight something disturbed the man as he slept; he turned over and, lo and behold, there was a woman lying 9 at his feet. 'Who are you?' he asked. 'I am your servant, Ruth', she replied. 'Now spread your skirt over your servant, because you are 10 my next-of-kin.' He said, 'The LORD has blessed you, my daughter. This last proof of your loyalty is greater than the first; you have not sought after any young man, rich 11 or poor. Set your mind at rest, my daughter. I will do whatever you ask; for, as the whole neighbour- hood knows, you are a capable wo- 12 man. Are you sure that I am the next-of-kin? There is a kinsman 13 even closer than I. Spend the night here and then in the morning, if he

is willing to act as your next-of- kin, well and good; but if he is not willing, I will do so; I swear it by the LORD. Now lie down till morn- ing.' So she lay at his feet till 14 morning, but rose before one man could recognize another; and he said, 'It must not be known that a woman has been to the threshing- floor.' Then he said, 'Bring me the 15 cloak you have on, and hold it out.' So she held it out, and he put in six measures of barley and lifted it on her back, and she went to the town. When she came to her mother-in- 16 law, Naomi asked, 'How did things go with you, my daughter?' Ruth told her all that the man had done for her. 'He gave me these six mea- 17 sures of barley,' she said; 'he would not let me come home to my mo- ther-in-law empty-handed.' Nao- 18 mi answered, 'Wait, my daughter, until you see what will come of it. He will not rest until he has settled the matter today.'

Now Boaz had gone up to the 4 city gate, and was sitting there; and, after a time, the next-of-kin of whom he had spoken passed by. 'Here,' he cried, calling him by name, 'come and sit down.' He came and sat down. Then Boaz 2 stopped ten elders of the town, and asked them to sit there, and they did so. Then he said to the next-of- 3 kin, 'You will remember the strip of field that belonged to our brother Elimelech. Naomi has returned from the Moabite country and is selling it. I promised to open the 4 matter with you, to ask you to ac- quire it in the presence of those who sit here, in the presence of the elders of my people. If you are going to do your duty as next-of-kin, then do so, but if not, someone must do it. So tell me, and then I shall know; for I come after you as next-of- kin.' He answered, 'I will act as next-of-kin.' Then Boaz said, 'On 5 the day when you acquire the field from Naomi, you also acquire Ruth the Moabitess, the dead man's

wife, so as to perpetuate the name of the dead man with his patri-
6 mony.' Thereupon the next-of-kin said, 'I cannot act myself, for I should risk losing my own patrimony. You must therefore do my duty as next-of-kin. I cannot act.'
7 Now in those old days, when property was redeemed or exchanged, it was the custom for a man to pull off his sandal and give it to the other party. This was the
8 form of attestation in Israel. So the next-of-kin said to Boaz, 'Acquire it for yourself', and pulled off his
9 sandal. Then Boaz declared to the elders and all the people, 'You are witnesses today that I have acquired from Naomi all that belonged to Elimelech and all that be-
10 longed to Mahlon and Chilion; and, further, that I have myself acquired Ruth the Moabitess, wife of Mahlon, to be my wife, to perpetuate the name of the deceased with his patrimony, so that his name may not be missing among his kindred and at the gate of his native place.
11 You are witnesses this day.' Then the elders and all who were at the gate said, 'We are witnesses. May the LORD make this woman, who has come to your home, like Rachel and Leah, the two who built up

the house of Israel. May you do great things in Ephrathah and keep a name alive in Bethlehem. May your house be like the house 12 of Perez, whom Tamar bore to Judah, through the offspring the LORD will give you by this girl.'

So Boaz took Ruth and made 13 her his wife. When they came together, the LORD caused her to conceive and she bore Boaz a son. Then 14 the women said to Naomi, 'Blessed be the LORD today, for he has not left you without a next-of-kin. May the dead man's name be kept alive in Israel. The child will give you new 15 life and cherish you in your old age; for your daughter-in-law who loves you, who has proved better to you than seven sons, has borne him.' Naomi took the child and laid him 16 in her lap and became his nurse. Her neighbours gave him a name: 17 'Naomi has a son,' they said; 'we will call him Obed.' He was the father of Jesse, the father of David.

THIS is the genealogy of Perez: 18 Perez was the father of Hezron, Hezron of Ram, Ram of Ammi- 19 nadab, Amminadab of Nahshon, 20 Nahshon of Salmon, Salmon of 21 Boaz, Boaz of Obed, Obed of Jesse, 22 and Jesse of David.

THE FIRST BOOK OF

SAMUEL

The birth and call of Samuel

1 THERE was a man from Ramathaim, a Zuphite from the hill-country of Ephraim, named Elkanah son of Jeroham, son of Elihu, son of Tohu, son of
2 Zuph an Ephraimite; and he had two wives named Hannah and

Peninnah. Peninnah had children, but Hannah was childless. This 3 man used to go up from his own town every year to worship and to offer sacrifice to the LORD of Hosts in Shiloh. There Eli's two sons, Hophni and Phinehas, were priests of the LORD. On the day 4 when Elkanah sacrificed, he gave

several shares of the meat to his wife Peninnah with all her sons
5 and daughters; but, although he loved Hannah, he gave her only one share, because the LORD had
6 not granted her children. Further, Hannah's rival used to torment her and humiliate her because she had
7 no children. Year after year this happened when they went up to the house of the LORD; her rival used to torment her. Once when she was in tears and would not
8 eat, her husband Elkanah said to her, 'Hannah, why are you crying and eating nothing? Why are you so miserable? Am I not more to
9-10 you than ten sons?' After they had finished eating and drinking at the sacrifice at Shiloh, Hannah rose in deep distress, and stood before the LORD and prayed to him, weeping bitterly. Meanwhile Eli the priest was sitting on his seat beside the door of the temple of the LORD.
11 Hannah made a vow in these words: 'O LORD of Hosts, if thou wilt deign to take notice of my trouble and remember me, if thou wilt not forget me but grant me offspring, then I will give the child to the LORD for his whole life, and no razor shall
12 ever touch his head.' For a long time she went on praying before the LORD, while Eli watched
13 her lips. Hannah was praying silently; but, although her voice could not be heard, her lips were moving and Eli took her for a
14 drunken woman. He said to her, 'Enough of this drunken behaviour! Go away till the wine has worn
15 off.' 'No, sir,' she answered, 'I am a sober person, I have drunk no wine or strong drink, and I have been pouring out my heart before
16 the LORD. Do not think me so degraded, sir; all this time I have been speaking out of the fullness
17 of my grief and misery.' 'Go in peace,' said Eli, 'and may the God of Israel answer the prayer you

have made to him.' Hannah said, 18 'May I be worthy of your kindness.' And she went away and took something to eat, no longer downcast. Next morning they were up early 19 and, after prostrating themselves before the LORD, returned to their own home at Ramah. Elkanah had intercourse with his wife Hannah, and the LORD remembered her. She 20 conceived, and in due time bore a son, whom she named Samuel, 'because', she said, 'I asked the LORD for him.'

Elkanah, with his whole house-21 hold, went up to make the annual sacrifice to the LORD and to redeem his vow. Hannah did not go with 22 them, but said to her husband, 'When the child is weaned I will come up with him to enter the presence of the LORD, and he shall[a] stay there always.' Her husband 23 Elkanah said to her, 'Do what you think best; stay at home until you have weaned him. Only, may the LORD indeed see your vow fulfilled.' So the woman stayed and nursed her son until she had weaned him; and when she had weaned him, she 24 took him up with her. She took also a bull three years old, an ephah of meal, and a flagon of wine, and she brought him, child as he was, into the house of the LORD at Shiloh. They slaughtered the bull, and 25 brought the boy to Eli. Hannah 26 said to him, 'Sir, as sure as you live, I am the woman who stood near you here praying to the LORD. It was this boy that I prayed for 27 and the LORD has given me what I asked. What I asked I have received; and now I lend him to the 28 LORD; for his whole life he is lent to the LORD.' And they prostrated themselves there before the LORD.

Then Hannah offered this prayer: 2

My heart rejoices in the LORD,
in the LORD I now hold my head
　high;

---

[a] come up . . . he shall: *or* bring him up, and he shall come into the presence of the LORD and . . .

my mouth is full of derision of my
  foes,
exultant because thou hast saved
  me.
2 There is none except thee,
  none so holy as the LORD,
  no rock like our God.
3 Cease your proud boasting,
  let no word of arrogance pass your
    lips;
  for the LORD is a god of all know-
    ledge:
  he governs all that men do.

4 Strong men stand in mute^a dis-
    may
  but those who faltered put on new
    strength.
5 Those who had plenty sell them-
    selves for a crust,
  and the hungry grow strong again.
  The barren woman has seven child-
    ren,
  and the mother of many sons is left
    to languish.

6 The LORD kills and he gives life,
  he sends down to Sheol, he can
    bring the dead up again.
7 The LORD makes a man poor, he
    makes him rich,
  he brings down and he raises up.
8 He lifts the weak out of the dust
  and raises the poor from the dung-
    hill;
  to give them a place among the
    great,
  to set them in seats of honour.

For the foundations of the earth
    are the LORD's,
  he has built the world upon them.
9 He will guard the footsteps of his
    saints,
  while the wicked sink into silence
    and gloom;
  not by mere strength shall a man
    prevail.
10 Those that stand against the LORD
    will be terrified
  when the High God^b thunders out
    of heaven.

The LORD is judge even to the ends
    of the earth,
he will give strength to his king
and raise high the head of his an-
    ointed prince.

Then Elkanah went to Ramah 11
with his household, but the boy
remained behind in the service of
the LORD under Eli the priest.
Now Eli's sons were scoundrels 12
and had no regard for the LORD.
The custom of the priests in their 13
dealings with the people was this:
when a man offered a sacrifice, the
priest's servant would come while
the flesh was stewing and would 14
thrust a three-pronged fork into
the cauldron or pan or kettle or
pot; and the priest would take
whatever the fork brought out.
This should have been their practice whenever Israelites came to
sacrifice at Shiloh; but now under 15
Eli's sons, even before the fat was
burnt, the priest's servant came
and said to the man who was
sacrificing, 'Give me meat to roast
for the priest; he will not accept
what has been already stewed, only
raw meat.' And if the man answer- 16
ed 'Let them burn the fat first, and
then take what you want', he said,
'No, give it to me now, or I will
take it by force.' The young men's 17
sin was very great in the LORD's
sight; for they brought the LORD's
sacrifice into general contempt.
Samuel continued in the service 18
of the LORD, a mere boy with a
linen ephod fastened round him.
Every year his mother made him 19
a little cloak and took it to him
when she went up with her husband
to offer the annual sacrifice. Eli 20
would give his blessing to Elkanah
and his wife and say, 'The LORD
grant you children by this woman
in place of the one for which you
asked him.'^c Then they went home
again.

---

^a in mute: *prob. rdg.*; *Heb. obscure.*
^b the High God: *prob. rdg.*; *Heb.* upon him.
^c for which...him: *or* which you lent him.

21 The Lord showed his care for Hannah, and she conceived and gave birth to three sons and two daughters; meanwhile the boy Samuel grew up in the presence of the Lord.

22 Eli, now a very old man, had heard how his sons were treating all the Israelites, and how they lay with the women who were serving at the entrance to the Tent of the

23 Presence. So he said to them, 'Why do you do such things? I hear from all the people how wickedly you

24 behave. Have done with it, my sons; for it is no good report that I hear spreading among the Lord's

25 people. If a man sins against another man, God will intervene; but if a man sins against the Lord, who can intercede for him?' For all this, they did not listen to their father's rebuke, for the Lord meant that

26 they should die. But the young Samuel, as he grew up, commended himself to the Lord and to men.

27 Now a man of God came to Eli and said, 'This is the word of the Lord: You know that I revealed myself to your forefather when he and his family were in Egypt in slavery in the house of Pharaoh.

28 You know that I chose him from all the tribes of Israel to be my priest, to mount the steps of my altar, to burn sacrifices and to carry*a* the ephod before me; and that I assigned all the food-offerings of the Israelites to your family.

29 Why then do you show disrespect for my sacrifices and the offerings which I have ordained? What makes you resent them? Why do you honour your sons more than me by letting them batten on the choicest offerings of my people Is-

30 rael? The Lord's word was, "I promise that your house and your father's house shall serve before me for all time"; but now his word is, "I will have no such thing: I will honour those who honour me, and

those who despise me shall meet with contempt. The time is coming 31 when I will lop off every limb of your own and of your father's family, so that no man in your house shall come to old age. You 32 will even resent*b* the prosperity I give to Israel; never again shall there be an old man in your house. If I allow any to survive to serve 33 my altar, his eyes will grow dim and his appetite fail, his issue will be weaklings and die off. The fate of 34 your two sons shall be a sign to you: Hophni and Phinehas shall both die on the same day. I will appoint 35 for myself a priest who will be faithful, who will do what I have in my mind and in my heart. I will establish his family to serve in perpetual succession before my anointed king. Any of your family that still live 36 will come and bow humbly before him to beg a fee, a piece of silver and a loaf, and will ask for a turn of priestly duty to earn a crust of bread."'

So the child Samuel was in the 3 Lord's service under his master Eli. Now in those days the word of the Lord was seldom heard, and no vision was granted. But one 2 night Eli, whose eyes were dim and his sight failing, was lying down in his usual place, while Samuel 3 slept in the temple of the Lord where the Ark of God was. Before the lamp of God had gone out, the 4 Lord called him, and Samuel answered, 'Here I am', and ran to 5 Eli saying, 'You called me: here I am.' 'No, I did not call you,' said Eli; 'lie down again.' So he went and lay down. The Lord called 6 Samuel again, and he got up and went to Eli. 'Here I am,' he said; 'surely you called me.' 'I did not call, my son,' he answered; 'lie down again.' Now Samuel had not 7 yet come to know the Lord, and the word of the Lord had not been disclosed to him. When the Lord 8 called him for the third time, he

_____
a Or wear.   *b* You...resent: *prob. rdg.*; Heb. *obscure.*

again went to Eli and said, 'Here I am; you did call me.' Then Eli understood that it was the LORD 9 calling the child; he told Samuel to go and lie down and said, 'If he calls again, say, "Speak, LORD; thy servant hears thee."' So Samuel went and lay down in his place.

10 The LORD came and stood there, and called, 'Samuel, Samuel', as before. Samuel answered, 'Speak; 11 thy servant hears thee.' The LORD said, 'Soon I shall do something in Israel which will ring in the ears of 12 all who hear it. When that day comes I will make good every word I have spoken against Eli and his 13 family from beginning to end. You are to*a* tell him that my judgement on his house shall stand for ever because*b* he knew of his sons' blasphemies against God*c* and 14 did not rebuke them. Therefore I have sworn to the family of Eli that their abuse of sacrifices and offerings shall never be expiated.'

15 Samuel lay down till morning and then opened the doors of the house of the LORD, but he was afraid to tell Eli about the vision. 16 Eli called Samuel: 'Samuel, my son', he said; and he answered, 17 'Here I am.' Eli asked, 'What did the LORD say to you? Do not hide it from me. God forgive you if you hide one word of all that he said 18 to you.' Then Samuel told him everything and hid nothing. Eli said, 'The LORD must do what is good in his eyes.'

19 As Samuel grew up, the LORD was with him, and none of his 20 words went unfulfilled. From Dan to Beersheba, all Israel recognized that Samuel was confirmed as a 21 prophet of the LORD. So the LORD continued to appear in Shiloh, because he had revealed himself there to Samuel.*d*

The struggle with the Philistines

So Samuel's word had authority 4 throughout Israel. And the time came when the Philistines mustered for battle against Israel, and the Israelites went out to meet them. The Israelites encamped at Eben-ezer and the Philistines at Aphek. The Philistines drew up 2 their lines facing the Israelites, and when they joined battle the Israelites were routed by the Philistines, who killed about four thousand men on the field. When the army 3 got back to the camp, the elders of Israel asked, 'Why did the LORD let us be routed today by the Philistines? Let us fetch the Ark of the Covenant of the LORD from Shiloh to go with us and deliver us from the power of our enemies.' So the 4 people sent to Shiloh and fetched the Ark of the Covenant of the LORD of Hosts, who is enthroned upon the cherubim; Eli's two sons, Hophni and Phinehas, were there with the Ark. When the Ark came 5 into the camp all the Israelites greeted it with a great shout, and the earth rang with the shouting. The Philistines heard the noise and 6 asked, 'What is this great shouting in the camp of the Hebrews?' When they knew that the Ark of the LORD had come into the camp, they were 7 afraid and cried, 'A god has come into the camp. We are lost! No such thing has ever happened before. We are utterly lost! Who can 8 deliver us from the power of these mighty gods? These are the very gods who broke the Egyptians and crushed them in the wilderness. Courage, Philistines, and act like 9 men, or you will become slaves to the Hebrews as they were yours. Be men, and fight!' The Philistines 10 then gave battle, and the Israelites were defeated and fled to their homes. It was a great defeat, and

---

a Prob. rdg.; Heb. I will.   *b* because: prob. rdg.; Heb. in guilt.
c against God: prob. original reading, altered in Heb. to to them.
d Prob. rdg.; Heb. adds according to the word of the LORD.

thirty thousand Israelite foot-
11 soldiers perished. The Ark of God
was taken, and Eli's two sons,
Hophni and Phinehas, were killed.
12 A Benjamite ran from the battlefield and reached Shiloh on the
same day, his clothes rent and dust
13 on his head. When he arrived Eli
was sitting on a seat by the road
to Mizpah, for he was deeply troubled about the Ark of God. The
man entered the city with his news,
and all the people cried out in
14 horror. When Eli heard it, he asked,
'What does this uproar mean?' The
man hurried to Eli and told him.
15 Eli was ninety-eight years old and
16 sat staring with sightless eyes; so
the man said to him, 'I am the
man who has just arrived from the
battle; this very day I have escaped
from the field.' Eli asked, 'What is
17 the news, my son?' The runner
answered, 'The Israelites have fled
from the Philistines; utter panic
has struck the army; your two sons,
Hophni and Phinehas, are killed,
18 and the Ark of God is taken.' At
the mention of the Ark of God, Eli
fell backwards from his seat by the
gate and broke his neck, for he was
old and heavy. So he died; he had
been judge over Israel for forty
19 years. His daughter-in-law, the
wife of Phinehas, was with child
and near her time, and when she
heard of the capture of the Ark and
the deaths of her father-in-law and
her husband, her labour suddenly
began and she crouched down and
20 was delivered. As she lay dying, the
women who attended her said, 'Do
not be afraid; you have a son.' But
she did not answer or heed what
21 they said. Then they named the
boy Ichabod,[a] saying, 'Glory has
departed from Israel' (in allusion
to the capture of the Ark of God
and the death of her father-in-
22 law and her husband); 'Glory
has departed from Israel,' they
said, 'because the Ark of God is
taken.'

After the Philistines had cap- 5
tured the Ark of God, they brought
it from Eben-ezer to Ashdod; and 2
there they carried it into the temple
of Dagon and set it beside Dagon
himself. When the people of Ash- 3
dod rose next morning, there was
Dagon fallen face downwards before the Ark of the LORD; so they
took him and put him back in his
place. Next morning when they 4
rose, Dagon had again fallen face
downwards before the Ark of the
LORD, with his head and his two
hands lying broken off beside his
platform; only Dagon's body remained on it. This is why from that 5
day to this the priests of Dagon
and all who enter the temple of
Dagon at Ashdod do not set foot
upon Dagon's platform.

Then the LORD laid a heavy hand 6
upon the people of Ashdod; he
threw them into distress and plagued them with tumours, and their
territory swarmed with rats.[b] There
was death and destruction all
through the city. When the men 7
of Ashdod saw this, they said, 'The
Ark of the God of Israel shall not
stay here, for he has laid a heavy
hand upon us and upon Dagon our
god.' So they sent and called all the 8
Philistine princes together to ask
what should be done with the Ark.
They said, 'Let the Ark of the God
of Israel be taken across to Gath.'
They took it there, and after its 9
arrival the hand of the LORD caused
great havoc in the city; he plagued
everybody, high and low alike,
with the tumours which broke out.
Then they sent the Ark of God on 10
to Ekron. When the Ark reached
Ekron, the people cried, 'They
have brought the Ark of the God
of Israel over to us, to kill us and
our families.' So they summoned 11
all the Philistine princes and said,
'Send the Ark of the God of Israel
away; let it go back to its own
place, or it will be the death of
us all.' There was death and de-

---

[a] *That is* No-glory.   [b] *Or* mice.

struction all through the city; for the hand of God lay heavy
12 upon it. Even those who did not die were plagued with tumours; the cry of the city went up to heaven.

6 When the Ark of the LORD had been in their territory for seven
2 months, the Philistines summoned the priests and soothsayers and asked, 'What shall we do with the Ark of the LORD? Tell us how we ought to send it back to its own
3 place.' They answered, 'If you send the Ark of the God of Israel back, do not let it go without a gift, but send it back with a gift for him by way of indemnity; then you will be healed and restored to favour; there is no reason why his hand should not be lifted from
4 you.' When they were asked, 'What gift shall we send back to him?', they answered, 'Send five tumours modelled in gold and five gold rats, one for each of the Philistine princes, for the same plague afflicted all of you and your princes.
5 Make models of your tumours and of the rats which are ravaging the land, and give honour to the God of Israel; perhaps he will relax the pressure of his hand on you, on
6 your god, and on your land. Why should you be stubborn like Pharaoh and the Egyptians? Remember how this god made sport of
7 them until they let Israel go. Now make a new wagon ready with two milch-cows which have never been yoked; harness the cows to the wagon, and take their calves from them and drive them back to their
8 stalls. Then take the Ark of the LORD and put it on the wagon, place in a casket, beside it, the gold offerings that you are sending to him as an indemnity, and
9 let it go where it will. Watch it: if it goes up towards its own territory to Beth-shemesh, then it is the LORD who has done us this great injury; but if not, then we shall know that his hand has not

touched us, but we have been the victims of chance.'

The men did this. They took 10 two milch-cows and harnessed them to a wagon, shutting up their calves in the stall, and they placed 11 the Ark of the LORD on the wagon together with the casket, the gold rats, and the models of their haemorrhoids. Then the cows went 12 straight in the direction of Beth-shemesh; they kept to the same road, lowing as they went and turning neither right nor left, while the Philistine princes followed them as far as the territory of Beth-shemesh. Now the people of Beth- 13 shemesh were harvesting their wheat in the Vale, and when they looked up and saw the Ark they rejoiced at the sight of it. The 14 wagon came to the farm of Joshua of Beth-shemesh and halted there. Close by stood a great stone; so they chopped up the wood of the wagon and offered the cows as a whole-offering to the LORD. Then 15 the Levites lifted down the Ark of the LORD and the casket containing the gold offerings, and laid them on the great stone; and the men of Beth-shemesh offered whole-offerings and shared-offerings that day to the LORD. The five princes 16 of the Philistines watched all this, and returned to Ekron the same day.

These golden haemorrhoids 17 which the Philistines sent back as a gift of indemnity to the LORD were for Ashdod, Gaza, Ashkelon, Gath, and Ekron, one for each city. The gold rats were for all the towns 18 of the Philistines governed by the five princes, both fortified towns and open settlements. The great stone where they deposited the Ark of the LORD stands witness on the farm of Joshua of Beth-shemesh to this very day.

But the sons of Jeconiah did not 19 rejoice with the rest of the men of Beth-shemesh when they welcomed the Ark of the LORD, and he

struck down seventy of them. The people mourned because the LORD had struck them so heavy a blow,
20 and the men of Beth-shemesh said, 'No one is safe in the presence of the LORD, this holy God. To whom can we send it, to be rid of him?'
21 So they sent this message to the inhabitants of Kiriath-jearim:'The Philistines have returned the Ark of the LORD; come down and take
7 charge of it.' Then the men of Kiriath-jearim came and took the Ark of the LORD away; they brought it into the house of Abinadab on the hill and consecrated his son Eleazar as its custodian.

Samuel judge over Israel

2 So for a long while the Ark was housed in Kiriath-jearim; and after some time, twenty years later, there was a movement throughout Israel to follow the
3 LORD. So Samuel addressed these words to the whole nation: 'If your return to the LORD is whole-hearted, banish the foreign gods and the Ashtaroth from your shrines; turn to the LORD with heart and mind, and worship him alone, and he will deliver you from the Philistines.'
4 The Israelites then banished the Baalim and the Ashtaroth, and worshipped the LORD alone.
5 Samuel summoned all Israel to an assembly at Mizpah, so that he might intercede with the LORD for
6 them. When they had assembled there, they drew water and poured it out before the LORD and fasted all day, confessing that they had sinned against the LORD. It was at Mizpah that Samuel acted as judge over Israel.
7 When the Philistines heard that the Israelites had assembled at Mizpah, their princes marched against them. The Israelites heard that the Philistines were advancing, and they were afraid. They
8 said to Samuel, 'Do not cease to pray for us to the LORD our God to save us from the power of the Philistines.' Thereupon Samuel
9 took a sucking lamb, offered it up complete as a whole-offering and prayed aloud to the LORD on behalf of Israel; and the LORD answered his prayer. As Samuel was
10 offering the sacrifice and the Philistines were advancing to battle with the Israelites, the LORD thundered loud and long over the Philistines and threw them into confusion. They fled in panic before the Israelites, who set out from
11 Mizpah in pursuit and kept up the slaughter of the Philistines till they reached a point below Beth-car.
12 There Samuel took a stone and set it up as a monument between Mizpah and Jeshanah,*a* naming it Eben-ezer,*b* 'for to this point', he said, 'the LORD has helped us.'
13 Thus the Philistines were subdued and no longer encroached on the territory of Israel; and the hand of the LORD was against them as
14 long as Samuel lived. The cities they had captured were restored to Israel, and from Ekron to Gath the borderland was freed from their control. Between Israel and the Amorites peace was maintained.
15 Samuel acted as judge in Israel as
16 long as he lived, and every year went on circuit to Bethel and Gilgal and Mizpah; he dispensed jus-
17 tice at all these places, returning always to Ramah. That was his home and the place from which he governed Israel, and there he built an altar to the LORD.

Saul anointed king

8 WHEN Samuel grew old, he appointed his sons to be judges in
2 Israel. The eldest son was named Joel and the second Abiah; they acted as judges in Beersheba.
3 His sons did not follow in their father's footsteps but were intent on their own profit, taking bribes

a Prob. rdg. (cp. 2 Chr. 13. 19); Heb. the tooth.　　　*b* That is Stone of Help.

and perverting the course of jus-
4 tice. So all the elders of Israel met,
and came to Samuel at Ramah
5 and said to him, 'You are now old
and your sons do not follow in your
footsteps; appoint us a king to
6 govern us, like other nations.' But
their request for a king to govern
them displeased Samuel, and he
7 prayed to the LORD. The LORD
answered Samuel, 'Listen to the
people and all that they are saying;
they have not rejected you, it is
I whom they have rejected, I whom
they will not have to be their king.
8 They are now doing to you just
what they have done to me since
I brought them up from Egypt:
they have forsaken me and wor-
9 shipped other gods. Hear what they
have to say now, but give them
a solemn warning and tell them
what sort of king will govern them.'
10 Samuel told the people who were
asking him for a king all that the
11 LORD had said to him. 'This will
be the sort of king who will govern
you', he said. 'He will take your
sons and make them serve in his
chariots and with his cavalry, and
will make them run before his
12 chariot. Some he will appoint
officers over units of a thousand
and units of fifty. Others will
plough his fields and reap his harvest; others again will make weapons of war and equipment for
13 mounted troops. He will take your
daughters for perfumers, cooks,
14 and confectioners, and will seize
the best of your cornfields, vineyards, and olive-yards, and give
15 them to his lackeys. He will take
a tenth of your grain and your
vintage to give to his eunuchs and
16 lackeys. Your slaves, both men
and women, and the best of your
cattle and your asses he will seize
17 and put to his own use. He will take
a tenth of your flocks, and you
yourselves will become his slaves.
18 When that day comes, you will cry
out against the king whom you
have chosen; but it will be too late,

the LORD will not answer you.' The 19
people refused to listen to Samuel;
'No,' they said, 'we will have a king
over us; then we shall be like other 20
nations, with a king to govern us,
to lead us out to war and fight our
battles.' So Samuel, when he had 21
heard what the people said, told
the LORD; and he answered, 'Take 22
them at their word and appoint
them a king.' Samuel then dismissed all the men of Israel to their
homes.

There was a man from the dis- 9
trict of Benjamin, whose name was
Kish son of Abiel, son of Zeror, son
of Bechorath, son of Aphiah a
Benjamite. He was a man of substance, and had a son named Saul, 2
a young man in his prime; there
was no better man among the
Israelites than he. He was a head
taller than any of his fellows.

One day some asses belonging 3
to Saul's father Kish had strayed,
so he said to his son Saul, 'Take one
of the servants with you, and go
and look for the asses.' They cross- 4
ed the hill-country of Ephraim
and went through the district of
Shalisha but did not find them;
they passed through the district
of Shaalim but they were not there;
they passed through the district
of Benjamin but again did not
find them. When they had entered 5
the district of Zuph, Saul said to
the servant with him, 'Come, we
ought to turn back, or my father
will stop thinking about the asses
and begin to worry about us.' The 6
servant answered, 'There is a man
of God in the city here, who has
a great reputation, because everything he says comes true. Suppose
we go there; he may tell us something about this errand of ours.'
Saul said, 'If we do go, what shall 7
we offer him? There is no food left
in our packs and we have no present for the man of God, nothing
at all.' The servant answered him 8
again, 'Wait! I have here a quarter-
shekel of silver. I can give that to

the man, to tell us what we should
10^a do.' Saul said, 'Good! let us go to
him.' So they went to the city
9 where the man of God was. (In days
gone by in Israel, when a man
wished to consult God, he would
say, 'Let us go to the seer.' For
what is nowadays called a prophet
11 used to be called a seer.) As they
were going up the hill to the city
they met some girls coming out to
draw water and asked, 'Shall we
12 find the seer there?' 'Yes,' they
said, 'the seer is ahead of you now;
he has just^b arrived in the city
because there is a feast at the hill-
13 shrine today. As you enter the city
you will meet him before he goes
up to the shrine to eat; the people
will not start until he comes, for
he has to bless the sacrifice before
the company can eat. Go up now,
14 and you will find him at once.' So
they went up to the city, and just
as they were going in, there was
Samuel coming towards them on
his way up to the shrine.

15 Now the day before Saul came,
the LORD had disclosed his intention to Samuel in these words:
16 'At this same time tomorrow I will
send you a man from the land of
Benjamin. Anoint him prince over
my people Israel, and then he shall
deliver my people from the Philistines. I have seen the sufferings
of my people and their cry has
17 reached my ears.' The moment
Saul appeared the LORD said to
Samuel, 'Here is the man of whom
I spoke to you. This man shall rule
18 my people.' Saul came up to
Samuel in the gateway and said,
'Would you tell me where the seer
19 lives?' Samuel replied, 'I am the
seer. Go on ahead of me to the
hill-shrine and you shall eat with
me today; in the morning I will
set you on your way, after telling
you what you have on your mind.
20 Trouble yourself no more about the

asses lost three days ago, for they
have been found. But what is it
that all Israel is wanting? It is you
and your ancestral house.' 'But I 21
am a Benjamite,' said Saul, 'from
the smallest of the tribes of Israel,
and my family is the least important of all the families of the tribe
of Benjamin. Why do you say this
to me?' Samuel then brought Saul 22
and his servant into the dining-hall
and gave them a place at the head
of the company, which numbered
about thirty. Then he said to the 23
cook, 'Bring the portion that I
gave you and told you to put on
one side.' So the cook took up the 24
whole haunch and leg and put it
before Saul; and Samuel said,
'Here is the portion of meat^c kept
for you. Eat it: it has been reserved
for you at this feast to which I have
invited the people.' So Saul dined
with Samuel that day, and when 25
they came down from the hill-
shrine to the city a bed was spread
on the roof for Saul, and he stayed 26
there that night. At dawn Samuel
called to Saul on the roof, 'Get up,
and I will set you on your way.'
When Saul rose, he and Samuel
went out together into the street.
As they came to the end of the 27
town, Samuel said to Saul, 'Tell
the boy to go on.' He did so, and
then Samuel said, 'Stay here a
moment, and I will tell you the
word of God.'

Samuel took a flask of oil and 10
poured it over Saul's head, and he
kissed him and said, 'The LORD
anoints you prince over his people
Israel; you shall rule the people of
the LORD and deliver them from
the enemies round about them.
You shall have a sign that the LORD
has anointed you prince to govern
his inheritance: when you leave me 2
today, you will meet two men by
the tomb of Rachel at Zelzah in
the territory of Benjamin. They

---

^a *Verses 9 and 10 transposed.*
^b the seer . . . just: *prob. rdg.*; *Heb.* he is ahead of you, hurry now, for he has today . . .
^c the portion of meat: *prob. rdg.*; *Heb.* what is left over.

will tell you that the asses you are looking for have been found and that your father is concerned for them no longer; he is anxious about you and says again and again, "What shall I do about my son?"

3 From there go across country as far as the terebinth of Tabor, where three men going up to Bethel to worship God will meet you. One of them will be carrying three kids, the second three loaves, and the 4 third a flagon of wine. They will greet you and will offer you two loaves, which you will accept from 5 them. Then when you reach the Hill of God, where the Philistine governor[a] resides, you will meet a company of prophets coming down from the hill-shrine, led by lute, harp, fife, and drum, and filled with 6 prophetic rapture. Then the spirit of the LORD will suddenly take possession of you, and you too will be rapt like a prophet and become 7 another man. When these signs happen, do whatever the occasion demands; God will be with you. 8 You shall go down to Gilgal ahead of me, and I will come to you to sacrifice whole-offerings and shared-offerings. Wait seven days until I join you; then I will tell you 9 what to do.' As Saul turned to leave Samuel, God gave him a new heart. On that same day all these signs 10 happened. When they reached the Hill there was a company of prophets coming to meet him, and the spirit of God suddenly took possession of him, so that he too was filled with prophetic rapture. 11 When people who had known him previously saw that he was rapt like the prophets, they said to one another, 'What can have happened to the son of Kish? Is Saul also 12 among the prophets?' One of the men of that place said, 'And whose sons are they?' Hence the proverb, 'Is Saul also among the prophets?' 13 When the prophetic rapture had 14 passed, he went home.[b] Saul's uncle

said to him and the boy, 'Where have you been?' Saul answered, 'To look for the asses, and when we could not find them, we went to Samuel.' His uncle said, 'Tell me 15 what Samuel said.' 'He told us that 16 the asses had been found', said Saul; but he did not repeat what Samuel had said about his being king.

Meanwhile Samuel summoned 17 the Israelites to the LORD at Mizpah and said to the people, 'This is 18 the word of the LORD the God of Israel: I brought Israel up from Egypt; I delivered you from the Egyptians and from all the kingdoms that oppressed you; but to- 19 day you have rejected your God who saved you from all your misery and distress; you have said, "No, set up a king over us." Now therefore take up your positions before the LORD tribe by tribe and clan by clan.' Samuel then presented 20 all the tribes of Israel, and Benjamin was picked by lot. Then he 21 presented the tribe of Benjamin, family by family, and the family of Matri was picked. Then he presented the family of Matri, man by man, and Saul son of Kish was picked; but when they looked for him he could not be found. They 22 went on to ask the LORD, 'Will the man be coming back?' The LORD answered, 'There he is, hiding among the baggage.' So someone 23 ran and fetched him out, and as he took his stand among the people, he was a head taller than anyone else. Samuel said to the people, 24 'Look at the man whom the LORD has chosen; there is no one like him in this whole nation.' They all acclaimed him, shouting, 'Long live the king!' Samuel then ex- 25 plained to the people the nature of a king, and made a written record of it on a scroll which he deposited before the LORD; he then dismissed them to their homes. Saul too went home to Gibeah, and 26 with him went some fighting men

---

[a] *Or garrison.*   [b] *Prob. rdg.; Heb. to the hill-shrine.*

27 whose hearts God had moved. But there were scoundrels who said, 'How can this fellow deliver us?' They thought nothing of him and brought him no gifts.

11 About a month later Nahash the Ammonite attacked and besieged Jabesh-gilead. The men of Jabesh said to Nahash, 'Come to terms with us and we will be your sub- 2 jects.' Nahash answered them, 'On one condition only will I come to terms with you: that I gouge out your right eyes and bring disgrace 3 on Israel.' The elders of Jabesh-gilead then said, 'Give us seven days' respite to send messengers throughout Israel and then, if no one relieves us, we will surrender 4 to you.' When the messengers came to Gibeah, where Saul lived, and delivered their message, all the 5 people broke into lamentation. Saul was just coming from the field driving in the oxen, and asked why the people were lamenting; and they repeated what the men of 6 Jabesh had said. When Saul heard this, the spirit of God suddenly 7 seized him. In his anger he took a pair of oxen and cut them in pieces, and sent messengers with the pieces all through Israel to proclaim that the same would be done to the oxen of any man who did not follow Saul and Samuel into battle. The fear of the LORD fell upon the people 8 and they came out, to a man. Saul mustered them in Bezek; there were three hundred thousand men from Israel and thirty thousand 9 from Judah. He said to the men who brought the message, 'Tell the men of Jabesh-gilead, "Victory will be yours tomorrow by the time the sun is hot."' The men of Jabesh heard what the messengers 10 reported and took heart; and they said to Nahash, 'Tomorrow we will surrender to you, and then you may deal with us as you think fit.' 11 Next day Saul drew up his men in three columns; they forced their way right into the enemy camp during the morning watch and massacred the Ammonites while the day grew hot, after which the survivors scattered until no two men were left together.

12 Then the people said to Samuel, 'Who said that Saul should not reign over us? Hand the men over 13 to us to be put to death.' But Saul said, 'No man shall be put to death on a day when the LORD has won such a victory in Israel.' Samuel 14 said to the people, 'Let us now go to Gilgal and there renew our allegiance to the kingdom.' So they 15 all went to Gilgal and invested Saul there as king in the presence of the LORD, sacrificing shared-offerings before the LORD; and Saul and all the Israelites celebrated the occasion with great joy.

12 THEN Samuel thus addressed the assembled Israelites: 'I have listened to your request and installed a king to rule over you. And the king 2 is now your leader, while I am old and white-haired and my sons are with you; but I have been your leader ever since I was a child. Here I am. Lay your complaints 3 against me in the presence of the LORD and of his anointed king. Whose ox have I taken, whose ass have I taken? Whom have I wronged, whom have I oppressed? From whom have I taken a bribe, to turn a blind eye? Tell me, and I will make restitution.' They answered, 4 'You have not wronged us, you have not oppressed us; you have not taken anything from any man.' Samuel then said to them, 'This 5 day the LORD is witness among you, his anointed king is witness, that you have found my hands empty.' They said, 'He is witness.' Samuel said to the people, 'Yes, the 6 LORD is witness, the LORD who gave you Moses and Aaron and brought your fathers out of Egypt. Now stand up, and here in the 7 presence of the LORD I will put the case against you and recite all the

victories which he has won for you
8 and for your fathers. After Jacob
and his sons had come down to
Egypt and the Egyptians had made
them suffer, your fathers cried to
the LORD for help, and he sent
Moses and Aaron, who brought
them out of Egypt and settled them
9 in this place. But they forgot the
LORD their God, and he abandoned
them to Sisera, commander-in-
chief of Jabin king of Hazor, to the
Philistines, and to the king of
Moab, and they had to fight against
10 them. Then your fathers cried to
the LORD for help: "We have sinned, we have forsaken the LORD
and we have worshipped the Baal
im and the Ashtaroth. But now,
if thou wilt deliver us from our
11 enemies, we will worship thee." So
the LORD sent Jerubbaal and Barak, Jephthah and Samson, and
delivered you from your enemies
on every side; and you lived in
peace and quiet.
12 'Then, when you saw Nahash
king of the Ammonites coming
against you, although the LORD
your God was your king, you said
to me, "No, let us have a king to
13 rule over us." Now, here is the king
you asked for; you chose him, and
the LORD has set a king over you.
14 If you will revere the LORD and
give true and loyal service, if you
do not rebel against his commands,
and if you and the king who reigns
over you are faithful to the LORD
15 your God, well and good; but if you
do not obey the LORD, and if you
rebel against his commands, then
he will set his face against you and
against your king.
16 'Stand still, and see the great
wonder which the LORD will do
17 before your eyes. It is now wheat
harvest; when I call upon the LORD
and he sends thunder and rain, you
will see and know how wicked it
was in the LORD's eyes for you to

ask for a king.' So Samuel called 18
upon the LORD and he sent thunder
and rain that day; and all the
people were in great fear of the
LORD and of Samuel. They said to 19
Samuel, 'Pray for us your servants
to the LORD your God, to save us
from death; for we have added to
all our other sins the great wickedness of asking for a king.' Samuel 20
said to the people, 'Do not be
afraid; although you have been so
wicked, do not give up the worship
of the LORD, but serve him with
all your heart. Give up the worship 21
of false gods which can neither
help nor save, because they are
false. For his name's sake the LORD 22
will not cast you off, because he
has resolved to make you his own
people. As for me, God forbid that 23
I should sin against the LORD and
cease to pray for you. I will show
you what is right and good: to re- 24
vere the LORD and worship him
faithfully with all your heart. Consider what great things he has done
for you; but if you persist in wicked- 25
ness, you shall be swept away, you
and your king.'

Saul was fifty years[a] old when 13
he became king, and he reigned
over Israel for twenty-two[b] years.
He picked three thousand men 2
from Israel, two thousand to be
with him in Michmash and the hill-
country of Bethel and a thousand
to be with Jonathan in Gibeah of
Benjamin; and he sent the rest of
the people home.

Jonathan killed the Philistine 3
governor[c] in Geba, and the news
spread among the Philistines that
the Hebrews were in revolt.[d] Saul
sounded the trumpet all through
the land; and when the Israelites 4
all heard that Saul had killed a
Philistine governor and that the
name of Israel stank among the
Philistines, they answered the call
to arms and came to join Saul at

[a] *fifty years: prob. rdg.; Heb.* a year.   [b] *Prob. rdg.; Heb.* two.   [c] *Or* garrison.
[d] *that...revolt: prob. rdg.; Heb. has* saying, Let the Hebrews hear *after* through
the land.

5 Gilgal.[a] The Philistines mustered to attack Israel; they had thirty thousand chariots and six thousand horse, with infantry as countless as sand on the sea-shore. They went up and camped at Michmash,
6 to the east of Beth-aven. The Israelites found themselves in sore straits, for the army was hard pressed, so they hid themselves in caves and holes and among the rocks, in
7 pits and cisterns. Some of them crossed the Jordan into the district of Gad and Gilead, but Saul remained at Gilgal, and all the peo-
8 ple at his back were in alarm.[b] He waited seven days for his meeting with Samuel, but Samuel did not come to Gilgal; so the people began
9 to drift away from Saul. He said therefore, 'Bring me the whole-offering and the shared-offerings', and he offered up the whole-offer-
10 ing. Saul had just finished the sacrifice, when Samuel arrived, and he
11 went out to greet him. Samuel said, 'What have you done?', and Saul answered, 'I saw that the people were drifting away from me, and you yourself had not come as you had promised, and the Philistines
12 were assembling at Michmash; and I thought, "The Philistines will now move against me at Gilgal, and I have not placated the LORD"; so I felt compelled to make the whole-
13 offering myself.' Samuel said to Saul, 'You have behaved foolishly. You have not kept the command laid on you by the LORD your God; if you had, he would have established your dynasty over Israel for
14 all time. But now your line will not endure; the LORD will seek a man after his own heart, and will appoint him prince over his people, because you have not kept the LORD's command.'
15 Samuel left Gilgal without more ado and went on his way. The rest of the people followed Saul, as he moved from Gilgal towards the enemy. At Gibeah of Benjamin he mustered the people who were with him; they were about six hundred
16 men. Saul and his son Jonathan and the men they had with them took up their quarters in Gibeah of Benjamin, while the Philistines
17 were encamped in Michmash. Raiding parties went out from the Philistine camp in three directions. One party turned towards Ophrah in
18 the district of Shual, another towards Beth-horon, and the third towards the range of hills overlooking the valley of Zeboim and the wilderness beyond.
19 No blacksmith was to be found in the whole of Israel, for the Philistines were determined to prevent the Hebrews from making swords
20 and spears. The Israelites had to go down to the Philistines for their ploughshares, mattocks, axes, and
21 sickles to be sharpened. The charge was two-thirds of a shekel for ploughshares and mattocks, and one-third of a shekel for sharpening the axes and setting the goads.[c]
22 So when war broke out none of the followers of Saul and Jonathan had either sword or spear; only Saul and Jonathan carried arms.

23 Now the Philistines had posted a force to hold the pass of Mich-
14 mash; and one day Saul's son Jonathan said to his armour-bearer, 'Come, let us go over to the Philistine post beyond that ridge';
2 but he did not tell his father. Saul, at the time, had his tent under the pomegranate-tree at Migron on the outskirts of Gibeah; and he had about six hundred men with him.
3 The ephod was carried by Ahijah son of Ahitub, Ichabod's brother, son of Phinehas son of Eli, the priest of the LORD at Shiloh. Nobody knew that Jonathan had
4 gone. On either side of the pass through which Jonathan tried to

---

[a] they answered...Gilgal: *or* they were summoned to follow Saul to Gilgal.
[b] but Saul...in alarm: *or* but Saul was still at Gilgal, and all the army joined him there.   [c] one-third...the goads: *prob. rdg.; Heb. obscure.*

make his way over to the Philistine post stood two sharp columns of rock, called Bozez[a] and Seneh;[b] 5 one of them was on the north towards Michmash, and the other on 6 the south towards Geba. Jonathan said to his armour-bearer, 'Now we will visit the post of those uncircumcised rascals. Perhaps the LORD will take a hand in it, and if he will, nothing can stop him. He can bring us safe through, 7 whether we are few or many.' The young man answered, 'Do what you will, go forward; I am with 8 you whatever you do.' 'Good!' said Jonathan, 'we will cross over and 9 let them see us. If they say, "Stay where you are till we come to you", then we will stay where we are and 10 not go up to them. But if they say, "Come up to us", we will go up; this will be the sign that the LORD 11 has put them into our power.' So they showed themselves to the Philistines, and the Philistines said, 'Look! Hebrews coming out of the holes where they have been hiding!' 12 And they called across to Jonathan and the young man, 'Come up to us; we have something to show you.' Jonathan said to the young man, 'Come on, the LORD has put them into the power of Israel.' 13 Jonathan climbed up on hands and feet, and the young man followed him. The Philistines fell in front of Jonathan, and the young man, coming behind him, dispatched 14 them. In that first attack Jonathan and his armour-bearer killed about twenty of them, like men cutting a furrow across a half-acre field. 15 Terror spread through the army in the field and through the whole people; the men at the post and the raiding parties were terrified; the very earth quaked, and there was panic.

16 Saul's men on the watch in Gibeah of Benjamin saw the mob of

Philistines surging to and fro in confusion; so he ordered the 17 people to call the roll and find out who was missing; and they called the roll and found that Jonathan and his armour-bearer were absent. Saul said to Ahijah, 'Bring forward 18 the ephod', for it was he who carried the ephod at that time before Israel. But while Saul was still 19 speaking, the confusion in the Philistine camp was increasing more and more, and he said to the priest, 'Hold your hand.' Then Saul and 20 all his men with shouting made for the battlefield, where they found the enemy fighting one another in complete disorder. The Hebrews 21 who up to now had been under the Philistines, and had been with them in camp, changed sides and joined the Israelites under Saul and Jonathan. All the Israelites in hiding in 22 the hill-country of Ephraim heard that the Philistines were in flight, and they also joined in and set off in hot pursuit. The LORD delivered 23 Israel that day, and the fighting passed on beyond Beth-aven.

Now the Israelites on that day 24 had been driven to exhaustion. Saul had adjured the people in these words: 'A curse be on the man who eats any food before nightfall until I have taken vengeance on my enemies.' So no one ate any food. Now there was honey- 25 comb[c] in the country-side; but 26 when his men came upon it, dripping with honey though it was, not one of them put his hand to his mouth for fear of the oath. But 27 Jonathan had not heard his father lay this solemn prohibition on the people, and he stretched out the stick that was in his hand, dipped the end of it in the honeycomb, put it to his mouth and was refreshed. One of the people said to him, 28 'Your father solemnly forbade this; he said, "A curse on the man who

[a] *That is* Shining. [b] *That is* Bramble-bush.
[c] Now...honeycomb: *prob. rdg.*; *Heb.* All the land went into the forest, and there was honey.

eats food today!'" Now the men
29 were faint with hunger. Jonathan said, 'My father has done the people nothing but harm; see how I am refreshed by this mere taste of
30 honey. How much better if the people had eaten today whatever they took from their enemies by way of spoil! Then there would indeed have been a great slaughter of Philistines.'

31 They defeated the Philistines that day, and pursued them from Michmash to Aijalon. But the peo-
32 ple were so faint with hunger that they turned to plunder and seized sheep, cattle, and bullocks; they slaughtered them on the bare ground, and ate the meat with the
33 blood in it. Someone told Saul that the people were sinning against the LORD by eating their meat with the blood in it. 'This is treason!' cried Saul. 'Roll a great stone here at
34 once.' He then said, 'Go about among the people and tell them to bring their oxen and sheep, and let each man slaughter his here and eat it; and so they will not sin against the LORD by eating meat with the blood in it.' So as night fell each man came, driving his own ox, and slaughtered it there.
35 Thus Saul came to build an altar to the LORD, and this was the first altar to the LORD that Saul built.

36 Saul said, 'Let us go down and make a night attack on the Philistines and harry them till daylight; we will not spare a man of them.' The people answered, 'Do what you think best', but the priest
37 said, 'Let us first consult God.' So Saul inquired of God, 'Shall I pursue the Philistines? Wilt thou put them into Israel's power?'; but this
38 time he received no answer. So he said, 'Let all the leaders of the people come forward and let us find out where the sin lies this day.
39 As the LORD lives, the deliverer of Israel, even if it lies in my son Jonathan, he shall die.' Not a soul

answered him. Then he said to the 40
Israelites, 'All of you stand on one side, and I and my son Jonathan will stand on the other.' The people answered, 'Do what you think best.' Saul said to the LORD the 41
God of Israel, 'Why hast thou not answered thy servant today? If this guilt lie in me or in my son Jonathan, O LORD God of Israel, let the lot be Urim; if it lie in thy people Israel, let it be Thummim.' Jonathan and Saul were taken, and the people were cleared. Then Saul said, 'Cast lots 42
between me and my son Jonathan'; and Jonathan was taken. Saul said to Jonathan, 'Tell me 43
what you have done.' Jonathan told him, 'True, I did taste a little honey on the tip of my stick. Here I am; I am ready to die.' Then Saul 44
swore a great oath that Jonathan should die. But the people said to 45
Saul, 'Shall Jonathan die, Jonathan who has won this great victory in Israel? God forbid! As the LORD lives, not a hair of his head shall fall to the ground, for he has been at work with God today.' So the people ransomed Jonathan and he did not die. Saul broke off the 46
pursuit of the Philistines because they had made their way home.

When Saul had made his throne 47
secure in Israel, he fought against his enemies on every side, the Moabites, the Ammonites, the Edomites, the king of Zobah, and the Philistines; and wherever he turned he was successful.[a] He dis- 48
played his strength by defeating the Amalekites and freeing Israel from hostile raids.

Saul's sons were: Jonathan, Ish- 49
yo and Malchishua. These were the names of his two daughters: Merab the elder and Michal the younger. His wife was Ahinoam daughter of 50
Ahimaaz, and his commander-in-chief was Abner son of his uncle Ner; Kish, Saul's father, and Ner, 51
Abner's father, were sons[b] of Abiel.

[a] Or he found ample provision.

[b] Prob. rdg.; Heb. son.

52 There was bitter warfare with the Philistines throughout Saul's lifetime; any strong man and any brave man that he found he took into his own service.

15 Samuel said to Saul, 'The LORD sent me to anoint you king over his people Israel. Now listen to the 2 voice of the LORD. This is the very word of the LORD of Hosts: "I am resolved to punish the Amalekites for what they did to Israel, how they attacked them on their way 3 up from Egypt." Go now and fall upon the Amalekites and destroy them, and put their property under ban. Spare no one; put them all to death, men and women, children and babes in arms, herds and flocks, 4 camels and asses.' Thereupon Saul called out the levy and mustered them in Telaim. There were two hundred thousand foot-soldiers and another ten thousand from 5 Judah.ᵃ He came to the Amalekite city and halted for a time in the 6 gorge. Meanwhile he sent word to the Kenites to leave the Amalekites and come down, 'or', he said, 'I shall destroy you as well as them; but you were friendly to Israel when they came up from Egypt.' So the Kenites left the Amalekites. 7 Then Saul cut the Amalekites to pieces, all the way from Havilah to Shur on the borders of Egypt. 8 Agag the king of the Amalekites he took alive, but he destroyed all the people, putting them to the sword. 9 Saul and his army spared Agag and the best of the sheep and cattle, the fat beasts and the lambs and everything worth keeping; they were unwilling to destroy them, but anything that was useless and of no value they destroyed.

10 Then the word of the LORD came 11 to Samuel: 'I repent of having made Saul king, for he has turned his back on me and has not obeyed my commands.' Samuel was angry; all night he cried aloud to the LORD.

Early next morning he went to 12 meet Saul, but was told that he had gone to Carmel; Saul had set up a monument for himself there, and had then turned and gone down to Gilgal. There Samuel found him, 13 and Saul greeted him with the words, 'The LORD's blessing upon you! I have obeyed the LORD's commands.' But Samuel said, 14 'What then is this bleating of sheep in my ears? Why do I hear the lowing of cattle?' Saul answered, 15 'The people have taken them from the Amalekites. These are what they spared, the best of the sheep and cattle, to sacrifice to the LORD your God. The rest we completely destroyed.' Samuel said to Saul, 16 'Let be, and I will tell you what the LORD said to me last night.' 'Tell me', said Saul. So Samuel 17 went on, 'Time was when you thought little of yourself, but now you are head of the tribes of Israel, and the LORD has anointed you king over Israel. The LORD sent 18 you with strict instructions to destroy that wicked nation, the Amalekites; you were to fight against them until you had wiped them out. Why then did you not obey 19 the LORD? Why did you pounce upon the spoil and do what was wrong in the eyes of the LORD?' Saul answered Samuel, 'But I did 20 obey the LORD; I went where the LORD sent me, and I have brought back Agag king of the Amalekites. The rest of them I destroyed. Out 21 of the spoil the people took sheep and oxen, the choicest of the animals laid under ban, to sacrifice to the LORD your God at Gilgal.' Samuel then said: 22

Does the LORD desire offerings and
   sacrifices
as he desires obedience?
Obedience is better than sacrifice,
and to listen to him than the fat of
   rams.

ᵃ *Prob. rdg.; Heb.* ten thousand with the men of Judah.

23 Defiance of him is sinful as witchcraft,
yielding to men*a* as evil as*b* idolatry.*c*
Because you have rejected the
word of the LORD,
the LORD has rejected you as
king.

24   Saul said to Samuel, 'I have sinned. I have ignored the LORD's
command and your orders: I was
afraid of the people and deferred
25 to them. But now forgive my sin,
I implore you, and come back with
me, and I will make my submission
26 before the LORD.' Samuel answered, 'I will not come back with you;
you have rejected the word of the
LORD and therefore the LORD has
rejected you as king over Israel.'
27 He turned to go, but Saul caught
the edge of his cloak and it tore.
28 And Samuel said to him, 'The LORD
has torn the kingdom of Israel from
your hand today and will give it to
another, a better man than you.
29 God who is the Splendour of Israel
does not deceive or change his
mind; he is not a man that he
30 should change his mind.' Saul said,
'I have sinned; but honour me this
once before the elders of my people
and before Israel and come back
with me, and I will make my sub-
31 mission to the LORD your God.' So
Samuel went back with Saul, and
Saul made his submission to the
32 LORD. Then Samuel said, 'Bring
Agag king of the Amalekites.' So
Agag came to him with faltering
step and said, 'Surely the bitter-
33 ness of death has passed.' Samuel
said, 'Your sword has made women
childless, and your mother of all
women shall be childless too.' Then
Samuel hewed Agag in pieces before
the LORD at Gilgal.

34   Saul went to his own home at
Gibeah, and Samuel went to
35 Ramah; and he never saw Saul
again to his dying day, but he

mourned for him, because the LORD
had repented of having made him
king over Israel.

Saul and David

THE LORD said to Samuel, 'How 16
long will you mourn for Saul
because I have rejected him as
king over Israel? Fill your horn
with oil and take it with you; I am
sending you to Jesse of Bethlehem; for I have chosen myself a
king among his sons.' Samuel an- 2
swered, 'How can I go? Saul will
hear of it and kill me.' 'Take a
heifer with you,' said the LORD;
'say you have come to offer a sacrifice to the LORD, and invite Jesse 3
to the sacrifice; then I will let you
know what you must do. You shall
anoint for me the man whom I
show you.' Samuel did as the LORD 4
had told him, and went to Bethlehem. The elders of the city came
in haste to meet him, saying, 'Why
have you come? Is all well?' 'All is 5
well,' said Samuel; 'I have come to
sacrifice to the LORD. Hallow yourselves and come with me to the
sacrifice.' He himself hallowed
Jesse and his sons and invited them
to the sacrifice also. They came, and 6
when Samuel saw Eliab he thought,
'Here, before the LORD, is his anointed king.' But the LORD said to 7
him, 'Take no account of it if he
is handsome and tall; I reject him.
The LORD does not see as man sees;
men judge by appearances but the
LORD judges by the heart.' Then 8
Jesse called Abinadab and made
him pass before Samuel, but he
said, 'No, the LORD has not chosen
this one.' Then he presented Sham- 9
mah, and Samuel said, 'Nor has
the LORD chosen him.' Seven of 10
his sons Jesse presented to Samuel,
but he said, 'The LORD has not
chosen any of these.' Then Samuel 11
asked, 'Are these all?' Jesse answered, 'There is still the youngest,

---

a yielding to men: *or* arrogance *or* obstinacy.
b as evil as: *prob. rdg.*; *Heb.* evil and . . .   *c* Or household gods; *Heb.* teraphim.

but he is looking after the sheep.'
Samuel said to Jesse, 'Send and
fetch him; we will not sit down
12 until he comes.' So he sent and
fetched him. He was handsome,
with ruddy cheeks and bright eyes.[a]
The LORD said, 'Rise and anoint
13 him: this is the man.' Samuel took
the horn of oil and anointed him
in the presence of his brothers.
Then the spirit of the LORD came
upon David and was with him from
that day onwards. And Samuel set
out on his way back to Ramah.

14   The spirit of the LORD had forsaken Saul, and at times an evil
spirit from the LORD would seize
15 him suddenly. His servants said to
him, 'You see, sir, how an evil
16 spirit from God seizes you; why do
you not command your servants
here to go and find some man who
can play the harp? – then, when
an evil spirit from God comes on
you, he can play and you will re-
17 cover.' Saul said to his servants,
'Find me a man who can play well
18 and bring him to me.' One of his
attendants said, 'I have seen a son
of Jesse of Bethlehem who can
play; he is a brave man and a good
fighter, wise in speech and handsome, and the LORD is with him.'
19 Saul therefore sent messengers to
Jesse and asked him to send him
his son David, who was with the
20 sheep. Jesse took a homer of bread,
a skin of wine, and a kid, and sent
them to Saul by his son David.
21 David came to Saul and entered
his service; and Saul loved him
dearly, and he became his armour-
22 bearer. So Saul sent word to Jesse:
'Let David stay in my service, for
23 I am pleased with him.' And whenever a spirit from God came upon
Saul, David would take his harp
and play on it, so that Saul found relief; he recovered and the evil spirit
left him alone.

17   The Philistines collected their
forces for war and massed at Socoh

in Judah; they camped between
Socoh and Azekah at Ephes-dammim. Saul and the Israelites also 2
massed, and camped in the Vale
of Elah. They drew up their lines
facing the Philistines, the Phili- 3
stines occupying a position on one
hill and the Israelites on another,
with a valley between them. A 4
champion came out from the Philistine camp, a man named Goliath,
from Gath; he was over nine feet in
height. He had a bronze helmet on 5
his head, and he wore plate-armour
of bronze, weighing five thousand
shekels. On his legs were bronze 6
greaves, and one of his weapons
was a dagger of bronze. The shaft 7
of his spear was like a weaver's
beam, and its head, which was of
iron, weighed six hundred shekels;
and his shield-bearer marched
ahead of him. The champion stood 8
and shouted to the ranks of Israel,
'Why do you come out to do battle,
you slaves of Saul? I am the Philistine champion; choose your man
to meet me. If he can kill me in 9
fair fight, we will become your
slaves; but if I prove too strong
for him and kill him, you shall be
our slaves and serve us. Here and 10
now I defy the ranks of Israel. Give
me a man,' said the Philistine, 'and
we will fight it out.' When Saul and 11
the Israelites heard what the Philistine said, they were shaken and
dismayed.

David was the son of an Ephra- 12
thite[b] called Jesse, who had eight
sons. By Saul's time he had become
a feeble old man, and his three 13
eldest sons had followed Saul to
the war. The eldest was called
Eliab, the next Abinadab, and
the third Shammah; David was 14
the youngest. The three eldest
followed Saul, while David used 15
to go to Saul's camp and back
to Bethlehem to mind his father's
flocks.

Morning and evening for forty 16

---

[a] *and bright eyes: prob. rdg.; Heb. obscure.*
[b] *Prob. rdg.; Heb. adds Is this the man from Bethlehem in Judah?*

17 days the Philistine came forward and took up his position. Then one day Jesse said to his son David, 'Take your brothers an ephah of this parched grain and these ten loaves of bread, and run with them

18 to the camp. These ten cream-cheeses are for you to take to the commanding officer. See if your brothers are well and bring back

19 some token from them.' Saul and the brothers and all the Israelites were in the Vale of Elah, fighting

20 the Philistines. Early next morning David left someone in charge of the sheep, set out on his errand and went as Jesse had told him. He reached the lines just as the army was going out to take up position

21 and was raising the war-cry. The Israelites and the Philistines drew up their ranks opposite each other.

22 David left his things in charge of the quartermaster, ran to the line and went up to his brothers to

23 greet them. While he was talking to them the Philistine champion, Goliath, came out from the Philistine ranks and issued his challenge in the same words as before; and

24 David heard him. When the Israelites saw the man they ran from him

25 in fear. 'Look at this man who comes out day after day to defy Israel', they said. 'The king is to give a rich reward to the man who kills him; he will give him his daughter in marriage too and will exempt his family from service due

26 in Israel.' Then David turned to his neighbours and said, 'What is to be done for the man who kills this Philistine and wipes out our disgrace? And who is he, an uncircumcised Philistine, to defy the

27 army of the living God?' The people told him how the matter stood and what was to be done for the man

28 who killed him. His elder brother Eliab overheard David talking with the men and grew angry. 'What are you doing here?' he asked. 'And who have you left to look after those few sheep in the

wilderness? I know you, you impudent young rascal; you have only come to see the fighting.' David 29 answered, 'What have I done now? I only asked a question.' And he 30 turned away from him to someone else and repeated his question, but everybody gave him the same answer.

What David had said was over- 31 heard and reported to Saul, who sent for him. David said to him, 32 'Do not lose heart, sir. I will go and fight this Philistine.' Saul answer- 33 ed, 'You cannot go and fight with this Philistine; you are only a lad, and he has been a fighting man all his life.' David said to Saul, 'Sir, I 34 am my father's shepherd; when a lion or bear comes and carries off a sheep from the flock, I go after it 35 and attack it and rescue the victim from its jaws. Then if it turns on me, I seize it by the beard and batter it to death. Lions I have 36 killed and bears, and this uncircumcised Philistine will fare no better than they; he has defied the army of the living God. The LORD 37 who saved me from the lion and the bear will save me from this Philistine.' 'Go then,' said Saul; 'and the LORD will be with you.' He put 38 his own tunic on David, placed a bronze helmet on his head and gave him a coat of mail to wear; he then 39 fastened his sword on David over his tunic. But David hesitated, because he had not tried them, and said to Saul, 'I cannot go with these, because I have not tried them.' So he took them off. Then 40 he picked up his stick, chose five smooth stones from the brook and put them in a shepherd's bag which served as his pouch. He walked out to meet the Philistine with his sling in his hand.

The Philistine came on towards 41 David, with his shield-bearer marching ahead; and he looked David 42 up and down and had nothing but contempt for this handsome lad with his ruddy cheeks and bright

43 eyes.*a* He said to David, 'Am I a dog that you come out against me with sticks?' And he swore at him
44 in the name of his god. 'Come on,' he said, 'and I will give your flesh
45 to the birds and the beasts.' David answered, 'You have come against me with sword and spear and dagger, but I have come against you in the name of the LORD of Hosts, the God of the army of Israel which
46 you have defied. The LORD will put you into my power this day; I will kill you and cut your head off and leave your carcass and the carcasses of the Philistines to the birds and the wild beasts; all the world shall know that there is a
47 God in Israel. All those who are gathered here shall see that the LORD saves neither by sword nor spear; the battle is the LORD's, and he will put you all into our power.'
48 When the Philistine began moving towards him again, David ran
49 quickly to engage him. He put his hand into his bag, took out a stone, slung it, and struck the Philistine on the forehead. The stone sank into his forehead, and he fell flat
50 on his face on the ground. So David proved the victor with his sling and stone; he struck Goliath down and gave him a mortal wound, though
51 he had no sword. Then he ran to the Philistine and stood over him, and grasping his sword, he drew it out of the scabbard, dispatched him and cut off his head. The Philistines, when they saw that their hero was dead, turned and ran.
52 The men of Israel and Judah at once raised the war-cry and hotly pursued them all the way to Gath and even to the gates of Ekron. The road that runs to Shaaraim, Gath, and Ekron was strewn with their
53 dead. On their return from the pursuit of the Philistines, the Israelites plundered their camp.
54 David took Goliath's head and carried it to Jerusalem, leaving his weapons in his tent.

Saul had said to Abner his com- 55 mander-in-chief, when he saw David going out against the Philistine, 'That boy there, Abner, whose son is he?' 'By your life, your majesty,' said Abner, 'I do not know.' The king said to Abner, 56 'Go and find out whose son the lad is.' When David came back 57 after killing the Philistine, Abner took him and presented him to Saul with the Philistine's head still in his hand. Saul asked him, 'Whose 58 son are you, young man?', and David answered, 'I am the son of your servant Jesse of Bethlehem.'

That same day, when Saul had 18 1–2 finished talking with David, he kept him and would not let him return any more to his father's house, for he saw that Jonathan had given his heart to David and had grown to love him as himself. So Jonathan and David made a 3 solemn compact because each loved the other as dearly as himself. And 4 Jonathan stripped off the cloak he was wearing and his tunic, and gave them to David, together with his sword, his bow, and his belt. David succeeded so well in every 5 venture on which Saul sent him that he was given a command in the army, and his promotion pleased the ordinary people, and even pleased Saul's officers.

At the home-coming of the army 6 when David returned from the slaughter of the Philistines, the women came out from all the cities of Israel to look on, and the dancers came out to meet King Saul with tambourines, singing, and dancing. The women as they made merry 7 sang to one another:

Saul made havoc among thousands but David among tens of thousands.

Saul was furious, and the words 8 rankled. He said, 'They have given David tens of thousands and me only thousands; what more can

---

a handsome...bright eyes: *prob. rdg.*; *Heb. obscure.*

9 they do but make him king?' From that day forward Saul kept a jealous eye on David.

10 Next day an evil spirit from God seized upon Saul; he fell into a frenzy^a in the house, and David played the harp to him as he had before. Saul had his spear in his 11 hand, and he hurled it at David, meaning to pin him to the wall; but twice David swerved aside. 12 After this Saul was afraid of David, because he saw that the LORD had forsaken him and was with David. 13 He therefore removed David from his household and appointed him to the command of a thousand men. David led his men into action, 14 and succeeded in everything that he undertook, because the LORD 15 was with him. When Saul saw how successful he was, he was more 16 afraid of him than ever; all Israel and Judah loved him because he took the field at their head.

17 Saul said to David, 'Here is my elder daughter Merab; I will give her to you in marriage, but in return you must serve me valiantly and fight the LORD's battles.' For Saul meant David to meet his end at the hands of the Philistines and 18 not himself. David answered Saul, 'Who am I and what are my father's people, my kinsfolk, in Israel, that I should become the king's son-in- 19 law?' However, when the time came for Saul's daughter Merab to be married to David, she had already been given to Adriel of 20 Meholah. But Michal, Saul's other daughter, fell in love with David, and when Saul was told of this, he 21 saw that it suited his plans. He said to himself, 'I will give her to him; let her be the bait that lures him to his death at the hands of the Philistines.' So Saul proposed a second time to make David his 22 son-in-law, and ordered his courtiers to say to David privately, 'The king is well disposed to you and you are dear to us all; now is the

time for you to marry into the king's family.' When Saul's people 23 spoke in this way to David, he said to them, 'Do you think that marrying the king's daughter is a matter of so little consequence that a poor man of no consequence, like myself, can do it?' Saul's courtiers reported 24 what David had said, and he re- 25 plied, 'Tell David this: all the king wants as the bride-price is the foreskins of a hundred Philistines, by way of vengeance on his enemies.' Saul was counting on David's death at the hands of the Philistines. The courtiers told David 26 what Saul had said, and marriage with the king's daughter on these terms pleased him well. Before the appointed time, David went out 27 with his men and slew two hundred Philistines; he brought their foreskins and counted them out to the king in order to be accepted as his son-in-law. So Saul married his daughter Michal to David. He saw 28 clearly that the LORD was with David, and knew that Michal his daughter had fallen in love with him; and so he grew more and more 29 afraid of David and was his enemy for the rest of his life.

The Philistine officers used to 30 come out to offer single combat; and whenever they did, David had more success against them than all the rest of Saul's men, and he won a great name for himself.

SAUL spoke to Jonathan his son 19 and all his household about killing David. But Jonathan was devoted to David and told him that his 2 father Saul was looking for an opportunity to kill him. 'Be on your guard tomorrow morning,' he said; 'conceal yourself, and remain in hiding. Then I will come out and 3 join my father in the open country where you are and speak to him about you, and if I discover anything I will tell you.' Jonathan 4 spoke up for David to his father

^a Or fell into prophetic rapture.

Saul and said to him, 'Sir, do not wrong your servant David; he has not wronged you; his conduct towards you has been beyond re-
5 proach. Did he not take his life in his hands when he killed the Philistine, and the LORD won a great victory for Israel? You saw it, you shared in the rejoicing; why should you wrong an innocent man and put David to death without cause?'
6 Saul listened to Jonathan and swore solemnly by the LORD that David should not be put to death.
7 So Jonathan called David and told him all this; then he brought him to Saul, and he was in attendance on the king as before.
8 War broke out again, and David attacked the Philistines and dealt them such a blow that they ran before him.
9 An evil spirit from the LORD came upon Saul as he was sitting in the house with his spear in his hand; and David was playing the
10 harp. Saul tried to pin David to the wall with the spear, but he avoided the king's thrust so that Saul drove the spear into the wall. David escaped and got safely away. That
11 night Saul sent servants to keep watch on David's house, intending to kill him in the morning, but David's wife Michal warned him to get away that night, 'or tomorrow', she said, 'you will be a dead
12 man.' She let David down through a window and he slipped away and
13 escaped. Michal took their household gods and put them on the bed; at its head she laid a goat's-hair rug and covered it all with a cloak.
14 When the men arrived to arrest David she told them he was ill.
15 Saul sent them back to see David for themselves. 'Bring him to me, bed and all,' he said, 'and I will
16 kill him.' When they came, there were the household gods on the bed and the goat's-hair rug at its
17 head. Then Saul said to Michal, 'Why have you played this trick on me and let my enemy get safe

away?' And Michal answered, 'He said to me, "Help me to escape or I will kill you."'

Meanwhile David made good his 18 escape and came to Samuel at Ramah, and told him how Saul had treated him. Then he and Samuel went to Naioth and stayed there. Saul was told that David 19 was there, and he sent a party of 20 men to seize him. When they saw the company of prophets in rapture, with Samuel standing at their head, the spirit of God came upon them and they fell into prophetic rapture. When this was reported to 21 Saul he sent another party. These also fell into a rapture, and when he sent more men a third time, they did the same. Saul him- 22 self then set out for Ramah and came to the great cistern in Secu. He asked where Samuel and David were and was told that they were at Naioth in Ramah. On his way 23 there the spirit of God came upon him too and he went on, in a rapture as he went, till he came to Naioth in Ramah. There he too stripped 24 off his clothes and like the rest fell into a rapture before Samuel and lay down naked all that day and all that night. That is why men say, 'Is Saul also among the prophets?'

Then David made his escape 20 from Naioth in Ramah and came to Jonathan. 'What have I done?' he asked. 'What is my offence? What does your father think I have done wrong, that he seeks my life?' Jonathan answered him, 'God for- 2 bid! There is no thought of putting you to death. I am sure my father will not do anything whatever without telling me. Why should my father hide such a thing from me? I cannot believe it!' David 3 said, 'I am ready to swear to it: your father has said to himself, "Jonathan must not know this or he will resent it", because he knows that you have a high regard for me. As the LORD lives, your life

upon it, there is only a step be-
4 tween me and death.' Jonathan
said to David, 'What do you want
5 me to do for you?' David answered,
'It is new moon tomorrow, and I
ought to dine with the king. Let
me go and lie hidden in the fields
6 until the third evening. If your
father happens to miss me, then
say, "David asked me for leave
to pay a rapid visit to his home in
Bethlehem, for it is the annual
sacrifice there for the whole fami-
7 ly." If he says, "Well and good",
that will be a good sign for me;
but if he flies into a rage, you will
know that he is set on doing me
8 wrong. My lord, keep faith with
me; for you and I have entered into
a solemn compact before the LORD.
Kill me yourself if I am guilty. Why
let me fall into your father's hands?'
9 'God forbid!' cried Jonathan. 'If I
find my father set on doing you
10 wrong I will tell you.' David answered Jonathan, 'How will you
let me know if he answers harshly?'
11 Jonathan said, 'Come with me into
the fields.' So they went together
12 into the fields, and Jonathan said
to David, 'I promise you, David,
in the sight of the LORD the God
of Israel, this time tomorrow I will
sound my father for the third time
and, if he is well disposed to you,
13 I will send and let you know. If my
father means mischief, the LORD
do the same to me and more, if I
do not let you know and get you
safely away. The LORD be with
you as he has been with my father!
14 I know that as long as I live you
will show me faithful friendship, as
the LORD requires; and if I should
15 die, you will continue loyal to my
family for ever. When the LORD
rids the earth of all David's ene-
16 mies, may the LORD call him to
account if he and his house are no
17 longer my friends.' Jonathan pledged himself afresh to David because
of his love for him, for he loved
18 him as himself. Then he said to
him, 'Tomorrow is the new moon,

and you will be missed when your
place is empty. So go down at night- 19
fall for the third time to the place
where you hid on the evening of the
feast and stay by the mound there.
Then I will shoot three arrows to- 20
wards it, as though I were aiming
at a mark. Then I will send my boy 21
to find the arrows. If I say to him,
"Look, the arrows are on this side
of you, pick them up", then you
can come out of hiding. You will
be quite safe, I swear it; for there
will be nothing amiss. But if I say 22
to the lad, "Look, the arrows are
on the other side of you, further
on", then the LORD has said that
you must go; the LORD stand wit- 23
ness between us for ever to the
pledges we have exchanged.'
So David hid in the fields. The 24
new moon came, the dinner was
prepared, and the king sat down
to eat. Saul took his customary 25
seat by the wall, and Abner sat
beside him; Jonathan too was present, but David's place was empty.
That day Saul said nothing, for he 26
thought that David was absent by
some chance, perhaps because he
was ritually unclean. But on the 27
second day, the day after the new
moon, David's place was still empty, and Saul said to his son Jonathan, 'Why has not the son of Jesse
come to the feast, either yesterday
or today?' Jonathan answered 28
Saul, 'David asked permission to
go to Bethlehem. He asked my 29
leave and said, "Our family is holding a sacrifice in the town and my
brother himself has ordered me to
be there. Now, if you have any
regard for me, let me slip away to
see my brothers." That is why he
has not come to dine with the king.'
Saul was angry with Jonathan, 30
'You son of a crooked and unfaithful mother! You have made friends
with the son of Jesse only to bring
shame on yourself and dishonour
on your mother; I see how it will
be. As long as Jesse's son remains 31
alive on earth, neither you nor your

crown will be safe. Send at once and fetch him; he deserves to die.'

32 Jonathan answered his father, 'Deserves to die! Why? What has he

33 done?' At that, Saul picked up his spear and threatened to kill him; and he knew that his father was

34 bent on David's death. Jonathan left the table in a rage and ate nothing on the second day of the festival; for he was indignant on David's behalf because his father had humiliated him.

35 Next morning, Jonathan went out into the fields to meet David at the appointed time, taking a

36 young boy with him. He said to the boy, 'Run and find the arrows; I am going to shoot.' The boy ran on, and he shot the arrows over his

37 head. When the boy reached the place where Jonathan's arrows had fallen, Jonathan called out after him, 'Look, the arrows are beyond

38 you. Hurry! No time to lose! Make haste!' The boy gathered up the arrows and brought them to his

39 master; but only Jonathan and David knew what this meant; the

40 boy knew nothing. Jonathan handed his weapons to the boy and told him to take them back to the city.

41 When the boy had gone, David got up from behind the mound and bowed humbly three times. Then they kissed one another and shed tears together, until David's grief was even greater than Jonathan's.

42 Jonathan said to David, 'Go in safety; we have pledged each other in the name of the LORD who is witness for ever between you and me and between your descendants and mine.'

David went off at once, while Jonathan returned to the city.

21 David made his way to the priest Ahimelech at Nob, who hurried out to meet him and said, 'Why have you come alone and no one

2 with you?' David answered Ahimelech, 'I am under orders from the king: I was to let no one know about the mission on which he was

sending me or what these orders were. When I took leave of my men I told them to meet me in such and such a place. Now, what have you

3 got by you? Let me have five loaves, or as many as you can find.' The

4 priest answered David, 'I have no ordinary bread available. There is only the sacred bread; but have the young men kept themselves from

women?' David answered the

5 priest, 'Women have been denied us hitherto, when I have been on campaign, even an ordinary campaign, and the young men's bodies have remained holy; and how much more will they be holy today?' So,

6 as there was no other bread there, the priest gave him the sacred bread, the Bread of the Presence, which had just been taken from the presence of the LORD to be replaced by freshly baked bread on the day that the old was removed. One of Saul's servants happened to

7 be there that day, detained before the LORD; his name was Doeg the Edomite, and he was the strongest of all Saul's herdsmen. David said

8 to Ahimelech, 'Have you a spear or sword here at hand? I have no sword or other weapon with me, because the king's business was urgent.' The priest answered, 'There

9 is the sword of Goliath the Philistine whom you slew in the Vale of Elah; it is wrapped up in a cloak behind the ephod. If you wish to take that, take it; there is no other weapon here.' David said, 'There is no sword like it; give it to me.'

That day, David went on his

10 way, eluding Saul, and came to Achish king of Gath. The ser-

11 vants of Achish said to him, 'Surely this is David, the king of his country, the man of whom they sang as they danced:

Saul made havoc among thousands
but David among tens of thousands.'

12 These words were not lost on David, and he became very much afraid of

13 Achish king of Gath. So he altered his behaviour in public and acted like a lunatic in front of them all, scrabbling on the double doors of the city gate and dribbling down

14 his beard. Achish said to his servants, 'The man is mad! Why bring

15 him to me? Am I short of madmen that you bring this one to plague me? Must I have this fellow in my house?'

22 DAVID made his escape and went from there to the cave of Adullam. When his brothers and all his family heard that he was there, they

2 joined him. Men in any kind of distress or in debt or with a grievance gathered round him, about four hundred in number, and he

3 became their chief. From there David went to Mizpeh in Moab and said to the king of Moab, 'Let my father and mother come and take shelter with you until I know what

4 God will do for me.' So he left them at the court of the king of Moab, and they stayed there as long as David was in his stronghold.

5 The prophet Gad said to David, 'You must not stay in your stronghold; go at once into Judah.' So David went as far as the forest of

6 Hareth. News that David and his men had been seen reached Saul while he was in Gibeah, sitting under the tamarisk-tree on the hilltop with his spear in his hand and all his retainers standing about

7 him. He said to them, 'Listen to me, you Benjamites: do you expect the son of Jesse to give you all fields and vineyards, or make you all officers over units of a thou-

8 sand and a hundred? Is that why you have all conspired against me? Not one of you told me when my son made a compact with the son of Jesse; none of you spared a thought for me or told me that my son had set my own servant against me, who is lying in wait for me now.'

9 Then Doeg the Edomite, who was standing with the servants of Saul, spoke: 'I saw the son of Jesse coming to Nob, to Ahimelech son

10 of Ahitub. Ahimelech consulted the LORD on his behalf, then gave him food and handed over to him the sword of Goliath the Philistine.'

11 The king sent for Ahimelech the priest and his family, who were priests at Nob, and they all came

12 into his presence. Saul said, 'Now listen, you son of Ahitub', and the man answered, 'Yes, my lord?'

13 Then Saul said to him, 'Why have you and the son of Jesse plotted against me? You gave him food and the sword too, and consulted God on his behalf; and now he has risen against me and is at this

14 moment lying in wait for me.' 'And who among all your servants', answered Ahimelech, 'is like David, a man to be trusted, the king's son-in-law, appointed to your staff and holding an honourable place

15 in your household? Have I on this occasion done something profane in consulting God on his behalf? God forbid! I trust that my lord the king will not accuse me or my family; for I know nothing what-

16 ever about it.' But the king said, 'Ahimelech, you must die, you and

17 all your family.' He then turned to the bodyguard attending him and said, 'Go and kill the priests of the LORD; for they are in league with David, and, though they knew that he was a fugitive, they did not tell me.' The king's men, however, were unwilling to raise a hand against the priests of the LORD.

18 The king therefore said to Doeg the Edomite, 'You, Doeg, go and fall upon the priests'; so Doeg went and fell upon the priests, killing that day with his own hand eighty-five men who could carry the ephod.

19 He put to the sword every living thing in Nob, the city of priests: men and women, children and babes in arms, oxen, asses, and

20 sheep. One son of Ahimelech named

Abiathar made his escape and join-
21 ed David. He told David how Saul
had killed the priests of the LORD.
22 Then David said to him, 'When
Doeg the Edomite was there that
day, I knew that he would inform
Saul. I have gambled with the lives
23 of all your father's family. Stay
here with me, have no fear; he who
seeks your life seeks mine, and you
will be safe with me.'

23 The Philistines were fighting a-
gainst Keilah and plundering the
threshing-floors; and when David
2 heard this, he consulted the LORD
and asked whether he should go
and attack the Philistines. The
LORD answered, 'Go, attack them,
3 and relieve Keilah.' But David's
men said to him, 'As we are now,
we have enough to fear from Judah.
How much worse if we challenge
the Philistine forces at Keilah!'
4 David consulted the LORD once
again and the LORD answered him,
'Go to Keilah; I will give the Phili-
5 stines into your hands.' So David
and his men went to Keilah and
fought the Philistines; they carried
off their cattle, inflicted a heavy
defeat on them and relieved the
6 inhabitants. Abiathar son of Ahimelech made good his escape and
joined David at Keilah, bringing
7 the ephod with him. Saul was told
that David had entered Keilah, and
he said, 'God has put him into my
hands; for he has walked into a
trap by entering a walled town
8 with gates and bars.' He called out
the levy to march on Keilah and
9 besiege David and his men. When
David learnt how Saul planned his
undoing, he told Abiathar the priest
10 to bring the ephod, and then he
prayed, 'O LORD God of Israel, I
thy servant have heard news that
Saul intends to come to Keilah and
destroy the city because of me.
11 Will the citizens of Keilah surrender me to him? Will Saul come
as I have heard? O LORD God of
Israel, I pray thee, tell thy servant.'
The LORD answered, 'He will come.'

12 Then David asked, 'Will the citizens of Keilah surrender me and
my men to Saul?', and the LORD
answered, 'They will.' Then David
13 left Keilah at once with his men,
who numbered about six hundred,
and moved about from place to
place. When the news reached Saul
that David had escaped from
Keilah, he made no further move.

While David was living in the
14 fastnesses of the wilderness of Ziph,
in the hill-country, Saul searched
for him day after day, but God did
not put him into his power. David
15 well knew that Saul had come out
to seek his life; and while he was at
Horesh in the wilderness of Ziph,
Saul's son Jonathan came to him
16 there and gave him fresh courage
in God's name: 'Do not be afraid,'
17 he said; 'my father's hand shall not
touch you. You will become king
of Israel and I shall hold rank after
you; and my father knows it.' The
18 two of them made a solemn compact before the LORD; then David
remained in Horesh and Jonathan
went home. While Saul was at
19 Gibeah the Ziphites brought him
this news: 'David, we hear, is in
hiding among us in the fastnesses
of Horesh on the hill of Hachilah,
south of Jeshimon. Come down,
20 your majesty, come whenever you
will, and we are able to surrender
him to you.' Saul said, 'The LORD
21 has indeed blessed you; you have
saved me a world of trouble. Go
22 now and make further inquiry, and
find out exactly where he is and
who saw him there. They tell me
that he by himself is crafty enough
to outwit me. Find out which of his
23 hiding-places he is using; then come
back to me at such and such a place,
and I will go along with you. So long
as he stays in this country, I will
hunt him down, if I have to go
through all the clans of Judah one
by one.' They set out for Ziph with-
24 out delay, ahead of Saul; David
and his men were in the wilderness
of Maon in the Arabah to the south

25 of Jeshimon. Saul set off with his men to look for him; but David got wind of it and went down to a refuge in the rocks, and there he stayed in the wilderness of Maon. Hearing of this, Saul went into the 26 wilderness after him; he was on one side of the hill, David and his men on the other. While David and his men were trying desperately to get away and Saul and his followers 27 were closing in for the capture, a runner brought a message to Saul: 'Come at once! the Philistines are 28 harrying the land.' So Saul called off the pursuit and turned back to face the Philistines. This is why that place is called the Dividing Rock. 29 David went up from there and lived in the fastnesses of En-gedi.

24 When Saul returned from the pursuit of the Philistines, he learnt that David was in the wilderness 2 of En-gedi. So he took three thousand men picked from the whole of Israel and went in search of David and his men to the east of 3 the Rocks of the Wild Goats. There beside the road were some sheepfolds, and near by was a cave, at the far end of which David and his men were sitting concealed. Saul came to the cave and went in to 4–7ᵃ relieve himself. His men said to David, 'The day has come: the LORD has put your enemy into your hands, as he promised he would, and you may do what you please with him.' David said to his men, 'God forbid that I should harm my master, the LORD's anointed, or lift a finger against him; he is the LORD's anointed.' So David reproved his men severely and would not let them attack Saul. He himself got up stealthily and cut off a piece of Saul's cloak; but when he had cut it off, his conscience smote him. Saul rose, left the cave 8 and went on his way; whereupon David also came out of the cave and called after Saul, 'My lord the king!' When Saul looked round,

David prostrated himself in obeisance and said to him, 'Why do you 9 listen when they say that David is out to do you harm? Today you 10 can see for yourself that the LORD put you into my power in the cave; I had a mind to kill you, but no, I spared your life and said, "I cannot lift a finger against my master, for he is the LORD's anointed." Look, my dear lord, look at this 11 piece of your cloak in my hand. I cut it off, but I did not kill you; this will show you that I have no thought of violence or treachery against you, and that I have done you no wrong; yet you are resolved to take my life. May the LORD 12 judge between us! but though he may take vengeance on you for my sake, I will never lift my hand against you; "One wrong begets 13 another", as the old saying goes, yet I will never lift my hand against you. Who has the king of 14 Israel come out against? What are you pursuing? A dead dog, a mere flea. The LORD will be judge and 15 decide between us; let him look into my cause, he will plead for me and will acquit me.'

When David had finished speak- 16 ing, Saul said, 'Is that you, David my son?', and he wept. Then he 17 said, 'The right is on your side, not mine; you have treated me so well, I have treated you so badly. Your 18 goodness to me this day has passed all bounds: the LORD put me at your mercy but you did not kill me. Not often does a man find his 19 enemy and let him go safely on his way; so may the LORD reward you well for what you have done for me today! I know now for certain 20 that you will become king, and that the kingdom of Israel will flourish under your rule. Swear to me by 21 the LORD then that you will not exterminate my descendants and blot out my name from my father's house.' David swore an oath to 22 Saul; and Saul went back to his

ᵃ *Verses 4–7 are re-arranged thus: 4a, 6, 7a, 4b, 5, 7b.*

home, while David and his men went up to their fastness.

25 SAMUEL died, and all Israel came together to mourn for him, and he was buried in his house in Ramah. Afterwards David went down to the wilderness of Paran.

2 There was a man at Carmel in Maon, who had great influence and owned three thousand sheep and a thousand goats; and he was shear-3 ing his flocks in Carmel. His name was Nabal and his wife's name Abigail; she was a beautiful and intelligent woman, but her husband, a Calebite, was surly and 4 mean. David heard in the wilderness that Nabal was shearing his 5 flocks, and sent ten of his men, saying to them, 'Go up to Carmel, find Nabal and give him my greet-6 ings. You are to say, "All good wishes for the year ahead! Prosperity to yourself, your household, 7 and all that is yours! I hear that you are shearing. Your shepherds have been with us lately and we did not molest them; nothing of 8 theirs was missing all the time they were in Carmel. Ask your own people and they will tell you. Receive my men kindly, for this is an auspicious day with us, and give what you can to David your son 9 and your servant."' David's servants came and delivered this message to Nabal in David's name. 10 When they paused, Nabal answered, 'Who is David? Who is this son of Jesse? In these days every slave who breaks away from his master 11 sets himself up as a chief.[a] Am I to take my food and my wine and the meat I have provided for my shearers and give it to men who come from I know not where?' 12 David's men turned and made their way back to him and told 13 him all this. He said to his men, 'Buckle on your swords, all of you.' So they buckled on their swords

and followed David, four hundred of them, while two hundred stayed behind with the baggage.

One of the young men said to 14 Abigail, Nabal's wife, 'David sent messengers from the wilderness to ask our master politely for a present, and he flew out[b] at them. The 15 men have been very good to us and have not molested us, nor did we miss anything all the time we were going about with them in the open country. They were as good as a 16 wall round us, night and day, while we were minding the flocks. Think 17 carefully what you had better do, for it is certain ruin for our master and his whole family; he is such a good-for-nothing that it is no good talking to him.' So Abigail hastily 18 collected two hundred loaves and two skins of wine, five sheep ready dressed, five measures of parched grain, a hundred bunches of raisins, and two hundred cakes of dried figs, and loaded them on asses, but 19 told her husband nothing about it. Then she said to her servants, 'Go on ahead, I will follow you.' As she 20 made her way on her ass, hidden by the hill, there were David and his men coming down towards her, and she met them. David had said, 21 'It was a waste of time to protect this fellow's property in the wilderness so well that nothing of his was missing. He has repaid me evil for good.' David swore a great 22 oath: 'God do the same to me and more if I leave him a single mother's son alive by morning!'

When Abigail saw David she 23 dismounted in haste and prostrated herself before him, bowing low to 24 the ground at his feet, and said, 'Let me take the blame, my lord, but allow me, your humble servant, to speak out and let my lord give me a hearing. How can you take 25 any notice of this good-for-nothing? He is just what his name Nabal means: "Churl" is his name, and

---

[a] Or In these days there are many slaves who break away from their master.
[b] flew out: or screamed.

churlish his behaviour. I did not myself, sir, see the men you sent.

26 And now, sir, the LORD has restrained you from bloodshed and from giving vent to your anger. As the LORD lives, your life upon it, your enemies and all who want to see you ruined will be like Nabal.

27 Here is the present which I, your humble servant, have brought; give it to the young men under

28 your command. Forgive me, my lord, if I am presuming; for the LORD will establish your family for ever, because you have fought his wars. No calamity shall overtake

29 you as long as you live. If any man sets out to pursue you and take your life, the LORD your God will wrap your life up and put it with his own treasure, but the lives of your enemies he will hurl away

30 like stones from a sling. When the LORD has made good all his promises to you, and has made you

31 ruler of Israel, there will be no reason why you should stumble or your courage falter because you have shed innocent blood or given way to your anger. Then when the LORD makes all you do prosper, you will remember me, your ser-

32 vant.' David said to Abigail, 'Blessed is the LORD the God of Israel who has sent you today to meet

33 me. A blessing on your good sense, a blessing on you because you have saved me today from the guilt of bloodshed and from giving way to

34 my anger. For I swear by the life of the LORD the God of Israel who has kept me from doing you wrong: if you had not come at once to meet me, not a man of Nabal's household, not a single mother's son, would have been left alive by

35 morning.' Then David took from her what she had brought him and said, 'Go home in peace, I have listened to you and I grant your request.'

36 On her return she found Nabal holding a banquet in his house, a banquet fit for a king. He grew

merry and became very drunk, so drunk that his wife said nothing to him, trivial or serious, till day-

37 break. In the morning, when the wine had worn off, she told him everything, and he had a seizure and lay there like a stone. Ten days

38 later the LORD struck him again and he died. When David heard

39 that Nabal was dead he said, 'Blessed be the LORD, who has himself punished Nabal for his insult, and has kept me his servant from doing wrong. The LORD has made Nabal's wrongdoing recoil on his own head.' David then sent to make proposals that Abigail should become his wife. And his servants came to

40 Abigail at Carmel and said to her, 'David has sent us to fetch you to be his wife.' She rose and prostrated

41 herself with her face to the ground, and said, 'I am his slave to command, I would wash the feet of my lord's servants.' So Abigail made

42 her preparations with all speed and, with her five maids in attendance, accompanied by David's messengers, rode away on an ass; and she became David's wife. David had also married Ahinoam

43 of Jezreel; both these women became his wives. Saul meanwhile

44 had given his daughter Michal, David's wife, to Palti son of Laish from Gallim.

THE Ziphites came to Saul at 26 Gibeah to report that David was in hiding on the hill of Hachilah overlooking Jeshimon. Saul went down 2 at once to the wilderness of Ziph, taking with him three thousand picked men, to search for David there. He encamped beside the 3 road on the hill of Hachilah overlooking Jeshimon, while David was still in the wilderness. As soon as David knew that Saul had come to the wilderness in pursuit of him, he sent out scouts and found that 4 Saul had reached such and such a place. Without delay, he went to 5 the place where Saul had pitched his camp and observed where Saul and Abner son of Ner, the commander-in-chief, were lying. Saul lay within the lines with his troops 6 encamped in a circle round him. David turned to Ahimelech the Hittite and Abishai son of Zeruiah, Joab's brother, and said, 'Who will venture with me into the camp, to go to Saul?' Abishai answered, 'I will.' 7 David and Abishai entered the camp at night and found Saul lying asleep within the lines with his spear thrust into the ground by his head. Abner and the army were lying all 8 round him. Abishai said to David, 'God has put your enemy into your power today; let me strike him and pin him to the ground with one thrust of the spear; I shall not have 9 to strike twice.' David said to him, 'Do him no harm; who has ever lifted a finger against the LORD's 10 anointed and gone unpunished? As the LORD lives,' went on David, 'the LORD will strike him down; either his time will come and he will die, or he will go down to battle 11 and meet his end. God forbid that I should lift a finger against the LORD's anointed! But now let us take the spear which is by his head, 12 and the water-jar, and go.' So David took the spear and the water-jar from beside Saul's head and they went. The whole camp was asleep; no one saw him, no one knew anything, no one even woke up. A heavy sleep sent by the LORD had fallen on them.

13   Then David crossed over to the other side and stood on the top of a hill a long way off; there was no 14 little distance between them. David shouted across to the army and hailed Abner, 'Answer me, Abner!' He answered, 'Who are you to 15 shout to the king?' David said to Abner, 'Do you call yourself a man? Is there anyone like you in Israel? Why, then, did you not keep watch over your lord the king, when someone came to harm your lord 16 the king? This was not well done.

As the LORD lives, you deserve to die, all of you, because you have not kept watch over your master the LORD's anointed. Look! Where are the king's spear and the water-jar that were by his head?'

Saul recognized David's voice 17 and said, 'Is that you, David my son?' 'Yes, sir, it is', said David. 'Why must your majesty pursue 18 me? What have I done? What mischief am I plotting? Listen, my 19 lord, to what I have to say. If it is the LORD who has set you against me, may an offering be acceptable to him; but if it is men, a curse on them in the LORD's name; for they have ousted me today from my share in the LORD's inheritance and have banished me to serve other gods! Do not let my blood 20 be shed on foreign soil, far from the presence of the LORD, just because the king of Israel came out to look for a flea, as one might hunt a partridge over the hills.' Saul 21 answered, 'I have done wrong; come back, David my son. You have held my life precious this day, and I will never harm you again. I have been a fool, I have been sadly in the wrong.' David answer- 22 ed, 'Here is the king's spear; let one of your men come across and fetch it. The LORD who rewards upright- 23 ness and loyalty will reward the man into whose power he put you today, when I refused to lift a finger against the LORD's anointed. As I held your life precious today, 24 so may the LORD hold mine precious and deliver me from every distress.' Then Saul said to David, 25 'A blessing is on you, David my son. You will do great things and be victorious.' So David went on his way and Saul returned home.

David thought, 'One of these 27 days I shall be killed by Saul. The best thing for me to do will be to escape into Philistine territory; then Saul will lose all further hope of finding me anywhere in Israel, search as he may, and I shall

2 escape his clutches.' So David and his six hundred men crossed the frontier forthwith to Achish son of 3 Maoch king of Gath. David settled in Gath with Achish, taking with him his men and their families and his two wives, Ahinoam of Jezreel and Abigail of Carmel, Nabal's 4 widow. Saul was told that David had escaped to Gath, and he gave 5 up the search. David said to Achish, 'If I stand well in your opinion, grant me a place in one of your country towns where I may settle. Why should I remain in the royal 6 city with your majesty?' Achish granted him Ziklag on that day: that is why Ziklag still belongs to the kings of Judah.

7 David spent a year and four 8 months in Philistine country. He and his men would sally out and raid the Geshurites, the Gizrites, and the Amalekites, for it was they who inhabited the country from Telaim[a] all the way to Shur and 9 Egypt. When David raided the country he left no one alive, man or woman; he took flocks and herds, asses and camels, and clothes too, and then came back 10 again to Achish. When Achish asked, 'Where was your raid today?', David would answer, 'The Negeb of Judah' or 'The Negeb of the Jerahmeelites' or 'The Negeb of 11 the Kenites'. Neither man nor woman did David bring back alive to Gath, for fear that they should denounce him and his men for what they had done. This was his practice as long as he remained with 12 the Philistines. Achish trusted David, thinking that he had won such a bad name among his own people the Israelites that he would remain his subject all his life.

Saul and his sons killed

28 IN those days the Philistines mustered their army for an attack on Israel. Achish said to David, 'You know that you and your men must take the field with me.' David an- 2 swered Achish, 'Good, you will learn what your servant can do.' And Achish said to David, 'I will make you my bodyguard for life.'

By this time Samuel was dead, 3 and all Israel had mourned for him and buried him in Ramah, his own city; and Saul had banished from the land all who trafficked with ghosts and spirits. The Philistines 4 mustered and encamped at Shunem, and Saul gathered all the Israelites and encamped on Gilboa; and when Saul saw the Philistine 5 force, fear struck him to the heart. He inquired of the LORD, but the 6 LORD did not answer him, whether by dreams or by Urim or by prophets. So he said to his servants, 7 'Find me a woman who has a familiar spirit, and I will go and inquire through her.' His servants told him that there was such a woman at En-dor. Saul put on 8 different clothes and went in disguise with two of his men. He came to the woman by night and said, 'Tell me my fortunes by consulting the dead, and call up the man I name to you.' But the woman an- 9 swered, 'Surely you know what Saul has done, how he has made away with those who call up ghosts and spirits; why do you press me to do what will lead to my death?' Saul swore her an oath: 'As the 10 LORD lives, no harm shall come to you for this.' The woman asked 11 whom she should call up, and Saul answered, 'Samuel.' When the wo- 12 man saw Samuel appear, she shrieked and said to Saul, 'Why have you deceived me? You are Saul!' The king said to her, 'Do 13 not be afraid. What do you see?' The woman answered, 'I see a ghostly form coming up from the earth.' 'What is it like?' he asked; 14 she answered, 'Like an old man coming up, wrapped in ·a cloak.' Then Saul knew it was Samuel, and

---

[a] from Telaim: *prob. rdg.*; Heb. from of old.

he bowed low with his face to the ground, and prostrated himself.
15 Samuel said to Saul, 'Why have you disturbed me and brought me up?' Saul answered, 'I am in great trouble; the Philistines are pressing me and God has turned away; he no longer answers me through prophets or through dreams, and I have summoned you to tell me
16 what I should do.' Samuel said, 'Why do you ask me, now that the LORD has turned from you and
17 become your adversary? He has done what he foretold through me. He has torn the kingdom from your hand and given it to another man,
18 to David. You have not obeyed the LORD, or executed the judgement of his fury against the Amalekites; that is why he has done
19 this to you today. For the same reason the LORD will let your people Israel fall into the hands of the Philistines and, what is more, tomorrow you and your sons shall be with me. Yes, indeed, the LORD will give the Israelite army into
20 the hands of the Philistines.' Saul was overcome and fell his full length to the ground, terrified by Samuel's words. He had no strength left, for he had eaten nothing all day and all night.
21 The woman went to Saul and saw that he was much disturbed, and she said to him, 'I listened to what you said and I risked my life
22 to obey you. Now listen to me: let me set before you a little food to give you strength for your journey.'
23 But he refused to eat anything. When his servants joined the woman in pressing him, he yielded, rose from the ground and sat on the
24 couch. The woman had a fatted calf at home, which she quickly slaughtered. She took some meal, kneaded it and baked unleavened
25 cakes, which she set before Saul and his servants. They ate the food and departed that same night.

The Philistines mustered all their 29 troops at Aphek, while the Israelites encamped at En-harod[a] in Jezreel. The Philistine princes were 2 advancing with their troops in units of a hundred and a thousand; David and his men were in the rear of the column with Achish. The Philistine commanders asked, 3 'Why are those Hebrews there?' Achish answered, 'This is David, the servant of Saul king of Israel who has been with me now for a year or more. I have had no fault to find in him ever since he came over to me.' The Philistine commanders 4 were indignant and said to Achish, 'Send the man back to the town which you allotted to him. He shall not fight side by side with us, or he may turn traitor in the battle. What better way to buy his master's favour, than at the price of our lives? This is that David of 5 whom they sang, as they danced:

Saul made havoc among thousands
but David among tens of thousands.'

Achish summoned David and 6 said to him, 'As the LORD lives, you are an upright man and your service with my troops has well satisfied me. I have had no fault to find with you ever since you joined me, but the other princes are not willing to accept you. Now go home 7 in peace, and you will then be doing nothing that they can regard as wrong.' David protested, 'What 8 have I done, or what fault have you found in me from the day I first entered your service till now, that I should not come and fight against the enemies of my lord the king?' Achish answered David, 'I agree 9 that you have been as true to me as an angel of God, but the Philistine commanders insist that you shall not fight alongside them. Now 10 rise early in the morning with those of your lord's subjects who have followed you, and go to the town which

---

[a] *Prob. rdg.; Heb.* at the spring.

I allotted to you; harbour no evil thoughts, for I am well satisfied with you. Rise early and start as 11 soon as it is light.' So David and his men rose early to start that morning on their way back to the land of the Philistines, while the Philistines went on to Jezreel.

30 On the third day David and his men reached Ziklag. Now the Amalekites had made a raid into the Negeb, attacked Ziklag and set 2 fire to it; they had carried off all the women, high and low, without putting one of them to death. These they drove with them and con- 3 tinued their march. When David and his men approached the town, they found it destroyed by fire, and their wives, their sons, and their 4 daughters carried off. David and the people with him wept aloud until they could weep no more. 5 David's two wives, Ahinoam of Jezreel and Abigail widow of Nabal of Carmel, were among the captives. 6 David was in a desperate position because the people, embittered by the loss of their sons and daughters, threatened to stone him. So David sought strength in the LORD his 7 God. He told Abiathar the priest, son of Ahimelech, to bring the ephod. When Abiathar had brought 8 the ephod, David inquired of the LORD, 'Shall I pursue these raiders? and shall I overtake them?' The answer came, 'Pursue them: you will overtake them and rescue 9 everyone.' So David and his six hundred men set out and reached 10 the ravine of Besor.*a* Two hundred of them who were too weary to cross the ravine stayed behind, and David with four hundred pressed on in pursuit.

11 In the open country they came across an Egyptian and took him to David. They gave him food to 12 eat and water to drink, also a lump of dried figs and two bunches of raisins. When he had eaten these he revived; for he had had nothing to eat or drink for three days and nights. David asked him, 'Whose 13 slave are you? and where have you come from?' 'I am an Egyptian boy,' he answered, 'the slave of an Amalekite, but my master left me behind because I fell ill three days ago. We had raided the Negeb of 14 the Kerethites, part of Judah, and the Negeb of Caleb; we also set fire to Ziklag.' David asked, 'Can 15 you guide me to this band?' 'Swear to me by God', he answered, 'that you will not put me to death or hand me back to my master, and I will guide you to them.' So he 16 led him down, and there they were scattered everywhere, eating and drinking and celebrating the capture of the great mass of spoil taken from Philistine and Judaean territory.

David attacked from dawn till 17 dusk and continued till next day; only four hundred young men mounted on camels made good their escape. David rescued all 18 those whom the Amalekites had taken, including his two wives. No one was missing, high or low, 19 sons or daughters, and none of the spoil, nor anything they had taken for themselves: David recovered everything. They took all the flocks 20 and herds, drove the cattle before him*b* and said, 'This is David's spoil.' When David returned to the 21 two hundred men who had been too weak to follow him and whom he had left behind at the ravine of Besor, they came forward to meet him and his men. David greeted them all, inquiring how things were with them. But some of those who 22 had gone with David, worthless men and scoundrels, broke in and said, 'These men did not go with us; we will not allot them any of the spoil that we have retrieved,

a Prob. rdg.; Heb. adds those who were left over remained.
b They took . . . before him: prob. rdg.; Heb. David took all the flocks and herds; they drove before that cattle.

except that each of them may take his own wife and children and then 23 go.' 'That you shall never do,' said David, 'considering what the LORD has given us, and how he has kept us safe and given the raiding party 24 into our hands. Who could agree with what you propose? Those who stayed with the stores shall have the same share as those who went into battle. They shall share and 25 share alike.' From that time onwards, this has been the established custom in Israel down to this day.

26 When David reached Ziklag, he sent some of the spoil to the elders of Judah and to his friends, with this message: 'This is a present for you out of the spoil taken from the 27 LORD's enemies.' He sent to those in Bethuel, in Ramoth-negeb, in 28 Jattir, in Ararah,*a* in Siphmoth, in 29 Eshtemoa, in Rachal, in the cities of the Jerahmeelites, in the cities 30 of the Kenites, in Hormah, in 31 Borashan, in Athak, in Hebron, and in all the places over which he and his men had ranged.

31 1*b* The Philistines fought a battle against Israel, and the men of Israel were routed, leaving their 2 dead on Mount Gilboa. The Philistines hotly pursued Saul and his sons and killed the three sons, Jonathan, Abinadab and Malchi-3 shua. The battle went hard for Saul, for some archers came upon him and he was wounded in the 4 belly by the archers. So he said to his armour-bearer, 'Draw your sword and run me through, so that

these uncircumcised brutes may not come and taunt me and make sport of me.' But the armour-bearer refused, he dared not; whereupon Saul took his own sword and fell on it. When the armour-bearer saw 5 that Saul was dead, he too fell on his sword and died with him. Thus 6 they all died together on that day, Saul, his three sons, and his armour-bearer, as well as his men. And all 7 the Israelites in the district of the Vale and of the Jordan, when they saw that the other Israelites had fled and that Saul and his sons had perished, fled likewise, abandoning their cities, and the Philistines went in and occupied them.

Next day, when the Philistines 8 came to strip the slain, they found Saul and his three sons lying dead on Mount Gilboa. They cut off his 9 head and stripped him of his weapons; then they sent messengers through the length and breadth of their land to take the good news to idols and people alike. They de-10 posited his armour in the temple of Ashtoreth and nailed his body on the wall of Beth-shan. When the 11 inhabitants of Jabesh-gilead heard what the Philistines had done to Saul, the bravest of them journey-12 ed together all night long and recovered the bodies of Saul and his sons from the wall of Beth-shan; they brought them back to Jabesh and anointed them there with spices. Then they took their bones 13 and buried them under the tamarisk-tree in Jabesh, and fasted for seven days.

---

a Prob. rdg.; Heb. Aroer.
b Verses 1–13: cp. 1 Chr. 10. 1–12.

THE SECOND BOOK OF

SAMUEL

David's rule at Hebron

1 WHEN David returned from his victory over the Amalekites, he spent two 2 days in Ziklag. And on the third day after Saul's death a man came from the army with his clothes rent and dust on his head. When he came into David's presence he fell to the 3 ground in obeisance, and David asked him where he had come from. He answered, 'I have escaped from 4 the army of Israel.' And David said to him, 'What news? Tell me.' 'The army has been driven from the field,' he answered, 'and many have fallen in battle. Saul and Jonathan 5 his son are dead.' David said to the young man who brought the news, 'How do you know that Saul and 6 Jonathan are dead?' The man answered, 'It so happened that I was on Mount Gilboa and saw Saul leaning on his spear with the chariots and horsemen closing in 7 upon him. He turned round and, seeing me, called to me. I said, 8 "What is it, sir?" He asked who I was, and I said, "An Amalekite." 9 Then he said to me, "Come and stand over me and dispatch me. I still live, but the throes of death 10 have seized me." So I stood over him and gave him the death-blow; for I knew that, broken as he was, he could not live. Then I took the crown from his head and the armlet from his arm, and I have brought 11 them here to you, sir.' At that David caught at his clothes and rent them, and so did all the men 12 with him. They beat their breasts and wept, because Saul and Jonathan his son and the people of the

LORD, the house of Israel, had fallen in battle; and they fasted till evening. David said to the young 13 man who brought the news, 'Where do you come from?', and he answered, 'I am the son of an alien, an Amalekite.' 'How is it', said David, 14 'that you were not afraid to raise your hand to slay the LORD's anointed?' And he summoned one of 15 his own young men and ordered him to fall upon the man. So the young man struck him down and killed him; and David said, 16 'Your blood be on your own head; for out of your own mouth you condemned yourself when you said, "I killed the LORD's anointed."'

David made this lament over 17 Saul and Jonathan his son; and he 18 ordered that this dirge over them should be taught to the people of Judah. It was written down and may be found in the Book of Jashar:[a]

O prince of Israel, laid low in 19
  death!
How are the men of war fallen!

Tell it not in Gath, 20
proclaim it not in the streets of
  Ashkelon,
lest the Philistine women rejoice,
lest the daughters of the uncircumcised exult.

Hills of Gilboa, let no dew or rain 21
  fall on you,
no showers on the uplands[b]!
For there the shields of the warriors
  lie tarnished,
and the shield of Saul, no longer
  bright with oil.

---

[a] Or the Book of the Upright.
[b] showers on the uplands: *prob. rdg.*; *Heb.* fields of offerings.

22 The bow of Jonathan never held
back
from the breast of the foeman, from
the blood of the slain;
the sword of Saul never returned
empty to the scabbard.

23 Delightful and dearly loved were
Saul and Jonathan;
in life, in death, they were not
parted.
They were swifter than eagles,
stronger than lions.

24 Weep for Saul, O daughters of
Israel!
who clothed you in scarlet and rich
embroideries,
who spangled your dress with
jewels of gold.

25 How are the men of war fallen,
fallen on the field!
O Jonathan, laid low in death!

26 I grieve for you, Jonathan my
brother;
dear and delightful you were to
me;
your love for me was wonderful,
surpassing the love of women.

27 Fallen, fallen are the men of war;
and their armour left on the field.

2 After this David inquired of the
LORD, 'Shall I go up into one of
the cities of Judah?' The LORD
answered, 'Go.' David asked, 'To
which city?', and the answer came,
2 'To Hebron.' So David went to
Hebron with his two wives, Ahinoam of Jezreel and Abigail widow
3 of Nabal of Carmel. David also
brought the men who had joined
him, with their families, and they
4 settled in the city*a* of Hebron. The
men of Judah came, and there they
anointed David king over the house
of Judah.
   Word came to David that the
men of Jabesh-gilead had buried
5 Saul, and he sent them this message: 'The LORD bless you because
you kept faith with Saul your lord
6 and buried him. For this may the

LORD keep faith and truth with
you, and I for my part will show
you favour too, because you have
done this. Be strong, be valiant, 7
now that Saul your lord is dead,
and the people of Judah have a-
nointed me to be king over them.'

   Meanwhile Saul's commander- 8
in-chief, Abner son of Ner, had
taken Saul's son Ishbosheth,
brought him across the Jordan to
Mahanaim, and made him king 9
over Gilead, the Asherites, Jezreel,
Ephraim, and Benjamin, and all
Israel. Ishbosheth was forty years 10
old when he became king over Israel, and he reigned two years. The
tribe of Judah, however, followed
David. David's rule over Judah in 11
Hebron lasted seven years and a
half.

   Abner son of Ner, with the 12
troops of Saul's son Ishbosheth,
marched out from Mahanaim to
Gibeon, and Joab son of Zeruiah 13
marched out with David's troops
from Hebron. They met at the
pool of Gibeon and took up their
positions one on one side of the
pool and the other on the other
side. Abner said to Joab, 'Let the 14
young men come forward and join
in single combat before us.' Joab
answered, 'Yes, let them.' So they 15
came up, one by one, and took
their places, twelve for Benjamin
and for Ishbosheth and twelve
from David's men. Each man 16
seized his opponent by the head
and thrust his sword into his side;
and thus they fell together. That
is why that place, which lies in
Gibeon, was called the Field of
Blades.

   There ensued a fierce battle that 17
day, and Abner and the men of
Israel were defeated by David's
troops. All three sons of Zeruiah 18
were there, Joab, Abishai and
Asahel. Asahel, who was swift as a
gazelle on the plains, ran straight 19
after Abner, swerving neither to
right nor left in his pursuit. Abner 20

a Prob. rdg.; Heb. cities.

311

turned and asked, 'Is it you, Asa-
21 hel?' Asahel answered, 'It is.' Abner said, 'Turn aside to right or
left, tackle one of the young men
and win his belt for yourself.' But
Asahel would not abandon the
22 pursuit. Abner again urged him to
give it up. 'Why should I kill you?'
he said. 'How could I look Joab
23 your brother in the face?' When
he still refused to turn aside, Abner
struck him in the belly with a
back-thrust of his spear[a] so that
the spear came out behind him, and
he fell dead in his tracks. All who
came to the place where Asahel lay
24 dead stopped there. But Joab and
Abishai kept up the pursuit of
Abner, until, at sunset, they reached the hill of Ammah, opposite
Giah on the road leading to the
pastures of Gibeon.
25 The Benjamites rallied to Abner
and, forming themselves into a
single company, took up their
stand on the top of the hill of
26 Ammah.[b] Abner called to Joab,
'Must the slaughter go on for ever?
Can you not see that it will be all
the more bitter in the end? Will
you never recall the people from
27 the pursuit of their kinsmen?' Joab
answered, 'As God lives, if you had
not spoken, the people would not
have given up the pursuit till morn-
28 ing.' Then Joab sounded the trumpet, and all the people abandoned
the pursuit of the men of Israel and
29 the fighting ceased. Abner and his
men moved along the Arabah all
that night, crossed the Jordan and
went on all the morning till they
30 reached Mahanaim. When Joab
returned from the pursuit of Abner, he assembled his troops and
found that, besides Asahel, nineteen of David's men were missing.
31 David's forces had routed the Benjamites and the followers of Abner,
killing three hundred and sixty of
32 them. They took up Asahel and

buried him in his father's tomb at
Bethlehem. Joab and his men
marched all night, and as day broke
they reached Hebron.

THE war between the houses of 3
Saul and David was long drawn
out, David growing steadily stronger while the house of Saul became
weaker and weaker.
Sons were born to David at 2[c]
Hebron. His eldest was Amnon,
whose mother was Ahinoam of
Jezreel; his second Chileab, whose 3
mother was Abigail widow of Nabal
of Carmel; the third Absalom,
whose mother was Maacah daughter of Talmai king of Geshur; the 4
fourth Adonijah, whose mother
was Haggith; the fifth Shephatiah,
whose mother was Abital; and the 5
sixth Ithream, whose mother was
David's wife Eglah. These were all
born to David at Hebron.
As the war between the houses 6
of Saul and David went on, Abner
made his position gradually stronger in the house of Saul. Now Saul 7
had had a concubine named Rizpah daughter of Aiah. Ishbosheth
asked Abner, 'Why have you slept
with my father's concubine?' Ab- 8
ner was very angry at this and
exclaimed, 'Am I a baboon in the
pay of Judah? Up to now I have
been loyal to the house of your
father Saul, to his brothers and
friends, and I have not betrayed
you into David's hands; yet you
choose this moment to charge me
with disloyalty over this woman.
But now, so help me God, I will do 9
all I can to bring about what the
LORD swore to do for David: I will 10
set to work to bring down the house
of Saul and to put David on the
throne over Israel and Judah from
Dan to Beersheba.' Ishbosheth 11
could not say another word; he was
too much afraid of Abner. Then 12
Abner, seeking to make friends

---

[a] a back-thrust of his spear: *prob. rdg.*; *Heb.* obscure.
[b] the hill of Ammah: *prob. rdg.*, *cp. verse* 24; *Heb.* a single hill.
[c] Verses 2–5: *cp.* 1 Chr. 3. 1–4.

where he could, instead of going to David himself sent envoys with this message: 'Let us come to terms, and I will do all I can to bring the whole of Israel over to 13 you.' David sent answer: 'Good, I will come to terms with you, but on this one condition, that you do not come into my presence without bringing Saul's daughter Michal 14 to me.' David also sent messengers to Saul's son Ishbosheth with the demand: 'Hand over to me my wife Michal to whom I was betrothed at the price of a hundred 15 Philistine foreskins.' Thereupon Ishbosheth sent and took her away from her husband, Paltiel son of 16 Laish. Paltiel followed her as far as Bahurim, weeping all the way, until Abner ordered him to go back home, and he went.

17 Abner now approached the elders of Israel and said, 'For some time past you have wanted David for 18 your king; now is the time to act, for this is the word of the LORD about David: "By the hand of my servant David I will deliver my people Israel from the Philistines 19 and from all their enemies."' Abner spoke also to the Benjamites and then went on to report to David at Hebron all that the Israelites and the Benjamites had agreed. 20 When Abner was admitted to David's presence, there were twenty men with him and David gave 21 a feast for them all. Then Abner said to David, 'I shall now go and bring the whole of Israel over to your majesty, and they shall make a covenant with you. Then you will be king over a realm after your own heart.' David dismissed Abner, granting him safe conduct. 22 David's men and Joab returned from a raid bringing a great deal of plunder with them, and by this time Abner, after his dismissal, was no longer with David in 23 Hebron. So when Joab and his raiding party arrived, they were greeted with the news that Abner

son of Ner had been with the king and had departed under safe conduct. Joab went in to the king and 24 said, 'What have you done? Here you have had Abner with you. How could you let him go? He has got clean away! You know Abner son 25 of Ner: he came meaning to deceive you, to learn all about your movements and to find out what you are doing.' When he left 26 David's presence, Joab sent messengers after Abner and they brought him back from the Pool of Sirah; but David knew nothing of all this. On Abner's return to 27 Hebron, Joab drew him aside in the gateway, as though to speak privately with him, and there, in revenge for his brother Asahel, stabbed him in the belly, and he died. When David heard the news 28 he said, 'I and my realm are for ever innocent in the sight of the LORD of the blood of Abner son of Ner. May it recoil upon the head 29 of Joab and upon all his family! May the house of Joab never be free from running sore or foul disease, nor lack a son fit only to ply the distaff or doomed to die by the sword or beg his bread!' So Joab 30 and Abishai his brother slew Abner because he had killed their brother Asahel in battle at Gibeon. Then 31 David ordered Joab and all the people with him to rend their clothes, put on sackcloth and beat their breasts for Abner, and the king himself walked behind the bier. They buried Abner in Hebron 32 and the king wept aloud at the tomb, while all the people wept with him. The king made this 33 lament for Abner:

Must Abner die so base a death?
Your hands were not bound, 34
your feet not thrust into fetters;
you fell as one who falls at a ruffian's hands.

And the people wept for him again.
They came to persuade David 35
to eat something; but it was still

day and he swore, 'So help me God! I will not touch food of any kind 36 before sunset.' The people took note of this and approved; indeed, everything the king did pleased 37 them. Everyone throughout Israel knew on that day that the king had had no hand in the murder of 38 Abner son of Ner. The king said to his servants, 'Do you not know that a warrior, a great man, has 39 fallen this day in Israel? King though I am, I feel weak and powerless in face of these ruthless sons of Zeruiah; they are too much for me; the LORD will requite the wrongdoer as he deserves.'

4 When Saul's son Ishbosheth heard that Abner had been killed in Hebron, his courage failed him 2 and all Israel was dismayed. Now Ishbosheth had*a* two officers, who were captains of raiding parties, and whose names were Baanah and Rechab; they were Benjamites, sons of Rimmon of Beeroth, Beeroth being reckoned part of 3 Benjamin; but the Beerothites had fled to Gittaim, where they have lived ever since.

4 (Saul's son Jonathan had a son lame in both feet. He was five years old when word of the death of Saul and Jonathan came from Jezreel. His nurse had picked him up and fled, but in her hurry to get away he fell and was crippled. His name was Mephibosheth.)

5 Rechab and Baanah, the sons of Rimmon of Beeroth, came to the house of Ishbosheth in the heat of the day and went in, while he 6 was taking his midday rest. Now the door-keeper had been sifting wheat, but she had grown drowsy and fallen asleep, so Rechab and 7 his brother Baanah crept in, found their way to the room where he was asleep on the bed, and struck him dead. They cut off his head and took it with them, and, making their way along the Arabah all 8 night, came to Hebron. They brought Ishbosheth's head to David at Hebron and said to the king, 'Here is the head of Ishbosheth son of Saul, your enemy, who sought your life. The LORD has avenged your majesty today on Saul and on his family.' David 9 answered Rechab and his brother Baanah, the sons of Rimmon of Beeroth, with an oath: 'As the LORD lives, who has rescued me from all my troubles! I seized the 10 man who brought me word that Saul was dead and thought it good news; I killed him in Ziklag, and that was how I rewarded him for his news. How much more when 11 ruffians have killed an innocent man on his bed in his own house? Am I not to take vengeance on you now for the blood you have shed, and rid the earth of you?' David 12 gave the word, and the young men killed them; they cut off their hands and feet and hung them up beside the pool in Hebron, but the head of Ishbosheth they took and buried in Abner's tomb at Hebron.

David king in Jerusalem

Now all the tribes of Israel 5 1*b* came to David at Hebron and said to him, 'We are your own flesh and blood. In the past, 2 while Saul was still king over us, you led the forces of Israel to war and you brought them home again. And the LORD said to you, "You shall be shepherd of my people Israel; you shall be their prince."' All the elders of Israel 3 came to the king at Hebron; there David made a covenant with them before the LORD, and they anointed David king over Israel. David 4 came to the throne at the age of thirty and reigned for forty years. In Hebron he had ruled over Judah 5 for seven years and a half, and for thirty-three years he reigned in Jerusalem over Israel and Judah together.

a had: *prob. rdg.*; *Heb. om.*

b *Verses 1–3, 6–10: cp. 1 Chr. 11. 1–9.*

6 The king and his men went to Jerusalem to attack the Jebusites, whose land it was. The Jebusites said to David, 'Never shall you come in here; not till you have disposed of the blind and the lame', meaning that David should never 7 come in. None the less David did capture the stronghold of Zion, and it is now known as the City of 8 David. David said on that day, 'Everyone who would kill a Jebusite, let him use his grappling-iron to reach the lame and the blind, David's bitter enemies.' That is why they say, 'No blind or lame man shall come into the LORD's house.'

9 David took up his residence in the stronghold and called it the City of David. He built the city[a] round it, starting at the Millo and 10 working inwards. So David steadily grew stronger, for the LORD the God of Hosts was with him.

11[b] Hiram king of Tyre sent an embassy to David; he sent cedar logs, and with them carpenters and stonemasons, who built David a 12 house. David knew by now that the LORD had confirmed him as king over Israel and had made his royal power stand higher for the sake of his people Israel.

13 After he had moved from Hebron he took more concubines and wives from Jerusalem; and more sons and daughters were born to 14[c] him. These are the names of the children born to him in Jerusalem: Shammua, Shobab, Nathan, Solo-15 mon, Ibhar, Elishua, Nepheg, 16 Japhia, Elishama, Eliada and Eliphelet.

17 When the Philistines learnt that David had been anointed king over Israel, they came up in force to seek him out. David, hearing of this, took refuge in the stronghold.

The Philistines had come and over-18 run the Vale of Rephaim. So David 19 inquired of the LORD, 'If I attack the Philistines, wilt thou deliver them into my hands?' And the LORD answered, 'Go, I will deliver the Philistines into your hands.' So he went up and attacked them 20 at Baal-perazim and defeated them there. 'The LORD has broken through my enemies' lines,' David said, 'as a river breaks its banks.' That is why the place was named Baal-perazim.[d] The Philistines left 21 their idols behind them there, and David and his men carried them off.

The Philistines made another 22 attack and overran the Vale of Rephaim. David inquired of the 23 LORD, who said, 'Do not attack now but wheel round and take them in the rear opposite the aspens. As soon as you hear a 24 rustling sound in the tree-tops, then act at once; for the LORD will have gone out before you to defeat the Philistine army.' David did as the LORD had com-25 manded, and drove the Philistines in flight all the way from Geba to Gezer.

After that David again sum-6 moned the picked men of Israel, thirty thousand in all, and went 2[e] with the whole army to Baalath-judah[f] to fetch the Ark of God which bears the name of the LORD of Hosts, who is enthroned upon the cherubim. They mounted the 3 Ark of God on a new cart and conveyed it from the house of Abinadab on the hill, with Uzzah and Ahio, sons of Abinadab, guiding the cart. They took it with the Ark 4 of God upon it from Abinadab's house on the hill, with Ahio walking in front. David and all Israel 5 danced for joy before the LORD without restraint to the sound of

---

[a] the city: *prob. rdg.*, *cp.* 1 Chr. 11. 8; Heb. *om.*
[b] Verses 11–25: *cp.* 1 Chr. 14. 1–16.   [c] Verses 14–16: *cp.* 1 Chr. 3. 5–8; 14. 4–7.
[d] That is Baal of Break-through.
[e] Verses 2–11: *cp.* 1 Chr. 13. 6–14.
[f] to Baalath-judah: *prob. rdg.*, *cp.* 1 Chr. 13. 6; Heb. from the lords of Judah.

singing,[a] of harps and lutes, of tambourines and castanets and 6 cymbals. But when they came to a certain threshing-floor, the oxen stumbled, and Uzzah reached out to the Ark of God and took hold 7 of it. The LORD was angry with Uzzah and struck him down there for his rash act. So he died there 8 beside the Ark of God. David was vexed because the LORD's anger had broken out upon Uzzah, and he called the place Perez-uzzah,[b] 9 the name it still bears. David was afraid of the LORD that day and said, 'How can I harbour the Ark 10 of the LORD after this?' He felt he could not take the Ark of the LORD with him to the City of David, but turned aside and carried it to the house of Obed-edom the Gittite. 11 Thus the Ark of the LORD remained at Obed-edom's house for three months, and the LORD blessed Obed-edom and all his family.

12[c] When they told David that the LORD had blessed Obed-edom's family and all that was his because of the Ark of God, he went and brought up the Ark of God from the house of Obed-edom to the City of David with much rejoicing. 13 When the bearers of the Ark of the LORD had gone six steps he sacri-14 ficed an ox and a buffalo. David, wearing a linen ephod, danced without restraint before the LORD. 15 He and all the Israelites brought up the Ark of the LORD with shouting and blowing of trumpets. 16 But as the Ark of the LORD was entering the City of David, Saul's daughter Michal looked down through a window and saw King David leaping and capering before the LORD, and she despised him in 17 her heart. When they had brought in the Ark of the LORD, they put it in its place inside the tent that David had pitched for it, and David offered whole-offerings and shared-offerings before the LORD. After 18 David had completed these sacrifices, he blessed the people in the name of the LORD of Hosts and 19 gave food to all the people, a flat loaf of bread, a portion of meat, and a cake of raisins, to every man and woman in the whole gathering of the Israelites. Then all the people went home. When David 20 returned to greet his household, Michal, Saul's daughter, came out to meet him and said, 'What a glorious day for the king of Israel, when he exposed his person in the sight of his servants' slave-girls like any empty-headed fool!' David 21 answered Michal, 'But it was done in the presence of the LORD, who chose me instead of your father and his family and appointed me prince over Israel, the people of the LORD. Before the LORD I will dance for joy, yes, and I will earn 22 yet more disgrace and lower myself still more in your eyes. But those girls of whom you speak, they will honour me for it.' Michal, Saul's 23 daughter, had no child to her dying day.

As soon as the king was estab- 7 1[d] lished in his house and the LORD had given him security from his enemies on all sides, he said to 2 Nathan the prophet, 'Here I live in a house of cedar, while the Ark of God is housed in curtains.' Na- 3 than answered the king, 'Very well, do whatever you have in mind, for the LORD is with you.' But that night the word of the 4 LORD came to Nathan: 'Go and 5 say to David my servant, "This is the word of the LORD: Are you the man to build me a house to dwell in? Down to this day I have never 6 dwelt in a house since I brought Israel up from Egypt; I made my journey in a tent and a tabernacle. Wherever I journeyed with Israel, 7 did I ever ask any of the judges[e]

---

[a] without...singing: *prob. rdg., cp. 1 Chr. 13. 8; Heb.* to the beating of batons.
[b] *That is* Outbreak on Uzzah.
[c] *Verses 12–19: cp. 1 Chr. 15. 25 – 16. 3.*
[d] *Verses 1–29: cp. 1 Chr. 17. 1–27.*
[e] *Prob. rdg., cp. 1 Chr. 17. 6; Heb.* tribes.

whom I appointed shepherds of my people Israel why they had not 8 built me a house of cedar?'' Then say this to my servant David: "This is the word of the LORD of Hosts: I took you from the pastures, and from following the sheep, to be prince over my people Israel. 9 I have been with you wherever you have gone, and have destroyed all the enemies in your path. I will make you a great name among the 10 great ones of the earth. I will assign a place for my people Israel; there I will plant them, and they shall dwell in their own land. They shall be disturbed no more, never again shall wicked men oppress them as 11 they did in the past, ever since the time when I appointed judges over Israel my people; and I will give you peace from all your enemies. The LORD has told you that he would build up your royal house. 12 When your life ends and you rest with your forefathers, I will set up one of your family, one of your own children, to succeed you and 13 I will establish his kingdom. It is he shall build a house in honour of my name, and I will establish his 14 royal throne for ever. I will be his father, and he shall be my son. When he does wrong, I will punish him as any father might, and not 15 spare the rod. My love will never be withdrawn from him as I withdrew it from Saul, whom I removed 16 from your path. Your family shall be established and your kingdom shall stand for all time in my sight, and your throne shall be established for ever.'''

17   Nathan recounted to David all that had been said to him and all 18 that had been revealed. Then King David went into the presence of the LORD and took his place there and said, 'What am I, Lord GOD, and what is my family, that thou hast brought me thus far? 19 It was a small thing in thy sight

to have planned for thy servant's house in days long past. But such, O Lord GOD, is the lot of a man embarked on a high career.[a] And 20 now what more can I say? for well thou knowest thy servant David, O Lord GOD. Thou hast made good 21 thy word; it was thy purpose to spread thy servant's fame, and so thou hast raised me to this greatness. Great indeed art thou, O Lord 22 GOD; we have never heard of one like thee; there is no god but thee. And thy people Israel, to whom 23 can they be compared? Is there any other nation on earth whom thou, O God, hast set out to redeem from slavery to be thy people? Any other for whom thou hast done great and terrible things to win fame for thyself? Any other whom thou hast redeemed for thyself from Egypt by driving out other nations and their gods to make way for them? Thou hast established 24 thy people Israel as thy own for ever, and thou, O LORD, hast become their God. But now, LORD 25 God, perform what thou hast promised for thy servant and his house, and for all time; make good what thou hast said. May thy fame be 26 great for evermore and let men say, "The LORD of Hosts is God over Israel." So shall the house of thy servant David be established before thee. O LORD of Hosts, God of 27 Israel, thou hast shown me thy purpose, in saying to thy servant, "I will build up your house"; and therefore I have made bold to offer this prayer to thee. Thou, O Lord 28 GOD, art God; thou hast made these noble promises to thy servant, and thy promises come true; be pleased now to bless thy servant's house that it may continue 29 always before thee; thou, O Lord GOD, hast promised, and thy blessing shall rest upon thy servant's house for evermore.'

    After this David defeated the 8 1[b]

---

[a] embarked on a high career: *prob. rdg., cp. 1 Chr. 17. 17; Heb. om.*
[b] *Verses 1–14: cp. 1 Chr. 18. 1–13.*

Philistines and conquered them, and took from them Metheg-ha-2 ammah. He defeated the Moabites, and he made them lie along the ground and measured them off with a length of cord; for every two lengths that were to be put to death one full length was spared. The Moabites became subject to 3 him and paid him tribute. David also defeated Hadadezer the Rehobite, king of Zobah, who was on his way to re-erect his monument of victory by*a* the river Euphrates. 4 From him David captured seventeen hundred horse and twenty thousand foot; he hamstrung all the chariot-horses, except a hun-5 dred which he retained. When the Aramaeans of Damascus came to the help of Hadadezer king of Zobah, David destroyed twenty-6 two thousand of them, and established garrisons among these Aramaeans; they became subject to him and paid him tribute. Thus the LORD gave David victory wherever 7 he went. David took the gold quivers borne by Hadadezer's servants and brought them to Jerusa-8 lem; and he also took a great quantity of bronze*b* from Hadadezer's cities, Betah and Berothai.

9 When Toi king of Hamath heard that David had defeated the entire 10 army of Hadadezer, he sent his son Joram to King David to greet him and to congratulate him on defeating Hadadezer in battle (for Hadadezer had been at war with Toi); and he brought with him vessels of silver, gold, and copper, 11 which King David dedicated to the LORD. He dedicated also the silver and gold taken from all the nations 12 he had subdued, from Edom and Moab, from the Ammonites, the Philistines, and Amalek, as well as part of the spoil taken from Hadadezer the Rehobite, king of Zobah.

David made a great name for 13 himself by the slaughter of eighteen thousand Edomites in the Valley of Salt, and on returning he stationed garrisons throughout 14 Edom, and all the Edomites were subject to him. Thus the LORD gave victory to David wherever he went.

David ruled over the whole of 15*e* Israel and maintained law and justice among all his people. Joab 16 son of Zeruiah was in command of the army; Jehoshaphat son of Ahilud was secretary of state; Zadok and Abiathar son of Ahi-17 melech, son of Ahitub,*d* were priests; Seraiah was adjutant-general; Benaiah son of Jehoiada 18 commanded the Kerethite and Pelethite guards. David's sons were priests.

David asked, 'Is any member of 9 Saul's family left, to whom I can show true kindness for Jonathan's sake?' There was a servant of Saul's 2 family named Ziba; and he was summoned to David. The king asked, 'Are you Ziba?', and he answered, 'Your servant, sir.' So 3 the king said, 'Is no member of Saul's family still alive to whom I may show the kindness that God requires?' 'Yes,' said Ziba, 'there is a son of Jonathan still alive; he is a cripple, lame in both feet.' 'Where is he?' said the king, and 4 Ziba answered, 'He is staying with Machir son of Ammiel in Lo-debar.' So the king sent and fetched him 5 from Lo-debar, from the house of Machir son of Ammiel, and when 6 Mephibosheth, son of Jonathan and Saul's grandson, entered David's presence, he prostrated himself and did obeisance. David said to him, 'Mephibosheth', and he answered, 'Your servant, sir.' Then 7 David said, 'Do not be afraid; I mean to show you kindness for your father Jonathan's sake, and

---

a re-erect...victory by: *or* recover control of the crossings of...
b Or copper.   *c* Verses 15–18: cp. 20. 23–26; 1 Kgs. 4. 2–6; 1 Chr. 18. 14–17.
d and Abiathar...Ahitub: *prob. rdg.*, cp. 1 Sam. 22. 11, 20; 2 Sam. 20. 25; *Heb.* son of Ahitub and Ahimelech son of Abiathar.

I will give you back the whole estate of your grandfather Saul; you shall have a place for yourself 8 at my table.' So Mephibosheth prostrated himself again and said, 'Who am I that you should spare a thought for a dead dog like me?' 9 Then David summoned Saul's servant Ziba to his presence and said to him, 'I assign to your master's grandson all the property that belonged to Saul and his fami- 10 ly. You and your sons and your slaves must cultivate the land and bring in the harvest to provide for your master's household, but Mephibosheth your master's grandson shall have a place at my table.' This man Ziba had fifteen sons and 11 twenty slaves. Then Ziba answered the king, 'I will do all that your majesty commands.' So Mephibosheth took his place in the royal household like one of the king's 12 sons. He had a young son, named Mica; and the members of Ziba's household were all Mephibosheth's 13 servants, while Mephibosheth lived in Jerusalem and had his regular place at the king's table, crippled as he was in both feet.

10 1[a] Some time afterwards the king of the Ammonites died and was 2 succeeded by his son Hanun. David said, 'I must keep up the same loyal friendship with Hanun son of Nahash as his father showed me', and he sent a mission to condole with him on the death of his father. But when David's envoys entered the country of the Am- 3 monites, the Ammonite princes said to Hanun their lord, 'Do you suppose David means to do honour to your father when he sends you his condolences? These men of his are spies whom he has sent to find 4 out how to overthrow the city.' So Hanun took David's servants, and he shaved off half their beards, cut off half their garments up to the buttocks, and dismissed them. 5 When David heard how they had

been treated, he sent to meet them, for they were deeply humiliated, and ordered them to wait in Jericho and not to return until their beards had grown again. The Am- 6 monites knew that they had fallen into bad odour with David, so they hired the Aramaeans of Beth-rehob and of Zobah to come to their help with twenty thousand infantry; they also hired the king of Maacah with a thousand men, and twelve thousand men from Tob. When 7 David heard of it, he sent out Joab and all the fighting men. The Am- 8 monites came and took up their position at the entrance to the city, while the Aramaeans of Zobah and of Rehob and the men of Tob and Maacah took up theirs in the open country. When Joab saw that he 9 was threatened both front and rear, he detailed some picked Israelite troops and drew them up facing the Aramaeans. The rest of 10 his forces he put under his brother Abishai, who took up a position facing the Ammonites. 'If the 11 Aramaeans prove too strong for me,' he said, 'you must come to my relief; and if the Ammonites prove too strong for you, I will come to yours. Courage! Let us fight brave- 12 ly for our people and for the cities[b] of our God. And the LORD's will be done.' But when Joab and his 13 men came to close quarters with the Aramaeans, they put them to flight; and when the Ammonites 14 saw them in flight, they too fled before Abishai and entered the city. Then Joab returned from the battle against the Ammonites and came to Jerusalem. The Aramaeans 15 saw that they had been worsted by Israel; but they rallied their forces, and Hadadezer sent to summon 16 other Aramaeans from the Great Bend of the Euphrates, and they advanced to Helam under Shobach, commander of Hadadezer's army. Their movement was report- 17 ed to David, who immediately

---

[a] *Verses 1–19: cp. 1 Chr. 19. 1–19.*   [b] *Or altars.*

mustered all the forces of Israel, crossed the Jordan and advanced to meet them at Helam. There the Aramaeans took up positions facing 18 David and engaged him, but were put to flight by Israel. David slew seven hundred Aramaeans in chariots and forty thousand horsemen, mortally wounding Shobach, who 19 died on the field. When all the vassal kings of Hadadezer saw that they had been worsted by Israel, they sued for peace and submitted to the Israelites. The Aramaeans never dared help the Ammonites again.

11 AT the turn of the year, when kings take the field, David sent Joab out with his other officers and all the Israelite forces, and they ravaged Ammon and laid siege to Rabbah, while David remained in 2 Jerusalem. One evening David got up from his couch and, as he walked about on the roof of the palace, he saw from there a woman bathing, and she was very beautiful. 3 He sent to inquire who she was, and the answer came, 'It must be Bathsheba daughter of Eliam and 4 wife of Uriah the Hittite.' So he sent messengers to fetch her, and when she came to him, he had intercourse with her, though she was still being purified after her period, 5 and then she went home. She conceived, and sent word to David 6 that she was pregnant. David ordered Joab to send Uriah the Hittite to him. So Joab sent him 7 to David, and when he arrived, David asked him for news of Joab and the troops and how the cam-8 paign was going; and then said to him, 'Go down to your house and wash your feet after your journey.' As he left the palace, a present 9 from the king followed him. But Uriah did not return to his house; he lay down by the palace gate 10 with the king's slaves. David heard that Uriah had not gone home, and

said to him, 'You have had a long journey, why did you not go home?' Uriah answered David, 'Israel and 11 Judah are under canvas,[a] and so is the Ark, and my lord Joab and your majesty's officers are camping in the open; how can I go home to eat and drink and to sleep with my wife? By your life, I cannot do this!' David then said to Uriah, 12 'Stay here another day, and tomorrow I will let you go.' So Uriah stayed in Jerusalem that day. The next day David invited him to eat 13 and drink with him and made him drunk. But in the evening Uriah went out to lie down in his blanket[b] among the king's slaves and did not go home.

The following morning David 14 wrote a letter to Joab and sent Uriah with it. He wrote in the let-15 ter, 'Put Uriah opposite the enemy where the fighting is fiercest and then fall back, and leave him to meet his death.' Joab had been 16 watching the city, and he stationed Uriah at a point where he knew they would put up a stout fight. The men of the city sallied out and 17 engaged Joab, and some of David's guards fell; Uriah the Hittite was also killed. Joab sent David a dis-18 patch with all the news of the battle and gave the messenger these 19 instructions: 'When you have finished your report to the king, if he is angry and asks, "Why did 20 you go so near the city during the fight? You must have known there would be shooting from the wall. Remember who killed Abimelech 21 son of Jerubbesheth. It was a woman who threw down an upper millstone on to him from the wall of Thebez and killed him! Why did you go so near the wall?" – if he asks this, then tell him, "Your servant Uriah the Hittite also is dead."'

So the messenger set out and, 22 when he came to David, he made his report as Joab had instructed.

[a] under canvas: *or* at Succoth.

[b] in his blanket: *or* on his pallet.

David was angry with Joab and said to the messenger, 'Why did you go so near the city during the fight? You must have known you would be struck down from the wall. Remember who killed Abimelech son of Jerubbesheth. Was it not a woman who threw down an upper millstone on to him from the wall of Thebez and killed him?
23 Why did you go near the wall?' He answered, 'The enemy massed against us and sallied out into the open; we pressed them back as far as the gateway. There the archers
24 shot down at us from the wall and some of your majesty's men fell; and your servant Uriah the Hittite
25 is dead.' David said to the man, 'Give Joab this message: "Do not let this distress you – there is no knowing where the sword will strike; press home your attack on the city, and you will take it and raze it to the ground"; and tell him to take heart.'
26 When Uriah's wife heard that her husband was dead, she mourn-
27 ed for him; and when the period of mourning was over, David sent for her and brought her into his house. She became his wife and bore him a son. But what David had done was wrong in the eyes of the LORD.

12 The LORD sent Nathan the prophet to David, and when he entered his presence, he said to him, 'There were once two men in the same city, one rich and the other
2 poor. The rich man had large flocks
3 and herds, but the poor man had nothing of his own except one little ewe lamb. He reared it himself, and it grew up in his home with his own sons. It ate from his dish, drank from his cup and nestled in his arms; it was like a daughter to him.
4 One day a traveller came to the rich man's house, and he, too mean to take something from his own flocks and herds to serve to his guest, took the poor man's lamb

and served up that.' David was 5 very angry, and burst out, 'As the LORD lives, the man who did this deserves to die! He shall pay for 6 the lamb four times over, because he has done this and shown no pity.' Then Nathan said to David, 7 'You are the man. This is the word of the LORD the God of Israel to you: "I anointed you king over Israel, I rescued you from the power of Saul, I gave you your 8 master's daughter*a* and his wives to be your own, I gave you the daughters of Israel and Judah; and, had this not been enough, I would have added other favours as great. Why then have you flouted the 9 word of the LORD by doing what is wrong in my eyes? You have struck down Uriah the Hittite with the sword; the man himself you murdered by the sword of the Ammonites, and you have stolen his wife. Now, therefore, since you 10 have despised me and taken the wife of Uriah the Hittite to be your own wife, your family shall never again have rest from the sword." This is the word of the 11 LORD: "I will bring trouble upon you from within your own family; I will take your wives and give them to another man before your eyes, and he will lie with them in broad daylight. What you did was 12 done in secret; but I will do this in the light of day for all Israel to see."' David said to Nathan, 'I 13 have sinned against the LORD.' Nathan answered him, 'The LORD has laid on another the consequences of your sin: you shall not die, but, because in this you have shown 14 your contempt for the LORD,*b* the boy that will be born to you shall die.'

When Nathan had gone home, 15 the LORD struck the boy whom Uriah's wife had borne to David, and he was very ill. David prayed 16 to God for the child; he fasted and

---

a *Prob. rdg.; Heb.* house.
b the LORD: *prob. rdg.; Heb.* the enemies of the LORD.

went in and spent the night fasting, lying on the ground. The older men of his household tried to get him to rise from the ground, but he refused and would eat no food with them. On the seventh day the boy died, and David's servants were afraid to tell him. 'While the boy was alive,' they said, 'we spoke to him, and he did not listen to us; how can we now tell him that the boy is dead? He may do something desperate.' But David saw his servants whispering among themselves and guessed that the boy was dead. He asked, 'Is the boy dead?', and they answered, 'He is dead.' Then David rose from the ground, washed and anointed himself, and put on fresh clothes; he entered the house of the LORD and prostrated himself there. Then he went home, asked for food to be brought, and when it was ready, he ate it. His servants asked him, 'What is this? While the boy lived you fasted and wept for him, but now that he is dead you rise up and eat.' He answered, 'While the boy was still alive I fasted and wept, thinking, "It may be that the LORD will be gracious to me, and the boy may live." But now that he is dead, why should I fast? Can I bring him back again? I shall go to him; he will not come back to me.' David consoled Bathsheba his wife; he went to her and had intercourse with her, and she gave birth to a son and called him Solomon. And because the LORD loved him, he sent word through Nathan the prophet that for the LORD's sake he should be given the name Jedidiah.[a]

Joab attacked the Ammonite city of Rabbah and took the King's Pool. He sent messengers to David with this report: 'I have attacked Rabbah and have taken the pool. You had better muster the rest of the army yourself, besiege the city and take it; otherwise I shall take the city and the name to be proclaimed over it will be mine.' David accordingly mustered his whole forces, marched to Rabbah, attacked it and took it. He took the crown from the head of Milcom, which weighed a talent of gold and was set with a precious stone, and this he placed on his own head. He also removed a great quantity of booty from the city; he took its inhabitants and set them to work with saws and other iron tools, sharp and toothed, and made them work in the brick-kilns. David did this to all the cities of the Ammonites; then he and all his people returned to Jerusalem.

Absalom's rebellion and other conflicts

Now David's son Absalom had a beautiful sister named Tamar, and Amnon, another of David's sons, fell in love with her. Amnon was so distressed that he fell sick with love for his half-sister; for he thought it an impossible thing to approach her since she was a virgin. But he had a friend named Jonadab, son of David's brother Shimeah, who was a very shrewd man. He said to Amnon, 'Why are you so low-spirited morning after morning, my lord? Will you not tell me?' So Amnon told him that he was in love with Tamar, his brother Absalom's sister. Jonadab said to him, 'Take to your bed and pretend to be ill. When your father comes to visit you, say to him, "Please let my sister Tamar come and give me my food. Let her prepare it in front of me, so that I may watch her and then take it from her own hands."' So Amnon lay down and pretended to be ill. When the king came to visit him, he said, 'Sir, let my sister Tamar come and make a few cakes in front of me, and serve them to me with her own hands.' So David sent a message to

That is Beloved of the LORD.   [b] Verses 26–31: *cp.* 1 Chr. 20. 1–3.

322

Tamar in the palace: 'Go to your brother Amnon's quarters and pre-
8 pare a meal for him.' Tamar came to her brother and found him lying down; she took some dough and kneaded it, made the cakes in
9 front of him and baked them. Then she took the pan and turned them out before him. But Amnon refused to eat and ordered everyone out of the room. When they had all left,
10 he said to Tamar, 'Bring the food over to the recess so that I may eat from your own hands.' Tamar took the cakes she had made and brought them to Amnon in the
11 recess. But when she offered them to him, he caught hold of her and said, 'Come to bed with me, sister.'
12 But she answered, 'No, brother, do not dishonour me, we do not do such things in Israel; do not be-
13 have like a beast. Where could I go and hide my disgrace? – and you would sink as low as any beast in Israel. Why not speak to the king for me? He will not refuse you leave
14 to marry me.' He would not listen, but overpowered her, dishonoured her and raped her.
15 Then Amnon was filled with utter hatred for her; his hatred was stronger than the love he had felt, and he said to her, 'Get up and
16 go.' She answered, 'No. It is wicked to send me away. This is harder to bear than all you have done to me.' He would not listen to her,
17 but summoned the boy who attended him and said, 'Get rid of this woman, put her out and bolt
18 the door after her.' She had on a long, sleeved robe, the usual dress of unmarried princesses; and the boy turned her out and bolted the
19 door. Tamar threw ashes over her head, rent the long, sleeved robe that she was wearing, put her hands on her head and went away, sob-
20 bing as she went. Her brother Absalom asked her, 'Has your brother Amnon been with you? Keep this to yourself, he is your brother; do

not take it to heart.' So Tamar remained in her brother Absalom's house, desolate. When King David 21 heard the whole story he was very angry; but he would not hurt Amnon because he was his eldest son and he loved him. Absalom did 22 not speak a single word to Amnon, friendly or unfriendly; he hated him for having dishonoured his sister Tamar.

Two years later Absalom invited 23 all the king's sons to his sheep-shearing at Baal-hazor, near Eph-ron.[a] He approached the king and 24 said, 'Sir, I am shearing; will your majesty and your servants come?' The king answered, 'No, my son, 25 we must not all come and be a burden to you.' Absalom pressed him, but David was still unwilling to go and dismissed him with his blessing. But Absalom said, 'If you 26 cannot, may my brother Amnon come with us?' 'Why should he go with you?' the king asked; but 27 Absalom pressed him again, so he let Amnon and all the other princes go with him.

Then Absalom prepared a feast 28 fit for a king. He gave his servants these orders: 'Bide your time, and when Amnon is merry with wine I shall say to you, "Strike." Then kill Amnon. You have nothing to fear, these are my orders; be bold and resolute.' Absalom's servants 29 did as he had told them, whereupon all the king's sons mounted their mules in haste and set off for home.

While they were on their way, a 30 rumour reached David that Absalom had murdered all the royal princes and that not one was left alive. The king stood up and rent 31 his clothes and then threw himself on the ground; all his servants were standing round him with their clothes rent. Then Jonadab, son of 32 David's brother Shimeah, said, 'Your majesty must not think that they have killed all the young

---

[a] *Prob. rdg.; Heb.* Ephraim.

princes; only Amnon is dead; Absalom has looked black ever since Amnon ravished his sister Tamar. 33 Your majesty must not pay attention to a mere rumour that all the princes are dead; only Amnon is dead.'

34 Absalom made good his escape. Meanwhile the sentry looked up and saw a crowd of people coming down the hill from the direction of Horonaim.[a] He came and reported to the king, 'I see men coming down 35 the hill from Horonaim.' Then Jonadab said to the king, 'Here come the royal princes, just as I 36 said they would.' As he finished speaking, the princes came in and broke into loud lamentations; the king and all his servants also wept bitterly.

37 But Absalom went to take refuge with Talmai son of Ammihur king of Geshur; and for a long while the king mourned for Am-38 non. Absalom, having escaped to Geshur, stayed there for three 39 years; and David's heart went out to him with longing, for he became reconciled to the death of Amnon.

14 Joab son of Zeruiah saw that the 2 king's heart was set on Absalom, so he sent to Tekoah and fetched a wise woman. He said to her, 'Pretend to be a mourner; put on mourning, go without anointing yourself, and behave like a bereaved woman who has been long 3 in mourning. Then go to the king and repeat what I tell you.' He then told her exactly what she was to say.

4 When the woman from Tekoah came into the king's presence, she threw herself, face downwards, on the ground and did obeisance, and 5 cried, 'Help, your majesty!' The king asked, 'What is it?' She answered, 'O sir, I am a widow; my 6 husband is dead. I had two sons; they came to blows out in the country where there was no one to part them, and one of them struck

the other and killed him. Now, sir, 7 the kinsmen have risen against me and they all cry, "Hand over the man who has killed his brother, so that we can put him to death for taking his brother's life, and so cut off the succession." If they do this, they will stamp out my last live ember and leave my husband no name and no descendant upon earth.' 'Go home,' said the king to 8 the woman, 'and I will settle your case.' But the woman continued, 9 'The guilt be on me, your majesty, and on my father's house; let the king and his throne be blameless.' The king said, 'If anyone says any- 10 thing more to you, bring him to me and he shall never molest you again.' Then the woman went on, 11 'Let your majesty call upon the LORD your God, to prevent his kinsmen bound to vengeance from doing their worst and destroying my son.' The king swore, 'As the LORD lives, not a hair of your son's head shall fall to the ground.'

The woman then said, 'May I 12 add one word more, your majesty?' 'Say on', said the king. So she con- 13 tinued, 'How then could it enter your head to do this same wrong to God's people? Out of your own mouth, your majesty, you condemn yourself: you have refused to bring back the man you have banished. We shall all die; we shall 14 be like water that is spilt on the ground and lost; but God will spare the man who does not set himself to keep the outlaw in banishment. I 15 came to say this to your majesty because the people have threatened me. I thought, "If I can only speak to the king, perhaps he will attend to my case; for he will listen, and 16 he will save me from the man who is seeking to cut off me and my son together from Israel, God's own possession." I thought too that the 17 words of my lord the king would be a comfort to me; for your majesty is like the angel of God and can de-

---

[a] *Prob. rdg.; Heb.* from a road behind him.

cide between right and wrong. The
18 LORD your God be with you!' Then
the king said to the woman, 'Tell
me no lies: I shall now ask you a
question.' 'Speak on, your majes-
19 ty', she said. So he asked, 'Is the
hand of Joab behind you in all
this?' 'Your life upon it, sir!' she
answered; 'when your majesty
asks a question, there is no way
round it, right or left. Yes, your
servant Joab did prompt me; it
was he who put the whole story
20 into my mouth. He did it to give a
new turn to this affair. Your majesty is as wise as the angel of God and
knows all that goes on in the land.'
21 The king said to Joab, 'You have
my consent; go and fetch back the
22 young man Absalom.' Then Joab
humbly prostrated himself, took
leave of the king with a blessing
and said, 'Now I know that I have
found favour with your majesty,
because you have granted my hum-
23 ble petition.' Joab went at once to
Geshur and brought Absalom to
24 Jerusalem, but the king said, 'Let
him go to his own quarters; he shall
not come into my presence.' So
Absalom went to his own quarters
and did not enter the king's presence.
25 No one in all Israel was so greatly admired for his beauty as Absalom; he was without flaw from the
crown of his head to the sole of his
26 foot. His hair, when he cut his hair
(as he had to do every year, for he
found it heavy), weighed two hundred shekels by the royal standard.
27 Three sons were born to Absalom,
and a daughter named Tamar, who
was a very beautiful woman.
28 Absalom remained in Jerusalem
for two whole years without enter-
29 ing the king's presence. He summoned Joab to send a message by
him to the king, but Joab refused
to come; he sent for him a second
30 time, but he still refused. Then
Absalom said to his servants, 'You
know that Joab has a field next to
mine with barley growing in it; go

and set fire to it.' So Absalom's
servants set fire to the field. Joab 31
promptly came to Absalom in his
own quarters and said to him, 'Why
have your servants set fire to my
field?' Absalom answered Joab, 'I 32
had sent for you to come here, so
that I could ask you to give the
king this message from me: "Why
did I leave Geshur? It would be
better for me if I were still there.
Let me now come into your majesty's presence and, if I have done
any wrong, put me to death."'
When Joab went to the king and 33
told him, he summoned Absalom,
who came and prostrated himself
humbly before the king; and he
greeted Absalom with a kiss.

AFTER this, Absalom provided 15
himself with a chariot and horses
and an escort of fifty men. He made 2
it a practice to rise early and stand
beside the road which runs through
the city gate. He would hail every
man who had a case to bring before
the king for judgement and would
ask him what city he came from.
When he answered, 'I come, sir,
from such and such a tribe of
Israel', Absalom would say to him, 3
'I can see that you have a very
good case, but you will get no
hearing from the king.' And he 4
would add, 'If only I were appointed judge in the land, it would
be my business to see that everyone who brought a suit or a claim
got justice from me.' Whenever a 5
man approached to prostrate himself, Absalom would stretch out his
hand, take hold of him and kiss
him. By behaving like this to every 6
Israelite who sought the king's
justice, Absalom stole the affections of the Israelites.

At the end of four years, Absa- 7
lom said to the king, 'May I have
leave now to go to Hebron to fulfil
a vow there that I made to the
LORD? For when I lived in Geshur, 8
in Aram, I made this vow: "If the
LORD brings me back to Jerusa-

9 lem, I will become a worshipper of the LORD in Hebron."' The king answered, 'Certainly you may go'; so he set off for Hebron at once.

10 Absalom sent runners through all the tribes of Israel with this message: 'As soon as you hear the sound of the trumpet, then say, "Absalom is king in Hebron."'

11 Two hundred men accompanied Absalom from Jerusalem; they were invited and went in all innocence, knowing nothing of the

12 affair. Absalom also sent to summon Ahithophel the Gilonite, David's counsellor, from Giloh his city, where he was offering the customary sacrifices. The conspiracy gathered strength, and Absalom's supporters increased in number.

13 When news reached David that the men of Israel had transferred

14 their allegiance to Absalom, he said to those who were with him in Jerusalem, 'We must get away at once; or there will be no escape from Absalom for any of us. Make haste, or else he will soon be upon us and bring disaster on us, showing no mercy to anyone in the city.'

15 The king's servants said to him, 'As your majesty thinks best; we are ready.'

16 When the king departed, all his household followed him except ten concubines, whom he left in charge

17 of the palace. At the Far House the king and all the people who were

18 with him halted. His own servants then stood[a] beside him, while the Kerethite and Pelethite guards and Ittai[b] with the six hundred Gittites under him marched past the king.

19 The king said to Ittai the Gittite, 'Are you here too? Why are you coming with us? Go back and stay with the new king, for you are a foreigner and, what is more, an

20 exile from your own country. You

came only yesterday, and today must you be compelled to share my wanderings? I do not know where I am going. Go back home and take your countrymen with you; and may the LORD ever be your steadfast friend.' Ittai swore to the king, 21 'As the LORD lives, your life upon it, wherever you may be, in life or in death, I, your servant, will be there.' David said to Ittai, 'It 22 is well, march on!' So Ittai the Gittite marched on with his whole company and all the dependants who were with him. The whole 23 country-side re-echoed with their weeping. And the king remained standing[c] while all the people crossed the gorge of the Kidron before him, by way of the olive-tree in the wilderness.[d]

Zadok also was there with all the 24 Levites; they were carrying the Ark of the Covenant of God, which they set down beside Abiathar[e] until all the people had passed out of the city. But the king said to 25 Zadok, 'Take the Ark of God back to the city. If I find favour with the LORD, he will bring me back and will let me see the Ark and its dwelling-place again. But if he 26 says he does not want me, then here I am; let him do what he pleases with me.' The king went on 27 to say to Zadok the priest, 'Can you make good use of your eyes? You may safely go back to the city, you and Abiathar,[f] and take with you the two young men, Ahimaaz your son and Abiathar's son Jonathan. Do not forget: I will 28 linger at the Fords of the Wilderness until you can send word to me.' Then Zadok and Abiathar 29 took the Ark of God back to Jerusalem and stayed there.

David wept as he went up the 30 slope of the Mount of Olives; he was bare-headed and went bare-

---

[a] *Prob. rdg.; Heb.* passed.　　[b] *and Ittai: prob. rdg.; Heb. om.*
[c] *Prob. rdg.; Heb.* passing.　　[d] *by way...wilderness: prob. rdg.; Heb. obscure.*
[e] *beside Abiathar: prob. rdg.; Heb.* and Abiathar went up.
[f] *you and Abiathar: prob. rdg., cp. verse 29; Heb. om.*

foot. The people with him all had their heads uncovered and wept as

31 they went. David had been told that Ahithophel was among the conspirators with Absalom, and he prayed, 'Frustrate, O LORD, the counsel of Ahithophel.'

32 As David was approaching the top of the ridge where it was the custom to prostrate oneself to God, Hushai the Archite was there to meet him with his tunic rent and

33 earth on his head. David said to him, 'If you come with me you will

34 only be a hindrance; but you can help me to frustrate Ahithophel's plans if you go back to the city and say to Absalom, "I will be your majesty's servant; up to now I have been your father's servant,

35 and now I will be yours." You will have with you, as you know, the priests Zadok and Abiathar; tell them everything that you hear in

36 the king's household. They have with them Zadok's son Ahimaaz and Abiathar's son Jonathan, and through them you may pass on to

37 me everything you hear.' So Hushai, David's friend, came to the city as Absalom was entering Jerusalem.

16 When David had moved on a little from the top of the ridge, he was met by Ziba the servant of Mephibosheth, who had with him a pair of asses saddled and loaded with two hundred loaves, a hundred clusters of raisins, a hundred bunches of summer fruit, and a

2 flagon of wine. The king said to him, 'What are you doing with these?' Ziba answered, 'The asses are for the king's family to ride on, the bread and the summer fruit are for the servants to eat, and the wine for anyone who becomes ex-

3 hausted in the wilderness.' The king asked, 'Where is your master's grandson?' 'He is staying in Jerusalem,' said Ziba, 'for he thought that the Israelites might now restore to him his grandfather's

4 throne.' The king said to Ziba, 'You shall have everything that belongs to Mephibosheth.' Ziba said, 'I am your humble servant, sir; may I continue to stand well with you.'

5 As King David approached Bahurim, a man of Saul's family, whose name was Shimei son of Gera, came out, cursing as he came.

6 He showered stones right and left on David and on all the king's servants and on everyone, soldiers and people alike. This is what Shi-

7 mei said as he cursed him: 'Get out, get out, you scoundrel! you man of blood! The LORD has taken ven-

8 geance on you for the blood of the house of Saul whose throne you stole, and he has given the kingdom to your son Absalom. You murderer, see how your crimes have overtaken you!'

9 Then Abishai son of Zeruiah said to the king, 'Why let this dead dog curse your majesty? I will go

10 across and knock off his head.' But the king said, 'What has this to do with you, you sons of Zeruiah? If he curses and if the LORD has told him to curse David, who can ques-

11 tion it?' David said to Abishai and to all his servants, 'If my son, my own son, is out to kill me, who can wonder at this Benjamite? Let him be, let him curse; for the LORD has

12 told him to do it. But perhaps the LORD will mark my sufferings and bestow a blessing on me in place of

13 the curse laid on me this day.' David and his men continued on their way, and Shimei moved along the ridge of the hill parallel to David's path, cursing as he went and hurling stones across the valley at him

14 and kicking up the dust. When the king and all the people with him reached the Jordan, they were worn out; and they refreshed themselves there.

15 By now Absalom and all his Israelites had reached Jerusalem,

16 and Ahithophel with him. When Hushai the Archite, David's friend, met Absalom he said to him, 'Long live the king! Long live the king!'

17 But Absalom retorted, 'Is this your loyalty to your friend? Why did you not go with him?' Hushai an-
18 swered Absalom, 'Because I mean to attach myself to the man chosen by the LORD, by this people, and by all the men of Israel, and with
19 him I will remain. After all, whom ought I to serve? Should I not serve the son? I will serve you as I
20 have served your father.' Then Absalom said to Ahithophel, 'Give us your advice: how shall we act?'
21 Ahithophel answered, 'Have intercourse with your father's concubines whom he left in charge of the palace. Then all Israel will come to hear that you have given great cause of offence to your father, and this will confirm the resolution of
22 your followers.' So they set up a tent for Absalom on the roof, and he lay with his father's concubines
23 in the sight of all Israel. In those days a man would seek counsel of Ahithophel as readily as he might make an inquiry of the word of God; that was how Ahithophel's counsel was esteemed by David and Absalom.

17 Ahithophel said to Absalom, 'Let me pick twelve thousand men, and I will pursue David tonight.
2 I shall overtake him when he is tired and dispirited; I will cut him off from his people and they will all scatter; and I shall kill no one but
3 the king. I will bring all the people over to you as a bride is brought to her husband. It is only one man's life that you are seeking; the rest of
4 the people will be unharmed.' Absalom and all the elders of Israel approved of Ahithophel's advice;
5 but Absalom said, 'Summon Hushai the Archite and let us hear
6 what he too has to say.' Hushai came, and Absalom told him all that Ahithophel had said and asked him, 'Shall we do what he says? If not, say what you think.'
7 Hushai said to Absalom, 'For once the counsel that Ahithophel
8 has given is not good. You know',

he went on, 'that your father and the men with him are hardened warriors and savage as a bear in the wilds robbed of her cubs. Your father is an old campaigner and will not spend the night with the main body; even now he will be 9 lying hidden in a pit or in some such place. Then if any of your men are killed at the outset, anyone who hears the news will say, "Disaster has overtaken the followers of Absalom." The courage of the most 10 resolute and lion-hearted will melt away, for all Israel knows that your father is a man of war and has determined men with him. My ad- 11 vice is this. Wait until the whole of Israel, from Dan to Beersheba, is gathered about you, countless as grains of sand on the sea-shore, and then you shall march with them in person. Then we shall come upon 12 him somewhere, wherever he may be, and descend on him like dew falling on the ground, and not a man of his family or of his followers will be left alive. If he retreats in- 13 to a city, all Israel will bring ropes to that city, and we will drag it in- to a ravine until not a stone can be found on the site.' Absalom and all 14 the men of Israel said, 'Hushai the Archite gives us better advice than Ahithophel.' It was the LORD's purpose to frustrate Ahithophel's good advice and so bring disaster upon Absalom.

Hushai told Zadok and Abiathar 15 the priests all the advice that Ahithophel had given to Absalom and the elders of Israel, and also his own. 'Now send quickly to David,' 16 he said, 'and warn him not to spend the night at the Fords of the Wilderness but to cross the river at once, before a blow can be struck at the king and his followers.' Jo- 17 nathan and Ahimaaz were waiting at En-rogel, and a servant girl would go and tell them what happened and they would pass it on to King David; for they could not risk being seen entering the city.

18 But this time a lad saw them and told Absalom; so the two of them hurried to the house of a man in Bahurim. He had a pit in his courtyard, and they climbed down into 19 it. The man's wife took a covering, spread it over the mouth of the pit and strewed grain over it, and no 20 one was any the wiser. Absalom's servants came to the house and asked the woman, 'Where are Ahimaaz and Jonathan?' She answered, 'They went beyond the pool.' The men searched but could not find them; so they went back 21 to Jerusalem. When they had gone the two climbed out of the pit and went off to report to King David and said, 'Over the water at once, make haste!', and they told him 22 Ahithophel's plan against him. So David and all his company began at once to cross the Jordan; by daybreak there was not one who had not reached the other bank.

23 When Ahithophel saw that his advice had not been taken he saddled his ass, went straight home to his own city, gave his last instructions to his household, and hanged himself. So he died and was buried in his father's grave.

24 By the time that Absalom had crossed the Jordan with the Israelites, David was already at Maha- 25 naim. Absalom had appointed Amasa as commander-in-chief instead of Joab; he was the son of a man named Ithra, an Ishmaelite, by Abigal daughter of Nahash and sister to Joab's mother Zeruiah. 26 The Israelites and Absalom camp- 27 ed in the district of Gilead. When David came to Mahanaim, he was met by Shobi son of Nahash from the Ammonite town Rabbah, Machir son of Ammiel from Lo-debar, and Barzillai the Gileadite from 28 Rogelim, bringing mattresses and blankets, bowls and jugs.[a] They brought also wheat and barley, meal and parched grain, beans and

lentils, honey and curds, sheep and 29 fat cattle, and offered them to David and his people to eat, knowing that the people must be hungry and thirsty and weary in the wilderness.

David mustered the people who 18 were with him, and appointed officers over units of a thousand and a hundred. Then he divided 2 the army in three, one division under the command of Joab, one under Joab's brother Abishai son of Zeruiah, and the third under Ittai the Gittite. The king announced to the army that he was coming out himself with them to battle. But they said, 'No, you 3 must not come out; if we turn and run, no one will take any notice, nor will they, even if half of us are killed; but you are worth ten thousand of us, and it would be better now for you to remain in the city in support.' 'I will do what you 4 think best', answered the king; and he then stood beside the gate, and the army marched past in their units of a thousand and a hundred. The king gave orders to Joab, Abi- 5 shai, and Ittai: 'Deal gently with the young man Absalom for my sake.' The whole army heard the king giving all his officers this order to spare Absalom.

The army took the field against 6 the Israelites and the battle was fought in the forest of Ephron.[b] There the Israelites were routed 7 before the onslaught of David's men; so great was the rout that twenty thousand men fell that day. The fighting spread over the whole 8 country-side, and the forest took toll of more people that day than the sword.

Now some of David's men caught 9 sight of Absalom. He was riding a mule and, as it passed beneath a great oak,[c] his head was caught in its boughs; he found himself in mid air and the mule went on from

---

[a] bringing . . . jugs: *prob. rdg.*; *Heb.* a couch, bowls and a potter's vessel.
[b] *Prob. rdg.*; *Heb.* Ephraim.   [c] *Or* terebinth.

10 under him. One of the men who saw it went and told Joab, 'I saw Absalom hanging from an oak.'

11 While the man was telling him, Joab broke in, 'You saw him? Why did you not strike him to the ground then and there? I would have given you ten pieces of silver

12 and a belt.' The man answered, 'If you were to put in my hands a thousand pieces of silver, I would not lift a finger against the king's son; for we all heard the king giving orders to you and Abishai and Ittai that whoever finds himself near the young man Absalom must take

13 great care of him. If I had dealt him a treacherous blow, the king would soon have known, and you would

14 have kept well out of it.' 'That is a lie!' said Joab. 'I will make a start and show you.'[a] So he picked up three stout sticks and drove them against Absalom's chest while he was held fast in the tree and still

15 alive. Then ten young men who were Joab's armour-bearers closed in on Absalom, struck at him and

16 killed him. Joab sounded the trumpet, and the army came back from the pursuit of Israel because he had

17 called it off. They took Absalom's body and flung it into a great pit in the forest, and raised over it a huge pile of stones. The Israelites all fled to their homes.

18 The pillar in the King's Vale had been set up by Absalom in his lifetime, for he said, 'I have no son to carry on my name.' He had named the pillar after himself; and to this day it is called Absalom's Monument.

19 Ahimaaz son of Zadok said, 'Let me run and take the news to the king that the LORD has avenged him and delivered him from his

20 enemies.' But Joab replied, 'This is no day for you to be the bearer of news. Another day you may have news to carry, but not today,

because the king's son is dead.'

21 Joab told a Cushite to go and report to the king what he had seen. The Cushite bowed low before Joab

22 and set off running. Ahimaaz pleaded again with Joab, 'Come what may,' he said, 'let me run after the Cushite.' 'Why should you, my son?' asked Joab. 'You will get no reward for your news.'

23 'Come what may,' he said, 'I will run.' 'Go, then', said Joab. So Ahimaaz ran by the road through the Plain of the Jordan and outstripped the Cushite.

24 David was sitting between the two gates when the watchman went up to the roof of the gatehouse by the wall and, looking out,

25 saw a man running alone. The watchman called to the king and told him. 'If he is alone,' said the king, 'then he has news.' The man

26 came nearer and nearer. Then the watchman saw another man running. He called down to the gatekeeper and said, 'Look, there is another man running alone.' The king said, 'He too brings news.'

27 The watchman said, 'I see by the way he runs that the first runner is Ahimaaz son of Zadok.' The king said, 'He is a good fellow and shall

28 earn the reward for good news.' Ahimaaz called out to the king, 'All is well!' He bowed low before him and said, 'Blessed be the LORD your God who has given into your hands the men who rebelled against

29 your majesty.' The king asked, 'Is all well with the young man Absalom?' Ahimaaz answered, 'Sir, your servant Joab sent me,[b] I saw a great commotion, but I did not

30 know what had happened.' The king told him to stand on one side; so he turned aside and stood there.

31 Then the Cushite came in and said, 'Good news, your majesty! The LORD has avenged you this day on all those who rebelled against you.'

---

[a] I will...show you: *or* I can waste no more time on you like this.
[b] Sir...sent me: *prob. rdg.; Heb.* At the sending of Joab the king's servant and your servant.

32 The king said to the Cushite, 'Is all well with the young man Absalom?' The Cushite answered, 'May all the king's enemies and all rebels who would do you harm be as that 33 young man is.' The king was deeply moved and went up to the roof-chamber over the gate and wept, crying out as he went, 'O, my son! Absalom my son, my son Absalom! If only I had died instead of you! O Absalom, my son, my son.'

19 Joab was told that the king was weeping and mourning for Absa-2 lom; and that day victory was turned to mourning for the whole army, because they heard how the 3 king grieved for his son; they stole into the city like men ashamed to show their faces after a defeat in 4 battle. The king hid his face and cried aloud, 'My son Absalom; O 5 Absalom, my son, my son.' But Joab came into the king's quarters and said to him, 'You have put to shame this day all your servants, who have saved you and your sons and daughters, your wives and 6 your concubines. You love those that hate you and hate those that love you; you have made us feel, officers and men alike, that we are nothing to you; for it is plain that if Absalom were still alive and all of us dead, you would be content. 7 Now go at once and give your servants some encouragement; if you refuse, I swear by the LORD that not a man will stay with you tonight, and that would be a worse disaster than any you have suffer-8 ed since your earliest days.' Then the king rose and took his seat in the gate; and when the army was told that the king was sitting in the gate, they all appeared before him.

Various events of David's reign

MEANWHILE the Israelites had all scattered to their homes. 9 Throughout all the tribes of Israel

people were discussing it among themselves and saying, 'The king has saved us from our enemies and freed us from the power of the Philistines, and now he has fled the country because of Absalom. But 10 Absalom, whom we anointed king, has fallen in battle; so now why have we no plans for bringing the king back?'

What all Israel was saying came 11 to the king's ears.*a* So he sent word to Zadok and Abiathar the priests: 'Ask the elders of Judah why they should be the last to bring the king back to his palace. Tell them, "You 12 are my brothers, my flesh and my blood; why are you last to bring me back?" And tell Amasa, "You 13 are my own flesh and blood. You shall be my commander-in-chief, so help me God, for the rest of your life in place of Joab."' David's 14 message won all hearts in Judah, and they sent to the king, urging him to return with all his men.

So the king came back to the 15 Jordan; and the men of Judah came to Gilgal to meet him and escort him across the river. Shimei 16 son of Gera the Benjamite from Bahurim hastened down among the men of Judah to meet King David with a thousand men from 17 Benjamin; Ziba was there too, the servant of Saul's family, with his fifteen sons and twenty servants. They rushed into the Jordan under the king's eyes and crossed to and 18 fro conveying his household in order to win his favour. Shimei son of Gera, when he had crossed the river, fell down before the king and 19 said to him, 'I beg your majesty not to remember how disgracefully your servant behaved when your majesty left Jerusalem; do not hold it against me or take it to heart. For I humbly acknowledge 20 that I did wrong, and today I am the first of all the house of Joseph to come down to meet your majes-

a What...ears: *prob. rdg.;* Heb. *has these words after* back to his palace *and adds* to his palace.

21 ty.' But Abishai son of Zeruiah objected, 'Ought not Shimei to be put to death because he cursed the
22 LORD's anointed prince?' David answered, 'What right have you, you sons of Zeruiah, to oppose me today? Why should any man be put to death this day in Israel? I know now that I am king of Israel.'
23 Then the king said to Shimei, 'You shall not die', and confirmed it with an oath.

24 Saul's grandson Mephibosheth also went down to meet the king. He had not dressed his feet, combed his beard or washed his clothes, from the day the king went out
25 until he returned victorious. When he came from Jerusalem to meet the king, David said to him, 'Why did you not go with me, Mephi-
26 bosheth?' He answered, 'Sir, my servant deceived me; I did intend to harness my ass and ride with the
27 king (for I am lame), but his stories set your majesty against me. Your majesty is like the angel of God; you must do what you think right.
28 My father's whole family, one and all, deserved to die at your majesty's hands, but you gave me, your servant, my place at your table. What further favour can I expect
29 of the king?' The king answered, 'You have said enough. My decision is that you and Ziba are to
30 share the estate.' Mephibosheth said, 'Let him have it all, now that your majesty has come home victorious.'

31 Barzillai the Gileadite too had come down from Rogelim, and he went as far as the Jordan with the
32 king to send him on his way. Now Barzillai was very old, eighty years of age; it was he who had provided for the king while he was at Mahanaim, for he was a man of high
33 standing. The king said to Barzillai, 'Cross over with me and I will provide for your old age in my
34 household in Jerusalem.' Barzillai answered, 'Your servant is far too old to go up with your majesty to

Jerusalem. I am already eighty; 35 and I cannot tell good from bad. I cannot taste what I eat or drink; I cannot hear the voices of men and women singing. Why should I be a burden any longer on your majesty? Your servant will attend 36 the king for a short way across the Jordan; and why should the king reward me so handsomely? Let me 37 go back and end my days in my own city near the grave of my father and mother. Here is my son Kimham; let him cross over with your majesty, and do for him what you think best.' The king answered, 38 'Kimham shall cross with me and I will do for him whatever you think best; and I will do for you whatever you ask.'

All the people crossed the Jor- 39 dan while the king waited. The king then kissed Barzillai and gave him his blessing. Barzillai went back to his own home; the king 40 crossed over to Gilgal, Kimham with him. All the people of Judah escorted the king over the river, and so did half the people of Israel.

The men of Israel came to the 41 king in a body and said, 'Why should our brothers of Judah have got possession of the king's person by joining King David's own men and then escorting him and his household across the Jordan?' The 42 men of Judah replied, 'Because his majesty is our near kinsman. Why should you resent it? Have we eaten at the king's expense? Have we received any gifts?' The men of 43 Israel answered, 'We have ten times your interest in the king and, what is more, we are senior to you; why do you disparage us? Were we not the first to speak of bringing the king back?' The men of Judah used language even fiercer than the men of Israel.

There happened to be a man 20 there, a scoundrel named Sheba son of Bichri, a man of Benjamin. He blew the trumpet and cried out:

What share have we in David?
We have no lot in the son of Jesse.
Away to your homes, O Israel.

2 The men of Israel all left David, to follow Sheba son of Bichri, but the men of Judah stood by their king and followed him from the Jordan to Jerusalem.

3 When David came home to Jerusalem he took the ten concubines whom he had left in charge of the palace and put them under guard; he maintained them but did not have intercourse with them. They were kept in confinement to the day of their death, widowed in the prime of life.

4 The king said to Amasa, 'Call up the men of Judah and appear before me again in three days' time.'

5 So Amasa went to call up the men of Judah, but it took longer than

6 the time fixed by the king. David said to Abishai, 'Sheba son of Bichri will give us more trouble than Absalom; take the royal bodyguard and follow him closely. If he has occupied some fortified cities,

7 he may escape us.' Abishai was followed by Joab*a* with the Kerethite and Pelethite guards and all the fighting men; they left Jerusalem in pursuit of Sheba son of

8 Bichri. When they reached the great stone in Gibeon, Amasa came towards them. Joab was wearing his tunic and over it a belt supporting a sword in its scabbard. He came forward, concealing his trea-

9 chery, and said to Amasa, 'I hope you are well, my brother', and with his right hand he grasped Amasa's

10 beard to kiss him. Amasa was not on his guard against the sword in Joab's hand. Joab struck him with it in the belly and his entrails poured out to the ground; he did not strike a second blow, for Amasa was dead. Joab and his bro-

ther Abishai went on in pursuit of Sheba son of Bichri. One of Joab's 11 young men stood over Amasa and called out, 'Follow Joab, all who are for Joab and for David!' Amasa's body lay soaked in blood 12 in the middle of the road, and when the man saw how all the people stopped, he rolled him off the road into the field and threw a cloak over him; for everyone who came by saw the body and stopped. When 13 he had been dragged from the road, they all went on after Joab in pursuit of Sheba son of Bichri.

Sheba passed through all the 14 tribes of Israel until he came to Abel-beth-maacah,*b* and all the clan of Bichri*c* rallied to him and followed him into the city. Joab's 15 forces came up and besieged him in Abel-beth-maacah, raised a siege-ramp against it and began undermining the wall to bring it down. Then a wise woman stood on the 16 rampart*d* and called from the city, 'Listen, listen! Tell Joab to step 17 forward and let me speak with him.' So he came forward and the woman said, 'Are you Joab?' He answered, 'I am.' 'Listen to what I have to say, sir', she went on, to which he replied, 'I am listening.' 'In the old days', she said, 'there 18 was a saying, "Go to Abel for the answer", and that settled the matter. My city is known to be one 19 of the most peaceable and loyal*e* in Israel; she is like a watchful mother in Israel, and you are seeking to kill her. Would you destroy the LORD's own possession?' Joab an- 20 swered, 'God forbid, far be it from me to ruin or destroy! That is not 21 our aim; but a man from the hill-country of Ephraim named Sheba son of Bichri has raised a revolt against King David; surrender this one man, and I will retire from the city.' The woman said to Joab,

---

a Abishai . . . Joab: *prob. rdg.*; *Heb.* Some men of Joab followed him.
b *Prob. rdg.*, *cp. verse 15*; *Heb.* Abel and Beth-maacah.
c *Prob. rdg.*; *Heb.* Beri.   *d* stood . . . rampart: *transposed from verse 15.*
e My city . . . loyal: *prob. rdg.*; *Heb.* I am the requited ones of the loyal ones.

'His head shall be thrown to you over the wall.' Then the woman 22 withdrew, and her wisdom won over the assembled people; they cut off Sheba's head and threw it to Joab. Then he sounded the trumpet and the whole army left the city and dispersed to their homes, while Joab went back to the king in Jerusalem.

23*[a]* Joab was in command of the army,*[b]* and Benaiah son of Jehoiada commanded the Kerethite 24 and Pelethite guards. Adoram was in charge of the forced levy, and Jehoshaphat son of Ahilud was 25 secretary of state. Sheva was adjutant-general, and Zadok and 26 Abiathar were priests; Ira the Jairite was David's priest.

21 IN David's reign there was a famine that lasted year after year for three years. So David consulted the LORD, and he answered, 'Bloodguilt rests on Saul and on his family because he put the Gibeon2 ites to death.' (The Gibeonites were not of Israelite descent; they were a remnant of Amorite stock whom the Israelites had sworn that they would spare. Saul, however, had sought to exterminate them in his zeal for Israel and Judah.) King David summoned the Gibeonites 3 therefore, and said to them, 'What can be done for you? How can I make expiation, so that you may have cause to bless the LORD's own 4 people?' The Gibeonites answered, 'Our feud with Saul and his family cannot be settled in silver and gold, and there is no one man in Israel whose death would content us.' 'Then what do you want me to 5 do for you?' asked David. They answered, 'Let us make an end of the man who caused our undoing and ruined us, so that he shall never again have his place within the 6 borders of Israel. Hand over to us seven of that man's sons, and we

will hurl them down to their death before*[c]* the LORD in Gibeah of Saul, the LORD's chosen king.' The king agreed to hand them over, but he 7 spared Mephibosheth son of Jonathan, son of Saul, because of the oath that had been taken in the LORD's name by David and Saul's son Jonathan. The king then took 8 the two sons whom Rizpah daughter of Aiah had borne to Saul, Armoni and Mephibosheth, and the five sons whom Merab, Saul's daughter, had borne to Adriel son of Barzillai of Meholah. He handed 9 them over to the Gibeonites, and they flung them down from the mountain before the LORD; the seven of them fell together. They were put to death in the first days of harvest at the beginning of the barley harvest. Rizpah daughter of 10 Aiah took sackcloth and spread it out as a bed for herself on the rock, from the beginning of harvest until the rains came and fell from heaven upon the bodies. She allowed no bird to set upon them by day nor any wild beast by night. When 11 David was told what Rizpah daughter of Aiah the concubine of Saul had done, he went and took 12 the bones of Saul and his son Jonathan from the citizens of Jabeshgilead, who had stolen them from the public square at Beth-shan, where the Philistines had hung them on the day they defeated Saul at Gilboa. He removed the bones of 13 Saul and Jonathan from there and gathered up the bones of the men who had been hurled to death. They 14 buried the bones of Saul and his son Jonathan in the territory of Benjamin at Zela, in the grave of his father Kish. Everything was done as the king ordered, and thereafter the LORD was willing to accept prayers offered for the country.

Once again war broke out be- 15 tween the Philistines and Israel.

---

[a] Verses 23–26: cp. 8. 16–18; 1 Kgs. 4. 2–6; 1 Chr. 18. 15–17.
[b] Prob. rdg., cp. 8. 16; Heb. adds Israel.   *[c]* Or for.

David and his men went down to the battle, but as he fought with the Philistines he fell exhausted.
16 Then Benob, one of the race of the Rephaim, whose bronze spear weighed three hundred shekels[a] and who wore a belt of honour, took David prisoner and was about
17 to kill him. But Abishai son of Zeruiah came to David's help, struck the Philistine down and killed him. Then David's officers took an oath that he should never again go out with them to war, for fear that the lamp of Israel might be extinguished.
18[b] Some time later war with the Philistines broke out again in Gob: it was then that Sibbechai of Hushah killed Saph, a descendant of
19 the Rephaim. In another war with the Philistines in Gob, Elhanan son of Jair[c] of Bethlehem killed Goliath of Gath, whose spear had
20 a shaft like a weaver's beam. In yet another war in Gath there appeared a giant with six fingers on each hand and six toes on each foot, twenty-four in all. He too was
21 descended from the Rephaim; and, when he defied Israel, Jonathan son of David's brother Shimeai
22 killed him. These four giants were the descendants of the Rephaim in Gath, and they all fell at the hands of David and his men.

22 THESE are the words of the song David sang to the LORD on the day when the LORD delivered him from the power of all his enemies and from the power of Saul:

2[d] The LORD is my stronghold, my fortress and my champion,
3 my God, my rock where I find safety;
my shield, my mountain fastness, my strong tower,
my refuge, my deliverer, who saves me from violence.

4 I will call on the LORD to whom all praise is due,
and I shall be delivered from my enemies.
5 When the waves of death swept round me,
and torrents of destruction overtook me,
6 the bonds of Sheol tightened about me,
the snares of death were set to catch me;
7 then in anguish of heart I cried to the LORD,
I called for help to my God;
he heard me from his temple,
and my cry rang in his ears.
8 The earth heaved and quaked,
heaven's foundations shook;
they heaved, because he was angry.
9 Smoke rose from his nostrils,
devouring fire came out of his mouth,
glowing coals and searing heat.
10 He swept the skies aside as he descended,
thick darkness lay under his feet.
11 He rode on a cherub, he flew through the air;
he swooped[e] on the wings of the wind.
12 He curtained himself in darkness and made dense vapour his canopy.
13 Thick clouds came out of the radiance before him;
glowing coals burned brightly.
14 The LORD thundered from the heavens
and the voice of the Most High spoke out.
15 He loosed his arrows, he sped them far and wide,
his lightning shafts, and sent them echoing.
16 The channels of the sea-bed were revealed,
the foundations of earth laid bare
at the LORD's rebuke,
at the blast of the breath of his nostrils.

---

[a] shekels: *prob. rdg.*; *Heb.* weight.   [b] Verses 18–22: *cp.* 1 Chr. 20. 4–7.
[c] Jair: *prob. rdg.*, *cp.* 1 Chr. 20. 5; *Heb.* Jaare-oregim.
[d] Verses 2–51: *cp.* Ps. 18. 2–50.   [e] Prob. rdg., *cp.* Ps. 18. 10; *Heb.* was seen.

17 He reached down from the height
    and took me,
   he drew me out of mighty waters,

18 he rescued me from my enemies,
    strong as they were,
   from my foes when they grew too
    powerful for me.

19 They confronted me in the hour of
    my peril,
   but the LORD was my buttress.

20 He brought me out into an open
    place,
   he rescued me because he de-
    lighted in me.

21 The LORD rewarded me as my
    righteousness deserved;
   my hands were clean, and he re-
    quited me.

22 For I have followed the ways of
    the LORD
   and have not turned wickedly from
    my God;

23 all his laws are before my eyes,
   I have not failed to follow his de-
    crees.

24 In his sight I was blameless
   and kept myself from wilful sin;

25 the LORD requited me as my
    righteousness deserved
   and my purity in his eyes.

26 With the loyal thou showest thy-
    self loyal
   and with the blameless man blame-
    less.

27 With the savage man thou showest
    thyself savage,
   and[a] tortuous with the perverse.

28 Thou deliverest humble folk,
   thou lookest with contempt upon
    the proud.

29 Thou, LORD, art my lamp,
   and the LORD will lighten my dark-
    ness.

30 With thy help I leap over a bank,
   by God's aid I spring over a wall.

31 The way of God is perfect,
   the LORD's word has stood the test;

he is the shield of all who take
   refuge in him.

32 What god is there but the LORD?
What rock but our God? –

33 the God who girds me[b] with
   strength
and makes my way blameless,[c]

34 who makes me swift as a hind
and sets me secure on the mountains;

35 who trains my hands for battle,
and my arms aim an arrow tipped
   with bronze.

36 Thou hast given me the shield of
   thy salvation,
in thy providence thou makest me
   great.

37 Thou givest me room for my steps,
my feet have not faltered.

38 I pursue my enemies and destroy
   them,
I do not return until I have made
   an end of them.

39 I make an end of them, I strike
   them down;
they rise no more, they fall beneath my feet.

40 Thou dost arm me with strength
   for the battle
and dost subdue my foes before me.

41 Thou settest[d] my foot on my
   enemies' necks,
and I bring to nothing those that
   hate me.

42 They cry out[e] and there is no one
   to help them,
they cry to the LORD and he does
   not answer.

43 I will pound them fine as dust on
   the ground,
like mud in the streets will I
   trample them.[f]

44 Thou dost deliver me from the
   clamour of the people,
and makest me master of the
   nations.
A people I never knew shall be my
   subjects.

---

[a] With the savage...savage, and: *or* With the pure thou showest thyself pure,
but...   [b] who girds me: *prob. rdg., cp.* Ps. 18. 32; *Heb.* my refuge *or* my strength.
[c] and makes...blameless: *prob. rdg., cp.* Ps. 18. 32; *Heb. unintelligible.*
[d] *Prob. rdg., cp.* Ps. 18. 40; *Heb. unintelligible.*
[e] cry out: *prob. rdg., cp.* Ps. 18. 41; *Heb.* look.
[f] *Prob. rdg., cp.* Ps. 18. 42; *Heb. adds* will I stamp them down.

45 Foreigners shall come cringing to
me;
as soon as they hear tell of me, they
shall obey me.

46 Foreigners shall be brought captive to me,
and come limping from their
strongholds.

47 The LORD lives, blessed is my rock,
high above all is God my rock and
safe refuge.

48 O God, who grantest me vengeance,
who dost subdue peoples under
me,

49 who dost snatch me from my foes
and set me over my enemies,
thou dost deliver me from violent
men.

50 Therefore, LORD, I will praise thee
among the nations
and sing psalms to thy name,

51 to one who gives his king great
victories
and in all his acts keeps faith with
his anointed king,
with David and his descendants
for ever.

23 These are the last words of
David:

The very word of David son of
Jesse,
the very word of the man whom
the High God raised up,
the anointed prince of the God of
Jacob,
and the singer of Israel's psalms:

2 the spirit of the LORD has spoken
through me,
and his word is on my lips.

3 The God of Israel spoke,
the Rock of Israel spoke of me:
'He who rules men in justice,
who rules in the fear of God,

4 is like the light of morning at sunrise,

a morning that is cloudless after
rain
and makes the grass sparkle from
the earth.'

5 Surely, surely my house is true to
God;
for he has made a pact with me for
all time,
its terms spelled out and faithfully
kept,
my whole salvation, all my[a] delight.

6 But the ungodly put forth no
shoots,
they are all like briars tossed aside;
none dare put out his hand to pick
them up,

7 none touch them but[b] with tool of
iron or of wood;
they are fit only for burning in the
fire.[c]

8[d] THESE are the names of David's
heroes. First came Ishbosheth the
Hachmonite,[e] chief of the three; it
was he who brandished his spear[f]
over eight hundred dead, all slain
at one time. Next to him was Elea-
9 zar son of Dodo the Ahohite,[g] one
of the heroic three. He was with
David at Pas-dammim where the
Philistines[h] had gathered for battle.
10 When the Israelites fell back, he
stood his ground and rained blows
on the Philistines until, from sheer
weariness, his hand stuck fast to
his sword; and so the LORD brought
about a great victory that day.
Afterwards the people rallied behind him, but it was only to strip
11 the dead. Next to him was Shammah son of Agee a Hararite. The
Philistines had gathered at Lehi,
where there was a field with a fine
crop of lentils; and, when the Phili-
12 stines put the people to flight, he
stood his ground in the field, saved

---

[a] Prob. rdg.; Heb. om.
[b] but: prob. rdg.; Heb. he shall be filled.
[c] Prob. rdg.; Heb. adds in sitting.
[d] Verses 8–39: cp. 1 Chr. 11. 10–41.
[e] Prob. rdg.; Heb. Josheb-basshebeth a Tahchemonite.
[f] who…spear: prob. rdg., cp. 1 Chr. 11. 11; Heb. unintelligible.
[g] the Ahohite: prob. rdg., cp. 1 Chr. 11. 12; Heb. son of Ahohi.
[h] He was…Philistines: prob. rdg., cp. 1 Chr. 11. 13; Heb. With David when they
taunted them among the Philistines.

it[a] and defeated them. So the LORD again brought about a great victory.

13 Three of the thirty went down towards the beginning of harvest to join David at the cave of Adullam, while a band of Philistines was encamped in the Vale of Rephaim. 14 At that time David was in the stronghold and a Philistine 15 garrison held Bethlehem. One day a longing came over David, and he exclaimed, 'If only I could have a drink of water from the well[b] by 16 the gate of Bethlehem!' At this the heroic three made their way through the Philistine lines and drew water from the well by the gate of Bethlehem and brought it to David. But David refused to drink it; he poured it out to the 17 LORD and said, 'God forbid that I should do such a thing! Can I drink[c] the blood of these men who risked their lives for it?' So he would not drink it. Such were the exploits of the heroic three.

18 Abishai the brother of Joab son of Zeruiah was chief of the thirty. He once brandished his spear over three hundred dead, and he was 19 famous among the thirty. Some think he even surpassed the rest of the thirty[d] in reputation, and he became their captain, but he did 20 not rival the three. Benaiah son of Jehoiada, from Kabzeel, was a hero of many exploits. It was he who smote the two champions of Moab, and who went down into a pit and killed a lion on a snowy day. 21 It was he who also killed the Egyptian, a man of striking appearance armed with a spear: he went to meet him with a club, snatched the spear out of the Egyptian's hand and killed him with his own wea-

pon. Such were the exploits of 22 Benaiah son of Jehoiada, famous among the heroic thirty.[d] He was 23 more famous than the rest of the thirty, but he did not rival the three. David appointed him to his household.

Asahel the brother of Joab was 24 one of the thirty, and Elhanan son of Dodo from Bethlehem; Sham- 25 mah from Harod, and Elika from Harod; Helez from Beth-pelet,[e] 26 and Ira son of Ikkesh from Tekoa; Abiezer from Anathoth, and Me- 27 bunnai from Hushah; Zalmon the 28 Ahohite, and Maharai from Netophah; Heled son of Baanah from 29 Netophah, and Ittai son of Ribai from Gibeah of Benjamin; Benai- 30 ah from Pirathon, and Hiddai from the ravines of Gaash; Abi- 31 albon from Beth-arabah,[f] and Azmoth from Bahurim;[g] Eliahba 32 from Shaalbon, and Hashem the Gizonite; Jonathan son of[h] Sham- 33 mah the Hararite, and Ahiam son of Sharar the Hararite;[i] Eliphelet 34 son of Ahasbai son of the Maacathite, and Eliam son of Ahithophel the Gilonite; Hezrai from Carmel, 35 and Paarai the Arbite; Igal son of 36 Nathan from Zobah, and Bani the Gadite; Zelek the Ammonite, and 37 Naharai from Beeroth, armourbearer to Joab son of Zeruiah; Ira the Ithrite, Gareb the Ithrite, 38 and Uriah the Hittite: there were 39 thirty-seven in all.

ONCE again the Israelites felt the 24 1[j] LORD's anger, when he incited David against them and gave him orders that Israel and Judah should be counted. So he instructed 2 Joab and the officers of the army[k] with him to go round all the tribes of Israel, from Dan to Beersheba,

---

[a] saved it: or cleared it of the Philistines.
[b] Or cistern.
[c] I drink: prob. rdg., cp. 1 Chr. 11. 19; Heb. om.
[d] Prob. rdg.; Heb. three.
[e] Prob. rdg., cp. Josh. 15. 27; Heb. from Pelet.
[f] Prob. rdg., cp. Josh. 18. 22; Heb. from Arabah.
[g] Prob. rdg., cp. 1 Chr. 11. 33; Heb. from Barhum.
[h] Hashem...son of: prob. rdg., cp. 1 Chr. 11. 34; Heb. the sons of Jashen, Jonathan.
[i] Prob. rdg., cp. 1 Chr. 11. 35; Heb. Ararite.
[j] Verses 1–25: cp. 1 Chr. 21. 1–27.
[k] Joab...army: prob. rdg., cp. 1 Chr. 21. 2; Heb. Joab the officer of the army.

and make a record of the people and report the number to him.
3 Joab answered, 'Even if the LORD your God should increase the people a hundredfold and your majesty should live to see it, what pleasure would that give your majesty?'
4 But Joab and the officers were overruled by the king and they left his presence in order to count the
5 people. They crossed the Jordan and began at Aroer and the level land of the gorge, proceeding to-
6 wards Gad[a] and Jazer. They came to Gilead and to the land of the Hittites, to Kadesh, and then to Dan and Iyyon[b] and so round to-
7 wards Sidon. They went as far as the walled city of Tyre and all the towns of the Hivites and Canaanites, and then went on to the Negeb
8 of Judah at Beersheba. They covered the whole country and arrived back at Jerusalem after nine
9 months and twenty days. Joab reported to the king the total number of people: the number of able-bodied men, capable of bearing arms, was eight hundred thousand in Israel and five hundred thousand in Judah.
10 After he had counted the people David's conscience smote him, and he said to the LORD, 'I have done a very wicked thing: I pray thee, LORD, remove thy servant's guilt,
11 for I have been very foolish.' He rose next morning, and meanwhile the command of the LORD had come to the prophet Gad, David's
12 seer, to go and speak to David: 'This is the word of the LORD: I have three things in store for you; choose one and I will bring it upon
13 you.' So Gad came to David and repeated this to him and said, 'Is it to be three years of famine in your land, or three months of flight with the enemy at your heels, or three days of pestilence in your land? Consider carefully what an-

swer I am to take back to him who sent me.' Thereupon David said to 14 Gad, 'I am in a desperate plight; let us fall into the hands of the LORD, for his mercy is great; and let me not fall into the hands of men.' So the LORD sent a pestilence 15 throughout Israel from morning till the hour of dinner, and from Dan to Beersheba seventy thousand of the people died. Then the 16 angel stretched out his arm towards Jerusalem to destroy it; but the LORD repented of the evil and said to the angel who was destroying the people, 'Enough! Stay your hand.' At that moment the angel of the LORD was standing by the threshing-floor of Araunah the Jebusite.

When David saw the angel who 17 was striking down the people, he said to the LORD, 'It is I who have done wrong, the sin is mine; but these poor sheep, what have they done? Let thy hand fall upon me and upon my family.' That same 18 day Gad came to David and said to him, 'Go and set up an altar to the LORD on the threshing-floor of Araunah the Jebusite.' David did 19 what Gad told him to do, and went up as the LORD had commanded. When Araunah looked down and 20 saw the king and his servants coming over towards him, he went out, prostrated himself low before the king and said, 'Why has your 21 majesty come to visit his servant?' David answered, 'To buy the threshing-floor from you to build an altar to the LORD, so that the plague which has attacked the people may be stopped.' Araunah 22 answered David, 'I beg your majesty to take it and sacrifice what you think fit. I have here the oxen for a whole-offering, and their harness and the threshing-sledges for the fuel.' Araunah[c] gave it all to 23 the king for his own use and said to

---

[a] *began at...Gad: prob. rdg.; Heb.* encamped in Aroer on the right of the level land of the gorge Gad.   [b] *Prob. rdg., cp.* 1 Kgs. 15. 20; *Heb.* Yaan.
[c] *Prob. rdg.; Heb. adds* the king.

him, 'May the LORD your God ac-
24 cept you.' But the king said to
Araunah, 'No, I will buy it from
you; I will not offer to the LORD
my God whole-offerings that
have cost me nothing.' So David
bought the threshing-floor and

the oxen for fifty shekels of silver.
He built an altar to the LORD 25
there and offered whole-offerings
and shared-offerings. Then the
LORD yielded to his prayer for
the land; and the plague in Israel
stopped.

THE FIRST BOOK OF

KINGS

The death of David and accession of Solomon

1 K ING David was now a very
old man and, though they
wrapped clothes round him,
2 he could not keep warm. So his
household said to him, 'Let us find
a young virgin for your majesty, to
attend you and take care of you;
and let her lie in your bosom, sir,
3 and make you warm.' So they
searched all over Israel for a beautiful maiden and found Abishag, a
Shunammite, and brought her to
4 the king. She was a very beautiful
girl, and she took care of the king
and waited on him, but he had no
intercourse with her.
5   Now Adonijah, whose mother
was Haggith, was boasting that he
was to be king; and he had already
provided himself with chariots and
horsemen[a] and fifty outrunners.
6 Never in his life had his father cor-
rected him or asked why he behaved as he did. He was a very
handsome man, too, and was next
7 in age to Absalom. He talked with
Joab son of Zeruiah and with Abiathar the priest, and they gave him
8 their strong support; but Zadok
the priest, Benaiah son of Jehoiada,
Nathan the prophet, Shimei, Rei,
and David's bodyguard of heroes,

did not take his side. Adonijah 9
then held a sacrifice of sheep, oxen,
and buffaloes at the stone Zoheleth
beside En-rogel, and he invited all
his royal brothers and all those
officers of the household who were
of the tribe of Judah. But he did 10
not invite Nathan the prophet,
Benaiah and the bodyguard, or
Solomon his brother.
     Then Nathan said to Bathsheba, 11
the mother of Solomon, 'Have you
not heard that Adonijah son of
Haggith has become king, all unknown to our lord David? Now 12
come, let me advise you what to do
for your own safety and for the
safety of your son Solomon. Go 13
in and see King David and say to
him, "Did not your majesty swear
to me, your servant, that my son
Solomon should succeed you as
king; that it was he who should sit
on your throne? Why then has
Adonijah become king?" Then 14
while you are still speaking there
with the king, I will follow you in
and tell the whole story.'
     So Bathsheba went to the king 15
in his private chamber; he was now
very old, and Abishag the Shunammite was waiting on him.
Bathsheba bowed before the king 16
and prostrated herself. 'What do
you want?' said the king. She an- 17

---

[a] Or a chariot and horses.

swered, 'My lord, you swore to me your servant, by the LORD your God, that my son Solomon should succeed you as king, and that he 18 should sit on your throne. But now, here is Adonijah become king, all 19 unknown to your majesty. He has sacrificed great numbers of oxen, buffaloes, and sheep, and has invited to the feast all the king's sons, and Abiathar the priest, and Joab the commander-in-chief, but he has not invited your servant Solo- 20 mon. And now, your majesty, all Israel is looking to you to announce who is to succeed you on the throne. 21 Otherwise, when you, sir, rest with your forefathers, my son Solomon and I shall be treated as criminals.' 22 She was still speaking to the king when Nathan the prophet arrived. 23 The king was told that Nathan was there; he came into the king's presence and prostrated himself with 24 his face to the ground. 'My lord,' he said, 'your majesty must, I suppose, have declared that Adonijah should succeed you and that he 25 should sit on your throne. He has today gone down and sacrificed great numbers of oxen, buffaloes, and sheep, and has invited to the feast all the king's sons, Joab the commander-in-chief, and Abiathar the priest; and at this very moment they are eating and drinking in his presence and shouting, "Long live 26 King Adonijah!" But he has not invited me your servant, Zadok the priest, Benaiah son of Jehoiada, or 27 your servant Solomon. Has this been done by your majesty's authority, while we*a* your servants have not been told who should 28 succeed you on the throne?' Thereupon King David said, 'Call Bathsheba', and she came into the king's presence and stood before him. 29 Then the king swore an oath to her: 'As the LORD lives, who has delivered me from all my troubles: 30 I swore by the LORD the God of

Israel that Solomon your son should succeed me and that he should sit on my throne, and this day I give effect to my oath.' Bathsheba bowed low to the king 31 and prostrated herself; and she said, 'May my lord King David live for ever!'

Then King David said, 'Call 32 Zadok the priest, Nathan the prophet, and Benaiah son of Jehoiada.' They came into the king's presence and he gave them these 33 orders: 'Take the officers of the household with you; mount my son Solomon on the king's mule and escort him down to Gihon. There 34 Zadok the priest and Nathan the prophet shall anoint him king over Israel. Sound the trumpet and shout, "Long live King Solomon!" Then escort him home again, and 35 he shall come and sit on my throne and reign in my place; for he is the man that I have appointed prince over Israel and Judah.' Benaiah son 36 of Jehoiada answered the king, 'It shall be done. And may the LORD, the God of my lord the king, confirm it! As the LORD has been with 37 your majesty, so may he be with Solomon; may he make his throne even greater than the throne of my lord King David.' So Zadok the 38 priest, Nathan the prophet, and Benaiah son of Jehoiada, together with the Kerethite and Pelethite guards, went down and mounted Solomon on King David's mule and escorted him to Gihon. Zadok 39 the priest took the horn of oil from the Tent of the LORD and anointed Solomon; they sounded the trumpet and all the people shouted, 'Long live King Solomon!' Then 40 all the people escorted him home in procession, with great rejoicing and playing of pipes, so that the very earth split with the noise.

Adonijah and his guests had 41 finished their banquet when the noise reached their ears. Joab,

---

a *Has this . . . while we:* or *If this has been done by your majesty's authority, then* we . . .

hearing the sound of the trumpet, exclaimed, 'What is all this uproar in the city? What has happened?' 42 While he was still speaking, Jonathan son of Abiathar the priest arrived. 'Come in', said Adonijah. 'You are an honourable man and 43 bring good news.' 'Far otherwise,' Jonathan replied; 'our lord King 44 David has made Solomon king and has sent with him Zadok the priest, Nathan the prophet, and Benaiah son of Jehoiada, together with the Kerethite and Pelethite guards; they have mounted him on the 45 king's mule, and Zadok the priest and Nathan the prophet have anointed him king at Gihon, and they have now escorted him home rejoicing, and the city is in an uproar. That was the noise you heard. 46 More than that, Solomon has taken 47 his seat on the royal throne. Yes, and the officers of the household have been to greet our lord King David with these words: "May your God make the name of Solomon your son more famous than your own and his throne even greater than yours", and the king 48 bowed upon his couch. What is more, he said this: "Blessed be the LORD the God of Israel who has set a successor on my throne this day while I am still alive to see it." 49 Then Adonijah's guests all rose in 50 panic and scattered. Adonijah himself, in fear of Solomon, sprang up and went to the altar and caught 51 hold of its horns. Then a message was sent to Solomon: 'Adonijah is afraid of King Solomon; he has taken hold of the horns of the altar and has said, "Let King Solomon first swear to me that he will not put his servant to the sword."' 52 Solomon said, 'If he proves himself a man of worth, not a hair of his head shall fall to the ground; but if he is found to be trouble- 53 some, he shall die.' Then King Solomon sent and had him brought down from the altar; he came in and prostrated himself before the king, and Solomon ordered him home.

When the time of David's death 2 drew near, he gave this last charge to his son Solomon: 'I am going the 2 way of all the earth. Be strong and show yourself a man. Fulfil your 3 duty to the LORD your God; conform to his ways, observe his statutes and his commandments, his judgements and his solemn precepts, as they are written in the law of Moses, so that you may prosper in whatever you do and whichever way you turn, and that 4 the LORD may fulfil this promise that he made about me: "If your descendants take care to walk faithfully in my sight with all their heart and with all their soul, you shall never lack a successor on the throne of Israel." You know how 5 Joab son of Zeruiah treated me and what he did to two commanders-in-chief in Israel, Abner son of Ner and Amasa son of Jether. He killed them both, breaking the peace by bloody acts of war; and with that blood he stained the belt about my waist and the sandals on my feet. Do as your wisdom prompts you, 6 and do not let his grey hairs go down to the grave in peace. Show 7 constant friendship to the family of Barzillai of Gilead; let them have their place at your table; they befriended me when I was a fugitive from your brother Absalom. Do not 8 forget Shimei son of Gera, the Benjamite from Bahurim, who cursed me bitterly the day I went to Mahanaim. True, he came down to meet me at the Jordan, and I swore by the LORD that I would not put him to death. But you do not need 9 to let him go unpunished now; you are a wise man and will know how to deal with him; bring down his grey hairs in blood to the grave.'

So David rested with his fore- 10 fathers and was buried in the city of David, having reigned over 11 Israel for forty years, seven in Hebron and thirty-three in Jeru-

12 salem; and Solomon succeeded his father David as king and was firmly established on the throne.

The reign of Solomon

13 THEN Adonijah son of Haggith came to Bathsheba, the mother of Solomon. 'Do you come as a friend?' she asked. 'As a friend,' he an- 14 swered; 'I have something to say to 15 you.' 'Tell me', she said. 'You know', he went on, 'that the throne was mine and that all Israel was looking to me to be king; but I was passed over and the throne has gone to my brother; it was his by 16 the LORD's will. And now I have one request to make of you; do not refuse me.' 'What is it?' she said. 17 He answered, 'Will you ask King Solomon (he will never refuse you) to give me Abishag the Shunam- 18 mite in marriage?' 'Very well,' said Bathsheba, 'I will speak for you to 19 the king.' So Bathsheba went in to King Solomon to speak for Adonijah. The king rose to meet her and kissed her, and seated himself on his throne. A throne was set for the king's mother and she sat at his 20 right hand. Then she said, 'I have one small request to make of you; do not refuse me.' 'What is it, mother?' he replied; 'I will not refuse 21 you.' 'It is this, that Abishag the Shunammite should be given to your brother Adonijah in marri- 22 age.' At that Solomon answered his mother, 'Why do you ask for Abishag the Shunammite as wife for Adonijah? you might as well ask for the throne, for he is my elder brother and has both Abia- thar the priest and Joab son of 23 Zeruiah on his side.' Then King Solomon swore by the LORD: 'So help me God, Adonijah shall pay 24 for this with his life. As the LORD lives, who has established me and set me on the throne of David my father and has founded a house for me as he promised, this very day Adonijah shall be put to death!'

Thereupon King Solomon gave 25 Benaiah son of Jehoiada his or- ders, and he struck him down and he died.

Abiathar the priest was told by 26 the king to go off to Anathoth to his own estate. 'You deserve to die,' he said, 'but in spite of this day's work I shall not put you to death, for you carried the Ark of the Lord GOD before my father David, and you shared in all the hardships that he endured.' So 27 Solomon dismissed Abiathar from his office as priest of the LORD, and so fulfilled the sentence that the LORD had pronounced against the house of Eli in Shiloh.

News of all this reached Joab, 28 and he fled to the Tent of the LORD and caught hold of the horns of the altar; for he had sided with Adoni- jah, though not with Absalom. When King Solomon learnt that 29 Joab had fled to the Tent of the LORD and that he was by the altar, he sent Benaiah son of Jehoiada with orders to strike him down. Be- 30 naiah came to the Tent of the LORD and ordered Joab in the king's name to come away; but he said, 'No; I will die here.' Benaiah re- ported Joab's answer to the king, and the king said, 'Let him have 31 his way; strike him down and bury him, and so rid me and my father's house of the guilt for the blood that he wantonly shed. The LORD will 32 hold him responsible for his own death, because he struck down two innocent men who were better men than he, Abner son of Ner, com- mander of the army of Israel, and Amasa son of Jether, commander of the army of Judah, and ran them through with the sword, without my father David's knowledge. The 33 guilt of their blood shall recoil on Joab and his descendants for all time; but David and his descen- dants, his house and his throne, will enjoy perpetual prosperity from the LORD.' So Benaiah son of Je- 34 hoiada went up to the altar and struck Joab down and killed him, and he was buried in his house on the 35 edge of the wilderness. Thereafter the king appointed Benaiah son of Jehoiada to command the army in his place, and installed Zadok the priest in place of Abiathar.

36 Next the king sent for Shimei and said to him, 'Build yourself a house in Jerusalem and stay there; you are not to leave the city for any 37 other place. If ever you leave it and cross the gorge of the Kidron, you shall die; make no mistake about that. Your blood will be on your 38 own head.' And Shimei said to the king, 'I accept your sentence; I will do as your majesty commands.' So for a long time Shimei remained in 39 Jerusalem; but three years later two of his slaves ran away to Achish son of Maacah, king of Gath. When Shimei heard that his slaves 40 were in Gath, he immediately saddled his ass and went there to Achish in search of his slaves; he came to Gath and returned with 41 them. When King Solomon was told that Shimei had gone from 42 Jerusalem to Gath and back, he sent for him and said, 'Did I not require you to swear by the LORD? Did I not give you this solemn warning: "If ever you leave this city for any other place, you shall die; make no mistake about it"? And you said, "I accept your sen- 43 tence; I obey." Why then have you not kept the oath which you swore by the LORD, and the order which 44 I gave you? Shimei, you know in your own heart all the mischief you did to my father David; the LORD is now making that mischief recoil 45 on your own head. But King Solomon is blessed and the throne of David will be secure before the 46 LORD for all time.' The king then gave orders to Benaiah son of Jehoiada, and he went out and struck Shimei down; and he died. Thus Solomon's royal power was secure-ly established.

Solomon allied himself to Pha- 3 raoh king of Egypt by marrying his daughter. He brought her to the City of David, until he had finished building his own house and the house of the LORD and the wall round Jerusalem. The people how- 2 ever continued to sacrifice at the hill-shrines, for till then no house had been built in honour of the name of the LORD. Solomon him- 3 self loved the LORD, conforming to the precepts laid down by his fa-ther David; but he too slaughtered and burnt sacrifices at the hill-shrines.

Now King Solomon went to Gi- 4 beon to offer a sacrifice, for that was the chief hill-shrine, and he used to offer a thousand whole-offerings on its altar. There that 5^a night the LORD God appeared to him in a dream and said, 'What shall I give you? Tell me.' And 6 Solomon answered, 'Thou didst show great and constant love to thy servant David my father, be-cause he walked before thee in loyalty, righteousness, and inte-grity of heart; and thou hast main-tained this great and constant love towards him and hast now given him a son to succeed him on the throne. Now, O LORD my God, 7 thou hast made thy servant king in place of my father David, though I am a mere child, unskilled in leadership. And I am here in the 8 midst of thy people, the people of thy choice, too many to be num-bered or counted. Give thy servant, 9 therefore, a heart with skill to listen, so that he may govern thy people justly and distinguish good from evil. For who is equal to the task of governing this great people of thine?' The LORD was well 10 pleased that Solomon had asked for this, and he said to him, 'Be- 11 cause you have asked for this, and not for long life for yourself, or for wealth, or for the lives of your ene-mies, but have asked for discern-

12 ment in administering justice, I grant your request; I give you a heart so wise and so understanding that there has been none like you before your time nor will be 13 after you. I give you furthermore those things for which you did not ask, such wealth and honour[a] as no 14 king of your time can match. And if you conform to my ways and observe my ordinances and commandments, as your father David 15 did, I will give you long life.' Then he awoke, and knew it was a dream.

Solomon came to Jerusalem and stood before the Ark of the Covenant of the Lord; there he sacrificed whole-offerings and brought shared-offerings, and gave a feast to all his household.

16 Then there came into the king's presence two women who were pro-17 stitutes and stood before him. The first said, 'My lord, this woman and I share the same house, and I gave birth to a child when she was there 18 with me. On the third day after my baby was born she too gave birth to a child. We were quite alone; no one else was with us in the house; only the two of us were there. 19 During the night this woman's child died because she overlaid it, 20 and she got up in the middle of the night, took my baby from my side while I, your servant, was asleep, and laid it in her bosom, putting 21 her dead child in mine. When I got up in the morning to feed my baby, I found him dead; but when I looked at him closely, I found that it was not the child that I had 22 borne.' The other woman broke in, 'No; the living child is mine; yours is the dead one', while the first re-torted, 'No; the dead child is yours; mine is the living one.' So they went on arguing in the king's pre-23 sence. The king thought to himself, 'One of them says, "This is my child, the living one; yours is the dead one." The other says, "No; it is your child that is dead and mine that is alive."' Then he said, 24 'Fetch me a sword.' They brought in a sword and the king gave the 25 order: 'Cut the living child in two and give half to one and half to the other.' At this the woman who was 26 the mother of the living child, moved with love for her child, said to the king, 'Oh! sir, let her have the baby; whatever you do, do not kill it.' The other said, 'Let neither of us have it; cut it in two.' Thereupon the king gave judge-27 ment: 'Give the living baby to the first woman; do not kill it. She is its mother.' When Israel heard the 28 judgement which the king had given, they all stood in awe of him; for they saw that he had the wisdom of God within him to administer justice.

KING Solomon reigned over Israel. **4** His officers were as follows: 2[b]

In charge of the calendar:[c] Azariah son of Zadok the priest.
Adjutant-general:[d] Ahijah son[e] of 3 Shisha.
Secretary of state: Jehoshaphat son of Ahilud.
Commander of the army: Benaiah 4 son of Jehoiada.
Priests: Zadok and Abiathar.
Superintendent of the regional 5 governors: Azariah son of Nathan.
King's Friend: Zabud son of Nathan.
Comptroller of the household: 6 Ahishar.
Superintendent of the forced levy: Adoniram son of Abda.

Solomon had twelve regional go-7 vernors over Israel and they supplied the food for the king and the royal household, each being responsible for one month's provision

---

[a] Or riches.   [b] Verses 2–6: cp. 2 Sam. 8. 16–18; 20. 23–26; 1 Chr. 18. 15–17.
[c] In...calendar: prob. rdg.; Heb. Elihoreph.
[d] Prob. rdg., cp. 1 Chr. 18. 16; Heb. Adjutants-general.   [e] Prob. rdg.; Heb. sons.

8 in the year. These were their names:

Ben-hur in the hill-country of Ephraim.

9 Ben-dekar in Makaz, Shaalbim, Beth-shemesh, Elon, and Beth-hanan.

10 Ben-hesed in Aruboth; he had charge also of Socoh and all the land of Hepher.

11 Ben-abinadab, who had married Solomon's daughter Taphath, in all the district of Dor.

12 Baana son of Ahilud in Taanach and Megiddo, all Beth-shean as far as Abel-meholah beside Zartanah, and from Beth-shean below Jezreel as far as Jokmeam.

13 Ben-geber in Ramoth-gilead, including the tent-villages of Jair son of Manasseh in Gilead and the region of Argob in Bashan, sixty large walled cities with gate-bars of bronze.

14 Ahinadab son of Iddo in Mahanaim.

15 Ahimaaz in Naphtali; he also had married a daughter of Solomon, Basmath.

16 Baanah son of Hushai in Asher and Aloth.

17 Jehoshaphat son of Paruah in Issachar.

18 Shimei son of Elah in Benjamin.

19 Geber son of Uri in Gilead, the land of Sihon king of the Amorites and of Og king of Bashan.

In addition, one governor over all the governors[a] in the land.

20 The people of Judah and Israel were countless as the sands of the sea; they ate and they drank, and

21 enjoyed life. Solomon ruled over all the kingdoms from the river Euphrates to Philistia and as far as the frontier of Egypt; they paid tribute and were subject to him all his life.

22 Solomon's provision for one day was thirty kor of flour and sixty

23 kor of meal, ten fat oxen and twenty oxen from the pastures and a

hundred sheep, as well as stags, gazelles, roebucks, and fattened fowl. For he was paramount over 24 all the land west of the Euphrates from Tiphsah to Gaza, ruling all the kings west of the river; and he enjoyed peace on all sides. All 25 through his reign Judah and Israel continued at peace, every man under his own vine and fig-tree, from Dan to Beersheba.

Solomon had forty thousand 26 chariot-horses in his stables and twelve thousand cavalry horses.

The regional governors, each for 27 a month in turn, supplied provisions for King Solomon and for all who came to his table; they never fell short in their deliveries. They 28 provided also barley and straw, each according to his duty, for the horses and chariot-horses where it was required.

And God gave Solomon depth of 29 wisdom and insight, and understanding as wide as the sand on the sea-shore, so that Solomon's wis- 30 dom surpassed that of all the men of the east and of all Egypt. For he 31 was wiser than any man, wiser than Ethan the Ezrahite, and Heman, Kalcol, and Darda, the sons of Mahol; his fame spread among all the surrounding nations. He 32 uttered three thousand proverbs, and his songs numbered a thousand and five. He discoursed of 33 trees, from the cedar of Lebanon down to the marjoram that grows out of the wall, of beasts and birds, of reptiles and fishes. Men of all 34 races came to listen to the wisdom of Solomon, and from all the kings of the earth who had heard of his wisdom he received gifts.

WHEN Hiram king of Tyre heard 5 that Solomon had been anointed king in his father's place, he sent envoys to him, because he had always been a friend of David. Solo- 2[b] mon sent this answer to Hiram: 'You know that my father David 3

---

[a] over...governors: *prob. rdg.*; *Heb. om.*   [b] *Verses 2–11: cp. 2 Chr. 2. 3–16.*

could not build a house in honour of the name of the LORD his God, because he was surrounded by armed nations until the LORD made 4 them subject to him. But now on every side the LORD my God has given me peace; there is no one to 5 oppose me, I fear no attack. So I propose to build a house in honour of the name of the LORD my God, following the promise given by the LORD to my father David: "Your son whom I shall set on the throne in your place will build the house in 6 honour of my name." If therefore you will now give orders that cedars be felled and brought from Lebanon, my men will work with yours, and I will pay you for your men whatever sum you fix; for, as you know, we have none so skilled at felling timber as your Sidonians.'

7 When Hiram received Solomon's message, he was greatly pleased and said, 'Blessed be the LORD to-day who has given David a wise son to rule over this great people.' 8 And he sent this reply to Solomon: 'I have received your message. In this matter of timber, both cedar and pine, I will do all you wish. 9 My men shall bring down the logs from Lebanon to the sea and I will make them up into rafts to be floated to the place you appoint; I will have them broken up there and you can remove them. You, on your part, will meet my wishes if you provide the food for my 10 household.' So Hiram kept Solomon supplied with all the cedar 11 and pine that he wanted, and Solomon supplied Hiram with twenty thousand kor of wheat as food for his household and twenty kor of oil of pounded olives; Solomon 12 gave this yearly to Hiram. (The LORD had given Solomon wisdom as he had promised him; there was peace between Hiram and Solomon and they concluded an alli-13 ance.) King Solomon raised a forced levy from the whole of

Israel amounting to thirty thousand men. He sent them to Leba- 14 non in monthly relays of ten thousand, so that the men spent one month in Lebanon and two at home; Adoniram was superintendent of the whole levy. Solomon 15 had also seventy thousand hauliers and eighty thousand quarrymen, 16 apart from the three thousand three hundred foremen in charge of the work who superintended the labourers. By the king's orders they 17 quarried huge, massive blocks for laying the foundation of the LORD's house in hewn stone. Solomon's 18 and Hiram's builders and the Gebalites shaped the blocks and prepared both timber and stone for the building of the house.

It was in the four hundred and 6 1[a] eightieth year after the Israelites had come out of Egypt, in the fourth year of Solomon's reign over Israel, in the second month of that year, the month of Ziv, that he began to build the house of the LORD.

The house which King Solomon 2 built for the LORD was sixty cubits long by twenty cubits broad, and its height was thirty cubits. The 3 vestibule in front of the sanctuary was twenty cubits long, spanning the whole breadth of the house, while it projected ten cubits in front of the house; and he furnished 4 the house with embrasures. Then 5 he built a terrace against its wall round both the sanctuary and the inner shrine. He made arcades all round: the lowest arcade was five 6 cubits in depth, the middle six, and the highest seven; for he made rebates all round the outside of the main wall so that the bearer beams might not be set into the walls. In 7 the building of the house, only blocks of undressed stone direct from the quarry were used; no hammer or axe or any iron tool whatever was heard in the house while it was being built.

8 The entrance to the lowest arcade was in the right-hand corner of the house; there was access by a spiral stairway from that to the middle arcade, and from the middle 9–10 arcade to the highest. So he built the house and finished it, having constructed the terrace five cubits high against the whole building, braced the house with struts of cedar and roofed it with beams and coffering of cedar.

11 Then the word of the LORD came 12 to Solomon, saying, 'As for this house which you are building, if you are obedient to my ordinances and conform to my precepts and loyally observe all my commands, then I will fulfil my promise to you, the promise I gave to your father 13 David, and I will dwell among the Israelites and never forsake my people Israel.'

14 So Solomon built the LORD's 15 house and finished it. He lined the inner walls of the house with cedar boards, covering the interior from floor to rafters with wood; the floor 16 he laid with boards of pine. In the innermost part of the house he partitioned off a space of twenty cubits with cedar boards from floor to rafters and made of it an inner shrine, to be the Most Holy Place. 17 The sanctuary in front of this was 18 forty cubits long. The cedar inside the house was carved with open flowers and gourds; all was cedar, no stone was left visible.

19 He prepared an inner shrine in the furthest recesses of the house to receive the Ark of the Covenant of 20 the LORD. This inner shrine was twenty cubits square and it stood twenty cubits high; he overlaid it with red gold and made an altar of 21 cedar. And Solomon overlaid the inside of the house with red gold and drew a Veil[a] with golden chains across in front of the inner shrine.[b] 22 The whole house he overlaid with gold until it was all covered; and

the whole of the altar by the inner shrine he overlaid with gold.

23[c] In the inner shrine he made two cherubim of wild olive, each ten 24 cubits high. Each wing of the cherubim was five cubits long, and from wing-tip to wing-tip was ten 25 cubits. Similarly the second cherub measured ten cubits; the two cherubim were alike in size and 26 shape, and each ten cubits high. 27 He put the cherubim within the shrine at the furthest recesses and their wings were outspread, so that a wing of the one cherub touched the wall on one side and a wing of the other touched the wall on the other side, and their other wings met in the middle; and he overlaid 28 the cherubim with gold.

29 Round all the walls of the house he carved figures of cherubim, palm-trees, and open flowers, both in the inner chamber and in the 30 outer. The floor of the house he overlaid with gold, both in the inner chamber and in the outer. 31 At the entrance to the inner shrine he made a double door of wild olive; the pilasters and the[d] door-32 posts were pentagonal. The doors were of wild olive, and he carved cherubim, palms, and open flowers on them, overlaying them with gold and hammering the gold upon 33 the cherubim and the palms. Similarly for the doorway of the sanctuary he made a square frame of wild 34 olive and a double door of pine, each leaf having two swivel-pins. 35 On them he carved cherubim, palms, and open flowers, overlaying them evenly with gold over the carving.

36 He built the inner court with three courses of dressed stone and one course of lengths of cedar.

37 In the fourth year of Solomon's reign the foundation of the house of the LORD was laid, in the month of Ziv; and in the eleventh year, in 38 the month of Bul, which is the

---

[a] a Veil: *prob. rdg.*; Heb. *om.*   [b] *Prob. rdg.*; Heb. *adds* and overlaid it with gold.
[c] *Verses 23–28: cp.* 2 *Chr.* 3. 10–13.   [d] and the: *prob. rdg.*; Heb. *om.*

eighth month, the house was finished in all its details according to the specification. It had taken seven years to build.

7 Solomon had been engaged on his building for thirteen years by 2 the time he had finished it. He built the House of the Forest of Lebanon, a hundred cubits long, fifty broad, and thirty high, constructed of four rows of cedar columns, over which were laid lengths 3 of cedar. It had a cedar roof, extending over the beams, which rested on the columns, fifteen in each row; and the number of the 4 beams was forty-five. There were three rows of window-frames, and the windows corresponded to each 5 other at three levels. All the doorways and the windows had square frames, and window corresponded to window at three levels.

6 He made also the colonnade, fifty cubits long and thirty broad,[a] with a cornice above.

7 He built the Hall of Judgement, the hall containing the throne where he was to give judgement; this was panelled in cedar from floor to rafters.

8 His own house where he was to reside, in a court set back from the colonnade, and the house he made for Pharaoh's daughter whom he had married, were constructed like the hall.

9 All these were made of heavy blocks of stone, hewn to measure and trimmed with the saw on the inner and outer sides, from foundation to coping and from the court of the house[b] as far as the great 10 court. At the base were heavy stones, massive blocks, some ten 11 and some eight cubits in size, and above were heavy stones dressed 12 to measure, and cedar. The great court had three courses of dressed stone all around and a course of lengths of cedar; so had the inner court of the house of the LORD, and so had the vestibule of the house.

King Solomon fetched from Tyre 13 Hiram, the son of a widow of the 14 tribe of Naphtali. His father, a native of Tyre, had been a worker in bronze, and he himself was a man of great skill and ingenuity, versed in every kind of craftsmanship in bronze. Hiram came to King Solomon and executed all his works.

He cast in a mould the two 15[c] bronze pillars. One stood eighteen cubits high and it took a cord twelve cubits long to go round it; it was hollow, and the metal was four fingers thick.[d] The second pillar was the same. He made two 16 capitals of solid copper to set on the tops of the pillars, each capital five cubits high. He made two bands 17 of ornamental network, in festoons of chain-work, for the capitals on the tops of the pillars, a band of network for each capital. Then he made pomegranates in 18 two rows all round on top of the ornamental network of the one pillar; he did the same with the other capital. (The capitals at the 19 tops of the pillars in the vestibule were shaped like lilies and were four cubits high.) Upon the capi- 20 tals at the tops of the two pillars, immediately above the cushion, which was beyond the network upwards, were two hundred pomegranates in rows all round on the two capitals.[e] Then he erected the 21 pillars at the vestibule of the sanctuary. When he had erected the pillar on the right side, he named it Jachin;[f] and when he had erected the one on the left side, he named it Boaz.[g] On the tops of the pillars 22 was lily-work. Thus the work of the pillars was finished.

---

[a] *Prob. rdg.; Heb. adds* and a colonnade and pillars in front of them.
[b] *Prob. rdg., cp. verse 12; Heb.* from outside.   [c] *Verses 15–21: cp. 2 Chr. 3. 15–17.*
[d] it was...thick: *prob. rdg., cp. Jer. 52. 21; Heb. om.*
[e] the two capitals: *prob. rdg.; Heb.* the second capital.
[f] *Or* Jachun, *meaning* It shall stand.   [g] *Or* Booz, *meaning* In strength.

23[a] He then made the Sea of cast metal; it was round in shape, the diameter from rim to rim being ten cubits; it stood five cubits high, and it took a line thirty cubits 24 long to go round it. All round the Sea on the outside under its rim, completely surrounding the thirty[b] cubits of its circumference, were two rows of gourds, cast in one 25 piece with the Sea itself. It was mounted on twelve oxen, three facing north, three west, three south, and three east, their hind quarters turned inwards; the Sea 26 rested on top of them. Its thickness was a hand-breadth; its rim was made like that of a cup, shaped like the calyx of a lily; it held two thousand bath of water.

27 He also made the ten trolleys of bronze; each trolley was four cubits long, four wide, and three high. 28 This was the construction of the trolleys. They had panels set in 29 frames; on these panels were portrayed lions, oxen, and cherubim, and similarly on the frames. Above and below the lions, oxen, and cherubim[c] were fillets of hammered 30 work of spiral design. Each trolley had four bronze wheels with axles of bronze; it also had four flanges and handles beneath the laver, and these handles were of cast metal with a spiral design on their sides. 31 The opening for the basin was set within a crown which projected one cubit; the opening was round with a level edge,[d] and it had decorations in relief. (The panels of the trolleys were square, not round.) 32 The four wheels were beneath the panels, and the wheel-forks were made in one piece with the trolleys; the height of each wheel was a 33 cubit and a half. The wheels were constructed like those of a chariot, their axles, hubs, spokes, and fel-

loes being all of cast metal. The 34 four handles were at the four corners of each trolley, of one piece with the trolley. At the top of the 35 trolley there was a circular band half a cubit high; the struts and panels on[e] the trolley were of one piece with it. On the plates, that is 36 on the panels,[f] he carved cherubim, lions, and palm-trees, wherever there was a blank space, with spiral work all round it. This is how 37 the ten trolleys were made; all of them were cast alike, having the same size and the same shape.

He then made ten bronze basins, 38 each holding forty bath and measuring four cubits; there was a basin for each of the ten trolleys. He put five trolleys on the right 39 side of the house and five on the left side; and he put the Sea in the south-east corner of it.

Hiram made also the pots, the 40[g] shovels, and the tossing-bowls. So he finished all the work which he had undertaken for King Solomon on the house of the LORD: the two 41 pillars; the two bowl-shaped capitals on the tops of the pillars; the two ornamental networks to cover the two bowl-shaped capitals on the tops of the pillars; the four 42 hundred pomegranates for the two networks, two rows of pomegranates for each network, to cover the bowl-shaped capitals on the two pillars; the ten trolleys and 43 the ten basins on the trolleys; the 44 one Sea and the twelve oxen which supported it; the pots, the shovels, 45 and the tossing-bowls – all these objects in the house of the LORD which Hiram made for King Solomon being of bronze, burnished work. In the Plain of the Jordan 46 the king cast them, in the foundry between Succoth and Zarethan.

Solomon put all these objects in 47

---

[a] Verses 23–26: cp. 2 Chr. 4. 2–5.
[b] Prob. rdg.; Heb. ten.
[c] and cherubim: prob. rdg.; Heb. om.
[d] Prob. rdg.; Heb. adds a cubit and a half (cp. verse 32).
[e] Prob. rdg.; Heb. adds the head of.
[f] Prob. rdg.; Heb. adds its struts.
[g] Verses 40–51: cp. 2 Chr. 4. 11 – 5. 1.

their places; so great was the quantity of bronze used in their making that the weight of it was beyond 48 all reckoning. He made also all the furnishings for the house of the LORD: the golden altar and the golden table upon which was set 49 the Bread of the Presence; the lamp-stands of red gold, five on the right side and five on the left side of the inner shrine; the flowers, 50 lamps, and tongs, of gold; the cups, snuffers, tossing-bowls, saucers, and firepans, of red gold; and the panels for the doors of the inner sanctuary, the Most Holy Place, and for the doors of the house,[a] of gold.

51 When all the work which King Solomon did for the house of the LORD was completed, he brought in the sacred treasures of his father David, the silver, the gold, and the vessels, and deposited them in the storehouses of the house of the LORD.

8 1[b] THEN Solomon summoned the elders of Israel, all the heads of the tribes who were chiefs of families in Israel, to assemble in Jerusalem, in order to bring up the Ark of the Covenant of the LORD from the City 2 of David, which is called Zion. All the men of Israel assembled in King Solomon's presence at the pilgrim-feast in the month Etha-3 nim, the seventh month. When the elders of Israel had all come, the priests took the Ark of the LORD 4 and carried it up with the Tent of the Presence and all the sacred furnishings of the Tent: it was the priests and the Levites together 5 who carried them up. King Solomon and the whole congregation of Israel, assembled with him before the Ark, sacrificed sheep and oxen in numbers past counting or reckon-6 ing. Then the priests brought in the Ark of the Covenant of the LORD to its place, the inner shrine

of the house, the Most Holy Place, beneath the wings of the cherubim. The cherubim spread their wings 7 over the place of the Ark; they formed a screen above the Ark and its poles. The poles projected, and 8 their ends could be seen from the Holy Place immediately in front of the inner shrine, but from nowhere else outside; they are there to this day. There was nothing inside the 9 Ark but the two tablets of stone which Moses had deposited there at Horeb, the tablets of the covenant which the LORD made with the Israelites when they left Egypt.

Then the priests came out of the 10 Holy Place, since the cloud was filling the house of the LORD, and 11 they could not continue to minister because of it, for the glory of the LORD filled his house. And Solo- 12[c] mon said:

O LORD who hast set the sun in heaven,
but hast chosen to dwell in thick darkness,
here have I built thee a lofty 13 house,
a habitation for thee to occupy for ever.

And as they stood waiting, the 14 king turned round and blessed all the assembly of Israel in these 15 words: 'Blessed be the LORD the God of Israel who spoke directly to my father David and has himself fulfilled his promise. For he said, "From the day when I brought my 16 people Israel out of Egypt, I chose no city out of all the tribes of Israel where I should build a house for my Name to be there, but I chose David to be over my people Israel." My father David had in 17 mind to build a house in honour of the name of the LORD the God of Israel, but the LORD said to him, 18 "You purposed to build a house in honour of my name; and your purpose was good. Nevertheless, you 19

[a] *Prob. rdg.; Heb. adds* for the temple.
[c] *Verses 12–50: cp. 2 Chr. 6. 1–39.*
[b] *Verses 1–9: cp. 2 Chr. 5. 2–10.*

shall not build it; but the son who is to be born to you, he shall build the house in honour of my name."

20 The LORD has now fulfilled his promise: I have succeeded my father David and taken his place on the throne of Israel, as the LORD promised; and I have built the house in honour of the name of the LORD

21 the God of Israel. I have assigned therein a place for the Ark containing the Covenant of the LORD, which he made with our forefathers when he brought them out of Egypt.'

22 Then Solomon, standing in front of the altar of the LORD in the presence of the whole assembly of Israel, spread out his hands to-

23 wards heaven and said, 'O LORD God of Israel, there is no god like thee in heaven above or on earth beneath, keeping covenant with thy servants and showing them constant love while they continue faithful to thee in heart and soul.

24 Thou hast kept thy promise to thy servant David my father; by thy deeds this day thou hast fulfilled what thou didst say to him in

25 words. Now therefore, O LORD God of Israel, keep this promise of thine to thy servant David my father: "You shall never want for a man appointed by me to sit on the throne of Israel, if only your sons look to their ways and walk before me as you have walked before me."

26 And now, O God of Israel, let the words which thou didst speak to thy servant David my father be confirmed.

27 'But can God indeed dwell on earth? Heaven itself, the highest heaven, cannot contain thee; how much less this house that I have

28 built! Yet attend to the prayer and the supplication of thy servant, O LORD my God, listen to the cry and the prayer which thy servant utters

29 this day, that thine eyes may ever be upon this house night and day, this place of which thou didst say, "My Name shall be there"; so

mayest thou hear thy servant when he prays towards this place.

30 Hear the supplication of thy servant and of thy people Israel when they pray towards this place. Hear thou in heaven thy dwelling and, when thou hearest, forgive.

31 'When a man wrongs his neighbour and he is adjured to take an oath, and the adjuration is made

32 before thy altar in this house, then do thou hear in heaven and act: be thou thy servants' judge, condemning the guilty man and bringing his deeds upon his own head, acquitting the innocent and rewarding him as his innocence may deserve.

33 'When thy people Israel are defeated by an enemy because they have sinned against thee, and they turn back to thee, confessing thy name and making their prayer and supplication to thee in this house,

34 do thou hear in heaven; forgive the sin of thy people Israel and restore them to the land which thou gavest to their forefathers.

35 'When the heavens are shut up and there is no rain because thy servant and thy people Israel have sinned against thee, and when they pray towards this place, confessing thy name and forsaking their sin

36 when they feel thy punishment, do thou hear in heaven and forgive their sin; so mayest thou teach them the good way which they should follow; and grant rain to thy land which thou hast given to thy people as their own possession.

37 'If there is famine in the land, or pestilence, or black blight or red, or locusts new-sloughed or fully grown; or if their enemies besiege them in any of their cities; or if plague or sickness befall them,

38 then hear the prayer or supplication of every man among thy people Israel, as each one, prompted by the remorse of his own heart, spreads out his hands towards this

39 house: hear it in heaven thy dwelling and forgive, and act. And, as

thou knowest a man's heart, reward him according to his deeds, for thou alone knowest the hearts

40 of all men; and so they will fear thee all their life in the land thou gavest to our forefathers.

41 'The foreigner too, the man who does not belong to thy people Israel, but has come from a distant

42 land because of thy fame (for men shall hear of thy great fame and thy strong hand and arm outstretched), when he comes and

43 prays towards this house, hear in heaven thy dwelling and respond to the call which the foreigner makes to thee, so that like thy people Israel all peoples of the earth may know thy fame and fear thee, and learn that this house which I have built bears thy name.

44 'When thy people go to war with an enemy, wherever thou dost send them, when they pray to the LORD, turning towards this city which thou hast chosen and towards this house which I have built in honour

45 of thy name, do thou in heaven hear their prayer and supplication, and grant them justice.

46 'Should they sin against thee (and what man is free from sin?) and shouldst thou in thy anger give them over to an enemy, who carries them captive to his own

47 land, far or near; if in the land of their captivity they learn their lesson and make supplication again to thee in that land and say, "We have sinned and acted per-

48 versely and wickedly", if they turn back to thee with heart and soul in the land of their captors, and pray to thee, turning towards their land which thou gavest to their forefathers and towards this city which thou didst choose and this house which I have built in

49 honour of thy name; then in heaven thy dwelling do thou hear their prayer and supplication, and grant

50 them justice. Forgive thy people their sins and transgressions against thee; put pity for them in

their captors' hearts. For they are 51 thy possession, thy people whom thou didst bring out of Egypt, from the smelting-furnace, and so 52 thine eyes are ever open to the entreaty of thy servant and of thy people Israel, and thou dost hear whenever they call to thee. Thou 53 thyself hast singled them out from all the peoples of the earth to be thy possession; so thou didst promise through thy servant Moses when thou didst bring our forefathers from Egypt, O Lord GOD.'

When Solomon had finished this 54 prayer and supplication to the LORD, he rose from before the altar of the LORD, where he had been kneeling with his hands spread out to heaven, stood up and in a loud 55 voice blessed the whole assembly of Israel: 'Blessed be the LORD who 56 has given his people Israel rest, as he promised: not one of the promises he made through his servant Moses has failed. The LORD our 57 God be with us as he was with our forefathers; may he never leave us nor forsake us. May he turn our 58 hearts towards him, that we may conform to all his ways, observing his commandments, statutes, and judgements, as he commanded our forefathers. And may the words of 59 my supplication to the LORD be with the LORD our God day and night, that, as the need arises day by day, he may grant justice to his servant and justice to his people Israel. So all the peoples of the 60 earth will know that the LORD is God, he and no other, and you will 61 be perfect in loyalty to the LORD our God as you are this day, conforming to his statutes and observing his commandments.'

When the king and all Israel 62 came to offer sacrifices before the LORD, Solomon offered as shared- 63 offerings to the LORD twenty-two thousand oxen and a hundred and twenty thousand sheep; thus it was that the king and the Israelites dedicated the house of the LORD.

64[a] On that day also the king consecrated the centre of the court which lay in front[b] of the house of the LORD; there he offered the whole-offering, the grain-offering, and the fat portions of the shared-offerings, because the bronze altar which stood before the LORD was too small to take them all, the whole-offering, the grain-offering, and the fat portions of the shared-offerings.

65 So Solomon and all Israel with him, a great assembly from Lebo-hamath to the Torrent of Egypt, celebrated the pilgrim-feast at that time before the LORD our God

66 for seven days. On the eighth day he dismissed the people; and they blessed the king, and went home happy and glad at heart for all the prosperity granted by the LORD to his servant David and to his people Israel.

9 1[c] WHEN Solomon had finished the house of the LORD and the royal palace and all the plans for building on which he had set his heart,

2 the LORD appeared to him a second time, as he had appeared to him at

3 Gibeon. The LORD said to him, 'I have heard the prayer and supplication which you have offered me; I have consecrated this house which you have built, to receive my Name for all time, and my eyes and my heart shall be fixed on it

4 for ever. And if you, on your part, live in my sight as your father David lived, in integrity and uprightness, doing all I command you and observing my statutes and my

5 judgements, then I will establish your royal throne over Israel for ever, as I promised your father David when I said, "You shall never want for a man upon the

6 throne of Israel." But if you or your sons turn back from following me and do not observe my commandments and my statutes which I have set before you, and if you go and serve other gods and prostrate yourselves before them, then I will 7 cut off Israel from the land which I gave them; I will renounce this house which I have consecrated in honour of my name, and Israel shall become a byword and an object lesson among all peoples. And 8 this house will become a ruin; every passer-by will be appalled and gasp at the sight of it; and they will ask, "Why has the LORD so treated this land and this house?" The answer will be, "Because they 9 forsook the LORD their God, who brought their forefathers out of Egypt, and clung to other gods, prostrating themselves before them and serving them; that is why the LORD has brought this great evil on them."'

Solomon had taken twenty years 10[d] to build the two houses, the house of the LORD and the royal palace. Hiram king of Tyre had supplied 11 him with all the timber, both cedar and pine, and all the gold, that he desired, and King Solomon gave Hiram twenty cities in the land of Galilee. But when Hiram went 12 from Tyre to inspect the cities which Solomon had given him, they did not satisfy him, and he 13 said, 'What kind of cities are these you have given me, my brother?' And so he called them the Land of Cabul,[e] the name they still bear. Hiram sent a hundred and twenty 14 talents of gold to the king.

This is the record of the forced 15 labour which King Solomon conscripted to build the house of the LORD, his own palace, the Millo, the wall of Jerusalem, and Hazor, Megiddo, and Gezer. Gezer had 16 been attacked and captured by Pharaoh king of Egypt, who had burnt it to the ground, put its Canaanite inhabitants to death,

---

[a] Verses 64–66: cp. 2 Chr. 7. 7–10.
[c] Verses 1–9: cp. 2 Chr. 7. 11–22.
[e] That is Sterile Land.

[b] Or to the east.
[d] Verses 10–28: cp. 2 Chr. 8. 1–18.

and given it as a marriage gift to
17 his daughter, Solomon's wife; and
Solomon rebuilt it. He also built
18 Lower Beth-horon, Baalath, and
19 Tamar in the wilderness, as well as
all his store-cities, and the towns
where he quartered his chariots
and horses; and he carried out all
his cherished plans for building in
Jerusalem, in the Lebanon, and
throughout his whole dominion.
20 All the survivors of the Amorites,
Hittites, Perizzites, Hivites, and
Jebusites, who did not belong to
21 Israel – that is their descendants
who survived in the land, wherever
the Israelites had been unable to
annihilate them – were employed
by Solomon on perpetual forced
22 labour, as they still are. But Solomon put none of the Israelites to
forced labour; they were his
fighting men,[a] his captains and
lieutenants, and the commanders
of his chariots and of his cavalry.
23 The number of officers in charge of
the foremen over Solomon's work
was five hundred and fifty; these
superintended the people engaged
on the work.
24 Then Solomon brought Pharaoh's daughter up from the City
of David to her own house which
he had built for her; later on he
built the Millo.
25 Three times a year Solomon
used to offer whole-offerings and
shared-offerings on the altar which
he had built to the LORD, making
smoke-offerings before the LORD.
So he completed the house.
26 King Solomon built a fleet of
ships at Ezion-geber, near Eloth[b]
on the shore of the Red Sea,[c] in
27 Edom. Hiram sent men of his own
to serve with the fleet, experienced
seamen, to work with Solomon's
28 men; and they went to Ophir and
brought back four hundred and
twenty talents of gold, which they
delivered to King Solomon.

THE queen of Sheba heard of 10
Solomon's fame[e] and came to test
him with hard questions. She ar- 2
rived in Jerusalem with a very
large retinue, camels laden with
spices, gold in great quantity, and
precious stones. When she came to
Solomon, she told him everything
she had in her mind, and Solomon 3
answered all her questions; not
one of them was too abstruse for
the king to answer. When the 4
queen of Sheba saw all the wisdom
of Solomon, the house which he had
built, the food on his table, the 5
courtiers sitting round him, and his
attendants standing behind in their
livery, his cupbearers, and the
whole-offerings which he used to
offer in the house of the LORD, there
was no more spirit left in her. Then 6
she said to the king, 'The report
which I heard in my own country
about you and your wisdom was
true, but I did not believe it until 7
I came and saw for myself. Indeed
I was not told half of it; your wisdom and your prosperity go far beyond the report which I had of
them. Happy are your wives, hap- 8
py these courtiers of yours who
wait on you every day and hear
your wisdom! Blessed be the LORD 9
your God who has delighted in you
and has set you on the throne of
Israel; because he loves Israel for
ever, he has made you their king to
maintain law and justice.' Then 10
she gave the king a hundred and
twenty talents of gold, spices in
great abundance, and precious
stones. Never again came such a
quantity of spices as the queen of
Sheba gave to King Solomon.

Besides all this, Hiram's fleet of 11
ships, which had brought gold from
Ophir, brought in also from Ophir
cargoes of almug wood and precious stones. The king used the 12
wood to make stools for the house
of the LORD and for the royal

---

[a] *Prob. rdg.; Heb. adds* and his servants.   [b] *Or* Elath.
[c] *Or the Sea of Reeds.*   [d] *Verses 1–25: cp.* 2 Chr. 9. 1–24.
[e] *Prob. rdg., cp.* 2 Chr. 9. 1; *Heb. adds* to the name of the LORD.

palace, as well as harps and lutes for the singers. No such almug wood has ever been imported or even seen since that time.

13 And King Solomon gave the queen of Sheba all she desired, whatever she asked, in addition to all that he gave her of his royal bounty. So she departed and returned with her retinue to her own land.

14 Now the weight of gold which Solomon received yearly was six
15 hundred and sixty-six talents, in addition to the tolls levied by the customs officers and profits on foreign trade, and the tribute of*a* the kings of Arabia and the regional governors.

16 King Solomon made two hundred shields of beaten gold, and six hundred shekels of gold went to the
17 making of each one; he also made three hundred bucklers of beaten gold, and three minas of gold went to the making of each buckler. The king put these into the House of the Forest of Lebanon.

18 The king also made a great throne of ivory and overlaid it with
19 fine gold. Six steps led up to the throne; at the back of the throne there was the head of a calf. There were arms on each side of the seat, with a lion standing beside each of
20 them, and twelve lions stood on the six steps, one at either end of each step. Nothing like it had ever
21 been made for any monarch. All Solomon's drinking vessels were of gold, and all the plate in the House of the Forest of Lebanon was of red gold; no silver was used, for it was reckoned of no value in the
22 days of Solomon. The king had a fleet of merchantmen at sea with Hiram's fleet; once every three years this fleet of merchantmen came home, bringing gold and silver, ivory, apes and monkeys.

23 Thus King Solomon outdid all the kings of the earth in wealth and wisdom, and all the world 24 courted him, to hear the wisdom which God had put in his heart. Each brought his gift with him, 25 vessels of silver and gold, garments, perfumes and spices, horses and mules, so much year by year.

And Solomon got together many 26*b* chariots and horses; he had fourteen hundred chariots and twelve thousand horses, and he stabled some in the chariot-towns and kept others at hand in Jerusalem. The 27 king made silver as common in Jerusalem as stones, and cedar as plentiful as sycomore-fig in the Shephelah. Horses were imported 28 from Egypt and Coa for Solomon; the royal merchants obtained them from Coa by purchase. Chariots 29 were imported from Egypt for six hundred silver shekels each, and horses for a hundred and fifty; in the same way the merchants obtained them for export from all the kings of the Hittites and the kings of Aram.

King Solomon was a lover of 11 women, and besides Pharaoh's daughter he married many foreign women, Moabite, Ammonite, Edomite, Sidonian, and Hittite, from 2 the nations with whom the LORD had forbidden the Israelites to intermarry, 'because', he said, 'they will entice you to serve their gods'. But Solomon was devoted to them and loved them dearly. He had seven hundred wives, who 3 were princesses, and three hundred concubines, and they turned his heart from the truth. When he 4 grew old, his wives turned his heart to follow other gods, and he did not remain wholly loyal to the LORD his God as his father David had been. He followed Ashtoreth, 5 goddess of the Sidonians, and Milcom, the loathsome god of the Ammonites. Thus Solomon did what 6 was wrong in the eyes of the LORD, and was not loyal to the LORD like

---

a and the tribute of: *prob. rdg.*; *Heb.* and all.
b Verses 26–29: cp. 2 Chr. 1. 14–17; 9. 25–28.

7 his father David. He built a hill-shrine for Kemosh, the loathsome god of Moab, on the height to the east of Jerusalem, and for Molech, the loathsome god of the Ammon-
8 ites. Thus he did for the gods to which all his foreign wives burnt
9 offerings and made sacrifices. The LORD was angry with Solomon because his heart had turned away from the LORD the God of Israel,
10 who had appeared to him twice and had strictly commanded him not to follow other gods; but he dis-
11 obeyed the LORD's command. The LORD therefore said to Solomon, 'Because you have done this and have not kept my covenant and my statutes as I commanded you, I will tear the kingdom from you and
12 give it to your servant. Nevertheless, for the sake of your father David I will not do this in your day; I will tear it out of your son's
13 hand. Even so not the whole kingdom; I will leave him one tribe for the sake of my servant David and for the sake of Jerusalem, my chosen city.'
14 　　Then the LORD raised up an adversary for Solomon, Hadad the Edomite, of the royal house of
15 Edom. At the time when David reduced Edom, his commander-in-chief Joab had destroyed every male in the country when he went
16 into it to bury the slain. He and the armies of Israel remained there for six months, until he had destroyed
17 every male in Edom. Then Hadad, who was still a boy, fled the country with some of his father's Edomite servants, intending to
18 enter Egypt. They set out from Midian, made their way to Paran and, taking some men from there, came to Pharaoh king of Egypt, who assigned Hadad a house and maintenance and made him a grant
19 of land. Hadad found great favour with Pharaoh, who gave him in marriage a sister of Queen Tah-
20 penes his wife. She bore him his son

Genubath; Tahpenes weaned the child in Pharaoh's house, and he lived there along with Pharaoh's children. When Hadad heard in 21 Egypt that David rested with his forefathers and that his commander-in-chief Joab was also dead, he said to Pharaoh, 'Let me go so that I may return to my own country.'
'What is it that you find wanting 22 in my country', said Pharaoh, 'that you want to go back to your own?' 'Nothing,' said Hadad, 'but do, pray, let me go.' He remained an 25 adversary for Israel all through Solomon's reign. This is the harm that Hadad caused: he maintained a stranglehold on Israel and became king of Edom.
　　Then God raised up another ad- 23 versary against Solomon, Rezon son of Eliada, who had fled from his master Hadadezer king of Zobah. He gathered men about him 24 and became a captain of free-booters, who came to Damascus and occupied it; he became king there.
　　Jeroboam son of Nebat, one of 26[a] Solomon's courtiers, an Ephrathite from Zeredah, whose widowed mother was named Zeruah, rebelled against the king. And this is 27 the story of his rebellion. Solomon had built the Millo and closed the breach in the wall of the city of his father David. Now this Jeroboam 28 was a man of great energy; and Solomon, seeing how the young man worked, had put him in charge of all the labour-gangs in the tribal district of Joseph. On one occasion 29 Jeroboam had left Jerusalem, and the prophet Ahijah from Shiloh met him on the road. The prophet was wrapped in a new cloak, and the two of them were alone in the open country. Then Ahijah took 30 hold of the new cloak he was wearing, tore it into twelve pieces and 31 said to Jeroboam, 'Take ten pieces, for this is the word of the LORD the God of Israel: "I am going to tear

[a] *Verse 25 transposed to follow verse 22.*

the kingdom from the hand of Solo-
32 mon and give you ten tribes. But
one tribe will remain his, for the
sake of my servant David and for
the sake of Jerusalem, the city I
have chosen out of all the tribes of
33 Israel. I have done this because
Solomon has forsaken me; he has
prostrated himself before Ashtoreth goddess of the Sidonians,
Kemosh god of Moab, and Milcom
god of the Ammonites, and has not
conformed to my ways. He has not
done what is right in my eyes or
observed my statutes and judgements as David his father did.
34 Nevertheless I will not take the
whole kingdom from him, but will
maintain his rule as long as he lives,
for the sake of my chosen servant
David, who did observe my com-
35 mandments and statutes. But I
will take the kingdom, that is the
ten tribes, from his son and give it
36 to you. One tribe I will give to his
son, that my servant David may
always have a flame burning before
me in Jerusalem, the city which I
37 chose to receive my Name. But I
will appoint you to rule over all
that you can desire, and to be king
38 over Israel. If you pay heed to all
my commands, if you conform to
my ways and do what is right in my
eyes, observing my statutes and
commandments as my servant
David did, then I will be with you.
I will establish your family for ever
as I did for David; I will give Israel
39 to you, and punish David's descendants as they have deserved,
but not for ever."'
40   After this Solomon sought to
kill Jeroboam, but he fled to King
Shishak in Egypt and remained
there till Solomon's death.
41[a] The other acts and events of
Solomon's reign, and all his wisdom, are recorded in the annals of
42 Solomon. The reign of King Solomon in Jerusalem over the whole of
43 Israel lasted forty years. Then he
rested with his forefathers and was

buried in the city of David his
father, and he was succeeded by
his son Rehoboam.

The divided kingdom

REHOBOAM went to Shechem, for 12 1[b]
all Israel had gone there to make
him king. When Jeroboam son of 2
Nebat, who was still in Egypt,
heard of it, he remained there, having taken refuge there to escape
King Solomon. They now recalled 3
him, and he and all the assembly of
Israel came to Rehoboam and said,
'Your father laid a cruel yoke upon 4
us; but if you will now lighten the
cruel slavery he imposed on us and
the heavy yoke he laid on us, we
will serve you.' 'Give me three 5
days,' he said, 'and come back
again.' So the people went away.
King Rehoboam then consulted 6
the elders who had been in attendance on his father Solomon while
he lived: 'What answer do you advise me to give to this people?'
And they said, 'If today you are 7
willing to serve this people, show
yourself their servant now and
speak kindly to them, and they will
be your servants ever after.' But 8
he rejected the advice which the
elders gave him. He next consulted
those who had grown up with him,
the young men in attendance, and 9
asked them, 'What answer do you
advise me to give to this people's
request that I should lighten
the yoke which my father laid on
them?' The young men replied, 10
'Give this answer to the people who
say that your father made their
yoke heavy and ask you to lighten
it; tell them: "My little finger is
thicker than my father's loins. My 11
father laid a heavy yoke on you; I
will make it heavier. My father
used the whip on you; but I will
use the lash."' Jeroboam and the 12
people all came back to Rehoboam
on the third day, as the king had
ordered. And the king gave them 13

[a] *Verses 41–43: cp. 2 Chr. 9. 29–31.*   [b] *Verses 1–19: cp. 2 Chr. 10. 1–19.*

a harsh answer. He rejected the advice which the elders had given

14 him and spoke to the people as the young men had advised: 'My father made your yoke heavy; I will make it heavier. My father used the whip

15 on you; but I will use the lash.' So the king would not listen to the people; for the LORD had given this turn to the affair, in order that the word he had spoken by Ahijah of Shiloh to Jeroboam son of Nebat might be fulfilled.

16 When all Israel saw that the king would not listen to them, they answered:

What share have we in David?
We have no lot in the son of Jesse.
Away to your homes, O Israel;
now see to your own house, David.

17 So Israel went to their homes, and Rehoboam ruled over those Israelites who lived in the cities of Judah.

18 Then King Rehoboam sent out Adoram, the commander of the forced levies, but the Israelites stoned him to death; thereupon King Rehoboam mounted his chariot in haste and fled to Jeru-

19 salem. From that day to this, the whole of Israel has been in rebellion against the house of David.

20 When the men of Israel heard that Jeroboam had returned, they sent and called him to the assembly and made him king over the whole of Israel. The tribe of Judah alone followed the house of David.

21ᵃ When Rehoboam reached Jerusalem, he assembled all the house of Judah, the tribe of Benjamin also, a hundred and eighty thousand chosen warriors, to fight against the house of Israel and re-

22 cover his kingdom. But the word of God came to Shemaiah the man of

23 God: 'Say to Rehoboam son of Solomon, king of Judah, and to the house of Judah and to Benjamin

24 and the rest of the people, "This is the word of the LORD: You shall not go up to make war on your

kinsmen the Israelites. Return to your homes, for this is my will."' So they listened to the word of the LORD and returned home, as the LORD had told them.

THEN Jeroboam rebuilt Shechem 25 in the hill-country of Ephraim and took up residence there; from there he went out and built Penuel. 'As things now stand,' he 26 said to himself, 'the kingdom will revert to the house of David. If 27 this people go up to sacrifice in the house of the LORD in Jerusalem, it will revive their allegiance to their lord Rehoboam king of Judah, and they will kill me and return to King Rehoboam.' After giving 28 thought to the matter he made two calves of gold and said to the people, 'It is too much trouble for you to go up to Jerusalem; here are your gods, Israel, that brought you up from Egypt.' One he set up at 29 Bethel and the other he put at Dan, and this thing became a sin 30 in Israel; the people went to Bethel to worship the one, and all the way to Dan to worship the other. He 31 set up shrines on the hill-tops also and appointed priests from every class of the people, who did not belong to the Levites. He instituted 32 a pilgrim-feast on the fifteenth day of the eighth month like that in Judah, and he offered sacrifices upon the altar. This he did at Bethel, sacrificing to the calves that he had made and compelling the priests of the hill-shrines, which he had set up, to serve at Bethel. So he went 33 up to the altar that he had made at Bethel on the fifteenth day of the eighth month; there, in a month of his own choosing, he instituted for the Israelites a pilgrim-feast and himself went up to the altar to burn the sacrifice.

As Jeroboam stood by the altar 13 to burn the sacrifice, a man of God from Judah, moved by the word of the LORD, appeared at Bethel. He 2

ᵃ *Verses 21–24: cp. 2 Chr. 11. 1–4.*

inveighed against the altar in the LORD's name, crying out, 'O altar, altar! This is the word of the LORD: "Listen! A child shall be born to the house of David, named Josiah. He will sacrifice upon you the priests of the hill-shrines who make offerings upon you, and he will burn human bones upon you."'

3 He gave a sign the same day: 'This is the sign which the LORD has ordained: This altar will be rent in pieces and the ashes upon it will be

4 spilt.' When King Jeroboam heard the sentence which the man of God pronounced against the altar at Bethel, he pointed to him from the altar and said, 'Seize that man!' Immediately the hand which he had pointed at him became paralysed, so that he could not draw it

5 back. The altar too was rent in pieces and the ashes were spilt, in fulfilment of the sign that the man of God had given at the LORD's

6 command. The king appealed to the man of God to pacify the LORD his God and pray for him that his hand might be restored. The man of God did as he asked; his hand was restored and became as it had

7 been before. Then the king said to the man of God, 'Come home and take refreshment at my table, and

8 let me give you a present.' But the man of God answered, 'If you were to give me half your house, I would not enter it with you: I will eat and

9 drink nothing in this place, for the LORD's command to me was to eat and drink nothing, and not to go

10 back by the way I came.' So he went back another way; he did not return by the road he had taken to Bethel.

11 At that time there was an aged prophet living in Bethel. His sons came and recounted to him all that the man of God had done in Bethel that day; they also told their father

12 what he had said to the king. Their father said to them, 'Which road did he take?' They pointed out the road taken by the man of God who

13 had come from Judah. He said to his sons, 'Saddle an ass for me.'

14 They saddled the ass, and he mounted it and went after the man of God. He found him seated under a terebinth and said to him, 'Are you the man of God who came from Judah?' And he said, 'Yes,

15 I am.' 'Come home and eat with

16 me', said the prophet. 'I cannot go back with you or enter your house,' said the other; 'I can neither eat nor drink with you in this place,

17 for it was told me by the word of the LORD: "You shall eat and drink nothing there, nor shall you

18 go back the way you came."' And the old man said to him, 'I also am a prophet, as you are; and an angel commanded me by the word of the LORD to bring you home with me to eat and drink with me.' He was

19 lying; but the man of Judah went back with him and ate and drank

20 in his house. While they were still seated at table the word of the LORD came to the prophet who had brought him back, and he cried out

21 to the man of God from Judah, 'This is the word of the LORD: "You have defied the word of the LORD your God and have not obeyed his

22 command; you have come back to eat and to drink in the place where he forbade it; therefore your body shall not be laid in the grave of your forefathers."'

23 After they had eaten and drunk, he saddled an ass for the prophet whom he had brought back. As he

24 went on his way a lion met him and killed him, and his body was left lying in the road, with the ass and the lion both standing beside it.

25 Some passers-by saw the body lying in the road and the lion standing beside it, and they brought the news to the city where

26 the old prophet lived. When the prophet who had caused him to break his journey heard it, he said, 'It is the man of God who defied the word of the LORD. The LORD has given him to the lion, and it has

broken his neck and killed him in fulfilment of the word of the LORD.' 27 He told his sons to saddle an ass 28 and, when they had saddled it, he set out and found the body lying in the road with the ass and the lion standing beside it; the lion had neither devoured the body nor 29 broken the back of the ass. Then the prophet lifted the body of the man of God, laid it on the ass and brought it back to his own city to 30 mourn over it and bury it. He laid the body in his own grave and they mourned for him, saying, 'My 31 brother, my brother!' After burying him, he said to his sons, 'When I die, bury me in the grave where the man of God lies buried; lay my 32 bones beside his; for the sentence which he pronounced at the LORD's command against the altar in Bethel and all the hill-shrines of Samaria shall be carried out.'

33 After this Jeroboam still did not abandon his evil ways but went on appointing priests for the hill-shrines from all classes of the people; any man who offered himself he would consecrate to be priest 34 of a hill-shrine. By doing this he brought guilt upon his own house and doomed it to utter destruction.

14 At that time Jeroboam's son 2 Abijah fell ill, and Jeroboam said to his wife, 'Come now, disguise yourself so that people may not be able to recognize you as my wife, and go to Shiloh. Ahijah the prophet is there, the man who said I was to be king over this people. 3 Take with you ten loaves, some raisins, and a flask of syrup, and go to him; he will tell you what will 4 happen to the child.' Jeroboam's wife did so; she set off at once for Shiloh and came to Ahijah's house. Now Ahijah could not see, for his eyes were fixed in the blindness of 5 old age, and the LORD had said to him, 'The wife of Jeroboam is on her way to consult you about her son, who is ill; you shall give her such and such an answer.' When

she came in, concealing who she was, and Ahijah heard her foot- 6 steps at the door, he said, 'Come in, wife of Jeroboam. Why conceal who you are? I have heavy news for you. Go and tell Jeroboam: 7 "This is the word of the LORD the God of Israel: I raised you out of the people and appointed you prince over my people Israel; I 8 tore away the kingdom from the house of David and gave it to you; but you have not been like my servant David, who kept my commands and followed me with his whole heart, doing only what was right in my eyes. You have out- 9 done all your predecessors in wickedness; you have provoked me to anger by making for yourself other gods and images of cast metal; and you have turned your back on me. For this I will bring 10 disaster on the house of Jeroboam and I will destroy them all, every mother's son, whether still under the protection of the family or not, and I will sweep away the house of Jeroboam in Israel, as a man sweeps up dung until none is left. Those of 11 that house who die in the city shall be food for the dogs, and those who die in the country shall be food for the birds. It is the word of the LORD."

'You must go home now; the 12 moment you set foot in the city, the child will die. All Israel will 13 mourn for him and bury him; he alone of all Jeroboam's family will have proper burial, because in him alone could the LORD the God of Israel find anything good. Then 14 the LORD will set up a king over Israel who shall put an end to the house of Jeroboam. This first; and what next? The LORD will strike 15 Israel, till it trembles like a reed in the water; he will uproot its people from this good land which he gave to their forefathers and scatter them beyond the Euphrates, because they have made their sacred poles and provoked the LORD's

16 anger. And he will abandon Israel for the sins that Jeroboam has committed and has led Israel to commit.' 17 Jeroboam's wife went home at once to Tirzah and, as she crossed the threshold of the house, 18 the boy died. They buried him, and all Israel mourned over him; and thus the word of the LORD was fulfilled which he had spoken through his servant Ahijah the prophet.

19 The other events of Jeroboam's reign, in war and peace, are recorded in the annals of the kings of 20 Israel. He reigned twenty-two years; then he rested with his forefathers and was succeeded by his son Nadab.

21 IN Judah Rehoboam son of Solomon had become king. He was forty-one years old when he came to the throne, and he reigned for seventeen years in Jerusalem, the city which the LORD had chosen out of all the tribes of Israel to receive his Name. Rehoboam's mother was a woman of Ammon 22 called Naamah. Judah did what was wrong in the eyes of the LORD, rousing his jealous indignation by the sins they committed, beyond anything that their forefathers had 23 done. They erected hill-shrines, sacred pillars, and sacred poles, on every high hill and under every 24 spreading tree. Worse still, all over the country there were male prostitutes attached to the shrines, and the people adopted all the abominable practices of the nations whom the LORD had dispossessed in favour of Israel.

25ᵃ In the fifth year of Rehoboam's reign Shishak king of Egypt at- 26 tacked Jerusalem. He removed the treasures of the house of the LORD and of the royal palace, and seized everything, including all the shields of gold that Solomon had made. 27 King Rehoboam replaced them

with bronze shields and entrusted them to the officers of the escort who guarded the entrance of the royal palace. Whenever the king 28 entered the house of the LORD, the escort carried them; afterwards they returned them to the guardroom.

The other acts and events of 29ᵇ Rehoboam's reign are recorded in the annals of the kings of Judah. There was continual fighting be- 30 tween him and Jeroboam. He 31 rested with his forefathers and was buried with them in the city of David. (His mother was a woman of Ammon, whose name was Naamah.) He was succeeded by his son Abijam.

In the eighteenth year of the 15 reign of Jeroboam son of Nebat, Abijam became king of Judah. He 2 reigned in Jerusalem for three years; his mother was Maacah granddaughter of Abishalom. All 3 the sins that his father had committed before him he committed too, nor was he faithful to the LORD his God as his ancestor David had been. But for David's sake the 4 LORD his God gave him a flame to burn in Jerusalem, by establishing his dynasty and making Jerusalem secure, because David had done 5 what was right in the eyes of the LORD and had not disobeyed any of his commandments all his life, except in the matter of Uriah the Hittite.ᶜ The other acts and events 7 of Abijam's reign are recorded in the annals of the kings of Judah. There was fighting between Abijam and Jeroboam. And Abijam 8 rested with his forefathers and was buried in the city of David; and he was succeeded by his son Asa.

In the twentieth year of Jero- 9 boam king of Israel, Asa became king of Judah. He reigned in Jeru- 10 salem for forty-one years; his grandmother was Maacah grand-

---

ᵃ *Verses 25–28: cp.* 2 Chr. 12. 9–11.   ᵇ *Verses 29–31: cp.* 2 Chr. 12. 13–16.
ᶜ *Prob. rdg.; Heb. adds* (6) There was war between Rehoboam and Jeroboam all his days (*cp.* 14. 30).

11 daughter of Abishalom. Asa did what was right in the eyes of the LORD, like his ancestor David.

12 He expelled from the land the male prostitutes attached to the shrines and did away with all the idols which his predecessors had made.

13[a] He even deprived his own grandmother Maacah of her rank as queen mother because she had an obscene object made for the worship of Asherah; Asa cut it down and burnt it in the gorge of the

14 Kidron. Although the hill-shrines were allowed to remain, Asa himself remained faithful to the LORD

15 all his life. He brought into the house of the LORD all his father's votive offerings and his own, gold and silver and sacred vessels.

16 Asa was at war with Baasha king of Israel all through their

17[b] reigns. Baasha king of Israel invaded Judah and fortified Ramah to cut off all access to Asa king of

18 Judah. So Asa took all the gold and silver that remained in the treasuries of the house of the LORD and of the royal palace, and sent his servants with them to Ben-hadad son of Tabrimmon, son of Hezion, king of Aram, whose capital was Damascus, with instructions to

19 say, 'There is an alliance between us, as there was between our fathers. I now send you this present of silver and gold; break off your alliance with Baasha king of Israel, so that he may abandon his cam-

20 paign against me.' Ben-hadad listened willingly to King Asa; he ordered the commanders of his armies to move against the cities of Israel, and they attacked Iyyon, Dan, Abel-beth-maacah, and that part of Kinnereth which marches

21 with the land of Naphtali. When Baasha heard of it, he stopped fortifying Ramah and fell back on

22 Tirzah. Then King Asa issued a proclamation requiring every man in Judah to join in removing the

stones of Ramah and the timbers with which Baasha had fortified it; no one was exempted; and he used them to fortify Geba of Benjamin and Mizpah.

All the other events of Asa's 23[c] reign, his exploits and his achievements, and the cities he built, are recorded in the annals of the kings of Judah. But in his old age his feet were crippled by disease. He 24 rested with his forefathers and was buried with them in the city of his ancestor David; and he was succeeded by his son Jehoshaphat.

Nadab son of Jeroboam became 25 king of Israel in the second year of Asa king of Judah, and he reigned for two years. He did what was 26 wrong in the eyes of the LORD and followed in his father's footsteps, repeating the sin which he had led Israel to commit. Baasha son of 27 Ahijah, of the house of Issachar, conspired against him and attacked him at Gibbethon, a Philistine city, which Nadab was besieging with all his forces. And Baasha slew 28 him and usurped the throne in the third year of Asa king of Judah. As soon as he became king, he 29 struck down all the family of Jeroboam, destroying every living soul and leaving not one survivor. Thus the word of the LORD was fulfilled which he spoke through his servant Ahijah the Shilonite. This hap- 30 pened because of the sins of Jeroboam and the sins which he led Israel to commit, and because he had provoked the anger of the LORD the God of Israel. The other 31 events of Nadab's reign and all his acts are recorded in the annals of the kings of Israel. Asa was at war 32 with Baasha king of Israel all through their reigns.

In the third year of Asa king of 33 Judah, Baasha son of Ahijah became king of all Israel in Tirzah and reigned twenty-four years. He did 34 what was wrong in the eyes of the

---

[a] *Verses 13–15: cp. 2 Chr. 15. 16–18.*
[c] *Verses 23, 24: cp. 2 Chr. 16. 11–14.*
[b] *Verses 17–22: cp. 2 Chr. 16. 1–6.*

LORD and followed in Jeroboam's footsteps, repeating the sin which
16 he had led Israel to commit. Then the word of the LORD came to Jehu son of Hanani concerning Baasha:
2 'I raised you from the dust and made you a prince over my people Israel, but you have followed in the footsteps of Jeroboam and have led my people Israel into sin, and have provoked me to anger with their
3 sins. Therefore I will sweep away Baasha and his house and will deal with it as I dealt with the house of
4 Jeroboam son of Nebat. Those of Baasha's family who die in the city shall be food for the dogs, and those who die in the country shall be
5 food for the birds.' The other events of Baasha's reign, his achievements and his exploits, are recorded in the annals of the kings of Israel.
6 Baasha rested with his forefathers and was buried in Tirzah; and he was succeeded by his son Elah.
7 Moreover the word of the LORD concerning Baasha and his family came through the prophet Jehu son of Hanani, because of all the wrong that he had done in the eyes of the LORD, thereby provoking his anger: because he had not only sinned like the house of Jeroboam, but had also brought destruction upon it.
8 In the twenty-sixth year of Asa king of Judah, Elah son of Baasha became king of Israel and he
9 reigned in Tirzah two years. Zimri, who was in his service commanding half the chariotry, plotted against him. The king was in Tirzah drinking himself drunk in the house of Arza, comptroller of the
10 household there, when Zimri broke in and attacked him, assassinated him and made himself king. This took place in the twenty-seventh
11 year of Asa king of Judah. As soon as he had become king and was enthroned, he struck down all the family of Baasha and left not a single mother's son alive, kinsman
12 or friend. He destroyed the whole family of Baasha, and thus fulfilled the word of the LORD concerning Baasha, spoken through the prophet Jehu. This was what
13 came of all the sins which Baasha and his son Elah had committed and the sins into which they had led Israel, provoking the anger of the LORD the God of Israel with their worthless idols. The other
14 events and acts of Elah's reign are recorded in the annals of the kings of Israel.

In the twenty-seventh year of
15 Asa king of Judah, Zimri reigned in Tirzah for seven days. At the time the army was investing the Philistine city of Gibbethon. When
16 the Israelite troops in the field heard of Zimri's conspiracy and the murder of the king, there and then in the camp they made their commander Omri king of Israel by common consent. Then Omri and
17 his whole force withdrew from Gibbethon and laid siege to Tirzah. Zimri, as soon as he saw that the
18 city had fallen, retreated to the keep of the royal palace, set the whole of it on fire over his head and so perished. This was what came
19 of the sin he had committed by doing what was wrong in the eyes of the LORD and following in the footsteps of Jeroboam, repeating the sin into which he had led Israel. The other events of Zimri's reign,
20 and his conspiracy, are recorded in the annals of the kings of Israel.

Thereafter the people of Israel
21 were split into two factions: one supported Tibni son of Ginath, determined to make him king; the other supported Omri. Omri's
22 party proved the stronger; Tibni lost his life and Omri became king.

It was in the thirty-first year of
23 Asa king of Judah that Omri became king of Israel and he reigned twelve years, six of them in Tirzah. He bought the hill of Samaria from
24 Shemer for two talents of silver and built a city on it which he named Samaria after Shemer the

25 owner of the hill. Omri did what was wrong in the eyes of the LORD; he outdid all his predecessors in
26 wickedness. He followed in the footsteps of Jeroboam son of Nebat, repeating the sins which he had led Israel to commit, so that they provoked the anger of the LORD their God with their worth-
27 less idols. The other events of Omri's reign, and his exploits, are recorded in the annals of the kings
28 of Israel. So Omri rested with his forefathers and was buried in Samaria; and he was succeeded by his son Ahab.

Ahab and Elijah

29 AHAB son of Omri became king of Israel in the thirty-eighth year of Asa king of Judah, and he reigned over Israel in Samaria for twenty-
30 two years. He did more that was wrong in the eyes of the LORD than
31 all his predecessors. As if it were not enough for him to follow the sinful ways of Jeroboam son of Nebat, he contracted a marriage with Jezebel daughter of Ethbaal king of Sidon, and went and worshipped Baal; he prostrated him-
32 self before him and erected an altar to him in the temple of Baal which
33 he built in Samaria. He also set up a sacred pole; indeed he did more to provoke the anger of the LORD the God of Israel than all the kings
34 of Israel before him. In his days Hiel of Bethel rebuilt Jericho; laying its foundations cost him his eldest son Abiram, and the setting up of its gates cost him Segub his youngest son. Thus was fulfilled what the LORD had spoken through Joshua son of Nun.

17   Elijah the Tishbite, of Tishbe in Gilead, said to Ahab, 'I swear by the life of the LORD the God of Israel, whose servant I am, that there shall be neither dew nor rain these coming years unless I give
2 the word.' Then the word of the
3 LORD came to him: 'Leave this place and turn eastwards; and go into hiding in the ravine of Kerith east of the Jordan. You shall drink 4 from the stream, and I have commanded the ravens to feed you there.' He did as the LORD had told 5 him: he went and stayed in the ravine of Kerith east of the Jordan, and the ravens brought him bread 6 and meat morning and evening, and he drank from the stream. After a while the stream dried up, 7 for there had been no rain in the land. Then the word of the LORD 8 came to him: 'Go now to Zare- 9 phath, a village of Sidon, and stay there; I have commanded a widow there to feed you.' So he went off to 10 Zarephath. When he reached the entrance to the village, he saw a widow gathering sticks, and he called to her and said, 'Please bring me a little water in a pitcher to drink.' As she went to fetch it, 11 he called after her, 'Bring me, please, a piece of bread as well.' But she said, 'As the LORD your 12 God lives, I have no food to sustain me except a handful of flour in a jar and a little oil in a flask. Here I am, gathering two or three sticks to go and cook something for my son and myself before we die.' 'Never fear,' said Elijah; 'go and 13 do as you say; but first make me a small cake from what you have and bring it out to me; and after that make something for your son and yourself. For this is the word of the 14 LORD the God of Israel: "The jar of flour shall not give out nor the flask of oil fail, until the LORD sends rain on the land."' She went 15 and did as Elijah had said, and there was food for him and for her and her family for a long time. The 16 jar of flour did not give out nor did the flask of oil fail, as the word of the LORD foretold through Elijah.

Afterwards the son of this wo- 17 man, the mistress of the house, fell ill and grew worse and worse, until at last his breathing ceased. Then 18 she said to Elijah, 'What made you

interfere, you man of God? You came here to bring my sins to light
19 and kill my son!' 'Give me your son', he said. He took the boy from her arms and carried him up to the roof-chamber where his lodging was, and laid him on his own bed.
20 Then he called out to the LORD, 'O LORD my God, is this thy care for the widow with whom I lodge, that thou hast been so cruel to her son?'
21 Then he breathed deeply[a] upon the child three times and called on the LORD, 'O LORD my God, let the breath of life, I pray, return to the
22 body of this child.' The LORD listened to Elijah's cry, and the breath of life returned to the child's
23 body, and he revived; Elijah lifted him up and took him down from the roof into the house, gave him to his mother and said, 'Look, your
24 son is alive.' Then she said to Elijah, 'Now I know for certain that you are a man of God and that the word of the LORD on your lips is truth.'

18 Time went by, and in the third year the word of the LORD came to Elijah: 'Go and show yourself to Ahab, and I will send rain upon the
2 land.' So he went to show himself to Ahab. At this time the famine in
3 Samaria was at its height, and Ahab summoned Obadiah, the comptroller of his household, a de-
4 vout worshipper of the LORD. When Jezebel massacred the prophets of the LORD, he had taken a hundred of them and hidden them in caves, fifty by fifty, giving them food and
5 drink to keep them alive. Ahab said to Obadiah, 'Let us go through the land, both of us, to every spring and gully; if we can find enough grass we may keep the horses and mules alive and lose
6 none of our cattle.' They divided the land between them for their survey, Ahab going one way by himself and Obadiah another.
7 As Obadiah was on his way, Elijah met him. Obadiah recog-

nized him and fell prostrate before him and said, 'Can it be you, my lord Elijah?' 'Yes,' he said, 'it is I; 8 go and tell your master that Elijah is here.' 'What wrong have I done?' 9 said Obadiah. 'Why should you give me into Ahab's hands? He will put me to death. As the LORD your 10 God lives, there is no nation or kingdom to which my master has not sent in search of you. If they said, "He is not here", he made that kingdom or nation swear on oath that they could not find you. Yet now you say, 'Go and tell your 11 master that Elijah is here.'' What 12 will happen? As soon as I leave you, the spirit of the LORD will carry you away, who knows where? I shall go and tell Ahab, and when he fails to find you, he will kill me. Yet I have been a worshipper of the LORD from boyhood. Have you not 13 been told, my lord, what I did when Jezebel put the LORD's prophets to death, how I hid a hundred of them in caves, fifty by fifty, and kept them alive with food and drink? And now you say, "Go and tell 14 your master that Elijah is here"! He will kill me.' Elijah answered, 15 'As the LORD of Hosts lives, whose servant I am, I swear that I will show myself to him this very day.' So Obadiah went to find Ahab and 16 gave him the message, and Ahab went to meet Elijah.

As soon as Ahab saw Elijah, he 17 said to him, 'Is it you, you troubler of Israel?' 'It is not I who have 18 troubled Israel,' he replied, 'but you and your father's family, by forsaking the commandments of the LORD and following Baal. But 19 now, send and summon all Israel to meet me on Mount Carmel, and the four hundred and fifty prophets of Baal with them and the four hundred prophets of the goddess Asherah, who are Jezebel's pensioners.' So Ahab sent out to all 20 the Israelites and assembled the prophets on Mount Carmel. Elijah 21

---

[a] *Or* stretched himself.

stepped forward and said to the people, 'How long will you sit on the fence? If the LORD is God, follow him; but if Baal, then follow him.' Not a word did they 22 answer. Then Elijah said to the people, 'I am the only prophet of the LORD still left, but there are four hundred and fifty prophets of 23 Baal. Bring two bulls; let them choose one for themselves, cut it up and lay it on the wood without setting fire to it, and I will prepare the other and lay it on the wood 24 without setting fire to it. You shall invoke your god by name and I will invoke the LORD by name; and the god who answers by fire, he is God.' And all the people shouted their approval.

25 Then Elijah said to the prophets of Baal, 'Choose one of the bulls and offer it first, for there are more of you; invoke your god by name, 26 but do not set fire to the wood.' So they took the bull provided for them and offered it, and they invoked Baal by name from morning until noon, crying, 'Baal, Baal, answer us'; but there was no sound, no answer. They danced wildly beside the altar they had set up. 27 At midday Elijah mocked them: 'Call louder, for he is a god; it may be he is deep in thought, or engaged, or on a journey; or he may have gone to sleep and must be 28 woken up.' They cried still louder and, as was their custom, gashed themselves with swords and spears 29 until the blood ran. All afternoon they raved and ranted till the hour of the regular sacrifice, but still there was no sound, no answer, no sign of attention. 30 Then Elijah said to all the people, 'Come here to me.' They all came, and he repaired the altar of the LORD which had been torn down. 31 He took twelve stones, one for each tribe of the sons of Jacob, the man named Israel by the word of 32 the LORD. With these stones he built an altar in the name of the LORD; he dug a trench round it big enough to hold two measures of seed; he arranged the wood, cut up 33 the bull and laid it on the wood. Then he said, 'Fill four jars with 34 water and pour it on the whole-offering and on the wood.' They did so, and he said, 'Do it again.' They did it again, and he said, 'Do it a third time.' They did it a third time, and the water ran all round 35 the altar and even filled the trench. At the hour of the regular sacrifice 36 the prophet Elijah came forward and said, 'LORD God of Abraham, of Isaac, and of Israel, let it be known today that thou art God in Israel and that I am thy servant and have done all these things at thy command. Answer me, O LORD, 37 answer me and let this people know that thou, LORD, art God and that it is thou that hast caused them to be backsliders.'[a] Then the fire of the 38 LORD fell. It consumed the whole-offering, the wood, the stones, and the earth, and licked up the water in the trench. When all the people 39 saw it, they fell prostrate and cried, 'The LORD is God, the LORD is God.' Then Elijah said to them, 40 'Seize the prophets of Baal; let not one of them escape.' They seized them, and Elijah took them down to the Kishon and slaughtered them there in the valley.

Elijah said to Ahab, 'Go back 41 now, eat and drink, for I hear the sound of coming rain.' He did so, 42 while Elijah himself climbed to the crest of Carmel. There he crouched on the ground with his face between his knees. He said to his 43 servant, 'Go and look out to the west.' He went and looked; 'There is nothing to see', he said. Seven times Elijah ordered him back, and seven times he went. The seventh 44 time he said, 'I see a cloud no bigger than a man's hand, coming up from the west.' 'Now go', said Elijah, 'and tell Ahab to harness his

---

[a] *Or* thou that dost bring them back to their allegiance.

45 chariot and be off, or the rain will stop him.' Meanwhile the sky had grown black with clouds, the wind rose, and heavy rain began to fall. Ahab mounted his chariot and set 46 off for Jezreel; but the power of the LORD had come upon Elijah: he tucked up his robe and ran before Ahab all the way to Jezreel.

19 Ahab told Jezebel all that Elijah had done and how he had put all the prophets to death with the 2 sword. Jezebel then sent a messenger to Elijah to say, 'The gods do the same to me and more, unless by this time tomorrow I have taken 3 your life as you took theirs.' He was afraid and fled for his life. When he reached Beersheba in Ju-4 dah, he left his servant there and himself went a day's journey into the wilderness. He came upon a broom-bush, and sat down under it and prayed for death: 'It is enough,' he said; 'now, LORD, take my life, for I am no better than my 5 fathers before me.' He lay down under the bush and, while he slept, an angel touched him and said, 6 'Rise and eat.' He looked, and there at his head was a cake baked on hot stones, and a pitcher of water. He ate and drank and lay 7 down again. The angel of the LORD came again and touched him a second time, saying, 'Rise and eat; the 8 journey is too much for you.' He rose and ate and drank and, sustained by this food, he went on for forty days and forty nights to Hor-9 eb, the mount of God. He entered a cave and there he spent the night.

Suddenly the word of the LORD came to him: 'Why are you here, 10 Elijah?' 'Because of my great zeal for the LORD the God of Hosts', he said. 'The people of Israel have forsaken thy covenant, torn down thy altars and put thy prophets to death with the sword. I alone am left, and they seek to take my life.' 11 The answer came: 'Go and stand on the mount before the LORD.'

For the LORD was passing by: a great and strong wind came rending mountains and shattering rocks before him, but the LORD was not in the wind; and after the wind there was an earthquake, but the LORD was not in the earthquake; and after the earthquake fire, but 12 the LORD was not in the fire; and after the fire a low murmuring sound. When Elijah heard it, he 13 muffled his face in his cloak and went out and stood at the entrance of the cave. Then there came a voice: 'Why are you here, Elijah?' 'Because of my great zeal for the 14 LORD the God of Hosts', he said. 'The people of Israel have forsaken thy covenant, torn down thy altars and put thy prophets to death with the sword. I alone am left, and they seek to take my life.'

The LORD said to him, 'Go back 15 by way of the wilderness of Damascus, enter the city and anoint Hazael to be king of Aram; anoint 16 Jehu son[a] of Nimshi to be king of Israel, and Elisha son of Shaphat of Abel-meholah to be prophet in your place. Anyone who escapes 17 the sword of Hazael Jehu will slay, and anyone who escapes the sword of Jehu Elisha will slay. But I will 18 leave seven thousand in Israel, all who have not bent the knee to Baal, all whose lips have not kissed him.'

Elijah departed and found Eli- 19 sha son of Shaphat ploughing; there were twelve pair of oxen ahead of him, and he himself was with the last of them. As Elijah passed, he threw his cloak over him, and Elisha, leaving his oxen, 20 ran after Elijah and said, 'Let me kiss my father and mother goodbye, and then I will follow you.' 'Go back,' he replied; 'what have I done to prevent you?' He followed 21 him no further but went home, took his pair of oxen, slaughtered them and burnt the wooden gear to cook the flesh, which he gave

[a] Or grandson (*cp.* 2 Kgs. 9. 2).

to the people to eat. Then he followed Elijah and became his disciple.

20 BEN-HADAD king of Aram, having mustered all his forces, and taking with him thirty-two kings with their horses and chariots, marched against Samaria to take 2 it by siege or assault. He sent envoys into the city to Ahab king of 3 Israel to say, 'Hear what Ben-hadad says: Your silver and gold are mine, your wives and your 4 splendid sons are mine.'[a] The king of Israel answered, 'As you say, my lord king, I am yours and all that I 5 have.' The envoys came again and said, 'Hear what Ben-hadad says: I demand that you hand over your silver and gold, your wives and 6 your sons. This time tomorrow I will send my servants to search your house and your subjects' houses and to take possession of everything you prize, and remove 7 it.' The king of Israel then summoned all the elders of the land and said, 'You see this? The man is plainly picking a quarrel; for I did not demur when he sent to claim my wives and my sons, my silver 8 and gold.' All the elders and all the people answered, 'Do not listen to 9 him; you must not consent.' So he gave this reply to Ben-hadad's envoys: 'Say to my lord the king: I accepted your majesty's demands on the first occasion; but what you now ask I cannot do.' The envoys went away and reported to their 10 master, and Ben-hadad sent back word: 'The gods do the same to me and more, if there is enough dust in Samaria to provide a handful for 11 each of my men.' The king of Israel made reply, 'Remind him of the saying: "The lame must not think himself a match for the 12 nimble."' This message reached Ben-hadad while he and the kings were drinking in their quarters.[b]

At once he ordered his men to attack the city, and they did so.

Meanwhile a prophet had come 13 to Ahab king of Israel and said to him, 'This is the word of the LORD: "You see this great rabble? Today I will give it into your hands and you shall know that I am the LORD."' 'Whom will you use for 14 that?' asked Ahab. 'The young men who serve the district officers', was the answer. 'Who will draw up the line of battle?' asked the king. 'You', said the prophet. Then Ahab called up these young 15 men, two hundred and thirty-two all told, and behind them the people of Israel, seven thousand in all. They went out at midday, while 16 Ben-hadad and his allies, those thirty-two kings, were drinking themselves drunk in their quarters.[b] The young men sallied out 17 first, and word was sent to Ben-hadad that a party had come out of Samaria. 'If they have come out 18 for peace,' he said, 'take them alive; if for battle, take them alive.'

So out of the city the young men 19 went, and the army behind them; each struck down his man, and the 20 Aramaeans fled. The Israelites pursued them, but Ben-hadad king of Aram escaped on horseback with some of the cavalry. Then the king 21 of Israel advanced and captured the horses and chariots, inflicting a heavy defeat on the Aramaeans.

Then the prophet came to the 22 king of Israel and said to him, 'Build up your forces; you know what you must do. At the turn of the year the king of Aram will renew the attack.' But the king of 23 Aram's ministers gave him this advice: 'Their gods are gods of the hills; that is why they defeated us. Let us fight them in the plain; and then we shall have the upper hand. What you must do is to relieve the 24 kings of their command and appoint other officers in their place.

---

[a] Or *are your wives and your sons any good to me?*
[b] *in their quarters: or at Succoth.*

25 Raise another army like the one you have lost. Bring your cavalry and chariots up to their former strength, and then let us fight them in the plain, and we shall have the upper hand.' He listened to their advice and acted on it.

26 At the turn of the year Ben-hadad mustered the Aramaeans and advanced to Aphek to attack

27 Israel. The Israelites too were mustered and formed into companies, and then went out to meet them and encamped opposite them. They seemed no better than a pair of new-born kids, while the Aramaeans covered the country-side.

28 The man of God came to the king of Israel and said, 'This is the word of the LORD: The Aramaeans may think that the LORD is a god of the hills and not a god of the valleys; but I will give all this great rabble into your hands and you shall know that I am the LORD.'

29 They lay in camp opposite one another for seven days; on the seventh day battle was joined and the Israelites destroyed a hundred thousand of the Aramaean infan-

30 try in one day. The survivors fled to Aphek, into the citadel, and the city wall fell upon the twenty-seven thousand men who were left. Ben-hadad took refuge in the citadel, retreating into an inner room;

31 and his attendants said to him, 'Listen; we have heard that the kings of Israel are men to be trusted. Let us therefore put sackcloth round our waists and wind rough cord round our heads and go out to the king of Israel. It may be that

32 he will spare your life.' So they fastened on the sackcloth and cord, and went to the king of Israel and said, 'Your servant Ben-hadad pleads for his life.' 'My royal cou-

33 sin,' he said, 'is he still alive?' The men, taking the word for a favourable omen, caught it up at once and said, 'Your cousin, yes, Ben-hadad.' 'Go and fetch him', he said.

Then Ben-hadad came out and A-hab invited him into his chariot.

34 And Ben-hadad said to him, 'I will restore the cities which my father took from your father, and you may establish for yourself a trading quarter in Damascus, as my father did in Samaria.' 'On these terms', said Ahab, 'I will let you go.' So he granted him a treaty and let him go.

35 One of a company of prophets, at the command of the LORD, ordered a certain man to strike him,

36 but the man refused. 'Because you have not obeyed the LORD,' said the prophet, 'when you leave me, a lion will attack you.' When the man left, a lion did meet him and

37 attacked him. The prophet fell in with another man and ordered him to strike him. He struck and wound-

38 ed him. Then the prophet went off, with a bandage over his eyes, and thus disguised waited by the

39 wayside for the king. As the king was passing, he called out to him, 'Sir, I went into the thick of the battle, and a soldier came over to me with a prisoner and said, "Take charge of this fellow. If by any chance he gets away, your life shall be forfeit, or you shall pay a talent

40 of silver." As I was busy with one thing and another, sir, he disappeared.' The king of Israel said to him, 'You deserve to die.' And he said to the king of Israel,*a* 'You have passed sentence on yourself.'

41 Then he tore the bandage from his eyes, and the king of Israel saw that he was one of the prophets.

42 And he said to the king, 'This is the word of the LORD: "Because you let that man go when I had put him under a ban, your life shall be forfeit for his life, your people for his people."' The king of Israel

43 went home sullen and angry and entered Samaria.

NABOTH of Jezreel had a vine- 21 yard near the palace of Ahab king

---

a You deserve...Israel: *prob. rdg.*; Heb. *om.*

2 of Samaria. One day Ahab made a proposal to Naboth: 'Your vineyard is close to my palace; let me have it for a garden; I will give you a better vineyard in exchange for it or, if you prefer, its value in silver.'

3 But Naboth answered, 'The LORD forbid that I should let you have land which has always been

4 in my family.' So Ahab went home sullen and angry because Naboth would not let him have his ancestral land. He lay down on his bed, covered his face and refused to eat.

5 His wife Jezebel came in to him and said, 'What makes you so sullen

6 and why do you refuse to eat?' He told her, 'I proposed to Naboth of Jezreel that he should let me have his vineyard at its value or, if he liked, in exchange for another; but he would not let me have the vine-

7 yard.' 'Are you or are you not king in Israel?' said Jezebel. 'Come, eat and take heart; I will make you a gift of the vineyard of Naboth of

8 Jezreel.' So she wrote a letter in Ahab's name, sealed it with his seal and sent it to the elders and notables of Naboth's city, who sat

9 in council with him. She wrote: 'Proclaim a fast and give Naboth the seat of honour among the

10 people. And see that two scoundrels are seated opposite him to charge him with cursing God and the king, then take him out and

11 stone him to death.' So the elders and notables of Naboth's city, who sat with him in council, carried out the instructions Jezebel had sent

12 them in her letter: they proclaimed a fast and gave Naboth the seat of

13 honour, and these two scoundrels came in, sat opposite him and charged him publicly with cursing God and the king. Then they took him outside the city and stoned

14 him, and sent word to Jezebel that Naboth had been stoned to death.

15 As soon as Jezebel heard that Naboth had been stoned and was dead, she said to Ahab, 'Get up and take possession of the vineyard which Naboth refused to sell you, for he is no longer alive; Naboth of Jezreel is dead.' When Ahab heard 16 that Naboth was dead, he got up and went to the vineyard to take possession. Then the word of the 17 LORD came to Elijah the Tishbite: 'Go down at once to Ahab king of 18 Israel, who is in Samaria; you will find him in Naboth's vineyard, where he has gone to take possession. Say to him, "This is the word 19 of the LORD: Have you killed your man, and taken his land as well?" Say to him, "This is the word of the LORD: Where dogs licked the blood of Naboth, there dogs shall lick your blood."' Ahab said to Elijah, 20 'Have you found me, my enemy?' 'I have found you', he said, 'because you have sold yourself to do what is wrong in the eyes of the LORD. I will bring*ᵃ* disaster upon 21 you; I will sweep you away and destroy every mother's son of the house of Ahab in Israel, whether under protection of the family or not. And I will deal with your house 22 as I did with the house of Jeroboam son of Nebat and of Baasha son of Ahijah, because you have provoked my anger and led Israel into sin.' And the LORD went on to say of 23 Jezebel, 'Jezebel shall be eaten by dogs by the rampart of Jezreel. Of 24 the house of Ahab, those who die in the city shall be food for the dogs, and those who die in the country shall be food for the birds.' (Never 25 was a man who sold himself to do what is wrong in the LORD's eyes as Ahab did, and all at the prompting of Jezebel his wife. He commit- 26 ted gross abominations in going after false gods, doing everything that the Amorites did, whom the LORD had dispossessed in favour of Israel.) When Ahab heard this, he 27 rent his clothes, put on sackcloth and fasted; he lay down in his sackcloth and went about muttering to himself. Then the word of the 28

ᵃ he said,. . .bring: *or* he said. 'Because you. . .LORD, I am bringing. . .

LORD came to Elijah the Tishbite:
29 'Have you seen how Ahab has
humbled himself before me? Because he has thus humbled himself, I will not bring disaster upon
his house in his own lifetime, but in
his son's.'

22 FOR three years there was no war
between the Aramaeans and the
2ᵃ Israelites, but in the third year
Jehoshaphat king of Judah went
down to visit the king of Israel.
3 The latter said to his courtiers,
'You know that Ramoth-gilead belongs to us, and yet we do nothing
to recover it from the king of A-
4 ram.' He said to Jehoshaphat,
'Will you join me in attacking
Ramoth-gilead?' Jehoshaphat said
to the king of Israel, 'What is mine
is yours: myself, my people, and
5 my horses.' Then Jehoshaphat said
to the king of Israel, 'First let us
6 seek counsel from the LORD.' The
king of Israel assembled the prophets, some four hundred of them,
and asked them, 'Shall I attack
Ramoth-gilead or shall I refrain?'
'Attack,' they answered; 'the Lord
will deliver it into your hands.' Je-
7 hoshaphat asked, 'Is there no other
prophet of the LORD here through
whom we may seek guidance?'
8 'There is one more', the king of
Israel answered, 'through whom we
may seek guidance of the LORD,
but I hate the man, because he
prophesies no good for me; never
anything but evil. His name is
Micaiah son of Imlah.' Jehoshaphat exclaimed, 'My lord king, let
9 no such word pass your lips!' So
the king of Israel called one of his
eunuchs and told him to fetch
Micaiah son of Imlah with all speed.
10   The king of Israel and Jehoshaphat king of Judah were seated on
their thrones, in shining armour, at
the entrance to the gate of Samaria, and all the prophets were pro-
11 phesying before them. One of them,
Zedekiah son of Kenaanah, made

himself horns of iron and said,
'This is the word of the LORD:
"With horns like these you shall
gore the Aramaeans and make an
end of them."' In the same vein all 12
the prophets prophesied, 'Attack
Ramoth-gilead and win the day;
the LORD will deliver it into your
hands.' The messenger sent to fetch 13
Micaiah told him that the prophets
had with one voice given the king a
favourable answer. 'And mind you
agree with them', he added. 'As 14
the LORD lives,' said Micaiah, 'I
will say only what the LORD tells
me to say.'
    When Micaiah came into the 15
king's presence, the king said to
him, 'Micaiah, shall we attack
Ramoth-gilead or shall we refrain?' 'Attack and win the day,'
he said; 'the LORD will deliver it
into your hands.' 'How often must 16
I adjure you', said the king, 'to tell
me nothing but the truth in the
name of the LORD?' Then Micaiah 17
said, 'I saw all Israel scattered on
the mountains, like sheep without
a shepherd; and I heard the LORD
say, "They have no master, let
them go home in peace."' The king 18
of Israel said to Jehoshaphat, 'Did
I not tell you that he never prophesies good for me, nothing but
evil?' Micaiah went on, 'Listen 19
now to the word of the LORD. I saw
the LORD seated on his throne,
with all the host of heaven in attendance on his right and on his
left. The LORD said, "Who will en- 20
tice Ahab to attack and fall onᵇ
Ramoth-gilead?" One said one
thing and one said another; then 21
a spirit came forward and stood
before the LORD and said, "I will
entice him." "How?" said the
LORD. "I will go out", he said, 22
"and be a lying spirit in the mouth
of all his prophets." 'You shall entice him," said the LORD, "and you
shall succeed; go and do it." You 23
see, then, how the LORD has put a
lying spirit in the mouth of all

ᵃ *Verses 2–35: cp. 2 Chr. 18. 2–34.*   ᵇ *Or at.*

these prophets of yours, because he
24 has decreed disaster for you.' Then
Zedekiah son of Kenaanah came
up to Micaiah and struck him in
the face: 'And how did the spirit
of the LORD pass from me to speak
25 to you?' he said. Micaiah answered,
'That you will find out on the day
when you run into an inner room to
26 hide yourself.' Then the king of
Israel ordered Micaiah to be arrested and committed to the custody of
Amon the governor of the city and
27 Joash the king's son.*a* 'Lock this
fellow up', he said, 'and give him
prison diet of bread and water un-
28 til I come home in safety.' Micaiah
retorted, 'If you do return in safety, the LORD has not spoken by me.'
29 So the king of Israel and Jehoshaphat king of Judah marched on
30 Ramoth-gilead, and the king of Israel said to Jehoshaphat, 'I will disguise myself to go into battle, but
you shall wear your royal robes.'
So he went into battle in disguise.
31 Now the king of Aram had commanded the thirty-two captains of
his chariots not to engage all and
sundry but the king of Israel alone.
32 When the captains saw Jehoshaphat, they thought he was the king
of Israel and turned to attack him.
33 But Jehoshaphat cried out and,
when the captains saw that he was
not the king of Israel, they broke
34 off the attack on him. But one man
drew his bow at random and hit
the king of Israel where the breast-
plate joins the plates of the armour.
So he said to his driver, 'Wheel
round and take me out of the line; I
35 am wounded.' When the day's
fighting reached its height, the
king was facing the Aramaeans
propped up in his chariot, and the
blood from his wound flowed down
upon the floor of the chariot; and
36 in the evening he died. At sunset
the herald went through the ranks,
crying, 'Every man to his city,
37 every man to his country.' Thus

died the king. He was brought to
Samaria and they buried him
there. The chariot was swilled out 38
at the pool of Samaria, and the
dogs licked up the blood, and the
prostitutes washed themselves in
it, in fulfilment of the word the
LORD had spoken.

Now the other acts and events 39
of Ahab's reign, the ivory house
and all the cities he built, are recorded in the annals of the kings of
Israel. So Ahab rested with his 40
forefathers and was succeeded by
his son Ahaziah.

Jehoshaphat son of Asa had be- 41*b*
come king of Judah in the fourth
year of Ahab king of Israel. He 42
was thirty-five years old when he
came to the throne, and he reigned
in Jerusalem for twenty-five years;
his mother was Azubah daughter
of Shilhi. He followed in the foot- 43
steps of Asa his father and did not
swerve from them; he did what was
right in the eyes of the LORD. But
the hill-shrines were allowed to remain; the people continued to
slaughter and burn sacrifices there.
Jehoshaphat remained at peace 44
with the king of Israel. The other 45
events of Jehoshaphat's reign, his
exploits and his wars, are recorded
in the annals of the kings of Judah.
But he did away with such of the 46
male prostitutes attached to the
shrines as were still left over from
the days of Asa his father.

There was no king in Edom, only*c* 47
a viceroy of Jehoshaphat; he built 48
merchantmen to sail to Ophir for
gold, but they never made the
journey because they were wrecked at Ezion-geber. Ahaziah son of 49
Ahab proposed to Jehoshaphat
that his own men should go to sea
with his; but Jehoshaphat would
not consent.

Jehoshaphat rested with his fore- 50
fathers and was buried with them
in the city of David his father, and
was succeeded by his son Joram.

---

a son: *or* deputy.   *b Verses 41–43: cp. 2 Chr. 20. 31–33.*
c only: *prob. rdg.*; Heb. om.

51 Ahaziah son of Ahab became king of Israel in Samaria in the seventeenth year of Jehoshaphat king of Judah, and reigned over 52 Israel for two years. He did what was wrong in the eyes of the LORD, following in the footsteps of his father and mother and in those of Jeroboam son of Nebat, who had led Israel into sin. He served Baal 53 and worshipped him, and provoked the anger of the LORD the God of Israel, as his father had done.

THE SECOND BOOK OF

KINGS

Elisha and the end of the house of Ahab

1 AFTER Ahab's death Moab rebelled against Israel. 2 Ahaziah fell through a latticed window in his roof-chamber in Samaria and injured himself; he sent messengers to inquire of Baal-zebub the god of Ekron whether he 3 would recover from his illness. The angel of the LORD ordered Elijah the Tishbite to go and meet the messengers of the king of Samaria and say to them, 'Is there no god in Israel, that you go to inquire of 4 Baal-zebub the god of Ekron? This is the word of the LORD to your master: "You shall not rise from the bed where you are lying; you will die."' Then Elijah departed. 5 The messengers went back to the king. When asked why they had 6 returned, they answered that a man had come to meet them and had ordered them to return and say to the king who had sent them, 'This is the word of the LORD: "Is there no god in Israel, that you send to inquire of Baal-zebub the god of Ekron? In consequence, you shall not rise from the bed where 7 you are lying; you will die."' The king asked them what kind of man it was who had met them and said 8 this. 'A hairy man', they answered, 'with a leather apron round his waist.' 'It is Elijah the Tishbite', said the king.

Then the king sent a captain to 9 him with his company of fifty. He went up and found the prophet sitting on a hill-top and said to him, 'Man of God, the king orders you to come down.' Elijah answered 10 the captain, 'If I am a man of God, may fire fall from heaven and consume you and your company!' Fire fell from heaven and consumed the officer and his fifty men. The king 11 sent another captain of fifty with his company, and he went up and said to the prophet, 'Man of God, this is the king's command: Come down at once.' Elijah answered, 'If 12 I am a man of God, may fire fall from heaven and consume you and your company!' God's fire fell from heaven and consumed the man and his company. The king sent the 13 captain of a third company with his fifty men, and this third captain went up the hill to Elijah and knelt down before him and pleaded with him: 'Man of God, consider me and these fifty servants of yours, and set some value on our lives. Fire fell from heaven and 14 consumed the other two captains of fifty and their companies; but let my life have some value in your eyes.' The angel of the LORD said 15 to Elijah, 'Go down with him. Do not be afraid.' So he rose and went 16 down with him to the king, and he said, 'This is the word of the LORD: "You have sent to inquire of Baal-zebub the god of Ekron, and therefore you shall not rise from the bed where you are lying; you will die."'

17 The word of the LORD which Elijah had spoken was fulfilled, and Aha-ziah died; and because he had no son, his brother Jehoram succeed-ed him in the second year of Joram son of Jehoshaphat king of Judah.

18 The other events of Ahaziah's reign are recorded in the annals of the kings of Israel.

2 The time came when the LORD would take Elijah up to heaven in a whirlwind. Elijah and Elisha left 2 Gilgal, and Elijah said to Elisha, 'Stay here; for the LORD has sent me to Bethel.' But Elisha said, 'As the LORD lives, your life upon it, I will not leave you.' So they went 3 down country to Bethel. There a company of prophets came out to Elisha and said to him, 'Do you know that the LORD is going to take your lord and master from you today?' 'I do know,' he re-4 plied; 'say no more.' Then Elijah said to him, 'Stay here, Elisha; for the LORD has sent me to Jericho.' But he replied, 'As the LORD lives, your life upon it, I will not leave you.' So they went to Jericho. 5 There a company of prophets came up to Elisha and said to him, 'Do you know that the LORD is going to take your lord and master from you today?' 'I do know,' he said; 6 'say no more.' Then Elijah said to him, 'Stay here; for the LORD has sent me to the Jordan.' The other replied, 'As the LORD lives, your life upon it, I will not leave you.' So the two of them went on.

7 Fifty of the prophets followed them, and stood watching from a distance as the two of them stop-8 ped by the Jordan. Elijah took his cloak, rolled it up and struck the water with it. The water divided to right and left, and they both cross-ed over on dry ground. While they 9 were crossing, Elijah said to Eli-sha, 'Tell me what I can do for you before I am taken from you.' Eli-sha said, 'Let me inherit a double share of your spirit.' 'You have 10 asked a hard thing', said Elijah. 'If you see me taken from you, may your wish be granted; if you do not, it shall not be granted.' They 11 went on, talking as they went, and suddenly there appeared chariots of fire and horses of fire, which separated them one from the other, and Elijah was carried up in the whirlwind to heaven. When Elisha 12 saw it, he cried, 'My father, my father, the chariots and the horse-men of Israel!', and he saw him no more. Then he took hold of his mantle and rent it in two, and he 13 picked up the cloak which had fall-en from Elijah, and came back and stood on the bank of the Jordan. There he too struck the water with 14 Elijah's cloak and said, 'Where is the LORD the God of Elijah?' When he struck the water, it was again divided to right and left, and he crossed over. The prophets from 15 Jericho, who were watching, saw him and said, 'The spirit of Elijah has settled on Elisha.' So they came to meet him, and fell on their faces before him and said, 'Your ser-16 vants have fifty stalwart men. Let them go and search for your mas-ter; perhaps the spirit of the LORD has lifted him up and cast him on some mountain or into some val-ley.' But he said, 'No, you must not send them.' They pressed him, 17 however, until he had not the heart to refuse. So they sent out the fifty men but, though they searched for three days, they did not find him. When they came 18 back to Elisha, who had remained at Jericho, he said to them, 'Did I not tell you not to go?'

The people of the city said to 19 Elisha, 'You can see how pleasant-ly our city is situated, but the

water is polluted and the country
20 is troubled with miscarriages.' He
said, 'Fetch me a new bowl and put
some salt in it.' When they had
21 fetched it, he went out to the
spring and, throwing the salt into
it, he said, 'This is the word of the
LORD: "I purify this water. It shall
cause no more death or miscar-
22 riage."' The water has remained
pure till this day, in fulfilment of
Elisha's word.

23 He went up from there to Bethel
and, as he was on his way, some
small boys came out of the city and
jeered at him, saying, 'Get along
24 with you, bald head, get along.' He
turned round and looked at them
and he cursed them in the name of
the LORD; and two she-bears came
out of a wood and mauled forty-
25 two of them. From there he went
on to Mount Carmel, and thence
back to Samaria.

3 In the eighteenth year of Jehoshaphat king of Judah, Jehoram
son of Ahab became king of Israel
in Samaria, and he reigned for
2 twelve years. He did what was
wrong in the eyes of the LORD,
though not as his father and his
mother had done; he did remove
the sacred pillar of the Baal which
3 his father had made. Yet he persisted in the sins into which Jeroboam son of Nebat had led Israel,
and did not give them up.

4 Mesha king of Moab was a sheep-
breeder, and he used to supply the
king of Israel regularly with the
wool of a hundred thousand lambs
and a hundred thousand rams.
5 When Ahab died, the king of Moab
rebelled against the king of Israel.
6 Then King Jehoram came from
Samaria and mustered all Israel.
7 He also sent this message to Jehoshaphat king of Judah: 'The king
of Moab has rebelled against me.
Will you join me in attacking
Moab?' 'I will,' he replied; 'what is
mine is yours: myself, my people,
8 and my horses.' 'From which direction shall we attack?' Jehoram

asked. 'Through the wilderness of
Edom', replied the other. So the 9
king of Israel set out with the king
of Judah and the king of Edom.
When they had been seven days on
the march, they had no water left
for the army or the pack-animals.
Then the king of Israel said, 'Alas, 10
the LORD has brought together
three kings, only to put us at the
mercy of the Moabites.' But Jeho- 11
shaphat said, 'Is there not a prophet of the LORD here through
whom we may seek guidance of the
LORD?' One of the officers of the
king of Israel answered, 'Elisha
son of Shaphat is here, the man
who poured water on Elijah's
hands.' 'The word of the LORD is 12
with him', said Jehoshaphat. So
the king of Israel and Jehoshaphat
and the king of Edom went down
to Elisha. Elisha said to the king of 13
Israel, 'Why do you come to me?
Go to the prophets of your father
and your mother.' But the king of
Israel said to him, 'No; the LORD
has called us three kings out to put
us at the mercy of the Moabites.'
'As the LORD of Hosts lives, whom 14
I serve,' said Elisha, 'I would not
spare a look or a glance for you, if it
were not for my regard for Jehoshaphat king of Judah. But now, 15
fetch me a minstrel.' They fetched
a minstrel, and while he was playing, the power of the LORD came
upon Elisha and he said, 'This is 16
the word of the LORD: "Pools will
form all over this ravine." The 17
LORD has decreed that you shall
see neither wind nor rain, yet this
ravine shall be filled with water for
you and your army and your pack-
animals to drink. But that is a mere 18
trifle in the sight of the LORD; what
he will also do, is to put Moab at
your mercy. You will raze to the 19
ground every fortified town and
every noble city; you will cut down
all their fine trees; you will stop up
all the springs of water; and you
will spoil every good piece of land
by littering it with stones.' In the 20

morning at the hour of the regular sacrifice they saw water flowing in from the direction of Edom, and the land was flooded.

21 Meanwhile all Moab had heard that the kings had come up to fight against them, and every man, young and old, who could carry arms, was called out and stationed 22 on the frontier. When they got up next morning and the sun had risen over the water, the Moabites saw the water in front of them red 23 like blood and cried out, 'It is blood. The kings must have quarrelled and attacked one another. 24 Now to the plunder, Moab!' When they came to the Israelite camp, the Israelites turned out and attacked them and drove the Moabites headlong in flight, and themselves entered the land of Moab, 25 destroying as they went. They razed the cities to the ground; they littered every good piece of land with stones, each man casting one stone on to it; they stopped up every spring of water; they cut down all their fine trees; and they harried Moab until only in Kirhareseth were any buildings left standing, and even this city the slingers surrounded and attacked. 26 When the king of Moab saw that the war had gone against him, he took seven hundred men with him, armed with swords, to cut a way through to the king of Aram, but 27 they failed in the attempt. Then he took his eldest son, who would have succeeded him, and offered him as a whole-offering upon the city wall. The Israelites were filled with such consternation at this sight,[a] that they struck camp and returned to their own land.

4 The wife of a member of a company of prophets appealed to Elisha. 'My husband, your servant, has died', she said. 'You know that he was a man who feared the LORD; but a creditor has come to take away my two boys as his slaves.' Elisha said to her, 'How 2 can I help you? Tell me what you have in the house.' 'Nothing at all', she answered, 'except a flask of oil.' 'Go out then', he said, 'and 3 borrow vessels from all your neighbours; get as many empty ones as you can. Then, when you come 4 home, shut yourself in with your sons, pour from the flask into all these vessels and, as they are filled, set them aside.' She left him and 5 shut herself in with her sons. As they brought her the vessels she filled them. When they were all 6 full, she said to one of her sons, 'Bring me another.' 'There is not one left', he said. Then the flow of oil ceased. She came out and told 7 the man of God, and he said, 'Go and sell the oil and redeem your boys who are being taken as pledges,[b] and you and they can live on what is left.'

It happened once that Elisha 8 went over to Shunem. There was a great lady there who pressed him to accept her hospitality, and so, whenever he came that way, he stopped to take food there. One day 9 she said to her husband, 'I know that this man who comes here regularly is a holy man of God. Why not 10 build up the wall to make him a little roof-chamber, and put in it a bed, a table, a seat, and a lamp, and let him stay there whenever he comes to us?' Once when he arrived 11 and went to this roof-chamber and lay down to rest, he said to Gehazi, 12 his servant, 'Call this Shunammite woman.' He called her and, when she appeared before the prophet, he said to his servant, 'Say to her, 13 "You have taken all this trouble for us. What can I do for you? Shall I speak for you to the king or to the commander-in-chief?"' But she replied, 'I am content where I am, among my own people.' He 14 said, 'Then what can be done for

---

[a] The Israelites...sight: *or* There was such great anger against the Israelites...
[b] redeem...pledges: *or* pay off your debt.

her?' Gehazi said, 'There is only this: she has no child and her husband is old.' 'Call her back', Elisha said. When she was called, she appeared in the doorway, and he said, 'In due season, this time next year, you shall have a son in your arms.' But she said, 'No, no, my lord, you are a man of God and would not lie to your servant.' Next year in due season the woman conceived and bore a son, as Elisha had foretold.

18 When the child was old enough, he went out one day to the reapers where his father was. All of a sudden he cried out to his father, 'O my head, my head!' His father told a servant to carry him to his mother. He brought him to his mother; the boy sat on her lap till midday, and then he died. She went up and laid him on the bed of the man of God, shut the door and went out. She called her husband and said, 'Send me one of the servants and a she-ass, I must go to the man of God as fast as I can, and come straight back.' 'Why go to him today?' he asked. 'It is neither new moon nor sabbath.'[a] 'Never mind that', she answered. When the ass was saddled, she said to her servant, 'Lead on and do not slacken pace unless I tell you.' So she set out and came to the man of God on Mount Carmel. The man of God spied her in the distance and said to Gehazi, his servant, 'That is the Shunammite woman coming. Run and meet her, and ask, "Is all well with you? Is all well with your husband? Is all well with the boy?"' She answered, 'All is well.' When she reached the man of God on the hill, she clutched his feet. Gehazi came forward to push her away, but the man of God said, 'Let her alone; she is in great distress, and the LORD has concealed it from me and not told me.' 'My lord,' she said, 'did I ask for a son? Did I not beg you not to raise my hopes and

then dash them?' Then he turned 29 to Gehazi: 'Hitch up your cloak; take my staff with you and run. If you meet anyone on the way, do not stop to greet him; if anyone greets you, do not answer him. Lay my staff on the boy's face.' But the 30 mother cried, 'As the LORD lives, your life upon it, I will not leave you.' So he got up and followed her.[b]

Gehazi went on ahead of them 31 and laid the staff on the boy's face, but there was no sound and no sign of life. So he went back to meet Elisha and told him that the boy had not roused. When Elisha entered the house, there was the boy 32 dead, on the bed where he had been laid. He went into the room, shut 33 the door on the two of them and prayed to the LORD. Then, getting 34 on to the bed, he lay upon the child, put his mouth to the child's mouth, his eyes to his eyes and his hands to his hands; and, as he pressed[c] upon him, the child's body grew warm. Elisha got up and 35 walked once up and down the room; then, getting on to the bed again, he pressed[c] upon him and breathed into him[d] seven times; and the boy opened his eyes. The 36 prophet summoned Gehazi and said, 'Call this Shunammite woman.' She answered his call and the prophet said, 'Take your child.' She came in and fell prostrate be- 37 fore him. Then she took up her son and went out.

Elisha returned to Gilgal at a 38 time when there was a famine in the land. One day, when a group of prophets was sitting at his feet, he said to his servant, 'Set the big pot on the fire and prepare some broth for the company.' One of them 39 went out into the fields to gather herbs and found a wild vine, and filled the skirt of his garment with bitter-apples.[e] He came back and sliced them into the pot, not know-

---

[a] Or full moon.   [b] Or went with her.   [c] Prob. rdg.; Heb. crouched.
[d] and breathed into him: or and the boy sneezed.   [e] Or poisonous wild gourds.

40 ing what they were. They poured it out for the men to eat, but, when they tasted it, they cried out, 'Man of God, there is death in the 41 pot', and they could not eat it. The prophet said, 'Fetch some meal.' He threw it into the pot and said, 'Now pour out for the men to eat.' This time there was no harm in the pot.

42 A man came from Baal-shalisha, bringing the man of God some of the new season's bread, twenty barley loaves, and fresh ripe ears of corn.[a] Elisha said, 'Give this to the 43 people to eat.' But his disciple protested, 'I cannot set this before a hundred men.' Still he repeated, 'Give it to the people to eat; for this is the word of the LORD: "They will eat and there will be 44 some left over."' So he set it before them, and they ate and left some over, as the LORD had said.

5 NAAMAN, commander of the king of Aram's army, was a great man highly esteemed by his master, because by his means the LORD had given victory to Aram; but he was 2 a leper.[b] On one of their raids the Aramaeans brought back as a captive from the land of Israel a little girl, who became a servant to 3 Naaman's wife. She said to her mistress, 'If only my master could meet the prophet who lives in Samaria, he would get rid of the disease 4 for him.' Naaman went in and reported to his master word for word what the girl from the land of Israel 5 had said. 'Very well, you may go,' said the king of Aram, 'and I will send a letter to the king of Israel.' So Naaman went, taking with him ten talents of silver, six thousand shekels of gold, and ten changes of 6 clothing. He delivered the letter to the king of Israel, which read thus: 'This letter is to inform you that I am sending to you my servant Naaman, and I beg you to rid him

of his disease.' When the king of 7 Israel read the letter, he rent his clothes and said, 'Am I a god[c] to kill and to make alive, that this fellow sends to me to cure a man of his disease? Surely you must see that he is picking a quarrel with me.' When Elisha, the man of God, 8 heard how the king of Israel had rent his clothes, he sent to him saying, 'Why did you rend your clothes? Let the man come to me, and he will know that there is a prophet in Israel.' So Naaman 9 came with his horses and chariots and stood at the entrance to Elisha's house. Elisha sent out a mes- 10 senger to say to him, 'If you will go and wash seven times in the Jordan, your flesh will be restored and you will be clean.' Naaman was 11 furious and went away, saying, 'I thought he would at least have come out and stood, and invoked the LORD his God by name, waved his hand over the place and so rid me of the disease. Are not Abana 12 and Pharpar, rivers of Damascus, better than all the waters of Israel? Can I not wash in them and be clean?' So he turned and went off in a rage. But his servants came up 13 to him and said, 'If the prophet had bidden you do something difficult, would you not do it? How much more then, if he tells you to wash and be clean?' So he went 14 down and dipped himself in the Jordan seven times as the man of God had told him, and his flesh was restored as a little child's, and he was clean.

Then he and his retinue went 15 back to the man of God and stood before him; and he said, 'Now I know that there is no god anywhere on earth except in Israel. Will you accept a token of gratitude from your servant?' 'As the LORD lives, 16 whom I serve,' said the prophet, 'I will accept nothing.' He was pressed to accept, but he refused. 'Then 17

---

[a] fresh...corn: *prob. rdg.*; *Heb. unintelligible.*
[b] he was a leper: *or* his skin was diseased.   [c] *Or* Am I God.

if you will not,' said Naaman, 'let me, sir, have two mules' load of earth. For I will no longer offer whole-offering or sacrifice to any
18 god but the LORD. In this one matter only may the LORD pardon me: when my master goes to the temple of Rimmon to worship, leaning on my arm, and I worship in the temple of Rimmon when he worships there, for this let the
19 LORD pardon me.' And Elisha bade him farewell.

20   Naaman had gone only a short distance on his way, when Gehazi, the servant of Elisha the man of God, said to himself, 'What? Has my master let this Aramaean, Naaman, go scot-free, and not accepted what he brought? As the LORD lives, I will run after him and
21 get something from him.' So Gehazi hurried after Naaman. When Naaman saw him running after him, he jumped down from his chariot to meet him and said, 'Is
22 anything wrong?' 'Nothing,' said Gehazi, 'but my master sent me to say that two young men of the company of prophets from the hill-country of Ephraim have just arrived. Could you provide them with a talent of silver and two
23 changes of clothing?' Naaman said, 'By all means; take two talents.' He pressed*a* him to take them; so he tied up the two talents of silver in two bags, and the two changes of clothing, and gave them to his two servants, and they walk-
24 ed ahead carrying them. When Gehazi came to the citadel*b* he took them from the two servants, deposited them in the house and dismissed the men; and they de-
25 parted. When he went in and stood before his master, Elisha said, 'Where have you been, Gehazi?'
26 'Nowhere', said Gehazi. But he said to him, 'Was I not with you in spirit when the man turned back

from his chariot to meet you? Is it not true that you have the money? You may buy gardens with it,*c d* and olive-trees and vineyards, sheep and oxen, slaves and slave-girls; but the disease of Naaman 27 will fasten on you and on your descendants for ever.' Gehazi left his presence, his skin diseased, white as snow.

A COMPANY of prophets said to 6 Elisha, 'You can see that this place where our community is living, under you as its head, is too small for us. Let us go to the Jordan and 2 each fetch a log, and make ourselves a place to live in.' The prophet agreed. Then one of them said, 3 'Please, sir, come with us.' 'I will', he said, and he went with them. 4 When they reached the Jordan, they began cutting down trees; but 5 it chanced that, as one man was felling a trunk, the head of his axe flew off into the water. 'Oh, master!' he exclaimed, 'it was a borrowed one.' 'Where did it fall?' 6 asked the man of God. When he was shown the place, he cut off a piece of wood and threw it in and made the iron float. Then he said, 7 'There you are, lift it out.' So he stretched out his hand and took it.

    Once, when the king of Aram 8 was making war on Israel, he held a conference with his staff at which he said, 'I mean to attack in such and such a direction.' But the man 9 of God warned the king of Israel: 'Take care to avoid this place, for the Aramaeans are going down that way.' So the king of Israel 10 sent to the place about which the man of God had given him this warning; and the king took special precautions every time he found himself near that place. The king of 11 Aram was greatly perturbed at this and, summoning his staff, he said to them, 'Tell me, one of you, who

---

a Prob. rdg; Heb. broke out on.   *b* Or hill.
c gardens with it: prob. rdg.; Heb. garments.
d Is it not...with it: or Was it a time to get the money and to get garments?

has betrayed us to the king of Is-
12 rael?' 'None of us, my lord king,'
said one of his staff; 'but Elisha,
the prophet in Israel, tells the king
of Israel the very words you speak
13 in your bedchamber.' 'Go and find
out where he is,' said the king, 'and
I will send and seize him.' He was
told that the prophet was at Doth-
14 an, and he sent a strong force there
with horses and chariots. They
came by night and surrounded the
city.

15 When the disciple of the man of
God rose early in the morning and
went out, he saw a force with
horses and chariots surrounding
the city. 'Oh, master,' he said,
16 'which way are we to turn?' He
answered, 'Do not be afraid, for
those who are on our side are more
17 than those on theirs.' Then Elisha
offered this prayer: 'O LORD, open
his eyes and let him see.' And the
LORD opened the young man's
eyes, and he saw the hills covered
with horses and chariots of fire all
18 round Elisha. As they came down
towards him, Elisha prayed to the
LORD: 'Strike this host, I pray
thee, with blindness'; and he struck
them blind as Elisha had asked.
19 Then Elisha said to them, 'You are
on the wrong road; this is not the
city. Follow me and I will lead you
to the man you are looking for.'
20 And he led them to Samaria. As
soon as they had entered Samaria,
Elisha prayed, 'O LORD, open the
eyes of these men and let them see
again.' And he opened their eyes
and they saw that they were inside
21 Samaria. When the king of Israel
saw them, he said to Elisha, 'My
22 father, am I to destroy them?' 'No,
you must not do that', he answered. 'You may destroy*a* those whom
you have taken prisoner with your
own sword and bow, but as for these
men, give them food and water,
and let them eat and drink, and
23 then go back to their master.' So he
prepared a great feast for them,

and they ate and drank and then
went back to their master. And
Aramaean raids on Israel ceased.

But later, Ben-hadad king of 24
Aram called up his entire army and
marched to the siege of Samaria.
The city was near starvation, and 25
they besieged it so closely that a
donkey's head was sold for eighty
shekels of silver, and a quarter of a
kab of locust-beans for five shekels.
One day, as the king of Israel was 26
walking along the city wall, a woman called to him, 'Help, my lord
king!' He said, 'If the LORD will 27
not bring you help, where can I
find any for you? From threshing-
floor or from winepress? What is 28
your trouble?' She replied, 'This
woman said to me, "Give up your
child for us to eat today, and we
will eat mine tomorrow." So we 29
cooked my son and ate him; but
when I said to her the next day,
"Now give up your child for us to
eat", she had hidden him.' When 30
he heard the woman's story, the
king rent his clothes. He was walking along the wall at the time, and
when the people looked, they saw
that he had sackcloth underneath,
next to his skin. Then he said, 'The 31
LORD do the same to me and more,
if the head of Elisha son of Shaphat
stays on his shoulders today.'

Elisha was sitting at home, the 32
elders with him. The king had dispatched one of his retinue but, before the messenger arrived, Elisha
said to the elders, 'See how this son
of a murderer has sent to behead
me! Take care, when the messenger comes, to shut the door and
hold it fast against him. Can you
not hear his master following on
his heels?' While he was still speak- 33
ing, the king*b* arrived and said,
'Look at our plight! This is the
LORD's doing. Why should I wait
any longer for him to help us?' But 7
Elisha answered, 'Hear this word
of the LORD: By this time tomorrow a shekel will buy a measure of

---

a Prob. rdg.; Heb. Would you destroy.   *b* Prob. rdg.; Heb. messenger.

flour or two measures of barley in
2 the gateway of Samaria.' Then the
lieutenant on whose arm the king
leaned said to the man of God,
'Even if the Lord were to open
windows in the sky, such a thing
could not happen!' He answered,
'You will see it with your own eyes,
but none of it will you eat.'
3   At the city gate were four lepers.[a]
They said to one another, 'Why
should we stay here and wait for
4 death? If we say we will go into the
city, there is famine there, and we
shall die; if we say we will stay
here, we shall die just the same.
Well then, let us go to the camp of
the Aramaeans and give ourselves
up: if they spare us, we shall live;
if they put us to death, we can but
5 die.' And so in the twilight they set
out for the Aramaean camp; but
when they reached the outskirts,
6 they found no one there; for the
Lord had caused the Aramaean
army to hear a sound like that of
chariots and horses and of a great
host, so that the word went round:
'The king of Israel has hired the
kings of the Hittites and the kings
7 of Egypt to attack us.' They had
fled at once in the twilight, abandoning their tents, their horses and
asses, and leaving the camp as it
stood, while they fled for their
8 lives. When the four men came to
the outskirts of the camp, they
went into a tent and ate and drank
and looted silver and gold and
clothing, and made off and hid
them. Then they came back, went
into another tent and rifled it, and
9 made off and hid the loot. Then
they said to one another, 'What we
are doing is not right. This is a day
of good news and we are keeping it
to ourselves. If we wait till morning, we shall be held to blame. We
must go now and give the news to
10 the king's household.' So they came
and called to the watch at the city
gate and described how they had

gone to the Aramaean camp and
found not a single man in it and
had heard no sound: nothing but
horses and asses tethered, and the
tents left as they were. Then the 11
watch called out and gave the
news to the king's household in the
palace. The king rose in the night 12
and said to his staff, 'I will tell you
what the Aramaeans have done.
They know that we are starving,
and they have left their camp to go
and hide in the open country, expecting us to come out, and then
they can take us alive and enter the
city.' One of his staff said, 'Send 13
out a party of men with some of
the horses that are left; if they live,
they will be as well off as all the
other Israelites who are still left; if
they die,[b] they will be no worse off
than all those who have already
perished. Let them go and see what
has happened.' So they picked two 14
mounted men, and the king dispatched them in the track of the
Aramaean army with the order to
go and find out what had happened.
They followed as far as the Jordan 15
and found the whole road littered
with clothing and equipment which
the Aramaeans had flung aside in
their haste. The messengers returned and reported this to the
king. Then the people went out and 16
plundered the Aramaean camp,
and a measure of flour was sold for
a shekel and two measures of barley
for a shekel, so that the word of the
Lord came true. Now the king had 17
appointed the lieutenant on whose
arm he leaned to take charge of the
gate, and the people trampled him
to death there, just as the man of
God had foretold when the king
visited him. For when the man of 18
God said to the king, 'By this time
tomorrow a shekel will buy two
measures of barley or one measure
of flour in the gateway of Samaria',
the lieutenant had answered, 'Even 19
if the Lord were to open windows

[a] Or men suffering from skin-disease.
[b] if they live...if they die: prob. rdg.; Heb. obscure.

in the sky, such a thing could not happen!' And the man of God had said, 'You will see it with your own eyes, but none of it will you eat.'

20 And this is just what happened to him: the people trampled him to death at the gate.

8 Elisha said to the woman whose son he had restored to life, 'Go away at once with your household and find lodging where you can, for the LORD has decreed a seven years' famine and it has already come

2 upon the land.' The woman acted at once on the word of the man of God and went away with her household; and she stayed in the Philistine country for seven years.

3 When she came back at the end of the seven years, she sought an audience of the king to appeal for the return of her house and land.

4 Now the king was questioning Gehazi, the servant of the man of God, about all the great things

5 Elisha had done; and, as he was describing to the king how he had brought the dead to life, the self-same woman began appealing to the king for her house and her land. 'My lord king,' said Gehazi, 'this is the very woman, and this is her son whom Elisha brought to life.'

6 The king asked the woman about it, and she told him. Then he entrusted the case to a eunuch and ordered him to restore all her property to her, with all the revenues from her land from the time she left the country till that day.

7 Elisha came to Damascus, at a time when Ben-hadad king of Aram was ill; and when he was told that the man of God had arrived,

8 he bade Hazael take a gift with him and go to the man of God and inquire of the LORD through him whether he would recover from his

9 illness. Hazael went, taking with him as a gift all kinds of wares of Damascus, forty camel-loads. When he came into the prophet's presence, he said, 'Your son Ben-

hadad king of Aram has sent me to you to ask whether he will recover from his illness.' 'Go and tell him 10 that he will recover,' he answered; 'but the LORD has revealed to me that in fact he will die.' The man 11 of God stood there with set face like a man stunned, until he could bear it no longer; then he wept. 'Why do you weep, my lord?' said 12 Hazael. He answered, 'Because I know the harm you will do to the Israelites: you will set their fortresses on fire and put their young men to the sword; you will dash their children to the ground and you will rip open their pregnant women.' But Hazael said, 'But I 13 am a dog, a mere nobody; how can I do this great thing?' Elisha answered, 'The LORD has revealed to me that you will be king of Aram.' Hazael left Elisha and returned to 14 his master, who asked him what Elisha had said. 'He told me that you would recover', he replied. But 15 the next day he took a blanket and, after dipping it in water, laid it over the king's face, and he died; and Hazael succeeded him.

In the fifth year of Jehoram son 16 of Ahab king of Israel, Joram son of Jehoshaphat king of Judah became king. He was thirty-two years 17[a] old when he came to the throne, and he reigned in Jerusalem for eight years. He followed the prac- 18 tices of the kings of Israel as the house of Ahab had done, for he had married Ahab's daughter; and he did what was wrong in the eyes of the LORD. But for his servant 19 David's sake the LORD was unwilling to destroy Judah, since he had promised to give him and his sons a flame, to burn for all time.

During his reign Edom revolted 20 against Judah and set up its own king. Joram crossed over to Zair 21 with all his chariots. He and his chariot-commanders set out by night, but they were surrounded

by the Edomites and defeated,[a] whereupon the people fled to
22 their tents. So Edom has remained independent of Judah to this day; Libnah also revolted at the same
23 time. The other acts and events of Joram's reign are recorded in the
24 annals of the kings of Judah. So Joram rested with his forefathers and was buried with them in the city of David, and his son Ahaziah succeeded him.

25[b] In the twelfth year of Jehoram son of Ahab king of Israel, Ahaziah son of Joram king of Judah
26 became king. Ahaziah was twenty-two years old when he came to the throne, and he reigned in Jerusalem for one year; his mother was Athaliah granddaughter of Omri
27 king of Israel. He followed the practices of the house of Ahab and did what was wrong in the eyes of the LORD like the house of Ahab, for he was connected with that
28 house by marriage. He allied himself with Jehoram son of Ahab to fight against Hazael king of Aram at Ramoth-gilead; but King Jehoram was wounded by the Ara-
29 maeans, and returned to Jezreel to recover from the wounds which were inflicted on him at Ramoth in battle with Hazael king of Aram; and because of his illness Ahaziah son of Joram king of Judah went down to Jezreel to visit him.

9 ELISHA the prophet summoned one of the company of prophets and said to him, 'Hitch up your cloak, take this flask of oil with you
2 and go to Ramoth-gilead. When you arrive, you will find Jehu son of Jehoshaphat, son of Nimshi; go in and call him aside from his fellow-officers, and lead him through
3 to an inner room. Then take the flask and pour the oil on his head and say, "This is the word of the LORD: I anoint you king over Israel"; then open the door and flee

for your life.' So the young prophet 4
went to Ramoth-gilead. When he 5
arrived, he found the officers sitting together and said, 'Sir, I have a word for you.' 'For which of us?' asked Jehu. 'For you, sir', he said. He rose and went into the house, 6
and the prophet poured the oil on his head, saying, 'This is the word of the LORD the God of Israel: "I anoint you king over Israel, the people of the LORD. You shall strike 7
down the house of Ahab your master, and I will take vengeance on Jezebel for the blood of my servants the prophets and for the blood of all the LORD's servants. All the house 8
of Ahab shall perish and I will destroy every mother's son of his house in Israel, whether under the protection of the family or not. And I will make the house of Ahab 9
like the house of Jeroboam son of Nebat and the house of Baasha son of Ahijah. Jezebel shall be de- 10
voured by dogs in the plot of ground at Jezreel and no one will bury her."' Then he opened the door and fled. When Jehu rejoined 11
the king's officers, they said to him, 'Is all well? What did this crazy fellow want with you?' 'You know him and the way his thoughts run', he said. 'Nonsense!' they replied; 12
'tell us what happened.' 'I will tell you exactly what he said: "This is the word of the LORD: I anoint you king over Israel."' They 13
snatched up their cloaks and spread them under him on the stones[c] of the steps, and sounded the trumpet and shouted, 'Jehu is king.'

Then Jehu son of Jehoshaphat, 14
son of Nimshi, laid his plans against Jehoram, while Jehoram and the Israelites were defending Ramoth-gilead against Hazael king of Aram. King Jehoram had returned to 15
Jezreel to recover from the wounds inflicted on him by the Aramaeans when he fought against Hazael

---

[a] *and defeated:* prob. rdg.; Heb. *and he defeated Edom.*
[b] *Verses 25–29:* cp. 2 Chr. 22. 1–6.   [c] Prob. rdg.; Heb. obscure.

king of Aram. Jehu said to them, 'If you are on my side, see that no one escapes from the city to tell 16 the news in Jezreel.' He mounted his chariot and drove to Jezreel, for Jehoram was laid up there, and Ahaziah king of Judah had gone down to visit him.

17 The watchman standing on the watch-tower in Jezreel saw Jehu and his troop approaching and called out, 'I see a troop of men.' Then Jehoram said, 'Fetch a horse-man and send to find out if they 18 come peaceably.' The horseman went to meet him and said, 'The king asks, "Is it peace?"' Jehu said, 'Peace? What is peace to you? Fall in behind me.' Thereupon the watchman reported, 'The messen-ger has met them but he is not 19 coming back.' A second horseman was sent; when he met them, he also said, 'The king asks, "Is it peace?"' 'Peace?' said Jehu. 'What is peace to you? Fall in behind me.' 20 Then the watchman reported, 'He has met them but he is not coming back. The driving is like the driv-ing of Jehu son*a* of Nimshi, for he 21 drives furiously.' 'Harness my cha-riot', said Jehoram. They harness-ed it, and Jehoram king of Israel and Ahaziah king of Judah went out each in his own chariot to meet Jehu, and met him by the plot of 22 Naboth of Jezreel. When Jehoram saw Jehu, he said, 'Is it peace, Jehu?' But he replied, 'Do you call it peace while your mother Jezebel keeps up her obscene idol-worship 23 and monstrous sorceries?' Jehoram wheeled about and fled, crying out to Ahaziah, 'Treachery, Ahaziah!' 24 Jehu seized his bow and shot Jeho-ram between the shoulders; the ar-row pierced his heart and he sank 25 down in his chariot. Then Jehu said to Bidkar, his lieutenant, 'Pick him up and throw him into the plot of land belonging to Naboth of Jezreel; remember how, when you and I were riding side by side

behind Ahab his father, the LORD pronounced this sentence against him: "It is the very word of the 26 LORD: as surely as I saw yesterday the blood of Naboth and the blood of his sons, I will requite you in this plot." So pick him up and throw him into it and thus fulfil the word of the LORD.' When Aha- 27 ziah king of Judah saw this, he fled by the road to Beth-haggan. Jehu went after him and said, 'Make sure of him too.' They shot him down in his chariot on the road up the valley*b* near Ibleam, but he es-caped to Megiddo and died there. His servants conveyed his body to 28 Jerusalem and buried him in his tomb with his forefathers in the city of David.

In the eleventh year of Jehoram 29 son of Ahab, Ahaziah became king over Judah.

Jehu came to Jezreel. Now Jeze- 30 bel had heard what had happened; she had painted her eyes and dress-ed her hair, and she stood looking down from a window. As Jehu en- 31 tered the gate, she said, 'Is it peace, you Zimri, you murderer of your master?' He looked up at the 32 window and said, 'Who is on my side, who?' Two or three eunuchs looked out, and he said, 'Throw her 33 down.' They threw her down, and some of her blood splashed on to the wall and the horses, which trampled her underfoot. Then he 34 went in and ate and drank. 'See to this accursed woman', he said, 'and bury her; for she is a king's daughter.' But when they went to 35 bury her they found nothing of her but the skull, the feet, and the palms of the hands; and they went 36 back and told him. Jehu said, 'It is the word of the LORD which his servant Elijah the Tishbite spoke, when he said, "In the plot of ground at Jezreel the dogs shall devour the flesh of Jezebel, and 37 Jezebel's corpse shall lie like dung upon the ground in the plot at

a Or grandson (*cp. verse 2*).   *b* the valley: *prob. rdg.*; *Heb.* to Gur.

Jezreel so that no one will be able to say: This is Jezebel.'''

10   Now seventy sons of Ahab were left in Samaria. Jehu therefore sent a letter to Samaria, to the elders, the rulers of the city, and to the tutors of Ahab's children, in which 2 he wrote: 'Now, when this letter reaches you, since you have in your care your master's family as well as his chariots and horses, for- 3 tified cities and weapons, choose the best and the most suitable of your master's family, set him on his father's throne, and fight for 4 your master's house.' They were panic-stricken and said, 'The two kings could not stand against him; what hope is there that we can?' 5 Therefore the comptroller of the household and the governor of the city, with the elders and the tutors, sent this message to Jehu: 'We are your servants. Whatever you tell us we will do; but we will not make anyone king. Do as you think fit.' 6 Then he wrote them a second let- ter: 'If you are on my side and will obey my orders, then bring the heads of your master's sons to me at Jezreel by this time tomorrow.' Now the royal princes, seventy in all, were with the nobles of the city 7 who were bringing them up. When the letter reached them, they took the royal princes and killed all seventy; they put their heads in baskets and sent them to Jehu in 8 Jezreel. When the messenger came to him and reported that they had brought the heads of the royal princes, he ordered them to be put in two heaps and left at the en- trance of the city gate till morning. 9 In the morning he went out, stood there and said to all the people, 'You are fair judges. If I conspired against my master and killed him, 10 who put all these to death? Be sure then that every word which the LORD has spoken against the house of Ahab shall be fulfilled, and that the LORD has now done what he

spoke through his servant Elijah.' So Jehu put to death all who were 11 left of the house of Ahab in Jezreel, as well as all his nobles, his close friends, and his priests, until he had left not one survivor.

Then he set out for Samaria, and 12 on the way there, when he had reached a shepherds' shelter,[a] he 13 came upon the kinsmen of Ahaziah king of Judah and said, 'Who are you?' 'We are kinsmen of Ahaziah,' they replied; 'and we have come down to greet the families of the king and of the queen mother.' 'Take them alive', he said. So they 14 took them alive; then they slew them and flung them into the pit that was there, forty-two of them; they did not leave a single survivor.

When he had left that place, he 15 found Jehonadab son of Rechab coming to meet him. He greeted him and said, 'Are you with me heart and soul, as I am with you?' 'I am', said Jehonadab. 'Then if you are,' said Jehu, 'give me your hand.' He gave him his hand and Jehu helped him up into his cha- riot. 'Come with me,' he said, 'and 16 you will see my zeal for the LORD.' So he took him with him in his chariot. When he came to Sam- 17 aria, he put to death all of Ahab's house who were left there and so blotted it out, in fulfilment of the word which the LORD had spoken to Elijah. Then Jehu called all the 18 people together and said to them, 'Ahab served the Baal a little; Jehu will serve him much. Now, sum- 19 mon all the prophets of Baal, all his ministers and priests; not one must be missing. For I am holding a great sacrifice to Baal, and no one who is missing from it shall live.' In this way Jehu outwitted the ministers of Baal in order to de- stroy them. So Jehu said, 'Let a 20 sacred ceremony for Baal be held.' They did so, and Jehu himself sent 21 word throughout Israel, and all the

_____

[a] a shepherds' shelter: *or* Beth-eker of the Shepherds.

ministers of Baal came; there was not a man left who did not come. They went into the temple of Baal and it was filled from end to end. 22 Then he said to the person who had charge of the wardrobe, 'Bring out robes for all the ministers of Baal'; 23 and he brought them out. Then Jehu and Jehonadab son of Rechab went into the temple of Baal and said to the ministers of Baal, 'Look carefully and make sure that there are no servants of the LORD here with you, but only the 24 ministers of Baal.' Then they went in to offer sacrifices and whole-offerings. Now Jehu had stationed eighty men outside and said to them, 'I am putting these men in your charge, and any man who lets one escape shall answer for it with 25 his life.' When he had finished offering the whole-offering, Jehu ordered the guards and the lieutenants to go and cut them all down, and let not one of them escape; so they slew them without quarter. The escort and the lieutenants then rushed into the keep of the 26 temple of Baal and brought out the sacred pole[a] from the temple of 27 Baal and burnt it; and they pulled down the sacred pillar of the Baal and the temple itself and made a 28 privy of it – as it is today. Thus Jehu stamped out the worship of 29 Baal in Israel. He did not however abandon the sins of Jeroboam son of Nebat who led Israel into sin, but he maintained the worship of the golden calves of Bethel and Dan. 30 Then the LORD said to Jehu, 'You have done well what is right in my eyes and have done to the house of Ahab all that it was in my mind to do. Therefore your sons to the fourth generation shall sit on 31 the throne of Israel.' But Jehu was not careful to follow the law of the LORD the God of Israel with all his heart; he did not abandon the sins of Jeroboam who led Israel into sin.

In those days the LORD began to 32 work havoc on Israel, and Hazael struck at them in every corner of their territory eastwards from the 33 Jordan: all the land of Gilead, Gad, Reuben, and Manasseh, from Aroer which is by the gorge of the Arnon, including Gilead and Bashan.

The other events of Jehu's reign, 34 his achievements and his exploits, are recorded in the annals of the kings of Israel. So Jehu rested 35 with his forefathers and was buried in Samaria; and he was succeeded by his son Jehoahaz. Jehu reigned 36 over Israel in Samaria for twenty-eight years.

Kings of Israel and Judah

As soon as Athaliah mother of 11 1[b] Ahaziah saw that her son was dead, she set out to destroy all the royal line. But Jehosheba daugh- 2 ter of King Joram, sister of Ahaziah, took Ahaziah's son Joash and stole him away from among the princes who were being murdered; she put[c] him and his nurse in a bedchamber where he was hidden from Athaliah and was not put to death. He remained concealed 3 with her in the house of the LORD for six years, while Athaliah ruled the country. In the seventh year 4 Jehoiada sent for the captains of units of a hundred, both of the Carites and of the guards, and he brought them into the house of the LORD; he made an agreement with them and put them on their oath in the house of the LORD, and showed them the king's son, and gave them 5 the following orders: 'One third of you who are on duty on the sabbath are to be on guard in the palace; the rest of you are to be on 6 special duty in the house of the LORD, one third at the Sur Gate and the other third at the gate with[d] the outrunners. Your two 7 companies who are off duty on the

---

[a] *Prob. rdg.; Heb. sacred pillars.*   [b] *Verses 1–20: cp. 2 Chr. 22. 10 – 23. 21.*
[c] *she put: prob. rdg., cp. 2 Chr. 22. 11; Heb. om.*   [d] *Or behind.*

8 sabbath shall be on duty for the king in the house of the LORD. So you shall be on guard round the king, each man with his arms at the ready, and anyone who comes near the ranks is to be put to death; you must be with the king wherever he goes.'

9 The captains carried out the orders of Jehoiada the priest to the letter. Each took his men, both those who came on duty on the sabbath and those who came off,

10 and came to Jehoiada. The priest handed out to the captains King David's spears and shields, which were in the house of the LORD.

11 Then the guards took up their stations, each man carrying his arms at the ready, from corner to corner of the house to north and

12 south,[a] surrounding the king. Then he brought out the king's son, put the crown on his head, handed him the warrant and anointed him king. The people clapped their hands and shouted, 'Long live the

13 king.' When Athaliah heard the noise made by the guards and the people, she came into the house of the LORD where the people were

14 and found the king standing, as was the custom, on the dais,[b] amidst outbursts of song and fanfares of trumpets in his honour, and all the populace rejoicing and blowing trumpets. Then Athaliah rent her clothes and cried, 'Trea-

15 son! Treason!' Jehoiada the priest gave orders to the captains in command of the troops: 'Bring her outside the precincts and put to the sword anyone in attendance on her'; for the priest said, 'She shall not be put to death in the house of

16 the LORD.' So they laid hands on her and took her out by the entry for horses to the royal palace, and there she was put to death.

17 Then Jehoiada made a covenant between the LORD and the king and

people that they should be the LORD's people, and also between the king and the people. And all 18 the people went into the temple of Baal and pulled it down; they smashed to pieces its altars and images, and they slew Mattan the priest of Baal before the altars. Then Jehoiada set a watch over the house of the LORD; he took the 19 captains of units of a hundred, the Carites and the guards and all the people, and they escorted the king from the house of the LORD through the Gate of the Guards to the royal palace, and seated him on the royal throne. The whole people rejoiced 20 and the city was tranquil. That is how Athaliah was put to the sword in the royal palace.

Joash was seven years old when 21[c] he became king. In the seventh 12 year of Jehu, Joash became king, and he reigned in Jerusalem for forty years; his mother was Zibiah of Beersheba. He did what was 2 right in the eyes of the LORD all his days, as Jehoiada the priest had taught him. The hill-shrines, how- 3 ever, were allowed to remain; the people still continued to sacrifice and make smoke-offerings there.

Then Joash ordered the priests 4 to take all the silver brought as holy-gifts into the house of the LORD, the silver for which each man was assessed,[d] the silver for the persons assessed under his name, and any silver which any man brought voluntarily to the house of the LORD. He ordered the 5 priests, also, each to make a contribution from his own funds, and to repair the house wherever it was found necessary. But in the twenty- 6 third year of the reign of Joash the priests had still not carried out the repairs to the house. King Joash 7 summoned Jehoiada the priest and the other priests and said to them, 'Why are you not repairing the

---

[a] *Prob. rdg.; Heb. adds* of the altar and the house.
[b] *Or* by the pillar.   [c] 11. 21 – 12. 15: *cp.* 2 *Chr.* 24. 1–14.
[d] the silver . . . assessed: *prob. rdg.; Heb. obscure.*

house? Henceforth you need not contribute from your own funds 8 for the repair of the house.' So the priests agreed neither to receive money from the people nor to undertake the repairs of the house. 9 Then Jehoiada the priest took a chest and bored a hole in the lid and put it beside the altar on the right side going into the house of the LORD, and the priests on duty at the entrance put in it all the money brought into the house of 10 the LORD. And whenever they saw that the chest was well filled, the king's secretary and the high priest came and melted down the silver found in the house of the LORD and 11 weighed it. When it had been checked, they gave the silver to the foremen over the work in the house of the LORD and they paid the carpenters and the builders working on 12 the temple and the masons and the stone-cutters; they used it also to buy timber and hewn stone for the repairs and for all other expenses 13 connected with them. They did not use the silver brought into the house of the LORD to make silver cups, snuffers, tossing-bowls, trumpets, or any gold or silver ves-14 sels; but they paid it to the workmen and used it for the repairs. 15 No account was demanded from the foremen to whom the money was given for the payment of the workmen, for they were acting on 16 trust. Money from guilt-offerings and sin-offerings was not brought into the house of the LORD: it belonged to the priests.

17 Then Hazael king of Aram came up and attacked Gath and took it; and he moved on against Jerusa-18 lem. But Joash king of Judah took all the holy-gifts that Jehoshaphat, Joram, and Ahaziah his forefathers, kings of Judah, had dedicated, and his own holy-gifts, and all the gold that was found in the treasuries of the house of the LORD

and in the royal palace, and sent them to Hazael king of Aram; and he withdrew from Jerusalem.

The other acts and events of the 19 reign of Joash are recorded in the annals of the kings of Judah. His 20[a] servants revolted against him and struck him down in the house of Millo on the descent to Silla. It was 21 his servants Jozachar son of Shimeath and Jehozabad son of Shomer who struck the fatal blow; and he was buried with his forefathers in the city of David. He was succeeded by his son Amaziah.

In the twenty-third year of Joash 13 son of Ahaziah king of Judah, Jehoahaz son of Jehu became king over Israel in Samaria and he reigned seventeen years. He did 2 what was wrong in the eyes of the LORD and continued the sinful practices of Jeroboam son of Nebat who led Israel into sin, and did not give them up. So the LORD was 3 roused to anger against Israel and he made them subject for some years to Hazael king of Aram and Ben-hadad son of Hazael. Then Je-4 hoahaz sought to placate the LORD, and the LORD heard his prayer, for he saw how the king of Aram oppressed Israel. The LORD 5 appointed a deliverer for Israel, who rescued them from the power of Aram, and the Israelites settled down again in their own homes. But 6 they did not give up the sinful practices of the house of Jeroboam who led Israel into sin, but continued in them; the goddess Asherah[b] remained in Samaria. Hazael 7 had left Jehoahaz no armed force except fifty horsemen, ten chariots, and ten thousand infantry; all the rest the king of Aram had destroyed and made like dust under foot.

The other events of the reign of 8 Jehoahaz, and all his achievements and his exploits, are recorded in the annals of the kings of Israel. So 9

---

[a] Verses 20, 21: cp. 2 Chr. 24. 25–27.
[b] the goddess Asherah: or the sacred pole.

Jehoahaz rested with his fore-fathers and was buried in Samaria; and he was succeeded by his son Jehoash.

10 In the thirty-ninth year of Joash king of Judah, Jehoash son of Je-hoahaz became king over Israel in Samaria and reigned sixteen years.

11 He did what was wrong in the eyes of the LORD; he did not give up any of the sinful practices of Jeroboam son of Nebat who led Israel into

12 sin, but continued in them. The other events of the reign of Jeho-ash, all his achievements, his ex-ploits and his war with Amaziah king of Judah, are recorded in the

13 annals of the kings of Israel. So Jehoash rested with his fore-fathers and was buried in Samaria with the kings of Israel, and Jero-boam sat upon his throne.

14 Elisha fell ill and lay on his deathbed, and Jehoash king of Is-rael went down to him and wept over him and said, 'My father! My father, the chariots and the horse-

15 men of Israel!' 'Take bow and arrows', said Elisha, and he took

16 bow and arrows. 'Put your hand to the bow', said the prophet. He did so, and Elisha laid his hands on

17 those of the king. Then he said, 'Open the window toward the east'; he opened it and Elisha told him to shoot, and he shot. Then the prophet said, 'An arrow for the LORD's victory, an arrow for vic-tory over Aram! You will defeat

18 Aram utterly at Aphek'; and he added, 'Now take up your arrows.' When the king had taken them, Elisha said, 'Strike the ground with them.' He struck three times

19 and stopped. The man of God was furious with him and said, 'You should have struck five or six times; then you would have de-feated Aram utterly; as it is, you will strike Aram three times and no more.'

20 Then Elisha died and was buried.

Year by year Moabite raiders used to invade the land. Once some 21 men were burying a dead man when they caught sight of the raiders. They threw the body into the grave of Elisha and made off; when the body touched the pro-phet's bones, the man came to life and rose to his feet.

All through the reign of Jeho- 22 ahaz, Hazael king of Aram op-pressed Israel. But the LORD was 23 gracious and took pity on them; because of his covenant with Abra-ham, Isaac, and Jacob, he looked on them with favour and was un-willing to destroy them; nor has he even yet banished them from his sight. When Hazael king of Aram 24 died and was succeeded by his son Ben-hadad, Jehoash son of Jeho- 25 ahaz recaptured the cities which Ben-hadad had taken in war from Jehoahaz his father; three times Jehoash defeated him and recover-ed the cities of Israel.

In the second year of Jehoash 14 1*a* son of Jehoahaz king of Israel, Am-aziah son of Joash king of Judah succeeded his father. He was 2 twenty-five years old when he came to the throne, and he reigned in Jerusalem for twenty-nine years; his mother was Jehoaddin of Jeru-salem. He did what was right in the 3 eyes of the LORD, yet not as his forefather David had done; he fol-lowed his father Joash in every-thing. The hill-shrines were allow- 4 ed to remain; the people continued to slaughter and burn sacrifices there. When the royal power was 5 firmly in his grasp, he put to death those of his servants who had mur-dered the king his father; but he 6 spared the murderers' children in obedience to the LORD's command written in the law of Moses: 'Fa-thers shall not be put to death for their children, nor children for their fathers; a man shall be put to death only for his own sin.' He 7 defeated ten thousand Edomites

a Verses 1–6: cp. 2 Chr. 25. 1–4.

in the Valley of Salt and captured Sela; he gave it the name Joktheel, which it still bears.

8[a] Then Amaziah sent messengers to Jehoash son of Jehoahaz, son of Jehu, king of Israel, to propose a 9 meeting. But Jehoash king of Israel sent this answer to Amaziah king of Judah: 'A thistle in Lebanon sent to a cedar in Lebanon to say, "Give your daughter in marriage to my son." But a wild beast in Lebanon, passing by, trampled 10 on the thistle. You have defeated Edom, it is true; and it has gone to your head. Stay at home and enjoy your triumph. Why should you involve yourself in disaster and bring yourself to the ground, and Judah with you?'

11 But Amaziah would not listen; so Jehoash king of Israel marched out, and he and Amaziah king of Judah met one another at Beth-12 shemesh in Judah. The men of Judah were routed by Israel and fled 13 to their homes. But Jehoash king of Israel captured Amaziah king of Judah, son of Joash, son of Ahaziah, at Beth-shemesh. He went to Jerusalem and broke down the city wall from the Gate of Ephraim to the Corner Gate, a distance of 14 four hundred cubits. He also took all the gold and silver and all the vessels found in the house of the LORD and in the treasuries of the royal palace, as well as hostages, and returned to Samaria.

15 The other events of the reign of Jehoash, and all his achievements, his exploits and his wars with Amaziah king of Judah, are recorded in the annals of the kings of Israel. 16 So Jehoash rested with his forefathers and was buried in Samaria with the kings of Israel; and he was succeeded by his son Jeroboam.

17[b] Amaziah son of Joash, king of Judah, outlived Jehoash son of Jehoahaz, king of Israel, by fifteen years. The other events of Ama-18 ziah's reign are recorded in the annals of the kings of Judah. A 19 conspiracy was formed against him in Jerusalem and he fled to Lachish; but they sent after him to Lachish and put him to death there. Then his body was conveyed 20 on horseback to Jerusalem, and there he was buried with his forefathers in the city of David. The 21 people of Judah took Azariah, now sixteen years old, and made him king in succession to his father Amaziah. It was he who built 22 Elath and restored it to Judah after the king rested with his forefathers.

In the fifteenth year of Amaziah 23 son of Joash king of Judah, Jeroboam son of Jehoash king of Israel became king in Samaria and reigned for forty-one years. He did 24 what was wrong in the eyes of the LORD; he did not give up the sinful practices of Jeroboam son of Nebat who led Israel into sin. He re-25 established the frontiers of Israel from Lebo-hamath to the Sea of the Arabah, in fulfilment of the word of the LORD the God of Israel spoken by his servant the prophet Jonah son of Amittai, of Gath-hepher. For the LORD had 26 seen how bitterly Israel had suffered; no one was safe, whether under the protection of his family or not, and Israel was left defenceless. But 27 the LORD had made no threat to blot out the name of Israel under heaven, and he saved them through Jeroboam son of Jehoash. The 28 other events of Jeroboam's reign, and all his achievements, his exploits, the wars he fought and how he recovered Damascus and Hamath in Jaudi for[c] Israel, are recorded in the annals of the kings of Israel. So Jeroboam rested with 29 his forefathers the kings of Israel; and he was succeeded by his son Zechariah.

---

[a] *Verses 8–14: cp.* 2 Chr. 25. 17–24.   [b] *Verses 17–22: cp.* 2 Chr. 25. 25 – 26. 2.
[c] in Jaudi for: *prob. rdg.; Heb.* to Judah in.

15 In the twenty-seventh year of Jeroboam king of Israel, Azariah[a] son of Amaziah king of Judah be-
2[b] came king. He was sixteen years old when he came to the throne, and he reigned in Jerusalem for fifty-two years; his mother was
3 Jecoliah of Jerusalem. He did what was right in the eyes of the LORD, as
4 Amaziah his father had done. But the hill-shrines were allowed to remain; the people still continued to slaughter and burn sacrifices there.
5[c] The LORD struck the king with leprosy,[d] which he had till the day of his death; he was relieved of all duties and lived in his own house, while his son Jotham was comptroller of the household and re-
6 gent. The other acts and events of Azariah's reign are recorded in the
7 annals of the kings of Judah. So he rested with his forefathers and was buried with them in the city of David; and he was succeeded by his son Jotham.
8 In the thirty-eighth year of Azariah king of Judah, Zechariah son of Jeroboam became king over Israel in Samaria and reigned six
9 months. He did what was wrong in the eyes of the LORD, as his forefathers had done; he did not give up the sinful practices of Jeroboam son of Nebat who led Israel into
10 sin. Shallum son of Jabesh formed a conspiracy against him, attacked him in Ibleam, killed him and
11 usurped the throne. The other events of Zechariah's reign are recorded in the annals of the kings of
12 Israel. Thus the word of the LORD spoken to Jehu was fulfilled: 'Your sons to the fourth generation shall sit on the throne of Israel.'
13 Shallum son of Jabesh became king in the thirty-ninth year of Uzziah king of Judah, and he reigned one full month in Samaria.
14 Then Menahem son of Gadi came up from Tirzah to Samaria, attack-

ed Shallum son of Jabesh there, killed him and usurped the throne. The other events of Shallum's 15 reign and the conspiracy that he formed are recorded in the annals of the kings of Israel.

Then Menahem, starting out 16 from Tirzah, destroyed Tappuah and everything in it and ravaged its territory; he ravaged it because it had not opened its gates to him, and he ripped open all the pregnant women.

In the thirty-ninth year of Aza- 17 riah king of Judah, Menahem son of Gadi became king over Israel and he reigned in Samaria for ten years. He did what was wrong in 18 the eyes of the LORD; he did not give up the sinful practices of Jeroboam son of Nebat who led Israel into sin. In his days Pul king of 19 Assyria invaded the country, and Menahem gave him a thousand talents of silver to obtain his help in strengthening his hold on the kingdom. Menahem laid a levy on 20 all the men of wealth in Israel, and each had to give the king of Assyria fifty silver shekels. Then the king of Assyria withdrew without occupying the country. The other 21 acts and events of Menahem's reign are recorded in the annals of the kings of Israel. So Menahem rested 22 with his forefathers; and he was succeeded by his son Pekahiah.

In the fiftieth year of Azariah 23 king of Judah, Pekahiah son of Menahem became king over Israel in Samaria and reigned for two years. He did what was wrong in 24 the eyes of the LORD; he did not give up the sinful practices of Jeroboam son of Nebat who led Israel into sin. Pekah son of Remaliah, 25 his lieutenant, formed a conspiracy against him and, with the help of fifty Gileadites, attacked him in Samaria in the citadel of the royal palace,[e] killed him and usurped

[a] Uzziah in verses 13, 30, 32, 34.　　[b] Verses 2, 3: cp. 2 Chr. 26. 3, 4.
[c] Verses 5–7: cp. 2 Chr. 26. 21–23.　　[d] Or a skin-disease.
[e] Prob. rdg.; Heb. adds Argob and Arieh.

26 the throne. The other acts and events of Pekahiah's reign are recorded in the annals of the kings of Israel.

27 In the fifty-second year of Azariah king of Judah, Pekah son of Remaliah became king over Israel in Samaria and reigned for twenty 28 years. He did what was wrong in the eyes of the LORD; he did not give up the sinful practices of Jeroboam son of Nebat who led Israel 29 into sin. In the days of Pekah king of Israel, Tiglath-pileser king of Assyria came and seized Iyyon, Abel-beth-maacah, Janoah, Kedesh, Hazor, Gilead, and Galilee, with all the land of Naphtali, and deported the people to Assyria. 30 Then Hoshea son of Elah formed a conspiracy against Pekah son of Remaliah, attacked him, killed him and usurped the throne in the twentieth year of Jotham 31 son of Uzziah. The other acts and events of Pekah's reign are recorded in the annals of the kings of Israel.

32 In the second year of Pekah son of Remaliah king of Israel, Jotham son of Uzziah king of Judah be-33ᵃ came king. He was twenty-five years old when he came to the throne, and he reigned in Jerusalem for sixteen years; his mother 34 was Jerusha daughter of Zadok. He did what was right in the eyes of the LORD, as his father Uzziah had 35 done; but the hill-shrines were allowed to remain and the people continued to slaughter and burn sacrifices there. It was he who constructed the upper gate of the house 36 of the LORD. The other acts and events of Jotham's reign are recorded in the annals of the kings of 37 Judah. In those days the LORD began to make Rezin king of Aram and Pekah son of Remaliah attack 38 Judah. And Jotham rested with his forefathers and was buried with them in the city of David his

forefather; and he was succeeded by his son Ahaz.

Downfall of the northern kingdom

IN the seventeenth year of Pekah 16 son of Remaliah, Ahaz son of Jotham king of Judah became king. Ahaz was twenty years old when 2ᵇ he came to the throne, and he reigned in Jerusalem for sixteen years. He did not do what was right in the eyes of the LORD his God like his forefather David, but 3 followed in the footsteps of the kings of Israel; he even passed his son through the fire, adopting the abominable practice of the nations whom the LORD had dispossessed in favour of the Israelites. He 4 slaughtered and burnt sacrifices at the hill-shrines and on the hill-tops and under every spreading tree.

Then Rezin king of Aram and 5 Pekah son of Remaliah king of Israel attacked Jerusalem and besieged Ahaz but could not bring him to battle. At that time the 6 king of Edomᶜ recovered Elath and drove the Judaeans out of it; so the Edomites entered the city and have occupied it to this day. Ahaz 7 sent messengers to Tiglath-pileser king of Assyria to say, 'I am your servant and your son. Come and save me from the king of Aram and from the king of Israel who are attacking me.' Ahaz took the silver 8 and gold found in the house of the LORD and in the treasuries of the royal palace and sent them to the king of Assyria as a bribe. The king 9 of Assyria listened to him; he advanced on Damascus, captured it, deported its inhabitants to Kir and put Rezin to death.

When King Ahaz went to meet 10 Tiglath-pileser king of Assyria at Damascus, he saw there an altar of which he sent a sketch and a detailed plan to Uriah the priest. Accordingly, Uriah built an altar, 11

ᵃ *Verses 33–35: cp. 2 Chr. 27. 1–3.* ᵇ *Verses 2–4: cp. 2 Chr. 28. 1–4.*
ᶜ the king of Edom: *prob. rdg.*; *Heb.* Rezin king of Aram.

following all the instructions that the king had sent him from Damascus, and had it ready against the 12 king's return. When the king returned from Damascus, he saw the altar, approached it and mounted 13 the steps; there he burnt his whole-offering and his grain-offering and poured out his drink-offering, and he flung the blood of his shared-14 offerings against it. The bronze altar that was before the LORD he removed from the front of the house, from between this altar and the house of the LORD, and put it 15 on the north side of this altar. Then King Ahaz gave these instructions to Uriah the priest: 'Burn on the great altar the morning whole-offering and the evening grain-offering, and the king's whole-offering and his grain-offering, and the whole-offering of all the people of the land, their grain-offering and their drink-offerings, and fling against it all the blood of the sacrifices. But the bronze altar shall be mine, to offer morning sacrifice.'
16 Uriah the priest did all that the 17 king told him. Then King Ahaz broke up the trolleys and removed the panels, and he took down the basin and the Sea of bronze from the oxen which supported it and 18 put it on a stone base. In the house of the LORD he turned round the structure they had erected for use on the sabbath, and the outer gate for the king, to satisfy the king of 19ᵃ Assyria. The other acts and events of the reign of Ahaz are recorded in the annals of the kings of Judah.
20 So Ahaz rested with his forefathers and was buried with them in the city of David; and he was succeeded by his son Hezekiah.
17 In the twelfth year of Ahaz king of Judah, Hoshea son of Elah became king over Israel in Samaria 2 and reigned nine years. He did what was wrong in the eyes of the LORD, but not as the previous

kings of Israel had done. Shalman-3 eser king of Assyria made war upon him and Hoshea became tributary to him. But when the king of Assy-4 ria discovered that Hoshea was being disloyal to him, sending messengers to the king of Egypt at So,ᵇ and withholding the tribute which he had been paying year by year, the king of Assyria arrested him and put him in prison. Then he 5 invaded the whole country and, reaching Samaria, besieged it for three years. In the ninth year of 6 Hoshea he captured Samaria and deported its people to Assyria and settled them in Halah and on the Habor, the river of Gozan, and in the cities of Media.

All this happened to the Israel-7 ites because they had sinned against the LORD their God who brought them up from Egypt, from the rule of Pharaoh king of Egypt; they paid homage to other gods and observed the laws and 8 customs of the nations whom the LORD had dispossessed before them and uttered blasphemies against 9 the LORD their God; they built hill-shrines for themselves in all their settlements, from watchtower to fortified city, and set up 10 sacred pillars and sacred poles on every high hill and under every spreading tree, and burnt sacri-11 fices at all the hill-shrines there, as the nations did whom the LORD had displaced before them. By this wickedness of theirs they provoked the LORD's anger. They worship-12 ped idols, a thing which the LORD had forbidden them to do. Still the 13 LORD solemnly charged Israel and Judah by every prophet and seer, saying, 'Give up your evil ways; keep my commandments and statutes given in the law which I enjoined on your forefathers and delivered to you through my servants the prophets.' They would not lis-14 ten, however, but were as stubborn

---

ᵃ *Verses 19, 20: cp. 2 Chr. 28. 26, 27.*
ᵇ to the king of Egypt at So: *prob. rdg.*; *Heb.* to So king of Egypt.

and rebellious as their forefathers had been, who refused to put their
15 trust in the LORD their God; they rejected his statutes and the covenant which he had made with their forefathers and the solemn warnings which he had given to them; they followed worthless idols and became worthless themselves; they imitated the nations round about them, a thing which the LORD had
16 forbidden them to do. Forsaking every commandment of the LORD their God, they made themselves images of cast metal, two calves, and also a sacred pole; they prostrated themselves to all the host of heaven and worshipped the
17 Baal, and they made their sons and daughters pass through the fire. They practised augury and divination; they sold themselves to do what was wrong in the eyes of the LORD and so provoked his anger.

18 Thus it was that the LORD was incensed against Israel and banished them from his presence; only
19 the tribe of Judah was left. Even Judah did not keep the commandments of the LORD their God but followed the practices adopted by
20 Israel; so the LORD rejected the whole race of Israel and punished them and gave them over to plunderers and finally flung them out of
21 his sight. When he tore Israel from the house of David, they made Jeroboam son of Nebat king, who seduced Israel from their allegiance to the LORD and led them into
22 grave sin. The Israelites persisted in all the sins that Jeroboam had committed and did not give them
23 up, until finally the LORD banished the Israelites from his presence, as he had threatened through his servants the prophets, and they were carried into exile from their own land to Assyria; and there they are to this day.

24 Then the king of Assyria brought people from Babylon, Cuthah, Av-

va, Hamath, and Sepharvaim, and settled them in the cities of Samaria in place of the Israelites; so they occupied Samaria and lived in its cities. In the early years of their 25 settlement they did not pay homage to the LORD; and the LORD sent lions among them, and the lions preyed upon them. The king 26 was told that the deported peoples whom he had settled in the cities of Samaria did not know the established usage of the god of the country, and that he had sent lions among them which were preying upon them because they did not know this. The king of Assyria, 27 therefore, gave orders that one of the priests deported from Samaria should be sent back to live there and teach the people the usage of the god of the country. So one of 28 the deported priests came and lived at Bethel, and taught them how they should pay their homage to the LORD. But each of the nations 29 made its own god, and they set them up within[a] the hill-shrines which the Samaritans had made, each nation in its own settlements. Succoth-benoth was worshipped 30 by the men of Babylon, Nergal by the men of Cuth, Ashima by the men of Hamath, Nibhaz and Tartak by the Avvites; and the Sepharvites burnt their children as offerings to Adrammelech and Anammelech, the gods of Sepharvaim. While still paying homage to the 32 LORD, they appointed people from every class to act as priests of the hill-shrines and they resorted to them there. They paid homage to 33 the LORD while at the same time they served their own gods, according to the custom of the nations from which they had been carried into exile.

They keep up these old practices 34 to this day; they do not pay homage to the LORD, for they do not keep his[b] statutes and his[b] judgements, the law and commandment,

_____
[a] *Or* in niches at.　　　[b] *Prob. rdg.; Heb.* their.

which he enjoined upon the descendants of Jacob whom he named 35 Israel. When the LORD made a covenant with them, he gave them this commandment: 'You shall not pay homage to other gods or bow down to them or serve them or 36 sacrifice to them, but you shall pay homage to the LORD who brought you up from Egypt with great power and with outstretched arm; to him you shall bow down, to him 37 you shall offer sacrifice. You shall faithfully keep the statutes, the judgements, the law, and the commandments which he wrote for you, and you shall not pay homage 38 to other gods. You shall not forget the covenant which I made with you; you shall not pay homage to 39 other gods. But to the LORD your God you shall pay homage, and he will preserve you from all your 40 enemies.' However, they would not listen but continued their for- 41 mer practices. While these nations paid homage to the LORD they continued to serve their images, and their children and their children's children have maintained the practice of their forefathers to this day.

18 1[a] IN the third year of Hoshea son of Elah king of Israel, Hezekiah son of Ahaz king of Judah became 2 king. He was twenty-five years old when he came to the throne, and he reigned in Jerusalem for twenty-nine years; his mother was Abi 3 daughter of Zechariah. He did what was right in the eyes of the LORD, as David his forefather had 4 done. It was he who suppressed the hill-shrines, smashed the sacred pillars, cut down every sacred pole and broke up the bronze serpent that Moses had made; for up to that time the Israelites had been burning sacrifices to it; they called 5 it Nehushtan. He put his trust in the LORD the God of Israel; there was nobody like him among all the

kings of Judah who succeeded him or among those who had gone before him. He remained loyal to the 6 LORD and did not fail in his allegiance to him, and he kept the commandments which the LORD had given to Moses. So the LORD 7 was with him and he prospered in all that he undertook; he rebelled against the king of Assyria and was no longer subject to him. He con- 8 quered the Philistine country as far as Gaza and its boundaries, alike the watch-tower and the fortified city.

In the fourth year of Hezekiah's 9 reign (that was the seventh year of Hoshea son of Elah king of Israel) Shalmaneser king of Assyria made an attack on Samaria, invested it and captured it after a siege of 10 three years; it was in the sixth year of Hezekiah (the ninth year of Hoshea king of Israel) that Samaria was captured. The king of Assyria 11 deported the Israelites to Assyria and settled them in Halah and on the Habor, the river of Gozan, and in the cities of Media, because they 12 did not obey the LORD their God but violated his covenant and every commandment that Moses the servant of the LORD had given them; they would not listen and they would not obey.

In the fourteenth year of the 13[b] reign of Hezekiah, Sennacherib king of Assyria attacked and took all the fortified cities of Judah. Hezekiah king of Judah sent a 14 message to the king of Assyria at Lachish: 'I have done wrong; withdraw from my land, and I will pay any penalty you impose upon me.' So the king of Assyria laid on Hezekiah king of Judah a penalty of three hundred talents of silver and thirty talents of gold; and 15 Hezekiah gave him all the silver found in the house of the LORD and in the treasuries of the royal palace. At that time Hezekiah broke 16

---

[a] Verses 1–3: cp. 2 Chr. 29. 1, 2.
[b] Verses 13–37: cp. Isa. 36. 1–22; 2 Chr. 32. 1–19.

up the doors of the temple of the LORD and the door-frames which he himself had plated, and gave them to the king of Assyria.

17 From Lachish the king of Assyria sent the commander-in-chief, the chief eunuch, and the chief officer[a] with a strong force to King Hezekiah at Jerusalem, and they went up and came to Jerusalem and halted by the conduit of the Upper Pool on the causeway which 18 leads to the Fuller's Field. When they called for the king, Eliakim son of Hilkiah, the comptroller of the household, came out to them, with Shebna the adjutant-general and Joah son of Asaph, the secret-19 ary of state. The chief officer said to them, 'Tell Hezekiah that this is the message of the Great King, the king of Assyria: "What ground have you for this confidence of 20 yours? Do you think fine words can take the place of skill and numbers? On whom then do you rely for support in your rebellion a-21 gainst me? On Egypt? Egypt is a splintered cane that will run into a man's hand and pierce it if he leans on it. That is what Pharaoh king of Egypt proves to all who rely on 22 him. And if you tell me that you are relying on the LORD your God, is he not the god whose hill-shrines and altars Hezekiah has suppressed, telling Judah and Jerusalem that they must prostrate themselves before this altar in Jerusalem?"
23 'Now, make a bargain with my master the king of Assyria: I will give you two thousand horses if 24 you can find riders for them. Will you reject the authority of even the least of my master's servants and rely on Egypt for chariots and 25 horsemen? Do you think that I have come to attack this place and destroy it without the consent of the LORD? No; the LORD himself said to me, "Attack this land and destroy it."'

Eliakim son of Hilkiah, Shebna, 26 and Joah said to the chief officer, 'Please speak to us in Aramaic, for we understand it; do not speak Hebrew to us within earshot of the people on the city wall.' The chief 27 officer answered, 'Is it to your master and to you that my master has sent me to say this? Is it not to the people sitting on the wall who, like you, will have to eat their own dung and drink their own urine?' Then he stood and shouted in 28 Hebrew, 'Hear the message of the Great King, the king of Assyria. These are the king's words: "Do 29 not be taken in by Hezekiah. He cannot save you from me. Do not 30 let him persuade you to rely on the LORD, and tell you that the LORD will save you and that this city will never be surrendered to the king of Assyria." Do not listen to Heze-31 kiah; these are the words of the king of Assyria: "Make peace with me. Come out to me, and then you shall each eat the fruit of his own vine and his own fig-tree, and drink the water of his own cistern, until I come and take you to a land 32 like your own, a land of grain and new wine, of corn and vineyards, of olives, fine oil, and honey – life for you all, instead of death. Do not listen to Hezekiah; he will only mislead you by telling you that the LORD will save you. Did the god of 33 any of these nations save his land from the king of Assyria? Where are the gods of Hamath and Arpad? Where are the gods of Sepharvaim, 34 Hena, and Ivvah? Where are the gods of Samaria? Did they save Samaria from me? Among all the 35 gods of the nations is there one who saved his land from me? And how is the LORD to save Jerusalem?"'

The people were silent and an-36 swered not a word, for the king had given orders that no one was to answer him. Eliakim son of 37

[a] the commander-in-chief, the chief eunuch, and the chief officer: *or* Tartan, Rab-saris, and Rab-shakeh.

Hilkiah, comptroller of the household, Shebna the adjutant-general, and Joah son of Asaph, secretary of state, came to Hezekiah with their clothes rent and reported what the chief officer had said.

19 1[a] When King Hezekiah heard their report, he rent his clothes and wrapped himself in sackcloth, and went into the house of the 2 LORD. He sent Eliakim comptroller of the household, Shebna the adjutant-general, and the senior priests, all covered in sackcloth, to 3 the prophet Isaiah son of Amoz, to give him this message from the king: 'This day is a day of trouble for us, a day of reproof and contempt. We are like a woman who has no strength to bear the child 4 that is coming to the birth. It may be that the LORD your God heard all the words of the chief officer whom his master the king of Assyria sent to taunt the living God, and will confute what he, the LORD your God, heard. Offer a prayer for those who still survive.' 5 King Hezekiah's servants came to 6 Isaiah, and he told them to say this to their master: 'This is the word of the LORD: "Do not be alarmed at what you heard when the lackeys of the king of Assyria blas- 7 phemed me. I will put a spirit in him and he shall hear a rumour and withdraw to his own country; and there I will make him fall by the sword."'

8 So the chief officer withdrew. He heard that the king of Assyria had left Lachish, and he found him 9 attacking Libnah. But when the king learnt that Tirhakah king of Cush was on the way to make war on him, he sent messengers again 10 to Hezekiah king of Judah, to say to him, 'How can you be deluded by your god on whom you rely when he promises that Jerusalem shall not fall into the hands of the 11 king of Assyria? Surely you have heard what the kings of Assyria

have done to all countries, exterminating their people; can you then hope to escape? Did their 12 gods save the nations which my forefathers destroyed, Gozan, Harran, Rezeph, and the people of Betheden living in Telassar? Where 13 are the kings of Hamath, of Arpad, and of Lahir, Sepharvaim, Hena, and Ivvah?'

Hezekiah took the letter from 14 the messengers and read it; then he went up into the house of the LORD, spread it out before the LORD and offered this prayer: 'O 15 LORD God of Israel, enthroned on the cherubim, thou alone art God of all the kingdoms of the earth; thou hast made heaven and earth. Turn thy ear to me, O LORD, and 16 listen; open thine eyes, O LORD, and see; hear the message that Sennacherib has sent to taunt the living God. It is true, O LORD, that 17 the kings of Assyria have ravaged the nations and their lands, that 18 they have consigned their gods to the fire and destroyed them; for they were no gods but the work of men's hands, mere wood and stone. But now, O LORD our God, save 19 us from his power, so that all the kingdoms of the earth may know that thou, O LORD, alone art God.'

Isaiah son of Amoz sent to Heze- 20 kiah and said, 'This is the word of the LORD the God of Israel: I have heard your prayer to me concerning Sennacherib king of Assyria. This is the word which the LORD 21 has spoken concerning him:

The virgin daughter of Zion disdains you,
she laughs you to scorn;
the daughter of Jerusalem tosses her head
as you retreat.
Whom have you taunted and 22 blasphemed?
Against whom have you clamoured, casting haughty glances at the Holy One of Israel?

[a] *Verses 1–37: cp. Isa. 37. 1–38; 2 Chr. 32. 20–22.*

23 You have sent your messengers to
   taunt the Lord,
   and said:
   I have mounted my chariot and
   done mighty deeds:
   I have gone high up in the
   mountains,
   into the recesses of Lebanon.
   I have cut down its tallest cedars,
   the best of its pines,
   I have reached its farthest corners,
   forest and meadow.
24 I have dug wells
   and drunk the waters of a foreign
   land,
   and with the soles of my feet I have
   dried up
   all the streams of Egypt.

25 Have you not heard long ago?
   I did it all.
   In days gone by I planned it
   and now I have brought it about,
   making fortified cities tumble
   down
   into heaps of rubble.*a*
26 Their citizens, shorn of strength,
   disheartened and ashamed,
   were but as plants in the field, as
   green herbs,
   as grass on the roof-tops blasted
   before the east wind.*b*
27 I know your rising up*c* and your
   sitting down,
   your going out and your coming in.
28 The frenzy of your rage against
   me*d* and your arrogance
   have come to my ears.
   I will put a ring in your nose
   and a hook in your lips,
   and I will take you back by the road
   on which you have come.

29 This shall be the sign for you: this
   year you shall eat shed grain and in
   the second year what is self-sown;
   but in the third year sow and reap,
   plant vineyards and eat their fruit.
30 The survivors left in Judah shall
   strike fresh root under ground and

yield fruit above ground, for a 31
remnant shall come out of Jerusalem and survivors from Mount
Zion. The zeal of the LORD will
perform this.
   'Therefore, this is the word of the 32
LORD concerning the king of Assyria:

He shall not enter this city
nor shoot an arrow there,
he shall not advance against it
   with shield
nor cast up a siege-ramp against it.
By the way on which he came he 33
   shall go back;
this city he shall not enter.
This is the very word of the LORD.
I will shield this city to deliver it, 34
for my own sake and for the sake of
   my servant David.'

   That night the angel of the 35
LORD went out and struck down a
hundred and eighty-five thousand
men in the Assyrian camp; when
morning dawned, they all lay
dead. So Sennacherib king of Assy- 36
ria broke camp, went back to Nineveh and stayed there. One day, 37
while he was worshipping in the
temple of his god Nisroch, Adrammelech and Sharezer his sons murdered him and escaped to the land
of Ararat. He was succeeded by
his son Esarhaddon.

   At this time Hezekiah fell dan- 20 1*e*
gerously ill and the prophet Isaiah
son of Amoz came to him and said,
'This is the word of the LORD: Give
your last instructions to your
household, for you are a dying
man and will not recover.' Heze- 2
kiah turned his face to the wall and
offered this prayer to the LORD:
'O LORD, remember how I have 3
lived before thee, faithful and loyal
in thy service, always doing what
was good in thine eyes.' And he
wept bitterly. But before Isaiah 4

---

a heaps of rubble: *prob. rdg., cp. Isa.* 37. 26; *Heb. obscure.*
b the east wind: *prob. rdg., cp. Isa.* 37. 27; *Heb. it is mature.*
c your rising up: *prob. rdg., cp. Isa.* 37. 28; *Heb. om.*
d *Prob. rdg., cp. Isa.* 37. 29; *Heb. repeats* the frenzy of your rage against me.
e *Verses* 1–11: *cp. Isa.* 38. 1–8, 21, 22.

had left the citadel, the word of the 5 LORD came to him: 'Go back and say to Hezekiah, the prince of my people: "This is the word of the LORD the God of your father David: I have heard your prayer and seen your tears; I will heal you and on the third day you shall go up to 6 the house of the LORD. I will add fifteen years to your life and deliver you and this city from the king of Assyria, and I will protect this city for my own sake and for 7 my servant David's sake."' Then Isaiah told them to apply a fig-plaster; so they made one and applied it to the boil, and he re-8 covered. Then Hezekiah asked Isaiah what sign the LORD would give him that he would be cured and would go up into the house of 9 the LORD on the third day. And Isaiah said, 'This shall be your sign from the LORD that he will do what he has promised; shall the shadow go forward ten steps or back ten 10 steps?' Hezekiah answered, 'It is an easy thing for the shadow to move forward ten steps; rather let 11 it go back ten steps.' Isaiah the prophet called to the LORD, and he made the shadow go back ten steps where it had advanced down the stairway of Ahaz.

12ᵃ At this time Merodach-baladan son of Baladan king of Babylon sent envoys with a gift to Hezekiah; for he had heard that he had been 13 ill. Hezekiah welcomed them and showed them all his treasury, silver and gold, spices and fragrant oil, his armoury and everything to be found among his treasures; there was nothing in his house and in all his realm that Hezekiah did 14 not show them. Then the prophet Isaiah came to King Hezekiah and asked him, 'What did these men say and where have they come from?' 'They have come from a far-off country,' Hezekiah answer-15 ed, 'from Babylon.' Then Isaiah asked, 'What did they see in your

house?' 'They saw everything,' Hezekiah replied; 'there was nothing among my treasures that I did not show them.' Then Isaiah 16 said to Hezekiah, 'Hear the word of the LORD: The time is coming, 17 says the LORD, when everything in your house, and all that your fore-fathers have amassed till the present day, will be carried away to Babylon; not a thing shall be left. And some of the sons who will be 18 born to you, sons of your own be-getting, shall be taken and shall be made eunuchs in the palace of the king of Babylon.' Hezekiah an-19 swered, 'The word of the LORD which you have spoken is good'; thinking to himself that peace and security would last out his lifetime.

The other events of Hezekiah's 20 reign, his exploits, and how he made the pool and the conduit and brought water into the city, are recorded in the annals of the kings of Judah. So Hezekiah rested with 21 his forefathers and was succeeded by his son Manasseh.

The last kings of Judah

MANASSEH was twelve years old 21 1ᵇ when he came to the throne, and he reigned in Jerusalem for fifty-five years; his mother was Hephzi-bah. He did what was wrong in the 2 eyes of the LORD, in following the abominable practices of the nations which the LORD had dis-possessed in favour of the Israel-ites. He rebuilt the hill-shrines 3 which his father Hezekiah had destroyed, he erected altars to the Baal and made a sacred pole as Ahab king of Israel had done, and prostrated himself before all the host of heaven and worshipped them. He built altars in the house 4 of the LORD, that house of which the LORD had said, 'Jerusalem shall receive my Name.' He built 5 altars for all the host of heaven in the two courts of the house of the

---

ᵃ *Verses 12–19: cp. Isa. 39. 1–8.*   ᵇ *Verses 1–9: cp. 2 Chr. 33. 1–9.*

6 LORD; he made his son pass through the fire, he practised soothsaying and divination, and dealt with ghosts and spirits. He did much wrong in the eyes of the LORD and 7 provoked his anger; and the image that he had made of the goddess Asherah he put in the house, the place of which the LORD had said to David and Solomon his son, 'This house and Jerusalem, which I chose out of all the tribes of Israel, shall receive my Name for all 8 time. I will not again make Israel outcasts from the land which I gave to their forefathers, if only they will be careful to observe all my commands and all the law that 9 my servant Moses gave them.' But they did not obey, and Manasseh misled them into wickedness far worse than that of the nations which the LORD had exterminated in favour of the Israelites.

10 Then the LORD spoke through 11 his servants the prophets: 'Because Manasseh king of Judah has done these abominable things, outdoing the Amorites before him in wickedness, and because he has led 12 Judah into sin with his idols, this is the word of the LORD the God of Israel: I will bring disaster on Jerusalem and Judah, disaster which will ring in the ears of all who hear 13 of it. I will mark down every stone of Jerusalem with the plumb-line of Samaria and the plummet of the house of Ahab; I will wipe away Jerusalem as when a man wipes his 14 plate and turns it upside down, and I will cast off what is left of my people, my own possession, and hand them over to their enemies. They shall be plundered and fall a 15 prey to all their enemies; for they have done what is wrong in my eyes and have provoked my anger from the day their forefathers left 16 Egypt up to the present day. And this Manasseh shed so much innocent blood that he filled Jerusalem

full to the brim, not to mention the sin into which he led Judah by doing what is wrong in my eyes.' The other events and acts of Man- 17 asseh's reign, and the sin that he committed, are recorded in the annals of the kings of Judah. So 18 Manasseh rested with his forefathers and was buried in the garden-tomb of his family, in the garden of Uzza; he was succeeded by his son Amon.

Amon was twenty-two years old 19[a] when he came to the throne, and he reigned in Jerusalem for two years; his mother was Meshullemeth daughter of Haruz of Jotbah. He 20 did what was wrong in the eyes of the LORD as his father Manasseh had done. He followed in his fa- 21 ther's footsteps and served the idols that his father had served and prostrated himself before them. He 22 forsook the LORD the God of his fathers and did not conform to his ways. King Amon's courtiers con- 23 spired against him and murdered him in his house; but the people of 24 the land killed all the conspirators and made his son Josiah king in his place. The other events of 25 Amon's reign are recorded in the annals of the kings of Judah. He 26 was buried in his grave in the garden of Uzza; he was succeeded by his son Josiah.

Josiah was eight years old when 22 1[b] he came to the throne, and he reigned in Jerusalem for thirty-one years; his mother was Jedidah daughter of Adaiah of Bozkath. He did what was right in the eyes 2 of the LORD; he followed closely in the footsteps of his forefather David, swerving neither right nor left.

In the eighteenth year of his 3[c] reign Josiah sent Shaphan son of Azaliah, son of Meshullam, the adjutant-general, to the house of the LORD. 'Go to the high priest 4 Hilkiah,' he said, 'and tell him to

---

[a] *Verses 19–24: cp.* 2 *Chr.* 33. 21–25.
[c] *Verses 3–20: cp.* 2 *Chr.* 34. 8–28.
[b] *Verses 1, 2: cp.* 2 *Chr.* 34. 1, 2.

melt down the silver that has been brought into the house of the LORD, which those on duty at the entrance have received from the 5 people, and to hand it over to the foremen in the house of the LORD, to pay the workmen who 6 are carrying out repairs in it, the carpenters, builders, and masons, and to purchase timber and hewn 7 stones for its repair. They are not to be asked to account for the money that has been given them; 8 they are acting on trust.' The high priest Hilkiah told Shaphan the adjutant-general that he had discovered the book of the law in the house of the LORD, and he gave it 9 to him, and Shaphan read it. Then Shaphan came to report to the king and told him that his servants had melted down the silver in the house of the LORD and handed it 10 over to the foremen. Then Shaphan the adjutant-general told the king that the high priest Hilkiah had given him a book, and he read it out in the king's presence. 11 When the king heard what was in the book of the law, he rent his 12 clothes, and ordered the priest Hilkiah, Ahikam son of Shaphan, Akbor son of Micaiah, Shaphan the adjutant-general, and Asaiah the 13 king's attendant, to go and seek guidance of the LORD for himself, for the people, and for all Judah, about what was written in this book that had been discovered. 'Great is the wrath of the LORD', he said, 'that has been kindled against us, because our forefathers did not obey the commands in this book and do all that is laid upon us.'

14   So Hilkiah the priest, Ahikam, Akbor, Shaphan, and Asaiah went to Huldah the prophetess, wife of Shallum son of Tikvah, son of Harhas, the keeper of the wardrobe, and consulted her at her home in the second quarter of 15 Jerusalem. 'This is the word of the LORD the God of Israel,' she answered: 'Say to the man who sent you to me, "This is the word of the 16 LORD: I am bringing disaster on this place and its inhabitants as foretold in the book which the king of Judah has read, because they 17 have forsaken me and burnt sacrifices to other gods, provoking my anger with all the idols they have made with their own hands; therefore, my wrath is kindled against this place and will not be quenched." This is what you shall say to 18 the king of Judah who sent you to seek guidance of the LORD: "This is the word of the LORD the God of Israel: You have listened to my words and shown a willing heart, 19 you humbled yourself before the LORD when you heard me say that this place and its inhabitants would become objects of loathing and scorn, you rent your clothes and wept before me. Because of all this, I for my part have heard you. This is the very word of the LORD. Therefore, I will gather you to your 20 forefathers, and you will be gathered to your grave in peace; you will not live to see all the disaster which I am bringing upon this place."' So they brought back word to the king.

Then the king sent and called all 23 1[a] the elders of Judah and Jerusalem together, and went up to the house 2 of the LORD; he took with him the men of Judah and the inhabitants of Jerusalem, the priests and the prophets, the whole population, high and low. There he read out to them all the book of the covenant discovered in the house of the LORD; and then, standing on the 3 dais,[b] the king made a covenant before the LORD to obey him and keep his commandments, his testimonies, and his statutes, with all his heart and soul, and so fulfil the terms of the covenant written in this book. And all the people pledged themselves to the covenant.

[a] *Verses 1–3: cp. 2 Chr. 34. 29–32.*   [b] *Or by the pillar.*

4   Next, the king ordered the high priest Hilkiah, the deputy high priest,*ᵃ* and those on duty at the entrance, to remove from the house of the LORD all the objects made for Baal and Asherah and all the host of heaven; he burnt these outside Jerusalem, in the open country by the Kidron, and carried 5 the ashes to Bethel. He suppressed the heathen priests whom the kings of Judah had appointed to burn sacrifices at the hill-shrines in the cities of Judah and in the neighbourhood of Jerusalem, as well as those who burnt sacrifices to Baal, to the sun and moon and planets 6 and all the host of heaven. He took the symbol of Asherah*ᵇ* from the house of the LORD to the gorge of the Kidron outside Jerusalem, burnt it there and pounded it to dust, which was then scattered over the common burial-ground. 7 He also pulled down the houses of the male prostitutes attached to the house of the LORD, where the women wove vestments in honour of Asherah.

8   He brought in all the priests from the cities of Judah and desecrated the hill-shrines where they had burnt sacrifices, from Geba to Beersheba, and dismantled the hill-shrines of the demons*ᵉ* in front of the gate of Joshua, the governor of the city, to the left of 9 the city gate. These priests, however, never came up to the altar of the LORD in Jerusalem but used to eat unleavened bread with the 10 priests of their clan. He desecrated Topheth in the Valley of Ben-hinnom, so that no one might make his son or daughter pass through 11 the fire in honour of Molech.*ᵈ* He destroyed the horses that the kings of Judah had set up in honour of the sun at the entrance to the house of the LORD, beside the room of Nathan-melek the eunuch in the

colonnade, and he burnt the chariots of the sun. He pulled down 12 the altars made by the kings of Judah on the roof by the upper chamber of Ahaz and the altars made by Manasseh in the two courts of the house of the LORD; he pounded them to dust and threw it into the gorge of the Kidron. Also, on the east of Jerusalem, to 13 the south of the Mount of Olives, the king desecrated the hill-shrines which Solomon the king of Israel had built for Ashtoreth the loathsome goddess of the Sidonians, and for Kemosh the loathsome god of Moab, and for Milcom the abominable god of the Ammonites; he 14 broke down the sacred pillars and cut down the sacred poles and filled the places where they had stood with human bones.

At Bethel he dismantled the 15 altar by*ᵉ* the hill-shrine made by Jeroboam son of Nebat who led Israel into sin, together with the hill-shrine itself; he broke its stones in pieces, crushed them to dust and burnt the sacred pole. When Josiah set eyes on the graves which 16 were there on the hill, he sent and took the bones from them and burnt them on the altar to desecrate it, thus fulfilling the word of the LORD announced by the man of God when Jeroboam stood by the altar at the feast. But when he caught sight of the grave of the man of God who had foretold these things, he asked, 'What is that 17 monument I see there?' The people of the city answered, 'The grave of the man of God who came from Judah and foretold all that you have done to the altar at Bethel.' 'Leave it alone,' he said; 'let no one 18 disturb his bones.' So they spared his bones and also those of the prophet who came from Samaria. Further, Josiah suppressed all the hill- 19 shrines in the cities of Samaria,

---

ᵃ Prob. rdg.; Heb. priests.
ᶜ Or satyrs.
ᵉ Prob. rdg.; Heb. om.
ᵇ symbol of Asherah: or sacred pole.
ᵈ in honour of Molech: or for an offering.

which the kings of Israel had set up and thereby provoked the LORD's anger, and he did to them 20 what he had done at Bethel. He slaughtered on the altars all the priests of the hill-shrines who were there, and he burnt human bones upon them. Then he went back to Jerusalem.

21 The king ordered all the people to keep the Passover to the LORD their God, as this book of the cove- 22 nant prescribed; no such Passover had been kept either when the judges were ruling Israel or during the times of the kings of Israel and 23 Judah. But in the eighteenth year of Josiah's reign this Passover was kept to the LORD in Jerusalem. 24 Further, Josiah got rid of all who called up ghosts and spirits, of all household gods and idols and all the loathsome objects seen in the land of Judah and in Jerusalem, so that he might fulfil the require- ments of the law written in the book which the priest Hilkiah had discovered in the house of the 25 LORD. No king before him had turned to the LORD as he did, with all his heart and soul and strength, following the whole law of Moses; nor did any king like him appear again.

26 Yet the LORD did not abate his fierce anger; it still burned against Judah because of all the provoca- tion which Manasseh had given 27 him. 'Judah also I will banish from my presence', he declared, 'as I banished Israel; and I will cast off this city of Jerusalem which once I chose, and the house where I pro- mised that my Name should be.'

28 The other events and acts of Jo- siah's reign are recorded in the 29 annals of the kings of Judah. It was in his reign that Pharaoh Necho king of Egypt set out for the river Euphrates to help the king of As- syria. King Josiah went to meet

him; and when they met at Megid- do, Pharaoh Necho slew him. His 30[a] attendants conveyed his body in a chariot from Megiddo to Jerusa- lem and buried him in his own burial place. Then the people of the land took Josiah's son Jehoahaz and anointed him king in place of his father.

Jehoahaz was twenty-three years 31 old when he came to the throne, and he reigned in Jerusalem for three months; his mother was Hamutal daughter of Jeremiah of Libnah. He did what was wrong in 32 the eyes of the LORD, as his fore- fathers had done. Pharaoh Necho 33 removed him from the throne[b] in Jerusalem, and imposed on the land a fine of a hundred talents of silver and one talent of gold. Pharaoh Necho made Josiah's son 34 Eliakim king in place of his father and changed his name to Jehoia- kim. He took Jehoahaz and brought him to Egypt, where he died. Je- 35 hoiakim paid the silver and gold to Pharaoh, taxing the country to meet Pharaoh's demands; he ex- acted it from the people, from every man according to his assess- ment, so that he could pay Pha- raoh Necho.

Jehoiakim was twenty-five years 36 old when he came to the throne, and he reigned in Jerusalem for eleven years; his mother was Zebi- dah daughter of Pedaiah of Ru- mah. He did what was wrong in the 37 eyes of the LORD, as his forefathers had done. During his reign Nebu- 24 chadnezzar king of Babylon took the field, and Jehoiakim became his vassal; but three years later he broke with him and revolted. The 2 LORD launched against him raid- ing-parties of Chaldaeans, Ara- maeans, Moabites, and Ammon- ites, letting them range through Judah and ravage it, as the LORD had foretold through his servants

---

[a] *Verses 30–34: cp. 2 Chr. 36. 1–4.*
[b] removed...throne: *prob. rdg., cp. 2 Chr. 36. 3; Heb.* bound him at Riblah in the land of Hamath when he was king...

3 the prophets. All this happened to Judah in fulfilment of the LORD's purpose to banish them from his presence, because of all the sin that
4 Manasseh had committed and because of the innocent blood that he had shed; he had drenched Jerusalem with innocent blood, and the
5 LORD would not forgive him. The other events and acts of Jehoiakim's reign are recorded in the
6 annals of the kings of Judah. He rested with his forefathers, and was succeeded by his son Jehoiachin.
7 The king of Egypt did not leave his own land again, because the king of Babylon had stripped him of all his possessions, from the Torrent of Egypt to the river Euphrates.

Downfall of the southern kingdom

8[a] JEHOIACHIN was eighteen years old when he came to the throne, and he reigned in Jerusalem for three months; his mother was Nehushta daughter of Elnathan of
9 Jerusalem. He did what was wrong in the eyes of the LORD, as his fa-
10 ther had done. At that time the troops of Nebuchadnezzar king of Babylon advanced on Jerusalem
11 and besieged the city. Nebuchadnezzar arrived while his troops
12 were besieging it, and Jehoiachin king of Judah, his mother, his courtiers, his officers, and his eunuchs, all surrendered to the king of Babylon. The king of Babylon, now in the eighth year of his reign,
13 took him prisoner; and, as the LORD had foretold, he carried off all the treasures of the house of the LORD and of the royal palace and broke up all the vessels of gold which Solomon king of Israel had made for the temple of the LORD.
14 He carried the people of Jerusalem into exile, the officers and the

fighting men, ten thousand in number, together with all the craftsmen and smiths; only the weakest class of people were left. He deport- 15 ed Jehoiachin to Babylon; he also took into exile from Jerusalem to Babylon the king's mother and his wives, his eunuchs and the foremost men of the land. He also de- 16 ported to Babylon all the men of substance, seven thousand in number, and a thousand craftsmen and smiths, all of them able-bodied men and skilled armourers. He 17 made Mattaniah, uncle of Jehoiachin, king in his place and changed his name to Zedekiah.

Zedekiah was twenty-one years 18[b] old when he came to the throne, and he reigned in Jerusalem for eleven years; his mother was Hamutal daughter of Jeremiah of Libnah. He did what was wrong in the 19 eyes of the LORD, as Jehoiakim had done. Jerusalem and Judah so 20 angered the LORD that in the end he banished them from his sight; and Zedekiah rebelled against the king of Babylon.

In the ninth year of his reign, in 25 1[c] the tenth month, on the tenth day of the month, Nebuchadnezzar king of Babylon advanced with all his army against Jerusalem, invested it and erected watch-towers against it on every side; the siege 2 lasted till the eleventh year of King Zedekiah. In the fourth 3 month of that year,[d] on the ninth day of the month, when famine was severe in the city and there was no food for the common people, the city was thrown open. When 4 Zedekiah king of Judah saw this,[e] he and all his armed escort left the city and fled by night through the gate called Between the Two Walls, near the king's garden. They escaped towards the Arabah, although the Chaldaeans were

[a] Verses 8–17: cp. 2 Chr. 36. 9, 10. [b] 24. 18–25. 21: cp. Jer. 52. 1–27.
[c] Verses 1–12: cp. Jer. 39. 1–10; verses 1–17: cp. 2 Chr. 36. 17–20.
[d] In...year: prob. rdg., cp. Jer. 52. 6; Heb. om.
[e] When...this: prob. rdg., cp. Jer. 39. 4; Heb. om.

5 surrounding the city. But the Chaldaean army pursued the king and overtook him in the lowlands of Jericho; and all his company was 6 dispersed. The king was seized and brought before the king of Babylon at Riblah, where he pleaded his 7 case before him. Zedekiah's sons were slain before his eyes; then his eyes were put out, and he was brought to Babylon in fetters of bronze.

8 In the fifth month, on the seventh day of the month, in the nineteenth year of Nebuchadnezzar king of Babylon, Nebuzaradan, captain of the king's bodyguard, 9 came to Jerusalem and set fire to the house of the LORD and the royal palace; all the houses in the city, including the mansion of 10 Gedaliah,[a] were burnt down. The Chaldaean forces with the captain of the guard pulled down the walls 11 all round Jerusalem. Nebuzaradan captain of the guard deported the rest of the people left in the city, those who had deserted to the king of Babylon and any remaining arti- 12 sans.[b] He left only the weakest class of people to be vine-dressers and labourers.

13 The Chaldaeans broke up the pillars of bronze in the house of the LORD, the trolleys, and the Sea of bronze, and took the metal to 14 Babylon. They took also the pots, shovels, snuffers, saucers, and all the vessels of bronze used in the 15 service of the temple. The captain of the guard took away the precious metal, whether gold or silver, of which the firepans and the 16 tossing-bowls were made. The bronze of the two pillars, the one Sea, and the trolleys, which Solomon had made for the house of the 17 LORD, was beyond weighing. The one pillar was eighteen cubits high and its capital was bronze; the capital was three cubits high, and

a decoration of network and pomegranates ran all round it, wholly of bronze. The other pillar, with its network, was exactly like it.

The captain of the guard took 18 Seraiah the chief priest and Zephaniah the deputy chief priest and the three on duty at the entrance; he took also from the city a eunuch 19 who was in charge of the fighting men, five of those with right of access to the king who were still in the city, the adjutant-general[c] whose duty was to muster the people for war, and sixty men of the people who were still there. These Nebuzaradan captain of the 20 guard brought to the king of Babylon at Riblah. There, in the land of 21 Hamath, the king of Babylon had them flogged and put to death. So Judah went into exile from their own land.

Nebuchadnezzar king of Baby- 22 lon appointed Gedaliah son of Ahikam, son of Shaphan, governor over the few people whom he had left in Judah. When the captains of 23 the armed bands and their men heard that the king of Babylon had appointed Gedaliah governor, they all came to him at Mizpah: Ishmael son of Nethaniah, Johanan son of Kareah, Seraiah son of Tanhumeth of Netophah, and Jaazaniah of Beth-maacah. Then Geda- 24 liah gave them and their men this assurance: 'Have no fear of the Chaldaean officers. Settle down in the land and serve the king of Babylon; and then all will be well with you.' But in the seventh 25 month Ishmael son of Nethaniah, son of Elishama, who was a member of the royal house, came with ten men and murdered Gedaliah and the Jews and Chaldaeans who were with him at Mizpah. There- 26 upon all the people, high and low, and the captains of the armed

[a] Gedaliah: *prob. rdg.*; *Heb.* a great man.
[b] any remaining artisans: *prob. rdg.*, *cp. Jer.* 52. 15; *Heb.* the remaining crowd.
[c] *Prob. rdg.*; *Heb. adds* commander-in-chief.

bands, fled to Egypt for fear of the Chaldaeans.

27[a] In the thirty-seventh year of the exile of Jehoiachin king of Judah, on the twenty-seventh day of the twelfth month, Evil-merodach[b] king of Babylon in the year of his accession showed favour to Jehoiachin king of Judah. He brought him out of prison, treated him 28 kindly and gave him a seat at table above the kings with him in Babylon. So Jehoiachin discarded 29 his prison clothes and lived as a pensioner of the king for the rest of his life. For his maintenance, a 30 regular daily allowance was given him by the king as long as he lived.

THE FIRST BOOK OF THE

CHRONICLES

Genealogies from Adam to Saul

1 1, 2[c] ADAM, Seth, Enosh, Kenan, 3 Mahalalel, Jared, Enoch, 4 Methuselah, Lamech, Noah. The sons of Noah: Shem, Ham and Japheth.

5[d] The sons of Japheth: Gomer, Magog, Madai, Javan,[e] Tubal, 6 Meshech and Tiras. The sons of Gomer: Ashkenaz, Diphath and 7 Togarmah. The sons of Javan: Elishah, Tarshish, Kittim[f] and Rodanim.

8[g] The sons of Ham: Cush, Miz-9 raim,[h] Put and Canaan. The sons of Cush: Seba, Havilah, Sabta, Raama and Sabtecha. The sons of Raama: Sheba and Dedan. 10 Cush was the father of Nimrod, who began to show himself a man 11[i] of might on earth. From Mizraim sprang the Lydians, Anamites, 12 Lehabites, Naphtuhites, Pathrusites, Casluhites, and the Caphtorites, from whom the Philistines were descended.

Canaan was the father of Sidon, 13 who was his eldest son, and Heth,[j] the Jebusites, the Amorites, the 14 Girgashites, the Hivites, the 15 Arkites, the Sinites, the Arva-16 dites, the Zemarites, and the Hamathites.

The sons of Shem: Elam, As-17[k] shur, Arphaxad, Lud[l] and Aram. The sons of Aram: Uz, Hul, Gether and Mash. Arphaxad was 18 the father of Shelah, and Shelah the father of Eber. Eber had two 19 sons: one was named Peleg,[m] because in his time the earth was divided, and his brother's name was Joktan. Joktan was the 20 father of Almodad, Sheleph, Hazarmoth, Jerah, Hadoram, Uzal, 21 Diklah, Ebal,[n] Abimael, Sheba, 22 Ophir, Havilah and Jobab. All 23 these were sons of Joktan.

The line of[o] Shem: Arphaxad, 24[p] Shelah, Eber, Peleg, Reu, Serug, 25, 26 Nahor, Terah, Abram, also known 27 as Abraham, whose sons were 28 Isaac and Ishmael.

[a] Verses 27–30: cp. Jer. 52. 31–34.   [b] Or Ewil-marduk.
[c] Verses 2–4: cp. Gen. 5. 9–32.   [d] Verses 5–7: cp. Gen. 10. 2–4.   [e] Or Greece.
[f] Or Tarshish of the Kittians.   [g] Verses 8–10: cp. Gen. 10. 6–8.   [h] Or Egypt.
[i] Verses 11–16: cp. Gen. 10. 13–18.   [j] Or the Hittites.
[k] Verses 17–23: cp. Gen. 10. 22–29.   [l] Or the Lydians.   [m] That is Division.
[n] Or Obal, cp. Gen. 10. 28.   [o] The line of: prob. rdg.; Heb. om.
[p] Verses 24–27: cp. Gen. 11. 10–26.

29[a] The sons of[b] Ishmael in the order of their birth: Nebaioth the eldest, then Kedar, Adbeel, Mibsam, 30 Mishma, Dumah, Massa, 31 Hadad, Teman, Jetur, Naphish and Kedemah. These were Ishmael's sons.

32[c] The sons of Keturah, Abraham's concubine: she bore him Zimran, Jokshan, Medan, Midian, Ishbak and Shuah. The sons of 33 Jokshan: Sheba and Dedan. The sons of Midian: Ephah, Epher, Enoch, Abida and Eldaah. All these were descendants of Keturah.

34 Abraham was the father of Isaac, and Isaac's sons were Esau 35[d] and Israel. The sons of Esau: Eliphaz, Reuel, Jeush, Jalam and 36 Korah. The sons of Eliphaz: Teman, Omar, Zephi, Gatam, Kenaz, 37 Timna and Amalek. The sons of Reuel: Nahath, Zerah, Shammah and Mizzah.

38[e] The sons of Seir: Lotan, Shobal, Zibeon, Anah, Dishon, Ezer and 39 Dishan. The sons of Lotan: Hori and Homam; and Lotan had a sister named Timna. 40 The sons of Shobal: Alvan, Manahath, Ebal, Shephi and Onam. The sons of 41 Zibeon: Aiah and Anah. The son[f] of Anah: Dishon. The sons of Dishon: Amram, Eshban, Ithran 42 and Cheran. The sons of Ezer: Bilhan, Zavan and Akan. The sons of Dishon: Uz and Aran.

43[g] These are the kings who ruled over Edom before there were kings in Israel: Bela son of Beor, whose 44 city was named Dinhabah. When he died, he was succeeded by Jobab 45 son of Zerah of Bozrah. When Jobab died, he was succeeded by 46 Husham of Teman. When Husham died, he was succeeded by Hadad son of Bedad, who defeated Midian in Moabite country. His city was named Avith. When Hadad died, 47 he was succeeded by Samlah of Masrekah. When Samlah died, he 48 was succeeded by Saul of Rehoboth on the River. When Saul died, 49 he was succeeded by Baal-hanan son of Akbor. When Baal-hanan 50 died, he was succeeded by Hadad. His city was named Pai; his wife's name was Mehetabel daughter of Matred a woman of Me-zahab.[h]

After Hadad died the chiefs in 51 Edom were: chief Timna, chief Aliah, chief Jetheth, chief Oholibamah, 52 chief Elah, chief Pinon, chief Kenaz, chief Teman, chief 53 Mibzar, chief Magdiel and chief 54 Iram. These were the chiefs of Edom.

These were the sons of Israel: 2 Reuben, Simeon, Levi, Judah, Issachar, Zebulun, Dan, Joseph, Benjamin, 2 Naphtali, Gad and Asher.

The sons of Judah: Er, Onan and 3 Shelah; the mother of these three was a Canaanite woman, Bathshua.[i] Er, Judah's eldest son, displeased the LORD and the LORD slew him. Then Tamar, Judah's 4 daughter-in-law, bore him Perez and Zerah, making in all five sons of Judah. The sons of Perez: 5 Hezron and Hamul. The sons of 6 Zerah: Zimri, Ethan, Heman, Calcol and Darda, five in all. The son 7 of Zimri: Carmi.[j] The son of Carmi: Achar, who troubled Israel by his violation of the sacred ban. The 8 son of Ethan: Azariah. The sons of 9 Hezron: Jerahmeel, Ram and Caleb. Ram was the father of 10 Amminadab, Amminadab father of Nahshon prince of Judah. Nah- 11 shon was the father of Salma, Salma father of Boaz, Boaz father of 12 Obed, Obed father of Jesse. The 13

---

[a] *Verses 29–31: cp. Gen. 25. 13–16.*
[b] *The sons of: prob. rdg., cp. Gen. 25. 13; Heb. om.*
[c] *Verses 32, 33: cp. Gen. 25. 1–4.*
[d] *Verses 35–37: cp. Gen. 36. 4, 5, 9–13.*   [e] *Verses 38–42: cp. Gen. 36. 20–28.*
[f] *Prob. rdg.; Heb. sons; the same correction is made in several other places in chs. 1–9.*
[g] *Verses 43–54: cp. Gen. 36. 31–43.*   [h] *Or daughter of Mezahab.*   [i] *Bathshua: or daughter of Shua.*   [j] *The son...Carmi: prob. rdg. (cp. Josh. 7. 1, 18); Heb. om.*

eldest son of Jesse was Eliab, the second Abinadab, the third Shi-14 mea, the fourth Nethaneel, the 15 fifth Raddai, the sixth Ozem, the 16 seventh David; their sisters were Zeruiah and Abigail. The sons of Zeruiah: Abishai, Joab and Asahel, 17 three in all. Abigail was the mother of Amasa; his father was Jether the Ishmaelite.

18 Caleb son of Hezron had Jerioth by Azubah his wife;[a] these were her sons: Jesher, Shobab and Ar-19 don. When Azubah died, Caleb married Ephrath, who bore him 20 Hur. Hur was the father of Uri, 21 and Uri father of Bezalel. Later, Hezron, then sixty years of age, had intercourse with the daughter of Machir father of Gilead, having married her, and she bore Segub. 22 Segub was the father of Jair, who had twenty-three cities in Gilead. 23 Geshur and Aram took from them Havvoth-jair, and Kenath and its dependent villages, a total of sixty towns. All these were descendants 24 of Machir father of Gilead. After the death of Hezron, Caleb had intercourse with Ephrathah and she bore him Ashhur the founder of Tekoa.

25 The sons of Jerahmeel eldest son of Hezron by[b] Ahijah were Ram the eldest, Bunah, Oren and Ozem. 26 Jerahmeel had another wife, whose name was Atarah; she was the 27 mother of Onam. The sons of Ram eldest son of Jerahmeel: Maaz, 28 Jamin and Eker. The sons of Onam: Shammai and Jada. The sons of Shammai: Nadab and Abi-29 shur. The name of Abishur's wife was Abihail; she bore him Ahban 30 and Molid. The sons of Nadab: Seled and Ephraim; Seled died 31 without children. Ephraim's son was Ishi, Ishi's son Sheshan, She-32 shan's son Ahlai. The sons of Jada brother of Shammai: Jether and Jonathan; Jether died without

children. The sons of Jonathan: 33 Peleth and Zaza. These were the descendants of Jerahmeel.

Sheshan had daughters but no 34 sons. He had an Egyptian servant named Jarha; he gave his daughter 35 in marriage to this Jarha, and she bore him Attai. Attai was the fa-36 ther of Nathan, Nathan father of Zabad, Zabad father of Ephlal, 37 Ephlal father of Obed, Obed father 38 of Jehu, Jehu father of Azariah, Azariah father of Helez, Helez fa-39 ther of Elasah, Elasah father of 40 Sisamai, Sisamai father of Shal-lum, Shallum father of Jekamiah, 41 and Jekamiah father of Elishama.

The sons of Caleb brother of 42 Jerahmeel: Mesha the eldest, foun-der of Ziph, and[c] Mareshah foun-der of Hebron. The sons of Hebron: 43 Korah, Tappuah, Rekem and She-ma. Shema was the father of Ra-44 ham father of Jorkoam, and Rek-em was the father of Shammai. The son of Shammai was Maon, 45 and Maon was the founder of Beth-zur. Ephah, Caleb's concu-46 bine, was the mother of Haran, Moza and Gazez; Haran was the father of Gazez. The sons of Jah-47 dai: Regem, Jotham, Geshan, Pel-et, Ephah and Shaaph. Maacah, 48 Caleb's concubine, was the mother of Sheber and Tirhanah; she bore 49 also Shaaph founder of Madman-nah, and Sheva founder of Mach-benah and Gibea. Caleb also had a daughter named Achsah.

The descendants of Caleb: the 50 sons of Hur, the eldest son of Eph-rathah: Shobal the founder of Kiriath-jearim, Salma the founder 51 of Bethlehem, and Hareph the founder of Beth-gader. Shobal the 52 founder of Kiriath-jearim was the father of Reaiah[d] and the ancestor of half the Manahethites.[e]

The clans of Kiriath-jearim: 53 Ithrites, Puhites, Shumathites, and Mishraites, from whom were

---

[a] his wife: prob. rdg.; Heb. a woman and.
[c] Prob. rdg.; Heb. adds the sons of.
[e] Prob. rdg., cp. verse 54; Heb. Menuhoth.

[b] by: prob. rdg.; Heb. om.
[d] Prob. rdg., cp. 4. 2; Heb. the seer.

descended the Zareathites and the Eshtaulites.

54 The descendants of Salma: Bethlehem, the Netophathites, Ataroth, Beth-joab, half the Manahethites, and the Zorites.
55 The clans of Sophrites[a] living at Jabez: Tirathites, Shimeathites, and Suchathites. These were Kenites who were connected by marriage with the ancestor of the Rechabites.

3 1[b] These were the sons of David, born at Hebron: the eldest Amnon, whose mother was Ahinoam of Jezreel; the second Daniel, whose
2 mother was Abigail of Carmel; the third Absalom, whose mother was Maacah daughter of Talmai king of Geshur; the fourth Adonijah,
3 whose mother was Haggith; the fifth Shephatiah, whose mother was Abital; the sixth Ithream, whose mother was David's wife
4 Eglah. These six were born at Hebron, where David reigned seven years and six months. In Jerusalem he reigned thirty-three years,
5[c] and there the following sons were born to him: Shimea, Shobab, Nathan and Solomon; these four were sons of Bathsheba daughter
6 of Ammiel. There were nine others:
7 Ibhar, Elishama, Eliphelet, No-
8 gah, Nepheg, Japhia, Elishama,
9 Eliada and Eliphelet. These were all the sons of David, with their sister Tamar, in addition to his sons by concubines.

10 Solomon's son was Rehoboam, his son Abia, his son Asa, his son
11 Jehoshaphat, his son Joram, his
12 son Ahaziah, his son Joash, his son Amaziah, his son Azariah, his son
13 Jotham, his son Ahaz, his son
14 Hezekiah, his son Manasseh, his
15 son Amon, and his son Josiah. The sons of Josiah: the eldest was Johanan, the second Jehoiakim,

the third Zedekiah, the fourth Shallum. The sons of Jehoiakim: 16 Jeconiah and Zedekiah. The sons 17 of Jeconiah, a prisoner:[d] Shealtiel, Malchiram, Pedaiah, Shenazzar, 18 Jekamiah, Hoshama and Nedabiah. The sons of Pedaiah: Zerub- 19 babel and Shimei. The sons of Zerubbabel: Meshullam and Hananiah; they had a sister, Shelomith. There were five others: 20 Hashubah, Ohel, Berechiah, Hasadiah and Jushab-hesed. The sons 21 of Hananiah: Pelatiah and Isaiah; his son was Rephaiah, his son Arnan, his son Obadiah, his son Shecaniah. The sons of Shecaniah: 22 Shemaiah,[e] Hattush, Igeal, Bariah, Neariah and Shaphat, six in all. The sons of Neariah: Elioenai, Hez- 23 ekiah and Azrikam, three in all. The sons of Elioenai: Hodaiah, 24 Eliashib, Pelaiah, Akkub, Johanan, Dalaiah and Anani, seven in all.

The sons of Judah: Perez, Hez- 4 ron, Carmi, Hur and Shobal. Reaiah son of Shobal was the 2 father of Jahath, Jahath father of Ahumai and Lahad. These were the clans of the Zorathites.

The sons of Etam: Jezreel, Ish- 3–4 ma, Idbash, Penuel the founder of Gedor, and Ezer the founder of Hushah; they had a sister named Hazelelponi. These were the sons of Hur: Ephrathah the eldest, the founder of Bethlehem.

Ashhur the founder of Tekoa 5 had two wives, Helah and Naarah. Naarah bore him Ahuzam, Heph- 6 er, Temeni and Haahashtari.[f] These were the sons of Naarah. The sons of Helah: Zereth, Jezoar, 7 Ethnan and Coz. Coz was the 8 father of Anub and Zobebah and the clans of Aharhel son of Harum.

Jabez ranked higher than his 9 brothers; his mother called him Jabez because, as she said, she had

---

a Or secretaries.   *b* Verses 1–4: cp. 2 Sam. 3. 2–5.
c Verses 5–8: cp. 14. 4–7; 2 Sam. 5. 14–16.
d Jeconiah, a prisoner: or Jeconiah: Assir,...
e Prob. rdg.; Heb. adds and the sons of Shemaiah.
f Temeni and Haahashtari: or the Temanite and the Ahashtarite.

10 borne him in pain. Jabez called upon the God of Israel and said, 'I pray thee, bless me and grant me wide territories. May thy hand be with me, and do me no harm, I pray thee, and let me be free from pain'; and God granted his petition.

11 Kelub brother of Shuah was the father of Mehir the father of Eshton.

12 Eshton was the father of Beth-rapha, Paseah, and Tehinnah father of Ir-nahash. These were the men of Rechah.

13 The sons of Kenaz: Othniel and Seraiah. The sons of Othniel: Hathath and Meonothai.

14 Meonothai was the father of Ophrah. Seraiah was the father of Joab founder of Ge-harashim,[a] for they were craftsmen.

15 The sons of Caleb son of Jephunneh: Iru, Elah and Naam. The son of Elah: Kenaz.

16 The sons of Jehaleleel: Ziph and Ziphah, Tiria and Asareel.

17-18 The sons of Ezra: Jether, Mered, Epher and Jalon. These were the sons of Bithiah daughter of Pharaoh, whom Mered had married; she conceived and gave birth to[b] Miriam, Shammai and Ishbah founder of Eshtemoa. His Jewish wife was the mother of Jered founder of Gedor, Heber founder of Soco, and Jekuthiel founder of

19 Zanoah. The sons of his[c] wife Hodiah sister of Naham were Daliah father of Keilah the Garmite, and Eshtemoa the Maacathite.

20 The sons of Shimon: Amnon, Rinnah, Ben-hanan and Tilon. The sons of Ishi: Zoheth and Ben-zoheth.

21 The sons of Shelah son of Judah: Er founder of Lecah, Laadah founder of Mareshah, the clans of the guild of linen-workers at Ashbea,

22 Jokim, the men of Kozeba, Joash, and Saraph who fell out with Moab and came back to Bethlehem.[d] (The records are ancient.) They 23 were the potters, and those who lived at Netaim and Gederah were there on the king's service.

24 The sons of Simeon: Nemuel, Jamin, Jarib, Zerah, Saul, his son 25 Shallum, his son Mibsam and his son Mishma. The sons of Mishma: 26 his son Hamuel, his son Zaccur and his son Shimei. Shimei had sixteen 27 sons and six daughters, but others of his family had fewer children, and the clan as a whole did not increase as much as the tribe of Judah. They lived at Beersheba, Mo-28 ladah, Hazar-shual, Bilhah, Ezem, 29 Tolad, Bethuel, Hormah, Ziklag, 30 Beth-marcaboth, Hazar-susim, 31 Beth-birei, and Shaaraim. These were their cities until David came to the throne. Their settlements[e] 32 were Etam, Ain, Rimmon, Tochen, and Ashan, five cities in all. They 33 had also hamlets round these cities as far as Baal. These were the places where they lived.

The names on their register 34 were: Meshobab, Jamlech, Joshah son of Amaziah, Joel, Jehu son of 35 Josibiah, son of Seraiah, son of Asiel, Elioenai, Jaakobah, Jesho-36 haiah, Asaiah, Adiel, Jesimiel, Benaiah, Ziza son of Shiphi, son of 37 Allon, son of Jedaiah, son of Shimri, son of Shemaiah, whose names 38 are recorded as princes in their clans, and their families had greatly increased. They then went from 39 the approaches to Gedor east of the valley in search of pasture for their flocks. They found rich and good 40 pasture in a wide stretch of open country where everything was quiet and peaceful; before then it had been occupied by Hamites. During the reign of Hezekiah king 41 of Judah these whose names are written above came and destroyed

---

[a] Or the Valley of Craftsmen.
[b] and gave birth to: *prob. rdg.*; *Heb. om.*
[c] his: *prob. rdg.*; *Heb. om.*
[d] and came...Bethlehem: *prob. rdg.*; *Heb. unintelligible.*
[e] *Prob. rdg.*; *Heb. hamlets.*

the tribes of Ham*a* and the Meunites whom they found there. They annihilated them so that no trace of them has remained to this day; and they occupied the land in their place, for there was pasture for 42 their flocks. Of their number five hundred Simeonites invaded the hill-country of Seir, led by Pelatiah, Neariah, Rephaiah, and 43 Uzziel, the sons of Ishi. They destroyed all who were left of the surviving Amalekites; and they live there still.

5   The sons of Reuben, the eldest of Israel's sons. (He was, in fact, the first son born, but because he had committed incest with a wife of his father's the rank of the eldest was transferred to the sons of Joseph, Israel's son, who, however, could not be registered as the eldest 2 son. Judah held the leading place among his brothers because he fathered a ruler, and the rank of the eldest was his, not*b* Joseph's.) 3 The sons of Reuben, the eldest of Israel's sons: Enoch, Pallu, Hez- 4 ron and Carmi. The sons of Joel: his son Shemaiah, his son Gog, his 5 son Shimei, his son Micah, his son 6 Reaia, his son Baal, his son Beerah, whom Tiglath-pileser king of Assyria carried away into exile; he 7 was a prince of the Reubenites. His kinsmen, family by family, as registered in their tribal lists: Jeiel the 8 chief, Zechariah, Bela son of Azaz, son of Shema, son of Joel. They lived in Aroer, and their lands stretched as far as Nebo and Baal-meon. 9 Eastwards they occupied territory as far as the edge of the desert which stretches from the river Euphrates, for they had large numbers 10 of cattle in Gilead. During Saul's reign they made war on the Hagarites, whom they conquered, occupying their encampments over all the country east of Gilead.

Adjoining them were the Gad- 11 ites, occupying the district of Bashan as far as Salcah: Joel the 12 chief; second in rank, Shapham; then Jaanai and Shaphat in Bashan. Their fellow-tribesmen be- 13 longed to the families of Michael, Meshullam, Sheba, Jorai, Jachan, Zia and Heber, seven in all. These 14 were the sons of Abihail son of Huri, son of Jaroah, son of Gilead, son of Michael, son of Jeshishai, son of Jahdo, son of Buz. Ahi son 15 of Abdiel, son of Guni, was head of their family; they lived in Gilead, 16 in Bashan and its villages, in all the common land of Sharon as far as it stretched. These registers were all 17 compiled in the reigns of Jotham king of Judah and Jeroboam king of Israel.

The sons of Reuben, Gad, and 18 half the tribe of Manasseh: of their fighting men armed with shield and sword, their archers and their battle-trained soldiers, forty-four thousand seven hundred and sixty were ready for active service. They 19 made war on the Hagarites, Jetur, Nephish, and Nodab. They were 20 given help against them, for they cried to their God for help in the battle, and because they trusted him he listened to their prayer, and the Hagarites and all their allies surrendered to them.*c* They drove 21 off their cattle, fifty thousand camels, two hundred and fifty thousand sheep, and two thousand asses, and they took a hundred thousand captives. Many had been 22 killed, for the war was of God's making, and they occupied the land instead of them until the exile.

Half the tribe of Manasseh lived 23 in the land from Bashan to Baal-hermon, Senir, and Mount Hermon, and were numerous also in Lebanon. The heads of their fami- 24

---

a the tribes of Ham: *prob. rdg., cp. verse 40*; *Heb.* their tribes.
b his, not: *prob. rdg.*; *Heb. om.*
c They were...surrendered to them: *or* They attacked them boldly, and the Hagarites and all their allies surrendered to them, for they cried...to their prayer.

lies were: Epher, Ishi, Eliel, Azriel, Jeremiah, Hodaviah, and Jahdiel, all men of ability and repute, 25 heads of their families. But they sinned against the God of their fathers, and turned wantonly to worship the gods of the peoples whom God had destroyed before 26 them. So the God of Israel stirred up Pul king of Assyria, that is Tiglath-pileser king of Assyria, and he carried into exile Reuben, Gad, and half the tribe of Manasseh. He took them to Halah, Habor, Hara, and the river Gozan, where they are to this day.

6 THE sons of Levi: Gershon,[a] Kohath 2 and Merari. The sons of Kohath: Amram, Izhar, Hebron and 3 Uzziel. The children of Amram: Aaron, Moses and Miriam. The sons of Aaron: Nadab, Abihu, 4[b] Eleazar and Ithamar. Eleazar was the father of Phinehas, Phinehas 5 father of Abishua, Abishua father of Bukki, Bukki father of Uzzi, 6 Uzzi father of Zerahiah, Zerahiah 7 father of Meraioth, Meraioth father of Amariah, Amariah father 8 of Ahitub, Ahitub father of Zadok, 9 Zadok father of Ahimaaz, Ahimaaz father of Azariah, Azariah 10 father of Johanan, and Johanan father of Azariah, the priest who officiated in the LORD's house which Solomon built at Jerusalem. 11 Azariah was the father of Amariah, 12 Amariah father of Ahitub, Ahitub father of Zadok, Zadok father of 13 Shallum, Shallum father of Hilkiah, Hilkiah father of Azariah, 14 Azariah father of Seraiah, and 15 Seraiah father of Jehozadak. Jehozadak went into exile when the LORD sent Judah and Jerusalem into exile under Nebuchadnezzar.

16[c] The sons of Levi: Gershom, Kohath 17 and Merari. The sons of Gershom: 18 Libni and Shimei. The sons of Kohath: Amram, Izhar, Hebron

and Uzziel. The sons of Merari: 19 Mahli and Mushi. The clans of Levi, family by family: Gershom: 20[d] his son Libni, his son Jahath, his son Zimmah, his son Joah, his son 21 Iddo, his son Zerah, his son Jeaterai. The sons of Kohath: his son 22[e] Amminadab, his son Korah, his son Assir, his son Elkanah, his son 23 Ebiasaph, his son Assir, his son 24 Tahath, his son Uriel, his son Uzziah, his son Saul. The sons of 25 Elkanah: Amasai and Ahimoth, his son Elkanah, his son Zophai, 26 his son Nahath, his son Eliab, his 27 son Jeroham, his son Elkanah. The 28 sons of Samuel: Joel the eldest and Abiah the second. The sons of 29 Merari: his son Mahli, his son Libni, his son Shimei, his son Uzza, his 30 son Shimea, his son Haggiah, his son Asaiah.

These are the men whom David 31 appointed to take charge of the music in the house of the LORD when the Ark should be deposited there. They performed their musi- 32 cal duties before the Tent of the Presence until Solomon built the house of the LORD in Jerusalem, and took their regular turns of duty there. The following, with 33 their descendants, took this duty. Of the line of Kohath: Heman the musician, son of Joel, son of Samuel, son of Elkanah, son of Jero- 34 ham, son of Eliel, son of Toah, son 35 of Zuph, son of Elkanah, son of Mahath, son of Amasai, son of 36 Elkanah, son of Joel, son of Azariah, son of Zephaniah, son of 37 Tahath, son of Assir, son of Ebiasaph, son of Korah, son of Izhar, 38 son of Kohath, son of Levi, son of Israel. Heman's colleague Asaph 39 stood at his right hand. He was the son of Berachiah, son of Shimea, son of Michael, son of Baaseiah, 40 son of Malchiah, son of Ethni, son 41[f] of Zerah, son of Adaiah, son of 42 Ethan, son of Zimmah, son of

---

[a] Gershom *in verses 16 and 17.*
[c] *Verses 16–19: cp. Exod. 6. 16–19.*
[e] *Verses 22–28: cp. verses 33–38.*
[b] *Verses 4–8: cp. verses 50–53.*
[d] *Verses 20, 21: cp. verses 41–43.*
[f] *Verses 41–43: cp. verses 20, 21.*

43 Shimei, son of Jahath, son of Ger-
44 shom, son of Levi. On their left
stood their colleague of the line of
Merari: Ethan son of Kishi, son of
45 Abdi, son of Malluch, son of Hashabiah, son of Amaziah, son of Hil-
46 kiah, son of Amzi, son of Bani, son
47 of Shamer, son of Mahli, son of
Mushi, son of Merari, son of Levi.
48 Their kinsmen the Levites were
dedicated to all the service of the
Tabernacle, the house of God.

49   But it was Aaron and his descendants who burnt the sacrifices
on the altar of whole-offering and
the altar of incense, in fulfilment of
all the duties connected with the
most sacred gifts, and to make expiation for Israel, exactly as Moses
the servant of God had com-
50ᵃ manded. The sons of Aaron: his
son Eleazar, his son Phinehas, his
51 son Abishua, his son Bukki, his son
52 Uzzi, his son Zerahiah, his son
Meraioth, his son Amariah, his
53 son Ahitub, his son Zadok, his son
Ahimaaz.

54   These are their settlements in
encampments in the districts assigned to the descendants of Aaron,
to the clan of Kohath, for it was to
55 them that the lot had fallen: they
gave them Hebron in Judah, with
56 the common land round it, but
they assigned to Caleb son of Jephunneh the open country belonging to the town and its ham-
57ᵇ lets. They gave to the sons of
Aaron: Hebron the cityᶜ of refuge,
58 Libnah, Jattir, Eshtemoa, Hilen,
59 Debir, Ashan, and Beth-shemesh,
60 each with its common land. And
from the tribe of Benjamin: Geba,
Alemeth, and Anathoth, each with
its common land, making thirteen
cities in all by their clans.
61   They gave to the remaining clans
of the sons of Kohath ten cities by
lot from the half tribe of Manasseh.

To the sons of Gershom according 62
to their clans they gave thirteen
cities from the tribes of Issachar,
Asher, Naphtali, and Manasseh in
Bashan. To the sons of Merari ac- 63
cording to their clans they gave by
lot twelve cities from the tribes of
Reuben, Gad, and Zebulun. Israel 64
gave these cities, each with its
common land, to the Levites. (The 65
cities mentioned above, from the
tribes of Judah, Simeon, and Benjamin, were assigned by lot.)

Some of the clans of Kohath had 66
cities allottedᵈ to them. They gave 67
them the cityᵉ of refuge, Shechem
in the hill-country of Ephraim,
Gezer, Jokmeam, Beth-horon, Ai- 68, 69
jalon, and Gath-rimmon, each
with its common land. From the 70
half tribe of Manasseh, Aner and
Bileam, each with its common
land, were given to the rest of the
clans of Kohath.

To the sons of Gershom they 71
gave from the half tribe of Manasseh: Golan in Bashan, and Ashtaroth, each with its common land.
From the tribe of Issachar: Ke- 72
desh, Daberath, Ramoth, and 73
Anem, each with its common land.
From the tribe of Asher: Mashal, 74
Abdon, Hukok, and Rehob, each 75
with its common land. From the 76
tribe of Naphtali: Kedesh in Galilee, Hammon, and Kiriathaim,
each with its common land.

To the rest of the sons of Merari 77
they gave from the tribe of Zebulun: Rimmon and Tabor, each with
its common land. On the east of 78
Jordan, opposite Jericho, from the
tribe of Reuben: Bezer-in-the-wilderness, Jahzah, Kedemoth, and 79
Mephaath, each with its common
land. From the tribe of Gad: Ra- 80
moth in Gilead, Mahanaim, Hesh- 81
bon, and Jazer, each with its common land.

ᵃ *Verses 50–53: cp. verses 4–8.*
ᵇ *Verses 57–81: cp. Josh. 21. 13–39.*
ᶜ *Prob. rdg., cp. Josh. 21. 13; Heb. cities.*
ᵈ allotted: *prob. rdg., cp. Josh. 21. 20; Heb. of their frontier.*
ᵉ *Prob. rdg., cp. Josh. 21. 21; Heb. cities.*

7 1[a] The sons of Issachar: Tola, Pua, 2 Jashub and Shimron, four. The sons of Tola: Uzzi, Rephaiah, Jeriel, Jahmai, Jibsam, and Samuel, all able men and heads of families by paternal descent from Tola according to their tribal lists; their number in David's time was twenty-two thousand six hundred. 3 The son of Uzzi: Izrahiah. The sons of Izrahiah: Michael, Obadiah, Joel and Isshiah, making a total of 4 five, all of them chiefs. In addition there were bands of fighting men recorded by families according to the tribal lists to the number of thirty-six thousand, for they had 5 many wives and children. Their fellow-tribesmen in all the clans of Issachar were able men, eighty-seven thousand; every one of them was registered.

6   The sons of Benjamin: Bela, 7 Becher and Jediael, three. The sons of Bela: Ezbon, Uzzi, Uzziel, Jerimoth and Iri, five. They were heads of their families and able men; the number registered was twenty-two thousand and thirty-8 four. The sons of Becher: Zemira, Joash, Eliezer, Elioenai, Omri, Jeremoth, Abiah, Anathoth and Alemeth; all these were sons of 9 Becher according to their tribal lists, heads of their families and able men; and the number registered was twenty thousand two hun-10 dred. The son of Jediael: Bilhan. The sons of Bilhan: Jeush, Benjamin, Ehud, Kenaanah, Zethan, 11 Tarshish and Ahishahar. All these were descendants of Jediael, heads of[b] families and able men. The number was seventeen thousand two hundred men, fit for active service in war.

12   The sons of Dan:[c] Hushim and the sons of Aher.[d]

The sons of Naphtali: Jahziel, 13 Guni, Jezer, Shallum. These were sons of Bilhah.

The sons of Manasseh,[e] born of 14[f] his concubine, an Aramaean: Machir father of Gilead. Machir married a woman whose name was[g] 15 Maacah. The second son was named Zelophehad, and Zelophehad had daughters. Maacah wife of Machir 16 had a son whom she named Peresh. His brother's name was Sheresh, and his sons were Ulam and Rakem. The son of Ulam: Bedan. 17 These were the sons of Gilead son of Machir, son of Manasseh. His 18 sister Hammoleketh was the mother of Ishhod, Abiezer and Mahalah. The sons of Shemida: Ahian, 19 Shechem, Likhi and Aniam.

The sons of Ephraim: Shuthe- 20 lah, his son Bered, his son Tahath, his son Eladah, his son Tahath, his son Zabad, his son Shuthelah. 21 Ephraim's other sons Ezer and Elead were killed by the native Gittites when they came down to lift their cattle. Their father Eph- 22 raim long mourned for them, and his kinsmen came to comfort him. Then he had intercourse with his 23 wife; she conceived and had a son whom he named Beriah (because disaster[h] had come on his family). He had a daughter named Sherah; 24 she built Lower and Upper Beth-horon and Uzzen-sherah. He also 25 had a son named Rephah; his son was Resheph, his son Telah, his son Tahan, his son Laadan, his son 26 Ammihud, his son Elishama, his 27 son Nun, his son Joshua.

Their lands and settlements were: 28 Bethel and its dependent villages, to the east Naaran, to the west Gezer, Shechem, and Gaza, with their villages. In the possession 29 of Manasseh were Beth-shean,

---

[a] Verses 1, 6, 13, 30 and 8. 1–5: cp. Gen. 46. 13, 17, 21–24.   [b] Prob. rdg.; Heb. to the heads of.   [c] The sons of Dan: prob. rdg., cp. Gen. 46. 23; Heb. And Shuppim and Huppim, the sons of Ir.   [d] Or another.   [e] Prob. rdg.; Heb. adds Asriel.   [f] Verses 14–19: cp. Num. 26. 29–33.   [g] whose name was: prob. rdg.; Heb. to Huppim and Shuppim, and his sister's name was...   [h] Heb. beraah.

Taanach, Megiddo, and Dor, with their villages. In all of these lived the descendants of Joseph the son of Israel.

30 The sons of Asher: Imnah, Ishvah, Ishvi and Beriah, together 31 with their sister Serah. The sons of Beriah: Heber and Malchiel father 32 of Birzavith. Heber was the father of Japhlet, Shomer, Hotham, and 33 their sister Shua. The sons of Japhlet: Pasach, Bimhal and Ashvath. These were the sons of Japh-34 let. The sons of Shomer: Ahi, Roh-35 gah, Jehubbah and Aram. The sons of his brother Hotham:[a] Zophah, Imna, Shelesh and Amal. 36 The sons of Zophah: Suah, Har-37 nepher, Shual, Beri, Imrah, Bezer, Hod, Shamma, Shilshah, Ithran 38 and Beera. The sons of Jether: 39 Jephunneh, Pispah and Ara. The sons of Ulla: Arah, Haniel and 40 Rezia. All these were descendants of Asher, heads of families, picked men of ability, leading princes. They were enrolled among the fighting troops; the total number was twenty-six thousand men.

8 The sons of Benjamin were: the eldest Bela, the second Ashbel, the 2 third Aharah, the fourth Nohah 3 and the fifth Rapha. The sons of Bela: Addar, Gera father of Ehud,[b] 4, 5 Abishua, Naaman, Ahoah, Gera, 6 Shephuphan and Huram. These were the sons of Ehud, heads of families living in Geba, who were re-7 moved to Manahath: Naaman, Ahiah, and Gera – he it was who removed them. He was the father 8 of Uzza and Ahihud. Shaharaim had sons born to him in Moabite country, after putting away his 9 wives Mahasham and Baara. By his wife Hodesh he had Jobab, Zi-10 bia, Mesha, Malcham, Jeuz, Shachia and Mirmah. These were his 11 sons, heads of families. By Mahasham he had had Abitub and El-12 paal. The sons of Elpaal: Eber,

Misham, Shamed who built Ono and Lod with its villages, also Be-13 riah and Shema who were heads of families living in Aijalon, having expelled the inhabitants of Gath. Ahio, Shashak, Jeremoth, Zeba-14, 15 diah, Arad, Ader, Michael, Ispah, 16 and Joha were sons of Beriah; Zebadiah, Meshullam, Hezeki, He-17 ber, Ishmerai, Jezliah, and Jobab 18 were sons of Elpaal; Jakim, Zi-19 chri, Zabdi, Elienai, Zilthai, Eliel, 20 Adaiah, Beraiah, and Shimrath 21 were sons of Shimei; Ishpan, He-22 ber, Eliel, Abdon, Zichri, Hanan, 23 Hananiah, Elam, Antothiah, Iphe-24, 25 deiah, and Penuel were sons of Shashak; Shamsherai, Shehariah, 26 Athaliah, Jaresiah, Eliah, and Zi-27 chri were sons of Jeroham. These 28 were enrolled in the tribal lists as heads of families, chiefs living in Jerusalem.

Jehiel founder of Gibeon lived 29[c] at Gibeon; his wife's name was Maacah. His eldest son was Ab-30 don, followed by Zur, Kish, Baal, Nadab, Gedor, Ahio, Zacher and 31 Mikloth. Mikloth was the father of 32 Shimeah; they lived alongside their kinsmen in Jerusalem.

Ner was the father of Kish, Kish 33 father of Saul, Saul father of Jonathan, Malchishua, Abinadab and Eshbaal. Jonathan's son was Me-34 ribbaal, and he was the father of Micah. The sons of Micah: Pithon, 35 Melech, Tarea and Ahaz. Ahaz was 36 the father of Jehoaddah, Jehoaddah father of Alemeth, Azmoth and Zimri. Zimri was the father of Moza, and Moza father of Binea; 37 his son was Raphah, his son Elasah, and his son Azel. Azel had six 38 sons, whose names were Azrikam, Bocheru, Ishmael, Sheariah, Obadiah and Hanan. All these were sons of Azel. The sons of his bro-39 ther Eshek: the eldest Ulam, the second Jeush, the third Eliphelet. The sons of Ulam were able men, 40 archers, and had many sons and

---

[a] *Prob. rdg., cp. verse 32; Heb. Helem. 3. 15; Heb. Abihud.*

[b] *father of Ehud: prob. rdg., cp. Judg.*
[c] *Verses 29–38: cp. 9. 35–44.*

grandsons, a hundred and fifty. All these were descendants of Benjamin.

The restored community

9 So all Israel were registered and recorded in the book of the kings of Israel; but Judah for their sins were carried away to exile in Baby-
2^a lon. The first to occupy their ancestral land in their cities were lay Israelites, priests, Levites, and
3 temple-servitors. Jerusalem was occupied partly by Judahites, partly by Benjamites, and partly by men of Ephraim and Manasseh.
4 Judahites:^b Uthai son of Ammihud, son of Omri, son of Imri, son of Bani, a descendant of Perez son
5 of Judah. Shelanites: Asaiah the
6 eldest and his sons. The sons of Zerah: Jeuel and six hundred and
7 ninety of their kinsmen. Benjamites: Sallu son of Meshullam, son of Hodaviah, son of Hassenuah,
8 Ibneiah son of Jeroham, Elah son of Uzzi, son of Micri, Meshullam son of Shephatiah, son of Reuel,
9 son of Ibniah, and their recorded kinsmen numbering nine hundred and fifty-six, all heads of families
10 Priests: Jedaiah, Jehoiarib, Ja-
11 chin, Azariah son of Hilkiah, son of Meshullam, son of Zadok, son of Meraioth, son of Ahitub, the officer in charge of the house of God,
12 Adaiah son of Jeroham, son of Pashhur, son of Malchiah, Maasai son of Adiel, son of Jahzerah, son of Meshullam, son of Meshillemith,
13 son of Immer, and their colleagues, heads of families numbering one thousand seven hundred and sixty, men of substance and fit for the work connected with the service of the house of God.
14 Levites: Shemaiah son of Hasshub, son of Azrikam, son of Hashabiah, a descendant of Merari,
15 Bakbakkar, Heresh, Galal, Mattaniah son of Mica, son of Zichri,

son of Asaph, Obadiah son of She- 16 maiah, son of Galal, son of Jeduthun, and Berechiah son of Asa, son of Elkanah, who lived in the hamlets of the Netophathites.

The door-keepers were Shallum, 17 Akkub, Talmon, and Ahiman; their brother Shallum was the chief. Until then they had all been door- 18 keepers in the quarters of the Levites at the king's gate, on the east. Shallum son of Kore, son of Ebia- 19 saph, son of Korah, and his kinsmen of the Korahite family were responsible for service as guards of the thresholds of the Tabernacle; their ancestors had performed the duty of guarding the entrances to the camp of the LORD. Phinehas 20 son of Eleazar had been their overseer in the past – the LORD be with him! Zechariah son of Meshele- 21 miah was the door-keeper of the Tent of the Presence. Those picked 22 to be door-keepers numbered two hundred and twelve in all, registered in their hamlets. David and Samuel the seer had installed them because they were trustworthy. They and their sons had 23 charge, by watches, of the gates of the house, the tent-dwelling of the LORD. The door-keepers were to be 24 on four sides, east, west, north, and south. Their kinsmen from their 25 hamlets had to come on duty with them for seven days at a time in turn. The four principal door- 26 keepers were chosen for their trustworthiness; they were Levites and had charge of the rooms and the stores in the house of God. They 27 always slept in the precincts of the house of God (for the watch was their duty) and they had charge of the key for opening the gates every morning. Some of them had charge 28 of the vessels used in the service of the temple, keeping count of them as they were brought in and taken out. Some of them were detailed to 29 take charge of the furniture and all the sacred vessels, the flour, the

---

^a *Verses 2–22: cp. Neh. 11. 3–22.*   ^b *Prob. rdg.; Heb. om.*

wine, the oil, the incense, and the spices.

30 Some of the priests compounded 31 the ointment for the spices. Mattithiah the Levite, the eldest son of Shallum the Korahite, was in charge of the preparation of the wafers because he was trustworthy. 32 Some of their Kohathite kinsmen were in charge of setting out the rows of the Bread of the Presence every sabbath.

33 These, the musicians, heads of Levite families, were lodged in rooms set apart for them, because they were liable for duty by day and by night.

34 These are the heads of Levite families, chiefs according to their tribal lists, living in Jerusalem.

35ᵃ Jehiel founder of Gibeon lived at Gibeon; his wife's name was 36 Maacah, and his sons were Abdon the eldest, Zur, Kish, Baal, Ner, 37 Nadab, Gedor, Ahio, Zechariah and 38 Mikloth. Mikloth was the father of Shimeam; they lived alongside 39 their kinsmen in Jerusalem.ᵇ Ner was the father of Kish, Kish father of Saul, Saul father of Jonathan, Malchishua, Abinadab and Esh-40 baal. The son of Jonathan was Meribbaal, and Meribbaal was the fa-41 ther of Micah. The sons of Micah: Pithon, Melech, Tahrea and Ahaz. 42 Ahaz was the father of Jarah, Jarah father of Alemeth, Azmoth, and Zimri; Zimri father of Moza, 43 and Moza father of Binea; his son was Rephaiah, his son Elasah, his 44 son Azel. Azel had six sons, whose names were Azrikam Bocheru, Ishmael, Sheariah, Obadiah and Hanan. These were the sons of Azel.

The death of Saul

10 1ᶜ THE Philistines fought a battle against Israel, and the men of Israel were routed, leaving their 2 dead on Mount Gilboa. The Phili-

stines hotly pursued Saul and his sons and killed the three sons, Jonathan, Abinadab and Malchishua. The battle went hard for Saul, for 3 some archers came upon him and he was wounded by them. So he 4 said to his armour-bearer, 'Draw your sword and run me through, so that these uncircumcised brutes may not come and make sport of me.' But the armour-bearer refused, he dared not; whereupon Saul took his own sword and fell on it. When the armour-bearer saw 5 that Saul was dead, he too fell on his sword and died. Thus Saul died 6 and his three sons; his whole house perished at one and the same time. And all the Israelites in the Vale, 7 when they saw that their army had fled and that Saul and his sons had perished, fled likewise, abandoning their cities, and the Philistines went in and occupied them.

Next day, when the Philistines 8 came to strip the slain, they found Saul and his sons lying dead on Mount Gilboa. They stripped him, 9 cut off his head and took away his armour; then they sent messengers through the length and breadth of their land to take the good news to idols and people alike. They de-10 posited his armour in the temple of their god,ᵈ and nailed up his skull in the temple of Dagon. When the 11 people of Jabesh-gilead heard all that the Philistines had done to Saul, the bravest of them set out 12 together to recover the bodies of Saul and his sons; they brought them back to Jabesh and buried their bones under the oak-tree there, and fasted for seven days. Thus Saul paid with his life for his 13 unfaithfulness: he had disobeyed the word of the LORD and had resorted to ghosts for guidance. He 14 had not sought guidance of the LORD, who therefore destroyed him and transferred the kingdom to David son of Jesse.

ᵃ *Verses 35–44: cp. 8. 29–38.*   ᵇ *Prob. rdg.; Heb. adds* with their kinsmen.
ᶜ *Verses 1–12: cp. 1 Sam. 31. 1–13.*   ᵈ *Or gods.*

David king over Israel

11 1[a] THEN all Israel assembled at Hebron to wait upon David. 'We are your own flesh and blood', they 2 said. 'In the past, while Saul was still king, you led the forces of Israel to war, and you brought them home again. And the LORD your God said to you, "You shall be shepherd of my people Israel, 3 you shall be their prince."' All the elders of Israel came to the king at Hebron; there David made a covenant with them before the LORD, and they anointed David king over Israel, as the LORD had said through the lips of Samuel.

4 Then David and all Israel went to Jerusalem (that is Jebus, where the Jebusites, the inhabitants of 5 the land, lived). The people of Jebus said to David, 'Never shall you come in here'; none the less David did capture the stronghold 6 of Zion, and it is now known as the City of David. David said, 'The first man to kill a Jebusite shall become a commander or an officer', and the first man to go up was Joab son of Zeruiah; so he was given the command.

7 David took up his residence in the stronghold: that is why they 8 called it the City of David. He built the city round it, starting at the Millo and including its neighbourhood, while Joab reconstruct-9 ed the rest of the city. So David steadily grew stronger, for the LORD of Hosts was with him.

10[b] Of David's heroes these were the chief, men who lent their full strength to his government and, with all Israel, joined in making him king; such was the LORD's 11 decree for Israel. First came Jashoboam the Hachmonite, chief of the three; he it was who brandished his spear over three hundred, all 12 slain at one time. Next to him was Eleazar son of Dodo the Ahohite, one of the heroic three. He was 13 with David at Pas-dammim where the Philistines had gathered for battle in a field carrying a good crop of barley; and when the people had fled from the Philistines he 14 stood his ground in the field, saved it[c] and defeated them. So the LORD brought about a great victory.

Three of the thirty chiefs went 15 down to the rock to join David at the cave of Adullam, while the Philistines were encamped in the Vale of Rephaim. At that time 16 David was in the stronghold, and a Philistine garrison held Bethlehem. One day a longing came over 17 David, and he exclaimed, 'If only I could have a drink of water from the well[d] by the gate of Bethlehem!' At this the three made their way 18 through the Philistine lines and drew water from the well by the gate of Bethlehem, and brought it to David. But David refused to drink it; he poured it out to the LORD and said, 'God forbid that I 19 should do such a thing! Can I drink the blood of these men? They have brought it at the risk of their lives.' So he would not drink it. Such were the exploits of the heroic three.

Abishai the brother of Joab was 20 chief of the thirty. He once brandished his spear over three hundred dead, and he was famous among the thirty. He held higher rank 21 than the rest of the thirty and became their captain, but he did not rival the three. Benaiah son of Jehoiada, from Kabzeel, was a hero 22 of many exploits. It was he who smote the two champions of Moab, and who went down into a pit and killed a lion on a snowy day. It was 23 he who also killed the Egyptian, a giant seven and a half feet high armed with a spear as big as the beam of a loom; he went to meet

---

[a] *Verses 1–9: cp. 2 Sam. 5. 1–3, 6–10.*
[b] *Verses 10–41: cp. 2 Sam. 23. 8–39.*　　[c] saved it: *or* cleared it of the Philistines.
[d] *Or* cistern.

him with a club, snatched the spear out of the Egyptian's hand and killed him with his own weapon. 24 Such were the exploits of Benaiah son of Jehoiada, famous among the 25 heroic thirty.[a] He was more famous than the rest of the thirty, but did not rival the three. David appointed him to his household.

26   These were his valiant heroes: Asahel the brother of Joab, and Elhanan son of Dodo from Bethle- 27 hem; Shammoth from Harod,[b] and 28 Helez from a place unknown; Ira son of Ikkesh from Tekoa, and 29 Abiezer from Anathoth; Sibbecai from Hushah, and Ilai the Aho- 30 hite; Maharai from Netophah, and Heled son of Baanah from Neto- 31 phah; Ithai son of Ribai from Gibeah of Benjamin, and Benaiah 32 from Pirathon; Hurai from the ravines of Gaash, and Abiel from 33 Beth-arabah; Azmoth from Bahurim, and Eliahba from Shaalbon; 34 Hashem the Gizonite, and Jonathan son of Shage the Hararite, 35 Ahiam son of Sacar the Hararite, 36 and Eliphal son of Ur; Hepher from Mecherah, and Ahijah from 37 a place unknown; Hezro from Carmel, and Naarai son of Ezbai; 38 Joel the brother of Nathan, and 39 Mibhar the son of Haggeri; Zelek the Ammonite, and Naharai from Beeroth, armour-bearer to Joab 40 son of Zeruiah; Ira the Ithrite, and 41 Gareb the Ithrite; Uriah the Hit- 42 tite, and Zabad son of Ahlai. Adina son of Shiza the Reubenite, a chief of the Reubenites, was over these 43 thirty. Also Hanan son of Maacah, 44 and Joshaphat the Mithnite; Uzzia from Ashtaroth, Shama and Jeiel the sons of Hotham from 45 Aroer; Jediael son of Shimri, and 46 Joha his brother, the Tizite; Eliel the Mahavite, and Jeribai and Joshaviah sons of Elnaam, and 47 Ithmah the Moabite; Eliel, Obed, and Jasiel, from Zobah.[c]

These are the men who joined 12 David at Ziklag while he was banned from the presence of Saul son of Kish. They ranked among the warriors valiant in battle. They 2 carried bows and could sling stones or shoot arrows with the left hand or the right; they were Benjamites, kinsmen of Saul. The foremost 3 were Ahiezer and Joash, the sons of Shemaah the Gibeathite; Jeziel and Pelet, men of Beth-azmoth; Berachah and Jehu of Anathoth; Ishmaiah the Gibeonite, a hero 4 among the thirty and a chief among them; Jeremiah, Jahaziel, Johanan, and Josabad of Gederah; Eluzai, Jerimoth, Bealiah, She- 5 mariah, and Shephatiah the Haruphite; Elkanah, Isshiah, Azareel, 6 Joezer, Jashobeam, the Korahites; and Joelah and Zebadiah sons of 7 Jeroham, of Gedor.

Some Gadites also joined David 8 at the stronghold in the wilderness, valiant men trained for war, who could handle the heavy shield and spear, grim as lions and swift as gazelles on the hills. Ezer was 9 their chief, Obadiah the second, Eliab the third; Mishmannah the 10 fourth and Jeremiah the fifth; Attai the sixth and Eliel the 11 seventh; Johanan the eighth and 12 Elzabad the ninth; Jeremiah the 13 tenth and Machbanai the eleventh. These were chiefs of the Gadites 14 in the army, the least of them a match for a hundred, the greatest a match for a thousand. These were 15 the men who in the first month crossed the Jordan, which was in full flood in all its reaches, and wrought havoc in the valleys, east and west.

Some men of Benjamin and 16 Judah came to David at the stronghold. David went out to 17 them and said, 'If you come as friends to help me, join me and welcome; but if you come to betray me to my enemies, innocent though

---

[a] *Prob. rdg.; Heb.* three.   [b] *Prob. rdg., cp. 2 Sam.* 23. 25; *Heb.* Haror.
[c] *from Zobah: prob. rdg.; Heb. obscure.*

I am of any crime of violence, may the God of our fathers see and 18 judge.' At that a spirit took possession of Amasai, the chief of the thirty, and he said:

We are on your side, David!
We are with you, son of Jesse!
Greetings, greetings to you
and greetings to your ally!
For your God is your ally.

So David welcomed them and attached them to the columns of his raiding parties.

19   Some men of Manasseh had deserted to David when he went with the Philistines to war against Saul, though he did not, in fact, fight on the side of the Philistines. Their princes brusquely dismissed him, saying to themselves that he would desert them for his master Saul, and that would cost them their 20 heads. The men of Manasseh who deserted to him when he went to Ziklag were these: Adnah, Jozabad, Jediael, Michael, Jozabad, Elihu, and Zilthai, each command-21 ing his thousand in Manasseh. It was they who stood valiantly by David against the raiders, for they were all good fighters, and they were given commands in his forces. 22 From day to day men came in to help David, until he had gathered an immense army.

23   These are the numbers of the armed bands which joined David at Hebron to transfer Saul's sovereignty to him, as the LORD had 24 said: men of Judah, bearing heavy shield and spear, six thousand eight hundred, drafted for active ser-25 vice; of Simeon, fighting men drafted for active service, seven 26 thousand one hundred; of Levi, 27 four thousand six hundred, together with Jehoiada prince of the house of Aaron and three thousand 28 seven hundred men, and Zadok a valiant fighter, with twenty-two 29 officers of his own clan; of Benjamin, Saul's kinsmen, three thou-

sand, though most of them had hitherto remained loyal to the house of Saul; of Ephraim, twenty 30 thousand eight hundred, fighting men, famous in their own clans; of the half tribe of Manasseh, 31 eighteen thousand, who had been nominated to come and make David king; of Issachar, whose 32 tribesmen were skilled in reading the signs of the times to discover what course Israel should follow, two hundred chiefs, with all their kinsmen under their command; of 33 Zebulun, fifty thousand troops well-drilled for battle, armed with every kind of weapon, bold and single-minded; of Naphtali, a 34 thousand officers with thirty-seven thousand men bearing heavy shield and spear; of the Danites, 35 twenty-eight thousand six hundred well-drilled for battle; of 36 Asher, forty thousand troops well-drilled for battle; of the Reuben-37 ites and the Gadites and the half tribe of Manasseh east of Jordan, a hundred and twenty thousand, armed with every kind of weapon.

All these warriors, bold men in 38 battle, came to Hebron, loyally determined to make David king over the whole of Israel; the rest of Israel, too, had but one thought, to make him king. They spent three 39 days there with David, eating and drinking, for their kinsmen made provision for them. Their neigh-40 bours also round about, as far away as Issachar, Zebulun, and Naphtali, brought food on asses and camels, on mules and oxen, supplies of meal, fig-cakes, raisin-cakes, wine and oil, oxen and sheep, in plenty; for there was rejoicing in Israel.

DAVID consulted the officers over 13 units of a thousand and a hundred on every matter brought forward. Then he said to the whole assembly 2 of Israel, 'If you approve, and if the LORD our God opens a way, let us[a] send to our kinsmen who have stayed behind, in all the districts of Israel, and also to the priests and Levites in the cities where they have common lands, bidding them 3 join us. Let us fetch the Ark of our God, for while Saul lived we never 4 resorted to it.' The whole assembly resolved to do this; the entire nation approved it.

5 So David assembled all Israel from the Shihor in Egypt to Lebo-hamath, in order to fetch the Ark 6[b] of God from Kiriath-jearim. Then David and all Israel went up to Baalah, to Kiriath-jearim, which belonged to Judah, to fetch the Ark of God, the LORD enthroned upon the cherubim, the Ark which 7 bore his name.[c] And they conveyed the Ark of God on a new cart from the house of Abinadab, with Uzza 8 and Ahio guiding the cart. David and all Israel danced for joy before God without restraint to the sound of singing, of harps and lutes, of tambourines, and cymbals and 9 trumpets. But when they came to the threshing-floor of Kidon, the oxen stumbled, and Uzza put out 10 his hand to hold the Ark. The LORD was angry with Uzza and struck him down because he had put out his hand to the Ark. So he 11 died there before God. David was vexed because the LORD's anger had broken out upon Uzza, and he called the place Perez-uzza,[d] the 12 name it still bears. David was afraid of God that day and said, 'How can I harbour the Ark of 13 God after this?' So he did not take the Ark with him into the City of David, but turned aside and carried it to the house of Obed-14 edom the Gittite. Thus the Ark of God remained beside the house of Obed-edom, in its tent,[e] for three months, and the LORD blessed the family of Obed-edom and all that he had.

Hiram king of Tyre sent an embassy to David; he sent cedar logs, and masons and carpenters with them to build him a house. David 2 knew by now that the LORD had confirmed him as king over Israel and had made his royal power stand higher for the sake of his people Israel.

David married more wives in 3 Jerusalem, and more sons and daughters were born to him. These 4[g] are the names of the children born to him in Jerusalem: Shammua, Shobab, Nathan, Solomon, Ibhar, 5 Elishua, Elpelet, Nogah, Nepheg, 6 Japhia, Elishama, Beeliada and 7 Eliphelet.

When the Philistines learnt that 8 David had been anointed king over the whole of Israel, they came up in force to seek him out. David, hearing of this, went out to face them. Now the Philistines had 9 come and raided the Vale of Rephaim. So David inquired of God, 10 'If I attack the Philistines, wilt thou deliver them into my hands?' And the LORD answered, 'Go; I will deliver them into your hands.' So he went up and attacked them 11 at Baal-perazim and defeated them there. 'God has used me to break through my enemies' lines,' David said, 'as a river breaks its banks'; that is why the place was named Baal-perazim.[h] The Philistines left 12 their gods behind them there, and by David's orders these were burnt.

The Philistines made another 13 raid on the Vale. Again David in-14 quired of God, and God said to him, 'No, you must go up towards their rear; wheel round without making contact and[i] come upon them

14 1[f]

---

[a] and if...let us: *or* and if it is from the LORD our God, let us seize the opportunity and...   [b] *Verses 6–14: cp.* 2 Sam. 6. 2–11.
[c] which bore his name: *prob. rdg.; Heb. obscure.*   [d] *That is* Outbreak on Uzza.
[e] *Or* in his tent.   [f] *Verses 1–16: cp.* 2 Sam. 5. 11–25.   [g] *Verses 4–7: cp.* 3. 5–8.
[h] *That is* Baal of Break-through.   [i] No...contact and: *or* Do not go up to the attack; withdraw from them and then...

15 opposite the aspens. Then, as soon as you hear a rustling sound in the tree-tops, you shall give battle, for God will have gone out before you to defeat the Philistine army.'

16 David did as God commanded, and they drove the Philistine army in flight all the way from Gibeon to

17 Gezer. So David's fame spread through every land, and the LORD inspired all nations with dread of him.

15 DAVID built himself quarters in the City of David, and prepared a place for the Ark of God and

2 pitched a tent for it. Then he decreed that only Levites should carry the Ark of God, since they had been chosen by the LORD to carry it and to serve him*a* for ever.

3 Next David assembled all Israel at Jerusalem, to bring up the Ark of the LORD to the place he had

4 prepared for it. He gathered together the sons of Aaron and the

5 Levites: of the sons of Kohath, Uriel the chief with a hundred and

6 twenty of his kinsmen; of the sons of Merari, Asaiah the chief with two hundred and twenty of his

7 kinsmen; of the sons of Gershom, Joel the chief with a hundred and

8 thirty of his kinsmen; of the sons of Elizaphan, Shemaiah the chief with two hundred of his kinsmen;

9 of the sons of Hebron, Eliel the

10 chief with eighty of his kinsmen; of the sons of Uzziel, Amminadab the chief with a hundred and twelve of

11 his kinsmen. And David summoned Zadok and Abiathar the priests, together with the Levites, Uriel, Asaiah, Joel, Shemaiah, Eliel, and

12 Amminadab, and said to them, 'You who are heads of families of the Levites, hallow yourselves, you and your kinsmen, and bring up the Ark of the LORD the God of Israel to the place which I have

13 prepared for it. It was because you

were not present the first time, that the LORD our God broke out upon us. For we had not sought his guidance as we should have done.'

So the priests and the Levites hal- 14 lowed themselves to bring up the Ark of the LORD the God of Israel, and the Levites carried the Ark of 15 God, bearing it on their shoulders with poles as Moses had prescribed at the command of the LORD.

David also ordered the chiefs of 16 the Levites to install as musicians those of their kinsmen who were players skilled in making joyful music on their instruments, lutes and harps and cymbals. So the Le- 17 vites installed Heman son of Joel and, from his kinsmen, Asaph son of Berechiah; and from their kinsmen the Merarites, Ethan son of Kushaiah, together with their kins- 18 men of the second degree, Zechariah, Jaaziel, Shemiramoth, Jehiel, Unni, Eliab, Benaiah, Maaseiah, Mattithiah, Eliphelehu, and Mikneiah, and the door-keepers Obededom and Jeiel. They installed the 19 musicians Heman, Asaph, and Ethan to sound the cymbals of bronze; Zechariah, Jaaziel, She- 20 miramoth, Jehiel, Unni, Eliab, Maaseiah, and Benaiah to play on lutes;*b* Mattithiah, Eliphelehu, 21 Mikneiah, Obed-edom, Jeiel, and Azaziah to play on harps.*c* Kena- 22 niah, officer of the Levites, was precentor in charge of the music because of his proficiency. Bere- 23 chiah and Elkanah were doorkeepers for the Ark, while the priests Shebaniah, Jehoshaphat, 24 Nethaneel, Amasai, Zechariah, Benaiah, and Eliezer sounded the trumpets before the Ark of God; and Obed-edom and Jehiah also were door-keepers for the Ark.

Then David and the elders of 25*d* Israel and the captains of units of a thousand went to bring up the Ark of the Covenant of the LORD

---

a Or it.   *b* Prob. rdg.; Heb. adds al alamoth, possibly a musical term.
c Prob. rdg.; Heb. adds al hashsheminith lenasseah, possibly musical terms.
d Verses 25–29: cp. 2 Sam. 6. 12–16.

with much rejoicing from the house
26 of Obed-edom. Because God had
helped the Levites who carried the
Ark of the Covenant of the LORD,
they sacrificed seven bulls and
seven rams.
27   Now David and all the Levites
who carried the Ark, and the
musicians, and Kenaniah the precentor,[a] were arrayed in robes of
fine linen; and David had on a
28 linen ephod. All Israel escorted the
Ark of the Covenant of the LORD
with shouts of acclamation, blowing on horns and trumpets, clash-
ing cymbals and playing on lutes
29 and harps. But as the Ark of the
Covenant of the LORD was entering the city of David, Saul's
daughter Michal looked down
through a window and saw King
David dancing and making merry,
and she despised him in her heart.

16 1[b]   When they had brought in the
Ark of God, they put it inside the
tent that David had pitched for it,
and they offered whole-offerings
and shared-offerings before God.
2 After David had completed these
sacrifices, he blessed the people in
3 the name of the LORD and gave
food, a loaf of bread, a portion of
meat, and a cake of raisins, to each
4 Israelite, man or woman. He appointed certain Levites to serve
before the Ark of the LORD, to
repeat the Name, to confess and to
praise the LORD the God of Israel.
5 Their leader was Asaph; second to
him was Zechariah; then came
Jaaziel,[c] Shemiramoth, Jehiel, Mattithiah, Eliab, Benaiah, Obed-
edom, and Jeiel, with lutes and
harps, Asaph, who sounded the
6 cymbals; and Benaiah and Jahaziel the priests, who blew the
trumpets before the Ark of the Cove-
7 nant of God continuously throughout that day. It was then that
David first ordained the offering of

thanks to the LORD by Asaph and
his kinsmen:

Give the LORD thanks and invoke 8[d]
   him by name,
make his deeds known in the world
   around.
Pay him honour with song and 9
   psalm
and think upon all his wonders.
Exult in his hallowed name; 10
let those who seek the LORD be joyful in heart.
Turn to the LORD, your strength,[e] 11
seek his presence always.
Remember the wonders that he 12
   has wrought,
his portents and the judgements he
   has given,
O offspring of Israel his servants, O 13
   chosen sons of Jacob.

He is the LORD our God; 14
his judgements fill the earth.
He called to mind his covenant 15
   from long ago,[f]
the promise he extended to a thousand generations –
the covenant made with Abraham, 16
his oath given to Isaac,
the decree by which he bound him- 17
   self for Jacob,
his everlasting covenant with
   Israel:
'I will give you the land of Ca- 18
   naan', he said,
'to be your possession, your patrimony.'
A small company it was, 19
few in number, strangers in that
   land,
roaming from nation to nation, 20
from one kingdom to another;
but he let no man ill-treat them, 21
for their sake he admonished kings:
'Touch not my anointed servants, 22
do my prophets no harm.'

Sing to the LORD, all men on earth, 23[g]
proclaim his triumph day by
   day.

[a] the precentor: *prob. rdg.*; *Heb. obscure.*
[c] *Prob. rdg.*, *cp.* 15. 18, 20; *Heb.* Jeiel.
[e] your strength: *or* the symbol of his strength; *lit.* and his strength.
[f] from long ago: *or* for ever.
[b] *Verses 1–3*: *cp.* 2 Sam. 6. 17–19.
[d] *Verses 8–22*: *cp.* Ps. 105. 1–15.
[g] *Verses 23–33*: *cp.* Ps. 96. 1–13.

24 Declare his glory among the nations,
    his marvellous deeds among all peoples.
25 Great is the LORD and worthy of all praise;
    he is more to be feared than all gods.
26 For the gods of the nations are idols every one;
    but the LORD made the heavens.
27 Majesty and splendour attend him,
    might and joy are in his dwelling.

28 Ascribe to the LORD, you families of nations,
    ascribe to the LORD glory and might;
29 ascribe to the LORD the glory due to his name,
    bring a gift and come before him.
    Bow down to the LORD in the splendour of holiness,[a]
30 and dance in his honour, all men on earth.
    He has fixed the earth firm, immovable.
31 Let the heavens rejoice and the earth exult,
    let men declare among the nations, 'The LORD is king.'
32 Let the sea roar and all the creatures in it,
    let the fields exult and all that is in them;
33 then let the trees of the forest shout for joy
    before the LORD when he comes to judge the earth.

34[b] It is good to give thanks to the LORD,
    for his love endures for ever.
35[c] Cry, 'Deliver us, O God our saviour,
    gather us in and save us from the nations
    that we may give thanks to thy holy name
    and make thy praise our pride.'

36 Blessed be the LORD the God of Israel
    from everlasting to everlasting.

And all the people said 'Amen' and 'Praise the LORD.'

37 David left Asaph and his kinsmen there before the Ark of the Covenant of the LORD, to perform regular service before the Ark as each day's duty required; 38 as door-keepers he left Obed-edom son of Jeduthun, and Hosah. (Obed-edom and his kinsmen were sixty-eight in number.) 39 He left Zadok the priest and his kinsmen the priests before the Tabernacle of the LORD at the hill-shrine in Gibeon, 40 to make offerings there to the LORD upon the altar of whole-offering regularly morning and evening, exactly as it is written in the law enjoined by the LORD upon Israel. 41 With them he left Heman and Jeduthun and the other men chosen and nominated to give thanks to the LORD, 'for his love endures for ever.' 42 They had trumpets and cymbals for the players, and the instruments used for sacred song. The sons of Jeduthun kept the gate.

43 So all the people went home, and David returned to greet his household.

17 1[d] As soon as David was established in his house, he said to Nathan the prophet, 'Here I live in a house of cedar, while the Ark of the Covenant of the LORD is housed in curtains.' 2 Nathan answered David, 'Do whatever you have in mind, for God is with you.' 3 But that night the word of God came to Nathan: 4 'Go and say to David my servant, "This is the word of the LORD: It is not you who shall build me a house to dwell in. 5 Down to this day I have never dwelt in a house since I brought Israel up from Egypt; I lived in a tent and a tabernacle.[e] 6 Wherever I journeyed with Israel, did I ever ask any of the judges whom I appointed

---

[a] Or in holy vestments.   [b] Verse 34: cp. Ps. 107. 1.   [c] Verses 35, 36: cp. Ps. 106. 47, 48.   [d] Verses 1–27: cp. 2 Sam. 7. 1–29.   [e] I lived...tabernacle: prob. rdg.; Heb. I have been from tent to tent and from a tabernacle.

shepherds of my people why they had not built me a house of cedar?"

7 Then say this to my servant David: "This is the word of the LORD of Hosts: I took you from the pastures, and from following the sheep, to be prince over my people Israel.

8 I have been with you wherever you have gone, and have destroyed all the enemies in your path. I will make you as famous as the great

9 ones of the earth. I will assign a place for my people Israel; there I will plant them, and they shall dwell in their own land. They shall be disturbed no more, never again shall wicked men wear them down

10 as they did from the time when I first appointed judges over Israel my people, and I will subdue all your enemies. But I will make you great and the LORD shall build up

11 your royal house. When your life ends and you go to join your forefathers, I will set up one of your family, one of your own sons, to succeed you, and I will establish

12 his kingdom. It is he shall build me a house, and I will establish his

13 throne for all time. I will be his father, and he shall be my son. I will never withdraw my love from him as I withdrew it from your

14 predecessor. But I will give him a sure place in my house and kingdom for all time, and his throne shall be established for ever.'"

15 Nathan recounted to David all that had been said to him and all

16 that had been revealed. Then King David went into the presence of the LORD and took his place there and said, 'What am I, LORD God, and what is my family, that thou

17 hast brought me thus far? It was a small thing in thy sight, O God, to have planned for thy servant's house in days long past, and now thou lookest upon me as a man already embarked on a high career,

18 O LORD God. What more can David say to thee of the honour thou hast done thy servant, well

though thou knowest him? For the 19 sake of thy servant, LORD, and according to thy purpose, thou hast brought me to all this greatness. O LORD, we have never heard of 20 one like thee; there is no god but thee. And thy people Israel, to 21 whom can they be compared? Is there any other nation on earth whom God has gone out to redeem from slavery, to make them his people? Thou hast won a name for thyself by great and terrible deeds, driving out nations before thy people whom thou didst redeem from Egypt. Thou hast made thy 22 people Israel thy own for ever, and thou, O LORD, hast become their God. But now, LORD, let what thou 23 hast promised for thy servant and his house stand fast for all time; make good what thou hast said. Let it stand fast, that thy fame 24 may be great for ever, and let men say, "The LORD of Hosts, the God of Israel, is Israel's God." So shall the house of thy servant David be established before thee. Thou, my 25 God, hast shown me thy purpose to build up thy servant's house; therefore I have been able to pray before thee. Thou, O LORD, art God, and 26 thou hast made these noble promises to thy servant; thou hast 27 been pleased to bless thy servant's house, that it may continue always before thee; thou it is who hast blessed it, and it shall be blessed for ever.'

After this David defeated the 18 1[a] Philistines and conquered them, and took from them Gath with its villages; he defeated the Moabites, 2 and they became subject to him and paid him tribute. He also de- 3 feated Hadadezer king of Zobahhamath, who was on his way to set up a monument of victory by the river Euphrates. From him David 4 captured a thousand chariots, seven thousand horsemen and twenty thousand foot; he hamstrung all the chariot-horses, ex-

[a] *Verses 1–13: cp. 2 Sam. 8. 1–14.*

cept a hundred which he retained.

5 When the Aramaeans of Damascus came to the help of Hadadezer king of Zobah, David destroyed 6 twenty-two thousand of them, and established garrisons among these Aramaeans; they became subject to him and paid him tribute. Thus the LORD gave David victory 7 wherever he went. David took the gold quivers borne by Hadadezer's servants and brought them to 8 Jerusalem. He also took a great quantity of bronze[a] from Hadadezer's cities, Tibhath and Kun; from this Solomon made the Sea of bronze,[a] the pillars, and the bronze[a] vessels.

9 When Tou king of Hamath heard that David had defeated the entire army of Hadadezer king of Zobah, 10 he sent his son Hadoram to King David to greet him and to congratulate him on defeating Hadadezer in battle (for Hadadezer had been at war with Tou); and he brought with him vessels of gold, 11 silver, and copper, which King David dedicated to the LORD. He dedicated also the silver and the gold which he had carried away from all the other nations, from Edom and Moab, from the Ammonites and the Philistines, and from Amalek.

12 Edom was defeated by Abishai son of Zeruiah, who destroyed eighteen thousand of them in the 13 Valley of Salt and stationed garrisons in the country. All the Edomites now became subject to David. Thus the LORD gave victory to David wherever he went.

14[b] David ruled over the whole of Israel and maintained law and jus-15 tice among all his people. Joab son of Zeruiah was in command of the army; Jehoshaphat son of Ahi-16 lud was secretary of state; Zadok and Abiathar son of Ahimelech, son of Ahitub,[c] were priests; Shavsha was adjutant-general; Benaiah son of Jehoiada com-17 manded the Kerethite and Pelethite guards. The eldest sons of David were in attendance on the king.

Some time afterwards Nahash 19 1[d] king of the Ammonites died and was succeeded by his son. David 2 said, 'I must keep up the same loyal friendship with Hanun son of Nahash as his father showed me', and he sent a mission to condole with him on the death of his father. But when David's envoys entered the country of the Ammonites to condole with Hanun, the Ammo-3 nite princes said to Hanun, 'Do you suppose David means to do honour to your father when he sends you his condolences? These men of his are spies whom he has sent to find out how to overthrow the country.' So Hanun took 4 David's servants, and he shaved them, cut off half their garments up to the hips, and dismissed them. When David heard how 5 they had been treated, he sent to meet them, for they were deeply humiliated, and ordered them to wait in Jericho and not to return until their beards had grown again. The Ammonites knew that they 6 had brought themselves into bad odour with David, so Hanun and the Ammonites sent a thousand talents of silver to hire chariots and horsemen from Aram-naharaim,[e] Maacah, and Aram-zobah.[f] They 7 hired thirty-two thousand chariots and the king of Maacah and his people, who came and encamped before Medeba, while the Ammonites came from their cities and mustered for battle. When David 8 heard of it, he sent out Joab and

---

[a] Or copper.   [b] *Verses 14–17: cp. 2 Sam. 8. 15–18; 20. 23–26; 1 Kgs. 4. 2–4.*
[c] and Abiathar...Ahitub: *prob. rdg., cp. 2 Sam. 8. 17; Heb.* son of Ahitub and Abimelech son of Abiathar.   [d] *Verses 1–19: cp. 2 Sam. 10. 1–19.*
[e] *That is* Aram of Two Rivers.
[f] Maacah, and Aram-zobah: *prob. rdg.; Heb.* Aram-maacah, and Zobah.

9 all the fighting men. The Ammonites came and took up their position at the entrance to the city, while the allied kings took up theirs 10 in the open country. When Joab saw that he was threatened both front and rear, he detailed some picked Israelite troops and drew them up facing the Aramaeans. 11 The rest of his forces he put under his brother Abishai, who took up a 12 position facing the Ammonites. 'If the Aramaeans prove too strong for me,' he said, 'you must come to my relief; and if the Ammonites prove too strong for you, I will 13 relieve you. Courage! Let us fight bravely for our people and for the cities*a* of our God. And the LORD's 14 will be done.' But when Joab and his men came to close quarters with the Aramaeans, they put 15 them to flight; and when the Ammonites saw them in flight, they too fled before his brother Abishai and entered the city. Then Joab 16 came to Jerusalem. The Aramaeans saw that they had been worsted by Israel, and they sent messengers to summon other Aramaeans from the Great Bend of the Euphrates under Shophach, commander of Hadadezer's army. 17 Their movement was reported to David, who immediately mustered all the forces of Israel, crossed the Jordan and advanced against them and took up battle positions. The Aramaeans likewise took up positions facing David and engaged 18 him, but were put to flight by Israel. David slew seven thousand Aramaeans in chariots and forty thousand infantry, killing Shophach the commander of the 19 army. When Hadadezer's men saw that they had been worsted by Israel, they sued for peace and submitted to David. The Aramaeans were never again willing to give support to the Ammonites.

AT the turn of the year, when 20 1*b* kings take the field, Joab led the army out and ravaged the Ammonite country. He came to Rabbah and laid siege to it, while David remained in Jerusalem; he reduced the city and razed it to the ground. David took the crown from the 2 head of Milcom and found that it weighed a talent of gold and was set with a precious stone, and this he placed on his own head. He also removed a great quantity of booty from the city; he took its inhabitants and set them to work with 3 saws and other iron tools, sharp and toothed. David did this to all the cities of the Ammonites; then he and all his people returned to Jerusalem.

Some time later war with the 4*c* Philistines broke out in Gezer; it was then that Sibbechai of Hushah killed Sippai, a descendant of the Rephaim, and the Philistines were reduced to submission. In another war with the Philistines, El- 5 hanan son of Jair killed Lahmi brother of Goliath of Gath, whose spear had a shaft like a weaver's beam. In yet another war in Gath, 6 there appeared a giant with six fingers on each hand and six toes on each foot, twenty-four in all; he too was descended from the Rephaim, and, when he defied 7 Israel, Jonathan son of David's brother Shimea killed him. These 8 giants were the descendants of the Rephaim in Gath, and they all fell at the hands of David and his men.

Now Satan, setting himself a- 21 1*d* gainst Israel, incited David to count the people. So he instructed 2 Joab and his public officers to go out and number Israel, from Beersheba to Dan, and to report the number to him. Joab answered, 3 'Even if the LORD should increase his people a hundredfold, would not your majesty still be king and

---

a Or altars.
c Verses 4–7: cp. 2 Sam. 21. 18–22.

b Verses 1–3: cp. 2 Sam. 12. 26–31.
d Verses 1–27: cp. 2 Sam. 24. 1–25.

all the people your slaves? Why should your majesty want to do this? It will only bring guilt on 4 Israel.' But Joab was overruled by the king; he set out and went up and down the whole country. He 5 then came to Jerusalem and reported to David the numbers recorded: those capable of bearing arms were one million one hundred thousand in Israel, and four hundred and seventy thousand in 6 Judah. Levi and Benjamin were not counted by Joab, so deep was his repugnance against the king's order.

7 God was displeased with all this and proceeded to punish Israel. 8 David said to God, 'I have done a very wicked thing: I pray thee remove thy servant's guilt, for I have 9 been very foolish.' And the LORD 10 said to Gad, David's seer, 'Go and tell David, "This is the word of the LORD: I have three things to offer you; choose one of them and I will 11 bring it upon you."' So Gad came to David and said to him, 'This is the word of the LORD: "Make your 12 choice: three years of famine, three months of harrying by your foes and close pursuit by the sword of your enemy, or three days of the LORD's own sword, bringing pestilence throughout the country, and the LORD's angel working destruction in all the territory of Israel." Consider now what answer I am to take back to him who sent me.' 13 Thereupon David said to Gad, 'I am in a desperate plight; let me fall into the hands of the LORD, for his mercy is very great; and let me 14 not fall into the hands of man.' So the LORD sent a pestilence throughout Israel, and seventy thousand 15 men of Israel died. And God sent an angel to Jerusalem to destroy it; but, as he was destroying it, the LORD saw and repented of the evil, and said to the destroying angel at the moment when he was standing

beside the threshing-floor of Ornan the Jebusite, 'Enough! Stay your hand.'

When David looked up and saw 16 the angel of the LORD standing between earth and heaven, with his sword drawn in his hand and stretched out over Jerusalem, he and the elders, clothed in sackcloth, fell prostrate to the ground; and 17 David said to God, 'It was I who gave the order to count the people. It was I who sinned, I, the shepherd,*a* who did wrong. But these poor sheep, what have they done? O LORD my God, let thy hand fall upon me and upon my family, but check this plague on the people.'*b*

The angel of the LORD, speaking 18 through the lips of Gad, commanded David to go to the threshing-floor of Ornan the Jebusite and to set up there an altar to the LORD. David went up as Gad had bidden 19 him in the LORD's name. Ornan's 20 four sons who were with him hid themselves, but he was busy threshing his wheat when he turned and saw the angel. As Da- 21 vid approached, Ornan looked up and, seeing the king, came out from the threshing-floor and prostrated himself before him. David 22 said to Ornan, 'Let me have the site of the threshing-floor that I may build on it an altar to the LORD; sell it me at the full price, that the plague which has attacked my people may be stopped.' Ornan 23 answered David, 'Take it and let your majesty do as he thinks fit; see, here are the oxen for whole-offerings, the threshing-sledges for the fuel, and the wheat for the grain-offering; I give you everything.' But King David said to 24 Ornan, 'No, I will pay the full price; I will not present to the LORD what is yours, or offer a whole-offering which has cost me nothing.' So David gave Ornan six 25 hundred shekels of gold for the

---

a I, the shepherd: *prob. rdg.*; *Heb.* doing wrong.
b check...people: *prob. rdg.*; *Heb.* among thy people, not for a plague.

26 site, and built an altar to the LORD there; on this he offered whole-offerings and shared-offerings, and called upon the LORD, who answered him with fire falling from heaven on the altar of whole-27 offering. Then, at the LORD's command, the angel sheathed his sword.

28 It was when David saw that the LORD had answered him at the threshing-floor of Ornan the Jebusite that he offered sacrifice there. 29 The tabernacle of the LORD and the altar of whole-offering which Moses had made in the wilderness were then at the hill-shrine in Gib-30 eon; but David had been unable to go there and seek God's guidance, so shocked and shaken was he at the sight of the angel's sword. 22 Then David said, 'This is to be the house of the LORD God, and this is to be an altar of whole-offering for Israel.'

The temple and its organization

2 DAVID now gave orders to assemble the aliens resident in Israel, and he set them as masons to dress hewn stones and to build the house 3 of God. He laid in a great store of iron to make nails and clamps for the doors, more bronze than could 4 be weighed and cedar-wood without limit; the men of Sidon and Tyre brought David an ample 5 supply of cedar. David said, 'My son Solomon is a boy of tender years, and the house that is to be built to the LORD must be exceedingly magnificent, renowned and celebrated in every land; therefore I must make preparations for it myself.' So David made abundant preparation before his death.

6 He sent for Solomon his son and charged him to build a house for 7 the LORD the God of Israel. 'Solomon, my son,' he said, 'I had intended to build a house in honour of the name of the LORD my God; but the LORD forbade me and said, 8 "You have shed much blood in my sight and waged great wars; for this reason you shall not build a house in honour of my name. But 9[a] you shall have a son who shall be a man of peace; I will give him peace from all his enemies on every side; his name shall be Solomon, 'Man of Peace', and I will grant peace and quiet to Israel in his days. He 10 shall build a house in honour of my name; he shall be my son and I will be a father to him, and I will establish the throne of his sovereignty over Israel for ever." Now, Solo-11 mon my son, the LORD be with you! May you prosper and build the house of the LORD your God, as he promised you should. But may the 12 LORD grant you wisdom and discretion, so that when he gives you authority in Israel you may keep the law of the LORD your God. You will prosper only if you are 13 careful to observe the decrees and ordinances which the LORD enjoined upon Moses for Israel; be strong and resolute, neither fainthearted nor dismayed.

'In spite of all my troubles, I 14 have here ready for the house of the LORD a hundred thousand talents of gold and a million talents of silver, with great quantities of bronze and iron, more than can be weighed; timber and stone, too, I have got ready; and you may add to them. Besides, you have a large 15 force of workmen, masons, sculptors, and carpenters, and countless men skilled in work of every kind, in gold and silver, bronze and iron. 16 So now to work, and the LORD be with you!'

David ordered all the officers of 17 Israel to help Solomon his son: 'Is not the LORD your God with 18 you? Will he not give you peace on every side? For he has given the inhabitants of the land into my power, and they will be subject to

---

a Verse 9: cp. 1 Kgs. 5. 4.

19 the LORD and his people. Devote yourselves, therefore, heart and soul, to seeking guidance of the LORD your God, and set about building his sanctuary, so that the Ark of the Covenant of the LORD and God's holy vessels may be brought into a house built in honour of his name.'

23 David was now an old man, weighed down with years, and he appointed Solomon his son king 2 over Israel. He gathered together all the officers of Israel, the priests, 3 and the Levites. The Levites were enrolled from the age of thirty upwards, their males being thirty-4 eight thousand in all. Of these, twenty-four thousand were to be responsible for the maintenance and service of the house of the LORD, six thousand to act as 5 officers and magistrates, four thousand to be door-keepers, and four thousand to praise the LORD on the musical instruments which David had made for the service of praise. 6 David organized them in divisions, called after Gershon, Kohath, and Merari, the sons of Levi.

7 The sons of Gershon: Laadan 8 and Shimei. The sons of Laadan: Jehiel the chief, Zetham and Joel, 9 three.[a] These were the heads of the families grouped under Laadan. 10 The sons of Shimei: Jahath, Ziza, 11 Jeush and Beriah, four. Jahath was the chief and Ziza the second, but Jeush and Beriah, having few children, were reckoned for duty as a single family. 12 The sons of Kohath: Amram, Izhar, Hebron and Uzziel, four. 13 The sons of Amram: Aaron and Moses. Aaron was set apart, he and his sons in perpetuity, to dedicate the most holy gifts,[b] to burn sacrifices before the LORD, to serve him, and to give the blessing in his name 14 for ever, but the sons of Moses, the man of God, were to keep the name 15 of Levite. The sons of Moses: Ger-

shom and Eliezer. The sons of Ger-16 shom: Shubael the chief. The sons 17 of Eliezer: Rehabiah the chief. Eliezer had no other sons, but Rehabiah had very many. The sons of 18 Izhar: Shelomoth the chief. The 19 sons of Hebron: Jeriah the chief, Amariah the second, Jahaziel the third and Jekameam the fourth. The sons of Uzziel: Micah the chief 20 and Isshiah the second.

The sons of Merari: Mahli and 21 Mushi. The sons of Mahli: Eleazar and Kish. When Eleazar died, he 22 left daughters but no sons, and their cousins, the sons of Kish, married them. The sons of Mushi: 23 Mahli, Eder and Jeremoth, three.

Such were the Levites, grouped 24 by families in the father's line whose heads were entered in the detailed list; they performed duties in the service of the house of the LORD, from the age of twenty upwards. For David said, 'The LORD 25 the God of Israel has given his people peace and has made his abode in Jerusalem for ever. The Levites 26 will no longer have to carry the Tabernacle or any of the vessels for its service.' By these last words of 27 David the Levites were enrolled from the age of twenty upwards. Their duty was to help the sons of 28 Aaron in the service of the house of the LORD: they were responsible for the care of the courts and the rooms, for the cleansing of all holy things, and the general service of the house of God; for the rows of 29 the Bread of the Presence, the flour for the grain-offerings, unleavened wafers, cakes baked on the griddle, and pastry, and for the weights and measures. They were to be on 30 duty continually before the LORD every morning and evening, giving thanks and praise to him, and at 31 every offering of whole-offerings to the LORD, on sabbaths, new moons and at the appointed seasons, according to their prescribed num-

---

[a] *Prob. rdg.*; *Heb. adds* The sons of Shimei: Shelomith, Haziel and Haran, three.
[b] to dedicate...gifts: *or* to be hallowed as most holy.

32 ber. The Levites were to have charge of the Tent of the Presence and of the sanctuary, but the sons of Aaron their kinsmen were charged with the service of worship in the house of the LORD.

24 The divisions of the sons of Aaron: his sons were Nadab and 2 Abihu, Eleazar and Ithamar. Nadab and Abihu died before their father, leaving no sons; therefore Eleazar and Ithamar held the 3 office of priest. David, acting with Zadok of the sons of Eleazar and with Ahimelech of the sons of Ithamar, organized them in divisions for the discharge of the duties of 4 their office. The male heads of families proved to be more numerous in the line of Eleazar than in that of Ithamar, so that sixteen heads of families were grouped under the line of Eleazar and eight under 5 that of Ithamar. He organized them by drawing lots among them, for there were sacred officers[a] and officers of God in the line of Elea- 6 zar and in that of Ithamar. Shemaiah the clerk, a Levite, son of Nethaneel, wrote down the names in the presence of the king, the officers, Zadok the priest, and Ahimelech son of Abiathar, and of the heads of the priestly and levitical families, one priestly family being taken from the line of Eleazar and 7 one from that of Ithamar. The first lot fell to Jehoiarib, the second to 8 Jedaiah, the third to Harim, the 9 fourth to Seorim, the fifth to Mal- 10 chiah, the sixth to Mijamin, the seventh to Hakkoz, the eighth to 11 Abiah, the ninth to Jeshua, the 12 tenth to Shecaniah, the eleventh to 13 Eliashib, the twelfth to Jakim, the thirteenth to Huppah, the four- 14 teenth to Jeshebeab, the fifteenth to Bilgah, the sixteenth to Immer, 15 the seventeenth to Hezir, the 16 eighteenth to Aphses, the nineteenth to Pethahiah, the twentieth 17 to Jehezekel, the twenty-first to Jachin, the twenty-second to Ga- mul, the twenty-third to Delaiah, 18 and the twenty-fourth to Maaziah. This was their order of duty for the 19 discharge of their service when they entered the house of the LORD, according to the rule prescribed for them by their ancestor Aaron, who had received his instructions from the LORD the God of Israel.

Of the remaining Levites: of the 20 sons of Amram: Shubael. Of the sons of Shubael: Jehdeiah. Of Re- 21 habiah: Isshiah, the chief of Rehabiah's sons. Of the line of Izhar: 22 Shelomoth. Of the sons of Shelo- 23 moth: Jahath. The sons of Hebron: Jeriah the chief, Amariah the second, Jahaziel the third and Jekameam the fourth. The sons of Uz- 24 ziel: Micah. Of the sons of Micah: Shamir; Micah's brother: Isshiah. 25 Of the sons of Isshiah: Zechariah. The sons of Merari: Mahli and 26 Mushi and also[b] Jaaziah his son. The sons of Merari: of Jaaziah: 27 Beno, Shoham, Zaccur and Ibri. Of Mahli: Eleazar, who had no 28 sons; of Kish: the sons of Kish: 29 Jerahmeel; and the sons of Mushi: 30 Mahli, Eder and Jerimoth. These were the Levites by families. These 31 also, side by side with their kinsmen the sons of Aaron, cast lots in the presence of King David, Zadok, Ahimelech, and the heads of the priestly and levitical families, the senior and junior houses casting lots side by side.

David and his chief officers as- 25 signed special duties to the sons of Asaph, of Heman, and of Jeduthun, leaders in inspired prophecy to the accompaniment of harps, lutes, and cymbals; the number of the men who performed this work in the temple was as follows. Of the 2 sons of Asaph: Zaccur, Joseph, Nethaniah and Asarelah; these were under Asaph, a leader in inspired prophecy under the king. Of the 3 sons of Jeduthun: Gedaliah, Izri,[c]

---

[a] sacred officers: *or* officers of the sanctuary.
[b] and also: *prob. rdg.*; *Heb.* the sons of.   [c] *Prob. rdg., cp. verse 11*; *Heb.* Zeri.

Isaiah, Shimei, Hashabiah, Mattithiah, these six under their father Jeduthun, a leader in inspired prophecy to the accompaniment of the harp, giving thanks and praise 4 to the Lord. Of the sons of Heman: Bukkiah, Mattaniah, Uzziel, Shubael, Jerimoth, Hananiah, Hanani, Eliathah, Giddalti, Romamti-ezer, Joshbekashah, Mallothi, 5 Hothir, and Mahazioth; all these were sons of Heman the king's seer, given to him through the promises of God for his greater glory. God had given Heman fourteen sons 6 and three daughters, and they all served under their father for the singing in the house of the Lord; they took part in the service of the house of God, with cymbals, lutes, and harps, while Asaph, Jeduthun, and Heman were under the king. 7 Reckoned with their kinsmen, trained singers of the Lord, they brought the total number of skilled musicians up to two hun- 8 dred and eighty-eight. They cast lots for their duties, young and old, master-singer and apprentice side by side.

9   The first lot fell[a] to Joseph: he and his brothers and his sons, twelve.[b] The second to Gedaliah: he and his brothers and his sons, 10 twelve. The third to Zaccur: his 11 sons and his brothers, twelve. The fourth to Izri: his sons and his bro- 12 thers, twelve. The fifth to Nethaniah: his sons and his brothers, 13 twelve. The sixth to Bukkiah: his 14 sons and his brothers, twelve. The seventh to Asarelah: his sons and 15 his brothers, twelve. The eighth to Isaiah: his sons and his brothers, 16 twelve. The ninth to Mattaniah: his 17 sons and his brothers, twelve. The tenth to Shimei: his sons and his 18 brothers, twelve. The eleventh to Azareel: his sons and his brothers, 19 twelve. The twelfth to Hashabiah: his sons and his brothers, twelve. 20 The thirteenth to Shubael: his sons

and his brothers, twelve. The four- 21 teenth to Mattithiah: his sons and his brothers, twelve. The fifteenth 22 to Jeremoth: his sons and his brothers, twelve. The sixteenth to 23 Hananiah: his sons and his brothers, twelve. The seventeenth to 24 Joshbekashah: his sons and his brothers, twelve. The eighteenth 25 to Hanani: his sons and his brothers, twelve. The nineteenth to 26 Mallothi: his sons and his brothers, twelve. The twentieth to Eliathah: 27 his sons and his brothers, twelve. The twenty-first to Hothir: his sons 28 and his brothers, twelve. The 29 twenty-second to Giddalti: his sons and his brothers, twelve. The 30 twenty-third to Mahazioth: his sons and his brothers, twelve. The 31 twenty-fourth to Romamti-ezer: his sons and his brothers, twelve.

26   The divisions of the door-keepers: Korahites: Meshelemiah son of Kore, son of Ebiasaph.[c] Sons of Meshelemiah: Zechariah 2 the eldest, Jediael the second, Zebediah the third, Jathniel the fourth, Elam the fifth, Jehohanan 3 the sixth, Elioenai the seventh. Sons of Obed-edom: Shemaiah the 4 eldest, Jehozabad the second, Joah the third, Sacar the fourth, Nethaneel the fifth, Ammiel the sixth, 5 Issachar the seventh, Peulthai the eighth (for God had blessed him). Shemaiah, his son, was the father 6 of sons who had authority in their family, for they were men of great ability. Sons of Shemaiah: Othni, 7 Rephael, Obed, Elzabad and his brothers Elihu and Semachiah, men of ability. All these belonged 8 to the family of Obed-edom; they, their sons and brothers, were men of ability, fit for service in the temple; total: sixty-two. Sons and 9 brothers of Meshelemiah, all men of ability, eighteen. Sons of Hosah, 10 a Merarite: Shimri the chief (he was not the eldest, but his father had made him chief), Hilkiah the 11

---

[a] *Prob. rdg.; Heb. adds* to Asaph.   [b] he . . . twelve: *prob. rdg.; Heb. om.*
[c] son of Ebiasaph: *prob. rdg.; Heb. from the sons of Asaph.*

second, Tebaliah the third, Zechariah the fourth. Total of Hosah's sons and brothers: thirteen.

12 The male heads of families constituted the divisions of the doorkeepers; their duty was to serve in the house of the LORD side by side 13 with their kinsmen. Young and old, family by family, they cast 14 lots for the gates. The lot for the east gate fell to Shelemiah; then lots were cast for his son Zechariah, a prudent counsellor, and he 15 was allotted the north gate. To Obed-edom was allotted the south gate, and the gatehouse to his sons. 16 Hosah[a] was allotted the west gate, together with the Shallecheth gate on the ascending causeway. Guard 17 corresponded to guard. Six Levites were on duty daily on the east side, four on the north and four on the south, and two at each gatehouse; 18 at the western colonnade there were four at the causeway and two 19 at the colonnade itself. These were the divisions of the door-keepers, Korahites and Merarites.

20 Fellow-Levites were in charge of the stores of the house of God and 21 of the stores of sacred gifts. Of the children of Laadan, descendants of the Gershonite line through Laadan, heads of families in the group 22 of Laadan the Gershonite, Jehiel and[b] his brothers Zetham and Joel were in charge of the stores of the 23 house of the LORD. Of the families of Amram, Izhar, Hebron and Uz- 24 ziel, Shubael son of Gershom, son of Moses, was overseer of the stores. 25 The line of Eliezer his brother: his son Rehabiah, his son Isaiah, his son Joram, his son Zichri, and his 26 son Shelomoth. This Shelomoth and his kinsmen were in charge of all the stores of the sacred gifts dedicated by David the king, the heads of families, the officers over units of a thousand and a hundred, 27 and other officers of the army. They

had dedicated some of the spoils taken in the wars for the upkeep of the house of the LORD. Everything 28 which Samuel the seer, Saul son of Kish, Abner son of Ner, and Joab son of Zeruiah had dedicated, in short every sacred gift, was under the charge of Shelomoth and his kinsmen. Of the family of Izhar, 29 Kenaniah and his sons acted as clerks and magistrates in the secular affairs of Israel. Of the family of 30 Hebron, Hashabiah and his kinsmen, men of ability to the number of seventeen hundred, had the oversight of Israel west of the Jordan, both in the work of the LORD and in the service of the king. Also of the family of Hebron, 31 Jeriah was the chief. (In the fortieth year of David's reign search was made in the family histories of the Hebronites, and men of great ability were found among them at Jazer in Gilead.) His kins- 32 men, all men of ability, two thousand seven hundred of them, heads of families, were charged by King David with the oversight of the Reubenites, the Gadites, and the half tribe of Manasseh, in religious and civil affairs alike.

THE number of the Israelites – 27 that is to say, of the heads of families, the officers over units of a thousand and a hundred, and the clerks who had their share in the king's service in the various divisions which took monthly turns of duty throughout the year – was twenty-four thousand in each division.

First, Jashobeam son of Zabdiel 2 commanded the division for the first month with twenty-four thousand in his division; a member of 3 the house of Perez, he was chief officer of the temple staff for the first month. Eleazar son of[c] Dodai the 4 Ahohite commanded the division

---

[a] *Hosah: prob. rdg.; Heb.* Shuppim and Hosah.
[b] *Jehiel and: prob. rdg.; Heb.* Jehieli. The sons of Jehieli...
[c] *Eleazar son of: prob. rdg., cp.* 11. 12; *Heb. om.*

for the second month with twenty-
5 four thousand in his division. Third,
Benaiah son of Jehoiada the chief
priest, commander of the army, was
the officer for the third month with
twenty-four thousand in his divi-
6 sion (he was the Benaiah who was
one of the thirty warriors and was a
chief among the thirty); but his
son Ammizabad commanded his
7 division. Fourth, Asahel, the brother of Joab, was the officer commanding for the fourth month with
twenty-four thousand in his division; and his successor was Zebe-
8 diah his son. Fifth, Shamhuth the
Zerahite[a] was the officer commanding for the fifth month with twenty-
9 four thousand in his division. Sixth,
Ira son of Ikkesh, a man of Tekoa,
was the officer commanding for the
sixth month with twenty-four
10 thousand in his division. Seventh,
Helez an Ephraimite, from a place
unknown, was the officer commanding for the seventh month
with twenty-four thousand in his
11 division. Eighth, Sibbecai the
Hushathite, of the family of Zerah,
was the officer commanding for the
eighth month with twenty-four
12 thousand in his division. Ninth,
Abiezer, from Anathoth in Benjamin, was the officer commanding
for the ninth month with twenty-
four thousand in his division.
13 Tenth, Maharai the Netophathite,
of the family of Zerah, was the
officer commanding for the tenth
month with twenty-four thousand
14 in his division. Eleventh, Benaiah
the Pirathonite, from Ephraim,
was the officer commanding for the
eleventh month with twenty-four
15 thousand in his division. Twelfth,
Heldai the Netophathite, of the
family of Othniel, was the officer
commanding for the twelfth month
with twenty-four thousand in his
division.
16　　The following were the principal
officers in charge of the tribes of
Israel: of Reuben, Eliezer son of

Zichri; of Simeon, Shephatiah son
of Maacah; of Levi, Hashabiah son 17
of Kemuel; of Aaron, Zadok; of 18
Judah, Elihu a kinsman of David;
of Issachar, Omri son of Michael;
of Zebulun, Ishmaiah son of Oba- 19
diah; of Naphtali, Jerimoth son of
Azriel; of Ephraim, Hoshea son of 20
Azaziah; of the half tribe of Manasseh, Joel son of Pedaiah; of the 21
half of Manasseh in Gilead, Iddo
son of Zechariah; of Benjamin,
Jassiel son of Abner; of Dan, Aza- 22
reel son of Jeroham. These were
the officers in charge of the tribes
of Israel.

David took no census of those 23
under twenty years of age, for the
LORD had promised to make the
Israelites as many as the stars in
the heavens. Joab son of Zeruiah 24
did begin to take a census but he
did not finish it; this brought harm
upon Israel, and the census was not
entered in the chronicle of King
David's reign.

Azmoth son of Adiel was in 25
charge of the king's stores; Jonathan son of Uzziah was in charge
of the stores in the country, in the
cities, in the villages and in the
fortresses. Ezri son of Kelub had 26
oversight of the workers on the
land; Shimei of Ramah was in 27
charge of the vine-dressers, while
Zabdi of Shephem had charge of
the produce of the vineyards for
the wine-cellars. Baal-hanan the 28
Gederite supervised the wild olives
and the sycomore-figs in the Shephelah; Joash was in charge of the
oil-stores. Shitrai of Sharon was in 29
charge of the herds grazing in Sharon, Shaphat son of Adlai of the
herds in the vales. Obil the Ish- 30
maelite was in charge of the camels,
Jehdeiah the Meronothite of the
asses. Jaziz the Hagerite was in 31
charge of the flocks. All these were
the officers in charge of King
David's possessions. David's fav- 32
ourite nephew Jonathan, a counsellor, a discreet and learned man,

---

[a] *the Zerahite: prob. rdg.; Heb. the Izrah.*

and Jehiel the Hachmonite, were
33 tutors to the king's sons. Ahithophel was a king's counsellor; Hushai the Archite was the King's
34 Friend. Ahithophel was succeeded
by Jehoiada son of Benaiah, and
Abiathar. Joab was commander
of the army.

28 DAVID assembled at Jerusalem all
the officers of Israel, the officers
over the tribes, over the divisions
engaged in the king's service, over
the units of a thousand and a hundred, and those in charge of all the
property and the cattle of the king
and of his sons, as well as the
eunuchs, the heroes and all the men
2 of ability. Then King David rose to
his feet and said, 'Hear me, kinsmen and people. I had in mind to
build a house as a resting-place for
the Ark of the Covenant of the
LORD which might serve as a footstool for the feet of our God, and I
3 made preparations to build it. But
God said to me, "You shall not
build a house in honour of my
name, for you have been a fighting
man and you have shed blood."
4 Nevertheless, the LORD the God of
Israel chose me out of all my father's family to be king over Israel
in perpetuity; for it was Judah
that he chose as ruling tribe, and,
out of the house of Judah, my
father's family; and among my
father's sons it was I whom he was
pleased to make king over all Israel.
5 And out of all my sons – for the
LORD gave me many sons – he
chose Solomon to sit upon the
throne of the LORD's sovereignty
6 over Israel; and he said to me, "It
is Solomon your son who shall
build my house and my courts, for
I have chosen him to be a son to me
7 and I will be a father to him. I will
establish his sovereignty in perpetuity, if only he steadfastly
obeys my commandments and my

laws as they are now obeyed."
Now, therefore, in the presence of 8
all Israel, the assembly of the LORD,
and within the hearing of our God,
I bid you all study carefully the
commandments of the LORD your
God, that you may possess this
good land and hand it down as an
inheritance for all time to your
children after you. And you, Solo- 9
mon my son, acknowledge your
father's God and serve him with
whole heart and willing mind, for
the LORD searches all hearts and
discerns every invention of men's
thoughts. If you search for him,
he will let you find him, but if you
forsake him, he will cast you off for
ever. Remember, then, that the 10
LORD has chosen you to build a
house for a sanctuary: be steadfast
and do it.'

David gave Solomon his son the 11
plan of the porch of the temple[a]
and its buildings, strong-rooms,
roof-chambers and inner courts,
and the shrine of expiation;[b] also 12
the plans of all he had in mind for
the courts of the house of the LORD
and for all the rooms around it, for
the stores of God's house and for
the stores of the sacred gifts, for 13
the divisions of the priests and the
Levites, for all the work connected
with the service of the house of the
LORD and for all the vessels used
in its service. He prescribed the 14
weight of gold for all the gold
vessels[c] used in the various services, and the weight of silver[d] for all
the silver vessels used in the various services; and the weight of gold 15
for the gold lamp-stands and their
lamps; and the weight of silver for
the silver lamp-stands, the weight
required for each lamp-stand and
its lamps according to the use of
each; and the weight of gold for 16
each of the tables for the rows of
the Bread of the Presence, and of
silver for the silver tables. He pre- 17

---

[a] of the temple: *prob. rdg.*; *Heb. om.*
[b] the shrine...expiation: *or* the place for the Ark with its cover.
[c] for...vessels: *prob. rdg.*; *Heb.* for gold.   [d] of silver: *prob. rdg.*; *Heb. om.*

scribed also the weight of pure gold for the forks, tossing-bowls and cups, the weight of gold for each of the golden dishes and of silver[a] for 18 each of the silver dishes; the weight also of refined gold for the altar of incense, and of gold for the model of the chariot, that is the cherubim with their wings outspread to screen the Ark of the Covenant of 19 the LORD. 'All this was drafted by the LORD's own hand,' said David; 'my part was to consider the detailed working out of the plan.'

20   Then David said to Solomon his son, 'Be steadfast and resolute and do it; be neither faint-hearted nor dismayed, for the LORD God, my God, will be with you; he will neither fail you nor forsake you, until you have finished all the work needed for the service of the house 21 of the LORD. Here are the divisions of the priests and the Levites, ready for all the service of the house of God. In all the work you will have the help of every willing craftsman for any task; and the officers and all the people will be entirely at your command.'

29   King David then said to the whole assembly, 'My son Solomon is the one chosen by God, Solomon alone, a boy of tender years; and this is a great work, for it is a palace not for man but for the LORD God.
2 Now to the best of my strength I have made ready for the house of my God gold for the gold work, silver for the silver, bronze for the bronze, iron for the iron, and wood for the woodwork, together with cornelian and other gems for setting, stones for mosaic work, precious stones of every sort, and 3 marble in plenty. Further, because I delight in the house of my God, I give my own private store of gold and silver for the house of my God – over and above all the store which I have collected for the sanc-4 tuary – namely three thousand

talents of gold, gold from Ophir, and seven thousand talents of fine silver for overlaying the walls of the buildings, for providing gold 5 for the gold work, silver for the silver, and for any work to be done by skilled craftsmen. Now who is willing to give with open hand to the LORD today?'

Then the heads of families, the 6 officers administering the tribes of Israel, the officers over units of a thousand and a hundred, and the officers in charge of the king's service, responded willingly and gave 7 for the work of the house of God five thousand talents of gold, ten thousand darics, ten thousand talents of silver, eighteen thousand talents of bronze, and a hundred thousand talents of iron. Further, those who possessed pre- 8 cious stones gave them to the treasury of the house of the LORD, into the charge of Jehiel the Gershonite. The people rejoiced at this 9 willing response, because in the loyalty of their hearts they had given willingly to the LORD; King David also was full of joy, and he 10 blessed the LORD in the presence of all the assembly and said, 'Blessed art thou, LORD God of our father Israel, from of old and for ever. Thine, O LORD, is the greatness, 11 the power, the glory, the splendour, and the majesty; for everything in heaven and on earth is thine;[b] thine, O LORD, is the sovereignty, and thou art exalted over all as head. Wealth and 12 honour come from thee; thou rulest over all; might and power are of thy disposing; thine it is to give power and strength to all. And now, we give thee thanks, 13 our God, and praise thy glorious name.

'But what am I, and what is my 14 people, that we should be able to give willingly like this? For everything comes from thee, and it is only of thy gifts that we give to

---

[a] of silver: *prob. rdg.*; *Heb. om.*   [b] is thine: *prob. rdg.*; *Heb. om.*

15 thee. We are aliens before thee and settlers, as were all our fathers; our days on earth are like a shadow, we
16 have no abiding place. O LORD our God, from thee comes all this wealth that we have laid up to build a house in honour of thy holy
17 name, and everything is thine. I know, O my God, that thou dost test the heart and that plain honesty pleases thee; with an honest heart I have given all these gifts willingly, and have rejoiced now to see thy people here present give
18 willingly to thee. O LORD God of Abraham, Isaac and Israel our fathers, maintain this purpose for ever in thy people's thoughts and direct their hearts toward thyself.
19 Grant that Solomon my son may loyally keep thy commandments, thy solemn charge, and thy statutes, that he may fulfil them all and build the palace for which I have prepared.'
20 Then, turning to the whole assembly, David said, 'Now bless the LORD your God.' So all the assembly blessed the LORD the God of their fathers, bowing low and prostrating themselves before the LORD
21 and the king. The next day they sacrificed to the LORD and offered whole-offerings to him, a thousand oxen, a thousand rams, a thousand lambs, with the prescribed drink-

offerings, and abundant sacrifices for all Israel. So they ate and drank 22 before the LORD that day with great rejoicing. They then appointed Solomon, David's son, king a second time and anointed him as the LORD's prince, and Zadok as priest. So Solomon sat on 23 the LORD's throne as king in place of his father David, and he prospered and all Israel obeyed him. All the officers and the warriors, as 24 well as all the sons of King David, swore fealty to King Solomon. The 25 LORD made Solomon stand very high in the eyes of all Israel, and bestowed upon him sovereignty such as no king in Israel had had before him.

David son of Jesse had ruled 26 over the whole of Israel, and the 27 length of his reign over Israel was forty years; he ruled for seven years in Hebron, and for thirty-three in Jerusalem. He died in ripe old age, 28 full of years, wealth, and honour; and Solomon his son ruled in his place. The events of King David's 29 reign from first to last are recorded in the books of Samuel the seer, of Nathan the prophet, and of Gad the seer, with a full account of his 30 reign, his prowess, and of the times through which he and Israel and all the kingdoms of the world had passed.

THE SECOND BOOK OF THE

CHRONICLES

The reign of Solomon and dedication of the temple

1 KING Solomon, David's son, strengthened his hold on the kingdom, for the LORD his God was with him and made him very great.

Solomon spoke to all Israel, to 2 the officers over units of a thousand and of a hundred, the judges and all the leading men of Israel, the heads of families; and he, together 3 with all the assembled people, went to the hill-shrine at Gibeon; for the Tent of God's Presence, which

Moses the LORD's servant had made
4 in the wilderness, was there. (But
David had brought up the Ark of
God from Kiriath-jearim to the
place which he had prepared for it,
for he had pitched a tent for it in
5 Jerusalem.) The altar of bronze
also, which Bezalel son of Uri, son
of Hur, had made, was there in
front of the Tabernacle of the
LORD; and Solomon and the as-
6 sembly resorted to it.[a] There Solomon went up to the altar of bronze
before the LORD in the Tent of the
Presence and offered on it a thou-
7[b] sand whole-offerings. That night
God appeared to Solomon and said,
'What shall I give you? Tell me.'
8 Solomon answered, 'Thou didst
show great and constant love to
David my father and thou hast
9 made me king in his place. Now,
O LORD God, let thy word to David
my father be confirmed, for thou
hast made me king over a people
as numerous as the dust on the
10 earth. Give me now wisdom and
knowledge, that I may lead this
people; for who is fit to govern this
11 great people of thine?' God answered Solomon, 'Because this is
what you desire, because you have
not asked for wealth or possessions
or honour[c] or the lives of your enemies or even long life for yourself,
but have asked for wisdom and
knowledge to govern my people
over whom I have made you king,
12 wisdom and knowledge are given
to you; I shall also give you wealth
and possessions and honour[c] such
as no king has had before you and
13 none shall have after you.' Then
Solomon returned from the hill-
shrine at Gibeon, from before the
Tent of the Presence, to Jerusalem
and ruled over Israel.
14[d]   Solomon got together many chariots and horses; he had fourteen
hundred chariots and twelve thousand horses, and he stabled some

in the chariot-towns and kept
others at hand in Jerusalem. The 15
king made silver and gold as common in Jerusalem as stones, and
cedar as plentiful as sycomore-fig
in the Shephelah. Horses were im- 16
ported from Egypt and Coa for
Solomon; the royal merchants obtained them from Coa by purchase.
Chariots were imported from Egypt 17
for six hundred silver shekels each,
and horses for a hundred and fifty;
in the same way the merchants obtained them for export from all the
kings of the Hittites and the kings
of Aram.

Solomon resolved to build a 2
house in honour of the name of the
LORD, and a royal palace for himself. He engaged seventy thousand 2
hauliers and eighty thousand
quarrymen, and three thousand six
hundred men to superintend them.
Then Solomon sent this message to 3[e]
Huram king of Tyre: 'You were so
good as to send my father David
cedar-wood to build his royal residence. Now I am about to build a 4
house in honour of the name of the
LORD my God and to consecrate it
to him, so that I may burn fragrant
incense in it before him, and present the rows of the Bread of the
Presence regularly, and whole-
offerings morning and evening, on
the sabbaths and the new moons
and the appointed festivals of the
LORD our God; for this is a duty
laid upon Israel for ever. The house 5
I am about to build will be a great
house, because our God is greater
than all gods. But who is able to 6
build him a house when heaven
itself, the highest heaven, cannot
contain him? And who am I that I
should build him a house, except
that I may burn sacrifices before
him? Send me then a skilled crafts- 7
man, a man able to work in gold
and silver, copper[f] and iron, and in
purple, crimson, and violet yarn,

---

[a] resorted to it: or worshipped him.
[c] Or riches.   [d] Verses 14–17: cp. 9. 25–28; 1 Kgs. 10. 26–29.
[e] Verses 3–16: cp. 1 Kgs. 5. 2–11.
[b] Verses 7–12: cp. 1 Kgs. 3. 5–14.
[f] Or bronze.

who is also an expert engraver and will work with my skilled workmen in Judah and in Jerusalem who were provided by David my father.

8 Send me also cedar, pine, and algum timber from Lebanon, for I know that your men are expert in felling the trees of Lebanon; my 9 men will work with yours to get an ample supply of timber ready for me, for the house which I shall build will be great and wonderful. 10 I will supply provisions for your servants, the woodmen who fell the trees: twenty thousand kor of wheat and twenty thousand kor of barley, with twenty thousand bath of wine and twenty thousand bath of oil.'

11 Huram king of Tyre sent this answer by letter to Solomon: 'It is because of the love which the LORD has for his people that he has made 12 you king over them.' The letter went on to say, 'Blessed is the LORD the God of Israel, maker of heaven and earth, who has given to King David a wise son, endowed with intelligence and understanding, to build a house for the LORD 13 and a royal palace for himself. I now send you a skilful and experienced craftsman, master Hu- 14 ram. He is the son of a Danite woman, his father a Tyrian; he is an experienced worker in gold and silver, copper[a] and iron, stone and wood, as well as in purple, violet, and crimson yarn, and in fine linen; he is also a trained engraver who will be able to work with your own skilled craftsmen and those of my lord David your father, to any 15 design submitted to him. Now then, let my lord send his servants the wheat and the barley, the oil and the wine, which he promised; 16 we will fell all the timber in Lebanon that you need and float it as rafts to the roadstead at Joppa, and you will convey it from there up to Jerusalem.'

Solomon took a census of all the 17 aliens resident in Israel, similar to the census which David his father had taken; these were found to be a hundred and fifty-three thousand six hundred. He made seventy 18 thousand of them hauliers and eighty thousand quarrymen, and three thousand six hundred superintendents to make the people work.

Then Solomon began to build 3 the house of the LORD in Jerusalem on Mount Moriah, where the LORD had appeared to his father David, on the site which David had prepared on the threshing-floor of Ornan the Jebusite. He began to 2[b] build in the second month of the fourth year of his reign. These are 3 the foundations which Solomon laid for building the house of God: the length, according to the old standard of measurement, was sixty cubits and the breadth twenty. The 4 vestibule in front of the house[c] was twenty cubits long, spanning the whole breadth of the house, and its height was twenty; on the inside he overlaid it with pure gold. He 5 panelled the large chamber with pine, covered it with fine gold and carved on it palm-trees and chainwork. He adorned the house with 6 precious stones for decoration, and the gold he used was from Parvaim. He covered the whole house with 7 gold, its rafters and frames, its walls and doors; and he carved cherubim on the walls.

He made the Most Holy Place 8 twenty cubits long, corresponding to the breadth of the house, and twenty cubits broad. He covered it all with six hundred talents of fine gold, and the weight of the nails 9 was fifty shekels of gold. He also covered the upper chambers with gold.

In the Most Holy Place he carved 10[d] two images of cherubim and overlaid them with gold. The total span 11

---

[a] Or bronze.
[c] house: *prob. rdg.*; *Heb.* length.

[b] *Verses 2–4: cp. 1 Kgs. 6. 1–3.*
[d] *Verses 10–13: cp. 1 Kgs. 6. 23–28.*

of the wings of the cherubim was twenty cubits. A wing of the one cherub extended five cubits to reach the wall of the house, while its other wing reached out five cubits to meet a wing of the other 12 cherub. Similarly, a wing of the second cherub extended five cubits to reach the other wall of the house, while its other wing met a wing of 13 the first cherub. The wings of these cherubim extended twenty cubits; they stood with their feet on the ground, facing the outer chamber. 14 He made the Veil of violet, purple, and crimson yarn, and fine linen, and embroidered cherubim on it.

15[a] In front of the house he erected two pillars eighteen cubits high, with an architrave five cubits high 16 on top of each. He made chain-work like a necklace[b] and set it round the tops of the pillars, and he carved a hundred pomegranates 17 and set them in the chain-work. He erected the two pillars in front of the temple, one on the right and one on the left; the one on the right he named Jachin[c] and the one on the left Boaz.[d]

4 He then made an altar of bronze, twenty cubits long, twenty cubits 2[e] broad, and ten cubits high. He also made the Sea of cast metal; it was round in shape, the diameter from rim to rim being ten cubits; it stood five cubits high, and it took a line thirty cubits long to go 3 round it. Under the Sea, on every side, completely surrounding the thirty[f] cubits of its circumference, were what looked like gourds,[g] two rows of them, cast in one piece with 4 the Sea itself. It was mounted on twelve oxen, three facing north, three west, three south, and three east, their hind quarters turned in-

wards; the Sea rested on top of them. Its thickness was a hand- 5 breadth; its rim was made like that of a cup, shaped like the calyx of a lily; when full it held three thousand bath. He also made ten basins 6 for washing, setting five on the left side and five on the right; in these they rinsed everything used for the whole-offering. The Sea was made for the priests to wash in.

He made ten golden lamp-stands 7 in the prescribed manner and set them in the temple, five on the right side and five on the left. He 8 also made ten tables and placed them in the temple, five on the right and five on the left; and he made a hundred golden tossing-bowls. He made the court of the 9 priests and the great precinct and the doors for it, and overlaid the doors of both with copper; he put 10 the Sea at the right side, at the south-east corner of the temple.

Huram made the pots, the 11[h] shovels, and the tossing-bowls. So he finished the work which he had undertaken for King Solomon on the house of God. The two pillars; 12 the two bowl-shaped capitals[i] on the tops of the pillars; the two ornamental networks to cover the two bowl-shaped capitals on the tops of the pillars; the four hundred pome- 13 granates for the two networks, two rows of pomegranates for each network, to cover the two bowl-shaped capitals on the two[j] pillars; the 14 ten[k] trolleys and the ten[k] basins on the trolleys; the one Sea and the 15 twelve oxen which supported it; the pots, the shovels, and the 16 tossing-bowls[l] – all these[m] objects master Huram made of bronze, burnished work for King Solomon for the house of the LORD. In the 17

---

[a] Verses 15–17: cp. 1 Kgs. 7. 15–21.
[c] Or Jachun, meaning It shall stand.
[e] Verses 2–5: cp. 1 Kgs. 7. 23–26.
[g] Prob. rdg., cp. 1 Kgs. 7. 24; Heb. oxen.
[i] bowl-shaped capitals: prob. rdg., cp. 1 Kgs. 7. 41; Heb. the bowls and the capitals.
[j] two: prob. rdg., cp. 1 Kgs. 7. 42; Heb. surface of the. [k] the ten: prob. rdg., cp. 1 Kgs. 7. 43; Heb. he made the...
7. 45; Heb. forks.

[b] necklace: prob. rdg.; Heb. obscure.
[d] Or Booz, meaning In strength.
[f] Prob. rdg.; Heb. ten.
[h] 4. 11 – 5. 1: cp. 1 Kgs. 7. 40–51.

[l] tossing-bowls: prob. rdg., cp. 1 Kgs.
[m] Prob. rdg., cp. 1 Kgs. 7. 45; Heb. their.

Plain of the Jordan the king cast them, in the foundry between 18 Succoth and Zeredah. Solomon made great quantities of all these objects; the weight of the copper[a] used was beyond reckoning.

19 Solomon made also all the furnishings for the house of God: the golden altar, the tables upon which was set the Bread of the Presence, 20 the lamp-stands of red gold whose lamps burned before the inner shrine in the prescribed manner, 21 the flowers and lamps and tongs of 22 solid gold, the snuffers, tossing-bowls, saucers, and firepans of red gold, and, at the entrance to the house, the inner doors leading to the Most Holy Place and those leading to the sanctuary, of gold.

5 When all the work which Solomon did for the house of the LORD was completed, he brought in the sacred treasures of his father David, the silver, the gold, and the vessels, and deposited them in the storehouses of the house of God.

2[b] THEN Solomon summoned the elders of Israel, and all the heads of the tribes who were chiefs of families in Israel, to assemble in Jerusalem, in order to bring up the Ark of the Covenant of the LORD from the City of David, which is 3 called Zion. All the men of Israel assembled in the king's presence at the pilgrim-feast in the seventh 4 month. When the elders of Israel had all come, the Levites took the 5 Ark and carried it up with the Tent of the Presence and all the sacred furnishings of the Tent: it was the priests and the Levites together 6 who carried them up. King Solomon and the whole congregation of Israel, assembled with him before the Ark, sacrificed sheep and oxen in numbers past counting or reckon-7 ing. Then the priests brought in the Ark of the Covenant of the LORD to

its place, the inner shrine of the house, the Most Holy Place, beneath the wings of the cherubim. The cherubim spread their wings 8 over the place of the Ark, and formed a covering above the Ark and its poles. The poles projected, 9 and their ends could be seen from the Holy Place immediately in front of the inner shrine, but from nowhere else outside; they are there to this day. There was no-10 thing inside the Ark but the two tablets which Moses had put there at Horeb, the tablets of the covenant[c] which the LORD made with the Israelites when they left Egypt.

Now when the priests came out 11 of the Holy Place (for all the priests who were present had hallowed themselves without keeping to their divisions), all the levitical 12 singers, Asaph, Heman, and Jeduthun, their sons and their kinsmen, clothed in fine linen, stood with cymbals, lutes, and harps, to the east of the altar, together with a hundred and twenty priests who blew trumpets. Now the trum-13 peters and the singers joined in unison to sound forth praise and thanksgiving to the LORD, and the song was raised with trumpets, cymbals, and musical instruments, in praise of the LORD, because 'that[d] is good, for his love endures for ever'; and the house was filled with the cloud of the glory of the LORD. The priests could not con-14 tinue to minister because of the cloud, for the glory of the LORD filled the house of God. Then Solo-6 1[e] mon said:

O LORD who hast chosen to dwell in thick darkness,
here have I built thee a lofty 2 house,
a habitation for thee to occupy for ever.

---

[a] Or bronze.
[b] *Verses 2–10: cp. 1 Kgs. 8. 1–9.*
[c] the tablets of the covenant: *prob. rdg.*, *cp. 1 Kgs. 8. 9; Heb. om.*
[d] Or he.
[e] *Verses 1–39: cp. 1 Kgs. 8. 12–50*

3　And as they stood waiting, the king turned round and blessed all 4 the assembly of Israel in these words: 'Blessed be the LORD the God of Israel who spoke directly to my father David and has himself fulfilled his promise. For he said, 5 "From the day when I brought my people out of Egypt, I chose no city out of all the tribes of Israel where I should build a house for my Name to be there, nor did I choose any man to be prince over my peo- 6 ple Israel. But I chose Jerusalem for my Name to be there, and I chose David to be over my people 7 Israel." My father David had in mind to build a house in honour of the name of the LORD the God of 8 Israel, but the LORD said to him, "You purposed to build a house in honour of my name; and your pur- 9 pose was good. Nevertheless, you shall not build it; but the son who is to be born to you, he shall build the house in honour of my name." 10 The LORD has now fulfilled his pro- mise: I have succeeded my father David and taken his place on the throne of Israel, as the LORD pro- mised; and I have built the house in honour of the name of the LORD 11 the God of Israel. I have installed there the Ark containing the cove- nant of the LORD which he made with Israel.'

12　Then Solomon, standing in front of the altar of the LORD, in the pre- sence of the whole assembly of 13 Israel, spread out his hands. He had made a bronze[a] platform, five cubits long, five cubits broad, and three cubits high, and had placed it in the centre of the precinct. He mounted it and knelt down in the presence of the assembly, and, spreading out his hands towards 14 heaven, he said, 'O LORD God of Israel, there is no god like thee in heaven or on earth, keeping cove- nant with thy servants and show- ing them constant love while they continue faithful to thee in heart and soul. Thou hast kept thy pro- 15 mise to thy servant David my father; by thy deeds this day thou hast fulfilled what thou didst say to him in words. Now, therefore, 16 O LORD God of Israel, keep this promise of thine to thy servant David my father: "You shall never want for a man appointed by me to sit on the throne of Israel, if only your sons look to their ways and conform to my law, as you have done in my sight." And now, O 17 LORD God of Israel, let the word which thou didst speak to thy ser- vant David be confirmed.

'But can God indeed dwell with 18 man on the earth? Heaven itself, the highest heaven, cannot con- tain thee; how much less this house that I have built! Yet attend to the 19 prayer and the supplication of thy servant, O LORD my God; listen to the cry and the prayer which thy servant utters before thee, that 20 thine eyes may ever be upon this house day and night, this place of which thou didst say, "It shall re- ceive my Name"; so mayest thou hear thy servant when he prays towards this place. Hear thou the 21 supplications of thy servant and of thy people Israel when they pray towards this place. Hear from hea- ven thy dwelling and, when thou hearest, forgive.

'When a man wrongs his neigh- 22 bour and he is adjured to take an oath, and the adjuration is made before thy altar in this house, then 23 do thou hear from heaven and act: be thou thy servants' judge, re- quiting the guilty man and bring- ing his deeds upon his own head, acquitting the innocent and re- warding him as his innocence may deserve.

'When thy people Israel are de- 24 feated by an enemy because they have sinned against thee, and they turn back to thee, confessing thy name and making their prayer and supplication before thee in this

---

[a] *Or* copper.

25 house, do thou hear from heaven; forgive the sin of thy people Israel and restore them to the land which thou gavest to them and to their forefathers.

26 'When the heavens are shut up and there is no rain, because thy servant and thy people Israel have sinned against thee, and when they pray towards this place, confessing thy name and forsaking their sin 27 when they feel thy punishment, do thou hear in heaven and forgive their sin; so mayest thou teach them the good way which they should follow, and grant rain to thy land which thou hast given to thy people as their own possession.

28 'If there is famine in the land, or pestilence, or black blight or red, or locusts new-sloughed or fully grown, or if their enemies besiege them in any*a* of their cities, or if plague or sickness befall them, 29 then hear the prayer or supplication of every man among thy people Israel, as each one, prompted by his own suffering and misery, spreads out his hands towards this 30 house; hear it from heaven thy dwelling and forgive. And, as thou knowest a man's heart, reward him according to his deeds, for thou alone knowest the hearts of all 31 men; and so they will fear and obey thee all their lives in the land thou gavest to our forefathers.

32 'The foreigner too, the man who does not belong to thy people Israel, but has come from a distant land because of thy great fame and thy strong hand and arm outstretched, when he comes and 33 prays towards this house, hear from heaven thy dwelling and respond to the call which the foreigner makes to thee, so that like thy people Israel all peoples of the earth may know thy fame and fear thee, and learn that this house which I have built bears thy name.

34 'When thy people go to war with their enemies, wherever thou dost send them, and they pray to thee, turning towards this city which thou hast chosen and towards this house which I have built in honour of thy name, do thou from heaven 35 hear their prayer and supplication, and grant them justice.

36 'Should they sin against thee (and what man is free from sin?) and shouldst thou in thy anger give them over to an enemy, who carries them captive to a land far or near; if in the land of their cap- 37 tivity they learn their lesson and turn back and make supplication to thee in that land and say, "We have sinned and acted perversely and wickedly", if they turn back to 38 thee with heart and soul in the land of their captivity to which they have been taken, and pray, turning towards their land which thou gavest to their forefathers and towards this city which thou didst choose and this house which I have built in honour of thy name; then 39 from heaven thy dwelling do thou hear their prayer and supplications and grant them justice. Forgive thy people their sins against thee. Now, O my God, let thine eyes be 40 open and thy ears attentive to the prayer made in this place. Arise 41 now, O LORD God, and come to thy place of rest, thou and the Ark of thy might. Let thy priests, O LORD God, be clothed with salvation and thy saints rejoice in prosperity. O LORD God, reject not thy an- 42 ointed prince; remember thy servant David's loyal service.'*b*

When Solomon had finished this 7 prayer, fire came down from heaven and consumed the whole-offering and the sacrifices, while the glory of the LORD filled the house. The priests were unable to 2 enter the house of the LORD because the glory of the LORD had filled it. All the Israelites were 3

a in any: *prob. rdg.*; *Heb.* in the land.
b thy servant...service: *or* thy constant love for David thy servant.

watching as the fire came down with the glory of the LORD on the house, and where they stood on the paved court they bowed low to the ground and worshipped and gave thanks to the LORD, because 'that[a] is good, for his love endures for ever.'

4 Then the king and all the people offered sacrifice before the LORD.

5 King Solomon offered a sacrifice of twenty-two thousand oxen and a hundred and twenty thousand sheep; in this way the king and all the people dedicated the house of

6 God. The priests stood at their appointed posts; so too the Levites with their musical instruments for the LORD's service, which King David had made for giving thanks to the LORD – 'for his love endures for ever' – whenever he rendered praise with their help; opposite them, the priests sounded their trumpets; and all the Israelites were standing there.

7[b] Then Solomon consecrated the centre of the court which lay in front[c] of the house of the LORD; there he offered the whole-offerings and the fat portions of the shared-offerings, because the bronze altar which he had made could not take the whole-offering, the grain-offer-

8 ing, and the fat portions. So Solomon and all Israel with him, a very great assembly from Lebo-hamath to the Torrent of Egypt, celebrated the pilgrim-feast at that time for

9 seven days. On the eighth day they held a closing ceremony; for they had celebrated the dedication of the altar for seven days; the pil-

10 grim-feast lasted seven days. On the twenty-third day of the seventh month he sent the people to their homes, happy and glad at heart for all the prosperity granted by the LORD to David and Solomon and to his people Israel.

11 When Solomon had finished the house of the LORD and the royal palace and had successfully carried out all that he had planned for the house of the LORD and the palace, the LORD appeared to him by 12 night and said, 'I have heard your prayer and I have chosen this place to be my place of sacrifice. When I shut up the heavens and 13 there is no rain, or command the locusts to consume the land, or send a pestilence against my people, if my people whom I have 14 named my own submit and pray to me and seek me and turn back from their evil ways, I will hear from heaven and forgive their sins and heal their land. Now my eyes 15 will be open and my ears attentive to the prayers which are made in this place. I have chosen and con- 16 secrated this house, that my Name may be there for all time and my eyes and my heart be fixed on it for ever. And if you, on your part, live 17 in my sight as your father David lived, doing all I command you, and observing my statutes and my judgements, then I will establish 18 your royal throne, as I promised by a covenant granted to your father David when I said, "You shall never want for a man to rule over Israel." But if you turn away and 19 forsake my statutes and my commandments which I have set before you, and if you go and serve other gods and prostrate yourselves before them, then I will uproot you 20 from my land which I gave you, I will reject this house which I have consecrated in honour of my name, and make it a byword and an object-lesson among all peoples. And this house will become a ruin; 21 every passer-by will be appalled at the sight of it, and they will ask, "Why has the LORD so treated this land and this house?" The answer 22 will be, "Because they forsook the LORD the God of their fathers, who brought them out of Egypt, and clung to other gods, prostrating

---

[a] *Or* he.
[b] *Verses 7–22: cp. 1 Kgs. 8. 64 – 9. 9.*
[c] *Or* to the east.

themselves before them and serving them; that is why the LORD has brought this great evil on them.'"

8 1[a] Solomon had taken twenty years to build the house of the LORD and 2 his own palace, and he rebuilt the cities which Huram had given him 3 and settled Israelites in them. He went to Hamath-zobah and seized 4 it, and rebuilt Tadmor in the wilderness and all the store-cities which he had built in Hamath. 5 He also built Upper Beth-horon and Lower Beth-horon as fortified cities with walls and barred gates, 6 and Baalath, as well as all his store-cities, and all the towns where he quartered his chariots and horses; and he carried out all his cherished plans for building in Jerusàlem, in the Lebanon, and throughout his 7 whole dominion. All the survivors of the Hittites, Amorites, Perizzites, Hivites, and Jebusites, who 8 did not belong to Israel – that is their descendants who survived in the land, wherever the Israelites had been unable to exterminate them – were employed by Solomon on forced labour, as they still 9 are. He put none of the Israelites to forced labour for his public works; they were his fighting men, his captains and lieutenants, and the commanders of his chariots and of 10 his cavalry. These were King Solomon's officers, two hundred and fifty of them, in charge of the foremen who superintended the people.

11 Solomon brought Pharaoh's daughter up from the City of David to the house he had built for her, for he said, 'No wife of mine shall live in the house of David king of Israel, because this place which the Ark of the LORD has entered is[b] holy.'

12 Then Solomon offered whole-offerings to the LORD on the altar which he had built to the east of the vestibule, according to what 13 was required for each day, making offerings according to the law of Moses for the sabbaths, the new moons, and the three annual appointed feasts – the pilgrim-feasts of Unleavened Bread, of Weeks, and of Tabernacles.[c] Following the 14 practice of his father David, he drew up the roster of service for the priests and that for the Levites for leading the praise and for waiting upon the priests, as each day required, and that for the doorkeepers at each gate; for such was the instruction which David the man of God had given. The in- 15 structions which David had given concerning the priests and the Levites and concerning the treasuries were not forgotten.

By this time all Solomon's work 16 was achieved, from the foundation of the house of the LORD to its completion; the house of the LORD was perfect. Then Solomon went to 17 Ezion-geber and to Eloth on the coast of Edom, and Huram sent 18 ships under the command of his own officers and manned by crews of experienced seamen; and these, in company with Solomon's servants, went to Ophir and brought back four hundred and fifty talents of gold, which they delivered to King Solomon.

THE queen of Sheba heard of 9 1[d] Solomon's fame and came to test him with hard questions. She arrived in Jerusalem with a very large retinue, camels laden with spices, gold in abundance, and precious stones. When she came to Solomon, she told him everything she had in her mind, and Solomon 2 answered all her questions; not one of them was too abstruse for him to answer. When the queen of Sheba 3 saw the wisdom of Solomon, the house which he had built, the food 4

---

[a] Verses 1–18: cp. 1 Kgs. 9. 10–28.
[b] this place which...is: *prob. rdg.*; *Heb.* those which...are.   [c] Or Booths.
[d] Verses 1–24: cp. 1 Kgs. 10. 1–25.

on his table, the courtiers sitting round him, his attendants and his cupbearers in their livery standing behind, and the stairs by which he went up to the house of the LORD, there was no more spirit left in her.

5 Then she said to the king, 'The report which I heard in my own country about you and your wis-
6 dom was true, but I did not believe what they told me until I came and saw for myself. Indeed, I was not told half of the greatness of your wisdom; you surpass the report
7 which I had of you. Happy are your wives, happy these courtiers of yours who wait on you every day
8 and hear your wisdom! Blessed be the LORD your God who has delighted in you and has set you on his throne as his king; because in his love your God has elected Israel to make it endure for ever, he has made you king over it to maintain
9 law and justice.' Then she gave the king a hundred and twenty talents of gold, spices in great abundance, and precious stones. There had never been any spices to equal those which the queen of Sheba gave to King Solomon.

10 Besides all this, the servants of Huram and of Solomon, who had brought gold from Ophir, brought also cargoes of algum wood and
11 precious stones. The king used the wood to make stands for the house of the LORD and for the royal palace, as well as harps and lutes for the singers. The like of them had never before been seen in the land of Judah.

12 King Solomon gave the queen of Sheba all she desired, whatever she asked, besides his gifts in return for*a* what she had brought him. Then she departed and returned with her retinue to her own land.

13 Now the weight of gold which Solomon received yearly was six
14 hundred and sixty-six talents, in addition to the tolls levied on merchants and on traders who imported goods; all the kings of Arabia and the regional governors also*b* brought gold and silver to the king.

15 King Solomon made two hundred shields of beaten gold, and six hundred shekels of gold went to the making of each one; he also
16 made three hundred bucklers of beaten gold, and three hundred shekels of gold went to the making of each buckler. The king put these into the House of the Forest of Lebanon.

17 The king also made a great throne of ivory and overlaid it with
18 pure gold. Six steps and a footstool for the throne were all encased in gold. There were arms on each side of the seat, with a lion standing beside each of them, and twelve
19 lions stood on the six steps, one at either end of each step. Nothing like it had ever been made for any
20 monarch. All Solomon's drinking vessels were of gold, and all the plate in the House of the Forest of Lebanon was of red gold; silver was reckoned of no value in the
21 days of Solomon. The king had a fleet of ships plying to Tarshish with Huram's men; once every three years this fleet of merchantmen came home, bringing gold and silver, ivory, apes, and monkeys.

22 Thus King Solomon outdid all the kings of the earth in wealth and
23 wisdom, and all the kings of the earth courted him, to hear the wisdom which God had put in his
24 heart. Each brought his gift with him, vessels of silver and gold, garments, perfumes and spices, horses and mules, so much year by year.

25*c* Solomon had standing for four thousand horses and chariots, and twelve thousand cavalry horses, and he stabled some in the chariot-towns and kept others at hand in

---

a his gifts...for: *prob. rdg.*; *Heb. om.*
b all...also: *or* and on all the kings of Arabia and the regional governors who...
c *Verses 25–28*: cp. 1. 14–17; 1 Kgs. 10. 26–29.

26 Jerusalem. He ruled over all the kings from the Euphrates to the land of the Philistines and the
27 border of Egypt. He made silver as common in Jerusalem as stones, and cedar as plentiful as sycomore-
28 fig in the Shephelah. Horses were imported from Egypt and from all countries for Solomon.

29ᵃ The rest of the acts of Solomon's reign, from first to last, are recorded in the history of Nathan the prophet, in the prophecy of Ahijah of Shiloh, and in the visions of Iddo the seer concerning Jero-
30 boam son of Nebat. Solomon ruled in Jerusalem over the whole of
31 Israel for forty years. Then he rested with his forefathers and was buried in the city of David his father, and he was succeeded by his son Rehoboam.

The kings of Judah from Rehoboam to Ahaz

10 1ᵇ REHOBOAM went to Shechem, for all Israel had gone there to
2 make him king. When Jeroboam son of Nebat heard of it in Egypt, where he had taken refuge to escape Solomon, he returned from
3 Egypt. They now recalled him, and he and all Israel came to Reho-
4 boam and said, 'Your father laid a cruel yoke upon us; but if you will now lighten the cruel slavery he imposed on us and the heavy yoke he laid on us, we will serve you.'
5 'Give me three days,' he said, 'and come back again.' So the people
6 went away. King Rehoboam then consulted the elders who had been in attendance on his father Solomon while he lived: 'What answer do you advise me to give to this
7 people?' And they said, 'If you show yourself well-disposed to this people and gratify them by speaking kindly to them, they will be
8 your servants ever after.' But he rejected the advice which the

elders gave him. He next consulted those who had grown up with him, the young men in attendance, and 9 asked them, 'What answer do you advise me to give to this people's request that I should lighten the yoke which my father laid on them?' The young men replied, 10 'Give this answer to the people who say that your father made their yoke heavy and ask you to lighten it; tell them: "My little finger is thicker than my father's loins. My father laid a heavy yoke 11 on you; I will make it heavier. My father used the whip on you; but I will use the lash."' Jeroboam and 12 the people all came back to Rehoboam on the third day, as the king had ordered. And the king gave 13 them a harsh answer. He rejected the advice which the elders had given him and spoke to the people 14 as the young men had advised: 'My father made your yoke heavy; I will make it heavier. My father used the whip on you; but I will use the lash.' So the king would not 15 listen to the people; for the LORD had given this turn to the affair, in order that the word he had spoken by Ahijah of Shiloh to Jeroboam son of Nebat might be fulfilled.

When all Israel sawᶜ that the 16 king would not listen to them, they answered:

What share have we in David?
We have no lot in the son of Jesse.
Away to your homes, O Israel;
now see to your own house, David.

So all Israel went to their homes, and Rehoboam ruled over those 17 Israelites who lived in the cities of Judah.

Then King Rehoboam sent out 18 Hadoram, the commander of the forced levies, but the Israelites stoned him to death; whereupon King Rehoboam mounted his chariot in haste and fled to Jerusalem. From that day to this, Israel 19

ᵃ Verses 29–31: cp. 1 Kgs. 11. 41–43.
ᶜ saw: prob. rdg., cp. 1 Kgs. 12. 16; Heb. om.

ᵇ Verses 1–19: cp. 1 Kgs. 12. 1–19.

has been in rebellion against the house of David.

11 1[a] When Rehoboam reached Jerusalem, he assembled the tribes of Judah and Benjamin, a hundred and eighty thousand chosen warriors, to fight against Israel and 2 recover his kingdom. But the word of the LORD came to Shemaiah the 3 man of God: 'Say to Rehoboam son of Solomon, king of Judah, and to all the Israelites in Judah and 4 Benjamin, "This is the word of the LORD: You shall not go up to make war on your kinsmen. Return to your homes, for this is my will."' So they listened to the word of the LORD and abandoned their campaign against Jeroboam.

5 Rehoboam resided in Jerusalem and built up the defences of certain 6 cities in Judah. The cities in Judah and Benjamin which he fortified were Bethlehem, Etam, Tekoa, 7, 8 Beth-zur, Soco, Adullam, Gath, 9 Mareshah, Ziph, Adoraim, La- 10 chish, Azekah, Zorah, Aijalon, and 11 Hebron. He strengthened the fortifications of these fortified cities, and put governors in them, as well as supplies of food, oil, and wine. 12 Also he stored shields and spears in every one of the cities, and strengthened their fortifications. Thus he retained possession of Judah and Benjamin.

13 Now the priests and the Levites throughout the whole of Israel resorted to Rehoboam from all their 14 territories; for the Levites had left all their common land and their own patrimony and had gone to Judah and Jerusalem, because Jeroboam and his successors rejected their services as priests of 15 the LORD, and he appointed his own priests for the hill-shrines, for the demons,[b] and for the calves 16 which he had made. Those, from all the tribes of Israel, who were resolved to seek the LORD the God of Israel followed the Levites to

Jerusalem to sacrifice to the LORD the God of their fathers. So they 17 strengthened the kingdom of Judah and for three years made Rehoboam son of Solomon secure, because he followed the example of David and Solomon during that time.

Rehoboam married Mahalath, 18 whose father was Jerimoth son of David and whose mother was Abihail daughter of Eliab son of Jesse. His sons by her were: Jeush, She- 19 mariah and Zaham. Next he 20 married Maacah granddaughter of Absalom, who bore him Abijah, Attai, Ziza and Shelomith. Of all 21 his wives and concubines, Rehoboam loved Maacah most; he had in all eighteen wives and sixty concubines and became the father of twenty-eight sons and sixty daughters. He appointed Abijah son of 22 Maacah chief among his brothers, making him crown prince and planning to make him his successor on the throne. He showed discre- 23 tion in detailing his sons to take charge of all the fortified cities throughout the whole territory of Judah and Benjamin; he also made generous provision for them and procured them[e] wives.

When the kingdom of Reho- 12 boam was on a firm footing and he became strong, he forsook the law of the LORD, he and all Israel with him. In the fifth year of Reho- 2 boam's reign, because of this disloyalty to the LORD, Shishak king of Egypt attacked Jerusalem with 3 twelve hundred chariots and sixty thousand horsemen, and brought with him from Egypt an innumerable following of Libyans, Sukkites, and Cushites.[d] He captured 4 the fortified cities of Judah and reached Jerusalem. Then She- 5 maiah the prophet came to Rehoboam and the leading men of Judah, who had assembled in Jerusalem before the advance of

---

[a] Verses 1–4: cp. 1 Kgs. 12. 21–24.
[e] procured them: prob. rdg.; Heb. asked for a multitude of...
[b] Or satyrs.
[d] Or Nubians.

Shishak, and said to them, 'This is the word of the LORD: You have abandoned me; therefore I now 6 abandon you to Shishak.' The princes of Israel and the king submitted and said, 'The LORD is just.' 7 When the LORD saw that they had submitted, there came from him this word to Shemaiah: 'Because they have submitted I will not destroy them, I will let them barely escape; my wrath shall not be poured out on Jerusalem by means 8 of Shishak, but they shall become his servants; then they will know the difference between serving me and serving the rulers of other 9[a] countries.' Shishak king of Egypt in his attack on Jerusalem removed the treasures of the house of the LORD and of the royal palace. He seized everything, including the shields of gold that Solomon 10 had made. King Rehoboam replaced them with bronze shields and entrusted them to the officers of the escort who guarded the 11 entrance of the royal palace. Whenever the king entered the house of the LORD, the escort entered, carrying the shields; afterwards they returned them to the guard- 12 room. Because Rehoboam submitted, the LORD's wrath was averted from him, and he was not utterly destroyed; Judah enjoyed prosperity.

13[b] Thus King Rehoboam increased his power in Jerusalem. He was forty-one years old when he came to the throne, and he reigned for seventeen years in Jerusalem, the city which the LORD had chosen out of all the tribes of Israel as the place to receive his Name. Rehoboam's mother was a woman of 14 Ammon called Naamah. He did what was wrong, he did not make a practice of seeking guidance of the 15 LORD. The events of Rehoboam's reign, from first to last, are recorded in the histories of She-

maiah the prophet and Iddo the seer.[c] There was continual fighting between Rehoboam and Jeroboam. 16 He rested with his forefathers and was buried in the city of David; and he was succeeded by his son Abijah.

IN the eighteenth year of King 13 Jeroboam's reign Abijah became king of Judah. He reigned in Jeru- 2 salem for three years; his mother was Maacah daughter of Uriel of Gibeah. There was fighting between Abijah and Jeroboam. Abi- 3 jah drew up his army of four hundred thousand picked troops in order of battle, while Jeroboam formed up against him with eight hundred thousand picked troops. Abijah took up position on the 4 slopes of Mount Zemaraim in the hill-country of Ephraim and called out, 'Hear me, Jeroboam and all Israel: Ought you not to know that 5 the LORD the God of Israel gave the kingship over Israel to David and his descendants in perpetuity by a covenant of salt? Yet Jero- 6 boam son of Nebat, the servant of Solomon son of David, rose in rebellion against his lord, and 7 certain worthless scoundrels gathered round him, who stubbornly opposed Solomon's son Rehoboam when he was young and inexperienced, and he was no match for them. Now you propose to match 8 yourselves against the kingdom of the LORD as ruled by David's sons, you and your mob of supporters and the golden calves which Jeroboam has made to be your gods. Have you not dismissed from 9 office the Aaronites, priests of the LORD, and the Levites, and followed the practice of other lands in appointing priests? Now, if any man comes for consecration with an offering of a young bull and seven rams, you accept him as a priest to a god that is no god. But 10

---

[a] *Verses 9–11: cp. 1 Kgs. 14. 25–28.*
[b] *Verses 13–16: cp. 1 Kgs. 14. 29–31.*
[c] *Prob. rdg.; Heb. adds to be enrolled by genealogy.*

as for us, the LORD is our God and we have not forsaken him; we have Aaronites as priests ministering to the LORD with the Levites, duly 11 discharging their office. Morning and evening, these burn whole-offerings and fragrant incense to the LORD and offer the Bread of the Presence arranged in rows on a table ritually clean; they also kindle the lamps on the golden lamp-stand every evening. Thus we do indeed keep the charge of the LORD our God, whereas you have 12 forsaken him. God is with us at our head, and his priests stand there with trumpets to signal the battle-cry against you. Men of Israel, do not fight the LORD the God of your fathers; you will have no success.'

13 Jeroboam sent a detachment of his troops to go round and lay an ambush in the rear, so that his main body faced Judah while the 14 ambush lay behind them. The men of Judah turned to find that they were engaged front and rear. Then they cried to the LORD for help. The priests sounded their trum-15 pets, and the men of Judah raised a shout, and when they did so, God put Jeroboam and all Israel to rout 16 before Abijah and Judah. The Israelites fled before the men of Judah, and God delivered them 17 into their power. So Abijah and his men defeated them with very heavy losses, and five hundred thousand picked Israelites fell in 18 the battle. After this, the Israelites were reduced to submission, and Judah prevailed because they re-lied on the LORD the God of their 19 fathers. Abijah followed up his victory over Jeroboam and cap-tured from him the cities of Bethel, Jeshanah, and Ephron, with their 20 villages. Jeroboam did not regain his power during the days of Abijah; finally the LORD struck him down and he died.

21 But Abijah established his posi-tion; he married fourteen wives and became the father of twenty-

two sons and sixteen daughters. The other events of Abijah's reign, 22 both what he said and what he did, are recorded in the story of the prophet Iddo. Abijah rested with 14 his forefathers and was buried in the city of David; and he was succeeded on the throne by his son Asa. In his days the land was at peace for ten years.

Asa did what was good and right 2 in the eyes of the LORD his God. He suppressed the foreign altars 3 and the hill-shrines, smashed the sacred pillars and hacked down the sacred poles, and ordered Judah to 4 seek guidance of the LORD the God of their fathers and to keep the law and the commandments. He also 5 suppressed the hill-shrines and the incense-altars in all the cities, and the kingdom was at peace under him. He built fortified cities in 6 Judah, for the land was at peace. He had no war to fight during those years, because the LORD had given him security. He said to the 7 men of Judah, 'Let us build these cities and fortify them, with walls round them, and towers and barred gates. The land still lies open be-fore us. Because we have sought guidance of the LORD our God, he has sought us and given us security on every side.' So they built and prospered.

Asa had an army equipped with 8 shields and spears; three hundred thousand men came from Judah, and two hundred and eighty thou-sand from Benjamin, shield-bear-ers and archers; all were valiant warriors. Zerah the Cushite came 9 out against them with an army a million strong and three hundred chariots. When he reached Mare-shah, Asa came out to meet him 10 and they took up position in the valley of Zephathah at Mareshah. Asa called upon the LORD his God 11 and said, 'There is none like thee, O LORD, to help men, whether strong or weak; help us, O LORD our God, for on thee we rely and in

thy name we have come out against this horde. O LORD, thou art our God, how can man vie with thee?'
12 So the LORD gave Asa and Judah victory over the Cushites and they
13 fled, and Asa and his men pursued them as far as Gerar. The Cushites broke before the LORD and his army, and many of them fell mortally wounded; and Judah
14 carried off great loads of spoil. They destroyed all the cities around Gerar, for the LORD had struck the people with panic; and they plundered the cities, finding rich spoil
15 in them all. They also killed the herdsmen and seized many sheep and camels, and then they returned to Jerusalem.

15 The spirit of God came upon
2 Azariah son of Oded, and he went out to meet Asa and said to him, 'Hear me, Asa and all Judah and Benjamin. The LORD is with you when you are with him; if you look for him, he will let himself be found; if you forsake him, he will
3 forsake you. For a long time Israel was without the true God, without a priest to interpret the law and
4 without law.*a* But when, in their distress, they turned to the LORD the God of Israel and sought him, he let himself be found by them.
5 At those times there was no safety for people as they went about their business; the inhabitants of every land had their fill of trouble; there
6 was ruin on every side, nation at odds with nation, city with city, for God harassed them with every
7 kind of distress. But now you must be strong and not let your courage fail; for your work will be re-
8 warded.' When Asa heard these words,*b* he resolutely suppressed the loathsome idols in all Judah and Benjamin and in the cities which he had captured in the hill-country of Ephraim; and he repaired the altar of the LORD which

stood before the vestibule of the LORD's house.*c* Then he assembled 9 all Judah and Benjamin and all who had come from Ephraim, Manasseh, and Simeon to reside among them; for great numbers had come over to him from Israel, when they saw that the LORD his God was with him. So they assembled 10 at Jerusalem in the third month of the fifteenth year of Asa's reign, and that day they sacrificed to the 11 LORD seven hundred oxen and seven thousand sheep from the spoil which they had brought. And 12 they entered into a covenant to seek guidance of the LORD the God of their fathers with all their heart and soul; all who would not seek 13 the LORD the God of Israel were to be put to death, young and old, men and women alike. Then they 14 bound themselves by an oath to the LORD, with loud shouts of acclamation while trumpets and horns sounded; and all Judah re- 15 joiced at the oath, because they had bound themselves with all their heart and had sought him earnestly, and he had let himself be found by them. So the LORD gave them security on every side. King Asa 16*d* also deprived Maacah his grandmother of her rank as queen mother because she had an obscene object made for the worship of Asherah; Asa cut it down, ground it to powder and burnt it in the gorge of the Kidron. Although the 17 hill-shrines were allowed to remain in Israel, Asa himself remained faithful all his life. He brought into 18 the house of God all his father's votive offerings and his own, gold and silver and sacred vessels. And 19 there was no more war until the thirty-fifth year of Asa's reign.

In the thirty-sixth year of the 16 1*e* reign of Asa, Baasha king of Israel invaded Judah and fortified Ramah to cut off all access to Asa king

---

a without law: or without the law. Oded the prophet.
b Prob. rdg.; Heb. adds and the prophecy,
c house: prob. rdg.; Heb. om.
d Verses 16–18: cp. 1 Kgs. 15. 13–15.
e Verses 1–6: cp. 1 Kgs. 15. 17–22.

2 of Judah. So Asa brought out silver and gold from the treasuries of the house of the LORD and the royal palace, and sent this request to Ben-hadad king of Aram, whose capital 3 was Damascus: 'There is an alliance between us, as there was between our fathers. I now send you herewith silver and gold; break off your alliance with Baasha king of Israel, so that he may abandon his 4 campaign against me.' Ben-hadad listened willingly to King Asa and ordered the commanders of his armies to move against the cities of Israel, and they attacked Iyyon, Dan, Abel-mayim, and all the 5 store-cities of Naphtali. When Baasha heard of it, he ceased fortifying Ramah and stopped all 6 work on it. Then King Asa took with him all the men of Judah and they carried away the stones of Ramah and the timbers with which Baasha had fortified it; and he used them to fortify Geba and Mizpah.

7 At that time the seer Hanani came to Asa king of Judah and said to him, 'Because you relied on the king of Aram and not on the LORD your God, the army of the king of 8 Israel has escaped. The Cushites and the Libyans, were they not a great army with a vast number of chariots and horsemen? Yet, because you relied on the LORD, he delivered them into your power. 9 The eyes of the LORD range through the whole earth, to bring aid and comfort to those whose hearts are loyal to him. You have acted foolishly in this affair; you 10 will have wars from now on.' Asa was angry with the seer and put him in the stocks; for these words of his had made the king very indignant. At the same time he treated some of the people with great brutality.

11[a] The events of Asa's reign, from first to last, are recorded in the annals of the kings of Judah and Israel. In the thirty-ninth year of 12 his reign Asa became gravely affected with gangrene in his feet; he did not seek guidance of the LORD but resorted to physicians. He rested with his forefathers. 13 the forty-first year of his reign, and 14 was buried in the tomb which he had bought[b] for himself in the city of David, being laid on a bier[c] which had been heaped with all kinds of spices skilfully compounded; and they kindled a great fire in his honour.

ASA was succeeded by his son 17 Jehoshaphat, who determined to resist Israel by force. He posted 2 troops in all the fortified cities of Judah and stationed officers[d] throughout Judah and in the cities of Ephraim which his father Asa had captured. The LORD was with 3 Jehoshaphat, for he followed the example his father had set in his early years and did not resort to the Baalim; he sought guidance of 4 the God of his father and obeyed his commandments and did not follow the practices of Israel. So 5 the LORD established the kingdom under his rule, and all Judah brought him gifts, and his wealth and fame[e] became very great. He 6 took pride in the service of the LORD; he also suppressed the hillshrines and the sacred poles in Judah.

In the third year of his reign he 7 sent his officers, Ben-hayil, Obadiah, Zechariah, Nethaneel, and Micaiah, to teach in the cities of Judah, together with the Levites, 8 Shemaiah, Nethaniah, Zebadiah, Asahel, Shemiramoth, Jehonathan, Adonijah, Tobiah, and To-badonijah,[f] accompanied by the priests Elishama and Jehoram. They taught in Judah, having with 9 them the book of the law of the LORD; they went round the cities of Judah, teaching the people.

---

[a] *Verses 11–14: cp. 1 Kgs. 15. 23, 24.*   [b] *Or dug.*   [c] *Or in a niche.*
[d] *Or garrisons.*   [e] *Or riches.*   [f] *Prob. rdg.; Heb. adds* the Levites.

10 So the dread of the LORD fell upon all the rulers of the lands surrounding Judah, and they did not 11 make war on Jehoshaphat. Certain Philistines brought a gift, a great quantity of silver, to Jehoshaphat; the Arabs too brought him seven thousand seven hundred rams and seven thousand seven hundred he-12 goats. Jehoshaphat became ever more powerful and built fortresses 13 and store-cities in Judah; and he had much work on hand in the cities of Judah. He had regular, 14 seasoned troops in Jerusalem, enrolled according to their clans in this way: of Judah, the officers over units of a thousand: Adnah the commander, together with three hundred thousand seasoned 15 troops; and next to him the commander Johanan, with two hun-16 dred and eighty thousand; and next to him Amasiah son of Zichri, who had volunteered for the service of the LORD, with two hundred 17 thousand seasoned troops; and of Benjamin: an experienced soldier Eliada, with two hundred thousand men armed with bows and 18 shields; next to him Jehozabad, with a hundred and eighty thou-19 sand fully-armed men. These were the men who served the king, apart from those whom the king had posted in the fortified cities throughout Judah.

18 When Jehoshaphat had become very wealthy and famous,[a] he allied himself with Ahab by mar-2[b] riage. Some years afterwards he went down to visit Ahab in Samaria, and Ahab slaughtered many sheep and oxen for him and his retinue, and incited him to 3 attack Ramoth-gilead. What Ahab king of Israel said to Jehoshaphat king of Judah was this: 'Will you join me in attacking Ramoth-gilead?' And he answered, 'What is mine is yours, myself and my people; I will join with you in the 4 war.' Then Jehoshaphat said to the

king of Israel, 'First let us seek counsel from the LORD.' The king 5 of Israel assembled the prophets, some four hundred of them, and asked them, 'Shall I attack Ramoth-gilead or shall I refrain?' 'Attack,' they answered; 'God will deliver it into your hands.' Jeho-6 shaphat asked, 'Is there no other prophet of the LORD here through whom we may seek guidance?' 'There is one more', the king of 7 Israel answered, 'through whom we may seek guidance of the LORD, but I hate the man, because he never prophesies any good for me; never anything but evil. His name is Micaiah son of Imla.' Jehoshaphat exclaimed, 'My lord king, let no such word pass your lips!' So 8 the king of Israel called one of his eunuchs and told him to fetch Micaiah son of Imla with all speed.

The king of Israel and Jehosha-9 phat king of Judah were seated on their thrones, clothed in their royal robes and in shining armour, at the entrance to the gate of Samaria, and all the prophets were prophesying before them. One of them, 10 Zedekiah son of Kenaanah, made himself horns of iron and said, 'This is the word of the LORD: "With horns like these you shall gore the Aramaeans and make an end of them."' In the same vein all the 11 prophets prophesied, 'Attack Ramoth-gilead and win the day; the LORD will deliver it into your hands.' The messenger sent to 12 fetch Micaiah told him that the prophets had with one voice given the king a favourable answer. 'And mind you agree with them', he added. 'As the LORD lives,' said 13 Micaiah, 'I will say only what my God tells me to say.'

When Micaiah came into the 14 king's presence, the king said to him, 'Micaiah, shall I attack Ramoth-gilead or shall I refrain?' 'Attack and win the day,' he said, 'and it will fall into your hands.'

---

[a] Or rich.　　　[b] Verses 2–34: cp. 1 Kgs. 22. 2–35.

15 'How often must I adjure you', said the king, 'to tell me nothing but the truth in the name of the LORD?'

16 Then Micaiah said, 'I saw all Israel scattered on the mountains, like sheep without a shepherd; and I heard the LORD say, "They have no master; let them go home in 17 peace."' The king of Israel said to Jehoshaphat, 'Did I not tell you that he never prophesies good for 18 me, nothing but evil?' Micaiah went on, 'Listen now to the word of the LORD: I saw the LORD seated on his throne, with all the host of heaven in attendance on his right 19 and on his left. The LORD said, "Who will entice Ahab to attack and fall on*a* Ramoth-gilead?" One said one thing and one said an- 20 other; then a spirit came forward and stood before the LORD and said, "I will entice him." "How?" 21 said the LORD. "I will go out", he said, "and be a lying spirit in the mouth of all his prophets." "You shall entice him," said the LORD, "and you shall succeed; go and do 22 it." You see, then, how the LORD has put a lying spirit in the mouth of all these prophets of yours, because he has decreed disaster for 23 you.' Then Zedekiah son of Ke- naanah came up to Micaiah and struck him in the face: 'And how did the spirit of the LORD pass from me to speak to you?' he said. 24 Micaiah answered, 'That you will find out on the day when you run into an inner room to hide your- 25 self.' Then the king of Israel ordered Micaiah to be arrested and committed to the custody of Amon the governor of the city and Joash 26 the king's son.*b* 'Lock this fellow up', he said, 'and give him prison diet of bread and water until I 27 come home in safety.' Micaiah re- torted, 'If you do return in safety, the LORD has not spoken by me.'*c* 28 So the king of Israel and Jeho- shaphat king of Judah marched on

Ramoth-gilead, and the king of 29 Israel said to Jehoshaphat, 'I will disguise myself to go into battle, but you shall wear your royal robes.' So he went into battle in disguise. Now the king of Aram had 30 commanded the captains of his chariots not to engage all and sundry but the king of Israel alone. When the captains saw Jehosha- 31 phat, they thought he was the king of Israel and wheeled to attack him. But Jehoshaphat cried out, and the LORD came to his help; and God drew them away from him. When the captains saw that he was 32 not the king of Israel, they broke off the attack on him. But one man 33 drew his bow at random and hit the king of Israel where the breast- plate joins the plates of the armour. So he said to his driver, 'Wheel round and take me out of the line; I am wounded.' When the day's 34 fighting reached its height, the king of Israel was facing the Ara- maeans, propped up in his chariot; he remained so till evening, and at sunset he died.

As Jehoshaphat king of Judah 19 returned in safety to his home in Jerusalem, Jehu son of Hanani, 2 the seer, went out to meet him and said, 'Do you take delight in helping the wicked and befriend- ing the enemies of the LORD? The LORD will make you suffer for this. Yet there is some good in you, for 3 you have swept away the sacred poles from the land and have made a practice of seeking guidance of God.'

Jehoshaphat had his residence 4 in Jerusalem, but he went out again among his people from Beer- sheba to the hill-country of Eph- raim and brought them back to the LORD the God of their fathers. He 5 appointed judges throughout the land, one in each of the fortified cities of Judah, and said to them, 6 'Be careful what you do; you are

---

a Or at.　　*b* son: *or* deputy.
c Prob. rdg.; Heb. adds and he said, 'Listen, peoples, all together.'

there as judges, to please not man but the LORD, who is with you 7 when you pass sentence. Let the dread of the LORD be upon you, then; take care what you do, for the LORD our God will not tolerate injustice, partiality, or bribery.'

8 In Jerusalem Jehoshaphat appointed some of the Levites and priests and some heads of families by paternal descent in Israel to administer the law of the LORD and to arbitrate in lawsuits among the 9 inhabitants[a] of the city, and he gave them these instructions: 'You must always act in the fear of the LORD, faithfully and with single-10 ness of mind. In every suit which comes before you from your kinsmen, in whatever city they live, whether cases of bloodshed or offences against the law or the commandments, against statutes or regulations, you shall warn them to commit no offence against the LORD; otherwise you and your kinsmen will suffer for it. If you act thus, you will be free of all 11 offence. Your authority in all matters which concern the LORD is Amariah the chief priest, and in those which concern the king it is Zebediah son of Ishmael, the prince of the house of Judah; the Levites are your officers. Be strong and resolute, and may the LORD be on the side of the good!'

20 It happened some time afterwards that the Moabites, the Ammonites, and some of the Meunites 2 made war on Jehoshaphat. News was brought to him that a great horde of them was attacking him from beyond the Dead Sea, from Edom, and was already at Haza-3 zon-tamar, which is En-gedi. Jehoshaphat in his alarm resolved to seek guidance of the LORD and proclaimed a fast for all Judah. 4 Judah gathered together to ask counsel of the LORD; from every city of the land they came to con-5 sult him. Jehoshaphat stood up in the assembly of Judah and Jerusalem in the house of the LORD, in front of the New Court, and said, 6 'O LORD God of our fathers, art not thou God in heaven? Thou rulest over all the kingdoms of the nations; in thy hand are strength and power, and there is none who can withstand thee. Didst not thou, O 7 God our God, dispossess the inhabitants of this land in favour of thy people Israel, and give it for ever to the descendants of Abraham thy friend? So they lived in it 8 and have built a sanctuary in it in honour of thy name and said, "Should evil come upon us, war or 9 flood,[b] pestilence or famine, we will stand before this house and before thee, for in this house is thy Name, and we will cry to thee in our distress and thou wilt hear and save." Thou didst not allow Israel, when 10 they came out of Egypt, to enter the land of the Ammonites, the Moabites, and the people of the hill-country of Seir, so they turned aside and left them alone and did not destroy them. Now see how 11 these people repay us: they are coming to drive us out of thy possession which thou didst give to us. Judge them, O God our God, for we 12 have no strength to face this great horde which is invading our land; we know not what we ought to do; we lift our eyes to thee.'

So all Judah stood there before 13 the LORD, with their dependants, their wives and their children. Then, in the midst of the assembly, 14 the spirit of the LORD came upon Jahaziel son of Zechariah, son of Benaiah, son of Jeiel, son of Mattaniah, a Levite of the line of Asaph, and he said, 'Attend, all 15 Judah, all inhabitants of Jerusalem, and King Jehoshaphat; this is the word of the LORD to you: "Have no fear; do not be dismayed by this great horde, for the battle is in God's hands, not yours. Go down 16 to meet them tomorrow; they will

---

[a] in...inhabitants: *prob. rdg.*; *Heb. obscure.*   [b] *Prob. rdg.*; *Heb. judgement.*

come up by the Ascent of Ziz. You will find them at the end of the valley, east of the wilderness of 17 Jeruel. It is not you who will fight this battle; stand firm and wait, and you will see the deliverance worked by the LORD: he is on your side, O Judah and Jerusalem. Do not fear or be dismayed; go out tomorrow to face them; for the 18 LORD is on your side.'' Jehoshaphat bowed his face to the ground, and all Judah and the inhabitants of Jerusalem fell down before the LORD to make obeisance to him. 19 Then the Levites of the lines of Kohath and Korah stood up and praised the LORD the God of Israel with a mighty shout.

20 So they rose early in the morning and went out to the wilderness of Tekoa; and, as they were starting, Jehoshaphat took his stand and said, 'Hear me, O Judah and inhabitants of Jerusalem: hold firmly to your faith in the LORD your God and you will be upheld; have faith in his prophets and you 21 will prosper.' After consulting with the people, he appointed men to sing to the LORD and praise the splendour of his holiness*a* as they went before the armed troops, and they sang:

Give thanks to the LORD, for his love endures for ever.

22 As soon as their loud shouts of praise were heard, the LORD deluded the Ammonites and Moabites and the men of the hill-country of Seir, who were invading Judah, 23 and they were defeated. It turned out that the Ammonites and Moabites had taken up a position against the men of the hill-country of Seir, and set themselves to annihilate and destroy them; and when they had exterminated the men of Seir, they savagely attacked one another. So when Judah came to the 24 watch-tower in the wilderness and looked towards the enemy horde, there they were all lying dead upon the ground; none had escaped. When Jehoshaphat and his men 25 came to collect the booty, they found a large number of cattle, goods, clothing, and precious things, which they plundered until they could carry away no more. They spent three days collecting the booty, there was so much of it. On the fourth day they assembled 26 in the Valley of Berakah,*b* the name that it bears to this day because they blessed the LORD there. Then 27 all the men of Judah and Jerusalem, with Jehoshaphat at their head, returned home to the city in triumph; for the LORD had given them cause to triumph over their enemies. They entered Jerusalem 28 with lutes, harps, and trumpets playing, and went into the house of the LORD. So the dread of God fell 29 upon the rulers of every country, when they heard that the LORD had fought against the enemies of Israel; and the realm of Jehoshaphat was at peace, God giving him 30 security on all sides.

Thus Jehoshaphat reigned over 31*c* Judah. He was thirty-five years old when he came to the throne, and he reigned in Jerusalem for twenty-five years; his mother was Azubah daughter of Shilhi. He followed in the footsteps of Asa his 32 father and did not swerve from them; he did what was right in the eyes of the LORD. But the hill-33 shrines were allowed to remain, and the people did not set their hearts upon the God of their fathers. The 34 other events of Jehoshaphat's reign, from first to last, are recorded in the history of Jehu son of Hanani, which is included in the annals of the kings of Israel.

Later Jehoshaphat king of Judah 35 allied himself with Ahaziah king of Israel; he did wrong in joining with 36 him to build ships for trade with

---

a Or singers in sacred vestments to praise the LORD.
b That is Valley of Blessing.
     c Verses 31–33: cp. 1 Kgs. 22. 41–43.

Tarshish; these were built in Ezion-
37 geber. But Eliezer son of Doda-
vahu of Mareshah denounced
Jehoshaphat with this prophecy:
'Because you have joined with
Ahaziah, the LORD will bring your
work to nothing.' So the ships were
wrecked and could not make the
voyage to Tarshish.

21 JEHOSHAPHAT rested with his
forefathers and was buried with
them in the city of David. He was
2 succeeded by his son Joram, whose
brothers were Azariah, Jehiel, Zechariah, Azariah, Michael, and
Shephatiah, sons of Jehoshaphat.
All of them were sons of Jehosha-
3 phat king of Judah, and their father gave them many gifts, silver
and gold and other costly things, as
well as fortified cities in Judah; but
the kingship he gave to Joram because he was the eldest.
4 When Joram was firmly established on his father's throne, he put
to the sword all his brothers and
also some of the princes of Israel.
5[a] He was thirty-two years old when
he came to the throne, and he
reigned in Jerusalem for eight
6 years. He followed the practices of
the kings of Israel as the house of
Ahab had done, for he had married
Ahab's daughter; and he did what
was wrong in the eyes of the LORD.
7 But for the sake of the covenant
which he had made with David, the
LORD was unwilling to destroy the
house of David, since he had promised to give him and his sons a
flame, to burn for all time.
8 During his reign Edom revolted
against Judah and set up its own
9 king. Joram, with his commanders
and all his chariots, advanced into
Edom. He and his chariot-commanders set out by night, but they
were surrounded by the Edomites
10 and defeated.[b] So Edom has remained independent of Judah to
this day. Libnah revolted against

him at the same time, because he
had forsaken the LORD the God of
his fathers, and because he had 11
built hill-shrines in the hill-country
of Judah and had seduced the inhabitants of Jerusalem into idolatrous practices and corrupted
Judah.
A letter reached Joram from 12
Elijah the prophet, which ran thus:
'This is the word of the LORD the
God of David your father: "You
have not followed in the footsteps
of Jehoshaphat your father and of
Asa king of Judah, but have fol- 13
lowed the kings of Israel and have
seduced Judah and the inhabitants
of Jerusalem, as the house of Ahab
did; and you have put to death
your own brothers, sons of your
father's house, men better than
yourself. Because of all this, the 14
LORD is about to strike a heavy
blow at your people, your children,
your wives, and all your possessions, and you yourself will suffer 15
from a chronic disease of the
bowels, until they prolapse and become severely ulcerated."' Then 16
the LORD aroused against Joram
the anger of the Philistines and of
the Arabs who live near the Cushites, and they invaded Judah 17
and made their way right through
it, carrying off all the property
which they found in the king's
palace, as well as his sons and
wives; not a son was left to him
except the youngest, Jehoahaz.
It was after all this that the LORD 18
struck down the king with an incurable disease of the bowels. It 19
continued for some time, and towards the end of the second year
the disease caused his bowels to
prolapse, and the painful ulceration brought on his death. But his
people kindled no fire in his honour
as they had done for his fathers.
He was thirty-two years old when 20
he became king, and he reigned in
Jerusalem for eight years. His

---

[a] Verses 5–10: cp. 2 Kgs. 8. 17–22.
[b] and defeated: prob. rdg.; Heb. and he defeated them.

passing went unsung, and he was buried in the city of David, but not in the burial-place of the kings.

22 1[a] Then the inhabitants of Jerusalem made Ahaziah, his youngest son, king in his place, for the raiders who had joined the Arabs in the campaign had killed all the elder sons. So Ahaziah son of Jo-2 ram became king of Judah. He was forty-two years old when he came to the throne, and he reigned in Jerusalem for one year; his mother was Athaliah granddaughter of 3 Omri. He too followed the practices of the house of Ahab, for his mother was his counsellor in wicked-4 ness. He did what was wrong in the eyes of the LORD like the house of Ahab, for they had been his counsellors after his father's death, to 5 his undoing. He followed their counsel also in the alliance he made with Jehoram son of Ahab king of Israel, to fight against Hazael king of Aram at Ramoth-gilead. But Jehoram was wounded by the Ara-6 maeans, and returned to Jezreel to recover from the wounds which were inflicted on him at Ramoth in battle with Hazael king of Aram. Because of Jehoram's illness Ahaziah son of Joram king of Judah went down to Jezreel to visit 7 him. It was God's will that the visit of Ahaziah to Jehoram should be the occasion of his downfall. During the visit he went out with Jehoram to meet Jehu son of Nimshi, whom the LORD had anointed to bring the house of Ahab to an 8 end. So it came about that Jehu, who was then at variance with the house of Ahab, found the officers of Judah and the kinsmen of Ahaziah who were his attendants, and 9 killed them. Then he searched out Ahaziah himself, and his men captured him in Samaria, where he had gone into hiding. They brought him to Jehu and put him to death; they gave him burial, for they said, 'He was a son of Jehoshaphat who

sought the guidance of the LORD with his whole heart.' Then the house of Ahaziah had no one strong enough to rule.

As soon as Athaliah mother of 10[b] Ahaziah saw that her son was dead, she set out to extirpate the royal line of the house of Judah. But 11 Jehosheba daughter of King Joram took Ahaziah's son Joash and stole him away from among the princes who were being murdered; she put him and his nurse in a bedchamber. Thus Jehosheba, daughter of King Joram and wife of Jehoiada the priest, because she was Ahaziah's sister, hid Joash from Athaliah so that she did not put him to death. He remained concealed with them 12 in the house of God for six years, while Athaliah ruled the country.

In the seventh year Jehoiada 23 felt himself strong enough to make an agreement with Azariah son of Jeroham, Ishmael son of Jehohanan, Azariah son of Obed, Maaseiah son of Adaiah, and Elishaphat son of Zichri, all captains of units of a hundred. They went all 2 through Judah and gathered to Jerusalem the Levites from the cities of Judah and the heads of clans in Israel, and they came to Jerusalem. All the assembly made 3 a compact with the king in the house of God, and Jehoiada said to them, 'Here is the king's son! He shall be king, as the LORD promised that the sons of David should be. This is what you must do: a third 4 of you, priests and Levites, as you come on duty on the sabbath, are to be on guard at the threshold gates, another third are to be in the 5 royal palace, and another third are to be at the Foundation Gate, while all the people will be in the courts of the house of the LORD. Let no one enter the house of the 6 LORD except the priests and the attendant Levites; they may enter, for they are holy, but all the people shall continue to keep the

----

[a] *Verses 1–6: cp. 2 Kgs. 8. 25–29.*

[b] *22. 10 – 23. 21: cp. 2 Kgs. 11. 1–20.*

7 LORD's charge. The Levites shall mount guard round the king, each with his weapons at the ready; anyone who tries to enter the house is to be put to death. They shall stay with the king wherever he goes.'

8 The Levites and all Judah carried out the orders of Jehoiada the priest to the letter. Each captain took his men, both those who came on duty on the sabbath and those who came off, for Jehoiada the priest had not released the out-
9 going divisions. And Jehoiada the priest handed out to the captains King David's spears, shields, and bucklers, which were in the house
10 of God; and he posted all the people, each man carrying his weapon at the ready, from corner to corner of the house to north and south,[a]
11 surrounding the king. Then they brought out the king's son, put the crown on his head, handed him the warrant and proclaimed him king, and Jehoiada and his sons anointed him; and a shout went up:
12 'Long live the king.' When Athaliah heard the noise of the people as they ran about cheering for the king, she came into the house of the LORD where the people were
13 and found the king standing on the dais[b] at the entrance, amidst outbursts of song and fanfares of trumpets in his honour; all the populace were rejoicing and blowing trumpets, and singers with musical instruments were leading the celebrations. Athaliah rent her clothes and cried, 'Treason! Trea-
14 son!' Jehoiada the priest gave orders to[c] the captains in command of the troops: 'Bring her outside the precincts and let anyone in attendance on her be put to the sword'; for the priest said, 'Do not kill her in the house of the LORD.'
15 So they laid hands on her and took her to the royal palace and killed

her there at the passage to the Horse Gate.

16 Then Jehoiada made a covenant between the LORD[d] and the whole people and the king, that they should be the LORD's people. And
17 all the people went into the temple of Baal and pulled it down; they smashed its altars and images, and they slew Mattan the priest of Baal before the altars. Then Jehoiada
18 committed the supervision of the house of the LORD to the charge of the priests and the Levites whom David had allocated to the house of the LORD, to offer whole-offerings to the LORD as prescribed in the law of Moses, with the singing and rejoicing as handed down from David. He stationed the door-
19 keepers at the gates of the house of the LORD, to prevent anyone entering who was in any way unclean. Then he took the captains of units
20 of a hundred, the nobles, and the governors of the people, and all the people of the land, and they escorted the king from the house of the LORD through the Upper Gate to the royal palace, and seated him on the royal throne. The whole people
21 rejoiced and the city was tranquil. That is how Athaliah was put to the sword.

Joash was seven years old when 24 1[e] he became king, and he reigned in Jerusalem for forty years; his mother was Zibiah of Beersheba. He did what was right in the eyes 2 of the LORD as long as Jehoiada the priest was alive. Jehoiada chose 3 him two wives, and he had a family of sons and daughters.

Some time after this, Joash de- 4 cided to repair the house of the LORD. So he assembled the priests 5 and the Levites and said to them, 'Go through the cities of Judah and collect the annual tax from all the Israelites for the restoration of

---

[a] *Prob. rdg.; Heb. adds* of the altar and the house.   [b] *Prob. rdg., cp.* 2 Kgs. 11. 14; *Heb.* by his pillar.   [c] *gave orders to: prob. rdg., cp.* 2 Kgs. 11. 15; *Heb.* brought out.   [d] *the* LORD: *prob. rdg., cp.* 2 Kgs. 11. 17; *Heb.* him. [e] *Verses* 1–14: *cp.* 2 Kgs. 11. 21–12. 15.

the house of your God, and do it quickly.' But the Levites did not 6 act quickly. The king then called for Jehoiada the chief priest and said to him, 'Why have you not required the Levites to bring in from Judah and Jerusalem the tax imposed by Moses the servant of the LORD and by the assembly of Israel for the Tent of the Tokens?' 7 For the wicked Athaliah and her adherents had broken into the house of God and had devoted all its holy things to the service of the 8 Baalim. So the king ordered them to make a chest and to put it outside the gate of the house of the 9 LORD; and proclamation was made throughout Judah and Jerusalem that the people should bring to the LORD the tax imposed on Israel in the wilderness by Moses the ser-10 vant of God. And all the leaders and all the people gladly brought their taxes and cast them into the 11 chest until it was full. Whenever the chest was brought to the king's officers by the Levites and they saw that it was well filled, the king's secretary and the chief priest's officer would come to empty it, after which it was carried back to its place. This they did daily, and they collected a great 12 sum of money. The king and Jehoiada gave it to those responsible for carrying out the work in the house of the LORD, and they hired masons and carpenters to do the repairs, as well as craftsmen in iron and copper[a] to restore the house. 13 So the workmen proceeded with their task and the new work progressed under their hands; they restored the house of God according to its original design and 14 strengthened it. When they had finished, they brought what was left of the money to the king and to Jehoiada, and it was made into vessels for the house of the LORD, both for service and for sacrificing, saucers and other vessels of gold

and silver. While Jehoiada lived, whole-offerings were offered in the house of the LORD continually.

Jehoiada, now old and weighed 15 down with years, died at the age of a hundred and thirty and was 16 buried with the kings in the city of David, because he had done good in Israel and served God and his house. After the death of Jehoiada the 17 leading men of Judah came and made obeisance to the king. He listened to them, and they forsook 18 the house of the LORD the God of their fathers and worshipped sacred poles and idols. And Judah and Jerusalem suffered for this wickedness. But the LORD sent prophets 19 to bring them back to himself, prophets who denounced them and were not heeded. Then the spirit of 20 God took possession of Zechariah son of Jehoiada the priest, and he stood looking down on the people and said to them, 'This is the word of God: "Why do you disobey the commands of the LORD and court disaster? Because you have forsaken the LORD, he has forsaken you."' But they made common 21 cause against him, and on orders from the king they stoned him to death in the court of the house of the LORD. King Joash did not re-22 member the loyalty of Zechariah's father Jehoiada but killed his son, who said as he was dying, 'May the LORD see this and exact the penalty.'

At the turn of the year an Aramaean army advanced against 23 Joash; they invaded Judah and Jerusalem and massacred all the officers, so that the army ceased to exist, and sent all their spoil to the king of Damascus. Although the 24 Aramaeans had invaded with a small force, the LORD delivered a very great army into their hands, because the people had forsaken the LORD the God of their fathers; and Joash suffered just punishment.

[a] Or bronze.

25^a When the Aramaeans had withdrawn, leaving the king severely wounded, his servants conspired against him to avenge the death of the son of Jehoiada the priest; and they killed him on his bed. Thus he died and was buried in the city of David, but not in the burial-place 26 of the kings. The conspirators were Zabad son of Shimeath an Ammonite woman and Jehozabad son of Shimrith a Moabite woman. 27 His children, the many oracles about him, and his reconstruction of the house of God are all on record in the story given in the annals of the kings. He was succeeded by his son Amaziah.

25 1^b AMAZIAH was twenty-five years old when he came to the throne, and he reigned in Jerusalem for twenty-nine years; his mother was 2 Jehoaddan of Jerusalem. He did what was right in the eyes of the LORD, but not whole-heartedly. 3 When the royal power was firmly in his grasp, he put to death those of his servants who had murdered 4 the king his father; but he spared their children, in obedience to the LORD's command written in the law of Moses: 'Fathers shall not die for their children, nor children for their fathers; a man shall die only for his own sin.'

5 Then Amaziah assembled the men of Judah and drew them up by families, all Judah and Benjamin as well, under officers over units of a thousand and a hundred. He mustered those of twenty years old and upwards and found their number to be three hundred thousand, all picked troops ready for service, 6 able to handle spear and shield. He also hired a hundred thousand seasoned troops from Israel for a 7 hundred talents of silver. But a man of God came to him and said, 'My lord king, do not let the Israelite army march with you; the LORD is not with Israel – all these Ephraimites! For, if you make 8 these people^c your allies in the war, God will overthrow you in battle; he has power to help or to overthrow.' Then Amaziah said to the 9 man of God, 'What am I to do about the hundred talents which I have spent on the Israelite army?' The man of God answered, 'It is in the LORD's power to give you much more than that.' So Amaziah de- 10 tached the troops which had come to him from Ephraim and sent them home; that infuriated them against Judah and they went home in a rage.

Then Amaziah took heart and 11 led his men to the Valley of Salt and there killed ten thousand men of Seir. The men of Judah captured 12 another ten thousand men alive, brought them to the top of a cliff^d and hurled them over so that they were all dashed to pieces. Mean- 13 while the troops which Amaziah had sent home without allowing them to take part in the battle raided the cities of Judah from Samaria to Beth-horon, massacred three thousand people in them and carried off quantities of booty.

After Amaziah had returned 14 from the defeat of the Edomites, he brought the gods of the people of Seir and, setting them up as his own gods, worshipped them and burnt sacrifices to them. The 15 LORD was angry with Amaziah for this and sent a prophet who said to him, 'Why have you resorted to gods who could not save their own people from you?' But while he 16 was speaking, the king said to him, 'Have we appointed you counsellor to the king? Stop! Why risk your life?' The prophet did stop, but first he said, 'I know that God has determined to destroy you because you have done this and have not listened to my counsel.'

---

^a Verses 25–27: cp. 2 Kgs. 12. 20, 21.
^c these people: prob. rdg.; Heb. obscure.
^b Verses 1–4: cp. 2 Kgs. 14. 1–6.
^d a cliff: or Sela.

17[a] Then Amaziah king of Judah, after consultation, sent messengers to Jehoash son of Jehoahaz, son of Jehu, king of Israel, to pro-
18 pose a meeting. But Jehoash king of Israel sent this answer to Amaziah king of Judah: 'A thistle in Lebanon sent to a cedar in Lebanon to say, "Give your daughter in marriage to my son." But a wild beast in Lebanon, passing by,
19 trampled on the thistle. You have defeated Edom, you say, but it has gone to your head. Enjoy your glory at home and stay there. Why should you involve yourself in disaster and bring yourself to the ground, and Judah with you?'
20 But Amaziah would not listen; and this was God's doing in order to give Judah into the power of Jehoash, because they had resort-
21 ed to the gods of Edom. So Jehoash king of Israel marched out, and he and Amaziah king of Judah met one another at Beth-shemesh in
22 Judah. The men of Judah were routed by Israel and fled to their
23 homes. But Jehoash king of Israel captured Amaziah king of Judah, son of Joash, son of Jehoahaz, at Beth-shemesh, and brought him to Jerusalem. There he broke down the city wall from the Gate of Ephraim to the Corner Gate, a distance
24 of four hundred cubits; he also took[b] all the gold and silver and all the vessels found in the house of God, in the care of Obed-edom, and the treasures of the royal palace, as well as hostages, and returned to Samaria.
25[c] Amaziah son of Joash, king of Judah, outlived Jehoash son of Jehoahaz, king of Israel, by fifteen
26 years. The other events of Amaziah's reign, from first to last, are recorded in the annals of the kings
27 of Judah and Israel. From the time when he turned away from the LORD, there was conspiracy against

him in Jerusalem and he fled to Lachish; but they sent after him to Lachish and put him to death there. Then his body was conveyed 28 on horseback to Jerusalem, and there he was buried with his forefathers in the city of David.

All the people of Judah took 26 Uzziah, now sixteen years old, and made him king in succession to his father Amaziah. It was he who 2 built Eloth and restored it to Judah after the king rested with his forefathers.

Uzziah was sixteen years old 3[d] when he came to the throne, and he reigned in Jerusalem for fifty-two years; his mother was Jecoliah of Jerusalem. He did what was 4 right in the eyes of the LORD, as Amaziah his father had done. He 5 set himself to seek the guidance of God in the days of Zechariah, who instructed him in the fear of God; as long as he sought guidance of the LORD, God caused him to prosper.

He took the field against the 6 Philistines and broke down the walls of Gath, Jabneh, and Ashdod; and he built cities in the territory of Ashdod and among the Philistines. God aided him against 7 them, against the Arabs who lived in Gur-baal, and against the Meunites. The Ammonites brought gifts 8 to Uzziah and his fame spread to the borders of Egypt, for he had become very powerful. Besides, he 9 built towers in Jerusalem at the Corner Gate, at the Valley Gate, and at the escarpment, and fortified them. He built other towers in 10 the wilderness and dug many cisterns, for he had large herds of cattle both in the Shephelah and in the plain. He also had farmers and vine-dressers in the hill-country and in the fertile lands, for he loved the soil.

Uzziah had an army of soldiers 11 trained and ready for service,

---

[a] *Verses 17–24: cp. 2 Kgs. 14. 8–14.*
[b] *he also took: prob. rdg., cp. 2 Kgs. 14. 14; Heb. om.*
[c] *25. 25 – 26. 2: cp. 2 Kgs. 14. 17–22.*
[d] *Verses 3, 4: cp. 2 Kgs. 15. 2, 3.*

grouped according to the census made by Jeiel the adjutant-general and Maaseiah the clerk under the direction of Hananiah, one of the 12 king's commanders. The total number of heads of families which supplied seasoned warriors was two 13 thousand six hundred. Under their command was an army of three hundred and seven thousand five hundred, a powerful fighting force to aid the king against his enemies. 14 Uzziah prepared for the whole army shields, spears, helmets, coats of mail, bows, and*a* sling-15 stones. In Jerusalem he had machines designed by engineers for use upon towers and bastions, made to discharge arrows and large stones. His fame spread far and wide, for he was so wonderfully gifted that he became very powerful.

16 But when he grew powerful his pride led to his own undoing:*b* he offended against the LORD his God by entering the temple of the LORD to burn incense on the altar 17 of incense. Azariah the priest and eighty others of the LORD's priests, courageous men, went in after 18 King Uzziah, confronted him and said, 'It is not for you, Uzziah, to burn incense to the LORD, but for the Aaronite priests who have been consecrated for that office. Leave the sanctuary; for you have offended, and that will certainly bring you no honour from the 19 LORD God.' The king, who had a censer in his hand ready to burn incense, was indignant; and because of his indignation at the priests, leprosy broke out on his forehead in the presence of the priests, there in the house of the LORD, beside the altar of incense. 20 When Azariah the chief priest and the other priests looked towards him, they saw that he had leprosy on his forehead and they hurried him out of the temple, and indeed

he himself hastened to leave, because the LORD had struck him with the disease. And King Uzziah 21*c* remained a leper till the day of his death; he lived in his own house as a leper, relieved of all duties and excluded from the house of the LORD, while his son Jotham was comptroller of the household and regent. The other events of Uz- 22 ziah's reign, from first to last, are recorded by the prophet Isaiah son of Amoz. So he rested with his 23 forefathers and was buried in a burial-ground, but not that of the kings; for they said, 'He is a leper'; and he was succeeded by his son Jotham.

Jotham was twenty-five years 27 1*d* old when he came to the throne, and he reigned in Jerusalem for sixteen years; his mother was Jerushah daughter of Zadok. He did 2 what was right in the eyes of the LORD, as his father Uzziah had done, but unlike him he did not enter the temple of the LORD; the people, however, continued their corrupt practices. He constructed 3 the upper gate of the house of the LORD and built extensively on the wall at Ophel. He built cities in the 4 hill-country of Judah, and forts and towers on the wooded hills. He made war on the king of the 5 Ammonites and defeated him; and that year the Ammonites gave him a hundred talents of silver, ten thousand kor of wheat and ten thousand of barley. They paid him the same tribute in the second and third years. Jotham became very 6 powerful because he maintained a steady course of obedience to the LORD his God. The other events of 7 Jotham's reign, all that he did in war and in peace, are recorded in the annals of the kings of Israel and Judah. He was twenty-five years 8 old when he came to the throne, and he reigned in Jerusalem for

---

a Prob. rdg.; Heb. adds for.   *b* his pride...undoing: *or* he became so proud that he acted corruptly.   *c* Verses 21–23: cp. 2 Kgs. 15. 5–7.
d Verses 1–3: cp. 2 Kgs. 15. 33–35.

9 sixteen years. He rested with his forefathers and was buried in the city of David; and he was succeeded by his son Ahaz.

28 1[a] AHAZ was twenty years old when he came to the throne, and he reigned in Jerusalem for sixteen years. He did not do what was right in the eyes of the LORD like 2 his forefather David, but followed in the footsteps of the kings of Israel, and cast metal images for 3 the Baalim. He also burnt sacrifices in the Valley of Ben-hinnom; he even burnt his sons in the fire according to the abominable practice of the nations whom the LORD had dispossessed in favour of the 4 Israelites. He slaughtered and burnt sacrifices at the hill-shrines and on the hill-tops and under every spreading tree.

5 The LORD his God let him suffer at the hands of the king of Aram, and the Aramaeans defeated him, took many captives and brought them to Damascus; he was also made to suffer at the hands of the king of Israel, who inflicted a 6 severe defeat on him. This was Pekah son of Remaliah, who killed in one day a hundred and twenty thousand men of Judah, seasoned troops, because they had forsaken the LORD the God of their fathers. 7 And Zichri, an Ephraimite hero, killed Maaseiah the king's son[b] and Azrikam the comptroller of the household and Elkanah the king's 8 chief minister. The Israelites took captive from their kinsmen two hundred thousand women and children; they also took a large amount of booty and brought it to Samaria.

9 A prophet of the LORD was there, Oded by name; he went out to meet the army as it returned to Samaria and said to them, 'It is because the LORD the God of your fathers is angry with Judah that he has given them into your power; and you

have massacred them in a rage that has towered up to heaven. Now you propose to force the 10 people of Judah and Jerusalem, male and female, into slavery. Are not you also guilty men before the LORD your God? Now, listen to me. 11 Send back those you have taken captive from your kinsmen, for the anger of the LORD is roused against you.' Next, some Ephraimite 12 chiefs, Azariah son of Jehohanan, Berechiah son of Meshillemoth, Hezekiah[c] son of Shallum, and Amasa son of Hadlai, met those who were returning from the war and 13 said to them, 'You must not bring these captives into our country; what you are proposing would make us guilty before the LORD and add to our sins and transgressions. We are guilty enough already, and there is fierce anger against Israel.' So the armed men left the captives 14 and the spoil with the officers and the assembled people. The captives 15 were put in charge of men nominated for this duty, who found clothes from the spoil for all who were naked. They clothed them and shod them, gave them food and drink, and anointed them; those who were tottering from exhaustion they conveyed on the backs of asses, and so brought them to their kinsmen in Jericho, in the Vale of Palm Trees. Then they themselves returned to Samaria.

At that time King Ahaz sent to 16 the king of Assyria for help. The 17 Edomites had invaded again and defeated Judah and taken away prisoners; and the Philistines had 18 raided the cities of the Shephelah and of the Negeb of Judah and had captured Beth-shemesh, Aijalon, and Gederoth, as well as Soco, Timnah, and Gimzo with their villages, and occupied them. The 19 LORD had reduced Judah to submission because of Ahaz king of Judah; for his actions in Judah had been unbridled and he had

_____

[a] Verses 1–4: cp. 2 Kgs. 16. 2–4.   [b] son: or deputy.   [c] Or Jehizkiah.

been grossly unfaithful to the
20 LORD. Then Tiglath-pileser king of
Assyria marched against him and,
so far from assisting him, pressed
21 him hard. Ahaz stripped the house
of the LORD, the king's palace and
the houses of his officers, and gave
the plunder to the king of Assyria;
but all to no purpose.

22 This King Ahaz, when hard
pressed, became more and more
23 unfaithful to the LORD; he sacrificed to the gods of Damascus who
had defeated him and said, 'The
gods of the kings of Aram helped
them; I will sacrifice to them so
that they may help me.' But in
fact they caused his downfall and
24 that of all Israel. Then Ahaz
gathered together the vessels of
the house of God and broke them
up, and shut the doors of the house
of the LORD; he made himself altars at every corner in Jerusalem,
25 and at every single city of Judah
he made hill-shrines to burn sacrifices to other gods and provoked
the anger of the LORD the God of
his fathers.
26ᵃ The other acts and all the events
of his reign, from first to last, are
recorded in the annals of the kings
27 of Judah and Israel. So Ahaz rested with his forefathers and was
buried in the city of Jerusalem, but
was not given burial with the kings
of Judah. He was succeeded by his
son Hezekiah.

The kings of Judah from Hezekiah to the exile

29 1ᵇ HEZEKIAH was twenty-five years
old when he came to the throne,
and he reigned in Jerusalem for
twenty-nine years; his mother was
2 Abijah daughter of Zechariah. He
did what was right in the eyes of
the LORD, as David his forefather
had done.

3 In the first year of his reign, in
the first month, he opened the
gates of the house of the LORD and

repaired them. He brought in the 4
priests and the Levites and gathered them together in the square on
the east side, and said to them, 5
'Levites, listen to me. Hallow yourselves now, hallow the house of the
LORD the God of your fathers, and
remove the pollution from the
sanctuary. For our forefathers 6
were unfaithful and did what was
wrong in the eyes of the LORD our
God: they forsook him, they would
have nothing to do with his
dwelling-place, they turned their
backs on it. They shut the doors of 7
the porch and extinguished the
lamps, they ceased to burn incense and offer whole-offerings in
the sanctuary to the God of Israel.
Therefore the anger of the LORD 8
fell upon Judah and Jerusalem and
he made them repugnant, an object of horror and derision, as you
see for yourselves. Hence it is that 9
our fathers have fallen by the
sword, our sons and daughters and
our wives are in captivity. Now I 10
intend that we should pledge ourselves to the LORD the God of Israel, in order that his anger may be
averted from us. So, my sons, let 11
no time be lost; for the LORD has
chosen you to serve him and to
minister to him, to be his ministers
and to burn sacrifices.'

Then the Levites set to work – 12
Mahath son of Amasai and Joel
son of Azariah of the family of Kohath; of the family of Merari, Kish
son of Abdi and Azariah son of
Jehalelel; of the family of Gershon,
Joah son of Zimmah and Eden son
of Joah; of the family of Elizaphan, 13
Shimri and Jeiel; of the family of
Asaph, Zechariah and Mattaniah;
of the family of Heman, Jehiel and 14
Shimei; and of the family of Jeduthun, Shemaiah and Uzziel. They 15
assembled their kinsmen and hallowed themselves, and then went
in, as the king had instructed them
at the LORD's command, to purify
the house of the LORD. The priests 16

ᵃ *Verses 26, 27: cp. 2 Kgs. 16. 19, 20.*   ᵇ *Verses 1, 2: cp. 2 Kgs. 18. 1–3.*

went inside to purify the house of the LORD; they removed all the pollution which they found in the temple into the court of the house of the LORD, and the Levites took it from them and carried it outside 17 to the gorge of the Kidron. They began the rites on the first day of the first month, and on the eighth day they reached the porch; then for eight days they consecrated the house of the LORD, and on the sixteenth day of the first month 18 they finished. Then they went into the palace and said to King Hezekiah, 'We have purified the whole of the house of the LORD, the altar of whole-offering with all its vessels, and the table for the Bread of the Presence arranged in rows 19 with all its vessels; and we have put in order and consecrated all the vessels which King Ahaz cast aside during his reign, when he was unfaithful. They are now in place before the altar of the LORD.'

20 Then King Hezekiah rose early, assembled the officers of the city and went up to the house of the 21 LORD. They brought seven bulls, seven rams, and seven lambs for the whole-offering,[a] and seven he-goats as a sin-offering for the kingdom, for the sanctuary, and for Judah; these he commanded the priests of Aaron's line to offer on 22 the altar of the LORD. So the bulls were slaughtered, and the priests took their blood and flung it against the altar; the rams were slaughtered, and their blood was flung against the altar; the lambs were slaughtered, and their blood was 23 flung against the altar. Then the he-goats for the sin-offering were brought before the king and the assembly, who laid their hands on 24 them; and the priests slaughtered them and used their blood as a sin-offering on the altar to make expiation for all Israel. For the king had commanded that the whole-

offering and the sin-offering should be made for all Israel.

He posted the Levites in the 25 house of the LORD with cymbals, lutes, and harps, according to the rule prescribed by David, by Gad the king's seer and Nathan the prophet; for this rule had come from the LORD through his prophets. The Levites stood ready with the 26 instruments of David, and the priests with the trumpets. Heze- 27 kiah gave the order that the whole-offering should be offered on the altar. At the moment when the whole-offering began, the song to the LORD began too, with the trumpets, led by the instruments of David king of Israel. The whole 28 assembly prostrated themselves, the singers sang and the trumpeters sounded; all this continued until the whole-offering was complete. When the offering was complete, 29 the king and all his company bowed down and prostrated themselves. And King Hezekiah and his 30 officers commanded the Levites to praise the LORD in the words of David and of Asaph the seer. So they praised him most joyfully and bowed down and prostrated themselves.

Then Hezekiah said, 'You have 31 now given to the LORD with open hands; approach with your sacrifices and thank-offerings for the house of the LORD.' So the assembly brought sacrifices and thank-offerings; and every man of willing spirit brought whole-offerings. The 32 number of whole-offerings which the assembly brought was seventy bulls, a hundred rams, and two hundred lambs; all these made a whole-offering to the LORD. And 33 the consecrated offerings were six hundred bulls and three thousand sheep. But the priests were too few 34 and could not flay all the whole-offerings; so their colleagues the Levites helped them until the work was completed and all the

---

[a] for the whole-offering: *prob. rdg.*; Heb. *om.*

priests had hallowed themselves – for the Levites had been more scrupulous than the priests in hal-
35 lowing themselves. There were indeed whole-offerings in abundance, besides the fat of the shared-offerings and the drink-offerings for the whole-offerings. In this way the service of the house of the
36 LORD was restored; and Hezekiah and all the people rejoiced over what God had done for the people and because it had come about so suddenly.

30 Then Hezekiah sent word to all Israel and Judah, and also wrote letters to Ephraim and Manasseh, inviting them to come to the house of the LORD in Jerusalem to keep the Passover of the LORD the God
2 of Israel. The king and his officers and all the assembly in Jerusalem had agreed to keep the Passover in
3 the second month, but they had not been able to keep it at that time, because not enough priests had hallowed themselves and the people had not assembled in Jeru-
4 salem. The proposal was acceptable to the king and the whole
5 assembly. So they resolved to make a proclamation throughout all Israel, from Beersheba to Dan, that the people should come to Jerusalem to keep the Passover of the LORD the God of Israel. Never before had so many kept it accord-
6 ing to the prescribed form. Couriers went throughout all Israel and Judah with letters from the king and his officers, proclaiming the royal command: 'Turn back, men of Israel, to the LORD the God of Abraham, Isaac, and Israel, so that he may turn back to those of you who escaped capture by the
7 kings of Assyria. Do not be like your forefathers and your kinsmen, who were unfaithful to the LORD the God of their fathers, so that he made them an object of
8 horror, as you yourselves saw. Do not be stubborn as your forefathers were; submit yourselves to the

LORD and enter his sanctuary which he has sanctified for ever, and worship the LORD your God, so that his anger may be averted from you. For when you turn back 9 to the LORD, your kinsmen and your children will win compassion from their captors and return to this land. The LORD your God is gracious and compassionate, and he will not turn away from you if you turn back to him.'

So the couriers passed from city 10 to city through the land of Ephraim and Manasseh and as far as Zebulun, but they were treated with scorn and ridicule. However, 11 a few men of Asher, Manasseh, and Zebulun submitted and came to Jerusalem. Further, the hand 12 of God moved the people in Judah with one accord to carry out what the king and his officers had ordered at the LORD's command.

Many people, a very great as- 13 sembly, came together in Jerusalem to keep the pilgrim-feast of Unleavened Bread in the second month. They began by removing 14 the altars in Jerusalem; they removed the altars for burning sacrifices and threw them into the gorge of the Kidron. They killed the 15 passover lamb on the fourteenth day of the second month; and the priests and the Levites were bitterly ashamed. They hallowed themselves and brought whole-offerings to the house of the LORD. They 16 took their accustomed places, according to the direction laid down for them in the law of Moses the man of God; the priests flung against the altar the blood which they received from the Levites. But many in the assembly had not 17 hallowed themselves; therefore the Levites had to kill the passover lamb for every one who was unclean, in order to hallow him to the LORD. For a majority of the 18 people, many from Ephraim, Manasseh, Issachar, and Zebulun, had not kept themselves ritually clean, and therefore kept the Passover irregularly. But Hezekiah prayed for them, saying, 'May the good 19 LORD grant pardon to every one who makes a practice of seeking guidance of God, the LORD the God of his fathers, even if he has not observed the rules for the 20 purification of the sanctuary.' The LORD heard Hezekiah and healed 21 the people. And the Israelites who were present in Jerusalem kept the feast of Unleavened Bread for seven days with great rejoicing, and the Levites and the priests praised the LORD every day with 22 unrestrained fervour.[a] Hezekiah spoke encouragingly to all the Levites who had shown true understanding in the service of the LORD. So they spent the seven days of the festival sacrificing shared-offerings and making confession to[b] the LORD the God of their fathers.

23   Then the whole assembly agreed to keep the feast for another seven days; so they kept it for another seven days with general rejoicing. 24 For Hezekiah king of Judah set aside for the assembly a thousand bulls and seven thousand sheep, and his officers set aside for the assembly a thousand bulls and ten thousand sheep; and priests hallowed themselves in great num- 25 bers. So the whole assembly of Judah, including the priests and the Levites, rejoiced, together with all the assembly which came out of Israel, and the resident aliens from Israel and those who 26 lived in Judah. There was great rejoicing in Jerusalem, the like of which had not been known there since the days of Solomon son of 27 David king of Israel. Then the priests and the Levites stood to bless the people; the LORD listened to their cry, and their prayer came to God's holy dwelling-place in heaven.

When this was over, all the Is- 31 raelites present went out to the cities of Judah and smashed the sacred pillars, hacked down the sacred poles and broke up the hill-shrines and the altars throughout Judah and Benjamin, Ephraim and Manasseh, until they had made an end of them. That done, the Israelites returned, each to his own patrimony in his own city.

Then Hezekiah installed the 2 priests and the Levites in office, division by division, allotting to each priest or Levite his own particular duty, for whole-offerings or shared-offerings, to give thanks or to sing praise, or to serve in the gates of the several quarters in the LORD's house.

The king provided from his own 3 resources, as the share due from him, the whole-offerings for both morning and evening, and for sabbaths, new moons, and appointed seasons, as prescribed in the law of the LORD. He ordered the people 4 living in Jerusalem to provide the share due from the priests and the Levites, so that they might devote themselves entirely to the law of the LORD. As soon as the king's 5 order was issued to the Israelites, they gave generously from the firstfruits of their corn and new wine, oil and honey, all the produce of their land; they brought a full tithe of everything. The Israel- 6 ites and the Judaeans living in the cities of Judah also brought a tithe of cattle and sheep, and a tithe of all produce as offerings dedicated to the LORD their God, and they stacked the produce in heaps. They began to deposit the heaps in 7 the third month and completed them in the seventh. When Heze- 8 kiah and his officers came and saw the heaps, they blessed the LORD with his people Israel. Hezekiah 9 asked the priests and the Levites about these heaps, and Azariah 10

---

[a] with unrestrained fervour: *prob. rdg.*; *Heb.* with powerful instruments.
[b] making confession to: *or* confessing.

the chief priest, who was of the line of Zadok, answered, 'From the time when the people began to bring their contribution into the house of the LORD, they have had enough to eat, enough and to spare; indeed, the LORD has so greatly blessed them that they have this great store left over.'

11 Then Hezekiah ordered storerooms to be prepared in the house of the LORD, and this was done; 12 and the people honestly brought in their contributions, the tithe, and their dedicated gifts. The overseer in charge of them was Conaniah the Levite, with Shimei his brother as 13 his deputy; Jehiel, Azaziah, Nahath, Asahel, Jerimoth, Jozabad, Eliel, Ismachiah, Mahath, and Benaiah were appointed by King Hezekiah and Azariah, the chief overseer of the house of God, to assist Conaniah and Shimei his 14 brother. And Kore son of Imnah the Levite, keeper of the East Gate, was in charge of the freewill offerings to God, to apportion the contributions made to the LORD and 15 the most sacred offerings. Eden, Miniamin, Jeshua, Shemaiah, Amariah, and Shecaniah in the priestly cities assisted him in the fair distribution of portions to their kinsmen, young and old[a] alike, by 16 divisions. Irrespective of their registration, shares were distributed to all males three years of age and upwards who entered the house of the LORD to take their daily part in the service, according to their divisions, as their office demanded. 17 The priests were registered by families, the Levites from twenty years of age and upwards by their 18 offices in their divisions. They were registered with all their dependants, their wives, their sons, and their daughters, the whole company of them, because in virtue of their permanent standing they had to keep themselves duly 19 hallowed. As for the priests of

Aaron's line in the common lands attached to their cities, in every city men were nominated to distribute portions to every male among the priests and to every one who was registered with the Levites.

20 Such was the action taken by Hezekiah throughout Judah; he did what was good and right and loyal in the sight of the LORD his God. Whatever he undertook in 21 the service of the house of God and in obedience to the law and the commandment to seek guidance of his God, he did with all his heart, and he prospered.

32 1[b] After these events and this example of loyal conduct, Sennacherib king of Assyria invaded Judah and encamped against the fortified cities, believing that he could attach them to himself. 2 When Hezekiah saw that he had come and was determined to attack Jerusalem, he consulted his 3 civil and military officers about blocking up the springs outside the city; and they encouraged him. 4 They gathered together a large number of people and blocked up all the springs and the stream which flowed through the land. 'Why', they said, 'should Assyrian kings come here and find plenty of water?' Then the king acted bold- 5 ly; he made good every breach in the city wall and erected towers on it; he built another wall outside it and strengthened the Millo of the city of David; he also collected a great quantity of weapons and shields. He appointed military 6 commanders over the people and assembled them in the square by the city gate and spoke encouragingly to them in these words: 'Be strong; be brave. Do not let 7 the king of Assyria or the rabble he has brought with him strike terror or panic into your hearts. We have more on our side than he has. He 8 has human strength; but we have

a Or high and low.   *b* Verses 1–19: cp. 2 Kgs. 18. 13–37; Isa. 36. 1–22.

470

the LORD our God to help us and to fight our battles.' So spoke Hezekiah king of Judah, and the people were buoyed up by his words.

9 After this, Sennacherib king of Assyria, while he and his high command were at Lachish, sent envoys to Jerusalem to deliver this message to Hezekiah king of Judah and to all the Judaeans in 10 Jerusalem: 'Sennacherib king of Assyria says, "What gives you confidence to stay in Jerusalem 11 under siege? Hezekiah is misleading you into risking death by famine or thirst where you are, when he tells you that the LORD your God will save you from the grip of 12 the Assyrian king. Was it not Hezekiah himself who suppressed the LORD's hill-shrines and altars and told the people of Judah and Jerusalem that they must prostrate themselves before one altar only 13 and burn sacrifices there? You know very well what I and my forefathers have done to all the peoples of the lands. Were the gods of these nations able to save their 14 lands from me? Not one of the gods of these nations, which my forefathers exterminated, was able to save his people from me. Much less 15 will your god save you! How, then, can Hezekiah deceive you or mislead you like this? How can you believe him, for no god of any nation or kingdom has been able to save his people from me or my forefathers? Much less will your gods save you!"'

16 The envoys of Sennacherib spoke still more against the LORD God and against his servant Hezekiah.

17 And the king himself wrote a letter to defy the LORD the God of Israel, in these terms: 'Just as the gods of other nations could not save their people from me, so the god of Hezekiah will not save his people 18 from me.' Then they shouted in

Hebrew at the top of their voices at the people of Jerusalem on the wall, to strike them with fear and terror, hoping thus to capture the city. They described the god[a] of 19 Jerusalem as being like the gods of the other peoples of the earth – things made by the hands of men.

In this plight King Hezekiah 20[b] and the prophet Isaiah son of Amoz cried to heaven in prayer. So the LORD sent an angel who cut 21 down all the fighting men, as well as the leaders and the commanders, in the camp of the king of Assyria, so that he went home disgraced to his own land. When he entered the temple of his god, certain of his own sons struck him down with their swords.

Thus the LORD saved Hezekiah 22 and the inhabitants of Jerusalem from Sennacherib king of Assyria and all their enemies; and he gave them respite on every side. Many 23 people brought to Jerusalem offerings for the LORD and costly gifts for Hezekiah king of Judah. From then on he was held in high honour by all the nations.

About this time Hezekiah fell 24 dangerously ill and prayed to the LORD; the LORD said, 'I will heal you,'[c] and granted him a sign. But, 25 being a proud man, he was not grateful for the good done to him, and Judah and Jerusalem suffered for it. Then, proud as he was, Heze- 26 kiah submitted, and the people of Jerusalem with him, and the LORD's anger did not fall on them again in Hezekiah's time.

Hezekiah enjoyed great wealth 27 and fame.[d] He built for himself treasuries for silver and gold, precious stones and spices, shields and other costly things; and barns for 28 the harvests of corn, new wine, and oil; and stalls for every kind of cattle, as well as sheepfolds. He 29 amassed[e] a great many flocks and

---

[a] Or gods.   [b] Verses 20–22: cp. 2 Kgs. 19. 1–37; Isa. 37. 1–38.
[c] I will heal you: prob. rdg., cp. 2 Kgs. 20. 5; Heb. om.   [d] Or riches.
[e] Prob. rdg.; Heb. adds cities.

herds; God had indeed given him vast riches. 30 It was this same Hezekiah who blocked the upper outflow of the waters of Gihon and directed them downwards and westwards to the city of David. In fact, Hezekiah was successful in everything he attempted, 31 even in the affair of the envoys sent by the king*a* of Babylon – the envoys who came to inquire about the portent which had been seen in the land at the time when God left him to himself, to test him and to discover all that was in his heart. 32 The other events of Hezekiah's reign, and his works of piety, are recorded in the vision of the prophet Isaiah son of Amoz and in the annals of the kings of Judah and Israel. 33 So Hezekiah rested with his forefathers and was buried in the uppermost of the graves of David's sons; all Judah and the people of Jerusalem paid him honour when he died, and he was succeeded by his son Manasseh.

33 1*b* MANASSEH was twelve years old when he came to the throne, and he reigned in Jerusalem for fifty-five years. 2 He did what was wrong in the eyes of the LORD, in following the abominable practices of the nations which the LORD had dispossessed in favour of the Israelites. 3 He rebuilt the hill-shrines which his father Hezekiah had dismantled, he erected altars to the Baalim and made sacred poles, he prostrated himself before all the host of heaven and worshipped them. 4 He built altars in the house of the LORD, that house of which the LORD had said, 'In Jerusalem shall my Name be for ever.' 5 He built altars for all the host of heaven in the two courts of the house 6 of the LORD; he made his sons pass through the fire in the Valley of Ben-hinnom, he practised soothsaying, divination, and sorcery, and dealt with ghosts and spirits.

He did much wrong in the eyes of the LORD and provoked his anger; and the image that he had had 7 carved in relief he put in the house of God, the place of which God had said to David and Solomon his son, 'This house and Jerusalem, which I chose out of all the tribes of Israel, shall receive my Name for all time. I will not again dis- 8 place Israel from the land which I assigned to their forefathers, if only they will be careful to observe all that I commanded them through Moses, all the law, the statutes, and the rules.' But Manasseh mis- 9 led Judah and the inhabitants of Jerusalem into wickedness far worse than that of the nations which the LORD had exterminated in favour of the Israelites.

The LORD spoke to Manasseh 10 and to his people, but they paid no heed. So the LORD brought against 11 them the commanders of the army of the king of Assyria; they captured Manasseh with spiked weapons, and bound him with fetters, and brought him to Babylon. In 12 his distress he prayed to the LORD his God and sought to placate him, and made his humble submission before the God of his fathers. He 13 prayed, and God accepted his petition and heard his supplication. He brought him back to Jerusalem and restored him to the throne; and thus Manasseh learnt that the LORD was God.

After this he built an outer wall 14 for the city of David, west of Gihon in the gorge, and extended it to the entrance by the Fish Gate, enclosing Ophel; and he raised it to a great height. He also put military commanders in all the fortified cities of Judah. He removed the 15 foreign gods and the carved image from the house of the LORD and all the altars which he had built on the temple mount and in Jerusalem, and threw them out of the city. Moreover, he repaired the altar of 16

a Prob. rdg., cp. 2 Kgs. 20. 12; Heb. officers.   *b* Verses 1–9: cp. 2 Kgs. 21. 1–9.

the LORD and sacrificed at it shared-offerings and thank-offerings, and commanded Judah to serve the LORD the God of Israel.

17 But the people still continued to sacrifice at the hill-shrines, though only to the LORD their God.

18 The rest of the acts of Manasseh, his prayer to his God, and the discourses of the seers who spoke to him in the name of the LORD the God of Israel, are recorded in the chronicles of the kings of Israel.

19 His prayer and the answer he received to it, and all his sin and unfaithfulness, and the places where he built hill-shrines and set up sacred poles and carved idols, before he submitted, are recorded

20 in the chronicles of the seers. So Manasseh rested with his forefathers and was buried in the garden-tomb of[a] his family; he was succeeded by his son Amon.

21[b] Amon was twenty-two years old when he came to the throne, and he reigned in Jerusalem for two years.

22 He did what was wrong in the eyes of the LORD as his father Manasseh had done. He sacrificed to all the images that his father Manasseh had made, and worshipped them.

23 He was not submissive before the LORD like his father Manasseh; his

24 guilt was much greater. His courtiers conspired against him and

25 murdered him in his house; but the people of the land killed all the conspirators and made his son Josiah king in his place.

34 1[c] JOSIAH was eight years old when he came to the throne, and he reigned in Jerusalem for thirty-one

2 years. He did what was right in the eyes of the LORD; he followed in the footsteps of his forefather David, swerving neither right nor

3 left. In the eighth year of his reign, when he was still a boy, he began to seek guidance of the God

of his forefather David; and in the twelfth year he began to purge Judah and Jerusalem of the hill-shrines and the sacred poles, and the carved idols and the images of metal. He saw to it that the altars 4 for the Baalim were destroyed and he hacked down the incense-altars which stood above them; he broke in pieces the sacred poles and the carved and metal images, grinding them to powder and scattering it on the graves of those who had sacrificed to them. He also burnt 5 the bones of the priests on their altars and purged Judah and Jerusalem. In the cities of Manasseh, 6 Ephraim, and Simeon, and as far as Naphtali, he burnt down their houses wherever he found them; he destroyed the altars and the 7 sacred poles, ground the idols to powder, and hacked down the incense-altars throughout the land of Israel. Then he returned to Jerusalem.

In the eighteenth year of his 8[d] reign, after he had purified the land and the house, he sent Shaphan son of Azaliah and Maaseiah the governor of the city and Joah son of Joahaz the secretary of state to repair the house of the LORD his God. They came to Hilkiah the 9 high priest and gave him the silver that had been brought to the house of God, the silver which the Levites, on duty at the threshold, had gathered from Manasseh, Ephraim, and all the rest of Israel, as well as from Judah and Benjamin and the inhabitants of Jerusalem. It was then handed over to the 10 foremen in charge of the work in the house of the LORD, and these men, working in the house, used it for repairing and strengthening the fabric; they gave it also to the 11 carpenters and builders to buy hewn stone, and timber for rafters and beams, for the buildings which

[a] the garden-tomb of: prob. rdg., cp. 2 Kgs. 21. 18; Heb. om.
[b] Verses 21–25: cp. 2 Kgs. 21. 19–24.
[c] Verses 1, 2: cp. 2 Kgs. 22. 1, 2.   [d] Verses 8–32: cp. 2 Kgs. 22. 3 – 23. 3.

the kings of Judah had allowed to
12–13 fall into ruin. The men did their
work honestly under the direction
of Jahath and Obadiah, Levites of
the line of Merari, and Zechariah
and Meshullam, members of the
family of Kohath. These also had
control of the porters and directed
the workmen of every trade. The
Levites were all skilled musicians,
and some of them were secretaries,
14 clerks, or door-keepers. When they
fetched the silver which had been
brought to the house of the LORD,
the priest Hilkiah discovered the
book of the law of the LORD which
had been given through Moses.
15 Then Hilkiah told Shaphan the
adjutant-general, 'I have discovered the book of the law in the house
of the LORD.' Hilkiah gave the
16 book to Shaphan, and he brought
it to the king and reported to him:
'Your servants are doing all that
17 was entrusted to them. They have
melted down the silver in the house
of the LORD and have handed it
over to the foremen and the work-
18 men.' Shaphan the adjutant-general also told the king that the
priest Hilkiah had given him a
book; and he read it out in the
19 king's presence. When the king
heard what was in the book of the
20 law, he rent his clothes, and ordered Hilkiah, Ahikam son of Shaphan, Abdon son of Micah, Shaphan
the adjutant-general, and Asaiah
21 the king's attendant, to go and
seek guidance of the LORD, for
himself and for all who still remained in Israel and Judah, about
the contents of the book that had
been discovered. 'Great is the
wrath of the LORD,' he said, 'and it
has been poured out upon us because our forefathers did not observe the command of the LORD
and do all that is written in this
book.'
2   So Hilkiah and those whom the
king had instructed went to Hul-

dah the prophetess, wife of Shallum son of Tikvah,[a] son of Hasrah,
the keeper of the wardrobe, and
consulted her at her home in the
second quarter of Jerusalem. 'This 23
is the word of the LORD the God of
Israel,' she answered: 'Say to the
man who sent you to me, "This is 24
the word of the LORD: I am bringing disaster on this place and its
inhabitants, fulfilling all the im-
precations recorded in the book
which was read in the presence of
the king of Judah, because they 25
have forsaken me and burnt sacrifices to other gods, provoking my
anger with all the idols they have
made with their own hands; therefore my wrath is poured out upon
this place and will not be quenched." This is what you shall say to 26
the king of Judah who sent you to
seek guidance of the LORD: "This
is the word of the LORD the God of
Israel: You have listened to my
words and shown a willing heart, 27
you humbled yourself before God
when you heard what I said about
this place and its inhabitants; you
humbled yourself and rent your
clothes and wept before me. Because of all this,[b] I for my part have
heard you. This is the very word of
the LORD. Therefore, I will gather 28
you to your forefathers, and you
will be gathered to your grave in
peace; you will not live to see all
the disaster which I am bringing
upon this place and upon its inhabitants."' So they brought back
word to the king.

Then the king sent and called all 29
the elders of Judah and Jerusalem
together, and went up to the house
of the LORD; he took with him all 30
the men of Judah and the inhabitants of Jerusalem, the priests and
the Levites, the whole population,
high and low. There he read them
the whole book of the covenant
discovered in the house of the
LORD; and then, standing on the 31

---

[a] *Prob. rdg., cp. 2 Kgs. 22. 14; Heb. Tokhath.*
[b] *Because of all this: prob. rdg.; Heb. om.*

dais, the king made a covenant before the LORD to obey him and keep his commandments, his testimonies, and his statutes, with all his heart and soul, and so fulfil the terms of the covenant written in 32 this book. Then he swore an oath with all who were present in Jerusalem to keep the covenant.[a] Thereafter the inhabitants of Jerusalem did obey the covenant of God, the 33 God of their fathers. Josiah removed all abominable things from all the territories of the Israelites, so that everyone living in Israel might serve the LORD his God. As long as he lived they did not fail in their allegiance to the LORD the God of their fathers.

35 Josiah kept a Passover to the LORD in Jerusalem, and the passover lamb was killed on the four-
2 teenth day of the first month. He appointed the priests to their offices and encouraged them to perform the service of the house of the
3 LORD. He said to the Levites, the teachers of Israel, who were dedicated to the LORD, 'Put the holy Ark in the house which Solomon son of David king of Israel built; it is not to be carried about on your shoulders. Now is the time to serve the LORD your God and his people
4 Israel: prepare yourselves by families according to your divisions, following the written instructions of David king of Israel and those of
5 Solomon his son; and stand in the Holy Place as representatives of the family groups of the lay people, your brothers, one division of Lev-
6 ites to each family group. Kill the passover lamb and hallow yourselves and prepare for your brothers to fulfil the word of the LORD given through Moses.'
7 Josiah contributed on behalf of all the lay people present thirty thousand small cattle, that is young rams and goats, for the Passover, in addition to three

thousand bulls; all these were from the king's own resources. And 8 his officers contributed willingly for the people, the priests, and the Levites. Hilkiah, Zechariah, and Jehiel, the chief officers of the house of God, gave on behalf of the priests two thousand six hundred small cattle for the Passover, in addition to three hundred bulls. And Conaniah, Shemaiah and 9 Nethaneel his brothers, and Hashabiah, Jeiel, and Jozabad, the chiefs of the Levites, gave on behalf of the Levites for the Passover five thousand small cattle in addition to five hundred bulls.

When the service had been ar- 10 ranged, the priests stood in their places and the Levites in their divisions, according to the king's command. They killed the pass- 11 over victim, and the priests flung the blood against the altar as the Levites flayed the animals. Then 12 they removed the fat flesh,[b] which they allocated to the people by groups of families for them to offer to the LORD, as prescribed in the book of Moses; and so with the bulls. They cooked the passover 13 victim over the fire according to custom, and boiled the holy offerings in pots, cauldrons, and pans, and served them quickly to all the people. After that they made the 14 necessary preparations for themselves and the priests, because the priests of Aaron's line were engaged till nightfall in offering whole-offerings and the fat portions; so the Levites made the necessary preparations for themselves and for the priests of Aaron's line. The singers, the sons of A- 15 saph, were in their places according to the rules laid down by David and by Asaph, Heman, and Jeduthun, the king's seers. The door-keepers stood, each at his gate; there was no need for them to leave their posts, because their

[a] to keep the covenant: prob. rdg., cp. 2 Kgs. 23. 3; Heb. and Benjamin.
[b] fat flesh: or whole-offering.

kinsmen the Levites had made the preparations for them.

16 In this manner all the service of the LORD was arranged that day, to keep the Passover and to offer whole-offerings on the altar of the LORD, according to the command 17 of King Josiah. The people of Israel who were present kept the Passover at that time and the pilgrim-feast of Unleavened Bread 18 for seven days. No Passover like it had been kept in Israel since the days of the prophet Samuel; none of the kings of Israel had ever kept such a Passover as Josiah kept, with the priests and Levites and all Judah and Israel who were present and the inhabitants of Jerusalem. 19 In the eighteenth year of Josiah's reign this Passover was kept.

20 After Josiah had thus organized all the service of the house, Necho king of Egypt marched up to attack Carchemish on the Euphrates; and Josiah went out to confront 21 him. But Necho sent envoys to him, saying, 'What do you want with me, king of Judah? I have no quarrel with you today, only with those with whom I am at war. God has purposed to speed me on my way, and God is on my side; do not stand in his way, or he will destroy 22 you.' Josiah would not be deflected from his purpose but insisted on fighting; he refused to listen to Necho's words spoken at God's command, and he sallied out to join battle in the vale of Megiddo. 23 The archers shot at him; he was severely wounded and told his 24 bodyguard to carry him off. They lifted him out of his chariot and carried him in his viceroy's chariot to Jerusalem. There he died and was buried among the tombs of his ancestors, and all Judah and Jeru- 25 salem mourned for him. Jeremiah also made a lament for Josiah; and to this day the minstrels, both men and women, commemorate Josiah in their lamentations. Such

laments have become traditional in Israel, and they are found in the written collections.

The other events of Josiah's 26 reign, and his works of piety, all performed in accordance with what is laid down in the law of the LORD, and his acts, from first to last, are 27 recorded in the annals of the kings of Israel and Judah.

THE people of the land took 36 1[a] Josiah's son Jehoahaz and made him king in place of his father in Jerusalem. He was twenty-three 2 years old when he came to the throne, and he reigned in Jerusalem for three months. Then Necho 3 king of Egypt deposed him and fined the country a hundred talents of silver and one talent of gold, and 4 made his brother Eliakim king over Judah and Jerusalem in his place, changing his name to Jehoiakim; he also carried away his brother Jehoahaz to Egypt. Je- 5 hoiakim was twenty-five years old when he came to the throne, and he reigned in Jerusalem for eleven years. He did what was wrong in the eyes of the LORD his God. So 6 Nebuchadnezzar king of Babylon marched against him and put him in fetters and took him to Babylon. He also removed to Babylon some 7 of the vessels of the house of the LORD and put them into his own palace there. The other events of 8 Jehoiakim's reign, including the abominations he committed, and everything of which he was held guilty, are recorded in the annals of the kings of Israel and Judah. He was succeeded by his son Jehoiachin.

Jehoiachin was eight years old 9[b] when he came to the throne, and he reigned in Jerusalem for three months and ten days. He did what was wrong in the eyes of the LORD. At the turn of the year King 10 Nebuchadnezzar sent and brought him to Babylon, together with the

---

[a] *Verses 1–4: cp. 2 Kgs. 23. 30–34.*   [b] *Verses 9, 10: cp. 2 Kgs. 24. 8–17.*

choicest vessels of the house of the LORD, and made his father's brother Zedekiah king over Judah and Jerusalem.

11 Zedekiah was twenty-one years old when he came to the throne, and he reigned in Jerusalem for 12 eleven years. He did what was wrong in the eyes of the LORD his God; he did not defer to the guidance of the prophet Jeremiah, the 13 spokesman of the LORD. He also rebelled against King Nebuchadnezzar, who had laid on him a solemn oath of allegiance. He was obstinate and stubborn and refused to return to the LORD the 14 God of Israel. All the chiefs of Judah and the priests and the people became more and more unfaithful, following all the abominable practices of the other nations; and they defiled the house of the LORD which he had hallowed in 15 Jerusalem. The LORD God of their fathers had warned them betimes through his messengers, for he took pity on his people and on his 16 dwelling-place; but they never ceased to deride his messengers, scorn his words and scoff at his prophets, until the anger of the LORD burst out against his people 17ᵃ and could not be appeased. So he brought against them the king of the Chaldaeans, who put their young men to the sword in the sanctuary and spared neither young man nor maiden, neither the old nor the weak; God gave them all 18 into his power. And he brought all

the vessels of the house of God, great and small, and the treasures of the house of the LORD and of the king and his officers – all these he brought to Babylon. And they 19 burnt down the house of God, razed the city wall of Jerusalem and burnt down all its stately mansions and all their precious possessions until everything was destroyed. Those who escaped the 20 sword he took captive to Babylon, and they became slaves to him and his sons until the sovereignty passed to the Persians, while the land 21 of Israel ran the full term of its sabbaths. All the time that it lay desolate it kept the sabbath rest, to complete seventy years in fulfilment of the word of the LORD by the prophet Jeremiah.

Now in the first year of Cyrus 22ᵇ king of Persia, so that the word of the LORD spoken through Jeremiah might be fulfilled, the LORD stirred up the heart of Cyrus king of Persia; and he issued a proclamation throughout his kingdom, both by word of mouth and in writing, to this effect:

'This is the word of Cyrus king of 23 Persia: The LORD the God of heaven has given me all the kingdoms of the earth, and he himself has charged me to build him a house at Jerusalem in Judah. To every man of his people now among you I say, the LORD his God beᶜ with him, and let him go up.'

ᵃ *Verses 17–20: cp. 2 Kgs. 25. 1–17.*
ᶜ be: *prob. rdg., cp. Ezra 1. 3; Heb. om.*

ᵇ *Verses 22, 23: cp. Ezra 1. 1–3.*

THE BOOK OF

EZRA

The return of the exiles to Jerusalem

1 NOW in the first year of Cyrus king of Persia, so that the word of the LORD spoken through Jeremiah might be fulfilled, the LORD stirred up the heart of Cyrus king of Persia; and he issued a proclamation throughout his kingdom, both by word of mouth and in writing, to this effect:

2 'This is the word of Cyrus king of Persia: The LORD the God of heaven has given me all the kingdoms of the earth, and he himself has charged me to build him a house at 3 Jerusalem in Judah. To every man of his people now among you I say, God be with him, and let him go up to Jerusalem in Judah, and rebuild the house of the LORD the God of Israel, the God whose city 4 is Jerusalem. And every remaining Jew, wherever he may be living, may claim aid from his neighbours in that place, silver and gold, goods[a] and cattle, in addition to the voluntary offerings for the house of God in Jerusalem.'

5 Thereupon the heads of families of Judah and Benjamin, and the priests and the Levites, answered the summons, all whom God had moved to go up to rebuild the house of the LORD in Jerusalem. 6 Their neighbours all assisted them with gifts of every kind, silver[b] and gold, goods[a] and cattle and valuable gifts in abundance,[c] in addition to any voluntary service.

Moreover, Cyrus king of Persia 7 produced the vessels of the house of the LORD which Nebuchadnezzar had removed from Jerusalem and placed in the temple of his god; and he handed them over into the 8 charge of Mithredath the treasurer, who made an inventory of them for Sheshbazzar the ruler of Judah. This was the list: thirty gold basins, 9 a thousand silver basins, twenty-nine vessels of various kinds, thirty golden bowls, four hundred 10 and ten silver bowls of various types, and a thousand other vessels. The vessels of gold and silver 11 amounted in all to five thousand four hundred; and Sheshbazzar took them all up to Jerusalem, when the exiles were brought back from Babylon.

Of the captives whom Nebu- 2 1[d] chadnezzar king of Babylon had taken into exile in Babylon, these were the people of the province who returned to Jerusalem and Judah, each to his own city, led by 2 Zerubbabel, Jeshua,[e] Nehemiah, Seraiah, Reelaiah, Mordecai, Bilshan, Mispar, Bigvai, Rehum and Baanah.

The roll of the men of the people 3 of Israel: the family of Parosh, two thousand one hundred and seventy-two; the family of Shephatiah, 4 three hundred and seventy-two; the family of Arah, seven hundred 5 and seventy-five; the family of 6 Pahath-moab, namely the families of Jeshua and[f] Joab, two thousand eight hundred and twelve; the 7 family of Elam, one thousand two

---

[a] Or pack-animals.
[b] with gifts...silver: prob. rdg., cp. 1 Esdras 2. 9; Heb. with vessels of silver.
[c] in abundance: prob. rdg., cp. 1 Esdras 2. 9; Heb. apart.
[d] Verses 1–70: cp. Neh. 7. 6–73.   [e] Or Joshua (cp. Hag. 1. 1).
[f] and: prob. rdg., cp. Neh. 7. 11; Heb. om.

8 hundred and fifty-four; the family of Zattu, nine hundred and forty-
9 five; the family of Zaccai, seven
10 hundred and sixty; the family of Bani, six hundred and forty-two;
11 the family of Bebai, six hundred
12 and twenty-three; the family of Azgad, one thousand two hundred
13 and twenty-two; the family of Adonikam, six hundred and sixty-
14 six; the family of Bigvai, two
15 thousand and fifty-six; the family of Adin, four hundred and fifty-
16 four; the family of Ater, namely
17 that of Hezekiah, ninety-eight; the family of Bezai, three hundred and
18 twenty-three; the family of Jorah,
19 one hundred and twelve; the family of Hashum, two hundred and
20 twenty-three; the family of Gibbar,
21 ninety-five. The men[a] of Bethlehem, one hundred and twenty-
22 three; the men of Netophah, fifty-
23 six; the men of Anathoth, one hun-
24 dred and twenty-eight; the men of
25 Beth-azmoth,[b] forty-two; the men of Kiriath-jearim,[c] Kephirah, and Beeroth, seven hundred and forty-
26 three; the men[d] of Ramah and Geba, six hundred and twenty-one;
27 the men of Michmas, one hundred
28 and twenty-two; the men of Bethel and Ai, two hundred and twenty-
29 three; the men[e] of Nebo, fifty-two;
30 the men of Magbish, one hundred
31 and fifty-six; the men of the other Elam, one thousand two hundred
32 and fifty-four; the men of Harim,
33 three hundred and twenty; the men of Lod, Hadid, and Ono, seven
34 hundred and twenty-five; the men of Jericho, three hundred and for-
35 ty-five; the men of Senaah, three thousand six hundred and thirty.
36 Priests: the family of Jedaiah, of the line of Jeshua, nine hundred
37 and seventy-three; the family of Immer, one thousand and fifty-

two; the family of Pashhur, one 38 thousand two hundred and forty-seven; the family of Harim, one 39 thousand and seventeen.

Levites: the families of Jeshua 40 and Kadmiel, of the line of Hoda-viah, seventy-four. Singers: the 41 family of Asaph, one hundred and twenty-eight. The guild of door- 42 keepers: the family of Shallum, the family of Ater, the family of Talmon, the family of Akkub, the family of Hatita, and the family of Shobai, one hundred and thirty-nine in all.

Temple-servitors: the family of 43 Ziha, the family of Hasupha, the family of Tabbaoth, the family of 44 Keros, the family of Siaha, the family of Padon, the family of 45 Lebanah, the family of Hagabah, the family of Akkub, the family of 46 Hagab, the family of Shamlai,[f] the family of Hanan, the family of Gid- 47 del, the family of Gahar, the family of Reaiah, the family of Rezin, the 48 family of Nekoda, the family of Gazzam, the family of Uzza, the 49 family of Paseah, the family of Besai, the family of Asnah, the 50 family of the Meunim,[g] the family of the Nephusim,[h] the family of 51 Bakbuk, the family of Hakupha, the family of Harhur, the family of 52 Bazluth, the family of Mehida, the family of Harsha, the family of 53 Barkos, the family of Sisera, the family of Temah, the family of 54 Neziah, and the family of Hatipha.

Descendants of Solomon's ser- 55 vants: the family of Sotai, the family of Hassophereth, the family of Peruda, the family of Jaalah, 56 the family of Darkon, the family of Giddel, the family of Shephatiah, 57 the family of Hattil, the family of Pochereth-hazzebaim, and the family of Ami.

[a] *Prob. rdg., cp. Neh. 7. 26; Heb. family.*
[b] *Prob. rdg., cp. Neh. 7. 28; Heb. the family of Azmoth.*
[c] *Prob. rdg., cp. Neh. 7. 29; Heb. the family of Kiriath-arim.*
[d] *Prob. rdg., cp. Neh. 7. 30; Heb. family.*
[e] *Prob. rdg.; Heb. family (also in verses 30–35).*   [f] *Or Shalmai (cp. Neh. 7. 48).*
[g] *Or Meinim.*   [h] *Or Nephisim.*

58 The temple-servitors and the descendants of Solomon's servants amounted to three hundred and ninety-two in all.

59 The following were those who returned from Tel-melah, Tel-harsha, Kerub, Addan, and Immer, but could not establish their father's family nor whether by descent they belonged to Israel:

60 the family of Delaiah, the family of Tobiah, and the family of Nekoda,

61 six hundred and fifty-two. Also of the priests: the family of Hobaiah, the family of Hakkoz, and the family of Barzillai who had married a daughter of Barzillai the Gileadite and went by his*a* name.

62 These searched for their names among those enrolled in the genealogies, but they could not be found; they were disqualified for

63 the priesthood as unclean, and the governor forbade them to partake of the most sacred food until there should be a priest able to consult the Urim and the Thummim.

64 The whole assembled people numbered forty-two thousand three

65 hundred and sixty, apart from their slaves, male and female, of whom there were seven thousand three hundred and thirty-seven; and they had two hundred singers,

66 men and women. Their horses numbered seven hundred and thirty-six, their mules two hun-

67 dred and forty-five, their camels four hundred and thirty-five, and their asses six thousand seven hundred and twenty.

68 When they came to the house of the LORD in Jerusalem, some of the heads of families volunteered to rebuild the house of God on its

69 original site. According to their resources they gave for the fabric fund a total of sixty-one thousand drachmas of gold, five thousand minas of silver, and one hundred priestly robes.

70 The priests, the Levites, and some of the people lived in Jerusalem and its suburbs;*b* the singers, the door-keepers, and temple-servitors,*c* and all other Israelites, lived in their own towns.

Worship restored and the temple rebuilt

3 WHEN the seventh month came, the Israelites now being settled in their towns, the people assembled as one man in Jerusalem. Then 2 Jeshua son of Jozadak and his fellow-priests, and Zerubbabel son of Shealtiel and his kinsmen, set to work and built the altar of the God of Israel, in order to offer upon it whole-offerings as prescribed in the law of Moses the man of God. They 3 put the altar in place first, because they lived in fear of the foreign population; and they offered upon it whole-offerings to the LORD, both morning and evening offerings. They kept the pilgrim-feast 4 of Tabernacles*d* as ordained, and offered whole-offerings every day in the number prescribed for each day, and, in addition to these, the 5 regular whole-offerings and the offerings for sabbaths,*e* for new moons and for all the sacred seasons appointed by the LORD, and all voluntary offerings brought to the LORD. The offering of whole-offer- 6 ings began from the first day of the seventh month, although the foundation of the temple of the LORD had not yet been laid. They gave 7 money for the masons and carpenters, and food and drink and oil for the Sidonians and the Tyrians to fetch cedar-wood from the Lebanon to the roadstead at Joppa, by licence from Cyrus king of Persia.

In the second year after their 8

---

a *Prob. rdg., cp. 1 Esdras 5. 38; Heb. their.*
b *in Jerusalem and its suburbs: prob. rdg., cp. 1 Esdras 5. 46; Heb. om.*
c *Prob. rdg.; Heb. adds in their towns.*   *d* *Or Booths.*
e *for sabbaths: prob. rdg., cp. 1 Esdras 5. 52; Heb. om.*

return to the house of God in Jerusalem, and in the second month, Zerubbabel son of Shealtiel and Jeshua son of Jozadak started work, aided by all their fellow-Israelites, the priests and the Levites and all who had returned from captivity to Jerusalem. They appointed Levites from the age of twenty years and upwards to supervise the work of the 9 house of the LORD. Jeshua with his sons and his kinsmen, Kadmiel, Binnui, and Hodaviah,[a] together assumed control of those responsible for the work on the house of God.[b]

10 When the builders had laid the foundation of the temple of the LORD, the priests in their robes took their places with their trumpets, and the Levites, the sons of Asaph, with their cymbals, to praise the LORD in the manner prescribed by David king of Israel; 11 and they chanted praises and thanksgiving to the LORD, singing, 'It is good to give thanks to the LORD,[c] for his love towards Israel endures for ever.' All the people raised a great shout of praise to the LORD because the foundation of the house of the LORD had been 12 laid. But many of the priests and Levites and heads of families, who were old enough to have seen the former house, wept and wailed aloud when they saw the foundation of this house laid, while many others shouted for joy at the top of 13 their voice. The people could not distinguish the sound of the shout of joy from that of the weeping and wailing, so great was the shout which the people were raising, and the sound could be heard a long way off.

4 When the enemies of Judah and Benjamin heard that the returned exiles were building a temple to the LORD the God of Israel, they ap- 2 proached Zerubbabel and Jeshua[d] and the heads of families and said to them, 'Let us join you in building, for like you we seek your God, and we have been sacrificing to him ever since the days of Esarhaddon king of Assyria, who brought us here.' But Zerubbabel 3 and Jeshua and the rest of the heads of families in Israel said to them, 'The house which we are building for our God is no concern of yours. We alone will build it for the LORD the God of Israel, as his majesty Cyrus king of Persia commanded us.'

Then the people of the land 4 caused the Jews to lose heart and made them afraid to continue building; and in order to defeat 5 their purpose they bribed officials at court to act against them. This continued throughout the reign of Cyrus and into the reign of Darius king of Persia.

At the beginning of the reign of 6 Ahasuerus, the people of the land brought a charge in writing against the inhabitants of Judah and Jerusalem.

And in the days of Artaxerxes 7 king of Persia, with the agreement of Mithredath, Tabeel and all his colleagues wrote to him; the letter was written in Aramaic and read aloud in Aramaic.

Rehum the high commissioner 8[e] and Shimshai the secretary wrote a letter to King Artaxerxes concerning Jerusalem in the following terms:

'From Rehum the high commis- 9 sioner, Shimshai the secretary, and all their colleagues, the judges, the commissioners, the overseers, and chief officers, the men of Erech and

---

[a] *Binnui, and Hodaviah: prob. rdg.; Heb. and his sons the family of Judah.*
[b] *Prob. rdg.; Heb. adds the family of Henadad, their family and their kinsmen the Levites.*   [c] *to give thanks to the LORD: prob. rdg., cp. Ps. 106. 1; Heb. om.*
[d] *and Jeshua: prob. rdg., cp. 1 Esdras 5. 68; Heb. om.*
[e] *From 4. 8 to 6. 18 the text is in Aramaic.*

481

Babylon, and the Elamites in Susa,
10 and the other peoples whom the great and renowned Asnappar[a] deported and settled in the city of Samaria and in the rest of the province of Beyond-Euphrates.'

11 Here follows the text of their letter:

'To King Artaxerxes from his servants, the men of the province of Beyond-Euphrates:

12 'Be it known to Your Majesty that the Jews who left you and came to these parts have reached Jerusalem and are rebuilding that wicked and rebellious city; they have surveyed[b] the foundations 13 and are completing the walls. Be it known to Your Majesty that, if their city is rebuilt and the walls are completed, they will pay neither general levy, nor poll-tax, nor land-tax, and in the end[c] they 14 will harm the monarchy. Now, because we eat the king's salt and it is not right that we should witness the king's dishonour, therefore we have sent to inform Your Majesty, 15 in order that search may be made in the annals of your predecessors. You will discover by searching through the annals that this has been a rebellious city, harmful to the monarchy and its provinces, and that sedition has long been rife within its walls. That is why the 16 city was laid waste. We submit to Your Majesty that, if it is rebuilt and its walls are completed, the result will be that you will have no more footing in the province of Beyond-Euphrates.'

17 The king sent this answer:

'To Rehum the high commissioner, Shimshai the secretary, and all your colleagues resident in Samaria and in the rest of the province of Beyond-Euphrates, greeting. 18 The letter which you sent to me has now been read clearly in my presence. I have given orders and 19 search has been made, and it has been found that the city in question has a long history of revolt against the monarchy, and that rebellion and sedition have been rife in it. Powerful kings have 20 ruled in Jerusalem, exercising authority over the whole province of Beyond-Euphrates, and general levy, poll-tax, and land-tax have been paid to them. Therefore, issue 21 orders that these men must desist. This city is not to be rebuilt until a decree to that effect is issued by me. See that you do not neglect 22 your duty in this matter, lest more damage and harm be done to the monarchy.'

When the text of the letter from 23 King Artaxerxes was read before Rehum the high commissioner, Shimshai the secretary, and their colleagues, they hurried to Jerusalem and forcibly compelled the Jews to stop work. From then onwards the work on the house of God 24 in Jerusalem stopped; and it remained at a standstill till the second year of the reign of Darius king of Persia.

But the prophets Haggai[d] and 5 Zechariah grandson of Iddo upbraided the Jews in Judah and Jerusalem, prophesying in the name of the God of Israel. Then 2 Zerubbabel son of Shealtiel and Jeshua son of Jozadak at once began to rebuild the house of God in Jerusalem, and the prophets of God were with them and supported them. Tattenai, governor of the 3 province of Beyond-Euphrates, Shethar-bozenai, and their colleagues promptly came to them and said, 'Who issued a decree permitting you to rebuild this house and complete its furnishings?' They also asked them for the 4

---

[a] Or Osnappar.   [b] have surveyed: *prob. rdg.*; *Aram.* are surveying.
[c] in the end: *or* certainly.
[d] *Prob. rdg.*, cp. 1 Esdras 6. 1; *Aram. adds* the prophet.

names of the men engaged in the building. But the elders of the Jews were under God's watchful eye, and they were not prevented from continuing the work, until such time as a report should reach Darius and a royal letter should be received in answer.

6 Here follows the text of the letter sent by Tattenai, governor of the province of Beyond-Euphrates, Shethar-bozenai, and his colleagues, the inspectors in the province of Beyond-Euphrates, to 7 King Darius. This is the written report that they sent:

8 'To King Darius, all greetings. Be it known to Your Majesty that we went to the province of Judah and found the house of the great God being rebuilt by the Jewish elders,[a] with massive stones and timbers laid in the walls. The work was being done thoroughly and was making good progress under their 9 direction. We asked these elders who had issued a decree for the rebuilding of this house and the 10 completion of the furnishings. We also asked them for their names, so that we might make a list of the 11 leaders for your information. This was their reply: "We are the servants of the God of heaven and earth, and we are rebuilding the house originally built many years ago; a great king of Israel built it 12 and completed it. But because our forefathers provoked the anger of the God of heaven, he put them into the power of Nebuchadnezzar the Chaldaean, king of Babylon, who pulled down this house and carried the people captive to Baby-13 lon. However, Cyrus king of Babylon in the first year of his reign issued a decree that this house of 14 God should be rebuilt. Moreover, there were gold and silver vessels of the house of God, which Nebuchadnezzar had taken from the temple in Jerusalem and put in the temple in Babylon; and these King Cyrus took out of the temple in Babylon. He gave them to a man named Sheshbazzar, whom he had appointed governor, and said to 15 him, 'Take these vessels; go and restore them to the temple in Jerusalem, and let the house of God there be rebuilt on its original site.' Then this Sheshbazzar came 16 and laid the foundation of the house of God in Jerusalem; and from that time until now the rebuilding has continued, but it is not yet finished." Now, therefore, 17 if it please Your Majesty, let search be made in the royal archives in Babylon, to discover whether a decree was issued by King Cyrus for the rebuilding of this house of God in Jerusalem. Then let the king send us his wishes in the matter.'

Then King Darius issued an 6 order, and search was made in the archives where the treasures were deposited in Babylon. But it was in 2 Ecbatana, in the royal residence in the province of Media, that a scroll was found, on which was written the following memorandum:

'In the first year of King Cyrus, the 3 king issued this decree concerning the house of God in Jerusalem: Let the house be rebuilt as a place where sacrifices are offered and fire-offerings brought. Its height shall be sixty cubits and its breadth sixty cubits, with three courses of 4 massive stones and one[b] course of timber, the cost to be defrayed from the royal treasury. Also the 5 gold and silver vessels of the house of God, which Nebuchadnezzar took out of the temple in Jerusalem and brought to Babylon, shall be restored; they shall all be taken back to the temple in Jerusalem, and restored each to its place in the house of God.'

---

[a] by...elders: *prob. rdg., cp.* 1 *Esdras* 6. 8; *Aram. om.*
[b] *Prob. rdg., cp.* 1 *Esdras* 6. 25; *Aram.* a new.

6 Then King Darius issued this order:[a]

'Now, Tattenai, governor of the province of Beyond-Euphrates, Shethar-bozenai, and your colleagues, the inspectors in the province of Beyond-Euphrates, you are to keep away from the place, 7 and to leave the governor of the Jews and their elders free to rebuild this house of God; let them 8 rebuild it on its original site. I also issue an order prescribing what you are to do for these elders of the Jews, so that the said house of God may be rebuilt. Their expenses are to be defrayed in full from the royal funds accruing from the taxes of the province of Beyond-Euphrates, so that the work may not be 9 brought to a standstill. And let them have daily without fail whatever they want, young bulls, rams, or lambs as whole-offerings for the God of heaven, or wheat, salt, wine, or oil, as the priests in Jerusalem 10 demand, so that they may offer soothing sacrifices to the God of heaven, and pray for the life of the 11 king and his sons. Furthermore, I decree that, if any man tampers with this edict, a beam shall be pulled out of his house and he shall be fastened erect to it and flogged; and, in addition, his house shall be 12 forfeit.[b] And may the God who made that place a dwelling for his Name overthrow any king or people that shall presume to tamper with this edict or to destroy this house of God in Jerusalem. I Darius have issued a decree; it is to be carried out to the letter.'

13 Then Tattenai, governor of the province of Beyond-Euphrates, Shethar-bozenai, and their colleagues carried out to the letter the instructions which King Darius 14 had sent them, and the elders of the Jews went on with the rebuilding. As a result of the prophecies of Haggai the prophet and Zechariah grandson of Iddo they had good success and finished the rebuilding as commanded by the God of Israel and according to the decrees of Cyrus and Darius;[c] and 15 the house was completed on the twenty-third[d] day of the month Adar, in the sixth year of King Darius.

16 Then the people of Israel, the priests and the Levites and all the other exiles who had returned, celebrated the dedication of the house of God with great rejoicing. 17 For its dedication they offered one hundred bulls, two hundred rams, and four hundred lambs, and as a sin-offering for all Israel twelve he-goats, corresponding to the number of the tribes of Israel. And they 18 re-established the priests in their groups and the Levites in their divisions for the service of God in Jerusalem, as prescribed in the book of Moses.

19 On the fourteenth day of the first month the exiles who had returned kept the Passover. The 20 priests and the Levites, one and all, had purified themselves; all of them were ritually clean, and they killed the passover lamb for all the exiles who had returned, for their fellow-priests and for themselves. 21 It was eaten by the Israelites who had come back from exile and by all who had separated themselves from the peoples of the land and their uncleanness and sought the LORD the God of Israel. And they 22 kept the pilgrim-feast of Unleavened Bread for seven days with rejoicing; for the LORD had given them cause for joy by changing the disposition of the king of Assyria towards them, so that he encouraged them in the work of the house of God, the God of Israel.

---

[a] Then... order: *prob. rdg.*, *cp.* 1 Esdras 6. 27; *Aram. om.*
[b] Or made into a dunghill (*mng. of Aram. word uncertain*).
[c] *Prob. rdg.*; *Aram. adds* and Artaxerxes king of Persia.
[d] *Prob. rdg.*, *cp.* 1 Esdras 7. 5; *Aram.* third.

Ezra's mission to Jerusalem

7 Now after these events, in the reign of Artaxerxes king of Persia, there came up from Babylon one Ezra son of Seraiah, son of Aza- 2 riah, son of Hilkiah, son of Shallum, son of Zadok, son*a* of Ahitub, 3 son of Amariah, son of Azariah, 4 son of Meraioth, son of Zerahiah, 5 son of Uzzi, son of Bukki, son of Abishua, son of Phinehas, son of Eleazar, son of Aaron the chief 6 priest. He was a scribe*b* learned in the law of Moses which the Lord the God of Israel had given them; and the king granted him all that he asked, for the hand of the Lord 7 his God was upon him. In the seventh year of King Artaxerxes, other Israelites, priests, Levites, singers, door-keepers, and temple-servitors went up with him to Jeru- 8 salem; and they reached Jerusalem in the fifth month, in the seventh 9 year of the king. On the first day of the first month Ezra fixed the day for departure from Babylon, and on the first day of the fifth month he arrived at Jerusalem, for the gracious hand of his God was upon 10 him. For Ezra had devoted himself to the study and observance of the law of the Lord and to teaching statute and ordinance in Israel.

11 This is a copy of the royal letter which King Artaxerxes had given to Ezra the priest and scribe, a scribe versed in questions concerning the commandments and the statutes of the Lord laid upon Israel:

12*c* 'Artaxerxes, king of kings, to Ezra the priest and scribe learned in the law of the God of heaven:

13 'This is my decision. I hereby issue a decree that any of the people of Israel or of its priests or Levites in my kingdom who volunteer to go to Jerusalem may go with you. 14 You are sent by the king and his seven counsellors to find out how things stand in Judah and Jerusalem with regard to the law of your God with which you are entrusted. You are also to convey the 15 silver and gold which the king and his counsellors have freely offered to the God of Israel whose dwelling is in Jerusalem, together with any 16 silver and gold that you may find throughout the province of Babylon, and the voluntary offerings of the people and of the priests which they freely offer for the house of their God in Jerusalem. In pur- 17 suance of this decree you shall use the money solely for the purchase of bulls, rams, and lambs, and the proper grain-offerings and drink-offerings, to be offered on the altar in the house of your God in Jerusalem. Further, should any silver and 18 gold be left over, you and your colleagues may use it at your discretion according to the will of your God. The vessels which have 19 been given you for the service of the house of your God you shall hand over to the God of Jerusalem; and if anything else should be 20 required for the house of your God, which it may fall to you to provide, you may provide it out of the king's treasury.

'And I, King Artaxerxes, issue 21 an order to all treasurers in the province of Beyond-Euphrates that whatever is demanded of you by Ezra the priest, a scribe learned in the law of the God of heaven, is to be supplied exactly, up to a hun- 22 dred talents of silver, a hundred kor of wheat, a hundred bath of wine, a hundred bath of oil, and salt without reckoning. Whatever 23 is demanded by the God of heaven, let it be diligently carried out for the house of the God of heaven; otherwise wrath may fall upon the realm of the king and his sons. We 24 also make known to you that you have no authority to impose

---

a Or grandson.　　　*b* Or doctor of the law.
c The text of verses 12–26 is in Aramaic.

general levy, poll-tax, or land-tax on any of the priests, Levites, musicians, door-keepers, temple-servitors, or other servants of this house of God.

25 'And you, Ezra, in accordance with the wisdom of your God with which you are entrusted, are to appoint arbitrators and judges to judge all your people in the province of Beyond-Euphrates, all who acknowledge the laws of your God;[a] and you and they are to instruct those who do not acknow-

26 ledge them. Whoever will not obey the law of your God and the law of the king, let judgement be rigorously executed upon him, be it death, banishment, confiscation of property, or imprisonment.'

27 Then Ezra said,[b] 'Blessed be the LORD the God of our fathers who has prompted the king thus to add glory to the house of the LORD in

28 Jerusalem, and has made the king and his counsellors and all his high officers well disposed towards me!' So, knowing that the hand of the LORD my God was upon me, I took courage and assembled leading men out of Israel to go up with me.

8 These are the heads of families, as registered, family by family, of those who went up with me from Babylon in the reign of King Artax-

2 erxes: of the family of Phinehas, Gershom; of the family of Ithamar, Daniel; of the family of David,

3 Hattush son of[c] Shecaniah; of the family of Parosh, Zechariah, and with him a hundred and fifty

4 males in the register; of the family of Pahath-moab, Elihoenai son of Zerahiah, and with him two hun-

5 dred males; of the family of Zattu,[d] Shecaniah son of Jahaziel, and

6 with him three hundred males; of

the family of Adin, Ebed son of Jonathan, and with him fifty males; of the family of Elam, Isaiah 7 son of Athaliah, and with him seventy males; of the family of 8 Shephatiah, Zebadiah son of Michael, and with him eighty males; of the family of Joab, Obadiah son 9 of Jehiel, and with him two hundred and eighteen males; of the 10 family of Bani,[e] Shelomith son of Josiphiah, and with him a hundred and sixty males; of the family of 11 Bebai, Zechariah son of Bebai, and with him twenty-eight males; of 12 the family of Azgad, Johanan son of Hakkatan, and with him a hundred and ten males. The last were 13 the family of Adonikam, and these were their names: Eliphelet, Jeiel, and Shemaiah, and with them sixty males; and the family of Bigvai, 14 Uthai and Zabbud, and with them seventy males.

I assembled them by the river 15 which flows toward Ahava; and we encamped there three days. When I reviewed the people and the priests, I found no Levite there. So 16 I sent Eliezer, Ariel, Shemaiah, Elnathan, Jarib, Elnathan, Nathan, Zechariah, and Meshullam, prominent men, and Joiarib and Elnathan, men of discretion, with 17 instructions to go to Iddo, the chief man of the settlement at Casiphia; and I gave them a message for him and his kinsmen, the temple-servitors there, asking for servitors for the house of our God to be sent to us. And, because the 18 gracious hand of our God was upon us, they let us have Sherebiah, a man of discretion, of the family of Mahli son of Levi, son of Israel, together with his sons and kinsmen, eighteen men; also Hashabiah, to- 19 gether with Isaiah of the family of

---

[a] to judge...your God: *or* all of them versed in the laws of your God, to judge all the people in the province of Beyond-Euphrates.
[b] Then Ezra said: *prob. rdg., cp.* 1 Esdras 8. 25; *Heb. om.*
[c] son of: *prob. rdg.; Heb.* of the family of.
[d] of Zattu: *prob. rdg., cp.* 1 Esdras 8. 32; *Heb. om.*
[e] of Bani: *prob. rdg., cp.* 1 Esdras 8. 36; *Heb. om.*

Merari, his kinsmen and their sons,
20 twenty men; besides two hundred
and twenty temple-servitors (this
was an order instituted by David
and his officers to assist the Levites). These were all indicated by
name.
21   Then I proclaimed a fast there
by the river Ahava, so that we
might mortify ourselves before our
God and ask from him a safe journey for ourselves, our dependants,
22 and all our possessions. For I was
ashamed to ask the king for an
escort of soldiers and horsemen to
help us against enemies on the
way, because we had said to the
king, 'The hand of our God is upon
all who seek him, working their
good; but his fierce anger is on all
23 who forsake him.' So we fasted and
asked our God for a safe journey,
and he answered our prayer.
24   Then I separated twelve of the
chiefs of the priests, together with[a]
Sherebiah and Hashabiah and ten
25 of their kinsmen, and handed over
to them the silver and gold and the
vessels which had been set aside by
the king, his counsellors and his
officers and all the Israelites who
were present, as their contribution
26 to the house of our God. I handed
over to them six hundred and fifty
talents of silver, a hundred silver
vessels weighing two talents, a
27 hundred talents of gold, twenty
golden bowls worth a thousand
drachmas, and two vessels of a fine
28 red copper,[b] precious as gold. And I
said to the men, 'You are dedicated
to the LORD, and the vessels too
are sacred; the silver and gold are a
voluntary offering to the LORD the
29 God of your fathers. Watch over
them and guard them, until you
hand them over in the presence of
the chiefs of the priests and the
Levites and the heads of families
of Israel in Jerusalem, in the rooms
of the house of the LORD.'
30   So the priests and Levites received the consignment of silver
and gold and vessels, to be taken
to the house of our God in Jerusalem; and on the twelfth day of the 31
first month we left the river Ahava
bound for Jerusalem. The hand of
our God was upon us, and he saved
us from enemy attack and from
ambush on the way. When we ar- 32
rived at Jerusalem, we rested for
three days. And on the fourth day 33
the silver and gold and the vessels
were deposited in the house of our
God in the charge of Meremoth son
of Uriah the priest, who had with
him Eleazar son of Phinehas, and
they had with them the Levites
Jozabad son of Jeshua and Noadiah son of Binnui. Everything 34
was checked as it was handed over,
and at the same time a written
record was made of the whole consignment. Then those who had 35
come home from captivity, the exiles who had returned, offered as
whole-offerings to the God of Israel twelve bulls for all Israel,
ninety-six rams and seventy-two[c]
lambs, with twelve he-goats as a
sin-offering; all these were offered
as a whole-offering to the LORD.
They also delivered the king's 36
commission to the royal satraps
and governors in the province of
Beyond-Euphrates; and these gave
support to the people and the house
of God.
    When all this had been done, 9
some of the leaders approached me
and said, 'The people of Israel, including priests and Levites, have
not kept themselves apart from
the foreign population and from
the abominable practices of the
Canaanites, the Hittites, the Perizzites, the Jebusites, the Ammonites, the Moabites, the Egyptians,
and the Amorites. They have taken 2
women of these nations as wives
for themselves and their sons, so
that the holy race has become mixed with the foreign population;

---

[a] *together with*: *prob. rdg.*, *cp.* 1 *Esdras* 8. 54; *Heb. om.*
[b] *red copper*: *or* orichalc.   [c] *Prob. rdg.*, *cp.* 1 *Esdras* 8. 65; *Heb.* seventy-seven.

and the leaders and magistrates have been the chief offenders.'

3 When I heard this news, I rent my robe and mantle, and tore my hair and my beard, and I sat dumb-
4 founded; and all who went in fear of the words of the God of Israel rallied to me because of the offence of these exiles. I sat there dumbfounded till the evening sacrifice.

5 Then, at the evening sacrifice, I rose from my humiliation and, in my rent robe and mantle, I knelt down and spread out my hands to
6 the LORD my God and said, 'O my God, I am humiliated, I am ashamed to lift my face to thee, my God; for we are sunk in our iniquities, and our guilt is so great that it
7 reaches high heaven. From the days of our fathers down to this present day our guilt has been great. For our iniquities we, our kings, and our priests have been subject to death, captivity, pillage, and shameful humiliation at the hands of foreign kings, and such is
8 our present plight. But now, for a brief moment, the LORD our God has been gracious to us, leaving us some survivors and giving us a foothold in his holy place. He has brought light to our eyes again and given us some chance to renew our
9 lives in our slavery. For slaves we are; nevertheless, our God has not forsaken us in our slavery, but has made the kings of Persia so well disposed towards us as to give us the means of renewal, so that we may repair the house of our God and rebuild its ruins, and to give us a wall of defence in[a] Judah and
10 Jerusalem. Now, O our God, what are we to say after this? For we have neglected the commands
11 which thou gavest through thy servants the prophets, when thou saidst, "The land which you are entering and will possess is a polluted land, polluted by the foreign population with their abominable practices, which have made it un-

clean from end to end. Therefore, 12 do not give your daughters in marriage to their sons, and do not marry your sons to their daughters, and never seek their welfare or prosperity. Thus you will be strong and enjoy the good things of the land, and pass it on to your children as an everlasting possession."
Now, after all that we have suffer- 13 ed for our evil deeds and for our great guilt – although thou, our God, hast punished us less than our iniquities deserved and hast allowed us to survive as now we do – shall we again disobey thy com- 14 mands and join in marriage with peoples who indulge in such abominable practices? Would not thy anger against us be unrelenting, until no remnant, no survivor was left? O LORD God of Israel, thou 15 art righteous; now as before, we are only a remnant that has survived. Look upon us, guilty as we are in thy sight; for because of our guilt none of us can stand in thy presence.'

While Ezra was praying and 10 making confession, prostrate in tears before the house of God, a very great crowd of Israelites assembled round him, men, women, and children, and they all wept bitterly. Then Shecaniah son of 2 Jehiel, one of the family of Elam, spoke up and said to Ezra, 'We have committed an offence against our God in marrying foreign wives, daughters of the foreign population. But in spite of this, there is still hope for Israel. Now, there- 3 fore, let us pledge ourselves to our God to dismiss all these women and their brood, according to your advice, my lord, and the advice of those who go in fear of the command of our God; and let us act as the law prescribes. Up now, the 4 task is yours, and we will support you. Take courage and act.'

Ezra stood up and made the 5 chiefs of the priests, the Levites,

---

[a] *Or* thereby giving us a wall of defence for...

and all the Israelites swear to do as had been said; and they took the 6 oath. Then Ezra left his place in front of the house of God and went to the room of Jehohanan grandson of Eliashib and lodged[a] there; he neither ate bread nor drank water, for he was mourning for the offence committed by the exiles 7 who had returned. Next, there was issued throughout Judah and Jerusalem a proclamation that all the exiles should assemble in Jeru- 8 salem, and that if anyone did not arrive within three days, it should be within the discretion of the chief officers and the elders to confiscate all his property and to exclude him from the community of the exiles. 9 So all the men of Judah and Benjamin assembled in Jerusalem within the three days; and on the twentieth day of the ninth month the people all sat in the forecourt of the house of God, trembling with apprehension and shivering 10 in the heavy rain. Ezra the priest stood up and said, 'You have committed an offence in marrying foreign wives and have added to 11 Israel's guilt. Make your confession now to the LORD the God of your fathers and do his will, and separate yourselves from the foreign population and from your 12 foreign wives.' Then all the assembled people shouted in reply, 'Yes; we must do what you say. 13 But there is a great crowd of us here, and it is the rainy season; we cannot go on standing out here in the open. Besides, this business will not be finished in one day or even two, because we have committed so grave an offence in this 14 matter. Let our leading men act for the whole assembly, and let all in our cities who have married foreign women present themselves at appointed times, each man with the elders and judges of his own city, until God's anger against us

on this account is averted.' Only 15 Jonathan son of Asahel and Jahzeiah son of Tikvah, supported by Meshullam and Shabbethai the Levite, opposed this.

So the exiles acted as agreed, and 16 Ezra the priest selected[b] certain men, heads of households representing their families, all of them designated by name. They began their formal inquiry into the matter on the first day of the tenth month, and by the first day of the 17 first month they had finished their inquiry into all the marriages with foreign women.

Among the members of priestly 18 families who had married foreign women were found Maaseiah, Eliezer, Jarib, and Gedaliah of the family of Jeshua son of Jozadak and his brothers. They pledged 19 themselves to dismiss their wives, and they brought a ram from the flock as a guilt-offering for their sins. Of the family of Immer: Han- 20 ani and Zebadiah. Of the family of 21 Harim: Maaseiah, Elijah, Shemaiah, Jehiel and Uzziah. Of the 22 family of Pashhur: Elioenai, Maaseiah, Ishmael, Nethaneel, Jozabad and Elasah.

Of the Levites: Jozabad, Shimei, 23 Kelaiah (that is Kelita), Pethahiah, Judah and Eliezer. Of the 24 singers: Eliashib. Of the doorkeepers: Shallum, Telem and Uri.

And of Israel: of the family of 25 Parosh: Ramiah, Izziah, Malchiah, Mijamin, Eleazar, Malchiah and Benaiah. Of the family of Elam: 26 Mattaniah, Zechariah, Jehiel, Abdi, Jeremoth and Elijah. Of the 27 family of Zattu: Elioenai, Eliashib, Mattaniah, Jeremoth, Zabad and Aziza. Of the family of Bebai: 28 Jehohanan, Hananiah, Zabbai and Athlai. Of the family of Bani: 29 Meshullam, Malluch, Adaiah, Jashub, Sheal and Jeremoth. Of the 30 family of Pahath-moab: Adna, Kelal, Benaiah, Maaseiah, Mattaniah,

---

[a] *Prob. rdg., cp. 1 Esdras 9. 2; Heb.* went.
[b] *and Ezra the priest selected: prob. rdg., cp. 1 Esdras 9. 16; Heb. obscure.*

31 Bezalel, Binnui and Manasseh. Of the family of Harim: Eliezer, Is-
shijah, Malchiah, Shemaiah, Sim-
32 eon, Benjamin, Malluch and She-
33 mariah. Of the family of Hashum:
Mattenai, Mattattah, Zabad, Eliphelet, Jeremai, Manasseh and
34 Shimei. Of the family of Bani:
35 Maadai, Amram and Uel, Benaiah,
36 Bedeiah and Keluhi, Vaniah, Me-
37 remoth, Eliashib, Mattaniah, Mattenai and Jaasau. Of the family of[a] 38
Binnui: Shimei, Shelemiah, Na- 39
than and Adaiah, Maknadebai, 40
Shashai and Sharai, Azareel, She- 41
lemiah and Shemariah, Shallum, 42
Amariah and Joseph. Of the family 43
of Nebo: Jeiel, Mattithiah, Zabad,
Zebina, Jaddai, Joel and Benaiah.
All these had married foreign wo- 44
men, and they dismissed them, together with their children.[b]

THE BOOK OF

NEHEMIAH

Nehemiah's commission

1 THE narrative of Nehemiah
son of Hacaliah.
    In the month Kislev in the
twentieth year, when I was in Susa
2 the capital city, it happened that
one of my brothers, Hanani, arrived with some others from Judah; and I asked them about Jerusalem and about the Jews, the
families still remaining of those
3 who survived the captivity. They
told me that those still remaining
in the province who had survived
the captivity were facing great
trouble and reproach; the wall of
Jerusalem was broken down and
the gates had been destroyed by
4 fire. When I heard this news, I sat
down and wept; I mourned for
some days, fasting and praying to
5 the God of heaven. This was my
prayer: 'O LORD God of heaven, O
great and terrible God who faithfully keepest covenant with those
who love thee and observe thy
6 commandments, let thy ear be
attentive and thine eyes open, to

hear my humble prayer which I
make to thee day and night on
behalf of thy servants the sons of
Israel. I confess the sins which we
Israelites have all committed a-
gainst thee, and of which I and my
father's house are also guilty. We 7
have wronged thee and have not observed the commandments, statutes, and rules which thou didst
enjoin upon thy servant Moses.
Remember what thou didst im- 8
press upon him in these words: "If
you are unfaithful, I will disperse
you among the nations; but if you 9
return to me and observe my commandments and fulfil them, I will
gather your children who have
been scattered to the ends of the
earth and will bring them home to
the place which I have chosen as a
dwelling for my Name." They are 10
thy servants and thy people, whom
thou hast redeemed with thy great
might and thy strong hand. O 11
Lord, let thy ear be attentive to
my humble prayer, and to the
prayer of thy servants who delight
to revere thy name. Grant me good

[a] Of the family of: prob. rdg., cp. 1 Esdras 9. 34; Heb. and Bani and.
[b] and they...children: prob. rdg., cp. 1 Esdras 9. 36; Heb. and some of them were
women; and they had borne sons.

success this day, and put it into this man's heart to show me kindness.'

2 Now I was the king's cupbearer, and one day, in the month Nisan, in the twentieth year of King Artaxerxes, when his wine was ready, I took it up and handed it to the king, and as I stood before him I was 2 feeling very unhappy. He said to me, 'Why do you look so unhappy? You are not ill; it can be nothing but unhappiness.' I was much a-3 fraid and answered, 'The king will live for ever. But how can I help looking unhappy when the city where my forefathers are buried lies waste and its gates are burnt?' 4 'What are you asking of me?' said the king. I prayed to the God of 5 heaven, and then I answered, 'If it please your majesty, and if I enjoy your favour, I beg you to send me to Judah, to the city where my forefathers are buried, so that I 6 may rebuild it.' The king, with the queen consort sitting beside him, asked me, 'How long will the journey last, and when will you return?' Then the king approved the request and let me go, and I told him 7 how long I should be. Then I said to the king, 'If it please your majesty, let letters be given me for the governors in the province of Beyond-Euphrates with orders to grant me all the help I need for my 8 journey to Judah. Let me have also a letter for Asaph, the keeper of your royal forests, instructing him to supply me with timber to make beams for the gates of the citadel, which adjoins the palace, and for the city wall, and for the palace which I shall occupy.' The king granted my requests, for the gracious hand of my God was upon 9 me. I came in due course to the governors in the province of Beyond-Euphrates and presented to them the king's letters; the king had given me an escort of army 10 officers with cavalry. But when Sanballat the Horonite and the

slave Tobiah, an Ammonite, heard this, they were much vexed that someone should have come to promote the interests of the Israelites.

The walls of Jerusalem rebuilt

WHEN I arrived in Jerusalem, I 11 waited three days. Then I set out 12 by night, taking a few men with me; but I told no one what my God was prompting me to do for Jerusalem. I had no beast with me except the one on which I myself rode. I went out by night through 13 the Valley Gate towards the Dragon Spring and the Dung Gate, and I inspected the places where the walls of Jerusalem had been broken down and her gates burnt. Then I passed on to the Fountain 14 Gate and the King's Pool; but there was no room for me to ride through. I went up the valley in 15 the night and inspected the city wall; then I re-entered the city by the Valley Gate. So I arrived back without the magistrates knowing 16 where I had been or what I was doing. I had not yet told the Jews, the priests, the nobles, the magistrates, or any of those who would be responsible for the work.

Then I said to them, 'You see 17 our wretched plight. Jerusalem lies in ruins, its gates destroyed by fire. Come, let us rebuild the wall of Jerusalem and be rid of the reproach.' I told them how the gra- 18 cious hand of my God had been upon me and also what the king had said to me. They replied, 'Let us start the rebuilding.' So they set about the work vigorously and to good purpose.

But when Sanballat the Horon- 19 ite, Tobiah the Ammonite slave, and Geshem the Arab heard of it, they jeered at us, asking contemptuously, 'What is this you are doing? Is this a rebellion against the king?' But I answered them, 20 'The God of heaven will give us success. We, his servants, are making a start with the rebuilding. You have no stake, or claim, or traditional right in Jerusalem.'

3 Eliashib the high priest and his fellow-priests started work and rebuilt the Sheep Gate. They laid its beams*a* and set its doors in place; they carried the work as far as the Tower of the Hundred, as far as the Tower of Hananel, and consecrated

2 it. Next to Eliashib the men of Jericho worked; and next to them Zaccur son of Imri.

3 The Fish Gate was built by the sons of Hassenaah; they laid its tie-beams and set its doors in place

4 with their bolts and bars. Next to them Meremoth son of Uriah, son of Hakkoz, repaired his section; next to them Meshullam son of Berechiah, son of Meshezabel; next to them Zadok son of Baana did

5 the repairs; and next again the men of Tekoa did the repairs, but their nobles would not demean themselves to serve their governor.

6 The Jeshanah Gate*b* was repaired by Joiada son of Paseah and Meshullam son of Besodeiah; they laid its tie-beams and set its doors in place with their bolts and bars.

7 Next to them Melatiah the Gibeonite and Jadon the Meronothite, the men of Gibeon and Mizpah, did the repairs as far as the seat of the governor of the province of Beyond-Euphrates. Next to them

8 Uzziel son of Harhaiah, a goldsmith, did the repairs, and next Hananiah, a perfumer; they reconstructed Jerusalem as far as the

9 Broad Wall. Next to them Rephaiah son of Hur, ruler of half the district of Jerusalem, did the re-

10 pairs. Next to them Jedaiah son of Harumaph did the repairs opposite his own house; and next Hattush

11 son of Hashabniah. Malchiah son of Harim and Hasshub son of Pahath-moab repaired a second section including the Tower of the

Ovens.*c* Next to them Shallum 12 son of Hallohesh, ruler of half the district of Jerusalem, did the repairs with the help of his daughters.

The Valley Gate was repaired 13 by Hanun and the inhabitants of Zanoah; they rebuilt it and set its doors in place with their bolts and bars, and they repaired a thousand cubits of the wall as far as the Dung Gate. The Dung Gate itself 14 was repaired by Malchiah son of Rechab, ruler of the district of Beth-hakkerem; he rebuilt*d* it and set its doors in place with their bolts and bars. The Fountain Gate 15 was repaired by Shallun son of Colhozeh, ruler of the district of Mizpah; he rebuilt*d* it and roofed it and set its doors in place with their bolts and bars; and he built the wall of the Pool of Shelah next to the king's garden and onwards as far as the steps leading down from the City of David.

After him Nehemiah son of Az- 16 buk, ruler of half the district of Beth-zur, did the repairs as far as a point opposite the burial-place of David, as far as the artificial pool and the House of the Heroes.*e* After him the Levites did the re- 17 pairs: Rehum son of Bani and next to him Hashabiah, ruler of half the district of Keilah, did the repairs for his district. After him their 18 kinsmen did the repairs: Binnui son of Henadad, ruler of half the district of Keilah; next to him 19 Ezer son of Jeshua, ruler of Mizpah, repaired a second section opposite the point at which the ascent meets the escarpment; after 20 him Baruch son of Zabbai repaired a second section, from the escarpment to the door of the house of Eliashib the high priest. After him 21 Meremoth son of Uriah, son of Hakkoz, repaired a second section, from the door of the house of Elia-

---

a laid its beams: *prob. rdg.*; *Heb.* consecrated it.
b The Jeshanah Gate: *or* The gate of the Old City.
d *Prob. rdg.*; *Heb.* he will rebuild.

c *Or* Furnaces.
e *Or* and the barracks.

shib to the end of the house of Eliashib.

22 After him the priests of the neighbourhood of Jerusalem did 23 the repairs. Next Benjamin and Hasshub did the repairs opposite their own house; and next Azariah son of Maaseiah, son of Ananiah, did the repairs beside his house. 24 After him Binnui son of Henadad repaired a second section, from the house of Azariah as far as the es-25 carpment and the corner. Palal son of Uzai worked opposite the escarpment and the upper tower which projects from the king's house and belongs to the court of the guard. After him Pedaiah son 26 of Parosh*a* worked as far as a point on the east opposite the Water Gate and the projecting tower. 27 Next the men of Tekoa repaired a second section, from a point opposite the great projecting tower as far as the wall of Ophel.

28 Above the Horse Gate the priests did the repairs opposite their own 29 houses. After them Zadok son of Immer did the repairs opposite his own house; after him Shemaiah son of Shecaniah, the keeper of the 30 East Gate, did the repairs. After him Hananiah son of Shelemiah and Hanun, sixth son of Zalaph, repaired a second section. After him Meshullam son of Berechiah did the repairs opposite his room. 31 After him Malchiah, a goldsmith, did the repairs as far as the house of the temple-servitors and the merchants, opposite the Mustering Gate, as far as the roof-chamber at 32 the corner. Between the roof-chamber at the corner and the Sheep Gate the goldsmiths and merchants did the repairs.

4 WHEN Sanballat heard that we were rebuilding the wall, he was very indignant; in his anger he 2 jeered at the Jews and said in front of his companions and of the garrison in Samaria, 'What do these feeble Jews think they are doing? Do they mean to reconstruct the place? Do they hope to offer sacrifice and finish the work in a day? Can they make stones again out of heaps of rubble, and burnt at that?' Tobiah the Ammonite, who was 3 beside him, said, 'Whatever it is they are building, if a fox climbs up their stone walls, it will break them down.'

Hear us, our God, for they treat 4 us with contempt. Turn back their reproach upon their own heads and let them become objects of contempt in a land of captivity. Do 5 not condone their guilt or let their sin be struck off the record, for they have openly provoked the builders.

We built up the wall until it was 6 continuous all round up to half its height; and the people worked with a will. But when Sanballat 7 and Tobiah, the Arabs and Ammonites and Ashdodites, heard that the new work on the walls of Jerusalem had made progress and that the filling of the breaches had begun, they were very angry; and 8 they all banded together to come and attack Jerusalem and to create confusion. So we prayed to our 9 God, and posted a guard day and night against them.

But the men of Judah said, 'The 10 labourers' strength has failed, and there is too much rubble; we shall never be able to rebuild the wall by ourselves.' And our adversaries 11 said, 'Before they know it or see anything, we shall be upon them and kill them, and so put an end to the work.' When the Jews who 12 lived among them came in to the city, they warned us many times that they would gather from every place where they lived to attack us, and that they would station them-13 selves on the lowest levels below the wall, on patches of open ground. Accordingly I posted my people by families, armed with

a Prob. rdg.; Heb. adds and the temple-servitors lodged on Ophel (cp. 11. 21).

14 swords, spears, and bows. Then I surveyed the position and at once addressed the nobles, the magistrates, and all the people. 'Do not be afraid of them', I said. 'Remember the Lord, great and terrible, and fight for your brothers, your sons and daughters, your 15 wives and your homes.' Our enemies heard that everything was known to us, and that God had frustrated their plans; and we all returned to our work on the wall.

16 From that day forward half the men under me were engaged in the actual building, while the other half stood by holding their spears, shields, and bows, and wearing coats of mail; and officers super- 17 vised all the people of Judah who were engaged on the wall. The porters carrying the loads had one hand on the load and a weapon in 18 the other. The builders had their swords attached to their belts as they built; the trumpeter was be- 19 side me. I addressed the nobles, the magistrates, and all the people: 'The work is great and covers much ground', I said. 'We are isolated on the wall, each man at some distance from his neighbour. 20 Wherever the trumpet sounds, rally to us there, and our God will 21 fight for us.' So we continued with the work, half the men holding the spears, from daybreak until the 22 stars came out. At the same time I had said to the people, 'Let every man and his servant pass the night in Jerusalem, to act as a guard for us by night and a working party by 23 day.' So neither I nor my kinsmen nor the men under me nor my bodyguard ever took off our clothes, each keeping his right hand on*a* his weapon.

5 THERE came a time when the common people, both men and women, raised a great outcry against their fellow-Jews. Some complain- 2 ed that they were giving their sons and daughters as pledges*b* for food to keep themselves alive; others 3 that they were mortgaging their fields, vineyards, and houses to buy corn in the famine; others 4 again that they were borrowing money on their fields and vineyards to pay the king's tax. 'But', 5 they said, 'our bodily needs are the same as other people's, our children are as good as theirs; yet here we are, forcing our sons and daughters to become slaves. Some of our daughters are already enslaved, and there is nothing we can do, because our fields and vineyards now belong to others.' I was very 6 angry when I heard their outcry and the story they told. I mastered 7 my feelings and reasoned with the nobles and the magistrates. I said to them, 'You are holding your fellow-Jews as pledges for debt.' I rebuked them severely and said, 8 'As far as we have been able, we have bought back our fellow-Jews who had been sold to other nations; but you are now selling your own fellow-countrymen, and they will have to be bought back by us!' They were silent and had not a word to say. I went on, 'What you 9 are doing is wrong. You ought to live so much in the fear of God that you are above reproach in the eyes of the nations who are our enemies. Speaking for myself, I and my kins- 10 men and the men under me are advancing them money and corn. Let us give up this taking of persons as pledges for debt. Give back 11 today to your debtors their fields and vineyards, their olive-groves and houses, as well as the income*c* in money, and in corn, new wine, and oil.' 'We will give them back', 12 they promised, 'and exact nothing more. We will do what you say.' So, summoning the priests, I put the

---

a keeping his right hand on: *prob. rdg.*; Heb. obscure.
b that they . . . as pledges: *prob. rdg.*; Heb. that they, their sons and daughters were many.　　　　　　　　*c* *Prob. rdg.*; Heb. hundredth.

offenders on oath to do as they had
13 promised. Then I shook out the
fold of my robe and said, 'So may
God shake out from his house and
from his property every man who
does not fulfil this promise. May he
be shaken out like this and emptied!' And all the assembled people
said 'Amen' and praised the LORD.
And they did as they had promised.

14 Moreover, from the time when I
was appointed governor in the land
of Judah, from the twentieth to the
thirty-second year of King Artaxerxes, a period of twelve years,
neither I nor my kinsmen drew the
15 governor's allowance of food. Former governors had laid a heavy
burden on the people, exacting
from them a daily toll*a* of bread and
wine to the value of forty shekels
of silver. Further, the men under
them had tyrannized over the
people; but, for fear of God, I did
16 not behave like this. I also put all
my energy into the work on this
wall, and I acquired no land; and
all my men were gathered there for
17 the work. Also I had as guests at
my table a hundred and fifty Jews,
including the magistrates, as well
as men who came to us from the
18 surrounding nations. The provision which had to be made each
day was an ox and six prime sheep;
fowls also were prepared for me,
and every ten days skins of wine in
abundance. Yet, in spite of all this,
I did not draw the governor's allowance, because the people were so
19 heavily burdened. Remember for
my good, O God, all that I have
done for this people.

6 When the news came to Sanballat, Tobiah, Geshem the Arab,
and the rest of our enemies, that I
had rebuilt the wall and that not a
single breach remained in it, although I had not yet set up the
2 doors in the gates, Sanballat and
Geshem sent me an invitation to
come and confer with them at
Hakkephirim in the plain of Ono;
this was a ruse on their part to do
me harm. So I sent messengers to 3
them with this reply: 'I have important work on my hands at the
moment; I cannot come down.
Why should the work be brought
to a standstill while I leave it and
come down to you?' They sent me 4
a similar invitation four times, and
each time I gave them the same
answer. On a fifth occasion San- 5
ballat made a similar approach,
but this time his messenger came
with an open letter. It ran as fol- 6
lows: 'It is reported among the
nations – and Gashmu*b* confirms
it – that you and the Jews are
plotting rebellion, and it is for this
reason that you are rebuilding the
wall, and – so the report goes –
that you yourself want to be king.
You are also said to have put up 7
prophets to proclaim in Jerusalem
that Judah has a king, meaning
yourself. The king will certainly
hear of this. So come at once and
let us talk the matter over.' Here is 8
the reply I sent: 'No such thing as
you allege has taken place; you
have made up the whole story.'
They were all trying to intimidate 9
us, in the hope that we should then
relax our efforts and that the work
would never be finished. So I applied myself to it with greater
energy.

One day I went to the house of 10
Shemaiah son of Delaiah, son of
Mehetabel, for he was confined to
his house. He said, 'Let us meet in
the house of God, within the sanctuary, and let us shut the doors, for
they are coming to kill you – they
are coming to kill you by night.'
But I said, 'Should a man like me 11
run away? And can a man like me
go into the sanctuary and survive*c*? I will not go in.' Then it 12
dawned on me: God had not sent
him. His prophecy aimed at harm-

---

a a daily toll: *prob. rdg.; Heb. obscure.*
c and survive: *or* to save his life.

b Geshem *in 2. 19 and 6. 1, 2.*

ing me, and Tobiah and Sanballat
13 had bribed him to utter it. He had
been bribed to frighten me into
compliance and into committing
sin; then they could give me a bad
14 name and discredit me. Remember
Tobiah and Sanballat, O God, for
what they have done, and also the
prophetess Noadiah and all the
other prophets who have tried to
intimidate me.

15 On the twenty-fifth day of the
month Elul the wall was finished;
16 it had taken fifty-two days. When
our enemies heard of it, and all
the surrounding nations saw it,[a]
they thought it a very wonderful
achievement,[b] and they recognized
that this work had been accomplished by the help of our God.
17 All this time the nobles in Judah
were sending many letters to Tobiah, and receiving replies from
18 him. For many in Judah were in
league with him, because he was a
son-in-law of Shecaniah son of
Arah, and his son Jehohanan had
married a daughter of Meshullam
19 son of Berechiah. They were always praising[c] him in my presence
and repeating to him what I said.
Tobiah also wrote to me to intimidate me.

7 Now when the wall had been rebuilt, and I had set the doors in
place and the gate-keepers[d] had
2 been appointed, I gave the charge
of Jerusalem to my brother Hanani, and to Hananiah, the governor
of the citadel, for he was trustworthy and God-fearing above
3 other men. And I said to them,
'The entrances to Jerusalem are
not to be left open during the heat
of the day; the gates must be kept
shut and barred while the gate-
keepers are standing at ease. Appoint guards from among the in-

habitants of Jerusalem, some on
sentry-duty and others posted in
front of their own homes.'
The city was large and spacious; 4
there were few people in it and no
houses had yet been rebuilt. Then 5
God prompted me to assemble the
nobles, the magistrates, and the
people, to be enrolled family by
family. And I found the book of
the genealogies of those who had
been the first to come back. This is
what I found written in it: Of the 6[e]
captives whom Nebuchadnezzar
king of Babylon had taken into
exile, these are the people of the
province who have returned to
Jerusalem and Judah, each to his
own town, led by Zerubbabel, 7
Jeshua,[f] Nehemiah, Azariah, Raa-
miah, Nahamani, Mordecai, Bilshan, Mispereth, Bigvai, Nehum
and Baanah.
The roll of the men of the people 8
of Israel: the family of Parosh, two
thousand one hundred and seventy-two; the family of Shephatiah, 9
three hundred and seventy-two;
the family of Arah, six hundred 10
and fifty-two; the family of Pa- 11
hath-moab, namely the families of
Jeshua and Joab, two thousand
eight hundred and eighteen; the 12
family of Elam, one thousand two
hundred and fifty-four; the family 13
of Zattu, eight hundred and forty-
five; the family of Zaccai, seven 14
hundred and sixty; the family of 15
Binnui, six hundred and forty-
eight; the family of Bebai, six 16
hundred and twenty-eight; the 17
family of Azgad, two thousand
three hundred and twenty-two;
the family of Adonikam, six hun- 18
dred and sixty-seven; the family of 19
Bigvai, two thousand and sixty-
seven; the family of Adin, six hun- 20
dred and fifty-five; the family of 21
Ater, namely that of Hezekiah,

[a] Or were afraid.
[b] they thought...achievement: *prob. rdg.*; Heb. they fell very much in their own
eyes.   [c] Or repeating rumours about...
[d] *Prob. rdg.*; Heb. *adds* the singers and the Levites.
[e] Verses 6–73: *cp. Ezra* 2. 1–70.   [f] Or Joshua (*cp. Hag.* 1. 1).

22 ninety-eight; the family of Hashum, three hundred and twenty-
23 eight; the family of Bezai, three
24 hundred and twenty-four; the family of Harif, one hundred and
25 twelve; the family of Gibeon,
26 ninety-five. The men of Bethlehem and Netophah, one hundred and
27 eighty-eight; the men of Anathoth,
28 one hundred and twenty-eight; the men of Beth-azmoth, forty-two;
29 the men of Kiriath-jearim, Kephirah, and Beeroth, seven hundred
30 and forty-three; the men of Ramah and Geba, six hundred and twenty-
31 one; the men of Michmas, one hun-
32 dred and twenty-two; the men of Bethel and Ai, one hundred and
33 twenty-three; the men of[a] Nebo,
34 fifty-two; the men[b] of the other Elam, one thousand two hundred
35 and fifty-four; the men of Harim,
36 three hundred and twenty; the men of Jericho, three hundred and
37 forty-five; the men of Lod, Hadid, and Ono, seven hundred and
38 twenty-one; the men of Senaah, three thousand nine hundred and thirty.

39 Priests: the family of Jedaiah, of the line of Jeshua, nine hundred
40 and seventy-three; the family of Immer, one thousand and fifty-
41 two; the family of Pashhur, one thousand two hundred and forty-
42 seven; the family of Harim, one thousand and seventeen.

43 Levites: the families of Jeshua and[c] Kadmiel, of the line of Hod-
44 vah, seventy-four. Singers: the family of Asaph, one hundred and
45 forty-eight. Door-keepers: the family of Shallum, the family of Ater, the family of Talmon, the family of Akkub, the family of Hatita, and the family of Shobai, one hundred and thirty-eight in all.

46 Temple-servitors: the family of Ziha, the family of Hasupha, the
47 family of Tabbaoth, the family of Keros, the family of Sia, the family
48 of Padon, the family of Lebanah, the family of Hagabah, the family
49 of Shalmai, the family of Hanan, the family of Giddel, the family of
50 Gahar, the family of Reaiah, the family of Rezin, the family of Ne-
51 koda, the family of Gazzam, the family of Uzza, the family of Pa-
52 seah, the family of Besai, the family of the Meunim, the family of the
53 Nephishesim,[d] the family of Bakbuk, the family of Hakupha, the
54 family of Harhur, the family of Bazlith,[e] the family of Mehida, the
55 family of Harsha, the family of Barkos, the family of Sisera, the
56 family of Temah, the family of Neziah, and the family of Hatipha.

57 Descendants of Solomon's servants: the family of Sotai, the family of Sophereth, the family of
58 Perida, the family of Jaalah, the family of Darkon, the family of
59 Giddel, the family of Shephatiah, the family of Hattil, the family of Pochereth-hazzebaim, and the family of Amon.

60 The temple-servitors and the descendants of Solomon's servants amounted to three hundred and ninety-two in all.

61 The following were those who returned from Tel-melah, Telharsha, Kerub, Addon, and Immer, but could not establish their father's family nor whether by descent they belonged to Israel:
62 the family of Delaiah, the family of Tobiah, the family of Nekoda, six hundred and forty-two. Also of the
63 priests: the family of Hobaiah, the family of Hakkoz, and the family of Barzillai who had married a daughter of Barzillai the Gileadite and went by his[f] name. These
64 searched for their names among those enrolled in the genealogies, but they could not be found; they were disqualified for the priest-

---

[a] Prob. rdg., cp. Ezra 2. 29; Heb. adds the other.
[b] Prob. rdg.; Heb. family (also in verses 35–38).
[c] and: prob. rdg., cp. Ezra 2. 40; Heb. to.
[d] Or Nephushesim.
[e] Or Bazluth (cp. Ezra 2. 52).
[f] Prob. rdg., cp. 1 Esdras 5. 38; Heb. their.

65 hood as unclean, and the governor forbade them to partake of the most sacred food until there should be a priest able to consult the Urim and the Thummim.

66 The whole assembled people numbered forty-two thousand three 67 hundred and sixty, apart from their slaves, male and female, of whom there were seven thousand three hundred and thirty-seven; and they had two hundred and forty-five singers, men and women.

68 Their horses numbered seven hundred and thirty-six, their mules 69 two hundred and forty-five, their camels four hundred and thirty-five, and their asses six thousand seven hundred and twenty.

70 Some of the heads of families gave contributions for the work. The governor gave to the treasury a thousand drachmas of gold, fifty tossing-bowls, and five hundred 71 and thirty priestly robes. Some of the heads of families gave for the fabric fund twenty thousand drachmas of gold and two thousand two 72 hundred minas of silver. What the rest of the people gave was twenty thousand drachmas of gold, two thousand minas of silver, and sixty-seven priestly robes.

73 The priests, the Levites, and some of the people lived in Jerusalem and its suburbs;[a] the doorkeepers, the singers, the templeservitors, and all other Israelites, lived in their own towns.

The law read by Ezra and the covenant renewed

WHEN the seventh month came, and the Israelites were now settled 8 in their towns, the people assembled as one man in the square in front of the Water Gate, and Ezra the scribe[b] was asked to bring the book of the law of Moses, which the LORD had enjoined upon Israel. On the first day of the seventh 2 month, Ezra the priest brought the law before the assembly, every man and woman, and all who were capable of understanding what they heard.[c] He read from it, 3 facing the square in front of the Water Gate, from early morning till noon, in the presence of the men and the women, and those who could understand;[d] all the people listened attentively to the book of the law. Ezra the scribe 4 stood on a wooden platform made for the purpose,[e] and beside him stood Mattithiah, Shema, Anaiah, Uriah, Hilkiah, and Maaseiah on his right hand; and on his left Pedaiah, Mishael, Malchiah, Hashum, Hashbaddanah, Zechariah and Meshullam. Ezra opened the book 5 in the sight of all the people, for he was standing above them; and when he opened it, they all stood. Ezra blessed the LORD, the great 6 God, and all the people raised their hands and answered, 'Amen, Amen'; and they bowed their heads and prostrated themselves humbly before the LORD. Jeshua, Bani, 7 Sherebiah, Jamin, Akkub, Shabbethai, Hodiah, Maaseiah, Kelita, Azariah, Jozabad, Hanan, Pelaiah, the Levites,[f] expounded the law to the people while they remained in their places. They read from the 8 book of the law of God clearly, made its sense plain and gave instruction in what was read.

Then Nehemiah the governor 9 and Ezra the priest and scribe, and the Levites who instructed the people, said to them all, 'This day is holy to the LORD your God; do not mourn or weep.' For all the people had been weeping while they listened to the words of the

---

[a] in Jerusalem and its suburbs: *prob. rdg.*, *cp.* 1 *Esdras* 5. 46; *Heb. om.*
[b] Or *doctor of the law.*
[c] *were capable...heard: or* would teach them to understand.
[d] could understand: *or* were to instruct.   [e] *Or* for the address.
[f] *Prob. rdg.*; *Heb.* and the Levites.

10 law. Then he said to them, 'You may go now; refresh yourselves with rich food and sweet drinks, and send a share to all who cannot provide for themselves; for this day is holy to our Lord. Let there be no sadness, for joy in the LORD 11 is your strength.' The Levites silenced the people, saying, 'Be quiet, for this day is holy; let there 12 be no sadness.' So all the people went away to eat and to drink, to send shares to others and to celebrate the day with great rejoicing, because they had understood what had been explained to them.

13 On the second day the heads of families of the whole people, with the priests and the Levites, assembled before Ezra the scribe to study 14 the law. And they found written in the law that the LORD had given commandment through Moses that the Israelites should live in arbours[a] during the feast of the seventh 15 month, and that they should make proclamation throughout all their cities and in Jerusalem: 'Go out into the hills and fetch branches of olive and wild olive, myrtle and palm, and other leafy boughs to 16 make arbours, as prescribed.' So the people went out and fetched them and made arbours for themselves, each on his own roof, and in their courts and in the courts of the house of God, and in the square at the Water Gate and the square at 17 the Ephraim Gate. And the whole community of those who had returned from the captivity made arbours and lived in them, a thing that the Israelites had not done from the days of Joshua son of Nun to that day; and there was 18 very great rejoicing. And day by day, from the first day to the last, the book of the law of God was read. They kept the feast for seven days, and on the eighth day there

was a closing ceremony, according to the rule.

ON the twenty-fourth day of this 9 month the Israelites assembled for a fast, clothed in sackcloth and with earth on their heads. Those 2 who were of Israelite descent separated themselves from all the foreigners; they took their places and confessed their sins and the iniquities of their forefathers. Then 3 they stood up in their places, and the book of the law of the LORD their God was read for one fourth of the day, and for another fourth they confessed and did obeisance to the LORD their God. Upon the 4 steps assigned to the Levites stood Jeshua, Bani, Kadmiel, Shebaniah, Bunni, Sherebiah, Bani, and Kenani, and they cried aloud to the LORD their God. Then the Lev- 5 ites, Jeshua, Kadmiel, Bani, Hashabniah, Sherebiah, Hodiah, Shebaniah, and Pethahiah, said, 'Stand up and bless the LORD your God, saying: From everlasting to everlasting thy glorious name is blessed[b] and exalted above all blessing and praise. Thou alone art the 6 LORD; thou hast made heaven, the highest heaven with all its host, the earth and all that is on it, the seas and all that is in them. Thou preservest all of them, and the host of heaven worships thee. Thou art 7 the LORD, the God who chose Abram and brought him out of Ur of the Chaldees and named him Abraham. Thou didst find him 8 faithful to thee and didst make a covenant with him to give to him and to his descendants the land of the Canaanites, the Hittites, the Amorites, the Perizzites, the Jebusites, and the Girgashites; and thou didst fulfil thy promise, for thou art just.

'And thou didst see the misery of 9 our forefathers in Egypt and didst

---

[a] Or tabernacles or booths.
[b] thy glorious name is blessed: *prob. rdg.*; *Heb.* and let them bless thy glorious name.

hear their cry for help at the Red
10 Sea,[a] and didst work signs and portents against Pharaoh, all his courtiers and all the people of his land, knowing how arrogantly they treated our forefathers, and thou didst win for thyself a name
11 that lives on to this day. Thou didst tear the sea apart before them so that they went through the middle of it on dry ground; but thou didst cast their pursuers into the depths, like a stone cast into turbulent
12 waters. Thou didst guide them by a pillar of cloud in the day-time and by a pillar of fire at night to give them light on the road by
13 which they travelled. Thou didst descend upon Mount Sinai and speak with them from heaven, and give them right judgements and true laws, and statutes and com-
14 mandments which were good, and thou didst make known to them thy holy sabbath and give them commandments, statutes, and laws
15 through thy servant Moses. Thou gavest them bread from heaven to stay their hunger and thou broughtest water out from a rock for them to quench their thirst, and thou didst bid them enter and take possession of the land which thou hadst solemnly sworn to give
16 them. But they, our forefathers, were arrogant and stubborn, and disobeyed thy commandments.
17 They refused to obey and did not remember the miracles which thou didst accomplish among them; they remained stubborn, and they appointed a man to lead them back to slavery in Egypt. But thou art a forgiving god, gracious and compassionate, long-suffering and ever constant, and thou didst not for-
18 sake them. Even when they made the image of a bull-calf in metal and said, "This is your god who brought you up from Egypt", and were guilty of great blasphemies,
19 thou in thy great compassion didst not forsake them in the wilderness.

The pillar of cloud did not fail to guide them on their journey by day nor the pillar of fire by night to give them light on the road by
20 which they travelled. Thou gavest thy good spirit to instruct them; thy manna thou didst not withhold from them, and thou gavest them
21 water to quench their thirst. Forty years long thou didst sustain them in the wilderness, and they lacked nothing; their clothes did not wear out and their feet were not swollen.

22 'Thou gavest them kingdoms and peoples, allotting these to them as spoils of war. Thus they took possession of the land of Sihon king of Heshbon and the land of Og king of
23 Bashan. Thou didst multiply their descendants so that they became countless as the stars in the sky, bringing them into the land which thou didst promise to give to their forefathers as their possession.
24 When their descendants entered the land and took possession of it, thou didst subdue before them the Canaanites who inhabited it and gavest these, kings and peoples alike, into their hands to do with
25 them whatever they wished. They captured fortified cities and a fertile land and took possession of houses full of all good things, rock-hewn cisterns, vineyards, olive-trees, and fruit-trees in abundance; so they ate and were satisfied and grew fat and found delight
26 in thy great goodness. But they were defiant and rebelled against thee; they turned their backs on thy law and killed thy prophets, who solemnly warned them to return to thee, and they were guilty of great blasphemies. Because of
27 this thou didst hand them over to their enemies who oppressed them. But when, in the time of their oppression, they cried to thee for help, thou heardest them from heaven and in thy great compassion didst send them saviours to
28 save them from their enemies. But

[a] Or the Sea of Reeds.

when they had had a respite, they once more did what was wrong in thine eyes; and thou didst abandon them to their enemies who held them in subjection. But again they cried to thee for help, and many times over thou heardest them from heaven and in thy compas-

29 sion didst save them. Thou didst solemnly warn them to return to thy law, but they grew arrogant and did not heed thy commandments; they sinned against thy ordinances, which bring life to him who keeps them. Stubbornly they turned away in mulish obstinacy

30 and would not obey. Many years thou wast patient with them and didst warn them by thy spirit through thy prophets; but they would not listen. Therefore thou didst hand them over to foreign

31 peoples. Yet in thy great compassion thou didst not make an end of them nor forsake them; for thou art a gracious and compassionate god.

32 'Now therefore, our God, thou great and mighty and terrible God, who faithfully keepest covenant, do not make light of the hardships that have befallen us – our kings, our princes, our priests, our prophets, our forefathers, and all thy people – from the days of the

33 kings of Assyria to this day. In all that has befallen us thou hast been just, thou hast kept faith, but we

34 have done wrong. Our kings, our princes, our priests, and our forefathers did not keep thy law nor heed thy commandments and the warnings which thou gavest them.

35 Even under their own kings, while they were enjoying the great prosperity which thou gavest them and the broad and fertile land which thou didst bestow upon them, they did not serve thee; they did not

36 abandon their evil ways. Today we are slaves, slaves here in the land which thou gavest to our fore-

fathers so that they might eat its

37 fruits and enjoy its good things. All its produce now goes to the kings whom thou hast set over us because of our sins. They have power over our bodies, and they do as they please with our beasts, while we are in dire distress.

38 'Because of all this we make a binding declaration in writing, and our princes, our Levites, and our priests witness the sealing.

10 'Those who witness the sealing are Nehemiah the governor, son of Hacaliah, Zedekiah, Seraiah, Az-

2 ariah, Jeremiah, Pashhur, Amar-

3 iah, Malchiah, Hattush, Sheban-

4 iah, Malluch, Harim, Meremoth,

5 Obadiah, Daniel, Ginnethon, Bar-

6 uch, Meshullam, Abiah, Mijamin,

7 Maaziah, Bilgai, Shemaiah; these

8 are the priests. The Levites: Je-

9 shua[a] son of Azaniah, Binnui of the family of Henadad, Kadmiel; and

10 their brethren, Shebaniah, Hodiah,[b] Kelita, Pelaiah, Hanan, Mica,

11 Rehob, Hashabiah, Zaccur, Shere-

12 biah, Shebaniah, Hodiah, Bani,

13 Beninu. The chiefs of the people:

14 Parosh, Pahath-moab, Elam, Zattu, Bani, Bunni, Azgad, Bebai,

15 Adonijah, Bigvai, Adin, Ater,

16, 17 Hezekiah, Azzur, Hodiah, Hash-

18 um, Bezai, Hariph, Anathoth,

19 Nebai,[c] Magpiash, Meshullam, He-

20 zir, Meshezabel, Zadok, Jaddua,

21 Pelatiah, Hanan, Anaiah, Hoshea,

22, 23 Hananiah, Hasshub, Hallohesh,

24 Pilha, Shobek, Rehum, Hashab-

25 nah, Maaseiah, Ahiah, Hanan, An-

26 an, Malluch, Harim, Baanah.

27 'The rest of the people, the

28 priests, the Levites, the doorkeepers, the singers, the temple-servitors, with their wives, their sons, and their daughters, all who are capable of understanding, all who for the sake of the law of God have kept themselves apart from

29 the foreign population, join with the leading brethren,[d] when the oath is put to them, in swearing to

---

[a] *Prob. rdg.; Heb.* and Jeshua.　　[b] *Or, with Ezra* 2. 40, Hodaviah.　　[c] *Or* Nobai.
[d] the leading brethren: *prob. rdg.; Heb.* their brethren, their leading men.

obey God's law given by Moses the servant of God, and to observe and fulfil all the commandments of the LORD our Lord, his rules and his statutes.

30 'We will not give our daughters in marriage to the foreign population or take their daughters for our

31 sons. If on the sabbath these people bring in merchandise, especially corn, for sale, we will not buy from them on the sabbath or on any holy day. We will forgo the crops of the seventh year and release every person still held as a pledge for debt.

32 'We hereby undertake the duty of giving yearly the third of a shekel for the service of the house

33 of our God, for the Bread of the Presence, the regular grain-offering and whole-offering, the sabbaths, the new moons, the appointed seasons, the holy-gifts, and the sin-offerings to make expiation on behalf of Israel, and for all else that has to be done in the house of

34 our God. We, the priests, the Levites, and the people, have cast lots for the wood-offering, so that it may be brought into the house of our God by each family in turn, at appointed times, year by year, to burn upon the altar of the LORD our God, as prescribed in the law.

35 We undertake to bring the first-fruits of our land and the firstfruits of every fruit-tree, year by year, to

36 the house of the LORD; also to bring to the house of our God, to the priests who minister in the house of our God, the first-born of our sons and of our cattle, as prescribed in the law, and the first-born of our herds and of our flocks;

37 and to bring to the priests the first kneading of our dough, and the first of the fruit of every tree, of the new wine and of the oil, to the store-rooms in the house of our God; and to bring to the Levites the tithes from our land, for it is the Levites who collect the tithes

38 in all our farming villages. The Aaronite priest shall be with the Levites when they collect the tithes; and the Levites shall bring up one tenth of the tithes to the house of our God, to the appro-

39 priate rooms in the storehouse. For the Israelites and the Levites shall bring the contribution of corn, new wine, and oil to the rooms where the vessels of the sanctuary are kept, and where the ministering priests, the door-keepers, and the singers are lodged. We will not neglect the house of our God.'

11 THE leaders of the people settled in Jerusalem; and the rest of the people cast lots to bring one in every ten to live in Jerusalem, the holy city, while the remaining nine

2 lived in other towns. And the people were grateful to all those who volunteered to live in Jerusalem.

3 These are the chiefs of the province who lived in Jerusalem; but, in the towns of Judah, other Israelites, priests, Levites, temple-servitors, and descendants of Solomon's servants lived on their own property, in their own towns.

4 Some members of the tribes of Judah and Benjamin lived in Jerusalem. Of Judah: Athaiah son of Uzziah, son of Zechariah, son of Amariah, son of Shephatiah, son of Mahalalel of the family of Perez,

6 all of whose family, to the number of four hundred and sixty-eight men of substance, lived in Jerusa-

5 lem; and Maaseiah son of Baruch, son of Col-hozeh, son of Hazaiah, son of Adaiah, son of Joiarib, son of Zechariah of the Shelanite family.

7 These were the Benjamites: Sallu son of Meshullam, son of Joed, son of Pedaiah, son of Kolaiah, son of Maaseiah, son of Ithiel, son of

8 Isaiah, and his kinsmen Gabbai and Sallai, nine hundred and twenty-eight in all. Joel son of Zichri was

9 their overseer, and Judah son of

Hassenuah was second over the city.[a]

10 Of the priests: Jedaiah son of 11 Joiarib, son of[b] Seraiah, son of Hilkiah, son of Meshullam, son of Zadok, son of Meraioth, son of Ahitub, supervisor of the house of 12 God, and his[c] brethren responsible for the work in the temple, eight hundred and twenty-two in all; and Adaiah son of Jeroham, son of Pelaliah, son of Amzi, son of Zechariah, son of Pashhur, son of Mal- 13 chiah, and his brethren, heads of fathers' houses, two hundred and forty-two in all; and Amasai[d] son of Azarel, son of Ahzai, son of 14 Meshillemoth, son of Immer, and his brethren, men of substance, a hundred and twenty-eight in all; their overseer was Zabdiel son of Haggedolim.

15 And of the Levites: Shemaiah son of Hasshub, son of Azrikam, son of Hashabiah, son of Bunni; 16 and Shabbethai and Jozabad of the chiefs of the Levites, who had charge of the external business of 17 the house of God; and Mattaniah son of Micah, son of Zabdi, son of Asaph, who as precentor led the prayer of thanksgiving, and Bakbukiah who held the second place among his brethren; and Abda son of Shammua, son of Galal, son of 18 Jeduthun. The number of Levites in the holy city was two hundred and eighty-four in all.

19 The gate-keepers who kept guard at the gates were Akkub, Talmon, and their brethren, a hundred and 20 seventy-two. The rest of the Israelites[e] were in all the towns of Judah, each man on his own in- 21 herited property. But the temple-servitors lodged on Ophel, and Ziha and Gishpa were in charge of them.

22 The overseer of the Levites in Jerusalem was Uzzi son of Bani, son of Hashabiah, son of Mattaniah, son of Mica, of the family of Asaph the singers, for the supervision of the business of the house of God. For they were under the 23 king's orders, and there was obligatory duty for the singers every day. Pethahiah son of Meshezabel, of 24 the family of Zerah son of Judah, was the king's adviser on all matters affecting the people.

As for the hamlets with their 25 surrounding fields: some of the men of Judah lived in Kiriath-arba and its villages, in Dibon and its villages, and in Jekabzeel and its hamlets, in Jeshua, Moladah, and 26 Bethpelet, in Hazar-shual, and in 27 Beersheba and its villages, in Zik- 28 lag and in Meconah and its villages, in Enrimmon, Zorah, and 29 Jarmuth, in Zanoah, Adullam, and 30 their hamlets, in Lachish and its fields and Azekah and its villages. Thus they occupied the country from Beersheba to the Valley of Hinnom.

The men of Benjamin lived in[f] 31 Geba, Michmash, Aiah, and Bethel with its villages, in Anathoth, Nob, 32 and Ananiah, in Hazor, Ramah, 33 and Gittaim, in Hadid, Zeboim, 34 and Neballat, in Lod, Ono, and[g] 35 Ge-harashim.[h] And certain divi- 36 sions of the Levites in Judah were attached to Benjamin.

These are the priests and the 12 Levites who came back with Zerubbabel son of Shealtiel, and Jeshua:[i] Seraiah, Jeremiah, Ezra, Amar- 2 iah, Malluch, Hattush, Shecaniah, 3 Rehum, Meremoth, Iddo, Ginne- 4 thon, Abiah, Mijamin, Maadiah, 5 Bilgah, Shemaiah, Joiarib, Jedai- 6 ah, Sallu, Amok, Hilkiah, Jedaiah. 7 These were the chiefs of the priests and of their brethren in the days of Jeshua.

---

[a] second over the city: *or* over the second quarter of the city.
[b] son of: *prob. rdg.; Heb. obscure.*   [c] *Prob. rdg.; Heb. their.*
[d] *Prob. rdg.; Heb. Amashsai.*   [e] *Prob. rdg.; Heb. adds* the levitical priests.
[f] *Prob. rdg.; Heb. from.*   [g] and: *prob. rdg.; Heb. om.*
[h] *Or* and the Valley of Woods *or* and the Valley of Craftsmen.   [i] *Or* Joshua.

503

8 And the Levites: Jeshua, Binnui, Kadmiel, Sherebiah, Judah, and Mattaniah, who with his brethren was in charge of the songs of 9 thanksgiving. And Bakbukiah and Unni their brethren stood opposite 10 them in the service. And Jeshua was the father of Joiakim, Joiakim the father of Eliashib, Eliashib of 11 Joiada, Joiada the father of Jonathan, and Jonathan the father of 12 Jaddua. And in the days of Joiakim the priests who were heads of families were: of Seraiah, Meraiah; 13 of Jeremiah, Hananiah; of Ezra, Meshullam; of Amariah, Jehohan- 14 an; of Malluch,[a] Jonathan; of She- 15 baniah, Joseph; of Harim, Adna; 16 of Meraioth, Helkai; of Iddo, Zechariah; of Ginnethon, Meshul- 17 lam; of Abiah, Zichri; of Minia- 18 min[b]; of Moadiah, Piltai; of Bilgah, Shammua; of Shemaiah, Jehona- 19 than; of Joiarib, Mattenai; of Je- 20 daiah, Uzzi; of Sallu,[c] Kallai; of 21 Amok, Eber; of Hilkiah, Hashabiah; of Jedaiah, Nethaneel. 22 [d]The heads of the priestly families[e] in the days of Eliashib, Joiada, Johanan, and Jaddua were recorded down to the reign of Darius 23 the Persian. The heads of the levitical families were recorded in the annals only down to the days of Johanan the grandson of Eliashib. 24 And the chiefs of the Levites: Hashabiah, Sherebiah, Jeshua, Binnui,[f] Kadmiel, with their brethren in the other turn of duty, to praise and to give thanks, according to the commandment of David the man of God, turn by turn. 25 Mattaniah, Bakbukiah, Obadiah, Meshullam, Talmon, and Akkub were gate-keepers standing guard 26 at the gatehouses. This was the arrangement in the days of Joiakim son of Jeshua, son of Jozadak,

and in the days of Nehemiah the governor and of Ezra the priest and scribe.

At the dedication of the wall of 27 Jerusalem they sought out the Levites in all their settlements, and brought them to Jerusalem to celebrate the dedication with[g] rejoicing, with thanksgiving and song, to the accompaniment of cymbals, lutes, and harps. And the Levites,[h] 28 the singers, were assembled from the district round Jerusalem and from the hamlets of the Netophathites; also from Beth-gilgal and 29 from the region of Geba and Bethazmoth;[i] for the singers had built themselves hamlets in the neighbourhood of Jerusalem. The priests 30 and the Levites purified themselves; and they purified the people, the gates, and the wall. Then I brought the leading men of 31 Judah up on to the city wall, and appointed two great choirs to give thanks. One went in procession[j] to the right, going along the wall to the Dung Gate; and after it went 32 Hoshaiah with half the leading men of Judah, and Azariah, Ezra, 33 Meshullam, Judah, Benjamin, She- 34 maiah, and Jeremiah; and certain 35 of the priests with trumpets: Zechariah son of Jonathan, son of Shemaiah, son of Mattanaiah, son of Micaiah, son of Zaccur, son of Asaph, and his kinsmen, Shemai- 36 ah, Azarel, Milalai, Gilalai, Maai, Nethaneel, Judah, and Hanani, with the musical instruments of David the man of God; and Ezra the scribe led them. They went 37 past the Fountain Gate and thence straight forward by the steps up to the City of David, by the ascent to the city wall, past the house of David, and on to the Water Gate on the east. The other thanks- 38

---

[a] *Prob. rdg.; Heb. Malluchi, or Melichu.* [b] *A name is missing here.*
[c] *Prob. rdg., cp. verse 7; Heb. Sallai.* [d] *Prob. rdg.; Heb. prefixes The Levites.*
[e] heads...families: *prob. rdg.; Heb. heads of the families and the priests.*
[f] *Jeshua, Binnui: prob. rdg.; Heb. and Jeshua son of.* [g] *Prob. rdg.; Heb. and.*
[h] *the Levites: prob. rdg.; Heb. the sons of.* [i] *Beth-azmoth: prob. rdg., cp. 7.*
28; *Heb. Azmoth.* [j] *One...procession: prob. rdg.; Heb. Processions.*

giving choir went to the left,[a] and I followed it with half the leading men of[b] the people, continuing along the wall, past the Tower of

39 the Ovens[c] to the Broad Wall, and past the Ephraim Gate, and over the Jeshanah Gate,[d] and over the Fish Gate, taking in the Tower of Hananel and the Tower of the Hundred, as far as the Sheep Gate; and they halted at the Gate of the

40 Guardhouse. So the two thanksgiving choirs took their place in the house of God, and I and half the

41 magistrates with me; and the priests Eliakim, Maaseiah, Miniamin, Micaiah, Elioenai, Zechariah,

42 and Hananiah, with trumpets; and Maaseiah, Shemaiah, Eleazar, Uzzi, Jehohanan, Malchiah, Elam, and Ezer. The singers, led by Izrahiah,

43 raised their voices. A great sacrifice was celebrated that day, and they all rejoiced because God had given them great cause for rejoicing; the women and children rejoiced with them. And the rejoicing in Jerusalem was heard a long way off.

44 On that day men were appointed to take charge of the store-rooms for the contributions, the firstfruits, and the tithes, to gather in the portions required by the law for the priests and Levites according to the extent of the farmlands round the towns; for all Judah was full of rejoicing at the ministry of

45 the priests and Levites. And they performed the service of their God and the service of purification, as did the singers and the doorkeepers, according to the rules laid down by David and his son Solo-

46 mon. For it was in the days of David that Asaph took the lead as chief of the singers and director[e] of praise and thanksgiving to God.

47 And in the days of Zerubbabel and of Nehemiah all Israel gave the portions for the singers and the door-keepers as each day required;

and they set apart the portion for the Levites, and the Levites set apart the portion for the Aaronites.

Nehemiah's reforms

13 ON that day at the public reading from the book of Moses, it was found to be laid down that no Ammonite or Moabite should ever en-

2 ter the assembly of God, because they did not meet the Israelites with food and water but hired Balaam to curse them, though our God turned the curse into a bless-

3 ing. When the people heard the law, they separated from Israel all who were of mixed blood.

4 But before this, Eliashib the priest, who was appointed over the store-rooms of the house of our God, and who was connected by marriage with Tobiah, had pro-

5 vided for his use a large room where formerly they had kept the grainoffering, the incense, the temple vessels, the tithes of corn, new wine, and oil prescribed for the Levites, singers, and door-keepers, and the contributions for the

6 priests. All this time I was not in Jerusalem because, in the thirtysecond year of Artaxerxes king of Babylon, I had gone to the king. Some time later, I asked permis-

7 sion from him and returned to Jerusalem. There I discovered the wicked thing that Eliashib had done for Tobiah's sake in providing him with a room in the courts of

8 the house of God. I was greatly displeased and threw all Tobiah's belongings out of the room. Then I

9 gave orders that the room should be purified, and that the vessels of the house of God, with the grainoffering and incense, should be put back into it.

10 I also learnt that the Levites had not been given their portions; both they and the singers, who were

---

[a] to the left: *prob. rdg.*; *Heb.* to the front.
[b] the leading men of: *prob. rdg.*; *Heb. om.*
[d] the Jeshanah Gate: *or* the gate of the Old City.
[c] *Or* Furnaces.
[e] *Prob. rdg.*; *Heb.* song.

responsible for their respective duties, had made off to their farms.

11 So I remonstrated with the magistrates and said, 'Why is the house of God deserted?' And I recalled the men and restored them to their

12 places. Then all Judah brought the tithes of corn, new wine, and oil

13 into the storehouses; and I put in charge of them Shelemiah the priest, Zadok the accountant, and Pedaiah a Levite, with Hanan son of Zaccur, son of Mattaniah, as their assistant, for they were considered trustworthy men; their duty was the distribution of their

14 shares to their brethren. Remember this, O God, to my credit, and do not wipe out of thy memory the devotion which I have shown in the house of my God and in his service.

15 In those days I saw men in Judah treading winepresses on the sabbath, collecting quantities of produce and piling it on asses – wine, grapes, figs, and every kind of load, which they brought into Jerusalem on the sabbath; and I protested to them about selling

16 food on that day. Tyrians living in Jerusalem also brought in fish and all kinds of merchandise and sold them on the sabbath to the people

17 of Judah, even in Jerusalem. Then I complained to the nobles of Judah and said to them, 'How dare you profane the sabbath in this

18 wicked way? Is not this just what your fathers did, so that our God has brought all this evil on us and on this city? Now you are bringing more wrath upon Israel by pro-

19 faning the sabbath.' When the entrances to Jerusalem had been cleared in preparation for the sabbath, I gave orders that the gates should be shut and not opened until after the sabbath. And I appointed some of the men under me to have charge of the gates so that no load

20 might enter on the sabbath. Then on one or two occasions the merchants and all kinds of traders camped just outside Jerusalem, but I cautioned them. 'Why are 21 you camping in front of the city wall?' I asked. 'If you do it again, I will take action against you.' After that they did not come on the sabbath again. And I commanded the 22 Levites who were to purify themselves and take up duty as guards at the gates, to ensure that the sabbath was kept holy. Remember this also to my credit, O God, and spare me in thy great love.

In those days also I saw that 23 some Jews had married women from Ashdod, Ammon, and Moab. Half their children spoke the lan- 24 guage of Ashdod or of the other peoples and could not speak the language of the Jews. I argued 25 with them and reviled them, I beat them and tore out their hair; and I made them swear in the name of God: 'We will not marry our daughters to their sons, or take any of their daughters in marriage for our sons or for ourselves.' 'Was it 26 not for such women', I said, 'that King Solomon of Israel sinned? Among all the nations there was no king like him; he was loved by his God, and God made him king over all Israel; nevertheless even he was led by foreign women into sin. Are 27 we then to follow your example and commit this grave offence, breaking faith with our God by marrying foreign women?'

Now one of the sons of Joiada son 28 of Eliashib the high priest had married a daughter of Sanballat the Horonite; therefore I drove him out of my presence. Remember, O God, 29 to their shame that they have defiled the priesthood and the covenant of the priests[a] and the Levites.

Thus I purified them from every- 30 thing foreign, and I made the Levites and the priests resume the duties of their office; I also made provision 31 for the wood-offering, at appointed times, and for the firstfruits. Remember me for my good, O God.

---

[a] *Or* priesthood.

ESTHER

Esther chosen as queen by the Persian king

1 THE events here related happened in the days of Ahasuerus, the Ahasuerus who ruled from India to Ethiopia, a hundred and twenty-seven pro-

2 vinces. At this time he sat on his royal throne in Susa the capital

3 city. In the third year of his reign he gave a banquet for all his officers and his courtiers; and when his army of Persians and Medes, with his nobles and provincial gov-

4 ernors, were in attendance, he displayed the wealth of his kingdom and the pomp and splendour of his majesty for many days, a

5 hundred and eighty in all. When these days were over, the king gave a banquet for all the people present in Susa the capital city, both high and low; it was held in the garden court of the royal pavil-

6 ion and lasted seven days. There were white curtains and violet hangings fastened to silver rings with bands of fine linen and purple;*a* there were alabaster pillars and couches of gold and silver set on a mosaic pavement of malachite and alabaster, of mother-of-

7 pearl and turquoise. Wine was served in golden cups of various patterns: the king's wine flowed

8 freely as befitted a king, and the law of the drinking was that there should be no compulsion, for the king had laid it down that all the stewards of his palace should re-

9 spect each man's wishes. In addition, Queen Vashti gave a banquet for the women in the royal apartments of King Ahasuerus.

10 On the seventh day, when he was merry with wine, the king ordered Mehuman, Biztha, Harbona, Bigtha, Abagtha, Zethar, and Carcas, the seven eunuchs who were in attendance on the king's person, to

11 bring Queen Vashti before him wearing her royal crown, in order to display her beauty to the people and the officers; for she was indeed

12 a beautiful woman. But Queen Vashti refused to come in answer to the royal command conveyed by the eunuchs. This greatly incensed the king, and he grew hot with anger.

13 Then the king conferred with his wise men versed in misdemeanours;*b* for it was his royal custom to consult all who were

14 versed in law and religion, those closest to him being Carshena, Shethar, Admatha, Tarshish, Meres, Marsena, and Memucan, the seven princes of Persia and Media who had access to the king and held first

15 place in the kingdom. He asked them, 'What does the law require to be done with Queen Vashti for disobeying the command of King Ahasuerus brought to her by the

16 eunuchs?' Then Memucan made answer before the king and the princes: 'Queen Vashti has done wrong, and not to the king alone, but also to all the officers and to all the peoples in all the provinces of King Ahasuerus. Every woman will

17 come to know what the queen has done, and this will make them treat their husbands with contempt; they will say, "King Ahasuerus ordered Queen Vashti to be brought before him and she did not come."

18 The great ladies of Persia and Media, who have heard of the queen's conduct, will tell all the

a bands...purple: *or* white and purple cords.   *b* Or times.

king's officers about this day, and there will be endless disrespect and 19 insolence! If it please your majesty, let a royal decree go out from you and let it be inscribed in the laws of the Persians and Medes, never to be revoked, that Vashti shall not again appear before King Ahasuerus; and let the king give her place as queen to another woman who is more worthy of it than 20 she. Thus when this royal edict is heard through the length and breadth of the kingdom, all women will give honour to their hus-21 bands, high and low alike.' Memucan's advice pleased the king and the princes, and the king did 22 as he had proposed. Letters were sent to all the royal provinces, to every province in its own script and to every people in their own language, in order that each man might be master in his own house and control all his own women-folk.[a]

2   Later, when the anger of King Ahasuerus had died down, he remembered Vashti and what she had done and what had been de-2 creed against her. So the king's attendants said, 'Let beautiful young virgins be sought out for 3 your majesty; and let your majesty appoint commissioners in all the provinces of your kingdom to bring all these beautiful young virgins into the women's quarters in Susa the capital city. Let them be committed to the care of Hegai, the king's eunuch in charge of the women, and let cosmetics be pro-4 vided for them; and let the one who is most acceptable to the king become queen in place of Vashti.' This idea pleased the king and he acted on it.

5   Now there was in Susa the capital city a Jew named Mordecai son of Jair, son of Shimei, son of Kish, 6 a Benjamite; he had been carried into exile from Jerusalem among those whom Nebuchadnezzar king of Babylon had carried away with Jeconiah king of Judah. He had a 7 foster-child Hadassah, that is Esther, his uncle's daughter, who had neither father nor mother. She was a beautiful and charming girl, and after the death of her father and mother Mordecai had adopted her as his own daughter. When the 8 king's order and his edict were published, and many girls were brought to Susa the capital city to be committed to the care of Hegai, Esther too was taken to the king's palace to be entrusted to Hegai, who had charge of the women. She attracted 9 his notice and received his special favour: he readily provided her with her cosmetics and her allowance of food, and also with seven picked maids from the king's palace, and he gave her and her maids privileges in the women's quarters.

Esther had not disclosed her 10 race or her family, because Mordecai had forbidden her to do so. Every day Mordecai passed along 11 by the forecourt of the women's quarters to learn how Esther was faring and what was happening to her.

The full period of preparation 12 prescribed for the women was twelve months, six months with oil and myrrh and six months with perfumes and cosmetics. When the period was complete, each girl's turn came to go to King Ahasuerus, and she was allowed to take 13 with her whatever she asked, when she went from the women's quarters to the king's palace. She went 14 into the palace in the evening and returned in the morning to another part of the women's quarters, to be under the care of Shaashgaz, the king's eunuch in charge of the concubines. She did not again go to the king unless he expressed a wish for her; then she was summoned by name.

When the turn came for Esther, 15

[a] *and control...womenfolk*: prob. rdg.; Heb. *and speak in his own language.*

daughter of Abihail the uncle of Mordecai her adoptive father, to go to the king, she asked for nothing to take with her except what was advised by Hegai, the king's eunuch in charge of the women; and Esther charmed all who saw 16 her. When she was taken to King Ahasuerus in the royal palace, in the seventh year of his reign, in the tenth month, that is the month Te-17 beth, the king loved her more than any of his other women and treated her with greater favour and kindness than the rest of the virgins. He put a royal crown on her head and made her queen in place of 18 Vashti. Then the king gave a great banquet for all his officers and courtiers, a banquet in honour of Esther. He also proclaimed a holiday[a] throughout the provinces and distributed gifts worthy of a king.

19 Mordecai was in attendance at 20 court; on his instructions Esther had not disclosed her family or her race, she had done what Mordecai told her, as she did when she was 21 his ward. One day when Mordecai was in attendance at court, Bigthan and Teresh, two of the king's eunuchs, keepers of the threshold, who were disaffected, were plotting to lay hands on King Ahasuerus. 22 This became known to Mordecai, who told Queen Esther; and she told the king, mentioning Morde-23 cai by name. The affair was investigated and the report confirmed; the two men were hanged on the gallows. All this was recorded in the royal chronicle in the presence of the king.

Haman's plot against the Jews

3 AFTER this, King Ahasuerus promoted Haman son of Hammedatha the Agagite, advancing him and giving him precedence above 2 all his fellow-officers. So the king's attendants at court all bowed down to Haman and did obeisance, for so the king had commanded; but Mordecai did not bow down to him or do obeisance. Then the attend-3 ants at court said to Mordecai, 'Why do you flout his majesty's command?' Day by day they 4 challenged him, but he refused to listen to them; so they informed Haman, in order to discover if Mordecai's refusal would be tolerated, for he had told them that he was a Jew. When Haman saw that 5 Mordecai was not bowing down to him or doing obeisance, he was infuriated. On learning who Mor-6 decai's people were, he scorned to lay hands on him alone, and looked for a way to destroy all the Jews throughout the whole kingdom of Ahasuerus, Mordecai and all his race.

In the twelfth year of King 7 Ahasuerus, in the first month, Nisan, they cast lots, Pur as it is called, in the presence of Haman, taking day by day and month by month, and the lot fell on the thirteenth day of the twelfth month,[b] the month Adar. Then Haman 8 said to King Ahasuerus, 'There is a certain people, dispersed among the many peoples in all the provinces of your kingdom, who keep themselves apart. Their laws are different from those of every other people; they do not keep your majesty's laws. It does not befit your majesty to tolerate them. If 9 it please your majesty, let an order be made in writing for their destruction; and I will pay ten thousand talents of silver to your majesty's officials, to be deposited in the royal treasury.' So the king 10 took the signet-ring from his hand and gave it to Haman son of Hammedatha the Agagite, the enemy of the Jews; and he said to him, 11 'The money and the people are yours; deal with them as you wish.'

---

[a] Or an amnesty.
[b] and the lot...twelfth month: *prob. rdg., cp. verse 13; Heb.* the twelfth.

12 On the thirteenth day of the first month the king's secretaries were summoned and, in accordance with Haman's instructions, a writ was issued to the king's satraps and the governor of every province, and to the officers over each separate people: for each province in its own script and for each people in their own language. It was drawn up in the name of King Ahasuerus and 13 sealed with the king's signet. Thus letters were sent by courier to all the king's provinces with orders to destroy, slay, and exterminate all Jews, young and old, women and children, in one day, the thirteenth day of the twelfth month, the month Adar, and to plunder their 14 possessions. A copy of the writ was to be issued as a decree in every province and to be published to all the peoples, so that they might be 15 ready for that day. The couriers were dispatched post-haste at the king's command, and the decree was issued in Susa the capital city. The king and Haman sat down to drink; but the city of Susa was thrown into confusion.

4 When Mordecai learnt all that had been done, he rent his clothes, put on sackcloth and ashes, and went through the city crying loud-2 ly and bitterly. He came within sight of the palace gate, because no one clothed with sackcloth was al-3 lowed to pass through the gate. In every province reached by the royal command and decree there was great mourning among the Jews, with fasting and weeping and beating of the breast. Most of them made their beds of sackcloth 4 and ashes. When Queen Esther's maids and eunuchs came and told her, she was distraught, and sent garments for Mordecai, so that they might take off the sackcloth and clothe him with them; but he 5 would not accept them. Then Esther summoned Hathach, one of the king's eunuchs who had been appointed to wait upon her, and ordered him to find out from Mordecai what the trouble was and what it meant. Hathach went to 6 Mordecai in the city square in front of the palace gate, and Mordecai 7 told him all that had happened to him and how much money Haman had offered to pay into the royal treasury for the destruction of the Jews. He also gave him a copy of 8 the writ for their destruction issued in Susa, so that he might show it to Esther and tell her about it, bidding her go to the king to plead for his favour and entreat him for her people. Hathach went 9 and told Esther what Mordecai had said, and she sent him back with 10 this message: 'All the king's cour-11 tiers and the people of the provinces are aware that if any person, man or woman, enters the king's presence in the inner court unbidden, there is one law only: that person shall be put to death, unless the king stretches out to him the golden sceptre; then and then only shall he live. It is now thirty days since I myself was called to go to the king.' But when they told Mor-12 decai what Esther had said, he 13 bade them go back to her and say, 'Do not imagine that you alone of all the Jews will escape because you are in the royal palace. If you 14 remain silent at such a time as this, relief and deliverance for the Jews will appear from another quarter, but you and your father's family will perish. Who knows whether it is not for such a time as this that you have come to royal estate?' Esther gave them this answer to 15 take back to Mordecai: 'Go and 16 assemble all the Jews to be found in Susa and fast for me; take neither food nor drink for three days, night or day, and I and my maids will fast as you do. After that I will go to the king, although it is against the law; and if I perish, I perish.' So Mordecai went away 17 and did exactly as Esther had bidden him.

5 On the third day Esther put on her royal robes and stood in the inner court of the king's palace, facing the palace itself; the king was seated on his royal throne in the palace, facing the entrance.
2 When the king caught sight of Queen Esther standing in the court, she won his favour and he stretched out to her the golden sceptre which he was holding. Thereupon Esther approached and touched the head of the sceptre.
3 Then the king said to her, 'What is it, Queen Esther? Whatever you ask of me, up to half my kingdom, shall be given to you.' 'If it please
4 your majesty,' said Esther, 'will you come today, sire, and Haman with you, to a banquet which I
5 have made ready for you?' The king gave orders that Haman should be fetched quickly, so that Esther's wish might be fulfilled; and the king and Haman went to the ban-
6 quet which she had prepared. Over the wine the king said to Esther, 'Whatever you ask of me shall be given to you. Whatever you request of me, up to half my kingdom, it
7 shall be done.' Esther said in answer, 'What I ask and request of
8 you is this. If I have won your majesty's favour, and if it please you, sire, to give me what I ask and to grant my request, will your majesty and Haman come tomorrow to the banquet which I shall prepare for you both? Tomorrow I will do as your majesty has said.'
9 So Haman went away that day in good spirits and well pleased with himself. But when he saw Mordecai in attendance at court and how he did not rise nor defer to him, he was filled with rage;
10 but he kept control of himself and went home. Then he sent for his
11 friends and his wife Zeresh and held forth to them about the splendour of his wealth and his many sons, and how the king had promoted him and advanced him above the other officers and cour-

tiers. 'That is not all,' said Haman; 12 'Queen Esther invited no one but myself to accompany the king to the banquet which she had prepared; and she has invited me again tomorrow with the king. Yet 13 all this means nothing to me so long as I see that Jew Mordecai in attendance at court.' Then his wife 14 Zeresh and all his friends said to him, 'Let a gallows seventy-five feet high be set up, and recommend to the king in the morning to have Mordecai hanged upon it. Then go with the king to the banquet in good spirits.' Haman thought this an excellent plan, and he set up the gallows.

Haman's downfall and Mordecai's triumph

THAT night sleep eluded the king, 6 so he ordered the chronicle of daily events to be brought; and it was read to him. Therein was recorded 2 that Mordecai had given information about Bigthana and Teresh, the two royal eunuchs among the keepers of the threshold who had plotted to lay hands on King Ahasuerus. Whereupon the king said, 3 'What honour or dignity has been conferred on Mordecai for this?' The king's courtiers who were in attendance told him that nothing had been done for Mordecai. The 4 king asked, 'Who is that in the court?' Now Haman had just entered the outer court of the palace to recommend to the king that Mordecai should be hanged on the gallows which he had prepared for him. The king's servants answered, 5 'It is Haman standing there'; and the king bade him enter. He came 6 in, and the king said to him, 'What should be done for the man whom the king wishes to honour?' Haman said to himself, 'Whom would the king wish to honour more than me?' And he said to the king, 'For 7 the man whom the king wishes to honour, let there be brought royal 8 robes which the king himself wears, and a horse which the king rides, with a royal crown upon its head.

9 And let the robes and the horse be delivered to one of the king's most honourable officers, and let him attire the man whom the king wishes to honour and lead him mounted on the horse through the city square, calling out as he goes: "See what is done for the man whom the king wishes to honour."'

10 Then the king said to Haman, 'Fetch the robes and the horse at once, as you have said, and do all this for Mordecai the Jew who is in attendance at court. Leave nothing undone of all that you have said.'

11 So Haman took the robes and the horse, attired Mordecai, and led him mounted through the city square, calling out as he went: 'See what is done for the man whom the king wishes to honour.'

12 Then Mordecai returned to court and Haman hurried off home mourning, with head uncovered.

13 He told his wife Zeresh and all his friends everything that had happened to him. And this was the reply of his friends and his wife Zeresh: 'If Mordecai, in face of whom your fortunes begin to fall, belongs to the Jewish race, you will not get the better of him; he will see your utter downfall.'

14 While they were still talking with Haman, the king's eunuchs arrived and hurried him away to the banquet which Esther had prepared.

7 So the king and Haman went to
2 dine with Queen Esther. Again on that second day, over the wine, the king said, 'Whatever you ask of me will be given to you, Queen Esther. Whatever you request of me, up to half my kingdom, it shall be done.'

3 Queen Esther answered, 'If I have found favour with your majesty, and if it please your majesty, my request and petition is that my own life and the lives of my people may be spared. For we have been sold, I 4 and my people, to be destroyed, slain, and exterminated. If it had been a matter of selling us, men and women alike, into slavery, I should have kept silence; for then our plight would not be such as to injure the king's interests.' Then 5 King Ahasuerus said to Queen Esther, 'Who is he, and where is he, who has presumed to do such a thing as this?' 'An adversary and 6 an enemy,' said Esther, 'this wicked Haman.' At that Haman was dumbfounded in the presence of the king and the queen. The king 7 rose from the banquet in a rage and went to the garden of the pavilion, while Haman remained where he was, to plead for his life with Queen Esther; for he saw that in the king's mind his fate was determined. When the king returned 8 from the garden to the banqueting hall, Haman had flung himself across the couch on which Esther was reclining. The king exclaimed, 'Will he even assault the queen here in my presence?' No sooner had the words left the king's mouth than Haman hid his face in despair.[a] Then Harbona, one of the 9 eunuchs in attendance on the king, said, 'At Haman's house stands the gallows, seventy-five feet high, which he himself has prepared for Mordecai, who once served the king well.' 'Hang Haman on it', said the king. So they hanged him 10 on the gallows that he himself had prepared for Mordecai. After that the king's rage abated.

On that day King Ahasuerus 8 gave Queen Esther the house of Haman, enemy of the Jews; and Mordecai came into the king's presence, for Esther had told him how he was related to her. Then the 2 king took off his signet-ring, which he had taken back from Haman, and gave it to Mordecai. And Esther put Mordecai in charge of Haman's house.

---

a Haman...despair: *prob. rdg.*; *Heb.* they covered Haman's face.

3 Once again Esther spoke before the king, falling at his feet in tears and pleading with him to avert the calamity planned by Haman the Agagite and to frustrate his plot 4 against the Jews. The king stretched out the golden sceptre to Esther, and she rose and stood before the 5 king, and said, 'May it please your majesty: if I have found favour with you, and if the proposal seems right to your majesty and I have won your approval, let a writ be issued to recall the letters which Haman son of Hammedatha the Agagite wrote in pursuance of his plan to destroy the Jews in all the 6 royal provinces. For how can I bear to see the calamity which is coming upon my race? Or how can I bear to see the destruction of my 7 family?' Then King Ahasuerus said to Queen Esther and to Mordecai the Jew, 'I have given Haman's house to Esther, and he has been hanged on the gallows, because he threatened the lives of the Jews. 8 Now you shall issue a writ concerning the Jews in my name, in whatever terms you think fit, and seal it with the royal signet; for an order written in the name of the king and sealed with the royal signet cannot be revoked.'

9 And so, on the twenty-third day of the third month, the month Sivan, the king's secretaries were summoned; and a writ was issued to the Jews, exactly as Mordecai directed, and to the satraps, the governors, and the officers in the provinces from India to Ethiopia, a hundred and twenty-seven provinces, for each province in its own script and for each people in their own language, and also for the Jews in their own script and lan- 10 guage. The writ was drawn up in the name of King Ahasuerus and sealed with the royal signet, and letters were sent by mounted couriers riding on horses from the 11 royal stables. By these letters the king granted permission to the Jews in every city to unite and defend themselves, and to destroy, slay, and exterminate the whole strength of any people or province which might attack them, women and children too, and to plunder their possessions, throughout all 12 the provinces of King Ahasuerus, in one day, the thirteenth day of the twelfth month, the month Adar. A copy of the writ was to be 13 issued as a decree in every province and published to all peoples, and the Jews were to be ready for that day, the day of vengeance on their enemies. So the couriers, 14 mounted on their royal horses, were dispatched post-haste at the king's urgent command; and the decree was issued also in Susa the capital city.

Mordecai left the king's presence 15 in royal robes of violet and white, wearing a great golden crown and a cloak of fine linen and purple, and all the city of Susa shouted for joy. For the Jews there was light and 16 joy, gladness and honour. In every 17 province and every city reached by the royal command and decree, there was joy and gladness for the Jews, feasting and holiday. And many of the peoples of the land professed themselves Jews, because fear of the Jews had seized them.

ON the thirteenth day of the 9 twelfth month, the month Adar, the time came for the king's command and his edict to be carried out. The very day on which the enemies of the Jews had hoped to gain the upper hand over them was to become the day when the Jews should gain the upper hand over those who hated them. On that 2 day the Jews united in their cities in all the provinces of King Ahasuerus to fall upon those who had planned their ruin. No one could resist them, because fear of them had seized all peoples. All the 3 officers of the provinces, the satraps and the governors, and all the royal officials, aided the Jews, because fear of Mordecai had 4 seized them. Mordecai had become a great personage in the royal palace; his fame had spread throughout all the provinces as the power of the man grew steadily 5 greater. So the Jews put their enemies to the sword, with great slaughter and destruction; they worked their will on those who 6 hated them. In Susa, the capital city, the Jews killed five hundred 7 men and destroyed them; and they killed also Parshandatha, Dal- 8 phon and Aspatha, Poratha, Ada- 9 lia and Aridatha, Parmashta, 10 Arisai, Aridai and Vaizatha, the ten sons of Haman son of Hammedatha, the enemy of the Jews; but they did not touch the plunder.

11 That day when the number of those killed in Susa the capital city 12 came to the notice of the king, he said to Queen Esther, 'In Susa, the capital city, the Jews have killed and destroyed five hundred men and the ten sons of Haman. What have they done in the rest of the king's provinces? Whatever you ask further will be given to you; whatever more you seek shall be 13 done.' Esther answered him, 'If it please your majesty, let tomorrow be granted to the Jews in Susa to do according to the edict for today; and let the bodies of Haman's ten sons be hung up on the gallows.' 14 The king gave orders for this to be done; the edict was issued in Susa and Haman's ten sons were hung 15 up on the gallows. The Jews in Susa united again on the fourteenth day of the month Adar and killed three hundred men in Susa; but they did not touch the plunder.

16 The rest of the Jews in the king's provinces had united to defend themselves; they took vengeance on[a] their enemies by killing seventy-five thousand of those who hated them; but they did not touch the plunder. This was on the thir- 17 teenth day of the month Adar, and they rested on the fourteenth day and made that a day of feasting and joy. The Jews in Susa had 18 united on the thirteenth and fourteenth days of the month, and rested on the fifteenth day and made that a day of feasting and joy. This is why isolated Jews who 19 live in remote villages keep the fourteenth day of the month Adar in joy and feasting, as a holiday on which they send presents of food to one another.

Then Mordecai set these things 20 on record and sent letters to all the Jews in all the provinces of King Ahasuerus, far and near, binding 21 them to keep the fourteenth and fifteenth days of the month Adar, year by year, as the days on which 22 the Jews obtained relief from their enemies and as the month which was changed for them from sorrow into joy, from a time of mourning to a holiday. They were to keep them as days of feasting and joy, days for sending presents of food to one another and gifts to the poor.

So the Jews undertook to con- 23 tinue the practice that they had begun in accordance with Mordecai's letter. This they did be- 24 cause Haman son of Hammedatha the Agagite, the enemy of all the Jews, had plotted to destroy the Jews and had cast lots, Pur as it is called, with intent to crush and destroy them. But when the matter 25 came before the king, he issued written orders that the wicked plot which Haman had devised against the Jews should recoil on his own head, and that he and his sons should be hanged on the gallows. Therefore, these days were 26 named Purim after the word Pur. Accordingly, because of all that was written in this letter, because of all they had seen and experienced in this affair, the Jews re- 27

---

[a] *Prob. rdg.; Heb.* got respite from.

solved and undertook, on behalf of themselves, their descendants, and all who should join them, that they would without fail keep these two days as a yearly festival in the prescribed manner and at the 28 appointed time; that these days should be remembered and kept, generation after generation, in every family, province, and city, that the days of Purim should always be observed among the Jews, and that the memory of them should never cease among their descendants.

29 Queen Esther daughter of Abihail gave full authority in writing to[a] Mordecai the Jew, to confirm this second letter about Purim.
30 Letters wishing peace and security were sent to all the Jews in the hundred and twenty-seven pro-
31 vinces of King Ahasuerus, making the observance of these days of Purim at their appointed time binding on them, as Mordecai the Jew[b] had prescribed. In the same way they had prescribed regulations for fasts and lamentations for themselves and their descendants. The command of Esther 32 confirmed these regulations for Purim, and the record is preserved in writing.

King Ahasuerus imposed forced 10 labour on the land and the coasts and islands. All the king's acts of 2 authority and power, and the dignities which he conferred on Mordecai, are written in the annals of the kings of Media and Persia. For Mordecai the Jew was second 3 only to King Ahasuerus; he was a great man among the Jews and was popular with the mass of his countrymen, for he sought the good of his people and promoted the welfare of all their descendants.[c]

THE BOOK OF

JOB

Prologue

1 THERE lived in the land of Uz a man of blameless and upright life named Job, who feared God and set his face against
2 wrongdoing. He had seven sons
3 and three daughters; and he owned seven thousand sheep and three thousand camels, five hundred yoke of oxen and five hundred asses, with a large number of slaves. Thus Job was the greatest man in all the East.
4 Now his sons used to foregather and give, each in turn, a feast in his own house; and they used to send and invite their three sisters to eat and drink with them. Then, 5 when a round of feasts was finished, Job sent for his children and sanctified them, rising early in the morning and sacrificing a whole-offering for each of them; for he thought that they might somehow have sinned against God and committed blasphemy in their hearts. This he always did.

The day came when the mem- 6 bers of the court of heaven took their places in the presence of the LORD, and Satan[d] was there among them. The LORD asked him 7 where he had been. 'Ranging over

---

a Prob. rdg.; Heb. and.   *b* Prob. rdg.; Heb. adds and Queen Esther.
c Or and was in friendly relations with all his race.   *d* Or the adversary.

the earth', he said, 'from end to
8 end.' Then the LORD asked Satan,
'Have you considered my servant
Job? You will find no one like him
on earth, a man of blameless and
upright life, who fears God and sets
9 his face against wrongdoing.' Satan
answered the LORD, 'Has not Job
good reason to be God-fearing?
10 Have you not hedged him round
on every side with your protection, him and his family and all his
possessions? Whatever he does
you have blessed, and his herds
have increased beyond measure.
11 But stretch out your hand and
touch all that he has, and then he
12 will curse you to your face.' Then
the LORD said to Satan, 'So be it.
All that he has is in your hands;
only Job himself you must not
touch.' And Satan left the LORD's
presence.

13 When the day came that Job's
sons and daughters were eating
and drinking in the eldest brother's
14 house, a messenger came running
to Job and said, 'The oxen were
ploughing and the asses were
15 grazing near them, when the Sabaeans swooped down and carried
them off, after putting the herdsmen to the sword; and I am the
only one to escape and tell the tale.'
16 While he was still speaking, another messenger arrived and said,
'God's fire flashed from heaven. It
struck the sheep and the shepherds
and burnt them up; and I am the
only one to escape and tell the tale.'
17 While he was still speaking, another arrived and said, 'The Chaldaeans, three bands of them, have
made a raid on the camels and
carried them off, after putting the
drivers to the sword; and I am the
only one to escape and tell the tale.'
18 While this man was speaking, yet
another arrived and said, 'Your
sons and daughters were eating and
drinking in the eldest brother's
19 house, when suddenly a whirlwind
swept across from the desert and
struck the four corners of the house,

and it fell on the young people and
killed them; and I am the only one
to escape and tell the tale.' At this 20
Job stood up and rent his cloak;
then he shaved his head and fell
prostrate on the ground, saying: 21

Naked I came from the womb,
naked I shall return whence I
came.
The LORD gives and the LORD
takes away;
blessed be the name of the LORD.

Throughout all this Job did not 22
sin; he did not charge God with
unreason.

Once again the day came when 2
the members of the court of heaven
took their places in the presence of
the LORD, and Satan was there
among them. The LORD asked him 2
where he had been. 'Ranging over
the earth', he said, 'from end to
end.' Then the LORD asked Satan, 3
'Have you considered my servant
Job? You will find no one like him
on earth, a man of blameless and
upright life, who fears God and sets
his face against wrongdoing. You
incited me to ruin him without a
cause, but his integrity is still unshaken.' Satan answered the LORD, 4
'Skin for skin! There is nothing the
man will grudge to save himself.
But stretch out your hand and 5
touch his bone and his flesh, and
see if he will not curse you to your
face.'

Then the LORD said to Satan, 'So 6
be it. He is in your hands; but spare
his life.' And Satan left the LORD's 7
presence, and he smote Job with
running sores from head to foot,
so that he took a piece of a broken 8
pot to scratch himself as he sat
among the ashes. Then his wife 9
said to him, 'Are you still unshaken
in your integrity? Curse God and
die!' But he answered, 'You talk as 10
any wicked fool of a woman might
talk. If we accept good from God,
shall we not accept evil?' Throughout all this, Job did not utter one
sinful word.

11 When Job's three friends, Eli-phaz of Teman, Bildad of Shuah, and Zophar of Naamah, heard of all these calamities which had over-taken him, they left their homes and arranged to come and condole 12 with him and comfort him. But when they first saw him from a distance, they did not recognize him; and they wept aloud, rent their cloaks and tossed dust into 13 the air over their heads. For seven days and seven nights they sat beside him on the ground, and none of them said a word to him; for they saw that his suffering was very great.

Job's complaint to God

3 1–2 After this Job broke silence and cursed the day of his birth:

3 Perish the day when I was born
and the night which said, 'A man is conceived'!
4 May that day turn to darkness;
may God above not look for it,
nor light of dawn shine on it.
5 May blackness sully it, and murk and gloom,
cloud smother that day, swift dark-ness eclipse its sun.
6 Blind darkness swallow up that night;
count it not among the days of the year,
reckon it not in the cycle of the months.
7 That night, may it be barren for ever,
no cry of joy be heard in it.
8 Cursed be it by those whose magic binds even the monster of the deep,
who are ready to tame Leviathan himself with spells.
9 May no star shine out in its twi-light;
may it wait for a dawn that never comes,
nor ever see the eyelids of the morning,

10 because it did not shut the doors of the womb that bore me
and keep trouble away from my sight.
11 Why was I not still-born,
why did I not die when I came out of the womb?
12 Why was I ever laid on my mo-ther's knees
or put to suck at her breasts?
16 Why was I not hidden like an un-timely birth,
like an infant that has not lived to see the light?
13 For then I should be lying in the quiet grave,
asleep in death, at rest,
14 with kings and their ministers
who built themselves palaces,
15 with princes rich in gold
who filled their houses with silver.
17ᵃ There the wicked man chafes no more,
there the tired labourer rests;
18 the captive too finds peace there
and hears no taskmaster's voice;
19 high and low are there,
even the slave, free from his master.

20 Why should the sufferer be born to see the light?
Why is life given to men who find it so bitter?
21 They wait for death but it does not come,
they seek it more eagerly thanᵇ hidden treasure.
22 They are glad when they reach the tomb,
and when they come to the grave they exult.
23 Why should a man be born to wander blindly,
hedged in by God on every side?
24 My sighing is all my food,
and groans pour from me in a torrent.
25 Every terror that haunted me has caught up with me,
and all that I feared has come up-on me.

ᵃ *Verse 16 transposed to follow verse 12.*   ᵇ *Or seek it among...*

26 There is no peace of mind nor quiet
   for me;
   I chafe in torment and have no rest.

First cycle of speeches

4 Then Eliphaz the Temanite began:

2 If one ventures to speak with you,
   will you lose patience?
   For who could hold his tongue any
   longer?
3 Think how once you encouraged
   those who faltered,
   how you braced feeble arms,
4 how a word from you upheld the
   stumblers
   and put strength into weak knees.
5 But now that adversity comes upon you, you lose patience;
   it touches you, and you are unmanned.
6 Is your religion no comfort to you?
   Does your blameless life give you
   no hope?
7 For consider, what innocent man
   has ever perished?
   Where have you seen the upright
   destroyed?
8 This I know, that those who
   plough mischief and sow trouble
   reap as they have sown;
9 they perish at the blast of God
   and are shrivelled by the breath of
   his nostrils.

10 The roar of the lion, the whimpering of his cubs, fall silent;
   the teeth of the young lions are
   broken;
11 the lion perishes for lack of prey
   and the whelps of the lioness are
   abandoned.

12 A word stole into my ears,
   and they caught the whisper of it;
13 in the anxious visions of the night,
   when a man sinks into deepest
   sleep,
14 terror seized me and shuddering;
   the trembling of my body frightened me.

A wind brushed my face   15
and made the hairs bristle on my
   flesh;
and a figure stood there whose   16
   shape I could not discern,
an apparition loomed before me,
and I heard the sound of a low
   voice:
'Can mortal man be more righteous   17
   than God,
or the creature purer than his
   Maker?
If God mistrusts his own servants   18
   and finds his messengers at fault,
how much more those that dwell in   19
   houses whose walls are clay,
   whose foundations are dust,
which can be crushed like a bird's
   nest
or torn down between dawn and   20
   dark,
how much more shall such men
   perish outright and unheeded,
*a*die, without ever finding wisdom?'   21

Call if you will; is there any to   5
   answer you?
To which of the holy ones will you
   turn?
The fool is destroyed by his own   2
   angry passions,
and the end of childish resentment
   is death.
I have seen it for myself: a fool   3
   uprooted,
his home in sudden ruin about him,*b*
his children past help,   4
browbeaten in court with none to
   save them;
*c*Their rich possessions are snatch-   5
   ed from them;
what they have harvested others
   hungrily devour;
the stronger man seizes it from the
   panniers,
panting, thirsting for their wealth.
Mischief does not grow out of the   6
   soil
nor trouble spring from the earth;
man is born to trouble,   7
   as surely as birds fly*d* upwards.

---

a *Prob. rdg., transposing* Their rich possessions are snatched from them *to follow*
5. 4.   *b* ruin about him: *prob. rdg.; Heb. obscure.*
c *Line transposed from 4. 21.*   *d* *Or* as sparks shoot.

8 For my part, I would make my petition to God
and lay my cause before him,

9 who does great and unsearchable things,
marvels without number.

10 He gives rain to the earth
and sends water on the fields;

11 he raises the lowly to the heights,
the mourners are uplifted by victory;

12 he frustrates the plots of the crafty,
and they win no success,

13 he traps the cunning in their craftiness,
and the schemers' plans are thrown into confusion.

14 In the daylight they run into darkness,
and grope at midday as though it were night.

15 He saves the destitute from their greed,
and the needy from the grip of the strong;

16 so the poor hope again,
and the unjust are sickened.

17 Happy the man whom God rebukes!
therefore do not reject the discipline of the Almighty.

18 For, though he wounds, he will bind up;
the hands that smite will heal.

19 You may meet disaster six times, and he will save you;
seven times, and no harm shall touch you.

20 In time of famine he will save you from death,
in battle from the sword.

21 You will be shielded from the lash of slander,[a]
and when violence comes you need not fear.

22 You will laugh at violence and starvation
and have no need to fear wild beasts;

23 for you have a covenant with the stones to spare your fields,
and the weeds have been constrained to leave you at peace.

24 You will know that all is well with your household,
you will look round your home and find nothing amiss;

25 you will know, too, that your descendants will be many
and your offspring like grass, thick upon the earth.

26 You will come in sturdy old age to the grave
as sheaves come in due season to the threshing-floor.

27 We have inquired into all this, and so it is;
this we have heard, and you may know it for the truth.

Then Job answered: 6

2 O that the grounds for my resentment might be weighed,
and my misfortunes set with them on the scales!

3 For they would outweigh the sands of the sea:
what wonder if my words are wild?[b]

4 The arrows of the Almighty find their mark in me,
and their poison soaks into my spirit;
God's onslaughts wear me away.

5 Does the wild ass bray when he has grass
or the ox low when he has fodder?

6 Can a man eat tasteless food unseasoned with salt,
or find any flavour in the juice of mallows?

7 Food that should nourish me sticks in my throat,
and my bowels rumble with an echoing sound.

8 O that I might have my request,
that God would grant what I hope for:

---

a from . . . slander: *or* when slander is rife.
b what . . . wild?: *or* therefore words fail me.

9 that he would be pleased to crush
me,
to snatch me away with his hand
and cut me off!

10 For that would bring me relief,
and in the face of unsparing anguish I would leap for joy.[a]

11 Have I the strength to wait?
What end have I to expect, that I
should be patient?

12 Is my strength the strength of stone,
or is my flesh bronze?

13 Oh how shall I find help within
myself?
The power to aid myself is put out
of my reach.

14 Devotion is due from his friends
to one who despairs and loses faith
in the Almighty;

15 but my brothers have been treacherous as a mountain stream,
like the channels of streams that
run dry,

16 which turn dark with ice
or are hidden with piled-up snow;

17 or they vanish the moment they
are in spate,
dwindle in the heat and are gone.

18 Then the caravans, winding hither
and thither,
go up into the wilderness and
perish;[b]

19 the caravans of Tema look for
their waters,
travelling merchants of Sheba
hope for them;

20 but they are disappointed, for all
their confidence,
they reach them only to be balked.

21 So treacherous have you now been
to me:[c]
you felt dismay and were afraid.

22 Did I ever say, 'Give me this or
that;
open your purses to save my life;

23 rescue me from my enemy;
ransom me out of the hands of
ruthless men'?

24 Tell me plainly, and I will listen in
silence;
show me where I have erred.

25 How harsh are the words of the upright man!
What do the arguments of wise
men[d] prove?

26 Do you mean to argue about
words
or to sift the utterance of a man
past hope?

27 Would you assail an orphan[e]?
Would you hurl yourselves on a
friend?

28 So now, I beg you, turn and look at
me:
am I likely to lie to your faces?

29 Think again, let me have no more
injustice;
think again, for my integrity is in
question.

30 Do I ever give voice to injustice?
Does my sense not warn me when
my words are wild?

7 Has not man hard service on
earth,
and are not his days like those of a
hired labourer,

2 like those of a slave longing for the
shade
or a servant kept waiting for his
wages?

3 So months of futility are my portion,
troubled nights are my lot.

4 When I lie down, I think,
'When will it be day that I may
rise?'
When the evening grows long and
I lie down,
I do nothing but toss till morning
twilight.

5 My body is infested with worms,
and scabs cover my skin.[f]

6 My days are swifter than a
shuttle[g]
and come to an end as the thread
runs out.[h]

---

[a] *Prob. rdg.; Heb. adds* I have not denied the words of the Holy One.
[b] *Or* and are lost.   [c] *So...to me: prob. rdg.; Heb. obscure.*
[d] *wise men: prob. rdg.; Heb. unintelligible.*   [e] *Or* a blameless man.
[f] *Prob. rdg.; Heb. adds* it is cracked and discharging.   [g] *Or* a fleeting odour.
[h] *as...out: or* without hope.

7 Remember, my life is but a breath
   of wind;
   I shall never again see good days.
8 Thou wilt behold me no more with
   a seeing eye;
   under thy very eyes I shall disappear.
9 As clouds break up and disperse,
   so he that goes down to Sheol never
   comes back;
10 he never returns home again,
   and his place will know him no
   more.[a]

11 But I will not hold my peace;
   I will speak out in the distress of
   my mind
   and complain in the bitterness of
   my soul.
12 Am I the monster of the deep, am
   I the sea-serpent,
   that thou settest a watch over me?
13 When I think that my bed will
   comfort me,
   that sleep will relieve my complaining,
14 thou dost terrify me with dreams
   and affright me with visions.
15 I would rather be choked outright;
   I would prefer death to all my
   sufferings.
16 I am in despair, I would not go on
   living;
   leave me alone, for my life is but
   a vapour.
17 What is man that thou makest
   much of him
   and turnest thy thoughts towards
   him,
18 only to punish him morning by
   morning
   or to test him every hour of the
   day?
19 Wilt thou not look away from me
   for an instant?
   Wilt thou not let me be while I
   swallow my spittle?
20 If I have sinned, how do I injure
   thee,
   thou watcher of the hearts of men?
   Why hast thou made me thy butt,
   and why have I become thy target?

21 Why dost thou not pardon my
   offence
   and take away my guilt?
   But now I shall lie down in the
   grave;
   seek me, and I shall not be.

8 Then Bildad the Shuhite began:

2 How long will you say such things,
   the long-winded ramblings of an
   old man?
3 Does God pervert judgement?
   Does the Almighty pervert justice?
4 Your sons sinned against him,
   so he left them to be victims of
   their own iniquity.
5 If only you will seek God betimes
   and plead for the favour of the Almighty,
6 if you are innocent and upright,
   then indeed will he watch over
   you
   and see your just intent fulfilled.
7 Then, though your beginnings
   were humble,
   your end will be great.

8 Inquire now of older generations
   and consider the experience of
   their fathers;
9 for we ourselves are of yesterday
   and are transient;
   our days on earth are a shadow.
10 Will not they speak to you and
   teach you
   and pour out the wisdom of their
   hearts?
11 Can rushes grow where there is no
   marsh?
   Can reeds flourish without water?
12 While they are still in flower and
   not ready to cut,[b]
   they wither earlier than[c] any green
   plant.
13 Such is the fate of all who forget
   God;
   the godless man's life-thread breaks
   off;
14 his confidence is gossamer,
   and the ground of his trust a
   spider's web.

[a] *Or* and he will not be noticed any more in his place.
[b] and...cut: *or* they are surely cut.   [c] *Or* wither like...

521

15 He leans against his house but it
    does not stand;
  he clutches at it but it does not
    hold firm.

16 His is the lush growth of a plant in
    the sun,
  pushing out shoots over the
    garden;

17 but its roots become entangled in
    a stony patch
  and run against a bed of rock.

18 Then someone uproots it from its
    place,
  which*a* disowns it and says, 'I have
    never known you.'

19 That is how its life withers
    away,
  and other plants spring up from
    the earth.

20 Be sure, God will not spurn the
    blameless man,
  nor will he grasp the hand of the
    wrongdoer.

21 He will yet fill your mouth with
    laughter,
  and shouts of joy will be on your
    lips;

22 your enemies shall be wrapped in
    confusion,
  and the tents of the wicked shall
    vanish away.

9 Then Job answered:

2 Indeed this I know for the truth,
  that no man can win his case
    against God.

3 If a man chooses to argue with
    him,
  God will not answer one question
    in a thousand.*b*

4 He is wise, he is powerful;
  what man has stubbornly resisted
    him and survived?

5 It is God who moves mountains,
    giving them no rest,
  turning them over in his wrath;

6 who makes the earth start from
    its place
  so that its pillars are convulsed;

7 who commands the sun's orb not
    to rise
  and shuts up the stars under his
    seal;

8 who by himself spread out the
    heavens
  and trod on the sea-monster's
    back;*c*

9 who made Aldebaran and Orion,
  the Pleiades and the circle of the
    southern stars;

10 who does great and unsearchable
    things,
  marvels without number.

11 He passes by me, and I do not see
    him;
  he moves on his way undiscerned
    by me;

12 if he hurries on, who can bring him
    back?
  Who will ask him what he does?

13 God does not turn back his wrath;
  the partisans of Rahab lie pros-
    trate at his feet.

14 How much less can I answer him
  or find words to dispute with him?

15 Though I am right, I get no answer,
  though I plead with my accuser
    for mercy.

16 If I summoned him to court and
    he responded,
  I do not believe that he would
    listen to my plea –

17 for he bears hard upon me for a
    trifle
  and rains blows on me without
    cause;

18 he leaves me no respite to recover
    my breath
  but fills me with bitter thoughts.

19 If the appeal is to force, see how
    strong he is;
  if to justice, who can compel him to
    give me a hearing?

20 Though I am right, he condemns
    me out of my own mouth;
  though I am blameless, he twists
    my words.

21 Blameless, I say; of myself
  I reck nothing, I hold my life cheap.

---

a Or and.
b If a man...thousand: *or* If God is pleased to argue with him, man cannot
answer one question in a thousand.   *c* Or on the crests of the waves.

22 But it is all one; therefore I say,
   'He destroys blameless and wicked
   alike.'
23 When a sudden flood brings
   death,
   he mocks the plight of the innocent.
24 The land is given over to the power
   of the wicked,
   and the eyes of its judges are
   blindfold.[a]

25 My days have been swifter than a
   runner,
   they have slipped away and seen
   no prosperity;
26 they have raced by like reed-built
   skiffs,
   swift as vultures swooping on
   carrion.
27 If I think, 'I will forget my
   griefs,
   I will show a cheerful face and
   smile',
28 I tremble in every nerve;[b]
   I know that thou wilt not hold me
   innocent.
29 If I am to be accounted guilty,
   why do I labour in vain?
30 Though I wash myself with soap
   or cleanse my hands with lye,
31 thou wilt thrust me into the
   mud
   and my clothes will make me
   loathsome.

32 He is not a man as I am, that I can
   answer him
   or that we can confront one another in court.
33 If only there were one to arbitrate
   between us
   and impose his authority on us
   both,
34 so that God might take his rod
   from my back,
   and terror of him might not come
   on me suddenly.
35 I would then speak without fear of
   him;
   for I know I am not what I am
   thought to be.

I am sickened of life;   10
I will give free rein to my griefs,
I will speak out in bitterness of
   soul.
I will say to God, 'Do not condemn 2
   me,
but tell me the ground of thy
   complaint against me.
Dost thou find any advantage in   3
   oppression,
in spurning the fruit of all thy
   labour
and smiling on the policy of wicked
   men?
Hast thou eyes of flesh   4
or dost thou see as mortal man
   sees?
Are thy days as those of a mortal 5
or thy years as the life of a man,
that thou lookest for guilt in me 6
and dost seek in me for sin,
though thou knowest that I am   7
   guiltless
and have none to save me from
   thee?

'Thy hands gave me shape and   8
   made me;
and dost thou at once turn and
   destroy me?
Remember that thou didst knead   9
   me like clay;
and wouldst thou turn me back
   into dust?
Didst thou not pour me out like   10
   milk
and curdle me like cheese,
clothe me with skin and flesh   11
and knit me together with bones
   and sinews?
Thou hast given me life and con-   12
   tinuing favour,
and thy providence has watched
   over my spirit.
Yet this was the secret purpose of 13
   thy heart,
and I know that this was thy intent:
that, if I sinned, thou wouldst be 14
   watching me
and wouldst not acquit me of my
   guilt.

[a] *Prob. rdg.; Heb. adds* if not he, then who?
[b] *Or* I am afraid of all that I must suffer.

15 If I indeed am wicked, the worse
    for me!
   If I am righteous, even so I may
    lift up my head;[a]
16 if I am proud as a lion, thou dost
    hunt me down
   and dost confront me again with
    marvellous power;
17 thou dost renew thy onslaught up-
    on me,
   and with mounting anger against
    me
   bringest fresh forces to the attack.
18 Why didst thou bring me out of the
    womb?
   O that I had ended there and no
    eye had seen me,
19 that I had been carried from the
    womb to the grave
   and were as though I had not been
    born.
20 Is not my life short and fleeting?
   Let me be, that I may be happy for
    a moment,
21 before I depart to a land of
    gloom,
   a land of deep darkness, never to
    return,
22 a land of gathering shadows, of
    deepening darkness,
   lit by no ray of light,[b] dark[c] upon
    dark.'

11 Then Zophar the Naamathite began:

2 Should this spate of words not be
    answered?
  Must a man of ready tongue be
    always right?
3 Is your endless talk to reduce men
    to silence?
  Are you to talk nonsense and no
    one rebuke you?
4 You claim that your opinions are
    sound;
  you say to God, 'I am spotless in
    thy sight.'
5 But if only he would speak
  and open his lips to talk with you,

and expound to you the secrets of 6
    wisdom,
for wonderful are its effects!
[Know then that God exacts from
    you less than your sin deserves.]
Can you fathom the mystery of 7
    God,
can you fathom the perfection of
    the Almighty?
It is higher than heaven; you can 8
    do nothing.
It is deeper than Sheol; you can
    know nothing.
Its measure is longer than the 9
    earth
and broader than the sea.
If he passes by, he may keep 10
    secret his passing;
if he proclaims it, who can turn
    him back?
He surely knows which men are 11
    false,
and when he sees iniquity, does he
    not take note of it?[d]
Can a fool grow wise?   12
can a wild ass's foal be born a
    man?
If only you had directed your 13
    heart rightly
and spread out your hands to
    pray to him!
If you have wrongdoing in hand, 14
    thrust it away;
let no iniquity make its home with
    you.
Then you could hold up your head 15
    without fault,
a man of iron, knowing no fear.
Then you will forget your trouble; 16
you will remember it only as flood-
    waters that have passed;
life will be lasting, bright as noon- 17
    day,
and darkness will be turned to
    morning.
You will be confident, because 18
    there is hope;
sure of protection, you will lie
    down in confidence;[e]
great men will seek your favour.   19

---

[a] *Prob. rdg.*; *Heb. adds* filled with shame and steeped in my affliction.
[b] lit...light: *or* a place of disorder.   [c] *Prob. rdg.*; *Heb. obscure.*
[d] does...of it?: *or* he does not stand aloof.
[e] *Prob. rdg.*; *Heb. adds* and you will lie down unafraid.

20 Blindness will fall on the wicked;
the ways of escape are closed to
them,
and their hope is despair.

12 Then Job answered:

2 No doubt you are perfect men*a*
and absolute wisdom is yours!
3 But I have sense as well as you;
in nothing do I fall short of you;
what gifts indeed have you that
others have not?
4 Yet I am a laughing-stock to my
friend –
a laughing-stock, though I am
innocent and blameless,
one that called upon God, and he
answered.*b*
5 Prosperity and ease look down on
misfortune,
on the blow that fells the man who
is already reeling,
6 while the marauders' tents are left
undisturbed
and those who provoke God live
safe and sound.*c*

7 Go and ask the cattle,
ask the birds of the air to inform
you,
8 or tell the creatures that crawl to
teach you,
and the fishes of the sea to give you
instruction.
9 Who cannot learn from all these
that the LORD's own hand has done
this?
11*d* (Does not the ear test what is
spoken
as the palate savours food?
12 There is wisdom, remember, in age,
and long life brings understanding.)

10 In God's hand are the souls of all
that live,
the spirits of all human kind.
13 Wisdom and might are his,
with him are firmness and understanding.

If he pulls down, there is no re- 14
building;
if he imprisons, there is no release.
If he holds up the waters, there is 15
drought;
if he lets them go, they turn the
land upside down.
Strength and success belong to 16
him,
deceived and deceiver are his to
use.
He makes counsellors behave like 17
idiots
and drives judges mad;
he looses the bonds imposed by 18
kings
and removes the girdle of office
from their waists;
he makes priests behave like idiots 19
and overthrows men long in office;
those who are trusted he strikes 20
dumb,
he takes away the judgement of
old men;
he heaps scorn on princes   21
and abates the arrogance of nobles.
He leads peoples astray and 23*e*
destroys them,
he lays them low, and there they
lie.
He takes away their wisdom from 24
the rulers of the nations
and leaves them wandering in a
pathless wilderness;
they grope in the darkness without 25
light
and are left to wander like a
drunkard.
He uncovers mysteries deep in 22
obscurity
and into thick darkness he brings
light.

All this I have seen with my own 13
eyes,
with my own ears I have heard it,
and understood it.
What you know, I also know;   2
in nothing do I fall short of
you.

---

a *Prob. rdg.; Heb.* No doubt you are people.   *b* *Or* and he afflicted me.
c *Prob. rdg.; Heb. adds* He brings it in full measure to whom he will (*cp. 21. 17*).
d *Verse 10 transposed to follow verse 12.*
e *Verse 22 transposed to follow verse 25.*

3 But for my part I would speak
  with the Almighty
  and am ready to argue with God,
4 while you like fools are smearing
  truth with your falsehoods,
  stitching a patchwork of lies, one
  and all.
5 Ah, if you would only be silent
  and let silence be your wisdom!
6 Now listen to my arguments
  and attend while I put my case.
7 Is it on God's behalf that you speak
  so wickedly,
  or in his defence that you allege
  what is false?
8 Must you take God's part,
  or put his case for him?
9 Will all be well when he examines
  you?
  Will you quibble with him as you
  quibble with a man?
10 He will most surely expose you
   if you take his part by falsely accusing me.
11 Will not God's majesty strike you
   with dread,
   and terror of him overwhelm
   you?
12 Your pompous talk is dust and
   ashes,
   your defences will crumble like
   clay.
13 Be silent, leave me to speak my
   mind,
   and let what may come upon me!
14 I will put my neck in the noose
   and take my life in my hands.
15 If he would slay me, I should not
   hesitate;
   I should still argue my cause to his
   face.
16 This at least assures my success,
   that no godless man may appear
   before him.
17 Listen then, listen to my words,
   and give a hearing to my exposi-
   tion.
18 Be sure of this: once I have stated
   my case
   I know that I shall be acquitted.

19 Who is there that can argue so
   forcibly with me
   that he could reduce me straight-
   way to silence and death?

20 Grant me these two conditions
   only,
   and then I will not hide myself out
   of thy sight:
21 take thy heavy hand clean away
   from me
   and let not the fear of thee strike
   me with dread.
22 Then summon me, and I will
   answer;
   or I will speak first, and do thou
   answer me.
23 How many iniquities and sins are
   laid to my charge?
   let me know my offences and my
   sin.
24 Why dost thou hide thy face
   and treat me as thy enemy?
25 Wilt thou chase a driven leaf,
   wilt thou pursue dry chaff,
26 prescribing punishment for me
   and making me heir to the iniquities of my youth,
27 putting my feet in the stocks[a]
   and setting a slave-mark on the
   arches of my feet?[b]

14 Man born of woman is short-lived
   and full of disquiet.
2 He blossoms like a flower and then
  he withers;
  he slips away like a shadow and
  does not stay;
  [c]he is like a wine-skin that perishes
  or a garment that moths have
  eaten.
3 Dost thou fix thine eyes on such a
  creature,
  and wilt thou bring him into court
  to confront thee?[d]
5 The days of his life are determined,
  and the number of his months is
  known to thee;
  thou hast laid down a limit, which
  he cannot pass.

[a] *Prob. rdg.; Heb. adds* keeping a close watch on all I do.
[b] *Prob. rdg.; Heb. adds verse 28, he is like. . .have eaten, now transposed to follow 14. 2.*
[c] he is like. . .have eaten: 13. 28 *transposed here.*
[d] *So one Heb. MS.; others add* (4) Who can produce pure out of unclean? No one.

6 Look away from him therefore and
   leave him alone
   counting the hours day by day like
   a hired labourer.

7 If a tree is cut down,
   there is hope that it will sprout
   again
   and fresh shoots will not fail.
8 Though its roots grow old in the
   earth,
   and its stump is dying in the
   ground,
9 if it scents water it may break into
   bud
   and make new growth like a young
   plant.
10 But a man dies, and he disappears;*a*
   man comes to his end, and where is
   he?

11 As the waters of a lake dwindle,
   or as a river shrinks and runs dry,
12 so mortal man lies down, never to
   rise
   until the very sky splits open.
   If a man dies, can he live again?*b*
   He shall never be roused from his
   sleep.
13 If only thou wouldst hide me in
   Sheol
   and conceal me till thy anger turns
   aside,
   if thou wouldst fix a limit for my
   time there, and then remember
   me!
14 *c*Then I would not lose hope, however long my service,
   waiting for my relief to come.
15 Thou wouldst summon me, and I
   would answer thee;
   thou wouldst long to see the creature thou hast made.
16 But now thou dost count every
   step I take,
   watching all my course.
17 Every offence of mine is stored in
   thy bag;
   thou dost keep my iniquity under
   seal.

Yet as a falling mountain-side is 18
swept away,
and a rock is dislodged from its
place,
as water wears away stones, 19
and a rain-storm scours the soil
from the land,
so thou hast wiped out the hope of
frail man;
thou dost overpower him finally, 20
and he is gone;
his face is changed, and he is
banished from thy sight.
His flesh upon him becomes black, 22*d*
and his life-blood dries up within
him.*e*
His sons rise to honour, and he sees 21
nothing of it;
they sink into obscurity, and he
knows it not.

Second cycle of speeches

Then Eliphaz the Temanite an- 15
swered:

Would a man of sense give vent to 2
such foolish notions
and answer with a bellyful of wind?
Would he bandy useless words 3
and arguments so unprofitable?
Why! you even banish the fear of 4
God from your mind,
usurping the sole right to speak in
his presence;
your iniquity dictates what you say, 5
and deceit is the language of your
choice.
You are condemned out of your 6
own mouth, not by me;
your own lips give evidence a-
gainst you.

Were you born first of mankind? 7
were you brought forth before the
hills?
Do you listen in God's secret 8
council
or usurp all wisdom for yourself
alone?

---

a Or and is powerless.
b *Line transposed from beginning of verse 14.*
c *See note on verse 12.*
d *Verses 21 and 22 transposed.*
e His flesh...within him: *or* His own kin, maybe, regret him, and his slaves
mourn his loss.

9 What do you know that we do not
   know?
   What insight have you that we do
   not share?
10 We have age and white hairs in our
   company,
   men older than your father.
11 Does not the consolation of God
   suffice you,
   a word whispered quietly in your
   ear?
12 What makes you so bold at heart,
   and why do your eyes flash,
13 that you vent your anger on God
   and pour out such a torrent of
   words?
14 What is frail man that he should
   be innocent,
   or any child of woman that he
   should be justified?
15 If God puts no trust in his holy
   ones,
   and the heavens are not innocent
   in his sight,
16 how much less so is man, who is
   loathsome and rotten
   and laps up evil like water!

17 I will tell you, if only you will
   listen,
   and I will describe what I have
   seen
18 [what has been handed down by
   wise men
   and was not concealed from them
   by their fathers;
19 to them alone the land was given,
   and no foreigner settled among
   them]:
20 the wicked are racked with anxiety all their days,
   the ruthless man for all the years
   in store for him.
21 The noise of the hunter's scare
   rings in his ears,
   and in time of peace the raider falls
   on him;
22 he cannot hope to escape from
   dark death;
   he is marked down for the sword;
23 he is flung out as food for vultures;
   such a man knows that his destruction is certain.

24 Suddenly a black day comes upon
   him,
distress and anxiety overwhelm
   him
[like a king ready for battle];
25 for he has lifted his hand against
   God
and is pitting himself against the
   Almighty,
26 charging him head down,
with the full weight of his bossed
   shield.

27 Heavy though his jowl is and gross,
and though his sides bulge with fat,
28 the city where he lives will lie in
   ruins,
his house will be deserted;
it will soon become a heap of rubble.
29 He will no longer be rich, his wealth
   will not last,
and he will strike no root in the
   earth;[a]
30 scorching heat will shrivel his
   shoots,
and his blossom will be shaken off
   by the wind.
31 He deceives himself, trusting in his
   high rank,
for all his dealings will come to
   nothing.
32 His palm-trees will wither un-
   seasonably,
and his branches will not spread;
33 he will be like a vine that sheds its
   unripe grapes,
like an olive-tree that drops its
   blossom.
34 For the godless, one and all, are
   barren,
and their homes, enriched by
   bribery, are destroyed by fire;
35 they conceive mischief and give
   birth to trouble,
and the child of their womb is
   deceit.

16 Then Job answered:

2 I have heard such things often
   before,
you who make trouble, all of you,
   with every breath,

---

[a] *Prob. rdg.; Heb. adds* he will not escape from darkness.

3 saying, 'Will this windbag never
　have done?
　What makes him so stubborn in
　argument?'
4 If you and I were to change places,
　I could talk like you;
　how I could harangue you
　and wag my head at you!
5 But no, I would speak words of en-
　couragement,
　and then my condolences would
　flow in streams.
6 If I speak, my pain is not eased;
　if I am silent, it does not leave
　me.
7 Meanwhile, my friend wearies me
　with false sympathy;
8 they tear me to pieces, he and his[a]
　fellows.
　He has come forward to give evi-
　dence against me;
　the liar testifies against me to my
　face,
9 in his wrath he wears me down, his
　hatred is plain to see;
　he grinds his teeth at me.

　My enemies look daggers at me,
10 they bare their teeth to rend me,
　they slash my cheeks with knives;
　they are all in league against me.
11 God has left me at the mercy of
　malefactors
　and cast me into the clutches of
　wicked men.
12 I was at ease, but he set upon me
　and mauled me,
　seized me by the neck and worried
　me.
　He set me up as his target;
13 his arrows rained upon me from
　every side;
　pitiless, he cut deep into my vitals,
　he spilt my gall on the ground.
14 He made breach after breach in my
　defences;
　he fell upon me like a fighting
　man.

15 I stitched sackcloth together to
　cover my body
　and I buried my forelock in the
　dust;

16 my cheeks were flushed with
　weeping
　and dark shadows were round my
　eyes,
17 yet my hands were free from vio-
　lence
　and my prayer was sincere.

18 O earth, cover not my blood
　and let my cry for justice find no
　rest!
19 For look! my witness is in heaven;
　there is one on high ready to an-
　swer for me.
20 My appeal will come before God,
　while my eyes turn again and again
　to him.
21 If only there were one to arbitrate
　between man and God,
　as between a man and his neigh-
　bour!
22 For there are but few years to
　come
　before I take the road from which
　I shall not return.

17 My mind is distraught, my days
　are numbered,
　and the grave is waiting for me.
2 Wherever I turn, men taunt
　me,
　and my day is darkened by their
　sneers.
3 Be thou my surety with thyself,
　for who else can pledge himself for
　me?
4 Thou wilt not let those men
　triumph,
　whose minds thou hast sunk in
　ignorance;
5 if such a man denounces his friends
　to their ruin,
　his sons' eyes shall grow dim.

6 I am held up as a byword in every
　land,
　a portent for all to see;
7 my eyes are dim with grief,
　my limbs wasted to a shadow.
8 Honest men are bewildered at
　this,
　and the innocent are indignant at
　my plight.

---

[a] *Prob. rdg.; Heb.* my.

9 In spite of all, the righteous man
maintains his course,
and he whose hands are clean
grows strong again.

10 But come on, one and all, try
again!
I shall not find a wise man among
you.

11 My days die away like an echo;
my heart-strings[a] are snapped.
12 Day is turned into night,
and morning[b] light is darkened before me.
13 If I measure Sheol for my house,
if I spread my couch in the darkness,
14 if I call the grave my father
and the worm my mother or my
sister,
15 where, then, will my hope be,
and who will take account of my
piety?
16 I cannot take them down to Sheol
with me,
nor can they descend with me into
the earth.

18 Then Bildad the Shuhite answered:

2 How soon will you bridle[c] your
tongue?
Do but think, and then we will talk.
3 What do you mean by treating us
as cattle?
Are we nothing but brute beasts to
you?[d]
4 Is the earth to be deserted to prove
you right,
or the rocks to be moved from their
place?

5 No, it is the wicked whose light is
extinguished,
from whose fire no flame will re-
kindle;
6 the light fades in his tent,
and his lamp dies down and fails
him.

In his iniquity his steps totter, 7
and his disobedience trips him
up;
he rushes headlong into a net 8
and steps through the hurdle that
covers a pit;
his heel is caught in a snare, 9
the noose grips him tight;
a cord lies hidden in the ground 10
for him
and a trap in the path.
The terrors of death suddenly be- 11
set him
and make him piss over his feet.
For all his vigour he is paralysed 12
with fear;
strong as he is, disaster awaits
him.
Disease eats away his skin, 13
Death's eldest child devours his
limbs.
He is torn from the safety of his 14
home,
and Death's terrors escort him to
their king.[e]
Magic herbs lie strewn about his 15
tent,
and his home is sprinkled with
sulphur to protect it.
His roots beneath dry up, 16
and above, his branches wither.
His memory vanishes from the face 17
of the earth
and he leaves no name in the
world.
He is driven from light into dark- 18
ness
and banished from the land of the
living.
He leaves no issue or offspring 19
among his people,
no survivor in his earthly home;
in the west men hear of his doom 20
and are appalled;
in the east they shudder with
horror.
Such is the fate of the dwellings of 21
evildoers,
and of the homes of those who care
nothing for God.

---

[a] *Prob. rdg.; Heb.* the desires of my heart.   [b] morning: *prob. rdg.; Heb.* near.
[c] bridle: *prob. rdg.; Heb. unintelligible.*
[d] *Prob. rdg.; Heb. adds* rending himself in his anger.
[e] *Or* and you conduct him to the king of terrors.

19 Then Job answered:

2 How long will you exhaust me
and pulverize me with words?

3 Time and time again you have insulted me
and shamelessly done me wrong.

4 If in fact I had erred,
the error would still be mine.

5 But if indeed you lord it over me
and try to justify the reproaches
levelled at me,

6 I tell you, God himself has put me
in the wrong,
he has drawn the net round me.

7 If I cry 'Murder!' no one answers;
if I appeal for help, I get no justice.

8 He has walled in my path so that
I cannot break away,
and he has hedged in the road before me.

9 He has stripped me of all honour
and has taken the crown from my
head.

10 On every side he beats me down
and I am gone;
he has pulled up my tent-rope[a]
like a tree.

11 His anger is hot against me
and he counts me his enemy.

12 His raiders gather in force[b]
and encamp about my tent.

13 My brothers hold aloof from me,
my friends are utterly estranged
from me;

14–15 my kinsmen and intimates fall
away,
my retainers have forgotten me;
my slave-girls treat me as a
stranger,
I have become an alien in their
eyes.

16 I summon my slave, but he does
not answer,
though I entreat him as a favour.

17 My breath is noisome to my wife,
and I stink in the nostrils of my
own family.

18 Mere children despise me
and, when I rise, turn their backs
on me;

19 my intimate companions loathe
me,
and those whom I love have turned
against me.

20 My bones stick out through my
skin,[c]
and I gnaw my under-lip with my
teeth.

21 Pity me, pity me, you that are my
friends;
for the hand of God has touched
me.

22 Why do you pursue me as God
pursues me?
Have you not had your teeth in me
long enough?

23 O that my words might be inscribed,
O that they might be engraved in
an inscription,

24 cut with an iron tool and filled with
lead
to be a witness[d] in hard rock!

25 But in my heart I know that my
vindicator lives
and that he will rise last to speak in
court;

26 and I shall discern my witness
standing at my side[e]
and see my defending counsel, even
God himself,

27 whom I shall see with my own
eyes,
I myself and no other.

28 My heart failed me when you said,
'What a train of disaster he has
brought on himself!
The root of the trouble lies in him.'

29 Beware of the sword that points at
you,
the sword that sweeps away all
iniquity;
then you will know that there is a
judge.[f]

---

[a] *Or* he has uprooted my hope.
[b] *Prob. rdg.; Heb. adds* they raise an earthwork against me.
[c] *Prob. rdg.; Heb. adds* and my flesh.   [d] to...witness: *or* for ever.
[e] my witness...side: *prob. rdg.; Heb. unintelligible.*
[f] *Or* judgement.

20 Then Zophar the Naamathite answered:

2 My distress of mind forces me to reply,
and this is why*a* I hasten to speak:

3 I have heard arguments that are a reproach to me,
a spirit beyond my understanding gives me the answers.

4 Surely you know that this has been so since time began,
since man was first set on the earth:

5 the triumph of the wicked is short-lived,
the glee of the godless lasts but a moment?

6 Though he stands high as heaven,
and his head touches the clouds,

7 he will be swept utterly away like his own dung,
and all that saw him will say, 'Where is he?'

8 He will fly away like a dream and be lost,
driven off like a vision of the night;

9 the eye which glimpsed him shall do so no more
and shall never again see him in his place.

11*b* The youth and strength which filled his bones
shall lie with him in the dust.

10 His sons will pay court to the poor,
and their*c* hands will give back his wealth.

12 Though evil tastes sweet in his mouth,
and he savours it, rolling it round his tongue,

13 though he lingers over it and will not let it go,
and holds it back on his palate,

14 yet his food turns in his stomach,
changing to asps' venom within him.

15 He gulps down wealth, then vomits it up,
or God makes him discharge it.

16 He sucks the poison of asps,
and the tongue of the viper kills him.

17 Not for him to swill down rivers of cream*d*
or torrents of honey and curds;

18 he must give back his gains without swallowing them,
and spew up his profit undigested;

19 for he has hounded and harassed the poor,
he has seized houses which he did not build.

20 Because his appetite gave him no rest,
and he cannot escape his own desires,

21 nothing is left for him to eat,
and so his well-being does not last;

22 with every need satisfied his troubles begin,
and the full force of hardship strikes him.

23 God vents his anger upon him
and rains on him cruel blows.

24 He is wounded by weapons of iron
and pierced by a bronze-tipped arrow;

25 out at his back the point comes,
the gleaming tip from his gall-bladder.

26 Darkness unrelieved awaits him,
a fire that needs no fanning will consume him.
[Woe betide any survivor in his tent!]

27 The heavens will lay bare his guilt,
and earth will rise up to condemn him.

28 A flood will sweep away his house,
rushing waters on the day of wrath.

29 Such is God's reward for the wicked man
and the lot appointed for the rebel*e* by God.

21 Then Job answered:

2 Listen to me, do but listen,
and let that be the comfort you offer me.

---

a this is why: *prob. rdg.*; Heb. obscure.
b Verses 10 and 11 transposed.
d rivers of cream: *prob. rdg.*; Heb. obscure.

c Prob. rdg.; Heb. his.
e the rebel: *prob. rdg.*; Heb. his word.

3 Bear with me while I have my say;
when I have finished, you may
mock.
4 May not I too voice[a] my thoughts?
Have not I as good cause to be impatient?
5 Look at my plight, and be aghast;
clap your hand to your mouth.
6 When I stop to think, I am filled
with horror,
and my whole body is convulsed.

7 Why do the wicked enjoy long life,
hale in old age, and great and
powerful?
8 They live to see their children
settled,
their kinsfolk and descendants
flourishing;
9 their families are secure and safe;
the rod of God's justice does not
reach them.
10 Their bull mounts and fails not of
its purpose;
their cow calves and does not miscarry.
11 Their children like lambs run out
to play,
and their little ones skip and
dance;
12 they rejoice with tambourine and
harp
and make merry to the sound of
the flute.
13 Their lives close in prosperity,
and they go down to Sheol in
peace.
14 To God they say, 'Leave us alone;
we do not want to know your ways.
15 What is the Almighty that we
should worship him,
or what should we gain by seeking
his favour?'

16 Is not the prosperity of the wicked
in their own hands?
Are not their purposes very different from God's[b]?
17 How often is the lamp of the
wicked snuffed out,
and how often does their ruin
come upon them?

How often does God in his anger
deal out suffering,
bringing it in full measure to whom
he will?[c]
How often is that man like a wisp 18
of straw before the wind,
like chaff which the storm-wind
whirls away?
You say, 'The trouble he has 19
earned, God will keep for his
sons';
no, let him be paid for it in full and
be punished.
Let his own eyes see damnation 20
come upon him,
and the wrath of the Almighty be
the cup he drinks.
What joy shall he have in his chil- 21
dren after him,
if his very months and days are
numbered?
Can any man teach God,   22
God who judges even those in heaven above?

One man, I tell you, dies crowned 23
with success,
lapped in security and comfort,
his loins full of vigour   24
and the marrow juicy in his bones;
another dies in bitterness of soul 25
and never tastes prosperity;
side by side they are laid in 26
earth,
and worms are the shroud of
both.

I know well what you are thinking 27
and the arguments you are mar-
shalling against me;
I know you will ask, 'Where is the 28
great man's home now,
what has become of the home of
the wicked?'
Have you never questioned tra- 29
vellers?
Can you not learn from the signs
they offer,
that the wicked is spared when 30
disaster comes
and conveyed to safety before the
day of wrath?

[a] May...voice: *prob. rdg.*; *Heb. obscure.*
[c] *Line transposed from* 12. 6.

[b] God's: *prob. rdg.*; *Heb. mine.*

31 No one denounces his conduct to
　his face,
　no one requites him for what he has
　done.

32-33 When he is carried to the grave,
　all the world escorts him, before
　and behind;
　the dust of earth is sweet to him,
　and thousands keep watch at his
　tomb.

34 How futile, then, is the comfort
　you offer me!
　How false your answers ring!

Third cycle of speeches

22 Then Eliphaz the Temanite an-
　swered:

2 Can man be any benefit to God?
　Can even a wise man benefit
　him?

3 Is it an asset to the Almighty if you
　are righteous?
　Does he gain if your conduct is
　perfect?

4 Do not think that he reproves you
　because you are pious,
　that on this count he brings you to
　trial.

5 No: it is because you are a very
　wicked man,
　and your depravity passes all
　bounds.

6 Without due cause you take a
　brother in pledge,
　you strip men of their clothes and
　leave them naked.

7 When a man is weary, you give
　him no water to drink
　and you refuse bread to the
　hungry.

8 Is the earth, then, the preserve of
　the strong
　and a domain for the favoured few?

9 Widows you have sent away
　empty-handed,
　orphans you have struck defence-
　less.

10 No wonder that there are pitfalls
　in your path,
　that scares are set to fill you with
　sudden fear.

11 The light is turned into darkness,
　and you cannot see;
　the flood-waters cover you.

12 Surely God is at the zenith of the
　heavens
　and looks down on all the stars,
　high as they are.

13 But you say, 'What does God
　know?
　Can he see through thick dark-
　ness to judge?

14 His eyes cannot pierce the curtain
　of the clouds
　as he walks to and fro on the vault
　of heaven.'

15 Consider the course of the wicked
　man,
　the path the miscreant treads:

16 see how they are carried off before
　their time,
　their very foundation flowing
　away like a river;

17 these men said to God, 'Leave us
　alone;
　what can the Almighty do to
　us?'

18 Yet it was he that filled their
　houses with good things,
　although their purposes and his
　were very different.

19 The righteous see their fate and
　exult,
　the innocent make game of
　them;

20 for their riches are swept away,
　and the profusion of their wealth
　is destroyed by fire.

21 Come to terms with God and you
　will prosper;
　that is the way to mend your
　fortune.

22 Take instruction from his mouth
　and store his words in your
　heart.

23 If you come back to the Almighty
　in true sincerity,
　if you banish wrongdoing from
　your home,

24 if you treat your precious metal as
　dust[a]
　and the gold of Ophir as stones
　from the river-bed,

---

[a] *Prob. rdg.; Heb.* if you put your precious metal on dust.

25 then the Almighty himself will be
   your precious metal;
   he will be your silver in double
   measure.
26 Then, with sure trust in[a] the Almighty,
   you will raise your face to God;
27 you will pray to him, and he will
   hear you,
   and you will have cause to fulfil
   your vows.
28 In all your designs you will
   succeed,
   and light will shine on your path;
29 but God brings down the pride of
   the haughty[b]
   and keeps safe the man of modest
   looks.
30 He will deliver the innocent,[c]
   and you will be delivered, because
   your hands are clean.

23 Then Job answered:

2 My thoughts today are resentful,
   for God's hand is heavy on me in
   my trouble.
3 If only I knew how to find him,
   how to enter his court,
4 I would state my case before him
   and set out my arguments in
   full;
5 then I should learn what answer he
   would give
   and find out what he had to say.
6 Would he exert his great power to
   browbeat me?
   No; God himself would never bring
   a charge against me.
7 There the upright are vindicated
   before him,
   and I shall win from my judge an
   absolute discharge.
8 If I go forward,[d] he is not there;
   if backward,[e] I cannot find him;
9 when I turn[f] left,[g] I do not descry
   him;
   I face right,[h] but I see him not.

But he knows me in action or at 10
   rest;
when he tests me, I prove to be
   gold.
My feet have kept to the path he 11
   has set me,
I have followed his way and not
   turned from it.
I do not ignore the commands that 12
   come from his lips,
I have stored in my heart what he
   says.
He decides,[i] and who can turn him 13
   from his purpose?
He does what his own heart desires.
What he determines, that he 14
   carries out;
his mind is full of plans like
   these.
Therefore I am fearful of meeting 15
   him;
when I think about him,[j] I am
   afraid;
it is God who makes me faint- 16
   hearted
and the Almighty who fills me with
   fear,
yet I am not reduced to silence by 17
   the darkness
nor[k] by the mystery which hides
   him.

[l]The day of reckoning is no secret 24
   to the Almighty,
though those who know him have
   no hint of its date.
Wicked men move boundary- 2
   stones
and carry away flocks and their
   shepherds.
In the field they reap what is not 6[m]
   theirs,
and filch the late grapes from the
   rich[n] man's vineyard.
They drive off the orphan's ass 3
   and lead away the widow's ox with
   a rope.

---

[a] with...in: *or* delighting in. [b] but...haughty: *prob. rdg.*; *Heb. obscure.*
[c] *Prob. rdg.*; *Heb.* the not innocent. [d] *Or* east. [e] *Or* west.
[f] *Prob. rdg.*; *Heb.* he turns. [g] *Or* north. [h] *Or* south.
[i] He decides: *prob. rdg.*; *Heb.* He in one. [j] when...him: *or* I stand aloof.
[k] yet I am not...nor: *or* indeed I am...and...
[l] *Prob. rdg.*; *Heb. prefixes* Why.
[m] *Verses 3–9 re-arranged to restore the natural order.* [n] *Or* wicked.

9 They snatch the fatherless infant from the breast
and take the poor man's child in pledge.

4 They jostle the poor out of the way;
the destitute huddle together, hiding from them.

5 The poor rise early like the wild ass,
when it scours the wilderness for food;
but though they work till nightfall,[a]
their children go hungry.[b]

7 Naked and bare they pass the night;
in the cold they have nothing to cover them.

8 They are drenched by rain-storms from the hills
and hug the rock, their only shelter.

10 Naked and bare they go about their work,
and hungry they carry the sheaves;

11 they press the oil in the shade where two walls meet,
they tread the winepress but themselves go thirsty.

12 Far from the city, they groan like dying men,
and like wounded men they cry out;
but God pays no heed to their prayer.

13 Some there are who rebel against the light of day,
who know nothing of its ways
and do not linger in the paths of light.

14 The murderer rises before daylight to kill some miserable wretch.[c]

15 The seducer watches eagerly for twilight,
thinking, 'No eye will catch sight of me.'

The thief prowls[d] by night,[e]
his face covered with a mask,
and in the darkness breaks into 16 houses
which he has marked down in the day.
One and all,[f] they are strangers to the daylight,
but dark night is morning to them; 17
and in the welter of night they are at home.

Such men are scum on the surface 18 of the water;
their fields have a bad name throughout the land,
and no labourer will go near their vineyards.

As drought and heat make away 19 with snow,
so the waters of Sheol[g] make away with the sinner.

The womb forgets him, the worm 20 sucks him dry;
he will not be remembered ever after.[h]

He may have wronged the barren 21 childless woman
and been no help to the widow;

yet God in his strength carries off 22 even the mighty;
they may rise, but they have no firm hope of life.

He lulls them into security and 23 confidence;
but his eyes are fixed on their ways.

For a moment they rise to the 24 heights, but are soon gone;
iniquity is snapped like a stick.[i]
They are laid low and wilt like a mallow-flower;
they droop like an ear of corn on the stalk.

If this is not so, who will prove me 25 wrong
and make nonsense of my argument?

---

[a] *Prob. rdg.; Heb.* Arabah.
[b] go hungry: *prob. rdg.; Heb.* to it food.
[c] *See note on verse 15.*
[d] The thief prowls: *prob. rdg.; Heb.* Let him be like a thief.
[e] *Line transposed from end of verse 14.*
[f] One and all: *transposed from after* but *in next verse.*
[g] snow...Sheol: *prob. rdg.; Heb.* snow-water, Sheol.
[h] *Prob. rdg.; Heb. here adds* iniquity is snapped like a stick (*see note on verse 24*).
[i] *Line transposed from end of verse 20.*

25 Then Bildad the Shuhite answered:

2 Authority and awe rest with him
who has established peace in his
realm on high.
3 His squadrons are without number;
at whom will they not spring from
ambush?
4 How then can a man be justified in
God's sight,
or one born of woman be innocent?
5 If the circling moon is found
wanting,
and the stars are not innocent in
his eyes,
6 much more so man who is but a
maggot,
mortal man who is only a worm.

26 Then Job answered:

2 What help you have given to the
man without resource,
what deliverance you have brought
to the powerless!
3 What counsel you offer to a man
at his wit's end,
what sound advice to the foolish!
4 Who has prompted you to say such
things,
and whose spirit is expressed in
your speech?

5 In the underworld the shades
writhe in fear,
the waters and all that live in them
are struck with terror.[a]
6 Sheol is laid bare,
and Abaddon uncovered before
him.
7 God spreads the canopy of the sky
over chaos
and suspends earth in the void.
8 He keeps the waters penned in
dense cloud-masses,
and the clouds do not burst open
under their weight.
9 He covers the face of the full
moon,[b]
unrolling his clouds across it.

10 He has fixed the horizon on the
surface of the waters
at the farthest limit of light and
darkness.
11 The pillars of heaven quake
and are aghast at his rebuke.
12 With his strong arm he cleft the
sea-monster,
and struck down the Rahab by his
skill.
13 At his breath the skies are clear,
and his hand breaks the twisting[c]
sea-serpent.
14 These are but the fringe of his
power;
and how faint the whisper that we
hear of him!
[Who could fathom the thunder of
his might?]

Then Job resumed his discourse: 27

2 I swear by God, who has denied me
justice,
and by the Almighty, who has
filled me with bitterness:
3 so long as there is any life left in me
and God's breath is in my nostrils,
4 no untrue word shall pass my lips
and my tongue shall utter no falsehood.
5 God forbid that I should allow you
to be right;
till death, I will not abandon my
claim to innocence.
6 I will maintain the rightness of my
cause, I will never give up;
so long as I live, I will not change.

7 May my enemy meet the fate of
the wicked,
and my antagonist the doom of the
wrongdoer!
8 What hope has a godless man, when
he is cut off,[d]
when God takes away his life?
9 Will God listen to his cry
when trouble overtakes him?
10 Will he trust himself to the Almighty
and call upon God at all times?

---

[a] *are struck with terror: prob. rdg.; Heb. om.*
[b] *Or He overlays the surface of his throne.*
[c] *Or primeval.*
[d] *Or What is a godless man's thread of life when it is cut . . .*

11 I will teach you what is in God's
power,
I will not conceal the purpose of
the Almighty.

12 If all of you have seen these things,
why then do you talk such empty
nonsense?

13 This is the lot prescribed by God
for the wicked,
and the ruthless man's reward from
the Almighty.

14 He may have many sons, but they
will fall by the sword,
and his offspring will go hungry;

15 the survivors will be brought to the
grave by pestilence,
and no widows will weep for them.

16 He may heap up silver like dirt
and get himself piles of clothes;

17 he may get them, but the righteous
will wear them,
and his silver will be shared among
the innocent.

18 The house he builds is flimsy as a
bird's nest
or a shelter put up by a watchman.

19 He may lie down rich one day, but
never again;
he opens his eyes and all is gone.

20 Disaster overtakes him like a flood,
and a storm snatches him away in
the night;

21 the east wind lifts him up and he is
gone;
it whirls him far from home;

22 it flings itself on him without
mercy,
and he is battered and buffeted by
its force;

23 it snaps its fingers at him
and whistles over him wherever he
may be.

God's unfathomable wisdom

28 There are mines for silver
and places where men refine gold;

2 where iron is won from the earth
and copper smelted from the ore;

3 the end of the seam lies in darkness,
and it is followed to its farthest
limit.[a]

4 Strangers cut the galleries;[b]
they are forgotten as they drive
forward far from men.[c]

5 While corn is springing from the
earth above,
what lies beneath is raked over
like a fire,

6 and out of its rocks comes lapis
lazuli,
dusted with flecks of gold.

7 No bird of prey knows the way
there,
and the falcon's keen eye cannot
descry it;

8 proud beasts do not set foot on it,
and no serpent comes that way.

9 Man sets his hand to the granite
rock
and lays bare the roots of the
mountains;

10 he cuts galleries in the rocks,
and gems of every kind meet his
eye;

11 he dams up the sources of the
streams
and brings the hidden riches of the
earth to light.

12 But where can wisdom be found?
And where is the source of understanding?

13 No man knows the way to it;
it is not found in the land of living
men.

14 The depths of ocean say, 'It is not
in us',
and the sea says, 'It is not with me.'

15 Red gold cannot buy it,
nor can its price be weighed out in
silver;

16 it cannot be set in the scales
against gold of Ophir,
against precious cornelian or lapis
lazuli;

17 gold and crystal are not to be
matched with it,
no work in fine gold can be bartered for it;

---

[a] *Prob. rdg.; Heb. adds* stones of darkness and deep darkness.
[b] Strangers...galleries: *prob. rdg.; Heb. obscure.*
[c] *Prob. rdg.; Heb. adds* languishing without foothold.

18 black coral and alabaster are not
   worth mention,
   and a parcel of wisdom fetches
   more than red coral;
19 topaz[a] from Ethiopia is not to be
   matched with it,
   it cannot be set in the scales
   against pure gold.
20 Where then does wisdom come
   from,
   and where is the source of understanding?
21 No creature on earth can see it,
   and it is hidden from the birds of
   the air.
22 Destruction and death say,
   'We know of it only by report.'
23 But God understands the way to it,
   he alone knows its source;
24 for he can see to the ends of the
   earth
   and he surveys everything under
   heaven.
25 When he made a counterpoise for
   the wind
   and measured out the waters in
   proportion,
26 when he laid down a limit for the
   rain
   and a path for the thunderstorm,
27 even then he saw wisdom and took
   stock of it,
   he considered it and fathomed its
   very depths.
28 And he said to man:
   The fear of the Lord is wisdom,
   and to turn from evil is understanding.

Job's final survey of his case

29 Then Job resumed his discourse:

2 If I could only go back to the old
   days,
   to the time when God was watching over me,
3 when his lamp shone above my
   head,
   and by its light I walked through
   the darkness!

If I could be as in the days of my 4
   prime,
when God protected my home,
while the Almighty was still there 5
   at my side,
and my servants stood round me,
while my path flowed with milk, 6
and the rocks streamed oil!
If I went through the gate out of 7
   the town
to take my seat in the public
   square,
young men saw me and kept out of 8
   sight;
old men rose to their feet,
men in authority broke off their 9
   talk
and put their hands to their lips;
the voices of the nobles died 10
   away,
and every man held his tongue.
They listened to me expectantly 21[b]
and waited in silence for my
   opinion.
When I had spoken, no one spoke 22
   again;
my words fell gently on them;
they waited for them as for rain 23
and drank them in like showers in
   spring.
When I smiled on them, they took 24
   heart;
when my face lit up, they lost their
   gloomy looks.
I presided over them, planning 25
   their course,
like a king encamped with his
   troops.[c]

Whoever heard of me spoke in my 11
   favour,
and those who saw me bore witness
   to my merit,
how I saved the poor man when he 12
   called for help
and the orphan who had no protector.
The man threatened with ruin 13
   blessed me,
and I made the widow's heart sing
   for joy.

[a] *Or* chrysolite.
[b] *Verses 21–25 transposed to this point.*
[c] *Prob. rdg.; Heb. adds* as when one comforts mourners.

14 I put on righteousness as a gar-
    ment and it clothed me;
    justice, like a cloak or a turban,
    wrapped me round.
15 I was eyes to the blind
    and feet to the lame;
16 I was a father to the needy,
    and I took up the stranger's cause.
17 I broke the fangs of the miscreant
    and rescued the prey from his
    teeth.
18 I thought, 'I shall die with my
    powers unimpaired
    and my days uncounted as the
    grains of sand,[a]
19 with my roots spreading out to the
    water
    and the dew lying on my branches,
20 with the bow always new in my
    grasp
    and the arrow ever ready to my
    hand.'[b]

30 But now I am laughed to scorn
    by men of a younger generation,
    men whose fathers I would have
    disdained
    to put with the dogs who kept my
    flock.
2 What use were their strong arms
    to me,
    since their sturdy vigour had
    wasted away?
3 They gnawed roots[c] in the desert,
    gaunt with want and hunger,[d]
4 they plucked saltwort and worm-
    wood
    and root of broom[e] for their food.
5 Driven out from the society of
    men,[f]
    pursued like thieves with hue and
    cry,
6 they lived in gullies and ravines,
    holes in the earth and rocky clefts;
7 they howled like beasts among the
    bushes,
    huddled together beneath the
    scrub,

vile base-born wretches, 8
hounded from the haunts of men.
Now I have become the target of 9
    their taunts,
my name is a byword among them.
They loathe me, they shrink from 10
    me,
they dare to spit in my face.
They run wild and savage[g] me; 11
at sight of me they throw off all
    restraint.
On my right flank they attack in a 12
    mob;[h]
they raise their siege-ramps a-
    gainst me,
they tear down my crumbling de- 13
    fences to my undoing,
and scramble up against me un-
    hindered;
they burst in through the gaping 14
    breach;
at the moment of the crash they
    come rolling in.
Terror upon terror overwhelms 15
    me,
it sweeps away my resolution like
    the wind,
and my hope of victory vanishes
    like a cloud.
So now my soul is in turmoil with- 16
    in me,
and misery has me daily in its grip.
By night pain pierces my very 17
    bones,
and there is ceaseless throbbing in
    my veins;
my garments are all bespattered 18
    with my phlegm,
which chokes me like the collar of
    a shirt.
God himself[i] has flung me down in 19
    the mud,
no better than dust or ashes.

I call for thy help, but thou dost 20
    not answer;
I stand up to plead, but thou sittest
    aloof;

---

[a] Or as those of the phoenix.   [b] *Verses 21–25 transposed to follow verse 10.*
[c] roots: *prob. rdg.*; *Heb. om.*   [d] *Prob. rdg.*; *Heb. adds* yesterday waste and
derelict land.   [e] root of broom: *probably* fungus on broom root.
[f] the society of men: *prob. rdg.*; *Heb. obscure.*
[g] They run...savage: *prob. rdg.*; *Heb.* He runs...savages.
[h] *Prob. rdg.*; *Heb. adds* they let loose my feet.
[i] God himself: *prob. rdg.*; *Heb. om.*

21 thou hast turned cruelly against
 me
 and with thy strong hand pursuest
 me in hatred;
22 thou dost snatch me up and set me
 astride the wind,
 and the tempest*a* tosses me up and
 down.
23 I know that thou wilt hand me
 over to death,
 to the place appointed for all
 mortal men.

24 Yet no beggar held out his hand
 but was relieved*b* by me in his
 distress.
25 Did I not weep for the man whose
 life was hard?
 Did not my heart grieve for the
 poor?
26 Evil has come though I expected
 good;
 I looked for light but there came
 darkness.
27 My bowels are in ferment and
 know no peace;
 days of misery stretch out before
 me.
28 I go about dejected and friendless;
 I rise in the assembly, only to
 appeal for help.
29 The wolf is now my brother,
 the owls of the desert have become
 my companions.
30 My blackened skin peels off,
 and my body is scorched by the
 heat.
31 My harp has been tuned for a dirge,
 my flute to the voice of those who
 weep.

31 2*c* What is the lot prescribed by God
 above,
 the reward from the Almighty on
 high?
 3 Is not ruin prescribed for the miscreant
 and calamity for the wrongdoer?
 4 Yet does not God himself see my
 ways
 and count my every step?

I swear I have had no dealings 5
 with falsehood
and have not embarked on a course
 of deceit.
I have come to terms with my eyes, 1
 never to take notice of a girl.
Let God weigh me in the scales of 6
 justice,
and he will know that I am innocent!
If my steps have wandered from 7
 the way,
if my heart has followed my eyes,
or any dirt stuck to my hands,
may another eat what I sow, 8
and may my crops be pulled up by
 the roots!
If my heart has been enticed by a 9
 woman
or I have lain in wait at my neighbour's door,
may my wife be another man's 10
 slave,
and may other men enjoy her.
[But that is a wicked act, an 11
 offence before the law;
it would be a consuming and 12
 destructive fire,
raging*d* among my crops.]
If I have ever rejected the plea of 13
 my slave
or of my slave-girl, when they
 brought their complaint to me,
what shall I do if God appears? 14
What shall I answer if he inter-
 venes?
Did not he who made me in the 15
 womb make them?
Did not the same God create us in
 the belly?
If I have withheld their needs from 16
 the poor
or let the widow's eye grow dim
 with tears,
if I have eaten my crust alone, 17
and the orphan has not shared it
 with me –
the orphan who from boyhood 18
 honoured me like a father,
whom I guided from the day of
 his*e* birth –

---

a the tempest: *prob. rdg.*; *Heb. unintelligible.* *b* was relieved: *prob. rdg.*; *Heb.
unintelligible.* *c* *Verse 1 transposed to follow verse 5.*
d *Prob. rdg.*; *Heb. uprooting.* *e* *Prob. rdg.*; *Heb. my.*

19 if I have seen anyone perish for
   lack of clothing,
   or a poor man with nothing to
   cover him,
20 if his body had no cause to bless
   me,
   because he was not kept warm
   with a fleece from my flock,
21 if I have raised[a] my hand against
   the innocent,[b]
   knowing that men would side
   with me in court,
22 then may my shoulder-blade be
   torn from my shoulder,
   my arm be wrenched out of its
   socket!
23 But the terror of God was heavy
   upon me,[c]
   and for fear of his majesty I could
   do none of these things.
24 If I have put my faith in gold
   and my trust in the gold of
   Nubia,
25 if I have rejoiced in my great
   wealth
   and in the increase of riches;
26 if I ever looked on the sun in
   splendour
   or the moon moving in her
   glory,
27 and was led astray in my secret
   heart
   and raised my hand in homage;
28 this would have been an offence
   before the law,
   for I should have been unfaithful
   to God on high.
38[d] If my land has cried out in reproach
   at me,
   and its furrows have joined in
   weeping,
39 if I have eaten its produce without
   payment
   and have disappointed my creditors,
40 may thistles spring up instead of
   wheat,
   and weeds instead of barley!

Have I rejoiced at the ruin of the 29
   man that hated me
or been filled with malice when
   trouble overtook me,
even though I did not allow my 30
   tongue to sin
by demanding his life with a curse?
Have the men of my household 31
   never said,
'Let none of us speak ill of him!
No stranger has spent the night in 32
   the street'?
For I have kept open house for the
   traveller.
Have I ever concealed my mis- 33
   deeds as men do,
keeping my guilt to myself,
because I feared the gossip of the 34
   town
or dreaded the scorn of my fellow-
   citizens?
Let me but call a witness in my 35
   defence!
Let the Almighty state his case
   against me!
If my accuser had written out his
   indictment,
I would not keep silence and remain indoors.[e]
No! I would flaunt it on my 36
   shoulder
and wear it like a crown on my
   head;
I would plead the whole record of 37
   my life
and present that in court as my
   defence.[f]

Job's speeches are finished.[g]

Speeches of Elihu

So these three men gave up an- 32
swering Job; for he continued to
think himself righteous. Then 2
Elihu son of Barakel the Buzite, of
the family of Ram, grew angry;
angry because Job had made himself out more righteous than God,[h]

---

[a] *Or waved.*   [b] *Or orphan.*
[c] *Prob. rdg.; Heb.* A fear towards me is a disaster from God.
[d] *Verses 38–40 transposed (but see note g).*
[e] *Line transposed from verse 34.*
[f] *Verses 38–40 transposed to follow verse 28 (but see note g).*
[g] *The last line of verse 40 retained here.*   [h] *Or had justified himself with God.*

3 and angry with the three friends
because they had found no answer
to Job and had let God appear
4 wrong.^a Now Elihu had hung back
while they were talking with Job
5 because they were older than he;
but, when he saw that the three
had no answer, he could no longer
6 contain his anger. So Elihu son of
Barakel the Buzite began to speak:

I am young in years,
and you are old;
that is why I held back and shrank
from displaying my knowledge in
front of you.
7 I said to myself, 'Let age speak,
and length of years expound
wisdom.'
8 But the spirit of God himself is in
man,
and the breath of the Almighty
gives him understanding;
9 it is not only the old who are wise
or the aged who understand what
is right.
10 Therefore I say: Listen to me;
I too will display my knowledge.
11 Look, I have been waiting upon
your words,
listening for the conclusions of
your thoughts,
while you sought for phrases;
12 I have been giving thought to your
conclusions,
but not one of you refutes Job or
answers his arguments.
13 Take care then not to claim that
you have found wisdom;
God will rebut him, not man.
14 I will not string^b words together
like you^c
or answer him as you have done.

15 If these men are confounded and
no longer answer,
if words fail them,
16 am I to wait because they do not
speak,
because they stand there and no
longer answer?

I, too, have a furrow to plough;   17
I will express my opinion;
for I am bursting with words,   18
a bellyful of wind gripes me.
My stomach is distended as if with   19
wine,
bulging like a blacksmith's bellows;
I must speak to find relief,   20
I must open my mouth and answer;
I will show no favour to anyone,   21
I will flatter no one, God or
man;^d
for I cannot use flattering titles,   22
or my Maker would soon do away
with me.

Come now, Job, listen to my words 33
and attend carefully to everything I say.
Look, I am ready to answer;   2
the words are on the tip of my
tongue.
My heart assures me that I speak   3
with knowledge,
and that my lips speak with
sincerity.
For the spirit of God made me,   4
and the breath of the Almighty
gave me life.
Answer me if you can,   5
marshal your arguments and confront me.
In God's sight^e I am just what you 6
are;
I too am only a handful of clay.
Fear of me need not abash you,   7
nor any pressure from me overawe
you.
You have said your say and I 8
heard you;
I have listened to the sound of
your words:
'I am innocent', you said, 'and free 9
from offence,
blameless and without guilt.
Yet God finds occasions to put me 10
in the wrong
and counts me his enemy;
he puts my feet in the stocks   11
and keeps a close watch on all I
do.'

^a *Prob. original rdg., altered in Heb. to* and had not proved Job wrong.
^b *Prob. rdg.; Heb.* He has not strung.
^d *Prob. rdg.; Heb.* I will not flatter man.
^c *Prob. rdg.; Heb.* towards me.
^e *In God's sight: or* In strength.

12 Well, this is my answer: You are wrong.
God is greater than man;

13 why then plead your case with him?
for no one can answer his arguments.

14 Indeed, once God has spoken
he does not speak a second time to confirm it.

15 In dreams, in visions of the night,
when deepest sleep falls upon men,

16 while they sleep on their beds,
God makes them listen,
and his correction strikes them with terror.

17 To turn a man from reckless conduct,
to check the pride*a* of mortal man,

18 at the edge of the pit he holds him back alive
and stops him from crossing the river of death.

19 Or again, man learns his lesson on a bed of pain,
tormented by a ceaseless ague in his bones;

20 he turns from his food with loathing
and has no relish for the choicest meats;

21 his flesh hangs loose upon him,
his bones are loosened and out of joint,

22 his soul draws near to the pit,
his life to the ministers of death.

23 Yet if an angel, one of thousands, stands by him,
a mediator between him and God,
to expound what he has done right
and to secure mortal man his due;*b*

24 if he speaks in the man's favour and says, 'Reprieve him,
let him not go down to the pit,
I have the price of his release';

25 then that man will grow sturdier*c* than he was in youth,
he will return to the days of his prime.

26 If he entreats God to show him favour,
to let him see his face and shout for joy;*d*

27 if he declares before all men, 'I have sinned,
turned right into wrong and thought nothing of it';

28 then he saves himself from going down to the pit,
he lives and sees the light.

29 All these things God may do to a man,
again and yet again,

30 bringing him back from the pit
to enjoy the full light of life.

31 Listen, Job, and attend to me;
be silent, and I myself will speak.

32 If you have any arguments, answer me;
speak, and I would gladly find you proved right;

33 but if you have none, listen to me:
keep silence, and I will teach you wisdom.

34 Then Elihu went on to say:

2 Mark my words, you wise men;
you men of long experience, listen to me;

3 for the ear tests what is spoken
as the palate savours food.

4 Let us then examine for ourselves what is right;
let us together establish the true good.

5 Job has said, 'I am innocent,
but God has deprived me of justice,

6 he has falsified my case;
my state is desperate, yet I have done no wrong.'

7 Was there ever a man like Job
with his thirst for irreverent talk,

8 choosing bad company to share his journeys,
a fellow-traveller with wicked men?

9 For he says that it brings a man no profit
to find favour with God.

10 But listen to me, you men of good sense.
Far be it from God to do evil
or the Almighty to play false!

---

a the pride: *prob. rdg.; Heb. obscure.*
c will grow sturdier: *prob. rdg.; Heb. unintelligible.*
b Line transposed from verse 26.
d See note on verse 23.

11 For he pays a man according to his
work
and sees that he gets what his conduct deserves.

12 The truth is, God does no wrong,
the Almighty does not pervert
justice.

13 Who committed the earth to his
keeping?
Who but he established the whole
world?

14 If he were to turn his thoughts inwards
and recall his life-giving spirit,

15 all that lives would perish on the
instant,
and man return again to dust.

16 Now Job, if you have the wit, consider this;
listen to the words I speak.

17 Can it be that a hater of justice
holds the reins?
Do you disparage a sovereign
whose rule is so fair,

18 who will say to a prince, 'You
scoundrel',
and call his magnates blackguards
to their faces;

19 who does not show special favour
to those in office
and thinks no more of rich than of
poor?
All alike are God's creatures,

20 who may die in a moment, in the
middle of the night;
at his touch the rich are no
more,
and the mighty vanish though no
hand is laid on them.

21 His eyes are on the ways of men,
and he sees every step they
take;

22 there is nowhere so dark, so deep
in shadow,
that wrongdoers may hide from
him.

25 Therefore he repudiates all that
they do;
he turns on them in the night, and
they are crushed.

There are no appointed days for 23
men
to appear before God for judgement.

He holds no inquiry, but breaks 24
the powerful
and sets up others in their place.

For their crimes he strikes them 26ᵃ
down*ᵇ*
and makes them disgorge their
bloated wealth,*ᶜ*

because they have ceased to obey 27
him
and pay no heed to his ways.

Then the cry of the poor reaches 28
his ears,
and he hears the cry of the distressed.

[Even if he is silent, who can con- 29–30
demn him?
If he looks away, who can find
fault?
What though he makes a godless
man king
over a stubborn nation and all its
people?]

But suppose you were to say to 31
God,
'I have overstepped the mark; I
will do no more*ᵈ* mischief.
Vile wretch that I am, be thou my 32
guide;
whatever wrong I have done, I will
do wrong no more.'

Will he, at these words, condone 33
your rejection of him?
It is for you to decide, not me:
but what can you answer?

Men of good sense will say, 34
any intelligent hearer will tell me,
'Job talks with no knowledge, 35
and there is no sense in what he
says.

If only Job could be put to the test 36
once and for all
for answers that are meant to
make mischief!

He is a sinner and a rebel as well*ᵉ* 37
with his endless ranting against
God.'

ᵃ Verse 25 transposed to follow verse 22.   *ᵇ he strikes them down: prob. rdg.; Heb. om.*
ᶜ Or and chastises them where people see.   *ᵈ more: prob. rdg.; Heb. obscure.*
ᵉ Prob. rdg.; Heb. adds between us it is enough.

35 Then Elihu went on to say:

2 Do you think that this is a sound
   plea
   or maintain that you are in the
   right against God? –
3 if you say, 'What would be the
   advantage to me?
   how much should I gain from
   sinning?'
4 I will bring arguments myself
   against you,
   you and your three friends.
5 Look up at the sky and then consider,
   observe the rain-clouds towering
   above you.
6 How does it touch him if you have
   sinned?
   However many your misdeeds,
   what does it mean to him?
7 If you do right, what good do you
   bring him,
   or what does he gain from
   you?
8 Your wickedness touches only
   men, such as you are;
   the right that you do affects none
   but mortal man.

9 Men will cry out beneath the
   burdens of oppression
   and call for help against the power
   of the great;
10 but none of them asks, 'Where is
   God my Maker
   who gives protection by night,
11 who grants us more knowledge than the beasts of the
   earth
   and makes us wiser than the birds
   of the air?'
12 So, when they cry out, he does not
   answer,
   because they are self-willed and
   proud.
13 All to no purpose! God does not
   listen,
   the Almighty does not see.

The worse for you when you say, 14
   'He does not see me'!
Humble yourself[a] in his presence
   and wait for his word.
But now, because God does not 15
   grow angry and punish
   and because he lets folly pass unheeded,
Job gives vent to windy nonsense 16
   and makes a parade of empty
   words.

Then Elihu went on to say: 36

Be patient a little longer, and let 2
   me enlighten you;
   there is still something more to be
   said on God's side.
I will search far and wide to sup- 3
   port my conclusions,
   as I defend the justice of my Maker.
There are no flaws in my reasoning; 4
   before you stands one whose conclusions are sound.

God,[b] I say, repudiates the high 5
   and[c] mighty
   and does not let the wicked pros- 6
   per,
   but allows the just claims of the
   poor and suffering;
he does not deprive the sufferer of 7
   his due.[d]
Look at kings on their thrones:
   when God gives them sovereign
   power, they grow arrogant.
Next you may see them loaded 8
   with fetters,
   held fast in captives' chains:
he denounces their conduct to 9
   them,
   showing how insolence and tyranny
   was their offence;
his warnings sound in their ears 10
   and summon them to turn back
   from their evil courses.
If they listen to him, they spend[e] 11
   their days in prosperity
   and their years in comfort.

---

[a] *Humble yourself: prob. rdg.; Heb. Judge.*
[b] *Prob. rdg.; Heb. adds* a mighty one and not.
[c] *and: prob. rdg.; Heb. om.*
[d] *deprive...due: or* withdraw his gaze from the righteous.
[e] *Prob. rdg.; Heb. adds* they end.

12 But, if they do not listen, they die,
their lesson unlearnt,
and cross the river of death.

13 Proud men rage against him
and do not cry to him for help when
caught in his toils;

14 so they die in their prime,
like male prostitutes,[a] worn out.[b]

15 Those who suffer he rescues
through suffering
and teaches them by the discipline
of affliction.

16 Beware, if you are tempted to exchange hardship for comfort,[c]
for unlimited plenty spread before
you, and a generous table;

17 if you eat your fill of a rich man's
fare
when you are occupied with the
business of the law,

18 do not be led astray by lavish gifts
of wine
and do not let bribery warp your
judgement.

19 Will that wealth of yours, however
great, avail you,
or all the resources of your high
position?

21[d] Take care not to turn to mischief;
for that is why you are tried by
affliction.

20 Have no fear if in the breathless
terrors of the night
you see nations vanish where they
stand.

22 God towers in majesty above us;
who wields such sovereign power
as he?

23 Who has prescribed his course for
him?
Who has said to him, 'Thou hast
done wrong'?

24 Remember then to sing the praises
of his work,
as men have always sung them.

All men stand back from[e] him;   25
the race of mortals look on from
afar.

Consider; God is so great that we   26
cannot know him;
the number of his years is beyond
reckoning.

He draws up drops of water from   27
the sea[f]
and distils rain from the mist he
has made;

the rain-clouds pour down in tor-   28
rents,[g]

they descend in showers on mankind;

thus he sustains the nations   31
and gives them food in plenty.

Can any man read the secret of the   29
sailing clouds,
spread like a carpet under[h] his
pavilion?

See how he unrolls the mist across   30
the waters,
and its streamers[i] cover the sea.

He charges the thunderbolts with   32[j]
flame
and launches them straight[k] at the
mark;

in his anger he calls up the tempest, 33
and the thunder is the herald of its
coming.[l]

This too makes my heart beat wildly 37
and start from its place.

Listen, listen to the thunder of   2
God's voice
and the rumbling of his utterance.

Under the vault of heaven he lets   3
it roll,
and his lightning reaches the ends
of the earth;

there follows a sound of roaring   4
as he thunders with the voice of
majesty.[m]

God's voice is marvellous in its   5
working;[n]
he does great deeds that pass our
knowledge.

---

[a] Cp. Deut. 23. 17.   [b] worn out: *prob. rdg.*; Heb. *unintelligible.*
[c] for comfort: *prob. rdg.*; Heb. *om.*   [d] *Verses 20 and 21 transposed.*   [e] *Or gaze at.*
[f] from the sea: *prob. rdg.*; Heb. *om.*   [g] in torrents: *prob. rdg.*; Heb. *which.*
[h] spread...under: *prob. rdg.*; Heb. *crashing noises.*   [i] its streamers: *prob. rdg.*;
Heb. the roots of.   [j] *Verse 31 transposed to follow verse 28.*   [k] and...straight:
prob. rdg.; Heb. *and gives orders concerning it.*   [l] in his anger...coming:
prob. rdg.; Heb. *obscure.*   [m] *See note on verse 6.*   [n] *Prob. rdg.*; Heb. *thundering.*

6 For he says to the snow, 'Fall to
earth',
and to the rainstorms, 'Be fierce.'
And when his voice is heard,
the floods of rain pour down unchecked.[a]

7 He shuts every man fast indoors,[b]
and all men whom he has made
must stand idle;

8 the beasts withdraw into their lairs
and take refuge in their dens.

9 The hurricane bursts from its
prison,
and the rain-winds bring bitter cold;

10 at the breath of God the ice-sheet
is formed,
and the wide waters are frozen
hard as iron.

11 He gives the dense clouds their
load of moisture,
and the clouds spread his mist
abroad,

12 as they travel round in their
courses,
steered by his guiding hand
to do his bidding
all over the habitable world.[c]

14 Listen, Job, to this argument;
stand still, and consider God's
wonderful works.

15 Do you know how God assigns
them their tasks,
how he sends light flashing from
his clouds?

16 Do you know why the clouds hang
poised overhead,
a wonderful work of his consum-
mate skill,

17 sweating there in your stifling
clothes,
when the earth lies sultry under
the south wind?

18 Can you beat out the vault of the
skies, as he does,
hard as a mirror of cast metal?

19 Teach us then what to say to him;
for all is dark, and we cannot
marshal our thoughts.

20 Can any man dictate to God when
he is[d] to speak?
or command him to make proclamation?

21 At one moment the light is not seen,
it is overcast with clouds and rain;
then the wind passes by and clears
them away,

22 and a golden glow comes from the
north.[e]

23 But the Almighty we cannot find;
his power is beyond our ken,
and his righteousness not slow to
do justice.

24 Therefore mortal men pay him
reverence,
and all who are wise look to him.

God's answer and
Job's submission

38 Then the LORD answered Job out
of the tempest:

2 Who is this whose ignorant words
cloud my design in darkness?

3 Brace yourself and stand up like
a man;
I will ask questions, and you shall
answer.

4 Where were you when I laid the
earth's foundations?
Tell me, if you know and understand.

5 Who settled its dimensions? Surely
you should know.
Who stretched his measuring-line
over it?

6 On what do its supporting pillars
rest?
Who set its corner-stone in place,

7 when the morning stars sang together
and all the sons of God shouted
aloud?

8 Who watched over the birth of the
sea,[f]
when it burst in flood from the
womb? —

---

[a] And when . . . unchecked: *prob. rdg.; some words in these lines transposed from verse 4.*
[b] indoors: *prob. rdg.; Heb. obscure.*   [c] *Prob. rdg.; Heb. adds* (13) whether he
makes him attain the rod, or his earth, or constant love.   [d] *Prob. rdg.; Heb.* I am.
[e] *Prob. rdg.; Heb. adds* this refers to God, terrible in majesty.
[f] Who . . . sea: *prob. rdg.; Heb.* And he held back the sea with two doors.

9 when I wrapped it in a blanket of
cloud
and cradled it in fog,
10 when I established its bounds,
fixing its doors and bars in place,
11 and said, 'Thus far shall you come
and no farther,
and here your surging waves shall
halt.'[a]
12 In all your life have you ever called
up the dawn
or shown the morning its place?
13 Have you taught it to grasp the
fringes of the earth
and shake the Dog-star from its
place;
14 to bring up the horizon in relief as
clay under a seal,
until all things stand out like the
folds of a cloak,
15 when the light of the Dog-star is
dimmed
and the stars of the Navigator's
Line go out one by one?
16 Have you descended to the springs
of the sea
or walked in the unfathomable
deep?
17 Have the gates of death been revealed to you?
Have you ever seen the door-
keepers of the place of darkness?
18 Have you comprehended the vast
expanse of the world?
Come, tell me all this, if you know.
19 Which is the way to the home of
light
and where does darkness dwell?
20 And can you then take each to its
appointed bound
and escort it on its homeward path?
21 Doubtless you know all this; for
you were born already,
so long is the span of your life!

22 Have you visited the storehouse
of the snow
or seen the arsenal where hail is
stored,
23 which I have kept ready for the
day of calamity,
for war and for the hour of battle?

By what paths is the heat spread 24
abroad
or the east wind carried far and
wide over the earth?
Who has cut channels for the down- 25
pour
and cleared a passage for the
thunderstorm,
for rain to fall on land where no 26
man lives
and on the deserted wilderness,
clothing lands waste and derelict 27
with green
and making grass grow on thirsty
ground[b]?
Has the rain a father? 28
Who sired the drops of dew?
Whose womb gave birth to the 29
ice,
and who was the mother of the
frost from heaven,
which lays a stony cover over the 30
waters
and freezes the expanse of ocean?
Can you bind the cluster of the 31
Pleiades
or loose Orion's belt?
Can you bring out the signs of the 32
zodiac in their season
or guide Aldebaran and its train?
Did you proclaim the rules that 33
govern the heavens,
or determine the laws of nature on
earth?
Can you command the dense 34
clouds
to cover you with their weight of
waters?
If you bid lightning speed on its 35
way,
will it say to you, 'I am ready'?
Who put wisdom in depths of 36
darkness
and veiled understanding in secrecy[c]?
Who is wise enough to marshal the 37
rain-clouds
and empty the cisterns of heaven,
when the dusty soil sets hard as 38
iron,
and the clods of earth cling together?

---

[a] *Prob. rdg.; Heb.* here one shall set on your surging waves.   [b] thirsty ground:
prob. rdg.; Heb. source.   [c] secrecy: *prob. rdg.; Heb. word unknown.*

39 Do you hunt her prey for the
    lioness
    and satisfy the hunger of young
    lions,
40 as they crouch in the lair
    or lie in wait in the covert?
41 Who provides the raven with its
    quarry
    when its fledglings croak[a] for lack
    of food?

39 Do you know when the mountain-
    goats are born
    or attend the wild doe when she is
    in labour?
2 Do you count the months that they
    carry their young
    or know the time of their delivery,
3 when they crouch down to open
    their wombs
    and bring their offspring to the
    birth,
4 when the fawns grow and thrive
    in the open forest,
    and go forth and do not return?
5 Who has let the wild ass of Syria
    range at will
    and given the wild ass of Arabia
    its freedom? –
6 whose home I have made in the
    wilderness
    and its lair in the saltings?
7 it disdains the noise of the city
    and is deaf to the driver's shout-
    ing;
8 it roams the hills as its pasture
    and searches for anything green.
9 Does the wild ox consent to serve
    you,
    does it spend the night in your
    stall?
10 Can you harness its strength[b] with
    ropes,
    or will it harrow the furrows[b] after
    you?
11 Can you depend on it, strong as it
    is,
    or leave your labour to it?
12 Do you trust it to come back
    and bring home your grain to the
    threshing-floor?

The wings of the ostrich are 13
    stunted;[c]
[d]her pinions and plumage are so
    scanty[e]
that she abandons her eggs to the 14
    ground,
letting them be kept warm by the
    sand.
She forgets that a foot may crush 15
    them,
or a wild beast trample on them;
she treats her chicks heartlessly as 16
    if they were not hers,
not caring if her labour is wasted
(for God has denied her wisdom 17
    and left her without sense),
while like a cock she struts over 18
    the uplands,
scorning both horse and rider.

Did you give the horse his 19
    strength?
Did you clothe his neck with a
    mane?
Do you make him quiver like a 20
    locust's wings,
when his shrill neighing strikes
    terror?
He shows his mettle as he paws 21
    and prances;
he charges the armoured line with
    all his might.
He scorns alarms and knows no 22
    dismay;
he does not flinch before the
    sword.
The quiver rattles at his side, 23
    the spear and sabre flash.
Trembling with eagerness, he de- 24
    vours the ground
and cannot be held in when he
    hears the horn;
at the blast of the horn he cries 25
    'Aha!'
and from afar he scents the
    battle.[f]
Does your skill teach the hawk to 26
    use its pinions
and spread its wings towards the
    south?

---

[a] *Prob. rdg.; Heb. adds* they cry to God.
[b] *Prob. rdg.; Heb. transposes*
strength *and* furrows.   [c] are stunted: *prob. rdg.; Heb. unintelligible.*
[d] *Prob. rdg.; Heb. prefixes* if.   [e] *Prob. rdg.; Heb.* godly *or* stork.
[f] *Prob. rdg.; Heb. adds* the thunder of the captains and the shouting.

27 Do you instruct the vulture to fly
high
and build its nest aloft?

28 It dwells among the rocks and
there it lodges;
its station is a crevice in the
rock;

29 from there it searches for food,
keenly scanning the distance,

30 that its brood may be gorged with
blood;
and where the slain are, there the
vulture is.

41 1[a] Can you pull out the whale[b] with
a gaff
or can you slip a noose round its
tongue?

2 Can you pass a cord through its
nose
or put a hook through its jaw?

3 Will it plead with you for mercy
or beg its life with soft words?

4 Will it enter into an agreement
with you
to become your slave for life?

5 Will you toy with it as with a
bird
or keep it on a string like a song-
bird for your maidens?

6 Do trading-partners haggle over it
or merchants share it out?

40 Then the LORD said to Job:

2 Is it for a man who disputes
with the Almighty to be stubborn?
Should he that argues with God
answer back?

3 And Job answered the LORD:

4 What reply can I give thee, I who
carry no weight?
I put my finger to my lips.

5 I have spoken once and now will
not answer again;
twice have I spoken, and I will do
so no more.

Then the LORD answered Job out 6
of the tempest:

Brace yourself and stand up like 7
a man;
I will ask questions, and you shall
answer.

Dare you deny that I am just   8
or put me in the wrong that you
may be right?

Have you an arm like God's 9
arm,
can you thunder with a voice like
his?

Deck yourself out, if you can, in 10
pride and dignity,
array yourself in pomp and splendour;

unleash the fury of your wrath,   11
look upon the proud man and
humble him;

look upon every proud man and 12
bring him low,
throw down the wicked where they
stand;

hide them in the dust together,   13
and shroud them in an unknown
grave.

Then I in my turn will acknow- 14
ledge
that your own right hand can save
you.

Consider the chief of the beasts, 15
the crocodile,[c]
who devours cattle as if they were
grass:[d]

what strength is in his loins!   16
what power in the muscles of his
belly!

His tail is rigid as[e] a cedar,   17
the sinews of his flanks are closely
knit,

his bones are tubes of bronze,   18
and his limbs like bars of
iron.

He is the chief of God's works,   19
made to be a tyrant over his
peers;[f]

---

[a] 41. 1–6 (in Heb. 40. 25–30) transposed to this point.   [b] Or Leviathan.
[c] chief...crocodile: prob. rdg.; Heb. beasts (behemoth) which I have made with
you.   [d] cattle...grass: prob. rdg.; Heb. grass like cattle.
[e] Or He bends his tail like...
[f] Prob. rdg.; Heb. his sword.

20 for he takes[a] the cattle of the hills
for his prey
and in his jaws he crunches all wild
beasts.

21 There under the thorny lotus he
lies,
hidden in the reeds and the marsh;

22 the lotus conceals him in its
shadow,
the poplars of the stream surround
him.

23 If the river is in spate, he is not
scared,
he sprawls at his ease though the
stream is in flood.

24 Can a man blind[b] his eyes and take
him
or pierce his nose with the teeth
of a trap?

41 7[c] Can you fill his skin with harpoons
or his head with fish-hooks?

8 If ever you lift your hand against
him,
think of the struggle that awaits
you, and let be.

9 No, such a man is in desperate
case,
hurled headlong at the very sight
of him.

10 How fierce he is when he is roused!
Who is there to stand up to him?

11 Who has ever attacked him[d] unscathed?
Not a man[e] under the wide heaven.

12 I will not pass over in silence his
limbs,
his prowess and the grace of his
proportions.

13 Who has ever undone his outer
garment
or penetrated his doublet of
hide?

14 Who has ever opened the portals
of his face?
for there is terror in his arching
teeth.

15 His back[f] is row upon row of
shields,
enclosed in a wall[g] of flints;

16 one presses so close on the other
that air cannot pass between
them,

17 each so firmly clamped to its neighbour
that they hold and cannot spring
apart.

18 His sneezing sends out sprays of
light,
and his eyes gleam like the shimmer
of dawn.

19 Firebrands shoot from his mouth,
and sparks come streaming out;

20 his nostrils pour forth smoke
like a cauldron on a fire blown to
full heat.

21 His breath sets burning coals a-
blaze,
and flames flash from his mouth.

22 Strength is lodged in his neck,
and untiring energy dances ahead
of him.

23 Close knit is his underbelly,
no pressure will make it yield.

24 His heart is firm as a rock,
firm as the nether millstone.

25 When he raises himself, strong
men[h] take fright,
bewildered at the lashings of his
tail.

26 Sword or spear, dagger or javelin,
if they touch him, they have no
effect.

27 Iron he counts as straw,
and bronze as rotting wood.

28 No arrow can pierce him,
and for him sling-stones are turned
into chaff;

29 to him a club is a mere reed,
and he laughs at the swish of the
sabre.

30 Armoured beneath with jagged
sherds,
he sprawls on the mud like a
threshing-sledge.

31 He makes the deep water boil like
a cauldron,
he whips up the lake like ointment
in a mixing-bowl.

---

[a] *Prob. rdg.; Heb.* they take.   [b] Can a man blind: *prob. rdg.; Heb. obscure.*
[c] *Verses 1–6 transposed to follow* 39. 30.   [d] *Prob. rdg.; Heb.* me.
[e] *Prob. rdg.; Heb.* He is mine.   [f] *Prob. rdg.; Heb.* pride.
[g] *Prob. rdg.; Heb.* seal.   [h] strong men: *or* leaders *or* gods.

32 He leaves a shining trail behind him,
and the great river is like white hair in his wake.
33 He has no equal on earth;
for he is made quite without fear.
34 He looks down on all creatures, even the highest;
he is king over all proud beasts.

42 Then Job answered the LORD:

2 I know that thou canst do all things and that no purpose is beyond thee.
3 But I have spoken of great things which I have not understood, things too wonderful for me to know.[a]
5 I knew of thee then only by report, but now I see thee with my own eyes.
6 Therefore I melt away;[b]
I repent in dust and ashes.

Epilogue

7 When the LORD had finished speaking to Job, he said to Eliphaz the Temanite, 'I am angry with you and your two friends, because you have not spoken as you ought about me, as my servant Job has 8 done. So now take seven bulls and seven rams, go to my servant Job and offer a whole-offering for yourselves, and he will intercede for you; I will surely show him favour by not being harsh with you because you have not spoken as you ought about me, as he has done.'
9 Then Eliphaz the Temanite and Bildad the Shuhite and Zophar the Naamathite went and carried out the LORD's command, and the LORD showed favour to Job when he had interceded for his friends.
10 So the LORD restored Job's fortunes and doubled all his possessions.

11 Then all Job's brothers and sisters and his former acquaintance came and feasted with him in his home, and they consoled and comforted him for all the misfortunes which the LORD had brought on him; and each of them gave him a sheep[c] and a gold ring. Further-12 more, the LORD blessed the end of Job's life more than the beginning; and he had fourteen thousand head of small cattle and six thousand camels, a thousand yoke of oxen and as many she-asses. 13 He had seven[d] sons and three daughters; and he named his 14 eldest daughter Jemimah, the second Keziah and the third Keren-15 happuch. There were no women in all the world so beautiful as Job's daughters; and their father gave them an inheritance with their brothers.
16 Thereafter Job lived another hundred and forty years, he saw his sons and his grandsons to four generations, and died at a very 17 great age.

---

[a] Prob. rdg.; Heb. adds (4) O listen, and let me speak; I will ask questions, and you shall answer.   [b] Or despise myself.
[c] Or piece of money.   [d] Or fourteen.

PSALMS

BOOK 1

1

1 Happy is the man
who does not take the wicked for
his guide
nor walk the road that sinners tread
nor take his seat among the scornful;
2 the law of the LORD is his delight,
the law his meditation night and
day.
3 He is like a tree
planted beside a watercourse,
which yields its fruit in season
and its leaf never withers:
in all that he does he prospers.
4 Wicked men are not like this;
they are like chaff driven by the
wind.
5 So when judgement comes the
wicked shall not stand firm,
nor shall sinners stand in the assembly of the righteous.
6 The LORD watches over the way
of the righteous,
but the way of the wicked is doomed.

2

1 Why are the nations in turmoil?
Why do the peoples hatch their
futile plots?
2 The kings of the earth stand ready,
and the rulers conspire together
against the LORD and his anointed
king.
3 'Let us break their fetters,' they
cry,
'let us throw off their chains!'
4 The Lord who sits enthroned in
heaven
laughs them to scorn;
5 then he rebukes them in anger,
he threatens them in his wrath.

Of me he says, 'I have enthroned 6
my king
on Zion my holy mountain.'
I will repeat the LORD's decree: 7
'You are my son,' he said;
'this day I become your father.
Ask of me what you will: 8
I will give you nations as your inheritance,
the ends of the earth as your possession.
You shall break them with a rod 9
of iron,
you shall shatter them like a clay
pot.'
Be mindful then, you kings; 10
learn your lesson, rulers of the
earth:
worship the LORD with reverence; 11-12
tremble, and kiss the king,[a]
lest the LORD be angry and you
are struck down in mid course;
for his anger flares up in a moment.
Happy are all who find refuge in
him.

3

LORD, how my enemies have 1
multiplied!
Many rise up against me,
many there are who say of me, 2
'God will not bring him victory.'
But thou, LORD, art a shield to 3
cover me:
thou art my glory, and thou dost
raise my head high.
I cry aloud to the LORD, 4
and he answers me from his holy
mountain.
I lie down and sleep, 5
and I wake again, for the LORD
upholds me.
I will not fear the nations in their 6
myriads
who set on me from all sides.

---

[a] tremble...king: *prob. rdg.*; *lit.* tremble and kiss the mighty one; *Heb. obscure.*

7 Rise up, LORD; save me, O my God.
Thou dost strike all my foes across
the face
and breakest the teeth of the
wicked.
8 Thine is the victory, O LORD,
and may[a] thy blessing rest upon
thy people.

4

1 Answer me when I call, O God,
maintainer of my right,
I was hard pressed, and thou didst
set me at large;
be gracious to me now and hear
my prayer.
2 Mortal men, how long will you pay
me not honour but dishonour,
or set your heart on trifles and run
after lies?
3 Know that the LORD has shown
me[b] his marvellous love;
the LORD hears when I call to him.
4 However angry your hearts, do not
do wrong;
though you lie abed resentful,[c] do
not break silence:
5 pay your due of sacrifice, and trust
in the LORD.

6 There are many who say, 'If only
we might be prosperous again!
But the light of thy presence has
fled from us, O LORD.'
7 Yet in my heart thou hast put
more happiness
than they enjoyed when there was
corn and wine in plenty.
8 Now I will lie down in peace, and
sleep;
for thou alone, O LORD, makest
me live unafraid.

5

1 Listen to my words, O LORD,
consider my inmost thoughts;
2 heed my cry for help, my king and
my God.

In the morning, when I say my 3
prayers,
thou wilt hear me.
I set out my morning sacrifice[d]
and watch for thee, O LORD.
For thou art not a God who wel- 4
comes wickedness;
evil can be no guest of thine.[e]
There is no place for arrogance 5
before thee;
thou hatest evildoers,
thou makest an end of all liars.   6

The LORD detests traitors and men
of blood.
But I, through thy great love, 7
may come into thy house,
and bow low toward thy holy
temple in awe of thee.
Lead me, LORD, in thy righteous- 8
ness,
because my enemies are on the
watch;
give me a straight path to follow.
There is no trusting what they say, 9
they are nothing but wind.
Their throats are an open[f] sepul-
chre;
smooth talk runs off their tongues.
Bring ruin on them, O God;   10
let them fall by their own devices.
Cast them out, after all their rebellions,
for they have defied thee.
But let all who take refuge in thee 11
rejoice,
let them for ever break into shouts
of joy;
shelter those who love thy name,
that they may exult in thee.
For thou, O LORD, wilt bless the 12
righteous;
thou wilt hedge him round with
favour as with a shield.

6

O LORD, do not condemn me in 1
thy anger,
do not punish me in thy fury.

---

[a] Thine...and may: or O LORD of salvation, may...   [b] Prob. rdg.; Heb. him.
[c] lie abed resentful: prob. rdg.; Heb. say on your beds.   [d] Or plea.
[e] who welcomes...thine: or who protects a wicked man; an evil man cannot be
thy guest.   [f] Or inscribed.

2 Be merciful to me, O LORD, for I
   am weak;
   heal me, my very bones are shaken;
3 my soul quivers in dismay.
   And thou, O LORD – how long?
4 Come back, O LORD; set my soul
   free,
   deliver me for thy love's sake.
5 None talk of thee among the dead;
   who praises thee in Sheol?

6 I am wearied with groaning;
   all night long my pillow is wet with
   tears,
   I soak my bed with weeping.
7 Grief dims my eyes;
   they are worn out with all my woes.
8 Away from me, all you evildoers,
   for the LORD has heard the sound
   of my weeping.
9 The LORD has heard my entreaty;
   the LORD will accept my prayer.
10 All my enemies shall be confound-
    ed and dismayed;
    they shall turn away in sudden
    confusion.

7

1 O LORD my God, in thee I find
   refuge;
   save me, rescue me from my
   pursuers,
2 before they tear at my throat like
   a lion
   and carry me off beyond hope of
   rescue.
3 O LORD my God, if I have done
   any of these things –
   if I have stained my hands with
   guilt,
4 if I have repaid a friend evil for
   good
   or set free an enemy who attacked
   me without cause,
5 may my adversary come after me
   and overtake me,
   trample my life to the ground
   and lay my honour in the dust!

6 Arise, O LORD, in thy anger,
   rouse thyself in wrath against my
   foes.

Awake, my God who hast ordered
   that justice be done;
let the peoples assemble around 7
   thee,
and take thou thy seat on high
   above them.
O LORD, thou who dost pass sen- 8
   tence on the nations,
O LORD, judge me as my righteousness deserves,
for I am clearly innocent.
Let wicked men do no more harm, 9
establish the reign of righteousness,[a]
thou who examinest both heart
   and mind,
thou righteous God.

God, the High God, is my shield   10
who saves men of honest heart.
God is a just judge,   11
every day he requites the raging
   enemy.

He sharpens his sword,   12
strings his bow and makes it ready.
He has prepared his deadly shafts 13
and tipped his arrows with fire.
But the enemy is in labour with   14
   iniquity;
he conceives mischief, and his
   brood is lies.
He has made a pit and dug it   15
   deep,
and he himself shall fall into the
   hole that he has made.
His mischief shall recoil upon him- 16
   self,
and his violence fall on his own
   head.

I will praise the LORD for his   17
   righteousness
and sing a psalm to the name of
   the LORD Most High.

8

O LORD our sovereign,   1
how glorious is thy name in all the
   earth!
Thy majesty is praised high as the
   heavens.

---

[a] the reign of righteousness: *or* the cause of the righteous.

2 Out of the mouths of babes, of
   infants at the breast,
   thou hast rebuked^a the mighty,
   silencing enmity and vengeance
   to teach thy foes a lesson.
3 When I look up at thy heavens,
   the work of thy fingers,
   the moon and the stars set in their
   place by thee,
4 what is man that thou shouldst
   remember him,
   mortal man that thou shouldst
   care for him?
5 Yet thou hast made him little less
   than a god,
   crowning him with glory and
   honour.
6 Thou makest him master over all
   thy creatures;
   thou hast put everything under his
   feet:
7 all sheep and oxen, all the wild
   beasts,
8 the birds in the air and the fish in
   the sea,
   and all that moves along the paths
   of ocean.
9 O LORD our sovereign,
   how glorious is thy name in all the
   earth!

9–10

1 I will praise thee, O LORD, with
   all my heart,
   I will tell the story of thy marvellous acts.
2 I will rejoice and exult in thee,
   I will praise thy name in psalms,
   O thou Most High,
3 when my enemies turn back,
   when they fall headlong and perish
   at thy appearing;
4 for thou hast upheld my right and
   my cause,
   seated on thy throne, thou righteous judge.
5 Thou hast rebuked the nations and
   overwhelmed the ungodly,
   thou hast blotted out their name
   for all time.

The strongholds of the enemy are 6
   thrown down for evermore;
   thou hast laid their cities in ruins,
   all memory of them is lost.
The LORD thunders,^b he sits en- 7
   throned for ever:
   he has set up his throne, his judge-
   ment-seat.
He it is who will judge the world 8
   with justice
   and try the cause of the peoples
   fairly.
So may the LORD be a tower of 9
   strength for the oppressed,
   a tower of strength in time of need,
   that those who acknowledge thy 10
   name may trust in thee;
   for thou, LORD, dost not forsake
   those who seek thee.
Sing psalms to the LORD who 11
   dwells in Zion,
   proclaim his deeds among the
   nations.
For the Avenger of blood has re- 12
   membered men's desire,
   and has not forgotten the cry of
   the poor.

Have pity on me, O LORD; look 13
   upon my affliction,
   thou who hast lifted me up^c and
   caught me back from the gates
   of death,
that I may repeat all thy praise 14
   and exult at this deliverance in the
   gates of Zion's city.

The nations have plunged into a 15
   pit of their own making;
   their own feet are entangled in the
   net which they hid.
Now the LORD makes himself 16
   known. Justice is done:
   the wicked man is trapped in his
   own devices.
They rush blindly down to Sheol, 17
   the wicked,
   all the nations who are heedless of
   God.
But the poor shall not always be 18
   unheeded

---

^a *Prob. rdg.*; *Heb.* founded.
^b thunders: *prob. rdg.*; *Heb.* unintelligible.
^c thou...me up: *prob. rdg.*; *Heb.* from those who hate me.

nor the hope of the destitute be
always vain.

19 Arise, LORD, give man no chance
to boast his strength;
summon the nations before thee
for judgement.

20 Strike them with fear, O LORD,
let the nations know that they are
but men.

10 Why stand so far off, LORD,
hiding thyself in time of need?

2 The wicked man in his pride hunts
down the poor:
may his crafty schemes be his own
undoing!

3 The wicked man is obsessed with
his own desires,
and in his greed gives wickedness
his blessing;

4 arrogant as he is, he scorns the
LORD
and leaves no place for God in all
his schemes.

5 His ways are always devious;
thy judgements are beyond his
grasp,[a]
and he scoffs at all restraint.

6 He says to himself, 'I shall never
be shaken;
no misfortune can check my
course.'[b]

7 His mouth is full of lies and
violence;
mischief and trouble lurk under
his tongue.

8 He lies in ambush in the villages
and murders innocent men by
stealth.
He is watching[c] intently for some
poor wretch;

9 he seizes him and drags him away
in his net;
he crouches stealthily, like a lion
in its lair
crouching to seize its victim;

10 the good man[d] is struck down and
sinks to the ground,
and poor wretches fall into his
toils.

11 He says to himself, 'God has forgotten;

he has hidden his face and has seen
nothing.'

Arise, LORD, set[e] thy hand to the 12
task;
do not forget the poor, O God.

Why, O God, has the wicked man 13
rejected thee
and said to himself that thou dost
not care?

Thou seest that mischief and 14
trouble are his companions,
thou takest the matter into thy
own hands.
The poor victim commits himself
to thee;
fatherless, he finds in thee his
helper.

Break the power of wickedness and 15
wrong;
hunt out all wickedness until thou
canst find no more.

The LORD is king for ever and ever; 16
the nations have vanished from
his land.
Thou hast heard the lament of the 17
humble, O LORD,
and art attentive to their heart's
desire,
bringing justice to the orphan and 18
the downtrodden
that fear may never drive men
from their homes again.

11

In the LORD I have found my 1
refuge; why do you say to me,
'Flee to the mountains like a bird;
see how the wicked string their 2
bows
and fit the arrow to the string,
to shoot down honest men out of
the darkness'?
When foundations are under- 3
mined, what can the good man do?
The LORD is in his holy temple, 4
the LORD's throne is in heaven.
His eye is upon mankind, he takes
their measure at a glance.

[a] beyond his grasp: *prob. rdg.*; *Heb.* on high before him.
[b] my course: *prob. rdg.*; *Heb.* which.
[d] the good man: *prob. rdg.*; *Heb. om.*
[c] *Prob. rdg.*; *Heb.* storing up.
[e] *Or* who settest.

5 The LORD weighs just and unjust
   and hates with all his soul the
   lover of violence.
6 He shall rain down red-hot coals
   upon the wicked;
   brimstone and scorching winds
   shall be the cup they drink.
7 For the LORD is just and loves just
   dealing;
   his face is turned towards the upright man.

12

1 Help, LORD, for loyalty is no more;
   good faith between man and man
   is over.
2 One man lies to another:
   they talk with smooth lip and
   double heart.
3 May the LORD make an end of such
   smooth lips
   and the tongue that talks so boast-
   fully!
4 They said, 'Our tongue can win
   the day.
   Words are our ally; who can
   master us?'
5 'For the ruin of the poor, for the
   groans of the needy,
   now I will arise,' says the LORD,
   'I will place him in the safety for
   which he longs.'

6 The words of the LORD are pure
   words:
   silver refined in a crucible,
   gold[a] seven times purified.
7 Do thou, LORD, protect us
   and guard us from a profligate and
   evil generation.[b]
8 The wicked flaunt themselves on
   every side,
   while profligacy stands high among
   mankind.

13

1 How long, O LORD, wilt thou quite
   forget me?
   How long wilt thou hide thy face
   from me?

How long must I suffer anguish in 2
   my soul,
   grief in my heart, day and night?
How long shall my enemy lord it
   over me?
Look now and answer me, O LORD 3
   my God.
Give light to my eyes lest I sleep
   the sleep of death,
lest my adversary say, 'I have 4
   overthrown him',
and my enemies rejoice at my
   downfall.
But for my part I trust in thy 5
   true love.
My heart shall rejoice, for thou
   hast set me free.
I will sing to the LORD, who has 6
   granted all my desire.

14

The impious fool says in his heart, 1[c]
   'There is no God.'
How vile men are, how depraved
   and loathsome;
not one does anything good!
The LORD looks down from heaven 2
   on all mankind
to see if any act wisely,
if any seek out God.
But all are disloyal, all are rotten 3
   to the core;
not one does anything good,
no, not even one.

Shall they not rue it,   4
all evildoers who devour my
   people
as men devour bread,
and never call upon the LORD?
There they were in dire alarm;   5
for God was in the brotherhood of
   the godly.
The resistance of their victim was 6
   too much for them,
because the LORD was his refuge.
If only Israel's deliverance might 7
   come out of Zion!
When the LORD restores his
   people's fortunes,
let Jacob rejoice, let Israel be glad.

---

[a] gold: prob. rdg.; Heb. to the earth.
rdg.; Heb. the generation which is for ever.
[b] a profligate and evil generation: prob.
[c] Verses 1–7: cp. Ps. 53. 1–6.

15

1 O Lord, who may lodge in thy
    tabernacle?
  Who may dwell on thy holy moun-
    tain?
2 The man of blameless life, who
    does what is right
  and speaks the truth from his
    heart;
3 who has no malice on his tongue,
  who never wrongs a friend
  and tells no tales against his neigh-
    bour;
4 the man who shows his scorn for
    the worthless
  and honours all who fear the Lord;
  who swears to his own hurt and
    does not retract;
5 who does not put his money out
    to usury
  and takes no bribe against an
    innocent man.
  He who does these things shall
    never be brought low.

16

1 Keep me, O God, for in thee have
    I found refuge.
2 I have said to the Lord,
  'Thou, Lord, art my felicity.'
3 The gods whom earth holds sacred
    are all worthless,
  and cursed are all who make them
    their delight;[a]
4 those who run after them[b] find
    trouble without end.
  I will not offer them libations of
    blood
  nor take their names upon my lips.
5 Thou, Lord, my allotted portion,
    thou my cup,
  thou dost enlarge my boundaries:
6 the lines fall for me in pleasant
    places,
  indeed I am well content with my
    inheritance.
7 I will bless the Lord who has given
    me counsel:
  in the night-time wisdom comes
    to me in my inward parts.

I have set the Lord continually 8
    before me:
with him[c] at my right hand I can-
    not be shaken.
Therefore my heart exults   9
and my spirit rejoices,
my body too rests unafraid;
for thou wilt not abandon me to 10
    Sheol
nor suffer thy faithful servant to
    see the pit.
Thou wilt show me the path of 11
    life;
in thy presence is the fullness of
    joy,
in thy right hand pleasures for
    evermore.

17

Hear, Lord, my plea for justice,   1
give my cry a hearing,
listen to my prayer,
for it is innocent of all deceit.
Let judgement in my cause issue 2
    from thy lips,
let thine eyes be fixed on justice.
Thou hast tested my heart and 3
    watched me all night long;
thou hast assayed me and found
    in me no mind to evil.
I will not speak of the deeds of 4
    men;
I have taken good note of all thy
    sayings.
I have not strayed from the course 5
    of duty;
I have followed thy path and
    never stumbled.
I call upon thee, O God, for thou 6
    wilt answer me.
Bend down thy ear to me, listen
    to my words.
Show me how marvellous thy true 7
    love can be,
who with thy hand dost save
all who seek sanctuary from their
    enemies.
Keep me like the apple of thine 8
    eye;
hide me in the shadow of thy wings
from the wicked who obstruct me, 9

---

[a] are all worthless...delight: *prob. rdg.*; *Heb. obscure.*
[b] after them: *prob. rdg.*; *Heb. obscure.*   [c] with him: *prob. rdg.*; *Heb. om.*

from deadly foes who throng round
   me.
10 They have stifled all compassion;
   their mouths are full of pride;
11 they press me hard,[a] now they hem
   me in,
   on the watch to bring me to the
    ground.
12 The enemy is like a lion eager for
   prey,
   like a young lion crouching in
    ambush.
13 Arise, LORD, meet him face to face
   and bring him down.
   Save my life from the wicked;
14 make an end of them[b] with thy
   sword.
   With thy hand, O LORD, make an
    end of them;[b]
   thrust them out of this world in
    the prime of their life,
   gorged as they are with thy good
    things,
   blest with many sons
   and leaving their children wealth
    in plenty.
15 But my plea is just: I shall see thy
   face,
   and be blest with a vision of thee
    when I awake.

18

1 I love thee, O LORD my strength.
2[c] The LORD is my stronghold, my
   fortress and my champion,
   my God, my rock where I find safe-
    ty,
   my shield, my mountain refuge,
   my strong tower.
3 I will call on the LORD to whom
   all praise is due,
   and I shall be delivered from my
    enemies.
4 When the bonds of death held me
   fast,
   destructive torrents overtook me,
5 the bonds of Sheol tightened
   round me,

the snares of death were set to
   catch me;
then in anguish of heart I cried to 6
   the LORD,
I called for help to my God;
he heard me from his temple,
and my cry reached his ears.
The earth heaved and quaked, 7
the foundations of the mountains
   shook;
they heaved, because he was angry.
Smoke rose from his nostrils, 8
devouring fire came out of his
   mouth,
glowing coals and searing heat.
He swept the skies aside as he 9
   descended,
thick darkness lay under his feet.
He rode on a cherub, he flew 10
   through the air;
he swooped on the wings of the
   wind.
He made darkness around him his 11
   hiding-place
and dense[d] vapour his canopy.[e]
Thick clouds came out of the 12
   radiance before him,
hailstones and glowing coals.
The LORD thundered from the 13
   heavens
and the voice of the Most High
   spoke out.[f]
He loosed his arrows, he sped them 14
   far and wide,
he shot forth lightning shafts and
   sent them echoing.
The channels of the sea-bed were 15
   revealed,
the foundations of earth laid bare
at the LORD's rebuke,
at the blast of the breath of his[g]
   nostrils.
He reached down from the height 16
   and took me,
he drew me out of mighty waters,
he rescued me from my enemies, 17
   strong as they were,
from my foes when they grew too
   powerful for me.

---

[a] they press me hard: *prob. rdg.*; *Heb.* our footsteps.   [b] make an end of
them: *prob. rdg.*; *Heb. unintelligible.*   [c] Verses 2–50: *cp.* 2 Sam. 22. 2–51.
[d] *Prob. rdg., cp.* 2 Sam. 22. 12; *Heb.* dark.   [e] *Prob. rdg.*; *Heb. adds* thick clouds.
[f] *Prob. rdg.*; *Heb. adds* hailstones and glowing coals.
[g] *Prob. rdg.*; *Heb.* thy.

18 They confronted me in the hour
   of my peril,
   but the LORD was my buttress.
19 He brought me out into an open
   place,
   he rescued me because he delighted
   in me.
20 The LORD rewarded me as my
   righteousness deserved;
   my hands were clean, and he requited me.
21 For I have followed the ways of
   the LORD
   and have not turned wickedly from
   my God;
22 all his laws are before my eyes,
   I have not failed to follow his
   decrees.
23 In his sight I was blameless
   and kept myself from wilful sin;
24 the LORD requited me as my
   righteousness deserved
   and the purity of my life in his eyes.

25 With the loyal thou showest thyself loyal
   and with the blameless man blameless.
26 With the savage man thou showest
   thyself savage,
   and[a] tortuous with the perverse.
27 Thou deliverest humble folk,
   and bringest proud looks down to
   earth.
28 Thou, LORD, dost make my lamp
   burn bright,
   and my God will lighten my darkness.
29 With thy help I leap over a bank,
   by God's aid I spring over a wall.

30 The way of God is perfect,
   the LORD's word has stood the test;
   he is the shield of all who take
   refuge in him.
31 What god is there but the LORD?
   What rock but our God? –
32 the God who girds me with strength
   and makes my way blameless,
33 who makes me swift as a hind
   and sets me secure on the mountains;

who trains my hands for battle,   34
and my arms aim an arrow tipped
   with bronze.

Thou hast given me the shield of   35
   thy salvation,
thy hand sustains me, thy providence makes me great.
Thou givest me room for my steps, 36
my feet have not faltered.
I pursue my enemies and overtake   37
   them,
I do not return until I have made
   an end of them.
I strike them down and they will   38
   never rise again;
they fall beneath my feet.
Thou dost arm me with strength   39
   for the battle
and dost subdue my foes before me.
Thou settest my foot on my   40
   enemies' necks,
and I bring to nothing those that
   hate me.
They cry out and there is no one   41
   to help them,
they cry to the LORD and he does
   not answer.
I will pound them fine as dust   42
   before the wind,
like mud in the streets will I
   trample them.[b]
Thou dost deliver me from the   43
   clamour of the people,
and makest me master of the
   nations.
A people I never knew shall be my
   subjects;
as soon as they hear tell of me, they 44
   shall obey me,
and foreigners shall come cringing
   to me.
Foreigners shall be brought cap-   45
   tive to me,
and emerge from their strongholds.

The LORD lives, blessed is my rock, 46
high above all is God who saves me.

O God, who grantest me vengeance, 47
who layest nations prostrate at my
   feet,

[a] With the savage...savage, and: *or* With the pure thou showest thyself pure,
but...   [b] *Prob. rdg., cp.* 2 Sam. 22. 43; *Heb.* will I empty them out.

48 who dost rescue me from my foes
and set me over my enemies,
thou dost deliver me from violent
men.

49 Therefore, LORD, I will praise thee
among the nations
and sing psalms to thy name,

50 to one who gives his king great
victories
and in all his acts keeps faith with
his anointed king,
with David and his descendants
for ever.

19

1 The heavens tell out the glory of
God,
the vault of heaven reveals his
handiwork.

2 One day speaks to another,
night with night shares its knowledge,

3 and this without speech or language
or sound of any voice.

4 Their music goes out through all
the earth,
their words reach to the end of the
world.
In them a tent is fixed for the
sun,

5 who comes out like a bridegroom
from his wedding canopy,
rejoicing like a strong man to run
his race.

6 His rising is at one end of the
heavens,
his circuit touches their farthest
ends;
and nothing is hidden from his
heat.

7 The law of the LORD is perfect and
revives the soul.
The LORD's instruction never fails,
and makes the simple wise.

8 The precepts of the LORD are right
and rejoice the heart.
The commandment of the LORD
shines clear
and gives light to the eyes.

9 The fear of the LORD is pure and
abides for ever.

The LORD's decrees are true and
righteous every one,

10 more to be desired than gold, pure
gold in plenty,
sweeter than syrup or honey from
the comb.

11 It is these that give thy servant
warning,
and he who keeps them wins a great
reward.

12 Who is aware of his unwitting sins?
Cleanse me of any secret fault.

13 Hold back thy servant also from
sins of self-will,
lest they get the better of me.
Then I shall be blameless
and innocent of any great transgression.

14 May all that I say and think be
acceptable to thee,
O LORD, my rock and my redeemer!

20

1 May the LORD answer you in the
hour of trouble!
The name of Jacob's God be your
tower of strength,

2 give you help from the sanctuary
and send you support from Zion!

3 May he remember all your offerings
and look with favour on your rich
sacrifices,

4 give you your heart's desire
and grant success to all your plans!

5 Let us sing aloud in praise of your
victory,
let us do homage to the name of
our God!
The LORD grant all you ask!

6 Now I know
that the LORD has given victory
to his anointed king:
he will answer him from his holy
heaven
with the victorious might of his
right hand.

7 Some boast of chariots and some
of horses,
but our boast is the name of the
LORD our God.

8 They totter and fall,
but we rise up and are full of
courage.
9 O LORD, save the king,
and answer us in the hour of our
calling.

21

1 The king rejoices in thy might, O
LORD:
well may he exult in thy victory,
2 for thou hast given him his heart's
desire
and hast not refused him what he
asked.
3 Thou dost welcome him with blessings and prosperity
and set a crown of fine gold upon
his head.
4 He asked of thee life, and thou
didst give it him,
length of days for ever and ever.
5 Thy salvation has brought him
great glory;
thou dost invest him with majesty
and honour,
6 for thou bestowest blessings on him
for evermore
and dost make him glad with joy
in thy presence.
7 The king puts his trust in the
LORD:
the loving care of the Most High
holds him unshaken.

8 Your hand shall reach all your
enemies:
your right hand shall reach those
who hate you;
9 at your coming you shall plunge
them into a fiery furnace;
the LORD in his anger will strike
them down,
and fire shall consume them.
10 It will exterminate their offspring
from the earth
and rid mankind of their posterity.
11 For they have aimed wicked blows
at you,
they have plotted mischief but
could not prevail;
12 but you will catch them round the
shoulders

and will aim with your bow-strings
at their faces.

Be exalted, O LORD, in thy might; 13
we will sing a psalm of praise to
thy power.

22

My God, my God, why hast thou 1
forsaken me
and art so far from saving me, from
heeding my groans?
O my God, I cry in the day-time 2
but thou dost not answer,
in the night I cry but get no respite.
And yet thou art enthroned in 3
holiness,
thou art he whose praises Israel
sings.
In thee our fathers put their trust; 4
they trusted, and thou didst rescue
them.
Unto thee they cried and were 5
delivered;
in thee they trusted and were not
put to shame.
But I am a worm, not a man, 6
abused by all men, scorned by the
people.
All who see me jeer at me, 7
make mouths at me and wag their
heads:
'He threw himself on the LORD for 8
rescue;
let the LORD deliver him, for he
holds him dear!'
But thou art he who drew me from 9
the womb,
who laid me at my mother's breast.
Upon thee was I cast at birth; 10
from my mother's womb thou hast
been my God.
Be not far from me, 11
for trouble is near, and I have no
helper.
A herd of bulls surrounds me, 12
great bulls of Bashan beset me.
Ravening and roaring lions 13
open their mouths wide against me.
My strength drains away like water 14
and all my bones are loose.
My heart has turned to wax and
melts within me.

15 My mouth*a* is dry as a potsherd,
and my tongue sticks to my jaw;
I am laid*b* low in the dust of death.
16 The huntsmen are all about me;
a band of ruffians rings me round,
and they have hacked off*c* my
hands and my feet.
17 I tell my tale of misery,
while they look on and gloat.
18 They share out my garments a-
mong them
and cast lots for my clothes.
19 But do not remain so far away, O
LORD;
O my help, hasten to my aid.
20 Deliver my very self from the
sword,
my precious life from the axe.
21 Save me from the lion's mouth,
my poor body*d* from the horns of
the wild ox.

22 I will declare thy fame to my
brethren;
I will praise thee in the midst of
the assembly.
23 Praise him, you who fear the LORD;
all you sons of Jacob, do him
honour;
stand in awe of him, all sons of
Israel.
24 For he has not scorned the downtrodden,
nor shrunk in loathing from his
plight,
nor hidden his face from him,
but gave heed to him when he
cried out.
25 Thou dost inspire my praise in the
full assembly;
and I will pay my vows before all
who fear thee.
26 Let the humble eat and be satisfied.
Let those who seek the LORD praise
him
and be in good heart for ever.
27 Let all the ends of the earth remember and turn again to the LORD;
let all the families of the nations
bow down before him.

For kingly power belongs to the 28
LORD,
and dominion over the nations is
his.
How can those buried in the earth 29
do him homage,
how can those who go down to the
grave bow before him?
But I shall live for his sake,
my posterity*e* shall serve him.   30
This shall be told of the Lord to
future generations;
and they shall justify him,   31
declaring to a people yet unborn
that this was his doing.

23

The LORD is my shepherd; I shall 1
want nothing.
He makes me lie down in green 2
pastures,
and leads me beside the waters of
peace;
he renews life within me,   3
and for his name's sake guides me
in the right path.
Even though I walk through a 4
valley dark as death
I fear no evil, for thou art with me,
thy staff and thy crook are my
comfort.

Thou spreadest a table for me in 5
the sight of my enemies;
thou hast richly bathed my head
with oil,
and my cup runs over.
Goodness and love unfailing, these 6
will follow me
all the days of my life,
and I shall dwell in the house of
the LORD
my whole life long.

24

The earth is the LORD's and all 1
that is in it,
the world and those who dwell
therein.

---

a Prob. rdg.; Heb. My strength.   *b* I am laid: prob. rdg.; Heb. thou wilt lay me.
c and they have hacked off: prob. rdg.; Heb. like a lion.   *d* my poor body: prob.
rdg.; Heb. thou hast answered me.   *e* But I...posterity: prob. rdg.; Heb. obscure.

2 For it was he who founded it upon
   the seas
   and planted it firm upon the waters
   beneath.

3 Who may go up the mountain of
   the LORD?
   And who may stand in his holy
   place?
4 He who has clean hands and a pure
   heart,
   who has not set his mind on falsehood,
   and has not committed perjury.
5 He shall receive a blessing from the
   LORD,
   and justice from God his saviour.
6 Such is the fortune of those who
   seek him,
   who seek the face of the God of
   Jacob.

7 Lift up your heads, you gates,
   lift yourselves up, you everlasting
   doors,
   that the king of glory may come
   in.
8 Who is the king of glory?
   The LORD strong and mighty,
   the LORD mighty in battle.
9 Lift up your heads, you gates,
   lift them up, you everlasting doors,
   that the king of glory may come in.
10 Who then is the king of glory?
   The king of glory is the LORD of
   Hosts.

25

1 Unto thee, O LORD my God, I lift
   up my heart.
2 In thee I trust: do not put me to
   shame,
   let not my enemies exult over me.
3 No man who hopes in thee is put
   to shame;
   but shame comes to all who break
   faith without cause.
4 Make thy paths known to me, O
   LORD;
   teach me thy ways.
5 Lead me in thy truth and teach me;
   thou art God my saviour.

For thee I have waited all the day
   long,
for the coming of thy goodness,
   LORD.[a]
Remember, LORD, thy tender care 6
   and thy love unfailing,
shown from ages past.
Do not remember the sins and 7
   offences of my youth,
but remember me in thy unfailing
   love.
The LORD is good and upright;   8
therefore he teaches sinners the
   way they should go.
He guides the humble man in doing 9
   right,
he teaches the humble his ways.
All the ways of the LORD are loving 10
   and sure
to men who keep his covenant and
   his charge.
For the honour of thy name, O 11
   LORD,
forgive my wickedness, great as it
   is.
If there is any man who fears the 12
   LORD,
he shall be shown the path that
   he should choose;
he shall enjoy lasting prosperity, 13
   and his children after him shall
   inherit the land.
The LORD confides his purposes to 14
   those who fear him,
and his covenant is theirs to know.
My eyes are ever on the LORD,   15
who alone can free my feet from
   the net.

Turn to me and show me thy 16
   favour,
for I am lonely and oppressed.
Relieve the sorrows of my heart 17
   and bring me out of my distress.
Look at my misery and my trouble 18
   and forgive me every sin.
Look at my enemies, see how many 19
   they are
and how violent their hatred for
   me.
Defend me and deliver me,   20
do not put me to shame when I take
   refuge in thee.

---

[a] for the coming...LORD: *transposed from end of verse* 7.

21 Let integrity and uprightness pro-
    tect me,
    for I have waited for thee, O LORD.
22 O God, redeem Israel from all his
    sorrows.

26

1 Give me justice, O LORD,
    for I have lived my life without
      reproach,
    and put unfaltering trust in the
      LORD.
2 Test me, O LORD, and try me;
    put my heart and mind to the proof.
3 For thy constant love is before my
      eyes,
    and I live in thy truth.
4 I have not sat among worthless
      men,
    nor do I mix with hypocrites;
5 I hate the company of evildoers
    and will not sit among the ungodly.
6 I wash my hands in innocence
    to join in procession round thy
      altar, O LORD,
7 singing of thy marvellous acts,
    recounting them all with thankful
      voice.
8 O LORD, I love the beauty of thy
      house,
    the place where thy glory dwells.
9 Do not sweep me away with sinners,
    nor cast me out with men who
      thirst for blood,
10 whose fingers are active in mis-
      chief,
    and their hands are full of bribes.
11 But I live my life without reproach;
    redeem me, O LORD, and show me
      thy favour.
12 When once my feet are planted on
      firm ground,
    I will bless the LORD in the full
      assembly.

27

1 The LORD is my light and my
      salvation;
    whom should I fear?
    The LORD is the refuge of my life;
    of whom then should I go in dread?

When evildoers close in on me to 2
    devour me,
it is my enemies, my assailants,
who stumble and fall.
If an army should encamp against 3
    me,
my heart would feel no fear;
if armed men should fall upon me,
even then I should be undismayed.
One thing I ask of the LORD, 4
    one thing I seek:
that I may be constant in the
    house of the LORD
all the days of my life,
to gaze upon the beauty of the LORD
and to seek him[a] in his temple.
For he will keep me safe beneath 5
    his roof
in the day of misfortune;
he will hide me under the cover of
    his tent;
he will raise me beyond reach of
    distress.
Now I can raise my head high 6
above the enemy all about me;
so will I acclaim him with sacrifice
    before his tent
and sing a psalm of praise to the
    LORD.

Hear, O LORD, when I call aloud; 7
    show me favour and answer me.
'Come,' my heart has said, 8
    'seek his face.'[b]
I will seek thy face, O LORD;
    do not hide it from me,
nor in thy anger turn away thy 9
    servant,
whose help thou hast been;
do not cast me off or forsake me,
    O God my saviour.
Though my father and my mother 10
    forsake me,
the LORD will take me into his care.
Teach me thy way, O LORD; 11–12
do not give me up to the greed of
    my enemies;
lead me by a level path
to escape my watchful foes;
liars stand up to give evidence
    against me,
breathing malice.

[a] Or and to pay my morning worship.
[b] seek his face: prob. rdg.; Heb. seek ye my face.

13 Well I know that I shall see the
goodness of the LORD
in the land of the living.

14 Wait for the LORD; be strong, take
courage,
and wait for the LORD.

28

1 To thee, O LORD, I call;
O my Rock, be not deaf to my
cry,
lest, if thou answer me with silence,
I become like those who go down
to the abyss.
2 Hear my cry for mercy
when I call to thee for help,
when I lift my hands to thy holy
shrine.
3 Do not drag me away with the
ungodly, with evildoers,
who speak civilly to neighbours,
with malice in their hearts.
4 Reward them for their works, their
evil deeds;
reward them for what their hands
have done;
give them their deserts.
5 Because they pay no heed to the
works of the LORD
or to what his hands have done,
may he tear them down and never
build them up!

6 Blessed be the LORD,
for he has heard my cry for mercy.
7 The LORD is my strength, my
shield,
in him my heart trusts;
so I am sustained, and my heart
leaps for joy,
and I praise him with my whole
body.[a]
8 The LORD is strength to his people,
a safe refuge for his anointed king.

9 O save thy people and bless thy
own,
shepherd them, carry them for
ever.

29

Ascribe to the LORD, you gods,   1
ascribe to the LORD glory and
might.
Ascribe to the LORD the glory due 2
to his name;
bow down to the LORD in the
splendour of holiness.[b]
The God of glory thunders: 3
the voice of the LORD echoes over
the waters,
the LORD is over the mighty
waters.
The voice of the LORD is power.   4
The voice of the LORD is majesty.
The voice of the LORD breaks the   5
cedars,
the LORD splinters the cedars of
Lebanon.
He makes Lebanon skip like a calf, 6
Sirion like a young wild ox.
The voice of the LORD makes   7
flames of fire burst forth,
the voice of the LORD makes the   8
wilderness writhe in travail;
the LORD makes the wilderness of
Kadesh writhe.
The voice of the LORD makes the   9
hinds calve
and brings kids early to birth;
and in his temple all cry, 'Glory!'
The LORD is king above[c] the   10
flood,
the LORD has taken his royal seat
as king for ever.
The LORD will give strength to his 11
people;
the LORD will bless his people with
peace.

30

I will exalt thee, O LORD;   1
thou hast lifted me up
and hast not let my enemies make
merry over me.
O LORD my God, I cried to thee   2
and thou didst heal me.
O LORD, thou hast brought me up   3
from Sheol

[a] with my whole body: *prob. rdg.*; *Heb.* from my song.
[b] the splendour of holiness: *or* holy vestments.
[c] *Or* since.

and saved my life as I was sinking
into the abyss.[a]

4 Sing a psalm to the LORD, all you
his loyal servants,
and give thanks to his holy name.

5 In his anger is disquiet, in his
favour there is life.
Tears may linger at nightfall,
but joy comes in the morning.

6 Carefree as I was, I had said,
'I can never be shaken.'

7 But, LORD, it was thy will to shake
my mountain refuge;
thou didst hide thy face, and I was
struck with dismay.

8 I called unto thee, O LORD,
and I pleaded with thee, Lord, for
mercy:

9 'What profit in my death if I go
down into the pit?
Can the dust confess thee or proclaim thy truth?

10 Hear, O LORD, and be gracious to
me;
LORD, be my helper.'

11 Thou hast turned my laments into
dancing;
thou hast stripped off my sackcloth and clothed me with joy,

12 that my spirit may sing psalms to
thee and never cease.
I will confess thee for ever, O LORD
my God.

31

1 With thee, O LORD, I have sought
shelter,
let me never be put to shame.
Deliver me in thy righteousness;

2 bow down and hear me,
come quickly to my rescue;
be thou my rock of refuge,
a stronghold to keep me safe.

3 Thou art to me both rock and
stronghold;
lead me and guide me for the
honour of thy name.

4 Set me free from the net men have
hidden for me;
thou art my refuge,

into thy keeping I commit my 5
spirit.
Thou hast redeemed me, O LORD
thou God of truth.
Thou hatest all who worship use- 6
less idols,
but I put my trust in the LORD.
I will rejoice and be glad in thy 7
unfailing love;
for thou hast seen my affliction
and hast cared for me in my distress.
Thou hast not abandoned me to 8
the power of the enemy
but hast set me free to range at
will.
Be gracious to me, O LORD, for 9
I am in distress,
and my eyes are dimmed with
grief.[b]
My life is worn away with sorrow 10
and my years with sighing;
strong as I am, I stumble under
my load of misery;
there is disease in all my bones.
I have such enemies that all men 11
scorn me;[c]
my neighbours find me a burden,
my friends shudder at me;
when they see me in the street they
turn quickly away.
I am forgotten, like a dead man 12
out of mind;
I have come to be like something
lost.
For I hear many men whispering 13
threats from every side,
in league against me as they are
and plotting to take my life.
But, LORD, I put my trust in thee; 14
I say, 'Thou art my God.'
My fortunes are in thy hand; 15
rescue me from my enemies and
those who persecute me.
Make thy face shine upon thy 16
servant;
save me in thy unfailing love.
O LORD, do not put me to shame 17
when I call upon thee;
let the wicked be ashamed, let
them sink into Sheol.

[a] and saved...abyss: or and rescued me alive from among those who go down to
the abyss.   [b] Prob. rdg.; Heb. adds my soul and my body.
[c] I have...scorn me: or I am scorned by all my enemies.

Strike dumb the lying lips
which speak with contempt against
the righteous
in pride and arrogance.

19 How great is thy goodness,
stored up for those who fear thee,
made manifest before the eyes of
men
for all who turn to thee for shelter.

20 Thou wilt hide them under the
cover of thy presence
from men in league together;
thou keepest them beneath thy
roof,
safe from contentious men.

21 Blessed be the LORD,
who worked a miracle of unfailing
love for me
when I was in sore straits.[a]

22 In sudden alarm I said,
'I am shut out from thy sight.'
But thou didst hear my cry for
mercy
when I called to thee for help.

23 Love the LORD, all you his loyal
servants.
The LORD protects the faithful
but pays the arrogant in full.

24 Be strong and take courage,
all you whose hope is in the LORD.

32

1 Happy the man whose disobedience
is forgiven,
whose sin is put away!

2 Happy is a man when the LORD
lays no guilt to his account,
and in his spirit there is no deceit.

3 While I refused to speak, my body
wasted away
with moaning all day long.

4 For day and night
thy hand was heavy upon me,
the sap in me dried up as in summer
drought.

5 Then I declared my sin, I did not
conceal my guilt.

I said, 'With sorrow I will confess
my disobedience to the LORD';
then thou didst remit the penalty
of my sin.

6 So every faithful heart shall pray
to thee
in the hour of anxiety,[b] when great
floods threaten.
Thou art a refuge for me from
distress
so that it cannot touch me;[c]

7 thou dost guard me[d] and enfold
me in salvation
beyond all reach of harm.[e]

8 I will teach you, and guide you in
the way you should go.
I will keep you under my eye.

9 Do not behave like horse or mule,
unreasoning creatures,
whose course must be checked with
bit and bridle.

10 Many are the torments of the ungodly;
but unfailing love enfolds him who
trusts in the LORD.

11 Rejoice in the LORD and be glad,
you righteous men,
and sing aloud, all men of upright
heart.

33

1 Shout for joy before the LORD, you
who are righteous;
praise comes well from the upright.

2 Give thanks to the LORD on the
harp;
sing him psalms to the ten-stringed
lute.

3 Sing to him a new song;
strike up with all your art and
shout in triumph.

4 The word of the LORD holds true,
and all his work endures.

5 The LORD loves righteousness and
justice,
his love unfailing fills the earth.

6 The LORD's word made the heavens,

---

[a] when...straits: prob. rdg.; Heb. like a city besieged.
[b] of anxiety: prob. rdg.; Heb. unintelligible.   [c] Prob. rdg.; Heb. him.
[d] Prob. rdg.; Heb. adds an unintelligible word.
[e] beyond...harm: transposed from end of verse 9.

all the host of heaven was made at his command.

7 He gathered the sea like water in a goatskin;
he laid up the deep in his store-chambers.

8 Let the whole world fear the LORD
and all men on earth stand in awe of him.

9 For he spoke, and it was;
he commanded, and it stood firm.

10 The LORD brings the plans of nations to nothing;
he frustrates the counsel of the peoples.

11 But the LORD's own plans shall stand for ever,
and his counsel endure for all generations.

12 Happy is the nation whose God is the LORD,
the people he has chosen for his own possession.

13 The LORD looks out from heaven,
he sees the whole race of men;

14 he surveys from his dwelling-place all the inhabitants of earth.

15 It is he who fashions the hearts of all men alike,
who discerns all that they do.

16 A king is not saved by a great army,
nor a warrior delivered by great strength.

17 A man cannot trust his horse to save him,
nor can it deliver him for all its strength.

18 The LORD's eyes are turned towards those who fear him,
towards those who hope for his unfailing love

19 to deliver them from death,
to keep them alive in famine.

20 We have waited eagerly for the LORD;
he is our help and our shield.

21 For in him our hearts are glad,
because we have trusted in his holy name.

22 Let thy unfailing love, O LORD, rest upon us,
as we have put our hope in thee.

34

1 I will bless the LORD continually;
his praise shall be always on my lips.

2 In the LORD I will glory;
the humble shall hear and be glad.

3 O glorify the LORD with me,
and let us exalt his name together.

4 I sought the LORD's help and he answered me;
he set me free from all my terrors.

5 Look towards him and shine with joy;
no longer hang your heads in shame.

6 Here was a poor wretch who cried to the LORD;
he heard him and saved him from all his troubles.

7 The angel of the LORD is on guard round those who fear him, and rescues them.

8 Taste, then, and see that the LORD is good.
Happy the man who finds refuge in him!

9 Fear the LORD, all you his holy people;
for those who fear him lack nothing.

10 Unbelievers suffer want and go hungry,
but those who seek the LORD lack no good thing.

11 Come, my children, listen to me:
I will teach you the fear of the LORD.

12 Which of you delights in life
and desires a long life to enjoy all good things?

13 Then keep your tongue from evil
and your lips from uttering lies;

14 turn from evil and do good,
seek peace and pursue it.

15 The eyes of the LORD are upon the righteous,
and his ears are open to their cries.

16 The LORD sets his face against evildoers
to blot out their memory from the earth.

17 When men cry for help, the LORD hears them
and sets them free from all their troubles.

18 The LORD is close to those whose
courage is broken
and he saves those whose spirit is
crushed.
19 The good man's misfortunes may
be many,
the LORD delivers him out of them
all.
20 He guards every bone of his body,
and not one of them is broken.
21 Their own misdeeds are death to
the wicked,
and those who hate the righteous
are brought to ruin.

22 The LORD ransoms the lives of his
servants,
and none who seek refuge in him
are brought to ruin.

35

1 Strive, O LORD, with those who
strive against me;
fight against those who fight me.
2 Grasp shield and buckler,
and rise up to help me.
3 Uncover the spear and bar the
way
against my pursuers.
Let me hear thee declare,
'I am your salvation.'
4 Shame and disgrace be on those
who seek my life;
and may those who plan to hurt
me retreat in dismay!
5 May they be like chaff before the
wind,
driven by the angel of the LORD!
6 Let their way be dark and slippery
as the angel of the LORD pursues
them!
7 For unprovoked they have hidden
a net[a] for me,
unprovoked they have dug a pit
to trap me.
8 May destruction unforeseen come
on him;
may the net which he hid catch
him;
may he crash headlong into it!

Then I shall rejoice in the LORD 9
and delight in his salvation.
My very bones cry out, 10
'LORD, who is like thee? –
thou saviour of the poor from those
too strong for them,
the poor and wretched from those
who prey on them.'
Malicious witnesses step forward; 11
they question me on matters of
which I know nothing.
They return me evil for good, 12
lying in wait[b] to take my life.
And yet when they were sick, I put 13
on sackcloth,
I mortified myself with fasting.
When my prayer came back unanswered,
I walked with head bowed in grief 14
as if for a brother;
as one in sorrow for his mother
I lay prostrate in mourning.
But when I stumbled, they crowd- 15
ed round rejoicing,
they crowded about me;
nameless ruffians[e] jeered at me
and nothing would stop them.
When I slipped, brutes who would 16
mock even a hunchback
ground their teeth at me.
O Lord, how long wilt thou look on 17
at those who hate me for no reason[d]?
Rescue me out of their cruel grasp,
save my precious life from the unbelievers.
Then I will praise thee before a 18
great assembly,
I will extol thee where many people
meet.
Let no treacherous enemy gloat 19
over me
nor leer at me in triumph.[e]
No friendly greeting do they give 20
to peaceable folk.
They invent lie upon lie,
they open their mouths at me: 21
'Hurrah!' they shout in their joy,
feasting their eyes on me.
Thou hast seen all this, O LORD, 22
do not keep silence;
O Lord, be not far from me.

---

[a] *Prob. rdg., transposing* a pit *from this line to follow* have dug.   [b] lying in wait:
prob. rdg.; Heb. bereavement.   [e] nameless ruffians: *or* ruffians who give me no rest.
[d] *Line transposed from verse 19.*   [e] *See note on verse 17.*

23 Awake, bestir thyself, to do me justice,
to plead my cause, my Lord and my God.
24 Judge me, O LORD my God, as thou art true;
do not let them gloat over me.
25 Do not let them say to themselves, 'Hurrah!
We have swallowed him up at one gulp.'
26 Let them all be disgraced and dismayed
who rejoice at my fall;
let them be covered with shame and dishonour
who glory over me.
27 But let all who would see me righted shout for joy,
let them cry continually,
'All glory to the LORD
who would see his servant thrive!'
28 So shall I talk of thy justice
and of thy praise all the day long.

36

1 Deep in his heart, sin whispers to the wicked man
who cherishes no fear of God.
2 For he flatters himself in his own opinion
and, when he is found out, he does not mend his ways.[a]
3 All that he says is mischievous and false;
he has turned his back on wisdom;
4 in his bed he plots how best to do mischief.
So set is he on his wrong courses
that he rejects nothing evil.
5 But thy unfailing love, O LORD, reaches to heaven,
thy faithfulness to the skies.
6 Thy righteousness is like the lofty mountains,
thy judgements are like the great abyss;
O LORD, who savest man and beast,
7 how precious is thy unfailing love!
Gods and men seek refuge in the shadow of thy wings.

They are filled with the rich plenty 8 of thy house,
and thou givest them water from the flowing stream of thy delights;
for with thee is the fountain of 9 life,
and in thy light we are bathed with light.
Maintain thy love unfailing over 10 those who know thee,
and thy justice toward men of honest heart.
Let not the foot of pride come near 11 me,
no wicked hand disturb me.
There they lie, the evildoers, 12
they are hurled down and cannot rise.

37

Do not strive to outdo the evil- 1 doers
or emulate those who do wrong.
For like grass they soon wither, 2
and fade like the green of spring.
Trust in the LORD and do good; 3
settle in the land and find safe pasture.
Depend upon the LORD, 4
and he will grant you your heart's desire.
Commit your life to the LORD; 5
trust in him and he will act.
He will make your righteousness 6 shine clear as the day
and the justice of your cause like the sun at noon.
Wait quietly for the LORD, be 7 patient till he comes;
do not strive to outdo the success- ful
nor envy him who gains his ends.
Be angry no more, have done with 8 wrath;
strive not to outdo in evildoing.
For evildoers will be destroyed, 9
but they who hope in the LORD shall possess the land.
A little while, and the wicked will 10 be no more;
look well, and you will find their place is empty.

[a] he does...ways: prob. rdg.; Heb. unintelligible.

11 But the humble shall possess the
     land
   and enjoy untold prosperity.
12 The wicked mutter against the
     righteous man
   and grind their teeth at the sight
     of him;
13 the Lord shall laugh at them,
   for he sees that their time is coming.
14 The wicked have drawn their
     swords
   and strung their bows
   to bring low the poor and needy
   and to slaughter honest men.
15 Their swords shall pierce their own
     hearts
   and their bows be broken.
16 Better is the little which the right-
     eous has
   than the great wealth of the wicked.
17 For the strong arm of the wicked
     shall be broken,
   but the Lord upholds the right-
     eous.
18 The Lord knows each day of the
     good man's life,
   and his inheritance shall last for
     ever.
19 When times are bad, he shall not
     be distressed,
   and in days of famine he shall have
     enough.
20 But the wicked shall perish,
   and their children shall beg their
     bread.[a]
   The enemies of the Lord, like fuel
     in a furnace,[b]
   are consumed in smoke.
21 The wicked man borrows and
     does not pay back,
   but the righteous is a generous
     giver.
22 All whom the Lord has blessed
     shall possess the land,
   and all who are cursed by him shall
     be destroyed.
23 It is the Lord who directs a man's
     steps,
   he holds him firm and watches over
     his path.

Though he may fall, he will not go 24
     headlong,
   for the Lord grasps him by the
     hand.
I have been young and am now 25
     grown old,
   and never have I seen a righteous
     man forsaken.[c]
Day in, day out, he lends generous- 26
     ly,
   and his children become a blessing.
Turn from evil and do good,   27
   and live at peace for ever;
for the Lord is a lover of justice 28
   and will not forsake his loyal
     servants.
The lawless are banished for ever
   and the children of the wicked
     destroyed.
The righteous shall possess the land 29
   and shall live there at peace for
     ever.
The righteous man utters words of 30
     wisdom
   and justice is always on his lips.
The law of his God is in his heart, 31
   his steps do not falter.
The wicked watch for the righteous 32
     man
   and seek to take his life;
but the Lord will not leave him 33
     in their power
   nor let him be condemned before
     his judges.
Wait for the Lord and hold to his 34
     way;
   he will keep you[d] safe from wicked
     men[e]
   and will raise you to be master of
     the land.
When the wicked are destroyed,
   you shall be there to see.
I have watched a wicked man at 35
     his work,
   rank as a spreading tree in its
     native soil.
I passed by one day, and he was 36
     gone;
   I searched for him, but he could
     not be found.

---

   [a] Line transposed from verse 25.
   [b] like...furnace: prob. rdg.; Heb. like the worth of rams.
   [c] See note on verse 20.   [d] Prob. rdg.; Heb. them.
   [e] he will...wicked men: transposed from verse 40.

37 Now look at the good man, watch
  him who is honest,
  for the man of peace leaves descendants;
38 but transgressors are wiped out
  one and all,
  and the descendants of the wicked
  are destroyed.
39 Deliverance for the righteous
  comes from the LORD,
  their refuge in time of trouble.
40 The LORD will help them and
  deliver them;[a]
  he will save them because they seek
  shelter with him.

38

1 O LORD, do not rebuke me in thy
  anger,
  nor punish me in thy wrath.
2 For thou hast aimed thy arrows[b]
  at me,
  and thy hand weighs heavy upon
  me.
3 Thy indignation has left no part
  of my body unscarred;
  there is no health in my whole
  frame because of my sin.
4 For my iniquities have poured over
  my head;
  they are a load heavier than I can
  bear.
5 My wounds fester and stink because of my folly.
6 I am bowed down and utterly
  prostrate.
  All day long I go about as if in
  mourning,
7 for my loins burn with fever,
  and there is no wholesome flesh in
  me.
8 All battered and benumbed,
  I groan aloud in my heart's longing.
9 O Lord, all my lament lies open
  before thee
  and my sighing is no secret to thee.
10 My heart beats fast, my strength
  has ebbed away,
  and the light has gone out of my
  eyes.

My friends and my companions 11
  shun me in my sickness,
and my kinsfolk keep far away.
Those who wish me dead defame 12
  me,
those who mean to injure me
  spread cruel gossip
and mutter slanders all day long.
But I am deaf, I do not listen; 13
I am like a dumb man who cannot
  open his mouth.
I behave like a man who cannot 14
  hear
and whose tongue offers no defence.
On thee, O LORD, I fix my hope; 15
  thou wilt answer, O Lord my God.
I said, 'Let them never rejoice over 16
  me
who exult when my foot slips.'
I am indeed prone to stumble, 17
and suffering is never far away.
I make no secret of my iniquity 18
and am anxious at the thought of
  my sin.
But many are my enemies, all 19
  without cause,[c]
and many those who hate me
  wrongfully.
Those who repay good with evil 20
oppose me because my purpose
  is good.
But, LORD, do not thou forsake 21
  me;
keep not far from me, my God.
Hasten to my help, O Lord my 22
  salvation.

39

I said: I will keep close watch over 1
  myself
that all I say may be free from sin.
I will keep a muzzle on my mouth,
so long as wicked men confront
  me.
In dumb silence I held my peace. 2
So my agony was quickened,
and my heart burned within me. 3
My mind wandered as the fever
  grew,
and I began to speak:

---

[a] See note on verse 34.
[b] thou...arrows: prob. rdg.; Heb. thy arrows have come down.
[c] all...cause: prob. rdg.; Heb. living.

4 LORD, let me know my end
  and the number of my days;
  tell me how short my life must be.
5 I know thou hast made my days
    a mere span long,
  and my whole life is nothing in thy
    sight.
  Man, though he stands upright, is
    but a puff of wind,
6 he moves like a phantom;
  the riches[a] he piles up are no more
    than vapour,
  he does not know who will enjoy
    them.
7 And now, Lord, what do I wait for?
  My hope is in thee.
8 Deliver me from all who do me
    wrong,
  make me no longer the butt of
    fools.
9 I am dumb, I will not open my
    mouth,
  because it is thy doing.
10 Plague me no more;
  I am exhausted by thy blows.
11 When thou dost rebuke a man to
    punish his sin,
  all his charm festers and drains
    away;
  indeed man is only a puff of wind.
12 Hear my prayer, O LORD;
  listen to my cry,
  hold not thy peace at my tears;
  for I find shelter with thee,
  I am thy guest, as all my fathers
    were.
13 Frown on me no more and let
    me smile again,
  before I go away and cease to be.

40

1 I waited, waited for the LORD,
  he bent down to me and heard my
    cry.
2 He brought me up out of the
    muddy pit,
  out of the mire and the clay;
  he set my feet on a rock
  and gave me a firm footing;
3 and on my lips he put a new song,
  a song of praise to our God.

Many when they see will be filled
    with awe
and will learn to trust in the LORD:
happy is the man   4
who makes the LORD his trust,
and does not look to brutal and
    treacherous men.
Great things thou hast done,   5
O LORD my God;
thy wonderful purposes are all for
    our good;
none can compare with thee;
I would proclaim them and speak
    of them,
but they are more than I can tell.
If thou hadst desired sacrifice and 6
    offering
thou wouldst have given me ears
    to hear.
If thou hadst asked for whole-
    offering and sin-offering
I would have said, 'Here I am.'[b]   7
My desire is to do thy will, O God, 8
and thy law is in my heart.
In the great assembly I have pro- 9
    claimed what is right,
I do not hold back my words,
as thou knowest, O LORD.
I have not kept thy goodness hid- 10
    den in my heart;
I have proclaimed thy faithfulness
    and saving power,
and not concealed thy unfailing
    love and truth
from the great assembly.
Thou, O LORD, dost not withhold 11
thy tender care from me;
thy unfailing love and truth for
    ever guard me.

For misfortunes beyond counting 12
press on me from all sides;
my iniquities have overtaken me,
and my sight fails;
they are more than the hairs of my
    head,
and my courage forsakes me.
Show me favour, O LORD, and save 13[c]
    me;
hasten to help me, O LORD.
Let those who seek to take my 14
    life

---

[a] the riches: *prob. rdg.; Heb.* they murmur.
scroll of a book it is prescribed for me.

[b] *Prob. rdg.; Heb. adds* in a
[c] *Verses 13–17: cp. Ps. 70. 1–5.*

be put to shame and dismayed
one and all;
let all who love to hurt me shrink
back disgraced;
15 let those who cry 'Hurrah!' at my
downfall
be horrified at their reward of
shame.
16 But let all those who seek thee
be jubilant and rejoice in thee;
and let those who long for thy
saving help ever cry,
'All glory to the LORD!'

17 But I am poor and needy;
O Lord, think of me.[a]
Thou art my help and my salvation;
O my God, make no delay.

41

1 Happy the man who has a concern
for the helpless!
The LORD will save him in time of
trouble.
2 The LORD protects him and gives
him life,
making him secure in the land;
the LORD never leaves him[b] to the
greed of his enemies.
3 He nurses him on his sick-bed;
he turns his bed when he is ill.

4 But I said, 'LORD, be gracious to me;
heal me, for I have sinned against
thee.'
5 'His case is desperate,' my enemies
say;
'when will he die, and his line
become extinct?'
6 All who visit me speak from an
empty heart,
alert to gather bad news;
then they go out to spread it
abroad.
7 All who hate me whisper together
about me
and love to make the worst of
everything:
8 'An evil spell is cast upon him;
he is laid on his bed, and will rise
no more.'

Even the friend whom I trusted, 9
who ate at my table,[c]
exults over my misfortune.
O LORD, be gracious and restore 10
me,
that I may pay them out to the
full.[d]
Then I shall know that thou de- 11
lightest in me
and that my enemy will not triumph over me.
But I am upheld by thee because 12
of my innocence;
thou keepest me for ever in thy
sight.

Blessed be the LORD, the God of 13
Israel,
from everlasting to everlasting.
Amen, Amen.

BOOK 2

42–43

As a hind longs for the running 1
streams,
so do I long for thee, O God.
With my whole being I thirst for 2
God, the living God.
When shall I come to God and
appear in his presence?
Day and night, tears are my food; 3
'Where is your God?' they ask me
all day long.
As I pour out my soul in distress, 4
I call to mind
how I marched in the ranks of the
great to the house of God,
among exultant shouts of praise,
the clamour of the pilgrims.
How deep I am sunk in misery, 5
groaning in my distress:
yet I will wait for God;
I will praise him continually,
my deliverer, my God.
I am sunk in misery, therefore will 6
I remember thee,
though from the Hermons and the
springs of Jordan,
and from the hill of Mizar,

[a] O Lord...me: *prob. rdg.*; *Heb.* may the Lord think of me.
[b] never leaves him: *prob. rdg.*; *Heb.* do thou not give him up...
[c] who...table: *or* slanders me.   [d] to the full: *transposed from end of verse 9.*

7 deep calls to deep in the roar of
thy cataracts,
and all thy waves, all thy breakers,
pass over me.

8 The LORD makes his unfailing love
shine forth[a]
alike by day and night;
his praise on my lips is a prayer
to the God of my life.

9 I will say to God my rock, 'Why
hast thou forgotten me?'
Why must I go like a mourner
because my foes oppress me?

10 My enemies taunt me, jeering[b] at
my misfortunes;
'Where is your God?' they ask me
all day long.

11 How deep I am sunk in misery,
groaning in my distress:
yet I will wait for God;
I will praise him continually,
my deliverer, my God.

43 Plead my cause and give me judgement against an impious race;
save me from malignant men and
liars, O God.

2 Thou, O God, art my refuge; why
hast thou rejected me?
Why must I go like a mourner
because my foes oppress me?

3 Send forth thy light and thy truth
to be my guide
and lead me to thy holy hill, to
thy tabernacle,

4 then shall I come to the altar of
God, the God of my joy,
and praise thee on the harp, O God,
thou God of my delight.

5 How deep I am sunk in misery,
groaning in my distress:
yet I will wait for God;
I will praise him continually,
my deliverer, my God.

44

1 O God, we have heard for ourselves,
our fathers have told us
all the deeds which thou didst in
their days,

2 all the work of thy hand in days
of old.

Thou didst plant them in the land
and drive the nations out,
thou didst make them strike root,
breaking up the peoples;

3 it was not our fathers' swords won
them the land,
nor their arm that gave them the
victory,
but thy right hand and thy arm
and the light of thy presence; such
was thy favour to them.

4 Thou art my king and my God;
at thy bidding Jacob is victorious.

5 By thy help we will throw back
our enemies,
in thy name we will trample down
our adversaries.

6 I will not trust in my bow,
nor will my sword win me the
victory;

7 for thou dost deliver us from our
foes
and put all our enemies to shame.

8 In God have we gloried all day
long,
and we will praise thy name for
ever.

9 But now thou hast rejected and
humbled us
and dost no longer lead our armies
into battle.

10 Thou hast hurled us back before
the enemy,
and our foes plunder us as they will.

11 Thou hast given us up to be
butchered like sheep
and hast scattered us among the
nations.

12 Thou hast sold thy people for next
to nothing
and had no profit from the sale.

13 Thou hast exposed us to the taunts
of our neighbours,
to the mockery and contempt of
all around.

14 Thou hast made us a byword
among the nations,
and the peoples shake their heads
at us;

15 so my disgrace confronts me all
day long,
and I am covered with shame

---

[a] makes...forth: *or* entrusts me to his unfailing love.
[b] jeering: *prob. rdg.; Heb. obscure.*

16 at the shouts of those who taunt
and abuse me
as the enemy takes his revenge.

17 All this has befallen us, but we do
not forget thee
and have not betrayed thy covenant;

18 we have not gone back on our
purpose,
nor have our feet strayed from thy
path.

19 Yet thou hast crushed us as the
sea-serpent was crushed
and covered us with the darkness
of death.

20 If we had forgotten the name of
our God
and spread our hands in prayer to
any other,

21 would not God find this out,
for he knows the secrets of the
heart?

22 Because of thee we are done to
death all day long,
and are treated as sheep for slaughter.

23 Bestir thyself, Lord; why dost
thou sleep?
Awake, do not reject us for ever.

24 Why dost thou hide thy face,
heedless of our misery and our
sufferings?

25 For we sink down to the dust
and lie prone on the earth.

26 Arise and come to our help;
for thy love's sake set us free.

45

1 My heart is stirred by a noble
theme,
in a king's honour I utter the song
I have made,
and my tongue runs like the pen
of an expert scribe.

2 You surpass all mankind in beauty,
your lips are moulded in grace,
so you are blessed by God for ever.

3 With your sword ready at your
side, warrior king,

your limbs resplendent[a] in their 4
royal armour,
ride on to execute true sentence
and just judgement.
Your right hand shall show you
a scene of terror:
your sharp arrows flying, nations 5
beneath your feet,
the courage of the king's foes melting away![b]

Your throne is like God's throne, 6
eternal,
your royal sceptre a sceptre of
righteousness.
You have loved right and hated 7
wrong;
so God, your God, has anointed
you
above your fellows with oil, the
token of joy.
Your robes are all fragrant with 8
myrrh and powder of aloes,
and the music of strings greets you
from a palace panelled with ivory.
A princess takes her place among 9
the noblest of your women,
a royal lady at your side in gold
of Ophir.

Listen, my daughter, hear my 10
words
and consider them:
forget your own people and your
father's house;
and, when the king desires your 11
beauty,
remember that he is your lord.
Do him obeisance, daughter of 12
Tyre,
and the richest in the land will
court you with gifts.

In the palace honour awaits her;[c] 13
she is a king's daughter,
arrayed in cloth-of-gold richly 14
embroidered.
Virgins shall follow her into the
presence of the king;
her companions shall be brought
to her,

---

[a] your limbs resplendent: *prob. rdg.*; *Heb.* and in your pomp prosper.
[b] the courage...away: *prob. rdg.*; *Heb. obscure.*
[c] honour awaits her: *prob. rdg.*; *Heb.* all honoured.

15 escorted with the noise of revels
and rejoicing
as they enter the king's palace.

16 You shall have sons, O king, in
place of your forefathers
and will make them rulers over
all the land.[a]

17 I will declare your fame to all
generations;
therefore the nations will praise
you for ever and ever.

46

1 God is our shelter and our refuge,
a timely help in trouble;

2 so we are not afraid when the earth
heaves
and the mountains are hurled into
the sea,

3 when its waters seethe in tumult
and the mountains quake before
his majesty.

4 There is a river whose streams
gladden the city of God,[b]
which the Most High has made
his holy dwelling;

5 God is in that city; she will not be
overthrown,
and he will help her at the break
of day.

6 Nations are in tumult, kingdoms
hurled down;
when he thunders, the earth surges
like the sea.

7 The LORD of Hosts is with us,
the God of Jacob our high stronghold.

8 Come and see what the LORD has
done,
the devastation he has brought
upon earth,

9 from end to end of the earth he
stamps out war:
he breaks the bow, he snaps the
spear
and burns the shield in the fire.

Let be then: learn that I am God, 10
high over the nations, high above
earth.

The LORD of Hosts is with us, 11
the God of Jacob our high stronghold.

47

Clap your hands, all you nations; 1
acclaim our God with shouts of joy.

How fearful is the LORD Most 2
High,
great sovereign over all the earth!

He lays the nations prostrate be- 3
neath us,
he lays peoples under our feet;

he chose our patrimony for us, 4
the pride of Jacob whom he loved.

God has gone up with shouts of 5
acclamation,
the LORD has gone up with a fan-
fare of trumpets.

Praise God,[c] praise him with 6
psalms;
praise our king, praise him with
psalms.

God is king of all the earth; 7
sing psalms with all your art.

God reigns over the nations, 8
God is seated on his holy throne.

The princes of the nations assemble 9
with the families of Abraham's
line;[d]
for the mighty ones of earth belong
to God,
and he is raised above them all.

48

The LORD is great and worthy of 1
our praise
in the city of our God, upon his
holy hill.

Fair and lofty, the joy of the whole 2
earth
is Zion's hill, like the farthest
reaches of the north,[e]
the hill of the great King's city.

---

[a] over all the land: or in all the earth.
[b] the city of God: or a wondrous city.
[c] Praise God: or Praise, you gods.
[d] the families of Abraham's line: prob. rdg.; Heb. the God of Abraham.
[e] Or of Zaphon.

3 In her palaces God is known for
  a tower of strength.
4 See how the kings all gather round
  her,
  marching on in company.
5 They are struck with amazement
  when they see her,
  they are filled with alarm and
  panic;
6 they are seized with trembling,
  they toss in pain like a woman in
  labour,
7 like the ships of Tarshish
  when an east wind wrecks them.
8 All we had heard we saw with
  our own eyes
  in the city of the LORD of Hosts,
  in the city of our God,
  the city which God plants firm for
  evermore.
9 O God, we re-enact the story of
  thy true love
  within thy temple;
10 the praise thy name deserves, O
  God,
  is heard at earth's farthest bounds.
  Thy hand is charged with justice,
11 and the hill of Zion rejoices,
  Judah's daughter-cities exult
  in thy judgements.

12 Make the round of Zion in procession,
  count the number of her towers,
13 take good note of her ramparts,
  pass her palaces in review,
  that you may tell generations yet
  to come:
14 Such is God,
  our God for ever and ever;
  he shall be our guide eternally.

49

1 Hear this, all you nations;
  listen, all who inhabit this world,
2 all mankind, every living man,
  rich and poor alike;
3 for the words that I speak are wise,
  my thoughtful heart is full of
  understanding.

I will set my ear to catch the moral 4
  of the story
and tell on the harp how I read the
  riddle;
why should I be afraid in evil times, 5
  beset by the wickedness of treacherous foes,
who trust in their riches 6
and boast of their great wealth?
Alas! no man can ever ransom 7
  himself
nor pay God the price of that
  release;
his ransom would cost too much, 8
for ever beyond his power to
  pay,
the ransom that would let him live 9
  on always
and never see the pit of death.

But remember this:[a] wise men 10
  must die;
stupid men, brutish men, all
  perish.[b]
The grave is their eternal home, 11
their dwelling for all time to come;
they may give their own names to
  estates,
but they must leave their riches to
  others.[c]
For men are like oxen whose life 12
  cannot last,
they are like cattle whose time is
  short.
Such is the fate of foolish men 13
and of all who seek to please them:
like sheep they run headlong into 14
  Sheol, the land of Death;
he is their shepherd and urges them
  on;
their flesh must rot away[d]
and their bodies be wasted by
  Sheol,
stripped of all honour.
But God will ransom my life, 15
he will take me from the power of
  Sheol.
Do not envy a man when he grows 16
  rich,
when the wealth of his family
  increases;

---

[a] But remember this: prob. rdg.; Heb. But he will remember this.
[b] Line transposed from here to follow verse 11.   [c] Line transposed from verse 10.
[d] and urges...rot away: prob. rdg.; Heb. obscure.

17 for he will take nothing when he
   dies,
   and his wealth will not go with him.
18 Though in his lifetime he counts
   himself happy
   and men praise him in his[a]
   prosperity,
19 he[b] will go to join the company of
   his forefathers
   who will never again see the light.
20 For men are like oxen whose life
   cannot last,
   they are like cattle whose time is
   short.

50

1 God, the LORD God, has spoken
   and summoned the world from the
   rising to the setting sun.
2 God shines out from Zion, perfect
   in beauty.
3 Our God is coming and will not
   keep silence:
   consuming fire runs before him
   and wreathes him closely round.[c]
4 He summons heaven on high and
   earth
   to the judgement of his people:
5 'Gather to me my loyal servants,
   all who by sacrifice have made a
   covenant with me.'
6 The heavens proclaim his justice,
   for God himself is the judge.

7 Listen, my people, and I will
   speak;
   I will bear witness against you, O
   Israel:
   I am God, your God,
8 shall I not[d] find fault with your
   sacrifices,
   though[e] your offerings are before
   me always?
9 I need take no young bull from
   your house,
   no he-goat from your folds;
10 for all the beasts of the forest are
   mine
   and the cattle in thousands on my
   hills.

11 I know every bird on those
   hills,
   the teeming life of the fields is my
   care.
12 If I were hungry, I would not tell
   you,
   for the world and all that is in it are
   mine.
13 Shall I eat the flesh of your bulls
   or drink the blood of he-goats?
14 Offer to God the sacrifice of
   thanksgiving
   and pay your vows to the Most
   High.
15 If you call upon me in time of
   trouble,
   I will come to your rescue, and you
   shall honour me.

16 God's word to the wicked man is
   this:
   What right have you to recite my
   laws
   and make so free with the words of
   my covenant,
17 you who hate correction
   and turn your back when I am
   speaking?
18 If you meet a thief, you choose him
   as your friend;
   you make common cause with
   adulterers;
19 you charge your mouth with
   wickedness
   and harness your tongue to slander.
20 You are for ever talking against
   your brother,
   stabbing your own mother's son in
   the back.
21 All this you have done, and shall I
   keep silence?
   You thought that I was another
   like yourself,
   but point by point I will rebuke
   you to your face.
22 Think well on this, you who forget
   God,
   or I will tear you in pieces and no
   one shall save you.
23 He who offers a sacrifice of
   thanksgiving

---

[a] him...his: prob. rdg.; Heb. you...your.   [b] he: prob. rdg.; Heb. you.
[c] and wreathes him closely round: or and rages round him.
[d] Or I will not.   [e] Or for.

does me due honour,
and to him who follows my way[a]
I will show the salvation of God.

51

1 Be gracious to me, O God, in thy
true love;
in the fullness of thy mercy blot
out my misdeeds.

2 Wash away all my guilt
and cleanse me from my sin.
3 For well I know my misdeeds,
and my sins confront me all the
day long.
4 Against thee, thee only, I have
sinned
and done what displeases thee,
so that thou mayest be proved
right in thy charge
and just in passing sentence.

5 In iniquity I was brought to birth
and my mother conceived me in
sin;
6 yet, though thou hast hidden the
truth in darkness,
through this mystery thou dost
teach me wisdom.
7 Take hyssop[b] and sprinkle me, that
I may be clean;
wash me, that I may become
whiter than snow;
8 let me hear the sounds of joy and
gladness,
let the bones dance which thou
hast broken.
9 Turn away thy face from my sins
and blot out all my guilt.

10 Create a pure heart in me, O God,
and give me a new and steadfast
spirit;
11 do not drive me from thy presence
or take thy holy spirit from me;
12 revive in me the joy of thy
deliverance
and grant me a willing spirit to
uphold me.

I will teach transgressors the ways 13
that lead to thee,
and sinners shall return to thee
again.
O LORD God, my deliverer, save 14
me from bloodshed,[c]
and I will sing the praises of thy
justice.
Open my lips, O Lord, 15
that my mouth may proclaim thy
praise.
Thou hast no delight in sacrifice; 16
if I brought thee an offering, thou
wouldst not accept it.
My sacrifice, O God, is a broken 17
spirit;
a wounded heart, O God, thou wilt
not despise.

Let it be thy pleasure to do good to 18
Zion,
to build anew the walls of Jerusalem.
Then only shalt thou delight in the 19
appointed sacrifices;[d]
then shall young bulls be offered on
thy altar.

52

Why make your wickedness your 1–2
boast, you man of might,
forging wild lies all day against
God's loyal servant?
Your slanderous tongue is sharp as
a razor.
You love evil and not good, 3
falsehood, not speaking the truth;
cruel gossip you love and slander- 4
ous talk.
So may God[e] pull you down to the 5
ground,
sweep you away, leave you ruined
and homeless,
uprooted from the land of the
living.
The righteous will look on, awe- 6
struck,
and laugh at his plight:

[a] him who follows my way: prob. rdg.; Heb. him who puts a way.
[b] Or marjoram.   [c] Or from punishment by death.
[d] Prob. rdg.; Heb. adds a whole-offering and one wholly consumed.
[e] Or So God will.

7 'This is the man', they say,
  'who does not make God his refuge,
  but trusts in his great wealth
  and takes refuge in wild lies.'

8 But I am like a spreading olive-tree
    in God's house;
  for I trust in God's true love for
    ever and ever.

9 I will praise thee for ever for what
    thou hast done,
  and glorify thy name among thy
    loyal servants;
  for that is good.

53

1[a] The impious fool says in his heart,
  'There is no God.'
  How vile men are, how depraved
    and loathsome;
  not one does anything good!

2 God looks down from heaven
    on all mankind
  to see if any act wisely,
  if any seek out God.

3 But all are unfaithful, all are rotten
    to the core;
  not one does anything good,
  no, not even one.

4 Shall they not rue it,
  these evildoers who devour my
    people
  as men devour bread,
  and never call upon God?

5 There they were in dire alarm
    when God scattered them.
  The crimes of the godless were
    frustrated;[b]
  for God had rejected them.

6 If only Israel's deliverance might
    come out of Zion!
  When God restores his people's
    fortunes,
  let Jacob rejoice, let Israel be glad.

54

1 Save me, O God, by the power of
    thy name,
  and vindicate me through thy
    might.

O God, hear my prayer,   2
listen to my supplication,
Insolent men rise to attack me,   3
ruthless men seek my life;
they give no thought to God.

But God is my helper,   4
the Lord the mainstay of my life.
May their own malice recoil on my   5
  watchful foes;
silence them by thy truth, O
  LORD.
I will offer thee a willing sacrifice   6
and praise thy name, for that is
  good;
God has rescued me from every   7
  trouble,
and I look on my enemies' downfall with delight.

55

Listen, O God, to my pleading,   1
do not hide thyself when I pray.
Hear me and answer,   2
for my cares give me no peace.
I am panic-stricken at the shouts   3
  of my enemies,
at the shrill clamour of the wicked;
for they heap trouble on me
and they revile me in their anger.
My heart is torn with anguish   4
and the terrors of death come upon
  me.
Fear and trembling overwhelm me   5
and I shudder from head to foot.
[c]Oh that I had the wings of a dove   6
to fly away and be at rest!
I should escape far away   7
and find a refuge in the wilderness;
soon I should find myself a   8
  sanctuary
from wind and storm,
from the blasts of calumny, O   9
  Lord,
from my enemies' contentious
  tongues.
I have seen violence and strife in
  the city;
day and night they encircle it,   10
all along its walls;
it is filled with trouble and mischief,

---

[a] *Verses 1–6: cp. Ps. 14. 1–7.*   [b] *The crimes...frustrated: prob. rdg.; Heb. obscure.*
[c] *Prob. rdg.; Heb. prefixes* And I said.

11 alive with rumour and scandal,
and its public square is never free
from violence and spite.

12 It was no enemy that taunted me,
or I should have avoided him;
no adversary that treated me with
scorn,
or I should have kept out of his
way.

13 It was you, a man of my own sort,
my comrade, my own dear friend,

14–15 with whom I kept pleasant
company
in the house of God.

May death strike them,
and may they[a] perish in confusion,
may they go down alive into
Sheol;
for their homes are haunts of evil!

16 But I will call upon God;
the LORD will save me.

17 Evening and morning and at noon
I nurse my woes, and groan.

18 He has heard my cry, he rescued
me
and gave me back my peace,
when they beset me like archers,[b]
massing against me,

19 like Ishmael and the desert tribes
and those who dwell in the East,
who have no respect for an oath
nor any fear of God.

20 Such men do violence to those at
peace with them
and break their promised word;

21 their speech is smoother than
butter
but their thoughts are of war;
their words are slippery as oil
but sharp as drawn swords.

22 Commit your fortunes to the
LORD,
and he will sustain you;
he will never let the righteous be
shaken.

Cast them, O God, into the pit of 23
destruction;
bloodthirsty and treacherous,
they shall not live out half their
days;
but I will put my trust in thee.

56

Be gracious to me, O God, for the 1
enemy persecute me,
my assailants harass me all day
long.
All the day long my watchful foes 2
persecute me;
countless are those who assail me.
Appear on high[c] in my day of fear; 3
I put my trust in thee.
With God to help me I will shout 4
defiance,
in God I trust and shall not be
afraid;
what can mortal men do to me?
All day long abuse of me is their 5
only theme,
all their thoughts are hostile.
In malice they are on the look-out, 6
and watch for me,
they dog my footsteps;
but, while they lie in wait for me,
it is they who will not[d] escape. 7
O God, in thy anger bring ruin on
the nations.

Enter my lament in thy book,[e] 8
store every tear in thy flask.[f]
Then my enemies will turn back 9
on the day when I call upon
thee;[g]
for this I know, that God is on my
side,
with God to help me I will shout 10
defiance.[h]
In God I trust and shall not be 11
afraid;
what can man do to me?
I have bound myself with vows to 12
thee, O God,

---

[a] *Prob. rdg.*; *Heb.* we.   [b] when...archers: *prob. rdg.*; *Heb. obscure.*
[c] Appear on high: *prob. rdg.*; *Heb.* Height.   [d] it is...not: *prob. rdg.*; *Heb.* for
iniquity.   [e] Enter...book: *prob. rdg.*; *Heb. obscure.*   [f] *Prob. rdg.*; *Heb. adds*
is it not in thy book?   [g] Enter...thee: *or* Thou hast entered my lament in thy
book, my tears are put in thy flask. Then my enemies turned back, when I called
upon thee.   [h] *Prob. rdg.*; *Heb. adds* With the LORD to help me I will shout defiance.

and will redeem them with due thank-offerings;

13 for thou hast rescued me from death[a]
to walk in thy presence, in the light of life.

57

1 Be gracious to me, O God, be gracious;
for I have made thee my refuge.
I will take refuge in the shadow of thy wings
until the storms are past.

2 I will call upon God Most High,
on God who fulfils his purpose for me.

3 He will send his truth and his love that never fails,
he will send from heaven and save me.
God himself will frustrate my persecutors;

4 for I lie down among lions, man-eaters,
whose teeth are spears and arrows
and whose tongues are sharp swords.

5 Show thyself, O God, high above the heavens;
let thy glory shine over all the earth.

6 Men have prepared a net to catch me as I walk,
but I bow my head to escape from it;
they have dug a pit in my path
but have fallen into it themselves.

7[b] My heart is steadfast, O God,
my heart is steadfast.
I will sing and raise a psalm;

8 awake, my spirit,
awake, lute and harp,
I will awake at dawn of day.[c]

9 I will confess thee, O Lord, among the peoples,

among the nations I will raise a psalm to thee,
for thy unfailing love is wide as the 10 heavens
and thy truth reaches to the skies.
Show thyself, O God, high above 11 the heavens;
let thy glory shine over all the earth.

58

Answer, you rulers:[d] are your 1 judgements just?
Do you decide impartially between man and man?
Never! Your hearts devise all 2 kinds of wickedness
and survey the violence that you have done on earth.

Wicked men, from birth they have 3 taken to devious ways;
liars, no sooner born than they go astray,
venomous with the venom of ser- 4 pents,
of the deaf asp which stops its ears
and will not listen to the sound of 5 the charmer,
however skilful his spells may be.

O God, break the teeth in their 6 mouths.
Break, O LORD, the jaws of the unbelievers.[e]
May they melt, may they vanish 7 like water,
may they wither like trodden grass,[f]
like an abortive birth which melts 8 away
or a still-born child which never sees[g] the sun!
All unawares, may they be rooted 9 up like[h] a thorn-bush,
like weeds which a man angrily[i] clears away!

---

[a] *Prob. rdg.; Heb. adds* is it not my feet from stumbling (*cp. Ps.* 116. 8).
[b] *Verses 7–11: cp. Ps.* 108. 1–5.   [e] at dawn of day: *or* the dawn.
[d] *Or* you gods.   [e] the jaws of the unbelievers: *or* the lions' fangs.
[f] like trodden grass: *prob. rdg.; Heb. obscure.*   [g] sees: *prob. rdg.; Heb.* they see
[h] may they be rooted up like: *prob. rdg.; Heb.* your pots.
[i] angrily: *prob. rdg.; Heb.* like anger.

10 The righteous shall rejoice that he
   has seen vengeance done
   and shall wash his feet in the blood
   of the wicked,
11 and men shall say,
   'There is after all a reward for the
   righteous;
   after all, there is a God that judges
   on earth.'

59

1 Rescue me from my enemies, O my
   God,
   be my tower of strength against
   all who assail me,
2 rescue me from these evildoers,
   deliver me from men of blood.
3 Savage men lie in wait for me,
   they lie in ambush ready to attack
   me;
   for no fault or guilt of mine, O
   Lord,
4–5 innocent as I am, they run to take
   post against me.
   But thou, Lord God of Hosts,
   Israel's God,
   do thou bestir thyself at my call,
   and look:
   awake, and punish all the nations.
   Have no mercy on villains and
   traitors,
6 who run wild at nightfall like
   dogs,
   snarling and prowling round the
   city,
15ᵃ wandering to and fro in search of
   food,
   and howling if they are not
   satisfied.
7 From their mouths comes a stream
   of nonsense;
   'But who will hear?' they murmur.
8 But thou, O Lord, dost laugh at
   them,
   and deride all the nations.
9 O my strength,ᵇ to thee I turn in
   the night-watches;
   for thou, O God, art my strong
   tower.

My God, in his true love, shall be 10
my champion;
with God's help, I shall gloat over
my watchful foes.
Wilt thou not kill them, lest my 11
people forget?
Scatter them by thy might and
bring them to ruin.
Deliver them,ᶜ O Lord, to be 12
destroyed
by their own sinful words;
let what they have spoken entrap
them in their pride.
Let them be cut off for their
cursing and falsehood;
bring them to an end in thy 13
wrath,
and they will be no more;
then they will know that God is
ruler in Jacob,
even to earth's farthest limits.ᵈ ᵉ
But I will sing of thy strength,   16
and celebrate thy love when
morning comes;
for thou hast been my strong
tower
and a sure retreat in days of
trouble.
O thou my strength, I will raise a 17
psalm to thee;
for thou, O God, art my strong
tower.

60

O God, thou hast cast us off and 1
broken us;
thou hast been angry and rebuked
us cruelly.
Thou hast made the land quake 2
and torn it open;
it gives way and crumbles into
pieces.
Thou hast made thy people drunk 3
with a bitter draught,
thou hast given us wine that makes
us stagger.
But thou hast given a warning to 4
those who fear thee,
to make their escape before the
sentence falls.

ᵃ Verse transposed.   ᵇ Or refuge.   ᶜ Deliver them: prob. rdg.; Heb. Our shield.
ᵈ Prob. rdg.; Heb. adds (14) who run wild at nightfall like dogs, snarling and
prowling round the city (cp. verse 6).   ᵉ Verse 15 transposed to follow verse 6.

5[a] Deliver those that are dear to thee;
save them with thy right hand, and
answer.

6 God has spoken from his sanc-
tuary:[b]
'I will go up now and measure out
Shechem;
I will divide the valley of Succoth
into plots;

7 Gilead and Manasseh are mine;
Ephraim is my helmet, Judah my
sceptre;

8 Moab is my wash-bowl, I fling my
shoes at Edom;
Philistia is the target of my anger.'

9 Who can bring me to the fortified
city,
who can guide me to Edom,

10 since thou, O God, hast abandoned
us
and goest not forth with our
armies?

11 Grant us help against the enemy,
for deliverance by man is a vain
hope.

12 With God's help we shall do
valiantly,
and God himself will tread our
enemies under foot.

61

1 Hear my cry, O God, listen to my
prayer.

2 From the end of the earth I call to
thee with fainting heart;
lift me up and set me upon a rock.

3 For thou hast been my shelter,
a tower for refuge from the enemy.

4 In thy tent will I make my home
for ever
and find my shelter under the
cover of thy wings.

5 For thou, O God, hast heard my
vows
and granted the wish[c] of all who
revere thy name.

6 To the king's life add length of
days,

year upon year for many generations;

may he dwell in God's presence for 7
ever,
may true and constant love preserve him.

So will I ever sing psalms in honour 8
of thy name
as I fulfil my vows day after day.

62

Truly my heart waits silently for 1
God;
my deliverance comes from him.

In truth he is my rock of deliver- 2
ance,
my tower of strength, so that I
stand unshaken.

How long will you assail a man 3
with your threats,
all battering on a leaning wall?

In truth men plan to topple him 4
from his height,
and stamp on the fallen stones.[d]
With their lips they bless him, the
hypocrites,
but revile him in their hearts.

Truly my heart waits silently for 5
God;
my hope of deliverance comes
from him.

In truth he is my rock of deliver- 6
ance,
my tower of strength, so that I am
unshaken.

My deliverance and my honour 7
depend upon God,
God who is my rock of refuge and
my shelter.

Trust always in God, my people, 8
pour out your hearts before him;
God is our shelter.

In very truth men are a puff of 9
wind,
all men are faithless;
put them in the balance and they
can only rise,
all of them lighter than wind.

[a] Verses 5–12: cp. Ps. 108. 6–13.   [b] from his sanctuary: or in his holiness.
[c] Prob. rdg.; Heb. the inheritance.
[d] the fallen stones: transposed from end of verse 3.

10 Put no trust in extortion,
   do not be proud of stolen goods;
   though wealth breeds wealth, set
      not your heart on it.
11 One thing God has spoken,
   two things I have learnt:
   'Power belongs to God'
12 and 'True love, O Lord, is thine';
   thou dost requite a man for his
      deeds.

63

1 O God, thou art my God, I seek
      thee early
   with a heart that thirsts for thee
   and a body wasted with longing
      for thee,
   like a dry and thirsty land that has
      no water.
2 So longing, I come before thee in
      the sanctuary
   to look upon thy power and
      glory.
3 Thy true love is better than life;
   therefore I will sing thy praises.
4 And so I bless thee all my life
   and in thy name lift my hands in
      prayer.
5 I am satisfied as with a rich and
      sumptuous feast
   and wake the echoes with thy
      praise.
6 When I call thee to mind upon my
      bed
   and think on thee in the watches
      of the night,
7 remembering how thou hast been
      my help
   and that I am safe in the shadow of
      thy wings,
8 then I humbly follow thee with all
      my heart,
   and thy right hand is my support.

9 Those who seek my life, bent on
      evil,
   shall sink into the depths of the
      earth;

they shall be given over to the 10
   sword;
they shall be carrion for jackals.

The king shall rejoice in God,   11
and whoever swears by God's
   name shall exult;
the voice of falsehood shall be
   silenced.

64

Hear me, O God, hear my lament; 1
keep me safe from the threats of
   the enemy.
Hide me from the factions of the 2
   wicked,
from the turbulent mob of evildoers,
who sharpen their tongues like 3
   swords
and wing their cruel words like
   arrows,[a]
to shoot down the innocent from 4
   cover,
shooting suddenly, themselves unseen.
They boldly[b] hide their snares,   5
sure that none will see them;
they hatch their secret plans[c] with 6
   skill and cunning,
with evil[d] purpose and deep
   design.
But God with his arrow shoots 7
   them down,
and sudden is their overthrow.

They may repeat their wicked 8
   tales,[e]
but their mischievous tongues[f] are
   their undoing.
All who see their fate take fright
   at it,
every man is afraid;   9
'This is God's work', they declare;
they learn their lesson from what
   he has done.
The righteous rejoice and seek 10
   refuge in the LORD
and all the upright exult.

---

[a] and wing...arrows: *prob. rdg.*; *Heb.* they tread their arrow a cruel word.
[b] *See first note on verse 8.*   [c] their secret plans: *prob. rdg.*; *Heb. unintelligible.*
[d] evil: *prob. rdg.*; *Heb.* man.
[e] They...tales: *transposed from after* boldly *in verse 5.*
[f] their mischievous tongues: *prob. rdg.*; *Heb.* against them their tongues.

65

1-2 We owe thee praise, O God, in Zion;
  thou hearest prayer, vows shall be paid to thee.
3 All men shall lay their guilt before thee:
  our sins are too heavy for us;
  only thou canst blot them out.
4 Happy is the man of thy choice, whom thou dost bring
  to dwell in thy courts;
  let us enjoy the blessing of thy house,
  thy holy temple.
5 By deeds of terror answer us with victory,
  O God of our deliverance,
  in whom men trust from the ends of the earth
  and far-off seas;
6 thou art girded with strength,
  and by thy might dost fix the mountains in their place,
7 dost calm the rage of the seas and their raging waves.ᵃ
8 The dwellers at the ends of the earth
  hold thy signs in awe;
  thou makest morning and evening sing aloud in triumph.

9 Thou dost visit the earth and give it abundance,
  as often as thou dost enrich it
  with the waters of heaven, brimming in their channels,
  providing rainᵇ for men.
  For this is thy provision for it,
10 watering its furrows, levelling its ridges,
  softening it with showers and blessing its growth.
11 Thou dost crown the year with thy good gifts
  and the palm-trees drip with sweet juice;
12 the pastures in the wild are rich with blessing
  and the hills wreathed in happiness,

the meadows are clothed with sheep 13
and the valleys mantled in corn,
so that they shout, they break into song.

66

Acclaim our God, all men on earth; 1
let psalms declare the glory of his name, 2
make glorious his praise.
Say unto God, 'How fearful are thy works! 3
Thy foes cower before the greatness of thy strength.
All men on earth fall prostrate in thy presence, 4
and sing to thee, sing psalms in honour of thy name.'
Come and see all that God has done, 5
tremendous in his dealings with mankind.
He turned the waters into dry land 6
so that his people passed through the sea on foot;
there did we rejoice in him.ᶜ

He rules for ever by his power, 7
his eye rests on the nations;
let no rebel rise in defiance.

Bless our God, all nations; 8
let his praise be heard far and near.
He set us in the land of the living; 9
he keeps our feet from stumbling.
For thou, O God, hast put us to the proof 10
and refined us like silver.
Thou hast caught us in a net, 11
thou hast bound our bodies fast;
thou hast let men ride over our heads. 12
We went through fire and water,
but thou hast brought us out into liberty.

I will bring sacrifices into thy temple 13
and fulfil my vows to thee,

ᵃ Prob. rdg.; Heb. adds and tumult of people.   ᵇ Or corn.
ᶜ there...him: or where we see this, we will rejoice in him.

14 vows which I made with my own
   lips
   and swore with my own mouth
   when in distress.
15 I will offer thee fat beasts as
   sacrifices
   and burn rams as a savoury
   offering;
   I will make ready oxen and he-
   goats.

16 Come, listen, all who fear God,
   and I will tell you all that he has
   done for me;
17 I lifted up my voice in prayer,
   his high praise was on my lips.
18 If I had cherished evil thoughts,
   the Lord would not have heard me;
19 but in truth God has heard
   and given heed to my prayer.
20 Blessed is God
   who has not withdrawn his love
   and care from me.

67

1 God be gracious to us and bless
  us,
  God make his face shine upon
  us,
2 that his ways may be known on
  earth
  and his saving power among all the
  nations.
3 Let the peoples praise thee, O God;
  let all peoples praise thee.
4 Let all nations rejoice and shout in
  triumph;
  for thou dost judge the peoples
  with justice
  and guidest the nations of the
  earth.
5 Let the peoples praise thee, O God;
  let all peoples praise thee.
6 The earth has given its increase
  and God, our God, will bless us.

7 God grant us his blessing,
  that all the ends of the earth may
  fear him.

68

God arises and his enemies are 1
scattered;
those who hate him flee before him,
driven away like smoke in the 2
wind;
like wax melting at the fire,
the wicked perish at the presence
of God.
But the righteous are joyful, they 3
exult before God,
they are jubilant and shout for
joy.

Sing the praises of God, raise a 4
psalm to his name,
extol him who rides over the
desert plains.[a]
Be joyful[b] and exult before him,
father of the fatherless, the 5
widow's champion –
God in his holy dwelling-place.
God gives the friendless a home   6
and brings out the prisoner safe
and sound;
but rebels must live in the
scorching desert.

O God, when thou didst go forth 7
before thy people,
marching across the wilderness,
earth trembled, the very heavens 8
quaked
before God the lord of Sinai,
before God the God of Israel.

Of thy bounty, O God, thou dost 9
refresh with rain
thy own land in its weariness,
the land which thou thyself didst
provide,
where thy own people made their 10
home,
which thou, O God, in thy goodness
providest for the poor.

The Lord proclaims good news:[c] 11–13
'Kings with their armies have fled
headlong.'

---

[a] over the desert plains: or on the plains.
[b] Be joyful: prob. rdg.; Heb. In the LORD is his name.
[c] proclaims good news: or gives the word, women bearing good news.

O mighty host, will you linger
  among the sheepfolds
while the women in your tents
  divide the spoil –
an image of a dove, its wings
  sheathed in silver
and its pinions in yellow gold –
14 while the Almighty scatters kings
  far and wide
like snowflakes falling on Zalmon?

15 The hill of Bashan is a hill of God
  indeed,
a hill of many peaks is Bashan's
  hill.
16 But, O hill of many peaks, why
  gaze in envy
at the hill where the LORD delights
  to dwell,
where the LORD himself will live
  for ever?
17 Twice ten thousand were God's
  chariots, thousands upon thousands,
when the Lord came in holiness
  from Sinai.[a]
18 Thou didst go up to thy lofty home
  with captives in thy train,
having received tribute from
  men;
in the presence of the LORD God no
  rebel could live.

19 Blessed is the Lord:
he carries us day by day,
God our salvation.
20 Our God is a God who saves us,
in the LORD God's hand lies
  escape from death.[b]
21 God himself will smite[c] the head of
  his enemies,
those proud sinners with their
  flowing locks.
22 The Lord says, 'I will return from
  the Dragon,[d]
I will return from the depths of the
  sea,

that you may dabble your feet in 23
  blood,
while the tongues of your dogs are
  eager[e] for it.'

Thy procession, O God, comes into 24
  view,
the procession of my God and King
  into the sanctuary:
at its head the singers, next come 25
  minstrels,
girls among them playing on
  tambourines.
In the great concourse they bless 26
  God,
all Israel assembled[f] bless the
  LORD.
There is the little tribe of Benjamin 27
  leading them,
there the company of Judah's
  princes,
the princes of Zebulun and of
  Naphtali.

O God, in virtue of thy power[g] – 28
that godlike power which has acted
  for us –
command kings to bring gifts to 29
  thee
for the honour of thy temple in
  Jerusalem.
Rebuke those wild beasts of the 30
  reeds, that herd of bulls,
the bull-calf warriors of the
  nations;[h]
scatter these nations which revel
  in war;
make them bring tribute from 31
  Egypt,
precious stones and silver from
  Pathros;[i]
let Nubia stretch out[j] her hands to
  God.

All you kingdoms of the world, 32
  sing praises to God,
sing psalms to the Lord,

---

[a] came...from Sinai: prob. rdg.; Heb. obscure.   [b] in the LORD God's
hand...death: or death is expelled by the LORD God.   [c] will smite: or smites.
[d] the Dragon: or Bashan.   [e] are eager: prob. rdg.; Heb. from enemies.
[f] assembled: prob. rdg.; Heb. obscure.   [g] O God...power: prob. rdg.; Heb.
Your God your power.   [h] See first note on verse 31.   [i] precious...Pathros:
prob. rdg., transposed from verse 30 and slightly altered.   [j] stretch out: prob.
rdg.; Heb. obscure.

33 to him who rides on the heavens,
      the ancient heavens.
   Hark! he speaks in the mighty
      thunder.
34 Ascribe all might to God, Israel's
      High God,
   Israel's pride and might throned in
      the skies.
35 Terrible is God as he comes from
      his sanctuary;
   he is Israel's own God,
   who gives to his people might and
      abundant power.

   Blessed be God.

69

1 Save me, O God;
   for the waters have risen up to my
      neck.
2 I sink in muddy depths and have
      no foothold;
   I am swept into deep water, and
      the flood carries me away.
3 I am wearied with crying out, my
      throat is sore,
   my eyes grow dim as I wait for
      God to help me.
4 Those who hate me without reason
      are more than the hairs of my
      head;
   they outnumber my hairs, those
      who accuse me falsely.
   How can I give back what I have
      not stolen?
5 O God, thou knowest how foolish
      I am,
   and my guilty deeds are not hidden
      from thee.
6 Let none of those who look to thee
      be shamed on my account,
   O Lord GOD of Hosts;
   let none who seek thee be humbled
      through my fault,
   O God of Israel.
7 For in thy service I have suffered
      reproach;
   I dare not show my face for
      shame.

I have become a stranger to my 8
      brothers,
an alien to my own mother's
      sons;
bitter enemies of thy temple tear 9
      me in pieces;[a]
those who reproach thee reproach
      me.
I have broken my spirit with 10
      fasting,
only to lay myself open to many
      reproaches.
I have made sackcloth my clothing 11
and have become a byword among
      them.
Those who sit by the town gate 12
      talk about me;
drunkards sing songs about me in
      their cups.
But I lift up this prayer to thee, O 13
      LORD:
accept me[b] now in thy great love,
answer me with thy sure deliver-
      ance, O God.
Rescue me from the mire, do not 14
      let me sink;
let me be rescued from the muddy
      depths,[c]
so that no flood may carry me 15
      away,
no abyss swallow me up,
no deep close over me.
Answer me, O LORD, in the good- 16
      ness of thy unfailing love,
turn towards me in thy great
      affection.
I am thy servant, do not hide thy 17
      face from me.
Make haste to answer me, for I am
      in distress.
Come near to me and redeem me; 18
ransom me, for I have many
      enemies.

Thou knowest what reproaches I 19
      bear,
all my anguish is seen by thee.
Reproach has broken my heart, 20
my shame and my dishonour[d] are
      past hope;

---

[a] bitter...pieces: or zeal for thy temple has eaten me up (cp. John 2. 17).
[b] Prob. rdg.; Heb. acceptance.
[c] from...depths: prob. rdg.; Heb. from my haters and from the depths.
[d] my shame and my dishonour: transposed from after reproaches in verse 19.

I looked for consolation and received none,
for comfort and did not find any.
21 They put poison in my food
and gave me vinegar when I was
thirsty.
22 May their own table be a snare to
them
and their sacred feasts lure them to
their ruin;
23 may their eyes be darkened so that
they do not see,
let a continual ague shake their
loins.
24 Pour out thine indignation upon
them
and let thy burning anger overtake
them.
25 May their settlements be desolate,
and no one living in their tents;
26 for they pursue him whom thou
hast struck down
and multiply the torments of those
whom thou hast wounded.
27 Give them the punishment their
sin deserves;[a]
exclude them from thy righteous
mercy;
28 let them be blotted out from the
book of life
and not be enrolled among the
righteous.

29 But by thy saving power, O God,
lift me high
above my pain and my distress,
30 then I will praise God's name in
song
and glorify him with thanksgiving;
31 that will please the LORD more
than the offering of a bull,
a young bull with horn and cloven
hoof.

32 See and rejoice, you humble folk,
take heart, you seekers after God;
33 for the LORD listens to the poor
and does not despise those bound
to his service.
34 Let sky and earth praise him,
the seas and all that move in
them,

for God will deliver Zion   35–36
and rebuild the cities of Judah.
His servants' children shall inherit
them;
they shall dwell there in their own
possession
and all who love his name shall
live in them.

70

Show me favour,[b] O God, and save 1[c]
me;
hasten to help me, O LORD.
Let all who seek my life be brought 2
to shame and dismay,
let all who love to hurt me shrink
back disgraced;
let those who cry 'Hurrah!' at my   3
downfall
turn back at the shame they incur,
but let all who seek thee   4
be jubilant and rejoice in thee,
and let those who long for thy
saving help ever cry,
'All glory to God!'

But I am poor and needy;   5
O God, hasten to my aid.
Thou art my help, my salvation;
O LORD, make no delay.

71

In thee, O LORD, I have taken   1
refuge;
never let me be put to shame.
As thou art righteous rescue me   2
and save my life;
hear me and set me free,
be a rock of refuge for me,   3
where I may ever find safety at thy
call;
for thou art my towering crag and
stronghold.
O God, keep my life safe from the   4
wicked,
from the clutches of unjust and
cruel men.

Thou art my hope, O Lord,   5
my trust, O LORD, since boyhood.

[a] Give them...deserves: or Add punishment to punishment.   [b] Show me
favour: prob. rdg., cp. Ps. 40. 13; Heb. om.   [c] Verses 1–5: cp. Ps. 40. 13–17.

6 From birth I have leaned upon thee,
my protector since I left[a] my mother's womb.[b]

7 To many I seem a solemn warning;
but I have thee for my strong refuge.

8 My mouth shall be full of thy praises,
I shall tell of thy splendour all day long.

9 Do not cast me off when old age comes,
nor forsake me when my strength fails,

10 when my enemies' rancour bursts upon me[c]
and those who watch me whisper together,

11 saying, 'God has forsaken him;
after him! seize him; no one will rescue him.'

12 O God, do not stand aloof from me;
O my God, hasten to my help.

13 Let all my traducers be shamed and dishonoured,
let all who seek my hurt be covered with scorn.

14 But I will wait in continual hope,
I will praise thee again and yet again;

15 all day long thy righteousness,
thy saving acts, shall be upon my lips.
Thou shalt ever be the theme of my praise,[d]
although I have not the skill of a poet.

16 I will begin with a tale of great deeds, O Lord GOD,
and sing of thy righteousness, thine alone.

17 O God, thou hast taught me from boyhood,
all my life I have proclaimed thy marvellous works;

18 and now that I am old and my hairs are grey,
forsake me not, O God,

when I extol thy mighty arm to future generations,
19 thy power and righteousness, O God, to highest heaven;
for thou hast done great things.
Who is like thee, O God?

20 Thou hast made me pass through bitter and deep distress,
yet dost revive me once again
and lift me again from earth's watery depths.

21 Restore me to honour, turn and comfort me,
22 then I will praise thee on the lute for thy faithfulness, O God;
I will sing psalms to thee with the harp,
thou Holy One of Israel;
23 songs of joy shall be on my lips;
I will sing thee psalms, because thou hast redeemed me.
24 All day long my tongue shall tell of thy righteousness;
shame and disgrace await those who seek my hurt.

72

1 O God, endow the king with thy own justice,
and give thy righteousness to a king's son,
2 that he may judge thy people rightly
and deal out justice to the poor and suffering.
3 May hills and mountains afford thy people
peace and prosperity in righteousness.
4 He shall give judgement for the suffering
and help those of the people that are needy;
he shall crush the oppressor.
5 He shall live as long as the sun endures,
long as the moon, age after age.
6 He shall be like rain falling on early crops,
like showers watering[e] the earth.

---

[a] my...left: or who didst bring me out from.   [b] See note on verse 15.
[c] enemies'...me: prob. rdg.; Heb. enemies say of me.   [d] Line transposed
from verse 6.   [e] like showers watering: prob. rdg.; Heb. unintelligible.

7 In his days righteousness shall
flourish,
prosperity abound until the moon
is no more.
8 May he hold sway from sea to sea,
from the River to the ends of the
earth.
9 Ethiopians shall crouch low before
him;
his enemies shall lick the dust.
10 The kings of Tarshish and the
islands shall bring gifts,
the kings of Sheba and Seba shall
present their tribute,
11 and all kings shall pay him homage,
all nations shall serve him.
12 For he shall rescue the needy from
their rich oppressors,
the distressed who have no protector.
13 May he have pity on the needy and
the poor,
deliver the poor from death;
14 may he redeem them from oppression and violence
and may their blood be precious in
his eyes.

15 May the king live long
and receive gifts of gold*a* from
Sheba;
prayer be made for him continually,
blessings be his all the day long.
16 May there be abundance of corn in
the land,
growing in plenty to the tops of the
hills;
may the crops flourish like
Lebanon,
and the sheaves*b* be numberless as
blades of grass.
17 Long may the king's name endure,
may it live for ever like the sun;
so shall all peoples pray to be
blessed as he was,
all nations tell of his happiness.

18 Blessed be the LORD God, the God
of Israel,

who alone does marvellous things;
blessed be his glorious name for 19
ever,
and may his glory fill all the earth.
Amen, Amen.

Here end the prayers of David son 20
of Jesse.

BOOK 3

73

How good God is to the upright!*c* 1
How good to those who are pure in
heart!

My feet had almost slipped, 2
my foothold had all but given way,
because the boasts of sinners 3
roused my envy
when I saw how they prosper.
No pain, no suffering is theirs; 4
they are sleek and sound in limb;
they are not plunged in trouble as 5
other men are,
nor do they suffer the torments of
mortal men.
Therefore pride is their collar of 6
jewels
and violence the robe that wraps
them round.
Their eyes gleam through folds of 7
fat;
while vain fancies pass through
their minds.
Their talk is all sneers and 8
malice;
scornfully they spread their calumnies.
Their slanders reach up to heaven, 9
while their tongues ply to and fro
on earth.
And so my people follow their 10
lead*d*
and find nothing to blame in them,*e*
even though they say, 'What does 11
God know?
The Most High neither knows nor
cares.'

a Or frankincense.   *b* the sheaves: *prob. rdg.*; *Heb.* from a city.
c How...upright: *prob. rdg.*; *Heb.* How good it is to Israel!
d their lead: *prob. rdg.*; *Heb.* hither.
e and find...in them: *prob. rdg.*; *Heb. obscure.*

12 So wicked men talk, yet still they
    prosper,
    and rogues*a* amass great wealth.

13 So it was all in vain that I kept my
    heart pure
    and washed my hands in innocence.
14 For all day long I suffer torment
    and am punished every morning.
15 Yet had I let myself talk on in this
    fashion,
    I should have betrayed the family
    of God.
16 So I set myself to think this out
    but I found it too hard for me,
17 until I went into God's sacred
    courts;
    there I saw clearly what their end
    would be.

18 How often thou dost set them on
    slippery ground
    and drive them headlong into ruin!
19 Then in a moment how dreadful
    their end,
    cut off root and branch by death
    with all its terrors,
20 like a dream when a man rouses
    himself, O Lord,
    like images in sleep which are
    dismissed on waking!

21 When my heart was embittered
    I felt the pangs of envy,
22 I would not understand, so brutish
    was I,
    I was a mere beast in thy sight, O
    God.
23 Yet I am always with thee,
    thou holdest my right hand;
24 thou dost guide me by thy counsel
    and afterwards wilt receive me
    with glory.
25 Whom have I in heaven but thee?
    And having thee,*b* I desire nothing
    else on earth.
26 Though heart and body fail,
    yet God is my possession for ever.

They who are far from thee are 27
    lost;
    thou dost destroy all who wanton-
    ly forsake thee.
But my chief good is to be near 28
    thee, O God;
    I have chosen thee, Lord GOD, to
    be my refuge.*c*

74

Why hast thou cast us off, O God? 1
    Is it for ever?
Why art thou so stern, so angry
    with the sheep of thy flock?
Remember the assembly of thy 2
    people,
    taken long since for thy own,*d*
    and Mount Zion, which was thy
    home.
Now at last*e* restore what was 3
    ruined beyond repair,
    the wreck that the foe has made of
    thy sanctuary.

The shouts of thy enemies filled the 4
    holy place,*f*
    they planted their standards there
    as tokens of victory.
They brought it crashing down,*g* 5
    like woodmen plying their axes in
    the forest;
they ripped the carvings clean 6
    out,
    they smashed them with hatchet
    and pick.
They set fire to thy sanctuary, 7
    tore down and polluted the shrine
    sacred to thy name.
They said to themselves, 'We will 8
    sweep them away',
    and all over the land they burnt
    God's holy places.*h*

We cannot see what lies before us,*i* 9
    we have no prophet now;
    we have no one who knows how
    long this is to last.

---

a yet...rogues: *prob. rdg.*; *Heb.* those at ease for ever.   *b* *Or* And compared
with thee.   *c* *Prob. rdg.*; *Heb. adds* to tell all thy works.   *d* *Prob. rdg.*; *Heb.*
adds thou didst redeem the tribe of thy possession.   *e* Now at last: *prob.*
rdg.; *Heb.* Thy steps.   *f* the holy place: *or* thy meeting place.
g They...down: *prob. rdg.*; *Heb. unintelligible.*   *h* holy places: *or* meeting places.
i what...us: *prob. rdg.*; *Heb.* our signs.

10 How long, O God, will the enemy
taunt thee?
Will the adversary pour scorn on
thy name for ever?

11 Why dost thou hold back thy
hand,
why keep thy right hand within
thy bosom?

12 But thou, O God, thou king from
of old,
thou mighty conqueror all the
world over,

13 by thy power thou didst cleave the
sea-monster in two
and break the sea-serpent's heads
above the waters;

14 thou didst crush Leviathan's many
heads
and throw him to the sharks[a] for
food.

15 Thou didst open channels for
spring and torrent;
thou didst dry up rivers never
known to fail.

16 The day is thine, and the night is
thine also,
thou didst ordain the light of moon
and sun;

17 thou hast fixed all the regions of
the earth;
summer and winter, thou didst
create them both.

18 Remember, O Lord, the taunts of
the enemy,
the scorn a savage nation pours on
thy name.

19 Cast not to the beasts the soul that
confesses thee;
forget not for ever the sufferings of
thy servants.

20 Look upon thy creatures:[b] they are
filled with hatred,
and earth is the haunt of violence.

21 Let not the oppressed be shamed
and turned away;
let the poor and the downtrodden
praise thy name.

22 Rise up, O God, maintain thy own
cause;

remember how brutal men taunt
thee all day long.
Ignore no longer the cries of thy 23
assailants,
the mounting clamour of those
who defy thee.

75

We give thee thanks, O God, we 1
give thee thanks;
thy name is brought very near to
us
in the story of thy wonderful
deeds.

I seize the appointed time 2
and then I judge mankind with
justice.
When the earth rocks, with all who 3
live on it,
I make its pillars firm.
To the boastful I say, 'Boast no 4
more',
and to the wicked, 'Do not toss
your proud horns:
toss not your horns against high 5
heaven
nor speak arrogantly against your
Creator.'
No power from the east nor from 6
the west,
no power from the wilderness, can
raise a man up.
For God is judge; 7
he puts one man down and raises
up another.
The Lord holds a cup in his hand, 8
and the wine foams in it, hot with
spice;
he offers it to every man for drink,
and all the wicked on earth must
drain it to the dregs.
But I will glorify him for ever; 9
I will sing praises to the God of
Jacob.

I will break off the horns of the 10
wicked,
but the horns of the righteous shall
be lifted high.

[a] to the sharks: *prob. rdg.*; *Heb.* to a people, desert-dwellers.
[b] thy creatures: *prob. rdg.*; *Heb.* the covenant, because.

76

1 In Judah God is known,
 his name is great in Israel;
2 his tent is pitched in Salem,
 in Zion his battle-quarters are set
 up.[a]
3 He has broken the flashing arrows,
 shield and sword and weapons of
 war.

4 Thou art terrible, O Lord, and
 mighty:
5 men that lust for plunder stand
 aghast,
 the boldest swoon away,
 and the strongest cannot lift a
 hand.
6 At thy rebuke, O God of Jacob,
 rider and horse fall senseless.
7 Terrible art thou, O Lord;
 who can stand in thy presence
 when thou art angry?
8 Thou didst give sentence out of
 heaven;
 the earth was afraid and kept
 silence.
9 O God, at thy rising[b] in judgement
 to deliver all humble men on the
 earth,
10 for all her fury Edom shall confess
 thee,
 and the remnant left in Hamath
 shall dance in worship.

11 Make vows to the LORD your God,
 and pay them duly;
 let the peoples all around him
 bring their tribute;[c]
12 for he breaks the spirit of princes,
 he is the terror of the kings on
 earth.

77

1 I cried aloud to God,
 I cried to God, and he heard me.
2 In the day of my distress I sought
 the Lord,

and by night I lifted[d] my outspread hands in prayer.
I lay sweating and nothing would
 cool me;
I refused all comfort.
When I called God to mind, I 3
 groaned;
as I lay thinking, darkness came
 over my spirit.
My eyelids were tightly closed; 4
I was dazed and I could not speak.
My thoughts went back to times 5
 long past,
I remembered forgotten years;
all night long I was in deep 6
 distress,
as I lay thinking, my spirit was
 sunk in despair.

Will the Lord reject us for ever- 7
 more
and never again show favour?
Has his unfailing love now failed 8
 us utterly,
must his promise time and again be
 unfulfilled?
Has God forgotten to be gracious, 9
 has he in anger withheld his
 mercies?
'Has his right hand', I said, 'lost 10
 its grasp?
Does it hang powerless,[e] the arm
 of the Most High?'

But then, O LORD, I call to mind 11
 thy deeds;[f]
I recall thy wonderful acts in
 times gone by.
I meditate upon thy works 12
and muse on all that thou hast done.
O God, thy way is holy; 13
what god is so great as our God?
Thou art the God who workest 14
 miracles;
thou hast shown the nations thy
 power.
With thy strong arm thou didst 15
 redeem thy people,
 the sons of Jacob and Joseph.

---

[a] are set up: prob. rdg.; Heb. thither (at beginning of verse 3).
[b] O God...rising: prob. rdg.; Heb. When God rises.
[c] Prob. rdg.; Heb. adds for the terror (cp. verse 12). [d] I lifted: prob. rdg.; Heb. om.
[e] lost...powerless: prob. rdg.; Heb. unintelligible.
[f] Prob. rdg.; Heb. then I call to mind the deeds of the LORD, for.

16 The waters saw thee, O God,
   they saw thee and writhed in
      anguish;
   the ocean was troubled to its
      depths.
17 The clouds poured water, the skies
      thundered,
   thy arrows flashed hither and
      thither.
18 The sound of thy thunder was in
      the whirlwind,[a]
   thy lightnings lit up the world,
   earth shook and quaked.
19 Thy path was through the sea, thy
      way through mighty waters,
   and no man marked thy footsteps.
20 Thou didst guide thy people like a
      flock of sheep,
   under the hand of Moses and
      Aaron.

78

1 Mark my teaching, O my people,
   listen to the words I am to speak.
2 I will tell you a story with a
      meaning,
   I will expound the riddle of things
      past,
3 things that we have heard and
      know,
   and our fathers have repeated to
      us.
4 From their sons we will not hide
   the praises of the LORD and his
      might
   nor the wonderful acts he has
      performed;
   then they shall repeat them to the
      next generation.
5 He laid on Jacob a solemn charge
   and established a law in Israel,
   which he commanded our fathers
      to teach their sons,
6 that it might be known to a future
      generation,
   to children yet unborn,
   and these would repeat it to their
      sons in turn.
7 He charged them to put their trust
      in God,
   to hold his great acts ever in mind
   and to keep all his commandments;

not to do as their fathers did,   8
a disobedient and rebellious race,
a generation with no firm purpose,
with hearts not fixed steadfastly
   on God.

The men of Ephraim, bowmen all 9
   and marksmen,
turned and ran in the hour of
   battle.
They had not kept God's covenant 10
and had refused to live by his law;
they forgot all that he had done   11
and the wonderful acts which he
   had shown them.

He did wonders in their fathers' 12
   sight
in the land of Egypt, the country
   of Zoan:
he divided the sea and took them 13
   through it,
making the water stand up like
   banks on either side.
He led them with a cloud by day 14
and all night long with a glowing
   fire.
He cleft the rock in the wilderness 15
and gave them water to drink,
   abundant as the sea;
he brought streams out of the cliff 16
and made water run down like
   rivers.
But they sinned against him yet 17
   again:
in the desert they defied the Most
   High,
they tried God's patience wilfully, 18
demanding food to satisfy their
   hunger.
They vented their grievance   19
   against God and said,
'Can God spread a table in the
   wilderness?'
When he struck a rock, water   20
   gushed out
until the gullies overflowed;
they said, 'Can he give bread as well,
can he provide meat for his people?'
When he heard this, the LORD was 21
   filled with fury:
fire raged against Jacob,
anger blazed up against Israel,

_____
[a] Or in the chariot-wheels.

22 because they put no trust in God
and had no faith in his power to
save.
23 Then he gave orders to the skies
above
and threw open heaven's doors,
24 he rained down manna for them to
eat
and gave them the grain of heaven.
25 So men ate the bread of angels;
he sent them food to their heart's
desire.
26 He let loose the east wind from
heaven
and drove the south wind by his
power;
27 he rained meat like a dust-storm
upon them,
flying birds like the sand of the
sea-shore,
28 which he made settle all over the
camp
round the tents where they lived.
29 So the people ate and were well
filled,
for he had given them what they
craved.
30 Yet they did not abandon their
complaints*a*
even while the food was in their
mouths.
31 Then the anger of God blazed up
against them;
he spread death among their
stoutest men
and brought the young men of
Israel to the ground.

32 In spite of all, they persisted in
their sin
and had no faith in his wonderful
acts.
33 So in one moment he snuffed out
their lives
and ended their years in calamity.
34 When he struck them, they began
to seek him,
they would turn and look eagerly
for God;
35 they remembered that God was
their Creator,
that God Most High was their
deliverer.

But still they beguiled him with 36
words
and deceived him with fine
speeches;
they were not loyal to him in their 37
hearts
nor were they faithful to his
covenant.
Yet he wiped out their guilt 38
and did not smother his own*b*
natural affection;
often he restrained his wrath
and did not rouse his anger to its
height.
He remembered that they were 39
only mortal men,
who pass by like a wind and never
return.

How often they rebelled against 40
him in the wilderness
and grieved him in the desert!
Again and again they tried God's 41
patience
and provoked the Holy One of
Israel.
They did not remember his 42
prowess
on the day when he saved them
from the enemy,
how he set his signs in Egypt, 43
his portents in the land of Zoan.
He turned their streams into blood, 44
and they could not drink the
running water.
He sent swarms of flies which 45
devoured them,
and frogs which brought devastation;
he gave their harvest over to 46
locusts
and their produce to the grubs;
he killed their vines with hailstones 47
and their figs with torrents of rain;
he abandoned their cattle to the 48
plague
and their beasts to the arrows of
pestilence.
He loosed upon them the violence 49
of his anger,
wrath and enmity and rage,
launching those messengers of evil
to open a way for his fury. 50–51

a Or craving.   *b* his own: *prob. rdg.*; Heb. om.

He struck down all the first-born
in Egypt,
the flower of their manhood in the
tents of Ham,
not shielding their lives from death
but abandoning their bodies to
the plague.

52 But he led out his own people like
sheep
and guided them like a flock in the
wilderness.

53 He led them in safety and they
were not afraid,
and the sea closed over their
enemies.

54 He brought them to his holy
mountain,
the hill which his right hand had
won;

55 he drove out nations before them,
he allotted their lands to Israel as a
possession
and settled his tribes in their
dwellings.

56 Yet they tried God's patience and
rebelled against him;
they did not keep the commands
of the Most High;

57 they were renegades, traitors like
their fathers,
they changed, they went slack like
a bow.

58 They provoked him to anger with
their hill-shrines
and roused his jealousy with their
carved images.

59 When God heard this, he put them
out of mind
and utterly rejected Israel.

60 He forsook his home at Shiloh,
the tabernacle in which he dwelt
among men;

61 he surrendered the symbol of his
strength into captivity
and his pride into enemy hands;

62 he gave his people over to the
sword
and put his own possession out of
mind.

63 Fire devoured his young men,
and his maidens could raise no
lament for them;

his priests fell by the sword, 64
and his widows could not weep.

Then the Lord awoke as a sleeper 65
awakes,
like a warrior heated with wine;
he struck his foes in the back parts 66
and brought perpetual shame upon
them.
He despised the clan of Joseph 67
and did not choose the tribe of
Ephraim;
he chose the tribe of Judah 68
and Mount Zion which he loved;
he built his sanctuary high as the 69
heavens,
founded like the earth to last for
ever.
He chose David to be his servant 70
and took him from the sheepfolds;
he brought him from minding the 71
ewes
to be the shepherd of his people
Jacob;[a]
and he shepherded them in single- 72
ness of heart
and guided them with skilful hand.

79

O God, the heathen have set foot in 1
thy domain,
defiled thy holy temple
and laid Jerusalem in ruins.
They have thrown out the dead 2
bodies of thy servants
to feed the birds of the air;
they have made thy loyal servants
carrion for wild beasts.
Their blood is spilled all round 3
Jerusalem like water,
and there they lie unburied.
We suffer the contempt of our 4
neighbours,
the gibes and mockery of all
around us.

How long, O Lord, wilt thou be 5
roused to such fury?
Must thy jealousy rage like a fire?
Pour out thy wrath over nations 6
which do not know thee

[a] *Prob. rdg.*; *Heb. adds* and Israel his possession.

and over kingdoms which do not invoke thee by name;

7 see how they have devoured Jacob and laid waste his homesteads.

8 Do not remember against us the guilt of past generations
but let thy compassion come swiftly to meet us,
we have been brought so low.

9 Help us, O God our saviour, for the honour of thy name;
for thy name's sake deliver us and wipe out our sins.

10 Why should the nations ask, 'Where is their God?'
Let thy vengeance for the bloody slaughter of thy servants
fall on those nations before our very eyes.

11 Let the groaning of the captives reach thy presence
and in thy great might set free death's prisoners.

12 As for the contempt our neighbours pour on thee, O Lord,
turn it back sevenfold on their own heads.

13 Then we thy people, the flock which thou dost shepherd,
will give thee thanks for ever
and repeat thy praise to every generation.

80

1 Hear us, O shepherd of Israel,
who leadest Joseph like a flock of sheep.
Show thyself, thou that art throned on the cherubim,

2 to Ephraim and to Benjamin.
Rouse thy victorious might from slumber,[a]
come to our rescue.

3 Restore us, O God,
and make thy face shine upon us that we may be saved.

4 O LORD God of Hosts,
how long wilt thou resist thy people's prayer?

Thou hast made sorrow their daily 5 bread
and tears of threefold grief their drink.

Thou hast humbled us before our 6 neighbours,
and our enemies mock us to their hearts' content.

O God of Hosts, restore us; 7
make thy face shine upon us that we may be saved.

Thou didst bring a vine out of 8 Egypt;
thou didst drive out nations and plant it;
thou didst clear the ground before 9 it,
so that it made good roots and filled the land.

The mountains were covered with 10 its shade,
and its branches were like those of mighty cedars.

It put out boughs all the way to 11 the Sea
and its shoots as far as the River.

Why hast thou broken down the 12 wall round it
so that every passer-by can pluck its fruit?

The wild boar from the thickets 13 gnaws it,
and swarming insects from the fields feed on it.

O God of Hosts, once more look 14 down from heaven,
take thought for this vine and tend it,
this stock that thy right hand has 15 planted.[b]

Let them that set fire to it or cut it 16 down
perish before thy angry face.

Let thy hand rest upon the man at 17 thy right side,
the man whom thou hast made strong for thy service.

We have not turned back from 18 thee,
so grant us new life, and we will invoke thee by name.

---

[a] from slumber: *prob. rdg.*; *Heb.* and Manasseh.   [b] *Prob. rdg.*; *Heb. adds*
and on the son whom thou hast made strong for thy service (*cp. verse 17*).

19 LORD God of Hosts, restore us;
   make thy face shine upon us that
   we may be saved.

81

1 Sing out in praise of God our
   refuge,*a*
   acclaim the God of Jacob.
2 Take pipe and tabor,
   take tuneful harp and lute.
3 Blow the horn for the new month,
   for the full moon on the day of our
   pilgrim-feast.
4 This is a law for Israel,
   an ordinance of the God of Jacob,
5 laid as a solemn charge on Joseph
   when he came out of Egypt.*b*

6 When I lifted the load from his
   shoulders,
   his hands let go the builder's
   basket.
7 When you cried to me in distress, I
   rescued you;
   unseen, I answered you in thunder.
   I tested you at the waters of
   Meribah,
   where I opened your mouths and
   filled them.*c*
16*d* I fed Israel*e* with the finest wheat-
   flour
   and satisfied him with honey from
   the rocks.
8 Listen, my people, while I give you
   a solemn charge –
   do but listen to me, O Israel:
9 you shall have no strange god
   nor bow down to any foreign god;
10 I am the LORD your God
   who brought you up from Egypt.*f*
11 But my people did not listen to
   my words
   and Israel would have none of
   me;
12 so I sent them off, stubborn as they
   were,
   to follow their own devices.

If my people would but listen to 13
me,
if Israel would only conform to my
ways,
I would soon bring their enemies to 14
their knees
and lay a heavy hand upon their
persecutors.
Let those who hate them*g* come 15
cringing to them,
and meet with everlasting
troubles.*h*

82

God takes his stand in the court of 1
heaven
to deliver judgement among the
gods themselves.

How long will you judge un- 2
justly
and show favour to the wicked?
You ought to give judgement for 3
the weak and the orphan,
and see right done to the destitute
and downtrodden,
you ought to rescue the weak and 4
the poor,
and save them from the clutches of
wicked men.
But you know nothing, you 5
understand nothing,
you walk in the dark
while earth's foundations are
giving way.
This is my sentence: Gods you 6
may be,
sons all of you of a high god,*i*
yet you shall die as men die;*j* 7
princes fall, every one of them, and
so shall you.

Arise, O God, and judge the 8
earth;
for thou dost pass all nations
through thy sieve.

---

a Or strength.   *b* Prob. rdg.; Heb. adds I hear an unfamiliar language.
c Line transposed from end of verse 10.   *d* Verse transposed.   *e* I fed Israel: prob.
rdg.; Heb. He fed him.   *f* See note on verse 7.   *g* those...them: prob. rdg.;
Heb. those who hate the LORD.   *h* Verse 16 transposed to follow verse 7.
i Or of the Most High.   *j* Or as Adam died.

83

1 Rest not, O God;
O God, be neither silent nor still,
2 for thy enemies are making a
tumult,
and those that hate thee carry
their heads high.
3 They devise cunning schemes
against thy people
and conspire against those thou
hast made thy treasure:
4 'Come, away with them,' they cry,
'let them be a nation no longer,
let Israel's name be remembered
no more.'
5 With one mind they have agreed
together
to make a league against thee:
6 the families of Edom, the Ishmaelites,
Moabites and Hagarenes,
7 Gebal, Ammon and Amalek,
Philistia and the citizens of Tyre,
8 Asshur too their ally,
all of them lending aid to the
descendants of Lot.
9 Deal with them as with Sisera,
as with Jabin by the torrent of
Kishon,
10 who fell vanquished as Midian*a* fell
at En-harod,*b*
and were spread on the battlefield
like dung.
11 Make their princes like Oreb and
Zeeb,
make all their nobles like Zebah
and Zalmunna;
12 for they said, 'We will seize for
ourselves
all the pastures of God's people.'
13 Scatter them, O God, like thistledown,
like chaff before the wind.
14 Like fire raging through the forest
or flames which blaze across the
hills,
15 hunt them down with thy tempest,
and dismay them with thy storm-
wind.

Heap shame upon their heads, O 16
LORD,
until they confess the greatness of
thy name.
Let them be abashed, and live in 17
perpetual dismay;
let them feel their shame and
perish.
So let them learn that thou alone 18
art LORD,
God Most High over all the earth.

84

How dear is thy dwelling-place,   1
thou LORD of Hosts!
I pine, I faint with longing   2
for the courts of the LORD's
temple;
my whole being cries out with joy
to the living God.
Even the sparrow finds a home,   3
and the swallow has her nest,
where she rears her brood beside
thy altars,
O LORD of Hosts, my King and my
God.
Happy are those who dwell in thy 4
house;
they never cease from praising
thee.
Happy the men whose refuge is in 5
thee,
whose hearts are set on the pilgrim
ways*c*!
As they pass through the thirsty 6
valley
they find water from a spring;
and the LORD provides even men
who lose their way
with pools to quench their thirst.*d*
So they pass on from outer wall to 7
inner,
and the God of gods shows himself
in Zion.

O LORD God of Hosts, hear my 8
prayer;
listen, O God of Jacob.
O God, look upon our lord the king 9

a as Midian: *transposed from previous verse.*   *b* En-harod: *prob. rdg., cp.*
Judg. 7. 1; *Heb.* Endor.   *c* are set...ways: *or* high praises fill.
d they find...thirst: *prob. rdg.; Heb. obscure.*

and accept thy anointed prince with favour.

10 Better one day in thy courts
than a thousand days at home;
better to linger by the threshold of God's house
than to live in the dwellings of the wicked.

11 The LORD God is a battlement and a shield;
grace and honour are his to give.
The LORD will hold back no good thing
from those whose life is blameless.

12 O LORD of Hosts,
happy the man who trusts in thee!

85

1 LORD, thou hast been gracious to thy land
and turned the tide of Jacob's fortunes.

2 Thou hast forgiven the guilt of thy people
and put away all their sins.

3 Thou hast taken back all thy anger
and turned from thy bitter wrath.

4 Turn back to us, O God our saviour,
and cancel thy displeasure.

5 Wilt thou be angry with us for ever?
Must thy wrath last for all generations?

6 Wilt thou not give us new life
that thy people may rejoice in thee?

7 O LORD, show us thy true love
and grant us thy deliverance.

8 Let me hear the words of the LORD:
are they not[a] words of peace,
peace to his people and his loyal servants
and to all who turn and trust in him?

9 Deliverance is near to those who worship him,
so that glory may dwell in our land.

10 Love and fidelity have come together;
justice and peace join hands.

11 Fidelity springs up from earth
and justice looks down from heaven.

12 The LORD will add prosperity,
and our land shall yield its harvest.

13 Justice shall go in front of him
and the path before his feet shall be peace.[b]

86

1 Turn to me, LORD, and answer;
I am downtrodden and poor.

2 Guard me, for I am constant and true;
save thy servant who puts his trust in thee.

3 O Lord my God,[c] show me thy favour;
I call to thee all day long.

4 Fill thy servant's heart with joy, O Lord,
for I lift up my heart to thee.

5 Thou, O Lord, art kind and forgiving,
full of true love for all who cry to thee.

6 Listen, O LORD, to my prayer
and hear my pleading.

7 In the day of my distress I call on thee;
for thou wilt answer me.

8 Among the gods not one is like thee, O Lord,
no deeds are like thine.

9 All the nations thou hast made, O Lord, will come,
will bow down before thee and honour thy name;

10 for thou art great, thy works are wonderful,
thou alone art God.

11 Guide me, O LORD,
that I may be true to thee and follow thy path;
let me be one in heart
with those who revere thy name.

---

[a] of the LORD: are they not: *prob. rdg.*; *Heb.* of God the LORD.
[b] and the path...peace: *prob. rdg.*; *Heb.* so that he may put his feet to the way.
[c] my God: *transposed from previous verse.*

12 I will praise thee, O Lord my God,
   with all my heart
   and honour thy name for ever.
13 For thy true love stands high
   above me;
   thou hast rescued my soul from
   the depths of Sheol.
14 O God, proud men attack me;
   a mob of ruffians seek my life
   and give no thought to thee.
15 Thou, Lord, art God, compassionate and gracious,
   forbearing, ever constant and true.
16 Turn towards me and show me thy
   favour;
   grant thy slave protection
   and rescue thy slave-girl's son.
17 Give me proof of thy kindness;
   let those who hate thee see to their
   shame
   that thou, O LORD, hast been my
   help and comfort.

87[a]

1-2 The LORD loves the gates of Zion
   more than all the dwellings of
   Jacob;
   her[b] foundations are laid upon
   holy hills,
4-5 and he has made her his home.[c]
   I will count Egypt and Babylon
   among my friends;
   Philistine, Tyrian and Nubian
   shall be[d] there;
   and Zion shall be called a mother
   in whom men of every race are born.
 6 The LORD shall write against each
   in the roll of nations:
   'This one was born in her.'
 7 Singers and dancers alike all chant[e]
   your praises,
 3 proclaiming glorious things of you,
   O city of God.

88

1 O LORD, my God, by day I call for
   help,[f]

by night I cry aloud in thy
presence.
Let my prayer come before thee,   2
hear my loud lament;
for I have had my fill of woes,   3
and they have brought me to the
threshold of Sheol.
I am numbered with those who go 4
down to the abyss
and have become like a man
beyond help,
like a man who lies dead[g]   5
or the slain who sleep in the grave,
whom thou rememberest no more
because they are cut off from thy
care.
Thou hast plunged me into the   6
lowest abyss,
in dark places, in the depths.
Thy wrath rises against me,   7
thou hast turned on me the full
force of thy anger.[h]
Thou hast taken all my friends far 8
from me,
and made me loathsome to them.
I am in prison and cannot escape;
my eyes are failing and dim with   9
anguish.
I have called upon thee, O LORD,
every day
and spread out my hands in prayer
to thee.

Dost thou work wonders for the   10
dead?
Shall their company rise up and
praise thee?
Will they speak of thy faithful   11
love in the grave,
of thy sure help in the place of
Destruction?
Will thy wonders be known in the 12
dark,
thy victories in the land of
oblivion?

But, LORD, I cry to thee,   13
my prayer comes before thee in the
morning.

---

[a] The text of this psalm is disordered, and several verses have been re-arranged.
[b] Prob. rdg.; Heb. his.   [c] his home: prob. rdg.; Heb. most high.   [d] Prob. rdg.;
Heb. adds this one was born (cp. verse 6).   [e] all chant: prob. rdg.; Heb. all
my springs.   [f] I call for help: prob. rdg.; Heb. my deliverance.
[g] who lies dead: prob. rdg.; Heb. obscure.   [h] anger: or waves.

14 Why hast thou cast me off, O
LORD,
why dost thou hide thy face
from me?

15 I have suffered from boyhood and
come near to death;
I have borne thy terrors, I cower
beneath thy blows.

16 Thy burning fury has swept over
me,
thy onslaughts have put me to
silence;

17 all the day long they surge round
me like a flood,
they engulf me in a moment.

18 Thou hast taken lover and friend
far from me,
and parted me from my companions.

89

1 I will sing the story of thy love, O
LORD, for ever;
I will proclaim thy faithfulness to
all generations.

2 Thy true love is firm as the ancient
earth,[a]
thy faithfulness fixed as the
heavens.

5[b] The heavens praise thy wonders, O
LORD,
and the council of the holy ones
exalts thy faithfulness.

6 In the skies who is there like the
LORD,
who like the LORD in the court of
heaven,

7 like God who is dreaded among the
assembled holy ones,
great and terrible above all who
stand about him?

8 O LORD God of Hosts, who is like
thee?
Thy strength[c] and faithfulness, O
LORD, surround thee.

9 Thou rulest the surging sea,
calming the turmoil[d] of its waves.

10 Thou didst crush the monster
Rahab with a mortal blow

and scatter thy enemies with thy
strong arm.

11 Thine are the heavens, the earth is
thine also;
the world with all that is in it is
of thy foundation.

12 Thou didst create Zaphon and
Amanus;[e]
Tabor and Hermon echo thy
name.

13 Strength of arm and valour are
thine;
thy hand is mighty, thy right hand
lifted high;

14 thy throne is built upon righteousness and justice,
true love and faithfulness herald
thy coming.

15 Happy the people who have learnt
to acclaim thee,
who walk, O LORD, in the light of
thy presence!

16 In thy name they shall rejoice all
day long;
thy righteousness shall lift them
up.

17 Thou art thyself the strength in
which they glory;
through thy favour we hold our
heads high.

18 The LORD, he is our shield;
the Holy One of Israel, he is our
king.

19 Then didst thou announce in a
vision
and declare to thy faithful servants:
I have made a covenant with him I
have chosen,
I have sworn to my servant David:

3 'I will establish your posterity for
ever,

4 I will make your throne endure for
all generations.'
I have endowed a warrior with
princely gifts,
so that the youth I have chosen
towers over his people.

----

[a] Thy...earth: *prob. rdg.*; *Heb.* Thou hast said for ever true love shall be made firm.
[b] *Verses 3 and 4 transposed to follow* servants *in verse 19*
[c] Thy strength: *prob. rdg.*; *Heb. obscure.*   [d] turmoil: *prob. rdg.*; *Heb. obscure.*
[e] Amanus: *prob. rdg.*; *Heb.* right hand *or* south.

20 I have discovered David my servant;
I have anointed him with my holy oil.
21 My hand shall be ready to help him
and my arm to give him strength.
22 No enemy shall strike at him
and no rebel bring him low;
23 I will shatter his foes before him
and vanquish those who hate him.
24 My faithfulness and true love shall be with him
and through my name he shall hold his head high.
25 I will extend his rule over the Sea
and his dominion as far as the River.
26 He will say to me, 'Thou art my father,
my God, my rock and my safe refuge.'
27 And I will name him my first-born, highest among the kings of the earth.
28 I will maintain my love for him for ever
and be faithful in my covenant with him.
29 I will establish his posterity for ever
and his throne as long as the heavens endure.
30 If his sons forsake my law
and do not conform to my judgements,
31 if they renounce my statutes
and do not observe my commands,
32 I will punish their disobedience with the rod
and their iniquity with lashes.
33 Yet I will not deprive him of my true love
nor let my faithfulness prove false;
34 I will not renounce my covenant
nor change my promised purpose.
35 I have sworn by my holiness once and for all,
I will not break my word to David:
36 his posterity shall continue for ever,

his throne before me like the sun;
it shall be sure for ever as the 37 moon's return,
faithful so long as the skies remain.ᵃ

Yet thou hast rejected thy anoint- 38 ed king,
thou hast spurned him and raged against him,ᵇ
thou hast denounced the covenant 39 with thy servant,
defiled his crown and flung it to the ground.
Thou hast breached his walls   40
and laid his fortresses in ruin;
all who pass by plunder him,   41
and he suffers the taunts of his neighbours.
Thou hast increased the power of 42 his enemies
and brought joy to all his foes;
thou hast let his sharp sword be 43 driven back
and left him without help in the battle.
Thou hast put an end to his 44 glorious ruleᶜ
and hurled his throne to the ground;
thou hast cut short the days of his 45 youth and vigour
and covered him with shame.

How long, O Lord, wilt thou hide 46 thyself from sight?
How long must thy wrath blaze like fire?
Remember that I shall not live for 47 ever;ᵈ
hast thou created man in vain?
What man shall live and not see 48 death
or save himself from the power of Sheol?
Where are those former acts of thy 49 love, O Lord,
those faithful promises given to David?
Remember, O Lord, the taunts 50 hurled at thy servant,

ᵃ so long...remain: *prob. rdg.*; *Heb.* a witness in the skies.   ᵇ raged against him: *or* put him out of mind.   ᶜ his glorious rule: *prob. rdg.*; *Heb.* from his purity.   ᵈ live for ever: *prob. rdg.*; *Heb. obscure.*

how I have borne in my heart the calumnies of the nations;[a]

51 so have thy enemies taunted us, O LORD,
taunted the successors of thy anointed king.

52 Blessed is the LORD for ever.

Amen, Amen.

BOOK 4

90

1 Lord, thou hast been our refuge from generation to generation.

2 Before the mountains were brought forth,
or earth and world were born in travail,
from age to age everlasting thou art God.

3 Thou turnest man back into dust; 'Turn back,' thou sayest, 'you sons of men';

4 for in thy sight a thousand years are as yesterday;

5 a night-watch passes, and thou hast cut them off;
they are like a dream at daybreak,

6 they fade like grass which springs up[b] with the morning
but when evening comes is parched and withered.

7 So we are brought to an end by thy anger
and silenced by thy wrath.

8 Thou dost lay bare our iniquities before thee
and our lusts in the full light of thy presence.

9 All our days go by under the shadow of thy wrath;
our years die away like a murmur.

10 Seventy years is the span of our life,
eighty if our strength holds;[c]
the hurrying years are labour and sorrow,
so quickly they pass and are forgotten.

11 Who feels the power of thy anger, who feels thy wrath like those that fear thee?

12 Teach us to order our days rightly, that we may enter the gate of wisdom.

13 How long, O LORD?
Relent, and take pity on thy servants.

14 Satisfy us with thy love when morning breaks,
that we may sing for joy and be glad all our days.

15 Repay us days of gladness for our days of suffering,
for the years thou hast humbled us.

16 Show thy servants thy deeds
and their children thy majesty.

17 May all delightful things be ours, O Lord our God;
establish firmly all we do.

91

1 You that live in the shelter of the Most High
and lodge under the shadow of the Almighty,

2 who say, 'The LORD is my safe retreat,
my God the fastness in which I trust';

3 he himself will snatch you away from fowler's snare or raging tempest.

4 He will cover you with his pinions, and you shall find safety beneath his wings;

5 you shall not fear the hunters' trap by night
or the arrow that flies by day,

6 the pestilence that stalks in darkness
or the plague raging at noonday.

7 A thousand may fall at your side, ten thousand close at hand,
but you it shall not touch;
his truth[d] will be your shield and your rampart.[e]

8 With your own eyes you shall see all this;

---

[a] the calumnies...nations: *prob. rdg.*; *Heb.* all of many peoples.
[b] *Prob. rdg.*; *Heb. adds* and passes away.   [c] *Or* eighty at the most.
[d] *Or* his arm.   [e] his truth...rampart: *transposed from end of verse 4.*

you shall watch the punishment of
the wicked.
9 For you, the LORD is a*a* safe retreat;
you have made the Most High your
refuge.
10 No disaster shall befall you,
no calamity shall come upon your
home.
11 For he has charged his angels
to guard you wherever you go,
12 to lift you on their hands
for fear you should strike your foot
against a stone.
13 You shall step on asp and cobra,
you shall tread safely on snake and
serpent.

14 Because his love is set on me, I will
deliver him;
I will lift him beyond danger, for
he knows me by my name.
15 When he calls upon me, I will
answer;
I will be with him in time of
trouble;
I will rescue him and bring him to
honour.
16 I will satisfy him with long life
to enjoy the fullness of my salvation.

92

1 O LORD, it is good to give thee
thanks,
to sing psalms to thy name, O Most
High,
2 to declare thy love in the morning
and thy constancy every night,
3 to the music of a ten-stringed lute,
to the sounding chords of the harp.
4 Thy acts, O LORD, fill me with
exultation;
I shout in triumph at thy mighty
deeds.
5 How great are thy deeds, O LORD!
How fathomless thy thoughts!

6 He who does not know this is a
brute,
a fool is he who does not understand
this:

that though the wicked grow like 7
grass
and every evildoer prospers,
they will be destroyed for ever.
While thou, LORD, dost reign on 8
high eternally,
thy foes will surely perish, 9
all evildoers will be scattered.

I lift my head high, like a wild ox 10
tossing its horn;
I am anointed richly with oil.
I gloat over all who speak ill of 11
me,
I listen for the downfall of my
cruel foes.
The righteous flourish like a 12
palm-tree,
they grow tall as a cedar on
Lebanon;
planted as they are in the house of 13
the LORD,
they flourish in the courts of our
God,
vigorous in old age like trees full of 14
sap,
luxuriant, wide-spreading,
eager to declare that the LORD is 15
just,
the LORD my rock,*b* in whom there
is no unrighteousness.

93

The LORD is king; he is clothed in 1
majesty;
the LORD clothes himself with
might and fastens on his belt of
wrath.

Thou hast fixed the earth immovable and firm,
thy throne firm from of old; 2
from all eternity thou art God.
O LORD, the ocean lifts up, the 3
ocean lifts up its clamour;
the ocean lifts up*c* its pounding
waves.
The LORD on high is mightier far 4
than the noise of great waters,
mightier than the breakers of the
sea.

---

a *Prob. rdg.; Heb.* my.   *b* *Or* creator.
c the ocean lifts up: *or* let the ocean lift up.

5 Thy law stands firm, and holiness
  is the beauty of thy temple,
  while time shall last, O LORD.

94

1 O LORD, thou God of vengeance,
  thou God of vengeance, show
  thyself.
2 Rise up, judge of the earth;
  punish the arrogant as they
  deserve.
3 How long shall the wicked, O
  LORD,
  how long shall the wicked exult?
4 Evildoers are full of bluster,
  boasting and swaggering;
5 they beat down thy people, O
  LORD,
  and oppress thy chosen nation;
6 they murder the widow and the
  stranger
  and do the fatherless to death;
7 they say, 'The LORD does not see,
  the God of Jacob pays no heed.'
8 Pay heed yourselves, most brutish
  of the people,
  you fools, when will you be wise?
9 Does he that planted the ear not
  hear,
  he that moulded the eye not see?
10 Shall not he that instructs the
   nations correct them?
   The teacher of mankind, has he no[a]
   knowledge?
11 The LORD knows the thoughts of
   man,
   that they are but a puff of wind.

12 Happy the man whom thou dost
   instruct, O LORD,
   and teach out of thy law,
13 giving him respite from adversity
   until a pit is dug for the wicked.
14 The LORD will not abandon his
   people
   nor forsake his chosen nation;
15 for righteousness still informs his
   judgement,[b]
   and all upright men follow it.

16 Who is on my side against these
   sinful men?
   Who will stand up for me against
   these evildoers?
17 If the LORD had not been my
   helper,
   I should soon have slept in the
   silent grave.
18 When I felt that my foot was
   slipping,
   thy love, O LORD, held me up.
19 Anxious thoughts may fill my
   heart,
   but thy presence is my joy and my
   consolation.
20 Shall sanctimonious calumny call
   thee partner,
   or he that contrives a mischief
   under cover of law?
21 For they put the righteous on
   trial[c] for his life
   and condemn to death innocent
   men.
22 But the LORD has been my strong
   tower,
   and God my rock of refuge;
23 our God requites the wicked for
   their injustice,
   the LORD puts them to silence for
   their misdeeds.

95

1 Come! Let us raise a joyful song to
  the LORD,
  a shout of triumph to the Rock of
  our salvation.
2 Let us come into his presence with
  thanksgiving,
  and sing him psalms of triumph.
3 For the LORD is a great God,
  a great king over all gods;
4 the farthest places of the earth are
  in his hands,
  and the folds of the hills are his;
5 the sea is his, he made it;
  the dry land fashioned by his hands
  is his.
6 Come! Let us throw ourselves at
  his feet in homage,

---

[a] no: *prob. rdg.*; *Heb. om.*   [b] for...judgement: *prob. rdg.*; *Heb.* for judgement
will return as far as righteousness.   [c] they put...trial: *prob. rdg.*; *Heb.* they
cut the righteous.

let us kneel before the LORD who
    made us;
7 for he is our God,
    we are his people, we the flock he
      shepherds.
    You shall know[a] his power today
    if you will listen to his voice.

8 Do not grow stubborn, as you were
    at Meribah,[b]
    as at the time of Massah[c] in the
      wilderness,
9 when your forefathers challenged
    me,
    tested me and saw for themselves
      all that I did.
10 For forty years I was indignant
    with that generation, and I said:
    They are a people whose hearts are
      astray,
    and they will not discern my ways.
11 As I swore in my anger:
    They shall never enter my rest.

96

1[d] Sing a new song to the LORD;
    sing to the LORD, all men on earth.
2 Sing to the LORD and bless his
    name,
    proclaim his triumph day by day.
3 Declare his glory among the
    nations,
    his marvellous deeds among all
      peoples.
4 Great is the LORD and worthy of all
    praise;
    he is more to be feared than all
      gods.
5 For the gods of the nations are
    idols every one;
    but the LORD made the heavens.
6 Majesty and splendour attend
    him,
    might and beauty are in his
      sanctuary.

7 Ascribe to the LORD, you families
    of nations,
    ascribe to the LORD glory and
      might;

ascribe to the LORD the glory due 8
    to his name,
    bring a gift and come into his
      courts.
Bow down to the LORD in the 9
    splendour of holiness,[e]
    and dance in his honour, all men on
      earth.
Declare among the nations, 'The 10
    LORD is king.
He has fixed the earth firm,
    immovable;
he will judge the peoples justly.'
Let the heavens rejoice and the 11
    earth exult,
let the sea roar and all the creatures
    in it,
let the fields exult and all that is in 12
    them;
then let all the trees of the forest
    shout for joy
before the LORD when he comes to 13
    judge the earth.
He will judge the earth with
    righteousness
and the peoples in good faith.

97

The LORD is king, let the earth be 1
    glad,
let coasts and islands all rejoice.
Cloud and mist enfold him,   2
righteousness and justice
are the foundation of his throne.
Fire goes before him   3
and burns up his enemies all
    around.
The world is lit up beneath his 4
    lightning-flash;
the earth sees it and writhes in pain.
The mountains melt like wax as 5
    the LORD approaches,
the Lord of all the earth.
The heavens proclaim his right- 6
    eousness,
and all peoples see his glory.
Let all who worship images, who 7
    vaunt their idols,
be put to shame;
bow down, all gods,[f] before him.

---

[a] You shall know: *prob. rdg.*; *Heb. om.*   [b] *That is* Dispute.
[c] *That is* Challenge.   [d] *Verses 1–13: cp. 1 Chr. 16. 23–33.*   [e] the splendour
of holiness: *or* holy vestments.   [f] bow...gods: *or* all gods bow down...

8 Zion heard and rejoiced, the cities
   of Judah were glad
at thy judgements, O LORD.
9 For thou, LORD, art most high over
   all the earth,
far exalted above all gods.

10 The LORD loves[a] those who hate
   evil;
he keeps his loyal servants safe
and rescues them from the wicked.
11 A harvest of light is sown for the
   righteous,
and joy for all good men.
12 You that are righteous, rejoice in
   the LORD
and praise his holy name.

98

1 Sing a new song to the LORD,
for he has done marvellous deeds;
his right hand and holy arm have
   won him victory.
2 The LORD has made his victory
   known;
he has displayed his righteousness
   to all the nations.
3 He has remembered his constancy,
his love for the house of Israel.
All the ends of the earth have seen
the victory of our God.

4 Acclaim the LORD, all men on
   earth,
break into songs of joy, sing
   psalms.
5 Sing psalms in the LORD's honour
   with the harp,
with the harp and with the music
   of the psaltery.
6 With trumpet and echoing horn
acclaim the presence of the LORD
   our king.
7 Let the sea roar and all its
   creatures,
the world and those who dwell in it.
8 Let the rivers clap their hands,
let the hills sing aloud together
9 before the LORD; for he comes
to judge the earth.

He will judge the world with
   righteousness
and the peoples in justice.

99

The LORD is king, the peoples are 1
   perturbed;
he is throned on the cherubim,
   earth quivers.
The LORD is great in Zion;   2
he is exalted above all the peoples.
They extol his[b] name as great and 3
   terrible;
he is holy, he is mighty,   4
a king who loves justice.

Thou hast established justice and
   equity;
thou hast dealt righteously in
   Jacob.
Exalt the LORD our God,   5
bow down before his footstool;
he is holy.

Moses and Aaron among his 6
   priests,
and Samuel among those who call
   on his name,
called to the LORD, and he answered.
He spoke to them in a pillar of 7
   cloud;
they followed his teaching and
   kept the law he gave them.
Thou, O LORD our God, thou didst 8
   answer them;
thou wast a God who forgave all
   their misdeeds
and held them innocent.
Exalt the LORD our God,   9
bow down towards his holy hill;
for the LORD our God is holy.

100

Acclaim the LORD, all men on 1
   earth,
worship the LORD in gladness;   2
enter his presence with songs of
   exultation.

[a] The LORD loves: *prob. rdg.*; *Heb.* Lovers of the LORD.
[b] *Prob. rdg.*; *Heb.* thy.

3 Know that the LORD is God;
he has made us and we are his own,
his people, the flock which he
  shepherds.
4 Enter his gates with thanksgiving
and his courts with praise.
Give thanks to him and bless his
  name;
5 for the LORD is good and his love is
  everlasting,
his constancy endures to all generations.

101

1 I sing of loyalty and justice;
I will raise a psalm to thee, O
  LORD.[a]

2 I will follow a wise and blameless
  course,
whatever may befall me.[b]
I will go about my house in purity
  of heart.
3 I will set before myself no sordid
  aim;
I will hate disloyalty, I will have
  none of it.
4 I will reject all crooked thoughts;
I will have no dealings with evil.
5 I will silence those who spread
  tales behind men's backs,
I will not sit at table with proud,
  pompous men,
6 I will choose the most loyal for my
  companions;
my servants shall be men whose
  lives are blameless.
7 No scandal-monger shall live in my
  household;
no liar shall set himself up where I
  can see him.
8 Morning after morning I will put
  all wicked men to silence
and will rid the LORD's city of all
  evildoers.

102

1 LORD, hear my prayer
and let my cry for help reach thee.

Hide not thy face from me   2
when I am in distress.
Listen to my prayer
and, when I call, answer me soon;
for my days vanish like smoke,   3
my body is burnt up as in an oven.
I am stricken, withered like grass;   4
I cannot find the strength to eat.
Wasted away,[c] I groan aloud   5
and my skin hangs on my bones.
I am like a desert-owl in the   6
  wilderness,
an owl that lives among ruins.
Thin and meagre, I wail in solitude,   7
like a bird that flutters on the roof-
  top.
My enemies insult me all the day   8
  long;
mad with rage, they conspire
  against me.
I have eaten ashes for bread   9
and mingled tears with my drink.
In thy wrath and fury   10
thou hast taken me up and flung
  me aside.
My days decline as the shadows   11
  lengthen,
and like grass I wither away.

But thou, LORD, art enthroned for   12
  ever
and thy fame shall be known to all
  generations.
Thou wilt arise and have mercy on   13
  Zion;
for the time is come[d] to pity her.
Her very stones are dear to thy   14
  servants,
and even her dust moves them
  with pity.
Then shall the nations revere thy   15
  name, O LORD;
and all the kings of the earth thy
  glory,
when the LORD builds up Zion again   16
and shows himself in his glory.
He turns to hear the prayer of the   17
  destitute
and does not scorn them when they
  pray.

---

[a] I sing...O LORD: *or* I will follow a course of justice and loyalty; I will hold thee
in awe, O LORD.   [b] whatever may befall me: *prob. rdg.*; *Heb.* when comest
thou to me?   [c] Wasted away: *transposed from previous verse.*
[d] *Prob. rdg.*; *Heb. adds* season.

18 This shall be written down for
future generations,
and a people yet unborn shall
praise the LORD.
19 The LORD looks down from his
sanctuary on high,
from heaven he surveys the earth
20 to listen to the groaning of the
prisoners
and set free men under sentence of
death;
21 so shall the LORD's name be on
men's lips in Zion
and his praise shall be told in
Jerusalem,
22 when peoples are assembled together,
peoples and kingdoms, to serve the
LORD.

23 My strength is broken in mid
course;
24 the time allotted me is short.
Snatch me not away before half
my days are done,
for thy years last through all
generations.
25 Long ago thou didst lay the
foundations of the earth,
and the heavens were thy handiwork.
26 They shall pass away, but thou
endurest;
like clothes they shall all grow old;
thou shalt cast them off like a
cloak,
and they shall vanish;
27 but thou art the same and thy
years shall have no end;
28 thy servants' children shall continue,
and their posterity shall be established in thy presence.

103

1 Bless the LORD, my soul;
my innermost heart, bless his holy
name.
2 Bless the LORD, my soul,
and forget none of his benefits.
3 He pardons all my guilt
and heals all my suffering.

He rescues me from the pit of death 4
and surrounds me with constant
love,
with tender affection;
he contents me with all good in the 5
prime of life,
and my youth is ever new like an
eagle's.

The LORD is righteous in his acts; 6
he brings justice to all who have
been wronged.
He taught Moses to know his way 7
and showed the Israelites what he
could do.
The LORD is compassionate and 8
gracious,
long-suffering and for ever constant;
he will not always be the accuser 9
or nurse his anger for all time.
He has not treated us as our sins 10
deserve
or requited us for our misdeeds.
For as the heaven stands high 11
above the earth,
so his strong love stands high over
all who fear him.
Far as east is from west, 12
so far has he put our offences away
from us.
As a father has compassion on his 13
children,
so has the LORD compassion on all
who fear him.
For he knows how we were made, 14
he knows full well that we are dust.

Man's days are like the grass; 15
he blossoms like the flowers of the
field:
a wind passes over them, and they 16
cease to be,
and their place knows them no
more.
But the LORD's love never fails 17
those who fear him;
his righteousness never fails their
sons and their grandsons
who listen to his voice[a] and keep 18
his covenant,
who remember his commandments
and obey them.

a who listen to his voice: transposed from end of verse 20.

19 The LORD has established his
   throne in heaven,
   his kingly power over the whole
   world.
20 Bless the LORD, all his angels,
   creatures of might who do his
   bidding.
21 Bless the LORD, all his hosts,
   his ministers who serve his will.
22 Bless the LORD, all created things,
   in every place where he has dominion.

   Bless the LORD, my soul.

104

1 Bless the LORD, my soul:
   O LORD my God, thou art great
   indeed,
   clothed in majesty and splendour,
2 and wrapped in a robe of light.
   Thou hast spread out the heavens
   like a tent
3 and on their waters laid the beams
   of thy pavilion;
   who takest the clouds for thy
   chariot,
   riding on the wings of the wind;
4 who makest the winds thy messengers
   and flames of fire thy servants;
5 thou didst fix the earth on its
   foundation
   so that it never can be shaken;
6 the deep overspread it like a cloak,
   and the waters lay above the
   mountains.
7 At thy rebuke they ran,
   at the sound of thy thunder they
   rushed away,
8 flowing over the hills,
   pouring down into the valleys
   to the place appointed for them.
9 Thou didst fix a boundary which
   they might not pass;
   they shall not return to cover the
   earth.

10 Thou dost make springs break out
   in the gullies,
   so that their water runs between
   the hills.

11 The wild beasts all drink from
   them,
   the wild asses quench their thirst;
12 the birds of the air nest on their
   banks
   and sing among the leaves.

13 From thy high pavilion thou dost
   water the hills;
   the earth is enriched by thy provision.
14 Thou makest grass grow for the
   cattle
   and green things for those who toil
   for man,
   bringing bread out of the earth
15 and wine to gladden men's hearts,
   oil to make their faces shine
   and bread to sustain their strength.
16 The trees of the LORD are green
   and leafy,
   the cedars of Lebanon which he
   planted;
17 the birds build their nests in
   them,
   the stork makes her home in their
   tops.[a]
18 High hills are the haunt of the
   mountain-goat,
   and boulders a refuge for the rock-
   badger.

19 Thou hast made the moon to measure the year
   and taught the sun where to
   set.
20 When thou makest darkness and
   it is night,
   all the beasts of the forest come
   forth;
21 the young lions roar for prey,
   seeking their food from God.
22 When thou makest the sun rise,
   they slink away
   and go to rest in their lairs;
23 but man comes out to his work
   and to his labours until evening.
24 Countless are the things thou hast
   made, O LORD.
   Thou hast made all by thy wisdom;
   and the earth is full of thy creatures,
25 beasts great and small.

[a] in their tops: *prob. rdg.*; *Heb.* the pine-trees.

Here is the great immeasurable sea,
in which move creatures beyond
number.

26 Here ships sail to and fro,
here is Leviathan whom thou hast
made thy plaything.[a]

27 All of them look expectantly to
thee
to give them their food at the
proper time;

28 what thou givest them they gather
up;
when thou openest thy hand, they
eat their fill.

29 Then thou hidest thy face, and
they are restless and troubled;
when thou takest away their
breath, they fail
[and they return to the dust from
which they came];

30 but when thou breathest into them,
they recover;
thou givest new life to the earth.

31 May the glory of the LORD stand
for ever
and may he rejoice in his works!

32 When he looks at the earth, it
quakes;
when he touches the hills, they
pour forth smoke.

33 I will sing to the LORD as long as I
live,
all my life I will sing psalms to my
God.

34 May my meditation please the
LORD,
as I show my joy in him!

35 Away with all sinners from the
earth
and may the wicked be no more!

Bless the LORD, my soul.

O praise the LORD.

105

1[b] Give the LORD thanks and invoke
him by name,

make his deeds known in the
world around.

2 Pay him honour with song and
psalm
and think upon all his wonders.

3 Exult in his hallowed name;
let those who seek the LORD be
joyful in heart.

4 Turn to the LORD, your strength,
seek his presence always.

5 Remember the wonders that he has
wrought,
his portents and the judgements he
has given,

6 O offspring of Abraham his servant, O chosen sons of Jacob.

7 He is the LORD our God;
his judgements fill the earth.

8 He called to mind his covenant
from long ago,[c]
the promise he extended to a thousand generations –

9 the covenant made with Abraham,
his oath given to Isaac,

10 the decree by which he bound himself for Jacob,
his everlasting covenant with
Israel:

11 'I will give you the land of Canaan', he said,
'to be your possession, your patrimony.'

12 A small company it was,
few in number, strangers in that
land,

13 roaming from nation to nation,
from one kingdom to another;

14 but he let no one ill-treat them,
for their sake he admonished kings:

15 'Touch not my anointed servants,
do my prophets no harm.'

16 He called down famine on the land
and cut short their daily bread.

17 But he had sent on a man before
them,
Joseph, who was sold into slavery;

18 he was kept a prisoner with fetters
on his feet
and an iron collar clamped on his
neck.

---

[a] thy plaything: *or* that it may sport in it.   [b] *Verses 1–15: cp. 1 Chr. 16. 8–22.*
[c] from long ago: *or* for ever.

19 He was tested by the LORD's command
   until what he foretold came true.
20 Then the king sent and set him free,
   the ruler of nations released him;
21 he made him master of his household
   and ruler over all his possessions,
22 to correct his officers at will
   and teach his counsellors wisdom.
23 Then Israel too went down into Egypt
   and Jacob came to live in the land of Ham.
24 There God made his people very fruitful,
   he made them stronger than their enemies,
25 whose hearts he turned to hatred of his people
   and double-dealing with his servants.
26 He sent his servant Moses
   and Aaron whom he had chosen.
27 They were his mouthpiece to announce his signs,
   his portents in the land of Ham.
28 He sent darkness, and all was dark,
   but still they resisted his commands.
29 He turned their waters into blood
   and killed all their fish.
30 Their country swarmed with frogs,
   even their princes' inner chambers.
31 At his command came swarms of flies
   and maggots the whole land through.
32 He changed their rain into hail
   and flashed fire over their country.
33 He blasted their vines and their fig-trees
   and splintered the trees throughout the land.
34 At his command came locusts,
   hoppers past all number,
35 they consumed every green thing in the land,
   consumed all the produce of the soil.
36 Then he struck down all the first-born in Egypt,
   the firstfruits of their manhood;

37 he led Israel out, laden with silver and gold,
   and among all their tribes no man fell.
38 The Egyptians were glad when they went,
   for fear of Israel had taken hold of them.
39 He spread a cloud as a screen,
   and fire to light up the night.
40 They asked, and he sent them quails,
   he gave them bread from heaven in plenty.
41 He opened a rock and water gushed out,
   a river flowing in a parched land;
42 for he had remembered his solemn promise
   given to his servant Abraham.
43 So he led out his people rejoicing,
   his chosen ones in triumph.
44 He gave them the lands of heathen nations
   and they took possession where others had toiled,
45 so that they might keep his statutes and obey his laws.

O praise the LORD.

106

O praise the LORD.   1

It is good to give thanks to the LORD;
for his love endures for ever.
Who will tell of the LORD's mighty acts   2
and make his praises heard?
Happy are they who act justly   3
and do right at all times!
Remember me, LORD, when thou   4
showest favour to thy people,
look upon me when thou savest them,
that I may see the prosperity of   5
thy chosen,
rejoice in thy nation's joy and
exult with thy own people.

We have sinned like our fore-   6
fathers,
we have erred and done wrong.

7 Our fathers in Egypt took no
account of thy marvels,
they did not remember thy many
acts of faithful love,
but in spite of all[a] they rebelled by
the Red Sea.[b]
8 Yet the LORD delivered them for
his name's sake
and so made known his mighty
power.
9 He rebuked the Red Sea and it
dried up,
he led his people through the deeps
as through the wilderness.
10 So he delivered them from those
who hated them,
and claimed them back from the
enemy's hand.
11 The waters closed over their adversaries,
not one of them survived.
12 Then they believed his promises
and sang praises to him.

13 But they quickly forgot all he had
done
and would not wait to hear his
counsel;
14 their greed was insatiable in the
wilderness,
they tried God's patience in the
desert.
15 He gave them what they asked
but sent a wasting sickness among
them.[c]

16 They were envious of Moses in the
camp,
and of Aaron, who was consecrated
to the LORD.
17 The earth opened and swallowed
Dathan,
it closed over the company of
Abiram;
18 fire raged through their company,
the wicked perished in flames.

19 At Horeb they made a calf
and bowed down to an image;
20 they exchanged their Glory[d]

for the image of a bull that feeds on
grass.
They forgot God their deliverer, 21
who had done great deeds in Egypt,
marvels in the land of Ham, 22
terrible things at the Red Sea.
So his purpose was to destroy them, 23
but Moses, the man he had chosen,
threw himself into the breach
to turn back his wrath lest it
destroy them.

They made light of the pleasant 24
land,
disbelieving his promise;
they muttered treason in their 25
tents
and would not obey the LORD.
So with uplifted hand he swore 26
to strike them down in the wilderness,
to scatter their descendants among 27
the nations
and disperse them throughout the
world.

They joined in worshipping the 28
Baal of Peor
and ate meat sacrificed to lifeless
gods.
Their deeds provoked the LORD to 29
anger,
and plague broke out amongst
them;
but Phinehas stood up and inter- 30
ceded,
so the plague was stopped.
This was counted to him as 31
righteousness
throughout all generations for
ever.

They roused the LORD to anger at 32
the waters of Meribah,
and Moses suffered because of
them;
for they had embittered his spirit 33
and he had spoken rashly.

They did not destroy the peoples 34
round about,

---

[a] in spite of all: prob. rdg.; Heb. obscure.   [b] Or the Sea of Reeds.
[c] among them: or in their throats.
[d] their Glory: or the glory of God (cp. Jer. 2. 11; Romans 1. 23).

as the LORD had commanded them
to do,
35 but they mingled with the nations,
learning their ways;
36 they worshipped their idols
and were ensnared by them.
37 Their sons and their daughters
they sacrificed to foreign demons;
38 they shed innocent blood,
the blood of sons and daughters
offered to the gods of Canaan,
and the land was polluted with
blood.
39 Thus they defiled themselves by
their conduct
and they followed their lusts and
broke faith with God.
40 Then the LORD grew angry with
his people
and loathed them, his own chosen
nation;
41 so he gave them into the hands of
the nations,
and they were ruled by their foes;
42 their enemies oppressed them
and made them subject to their
power.
43 Many times he came to their rescue,
but they were disobedient and rebellious still.[a]
44 And yet, when he heard them wail
and cry aloud,
he looked with pity on their
distress;
45 he called to mind his covenant
with them
and, in his boundless love, relented;
46 he roused compassion for them
in the hearts of all their captors.

47 Deliver us, O LORD our God,
and gather us in from among the
nations
that we may give thanks to thy
holy name
and make thy praise our pride.

48 Blessed be the LORD the God of
Israel
from everlasting to everlasting;
and let all the people say 'Amen.'

O praise the LORD.

BOOK 5

107

It is good to give thanks to the 1
LORD,
for his love endures for ever.
So let them say who were redeemed 2
by the LORD,
redeemed by him from the power
of the enemy
and gathered out of every land, 3
from east and west, from north and
south.

Some lost their way in desert 4
wastes;
they found no road to a city to live
in;
hungry and thirsty, 5
their spirit sank within them.
So they cried to the LORD in their 6
trouble,
and he rescued them from their
distress;
he led them by a straight and easy 7
way
until they came to a city to live in.
Let them thank the LORD for his 8
enduring love
and for the marvellous things he
has done for men:
he has satisfied the thirsty 9
and filled the hungry with good
things.

Some sat in darkness, dark as 10
death,
prisoners bound fast in iron,
because they had rebelled against 11
God's commands
and flouted the purpose of the
Most High.
Their spirit was subdued by hard 12
labour;
they stumbled and fell with none
to help them.
So they cried to the LORD in their 13
trouble,
and he saved them from their
distress;
he brought them out of darkness, 14
dark as death,
and broke their chains.

[a] *Prob. rdg.; Heb. adds* and were brought low by their guilt.

15 Let them thank the LORD for his
enduring love
and for the marvellous things he
has done for men:
16 he has shattered doors of bronze,
bars of iron he has snapped in two.

17 Some were fools, they took to rebellious ways,
and for their transgression they
suffered punishment.
18 They sickened at the sight of food
and drew near to the very gates of
death.
19 So they cried to the LORD in their
trouble,
and he saved them from their
distress;
20 he sent his word to heal them
and bring them alive out of the pit
of death.[a]
21 Let them thank the LORD for his
enduring love
and for the marvellous things he
has done for men.
22 Let them offer sacrifices of thanksgiving
and recite his deeds with shouts of
joy.

23 Others there are who go to sea in
ships
and make their living on the wide
waters.
24 These men have seen the acts of
the LORD
and his marvellous doings in the
deep.
25 At his command the storm-wind
rose
and lifted the waves high.
26 Carried up to heaven, plunged
down to the depths,
tossed to and fro in peril,
27 they reeled and staggered like
drunken men,
and their seamanship was all in
vain.
28 So they cried to the LORD in their
trouble,
and he brought them out of their
distress.
29 The storm sank to a murmur

and the waves of the sea were
stilled.
30 They were glad then that all was
calm,
as he guided them to the harbour
they desired.
31 Let them thank the LORD for his
enduring love
and for the marvellous things he
has done for men.
32 Let them exalt him in the assembly of the people
and praise him in the council of the
elders.

33 He turns rivers into desert
and springs of water into thirsty
ground;
34 he turns fruitful land into salt
waste,
because the men who dwell there
are so wicked.
35 Desert he changes into standing
pools,
and parched land into springs of
water.
36 There he gives the hungry a home,
and they build themselves a city
to live in;
37 they sow fields and plant vineyards
and reap a fruitful harvest.
38 He blesses them and their numbers
increase,
and he does not let their herds lose
strength.
39 Tyrants[b] lose their strength and
are brought low
in the grip of misfortune and
sorrow;
40 he brings princes into contempt
and leaves them wandering in a
trackless waste.
41 But the poor man he lifts clear of
his troubles
and makes families increase like
flocks of sheep.
42 The upright see it and are glad,
while evildoers are filled with
disgust.
43 Let the wise man lay these things
to heart,
and ponder the record of the
LORD's enduring love.

[a] alive...death: *prob. rdg.*; *Heb.* from their corruption.   [b] *Prob. rdg.*; *Heb. om.*

108

1[a] My heart is steadfast, O God,
my heart is steadfast.
I will sing and raise a psalm;
awake,[b] my spirit,

2 awake, lute and harp,
I will awake at dawn of day.[c]

3 I will confess thee, O LORD, among
the peoples,
among the nations I will raise a
psalm to thee;

4 for thy unfailing love is wider than
the heavens
and thy truth reaches to the skies.

5 Show thyself, O God, high above
the heavens;
let thy glory shine over all the earth.

6[d] Deliver those that are dear to thee;
save with thy right hand and
answer.

7 God has spoken from his sanc-
tuary:[e]
'I will go up now and measure out
Shechem;
I will divide the valley of Succoth
into plots;

8 Gilead and Manasseh are mine;
Ephraim is my helmet, Judah my
sceptre;

9 Moab is my wash-bowl, I fling my
shoes at Edom;
Philistia is the target of my anger.'

10 Who can bring me to the impregnable city,
who can guide me to Edom,

11 since thou, O God, hast abandoned
us
and goest not forth with our
armies?

12 Grant us help against the enemy,
for deliverance by man is a vain
hope.

13 With God's help we shall do
valiantly,
and God himself will tread our
enemies under foot.

109

O God of my praise, be silent no 1
longer,
for wicked men heap calumnies 2
upon me.
They have lied to my face
and ringed me round with words of 3
hate.
They have attacked me without a
cause[f]
and accused me though I have 4
done nothing unseemly.[g]
They have repaid me evil for 5
good
and hatred in return for my love.
They say, 'Put up some rascal to 6
denounce him,
an accuser to stand at his right
side.'
But when judgement is given, that 7
rascal will be exposed
and his follies accounted a sin.
May his days be few; 8
may his hoarded wealth[h] fall to
another!
May his children be fatherless, 9
his wife a widow!
May his children be vagabonds and 10
beggars,
driven from their homes!
May the money-lender distrain on 11
all his goods
and strangers seize his earnings!
May none remain loyal to him, 12
and none have mercy on his fatherless children!
May his line be doomed to extinc- 13
tion,
may their name be wiped out within a generation!
May the sins of his forefathers be 14
remembered
and his mother's wickedness never
be wiped out!
May they remain on record before 15
the LORD,
but may he extinguish their name
from the earth!

---

[a] Verses 1–5: cp. Ps. 57. 7–11.   [b] awake: prob. rdg.; Heb. also.
[c] at dawn of day: or the dawn.   [d] Verses 6–13: cp. Ps. 60. 5–12.
[e] from his sanctuary: or in his holiness.   [f] Prob. rdg.; Heb. adds in return
for my love.   [g] though...unseemly: prob. rdg.; Heb. obscure.
[h] hoarded wealth: or charge, cp. Acts 1. 20.

16 For that man never set himself
   to be loyal to his friend
   but persecuted the downtrodden
   and the poor
   and hounded the broken-hearted
   to their death.
17 Curses he loved: may the curse fall
   on him!
   He took no pleasure in blessing:
   may no blessing be his!
18 He clothed himself in cursing like
   a garment:
   may it seep into his body like water
   and into his bones like oil!
19 May it wrap him round like the
   clothes he puts on,
   like the belt which he wears every
   day!
20 May the LORD so requite my
   accusers
   and those who speak evil against
   me!

21 But thou, O LORD God,
   deal with me as befits thy honour;
   in the goodness of thy unfailing
   love deliver me,
22 for I am downtrodden and poor,
   and my heart within me is distracted.
23 I fade like a passing shadow,
   I am shaken off like a locust.
24 My knees are weak with fasting
   and my flesh wastes away, so
   meagre is my fare.
25 I have become the victim of their
   taunts;
   when they see me they toss their
   heads.
26 Help me, O LORD my God;
   save me, by thy unfailing love,
27 that men may know this is thy
   doing
   and thou alone, O LORD, hast done
   it.
28 They may curse, but thou dost
   bless;

may my opponents be put to
shame,
but may thy servant rejoice!
May my accusers be clothed with 29
dishonour,
wrapped in their shame as in a
cloak!
I will lift up my voice to extol the 30
LORD,
and before a great company I will
praise him.
For he stands at the poor man's 31
right side
to save him from his adversaries.[a]

110

The LORD said to my lord,   1
'You shall sit[b] at my right hand
when[c] I make your enemies the
footstool under your feet.'
When the LORD from Zion hands 2
you the sceptre, the symbol of
your power,
march forth through the ranks of[d]
your enemies.
At birth[e] you were endowed with 3
princely gifts
and[f] resplendent[g] in holiness.
You have shone with the dew of
youth since your mother bore
you.
The LORD has sworn and will not 4
change his purpose:
'You are a priest for ever,
in the succession of Melchizedek.'
The Lord at your right hand   5
has broken kings in the day of his
anger.
So the king in his majesty,[h] sove- 6
reign of a mighty land,
will punish nations;[i]
he will drink from the torrent 7
beside the path
and therefore will hold his head
high.

---

[a] Prob. rdg.; Heb. his judges.   [b] You shall sit: or Sit.   [c] Or until or while.
[d] Or reign in the midst of.   [e] At birth: or On the day of your power.
[f] you were...and: or your people offered themselves willingly; mng. of Heb.
uncertain.   [g] Or apparelled.
[h] So...majesty: poss. rdg.; Heb. full of corpses, he crushed.
[i] So...nations: or He shall punish the nations – heaps of corpses, broken heads –
over a wide expanse.

111

1 O praise the LORD.

With all my heart will I praise the LORD
in the company of good men, in the whole congregation.

2 Great are the doings of the LORD;
all men study them for their delight.

3 His acts are full of majesty and splendour;
righteousness is his for ever.

4 He has won a name by his marvellous deeds;
the LORD is gracious and compassionate.

5 He gives food to those who fear him,
he keeps his covenant always in mind.

6 He showed his people what his strength could do,
bestowing on them the lands of other nations.

7 His works are truth and justice;
his precepts all stand on firm foundations,

8 strongly based to endure for ever,
their fabric goodness and truth.

9 He sent and redeemed his people;
he decreed that his covenant should always endure.
Holy is his name, inspiring awe.

10 The fear of the LORD is the beginning[a] of wisdom,
and they who live by it grow in understanding.
Praise will be his for ever.

112

1 O praise the LORD.

Happy is the man who fears the LORD
and finds great joy in his commandments.

2 His descendants shall be the mightiest in the land,
a blessed generation of good men.

3 His house shall be full of wealth and riches;
righteousness shall be his for ever.

4 He is gracious, compassionate, good,
a beacon in darkness for honest men.

5 It is right for a man to be gracious in his lending,
to order his affairs with judgement.

6 Nothing shall ever shake him;
his goodness shall be remembered for all time.

7 Bad news shall have no terrors for him,
because his heart is steadfast, trusting in the LORD.

8 His confidence is strongly based, he will have no fear;
and in the end he will gloat over his enemies.

9 He gives freely to the poor;
righteousness shall be his for ever;
in honour he carries his head high.

10 The wicked man shall see it with rising anger
and grind his teeth in despair;
the hopes of wicked men shall come to nothing.

113

1 O praise the LORD.

Praise the LORD, you that are his servants,
praise the name of the LORD.

2 Blessed be the name of the LORD
now and evermore.

3 From the rising of the sun to its setting
may the LORD's name be praised.

4 High is the LORD above all nations,
his glory above the heavens.

5–6 There is none like the LORD our God
in heaven or on earth,
who sets his throne so high
but deigns to look down so low;

7 who lifts the weak out of the dust
and raises the poor from the dung-hill,

[a] Or chief part.

8 giving them a place among princes,
among the princes of his people;
9 who makes the woman in a childless house
a happy mother of children.[a]

114

1 O praise the LORD.[b]

When Israel came out of Egypt,
Jacob from a people of outlandish
speech,
2 Judah became his sanctuary,
Israel his dominion.
3 The sea looked and ran away;
Jordan turned back.
4 The mountains skipped like rams,
the hills like young sheep.
5 What was it, sea? Why did you
run?
Jordan, why did you turn back?
6 Why, mountains, did you skip like
rams,
and you, hills, like young sheep?
7 Dance, O earth, at the presence of
the Lord,
at the presence of the God of
Jacob,
8 who turned the rock into a pool of
water,
the granite cliff into a fountain.

115

1 Not to us, O LORD, not to us,
but to thy name ascribe the glory,
for thy true love and for thy
constancy.

2 Why do the nations ask,
'Where then is their God?'
3 Our God is in high heaven;
he does whatever pleases him.
4 Their idols are silver and gold,
made by the hands of men.
5 They have mouths that cannot
speak,
and eyes that cannot see;
6 they have ears that cannot hear,
nostrils, and cannot smell;
7 with their hands they cannot feel,

with their feet they cannot walk,
and no sound comes from their
throats.
Their makers grow to be like them, 8
and so do all who trust in them.

But Israel trusts in the LORD; 9
he is their helper and their shield.
The house of Aaron trusts in the 10
LORD;
he is their helper and their shield.
Those who fear the LORD trust in 11
the LORD;
he is their helper and their shield.
The LORD remembers us, and he 12
will bless us;
he will bless the house of Israel,
he will bless the house of Aaron.
The LORD will bless all who fear 13
him,
high and low alike.

May the LORD give you increase, 14
both you and your sons.
You are blessed by the LORD, 15
the LORD who made heaven and
earth.
The heavens, they are the LORD's; 16
the earth he has given to all mankind.
It is not the dead who praise the 17
LORD,
not those who go down into silence;
but we, the living, bless the LORD, 18
now and for evermore.

O praise the LORD.

116

I love the LORD, for he has heard 1
me
and listens to my prayer;
for he has given me a hearing 2
whenever I have cried to him.
The cords of death bound me, 3
Sheol held me in its grip.
Anguish and torment held me fast;
so I invoked the LORD by name, 4
'Deliver me, O LORD, I beseech
thee;
for I am thy slave.'[c]

---

[a] O praise the LORD transposed to the beginning of Ps. 114.   [b] See note on Ps. 113. 9.
[c] for . . . slave: transposed from the beginning of verse 16; Heb. adds O LORD.

5 Gracious is the LORD and righteous,
  our God is full of compassion.
6 The LORD preserves the simple-
  hearted;
  I was brought low and he saved me.
7 Be at rest once more, my heart,
  for the LORD has showered gifts
  upon you.
8 He has rescued me from death
  and my feet from stumbling.
9 I will walk in the presence of the
  LORD
  in the land of the living.

10 I was sure that I should be swept
   away,
   and my distress was bitter.
11 In panic I cried,
   'How faithless all men are!'
12 How can I repay the LORD
   for all his gifts to me?
13 I will take in my hands the cup of
   salvation
   and invoke the LORD by name.
14 I will pay my vows to the LORD
   in the presence of all his people.
15 A precious thing in the LORD's
   sight
   is the death of those who die faithful to him.
16 *a*I am thy slave, thy slave-girl's son;
   thou hast undone the bonds that
   bound me.
17 To thee will I bring a thank-
   offering
   and invoke the LORD by name.
18 I will pay my vows to the LORD
   in the presence of all his people,
19 in the courts of the LORD's house,
   in the midst of you, Jerusalem.

O praise the LORD.

117

1 Praise the LORD, all nations,
  extol him, all you peoples;
2 for his love protecting us is strong,
  the LORD's constancy is everlasting.

O praise the LORD.

118

1 It is good to give thanks to the
  LORD,
  for his love endures for ever.
2 Declare it, house of Israel:
  his love endures for ever.
3 Declare it, house of Aaron:
  his love endures for ever.
4 Declare it, you that fear the LORD:
  his love endures for ever.
5 When in my distress I called to the
  LORD,
  his answer was to set me free.
6 The LORD is on my side, I have no
  fear;
  what can man do to me?
7 The LORD is on my side, he is my
  helper,
  and I shall gloat over my enemies.
8 It is better to find refuge in the
  LORD
  than to trust in men.
9 It is better to find refuge in the
  LORD
  than to trust in princes.
10 All nations surround me,
   but in the LORD's name I will drive
   them away.
11 They surround me on this side and
   on that,
   but in the LORD's name I will drive
   them away.
12 They surround me like bees at the
   honey;
   they attack me, as fire attacks
   brushwood,
   but in the LORD's name I will drive
   them away.
13 They thrust hard against me so
   that I nearly fall;
   but the LORD has helped me.
14 The LORD is my refuge and defence,
   and he has become my deliverer.
15 Hark! Shouts of deliverance
   in the camp of the victors*b*!
   With his right hand the LORD does
   mighty deeds,
16 the right hand of the LORD raises
   up.
17 I shall not die but live
   to proclaim the works of the LORD.

---

a Prob. rdg.; Heb. prefixes For I am thy slave, O LORD; see note on verse 4.
b Or righteous.

18 The LORD did indeed chasten me,
but he did not surrender me to
Death.

19 Open to me the gates of victory;*a*
I will enter by them and praise the
LORD.

20 This is the gate of the LORD;
the victors*b* shall make their entry
through it.

21 I will praise thee, for thou hast
answered me
and hast become my deliverer.

22 The stone which the builders rejected
has become the chief corner-stone.

23 This is the LORD's doing;
it is marvellous in our eyes.

24 This is the day on which the LORD
has acted:*c*
let us exult and rejoice in it.

25 We pray thee, O LORD, deliver us;
we pray thee, O LORD, send us
prosperity.

26 Blessed in the name of the LORD
are all who come;
we bless you from the house of the
LORD.

27 The LORD is God; he has given
light to us,
the ordered line of pilgrims by the
horns of the altar.

28 Thou art my God and I will praise
thee;
my God, I will exalt thee.

29 It is good to give thanks to the
LORD,
for his love endures for ever.

119

1 Happy are they whose life is blameless,
who conform to the law of the LORD.

2 Happy are they who obey his instruction,
who set their heart on finding him;

3 who have done no wrong
and have lived according to his will.

4 Thou, Lord, hast laid down thy
precepts
for men to keep them faithfully.

5 If only I might hold a steady
course,
keeping thy statutes!

6 I shall never be put to shame
if I fix my eyes on thy commandments.

7 I will praise thee in sincerity of
heart
as I learn thy just decrees.

8 Thy statutes will I keep faithfully;
O do not leave me forsaken.

9 How shall a young man steer an
honest course?
By holding to thy word.

10 With all my heart I strive to find
thee;
let me not stray from thy commandments.

11 I treasure thy promise in my heart,
for fear that I might sin against
thee.

12 Blessed art thou, O LORD;
teach me thy statutes.

13 I say them over, one by one,
the decrees that thou hast proclaimed.

14 I have found more joy along the
path of thy instruction
than in any kind of wealth.

15 I will meditate on thy precepts
and keep thy paths ever before my
eyes.

16 In thy statutes I find continual delight;
I will not forget thy word.

17 Grant this to me, thy servant: let
me live
and, living, keep thy word.

18 Take the veil from my eyes, that I
may see
the marvels that spring from thy
law.

19 I am but a stranger here on earth,*d*
do not hide thy commandments
from me.

20 My heart pines with longing
day and night for thy decrees.

21 The proud have felt thy rebuke;
cursed are those who turn from thy
commandments.

a Or *righteousness.*
b Or *righteous.*
c Or *which the* LORD *has made.*
d Or *in the land.*

22 Set me free from scorn and insult,
   for I have obeyed thy instruction.
23 The powers that be sit scheming together against me;
   but I, thy servant, will study thy
   statutes.
24 Thy instruction is my continual
   delight;
   I turn to it for counsel.

25 I lie prone in the dust;
   grant me life according to thy
   word.
26 I tell thee all I have done and thou
   dost answer me;
   teach me thy statutes.
27 Show me the way set out in thy
   precepts,
   and I will meditate on thy wonders.
28 I cannot rest for misery;
   renew my strength in accordance
   with thy word.
29 Keep falsehood far from me
   and grant me the grace of living by
   thy law.
30 I have chosen the path of truth
   and have set thy decrees before me.
31 I hold fast to thy instruction;
   O LORD, let me not be put to shame.
32 I will run the course set out in thy
   commandments,
   for they gladden my heart.

33 Teach me, O LORD, the way set out
   in thy statutes,
   and in keeping them I shall find
   my reward.
34 Give me the insight to obey thy law
   and to keep it with all my heart;
35 make me walk in the path of thy
   commandments,
   for that is my desire.
36 Dispose my heart toward thy instruction
   and not toward ill-gotten gains;
37 turn away my eyes from all that is
   vile,
   grant me life by thy word.
38 Fulfil thy promise for thy servant,
   the promise made to those who
   fear thee.
39 Turn away the censure which I
   dread,

for thy decrees are good.
How I long for thy precepts!   40
In thy righteousness grant me life.

Thy love never fails; let it light on   41
me, O LORD,
and thy deliverance, for that was
thy promise;
then I shall have my answer to the   42
man who taunts me,
because I trust in thy word.
Rob me not of my power to speak   43
the truth,
for I put my hope in thy decrees.
I will heed thy law continually,   44
for ever and ever;
I walk in freedom wherever I will,   45
because I have studied thy pre-
cepts.
I will speak of thy instruction   46
before kings
and will not be ashamed;
in thy commandments I find con-   47
tinuing delight;
I love them with all my heart.
I will welcome thy commandments[a]   48
and will meditate on thy statutes.

Remember the word spoken to me,   49
thy servant,
on which thou hast taught me to
fix my hope.
In time of trouble my consolation   50
is this,
that thy promise has given me life.
Proud men treat me with insolent   51
scorn,
but I do not swerve from thy law.
I have cherished thy decrees all my   52
life long,
and in them I find consolation, O
LORD.
Gusts of anger seize me as I think   53
of evil men
who forsake thy law.
Thy statutes are the theme of my   54
song[b]
wherever I make my home.
In the night I remember thy name,   55
O LORD,
and dwell upon thy law.
This is true of me,   56
that I have kept thy precepts.

[a] *Prob. rdg.; Heb. adds* which I love.   [b] the theme of my song: *or* wonderful to me.

57 Thou, LORD, art all I have;
  I have promised to keep thy word.
58 With all my heart I have tried to
  please thee;
  fulfil thy promise and be gracious
  to me.
59 I have thought much about the
  course of my life
  and always turned back to thy
  instruction;
60 I have never delayed but always
  made haste
  to keep thy commandments.
61 Bands of evil men close round me,
  but I do not forget thy law.
62 At midnight I rise to give thee
  thanks
  for the justice of thy decrees.
63 I keep company with all who fear
  thee,
  with all who follow thy precepts.
64 The earth is full of thy never-
  failing love;
  O LORD, teach me thy statutes.

65 Thou hast shown thy servant
  much kindness,
  fulfilling thy word, O LORD.
66 Give me insight, give me knowledge,
  for I put my trust in thy commandments.
67 I went astray before I was punished;
  but now I pay heed to thy promise.
68 Thou art good and thou doest good;
  teach me thy statutes.
69 Proud men blacken my name with
  lies,
  yet I follow thy precepts with all
  my heart;
70 their hearts are thick and gross;
  but I continually delight in thy law.
71 How good it is for me to have been
  punished,
  to school me in thy statutes!
72 The law thou hast ordained means
  more to me
  than a fortune in gold and silver.

73 Thy hands moulded me and made
  me what I am;
  show me how I may learn thy
  commandments.

74 Let all who fear thee be glad when
  they see me,
  because I hope for the fulfilment of
  thy word.
75 I know, O LORD, that thy decrees
  are just
  and even in punishing thou keepest
  faith with me.
76 Let thy never-failing love console
  me,
  as thou hast promised me, thy
  servant.
77 Extend thy compassion to me,
  that I may live;
  for thy law is my continual delight.
78 Put the proud to shame, for with
  their lies they wrong me;
  but I will meditate on thy precepts.
79 Let all who fear thee turn to me,
  all who cherish thy instruction.
80 Let me give my whole heart to thy
  statutes,
  so that I am not put to shame.

81 I long with all my heart for thy
  deliverance,
  hoping for the fulfilment of thy
  word;
82 my sight grows dim with looking
  for thy promise
  and still I cry, 'When wilt thou
  comfort me?'
83 Though I shrivel like a wine-skin in
  the smoke,
  I do not forget thy statutes.
84 How long has thy servant to wait
  for thee to fulfil thy decree against
  my persecutors?
85 Proud men who flout thy law
  spread tales about me.
86 Help me, for they hound me with
  their lies,
  but thy commandments all stand
  for ever.
87 They had almost swept me from
  the earth,
  but I did not forsake thy precepts;
88 grant me life, as thy love is unchanging,
  that I may follow all thy instruction.

89 Eternal is thy word, O LORD,
  planted firm in heaven.

90 Thy promise[a] endures for all time,
  stable as the earth which thou hast
  fixed.
91 This day, as ever, thy decrees
  stand fast;
  for all things serve thee.
92 If thy law had not been my continual delight,
  I should have perished in all my
  troubles.
93 never will I forget thy precepts,
  for through them thou hast given
  me life.
94 I am thine; O save me,
  for I have pondered thy precepts.
95 Evil men lie in wait to destroy
  me;
  but I will give thought to thy
  instruction.
96 I see that all things come to an end,
  but thy commandment has no
  limit.

97 O how I love thy law!
  It is my study all day long.
98 Thy commandments are mine for
  ever;
  through them I am wiser than my
  enemies.
99 I have more insight than all my
  teachers,
  for thy instruction is my study;
100 I have more wisdom than the old,
  because I have kept thy precepts.
101 I set no foot on any evil path
  in my obedience to thy word;
102 I do not swerve from thy decrees,
  for thou thyself hast been my
  teacher.
103 How sweet is thy promise in my
  mouth,
  sweeter on my tongue than honey!
104 From thy precepts I learn wisdom;
  therefore I hate the paths of falsehood.

105 Thy word is a lamp to guide my
  feet
  and a light on my path;
106 I have bound myself by oath and
  solemn vow
  to keep thy just decrees.
107 I am cruelly afflicted;

O LORD, revive me and make good
  thy word.
Accept, O LORD, the willing tribute 108
  of my lips
and teach me thy decrees.
Every day I take my life in my 109
  hands,
yet I never forget thy law.
Evil men have set traps for me, 110
but I do not stray from thy precepts.
Thy instruction is my everlasting 111
  inheritance;
it is the joy of my heart.
I am resolved to fulfil thy statutes; 112
they are a reward that never fails.

I hate men who are not single- 113
  minded,
but I love thy law.
Thou art my shield and hiding- 114
  place;
I hope for the fulfilment of thy word.
Go, you evildoers, and leave me to 115
  myself,
that I may keep the commandments of my God.
Support me as thou hast promised, 116
  that I may live;
do not disappoint my hope.
Sustain me, that I may see de- 117
  liverance;
so shall I always be occupied with
  thy statutes.
Thou dost reject those who stray 118
  from thy statutes,
for their talk is all malice and lies.
In thy sight all the wicked on earth 119
  are scum;
therefore I love thy instruction.
The dread of thee makes my flesh 120
  creep,
and I stand in awe of thy decrees.

I have done what is just and right; 121
thou wilt not abandon me to my
  oppressors.
Stand surety for the welfare of thy 122
  servant;
let not the proud oppress me.[b]
My sight grows dim with looking 123
  for thy deliverance
and waiting for thy righteous promise.

---

[a] *Prob. rdg.; Heb.* Thy constancy.   [b] oppress me: *or* charge me falsely.

124 In all thy dealings with me, LORD,
    show thy true love
    and teach me thy statutes.
125 I am thy servant; give me insight
    to understand thy instruction.
126 It is time to act, O LORD;
    for men have broken thy law.
127 Truly I love thy commandments
    more than the finest gold.
128 It is by thy precepts that I find the
    right way;
    I hate the paths of falsehood.

129 Thy instruction is wonderful;
    therefore I gladly keep it.
130 Thy word is revealed, and all is
    light;
    it gives understanding even to the
    untaught.
131 I pant, I thirst,
    longing for thy commandments.
132 Turn to me and be gracious,
    as thou hast decreed for those who
    love thy name.
133 Make my step firm according to
    thy promise,
    and let no wrong have the mastery
    over me.
134 Set me free from man's oppression,
    that I may observe thy precepts.
135 Let thy face shine upon thy servant
    and teach me thy statutes.
136 My eyes stream with tears
    because men do not heed thy law.

137 How just thou art, O LORD!
    How straight and true are thy
    decrees!
138 How just is the instruction thou
    givest!
    It is fixed firm and sure.
139 I am speechless with resentment,
    for my enemies have forgotten thy
    words.
140 Thy promise has been tested
    through and through,
    and thy servant loves it.
141 I may be despised and of little
    account,
    but I do not forget thy precepts.
142 Thy justice is an everlasting justice,
    and thy law is truth.
143 Though I am oppressed by trouble
    and anxiety,

thy commandments are my con-
    tinual delight.
Thy instruction is ever just;   144
give me understanding that I may
    live.

I call with my whole heart; answer 145
    me, LORD.
I will keep thy statutes.
I call to thee; O save me   146
that I may heed thy instruction.
I rise before dawn and cry for help; 147
I hope for the fulfilment of thy
    word.
Before the midnight watch also my 148
    eyes are open
for meditation on thy promise.
Hear me, as thy love is unchanging, 149
and give me life, O LORD, by thy
    decree.
My pursuers in their malice are 150
    close behind me,
but they are far from thy law.
Yet thou art near, O LORD,   151
and all thy commandments are
    true.
I have long known from thy in- 152
    struction
that thou hast given it eternal
    foundations.

See in what trouble I am and set me 153
    free,
for I do not forget thy law.
Be thou my advocate and win 154
    release for me;
true to thy promise, give me life.
Such deliverance is beyond the 155
    reach of wicked men,
because they do not ponder thy
    statutes.
Great is thy compassion, O LORD; 156
grant me life by thy decree.
Many are my persecutors and 157
    enemies,
but I have not swerved from thy
    instruction.
I was cut to the quick when I saw 158
    traitors
who had no regard for thy promise.
See how I love thy precepts, O 159
    LORD!
Grant me life, as thy love is un-
    changing.

160 Thy word is founded in truth,
and thy just decrees are everlasting.

161 The powers that be persecute me
without cause,
yet my heart thrills at thy word.

162 I am jubilant over thy promise,
like a man carrying off much booty.

163 Falsehood I detest and loathe,
but I love thy law.

164 Seven times a day I praise thee
for the justice of thy decrees.

165 Peace is the reward of those who
love thy law;
no pitfalls beset their path.

166 I hope for thy deliverance, O LORD,
and I fulfil thy commandments;

167 gladly I heed thy instruction
and love it greatly.

168 I heed thy precepts and thy
instruction,
for all my life lies open before thee.

169 Let my cry of joy reach thee, O
LORD;
give me understanding of thy word.

170 Let my supplication reach thee;
be true to thy promise and save me.

171 Let thy praise pour from my lips,
because thou teachest me thy
statutes;

172 let the music of thy promises be on
my tongue,
for thy commandments are justice
itself.

173 Let thy hand be prompt to help me,
for I have chosen thy precepts.

174 I long for thy deliverance, O LORD,
and thy law is my continual
delight.

175 Let me live and I will praise thee;
let thy decrees be my support.

176 I have strayed like a lost sheep;
come, search for thy servant,
for I have not forgotten thy
commandments.

120

1 I called to the LORD in my distress,
and he answered me.

2 'O LORD,' I cried, 'save me from
lying lips
and from the tongue of slander.'

What has he in store for you, 3
slanderous tongue?
What more has he for you?

Nothing but a warrior's sharp 4
arrows
or red-hot charcoal.

Hard is my lot, exiled in Meshech, 5
dwelling by the tents of Kedar.

All the time that I dwelt 6
among men who hated peace,

I sought peace; but whenever I 7
spoke of it,
they were for war.

121

If I lift up my eyes to the hills, 1
where shall I find help?

Help comes only from the LORD, 2
maker of heaven and earth.

How could he let your foot 3
stumble?
How could he, your guardian, sleep?

The guardian of Israel 4
never slumbers, never sleeps.

The LORD is your guardian, 5
your defence at your right hand;

the sun will not strike you by day 6
nor the moon by night.

The LORD will guard you against 7
all evil;
he will guard you, body and soul.

The LORD will guard your going 8
and your coming,
now and for evermore.

122

I rejoiced when they said to me, 1
'Let us go to the house of the
LORD.'

Now we stand within your gates, 2
O Jerusalem:

Jerusalem that is built to be a city 3
where people come together in
unity;

to which the tribes resort, the 4
tribes of the LORD,

to give thanks to the LORD himself,
the bounden duty of Israel.

For in her are set the thrones of 5
justice,
the thrones of the house of David.

6 Pray for the peace of Jerusalem:
'May those who love you prosper;
7 peace be within your ramparts
and prosperity in your palaces.'
8 For the sake of these my brothers
and my friends,
I will say, 'Peace be within you.'
9 For the sake of the house of the
LORD our God
I will pray for your good.

123

1 I lift my eyes to thee
whose throne is in heaven.
2 As the eyes of a slave follow his
master's hand
or the eyes of a slave-girl her
mistress,
so our eyes are turned to the LORD
our God
waiting for kindness from him.
3 Deal kindly with us, O LORD, deal
kindly,
for we have suffered insult enough;
4 too long have we had to suffer
the insults of the wealthy,
the scorn of proud men.

124

1 If the LORD had not been on our
side,
Israel may now say,
2 if the LORD had not been on our
side
when they assailed us,
3 they would have swallowed us
alive
when their anger was roused
against us.
4 The waters would have carried us
away
and the torrent swept over us;
5 over us would have swept
the seething waters.
6 Blessed be the LORD, who did not
leave us
to be the prey between their
teeth.
7 We have escaped like a bird
from the fowler's trap;
the trap broke, and so we escaped.

Our help is in the name of the LORD, 8
maker of heaven and earth.

125

Those who trust in the LORD are 1
like Mount Zion,
which cannot be shaken but stands
fast for ever.
As the hills enfold Jerusalem, 2
so the LORD enfolds his people,
now and evermore.
The sceptre of wickedness shall 3
surely find no home
in the land allotted to the righteous,
so that the righteous shall not set
their hands to injustice.
Do good, O LORD, to those who are 4
good
and to those who are upright in
heart.
But those who turn aside into 5
crooked ways,
may the LORD destroy them, as he
destroys all evildoers!

Peace be upon Israel!

126

When the LORD turned the tide of 1
Zion's fortune,
we were like men who had found
new health.[a]
Our mouths were full of laughter 2
and our tongues sang aloud for joy.
Then word went round among the
nations,
'The LORD has done great things
for them.'
Great things indeed the LORD then 3
did for us,
and we rejoiced.

Turn once again our fortune, LORD, 4
as streams return in the dry south.
Those who sow in tears 5
shall reap with songs of joy.
A man may go out weeping, 6
carrying his bag of seed;
but he will come back with songs
of joy,
carrying home his sheaves.

_a_ like...health: _or_ like dreamers.

127

1 Unless the LORD builds the house,
its builders will have toiled in vain.
Unless the LORD keeps watch over
  a city,
in vain the watchman stands on
  guard.
2 In vain you rise up early
and go late to rest,
toiling for the bread you eat;
he supplies the need of those he
  loves.[a]
3 Sons are a gift from the LORD
and children a reward from him.
4 Like arrows in the hand of a
  fighting man
are the sons of a man's youth.
5 Happy is the man
who has his quiver full of them;
such men shall not be put to shame
when they confront their enemies
  in court.

128

1 Happy are all who fear the LORD,
who live according to his will.
2 You shall eat the fruit of your own
  labours,
you shall be happy and you shall
  prosper.
3 Your wife shall be like a fruitful vine
in the heart of your house;
your sons shall be like olive-shoots
round about your table.
4 This is the blessing in store for the
  man
who fears the LORD.
5 May the LORD bless you from Zion;
may you share the prosperity of
  Jerusalem
all the days of your life,
6 and live to see your children's
  children!

Peace be upon Israel!

129

1 Often since I was young have men
  attacked me –
let Israel now say –

often since I was young have men 2
  attacked me,
but never have they prevailed.
They scored my back with scourges, 3
like ploughmen driving long furrows.
Yet the LORD in his justice 4
has cut me loose from the bonds of
  the wicked.
Let all enemies of Zion 5
be thrown back in shame;
let them be like grass growing on 6
  the roof,
which withers before it can shoot,
which will never fill a mower's hand 7
nor yield an armful for the harvester,
so that passers-by will never say to 8
  them,
'The blessing of the LORD be upon
  you!
We bless you in the name of the
  LORD.'

130

Out of the depths have I called to 1
  thee, O LORD;
Lord, hear my cry. 2
Let thy ears be attentive
to my plea for mercy.
If thou, LORD, shouldest keep 3
  account of sins,
who, O Lord, could hold up his
  head?
But in thee is forgiveness, 4
and therefore thou art revered.
I wait for the LORD with all my 5
  soul,
I hope for the fulfilment of his
  word.
My soul waits[b] for the Lord 6
more eagerly than watchmen for
  the morning.
Like men who watch for the
  morning,
O Israel, look for the LORD. 7
For in the LORD is love unfailing,
and great is his power to set men
  free.
He alone will set Israel free 8
from all their sins.

[a] Prob. rdg.; Heb. adds an unintelligible word.
[b] waits: transposed from after the LORD in verse 5.

131

1 O Lord, my heart is not proud,
nor are my eyes haughty;
I do not busy myself with great
  matters
or things too marvellous for me.
2 No; I submit myself, I account myself lowly,
as a weaned child clinging to its
  mother.*a*
3 O Israel, look for the Lord
now and evermore.

132

1 O Lord, remember David
in the time of his adversity,
2 how he swore to the Lord
and made a vow to the Mighty One
  of Jacob:
3 'I will not enter my house
nor will I mount my bed,
4 I will not close my eyes in sleep
or my eyelids in slumber,
5 until I find a sanctuary for the
  Lord,
a dwelling for the Mighty One of
  Jacob.'
6 We heard of it in Ephrathah;
we came upon it in the region of
  Jaar.
7 Let us enter his dwelling,
let us fall in worship at his footstool.
8 Arise, O Lord, and come to thy
  resting-place,
thou and the ark of thy power.
9 Let thy priests be clothed in
  righteousness
and let thy loyal servants shout for
  joy.
10 For thy servant David's sake
reject not thy anointed king.
11 The Lord swore to David
an oath which he will not break:
'A prince of your own line
will I set upon your throne.
12 If your sons keep my covenant
and heed the teaching that I give
  them,

their sons in turn for all time
shall sit upon your throne.'
For the Lord has chosen Zion   13
and desired it for his home:
'This is my resting-place for   14
  ever;
here will I make my home, for such
  is my desire.
I will richly bless her destitute*b*   15
and satisfy her needy with
  bread.
With salvation will I clothe her 16
  priests;
her loyal servants shall shout for
  joy.
There will I renew the line of   17
  David's house
and light a lamp for my anointed
  king;
his enemies will I clothe with   18
  shame,
but on his head shall be a shining
  crown.'

133

How good it is and how pleasant   1
for brothers to live*c* together!
It is fragrant as oil poured upon 2
  the head
and falling over the beard,
Aaron's beard, when the oil runs
  down
over the collar of his vestments.
It is like the dew of Hermon falling 3
upon the hills of Zion.
There the Lord bestows his
  blessing,
life for evermore.

134

Come, bless the Lord,   1
all you servants of the Lord,
who stand night after night
in the house of the Lord.
Lift up your hands in the sanctuary 2
and bless the Lord.
The Lord, maker of heaven and   3
  earth,
bless you from Zion!

---

a Prob. rdg.; Heb. adds as a weaned child clinging to me.
b her destitute: prob. rdg.; Heb. her provisions.
c Or to worship.

135

1 O praise the LORD.

Praise the name of the LORD;
praise him, you servants of the
LORD,
2 who stand in the house of the LORD,
in the temple courts of our God.
3 Praise the LORD, for that is good;
honour his name with psalms, for
that is pleasant.
4 The LORD has chosen Jacob to be
his own
and Israel as his special treasure.
5 I know that the LORD is great,
that our Lord is above all gods.
6 Whatever the LORD pleases,
that he does, in heaven and on
earth,
in the sea, in the depths of ocean.
7 He brings up the mist from the
ends of the earth,
he opens rifts[a] for the rain,
and brings the wind out of his
storehouses.
8 He struck down all the first-born
in Egypt,
both man and beast.
9 In Egypt he sent signs and portents
against Pharaoh and all his subjects.
10 He struck down mighty nations
and slew great kings,
11 Sihon king of the Amorites, Og the
king of Bashan,
and all the princes of Canaan,
12 and gave their land to Israel,
to Israel his people as their patrimony.
13 O LORD, thy name endures for ever;
thy renown, O LORD, shall last for
all generations.
14 The LORD will give his people
justice
and have compassion on his servants.
15 The gods of the nations are idols of
silver and gold,
made by the hands of men.
16 They have mouths that cannot
speak
and eyes that cannot see;

17 they have ears that do not hear,
and there is no breath in their
nostrils.[b]
18 Their makers grow like them,
and so do all who trust in them.
19 O house of Israel, bless the LORD;
O house of Aaron, bless the LORD.
20 O house of Levi, bless the LORD;
you who fear the LORD, bless the
LORD.
21 Blessed from Zion be the LORD
who dwells in Jerusalem.

O praise the LORD.

136

1 It is good to give thanks to the
LORD,
for his love endures for ever.
2 Give thanks to the God of gods;
his love endures for ever.
3 Give thanks to the Lord of lords;
his love endures for ever.
4 Alone he works great marvels;
his love endures for ever.
5 In wisdom he made the heavens;
his love endures for ever.
6 He laid the earth upon the waters;
his love endures for ever.
7 He made the great lights,
his love endures for ever,
8 the sun to rule by day,
his love endures for ever,
9 the moon and the stars to rule by
night;
his love endures for ever.
10 He struck down the first-born of
the Egyptians,
his love endures for ever,
11 and brought Israel from among
them;
his love endures for ever.
12 With strong hand and outstretched arm,
his love endures for ever,
13 he divided the Red Sea in two,
his love endures for ever,
14 and made Israel pass through it,
his love endures for ever;
15 but Pharaoh and his host he swept
into the sea;
his love endures for ever.

[a] Prob. rdg.; Heb. lightnings.

[b] Prob. rdg.; Heb. mouths.

16 He led his people through the
  wilderness;
  his love endures for ever.
17 He struck down great kings;
  his love endures for ever.
18 He slew mighty kings,
  his love endures for ever,
19 Sihon king of the Amorites,
  his love endures for ever,
20 and Og the king of Bashan;
  his love endures for ever.
21 He gave their land to Israel,
  his love endures for ever,
22 to Israel his servant as their patrimony;
  his love endures for ever.
23 He remembered us when we were
  cast down,
  his love endures for ever,
24 and rescued us from our enemies;
  his love endures for ever.
25 He gives food to all his creatures;
  his love endures for ever.
26 Give thanks to the God of heaven,
  for his love endures for ever.

137

1 By the rivers of Babylon we sat
  down and wept
  when we remembered Zion.
2 There on the willow-trees*a*
  we hung up our harps,
3 for there those who carried us off
  demanded music and singing,
  and our captors called on us to be
  merry:
  'Sing us one of the songs of Zion.'
4 How could we sing the LORD's song
  in a foreign land?

5 If I forget you, O Jerusalem,
  let my right hand wither away;
6 let my tongue cling to the roof of
  my mouth
  if I do not remember you,
  if I do not set Jerusalem
  above my highest joy.
7 Remember, O LORD, against the
  people of Edom

the day of Jerusalem's fall,
when they said, 'Down with it,
  down with it,
down to its very foundations!'
O Babylon, Babylon the destroyer, 8
happy the man who repays you
for all that you did to us!
Happy is he who shall seize your 9
  children
and dash them against the rock.

138

I will praise thee, O LORD, with all 1
  my heart;
boldly, O God, will I sing psalms to
  thee.*b*
I will bow down towards thy holy 2
  temple,
for thy love and faithfulness I will
  praise thy name;
for thou hast made thy promise
  wide as the heavens.
When I called to thee thou didst 3
  answer me
and make me bold and valiant-
  hearted.
Let all the kings of the earth 4
  praise*c* thee, O LORD,
when they hear the words thou
  hast spoken;
and let them sing of*d* the LORD's 5
  ways,
for great is the glory of the
  LORD.
For the LORD, high as he is, cares 6
  for the lowly,
and from afar he humbles the
  proud.
Though I walk among foes thou 7
  dost preserve my life,
exerting thy power against the
  rage of my enemies,
and with thy right hand thou
  savest me.
The LORD will accomplish his pur- 8
  pose for me.
Thy true love, O LORD, endures
  for ever;
leave not thy work unfinished.

a Or poplars.
b boldly...thee: or I will sing psalms to thee before the gods.
c Or confess.
d Or walk in.

139

1 LORD, thou hast examined me and
knowest me.
2 Thou knowest all, whether I sit
down or rise up;
thou hast discerned my thoughts
from afar.
3 Thou hast traced my journey and
my resting places,
and art familiar with all my paths.
4 For there is not a word on my
tongue
but thou, LORD, knowest them all.[a]
5 Thou hast kept close guard before
me and behind
and hast spread thy hand over me.
6 Such knowledge is beyond my
understanding,
so high that I cannot reach it.
7 Where can I escape from thy spirit?
Where can I flee from thy presence?
8 If I climb up to heaven, thou art
there;
if I make my bed in Sheol, again
I find thee.
9 If I take my flight to the frontiers
of the morning
or dwell at the limit of the western
sea,
10 even there thy hand will meet me
and thy right hand will hold me fast.
11 If I say, 'Surely darkness will steal
over me,
night will close around me',
12 darkness is no darkness for thee
and night is luminous as day;
to thee both dark and light are one.

13 Thou it was who didst fashion my
inward parts;
thou didst knit me together in my
mother's womb.
14 I will praise thee, for thou dost fill
me with awe;
wonderful thou art, and wonderful
thy works.
Thou knowest me through and
through:
15 my body is no mystery to thee,
how I was secretly kneaded into
shape

and patterned in the depths of the
earth.
Thou didst see my limbs unformed 16
in the womb,
and in thy book they are all
recorded;
day by day they were fashioned,
not one of them was late in
growing.[b]
How deep I find thy thoughts, O 17
God,
how inexhaustible their themes!
Can I count them? They out- 18
number the grains of sand;
to finish the count, my years must
equal thine.

O God, if only thou wouldst slay 19
the wicked!
If those men of blood would but
leave me in peace –
those who provoke thee with 20
deliberate evil
and rise in vicious rebellion
against thee!
How I hate them, O LORD, that 21
hate thee!
I am cut to the quick when they
oppose thee;
I hate them with undying hatred; 22
I hold them all my enemies.

Examine me, O God, and know my 23
thoughts;
test me, and understand my mis-
givings.
Watch lest I follow any path that 24
grieves thee;
guide me in the ancient[c] ways.

140

Rescue me, O LORD, from evil 1
men;
keep me safe from violent men,
whose heads are full of wicked 2
schemes,
who stir up contention day after
day.
Their tongues are sharp as ser- 3
pents' fangs;
on their lips is spiders' poison.

[a] For...them all: or If there is any offence on my tongue, thou, LORD, knowest it all.
[b] was late in growing: prob. rdg.; Heb. om.　　　　[c] Or everlasting.

4 Guard me, O Lord, from wicked
   men;
keep me safe from violent men,
who plan to thrust me out of the
   way.
5 Arrogant men set hidden traps for
   me,
rogues spread their nets
and lay snares for me along the path.
6 I said, 'O Lord, thou art my God;
O Lord, hear my plea for mercy.
7 O Lord God, stronghold of my
   safety,
thou hast shielded my head in the
   day of battle.
8–9 Frustrate, O Lord, their designs
   against me;
never let the wicked gain their purpose.
If any of those at my table rise
   against me,
let their own conspiracies be their
   undoing.
10 Let burning coals be tipped upon
   them;
let them be plunged into the miry
   depths,
never to rise again.
11 Slander shall find no home in the
   land;
evil and violence shall be hounded
   to destruction.'

12 I know that the Lord will give
   their due to the needy
and justice to the downtrodden.
13 Righteous men will surely give
   thanks to thy name;
the upright will worship in thy
   presence.

141

1 O Lord, I call to thee, come quickly to my aid;
listen to my cry when I call to thee.
2 Let my prayer be like incense duly
   set before thee
and my raised hands like the
   evening sacrifice.
3 Set a guard, O Lord, over my
   mouth;
keep watch at the door of my lips.

Turn not my heart to sinful 4
   thoughts
nor to any pursuit of evil courses.
The evildoers appal me;[a]
not for me the delights of their
   table.
I would rather be buffeted by the 5
   righteous
and reproved by good men.
My head shall not be anointed with
   the oil of wicked men,
for that would make me a party to
   their crimes.
They shall founder on the rock of 6
   justice
and shall learn how acceptable my
   words are.
Their bones shall be scattered at 7
   the mouth of Sheol,
like splinters of wood or stone on
   the ground.
But my eyes are fixed on thee, O 8
   Lord God;
thou art my refuge; leave me not
   unprotected.
Keep me from the trap which they 9
   have set for me,
from the snares of evildoers.
Let the wicked fall into their own 10
   nets,
whilst I pass in safety, all alone.

142

I cry aloud to the Lord;   1
to the Lord I plead aloud for
   mercy.
I pour out my complaint before him 2
and tell over my troubles in his
   presence.
When my spirit is faint within me, 3
thou art there to watch over my
   steps.
In the path that I should take
they have hidden a snare.
I look to my right hand,   4
I find no friend by my side;
no way of escape is in sight,
no one comes to rescue me.
I cry to thee, O Lord,   5
and say, 'Thou art my refuge;
thou art all I have
in the land of the living.

---

[a] appal me: *prob. rdg.*; *Heb.* with men.

6 Give me a hearing when I cry,
  for I am brought very low;
  save me from my pursuers,
  for they are too strong for me.
7 Set me free from my prison,
  so that I may praise thy name.'
  The righteous shall crown me with
    garlands,[a]
  when thou givest me my due
    reward.

143

1 LORD, hear my prayer;
  be true to thyself, and listen to my
    pleading;
  then in thy righteousness answer
    me.
2 Bring not thy servant to trial
    before thee;
  against thee no man on earth can
    be right.
3 An enemy has hunted me down,
  has ground my living body under
    foot
  and plunged me into darkness like
    a man long dead,
4 so that my spirit fails me
  and my heart is dazed with despair.
5 I dwell upon the years long past,
  upon the memory of all that thou
    hast done;
  the wonders of thy creation fill my
    mind.
6 To thee I lift my outspread hands,
  athirst for thee in a thirsty land.
7 LORD, make haste to answer,
  for my spirit faints.
  Do not hide thy face from me
  or I shall be like those who go down
    to the abyss.
8 In the morning let me know thy
    true love;
  I have put my trust in thee.
  Show me the way that I must take;
  to thee I offer all my heart.
9 Deliver me, LORD, from my ene-
    mies,
  for with thee have I sought refuge.
10 Teach me to do thy will, for thou
    art my God;

in thy gracious kindness, show me
  the level road.
Keep me safe, O LORD, for the 11
  honour of thy name
and, as thou art just, release me
  from my distress.
In thy love for me, reduce my ene- 12
  mies to silence
and bring destruction on all who
  oppress me;
for I am thy servant.

144

Blessed is the LORD, my rock,   1
who trains my hands for war,
my fingers for battle;
my help that never fails, my 2
  fortress,
my strong tower and my refuge,
my shield in which I trust,
he who puts nations under my feet.

O LORD, what is man that thou 3
  carest for him?
What is mankind? Why give a
  thought to them?
Man is no more than a puff of wind, 4
his days a passing shadow.
If thou, LORD, but tilt the hea- 5
  vens, down they come;
touch the mountains, and they
  smoke.
Shoot forth thy lightning flashes, 6
  far and wide,
and send thy arrows whistling.
Stretch out thy hands from on high 7
  to rescue me
and snatch me from great waters.[b]

I will sing a new song to thee, O God, 9
psalms to the music of a ten-
  stringed lute.
O God who gavest victory to kings 10
and deliverance to thy servant
  David,
rescue me from the cruel sword;
snatch me from the power of for- 11
  eign foes,
whose every word is false
and all their oaths are perjury.

---

[a] crown me with garlands: or crowd round me.
[b] Prob. rdg.; Heb. adds from the power of foreign foes, (8) whose every word is false
and all their oaths are perjury (cp. verse 11).

12 Happy[a] are we whose sons in their
early prime
stand like tall towers,
our daughters like sculptured
pillars
at the corners of a palace.
13 Our barns are full and furnish
plentiful provision;
our sheep bear lambs in thousands
upon thousands;
14 the oxen in our fields are fat and
sleek;
there is no miscarriage or untimely
birth,
no cries of distress in our public
places.
15 Happy are the people in such a
case as ours;
happy the people who have the
LORD for their God.

145

1 I will extol thee, O God my king,
and bless thy name for ever and
ever.
2 Every day will I bless thee
and praise thy name for ever and
ever.
3 Great is the LORD and worthy of
all praise;
his greatness is unfathomable.
4 One generation shall commend thy
works to another
and set forth thy mighty deeds.
5 My theme shall be thy marvellous
works,
the glorious splendour of thy
majesty.
6 Men shall declare thy mighty acts
with awe
and tell of thy great deeds.
7 They shall recite the story of thy
abounding goodness
and sing of thy righteousness with
joy.

8 The LORD is gracious and compassionate,
forbearing, and constant in his love.
9 The LORD is good to all men,
and his tender care rests upon all
his creatures.

All thy creatures praise thee, LORD, 10
and thy servants bless thee.
They talk of the glory of thy king- 11
dom
and tell of thy might,
they proclaim to their fellows how 12
mighty are thy deeds,
how glorious the majesty of thy
kingdom.
Thy kingdom is an everlasting 13
kingdom,
and thy dominion stands for all
generations.

In all his promises the LORD keeps 14
faith,
he is unchanging in all his works;
the LORD holds up those who
stumble
and straightens backs which are
bent.
The eyes of all are lifted to thee in 15
hope,
and thou givest them their food
when it is due;
with open and bountiful hand 16
thou givest what they desire[b] to
every living creature.
The LORD is righteous in all his 17
ways,
unchanging in all that he does;
very near is the LORD to those who 18
call to him,
who call to him in singleness of
heart.
He fulfils their desire if only they 19
fear him;
he hears their cry and saves them.
The LORD watches over all who 20
love him
but sends the wicked to their doom.
My tongue shall speak out the 21
praises of the LORD,
and all creatures shall bless his
holy name
for ever and ever.

146

O praise the LORD.   1

Praise the LORD, my soul.
As long as I live I will praise the 2
LORD;

Prob. rdg.; Heb. Who.   [b] they desire: _or_ thou wilt.

I will sing psalms to my God all my
life long.

3 Put no faith in princes,
in any man, who has no power to
save.

4 He breathes his last breath,
he returns to the dust;
and in that same hour all his
thinking ends.

5 Happy the man whose helper is
the God of Jacob,
whose hopes are in the LORD his
God,

6 maker of heaven and earth,
the sea, and all that is in them;
who serves wrongdoers as he has
sworn

7 and deals out justice to the
oppressed.
The LORD feeds the hungry
and sets the prisoner free.

8 The LORD restores sight to the blind
and straightens backs which are
bent;
the LORD loves the righteous

9 and watches over the stranger;
the LORD gives heart to the orphan
and widow
but turns the course of the wicked
to their ruin.

10 The LORD shall reign for ever,
thy God, O Zion, for all generations.

O praise the LORD.

147

1 O praise the LORD.

How good it is to sing psalms to
our God!
How pleasant to praise him!

2 The LORD is rebuilding Jerusalem;
he gathers in the scattered sons of
Israel.

3 It is he who heals the broken in
spirit
and binds up their wounds,

4 he who numbers the stars one by
one
and names them one and all.

5 Mighty is our Lord and great his
power,
and his wisdom beyond all telling.

The LORD gives new heart to the 6
humble
and brings evildoers down to the
dust.

Sing to the LORD a song of thanks- 7
giving,
sing psalms to the harp in honour
of our God.

He veils the sky in clouds 8
and prepares rain for the earth;
he clothes the hills with grass
and green plants for the use of man.

He gives the cattle their food 9
and the young ravens all that they
gather.

The LORD sets no store by the 10
strength of a horse
and takes no pleasure in a runner's
legs;

his pleasure is in those who fear 11
him,
who wait for his true love.

Sing to the LORD, Jerusalem; 12
O Zion, praise your God,

for he has put new bars in your 13
gates;
he has blessed your children within
them.

He has brought peace to your 14
realm
and given you fine wheat in plenty.

He sends his command to the ends 15
of the earth,
and his word runs swiftly.

He showers down snow, white as 16
wool,
and sprinkles hoar-frost thick as
ashes;

crystals of ice he scatters like 17
bread-crumbs;
he sends the cold, and the water
stands frozen,

he utters his word, and the ice is 18
melted;
he blows with his wind and the
waters flow.

To Jacob he makes his word known, 19
his statutes and decrees to Israel;

he has not done this for any other 20
nation,
nor taught them his decrees.

O praise the LORD.

148

1 O praise the LORD.

Praise the LORD out of heaven;
praise him in the heights.
2 Praise him, all his angels;
praise him, all his host.
3 Praise him, sun and moon;
praise him, all you shining stars;
4 praise him, heaven of heavens,
and you waters above the heavens.
5 Let them all praise the name of the
LORD,
for he spoke the word and they
were created;
6 he established them for ever and
ever
by an ordinance which shall never
pass away.

7 Praise the LORD from the earth,
you water-spouts and ocean
depths;
8 fire and hail, snow and ice,
gales of wind obeying his voice;
9 all mountains and hills,
all fruit-trees and all cedars;
10 wild beasts and cattle,
creeping things and winged birds;
11 kings and all earthly rulers,
princes and judges over the whole
earth;
12 young men and maidens,
old men and young together.
13 Let all praise the name of the LORD,
for his name is high above all
others,
and his majesty above earth and
heaven;
14 he has exalted his people in the
pride of power
and crowned with praise his loyal
servants,
all Israel, the people nearest him.

O praise the LORD.

149

1 O praise the LORD.

Sing to the LORD a new song,
sing his praise in the assembly of
the faithful;

let Israel rejoice in his maker   2
and the sons of Zion exult in their
king.
Let them praise his name in the   3
dance,
and sing him psalms with tambourine and harp.
For the LORD accepts the service   4
of his people;
he crowns his humble folk with
victory.
Let his faithful servants exult in   5
triumph;
let them shout for joy as they kneel
before him.
Let the high praises of God be on   6
their lips
and a two-edged sword in their
hand,
to wreak vengeance on the nations   7
and to chastise the heathen;
to load their kings with chains   8
and put their nobles in irons;
to execute the judgement decreed   9
against them –
this is the glory of all his faithful
servants.

O praise the LORD.

150

O praise the LORD.   1

O praise God in his holy place,
praise him in the vault of heaven,
the vault of his power;
praise him for his mighty works, 2
praise him for his immeasurable
greatness.
Praise him with fanfares on the 3
trumpet,
praise him upon lute and harp;
praise him with tambourines and 4
dancing,
praise him with flute and strings;
praise him with the clash of 5
cymbals,
praise him with triumphant cymbals;
let everything that has breath 6
praise the LORD!

O praise the LORD.

PROVERBS

Advice to the reader

1 The proverbs of Solomon son of David, king of Israel,

2 by which men will come to wisdom and instruction
and will understand words that bring understanding,

3 and by which they will gain a well-instructed intelligence,
righteousness, justice, and probity.

4 The simple will be endowed with shrewdness
and the young with knowledge and prudence.

5 If the wise man listens, he will increase his learning,
and the man of understanding will acquire skill

6 to understand proverbs and parables,
the sayings of wise men and their riddles.

7 The fear of the LORD is the beginning[a] of knowledge,
but fools scorn wisdom and discipline.

8 Attend, my son, to your father's instruction
and do not reject the teaching of your mother;

9 for they are a garland of grace on your head
and a chain of honour round your neck.

10 My son, bad men may tempt you[b]
11 and say,
'Come with us; let us lie in wait for someone's blood;

let us waylay[c] an innocent man who has done us no harm.

12 Like Sheol we will swallow them alive;
though blameless, they shall be like men who go down to the abyss.

13 We shall take rich treasure of every sort
and fill our homes with booty;

14 throw in your lot with us,
and we will have a common purse.'

15 My son, do not go along with them,
keep clear of their ways;

16 they hasten hot-foot into crime,
impatient to shed blood.

17 In vain is a net spread wide
if any bird that flies can see it.

18 These men lie in wait for their own blood
and waylay[c] no one but themselves.

19 This is the fate[d] of men eager for ill-gotten gain:
it robs those who get it of their lives.

20 Wisdom cries aloud in the open air,
she raises her voice in public places;

21 she calls at the top of the busy street
and proclaims at the open gates of the city:

22 'Simple fools, how long will you be content with your simplicity?[e]

23 If only you would respond to my reproof,
I would give you my counsel
and teach you my precepts.

24 But because you refused to listen when I called,

---

[a] Or chief part.
[b] Prob. rdg.; Heb. adds do not come, or, with some MSS., do not consent.
[c] Prob. rdg.; Heb. store up.
[d] This...fate: prob. rdg.; Heb. Such are the courses.
[e] The rest of verse 22 transposed to follow verse 27.

because no one attended when I
stretched out my hand,
25 because you spurned all my advice
and would have nothing to do with
my reproof,
26 I in my turn will laugh at your
doom
and deride you when terror comes
upon you,
27 when terror comes upon you like a
hurricane
and your doom descends like a
whirlwind.[a]
Insolent men delight in their insolence;
stupid men hate knowledge.[b]
28 When they call upon me, I will not
answer them;
when they search for me, they shall
not find me.
29 Because they hate knowledge
and have not chosen to fear the
LORD,
30 because they have not accepted my
counsel
and have spurned all my reproof,
31 they shall eat the fruits of their behaviour
and have a surfeit of their own
devices;
32 for the simpleton turns a deaf ear
and comes to grief,
and the stupid are ruined by their
own complacency.
33 But whoever listens to me shall
live without a care,
undisturbed by fear of misfortune.'

2 My son, if you take my words to
heart
and lay up my commands in your
mind,
2 giving your attention to wisdom
and your mind to understanding,
3 if you summon discernment to
your aid
and invoke understanding,
4 if you seek her out like silver
and dig for her like buried treasure,
5 then you will understand the fear
of the LORD

and attain to the knowledge of
God;
for the LORD bestows wisdom   6
and teaches knowledge and understanding.
Out of his store he endows the up- 7
right with ability
as a shield for those who live
blameless lives;
for he guards the course of justice 8
and keeps watch over the way of
his loyal servants.

Then you will understand what is   9
right and just
and keep[c] only to the good man's
path;
for wisdom will sink into your   10
mind,
and knowledge will be your heart's
delight.
Prudence will keep watch over you, 11
understanding will guard you,
it will save you from evil ways   12
and from men whose talk is subversive,
who forsake the honest course   13
to walk in ways of darkness,
who rejoice in doing evil   14
and exult in evil and subversive
acts,
whose own ways are crooked,   15
whose tracks are devious.
It will save you from the adul-   16
teress,
from the loose woman with her
seductive words,
who forsakes the teaching of her   17
childhood
and has forgotten the covenant of
her God;
for her path[d] runs downhill to- 18
wards death,
and her course is set for the land of
the dead.
No one who resorts to her[e] finds his 19
way back
or regains the path to life.

See then that you follow the foot- 20
steps of good men

---

[a] Prob. rdg.; Heb. adds when anguish and distress come upon you.
[b] Insolent...knowledge: transposed from end of verse 22.   [c] keep: prob. rdg.;
Heb. uprightness.   [d] Prob. rdg.; Heb. house.   [e] resorts to her: or takes to them.

and keep to the course of the righteous;

21 for the upright shall dwell on earth
and blameless men remain there;

22 but the wicked shall be uprooted from it
and traitors weeded out.

3 My son, do not forget my teaching,
but guard my commands in your heart;

2 for long life and years in plenty
will they bring you, and prosperity as well.

3 Let your good faith and loyalty never fail,
but bind them about your neck.

4 Thus will you win favour and success
in the sight of God and man.

5 Put all your trust in the LORD
and do not rely on your own understanding.

6 Think of him in all your ways,
and he will smooth your path.

7 Do not think how wise you are,
but fear the LORD and turn from evil.

8 Let that be the medicine to keep you in health,
the liniment for your limbs.

9 Honour the LORD with your wealth
as the first charge on all your earnings;

10 then your granaries will be filled with corn[a]
and your vats bursting with new wine.

11 My son, do not spurn the LORD's correction
or take offence at his reproof;

12 for those whom he loves the LORD reproves,
and he punishes a favourite son.

13 Happy he who has found wisdom,
and the man who has acquired understanding;

14 for wisdom is more profitable than silver,
and the gain she brings is better than gold.

15 She is more precious than red coral,
and all your jewels are no match for her.

16 Long life is in her right hand,
in her left hand are riches and honour.

17 Her ways are pleasant ways
and all her paths lead to prosperity.

18 She is a staff of life to all who grasp her,
and those who hold her fast are safe.

19 In wisdom the LORD founded the earth
and by understanding he set the heavens in their place;

20 by his knowledge the depths burst forth
and the clouds dropped dew.

21 My son, keep watch over your ability and prudence,
do not let them slip from sight;

22 they shall be a charm hung about your neck
and an ornament on your breast.

23 Then you will go your way without a care,
and your feet will not stumble.

24 When you sit, you need have no fear;
when you lie down, your sleep will be pleasant.

25 Do not be afraid when fools are frightened
or when ruin comes upon the wicked;

26 for the LORD will be at your side,
and he will keep your feet clear of the trap.

27 Refuse no man any favour that you owe him
when it lies in your power to pay it.

28 Do not say to your friend, 'Come back again;
you shall have it tomorrow' – when you have it already.

29 Plot no evil against your friend,
your unsuspecting neighbour.

30 Do not pick a quarrel with a man for no reason,
if he has not done you a bad turn.

---

[a] *with corn: or* to overflowing.

31 Do not emulate a lawless man,
do not choose to follow his footsteps;
32 for one who is not straight is detestable to the LORD,
but upright men are in God's confidence.
33 The LORD's curse rests on the
house of the evildoer,
while he blesses the home of the
righteous.
34 Though God himself meets the
arrogant with arrogance,
yet he bestows his favour on the
meek.*a*
35 Wise men are adorned with*b*
honour,
but the coat*c* on a fool's back is
contempt.

4 Listen, my sons, to a father's instruction,
consider attentively how to gain
understanding;
2 for it is sound learning I give you;
so do not forsake my teaching.
3 I too have been a father's son,
tender in years, my mother's only
child.
4 He taught me and said to me:
Hold fast to my words with all your
heart,
keep my commands and you will
have life.
5 Do not forget or turn a deaf ear to
what I say.

7 The first thing*d* is to acquire wisdom;
gain understanding though it cost
you all you have.
6 Do not forsake her, and she will
keep you safe;
love her, and she will guard you;
8 cherish her, and she will lift you
high;
if only you embrace her, she will
bring you to honour.
9 She will set a garland of grace on
your head
and bestow on you a crown of
glory.

Listen, my son, take my words to 10
heart,
and the years of your life shall be
multiplied.
I will guide you in the paths of 11
wisdom
and lead you in honest ways.
As you walk you will not slip, 12
and, if you run, nothing will bring
you down.
Cling to instruction and never let it 13
go;
observe it well, for it is your life.
Do not take to the course of the 14
wicked
or follow the way of evil men;
do not set foot on it, but avoid it; 15
turn aside and go on your way.
For they cannot sleep unless they 16
have done some wrong;
unless they have been someone's
downfall they lose their sleep.
The bread they eat is the fruit of 17
crime
and they drink wine got by violence.
The course of the righteous is like 18
morning light,
growing brighter till it is broad
day;
but the ways of the wicked are 19
like darkness at night,
and they do not know what has
been their downfall.

My son, attend to my speech, 20
pay heed to my words;
do not let them slip out of your 21
mind,
keep them close in your heart;
for they are life to him who finds 22
them,
and health to his whole body.
Guard your heart more than any 23
treasure,
for it is the source of all life.
Keep your mouth from crooked 24
speech
and your lips from deceitful talk.
Let your eyes look straight before 25
you,
fix your gaze upon what lies ahead.

a Or *wretched.*   *b* are adorned with: *prob. rdg.*; *Heb.* shall inherit.
c the coat: *prob. rdg.*; *Heb. obscure.*   *d Prob. rdg.*; *Heb. adds* wisdom.

26 Look out for the path that your
feet must take,
and your ways will be secure.
27 Swerve neither to right nor left,
and keep clear of every evil thing.

5 My son, attend to my wisdom
and listen to my good counsel,
2 so that you may observe proper
prudence
and your speech be informed with
knowledge.
3 For though the lips of an adulteress
drip honey
and her tongue is smoother than oil,
4 yet in the end she is more bitter
than wormwood,
and sharp as a two-edged sword.
5 Her feet go downwards on the path
to death,
her course is set for Sheol.
6 She does not watch for the road
that leads to life;
her course turns this way and that,
and what does she care?[a]

7 Now, my son, listen to me
and do not ignore what I say:
8 keep well away from her
and do not go near the door of her
house;
9 or you will lose your dignity in the
eyes of others
and your honour before strangers;
10 strangers will batten on your
wealth,
and your hard-won gains pass to
another man's family.
11 The end will be that you will starve,
you will shrink to mere skin and
bones.
12 Then you will say, 'Why did I hate
correction
and set my heart against reproof?
13 I did not listen to the voice of my
teachers
or pay attention to my masters.
14 I soon earned[b] a bad name
and was despised in the public
assembly.'

15 Drink water from your own cistern

and running water from your own
spring;
do not let your[c] well overflow into 16
the road,
your runnels of water pour into
the street;
let them be yours alone, 17
not shared with strangers.
Let your fountain, the wife of your 18
youth,
be blessed, rejoice in her,
a lovely doe, a graceful hind, let 19
her be your companion;
you will at all times be bathed in
her love,
and her love will continually wrap
you round.
Wherever you turn, she will guide
you;
when you lie in bed, she will watch
over you,
and when you wake she will talk
with you.[d]
Why, my son, are you wrapped up 20
in the love of an adulteress?
Why do you embrace a loose woman?
For a man's ways are always in 21
the LORD's sight
who watches for every path that
he must take.
The wicked man is caught in his 22
own iniquities
and held fast in the toils of his
own sin;
he will perish for want of discipline, 23
wrapped in the shroud of his boundless folly.

My son, if you pledge yourself to 6
another man
and stand surety for a stranger,
if you are caught by your promise, 2
trapped by some promise you have
made,
do what I now tell you 3
and save yourself, my son:
when you fall into another man's
power,
bestir yourself, go and pester the
man,

---

[a] what...care?: *or* she is restless.   [b] *Or* I almost earned.
[c] do not let your: *prob. rdg.; Heb.* shall your.
[d] Wherever...with you: *transposed from ch. 6 (verse 22).*

4 give yourself no rest,
  allow yourself no sleep.
5 Save yourself like a gazelle from
  the toils,
  like a bird from the grasp of the
  fowler.

6 Go to the ant, you sluggard,
  watch her ways and get wisdom.
7 She has no overseer,
  no governor or ruler;
8 but in summer she prepares her
  store of food
  and lays in her supplies at harvest.
9 How long, you sluggard, will you
  lie abed?
  When will you rouse yourself from
  sleep?
10 A little sleep, a little slumber,
   a little folding of the hands in rest,
11 and poverty will come upon you
   like a robber,
   want like a ruffian.

12 A scoundrel, a mischievous man,
   is he
   who prowls about with crooked
   talk –
13 a wink of the eye,
   a touch with the foot,
   a sign with the fingers.
14 Subversion is the evil that he is
   plotting,
   he stirs up quarrels all the time.
15 Down comes disaster suddenly
   upon him;
   suddenly he is broken beyond all
   remedy.

16 Six things the LORD hates,
   seven things are detestable to him:
17 a proud eye, a false tongue,
   hands that shed innocent blood,
18 a heart that forges thoughts of
   mischief,
   and feet that run swiftly to do evil,
19 a false witness telling a pack of lies,
   and one who stirs up quarrels between brothers.

20 My son, observe your father's commands
   and do not reject the teaching of
   your mother;

wear them always next your 21
heart
and bind them close about your
neck;
for a command is a lamp, and 23*a*
teaching a light,
reproof and correction point the
way of life,
to keep you from the wife of 24
another man,
from the seductive tongue of the
loose woman.
Do not desire her beauty in your 25
heart
or let her glance provoke you;
for a prostitute can be had for the 26
price of a loaf,
but a married woman is out for
bigger game.

Can a man kindle fire in his bosom 27
without burning his clothes?
If a man walks on hot coals, 28
will his feet not be scorched?
So is he who sleeps with his neigh- 29
bour's wife;
no one can touch such a woman
and go free.
Is not a thief contemptible when 30
he steals
to satisfy his appetite, even if he
is hungry?
And, if he is caught, must he not 31
pay seven times over
and surrender all that his house
contains?
So one who commits adultery is 32
a senseless fool:
he dishonours the woman and ruins
himself;
he will get nothing but blows and 33
contumely
and will never live down the disgrace;
for a husband's anger is a jealous 34
anger
and in the day of vengeance he
will show no mercy;
compensation will not buy his 35
forgiveness;*b*
no bribe, however large, will purchase his connivance.

a Verse 22 transposed to follow wrap you round *in 5. 19.*
b compensation...forgiveness: *prob. rdg.; Heb. obscure.*

7 My son, keep my words,
store up my commands in your
mind.

2 Keep my commands if you would
live,
and treasure my teaching as the
apple of your eye.

3 Wear them like a ring on your
finger;
write them on the tablet of your
memory.

4 Call Wisdom your sister,
greet Understanding as a familiar
friend;

5 then they will save you from the
adulteress,
from the loose woman with her
seductive words.

6 I glanced[a] out of the window of
my house,
I looked down through the lattice,

7 and I saw among simple youths,
there amongst the boys I noticed
a lad, a foolish lad,

8 passing along the street, at the
corner,
stepping out in the direction of
her house

9 at twilight, as the day faded,
at dusk as the night grew dark;

10 suddenly a woman came to meet
him,
dressed like a prostitute, full of
wiles,

11 flighty and inconstant,
a woman never content to stay at
home,

12 lying in wait at every corner,
now in the street, now in the public
squares.

13 She caught hold of him and kissed
him;
brazenly she accosted him and
said,

14 'I have had a sacrifice, an offering,
to make
and I have paid my vows today;

15 that is why I have come out to
meet you,
to watch for you and find you.

16 I have spread coverings on my bed
of coloured linen from Egypt.

I have sprinkled my bed with 17
myrrh,
my clothes[b] with aloes and cassia.

Come! Let us drown ourselves in 18
pleasure,
let us spend a whole night of love;

for the man of the house is away, 19
he has gone on a long journey,

he has taken a bag of silver with 20
him;
until the moon is full he will not be
home.'

Persuasively she led him on, 21
she pressed him with seductive
words.

Like a simple fool he followed her, 22
like an ox on its way to the
slaughter-house,
like an antelope bounding into the
noose,

like a bird hurrying into the trap; 23
he did not know that he was risking
his life
until the arrow pierced his vitals.

But now, my son, listen to me, 24
attend to what I say.

Do not let your heart entice you 25
into her ways,
do not stray down her paths;

many has she pierced and laid low, 26
and her victims are without
number.

Her house is the entrance to Sheol, 27
which leads down to the halls of
death.

Wisdom and folly contrasted

Hear how Wisdom lifts her voice **8**
and Understanding cries out.

She stands at the cross-roads, 2
by the wayside, at the top of the hill;

beside the gate, at the entrance 3
to the city,
at the entry by the open gate she
calls aloud:

'Men, it is to you I call, 4
I appeal to every man:

understand, you simple fools, what 5
it is to be shrewd;
you stupid people, understand
what sense means.

---

[a] I glanced: *prob. rdg.*; *Heb. om.*   [b] my clothes: *prob. rdg.*; *Heb. om.*

6 Listen! For I will speak clearly,
   you will have plain speech from
   me;
7 for I speak nothing but truth
   and my lips detest wicked talk.
8 All that I say is right,
   not a word is twisted or crooked.
9 All is straightforward to him who
   can understand,
   all is plain to the man who has
   knowledge.
10 Accept instruction and not silver,
   knowledge rather than pure gold;
11 for wisdom is better than red coral,
   no jewels can match her.
12 I am Wisdom, I bestow shrewdness
   and show the way to knowledge
   and prudence.
13 *a*Pride, presumption, evil courses,
   subversive talk, all these I hate.
14 I have force, I also have ability;
   understanding and power are mine.
15 Through me kings are sovereign
   and governors make just laws.
16 Through me princes act like
   princes,
   from me all rulers on earth derive
   their nobility.
17 Those who love me I love,
   those who search for me find me.
18 In my hands are riches and honour,
   boundless wealth and the rewards
   of virtue.
19 My harvest is better than gold,
   fine gold,
   and my revenue better than pure
   silver.
20 I follow the course of virtue,
   my path is the path of justice;
21 I endow with riches those who
   love me
   and I will fill their treasuries.

22 'The LORD created me the beginning of his works,
   before all else that he made, long
   ago.
23 Alone, I was fashioned in times
   long past,
   at the beginning, long before earth
   itself.

When there was yet no ocean I was 24
   born,
   no springs brimming with water.
Before the mountains were settled 25
   in their place,
   long before the hills I was born,
when as yet he had made neither 26
   land nor lake
   nor the first clod*b* of earth.
When he set the heavens in their 27
   place I was there,
   when he girdled the ocean with
   the horizon,
when he fixed the canopy of clouds 28
   overhead
   and set the springs of ocean firm
   in their place,
when he prescribed its limits for 29
   the sea*c*
   and knit together earth's foundations.
Then I was at his side each day,   30
   his darling and delight,
   playing in his presence continually,
   playing on the earth, when he had 31
   finished it,
   while my delight was in mankind.

'Now, my sons, listen to me,   32–33
   listen to instruction and grow wise,
   do not reject it.
Happy is the man who keeps to
   my ways,
   happy the man who listens to me, 34
   watching daily at my threshold
   with his eyes on the doorway;
   for he who finds me finds life   35
   and wins favour with the LORD,
   while he who finds me not, hurts 36
   himself,
   and all who hate me are in love
   with death.'

Wisdom has built her house,   9
   she has hewn her seven pillars;
   she has killed a beast and spiced 2
   her wine,
   and she has spread her table.
She has sent out her maidens to 3
   proclaim
   from the highest part of the town,

---

a *Prob. rdg.; Heb. prefixes* The fear of the LORD is to hate evil.
b the first clod: *or* the sum of the clods.
c *Prob. rdg.; Heb. adds* and the water shall not disobey his command.

4 'Come in, you simpletons.'
  She says also to the fool,
5 'Come, dine with me
  and taste the wine that I have
  spiced.
6 Cease to be silly, and you will
  live,
  you will grow in understanding.'

7 Correct an insolent man, and be
  sneered at for your pains;
  correct a bad man, and you will
  put yourself in the wrong.
8 Do not correct the insolent or they
  will hate you;
  correct a wise man, and he will be
  your friend.
9 Lecture a wise man, and he will
  grow wiser;
  teach a righteous man, and his
  learning will increase.

10 The first step to wisdom is the fear
   of the LORD,
   and knowledge of the Holy One is
   understanding;
11 for through me your days will be
   multiplied
   and years will be added to your life.
12 If you are wise, it will be to your
   own advantage;
   if you are haughty, you alone are
   to blame.
13 The Lady Stupidity is a flighty
   creature;
   the simpleton, she cares for nothing.
14 She sits at the door of her house,
   on a seat in the highest part of the
   town,
15 to invite the passers-by indoors
   as they hurry on their way:
16 'Come in, you simpletons', she
   says.
   She says also to the fool,
17 'Stolen water is sweet
   and bread got by stealth tastes
   good.'
18 Little does he know that death
   lurks there,
   that her guests are in the depths
   of Sheol.

A collection of wise sayings

The proverbs of Solomon: 10

A wise son brings joy to his
father;
a foolish son is his mother's bane.
Ill-gotten wealth brings no profit; 2
uprightness is a safeguard against
death.
The LORD does not let the righteous 3
go hungry,*a*
but he disappoints the cravings*b*
of the wicked.
Idle hands make a man poor;   4
busy hands grow rich.
A thoughtful son puts by in sum- 5
mer;
a son who sleeps at harvest is a
disgrace.
Blessings are showered on the 6
righteous;
the wicked are choked by their own
violence.
The righteous are remembered in 7
blessings;
the name of the wicked turns rotten.
A wise man takes a command to 8
heart;
a foolish talker comes to grief.
A blameless life makes for security; 9
crooked ways bring a man down.
To wink at a fault causes trouble; 10
a frank rebuke leads to peace.
The words of good men are a 11
fountain of life;
the wicked are choked by their
own violence.
Hate is always picking a quarrel, 12
but love turns a blind eye to every
fault.
The man of understanding has 13
wisdom on his lips;
a rod is in store for the back of the
fool.
Wise men lay up knowledge;   14
when a fool speaks, ruin is near.
A rich man's wealth is his strong 15
city,
but poverty is the undoing of the
helpless.

a Or be afraid.
b Or the clamour.

16 The good man's labour is his livelihood;
the wicked man's earnings bring
him to a bad end.

17 Correction is the high road to life;
neglect reproof and you miss the
way.

18 There is no spite in a just man's
talk;
it is the stupid who are fluent with
calumny.

19 When men talk too much, sin is
never far away;
common sense holds its tongue.

20 A good man's tongue is pure silver;
the heart of the wicked is trash.

21 The lips of a good man teach many,
but fools perish for want of sense.

22 The blessing of the LORD brings
riches
and he sends no sorrow with them.

23 Lewdness is sport for the stupid;
wisdom a delight to men of understanding.

24 The fears of the wicked will overtake them;
the desire of the righteous will be
granted.

25 When the whirlwind has passed
by, the wicked are gone;
the foundations of the righteous
are eternal.

26 Like vinegar on the teeth or smoke
in the eyes,
so is the lazy servant to his master.

27 The fear of the LORD brings length
of days;
the years of the wicked are few.

28 The hope of the righteous blossoms;
the expectation of the wicked
withers away.

29 The way of the LORD gives refuge
to the honest man,
but dismays those who do evil.

30 The righteous man will never be
shaken;
the wicked shall not remain on
earth.

31 Wisdom flows from the mouth of
the righteous;
the subversive tongue will be rooted
out.

32 The righteous man can suit his
words to the occasion;

the wicked know only subversive
talk.

False scales are the LORD's abomi- 11
nation;
correct weights are dear to his
heart.

When presumption comes in, in 2
comes contempt,
but wisdom goes with sagacity.

Honesty is a guide to the upright, 3
but rogues are balked by their own
perversity.

Wealth is worth nothing in the day 4
of wrath,
but uprightness is a safeguard
against death.

By uprightness the blameless keep 5
their course,
but the wicked are brought down
by their wickedness.

Uprightness saves the righteous,   6
but rogues are trapped in their own
greed.

When a man dies, his thread of 7
life ends,
and with it ends the hope of
affluence.

A righteous man is rescued from 8
disaster,
and the wicked man plunges into
it.

By his words a godless man tries 9
to ruin others,
but they are saved when the
righteous plead for them.

A city rejoices in the prosperity of 10
the righteous;
there is jubilation when the wicked
perish.

By the blessing of the upright a 11
city is built up;
the words of the wicked tear it
down.

A man without sense despises 12
others,
but a man of understanding holds
his peace.

A gossip gives away secrets,   13
but a trusty man keeps his own
counsel.

For want of skilful strategy an 14
army is lost;
victory is the fruit of long planning.

15 Give a pledge for a stranger and
   know no peace;
   refuse to stand surety and be safe.
16 Grace in a woman wins honour,
   but she who hates virtue makes
   a home for dishonour.
   Be timid in business and come to
   beggary;
   be bold and make a fortune.
17 Loyalty brings its own reward;
   a cruel man makes trouble for his
   kin.
18 A wicked man earns a fallacious[a]
   profit;
   he who sows goodness reaps a sure
   reward.[b]
19 A man set on righteousness finds
   life,
   but the pursuit of evil leads to
   death.
20 The LORD detests the crooked
   heart,
   but honesty is dear to him.
21 Depend upon it: an evil man shall
   not escape punishment;
   the righteous and all their offspring
   shall go free.
22 Like a gold ring in a pig's snout
   is a beautiful woman without good
   sense.
23 The righteous desire only what is
   good;
   the hope of the wicked comes to
   nothing.
24 A man may spend freely and yet
   grow richer;
   another is sparing beyond measure,
   yet ends in poverty.
25 A generous man grows fat and
   prosperous,
   and he who refreshes others will
   himself be refreshed.
26 He who withholds his grain is
   cursed by the people,
   but he who sells his corn is
   blessed.
27 He who eagerly seeks what is good
   finds much favour,
   but if a man pursues evil it turns
   upon him.
28 Whoever relies on his wealth is
   riding for a fall,

but the righteous flourish like the
green leaf.
He who brings trouble on his 29
family inherits the wind,
and a fool becomes slave to a wise
man.
The fruit of righteousness is a tree 30
of life,
but violence means the taking
away of life.
If the righteous in the land get 31
their deserts,
how much more the wicked man
and the sinner!

He who loves correction loves 12
knowledge;
he who hates reproof is a mere
brute.
A good man earns favour from the 2
LORD;
the schemer is condemned.
No man can establish himself by 3
wickedness,
but good men have roots that
cannot be dislodged.
A capable wife is her husband's 4
crown;
one who disgraces him is like rot
in his bones.
The purposes of the righteous are 5
lawful;
the designs of the wicked are full
of deceit.
The wicked are destroyed[c] by their 6
own words;
the words of the good man are his
salvation.
Once the wicked are down, that is 7
the end of them,
but the good man's line continues.
A man is commended for his in- 8
telligence,
but a warped mind is despised.
It is better to be modest[d] and earn 9
one's living
than to be conceited[e] and go
hungry.
A righteous man cares for his beast, 10
but a wicked man is cruel at heart.
He who tills his land has enough to 11
eat,

---

[a] *Or* fraudulent.   [b] a sure reward: *or* the reward of honesty.
[c] *Prob. rdg.; Heb.* are an ambush for blood.   [d] *Or* scorned.   [e] *Or* honoured.

but to follow idle pursuits is foolishness.

12 The stronghold of the wicked crumbles like clay,[a]
but the righteous take lasting root.

13 The wicked man is trapped by his own falsehoods,
but the righteous comes safe through trouble.

14 One man wins success by his words;
another gets his due reward by the work of his hands.

15 A fool thinks that he is always right;
wise is the man who listens to advice.

16 A fool shows his ill humour at once;
a clever man slighted conceals his feelings.

17 An honest speaker comes out with the truth,
but the false witness is full of deceit.

18 Gossip can be sharp as a sword,
but the tongue of the wise heals.

19 Truth spoken stands firm for ever,
but lies live only for a moment.

20 Those who plot evil delude themselves,
but there is joy for those who seek the common good.

21 No mischief will befall the righteous,
but wicked men get their fill of adversity.

22 The LORD detests a liar
but delights in the honest man.

23 A clever man conceals his knowledge,
but a stupid man broadcasts his folly.

24 Diligence brings a man to power,
but laziness to forced labour.

25 An anxious heart dispirits a man,
and a kind word fills him with joy.

26 A righteous man recoils from evil,[b]
but the wicked take a path that leads them astray.

27 The lazy hunter puts up no game,
but the industrious man reaps a rich harvest.[c]

28 The way of honesty leads to life,
but there is a well-worn path to death.

13 A wise man sees the reason for his father's correction;
an arrogant man will not listen to rebuke.

2 A good man enjoys the fruit of righteousness,
but violence is meat and drink for the treacherous.

3 He who minds his words preserves his life;
he who talks too much comes to grief.

4 A lazy man is torn by appetite unsatisfied,
but the diligent grow fat and prosperous.

5 The righteous hate falsehood;
the doings of the wicked are foul and deceitful.

6 To do right is the protection of an honest man,
but wickedness brings sinners to grief.[d]

7 One man pretends to be rich, although he has nothing;
another has great wealth but goes in rags.[e]

8 A rich man must buy himself off,
but a poor man is immune from threats.

9 The light of the righteous burns brightly;
the embers of the wicked will be put out.

10 A brainless fool causes strife by his presumption;
wisdom is found among friends in council.

11 Wealth quickly come by dwindles away,
but if it comes little by little, it multiplies.

---

[a] *Prob. rdg.; Heb.* A wicked man covets a stronghold of crumbling earth.
[b] recoils from evil: *prob. rdg.; Heb.* let him spy out his friend.
[c] but...harvest: *prob. rdg.; Heb. obscure.*   [d] brings...grief: *or* plays havoc with a man.   [e] One man...rags: *or* One man may grow rich though he has nothing; another may grow poor though he has great wealth.

12 Hope deferred makes the heart sick;
a wish come true is a staff of life.

13 To despise a word of advice is to
ask for trouble;
mind what you are told, and you
will be rewarded.

14 A wise man's teaching is a fountain
of life
for one who would escape the
snares of death.

15 Good intelligence wins favour,
but treachery leads to disaster.

16 A clever man is wise and conceals
everything,
but the stupid parade their folly.

17 An evil messenger causes trouble,[a]
but a trusty envoy makes all go
well again.

18 To refuse correction brings poverty
and contempt;
one who takes a reproof to heart
comes to honour.

19 Lust indulged sickens a man;[b]
stupid people loathe to mend their
ways.

20 Walk with the wise and be wise;
mix with the stupid and be misled.

21 Ill fortune follows the sinner close
behind,
but good rewards the righteous.

22 A good man leaves an inheritance
to his descendants,
but the sinner's hoard passes to
the righteous.

23 Untilled land might yield food
enough for the poor,
but even that may be lost through
injustice.

24 A father who spares the rod hates
his son,
but one who loves him keeps him
in order.

25 A righteous man eats his fill,
but the wicked go hungry.

14 The wisest women build up their
homes;
the foolish pull them down with
their own hands.

2 A straightforward man fears the
LORD;
the double-dealer scorns him.

The speech of a fool is a rod for his 3
back;[c]
a wise man's words are his safeguard.

Where there are no oxen the barn 4
is empty,
but the strength of a great ox
ensures rich crops.

A truthful witness is no liar; 5
a false witness tells a pack of
lies.

A conceited man seeks wisdom, yet 6
finds none;
to one of understanding, knowledge
comes easily.

Avoid a stupid man, 7
you will hear not a word of sense
from him.

A clever man has the wit to find 8
the right way;
the folly of stupid men misleads
them.

A fool is too arrogant to make 9
amends;
upright men know what reconciliation means.

The heart knows its own bitter- 10
ness,
and a stranger has no part in its
joy.

The house of the wicked will be 11
torn down,
but the home of the upright
flourishes.

A road may seem straightforward 12
to a man,
yet may end as the way to death.

Even in laughter the heart may 13
grieve,
and mirth may end in sorrow.

The renegade reaps the fruit of 14
his conduct,
a good man the fruit of his own
achievements.

A simple man believes every word 15
he hears;
a clever man understands the need
for proof.

A wise man is cautious and turns 16
his back on evil;
the stupid is heedless and falls
headlong.

---

[a] *causes trouble: or is unsuccessful.
is pleasant to the appetite.*

[b] *Lust . . . a man: or Desire fulfilled*
[c] *his back: prob. rdg.; Heb. pride.*

17 Impatience runs into folly;
   distinction comes by careful thought.[a]
18 The simple wear the trappings of folly;
   the clever are crowned with knowledge.
19 Evil men cringe before the good,
   wicked men at the righteous man's door.
20 A poor man is odious even to his friend;
   the rich have friends in plenty.
21 He who despises a hungry man does wrong,
   but he who is generous to the poor is happy.
22 Do not those who intend evil go astray,
   while those with good intentions are loyal and faithful?
23 The pains of toil bring gain,
   but mere talk brings nothing but poverty.
24 Insight is the crown of the wise;
   folly the chief ornament of the stupid.
25 A truthful witness saves life;
   the false accuser utters nothing but lies.
26 A strong man who trusts in the fear of the LORD
   will be a refuge for his sons.
27 The fear of the LORD is the fountain of life
   for the man who would escape the snares of death.
28 Many subjects make a famous king;
   with none to rule, a prince is ruined.
29 To be patient shows great understanding;
   quick temper is the height of folly.
30 A tranquil mind puts flesh on a man,
   but passion rots his bones.
31 He who oppresses[b] the poor insults his Maker;
   he who is generous to the needy honours him.
32 An evil man is brought down by his wickedness;
   the upright man is secure in his own honesty.
33 Wisdom is at home in a discerning mind,
   but is ill at ease in the heart of a fool.
34 Righteousness raises a people to honour;
   to do wrong is a disgrace to any nation.
35 A king shows favour to an intelligent servant,
   but his displeasure strikes down those who fail him.

15 A soft answer turns away anger,
   but a sharp word makes tempers hot.
2 A wise man's tongue spreads knowledge;
   stupid men talk nonsense.
3 The eyes of the LORD are everywhere,
   surveying evil and good men alike.
4 A soothing word is a staff of life,
   but a mischievous tongue breaks the spirit.
5 A fool spurns his father's correction,
   but to take a reproof to heart shows good sense.
6 In the righteous man's house there is ample wealth;
   the gains of the wicked bring trouble.
7 The lips of a wise man promote knowledge;
   the hearts of the stupid are dishonest.
8 The wicked man's sacrifice is abominable to the LORD;
   the good man's prayer is his delight.
9 The conduct of the wicked is abominable to the LORD,
   but he loves the seeker after righteousness.
10 A man who leaves the main road resents correction,
   and he who hates reproof will die.
11 Sheol and Abaddon lie open before the LORD,
   how much more the hearts of men!

---

[a] distinction...thought: *prob. rdg.*; *Heb.* a man of careful thought is hated.
[b] *Or* slanders.

12 The conceited man does not take kindly to reproof
and he will not consult the wise.

13 A merry heart makes a cheerful face;
heartache crushes the spirit.

14 A discerning mind seeks knowledge, but the stupid man feeds on folly.

15 In the life of the downtrodden every day is wretched,
but to have a glad heart is a perpetual feast.

16 Better a pittance with the fear of the LORD
than great treasure and trouble in its train.

17 Better a dish of vegetables if love go with it
than a fat ox eaten in hatred.

18 Bad temper provokes a quarrel, but patience heals discords.

19 The path of the sluggard is a tangle of weeds,
but the road of the diligent is a highway.

20 A wise son brings joy to his father; a young fool despises his mother.

21 Folly may amuse the empty-headed;
a man of understanding makes straight for his goal.

22 Schemes lightly made come to nothing,
but with long planning they succeed.

23 A man may be pleased with his own retort;
how much better is a word in season!

24 For men of intelligence the path of life leads upwards
and keeps them clear of Sheol below.

25 The LORD pulls down the proud man's home
but fixes the widow's boundary-stones.

26 A bad man's thoughts are the LORD's abomination,
but the words of the pure are a delight.[a]

27 A grasping man brings trouble on his family,

but he who spurns a bribe will enjoy long life.

28 The righteous think before they answer;
a bad man's ready tongue is full of mischief.

29 The LORD stands aloof from the wicked,
he listens to the righteous man's prayer.

30 A bright look brings joy to the heart,
and good news warms a man's marrow.

31 Whoever listens to wholesome reproof
shall enjoy the society of the wise.

32 He who refuses correction is his own worst enemy,
but he who listens to reproof learns sense.

33 The fear of the LORD is a training in wisdom,
and the way to honour is humility.

16 A man may order his thoughts, but the LORD inspires the words he utters.

2 A man's whole conduct may be pure in his own eyes,
but the LORD fixes a standard for the spirit of man.

3 Commit to the LORD all that you do,
and your plans will be fulfilled.

4 The LORD has made each thing for its own end;
he made even the wicked for a day of disaster.

5 Proud men, one and all, are abominable to the LORD;
depend upon it: they will not escape punishment.

6 Guilt is wiped out by faith and loyalty,
and the fear of the LORD makes men turn from evil.

7 When the LORD is pleased with a man and his ways,
he makes even his enemies live at peace with him.

8 Better a pittance honestly earned than great gains ill gotten.

---

[a] the words...delight: *or* gracious words are pure.

9 Man plans his journey by his own wit,
but it is the LORD who guides his steps.

10 The king's mouth is an oracle,
he cannot err when he passes sentence.

11 Scales[a] and balances[b] are the LORD's concern;
all the weights in the bag are his business.

12 Wickedness is abhorrent to kings,
for a throne rests firm on righteousness.

13 Honest speech is the desire of kings,
they love a man who speaks the truth.

14 A king's anger is a messenger of death,
and a wise man will appease it.

15 In the light of the king's countenance is life,
his favour is like a rain-cloud in the spring.

16 How much better than gold it is to gain wisdom,
and to gain discernment is better than pure silver.

17 To turn from evil is the highway of the upright;
watch your step and save your life.

18 Pride comes before disaster,
and arrogance before a fall.

19 Better sit humbly with those in need
than divide the spoil with the proud.

20 The shrewd man of business will succeed well,
but the happy man is he who trusts in the LORD.

21 The sensible man seeks advice from the wise,
he drinks it in and increases his knowledge.[c]

22 Intelligence is a fountain of life to its possessors,
but a fool is punished by his own folly.

23 The wise man's mind guides his speech,
and what his lips impart increases learning.[d]

24 Kind words are like dripping honey,
sweetness on the tongue and health for the body.

25 A road may seem straightforward to a man,
yet may end as the way to death.

26 The labourer's appetite is always plaguing him,
his hunger spurs him on.

27 A scoundrel repeats evil gossip;
it is like a scorching fire on his lips.

28 Disaffection stirs up quarrels,
and tale-bearing breaks up friendship.

29 A man of violence draws others on
and leads them into lawless ways.

30 The man who narrows his eyes is disaffected at heart,
and a close-lipped man is bent on mischief.

31 Grey hair is a crown of glory,
and it is won by a virtuous life.

32 Better be slow to anger than a fighter,
better govern one's temper than capture a city.

33 The lots may be cast into the lap,
but the issue depends wholly on the LORD.

17 Better a dry crust and concord with it
than a house full of feasting and strife.

2 A wise slave may give orders to a disappointing son
and share the inheritance with the brothers.

3 The melting-pot is for silver and the crucible for gold,
but it is the LORD who assays the hearts of men.

4 A rogue gives a ready ear to mischievous talk,
and a liar listens to slander.

---

[a] Or Pointer.   [b] Prob. rdg.; Heb. balances of justice.
[c] he drinks...knowledge: or and he whose speech is persuasive increases learning.
[d] and what...learning: or and increases the learning of his utterance.

5 A man who sneers at the poor insults his Maker,
and he who gloats over another's ruin will answer for it.

6 Grandchildren are the crown of old age,
and sons are proud of their fathers.

7 Fine talk is out of place in a boor,
how much more is falsehood in the noble!

8 He who offers a bribe finds it work like a charm,
he prospers in all he undertakes.

9 He who conceals another's offence seeks his goodwill,
but he who harps on something breaks up friendship.

10 A reproof is felt by a man of discernment
more than a hundred blows by a stupid man.

11 An evil man is set only on disobedience,
but a messenger without mercy will be sent against him.

12 Better face a she-bear robbed of her cubs
than a stupid man in his folly.

13 If a man repays evil for good,
evil will never quit his house.

14 Stealing water starts a quarrel;
drop a dispute before you bare your teeth.

15 To acquit the wicked and condemn the righteous,
both are abominable in the LORD's sight.

16 What use is money in the hands of a stupid man?
Can he buy wisdom if he has no sense?

17 A friend is a loving companion at all times,
and a brother is born to share troubles.

18 A man is without sense who gives a guarantee
and surrenders himself to another as surety.

19 He who loves strife loves sin.
He who builds a lofty entrance invites thieves.

20 A crooked heart will come to no good,
and a mischievous tongue will end in disaster.

21 A stupid man is the bane of his parent,
and his father has no joy in a boorish son.

22 A merry heart makes a cheerful countenance,
but low spirits sap a man's strength.

23 A wicked man accepts a bribe under his cloak
to pervert the course of justice.

24 Wisdom is never out of sight of a discerning man,
but a stupid man's eyes are roving everywhere.

25 A stupid son exasperates his father
and is a bitter sorrow to the mother who bore him.

26 Again, to punish the righteous is not good
and it is wrong to inflict blows on men of noble mind.

27 Experience uses few words;
discernment keeps a cool head.

28 Even a fool, if he holds his peace, is thought wise;
keep your mouth shut and show your good sense.

18 The man who holds aloof seeks every pretext
to bare his teeth in scorn at competent people.

2 The foolish have no interest in seeking to understand,
but prefer to display their wit.

3 When wickedness comes in, in comes contempt;
with loss of honour comes reproach.

4 The words of a man's mouth are a gushing torrent,
but deep is the water in the well of wisdom.[a]

5 It is not good to show favour to the wicked
or to deprive the righteous of justice.

6 When the stupid man talks, contention follows;

[a] *The words...wisdom: prob. rdg., inverting phrases.*

his words provoke blows.

7 The stupid man's tongue is his
undoing;
his lips put his life in jeopardy.

8 A gossip's whispers are savoury
morsels,
gulped down into the inner man.

9 Again, the lazy worker is own
brother
to the man who enjoys destruction.

10 The name of the LORD is a tower
of strength,
where the righteous may run for
refuge.

11 A rich man's wealth is his strong
city,
a towering wall, so he supposes.

12 Before disaster comes, a man is
proud,
but the way to honour is humility.

13 To answer a question before you
have heard it out
is both stupid and insulting.

14 A man's spirit may sustain him
in sickness,
but if the spirit is wounded, who
can mend it?

15 Knowledge comes to the discerning
mind;
the wise ear listens to get knowledge.

16 A gift opens the door to the giver
and gains access to the great.

17 In a lawsuit the first speaker seems
right,
until another steps forward and
cross-questions him.

18 Cast lots, and settle a quarrel,
and so keep litigants apart.

19 A reluctant brother is more un-
yielding than a fortress,
and quarrels are stubborn as the
bars of a castle.

20 A man may live by the fruit of his
tongue,
his lips may earn him a livelihood.

21 The tongue has power of life and
death;
make friends with it and enjoy its
fruits.

22 Find a wife, and you find a good
thing;
so you will earn the favour of the
LORD.

23 The poor man speaks in a tone of
entreaty,
and the rich man gives a harsh
answer.

24 Some companions are good only
for idle talk,
but a friend may stick closer than
a brother.

19 Better be poor and above reproach
than rich and crooked in speech.

2 Again, desire without knowledge
is not good;
the man in a hurry misses the
way.

3 A man's own folly wrecks his life,
and then he bears a grudge against
the LORD.

4 Wealth makes many friends,
but a man without means loses the
friend he has.

5 A false witness will not escape
punishment,
and one who utters nothing but
lies will not go free.

6 Many curry favour with the great;
a lavish giver has the world for
his friend.

7 A poor man's brothers all dislike
him,
how much more is he shunned by
his friends!
Practice in evil makes the perfect
scoundrel;
the man who talks too much meets
his deserts.

8 To learn sense is true self-love;
cherish discernment and make sure
of success.

9 A false witness will not escape
punishment,
and one who utters nothing but lies
will perish.

10 A fool at the helm is out of place,
how much worse a slave in command of men of rank!

11 To be patient shows intelligence;
to overlook faults is a man's glory.

12 A king's rage is like a lion's roar,
his favour like dew on the grass.

13 A stupid son is a calamity to his
father;
a nagging wife is like water dripping endlessly.

14 Home and wealth may come down from ancestors,
but an intelligent wife is a gift from the LORD.

15 Laziness is the undoing of the worthless;
idlers must starve.

16 To keep the commandments keeps a man safe,
but scorning the way of the LORD brings death.

17 He who is generous to the poor lends to the LORD;
he will repay him in full measure.

18 Chastise your son while there is hope for him,
but be careful not to flog him to death.

19 A man's ill temper brings its own punishment;
try to save him, and you make matters worse.

20 Listen to advice and accept instruction,
and you will die a wise man.

21 A man's heart may be full of schemes,
but the LORD's purpose will prevail.

22 Greed is a disgrace to a man;
better be a poor man than a liar.

23 The fear of the LORD is life;
he who is full of it will rest untouched by evil.

24 The sluggard plunges his hand in the dish
but will not so much as lift it to his mouth.

25 Strike an arrogant man, and he resents it like a fool;
reprove an understanding man, and he understands what you mean.

26 He who talks his father down vexes his mother;
he is a son to bring shame and disgrace on them.

27 A son who ceases to accept correction
is sure to turn his back on the teachings of knowledge.

28 A rascally witness perverts justice,
and the talk of the wicked fosters mischief.

29 There is a rod in pickle for the arrogant,
and blows ready for the stupid man's back.

20 Wine is an insolent fellow, and strong drink makes an uproar;
no one addicted to their company grows wise.

2 A king's threat is like a lion's roar;
one who ignores it is his own worst enemy.

3 To draw back from a dispute is honourable;
it is the fool who bares his teeth.

4 The sluggard who does not plough in autumn
goes begging at harvest and gets nothing.

5 Counsel in another's heart is like deep water,
but a discerning man will draw it up.

6 Many a man protests his loyalty,
but where will you find one to keep faith?

7 If a man leads a good and upright life,
happy are the sons who come after him!

8 A king seated on the judgement-throne
has an eye to sift all that is evil.

9 Who can say, 'I have a clear conscience;
I am purged from my sin'?

10 A double standard in weights and measures
is an abomination to the LORD.

11 Again, a young man is known by his actions,
whether his conduct is innocent or guilty.[a]

12 The ear that hears, the eye that sees,
the LORD made them both.

13 Love sleep, and you will end in poverty;
keep your eyes open, and you will eat your fill.

14 'A bad bargain!' says the buyer to the seller,
but off he goes to brag about it.

---

[a] *Prob. rdg.*; *Heb.* upright.

15 There is gold in plenty and coral too,
but a wise word is a rare jewel.
16 Take a man's garment when he pledges his word for a stranger
and hold that as a pledge for the unknown person.
17 Bread got by fraud tastes good,
but afterwards it fills the mouth with grit.
18 Care is the secret of good planning;
wars are won by skilful strategy.
19 A gossip will betray secrets;[a]
have nothing to do with a tattler.
20 If a man reviles father and mother,
his lamp will go out when darkness comes.
21 If you begin by piling up property in haste,
it will bring you no blessing in the end.
22 Do not think to repay evil for evil,
wait for the LORD to deliver you.
23 A double standard in weights is an abomination to the LORD,
and false scales are not good in his sight.
24 It is the LORD who directs a man's steps;
how can mortal man understand the road he travels?
25 It is dangerous to dedicate a gift rashly
or to make a vow and have second thoughts.
26 A wise king sifts out the wicked
and turns back for them the wheel of fortune.
27 The LORD shines into a man's very soul,
searching out his inmost being.
28 A king's guards are loyalty and good faith,
his throne is upheld by righteousness.
29 The glory of young men is their strength,
the dignity of old men their grey hairs.
30 A good beating purges the mind,
and blows chasten the inmost being.

21 The king's heart is under the LORD's hand;
like runnels of water, he turns it wherever he will.
2 A man may think that he is always right,
but the LORD fixes a standard for the heart.
3 Do what is right and just;
that is more pleasing to the LORD than sacrifice.
4 Haughty looks and a proud heart –
these sins mark a wicked man.
5 Forethought and diligence are sure of profit;
the man in a hurry is as sure of poverty.
6 He who makes a fortune by telling lies
runs needlessly into the toils of death.
7 The wicked are caught up in their own violence,
because they refuse to do what is just.
8 The criminal's conduct is tortuous;
straight dealing is a sign of integrity.
9 Better to live in a corner of the house-top
than have a nagging wife and a brawling household.
10 The wicked man is set on evil;
he has no pity to spare for his friend.
11 The simple man is made wise when he sees the insolent punished,
and learns his lesson when the wise man prospers.
12 The just God[b] makes the wicked man's home childless;[c]
he overturns the wicked and ruins them.
13 If a man shuts his ears to the cry of the helpless,
he will cry for help himself and not be heard.
14 A gift in secret placates an angry man;
a bribe slipped under the cloak pacifies great wrath.

---

[a] *Or* He who betrays secrets is a gossip.   [b] *Or* The just man.
[c] makes...childless: *prob. rdg.*; *Heb.* considers the wicked man's home.

15 When justice is done, all good men rejoice,
but it brings ruin to evildoers.
16 A man who takes leave of common sense
comes to rest in the company of the dead.
17 Love pleasure and you will beg your bread;
a man who loves wine and oil will never grow rich.
18 The wicked man serves as a ransom for the righteous,
so does a traitor for the upright.
19 Better to live alone in the desert than with a nagging and ill-tempered wife.
20 The wise man has his home full of fine and costly treasures;
the stupid man is a mere spendthrift.
21 Persevere in right conduct and loyalty
and you shall find life and honour.
22 A wise man climbs into a city full of armed men
and undermines its strength and its confidence.
23 Keep a guard over your lips and tongue
and keep yourself out of trouble.
24 The conceited man is haughty, his name is insolence;
conceit and impatience are in all he does.
25 The sluggard's cravings will be the death of him,
because his hands refuse to work;
26 all day long his cravings go unsatisfied,
while the righteous man gives without stint.
27 The wicked man's sacrifice is an abomination to the LORD;
how much more when he offers it with vileness at heart!
28 A lying witness will perish,
but he whose words ring true will leave children behind him.
29 A wicked man puts a bold face on it,
whereas the upright man secures his line of retreat.
30 Face to face with the LORD,

wisdom, understanding, counsel go for nothing.
31 A horse may be made ready for the day of battle,
but victory comes from the LORD.

22 A good name is more to be desired than great riches;
esteem is better than silver or gold.
2 Rich and poor have this in common: the LORD made them both.
3 A shrewd man sees trouble coming and lies low;
the simple walk into it and pay the penalty.
4 The fruit of humility is the fear of God
with riches and honour and life.
5 The crooked man's path is set with snares and pitfalls;
the cautious man will steer clear of them.
6 Start a boy on the right road,
and even in old age he will not leave it.
7 The rich lord it over the poor;
the borrower becomes the lender's slave.
8 The man who sows injustice reaps trouble,
and the end of his work will be the rod.[a]
9 The kindly man will be blessed,
for he shares his food with the poor.
10 Drive out the insolent man, and strife goes with him;
if he sits on the bench, he makes a mockery of justice.
11 The LORD loves a sincere man;
but you will make a king your friend with your fine phrases.
12 The LORD keeps watch over every claim at law,
and overturns the scoundrel's case.
13 The sluggard protests, 'There's a lion outside;
I shall get myself killed in the street.'
14 The words of an adulteress are like a deep pit;
those whom the LORD has cursed will fall into it.

---

[a] *the rod: or* the threshing.

15 Folly is deep-rooted in the heart of a boy;
a good beating will drive it right out of him.
16 Oppression of the poor may bring gain to a man,
but giving to the rich leads only to penury.

Thirty wise sayings

17 The sayings of the wise:
Pay heed and listen to my words,
open your mind to the knowledge I impart;
18 to keep them in your heart will be a pleasure,
and then you will always have them ready on your lips.
19 I would have you trust in the LORD
and so I tell you these things this day for your own good.
20 Here I have written out for you thirty sayings,
full of knowledge and wise advice,
21 to impart to you a knowledge of the truth,
that you may take back a true report[a] to him who sent you.

22 Never rob a helpless man because he is helpless,
nor ill-treat a poor wretch in court;
23 for the LORD will take up their cause
and rob him who robs them of their livelihood.
24 Never make friends with an angry man
nor keep company with a bad-tempered one;
25 be careful not to learn his ways,
or you will find yourself caught in a trap.
26 Never be one to give guarantees,
or to pledge yourself as surety for another;
27 for if you cannot pay, beware:
your bed will be taken from under you.

28 Do not move the ancient boundary-stone
which your forefathers set up.
29 You see a man skilful at his craft:
he will serve kings, he will not serve common men.

23 When you sit down to eat with a ruling prince,
be sure to keep your mind on what is before you,
2 and if you are a greedy man,
cut your throat first.
3 Do not be greedy for his dainties,
for they are not what they seem.
4 Do not slave to get wealth;[b]
be a sensible man, and give up.
5 Before you can look round, it will be gone:
it will surely grow wings
like an eagle, like a bird in the sky.
6 Do not go to dinner with a miser,[c]
do not be greedy for his dainties;
7 for they will stick in your[d] throat like a hair.
He will bid you eat and drink,
but his heart is not with you;
8 you will bring up the mouthful you have eaten,
and your winning words will have been wasted.

9 Hold your tongue in the hearing of a stupid man;
for he will despise your words of wisdom.
10 Do not move the ancient boundary-stone
or encroach on the land of orphans:
11 they have a powerful guardian who will take up their cause against you.
12 Apply your mind to instruction and open your ears to knowledge when it speaks.
13 Do not withhold discipline from a boy;
take the stick to him, and save him from death.
14 If you take the stick to him yourself,
you will preserve him from the jaws of death.

---

[a] *Prob. rdg.; Heb. adds* words of truth. to a feast.
[b] to get wealth: *or* for an invitation
[c] *Or* a man with an evil eye.
[d] *Prob. rdg.; Heb.* his.

15 My son, if you are wise at heart,
my heart in its turn will be glad;
16 I shall rejoice with all my soul
when you speak plain truth.

17 Do not try to emulate sinners;
envy only those who fear the LORD
day by day;
18 do this, and you may look forward
to the future,
and your thread of life will not be
cut short.

19 Listen, my son, listen, and become
wise;
set your mind on the right course.
20 Do not keep company with drunkards
or those who are greedy for the
fleshpots;
21 for drink and greed will end in
poverty,
and drunken stupor goes in rags.

22 Listen to your father, who gave
you life,
and do not despise your mother
when she is old.
23 Buy truth, never sell it;
buy wisdom, instruction, and
understanding.
24 A good man's father will rejoice
and he who has a wise son will
delight in him.
25 Give your father and your mother
cause for delight,
let her who bore you rejoice.

26 My son, mark my words,
and accept my guidance with a will.
27 A prostitute is a deep pit,
a loose woman a narrow well;
28 she lies in wait like a robber
and betrays her husband with man
after man.

29 Whose is the misery? whose the
remorse?
Whose are the quarrels and the
anxiety?
Who gets the bruises without
knowing why?

Whose eyes are bloodshot?
Those who linger late over their 30
wine,
those who are always trying some
new spiced liquor.
Do not gulp down the wine, the 31
strong red wine,
when the droplets form on the side
of the cup;[a]
in the end it will bite like a snake 32
and sting like a cobra.
Then your eyes see strange sights, 33
your wits and your speech are
confused;
you become like a man tossing out 34
at sea,
like one who clings to[b] the top of
the rigging;
you say, 'If it lays me flat, what 35
do I care?
If it brings me to the ground, what
of it?
As soon as I wake up,
I shall turn to it again.'

Do not emulate wicked men   24
or long to make friends with them;
for violence is all they think of, 2
and all they say means mischief.

Wisdom builds the house, 3
good judgement makes it secure,
knowledge furnishes the rooms 4
with all the precious and pleasant
things that wealth can buy.

Wisdom prevails over strength, 5
knowledge over brute force;
for wars are won by skilful strategy, 6
and victory is the fruit of long
planning.

Wisdom is too high for a fool; 7
he dare not open his mouth in
court.

A man who is bent on mischief 8
gets a name for intrigue;
the intrigues of foolish men mis- 9
fire,
and the insolent man is odious to
his fellows.

---

[a] *Prob. rdg.; Heb. adds* it runs smoothly to and fro.
[b] clings to: *prob. rdg.; Heb.* lies on.

10 If your strength fails on a lucky[a]
    day,
    how helpless will you be on a day
    of disaster!

11 When you see a man being dragged
    to be killed, go to his rescue,
    and save those being hurried away
    to their death.

12 If you say, 'But I do not know
    this man',
    God, who fixes a standard for the
    heart, will take note.
    God who watches you – be sure he
    will know;
    he will requite every man for what
    he does.

13 Eat honey, my son, for it is good,
    and the honeycomb so sweet upon
    the tongue.

14 Make wisdom too your own;
    if you find it, you may look forward
    to the future,
    and your thread of life will not be
    cut short.

15 Do not lie in wait like a felon at
    the good man's house,
    or raid his farm.

16 Though the good man may fall
    seven times, he is soon up again,
    but the rascal is brought down by
    misfortune.

17 Do not rejoice when your enemy
    falls,
    do not gloat when he is brought
    down;

18 or the Lord will see and be dis-
    pleased with you,
    and he will cease to be angry with
    him.

19 Do not vie with evildoers
    or emulate the wicked;

20 for wicked men have no future to
    look forward to;
    their embers will be put out.

21 My son, fear the Lord and grow
    rich,

but have nothing to do with men
of rank,
they will bring about disaster 22
without warning;
who knows what ruin such men
may cause[b]?

More sayings of wise men: 23

Partiality in dispensing justice is
not good.
A judge who pronounces a guilty 24
man innocent
is cursed by all nations, all peoples
execrate him;
but for those who convict the 25
guilty all will go well,
they will be blessed with prosperity.
A straightforward answer   26
is as good as a kiss of friendship.

First put all in order out of doors 27
and make everything ready on the
land;
then establish your house and
home.

Do not be a witness against your 28
neighbour without good reason
nor misrepresent him in your
evidence.
Do not say,   29
'I will do to him what he has done
to me;
I will requite him for what he has
done.'

I passed by the field of an idle man, 30
by the vineyard of a man with no
sense.
I looked, and it was all dried up, 31
it was overgrown with thistles
and covered with weeds,
and the stones of its walls had been
torn down.
I saw and I took good note,   32
I considered and learnt the lesson:
a little sleep, a little slumber, 33
a little folding of the hands in rest,
and poverty will come upon you 34
like a robber,
want like a ruffian.

[a] lucky: *prob. rdg.*; Heb. *om.*
[b] they...cause: *or* they will come to sudden disaster; who knows what the ruin
of such men will be.

Other collections of wise sayings

25 More proverbs of Solomon transcribed by the men of Hezekiah king of Judah:

2 The glory of God is to keep things hidden
but the glory of kings is to fathom them.

3 The heavens for height, the earth[a] for depth:
unfathomable is the heart of a king.

4 Rid silver of its impurities,
then it may go to[b] the silversmith;

5 rid the king's presence of wicked men,
and his throne will rest firmly on righteousness.

6 Do not put yourself forward in the king's presence
or take your place among the great;

7 for it is better that he should say to you, 'Come up here',
than move you down to make room for a nobleman.

8 Be in no hurry to tell everyone what you have seen,
or it will end in bitter reproaches from your friend.

9 Argue your own case with your neighbour,
but do not reveal another man's secrets,

10 or he will reproach you when he hears of it
and your indiscretion will then be beyond recall.

11 Like apples of gold set in silver filigree
is a word spoken in season.

12 Like a golden earring or a necklace of Nubian gold
is a wise man whose reproof finds attentive ears.

13 Like the coolness of snow in harvest
is a trusty messenger to those who send him.[c]

14 Like clouds and wind that bring no rain

is the man who boasts of gifts he never gives.

15 A prince may be persuaded by patience,
and a soft tongue may break down solid bone.[d]

16 If you find honey, eat only what you need,
too much of it will make you sick;

17 be sparing in visits to your neighbour's house,
if he sees too much of you, he will dislike you.

18 Like a club or a sword or a sharp arrow
is a false witness who denounces his friend.

19 Like a tooth decayed or a foot limping
is a traitor relied on in the day of trouble.

20 Like one who dresses[e] a wound with vinegar,
so is the sweetest of singers to the heavy-hearted.

21 If your enemy is hungry, give him bread to eat;
if he is thirsty, give him water to drink;

22 so you will heap glowing coals on his head,
and the LORD will reward you.

23 As the north wind holds back the rain,
so an angry glance holds back slander.

24 Better to live in a corner of the house-top
than have a nagging wife and a brawling household.

25 Like cold water to the throat when it is dry
is good news from a distant land.

26 Like a muddied spring or a tainted well
is a righteous man who gives way to a wicked one.

27 A surfeit of honey is bad for a man,
and the quest for honour is burdensome.

---

[a] Or the underworld.   [b] then it may go to: or and it will come out bright for.
[c] Prob. rdg.; Heb. adds refreshing his master.   [d] solid bone: or authority.
[e] Prob. rdg.; Heb. adds a garment on a cold day.

28 Like a city that has burst out of
　　its confining walls[a]
　　is a man who cannot control his
　　temper.

26 Like snow in summer or rain at
　　harvest,
　　honour is unseasonable in a stupid
　　man.

2 Like a fluttering sparrow or a
　　darting swallow,
　　groundless abuse gets nowhere.

3 The whip for a horse, the bridle for
　　an ass,
　　the rod for the back of a fool!

4 Do not answer a stupid man in the
　　language of his folly,
　　or you will grow like him;

5 answer a stupid man as his folly
　　deserves,
　　or he will think himself a wise man.

6 He who sends a fool on an errand
　　cuts his own leg off and displays
　　the stump.

7 A proverb in the mouth of stupid
　　men
　　dangles helpless as a lame man's
　　legs.

8 Like one who gets the stone caught
　　in his sling
　　is he who bestows honour on a fool.

9 Like a thorn that pierces a drunk-
　　ard's hand
　　is a proverb in a stupid man's
　　mouth.

10 Like an archer who shoots at any
　　passer-by[b]
　　is one who hires a stupid man or
　　a drunkard.

11 Like a dog returning to its vomit
　　is a stupid man who repeats his
　　folly.

12 Do you see that man who thinks
　　himself so wise?
　　There is more hope for a fool than
　　for him.

13 The sluggard protests, 'There is a
　　lion[c] in the highway,
　　a lion at large in the streets.'

14 A door turns on its hinges,
　　a sluggard on his bed.

A sluggard plunges his hand in the 15
dish
but is too lazy to lift it to his mouth.

A sluggard is wiser in his own eyes 16
than seven men who answer
sensibly.

Like a man who seizes a passing 17
cur by the ears
is he who meddles in another's
quarrel.

A man who deceives another 19[d]
and then says, 'It was only a joke',
is like a madman shooting at 18
random
his deadly darts and arrows.

For lack of fuel a fire dies down 20
and for want of a tale-bearer a
quarrel subsides.

Like bellows for the coal and fuel 21
for the fire
is a quarrelsome man for kindling
strife.

A gossip's whispers are savoury 22
morsels
gulped down into the inner man.

Glib speech that covers a spiteful 23
heart
is like glaze spread on earthenware.

With his lips an enemy may speak 24
you fair
but inwardly he harbours deceit;

when his words are gracious, do 25
not trust him,
for seven abominations fill his
heart;

he may cloak his enmity in dis- 26
simulation,
but his wickedness is shown up
before the assembly.

If he digs a pit, he will fall into it; 27
if he rolls a stone, it will roll back
upon him.

A lying tongue makes innocence 28
seem guilty,
and smooth words conceal their
sting.

Do not flatter yourself about to- 27
morrow,
for you never know what a day
will bring forth.

---

[a] *Or that is breached and left unwalled.*　[b] passer-by: *transposed from end of*
verse.　　　[c] *Or snake.*　[d] *Verses 18 and 19 transposed.*

2 Let flattery come from a stranger,
not from yourself,
from the lips of an outsider and
not from your own.
3 Stone is a burden and sand a dead
weight,
but to be vexed by a fool is more
burdensome than either.
4 Wrath is cruel and anger is a
deluge;
but who can stand up to jealousy?
5 Open reproof is better
than love concealed.
6 The blows a friend gives are well
meant,
but the kisses of an enemy are
perfidious.
7 A man full-fed refuses honey,
but even bitter food tastes sweet
to a hungry man.
8 Like a bird that strays far from its
nest
is a man far from his home.
9 Oil and perfume bring joy to the
heart,
but cares torment a man's very
soul.
10 Do not neglect your own friend or
your father's;*a*
a neighbour at hand is better than
a brother far away.
11 Be wise, my son, then you will
bring joy to my heart,
and I shall be able to forestall my
critics.
12 A shrewd man sees trouble coming
and lies low;
the simple walk into it and pay
the penalty.
13 Take a man's garment when he
pledges his word for a stranger
and hold that as a pledge for the
unknown person.
14 If one man greets another too
heartily,
he may give great offence.
15 Endless dripping on a rainy day –
that is what a nagging wife is
like.
16 As well try to control the wind as
to control her!

As well try to pick up oil in one's
fingers!
As iron sharpens iron, 17
so one man sharpens the wits of
another.
He who guards the fig-tree will eat 18
its fruit,
and he who watches his master's
interests will come to honour.
As face answers face reflected in 19
the water,
so one man's heart answers another's.
Sheol and Abaddon are insatiable; 20
a man's eyes too are never satisfied.
The melting-pot is for silver and 21
the crucible for gold,
but praise is the test of character.
Pound a fool with pestle and 22
mortar,*b*
his folly will never be knocked out
of him.

Be careful to know your own sheep 23
and take good care of your flocks;
for possessions do not last for 24
ever,
nor will a crown endure to endless
generations.
The grass disappears, new shoots 25
are seen
and the green growth on the hills
is gathered in;
the lambs clothe you, 26
the he-goats are worth the price
of a field,
while the goats' milk is enough for 27
your food
and nourishment for your maidens.

The wicked man runs away with 28
no one in pursuit,
but the righteous is like a young
lion in repose.
It is the fault of a violent man 2
that quarrels start,
but they are settled by a man of
discernment.
A tyrant oppressing the poor 3
is like driving rain which ruins the
crop.

---

a *Prob. rdg.; Heb. adds* or how should you enter your brother's house in the day
of your ruin?   *b* *Prob. rdg.; Heb. adds* with groats.

4 The lawless praise wicked men;
the law-abiding contend with
them.

5 Bad men do not know what justice
is,
but those who seek the LORD know
everything good.

6 Better be poor and above reproach
than rich and crooked.

7 A discerning son observes the law,
but one who keeps riotous company
wounds his father.

8 He who grows rich by lending at
discount or at interest
is saving for another who will be
generous to the poor.

9 If a man turns a deaf ear to the law,
even his prayers are an abomination.

10 He who tempts the upright into
evil courses
will himself fall into the pit he has
dug.
The honest shall inherit a fortune,
but the wicked shall inherit nothing.

11 The rich man may think himself
wise,
but a poor man of discernment sees
through him.

12 When the just are in power, there
are great celebrations,[a]
but when the wicked come to the
top, others are downtrodden.

13 Conceal your faults, and you will
not prosper;
confess and give them up, and you
will find mercy.

14 Happy the man who is scrupulous
in conduct,
but he who hardens his heart falls
into misfortune.

15 Like a starving lion or a thirsty
bear
is a wicked man ruling a helpless
people.

16 The man who is stupid and grasping
will perish,
but he who hates ill-gotten gain
will live long.

17 A man charged with bloodshed

will jump into a well to escape
arrest.

18 Whoever leads an honest life will
be safe,
but a rogue will fail, one way or
another.

19 One who cultivates his land has
plenty to eat;
idle pursuits lead to poverty.

20 A man of steady character will
enjoy many blessings,
but one in a hurry to grow rich
will not go unpunished.

21 To show favour is not good;
but men will do wrong for a mere
crust of bread.

22 The miser[b] is in a hurry to grow
rich,
never dreaming that want will
overtake him.

23 Take a man to task and in the
end win more thanks
than the man with a flattering
tongue.

24 To rob your father or mother and
say you do no wrong
is no better than wanton destruction.

25 A self-important[c] man provokes
quarrels,
but he who trusts in the LORD
grows fat and prosperous.

26 It is plain stupidity to trust in one's
own wits,
but he who walks the path of wisdom will come safely through.

27 He who gives to the poor will never
want,
but he who turns a blind eye gets
nothing but curses.

28 When the wicked come to the top,
others are pulled down;[d]
but, when they perish, the righteous
come into power.

29 A man who is still stubborn after
much reproof
will suddenly be broken past
mending.

2 When the righteous are in power
the people rejoice,

---

[a] Or there is great pageantry.
[c] Or grasping.

[b] Or The man with the evil eye.
[d] are pulled down: or hide themselves.

but they groan when the wicked hold office.

3 A lover of wisdom brings joy to his father,
but one who keeps company with harlots squanders his wealth.

4 By just government a king gives his country stability,
but by forced contributions he reduces it to ruin.

5 A man who flatters his neighbour is spreading a net for his feet.

6 An evil man is ensnared by his sin,[a]
but a righteous man lives and flourishes.

7 The righteous man is concerned for the cause of the helpless,
but the wicked understand no such concern.

8 Arrogance can inflame a city,
but wisdom averts the people's anger.

9 If a wise man goes to law with a fool, he will meet abuse or derision, but get no remedy.

10 Men who have tasted blood hate an honest man,
but the upright set much store by his life.

11 A stupid man gives free rein to his anger;
a wise man waits and lets it grow cool.

12 If a prince listens to falsehood, all his servants will be wicked.

13 Poor man and oppressor have this in common:
what happiness each has comes from the LORD.

14 A king who steadfastly deals out justice to the weak
will be secure for ever on his throne.

15 Rod and reprimand impart wisdom,
but a boy who runs wild brings shame on his mother.

16 When the wicked are in power, sin is in power,
but the righteous will gloat over their downfall.

17 Correct your son, and he will be a comfort to you
and bring you delights of every kind.

18 Where there is no one in authority,[b] the people break loose,
but a guardian of the law keeps them on the straight path.

19 Mere words will not keep a slave in order;
he may understand, but he will not respond.

20 When you see someone over-eager to speak,[c]
there will be more hope for a fool than for him.

21 Pamper a slave from boyhood,
and in the end he will prove ungrateful.

22 A man prone to anger provokes a quarrel
and a hot-head is always doing wrong.

23 Pride will bring a man low;
a man lowly in spirit wins honour.

24 He who goes shares with a thief is his own enemy:
he hears himself put on oath and dare not give evidence.

25 A man's fears will prove a snare to him,
but he who trusts in the LORD has a high tower of refuge.

26 Many seek audience of a prince,
but in every case the LORD decides.

27 The righteous cannot abide an unjust man,
nor the wicked a man whose conduct is upright.

Sayings of Agur son of Jakeh from 30 Massa:[d]

This is the great man's very word:
I am weary, O God,
I am weary and worn out;

2 I am a dumb brute, scarcely a man,
without a man's powers of understanding;

---

[a] An evil...sin: *or* When an evil man steps out a trap awaits him.
[b] Or no vision.　　　　[c] Or someone hasty in business.
[d] from Massa: *prob. rdg.* (*cp.* 31. 1); *Heb.* the oracle.

3 I have not learnt wisdom
nor have I received knowledge
from the Holy One.
4 Who has ever gone up to heaven
and come down again?
Who has cupped the wind in the
hollow of his hands?
Who has bound up the waters in
the fold of his garment?
Who has fixed the boundaries of
the earth?
What is his name or his son's name,
if you know it?

5 God's every promise has stood the
test:
he is a shield to all who seek refuge
with him.
6 Add nothing to his words,
or he will expose you for a liar.
7 Two things I ask of thee;
do not withhold them from me
before I die.
8 Put fraud and lying far from me;
give me neither poverty nor wealth,
provide me only with the food I
need.
9 If I have too much, I shall deny
thee
and say, 'Who is the LORD?'
If I am reduced to poverty, I shall
steal
and blacken the name of my God.

10 Never disparage a slave to his
master,
or he will speak ill of you, and you
will pay for it.

11 There is a sort of people who defame
their fathers
and do not speak well of their own
mothers;
12 a sort who are pure in their own
eyes
and yet are not cleansed of their
filth;
13 a sort – how haughty are their
looks,
how disdainful their glances!
14 A sort whose teeth are swords,
their jaws are set with knives,

they eat the wretched out of the
country
and the needy out of house and
home.[a]

The leech has two daughters;   15
'Give', says one, and 'Give', says
the other.

Three things there are which will
never be satisfied,
four which never say, 'Enough!'
The grave and a barren womb,[b]   16
a land thirsty for water
and fire that never says, 'Enough!'

The eye that mocks a father or 17
scorns a mother's old age[c]
will be plucked out by magpies
or eaten by the vulture's young.

Three things there are which are 18
too wonderful for me,
four which I do not understand:
the way of a vulture in the sky,   19
the way of a serpent on the rock,
the way of a ship out at sea,
and the way of a man with a girl.

The way of an unfaithful wife is 20
this:
she eats, then she wipes her mouth
and says, 'I have done no harm.'

At three things the earth shakes,   21
four things it cannot bear:
a slave turned king,   22
a churl gorging himself,
a woman unloved when she is 23
married,
and a slave-girl displacing her
mistress.

Four things there are which are 24
smallest on earth
yet wise beyond the wisest:
ants, a people with no strength,   25
yet they prepare their store of food
in the summer;
rock-badgers, a feeble folk,   26
yet they make their home among
the rocks;

---

[a] house and home: *prob. rdg.*; Heb. *man.*   [b] *Or* a woman's desire.
[c] old age: *prob. rdg.*; Heb. *unintelligible.*

27 locusts, which have no king,
yet they all sally forth in detachments;
28 the lizard, which can be grasped in the hand,
yet is found in the palaces of kings.

29 Three things there are which are stately in their stride,
four which are stately as they move:
30 the lion, a hero among beasts,
which will not turn tail for anyone;
31 the strutting cock and the he-goat;
and a king going forth to lead his army.[a]

32 If you are churlish and arrogant and fond of filthy talk, hold your tongue;
33 for wringing out the milk produces curd
and wringing the nose produces blood,
so provocation leads to strife.

31 Sayings of Lemuel king of Massa, which his mother taught him:

2 What, O my son, what shall I say to you,
you, the child of my womb and answer to my prayers?
3 Do not give the vigour of your manhood to women
nor consort with those who make eyes at[b] kings.
4 It is not for kings, O Lemuel, not for kings to drink wine
nor for princes to crave strong drink;
5 if they drink, they will forget rights and customs
and twist the law against their wretched victims.
6 Give strong drink to the desperate and wine to the embittered;
7 such men will drink and forget their poverty
and remember their trouble no longer.

Open your mouth and speak up 8 for the dumb,
against the suit of any that oppose them;
open your mouth and pronounce 9 just sentence
and give judgement for the wretched and the poor.

A capable wife

Who can find a capable wife? 10
Her worth is far beyond coral.
Her husband's whole trust is in 11 her,
and children are not lacking.
She repays him with good, not evil, 12 all her life long.
She chooses wool and flax 13
and toils at her work.
Like a ship laden with merchandise, 14
she brings home food from far off.
She rises while it is still night 15
and sets meat before her household.[c]
After careful thought she buys a 16 field
and plants a vineyard out of her earnings.
She sets about her duties with 17 vigour
and braces herself for the work.
She sees that her business goes 18 well,
and never puts out her lamp at night.
She holds the distaff in her hand, 19
and her fingers grasp the spindle.
She is open-handed to the wretched 20
and generous to the poor.
She has no fear for her household 21 when it snows,
for they are wrapped in two cloaks.
She makes her own coverings, 22
and clothing of fine linen and purple.
Her husband is well known in the 23 city gate
when he takes his seat with the elders of the land.

---

[a] going forth to lead his army: *prob. rdg.*; *Heb. unintelligible.*
[b] who make eyes at: *prob. rdg.*; *Heb. unintelligible.*
[c] *Prob. rdg.*; *Heb. adds and a prescribed portion for her maidens.*

24 She weaves linen and sells it,
and supplies merchants with their
sashes.

25 She is clothed in dignity and
power
and can afford to laugh at tomorrow.

26 When she opens her mouth, it is
to speak wisely,
and loyalty is the theme of her
teaching.

27 She keeps her eye on the doings of
her household
and does not eat the bread of idleness.

Her sons with one accord call her 28
happy;
her husband too, and he sings her
praises:

'Many a woman shows how capable 29
she is;[a]
but you excel them all.'

Charm is a delusion and beauty 30
fleeting;
it is the God-fearing woman who
is honoured.

Extol her for the fruit of all her 31
toil,
and let her labours bring her
honour in the city gate.

ECCLESIASTES

The emptiness of all endeavour

1 THE words of the Speaker,
the son of David, king in
Jerusalem.

2 Emptiness, emptiness, says the
Speaker, emptiness, all is empty.

3 What does man gain from all his
labour and his toil here under the

4 sun? Generations come and generations go, while the earth endures
for ever.

5 The sun rises and the sun goes
down; back it returns to its place[b]

6 and rises there again. The wind
blows south, the wind blows north,
round and round it goes and re-

7 turns full circle. All streams run
into the sea, yet the sea never
overflows; back to the place from
which the streams ran they return
to run again.

8 All things are wearisome;[c] no
man can speak of them all. Is not
the eye surfeited with seeing, and

9 the ear sated with hearing? What
has happened will happen again,
and what has been done will be
done again, and there is nothing

new under the sun. Is there any- 10
thing of which one can say, 'Look,
this is new'? No, it has already
existed, long ago before our time.
The men of old are not remembered, 11
and those who follow will not be
remembered by those who follow
them.

I, the Speaker, ruled as king 12
over Israel in Jerusalem; and in 13
wisdom I applied my mind to study
and explore all that is done under
heaven. It is a sorry business that
God has given men to busy themselves with. I have seen all the 14
deeds that are done here under the
sun; they are all emptiness and
chasing the wind. What is crooked 15
cannot become straight; what is
not there cannot be counted. I said 16
to myself, 'I have amassed great
wisdom, more than all my predecessors on the throne in Jerusalem; I have become familiar with
wisdom and knowledge.' So I ap- 17
plied my mind to understand wisdom and knowledge, madness and
folly, and I came to see that this
too is chasing the wind. For in 18

---

[a] *Or* Many daughters show how capable they are.
rdg.; Heb. to its place panting.

[b] back...place: *prob.*
[c] *Prob. rdg.; Heb.* weary.

much wisdom is much vexation, and the more a man knows, the more he has to suffer.

2 I said to myself, 'Come, I will plunge into pleasures and enjoy myself'; but this too was emptiness. 2 Of laughter I said, 'It is madness!' And of pleasure, 'What is the good 3 of that?' So I sought to stimulate myself with wine, in the hope of finding out what was good for men to do under heaven throughout the brief span of their lives. But my mind was guided by wisdom, not blinded by[a] folly.

4 I undertook great works; I built myself houses and planted vine- 5 yards; I made myself gardens and parks and planted all kinds of 6 fruit-trees in them; I made myself pools of water to irrigate a grove 7 of growing trees; I bought slaves, male and female, and I had my home-born slaves as well; I had possessions, more cattle and flocks than any of my predecessors in 8 Jerusalem; I amassed silver and gold also, the treasure of kings and provinces; I acquired singers, men and women, and all that man de- 9 lights in.[b] I was great, greater than all my predecessors in Jerusalem; and my wisdom stood me in good 10 stead. Whatever my eyes coveted, I refused them nothing, nor did I deny myself any pleasure. Yes indeed, I got pleasure from all my labour, and for all my labour this 11 was my reward. Then I turned and reviewed all my handiwork, all my labour and toil, and I saw that everything was emptiness and chasing the wind, of no profit under the sun.

12 I set myself to look at wisdom 13 and at madness and folly.[c] Then I perceived that wisdom is more profitable than folly, as light is 14 more profitable than darkness: the wise man has eyes in his head, but the fool walks in the dark. Yet I saw also that one and the same fate overtakes them both. So I said 15 to myself, 'I too shall suffer the fate of the fool. To what purpose have I been wise? What[d] is the profit of it? Even this', I said to myself, 'is emptiness. The wise 16 man is remembered no longer than the fool, for, as the passing days multiply,[e] all will be forgotten. Alas, wise man and fool die the same death!' So I came to hate life, 17 since everything that was done here under the sun was a trouble to me; for all is emptiness and chasing the wind. So I came to hate 18 all my labour and toil here under the sun, since I should have to leave its fruits to my successor. What sort of a man will he be who succeeds me, who inherits what others have acquired?[f] Who knows 19 whether he will be a wise man or a fool? Yet he will be master of all the fruits of my labour and skill here under the sun. This too is emptiness.

Then I turned and gave myself 20 up to despair, reflecting upon all my labour and toil here under the sun. For anyone who toils with 21 wisdom, knowledge, and skill must leave it all to a man who has spent no labour on it. This too is emptiness and utterly wrong. What re- 22 ward has a man for all his labour, his scheming, and his toil here under the sun? All his life long his 23 business is pain and vexation to him; even at night his mind knows no rest. This too is emptiness. There 24 is nothing better for a man to do than to eat and drink and enjoy himself in return for his labours. And yet I saw that this comes from the hand of God. For without him 25 who can enjoy his food, or who can be anxious? God gives wisdom and 26 knowledge and joy to the man who

---

[a] not blinded by: *prob. rdg.*; *Heb* to grasp.   [b] *Prob. rdg.*; *Heb. adds two unintelligible words.*   [c] *The rest of verse 12 transposed to follow verse 18.*   [d] *Prob. rdg.*; *Heb.* Then.   [e] for...multiply: *prob. rdg.*; *Heb.* because already.   [f] What sort...acquired: *see note on verse 12.*

pleases him, while to the sinner is given the trouble of gathering and amassing wealth only to hand it over to someone else who pleases God. This too is emptiness and chasing the wind.

3 FOR everything its season, and for every activity under heaven its time:

2 a time to be born and a time to die;
   a time to plant and a time to uproot;
3 a time to kill and a time to heal;
   a time to pull down and a time to build up;
4 a time to weep and a time to laugh;
   a time for mourning and a time for dancing;
5 a time to scatter stones and a time to gather them;
   a time to embrace and a time to refrain from embracing;
6 a time to seek and a time to lose;
   a time to keep and a time to throw away;
7 a time to tear and a time to mend;
   a time for silence and a time for speech;
8 a time to love and a time to hate;
   a time for war and a time for peace.

9 What profit does one who works
10 get from all his labour? I have seen the business that God has given
11 men to keep them busy. He has made everything to suit its time; moreover he has given men a sense of time past and future, but no comprehension of God's work from
12 beginning to end. I know that there is nothing good for man[a] except to be happy and live the best life he
13 can while he is alive. Moreover, that a man should eat and drink and enjoy himself, in return for all
14 his labours, is a gift of God. I know that whatever God does lasts for ever; to add to it or subtract from it is impossible. And he has done it all in such a way that men must
15 feel awe in his presence. Whatever

is has been already,[b] and whatever is to come has been already, and God summons each event back in its turn. Moreover I saw here under 16 the sun that, where justice ought to be, there was wickedness, and where righteousness ought to be, there was wickedness. I said to 17 myself, 'God will judge the just man and the wicked equally; every activity and[c] every purpose has its proper time.' I said to myself, 'In 18 dealing with men it is God's purpose[d] to test them and to see what they truly are.[e] For man is a crea- 19 ture of chance and the beasts are creatures of chance, and one mischance awaits them all: death comes to both alike. They all draw the same breath. Men have no advantage over beasts; for everything is emptiness. All go to the same 20 place: all came from the dust, and to the dust all return. Who knows 21 whether the spirit[f] of man goes upward or whether the spirit[f] of the beast goes downward to the earth?' So I saw that there is 22 nothing better than that a man should enjoy his work, since that is his lot. For who can bring him through to see what will happen next?

Again, I considered all the acts 4 of oppression here under the sun; I saw the tears of the oppressed, and I saw that there was no one to comfort them. Strength was on the side of their oppressors, and there was no one to avenge them. I count- 2 ed the dead happy because they were dead, happier than the living who are still in life. More fortunate 3 than either I reckoned the man yet unborn, who had not witnessed the wicked deeds done here under the sun. I considered all toil and all 4 achievement and saw that it comes from rivalry between man and man. This too is emptiness and chasing the wind. The fool folds his arms 5

---

[a] for man: *prob. rdg., cp. 2. 24; Heb.* in them.   [b] *Or* Whatever has been already is.
[c] *Prob. rdg.; Heb.* and upon.   [d] it is God's purpose: *prob. rdg.; Heb. obscure.*
[e] *Prob. rdg.; Heb. adds* they to them.   [f] *Or* breath.

6 and wastes away. Better one hand full and peace of mind, than both fists full and toil that is chasing the wind.

7 Here again, I saw emptiness
8 under the sun: a lonely man without a friend, without son or brother, toiling endlessly yet never satisfied with his wealth – 'For whom', he asks, 'am I toiling and denying myself the good things of life?' This too is emptiness, a sorry busi-
9 ness. Two are better than one; they receive a good reward for their
10 toil, because, if one falls, the other[a] can help his companion up again; but alas for the man who falls alone with no partner to help him up.
11 And, if two lie side by side, they keep each other warm; but how can one keep warm by himself?
12 If a man is alone, an assailant may overpower him, but two can resist; and a cord of three strands is not quickly snapped.

13 Better a young man poor and wise than a king old and foolish who will listen to advice no longer.
14 A man who leaves prison may well come to be king, though born a
15 pauper in his future kingdom. But I have studied all life here under the sun, and I saw his place taken
16 by yet another young man, and no limit set to the number of the subjects whose master he became. And he in turn will be no hero to those who come after him. This too is emptiness and chasing the wind.

5 Go carefully when you visit the house of God. Better draw near in obedience than offer the sacrifice of fools, who sin without a thought.
2 Do not rush into speech, let there be no hasty utterance in God's presence. God is in heaven, you are on earth; so let your words be few.
3 The sensible man has much business on his hands; the fool talks
4 and it is so much chatter. When

you make a vow to God, do not be slow to pay it, for he has no use for fools; pay whatever you vow. Bet- 5 ter not vow at all than vow and fail to pay. Do not let your tongue 6 lead you into sin, and then say before the angel of God that it was a mistake; or God will be angry at your words, and all your achievements will be brought to nothing.[b] You must fear God. 7

If you witness in some province 8 the oppression of the poor and the denial of right and justice, do not be surprised at what goes on, for every official has a higher one set over him, and the highest[c] keeps watch over them all. The best 9 thing for a country is a king whose[d] own lands are well tilled.

The man who loves money can 10 never have enough, and the man who is in love with great wealth enjoys no return from it. This too is emptiness. When riches multiply, 11 so do those who live off them; and what advantage has the owner, except to look at them? Sweet is 12 the sleep of the labourer whether he eats little or much; but the rich man owns too much and cannot sleep. There is a singular evil here 13 under the sun which I have seen: a man hoards wealth to his own hurt, and then that wealth is lost 14 through an unlucky venture, and the owner's son left with nothing. As he came from the womb of 15 mother earth, so must he return, naked as he came; all his toil produces nothing which he can take away with him. This too is a 16 singular evil: exactly as he came, so shall he go, and what profit does he get when his labour is all for the wind? What is more, all his days 17 are overshadowed; gnawing anxiety and great vexation are his lot, sickness[e] and resentment. What I 18 have seen is this: that it is good and

---

[a] if one falls, the other: *prob. rdg.*; *Heb. obscure.*　　[b] *Prob. rdg.*; *Heb. adds* for in a multitude of dreams and empty things and many words.
[c] for every...the highest: *or* though every...over him, the Highest...
[d] whose: *prob. rdg.*; *Heb.* for.　　[e] sickness: *prob. rdg.*; *Heb.* and his sickness.

proper for a man to eat and drink and enjoy himself in return for his labours here under the sun, throughout the brief span of life 19 which God has allotted him. Moreover, it is a gift of God that every man to whom he has granted wealth and riches and the power to enjoy them should accept his 20 lot and rejoice in his labour. He will not dwell overmuch upon the passing years; for God fills his[a] time with joy of heart.

6 Here is an evil under the sun which I have seen, and it weighs 2 heavy upon men. Consider the man to whom God grants wealth, riches, and substance,[b] and who lacks nothing that he has set his heart on: if God has not given him the power to enjoy these things, but a stranger enjoys them instead, that is emptiness and a grave dis- 3 order. A man may have a hundred children and live a long life; but however many his days may be, if he does not get satisfaction from the good things of life and in the end receives no burial, then I maintain that the still-born child is in 4 better case than he. Its coming is an empty thing, it departs into darkness, and in darkness its name 5 is hidden; it has never seen the sun or known anything,[c] yet its state 6 is better than his. What if a man should live a thousand years twice over, and never prosper? Do not both go to one place?

7 The end of all man's toil is but to fill his belly, yet his appetite is 8 never satisfied. What advantage then in facing life has the wise man over the fool, or the poor man for 9 all his experience? It is better to be satisfied with what is before your eyes than give rein to desire; this too is emptiness and chasing 10 the wind. Whatever has already existed has been given a name, its nature is known; a man cannot contend with what is stronger than

he. The more words one uses the 11 greater is the emptiness of it all; and where is the advantage to a man? For who can know what is 12 good for a man in this life, this brief span of empty existence through which he passes like a shadow? Who can tell a man what is to happen next here under the sun?

Wisdom and folly compared

A GOOD name smells sweeter than 7 the finest ointment, and the day of death is better than the day of birth. Better to visit the house of 2 mourning than the house of feasting; for to be mourned is the lot of every man, and the living should take this to heart. Grief is 3 better than laughter: a sad face may go with a cheerful heart. Wise men's thoughts are at home 4 in the house of mourning, but a fool's thoughts in the house of mirth. It is better to listen to a 5 wise man's rebuke than to the praise of fools. For the laughter of 6 a fool is like the crackling of thorns under a pot. This too is emptiness. Slander drives a wise man crazy 7 and breaks a strong man's[d] spirit. Better the end of anything than its 8 beginning; better patience than pride. Do not be quick to show re- 9 sentment; for resentment is nursed by fools. Do not ask why the old 10 days were better than these; for that is a foolish question. Wis- 11 dom is better than possessions and an advantage to all who see the sun. Better have wisdom behind 12 you than money; wisdom profits men by giving life to those who know her.

Consider God's handiwork; who 13 can straighten what he has made crooked? When things go well, be 14 glad; but when things go ill, consider this: God has set the one alongside the other in such a way

---

[a] his: *prob. rdg.*; Heb. *om.*   [b] Or *honour.*
[c] Or *it.*   [d] strong man's: *prob. rdg.*; Heb. *obscure.*

that no one can find out what is to
15 happen next.ᵃ In my empty existence I have seen it all, from a righteous man perishing in his righteousness to a wicked man growing old
16 in his wickedness. Do not be over-
righteous and do not be over-wise.
Why make yourself a laughing-
17 stock? Do not be over-wicked and
do not be a fool. Why should you
18 die before your time? It is good to
hold on to the one thing and not
lose hold of the other; for a man
who fears God will succeed both
19 ways. Wisdom makes the wise man
stronger than the ten rulers of a
20 city. The world contains no man so
righteous that he can do right al-
21 ways and never do wrong.ᵇ Moreover, do not pay attention to
everything men say, or you may
hear your servant disparage you;
22 for you know very well how many
times you yourself have disparaged
23 others. All this I have put to the
test of wisdom. I said, 'I am resolved to be wise', but wisdom was
24 beyond my grasp – whatever has
happened lies beyond our grasp,
deep down, deeper than man can
fathom.

25   I went on to reflect, I set my
mindᶜ to inquire and search for
wisdom and for the reason in
things, only to discover that it is
folly to be wicked and madness to
26 act like a fool. The wiles of a woman
I find mightierᵈ than death; her
heart is a trap to catch you and her
arms are fetters. The man who is
pleasing to God may escape her,
27 but she will catch a sinner. 'See,'
says the Speaker, 'this is what I
have found, reasoning things out
28 one by one, after searching long
without success: I have found one
man in a thousand worth the name,
but I have not found one woman
29 among them all. This alone I have

found, that God, when he made
man, made him straightforward,
but man invents endless subtleties
of his own.'
Who is wise enough for all this? 8
Who knows the meaning of anything? Wisdom lights up a man's
face, but grim looks make a man
hated.ᵉ Do as the king commands 2
you, and if you have to swear by
God, do not be precipitate. Leave 3
the king's presence and do not persist in a thing which displeases
him; he does what he chooses. For 4
the king's word carries authority.
Who can question what he does?
Whoever obeys a command will 5
come to no harm. A wise man
knows in his heart the right time
and method for action. There is a 6
time and a method for every enterprise, although man is greatly
troubled by ignorance of the future; 7
who can tell him what it will bring?
It is not in man's power to restrain 8
the wind,ᶠ and no one has power
over the day of death. In war no
one can lay aside his arms, no
wealth will save its possessor. All 9
this I have seen, having applied
my mind to everything done under
the sun. There was a time when
one man had power over another
and could make him suffer. It was 10
then that I saw wicked men approaching and even enteringᵍ the
holy place; and they went about
the city priding themselves on
having done right. This too is
emptiness. It is because sentence 11
upon a wicked act is not promptly
carried out that men do evil so
boldly. A sinner may do wrongʰ 12
and live to old age, yet I know that
it will be well with those who fear
God: their fear of him ensures this,
but it will not be well with a wicked 13
man nor will he live long; the man
who does not fear God is a mere

14 shadow. There is an empty thing found on earth: when the just man gets what is due to the unjust, and the unjust what is due to the just. I maintain that this too is empti-
15 ness. So I commend enjoyment, since there is nothing good for a man to do here under the sun but to eat and drink and enjoy himself; this is all that will remain with him to reward his toil throughout the span of life which God grants him
16 here under the sun. I applied my mind to acquire wisdom and to observe the business which goes on upon earth, when man never closes an eye in sleep day or night;
17 and always I perceived that God has so ordered it that man should not be able to discover what is happening here under the sun. However hard a man may try, he will not find out; the wise man may think that he knows, but he will be unable to find the truth of it.

9 I applied my mind to all this, and I understood that the righteous and the wise and all their doings are under God's control; but is it love or hatred? No man knows. Everything that confronts him,
2 everything is empty, since one and the same fate befalls every one, just and unjust alike, good and bad, clean and unclean, the man who offers sacrifice and the man who does not. Good man and sinner fare alike, the man who can take an oath and the man who dares
3 not. This is what is wrong in all that is done here under the sun: that one and the same fate befalls every man. The hearts of men are full of evil; madness fills their hearts all through their lives, and after that they go down to join the
4 dead. But for a man who is counted among the living there is still hope: remember, a live dog is better than
5 a dead lion. True, the living know that they will die; but the dead know nothing. There are no more rewards for them; they are utterly

forgotten. For them love, hate, 6 ambition,[a] all are now over. Never again will they have any part in what is done here under the sun.

Go to it then, eat your food and 7 enjoy it, and drink your wine with a cheerful heart; for already God has accepted what you have done. Always be dressed in white and 8 never fail to anoint your head. Enjoy life with a woman you love 9 all the days of your allotted span here under the sun, empty as they are;[b] for that is your lot while you live and labour here under the sun. Whatever task lies to your hand, 10 do it with all your might; because in Sheol, for which you are bound, there is neither doing nor thinking, neither understanding nor wisdom. One more thing I have observed 11 here under the sun: speed does not win the race nor strength the battle. Bread does not belong to the wise, nor wealth to the intelligent, nor success to the skilful; time and chance govern all. Moreover, no 12 man knows when his hour will come; like fish caught in a net, like a bird taken in a snare, so men are trapped when bad times come suddenly.

This too is an example of wisdom 13 as I have observed it here under the sun, and notable I find it. There 14 was a small town with few inhabitants, and a great king came to attack it; he besieged it and constructed great siege-works against it. There was in it a poor wise man, 15 and he alone might have saved the town by his wisdom, but no one remembered that poor wise man. 'Surely', I said to myself, 'wisdom 16 is better than strength.' But the poor man's wisdom was despised, and his words went unheeded. A 17 wise man who speaks his mind calmly is more to be heeded than a commander shouting orders among fools. Wisdom is better than 18 weapons of war, and one mistake can undo many things done well.

---

[a] Or passion.   [b] *Prob. rdg.*; *Heb. adds* all your days, empty as they are.

10 Dead flies make the perfumer's sweet ointment turn rancid and ferment; so can a little folly make
2 wisdom lose its worth. The mind of the wise man faces right, but
3 the mind of the fool faces left. Even when he walks along the road, the fool shows no sense and calls every-
4 one else[a] a fool. If your ruler breaks out in anger against you, do not resign your post; submission makes
5 amends for great mistakes. There is an evil that I have observed here under the sun, an error for which
6 a ruler is responsible: the fool given high office, but[b] the great and the
7 rich in humble posts. I have seen slaves on horseback and men of high rank going on foot like slaves.
8 The man who digs a pit may fall into it, and he who pulls down a
9 wall may be bitten by a snake. The man who quarries stones may strain himself, and the woodcutter
10 runs a risk of injury. When the axe is blunt and has not first[c] been sharpened, then one must use more force; the wise man has a better
11 chance of success. If a snake bites before it is charmed, the snake-charmer loses his fee.
12 A wise man's words win him favour, but a fool's tongue is his
13 undoing. He begins by talking nonsense and ends in mischief run
14 mad. The fool talks on and on; but no man knows what is coming, and who can tell him what will come
15 after that? The fool wearies himself to death[d] with all his labour, for he does not know the way to town.
16 Woe betide the land when a slave has become its king, and its
17 princes feast in the morning. Happy the land when its king is nobly born, and its princes feast at the right time of day, with self-control,
18 and not as drunkards. If the owner is negligent the rafters collapse, and if he is idle the house crumbles

away. The table has its pleasures, 19 and wine makes a cheerful life; and money is behind it all. Do not 20 speak ill of the king in your ease, or of a rich man in your bedroom; for a bird may carry your voice, and a winged messenger may repeat what you say.

Send your grain across the seas, 11 and in time you will get a return. Divide your merchandise among 2 seven ventures, eight maybe, since you do not know what disasters may occur on earth.[e] If the clouds 3 are heavy with rain, they will discharge it on the earth; whether a tree falls south or north, it must lie as it falls. He who watches the 4 wind will never sow, and he who keeps an eye on the clouds will never reap. You do not know how 5 a pregnant woman comes to have a body and a living spirit in her womb; nor do you know how God, the maker of all things, works. In 6 the morning sow your seed betimes, and do not stop work until evening, for you do not know whether this or that sowing will be successful, or whether both alike will do well.

Advice to a young man

THE light of day is sweet, and 7 pleasant to the eye is the sight of the sun; if a man lives for many 8 years, he should rejoice in all of them. But let him remember that the days of darkness will be many. Everything that is to come will be emptiness. Delight in your boy- 9 hood, young man, make the most of the days of your youth; let your heart and your eyes show you the way; but remember that for all these things God will call you to account. Banish discontent from 10 your mind, and shake off the troubles of the body; boyhood and the prime of life are mere emptiness.

---

[a] calls everyone else: *or* tells everyone he is.   [b] but: *prob. rdg.; Heb. om.*
[c] first: *prob. rdg.; Heb. face.*   [d] fool...death: *prob. rdg.; Heb. obscure.*
[e] *Or on land.*

12 Remember your Creator in the days of your youth, before the time of trouble comes and the years draw near when you will say, 'I see 2 no purpose in them.'*a* Remember him before the sun and the light of day give place to darkness, before the moon and the stars grow dim, and the clouds return with 3 the rain – when the guardians of the house tremble, and the strong men stoop, when the women grinding the meal cease work because they are few, and those who look through the windows look no long- 4 er, when the street-doors are shut, when the noise of the mill is low, when the chirping of the sparrow grows faint*b* and the song-birds 5 fall silent;*c* when men are afraid of a steep place and the street is full of terrors, when the blossom whitens on the almond-tree and the locust's paunch is swollen and caper-buds have no more zest. For man goes to his everlasting home, and the mourners go about the 6 streets. Remember him before the silver cord is snapped*d* and the golden bowl is broken, before the pitcher is shattered at the spring and the wheel broken at the well, before the dust returns to the earth 7 as it began and the spirit*e* returns to God who gave it. Emptiness, 8 emptiness, says the Speaker, all is empty.

So the Speaker, in his wisdom, 9 continued to teach the people what he knew. He turned over many maxims in his mind and sought how best to set them out. He chose 10 his words to give pleasure, but what he wrote was the honest truth. The sayings of the wise are sharp 11 as goads, like nails driven home; they lead the assembled people, for they come from one shepherd. One 12 further warning, my son: the use of books is endless, and much study is wearisome.

This is the end of the matter: you 13 have heard it all. Fear God and obey his commands; there is no more to man than this. For God 14 brings everything we do to judge-ment, and every secret, whether good or bad.

THE SONG OF SONGS

Bride*f*

1 I will sing the song of all songs to Solomon
2 that he may*g* smother me with kisses.

Your love is more fragrant than wine,

fragrant is*h* the scent of your per- 3 fume,
and your name like perfume pour-ed out;*i*
for this the maidens love you.
Take me with you, and we will run 4 together;
bring me into your chamber, O king.

---

a Or I have no pleasure in them.   *b* grows faint: *prob. rdg.*; *Heb. obscure.*
c *Prob. rdg.*; *Heb. sink low.*   *d* is snapped: *prob. rdg.*; *Heb. unintelligible.*
e Or breath.   *f* *The Hebrew text implies, by its pronouns, different speakers, but does not indicate them; they are given, however, in two MSS. of Sept.*
g I will...that he may: *or* The song of all songs which was Solomon's; may he...
h Or more fragrant than.   *i* poured out: *prob. rdg.*; *Heb. word uncertain.*

Companions
Let us rejoice and be glad for you;
let us praise your love more than
  wine,
and your caresses more than any
  song.

Bride
5 I am dark but lovely, daughters
   of Jerusalem,
like the tents of Kedar
or the tent-curtains of Shalmah.
6 Do not look down on me; a little
   dark I may be
because I am scorched by the sun.
My mother's sons were displeased
   with me,
they sent me to watch over the
   vineyards;
so I did not watch over my own
   vineyard.
7 Tell me, my true love,
where you mind your flocks,
where you rest them at midday,
that I may not be left picking lice
as I sit among your companions'
   herds.

Bridegroom
8 If you yourself do not know,
   O fairest of women,
go, follow the tracks of the sheep
and mind your kids by the shepherds' huts.

9 I would compare you, my dearest,
   to Pharaoh's chariot-horses.
10 Your cheeks are lovely between
   plaited tresses,
your neck with its jewelled chains.

Companions
11 We will make you braided plaits
   of gold
set with beads of silver.

Bride
12 While the king reclines on his
   couch,
my spikenard gives forth its scent.

My beloved is for me a bunch of 13
  myrrh
as he lies on my breast,
my beloved is for me a cluster of 14
  henna-blossom
from the vineyards of En-gedi.

Bridegroom
How beautiful you are, my dearest, 15
O how beautiful,
your eyes are like doves!

Bride
How beautiful you are, O my love, 16
and how pleasant!

Bridegroom
Our couch is shaded with branches;
the beams of our house are of cedar, 17
our ceilings are all of fir.

Bride
I am an asphodel in Sharon,   2
a lily growing in the valley.

Bridegroom
No, a lily among thorns   2
is my dearest among girls.

Bride
Like an apricot-tree among the 3
   trees of the wood,
so is my beloved among boys.
To sit in its shadow was my delight,
and its fruit was sweet to my taste.
He took me into the wine-garden 4
and gave me loving glances.
He refreshed me with raisins, he 5
   revived me with apricots;
for I was faint with love.
His left arm was under my head, 6
   his right arm was round me.

Bridegroom
I charge you, daughters of Jerusa- 7
   lem,
by the spirits and the goddesses[a]
   of the field:
Do not rouse her, do not disturb
   my love
until she is ready.[b]

---

[a] by...goddesses: *or* by the gazelles and the hinds.
[b] until...ready: *or* while she is resting.

Bride

8 Hark! My beloved! Here he comes,
  bounding over the mountains,
  leaping over the hills.

9 My beloved is like a gazelle
  or a young wild goat:
  there he stands outside our wall,
  peeping in at the windows, glanc-
  ing through the lattice.

10 My beloved answered, he said to
  me:
  Rise up, my darling;
  my fairest, come away.

11 For now the winter is past,
  the rains are over and gone;

12 the flowers appear in the country-
  side;
  the time is coming when the birds
  will sing,
  and the turtle-dove's cooing will
  be heard in our land;

13 when the green figs will ripen on
  the fig-trees
  and the vines[a] give forth their
  fragrance.
  Rise up, my darling;
  my fairest, come away.

Bridegroom

14 My dove, that hides in holes in the
  cliffs
  or in crannies on the high ledges,
  let me see your face, let me hear
  your voice;
  for your voice is pleasant, your
  face is lovely.

Companions

15 Catch for us the jackals, the little
  jackals,[b]
  that spoil our vineyards, when the
  vines are in flower.

Bride

16 My beloved is mine and I am
  his;
  he delights in the lilies.

17 While the day is cool and the
  shadows are dispersing,

turn, my beloved, and show yourself
a gazelle or a young wild goat
on the hills where cinnamon grows.[c]

3 Night after night on my bed
I have sought my true love;
I have sought him but not found
  him,
I have called him but he has not
  answered.

2 I said, 'I will rise and go the rounds
  of the city,
through the streets and the squares,
  seeking my true love.'
I sought him but I did not find him,
I called him but he did not answer.

3 The watchmen, going the rounds
  of the city, met me,
and I asked, 'Have you seen my
  true love?'

4 Scarcely had I left them behind me
when I met my true love.
I seized him and would not let him
  go
until I had brought him to my
  mother's house,
to the room of her who conceived
  me.

Bridegroom

5 I charge you, daughters of Jerusalem,
by the spirits and the goddesses[d] of
  the field:
Do not rouse her, do not disturb
  my love
until she is ready.[e]

Companions

6 What is this coming up from the
  wilderness
like a column of smoke
from burning myrrh or frankincense,
from all the powdered spices that
  merchants bring?

7 Look; it is Solomon carried in his
  litter;
sixty of Israel's chosen warriors
  are his escort,

---

[a] *Prob. rdg.; Heb. adds* blossom.   [b] *Or* fruit-bats.   [c] on...grows: *or*
on the rugged hills *or* on the hills of Bether.   [d] *by...goddesses: or by the*
gazelles and the hinds.   [e] *until...ready: or while she is resting.*

8 all of them skilled swordsmen,
all trained to handle arms,
each with his sword ready at his side
to ward off the demon of the night.

9 The palanquin which King Solomon had made for himself
was of wood from Lebanon.
10 Its poles he had made of silver,
its head-rest of gold;
its seat was of purple stuff,
and its lining was of leather.

11 Come out, daughters of Jerusalem;
you daughters of Zion, come out
and welcome King Solomon,
wearing the crown with which his
mother has crowned him,
on his wedding day, on his day of
joy.

Bridegroom

4 How beautiful you are, my dearest,
how beautiful!
Your eyes behind your veil are like
doves,
your hair like a flock of goats
streaming down Mount Gilead.
2 Your teeth are like a flock of ewes
just shorn
which have come up fresh from the
dipping;
each ewe has twins and none has
cast a lamb.
3 Your lips are like a scarlet thread,
and your words are delightful;[a]
your parted lips behind your veil
are like a pomegranate cut open.
4 Your neck is like David's tower,
which is built with winding courses;
a thousand bucklers hang upon it,
and all are warriors' shields.
5 Your two breasts are like two
fawns,
twin fawns of a gazelle.[b]
6 While the day is cool and the
shadows are dispersing,
I will go to the mountains of myrrh
and to the hills of frankincense.

You are beautiful, my dearest, 7
beautiful without a flaw.

Come from Lebanon, my bride; 8
come with me from Lebanon.
Hurry down from the top of
Amana,
from Senir's top and Hermon's,
from the lions' lairs, and the hills
the leopards haunt.

You have stolen my heart,[c] my 9
sister,
you have stolen it,[d] my bride,
with one of your eyes, with one
jewel of your necklace.
How beautiful are your breasts, 10
my sister, my bride!
Your love is more fragrant than
wine,
and your perfumes sweeter than
any spices.
Your lips drop sweetness like the 11
honeycomb, my bride,
syrup and milk are under your
tongue,
and your dress has the scent of
Lebanon.
Your two cheeks[e] are an orchard of 13[f]
pomegranates,
an orchard full of rare fruits:[g]
spikenard and saffron, sweet-cane 14
and cinnamon
with every incense-bearing tree,
myrrh and aloes
with all the choicest spices.
My sister, my bride, is a garden 12
close-locked,
a garden close-locked, a fountain
sealed.

Bride

The fountain in my garden[h] is a 15
spring of running water
pouring down from Lebanon.
Awake, north wind, and come, 16
south wind;
blow upon my garden that its
perfumes may pour forth,

---

[a] Or and your mouth is lovely.   [b] Prob. rdg.; Heb. adds which delight in
the lilies.   [c] stolen my heart: or put heart into me.   [d] stolen it: or put
heart into me.   [e] Your two cheeks: prob. rdg.; Heb. Your shoots.   [f] Verse
12 transposed to follow verse 14.   [g] Prob. rdg.; Heb. adds henna with spikenard.
[h] my garden: prob. rdg.; Heb. gardens.

that my beloved may come to his
garden
and enjoy its rare fruits.

Bridegroom

5 I have come to my garden, my
sister and bride,
and have plucked my myrrh with
my spices;
I have eaten my honey and my
syrup,
I have drunk my wine and my
milk.
Eat, friends, and drink,
until you are drunk with love.

Bride

2 I sleep but my heart is awake.
Listen! My beloved is knocking:

'Open to me, my sister, my dearest,
my dove, my perfect one;
for my head is drenched with dew,
my locks with the moisture of the
night.'

3 'I have stripped off my dress; must
I put it on again?
I have washed my feet; must I soil
them again?'

4 When my beloved slipped his hand
through the latch-hole,
my bowels stirred within me.

5 When I arose to open for my
beloved,
my hands dripped with myrrh;
the liquid myrrh from my fingers
ran over the knobs of the bolt.

6 With my own hands I opened to
my love,
but my love had turned away and
gone by;
my heart sank when he turned his
back.
I sought him but I did not find him,
I called him but he did not answer.

7 The watchmen, going the rounds
of the city, met me;
they struck me and wounded me;
the watchmen on the walls took
away my cloak.

I charge you, daughters of Jeru- 8
salem,
if you find my beloved, will you
not tell him[a]
that I am faint with love?

Companions

What is your beloved more than 9
any other,
O fairest of women?
What is your beloved more than
any other,
that you give us this charge?

Bride

My beloved is fair and ruddy,   10
a paragon among ten thousand.
His head is gold, finest gold;   11
his locks are like palm-fronds.[b]
His eyes are like doves beside 12
brooks of water,
splashed by the milky water
as they sit where it is drawn.
His cheeks are like beds of spices or 13
chests full of perfumes;
his lips are lilies, and drop liquid
myrrh;
his hands are golden rods set in 14
topaz;
his belly a plaque of ivory overlaid
with lapis lazuli.
His legs are pillars of marble in 15
sockets of finest gold;
his aspect is like Lebanon, noble as
cedars.
His whispers are[c] sweetness itself, 16
wholly desirable.
Such is my beloved, such is my
darling,
daughters of Jerusalem.

Companions

Where has your beloved gone,   6
O fairest of women?
Which way did your beloved go,
that we may help you to seek him?

Bride

My beloved has gone down to his 2
garden,
to the beds where balsam grows,

---

[a] will you...him: *or* what will you tell him?
[b] *Prob. rdg.; Heb. adds* black as the raven.   [c] *Or* His nature is.

to delight in the garden*a* and to pick the lilies.

3 I am my beloved's, and my beloved is mine,
he who delights in the lilies.

Bridegroom

4 You are beautiful, my dearest, as Tirzah,
lovely as Jerusalem.*b*

5 Turn your eyes away from me; they dazzle me.
Your hair is like a flock of goats streaming down Mount Gilead;

6 your teeth are like a flock of ewes come up fresh from the dipping,
each ewe has twins and none has cast a lamb.

7 Your parted lips behind your veil are like a pomegranate cut open.

8 There may be sixty princesses, eighty concubines, and young women past counting,

9 but there is one alone, my dove, my perfect one,
her mother's only child,
devoted to the mother who bore her;
young girls see her and call her happy,
princesses and concubines praise her.

10 Who is this that looks out like the dawn,
beautiful as the moon, bright as the sun,
majestic as the starry heavens?

11 I went down to a garden of nut-trees
to look at the rushes by the stream,
to see if the vine had budded
or the pomegranates were in flower.

12 I did not know myself;
she made me feel more than a prince
reigning over the myriads*c* of his people.

Companions

Come back, come back, Shulam- 13 mite maiden,
come back, that we may gaze upon you.

Bridegroom

How you love to gaze on the Shulammite maiden,
as she moves between the lines of dancers!

How beautiful are your sandalled 7 feet, O prince's daughter!
The curves of your thighs are like jewels,
the work of a skilled craftsman.
Your navel is a rounded goblet   2
that never shall want for spiced wine.
Your belly is a heap of wheat fenced in by lilies.
Your two breasts are like two 3 fawns,
twin fawns of a gazelle.
Your neck is like a tower of ivory. 4
Your eyes are the pools in Heshbon,
beside the gate of the crowded city.*d*
Your nose is like towering Lebanon
that looks towards Damascus.
You carry your head like Carmel; 5
the flowing hair on your head is lustrous black,
your tresses are braided with ribbons.
How beautiful, how entrancing 6 you are,
my loved one, daughter of delights!
You are stately as a palm-tree,   7
and your breasts are the clusters of dates.
I said, 'I will climb up into the 8 palm
to grasp its fronds.'
May I find your breasts like clusters of grapes on the vine,

a Prob. rdg.; Heb. gardens.
b Prob. rdg.; Heb. *adds* majestic as the starry heavens (*see verse* 10).
c Prob. rdg.; Heb. chariots.   *d* Or the gate of Beth-rabbim.

the scent of your breath like apricots,

9 and your whispers like spiced wine
flowing smoothly to welcome my caresses,
gliding down through lips and teeth.

Bride

10 I am my beloved's, his longing is all for me.

11 Come, my beloved, let us go out into the fields
to lie among the henna-bushes;

12 let us go early to the vineyards
and see if the vine has budded or its blossom opened,
if the pomegranates are in flower.
There will I give you my love,

13 when the mandrakes give their perfume,
and all rare fruits are ready at our door,
fruits new and old
which I have in store for you, my love.

8 If only you were my own true brother
that sucked my mother's breasts!
Then, if I found you outside, I would kiss you,
and no man would despise me.

2 I would lead you to the room of the mother who bore me,
bring you to her house for you to embrace me;[a]
I would give you mulled wine to drink
and the fresh juice of pomegranates,

3 your[b] left arm under my head and your[b] right arm round me.

Bridegroom

4 I charge you, daughters of Jerusalem:
Do not rouse her, do not disturb my love
until she is ready.[c]

Companions

Who is this coming up from the 5 wilderness
leaning on her beloved?

Bridegroom

Under the apricot-trees I roused you,
there where your mother was in labour with you,
there where she who bore you was in labour.
Wear me as a seal upon your 6 heart,
as a seal upon your arm;
for love is strong as death,
passion cruel as the grave;
it blazes up like blazing fire,
fiercer than any flame.
Many waters cannot quench love, 7
no flood can sweep it away;
if a man were to offer for love
the whole wealth of his house,
it would be utterly scorned.

Companions

We have a little sister 8
who has no breasts;
what shall we do for our sister
when she is asked in marriage?
If she is a wall, 9
we will build on it a silver parapet,
but[d] if she is a door,
we will close it up with planks of cedar.

Bride

I am a wall and my breasts are like 10 towers;
so in his eyes I am as one who brings contentment.
Solomon has a vineyard at Baal- 11 hamon;
he has let out his vineyard to guardians,
and each is to bring for its fruit
a thousand pieces of silver.

---

[a] for you to embrace me: *or* to teach me how to love you.
[b] *Prob. rdg.; Heb.* his.   [c] until...ready: *or* while she is resting.
[d] *Or* and.

12 But my vineyard is mine to give;
the thousand pieces are yours, O
Solomon,
and the guardians of the fruit shall
have two hundred.

Bridegroom

13 My bride, you who sit in my
garden,

what is it that my friends[a] are
listening to?
Let me also hear your voice.

Bride

Come into the open, my beloved, 14
and show yourself like a gazelle or
a young wild goat
on the spice-bearing mountains.

THE BOOK OF THE PROPHET

ISAIAH

Judah arraigned

1 THE vision received by
Isaiah son of Amoz con-
cerning Judah and Jerusa-
lem during the reigns of Uzziah,
Jotham, Ahaz, and Hezekiah,
kings of Judah.

2 Hark you heavens, and earth give
ear,
for the LORD has spoken:
I have sons whom I reared and
brought up,
but they have rebelled against me.
3 The ox knows its owner
and the ass its master's stall;
but Israel, my own people,
has no knowledge, no discernment.

4 O sinful nation, people loaded with
iniquity,
race of evildoers, wanton destructive children
who have deserted the LORD,
spurned the Holy One of Israel
and turned your backs on him.
5 Where can you still be struck
if you will be disloyal still?
Your head is covered with sores,
your body diseased;

from head to foot there is not a 6
sound spot in you –
nothing but bruises and weals and
raw wounds
which have not felt compress or
bandage
or soothing oil.
Your country is desolate, your 7
cities lie in ashes.
Strangers devour your land before
your eyes;
it is desolate as Sodom[b] in its
overthrow.
Only Zion is left, 8
like a watchman's shelter in a
vineyard,
a shed in a field of cucumbers,
a city well guarded.
If the LORD of Hosts had not left 9
us a remnant,
we should soon have been like
Sodom,
no better than Gomorrah.

Hear the word of the LORD, you 10
rulers of Sodom;
attend, you people of Gomorrah,
to the instruction of our God:
Your countless sacrifices, what are 11
they to me?
says the LORD.

[a] my garden...friends: *prob. rdg.*; *Heb.* the gardens, friends.
[b] Sodom: *prob. rdg.*; *Heb.* strangers.

691

I am sated with whole-offerings of
rams
and the fat of buffaloes;
I have no desire for the blood of
bulls,
of sheep and of he-goats.

12–13 Whenever you come to enter my
presence –
who asked you for this?
No more shall you trample my
courts.
The offer of your gifts is useless,
the reek of sacrifice is abhorrent to
me.
New moons and sabbaths and
assemblies,
sacred seasons and ceremonies, I
cannot endure.

14 I cannot tolerate your new moons
and your festivals;
they have become a burden to me,
and I can put up with them no
longer.

15 When you lift your hands out-
spread in prayer,
I will hide my eyes from you.
Though you offer countless prayers,
I will not listen.
There is blood on your hands;

16 wash yourselves and be clean.
Put away the evil of your deeds,
away out of my sight.

17 Cease to do evil and learn to do
right,
pursue justice and champion the
oppressed;
give the orphan his rights, plead
the widow's cause.

18 Come now, let us argue it out,
says the LORD.
Though your sins are scarlet,
they may become white as snow;
though they are dyed crimson,
they may yet be like wool.

19 Obey with a will,
and you shall eat the best that
earth yields;

20 but, if you refuse and rebel,
locust-beans shall be your only
food.*a*
The LORD himself has spoken.

21 How the faithful city has played
the whore,
once the home of justice where
righteousness dwelt –
but now murderers!

22 Your silver has turned into base
metal
and your liquor is diluted with
water.

23 Your very rulers are rebels, confederate with thieves;
every man of them loves a bribe
and itches for a gift;
they do not give the orphan his
rights,
and the widow's cause never
comes before them.

24 This therefore is the word of the
Lord, the LORD of Hosts, the
Mighty One of Israel:

Enough! I will secure a respite
from my foes
and take vengeance on my enemies.

25 Once again I will act against you
to refine away your base metal as
with potash
and purge all your impurities;

26 I will again make your judges what
once they were
and your counsellors like those of
old.
Then at length you shall be called
the home of righteousness, the
faithful city.

27 Justice shall redeem Zion
and righteousness her repentant
people.

28 Rebels and sinners shall be broken
together
and those who forsake the LORD
shall cease to be.

29 For the sacred oaks in which you
delighted shall fail you,
the garden-shrines of your fancy
shall disappoint you.

30 You shall be like a terebinth whose
leaves have withered,
like a garden without water;

31 the strongest tree*b* shall become
like tow,

---

a locust-beans...food: *or, with Scroll,* you shall be eaten by the sword.
b Or the strong man.

and what is made of it[a] shall go up
  in sparks,
and the two shall burst into flames
  together
with no one to quench them.

2   This is the word which Isaiah
son of Amoz received in a vision
concerning Judah and Jerusalem.

2[b] In days to come
  the mountain of the LORD's house
shall be set over all other mountains,
lifted high above the hills.
All the nations shall come streaming to it,
3 and many peoples shall come and
  say,
  'Come, let us climb up on to the
    mountain of the LORD,
to the house of the God of Jacob,
that he may teach us his ways
and we may walk in his paths.'
For instruction issues from Zion,
and out of Jerusalem comes the
  word of the LORD;
4 he will be judge between nations,
arbiter among many peoples.
They shall beat their swords into
  mattocks
and their spears into pruning-
  knives;[c]
nation shall not lift sword against
  nation
nor ever again be trained for war.

5 O people of Jacob, come,
let us walk in the light of the
  LORD.
6 Thou hast abandoned thy people
  the house of Jacob;
for they are crowded with traders[d]
and barbarians like the Philistines,
and with the children of foreigners
  everywhere.
7 Their land is filled with silver and
  gold,
and there is no end to their
  treasure;
their land is filled with horses,

and there is no end to their chariots;
their land is filled with idols,   8
and they bow down to the work
  of their own hands,
to what their fingers have made.
Mankind shall be brought low,   9
all men shall be humbled;
and how can they raise themselves?[e]
Get you into the rocks and hide 10
  yourselves in the ground
from the dread of the LORD and
  the splendour of his majesty.
Man's proud eyes shall be humbled, 11
the loftiness of men brought low,
and the LORD alone shall be
  exalted
on that day.

For the LORD of Hosts has a day of 12
  doom waiting
for all that is proud and lofty,
for all that is high and lifted up,
for all the cedars of Lebanon, lofty 13
  and high,
and for all the oaks of Bashan,
for all lofty mountains and for all 14
  high hills,
for every high tower and for every 15
  sheer wall,
for all ships of Tarshish and all the 16
  dhows of Arabia.
Then man's pride shall be brought 17
  low,
and the loftiness of man shall be
  humbled,
and the LORD alone shall be
  exalted
on that day,
while the idols shall pass away 18
  utterly.
Get you into caves in the rocks   19
and crevices in the ground
from the dread of the LORD and the
  splendour of his majesty,
when he rises to inspire the earth
  with fear.
On that day a man shall fling 20
  away
his idols of silver and his idols of
  gold

---

[a] Or what he makes.   [b] Verses 2–4: cp. Mic. 4. 1–3.
[c] They shall beat...pruning-knives: cp. Joel 3. 9–12.   [d] Or hawkers.
[e] Prob. rdg.; Heb. and do not forgive them.

which he has made for himself to
   worship;
he shall fling them to the dung-
   beetles and the bats,
21 and creep into clefts in the rocks
   and crannies in the cliffs
from the dread of the LORD and the
   splendour of his majesty,
when he rises to inspire the earth
   with fear.
22 Have no more to do with man, for
   what is he worth?
He is no more than the breath in
   his nostrils.

3 Be warned: the Lord, the LORD of
   Hosts,
is stripping Jerusalem and Judah
   of every prop and stay,[a]
2 warrior and soldier,
judge and prophet, diviner and
   elder,
3 captains of companies and men of
   rank,
counsellor, magician, and cunning
   enchanter.
4 Then I will appoint mere boys to
   be their captains,
who shall govern as the fancy
   takes them;
5 the people shall deal harshly
each man with his fellow and with
   his neighbour;
children shall break out against
   their elders,
and nobodies against men of substance.
6 If a man takes hold of his brother
   in his father's house,
saying, 'You have a cloak, you
   shall be our chief;
our stricken family shall be under
   you,'
7 he will cry out that day and
   say,
'I will not be your master;
there is neither bread nor cloak in
   my house,
and you shall not make me head of
   the clan.'

Jerusalem is stricken and Judah 8
   fallen
because they have spoken and
   acted against the LORD,
rebelling against the glance of his
   glorious eye.
The look on their faces testifies 9
   against them;
like Sodom they proclaim their
   sins
and do not conceal them.[b]
Woe upon them! they have earned
   their own disaster.
Happy[c] the righteous man! all 10
   goes well with him,
for such men enjoy the fruit of
   their actions.
Woe betide the wicked! with him 11
   all goes ill,
for he reaps the reward that he has
   earned.
Money-lenders strip my people 12
   bare,
and usurers lord it over them.
O my people! your guides lead you
   astray
and confuse the path that you
   should take.
The LORD comes forward to argue 13
   his case
and stands to judge his people.
The LORD opens the indictment   14
   against the elders of his people and
   their officers:
You have ravaged the vineyard,
and the spoils of the poor are in
   your houses.
Is it nothing to you that you crush 15
   my people
and grind the faces of the poor?
This is the very word of the Lord,
   the LORD of Hosts.

Then the LORD said: 16
Because the women of Zion hold
   themselves high
and walk with necks outstretched
   and wanton glances,
moving with mincing gait
and jingling feet,

---

[a] *Prob. rdg.; Heb. adds* all stay of bread and all stay of water.
[b] like...them: *or* and their sins, like those of Sodom, denounce them; they do not deny them.
[c] *Prob. rdg.; Heb.* Say.

17 the Lord will give the women of
Zion bald heads,
the LORD will strip the hair from
their foreheads.

18   In that day the Lord will take
away all finery: anklets, discs,
19 crescents, pendants, bangles, coro-
20 nets, head-bands, armlets, neck-
21 laces, lockets, charms, signets,
22 nose-rings, fine dresses, mantles,
23 cloaks, flounced skirts, scarves of
gauze, kerchiefs of linen, turbans,
and flowing veils.

24 So instead of perfume you shall
have the stench of decay,
and a rope in place of a girdle,
baldness instead of hair elegantly
coiled,
a loin-cloth of sacking instead of a
mantle,
and branding instead of beauty.
25 Your men shall fall by the sword,
and your warriors in battle;
26 then Zion's gates shall mourn and
lament,
and she shall sit on the ground
stripped bare.

4 Then on that day
seven women shall take hold of one
man and say,
'We will eat our own bread and
wear our own clothes
if only we may be called by your
name;
take away our disgrace.'

2 On that day the plant that the
LORD has grown
shall become glorious in its beauty,
and the fruit of the land shall be
the pride and splendour
of the survivors of Israel.

3   Then those who are left in Zion,
who remain in Jerusalem, every
one enrolled in the book of life,
4 shall be called holy. If the Lord
washes away the filth of the women
of Zion and cleanses Jerusalem
from the blood that is in it by a

spirit of judgement, a consuming
spirit, then over every building on 5
Mount Zion and on all her places of
assembly the LORD will create a
cloud of smoke by day and a bright
flame of fire by night; for glory
shall be spread over all as a covering and a canopy, a shade from the 6
heat by day, a refuge and a shelter
from rain and tempest.

I will sing for my beloved   5
my love-song about his vineyard:
My beloved had a vineyard
high up on a fertile hill-side.
He trenched it and cleared it of 2
stones
and planted it with red vines;
he built a watch-tower in the middle
and then hewed out a winepress in
it.
He looked for it to yield grapes,
but it yielded wild grapes.
Now, you who live in Jerusalem, 3
and you men of Judah,
judge between me and my vineyard.
What more could have been done 4
for my vineyard
that I did not do in it?
Why, when I looked for it to yield
grapes,
did it yield wild grapes?
Now listen while I tell you   5
what I will do to my vineyard:
I will take away its fences and let it
be burnt,
I will break down its walls and let
it be trampled underfoot,
and so I will leave it derelict;   6
it shall be neither pruned nor
hoed,
but shall grow thorns and briars.
Then I will command the clouds
to send no more rain upon it.
The vineyard of the LORD of Hosts 7
is Israel,
and the men of Judah are the
plant he cherished.
He looked for justice and found it
denied,
for righteousness but heard cries
of distress.

8 Shame on you! you who add house
    to house
    and join field to field,
    until not an acre remains,
    and you are left to dwell alone in
    the land.
9 The LORD of Hosts has sworn[a] in
    my hearing:
    Many houses shall go to ruin,
    fine large houses shall be un-
    inhabited.
10 Five acres of vineyard shall yield
    only a gallon,
    and ten bushels of seed return only
    a peck.
11 Shame on you! you who rise early
    in the morning
    to go in pursuit of liquor
    and draw out the evening in-
    flamed with wine,
12 at whose feasts there are harp and
    lute,
    tabor and pipe and wine,
    who have no eyes for the work of
    the LORD,
    and never see the things that he
    has done.
13 Therefore my people are dwindling
    away
    all unawares;
    the nobles are starving to death,
    and the common folk die of
    thirst.
14 Therefore Sheol gapes with strain-
    ing throat
    and has opened her measureless
    jaws:
    down go nobility and common
    people,
    their noisy bustling mob.[b]
15 Mankind is brought low, men are
    humbled,
    humbled are haughty looks.
16 But the LORD of Hosts sits high in
    judgement,
    and by righteousness the holy God
    shows himself holy.
17 Young rams shall feed where fat
    bullocks once pastured,
    and kids shall graze broad acres
    where cattle grew fat.[c]

Shame on you! you who drag 18
    wickedness along like a tethered
    sheep
    and sin like a heifer on a rope,
who say, 'Let the LORD make 19
    haste,
let him speed up his work for us to
    see it,
let the purpose of the Holy One of
    Israel
be soon fulfilled, so that we may
    know it.'
Shame on you! you who call evil 20
    good and good evil,
who turn darkness into light and
    light into darkness,
who make bitter sweet and sweet
    bitter.
Shame on you! you who are wise in 21
    your own eyes
    and prudent in your own esteem.
Shame on you! you mighty topers, 22
    valiant mixers of drink,
who for a bribe acquit the guilty 23
    and deny justice to those in the
    right.

So he will hoist a signal to a nation 26[d]
    far away,
he will whistle to call them from
    the end of the earth;
and see, they come, speedy and
    swift;
none is weary, not one of them 27
    stumbles,
not one slumbers or sleeps.
None has his belt loose about his
    waist
or a broken thong to his sandals.
Their arrows are sharpened and 28
    their bows all strung,
their horses' hooves flash like
    shooting stars,
their chariot-wheels are like the
    whirlwind.
Their growling is the growling of a 29
    lioness,
they growl like young lions,
which roar as they seize the prey
and carry it beyond reach of
    rescue.

---

[a] has sworn: *prob. rdg.*; Heb. *om.*   [b] nobility...mob: *or* nobility, common
people, and noisy mob, and are restless there.   [c] Young...grew fat: *prob.
rdg.*; Heb. *unintelligible.*   [d] *Verses 24 and 25 transposed to follow 10. 4.*

30 They shall roar over it on that day
like the roaring of the sea.
If a man looks over the earth,
behold, darkness closing in,
and the light darkened on the
hill-tops[a]!

The call of Isaiah

6 IN the year of King Uzziah's
death I saw the Lord seated on a
throne, high and exalted, and the
skirt of his robe filled the temple.
2 About him were attendant seraphim, and each had six wings; one
pair covered his face and one pair
his feet, and one pair was spread in
3 flight. They were calling ceaselessly to one another,

Holy, holy, holy is the LORD of
Hosts:
the whole earth is full of his glory.

4 And, as each one called, the threshold shook to its foundations, while
the house was filled with smoke.
5 Then I cried,

Woe is me! I am lost,
for I am a man of unclean lips
and I dwell among a people of
unclean lips;
yet with these eyes I have seen the
King, the LORD of Hosts.

6 Then one of the seraphim flew to
me carrying in his hand a glowing
coal which he had taken from the
7 altar with a pair of tongs. He
touched my mouth with it and
said,

See, this has touched your lips;
your iniquity is removed,
and your sin is wiped away.

8 Then I heard the Lord saying,
Whom shall I send? Who will go
for me? And I answered, Here am
9 I; send me. He said, Go and tell
this people:

You may listen and listen, but you
will not understand.[b]
You may look and look again, but
you will never know.[c]
This people's wits are dulled,   10
their ears are deafened and their
eyes blinded,
so that they cannot see with their
eyes
nor listen with their ears
nor understand with their wits,
so that they may turn and be
healed.

Then I asked, How long, O Lord? 11
And he answered,

Until cities fall in ruins and are
deserted,
houses are left without people,
and the land goes to ruin and lies
waste,
until the LORD has sent all man- 12
kind far away,
and the whole country is one vast
desolation.
Even if a tenth part of its people 13
remain there,
they too will be exterminated
[like an oak or a terebinth,
a sacred pole thrown out from its
place in a hill-shrine[d]].

Prophecies during the Syro-Ephraimite war

WHILE Ahaz son of Jotham and 7
grandson of Uzziah was king of
Judah, Rezin king of Aram with
Pekah son of Remaliah, king of
Israel, marched on Jerusalem, but
could not force a battle. When the 2
house of David heard that the
Aramaeans had come to terms
with the Ephraimites, king and
people were shaken like forest
trees in the wind. Then the LORD 3
said to Isaiah, Go out with your
son Shear-jashub[e] to meet Ahaz at
the end of the conduit of the Upper

---

[a] hill-tops: *or* clouds.   [b] *Or* but how will you understand?
[c] *Or* but how will you know?
[d] a sacred pole...hill-shrine: *prob. rdg.; Heb. obscure.*
[e] *That is* A remnant shall return.

Pool by the causeway leading to
4 the Fuller's Field, and say to him,
Be on your guard, keep calm; do
not be frightened or unmanned by
these two smouldering stumps of
firewood, because Rezin and his
Aramaeans with Remaliah's son
5 are burning with rage. The Aramaeans with Ephraim and Remaliah's son have laid their plans
6 against you, saying, Let us invade
Judah and break her spirit;[a] let us
make her join with us, and set the
son of Tabeal on the throne.
7 Therefore the Lord GOD has said:

This shall not happen now, and
never shall,
8 for all that the chief city of Aram is
Damascus,
and Rezin is the chief of Damascus;
within sixty-five years
Ephraim shall cease to be a nation,
9 for all that Samaria is the chief city
of Ephraim,
and Remaliah's son the chief of
Samaria.
Have firm faith, or you will not
stand firm.

10 Once again the LORD spoke to
11 Ahaz and said, Ask the LORD your
God for a sign, from lowest Sheol or
12 from highest heaven. But Ahaz
said, No, I will not put the LORD
to the test by asking for a sign.
13 Then the answer came: Listen,
house of David. Are you not content to wear out men's patience?
Must you also wear out the
14 patience of my God? Therefore the
Lord himself shall give you a sign:
A young woman is with child, and
she will bear a son, and will[b] call him
15 Immanuel.[c] By the time that he
has learnt to reject evil and choose
good, he will be eating curds and
16 honey;[d] before that child has
learnt to reject evil and choose
good, desolation will come upon

the land before whose two kings
you cower now. The LORD will 17
bring on you, your people, and
your house, a time the like of
which has not been seen since
Ephraim broke away from Judah.[e]
On that day the LORD will 18
whistle for the fly from the distant
streams of Egypt and for the bee
from Assyria. They shall all come 19
and settle in the precipitous ravines and in the clefts of the rock;
camel-thorn and stink-wood shall
be black with them. On that day 20
the Lord shall shave the head and
body with a razor hired on the
banks of the Euphrates,[f] and it
shall remove the beard as well. On 21
that day a man shall save alive a
young cow and two ewes; and he 22
shall get so much milk that he eats
curds; for all who are left in the
land shall eat curds and honey. On 23
that day every place where there
used to be a thousand vines worth
a thousand pieces of silver shall be
given over to thorns and briars. A 24
man shall go there only to hunt
with bow and arrows, for thorns
and briars cover the whole land;
and no one who fears thorns and 25
briars shall set foot on any of those
hills once worked with the hoe.
Oxen shall be turned loose on them,
and sheep shall trample them.

The LORD said to me, Take a 8
large tablet and write on it in common writing,[g] Maher-shalal-hash-
baz;[h] and fetch Uriah the priest 2
and Zechariah son of Jeberechiah
for me as trustworthy witnesses.
Then I lay with the prophetess, 3
and she conceived and bore a son;
and the LORD said to me, Call him
Maher-shalal-hash-baz. Before the 4
boy can say Father or Mother, the
wealth of Damascus and the spoils
of Samaria shall be carried off and
presented to the king of Assyria.

---

[a] *Or* and parley with her.   [b] *Or* you will.   [c] *That is* God is with us.
[d] he will...honey: *or* curds and honey will be eaten.   [e] *Prob. rdg.*; *Heb.*
adds the king of Assyria.   [f] *Prob. rdg.*; *Heb. adds* with the king of Assyria.
[g] in common writing: *or* with an ordinary stylus.
[h] *That is* Speed-spoil-hasten-plunder.

5   Once again the LORD said to me:

6 Because this nation has rejected the waters of Shiloah, which run so softly and gently,[a]

7 therefore the Lord will bring up against it
the strong, flooding waters of the Euphrates,
the king of Assyria and all his glory;
it shall run up all its channels
and overflow all its banks;

8 it shall sweep through Judah in a flood,
pouring over it and rising shoulder-high.
The whole expanse of the land shall be filled,
so wide he spreads his wings; for God is with us.[b]

9 Take note, you nations, and be dismayed.
Listen, all you distant parts of the earth:
you may arm yourselves but will be dismayed;
you may arm yourselves but will be dismayed.

10 Make your plans, but they will be foiled,
propose what you please, but it shall not stand;
for God is with us.[b]

11   These were the words of the LORD to me, for his hand was strong upon me; and he warned me not to follow[c] the ways of this

12 people: You shall not say 'too hard' of everything that this people calls hard; you shall neither dread nor fear that which they

13 fear. It is the LORD of Hosts whom you must count 'hard';[d] he it is whom you must fear and

14 dread. He shall become your 'hardship',[d] a boulder and a rock which the two houses of Israel shall run against and over which

they shall stumble, a trap and a snare to those who live in Jerusalem; and many shall stumble over 15 them, many shall fall and be broken, many shall be snared and caught.

Fasten up the message, 16
seal the oracle with my teaching;[e]
and I will wait for the LORD 17
who hides his face from the house of Jacob;
I will watch for him.
See, I and the sons whom the 18 LORD has given me
are to be signs and portents in Israel,
sent by the LORD of Hosts who dwells on Mount Zion.
But men will say to you, 19
'Seek guidance of ghosts and familiar spirits
who squeak and gibber;
a nation may surely seek guidance of its gods,
of the dead on behalf of the living,
for an oracle or a message?' 20
They will surely say some such thing as this;
but what they say is futile.
So despondency and fear will come 21 over them,
and then, when they are afraid and fearful,
they will turn against their king and their gods.
Then, whether they turn their 22 gaze upwards or look down,
everywhere is distress and darkness inescapable,
constraint and gloom that cannot be avoided;
for there is no escape for an 9 oppressed people.

For, while the first invader has dealt lightly with the land of Zebulun and the land of Naphtali, the second has dealt heavily with

---

[a] *Prob. rdg.*; *Heb. adds* Rezin and the son of Remaliah.
[b] God is with us: *Heb.* Immanuel.   [c] *Or* and he turned me from following...
[d] 'hard' *and* 'hardship': *prob. rdg.*; *Heb. unintelligible in this context.*
[e] *Or* among my disciples.

Galilee of the Nations on the road
beyond Jordan to the sea.

2 The people who walked in darkness
have seen a great light:
light has dawned upon them,
dwellers in a land as dark as death.
3 Thou hast increased their joy and[a]
given them great gladness;
they rejoice in thy presence as men
rejoice at harvest,
or as they are glad when they
share out the spoil;
4 for thou hast shattered the yoke
that burdened them,
the collar that lay heavy on their
shoulders,
the driver's goad, as on the day of
Midian's defeat.
5 All the boots of trampling soldiers
and the garments fouled with
blood
shall become a burning mass, fuel
for fire.
6 For a boy has been born for us, a
son given to us
to bear the symbol of dominion on
his shoulder;
and he shall be called
in purpose wonderful, in battle
God-like,
Father for all time,[b] Prince of
peace.
7 Great shall the dominion be,
and boundless the peace
bestowed on David's throne and
on his kingdom,
to establish it and sustain it
with justice and righteousness
from now and for evermore.
The zeal of the Lord of Hosts shall
do this.

Prophecies addressed to Israel

8 The Lord has sent forth his word
against Jacob
and it shall fall on Israel;
9 all the people shall be humbled,
Ephraim and the dwellers in
Samaria,
though in their pride and arrogance they say,
10 The bricks are fallen, but we will
build in hewn stone;
the sycomores are hacked down,
but we will use cedars instead.
11 The Lord has raised their foes[c]
high against them
and spurred on their enemies,
12 Aramaeans from the east and
Philistines from the west,
and they have swallowed Israel in
one mouthful.
For all this his anger has not
turned back,
and his hand is stretched out
still.
13 Yet the people did not come back
to him who struck them,
or seek guidance of the Lord of
Hosts;
14 therefore on one day the Lord cut
off from Israel
head and tail, palm and reed.[d]
16 This people's guides have led them
astray;
those who should have been guided
are in confusion.
17 Therefore the Lord showed no
mercy to their young men,
no tenderness to their orphans and
widows;
all were godless and evildoers,
every one speaking profanity.
For all this his anger has not
turned back,
and his hand is stretched out still.

18 Wicked men have been set ablaze
like a fire
fed with briars and thorns,
kindled in the forest thickets;
they are wrapped in a murky pall
of smoke.
19 The land is scorched by the fury of
the Lord of Hosts,
and the people have become fuel
for the fire.[e]

[a] *their joy and*: *prob. rdg.*; *Heb.* the nation, not.   [b] *Or of a wide realm.*
[c] *their foes*: *prob. rdg.*; *Heb.* the foes of Rezin.   [d] *Prob. rdg.*; *Heb.* adds (15)
The aged and honoured are the head, and the prophet who gives false instruction
is the tail.   [e] *See note on verse 20.*

20 On the right, one man eats his fill
  but yet is hungry;
on the left, another devours but is
  not satisfied;
each feeds on his own children's
  flesh,
and neither spares his own brother.[a]
21 [b]For all this his anger has not
  turned back,
and his hand is stretched out still.

10 Shame on you! you who make
  unjust laws
and publish burdensome decrees,
2 depriving the poor of justice,
  robbing the weakest of my people
    of their rights,
  despoiling the widow and plunder-
    ing the orphan.
3 What will you do when called to
  account,
when ruin from afar confronts
  you?
To whom will you flee for help
and where will you leave your
  children,
4 so that they do not cower before
  the gaoler
or fall by the executioner's hand?
For all this his anger has not
  turned back,
and his hand is stretched out still.

[24[c]] So, as tongues of fire lick up the
  stubble
and the heat of the flame dies
  down,
their root shall moulder away,
and their shoots vanish like dust;
for they have spurned the instruction of the LORD of Hosts
and have rejected the word of the
  Holy One of Israel.
[25[c]] So the anger of the LORD is roused
  against his people,
he has stretched out his hand
  against them and struck them
    down;
the mountains trembled,

and their corpses lay like offal in
  the streets.
For all this his anger has not
  turned back,
and his hand is stretched out still.

The Assyrian! He is the rod that I 5
  wield in my anger,
and the staff of my wrath is in his
  hand.[d]
I send him against a godless 6
  nation,
I bid him march against a people
  who rouse my wrath,
to spoil and plunder at will
and trample them down like mud
  in the streets.
But this man's purpose is lawless, 7
lawless are the plans in his mind;
for his thought is only to destroy
and to wipe out nation after nation.
'Are not my officers all kings?' he 8
  says;
'see how Calno has suffered the 9
  fate of Carchemish.
Is not Hamath like Arpad, and
  Samaria li! Damascus?
Before now I have found kingdoms 10
  full of idols,
with more images than Jerusalem
  and Samaria,
and now, what I have done to 11
  Samaria and her worthless gods,
I will do also to Jerusalem and her
  idols.'

When the Lord has finished all 12
that he means to do on Mount
Zion and in Jerusalem, he will
punish the king of Assyria for this
fruit of his pride and for his arrogance and vainglory, because he 13
said:

By my own might I have acted
and in my own wisdom I have laid
  my schemes;
I have removed the frontiers of
  nations
and plundered their treasures,

---

[a] and neither...brother: *transposed from end of verse 19.*   [b] *Prob. rdg.; Heb.*
prefixes Manasseh devours Ephraim, *and* Ephraim Manasseh; *together they are*
against Judah.   [c] *These are verses 24 and 25 of ch. 5, transposed to this point.*
[d] and...hand: *prob. rdg.; Heb. obscure.*

like a bull I have trampled on their
inhabitants.

14 My hand has found its way to the
wealth of nations,
and, as a man takes the eggs from a
deserted nest,
so have I taken every land;
not a wing fluttered,
not a beak gaped, no chirp was
heard.

15 Shall the axe set itself up against
the hewer,
or the saw claim mastery over the
sawyer,
as if a stick were to brandish him
who wields it,
or a staff of wood to wield one who
is not wood?

16 Therefore the Lord, the LORD of
Hosts, will send disease
on his sturdy frame, from head to
toe,[a]
and within his flesh[b] a fever like
fire shall burn.

17 The light of Israel shall become a
fire
and his Holy One a flame,
which in one day shall burn up and
consume
his thorns and his briars;

18 the glory of forest and meadow
shall be destroyed
as when a man falls in a fit;

19 and the remnant of trees in the
forest shall be so few
that a child may count them one
by one.

20 On that day the remnant of
Israel, the survivors of Jacob, shall
cease to lean on him that proved
their destroyer, but shall loyally
lean on the LORD, the Holy One of
Israel.

21 A remnant shall turn again, a
remnant of Jacob,
to God their champion.

22 Your people, Israel, may be many
as the sands of the sea,
but only a remnant shall turn
again,
the instrument of final destruction,
justice in full flood;[c]

23 for the Lord, the LORD of Hosts,
will bring final destruction
upon all the earth.

24 Therefore these are the words of
the Lord, the LORD of Hosts: My
people who live in Zion, you must
not be afraid of the Assyrians,
though they beat you with their
rod and lift their staff against you
as the Egyptians did; for soon,
25 very soon, my anger will come to
an end, and my wrath will all be
spent.[d] Then the LORD of Hosts
26 will brandish his whip over them
as he did when he struck Midian at
the Rock of Oreb, and will lift his
staff against the River as he did
against Egypt.

On that day   27
the burden they laid on your
shoulder shall be removed
and their yoke shall be broken
from your neck.

28 An invader from Rimmon[e] has
come to Aiath,
has passed by Migron,
and left his baggage-train at Michmash;

29 he has passed by Maabarah
and camped for the night at
Geba.
Ramah is anxious, Gibeah of Saul
is in panic.

30 Raise a shrill cry, Bath-gallim;
hear it, Laish, and answer her,
Anathoth:

31 'Madmenah is in flight; take refuge, people of Gebim.'

32 Today he is due to pitch his camp
in Nob;
he gives the signal to advance

---

[a] from...toe: *transposed from verse 18.* [b] within his flesh: *or* in his strong body.
[c] the instrument...flood: *or* wasting with sickness, yet overflowing with
righteousness. [d] will...spent: *prob. rdg.; Heb. obscure.* [e] and their
yoke...Rimmon: *prob. rdg.; Heb.* and their yoke from upon your neck, and a
yoke shall be broken because of oil. He...

against the mount of the daughter
of Zion,
the hill of Jerusalem.

33 Look, the Lord, the LORD of
Hosts,
cleaves the trees with a flash of
lightning,
the tallest are hewn down, the
lofty laid low,
34 the heart of the forest is felled
with the axe,
and Lebanon with its noble trees
has fallen.

11 Then a shoot shall grow from the
stock of Jesse,
and a branch shall spring from his
roots.
2 The spirit of the LORD shall rest
upon him,
a spirit of wisdom and understanding,
a spirit of counsel*a* and power,
a spirit of knowledge and the fear
of the LORD.*b*
3 He shall not judge by what he
sees
nor decide by what he hears;
4 he shall judge the poor with
justice
and defend the humble in the land
with equity;
his mouth shall be a rod to strike
down the ruthless,*c*
and with a word he shall slay the
wicked.
5 Round his waist he shall wear the
belt of justice,
and good faith shall be the girdle
round his body.
6 Then the wolf shall live with the
sheep,
and the leopard lie down with the
kid;
the calf and the young lion shall
grow up together,
and a little child shall lead them;
7 the cow and the bear shall be
friends,
and their young shall lie down
together.
The lion shall eat straw like cattle.

the infant shall play over the hole 8
of the cobra,
and the young child dance over the
viper's nest.
They shall not hurt or destroy in 9
all my holy mountain;
for as the waters fill the sea,
so shall the land be filled with the
knowledge of the LORD.

On that day a scion from the root 10
of Jesse
shall be set up as a signal to the
peoples;
the nations shall rally to it,
and its resting-place shall be
glorious.

On that day the Lord will make 11
his power more glorious by recovering the remnant of his people,
those who are still left, from Assyria and Egypt, from Pathros, from
Cush and Elam, from Shinar, Hamath and the islands of the sea.

Then he will raise a signal to the 12
nations
and gather together those driven
out of Israel;
he will assemble Judah's scattered
people
from the four corners of the earth.
Ephraim's jealousy shall vanish,   13
and Judah's enmity shall be done
away.
Ephraim shall not be jealous of
Judah,
nor Judah the enemy of Ephraim.
They shall swoop down on the 14
Philistine flank in the west
and together they shall plunder
the tribes of the east;
Edom and Moab shall be within
their grasp,
and Ammon shall obey them.
The LORD will divide the tongue of 15
the Egyptian sea
and wave his hand over the River
to bring a scorching wind;
he shall split it into seven channels
and let men go across dry-shod.

a *Or* force.   *b* *Prob. rdg.; Heb. adds* and his delight shall be in the fear of
the LORD.   *c* *Prob. rdg.; Heb.* land.

16 So there shall be a causeway for the
   remnant of his people,
   for the remnant rescued from
   Assyria,
   as there was for Israel when they
   came up out of Egypt.

12 You shall say on that day:
   I will praise thee, O LORD,
   though thou hast been angry with
   me;
   thy anger has turned back,
   and thou hast comforted me.
2 God is indeed my deliverer.
   I am confident and unafraid;
   for the LORD is my refuge and
   defence
   and has shown himself my deliverer.
3 And so you shall draw water with
   joy
   from the springs of deliverance.

4 You shall all say on that day:
   Give thanks to the LORD and invoke him by name,
   make his deeds known in the
   world around;
   declare that his name is supreme.
5 Sing psalms to the LORD, for he has
   triumphed,
   and this must be made known in all
   the world.
6 Cry out, shout aloud, you that
   dwell in Zion,
   for the Holy One of Israel is among
   you in majesty.

*Prophecies relating to
foreign nations*

13 BABYLON: an oracle which Isaiah
son of Amoz received in a vision.

2 Raise the standard on a windy
   height,
   roar out your summons,
   beckon with arm upraised to the
   advance,
   draw your swords, you nobles.
3 I have given my warriors their
   orders

and summoned my fighting men to
launch my anger;
they are eager for my triumph.
Hark, a tumult in the mountains, 4
the sound of a vast multitude;
hark, the roar of kingdoms, of
nations gathering!
The LORD of Hosts is mustering a
host for war,
men from a far country, from be- 5
yond the horizon.
It is the LORD with the weapons of
his wrath
coming to lay the whole land
waste.
Howl, for the Day of the LORD is at 6
hand;
it comes, a mighty blow from
Almighty God.
Thereat shall every hand hang 7
limp,
every man's courage shall melt
away,
his stomach hollow with fear; 8
anguish shall grip them, like a
woman in labour.
One man shall look aghast at
another,
and their faces shall burn with
shame.
The Day of the LORD is coming 9
indeed,
that cruel day of wrath and fury,
to make the land a desolation
and exterminate its wicked people.
The stars of heaven in their con- 10
stellations shall give no light,
the sun shall be darkened at its
rising,
and the moon refuse to shine.
I will bring disaster upon the 11
world
and their due punishment upon
the wicked.
I will check the pride of the
haughty
and bring low the arrogance of
ruthless men.
I will make men scarcer than fine 12
gold,
rarer than gold of Ophir.
Then the heavens shall shudder,[a] 13

---

[a] Prob. rdg.; Heb. Then I will make the heavens shudder.

and the earth shall be shaken from
    its place
at the fury of the LORD of Hosts,
    on the day of his anger.
14 Then, like a gazelle before the
    hunter
or a flock with no man to round it
    up,
each man will go back to his own
    people,
every one will flee to his own land.
15 All who are found will be stabbed,
all who are taken will fall by the
    sword;
16 their infants will be dashed to the
    ground before their eyes,
their houses rifled and their wives
    ravished.
17 I will stir up against them the
    Medes,
who care nothing for silver and are
    not tempted by gold,[a]
18 who have no pity on little children
and spare no mother's son;
19 and Babylon, fairest of kingdoms,
proud beauty of the Chaldaeans,
shall be like Sodom and Gomorrah
when God overthrew them.
20 Never again shall she be inhabited,
no man shall dwell in her through
    all the ages;
there no Arab shall pitch his tent,
no shepherds fold their flocks.
21 There marmots shall have their
    lairs,
and porcupines shall overrun her
    houses;
there desert owls shall dwell,
and there he-goats shall gambol;
22 jackals shall occupy her mansions,[b]
and wolves her gorgeous palaces.
Her time draws very near,
and her days have not long to run.

14   The LORD will show compassion
for Jacob and will once again make
Israel his choice. He will settle
them on their own soil, and
strangers will come to join them
and attach themselves to Jacob.

Many nations shall escort Israel to 2
her place, and she shall employ
them as slaves and slave-girls on
the land of the LORD; she shall take
her captors captive and rule over
her task-masters.

When the LORD gives you relief 3
from your pain and your fears and
from the cruel slavery laid upon
you, you will take up this song of 4
derision over the king of Babylon:

See how the oppressor has met his
    end and his frenzy ceased!
The LORD has broken the rod of 5
    the wicked,
the sceptre of the ruler
who struck down peoples in his 6
    rage
with unerring blows,
who crushed nations in anger
and persecuted them unceasingly.
The whole world has rest and is at 7
    peace;
it breaks into cries of joy.
The pines themselves and the 8
    cedars of Lebanon exult over
    you:
Since you have been laid low, they
    say,
no man comes up to fell us.

Sheol below was all astir   9
to meet you at your coming;
she roused the ancient dead to
    meet you,
all who had been leaders on earth;
she made all who had been kings of
    the nations
rise from their thrones.
One and all they greet you with 10
    these words:
So you too are weak as we are,
and have become one of us!
Your pride and all the music of 11
    your lutes
have been brought down to Sheol;[c]
maggots are the pallet beneath
    you,
and worms your coverlet.

[a] *Prob. rdg.; Heb. adds* bows shall dash young men to the ground.
[b] *Prob. rdg.; Heb.* her widows.
[c] *Or* Your pride has been brought down to Sheol to the crowding throng of your dead.

12 How you have fallen from heaven,
      bright morning star,
   felled to the earth, sprawling help-
      less across the nations!
13 You thought in your own mind,
      I will scale the heavens;
   I will set my throne high above the
      stars of God,
   I will sit on the mountain where
      the gods meet
   in the far recesses of the north.
14 I will rise high above the cloud-
      banks
   and make myself like the Most
      High.
15 Yet you shall be brought down to
      Sheol,
   to the depths of the abyss.
16 Those who see you will stare at
      you,
   they will look at you and ponder:
   Is this, they will say, the man who
      shook the earth,
   who made kingdoms quake,
17 who turned the world into a
      desert
   and laid its cities in ruins,
   who never let his prisoners go free
      to their homes,
18 the kings of every land?
   Now they lie all of them in honour,
   each in his last home.
19 But you have been flung out
      unburied,
   mere loathsome carrion,
   a companion to the slain pierced by
      the sword
   who have gone down to the stony
      abyss.
   And you, a corpse trampled under-
      foot,
20 shall not share burial with them,
   for you have ruined your land and
      slaughtered your people.
   Such a brood of evildoers shall
      never be seen again.
21 Make the shambles ready for his
      sons
   butchered for their fathers' sin;
   they shall not rise up and possess
      the world
   nor cover the face of the earth with
      cities.

22 I will rise against them, says the
   LORD of Hosts; I will destroy the
   name of Babylon and what remains of her, her offspring and
23 posterity, says the LORD; I will
   make her a haunt of the bustard, a
   waste of fen, and sweep her with
   the besom of destruction. This is
   the very word of the LORD of
   Hosts.

24 The LORD of Hosts has sworn:
   In very truth, as I planned, so shall
      it be;
   as I designed, so shall it fall out:
25 I will break the Assyrian in my
      own land
   and trample him underfoot upon
      my mountains;
   his yoke shall be lifted from you,
   his burden taken from your shoul-
      ders.
26 This is the plan prepared for the
      whole earth,
   this the hand stretched out over all
      the nations.
27 For the LORD of Hosts has pre-
      pared his plan:
   who shall frustrate it?
   His is the hand stretched out, and
   who shall turn it back?

28 In the year that King Ahaz died
   this oracle came from God:

29 Let none of you rejoice, you
      Philistines,
   because the rod that chastised you
      is broken;
   for a viper shall be born of a snake
      as a plant from the root,
   and its fruit shall be a flying serpent.
30 But the poor shall graze their
      flocks in my meadows,
   and the destitute shall lie down in
      peace;
   but the offspring of your roots I
      will kill by starvation,
   and put the remnant of you to
      death.
31 Howl in the gate, cry for help in
      the city,
   let all Philistia be in turmoil;

for a great enemy is coming from
the north,
not a man straying from his
ranks.
32 What answer is there for the envoys of the nation?
This, that the LORD has fixed Zion
in her place,
and the afflicted among his people
shall take refuge there.

15   Moab: an oracle.

On the night when Ar is sacked,
Moab meets her doom;
on the night when Kir is sacked,
Moab meets her doom.
2 The people of Dibon go up[a] to the
hill-shrines to weep;
Moab howls over Nebo and over
Medeba.
The hair is torn from every head,
and every beard shaved off.
3 In the streets men go clothed with
sackcloth,
they cry out on the roofs;
in the public squares every man
howls,
weeping as he goes through them.
4 Heshbon and Elealeh cry for help,
their voices are heard as far as
Jahaz.
Thus Moab's stoutest warriors become cowards,
and her courage ebbs away.
5 My heart cries out for Moab,
whose nobles have fled[b] as far as
Zoar.[c]
On the ascent to Luhith men go up
weeping;
on the road to Horonaim there are
cries of 'Disaster!'
6 The waters of Nimrim are desolate
indeed;
the grass is parched, the herbage
dead,
not a green thing is left;
7 and so the people carry off across
the gorge of the Arabim
their hard-earned wealth and all
their savings.

The cry for help echoes round the 8
frontiers of Moab,
their howling reaches Eglaim and
Beer-elim.
The waters of Dimon already run 9
with blood;
yet I have more troubles in store
for Dimon,
for I have a vision[d] of the survivors
of Moab,
of the remnant of Admah.
The rulers of the country send a 16
present of lambs
from Sela in the wilderness
to the hill of the daughter of Zion;
the daughters of Moab at the fords 2
of the Arnon
shall be like fluttering birds, like
scattered nestlings.
'Take up our cause with all your 3
might;
let your shadow shield us at high
noon, dark as night.
Shelter the homeless, do not betray
the fugitive;
let the homeless people of Moab 4
find refuge with you;
hide them from the despoiler.'

When extortion has done its work
and the looting is over,
when the heel of the oppressor has
vanished from the land,
a throne shall be set up in mutual 5
trust in David's tent,
and on it there shall sit a true judge,
one who seeks justice and is swift
to do right.

We have heard tell of Moab's 6
pride, how great it is,
we have heard of his pride, his
overweening pride;
his talk is full of lies.
For this all Moab shall howl;   7
Moab shall howl indeed;
he[e] shall mourn for the prosperous
farmers of Kir-hareseth,
utterly ruined;
the orchards of Heshbon,   8
the vines of Sibmah languish,

---

[a] The people...go up: *prob. rdg.*; *Heb.* He has gone up to the house and Dibon.
[b] have fled: *prob. rdg.*; *Heb. om.*   [c] *Prob. rdg.*; *Heb. adds* Eglath Shelishiya.
[d] I have a vision: *prob. rdg.*; *Heb.* a lion.   [e] *Prob. rdg.*; *Heb.* you.

though their red grapes once laid
low the lords of the nations,
though they reached as far as
Jazer
and trailed out to the wilderness,
though their branches spread a-
broad and crossed the sea.
9 Therefore I will weep for Sibmah's
vines as I weep for Jazer.
I will drench you with my tears,
Heshbon and Elealeh;
for over your summer-fruits and
your harvest
the shouts of the harvesters are
ended.
10 Joy and gladness shall be banished
from the meadows,
no more shall men shout and sing
in the vineyards,
no more shall they tread wine in
the winepresses;
I have silenced the shouting of the
harvesters.
11 Therefore my heart throbs
like a harp for Moab,
and my very soul for Kir-hareseth.[a]
12 When Moab comes to worship
and wearies himself at the hill-
shrines,
when he enters his sanctuary to
pray,
he will gain nothing.

13   These are the words which the
LORD spoke long ago about Moab;
14 and now he says, In three years, as
a hired labourer counts them off,
the glory of Moab shall become
contemptible for all his vast numbers; a handful shall be left and
those of no account.

17   Damascus: an oracle.

Damascus shall be a city no longer,
she shall be but a heap of ruins.
2 For ever desolate, flocks shall have
her for their own,
and lie there undisturbed.
3 No longer shall Ephraim boast a
fortified city,
or Damascus a kingdom;

the remnant of Aram and the glory
of Israel, their fate is one.
This is the very word of the LORD
of Hosts.

On that day Jacob's weight shall 4
dwindle
and the fat on his limbs waste
away,
as when the harvester gathers up 5
the standing corn
and reaps the ears in armfuls,
or as when a man gleans the ears in
the Vale of Rephaim,
or as when one beats an olive-tree 6
and only gleanings are left on it,
two or three berries on the top of a
branch,
four or five on the boughs of the
fruiting tree.
This is the very word of the LORD
the God of Israel.

On that day men shall look to 7
their Maker and turn their eyes to
the Holy One of Israel; they shall 8
not look to the altars made by
their own hands nor to anything
that their fingers have made,
sacred poles or incense-altars.
On that day their strong cities 9
shall be deserted like the cities of
the Hivites and the Amorites,
which they abandoned when Israel
came in; all shall be desolate.

For you forgot the God who 10
delivered you,
and did not remember the rock,
your stronghold.
Plant then, if you will, your gardens in honour of Adonis,
strike your cuttings for a foreign
god;
protect your gardens on the day 11
you plant them,
and next day make the seed sprout.
But the crop will be scorched when
wasting disease comes
in the day of incurable pain.

Listen! it is the thunder of many 12
peoples,

[a] *Prob. rdg.; Heb.* Kir-hares.

they thunder with the thunder of
  the sea.
Listen! it is the roar of nations
roaring with the roar of mighty
  waters.
13 When he rebukes them, away they
    fly,
  driven like chaff on the hills before
    the wind,
  like thistledown before the storm.
14 At evening all is confusion,
  and before morning they are gone.
  Such is the fate of our plunderers,
  the lot of those who despoil us.

18 There is a land of sailing ships,
  a land beyond the rivers of Cush
 2 which sends its envoys by the
    Nile,
  journeying on the waters in vessels
    of reed.
  Go, swift messengers,
  go to a people tall and smooth-
    skinned,
  to a people dreaded near and far,
  a nation strong and proud,
  whose land is scoured by rivers.
 3 All you who dwell in the world,
    inhabitants of earth,
  shall see when the signal is hoisted
    on the mountains
  and shall hear when the trumpet
    sounds.

 4 These were the words of the LORD
   to me:

  From my dwelling-place I will
    look quietly down
  when the heat shimmers in the
    summer sun,
  when the dew is heavy at harvest
    time.
 5 Before the vintage, when the bud-
    ding is over
  and the flower ripens into a berry,
  the shoots shall be cut down with
    knives,
  the branches struck off and cleared
    away.
 6 All shall be left to birds of prey on
    the hills
  and to beasts of the earth;

in summer the birds shall make
  their home there,
in winter every beast of the earth.

At that time tribute shall be 7
brought to the LORD of Hosts
from a people tall and smooth-
skinned, dreaded near and far, a
nation strong and proud, whose
land is scoured by rivers. They
shall bring it to Mount Zion, the
place where men invoke the name
of the LORD of Hosts.

Egypt: an oracle.   19

See how the LORD comes riding
  swiftly upon a cloud,
he shall descend upon Egypt;
the idols of Egypt quail before
  him,
Egypt's courage melts within her.
I will set Egyptian against Egyp- 2
  tian,
and they shall fight one against
  another,
neighbour against neighbour,
city against city and kingdom
  against kingdom.
Egypt's spirit shall sink within 3
  her,
and I will throw her counsels into
  confusion.
They may resort to idols and
  oracle-mongers,
to ghosts and spirits,
but I will hand Egypt over to a 4
  hard master,
and a cruel king shall rule over
  them.
This is the very word of the Lord,
  the LORD of Hosts.

The waters of the Nile shall drain 5
  away,
the river shall be parched and run
  dry;
its channels shall stink,   6
the streams of Egypt shall be
  parched and dry up;
reeds and rushes shall wither
  away;
the lotus too beside the Nile*a*   7

---

a *Prob. rdg.; Heb. adds* on the mouth of the Nile.

and all that is sown along the Nile
  shall dry up,
shall be blown away and vanish.
8 The fishermen shall groan and
  lament,
all who cast their hooks into the
  Nile
and those who spread nets on the
  water shall lose heart.
9 The flax-dressers shall hang their
  heads,
the women carding and the
  weavers shall grow pale,
10 Egypt's spinners shall be downcast,
and all her artisans sick at heart.

11 Fools that you are, you princes of
  Zoan!
Wisest of Pharaoh's counsellors
  you may be,
but stupid counsellors you are.
How can you say to Pharaoh,
'I am the heir of wise men and
  spring from ancient kings'?
12 Where are your wise men, Pharaoh,
to teach you and make known to
  you
what the LORD of Hosts has
  planned for Egypt?
13 Zoan's princes are fools, the princes
  of Noph are dupes;
the chieftains of her clans have led
  Egypt astray.
14 The LORD has infused into them
a spirit that warps their judgement;
they make Egypt miss her way in
  all she does,
as a drunkard will miss his footing
  as he vomits.
15 There shall be nothing in Egypt
  that any man can do,
head or tail, palm or rush.

16   When that day comes the Egyptians shall become weak as women; they shall fear and tremble
when they see the LORD of Hosts
raise his hand against them, as
17 raise it he will. The land of Judah

shall strike terror into Egypt; its
very name shall cause dismay, because of the plans that the LORD of
Hosts has laid against them.

   When that day comes there shall 18
be five cities in Egypt speaking the
language of Canaan and swearing
allegiance to the LORD of Hosts,
and one of them shall be called the
City of the Sun.[a]

   When that day comes there shall 19
be an altar to the LORD in the heart
of Egypt, and a sacred pillar set up
for the LORD upon her frontier. It 20
shall stand as a token and a reminder to the LORD of Hosts in
Egypt, so that when they appeal
to him against their oppressors, he
may send a deliverer to champion
their cause, and he shall rescue
them. The LORD will make him- 21
self known to the Egyptians; on
that day they shall acknowledge
the LORD and do him service with
sacrifice and grain-offering, make
vows to him and pay them. The 22
LORD will strike down Egypt,
healing as he strikes; then they
will turn back to him and he will
hear their prayers and heal them.

   When that day comes there shall 23
be a highway between Egypt and
Assyria; Assyrians shall come to
Egypt and Egyptians to Assyria;
then Egyptians shall worship with[b]
Assyrians.

   When that day comes Israel 24
shall rank with Egypt and Assyria,
those three, and shall be a blessing
in the centre of the world. So the 25
LORD of Hosts will bless them: A
blessing be upon Egypt my people,
upon Assyria the work of my
hands, and upon Israel my possession.

SARGON king of Assyria sent his 20
commander-in-chief[c] to Ashdod,
and he took it by storm. At that 2
time the LORD said to Isaiah son of
Amoz, Come, strip the sackcloth

---

[a] the City of the Sun: or Heliopolis.
[b] Or shall be slaves to.   [c] Or sent Tartan.

from your waist and take your sandals off. He did so, and went about
3 naked and barefoot. The LORD said, My servant Isaiah has gone naked and barefoot for three years as a sign and a warning to Egypt
4 and Cush; just so shall the king of Assyria lead the captives of Egypt and the exiles of Cush naked and barefoot, their buttocks shamefully exposed, young and old alike.
5 All men shall be dismayed, their hopes in Cush and their pride in
6 Egypt humbled. On that day those who dwell along this coast will say, So much for all our hopes on which we relied for help and deliverance from the king of Assyria; what escape have we now?

21   A wilderness: an oracle.

Rough weather, advancing like a storm in the south,
coming from the wilderness, from a land of terror!
2 Grim is the vision shown to me:
the traitor betrayed, the spoiler himself despoiled.
Up, Elam; up, Medes, to the siege, no time for weariness!
3 At this my limbs writhe in anguish,
I am gripped by pangs like a woman in labour.
I am distraught past hearing, dazed past seeing,
4 my mind reels, sudden convulsions seize me.

The cool twilight I longed for has become a terror:
5 the banquet is set out, the rugs are spread;
they are eating and drinking –
rise, princes, burnish your shields.
6 For these were the words of the Lord to me:
Go, post a watchman to report what he sees.
7 He sees chariots, two-horsed chariots,
riders on asses, riders on camels.

He is alert, alert, always on the alert.
Then the look-out cried: 8
All day long I stand on the Lord's watch-tower
and night after night I keep my station.
See, there come men in a chariot, a 9
two-horsed chariot.
And a voice calls back:
Fallen, fallen is Babylon,
and all the images of her gods lie shattered on the ground.
O my people,   10
once trodden out and winnowed on the threshing-floor,
what I have heard from the LORD of Hosts,
from the God of Israel, I have told you.

Dumah: an oracle.   11

One calls to me from Seir:
Watchman, what is left of the night?
Watchman, what is left?
The watchman answered: 12
Morning comes, and also night.*
Ask if you must; then come back again.

With the Arabs: an oracle.   13

You caravans of Dedan, that camp in the scrub with the Arabs,
bring water to meet the thirsty.   14
You dwellers in Tema, meet the fugitives with food,
for they flee from the sword, the 15
sharp edge of the sword,
from the bent bow, and from the press of battle.

For these are the words of the 16
Lord to me: Within a year, as a hired labourer counts off the years, all the glory of Kedar shall come to an end; few shall be the bows left to 17 the warriors of Kedar.
The LORD the God of Israel has spoken.

---

a and also night: *or* and the night is full spent.

22 The Valley of Vision:[a] an oracle.

Tell me, what is amiss
that you have all climbed on to the
  roofs,
2 O city full of tumult, town in
  ferment
and filled with uproar,
whose slain were not slain with the
  sword
and did not die in battle?
3 Your commanders are all in flight,
huddled together out of bowshot;
all your stoutest warriors are
  huddled together,
they have taken to their heels.
4 Then I said, Turn your eyes away
  from me;
leave me to weep in misery.
Do not thrust consolation on me
for the ruin of my own people.

5   For the Lord, the LORD of
Hosts, has ordained a day of tumult, a day of trampling and turmoil in the Valley of Vision,[a]
rousing cries for help that echo
among the mountains.

6 Elam took up his quiver,
horses were harnessed to the chariots of Aram,[b]
Kir took the cover from his shield.
7 Your fairest valleys were overrun
  by chariots and horsemen,
the gates were hard beset,
8 the heart of Judah's defence was
  laid open.

  On that day you looked to the
weapons stored in the House of the
9 Forest; you filled all the many
pools in the City of David, collecting water from the Lower Pool.[c]
10 Then you surveyed the houses in
Jerusalem, tearing some down to
11 make the wall inaccessible, and
between the two walls you made a
cistern for the Waters of the Old
Pool;

but you did not look to the Maker
  of it all
or consider him who fashioned it
  long ago.
On that day the Lord, the LORD of 12
  Hosts,
called for weeping and beating the
  breast,
for shaving the head and putting
  on sackcloth;
but instead there was joy and 13
  merry-making,
slaughtering of cattle and killing of
  sheep,
eating of meat and drinking of
  wine, as you thought,
Let us eat and drink; for tomorrow
  we die.

  The LORD of Hosts has revealed 14
himself to me; in my hearing he
swore:

Your wickedness shall never be
  purged
until you die.
This is the word of the Lord, the
  LORD of Hosts.

These were the words of the Lord, 15
the LORD of Hosts:

Go to this steward,
to Shebna, comptroller of the
  household, and say:
What right, what business, have 16
  you here,
that you have dug yourself a grave
  here,
cutting out your grave on a
  height
and carving yourself a resting-
  place in the rock?
The LORD will shake you out,   17
shake you as a garment[d] is shaken
  out
to rid it of lice;
then he will bundle you tightly and 18
  throw you
like a ball into a great wide land.
There you shall die,

---

[a] Or of Calamity.   [b] Prob. rdg.; Heb. man.
[c] you filled...Lower Pool: or you took note of the cracks, many as they were, in
the wall of the City of David, and you collected water from the Lower Pool.
[d] Prob. rdg.; Heb. man.

and there shall lie your chariot of honour,
an object of contempt to your master's household.

19 I will remove you from office and drive you from your post.

20 On that day I will send for my
21 servant Eliakim son of Hilkiah; I will invest him with your robe, gird him with your sash; and hand over your authority to him. He shall be a father to the inhabitants of Jerusalem and the people of
22 Judah. I will lay the key of the house of David on his shoulder; what he opens no man shall shut, and what he shuts no man shall
23 open. He shall be a seat of honour for his father's family; I will fasten
24 him firmly in place like a peg. On him shall hang all the weight of the family, down to the lowest dregs – all the little vessels, both bowls
25 and pots. On that day, says the LORD of Hosts, the peg which was firmly fastened in its place shall be removed; it shall be hacked out and shall fall, and the load of things hanging on it shall be destroyed. The LORD has spoken.

23   Tyre: an oracle.

The ships of Tarshish howl, for the harbour is sacked;
the port of entry from Kittim is swept away.

2-3 The people of the sea-coast, the merchants of Sidon, wail,
people whose agents cross the great waters,
whose harvest[a] is the grain of the Shihor
and their revenue the trade of nations.

4 Sidon, the sea-fortress,[b] cries in her disappointment,[c]
I no longer feel the anguish of labour or bear children;

I have no young sons to rear, no daughters to bring up.
When the news is confirmed in 5 Egypt
her people sway in anguish at the fate of Tyre.

Make your way to Tarshish, they 6 say,
howl, you who dwell by the sea-coast.
Is this your busy city, ancient in 7 story,
on whose voyages you were carried to settle far away?

Whose plan was this against Tyre, 8 the city of battlements,
whose merchants were princes
and her traders the most honoured men on earth?
The LORD of Hosts planned it to 9 prick every noble's pride
and bring all the most honoured men on earth into contempt.
Take to the tillage of your fields, 10 you people of Tarshish;
for your market[d] is lost.
The LORD has stretched out his 11 hand over the sea
and shaken kingdoms,
he has given his command to destroy the marts of Canaan;
and he has said, You shall busy 12 yourselves no more,
you, the sorely oppressed virgin city of Sidon.
Though you arise and cross over to Kittim,
even there you shall find no rest.

Look at this land, the destined 13 home of ships[e]! The Chaldaeans[f] erected their[g] siege-towers, dismantled its palaces and laid it in ruins.

Howl, you ships of Tarshish;   14 for your haven is sacked.

---

[a] *whose harvest: prob. rdg.; Heb.* the harvest of the Nile.   [b] *the sea-fortress: prob. rdg.; Heb.* the sea, sea-fortress, saying.   [c] *in her disappointment: prob. rdg.; Heb.* be disappointed.   [d] *Prob. rdg.; Heb.* girdle.   [e] *Or* marmots.
[f] *Prob. rdg.; Heb. adds* this was the people; it was not Assyria.
[g] *Prob. rdg.; Heb.* his.

15 From that day Tyre shall be forgotten for seventy years, the span of one king's life. At the end of the seventy years her plight shall be that of the harlot in the song:

16 Take your harp, go round the city, poor forgotten harlot;
touch the strings sweetly, sing all your songs,
make men remember you again.

17 At the end of seventy years, the LORD will turn again to Tyre; she shall go back to her old trade and hire herself out to every kingdom
18 on earth. The profits of her trading will be dedicated to the LORD; they shall not be hoarded or stored up, but shall be given to those who worship the LORD, to purchase food in plenty and fine attire.

The LORD's judgement on the earth

24 Beware, the LORD will empty the earth,
split it open and turn it upside down,
and scatter its inhabitants.
2 Then it will be the same for priest and people,
the same for master and slave, mistress and slave-girl,
seller and buyer,
borrower and lender, debtor and creditor.
3 The earth is emptied clean away and stripped clean bare.
For this is the word that the LORD has spoken.
4 The earth dries up and withers, the whole world withers and grows sick;
the earth's high places sicken,
5 and earth itself is desecrated by the feet of those who live in it, because they have broken the laws, disobeyed the statutes and violated the eternal covenant.
6 For this a curse has devoured the earth
and its inhabitants stand aghast.

For this those who inhabit the earth dwindle
and only a few men are left.

The new wine dries up, the vines 7 sicken,
and all the revellers turn to sorrow.
Silent the merry beat of tam- 8 bourines,
hushed the shouts of revelry,
the merry harp is silent.
No one shall drink wine to the 9 sound of song;
the liquor will be bitter to the man who drinks it.
The city of chaos is a broken city, 10 every house barred, that no one may enter.
Men call for wine in the streets; 11 all revelry is darkened,
and mirth is banished from the land.

Desolation alone is left in the city 12 and the gate is broken into pieces.
So shall it be in all the world, in 13 every nation,
as when an olive-tree is beaten and stripped,
as when the vintage is ended.

Men raise their voices and cry 14 aloud,
they shout in the west,[a] so great is the LORD's majesty.
Therefore let the LORD be glorified 15 in the regions of the east,
and the name of the LORD the God of Israel
in the coasts and islands of the west.

From the ends of the earth we 16 have heard them sing,
How lovely is righteousness!
But I thought, Villainy, villainy!
Woe to the traitors and their treachery!
Traitors double-dyed they are indeed!
The hunter's scare, the pit, and the 17 trap
threaten all who dwell in the land;

[a] in the west: or more loudly than the sea.

18 if a man runs from the rattle of the scare
he will fall into the pit;
if he climbs out of the pit
he will be caught in the trap.
When the windows of heaven above are opened
and earth's foundations shake,
19 the earth is utterly shattered,
it is convulsed and reels wildly.
20 The earth reels to and fro like a drunken man
and sways like a watchman's shelter;
the sins of men weigh heavy upon it,
and it falls to rise no more.

21 On that day the LORD will punish the host of heaven in heaven,
and on earth the kings of the earth,
22 herded together, close packed like prisoners in a dungeon;
shut up in gaol, after a long time they shall be punished.
23 The moon shall grow pale and the sun hide its face in shame;
for the LORD of Hosts has become king
on Mount Zion and in Jerusalem,
and shows his glory before their elders.

The deliverance and ingathering of Judah

25 O LORD, thou art my God;
I will exalt thee and praise thy name;
for thou hast accomplished a wonderful purpose,
certain and sure, from of old.
2 For thou hast turned cities into heaps of ruin,
and fortified towns into rubble;
every mansion in the cities is swept away,
never to be rebuilt.
3 For this a cruel nation holds thee in honour,
the cities of ruthless nations fear thee.

Truly thou hast been a refuge to 4 the poor,
a refuge to the needy in his trouble,
shelter from the tempest and shade from the heat.
For the blast of the ruthless is like an icy storm
or a scorching drought; 5
thou subduest the roar of the foe,[a]
and the song of the ruthless dies away.

On this mountain the LORD of 6 Hosts will prepare
a banquet of rich fare for all the peoples,
a banquet of wines well matured and richest fare,
well-matured wines strained clear.
On this mountain the LORD will 7 swallow up
that veil that shrouds all the peoples,
the pall thrown over all the nations;
he will swallow up death for ever. 8
Then the Lord GOD will wipe away the tears
from every face
and remove the reproach of his people from the whole earth.
The LORD has spoken.

On that day men will say, 9
See, this is our God
for whom we have waited to deliver us;
this is the LORD for whom we have waited;
let us rejoice and exult in his deliverance.
For the hand of the LORD will rest 10 on this mountain,
but Moab shall be trampled under his feet
as straw is trampled into a midden.
In it Moab shall spread out his 11 hands
as a swimmer spreads his hands to swim,
but he shall sink his pride with every stroke of his hands.

[a] *Prob. rdg.; Heb. adds* heat in the shadow of a cloud.

12 The LORD has thrown down the
high defences of your walls,
has levelled them to the earth
and brought them down to the
dust.

26 On that day this song shall be sung
in Judah:

We have a strong city
whose walls and ramparts are our
deliverance.
2 Open the gates to let a righteous
nation in,
a nation that keeps faith.
3 Thou dost keep in peace men of
constant mind,
in peace because they trust in thee.
4 Trust in the LORD for ever;
for the LORD himself is an everlasting rock.
5 He has brought low all who dwell
high in a towering city;
he levels it to the ground and lays
it in the dust,
6 that the oppressed and the poor
may tread it underfoot.
7 The path of the righteous is level,
and thou markest out the right
way for the upright.
8 We too look to the path prescribed
in thy laws, O LORD;
thy name and thy memory are our
heart's desire.
9 With all my heart I long for thee in
the night,
I seek thee eagerly when dawn
breaks;
for, when thy laws prevail in the
land,
the inhabitants of the world learn
justice.
10 The wicked are destroyed, they
have never learnt justice;
corrupt in a land of honest ways,
they do not regard the majesty of
the LORD.

11 O LORD, thy hand is lifted high,
but the bitter enemies of thy
people do not see it;[a]
let the fire of thy enmity destroy
them.

O LORD, thou wilt bestow pros- 12
perity on us;
for in truth all our works are thy
doing.
O LORD our God, 13
other lords than thou have been
our masters,
but thee alone do we invoke by
name.
The dead will not live again, 14
those long in their graves will not
rise;
to this end thou hast punished
them and destroyed them,
and made all memory of them
perish.
Thou hast enlarged the nation, O 15
LORD,
enlarged it and won thyself
honour,
thou hast extended all the frontiers
of the land.
In our distress, O LORD, we[b] 16
sought thee out,
chastened by the mere whisper of
thy rebuke.
As a woman with child, when her 17
time is near,
is in labour and cries out in her
pains,
so were we in thy presence, O
LORD.
We have been with child, we have 18
been in labour,
but have brought forth wind.
We have won no success for the
land,
and no one will be born to inhabit
the world.
But thy dead live, their bodies will 19
rise again.
They that sleep in the earth will
awake and shout for joy;
for thy dew is a dew of sparkling
light,
and the earth will bring those long
dead to birth again.

Go, my people, enter your rooms 20
and shut your doors behind
you;
withdraw for a brief while, until
wrath has gone by.

---

[a] *Prob. rdg.; Heb. adds* let them see and be ashamed.   [b] *Prob. rdg.; Heb.* they.

21 For see, the LORD is coming from
his place
to punish the inhabitants of the
earth for their sins;
then the earth shall uncover her
blood-stains
and hide her slain no more.

27 On that day the LORD will punish
with his cruel sword, his mighty
and powerful sword,
Leviathan that twisting[a] sea-
serpent,
that writhing serpent Leviathan,
and slay the monster of the
deep.

2 On that day sing to the pleasant
vineyard,
3 I the LORD am its keeper,
moment by moment I water it for
fear its green leaves fail.
Night and day I tend it,
4 but I get no wine;
I would as soon have briars and
thorns,
then I would wage war upon it and
burn it all up,
5 unless it grasps me as its refuge and
makes peace with me –
unless it makes peace with me.

6 In time to come Jacob's offspring
shall take root
and Israel shall bud and blossom,
and they shall fill the whole earth
with fruit.

7 Has God struck him down as he
struck others down?
Has the slayer been slain as he slew
others?
8–10[b] This then purges Jacob's iniquity,
this[c] has removed his sin:
that he grinds all altar stones to
powder like chalk;
no sacred poles and incense-altars
are left standing.

The fortified city is left solitary,
and his quarrel with her ends in
brushing her away,[d]

removing her by a cruel blast when
the east wind blows;
it is a homestead stripped bare,
deserted like a wilderness;
there the calf grazes and there lies
down,
and crops every twig.
Its boughs snap off when they 11
grow dry,
and women come and light their
fires with them.
For they are a people without
sense;
therefore their maker will show
them no mercy,
he who formed them will show
them no favour.

On that day the LORD will beat out 12
the grain,
from the streams of the Euphrates
to the Torrent of Egypt;
but you Israelites will be gleaned
one by one.

On that day 13
a blast shall be blown on a great
trumpet,
and those who are lost in Assyria
and those dispersed in Egypt will
come in
and worship the LORD on the holy
mountain, in Jerusalem.

Assyria and Judah

Oh, the proud garlands of the 28
drunkards of Ephraim
and the flowering sprays, so lovely
in their beauty,
on the heads of revellers dripping
with perfumes,
overcome with wine!
See, the Lord has one at his 2
bidding, mighty and strong,
whom he sets to work with violence
against the land,
like a sweeping storm of hail, like a
destroying tempest,
like a torrent of water in overwhelming flood.

---

[a] Or *primeval.*
[c] *Prob. rdg.; Heb. adds* all fruit.
[b] *Verses 8–10 re-arranged thus:* 9, 10a, 8, 10b.
[d] *Prob. rdg.; Heb. adds* by dismissing her.

3 The proud garlands of Ephraim's
   drunkards
   shall be trampled underfoot,
4 and the flowering sprays, so lovely
   in their beauty
   on the heads dripping with perfumes,
   shall be like early figs ripe before
   summer;
   he who sees them plucks them,
   and their bloom is gone while they
   lie in his hand.
5 On that day the LORD of Hosts
   shall be a lovely garland,
   a beautiful diadem for the remnant
   of his people,
6 a spirit of justice for one who pre-
   sides in a court of justice,
   and of valour for*a* those who repel
   the enemy at the gate.

7 These too are addicted to wine,
   clamouring in their cups:
   priest and prophet are addicted to
   strong drink
   and bemused with wine;
   clamouring in their cups, confirmed topers,*b*
   hiccuping in drunken stupor;
8 every table is covered with vomit,
   filth that leaves no clean spot.
9 Who is it that the prophet hopes to
   teach,
   to whom will what they hear make
   sense?
   Are they babes newly weaned, just
   taken from the breast?
10 It is all harsh cries and raucous
   shouts,
   'A little more here, a little there!'
11 So it will be with barbarous speech
   and strange tongue
   that this people will hear God
   speaking,
12 this people to whom he once
   said,
   'This is true rest; let the exhausted
   have rest.
   This is repose', and they refused to
   listen.

Now to them the word of the LORD 13
   will be
   harsh cries and raucous shouts,
   'A little more here, a little there!' –
   and so, as they walk, they will
   stumble backwards,
   they will be injured, trapped and
   caught.
Listen then to the word of the 14
   LORD, you arrogant men
   who rule this people in Jerusalem.
You say, 'We have made a treaty 15
   with Death
   and signed a pact with Sheol:
   so that, when the raging flood
   sweeps by, it shall not touch
   us;
   for we have taken refuge in lies
   and sheltered behind falsehood.'
These then are the words of the 16
   Lord GOD:
Look, I am laying a stone in Zion,
   a block of granite,
   a precious corner-stone for a firm
   foundation;
   he who has faith shall not waver.
I will use justice as a plumb-line 17
   and righteousness as a plummet;
   hail shall sweep away your refuge
   of lies,
   and flood-waters carry away your
   shelter.
Then your treaty with Death shall 18
   be annulled
   and your pact with Sheol shall not
   stand;
   the raging waters will sweep by,
   and you will be like land swept by
   the flood.
As often as it sweeps by, it will take 19
   you;
   morning after morning it will
   sweep by,
   day and night.
The very thought of such tidings
   will bring nothing but dismay;
   for 'The bed is too short for a man 20
   to stretch,
   and the blanket too narrow to
   cover him.'

a for: *prob. rdg.*; *Heb. om.*   *b* These too. . .topers: *or* These too lose their way
through wine and are set wandering by strong drink: priest and prophet lose their
way through strong drink and are fuddled with wine; are set wandering by strong
drink, lose their way through tippling.

21 But the LORD shall arise as he rose
   on Mount Perazim
   and storm with rage as he did in
   the Vale of Gibeon
   to do what he must do – how
   strange a deed!
   to perform his work – how outlandish a work!
22 But now have done with your
   arrogance,
   lest your bonds grow tighter;
   for I have heard destruction decreed
   by the Lord GOD of Hosts for the
   whole land.

23 Listen and hear what I say,
   attend and hear my words.
24 Will the ploughman continually
   plough for the sowing,
   breaking his ground and harrowing
   it?
25 Does he not, once he has levelled it,
   broadcast the dill and scatter the
   cummin?
   Does he not plant the wheat in
   rows
   with barley[a] and spelt along the
   edge?
26 Does not his God instruct him and
   train him aright?
27 Dill is not threshed with a sledge,
   and the cartwheel is not rolled over
   cummin;
   dill is beaten with a rod,
   and cummin with a flail.
28 Corn is crushed, but not to the
   uttermost,
   not with a final crushing;
   his cartwheels rumble over it and
   break it up,
   but they do not grind it fine.
29 This message, too, comes from the
   LORD of Hosts,
   whose purposes are wonderful
   and his power great.

29 Alas for Ariel! Ariel,
   the city where David encamped.
   Add year to year,
   let the pilgrim-feasts run their
   round,
2 and I will bring Ariel to sore straits,

when there shall be moaning and
   lamentation.
I will make her my Ariel indeed,
   my fiery altar.
I will throw my army round you 3
   like a wall;
I will set a ring of outposts all
   round you
and erect siege-works against you.
You shall be brought low, you 4
   will speak out of the ground
and your words will issue from the
   earth;
your voice will come like a ghost's
   from the ground,
and your words will squeak out of
   the earth.
Yet the horde of your enemies 5
   shall crumble into dust,
the horde of ruthless foes shall fly
   like chaff.
Then suddenly, all in an instant,
punishment shall come from the 6
   LORD of Hosts
with thunder and earthquake and
   a great noise,
with storm and tempest and a
   flame of devouring fire;
and the horde of all the nations 7
   warring against Ariel,
all their baggage-trains and siege-
   works,
and all her oppressors themselves,
   shall fade as a dream, a vision of
   the night.
Like a starving man who dreams 8
   and thinks that he is eating,
but wakes up to find himself
   empty,
or a thirsty man who dreams
   and thinks that he is drinking,
but wakes up to find himself thirsty and dry,
so shall the horde of all the nations
   be
that war against Mount Zion.

Loiter and be dazed, enjoy your- 9
   selves and be blinded,
be drunk but not with wine, reel
   but not with strong drink;
for the LORD has poured upon you 10
   a spirit of deep stupor;

---

[a] *Prob. rdg.; Heb. adds an unintelligible word.*

he has closed your eyes, the pro-
    phets,
and muffled your heads, the seers.

11   All prophetic vision has become
for you like a sealed book. Give
such a book to one who can read
and say, 'Come, read this'; he will
answer, 'I cannot', because it is
12 sealed. Give it to one who cannot
read and say, 'Come, read this'; he
will answer, 'I cannot read.'
13   Then the Lord said:

Because this people approach me
    with their mouths
and honour me with their lips
while their hearts are far from
    me,
and their religion is but a precept
    of men, learnt by rote,
14 therefore I will yet again shock
    this people,
adding shock to shock:
the wisdom of their wise men shall
    vanish
and the discernment of the discern-
    ing shall be lost.

15 Shame upon those who seek to hide
    their purpose
too deep for the LORD to see,
and who, when their deeds are
    done in the dark,
say, 'Who sees us? Who knows of
    us?'
16 How you turn things upside down,
as if the potter ranked no higher
    than the clay!
Shall the thing made say of its
    maker, 'He did not make me'?
Shall the pot say of the potter, 'He
    has no skill'?
17 The time is but short
before Lebanon goes back to
    grassland
and the grassland is no better than
    scrub.

18 On that day deaf men shall hear
    when a book is read,
and the eyes of the blind shall see
    out of impenetrable darkness.
19 The lowly shall once again rejoice
    in the LORD,

and the poorest of men exult in the
    Holy One of Israel.
20 The ruthless shall be no more, the
    arrogant shall cease to be;
those who are quick to see mis-
    chief,
21 those who charge others with a
    sin
or lay traps for him who brings the
    wrongdoer into court
or by falsehood deny justice to the
    righteous –
all these shall be exterminated.

22   Therefore these are the words of
the LORD the God of the house of
Jacob, the God who ransomed
Abraham:

This is no time for Jacob to be
    shamed,
no time for his face to grow pale;
23 for his descendants will hallow my
    name
when they see what I have done in
    their nation.
They will hallow the Holy One of
    Jacob
and hold the God of Israel in
    awe;
24 those whose minds are confused
    will gain understanding,
and the obstinate will receive
    instruction.

30 Oh, rebel sons! says the LORD,
you make plans, but not of my
    devising,
you weave schemes, but not in-
    spired by me,
piling sin upon sin;
2 you hurry down to Egypt without
    consulting me,
to seek protection under Pha-
    raoh's shelter
and take refuge under Egypt's
    wing.
3 Pharaoh's protection will bring
    you disappointment
and refuge under Egypt's wing
    humiliation;
4 for, though his officers are at Zoan
and his envoys reach as far as
    Hanes,

5 all are left in sorry plight by that
    unprofitable nation,
no help they find, no profit, only
    disappointment and disgrace.

6   The Beasts of the South:
            an oracle.

Through a land of hardship and
    distress
the tribes of lioness and roaring lion,
sand-viper and venomous flying
    serpent,
carry their wealth on the backs of
    asses
and their treasures on camels'
    humps
to an unprofitable people.

7 Vain and worthless is the help of
    Egypt;
therefore have I given her this
    name,
Rahab Quelled.

8 Now come and write it on a tablet,
    engrave it as an inscription before
    their eyes,
that it may be there in future days,
a testimony for all time.

9 For they are a race of rebels,
    disloyal sons,
sons who will not listen to the
    LORD's instruction;

10 they say to the seers, 'You shall
    not see',
and to the visionaries, 'You shall
    have no true visions;
give us smooth words and seduc-
    tive visions.

11 Turn aside, leave the straight path,
    and rid us for ever of the Holy One
    of Israel.'

12 These are the words of the Holy
    One of Israel:

Because you have rejected this
    warning
and trust in devious and dishonest
    practices,
resting on them for support,

13 therefore you shall find this ini-
    quity will be
like a crack running down
a high wall, which bulges

and suddenly, all in an instant,
    comes crashing down,
as an earthen jar is broken with a 14
    crash,
mercilessly shattered,
so that not a shard is found among
    the fragments
to take fire from the glowing
    embers,
or to scoop up water from a pool.

These are the words of the Lord 15
GOD the Holy One of Israel:

Come back, keep peace, and you
    will be safe;
in stillness and in staying quiet,
    there lies your strength.
But you would have none of it; you 16
    said, No,
we will take horse and flee;
therefore you shall be put to flight:
We will ride apace;
therefore swift shall be the pace of
    your pursuers.
When a thousand flee at the 17
    challenge of one,
you shall all flee at the challenge of
    five, until you are left
like a pole on a mountain-top, a
    signal post on a hill.
Yet the LORD is waiting to show 18
    you his favour,
yet he yearns to have pity on you;
for the LORD is a God of justice.
Happy are all who wait for him!

O people of Zion who dwell in 19
Jerusalem, you shall weep no more.
The LORD will show you favour
and answer you when he hears
your cry for help. The Lord may 20
give you bread of adversity and
water of affliction, but he who
teaches you shall no longer be
hidden out of sight, but with your
own eyes you shall see him always.
If you stray from the road to right 21
or left you shall hear with your
own ears a voice behind you saying, This is the way; follow it. You 22
will reject, as things unclean, your
silvered images and your idols
sheathed in gold; you will loathe

them like a foul discharge and call
23 them ordure.[a] The Lord will give
you rain for the seed you sow, and
as the produce of your soil he will
give you heavy crops of corn in
plenty. When that day comes the
cattle shall graze in broad pas-
24 tures; the oxen and asses that
work your land shall be fed with
well-seasoned fodder, winnowed
25 with shovel and fork. On each high
mountain and each lofty hill shall
be streams of running water, on
the day of massacre when the
26 highest in the land fall. The moon
shall shine with a brightness like
the sun's, and the sun with seven
times his wonted brightness, seven
days' light in one, on the day when
the Lord binds up the broken
limbs of his people and heals their
wounds.

27 See, the name of the Lord comes
from afar,
his anger blazing and his doom
heavy.
His lips are charged with wrath
and his tongue is a devouring fire.
28 His breath is like a torrent in spate,
rising neck-high,
a yoke to force the nations to their
ruin,
a bit in the mouth to guide the
peoples astray.
29 But for you there shall be songs,
as on a night of sacred pilgrimage,
your hearts glad, as the hearts of
men who walk to the sound of the
pipe
on their way to the Lord's hill, to
the rock of Israel.
30 Then the Lord shall make his
voice heard in majesty
and show his arm sweeping down
in fierce anger
with devouring flames of fire,
with cloudburst and tempests of
rain and hailstones;
31 for at the voice of the Lord
Assyria's heart fails her,
as she feels the stroke of his rod.

32 Tambourines and harps and shaking sistrums
shall keep time
with every stroke of his rod,
of the chastisement which the
Lord inflicts on her.
33 Long ago was Topheth made
ready,[b]
made deep and broad,
its fire-pit a blazing mass of logs,
and the breath of the Lord like a
stream of brimstone
blazing in it.

31 Shame upon those who go down to
Egypt for help
and rely on horses,
putting their trust in chariots
many in number
and in horsemen in their thousands,
but do not look to the Holy One of
Israel
or seek guidance of the Lord!
2 Yet the Lord too in his wisdom
can bring about trouble
and he does not take back his
words;
he will rise up against the league of
evildoers,
against all who help those who do
wrong.
3 The Egyptians are men, not God,[c]
their horses are flesh, not spirit;
and, when the Lord stretches out
his hand,
the helper will stumble and he who
is helped will fall,
and they will all vanish together.

4 This is what the Lord has said
to me:

As a lion or a young lion growls
over its prey
when the muster of shepherds is
called out against it,
and is not scared at their noise
or cowed by their clamour,
so shall the Lord of Hosts come
down to do battle
for Mount Zion and her high
summit.

---

[a] call them ordure: *or* say to them, Be off.
[b] *Prob. rdg.; Heb. adds* is that prepared also for the king?   [c] *Or* gods.

5 Thus the LORD of Hosts, like a
   bird hovering over its young,
   will be a shield over Jerusalem;
   he will shield her and deliver her,
   standing over her and delivering
   her.
6 O Israel, come back to him whom
   you have so deeply offended,
7 for on that day when you spurn,
   one and all,
   the idols of silver and the idols of
   gold
   which your own sinful hands have
   made,
8 Assyria shall fall by the sword, but
   by no sword of man;
   a sword that no man wields shall
   devour him.
   He shall flee before the sword,
   and his young warriors shall be put
   to forced labour,
9 his officers shall be helpless from
   terror
   and his captains too dismayed to
   flee.
   This is the very word of the LORD
   whose fire blazes in Zion,
   and whose furnace is set up in
   Jerusalem.

32 Behold, a king shall reign in
    righteousness
    and his rulers rule with justice,
2 and a man shall be a refuge from
   the wind
   and a shelter from the tempest,
   or like runnels of water in dry
   ground,
   like the shadow of a great rock in a
   thirsty land.
3 The eyes that can see will not be
   clouded,
   and the ears that can hear will
   listen;
4 the anxious heart will understand
   and know,
   and the man who stammers will at
   once speak plain.
5 The scoundrel will no longer be
   thought noble,
   nor the villain called a prince;
6 for the scoundrel will speak like a
   scoundrel

and will hatch evil in his heart;
he is an impostor in all his actions,
and in his words a liar even to the
   LORD;
he starves the hungry of their food
and refuses drink to the thirsty.
The villain's ways are villainous 7
and he devises infamous plans
to ruin the poor with his lies
and deny justice to the needy.
But the man of noble mind forms 8
   noble designs
and stands firm in his nobility.

You women that live at ease, 9
   stand up
and hear what I have to say.
You young women without a care,
   mark my words.
You have no cares now, but when 10
   the year is out, you will tremble,
for the vintage will be over and no
   produce gathered in.
You who are now at ease, be 11
   anxious;
tremble, you who have no cares.
Strip yourselves bare;
put a cloth round your waists
and beat your breasts 12
for the pleasant fields and fruitful
   vines.
On the soil of my people shall 13
   spring up thorns and briars,
in every happy home and in the
   busy town,
for the palace is forsaken and the 14
   crowded streets deserted;
citadel[a] and watch-tower are
   turned into open heath,
the joy of wild asses ever after and
   pasture for the flocks,
until a spirit from on high is 15
   lavished upon us.
Then the wilderness will become
   grassland
and grassland will be cheap as
   scrub;
then justice shall make its home in 16
   the wilderness,
and righteousness dwell in the
   grassland;
when righteousness shall yield 17
   peace

a Or hill; Heb. Ophel.

and its fruit be quietness and confidence for ever.

18 Then my people shall live in a tranquil country,
dwelling in peace, in houses full of ease;

19 it will be cool on the slopes of the forest then,
and cities shall lie peaceful in the plain.

20 Happy shall you be, sowing every man by the water-side,
and letting ox and ass run free.

33 Ah! you destroyer, yourself undestroyed,
betrayer still unbetrayed,
when you cease to destroy you will be destroyed,
after all your betrayals, you will be betrayed yourself.

2 O LORD, show us thy favour; we hope in thee.
Uphold us every morning,
save us when troubles come.

3 At the roar of the thunder the peoples flee,
at thy rumbling nations are scattered;

4 their spoil is swept up as if young locusts had swept it,
like a swarm of locusts men swarm upon it.

5 The LORD is supreme, for he dwells on high;
if you fill Zion with justice and with righteousness,

6 then he will be the mainstay of the age:[a]
wisdom and knowledge are the assurance of salvation;
the fear of the LORD is her[b] treasure.

7 Hark, how the valiant cry aloud for help,
and those sent to sue for peace weep bitterly!

8 The highways are deserted, no travellers tread the roads.

Covenants are broken, treaties are flouted;
man is of no account.

9 The land is parched and wilting,
Lebanon is eaten away and crumbling;
Sharon has become a desert,
Bashan and Carmel are stripped bare.

10 Now, says the LORD, I will rise up.
Now I will exalt myself, now lift myself up.

11 What you conceive and bring to birth is chaff and stubble;
a wind like fire shall devour you.

12 Whole nations shall be heaps of white ash,
or like thorns cut down and set on fire.

13 You who dwell far away, hear what I have done;
acknowledge my might, you who are near.

14 In Zion sinners quake with terror,
the godless are seized with trembling and ask,
Can any of us live with a devouring fire?
Can any live in endless burning?

15 The man who lives an upright life and speaks the truth,
who scorns to enrich himself by extortion,
who snaps his fingers at a bribe,
who stops his ears to hear nothing of bloodshed,
who closes his eyes to the sight of evil –

16 that is the man who shall dwell on the heights,
his refuge a fastness in the cliffs,
his bread secure and his water never failing.

17 Your eyes shall see a king in his splendour
and will look upon a land of far distances.

18 You will call to mind what once you feared:
'Where then is he that counted, where is he that weighed,

[a] the age: *prob. rdg.; Heb.* your times.   [b] *Prob. rdg.; Heb.* his.

where is he that counted the treasures?'

19 You will no longer see that barbarous people,
that people whose speech was so hard to catch,
whose stuttering speech you could not understand.

20 Look upon Zion, city of our solemn feasts,
let your eyes rest on Jerusalem,
a land of comfort, a tent that shall never be shifted,
whose pegs shall never be pulled up,
not one of its ropes cast loose.

21 There we have the LORD's majesty;[a]
it will be a place[b] of rivers and broad streams;
but[c] no galleys shall be rowed there,
no stately ship sail by.

22 For the LORD our judge, the LORD our law-giver,
the LORD our king – he himself will save us.

23 [Men may say, Your rigging is slack;
it will not hold the mast firm in its socket,
nor can the sails be spread.]
Then the blind man shall have a full share of the spoil
and the lame shall take part in the pillage;

24 no man who dwells there shall say, 'I am sick';
and the sins of the people who live there shall be pardoned.

Edom and Israel

34 Approach, you nations, to listen, and attend, you peoples;
let the earth listen and everything in it,
the world and all that it yields;

2 for the LORD's anger is turned against all the nations

and his wrath against all the host of them:
he gives them over to slaughter and destruction.

3 Their slain shall be flung out,
the stench shall rise from their corpses,
and the mountains shall stream with their blood.

4 All the host of heaven shall crumble into nothing,
the heavens shall be rolled up like a scroll,
and the starry host fade away,
as the leaf withers from the vine
and the ripening fruit from the fig-tree;

5 for the sword of the LORD[d] appears in heaven.
See how it descends in judgement on Edom,
on the people whom he dooms[e] to destruction.

6 The LORD has a sword steeped in blood,
it is gorged with fat,
the fat of rams' kidneys, and the blood of lambs and goats;
for he has a sacrifice in Bozrah,
a great slaughter in Edom.

7 Wild oxen shall come down and buffaloes[f] with them,
bull and bison together,
and the land shall drink deep of blood
and the soil be sated with fat.

8 For the LORD has a day of vengeance,
the champion of Zion has a year when he will requite.

9 Edom's torrents shall be turned into pitch
and its soil into brimstone,
and the land shall become blazing pitch,

10 which night and day shall never be quenched,
and its smoke shall go up for ever.
From generation to generation it shall lie waste,

---

[a] Or threshing-floor.   [b] it...place: or instead.   [c] Or and.
[d] the sword of the LORD: prob. rdg.; Heb. my sword.   [e] Prob. rdg.; Heb. I doom.
[f] and buffaloes: prob. rdg.; Heb. om.

and no man shall pass through it ever again.

11 Horned owl and bustard shall make their home in it,
screech-owl and raven shall haunt it.
He has stretched across it a measuring-line of chaos,

12 and its frontiers shall be a jumble of stones.
No king shall be acclaimed there, and all its princes shall come to nought.

13 Thorns shall sprout in its palaces; nettles and briars shall cover its walled towns.
It shall be rough land fit for wolves, a haunt of desert-owls.

14 Marmots shall consort with jackals, and he-goat shall encounter he-goat.
There too the nightjar shall rest and find herself a place for repose.

15 There the sand-partridge shall make her nest,
lay her eggs and hatch them and gather her brood under her wings;
there shall the kites gather, one after another.

16 Consult the book of the LORD and read it:
not one of these shall be lacking, not one miss its fellow,
for with his own mouth he has ordered it
and with his own breath he has brought them together.

17 He it is who has allotted each its place,
and his hand has measured out their portions;
they shall occupy it for ever
and dwell there from generation to generation.

35 Let the wilderness and the thirsty land be glad,
let the desert rejoice and burst into flower.

2 Let it flower with fields of asphodel,
let it rejoice and shout for joy.
The glory of Lebanon is given to it,
the splendour too of Carmel and Sharon;
these shall see the glory of the LORD, the splendour of our God.

3 Strengthen the feeble arms, steady the tottering knees;

4 say to the anxious, Be strong and fear not.
See, your God comes with vengeance,
with dread retribution he comes to save you.

5 Then shall blind men's eyes be opened,
and the ears of the deaf unstopped.

6 Then shall the lame man leap like a deer,
and the tongue of the dumb shout aloud;
for water springs up in the wilderness,
and torrents flow in dry land.

7 The mirage becomes a pool, the thirsty land bubbling springs;
instead of reeds and rushes, grass shall grow
in the rough land where wolves now lurk.

8 And there shall be a causeway there which shall be called the Way of Holiness,
and the unclean shall not pass along it;
it shall become a pilgrim's way,[a]
no fool shall trespass on it.

9 No lion shall come there, no savage beast climb on to it;
not one shall be found there.
By it those he has ransomed shall return

10 and the LORD's redeemed come home;
they shall enter Zion with shouts of triumph,
crowned with everlasting gladness.
Gladness and joy shall be their escort,
and suffering and weariness shall flee away.

[a] a pilgrim's way: *prob. rdg.; Heb. unintelligible.*

Jerusalem delivered from Sennacherib

36 1[a] IN the fourteenth year of the reign of Hezekiah, Sennacherib king of Assyria attacked and took all the fortified cities of Judah. 2 From Lachish he sent the chief officer[b] with a strong force to King Hezekiah at Jerusalem; and he halted by the conduit of the Upper Pool on the causeway which leads to the Fuller's 3 Field. There Eliakim son of Hilkiah, the comptroller of the household, came out to him, with Shebna the adjutant-general and Joah son of Asaph, the secretary of state. 4 The chief officer said to them, 'Tell Hezekiah that this is the message of the Great King, the king of Assyria: "What ground have you for 5 this confidence of yours? Do you think fine words can take the place of skill and numbers? On whom then do you rely for support in your 6 rebellion against me? On Egypt? Egypt is a splintered cane that will run into a man's hand and pierce it if he leans on it. That is what Pharaoh king of Egypt proves to all 7 who rely on him. And if you tell me that you are relying on the LORD your God, is he not the god whose hill-shrines and altars Hezekiah has suppressed, telling Judah and Jerusalem that they must prostrate themselves before this altar alone?" 8 'Now, make a bargain with my master the king of Assyria: I will give you two thousand horses if 9 you can find riders for them. Will you reject the authority of even the least of my master's servants and rely on Egypt for chariots and 10 horsemen? Do you think that I have come to attack this land and destroy it without the consent of the LORD? No; the LORD himself said to me, "Attack this land and destroy it."'

11 Eliakim, Shebna, and Joah said to the chief officer, 'Please speak to us in Aramaic, for we understand it; do not speak Hebrew to us within earshot of the people on the city wall.' The chief officer answered, 12 'Is it to your master and to you that my master has sent me to say this? Is it not to the people sitting on the wall who, like you, will have to eat their own dung and drink their own urine?' Then he stood 13 and shouted in Hebrew, 'Hear the message of the Great King, the king of Assyria. These are the 14 king's words: "Do not be taken in by Hezekiah. He cannot save you. Do not let him persuade you to 15 rely on the LORD, and tell you that the LORD will save you and that this city will never be surrendered to the king of Assyria." Do not 16 listen to Hezekiah; these are the words of the king of Assyria: "Make peace with me. Come out to me, and then you shall each eat the fruit of his own vine and his own fig-tree, and drink the water of his own cistern, until I come and take 17 you to a land like your own, a land of grain and new wine, of corn and vineyards. Beware lest Hezekiah 18 mislead you by telling you that the LORD will save you. Did the god of any of these nations save his land from the king of Assyria? Where 19 are the gods of Hamath and Arpad? Where are the gods of Sepharvaim? Where are the gods of Samaria? Did they save Samaria from me? Among all 20 the gods of these nations is there one who saved his land from me? And how is the LORD to save Jerusalem?"'

21 The people were silent and answered not a word, for the king had given orders that no one was to answer him. Eliakim son of Hilkiah, comptroller of the household, 22 Shebna the adjutant-general, and Joah son of Asaph, secretary of state, came to Hezekiah with their clothes rent and reported what the chief officer had said.

---

[a] *Verses 1–22: cp. 2 Kgs. 18. 13–37; 2 Chr. 32. 1–19.*　　　[b] *Or sent Rab-shakeh.*

37 1[a] When King Hezekiah heard their report, he rent his clothes and wrapped himself in sackcloth, and went into the house of the LORD. 2 He sent Eliakim comptroller of the household, Shebna the adjutant-general, and the senior priests, all covered in sackcloth, to the pro-3 phet Isaiah son of Amoz, to give him this message from the king: 'This day is a day of trouble for us, a day of reproof and contempt. We are like a woman who has no strength to bear the child that is 4 coming to the birth. It may be that the LORD your God heard the words of the chief officer whom his master the king of Assyria sent to taunt the living God, and will confute what he, the LORD your God, heard. Offer a prayer for those who 5 still survive.' King Hezekiah's ser-6 vants came to Isaiah, and he told them to say this to their master: 'This is the word of the LORD: "Do not be alarmed at what you heard when the lackeys of the king of 7 Assyria blasphemed me. I will put a spirit in him, and he shall hear a rumour and withdraw to his own country; and there I will make him fall by the sword."'

8 So the chief officer withdrew. He heard that the king of Assyria had left Lachish, and he found him at-9 tacking Libnah. But when the king learnt that Tirhakah king of Cush was on the way to make war on him, he sent messengers again[b] to 10 Hezekiah king of Judah, to say to him, 'How can you be deluded by your god on whom you rely when he promises that Jerusalem shall not fall into the hands of the king 11 of Assyria? Surely you have heard what the kings of Assyria have done to all countries, exterminating their people; can you then hope 12 to escape? Did their gods save the nations which my forefathers destroyed, Gozan, Harran, Rezeph, and the people of Beth-eden living

in Telassar? Where are the kings of 13 Hamath, of Arpad, and of Lahir, Sepharvaim, Hena, and Ivvah?'

Hezekiah took the letter from 14 the messengers and read it; then he went up into the house of the LORD, spread it out before the LORD and 15 offered this prayer: 'O LORD of 16 Hosts, God of Israel, enthroned on the cherubim, thou alone art God of all the kingdoms of the earth; thou hast made heaven and earth. Turn thy ear to me, O LORD, and 17 listen; open thine eyes, O LORD, and see; hear the message that Sennacherib has sent to taunt the living God. It is true, O LORD, that 18 the kings of Assyria have laid waste every country, that they 19 have consigned their gods to the fire and destroyed them; for they were no gods but the work of men's hands, mere wood and stone. But 20 now, O LORD our God, save us from his power, so that all the kingdoms of the earth may know that thou, O LORD, alone art God.'

Isaiah son of Amoz sent to Heze-21 kiah and said, 'This is the word of the LORD the God of Israel: I have heard your prayer to me concerning Sennacherib king of Assyria. This is the word which the LORD 22 has spoken concerning him:

The virgin daughter of Zion disdains you,
she laughs you to scorn;
the daughter of Jerusalem tosses
  her head
as you retreat.
Whom have you taunted and 23
  blasphemed?
Against whom have you clamoured,
casting haughty glances at the
  Holy One of Israel?
You have sent your servants to 24
  taunt the Lord,
and said:
With my countless chariots I have
  gone up

[a] Verses 1–38: cp. 2 Kgs. 19. 1–37; 2 Chr. 32. 20–22.
[b] again: prob. rdg., cp. 2 Kgs. 19. 9; Heb. and he heard.

high in the mountains, into the recesses of Lebanon.
I have cut down its tallest cedars,
the best of its pines,
I have reached its highest limit of forest and meadow.[a]

25 I have dug wells
and drunk the waters of a foreign land,
and with the soles of my feet I have dried up
all the streams of Egypt.

26 Have you not heard long ago?
I did it all.
In days gone by I planned it
and now I have brought it about,
making fortified cities tumble down into heaps of rubble.

27 Their citizens, shorn of strength,
disheartened and ashamed,
were but as plants in the field, as green herbs,
as grass on the roof-tops blasted before the east wind.

28 I know your rising up and your sitting down,
your going out and your coming in.

29 The frenzy of your rage against me and your arrogance
have come to my ears.
I will put a ring in your nose
and a hook in your lips,
and I will take you back by the road
on which you have come.

30 This shall be the sign for you: this year you shall eat shed grain and in the second year what is self-sown; but in the third year sow and reap, plant vineyards and eat their fruit.

31 The survivors left in Judah shall strike fresh root under ground and

32 yield fruit above ground, for a remnant shall come out of Jerusalem and survivors from Mount Zion. The zeal of the LORD of Hosts will perform this.

33 'Therefore, this is the word of the LORD concerning the king of Assyria:

He shall not enter this city
nor shoot an arrow there,
he shall not advance against it with shield
nor cast up a siege-ramp against it.

34 By the way on which he came he shall go back;
this city he shall not enter.
This is the very word of the LORD.

35 I will shield this city to deliver it, for my own sake and for the sake of my servant David.'

36 The angel of the LORD went out and struck down a hundred and eighty-five thousand men in the Assyrian camp; when morning dawned, they all lay dead. So Sen-

37 nacherib king of Assyria broke camp, went back to Nineveh and

38 stayed there. One day, while he was worshipping in the temple of his god Nisroch, Adrammelech and Sharezer his sons murdered him and escaped to the land of Ararat. He was succeeded by his son Esarhaddon.

38 1[b] At this time Hezekiah fell dangerously ill and the prophet Isaiah son of Amoz came to him and said, 'This is the word of the LORD: Give your last instructions to your household, for you are a dying man and will not recover.' Hezekiah

2 turned his face to the wall and

3 offered this prayer to the LORD: 'O LORD, remember how I have lived before thee, faithful and loyal in thy service, always doing what was good in thine eyes.' And he wept

4 bitterly. Then the word of the

5 LORD came to Isaiah: 'Go and say to Hezekiah: "This is the word of the LORD the God of your father David: I have heard your prayer and seen your tears; I will add fifteen years to your life. I will

6 deliver you and this city from the king of Assyria and will protect this city."' Then Isaiah told them

21[c] to apply a fig-plaster; so they made one and applied it to the boil, and

---

[a] and meadow: *prob. rdg.*; *Heb.* its meadow.
[b] Verses 1–8, 21, 22: cp. 2 Kgs. 20. 1–11.
[c] Verses 21, 22 transposed.

22 he recovered. Then Hezekiah said, 'By what sign shall I know that I shall go up into the house of the 7 LORD?' And Isaiah said,[a] 'This shall be your sign from the LORD that he will do what he has pro- 8 mised. Watch the shadow cast by the sun on the stairway of Ahaz: I will bring backwards ten steps the shadow which has gone down on the stairway.' And the sun went back ten steps on the stairway down which it had gone.

9   A poem of Hezekiah king of Judah after his recovery from his illness, as it was written down:

10 I thought: In the prime of life I
     must pass away;
     for the rest of my years I am con-
     signed to the gates of Sheol.
11 I said: I shall no longer see the
     LORD
     in the land of the living;
     never again, like those who live in
     the world,
     shall I look on a man.
12 My dwelling is taken from me,
     pulled up like a shepherd's tent;
     thou hast cut short my life like a
     weaver
     who severs the web from the thrum.
     From morning to night thou tor-
     mentest me.
13 then I am racked with pain till the
     morning.
     All my bones are broken, as a lion
     would break them;
     from morning to night thou tor-
     mentest me.
14 I twitter as if I were a swallow,
     I moan like a dove.
     My eyes falter as I look up to the
     heights;
     O Lord, pay heed, stand surety for
     me.
15 How can I complain, what can I
     say to the LORD
     when he himself has done this?
     I wander to and fro all my life long
     in the bitterness of my soul.

Yet, O Lord, my soul shall live 16
     with thee;
do thou give my spirit rest.[b]
Restore me and give me life.
Bitterness had indeed been my lot 17
     in place of prosperity;
but thou by thy love hast brought
     me back
from the pit of destruction;
for thou hast cast all my sins be-
     hind thee.
Sheol cannot confess thee, 18
Death cannot praise thee,
nor can they who go down to the
     abyss
hope for thy truth.
The living, the living alone can 19
     confess thee
as I do this day,
as a father makes thy truth known,
     O God, to his sons.
The LORD is at hand to save me; 20
so let us sound the music of our
     praises
all our life long in the house of the
     LORD.[c]

     At this time Merodach-baladan 39 1[d] son of Baladan king of Babylon sent envoys with a gift to Heze- kiah; for he had heard that he had been ill and was well again. Heze- 2 kiah welcomed them and showed them all his treasury, silver and gold, spices and fragrant oil, his entire armoury and everything to be found among his treasures; there was nothing in his house and in all his realm that Hezekiah did not show them. Then the prophet 3 Isaiah came to King Hezekiah and asked him, 'What did these men say and where have they come from?' 'They have come from a far- off country,' Hezekiah answered, 'from Babylon.' Then Isaiah asked, 4 'What did they see in your house?' 'They saw everything,' Hezekiah replied; 'there was nothing among my treasures that I did not show them.' Then Isaiah said to Heze- 5

---

[a] *And Isaiah said: prob. rdg., cp.* 2 Kgs. 20. 9; *Heb. om.*
[b] Yet...rest: *prob. rdg.; Heb. unintelligible.*
[c] *Verses 21, 22 transposed to follow verse 6.*   [d] *Verses 1–8: cp.* 2 Kgs. 20. 12–19.

kiah, 'Hear the word of the LORD
6 of Hosts: The time is coming, says
the LORD, when everything in your
house, and all that your forefathers
have amassed till the present day,
will be carried away to Babylon;
7 not a thing shall be left. And some
of the sons who will be born to you,
sons of your own begetting, shall be
taken and shall be made eunuchs
in the palace of the king of Baby-
8 lon.' Hezekiah answered, 'The
word of the LORD which you have
spoken is good'; thinking to himself that peace and security would
last out his lifetime.

News of the returning exiles

40 Comfort, comfort my people;[a]
   – it is the voice of your God;
2 speak tenderly to Jerusalem[b]
and tell her this,
   that she has fulfilled her term of
      bondage,
   that her penalty is paid;
   she has received at the LORD's
      hand
   double[c] measure for all her sins.

3 There is a voice that cries:
   Prepare a road for the LORD
      through the wilderness,
   clear a highway across the desert
      for our God.
4 Every valley shall be lifted up,
   every mountain and hill brought
      down;
   rugged places shall be made smooth
   and mountain-ranges become a
      plain.
5 Thus shall the glory of the LORD
      be revealed,
   and all mankind together shall see
      it;
   for the LORD himself has spoken.

6 A voice says, 'Cry',
   and another asks, 'What shall I
      cry?'

'That all mankind is grass,
   they last no longer than a flower of
      the field.
The grass withers, the flower fades, 7
   when the breath of[d] the LORD
      blows upon them;[e]
the grass withers, the flowers fade, 8
   but the word of our God endures
      for evermore.'

You who bring Zion good news,[f] up 9
   with you to the mountain-top;
lift up your voice and shout,
you who bring good news to Jeru-
      salem,[g]
lift it up fearlessly;
cry to the cities of Judah, 'Your
      God is here.'
Here is the Lord GOD coming in 10
      might,
coming to rule with his right arm.
His recompense comes with him,
he carries his reward before him.
He will tend his flock like a 11
      shepherd
and gather them together with his
      arm;
he will carry the lambs in his bosom
and lead the ewes to water.

Israel delivered and redeemed

Who has gauged the waters in the 12
   palm of his hand,
or with its span set limits to the
   heavens?
Who has held all the soil of earth
   in a bushel,
or weighed the mountains on a
   balance
and the hills on a pair of scales?
Who has set limits to the spirit of 13
   the LORD?
What counsellor stood at his side
   to instruct him?
With whom did he confer to gain 14
   discernment?
Who taught him how to do justice
or gave him lessons in wisdom?

[a] Comfort...people: *or* Comfort, O my people, comfort.
[b] speak...Jerusalem: *or* bid Jerusalem be of good heart. [c] double: *or* full.
[d] the breath of: *or* a wind from. [e] *Prob. rdg.*; *Heb. adds* surely the people
are grass. [f] You...news: *or* O Zion, bringer of good news.
[g] you...Jerusalem: *or* O Jerusalem, bringer of good news.

15 Why, to him nations are but drops
   from a bucket,
no more than moisture on the
   scales;
coasts and islands weigh as light as
   specks of dust.
16 All Lebanon does not yield wood
   enough for fuel
or beasts enough for a sacrifice.
17 All nations dwindle to nothing
   before him,
he reckons them mere nothings,
   less than nought.

18 What likeness will you find for
   God
or what form to resemble his?
19 Is it an image which a craftsman
   sets up,
and a goldsmith covers with plate
and fits with studs of silver as a
   costly gift?
20 Or is it mulberry-wood that will
   not rot which a man chooses,
seeking out a skilful craftsman for
   it,
to mount an image that will not
   fall?

[6*a*] Each workman helps the others,
each man encourages his fellow.
[7*a*] The craftsman urges on the goldsmith,
the gilder urges the man who beats
   the anvil,
he declares the soldering to be
   sound;
he fastens the image with nails
so that it will not fall down.

21 Do you not know, have you not
   heard,
were you not told long ago,
have you not perceived ever since
   the world began,
22 that God sits throned on the vaulted
   roof of earth,
whose inhabitants are like grasshoppers*b*?
He stretches out the skies like a
   curtain,

he spreads them out like a tent to
   live in;
he reduces the great to nothing   23
and makes all earth's princes less
   than nothing.
Scarcely are they planted, scarcely 24
   sown,
scarcely have they taken root in
   the earth,
before he blows upon them and
   they wither away,
and a whirlwind carries them off
   like chaff.
To whom then will you liken me,   25
   whom set up as my equal?
asks the Holy One.
Lift up your eyes to the heavens;   26
   consider who created it all,
led out their host one by one
and called them all by their names;
through his great might, his might
   and power,
not one is missing.
Why do you complain, O Jacob,   27
and you, Israel, why do you say,
'My plight is hidden from the LORD
and my cause has passed out of
   God's notice'?
Do you not know, have you not   28
   heard?
The LORD, the everlasting God,
   creator of the wide world,
grows neither weary nor faint;
no man can fathom his understanding.
He gives vigour to the weary,   29
new strength to the exhausted.
Young men may grow weary and   30
   faint,
even in their prime they may
   stumble and fall;
but those who look to the LORD   31
   will win new strength,
they will grow wings like eagles;
they will run and not be weary,
they will march on and never grow
   faint.

Keep silence before me, all you   41
   coasts and islands;
let the peoples come to meet me.*c*

---

a *These are verses 6 and 7 of ch. 41, transposed to this point.*   *b Or locusts.*
c come to meet me: *prob. rdg., transposing, with slight change, from end of verse 5;*
Heb. win new strength *(repeated from* 40. 31*).*

Let them come near, then let them
  speak;
we will meet at the place of judgement, I and they.
2 Tell me, who raised up that one
  from the east,
one greeted by victory wherever he
  goes?
Who is it that puts nations into his
  power
and makes kings go down before
  him,[a]
he scatters them with his sword
  like dust
and with his bow like chaff before
  the wind;
3 he puts them to flight and passes
  on unscathed,
swifter than any traveller on foot?
4 Whose work is this, I ask, who has
  brought it to pass?
Who has summoned the generations from the beginning?
It is I, the LORD, I am the first,
and to the last of them I am He.
5 Coasts and islands saw it and were
  afraid,
the world trembled from end to
  end.[b]

8[c] But you, Israel my servant,
you, Jacob whom I have chosen,
race of Abraham my friend,
9 I have taken you up,
have fetched you from the ends of
  the earth,
and summoned you from its farthest corners,
I have called you my servant,
have chosen you and not cast you
  off:
10 fear nothing, for I am with you;
be not afraid, for I am your God.
I strengthen you, I help you,
I support you with my victorious
  right hand.

11 Now shall all who defy you
be disappointed and put to shame;
all who set themselves against you
shall be as nothing; they shall
  vanish.

You will look for your assailants 12
  but not find them;
all who take up arms against you
shall be as nothing, nothing at all.
For I, the LORD your God, 13
take you by the right hand;
I say to you, Do not fear;
it is I who help you,
fear not, Jacob you worm and 14
  Israel poor louse.
It is I who help you, says the
  LORD,
your ransomer, the Holy One of
  Israel.
See, I will make of you a sharp 15
  threshing-sledge,
new and studded with teeth;
you shall thresh the mountains
  and crush them
and reduce the hills to chaff;
you shall winnow them, the wind 16
  shall carry them away
and a great gale shall scatter them.
Then shall you rejoice in the LORD
and glory in the Holy One of Israel.

The wretched and the poor look 17
  for water and find none,
their tongues are parched with
  thirst;
but I the LORD will give them an
  answer,
I, the God of Israel, will not forsake
  them.
I will open rivers among the sand- 18
  dunes
and wells in the valleys;
I will turn the wilderness into pools
and dry land into springs of water;
I will plant cedars in the wastes, 19
and acacia and myrtle and wild
  olive;
the pine shall grow on the barren
  heath
side by side with fir and box,
that men may see and know, 20
may once for all give heed and
  understand
that the LORD himself has done
  this,
that the Holy One of Israel has
  performed it.

[a] before him: *prob. rdg.*; *Heb. om.*   [b] *See note on verse 1.*
[c] *Verses 6 and 7 transposed to follow 40. 20.*

21 Come, open your plea, says the
   LORD,
   present your case, says Jacob's
      King;
22 let them come forward, these idols,
   let them foretell the future.
   Let them declare the meaning of
      past events
   that we may give our minds to it;
   let them predict things that are to
      be
   that we may know their outcome.
23 Declare what will happen here-
      after;
   then we shall know you are gods.
   Do what you can, good or ill,
   anything that may grip us with
      fear and awe.
24 You cannot! You are sprung from
      nothing,
   your works are rotten;
   whoever chooses you is vile as you
      are.
25 I roused one from the north, and he
      obeyed;
   I called one from the east, sum-
      moned him in[a] my name,
   he marches over viceroys as if they
      were mud,
   like a potter treading his clay.
26 Tell us, who declared this from the
      beginning, that we might know it,
   or told us beforehand so that we
      could say, 'He was right'?
   Not one declared, not one foretold,
   not one heard a sound from you.
27 Here is one who will speak first as
      advocate for Zion,
   here I appoint defending counsel
      for Jerusalem;
28 but from the other side no advo-
      cate steps forward
   and, when I look, there is no one
      there.
   I ask a question and no one answers;
29 see what empty things they are!
   Nothing that they do has any
      worth,
   their effigies are wind, mere
      nothings.

Here is my servant, whom I up- 42
   hold,
my chosen one in whom I delight,
I have bestowed my spirit upon
   him,
and he will make justice shine on
   the nations.
He will not call out or lift his voice 2
   high,
or[b] make himself heard in the open
   street.
He will not break a bruised reed, 3
or snuff out a smouldering wick;
he will make justice shine on every
   race,[c]
never faltering, never breaking 4
   down,[d]
he will plant justice on earth,
while coasts and islands wait for
   his teaching.

Thus speaks the LORD who is God, 5
he who created the skies and
   stretched them out,
who fashioned the earth and all
   that grows in it,
who gave breath to its people,
the breath of life to all who walk
   upon it:
I, the LORD, have called you with 6
   righteous purpose
and taken you by the hand;
I have formed you, and appointed
   you
to be a light[e] to all peoples,
a beacon for the nations,
to open eyes that are blind, 7
to bring captives out of prison,
out of the dungeons where they lie
   in darkness.
I am the LORD; the LORD[f] is my 8
   name;
I will not give my glory to another
   god,
nor my praise to any idol.
See how the first prophecies have 9
   come to pass,
and now I declare new things;
before they break from the bud I
   announce them to you.

---

[a] summoned him in: *or* who will call on.
he will call out and lift his voice high, and...
[d] never faltering...down: *or* he will neither rebuke nor wound.
[e] Or a covenant.

[b] He will not...or: *or* In very truth
      [c] on every race: *or* in truth.

[f] the LORD: *or* He.

10 Sing a new song to the LORD,
   sing his praise throughout the
     earth,
   you that sail the sea, and all sea-
     creatures,
   and you that inhabit the coasts
     and islands.
11 Let the wilderness and its towns
     rejoice,
   and the villages of the tribe of
     Kedar.
   Let those who live in Sela shout
     for joy
   and cry out from the hill-tops.
12 You coasts and islands, all uplift
     his praises;
   let all ascribe glory to the LORD.
13 The LORD will go forth as a warrior,
   he will rouse the frenzy of battle
     like a hero;
   he will shout, he will raise the
     battle-cry
   and triumph over his foes.
14 Long have I lain still,
   I kept silence and held myself in
     check;
   now I will cry like a woman in
     labour,
   whimpering, panting and gasping.
15 I will lay waste mountains and
     hills
   and shrivel all their green herbs;
   I will turn rivers into desert wastes[a]
   and dry up all the pools.
16 Then will I lead blind men on their
     way[b]
   and guide them by paths they do
     not know;
   I will turn darkness into light
     before them
   and straighten their twisting roads.
   All this I will do and leave nothing
     undone.
17 Those who trust in an image,
   those who take idols for their gods
   turn tail in bitter shame.

18 Hear now, you that are deaf;
   you blind men, look and see:
19 yet who is blind but my servant,
   who so deaf as the messenger whom
     I send?

Who so blind as the one who holds
   my commission,
so deaf as the servant of the
   LORD?
You have seen much but re- 20
   membered little,
your ears are wide open but nothing is heard.
It pleased the LORD, for the fur- 21
   therance of his justice,
to make his law a law of surpassing
   majesty;
yet here is a people plundered and 22
   taken as prey,
all of them ensnared, trapped in
   holes,
lost to sight in dungeons,
carried off as spoil without hope of
   rescue,
as plunder with no one to say,
   'Give it back.'
Hear this, all of you who will,   23
listen henceforward and give me a
   hearing:
who gave away Jacob for plunder, 24
who gave Israel away for spoil?
Was it not the LORD? They sinned
   against him,
they would not follow his ways
and refused obedience to his law;
so in his anger he poured out upon 25
   Jacob
his wrath and the fury of battle.
It wrapped him in flames, yet still
   he did not learn the lesson,
scorched him, yet he did not lay it
   to heart.

But now this is the word of the 43
   LORD,
the word of your creator, O Jacob,
of him who fashioned you, Israel:
Have no fear; for I have paid your
   ransom;
I have called you by name and you
   are my own.
When you pass through deep 2
   waters, I am with you,
when you pass through rivers,
   they will not sweep you away;
walk through fire and you will not
   be scorched,

---

[a] desert wastes: *prob. rdg.*; *Heb.* coasts and islands.
[b] *Prob. rdg.*; *Heb. adds* which they do not know.

through flames and they will not
burn you.

3 For I am the LORD your God,
the Holy One of Israel, your
deliverer;
for your ransom I give Egypt,
Nubia and Seba are your price.

4 You are more precious to me than
the Assyrians,
you are honoured and I have
loved you,
I would give the Edomites in exchange for you,
and the Leummim for your life.

5 Have no fear; for I am with you;
I will bring your children from the
east
and gather you all from the west.

6 I will say to the north, 'Give them
up',
and to the south, 'Do not hold
them back.
Bring my sons and daughters from
afar,
bring them from the ends of the
earth;

7 bring every one who is called by
my name,
all whom I have created, whom I
have formed,
all whom I have made for my
glory.'

8 Bring out this people,
a people who have eyes but are
blind,
who have ears but are deaf.

9 All the nations are gathered together
and the peoples assembled.
Who amongst them can expound
this thing
and interpret for us all that has
gone before?
Let them produce witnesses to
prove their case,
or let them listen and say, 'That is
the truth.'

10 My witnesses, says the LORD, are
you, my servants,
you whom I have chosen
to know me and put your faith in
me
and understand that I am He.

Before me there was no god
fashioned
nor ever shall be after me.
I am the LORD, I myself,   11
and none but I can deliver.
I myself have made it known in   12
full, and declared it,
I and no alien god amongst you,
and you are my witnesses, says the
LORD.
I am God; from this very day I am   13
He.
What my hand holds, none can
snatch away;
what I do, none can undo.

Thus says the LORD your ran-   14
somer, the Holy One of Israel:
For your sakes I have sent to
Babylon;
I will lay the Chaldaeans prostrate
as they flee,
and their cry of triumph will turn
to groaning.
I am the LORD, your Holy One,   15
your creator, Israel, and your
King.

Thus says the LORD,   16
who opened a way in the sea
and a path through mighty waters,
who drew on chariot and horse to   17
their destruction,
a whole army, men of valour;
there they lay, never to rise again;
they were crushed, snuffed out like
a wick:
Cease to dwell on days gone by   18
and to brood over past history.
Here and now I will do a new   19
thing;
this moment it will break from the
bud.
Can you not perceive it?
I will make a way even through the
wilderness
and paths in the barren desert;
the wild beasts shall do me honour, 20
the wolf and the ostrich;
for I will provide water in the wilderness
and rivers in the barren desert,
where my chosen people may
drink.

21 I have formed this people for myself
and they shall proclaim my praises.
22 Yet you did not call upon me, O
Jacob;
much less did you weary yourself
in my service, O Israel.
23 You did not bring me sheep as
whole-offerings
or honour me with sacrifices;
I asked you for no burdensome
offerings
and wearied you with no demands
for incense.
24 You did not buy me sweet-cane
with your money
or glut me with the fat of your
sacrifices;
rather you burdened me with your
sins
and wearied me with your iniquities.
25 I alone, I am He,
who for his own sake wipes out
your transgressions,
who will remember your sins no
more.
26 Cite me by name, let us argue it out;
set forth your pleading and justify
yourselves.
27 Your first father transgressed,
your spokesmen rebelled against
me,
28 and your princes profaned my
sanctuary;
so I sent Jacob to his doom
and left Israel to execration.

44 Hear me now, Jacob my servant,
hear me, my chosen Israel.
2 Thus says the LORD your maker,
your helper, who fashioned you
from birth:
have no fear, Jacob my servant,
Jeshurun whom I have chosen,
3 for I will pour down rain on a
thirsty land,
showers on the dry ground.
I will pour out my spirit on your
offspring
and my blessing on your children.

They shall spring up like a green 4
tamarisk,
like poplars by a flowing stream.
This man shall say, 'I am the 5
LORD's man',
that one shall call himself a son of
Jacob,
another shall write the LORD's
name on his hand
and shall add the name of Israel to
his own.

Thus says the LORD, Israel's King, 6
the LORD of Hosts, his ransomer:
I am the first and I am the last,
and there is no god but me.
Who is like me? Let him stand 7
up,
let him declare himself and speak
and show me his evidence,
let him announce beforehand[a]
things to come,
let him[b] declare what is yet to
happen.
Take heart, do not be afraid. 8
Did I not foretell this long ago?
I declared it, and you are my
witnesses.
Is there any god beside me,
or any creator, even one that I do
not know?
Those who make idols are less than 9
nothing;
all their cherished images profit
nobody;
their worshippers are blind,
sheer ignorance makes fools of
them.
If a man makes a god or casts an 10
image,
his labour is wasted.
Why! its votaries show their folly; 11
the craftsmen too are but men.
Let them all gather together and
confront me,
all will be afraid and look the fools
they are.

The blacksmith sharpens a grav- 12
ing tool and hammers out his work[c]
hot from the coals and shapes it

---

[a] *let him announce beforehand*: *prob. rdg.*; *Heb.* since my appointing an ancient
people and...   [b] *Prob. rdg.*; *Heb.* them.
[c] *his work*: *prob. rdg.*; *Heb.* he works.

with his strong arm; when he grows hungry his strength fails, if he has 13 no water to drink he tires. The woodworker draws his line taut and marks out a figure with a scriber; he planes the wood and measures it with callipers, and he carves it to the shape of a man, comely as the human form, to be set up presently in a house.[a]

14 A man plants a cedar and the rain makes it grow, so that later on he will have cedars to cut down; or he chooses an ilex or an oak to raise a stout tree for himself in the 15 forest. It becomes fuel for his fire: some of it he takes and warms himself, some he kindles and bakes bread on it, and some he makes into a god and prostrates himself, shaping it into an idol and bowing 16 down before it. The one half of it he burns in the fire and on this he roasts meat, so that he may eat his roast and be satisfied; he also warms himself at it and he says, 'Good! I can feel the heat, I am 17 growing warm.' Then what is left of the wood he makes into a god by carving it into shape; he bows down to it and prostrates himself and prays to it, saying, 'Save me; for 18 thou art my god.' Such people neither know nor understand, their eyes made too blind to see, their 19 minds too narrow to discern. Such a man will not use his reason, he has neither the wit nor the sense to say, 'Half of it I have burnt, yes, and used its embers to bake bread; I have roasted meat on them too and eaten it; but the rest of it I turn into this abominable thing and so I am worshipping a log of 20 wood.' He feeds on ashes indeed! His own deluded mind has misled him, he cannot recollect himself so far as to say, 'Why! this thing in my hand is a sham.'

21 Remember all this, Jacob, remember, Israel, for you are my servant,

I have fashioned you, and you are to serve me; you shall not forget me, Israel. I have swept away your sins like a 22 dissolving mist, and your transgressions are dispersed like clouds; turn back to me; for I have ransomed you. Shout in triumph, you heavens, for 23 it is the LORD's doing; cry out for joy, you lowest depths of the earth; break into songs of triumph, you mountains, you forest and all your trees; for the LORD has ransomed Jacob and made Israel his masterpiece.

Thus says the LORD, your ran- 24 somer, who fashioned you from birth: I am the LORD who made all things, by myself I stretched out the skies, alone I hammered out the floor of the earth. I frustrate false prophets and their 25 signs and make fools of diviners; I reverse what wise men say and make nonsense of their wisdom. I make my servants' prophecies 26 come true and give effect to my messengers' designs. I say of Jerusalem, 'She shall be inhabited once more', and of the cities of Judah, 'They shall be rebuilt; all their ruins I will restore.' I say to the deep waters, 'Be dried 27 up; I will make your streams run dry.' I say to Cyrus, 'You shall be my 28 shepherd to carry out all my purpose, so that Jerusalem may be rebuilt and the foundations of the temple may be laid.'

Thus says the LORD to Cyrus his 45 anointed,

---

[a] *Or* a shrine.

Cyrus whom he has taken by the hand
to subdue nations before him
and undo the might of kings;
before whom gates shall be opened
and no doors be shut:
2 I will go before you
and level the swelling hills;
I will break down gates of bronze
and hack through iron bars.
3 I will give you treasures from dark vaults,
hoarded in secret places,
that you may know that I am the LORD,
Israel's God who calls you by name.
4 For the sake of Jacob my servant
and Israel my chosen
I have called you by name
and given you your title, though you have not known me.
5 I am the LORD, there is no other;
there is no god beside me.
I will strengthen you though you have not known me,
6 so that men from the rising and the setting sun
may know that there is none but I:
I am the LORD, there is no other;
7 I make the light, I create darkness, author alike of prosperity and trouble.
I, the LORD, do all these things.

8 Rain righteousness, you heavens,
let the skies above pour down;
let the earth open to receive it,
that it may bear the fruit of salvation
with righteousness in blossom at its side.
All this I, the LORD, have created.

9 Will the pot contend[a] with the potter,
or the earthenware[b] with the hand that shapes it?
Will the clay ask the potter what he is making?

or his[c] handiwork say to him, 'You have no skill'?
Will the babe say[d] to his father, 10 'What are you begetting?',
or to his mother, 'What are you bringing to birth?'
Thus says the LORD, Israel's Holy 11 One, his maker:
Would you dare question me concerning my children,
or instruct me in my handiwork?
I alone, I made the earth 12 and created man upon it;
I, with my own hands, stretched out the heavens
and caused all their host to shine.
I alone have roused this man in 13 righteousness,
and I will smooth his path before him;
he shall rebuild my city
and let my exiles go free –
not for a price nor for a bribe,
says the LORD of Hosts.

Thus says the LORD: 14
Toilers of Egypt and Nubian merchants
and Sabaeans bearing tribute[e]
shall come into your power and be your slaves,
shall come and march behind you in chains;
they shall bow down before you in supplication, saying,
'Surely God is among you and there is no other,
no other god.
How then canst thou be a god that 15 hidest thyself,
O God of Israel, the deliverer?'

Those who defy him are con- 16 founded and brought to shame,
those who make idols perish in confusion.
But Israel has been delivered by 17 the LORD,
delivered for all time to come;
they shall not be confounded or put to shame for all eternity.

---

[a] Will...contend: *prob. rdg.*; *Heb.* Ho! he has contended.　　　　[b] *Or* shard.
[c] *Prob. rdg.*; *Heb.* your.　　　[d] Will...say: *prob. rdg.*; *Heb.* Ho! you that say.
[e] bearing tribute: *or* men of stature.

18 Thus says the LORD, the creator of
   the heavens,
he who is God,
who made the earth and fashioned
   it
and himself fixed it fast,
who created it no empty void,
but made it for a place to dwell in:
I am the LORD, there is no other.

19 I do not speak in secret, in realms
   of darkness,
I do not say to the sons of Jacob,
'Look for me in the empty void.'
I the LORD speak what is right,
   declare what is just.

20 Gather together, come, draw near,
all you survivors of the nations,
you fools, who carry your wooden
   idols in procession
and pray to a god that cannot save
   you.

21 Come forward and urge your case,
   consult together:
who foretold this in days of old,
who stated it long ago?
Was it not I the LORD?
There is no god but me;
there is no god other than I, victorious and able to save.

22 Look to me and be saved,
you peoples from all corners of the
   earth;
for I am God, there is no other.

23 By my life I have sworn,
I have given a promise of victory,
a promise that will not be broken,
that to me every knee shall bend
and by me every tongue shall
   swear.

24 In the LORD alone, men shall say,
   are victory and might;
and all who defy him
shall stand ashamed in his presence,

25 but all the sons of Israel shall stand
   victorious
and find their glory in the LORD.

46 Bel has crouched down, Nebo has
   stooped low:
their images, once carried in your
   processions,
have been loaded on to beasts and
   cattle,

a burden for the weary creatures;
they stoop and they crouch;   2
not for them to bring the burden to
   safety;
the gods themselves go into captivity.

Listen to me, house of Jacob   3
and all the remnant of the house of
   Israel,
a load on me from your birth,
   carried by me from the womb:
till you grow old I am He,   4
and when white hairs come, I will
   carry you still;
I have made you and I will bear
   the burden,
I will carry you and bring you to
   safety.

To whom will you liken me? Who   5
   is my equal?
With whom can you compare me?
   Where is my like?
Those who squander their bags of   6
   gold
and weigh out their silver with a
   balance
hire a goldsmith to fashion them
   into a god;
then they worship it and fall
   prostrate before it;
they hoist it shoulder-high and   7
   carry it home;
they set it down on its base;
there it must stand, it cannot stir
   from its place.
Let a man cry to it as he will, it
   never answers him;
it cannot deliver him from his
   troubles.

Remember this, you rebels,   8
consider it well, and abandon hope,
remember all that happened long   9
   ago;
for I am God, there is no other,
I am God, and there is no one like
   me;
I reveal the end from the be-   10
   ginning,
from ancient times I reveal what is
   to be;
I say, 'My purpose shall take effect,
I will accomplish all that I please.'

11 I summon a bird of prey[a] from the
      east,
   one from a distant land to fulfil my
      purpose.
   Mark this; I have spoken, and I will
      bring it about,
   I have a plan to carry out, and
      carry it out I will.
12 Listen to me, all you stubborn
      hearts,
   for whom victory is far off:
13 I bring my victory near, it is not
      far off,
   and my deliverance shall not be
      delayed;
   I will grant deliverance in Zion
   and give my glory to Israel.[b]

47 Down with you, sit in the dust,
      virgin daughter of Babylon.
   Down from your throne, sit on the
      ground,
   daughter of the Chaldaeans;
   never again shall men call you
      soft-skinned and delicate.
 2 Take up the millstone, grind meal,
      uncover your tresses;
   strip off your skirt, bare your
      thighs, wade through rivers,
 3 so that your nakedness may be
      plain to see
   and your shame exposed.
   I will take vengeance, I will treat
      with none of you,
 4 says the Holy One of Israel, our
      ransomer,
   whose name is the LORD of Hosts.

 5 Sit silent,
   be off into the shadows, daughter
      of the Chaldaeans;
   for never again shall men call
      you
   queen of many kingdoms.
 6 When I was angry with my people,
   I dishonoured my own possession
   and gave them into your power.
   You showed them no mercy,
   you made your yoke weigh heavy
      on the aged.

You said then, 'I shall reign a 7
   queen for ever',
while[c] you gave no thought to
   this
and did not consider how it would
   end.
Now therefore listen to this,   8
you lover of luxury, carefree on
   your throne.
You say to yourself,
'I am, and who but I?
No widow's weeds for me, no
   deaths of children.'
Yet suddenly, in a single day,   9
these two things shall come upon
   you;
they shall both come upon you in
   full measure:[d]
children's deaths and widowhood,
for all your monstrous sorceries,
   your countless spells.
Secure in your wicked ways you   10
   thought, 'No one is looking.'
Your wisdom betrayed you, omniscient as you were,
and you said to yourself,
'I am, and who but I?'
Therefore evil shall come upon you, 11
and you will not know how to
   master it;
disaster shall befall you,
and you will not be able to charm
   it away;
ruin all unforeseen
shall come suddenly upon you.
Persist in your spells and your   12
   monstrous sorceries,[e]
maybe you can get help from them,
maybe you will yet inspire awe.
But no! in spite of your many wiles 13
   you are powerless.
Let your astrologers, your star-
   gazers
who foretell your future month by
   month,
persist, and save you!
But look, they are gone like chaff; 14
fire burns them up;
they cannot snatch themselves
   from the flames;

---

[a] a bird of prey: *or* a massed host.   [b] and give my glory to Israel: *or* for
Israel my glory.   [c] for ever', while: *or* of a wide realm, for all time'; but.
[d] in full measure: *or* at random.
[e] *Prob. rdg.*; *Heb. adds* with which you have trafficked all your life (*cp. verse* 15).

this is no glowing coal to warm
them,
no fire for them to sit by.
So much for your magicians
with whom you have trafficked all
your life:
they have stumbled off, each his
own way,
and there is no one to save you.

48 Hear this, you house of Jacob,
you who are called by the name of
Israel,
you who spring from the seed of
Judah;
who swear by the name of the LORD
and boast in the God of Israel,
but not in honesty or sincerity,
2 although you call yourselves citizens of a holy city
and lean for support on the God of
Israel;
his name is the LORD of Hosts.
3 Long ago I announced what would
first happen,
I revealed it with my own mouth;
suddenly I acted and it came about.
4 I knew that you were stubborn,
your neck stiff as iron, your brow
like bronze,
5 therefore I told you of these things
long ago,
and declared them before they
came about,
so that you could not say, 'This
was my idol's doing;
my image, the god that I fashioned,
he ordained them.'
6 You have heard what I said; consider it well,
and you must admit the truth of it.
Now I show you new things,
hidden things which you did not
know before.
7 They were not created long ago,
but in this very hour;
you had never heard of them before
today.
You cannot say, 'I know them already.'
8 You neither heard nor knew,
long ago your ears were closed;

for I knew that you were un-
trustworthy, treacherous,
a notorious rebel from your birth.
For the sake of my own name I was 9
patient,[a]
rather than destroy you I held myself in check.
See how I tested you, not as silver 10
is tested,
but in the furnace of affliction;
there I purified you.
For my honour, for my own 11
honour I did it;
let them disparage my past
triumphs[b] if they will:
I will not give my glory to any
other god.

Hear me, Jacob,   12
and Israel whom I called:
I am He; I am the first,
I am the last also.
With my own hands I founded the 13
earth,
with my right hand I formed the
expanse of sky;
when I summoned them,
they sprang at once into being.
Assemble, all of you, and listen to 14
me;
which of you has declared what is
coming,
that he whom I love shall wreak
my[c] will on Babylon
and the Chaldaeans shall be scattered?
I, I myself, have spoken, I have 15
called him,
I have made him appear, and
wherever he goes he shall prosper.
Draw near to me and hear this: 16
from the beginning I have never
spoken in secret;
from the moment of its first happening I was there.[d]

Thus says the LORD your ran- 17
somer, the Holy One of Israel:
I am the LORD your God:
I teach you for your own advantage
and lead you in the way you must
go.

---

[a] *See note on verse 11.*   [b] my past triumphs: *transposed from verse 9.*   [c] *Or his.*
[d] *Prob. rdg.; Heb. adds* and now the Lord GOD has sent me, and his spirit.

18 If only you had listened to my
   commands,
   your prosperity would have rolled
   on like a river in flood
   and your just success like the
   waves of the sea;
19 in number your children would
   have been like the sand
   and your descendants countless as
   its grains;
   their name would never be erased
   or blotted from my sight.
20 Come out of Babylon, hasten
   away from the Chaldaeans;
   proclaim it with loud songs of
   triumph,
   crying the news to the ends of the
   earth;
   tell them, 'The LORD has ransomed his servant Jacob.'
21 Though he led them through
   desert places they suffered no
   thirst,
   for them he made water run from
   the rock,
   for them he cleft the rock and
   streams gushed forth.

22 There is no peace for the wicked,
   says the LORD.

Israel a light to the nations

49 Listen to me, you coasts and
   islands,
   pay heed, you peoples far away:
   from birth the LORD called me,
   he named me from my mother's
   womb.
2 He made my tongue his sharp
   sword
   and concealed me under cover of
   his hand;
   he made me a polished arrow
   and hid me out of sight in his
   quiver.
3 He said to me, 'You are my servant,
   Israel through whom I shall win
   glory';

so I rose to honour in the LORD's
   sight
and my God became my strength.[a]
Once I said, 'I have laboured in 4
   vain;
I have spent my strength for nothing, to no purpose';
yet in truth my cause is with the
   LORD
and my reward is in God's hands.
And now the LORD who formed me 5
   in the womb to be his servant,
to bring Jacob back to him
that Israel should be gathered to
   him,[b]
now the LORD calls me again:[c]
it is too slight a task for you, as my 6
   servant,
to restore the tribes of Jacob,
to bring back the descendants of
   Israel:
I will make you a light to the
   nations,
to be my salvation[d] to earth's
   farthest bounds.

Thus says the Holy One, the LORD 7
   who ransoms Israel,
to one who thinks little of himself,
whom every nation abhors,
the slave of tyrants:
When they see you kings shall
   rise,
princes shall rise and bow down,
because of the LORD who is faithful,
because of the Holy One of Israel
   who has chosen you.

Thus says the LORD: 8
In the hour of my favour I answered you,
and I helped you on the day of
   deliverance,[e]
putting the land to rights
and sharing out afresh its desolate
   fields;
I said to the prisoners, 'Go free',   9
and to those in darkness, 'Come
   out and be seen.'

[a] so I rose...strength: *transposed from end of verse 5.*   [b] be gathered to him:
or not be swept away.   [c] *See note on verse 3.*   [d] to be my salvation: *or that
my salvation may reach.*   [e] *Prob. rdg.; Heb. adds* I have formed you, and
appointed you to be a light to all peoples (*cp. 42. 6*).

They shall find pasture in the desert sands[a]
and grazing on all the dunes.

10 They shall neither hunger nor thirst,
no scorching heat or sun shall distress them;
for one who loves them shall lead them
and take them to water at bubbling springs.

11 I will make every hill a path
and build embankments for my highways.

12 See, they come; some from far away,
these from the north and these from the west
and those from the land of Syene.

13 Shout for joy, you heavens, rejoice, O earth,
you mountains, break into songs of triumph,
for the LORD has comforted his people
and has had pity on his own in their distress.

14 But Zion says,
'The LORD has forsaken me; my God has forgotten me.'

15 Can a woman forget the infant at her breast,
or a loving mother the child of her womb?
Even these forget, yet I will not forget you.

16 Your walls are always before my eyes,
I have engraved them on the palms of my hands.

17 Those who are to rebuild you make better speed
than those who pulled you down,
while those who laid you waste depart.

18 Raise your eyes and look around you:
see how they assemble, how they are flocking back to you.
By my life I, the LORD, swear it,

you shall wear them proudly as your jewels,
and adorn yourself with them like a bride;

19 I did indeed make you waste and desolate,
I razed you to the ground,
but your boundaries[b] shall now be too narrow
for your inhabitants –
and those who laid you in ruins are far away.

20 The children born in your bereavement shall yet say in your hearing,
'This place is too narrow; make room for me to live in.'

21 Then you will say to yourself,
'All these children, how did I come by them,
bereaved and barren as I was?
Who reared them
when I was left alone, left by myself;
where did I get them all?'

22 The Lord GOD says,
Now is the time: I will beckon to the nations
and hoist a signal to the peoples,
and they shall bring your sons in their arms
and carry your daughters on their shoulders;

23 kings shall be your foster-fathers
and their princesses shall be your nurses.
They shall bow to the earth before you
and lick the dust from your feet;
and you shall know that I am the LORD
and that none who look to me will be disappointed.

24 Can his prey be taken from the strong man,
or the captive be rescued from the ruthless?

25 And the LORD answers,
The captive shall be taken even from the strong,
and the prey of the ruthless shall be rescued;

---

[a] desert sands: *prob. rdg.*; *Heb.* ways.
[b] I did...boundaries: *or* your wasted and desolate land, your ruined countryside.

I will contend with all who contend
  against you
and save your children from them.
26 I will force your oppressors to feed
  on their own flesh
and make them drunk with their
  own blood as if with fresh wine,
and all mankind shall know
that it is I, the LORD, who save
  you,
I your ransomer, the Mighty One
  of Jacob.

50 The LORD says,
  Is there anywhere a deed of di-
    vorce
by which I have put your mother
  away?
Was there some creditor of mine
to whom I sold you?
No; it was through your own
  wickedness that you were sold
and for your own misconduct that
  your mother was put away.
2 Why, then, did I find no one when
  I came?
Why, when I called, did no one
  answer?
Did you think my arm too short to
  redeem,
did you think I had no power to
  save?
Not so. By my rebuke I dried up
  the sea
  and turned rivers into desert;
their fish perished for lack of
  water
and died on the thirsty ground;
3 I clothed the skies in mourning
and covered them with sackcloth.

4 The Lord GOD has given me
the tongue of a teacher
and skill to console the weary
with a word in the morning;
he sharpened my hearing
that I might listen like one who is
  taught.
5 The Lord GOD opened my ears
and I did not disobey or turn back
  in defiance.
6 I offered my back to the lash,
and let my beard be plucked from
  my chin,

I did not hide my face from spitting
  and insult;
but the Lord GOD stands by to 7
  help me;
therefore no insult can wound me.
I have set my face like flint,
for I know that I shall not be put
  to shame,
because one who will clear my 8
  name is at my side.
Who dare argue against me? Let us
  confront one another.
Who will dispute my cause? Let
  him come forward.
The Lord GOD will help me; 9
who then can prove me guilty?
They will all wear out like a
  garment,
the moths will eat them up.

Which of you fears the LORD and 10
  obeys his servant's commands?
The man who walks in dark places
  with no light,
yet trusts in the name of the LORD
  and leans on his God.
But you who kindle a fire and set 11
  fire-brands alight,
go, walk into your own fire
and among the fire-brands you
  have set ablaze.
This is your fate at my hands:
you shall lie down in torment.

Listen to me, all who follow the 51
  right and seek the LORD:
look to the rock from which you
  were hewn,
to the quarry from which you were
  dug;
look to your father Abraham 2
and to Sarah who gave you birth:
when I called him he was but one,
I blessed him and made him many.
The LORD has indeed comforted 3
  Zion,
comforted all her ruined homes,
turning her wilderness into an
  Eden,
her thirsty plains into a garden of
  the LORD.
Joy and gladness shall be found in
  her,
thanksgiving and melody.

4 Pay heed to me, my people,
and hear me, O my nation;
for my law shall shine forth
and I will flash the light of my
judgement over the nations.
5 My victory is near, my deliverance
has gone*a* forth
and my arm shall rule the nations;
for me coasts and islands shall
wait
and they shall look to me for protection.
6 Lift your eyes to the heavens,
look at the earth beneath:
the heavens grow murky as smoke;
the earth wears into tatters like a
garment,
and those who live on it die like
maggots;
but my deliverance is everlasting
and my saving power shall never
wane.

7 Listen to me, my people who know
what is right,
you who lay my law to heart:
do not fear the taunts of men,
let no reproaches dismay you;
8 for the grub will devour them like
a garment
and the moth as if they were wool,
but my saving power shall last for
ever
and my deliverance to all generations.

9 Awake, awake, put on your
strength, O arm of the LORD,
awake as you did long ago, in days
gone by.
Was it not you
who hacked the Rahab in pieces
and ran the dragon through?
10 Was it not you
who dried up the sea, the waters of
the great abyss,
and made the ocean depths a path
for the ransomed?
11 So the LORD's people shall come
back, set free,
and enter Zion with shouts of
triumph,
crowned with everlasting joy;

joy and gladness shall overtake
them as they come,
and sorrow and sighing shall flee
away.
I, I myself, am he that comforts 12
you.
Why then fear man, man who must
die,
man frail as grass?
Why have you forgotten the LORD 13
your maker,
who stretched out the skies and
founded the earth?
Why are you continually afraid,
all the day long,
why dread the fury of oppressors
ready to destroy you?
Where is that fury?
He that cowers under it shall soon 14
stand upright and not die,
he shall soon reap the early crop
and not lack bread.

I am the LORD your God, the 15
LORD of Hosts is my name. I cleft
the sea and its waves roared, that 16
I might fix the heavens in place and
form the earth and say to Zion,
'You are my people.' I have put my
words in your mouth and kept you
safe under the shelter of my hand.

Awake, awake; rise up, Jerusalem. 17
You have drunk from the LORD's
hand
the cup of his wrath,
drained to its dregs the bowl of
drunkenness;
of all the sons you have borne 18
there is not one to guide you,
of all you have reared, not one to
take you by the hand.
These two disasters have over- 19
taken you;
who can console you? –
havoc and ruin, famine and the
sword;
who can comfort you?
Your sons are in stupor, they lie at 20
the head of every street,
like antelopes caught in the net,
glutted with the wrath of the LORD,
the rebuke of your God.

a Or shone.

21 Therefore listen to this, in your
   affliction,
   drunk that you are, but not with
   wine:
22 thus says the LORD, your Lord and
   your God,
   who will plead his people's cause:
   Look, I take from your hand
   the cup of drunkenness;
   you shall never again drink from
   the bowl of my wrath,
23 I will give it instead to your tor-
   mentors and oppressors,
   those who said to you, 'Lie down
   and we will walk over you';
   and you made your backs like the
   ground beneath them,
   like a roadway for passers-by.

52 Awake, awake, put on your
   strength, O Zion,
   put on your loveliest garments,
   holy city of Jerusalem;
   for never shall the uncircumcised
   and the unclean enter you again.
2 Rise up, captive Jerusalem, shake
   off the dust;
   loose your neck from the collar
   that binds it,
   O captive daughter of Zion.

3   The LORD says, You were sold
   but no price was paid, and without
   payment you shall be ransomed.
4 The Lord GOD says, At the beginning my people went down into
   Egypt to live there, and at the end
   it was the Assyrians who oppress-
5 ed them; but now what do I find
   here? says the LORD. My people
   carried off and no price paid, their
   rulers derided, and my name reviled all day long, says the LORD.
6 But on that day my people shall
   know my name; they shall know
   that it is I who speak; here I am.

7 How lovely on the mountains are
   the feet of the herald
   who comes to proclaim prosperity
   and bring good news,
   the news of deliverance,
   calling to Zion, 'Your God is king.'

Hark, your watchmen raise their 8
   voices
and shout together in triumph;
for with their own eyes they shall
   see
the LORD returning in pity to
   Zion.
Break forth together in shouts of 9
   triumph,
you ruins of Jerusalem;
for the LORD has taken pity on his
   people
and has ransomed Jerusalem.
The LORD has bared his holy arm 10
in the sight of all nations,
and the whole world from end to
   end
shall see the deliverance of our
   God.
Away from Babylon; come out, 11
   come out,
touch nothing unclean.
Come out from Babylon, keep
   yourselves pure,
you who carry the vessels of the
   LORD.
But you shall not come out in 12
   urgent haste
nor leave like fugitives;
for the LORD will march at your
   head,
your rearguard will be Israel's
   God.

Behold, my servant shall prosper, 13
he shall be lifted up, exalted to the
   heights.

Time was when many[a] were aghast 14
   at you, my people;[b]
so now many nations[c] recoil at 15
   sight of him,
and kings curl their lips in disgust.
For they see what they had never
   been told
and things unheard before fill their
   thoughts.

Who could have believed what we 53
   have heard,
and to whom has the power of the
   LORD been revealed?

---

[a] *Or the great.*   [b] *See note on 53. 2.*   [c] *Or great nations.*

2 He grew up before the LORD like a
   young plant
whose roots are in parched ground;
he had no beauty, no majesty to
   draw our eyes,
no grace to make us delight in him;
his form, disfigured, lost all the
   likeness of a man,
his beauty changed beyond human
   semblance.[a]

3 He was despised, he shrank from
   the sight of men,
tormented and humbled by suffering;
we despised him, we held him of no
   account,
a thing from which men turn away
   their eyes.

4 Yet on himself he bore our sufferings,
our torments he endured,
while we counted him smitten by
   God,
struck down by disease and misery;

5 but he was pierced for our transgressions,
tortured for our iniquities;
the chastisement he bore is health
   for us
and by his scourging we are healed.

6 We had all strayed like sheep,
each of us had gone his own way;
but the LORD laid upon him
the guilt of us all.

7 He was afflicted, he submitted to
   be struck down
and did not open his mouth;
he was led like a sheep to the
   slaughter,
like a ewe that is dumb before the
   shearers.[b]

8 Without protection, without justice,[c] he was taken away;
and who gave a thought to his
   fate,
how he was cut off from the world
   of living men,
stricken to the death for my people's transgression?

9 He was assigned a grave with the
   wicked,
a burial-place among the refuse of
   mankind,
though he had done no violence
and spoken no word of treachery.

10 Yet the LORD took thought for his
   tortured servant
and healed him who had made himself[d] a sacrifice for sin;
so shall he enjoy long life and see
   his children's children,
and in his hand the LORD's cause
   shall prosper.

11 After all his pains he shall be
   bathed in light,
after his disgrace he shall be fully
   vindicated;
so shall he, my servant, vindicate
   many,
himself bearing the penalty of
   their guilt.

12 Therefore I will allot him a portion
   with the great,
and he shall share the spoil with
   the mighty,
because he exposed himself to face
   death[e]
and was reckoned among transgressors,
because he bore the sin of many
and interceded for their transgressions.

54 Sing aloud, O barren woman who
   never bore a child,
break into cries of joy, you who
   have never been in labour;
for the deserted wife has more sons
   than she who lives in wedlock,
says the LORD.

2 Enlarge the limits of your home,
spread wide the curtains of your
   tent;
let out its ropes to the full
and drive the pegs home;

3 for you shall break out of your con-
   fines right and left,

---

[a] his form...semblance: *transposed from end of 52. 14.*
[b] *Prob. rdg.*; *Heb. adds* and he would not open his mouth.
[c] Without protection, without justice: *or* After arrest and sentence.
[d] healed...himself: *prob. rdg.*; *Heb.* he made sick, if you make.
[e] *Or because he poured out his life to the death.*

your descendants shall dispossess
wide regions,[a]
and re-people cities now desolate.

4 Fear not; you shall not be put to
shame,
you shall suffer no insult, have no
cause to blush.
It is time to forget the shame of
your younger days
and remember no more the reproach of your widowhood;

5 for your husband is your maker,
whose name is the LORD of Hosts;
your ransomer is the Holy One of
Israel
who is called God of all the earth.

6 The LORD has acknowledged you a
wife again,
once deserted and heart-broken,
your God has called you a bride
still young
though once rejected.

7 On the impulse of a moment I forsook you,
but with tender affection I will
bring you home again.

8 In sudden anger
I hid my face from you for a
moment;
but now have I pitied you with a
love which never fails,
says the LORD who ransoms you.

9 These days recall for me the days
of Noah:
as I swore that the waters of
Noah's flood
should never again pour over the
earth,
so now I swear to you
never again to be angry with you
or reproach you.

10 Though the mountains move and
the hills shake,
my love shall be immovable and
never fail,
and my covenant of peace shall
not be shaken.
So says the LORD who takes pity
on you.

11 O storm-battered city, distressed
and disconsolate,

now I will set your stones in the
finest mortar
and your foundations in lapis
lazuli;
I will make your battlements of 12
red jasper[b]
and your gates of garnet;[c]
all your boundary-stones shall be
jewels.
Your masons shall all be instructed 13
by the LORD,
and your sons shall enjoy great
prosperity;
and in triumph[d] shall you be 14
restored.
You shall be free from oppression
and have no fears,
free from terror, and it shall not
come near you;
should any attack you, it will not 15
be my doing,
the aggressor, whoever he be, shall
perish for his attempt.
It was I who created the smith 16
to fan the coals in the furnace
and forge weapons each for its
purpose,
and I who created the destroyer to
lay waste;
but now no weapon made to harm 17
you shall prevail,
and you shall rebut every charge
brought against you.
Such is the fortune of the servants
of the LORD;
their vindication comes from me.
This is the very word of the LORD.

Come, all who are thirsty, come, 55
fetch water;
come, you who have no food, buy
corn and eat;
come and buy, not for money, not
for a price.[e]
Why spend money and get what is 2
not bread,
why give the price of your labour
and go unsatisfied?
Only listen to me and you will have
good food to eat,
and you will enjoy the fat of the
land.

---

[a] wide regions: *or* the nations.   [b] *Or* carbuncle.   [c] *Or* firestone.
[d] *Or* in righteousness.   [e] *Prob. rdg.; Heb. adds* wine and milk.

3 Come to me and listen to my words,
hear me, and you shall have life:
I will make a covenant with you,
this time for ever,
to love you faithfully as I loved
David.

4 I made him a witness to all races,
a prince and instructor of peoples;

5 and you in turn shall summon
nations you do not know,
and nations that do not know you
shall come running to you,
because the LORD your God,
the Holy One of Israel, has
glorified you.

6 Inquire of the LORD while he is
present,
call upon him when he is close at
hand.

7 Let the wicked abandon their ways
and evil men their thoughts:
let them return to the LORD, who
will have pity on them,
return to our God, for he will freely
forgive.

8 For my thoughts are not your
thoughts,
and your ways are not my ways.
This is the very word of the LORD.

9 For as the heavens are higher than
the earth,
so are my ways higher than your
ways
and my thoughts than your
thoughts;

10 and as the rain and the snow come
down from heaven
and do not return until they have
watered the earth,
making it blossom and bear fruit,
and give seed for sowing and bread
to eat,

11 so shall the word which comes from
my mouth prevail;
it shall not return to me fruitless
without accomplishing my purpose
or succeeding in the task I gave it.

12 You shall indeed go out with joy
and be led forth in peace.
Before you mountains and hills
shall break into cries of joy,
and all the trees of the wild shall
clap their hands,

13 pine-trees shall shoot up in place
of camel-thorn,
myrtles instead of briars;
all this shall win the LORD a great
name,
imperishable, a sign for all time.

Warnings to keep the moral law

56 These are the words of the LORD:
Maintain justice, do the right;
for my deliverance is close at hand,
and my righteousness will show
itself victorious.

2 Happy is the man who follows
these precepts,
happy the mortal who holds them
fast,
who keeps the sabbath undefiled,
who refrains from all wrong-doing!

3 The foreigner who has given his
allegiance to the LORD must not
say,
'The LORD will keep me separate
from his people for ever';
and the eunuch must not say,
'I am nothing but a barren tree.'

4 For these are the words of the
LORD:
The eunuchs who keep my sabbaths,
who choose to do my will and hold
fast to my covenant,

5 shall receive from me something
better than sons and daughters,
a memorial and a name in my own
house and within my walls:
I will give them an everlasting
name,
a name imperishable for all time.

6 So too with the foreigners who give
their allegiance to me, the LORD,
to minister to me and love my name
and to become my servants,
all who keep the sabbath undefiled
and hold fast to my covenant:

7 them will I bring to my holy hill
and give them joy in my house of
prayer.
Their offerings and sacrifices shall
be acceptable on my altar;
for my house shall be called
a house of prayer for all nations.

8 This is the very word of the Lord
  God,
  who brings home the outcasts of
    Israel:
  I will yet bring home all that re-
    main to be brought in.

9 Come, beasts of the plain, beasts of
    the forest,
  come, eat your fill,
10 for Israel's watchmen are blind, all
    of them unaware.
  They are all dumb dogs who
    cannot bark,
  stretched on the ground, dream-
    ing, lovers of sleep,
11 greedy dogs that can never have
    enough.
  They are shepherds who under-
    stand nothing,
  absent each of them on his own
    pursuits,
  each intent on his own gain
    wherever he can find it.
12 'Come,' says each of them, 'let me
    fetch wine,
  strong drink, and we will drain it
    down;
  let us make tomorrow like today,
    or greater far!'
57 The righteous perish,
  and no one takes it to heart;
  men of good faith are swept away,
    but no one cares,
  the righteous are swept away be-
    fore the onset of evil,
2 but they enter into peace;
  they have run a straight course
  and rest in their last beds.

3 Come, stand forth, you sons of a
    soothsayer.
  You spawn of an adulterer and a
    harlot,
4 who is the target of your jests?
  Against whom do you open your
    mouths
  and wag your tongues,
  children of sin that you are, spawn
    of a lie,
5 burning with lust under the tere-
    binths,
  under every spreading tree,

and sacrificing children in the
    gorges,
under the rocky clefts?
And you, woman,   6
your place is with the creatures of
    the gorge;
that is where you belong.
To them you have dared to pour a
    libation
and present an offering of grain.[a]
On a high mountain-top   7
you have made your bed;
there too you have gone up to offer
    sacrifice.
In spite of all this am I to relent?[b]
Beside door and door-post you 8
  have put up your sign.
Deserting me, you have stripped
    and lain down
on the wide bed which you have
    made,
and you drove bargains with men
for the pleasure of sleeping to-
    gether,
and you have committed countless
    acts of fornication
in the heat of your lust.
You drenched your tresses in 9
    oil
blended with many perfumes;
you sent out your procurers far
    and wide
even down to the gates of Sheol.
Worn out by your unending ex- 10
    cesses,
even so you never said, 'I am past
    hope.'
You earned a livelihood
and so you had no anxiety.
Whom do you fear so much, that 11
  you should be false,
that you never remembered me or
    gave me a thought?
Did I not hold my peace and seem
    not to see
while you showed no fear of me?
Now I will denounce your conduct 12
that you think so righteous.
These idols of yours shall not help 13
    when you cry;
no idol shall save you.
The wind shall carry them off, one
    and all,

---

[a] *See note on verse 7.*   [b] *Line transposed from end of verse 6.*

a puff of air shall blow them
away;
but he who makes me his refuge
shall possess the earth
and inherit my holy hill.

14 Then a voice shall be heard:
Build up a highway, build it and
clear the track,
sweep away all that blocks my
people's path.

15 Thus speaks the high and exalted
one,
whose name is holy, who lives for
ever:
I dwell in a high and holy place
with him who is broken and
humble in spirit,
to revive the spirit of the humble,
to revive the courage of the broken.

16 I will not be always accusing,
I will not continually nurse my
wrath.
For a breath of life passed out from
me,
and by my own act I created
living creatures.

17 For a time I was angry at the guilt
of Israel;
I smote him in my anger and withdrew my favour.
But he ran wild and went his
wilful way.

18 Then I considered his ways,
I cured him and gave him relief,
and I brought him comfort in full
measure,

19 brought peace to those who
mourned for him,
by the words that issue from my
lips,
peace for all men, both near and far,
and so I cured him, says the LORD.

20 But the wicked are like a troubled
sea,
a sea that cannot rest,
whose troubled waters cast up mud
and filth.

21 There is no peace for the wicked,
says the LORD.

58 Shout aloud without restraint;
lift up your voice like a trumpet.

Call my people to account for their
transgression
and the house of Jacob for their
sins,
although they ask counsel of me 2
day by day
and say they delight in knowing
my ways,
although, like nations which have
acted rightly
and not forsaken the just laws of
their gods,
they ask me for righteous laws
and say they delight in approaching God.

Why do we fast, if thou dost not 3
see it?
Why mortify ourselves, if thou
payest no heed?
Since you serve your own interest
only on your fast-day
and make all your men work the
harder,
since your fasting leads only to 4
wrangling and strife
and dealing vicious blows with the
fist,
on such a day you are keeping no
fast
that will carry your cry to heaven.
Is it a fast like this that I require, 5
a day of mortification such as this,
that a man should bow his head
like a bulrush
and make his bed on sackcloth and
ashes?
Is this what you call a fast,
a day acceptable to the LORD?
Is not this what I require of you as 6
a fast:
to loose the fetters of injustice,
to untie the knots of the yoke,
to snap every yoke
and set free those who have been
crushed?
Is it not sharing your food with the 7
hungry,
taking the homeless poor into your
house,
clothing the naked when you meet
them
and never evading a duty to your
kinsfolk?

8 Then shall your light break forth
like the dawn
and soon you will grow healthy
like a wound newly healed;
your own righteousness shall be
your vanguard
and the glory of the LORD your
rearguard.

9 Then, if you call, the LORD will
answer;
if you cry to him, he will say, 'Here
I am.'
If you cease to pervert justice,
to point the accusing finger and
lay false charges,

10 if you feed the hungry from your
own plenty
and satisfy the needs of the
wretched,
then your light will rise like dawn
out of darkness
and your dusk be like noonday;

11 the LORD will be your guide continually
and will satisfy your needs in the
shimmering heat;
he will give you strength of limb;
you will be like a well-watered
garden,
like a spring whose waters never
fail.

12 The ancient ruins will be restored
by your own kindred
and you will build once more on
ancestral foundations;
you shall be called Rebuilder of
broken walls,
Restorer of houses in ruins.

13 If you cease to tread the sabbath
underfoot,
and keep my holy day free from
your own affairs,
if you call the sabbath a day of joy
and the LORD's holy day a day to be
honoured,
if you honour it by not plying
your trade,
not seeking your own interest
or attending to your own affairs,

14 then you shall find your joy in the
LORD,
and I will set you riding on the
heights of the earth,

and your father Jacob's patrimony shall be yours to enjoy;
the LORD himself has spoken it.

The LORD's arm is not so short 59
that he cannot save
nor his ear too dull to hear;
it is your iniquities that raise a 2
barrier
between you and your God,
because of your sins he has hidden
his face
so that he does not hear you.
Your hands are stained with blood 3
and your fingers with crime;
your lips speak lies
and your tongues utter injustice.
No man sues with just cause, 4
no man goes honestly to law;
all trust in empty words, all tell
lies,
conceive mischief and give birth to
trouble.
They hatch snakes' eggs, they 5
weave cobwebs;
eat their eggs and you will die,
for rotten eggs hatch only rotten-
ness.
As for their webs, they will never 6
make cloth,
no one can use them for clothing;
their works breed trouble
and their hands are busy with
deeds of violence.
They rush headlong into crime 7
in furious haste to shed innocent
blood;
their schemes are schemes of
mischief
and leave a trail of ruin and devastation.
They do not know the way to peace, 8
no justice guides their steps;
all the paths they follow are
crooked;
no one who walks in them enjoys
true peace.

Therefore justice is far away from 9
us,
right does not reach us;
we look for light but all is darkness,
for the light of dawn, but we walk
in deep gloom.

10 We grope like blind men along a
   wall,
   feeling our way like men without
   eyes;
   we stumble at noonday as if it
   were twilight,
   like dead men in the ghostly
   underworld.
11 We growl like bears,
   like doves we moan incessantly,
   waiting for justice, and there is
   none;
   for deliverance, but it is still far
   away.

12 Our acts of rebellion against thee
   are past counting
   and our sins bear witness against
   us;
   we remember our many rebellions,
   we know well our guilt:
13 we have rebelled and broken faith
   with the LORD,
   we have relapsed and forsaken our
   God;
   we have conceived lies in our
   hearts and repeated them
   in slanderous and treacherous
   words.
14 Justice is rebuffed and flouted
   while righteousness stands aloof;
   truth stumbles in the market-place
   and honesty is kept out of court,
15 so truth is lost to sight,
   and whoever shuns evil is thought
   a madman.

   The LORD saw, and in his eyes it
   was an evil thing,
   that there was no justice;
16 he saw that there was no man to
   help
   and was outraged that no one
   intervened;
   so his own arm brought him
   victory
   and his own integrity upheld him.
17 He put on integrity as a coat of
   mail
   and the helmet of salvation on his
   head;
   he put on garments of vengeance
   and wrapped himself in a cloak of
   jealous anger.

High God of retribution that he is, 18
he pays in full measure,
wreaking his anger on his foes,
   retribution on his enemies.
So from the west men shall fear his 19
   name,
fear his glory from the rising of the
   sun;
for it shall come like a shining river,
the spirit of the LORD hovering
   over it,
come as the ransomer of Zion   20
and of all in Jacob who repent of
   their rebellion.
This is the very word of the LORD.

   This, says the LORD, is my cove- 21
nant, which I make with them: My
spirit which rests on you and my
words which I have put into your
mouth shall never fail you from
generation to generation of your
descendants from now onward for
ever. The LORD has said it.

Promise of the new Jerusalem

Arise, Jerusalem,   60
rise clothed in light; your light has
   come
and the glory of the LORD shines
   over you.
For, though darkness covers the   2
   earth
and dark night the nations,
the LORD shall shine upon you
and over you shall his glory appear;
and the nations shall march to-   3
   wards your light
and their kings to your sunrise.

Lift up your eyes and look all   4
   around:
they flock together, all of them,
   and come to you;
your sons also shall come from afar,
your daughters walking beside
   them leading the way.
Then shall you see, and shine with 5
   joy,
then your heart shall thrill with
   pride:
the riches of the sea shall be
   lavished upon you

and you shall possess the wealth of nations.

6 Camels in droves shall cover the land,
dromedaries of Midian and Ephah,
all coming from Sheba
laden with golden spice[a] and frankincense,
heralds of the LORD's praise.
7 All Kedar's flocks shall be gathered for you,
rams of Nebaioth shall serve your need,
acceptable offerings on my altar,
and glory shall be added to glory in my temple.

8 Who are these that sail along like clouds,
that fly like doves to their dovecotes?
9 They are vessels assembling from the coasts and islands,
ships from Tarshish leading the convoy;
they bring your sons from afar,
their gold and their silver with them,
to the honour of the LORD your God,
the Holy One of Israel;
for he has made you glorious.

10 Foreigners shall rebuild your walls
and their kings shall be your servants;
for though in my wrath I struck you down,
now I have shown you pity and favour.
11 Your gates shall be open continually,
they shall never be shut day or night,
that through them may be brought the wealth of nations
and their kings under escort.

12   For the nation or kingdom which refuses to serve you shall perish, and wide regions shall be laid utterly waste.

The wealth of Lebanon shall come 13 to you,
pine, fir,[b] and boxwood,[c] all together,
to bring glory to my holy sanctuary,
to honour the place where my feet rest.
The sons of your oppressors shall 14 come forward to do homage,
all who reviled you shall bow low at your feet;
they shall call you the City of the LORD,
the Zion of the Holy One of Israel.

No longer will you be deserted, 15
a wife hated and unvisited;[d]
I will make you an eternal pride
and a never-ending joy.
You shall suck the milk of nations 16
and be suckled at the breasts of kings.
So you shall know that I the LORD am your deliverer,
your ransomer the Mighty One of Jacob.

For bronze[e] I will bring you gold 17
and for iron I will bring silver,
bronze[e] for timber and iron for stone;
and I will make your government be peace
and righteousness rule over you.
The sound of violence shall be 18 heard no longer in your land,
or ruin and devastation within your borders;
but you shall call your walls Deliverance
and your gates Praise.

The sun shall no longer be your 19 light by day,
nor the moon shine on you when evening falls;
the LORD shall be your everlasting light,
your God shall be your glory.
Never again shall your sun set 20
nor your moon withdraw her light;

---

[a] golden spice: *or* gold.   [b] *Or* elm.   [c] *Or* cypress.
[d] *Or* divorced and unmated.   [e] *Or* copper.

but the LORD shall be your everlasting light
and the days of your mourning
shall be ended.

21 Your people shall all be righteous
and shall for ever possess the land,
a shoot of my own planting,
a work of my own hands to bring
me glory.
22 The few shall become ten thousand,
the little nation great.
I am the LORD;
soon, in the fullness of time, I will
bring this to pass.

61 The spirit of the Lord GOD is upon
me
because the LORD has anointed me;
he has sent me to bring good news
to the humble,
to bind up the broken-hearted,
to proclaim liberty to captives
and release to those in prison;
2 to proclaim a year of the LORD's
favour
and a day of the vengeance of our
God;
to comfort all who mourn,*a*
3 to give them garlands instead of
ashes,
oil of gladness instead of mourners'
tears,
a garment of splendour for the
heavy heart.
They shall be called Trees of
Righteousness,
planted by the LORD for his glory.
4 Ancient ruins shall be rebuilt
and sites long desolate restored;
they shall repair the ruined cities
and restore what has long lain
desolate.
5 Foreigners shall serve as shepherds
of your flocks,
and aliens shall till your land and
tend your vines;
6 but you shall be called priests of
the LORD
and be named ministers of our
God;

you shall enjoy the wealth of other
nations
and be furnished*b* with their riches.
And so, because shame in double 7
measure
and jeers and insults*c* have been
my people's lot,
they shall receive in their own land
a double measure of wealth,
and everlasting joy shall be theirs.
For I, the LORD, love justice   8
and hate robbery and wrong-
doing;
I will grant them a sure reward
and make an everlasting covenant
with them;
their posterity will be renowned 9
among the nations
and their offspring among the
peoples;
all who see them will acknowledge
in them
a race whom the LORD has blessed.

Let me rejoice in the LORD with all 10
my heart,
let me exult in my God;
for he has robed me in salvation as
a garment
and clothed me in integrity as a
cloak,
like a bridegroom with his priestly
garland,
or a bride decked in her jewels.
For, as the earth puts forth her 11
blossom
or bushes in the garden burst into
flower,
so shall the Lord GOD make
righteousness and praise
blossom before all the nations.

For Zion's sake I will not keep 62
silence,
for Jerusalem's sake I will speak
out,
until her right shines forth like the
sunrise,
her deliverance like a blazing torch,
until the nations see the triumph of 2
your right
and all kings see your glory.

---

*a Prob. rdg.; Heb. adds to appoint to Zion's mourners.   b be furnished: prob.
rdg.; Heb. unintelligible.   c and insults: prob. rdg.; Heb. they shout in triumph.*

Then you shall be called by a new
name
which the LORD shall pronounce
with his own lips;

3 you will be a glorious crown in the
LORD's hand,
a kingly diadem in the hand of
your God.

4 No more shall men call you Forsaken,
no more shall your land be called
Desolate,
but you shall be named Hephzi-
bah[a]
and your land Beulah;[b]
for the LORD delights in you
and to him your land is wedded.

5 For, as a young man weds a
maiden,
so you shall wed him who rebuilds
you,
and your God shall rejoice over you
as a bridegroom rejoices over the
bride.

6 I have posted watchmen on your
walls, Jerusalem,
who shall not keep silence day or
night:
'You who invoke the LORD's name,
7 take no rest, give him no rest
until he makes Jerusalem
a theme of endless praise on earth.'

8 The LORD has sworn with raised
right hand and mighty arm:
Never again will I give your grain
to feed your foes
or let foreigners drink the new wine
for which you have toiled;
9 but those who bring in the corn
shall eat and praise the LORD,
and those who gather the grapes
shall drink in my holy courts.

10 Go out of the gates, go out,
prepare a road for my people;
build a highway, build it up,
clear away the boulders;
raise a signal to the peoples.
11 This is the LORD's proclamation
to earth's farthest bounds:
Tell the daughter of Zion,
Behold, your deliverance has come.

His recompense comes with him;
he carries his reward before him;
and they shall be called a Holy 12
People,
the Ransomed of the LORD,
a People long-sought, a City not
forsaken.

'Who is this coming from Edom, 63
coming from Bozrah, his garments
stained red?
Under his clothes his muscles
stand out,
and he strides, stooping in his
might.'
It is I, who announce that right
has won the day,
I, who am strong to save.
'Why is your clothing all red, 2
like the garments of one who
treads grapes in the vat?'
I have trodden the winepress alone; 3
no man, no nation was with me.
I trod them down in my rage,
I trampled them in my fury;
and their life-blood spurted over
my garments
and stained all my clothing.
For I resolved on a day of ven- 4
geance;
the year for ransoming my own
had come.
I looked for a helper but found no 5
one,
I was amazed that there was no one
to support me;
yet my own arm brought me
victory,
alone my anger supported me.
I stamped on nations in my fury, 6
I pierced them in my rage
and let their life-blood run out
upon the ground.

I will recount the LORD's acts of 7
unfailing love
and the LORD's praises as High God,
all that the LORD has done for us
and his great goodness to the house
of Israel,
all that he has done for them in his
tenderness
and by his many acts of love.

----

[a] *That is* My delight is in her.   [b] *That is* Wedded.

8 He said, 'Surely they are my
people,
my sons who will not play me
false';
9 and he became their deliverer in all
their troubles.
It was no envoy, no angel, but he
himself that delivered them;
he himself ransomed them by his
love and pity,
lifted them up and carried them
through all the years gone by.
10 Yet they rebelled and grieved his
holy spirit;
only then was he changed into
their enemy
and himself fought against them.
11 Then men remembered days long
past
and him who drew out[a] his
people:
Where is he who brought them up
from the Nile
with the shepherd[b] of his flock?
Where is he who put within him
his holy spirit,
12 who made his glorious power march
at the right hand of Moses,
dividing the waters before them,
to win for himself an everlasting
name,
13 causing them to go through the
depths
sure-footed as horses in the wilderness,
14 like cattle moving down into a
valley without stumbling,
guided by the spirit of the LORD?
So didst thou lead thy people
to win thyself a glorious name.

15 Look down from heaven and behold
from the heights where thou
dwellest holy and glorious.
Where is thy zeal, thy valour,
thy burning and tender love?
16 Stand not aloof;[c] for thou art our
father,

though Abraham does not know us
nor Israel acknowledge us.
Thou, LORD, art our father;
thy name is our Ransomer[d] from
of old.
Why, LORD, dost thou let us 17
wander from thy ways
and harden our hearts until we
cease to fear thee?
turn again for the sake of thy
servants,
the tribes of thy patrimony.
Why have wicked men trodden 18
down thy sanctuary,[e]
why have our enemies trampled on
thy shrine?
We have long been reckoned as 19
beyond thy sway,
as if we had not been named thy
own.

Why didst thou not rend the 64
heavens and come down,
and make the mountains shudder
before thee
as when fire blazes up in brushwood 2
or fire makes water boil?
then would thy name be known to
thy enemies
and nations tremble at thy coming.
When thou didst terrible things 3
that we did not look for,
the mountains shuddered before
thee.
Never has ear heard[f] or eye seen 4
any other god taking the part of
those who wait for him.
Thou dost welcome him who re- 5
joices to do what is right,
who remembers thee in thy ways.
Though thou wast angry, yet we
sinned,
in spite of it we have done evil from
of old,
we all became like a man who is 6
unclean
and all our righteous deeds like a
filthy rag;
we have all withered[g] like leaves

---

^a *That is Moses* whose name resembles the Heb. verb meaning draw out, *cp. Exod. 2. 10
and the note there.* ^b *Or* shepherds. ^c *Stand not aloof: prob. rdg.;
Heb. obscure in context.* ^d *Or our Kinsman.* ^e *Why...sanctuary:
prob. rdg.; Heb.* For a little while they possessed thy holy people.
^f *Never...heard: prob. rdg.; Heb.* They have never heard or listened.
^g *have all withered: or* are all carried away.

and our iniquities sweep us away
　like the wind.

7 There is no one who invokes thee
　by name
　or rouses himself to cling to thee;
　for thou hast hidden thy face from
　us
　and abandoned us to our iniquities.

8 But now, Lord, thou art our father;
　we are the clay, thou the potter,
　and all of us are thy handiwork.

9 Do not be angry beyond measure,
　O Lord,
　and do not remember iniquity for
　ever;
　look on us all, look on thy people.

10 Thy holy cities are a wilderness,
　Zion a wilderness, Jerusalem deso-
　late;

11 our sanctuary, holy and glorious,
　where our fathers praised thee,
　has been burnt to the ground
　and all that we cherish is a ruin.

12 After this, O Lord, wilt thou hold
　back,
　wilt thou keep silence and punish
　us beyond measure?

65 I was there to be sought by a
　people who did not ask,
　to be found by men who did not
　seek me.
　I said, 'Here am I, here am I',
　to a nation that did not invoke me
　by name.

2 I spread out my hands all day
　appealing to an unruly people
　who went their evil way,
　following their own devices,

3 a people who provoked me
　continually to my face,
　offering sacrifice in gardens, burn-
　ing incense on brick altars,

4 crouching among graves, keeping
　vigil all night long,
　eating swine's flesh, their cauldrons
　full of a tainted brew.

5 'Stay where you are,' they cry,
　'do not dare touch me; for I am too
　sacred for you.'
　Such people are a smouldering fire,
　smoking in my nostrils all day
　long.

All is on record before me; I will 6
　not keep silence;

I will repay[a] your iniquities, 7
　yours and your fathers', all at
　once, says the Lord,
　because they burnt incense[b] on the
　mountains
　and defied me on the hills;
　I will first measure out their
　reward
　and then pay them in full.

These are the words of the Lord: 8
　As there is new wine in a cluster of
　grapes
　and men say, 'Do not destroy it;
　there is a blessing in it',
　so will I do for my servants' sake:
　I will not destroy the whole nation.

I will give Jacob children to come 9
　after him
　and Judah heirs who shall possess
　my mountains;
　my chosen shall inherit them
　and my servants shall live there.

Flocks shall range over Sharon, 10
　and the Vale of Achor be a pasture
　for cattle;
　they shall belong to my people who
　seek me.

But you that forsake the Lord and 11
　forget my holy mountain,
　who spread a table for the god of
　Fate,
　and fill bowls of spiced wine in
　honour of Fortune,

I will deliver you to your fate, to 12
　execution,
　and you shall all bend the neck to
　the sword,
　because I called and you did not
　answer,
　I spoke and you did not listen;
　and you did what was wrong in my
　eyes
　and you chose what was against
　my will.

Therefore these are the words of 13
　the Lord God:
　My servants shall eat but you shall
　starve;
　my servants shall drink but you
　shall go thirsty;

---

[a] *Prob. rdg., transposing* and then pay *to follow* reward.　　　　[b] *Or* sacrifices.

my servants shall rejoice but you
   shall be put to shame;
14 my servants shall shout in triumph
   in the gladness of their hearts,
but you shall cry from sorrow
and wail from anguish of spirit;
15 your name shall be used as an oath
   by my chosen,
and the Lord GOD shall give you
   over to death;
but his servants he shall call by
   another name.
16 He who invokes a blessing on
   himself in the land
shall do so by the God whose name
   is Amen,
and he who utters an oath in the
   land
shall do so by the God of Amen;
the former troubles are forgotten
and they are hidden from my
   sight.
17 For behold, I create
   new heavens and a new earth.
Former things shall no more be
   remembered
nor shall they be called to mind.
18 Rejoice and be filled with delight,
   you boundless realms which I
   create;
for I create Jerusalem to be a
   delight
and her people a joy;
19 I will take delight in Jerusalem
   and rejoice in my people;
weeping and cries for help
shall never again be heard in her.
20 There no child shall ever again die
   an infant,
no old man fail to live out his
   life;
every boy shall live his hundred
   years before he dies,
whoever falls short of a hundred
   shall be despised.[a]
21 Men shall build houses and live to
   inhabit them,
plant vineyards and eat their fruit;
22 they shall not build for others to
   inhabit
nor plant for others to eat.

My people shall live the long life of
   a tree,
and my chosen shall enjoy the
   fruit of their labour.
They shall not toil in vain or raise 23
   children for misfortune.
For they are the offspring of the
   blessed of the LORD
and their issue after them;
before they call to me, I will 24
   answer,
and while they are still speaking I
   will listen.
The wolf and the lamb shall feed 25
   together
and the lion shall eat straw like
   cattle.[b]
They shall not hurt or destroy in
   all my holy mountain,
says the LORD.

These are the words of the LORD: 66
Heaven is my throne and earth my
   footstool.
Where will you build a house for
   me,
where shall my resting-place be?
All these are of my own making 2
and all these are mine.
This is the very word of the LORD.

The man I look to is a man downtrodden and distressed,
one who reveres my words.
But to sacrifice an ox or to[c] kill a 3
   man,
slaughter a sheep or break a dog's
   neck,
offer grain or offer pigs' blood,
burn incense as a token and worship an idol –
all these are the chosen practices of
   men
who[d] revel in their own loathsome
   rites.
I too will practise those wanton 4
   rites of theirs
and bring down on them the very
   things they dread;
for I called and no one answered,
I spoke and no one listened.

[a] *Or* cursed.   [b] *Prob. rdg.; Heb. adds* and the food of the snake shall be dust.
[c] to sacrifice an ox or to: *or* those who sacrifice an ox and...
[d] are the chosen practices of men who: *or* have chosen their own devices and...

They did what was wrong in my eyes
and chose practices not to my liking.

5 Hear the word of the LORD, you who revere his word:
Your fellow-countrymen who hate you,
who spurn you because you bear my name, have said,
'Let the LORD show his glory,
then we shall see you rejoice';
but they shall be put to shame.
6 That roar from the city, that uproar in the temple,
is the sound of the LORD dealing retribution to his foes.

7 Shall a woman bear a child without pains?
give birth to a son before the onset of labour?
8 Who has heard of anything like this?
Who has seen any such thing?
Shall a country be born after one day's labour,
shall a nation be brought to birth all in a moment?
But Zion, at the onset of her pangs, bore her sons.
9 Shall I bring to the point of birth and not deliver?
the LORD says;
shall I who deliver close the womb?
your God has spoken.

10 Rejoice with Jerusalem and exult in her,
all you who love her;
share her joy with all your heart,
all you who mourn over her.
11 Then you may suck and be fed from the breasts that give comfort,
delighting in her plentiful milk.
12 For thus says the LORD:
I will send peace flowing over her like a river,
and the wealth of nations like a stream in flood;
it shall suckle you,

and you shall be carried in their arms
and dandled on their knees.
As a mother comforts her son, 13
so will I myself comfort you,
and you shall find comfort in Jerusalem.
This you shall see and be glad at 14 heart,
your limbs shall be as fresh as grass in spring;
the LORD shall make his power known among his servants
and his indignation felt among his foes.
For see, the LORD is coming in 15 fire,
with his chariots like a whirlwind,
to strike home with his furious anger
and with the flaming fire of his reproof.
The LORD will judge by fire, 16
with fire he will test all living men,
and many will be slain by the LORD;
those who hallow and purify 17 themselves in garden-rites,
one after another in a magic ring,
those who eat the flesh of pigs and rats[a] and all vile vermin,
shall meet their end, one and all, says the LORD,
for I know their deeds and their 18 thoughts.

Then I myself will come to gather all nations and races,
and they shall come and see my glory;
and I will perform a sign among 19 them.
I will spare some of them and send them to the nations,
to Tarshish, Put, and Lud,[b]
to Meshek, Rosh,[c] Tubal, and Javan,[d]
distant coasts and islands which have never yet heard of me
and have not seen my glory;
these shall announce that glory among the nations.

[a] Or jerboas.   [b] Or Lydia.
[c] Meshek, Rosh: *prob. rdg.*; *Heb.* those who draw the bow.   [d] Or Greece.

20 From every nation they shall
    bring your countrymen
    on horses, in chariots and wagons,
    on mules and dromedaries,
    as an offering to the LORD,
    on my holy mountain Jerusalem,
    says the LORD,
    as the Israelites bring offerings
    in pure vessels to the LORD's house;
21 and some of them I will take for
    priests, for Levites,
    says the LORD.
22 For, as the new heavens and the
    new earth
    which I am making shall endure in
    my sight,

says the LORD,
so shall your race and your name
    endure;
and month by month at the new 23
    moon,
week by week on the sabbath,
all mankind shall come to bow
    down before me,
says the LORD;
and they shall come out and see 24
    the dead bodies of those who have
    rebelled against me;
their worm shall not die nor their
    fire be quenched,
and they shall be abhorred by all
    mankind.

THE BOOK OF THE PROPHET

JEREMIAH

1 T H E words of Jeremiah son
    of Hilkiah, one of the priests
    at Anathoth in Benjamin.
2 The word of the LORD came to
him in the thirteenth year of the
reign of Josiah son of Amon,
3 king of Judah; also during the
reign of Jehoiakim son of Josiah,
king of Judah, until the eleventh
year of Zedekiah son of Josiah,
king of Judah, was completed.
In the fifth month the people of
Jerusalem were carried away into
exile.

Jeremiah's call and two visions

4 T H E word of the LORD came to me:
5 'Before I formed you in the womb I
knew you for my own; before you
were born I consecrated you, I
appointed you a prophet to the
6 nations.' 'Ah! Lord GOD,' I answered, 'I do not know how to
7 speak; I am only a child.' But the
LORD said, 'Do not call yourself a

child; for you shall go to whatever
people I send you and say whatever I tell you to say. Fear none of 8
them, for I am with you and will
keep you safe.' This was the very
word of the LORD. Then the LORD 9
stretched out his hand and touched
my mouth, and said to me, 'I put
my words into your mouth. This 10
day I give you authority over
nations and over kingdoms, to
pull down and to uproot, to destroy and to demolish, to build and
to plant.'
    The word of the LORD came to 11
me: 'What is it that you see, Jeremiah?' 'An almond in early bloom',ᵃ
I answered. 'You are right,' said 12
the LORD to me, 'for I am early on
the watchᵇ to carry out my purpose.' The word of the LORD came 13
to me a second time: 'What is it
that you see?' 'A cauldron', I said,
'on a fire, fanned by the wind; it is
tilted away from the north.' The 14
LORD said:

ᵃ *Heb.* shaked.   ᵇ *Heb.* shoked.

From the north disaster shall flare
  up
against all who live in this land;
15 for now I summon all peoples and
  kingdoms of the north,
says the LORD.
Their kings shall come and each
  shall set up his throne
before the gates of Jerusalem,
against her walls on every side,
and against all the cities of Judah.
16 I will state my case against my
  people
for all the wrong they have done in
  forsaking me,
in burning sacrifices to other gods,
worshipping the work of their
  own hands.
17 Brace yourself, Jeremiah;
stand up and speak to them.
Tell them everything I bid you,
do not let your spirit break at sight
  of them,
or I will break you before their
  eyes.
18 This day I make you a fortified
  city,
a pillar of iron, a wall of bronze,
to stand fast against the whole
  land,
against the kings and princes of
  Judah,
its priests and its people.
19 They will make war on you but
  shall not overcome you,
for I am with you and will keep
  you safe.
This is the very word of the LORD.

Exhortations to Israel and Judah

2 THE word of the LORD came to me:
2 Go, make a proclamation that all
Jerusalem shall hear: These are
the words of the LORD:

I remember the unfailing devotion
  of your youth,
the love of your bridal days,
when you followed me in the
  wilderness,
through a land unsown.
3 Israel then was holy to the LORD,
the firstfruits of his harvest;

no one who devoured her went
  unpunished,
evil always overtook them.
This is the very word of the
  LORD.

Listen to the word of the LORD, 4
people of Jacob, families of Israel, one and all. These are the 5
words of the LORD:

What fault did your forefathers
  find in me,
that they wandered far from me,
pursuing empty phantoms and
  themselves becoming empty;
that they did not ask, 'Where is the 6
  LORD,
who brought us up from Egypt,
and led us through the wilderness,
through a country of deserts and
  shifting sands,
a country barren and ill-omened,
where no man ever trod,
no man made his home?'
I brought you into a fruitful land 7
to enjoy its fruit and the goodness
  of it;
but when you entered upon it you
  defiled it
and made the home I gave you
  loathsome.
The priests no longer asked, 'Where 8
  is the LORD?'
Those who handled the law had no
  thought of me,
the shepherds of the people rebelled against me;
the prophets prophesied in the
  name of Baal
and followed gods powerless to
  help.
Therefore I will bring a charge 9
  against you once more,
says the LORD,
against you and against your descendants.
Cross to the coasts and islands of 10
  Kittim and see,
send to Kedar and consider well,
see whether there has been anything like this:
has a nation ever changed its gods, 11
although they were no gods?

But my people have exchanged
their Glory
for a god altogether powerless.

12 Stand aghast at this, you heavens,
tremble in utter despair,
says the LORD.

13 Two sins have my people committed:
they have forsaken me,
a spring of living water,
and they have hewn out for themselves cisterns,
cracked cisterns that can hold no
water.

14 Is Israel a slave? Was he born in
slavery?
If not, why has he been despoiled?

15 Why do lions roar and growl at
him?
Why has his land been laid waste,
why are his cities razed to the
ground and abandoned?

16 Men of Noph and Tahpanhes
will break your heads.

17 Is it not your desertion of the LORD
your God
that brings all this upon you?

18 And now, why should you make off
to Egypt
to drink the waters of the Shihor?
Or why make off to Assyria
to drink the waters of the River?

19 It is your own wickedness that will
punish you,
your own apostasy that will condemn you.
See for yourselves how bitter a
thing it is and how evil,
to forsake the LORD your God and
revere me no longer.
This is the very word of the Lord
GOD of Hosts.

20 Ages ago you broke your yoke and
snapped your traces,
crying, 'I will not be your slave';
and you sprawled in promiscuous
vice
on all the hill-tops, under every
spreading tree.

21 I planted you as a choice red vine,
true stock all of you,

yet now you are turned into a
vine
debased and worthless!

22 The stain of your sin is still there
and I see it,
though you wash with soda and do
not stint the soap.
This is the very word of the Lord
GOD.

23 How can you say, 'I am not polluted, not I!
I have not followed the Baalim'?
Look how you conducted yourself
in the valley;
remember what you have done.
You have been like a she-camel,
twisting and turning as she runs,

24 rushing alone into*a* the wilderness,
snuffing the wind in her lust;
who can restrain her in her heat?
No one need tire himself out in
pursuit of her;
she is easily found at mating time.

25 Why not save your feet from stony
ground
and your throats from thirst?
But you said, 'No; I am desperate.
I love foreign gods and I must go
after them.'

26 As a thief is ashamed when he is
found out,
so the people of Israel feel ashamed,
they, their kings, their princes,
their priests and their prophets;

27 they say 'You are our father' to a
block of wood
and cry 'Mother' to a stone.
But on me they have turned their
backs
and averted their faces from me.
And now on the day of disaster
they say,
'Rise up and save us.'

28 Where are they, those gods you
made for yourselves?
Let them come and save you in the
day of disaster.
For you, Judah, have as many
gods as you have towns.*b*

29 The LORD answers,
Why argue your case with me?
You are rebels, every one of you.

---

a rushing alone into: *prob. rdg.*; *Heb.* a wild-ass taught in.
b towns: *or* blood-spattered altars.

30 In vain I struck down your sons,
the lesson was not learnt;
still your own sword devoured
your prophets
like a ravening lion.
31 ^aHave I shown myself inhospitable
to Israel
like some wilderness or waterless
land?
Why do my people say, 'We have
broken away;
we will never come back to thee'?

32 Will a girl forget her finery
or a bride her ribbons?
Yet my people have forgotten me
over and over again.
33 How well you pick your way in
search of lovers!
Why! even the worst of women
can learn from you.
34 Yes, and there is blood on the
corners of your robe –
the life-blood of the innocent poor.
You did not get it by house-
breaking
but by your sacrifices under every
oak.
35 You say, 'I am innocent;
surely his anger has passed away.'
But I will challenge your claim
to have done no sin.
36 Why do you so lightly change your
course?
Egypt will fail you as Assyria did;
37 you shall go out from here,
each of you with his hands above
his head,
for the LORD repudiates those in
whom you trusted,
and from them you shall gain
nothing.

3 If a man puts away his wife
and she leaves him,
and if she then becomes another's,
may he go back to her again?
Is not that woman defiled,
a forbidden thing?
You have played the harlot with
many lovers;
can you come back to me?
says the LORD.

Look up to the high bare places 2
and see:
where have you not been ravished?
You sat by the wayside to catch
lovers,
like an Arab lurking in the desert,
and defiled the land
with your fornication and your
wickedness.
Therefore the showers were with- 3
held
and the spring rain failed.
But yours was a harlot's brow,
and you were resolved to show no
shame.
Not so long since, you called me 4
'Father,
dear friend of my youth',
thinking, 'Will he be angry for 5
ever?
Will he rage eternally?'
This is how you spoke; you have
done evil
and gone unchallenged.

In the reign of King Josiah, the 6
LORD said to me, Do you see what
apostate Israel did? She went up to
every hill-top and under every
spreading tree, and there she played the whore. Even after she had 7
done all this, I said to her, Come
back to me, but she would not.
That faithless woman, her sister
Judah, saw it all; she saw too that I 8
had put apostate Israel away and
given her a note of divorce because
she had committed adultery. Yet
that faithless woman, her sister
Judah, was not afraid; she too
has gone and played the whore.
She defiled the land with her 9
thoughtless harlotry and her adulterous worship of stone and wood.
In spite of all this that faithless 10
woman, her sister Judah, has not
come back to me in good faith,
but only in pretence. This is the
very word of the LORD.
The LORD said to me, Apostate 11
Israel is less to blame than that
faithless woman Judah. Go and 12
proclaim this message to the north:

---

^a *Prob. rdg.; Heb. prefixes* You, O generation, see the word of the LORD.

Come back to me, apostate Israel,
says the LORD,
I will no longer frown on you.
For my love is unfailing, says the
LORD,
I will not be angry for ever.

13 Only you must acknowledge your
wrongdoing,
confess your rebellion against the
LORD your God.
Confess your promiscuous traffic
with foreign gods
under every spreading tree,
confess that you have not obeyed
me.
This is the very word of the LORD.

14 Come back to me, apostate children, says the LORD, for I am
patient with you, and I will take
you, one from a city and two from
a clan, and bring you to Zion.
15 There will I give you shepherds
after my own heart, and they shall
lead you with knowledge and un-
16 derstanding. In those days, when
you have increased and become
fruitful in the land, says the LORD,
men shall speak no more of the Ark
of the Covenant of the LORD; they
shall not think of it nor remember
it nor resort to it; it will be needed
17 no more. At that time Jerusalem
shall be called the Throne of the
LORD. All nations shall gather in
Jerusalem to honour the LORD's
name; never again shall they follow
the promptings of their evil and
18 stubborn hearts. In those days
Judah shall join Israel, and together they shall come from a
northern land into the land I gave
their fathers as their patrimony.

19 I said, How gladly would I treat
you as a son,
giving you a pleasant land,
a patrimony fairer than that of any
nation!
I said, You shall call me Father
and never cease to follow me.
20 But like a woman who is unfaithful
to her lover,

so you, Israel, were unfaithful to
me.
This is the very word of the LORD.
Hark, a sound of weeping on the 21
bare places,
Israel's people pleading for mercy!
For they have taken to crooked
ways
and ignored the LORD their God.
Come back to me, wayward^a sons; 22
I will heal your apostasy.

O LORD, we come! We come to
thee;
for thou art our God.
There is no help in worship on the 23
hill-tops,
no help from clamour on the
heights;
truly in the LORD our God
is Israel's only salvation.
From our early days 24
Baal, god of shame, has devoured
the fruits of our fathers' labours,
their flocks and herds, their sons
and daughters.
Let us lie down in shame, wrapped 25
round by our dishonour,
for we have sinned against the
LORD our God,
both we and our fathers,
from our early days till now,
and we have not obeyed the LORD
our God.

If you will but come back, O Israel, 4
if you will but come back to me,
says the LORD,
if you will banish your loathsome
idols from my sight,
and stray no more,
if you swear by the life of the 2
LORD,
in truth, in justice and uprightness,
then shall the nations pray to be
blessed like you^b
and in you^b shall they boast.

These are the words of the LORD to 3
the men of Judah and Jerusalem:

Break up your fallow ground,
do not sow among thorns,

---

^a *Or* apostate.   ^b *Prob. rdg.*; *Heb.* him.

4 circumcise yourselves to the service of the LORD,
circumcise your hearts,
men of Judah and dwellers in Jerusalem,
lest the fire of my fury blaze up and burn unquenched,
because of your evil doings.

5 Tell this in Judah,
proclaim it in Jerusalem,
blow the trumpet throughout the land,
sound the muster,
give the command, Stand to! –
and let us fall back
on the fortified cities.

6 Raise the signal – To Zion!
make for safety, lose no time,
for I bring disaster out of the north,
and dire destruction.

7 A lion has come out from his lair,
the destroyer of nations;
he has struck his tents, he has broken camp,
to harry your land
and lay your cities waste and unpeopled.

8 Well may you put on sackcloth,
beat the breast and wail,
for the anger of the LORD
is not averted from us.

9 On that day, says the LORD,
the hearts of the king and his officers shall fail them,
priests shall be struck with horror
and prophets dumbfounded.

10 And I said, O Lord GOD, thou surely didst deceive this people and Jerusalem in saying, 'You shall have peace', while the sword is at our throats.

11 At that time this people and Jerusalem shall be told:

A scorching wind from the high bare places in the wilderness
sweeps down upon my people,
no breeze for winnowing or for cleansing;

12 a wind too strong for these will come at my bidding,

and now I will state my case against them.

Like clouds the enemy advances 13
with a whirlwind of chariots;
his horses are swifter than eagles –
alas, we are overwhelmed!
O Jerusalem, wash the wrongdoing 14
from your heart
and you may yet be saved;
how long will you cherish
your evil schemes?
Hark, a runner from Dan, 15
tidings of evil from Mount Ephraim!
Tell all this to the nations, 16
proclaim the doom of Jerusalem:
hordes of invaders come from a distant land,
howling against the cities of Judah.
Their pickets are closing in all 17
round her,
because she has rebelled against me.
This is the very word of the LORD.
Your own ways, your own deeds 18
have brought all this upon you;
this is your punishment,
and all this comes of your rebellion.[a]
Oh, the writhing of my bowels 19
and the throbbing of my heart!
I cannot keep silence.
I hear the sound of the trumpet,
the sound of the battle-cry.
Crash upon crash, 20
the land goes down in ruin,
my tents are thrown down,
their coverings torn to shreds.
How long must I see the standard 21
raised
and hear the trumpet call?
My people are fools, they know 22
nothing of me;
silly children, with no understanding,
they are clever only in wrongdoing,
and of doing right they know nothing.

I saw the earth, and it was without 23
form and void;
the heavens, and their light was gone.

[a] *your rebellion: prob. rdg.; Heb. obscure.*

24 I saw the mountains, and they
      reeled;
   all the hills rocked to and fro.
25 I saw, and there was no man,
   and the very birds had taken
      flight.
26 I saw, and the farm-land was
      wilderness,
   and the towns all razed to the
      ground,
   before the LORD in his anger.
27 These are the words of the LORD:
   The whole land shall be desolate,
   though I will not make an end of
      it.
28 Therefore the earth will mourn
   and the heavens above turn black.
   For I have made known my
      purpose;
   I will not relent or change my
      mind.

29 At the sound of the horsemen and
      archers
   the whole country is in flight;
   they creep into caves, they hide in
      thickets,
   they scramble up the crags.
   Every town is forsaken,
   no one dwells there.

30 And you, what are you doing?
   When you dress yourself in scarlet,
   deck yourself out with golden
      ornaments,
   and make your eyes big with
      antimony,
   you are beautifying yourself to no
      purpose.
   Your lovers spurn you
   and are out for your life.
31 I hear a sound as of a woman in
      labour,
   the sharp cry of one bearing her
      first child.
   It is Zion, gasping for breath,
   clenching her fists.
   Ah me! I am weary,
   weary of slaughter.

5 Go up and down the streets of
      Jerusalem
   and see for yourselves;
   search her wide squares:

can you find any man who acts
      justly,
who seeks the truth,
that I may forgive that city?
Men may swear by the life of the 2
      LORD,
but they only perjure themselves.
O LORD, are thine eyes not set 3
      upon the truth?
Thou didst strike them down,
but they took no heed;
didst pierce them to the heart,
but they refused to learn.
They set their faces harder than
      flint
and refused to come back.
I said, 'After all, these are the poor, 4
these are stupid folk,
who do not know the way of the
      LORD,
the ordinances of their God.
I will go to the great   5
and speak with them;
for they will know the way of the
      LORD,
the ordinances of their God.'
But they too have broken the yoke
and snapped their traces.
Therefore a lion out of the scrub 6
      shall strike them down,
a wolf from the plains shall ravage
      them;
a leopard shall prowl about their
      cities
and maul any who venture out.
For their rebellious deeds are
      many,
their apostasies past counting.
How can I forgive you for all this? 7
Your sons have forsaken me and
      sworn by gods
that are no gods.
I gave them all they needed, yet
      they preferred adultery,
and haunted the brothels;
each neighs after another man's 8
      wife,
like a well-fed and lusty stallion.
Shall I not punish them for this? 9
the LORD asks.
Shall I not take vengeance
on such a people?
Go along her rows of vines and 10
      slash them,

yet do not make an end of them.
Hack away her green branches,
for they are not the LORD's.

11 Faithless are Israel and Judah,
both faithless to me.
This is the very word of the LORD.

12 They have denied the LORD,
saying, 'He does not exist.
No evil shall come upon us;
we shall never see sword or famine.

13 The prophets will prove mere
wind,
the word not in them.'

14 And so, because you talk in this
way, these are the words of the
LORD the God of Hosts to me:

I will make my words a fire in your
mouth;
and it shall burn up this people
like brushwood.

15 I bring against you, Israel, a nation from afar,
an ancient people established long
ago,
says the LORD.
A people whose language you do
not know,
whose speech you will not understand;

16 they are all mighty warriors,
their jaws are a grave, wide open,

17 to devour your harvest and your
bread,
to devour your sons and your
daughters,
to devour your flocks and your
herds,
to devour your vines and your
fig-trees.
They shall batter down the cities in
which you trust,[a]
walled though they are.

18 But in those days, the LORD
declares, I will still not make an

19 end of you. When you ask, 'Why
has the LORD our God done all this
to us?' I shall answer, 'As you have
forsaken me and served alien gods

in your own land, so shall you serve
foreigners[b] in a land that is not
yours.'

20 Tell this to the people of Jacob,
proclaim it in Judah:

21 Listen, you foolish and senseless
people,
who have eyes and see nothing,
ears and hear nothing.

22 Have you no fear of me? says the
LORD;
will you not shiver before me,
before me, who made the shivering
sand to bound the sea,
a barrier it never can pass?
Its waves heave and toss but they
are powerless;
roar as they may, they cannot
pass.

23 But this people has a rebellious
and defiant heart,
rebels they have been and now
they are clean gone.

24 They did not say to themselves,
'Let us fear the LORD our God,
who gives us the rains of autumn
and spring showers in their turn,
who brings us unfailingly
fixed seasons of harvest.'

25 But your wrongdoing has upset
nature's order,
and your sins have kept from you
her kindly gifts.

26 For among my people there are
wicked men,
who lay snares like a fowler's net[c]
and set deadly traps to catch men.

27 Their houses are full of fraud,
as a cage is full of birds.
They grow rich and grand,

28 bloated and rancorous;
their thoughts are all of evil,
and they refuse to do justice,
the claims of the orphan they do
not put right
nor do they grant justice to the
poor.

29 Shall I not punish them for this?
says the LORD;
shall I not take vengeance
on such a people?

---

[a] *Prob. rdg.; Heb. adds* with the sword.
[b] *Or* foreign gods.
[c] who...net: *prob. rdg.; Heb. unintelligible.*

30 An appalling thing, an outrage,
   has appeared in this land:
31 prophets prophesy lies and priests
   go hand in hand with them,
   and my people love to have it so.
   How will you fare at the end of it
   all?

6 Save yourselves, men of Benjamin,
   come out of Jerusalem,
   blow the trumpet in Tekoa,
   fire the beacon on Beth-hakkerem,
   for calamity looms from the north
   and great disaster.
2 Zion, delightful and lovely:
   her end is near –
3 she to whom the shepherds come
   and bring their flocks with them.
   There they pitch their tents all
   round her,
   each grazing his own strip of
   pasture.
4 Declare war solemnly against her;
   come, let us attack her at noon.
   Too late! the day declines
   and the shadows lengthen.
5 Come then, let us attack her by
   night
   and destroy her palaces.
6 These are the words of the LORD
   of Hosts:
   Cut down the trees of Jerusalem
   and raise siege-ramps against her,
   the city whose name is Licence,
   oppression is rampant in her.
7 As a well keeps its water fresh,
   so she keeps her evil fresh.
   Violence and outrage echo in her
   streets;
   sickness and wounds stare me in
   the face.
8 Learn your lesson, Jerusalem,
   lest my love for you be torn from
   my heart,
   and I leave you desolate,
   a land where no one can live.
9 These are the words of the LORD of
   Hosts:
   Glean the remnant of Israel
   like a vine,
   pass your hand like a vintager one
   last time
   over the branches.

To whom can I address myself,   10
   to whom give solemn warning?
   Who will hear me?
Their ears are uncircumcised;
   they cannot listen;
   they treat the LORD's word as a
   reproach;
   they show no concern with it.
But I am full of the anger of the   11
   LORD,
   I cannot hold it in.
   I must pour it out on the children
   in the street
   and on the young men in their
   gangs.
Man and wife alike shall be caught
   in it,
   the greybeard and the very old.
Their houses shall be turned over   12
   to others,
   their fields and their women alike.
For I will raise my hand, says the
   LORD,
   against the people of the country.
For all, high and low,   13
   are out for ill-gotten gain;
   prophets and priests are frauds,
   every one of them;
   they dress my people's wound, but   14
   skin-deep only,
   with their saying, 'All is well.'
   All well? Nothing is well!
Are they ashamed when they prac-   15
   tise their abominations?
   Ashamed? Not they!
   They can never be put out of
   countenance.
   Therefore they shall fall with a
   great crash,[a]
   and be brought to the ground on
   the day of my reckoning.
   The LORD has said it.

These are the words of the LORD: 16
   Stop at the cross-roads; look for
   the ancient paths; ask, 'Where is
   the way that leads to what is good?'
   Then take that way, and you will
   find rest for yourselves. But they
   said, 'We will not.' Then I will   17
   appoint watchmen to direct you;
   listen for their trumpet-call. But
   they said, 'We will not.' Therefore   18

---

[a] with a great crash: *or* where they fall *or* among the fallen.

hear, you nations, and take note,
all you who witness it, of the plight
19 of this people. Listen, O earth, I
bring ruin on them, the harvest of
all their scheming; for they have
given no thought to my words and
20 have spurned my instruction. What
good is it to me if frankincense is
brought from Sheba and fragrant
spices from distant lands? I will
not accept your whole-offerings,
your sacrifices do not please me.
21 Therefore these are the words of
the LORD:

I will set obstacles before this
people
which shall bring them to the
ground;
fathers and sons, friends and neighbours
shall all perish together.

22 These are the words of the LORD:

See, a people is coming from a
northern land,
a great nation rouses itself from
earth's farthest corners.
23 They come with bow and sabre,
cruel men and pitiless,
bestriding their horses, they sound
like the thunder of the sea,
they are like men arrayed for
battle against you, Zion.
24 We have heard tell of them
and our hands hang limp,
agony grips us, the anguish of a
woman in labour.
25 Do not go out into the country,
do not walk by the high road;
for the foe, sword in hand,
is a terror let loose.
26 Daughter of my people, wrap
yourself in sackcloth,
sprinkle ashes over yourself, wail
bitterly,
as one who mourns an only son;
in an instant shall the marauder be
upon us.

27 I have appointed you an assayer of
my people;

you will know how to test them
and will assay their conduct;
arch-rebels all of them,　　　　　　28
mischief-makers, corrupt to a man.
The bellows puff and blow, the　29
furnace glows;
in vain does the refiner smelt the
ore,
lead, copper and iron*a* are not
separated out.
Call them spurious silver;　　　　　30
for the LORD has spurned them.

False religion and its punishment

THIS word came from the LORD to　7
Jeremiah. Stand at the gate of the　2
LORD's house and there make your
proclamation: Listen to the words
of the LORD, all you men of Judah
who come in through these gates
to worship him. These are the　3
words of the LORD of Hosts the
God of Israel: Mend your ways and
your doings, that I may let you
live in this place. You keep saying,　4
'This place*b* is the temple of the
LORD, the temple of the LORD, the
temple of the LORD!' This catch-
word of yours is a lie; put no trust
in it. Mend your ways and your　5
doings, deal fairly with one another, do not oppress the alien, the　6
orphan, and the widow, shed no
innocent blood in this place, do not
run after other gods to your own
ruin. Then will I let you live in this　7
place, in the land which I gave long
ago to your forefathers for all time.
You gain nothing by putting your　8
trust in this lie. You steal, you　9
murder, you commit adultery and
perjury, you burn sacrifices to
Baal, you run after other gods
whom you have not known; then　10
you come and stand before me in
this house, which bears my name,
and say, 'We are safe'; safe, you
think, to indulge in all these abominations. Do you think that this　11
house, this house which bears my
name, is a robbers' cave? I myself

---

a copper and iron: *transposed from after* mischief-makers *in verse* 28.
b This place: *prob. rdg.; Heb.* Those.

have seen all this, says the LORD.

12 Go to my shrine at Shiloh, which once I made a dwelling for my Name, and see what I did to it because of the wickedness of my 13 people Israel. And now you have done all these things, says the LORD; though I took pains to speak to you, you did not listen, and though I called, you gave no 14 answer. Therefore what I did to Shiloh I will do to this house which bears my name, the house in which you put your trust, the place I gave to you and your fore- 15 fathers; I will fling you away out of my sight, as I flung away all your kinsfolk, the whole brood of Ephraim.

16 Offer up no prayer, Jeremiah, for this people, raise no plea or prayer on their behalf, and do not intercede with me; for I will not 17 listen to you. Do you not see what is going on in the cities of Judah and in the streets of Jerusalem? 18 Children are gathering wood, fathers lighting fires, women kneading dough to make crescent-cakes in honour of the queen of heaven; and drink-offerings are poured out to other gods than me – all to pro- 19 voke and hurt me. But is it I, says the LORD, whom they hurt? No; it is themselves, covering their own 20 selves with shame. Therefore, says the Lord GOD, my anger and my fury shall fall on this place, on man and beast, on trees and crops, and it shall burn unquenched.

21 These are the words of the LORD of Hosts the God of Israel: Add whole-offerings to sacrifices and 22 eat the flesh if you will. But when I brought your forefathers out of Egypt, I gave them no commands about whole-offering and sacrifice; I said not a word about them. 23 What I did command them was this: If you obey me, I will be your God and you shall be my people. You must conform to all my com- 24 mands, if you would prosper. But they did not listen; they paid no

heed, and persisted in disobedience with evil and stubborn hearts; they looked backwards and not forwards, from the day when your 25 forefathers left Egypt until now. I took pains to send to them all my servants the prophets; they did 26 not listen to me, they paid no heed, but were obstinate and proved even more wicked than their forefathers. When you tell them this, 27 they will not listen to you; if you call them, they will not answer. Then you shall say to them, This is 28 the nation that did not obey the LORD its God nor accept correction; truth has perished, it is heard no more on their lips.

O Jerusalem, cut off your hair, 29
the symbol of your dedication, and throw it away;
raise up a lament on the high bare places.

For the LORD has spurned the generation which has roused his wrath, and has abandoned them. For the men of Judah have done 30 what is wrong in my eyes, says the LORD. They have defiled with their loathsome idols the house that bears my name, they have built a 31 shrine of Topheth in the Valley of Ben-hinnom, at which to burn their sons and daughters; that was no command of mine, nor did it ever enter my thought. Therefore a 32 time is coming, says the LORD, when it shall no longer be called Topheth or the Valley of Ben-hinnom, but the Valley of Slaughter; for the dead shall be buried in Topheth because there is no room elsewhere. So the bodies of this 33 people shall become food for the birds of the air and the wild beasts, and there will be no one to scare them away. From the cities of 34 Judah and the streets of Jerusalem I will banish all sounds of joy and gladness, the voice of the bridegroom and the bride; for the land shall become desert.

8 At that time, says the LORD, men shall bring out from their graves the bones of the kings of Judah, of the officers, priests, and prophets, and of all who lived in
2 Jerusalem. They shall expose them to the sun, the moon, and all the host of heaven, whom they loved and served and adored, to whom they resorted and bowed in worship. Those bones shall not be gathered up nor buried but shall
3 become dung on the ground. All the survivors of this wicked race, wherever I have banished them, would rather die than live. This is the very word of the LORD of Hosts.

4 You shall say to them, These are the words of the LORD:

If men fall, can they not also rise?
If a man breaks away, can he not return?
5 Then why are this people so wayward,
incurable in their waywardness?
Why have they clung to their treachery
and refused to return to their obedience?
6 I have listened to them
and heard not one word of truth,
not one sinner crying remorsefully,
'Oh, what have I done?'
Each one breaks away[a] in headlong career
as a war-horse plunges in battle.

7 The stork in the sky
knows the time to migrate,
the dove and the swift and the wryneck
know the season of return;
but my people do not know the ordinances of the LORD.
8 How can you say, 'We are wise,
we have the law of the LORD',
when scribes with their lying pens have falsified it?
9 The wise are put to shame, they are dismayed and have lost their wits.

They have spurned the word of the LORD,
and what sort of wisdom is theirs?
Therefore will I give their wives to 10 other men
and their lands to new owners.
For all, high and low,
are out for ill-gotten gain;
prophets and priests are frauds,
every one of them;
they dress my people's wound, but 11 skin-deep only,
with their saying, 'All is well.'
All well? Nothing is well!
Are they ashamed when they prac- 12 tise their abominations?
Ashamed? Not they!
They can never be put out of countenance.
Therefore they shall fall with a great crash,[b]
and be brought to the ground on the day of my reckoning.
The LORD has said it.
I would gather their harvest, says 13 the LORD,
but there are no grapes on the vine,
no figs on the fig-tree;
even their leaves are withered.
Why do we sit idle? Up, all of you 14 together,
let us go into our walled cities and there meet our doom.
For the LORD our God has struck us down,
he has given us a draught of bitter poison;
for we have sinned against the LORD.
Can we hope to prosper when 15 nothing goes well?
Can we hope for respite when the terror falls suddenly?
The snorting of his horses is heard 16 from Dan;
at the neighing of his stallions the whole land trembles.
The enemy come; they devour the land and all its store,
city and citizens alike.
Beware, I am sending snakes 17 against you,

[a] breaks away: *or* is wayward.
[b] with a great crash: *or* where they fall *or* among the fallen.

vipers, such as no man can
charm,
and they shall bite you.
This is the very word of the
LORD.

18 How can I bear my sorrow?[a]
I am sick at heart.
19 Hark, the cry of my people
from a distant land:
'Is the LORD not in Zion?
Is her King no longer there?'
Why do they provoke me with
their images
and foreign gods?
20 Harvest is past, summer is over,
and we are not saved.
21 I am wounded at the sight of my
people's wound;
I go like a mourner, overcome with
horror.
22 Is there no balm in Gilead,
no physician there?
Why has no new skin grown over
their wound?

9 Would that my head were all
water,
my eyes a fountain of tears,
that I might weep day and night
for my people's dead!

2 Oh that I could find in the wilderness a shelter by the wayside,
that I might leave my people and
depart!
Adulterers are they all, a mob of
traitors.
3 The tongue is their weapon, a bow
ready bent.
Lying, not truth, is master in the
land.
They run from one sin to another,
and for me they care nothing.
This is the very word of the LORD.

4 Be on your guard, each man
against his friend;
put no trust even in a brother.
Brother supplants brother,[b]
and friend slanders friend.

They make game of their friends 5
but never speak the truth;
they have trained their tongues to
lies;
deep in their sin, they cannot re-
trace their steps.
Wrong follows wrong, deceit fol- 6
lows deceit;
they refuse to acknowledge me.
This is the very word of the LORD.
Therefore these are the words of 7
the LORD of Hosts:
I am their refiner and will assay
them.
How can I disregard my people?
Their tongue is a cruel arrow, 8
their mouths speak lies.
One speaks amicably to another,
while inwardly he plans a trap for
him.
Shall I not punish them for this? 9
says the LORD;
shall I not take vengeance
on such a people?

Over the mountains will I raise 10
weeping and wailing,
and over the desert pastures will I
chant a dirge.
They are scorched and untrodden,
they hear no lowing of cattle;
birds of the air and beasts have
fled and are gone.

I will make Jerusalem a heap of 11
ruins, a haunt of wolves,
and the cities of Judah an unpeopled waste.

What man is wise enough to 12
understand this, to understand
what the LORD has said and to
proclaim it? Why has the land
become a dead land, scorched like
the desert and untrodden? The 13
LORD said, It is because they forsook my law which I set before
them; they neither obeyed me nor
conformed to it. They followed the 14
promptings of their own stubborn
hearts, they followed the Baalim as

---

[a] How...sorrow?: *prob. rdg.*; *Heb. unintelligible.*
[b] Brother supplants brother: *or* Every brother is a supplanter like Jacob (*cp. Gen.
27. 35 and note*).

their forefathers had taught them.

15 Therefore these are the words of the LORD of Hosts the God of Israel: I will feed this people with wormwood and give them bitter

16 poison to drink. I will scatter them among nations whom neither they nor their forefathers have known; I will harry them with the sword until I have made an end of them.

17 These are the words of the LORD of Hosts:

Summon the wailing women to come,
send for the women skilled in keening

18 to come quickly and raise a lament for us,
that our eyes may run with tears
and our eyelids be wet with weeping.

19 Hark, hark, lamentation is heard in Zion:
How fearful is our ruin! How great our shame!
We have left our lands, our houses have been pulled down.

20 Listen, you women, to the words of the LORD,
that your ears may catch what he says.
Teach your daughters the lament,
let them teach one another this dirge:

21 Death has climbed in through our windows,
it has entered our palaces,
it sweeps off the children in the open air
and drives young men from the streets.

22 This is the word of the LORD:

The corpses of men shall fall and lie like dung in the fields,
like swathes behind the reaper, but no one shall gather them.

23 These are the words of the LORD:

Let not the wise man boast of his wisdom

nor the valiant of his valour;
let not the rich man boast of his riches;

24 but if any man would boast, let him boast of this,
that he understands and knows me.
For I am the LORD, I show unfailing love,
I do justice and right upon the earth;
for on these I have set my heart.
This is the very word of the LORD.

25 The time is coming, says the LORD, when I will punish all the

26 circumcised, Egypt and Judah, Edom and Ammon, Moab, and all who haunt the fringes of the desert;[a] for all alike, the nations and Israel, are uncircumcised in heart.

10 Listen, Israel, to this word that the LORD has spoken against you:

2 Do not fall into the ways of the nations,
do not be awed by signs in the heavens;
it is the nations who go in awe of these.

3 For the carved images of the nations are a sham,
they are nothing but timber cut from the forest,
worked with his chisel by a craftsman;

4 he adorns it with silver and gold, fastening them on with hammer and nails
so that they do not fall apart.

5 They can no more speak than a scarecrow in a plot of cucumbers;
they must be carried, for they cannot walk.
Do not be afraid of them: they can do no harm,
and they have no power to do good.

6 Where can one be found like thee, O LORD?
Great thou art and great the might of thy name.

7 Who shall not fear thee, king of the nations?
for fear is thy fitting tribute.

[a] who...desert: *or* the dwellers in the desert who clip the hair on their temples.

Where among the wisest of the
nations and all their royalty
can one be found like thee?

8 They are fools and blockheads one
and all,
learning their nonsense from a log
of wood.

9 The beaten silver is brought from
Tarshish
and the gold from Ophir;
all are the work of craftsmen and
goldsmiths.
They are draped in violet and
purple,
all the work of skilled men.

10 But the LORD is God in truth,
a living god, an eternal king.
The earth quakes under his wrath,
nations cannot endure his fury.

11 [You shall say this to them: The
gods who did not make heaven and
earth shall perish from the earth
and from under these heavens.]

12*a* God made the earth by his
power,
fixed the world in place by his
wisdom,
unfurled the skies by his understanding.

13 At the thunder of his voice the
waters in heaven are amazed;*b*
he brings up the mist from the ends
of the earth,
he opens rifts*c* for the rain
and brings the wind out of his
storehouses.

14 All men are brutish and ignorant;
every goldsmith is discredited by
his idol;
for the figures he casts are a
sham,
there is no breath in them.

15 They are worth nothing, mere
mockeries,
which perish when their day of
reckoning comes.

16 God, Jacob's creator, is not like
these;
for he is the maker of all.

Israel is the people he claims as his
own;
the LORD of Hosts is his name.

Put your goods together and carry 17
them out of the country,
living as you are under siege.

For these are the words of the 18
LORD:
This time I will uproot
the whole population of the land,
and I will press them hard and
squeeze them dry.

O the pain of my wounds! 19
Cruel are the blows I suffer.
But this is my plight, I said, and I
must endure it.

My home is ruined, my tent-ropes 20
all severed,
my sons have left me and are gone,
there is no one to pitch my tent
again,
no one to put up its curtains.

The shepherds of the people are 21
mere brutes;
they never consult the LORD,
and so they do not prosper,
and all their flocks at pasture are
scattered.

Hark, a rumour comes flying, 22
then a mounting uproar from the
land of the north,
an army to make Judah's cities
desolate, a haunt of wolves.

I know, O LORD, 23
that man's ways are not of his own
choosing;
nor is it for a man to determine his
course in life.

Correct us, O LORD, but with 24
justice, not in anger,
lest thou bring us almost to
nothing.

Pour out thy fury on nations 25
that have not acknowledged thee,
on tribes that have not invoked
thee by name;
for they have devoured Jacob and
made an end of him
and have left his home a waste.

---

a *Verses 12–16: cp. 51. 15–19.*   *b* At the thunder...amazed: *prob. rdg.*; *Heb.*
At the sound of his giving tumult of waters in heaven.
c rifts: *prob. rdg.*; *Heb.* lightnings.

Warnings and punishment

11 THE word which came to Jeremiah
2 from the LORD: Listen to the terms
of this covenant and repeat them
to the men of Judah and the in-
3 habitants of Jerusalem. Tell them,
These are the words of the LORD
the God of Israel: A curse on the
man who does not observe the
4 terms of this covenant by which I
bound your forefathers when I
brought them out of Egypt, from
the smelting-furnace. I said, If you
obey me and do all that I tell you,
you shall become my people and I
5 will become your God. And I will
thus make good the oath I swore
to your forefathers, that I would
give them a land flowing with
milk and honey, the land you now
possess. I answered, 'Amen, LORD.'
6 Then the LORD said: Proclaim all
these terms in the cities of Judah
and in the streets of Jerusalem.
Say, Listen to the terms of this
7 covenant and carry them out. I
have protested to your forefathers
since I brought them out of Egypt,
till this day; I took pains to warn
8 them: Obey me, I said. But they
did not obey; they paid no attention to me, but each followed the
promptings of his own stubborn
and wicked heart. So I brought on
them all the penalties laid down in
this covenant by which I had bound
them, whose terms they did not
observe.
9   The LORD said to me, The men
of Judah and the inhabitants of
Jerusalem have entered into a
10 conspiracy: they have gone back to
the sins of their earliest forefathers
and refused to listen to me. They
have followed other gods and worshipped them; Israel and Judah
have broken the covenant which I
11 made with their fathers. Therefore
these are the words of the LORD: I
now bring on them disaster from
which they cannot escape; though

they cry to me for help I will not
listen. The inhabitants of the cities 12
of Judah and of Jerusalem may go
and cry for help to the gods to
whom they have burnt sacrifices;
they will not save them in the hour
of disaster. For you, Judah, have 13
as many gods as you have towns;
you have set up as many altars to
burn sacrifices to Baal as there are
streets in Jerusalem. So offer up no 14
prayer for this people; raise no cry
or prayer on their behalf, for I will
not listen when they call to me in
the hour of disaster.

What right has my beloved in my 15
house
with her shameless ways?
Can the flesh of fat offerings on the
altar
ward off the disaster that threatens
you?
Once the LORD called you an 16
olive-tree,
leafy and fair;
but now with a great roaring noise
you will feel sharp anguish;[a]
fire sets its leaves alight
and consumes[b] its branches.

The LORD of Hosts who planted 17
you has threatened you with disaster, because of the harm Israel
and Judah brought on themselves
when they provoked me to anger
by burning sacrifices to Baal.
It was the LORD who showed me, 18
and so I knew; he opened my eyes
to what they were doing. I had 19
been like a sheep led obedient to
the slaughter; I did not know that
they were hatching plots against
me and saying, 'Let us cut down
the tree while the sap is in it; let us
destroy him out of the living, so
that his very name shall be forgotten.'

O LORD of Hosts who art a right- 20
eous judge,
testing the heart and mind,

---

[a] you will feel sharp anguish: *transposed from end of verse 15.*
[b] consumes: *prob. rdg.; Heb.* they consume.

I have committed my cause to
thee;
let me see thy vengeance upon
them.

21 Therefore these are the words of
the LORD about the men of Anathoth who seek to take my life, and
say, 'Prophesy no more in the
name of the LORD or we will kill
22 you' – these are his words: I will
punish them: their young men
shall die by the sword, their sons
and daughters shall die by famine.
23 Not one of them shall survive; for
in the year of their reckoning I
will bring ruin on the men of Anathoth.

12 O LORD, I will dispute with thee,
for thou art just;
yes, I will plead my case before
thee.
Why do the wicked prosper
and traitors live at ease?
2 Thou hast planted them and their
roots strike deep,
they grow up and bear fruit.
Thou art ever on their lips,
yet far from their hearts.
3 But thou knowest me, O LORD,
thou seest me;
thou dost test my devotion to
thyself.
Drag them away like sheep to the
shambles;
set them apart for the day of
slaughter.

4 How long must the country lie
parched
and its green grass wither?
No birds and beasts are left, because its people are so wicked,
because they say, 'God will not see
what we are doing.'

5 If you have raced with men and
the runners have worn you down,
how then can you hope to vie with
horses?

If you fall headlong in easy country,
how will you fare in Jordan's dense
thickets?
All men, your brothers and kins- 6
men, are traitors to you,
they are in full cry after you;
trust them not, for all the fine
words they give you.

I have forsaken the house of Israel, 7
I have cast off my own people.
I have given my beloved into the
power of her foes.
My own people have turned on me 8
like a lion from the scrub,
roaring against me; therefore I
hate them.
Is this land of mine a hyena's lair, 9
with birds of prey hovering all
around it?
Come, you wild beasts; come, all of
you, flock to the feast.

Many shepherds have ravaged my 10
vineyard
and trampled down my field,
they have made my pleasant field a
desolate wilderness,
made it a waste land, waste and 11
waterless, to my sorrow.
The whole land is waste, and no
one cares.

Plunderers have swarmed across 12
the high bare places in the wilderness, a sword of the LORD devouring the land from end to end; no
creature can find peace.

Men sow wheat and reap thistles; 13
they sift but get no grain.
They are disappointed of their[a]
harvest
because of the anger of the LORD.

These are the words of the LORD 14
about all those evil neighbours
who are laying hands on the land
which I gave to my people Israel as
their patrimony: I will uproot
them from that[b] soil. Yet, if they 16[c]
will learn the ways of my people,

---

[a] *Prob. rdg.*; *Heb.* your.
[b] *Prob. rdg.*; *Heb.* their.
[c] *The rest of verse 14 and verse 15 transposed to follow* destroy them *in verse 17.*

swearing by my name, 'By the life of the LORD', as they taught my people to swear by the Baal, they shall form families among my 17 people. But if they will not listen, I will uproot that people, uproot and destroy them. Also I will uproot 15 Judah from among them; but after I have uprooted them, I will have pity on them again and will bring each man back to his patrimony and his land. This is the very word of the LORD.

13 These were the words of the LORD to me: Go and buy yourself a linen girdle and put it round your waist, but do not let it come near 2 water. So I bought it as the LORD had told me and put it round my 3 waist. The LORD spoke to me a 4 second time: Take the girdle which you bought and put round your waist; go at once to Perath and hide it in a crevice among the 5 rocks. So I went and hid the girdle at[a] Perath, as the LORD had told 6 me. After a long time the LORD said to me: Go at once to Perath and fetch back the girdle which I 7 told you to hide there. So I went to Perath and looked for the place where I had hidden it, but when I picked it up, I saw that it was spoilt, and no good for anything. 8, 9 Again the LORD spoke to me and these were his words: Thus will I spoil the gross pride of Judah, the 10 gross pride of Jerusalem. This wicked nation has refused to listen to my words; they have followed other gods, serving them and bowing down to them. So it shall be[b] like this girdle, no good for any- 11 thing. For, just as a girdle is bound close to a man's waist, so I bound all Israel and all Judah to myself, says the LORD, so that they should become my people to win a name for me, and praise and glory; but they did not listen.

You shall say this to them: These 12 are the words of the LORD the God of Israel: Wine-jars should be filled with wine. They will answer, 'We know quite well that wine-jars should be filled with wine.' Then 13 you shall say to them, These are the words of the LORD: I will fill all the inhabitants of this land with wine until they are drunk – kings of David's line who sit on his throne, priests, prophets, and all who live in Jerusalem. I will dash 14 them to pieces one against an-other, fathers and sons alike, says the LORD, I will show them no compassion or pity or tenderness; nor refrain from destroying them.[c]

Hear and attend. Be not too proud 15
  to listen,
for it is the LORD who speaks.
Ascribe glory to the LORD your 16
  God
before the darkness falls,
before your feet stumble
on the twilit hill-sides,
before he turns the light you look
  for
to deep gloom and thick darkness.
If in those depths of gloom you 17
  will not listen,
then for very anguish I can only
  weep and shed tears,[d]
my eyes must stream with tears;
for the LORD's flock is carried away
  into captivity.
Say to the king and the queen 18
  mother:[e]
Down, take a humble seat,
for your proud crowns are fallen
  from your heads.
Your cities in the Negeb are be- 19
  sieged,
and no one can relieve them;
all Judah has been swept into exile,
  swept clean away.
Lift up your eyes and see   20
those who are coming from the
  north.

---

[a] Or by.   [b] Prob. rdg.; Heb. And let it be.
[c] nor refrain...them: or so corrupt are they.
[d] If...shed tears: or If you will not listen to this, for very anguish I must weep in secret.   [e] Or queen.

Where is the flock that was entrusted to you,
the flock you were so proud of?

21 What will you say when you
suffer
because your leaders[a] cannot be
found,
though it was you who trained
them
to be your head?
Will not pangs seize you,
like the pangs of a woman in
labour,

22 when you wonder,
'Why has this come upon me?'
For your many sins your skirts are
torn off you,
your limbs uncovered.

23 Can the Nubian change his skin,
or the leopard its spots?
And you? Can you do good,
you who are schooled in evil?

24 Therefore I will scatter you[b] like
chaff
driven by the desert wind.

25 This is your lot, the portion of the
rebel,
measured out by me, says the
LORD,
because you have forsaken me
and trusted in false gods.

26 So I myself have stripped off your
skirts
and laid bare your shame.

27 Your adulteries, your lustful
neighing,
your wanton lewdness, are an
offence to me.[c]
On the hills and in the open country
I have seen your foul deeds.
Alas, Jerusalem, unclean that you
are!
How long, how long will you delay?[d]

14 This came to Jeremiah as the
word of the LORD concerning the
drought:

Judah droops, her cities languish, 2
her men sink to the ground;
Jerusalem's cry goes up.
Their flock-masters send their boys 3
for water;
they come to the pools but find no
water there.
Back they go, with empty vessels;
the produce[e] of the land has failed, 4
because there is no rain.
The farmers' hopes are wrecked,
they uncover their heads for grief.
The hind calves in the open 5
country
and forsakes her young
because there is no grass;
for lack of herbage, wild asses 6
stand on the high bare places
and snuff the wind for moisture,
as wolves do, and their eyes begin
to fail.
Though our sins testify against us, 7
yet act,[f] O LORD, for thy own
name's sake.
Our disloyalties indeed are many;
we have sinned against thee.
O hope of Israel, their saviour in 8
time of trouble,
must thou be a stranger in the
land,
a traveller pitching his tent for a
night?
Must thou be like a man suddenly 9
overcome,
like a man powerless to save
himself?
Thou art in our midst, O LORD,
and thou hast named us thine; do
not forsake us.

The LORD speaks thus of this 10
people: They love to stray from my
ways, they wander where they
will. Therefore he has no more
pleasure in them; he remembers
their guilt now, and punishes their
sins. Then the LORD said to me, Do 11
not pray for the well-being of this
people. When they fast, I will not 12
listen to their cry; when they

---

[a] leaders: *transposed from next line.*
[b] *Prob. rdg.; Heb.* them.
[c] an offence to me (*Heb.* you): *transposed from verse 26.*
[d] How...delay?: *prob. rdg.; Heb.* unintelligible.
[e] the produce: *prob. rdg.; Heb. obscure.*
[f] *Or* turn away.

sacrifice whole-offering and grain-offering, I will not accept them. I will make an end of them with sword, with famine and pestilence.

13 But I said, O Lord GOD, the prophets tell them that they shall see no sword and suffer no famine; for thou wilt give them lasting pro-

14 sperity in this place. The LORD answered me, The prophets are prophesying lies in my name. I have not sent them; I have given them no charge; I have not spoken to them. The prophets offer them false visions, worthless augury, and their own deluding fancies.

15 Therefore these are the words of the LORD about the prophets who, though not sent by me, prophesy in my name and say that neither sword nor famine shall touch this land: By sword and by famine shall those prophets meet their

16 end. The people to whom they prophesy shall be flung out into the streets of Jerusalem, victims of famine and sword; they, their wives, their sons, and their daughters, with no one to bury them: I will pour down upon them the evil they deserve.

17 So this is what you shall say to them:
Let my eyes stream with tears, ceaselessly, day and night.
For the virgin daughter of my people
has been broken in pieces, struck by a cruel blow.

18 If I go out into the country, I see men slain by the sword; if I enter the city, I see the ravages of famine; prophet and priest alike go begging round the land and are never at rest.

19 Hast thou spurned Judah utterly? Dost thou loathe Zion?
Why hast thou wounded us, and there is no remedy;
why let us hope for better days, and we find nothing good,

for a time of healing, and all is disaster?

20 We acknowledge our wickedness, the guilt of our forefathers;
O LORD, we have sinned against thee.

21 Do not despise the place where thy name dwells
nor bring contempt on the throne of thy glory.
Remember thy covenant with us and do not make it void.

22 Can any of the false gods of the nations give rain?
Or do the heavens send showers of themselves?
Art thou not God, O LORD,
that we may hope in thee?
It is thou only who doest[a] all these things.

The LORD said to me, Even if 15 Moses and Samuel stood before me, I would not be moved to pity this people. Banish them from my presence; let them be gone. When 2 they ask where they are to go, you shall say to them, These are the words of the LORD:

Those who are for death shall go to their death,
and those for the sword to the sword;
those who are for famine to famine, and those for captivity to captivity.

Four kinds of doom do I ordain 3 for them, says the LORD: the sword to kill, dogs to tear, birds of prey from the skies and beasts from their lairs to devour and destroy. I will make them repugnant to all 4 the kingdoms of the earth, because of the crimes of Manasseh son of Hezekiah, king of Judah, in Jerusalem.

Who will take pity on you, Jeru- 5 salem,
who will offer you consolation?
Who will turn aside to wish you well?

---

[a] Or madest.

6 You cast me off, says the LORD,
you turned your backs on me.
So I stretched out my hand and
ruined you;
I was weary of relenting.

7 I winnowed them and scattered
them
through the cities of the land;
I brought bereavement on them, I
destroyed my people,
for they would not abandon their
ways.

8 I made widows among them more
in number
than the sands of the sea;
I brought upon them a horde of
raiders[a]
to plunder at high noon.
I made the terror of invasion fall
upon them
all in a moment.

9 The mother of seven sons grew
faint,
she sank into a swoon;
her light was quenched while it was
yet day;
she was left humbled and shamed.
All the remnant I gave to perish by
the sword
at the hand of their enemies.
This is the very word of the LORD.

Confessions and addresses

10 Alas, alas, my mother, that you
ever gave me birth!
a man doomed to strife, with the
whole world against me.
I have borrowed from no one, I
have lent to no one,
yet all men abuse me.

11 The LORD answered,

But I will greatly strengthen you;
in time of distress and in time of
disaster
I will bring the enemy to your feet.

12 Can iron break steel from the
north?[b]

LORD, thou knowest;   15
remember me, LORD, and come to
visit me,
take vengeance for me on my
persecutors.
Be patient with me and take me
not away,
see what reproaches I endure for
thy sake.
I have to suffer those who despise   16
thy words,
but thy word is joy and happiness
to me,
for thou hast named me thine,
O LORD, God of Hosts.
I have never kept company with   17
any gang of roisterers,
or made merry with them;
because I felt thy hand upon me I
have sat alone;
for thou hast filled me with indignation.
Why then is my pain unending,   18
my wound desperate and incurable?
Thou art to me like a brook that is
not to be trusted,
whose waters fail.

This was the LORD's answer: 19

If you will turn back to me, I will
take you back
and you shall stand before me.
If you choose noble utterance and
reject the base,
you shall be my spokesman.
This people will turn again to
you,
but you will not turn to them.
To withstand them I will make you 20
impregnable,
a wall of bronze.
They will attack you but they will
not prevail,
for I am with you to deliver you
and save you, says the LORD;
I will deliver you from the wicked, 21
I will rescue you from the ruthless.

---

[a] I brought...raiders: *prob. rdg.*; *Heb. obscure.*   [b] *Prob. rdg.*; *Heb. adds* and
bronze. *Heb. also adds* (13) I will give away your wealth as spoil, and your treasure
for no payment, because of your sin throughout your country. (14) I will make
your enemies pass through a land you do not know; for my anger is a blazing fire
and it shall burn for ever (*cp.* 17. 3, 4).

16 The word of the LORD came to
2 me: You shall not marry a wife;
you shall have neither son nor
3 daughter in this place. For these
are the words of the LORD concerning sons and daughters born in
this place, the mothers who bear
them and the fathers who beget
4 them in this land: When men die,
struck down by deadly ulcers,
there shall be no wailing for them
and no burial; they shall be like
dung lying upon the ground. When
men perish by sword or famine,
their corpses shall become food for
birds and for beasts.

5 For these are the words of the
LORD: Enter no house where there
is a mourning-feast; do not go in to
wail or to bring comfort, for I have
withdrawn my peace from this
people, says the LORD, my love
6 and affection. High and low shall
die in this land, but there shall be
no burial, no wailing for them; no
one shall gash himself, or shave
7 his head. No one shall give the
mourner a portion of bread to console him for the dead, nor give him
the cup of consolation, even for
8 his father or mother. Nor shall you
enter a house where there is feasting, to sit eating and drinking
9 there. For these are the words of
the LORD of Hosts, the God of
Israel: In your own days, in the
sight of you all, and in this very
place, I will silence all sounds of
joy and gladness, and the voice of
bridegroom and bride.
10 When you tell this people all
these things they will ask you,
'Why has the LORD decreed that
this great disaster is to come upon
us? What wrong have we done?
What sin have we committed
11 against the LORD our God?' You
shall answer, Because your forefathers forsook me, says the LORD,
and followed other gods, serving
them and bowing down to them.
They forsook me and did not keep
12 my law. And you yourselves have

done worse than your forefathers;
for each of you follows the promptings of his wicked and stubborn
heart instead of obeying me. So I 13
will fling you headlong out of this
land into a country unknown to
you and to your forefathers; there
you can serve other gods day and
night, for I will show you no favour. Therefore, says the LORD, 14
the time is coming when men shall
no longer swear, 'By the life of the
LORD who brought the Israelites
up from Egypt', but, 'By the life of 15
the LORD who brought the Israelites back from a northern land and
from all the lands to which he had
dispersed them'; and I will bring
them back to the soil which I gave
to their forefathers.

I will send for many fishermen, 16
says the LORD, and they shall fish
for them. After that I will send for
many hunters, and they shall hunt
them out from every mountain
and hill and from the crevices in
the rocks. For my eyes are on all 17
their ways; they are not hidden
from my sight, nor is their wrongdoing concealed from me. I will 18
first make them pay in full[a] for the
wrong they have done and the sin
they have committed by defiling
with the dead lumber of their idols
the land which belongs to me, and
by filling it with their abominations.

O LORD, my strength and my 19
stronghold,
my refuge in time of trouble,
to thee shall the nations come
from the ends of the earth and say,
Our forefathers inherited only a
sham,
an idol vain and useless.
Can man make gods for himself? 20
They would be no gods.
Therefore I am teaching them, 21
once for all will I teach them
my power and my might,
and they shall learn that my name
is the LORD.

---

[a] *in full: or* double.

17 The sin of Judah is recorded with an iron tool, engraved on the tablet of their heart with a point of adamant and carved on the horns 2 of their altars to bear witness against them.[a] Their altars and their sacred poles stand by every 3 spreading tree, on the heights and the hills in the mountain country. I will give away your wealth as spoil, and all your treasure for no payment,[b] because of your[c] sin 4 throughout your country. You will lose possession[d] of the patrimony which I gave you. I will make you serve your enemies as slaves in a land you do not know; for my anger is a blazing fire[e] and it shall burn for ever.

5 These are the words of the LORD:

A curse on the man who trusts in man
and leans for support on human kind,
while his heart is far from the LORD!
6 He shall be like a juniper in the desert;
when good comes he shall not see it.
He shall dwell among the rocks in the wilderness,
in a salt land where no man can live.
7 Blessed is the man who trusts in the LORD,
and rests his confidence upon him.
8 He shall be like a tree planted by the waterside,
that stretches its roots along the stream.
When the heat comes it has nothing to fear;
its spreading foliage stays green.
In a year of drought it feels no care,
and does not cease to bear fruit.

The heart is the most deceitful of 9 all things,
desperately sick;[f] who can fathom it?
I, the LORD, search the mind 10
and test the heart,
requiting man for his conduct,
and as his deeds deserve.
Like a partridge which gathers 11 into its nest
eggs which it has not laid,
so is the man who amasses wealth unjustly.
Before his days are half done he must leave it,
and prove but a fool at the last.

O throne of glory, exalted from the 12 beginning,
the place of our sanctuary,
O LORD on whom Israel's hope is 13 fixed,
all who reject thee shall be put to shame;
all in this land who forsake thee shall be humbled,[g]
for they have rejected the fountain of living water.[h]
Heal me, O LORD, and I shall be 14 healed,
save me and I shall be saved;
for thou art my praise.
They say to me, 'Where is the 15 word of the LORD?
Let it come if it can!'
It is not the thought of disaster 16 that makes me press after thee;
never did I desire this day of despair.
Thou knowest all that has passed my lips;
it was approved by thee.
Do not become a terror to me; 17
thou art my only refuge on the day of disaster.
May my persecutors be foiled, not 18 I;
may they be terrified, not I.

---

[a] to bear...them: *prob. rdg.*; *Heb.* as their sons remember.
[b] for no payment: *prob. rdg., cp.* 15. 13; *Heb.* your hill-shrines.
[c] your: *prob. rdg., cp.* 15. 13; *Heb. om.*   [d] You...possession: *prob. rdg.*; *Heb. obscure.*
[e] for...fire: *prob. rdg., cp.* 15. 14; *Heb.* for you have kindled a fire in my anger.
[f] the most...sick: *or* too deceitful for any man.
[g] humbled: *prob. rdg.*; *Heb.* written.   [h] *Prob. rdg.*; *Heb. adds* the LORD.

Bring on them the day of disaster;
destroy them, destroy them utterly.

19 These were the words of the
LORD to me: Go and stand in the
Benjamin[a] Gate, through which
the kings of Judah go in and out,
and in all the gates of Jerusalem.
20 Say, Hear the words of the LORD,
you princes of Judah, all you men
of Judah, and all you inhabitants
of Jerusalem who come in through
21 these gates. These are the words of
the LORD: Observe this with care,
that you do not carry any load on
the sabbath or bring it through the
22 gates of Jerusalem. You shall not
bring any load out of your houses
or do any work on the sabbath, but
you shall keep the sabbath day
holy as I commanded your fore-
23 fathers. Yet they did not obey or
pay attention, but obstinately refused to hear or learn their lesson.
24 Now if you will obey me, says the
LORD, and refrain from bringing
any load through the gates of this
city on the sabbath, and keep that
day holy by doing no work on it,
25 then kings shall come through the
gates of this city, kings[b] who shall
sit on David's throne. They shall
come riding in chariots or on
horseback, escorted by their captains, by the men of Judah and the
inhabitants of Jerusalem; and this
city shall be inhabited for ever.
26 People shall come from the cities
of Judah, the country round Jerusalem, the land of Benjamin, the
Shephelah, the hill-country and
the Negeb, bringing whole-offerings, sacrifices, grain-offerings, and
frankincense, bringing also thank-
offerings to the house of the LORD.
27 But if you do not obey me by
keeping the sabbath day holy and
by not carrying any load as you
come through the gates of Jerusalem on the sabbath, then I will set
fire to those gates; it shall consume
the palaces of Jerusalem and shall
not be put out.

18 These are the words which came
2 to Jeremiah from the LORD: Go
down at once to the potter's house,
and there I will tell you what I
3 have to say. So I went down to the
potter's house and found him work-
4 ing at the wheel. Now and then a
vessel he was making out of the
clay would be spoilt in his hands,
and then he would start again and
mould it into another vessel to his
5 liking. Then the word of the LORD
6 came to me: Can I not deal with
you, Israel, says the LORD, as the
potter deals with his clay? You are
clay in my hands like the clay in
7 his, O house of Israel. At any
moment I may threaten to uproot
a nation or a kingdom, to pull it
8 down and destroy it. But if the
nation which I have threatened
turns back from its wicked ways,
then I shall think better of the evil
9 I had in mind to bring on it. Or at
any moment I may decide to build
or to plant a nation or a kingdom.
10 But if it does evil in my sight and
does not obey me, I shall think
better of the good I had in mind
11 for it. Go now and tell the men of
Judah and the inhabitants of Jerusalem that these are the words of
the LORD: I am the potter; I am
preparing evil for you and per-
fecting my designs against you.
Turn back, every one of you, from
his evil course; mend your ways
12 and your doings. But they answer,
'Things are past hope. We will do
as we like, and each of us will follow the promptings of his own
13 wicked and stubborn heart.' Therefore these are the words of the
LORD:

Inquire   among   the   nations:
who ever heard the like of
this?
The virgin Israel has done a thing
most horrible.

---

[a] Benjamin: *prob. rdg.*; *Heb.* sons of the people.
[b] *Prob. rdg.*; *Heb. adds* and officers.

14 Will the snow cease to fall on the
    rocky slopes of Lebanon?
    Will the cool rain streaming in
    torrents ever fail?
15 No, but my people have forgotten
    me;
    they burn sacrifices to a mere
    idol,
    so they stumble in their paths, the
    ancient ways,
    and they take to byways and un-
    made roads;
16 their own land they lay waste,
    and men will jeer at it for ever in
    contempt.
    All who go by will be horror-struck
    and shake their heads.
17 Like a wind from the east
    I will scatter them before their
    enemies.
    In the hour of their downfall
    I will turn my back towards them
    and not my face.

18 'Come, let us decide what to do
    with Jeremiah', men say. 'There
    will still be priests to guide us, still
    wise men to advise, still prophets
    to proclaim the word. Come, let us
    invent some charges against him;
    let us pay no attention to his
    message.'

19 But do thou, O LORD, pay atten-
    tion,
    and hear what my opponents are
    saying against me.
20 Is good to be repaid with evil?[a]
    Remember how I stood before
    thee,
    pleading on their behalf
    to avert thy wrath from them.
21 Therefore give their sons over to
    famine,
    leave them at the mercy of the
    sword.
    Let their women be childless and
    widowed,
    let death carry off their men,
    let their young men be cut down in
    battle.
22 Bring raiders upon them without
    warning,

and let screams of terror ring out
    from their houses.
For they have dug a pit to catch
    me
and have hidden snares for my
    feet.
Well thou knowest, O LORD,   23
all their murderous plots against
    me.
Do not blot out their wrongdoing
    or annul their sin;
when they are brought stumbling
    into thy presence,
deal with them on the day of thy
    anger.

These are the words of the LORD: 19
Go and buy an earthenware jar.
Then take with you some of the
elders of the people and of the
priests, and go out to the Valley of 2
Ben-hinnom, on which the Gate of
the Potsherds opens, and there
proclaim what I tell you. Say, 3
Hear the word of the LORD, you
princes of Judah and inhabitants
of Jerusalem. These are the words
of the LORD of Hosts the God of
Israel: I will bring on this place a
disaster which shall ring in the ears
of all who hear of it. For they have 4
forsaken me, and treated this place
as if it were not mine, burning
sacrifices to other gods whom neither they nor their fathers nor the
kings of Judah have known, and
filling this place with the blood of
the innocent. They have built 5
shrines to Baal, where they burn
their sons as whole-offerings to
Baal. It was no command of mine;
I never spoke of it; it never entered
my thought. Therefore, says the 6
LORD, the time is coming when
this place shall no longer be called
Topheth or the Valley of Ben-
hinnom, but the Valley of Slaughter. In this place I will shatter the 7
plans of Judah and Jerusalem as a
jar is shattered; I will make the
people fall by the sword before
their enemies, at the hands of
those who would kill them, and I

---

[a] *Prob. rdg.; Heb. adds* they have dug a pit for me (*cp. verse* 22).

will give their corpses to the birds
8 and beasts to devour. I will make
this city a scene of horror and
contempt, so that every passer-by
will be horror-struck and jeer in
contempt at the sight of its wounds.
9 I will compel men to eat the flesh of
their sons and their daughters;
they shall devour one another's
flesh in the dire straits to which
their enemies and those who would
kill them will reduce them in the
10 siege. Then you must shatter the
jar before the eyes of the men who
11 have come with you and say to
them, These are the words of the
LORD of Hosts: Thus will I shatter
this people and this city as one
shatters an earthen vessel so that
it cannot be mended, and the dead
shall be buried in Topheth because
there is no room elsewhere to bury
12 them. This is what I will do to this
place, says the LORD, and to those
who live there: I will make this city
13 like Topheth. Because of their defilement, the houses of Jerusalem
and those of the kings of Judah
shall be like Topheth, every one of
the houses on whose roofs men
have burnt sacrifices to the host of
heaven and poured drink-offerings
to other gods.

14 Jeremiah came in from Topheth,
where the LORD had sent him to
prophesy, and stood in the court of
the LORD's house. He said to all the
15 people, These are the words of the
LORD of Hosts the God of Israel: I
am bringing on this city and on all
its blood-spattered altars every
disaster with which I have threatened it, for its people have remained obstinate and refused to
listen to me.

20 When Pashhur son of Immer the
priest, the chief officer in the house
of the LORD, heard Jeremiah pro-
2 phesying these things, he had him
flogged[a] and put him into the
stocks at the Upper Gate of Benjamin, in the house of the LORD.

The next morning he released him, 3
and Jeremiah said to him, The
LORD has called you not Pashhur
but Magor-missabib.[b] For these 4
are the words of the LORD: I will
make you a terror to yourself and
to all your friends; they shall fall
by the sword of the enemy before
your very eyes. I will hand over all
Judah to the king of Babylon, and
he will deport them to Babylon
and put them to the sword. I will 5
give all this city's store of wealth
and riches and all the treasures of
the kings of Judah to their enemies; they shall seize them as spoil
and carry them off to Babylon.
You, Pashhur, and all your house- 6
hold shall go into captivity and
come to Babylon. There shall you
die and there shall you be buried,
you and all your friends to whom
you have been a false prophet.

O LORD, thou hast duped me, and I 7
have been thy dupe;
thou hast outwitted me and hast
prevailed.
I have been made a laughing-stock
all the day long,
everyone mocks me.
Whenever I speak I must needs 8
cry out
and proclaim violence and destruction.
I am reproached and mocked all
the time
for uttering the word of the LORD.
Whenever I said, 'I will call him to 9
mind no more,
nor speak in his name again',
then his word was imprisoned in
my body,
like a fire blazing in my heart,
and I was weary with holding it
under,
and could endure no more.
For I heard many whispering,[c]   10
'Denounce him! we will denounce
him.'
All my friends were on the watch
for a false step,

---

[a] *had him flogged: or* struck him.   [b] *That is* Terror let loose.
[c] *Prob. rdg.; Heb. adds* Terror let loose.

saying, 'Perhaps he may be tricked, then we can catch him
and take our revenge.'

11 But the LORD is on my side, strong
and ruthless,
therefore my persecutors shall
stumble and fall powerless.
Bitter shall be their abasement
when they fail,
and their shame shall long be
remembered.

12 O LORD of Hosts, thou dost test
the righteous
and search the depths of the heart;
to thee have I committed my cause,
let me see thee take vengeance on
them.

13 Sing to the LORD, praise the LORD;
for he rescues the poor from those
who would do them wrong.

14 A curse on the day when I was
born!
Be it for ever unblessed,
the day when my mother bore me!

15 A curse on the man who brought
word to my father,
'A child is born to you, a son',
and gladdened his heart!

16 That man shall fare like the cities
which the LORD overthrew without mercy.
He shall hear cries of alarm in the
morning
and uproar at noon,

17 because death did not claim me
before birth,
and my mother did not become my
grave,
her womb great with me for ever.

18 Why did I come forth from the
womb
to know only sorrow and toil,
to end my days in shame?

Kings and prophets denounced

21 THE word which came from the
LORD to Jeremiah when King Zedekiah sent to him Pashhur son of
Malchiah and Zephaniah the priest,
son of Maaseiah, with this request:

2 'Nebuchadrezzar king of Babylon
is making war on us; inquire of the

LORD on our behalf. Perhaps the
LORD will perform a miracle as he
has done in past times, so that
Nebuchadrezzar may raise the
siege.' But Jeremiah answered 3
them, Tell Zedekiah, these are the 4
words of the LORD the God of
Israel: I will turn back upon you
your own weapons with which you
are fighting the king of Babylon
and the Chaldaeans besieging you
outside the wall; and I will bring
them into the heart of this city. I 5
myself will fight against you in
burning rage and great fury, with
an outstretched hand and a strong
arm. I will strike down those who 6
live in this city, men and cattle
alike; they shall die of a great pestilence. After that, says the LORD, 7
I will take Zedekiah king of Judah,
his courtiers and the people, all in
this city who survive pestilence,
sword, and famine, and hand them
over to Nebuchadrezzar the king
of Babylon, to their enemies and
those who would kill them. He
shall put them to the sword and
shall show no pity, no mercy or
compassion.

You shall say further to this 8
people, These are the words of the
LORD: I offer you now a choice between the way of life and the way
of death. Whoever remains in this 9
city shall die by sword, by famine,
or by pestilence, but whoever goes
out to surrender to the Chaldaeans,
who are now besieging you, shall
survive; he shall take home his life,
and nothing more. I have set my 10
face against this city, meaning to
do them harm, not good, says the
LORD. It shall be handed over to
the king of Babylon, and he shall
burn it to the ground.

To the royal house of Judah. 11
Listen to the word of the LORD:
O house of David, these are the 12
words of the LORD:
Administer justice betimes,
rescue the victim from his oppressor,

lest the fire of my fury blaze up and
  burn unquenched
because of your evil doings.

13 The LORD says,
  I am against you who lie in the
    valley,
  you, the rock in the plain,
  you who say, 'Who can come down
    upon us?
  Who can penetrate our lairs?'
14 I will punish you as you deserve,
    says the LORD,
  I will kindle fire on the heathland
    around you,
  and it shall consume everything
    round about.

22 These were the words of the
  LORD: Go down to the house of the
2 king of Judah and say this: Listen
  to the words of the LORD, O king of
  Judah, you who sit on David's
  throne, you and your courtiers and
  your people who come in at these
3 gates. These are the words of the
  LORD: Deal justly and fairly, rescue the victim from his oppressor,
  do not ill-treat or do violence to the
  alien, the orphan or the widow, do
  not shed innocent blood in this
4 place. If you obey, and only if you
  obey, kings who sit on David's
  throne shall yet come riding
  through these gates in chariots and
  on horses, with their retinue of cour-
5 tiers and people. But if you do not
  listen to my words, then by myself I swear, says the LORD, this
  house shall become a desolate ruin.
6 For these are the words of the
  LORD about the royal house of
  Judah:

  Though you are dear to me as
    Gilead
  or as the heights of Lebanon,
  I swear that I will make you a
    wilderness,
  a land of unpeopled cities.
7 I will dedicate an armed host to
    fight against you,
  a ravening horde;

they shall cut your choicest cedars
    down
  and fling them on the fire.

  Men of many nations shall pass 8
by this city and say to one another,
'Why has the LORD done this to
such a great city?' The answer will 9
be, 'Because they forsook their
covenant with the LORD their God;
they worshipped other gods and
served them.'

Weep not for the dead nor brood 10
    over his loss.
Weep rather for him who has gone
    away,
for he shall never return,
never again see the land of his
    birth.

  For these are the words of the 11
LORD concerning Shallum son of
Josiah, king of Judah, who succeeded his father on the throne and
has gone away: He shall never return; he shall die in the place of his 12
exile and never see this land again.

Shame on the man who builds his 13
    house by unjust means
and completes its roof-chambers
    by fraud,
making his countrymen work with-
    out payment,
giving them no wage for their
    labour!
Shame on the man who says, 'I 14
    will build a spacious house
with airy roof-chambers,
set windows in it, panel it with
    cedar
and paint it with vermilion'!
If your cedar is more splendid,   15
does that prove you a king?
Think of your father: he ate and
    drank,
dealt justly and fairly; all went
    well with him.
He dispensed justice to the lowly 16
    and poor;[a]
did not this show he knew me? says
    the LORD.

---

[a] *Prob. rdg.; Heb. adds* all went well (*repeated from verse 15*).

17 But you have no eyes, no thought
for anything but gain,
set only on the innocent blood you
can shed,
on cruel acts of tyranny.

18 Therefore these are the words of
the LORD concerning Jehoiakim
son of Josiah, king of Judah:

For him no mourner shall say,
'Alas, brother, dear brother!'
no one say, 'Alas, lord and master!'
19 He shall be buried like a dead ass,
dragged along and flung out
beyond the gates of Jerusalem.

20 Get up into Lebanon and cry aloud,
make your voice heard in Bashan,
cry aloud from Abarim, for all who
befriend you are broken.
21 I spoke to you in your days of
prosperous ease,
but you said, 'I will not listen.'
This is how you behaved since
your youth;
never have you obeyed me.
22 The wind shall carry away all your
friends,[a]
your lovers shall depart into exile.
Then you will be put to shame and
abashed
for all your evil deeds.[b]
23 You dwellers in Lebanon, who
make your nests among the
cedars,
how you will groan when the pains
come upon you,
like the pangs of a woman in
labour!

24 By my life, says the LORD, Coniah son of Jehoiakim, king of Judah, shall be the signet-ring on my
right hand no longer. Yes, Coniah,
25 I will pull you off. I will hand you
over to those who seek your life, to
those you fear, to Nebuchadrezzar
king of Babylon and to the Chal-
26 daeans. I will fling you headlong,
you and the mother who gave you
birth, into another land, a land
where you were not born; and

there shall you both die. They shall 27
never come back to their own land,
the land for which they long.
This man, Coniah, then, is he a 28
mere puppet, contemptible and
broken, only a thing unwanted?
Why else are he and his children
flung out headlong and hurled into
a country they do not know?
O land, land, land, hear the 29
words of the LORD: These are the 30
words of the LORD: Write this
man down as stripped of all honour, one who in his own life shall
not prosper, nor shall he leave
descendants to sit in prosperity on
David's throne or rule again in
Judah.

Shame on the shepherds who let 23
the sheep of my flock scatter and
be lost! says the LORD. Therefore 2
these are the words of the LORD the
God of Israel about the shepherds
who tend my people: You have
scattered and dispersed my flock.
You have not watched over them;
but I am watching you to punish
you for your evil doings, says the
LORD. I will myself gather the 3
remnant of my sheep from all the
lands to which I have dispersed
them. I will bring them back to
their homes, and they shall be
fruitful and increase. I will appoint 4
shepherds to tend them; they shall
never again know fear or dismay or
punishment. This is the very word
of the LORD.

The days are now coming, says the 5
LORD,
when I will make a righteous
Branch spring from David's
line,
a king who shall rule wisely,
maintaining law and justice in the
land.
In his days Judah shall be kept 6
safe,
and Israel shall live undisturbed.
This is the name to be given to
him:
The LORD is our Righteousness.

[a] *Or* shepherds.   [b] *Or* calamities.

7   Therefore the days are coming, says the LORD, when men shall no longer swear, 'By the life of the LORD who brought Israel up from
8 Egypt', but, 'By the life of the LORD who brought the descendants of the Israelites back from a northern land and from all the lands to which he had dispersed them, to live again on their own soil.'

9 On the prophets.
Deep within me my heart is broken,
there is no strength in my bones;
because of the LORD, because of his dread words
I have become like a drunken man,
like a man overcome with wine.
10 For the land is full of adulterers,
and because of them the earth lies parched,
the wild pastures have dried up.
The course that they run is evil,
and their powers are misused.
11 For prophet and priest alike are godless;
I have come upon the evil they are doing even in my own house.
This is the very word of the LORD.

12 Therefore the path shall turn slippery beneath their feet;
they shall be dispersed in the dark and shall fall there.
For I will bring disaster on them when their day of reckoning comes.
This is the very word of the LORD.
13 I found the prophets of Samaria men of no sense:
they prophesied in Baal's name and led my people Israel astray.
14 In the prophets of Jerusalem I see a thing most horrible:
adulterers and hypocrites that they are,
they encourage evildoers,
so that no man turns back from his sin;
to me all her inhabitants are like Sodom and Gomorrah.

These then are the words of the 15 LORD of Hosts concerning the prophets:

I will give them wormwood to eat and a bitter poison to drink;
for a godless spirit has spread over all the land
from the prophets of Jerusalem.

These are the words of the LORD of 16 Hosts:

Do not listen to what the prophets say,
who buoy you up with false hopes;
the vision they report springs from their own imagination,
it is not from the mouth of the LORD.
They say to those who spurn the 17 word of the LORD,
'Prosperity shall be yours';
and to all who follow the promptings of their own stubborn heart they say,
'No disaster shall befall you.'
But which of them has stood in the 18 council of the LORD,
seen him and heard his word?
Which of them has listened to his word and obeyed?
See what a scorching wind has 19 gone out from the LORD,
a furious whirlwind;
it whirls round the heads of the wicked.
The LORD's anger is not to be 20 turned aside,
until he has accomplished and fulfilled his deep designs.
In days to come you will fully understand.
I did not send these prophets, yet 21 they went in haste;
I did not speak to them, yet they prophesied.
If they have stood in my council, 22 let them proclaim my words to my people
and turn them from their evil course and their evil doings.
Am I a god only near at hand, not 23 far away?

24 Can a man hide in any secret place
and I not see him?
Do I not fill heaven and earth?
This is the very word of the LORD.

25   I have heard what the prophets
say, the prophets who speak lies in
my name and cry, 'I have had a
26 dream, a dream!' How long will it
be till they change their tune, these
prophets who prophesy lies and
give voice to their own inventions?
27 By these dreams which they tell
one another these men think they
will make my people forget my
name, as their fathers forgot my
28 name for the name of*[a]* Baal. If a
prophet has a dream, let him tell
his dream; if he has my word, let
him speak my word in truth. What
has chaff to do with grain? says the
29 LORD. Do not my words scorch*[b]*
like fire? says the LORD. Are they
not like a hammer that splinters
30 rock? I am against the prophets,
says the LORD, who steal my words
from one another for their own use.
31 I am against the prophets, says the
LORD, who concoct words of their
own and then say, 'This is his very
32 word.' I am against the prophets,
says the LORD, who dream lies and
retail them, misleading my people
with wild and reckless falsehoods.
It was not I who sent them or commissioned them, and they will do
this people no good. This is the
very word of the LORD.
33   When you are asked by this
people or by a prophet or priest
what the burden of the LORD's message is, you shall answer, You are
his burden, and I shall throw you
34 down, says the LORD. If prophet
or priest or layman uses the term
'the LORD's burden', I will punish
35 that man and his family. The form
of words you shall use in speaking
amongst yourselves is: 'What answer has the LORD given?' or,
36 'What has the LORD said?' You
shall never again mention 'the

burden of the LORD'; that is reserved for the man to whom he
entrusts his message. If you do,
you will make nonsense of the
words of the living God, the LORD
of Hosts our God. This is the form 37
you shall use in speaking to a prophet: 'What answer has the LORD
given?' or, 'What has the LORD
said?' But to any of you who do 38
say, 'the burden of the LORD', the
LORD speaks thus: Because you
say, 'the burden of the LORD',
though I sent to tell you not to say
it, therefore I myself will carry you 39
like a burden and throw you down,
casting out of my sight both you
and the city which I gave to you
and to your forefathers. I will in- 40
flict on you endless reproach, endless shame which shall never be
forgotten.

Two visions

THIS is what the LORD showed me: 24
I saw two baskets of figs set out in
front of the sanctuary of the LORD.
This was after Nebuchadrezzar
king of Babylon had deported from
Jerusalem Jeconiah son of Jehoiakim, king of Judah, with the officers of Judah, the craftsmen and
the smiths,*[c]* and taken them to
Babylon. In one basket the figs 2
were very good, like the figs that
are first ripe; in the other the figs
were very bad, so bad that they
were not fit to eat. The LORD said 3
to me, 'What are you looking at,
Jeremiah?' 'Figs,' I answered, 'the
good very good, and the bad so bad
that they are not fit to eat.' Then 4
this word came to me from the
LORD: These are the words of the 5
LORD the God of Israel: I count the
exiles of Judah whom I sent away
from this place to the land of the
Chaldaeans as good as these good
figs. I will look upon them meaning 6
to do them good, and I will restore
them to their land; I will build

---

[a] for the name of: *or* by their worship of.   *[b]* scorch: *prob. rdg.*; *Heb.* thus.
[c] the smiths: *or* the harem.

them up and not pull them down,
7 plant them and not uproot them. I
will give them the wit to know me,
for I am the LORD; they shall become my people and I will become
their God, for they will come back
8 to me with all their heart. But
Zedekiah king of Judah, his officers and the survivors of Jerusalem, whether they remain in this
land or live in Egypt – all these I
will treat as bad figs, says the
LORD, so bad that they are not fit
9 to eat. I will make them repugnant
to all the kingdoms of the earth, a
reproach, a by-word, an object-
lesson and a thing of ridicule
10 wherever I drive them. I will send
against them sword, famine, and
pestilence until they have vanished from the land which I gave to
them and to their forefathers.

25 This came to Jeremiah as the
word concerning all the people of
Judah in the fourth year of Jehoiakim son of Josiah, king of Judah
(that is the first year of Nebuchad-
2 rezzar king of Babylon). This is
what the prophet Jeremiah said to
all Judah and all the inhabitants of
3 Jerusalem: For twenty-three years,
from the thirteenth year of Josiah
son of Amon, king of Judah, to the
present day, I have been receiving the words of the LORD and
taking pains to speak to you, but
4 you have not listened. The LORD
has taken pains to send you his
servants the prophets, but you
have not listened or shown any
5 inclination to listen. If each of you
will turn from his wicked ways and
evil courses, he has said, then you
shall for ever live on the soil which
the LORD gave to you and to your
6 forefathers. You must not follow
other gods, serving and worshipping them, nor must you provoke
me to anger with the idols your
hands have made; then I will not
7 do you harm. But you did not
listen to me, says the LORD; you
provoked me to anger with the

idols your hands had made and so
brought harm upon yourselves.
Therefore these are the words of 8
the LORD of Hosts: Because you
have not listened to my words, I 9
will summon all the tribes of the
north, says the LORD: I will send
for my servant Nebuchadrezzar
king of Babylon. I will bring them
against this land and all its inhabitants and all these nations round
it; I will exterminate them and
make them a thing of horror and
derision, a scandal for ever. I will 10
silence all sounds of joy and gladness among them, the voices of
bridegroom and bride, and the
sound of the handmill; I will
quench the light of every lamp.
For seventy years this whole coun- 11
try shall be a scandal and a horror;
these nations shall be in subjection
to the king of Babylon. When those 12
seventy years are completed, I
will punish the king of Babylon
and his people, says the LORD, for
all their misdeeds and make the
land of the Chaldaeans a waste for
ever. I will bring upon that coun- 13
try all I have said, all that is
written in this book, all that Jeremiah has prophesied against these
peoples. They will be the victims*a* 14
of mighty nations and great kings,
and thus I will repay them for
their actions and their deeds.
These were the words of the 15
LORD the God of Israel to me: Take
from my hand this cup of fiery
wine and make all the nations to
whom I send you drink it. When 16
they have drunk it they will vomit
and go mad; such is the sword
which I am sending among them.
Then I took the cup from the 17
LORD'S hand, gave it to all the
nations to whom he sent me and
made them drink it: to Jerusalem, 18
the cities of Judah, its kings and
officers, making them a scandal, a
thing of horror and derision and an
object of ridicule, as they still are:
to Pharaoh king of Egypt, his 19

a They...victims: *prob. rdg.*; *Heb.* They were the victims.

courtiers, his officers, all his people,
20 and all his rabble of followers, all
the kings of the land of Uz, all the
kings of the Philistines: to Ashkelon, Gaza, Ekron, and the rem-
21 nant of Ashdod: also to Edom,
22 Moab, and the Ammonites, all the
kings of Tyre, all the kings of
Sidon, and the kings of the coasts
23 and islands: to Dedan, Tema, Buz,
and all who roam the fringes of the
24 desert,*a* all the kings of Arabia
25 living in the wilderness, all the
kings of Zamri, all the kings of
Elam, and all the kings of the
26 Medes, all the kings of the north,
neighbours or far apart, and all the
kingdoms on the face of the earth.
Last of all the king of Sheshak*b*
27 shall drink. You shall say to them,
These are the words of the LORD of
Hosts the God of Israel: Drink
this, get drunk and be sick; fall, to
rise no more, before the sword
28 which I am sending among you. If
they refuse to take the cup from
you and to drink, say to them,
These are the words of the LORD of
Hosts: You must and shall drink.
29 I will first punish the city which
bears my name; do you think that
you can be exempt? No, you cannot be exempt, for I am invoking
the sword against all that inhabit
the earth. This is the very word of
the LORD of Hosts.
30   Prophesy to them and tell them
all I have said:

The LORD roars from Zion on high
and thunders from his holy
dwelling-place.
Yes, he roars across the heavens,
his home;
an echo comes back like the shout
of men treading grapes.
31 The great noise reaches to the ends
of the earth
and all its inhabitants.
For the LORD brings a charge
against the nations,
he goes to law with all mankind

and has handed the wicked over to
the sword.
This is the very word of the LORD.

These are the words of the LORD 32
of Hosts:
Ruin spreads from nation to nation,
a mighty tempest is blowing up
from the ends of the earth.

In that day those whom the 33
LORD has slain shall lie like dung
on the ground from one end of the
earth to the other; no one shall wail
for them, they shall not be taken
up and buried.

Howl, shepherds, cry aloud,   34
sprinkle yourselves with ashes,
you masters of the flock.
It is your turn to go to the slaughter,
and you shall fall like fine rams.
The shepherds shall have nowhere 35
to flee,
the flockmasters no way of escape.
Hark, the shepherds cry out, the 36
flockmasters howl,
for the LORD is ravaging their
pasture,
and their peaceful homesteads lie 37
in ruins beneath his anger.
They flee like a young lion aban- 38
doning his lair,
for their land has become a
waste,
wasted by the cruel sword and by
his anger.

Jerusalem laid under a curse

AT the beginning of the reign of 26
Jehoiakim son of Josiah, king of
Judah, this word came to Jeremiah
from the LORD: These are the 2
words of the LORD: Stand in the
court of the LORD's house and
speak to the inhabitants of all the
cities of Judah who come to worship there. You shall tell them
everything that I command you to

---

a who roam...desert: *or* who clip the hair on their temples.
b A name for Babylon.

say to them, keeping nothing back.
3 Perhaps they may listen, and every man may turn back from his evil courses. Then I will relent, and give up my purpose to bring disaster on them for their evil deeds.
4 You shall say to them, These are the words of the LORD: If you do not obey me, if you do not follow
5 the law I have set before you, and listen to the words of my servants the prophets, the prophets whom I have taken pains to send to you, but you have never listened to
6 them, then I will make this house like Shiloh and this city an object of ridicule to all nations on earth.
7 The priests, the prophets, and all the people heard Jeremiah say
8 this in the LORD's house and, when he came to the end of what the LORD had commanded him to say to them, priests, prophets, and people seized him and threatened
9 him with death. 'Why,' they demanded, 'have you prophesied in the LORD's name that this house shall become like Shiloh and this city waste and uninhabited?' The people all gathered against Jere-
10 miah in the LORD's house. The officers of Judah heard what was happening, and they went up from the royal palace to the LORD's house and took their places there at the entrance of the new gate.
11 Then the priests and the prophets said to the officers and all the people, 'Condemn this fellow to death. He has prophesied against this city: you have heard it with
12 your own ears.' Then Jeremiah said to the officers and the people, 'The LORD sent me to prophesy against this house and this city all
13 that you have heard. If you now mend your ways and your doings and obey the LORD your God, then he may relent and revoke the disaster with which he has threatened
14 you. But I am in your hands; do with me whatever you think right
15 and proper. Only you may be certain that, if you put me to

death, you and this city and all who live in it will be guilty of murdering an innocent man; for in very truth the LORD has sent me to you to say all this in your hearing.'
16 Then the officers and all the people said to the priests and the prophets, 'This man ought not to be condemned to death, for he has spoken to us in the name of the LORD our God.' Some of the elders
17 of the land also stood up and said to the assembled people, 'In the
18 time of Hezekiah king of Judah, Micah of Moresheth was prophesying and said to all the people of Judah: "These are the words of the LORD of Hosts:

Zion shall become a ploughed field,
Jerusalem a heap of ruins,
and the temple-hill rough heath."

Did King Hezekiah and all Judah
19 put him to death? Did not the king show reverence for the LORD and seek to placate him? Then the LORD relented and revoked the disaster with which he had threatened them. Are we to bring great disaster on ourselves?'

There was another man who
20 prophesied in the name of the LORD, Uriah son of Shemaiah, from Kiriath-jearim. He also prophesied against this city and this land, just as Jeremiah had done. King Jehoiakim with all his officers
21 and his bodyguard heard what he said and sought to put him to death. When Uriah heard of it, he was afraid and fled to Egypt. King
22 Jehoiakim sent Elnathan son of Akbor with others to fetch Uriah
23 from Egypt, and they brought him to the king. He had him put to death by the sword, and his body flung into the burial-place of the common people. But Ahikam son
24 of Shaphan used his influence on Jeremiah's behalf to save him from death at the hands of the people.

A rising against Nebuchadrezzar checked

27 AT the beginning of the reign of Zedekiah son of Josiah, king of Judah, this word came from the 2 LORD to Jeremiah: These are the words of the LORD to me: Take the cords and bars of a yoke and put 3 them on your neck. Then send to the kings of Edom, Moab, Ammon, Tyre, and Sidon by the envoys who have come from them to Zedekiah king of Judah in Jerusa- 4 lem, and give them the following message for their masters: These are the words of the LORD of Hosts the God of Israel: Say to your 5 masters: I made the earth with my great strength and with outstretched arm, I made man and beast on the face of the earth, and I 6 give it to whom I see fit. I now give all these lands to my servant Nebuchadrezzar king of Babylon, and I give him also all the beasts 7 of the field to serve him. All nations shall serve him, and his son and his grandson, until the destined hour of his own land comes, and then mighty nations and great kings shall use him as they please. 8 If any nation or kingdom will not serve Nebuchadrezzar king of Babylon or submit to his yoke, I will punish them with sword, famine, and pestilence, says the LORD, until I leave them entirely in his 9 power. Therefore do not listen to your prophets, your diviners, your wise women, your soothsayers, and your sorcerers when they tell you not to serve the king of Baby- 10 lon. They are prophesying falsely to you; and so you will be carried far from your own land, and I shall banish you and you will perish. 11 But if any nation submits to the yoke of the king of Babylon and serves him, I will leave them on their own soil, says the LORD; they shall cultivate it and live there.

12 I have said all this to Zedekiah king of Judah: If you will submit to the yoke of the king of Babylon and serve him and his people, then you shall save your lives. Why 13 should you and your people die by sword, famine, and pestilence, the fate with which the LORD has threatened any nation which does not serve the king of Babylon? Do 14 not listen to the prophets who tell you not to become subject to the king of Babylon; they are prophesying falsely to you. I have not 15 sent them, says the LORD; they are prophesying falsely in my name, and so I shall banish you and you will perish, you and these prophets who prophesy to you.

I said to the priests and all the 16 people, These are the words of the LORD: Do not listen to your prophets who tell you that the vessels of the LORD's house will very soon be brought back from Babylon; they are only prophesying falsely to you. Do not listen to them; 17 serve the king of Babylon, and save your lives. Why should this city become a ruin? If they are 18 prophets, and if they have the word of the LORD, let them intercede with the LORD of Hosts to grant that the vessels still left in the LORD's house, in the royal palace, and in Jerusalem, may not be carried off to Babylon. For these 19 are the words of the LORD of Hosts concerning the pillars, the sea, the trolleys, and all the other vessels still left in this city, which Nebu- 20 chadrezzar king of Babylon did not take when he deported Jeconiah son of Jehoiakim, king of Judah, from Jerusalem to Babylon, together with all the nobles of Judah and Jerusalem. These indeed are 21 the words of the LORD of Hosts the God of Israel concerning the vessels still left in the LORD's house, in the royal palace, and in Jerusalem: They shall be taken to Babylon and 22 stay there until I recall them, says the LORD; then I will bring them back and restore them to this place.

28 That same year,[a] in the fifth month of the first[b] year of the reign of Zedekiah king of Judah, Hananiah son of Azzur, the prophet from Gibeon, said to me in the house of the LORD, in the presence of the priests and all the people, 2 'These are the words of the LORD of Hosts the God of Israel: I have broken the yoke of the king of 3 Babylon. Within two years I will bring back to this place all the vessels of the LORD's house which Nebuchadrezzar king of Babylon took from here and carried off to 4 Babylon. I will also bring back to this place, says the LORD, Jeconiah son of Jehoiakim, king of Judah, and all the exiles of Judah who went to Babylon; for I will break the yoke of the king of Babylon.' 5 The prophet Jeremiah said to Hananiah the prophet in the presence of the priests and all the people standing in the LORD's 6 house: 'May it be so! May the LORD indeed do this: may he fulfil all that you have prophesied, by bringing back the vessels of the LORD's house and all the exiles 7 from Babylon to this place! Only hear what I have to say to you and 8 to all the people: the prophets who preceded you and me from earliest times have foretold war, famine, and pestilence for many lands and 9 for great kingdoms. If a prophet foretells prosperity, when his words come true it will be known that the LORD has sent him.' 10 Then the prophet Hananiah took the yoke from the neck of the prophet Jeremiah and broke it, 11 saying before all the people, 'These are the words of the LORD: Thus will I break the yoke of Nebuchadrezzar king of Babylon; I will break it off the necks of all nations within two years';[c] and the pro- 12 phet Jeremiah went his way. After Hananiah had broken the yoke

which had been on Jeremiah's neck, the word of the LORD came to Jeremiah: Go and say to Hanan- 13 iah, These are the words of the LORD: You have broken bars of wood; in their place you shall get bars of iron. For these are the 14 words of the LORD of Hosts the God of Israel: I have put a yoke of iron on the necks of all these nations, making them serve Nebuchadrezzar king of Babylon. They shall serve him, and I have given him even the beasts of the field. Then Jeremiah said to Hananiah, 15 'Listen, Hananiah. The LORD has not sent you, and you have led this nation to trust in false prophecies. Therefore these are the words of 16 the LORD: Beware, I will remove you from the face of the earth; you shall die within the year, because you have preached rebellion a- gainst the LORD.' The prophet 17 Hananiah died that same year, in the seventh month.

Jeremiah sent a letter from 29 Jerusalem to the remaining elders among the exiles, to the priests and prophets, and to all the people whom Nebuchadrezzar had de- ported from Jerusalem to Baby- lon, after King Jeconiah had left 2 Jerusalem with the queen mother and the eunuchs, the officers of Judah and Jerusalem, the crafts- men and the smiths.[d] The prophet 3 entrusted the letter to Elasah son of Shaphan and Gemariah son of Hilkiah, whom Zedekiah king of Judah had sent to Babylon to King Nebuchadrezzar. This is what he wrote: These are the words 4 of the LORD of Hosts the God of Israel: To all the exiles whom I have carried off from Jerusalem to Babylon: Build houses and live in 5 them; plant gardens and eat their produce. Marry wives and beget 6 sons and daughters; take wives for your sons and give your daughters

---

[a] Prob. rdg.; Heb. adds at the beginning of the reign.   [b] Prob. rdg.; Heb. fourth.
[c] within two years: or while there are still two full years to run.
[d] the smiths: or the harem

to husbands, so that they may bear sons and daughters and you may increase there and not dwindle 7 away. Seek the welfare of any city to which I have carried you off, and pray to the LORD for it; on its welfare your welfare will depend. 8 For these are the words of the LORD of Hosts the God of Israel: Do not be deceived by the prophets or the diviners among you, and do not listen to the wise women whom you set to dream dreams. 9 They prophesy falsely to you in my name; I did not send them. This is the very word of the LORD.

10 These are the words of the LORD: When a full seventy years has passed over Babylon, I will take up your cause and fulfil the promise of good things I made you, by 11 bringing you back to this place. I alone know my purpose for you, says the LORD: prosperity and not misfortune, and a long line of child-12 ren after you. If you invoke me and pray to me, I will listen to you: 13 when you seek me, you shall find me; if you search with all your 14 heart, I will let you find me, says the LORD. I will restore your fortunes and gather you again from all the nations and all the places to which I have banished you, says the LORD, and bring you back to the place from which I have carried you into exile.

15 You say that the LORD has raised up prophets for you in Baby-16 lon. These are the words of the LORD concerning the king who sits on the throne of David and all the people who live in this city, your fellow-countrymen who have not 17 gone into exile with you. These are the words of the LORD of Hosts: I bring upon them sword, famine, and pestilence, and make them like rotten figs, too bad to be eaten. 18 I pursue them with sword, famine, and pestilence, and make them repugnant to all the kingdoms of the earth, an object of execration

and horror, of derision and reproach, among all the nations to which I have banished them. Just 19 as they did not listen to my words, says the LORD, when I took pains to send them my servants the prophets, so you did not listen, says the LORD. But now, you exiles 20 whom I have sent from Jerusalem to Babylon, listen to the words of the LORD. These are the words of 21 the LORD of Hosts the God of Israel concerning Ahab son of Kolaiah and Zedekiah son of Maaseiah, who prophesy falsely to you in my name. I will hand them over to Nebuchadrezzar king of Babylon, and he will put them to death before your eyes. Their names shall be 22 used by all the exiles of Judah in Babylon when they curse a man; they shall say, May the LORD treat you like Zedekiah and Ahab, whom the king of Babylon roasted in the fire! For their conduct in Israel was 23 an outrage: they committed adultery with other men's wives, and without my authority prophesied in my name, and what they prophesied was false. I know; I can testify. This is the very word of the LORD.

To Shemaiah the Nehelamite.*a* 24 These are the words of the LORD of 25 Hosts the God of Israel: You have sent a letter in your own name to Zephaniah son of Maaseiah the priest, in which you say: 'The 26 LORD has appointed you to be priest in place of Jehoiada the priest, and it is your duty, as officer in charge of the LORD's house, to put every madman who sets up as a prophet into the stocks and the pillory. Why, then, have you not 27 reprimanded Jeremiah of Anathoth, who poses as a prophet before you? On the strength of this 28 he has sent to us in Babylon and said, "Your exile will be long; build houses and live in them, plant gardens and eat their produce."' Zephaniah the priest read this 29

a Prob. rdg.; Heb. adds you shall say, saying.

30 letter to Jeremiah the prophet, and the word of the LORD came to 31 Jeremiah: Send and tell all the exiles that these are the words of the LORD concerning Shemaiah the Nehelamite: Because Shemaiah has prophesied to you, though I did not send him, and has led you 32 to trust in false prophecies, these are now the words of the LORD: I will punish Shemaiah and his children. He shall have no one to take his place in this nation and enjoy the prosperity which I will bestow on my people, says the LORD, because he has preached rebellion against me.

Hopes for the restoration of Jerusalem

30 THE word which came to Jeremiah 2 from the LORD. These are the words of the LORD the God of Israel: Write in a book all that 3 I have said to you, for this is the very word of the LORD: The time is coming when I will restore the fortunes of my people Israel and Judah, says the LORD, and bring them back to the land which I gave to their forefathers; and it shall be their possession. 4 This is what the LORD has said 5 to Israel and Judah. These are the words of the LORD:

You shall hear a cry of terror, of fear without relief.
6 Ask and see: can a man bear a child? Why then do I see every man gripping his sides like a woman in labour,
every face changed, all turned pale?
7 Awful is that day:
when has there been its like?
A time of anguish for Jacob,
yet he shall come through it safely.

8 In that day, says the LORD of Hosts, I will break their yoke off their necks and snap their cords;

foreigners shall no longer use them as they please; they shall serve the 9 LORD their God and David their king, whom I will raise up for them.

And you, Jacob my servant, have 10 no fear;
despair not, O Israel, says the LORD.
For I will bring you back safe from afar
and your offspring from the land where they are captives;
and Jacob shall be at rest once more, prosperous and unafraid.
For I am with you and will save 11 you, says the LORD.
I will make an end of all the nations amongst whom I have scattered you,
but I will not make an end of you; though I punish you as you deserve, I will not sweep you clean away.

For these are the words of the 12 LORD to Zion:

Your injury is past healing, cruel was the blow you suffered.
There can be no[a] remedy for your 13 sore,
the new skin cannot grow.
All your lovers have forgotten you; 14 they look for you no longer.
I have struck you down
as an enemy strikes, and punished you cruelly;
for your wickedness is great and your sins are many.
Why complain of your injury, 15 that your sore cannot be healed?[b]
I have done this to you,
because your wickedness is great and your sins are many.

Yet all who devoured you shall 16 themselves be devoured,
all your oppressors shall go into captivity.
Those who plunder you shall be plundered,
and those who despoil you I will give up to be spoiled.

---

[a] Prob. rdg.; Heb. adds one judging your case.
[b] Why...healed?: or Cry not for help in your injury. Your sore cannot be healed.

17 I will cause the new skin to grow
and heal your wounds, says the
LORD,
although men call you the Outcast,
Zion, nobody's friend.

18 These are the words of the LORD:

Watch; I will restore the fortunes
of Jacob's clans
and show my love for all his dwellings.
Every city shall be rebuilt on its
mound of ruins,
every mansion shall have its familiar household.
19 From them praise shall be heard
and sounds of merrymaking.
I will increase them, they shall not
diminish,
I will raise them to honour, they
shall no longer be despised.
20 Their sons shall be what they once
were,
and their community shall be
established in my sight.
I will punish all their oppressors;
21 a ruler shall appear, one of themselves,
a governor shall arise from their
own number.
I will myself bring him[a] near and
so he[b] shall approach me;
for no one ventures of himself to
approach me,
says the LORD.
22 So you shall be my people,
and I will be your God.
23 See what a scorching wind has gone
out from the LORD,
a sweeping whirlwind.
It whirls round the heads of the
wicked;
24 the LORD's anger is not to be turned aside,
till he has finished and achieved
his heart's desire.
In days to come you will understand.

31   At that time, says the LORD, I
will become God of all the families
of Israel, and they shall become

my people. These are the words of 2
the LORD:

A people that survived the sword
found favour in the wilderness;
Israel journeyed to find rest;
long ago[c] the LORD appeared to 3
them:
I have dearly loved you from of
old,
and still I maintain my unfailing
care for you.
I will build you up again, O virgin 4
Israel,
and you shall be rebuilt.
Again you shall adorn yourself
with jingles,
and go forth with the merry throng
of dancers.
Again you shall plant vineyards 5
on the hills of Samaria,
vineyards which those who planted
them defiled;
for a day will come when the watch- 6
men on Ephraim's hills cry out,
Come, let us go up to Zion, to the
LORD our God.

For these are the words of the 7
LORD:

Break into shouts of joy for Jacob's
sake,
lead the nations, crying loud and
clear,
sing out your praises and say,
The LORD has saved his people,
and preserved a remnant of
Israel.
See how I bring them from the 8
land of the north;
I will gather them from the ends
of the earth,
their blind and lame among them,
women with child and women in
labour,
a great company.
They come home, weeping as they 9
come,
but I will comfort them and be
their escort.
I will lead them to flowing streams;
they shall not stumble, their path
will be so smooth.

---

[a] *Or* them.   [b] *Or* they.   [c] long ago: *or* from afar.

For I have become a father to
Israel,
and Ephraim is my eldest son.

10 Listen to the word of the LORD,
you nations,
announce it, make it known to
coasts and islands far away:
He who scattered Israel shall gather
them again
and watch over them as a shepherd
watches his flock.

11 For the LORD has ransomed Jacob
and redeemed him from a foe too
strong for him.

12 They shall come with shouts of joy
to Zion's height,
shining with happiness at the
bounty of the LORD,
the corn, the new wine, and the oil,
the young of flock and herd.
They shall become like a watered
garden
and they shall never want again.

13 Then shall the girl show her joy in
the dance,
young men and old shall rejoice;
I will turn their mourning into
gladness,
I will relent and give them joy to
outdo their sorrow.

14 I will satisfy the priests with the
fat of the land
and fill my people with my bounty.
This is the very word of the LORD.

15 These are the words of the LORD:

Hark, lamentation is heard in
Ramah, and bitter weeping,
Rachel weeping for her sons.
She refuses to be comforted: they
are no more.

16 These are the words of the LORD:

Cease your loud weeping,
shed no more tears;
for there shall be a reward for your
toil,
they shall return from the land of
the enemy.

You shall leave descendants after 17
you;[a]
your sons shall return to their own
land.
I listened; Ephraim was rocking 18
in his grief:
'Thou hast trained me to the yoke
like an unbroken calf,
and now I am trained;
restore me, let me return,
for thou, LORD, art my God.
Though I broke loose I have 19
repented:
now that I am tamed I beat my
breast;
in shame and remorse
I reproach myself for the sins of
my youth.'
Is Ephraim still my dear son, 20
a child in whom I delight?
As often as I turn my back on
him
I still remember him;
and so my heart yearns for him,
I am filled with tenderness towards
him.
This is the very word of the LORD.
Build cairns to mark your way, 21
set up sign-posts;
make sure of the road,
the path which you will tread.
Come back, virgin Israel,
come back to your cities.
How long will you twist and turn, 22
my wayward child?
For the LORD has created a new
thing in the earth:
a woman turned into a man.

These are the words of the LORD 23
of Hosts the God of Israel: Once
more shall these words be heard
in the land of Judah and in her
cities, when I restore their fortunes:

The LORD bless you,
the LORD, your true goal,[b] your
holy mountain.
Ploughmen and shepherds who 24
wander with their flocks
shall live together there.[c]

---

[a] You shall...you: *or* There shall be hope for your posterity.
[b] the LORD...goal: *or* O home of righteousness.
[c] *Prob. rdg.*; Heb. *adds* Judah and all his cities.

25 For I have given deep draughts to
the thirsty,
and satisfied those who were faint
with hunger.

26 Thereupon I woke and looked
about me, and my dream*a* had
been pleasant.

27 The time is coming, says the
LORD, when I will sow Israel and
Judah with the seed of man and
28 the seed of cattle. As I watched
over them with intent to pull down
and to uproot, to demolish and
destroy and harm, so now will I
watch over them to build and to
plant. This is the very word of the
LORD.

29 In those days it shall no longer
be said,

'The fathers have eaten sour grapes
and the children's teeth are set on
edge';

30 for a man shall die for his own
wrongdoing; the man who eats
sour grapes shall have his own
teeth set on edge.

31 The time is coming, says the
LORD, when I will make a new
covenant with Israel and Judah.
32 It will not be like the covenant I
made with their forefathers when
I took them by the hand and led
them out of Egypt. Although they
broke my covenant, I was patient
33 with them, says the LORD. But
this is the covenant which I will
make with Israel after those days,
says the LORD; I will set my law
within them and write it on their
hearts; I will become their God and
34 they shall become my people. No
longer need they teach one another
to know the LORD; all of them, high
and low alike, shall know me, says
the LORD, for I will forgive their
wrongdoing and remember their
sin no more.

35 These are the words of the LORD,
who gave the sun for a light by day
and the moon and stars for a light
by night, who cleft the sea and its

waves roared; the LORD of Hosts
is his name:

36 If this fixed order could vanish out
of my sight,
says the LORD,
then the race of Israel too could
cease for evermore
to be a nation in my sight.

37 These are the words of the LORD:
If any man could measure the
heaven above or fathom the depths
of the earth beneath, then I could
spurn the whole race of Israel
because of all they have done.
This is the very word of the
LORD.

38 The time is coming, says the
LORD, when the city shall be rebuilt in the LORD's honour from
the Tower of Hananel to the Corner
39 Gate. The measuring line shall then
be laid straight out over the hill of
40 Gareb and round Goath.*b* All the
valley and every field as far as the
gorge of the Kidron to the corner
by the Horse Gate eastwards shall
be holy to the LORD. It shall never
again be pulled down or demolished.

32 The word which came to Jeremiah from the LORD in the tenth
year of Zedekiah king of Judah
(the eighteenth year of Nebu-
2 chadrezzar). At that time the forces
of the Babylonian king were besieging Jerusalem, and the prophet
Jeremiah was imprisoned in the
court of the guard-house attached
3 to the royal palace. Zedekiah king
of Judah had imprisoned him after
demanding what he meant by this
prophecy: 'These are the words of
the LORD: I will deliver this city
into the hands of the king of Babylon, and he shall take it. Zedekiah
4 king of Judah will not escape from
the Chaldaeans but will be surrendered to the king of Babylon;
he will speak with him face to face
and see him with his own eyes.
5 Zedekiah will be taken to Babylon
and will remain there until I turn
my thoughts to him, says the LORD.

a Or sleep.   *b* Or Goah.

However much you fight against the Chaldaeans you will have no success.'

6 Jeremiah said, The word of the 7 LORD came to me: Hanamel son of your uncle Shallum is coming to see you and will say, 'Buy my field at Anathoth; you have the right of redemption, as next of 8 kin, to buy it.' As the LORD had foretold, my cousin Hanamel came to the court of the guard-house and said, 'Buy my field at Anathoth in Benjamin. You have the right of redemption and possession as next of kin; buy it.' I knew that this was 9 the LORD's message; so I bought the field at Anathoth from my cousin Hanamel and weighed out the price, seventeen shekels of 10 silver. I signed and sealed the deed and had it witnessed; then I weighed out the money on the scales. 11 I took my copies of the deed of purchase, both the sealed and the 12 unsealed, and gave them to Baruch son of Neriah, son of Mahseiah, in the presence of Hanamel my cousin, of the witnesses whose names were on the deed of purchase, and of the Judaeans sitting in the court 13 of the guard-house. In the presence of them all I gave my instructions 14 to Baruch: These are the words of the LORD of Hosts the God of Israel: Take these copies of the deed of purchase, the sealed and the unsealed, and deposit them in an earthenware jar so that they may be preserved for a long time. 15 For these are the words of the LORD of Hosts the God of Israel: The time will come when houses, fields, and vineyards will again be 16 bought and sold in this land. After I had given the deed of purchase to Baruch son of Neriah, I prayed 17 to the LORD: O Lord GOD, thou hast made the heavens and the earth by thy great strength and with thy outstretched arm; nothing 18 is impossible for thee. Thou keepest faith with thousands and thou dost requite the sins of fathers on to

the heads of their sons. O great and mighty God whose name is the LORD of Hosts, great are thy pur- 19 poses and mighty thy actions. Thine eyes watch all the ways of men, and thou rewardest each according to his ways and as his deeds deserve. Thou didst work 20 signs and portents in Egypt and hast continued them to this day, both in Israel and amongst all men, and hast won for thyself a name that lives on to this day. Thou 21 didst bring thy people Israel out of Egypt with signs and portents, with a strong hand and an outstretched arm, and with terrible power. Thou didst give them this 22 land which thou didst promise with an oath to their forefathers, a land flowing with milk and honey. They 23 came and took possession of it, but they did not obey thee or follow thy law, they disobeyed all thy commands; and so thou hast brought this disaster upon them. Look at the siege-ramps, the men 24 who are advancing to take the city, and the city given over to its assailants from Chaldaea, the victim of sword, famine, and pestilence. The word thou hast spoken is fulfilled and thou dost see it. And 25 yet thou hast bidden me buy the field, O Lord GOD, and have the deed witnessed, even though the city is given to the Chaldaeans.

These are the words of the LORD 26 to Jeremiah: I am the LORD, the 27 God of all flesh; is anything impossible for me? Therefore these are 28 the words of the LORD: I will deliver this city into the hands of the Chaldaeans and of Nebuchadrezzar king of Babylon, and he shall take it. The Chaldaeans who 29 are fighting against this city will enter it, set it on fire and burn it down, with the houses on whose roofs sacrifices have been burnt to Baal and drink-offerings poured out to other gods, by which I was provoked to anger.

From their earliest days Israel 30

and Judah have been doing what is wrong in my eyes, provoking me to anger by their actions, says 31 the LORD. For this city has so roused my anger and my fury, from the time it was built down to this day, that I would rid myself 32 of it. Israel and Judah, their kings, officers, priests, prophets, and everyone living in Jerusalem and Judah have provoked me to anger 33 by their wrongdoing. They have turned their backs on me and averted their faces; though I took pains to teach them, they would 34 not hear or learn their lesson. They set up their loathsome idols in the house which bears my name and 35 so defiled it. They built shrines to Baal in the Valley of Ben-hinnom, to surrender their sons and daughters to Molech. It was no command of mine, nor did it ever enter my thought to do this abominable thing and lead Judah into sin.

36   Now, therefore, these are the words of the LORD the God of Israel to this city of which you say, 'It is being given over to the king of Babylon, with sword, famine, and 37 pestilence': I will gather them from all the lands to which I banished them in my anger, rage, and fury, and I will bring them back to this place and let them dwell there un- 38 disturbed. They shall become my people and I will become their God. 39 I will give them one heart and one way of life so that they shall fear me at all times, for their own good and the good of their children after 40 them. I will enter into an eternal covenant with them, to follow them unfailingly with my bounty; I will fill their hearts with fear of me, and so they will not turn away 41 from me. I will rejoice over them, rejoice to do them good, and faithfully with all my heart and soul 42 I will plant them in this land. For these are the words of the LORD: As I brought on this people such great disaster, so will I bring them all the prosperity which I now promise them. Fields shall again 43 be bought and sold in this land of which you now say, 'It is desolate, without man or beast; it is given over to the Chaldaeans.' Fields 44 shall be bought and sold, deeds signed, sealed, and witnessed, in Benjamin, in the neighbourhood of Jerusalem, in the cities of Judah, of the hill-country, of the Shephelah, and of the Negeb; for I will restore their fortunes. This is the very word of the LORD.

The word of the LORD came to 33 Jeremiah a second time while he was still imprisoned in the court of the guard-house: These are the 2 words of the LORD who made the earth, who formed it and established it; the LORD is his name: If you 3 call to me I will answer you, and tell you great and mysterious things which you do not understand. These are the words of the 4 LORD the God of Israel concerning the houses in this city and the royal palace, which are to be razed to the ground, concerning siege-ramp and sword, and attackers[a] who fill 5 the houses with the corpses of those whom he struck down in his furious rage: I hid my face from this city because of their wicked ways, but 6 now I will bring her healing; I will heal and cure Judah and Israel, and will let my people see an age of peace and security. I will restore 7 their fortunes and build them again as once they were. I will 8 cleanse them of all the wickedness and sin that they have committed; I will forgive all the evil deeds they have done in rebellion against me. This city will win me a name[b] and 9 praise and glory before all the nations on earth, when they hear of all the blessings I bestow on her; and they shall be moved and filled with awe because of the blessings and the peace which I have brought upon her.

These are the words of the LORD: 10

---

[a] *Prob. rdg.; Heb. adds* the Chaldaeans.

[b] *Prob. rdg.; Heb. adds* of joy.

You say of this place, 'It is in ruins, and neither man nor beast lives in the cities of Judah or in the streets of Jerusalem. It is all a waste, inhabited by neither man nor beast.' Yet in this place shall 11 be heard once again the sounds of joy and gladness, the voice of the bridegroom and the bride; here too shall be heard voices shouting, 'Praise the LORD of Hosts, for he is good, for his love endures for ever', as they offer praise and thanksgiving in the house of the LORD. For I will restore the fortunes of the land as once they were. This is the word of the LORD.

12 These are the words of the LORD of Hosts: In this place and in all its cities, now ruined and inhabited by neither man nor beast, there shall once more be a refuge where shepherds may fold their flocks. 13 In the cities of the hill-country, of the Shephelah, of the Negeb, in Benjamin, in the neighbourhood of Jerusalem and the cities of Judah, flocks will once more pass under the shepherd's hand as he counts them. This is the word of the LORD.

14 Wait, says the LORD, the days are coming when I will bestow on Israel and Judah all the blessings 15 I have promised them. In those days, at that time, I will make a righteous Branch of David spring up; he shall maintain law and 16 justice in the land. In those days Judah shall be kept safe and Jerusalem shall live undisturbed; and this shall be her name: The LORD is our Righteousness.

17 For these are the words of the LORD: David will never lack a successor on the throne of Israel, 18 nor will the levitical priests lack a man who shall come before me continually to present whole-offerings, to burn grain-offerings and to make other offerings.

19 This word came from the LORD 20 to Jeremiah: These are the words of the LORD: If the law that I made for the day and the night could be annulled so that they fell out of their proper order, then my cove- 21 nant with my servant David could be annulled so that none of his line should sit upon his throne; so also could my covenant with the leviti- cal priests who minister to me. Like the innumerable host of hea- 22 ven or the countless sands of the sea, I will increase the descendants of my servant David and the Levites who minister to me.

The word of the LORD came to 23 Jeremiah: Have you not observed 24 how this people have said, 'It is the two families whom he chose that the LORD has spurned'? So others will despise my people and no longer regard them as a nation. These are the words of the LORD: 25 If I had not made my law for day and night nor established a fixed order in heaven and earth, then I 26 would spurn the descendants of Jacob and of my servant David, and would not take any of David's line to be rulers over the descend- ants of Abraham, Isaac and Jacob. But now I will restore their for- tunes and have compassion upon them.

Events under Jehoiakim and Zedekiah

THE word which came to Jeremiah 34 from the LORD when Nebuchad- rezzar king of Babylon and his army, with all his vassal kingdoms and nations, were fighting against Jerusalem and all her towns: These are the words of the LORD 2 the God of Israel: Go and say to Zedekiah king of Judah, These are the words of the LORD: I will give this city into the hands of the king of Babylon and he will burn it down. You shall not escape, you 3 will be captured and handed over to him. You will see him face to face, and he will speak to you in person; and you shall go to Baby- lon. But listen to the LORD's word 4 to you, Zedekiah king of Judah.

This is his word: You shall not die
5 by the sword; you will die a peaceful death, and they will kindle fires in your honour like the fires kindled in former times for the kings your ancestors who preceded you. 'Alas, my lord!' they will say as they beat their breasts in mourning for you. This I have spoken. This is the very word of the LORD.
6 The prophet Jeremiah repeated all this to Zedekiah king of Judah in
7 Jerusalem when the army of the king of Babylon was attacking Jerusalem and the remaining cities of Judah, namely Lachish and Azekah. These were the only fortified cities left in Judah.

8   The word that came to Jeremiah from the LORD after Zedekiah had made a covenant with all the people in Jerusalem to proclaim an act of freedom for the slaves.
9 All who had Hebrew slaves, male or female, were to set them free; they were not to keep their fellow
10 Judaeans in servitude. All the officers and people, having made this covenant to set free their slaves, both male and female, and not to keep them in servitude any longer, fulfilled its terms and let
11 them go. Afterwards, however, they changed their minds and forced back again into slavery the men and women whom they had
12 freed. Then this word came from
13 the LORD to Jeremiah: These are the words of the LORD the God of Israel: I made a covenant with your forefathers on the day that I brought them out of Egypt, out of the land of slavery. These were
14 its terms: 'Within seven years each of you shall set free any Hebrew who has sold himself to you as a slave and has served you for six years; you shall set him free.' Your forefathers did not listen to me
15 or obey me. You, on the contrary, recently proclaimed an act of freedom for the slaves and made a covenant in my presence, in the house that bears my name, and so

have done what is right in my eyes.
But you too have profaned my 16 name. You have all taken back the slaves you had set free and you have forced them, both male and female, to be your slaves again. Therefore these are the words of 17 the LORD: After you had proclaimed an act of freedom, a deliverance for your kinsmen and your neighbours, you did not obey me; so I will proclaim a deliverance for you, says the LORD, a deliverance over to sword, to pestilence, and to famine, and I will make you repugnant to all the kingdoms of the earth. You have disregarded my 18 covenant and have not fulfilled the terms to which you yourselves had agreed; so I will make you like the calf of the covenant when they cut it into two and passed between the pieces. Those who passed be- 19 tween the pieces of the calf were the officers of Judah and Jerusalem, the eunuchs and priests and all the people of the land. I will give 20 them up to their enemies who seek their lives, and their bodies shall be food for birds of prey and wild beasts. I will deliver Zedekiah king 21 of Judah and his officers to their enemies who seek their lives and to the army of the king of Babylon, which is now raising the siege. I 22 will give the command, says the LORD, and will bring them back to this city. They shall attack it and take it and burn it down, and I will make the cities of Judah desolate and unpeopled.

The word which came to Jere- 35 miah from the LORD in the days of Jehoiakim son of Josiah, king of Judah: Go and speak to the 2 Rechabites, bring them to one of the rooms in the house of the LORD and offer them wine to drink. So 3 I fetched Jaazaniah son of Jeremiah, son of Habaziniah, with his brothers and all his sons and all the family of the Rechabites. I 4 brought them into the house of the LORD to the room of the sons of Hanan son of Igdaliah, the man of God; this adjoins the officers' room above that of Maaseiah son of Shallum, the keeper 5 of the threshold. I set bowls full of wine and drinking-cups before the Rechabites and invited them 6 to drink wine; but they said, 'We will not drink wine, for our forefather Jonadab son of Rechab laid this command on us: "You shall never drink wine, neither 7 you nor your children. You shall not build houses or sow seed or plant vineyards; you shall have none of these things. Instead, you shall remain tent-dwellers all your lives, so that you may live long in the land where you are sojourn- 8 ers." We have honoured all the commands of our forefather Jonadab son of Rechab and have drunk no wine all our lives, neither we nor our wives, nor our sons, nor 9 our daughters. We have not built houses to live in, nor have we possessed vineyards or sown fields. 10 We have lived in tents, obeying and observing all the commands 11 of our forefather Jonadab. But when Nebuchadrezzar king of Babylon invaded the land we said, "Come, let us go to Jerusalem before the advancing Chaldaean and Aramaean armies." And we have stayed in Jerusalem.'

12   Then the word of the LORD came 13 to Jeremiah: These are the words of the LORD of Hosts the God of Israel: Go and say to the men of Judah and the inhabitants of Jerusalem, You must accept correction and obey my words, says the 14 LORD. The command of Jonadab son of Rechab to his descendants not to drink wine has been honoured; they have not drunk wine to this day, for they have obeyed their ancestor's command. But I have taken especial pains to warn you and yet you have not obeyed 15 me. I sent my servants the prophets especially to say to you, 'Turn back every one of you from his evil course, mend your ways and cease to follow other gods and worship them; then you shall remain on the land that I have given to you and to your forefathers.' Yet you did not obey or listen to me. The sons of Jonadab son of 16 Rechab have honoured their ancestor's command laid on them, but this people have not listened to me. Therefore, these are the 17 words of the LORD the God of Hosts, the God of Israel: Because they did not listen when I spoke to them, nor answer when I called them, I will bring upon Judah and upon all the inhabitants of Jerusalem the disaster with which I threatened them. To the Recha- 18 bites Jeremiah said, These are the words of the LORD of Hosts the God of Israel: Because you have kept the command of Jonadab your ancestor and obeyed all his instructions and carried out all that he told you to do, therefore these 19 are the words of the LORD of Hosts the God of Israel: Jonadab son of Rechab shall not want a descendant to stand before me for all time.

IN the fourth year of Jehoiakim 36 son of Josiah, king of Judah, this word came to Jeremiah from the LORD: Take a scroll and write on 2 it every word that I have spoken to you about Jerusalem and Judah and all the nations, from the day that I first spoke to you in the reign of Josiah down to the present day. Perhaps the house of Judah 3 will be warned of the calamity that I am planning to bring on them, and every man will abandon his evil course; then I will forgive their wrongdoing and their sin. So Jere- 4 miah called Baruch son of Neriah, and he wrote on the scroll at Jeremiah's dictation all the words which the LORD had spoken to him. He gave Baruch this instruction: 5 'I am prevented from going to the LORD's house. You must go there in 6 my place on a fast-day and read the words of the LORD in the hearing of the people from the scroll you have written at my dictation. You shall read them in the hearing of all the men of Judah who come in 7 from their cities. Then perhaps they will present a petition to the LORD and every man will abandon his evil course; for the LORD has spoken against this people in great 8 anger and wrath.' Baruch son of Neriah did all that the prophet Jeremiah had told him to do, and read the words of the LORD in the LORD's house out of the book.

9 In the ninth month of the fifth year of the reign of Jehoiakim son of Josiah, king of Judah, all the people in Jerusalem and all who came there from the cities of Judah proclaimed a fast before the LORD. 10 Then Baruch read Jeremiah's words in the house of the LORD out of the book in the hearing of all the people; he read them from the room of Gemariah son of the adjutant-general Shaphan in the upper court at the entrance to the new gate of the LORD's house. 11 Micaiah son of Gemariah, son of Shaphan, heard all the words of 12 the LORD out of the book and went down to the palace, to the adjutant-general's room where all the officers were gathered – Elishama the adjutant-general, Delaiah son of Shemaiah, Elnathan son of Akbor, Gemariah son of Shaphan, Zedekiah son of Hananiah and all the other officers. 13 There Micaiah repeated all the words he had heard when Baruch read out of the book in the people's 14 hearing. Then the officers sent Jehudi son of Nethaniah, son of Shelemiah, son of Cushi, to Baruch with this message: 'Come here and bring the scroll from which you read in the people's hearing.' So Baruch son of Neriah brought the 15 scroll to them, and they said, 'Sit 16 down and*a* read it to us.' When they heard what he read, they

turned to each other trembling and said, 'We must report this to the king.' They asked Baruch to tell 17 them how he had come to write all this. He said to them, 'Jeremiah 18 dictated every word of it to me, and I wrote it down in ink in the book.' The officers said to Baruch, 19 'You and Jeremiah must go into hiding so that no one may know where you are.' When they had 20 deposited the scroll in the room of Elishama the adjutant-general, they went to the court and reported everything to the king.

The king sent Jehudi to fetch 21 the scroll. When he had fetched it from the room of Elishama the adjutant-general, he read it to the king and to all the officers in attendance. It was the ninth month 22 of the year, and the king was sitting in his winter apartments with a fire burning in a brazier in front of him. When Jehudi had read 23 three or four columns of the scroll, the king cut them off with a penknife and threw them into the fire in the brazier. He went on doing so until the whole scroll had been thrown on the fire. Neither the 24 king nor any of his courtiers who heard these words showed any fear or rent their clothes; and though 25 Elnathan, Delaiah, and Gemariah begged the king not to burn the scroll, he would not listen to them. The king then ordered Jerahmeel, 26 a royal prince,*b* Seraiah son of Azriel, and Shelemiah son of Abdeel to fetch the scribe Baruch and the prophet Jeremiah; but the LORD had hidden them.

After the king had burnt the 27 scroll with all that Baruch had written on it at Jeremiah's dictation, the word of the LORD came to Jeremiah: Now take another 28 scroll and write on it all the words that were on the first scroll which Jehoiakim king of Judah burnt. You shall say to Jehoiakim king 29 of Judah, These are the words of

---

a Sit down and: *or* This time.   *b* a royal prince: *or* the king's deputy.

the LORD: You burnt this scroll and said, Why have you written here that the king of Babylon shall come and destroy this land and exterminate both men and beasts? 30 Therefore these are the words of the LORD about Jehoiakim king of Judah: He shall have no one to succeed him on the throne of David, and his dead body shall be exposed to scorching heat by day 31 and frost by night. I will punish him and also his offspring and his courtiers for their wickedness, and I will bring down on them and on the inhabitants of Jerusalem and on the men of Judah all the calamities with which I threatened them, and to which they turned a deaf 32 ear. Then Jeremiah took another scroll and gave it to the scribe Baruch son of Neriah, who wrote on it at Jeremiah's dictation all the words of the book which Jehoiakim king of Judah had burnt; and much else was added to the same effect.

37 King Zedekiah son of Josiah was set on the throne of Judah by Nebuchadrezzar king of Babylon, in succession to Coniah son of 2 Jehoiakim. Neither he nor his courtiers nor the people of the land listened to the words which the LORD spoke through the prophet Jeremiah.

3 King Zedekiah sent Jehucal son of Shelemiah and the priest Zephaniah son of Maaseiah to the prophet Jeremiah to say to him, 'Pray 4 for us to the LORD our God.' At the time Jeremiah was free to come and go among the people; he had not yet been thrown into prison. 5 Meanwhile, Pharaoh's army had marched out of Egypt, and when the Chaldaeans who were besieging Jerusalem heard of it they raised 6 the siege. Then this word came from the LORD to the prophet 7 Jeremiah: These are the words of the LORD the God of Israel: Say to the king of Judah who sent you to consult me, Pharaoh's army

which marched out to help you is on its way back to Egypt, its own land, and the Chaldaeans will 8 return to the attack. They will capture this city and burn it to the ground. These are the words 9 of the LORD: Do not deceive yourselves, do not imagine that the Chaldaeans will go away and leave you alone. They will not go; for 10 even if you defeated the whole Chaldaean force with which you are now fighting, and only the wounded were left lying in their tents, they would rise and burn down the city.

When the Chaldaean army had 11 raised the siege of Jerusalem because of the advance of Pharaoh's army, Jeremiah was on the point 12 of leaving Jerusalem to go into Benjamite territory and take possession of his patrimony in the presence of the people there. Irijah 13 son of Shelemiah, son of Hananiah, the officer of the guard, was in the Benjamin Gate when Jeremiah reached it, and he arrested the prophet, accusing him of going over to the Chaldaeans. 'It is a lie,' 14 said Jeremiah; 'I am not going over to the Chaldaeans.' Irijah would not listen to him but arrested him and brought him before the officers. The officers were indignant 15 with Jeremiah; they flogged him and imprisoned him in the house of Jonathan the scribe, which they had converted into a prison; for 16 Jeremiah had been put into a vaulted pit beneath the house, and here he remained for a long time.

King Zedekiah had Jeremiah 17 brought to him and consulted him privately in the palace, asking him if there was a word from the LORD. 'Indeed there is,' said Jeremiah; 'you shall fall into the hands of the king of Babylon.' Then Jere- 18 miah said to King Zedekiah, 'What wrong have I done to you or your courtiers or this people? Why have you thrown me into prison? Where 19 are your prophets who prophesied that the king of Babylon would not attack you or your country? 20 I pray you now, my lord king, give me a hearing and let my petition be presented: do not send me back to the house of Jonathan the scribe, 21 or I shall die there.' Then King Zedekiah gave the order and Jeremiah was committed to the court of the guard-house and was granted a daily ration of one loaf from the Street of the Bakers, until the bread in the city was all gone. So Jeremiah remained in the court of the guard-house.

38 Shephatiah son of Mattan, Gedaliah son of Pashhur, Jucal son of Shelemiah, and Pashhur son of Malchiah heard what Jeremiah 2 was saying to all the people: These are the words of the LORD: Whoever remains in this city shall die by sword, by famine, or by pestilence, but whoever goes out to surrender to the Chaldaeans shall survive; he shall survive, he shall take home his life and nothing more. 3 These are the words of the LORD: This city will fall into the hands of the king of Babylon's army, and 4 they will capture it. Then the officers said to the king, 'The man must be put to death. By talking in this way he is discouraging the soldiers and the rest of the people left in the city. He is pursuing not the people's welfare but their ruin.' 5 King Zedekiah said, 'He is in your hands; the king is powerless against 6 you.' So they took Jeremiah and threw him into the pit,[a] in the court of the guard-house, letting him down with ropes. There was no water in the pit, only mud, and Jeremiah 7–8 sank in the mud. Now Ebed-melech the Cushite, a eunuch, who was in the palace, heard that they had thrown Jeremiah into the pit and went to tell the king, who was 9 seated in the Benjamin Gate. 'Your majesty,' he said, 'these men have shown great wickedness in their treatment of the prophet Jeremiah. They have thrown him into the pit, and when there is no more bread in the city he will die of hunger where he lies.' Thereupon 10 the king told Ebed-melech the Cushite to take three men with him and hoist Jeremiah out of the pit before he died. So Ebed-melech 11 went to the palace with the men and took some tattered, cast-off clothes from the wardrobe[b] and let them down with ropes to Jeremiah in the pit. Ebed-melech 12 the Cushite said to Jeremiah, 'Put these old clothes under your armpits to ease the ropes.' Jeremiah did this, and they pulled him up 13 out of the pit with the ropes; and he remained in the court of the guard-house.

King Zedekiah had the prophet 14 Jeremiah brought to him by the third entrance to the LORD's house and said to him, 'I want to ask you something; hide nothing from me.' Jeremiah answered, 'If I speak 15 out, you will certainly put me to death; if I offer you any advice, you will not take it.' But King 16 Zedekiah swore to Jeremiah privately, 'By the life of the LORD who gave us our lives, I will not put you to death, nor will I hand you over to these men who are seeking to take your life.' Jeremiah 17 said to Zedekiah, 'These are the words of the LORD the God of Hosts, the God of Israel: If you go out and surrender to the officers of the king of Babylon, you shall live and this city shall not be burnt down; you and your family shall live. But if you do not surrender 18 to the officers of the king of Babylon, the city shall fall into the hands of the Chaldaeans, and they shall burn it down, and you will not escape them.' King Zedekiah 19 said to Jeremiah, 'I am afraid of the Judaeans who have gone over to the enemy. I fear the Chaldaeans

[a] *Prob. rdg.; Heb. adds* Malchiah son (*or* deputy) of the king.
[b] the wardrobe: *prob. rdg.; Heb.* underneath the treasury.

will give me up to them and I shall
20 be roughly handled.' Jeremiah answered, 'They will not give you up.
If you obey the LORD in everything
I tell you, all will be well with you
21 and you shall live. But if you refuse
to go out and surrender, this is
22 what the LORD has shown me: all
the women left in the king of
Judah's palace will be led out to
the officers of the king of Babylon
and they will say:

Your own friends have misled you
and have been too strong for you;
they have let your feet sink in the
mud
and have turned away and left you.

23 All your women and children will
be led out to the Chaldaeans, and
you will not escape; you will be
seized by the king of Babylon and
this city will be burnt down.'
24 Zedekiah said to Jeremiah, 'Let
no one know about this, and you
25 shall not be put to death. If the
officers hear that I have been
speaking with you and they come
to you and say, "Tell us what you
said to the king and what he said
to you; hide nothing from us, and
26 we will not put you to death", then
answer, "I was presenting a petition
to the king not to send me back
to the house of Jonathan to die
27 there."' The officers all came to
Jeremiah and questioned him, and
he said to them just what the king
had told him to say; so their talk
came to an end and they were none
28 the wiser. Jeremiah remained in
the court of the guard-house till
the day Jerusalem fell.

39 1ᵃ IN the tenth month of the ninth
year of the reign of Zedekiah king
of Judah, Nebuchadrezzar advanced with all his army against
Jerusalem, and they laid siege to
2 it. In the fourth month of the

eleventh year of Zedekiah, on the
ninth day of the month, the city
was thrown open. All the officers 3
of the king of Babylon came in and
took their seats in the middle gate:
Nergalsarezer of Simmagir, Nebu-
sarsekimᵇ the chief eunuch,ᶜ Nergalsarezer the commander of the
frontier troops,ᵈ and all the other
officers of the king of Babylon.
When Zedekiah king of Judah saw 4
them, he and all his armed escort
left the city and fled by night by
way of the king's garden through
the gate called Between the Two
Walls. They escaped towards the
Arabah, but the Chaldaean army 5
pursued them and overtook Zedekiah in the lowlands of Jericho.
The king was seized and brought
before Nebuchadrezzar king of
Babylon at Riblah in the land of
Hamath, and he pleaded his case
before him. The king of Babylon 6
slew Zedekiah's sons before his
eyes at Riblah; he also put to death
the nobles of Judah. Then Zede- 7
kiah's eyes were put out, and he
was bound in fetters of bronze to
be brought to Babylon. The Chal- 8
daeans burnt the royal palace and
the house of the LORD and the
housesᵉ of the people, and pulled
down the walls of Jerusalem. Ne- 9
buzaradan captain of the bodyguard deported to Babylon the
rest of the people left in the city,
those who had deserted to him
and any remaining artisans.ᶠ At 10
the same time the captain of the
guard left behind the weakest class
of the people, those who owned
nothing at all, and made them
vine-dressers and labourers.

Nebuchadrezzar king of Baby- 11
lon sent orders about Jeremiah to
Nebuzaradan captain of the guard.
'Take him,' he said; 'take special 12
care of him, and do him no harm
of any kind, but do for him what-

ᵃ Verses 1–10: cp. 52. 4–16 and 2 Kgs. 25. 1–12. ᵇ Probably a different form of
Nebushazban (verse 13). ᶜ the chief eunuch: or Rab-saris. ᵈ the commander
...troops: or Rab-mag. ᵉ of the LORD and the houses: prob. rdg.; Heb. om.
ᶠ artisans: prob. rdg., cp. 52. 15; Heb. people who were left.

13 ever he says.' So Nebuzaradan captain of the guard sent Nebushazban the chief eunuch, Nergalsarezer the commander of the frontier troops, and all the chief 14 officers of the king of Babylon, and they fetched Jeremiah from the court of the guard-house and handed him over to Gedaliah son of Ahikam, son of Shaphan, to take him out to the Residence. So he stayed with his own people.

15   The word of the LORD had come to Jeremiah while he was under arrest in the court of the guard-16 house: Go and say to Ebed-melech the Cushite, These are the words of the LORD of Hosts the God of Israel: I will make good the words I have spoken against this city, foretelling ruin and not prosperity, and when that day comes you will 17 be there to see it. But I will preserve you on that day, says the LORD, and you shall not be handed 18 over to the men you fear. I will keep you safe and you shall not fall a victim to the sword; because you trusted in me you shall escape, you shall take home your life and nothing more. This is the very word of the LORD.

Jeremiah after the capture of Jerusalem

40 THE word which came from the LORD concerning Jeremiah: Nebuzaradan captain of the guard had taken him in chains to Ramah along with the other exiles from Jerusalem and Judah who were being deported to Babylon; and 2 there he set him free, and took it upon himself to say to Jeremiah, 'The LORD your God threatened 3 this place with disaster, and has duly carried out his threat that this should happen to all of you because you have sinned against the LORD and not obeyed him. 4 But as for you, Jeremiah, today I remove the fetters from your wrists. Come with me to Babylon if you wish, and I will take special care of you; but if you prefer not to come, well and good. The whole country lies before you; go wherever you think best.' Jeremiah 5 had not yet answered when Nebuzaradan went on,*a* 'Go back to Gedaliah son of Ahikam, son of Shaphan, whom the king of Babylon has appointed governor of the cities of Judah, and stay with him openly; or else go wherever you choose.' Then the captain of the guard granted him an allowance of food, and gave him a present, and so took leave of him. Jeremiah 6 then came to Gedaliah son of Ahikam at Mizpah and stayed with him among the people left in the land.

When all the captains of the 7 armed bands in the country-side and their men heard that the king of Babylon had appointed Gedaliah son of Ahikam governor of the land, and had put him in charge of the weakest class of the population, men, women, and children, who had not been deported to Babylon, they came to him at 8 Mizpah; Ishmael son of Nethaniah came, and Johanan and Jonathan sons of Kareah, Seraiah son of Tanhumeth, the sons of Ephai*b* from Netophah, and Jezaniah of Beth-maacah, with their men. Gedaliah son of Ahikam, son of 9 Shaphan, gave them all this assurance: 'Have no fear of the Chaldaean officers. Settle down in the land and serve the king of Babylon; and then all will be well with you. I am to stay in Mizpah and attend 10 upon the Chaldaeans whenever they come, and you are to gather in the summer-fruits, wine, and oil, store them in jars, and settle in the towns you have taken over.' The Judaeans also, in Moab, Am-11 mon, Edom and other countries, heard that the king of Babylon had left a remnant in Judah and that

---

a Jeremiah...went on: *prob. rdg.; Heb. unintelligible in context.*   *b* Or Ophai.

he had set over them Gedaliah son
12 of Ahikam, son of Shaphan. The
Judaeans, therefore, from all the
places where they were scattered,
came back to Judah and presented
themselves before Gedaliah at
Mizpah; and they gathered in a
considerable store of fruit and
wine.

13   Johanan son of Kareah and all
the captains of the armed bands
from the country-side came to
14 Gedaliah at Mizpah and said to
him, 'Do you know that Baalis
king of the Ammonites has sent
Ishmael son of Nethaniah to assassinate you?' But Gedaliah son
of Ahikam did not believe them.
15 Then Johanan son of Kareah said
in private to Gedaliah, 'Let me
go, unknown to anyone else, and
kill Ishmael son of Nethaniah.
Why allow him to assassinate you,
and so let all the Judaeans who
have rallied round you be scattered
and the remnant of Judah lost?'
16 Gedaliah son of Ahikam answered
him, 'Do no such thing. Your story
about Ishmael is a lie.'

41   In the seventh month Ishmael
son of Nethaniah, son of Elishama,
who was a member of the royal
house, came with ten men to Gedaliah son of Ahikam at Mizpah.
While they were at table with him
2 there, Ishmael son of Nethaniah
and the ten men with him rose to
their feet and assassinated Gedaliah son of Ahikam, son of Shaphan,
whom the king of Babylon had
appointed governor of the land.
3 They also murdered the Judaeans
with him in Mizpah and the Chaldaeans who happened to be there.
4 The second day after the murder
of Gedaliah, while it was not yet
5 common knowledge, there came
eighty men from Shechem, Shiloh,
and Samaria. They had shaved off
their beards, their clothes were
rent and their bodies gashed, and
they were carrying grain-offerings
and frankincense to take to the
6 house of the LORD. Ishmael son of

Nethaniah came out weeping from
Mizpah to meet them and, when
he met them, he said, 'Come to
Gedaliah son of Ahikam.' But as 7
soon as they reached the centre
of the town, Ishmael son of Nethaniah and his men murdered them
and threw their bodies into a pit,
all except ten of them who said to 8
Ishmael, 'Do not kill us, for we
have a secret hoard in the country,
wheat and barley, oil and honey.'
So he held his hand and did not
kill them with the others. The pit 9
into which he threw the bodies of
those whose death he had caused
by using Gedaliah's name was the
pit which King Asa had made
when threatened by Baasha king
of Israel; and the dead bodies filled
it. He rounded up the rest of the 10
people in Mizpah, that is the king's
daughters and all who remained in
Mizpah when Nebuzaradan captain of the guard appointed Gedaliah son of Ahikam governor; and
with these he set out to cross over
into Ammon. When Johanan son 11
of Kareah and all the captains of
the armed bands heard of the
crimes committed by Ishmael son
of Nethaniah, they took all the 12
men they had and went to attack
him. They found him by the great
pool in Gibeon. The people with 13
Ishmael were glad when they saw
Johanan son of Kareah and the
captains of the armed bands with
him; and all whom Ishmael had 14
taken prisoner at Mizpah turned
and joined Johanan son of Kareah.
But Ishmael son of Nethaniah 15
escaped from Johanan with eight
men, and they made their way to
the Ammonites.

    Johanan son of Kareah and all 16
the captains of the armed bands
took from Mizpah the survivors
whom he had rescued from Ishmael
son of Nethaniah after the murder
of Gedaliah son of Ahikam – men,
armed and unarmed, women, children, and eunuchs, whom he had
brought back from Gibeon. They 17

started out and broke their journey at Kimham's holding near Bethlehem, on their way into E-
18 gypt to escape the Chaldaeans. They were afraid because Ishmael son of Nethaniah had assassinated Gedaliah son of Ahikam, whom the king of Babylon had appointed governor of the country.

42 All the captains of the armed bands, including Johanan son of Kareah and Azariah son of Hoshaiah, together with the people, high and low, came to the prophet
2 Jeremiah and said to him, 'May our petition be acceptable to you: Pray to the LORD your God on our behalf and on behalf of this remnant; for, as you see for yourself, only a few of us remain out of
3 many. Pray that the LORD your God may tell us which way we ought to go and what we ought to
4 do.' Then the prophet Jeremiah said to them, 'I have heard your request and will pray to the LORD your God as you desire, and whatever answer the LORD gives I will tell you; I will keep nothing back.'
5 They said to Jeremiah, 'May the LORD be a true and faithful witness against us if we do not keep our oath! We swear that we will do whatever the LORD your God
6 sends you to tell us. Whether we like it or not, we will obey the LORD our God to whom we send you, in order that it may be well with us; we will obey the LORD our God.'
7 Within ten days the word of the
8 LORD came to Jeremiah; so he summoned Johanan son of Kareah, all the captains of the armed bands with him, and all the people, both
9 high and low. He said to them, These are the words of the LORD the God of Israel, to whom you sent me to present your petition:
10 If you will stay in this land, then I will build you up and not pull you down, I will plant you and not uproot you; I grieve for the disaster which I have brought

upon you. Do not be afraid of the 11 king of Babylon whom you now fear. Do not be afraid of him, says the LORD; for I am with you, to save you and deliver you from his power. I will show you compassion, 12 and he too will have compassion on you; he will let you stay on your own soil. But it may be that 13 you will disobey the LORD your God and say, 'We will not stay in this land. No, we will go to Egypt, 14 where we shall see no sign of war, never hear the sound of the trumpet, and not starve for want of bread; and there we will live.' Then 15 hear the word of the LORD, you remnant of Judah. These are the words of the LORD of Hosts the God of Israel: If you are bent on going to Egypt, if you do settle there, then the sword you fear will 16 overtake you in Egypt, and the famine you dread will still be with you, even in Egypt, and there you will die. All the men who are bent 17 on going to Egypt and settling there will die by sword, by famine, or by pestilence; not one shall escape or survive the calamity which I will bring upon them. These are the words of the LORD 18 of Hosts the God of Israel: As my anger and my wrath were poured out upon the inhabitants of Jerusalem, so will my wrath be poured out upon you when you go to Egypt; you will become an object of execration and horror, of ridicule and reproach; you will never see this place again. To you, then, rem- 19 nant of Judah, the LORD says, Do not go to Egypt. Make no mistake, I can bear witness against you this day. You deceived yourselves when 20 you sent me to the LORD your God and said, 'Pray for us to the LORD our God; tell us all that the LORD our God says and we will do it.' I 21 have told you everything today; but you have not obeyed the LORD your God in what he sent me to tell you. So now be sure of this: you 22 will die by sword, by famine, and by pestilence in the place where you desire to go and make your home.

43 When Jeremiah had finished reciting to the people all that the LORD their God had sent him to 2 say, Azariah son of Hoshaiah and Johanan son of Kareah and their party had the effrontery to say to[a] Jeremiah, 'You are lying; the LORD our God has not sent you to forbid us to go and make our home in 3 Egypt. Baruch son of Neriah has incited you against us in order to put us in the power of the Chaldaeans, so that they may kill us 4 or deport us to Babylon.' Johanan son of Kareah and the captains of the armed bands and all the people refused to obey the LORD and stay 5 in Judah. So Johanan son of Kareah and the captains collected the remnant of Judah, all who had returned from the countries among which they had been scattered to 6 make their home in Judah – men, women and children, including the king's daughters, all the people whom Nebuzaradan captain of the guard had left with Gedaliah son of Ahikam, son of Shaphan, as well as the prophet Jeremiah 7 and Baruch son of Neriah; these all went to Egypt and came to Tahpanhes, disobeying the LORD.

8 The word of the LORD came to 9 Jeremiah at Tahpanhes: Take some large stones and set them in cement in the pavement at the entrance to Pharaoh's palace in Tahpanhes. Let the Judaeans see 10 you do it and say to them, These are the words of the LORD of Hosts the God of Israel: I will send for my servant Nebuchadrezzar king of Babylon, and he will place his throne on these stones that I have set there, and spread his canopy 11 over them. He will then proceed to strike Egypt down, killing those doomed to death, taking captive those who are for captivity, and

putting to the sword those who are for the sword. He will set fire 12 to the temples of the Egyptian gods, burning the buildings and carrying the gods into captivity. He will scour the land of Egypt as a shepherd scours his clothes to rid them of lice. He will leave Egypt with his purpose achieved. He will smash the sacred pillars 13 of Beth-shemesh in Egypt and burn down the temples of the Egyptian gods.

The word that came to Jeremiah 44 for all the Judaeans who were living in Egypt, in Migdol, Tahpanhes, Noph, and the district of Pathros: These are the words of 2 the LORD of Hosts the God of Israel: You have seen the calamity that I brought upon Jerusalem and all the cities of Judah: today they are laid waste and left uninhabited, all because of the wicked- 3 ness of those who provoked me to anger by going after other gods, gods unknown to them, by burning sacrifices to them. It was you and your fathers who did this. I took 4 pains to send all my servants the prophets to you with this warning: 'Do not do this abominable thing which I hate.' But your fathers 5 would not listen; they paid no heed. They did not give up their wickedness or cease to burn sacrifices to other gods; so my anger and wrath 6 raged like a fire through the cities of Judah and the streets of Jerusalem, and they became the desolate ruin that they are today.

Now these are the words of the 7 LORD the God of Hosts, the God of Israel: Why bring so great a disaster upon yourselves? Why bring destruction upon Judaeans, men and women, children and babes, and leave yourselves without a survivor? This is what comes 8 of your provoking me by all your idolatry in burning sacrifices to other gods in Egypt where you have made your home. You will

---

[a] *to say to: or* to say: It is being said to.

destroy yourselves and become an object of ridicule and reproach to 9 all the nations of the earth. Have you forgotten all the wickedness committed by your forefathers, by the kings of Judah and their wives, by yourselves and your wives in the land of Judah and in the streets 10 of Jerusalem? To this day you have shown no remorse, no reverence; you have not conformed to the law and the statutes which I set before 11 you and your forefathers. These, therefore, are the words of the LORD of Hosts the God of Israel: I have made up my mind to bring calamity upon you and extermi-12 nate the people of Judah. I will deal with the remnant of Judah who were bent on going to make their home in Egypt; in Egypt they shall all meet their end. Some shall fall by the sword, others will meet their end by famine. High and low alike will die by sword or by famine and will be an object of execration and horror, of ridi-13 cule and reproach. I will punish those who live in Egypt as I punished those in Jerusalem, by sword, 14 famine, and pestilence. Those who had remained in Judah came to make their home in Egypt, confident that they would return and live once more in Judah. But they shall not return;[a] not one of them shall survive, not one escape.

15   Then all the men who knew that their wives were burning sacrifices to other gods and the crowds of women standing by[b] answered 16 Jeremiah, 'We will not listen to what you tell us in the name of the 17 LORD. We intend to fulfil all the promises by which we have bound ourselves: we will burn sacrifices to the queen of heaven and pour drink-offerings to her as we used to do, we and our fathers, our kings and our princes, in the cities of Judah and in the streets of Jerusalem. We then had food in plenty and were content; no cala-mity touched us. But from the time 18 we left off burning sacrifices to the queen of heaven and pouring drink-offerings to her, we have been in great want, and in the end we have fallen victims to sword and famine.' And the women said, 'When we 19 burnt sacrifices to the queen of heaven and poured drink-offerings to her, our husbands knew full well that we were making crescent-cakes marked with her image and pour-ing drink-offerings to her.' When 20 Jeremiah received this answer from these men and women and all the people, he said, 'The LORD did not 21 forget those sacrifices which you and your fathers, your kings and princes and the people of the land burnt in the cities of Judah and in the streets of Jerusalem, and they mounted up in his mind until 22 he could no longer tolerate them, so wicked were your deeds and so abominable the things you did. Your land became a desolate waste, an object of horror and ridicule, with no inhabitants, as it still is. This calamity has come upon you 23 because you burnt these sacrifices and sinned against the LORD and did not obey the LORD or conform to his laws, statutes, and teach-ings.'

Jeremiah further said to all the 24 people and to the women, Listen to the word of the LORD, all you from Judah who live in Egypt. These are the words of the LORD 25 of Hosts the God of Israel: You women have made your actions match your words. 'We will carry out our vows', you said, 'to burn sacrifices to the queen of heaven and to pour drink-offerings to her.' Well then, fulfil your vows by all means, and make your words good. But listen to the word of the LORD, 26 all you from Judah who live in Egypt. I have sworn by my great

---

[a] *Prob. rdg.*; *Heb. adds* except fugitives.
[b] *Prob. rdg.*; *Heb. adds* and all the people who lived in Egypt, in Pathros.

name, says the LORD, that my name shall never again be on the lips of the men of Judah; they shall no longer swear in Egypt, 'By the life of the Lord GOD.' I am on the watch to bring you evil and not good, and all the men of Judah who are in Egypt shall meet their end by sword and by famine until not one is left.[a] It is then that all the survivors of Judah who have made their home in Egypt shall know whose word prevails, theirs or mine.

27

28

29 This is the sign I give you, says the LORD, that I intend to punish you in this place, so that you may learn that my words against you will prevail to bring evil upon you:

30 These are the words of the LORD: I will hand over Pharaoh Hophra king of Egypt to his enemies and to those who seek his life, just as I handed over Zedekiah king of Judah to his enemy Nebuchadrezzar king of Babylon who was seeking to take his life.

45 THE word which the prophet Jeremiah spoke to Baruch son of Neriah when he wrote these words in a book at Jeremiah's dictation in the fourth year of Jehoiakim son of Josiah, king of Judah: These are the words of the LORD the God of Israel concerning you, Baruch:

2

3 You said, 'Woe is me, for the LORD has added grief to all my trials. I have worn myself out with my labours and have had no respite.' This is what you shall say to Baruch, These are the words of the LORD: What I have built, I demolish; what I have planted, I uproot. So it will be with the whole earth. You seek great things for yourself. Leave off seeking them; for I will bring disaster upon all mankind, says the LORD, and I will let you live wherever you go, but you shall save your life and nothing more.

4

5

Prophecies against the nations

THIS came to the prophet Jeremiah as the word of the LORD concerning the nations.

46

Of Egypt: concerning the army of Pharaoh Necho king of Egypt at Carchemish on the river Euphrates, which Nebuchadrezzar king of Babylon defeated in the fourth year of Jehoiakim son of Josiah, king of Judah.

2

Hold shield and buckler ready and advance to battle;   3
harness the horses, let the riders mount;   4
form up, your helmets on, your lances burnished;
on with your coats of mail!
But now, what sight is this?   5
They are broken and routed, their warriors beaten down;
they have turned to flight and do not look behind them.
Terror let loose!
This is the very word of the LORD.

Can the swift escape, can the warrior save himself?   6
In the north, by the river Euphrates,
they stumble and fall.

Who is this rising like the Nile,   7
like its streams turbulent in flood?
Egypt is rising like the Nile,   8
like its streams turbulent in flood.

He[b] says:

I will rise and cover the earth,
I will destroy both city and people.

Charge, horsemen! On, you flashing chariots, on!   9
Forward, the warriors,
Cushites and men of Put carrying shields,
Lydians grasping their bent bows!

[a] *Prob. rdg.; Heb. adds* Few will escape the sword in Egypt to return to Judah.
[b] *Or* It.

10 This is the day of the Lord, the
GOD of Hosts,
a day of vengeance, vengeance on
his enemies;
the sword shall devour and be
sated,
drunk with their blood.
For the GOD of Hosts, the Lord,
holds sacrifice
in a northern land, by the river
Euphrates.

11 Go up into Gilead and fetch balm,
O virgin people of Egypt.
You have tried many remedies, all
in vain;
no skin shall grow over your
wounds.

12 The nations have heard your cry,
and the earth echoes with your
screams;
warrior stumbles against warrior
and both fall together.

13   The word which the LORD spoke
to the prophet Jeremiah when Nebuchadrezzar king of Babylon
was coming to harry the land of
Egypt:

14 Announce it in Egypt, proclaim it
in Migdol,
proclaim it in Noph and Tahpanhes.
Say, Stand to! Be ready!
for a sword devours all around you.

15 Why does Apis flee, why does your
bull-god not[a] stand fast?
The LORD has thrust him out.

16 The rabble of Egypt stumbles and
falls,
man against man;
each says, 'Quick, back to our
people,
to the land of our birth, far from
the cruel sword!'

17 Give Pharaoh of Egypt the title
King Bombast,
the man who missed his moment.

18 By my life, says the King
whose name is the LORD of Hosts,
one shall come mighty as Tabor
among the hills,
as Carmel by the sea.

19 Make ready your baggage for exile,
you native people of Egypt;
for Noph shall become a waste,
ruined and unpeopled.

20 Egypt was a lovely heifer,
but a gadfly from the north descended on her.

21 The mercenaries in her land were
like stall-fed calves;
but they too turned and fled,
not one of them stood his ground.
The hour of their downfall has
come upon them,
their day of reckoning.

22 Hark, she is hissing like a snake,
for the enemy has come in all his
force.
They fall upon her with axes
like woodcutters at their work.

23 They cut down her forest, says the
LORD,
and it flaunts itself no more;
for they are many as locusts and
past counting.

24 The Egyptians are put to shame,
enslaved to a northern race.

25 The LORD of Hosts the God of
Israel has spoken:
I will punish Amon god of No,[b]
Egypt with her gods and her
princes,
Pharaoh and all who trust in
him.

26 I will deliver them to those bent
on their destruction,
to Nebuchadrezzar king of Babylon and his troops;
yet in after time the land shall be
peopled as of old.
This is the very word of the LORD.

27 But you, Jacob my servant, have
no fear,
despair not, O Israel;
for I will bring you back safe from
afar
and your offspring from the land
where they are captives;
and Jacob shall be at rest once
more,
prosperous and unafraid.

---

[a] Why does Apis...not: or Why is your bull-god routed, why does he not...
[b] Prob. rdg.; Heb. adds and Pharaoh.

28 O Jacob my servant, have no fear,
says the LORD; for I am with you.
I will make an end of all the nations
amongst whom I have banished
you;
but I will not make an end of you;
though I will punish you as you deserve,
I will not sweep you clean away.

47 This came to the prophet
Jeremiah as the word of the LORD
concerning the Philistines before
2 Pharaoh's harrying of Gaza: The
LORD has spoken:

See how waters are rising from
the north
and swelling to a torrent in spate,
flooding the land and all that is in it,
cities and all who live in them.
Men shall shriek in alarm
and all who live in the land shall
howl.
3 Hark, the pounding of his chargers'
hooves,
the rattle of his chariots and their
rumbling wheels!
Fathers spare no thought for their
children;
their hands hang powerless,
4 because the day is upon them when
Philistia will be despoiled,
and Tyre and Sidon destroyed to
the last defender;
for the LORD will despoil the Philistines,
that remnant of the isle of Caphtor.
5 Gaza is shorn bare, Ashkelon ruined.
Poor remnant of their strength,
how long will you gash yourselves
and cry:
6 Ah, sword in the hand of the LORD,
how long will it be before you rest?
Sheathe yourself, rest and be quiet.
7 How can it rest? for the LORD has
given it work to do
against Ashkelon and the plain by
the sea;
there he has assigned the sword its
task.

Of Moab. The LORD of Hosts 48
the God of Israel has spoken:

Alas for Nebo! it is laid waste;
Kiriathaim is put to shame and
captured,
Misgab reduced to shame and dis-
may;
Moab is renowned no longer.   2
In Heshbon they plot evil against
her:
Come, destroy her, and leave her
no longer a nation.
And you who live in Madmen shall
be struck down,
your people pursued by the sword.
Hark to the cries of anguish from 3
Horonaim,
great havoc and disaster!
Moab is broken.   4
Their cries are heard as far as Zoar.
On the ascent of Luhith   5
men go up weeping bitterly;
on the descent of Horonaim
cries of 'Disaster!' are heard.
Flee, flee for your lives   6
like a sand-grouse in the wilderness.
Because you have trusted in your 7
defences and your arsenals,
you too will be captured,
and Kemosh will go into exile,
his priests and his captains with
him;
and a spoiler shall descend on 8
every city.
No city shall escape,
valley and tableland will be laid
waste and plundered;
the LORD has spoken.

Let a warning flash to Moab,[a]   9
for she shall be laid in ruins[b]
and her cities shall become waste
places
with no inhabitant.
A curse on him who is slack in 10
doing the LORD'S work!
A curse on him who withholds his
sword from bloodshed!

All his life long, Moab has lain un- 11
disturbed
like wine settled on its lees,

---

[a] Let...Moab: *or* Doom Moab to become saltings.
[b] laid in ruins: *prob. rdg.*; Heb. obscure.

not emptied from vessel to vessel;
he has not gone into exile.
Therefore the taste of him is un-
altered,
and the flavour stays unchanged.
12 Therefore the days are coming,
says the LORD,
when I will send men to tilt the
jars; they shall tilt them
and empty his vessels and smash
his jars;
13 and Moab shall be betrayed by
Kemosh,
as Israel was betrayed by Bethel,
a god in whom he trusted.

14 How can you say, 'We are warriors
and men valiant in battle'?
15 The spoiler of Moab and her cities
has come up,
and the flower of her army goes
down to the slaughter.

This is the very word of the King
whose name is the LORD of
Hosts.

16 The downfall of Moab is near at
hand,
disaster rushes swiftly upon him.
17 Grieve for him, all you his neighbours
and all you who acknowledge him,
and say, 'Alas! The commander's
staff is broken,
broken is the baton of honour.'
18 Come down from your place of
honour,
sit on the thirsty ground, you
natives of Dibon;
for the spoiler of Moab has come
upon you
and destroyed your citadels.
19 You that live in Aroer, stand on
the roadside and watch,
ask the fugitives, the man running,
the woman escaping,
ask them, 'What has happened?'

20 Moab is reduced to shame and
dismay:
howl and shriek,
proclaim by the Arnon that Moab
is despoiled,

and that judgement has come to 21
the tableland, to Holon and Jaha-
zah, Mephaath and Dibon, Nebo 22
and Beth-diblathaim and Kiria- 23
thaim, Beth-gamul, Beth-meon,
Kirioth and Bozrah, and to all the 24
cities of Moab far and near.

Moab's horn is hacked off   25
and his strong arm is broken,
says the LORD.

Make Moab drunk – he has defied 26
the LORD –
until he overflows with his vomit
and even he becomes a butt for
derision.
But was Israel ever your butt?   27
Was he ever in company with
thieves,
that whenever you spoke of him
you should shake your head?
Leave your cities, you inhabitants 28
of Moab,
and find a home among the
crags;
become like a dove which nests
in the rock-face at the mouth of a
cavern.

We have heard of Moab's pride, 29
and proud indeed he is,
proud, presumptuous, overbearing,
insolent.
I know his arrogance, says the 30
LORD;
his boasting is false, false are his
deeds.
Therefore I will howl over Moab   31
and cry in anguish at the fate of
every soul in Moab;
I will moan over the men of Kir-
heres.
I will weep for you more than I 32
wept for Jazer,
O vine of Sibmah
whose branches spread out to the
sea
and stretch as far as Jazer.
The despoiler has fallen on your
fruit and on your vintage,
gladness and joy are taken away 33
from the meadows of Moab,

and I have stopped the flow of
wine from the vats;
nor shall shout follow shout
from the harvesters – not one
shout.

34 Heshbon and[a] Elealeh utter cries
of anguish which are heard in
Jahaz; the sound carries from Zoar
to Horonaim and Eglath-shelishi-
yah; for the waters of Nimrim have
35 become a desolate waste. In Moab
I will stop their sacrificing at hill-
shrines and burning of offerings to
36 their gods, says the LORD. Therefore my heart wails for Moab like
a reed-pipe, wails like a pipe for
the men of Kir-heres. Their hard-
37 earned wealth has vanished. Every
man's head is shorn in mourning,
every beard shaved, every hand
gashed, and every waist girded
38 with sackcloth. On Moab's roofs
and in her broad streets nothing is
heard but lamentation; for I have
broken Moab like a useless thing.[b]
39 Moab in her dismay has shamefully
turned to flight. Moab has become
a butt of derision and a cause of
dismay to all her neighbours.
40 For the LORD has spoken:

A vulture shall swoop down
and spread out his wings over
Moab.
41 The towns are captured, the
strongholds taken;
on that day the spirit of Moab's
warriors shall fail
like the spirit of a woman in childbirth.
42 Then Moab shall be destroyed, no
more to be a nation;
for he defied the LORD.
43 The hunter's scare, the pit, and
the trap
threaten all who dwell in Moab,
says the LORD.
44 If a man runs from the scare
he will fall into the pit;
if he climbs out of the pit
he will be caught in the trap.

All this will I bring on Moab in the
year of their reckoning.
This is the very word of the LORD.

In the shadow of Heshbon the 45
fugitives stand helpless;
for fire has blazed out from Heshbon,
flames have shot out from the
palace of Sihon;
they devour the homeland of Moab
and the country of the sons of
tumult.
Alas for you, Moab! the people of 46
Kemosh have vanished,
for your sons are taken into captivity
and your daughters led away
captive.
Yet in days to come I will restore 47
Moab's fortunes.
This is the very word of the LORD.

Here ends the sentence on Moab.

Of the people of Ammon. Thus 49
says the LORD:

Has Israel no sons? Has he no
heir?
Why has Milcom inherited the land
of Gad,
and why do his people live in the
cities of Gad?
Look, therefore, a time is coming, 2
says the LORD,
when I will make Rabbath Ammon
hear the battle-cry,
when it will become a desolate
mound of ruins
and its villages will be burnt to
ashes,
and Israel shall disinherit those
who disinherited him,
says the LORD.

Howl, Heshbon, for Ai is despoiled. 3
Cry aloud, you villages round Rabbath Ammon,
put on sackcloth and beat your
breast,
and score your bodies with gashes.
For Milcom will go into exile,

---

[a] and: *prob. rdg., cp. Isa. 15. 4;* Heb. *as far as.*
[b] *Prob. rdg.;* Heb. *adds* says the LORD.

and with him his priests and officers.

4 Why do you boast of your resources,
you whose resources are melting away,
you wayward people who trust in your arsenals,
and say, 'Who will dare attack me?'

5 Beware, I am bringing fear upon you from every side,[a]
and every one of you shall be driven headlong
with no man to round up the stragglers.

6 Yet after this I will restore the fortunes of Ammon.
This is the very word of the LORD.

7 Of Edom. The LORD of Hosts has said:

Is wisdom no longer to be found in Teman?
Have her sages no skill in counsel?
Has their wisdom decayed?

8 The people of Dedan have turned and fled
and taken refuge in remote places;
for I will bring Esau's calamity upon him
when his day of reckoning comes.

9[b] When the vintagers come to you they will surely leave gleanings;
and if thieves raid your early crop in the night,
they will take only as much as they want.

10 But I have ransacked Esau's treasure,
I have uncovered his hiding-places,
and he has nowhere to conceal himself;
his children, his kinsfolk and his neighbours are despoiled;
there is no one to help him.

11 What! am I to save alive your fatherless children?
Are your widows to trust in me?

12 For the LORD has spoken: Those who were not doomed to drink the cup shall drink it none the less. Are you alone to go unpunished? You shall not go unpunished; you shall drink it. For by my life, says 13 the LORD, Bozrah shall become a horror and reproach, a byword and a thing of ridicule; and all her towns shall be a byword for ever.

When a herald was sent among the 14[c] nations, crying,
'Gather together and march against her,
rouse yourselves for battle',
I heard this message from the LORD:

Look, I make you the least of all 15 nations,
an object of all men's contempt.
Your overbearing arrogance and 16 your insolent heart
have led you astray,
you who haunt the crannies among the rocks
and keep your hold on the heights of the hills.
Though you build your nest high as a vulture,
thence I will bring you down.
This is the very word of the LORD.
Edom shall become a scene of 17 horror,
all who pass that way shall be horror-struck
and shall jeer in derision at the blows she has borne,
overthrown like Sodom and Go- 18 morrah and their neighbours,[d]
says the LORD.
No man shall live there,
no mortal make a home in her.
Look, like a lion coming up 19 from Jordan's dense thickets to the perennial pastures,
in a moment I will chase every one away
and round up the choicest of[e] her rams.

---

[a] *Prob. rdg.; Heb. adds* says the Lord GOD of Hosts.
[b] *Verses 9 and 10: cp. Obad. 5, 6.*   [c] *Verses 14–16: cp. Obad. 1–4.*
[d] *Or* inhabitants.   [e] the choicest of: *prob. rdg.; Heb.* who is chosen?

For who is like me? Who is my
  equal?
What shepherd can stand his
  ground before me?

20 Therefore listen to the LORD's
whole purpose against Edom and
all his plans against the people
of Teman:

The young ones of the flock shall
  be carried off,
and their pasture shall be horrified
  at their fate.
21 At the sound of their fall the land
  quakes;
it cries out, and the cry is heard
  at the Red Sea.[a]

22 A vulture shall soar and swoop
  down
and spread out his wings over
  Bozrah,
and on that day the spirit of
  Edom's warriors shall fail
like the spirit of a woman in labour.

23 Of Damascus.

Hamath and Arpad are in confusion,
for they have heard news of
  disaster;
they are tossed up and down in
  anxiety
like the unresting sea.
24 Damascus has lost heart and turns
  to flight;
trembling has seized her,
the pangs of childbirth have
  gripped her.
25 How forlorn is the town of joyful
  song,
the city of gladness!
26 Therefore her young men shall fall
  in her streets
and all her warriors lie still in
  death that day.
This is the very word of the LORD
of Hosts.
27 Then will I kindle a fire against the
  wall of Damascus
and it shall consume the palaces
  of Ben-hadad.

Of Kedar and the royal princes[b] 28
of Hazer which Nebuchadrezzar
king of Babylon subdued. The
LORD has said:

Come, attack Kedar,
despoil the Arabs of the east.
Carry off their tents and their 29
  flocks,
their tent-hangings and all their
  vessels,
drive off their camels too,
and a cry shall go up: 'Terror let
  loose!'
Flee, flee; make haste,   30
take refuge in remote places, O
  people of Hazer,
for the king of Babylon has laid
  his plans
and formed a design against you,
says the LORD.
Come, let us attack a nation living 31
  at peace,
in fancied security,
with neither gates nor bars,
sufficient to themselves.
Their camels shall be carried off as 32
  booty,
their vast herds of cattle as plunder;
I will scatter them before the wind
  to roam the fringes of the desert,[c]
and bring ruin upon them from
  every side.
Hazer shall become a haunt of 33
  wolves,
for ever desolate;
no man shall live there,
no mortal make a home in her.
This is the very word of the LORD.

This came to the prophet Jere- 34
miah as the word of the LORD
concerning Elam, at the beginning
of the reign of Zedekiah king of
Judah: Thus says the LORD of 35
Hosts:

Listen, I will break the bow of
  Elam,
the chief weapon of their might;
I will bring four winds against 36
  Elam
from the four quarters of heaven;

---

[a] Or *the Sea of Reeds.*
[b] *royal princes: or* kingdom.
[c] *them...desert: or* to the wind those who clip the hair on their temples.

I will scatter them before these
four winds,
and there shall be no nation
to which the exiles from Elam shall
not come.
37 I will break Elam before their foes,
before those who are bent on their
destruction;
I will vent my anger upon them
in disaster;
I will harry them with the sword
until I make an end of them.
38 Then I will set my throne in Elam,
and there I will destroy the king
and his officers.
This is the very word of the LORD.
39 Yet in days to come I will restore
the fortunes of Elam.
This is the very word of the LORD.

50   The word which the LORD spoke
concerning Babylon, concerning
the land of the Chaldaeans, through
the prophet Jeremiah:

2 Declare and proclaim among the
nations,
keep nothing back, spread the
news:
Babylon is taken,
Bel is put to shame, Marduk is in
despair;
the idols of Babylon are put to
shame,
her false gods are in despair.
3 For a nation out of the north has
fallen upon her;
they will make her land a desolate
waste
where neither man nor beast shall
live.

4   In those days, at that time, says
the LORD, the people of Israel and
the people of Judah shall come
together and go in tears to seek
5 the LORD their God; they shall ask
after Zion, turning their faces towards her, and they shall come
and join themselves to the LORD
in an everlasting covenant which
shall not be forgotten.
6   My people were lost sheep, whose
shepherds let them stray and run

wild on the mountains; they went
from mountain to hill and forgot
their fold. Whoever found them 7
devoured them, and their enemies
said, 'We incur no guilt, because
they have sinned against the LORD,
the LORD who is the true goal and
the hope of all their fathers.'

Flee from Babylon, from the 8
land of the Chaldaeans;
go forth, and be like he-goats
leading the flock.
For I will stir up a host of mighty 9
nations
and bring them against Babylon,
marshalled against her from a
northern land;
and from the north she shall be
captured.
Their arrows shall be like a practised warrior
who never comes back empty-
handed;
the Chaldaeans shall be plundered, 10
and all who plunder them shall
take their fill.
This is the very word of the LORD.
You ravaged my patrimony; but 11
though you rejoice and exult,
though you run free like a heifer
after threshing,
though you neigh like a stallion,
your mother shall be cruelly dis- 12
graced,
she who bore you shall be put to
shame.
Look at her, the mere rump of the
nations,
a wilderness, parched and desert,
unpeopled through the wrath of 13
the LORD,
nothing but a desolate waste;
all who pass by Babylon shall be
horror-struck
and jeer in derision at the sight
of her wounds.

Marshal your forces against Baby- 14
lon, on every side,
you whose bows are ready strung;
shoot at her, spare no arrows.
Shout in triumph over her, she has 15
thrown up her hands,

her bastions are down, her walls
  demolished;
this is the vengeance of the LORD.
Take vengeance on her;
  as she has done, so do to her.
16 Destroy every sower in Babylon,
  every reaper with his sickle at
    harvest-time.
Before the cruel sword every man
  will go back to his people,
  every man flee to his own land.

17 Israel is a scattered flock
  harried and chased by lions:
as the king of Assyria was the first
  to feed on him,
so the king of Babylon was the
  last to gnaw his bones.

18 Therefore the LORD of Hosts the
  God of Israel says this:

I will punish the king of Babylon
  and his country
as I have punished the king of
  Assyria.
19 I will bring Israel back to his
  pasture,
and he shall graze on Carmel and
  Bashan;
in the hills of Ephraim and Gilead
  he shall eat his fill.

20   In those days, says the LORD,
when that time comes, search shall
be made for the iniquity of Israel
but there shall be none, and for the
sin of Judah but it shall not be
found; for those whom I leave as
a remnant I will forgive.

21 Attack the land of Merathaim;
attack it and the inhabitants of
  Pekod;
put all to the sword and destroy
  them,
and do whatever I bid you.
This is the very word of the LORD.

22 Hark, the sound of war in the land
and great destruction!
23 See how the hammer of all the
  earth
  is hacked and broken in pieces,

how Babylon has become
  a horror among the nations.
O Babylon, you have laid a snare 24
  to be your own undoing;
you have been trapped, all unawares;
there you are, you are caught,
because you have challenged the
  LORD.
The LORD has opened his arsenal 25
and brought out the weapons of
  his wrath;
for this is work for the Lord the
  GOD of Hosts
in the land of the Chaldaeans.
Her harvest-time has come; 26
throw open her granaries,*a* pile her
  in heaps;
destroy her, let no survivor be
  left.
Put all her warriors to the sword; 27
let them be led to the slaughter.
Woe upon them! for their time has
  come,
their day of reckoning.
I hear the fugitives escaping from 28
  the land of Babylon
to proclaim in Zion the vengeance
  of the LORD our God.

Let your arrows be heard whistling 29
  against Babylon,
all you whose bows are ready
  strung.
Pitch your tents all around her
so that no one escapes.
Pay her back for all her misdeeds;
as she has done, so do to her,
for she has insulted the LORD the
  Holy One of Israel.
Therefore her young men shall fall 30
  in her streets,
and all her warriors shall lie still
  in death that day.
This is the very word of the LORD.

I am against you, insolent city; 31
for your time has come, your day
  of reckoning.
This is the very word of the Lord
  GOD of Hosts.
Insolence shall stumble and fall 32
and no one shall lift her up,

a Or cattle-pens.

and I will kindle fire in the heath
around her
and it shall consume everything
round about.

33   The LORD of Hosts has said this:

The peoples of Israel and Judah
together are oppressed;
their captors hold them firmly and
refuse to release them.
34 But they have a powerful advocate,
whose name is the LORD of Hosts;
he himself will plead their cause,
bringing distress on Babylon and
turmoil on its people.

35 A sword hangs over the Chaldaeans,
over the people of Babylon, her
officers and her wise men,
says the LORD.
36 A sword over the false prophets,
and they are made fools,
a sword over her warriors, and they
despair,
37 a sword over her horses and her
chariots
and over all the rabble within
her,
and they shall become like women;
a sword over her treasures, and
they shall be plundered,
38 a sword over her waters, and they
shall dry up;
for it is a land of idols
that glories in its dreaded gods.*a*

39 Therefore marmots and jackals
shall skulk in it, desert-owls shall
haunt it, nevermore shall it be
inhabited by men and no one shall
dwell in it through all the ages.
40 As when God overthrew Sodom
and Gomorrah and their neighbours,*b* says the LORD, no man
shall live there, no mortal make
a home in her.

41 See, a people is coming from the
north, a great nation,
mighty*c* kings rouse themselves
from earth's farthest corners;

armed with bow and sabre, they 42
are cruel and pitiless;
bestriding horses, they sound like
the thunder of the sea;
they are like men arrayed for
battle against you, Babylon.
The king of Babylon has heard 43
news of them
and his hands hang limp;
agony grips him, anguish as of a
woman in labour.
Look, like a lion coming up 44
from Jordan's dense thickets to
the perennial pastures,
in a moment I will chase every
one away
and round up the choicest of*d* the
rams.
For who is like me? Who is my
equal?
What shepherd can stand his
ground before me?

Therefore listen to the LORD's 45
whole purpose against Babylon
and all his plans against the land
of the Chaldaeans:

The young ones of the flock shall
be carried off
and their pasture shall be horrified
at their fate.
At the sound of the capture of 46
Babylon
the land quakes and her cry is
heard among the nations.

For thus says the LORD: 51

I will raise a destroying wind
against Babylon and those who
live in Kambul,*e*
and I will send winnowers to Baby- 2
lon,
who shall winnow her and empty
her land;
for they shall assail her on all sides
on the day of disaster.
How shall the archer then string 3
his bow
or put on his coat of mail?

---

a dreaded gods: *or* dire portents.   *b* Or inhabitants.   *c* Or many.
d the choicest of: *prob. rdg.*; *Heb.* who is chosen?
e Kambul: *prob. rdg.*; *Heb.* the heart of my opponents.

Spare none of her young men,
　destroy all her host,
4 and let them fall dead in the land
　of the Chaldaeans,
　pierced through in her streets.
5 Israel and Judah are not left
　widowed
　by their God, by the LORD of Hosts;
　but the land of the Chaldaeans is
　full of guilt,
　condemned by the Holy One of
　Israel.

6 Flee out of Babylon, every man
　for himself,
　or you will be struck down for her
　sin;
　for this is the LORD's day of ven-
　geance,
　and he is paying her full recom-
　pense.
7 Babylon has been a gold cup in
　the LORD's hand
　to make all the earth drunk;
　the nations have drunk of her wine,
　and that has made them mad.
8 Babylon falls suddenly and is
　broken.
　Howl over her,
　fetch balm for her wound;
　perhaps she will be healed.
9 We would have healed Babylon,
　but she would not be[a] healed.
　Leave her and let us be off, each
　to his own country;
　for her doom reaches to heaven
　and mounts up to the skies.
10 The LORD has made our innocence
　plain to see;
　come, let us proclaim in Zion
　what the LORD our God has done.

11 Sharpen the arrows, fill the quivers.
　The LORD has roused the spirit of
　the king of the Medes;
　for the LORD's purpose against
　Babylon is to destroy it,
　and his vengeance is the avenging
　of his temple.
12 Raise the standard against Baby-
　lon's walls,

mount a strong guard, post a
　watch, set an ambush;
for the LORD has both planned and
　carried out
what he threatened to do to the
　people of Babylon.
O opulent city, standing beside 13
　great waters,
your end has come, your destiny is
　certain.
The LORD of Hosts has sworn by 14
　himself, saying,
Once I filled you with men, count-
　less as locusts,
yet a song of triumph shall be
　chanted over you.

God made the earth by his power, 15[b]
fixed the world in place by his
　wisdom,
unfurled the skies by his under-
　standing.
At the thunder of his voice the 16
　waters in heaven are amazed;[c]
he brings up the mist from the
　ends of the earth,
he opens rifts[d] for the rain
and brings the wind out of his
　storehouses.
All men are brutish and ignorant, 17
every goldsmith is discredited by
　his idol;
for the figures he casts are a sham,
there is no breath in them.
They are worth nothing, mere 18
　mockeries,
which perish when their day of
　reckoning comes.
God, Jacob's creator, is not like 19
　these;
for he is the maker of all.
Israel is the people he claims as
　his own;
the LORD of Hosts is his name.

You are my battle-axe, my weapon 20
　of war;
with you I will break nations in
　pieces,
and with you I will destroy king-
　doms.

---

[a] would not be: *or* was not.
[c] At the thunder...amazed: *prob. rdg.*; *Heb.* At the sound of his giving tumult of waters in heaven.
[b] *Verses 15–19*: *cp. 10. 12–16.*
[d] rifts: *prob. rdg.*; *Heb.* lightnings.

21 With you I will break horse and
      rider,
   with you I will break chariot and
      rider,
22 with you I will break man and
      woman,
   with you I will break young and
      old,
   with you I will break young man
      and maiden,
23 with you I will break shepherd
      and flock,
   with you I will break ploughman
      and team,
   with you I will break viceroys and
      governors.
24 So will I repay Babylon and the
      people of Chaldaea
   for all the wrong which they did
      in Zion in your sight.
   This is the very word of the
      LORD.

25 I am against you, O destroying
      mountain,*a*
   you who destroy the whole
      earth,
   and I will stretch out my hand
      against you
   and send you tumbling from your
      terraces
   and make you a burnt-out moun-
      tain.
26 No stone of yours shall be used as
      a corner-stone,
   no stone for a foundation;
   but you shall be desolate, for ever
      waste.
   This is the very word of the
      LORD.

27 Raise a standard in the land,*b*
   blow the trumpet among the
      nations,
   hallow the nations for war against
      her,
   summon the kingdoms of Ararat,
      Minni, and Ashkenaz,
   appoint a commander-in-chief a-
      gainst her,
   bring up the horses like a dark
      swarm of locusts;*c*

28 hallow the nations for war against
      her,
   the king of the Medes, his viceroys
      and governors,
   and all the lands of his realm.
29 The earth quakes and writhes;
   for the LORD's designs against
      Babylon are fulfilled,
   to make the land of Babylon deso-
      late and unpeopled.
30 Babylon's warriors have given up
      the fight,
   they skulk in the forts;
   their courage has failed, they have
      become like women.
   Her buildings are set on fire, the
      bars of her gates broken.
31 Runner speeds to meet runner,
   messenger to meet messenger,
   bringing news to the king of
      Babylon
   that every quarter of his city is
      taken,
32 the river-crossings are seized,
   the guard-towers set on fire
   and the garrison stricken with
      panic.

33 For the LORD of Hosts the God of
   Israel has spoken:

   Babylon is like a threshing-floor
      when it is trodden;
   soon, very soon, harvest-time will
      come.

34 'Nebuchadrezzar king of Babylon
      has devoured me
   and sucked me dry,
   he has set me aside like an empty
      jar.
   Like a dragon he has gulped me
      down;
   he has filled his maw with my
      delicate flesh
   and spewed me up.
35 On Babylon be the violence done
      to me,
   the vengeance taken upon me!',
      Zion's people shall say.
   'My blood be upon the Chal-
      daeans!',
      Jerusalem shall say.

a Or O Mount of the Destroyer.
c Or hoppers.

b Or earth.

36 Therefore the LORD says:

I will plead your cause, I will
   avenge you;
I will dry up her sea[a] and make her
   waters fail;
37 and Babylon shall become a heap
   of ruins, a haunt of wolves,
a scene of horror and derision, with
   no inhabitant.

38 Together they roar like young lions,
they growl like the whelps of a
   lioness.
39 I will cause their drinking bouts
   to end in fever
and make them so drunk that they
   will writhe and toss,
then sink into unending sleep,
   never to wake.
This is the very word of the LORD.
40 I will bring them like lambs to the
   slaughter,
rams and he-goats together.
41 Sheshak[b] is captured,
the pride of the whole earth taken;
Babylon has become a horror
   amongst the nations!
42 The sea has surged over Babylon,
she is covered by its roaring waves.
43 Her cities have become waste
   places,
a land dried up and desert,
a land in whose cities no man lives
and through which no mortal
   travels.
44 I will punish Bel in Babylon
and make him bring up what he
   has swallowed;
nations shall never again come
   streaming to him.
The wall of Babylon has fallen;
45 come out of her, O my people,
and let every man save himself
from the anger of the LORD.
46 Then beware of losing heart,
fear no rumours spread abroad in
   the land,
as rumour follows rumour,
each year a new one:
violence on earth and ruler against
   ruler.
47 Therefore a time is coming

when I will punish Babylon's idols,
and all her land shall be put to
   shame,
and all her slain shall lie fallen in
   her midst.
48 Heaven and earth and all that is
   in them
shall sing in triumph over Babylon;
for marauders from the north shall
   overrun her.
This is the very word of the LORD.
49 Babylon must fall for the sake of[c]
   Israel's slain,
as the slain of all the world fell for
   the sake of Babylon.
50 You who have escaped from her
sword, off with you, do not linger.
Remember the LORD from afar
and call Jerusalem to mind.
51 We are put to shame by the reproaches we have heard,
and our faces are covered with
   confusion:
strangers have entered the sacred
   courts of the LORD's house.

52 A time is coming therefore, says
   the LORD,
when I will punish her idols,
and all through the land there shall
   be the groaning of the wounded.
53 Though Babylon should reach to
   the skies
and make her high towers inaccessible,
I will send marauders to overrun
   her.
This is the very word of the LORD.
54 Hark, cries of agony from Babylon!
Sounds of destruction from the
   land of the Chaldaeans!
55 For the LORD is despoiling Babylon
and will silence the hum of the city,
before the advancing wave that
   booms and roars
like mighty waters.
56 For marauders march on Babylon
   herself,
her warriors are captured and their
   bows are broken;
for the LORD, a God of retribution,
   will repay in full.

---

[a] *Possibly the Euphrates.*
[c] *for the sake of:* prob. rdg.; *Heb. om.*

[b] *A name for Babylon.*

57 I will make her princes and her
  wise men drunk,
  her viceroys and governors and
  warriors,
  and they shall sink into unending
  sleep, never to wake.
  This is the very word of the
  King,
  whose name is the LORD of
  Hosts.

58 The LORD of Hosts says:

  The walls of broad Babylon shall
  be razed to the ground,
  her lofty gates shall be set on
  fire.
  Worthless now is the thing for
  which the nations toiled;
  the peoples wore themselves out
  for a mere nothing.

59 The instructions given by the
  prophet Jeremiah to the quartermaster Seraiah son of Neriah and
  grandson of Mahseiah, when he
  went to Babylon with Zedekiah
  king of Judah in the fourth year
  of his reign.
60 Jeremiah, having written down
  in a*a* book*b* a full description of the
  disaster which would come upon
61 Babylon, said to Seraiah, 'When
  you come to Babylon, look at this,
62 read it all and then say, "Thou, O
  LORD, hast declared thy purpose
  to destroy this place and leave it
  with no one living in it, man or
  beast; it shall be desolate, for ever
63 waste." When you have finished
  reading the book, tie a stone to
  it and throw it into the Euphrates,
64 and then say, "So shall Babylon
  sink, never to rise again after the
  disaster which I shall bring upon
  her."'

  Thus far are the collected sayings of Jeremiah.

Historical note about the fall of Jerusalem

ZEDEKIAH was twenty-one years 52 1*c*
old when he came to the throne,
and he reigned in Jerusalem for
eleven years; his mother was
Hamutal daughter of Jeremiah of
Libnah. He did what was wrong 2
in the eyes of the LORD, as Jehoiakim had done. Jerusalem and 3
Judah so angered the LORD that
in the end he banished them
from his sight; and Zedekiah
rebelled against the king of Babylon.
  In the ninth year of his reign, 4
in the tenth month, on the tenth
day of the month, Nebuchadrezzar
king of Babylon advanced with
all his army against Jerusalem, invested it and erected watch-towers
against it on every side; the siege 5
lasted till the eleventh year of King
Zedekiah. In the fourth month of 6
that year, on the ninth day of the
month, when famine was severe
in the city and there was no food
for the common people, the city 7
was thrown open. When Zedekiah
king of Judah saw this, he and*d*
all his armed escort left the city
and fled by night through the gate
called Between the Two Walls, near
the king's garden. They escaped
towards the Arabah, although the
Chaldaeans were surrounding the
city. But the Chaldaean army 8
pursued the king and overtook him
in the lowlands of Jericho; and
all his company was dispersed. The 9
king was seized and brought before
the king of Babylon at Riblah in
the land of Hamath, where he
pleaded his case before him. The 10
king of Babylon slew Zedekiah's
sons before his eyes; he also put
to death all the princes of Judah
in Riblah. Then the king of Baby- 11

a Or one.
b *Prob. rdg.*; *Heb. adds* all these things which are written concerning
Babylon.
c *Verses 1–27: cp. 39. 1–10 and 2 Kgs. 24. 18 – 25. 21.*
d *When Zedekiah...and: prob. rdg., cp. 39. 4; Heb. om.*

lon put Zedekiah's eyes out, bound him with fetters of bronze, brought him to Babylon and committed him to prison till the day of his death.

12 In the fifth month, on the tenth day of the month, in the nineteenth year of Nebuchadrezzar king of Babylon, Nebuzaradan, captain of the king's bodyguard,[a] came to 13 Jerusalem and set fire to the house of the LORD and the royal palace; all the houses in the city, including the mansion of Gedaliah,[b] were 14 burnt down. The Chaldaean forces with the captain of the guard pulled down the walls all round 15 Jerusalem. [c]Nebuzaradan captain of the guard deported the rest of the people left in the city, those who had deserted to the king of Babylon and any remaining arti-16 sans. The captain of the guard left only the weakest class of people to be vine-dressers and labourers.

17 The Chaldaeans broke up the pillars of bronze in the house of the LORD, the trolleys, and the sea of bronze, and took the metal to 18 Babylon. They took also the pots, shovels, snuffers, tossing-bowls, saucers, and all the vessels of bronze used in the service of the 19 temple. The captain of the guard took away the precious metal, whether gold or silver, of which the cups, firepans, tossing-bowls, pots, lamp-stands, saucers, and 20 flagons were made. The bronze of the two pillars, of the one sea and of the twelve oxen supporting it, which King Solomon had made for the house of the LORD, was 21 beyond weighing. The one pillar was eighteen cubits high and twelve cubits in circumference; it was hollow and the metal was 22 four fingers thick. It had a capital

of bronze, five cubits high, and a decoration of network and pomegranates ran all round it, wholly of bronze. The other pillar, with its pomegranates, was exactly like it. Ninety-six pomegranates were 23 exposed to view and there were a hundred in all on the network all round.

The captain of the guard took 24 Seraiah the chief priest and Zephaniah the deputy chief priest and the three on duty at the entrance; he took also from the city a eunuch 25 who was in charge of the fighting men, seven of those with right of access to the king who were still in the city, the adjutant-general[d] whose duty was to muster the people for war, and sixty men of the people who were still there. These Nebuzaradan captain of the 26 guard brought to the king of Babylon at Riblah. There, in the land 27 of Hamath, the king of Babylon had them flogged and put to death. So Judah went into exile from their own land.

These were the people deported 28 by Nebuchadrezzar in the seventeenth[e] year: three thousand and twenty-three Judaeans. In his 29 eighteenth year, eight hundred and thirty-two people from Jerusalem; in his twenty-third year, seven 30 hundred and forty-five Judaeans were deported by Nebuzaradan the captain of the bodyguard: all together four thousand six hundred people.

In the thirty-seventh year of 31[f] the exile of Jehoiachin king of Judah, on the twenty-fifth day of the twelfth month, Evil-merodach king of Babylon in the year of his accession showed favour to Jehoiachin king of Judah. He brought him out of prison, treated him 32

---

[a] captain....bodyguard: *prob. rdg., cp.* 2 *Kgs.* 25. 8; *Heb.* captain of the bodyguard stood before the king of Babylon.
[b] Gedaliah: *prob. rdg.*; *Heb.* the great man.
[c] *Prob. rdg., cp.* 39. 9 *and* 2 *Kgs.* 25. 11; *Heb. prefixes* The weakest class of the people (*cp. verse* 16).   [d] *Prob. rdg.*; *Heb. adds* commander-in-chief.
[e] *Prob. rdg.*; *Heb.* seventh.   [f] *Verses* 31–34: *cp.* 2 *Kgs.* 25. 27–30.

kindly and gave him a seat at table above the kings with him in Baby-
33 lon. So Jehoiachin discarded his prison clothes and lived as a pen-sioner of the king for the rest of his life. For his maintenance a 34 regular daily allowance was given him by the king of Babylon as long as he lived, to the day of his death.

LAMENTATIONS

Sorrows of captive Zion

1 How solitary lies the city, once so
full of people!
Once great among nations, now
become a widow;
once queen among provinces, now
put to forced labour!
2 Bitterly she weeps in the night,
tears run down her cheeks;
she has no one to bring her comfort
among all that love her;
all her friends turned traitor
and became her enemies.
3 Judah went into the misery of
exile
and endless servitude.
Settled among the nations,
she found no resting-place;
all her persecutors fell upon her
in her sore straits.
4 The paths to Zion mourn,
for none attend her sacred feasts;
all her gates are desolate.
Her priests groan and sigh,
her virgins are cruelly treated.
How bitter is her fate!
5 Her adversaries have become her
masters,
her enemies take their ease,
for the LORD has cruelly punished
her
because of misdeeds without number;
her young children have gone,
driven away captive by the enemy.
6 All majesty has vanished
from the daughter of Zion.
Her princes have become like deer
that can find no pasture

and run on, their strength all spent,
pursued by the hunter.
Jerusalem has remembered 7
her days of misery and wandering,[a]
when her people fell into the power
of the adversary
and there was no one to help her.
The adversary saw and mocked
at her fallen state.
Jerusalem had sinned greatly, 8
and so she was treated like a filthy
rag;
all those who had honoured her
held her cheap,
for they had seen her nakedness.
What could she do but sigh
and turn away?
Uncleanness clung to her skirts, 9
and she gave no thought to her
fate.
Her fall was beyond belief
and there was no one to comfort
her.
Look, LORD, upon her misery,
see how the enemy has triumphed.
The adversary stretched out his 10
hand
to seize all her treasures;
then it was that she saw Gentiles
entering her sanctuary,
Gentiles forbidden by thee to
enter
the assembly, for it was thine.
All her people groaned, 11
they begged for bread;
they sold their treasures for food
to give them strength again.

Look, O LORD, and see
how cheap I am accounted.

---

[a] *Prob. rdg.; Heb. adds* all her treasures which have been from days of old.

12 Is it of no concern to you who
   pass by?
   If only you would look and see:
   is there any agony like mine,
   like these my torments
   with which the LORD has cruelly
   punished me
   in the day of his anger?

13 He sent down fire from heaven,
   it ran through my bones;
   he spread out a net to catch my
   feet,
   and turned me back;
   he made me an example of desolation,
   racked with sickness all day long.

14 My transgressions were bound[a]
   upon me,
   his own hand knotted them round
   me;
   his yoke was lifted on to my neck,
   my strength failed beneath its
   weight;
   the Lord abandoned me to its
   hold,[b]
   and I could not stand.

15 The Lord treated with scorn
   all the mighty men within my walls;
   he marshalled rank on rank against
   me
   to crush my young warriors.
   The Lord trod down, like grapes in
   the press,
   the virgin daughter of Judah.

16 For these things I weep over my
   plight,[c]
   my eyes run with tears;
   for any to comfort me and renew
   my strength
   are far to seek;
   my sons are an example of desolation,
   for the enemy is victorious.

17 Zion lifted her hands in prayer,
   but there was no one to comfort
   her;
   the LORD gave Jacob's enemies
   the order
   to beset him on every side.
   Jerusalem became a filthy rag in
   their midst.

18 The LORD was in the right;
   it was I who rebelled against his
   commands.
   Listen, O listen, all you nations,
   and look on my agony:
   my virgins and my young men are
   gone into captivity.

19 I called to my lovers, they broke
   faith with me;
   my priests and my elders in the
   city
   went hungry and could find nothing,
   although they sought food for
   themselves
   to renew their strength.

20 See, LORD, how sorely I am distressed.
   My bowels writhe in anguish
   and my stomach turns within
   me,
   because I wantonly rebelled.
   The sword makes orphans in the
   streets,
   as plague does within doors.

21 Hear me when I groan
   with no one to comfort me.
   All my enemies, when they heard
   of my calamity,
   rejoiced at what thou hadst
   done;
   but hasten the day thou hast
   promised
   when they shall become like me.

22 Let all their evil deeds come before
   thee;
   torment them in their turn,
   as thou hast tormented me
   for all my transgressions;
   for my sighs are many and my
   heart is faint.

*Zion's hope of relief after
punishment*

2 What darkness the Lord in his
   anger
   has brought upon the daughter of
   Zion!
   He hurled down from heaven to
   earth
   the glory of Israel,

---

[a] bound: *prob. rdg.*; *Heb. word unknown.*
[c] my plight: *prob. rdg.*; *Heb.* my eye.
[b] its hold: *prob. rdg.*; *Heb. obscure.*

and did not remember in the day
  of his anger
that Zion was his footstool.

2 The Lord overwhelmed without
  pity
all the dwellings of Jacob.
In his wrath he tore down
the strongholds of the daughter of
  Judah;
he levelled with the ground and
  desecrated
the kingdom and its rulers.

3 In his anger he hacked down
the horn of Israel's pride,
he withdrew his helping hand
when the enemy came on;
and he blazed in Jacob like flaming
  fire
that rages far and wide.

4 In enmity he strung his bow;
he took his stand like an adversary
and with his strong arm he slew
all those who had been his delight;
he poured his fury out like fire
on the tent of the daughter of Zion.

5 The Lord played an enemy's part
and overwhelmed Israel.
He overwhelmed all their towered
  mansions
and brought down their strongholds in ruins;
sorrow upon sorrow he brought
to the daughter of Judah.

6 He stripped his tabernacle as a vine
  is stripped,
and made the place of assembly a
  ruin.
In Zion the Lord blotted out all
  memory
of festal assembly[a] and of sabbath;
king and priest alike he scorned
in the grimness of his anger.

7 The Lord spurned his own altar
and laid a curse upon his sanctuary.
He delivered the walls of her
  mansions
into the power of the enemy;
in the Lord's very house they
  raised shouts of victory
as on a day of festival.

8 The Lord was minded to bring
  down in ruins
the walls of the daughter of Zion;

he took their measure with his
  line
and did not scruple to demolish
  her;
he made rampart and wall lament,
and both together lay dejected.
Her gates are sunk into the earth, 9
he has shattered and broken their
  bars;
her king and her rulers are among
  the Gentiles,
and there is no law;
her prophets too have received
no vision from the Lord.
The elders of the daughter of 10
  Zion
sit on the ground and sigh;
they have cast dust on their
  heads
and clothed themselves in sackcloth;
the virgins of Jerusalem
bow their heads to the ground.
My eyes are blinded with tears, 11
my bowels writhe in anguish.
In my bitterness my bile is spilt on
  the earth
because of my people's wound,
when children and infants faint
in the streets of the town
and cry to their mothers, 12
'Where can we get corn and wine?'–
when they faint like wounded
  things
in the streets of the city,
gasping out their lives
in their mothers' bosom.

How can I cheer you? Whose 13
  plight is like yours,
daughter of Jerusalem?
To what can I compare you for
  your comfort,
virgin daughter of Zion?
For your wound gapes wide as the
  ocean;
who can heal you?
The visions that your prophets saw 14
  for you
were false and painted shams;
they did not bring home to you
  your guilt
and so reverse your fortunes.

---

[a] festal assembly: or appointed seasons.

The visions that they saw for you
were delusions,
false and fraudulent.[a]
15 All those who pass by
snap their fingers at you;
they hiss and wag their heads at
you,
daughter of Jerusalem:
'Is this the city once called Perfect
in beauty,
Joy of the whole earth?'
16 All your enemies
make mouths and jeer at you;
they hiss and grind their teeth,
saying, 'Here we are,
this is the day we have waited for;
we have lived to see it.'

17 The LORD has done what he planned to do,
he has fulfilled his threat,
all that he ordained from days of
old.
He has demolished without pity
and let the enemy rejoice over you,
filling your adversaries with pride.
18 Cry with a full heart[b] to the Lord,
O wall of the daughter of Zion;
let your tears run down like a torrent
by day and by night.
Give yourself not a moment's rest,
let your tears never cease.
19 Arise and cry aloud in the night;
at the beginning of every watch
pour out your heart like water
in the Lord's very presence.
Lift up your hands to him
for the lives of your children.[c]
20 Look, LORD, and see:
who is it that thou hast thus tormented?
Must women eat the fruit of their
wombs,
the children they have brought
safely to birth?
Shall priest and prophet be slain
in the sanctuary of the Lord?
21 There in the streets young men
and old
lie on the ground.

My virgins and my young men
have fallen
by sword and by famine;
thou hast slain them in the day
of thy anger,
slaughtered them without pity.
Thou didst summon my enemies 22
against me from every side,
like men assembling for a festival;
not a man escaped, not one survived
in the day of the LORD's anger.
All whom I brought safely to birth
and reared
were destroyed by my enemies.

I am the man who has known 3
affliction,
I have felt the rod of his wrath.
It was I whom he led away and 2
left to walk
in darkness, where no light is.
Against me alone he has turned 3
his hand,
and so it is all day long.
He has wasted away my flesh and 4
my skin
and broken all my bones;
he has built up walls around me, 5
behind and before,
and has cast me into a place of 6
darkness
like a man long dead.
He has walled me in so that I cannot escape, 7
and weighed me down with fetters;
even when I cry out and call for 8
help,
he rejects my prayer.
He has barred my road with blocks 9
of stone
and tangled up my way.
He lies in wait for me like a bear 10
or a lion lurking in a covert.
He has made my way refractory 11
and lamed me
and left me desolate.
He has strung his bow 12
and made me the target for his
arrows;

---

[a] fraudulent: *or* causing banishment.
[b] Cry...heart: *prob. rdg.*; *Heb.* Their heart cried.
[c] *Prob. rdg.*; *Heb. adds* who faint with hunger at every street-corner.

835

13 he has pierced my kidneys with
    shafts
    drawn from his quiver.
14 I have become a laughing-stock
    to all nations,
    the target of their mocking songs
    all day.
15 He has given me my fill of bitter
    herbs
    and made me drunk with worm-
    wood.
16 He has broken my teeth on gravel;
    fed on ashes, I am racked with
    pain;
17 peace has gone out of my life,
    and I have forgotten what pros-
    perity means.
18 Then I cry out that my strength
    has gone
    and so has my hope in the LORD.

19 The memory of my distress and
    my wanderings
    is[a] wormwood and gall.
20 Remember, O remember,
    and stoop down to me.[b][c]
21 All this I take to heart
    and therefore I will wait patiently:
22 the LORD's true love is surely not
    spent,[d]
    nor has his compassion failed;
23 they are new every morning,
    so great is his constancy.
24 The LORD, I say, is all that I
    have;
    therefore I will wait for him
    patiently.
25 The LORD is good to those who
    look for him,
    to all who seek him;
26 it is good to wait in patience and
    sigh
    for deliverance by the LORD.
27 It is good, too, for a man
    to carry the yoke in his youth.
28 Let him sit alone and sigh
    if it is heavy upon him;
29 let him lay his face in the dust,
    and there may yet be hope.

30 Let him turn his cheek to the
    smiter
    and endure full measure of abuse;
31 for the Lord will not cast off
    his servants[e] for ever.
32 He may punish cruelly, yet he will
    have compassion
    in the fullness of his love;
33 he does not willingly afflict
    or punish any mortal man.

34 To trample underfoot
    any prisoner in the land,
35 to deprive a man of his rights
    in defiance of the Most High,
36 to pervert justice in the courts –
    such things the Lord has never
    approved.

37 Who can command and it is done,
    if the Lord has forbidden it?
38 Do not both bad and good proceed
    from the mouth of the Most High?
39 Why should any man living com-
    plain,
    any mortal who has sinned?
40 Let us examine our ways and put
    them to the test
    and turn back to the LORD;
41 let us lift up our hearts, not our
    hands,
    to God in heaven.
42 We ourselves have sinned and re-
    belled,
    and thou hast not forgiven.
43 In anger thou hast turned[f] and
    pursued us
    and slain without pity;
44 thou hast hidden thyself behind
    the clouds
    beyond reach of our prayers;
45 thou hast treated us as offscouring
    and refuse
    among the nations.
46 All our enemies make mouths
    and jeer at us.
47 Before us lie hunter's scare and
    pit,
    devastation and ruin.

---

[a] The memory...is: *or* Remember my distress and my wanderings, the...
[b] stoop down to me: *prob. original rdg., altered in Heb. to* I sink down.
[c] Remember...me: *or* I remember, I remember them and sink down.
[d] spent: *prob. rdg.; Heb. unintelligible.*   [e] his servants: *prob. rdg.; Heb. om.*
[f] *Prob. rdg.; Heb. hidden.*

48 My eyes run with streams of water
because of my people's wound.
49 My eyes stream with unceasing tears
and refuse all comfort,
50 while the LORD in heaven looks down
and watches my affliction,[a]
51 while the LORD torments[b] me
with the fate of all the daughters of my city.

52 Those who for no reason were my enemies
drove me cruelly like a bird;
53 they thrust me alive into the silent pit,
and they closed it over me with a stone;
54 the waters rose high above my head,
and I said, 'My end has come.'
55 But I called on thy name, O LORD,
from the depths of the pit;
56 thou heardest my voice; do not turn a deaf ear
when I cry, 'Come to my relief.'
57 Thou wast near when I called to thee;
thou didst say, 'Have no fear.'
58 Lord, thou didst plead my cause
and ransom my life;
59 thou sawest, LORD, the injustice done to me
and gavest judgement in my favour;
60 thou sawest their vengeance,
all their plots against me.
61 Thou didst hear their bitter taunts, O LORD,
their many plots against me,
62 the whispering, the murmurs of my enemies
all the day long.
63 See how, whether they sit or stand,
they taunt me bitterly.
64 Pay them back for their deeds, O LORD,
pay them back what they deserve.

65 Show them how hard thy heart can be,
how little concern thou hast for them.
66 Pursue them in anger and exterminate them
from beneath thy heavens, O LORD.

4 How dulled is the gold,
how tarnished the fine gold!
The stones of the sanctuary[c] lie strewn
at every street-corner.
2 See Zion's precious sons,
once worth their weight in finest gold,
now counted as pitchers of earthenware
made by any potter's hand.
3 Even whales[d] uncover the teat
and suckle their young;
but the daughters of my people are cruel
as ostriches in the desert.
4 The sucking infant's tongue
cleaves to its palate from thirst;
young children beg for bread
but no one offers them a crumb.
5 Those who once fed delicately
are desolate in the streets,
and those nurtured in purple
now grovel on dunghills.
6 The punishment[e] of my people is worse
than the penalty[f] of Sodom,
which was overthrown in a moment
and no one wrung his hands.
7 Her crowned princes[g] were once
purer than snow,
whiter than milk;
they were ruddier than branching coral,[h]
and their limbs were lapis lazuli.
8 But their faces turned blacker than soot,
and no one knew them in the streets;

---

[a] *my affliction: prob. rdg.; Heb.* my eye.
[b] *the* LORD *torments: prob. rdg.; Heb.* tormenting.
[c] *The stones of the sanctuary: or* Bright gems.   [d] *Prob. rdg.; Heb.* jackals.
[e] *Or* iniquity.   [f] *Or* sin.   [g] *crowned princes: or* Nazirites.
[h] *than...coral: prob. rdg.; Heb.* branch than coral.

the skin was drawn tight over their
  bones,
dry as touchwood.
9 Those who died by the sword were
    more fortunate
than those who died of hunger;
these wasted away, deprived
of the produce of the field.
10 Tender-hearted women with their
    own hands
boiled their own children;
their children became their food
in the day of my people's wounding.
11 The LORD glutted his rage
and poured forth his anger;
he kindled a fire in Zion,
and it consumed her foundations.
12 This no one believed, neither the
    kings of the earth
nor anyone that dwelt in the world:
that enemy or invader would enter
the gates of Jerusalem.
13 It was for the sins of her prophets
and for the iniquities of her priests,
who shed within her walls
the blood of the righteous.
14 They wandered blindly in the
    streets,
so stained with blood
that men would not touch
even their garments.
15 'Away, away; unclean!' men cried
    to them.
'Away, do not come near.'
They hastened away, they wandered among the nations,[a]
unable to find any resting-place.
16 The LORD himself scattered them,
he thought of them no more;
he showed no favour to priests,
no pity for elders.

17 Still we strain our eyes,
looking in vain for help.
We have watched and watched
for a nation powerless to save us.
18 When we go out, we take to by-
  ways
to avoid the public streets;
our days are all but finished,[b]
our end has come.

19 Our pursuers have shown themselves swifter
than vultures in the sky;
they are hot on our trail over the
  hills,
they lurk to catch us in the wilderness.
20 The LORD'S anointed, the breath of
  life to us,
was caught in their machinations;
although we had thought to
  live
among the nations, safe under his
  protection.

21 Rejoice and be glad, daughter of
  Edom,
you who live in the land of Uz.
Yet the cup shall pass to you in
  your turn,
and when you are drunk you will
expose yourself to shame.
22 The punishment for your sin,
  daughter of Zion, is now complete,
and never again shall you be
carried into exile.
But you, daughter of Edom, your
sin shall be punished,
and your guilt revealed.

*A prayer for remembrance and
restoration*

5 Remember, O LORD, what has befallen us;
look, and see how we are scorned.
2 Our patrimony is turned over to
  strangers
and our homes to foreigners.
3 We are like orphans, without a
  father;
our mothers are like widows.
4 We must buy our own water to
  drink,
our own wood can only be had at
  a price.
5 The yoke is on our necks, we are
  overdriven;
we are weary and are given no
  rest.

[a] *Prob. rdg.; Heb. adds* they said.
[b] our...finished: *prob. rdg.; Heb.* our end has drawn near, our days are complete.

6 We came to terms, now with the
Egyptians,
now with the Assyrians, to provide
us with food.
7 Our fathers sinned and are no
more,
and we bear the burden of their
guilt.
8 Slaves have become our rulers,
and there is no one to rescue us
from them.
9 We must bring in our food from
the wilderness,
risking our lives in the scorching
heat.[a]
10 Our skins are blackened as in a
furnace
by the ravages of starvation.
11 Women were raped in Zion,
virgins raped in the cities of Judah.
12 Princes were hung up by their
hands,
and elders received no honour.
13 Young men toil to grind corn,
and boys stumble under loads of
wood.
14 Elders have left off their sessions
in the gate,

and young men no longer pluck
the strings.
Joy has fled from our hearts,   15
and our dances are turned to
mourning.
The garlands have fallen from our   16
heads;
woe betide us, sinners that we
are.
For this we are sick at heart,   17
for all this our eyes grow dim:
because Mount Zion is desolate   18
and over it the jackals run wild.

O LORD, thou art enthroned for 19
ever,
thy throne endures from one
generation to another.
Why wilt thou quite forget us   20
and forsake us these many days?
O LORD, turn us back to thyself, 21
and we will come back;
renew our days as in times long
past.
For if thou hast utterly rejected 22
us,
then great indeed has been thy
anger against us.

THE BOOK OF THE PROPHET

EZEKIEL

Ezekiel's call to be a prophet

1 ON the fifth day of the fourth
month in the thirtieth year,
while I was among the exiles
by the river Kebar,[b] the heavens
were opened and I saw a vision of
2 God. On the fifth day of the month
in the fifth year of the exile of King
3 Jehoiachin, the word of the LORD
came to Ezekiel son of Buzi the
priest, in Chaldaea, by the river
Kebar, and there the hand of the
LORD came upon him.

I saw a storm wind coming from 4
the north, a vast cloud with flashes
of fire and brilliant light about it;
and within was a radiance like
brass, glowing in the heart of the
flames. In the fire was the sem- 5
blance of four living creatures in
human form. Each had four faces 6
and each four wings; their legs 7
were straight, and their hooves
were like the hooves of a calf,
glittering like a disc of bronze.
Under the wings on each of the 8
four sides were human hands; all

---

[a] in the scorching heat: *or* by the sword.   [b] *Or* the Kebar canal.

four creatures had faces and wings,
9 and their wings touched one another. They did not turn as they
moved; each creature went straight
10 forward. Their faces were like this:
all four had the face of a man and
the face of a lion on the right, on
the left the face of an ox and the
11 face of an eagle. Their wings were
spread; each living creature had
one pair touching its neighbours',[a]
while one pair covered its body.
12 They moved straight forward in
whatever direction the spirit[b]
would go; they never swerved in
13 their course. The appearance of
the creatures was as if fire from
burning coals or torches were darting to and fro among them; the fire
was radiant, and out of the fire
came lightning.[c]
15 As I looked at the living creatures, I saw wheels on the ground,
16 one beside each of the four.[d] The
wheels sparkled like topaz, and
they were all alike: in form and
working they were like a wheel in-
17 side a wheel, and when they moved
in any of the four directions they
18 never swerved in their course. All
four had hubs and each hub had a
projection which had the power of
sight,[e] and the rims of the wheels
19 were full of eyes all round. When
the living creatures moved, the
wheels moved beside them; when
the creatures rose from the ground,
20 the wheels rose; they moved in
whatever direction the spirit[b]
would go; and the wheels rose together with them, for the spirit of
the living creatures was in the
21 wheels. When the one moved, the
other moved; when the one halted,
the other halted; when the creatures rose from the ground, the
wheels rose together with them,
for the spirit of the creatures was
in the wheels.

Above the heads of the living 22
creatures was, as it were, a vault
glittering like a sheet of ice, awe-
inspiring, stretched over their
heads above them. Under the vault 23
their wings were spread straight
out, touching one another, while
one pair covered the body of each.
I heard, too, the noise of their 24
wings; when they moved it was
like the noise of a great torrent or
of a cloud-burst,[f] like the noise of a
crowd or of an armed camp; when
they halted their wings dropped. A 25
sound was heard above the vault
over their heads, as they halted
with drooping wings. Above the 26
vault over their heads there appeared, as it were, a sapphire[g] in
the shape of a throne, and high
above all, upon the throne, a form
in human likeness. I saw what 27
might have been brass glowing like
fire in a furnace from the waist upwards; and from the waist downwards I saw what looked like fire
with encircling radiance. Like a 28
rainbow in the clouds on a rainy
day was the sight of that encircling
radiance; it was like the appearance of the glory of the LORD.

When I saw this I threw myself
on my face, and heard a voice
speaking to me: Man, he said, 2
stand up, and let me talk with you.
As he spoke, a spirit came into me 2
and stood me on my feet, and I
listened to him speaking. He said 3
to me, Man, I am sending you to
the Israelites, a nation of rebels
who have rebelled against me. Past
generations of them have been in
revolt against me to this very day,
and this generation to which I am 4
sending you is stubborn and obstinate. When you say to them, 'These
are the words of the Lord GOD',
they will know that they have a 5
prophet among them, whether they

---

[a] its neighbours': *prob. rdg.*; *Heb. unintelligible.*　　　　　　[b] *Or wind.*
[c] *Prob. rdg., cp. Sept.*; *Heb. adds* (14) and the living creatures went out (*prob. rdg.*;
Heb. obscure) and in like rays of light.　　　[d] one...four: *prob. rdg.*; *Heb. obscure.*
[e] the power of sight: *prob. rdg.*; *Heb. fear.*
[f] *Or of the Almighty.*　　　　　　　　　[g] *Or lapis lazuli.*

listen or whether they refuse to
6 listen, because they are rebels. But
you, man, must not be afraid of
them or of what they say, though
they are rebels against you and
renegades, and you find yourself
sitting on scorpions. There is nothing to fear in what they say, and
nothing in their looks to terrify
7 you, rebels though they are. You
must speak my words to them,
whether they listen or whether
they refuse to listen, rebels that
8 they are. But you, man, must listen
to what I say and not be rebellious
like them. Open your mouth and
eat what I give you.

9 Then I saw a hand stretched out
10 to me, holding a scroll. He unrolled it before me, and it was
written all over on both sides with
dirges and laments and words of
3 woe. Then he said to me, 'Man, eat
what is in front of you, eat this
scroll; then go and speak to the
2 Israelites.' So I opened my mouth
and he gave me the scroll to eat.
3 Then he said, 'Man, swallow this
scroll I give you, and fill yourself
full.' So I ate it, and it tasted as
sweet as honey.

4 Man, he said to me, go and tell
the Israelites what I have to say
5 to them. You are sent not to people
whose speech is thick and difficult,
6 but to Israelites. No; I am not
sending you to great nations whose
speech is thick and so difficult
that you cannot make out what
they say; if however I had sent you
to them they would have listened
7 to you. But the Israelites will refuse to listen to you, for they refuse
to listen to me, so brazen are they
8 all and stubborn. But I will make
you a match for them. I will make
you as brazen as they are and as
9 stubborn as they are. I will make
your brow like adamant, harder
than flint. Never fear them, never
be terrified by them, rebels though
10 they are. And he said to me, Listen

carefully, man, to all that I have
to say to you, and take it to heart.
Go to your fellow-countrymen in 11
exile and speak to them. Whether
they listen or refuse to listen, say,
'These are the words of the Lord
GOD.'

Then a spirit*a* lifted me up, and I 12
heard behind me a fierce rushing
sound as the glory of the LORD rose*b*
from his place. I heard the sound of 13
the living creatures' wings brushing against one another, the sound
of the wheels beside them, and a
fierce rushing sound. A spirit*a* lifted 14
me and carried me along, and I
went full of exaltation, the hand of
the LORD strong upon me. So I 15
came to the exiles at Tel-abib who
were settled by the river Kebar.
For seven days I stayed with them,
dumbfounded.

At the end of seven days the 16
word of the LORD came to me:
Man, I have made you a watchman 17
for the Israelites; you will take
messages from me and carry my
warnings to them. It may be that I 18
pronounce sentence of death on a
wicked man:*c* if you do not warn
him to give up his wicked ways and
so save his life, the guilt is his; because of his wickedness he shall die,
but I will hold you answerable for
his death. But if you have warned 19
him and he still continues in his
wicked and evil ways, he shall die
because of his wickedness, but you
will have saved yourself. Or it may 20
be that a righteous man turns
away and does wrong, and I let
that be the cause of his downfall;
he will die because you have not
warned him. He will die for his sin;
the righteous deeds he has done
will not be taken into account, and
I will hold you answerable for his
death. But if you have warned the 21
righteous man not to sin and he has
not sinned, then he will have saved
his life because he has been warned,
and you will have saved yourself.

a Or wind.   *b* rose: *prob. rdg.*; *Heb. obscure.*
c *Prob. rdg.*; *Heb. adds* if you do not warn him.

22 THE hand of the LORD came upon me there, and he said to me, Rise up; go out into the plain, and there 23 I will speak to you. So I rose and went out into the plain; the glory of the LORD was there, like the glory which I had seen by the river Kebar, and I threw myself down 24 on my face. Then a spirit came into me and stood me on my feet, and spoke to me: Go, he said, and shut 25 yourself up in your house. You shall be tied and bound with ropes, man, so that you cannot go out 26 among the people. I will fasten your tongue to the roof of your mouth and you will be unable to speak; you will not be the one to rebuke them, rebels though they 27 are. But when I have something to say to you, I will give you back the power of speech. Then you will say to them, 'These are the words of the Lord GOD.' If anyone will listen, he may listen, and, if he refuses to listen, he may refuse; for they are rebels.

4 Man, take a tile and set it before you. Draw a city on it, the city of 2 Jerusalem: lay siege to it, erect watch-towers against it, raise a siege-ramp, put mantelets in position, and bring battering-rams a-3 gainst it all round. Then take an iron griddle, and put it as a wall of iron between you and the city. Keep your face turned towards the city; it will be the besieged and you the besieger. This will be a sign to the Israelites.

4 Now lie on your left side, and I will lay Israel's iniquity on you; you shall bear their iniquity for as many days as you lie on that side. 5 Allowing one day for every year of their iniquity, I ordain that you bear it for one hundred and ninety days; thus you shall bear Israel's 6 iniquity. When you have completed all this, lie down a second time on your right side, and bear Judah's iniquity for forty days; I

count one day for every year. Then 7 turn your face towards the siege of Jerusalem and bare your arm, and prophesy against it. See how I tie 8 you with ropes so that you cannot turn over from one side to the other until you complete the days of your distress.

Then take wheat and barley, 9 beans and lentils, millet and spelt. Mix them all in one bowl and make your bread out of them. You are to eat it during the one hundred and ninety days you spend lying on your side. And you must weigh out 10 your food; you may eat twenty shekels' weight a day, taking it from time to time. Measure out 11 your drinking water too; you may drink a sixth of a hin a day, taking it from time to time. You are to eat 12 your bread baked like barley cakes, using human dung as fuel, and you must bake it where people can see you. Then the LORD said, 'This is 13 the kind of bread, unclean bread, that the Israelites will eat in the foreign lands into which I shall drive them.' But I said, 'O Lord 14 GOD, I have never been made unclean, never in my life have I eaten what has died naturally or been killed by wild beasts; no tainted meat has ever passed my lips.' So 15 he allowed me to use cow-dung instead of human dung to bake my bread.

Then he said to me, Man, I am 16 cutting short their daily bread in Jerusalem; people will weigh out anxiously the bread they eat, and measure with dismay the water they drink. So their food and their 17 water will run short until they are dismayed at the sight of one another; they will waste away because of their iniquity.

Man, take a sharp sword, take it 5 like a barber's razor and run it over your head and your chin. Then take scales and divide the hair into three. When the siege comes to an 2 end, burn one third of the hair in a fire in the centre of the city; cut up one third with the sword all round the city; scatter one third to the wind, and I will follow it with 3 drawn sword. Take a few of these hairs and tie them up in a fold of 4 your robe. Then take others of them, throw them into the fire and burn them, and out of them fire will come upon all Israel.

5 These are the words of the Lord GOD: This city of Jerusalem I have set among the nations, with other 6 countries around her, and she has rebelled against my laws and my statutes more wickedly than those nations and countries; for her people have rejected my laws and refused to conform to my statutes.

7 Therefore the Lord GOD says: Since you have been more ungrateful than the nations around you and have not conformed to my statutes and have not kept my laws or even the laws of the na-8 tions around you, therefore, says the Lord GOD, I, in my turn, will be against you; I will execute judgements in your midst for the nations 9 to see, such judgements as I have never executed before nor ever will again, so abominable have your 10 offences been. Therefore, O Jerusalem, fathers will eat their children and children their fathers in your midst; I will execute judgements on you, and any who are left in you I will scatter to the four 11 winds. As I live, says the Lord GOD, because you have defiled my holy place with all your vile and abominable rites, I in my turn will consume you without pity; I in my 12 turn will not spare you. One third of your people shall die by pestilence and perish by famine in your midst; one third shall fall by the sword in the country round about; and one third I will scatter to the four winds and follow with drawn 13 sword. Then my anger will be spent, I will abate my fury against them and be calm; when my fury is

spent they will know that it is I, the LORD, who spoke in jealous passion. I have made you a scandal[a] 14 and a reproach to the nations around you, and all who pass by will see it. You will be an object of re- 15 proach and abuse, a terrible lesson to the nations around you, when I pass sentence on you and do judgement in anger and fury. I, the LORD, have spoken. When I shoot 16 the deadly arrows of famine against you,[b] arrows of destruction, I will shoot to destroy you. I will bring famine upon you and cut short your daily bread; I will un- 17 leash famine and beasts of prey upon you, and they will leave you childless. Pestilence and slaughter will sweep through you, and I will bring the sword upon you. I, the LORD, have spoken.

These were the words of the 6 LORD to me: Man, look towards the 2 mountains of Israel, and prophesy to them: Mountains of Israel, hear 3 the word of the Lord GOD. This is his word to mountains and hills, water-courses and valleys: I am bringing a sword against you, and I will destroy your hill-shrines. Your altars will be made desolate, 4 your incense-altars shattered, and I will fling down your slain before your idols. I will strew the corpses 5 of the Israelites before their idols, and I will scatter your bones about your altars. In all your settlements 6 the blood-spattered altars[c] shall be laid waste and the hill-shrines made desolate. Your altars will be waste and desolate and your idols shattered and useless, your incense-altars hewn down, and all your works wiped out; with the 7 slain falling about you, you shall know that I am the LORD. But 8 when they fall,[d] I will leave you, among the nations, some who survive the sword. When you are scattered in foreign lands, these 9 survivors, in captivity among the

---

[a] Or desolation.   [b] Prob. rdg.; Heb. them.   [c] blood-spattered altars: or cities.
[d] when they fall: prob. rdg.; Heb. obscure.

nations, will remember how I was grieved because their hearts had turned wantonly from me and their eyes had gone roving wantonly after idols. Then they will loathe themselves for all the evil they have done with their abomin-
10 ations. So they will know that I am the LORD, that I was uttering no vain threat when I said that I would bring this evil upon them.

11   These are the words of the Lord GOD: Beat your hands together, stamp with your foot, bemoan your vile abominations, people of Israel. Men will fall by sword, famine, and
12 pestilence. Far away they will die by pestilence; at home they will fall by the sword; any who survive or are spared will die by famine, and so at last my anger will be
13 spent. You will know that I am the LORD when their slain fall among the idols round their altars, on every high hill, on all mountaintops, under every spreading tree, under every leafy terebinth, wherever they have brought offerings of soothing odour for their idols one
14 and all. So I will stretch out my hand over them and make the land a desolate waste in all their settlements, more desolate than the desert of Riblah.[a] They shall know that I am the LORD.

7   The word of the LORD came to
2 me: Man, the Lord GOD says this to the land of Israel: An end is coming, the end is coming upon the
3 four corners of the land.[b] The end is now upon you; I will unleash my anger against you; I will call you to account for your doings and bring your abominations upon your own
4 heads. I will neither pity nor spare you: I will make you suffer for your doings and the abominations that continue in your midst. So you shall know that I am the LORD.

5   These are the words of the Lord GOD: Behold, it comes, disasters
6 one upon another; the end, the end,

it comes, it comes.[c] Doom is com- 7 ing upon you, dweller in the land; the time is coming, the day is near, with confusion and the crash of thunder.[d] Now, in an instant, I will 8 vent my rage upon you and let my anger spend itself. I will call you to account for your doings and bring your abominations upon your own heads. I will neither pity nor spare; 9 I will make you suffer for your doings and the abominations that continue in your midst. So you shall know that it is I, the LORD, who strike the blow.

Behold, the day! the doom is 10 here, it has burst upon them. Injustice buds, insolence blossoms, violence shoots up into injustice 11 and wickedness. And it is all their fault, the fault of their turmoil and tumult and all their restless ways. The time has come, the day has 12 arrived; the buyer has no reason to be glad, and the seller none for regret, for I am angry at all their turmoil. The seller will never go 13 back on his bargain while either of them lives; for the bargain will never be reversed because of the turmoil, and no man will exert himself, even in his iniquity, as long as he lives. The trumpet has sounded 14 and all is ready, but no one goes out to war.

Outside is the sword, inside are 15 pestilence and famine; in the country men will die by the sword, in the city famine and pestilence will carry them off. If any escape 16 and take to the mountains, like moaning doves, there will I slay them, each for his iniquity, while 17 their hands hang limp and their knees run with urine. They will go 18 in sackcloth, shuddering from head to foot, with faces downcast and heads close shaved. They shall fling 19 their silver into the streets and cast aside their gold like filth; their silver and their gold will be powerless to save them on the day of the

---

[a] *Prob. rdg.*; *Heb.* Diblah.   [b] *Or* earth.   [c] *Prob. rdg.*; *Heb. adds* it wakes up, behold it comes.   [d] *and the crash of thunder*: *prob. rdg.*; *Heb. unintelligible.*

LORD's fury. Their hunger will not be satisfied nor their bellies filled; for their iniquity will be the cause 20 of their downfall. They have fed their pride on their beautiful jewels, which they made into vile and abominable images. Therefore I will 21 treat their jewels like filth, I will hand them over as plunder to foreigners and as booty to the most evil people on earth, and these will 22 defile them. I will turn my face from them and let my treasured land be profaned; brigands will come in and defile it.

23   Clench your fists, for the land is full of bloodshed[a] and the city full 24 of violence. I will let in the scum of nations to take possession of their houses; I will quell the pride of the strong, and their sanctuaries shall 25 be profaned. Shuddering will come over them, and they will look in 26 vain for peace. Tempest shall follow upon tempest and rumour upon rumour. Men will go seeking a vision from a prophet; there will be no more guidance from a priest, 27 no counsel from elders. The king will mourn, the prince will be clothed with horror, the hands of the common people will shake with fright. I will deal with them as they deserve, and call them to account for their doings; and so they shall know that I am the LORD.

Jerusalem's guilt and punishment

8 ON the fifth day of the sixth month in the sixth year, I was sitting at home and the elders of Judah were with me. Suddenly the hand of the 2 Lord GOD came upon me, and I saw what looked like a man. He seemed to be all fire from the waist down and to shine and glitter like 3 brass from the waist up. He stretched out what seemed a hand and seized me by the forelock. A spirit[b] lifted me up between heaven and earth, carried me to Jerusalem in a vision of God and put me down at the entrance to the inner gate facing north, where stands the image of Lust to rouse lustful passion. The glory of the God of 4 Israel was there, like the vision I had seen in the plain. The LORD 5 said to me, 'Man, look northwards.' I did so, and there to the north of the altar gate, at the entrance, was that image of Lust. 'Man,' he said, 'do you see what 6 they are doing? The monstrous abominations which the Israelites practise here are driving me far from my sanctuary, and you will see even more such abominations.'

Then he brought me to the en- 7 trance of the court, and I looked and found a hole in the wall. 'Man,' 8 he said to me, 'dig through the wall.' I did so, and it became an opening. 'Go in,' he said, 'and see 9 the vile abominations they practise here.' So I went in and saw 10 figures of reptiles, beasts, and vermin, and all the idols of the Israelites, carved round the walls. Seventy elders of Israel were stand- 11 ing in front of them, with Jaazaniah son of Shaphan in the middle, and each held a censer from which rose the fragrant smoke of incense. 'Man,' he said to 12 me, 'do you see what the elders of Israel are doing in darkness, each at the shrine of his own carved image? They think that the LORD does not see them, or that he has forsaken the country. You will see', 13 he said, 'yet more monstrous abominations which they practise.'

Then he brought me to that gate- 14 way of the LORD's house which faces north; and there I saw women sitting and wailing for Tammuz. 'Man, do you see that?' he asked 15 me. 'But you will see abominations more monstrous than these.' So he 16 took me to the inner court of the LORD's house, and there, by the entrance to the sanctuary of the LORD, between porch and altar,

---

[a] bloodshed: *prob. rdg.*; *Heb.* the judgement of bloodshed.   [b] *Or* wind.

were some twenty-five men with their backs to the sanctuary and their faces to the east, prostrating
17 themselves to the rising sun. He said to me, 'Man, do you see that? Is it because they think these abominations a trifle, that the Jews have filled the country with violence? They provoke me further to anger, even while they seek to
18 appease me; I will turn upon them in my rage; I will neither pity nor spare. Loudly as they may cry to me, I will not listen.'

9   A loud voice rang in my ears: 'Here they come, those appointed to punish the city, each carrying
2 his weapon of destruction.' Then I saw six men approaching from the road that leads to the upper northern gate, each carrying a battle-axe, one man among them dressed in linen, with pen and ink at his waist; and they halted by the
3 altar of bronze. Then the glory of the God of Israel rose from above the cherubim. He came to the terrace of the temple and called to the man dressed in linen with pen
4 and ink at his waist. 'Go through the city, through Jerusalem,' said the LORD, 'and put a mark on the foreheads of those who groan and lament over the abominations
5 practised there.' Then I heard him say to the others, 'Follow him through the city and kill without
6 pity; spare no one. Kill and destroy them all, old men and young, girls, little children and women, but touch no one who bears the mark. Begin at my sanctuary.' So they began with the elders in front of
7 the temple. 'Defile the temple,' he said, 'and fill the courts with dead bodies; then go out into the city and kill.'
8   While they did their work, I was left alone; and I threw myself upon my face, crying out, 'O Lord GOD, must thou destroy all the Israelites who are left, pouring out
9 thy anger on Jerusalem?' He an-

swered, 'The iniquity of Israel and Judah is great indeed; the land is full of murder, the city is filled with injustice. They think the LORD has forsaken this country; they think he sees nothing. But I 10 will neither pity nor spare them; I will make them answer for all they have done.' Then the man 11 dressed in linen with pen and ink at his waist came and made his report: 'I have done what thou hast commanded.'

Then I saw, above the vault over 10 the heads of the cherubim, as it were a throne of sapphire*a* visible above them. The LORD said to the 2 man dressed in linen, 'Come in between the circling wheels under the cherubim, and take a handful of the burning embers lying among the cherubim; then toss them over the city.' So he went in before my eyes.

The cherubim stood on the right 3 side of the temple as a man enters, and a cloud filled the inner court. The glory of the LORD rose high 4 from above the cherubim and moved on to the terrace; and the temple was filled with the cloud, while the radiance of the glory of the LORD filled the court. The 5 sound of the wings of the cherubim could be heard as far as the outer court, as loud as if God Almighty were speaking. Then he told the 6 man dressed in linen to take fire from between the circling wheels and among the cherubim; the man came and stood by a wheel, and a 7 cherub from among the cherubim put its hand into the fire that lay among them, and, taking some fire, gave it to the man dressed in linen; and he received it and went out.

Under the wings of the cheru- 8 bim there appeared what seemed a human hand. And I saw four 9 wheels beside the cherubim, one wheel beside each cherub. They had the sparkle of topaz, and all 10 four were alike, like a wheel inside

a Or lapis lazuli.

11 a wheel. When the cherubim moved in any of the four directions, they never swerved in their course; they went straight on in the direction in which their heads were turned, never swerving in their 12 course. Their whole bodies, their backs and hands and wings, as well as the wheels, were full of eyes 13 all round the four of them.[a] The whirring of the wheels sounded in 14 my ears. Each had four faces: the first was that of a cherub, the second that of a man, the third that of a lion, and the fourth that of an eagle.

15 Then the cherubim raised themselves up, those same living creatures I had seen by the river Kebar. 16 When the cherubim moved, the wheels moved beside them; when the cherubim lifted their wings and rose from the ground, the wheels did not turn away from them. 17 When the one halted, the other halted; when the one rose, the other rose; for the spirit of the 18 creatures was in the wheels. Then the glory of the LORD left the temple terrace and halted above 19 the cherubim. The cherubim lifted their wings and raised themselves from the ground; I watched them go with the wheels beside them. They halted at the eastern gateway of the LORD's house, and the glory of the God of Israel was over them.

20 These were the living creatures I had seen beneath the God of Israel at the river Kebar; I knew that 21 they were cherubim. Each had four faces and four wings, and the semblance of human hands under 22 their wings. Their faces were like those I had seen in vision by the river Kebar;[b] they moved, each one of them, straight forward.

11 A spirit[c] lifted me up and brought me to the eastern gate of the LORD's house, the gate that faces east. By the doorway were twenty-five men,

and I saw among them two of high office, Jaazaniah son of Azzur and Pelatiah son of Benaiah. The LORD 2 said to me, Man, it is these who are planning mischief and plotting trouble in this city, saying to them- 3 selves, 'There will be no building of houses yet awhile; the city is a stewpot and we are the meat in it.' Therefore, said he, prophesy a- 4 gainst them, prophesy, O man. Then the spirit of the LORD came 5 suddenly upon me, and he told me to say, These are the words of the LORD: This is what you are saying to yourselves, you men of Israel; well do I know the thoughts that rise in your mind. You have killed 6 and killed in this city and heaped the streets with the slain. These, 7 therefore, are the words of the Lord GOD: The bodies of the slain that you have put there, it is they that are the meat. The city is indeed the stewpot, but I will take you out of it. It is a sword that you fear, and 8 a sword I will bring upon you, says the Lord GOD. I will take you out 9 of it; I will give you over to a foreign power; I will bring you to justice. You too shall fall by the 10 sword when I judge you on the frontier of Israel; thus you shall know that I am the LORD. So the 11 city will not be your stewpot, nor you the meat in it. On the frontier of Israel I will judge you; thus you 12 shall know that I am the LORD. You have not conformed to my statutes nor kept my laws, but you have followed the laws of the nations around you.

While I was prophesying, Pe- 13 latiah son of Benaiah fell dead; and I threw myself upon my face, crying aloud, 'O Lord GOD, must thou make an end of all the Israelites who are left?'

The word of the LORD came to 14 me: Man, they are your brothers, 15 your brothers and your kinsmen, this whole people of Israel, to whom

---

[a] *Prob. rdg.; Heb. adds* their wheels.
[c] *Or* wind.

[b] *Prob. rdg.; Heb. adds* and them.

the men who now live in Jerusalem have said, 'Keep your distance from the LORD; the land has been made over to us as our property.'

16 Say therefore, These are the words of the Lord GOD: When I sent them far away among the nations and scattered them in many lands, for a while I became their sanctuary in the countries to which they had

17 gone. Say therefore, These are the words of the Lord GOD: I will gather them from among the nations and assemble them from the countries over which I have scattered them, and I will give them

18 the soil of Israel. When they come into it, they will do away with all their vile and abominable prac-

19 tices. I will give them a different heart and put a new spirit into them; I will take the heart of stone out of their bodies and give them

20 a heart of flesh. Then they will conform to my statutes and keep my laws. They will become my people, and I will become their

21 God. But as for those whose heart is set upon[a] their vile and abominable practices, I will make them answer for all they have done. This is the very word of the Lord GOD.

22 Then the cherubim lifted their wings, with the wheels beside them and the glory of the God of Israel

23 above them. The glory of the LORD rose up and left the city, and halted on the mountain to the east of it.

24 And a spirit[b] lifted me up and brought me to the exiles in Chaldaea. All this came in a vision sent by the spirit of God, and then the

25 vision that I had seen left me. I told the exiles all that the LORD had revealed to me.

Jerusalem's downfall certain

12 THE word of the LORD came to me:
2 Man, you live among a rebellious people. Though they have eyes they will not see, though they have

ears they will not hear, because they are a rebellious people. There- 3 fore, man, pack up what you need for a journey into exile, by day before their eyes; then set off on your journey. When you leave home and go off into exile before their eyes, it may be they will see that they are rebels. Bring out 4 your belongings, packed as for exile; do it by day, before their eyes, and then at evening, still before their eyes, leave home, as if you were going into exile. Next, 5 before their eyes, break a hole through the wall, and carry your belongings out through it. When 6 dusk falls, take your pack on your shoulder, before their eyes, and carry it out, with your face covered so that you cannot see the ground. I am making you a warning sign for the Israelites.

I did exactly as I had been told. 7 By day I brought out my belongings, packed as for exile, and at evening I broke through the wall with my hands. When dusk fell, I shouldered my pack and carried it out before their eyes.

Next morning, the word of the 8 LORD came to me: Man, he said, 9 have not the Israelites, that rebellious people, asked you what you are doing? Tell them that these are 10 the words of the Lord GOD: This oracle concerns the prince in Jerusalem, and all the Israelites therein.[c] Tell them that you are a sign 11 to warn them; what you have done will be done to them; they will go into exile and captivity. Their 12 prince will shoulder his pack in the dusk and go through a hole made to let him out, with his face covered so that he cannot be seen nor himself see the ground. But I will 13 cast my net over him, and he will be caught in the meshes. I will bring him to Babylon, the land of the Chaldaeans, though he will not see it; and there he will die. I will 14

---

[a] *Prob. rdg.*; *Heb. adds* the heart of.   [b] *Or* wind.
[c] therein: *prob. rdg.*; *Heb.* among them.

scatter his bodyguard and drive all his squadrons to the four winds; I will follow them with drawn sword.

15 Then they shall know that I am the LORD, when I disperse them among the nations and scatter them 16 through many lands. But I will leave a few of them who will escape sword, famine, and pestilence, to tell the whole story of their abominations to the peoples among whom they go; and they shall know that I am the LORD.

17 And the word of the LORD came 18 to me: Man, he said, as you eat you must tremble, and as you drink 19 you must shudder with dread. Say to the common people, These are the words of the Lord GOD about those who live in Jerusalem and about the land of Israel: They will eat with dread and be filled with horror as they drink; the land shall be filled with horror because it is sated with the violence of all who 20 live there. Inhabited cities shall be deserted, and the land shall become a waste. Thus you shall know that I am the LORD.

21 The word of the LORD came to 22 me: Man, he said, what is this proverb current in the land of Israel: 'Time runs on, visions die away'? 23 Say to them, These are the words of the Lord GOD: I have put an end to this proverb; it shall never be heard in Israel again. Say rather to them, The time, with all the vision 24 means, is near. There will be no more false visions, no specious divi-25 nation among the Israelites, for I, the LORD, will say what I will, and it shall be done. It shall be put off no longer: in your lifetime, you rebellious people, I will speak, I will act. This is the very word of the Lord GOD.

26 The word of the LORD came to 27 me: Man, he said, the Israelites say that the vision you now see is not to be fulfilled for many years: you are prophesying of a time far 28 off. Say to them, These are the words of the Lord GOD: No word

of mine shall be delayed; even as I speak it shall be done. This is the very word of the Lord GOD.

The LORD said to me, Man, pro- 13 1, 2 phesy of the prophets of Israel; prophesy, and say to those who prophesy out of their own hearts, Hear what the LORD says: These 3 are the words of the Lord GOD: Oh, the wicked folly of the prophets! Their inspiration comes from themselves; they have seen no vision. Your prophets, Israel, have been 4 like jackals among ruins. They 5 have not gone up into the breach to repair the broken wall round the Israelites, that they may stand firm in battle on the day of the LORD. Oh, false vision and lying 6 divination! Oh, those prophets who say, 'It is the very word of the LORD', when it is not the LORD who has sent them; yet they expect their words to control the event. Is it not a false vision that you 7 prophets have seen? Is not your divination a lie? You call it the very word of the LORD, but it is not I who have spoken.

These, then, are the words of the 8 Lord GOD: Because your words are false and your visions a lie, I am against you, says the Lord GOD. I 9 will raise my hand against the prophets whose visions are false, whose divinations are a lie. They shall have no place in the counsels of my people; they shall not be entered in the roll of Israel nor set foot upon its soil. Thus you shall know that I am the Lord GOD. Rightly, for they have misled my 10 people by saying that all is well when all is not well. It is as if they were building a wall and used whitewash for the daubing. Tell 11 these daubers that it will fall; rain will pour down in torrents, and I will send hailstones hard as rock streaming down and I will unleash a stormy wind. When the building 12 falls, men will ask, 'Where is the plaster you should have used?' So 13 these are the words of the Lord

GOD: In my rage I will unleash a stormy wind; rain will come in torrents in my anger, hailstones hard as rock in my fury, until all is 14 destroyed. I will demolish the building which you have daubed with whitewash and level it to the ground, so that its foundations are laid bare. It shall fall, and you shall be destroyed within it; thus you 15 shall know that I am the LORD. I will spend my rage on the building and on those who daubed it with wash; and people[a] will say, 'The building is gone and the men who 16 daubed it are gone, those prophets of Israel who prophesied to Jerusalem, who saw visions of prosperity when there was no prosperity.' This is the very word of the Lord GOD.

17   Now turn, man, to the women of your people who prophesy out of their own hearts, and prophesy to 18 them. Say to them, These are the words of the Lord GOD: I loathe you, you women who hunt men's lives by sewing magic bands upon the wrists and putting veils over the heads of persons of every age; are you to hunt the lives of my people and keep your own lives 19 safe? You have violated my sanctity before my people with handfuls of barley and scraps of bread. You bring death to those who should not die, and life to those who should not live, by lying to this people of mine who listen to 20 lies. So these are the words of the Lord GOD: I am against your magic bands with which you hunt men's lives for the excitement of it. I will tear them from your arms and set those lives at liberty, lives that you 21 hunt for the excitement of it. I will tear up your long veils and save my people from you; you shall no longer have power to hunt them. Thus you shall know that I am the 22 LORD. You discouraged the righteous man with lies, when I meant him no hurt; you so strengthened

the wicked that he would not abandon his evil ways and be saved; and therefore you shall 23 never see your false visions again nor practise your divination any more. I will rescue my people from your power; and thus you shall know that I am the LORD.

Some of the elders of Israel came 14 to visit me, and while they sat with me the LORD said to me, Man, 2, 3 these people have set their hearts on their idols and keep their eyes fixed on the sinful things that cause their downfall. Am I to let such men consult me? Speak to them 4 and tell them that these are the words of the Lord GOD: If any Israelite, with his heart set on his idols and his eyes fixed on the sinful things that cause his downfall, comes to a prophet, I, the LORD, in my own person, shall be constrained to answer him, despite his many idols. My answer will grip the 5 hearts of the Israelites, estranged from me as they are, one and all, through their idols. So tell the 6 Israelites that these are the words of the Lord GOD: Turn away, turn away from your idols; turn your backs on all your abominations. If any man, Israelite or alien, re- 7 nounces me, sets his heart upon idols and fixes his eyes upon the vile thing that is his downfall – if such a man comes to consult me through a prophet, I, the LORD, in my own person, shall be constrained to answer him. I will set my face 8 against that man; I will make him an example and a byword; I will rid my people of him. Thus you shall know that I am the LORD. If a 9 prophet is seduced into making a prophecy, it is I the LORD who have seduced him; I will stretch out my hand and rid my people Israel of him. Both shall be pun- 10 ished; the prophet and the man who consults him alike are guilty. And never again will the Israelites 11 stray from their allegiance, never

[a] *Prob. rdg.; Heb.* I.

850

again defy my will and bring pollution upon themselves; they will become my people, and I will become their God. This is the very word of the Lord GOD.

12 These were the words of the
13 LORD to me: Man, when a country sins by breaking faith with me, I will stretch out my hand and cut short its daily bread. I will send famine upon it and destroy both
14 men and cattle. Even if those three men were living there, Noah, Danel[a] and Job, they would save none but themselves by their righteousness. This is the very
15 word of the Lord GOD. If I should turn wild beasts loose in a country to destroy its inhabitants, until it became a waste through which no man would pass for fear of the
16 beasts, then, if those three men were living there, as I live, says the Lord GOD, they would not save even their own sons and daughters; they would save themselves alone, and the country would become a
17 waste. Or if I should bring the sword upon that country and command it to go through the land and should destroy men and cattle,
18 then, if those three men were living there, as I live, says the Lord GOD, they could save neither son nor daughter; they would save
19 themselves alone. Or if I should send pestilence on that land and pour out my fury upon it in blood,
20 to destroy men and cattle, then, if Noah, Danel and Job were living there, as I live, says the Lord GOD, they would save neither son nor daughter; they would save themselves alone by their righteousness.
21 These were the words of the Lord GOD: How much less hope is there for Jerusalem when I inflict on her these four punishments of mine, sword and famine, wild beasts and pestilence, to destroy both men
22 and cattle! Some will be left in her, some survivors to be brought out, both sons and daughters. Look at

them as they come out to you, and see how they have behaved and what they have done. This will be some comfort to you for all the harm I have done to Jerusalem and all I have inflicted upon her. It will bring you comfort when you 23 see how they have behaved and what they have done; for you will know that it was not without reason that I dealt thus with her. This is the very word of the Lord GOD.

These were the words of the 15 LORD to me:

Man, how is the vine better than 2
　　any other tree,
than a branch from a tree in the
　　forest?
Is wood got from it 3
fit to make anything useful?
Can men make it into a peg
and hang things on it?
If it is put on the fire for fuel, 4
if its two ends are burnt by the
　　fire
and the middle is charred,
is it fit for anything useful?
Nothing useful could be made of it 5
　　even when whole;
how much less, when it is burnt by
　　the fire and charred,
can it be made into anything
　　useful!

So these are the words of the Lord 6
GOD:

I treat the vine, as against forest-
　　trees,
only as fuel for the fire,
even so I treat the people of Jeru-
　　salem;
I set my face against them. 7
Though they escape from the fire,
　　fire shall burn them up.
Thus you shall know that I am
　　the LORD
when I set my face against them,
making the land a waste 8
because they have broken faith.
This is the very word of the Lord
GOD.

---

[a] Or, *as otherwise read,* Daniel.

16 The word of the LORD came to
2 me: Man, he said, make Jerusalem
3 see her abominable conduct. Tell
her that these are the words of the
Lord GOD to her: Canaan is the
land of your ancestry and there you
were born; an Amorite was your
father and a Hittite your mother.
4 This is how you were treated
at birth: when you were born,
your navel-string was not tied,
you were not bathed in water ready
for the rubbing, you were not
salted as you should have been nor
5 wrapped in swaddling clothes. No
one cared for you enough to do any
of these things or, indeed, to have
any pity for you; you were thrown
out on the bare ground in your own
6 filth on the day of your birth. Then
I came by and saw you kicking
helplessly in your own blood; I
spoke to you, there in your blood,
7 and bade you live. I tended you
like an evergreen plant, like something growing in the fields; you
throve and grew. You came to full
womanhood; your breasts became
firm and your hair grew, but still
you were naked and exposed.
8 Again I came by and saw that
you were ripe for love. I spread the
skirt of my robe over you and
covered your naked body. Then I
plighted my troth and entered into
a covenant with you, says the Lord
9 GOD, and you became mine. Then
I bathed you in water and washed
off the blood and anointed you with
10 oil. I gave you robes of brocade and
sandals of stout hide; I fastened a
linen girdle round you and dressed
11 you in lawn. For jewellery I put
bracelets on your arms and a chain
12 round your neck; I gave you a
nose-ring, I put pendants in your
ears and a beautiful coronet on
13 your head. You had ornaments of
gold and silver, your dresses were
of linen, lawn, and brocade. You
had flour and honey and olive oil
for food, and you grew very
beautiful, you grew into a queen.

The fame of your beauty went all 14
over the world, for the splendour
with which I decked you made it
perfect. This is the very word of
the Lord GOD.

But you trusted to your beauty 15
and prostituted your fame; you
committed fornication, offering
yourself freely to any passer-by
for your beauty to become his. You 16
took some of your clothes and
decked a platform for yourself in
gay colours and there you committed fornication; you had intercourse with him for your beauty to
become his.*a* You took the splen- 17
did ornaments of gold and silver
which I had given you, and made
for yourself male images with which
you committed fornication. You 18
covered them with your robes of
brocade and offered up my oil and
my incense before them. You took 19
the food I had given you, the flour,
the oil, and the honey, with which
I had fed you, and set it before
them as an offering of soothing
odour. This is the very word of the
Lord GOD.

You took the sons and daughters 20
whom you had borne to me, and
sacrificed them to these images for
their food. Was this of less account
than your fornication? No! you 21
slaughtered my children and handed them over, you surrendered
them to your images. With all your 22
abominable fornication you forgot
those early days when you lay
naked and exposed, kicking helplessly in your own blood.

After all the evil you had done 23
(Oh! the pity of it, says the Lord
GOD), you built yourself a couch 24
and constructed a high-stool in
every open place. You built up your 25
high-stools at the top of every
street and disgraced your beauty,
offering your body to any passer-
by in countless acts of fornication.
You committed fornication with 26
your gross neighbours, the Egyptians, and you provoked me to

a you had intercourse...his: prob. rdg.; Heb. obscure.

anger by your countless acts of fornication.

27 I stretched out my hand against you and cut down your portion. Then I gave you up to women who hated you, Philistine women, who were so disgusted by your lewd

28 ways. Not content with this, you committed fornication with the Assyrians, led them into fornication and still were not content.

29 You committed countless acts of fornication in Chaldaea, the land of commerce, and even with this you were not content.

30 How you anger me! says the Lord GOD. You have done all this like the imperious whore you are.

31 You have built your couch at the top of every street and constructed your stool in every open place, but, unlike the common prostitute,

32 you have scorned a fee. An adulterous wife who owes obedience to her husband takes a fee from[a]

33 strangers. The prostitute also takes her fee; but you give presents to all your lovers, you bribe them to come from all quarters to commit forni-

34 cation with you. You are the very opposite of other women in your fornication: no one runs after you, you do not receive a fee, you give it. You are the very opposite.

35 Listen to the words of the LORD,

36 whore that you are. These are the words of the Lord GOD: You have been prodigal in your excesses, you have exposed your naked body in fornication with your lovers. In return for your abominable idols and for the slaughter of the chil-

37 dren you have given them, I will gather all those lovers to whom you made advances,[b] all whom you loved and all whom you hated. I will gather them in from all quarters against you; I will strip you naked before them, and they

38 shall see your whole body naked. I will put you on trial for adultery

and murder, and I will charge you with[c] blood shed in jealousy and fury. Then I will hand you over to 39 them. They will demolish your couch and pull down your highstool; they will strip your clothes off, take away your splendid ornaments, and leave you naked and exposed. They will bring up the 40 mob against you and stone you, they will hack you to pieces with their swords. They will burn down 41 your houses and execute judgement on you, and many women shall see it. I will put an end to your fornication, and you shall never again give a fee to your lovers. Then I will abate my fury, 42 and my jealousy will turn away from you. I will be calm and will no longer be provoked to anger. For 43 you had forgotten the days of your youth and exasperated me with all your doings: so I in my turn brought retribution upon you for your deeds. This is the very word of the Lord GOD.

Did you not commit these obscenities, as well as all your other abominations? Dealers in pro- 44 verbs will say of you, 'Like mother, like daughter.' You are a true 45 daughter of a mother who loathed her husband and children. You are a true sister of your sisters who loathed their husbands and children. You are all daughters of a Hittite mother and an Amorite father. Your elder sister was Sa- 46 maria, who lived with her daughters to the north of you; your younger sister, who lived with her daughters to the south of you, was Sodom. Did you not behave as 47 they did and commit the same abominations? You came very near to doing even worse than they. As I 48 live, says the Lord GOD, your sister Sodom and her daughters never behaved as you and your daughters have done. This was the 49

---

[a] a fee from: *prob. rdg.*; Heb. om.
[b] to whom...advances: *or* whom you charmed.
[c] charge you with: *prob. mng.*; Heb. give you.

iniquity of your sister Sodom: she and her daughters had pride of wealth and food in plenty, comfort and ease, and yet she never helped 50 the poor and wretched. They grew haughty and did deeds abominable in my sight, and I made away 51 with them, as you have seen. Samaria was never half the sinner you have been; you have committed more abominations than she, abominations which have made your sister seem innocent. 52 You must bear the humiliation which you thought your sisters deserved. Your sins are so much more abominable than theirs that they appear innocent in comparison with you; and now you must bear your shame and humiliation and make your sisters seem innocent. 53 But I will restore the fortunes of Sodom and her daughters and of Samaria and her daughters, and I will restore yours at the same time. 54 Even though you bring them comfort, you will bear your shame, you will be disgraced for all you have 55 done; but when your sister Sodom and her daughters become what they were of old, and when your sister Samaria and her daughters become what they were of old, then you and your daughters will be 56 restored. Did you not hear and talk much of your sister Sodom in the 57 days of your pride, before your wickedness was exposed, in the days when the daughters of Aram with those about her were disgraced, and the daughters of the Philistines round about, who so 58 despised you? Now you too must bear the consequences of your lewd and abominable conduct. This is the very word of the LORD.

59 These are the words of the Lord GOD: I will treat you as you have deserved, because you violated a covenant and made light of a sol- 60 emn oath. But I will remember the covenant I made with you when you were young, and I will establish with you a covenant which shall last for ever. And you will re- 61 member your past ways and feel ashamed when you receive your sisters, the elder and the younger. For I will give them to you as daughters, and they shall not be outside your covenant.[a] Thus I will 62 establish my covenant with you, and you shall know that I am the LORD. You will remember, and will 63 be so ashamed and humiliated that you will never open your mouth again once I have accepted expiation for all you have done. This is the very word of the Lord GOD.

These were the words of the 17 LORD to me: Man, speak to the 2 Israelites in allegory and parable. Tell them that these are the words 3 of the Lord GOD:

A great eagle
with broad wings and long pinions,
in full plumage, richly patterned,
came to Lebanon.
He took the very top of a cedar-
tree,
he plucked its highest twig;   4
he carried it off to a land of commerce,
and planted it in a city of merchants.
Then he took a native seed   5
and put it in nursery-ground;
he set it like a willow,
a shoot beside abundant water.
It sprouted and became a vine,   6
sprawling low along the ground
and bending its trailing boughs
towards him[b]
with its roots growing beneath
him.
So it became a vine, it branched
out
and put forth shoots.
But there was another great eagle 7
with broad wings and thick
plumage;
and this vine gave its roots
a twist towards him;[b]

---

[a] and they...covenant: *or* though not on the ground of your covenant.
[b] *Or* inwards.

it pushed out its trailing boughs
  towards him,
seeking drink from the bed where
  it was planted,
8 though it had been set
in good ground beside abundant
  water
that it might bear shoots and be
  fruitful
and become a noble vine.

9 Tell them that these are the words
of the Lord GOD:

Can such a vine flourish?
Will not its roots be broken off
and its fruit be stripped,
and all its fresh sprouting leaves
  wither,
until it is uprooted and carried
  away
with little effort and few hands?
10 If it is transplanted, can it
  flourish?
Will it not be utterly shrivelled,
as though by the touch of the east
  wind,
on the bed where it ought to sprout?

11   These were the words of the
12 LORD to me: Say to that rebellious
people, Do you not know what this
means? The king of Babylon came
to Jerusalem, took its king and its
officers and had them brought to
13 him at Babylon. He took a prince
of the royal line and made a treaty
with him, putting him on his oath.
He took away the chief men of the
14 country, so that it should become
a humble kingdom unable to raise
itself but ready to observe its
15 treaty and keep it in force. But the
prince rebelled against him and
sent messengers to Egypt, asking
for horses and men in plenty. Can
such a man prosper? Can he escape
destruction if he acts in this way?
Can he violate a covenant and
16 escape? As I live, says the Lord
GOD, I swear that he shall die in
the land of the king who put him
on the throne; he made light of his
oath and violated the covenant he
made with him. He shall die in

Babylon. Pharaoh will send no 17
large army, no great host, to protect him in battle; no siege-ramp
will be raised, no watch-tower put
up, nor will the lives of many men
be lost. He has violated a covenant 18
and has made light of his oath. He
had submitted, and yet he did all
these things; he shall not escape.

These then are the words of the 19
Lord GOD: As I live, he has made
light of the oath he took by me and
has violated the covenant I made
with him. I will bring retribution
upon him; I will cast my net over 20
him, and he shall be caught in its
meshes. I will carry him to Babylon and bring him to judgement
there, because he has broken faith
with me. In all his squadrons every 21
commander shall fall by the sword;
those who are left will be scattered
to the four winds. Thus you shall
know that it is I, the LORD, who
have spoken.

These are the words of the Lord 22
GOD:

I, too, will take a slip
from the lofty crown of the cedar
and set it in the soil;
I will pluck a tender shoot from
  the topmost branch
and plant it.
I will plant it high on a lofty moun- 23
  tain,
the highest mountain in Israel.
It will put out branches, bear its
  fruit,
and become a noble cedar.
Winged birds of every kind will
  roost under it,
they will roost in the shelter of its
  sweeping boughs.
All the trees of the country-side 24
  will know
that it is I, the LORD,
who bring low the tall tree
and raise the low tree high,
who dry up the green tree
and make the dry tree put forth
  buds.
I, the LORD, have spoken and will
  do it.

18 THESE were the words of the
2 LORD to me: What do you all mean
by repeating this proverb in the
land of Israel:

'The fathers have eaten sour
  grapes,
and the children's teeth are set on
  edge'?

3 As I live, says the Lord GOD, this
proverb shall never again be used
4 in Israel. Every living soul belongs
to me; father and son alike are
mine. The soul that sins shall die.
5 Consider the man who is righteous and does what is just and
6 right. He never feasts at mountain-shrines, never lifts his eyes to
the idols of Israel, never dishonours another man's wife, never
approaches a woman during her
7 periods. He oppresses no man, he
returns the debtor's pledge, he
never robs. He gives bread to the
hungry and clothes to those who
8 have none. He never lends either
at discount or at interest. He shuns
injustice and deals fairly between
9 man and man. He conforms to my
statutes and loyally observes my
laws. Such a man is righteous: he
shall live, says the Lord GOD.
10 He may have a son who is a man
of violence and a cut-throat who
11 turns his back on these rules.[a] He
obeys none of them, he feasts at
mountain-shrines, he dishonours
12 another man's wife, he oppresses
the unfortunate and the poor, he is
a robber, he does not return the
debtor's pledge, he lifts his eyes to
idols and joins in abominable rites;
13 he lends both at discount and at
interest. Such a man shall not live.
Because he has committed all these
abominations he shall die, and his
blood will be on his own head.
14 This man in turn may have a son
who sees all his father's sins; he
sees, but he commits none of them.
15 He never feasts at mountain-
shrines, never lifts his eyes to the
idols of Israel, never dishonours

another man's wife. He oppresses 16
no man, takes no pledge, does not
rob. He gives bread to the hungry
and clothes to those who have none.
He shuns injustice, he never lends 17
either at discount or at interest. He
keeps my laws and conforms to my
statutes. Such a man shall not die
for his father's wrongdoing; he
shall live.
His father may have been guilty 18
of oppression and robbery and may
have lived an evil life among his
kinsfolk, and so has died because of
his iniquity. You may ask, 'Why is 19
the son not punished for his father's iniquity?' Because he has
always done what is just and right
and has been careful to obey all my
laws, therefore he shall live. It is 20
the soul that sins, and no other,
that shall die; a son shall not share
a father's guilt, nor a father his
son's. The righteous man shall reap
the fruit of his own righteousness,
and the wicked man the fruit of his
own wickedness.
It may be that a wicked man 21
gives up his sinful ways and keeps
all my laws, doing what is just
and right. That man shall live; he
shall not die. None of the offences 22
he has committed shall be remembered against him; he shall
live because of his righteous deeds.
Have I any desire, says the Lord 23
GOD, for the death of a wicked
man? Would I not rather that he
should mend his ways and live?
It may be that a righteous man 24
turns back from his righteous
ways and commits every kind of
abomination that the wicked practise; shall he do this and live? No,
none of his former righteousness
will be remembered in his favour;
he has broken his faith, he has
sinned, and he shall die. You say 25
that the Lord acts without principle? Listen, you Israelites, it is
you who act without principle, not
I. If a righteous man turns from 26
his righteousness, takes to evil

---

[a] who turns...rules: *prob. rdg.*; Heb. *unintelligible.*

856

ways and dies,[a] it is because of
27 these evil ways that he dies. Again,
if a wicked man turns from his
wicked ways and does what is just
28 and right, he will save his life. If he
sees his offences as they are and
turns his back on them all, then he
shall live; he shall not die.
29 'The Lord acts without principle', say the Israelites. No, Israelites, it is you who act without
30 principle, not I. Therefore, Israelites, says the Lord GOD, I will
judge every man of you on his
deeds. Turn, turn from your offences, or your iniquity will be
31 your downfall. Throw off the load
of your past misdeeds; get yourselves a new heart and a new spirit.
Why should you die, you men of
32 Israel? I have no desire for any
man's death. This is the very word
of the Lord GOD.

19   Raise a lament over the princes
2 of Israel and say:

Your mother was a lioness
among the lions!
She made her lair among the young
lions
and many were the cubs she bore.
3 One of her cubs she raised,
and he grew into a young lion.
He learnt to tear his prey,
he devoured men.
4 Then the nations shouted at[b] him
and he was caught in their pit,
and they dragged him with hooks
to the land of Egypt.
5 His case, she saw, was desperate,
her hope was lost;
so she took another of her cubs
and made him a young lion.
6 He prowled among the lions
and acted like a young lion.
He learnt to tear his prey,
he devoured men;
7 he broke down their palaces, laid
their cities in ruins.
The land and all that was in it
was aghast at the noise of his
roaring.

From the provinces all round   8
the nations raised the hue and cry;
they cast their net over him
and he was caught in their pit.
With hooks they drew him into a 9
cage
and brought him to the king of
Babylon,
who flung him into prison,
that his voice might never again be
heard
on the mountains of Israel.

Your mother was a vine in a vine- 10
yard[c]
planted by the waterside.
It grew fruitful and luxuriant,
for there was water in plenty.
It had stout branches,   11
fit to make sceptres for those who
bear rule.
It grew tall, finding its way
through the foliage,
and conspicuous for its height and
many trailing boughs.
But it was torn up in anger and 12
thrown to the ground;
the east wind blighted it,
its fruit was blown off,
its strong branches were blighted,
and fire burnt it.
Now it is replanted in the wilder- 13
ness,
in a dry and thirsty land;
and fire bursts forth from its own 14
branches
and burns up its shoots.[d]
It has no strong branch any more
to make a sceptre for those who
bear rule.

This is the lament and as a lament
it passed into use.

ON the tenth day of the fifth 20
month in the seventh year, some of
the elders of Israel came to consult
the LORD and were sitting with me.
Then this word came to me from 2
the LORD: Man, say to the elders of 3
Israel, This is the word of the Lord
GOD: Do you come to consult me?
As I live, I will not be consulted by

---

[a] *Prob. rdg.; Heb. adds* because of them.   [b] shouted at: *or* heard a report about.
[c] in a vineyard: *prob. rdg.; Heb. obscure in context.*   [d] *Prob. rdg.; Heb. adds* its fruit.

you. This is the very word of the Lord GOD.

4 Will you judge them? Will you judge them, O man? Then tell them of the abominations of their fore-
5 fathers and say to them, These are the words of the Lord GOD: When I chose Israel, with uplifted hand I bound myself by oath to the race of Jacob and revealed myself to them in Egypt; I lifted up my hand and declared: I am the LORD your
6 God. On that day I swore with hand uplifted that I would bring them out of Egypt into the land I had sought out for them, a land flowing with milk and honey, fairest of all
7 lands. I told them, every one, to cast away the loathsome things on which they feasted their eyes and not to defile themselves with the idols of Egypt. I am the LORD your God, I said.

8 But they rebelled against me, they refused to listen to me, and not one of them cast away the loathsome things on which he feasted his eyes or forsook the idols of Egypt. I had thought to pour out my wrath and exhaust my
9 anger on them in Egypt. I acted for the honour of my name, that it might not be profaned in the sight of the nations among whom Israel was living: I revealed myself to them by bringing Israel out of
10 Egypt. I brought them out of Egypt and led them into the wil-
11 derness. There I gave my statutes to them and taught them my laws, so that by keeping them men
12 might have life. Further, I gave them my sabbaths as a sign be-tween us, so that they should know that I, the LORD, was hallowing
13 them for myself. But the Israelites rebelled against me in the wilder-ness; they did not conform to my statutes, they rejected my laws, though by keeping them men might have life, and they utterly desecrated my sabbaths. So again I thought to pour out my wrath on them in the wilderness to destroy

them. I acted for the honour of my 14 name, that it might not be pro-faned in the sight of the nations who had seen me bring them out.

Further, I swore to them in the 15 wilderness with uplifted hand that I would not bring them into the land I had given them, that land flowing with milk and honey, fairest of all lands. For they had rejected 16 my laws, they would not conform to my statutes and they desecrated my sabbaths, because they loved to follow idols of their own. Yet I 17 pitied them too much to destroy them and did not make an end of them in the wilderness. I com- 18 manded their sons in the wilder-ness not to conform to their fathers' statutes, nor observe their laws, nor defile themselves with their idols. I said, I am the LORD your 19 God, you must conform to my statutes; you must observe my laws and act according to them. You must keep my sabbaths holy, 20 and they will become a sign be-tween us; so you will know that I am the LORD your God.

But the sons too rebelled against 21 me. They did not conform to my statutes or observe my laws, though any who had done so would have had life through them, and they desecrated my sabbaths. Again I thought to pour out my wrath and exhaust my anger on them in the wilderness. I acted for 22 the honour of my name, that it might not be profaned in the sight of the nations who had seen me bring them out. Yes, and in the 23 wilderness I swore to them with up-lifted hand that I would disperse them among the nations and scat-ter them abroad, because they had 24 disobeyed my laws, rejected my statutes, desecrated my sabbaths, and turned longing eyes toward the idols of their forefathers. I did 25 more; I imposed on them statutes that were not good statutes, and laws by which they could not win life. I let them defile themselves 26 with gifts to idols; I made them surrender their eldest sons to them so that I might fill them with horror. Thus they would know that I am the LORD.

27 Speak then, O man, to the Israelites and say to them, These are the words of the Lord GOD: Once again your forefathers insulted me

28 and broke faith with me: when I brought them into the land which I had sworn with uplifted hand to give them, they marked down every hill-top and every leafy tree, and there they offered their sacrifices, they made the gifts which roused my anger, they set out their offerings of soothing odour and poured out their drink-offerings.

29 I asked them, What is this hill-shrine to which you are going up? And 'hill-shrine' has been its name ever since.

30 So tell the Israelites, These are the words of the Lord GOD: Are you defiling yourselves as your forefathers did? Are you wantonly giving yourselves to their loath-

31 some gods? When you bring your gifts, when you pass your sons through the fire, you are still defiling yourselves in the service of your crowd of idols. How can I let you consult me, men of Israel? As I live, says the Lord GOD, I will not

32 be consulted by you. When you say to yourselves, 'Let us become like the nations and tribes of other lands and worship wood and stone', you are thinking of something that

33 can never be. As I live, says the Lord GOD, I will reign over you with a strong hand, with arm outstretch-

34 ed and wrath outpoured. I will bring you out from the peoples and gather you from the lands over which you have been scattered by my strong hand, my outstretched

35 arm and outpoured wrath. I will bring you into the wilderness of the peoples; there will I confront you, and there will I state my case

36 against you. Even as I did in the wilderness of Egypt against your forefathers, so will I state my case against you. This is the very word of the Lord GOD.

37 I will pass you under the rod and bring you within the bond*a* of the covenant. I will rid you of those who revolt and rebel against me.

38 I will take them out of the land where they are now living, but they shall not set foot on the soil of Israel. Thus shall you know that I am the LORD.

39 Now, men of Israel, these are the words of the Lord GOD: Go, sweep away your idols, every man of you. So in days to come you will never be disobedient to me or desecrate my holy name with your gifts and your idolatries. But on

40 my holy hill, the lofty hill of Israel, says the Lord GOD, there shall the Israelites serve me in the land, every one of them. There will I receive them with favour; there will I demand your contribution and the best of your offerings, with all your consecrated gifts. I will re-

41 ceive your offerings of soothing odour, when I have brought you out from the peoples and gathered you from the lands where you have been scattered. I, and only I, will have your worship, for all the nations to see.

42 You will know that I am the LORD, when I bring you home to the soil of Israel, to the land which I swore with uplifted hand to give your forefathers. There you will

43 remember your past ways and all the wanton deeds with which you have defiled yourselves, and will loathe yourselves for all the evils you have done. You will know that

44 I am the LORD, when I have dealt with you, O men of Israel, not as your wicked ways and your vicious deeds deserve but for the honour of my name. This is the very word of the Lord GOD.

45 These were the words of the

46 LORD to me: Man, turn and face

---

a Or muster.

towards Teman*a* and pour out your words to the south; prophesy to the rough country of the Negeb.

47 Say to it, Listen to the words of the LORD. These are the words of the Lord GOD: I will set fire to you, and the fire will consume all the wood, green and dry alike. Its fiery flame shall not be put out, but from the Negeb northwards every face will

48 be scorched by it. All men will see that it is I, the LORD, who have set it ablaze; it shall not be put out.

49 'Ah no! O Lord GOD,' I cried; 'they say of me, "He deals only in parables."'

21 These were the words of the
2 LORD to me: Man, turn and face towards Jerusalem, and pour out your words against her sanctuary;*b* prophesy against the land of Israel.

3 Say to the land of Israel, These are the words of the LORD: I am against you; I will draw my sword from the scabbard and cut off from

4 you both righteous and wicked. It is because I would cut off your righteous and your wicked equally that my sword will be drawn from the scabbard against all men, from

5 the Negeb northwards. All men shall know that I the LORD have drawn my sword; it shall never

6 again be sheathed. Groan in their presence, man, groan bitterly until

7 your lungs are bursting. When they ask you why you are groaning, say to them, 'I groan at the thing I have heard; when it comes, all hearts melt, all courage fails, all hands fall limp, all men's knees run with urine. It is coming. It is here.' This is the very word of the Lord GOD.

8 These were the words of the
9 LORD to me: Prophesy, man, and say, This is the word of the Lord:

A sword, a sword is sharpened and burnished,
10 sharpened to kill and kill again,

burnished to flash*c* like lightning.
Ah! the club is brandished, my son,
to defy all wooden idols!
The sword is given to be burnished 11
ready for the hand to grasp.
The sword – it is sharpened,
it is burnished,
ready to be put into the slayer's
hand.

Cry, man, and howl; for all this 12
falls on my people, it falls on
Israel's princes who are delivered
over to the sword and are slain
with my people. Therefore beat
your breast in remorse, for it is the 13
test – and what if it is not in truth
the club of defiance? This is the
very word of the Lord GOD.

But you, man, prophesy and clap 14
your hands together;
swing the sword twice, thrice:
it is the sword of slaughter,
the great sword of slaughter
whirling about them.
That their hearts may be troubled 15
and many stumble and fall,
I have set the threat of the sword
at all their gates,
the threat of the sword*d* made to
flash like lightning
and drawn to kill.
Be sharpened, turn right; be un- 16
sheathed, turn left,
wherever your point is aimed.

I, too, will clap my hands together 17
and abate my anger. I, the LORD,
have spoken.

These were the words of the 18
LORD to me: Man, trace out two 19
roads by which the sword of the
king of Babylon may come, starting both of them from the same
land. Then carve a signpost, carve
it at the point where the highway
forks. Mark out a road for the 20
sword to come to the Ammonite
city of Rabbah, to Judah, and to
Jerusalem at the heart of it. For 21
the king of Babylon halts to take

---

a Or face southward.   *b* her sanctuary: *prob. rdg.*; *Heb.* sanctuaries.
c to flash: *prob. rdg.*; *Heb. unintelligible.*
d the threat of the sword: *prob. rdg.*; *Heb. obscure in context.*

the omens at the parting of the ways, where the road divides. He casts lots with arrows, consults teraphim[a] and inspects the livers
22 of beasts. The augur's arrow marked 'Jerusalem' falls at his right hand: here, then,[b] he must raise a shout and sound the battle-cry, set battering-rams against the gates, pile siege-ramps and build
23 watch-towers. It may well seem to the people that the auguries are false, whereas they will put me in mind of their wrongdoing, and they will fall into the enemies'
24 hand. These therefore are the words of the Lord GOD: Because you have kept me mindful of your wrongdoing by your open rebellion, and your sins have been revealed in all your acts, because you have kept yourselves in my mind, you will fall into the enemies' hand by force.
25 You, too, you impious and wicked prince of Israel, your fate has come upon you in the hour of
26 final punishment. These are the words of the Lord GOD: Put off your diadem, lay aside your crown. All is changed; raise the low and
27 bring down the high. Ruin! Ruin! I will bring about such ruin as never was before, until the rightful sovereign comes. Then I will give him all.
28 Man, prophesy and say, These are the words of the Lord GOD to the Ammonites and to their shameful god:

A sword, a sword drawn for slaughter,
burnished for destruction,[c]
to flash like lightning!
29 Your visions are false, your auguries a lie,
which bid you bring it[d] down upon the necks of impious and wicked men,
whose fate has come upon them in the hour of final punishment.

Sheathe it again.   30
I will judge you in the place where you were born,
the land of your origin.
I will pour out my rage upon you; 31
I will breathe out my blazing wrath over you.
I will hand you over to brutal men, skilled in destruction.
You shall become fuel for fire,   32
your blood shall be shed within the land
and you shall leave no memory behind.

For I, the LORD, have spoken.

These were the words of the 22
LORD to me: Man, will you judge 2
her, will you judge the murderous city and bring home to her all her abominable deeds? Say to her, 3
These are the words of the Lord GOD: Alas for the city that sheds blood within her walls and brings her fate upon herself, the city that makes herself idols and is defiled thereby! The guilt is yours for the 4
blood you have shed, the pollution is on you for the idols you have made. You have shortened your days by this and brought the end of your years nearer. This is why I exposed you to the contempt of the nations and the mockery of every country. Lands far and near will 5
taunt you with your infamy and gross disorder. In you the princes 6
of Israel, one and all, have used their power to shed blood; men 7
have treated their fathers and mothers with contempt, they have oppressed the alien and ill-treated the orphan and the widow. You 8
have disdained what is sacred to me and desecrated my sabbaths. In you, Jerusalem, informers have 9
worked to procure bloodshed; in you are men who have feasted at mountain-shrines and have committed lewdness. In you men have 10
exposed their fathers' nakedness;

---

[a] *Or* household gods.   [b] *Prob. rdg.*; *Heb. adds* he must set battering-rams.
[c] for destruction: *prob. rdg.*; *Heb. obscure.*   [d] *Prob. rdg.*; *Heb.* you.

11 they have violated women during their periods; they have committed an outrage with their neighbours' wives and have lewdly defiled their daughters-in-law; they have ravished their sisters, their own fa-
12 thers' daughters. In you men have accepted bribes to shed blood, and they have exacted discount and interest on their loans. You have oppressed your fellows for gain, and you have forgotten me. This is the very word of the Lord GOD.

13 See, I strike with my clenched fist in anger at your ill-gotten gains and at the bloodshed within your
14 walls. Will your strength or courage stand when I deal with you? I, the LORD, have spoken and I will
15 act. I will disperse you among the nations and scatter you abroad; thus will I rid you altogether of
16 your defilement. I will sift you[a] in the sight of the nations, and you will know that I am the LORD.

17 These were the words of the
18 LORD to me: Man, to me all Israelites are an alloy, their silver alloyed with copper, tin, iron, and lead.[b]
19 Therefore, these are the words of the Lord GOD: Because you have all become alloyed, I will gather
20 you together into Jerusalem, as a mass of silver, copper, iron, lead, and tin is gathered into a crucible for the fire to be blown to full heat to melt them. So will I gather you in my anger and wrath, set you
21 there and melt you; I will collect you and blow up the fire of my anger until you are melted within
22 it. You will be melted as silver is melted in a crucible, and you will know that I, the LORD, have poured out my anger upon you.

23 These were the words of the
24 LORD to me: Man, say to Jerusalem, You are like a land on which no rain has fallen; no shower has come down upon you[c] in the days
25 of indignation. The princes within

her are like lions growling as they tear their prey. They have devoured men, and seized their treasure and all their wealth; they have widowed many women within her walls. Her priests have done vio- 26 lence to my law[d] and profaned what is sacred to me. They make no distinction between sacred and common, and lead men to see no difference between clean and unclean. They have disregarded my sabbaths, and I am dishonoured among them. Her officers within 27 her are like wolves tearing their prey, shedding blood and destroying men's lives to acquire ill-gotten gain. Her prophets use whitewash 28 instead of plaster;[e] their vision is false and their divination a lie. They say, 'This is the word of the Lord GOD', when the LORD has not spoken. The common people are 29 bullies and robbers; they ill-treat the unfortunate and the poor, they are unjust and cruel to the alien. I 30 looked for a man among them who could build up a barricade, who could stand before me in the breach to defend the land from ruin; but I found no such man. I poured out 31 my indignation upon them and utterly destroyed them in the fire of my wrath. Thus I brought on them the punishment they had deserved. This is the very word of the Lord GOD.

The word of the LORD came to 23 me: Man, he said, there were once 2 two women, daughters of the same mother. They played the whore in 3 Egypt, played the whore while they were still girls; for there they let their virgin breasts be fondled and their virgin bosoms pressed. The 4 elder was named Oholah, her sister Oholibah. They became mine and bore me sons and daughters. 'Oholah' is Samaria, 'Oholibah' Jerusalem. While she owed me 5 obedience Oholah played the

---

[a] I will sift you: *or* You will be profaned.   [b] their silver...lead: *prob. rdg.*;
Heb. copper, tin, iron, and lead inside a crucible; they are an alloy, silver.
[c] *Prob. rdg.*; *Heb.* it.   [d] *Or* instruction.   [e] *Cp. 13. 8–16.*

whore and was infatuated with her
6 Assyrian lovers, staff officers in
blue,[a] viceroys and governors,
handsome young cavaliers all of
7 them, riding on horseback. She
played the whore with all of them,
the flower of the Assyrian youth;
and she let herself be defiled with
all their idols, wherever her lust
8 led her. She never gave up the
whorish ways she had learnt in
Egypt, where men had lain with
her when young, had pressed her
virgin bosom and overwhelmed her
9 with their fornication. So I abandoned her to her lovers, the Assyrians, with whom she was
10 infatuated. They ravished her,
they took her sons and daughters,
and they killed her with the sword.
She became a byword among women, and judgement was passed
upon her.
11   Oholibah, her sister, had watched her, and she gave herself up to
lust and played the whore worse
12 than her sister. She, too, was
infatuated with Assyrians, viceroys, governors and staff officers,
all handsome young cavaliers, in
full dress, riding on horseback.
13 I found that she too had let herself
be defiled; both had gone the same
14 way; but she carried her fornication to greater lengths; she saw
male figures carved on the wall,
sculptured forms of Chaldaeans,
15 picked out in vermilion. Belts were
round their waists, and on their
heads turbans with dangling ends.
All seemed to be high officers and
looked like Babylonians, natives of
16 Chaldaea. As she looked she was
infatuated with them, so she sent
messengers to Chaldaea for them.
17 And the Babylonians came to her
to share her bed, and defiled her
with fornication; she was defiled by
them until she was filled with re-
18 vulsion. She made no secret that

she was a whore but let herself be
ravished until I was filled with revulsion against her as I was against
her sister. She played the whore 19
again and again, remembering how
in her youth she had played the
whore in Egypt. She was infatu- 20
ated with their male prostitutes,
whose members were like those of
asses and whose seed came in floods
like that of horses. So, Oholibah, 21
you relived the lewdness of your
girlhood in Egypt when you let
your bosom be pressed and your
breasts fondled.[b]

Therefore these are the words 22
of the Lord GOD: I will rouse them
against you, Oholibah, those lovers
of yours who have filled you with
revulsion, and bring them upon
you from every side, the Baby- 23
lonians and all those Chaldaeans,
men of Pekod, Shoa, and Koa, and
all the Assyrians with them. Handsome young men they are, viceroys
and governors, commanders and
staff officers,[c] riding on horseback.
They will come against you with 24
war-horses, with chariots and
wagons, with a host drawn from
the nations, armed with shield,
buckler, and helmet; they will beset you on every side. I will give
them authority to judge, and they
will use that authority to judge
you. I will turn my jealous wrath 25
loose on you, and they will make
you feel their fury. They will cut
off your nose and your ears, and in
the end you[d] will fall by the sword.[e]
They will strip you of your clothes 26
and take away all your finery. So I 27
will put a stop to your lewdness
and the way in which you learnt to
play the whore in Egypt. You will
never cast longing eyes on such
things again, never remember
Egypt any more.

These are the words of the Lord 28
GOD: I am handing you over to

---

[a] *Or* violet.   [b] fondled: *prob. rdg.*; *Heb. unintelligible.*
[c] staff officers: *prob. rdg., cp. verses 5 and 12*; *Heb. obscure.*   [d] in the end you:
or your successors.   [e] *Prob. rdg.*; *Heb. adds* They will take your sons and
daughters, and in the end you will be burnt.

29 those whom you hate, those who have filled you with revulsion; and they will make you feel their hatred. They will take all you have earned and leave you naked and exposed; that body with which you have played the whore will be ravished. It is your lewdness and your forni-

30 cation that have brought this upon you, it is because you have followed alien peoples and played the whore and have allowed yourself to

31 be defiled with their idols. You have followed in your sister's footsteps, and I will put her cup into your hand.

32 These are the words of the Lord God:

You shall drink from your sister's cup,
a cup deep and wide,
charged with mockery and scorn,
more than ever cup can hold.

33 It[a] will be full of drunkenness and grief,
a cup of ruin and desolation,
the cup of your sister Samaria;

34 and you shall drink it to the dregs.
Then you will chew[b] it in pieces
and tear out your breasts.
This is my verdict, says the Lord God.

35 Therefore, these are the words of the Lord God: Because you have forgotten me and flung me behind your back, you must bear the guilt of your lewdness and your fornication.

36 The Lord said to me, Man, will you judge Oholah and Oholibah? Then tax them with their vile of-

37 fences. They have committed adultery, and there is blood on their hands. They have committed adultery with their idols and offered my children to them for food, the children they had borne

38 me. This too they have done to me: they have polluted my sanctuary

39 and desecrated my sabbaths. They came into my sanctuary and desecrated it by slaughtering their sons as an offering to their idols; this they did in my own house. They

40 would send for men from a far-off country; and the men came at the messenger's bidding. You bathed your body for these men, you painted your eyes, decked yourself in your finery, you sat yourself

41 upon a bed of state and had a table put ready before it and laid my own incense and my own oil on it.

42 Loud were the voices of the light-hearted crowd; and besides ordinary folk Sabaeans were there, brought from the wilderness; they put bracelets on the women's hands and beautiful garlands on their

43 heads. I thought: Ah that woman, grown old in adultery! Now they will commit fornication with her –

44 with her of all women! They resorted to her as a prostitute; they resorted to Oholah and Oholibah,

45 those lewd women. Upright men will condemn them for their adultery and bloodshed; for adulterous they are, and blood is on their hands.

46 These are the words of the Lord God: Summon the invading host; abandon them to terror and rapine.

47 Let the host stone them and hack them to pieces with their swords, kill their sons and daughters and

48 burn down their houses. Thus I will put an end to lewdness in the land, and other women shall be taught not to be as lewd as they. You shall

49 pay the penalty for your lewd conduct and be punished for your idolatries, and you will know that I am the Lord God.

24 These were the words of the Lord, spoken to me on the tenth day of the tenth month in the

2 ninth year: Man, write down a name for this day, this very day: This is the day the king of Babylon

3 invested Jerusalem. Sing a song of derision to this people of rebels;

---

[a] Prob. rdg.; *Heb.* You.
[b] Or dash.

say to them, These are the words
of the Lord GOD:

Set a cauldron on the fire,
set it on and pour water into it.

4 Into it collect the pieces,
all the choice pieces,
cram it with leg and shoulder and
the best of the bones;

5 take the best of the flock.
Pack the logs[a] round it underneath;
seethe the stew
and boil the bones in it.

6 O city running with blood,
O pot green with corrosion,
corrosion that will never be clean!

Therefore these are the words of
the Lord GOD:

Empty it, piece after piece,
though no lot is cast for any of
them.

7 The city had blood in her midst
and she poured it out on the
gleaming rock,
not on the ground: she did not pour
it there
for the dust to cover it.

8 But I too have spilt blood on the
gleaming white rock
so that it cannot be covered,
to make anger flare up and to call
down vengeance.

9 Therefore these are the words of
the Lord GOD:

O city running with blood,
I too will make a great fire-pit.

10 Fill it with logs, light the fire;
make an end of the meat,
pour out all the broth[b] and the
bones with it.[c]

11 Then set the pot empty on the coals
so that its copper may be heated
red-hot,
and then the impurities in it may
be melted
and its corrosion burnt off.

Try as you may,[d]   12
the corrosion is so deep that it will
not come off;
only fire will rid it of corrosion for
you.
Even so, when I cleansed you in   13
your filthy lewdness,
you did not become clean from it,
and therefore you shall never again
be clean
until I have satisfied my anger
against you.

I, the LORD, have spoken; the   14
time is coming, I will act. I will not
refrain nor pity nor relent; I will
judge you for your conduct and
for all that you have done. This is
the very word of the Lord GOD.

These were the words of the   15
LORD to me: Man, I am taking   16
from you at one blow the dearest
thing you have, but you must not
wail or weep or give way to tears.
Keep in good heart; be quiet, and   17
make no mourning for the dead;
cover your head as usual and put
sandals on your feet. You shall not
cover your upper lip in mourning
nor eat the bread of despair.

I spoke to the people in the   18
morning; and that very evening
my wife died. Next morning I did
as I was told. The people asked me   19
to say what meaning my behaviour
had for them. I answered, These   20
were the words of the LORD to me:
Tell the Israelites, This is the word   21
of the Lord GOD: I will desecrate
my sanctuary, which has been the
pride of your strength, the delight
of your eyes and your heart's
desire; and the sons and daughters
whom you have left behind shall
fall by the sword. But, I said, you   22
shall do as I have done: you shall
not cover your upper lip in mourning nor eat the bread of despair.
You shall cover your head and put   23
sandals on your feet; you shall not
wail nor weep. Because of your

---

[a] *Prob. rdg., cp. verse 10; Heb.* bones.
[b] pour...broth: *prob. rdg.; Heb.* mix ointment.   [c] with it: *prob. rdg.; Heb.*
will be scorched.   [d] Try as you may: *prob. rdg.; Heb. obscure.*

wickedness you will pine away and
24 will lament to^a one another. The
LORD says, Ezekiel will be a sign to
warn you, and when it happens
you will do as he has done, and you
will know that I am the Lord GOD.
25 And now, man, a word for you:
I am taking from them that fortress
whose beauty so gladdened them,
the delight of their eyes, their
heart's desire; I am taking their
26 sons and their daughters. Soon
fugitives will come and tell you
27 their news by word of mouth. At
once you will recover the power of
speech and speak with the fugitives; you will no longer be dumb.
So will you be a portent to them,
and they shall know that I am the
LORD.

Prophecies against foreign nations

25 THESE were the words of the
2 LORD to me: Man, look towards
the Ammonites and prophesy a-
3 gainst them. Say to the Ammonites, Listen to the word of the
Lord GOD. These are his words:
Because you cried 'Aha!' when you
saw my holy place desecrated, the
soil of Israel laid waste and the
people of Judah sent into exile,
4 I will hand you over as a possession
to the tribes of the east. They shall
pitch their camps and put up their
dwellings among you; they shall
eat your crops; they shall drink
5 your milk. I will make Rabbah a
camel-pasture and Ammon a sheep-
walk. Thus you shall know that I
6 am the LORD. These are the words
of the Lord GOD: Because you
clapped your hands and stamped
your feet, and exulted over the
land of Israel with single-minded
7 scorn, I will stretch out my hand
over you and make you the prey of
the nations and cut you off from all
other peoples; in every land I will
exterminate you and bring you to
utter ruin. Thus you shall know
that I am the LORD.

These are the words of the Lord 8
GOD: Because Moab said, 'Judah
is like all the rest', I will expose the 9
flank of Moab and lay open its
cities,^b from one end to the other –
the fairest of its cities: Beth-jeshimoth, Baal-meon and Kiriathaim.
I will hand over Moab and Ammon 10
together to the tribes of the east to
be their possession, so that the
Ammonites shall not be remembered among the nations, and so 11
that I may execute judgement upon Moab. Thus they shall know that
I am the LORD.

These are the words of the Lord 12
GOD: Because Edom took deliberate revenge on Judah and by so
doing incurred lasting guilt, I will 13
stretch my hand out over Edom,
says the Lord GOD, and destroy
both man and beast in it, laying
waste the land from Teman as far
as Dedan; they shall fall by the
sword. I will wreak my vengeance 14
upon Edom through my people
Israel. They will deal with Edom
as my anger and fury demand,
and it shall feel my vengeance.
This is the very word of the Lord
GOD.

These are the words of the Lord 15
GOD: Because the Philistines have
taken deliberate revenge and have
avenged themselves with single-
minded scorn, giving vent to their
age-long enmity in destruction, I 16
will stretch out my hand over the
Philistines, says the Lord GOD, I
will wipe out the Kerethites and
destroy all the rest of the dwellers
by the sea. I will take fearful ven- 17
geance upon them and punish them
in my fury. When I take my vengeance, they shall know that I am
the LORD.

These were the words of the 26
LORD to me on the first day of the

---

^a Or for.   ^b and lay...cities: *prob. rdg.*; *Heb.* from the cities, from its cities.

first month in the eleventh year:

2 Man, Tyre has said of Jerusalem,

Aha! she that was the gateway of
  the nations
is broken,
her gates swing open to me;
I grow rich, she lies in ruins.

3 Therefore these are the words of
  the Lord GOD:

I am against you, Tyre,
and will bring up many nations
  against you
as the sea brings up its waves;
4 they will destroy the walls of Tyre
  and pull down her towers.
I will scrape the soil off her
and make her a gleaming rock,
5 she shall be an islet where men
  spread their nets;
I have spoken, says the Lord GOD.
She shall become the prey of
  nations,
6 and her daughters[a] shall be slain
  by the sword in the open country.

Thus they shall know that I am the
  LORD.

7 These are the words of the Lord
GOD: I am bringing against Tyre
from the north Nebuchadrezzar
king of Babylon, king of kings. He
will come with horses and chariots,
with cavalry and a great army.

8 Your daughters in the open country
he will put to the sword.
He will set up watch-towers
  against you,
pile up siege-ramps against you
and raise against you a screen of
  shields.
9 He will launch his battering-rams
  on your walls
and break down your towers with
  his axes.
10 He will cover you with dust from
  the thousands of his cavalry;
at the thunder of his horses
and of his chariot-wheels

your walls will quake when he
  enters your gates
as men enter a city that is breached.
He will trample all your streets   11
with the hooves of his horses
and put your people to the
  sword,
and your strong pillars will fall of
  the ground.
Your wealth will become spoil,   12
your merchandise will be plundered,
your walls levelled,
your pleasant houses pulled down,
your stones, your timber and your
  rubble
will be dumped into the sea.
So I will silence the clamour of   13
  your songs,
and the sound of your harps shall
  be heard no more.
I will make you a gleaming   14
  rock,
a place for fishermen to spread
  their nets,
and you shall never be rebuilt.
I, the LORD, have spoken.
This is the very word of the Lord
  GOD.

These are the words of the Lord   15
GOD to Tyre: How the coasts and
islands will shake at the sound of
your downfall, while the wounded
groan, and the slaughter goes on in
your midst! Then all the sea-kings   16
will come down from their thrones,
and lay aside their cloaks, and
strip off their brocaded robes. They
will wear coarse loin-cloths; they
will sit on the ground, shuddering
at every moment, horror-struck at
your fate. Then they will raise this   17
dirge over you:

How you are undone, swept from
  the sea,
O famous city!
You whose strength lay in the sea,
you and your inhabitants,
who spread their terror throughout the mainland.[b]

[a] Or daughter-towns.
[b] the mainland: *prob. rdg.*; *Heb.* her inhabitants.

18 Now the coast-lands tremble on
the day of your downfall,
and the isles of the sea are appalled
at your passing.

19   For these are the words of the
Lord GOD: When I make you a
desolate city, like a city where no
man can live, when I bring up the
primeval ocean against you and
20 the great waters cover you, I will
thrust you down with those that
descend to the abyss, to the dead
of all the ages. I will make you
dwell in the underworld as in
places long desolate, with those
that go down to the abyss. So you
will never again be inhabited or
take your place in the land of the
21 living. I will bring you to a fearful
end, and you shall be no more; men
may look for you but will never
find you again. This is the very
word of the Lord GOD.

27   These were the words of the
2 LORD to me: Man, raise a dirge
3 over Tyre and say, Tyre, throned
above your harbours, you who
carry the trade of the nations to
many coasts and islands, these are
the words of the Lord GOD:

O Tyre, you said,
'I am perfect in beauty.'
4 Your frontiers are on the high seas,
your builders made your beauty
perfect;
5 they fashioned all your timbers
of pine from Senir;
they took a cedar from Lebanon
to raise up a mast over you.
6 They made your oars of oaks from
Bashan;
they made your deck strong[a] with
box-wood
from the coasts of Kittim.
7 Your canvas was linen,
patterned linen from Egypt
to make your sails;
your awnings were violet and
purple
from the coasts of Elishah.

Men of Sidon and Arvad became 8
your oarsmen;
you had skilled men within you,
O Tyre,
who served as your helmsmen.
You had skilled veterans from 9
Gebal
caulking your seams.
You had all sea-going ships and
their sailors
to market your wares;
men of Pharas,[b] Lud,[c] and Put, 10
served
as warriors in your army;
they hung shield and helmet
around you,
and it was they who gave you your
glory.
Men of Arvad and Cilicia manned 11
all your walls,
men of Gammad were posted on
your towers
and hung their shields around your
battlements;
it was they who made your beauty
perfect.

Tarshish was a source of your 12
commerce, from its abundant resources offering silver and iron, tin
and lead, as your staple wares. Ja- 13
van,[d] Tubal, and Meshech dealt
with you, offering slaves and
vessels of bronze as your imports.
Men from Togarmah offered horses, 14
mares, and mules as your staple
wares. Rhodians dealt with you, 15
great islands were a source of your
commerce, paying what was due to
you in ivory and ebony. Edom was 16
a source of your commerce, so many
were your undertakings, and offered purple garnets, brocade and fine
linen, black coral and red jasper,[e]
for your staple wares. Judah and 17
Israel dealt with you, offering
wheat from Minnith, and meal,
syrup, oil, and balsam, as your
imports. Damascus was a source of 18
your commerce, so many were your
undertakings, from its abundant
resources offering wine of Helbon

---

[a] strong: *prob. rdg.*; *Heb.* ivory.
[c] *Or* Lydia.   [d] *Or* Ionia.
[b] *Or* Persia.
[e] *Or* and carbuncles.

19 and wool of Suhar, and casks of wine from Izalla,[a] for your staple wares; wrought iron, cassia, and sweet cane were among your im-
20 ports. Dedan dealt with you in coarse woollens for saddle-cloths.
21 Arabia and all the chiefs of Kedar were the source of your commerce in lambs, rams, and he-goats; this
22 was your trade with them. Dealers from Sheba and Raamah dealt with you, offering the choicest spices, every kind of precious stone and gold, as your staple wares.
23 Harran, Kanneh, and Eden, dealers from Asshur and all Media,
24 dealt with you; they were your dealers in gorgeous stuffs, violet cloths and brocades, in stores of coloured fabric rolled up and tied with cords; your dealings with them were in these.

25 Ships of Tarshish were the caravans for your imports;
you were deeply laden with full cargoes
on the high seas.
26 Your oarsmen brought you into many waters,
but on the high seas an east wind wrecked you.
27 Your wealth, your staple wares, your imports,
your sailors and your helmsmen,
your caulkers, your merchants, and your warriors,
all your ship's company,
all who were with you,
were flung into the sea on the day of your disaster;
28 at the cries of your helmsmen the troubled waters tossed.

29 When all the rowers disembark from their ships,
when the sailors, the helmsmen all together, go ashore,
30 they exclaim over your fate,
they cry out bitterly;
they throw dust on their heads
and sprinkle themselves with ashes.

31 They tear out their hair at your plight
and put on sackcloth;
they weep bitterly over you,
bitterly wailing.
32 In their lamentation they raise a dirge over you,
and this is their dirge:
Who was like Tyre,
with her buildings piled[b] off shore?
33 When your wares were unloaded off the sea
you met the needs of many nations;
with your vast resources and your imports
you enriched the kings of the earth.
34 Now you are broken by the sea in deep water;
your wares and all your company are gone overboard.
35 All who dwell on the coasts and islands
are aghast at your fate;
horror is written on the faces of their kings
and their hair stands on end.
36 Among the nations the merchants jeer in derision at you;
you have come to a fearful end and shall be no more for ever.

28 These were the words of the LORD to me: Man, say to the prince 2 of Tyre, This is the word of the Lord GOD:

In your arrogance you say,
'I am a god;
I sit throned like a god on the high seas.'
Though you are a man and no god,
you try to think the thoughts of a god.
3 What? are you wiser than Danel[c]?
Is no secret too dark for you?
4 Clever and shrewd as you are,
you have amassed wealth for yourself,
you have amassed gold and silver in your treasuries;

---

[a] casks . . . Izalla: *prob. rdg.*; *Heb. obscure.*
prob. rdg.; *Heb. obscure.*   [b] with her buildings piled: *prob. rdg.*; *Heb. obscure.*   [c] Or, *as otherwise read,* Daniel; *cp. 14. 14, 20.*

5 by great cleverness in your trading
you have heaped up riches,
and with your riches your arrogance has grown.

6 Therefore these are the words of
the Lord GOD:

Because you try to think the
thoughts of a god
7 I will bring strangers against you,
the most ruthless of nations,
who will draw their swords against
your fine wisdom
and lay your pride in the dust,
8 sending you down to the pit[a] to die
a death of disgrace on the high
seas.
9 Will you dare to say that you are a
god
when you face your assailants,
though you are a man and no god
in the hands of those who lay you
low?
10 You will die strengthless
at the hands of strangers.

For I have spoken. This is the very
word of the Lord GOD.

11 These were the words of the
12 LORD to me: Man, raise this dirge
over the king of Tyre, and say to
him, This is the word of the Lord
GOD:

You set the seal on perfection;
full of wisdom you were and altogether beautiful.
13 You were in an Eden, a garden of
God,
adorned with gems of every kind:
sardin and chrysolite and jade,
topaz, cornelian and green jasper,
lapis lazuli,[b] purple garnet and
green felspar.
Your jingling beads were of gold,
and the spangles you wore were
made for you
on the day of your birth.
14 I set you with a towering cherub[c]
as guardian;
you were on God's holy hill

and you walked proudly among
stones that flashed with fire.
You were blameless in all your 15
ways
from the day of your birth
until your iniquity came to light.
Your commerce grew so great, 16
lawlessness filled your heart and
you went wrong,
so I brought you down in disgrace
from the mountain of God,
and the guardian cherub banished
you[d]
from among the stones that flashed
like fire.
Your beauty made you arrogant, 17
you misused your wisdom to increase your dignity.
I flung you to the ground,
I left you there, a sight for kings to
see.
So great was your sin in your 18
wicked trading
that you desecrated your sanctuaries.
So I kindled a fire within you,
and it devoured you.
I left you as ashes on the ground
for all to see.
All among the nations who knew 19
you were aghast:
you came to a fearful end and shall
be no more for ever.

These were the words of the 20
LORD to me: Man, look towards 21
Sidon and prophesy against her.
These are the words of the Lord 22
GOD:

Sidon, I am against you
and I will show my glory in your
midst.

Men will know that I am the LORD
when I execute judgement upon
her
and thereby prove my holiness.
I will let loose pestilence upon her 23
and bloodshed in her streets;
the slain will fall in her streets,

---

[a] Or to destruction.   [b] Or sapphire.
[c] I set...cherub: *prob. rdg.*; *Heb.* You were a towering cherub whom I set.
[d] and the...you: *or* and I parted you, O guardian cherub,...

beset on all sides by the sword;
then men will know that I am the
LORD.

24 No longer shall the Israelites
suffer from the scorn of their neighbours, the pricking of briars and
scratching of thorns, and they shall
know that I am the Lord GOD.

25 These are the words of the Lord
GOD: When I gather the Israelites
from the peoples among whom
they are scattered, I shall thereby
prove my holiness in the sight of all
nations. They shall live on their
native soil, which I gave to my

26 servant Jacob. They shall live
there in peace of mind, build
houses and plant vineyards; they
shall live there in peace of mind
when I execute judgement on all
their scornful neighbours. Thus
they shall know that I am the
LORD their God.

29 These were the words of the
LORD to me on the twelfth day of
the tenth month in the tenth year:

2 Man, look towards Pharaoh king
of Egypt and prophesy against him

3 and all his country. Say, These are
the words of the Lord GOD:

I am against you,
Pharaoh king of Egypt,
you great monster,
lurking in the streams of the Nile.
You have said, 'My Nile is my own;
it was I who made it.'

4 I will put hooks in your jaws
and make them cling[a] to your
scales.
I will hoist you out of its streams
with all its fish clinging to your
scales.

5 I will fling you into the wilderness,
you and all the fish in your
streams;
you will fall on the bare ground
with none to pick you up and bury
you;
I will make you food
for beasts and for birds.

So all who live in Egypt will know 6
that I am the LORD,
for the support that you gave to the
Israelites
was no better than a reed,
which splintered in the hand when 7
they grasped you,
and tore their armpits;
when they leaned upon you, you
snapped
and their limbs gave way.

This therefore is the word of the 8
Lord GOD: I am bringing a sword
upon you to destroy both man and
beast. The land of Egypt shall be- 9
come a desolate waste, and they
shall know that I am the LORD,
because you said, 'The Nile is
mine; it was I who made it.' I am 10
against you therefore, you and
your Nile, and I will make Egypt
desolate, wasted by drought, from
Migdol to Syene and up to the very
frontier of Cush. No foot of man 11
shall pass through it, no foot of
beast; it shall lie uninhabited for
forty years. I will make the land of 12
Egypt the most desolate of desolate lands; her cities shall lie
derelict among the ruined cities.
For forty years shall they lie derelict, and I will scatter the Egyptians among the nations and disperse them among the lands.

These are the words of the Lord 13
GOD: At the end of forty years I
will gather the Egyptians from the
peoples among whom they are
scattered. I will turn the fortunes of 14
Egypt and bring them back to
Pathros, the land of their origin,
where they shall become a petty
kingdom. She shall be the most 15
paltry of kingdoms and never again
exalt herself over the nations, for I
will make the Egyptians too few to
rule over them. The Israelites will 16
never trust Egypt again; this will
be a reminder to them of their sin
in turning to Egypt for help. They
shall know that I am the Lord
GOD.

---

[a] make them cling: *prob. rdg.*; *Heb.* make the fish of your streams cling.

17 These were the words of the LORD to me on the first day of the first month in the twenty-seventh
18 year: Man, long did Nebuchadrezzar king of Babylon keep his army in the field against Tyre, until every head was rubbed bare and every shoulder chafed. But neither he nor his army gained anything from Tyre for their long ser-
19 vice against her. This, therefore, is the word of the Lord GOD: I am giving the land of Egypt to Nebuchadrezzar king of Babylon. He shall carry off its wealth, he shall spoil and plunder it, and so his
20 army will be paid. I have given him the land of Egypt as the wages for his service because they have disregarded me. This is the very word of the Lord GOD.

21 At that time I will make Israel put out fresh shoots, and give you back the power to speak among them, and they will know that I am the LORD.

30 These were the words of the
2 LORD to me: Man, prophesy and say, These are the words of the Lord GOD:

Woe, woe for the day!
3 for a day is near,
a day of the LORD is near,
a day of cloud, a day of reckoning for the nations.
4 Then a sword will come upon Egypt,
and there will be anguish in Cush,
when the slain fall in Egypt,
when its wealth is taken and its foundations are torn up.
5 Cush and Put and Lud,[a]
all the Arabs and Libyans and the peoples of allied lands,
shall fall with them by the sword.

6 These are the words of the LORD:

All who support Egypt shall fall
and her boasted might be brought low;

from Migdol to Syene men shall fall by the sword.
This is the very word of the Lord GOD.

They shall be the most desolate 7 of desolate lands, and their cities shall lie derelict among the ruined cities. When I set Egypt on fire 8 and all her helpers are broken, they will know that I am the LORD. When that time comes messengers 9 shall go out in haste from my presence to alarm Cush, still without a care, and anguish shall come upon her in Egypt's hour. Even now it is on the way.

These are the words of the Lord 10 GOD:

I will make an end of Egypt's hordes
by the hands of Nebuchadrezzar king of Babylon.
He and his people with him, the 11 most ruthless of nations,
will be brought to ravage the land.
They will draw their swords against Egypt
and fill the land with the slain.
I will make the streams of the Nile 12 dry land
and sell Egypt to evil men;
I will lay waste the land and everything in it by foreign hands.
I, the LORD, have spoken.

These are the words of the Lord 13 GOD:

I will make an end of the lordlings[b]
and wipe out the princelings[c] of Noph;
and never again shall a prince arise in Egypt.
Then I will put fear in that land,
I will lay Pathros waste and set fire 14 to Zoan
and execute judgement on No.
I will pour out my rage upon Sin, 15 the bastion of Egypt,
and destroy the horde of Noph.
I will set Egypt on fire, 16
and Syene shall writhe in anguish;

[a] *Or Lydia.*   [b] *Or idols.*   [c] *Or false gods.*

the walls of No shall be breached
and flood-waters shall burst into it.
17 The young men of On and Pi-
beseth[a] shall fall by the sword
and the cities themselves go into
captivity.
18 Daylight shall fail in Tahpanhes
when I break the yoke of Egypt
there;
then her boasted might shall be
subdued;
a cloud shall cover her,
and her daughters[b] shall go into
captivity.
19 Thus I will execute judgement on
Egypt,
and they shall know that I am the
LORD.

20　　This was the word of the LORD
to me on the seventh day of the
first month in the eleventh year:
21 Man, I have broken the arm of
Pharaoh king of Egypt. See, it has
not been bound up with dressings
and bandage to give it strength to
22 wield a sword. These, therefore,
are the words of the Lord GOD: I am
against Pharaoh king of Egypt; I
will break both his arms, the sound
and the broken, and make the
23 sword drop from his hand. I will
scatter the Egyptians among the
nations and disperse them over
24 many lands. Then I will strengthen
the arms of the king of Babylon and
put my sword in his hand; but I
will break Pharaoh's arms, and he
shall lie wounded and groaning
25 before him. I will give strength to
the arms of the king of Babylon,
but the arms of Pharaoh will fall.
Men will know that I am the LORD,
when I put my sword in the hand
of the king of Babylon, and he
stretches it out over the land of
26 Egypt. I will scatter the Egyptians
among the nations and disperse
them over many lands, and they
shall know that I am the LORD.

31　　On the first day of the third
month in the eleventh year this
word came to me from the LORD:

Man, say to Pharaoh king of 2
Egypt and all his horde:

What are you like in your greatness?

Look at Assyria: it was a cedar in 3
Lebanon,
whose fair branches overshadowed
the forest,
towering high with its crown
finding a way through the foliage.
Springs nourished it, underground 4
waters gave it height,
their streams washed the soil all
round it
and sent forth their rills to every
tree in the country.
So it grew taller than every other 5
tree.
Its boughs were many, its branches
spread far;
for water was abundant in the
channels.
In its boughs all the birds of the air 6
had their nests,
under its branches all wild creatures bore their young,
and in its shadow all great nations
made their home.
A splendid great tree it was, with 7
its long spreading boughs,
for its roots were beside abundant
waters.
No cedar in God's garden over- 8
shadowed it,
no fir could compare with its
boughs,
and no plane-tree had such
branches;
not a tree in God's garden
could rival its beauty.
I, the LORD, gave it beauty 9
with its mass of spreading boughs,
the envy of all the trees in Eden,
the garden of God.

Therefore these are the words of 10
the Lord GOD: Because it grew so
high and pushed its crown up
through the foliage, and its pride
mounted as it grew, therefore I 11
handed it over to a prince of the

---

[a] *Or* Bubastis.　　[b] *Or* daughter-towns.

nations to deal with it; I made an example of it as its wickedness de-
12 served. Strangers from the most ruthless of nations hewed it down and flung it away. Its sweeping boughs fell on the mountains and in all the valleys, and its branches lay broken beside all the streams in the land. All nations of the earth came out from under its shade and
13 left it. All the birds of the air settled on its fallen trunk; the wild creatures all stood by its branches.
14 Never again, therefore, shall the well-watered trees grow so high or push their crowns up through the foliage. Nor shall the strongest of them, well watered though they be, stand erect in their full height; for all have been given over to death, to the world below, to share the common doom and go down to the abyss.
15 These are the words of the Lord GOD: When he went down to Sheol, I closed the deep over him as a gate, I dammed its rivers, the great waters were held back. I put Lebanon in mourning for him, and all the trees of the country-side
16 wilted. I made nations shake with the crash of his fall, when I brought him down to Sheol with those who go down to the abyss. From this all the trees of Eden, all the choicest and best of Lebanon, all the well-watered trees, drew comfort in the
17 world below. They too like him had gone down to Sheol, to those slain with the sword; and those who had lived in his shadow were scattered
18 among the nations. Which among the trees of Eden was like you in glory and greatness? Yet you will be brought down with the trees of Eden to the world below; you will lie with those who have been slain by the sword, in the company of the strengthless dead. This stands for Pharaoh and all his horde. This is the very word of the Lord GOD.

On the first day of the twelfth 32 month in the twelfth year the word of the LORD came to me: Man, raise 2 a dirge over Pharaoh king of Egypt and say to him:

Young lion of the nations, you are undone.
You were like a monster in the waters of the Nile
scattering the water with its snout,[a] [b]
churning the water with its feet and fouling the streams.

These are the words of the Lord 3 GOD: When many nations are gathered together I will spread my net over you, and you will be dragged up in its meshes. I will 4 fling you on land, dashing you down on the bare ground. I will let all the birds of the air settle upon you and all the wild beasts gorge themselves on your flesh. Your flesh 5 I will lay on the mountains, and fill the valleys with the worms that feed on it. I will drench the land 6 with your discharge, drench it with your blood to the very mountain-tops, and the watercourses shall be full of you. When I put out 7 your light I will veil the sky and blacken its stars; I will veil the sun with a cloud, and the moon shall not give its light. I will darken all 8 the shining lights of the sky above you and bring darkness over your land. This is the very word of the Lord GOD.

I will disquiet many peoples 9 when I bring your broken army among the nations into lands you have never known. I will appal 10 many peoples with your fate; when I brandish my sword in the faces of their kings, their hair shall stand on end. In the day of your downfall each shall tremble for his own fate from moment to moment. For 11 these are the words of the Lord GOD: The sword of the king of

---

[a] snout: *prob. rdg.*; *Heb.* streams.
[b] scattering...snout: *or* heaving itself up in the streams.

12 Babylon shall come upon you. I will make the whole horde of you fall by the sword of warriors who are of all men the most ruthless. They shall make havoc of the pride of Egypt, and all its horde shall be 13 wiped out. I will destroy all their cattle beside many waters. No foot of man, no hoof of beast, shall ever 14 churn them up again. Then will I let their waters settle and their streams run smooth as oil. This is the very word of the Lord GOD. 15 When I have laid Egypt waste, and the whole land is devastated, when I strike down all who dwell there, they shall know that I am the LORD.

16 This is a dirge, and the women of the nations shall sing it as a dirge. They shall sing it as a dirge, as a dirge over Egypt and all its horde. This is the very word of the Lord GOD.

17 On the fifteenth day of the first month in the twelfth year, the word of the LORD came to me:

18 Man, raise a lament, you and the daughters of the nations,
over the hordes of Egypt and her nobles,
whom I will bring down[a] to the world below
with those that go down to the abyss.

19 Are you better favoured than others?
Go down and be laid to rest with the strengthless dead.

20 A sword stands ready. Those who marched with her, and all her horde, shall fall into the midst of 21 those slain by the sword. Warrior chieftains in Sheol speak to Pharaoh and those who aided him:
The strengthless dead, slain by the sword, have come down and 22 are laid to rest. There is Assyria

with all her company, her buried around her, all of them slain and fallen by the sword. Her graves are 23 set in the recesses of the abyss, with her company buried around her, all of them slain, fallen by the sword, men who once filled the land of the living with terror. There is 24 Elam, with all her hordes buried around her, all of them slain, fallen by the sword; they have gone down strengthless to the world below, men who struck terror into the land of the living but now share the disgrace of those that go down to the abyss. In the midst of the slain 25 a resting-place has been made for her, with all her hordes buried a-round her; all of them strength-less, slain by the sword. For they who once struck terror into the land of the living now share the disgrace of those that go down to the abyss; they are assigned a place in the midst of the slain. There are Meshech and Tubal with 26 all their hordes, with their buried around them, all of them strength-less and slain by the sword, men who once struck terror into the land of the living. Do they not rest 27 with warriors fallen strengthless,[b] who have gone down to Sheol with their weapons, their swords under their heads and their shields over their bones,[c] though the terror of their prowess once lay on the land of the living? You also, Pharaoh, 28 shall lie broken in the company of the strengthless dead, resting with those slain by the sword. There is 29 Edom, her kings and all her princes, who, for all their prowess, have been lodged with those slain by the sword; they shall rest with the strengthless dead and with those that go down to the abyss. There are all the princes of the 30 North and all the Sidonians, who have gone down in shame with the slain, for all the terror they

---

[a] her nobles...down: *prob. rdg.*; *Heb. obscure.*
[b] *Prob. rdg.*; *Heb.* from strengthless ones.
[c] and...bones: *prob. rdg.*; *Heb. unintelligible.*

inspired by their prowess. They rest strengthless with those slain by the sword, and they share the disgrace of those that go down to the abyss.

31 Pharaoh will see them and will take comfort for his lost hordes – Pharaoh who, with all his army, is slain by the sword, says the Lord

32 GOD; though he spread*ᵃ* terror throughout the land of the living, yet he with all his horde is laid to rest with those that are slain by the sword, in the company of the strengthless dead. This is the very word of the Lord GOD.

The remnant of Israel in the land

33 THESE were the words of the

2 LORD to me: Man, say to your fellow-countrymen, When I set armies in motion against a land, its people choose one of them-

3 selves to be a watchman. When he sees the enemy approaching and blows his trumpet to warn the

4 people, then if anyone does not heed the warning and is overtaken by the enemy, he is responsible for

5 his own fate. He is responsible because, when he heard the alarm, he paid no heed to it; if he had heeded

6 it, he would have escaped. But if the watchman does not blow his trumpet or warn the people when he sees the enemy approaching, then any man who is killed is caught with all his sins upon him; but I will hold the watchman answerable for his death.

7 Man, I have appointed you a watchman for the Israelites. You will take messages from me and

8 carry my warnings to them. It may be that I pronounce sentence of death on a man because he is wicked; if you do not warn him to give up his ways, the guilt is his and because of his wickedness he shall die, but I will hold you an-

9 swerable for his death. But if you have warned him to give up his ways, and he has not given them up, he will die because of his wickedness, but you will have saved yourself.

10 Man, say to the Israelites, You complain, 'We are burdened by our sins and offences; we are pining away because of them; we despair of life.' So tell them: As I live, says

11 the Lord GOD, I have no desire for the death of the wicked. I would rather that a wicked man should mend his ways and live. Give up your evil ways, give them up; O Israelites, why should you die?

12 Man, say to your fellow-countrymen, When a righteous man goes wrong, his righteousness shall not save him. When a wicked man mends his ways, his former wickedness shall not bring him down. When a righteous man sins, all his righteousness cannot save his life.

13 It may be that, when I tell the righteous man that he will save his life, he presumes on his righteousness and does wrong; then none of his righteous acts will be remembered: he will die for the wrong he

14 has done. It may be that when I pronounce sentence of death on the wicked, he mends his ways and

15 does what is just and right: if he then restores the pledges he has taken, repays what he has stolen, and, doing no more wrong, follows the rules that ensure life, he shall

16 live and not die. None of the sins he has committed shall be remembered against him; he shall live, because he does what is just and right.

17 Your fellow-countrymen are saying, 'The Lord acts without principle', but it is their ways that

18 are unprincipled. When a righteous man gives up his righteousness and does wrong, he shall die

19 because of it; and when a wicked man gives up his wickedness and does what is just and right, he shall

20 live. How, Israel, can you say that the Lord acts without principle,

---

ᵃ Prob. rdg.; Heb. I have spread.

when I judge every man of you on his deeds?

21 On the fifth day of the tenth month in the twelfth year of our captivity, fugitives came to me from Jerusalem and told me that 22 the city had fallen. The evening before they arrived, the hand of the LORD had come upon me, and by the time they reached me in the morning the LORD had given me back my speech. My speech was restored and I was no longer dumb.

23 These were the words of the 24 LORD to me: Man, the inhabitants of these wastes on the soil of Israel say, 'When Abraham took possession of the land he was but one; now we are many, and the land has been granted to us in possession.' 25 Tell them, therefore, that these are the words of the Lord GOD: You eat meat with the blood in it, you lift up your eyes to idols, you shed[a] blood; and yet you expect to 26 possess the land! You trust to the sword, you commit abominations, you defile one another's wives; and you expect to possess the land! 27 Tell them that these are the words of the Lord GOD: As I live, among the ruins they shall fall by the sword; in the open country I will give them for food to beasts; in dens and caves they shall die by 28 pestilence. I will make the land a desolate waste; her boasted might shall be brought to nothing, and the mountains of Israel shall be an 29 untrodden desert. When I make the land a desolate waste because of all the abominations they have committed, they will know that I am the LORD.

30 Man, your fellow-countrymen gather in groups and talk of you under walls and in doorways and say to one another, 'Let us go and see what message there is from the 31 LORD.' So my people will come crowding in, as people do, and sit down in front of you. They will hear what you have to say, but they will not do it. 'Fine words[b]!' they will say, but their hearts are set on selfish gain. You are no more 32 to them than a singer of fine songs[c] with a lovely voice, or a clever harpist; they will listen to what you say but will certainly not do it. But when it comes, as come it will, 33 they will know that there has been a prophet in their midst.

These were the words of the 34 LORD to me: Prophesy, man, a- 2 gainst the shepherds of Israel; prophesy and say to them, You shepherds, these are the words of the Lord GOD: How I hate the shepherds of Israel who care only for themselves! Should not the shepherd care for the sheep? You con- 3 sume the milk, wear the wool, and slaughter the fat beasts, but you do not feed the sheep. You have not 4 encouraged the weary, tended the sick, bandaged the hurt, recovered the straggler, or searched for the lost; and even the strong you have driven with ruthless severity. They 5 are scattered, they have no shepherd, they have become the prey of wild beasts. My sheep go stray- 6 ing over the mountains and on every high hill, my flock is dispersed over the whole country, with no one to ask after them or search for them.

Therefore, you shepherds, hear 7 the words of the LORD. As surely 8 as I live, says the Lord GOD, because my sheep are ravaged by wild beasts and have become their prey for lack of a shepherd, because my shepherds have not asked after the sheep but have cared only for themselves and not for the sheep – therefore, you shep- 9 herds, hear the words of the LORD. These are the words of the Lord 10 GOD: I am against the shepherds and will demand my sheep from them. I will dismiss those shepherds: they shall care only for

---

[a] *Or* pour out.
[c] fine songs: *or* love songs.
[b] Fine words: *or* Love songs.

themselves no longer; I will rescue my sheep from their jaws, and they shall feed on them no more.

11 For these are the words of the Lord GOD: Now I myself will ask after my sheep and go in search of 12 them. As a shepherd goes in search of his sheep when his flock is dispersed all around him, so I will go in search of my sheep and rescue them, no matter where they were scattered in dark and cloudy days. 13 I will bring them out from every nation, gather them in from other lands, and lead them home to their own soil. I will graze them on the mountains of Israel, by her streams 14 and in all her green fields. I will feed them on good grazing-ground, and their pasture shall be the high mountains of Israel. There they will rest, there in good pasture, and find rich grazing on the mountains 15 of Israel. I myself will tend my flock, I myself will pen them in their 16 fold, says the Lord GOD. I will search for the lost, recover the straggler, bandage the hurt, strengthen the sick, leave the healthy and strong to play, and give them their proper food.

17 As for you, my flock, these are the words of the Lord GOD: I will judge between one sheep and an- 18 other. You rams and he-goats! Are you not satisfied with grazing on good herbage, that you must trample down the rest with your feet? Or with drinking clear water, that you must churn up the rest 19 with your feet? My flock has to eat what you have trampled and drink 20 what you have churned up. These, therefore, are the words of the Lord GOD to them: Now I myself will judge between the fat sheep and 21 the lean. You hustle the weary with flank and shoulder, you butt them with your horns until you have driven them away and scat- 22 tered them abroad. Therefore I will save my flock, and they shall be ravaged no more; I will judge between one sheep and another.

Then I will set over them one shep- 23 herd to take care of them, my servant David; he shall care for them and become their shepherd. I, the 24 LORD, will become their God, and my servant David shall be a prince among them. I, the LORD, have spoken. I will make a covenant 25 with them to ensure prosperity; I will rid the land of wild beasts, and men shall live in peace of mind on the open pastures and sleep in the woods. I will settle them in the 26 neighbourhood of my hill and send them rain in due season, blessed rain. Trees in the country-side shall 27 bear their fruit, the land shall yield its produce, and men shall live in peace of mind on their own soil. They shall know that I am the LORD when I break the bars of their yokes and rescue them from those who have enslaved them. They shall never be ravaged by the 28 nations again nor shall wild beasts devour them; they shall live in peace of mind, with no one to alarm them. I will give prosperity to their 29 plantations; they shall never again be victims of famine in the land nor any longer bear the taunts of the nations. They shall know that I, 30 the LORD their God, am with them, and that they are my people Israel, says the Lord GOD. You are my 31 flock, my people, the flock I feed, and I am your God. This is the very word of the Lord GOD.

These were the words of the 35 LORD to me: Man, look towards the 2 hill-country of Seir and prophesy against it. Say, These are the words 3 of the Lord GOD:

O hill-country of Seir, I am against you:
I will stretch out my hand over you and make you a desolate waste.
I will lay your cities in ruins 4
and you shall be made desolate;
thus you shall know that I am the LORD.
For you have maintained an im- 5
memorial feud

and handed over the Israelites to
the sword
in the hour of their doom,
at the time of their final punishment.

6 Therefore, as I live, says the Lord
GOD,
I make blood your destiny, and
blood shall pursue you;
you are most surely guilty of
blood,
and blood shall pursue you.
7 I will make the hill-country of Seir
a desolate waste
and put an end to all in it who pass
to and fro;
8 I will fill your hills and your valleys with its slain,
and those slain by the sword shall
fall into your streams.
9 I will make you desolate for ever,
and your cities shall not be inhabited;
thus you shall know that I am the
LORD.

10   You say, The two nations and
the two countries shall be mine
and I will take possession of them,
11 though the LORD is[a] there. Therefore, as I live, says the Lord GOD,
your anger and jealousy shall be
requited, for I will do to you what
you have done in your hatred
against them. I shall be known
12 among you when I judge you; you
shall know that I am the LORD. I
have heard all your blasphemies;
you have said, 'The mountains of
Israel are desolate and have been
13 given to us to devour.' You have
set yourselves up against me and
spoken recklessly against me. I
14 myself have heard you. These are
the words of the Lord GOD: I will
make you so desolate that the
15 whole world will gloat over you. I
will do to you as you did to Israel
my own possession when you
gloated over its desolation. O hill-
country of Seir, you will be desolate, and it will be the end of all

Edom. Thus men will know that I
am the LORD.
And do you, man, prophesy to 36
the mountains of Israel and say,
Mountains of Israel, hear the words
of the LORD. These are the words 2
of the Lord GOD: The enemy has
said, 'Aha! now the everlasting
highlands are ours.' Therefore pro- 3
phesy and say, These are the words
of the Lord GOD: You mountains
of Israel, all round you men gloated over you and trampled you
down when you were seized and
occupied by the rest of the nations; your name was bandied
about in the common talk of men.
Therefore, listen to the words of 4
the Lord GOD when he speaks to
the mountains and hills, to the
streams and valleys, to the desolate palaces and deserted cities, all
plundered and despised by the
rest of the nations round you.
These are the words of the Lord 5
GOD: In the fire of my jealousy I
have spoken plainly against the
rest of the nations, and against
Edom above all. For Edom, swollen with triumphant scorn, seized
on my land to hold it up to public
contempt. Therefore prophesy over 6
the soil of Israel and say to the
mountains and hills, the streams
and valleys, These are the words
of the Lord GOD: I have spoken
my mind in jealousy and anger because you have had to endure the
taunts of all nations. Therefore, 7
says the Lord GOD, I have sworn
with uplifted hand that the nations round about shall be punished for[b] their taunts. But you, 8
mountains of Israel, you shall put
forth your branches and yield your
fruit for my people Israel, for their
home-coming is near. See now, I 9
am for you, I will turn to you, and
you shall be tilled and sown. I will 10
plant many men upon you – the
whole house of Israel. The cities
shall again be inhabited and the
palaces rebuilt. I will plant many 11

_____

[a] Or has been.   [b] be punished for: or bear.

men and beasts upon you; they shall increase and be fruitful. I will make you populous as in days of old and more prosperous than you were at first. Thus you will 12 know that I am the LORD. I will make men – my people Israel – tread your paths again. They shall settle in you, and you shall be their possession; but you shall never again rob them of their children.

13 These are the words of the Lord GOD: People say that you are a land that devours men and robs 14 your tribes of their children. But you shall never devour men any more nor rob your tribes of their 15 children, says the Lord GOD. I will never let you hear the taunts of the nations again nor shall you have to endure the reproaches of the peoples. This is the very word of the Lord GOD.

16 These were the words of the 17 LORD to me: Man, when the Israelites lived on their own soil they defiled it with their ways and deeds; their ways were foul and 18 disgusting in my sight. I poured out my fury upon them because of the blood they had poured out upon the land, and the idols with 19 which they had defiled it. I scattered them among the nations, and they were dispersed among different countries; I passed on them the sentence which their ways and 20 deeds deserved. When they came among those nations, they caused my holy name to be profaned wherever they came: men said of them, 'These are the people of the LORD, and it is from his land that 21 they have come.' And I spared them for the sake of my holy name which the Israelites had profaned among the nations to whom they had gone.

22 Therefore tell the Israelites that these are the words of the Lord GOD: It is not for your sake, you Israelites, that I am acting, but for the sake of my holy name, which you have profaned among the peoples where you have gone. I 23 will hallow my great name, which has been profaned among those nations. When they see that I reveal my holiness through you, the nations will know that I am the LORD, says the Lord GOD. I will 24 take you out of the nations and gather you from every land and bring you to your own soil. I will 25 sprinkle clean water over you, and you shall be cleansed from all that defiles you; I will cleanse you from the taint of all your idols. I will 26 give you a new heart and put a new spirit within you; I will take the heart of stone from your body and give you a heart of flesh. I will 27 put my spirit into you and make you conform to my statutes, keep my laws and live by them. You 28 shall live in the land which I gave to your ancestors; you shall become my people, and I will become your God. I will save you 29 from all that defiles you; I will call to the corn and make it plentiful; I will bring no more famine upon you. I will make the trees bear 30 abundant fruit and the ground yield heavy crops, so that you will never again have to bear the reproach of famine among the nations. You will recall your wick- 31 ed ways and evil deeds, and you will loathe yourselves because of your wickedness and your abominations. It is not for your sake 32 that I am acting; be sure of that, says the Lord GOD. Feel, then, the shame and disgrace of your ways, men of Israel.

These are the words of the Lord 33 GOD: When I cleanse you of all your wickedness, I will re-people the cities, and the palaces shall be rebuilt. The land now desolate shall 34 be tilled, instead of lying waste for every passer-by to see. Men will 35 say that this same land which was waste has become like a garden of Eden, and people will make their homes in the cities once ruined,

wasted, and shattered, but now
36 well fortified. The nations still left
around you will know that it is I,
the LORD, who have rebuilt the
shattered cities and planted anew
the waste land; I, the LORD, have
spoken and will do it.

37   These are the words of the Lord
GOD: Yet again will I let the Israelites ask me to act in their behalf. I
will make their men numerous as
38 sheep, like the sheep offered as
holy-gifts, like the sheep in Jerusalem at times of festival. So shall
their ruined cities be filled with
human flocks, and they shall know
that I am the LORD.

37   The hand of the LORD came
upon me, and he carried me out by
his spirit and put me down in a
2 plain full of bones. He made me go
to and fro across them until I had
been round them all;[a] they covered
the plain, countless numbers of
3 them, and they were very dry. He
said to me, 'Man, can these bones
live again?' I answered, 'Only thou
4 knowest that, Lord GOD.' He said
to me, 'Prophesy over these bones
and say to them, O dry bones, hear
5 the word of the LORD. This is the
word of the Lord GOD to these
bones: I will put breath[b] into you,
6 and you shall live. I will fasten
sinews on you, bring flesh upon
you, overlay you with skin, and
put breath in you, and you shall
live; and you shall know that I am
7 the LORD.' I began to prophesy as
he had bidden me, and as I prophesied there was a rustling sound
and the bones fitted themselves
8 together. As I looked, sinews appeared upon them, flesh covered
them, and they were overlaid with
skin, but there was no breath in
9 them. Then he said to me, 'Prophesy to the wind, prophesy, man,
and say to it, These are the words
of the Lord GOD: Come, O wind,
come from every quarter and

breathe into these slain, that they
may come to life.' I began to pro- 10
phesy as he had bidden me: breath
came into them; they came to life
and rose to their feet, a mighty
host. He said to me, 'Man, these 11
bones are the whole people of Israel. They say, "Our bones are dry,
our thread of life is snapped, our
web is severed from the loom."[c]
Prophesy, therefore, and say to 12
them, These are the words of the
Lord GOD: O my people, I will
open your graves and bring you up
from them, and restore you to the
land of Israel. You shall know that 13
I am the LORD when I open your
graves and bring you up from
them, O my people. Then I will 14
put my spirit[d] into you and you
shall live, and I will settle you on
your own soil, and you shall know
that I the LORD have spoken and
will act. This is the very word of
the LORD.'

These were the words of the 15
LORD to me: Man, take one leaf of 16
a wooden tablet and write on it,
'Judah and his associates of Israel.' Then take another leaf and
write on it, 'Joseph, the leaf of
Ephraim and all his associates of
Israel.' Now bring the two to- 17
gether to form one tablet; then
they will be a folding tablet in your
hand. When your fellow-country- 18
men ask you to tell them what you
mean by this, say to them, These 19
are the words of the Lord GOD: I
am taking the leaf of Joseph,
which belongs to Ephraim and his
associate tribes of Israel, and joining[e] to it the leaf of Judah. Thus I
shall make them one tablet, and
they shall be one in my hand. The 20
leaves on which you write shall be
visible in your hand for all to see.

Then say to them, These are the 21
words of the Lord GOD: I am
gathering up the Israelites from
their places of exile among the

---

[a] He made...all: or He made me pass all round them.   [b] Or wind or spirit.
[c] our web...loom: prob. rdg.; Heb. we are completely cut off.   [d] Or breath.
[e] Prob. rdg.; Heb. adds them.

nations; I will assemble them from every quarter and restore them to 22 their own soil. I will make them one single nation in the land, on the mountains of Israel, and they shall have one king; they shall no longer be two nations or divided 23 into two kingdoms. They shall never again be defiled with their idols, their loathsome ways and all their disloyal acts; I will rescue them from all their sinful backsliding and purify them. Thus they shall become my people, and I will 24 become their God. My servant David shall become king over them, and they shall have one shepherd. They shall conform to my laws, they shall observe and carry out 25 my statutes. They shall live in the land which I gave my servant Jacob, the land where your fathers lived. They and their descendants shall live there for ever, and my servant David shall for ever be 26 their prince. I will make a covenant with them to bring them prosperity; this covenant shall be theirs for ever.*a* I will greatly increase their numbers, and I will put my sanctuary for ever in their midst. 27 They shall live under the shelter of my dwelling; I will become their God and they shall become my 28 people. The nations shall know that I the LORD am keeping Israel sacred to myself, because my sanctuary is in the midst of them for ever.

God's triumph over the world

38 THESE were the words of the 2 LORD to me: Man, look towards Gog, the prince of Rosh, Meshech, and Tubal, in the land of Magog, 3 and prophesy against him. Say, These are the words of the Lord GOD: I am against you, Gog, prince 4 of Rosh, Meshech, and Tubal. I will turn you about, I will put hooks in your jaws. I will lead you

out, you and your whole army, horses and horsemen, all fully equipped, a great host with shield and buckler, every man wielding a sword, and with them the men of 5 Pharas, Cush, and Put, all with shield and helmet; Gomer and all 6 its squadrons, Beth-togarmah with its squadrons from the far recesses of the north – a great concourse of peoples with you. Be prepared; 7 make ready, you and all the host which has gathered to join you, and hold yourselves in reserve for me.*b* After many days you will be 8 summoned; in years to come you will enter a land restored from ruin, whose people are gathered from many nations upon the mountains of Israel that have been desolate so long. The Israelites, brought out from the nations, will all be living undisturbed; and you 9 will come up, driving in like a hurricane; you will cover the land like a cloud, you and all your squadrons, a great concourse of peoples.

This is the word of the Lord 10 GOD: At that time a thought will enter your head and you will plan evil. You will say, 'I will attack a 11 land of open villages, I will fall upon a people living quiet and undisturbed, undefended by walls, with neither gates nor bars.' You 12 will expect to come plundering, spoiling, and stripping bare the ruins where men now live again, a people gathered out of the nations, a people acquiring cattle and goods, and making their home at the very centre of the world. Sheba 13 and Dedan, the traders of Tarshish and her leading merchants, will say to you, 'Is it for plunder that you have come? Have you gathered your host to get spoil, to carry off silver and gold, to seize cattle and goods, to collect rich spoil?'

Therefore, prophesy, man, and 14 say to Gog, These are the words of the Lord GOD: In that day when

---

a Prob. rdg.; Heb. adds and I will put them.
b and hold...me: or and you shall be their rallying-point.

my people Israel is living un-
15 disturbed, will you not awake and
come with many nations from
your home in the far recesses of the
north, all riding on horses, a great
16 host, a mighty army? You will
come up against my people Israel;
and in those future days you will
be like a cloud covering the earth. I
will bring you against my land,
that the nations may know me,
when they see me prove my holiness at your expense, O Gog.
17   This is the word of the Lord
GOD: When I spoke in days of old
through my servants the prophets,
who prophesied in those days unceasingly, it was you whom I
threatened to bring against Israel.
18 On that day, when at length Gog
comes against the land of Israel,
says the Lord GOD, my wrath will
19 boil over. In my jealousy and in
the heat of my anger I swear that
on that day there shall be a great
earthquake throughout the land of
20 Israel. The fish in the sea and the
birds in the air, the wild animals
and all reptiles that move on the
ground, all mankind on the face of
the earth, all shall be shaken before me. Mountains shall be torn
up, the terraced hills collapse, and
21 every wall crash to the ground. I
will summon universal terror a-
gainst Gog, says the Lord GOD,
and his men shall turn their swords
22 against one another. I will bring
him to judgement with pestilence
and bloodshed; I will pour down
teeming rain, hailstones hard as
rock, and fire and brimstone, upon
him, upon his squadrons, upon the
whole concourse of peoples with
23 him. Thus will I prove myself great
and holy and make myself known
to many nations; they shall know
that I am the LORD.
39   And you, man, prophesy against
Gog and say, These are the words
of the Lord GOD: I am against you,
Gog, prince of Rosh, Meshech, and
2 Tubal. I will turn you about and

drive you, I will fetch you up from
the far recesses of the north and
bring you to the mountains of
Israel. I will strike the bow from 3
your left hand and dash the arrows
from your right hand. There on the 4
mountains of Israel you shall fall,
you, all your squadrons, and your
allies; I will give you as food to the
birds of prey and the wild beasts.
You shall fall on the bare ground, 5
for it is I who have spoken. This
is the very word of the Lord GOD. I 6
will send fire on Magog and on those
who live undisturbed in the coasts
and islands, and they shall know
that I am the LORD. My holy name 7
I will make known in the midst of
my people Israel and will no longer
let it be profaned; the nations shall
know that in Israel I, the LORD, am
holy.
    Behold, it comes; it shall be, says 8
the Lord GOD, the day of which I
have spoken. The dwellers in the 9
cities of Israel shall come out and
gather weapons to light their fires,
buckler and shield, bow and arrows, throwing-stick and lance,
and they shall kindle fires with
them for seven years. They shall 10
take no wood from the fields nor
cut it from the forests but shall
light their fires with the weapons.
Thus they will plunder their plunderers and spoil their spoilers. This
is the very word of the Lord GOD.
    In that day I will give to Gog, 11
instead of[a] a burial-ground in Israel, the valley of Abarim east of
the Sea.[b] There they shall bury
Gog and all his horde, and all Abarim will be blocked; and they shall
call it the Valley of Gog's Horde.
For seven months the Israelites 12
shall bury them and purify the
land; all the people shall take their 13
share in the burying. The day that
I win myself honour shall be a
memorable day for them. This is
the very word of the Lord GOD.
Men shall be picked for the regular 14
duty of going through the country

_____

[a] Prob. rdg.; Heb. adds there.   [b] That is the Dead Sea.

and searching for[a] any left above ground, to purify the land; they shall begin their search at the end 15 of the seven months. They shall go through the country, and whenever one of them sees a human bone he shall put a marker beside it, until it has been buried in the 16 Valley of Gog's Horde. So no more shall be heard of that great horde,[b] and the land will be purified.

17   Man, these are the words of the Lord GOD: Cry to every bird that flies and to all the wild beasts: Come, assemble, gather from every side to my sacrifice, the great sacrifice I am making for you on the mountains of Israel; eat flesh 18 and drink blood, eat the flesh of warriors and drink the blood of princes of the earth; all these are your rams and sheep, he-goats and bulls, and buffaloes of Bashan. 19 You shall cram yourselves with fat and drink yourselves drunk on blood at the sacrifice which I am 20 preparing for you. At my table you shall eat your fill of horses and riders, of warriors and all manner of fighting men. This is the very word of the Lord GOD.

21   I will show my glory among the nations; all shall see the judgement that I execute and the heavy hand 22 that I lay upon them. From that day forwards the Israelites shall know that I am the LORD their 23 God. The nations shall know that the Israelites went into exile for their iniquity, because they were faithless to me. So I hid my face from them and handed them over to their enemies, and they fell, every one of them, by the sword. 24 I dealt with them as they deserved, defiled and rebellious as they were, and hid my face from them.

25   These, therefore, are the words of the Lord GOD: Now I will restore the fortunes of Jacob and show my affection for all Israel, and I will be jealous for my holy

name. They shall forget their 26 shame and all their unfaithfulness to me, when they are at home again on their own soil, undisturbed, with no one to alarm them. When I bring them home out of the 27 nations and gather them from the lands of their enemies, I will make them an example of my holiness, for many nations to see. They will 28 know that I am the LORD their God, because I who sent them into exile among the nations will bring them together again on the soil of their own land and leave none of them behind. No longer will I hide 29 my face from them, I who have poured out my spirit upon Israel. This is the very word of the Lord GOD.

The restored theocracy

AT the beginning of the year, on 40 the tenth day of the month, in the twenty-fifth year of our exile, that is fourteen years after the destruction of the city, on that very day, the hand of the LORD came upon me and he brought me there. In a 2 vision God brought me to the land of Israel and set me on a very high mountain, where I saw what seemed the buildings of a city facing me. He led me towards it, and I saw a 3 man like a figure of bronze holding a cord of linen thread and a measuring-rod, and standing at the gate. 'Man,' he said to me, 'look 4 closely and listen carefully; mark well all that I show you, for this is why you have been brought here. Tell the Israelites all that you see.'

Round the outside of the temple 5 ran a wall. The length of the rod which the man was holding was six cubits, reckoning by the long cubit which was one cubit and a hand's breadth. He measured the thickness and the height of the wall; each was one rod. He came to a 6 gate which faced eastwards, went

---

[a] searching for: *prob. rdg.*; *Heb.* burying those who are passing through.
[b] So...horde: *prob. rdg.*; *Heb. obscure.*

up its steps and measured the threshold of the gateway; its depth 7 was one rod. Each cell was one rod long and one rod wide; the space between the cells five cubits, and the threshold of the gateway at the end of the vestibule on the side 8 facing the temple one rod. He measured the vestibule of the gate 9 and found it eight cubits, with pilasters two cubits thick; the vestibule of the gateway lay at the end 10 near the temple. Now the cells of the gateway, looking back eastwards, were three in number on each side; all three of the same size, and their pilasters on each 11 side of the same size also. He measured the entrance into the gateway; it was ten cubits wide, and the gateway itself throughout its 12 length thirteen cubits wide. In front of the cells on each side lay a kerb, one cubit wide; each cell was 13 six cubits by six. He measured the width of the gateway through the cell doors which faced one another, from the back of one cell to the back of the opposite cell; he made 14 it twenty-five cubits, and the vestibule twenty cubits, across; the gateway on every side projected 15 into[a] the court. From the front of the entrance-gate to the outer face of the vestibule of the inner gate 16 the distance was fifty cubits. Both cells and pilasters had loopholes all round inside the gateway, and the vestibule had windows all round within and palms carved on each pilaster.

17 He brought me to the outer court, and I saw rooms and a pavement all round the court: in all, 18 thirty rooms on the pavement. The pavement ran up to the side of the gateways, as wide as they were long; this was the lower pavement. 19 He measured the width of the court from the front of the lower gateway to the outside of the inner

gateway; it was a hundred cubits. He led me round to the north and I 20 saw a gateway facing northwards, belonging to the outer court, and he measured its length and its breadth. Its cells, three on each 21 side, together with its pilasters and its vestibule, were the same size as those of the first gateway, fifty cubits long by twenty-five wide. So too its windows, and those of[b] 22 its vestibule, and its palms were the same size as those of the gateway which faced east; it was approached by seven steps with its vestibule facing them. A gate like 23 that on the east side led to the inner court opposite the northern gateway; he measured from gateway to gateway, and it was a hundred cubits. Then he led me round 24 to the south, and I found a gateway facing southwards. He measured its cells, its pilasters, and its vestibule, and found it the same size as the others, fifty cubits long 25 by twenty-five wide. Both gateway and vestibule had windows all round like the others. It was approached by seven steps with a 26 vestibule facing them and palms carved on each pilaster. The inner 27 court had a gateway facing southwards, and he measured from gateway to gateway; it was a hundred cubits.

He brought me into the inner 28 court through the southern gateway, measured it and found it the same size as the others. So were its 29 cells, pilasters, and vestibule, fifty cubits long by twenty-five wide. It and its vestibule had windows all round.[c] Its vestibule faced the 31 outer court; it had palms carved on its pilasters, and eight steps led up to it.

Then he brought me into the 32 inner court, towards the east, and measured the gateway and found it the same size as the others. So 33

---

[a] *Prob. rdg.; Heb. adds* pilaster.   [b] those of: *prob. rdg.; Heb. om.*
[c] *So some MSS.; others add* (30) It had vestibules all round, and it was twenty-five cubits long by five wide.

too were its cells, pilasters, and vestibule; it and its vestibule had windows all round, and it was fifty cubits long by twenty-five wide.

34 Its vestibule faced the outer court and had a palm carved on each pilaster; eight steps led up to it.

35 Then he brought me to the north gateway and measured it and found it the same size as the others.

36 So were its cells, pilasters, and vestibule, and it had windows all round; it was fifty cubits long by

37 twenty-five wide. Its vestibule faced the outer court and had palms carved on the pilaster at each side; eight steps led up to it.

38 There was a room opening out from the vestibule of the gateway;[a] here the whole-offerings were wash-

39 ed. In the vestibule of the gateway were two tables on each side, at which to slaughter the whole-offering, the sin-offering, and the guilt-

40 offering. At the corner on the outside, as one goes up to the opening of the northern gateway, stood two tables, and two more at the other corner of the vestibule of the gate-

41 way. Another four stood on each side at the corner of the gateway, eight tables in all at which slaugh-

42 tering was done. Four tables used for the whole-offering were of hewn stone, each a cubit and a half long by a cubit and a half wide and a cubit high; and on them they put the instruments used for the whole-

43 offering and other sacrifices. The flesh of the offerings was on the tables, and ledges a hand's breadth in width were fixed all round facing inwards.

44 Then he brought me right into the inner court, and I saw two rooms in the inner court, one at the corner of the northern gateway, facing south, and one at the corner of the southern gateway, facing

45 north. This room facing south, he told me, is for the priests who have

46 charge of the temple. The room facing north is for the priests who

have charge of the altar; these are the sons of Zadok, who alone of the Levites may come near to serve the LORD. He measured the court; it 47 was square, a hundred cubits each way, and the altar lay in front of the temple.

Then he brought me into the 48 vestibule of the temple, and measured a pilaster of the vestibule; it was five cubits on each side, the width of the gateway fourteen cubits and that of the corners of the gateway three cubits in each direction. The vestibule was twen- 49 ty cubits long by twelve wide; ten steps led up to it, and by the pilasters rose pillars, one on each side.

Then he brought me into the 41 sanctuary and measured the pilasters; they were six cubits wide on each side. The opening was ten 2 cubits wide and its corners five cubits wide in each direction. He measured its length; it was forty cubits, and its width twenty. He 3 went inside and measured the pilasters at the opening: they were two cubits; the opening itself was six cubits, and the corners of the opening were seven cubits in each direction. Then he measured the 4 room at the far end of the sanctuary; its length and its breadth were each twenty cubits. He said to me, 'This is the Holy of Holies.'

He measured the wall of the 5 temple; it was six cubits high, and each arcade all round the house was four cubits wide. The arcades 6 were arranged in three tiers, each tier in thirty sections. In the wall all round the temple there were intakes for the arcades, so that they could be supported without being fastened into the wall of the temple. The higher up the arcades 7 were, the broader they were all round by the addition of the intakes, one above the other all round the temple; the temple itself had a ramp running upwards on a base, and in this way one

---

[a] *the vestibule of the gateway: prob. rdg.; Heb. pilasters, the gates.*

went up from the lowest to the highest tier by way of the middle tier.

8 Then I saw a raised pavement all round the temple, and the foundations of the arcades were flush with it and measured a full rod, six 9 cubits high. The outer wall of the arcades was five cubits thick. There was an unoccupied area beside the terrace[a] which was adja-11[b] cent to the temple, and the arcades opened on to this area, one opening facing northwards and one southwards; the unoccupied area was 10 five cubits wide on all sides. There was a free space[e] twenty cubits 12 wide all round the temple. On the western side, at the far end of the free space, stood a building seventy cubits wide; its wall was five cubits thick all round, and its length ninety cubits.

13 He measured the temple; it was a hundred cubits long; and the free space, the building, and its walls, a 14 hundred cubits in all. The eastern front of the temple and the free space was a hundred cubits wide. 15 He measured the length of the building at the far end of the free space to the west of the temple, and its corridors on each side: a hundred cubits.

The sanctuary, the inner shrine and the outer vestibule were pan-16 elled; the embrasures all round the three of them were framed with 17 wood all round. From the ground up to the windows and above the door, both in the inner and outer chambers, round all the walls, in-18 side and out, were carved figures,[d] cherubim and palm-trees, a palm between every pair of cherubim. 19 Each cherub had two faces: one the face of a man, looking towards one palm-tree, and the other the face of a lion, looking towards

another palm-tree. Such was the carving round the whole of the temple. The cherubim and the 20 palm-trees were carved from the ground up to the top of the doorway and on the wall of the sanctuary. The door-posts of the sanc-21 tuary were square.[e]

In front of[f] the Holy Place was 22 what seemed an altar of wood, three cubits high and two cubits long; it was fitted with cornerposts, and its base and sides also were of wood. He told me that this was the table which stood before the LORD. The sanctuary had a 23 double door, and the Holy Place also had a double door: the double 24 doors had swinging leaves, a pair for each door. Cherubim and palm-25 trees like those on the walls were carved on them.[g] Outside there was a wooden cornice over the vestibule; on both sides of the 26 vestibule were loopholes, with palm-trees carved at the corners.[h]

Then he took me to the outer 42 court round by the north and brought me to the rooms facing the free space and facing the buildings to the north. The length along the 2 northern side was a hundred cubits, and the breadth fifty. Facing 3 the free space measuring twenty cubits, which adjoined the inner court, and facing the pavement of the outer court, were corridors at three levels corresponding to each other. In front of the rooms a pas-4 sage, ten cubits wide and a hundred cubits long, ran towards the inner court; their entrances faced northwards. The upper rooms were 5 shorter than the lower and middle rooms, because the corridors took building space from them. For 6 they were all at three levels and had no pillars as the courts had, so that the lower and middle levels

---

[a] *beside the terrace: prob. rdg.; Heb. between the arcades.*   [b] *Verses 10 and 11 transposed.*   [c] *There...space: prob. rdg.; Heb. Between the rooms.*
[d] *carved figures: prob. rdg.; Heb. measures and carving.*
[e] *The door-posts...square: prob. rdg.; Heb. unintelligible.*   [f] *In front of: prob. rdg.; Heb. The face of.*   [g] *Prob. rdg.; Heb. adds on the doors of the sanctuary.*
[h] *Prob. rdg.; Heb. adds and the arcades of the temple and the cornices.*

were recessed from the ground upwards.

7 An outside wall, fifty cubits long, ran parallel to the rooms and in front of them, on the side of

8 the outer court. The rooms adjacent to the outer court were fifty cubits long, and those facing the

9 sanctuary a hundred cubits. Below these rooms was an entry from the east as one entered them from

10 the outer court where the wall of the court began.[a] On the south side, passing by the free space and the building, were other rooms

11 with a passage in front of them. These rooms corresponded, in length and breadth and in general character, to those facing north,

12 whose exits and entrances were the same as those of the rooms on the south. As one[b] went eastwards, where the passages began, there was an entrance in the face of the

13 inner[c] wall. Then he said to me, 'The northern and southern rooms facing the free space are the consecrated rooms where the priests who approach the LORD may eat the most sacred offerings. There they shall put these offerings as well as the grain-offering, the sin-offering, and the guilt-offering; for

14 the place is holy. When the priests have entered the Holy Place they shall not go into the outer court again without leaving here the garments they have worn while performing their duties, for these are holy. They shall put on other garments when they approach the place assigned to the people.'

15 When he had finished measuring the inner temple, he brought me out towards the gateway which faces eastwards and measured the

16 whole area. He measured the east side with the measuring-rod, and it was five hundred cubits. He turned

17 and measured the north side with his rod, and it was five hundred

18 cubits. He turned to the south side and measured it with his rod; it was five hundred cubits. He turned

19 to the west and measured it with his rod; it was five hundred cubits. So he measured all four sides; in

20 each direction the surrounding wall measured five hundred cubits. This marked off the sacred area from the profane.

He led me to the gate, the gate 43 facing eastwards, and I beheld the 2 glory of the God of Israel coming from the east. His voice was like the sound of a mighty torrent, and the earth shone with his glory. The 3 form that I saw was the same as that which I had seen when he came to destroy the city, and as that which I had seen by the river Kebar,[d] and I fell on my face. The 4 glory of the LORD came up to the temple towards the gate which faced eastwards. A spirit[e] lifted me 5 up and brought me into the inner court, and the glory of the LORD filled the temple. Then I heard one 6 speaking to me from the temple, and the man was standing at my side. He said, Man, do you see the 7 place of my throne, the place where I set my feet, where I will dwell among the Israelites for ever? Neither they nor their kings shall ever defile my holy name again with their wanton disloyalty, and with the corpses[f] of their kings when they die. They set their 8 threshold by mine and their door-post beside mine, with a wall between me and them, and they defiled my holy name with the abominations they committed, and I destroyed them in my anger. But 9 now they shall abandon their wanton disloyalty and remove the corpses[f] of their kings far from me, and I will dwell among them for ever. So tell the Israelites, man, 10 about this temple, its appearance and proportions, that they may be ashamed of their iniquities. If they 11

---

[a] began: *prob. rdg.*; *Heb.* breadth.
[c] *Prob. rdg.*; *Heb. word unknown.*
[e] Or wind.

[b] *Prob. rdg.*; *Heb.* they.
[d] Or the Kebar canal.
[f] Or effigies.

are ashamed of all they have done, you shall describe to them the temple and its fittings, its exits and entrances, all the details and particulars of its elevation and plan; explain them and draw them before their eyes, so that they may keep them in mind and carry 12 them out. This is the plan of the temple to be built on the top of the mountain; all its precincts on every side shall be most holy.

13   These were the dimensions of the altar in cubits (the cubit that is a cubit and a hand's breadth). This was the height of the altar: the base was a cubit high[a] and projected a cubit; on its edge was a rim one 14 span deep. From the base to the cubit-wide ridge of the lower pedestal-block was two cubits, and from this shorter pedestal-block to the cubit-wide ridge of the taller pedestal-block was four cubits. 15 The altar-hearth was four cubits high and was surmounted by four 16 horns a cubit high. The hearth was twelve cubits long and twelve cubits wide, being a perfect square. 17 The upper pedestal-block was fourteen cubits long and fourteen cubits wide along its four sides, and the rim round it was half a cubit deep. The base of the altar projected a cubit, and there were steps facing eastwards.

18   He said to me, Man, these are the words of the Lord GOD: These are the regulations for the altar when it has been made, for sacrificing whole-offerings on it and 19 flinging the blood against it. The levitical priests of the family of Zadok, and they alone, may come near to me to serve me, says the Lord GOD. You shall assign them a 20 young bull for a sin-offering; you shall take some of the blood and put it on the four horns of the altar, on the four corners of the upper pedestal and all round the rim, and so purify it and make 21 expiation for it. Then take the bull

assigned as the sin-offering, and they shall destroy it by fire in the proper place within the precincts but outside the Holy Place. On the 22 second day you shall present a he-goat without blemish as a sin-offering, and with it they shall purify the altar as they did with the bull. When you have com- 23 pletely purified the altar, you shall present a young bull without blemish and a ram without blemish from the flock. You shall present 24 them before the LORD; the priests shall throw salt on them and sacrifice them as a whole-offering to the LORD. For seven days you 25 shall provide as a daily sin-offering a goat, a young bull, and a ram from the flock; all of them shall be provided free from blemish. For 26 seven days they shall make expiation for the altar, and pronounce it ritually clean, and consecrate it. At the end of that time, on the 27 eighth day and onwards, the priests shall sacrifice on the altar your whole-offerings and your shared-offerings, and I will accept you. This is the very word of the Lord GOD.

He again brought me round to 44 the outer gate of the sanctuary facing eastwards, and it was shut. The LORD said to me, This gate 2 shall be kept shut; it must not be opened. No man may enter by it, for the LORD the God of Israel has entered by it. It shall be kept shut. The prince, however, when he is 3 here as prince, may sit there to eat food in the presence of the LORD; he shall come in and go out by the vestibule of the gate.

He brought me round to the 4 northern gate facing the temple, and I saw the glory of the LORD filling the LORD's house, and I fell on my face. The LORD said to me, 5 Mark well, man, look closely, and listen carefully to all that I say to you, to all the rules and regulations for the house of the LORD. Mark

---

[a] the base...high: *prob. rdg.*; *Heb.* the base of the cubit.

well the entrance to the house of the LORD and all the exits from the 6 sanctuary. Say to that rebel people of Israel, These are the words of the Lord GOD: Enough of all these abominations of yours, you Israel- 7 ites! You have added to them by bringing foreigners, uncircumcised in mind and body, to stand in my sanctuary and defile my house when you present my food to me, both fat and blood, and they have 8 made my covenant void. Instead of keeping charge of my holy things yourselves, you have chosen to put these men in charge of my sanc- tuary.

9 These are the words of the Lord GOD: No foreigner, uncircumcised in mind and body, shall enter my sanctuary, not even a foreigner 10 living among the Israelites. But the Levites, though they deserted me when the Israelites went astray after their idols and had to bear the 11 punishment of their iniquity, shall yet do service in my sanctuary. They shall take charge of the gates of the temple and do service there. They shall slaughter the whole- offering and the sacrifice for the people and shall be in attendance 12 to serve them. Because they serv- ed them in the presence of their idols and brought Israel to the ground by their iniquity, says the Lord GOD, I have sworn with up- lifted hand that they shall bear the 13 punishment of their iniquity. They shall not have access to me, to serve me as priests; they shall not come near to my holy things or to the Holy of Holies; they shall bear the shame of the abominable deeds 14 they have done. I will put them in charge of the temple with all the service which must be performed there.

15 But the levitical priests of the family of Zadok remained in charge of my sanctuary when the Israelites went astray from me; these shall approach me to serve me. They shall be in attendance on me, presenting the fat and the blood, says the Lord GOD. It is 16 they who shall enter my sanctuary and approach my table to serve me and observe my charge. When 17 they come to the gates of the inner court they shall dress in linen; they shall wear no wool when they serve me at the gates of the inner court and within. They shall wear linen 18 turbans, and linen drawers on their loins; they shall not fasten their clothes with a belt so that they sweat. When they go out to 19 the people in the outer court, they shall take off the clothes they have worn while serving, leave them in the sacred rooms and put on other clothes; otherwise they will trans- mit the sacred influence to the people through their clothing.

They shall neither shave their 20 heads nor let their hair grow long; they shall only clip their hair. No 21 priest shall drink wine when he is to enter the inner court. He may 22 not marry a widow or a divorced woman; he may marry a virgin of Israelite birth. He may, however, marry the widow of a priest.

They shall teach my people to 23 distinguish the sacred from the profane, and show them the differ- ence between clean and unclean. When disputes break out, they 24 shall take their place in court, and settle the case according to my rules. At all my appointed seasons they shall observe my laws and statutes. They shall keep my sab- baths holy.

They shall not defile themselves 25 by contact with any dead person, except[a] father or mother, son or daughter, brother or unmarried sister. After purification, they 26 shall count seven days and then be clean. When they enter the inner 27 court to serve in the Holy Place, they shall present their sin-offer- ing, says the Lord GOD.

They shall own no patrimony in 28

---

[a] any...except: *or* anyone else's dead, but only their own...

Israel; I am their patrimony. You shall grant them no holding in 29 Israel; I am their holding. The grain-offering, the sin-offering, and the guilt-offering shall be eaten by them, and everything in Israel 30 devoted to God shall be theirs. The first of all the first-fruits and all your contributions of every kind shall belong wholly to the priests. You shall give the first lump of your dough to the priests, that a blessing may rest upon your home. 31 The priests shall eat no carrion, bird or beast, whether it has died naturally or been killed by a wild animal.

45 When you divide the land by lot among the tribes for their possession, you shall set apart from it a sacred reserve for the LORD, twenty-five thousand cubits in length and twenty thousand in width; the whole enclosure shall be 2 sacred. Of this a square plot, five hundred cubits each way, shall be devoted to the sanctuary, with fifty cubits of open land round it. 3 From this area you shall measure out a space twenty-five thousand by ten thousand cubits, in which the sanctuary, the holiest place of 4 all, shall stand. This space is for the priests who serve in the sanctuary and who come nearest in serving the LORD. It shall include space for their houses and a sacred 5 plot for the sanctuary. An area of twenty-five thousand by ten thousand cubits shall belong to the Levites, the temple servants; on this shall stand the towns in which 6 they live. You shall give to each town an area of five thousand by twenty-five thousand cubits alongside the sacred reserve; this shall 7 belong to all Israel. On either side of the sacred reserve and of the city's holding the prince shall have a holding facing the sacred reserve and the city's holding, running westwards on the west and east-

wards on the east. It shall run alongside one of the tribal portions, and stretch to the western limit of the land and to the eastern. It shall be his holding in Israel; the 8 princes of Israel shall never oppress my people again but shall give the land to Israel, tribe by tribe.

THESE are the words of the Lord 9 GOD: Enough, princes of Israel! Put an end to lawlessness and robbery; maintain law and justice; relieve my people and stop your evictions, says the Lord GOD. Your scales 10 shall be honest, your bushel and your gallon shall be honest. There 11 shall be one standard for each, taking each as the tenth of a homer, and the homer shall have its fixed standard. Your shekel weight 12 shall contain twenty gerahs; your mina shall contain weights of ten[a] and twenty-five and fifteen shekels.

These are the contributions you 13 shall set aside: out of every homer of wheat or of barley, one sixth of an ephah. For oil the rule is[b] one 14 tenth of a bath from every kor (at ten bath to the kor); one sheep in 15 every flock of two hundred is to be reserved by every Israelite clan. For a grain-offering, a whole-offering, and a shared-offering, to make expiation for them, says the Lord GOD, all the people of the land shall 16 bring[c] this contribution to the prince in Israel; and the prince 17 shall be responsible for the whole-offering, the grain-offering, and the drink-offering, at pilgrim-feasts, new moons, sabbaths, and every sacred season observed by Israel. He himself is to provide the sin-offering and the grain-offering, the whole-offering and the shared-offering, needed to make expiation for Israel.

These are the words of the Lord 18 GOD: On the first day of the first month you shall take a young bull

[a] Prob. rdg.; Heb. twenty.   [b] Prob. rdg.; Heb. adds the bath, the oil.
[c] all...bring: prob. rdg.; Heb. unintelligible.

without blemish, and purify the
19 sanctuary. The priest shall take
some of the blood from the sin-
offering and put it on the door-
posts of the temple, on the four
corners of the altar pedestal and on
the gate-posts of the inner court.
20 You shall do the same on the
seventh day of the month;[a] in this
way you shall make expiation for
the temple.
21 On the fourteenth day of the
first month you shall hold the
Passover, the pilgrim-feast of sev-
en days; bread must be eaten un-
22 leavened. On that day the prince
shall provide a bull as a sin-offering
for himself and for all the people.
23 During the seven days of the feast
he shall offer daily as a whole-
offering to the LORD seven bulls
and seven rams without blemish,
and a he-goat as a daily sin-offer-
24 ing. With every bull and ram he
shall provide a grain-offering of
one ephah, together with a hin of
25 oil for each ephah. He shall do the
same thing also on the fifteenth
day of the seventh month at the
pilgrim-feast; this also shall last
seven days, and he shall provide
the same sin-offering and whole-
offering and the same quantity of
grain and oil.

46 These are the words of the Lord
GOD: The eastern gate of the inner
court shall remain closed for the
six working days; it may be opened
only on the sabbath and at new
2 moon. When the prince comes
through the porch of the gate from
the outside, he shall halt at the
door-post, and the priests shall
sacrifice his whole-offering and
shared-offerings. On the terrace he
shall bow down at the gate and
then go out, but the gate shall not
3 be shut till the evening. On sabbaths and at new moons the people
also shall bow down before the

LORD at the entrance to that
gate.
The whole-offering which the 4
prince sacrifices to the LORD shall
be as follows: on the sabbath, six
sheep without blemish and a ram
without blemish; the grain-offer- 5
ing shall be an ephah with the ram
and as much as he likes with the
sheep, together with a hin of oil for
every ephah. At the new moon it 6
shall be a young bull without
blemish, six sheep and a ram, all
without blemish. He shall provide 7
as the grain-offering to go with the
bull one ephah and with the ram
one ephah, with the sheep as much
as he can afford, adding a hin of oil
for every ephah.
When the prince comes in, he 8
shall enter through the porch of
the gate and come out by the same
way. But on festal days when the 9
people come before the LORD, a
man who enters by the northern
gate to bow down shall leave by
the southern gate, and a man who
enters by the southern gate shall
leave by the northern gate. He
shall not turn back and go out
through the gate by which he came
in but shall go straight on. The 10
prince shall then be among them,
going in when they go in and
coming out when they come out.
At pilgrim-feasts and on festal 11
days the grain-offering shall be an
ephah with a bull, an ephah with a
ram and as much as he likes with a
sheep, together with a hin of oil for
every ephah.
When the prince provides a 12
whole-offering or shared-offerings
as a voluntary sacrifice to the
LORD, the eastern gate shall be
opened for him,[b] and he shall make
his whole-offering and his shared-
offerings as he does on the sabbath; when he goes out the gate
shall be closed[c] behind him.

---

[a] *Prob. rdg.; Heb. adds* This comes from a man who is wrong and foolish. *Cp. Lev.*
23. 24; *Num.* 29. 1.
[b] the eastern...him: *or* he shall open the gate facing east.
[c] the gate...closed: *or* he shall close the gate.

13 You shall provide a yearling sheep without blemish daily as a whole-offering to the LORD; you shall provide it morning by morn- 14 ing. With it every morning you shall provide as a grain-offering one sixth of an ephah with a third of a hin of oil to moisten the flour; the LORD's grain-offering is an observance prescribed for all time. 15 Morning by morning, as a regular whole-offering, they shall offer a sheep with the grain-offering and the oil.

16 These are the words of the Lord GOD: When the prince makes a gift out of his property to any of his sons, it shall belong to his sons, since it is part of the family pro- 17 perty. But when he makes such a gift to one of his slaves, it shall be his only till the year of manumission, when it shall revert to the prince; it is the property of his sons and shall belong to them.

18 The prince shall not oppress the people by taking part of their holdings; he shall give his sons an inheritance from his own holding of land, so that my people may not be scattered and separated from their holdings.

19 Then he brought me through the entrance by the side of the gate to the rooms which face north (the sacred rooms reserved for the priests), and, pointing to a place on 20 their western side, he said to me, 'This is the place where the priests shall boil the guilt-offering and the sin-offering and bake the grain-offering; they shall not take it into the outer court for fear they transmit the sacred influence to the 21 people.' Then he brought me into the outer court and took me across to the four corners of the court, at each of which there was a further 22 court. These four courts were vaulted and were the same size, forty cubits long by thirty cubits 23 wide. Round each of the four was a row of stones, with fire-places constructed close up against the rows.

He said to me, 'These are the kit- 24 chens where the attendants shall boil the people's sacrifices.'

He brought me back to the gate 47 of the temple, and I saw a spring of water issuing from under the terrace of the temple towards the east; for the temple faced east. The water was running down along the right side, to the south of the altar. He took me out through the nor- 2 thern gate and brought me round by an outside path to the eastern gate of the court, and water was trickling from the right side. When 3 the man went out eastwards he had a line in his hand. He measured a thousand cubits and made me walk through the water; it came up to my ankles. He measured an- 4 other thousand and made me walk through the water; it came up to my knees. He measured another thousand and made me walk through the water; it was up to my waist. Another thousand, and it 5 was a torrent I could not cross, for the water had risen and was now deep enough to swim in; it had become a torrent that could not be crossed. 'Mark this, man', he said, 6 and led me back to the bank of the torrent. When we came back to the 7 bank I saw a great number of trees on each side. He said to me, 'This 8 water flows out to the region lying east, and down to the Arabah; at last it will reach that sea whose waters are foul, and they will be sweetened. When any one of the 9 living creatures that swarm upon the earth comes where the torrent flows, it shall draw life from it. The fish shall be innumerable; for these waters come here so that the others may be sweetened, and where the torrent flows everything shall live. From En-gedi as far as 10 En-eglaim fishermen shall stand on its shores, for nets shall be spread there. Every kind of fish shall be there in shoals, like the fish of the Great Sea; but its swamps and 11 pools shall not have their waters

sweetened but shall be left as salt-
12 pans. Beside the torrent on either
bank all trees good for food shall
spring up. Their leaves shall not
wither, their fruit shall not cease;
they shall bear early every month.
For their water comes from the
sanctuary; their fruit is for food
and their foliage for enjoyment.'

13　　These are the words of the Lord
GOD: These are the boundary lines
within which the twelve tribes of
Israel shall enter into possession of
the land, Joseph receiving two
14 portions. The land which I swore
with hand uplifted to give to your
fathers you shall divide with each
other; it shall be assigned to you by
15 lot as your patrimony. This is the
frontier: on its northern side, from
the Great Sea through Hethlon,
16 Lebo-hamath, Zedad, Berutha,
and Sibraim, which are between
the frontiers of Damascus and
Hamath, to Hazar-enan, near the
17 frontier of Hauran. So the frontier
shall run from the sea to Hazar-
enan on the frontier of Damascus
and northwards; this is its north-
18 ern side. The eastern side runs
alongside the territories of Hauran, Damascus, and Gilead, and
alongside the territory of Israel;
Jordan sets the boundary to the
eastern sea, to Tamar. This is the
19 eastern side. The southern side
runs from Tamar to the waters of
Meribah-by-Kadesh; the region assigned to you reaches the Great
Sea. This is the southern side to-
20 wards the Negeb. The western side
is the Great Sea, which forms a
boundary as far as a point opposite Lebo-hamath. This is the
21 western side. You shall distribute
this land among the tribes of Israel
22 and assign it by lot as a patrimony
for yourselves and for any aliens
living in your midst who leave
sons among you. They shall be
treated as native-born in Israel
and with you shall receive a patrimony by lot among the tribes of

Israel. You shall give the alien his 23
patrimony with the tribe in which
he is living. This is the very word
of the Lord GOD.

These are the names of the 48
tribes: In the extreme north, in the
direction of Hethlon, to Lebo-
hamath and Hazar-enan, with
Damascus on the northern frontier in the direction of Hamath,
and so from the eastern side to
the western, shall be Dan: one
portion.

Bordering on Dan, from the 2
eastern side to the western, shall be
Asher: one portion.

Bordering on Asher, from the 3
eastern side to the western, shall be
Naphtali: one portion.

Bordering on Naphtali, from the 4
eastern side to the western, shall be
Manasseh: one portion.

Bordering on Manasseh, from 5
the eastern side to the western,
shall be Ephraim: one portion.

Bordering on Ephraim, from the 6
eastern side to the western, shall be
Reuben: one portion.

Bordering on Reuben, from the 7
eastern side to the western, shall be
Judah: one portion.

Bordering on Judah, from the 8
eastern side to the western, shall be
the reserve which you shall set
apart. Its breadth shall be twenty-
five thousand cubits and its length
the same as that of the other portions, from the eastern side to the
western, and the sanctuary shall
be in the middle of it.

The reserve which you shall set 9
apart for the LORD shall measure
twenty-five thousand cubits by
twenty[a] thousand. The reserve 10
shall be apportioned thus: the
priests shall have an area measuring twenty-five thousand cubits on the north side, ten thousand
on the west, ten thousand on the
east, and twenty-five thousand on
the south side; the sanctuary of the
LORD shall be in the middle of it. It 11
shall be for the consecrated priests,

[a] *Prob. rdg.; Heb.* ten.

the sons of Zadok, who kept my charge and did not follow the Israelites when they went astray, as 12 the Levites did. The area set apart for the priests from the reserved territory shall be most sacred, reaching the frontier of the Levites.

13 The Levites shall have a portion running parallel to the border of the priests. It shall be twenty-five thousand cubits long by ten thousand wide; altogether, the length shall be twenty-five thousand cubits and the breadth ten thousand.

14 They shall neither sell nor exchange any part of it, nor shall the best of the land be alienated; for it is holy to the LORD.

15 The strip which is left, five thousand cubits in width by twenty-five thousand, is the city's secular land for dwellings and common land, and the city shall be in the 16 middle of it. These shall be its dimensions: on the northern side four thousand five hundred cubits, on the southern side four thousand five hundred cubits, on the eastern side four thousand five hundred cubits, on the western side four 17 thousand five hundred cubits. The common land belonging to the city shall be two hundred and fifty cubits to the north, two hundred and fifty to the south, two hundred and fifty to the east, and two hun- 18 dred and fifty to the west. What is left parallel to the reserve, ten thousand cubits to the east and ten thousand to the west,*a* shall provide food for those who work in the 19 city. Those who work in the city shall cultivate it; they may be drawn from any of the tribes of Israel.

20 You shall set apart the whole reserve, twenty-five thousand cubits square, as sacred, as far as the 21 holding of the city. What is left over on each side of the sacred reserve and the holding of the city

shall be assigned to the prince. Eastwards, what lies over against the reserved twenty-five thousand cubits, as far as the eastern side, and westwards, what lies over against the twenty-five thousand cubits to the western side, parallel to the tribal portions, shall be assigned to the prince; the sacred reserve and the sanctuary itself shall be in the centre. The*b* holding 22 of the Levites and the*b* holding of the city shall be in the middle of that which is assigned to the prince; it shall be between the frontiers of Judah and Benjamin.

The rest of the tribes: from the 23 eastern side to the western shall be Benjamin: one portion.

Bordering on Benjamin, from 24 the eastern side to the western, shall be Simeon: one portion.

Bordering on Simeon, from the 25 eastern side to the western, shall be Issachar: one portion.

Bordering on Issachar, from the 26 eastern side to the western, shall be Zebulun: one portion.

Bordering on Zebulun, from the 27 eastern side to the western, shall be Gad: one portion.

Bordering on Gad, on the side 28 of the Negeb, the border on the south stretches from Tamar to the waters of Meribah-by-Kadesh, to the Brook as far as the Great Sea.

This is the land which you shall 29 allot as a patrimony to the tribes of Israel, and these shall be their lots. This is the very word of the Lord GOD.

These are to be the ways out of 30–31 the city, and they are to be named after the tribes of Israel. The northern side, four thousand five hundred cubits long, shall have three gates, those of Reuben, Judah, and Levi; the eastern side, four thou- 32 sand five hundred cubits long, three gates, those of Joseph, Benjamin, and Dan; the southern side, 33

---

a Prob. rdg.; Heb. adds and it shall be parallel to the sacred reserve.
b Prob. rdg.; Heb. Some of the.

four thousand five hundred cubits long, three gates, those of Simeon, 34 Issachar, and Zebulun; the western side, four thousand five hundred cubits long, three gates, those of Gad, Asher, and Naphtali. The 35 perimeter of the city shall be eighteen thousand cubits, and the city's name for ever after shall be Jehovah-shammah.[a]

THE BOOK OF
DANIEL

Jews at the court of Nebuchadnezzar

1 IN the third year of the reign of Jehoiakim king of Judah, Nebuchadnezzar king of Babylon came to Jerusalem and laid siege to 2 it. The Lord delivered Jehoiakim king of Judah into his power, together with all that was left of the vessels of the house of God; and he carried them off to the land of Shinar, to the temple of his god, where he deposited the vessels in 3 the treasury. Then the king ordered Ashpenaz, his chief eunuch, to take certain of the Israelite exiles, of the blood royal and of the nobi- 4 lity, who were to be young men of good looks and bodily without fault, at home in all branches of knowledge, well-informed, intelligent, and fit for service in the royal court; and he was to instruct them in the literature and lan- 5 guage of the Chaldaeans. The king assigned them a daily allowance of food and wine from the royal table. Their training was to last for three years, and at the end of that time they would[b] enter the royal service.

6 Among them there were certain young men from Judah called Daniel, Hananiah, Mishael and 7 Azariah; but the master of the eunuchs gave them new names: Daniel he called Belteshazzar, Hananiah Shadrach, Mishael Meshach and Azariah Abed-nego. Now Daniel determined not to con- 8 taminate himself by touching the food and wine assigned to him by the king, and he begged the master of the eunuchs not to make him do so. God made the master show 9 kindness and goodwill to Daniel, and he said to him, 'I am afraid of 10 my lord the king: he has assigned you your food and drink, and if he sees you looking dejected, unlike the other young men of your own age, it will cost me my head.' Then 11 Daniel said to the guard whom the master of the eunuchs had put in charge of Hananiah, Mishael, Azariah and himself, 'Submit us to 12 this test for ten days. Give us only vegetables to eat and water to drink; then compare our looks 13 with those of the young men who have lived on the food assigned by the king, and be guided in your treatment of us by what you see.'[c] The guard listened to what they 14 said and tested them for ten days. At the end of ten days they looked 15 healthier and were better nourished than all the young men who had lived on the food assigned them by the king. So the guard took away 16 the assignment of food and the

---

[a] *That is* the LORD *is there.*   [b] *at the end...would: or* all of them were to.
[c] *be guided...see: or* treat us as you see fit.

wine they were to drink, and gave them only the vegetables.

17 To all four of these young men God had given knowledge and understanding of books and learning of every kind, while Daniel had a gift for interpreting visions and 18 dreams of every kind. The time came which the king had fixed for introducing the young men to court, and the master of the eunuchs brought them into the pres- 19 ence of Nebuchadnezzar. The king talked with them and found none of them to compare with Daniel, Hananiah, Mishael and Azariah; so they entered the royal service. 20 Whenever the king consulted them on any matter calling for insight and judgement, he found them ten times better than all the magicians and exorcists in his whole king- 21 dom. Now Daniel was there till the first year of King Cyrus.

2 In the second year of his reign Nebuchadnezzar had dreams, and his mind was so troubled that he 2 could not sleep. Then the king gave orders to summon the magicians, exorcists, sorcerers, and Chaldaeans to tell him what he had dreamt. They came in and stood in 3 the royal presence, and the king said to them, 'I have had a dream and my mind has been troubled to 4 know what my dream was.' The Chaldaeans, speaking in Aramaic, said, *a*'Long live the king! Tell us what you dreamt and we will tell 5 you the interpretation.' The king answered, 'This is my declared intention. If you do not tell me both dream and interpretation, you shall be torn in pieces and your 6 houses shall be forfeit.*b* But if you can tell me the dream and the interpretation, you will be richly rewarded and loaded with honours. Tell me, therefore, the dream 7 and its interpretation.' They answered a second time, 'Let the king tell his servants the dream, and we

will tell him the interpretation.' The king answered, 'It is clear to 8 me that you are trying to gain time, because you see that my intention has been declared. If you 9 do not make known to me the dream, there is one law that applies to you, and one only. What is more, you have agreed among yourselves to tell me a pack of lies to my face in the hope that with time things may alter. Tell me the dream, therefore, and I shall know that you can give me the interpretation.' The Chaldaeans an- 10 swered in the presence of the king, 'Nobody on earth can tell your majesty what you wish to know; no great king or prince has ever made such a demand of magician, exorcist, or Chaldaean. What your 11 majesty requires of us is too hard; there is no one but the gods, who dwell remote from mortal men, who can give you the answer.' At 12 this the king lost his temper and in a great rage ordered the death of all the wise men of Babylon. A 13 decree was issued that the wise men were to be executed, and accordingly men were sent to fetch Daniel and his companions for execution.

When Arioch, the captain of the 14 king's bodyguard, was setting out to execute the wise men of Babylon, Daniel approached him cau- 15 tiously and with discretion and said, 'Sir, you represent the king; why has his majesty issued such a peremptory decree?' Arioch explained everything; so Daniel went 16 in to the king's presence and begged for a certain time by which he would give the king the interpretation. Then Daniel went home and 17 told the whole story to his companions, Hananiah, Mishael and Azariah. They should ask the God 18 of heaven in his mercy, he said, to disclose this secret, so that they and he with the rest of the wise

a The Aramaic text begins here and continues to the end of ch. 7.
b Or made into a dunghill (*mng. of Aram. word uncertain*).

men of Babylon should not be put
19 to death. Then in a vision by night
the secret was revealed to Daniel,
and he blessed the God of heaven
20 in these words:

Blessed be God's name from age to
age,
for all wisdom and power are
his.

21 He changes seasons and times;
he deposes kings and sets them
up;
he gives wisdom to the wise
and all their store of knowledge to
the men who know;

22 he reveals deep mysteries;
he knows what lies in darkness,
and light has its dwelling with
him.

23 To thee, God of my fathers, I give
thanks and praise,
for thou hast given me wisdom and
power;
thou hast now revealed to me what
we asked,
and told us what the king is concerned to know.

24 Daniel therefore went to Arioch
who had been charged by the king
to put to death the wise men of
Babylon and said to him, 'Do not
put the wise men of Babylon to
death. Take me into the king's
presence, and I will now tell him
the interpretation of the dream.'

25 Arioch in great trepidation brought
Daniel before the king and said to
him, 'I have found among the
Jewish exiles a man who will make
known to your majesty the inter-

26 pretation of your dream.' Thereupon the king said to Daniel (who
was also called Belteshazzar), 'Can
you tell me what I saw in my dream

27 and interpret it?' Daniel answered
in the king's presence, 'The secret
about which your majesty in-
quires no wise man, exorcist, magician, or diviner can disclose to you.

28 But there is in heaven a god who
reveals secrets, and he has told

King Nebuchadnezzar what is to
be at the end of this age. This is the
dream and these the visions that
came into your head: the thoughts 29
that came to you, O king, as you lay
on your bed, were thoughts of
things to come, and the revealer of
secrets has made known to you
what is to be. This secret has been 30
revealed to me not because I am
wise beyond all living men, but because your majesty is to know the
interpretation and understand the
thoughts which have entered your
mind.

'As you watched, O king, you 31
saw a great image. This image,
huge and dazzling, towered before
you, fearful to behold. The head of 32
the image was of fine gold, its breast
and arms of silver, its belly and
thighs of bronze,[a] its legs of iron, 33
its feet part iron and part clay.
While you looked, a stone was 34
hewn from a mountain, not by
human hands; it struck the image
on its feet of iron and clay and
shattered them. Then the iron, the 35
clay, the bronze, the silver, and the
gold, were all shattered to fragments and were swept away like
chaff before the wind from a
threshing-floor in summer, until no
trace of them remained. But the
stone which struck the image grew
into a great mountain filling the
whole earth. That was the dream. 36
We shall now tell your majesty the
interpretation. You, O king, king 37
of kings, to whom the God of heaven has given the kingdom with all
its power, authority, and honour;
in whose hands he has placed men 38
and beasts and birds of the air,
wherever they dwell, granting you
sovereignty over them all – you
are that head of gold. After you 39
there shall arise another kingdom,
inferior to yours, and yet a third
kingdom, of bronze, which shall
have sovereignty over the whole
world. And there shall be a fourth 40
kingdom, strong as iron; as iron

a Or copper.

shatters and destroys all things, it shall break and shatter the whole
41 earth.*ᵃ* As, in your vision, the feet and toes were part potter's clay and part iron, it shall be a divided kingdom. Its core shall be partly of iron just as you saw iron mixed
42 with the common clay; as the toes were part iron and part clay, the kingdom shall be partly strong and
43 partly brittle. As, in your vision, the iron was mixed with common clay, so shall men mix with each other by intermarriage, but such alliances shall not be stable: iron
44 does not mix with clay. In the period of those kings the God of heaven will establish a kingdom which shall never be destroyed; that kingdom shall never pass to another people; it shall shatter and make an end of all these kingdoms, while it shall itself endure
45 for ever. This is the meaning of your vision of the stone being hewn from a mountain, not by human hands, and then shattering the iron, the bronze, the clay, the silver, and the gold. The mighty God has made known to your majesty what is to be hereafter. The dream is sure and the interpretation to be trusted.'
46 Then King Nebuchadnezzar prostrated himself and worshipped Daniel, and gave orders that sacrifices and soothing offerings should
47 be made to him. 'Truly,' he said, 'your god is indeed God of gods and Lord over kings, a revealer of secrets, since you have been able
48 to reveal this secret.' Then the king promoted Daniel, bestowed on him many rich gifts, and made him regent over the whole province of Babylon and chief prefect over all
49 the wise men of Babylon. Moreover at Daniel's request the king put Shadrach, Meshach and Abednego in charge of the administration of the province of Babylon. Daniel himself, however, remained at court.

KING Nebuchadnezzar made an 3 image of gold, ninety feet high and nine feet broad. He had it set up in the plain of Dura in the province of Babylon. Then he sent out 2 a summons to assemble the satraps, prefects, viceroys, counsellors, treasurers, judges, chief constables, and all governors of provinces to attend the dedication of the image which he had set up. So 3 they assembled – the satraps, prefects, viceroys, counsellors, treasurers, judges, chief constables, and all governors of provinces – for the dedication of the image which King Nebuchadnezzar had set up; and they stood before the image which Nebuchadnezzar had set up. Then the herald loudly 4 proclaimed, 'O peoples and nations of every language, you are commanded, when you hear the sound 5 of horn, pipe, zither, triangle, dulcimer, music, and singing of every kind, to prostrate yourselves and worship the golden image which King Nebuchadnezzar has set up. Whoever does not prostrate him- 6 self and worship shall forthwith be thrown into a blazing furnace.' Accordingly, no sooner did all the 7 peoples hear the sound of horn, pipe, zither, triangle, dulcimer, music, and singing of every kind, than all the peoples and nations of every language prostrated themselves and worshipped the golden image which King Nebuchadnezzar had set up.

It was then that certain Chal- 8 daeans came forward and brought a charge against the Jews. They 9 said to King Nebuchadnezzar, 'Long live the king! Your maj- 10 esty has issued an order that every man who hears the sound of horn, pipe, zither, triangle, dulcimer, music, and singing of every kind shall fall down and worship the image of gold. Whoever does 11 not do so shall be thrown into a blazing furnace. There are certain 12

ᵃ the whole earth: *prob. rdg.; Aram.* and like iron which shatters all these.

Jews, Shadrach, Meshach and Abed-nego, whom you have put in charge of the administration of the province of Babylon. These men, your majesty, have taken no notice of your command; they do not serve your god, nor do they worship the golden image which you 13 have set up.' Then in rage and fury Nebuchadnezzar ordered Shadrach, Meshach and Abed-nego to be fetched, and they were brought in- 14 to the king's presence. Nebuchadnezzar said to them, 'Is it true, Shadrach, Meshach and Abed-nego, that you do not serve my god or worship the golden image which 15 I have set up? If you are ready at once to prostrate yourselves when you hear the sound of horn, pipe, zither, triangle, dulcimer, music, and singing of every kind, and to worship the image that I have set up, well and good. But if you do not worship it, you shall forthwith be thrown into the blazing furnace; and what god is there that can save 16 you from my power?' Shadrach, Meshach and Abed-nego said to King Nebuchadnezzar, 'We have no need to answer you on this 17 matter. If there is a god who is able to save us from the blazing furnace, it is our God whom we serve, and he will save us from your 18 power, O king; but if not, be it known to your majesty that we will neither serve your god nor worship the golden image that you have set up.'

19 Then Nebuchadnezzar flew into a rage with Shadrach, Meshach and Abed-nego, and his face was distorted with anger. He gave orders that the furnace should be heated up to seven times its usual 20 heat, and commanded some of the strongest men in his army to bind Shadrach, Meshach and Abed-nego and throw them into the 21 blazing furnace. Then those men in their trousers, their shirts, and their hats and all their other clothes, were bound and thrown into the blazing furnace. Because 22 the king's order was urgent and the furnace exceedingly hot, the men who were carrying Shadrach, Meshach and Abed-nego were killed by the flames that leapt out; and 23 those three men, Shadrach, Meshach and Abed-nego, fell bound into the blazing furnace.

Then King Nebuchadnezzar was 24 amazed and sprang to his feet in great trepidation. He said to his courtiers, 'Was it not three men whom we threw bound into the fire?' They answered the king, 'Assuredly, your majesty.' He an- 25 swered,'Yet I see four men walking about in the fire free and unharmed; and the fourth looks like a god.' Nebuchadnezzar approached the 26 door of the blazing furnace and said to the men, 'Shadrach, Meshach and Abed-nego, servants of the Most High God, come out, come here.' Then Shadrach, Meshach and Abed-nego came out from the fire. And the satraps, pre- 27 fects, viceroys, and the king's courtiers gathered round and saw how the fire had had no power to harm the bodies of these men; the hair of their heads had not been singed, their trousers were untouched, and no smell of fire lingered about them.

Then Nebuchadnezzar spoke 28 out, 'Blessed is the God of Shadrach, Meshach and Abed-nego. He has sent his angel to save his servants who put their trust in him, who disobeyed the royal command and were willing to yield themselves to the fire rather than to serve or worship any god other than their own God. I therefore 29 issue a decree that any man, to whatever people or nation he belongs, whatever his language, if he speaks blasphemy against the God of Shadrach, Meshach and Abed-nego, shall be torn to pieces and his house shall be forfeit;[a] for there is

a Or made into a dunghill (mng. of Aram. word uncertain).

no other god who can save men in
30 this way.' Then the king advanced
the fortunes of Shadrach, Meshach
and Abed-nego in the province of
Babylon.

4 KING Nebuchadnezzar to all
peoples and nations of every language living in the whole world!
2 May all prosperity be yours! It is
my pleasure to recount the signs
and marvels which the Most High
God has worked for me:

3 How great are his signs,
and his marvels overwhelming!
His kingdom is an everlasting
kingdom,
his sovereignty stands to all generations.

4 I, Nebuchadnezzar, was living
peacefully at home in the luxury of
5 my palace. As I lay on my bed, I
saw a dream which terrified me;
and fantasies and visions which
came into my head dismayed me.
6 So I issued an order summoning
into my presence all the wise men
of Babylon to make known to me
the interpretation of the dream.
7 Then the magicians, exorcists,
Chaldaeans, and diviners came in,
and in their presence I related my
dream. But they could not inter-
8 pret it. And yet another came into
my presence, Daniel, who is called
Belteshazzar after the name of my
god, a man possessed by the spirit
of the holy gods. To him, too, I
9 related the dream: 'Belteshazzar,
chief of the magicians, whom I myself know to be possessed by the
spirit of the holy gods, and whom
no secret baffles, listen to the
vision I saw in a dream, and tell me
its interpretation.
10 'Here is the vision which came
into my head as I was lying upon
my bed:

As I was looking,
I saw a tree of great height at the
centre of the earth;

the tree grew and became strong, 11
reaching with its top to the sky
and visible to earth's farthest
bounds.
Its foliage was lovely, 12
and its fruit abundant;
and it yielded food for all.
Beneath it the wild beasts found
shelter,
the birds lodged in its branches,
and from it all living creatures fed.

'Here is another vision which 13
came into my head as I was lying
upon my bed:

As I was watching, there was a
Watcher,
a Holy One coming down from
heaven.
He cried aloud and said, 14
"Hew down the tree, lop off the
branches,
strip away the foliage, scatter the
fruit.
Let the wild beasts flee from its
shelter
and the birds from its branches,
but leave the stump with its roots 15
in the ground.
So, tethered with an iron ring,
let him eat his fill of the lush grass;
let him be drenched with the dew
of heaven
and share the lot of the beasts in
their pasture;
let his mind cease to be a man's 16
mind,
and let him be given the mind of a
beast.
Let seven times pass over him.
The issue has been determined by 17
the Watchers
and the sentence pronounced by
the Holy Ones.

Thereby the living will know
that the Most High is sovereign in
the kingdom of men: he gives the
kingdom to whom he will and he
may set over it the humblest of
mankind."
'This is the dream which I, King 18
Nebuchadnezzar, have dreamed;

now, Belteshazzar, tell me its interpretation; for, though all the wise men of my kingdom are unable to tell me what it means, you can tell me, since the spirit of the holy gods is in you.'

19 Daniel, who was called Belteshazzar, was dumbfounded for a moment, dismayed by his thoughts; but the king said, 'Do not let the dream and its interpretation dismay you.' Belteshazzar answered, 'My lord, if only the dream were for those who hate you and its inter- 20 pretation for your enemies! The tree which you saw grow and become strong, reaching with its top to the sky and visible to earth's 21 farthest bounds, its foliage lovely and its fruit abundant, a tree which yielded food for all, beneath which the wild beasts dwelt and in whose branches the birds lodged, 22 that tree, O king, is you. You have grown and become strong. Your power has grown and reaches the sky; your sovereignty stretches to 23 the ends of the earth. Also, O king, you saw a Watcher, a Holy One, coming down from heaven and saying, "Hew down the tree and destroy it, but leave its stump with its roots in the ground. So, tethered with an iron ring, let him eat his fill of the lush grass; let him be drenched with the dew of heaven and share the lot of the beasts until 24 seven times pass over him." This is the interpretation, O king – it is a decree of the Most High which 25 touches my lord the king. You will be banished from the society of men; you will have to live with the wild beasts; you will feed on grass like oxen and you will be drenched with the dew of heaven. Seven times will pass over you until you have learnt that the Most High is sovereign over the kingdom of men and gives it to whom he will. 26 The command was given to leave the stump of the tree with its

roots. By this you may know that from the time you acknowledge the sovereignty of heaven your rule will endure. Be advised by me, 27 O king: redeem your sins by charity and your iniquities by generosity to the wretched. So may you long enjoy peace of mind.'

All this befell King Nebuchad- 28 nezzar. At the end of twelve 29 months the king was walking on the roof of the royal palace at Babylon, and he exclaimed, 'Is not 30 this Babylon the great which I have built as a royal residence by my own mighty power and for the honour of my majesty?' The words 31 were still on his lips, when a voice came down from heaven: 'To you, King Nebuchadnezzar, the word is spoken: the kingdom has passed from you. You are banished from 32 the society of men and you shall live with the wild beasts; you shall feed on grass like oxen, and seven times will pass over you until you have learnt that the Most High is sovereign over the kingdom of men and gives it to whom he will.' At 33 that very moment this judgement came upon Nebuchadnezzar. He was banished from the society of men and ate grass like oxen; his body was drenched by the dew of heaven, until his hair grew long like goats' hair and his nails like eagles' talons.[a]

At the end of the appointed time, 34 I, Nebuchadnezzar, raised my eyes to heaven and I returned to my right mind. I blessed the Most High, praising and glorifying the Ever-living One:

His sovereignty is never-ending
and his rule endures through all
    generations;
all dwellers upon earth count for 35
    nothing
and he deals as he wishes with the
    host of heaven;[b]

---

[a] goats' hair...eagles' talons: *prob. rdg.*; *Aram.* eagles' and his nails like birds'.
[b] *Prob. rdg.*; *Aram. adds* and the dwellers upon earth.

no one may lay hand upon him and ask him what he does.

36 At that very time I returned to my right mind and my majesty and royal splendour were restored to me for the glory of my kingdom. My courtiers and my nobles sought audience of me. I was established in my kingdom and my power 37 was greatly increased. Now I, Nebuchadnezzar, praise and exalt and glorify the King of heaven; for all his acts are right and his ways are just and those whose conduct is arrogant he can bring low.

Belshazzar's feast

5 BELSHAZZAR the king gave a banquet for a thousand of his nobles and was drinking wine in the presence of the thousand. 2 Warmed by the wine, he gave orders to fetch the vessels of gold and silver which his father Nebuchadnezzar had taken from the sanctuary at Jerusalem, that he and his nobles, his concubines and his courtesans, might drink from 3 them. So the vessels of gold and silver from the sanctuary in the house of God at Jerusalem were brought in, and the king and his nobles, his concubines and his 4 courtesans, drank from them. They drank wine and praised the gods of gold and silver, of bronze and iron, 5 and of wood and stone. Suddenly there appeared the fingers of a human hand writing on the plaster of the palace wall opposite the lamp, and the king could see the 6 back of the hand as it wrote. At this the king's mind was filled with dismay and he turned pale, he became limp in every limb and his 7 knees knocked together. He called loudly for the exorcists, Chaldaeans, and diviners to be brought in; then, addressing the wise men of Babylon, he said, 'Whoever can read this writing and tell me its

interpretation shall be robed in purple and honoured with a chain of gold round his neck and shall rank as third in the kingdom.' Then 8 all the king's wise men came in, but they could not read the writing or interpret it to the king. King 9 Belshazzar sat there pale and utterly dismayed, while his nobles were perplexed.

The king and his nobles were 10 talking when the queen entered the banqueting-hall: 'Long live the king!' she said. 'Why this dismay, and why do you look so pale? There is a man in your kingdom 11 who has in him the spirit of the holy gods, a man who was known in your father's time to have a clear understanding and godlike wisdom. King Nebuchadnezzar, your father, appointed him chief of the magicians, exorcists, Chaldaeans, and diviners. This same 12 Daniel, whom the king named Belteshazzar, is known to have a notable spirit, with knowledge and understanding, and the gift of interpreting dreams, explaining riddles and unbinding spells;[a] let him be summoned now and he will give the interpretation.' Daniel 13 was then brought into the king's presence and the king said to him, 'So you are Daniel, one of the Jewish exiles whom the king my father brought from Judah. I have 14 heard that you possess the spirit of the holy gods and that you are a man of clear understanding and peculiar wisdom. The wise men, 15 the exorcists, have just been brought into my presence to read this writing and tell me its interpretation, and they have been unable to interpret it. But I have 16 heard it said of you that you are able to give interpretations and to unbind spells.[b] So now, if you are able to read the words and tell me what they mean, you shall be robed in purple and honoured with a chain of gold round your neck and

---

[a] *Or and solving problems.*

[b] *Or and to solve problems.*

shall rank as third in the kingdom.'
17 Then Daniel answered in the king's presence, 'Your gifts you may keep for yourself; or else give your rewards to another. Nevertheless I will read the writing to your majesty and tell you its interpretation.
18 My lord king, the Most High God gave your father Nebuchadnezzar a kingdom and power and glory
19 and majesty; and, because of this power which he gave him, all peoples and nations of every language trembled before him and were afraid. He put to death whom he would and spared whom he would, he promoted them at will
20 and at will degraded them. But, when he became haughty, stubborn and presumptuous, he was deposed from his royal throne and
21 his glory was taken from him. He was banished from the society of men, his mind became like that of a beast, he had to live with the wild asses and to eat grass like oxen, and his body was drenched with the dew of heaven, until he came to know that the Most High God is sovereign over the kingdom of men and sets up over it whom he will.
22 But you, his son Belshazzar, did not humble your heart, although
23 you knew all this. You have set yourself up against the Lord of heaven. The vessels of his temple have been brought to your table; and you, your nobles, your concubines, and your courtesans have drunk from them. You have praised the gods of silver and gold, of bronze and iron, of wood and stone, which neither see nor hear nor know, and you have not given glory to God, in whose charge is your very breath and in whose
24 hands are all your ways. This is why that hand was sent from his very presence and why it wrote this
25 inscription. And these are the words of the writing which was inscribed: *Mene mene tekel u-*

pharsin. Here is the interpreta- 26 tion: *mene:*[a] God has numbered the days of your kingdom and brought it to an end; *tekel:*[b] you have been 27 weighed in the balance and found wanting; *u-pharsin:*[c] and your 28 kingdom has been divided and given to the Medes and Persians.' Then Belshazzar gave the order 29 and Daniel was robed in purple and honoured with a chain of gold round his neck, and proclamation was made that he should rank as third in the kingdom.

That very night Belshazzar king 30 of the Chaldaeans was slain, and 31 Darius the Mede took the kingdom, being then sixty-two years old.

Daniel in the lions' pit

It pleased Darius to appoint sat- 6 raps over the kingdom, a hundred and twenty in number in charge of the whole kingdom, and over them 2 three chief ministers, to whom the satraps should send reports so that the king's interests might not suffer; of these three, Daniel was one. In the event Daniel outshone 3 the other ministers and the satraps because of his ability, and the king had it in mind to appoint him over the whole kingdom. Then the chief 4 ministers and the satraps began to look round for some pretext to attack Daniel's administration of the kingdom, but they failed to find any malpractice on his part; for he was faithful to his trust. Since they could discover no neg- 5 lect of duty or malpractice, they said, 'There will be no charge to bring against this Daniel unless we find one in his religion.' These chief 6 ministers and satraps watched for an opportunity to approach the king, and said to him, 'Long live King Darius! All we, the ministers 7 of the kingdom, prefects, satraps, courtiers, and viceroys, have taken

---

[a] *That is* numbered.   [b] *That is* shekel *or* weight.   [c] *Prob. rdg.; Aram.* pheres. *There is a play on three possible meanings:* halves *or* divisions *or* Persians.

counsel and agree that the king should issue a decree and bring an ordinance into force, that whoever within the next thirty days shall present a petition to any god or man other than the king shall be 8 thrown into the lions' pit. Now, O king, issue the ordinance and have it put in writing, so that it may be unalterable, for the law of the Medes and Persians stands for ever.' 9 Accordingly King Darius issued the ordinance in written form.

10 When Daniel learnt that this decree had been issued, he went into his house. He had had windows made in his roof-chamber looking towards Jerusalem; and there he knelt down three times a day and offered prayers and praises to his God as his custom had al- 11 ways been. His enemies watched for an opportunity to catch Daniel and found him at his prayers making supplication to his God. 12 Then they came into the king's presence and reminded him of the ordinance. 'Your majesty,' they said, 'have you not issued an ordinance that any person who, within the next thirty days, shall present a petition to any god or man other than your majesty shall be thrown into the lions' pit?' The king answered, 'Yes, it is fixed. The law of the Medes and Persians stands for 13 ever.' So in the king's presence they said, 'Daniel, one of the Jewish exiles, has ignored the ordinance issued by your majesty, and is making petition to his god three 14 times a day.' When the king heard this, he was greatly distressed. He tried to think of a way to save Daniel, and continued his efforts 15 till sunset; then those same men watched for an opportunity to approach the king, and said to him, 'Your majesty must know that by the law of the Medes and Persians no ordinance or decree issued by 16 the king may be altered.' So the king gave orders and Daniel was brought and thrown into the lions' pit; but he said to Daniel, 'Your own God, whom you serve continually, will save you.' A stone 17 was brought and put over the mouth of the pit, and the king sealed it with his signet and with the signets of his nobles, so that no one might intervene to rescue Daniel.

The king went back to his palace 18 and spent the night fasting; no woman was brought to him and sleep eluded him. At dawn, as soon 19 as it was light, he rose and went in fear and trembling to the pit. When the king reached it, he called 20 anxiously to Daniel, 'Daniel, servant of the living God, has your God whom you serve continually been able to save you from the lions?' Then Daniel answered, 21 'Long live the king! My God sent 22 his angel to shut the lions' mouths so that they have done me no injury, because in his judgement I was found innocent;[a] and moreover, O king, I had done you no injury.' The king was overjoyed 23 and gave orders that Daniel should be lifted out of the pit. So Daniel was lifted out and no trace of injury was found on him, because he had put his faith in his God. By 24 order of the king Daniel's accusers were brought and thrown into the lions' pit with their wives and children, and before they reached the floor of the pit the lions were upon them and crunched them up, bones and all.

Then King Darius wrote to all 25 peoples and nations of every language throughout the whole world: 'May your prosperity increase! I 26 have issued a decree that in all my royal domains men shall fear and reverence the God of Daniel;

for he is the living God, the everlasting,
whose kingly power shall not be weakened;

---

[a] *in his judgement...innocent: or before him success was granted me.*

whose sovereignty shall have no end –

27 a saviour, a deliverer, a worker of signs and wonders
in heaven and on earth,
who has delivered Daniel from the power of the lions.'

28 So this Daniel prospered during the reigns of Darius and Cyrus the Persian.

Daniel's visions

7 IN the first year of Belshazzar king of Babylon, as Daniel lay on his bed, dreams and visions came into his head. Then he wrote down the dream, and here his account begins:

2 In my visions of the night I, Daniel, was gazing intently and I saw a great sea churned up by the
3 four winds of heaven, and four huge beasts coming up out of the sea, each one different from the
4 others. The first was like a lion but had an eagle's wings. I watched until its wings were plucked off and it was lifted from the ground and made to stand on two feet like a man; it was also given the mind of
5 a man. Then I saw another, a second beast, like a bear. It was half crouching and had three ribs in its mouth, between its teeth. The command was given: 'Up,
6 gorge yourself with flesh.' After this as I gazed I saw another, a beast like a leopard with four bird's wings on its back; this creature had four heads, and it was invested with sovereign power.
7 Next in my visions of the night I saw a fourth beast, dreadful and grisly, exceedingly strong, with great iron teeth and bronze claws.[a] It crunched and devoured, and trampled underfoot all that was left. It differed from all the beasts which preceded it in having ten
8 horns. While I was considering the horns I saw another horn, a little

one, springing up among them, and three of the first horns were uprooted to make room for it. And in that horn were eyes like the eyes of a man, and a mouth that spoke proud words. I kept looking, and 9 then

thrones were set in place and one ancient in years took his seat,
his robe was white as snow and the hair of his head like cleanest wool.
Flames of fire were his throne and its wheels blazing fire;
a flowing river of fire streamed out 10 before him.[b]
Thousands upon thousands served him
and myriads upon myriads attended his presence.
The court sat, and the books were opened.

Then because of the proud words 11 that the horn was speaking, I went on watching until the beast was killed and its carcass destroyed: it was given to the flames. The rest of 12 the beasts, though deprived of their sovereignty, were allowed to remain alive for a time and a season. I was still watching in visions 13 of the night and I saw one like a man coming with the clouds of heaven; he approached the Ancient in Years and was presented to him. Sovereignty and glory and 14 kingly power were given to him, so that all people and nations of every language should serve him; his sovereignty was to be an everlasting sovereignty which should not pass away, and his kingly power such as should never be impaired.

My spirit within me was troubled, 15 and, dismayed by the visions which came into my head, I, 16 Daniel, approached one of those who stood there and inquired from him what all this meant; and he told me the interpretation. 'These 17 great beasts, four in number,' he

_____
[a] *and bronze claws:* prob. rdg., cp. verse 19; Aram. om.   [b] Or it.

said, 'are four kingdoms which
18 shall rise from the ground. But the
saints[a] of the Most High shall receive the kingly power and shall retain it for ever, for ever and ever.'
19 Then I desired to know what the
fourth beast meant, the beast that
was different from all the others,
very dreadful with its iron teeth
and bronze claws, crunching and
devouring and trampling under-
20 foot all that was left. I desired also
to know about the ten horns on its
head and the other horn which
sprang up and at whose coming
three of them fell – the horn that
had eyes and a mouth speaking
proud words and appeared larger
21 than the others. As I still watched,
that horn was waging war with the
22 saints and overcoming them until
the Ancient in Years came. Then
judgement was given in favour of
the saints of the Most High, and
the time came when the saints
gained possession of the kingly
23 power. He gave me this answer:
'The fourth beast signifies a fourth
kingdom which shall appear upon
earth. It shall differ from the other
kingdoms and shall devour the
whole earth, tread it down and
24 crush it. The ten horns signify the
appearance of ten kings in this
kingdom, after whom another king
shall arise, differing from his predecessors; and he shall bring low
25 three kings. He shall hurl defiance
at the Most High and shall wear
down the saints of the Most High.
He shall plan to alter the customary times and law; and the saints
shall be delivered into his power
for a time and times and half a
26 time. Then the court shall sit, and
he shall be deprived of his sovereignty, so that in the end it may be
27 destroyed and abolished. The kingly power, sovereignty, and greatness of all the kingdoms under
heaven shall be given to the people
of the saints of the Most High.
Their kingly power is an everlast-

ing power and all sovereignties
shall serve them and obey them.'
Here the account ends. As for 28
me, Daniel, my thoughts dismayed me greatly and I turned
pale; and I kept these things in my
mind.

[b]In the third year of the reign of 8 1–2
King Belshazzar, while I was in
Susa the capital city of the province of Elam, a vision appeared
to me, Daniel, similar to my former vision. In this vision I was
watching beside the stream of the
Ulai. I raised my eyes and there I 3
saw a ram with two horns standing
between me and the stream. The
two horns were long, the one longer
than the other, growing up behind.
I watched the ram butting west 4
and north and south. No beasts
could stand before it, no one could
rescue from its power. It did what
it liked, making a display of its
strength. While I pondered this, 5
suddenly a he-goat came from the
west skimming over the whole
earth without touching the ground;
it had a prominent horn between
its eyes. It approached the two- 6
horned ram which I had seen
standing between me and the
stream and rushed at it with impetuous force. I saw it advance on 7
the ram, working itself into a fury
against it, then strike the ram and
break its two horns; the ram had
no strength to resist. The he-goat
flung it to the ground and trampled
on it, and there was no one to save
the ram.

Then the he-goat made a great 8
display of its strength. Powerful as
it was, its great horn snapped and
in its place there sprang out towards the four quarters of heaven
four prominent horns. Out of one of 9
them there issued one small horn,
which made a prodigious show of
strength south and east and towards the fairest of all lands. It 10
aspired to be as great as the host of
heaven, and it cast down to the

---

[a] *Or* holy ones.   [b] *Here the Hebrew text resumes (see note at 2. 4).*

earth some of the host and some of the stars and trod them underfoot.

11 It aspired to be as great as the Prince of the host, suppressed his regular offering and even threw

12 down his sanctuary. The heavenly hosts were delivered up, and it raised itself[a] impiously against the regular offering and threw true religion to the ground; in all that it

13 did it succeeded. I heard a holy one speaking and another holy one answering him, whoever he was. The one said, 'For how long will the period of this vision last? How long will the regular offering be suppressed, how long will impiety cause desolation,[b] and both the Holy Place and the fairest of all lands[c] be given over to be trodden

14 down?' The answer came, 'For two thousand three hundred evenings and mornings; then the Holy Place shall emerge victorious.'

15   All the while that I, Daniel, was seeing the vision, I was trying to understand it. Suddenly I saw standing before me one with the

16 semblance of a man; at the same time I heard a human voice calling to him across the bend of the Ulai, 'Gabriel, explain the vision to this

17 man.' He came up to where I was standing; I was seized with terror at his approach and threw myself on my face. But he said to me, 'Understand, O man: the vision points to the time of the end.'

18 When he spoke to me, I fell to the ground in a trance; but he grasped me and made me stand up where I

19 was. And he said, 'I shall make known to you what is to happen at the end of the wrath; for there is an

20 end to the appointed time. The two-horned ram which you saw signifies the kings of Media and

21 Persia, the he-goat is the kingdom[d] of the Greeks and the great horn on

22 his forehead is the first king. As for the horn which was snapped off

and replaced by four horns: four kingdoms shall rise out of that nation, but not with power comparable to his.

In the last days of those kingdoms, 23
when their sin is at its height,
a king shall appear, harsh and grim, a master of stratagem.
His power shall be great, he shall 24
work havoc untold;
he shall succeed in whatever he does.
He shall work havoc among great nations and upon a holy people.
His mind shall be ever active, 25
and he shall succeed in his crafty designs;
he shall conjure up great plans
and, when they least expect it, work havoc on many.
He shall challenge even the Prince of princes
and be broken, but not by human hands.
This revelation which has been 26
given
of the evenings and the mornings is true;
but you must keep the vision secret,
for it points to days far ahead.'

As for me, Daniel, my strength 27
failed me and I lay sick for a while.
Then I rose and attended to the king's business. But I was perplexed by the revelation and no one could explain it.

IN the first year of the reign of 9
Darius son of Ahasuerus (a Mede by birth, who was appointed king over the kingdom of the Chaldaeans) I, Daniel, was reading the 2
scriptures and reflecting on the seventy years which, according to the word of the LORD to the prophet Jeremiah, were to pass while Jerusalem lay in ruins. Then I 3
turned to the Lord God in earnest

---

[a] *and it raised itself: prob. rdg.; Heb. om.*
[b] *will impiety cause desolation: prob. rdg.; Heb. obscure.*   [c] *fairest of all lands: prob. rdg., cp. verse 9; Heb. host.*   [d] *Prob. rdg.; Heb. king.*

prayer and supplication with fast-
4 ing and sackcloth and ashes. I
prayed to the LORD my God, making confession thus:

'Lord, thou great and terrible
God who faithfully keepest the
covenant with those who love thee
and observe thy commandments,
5 we have sinned, we have done what
was wrong and wicked; we have
rebelled, we have turned our backs
on thy commandments and thy
6 decrees. We have not listened to
thy servants the prophets, who
spoke in thy name to our kings and
princes, to our forefathers and to
7 all the people of the land. O Lord,
the right is on thy side; the shame,
now as ever, belongs to us, the men
of Judah and the citizens of Jerusalem, and to all the Israelites near
and far in every land to which thou
hast banished them for their
8 treachery towards thee. O LORD,
the shame falls on us as on our
kings, our princes and our forefathers; we have all sinned against
9 thee. Compassion and forgiveness
belong to the Lord our God,
though we have rebelled against
10 him. We have not obeyed the
LORD our God, we have not conformed to the laws which he laid
down for us through his servants
11 the prophets. All Israel has broken
thy law and not obeyed thee, so
that the curses set out in the law of
Moses thy servant in the adjuration and the oath have rained
down upon us; for we have sinned
12 against him. He has fulfilled all
that he said about us and about our
rulers, by bringing upon us and
upon Jerusalem a calamity greater
than has ever happened in all the
13 world. It was all foreshadowed in
the law of Moses, this calamity
which has come upon us; yet we
have done nothing to propitiate
the LORD our God; we have neither
repented of our wrongful deeds nor
remembered that thou art true to
14 thy word. The LORD has been

biding his time and has now brought
this calamity upon us. In all that
he has done the LORD our God has
been right; yet we have not obeyed
him.

'And now, O Lord our God who 15
didst bring thy people out of Egypt
by a strong hand, winning for
thyself a name that lives on to this
day, we have sinned, we have done
wrong. O Lord, by all thy saving 16
deeds we beg that thy wrath and
anger may depart from Jerusalem,
thy city, thy holy hill; through our
own sins and our fathers' guilty
deeds Jerusalem and thy people
have become a byword among all
our neighbours. And now, our 17
God, listen to thy servant's prayer
and supplication; for thy own sake,
O Lord, make thy face shine upon
thy desolate sanctuary. Lend thy 18
ear, O God, and hear, open thine
eyes and look upon our desolation
and upon the city that bears thy
name; it is not by virtue of our own
saving acts but by thy great mercy
that we present our supplications
before thee. O Lord, hear; O Lord,
forgive; O Lord, listen and act; for 19
thy own sake do not delay, O God,
for thy city and thy people bear
thy name.'

Thus I was speaking and pray- 20
ing, confessing my own sin and my
people Israel's sin, and presenting
my supplication before the LORD
my God on behalf of his holy hill.
While I was praying, the man 21
Gabriel, whom I had already seen
in the vision, came close to[a] me at
the hour of the evening sacrifice,
flying swiftly.[b] He spoke clearly to 22
me and said, 'Daniel, I have now
come to enlighten your understanding. As you were beginning 23
your supplications a word went
forth; this I have come to pass on
to you, for you are a man greatly
beloved. Consider well the word,
consider the vision: Seventy weeks 24
are marked out for your people and
your holy city; then rebellion shall

---

[a] Or touched.   [b] flying swiftly: *prob. rdg.*; *Heb.* thoroughly wearied.

be stopped,[a] sin brought to an end,[b] iniquity expiated, everlasting right ushered in, vision and prophecy sealed, and the Most Holy Place
25 anointed. Know then and understand: from the time that the word went forth that Jerusalem should be restored and rebuilt, seven weeks shall pass till the appearance of one anointed, a prince; then for sixty-two weeks it shall remain restored, rebuilt with streets
26 and conduits. At the critical time, after the sixty-two weeks, one who is anointed shall be removed with no one to take his part; and the horde of an invading prince shall work havoc on city and sanctuary. The end of it shall be a deluge, inevitable war with all its horrors.
27 He shall make a firm league with the mighty[c] for one week; and, the week half spent, he shall put a stop to sacrifice and offering. And in the train of these abominations shall come an author of desolation; then, in the end, what has been decreed concerning the desolation will be poured out.'

10 IN the third year of Cyrus king of Persia a word was revealed to Daniel who had been given the name Belteshazzar. Though this word was true, it cost him[d] much toil to understand it; nevertheless understanding came to him in the course of the vision.
2   In those days I, Daniel, mourn-
3 ed for three whole weeks. I refrained from all choice food; no meat or wine passed my lips, and I did not anoint myself until the
4 three weeks had gone by. On the twenty-fourth day of the first month, I found myself on the bank of the great river, that is the Tig-
5 ris; I looked up and saw a man clothed in linen with a belt of gold
6 from Ophir round his waist. His body gleamed like topaz, his face shone like lightning, his eyes flamed like torches, his arms and feet

sparkled like a disc of bronze; and when he spoke his voice sounded like the voice of a multitude. I, 7 Daniel, alone saw the vision, while those who were near me did not see it, but great fear fell upon them and they stole away, and I was left 8 alone gazing at this great vision. But my strength left me; I became a sorry figure of a man, and retained no strength. I heard the 9 sound of his words and, when I did so, I fell prone on the ground in a trance. Suddenly a hand grasped 10 me and pulled me up on to my hands and knees. He said to me, 11 'Daniel, man greatly beloved, attend to the words I am speaking to you and stand up where you are, for I am now sent to you.' When he addressed me, I stood up trembling and he said, 'Do not be afraid, 12 Daniel, for from the very first day that you applied your mind to understand and to mortify yourself before your God, your prayers have been heard, and I have come in answer to them. But the angel 13 prince of the kingdom of Persia resisted me for twenty-one days, and then, seeing that I had held out there, Michael, one of the chief princes, came to help me against the prince of the kingdom of Persia. And I have come to explain to 14 you what will happen to your people in days to come; for this too is a vision for those days.'

While he spoke to me I hung my 15 head and was struck dumb. Sud- 16 denly one like a man touched my lips. Then I opened my mouth to speak and addressed him as he stood before me: 'Sir, this has pierced me to the heart, and I retain no strength. How can my 17 lord's servant presume to talk with such as my lord, since my strength has failed me and no breath is left in me?' Then the 18 figure touched me again and restored my strength. He said, 'Do 19 not be afraid, man greatly beloved;

---

[a] *Or* restrained.   [b] *Or* sealed.   [c] *Or* many.   [d] him: *prob. rdg.; Heb. om.*

all will be well with you. Be strong, be strong.' When he had spoken to me, I recovered strength and said, 'Speak, sir, for you have given me 20 strength.' He said, 'Do you know why I have come to you? I am first going back to fight with the prince of Persia, and, as soon as I have left, the prince of Greece will 21–11 appear: I have no ally on my side to help and support me, except Michael your prince.[a] However I will tell you what is written in the 2 Book of Truth. Here and now I will tell you what is true:

'Three more kings will appear in Persia, and the fourth will far surpass all the others in wealth; and when he has extended his power through his wealth, he will rouse the whole world against the king- 3 dom of Greece. Then there will appear a warrior king. He will rule a vast kingdom and will do what he 4 chooses. But as soon as he is established, his kingdom will be shattered and split up north, south, east and west. It will not pass to his descendants, nor will any of his successors have an empire like his; his kingdom will be torn up by the roots and given to others as well as 5 to them. Then the king of the south will become strong; but another of the captains will surpass him in strength and win a greater 6 kingdom. In due course the two will enter into a friendly alliance; to redress the balance the daughter of the king of the south will be given in marriage to the king of the north, but she will not maintain her influence and their line will not last. She and her escort, her child, and also her lord and master, will all be the victims of foul play. 7 Then another shoot from the same stock as hers will appear in his father's place, will penetrate the defences of the king of the north and enter his fortress, and will win a decisive victory over his people.

He will take back as booty to 8 Egypt even the images of their gods cast in metal and their precious vessels of silver and gold. Then for some years he will refrain from attacking the king of the north. After that the king of 9 the north will overrun the southern kingdom but will retreat to his own land.

'His sons will press on to as- 10 semble a great armed horde. One of them will sweep on and on like an irresistible flood. And after that he will press on as far as his enemy's stronghold. The king of 11 the south, his anger roused, will march out to do battle with the king of the north who, in turn, will raise a great horde, but it will be delivered into the hands of his enemy. When this horde has been 12 captured, the victor will be elated and he will slaughter tens of thousands, yet he will not maintain his advantage. Then the king of the 13 north will once more raise a horde even greater than the last and, when the years come round, will advance with a great army and a large baggage-train. During these 14 times many will resist the king of the south, but some hotheads among your own people will rashly attempt to give substance to a vision and will come to disaster. Then the king of the north will 15 come and throw up siege-ramps and capture a fortified town, and the forces of the south will not stand up to him; even the flower of their army will not be able to hold their ground. And so his adversary 16 will do as he pleases and meet with no opposition. He will establish himself in the fairest of all lands and it will come wholly into his power. He will resolve to subjugate 17 all the dominions of the king of the south; and he will come to fair terms with him,[b] and he will give him a young woman in marriage,

---

[a] *Prob. rdg.*; *Heb. adds* and as for me, in the first year of Darius the Mede.
[b] and he...with him: *prob. rdg.*; *Heb. obscure.*

for the destruction of the kingdom; but she will not persist nor serve 18 his purpose. Then he will turn to the coasts and islands and take many prisoners, but a foreign commander*ᵃ* will put an end to his challenge by wearing him down;*ᵇ* thus he will throw back his challenge 19 on to him. He will fall back upon his own strongholds; there he will come to disaster and be overthrown and be seen no more.

20 'He will be succeeded by one who will send out an officer with a royal escort to extort tribute; after a short time this king too will meet his end, yet neither openly nor in battle.

21 'A contemptible creature will succeed but will not be given recognition as king; yet he will seize the kingdom by dissimulation and 22 intrigue in time of peace. He will sweep away all forces of opposition as he advances, and even the Prince of the Covenant will be 23 broken. He will enter into fraudulent alliances and, although the people behind him are but few, he will rise to power and establish 24 himself in time of peace. He will overrun the richest districts of the province and succeed in doing what his fathers and forefathers failed to do, distributing spoil, booty, and property to his followers. He will lay his plans against fortresses, but only for a time.

25 'He will rouse himself in all his strength and courage and lead a great army against the king of the south, but the king of the south will press the campaign against him with a very great and numerous army; yet the king of the south will not persist, for traitors will lay 26 their plots. Those who eat at his board will be his undoing; his army will be swept away, and many will 27 fall on the field of battle. The two kings will be bent on mischief and, sitting at the same table, they will lie to each other with advantage to

neither. Yet there will still be an end to the appointed time. Then 28 one will return home with a long baggage-train, and with anger in his heart against the Holy Covenant; he will work his will and return to his own land.

'At the appointed time he will 29 once more overrun the south, but he will not succeed as he did before. Ships from the west will sail a- 30 gainst him, and he will receive a rebuff. He will turn and vent his fury against the Holy Covenant; on his way back he will take due note of those who have forsaken it. Armed forces dispatched by him 31 will desecrate the sanctuary and the citadel and do away with the regular offering. And there they will set up "the abominable thing that causes desolation". He will 32 win over by plausible promises those who are ready to condemn the covenant, but the people who are faithful to their God will hold firm and fight back. Wise leaders 33 of the nation will give guidance to the common people; yet for a while they will fall victims to fire and sword, to captivity and pillage. But these victims will not want 34 for help, though small, even if many who join them are insincere. Some of these leaders will them- 35 selves fall victims for a time so that they may be tested, refined and made shining white. Yet there will still be an end*ᶜ* to the appointed time. The king will do what he 36 chooses; he will exalt and magnify himself above every god and against the God of gods he will utter monstrous blasphemies. All will go well for him until the time of wrath ends, for what is determined must be done. He will ignore his an- 37 cestral gods, and the god beloved of women; to no god will he pay heed but will exalt himself above them all. Instead he will honour 38 the god of the citadel, a god un-

ᵃ Or consul or legate.   *ᵇ by wearing him down: prob. rdg.; Heb. obscure.*
ᶜ Yet...end: prob. rdg.; Heb. has different word order.

known to his ancestors, with gold and silver, gems and costly gifts.

39 He will garrison his strongest fortresses with aliens, the people of a foreign god. Those whom he favours he will load with honour, putting them in office over the common people and distributing land at a price.

40 'At the time of the end, he and the king of the south will make feints at one another, and the king of the north will come storming against him with chariots and cavalry and many ships. He will overrun land after land, sweeping over

41 them like a flood, amongst them the fairest of all lands, and tens of thousands shall fall victims. Yet all these lands [including Edom and Moab and the remnant of the Ammonites] will survive his at-

42 tack. He will reach out to land after land, and Egypt will not

43 escape. He will gain control of her hidden stores of gold and silver and of all her treasures; Libyans and Cushites will follow in his train.

44 Then rumours from east and north will alarm him, and he will depart in a great rage to destroy and to

45 exterminate many. He will pitch his royal pavilion between the sea and the holy hill, the fairest of all hills; and he will meet his end with no one to help him.

12 At that moment Michael shall appear,
Michael the great captain,
who stands guard over your fellow-countrymen;
and there will be a time of distress such as has never been
since they became a nation till that moment.
But at that moment your people will be delivered,[a]
every one who is written in the book:

2 many of those who sleep in the dust of the earth will wake,
some to everlasting life

and some to the reproach of eternal abhorrence.

3 The wise leaders shall shine like the bright vault of heaven,
and those who have guided the people in the true path
shall be like the stars for ever and ever.

4 But you, Daniel, keep the words secret and seal the book till the time of the end. Many will be at their wits' end, and punishment will be heavy.'

5 And I, Daniel, looked and saw two others standing, one on this bank of the river and the other on

6 the opposite bank. And I said to the man clothed in linen who was above the waters of the river, 'How long will it be before these portents

7 cease?' The man clothed in linen above the waters lifted to heaven his right hand and his left, and I heard him swear by him who lives for ever: 'It shall be for a time, times, and a half. When the power of the holy people ceases to be dispersed, all these things shall come

8 to an end.' I heard but I did not understand, and so I said, 'Sir, what will the issue of these things

9 be?' He replied, 'Go your way, Daniel, for the words are kept secret and sealed till the time of the

10 end. Many shall purify themselves and be refined, making themselves shining white, but the wicked shall continue in wickedness and none of them shall understand; only the wise leaders shall understand.

11 From the time when the regular offering is abolished and "the abomination of desolation" is set up, there shall be an interval of one thousand two hundred and ninety

12 days. Happy the man who waits and lives to see the completion of one thousand three hundred and

13 thirty-five days! But go your way to the end and rest, and you shall arise to your destiny at the end of the age.'

a Or will escape.

HOSEA

1 THE word of the LORD which came to Hosea son of Beeri during the reigns of Uzziah, Jotham, Ahaz, and Hezekiah, kings of Judah, and during the reign of Jeroboam son of Jehoash king of Israel.

Hosea's unfaithful wife

2 THIS is the beginning of the LORD'S message by Hosea. He said, Go, take a wanton for your wife and get children of her wantonness; for like a wanton this land

3 is unfaithful to the LORD. So he went and took Gomer, a worthless woman;[a] and she conceived and

4 bore him a son. And the LORD said to him,

Call him Jezreel;[b] for in a little while
I will punish the line of Jehu for the blood shed in Jezreel
and put an end to the kingdom of Israel.

5 On that day
I will break Israel's bow in the Vale of Jezreel.

6 She conceived again and bore a daughter, and the LORD said to him,

Call her Lo-ruhamah;[c]
for I will never again show love to Israel,
never again forgive them.[d]

8 After weaning Lo-ruhamah, she

9 conceived and bore a son; and the LORD said,

Call him Lo-ammi;[e]
for you are not my people,
and I will not be your God.

10 The Israelites shall become countless as the sands of the sea
which can neither be measured nor numbered;
it shall no longer be said, 'They are not my people',
they shall be called Sons of the Living God.

11 Then the people of Judah and of Israel shall be reunited
and shall choose for themselves a single head,
and they shall become masters of the earth;
for great shall be the day of Jezreel.

2 Then you will say to your brothers, 'You are my people',
and to your sisters, 'You are loved.'

2 Plead my cause with your mother;
is she not my wife and I her husband?[f]
Plead with her to forswear those wanton looks,
to banish the lovers from her bosom.

3 Or I will strip her and expose her naked as the day she was born;
I will make her bare as the wilderness,
parched as the desert,
and leave her to die of thirst.

4 I will show no love for her children;
they are the offspring of wantonness,

5 and their mother is a wanton.
She who conceived them is shameless;

[a] a worthless woman: or daughter of Diblaim.   [b] That is God shall sow.
[c] That is Not loved.   [d] Prob. rdg.; Heb. adds (7) Then I will love Judah and will save them. I will save them not by bow or sword or weapon of war, by horses or by horsemen, but by the LORD their God.   [e] That is Not my people.
[f] is she...husband?: or for she is no longer my wife nor I her husband.

she says, 'I will go after my
lovers;
they give me my food and drink,
my wool and flax, my oil and my
perfumes.'

6 Therefore I will block her road
with thorn-bushes
and obstruct her path with a wall,
so that she can no longer follow her
old ways.

7 When she pursues her lovers she
will not overtake them,
when she looks for them she will
not find them;
then she will say,
'I will go back to my husband
again;
I was better off with him than I am
now.'

8 For she does not know that it is I
who gave her
corn, new wine, and oil,
I who lavished upon her silver and
gold
which they spent on the Baal.

9 Therefore I will take back
my corn at the harvest and my new
wine at the vintage,
and I will take away the wool and
the flax
which I gave her to cover her naked
body;

10 so I will show her up for the lewd
thing she is,
and no lover will want to steal her
from me.

12ᵃ I will ravage the vines and the fig-
trees,
which she says are the fee
with which her lovers have hired
her,
and turn them into jungle where
wild beasts shall feed.

11 I will put a stop to her merry-
making,
her pilgrimages and new moons,
her sabbathsᵇ and festivals.

13 I will punish her for the holy days
when she burnt sacrifices to the
Baalim,

when she decked herself with earrings and necklaces,
ran after her lovers and forgot me.
This is the very word of the LORD.

But now listen, 14
I will woo her, I will go with her
into the wilderness
and comfort her:
there I will restore her vineyards, 15
turning the Vale of Trouble into
the Gate of Hope,ᶜ
and there she will answer as in her
youth,
when she came up out of Egypt.
On that day she shall call me 'My 16
husband'
and shall no more call me 'My
Baal';ᵈ
and I will wipe from her lips the 17
very names of the Baalim;
never again shall their names be
heard.
This is the very word of the LORD.ᵉ

Then I will make a covenant on 18
behalf of Israel with the wild
beasts, the birds of the air, and the
things that creep on the earth, and
I will break bow and sword and
weapon of war and sweep them off
the earth, so that all living creatures may lie down without fear. I 19
will betroth you to myself for ever,
betroth you in lawful wedlock with
unfailing devotion and love; I will 20
betroth you to myself to have and
to hold, and you shall know the
LORD. At that time I will give 21
answer, says the LORD, I will answer for the heavens and they will
answer for the earth, and the earth 22
will answer for the corn, the new
wine, and the oil, and they will
answer for Jezreel. Israel shall be 23
my new sowing in the land, and I
will show love to Lo-ruhamah and
say to Lo-ammi, 'You are my
people', and he will say, 'Thou art
my God.'

ᵃ *Verses 11 and 12 transposed.*　　　ᵇ *Or her full moons.*
ᶜ turning...Hope: *or Emek-achor to Pethah-tikvah.*
ᵈ *Also means My husband.*
ᵉ This...LORD: *transposed from after* On that day *in verse 16.*

3   The LORD said to me,

Go again and love a woman
loved by another man, an adulter-
    ess,
and love her as I, the LORD, love
    the Israelites
although they resort to other gods
and love the raisin-cakes offered to
    their idols.

2 So I got her back[a] for fifteen pieces
of silver, a homer of barley and a
3 measure of wine; and I said to her,

Many a long day you shall live in
    my house
and not play the wanton,
and have no intercourse with a
    man, nor I with you.

4 For the Israelites shall live many a
    long day
without king or prince,
without sacrifice or sacred pillar,
without image or household gods;
5 but after that they will again seek
    the LORD their God and David
    their king,
and turn anxiously to the LORD for
    his bounty in days to come.

God's case against Israel

4 Hear the word of the LORD, O
    Israel;
for the LORD has a charge to
    bring against the people of the
    land:
There is no good faith or mutual
    trust,
no knowledge of God in the land,
2 oaths are imposed and broken,
    they kill and rob;
there is nothing but adultery and
    licence,[b]
one deed of blood after another.
3 Therefore the land shall be dried
    up,

and all who live in it shall pine
    away,
and with them the wild beasts and
    the birds of the air;
even the fish shall be swept from
    the sea.
But it is not for any man to bring a 4
    charge,
it is not for him to prove a case;
the quarrel with you, false priest,
    is mine.

Priest?[c] By day and by night you 5
    blunder on,
you and the prophet with you.
My people are ruined for lack of 6
    knowledge;
your own countrymen are brought
    to ruin.[d]
You have rejected knowledge,
and I will reject you from serving
    me as priest.
You have forgotten the teaching of
    God,
and I, your God, will forget your
    sons.

The more priests there are, the 7
    more they sin against me;
their dignity I will turn into dis-
    honour.
They feed on the sin of my people 8
and batten on their iniquity.
But people and priest shall be 9
    treated alike.
I will punish them for their con-
    duct
and repay them for their deeds:
they shall eat but never be satisfied, 10
behave wantonly but their lust
    will never be overtaken,
for they have forsaken the LORD
to give themselves to sacred prosti- 11
    tution.
New wine and old steal my people's 12
    wits:[e]
they ask advice from a block of
    wood
and take their orders from a fetish;

---

[a] got her back: *or* bought her.   [b] and licence: *prob. rdg.*; *Heb.* they exceed.
[c] the quarrel...Priest?: *prob. rdg.*; *Heb.* and your people are like those who
quarrel with a priest.   [d] My people...ruin: *or* Your mother (Israel) is
destroyed, my people destroyed for lack of knowledge.
[e] steal...wits: *or* embolden my people.

for a spirit of wantonness has led
them astray
and in their lusts they are unfaithful to their God.
13 Your men sacrifice on mountain-
tops
and burn offerings on the hills,
under oak and poplar
and the terebinth's pleasant shade.
Therefore your daughters play the
wanton
and your sons' brides commit
adultery.
14 I will not punish your daughters
for playing the wanton
nor your sons' brides for their
adultery,
because your men resort to wanton
women
and sacrifice with temple-prosti-
tutes.
A people without understanding
comes to grief;
15 they are a mother turned wanton.
Bring no guilt-offering,[a] Israel;
do not come to Gilgal, Judah,
do not go up to Beth-aven to swear
by the life of the LORD,
16 since Israel has run wild, wild as a
heifer;
and will the LORD now feed this
people
like lambs in a broad meadow?
17 Ephraim, keeping company with
idols,
18 has held a drunken orgy,[b]
they have practised sacred prosti-
tution,
they have preferred dishonour to
glory.
19 The wind shall sweep them away,
wrapped in its wings,
and they will find their sacrifices a
delusion.

5 Hear this, you priests,
and listen, all Israel; let the royal
house mark my words.
Sentence is passed on you;
for you have been a snare at Mizpah,
and a net spread out on Tabor.

The rebels! they have shown base 2
ingratitude,
but I will punish them all.
I have cared for Ephraim 3
and I have not neglected Israel;
but now Ephraim has played the
wanton
and Israel has defiled himself.
Their misdeeds have barred their 4
way back to their God;
for a wanton spirit is in them,
and they care nothing for the LORD.
Israel's arrogance cries out against 5
him;
[c]Ephraim's guilt is his undoing,
and Judah no less is undone.
They go with sacrifices of sheep 6
and cattle
to seek the LORD, but do not find
him.
He has withdrawn himself from
them;
for they have been unfaithful to 7
him,
and their sons are bastards.
Now an invader shall devour their
fields.
Blow the trumpet in Gibeah, 8
the horn in Ramah,
raise the battle-cry in Beth-aven:
'Benjamin, we are with you!'
On the tribes of Israel I have pro- 9
claimed this unalterable doom:
on the day of punishment Ephraim
shall be laid waste.
The rulers of Judah act like men 10
who move their neighbour's
boundary;
on them will I pour out my wrath
like a flood.
Ephraim is an oppressor trampling 11
on justice,
doggedly pursuing what is worthless.
But I am a festering sore to Eph- 12
raim,
a canker to the house of Judah.
So when Ephraim found that he 13
was sick,
Judah that he was covered with
sores,
Ephraim went to Assyria,

[a] Bring no guilt-offering: *prob. rdg.*; *Heb.* Let him not be guilty.   [b] a drunken
orgy: *prob. rdg.*; *Heb. unintelligible.*   [c] *Prob. rdg.*; *Heb. prefixes* Israel.

he went in haste to the Great
  King;
but he has no power to cure you
  or to heal your sores.
14 Yes indeed, I will be fierce as a
  panther to Ephraim,
fierce as a lion to Judah –
I will maul the prey and go,
carry it off beyond hope of rescue –
  I, the LORD.
15 I will go away and return to my
  place
until in their horror they seek me,
and look earnestly for me in their
  distress.

6 Come, let us return to the LORD;
for he has torn us and will heal
  us,
he has struck us and he will bind
  up our wounds;
2 after two days he will revive us,
on the third day he will restore us,
that in his presence we may live.
3 Let us humble ourselves, let us
  strive to know the LORD,
whose justice dawns like morning
  light,[a]
and its dawning is as sure as the
  sunrise.
It will come to us like a shower,
like spring rains that water the
  earth.

4 O Ephraim, how shall I deal with
  you?
How shall I deal with you, Judah?
Your loyalty to me is like the
  morning mist,
like dew that vanishes early.
5 Therefore have I lashed you
  through the prophets
and torn you[b] to shreds with my
  words;
6 loyalty is my desire, not sacrifice,
not whole-offerings but the knowledge of God.

7 At Admah[c] they have broken my
  covenant,
there they have played me false.

Gilead is a haunt of evildoers,   8
marked by a trail of blood;
like robbers lying in wait for a 9
  man,
priests are banded together
to do murder on the road to Shechem;
their deeds are outrageous.
At Israel's sanctuary I have seen a 10
  horrible thing:
there Ephraim played the wanton
and Israel defiled himself.
And for you, too, Judah, comes a 11
  harvest of reckoning.

When I would reverse the fortunes
  of my people,
when I would heal Israel,   7
then the guilt of Ephraim stands
  revealed,
and all the wickedness of Samaria;
they have not kept faith.
They are thieves, they break into
  houses;[d]
they are robbers, they strip people
  in the street,
little thinking that I have their 2
  wickedness ever in mind.
Now their misdeeds beset them
and stare me in the face.
They win over the king with their 3
  wickedness
and princes with their treachery,
lecherous all of them, hot as an 4
  oven over the fire
which the baker does not stir
after kneading the dough until it is
  proved.
On their king's festal day the 5
  officers
begin to be inflamed with wine,
and he joins in the orgies of arrogant men;
for their hearts are heated by it[e] 6
  like an oven.
While they are relaxed all night
  long
their passion slumbers,
but in the morning it flares up
like a blazing fire;

[a] *Line transposed from end of verse 5.*
[c] *At Admah: prob. rdg.; Heb.* Like Adam.
[e] *are heated by it: prob. rdg.; Heb.* draw near.

[b] *Prob. rdg.; Heb.* them.
[d] *houses: prob. rdg.; Heb. om.*

7 they all grow feverish, hot as an
  oven,
  and devour their rulers.
  King after king falls from power,
  but not one of them calls upon
  me.
8 Ephraim and his aliens make a
  sorry mixture;
  Ephraim has become a cake half-
  baked.
9 Foreigners fed on his strength,
  but he was unaware;
  even his grey hairs turned white,
  but he was unaware.
10 So Israel's arrogance cries out
  against them;
  but they do not return to the
  LORD their God
  nor seek him, in spite of it all.
11 Ephraim is a silly senseless pigeon,
  now calling upon Egypt, now turning to Assyria for help.
12 Wherever they turn, I will cast my
  net over them
  and will bring them down like
  birds on the wing;
  I will take them captive as soon as
  I hear them flocking.
13 Woe betide them, for they have
  strayed from me!
  May disaster befall them for rebelling against me!
  I long to deliver them,
  but they tell lies about me.
14 There is no sincerity in their cry to
  me;
  for all their howling on their pal-
  lets
  and gashing of themselves over
  corn and new wine,
  they are turning away from me.
15 Though I support them, though I
  give them strength of arm,
  they plot evil against me.
16 Like a bow gone slack,
  they relapse into the worship of
  their high god;[a]
  their talk is all lies,[b]
  and so their princes shall fall by the
  sword.

Put the trumpet to your lips!   8
A[c] vulture hovers over the sanctuary of the LORD:
they have broken my covenant
and rebelled against my instruction.
They cry to me for help: 2
'We know thee, God of Israel.'[d]
But Israel is utterly loathsome;   3
and therefore he shall run before
  the enemy.
They make kings, but not by my   4
  will;
they set up officers, but without
  my knowledge;
they have made themselves idols
  of their silver and gold.[e]

Your calf-gods stink, O Samaria;   5
my anger flares up against them.
Long will it be before they prove
  innocent.
For what sort of a god is this bull?   6
It is no god,
a craftsman made it;
the calf of Samaria will be broken
  in fragments.

Israel sows the wind and reaps the   7
  whirlwind;
there are no heads on the standing
  corn, it yields no grain;
and, if it yielded any, strangers
  would swallow it up.
Israel is now swallowed up,   8
lost among the nations,
a worthless nothing.
For, like a wild ass that has left the 9
  herd,
they have run to Assyria.
Ephraim has bargained for lovers;
and, because they have bargained   10
  among the nations,
I will now round them up,
and then they will soon abandon
this setting up of kings and
  princes.
For Ephraim in his sin has multi-   11
  plied altars,
altars have become his sin.

---

[a] they relapse...god: *prob. rdg.*; *Heb. obscure.*   [b] *Prob. rdg.*; *Heb. adds that*
is their stammering speech in Egypt.   [c] *Prob. rdg.*; *Heb. Like a.*
[d] We...Israel: *prob. rdg.*; *Heb. O my God, we know thee, Israel.*
[e] *Prob. rdg.*; *Heb. adds so that he may be cut off.*

12 Though I give him countless rules in writing,
they are treated as invalid.
13 Though they sacrifice flesh as offerings to me and eat them,
I,[a] the LORD, will not accept them.
Their guilt will be remembered and their sins punished.
They shall go back to Egypt,
or in Assyria they shall eat unclean food.

14 Israel has forgotten his Maker and built palaces,
Judah has multiplied walled cities;
but I will set fire to his cities,
and it shall devour his castles.

9 Do not rejoice, Israel, do not exult like other peoples;
for like a wanton you have forsaken your God,
you have loved an idol[b]
on every threshing-floor heaped with corn.
2 Threshing-floor and winepress shall know them no more,
new wine shall disown[c] them.
3 They shall not dwell in the LORD's land;
Ephraim shall go back to Egypt,
or in Assyria they shall eat unclean food.
4 They shall pour out no wine to the LORD,
they shall not bring their sacrifices to him;
that would be mourners' fare for them,
and all who ate it would be polluted.
For their food shall only stay their hunger;
it shall not be offered in the house of the LORD.
5 What will you do for the festal day, the day of the LORD's pilgrim-feast?
6 For look, they have fled from a scene of devastation:
Egypt shall receive them,
Memphis shall be their grave;

the sands of Syrtes shall wreck them,
weeds shall inherit their land,
thorns shall grow in their dwellings.
The days of punishment are come, 7
the days of vengeance are come
when Israel shall be humbled.
Then the prophet shall be made a fool
and the inspired seer a madman
by your great guilt.
With great enmity Ephraim lies in 8
wait for God's people
while the prophet is a fowler's trap by all their paths,
a snare in the very temple of God.
They lead them deep into sin as at 9
the time of Gibeah.
Their guilt will be remembered and their sins punished.

I came upon Israel like grapes in 10
the wilderness,
I looked on their forefathers
with joy like the first ripe figs;
but they resorted to Baal-peor
and consecrated themselves to a thing of shame,
and Ephraim became as loathsome 11
as the thing he loved.
Their honour shall fly away like a bird:
no childbirth, no fruitful womb, no conceiving;
even if they rear their children, 12
I will make them childless, without posterity.
Woe to them indeed when I turn away from them!

As lion-cubs emerge only to be 13
hunted,[d]
so must Ephraim bring out his children for slaughter.
Give them, O LORD – what wilt 14
thou give them?
Give them a womb that miscarries and dry breasts.
All their wickedness was seen at 15
Gilgal; there did I hate them.
For their evil deeds I will drive them from my house,

---

[a] *Prob. rdg.; Heb.* he.   [b] *an idol: or* a harlot's fee.   [c] *Or* fail.
[d] *As lion-cubs...hunted: prob. rdg.; Heb. unintelligible.*

I will love them no more: all their
    princes are in revolt.
16 Ephraim is struck down:
    their root is withered, and they
      yield no fruit;
    if ever they give birth,
    I will slay the dearest offspring of
      their womb.

17 My God shall reject them,
    because they have not listened to
      him,
    and they shall become wanderers
      among the nations.

God's judgement on Israel

10 Israel is like a rank vine
    ripening its fruit:
    his fruit grows more and more, and
      more and more his altars;
    the fairer his land becomes, the
      fairer he makes his sacred pillars.
2 They are crazy now, they are mad.
    God himself will hack down their
      altars
    and wreck their sacred pillars.
3 Well may they say, 'We have no
      king,
    for we do not fear the LORD;
    and what can the king do for us?'
4 There is nothing but talk,
    imposing of oaths and making of
      treaties, all to no purpose;
    and litigation spreads like a poi-
      sonous weed
    along the furrows of the fields.
5 The inhabitants of Samaria tremble
    for the calf-god of Beth-aven;
    the people mourn over it[a] and its
      priestlings howl,
    distressed for their image, their
      glory,
    which is carried away into exile.
6 It shall be carried to Assyria
    as tribute to the Great King;
    disgrace shall overtake Ephraim
    and Israel shall feel the shame of
      their disobedience.
7 Samaria and her king are swept
      away
    like flotsam on the water;

the hill-shrines of Aven are wiped 8
      out,
    the shrines where Israel sinned;
    thorns and thistles grow over her
      altars.
So they will say to the mountains,
    'Cover us',
    and to the hills, 'Fall on us.'

Since the day of Gibeah Israel has 9
      sinned;
    there they took their stand in
      rebellion.
Shall not war overtake them in
      Gibeah?
I have come against the rebels to 10
      chastise them,
    and the peoples shall mass against
      them
    in hordes for their two deeds of
      shame.
Ephraim is like a heifer broken in, 11
    which loves to thresh corn,
    across whose fair neck I have laid a
      yoke;[b]
I have harnessed Ephraim to the
      pole that he[c] may plough,
    that Jacob may harrow his land.
Sow for yourselves in justice,   12
    and you will reap what loyalty
      deserves.
Break up your fallow;
    for it is time to seek the LORD,
    seeking him till he comes and gives
      you just measure of rain.
You have ploughed wickedness into 13
      your soil,
    and the crop is mischief;
    you have eaten the fruit of
      treachery.

Because you have trusted in your
      chariots,
    in the number of your warriors,
    the tumult of war shall arise 14
      against your people,
    and all your fortresses shall be
      razed
    as Shalman razed Beth-arbel in the
      day of battle,
    dashing the mother to the ground
      with her babes.

_____
[a] the people mourn over it: or the high god and his people mourn.
[b] a yoke: prob. rdg.; Heb. om.   [c] he: prob. rdg.; Heb. Judah.

15 So it shall be done to you, Bethel,
   because of your evil scheming;
   as sure as day dawns, the king of
   Israel shall be swept away.

11 When Israel was a boy, I loved
   him;
   I called my son out of Egypt;
2 but the more I called, the further
   they went from me;
   they must needs sacrifice to the
   Baalim
   and burn offerings before carved
   images.
3 It was I who taught Ephraim to
   walk,
   I who had taken them in my arms;
4 but they did not know that I
   harnessed them in leading-strings[a]
   and led them with bonds of love[b] –
   that I had lifted them like a little
   child[c] to my cheek,
   that I had bent down to feed them.
5 Back they shall go to Egypt,
   the Assyrian shall be their king;
   for they have refused to return to
   me.
6 The sword shall be swung over
   their blood-spattered altars
   and put an end to their prattling
   priests
7 and devour my people in return for
   all their schemings,
   bent on rebellion as they are.
   Though they call on their high
   god,
   even then he will not reinstate
   them.
8 How can I give you up, Ephraim,
   how surrender you, Israel?
   How can I make you like Admah
   or treat you as Zeboyim?
   My heart is changed within me,
   my remorse kindles already.
9 I will not let loose my fury,
   I will not turn round and destroy
   Ephraim;
   for I am God and not a man,
   the Holy One in your midst;

I will not come with threats[d] like a 10
   roaring lion.
No; when I roar, I who am God,
   my sons shall come with speed out
   of the west.
They will come speedily, flying 11
   like birds out of Egypt,
   like pigeons from Assyria,
   and I will settle them in their own
   homes.
This is the very word of the LORD.
Ephraim besets me with treachery, 12
   the house of Israel besets me with
   deceit;
   and Judah is still restive under God,
   still loyal to the idols he counts
   holy.
Ephraim is a shepherd whose flock 12
   is but[e] wind,
   a hunter chasing the east wind all
   day;[f]
   he makes a treaty with Assyria
   and carries tribute of oil to Egypt.

The LORD has a charge to bring 2
   against Judah
   and is resolved to punish Jacob for
   his conduct;
   he will requite him for his misdeeds.
Even in the womb Jacob over- 3
   reached his brother,
   and in manhood he strove with
   God.
The divine angel stood firm and 4
   held his own;[g]
   Jacob wept and begged favour for
   himself.
Then God met him at Bethel
   and there spoke with him.
The LORD the God of Hosts, the 5
   LORD is his name.

Turn back all of you by God's help; 6
   practise loyalty and justice
   and wait always upon your God.
False scales are in merchants' 7
   hands,
   and they love to cheat;
   so Ephraim says,   8

---

[a] leading-strings: *or* cords of leather.   [b] bonds of love: *or* reins of hide.
[c] I had...child: *prob. rdg.*; *Heb.* like those who lift up a yoke.
[d] *Prob. rdg.*; *Heb. adds* they shall go after the LORD.   [e] is a...but: *or* feeds on.
[f] *Prob. rdg.*; *Heb. adds* piling up treachery and havoc.
[g] The divine...own: *or* He stood firm against an angel, but flagged.

'Surely I have become a rich man,
  I have made my fortune';
but all his gains will not pay
  for the guilt*a* of his sins.
9 Yet I have been the LORD your
  God since your days in Egypt;
I will make you live in tents yet
  again, as in the old days.

10 I spoke to the prophets,
  it was I who gave vision after
  vision;
I spoke through the prophets in
  parables.

11 Was there idolatry in Gilead?
  Yes: they were worthless
and sacrificed to bull-gods in
  Gilgal;
their altars were common as heaps
  of stones beside a ploughed field.

12 Jacob fled to the land of Aram;
Israel did service to win a wife,
to win a wife he tended sheep.

13 By a prophet the LORD brought up
  Israel out of Egypt
and by a prophet he was tended.

14 Ephraim has given bitter provocation;
therefore his Lord will make him
  answerable
for his own death
and bring down upon his own head
  the blame
for all that he has done.

13 When the Ephraimites mumbled
  their prayers,
God himself denounced Israel;
they were guilty of Baal-worship
  and died.
2 Yet now they sin more and more;
they have made themselves an
  image of cast metal,
they have fashioned their silver
  into idols,
nothing but the work of craftsmen;
men say of them,
'Those who kiss calf-images offer
  human sacrifice.'

Therefore they shall be like the 3
  morning mist
or like dew that vanishes early,
like chaff blown from the threshing-floor
or smoke from a chimney.
But I have been the LORD your 4
  God since your days in Egypt,
when you knew no other saviour
  than me,
no god but me.
I cared for you in the wilderness, 5
in a land of burning heat, as if you 6
  were in pasture.
So they were filled,
and, being filled, grew proud;
and so they forgot me.
So now I will be like a panther to 7
  them,
I will prowl like a leopard by the
  wayside;
I will meet them like a she-bear 8
  robbed of her cubs
and tear their ribs apart,
like a lioness I will devour them on
  the spot,
I will rip them up like a wild beast.
I have destroyed you, O Israel; 9
  who is there to help you?
Where now is your king that he 10
  may save you,
or the rulers in all your cities
for whom you asked me,
begging for king and princes?
I gave you a king in my anger, 11
and in my fury took him away.

Ephraim's guilt is tied up in a 12
  scroll,
his sins are kept on record.
When the pangs of his birth came 13
  over his mother,
he showed himself a senseless
  child;
for at the proper time he could not
  present himself
at the mouth of the womb.
Shall I redeem him from Sheol? 14
Shall I ransom him from death?
Oh, for your plagues, O death! Oh,
  for your sting, Sheol!
I will put compassion out of my
  sight.

a for the guilt: *prob. rdg.*; Heb. for me, guilt.

15 Though he flourishes among the
reeds,[a]
  an east wind shall come, a blast
from the LORD,
  rising over the desert;
  Ephraim's spring will fail and his
fountain run dry.
  It will carry away as spoil
  his whole store of costly treasures.
16 Samaria will become desolate because she has rebelled against her
God;
  her babes will fall by the sword and
be dashed to the ground,
  her women with child shall be
ripped up.

Repentance, forgiveness, and restoration

14 Return, O Israel, to the LORD your
God;
  for you have stumbled in your evil
courses.
2 Come with your words ready,
  come back to the LORD;
  say to him, 'Thou dost not endure
iniquity.[b]
  Accept our plea,
  and we will pay our vows with
cattle from our pens.
3 Assyria shall not save us, nor will
we seek horses to ride;

what we have made with our own
hands
we will never again call gods;
for in thee the fatherless find a
father's love.'

I will heal their apostasy; of my 4
own bounty will I love them;
for my anger is turned away from
them.
I will be as dew to Israel 5
that he may flower like the lily,
strike root like the poplar[c]
and put out fresh shoots, 6
that he may be as fair as the olive
and fragrant as Lebanon.
Israel shall again dwell in my[d] 7
shadow
and grow corn in abundance;
they shall flourish like a vine
and be famous as the wine of
Lebanon.
What has Ephraim any more to do 8
with idols?
I have spoken and I affirm it:
I am the pine-tree that shelters you;
to me you owe your fruit.

Let the wise consider these 9
things and let him who considers
take note; for the LORD's ways are
straight and the righteous walk in
them, while sinners stumble.

JOEL

1 The word of the LORD which came
to Joel son of Pethuel.

The day of the LORD

2 Listen, you elders;
  hear me, all you who live in the land:
  has the like of this happened in all
your days
  or in your fathers' days?

Tell it to your sons and they may 3
tell theirs;
let them pass it on from generation
to generation.
What the locust has left the swarm 4
eats,
what the swarm has left the hopper
eats,
and what the hopper has left the
grub eats.

---

[a] among the reeds: *prob. rdg.*; *Heb.* between (*or* a son of) brothers.
[b] Thou...iniquity: *or* Thou wilt surely take away iniquity.
[c] *Prob. rdg.*; *Heb.* like Lebanon.   [d] *Prob. rdg.*; *Heb.* its.

5 Wake up, you drunkards, and
  lament your fate;
  mourn for the fresh wine, all you
  wine-drinkers,
  because it is lost to you.
6 For a horde has overrun my land,
  mighty and past counting;
  their teeth are a lion's teeth;
  they have the fangs of a lioness.
7 They have ruined my vines
  and left my fig-trees broken and
  leafless,
  they have plucked them bare
  and stripped them of their bark;
  they have left the branches white.

8 Wail like a virgin wife in sackcloth,
  wailing over the bridegroom of her
  youth;
9 the drink-offering and grain-offering are lost
  to the house of the L<small>ORD</small>.
  Mourn, you priests, ministers of the
  L<small>ORD</small>.
10 the fields are ruined, the parched
  earth mourns;
  for the corn is ruined, the new wine
  is desperate,
  the oil has failed.
11 Despair, you husbandmen; you
  vinedressers, lament,
  because the wheat and the barley,
  the harvest of the field, is lost.
12 The vintage is desperate, and the
  fig-tree has failed;
  pomegranate, palm, and apple,
  all the trees of the country-side are
  parched,
  and none make merry over harvest.

13 Priests, put on sackcloth and beat
  your breasts;
  lament, you ministers of the altar;
  come, lie in sackcloth all night
  long, you ministers of my God;
  for grain-offering and drink-offering
  are withheld from the house of
  your God.
14 Proclaim a solemn fast, appoint a
  day of abstinence.
  You elders, summon all that live
  in the land

to come together in the house of
  your God,
  and cry to the L<small>ORD</small>.
Alas! the day is near,   15
  the day of the L<small>ORD</small>: it comes,
  a mighty destruction from the Almighty.
Look! it stares us in the face;   16
  the house of our God has lost its
  food,
  lost all its joy and gladness.
The soil is parched,   17
  the dykes are dry,
  the granaries are deserted,
  the barns ruinous;
  for the rains have failed.
The cattle are exhausted,   18
  the herds of oxen distressed
  because they have no pasture;
  the flocks of sheep waste away.
To thee I cry, O L<small>ORD</small>;   19
  for fire has devoured the open
  pastures
  and the flames have burnt up all
  the trees of the country-side.
The very cattle in the field look up 20
  to thee;
  for the water-channels are dried
  up,
  and fire has devoured the open
  pastures.

Blow the trumpet in Zion,   2
sound the alarm upon my holy
  hill;
let all that live in the land tremble,
for the day of the L<small>ORD</small> has come,
surely a day of darkness and gloom 2
  is upon us,
a day of cloud and dense fog;
like a blackness spread over the
  mountains
a mighty, countless host appears;
their like has never been known,
nor ever shall be in ages to come;
their vanguard a devouring fire,   3
their rearguard leaping flame;
before them the land is a garden of
  Eden,
behind them a wasted wilderness;
nothing survives their march.
On they come, like squadrons of 4
  horse,
like war-horses they charge;

5 bounding over the peaks they advance with the rattle of chariots,
  like flames of fire burning up the
  stubble,
  like a countless host in battle
  array.
6 Before them nations tremble,
  every face turns pale.
7 Like warriors they charge,
  they mount the walls like men at
  arms,
  each marching in line,
  no confusion in the ranks,
8 none jostling his neighbour,
  none breaking line.
  They plunge through streams without halting their advance;
9 they burst into the city, leap on to
  the wall,
  climb into the houses,
  entering like thieves through the
  windows.
10 Before them the earth shakes,
  the heavens shudder,
  sun and moon are darkened,
  and the stars forbear to shine.
11 The Lord thunders before his
  host;
  his is a mighty army,
  countless are those who do his
  bidding.
  Great is the day of the Lord and
  terrible,
  who can endure it?
12 And yet, the Lord says, even
  now
  turn back to me with your whole
  heart,
  fast, and weep, and beat your
  breasts.
13 Rend your hearts and not your
  garments;
  turn back to the Lord your God;
  for he is gracious and compassionate,
  long-suffering and ever constant,
  always ready to repent of the
  threatened evil.
14 It may be he will turn back and
  repent
  and leave a blessing behind him,
  blessing enough for grain-offering
  and drink-offering
  for the Lord your God.

Blow the trumpet in Zion,   15
proclaim a solemn fast, appoint a
  day of abstinence;
gather the people together, pro- 16
  claim a solemn assembly;
summon the elders,
gather the children, yes, babes at
  the breast;
bid the bridegroom leave his
  chamber
and the bride her bower.
Let the priests, the ministers of the 17
  Lord,
stand weeping between the porch
  and the altar
and say, 'Spare thy people, O
  Lord, thy own people,
expose them not to reproach,
lest other nations make them a byword
and everywhere men ask,
"Where is their God?"'

Israel forgiven and restored

Then the Lord's love burned with 18
  zeal for his land,
and he was moved with compassion for his people.
He answered their appeal and said, 19
I will send you corn, and new wine,
  and oil,
and you shall have your fill;
I will expose you no longer
to the reproach of other nations.
I will remove the northern peril 20
  far away from you
and banish them into a land
  parched and waste,
their vanguard into the eastern sea
and their rear into the western,
and the stench shall rise from their
  rotting corpses
because of their proud deeds!
Earth, be not afraid, rejoice and be 21
  glad;
for the Lord himself has done a
  proud deed.
Be not afraid, you cattle in the 22
  field;
for the pastures shall be green,
the trees shall bear fruit,
the fig and the vine yield their
  harvest.

23 O people of Zion,
rejoice and be glad in the LORD
your God,
who gives you good food in due
measure[a]
and sends down rain[b] as of old.

24 The threshing-floors shall be heaped with grain,
the vats shall overflow with new
wine and oil.

25 So I will make good the years
that the swarm has eaten,
hopper and grub and locust,
my great army which I sent
against you;

26 and you shall eat, you shall eat
your fill
and praise the name of the LORD
your God
who has done wonders for you,[c]

27 and you shall know that I am
present in Israel,
that I and no other am the LORD
your God;
and my people shall not again be
brought to shame.

28 Thereafter the day shall come
when I will pour out my spirit on
all mankind;
your sons and your daughters shall
prophesy,
your old men shall dream dreams
and your young men see visions;

29 I will pour out my spirit in those
days
even upon slaves and slave-girls.

30 I will show portents in the sky and
on earth,
blood and fire and columns of
smoke;

31 the sun shall be turned into darkness
and the moon into blood
before the great and terrible day
of the LORD comes.

32 Then everyone who invokes the
LORD by name
shall be saved:

for when the LORD gives the
word
there shall yet be survivors on
Mount Zion
and in Jerusalem a remnant[d]
whom the LORD will call.[e]

3 When that time comes, on that day
when I reverse the fortunes of
Judah and Jerusalem,
2 I will gather all the nations together
and lead them down to the Valley
of the LORD's Judgement
and there bring them to judgement
on behalf of Israel, my own possession;
for they have scattered my people
throughout their own countries,
have taken each their portion of
my land
3 and shared out my people by lot,
bartered a boy for a whore,
and sold a girl for wine and drunk
it down.

4 What are you to me, Tyre and
Sidon and all the districts of
Philistia? Can you pay me back for
anything I have done? Is there
anything that you can do to me?
Swiftly and speedily I will make
your deeds recoil upon your own
5 heads; for you have taken my
silver and my gold and carried off
my costly treasures into your
6 temples; you have sold the people
of Judah and Jerusalem to the
Greeks, and removed them far be-
7 yond their own frontiers. But I will
rouse them to leave the places to
which you have sold them. I will
make your deeds recoil upon your
8 own heads: I will sell your sons and
your daughters to the people of
Judah, and they shall sell them to
the Sabaeans, a nation far away.
The LORD has spoken.

[a] *Or* gives you a sign pointing to prosperity.
[b] *Prob. rdg.; Heb. adds* spring rain and autumn rain.
[c] *Prob. rdg.; Heb. adds* and my people shall not again be brought to shame (*cp.* verse 27).
[d] a remnant: *prob. rdg.; Heb.* among the remnant.
[e] *Or* when the LORD calls.

9–12[a] Proclaim this amongst the nations:
Declare a holy war, call your troops
   to arms!
Beat your mattocks into swords
and your pruning-hooks into
   spears.[b]
Rally to each other's help, all you
   nations round about.
Let the weakling say, 'I am
   strong',
and let the coward show himself
   brave.[c]
Let all the nations hear the call to
   arms
and come to the Valley of the
   Lord's Judgement;
let all the warriors come and draw
   near
and muster there;
for there I will take my seat
and judge all the nations round
   about.

13 Ply the sickle, for the harvest is
   ripe;
come, tread the grapes,
for the press is full and the vats
   overflow;
great is the wickedness of the
   nations.
14 The roar of multitudes, multitudes,
   in the Valley of Decision!
The day of the Lord is at hand
in the Valley of Decision;
15 sun and moon are darkened
and the stars forbear to shine.

The Lord roars from Zion   16
and thunders from Jerusalem;
heaven and earth shudder,
but the Lord is a refuge for his
   people
and the defence of Israel.

Thus you shall know that I am the   17
   Lord your God,
dwelling in Zion my holy mountain;
Jerusalem shall be holy,
and no one without the right shall
   pass through her again.
When that day comes,   18
the mountains shall run with fresh
   wine
and the hills flow with milk.
All the streams of Judah shall be
   full of water,
and a fountain shall spring from
   the Lord's house
and water the gorge of Shittim,
but Egypt shall become a desert   19
and Edom a deserted waste,
because of the violence done to
   Judah
and the innocent blood shed in her
   land;
and I will spill their blood,   20–21
the blood I have not yet spilt.
Then there shall be people living in
   Judah for ever,
in Jerusalem generation after generation;
and the Lord will dwell in Zion.

AMOS

1   THE words of Amos, one of
the sheep-farmers of Tekoa,
which he received in visions
concerning Israel during the reigns
of Uzziah king of Judah and Jeroboam son of Jehoash king of Israel,
two years before the earthquake.

He said,   2

The Lord roars from Zion
and thunders from Jerusalem;
the shepherds' pastures are scorched
and the top of Carmel[d] is dried up.

---

[a] *The order of lines in verses 9–12 has been re-arranged in several places.*
[b] Beat . . .spears: cp. Isa. 2. 4; Mic. 4. 3.
   O Lord bring down thy warriors.
[c] and let. . .brave: *prob. rdg.; Heb.*
[d] top of Carmel: *or* choicest farmland.

*The sins of Israel and
her neighbours*

3 These are the words of the LORD:

For crime after crime of Damascus
I will grant them no reprieve,
because they threshed Gilead under
threshing-sledges spiked with
iron.
4 Therefore will I send fire upon the
house of Hazael,
fire that shall eat up Ben-hadad's
palaces;
5 I will crush the great men of
Damascus
and wipe out those who live in the
Vale of Aven
and the sceptred ruler of Beth-
eden;
the people of Aram shall be exiled
to Kir.
It is the word of the LORD.

6 These are the words of the LORD:

For crime after crime of Gaza
I will grant them no reprieve,
because they deported a whole
band of exiles
and delivered them up to Edom.
7 Therefore will I send fire upon the
walls of Gaza,
fire that shall consume its palaces.
8 I will wipe out those who live in
Ashdod
and the sceptred ruler of Ashkelon;
I will turn my hand against
Ekron,
and the remnant of the Philistines
shall perish.
It is the word of the Lord GOD.

9 These are the words of the LORD:

For crime after crime of Tyre
I will grant them no reprieve,
because, forgetting the ties of kin-
ship,
they delivered a whole band of
exiles to Edom.
10 Therefore will I send fire upon the
walls of Tyre,
fire that shall consume its palaces.

These are the words of the LORD: 11

For crime after crime of Edom
I will grant them no reprieve,
because, sword in hand, they
hunted their kinsmen down,
stifling their natural affections.
Their anger raged unceasing,
their fury stormed unchecked.
Therefore will I send fire upon 12
Teman,
fire that shall consume the palaces
of Bozrah.

These are the words of the LORD: 13

For crime after crime of the Ammonites
I will grant them no reprieve,
because in their greed for land
they invaded the ploughlands of
Gilead.
Therefore will I set fire to the walls 14
of Rabbah,
fire that shall consume its palaces
amid war-cries on the day of
battle,
with a whirlwind on the day of
tempest;
then their king shall be carried into 15
exile,
he and his officers with him.
It is the word of the LORD.

These are the words of the LORD: 2

For crime after crime of Moab
I will grant them no reprieve,
because they burnt the bones of
the king of Edom to ash.[a]
Therefore will I send fire upon 2
Moab,
fire that shall consume the palaces
in their towns;
Moab shall perish in uproar,
with war-cries and the sound of
trumpets,
and I will cut off the ruler from 3
among them
and kill all their officers with
him.
It is the word of the LORD.

[a] to ash: *or* for lime.

4 These are the words of the LORD:

For crime after crime of Judah
I will grant them no reprieve,
because they have spurned the law
of the LORD
and have not observed his decrees,
and have been led astray by the
false gods
that their fathers followed.

5 Therefore will I send fire upon
Judah,
fire that shall consume the palaces
of Jerusalem.

6 These are the words of the LORD:

For crime after crime of Israel
I will grant them no reprieve,
because they sell the innocent for
silver
and the destitute for a pair of shoes.

7 They grind the heads of the poor
into the earth
and thrust the humble out of their
way.
Father and son resort to the same
girl,
to the profanation of my holy
name.

8 Men lie down beside every altar
on garments seized in pledge,
and in the house of their God[a] they
drink liquor
got by way of fines.

9 Yet it was I who destroyed the
Amorites before them,
though they were tall as cedars,
though they were sturdy as oaks,
I who destroyed their fruit above
and their roots below.

10 It was I who brought you up from
the land of Egypt,
I who led you in the wilderness
forty years,
to take possession of the land of
the Amorites;

11 I raised up prophets from your sons,
Nazirites from your young men.
Was it not so indeed, you men of
Israel?
says the LORD.

But you made the Nazirites drink 12
wine,
and said to the prophets, 'You shall
not prophesy.'
Listen, I groan under the burden 13
of you,
as a wagon creaks under a full load.
Flight shall not save the swift, 14
the strong man shall not rally his
strength.
The warrior shall not save himself,
the archer shall not stand his 15
ground;
the swift of foot shall not be saved,
nor the horseman escape;
on that day the bravest of warriors 16
shall be stripped of his arms and
run away.
This is the very word of the LORD.

Israel's sins and threatened punishment

LISTEN, Israelites, to these words 3
that the LORD addresses to you, to
the whole nation which he brought
up from Egypt:

For you alone have I cared 2
among all the nations of the world;
therefore will I punish you
for all your iniquities.
Do two men travel together 3
unless they have agreed?
Does a lion roar in the forest 4
if he has no prey?
Does a young lion growl in his den
if he has caught nothing?
Does a bird fall into a trap on the 5
ground
if the striker is not set for it?
Does a trap spring from the ground
and take nothing?
If a trumpet sounds the alarm, 6
are not the people scared?
If disaster falls on a city,
has not the LORD been at work?[b]
For the Lord GOD does nothing 7
without giving to his servants the
prophets knowledge of his plans.
The lion has roared; who is not 8
terrified?

---

[a] Or gods.
[b] If disaster...work?: or If there is evil in a city, will not the LORD act?

The Lord GOD has spoken; who will not prophesy?

9 Stand upon the palaces in Ashdod
and upon the palaces of Egypt,
and proclaim aloud:
'Assemble on the hills of Samaria,
look at the tumult seething among her people
and at the oppression in her midst;
10 what do they care for honesty
who hoard in their palaces the gains of crime and violence?'
This is the very word of the LORD.

11 Therefore these are the words of the Lord GOD:

An enemy shall surround*a* the land;
your stronghold shall be thrown down
and your palaces sacked.

12 These are the words of the LORD:

As a shepherd rescues out of the jaws of a lion
two shin bones or the tip of an ear,
so shall the Israelites who live in Samaria be rescued
like a corner of a couch or a chip from the leg of a bed.*b*
13 Listen and testify against the family of Jacob.
This is the very word of the Lord GOD, the God of Hosts.

14 On the day when I deal with Israel for all their crimes,
I will most surely deal with the altars of Bethel:
the horns of the altar shall be hacked off
and shall fall to the ground.
15 I will break down both winter-house and summer-house;
houses of ivory shall perish,
and great houses be demolished.
This is the very word of the LORD.

Listen to this,   4
you cows of Bashan who live on the hill of Samaria,
you who oppress the poor and crush the destitute,
who say to your lords, 'Bring us drink':
the Lord GOD has sworn by his 2 holiness
that your time is coming
when men shall carry you away on their shields*c*
and your children in fish-baskets.
You shall each be carried straight 3 out
through the breaches in the walls
and pitched on a dunghill.*d*
This is the very word of the LORD.

Come to Bethel – and rebel!   4
Come to Gilgal – and rebel the more!
Bring your sacrifices for the morning,
your tithes within three days.
Burn your thank-offering without 5 leaven;
announce, proclaim your freewill offerings;
for you love to do what is proper, you men of Israel!
This is the very word of the Lord GOD.

It was I who kept teeth idle   6
in all your cities,
who brought famine on all your settlements;
yet you did not come back to me.
This is the very word of the LORD.

It was I who withheld the showers 7
from you
while there were still three months to harvest.
I would send rain on one city
and no rain on another;
rain would fall on one field,
and another would be parched for lack of it.

---

a shall surround: *prob. rdg.*; *Heb.* and round.
b or a chip...bed: *prob. rdg.*; *Heb. obscure.*
c Or baskets.   *d* a dunghill: *prob. rdg.*; *Heb.* the Harmon.

8 From this city and that, men would
stagger to another
for water to drink, but would not
find enough;
yet you did not come back to me.
This is the very word of the LORD.

9 I blasted you with black blight and
red;
I laid waste[a] your gardens and
vineyards;
the locust devoured your fig-trees
and your olives;
yet you did not come back to me.
This is the very word of the LORD.

10 I sent plague upon you like the
plagues of Egypt;
I killed with the sword
your young men and your troops
of horses.
I made your camps stink in your
nostrils;
yet you did not come back to me.
This is the very word of the LORD.

11 I brought destruction amongst you
as God destroyed Sodom and Gomorrah;
you were like a brand snatched
from the fire;
yet you did not come back to me.
This is the very word of the LORD.

12 Therefore, Israel, this is what I will
do to you;
and, because this is what I will do
to you,
Israel, prepare to meet your God.
13 It is he who forges the thunder and
creates the wind,
who showers abundant rain on the
earth,[b]
who darkens the dawn with thick
clouds
and marches over the heights of
the earth –
his name is the LORD the God of
Hosts.

Listen to these words; I raise a 5
dirge over you, O Israel:

She has fallen to rise no more, 2
the virgin Israel,
prostrate on her own soil, with no
one to lift her up.

These are the words of the Lord 3
GOD:

The city that marched out to war a
thousand strong
shall have but a hundred left,
that which marched out a hundred
strong
shall have but ten men of Israel
left.

These are the words of the LORD 4
to the people of Israel:

Resort to me, if you would live, not 5
to Bethel;
go not to Gilgal, nor pass on to
Beersheba;
for Gilgal shall be swept away
and Bethel brought to nothing.
If you would live, resort to the 6
LORD,
or he will break out against Joseph
like fire,
fire which will devour Israel with
no one to quench it;
he who made the Pleiades and 8[c]
Orion,
who turned darkness into morning
and darkened day into night,
who summoned the waters of the
sea
and poured them over the earth,
who makes Taurus rise after 9
Capella
and Taurus set hard on the rising
of the Vintager[d] –
he who does this, his name is the
LORD.[e]
You that turn justice upside down[f] 7
and bring righteousness to the
ground,

---

[a] *I laid waste: prob. rdg.; Heb.* to increase.
Heb. who tells his thoughts to mankind.   [b] *who showers...earth: prob. rdg.;*
[d] *who makes...Vintager: prob. rdg.; Heb.* who smiles destruction on the strong,
and destruction comes on the fortified city.   [e] *his...LORD: transposed from*
end of verse 8.   [f] upside down: *prob. rdg.; Heb.* poison.   [c] *Verse 7 transposed to follow verse 9.*

10 you that hate a man who brings
   the wrongdoer to court
  and loathe him who speaks the
   whole truth:
11 for all this, because you levy taxes
   on the poor
  and extort a tribute of grain from
   them,
  though you have built houses of
   hewn stone,
  you shall not live in them,
  though you have planted pleasant
   vineyards,
  you shall not drink wine from them.
12 For I know how many your crimes
   are
  and how countless your sins,
  you who persecute the guiltless,
   hold men to ransom
  and thrust the destitute out of
   court.
13 At that time, therefore, a prudent
   man will stay quiet,
  for it will be an evil time.

14 Seek good and not evil,
  that you may live,
  that the LORD the God of Hosts
   may be firmly on your side,
  as you say he is.
15 Hate evil and love good;
  enthrone justice in the courts;
  it may be that the LORD the God
   of Hosts
  will be gracious to the survivors of
   Joseph.

16   Therefore these are the words of
  the LORD the God of Hosts:

  There shall be wailing in every
   street,
  and in all open places cries of woe.
  The farmer shall be called to
   mourning,
  and those skilled in the dirge to[a]
   wailing;
17 there shall be lamentation in every
   vineyard;
  for I will pass through the midst of
   you,
  says the LORD.

Fools who long for the day of the 18
  LORD,
what will the day of the LORD mean
  to you?
It will be darkness, not light.
It will be as when a man runs from 19
  a lion,
and a bear meets him,
or turns into a house and leans his
  hand on the wall,
and a snake bites him.
The day of the LORD is indeed 20
  darkness, not light,
a day of gloom with no dawn.

I hate, I spurn your pilgrim-feasts; 21
I will not delight in your sacred
  ceremonies.
When you present your sacrifices 22
  and offerings
I will not accept them,
nor look on the buffaloes of your
  shared-offerings.
Spare me the sound of your songs; 23
I cannot endure the music of your
  lutes.
Let justice roll on like a river   24
and righteousness like an ever-
  flowing stream.
Did you bring me sacrifices and 25
  gifts,
you people of Israel, those forty
  years in the wilderness?
No! but now you shall take up   26
the shrine of your idol king
and the pedestals of your images,[b]
which you have made for yourselves,
and I will drive you into exile be- 27
  yond Damascus.

So says the LORD; the God of Hosts
is his name.

Shame on you who live at ease in 6
  Zion,
and you, untroubled on the hill of
  Samaria,
men of mark in the first of nations,
you to whom the people of Israel
  resort!

---

[a] *Prob. rdg.; Heb. places to before those skilled.*
[b] *Prob. rdg.; Heb. adds the star of your gods.*

2 Go, look at Calneh,
   travel on to Hamath the great,
   then go down to Gath of the
     Philistines –
   are you better than these king-
     doms?
   Or is your[a] territory greater than
     theirs[b]?
3 You who thrust the evil day aside
   and make haste to establish vio-
     lence.[c]
4 You who loll on beds inlaid with
     ivory
   and sprawl over your couches,
   feasting on lambs from the flock
   and fatted calves,
5 you who pluck the strings of the
     lute
   and invent musical instruments
     like David,
6 you who drink wine by the bowlful
   and lard yourselves with the
     richest of oils,
   but are not grieved at the ruin of
     Joseph –
7 now, therefore,
   you shall head the column of
     exiles;
   that will be the end of sprawling
     and revelry.

8   The Lord GOD has sworn by
   himself:

   I loathe the arrogance of Jacob,
   I loathe his palaces;
   city and all in it I will abandon to
     their fate.

9 If ten men are left in one house,
   they shall die,
10 and a man's uncle and the em-
     balmer shall take him up
   to carry his body out of the house
     for burial,
   and they shall call to someone in a
     corner of the house,
   'Any more there?', and he shall
     answer, 'No.'
   Then he will add, 'Hush!' –

for the name of the LORD must not
  be mentioned.
For the LORD will command,   11
and at the shock the great house
  will be rubble
and the cottage matchwood.

Can horses gallop over rocks?   12
Can the sea be ploughed with
  oxen?
Yet you have turned into venom
  the process of law
and justice itself into poison,
you who are jubilant over a no-   13
  thing[d] and boast,
'Have we not won power[d] by our
  own strength?'
O Israel, I am raising a nation   14
  against you,
and they shall harry your land
from Lebo-hamath to the gorge of
  the Arabah.
This is the very word of the LORD
  the God of Hosts.

Visions foretelling doom upon Israel

THIS was what the Lord GOD   7
showed me: a swarm of locusts
hatched out when the late corn,
which comes after the king's early
crop, was beginning to sprout. As   2
they were devouring the last of the
herbage in the land, I said, 'O
Lord GOD, forgive; what will Jacob
be after this? He is so small.' Then 3
the LORD relented and said, 'This
shall not happen.'
   This was what the Lord GOD   4
showed me: the Lord GOD was
summoning a flame of fire[e] to
devour the great abyss, and to
devour all creation. I said, 'O Lord   5
GOD, I pray thee, cease; what will
Jacob be after this? He is so small.'
The LORD relented and said, 'This   6
also shall not happen.'
   This was what the LORD showed   7
me: there was a man standing by a

---

[a] *Prob. rdg.*; *Heb.* their.   [b] *Prob. rdg.*; *Heb.* yours.   [c] *You . . . violence: or*
You who invoke the day of wrongdoing and bring near the sabbath of violence.
[d] a nothing *and* power: *Heb.* Lo-debar *and* Karnaim, *making a word-play on the*
two place-names.   [e] a flame of fire: *prob. rdg.*; *Heb.* to contend with fire.

wall[a] with a plumb-line in his hand.
8 The LORD said to me, 'What do you see, Amos?' 'A plumb-line', I answered, and the Lord said, 'I am setting a plumb-line to the heart of my people Israel; never again will
9 I pass them by. The hill-shrines of Isaac shall be desolated and the sanctuaries of Israel laid waste; I will rise, sword in hand, against the house of Jeroboam.'
10 Amaziah, the priest of Bethel, reported to Jeroboam king of Israel: 'Amos is conspiring against you in Israel; the country cannot
11 tolerate what he is saying. He says, "Jeroboam shall die by the sword, and Israel shall be deported far
12 from their native land."' To Amos himself Amaziah said, 'Be off, you seer! Off with you to Judah! You can earn your living and do your
13 prophesying there. But never prophesy again at Bethel, for this is the king's sanctuary, a royal
14 palace.' 'I am[b] no prophet,' Amos replied to Amaziah, 'nor am I a prophet's son; I am[b] a herdsman and a dresser of sycomore-figs.
15 But the LORD took me as I followed the flock and said to me, "Go and prophesy to my people
16 Israel." So now listen to the word of the LORD. You tell me I am not to prophesy against Israel or go drivelling on against the people of
17 Isaac. Now these are the words of the LORD: Your wife shall become a city strumpet[c] and your sons and daughters shall fall by the sword. Your land shall be divided up with a measuring-line, you yourself shall die in a heathen country, and Israel shall be deported far from their native land and go into exile.'

8   This was what the Lord GOD showed me: there was a basket of
2 summer fruit, and he said, 'What are you looking at, Amos?' I answered, 'A basket of ripe summer[d] fruit.' Then the LORD said to me,

'The time is ripe[d] for my people Israel. Never again will I pass them
3 by. In that day, says the Lord GOD, the singing women in the palace shall howl, "So many dead men, flung out everywhere! Silence!"'

Listen to this, you who grind the 4 destitute and plunder[e] the humble, you who say, 'When will the 5 new moon be over so that we may sell corn? When will the sabbath be past so that we may open our wheat again, giving short measure in the bushel and taking overweight in the silver, tilting the scales fraudulently, and selling the 6 dust of the wheat; that we may buy the poor for silver and the destitute for a pair of shoes?' The LORD 7 has sworn by the pride of Jacob: I will never forget any of their doings.

Shall not the earth shake for this? 8
Shall not all who live on it grieve?
All earth shall surge and seethe like the Nile
and subside like the river of Egypt.

On that day, says the Lord GOD, 9
I will make the sun go down at noon
and darken the earth in broad daylight.
I will turn your pilgrim-feasts into 10 mourning
and all your songs into lamentation.
I will make you all put sackcloth round your waists
and have all your heads shaved.
I will make it like mourning for an only son
and the end of it a bitter day.

The time is coming, says the Lord 11 GOD,
when I will send famine on the land, not hunger for bread or thirst for water,
but for hearing the word of the LORD.

---

12 Men shall stagger from north to
   south,[a]
   they shall range from east to west,
   seeking the word of the LORD,
   but they shall not find it.
13 On that day fair maidens and young
   men
   shall faint from thirst;
14 all who take their oath by Ashi-
   mah, goddess of Samaria,
   all who swear, 'By the life of your
   god, O Dan',
   and, 'By the sacred way to Beersheba',
   shall fall to rise no more.

9   I saw the LORD standing by the
     altar, and he said:

   Strike the capitals so that the
     whole porch is shaken;
   I will smash them all into pieces[b]
   and I will kill them to the last man[c]
     with the sword.
   No fugitive shall escape,
   no survivor find safety;
 2 if they dig down to Sheol,
   thence shall my hand take them;
   if they climb up to heaven,
   thence will I bring them down.
 3 If they hide on the top of Carmel,
   there will I search out and take
     them;
   if they conceal themselves from me
     in the depths of the sea,
   there will I bid the sea-serpent bite
     them.
 4 If they are herded into captivity
     by their enemies,
   there will I bid the sword slay them,
   and I will fix my eye on them
   for evil and not for good.

 5 The Lord the GOD of Hosts,
   at whose touch the earth heaves,
   and all who dwell on it wither,[d]
   it surges like the Nile,
   and subsides like the river of
     Egypt,
 6 who builds his stair up to the
   heavens

and arches his ceiling over the
   earth,
who summons the waters of the sea
and pours them over the land –
his name is the LORD.

Are not you Israelites like Cushites 7
   to me?
says the LORD.
Did I not bring Israel up from
   Egypt,
the Philistines from Caphtor, the
   Aramaeans from Kir?
Behold, I, the Lord GOD,   8
have my eyes on this sinful kingdom,
and I will wipe it off the face of the
   earth.

A remnant spared and restored

Yet I will not wipe out the family
   of Jacob root and branch,
says the LORD.
No; I will give my orders,   9
I will shake Israel to and fro
   through all the nations
as a sieve is shaken to and fro
and not one pebble falls to the
   ground.
They shall die by the sword, all the 10
   sinners of my people,
who say, 'Thou wilt not let
   disaster come near us
or overtake us.'
On that day I will restore   11
David's fallen house;
I will repair its gaping walls and
   restore its ruins;
I will rebuild it as it was long ago,
that they may possess what is left 12
   of Edom
and all the nations who were once
   named mine.

This is the very word of the LORD,
who will do this.

A time is coming, says the LORD,   13
when the ploughman shall follow
   hard on the vintager,[e]

---

[a] south: *prob. rdg.; Heb.* west.
[b] I will...pieces: *prob. rdg.; Heb.* I will hack them on the heads of them all.
[c] them to the last man: *or* their children.   [d] *Or* mourn.   [e] *Or* reaper.

and he who treads the grapes after
him who sows the seed.
The mountains shall run with fresh
wine,
and every hill shall wave with
corn.
14 I will restore the fortunes of my
people Israel;
they shall rebuild deserted cities
and live in them,

they shall plant vineyards and
drink their wine,
make gardens and eat the fruit.
Once more I will plant them on 15
their own soil,
and they shall never again be uprooted
from the soil I have given them.
It is the word of the LORD your
God.

OBADIAH

Edom's pride and downfall

1[a] The vision of Obadiah: what the
Lord GOD has said concerning
Edom.

When a herald was sent out among
the nations, crying,
'Rouse yourselves;
let us rouse ourselves to battle
against Edom',
I heard this message from the
LORD:

2 Look, I make you the least of all
nations,
an object of contempt.
3 Your proud, insolent heart has led
you astray;
you who haunt the crannies
among the rocks,
making your home on the heights,
you say to yourself, 'Who can
bring me to the ground?'
4 Though you soar as high as a vulture
and your nest is set among the
stars,
thence I will bring you down.
This is the very word of the LORD.

5[b] If thieves or robbers come to you
by night,
though your loss be heavy,
they will steal only what they want;

if vintagers come to you,
will they not leave gleanings?
But see how Esau's treasure is ran- 6
sacked,
his secret wealth hunted out!
All your former allies march you to 7
the frontier,
your confederates mislead you and
bring you low,
your own kith and kin lay a snare
for your feet,
a snare that works blindly, without wisdom.
And on that very day 8
I will destroy all the sages of
Edom
and leave no wisdom on the mount
of Esau.
This is the very word of the LORD.
Then shall your warriors, O Te- 9
man, be so enfeebled,
that every man shall be cut down
on the mount of Esau.
For the murderous violence done 10
to your brother Jacob
you shall be covered with shame
and cut off for ever.
On the day when you stood aloof, 11
on the day when strangers carried
off his wealth,
when foreigners trooped in by his
gates
and parcelled out Jerusalem by lot,
you yourselves were of one mind
with them.

[a] *Verses 1–4: cp. Jer. 49. 14–16.*   [b] *Verses 5 and 6: cp. Jer. 49. 9, 10.*

12 Do not gloat over your brother on
  the day of his misfortune,
  nor rejoice over Judah on his day
  of ruin;
  do not boast on the day of distress,
13 nor enter my people's gates on the
  day of his downfall.
  Do not gloat over his fall on the
  day of his downfall
  nor seize his treasure on the day
  of his downfall.
14 Do not wait at the cross-roads to
  cut off his fugitives
  nor betray the survivors on the day
  of distress.

15 For soon the day of the LORD will
  come on all the nations:
  you shall be treated as you have
  treated others,
  and your deeds will recoil on your
  own head.
16 The draught that you have drunk
  on my holy mountain
  all the nations shall drink continually;
  they shall drink and gulp down
  and shall be as though they had
  never been;
17 but on Mount Zion there shall be
  those that escape,

and it shall be holy,
and Jacob shall dispossess those
  that dispossessed them.
Then shall the house of Jacob be 18
  fire,
the house of Joseph flame,
and the house of Esau shall be
  chaff;
they shall blaze through it and
  consume it,
and the house of Esau shall have
  no survivor.
The LORD has spoken.
Then they shall possess the Negeb, 19
  the mount of Esau,
and the Shephelah of the Philistines;
they shall possess the country-side
  of Ephraim and Samaria,
and Benjamin shall possess Gilead.
Exiles of Israel[a] shall possess[b] 20
  Canaan as far as Zarephath,
exiles of Jerusalem[c] shall possess
  the cities of the Negeb.
Those who find safety on Mount 21
  Zion shall go up
to hold sway over the mount of
  Esau,
and dominion shall belong to the
  LORD.

JONAH

Jonah's mission to Nineveh

1 THE word of the LORD came
2 to Jonah son of Amittai: 'Go
   to the great city of Nineveh,
go now and denounce it, for its
wickedness stares me in the face.'
3 But Jonah set out for Tarshish to
escape from the LORD. He went
down to Joppa, where he found a
ship bound for Tarshish. He paid
his fare and went on board, meaning to travel by it to Tarshish out

of reach of the LORD. But the LORD 4
let loose a hurricane, and the sea
ran so high in the storm that the
ship threatened to break up. The 5
sailors were afraid, and each cried
out to his god for help. Then they
threw things overboard to lighten
the ship. Jonah had gone down into
a corner of the ship and was lying
sound asleep when the captain 6
came upon him. 'What, sound a-
sleep?' he said. 'Get up, and call on
your god; perhaps he will spare

[a] *Prob. rdg.*; *Heb. adds* this army.
[c] *Prob. rdg.*; *Heb. adds* who are in Sepharad.

[b] shall possess: *prob. rdg.*; *Heb.* which.

us a thought and we shall not perish.'

7 At last the sailors said to each other, 'Come and let us cast lots to find out who is to blame for this bad luck.' So they cast lots, and 8 the lot fell on Jonah. 'Now then,' they said to him, 'what is your business? Where do you come from? What is your country? Of 9 what nation are you?' 'I am a Hebrew,' he answered, 'and I worship the LORD the God of heaven, who 10 made both sea and land.' At this the sailors were even more afraid. 'What can you have done wrong?' they asked. They already knew that he was trying to escape from the LORD, for he had told them so. 11 'What shall we do with you,' they asked, 'to make the sea go down?' For the storm grew worse and 12 worse. 'Take me and throw me overboard,' he said, 'and the sea will go down. I know it is my fault that this great storm has struck 13 you.' The crew rowed hard to put back to land but in vain, for the sea 14 ran higher and higher. At last they called on the LORD and said, 'O LORD, do not let us perish at the price of this man's life; do not charge us with the death of an innocent man. All this, O LORD, is 15 thy set purpose.' Then they took Jonah and threw him overboard, 16 and the sea stopped raging. So the crew were filled with the fear of the LORD and offered sacrifice and 17 made vows to him. But the LORD ordained that a great fish should swallow Jonah, and for three days and three nights he remained in its belly.

2 Jonah prayed to the LORD his God from the belly of the fish:

2 I called to the LORD in my distress,
and he answered me;
out of the belly of Sheol I cried for help,
and thou hast heard my cry.
3 Thou didst cast me into the depths,
far out at sea,

and the flood closed round me;
all thy waves, all thy billows,
passed over me.
4 I thought I was banished from thy sight
and should never see thy holy temple again.
5 The water about me rose up to my neck;
the ocean was closing over me.
Weeds twined about my head
6 in the troughs of the mountains;
I was sinking into a world
whose bars would hold me fast for ever.
But thou didst bring me up alive
from the pit, O LORD my God.
7 As my senses failed me I remembered the LORD,
and my prayer reached thee in thy holy temple.
8 Men who worship false gods may abandon their loyalty,
9 but I will offer thee sacrifice with words of praise;
I will pay my vows; victory is the LORD's.

10 Then the LORD spoke to the fish and it spewed Jonah out on to the dry land.

3 The word of the LORD came to 2 Jonah a second time: 'Go to the great city of Nineveh, go now and denounce it in the words I give 3–4 you.' Jonah obeyed at once and went to Nineveh. He began by going a day's journey into the city, a vast city, three days' journey across, and then proclaimed: 'In forty days Nineveh shall be over-5 thrown!' The people of Nineveh believed God's word. They ordered a public fast and put on sackcloth, 6 high and low alike. When the news reached the king of Nineveh he rose from his throne, stripped off his robes of state, put on sackcloth 7 and sat in ashes. Then he had a proclamation made in Nineveh: 'This is a decree of the king and his nobles. No man or beast, herd or flock, is to taste food, to graze or to 8 drink water. They are to clothe

themselves in sackcloth and call on God with all their might. Let every man abandon his wicked ways and

9 his habitual violence. It may be that God will repent and turn away from his anger: and so we

10 shall not perish.' God saw what they did, and how they abandoned their wicked ways, and he repented and did not bring upon them the disaster he had threatened.

4 Jonah was greatly displeased
2 and angry, and he prayed to the LORD: 'This, O LORD, is what I feared when I was in my own country, and to forestall it I tried to escape to Tarshish; I knew that thou art "a god gracious and compassionate, long-suffering and ever constant, and always willing to

3 repent of the disaster".*a* And now, LORD, take my life: I should be

4 better dead than alive.' 'Are you so

5 angry?' said the LORD. Jonah went out and sat down on the east of the city. There he made himself a shelter and sat in its shade, waiting

to see what would happen in the city. Then the LORD God ordained 6 that a climbing gourd*b* should grow up over his head to throw its shade over him and relieve his distress, and Jonah was grateful for the gourd. But at dawn the next day 7 God ordained that a worm should attack the gourd, and it withered; and at sunrise God ordained that a 8 scorching wind should blow up from the east. The sun beat down on Jonah's head till he grew faint. Then he prayed for death and said, 'I should be better dead than alive.' At this God said to Jonah, 'Are you 9 so angry over the gourd?' 'Yes,' he answered, 'mortally angry.' The 10 LORD said, 'You are sorry for the gourd, though you did not have the trouble of growing it, a plant which came up in a night and withered in a night. And should not 11 I be sorry for the great city of Nineveh, with its hundred and twenty thousand who cannot tell their right hand from their left, and cattle without number?'

MICAH

1 THIS is the word of the LORD which came to Micah of Moresheth during the reigns of Jotham, Ahaz, and Hezekiah, kings of Judah; which he received in visions concerning Samaria and Jerusalem.

The rulers of Israel and Judah denounced

2 Listen, you peoples, all together; attend, O earth and all who are in it,
that the Lord GOD, the Lord from his holy temple,

may bear witness against you.
For look, the LORD is leaving his 3 dwelling-place;
down he comes and walks on the heights of the earth.
Beneath him mountains dissolve 4 like wax before the fire,
valleys are torn open,
as when torrents pour down the hill-side –
and all for the crime of Jacob and 5 the sin of Israel.
What is the crime of Jacob? Is it not Samaria?
What is the hill-shrine of Judah? Is it not Jerusalem?

a a god...disaster: *cp.* Exod. 34. 6.   *b* a climbing gourd: *or* a castor-oil plant.

6 So I will make Samaria
a heap of ruins in open country,
a place for planting vines;
I will pour her stones down into the
valley
and lay her foundations bare.
7 All her carved figures shall be
shattered,
her images burnt one and all;
I will make a waste heap of all her
idols.
She amassed them out of fees for
harlotry,
and a harlot's fee shall they become once more.
8 Therefore I must howl and wail,
go naked and distraught;
I must howl like a wolf, mourn like
a desert-owl.
9 Her wound cannot be healed;
for the stroke has bitten deep into
Judah,
it has fallen on the gate of my
people,
upon Jerusalem itself.
10 Will you not weep your fill, weep
your eyes out in Gath?
In Beth-aphrah sprinkle yourselves with dust;
11 take the road, you that dwell in
Shaphir;
have not the people of Zaanan
gone out in shame from their
city?
Beth-ezel is a place of lamentation,
she can lend you support no longer.
12 The people of Maroth are greatly
alarmed,
for disaster has come down from
the LORD
to the very gate of Jerusalem.
13 Harness the steeds to the chariot,
O people of Lachish,
for you first led the daughter of
Zion into sin;
to you must the crimes of Israel be
traced.
14 Let Moresheth-gath be given her
dismissal.
Beth-achzib has*a* disappointed*b*
the kings of Israel.

And you too, O people of Mare- 15
shah,
I will send others to take your
place;
and the glory of Israel shall hide
in the cave of Adullam.
Shave the hair from your head in 16
mourning
for the children of your delight;
make yourself bald as a vulture,
for they have left you and gone
into exile.

Shame on those who lie in bed 2
planning evil and wicked deeds
and rise at daybreak to do them,
knowing that they have the power!
They covet land and take it by 2
force;
if they want a house they seize it;
they rob a man of his home
and steal every man's inheritance.

Therefore these are the words of 3
the LORD:

Listen, for this whole brood I am
planning disaster,
whose yoke you cannot shake from
your necks
and walk upright; it shall be your
hour of disaster.

On that day 4
they shall take up a poem about
you
and raise a lament thrice told,
saying, 'We are utterly despoiled:
the land of the LORD's*c* people
changes hands.
How shall a man have power*d*
to restore our fields, now parcelled
out*e*?'
Therefore there shall be no one to 5
assign to you
any portion by lot in the LORD's
assembly.

How they rant! They may say, 'Do 6
not rant';
but this ranting is all their own,

---

a Beth-achzib has: *prob. rdg.*; *Heb.* The houses of Achzib have.   *b Heb.* achzab.
c the LORD's: *prob. rdg.*; *Heb.* my.   *d* have power: *prob. rdg.*; *Heb.* remove
from me.   *e* now parcelled out: *prob. rdg.*; *Heb.* he will parcel out.

these insults are their*a* own invention.

7 Can one ask, O house of Jacob,
'Is the LORD's patience truly at an end?
Are these his deeds?
Does not good come of the LORD's words?
He is the upright man's best friend.'
8 But you are no*b* people for me,
rising up as my enemy to my*c* face,
to strip the cloak from him that was safe*d*
and take away the confidence of returning warriors,
9 to drive the women of my people from their pleasant homes
and rob the children of my glory for ever.
10 Up and be gone; this is no resting-place for you,
you that to defile yourselves would commit any mischief,
mischief however cruel.

11 If anyone had gone about in a spirit of falsehood and lies, saying,
'I will rant to you of wine and strong drink', his ranting would be what this people like.

12 I will assemble you, the whole house of Jacob;
I will gather together those that are left in Israel.
I will herd them like sheep in a fold,
like a grazing flock which stampedes at the sight of a man.
13 So their leader breaks out before them,
and they all break through the gate and escape,
and their king goes before them,
and the LORD leads the way.

3 And I said:

Listen, you leaders of Jacob, rulers of Israel,

should you not know what is right?
You hate good and love evil, 2
you flay men alive and tear the very flesh from their bones;
you devour the flesh of my people, 3
strip off their skin,
splinter their bones;
you shred them like flesh into a pot,
like meat into a cauldron.

Then they will call to the LORD, 4
and he will give them no answer;
when that time comes he will hide his face from them,
so wicked are their deeds.

These are the words of the LORD 5
concerning the prophets who lead my people astray, who promise prosperity in return for a morsel of food, who proclaim a holy war against them if they put nothing into their mouths:

Therefore night shall bring you no 6
vision,
darkness no divination;
the sun shall go down on the prophets,
the day itself shall be black above them.
Seers and diviners alike shall blush 7
for shame;
they shall all put their hands over their mouths,
because there is no answer from God.

But I am full of strength,*e* of 8
justice and power,
to denounce his crime to Jacob
and his sin to Israel.
Listen to this, leaders of Jacob, 9
rulers of Israel,
you who make justice hateful
and wrest it from its straight course,
building Zion in bloodshed 10
and Jerusalem in iniquity.

---

a *Prob. rdg.*; *Heb.* his. *b* But...no: *prob. rdg.*; *Heb.* But yesterday.
c my: *prob. rdg.*; *Heb. om.* *d* the cloak...safe: *prob. rdg.*; *Heb.* mantle, cloak.
e *Prob. rdg.*; *Heb. adds* the spirit of the LORD.

11 Her rulers sell justice,
  her priests give direction in return
    for a bribe,
  her prophets take money for their
    divination,
  and yet men rely on the LORD.
  'Is not the LORD among us?' they
    say;
  'then no disaster can befall us.'
12 Therefore, on your account
  Zion shall become a ploughed
    field,
  Jerusalem a heap of ruins,
  and the temple hill rough heath.

A remnant restored in an age of peace

4 1ᵃ In days to come
  the mountain of the LORD's house
    shall be set over all other moun-
    tains,
  lifted high above the hills.
  Peoples shall come streaming to it,
2 and many nations shall come and
    say,
  'Come, let us climb up on to the
    mountain of the LORD,
  to the house of the God of Jacob,
  that he may teach us his ways
  and we may walk in his paths.'
  For instruction issues from Zion,
  and out of Jerusalem comes the
    word of the LORD;
3 he will be judge between many
    peoples
  and arbiter among mighty nations
    afar.
  They shall beat their swords into
    mattocks
  and their spears into pruning-
    knives;
  nation shall not lift sword against
    nation
  nor ever again be trained for war,
4 and each man shall dwell under his
    own vine,
  under his own fig-tree, undisturbed.
  For the LORD of Hosts himself has
    spoken.

5 All peoples may walk, each in the
    name of his god,
but we will walk in the name of the
    LORD our God
for ever and ever.

On that day, says the LORD,   6
I will gather those who are lost;
I will assemble the exiles and I will
    strengthen the weaklings.
I will preserve the lost as a 7
    remnant
and turn the derelict into a mighty
    nation.
The LORD shall be their king on
    Mount Zion
now and for ever.
And you, rocky bastion, hill of 8
    Zion's daughter,
the promises to you shall be ful-
    filled;
and your former sovereignty shall
    come again,
the dominion of the daughter of
    Jerusalem.

Why are you now filled with alarm? 9
Have you no king?
Have you no counsellor left,
that you are seized with writhing
    like a woman in labour?
Lie writhing on the ground like a 10
    woman in childbirth,
O daughter of Zion;
for now you must leave the city
and camp in the open country;
and so you will come to Babylon.
There you shall be saved,
there the LORD will deliver you
    from your enemies.
But now many nations are massed 11
    against you;
they say, 'Let her suffer outrage,
let us gloat over Zion.'
But they do not know the LORD's 12
    thoughts
nor understand his purpose;
for he has gathered them like
    sheaves to the threshing-floor.
Start your threshing, daughter of 13
    Zion;
for I will make your horns of
    iron,
your hooves will I make of bronze,
and you shall crush many peoples.

ᵃ Verses 1–3: cp. Isa. 2. 2–4.

You shall devote their ill-gotten
  gain to the LORD,
their wealth to the Lord of all the
  earth.

5 Get you behind your walls, you
  people of a walled city;
the siege is pressed home against
  you:
Israel's ruler shall be struck on the
  cheek with a rod.

2 But you, Bethlehem in Ephrathah,
small as you are to be among
  Judah's clans,
out of you shall come forth a
  governor for Israel,
one whose roots are far back in the
  past, in days gone by.

3 Therefore only so long as a woman
  is in labour
shall he give up Israel;
and then those that survive of his
  race
shall rejoin their brethren.

4 He shall appear and be their shepherd
in the strength of the LORD,
in the majesty of the name of the
  LORD his God.
And they shall continue, for now
  his greatness shall reach
to the ends of the earth;

5 and he shall be a man of peace.

When the Assyrian comes into our
  land,
when he tramples our castles,
we will raise against him seven men
  or eight
to be shepherds and princes.

6 They shall shepherd Assyria with
  the sword
and the land of Nimrod with bare
  blades;
they shall deliver us from the
  Assyrians
when they come into our land,
when they trample our frontiers.

7 All that are left of Jacob, surrounded by many peoples,
shall be like dew from the LORD,
like copious showers on the
  grass,

which do not wait for man's command
or linger for any man's bidding.
All that are left of Jacob among the 8
  nations,
surrounded by many peoples,
shall be like a lion among the beasts
  of the forest,
like a young lion loose in a flock of
  sheep;
as he prowls he will trample and
  tear them,
with no rescuer in sight.
Your hand shall be raised high 9
  over your foes,
and all who hate you shall be
  destroyed.

On that day, says the LORD,   10
I will destroy all your horses among
  you
and make away with your chariots.
I will destroy the cities of your 11
  land
and raze your fortresses.
I will destroy all your sorcerers,   12
and there shall be no more soothsayers among you.
I will destroy your images and all 13
  the sacred pillars in your land;
you shall no longer bow in reverence before things your own hands
  made.
I will pull down the sacred poles in 14
  your land,
and demolish your blood-spattered
  altars.
In anger and fury will I take 15
  vengeance
on all nations who disobey me.

*Israel denounced for her
people's sins*

Hear now what the LORD is saying: 6

Up, state your case to the mountains;
let the hills hear your plea.
Hear the LORD's case, you moun- 2
  tains,
you everlasting pillars that bear
  up the earth;

for the LORD has a case against his people,
and will argue it with Israel.

3 O my people, what have I done to you?
Tell me how I have wearied you; answer me this.

4 I brought you up from Egypt,
I ransomed you from the land of slavery,
I sent Moses and Aaron and Miriam to lead you.

5 Remember, my people,
what Balak king of Moab schemed against you,
and how Balaam son of Beor answered him;
consider the journey*a* from Shittim to Gilgal,
in order that you may know the triumph of the LORD.

6 What shall I bring when I approach the LORD?
How shall I stoop before God on high?
Am I to approach him with whole-offerings or yearling calves?

7 Will the LORD accept thousands of rams
or ten thousand rivers of oil?
Shall I offer my eldest son for my own wrongdoing,
my children for my own sin?

8 God*b* has told you what is good;
and what is it that the LORD asks of you?
Only to act justly, to love loyalty,
to walk wisely before your God.

9 Hark, the LORD, the fear of whose name brings success,
the LORD calls to the city.

10 Listen, O tribe of Judah and citizens in assembly,*c*
can I overlook*d* the infamous false measure,*e*
the accursed short bushel?

11 Can I connive at false scales or a bag of light weights?

12 Your rich men are steeped in violence,
your townsmen are all liars,
and their tongues frame deceit.

13 But now I will inflict a signal punishment on you
to lay you waste for your sins:

14 you shall eat but not be satisfied,
your food shall lie heavy on your stomach;
you shall come to labour but not bring forth,
and even if you bear a child
I will give it to the sword;

15 you shall sow but not reap,
you shall press the olives but not use the oil,
you shall tread the grapes but not drink the wine.

16 You have kept the precepts of Omri;
what the house of Ahab did, you have done;
you have followed all their ways.
So I will lay you utterly waste;
the nations shall jeer at your citizens,
and their insults you shall bear.

Disappointment turned to hope

7 Alas! I am now like the last gatherings of summer fruit,
the last gleanings of the vintage,
when there are no grapes left to eat,
none of those early figs that I love.

2 Loyal men have vanished from the earth,
there is not one upright man.
All lie in wait to do murder,
each man drives his own kinsman like a hunter into the net.

3 They are bent eagerly on wrong-doing,
the officer who presents the requests,*f*
the judge who gives judgement*g* for reward,

---

a consider the journey: *prob. rdg.; Heb. om.*   *b* God: *prob. rdg.; Heb. obscure.*
c citizens in assembly: *prob. rdg.; Heb. unintelligible.*   *d* can I overlook: *prob. rdg.; Heb. obscure.*   *e* *Prob. rdg.; Heb. adds infamous treasures.*
f the requests: *prob. rdg.; Heb. om.*   *g* who gives judgement: *prob. rdg.; Heb. om.*

and the nobleman who harps on
his desires.
4 Thus their goodness is twisted[a]
like rank weeds
and their honesty like briars.[b]
As soon as thine eye sees, thy
punishment falls;
at that moment bewilderment
seizes them.
5 Trust no neighbour, put no confidence in your closest friend;
seal your lips even from the wife
of your bosom.
6 For son maligns father,
daughter rebels against mother,
daughter-in-law against mother-
in-law,
and a man's enemies are his own
household.
7 But I will look for the LORD,
I will wait for God my saviour; my
God will hear me.
8 O my enemies, do not exult over
me;
I have fallen, but shall rise again;
though I dwell in darkness, the
LORD is my light.
9 I will bear the anger of the LORD,
for I have sinned against him,
until he takes up my cause and
gives judgement for me,
until he brings me out into light,
and I see his justice.
10 Then may my enemies see and be
abashed,
those who said to me, 'Where is he,
the LORD your God?'
Then shall they be trampled like
mud in the streets;
I shall gloat over them;
11 that will be a day for rebuilding
your walls,
a day when your frontiers will be
extended,
12 a day when men will come seeking
you

from Assyria to Egypt
and from Egypt to the Euphrates,
from every sea and every mountain;
and the earth with its inhabitants 13
shall be waste.
This shall be the fruit of their deeds.

Shepherd thy people with thy 14
crook,
the flock that is thy very own,
that dwells by itself on the heath
and in the meadows;
let them graze in Bashan and
Gilead, as in days gone by.
Show us[c] miracles as in the days 15
when thou camest out of Egypt;
let the nations see and be taken a- 16
back for all their might,
let them keep their mouths shut,
make their ears deaf,
let them lick the dust like snakes, 17
like creatures that crawl upon the
ground.
Let them come trembling and fearful from their strongholds,
let them fear thee, O LORD our God.

Who is a god like thee? Thou takest 18
away guilt,
thou passest over the sin of the
remnant of thy own people,
thou dost not let thy anger rage for
ever
but delightest in love that will not
change.
Once more thou wilt show us 19
tender affection
and wash out our guilt,
casting all our sins into the depths
of the sea.
Thou wilt show good faith to 20
Jacob,
unchanging love to Abraham,
as thou didst swear to our fathers
in days gone by.

[a] twisted: *prob. rdg.*; *Heb. obscure.*
[b] their honesty like briars: *prob. rdg.*; *Heb. obscure.*
[c] *Prob. rdg.*; *Heb.* I will show him.

NAHUM

1 An oracle about Nineveh: the book of the vision of Nahum the Elkoshite.

The vengeance of the LORD on his enemies

2[a] The LORD is a jealous god, a god of vengeance;
the LORD takes vengeance and is quick to anger.[b]

3 [c]In whirlwind and storm he goes on his way,
and the clouds are the dust beneath his feet.

4 He rebukes the sea and dries it up and makes all the streams fail.
Bashan and Carmel languish,
and on Lebanon the young shoots wither.

5 The mountains quake before him, the hills heave and swell,
and the earth, the world and all that lives in it,
are in tumult at his presence.

6 Who can stand before his wrath? Who can resist his fury?
His anger pours out[d] like a stream of fire,
and the rocks melt[e] before him.

7 The LORD is a sure refuge
for those who look to him in time of distress;
he cares for all who seek his protection

8 and brings them safely[f] through the sweeping flood;
he makes a final end of all who oppose him
and pursues his enemies into darkness.

No adversaries dare oppose him 9-11 twice;
all are burnt up[g] like tangled briars.
Why do you make plots against the LORD?
He himself will make an end of you all.
From you has come forth a wicked counsellor,
plotting evil against the LORD.
The LORD takes vengeance on his adversaries,
against his enemies he directs his wrath;
with skin scorched black, they are consumed
like stubble that is parched and dry.

Israel and Judah rid of the invaders

These are the words of the LORD:

Now I will break his yoke from 13 your necks
and snap the cords that bind you.
Image and idol will I hew down in 14 the house of your God.
This is what the LORD has ordained for you:
never again shall your offspring be scattered;
and I will grant you burial, fickle though you have been.
Has the punishment been so great? 12
Yes, but it has passed away and is gone.
I have afflicted you, but I will not afflict you again.

[a] Verses 2–14 are an incomplete alphabetic acrostic poem; some parts have been rearranged accordingly.   [b] The rest of verse 2, The LORD takes...wrath, transposed to verse 11.   [c] Prob. rdg.; Heb. inserts two lines The LORD is long-suffering and of great might, but the LORD does not sweep clean away.   [d] pours out: or fuses or melts.   [e] Prob. rdg.; Heb. are torn down.   [f] brings them safely: prob. rdg.; Heb. om.   [g] all are burnt up: prob. rdg.; Heb. for until.

15 See on the mountains the feet of
the herald
who brings good news.
Make your pilgrimages, O Judah,
and pay your vows.
For wicked men shall never again
overrun you;
they are totally destroyed.

2 2ª The LORD will restore the pride of
Jacob and Israel alike,
although plundering hordes have
stripped them bare
and pillaged their vines.

Nineveh's enemies triumphant

1 The battering-ram is mounted
against your bastions,
the siege is closing in.
Watch the road and brace yourselves;
put forth all your strength.

3 The shields of their warriors are
gleaming red,
their soldiers are all in scarlet;
their chariots, when the line is
formed,
are like flickeringᵇ fire;

4 squadrons of horse advance on the
city in mad frenzy;ᶜ
they jostle one another in the outskirts, like waving torches;

5 the leaders display their prowessᵈ
as they dash to and fro like
lightning,
rushingᵉ in headlong career;
they hasten to the wall, and mantelets are set in position.

6 The sluices of the rivers are
opened, the palace topples down;

7 the train of captives goes into
exile,
their slave-girls are carried off,
moaning like doves and beating
their breasts;

8 and Nineveh has become like a
pool of water,
like the waters round her, which
are ebbing away.

'Stop! Stop!' they cry; but none
turns back.

9 Spoil is taken, spoil of silver and
gold;
there is no end to the store,
treasure beyond the costliest that
man can desire.

10 Plundered, pillaged, stripped bare!
Courage melting and knees giving
way,
writhing limbs, and faces drained
of colour!

11 Where now is the lions' den,
the caveᶠ where the lion cubs
lurked,
where the lion andᵍ lioness and
young cubs
went unafraid,

12 the lion which killed to satisfy its
whelps
and for its mate broke the neck of
the kill,
mauling its prey to fill its lair,
filling its den with the mauled
prey?

13 I am against you, says the LORD of
Hosts,
I will smoke out your pride,ʰ
and a sword shall devour your cubs.
I will leave you no more prey on
the earth,
and the sound of your feedingⁱ shall
no more be heard.

3 Ah! blood-stained city, steeped in
deceit,
full of pillage, never empty of prey!

2 Hark to the crack of the whip,
the rattle of wheels and stamping
of horses,

3 bounding chariots, chargers rearing,
swords gleaming, flash of spears!
The dead are past counting, their
bodies lie in heaps,
corpses innumerable, men stumbling over corpses –

ª *Verses 1 and 2 transposed.*   ᵇ flickering: *prob. rdg.*; *Heb.* obscure.
ᶜ *Prob. rdg.*; *Heb.* adds chariots.   ᵈ display their prowess: *or* shout their
own names.   ᵉ *Prob. rdg.*; *Heb.* stumbling.   ᶠ *Prob. rdg.*; *Heb.* pasture.
ᵍ and: *prob. rdg.*; *Heb. om.*   ʰ your pride: *prob. rdg.*; *Heb.* her chariot.
ⁱ your feeding: *prob. rdg.*; *Heb.* your messenger.

4 all for a wanton's monstrous wan-
    tonness,
  fair-seeming, a mistress of sorcery,
  who beguiled nations and tribes
  by her wantonness and her sor-
    ceries.

5 I am against you, says the LORD of
    Hosts,
  I will uncover your breasts to your
    disgrace
  and expose your naked body to
    every nation,
  to every kingdom your shame.

6 I will cast loathsome filth over
    you,
  I will count you obscene and treat
    you like excrement.

7 Then all who see you will shrink
    from you and say,
  'Nineveh is laid waste; who will
    console her?'
  Where shall I look for anyone to
    comfort you?

8 Will you fare better than No-
    amon? –
  she that lay by the streams of the
    Nile,
  surrounded by water,
  whose rampart was the Nile,
    waters her wall;

9 Cush and Egypt were her strength,
    and it was boundless,
  Put and the Libyans brought her
    help.

10 She too became an exile and went
    into captivity,
  her infants too were dashed to the
    ground at every street-corner,
  her nobles were shared out by
    lot,
  all her great men were thrown into
    chains.

11 You too shall hire yourself out,
    flaunting your sex;
  you too shall seek refuge from the
    enemy.

Your fortifications are like figs 12
    when they ripen:
  if they are shaken, they fall into
    the mouth of the eater.

The troops[a] in your midst are a 13
    pack of women,
  the gates of your country stand
    open to the enemy,
  and fire consumes their bars.

Draw yourselves water for the 14
    siege,
  strengthen your fortifications;
  down into the clay, trample the
    mortar,
  repair the brickwork.

Even then the fire will consume 15
    you,
  and the sword will cut you down.[b]
  Make yourselves many as the
    locusts,
  make yourselves many as the
    hoppers,
  a swarm which spreads out and 16
    then flies away.

You have spies as numerous as the
    stars in the sky;
  your secret agents are like locusts, 17
  your commanders like the hoppers
  which lie dormant in the walls on
    a cold day;
  but when the sun rises, they scurry
    off,
  and no one knows where they have
    gone.

Your shepherds slumber, O king of 18
    Assyria,
  your flock-masters lie down to
    rest;
  your troops[a] are scattered over the
    hills,
  and no one rounds them up.

Your wounds cannot be assuaged, 19
    your injury is mortal;
  all who have heard of your fate
    clap their hands in joy.
  Are there any whom your ceaseless
    cruelty has not borne down?

---

[a] Or people.
[b] Prob. rdg.; Heb. adds and consume you like the locust (or hopper).

HABAKKUK

1 An oracle which the prophet Habakkuk received in a vision.

Divine justice

2 How long, O LORD, have I cried to thee, unanswered?
I cry, 'Violence!', but thou dost not save.
3 Why dost thou let me see such misery,
why countenance[a] wrongdoing?

Devastation and violence confront me;
strife breaks out, discord raises its head,
4 and so law grows effete;
justice does not come forth victorious;
for the wicked outwit the righteous,
and so justice comes out perverted.

5 Look, you treacherous people, look:
here is what will astonish you and stun you,
for there is work afoot in your days which you will not believe when it is told you.
6 It is this: I am raising up the Chaldaeans,
that savage and impetuous nation,
who cross the wide tracts of the earth
to take possession of homes not theirs.
7 Terror and awe go with them;
their justice and judgement are of their own making.
8 Their horses are swifter than hunting-leopards,
keener than wolves of the plain;[b]
their cavalry wait ready, they spring forward,

they come flying from afar
like vultures swooping to devour the prey.
9 Their whole army advances, violence in their hearts;
a sea of faces rolls on;
they bring in captives countless as the sand.
10 Kings they hold in derision, rulers they despise;
they despise every fortress,
they raise siege-works and capture it.
11 Then they pass on like the wind and are gone;
and dismayed are all those whose strength was their god.

12 Art thou not from of old, O LORD? –
my God, the holy, the immortal.[c]
O LORD, it is thou who hast appointed them to execute judgement;
O mighty God, thou who hast destined them to chastise,
13 thou whose eyes are too pure to look upon evil,
and who canst not countenance wrongdoing,
why dost thou countenance the treachery of the wicked?
Why keep silent when they devour men more righteous than they?
14 Why dost thou make men like the fish of the sea,
like gliding creatures that obey no ruler?
15 They haul them up with hooks, one and all,
they catch them in nets
and drag them in their trawls;
then they make merry and rejoice,

---

[a] Or dost thou let me see.   [b] Or evening.
[c] the immortal: *prob. original rdg., altered in Heb. to* we shall not die.

16 sacrificing to their nets
and burning offerings*a* to their
trawls;
for by these they live sumptuously
and enjoy rich fare.

17 Are they then to unsheathe the
sword every day,
to slaughter the nations without
pity?

2 I will stand at my post,
I will take up my position on the
watch-tower,
I will watch to learn what he will
say through me,
and what I shall reply when I am
challenged.*b*

2 Then the LORD made answer:
Write down the vision, inscribe it
on tablets,
ready for a herald to carry it with
speed;*c*

3 for there is still a vision for the
appointed time.
At the destined hour it will come in
breathless haste,
it will not fail.
If it delays, wait for it;
for when it comes will be no time
to linger.

4 The reckless will be unsure of himself,
while the righteous man will live
by being faithful;*d*

5 as for the traitor in his over-
confidence,
still less will he ride out the storm,
for all his bragging.
Though he opens his mouth as wide
as Sheol
and is insatiable as Death,
gathering in all the nations,
making all peoples his own harvest,

6 surely they will all turn upon him
with insults and abuse, and say,
'Woe betide you who heap up
wealth that is not yours*e*
and enrich yourself with goods
taken in pledge!'

Will not your creditors suddenly 7
start up,
will not all awake who would shake
you till you are empty,
and will you not fall a victim to
them?

Because you yourself have plun- 8
dered mighty*f* nations,
all the rest of the world will
plunder you,
because of bloodshed and violence
done in the land,
to the city and all its inhabitants.

Woe betide you who seek unjust 9
gain for your house,
to build your nest on a height,
to save yourself from the grasp of
wicked men!

Your schemes to overthrow 10
mighty*f* nations
will bring dishonour to your house
and put your own life in jeopardy.

The very stones will cry out from 11
the wall,
and from the timbers a beam will
answer them.

Woe betide you who have built a 12
town with bloodshed
and founded a city on fraud,

so that nations toil for a pittance, 13
and peoples weary themselves for
a mere nothing!
Is not all this the doing of the LORD
of Hosts?

For the earth shall be full of the 14
knowledge of the glory of the
LORD
as the waters fill the sea.

Woe betide you who make your*g* 15
companions drink the outpouring
of your wrath,
making them drunk, that you may
watch their naked orgies!

Drink deep draughts of shame, not 16
of glory;
you too shall drink until you
stagger.

---

a Or incense.   *b* when I am challenged: *or* concerning my complaint.
c ready...speed: *or* so that a man may read it easily.
d Or by his faithfulness (*cp. Romans* 1. 17; *Galatians* 3. 11).
e *Prob. rdg.*; *Heb. adds* till when.   *f* Or many.   *g* *Prob. rdg.*; *Heb.* his.

The cup in the LORD's right hand is
passed to you,
and your shame will exceed[a] your
glory.

17 The violence done to Lebanon shall
sweep over you,
the havoc done to its beasts shall
break your own spirit,
because of bloodshed and violence
done in the land,
to the city and all its inhabitants.

18 What use is an idol when its maker
has shaped it? –
it is only an image, a source of
lies;
or when the maker trusts what he
has made? –
he is only making dumb idols.

19 Woe betide him who says to the
wood, 'Wake up',
to the dead stone, 'Bestir yourself'![b]
Why, it is firmly encased in gold
and silver
and has no breath in it.

20 But the LORD is in his holy
temple;
let all the earth be hushed in his
presence.

A prayer for mercy

3 A prayer of the prophet Habakkuk.

2 O LORD, I have heard tell of thy
deeds;
I have seen, O LORD, thy work.[c]
In the midst of the years thou didst
make thyself known,
and in thy wrath thou didst remember mercy.

3 God comes from Teman,
the Holy One from Mount Paran;
his radiance overspreads the skies,
and his splendour fills the earth.

He rises like the dawn,   4
with twin rays starting forth at his
side;
the skies are[d] the hiding-place of
his majesty,
and the everlasting[e] ways are for[f]
his swift flight.[g]
Pestilence stalks before him,   5
and plague comes forth behind.
He stands still and shakes the 6
earth,
he looks and makes the nations
tremble;
the eternal mountains are riven,
the everlasting[e] hills subside,
the tents of Cushan are snatched 7
away,[h]
the tent-curtains of Midian flutter.
Art thou angry with the streams? 8
Is thy wrath against the sea, O
LORD?
When thou dost mount thy horses,
thy riding is to victory.
Thou dost draw thy bow from its 9
case[i]
and charge thy quiver with shafts.
Thou cleavest the earth with
rivers;
the mountains see thee and writhe 10–11
with fear.
The torrent of water rushes by,
and the deep sea thunders aloud.
The sun forgets to turn in his
course,[j]
and the moon stands still at her
zenith,
at the gleam of thy speeding
arrows
and the glance of thy flashing
spear.
With threats thou dost bestride 12
the earth
and trample down the nations in
anger.
Thou goest forth to save thy 13
people,
thou comest to save thy anointed;

[a] will exceed: *prob. rdg.*; *Heb. unintelligible.*   [b] *Prob. rdg.*; *Heb. adds* he
will teach.   [c] *Prob. rdg.*; *Heb. adds* in the midst of the years quicken it.
[d] the skies are: *prob. rdg.*; *Heb.* there is.   [e] *Or* ancient.   [f] and...are
for: *transposed from end of verse 6.*   [g] his swift flight: *transposed, with slight
change, from verse 7.*   [h] are snatched away: *prob. rdg.*; *Heb.* under wickedness.
[i] Thou...case: *prob. rdg.*; *Heb.* Thy bow was quite bared.
[j] The sun...course: *prob. rdg.*; *Heb.* The sun raised the height of his hands.

thou dost shatter the wicked man's
house from the roof down,[a]
uncovering its foundations to the
bare rock.[b]

14 Thou piercest their[c] chiefs with
thy[d] shafts,
and their leaders are torn from
them by the whirlwind,
as they open[e] their jaws
to devour their wretched victims
in secret.

15 When thou dost tread the sea with
thy horses
the mighty waters boil.

16 I hear, and my belly quakes;
my lips quiver at the sound;
trembling comes over my bones,

and my feet totter in their tracks;
I sigh for the day of distress
to dawn over my assailants.

Although the fig-tree does not 17
burgeon,
the vines bear no fruit,
the olive-crop fails,
the orchards yield no food,
the fold is bereft of its flock
and there are no cattle in the
stalls,
yet I will exult in the LORD   18
and rejoice in the God of my
deliverance.
The LORD God is my strength,   19
who makes my feet nimble as a
hind's
and sets me to range the heights.

ZEPHANIAH

1 THIS is the word of the LORD
which came to Zephaniah
son of Cushi, son of Gedaliah, son of Amariah, son of Hezekiah, in the time of Josiah son of
Amon king of Judah.

Doom on Judah and her neighbours

2 I will sweep the earth clean of all
that is on it,
says the LORD.

3 I will sweep away both man and
beast,
I will sweep the birds from the air
and the fish from the sea,
and I will bring the wicked to their
knees[f]
and wipe out mankind from the
earth.
This is the very word of the LORD.

4 I will stretch my hand over Judah
and all who live in Jerusalem;

I will wipe out from this place the
last remnant of Baal
and the very name of the heathen
priests,
those who bow down upon the 5
house-tops
to worship the host of heaven
and who swear by Milcom,
those who have turned their backs 6
on the LORD,
who have not sought the LORD or
consulted him.

Silence before the Lord GOD!   7
for the day of the LORD is near.
The LORD has prepared a sacrifice
and has hallowed his guests.
On the day of the LORD's sacrifice 8
I will punish the royal house and
its chief officers
and all who ape outlandish
fashions.
On that day   9
I will punish all who dance on the
temple terrace,

[a] the wicked...down: *prob. rdg.*; *Heb.* a head from the house of the wicked.
[b] bare rock: *prob. rdg.*; *Heb.* neck.   [c] their: *prob. rdg.*; *Heb. om.*
[d] *Prob. rdg.*; *Heb.* his.   [e] from them...open: *prob. rdg.*; *Heb. obscure.*
[f] I will bring...knees: *prob. rdg.*; *Heb.* the ruins with the wicked.

who fill their master's[a] house with
crimes of violence and fraud.

10 On that day, says the LORD,
an outcry shall be heard from the
Fish Gate,
wailing from the second quarter of
the city,
a loud crash from the hills;
11 and[b] those who live in the Lower
Town shall wail.
For it is all over with the merchants,
and all the dealers in silver are
wiped out.

12 At that time
I will search Jerusalem with a
lantern
and punish all who sit in stupor
over the dregs of their wine,
who say to themselves,
'The LORD will do nothing, good or
bad.'
13 Their wealth shall be plundered,
their houses laid waste;
they shall build houses but not
live in them,
they shall plant vineyards but not
drink the wine from them.
14 The great day of the LORD is near,
it comes with speed;
no runner so fast as that day,
no raiding band so swift.[c]
15 That day is a day of wrath,
a day of anguish and affliction,
a day of destruction and devastation,
a day of murk and gloom,
a day of cloud and dense fog,
16 a day of trumpet and battle-cry
over fortified cities and lofty
battlements.
17 I will bring dire distress upon men;
they shall walk like blind men for
their sin against the LORD.
Their blood shall be spilt like dust
and their bowels like dung;

neither their silver nor their gold 18
shall avail to save them.
On the day of the LORD's wrath, by
the fire of his jealousy
the whole land shall be consumed;
for he will make an end, a swift end,
of all who live in the land.

Gather together, you unruly na- 2
tion, gather together,
before you are sent far away and 2
vanish[d] like chaff,
before the burning anger of the
LORD comes upon you,
before the day of the LORD's anger
comes upon you.
Seek the LORD, 3
all in the land who live humbly by
his laws,
seek righteousness, seek a humble
heart;
it may be that you will find shelter
in the day of the LORD's anger.
For Gaza shall be deserted, 4
Ashkelon left desolate,
the people of Ashdod shall be
driven out[e] at noonday
and Ekron uprooted.

Listen, you who live by the coast, 5
you Kerethite settlers.
The word of the LORD is spoken
against you;
I will subdue you,[f] land of the
Philistines,
I will lay you waste and leave you
without inhabitants,
and you, Kereth, shall be all shep- 6
herds' huts[g] and sheepfolds;
and the coastland shall belong to 7
the survivors of Judah.
They shall pasture their flocks by
the sea[h]
and lie down at evening in the
houses of Ashkelon,
for the LORD their God will turn
to them
and restore their fortunes.

---

[a] Or their Lord's.   [b] and: prob. rdg.; Heb. om.   [c] no runner...swift: prob.
rdg.; Heb. hark, the day of the LORD is bitter, there the warrior cries aloud.
[d] you are...vanish: prob. rdg.; Heb. obscure.   [e] the people...out: or Ashdod
shall be made an example.   [f] I...you: prob. rdg.; Heb. Canaan.
[g] you...huts: Heb. has these words in a different order.
[h] by the sea: prob. rdg.; Heb. upon them.

8 I have heard the insults of Moab,
the taunts of Ammon,
how they have insulted my people
and encroached on their frontiers.
9 Therefore, by my life,
says the LORD of Hosts, the God of
Israel,
Moab shall be like Sodom,
Ammon like Gomorrah,
a pile of weeds, a rotting heap of
saltwort,
waste land for evermore.
The survivors of my people shall
plunder them,
the remnant of my nation shall
possess their land.

10 This will be retribution for their
pride, because they have insulted
the people of the LORD of Hosts
and encroached upon their rights.
11 The LORD will appear against them
with all his terrors; for he will reduce to beggary all the gods of the
earth, and all the coasts and islands
of the nations will worship him,
every man in his own home.

12 You Cushites also shall be killed
by the sword of the LORD.[a]
13 So let him stretch out his hand
over the north
and destroy Assyria,
make Nineveh desolate,
arid as the wilderness.
14 Flocks shall couch there,
and all the beasts of the wild.
Horned owl and ruffed bustard
shall roost on her capitals;
the tawny owl shall hoot in the
window,
and the bustard stand in the
porch.[b]
15 This is the city that exulted in
fancied security,
saying to herself, 'I am, and I
alone.'
And what is she now? A waste, a
haunt for wild beasts,
at which every passer-by shall hiss
and shake his fist.

Shame on the tyrant city, filthy 3
and foul!
No warning voice did she heed, she 2
took no rebuke to heart,
she did not trust in the LORD or
come near to her God.
Her officers were lions roaring in 3
her midst,
her rulers wolves of the plain[c]
that did not wait[d] till morning,
her prophets were reckless, no true 4
prophets.
Her priests profaned the sanctuary
and did violence to the law.
But the LORD in her midst is just; 5
he does no wrong;
morning by morning he gives
judgement,
without fail at daybreak.[e]

I have wiped out the proud; 6
their battlements are laid in ruin.
I have made their streets a desert
where no one passes.
Their cities are laid waste, deserted, unpeopled.
In the hope that she would re- 7
member all my instructions,
I said, 'Do but fear me
and take my rebuke to heart';
but they were up betimes and went
about their evil deeds.

Wait for me, therefore, says the 8
LORD,
wait for the day when I stand up to
accuse you;
for mine it is to gather nations
and assemble kingdoms,
to pour out on them my indignation,
all the heat of my anger;
the whole earth shall be consumed
by the fire of my jealousy.
I will give all peoples once again 9
pure lips,
that they may invoke the LORD by
name
and serve him with one consent.
From beyond the rivers of Cush 10
my suppliants of the Dispersion
shall bring me tribute.

---

[a] *the sword of the* LORD: *prob. rdg.; Heb.* my sword.
[b] *Prob. rdg.; Heb. adds an unintelligible phrase.*   [c] *Or* evening.   [d] *Or* carry off.
[e] *Prob. rdg.; Heb. adds* but the wrongdoer knows no shame.

11 On that day, Jerusalem,
   you shall not be put to shame for
      all your deeds
   by which you have rebelled against
      me;
   for then I will rid you
   of your proud and arrogant citi-
      zens,
   and never again shall you flaunt
      your pride
   on my holy hill.
12 But I will leave in you a people
   afflicted and poor.
13 The survivors in Israel shall find
      refuge in the name of the LORD;
   they shall no longer do wrong or
      speak lies,
   no words of deceit shall pass their
      lips;
   for they shall feed and lie down
   with no one to terrify them.

14 Zion, cry out for joy;
   raise the shout of triumph, Israel;
   be glad, rejoice with all your heart,
   daughter of Jerusalem.
15 The LORD has rid you of your ad-
      versaries,
   he has swept away your foes;
   the LORD is among you as king, O
      Israel;
   never again shall you fear disaster.

16 On that day this shall be the
   message to Jerusalem:
   Fear not, O Zion; let not your hands
      fall slack.
17 The LORD your God is in your
      midst,
   like a warrior, to keep you safe;
   he will rejoice over you and be glad;
   he will show you his love once
      more;
   he will exult over you with a shout
      of joy
18 as in days long ago.[a]

   I will take your cries of woe[b] away
      from you;
   and you shall no longer endure re-
      proach for her.
19 When that time comes, see,
   I will deal with all your oppressors.
   I will rescue the lost and gather the
      dispersed;
   I will win my people praise and
      renown
   in all the world where once they
      were despised.
20 When the time comes for me to
      gather you,[c]
   I will bring you home.
   I will win you renown and praise
   among all the peoples of the earth,
   when I bring back your pros-
      perity; and you shall see it.
   It is the LORD who speaks.

HAGGAI

Zerubbabel restorer of the temple

1 IN the second year of King
   Darius, on the first day of the
   sixth month, the word of the
LORD came through the prophet
Haggai to Zerubbabel son of Shealtiel, governor of Judah, and to
Joshua son of Jehozadak, the high
2 priest: These are the words of the
LORD of Hosts: This nation says to
itself that it is not yet time for the
house of the LORD to be rebuilt.
Then this word came through 3
Haggai the prophet: Is it a time for 4
you to live in your own well-roofed
houses, while this house lies in
ruins? Now these are the words of 5
the LORD of Hosts: Consider your
way of life. You have sown much 6

[a] as...ago: *prob. rdg.*; *Heb. obscure.*   [b] cries of woe: *prob. rdg.*; *Heb. obscure.*
[c] When...you: *prob. rdg.*; *Heb.* and in the time, my gathering you.

but reaped little; you eat but never as much as you wish, you drink but never more than you need, you are clothed but never warm, and the labourer puts his wages into a purse with a hole in 7 it. These are the words of the LORD of Hosts: Consider your way of 8 life. Go up into the hills, fetch timber, and build a house acceptable to me, where I can show my 9 glory,[a] says the LORD. You look for much and get little. At the moment when you would bring home the harvest, I blast it. Why? says the LORD of Hosts. Because my house lies in ruins, while each of you has a house that he can run to. 10 It is your fault that the heavens withhold their dew and the earth 11 its produce. So I have proclaimed a drought against land and mountain, against corn, new wine, and oil, and all that the ground yields, against man and cattle and all the products of man's labour.

12 Zerubbabel son of Shealtiel, Joshua son of Jehozadak, the high priest, and the rest of the people listened to what the LORD their God had said and what the prophet Haggai said when the LORD their God sent him, and they were filled 13 with fear because of the LORD. So Haggai the LORD'S messenger, as the LORD had commissioned him, said to the people: I am with you, 14 says the LORD. Then the LORD stirred up the spirit of Zerubbabel son of Shealtiel, governor of Judah, of Joshua son of Jehozadak, the high priest, and of the rest of the people; they came and began work on the house of the LORD of 15 Hosts their God on the twenty-fourth day of the sixth month.

2 In the second year of King Darius, on the twenty-first day of the seventh month, these words came from the LORD through the pro- 2 phet Haggai: Say to Zerubbabel son of Shealtiel, governor of Judah, to Joshua son of Jehozadak,

the high priest, and to the rest of the people: Is there anyone still 3 among you who saw this house in its former glory? How does it appear to you now? Does it not seem to you as if it were not there? But 4 now, Zerubbabel, take heart, says the LORD; take heart, Joshua son of Jehozadak, high priest. Take heart, all you people, says the LORD. Begin the work, for I am with you, says the LORD of Hosts, and my spirit is present among you. 5 Have no fear. For these are the 6 words of the LORD of Hosts: One thing more: I will shake heaven and earth, sea and land, I will 7 shake all nations; the treasure of all nations shall come hither, and I will fill this house with glory;[b] so says the LORD of Hosts. Mine is the 8 silver and mine the gold, says the LORD of Hosts, and the glory[b] of 9 this latter house shall surpass the glory[b] of the former, says the LORD of Hosts. In this place will I grant prosperity and peace. This is the very word of the LORD of Hosts.

In the second year of Darius, on 10 the twenty-fourth day of the ninth month, this word came from the LORD to the prophet Haggai: These are the words of the LORD of 11 Hosts: Ask the priests to give their ruling: If a man is carrying con- 12 secrated flesh in a fold of his robe, and he lets the fold touch bread or broth or wine or oil or any other kind of food, will that also become consecrated? And the priests answered, 'No.' Haggai went on, But 13 if a person defiled by contact with a corpse touches any one of these things, will that also become defiled? 'It will', answered the priests. Haggai replied, So it is with this 14 people and nation and all that they do, says the LORD; whatever offering they make here is defiled in my sight. And now look back over re- 15 cent times down to this day: before one stone was laid on another in

[a] *show my glory: or* be honoured.   [b] *Or* wealth.

16 the LORD's temple, what was your plight? If a man came to a heap of corn expecting twenty measures, he found but ten; if he came to a wine-vat to draw fifty measures, he 17 found but twenty. I blasted you and all your harvest with black blight and red and with hail, and yet you had no mind to return to 18 me, says the LORD. Consider, from this day onwards, from this twenty-fourth day of the ninth month, the day when the foundations of the temple of the LORD are 19 laid, consider: will the seed still be diminished[a] in the barn? Will the vine and the fig, the pomegranate and the olive, still bear no fruit?

Not so, from this day I will bless you.

On that day, the twenty-fourth 20 day of the month, the word of the LORD came to Haggai a second time: Tell Zerubbabel, governor of 21 Judah, I will shake heaven and earth; I will overthrow the thrones 22 of kings, break the power of heathen realms, overturn chariots and their riders; horses and riders shall fall by the sword of their comrades. On that day, says the LORD of 23 Hosts, I will take you, Zerubbabel son of Shealtiel, my servant, and will wear you as a signet-ring; for you it is that I have chosen. This is the very word of the LORD of Hosts.

ZECHARIAH

Zechariah's commission

1 IN the eighth month of the second year of Darius, the word of the LORD came to the prophet Zechariah son of Berechiah, 2 son of Iddo: The LORD was very 3 angry with your forefathers. Say to the people, These are the words of the LORD of Hosts: Come back to me, and I will come back to you, 4 says the LORD of Hosts. Do not be like your forefathers. They heard the prophets of old proclaim, 'These are the words of the LORD of Hosts: Turn back from your evil ways and your evil deeds.' But they did not listen or pay heed to 5 me, says the LORD. And where are your forefathers now? And the prophets, do they live for ever? 6 But the warnings and the decrees with which I charged my servants the prophets – did not these overtake your forefathers? Did they not then repent and say, 'The LORD of Hosts has treated us as he

purposed; as our lives and as our deeds deserved, so has he treated us'?

Eight visions with their interpretations

ON the twenty-fourth day of the 7 eleventh month, the month Shebat, in the second year of Darius, the word of the LORD came to the prophet Zechariah son of Berechiah, son of Iddo.

Last night I had a vision. I saw 8 a man on a bay horse standing among the myrtles in a hollow; and behind him were other horses, black, dappled, and white. 'What 9 are these, sir?' I asked, and the angel who talked with me answered, 'I will show you what they are.' Then the man standing among the 10 myrtles said, 'They are those whom the LORD has sent to range through the world.' They reported to the 11 angel of the LORD as he stood among the myrtles: 'We have

[a] diminished: *prob. rdg.*; *Heb. om.*

ranged through the world; the whole world is still and at peace.'

12 Thereupon the angel of the LORD said, 'How long, O LORD of Hosts, wilt thou withhold thy compassion from Jerusalem and the cities of Judah, upon whom thou hast vented thy wrath these seventy years?'

13 Then the LORD spoke kind and comforting words to the angel who

14 talked with me, and the angel said to me, Proclaim, These are the words of the LORD of Hosts: I am very jealous for Jerusalem and

15 Zion. I am full of anger against the nations that enjoy their ease, because, while my anger was but mild, they heaped evil on evil.

16 Therefore these are the words of the LORD: I have come back to Jerusalem with compassion, and my house shall be rebuilt in her, says the LORD of Hosts, and the measuring-line shall be stretched

17 over Jerusalem. Proclaim once more, These are the words of the LORD of Hosts: My cities shall again overflow with good things; once again the LORD will comfort Zion, once again he will make Jerusalem the city of his choice.

18 I lifted my eyes and there I saw

19 four horns. I asked the angel who talked with me what they were, and he answered, 'These are the horns which scattered Judah[a] and

20 Jerusalem.' Then the LORD show-

21 ed me four smiths. I asked what they were coming to do, and he said, 'Those horns scattered Judah and Jerusalem so completely that no man could lift his head. But these smiths have come to reunite them and to throw down the horns of the nations which had raised them against the land of Judah and scattered its people.'

2 I lifted my eyes and there I saw a

2 man carrying a measuring-line. I asked him where he was going, and he said, 'To measure Jerusalem and see what should be its breadth

and length.' Then, as the angel who 3 talked with me was going away, another angel came out to meet him and said to him, Run to the 4 young man there and tell him that Jerusalem shall be a city without walls, so numerous shall be the men and cattle within it. I will be a 5 wall of fire round her, says the LORD, and a glory in the midst of her.

Away, away; flee from the land 6 of the north, says the LORD, for I will make you spread your wings like the four winds of heaven, says the LORD. Away, escape, you 7 people of Zion who live in Babylon.

For these are the words of the 8 LORD of Hosts, spoken when he sent me on a glorious mission[b] to the nations who have plundered you, for whoever touches you touches the apple of his eye: I 9 raise[c] my hand against them; they shall be plunder for their own slaves. So you shall know that the LORD of Hosts has sent me. Shout 10 aloud and rejoice, daughter of Zion; I am coming, I will make my dwelling among you, says the LORD. Many nations shall come 11 over to the LORD on that day and become his people, and he will make his dwelling with you. Then you shall know that the LORD of Hosts has sent me to you. The 12 LORD will once again claim Judah as his own possession in the holy land, and make Jerusalem the city of his choice.

Silence, all mankind, in the pre- 13 sence of the LORD! For he has bestirred himself out of his holy dwelling-place.

The angel who talked with me 4 1[d] came back and roused me as a man is roused from sleep. He asked me 2 what I saw, and I answered, 'A lamp-stand all of gold with a bowl on it; it holds seven lamps, and there are seven pipes for the lamps on top of it, with two olive-trees 3

---

a Prob. rdg.; Heb. adds Israel. glory.   *c* Or wave.   *b* on a glorious mission: prob. rdg.; Heb. after   *d* 3. 1–10 transposed to follow 4. 14.

standing by it, one on the right of the bowl and another on the left.'

11[a] I asked him, "What are these two olive-trees, the one on the right and the other on the left of the lamp-

12 stand?' I asked also another question, 'What are the two sprays of olive beside the golden pipes which discharge the golden oil

13 from their bowls?' He said, 'Do you not know what these mean?'

14 'No, sir', I answered. 'These two', he said, 'are the two consecrated with oil who attend the Lord of all the earth.'

3 1   Then he showed me Joshua the high priest standing before the angel of the Lord, with the Adversary[b] standing at his right hand to

2 accuse him. The Lord said to the Adversary, 'The Lord rebuke you, Satan, the Lord rebuke you who are venting your spite on Jerusalem.[c] Is not this man a brand

3 snatched from the fire?' Now Joshua was wearing filthy clothes

4 as he stood before the angel; and the angel turned and said to those in attendance on him, 'Take off his filthy clothes.' Then he turned to him and said, 'See how I have taken away your guilt from you; I will clothe you in fine vestments';

5 and he added, 'Let a clean turban be put on his head.' So they put a clean turban on his head and clothed him in clean garments,

6 while the angel of the Lord stood by. Then the angel of the Lord gave Joshua this solemn charge:

7 These are the words of the Lord of Hosts: If you will conform to my ways and carry out your duties, you shall administer my house and be in control of my courts, and I grant you the right to come and go amongst these in attendance

8 here. Listen, Joshua the high priest, you and your colleagues seated here before you, all you who

are an omen of things to come: I will now bring my servant, the Branch. In one day I will wipe 9–10 away the guilt of the land. On that day, says the Lord of Hosts, you shall all of you invite one another to come and sit each under his vine and his fig-tree.

Here is the stone that I set before Joshua, a stone in which are seven eyes. I will reveal its meaning to you, says the Lord of Hosts. Then I asked the angel of the Lord 4 4[d] who talked with me, 'Sir, what are these?' And he answered, 'Do you 5 not know what these mean?' 'No, sir', I answered. 'These seven', he said, 'are the eyes of the Lord ranging over the whole earth.'[e]

Then he turned and said to me, 6 This is the word of the Lord concerning Zerubbabel: Neither by force of arms nor by brute strength, but by my spirit! says the Lord of Hosts. How does a mountain, the 7 greatest mountain, compare with Zerubbabel? It is no higher than a plain. He shall bring out the stone called Possession[f] while men acclaim its beauty. This word came 8 to me from the Lord: Zerubbabel 9 with his own hands laid the foundation of this house and with his own hands he shall finish it. So shall you know that the Lord of Hosts has sent me to you. Who 10 has despised the day of small things? He shall rejoice when he sees Zerubbabel holding the stone called Separation.[f]

I looked up again and saw a 5 flying scroll. He asked me what I 2 saw, and I answered, 'A flying scroll, twenty cubits long and ten cubits wide.' This, he told me, is 3 the curse which goes out over the whole land; for by the writing on one side every thief shall be swept clean away, and by the writing on the other every perjurer shall be

---

[a] 4. 4–10 transposed to follow 3. 10.   [b] *Heb.* the Satan.
[c] the Lord...Jerusalem: *or* the Lord who has chosen Jerusalem rebuke you.
[d] *See note on* 4. 11 *above.*
[e] These seven...earth: *transposed from verse* 10.   [f] Cp. Lev. 20. 24–26.

4 swept clean away. I have sent it out, the LORD of Hosts has said, and it shall enter the house of the thief and the house of the man who has perjured himself in my name; it shall stay inside that house and demolish it, timbers and stones and all.

5 The angel who talked with me came out and said to me, 'Raise your eyes and look at this thing 6 that comes forth.' I asked what it was, and he said, 'It is a great barrel coming forth,' and he added, 'so great is their guilt in all the 7 land.' Then a round slab of lead was lifted, and a woman was sit-8 ting there inside the barrel. He said, 'This is Wickedness', and he thrust her down into the barrel and rammed the leaden weight upon 9 its mouth. I looked up again and saw two women coming forth with the wind in their wings (for they had wings like a stork's), and they carried the barrel between earth 10 and sky. I asked the angel who talked with me where they were 11 taking the barrel, and he answer-ed, 'To build a house for it[a] in the land of Shinar; when the house is ready, it[b] shall be set on the place prepared for it[a] there.'

6 I looked up again and saw four chariots coming out between two mountains, and the mountains 2 were made of copper.[c] The first chariot had bay horses, the second 3 black, the third white, and the 4 fourth dappled. I asked the angel who talked with me, 'Sir, what are 5 these?' He answered, 'These are the four winds of heaven which have been attending the Lord of the whole earth, and they are now 6 going forth. The chariot with the black horses is going to the land of the north, that with the white to the far west,[d] that with the 7 dappled to the south, and that

with the roan to the land of the east.'[e] They were eager to go and range over the whole earth; so he said, 'Go and range over the earth', and the chariots did so. Then he 8 called me to look and said, 'Those going to the land of the north have given my spirit rest in the land of the north.'

9 The word of the LORD came to me: Take silver and gold from the 10 exiles, from Heldai, Tobiah, Jeda-iah, and[f] Josiah son of Zephaniah, who have come back from Baby-lon. Take it and make a crown; put 11 the crown on the head of Joshua son of Jehozadak, the high priest,[g] and say to him, These are the 12 words of the LORD of Hosts: Here is a man named the Branch; he will shoot up from the ground where he is and will build the temple of the LORD. It is he who 13 will build the temple of the LORD, he who will assume royal dignity, will be seated on his throne and govern, with a priest at his right side, and concord shall prevail be-tween them. The crown shall be in 14 the charge of Heldai, Tobiah, Jeda-iah, and Josiah son of Zephaniah, as a memorial in the temple of the LORD.

Men from far away shall come 15 and work on the building of the temple of the LORD; so shall you know that the LORD of Hosts has sent me to you. If only you will obey the LORD your God!

Joy and gladness in the coming age

THE word of the LORD came to 7 Zechariah in the fourth year of the reign of King Darius, on the fourth day of Kislev, the ninth month. Bethel-sharezer sent Regem-mel- 2 ech with his men to seek the favour of the LORD. They were to say to 3

[a] Or her.   [b] Or she.   [c] Or bronze.   [d] to the far west: *prob. rdg.; Heb.* behind them.   [e] to the land of the east: *prob. rdg.; Heb. om.*
[f] and: *prob. rdg.; Heb.* and go on that day yourself and go to the house of...
[g] Joshua...priest: *possibly an error for* Zerubbabel son of Shealtiel, cp. 3. 5; 4. 9.

the priests in the house of the LORD of Hosts and to the prophets, 'Am I to lament and abstain in the fifth month as I have done for so 4 many years?' Then the word of the 5 LORD of Hosts came to me: Say to all the people of the land and to the priests, When you fasted and lamented in the fifth and seventh months these seventy years, was it indeed in my honour that you 6 fasted? And when you ate and drank, was it not to please your- 7 selves? Was it not this that the LORD proclaimed through the prophets of old, while Jerusalem was populous and peaceful, as were the cities round her, and the Negeb and the Shephelah?

8 The word of the LORD came to 9 Zechariah: These are the words of the LORD of Hosts: Administer true justice, show loyalty and 10 compassion to one another, do not oppress the orphan and the widow, the alien and the poor, do not contrive any evil one against an- 11 other. But they refused to listen, they turned their backs on me in defiance, they stopped their ears 12 and would not hear. Their hearts were adamant; they refused to accept instruction and all that the LORD of Hosts had taught them by his spirit through the prophets of old; and they suffered under the 13 anger of the LORD of Hosts. As they did not listen when I*a* called, so I did not listen when they called, 14 says the LORD of Hosts, and I drove them out among all the nations to whom they were strangers, leaving their land a waste behind them, so that no one came and went. Thus they made their pleasant land a waste.

8 The word of the LORD of Hosts 2 came to me: These are the words of the LORD of Hosts: I have been very jealous for Zion, fiercely jea- 3 lous for her. Now, says the LORD, I have come back to Zion and I will

dwell in Jerusalem. Jerusalem shall be called the City of Truth, and the mountain of the LORD of Hosts shall be called the Holy Mountain. These are the words of the LORD of 4 Hosts: Once again shall old men and old women sit in the streets of Jerusalem, each leaning on a stick because of their great age; and the 5 streets of the city shall be full of boys and girls, playing in the streets. These are the words of the 6 LORD of Hosts: Even if it may seem impossible*b* to the survivors of this nation on that day, will it also seem impossible to me?*c* This is the very word of the LORD of Hosts. These are the words of the 7 LORD of Hosts: See, I will rescue my people from the countries of the east and the west, and bring 8 them back to live in Jerusalem. They shall be my people, and I will be their God, in truth and justice.

These are the words of the LORD 9 of Hosts: Take courage, you who in these days hear, from the prophets who were present when the found-ations were laid for the house of the LORD of Hosts, their promise that the temple is to be rebuilt. Till that 10 time there was no hiring either of man or of beast, no one could safely go about his business because of his enemies, and I set all men one against another. But now I am not 11 the same towards the survivors of this people as I was in former days, says the LORD of Hosts. For they 12 shall sow in safety; the vine shall yield its fruit and the soil its pro-duce, the heavens shall give their dew; with all these things I will endow the survivors of this people. You, house of Judah and house of 13 Israel, have been the very symbol of a curse to all the nations; and now I will save you, and you shall become the symbol of a blessing. Courage! Do not be afraid.

For these are the words of the 14

---

a Prob. rdg.; Heb. he. *b* Or wonderful.
c will...me?: or it will seem wonderful also to me.

LORD of Hosts: Whereas I resolved to ruin you because your ancestors roused me to anger, says the LORD of Hosts, and I did not 15 relent, so in these days I have once more[a] resolved to do good to Jerusalem and to the house of 16 Judah; do not be afraid. This is what you shall do: speak the truth to each other, administer true and 17 sound justice in the city gate. Do not contrive any one evil against another, and do not love perjury, for all this I hate. This is the very word of the LORD.

18   The word of the LORD of Hosts 19 came to me: These are the words of the LORD of Hosts: The fasts of the fourth month and of the fifth, the seventh, and the tenth, shall become festivals of joy and gladness for the house of Judah. Love truth and peace.

20   These are the words of the LORD of Hosts: Nations and dwellers in 21 great cities shall yet come; people of one city shall come to those of another and say, 'Let us go and entreat the favour of the LORD, and resort to the LORD of Hosts; 22 and I will come too.' So great nations and mighty peoples shall resort to the LORD of Hosts in Jerusalem and entreat his favour. 23 These are the words of the LORD of Hosts: In those days, when ten men from nations of every language pluck up courage, they shall pluck the robe of a Jew and say, 'We will go with you because we have heard that God is with you.'

Judah's triumph over her enemies

9 An oracle: the word of the LORD.

He has come to the land of Hadrach
and[b] established himself in Damascus;

for the capital city[c] of Aram is the LORD's,
as are all the tribes of Israel.
[d]Sidon has closed her frontier 2
against Hamath,
for she is very wary.
Tyre has built herself a rampart; 3
she has heaped up silver like dust
and gold like mud in the streets.
But wait, the Lord will dispossess 4
her
and strike down the power of her ships,
and the city itself will be destroyed by fire.
Let Ashkelon see it and be afraid; 5
Gaza shall writhe in terror,
and Ekron's hope shall be extinguished;
kings shall vanish from Gaza,
and Ashkelon shall be unpeopled;
half-breeds shall settle in Ashdod, 6
and I will uproot the pride of the Philistine.
I will dash the blood of sacrifices 7
from his mouth
and his loathsome offerings from his teeth;
and his survivors shall belong[e] to our God
and become like a clan in Judah,
and Ekron like a Jebusite.
And I will post a garrison for my 8
house
so that no one may pass in or out,
and no oppressor shall ever overrun them.
[This I have lived to see with my own eyes.]

Rejoice, rejoice, daughter of Zion, 9
shout aloud, daughter of Jerusalem;
for see, your king is coming to you,
his cause won, his victory gained,
humble and mounted on an ass,
on a foal, the young of a she-ass.
He shall banish chariots from 10
Ephraim
and war-horses from Jerusalem;

---

[a] *once more: or* changed my mind and.
[b] *He has come...and: prob. rdg.; Heb.* In the land of Hadrach he has...
[c] *capital city: or* chief part.   [d] *Prob. rdg.; Heb. prefixes* Tyre and.
[e] *his survivors shall belong: or* he shall become kin.

the warrior's bow shall be banished.
He shall speak peaceably to every
nation,
and his rule shall extend from sea
to sea,
from the River to the ends of the
earth.

11 And as for you, by your covenant
with me sealed in blood
I release your prisoners from the
dungeon.[a]
12 (Come back to the stronghold, you
prisoners who wait in hope.)
Now is the day announced
when I will grant you twofold[b]
reparation.
13 For my bow is strung, O Judah;
I have laid the arrow to it, O
Ephraim;
I have roused your sons, O Zion,[c]
and made you into the sword of a
warrior.
14 The LORD shall appear above them,
and his arrow shall flash like
lightning;
the Lord GOD shall blow a blast on
the horn
and march with the storm-winds
of the south.
15 The LORD of Hosts will be their
shield;
they shall prevail, they shall
trample on the sling-stones;
they shall be roaring drunk as if
with wine,
brimful as a bowl, drenched like
the corners of the altar.
16 So on that day the LORD their God
will save them, his own people, like
sheep,
setting them all about his land,
like[d] jewels set to sparkle in a
crown.

17 What wealth, what beauty, is
theirs:
corn to strengthen young men,
and new wine for maidens!

Ask of the LORD rain in the au- 10
tumn,
ask him for rain in the spring,
the LORD who makes the storm-
clouds,
and he will give you showers of
rain
and to every man grass in his field;
for the household gods make mis- 2
chievous promises;
diviners see false signs,
they tell lying dreams[e]
and talk raving nonsense.
Men wander about like sheep
in distress for lack of a shepherd.
My anger is turned against the 3
shepherds,
and I will visit with punishment
the leaders of the flock;
but the LORD of Hosts will visit his
flock,
the house of Judah,
and make them his royal war-
horses.
They shall be corner-stone and 4
tent-peg,
they shall be the bow ready for
battle,
and from them shall come every
commander.
Together they shall be like war- 5
riors
who tramp the muddy ways in
battle,
and they will fight because the
LORD is with them;
they will put horsemen shamefully
to rout.
And I will give strength to the 6
house of Judah
and grant victory to[f] the house of
Joseph;
I will restore them, for I have pitied them,
and they shall be as though I had
never cast them off;
for I am the LORD their God and I
will answer them.
So Ephraim shall be like warriors, 7
glad like men cheerful with wine,

---

[a] *Prob. rdg.*; *Heb. adds* no water in it.   [b] *Or* equal.   [c] *Prob. rdg.*; *Heb. adds*
against your sons, O Javan (*or* Greece).   [d] like: *prob. rdg.*; *Heb.* for.
[e] they...dreams: *or* dreaming women make empty promises.
[f] grant victory to: *or* expand.

and their sons shall see and be
glad;
so let their hearts exult in the
LORD.

8 I will whistle to call them in, for I
have redeemed them;
and they shall be as many as once
they were.

9 If I disperse them*a* among the
nations,
in far-off lands they will remember
me
and will rear their sons and then
return.

10 Then will I fetch them home from
Egypt
and gather them in from Assyria;
I will lead them into Gilead and
Lebanon
until there is no more room for
them.

11 Dire distress*b* shall come upon the
Euphrates
and shall beat down its turbulent
waters;
all the depths of the Nile shall run
dry.
The pride of Assyria shall be
brought down,
and the sceptre of Egypt shall pass
away;

12 but Israel's strength shall be in the
LORD,
and they shall march proudly in
his name.
This is the very word of the LORD.

11 Throw open your gates, O Lebanon,
that fire may feed on your cedars.

2 Howl, every pine-tree; for the
cedars have fallen,
mighty trees are ravaged.
Howl, every oak of Bashan;
for the impenetrable forest is laid
low.

3 Hark to the howling of the shepherds,
for their rich pastures are ravaged.
Hark to the roar of the young lions,
for Jordan's dense thickets are
ravaged.

These were the words of the 4
LORD my God: Fatten the flock for
slaughter. Those who buy will 5
slaughter it and incur no guilt;
those who sell will say, 'Blessed be
the LORD, I am rich!' Its shepherds
will have no pity for it. For I will 6
never again pity the inhabitants of
the earth, says the LORD. I will put
every man in the power of his
neighbour and his king, and as
each country is crushed I will not
rescue him from their hands.

So I fattened the flock for 7
slaughter for the dealers. I took
two staves: one I called Favour
and the other Union, and so I
fattened the flock. In one month 8
I got rid of the three shepherds, for
I had lost patience with them and
they had come to abhor me. Then I 9
said to the flock, 'I will not fatten
you any more. Any that are to die,
let them die; any that stray, let
them stray; and the rest can devour one another.' I took my staff 10
called Favour and snapped it in
two, annulling the covenant which
the LORD*c* had made with all nations. So it was annulled that day, 11
and the dealers who were watching
me knew that all this was the word
of the LORD. I said to them, 'If it 12
suits you, give me my wages;
otherwise keep them.' Then they
weighed out my wages, thirty
pieces of silver. The LORD said to 13
me, 'Throw it into the treasury.' I
took the thirty pieces of silver –
that noble sum at which I was
valued and rejected by them! –
and threw them into the house of
the LORD, into the treasury. Then 14
I snapped in two my second staff
called Union, annulling the brotherhood between Judah and Israel.

Then the LORD said to me, Equip 15
yourself again as a shepherd, a
worthless one; for I am about to 16
install a shepherd in the land who
will neither miss any that are lost

---

a Or scatter them like seed.
c the LORD: *prob. rdg.*; *Heb.* I.

b Dire distress: *or* An enemy.

nor search for those that have gone astray nor heal the injured nor nurse the sickly, but will eat the flesh of the fat beasts and throw away their broken bones.

17 Alas for the worthless shepherd who abandons the sheep!
A sword shall fall on his arm and on his right eye;
his arm shall be shrivelled
and his right eye blinded.
13 7*a* This is the very word of the Lord of Hosts:
O sword, awake against my shepherd
and against him who works with me.
Strike the shepherd, and the sheep will be scattered,
and I will turn my hand against the shepherd boys.
8 This also is the very word of the Lord:
It shall happen throughout the land
that two thirds of the people shall be struck down and die,
while one third of them shall be left there.
9 Then I will pass this third through the fire
and I will refine them as silver is refined,
and assay them as gold is assayed.
Then they will invoke me by my name,
and I myself will answer them;
I will say, 'They are my people',
and they shall say, 'The Lord is our God.'

Jerusalem a centre of worship for all men

12 An oracle. This is the word of the Lord concerning Israel, the very word of the Lord who stretched out the heavens and founded the earth, and who formed the spirit of 2 man within him: I am making the steep approaches to Jerusalem slippery for all the nations pressing round her; and Judah will be caught up in the siege of Jerusalem. On that day, when all the 3 nations of the earth will be gathered against her, I will make Jerusalem a rock too heavy for any people to remove, and all who try to lift it shall injure themselves. On that 4 day, says the Lord, I will strike every horse with panic and its rider with madness; I will keep watch over Judah, but I will strike all the horses of the other nations with blindness. Then the clans of 5 Judah shall say to themselves, 'The inhabitants of Jerusalem find their strength*b* in the Lord of Hosts their God.'

On that day I will make the clans 6 of Judah like a brazier in woodland, like a torch blazing among sheaves of corn. They shall devour all the nations round them, right and left, while the people of Jerusalem remain safe in their city. The Lord will first set free all the 7 families*c* of Judah, so that the glory of David's line and of the inhabitants of Jerusalem may not surpass that of Judah.

On that day the Lord will shield 8 the inhabitants of Jerusalem; on that day the very weakest of them shall be like David, and the line of David like God, like the angel of the Lord going before them.

On that day I will set about 9 destroying all the nations that come against Jerusalem, but I will 10 pour a spirit of pity and compassion into the line of David and the inhabitants of Jerusalem. Then

They shall look on me, on him whom they have pierced,

and shall wail over him as over an only child, and shall grieve for him bitterly as for a first-born son. On that day the mourning in 11 Jerusalem shall be as great as the

a 13. 7–9 transposed to this point.
O inhabitants of Jerusalem, I am strong.

b The...strength: prob. rdg.; Heb.
c Or tents.

mourning over Hadad-rimmon in
12 the vale of Megiddo. The land shall
wail, each family by itself: the
family of David by itself and its
13 women by themselves; the family
of Nathan by itself and its women
by themselves; the family of Levi
by itself and its women by themselves; the family of Shimei by
itself and its women by them-
14 selves; all the remaining families
by themselves and their women by
themselves.

13 On that day a fountain shall be
opened for the line of David and
for the inhabitants of Jerusalem,
to remove all sin and impurity.

2 On that day, says the LORD of
Hosts, I will erase the names of the
idols from the land, and they shall
be remembered no longer; I will
also remove the prophets and the
spirit of uncleanness from the land.

3 Thereafter, if a man continues to
prophesy, his parents, his own
father and mother, will say to him,
'You shall live no longer, for you
have spoken falsely in the name of
the LORD.' His own father and
mother will pierce him through
4 because he has prophesied. On that
day every prophet shall be ashamed of his vision when he prophesies,
nor shall he wear a robe of coarse
5 hair in order to deceive. He will
say, 'I am no prophet, I am a tiller
of the soil who has been schooled in
6 lust from boyhood.' 'What', someone will ask, 'are these scars on
your chest?' And he will answer, 'I
got them in the house of my lovers.'[a]

14 A day is coming for the LORD to
act, and the plunder taken from
you shall be shared out while you
2 stand by. I will gather all the
peoples to fight against Jerusalem;
the city shall be taken, the houses
plundered and the women raped.
Half the city shall go into exile, but
the rest of the nation in the city
3 shall not be wiped out. The LORD
will come out and fight against
those peoples, as in the days of his

prowess on the field of battle. On 4
that day his feet will stand on the
Mount of Olives, which is opposite
Jerusalem to the east, and the
mountain shall be cleft in two by
an immense valley running east
and west; half the mountain shall
move northwards and half southwards. The valley between the 5
hills[b] shall be blocked, for the new
valley between them will reach as
far as Asal. Blocked it shall be as it
was blocked by the earthquake in
the time of Uzziah king of Judah,
and the LORD my God will appear
with all the holy ones.

On that day there shall be nei- 6
ther heat nor cold nor frost. It shall 7
be all one day, whose coming is
known only to the LORD, without
distinction of day or night, and at
evening-time there shall be light.

On that day living water shall 8
issue from Jerusalem, half flowing
to the eastern sea and half to the
western, in summer and winter
alike. Then the LORD shall become 9
king over all the earth; on that day
the LORD shall be one LORD and
his name the one name. The whole 10
land shall be levelled, flat as the
Arabah from Geba to Rimmon
southwards; but Jerusalem shall
stand high in her place, and shall
be full of people from the Benjamin
Gate [to the point where the former gate stood,] to the Corner
Gate, and from the Tower of Hananel to the king's wine-vats. Men 11
shall live in Jerusalem, and never
again shall a solemn ban be laid
upon her; men shall live there in
peace. The LORD will strike down 12
all the nations who warred against
Jerusalem, and the plague shall be
this: their flesh shall rot while they
stand on their feet, their eyes shall
rot in their sockets, and their
tongues shall rot in their mouths.

On that day a great panic, sent 13
by the LORD, shall fall on them. At
the very moment when a man
would encourage his comrade his

---

[a] *Verses 7–9 transposed to follow 11. 17.*   [b] *Prob. rdg.; Heb. my hills.*

hand shall be raised to strike him
14 down. Judah too shall join in the
fray in Jerusalem, and the wealth
of the surrounding nations will be
swept away – gold and silver and
15 apparel in great abundance. And
slaughter shall be the fate of horse
and mule, camel and ass, the fate
of every beast in those armies.

16   All who survive of the nations
which attacked Jerusalem shall
come up year by year to worship
the King, the LORD of Hosts, and
to keep the pilgrim-feast of Taber-
17 nacles. If any of the families of the
earth do not go up to Jerusalem to
worship the King, the LORD of
Hosts, no rain shall fall upon them.
18 If any family of Egypt does not go
up and enter the city, then the

same disaster shall overtake it as
that which the LORD will inflict on
any nation which does not go up to
keep the feast. This shall be the 19
punishment of Egypt and of any
nation which does not go up to
keep the feast of Tabernacles.

On that day, not a bell on a war- 20
horse but shall be inscribed 'Holy
to the LORD', and the pots in the
house of the LORD shall be like the
bowls before the altar. Every pot 21
in Jerusalem and Judah shall be
holy to the LORD of Hosts, and all
who sacrifice shall come and shall
take some of them and boil the
flesh in them. So when that time
comes, no trader shall again be
seen in the house of the LORD of
Hosts.

MALACHI

1 An oracle. The word of the LORD to
Israel through Malachi.[a]

Religious decline and hope
of recovery

2 I LOVE you, says the LORD. You
ask, 'How hast thou shown love to
us?' Is not Esau Jacob's brother?
the LORD answers. I love Jacob,
3 but I hate Esau; I have turned his
mountains into a waste and his
ancestral home into a lodging in
4 the wilderness. When Edom says,
'We are beaten down; let us rebuild our ruined homes', these are
the words of the LORD of Hosts: If
they rebuild, I will pull down. They
shall be called a realm of wickedness, a people whom the LORD has
5 cursed for ever. You yourselves
will see it with your own eyes; you
yourselves will say, 'The LORD's
greatness reaches beyond the realm
of Israel.'

A son honours his father, and a 6
slave goes in fear of his master. If I
am a father, where is the honour
due to me? If I am a master, where
is the fear due to me? So says the
LORD of Hosts to you, you priests
who despise my name. You ask,
'How have we despised thy name?'
Because you have offered defiled 7
food on my altar. You ask, 'How
have we defiled thee?' Because you
have thought that the table of the
LORD may be despised, that if you 8
offer a blind victim, there is nothing wrong, and if you offer a victim lame or diseased, there is
nothing wrong. If you brought
such a gift to the governor, would
he receive you or show you favour?
says the LORD of Hosts. But now, 9
if you placate God, he may show
you mercy; if you do this, will he
withhold his favour from you? So
the LORD of Hosts has spoken.
Better far that one of you should 10

***

[a] Malachi: *or* my messenger.

close the great door altogether, so that the light might not fall thus all in vain upon my altar! I have no pleasure in you, says the LORD of Hosts; I will accept no offering 11 from you. From furthest east to furthest west my name is great among the nations. Everywhere fragrant sacrifice and pure gifts are offered in my name; for my name is great among the nations, says 12 the LORD of Hosts. But you profane it by thinking that the table of the LORD may be defiled, and that you can offer on it food you 13 yourselves despise. You sniff at it, says the LORD of Hosts, and say, 'How irksome!' If you bring as your offering victims that are mutilated, lame, or diseased, shall I accept them from you? says the 14 LORD. A curse on the cheat who pays his vows by sacrificing a damaged victim to the Lord, though he has a sound ram in his flock! I am the great king, says the LORD of Hosts, and my name is held in awe among the nations.

2 And now, you priests, this de- 2 cree is for you: if you will not listen to me and pay heed to the honouring of my name, says the LORD of Hosts, then I will lay a curse upon you. I will turn your blessings into a curse; yes, into a curse, because 3 you pay no heed. I will cut off your arm,[a] fling offal in your faces, the offal of your pilgrim-feasts, and I will banish you from my presence. 4 Then you will know that I have issued this decree against you: my covenant with Levi falls to the ground, says the LORD of Hosts. 5 My covenant was with him: I bestowed life and prosperity on him; I laid on him the duty of reverence, he revered me and lived in awe of 6 my name. The instruction he gave was true, and no word of injustice fell from his lips; he walked in harmony with me and in uprightness, and he turned many back from sin. 7 For men hang upon the words of

the priest and seek knowledge and instruction from him, because he is the messenger of the LORD of Hosts. But you have turned away 8 from that course; you have made many stumble with your instruction; you have set at nought the covenant with the Levites, says the LORD of Hosts. So I, in my 9 turn, have made you despicable and mean in the eyes of the people, in so far as you disregard my ways and show partiality in your instruction.

Have we not all one father? Did 10 not one God create us? Why do we violate the covenant of our forefathers by being faithless to one another? Judah is faithless, and 11 abominable things are done in Israel and in Jerusalem; Judah has violated the holiness of the LORD by loving and marrying daughters of a foreign god. May the LORD 12 banish any who do this from the dwellings of Jacob, nomads or settlers, even though they bring offerings to the LORD of Hosts.

Here is another thing that you 13 do: you weep and moan, and you drown the altar of the LORD with tears, but he still refuses to look at the offering or receive an acceptable gift from you. You ask why. It 14 is because the LORD has borne witness against you on behalf of the wife of your youth. You have been unfaithful to her, though she is your partner and your wife by solemn covenant. Did not the one 15 God make her, both flesh and spirit? And what does the one God require but godly children? Keep watch on your spirit, and do not be unfaithful to the wife of your youth. If a man divorces or puts 16 away his spouse, he overwhelms her with cruelty, says the LORD of Hosts the God of Israel. Keep watch on your spirit, and do not be unfaithful.

You have wearied the LORD 17 with your talk. You ask, 'How

[a] *Or* posterity.

have we wearied him?' By saying that all evildoers are good in the eyes of the LORD, that he is pleased with them, or by asking, 'Where is
3 the God of justice?' Look, I am sending my messenger[a] who will clear a path before me. Suddenly the Lord whom you seek will come to his temple; the messenger of the covenant in whom you delight is here, here already, says the LORD
2 of Hosts. Who can endure the day of his coming? Who can stand firm when he appears? He is like a
3 refiner's fire, like fuller's soap; he will take his seat, refining and purifying;[b] he will purify the Levites and cleanse them like gold and silver, and so they shall be fit to
4 bring offerings to the LORD. Thus the offerings of Judah and Jerusalem shall be pleasing to the LORD as they were in days of old, in
5 years long past. I will appear before you in court, prompt to testify against sorcerers, adulterers, and perjurers, against those who wrong[c] the hired labourer, the widow, and the orphan, who thrust the alien aside and have no fear of me, says the LORD of Hosts.
6 I am the LORD, unchanging; and you, too, have not ceased to be
7 sons of Jacob. From the days of your forefathers you have been wayward and have not kept my laws. If you will return to me, I will return to you, says the LORD of Hosts. You ask, 'How can we
8 return?' May man defraud God, that you defraud me? You ask, 'How have we defrauded thee?' Why, in tithes and contributions.
9 There is a curse, a curse on you all, the whole nation of you, because
10 you defraud me. Bring the tithes into the treasury, all of them; let there be food in my house. Put me to the proof, says the LORD of Hosts, and see if I do not open windows in the sky and pour a blessing on you as long as there is

need. I will forbid pests to destroy 11 the produce of your soil or make your vines barren, says the LORD of Hosts. All nations shall count 12 you happy, for yours shall be a favoured land, says the LORD of Hosts.

Murmurers warned, the righteous triumphant

YOU have used hard words about 13 me, says the LORD, and then you ask, 'How have we spoken against thee?' You have said, 'It is useless 14 to serve God; what do we gain from the LORD of Hosts by observing his rules and behaving with deference? We ourselves count 15 the arrogant happy; it is evildoers who are successful; they have put God to the proof and come to no harm.'

Then those who feared the 16 LORD talked together, and the LORD paid heed and listened. A record was written before him of those who feared him and kept his name in mind. They shall be mine, 17 says the LORD of Hosts, my own possession against the day that I appoint, and I will spare them as a man spares the son who serves him. You will again tell good men 18 from bad, the servant of God from the man who does not serve him.

The day comes, glowing like a 4 furnace; all the arrogant and the evildoers shall be chaff, and that day when it comes shall set them ablaze, says the LORD of Hosts, it shall leave them neither root nor branch. But for you who fear my 2 name, the sun of righteousness shall rise with healing in his wings, and you shall break loose like calves released from the stall. On 3 the day that I act, you shall trample down the wicked, for they will be ashes under the soles of your feet, says the LORD of Hosts.

---

[a] my messenger: *Heb.* Malachi.
[b] *Prob. rdg.; Heb. adds* silver.
[c] *Prob. rdg.; Heb. adds* the wages of.

4   Remember the law of Moses my servant, the rules and precepts which I bade him deliver to all Israel at Horeb.

5   Look, I will send you the prophet Elijah before the great and terrible day of the LORD comes. He will reconcile fathers to sons and sons to fathers, lest I come and put the land under a ban to destroy it. 6

APPENDIX

MEASURES OF LENGTH

	span	cubit	rod[a]
span	1	..	..
cubit	2	1	..
rod[a]	12	6	1

The 'short cubit' was traditionally the measure from the elbow to the knuckles of the closed fist; and what seems to be intended as a 'long cubit' measured a 'cubit and a hand-breadth', i.e. 7 instead of 6 hand-breadths (Ezek. 40. 5). What is meant by cubits 'according to the old standard of measurement' (2 Chr. 3. 3) is presumably this pre-exilic cubit of 7 hand-breadths. Modern estimates of the Hebrew cubit range from 12 to 25·2 inches, without allowing for varying local standards.

MEASURES OF CAPACITY

liquid measures	equivalences	dry measures
'log'	1 'log'	..
..	4 'log'	'kab'
..	7½ 'log'	'omer'
'hin'	12 'log'	..
'bath'	72 'log'	'ephah'
'kor'	720 'log'	'homer' or 'kor'

According to ancient authorities the Hebrew 'log' was of the same capacity as the Roman *sextarius*; this according to the best available evidence was equivalent to 0·99 pint of the English standard.

[a] Hebrew literally 'reed', the length of Ezekiel's measuring-rod.

APPENDIX

WEIGHTS AND COINS

	heavy (Phoenician) standard			light (Babylonian) standard		
	shekel	mina	talent	shekel	mina	talent
shekel	1	..	..	1	..	..
mina	50	1	..	60	1	..
talent	3,000	60	1	3,600	60	1

The 'gerah' was 1/20 of the sacred or heavy shekel and probably 1/24 of the light shekel.

The 'sacred shekel' according to tradition was identical with the heavy shekel; while the 'shekel of the standard recognized by merchants' (Gen. 23. 16) was perhaps a weight stamped with its value as distinct from one not so stamped and requiring to be weighed on the spot.

The weight and value of the shekel varied so greatly according to the district and with the passing centuries that its evaluation in modern terms is impossible. Recent discoveries suggest that it may have weighed approximately 11·5 grammes.

Coins are not mentioned before the Exile. Only the 'daric' (1 Chr. 29. 7) and the 'drachma' (Ezra 2. 69; Neh. 7. 70–72), if this is a distinct coin, are found in the Old Testament; the former is said to have been a month's pay for a soldier in the Persian army, while the latter will have been the Greek silver drachma, estimated at approximately 4·4 grammes. The 'shekel' of this period (Neh. 5. 15) as a coin was probably the Graeco-Persian *siglos* weighing 5·6 grammes.

THE NEW
ENGLISH BIBLE

THE NEW TESTAMENT

CONTENTS

Introduction to the New Testament   *page* v

Marginal Numbers   viii

THE GOSPEL

According to Matthew   3
According to Mark   39
According to Luke   62
According to John   101

ACTS OF THE APOSTLES   135

LETTERS

The Letter of Paul to the Romans   177
The First Letter of Paul to the Corinthians   194
The Second Letter of Paul to the Corinthians   210
The Letter of Paul to the Galatians   221
The Letter of Paul to the Ephesians   227
The Letter of Paul to the Philippians   232
The Letter of Paul to the Colossians   237
The First Letter of Paul to the Thessalonians   241
The Second Letter of Paul to the Thessalonians   244
The First Letter of Paul to Timothy   246
The Second Letter of Paul to Timothy   251
The Letter of Paul to Titus   254
The Letter of Paul to Philemon   257
A Letter to Hebrews   258
A Letter of James   270
The First Letter of Peter   274
The Second Letter of Peter   279
The First Letter of John   282
The Second Letter of John   286
The Third Letter of John   287
A Letter of Jude   288

THE REVELATION OF JOHN   293

32-2

INTRODUCTION

TO THE NEW TESTAMENT

THIS translation of the New Testament was undertaken with the object of providing English readers, whether familiar with the Bible or not, with a faithful rendering of the best available Greek text into the current speech of our own time, and a rendering which should harvest the gains of recent biblical scholarship.

It is now some three centuries and a half since King James's men put out what we have come to know as the Authorized Version. Two hundred and seventy years later the New Testament was revised. The Revised Version of the New Testament, which appeared in 1881, marked a new departure especially in that it abandoned the so-called Received Text, which had reigned ever since printed editions of the New Testament began, but which the advance of textual criticism had antiquated. The Revisers no longer followed (as their predecessors had done) the text of the majority of manuscripts, which, being for the most part of late date, had been exposed not only to the accidental corruptions of long-continued copying, but also in part to deliberate correction and 'improvement'. Instead, they followed a very small group of manuscripts, the earliest, and in their judgement the best, of those which had survived. During the years which have passed since their time, textual criticism has not stood still. Manuscripts have been discovered of substantially earlier date than any which the Revisers knew. Other important sources of evidence have been either freshly discovered or made more fully available. Meanwhile the methods of textual criticism have themselves been refined and estimates of the value of particular manuscripts have sometimes been reconsidered. The problem of restoring a form of text as near as possible to the vanished autographs now appears less simple than it did to our predecessors. There is not at the present time any critical text which would command the same degree of general acceptance as the Revisers' text did in its day. Nor has the time come, in the judgement of most scholars, to construct such a text, since new material constantly comes to light, and the debate continues. The present translators therefore could do no other than consider variant readings on their merits, and, having weighed the evidence for themselves, select for translation in each passage the reading which to the best of their judgement seemed most likely to represent what the author wrote. Where other readings seemed to deserve serious consideration they have been recorded in footnotes. In assessing the evidence, the translators have taken into account (a) ancient manuscripts of the New Testament in Greek, (b) manuscripts of early translations into other languages, and (c) quotations from the New Testament by early Christian writers. These three sources of evidence are collectively referred to as 'witnesses'. A large number of variants, however, are such as could make no appreciable difference to the meaning so far as it could be represented in translation, and these have been passed over in silence. The translators are well aware that their judgement is at best provisional, but they believe the text they have followed to be an improvement on that underlying the earlier translations. This text can now be read in *The Greek New Testament*, edited by

INTRODUCTION

R. V. G. Tasker (Oxford and Cambridge University Presses, 1964).

So much for the text. The next step was the effort to understand the original as accurately as possible, as a preliminary to turning it into English. The Revisers of 1881 believed that a better knowledge of the Greek language made it possible to correct a number of mistranslations in the older version, though in doing so they were somewhat limited by the instruction 'to introduce as few alterations as possible...consistently with faithfulness'. Since their time the study of the Greek language has no more stood still than has textual criticism. In particular, our knowledge of the kind of Greek used by most of the New Testament writers has been greatly enriched since 1881 by the discovery of many thousands of papyrus documents in popular or non-literary Greek of about the same period as the New Testament. It would be wrong to suggest that they lead to any far-reaching change in our understanding of the Greek of the New Testament period, but they have often made possible a better appreciation of the finer shades of idiom, which sometimes clarifies the meaning of passages in the New Testament. Its language is indeed in many respects more flexible and easy-going than the Revisers were ready to allow, and invites the translator to use a larger freedom.

Our task, however, differed in an important respect from that of the Revisers of 1881. They were instructed not only to introduce as few alterations as possible, but also 'to limit, as far as possible, the expression of such alterations to the language of the Authorised and earlier English Versions'. The present translators were subject to no such limitation. In accordance with the original decision of the Joint Committee they were to make the attempt to use consistently the idiom of contemporary English to convey the meaning of the Greek.

The older translators, on the whole, considered that fidelity to the original demanded that they should reproduce, as far as possible, characteristic features of the language in which it was written, such as the syntactical order of words, the structure and division of sentences, and even such irregularities of grammar as were indeed natural enough to authors writing in the easy idiom of popular Hellenistic Greek, but less natural when turned into English. The present translators were enjoined to replace Greek constructions and idioms by those of contemporary English.

This meant a different theory and practice of translation, and one which laid a heavier burden on the translators. Fidelity in translation was not to mean keeping the general framework of the original intact while replacing Greek words by English words more or less equivalent. A word, indeed, in one language is seldom the exact equivalent of a word in a different language. Each word is the centre of a whole cluster of meanings and associations, and in different languages these clusters overlap but do not often coincide. The place of a word in the clause or sentence, or even in a larger unit of thought, will determine what aspect of its total meaning is in the foreground. The translator can hardly hope to convey in another language every shade of meaning that attaches to the word in the original, but if he is free to exploit a wide range of English words covering a similar area of meaning and association he may hope to carry over the meaning of the sentence as a whole. Thus we have not felt obliged (as did the Revisers of 1881) to make an effort to render the same Greek word everywhere by the same English word. We have in this respect returned to the wholesome practice of King James's men, who (as they expressly state in their preface) recognized no such obligation.

We have conceived our task to be that of understanding the original as precisely as we could (using all available aids), and then saying again in our own native idiom what we be-

vi

lieved the author to be saying in his. We have found that in practice this frequently compelled us to make decisions where the older method of translation allowed a comfortable ambiguity. In such places we have been aware that we take a risk, but we have thought it our duty to take the risk rather than remain on the fence.

In doing our work, we have constantly striven to follow our instructions and render the Greek, as we understood it, into the English of the present day, that is, into the natural vocabulary, constructions, and rhythms of contemporary speech. We have sought to avoid archaism, jargon, and all that is either stilted or slipshod.

It should be said that our intention has been to offer a translation in the strict sense, and not a paraphrase, and we have not wished to encroach on the field of the commentator. But if the best commentary is a good translation, it is also true that every intelligent translation is in a sense a paraphrase. The line between translation and paraphrase is a fine one. But we have had recourse to deliberate paraphrase with great caution, and only in a few passages where without it we could see no way to attain our aim of making the meaning as clear as it could be made. Taken as a whole, our version claims to be a translation, free, it may be, rather than literal, but a faithful translation nevertheless, so far as we could compass it.

For this edition, the translation of the New Testament has been given a careful revision, in which account has been taken of numerous criticisms and suggestions which have come in from various quarters. It is hoped that the modifications introduced, mostly in minor details and seldom reflecting any substantial change of view about the meaning of a passage, will be found to be in the direction of improvement.

In the course of revision, consideration has been given to passages from the Old Testament quoted in the New. These have now been harmonized with the present version of the Old Testament, where this seemed desirable, and practicable. But the quotations are in Greek, and the Greek is by no means always an exact equivalent of the Hebrew. Where it is not, we have deemed it our duty to render the Greek as it lay before us, and not to attempt to reproduce the underlying Hebrew. On this point there has been consultation between representatives of the Old and the New Testament panels.

The translators are as conscious as anyone can be of the limitations and imperfections of their work. No one who has not tried it can know how impossible an art translation is. Only those who have meditated long upon the Greek original are aware of the richness and subtlety of meaning that may lie even within the most apparently simple sentence, or know the despair that attends all efforts to bring it out through the medium of a different language. Yet we may hope that we have been able to convey to our readers something at least of what the New Testament has said to us during these years of work, and trust that under the providence of Almighty God this translation may open the truth of the Scriptures to many who have been hindered in their approach to it by barriers of language.

C.H.D.

MARGINAL NUMBERS

THE conventional verse divisions in the New Testament date only from 1551 and have no basis in the manuscripts. Any system of division into numbered verses is foreign to the spirit of this translation, which is intended to convey the meaning in continuous natural English rather than to correspond sentence by sentence with the Greek.

For purposes of reference, and of comparison with other translations, verse numbers are placed in the margin opposite the line in which the first word belonging to the verse in question appears. Sometimes, however, successive verses are combined in a continuous English sentence, so that the precise point where a new verse begins cannot be fixed; occasionally in the interests of clarity the order of successive verses is reversed (e.g. at John 4. 7, 8).

THE GOSPEL

THE GOSPEL ACCORDING TO
MATTHEW

The coming of Christ

1 A TABLE of the descent of Jesus Christ, son of David, son of Abraham.

2 Abraham was the father of Isaac, Isaac of Jacob, Jacob of 3 Judah and his brothers, Judah of Perez and Zarah (their mother was Tamar), Perez of Hezron, Hezron 4 of Ram, Ram of Amminadab, Amminadab of Nahshon, Nahshon 5 of Salma, Salma of Boaz (his mother was Rahab), Boaz of Obed (his mother was Ruth), Obed of 6 Jesse; and Jesse was the father of King David.

David was the father of Solomon (his mother had been the wife 7 of Uriah), Solomon of Rehoboam, Rehoboam of Abijah, Abijah of 8 Asa, Asa of Jehoshaphat, Jehoshaphat of Joram, Joram of Azar- 9 iah, Azariah of Jotham, Jotham of 10 Ahaz, Ahaz of Hezekiah, Hezekiah of Manasseh, Manasseh of Amon, 11 Amon of Josiah; and Josiah was the father of Jeconiah and his brothers at the time of the deportation to Babylon.

12 After the deportation Jeconiah was the father of Shealtiel, Sheal- 13 tiel of Zerubbabel, Zerubbabel of Abiud, Abiud of Eliakim, Eliakim 14 of Azor, Azor of Zadok, Zadok of 15 Achim, Achim of Eliud, Eliud of Eleazar, Eleazar of Matthan, Mat- 16 than of Jacob, Jacob of Joseph, the husband of Mary, who gave birth to[a] Jesus called Messiah.

17 There were thus fourteen generations in all from Abraham to David, fourteen from David until the deportation to Babylon, and fourteen from the deportation until the Messiah.

THIS is the story of the birth of the 18 Messiah. Mary his mother was betrothed to Joseph; before their marriage she found that she was with child by the Holy Spirit. Being a 19 man of principle, and at the same time wanting to save her from exposure, Joseph desired to have the marriage contract set aside quietly. He had resolved on this, 20 when an angel of the Lord appeared to him in a dream. 'Joseph son of David,' said the angel, 'do not be afraid to take Mary home with you as your wife. It is by the Holy Spirit that she has conceived this child. She will bear a son; and you 21 shall give him the name Jesus (Saviour), for he will save his people from their sins.' All this happened 22 in order to fulfil what the Lord declared through the prophet: 'The virgin will conceive and bear 23 a son, and he shall be called Emmanuel', a name which means 'God is with us'. Rising from sleep 24 Joseph did as the angel had directed him; he took Mary home to be his wife, but had no intercourse 25 with her until her son was born. And he named the child Jesus.

JESUS was born at Bethlehem in 2 Judaea during the reign of Herod. After his birth astrologers from the east arrived in Jerusalem, asking, 2 'Where is the child who is born to be king of the Jews?[b] We observed the rising of his star, and we have

---

[a] Some witnesses read Joseph, to whom was betrothed Mary, a virgin, who gave birth to...; one witness has Joseph, and Joseph, to whom Mary, a virgin, was betrothed, was the father of...

[b] Or Where is the king of the Jews who has just been born?

3 come to pay him homage.' King Herod was greatly perturbed when he heard this; and so was the whole 4 of Jerusalem. He called a meeting of the chief priests and lawyers of the Jewish people, and put before them the question: 'Where is it that the Messiah is to be born?' 5 'At Bethlehem in Judaea', they replied; and they referred him to 6 the prophecy which reads: 'Bethlehem in the land of Judah, you are far from least in the eyes of*[a]* the rulers of Judah; for out of you shall come a leader to be the shepherd of my people Israel.'

7 Herod next called the astrologers to meet him in private, and ascertained from them the time 8 when the star had appeared. He then sent them on to Bethlehem, and said, 'Go and make a careful inquiry for the child. When you have found him, report to me, so that I may go myself and pay him homage.' 9 They set out at the king's bidding; and the star which they had seen at its rising went ahead of them until it stopped above the 10 place where the child lay. At the sight of the star they were over- 11 joyed. Entering the house, they saw the child with Mary his mother, and bowed to the ground in homage to him; then they opened their treasures and offered him gifts: gold, frankincense, and 12 myrrh. And being warned in a dream not to go back to Herod, they returned home another way.

13 After they had gone, an angel of the Lord appeared to Joseph in a dream, and said to him, 'Rise up, take the child and his mother and escape with them to Egypt, and stay there until I tell you; for Herod is going to search for the 14 child to do away with him.' So Joseph rose from sleep, and taking mother and child by night he went 15 away with them to Egypt, and there he stayed till Herod's death.

This was to fulfil what the Lord had declared through the prophet: 'I called my son out of Egypt.'

When Herod saw how the astro- 16 logers had tricked him he fell into a passion, and gave orders for the massacre of all children in Bethlehem and its neighbourhood, of the age of two years or less, corresponding with the time he had ascertained from the astrologers. So the 17 words spoken through Jeremiah the prophet were fulfilled: 'A voice 18 was heard in Rama, wailing and loud laments; it was Rachel weeping for her children, and refusing all consolation, because they were no more.'

The time came that Herod died; 19 and an angel of the Lord appeared in a dream to Joseph in Egypt and 20 said to him, 'Rise up, take the child and his mother, and go with them to the land of Israel, for the men who threatened the child's life are dead.' So he rose, took 21 mother and child with him, and came to the land of Israel. Hearing, 22 however, that Archelaus had succeeded his father Herod as king of Judaea, he was afraid to go there. And being warned by a dream, he withdrew to the region of Galilee; there he settled in a town called 23 Nazareth. This was to fulfil the words spoken through the prophets: 'He shall be called a Nazarene.'

ABOUT that time John the Bap- **3** tist appeared as a preacher in the Judaean wilderness; his theme was: 2 'Repent; for the kingdom of Heaven is upon you!' It is of him that 3 the prophet Isaiah spoke when he said, 'A voice crying aloud in the wilderness, "Prepare a way for the Lord; clear a straight path for him."'

John's clothing was a rough coat 4 of camel's hair, with a leather belt round his waist, and his food was locusts and wild honey. They 5

[a] Or least among.

flocked to him from Jerusalem, from all Judaea, and the whole 6 Jordan valley, and were baptized by him in the River Jordan, confessing their sins.

7 When he saw many of the Pharisees and Sadducees coming for baptism he said to them: 'You vipers' brood! Who warned you to escape from the coming retribu- 8 tion? Then prove your repentance 9 by the fruit it bears; and do not presume to say to yourselves, "We have Abraham for our father." I tell you that God can make children for Abraham out of these 10 stones here. Already the axe is laid to the roots of the trees; and every tree that fails to produce good fruit is cut down and thrown on the fire. 11 I baptize you with water, for repentance; but the one who comes after me is mightier than I. I am not fit to take off his shoes. He will baptize you with the Holy Spirit 12 and with fire. His shovel is ready in his hand and he will winnow his threshing-floor; the wheat he will gather into his granary, but he will burn the chaff on a fire that can never go out.'

13 Then Jesus arrived at the Jordan from Galilee, and came to John 14 to be baptized by him. John tried to dissuade him. 'Do you come to me?' he said; 'I need rather to be 15 baptized by you.' Jesus replied, 'Let it be so for the present; we do well to conform in this way with all that God requires.' John then allowed 16 him to come. After baptism Jesus came up out of the water at once, and at that moment heaven opened; he saw the Spirit of God descending like a dove to alight upon 17 him; and a voice from heaven was heard saying, 'This is my Son, my Beloved,[a] on whom my favour rests.'

4 JESUS was then led away by the Spirit into the wilderness, to be tempted by the devil.

For forty days and nights he 2 fasted, and at the end of them he was famished. The tempter ap- 3 proached him and said, 'If you are the Son of God, tell these stones to become bread.' Jesus answered, 4 'Scripture says, "Man cannot live on bread alone; he lives on every word that God utters."'

The devil then took him to the 5 Holy City and set him on the parapet of the temple. 'If you are the 6 Son of God,' he said, 'throw yourself down; for Scripture says, "He will put his angels in charge of you, and they will support you in their arms, for fear you should strike your foot against a stone."' Jesus 7 answered him, 'Scripture says again, "You are not to put the Lord your God to the test."'

Once again, the devil took him 8 to a very high mountain, and showed him all the kingdoms of the world in their glory. 'All these', he 9 said, 'I will give you, if you will only fall down and do me homage.' But Jesus said, 'Begone, Satan! 10 Scripture says, "You shall do homage to the Lord your God and worship him alone."'

Then the devil left him; and 11 angels appeared and waited on him.

When he heard that John had 12 been arrested, Jesus withdrew to Galilee; and leaving Nazareth he 13 went and settled at Capernaum on the Sea of Galilee, in the district of Zebulun and Naphtali. This was to 14 fulfil the passage in the prophet Isaiah which tells of 'the land of 15 Zebulun, the land of Naphtali, the Way of the Sea, the land beyond Jordan, heathen Galilee', and says:

'The people that lived in darkness 16
  saw a great light;
light dawned on the dwellers in the
  land of death's dark shadow.'

From that day Jesus began to pro- 17 claim the message: 'Repent; for[b]

---

[a] Or This is my only Son.   [b] Some witnesses omit Repent; for.

the kingdom of Heaven is upon you.'

18 JESUS was walking by the Sea of Galilee when he saw two brothers, Simon called Peter and his brother Andrew, casting a net into the 19 lake; for they were fishermen. Jesus said to them, 'Come with me, and I will make you fishers of men.' 20 And at once they left their nets and followed him.

21 He went on, and saw another pair of brothers, James son of Zebedee and his brother John; they were in the boat with their father Zebedee, overhauling their 22 nets. He called them, and at once they left the boat and their father, and followed him.

23 He went round the whole of Galilee, teaching in the synagogues, preaching the gospel of the Kingdom, and curing whatever illness or infirmity there was among the 24 people. His fame reached the whole of Syria; and sufferers from every kind of illness, racked with pain, possessed by devils, epileptic, or paralysed, were all brought to 25 him, and he cured them. Great crowds also followed him, from Galilee and the Ten Towns,[a] from Jerusalem and Judaea, and from Transjordan.

The Sermon on the Mount

5 WHEN he saw the crowds he went up the hill. There he took his seat, and when his disciples had gather- 2 ed round him he began to address them. And this is the teaching he gave:

3 'How blest are those who know their need of God;
the kingdom of Heaven is theirs.
4 How blest are the sorrowful;
they shall find consolation.
5 How blest are those of a gentle spirit;

they shall have the earth for their possession.
How blest are those who hunger 6 and thirst to see right prevail;[b]
they shall be satisfied.
How blest are those who show 7 mercy;
mercy shall be shown to them.
How blest are those whose hearts 8 are pure;
they shall see God.
How blest are the peacemakers; 9
God shall call them his sons.
How blest are those who have 10 suffered persecution for the cause of right;
the kingdom of Heaven is theirs.

'How blest you are, when you 11 suffer insults and persecution and every kind of calumny for my sake. Accept it with gladness and 12 exultation, for you have a rich reward in heaven; in the same way they persecuted the prophets before you.

'You are salt to the world. And if 13 salt becomes tasteless, how is its saltness to be restored? It is now good for nothing but to be thrown away and trodden underfoot.

'You are light for all the world. 14 A town that stands on a hill cannot be hidden. When a lamp is lit, it is 15 not put under the meal-tub, but on the lamp-stand, where it gives light to everyone in the house. And you, 16 like the lamp, must shed light among your fellows, so that, when they see the good you do, they may give praise to your Father in heaven.

'Do not suppose that I have come 17 to abolish the Law and the prophets; I did not come to abolish, but to complete. I tell you this: so 18 long as heaven and earth endure, not a letter, not a stroke, will disappear from the Law until all that must happen has happened.[c] If any 19 man therefore sets aside even the

---

[a] *Greek* Decapolis.   [b] *Or* to do what is right.
[c] *Or* before all that it stands for is achieved.

least of the Law's demands, and teaches others to do the same, he will have the lowest place in the kingdom of Heaven, whereas anyone who keeps the Law, and teaches others so, will stand high
20 in the kingdom of Heaven. I tell you, unless you show yourselves far better men than the Pharisees and the doctors of the law, you can never enter the kingdom of Heaven.
21 'You have learned that our fore-fathers were told, "Do not commit murder; anyone who commits murder must be brought to judge-
22 ment." But what I tell you is this: Anyone who nurses anger against his brother[a] must be brought to judgement. If he abuses his brother he must answer for it to the court; if he sneers at him he will have to answer for it in the fires of hell.
23 'If, when you are bringing your gift to the altar, you suddenly remember that your brother has a
24 grievance against you, leave your gift where it is before the altar. First go and make your peace with your brother, and only then come back and offer your gift.
25 'If someone sues you, come to terms with him promptly while you are both on your way to court; otherwise he may hand you over to the judge, and the judge to the constable, and you will be put in
26 jail. I tell you, once you are there you will not be let out till you have paid the last farthing.
27 'You have learned that they were told, "Do not commit adul-
28 tery." But what I tell you is this: If a man looks on a woman with a lustful eye, he has already com-mitted adultery with her in his heart.
29 'If your right eye is your un-doing, tear it out and fling it away; it is better for you to lose

one part of your body than for the whole of it to be thrown into hell.
30 And if your right hand is your un-doing, cut it off and fling it away; it is better for you to lose one part of your body than for the whole of it to go to hell.
31 'They were told, "A man who divorces his wife must give her a
32 note of dismissal." But what I tell you is this: If a man divorces his wife for any cause other than un-chastity he involves her in adul-tery; and anyone who marries a divorced woman commits adul-tery.
33 'Again, you have learned that our forefathers were told, "Do not break your oath", and, "Oaths sworn to the Lord must be kept."
34 But what I tell you is this: You are not to swear at all – not by heaven,
35 for it is God's throne, nor by earth, for it is his footstool, nor by Jeru-salem, for it is the city of the great
36 King, nor by your own head, be-cause you cannot turn one hair of
37 it white or black. Plain "Yes" or "No" is all you need to say; any-thing beyond that comes from the devil.
38 'You have learned that they were told, "Eye for eye, tooth for
39 tooth." But what I tell you is this: Do not set yourself against the man who wrongs you. If someone slaps you on the right cheek, turn and offer him your left. If a man
40 wants to sue you for your shirt, let him have your coat as well. If a
41 man in authority makes you go one mile, go with him two. Give
42 when you are asked to give; and do not turn your back on a man who wants to borrow.
43 'You have learned that they were told, "Love your neighbour, hate your enemy." But what I tell
44 you is this: Love your enemies[b] and pray for your persecutors;[c] only so can you be children of your
45

---

[a] *Some witnesses insert* without good cause.
[b] *Some witnesses insert* bless those who curse you, do good to those who hate you.
[c] *Some witnesses insert* and those who treat you spitefully.

heavenly Father, who makes his sun rise on good and bad alike, and sends the rain on the honest and 46 the dishonest. If you love only those who love you, what reward can you expect? Surely the tax-47 gatherers do as much as that. And if you greet only your brothers, what is there extraordinary about that? Even the heathen do as 48 much. There must be no limit to your goodness, as your heavenly Father's goodness knows no bounds.

6 'BE careful not to make a show of your religion before men; if you do, no reward awaits you in your Father's house in heaven.
2   'Thus, when you do some act of charity, do not announce it with a flourish of trumpets, as the hypocrites do in synagogue and in the streets to win admiration from men. I tell you this: they have 3 their reward already. No; when you do some act of charity, do not let your left hand know what your 4 right is doing; your good deed must be secret, and your Father who sees what is done in secret will reward you.*a*
5   'Again, when you pray, do not be like the hypocrites; they love to say their prayers standing up in synagogue and at the street-corners, for everyone to see them. I tell you this: they have their re-6 ward already. But when you pray, go into a room by yourself, shut the door, and pray to your Father who is there in the secret place; and your Father who sees what is secret will reward you.*a*
7   'In your prayers do not go babbling on like the heathen, who imagine that the more they say the more likely they are to be heard. 8 Do not imitate them. Your Father knows what your needs are before you ask him.

'This is how you should pray: 9

"Our Father in heaven,
thy name be hallowed;
thy kingdom come, 10
thy will be done,
on earth as in heaven.
Give us today our daily bread.*b* 11
Forgive us the wrong we have done, 12
as we have forgiven those who
have wronged us.
And do not bring us to the test, 13
but save us from the evil one."*cd*

For if you forgive others the 14 wrongs they have done, your heavenly Father will also forgive you; but if you do not forgive 15 others, then the wrongs you have done will not be forgiven by your Father.
'So too when you fast, do not 16 look gloomy like the hypocrites: they make their faces unsightly so that other people may see that they are fasting. I tell you this: they have their reward already. But when you fast, anoint your 17 head and wash your face, so that 18 men may not see that you are fasting, but only your Father who is in the secret place; and your Father who sees what is secret will give you your reward.

'Do not store up for yourselves 19 treasure on earth, where it grows rusty and moth-eaten, and thieves break in to steal it. Store up trea-20 sure in heaven, where there is no moth and no rust to spoil it, no thieves to break in and steal. For 21 where your treasure is, there will your heart be also.
'The lamp of the body is the eye. 22 If your eyes are sound, you will have light for your whole body; if 23 the eyes are bad, your whole body will be in darkness. If then the only light you have is darkness, the darkness is doubly dark.

a Some witnesses add openly.   *b Or* our bread for the morrow.   *c Or* from evil.
d Some witnesses add For thine is the kingdom and the power and the glory, for ever. Amen.

24 'No servant can be the slave of two masters; for either he will hate the first and love the second, or he will be devoted to the first and think nothing of the second. You cannot serve God and Money.

25 'Therefore I bid you put away anxious thoughts about food and drink to keep you alive, and clothes to cover your body. Surely life is more than food, the body

26 more than clothes. Look at the birds of the air; they do not sow and reap and store in barns, yet your heavenly Father feeds them. You are worth more than the

27 birds! Is there a man of you who by anxious thought can add a foot to

28 his height*ᵃ*? And why be anxious about clothes? Consider how the lilies grow in the fields; they do not

29 work, they do not spin;*ᵇ* and yet, I tell you, even Solomon in all his splendour was not attired like one

30 of these. But if that is how God clothes the grass in the fields, which is there today, and tomorrow is thrown on the stove, will he not all the more clothe you? How little

31 faith you have! No, do not ask anxiously, "What are we to eat? What are we to drink? What shall

32 we wear?" All these are things for the heathen to run after, not for you, because your heavenly Father

33 knows that you need them all. Set your mind on God's kingdom and his justice before everything else, and all the rest will come to you as

34 well. So do not be anxious about tomorrow; tomorrow will look after itself. Each day has troubles enough of its own.

7 'PASS no judgement, and you will
2 not be judged. For as you judge others, so you will yourselves be judged, and whatever measure you deal out to others will be dealt
3 back to you. Why do you look at

the speck of sawdust in your brother's eye, with never a thought for the great plank in your own? Or how can you say to your bro- 4 ther, "Let me take the speck out of your eye", when all the time there is that plank in your own? You 5 hypocrite! First take the plank out of your own eye, and then you will see clearly to take the speck out of your brother's.

'Do not give dogs what is holy; 6 do not throw your pearls to the pigs: they will only trample on them, and turn and tear you to pieces.

'Ask, and you will receive; seek, 7 and you will find; knock, and the door will be opened. For everyone 8 who asks receives, he who seeks finds, and to him who knocks, the door will be opened.

'Is there a man among you who 9 will offer his son a stone when he asks for bread, or a snake when 10 he asks for fish? If you, then, bad 11 as you are, know how to give your children what is good for them, how much more will your heavenly Father give good things to those who ask him!

'Always treat others as you 12 would like them to treat you: that is the Law and the prophets.

'Enter by the narrow gate. The 13 gate is wide that leads to perdition, there is plenty of room on the road,*ᶜ* and many go that way; but 14 the gate that leads to life is small and the road is narrow,*ᵈ* and those who find it are few.

'Beware of false prophets, men 15 who come to you dressed up as sheep while underneath they are savage wolves. You will recognize 16 them by the fruits they bear. Can grapes be picked from briars, or figs from thistles? In the same way, 17 a good tree always yields good fruit, and a poor tree bad fruit. A 18 good tree cannot bear bad fruit, or

---

ᵃ Or a day to his life.
ᵇ One witness reads Consider the lilies: they neither card nor spin, nor labour.
ᶜ Some witnesses read The road that leads to perdition is wide with plenty of room.
ᵈ Some witnesses read but the road that leads to life is small and narrow.

19 a poor tree good fruit. And when a
20 tree does not yield good fruit it is
cut down and burnt. That is why I
say you will recognize them by
their fruits.

21   'Not everyone who calls me
"Lord, Lord" will enter the kingdom of Heaven, but only those
who do the will of my heavenly
22 Father. When that day comes,
many will say to me, "Lord, Lord,
did we not prophesy in your name,
cast out devils in your name, and
in your name perform many
23 miracles?" Then I will tell them to
their face, "I never knew you; out
of my sight, you and your wicked
ways!"

24   'What then of the man who
hears these words of mine and acts
upon them? He is like a man who
had the sense to build his house on
25 rock. The rain came down, the
floods rose, the wind blew, and
beat upon that house; but it did
not fall, because its foundations
26 were on rock. But what of the man
who hears these words of mine and
does not act upon them? He is like
a man who was foolish enough to
27 build his house on sand. The rain
came down, the floods rose, the
wind blew, and beat upon that
house; down it fell with a great
crash.'

28   When Jesus had finished this
discourse the people were astound-
29 ed at his teaching; unlike their own
teachers he taught with a note of
authority.

Teaching and healing

8 AFTER he had come down from
the hill he was followed by a great
2 crowd. And now a leper[a] approached him, bowed low, and said, 'Sir,
if only you will, you can cleanse
3 me.' Jesus stretched out his hand,
touched him, and said, 'Indeed I

will; be clean again.' And his leprosy was cured immediately. Then 4
Jesus said to him, 'Be sure you tell
nobody; but go and show yourself
to the priest, and make the offering
laid down by Moses for your cleansing; that will certify the cure.'

When he had entered Caper- 5
naum a centurion came up to ask
his help. 'Sir,' he said, 'a boy of 6
mine lies at home paralysed and
racked with pain.' Jesus said, 'I 7
will come and cure him.'[b] But the 8
centurion replied, 'Sir, who am I to
have you under my roof? You
need only say the word and the boy
will be cured. I know, for I am 9
myself under orders, with soldiers
under me. I say to one, "Go", and
he goes; to another, "Come here",
and he comes; and to my servant,
"Do this", and he does it.' Jesus 10
heard him with astonishment, and
said to the people who were following him, 'I tell you this: nowhere,
even in Israel, have I found such
faith.

'Many, I tell you, will come from 11
east and west to feast with Abraham, Isaac, and Jacob in the kingdom of Heaven. But those who 12
were born to the kingdom will be
driven out into the dark, the place
of wailing and grinding of teeth.'
Then Jesus said to the centurion, 13
'Go home now; because of your
faith, so let it be.' At that moment
the boy recovered.

Jesus then went to Peter's house 14
and found Peter's mother-in-law
in bed with fever. So he took her by 15
the hand; the fever left her, and she
got up and waited on him.

When evening fell, they brought 16
to him many who were possessed
by devils; and he drove the spirits
out with a word and healed all who
were sick, to fulfil the prophecy of 17
Isaiah: 'He took away our illnesses
and lifted our diseases from us.'[c]

---

[a] *The words* leper, leprosy, *as used in this translation, refer to some disfiguring skin disease which entailed ceremonial defilement. It is different from what is now called* leprosy.   [b] *Or* Am I to come and cure him?
[c] *Or and bore the burden of our diseases.*

18 AT the sight of the crowds surrounding him Jesus gave word to
19 cross to the other shore. A doctor
of the law came up, and said,
'Master, I will follow you wher-
20 ever you go.' Jesus replied, 'Foxes
have their holes, and the birds their
roosts; but the Son of Man has
21 nowhere to lay his head.' Another
man, one of his disciples, said to
him, 'Lord, let me go and bury my
22 father first.' Jesus replied, 'Follow
me, and leave the dead to bury
their dead.'

23 Jesus then got into the boat, and
24 his disciples followed. All at once a
great storm arose on the lake, till
the waves were breaking right over
the boat; but he went on sleeping.
25 So they came and woke him up,
crying: 'Save us, Lord; we are
26 sinking!' 'Why are you such cowards?' he said; 'how little faith you
have!' Then he stood up and rebuked the wind and the sea, and
27 there was a dead calm. The men
were astonished at what had
happened, and exclaimed, 'What
sort of man is this? Even the wind
and the sea obey him.'

28 When he reached the other side,
in the country of the Gadarenes, he
was met by two men who came out
from the tombs; they were possessed by devils, and so violent that
29 no one dared pass that way. 'You
son of God,' they shouted, 'what
do you want with us? Have you
come here to torment us before our
30 time?' In the distance a large herd
31 of pigs was feeding; and the devils
begged him: 'If you drive us out,
send us into that herd of pigs.'
32 'Begone!' he said. Then they came
out and went into the pigs; the
whole herd rushed over the edge
into the lake, and perished in the
water.
33 The men in charge of them took
to their heels, and made for the
town, where they told the whole
story, and what had happened to
34 the madmen. Thereupon all the
town came out to meet Jesus; and

when they saw him they begged
him to leave the district and go. So 9
he got into the boat and crossed
over, and came to his own town.

And now some men brought 2
him a paralysed man lying on a
bed. Seeing their faith Jesus said to
the man, 'Take heart, my son;
your sins are forgiven.' At this 3
some of the lawyers said to themselves, 'This is blasphemous talk.'
Jesus knew what they were think- 4
ing, and said, 'Why do you harbour these evil thoughts? Is it 5
easier to say, "Your sins are forgiven", or to say, "Stand up and
walk"? But to convince you that 6
the Son of Man has the right on
earth to forgive sins' – he turned
to the paralysed man – 'stand up,
take your bed, and go home.'
Thereupon the man got up, and 7
went off home. The people were 8
filled with awe at the sight, and
praised God for granting such
authority to men.

As he passed on from there Jesus 9
saw a man named Matthew at his
seat in the custom-house, and said
to him, 'Follow me'; and Matthew
rose and followed him.

When Jesus was at table in the 10
house, many bad characters – tax-
gatherers and others – were seated
with him and his disciples. The 11
Pharisees noticed this, and said to
his disciples, 'Why is it that your
master eats with tax-gatherers and
sinners?' Jesus heard it and said, 12
'It is not the healthy that need a
doctor, but the sick. Go and learn 13
what that text means, "I require
mercy, not sacrifice." I did not
come to invite virtuous people, but
sinners.'

Then John's disciples came to 14
him with the question: 'Why do we
and the Pharisees fast, but your
disciples do not?' Jesus replied, 15
'Can you expect the bridegroom's
friends to go mourning while the
bridegroom is with them? The
time will come when the bride-

groom will be taken away from them; that will be the time for them to fast.

16 'No one sews a patch of unshrunk cloth on to an old coat; for then the patch tears away from the coat, and leaves a bigger hole.
17 Neither do you put new wine into old wine-skins; if you do, the skins burst, and then the wine runs out and the skins are spoilt. No, you put new wine into fresh skins; then both are preserved.'

18 Even as he spoke, there came a president of the synagogue, who bowed low before him and said, 'My daughter has just died; but come and lay your hand on her,
19 and she will live.' Jesus rose and went with him, and so did his disciples.
20 Then a woman who had suffered from haemorrhages for twelve years came up from behind, and
21 touched the edge of his cloak; for she said to herself, 'If I can only touch his cloak, I shall be cured.'
22 But Jesus turned and saw her, and said, 'Take heart, my daughter; your faith has cured you.' And from that moment she recovered.
23 When Jesus arrived at the president's house and saw the flute-players and the general commo-
24 tion, he said, 'Be off! The girl is not dead: she is asleep'; and they only
25 laughed at him. But, when everyone had been turned out, he went into the room and took the girl by
26 the hand, and she got up. This story became the talk of all the country round.
27 As he passed on Jesus was followed by two blind men, who cried
28 out, 'Son of David, have pity on us!' And when he had gone indoors they came to him. Jesus asked, 'Do you believe that I have the power to do what you want?' 'Yes,
29 sir', they said. Then he touched their eyes, and said, 'As you have

30 believed, so let it be'; and their sight was restored. Jesus said to them sternly, 'See that no one
31 hears about this.' But as soon as they had gone out they talked about him all over the countryside.

32 They were on their way out when a man was brought to him, who was dumb and possessed by a
33 devil; the devil was cast out and the patient recovered his speech. Filled with amazement the onlookers said, 'Nothing like this has ever been seen in Israel.'[a]

35 So Jesus went round all the towns and villages teaching in their synagogues, announcing the good news of the Kingdom, and curing every
36 kind of ailment and disease. The sight of the people moved him to pity: they were like sheep without a shepherd, harassed and helpless;
37 and he said to his disciples, 'The crop is heavy, but labourers are
38 scarce; you must therefore beg the owner to send labourers to harvest his crop.'
10 Then he called his twelve disciples to him and gave them authority to cast out unclean spirits and to cure every kind of ailment and disease.
2 These are the names of the twelve apostles: first Simon, also called Peter, and his brother Andrew; James son of Zebedee, and
3 his brother John; Philip and Bartholomew, Thomas and Matthew the tax-gatherer, James son of Al-
4 phaeus, Lebbaeus,[b] Simon, a member of the Zealot party, and a Judas Iscariot, the man who betrayed him.
5 These twelve Jesus sent out with the following instructions: 'Do not take the road to gentile lands, and do not enter any Sam-
6 aritan town; but go rather to the lost sheep of the house of Israel.
7 And as you go proclaim the mes-

---

[a] *Some witnesses add* (34) But the Pharisees said, 'He casts out devils by the prince of devils.'   [b] *Some witnesses read* Thaddaeus.

sage: "The kingdom of Heaven is
8 upon you." Heal the sick, raise the
dead, cleanse lepers, cast out
devils. You received without cost;
give without charge.

9 'Provide no gold, silver, or cop-
10 per to fill your purse, no pack for
the road, no second coat, no shoes,
no stick; the worker earns his
keep.

11 'When you come to any town or
village, look for some worthy person in it, and make your home
12 there until you leave. Wish the
13 house peace as you enter it, so
that, if it is worthy, your peace
may descend on it; if it is not
worthy, your peace can come back
14 to you. If anyone will not receive
you or listen to what you say, then
as you leave that house or that
town shake the dust of it off your
15 feet. I tell you this: on the day of
judgement it will be more bearable
for the land of Sodom and Gomorrah than for that town.

16 'Look, I send you out like sheep
among wolves; be wary as serpents, innocent as doves.

17 'And be on your guard, for men
will hand you over to their courts,
they will flog you in the syna-
18 gogues, and you will be brought
before governors and kings, for my
sake, to testify before them and
19 the heathen. But when you are
arrested, do not worry about what
you are to say; when the time
comes, the words you need will be
20 given you; for it is not you who will
be speaking: it will be the Spirit
of your Father speaking in you.

21 'Brother will betray brother to
death, and the father his child;
children will turn against their
parents and send them to their
22 death. All will hate you for your
allegiance to me; but the man who
holds out to the end will be saved.
23 When you are persecuted in one
town, take refuge in another; I tell
you this: before you have gone
through all the towns of Israel the
Son of Man will have come.

'A pupil does not rank above 24
his teacher, or a servant above his
master. The pupil should be con- 25
tent to share his teacher's lot, the
servant to share his master's. If the
master has been called Beelzebub,
how much more his household!

'So do not be afraid of them. 26
There is nothing covered up that
will not be uncovered, nothing
hidden that will not be made
known. What I say to you in the 27
dark you must repeat in broad
daylight; what you hear whispered
you must shout from the house-
tops. Do not fear those who kill the 28
body, but cannot kill the soul.
Fear him rather who is able to
destroy both soul and body in hell.

'Are not sparrows two a penny? 29
Yet without your Father's leave
not one of them can fall to the
ground. As for you, even the hairs 30
of your head have all been counted.
So have no fear; you are worth more 31
than any number of sparrows.

'Whoever then will acknow- 32
ledge me before men, I will acknowledge him before my Father in
heaven; and whoever disowns me 33
before men, I will disown him before my Father in heaven.

'You must not think that I have 34
come to bring peace to the earth; I
have not come to bring peace, but
a sword. I have come to set a man 35
against his father, a daughter a-
gainst her mother, a son's wife
against her mother-in-law; and a 36
man will find his enemies under
his own roof.

'No man is worthy of me who 37
cares more for father or mother
than for me; no man is worthy of
me who cares more for son or
daughter; no man is worthy of me 38
who does not take up his cross and
walk in my footsteps. By gaining 39
his life a man will lose it; by losing
his life for my sake, he will gain it.

'To receive you is to receive me, 40
and to receive me is to receive the
One who sent me. Whoever re- 41
ceives a prophet as a prophet will

be given a prophet's reward, and whoever receives a good man because he is a good man will be

42 given a good man's reward. And if anyone gives so much as a cup of cold water to one of these little ones, because he is a disciple of mine, I tell you this: that man will assuredly not go unrewarded.'

11 When Jesus had finished giving his twelve disciples their instructions, he left that place and went to teach and preach in the neighbouring towns.

2 JOHN, who was in prison, heard what Christ was doing, and sent his

3 own disciples to him with this message: 'Are you the one who is to come, or are we to expect some

4 other?' Jesus answered, 'Go and tell John what you hear and see:

5 the blind recover their sight, the lame walk, the lepers are made clean, the deaf hear, the dead are raised to life, the poor are hearing

6 the good news – and happy is the man who does not find me a stumbling-block.'

7 When the messengers were on their way back, Jesus began to speak to the people about John: 'What was the spectacle that drew you to the wilderness? A

8 reed-bed swept by the wind? No? Then what did you go out to see? A man dressed in silks and satins? Surely you must look in palaces

9 for that. But why did you go out? To see a prophet? Yes indeed, and

10 far more than a prophet. He is the man of whom Scripture says,

"Here is my herald, whom I send on ahead of you,
and he will prepare your way before you."

11 I tell you this: never has there appeared on earth a mother's son greater than John the Baptist, and yet the least in the kingdom of Heaven is greater than he.

'Ever since the coming of John 12 the Baptist the kingdom of Heaven has been subjected to violence and violent men[a] are seizing it. For all the prophets and the Law 13 foretold things to come until John appeared, and John is the destined 14 Elijah, if you will but accept it. If 15 you have ears, then hear.

'How can I describe this genera- 16 tion? They are like children sitting in the market-place and shouting at each other,

"We piped for you and you would 17 not dance."
"We wept and wailed, and you would not mourn."

For John came, neither eating nor 18 drinking, and they say, "He is possessed." The Son of Man came eat- 19 ing and drinking, and they say, "Look at him! a glutton and a drinker, a friend of tax-gatherers and sinners!" And yet God's wisdom is proved right by its results.'

THEN he spoke of the towns in 20 which most of his miracles had been performed, and denounced them for their impenitence. 'Alas 21 for you, Chorazin!' he said; 'alas for you, Bethsaida! If the miracles that were performed in you had been performed in Tyre and Sidon, they would have repented long ago in sackcloth and ashes. But it will 22 be more bearable, I tell you, for Tyre and Sidon on the day of judgement than for you. And as for 23 you, Capernaum, will you be exalted to the skies? No, brought down to the depths! For if the miracles had been performed in Sodom which were performed in you, Sodom would be standing to this day. But it will be more bearable, I 24 tell you, for the land of Sodom on the day of judgement than for you.'

At that time Jesus spoke these 25 words: 'I thank thee, Father, Lord

---

[a] *Or* has been forcing its way forward, and men of force...

of heaven and earth, for hiding these things from the learned and wise, and revealing them to the
26 simple. Yes, Father, such*ᵃ* was thy
27 choice. Everything is entrusted to me by my Father; and no one knows the Son but the Father, and no one knows the Father but the Son and those to whom the Son may choose to reveal him.

28 'Come to me, all whose work is hard, whose load is heavy; and I
29 will give you relief. Bend your necks to my yoke, and learn from me, for I am gentle and humble-hearted; and your souls will find
30 relief. For my yoke is good to bear, my load is light.'

Controversy

12 ONCE about that time, Jesus went through the cornfields on the Sabbath; and his disciples, feeling hungry, began to pluck some ears
2 of corn and eat them. The Pharisees noticed this, and said to him, 'Look, your disciples are doing something which is forbidden on
3 the Sabbath.' He answered, 'Have you not read what David did when
4 he and his men were hungry? He went into the House of God and ate the sacred bread, though neither he nor his men had a right to
5 eat it, but only the priests. Or have you not read in the Law that on the Sabbath the priests in the temple break the Sabbath and it is not
6 held against them? I tell you, there is something greater than the
7 temple here. If you had known what that text means, "I require mercy, not sacrifice", you would not have condemned the innocent.
8 For the Son of Man is sovereign over the Sabbath.'

9 He went on to another place,
10 and entered their synagogue. A man was there with a withered arm, and they asked Jesus, 'Is it permitted to heal on the Sabbath?' (They wanted to frame a charge

against him.) But he said to them, 11 'Suppose you had one sheep, which fell into a ditch on the Sabbath; is there one of you who would not catch hold of it and lift it out? And 12 surely a man is worth far more than a sheep! It is therefore permitted to do good on the Sabbath.' Turning to the man he said, 13 'Stretch out your arm.' He stretched it out, and it was made sound again like the other. But the Phari- 14 sees, on leaving the synagogue, laid a plot to do away with him.

Jesus was aware of it and with- 15 drew. Many followed, and he cured all who were ill; and he gave strict 16 injunctions that they were not to make him known. This was to fulfil 17 Isaiah's prophecy:

'Here is my servant, whom I have 18 chosen,
my beloved, on whom my favour rests;
I will put my Spirit upon him,
and he will proclaim judgement among the nations.
He will not strive, he will not 19 shout,
nor will his voice be heard in the streets.
He will not snap off the broken 20 reed,
nor snuff out the smouldering wick,
until he leads justice on to victory.
In him the nations shall place their 21 hope.'

THEN they brought him a man 22 who was possessed; he was blind and dumb; and Jesus cured him, restoring both speech and sight. The bystanders were all amazed, 23 and the word went round: 'Can this be the Son of David?' But 24 when the Pharisees heard it they said, 'It is only by Beelzebub prince of devils that this man drives the devils out.'

He knew what was in their 25 minds; so he said to them, 'Every

---

ᵃ Or Yes, I thank thee, Father, that such...

kingdom divided against itself goes to ruin; and no town, no household, that is divided against 26 itself can stand. And if it is Satan who casts out Satan, Satan is divided against himself; how then 27 can his kingdom stand? And if it is by Beelzebub that I cast out devils, by whom do your own people drive them out? If this is your argument, they themselves will re- 28 fute you. But if it is by the Spirit of God that I drive out the devils, then be sure the kingdom of God has already come upon you.

29 'Or again, how can anyone break into a strong man's house and make off with his goods, unless he has first tied the strong man up before ransacking the house?

30 'He who is not with me is against me, and he who does not gather with me scatters.

31 'And so I tell you this: no sin, no slander, is beyond forgiveness for men, except slander spoken against the Spirit, and that will not 32 be forgiven. Any man who speaks a word against the Son of Man will be forgiven; but if anyone speaks against the Holy Spirit, for him there is no forgiveness, either in this age or in the age to come.

33 'Either make the tree good and its fruit good, or make the tree bad and its fruit bad; you can tell a tree 34 by its fruit. You vipers' brood! How can your words be good when you yourselves are evil? For the words that the mouth utters come from the overflowing of the heart. 35 A good man produces good from the store of good within himself; and an evil man from evil within produces evil.

36 'I tell you this: there is not a thoughtless word that comes from men's lips but they will have to account for it on the day of judge- 37 ment. For out of your own mouth you will be acquitted; out of your own mouth you will be condemned.'

At this some of the doctors of the 38 law and the Pharisees said, 'Master, we should like you to show us a sign.' He answered: 'It is a wicked, 39 godless generation that asks for a sign; and the only sign that will be given it is the sign of the prophet Jonah. Jonah was in the sea- 40 monster's belly for three days and three nights, and in the same way the Son of Man will be three days and three nights in the bowels of the earth. At the Judgement, when 41 this generation is on trial, the men of Nineveh will appear against it[a] and ensure its condemnation, for they repented at the preaching of Jonah; and what is here is greater than Jonah. The Queen of the 42 South will appear at the Judgement when this generation is on trial,[b] and ensure its condemnation, for she came from the ends of the earth to hear the wisdom of Solomon; and what is here is greater than Solomon.

'When an unclean spirit comes 43 out of a man it wanders over the deserts seeking a resting-place, and finds none. Then it says, "I 44 will go back to the home I left." So it returns and finds the house unoccupied, swept clean, and tidy. Off it goes and collects seven other 45 spirits more wicked than itself, and they all come in and settle down; and in the end the man's plight is worse than before. That is how it will be with this wicked generation.'

He was still speaking to the 46 crowd when his mother and brothers appeared; they stood outside, wanting to speak to him. Someone said, 'Your mother and 47 your brothers are here outside; they want to speak to you.' Jesus 48 turned to the man who brought the message, and said, 'Who is my mother? Who are my brothers?'; and pointing to the disciples, he 49 said, 'Here are my mother and my

---

[a] *Or* will rise again together with it.   [b] *Or* At the Judgement the Queen of the South will be raised to life together with this generation.

50 brothers. Whoever does the will of my heavenly Father is my brother, my sister, my mother.'

13 THAT same day Jesus went out 2 and sat by the lake-side, where so many people gathered round him that he had to get into a boat. He sat there, and all the people stood 3 on the shore. He spoke to them in parables, at some length.

He said: 'A sower went out to 4 sow. And as he sowed, some seed fell along the footpath; and the 5 birds came and ate it up. Some seed fell on rocky ground, where it had little soil, and it sprouted quickly because it had no depth of 6 earth; but when the sun rose the young corn was scorched, and as it had no root it withered away. 7 Some seed fell among thistles; and the thistles shot up, and choked 8 the corn. And some of the seed fell into good soil, where it bore fruit, yielding a hundredfold or, it might 9 be, sixtyfold or thirtyfold. If you have ears, then hear.'

10 The disciples went up to him and asked, 'Why do you speak to them 11 in parables?' He replied, 'It has been granted to you to know the secrets of the kingdom of Heaven; but to those others it has not been 12 granted. For the man who has will be given more, till he has enough and to spare; and the man who has not will forfeit even what he has. 13 That is why I speak to them in parables; for they look without seeing, and listen without hearing 14 or understanding. There is a prophecy of Isaiah which is being fulfilled for them: "You may hear and hear, but you will never understand; you may look and look, but 15 you will never see. For this people's mind has become gross; their ears are dulled, and their eyes are closed. Otherwise, their eyes might see, their ears hear, and their mind understand, and then they might turn again, and I would heal them."

'But happy are your eyes be- 16 cause they see, and your ears because they hear! Many pro- 17 phets and saints, I tell you, desired to see what you now see, yet never saw it; to hear what you hear, yet never heard it.

'You, then, may hear the par- 18 able of the sower. When a man 19 hears the word that tells of the Kingdom but fails to understand it, the evil one comes and carries off what has been sown in his heart. There you have the seed sown along the footpath. The seed sown 20 on rocky ground stands for the man who, on hearing the word, accepts it at once with joy; but as it 21 strikes no root in him he has no staying-power, and when there is trouble or persecution on account of the word he falls away at once. The seed sown among thistles re- 22 presents the man who hears the word, but worldly cares and the false glamour of wealth choke it, and it proves barren. But the seed 23 that fell into good soil is the man who hears the word and understands it, who accordingly bears fruit, and yields a hundredfold or, it may be, sixtyfold or thirtyfold.'

Here is another parable that he 24 put before them: 'The kingdom of Heaven is like this. A man sowed 25 his field with good seed; but while everyone was asleep his enemy came, sowed darnel among the wheat, and made off. When the 26 corn sprouted and began to fill out, the darnel could be seen among it. The farmer's men went to their 27 master and said, "Sir, was it not good seed that you sowed in your field? Then where has the darnel come from?" "This is an enemy's 28 doing", he replied. "Well then," they said, "shall we go and gather the darnel?" "No," he answered; 29 "in gathering it you might pull up the wheat at the same time. Let 30 them both grow together till harvest; and at harvest-time I will tell the reapers, 'Gather the darnel first, and tie it in bundles for burning; then collect the wheat into my barn.'"'

31 And this is another parable that he put before them: 'The kingdom of Heaven is like a mustard-seed, which a man took and sowed in his 32 field. As a seed, mustard is smaller than any other; but when it has grown it is bigger than any garden-plant; it becomes a tree, big enough for the birds to come and roost among its branches.'

33 He told them also this parable: 'The kingdom of Heaven is like yeast, which a woman took and mixed with half a hundredweight of flour till it was all leavened.'

34 In all this teaching to the crowds Jesus spoke in parables; in fact he never spoke to them without 35 a parable. This was to fulfil the prophecy of Isaiah:[a]

'I will open my mouth in parables;
I will utter things kept secret since the world was made.'

36 He then dismissed the people, and went into the house, where his disciples came to him and said, 'Explain to us the parable of the 37 darnel in the field.' And this was his answer: 'The sower of the good 38 seed is the Son of Man. The field is the world; the good seed stands for the children of the Kingdom, the darnel for the children of the evil 39 one. The enemy who sowed the darnel is the devil. The harvest is the end of time. The reapers are 40 angels. As the darnel, then, is gathered up and burnt, so at the 41 end of time the Son of Man will send out his angels, who will gather out of his kingdom whatever makes men stumble, and all whose 42 deeds are evil, and these will be thrown into the blazing furnace, the place of wailing and grinding 43 of teeth. And then the righteous will shine as brightly as the sun in the kingdom of their Father. If you have ears, then hear.

44 'The kingdom of Heaven is like treasure lying buried in a field. The man who found it, buried it again; and for sheer joy went and sold everything he had, and bought that field.

45 'Here is another picture of the kingdom of Heaven. A merchant 46 looking out for fine pearls found one of very special value; so he went and sold everything he had, and bought it.

47 'Again the kingdom of Heaven is like a net let down into the sea, where fish of every kind were 48 caught in it. When it was full, it was dragged ashore. Then the men sat down and collected the good fish into pails and threw the 49 worthless away. That is how it will be at the end of time. The angels 50 will go forth, and they will separate the wicked from the good, and throw them into the blazing furnace, the place of wailing and grinding of teeth.

51 'Have you understood all this?' he asked; and they answered, 52 'Yes.' He said to them, 'When, therefore, a teacher of the law has become a learner in the kingdom of Heaven, he is like a householder who can produce from his store both the new and the old.'

53 WHEN he had finished these par-54 ables Jesus left that place, and came to his home town, where he taught the people in their synagogue. In amazement they asked, 'Where does he get this wisdom from, and these miraculous pow-55 ers? Is he not the carpenter's son? Is not his mother called Mary, his brothers James, Joseph, Simon, 56 and Judas? And are not all his sisters here with us? Where then has 57 he got all this from?' So they fell foul of him, and this led him to say, 'A prophet will always be held in honour, except in his home town,

[a] *Some witnesses omit* of Isaiah.

58 and in his own family.' And he did not work many miracles there: such was their want of faith.

14 It was at that time that reports about Jesus reached the ears of 2 Prince Herod. 'This is John the Baptist,' he said to his attendants; 'John has been raised to life, and that is why these miraculous powers are at work in him.'

3 N o w Herod had arrested John, put him in chains, and thrown him into prison, on account of Herodias, his 4 brother Philip's wife; for John had told him: 'You have no right to 5 her.' Herod would have liked to put him to death, but he was afraid of the people, in whose eyes John 6 was a prophet. But at his birthday celebrations the daughter of He-rodias danced before the guests, 7 and Herod was so delighted that he took an oath to give her any-8 thing she cared to ask. Prompted by her mother, she said, 'Give me here on a dish the head of John the 9 Baptist.' The king was distressed when he heard it; but out of regard for his oath and for his guests, he ordered the request to 10 be granted, and had John behead-11 ed in prison. The head was brought in on a dish and given to the girl; and she carried it to her mother. 12 Then John's disciples came and took away the body, and buried it; and they went and told Jesus.

13 W H E N he heard what had hap-pened Jesus withdrew privately by boat to a lonely place; but people heard of it, and came after him in crowds by land from the towns. 14 When he came ashore, he saw a great crowd; his heart went out to them, and he cured those of them 15 who were sick. When it grew late the disciples came up to him and said, 'This is a lonely place, and the day has gone; send the people off to the villages to buy themselves 16 food.' He answered, 'There is no

need for them to go; give them something to eat yourselves.' 'All 17 we have here', they said, 'is five loaves and two fishes.' 'Let me 18 have them', he replied. So he told 19 the people to sit down on the grass; then, taking the five loaves and the two fishes, he looked up to heaven, said the blessing, broke the loaves, and gave them to the disciples; and the disciples gave them to the people. They all ate to 20 their hearts' content; and the scraps left over, which they picked up, were enough to fill twelve great baskets. Some five thousand 21 men shared in this meal, to say nothing of women and children.

Then he made the disciples em- 22 bark and go on ahead to the other side, while he sent the people away; after doing that, he went up 23 the hill-side to pray alone. It grew late, and he was there by himself. The boat was already some fur- 24 longs from the shore,*a* battling with a head-wind and a rough sea. Between three and six in the morn- 25 ing he came to them, walking over the lake. When the disciples saw 26 him walking on the lake they were so shaken that they cried out in terror: 'It is a ghost!' But at once 27 he spoke to them: 'Take heart! It is I; do not be afraid.'

Peter called to him: 'Lord, if it is 28 you, tell me to come to you over the water.' 'Come', said Jesus. 29 Peter stepped down from the boat, and walked over the water towards Jesus. But when he saw the 30 strength of the gale he was seized with fear; and beginning to sink, he cried, 'Save me, Lord.' Jesus at 31 once reached out and caught hold of him, and said, 'Why did you hesitate? How little faith you have!' They then climbed into the 32 boat; and the wind dropped. And 33 the men in the boat fell at his feet, exclaiming, 'Truly you are the Son of God.'

So they finished the crossing and 34

---

a Some witnesses read already well out on the water.

35 came to land at Gennesaret. There Jesus was recognized by the people of the place, who sent out word to all the country round. And all who
36 were ill were brought to him, and he was begged to allow them simply to touch the edge of his cloak. And everyone who touched it was completely cured.

15 THEN Jesus was approached by a group of Pharisees and lawyers from Jerusalem, with the question:
2 'Why do your disciples break the ancient tradition? They do not
3 wash their hands before meals.' He answered them: 'And what of you? Why do you break God's commandment in the interest of your
4 tradition? For God said, "Honour your father and mother", and, "The man who curses his father or
5 mother must suffer death." But you say, "If a man says to his father or mother, 'Anything of mine which might have been used for your benefit is set apart for
6 God", then he must not honour his father or his mother." You have made God's law null and void out
7 of respect for your tradition. What hypocrisy! Isaiah was right when
8 he prophesied about you: "This people pays me lip-service, but
9 their heart is far from me; their worship of me is in vain, for they teach as doctrines the commandments of men."'
10 He called the crowd and said to them, 'Listen to me, and under-
11 stand this: a man is not defiled by what goes into his mouth, but by what comes out of it.'
12 Then the disciples came to him and said, 'Do you know that the Pharisees have taken great offence at what you have been saying?'
13 His answer was: 'Any plant that is not of my heavenly Father's plant-
14 ing will be rooted up. Leave them alone; they are blind guides,[a] and if one blind man guides another they will both fall into the ditch.'

Then Peter said, 'Tell us what 15 that parable means.' Jesus answer- 16 ed, 'Are you still as dull as the rest? Do you not see that whatever 17 goes in by the mouth passes into the stomach and so is discharged into the drain? But what comes 18 out of the mouth has its origins in the heart; and that is what defiles a man. Wicked thoughts, murder, 19 adultery, fornication, theft, perjury, slander – these all proceed from the heart; and these are the 20 things that defile a man; but to eat without first washing his hands, that cannot defile him.'

Jesus and his disciples

JESUS then left that place and 21 withdrew to the region of Tyre and Sidon. And a Canaanite woman 22 from those parts came crying out, 'Sir! have pity on me, Son of David; my daughter is tormented by a devil.' But he said not a word 23 in reply. His disciples came and urged him: 'Send her away; see how she comes shouting after us.' Jesus replied, 'I was sent to the 24 lost sheep of the house of Israel, and to them alone.' But the wo- 25 man came and fell at his feet and cried, 'Help me, sir.' To this 26 Jesus replied, 'It is not right to take the children's bread and throw it to the dogs.' 'True, sir,' 27 she answered; 'and yet the dogs eat the scraps that fall from their masters' table.' Hearing this Jesus 28 replied, 'Woman, what faith you have! Be it as you wish!' And from that moment her daughter was restored to health.

After leaving that region Jesus 29 took the road by the Sea of Galilee and went up to the hills. When he was seated there, crowds flocked to 30 him, bringing with them the lame, blind, dumb, and crippled, and many other sufferers; they threw them down at his feet, and he healed them. Great was the amaze- 31

[a] *Some witnesses insert* of blind men.

ment of the people when they saw the dumb speaking, the crippled strong, the lame walking, and sight restored to the blind; and they gave praise to the God of Israel.

32 Jesus called his disciples and said to them, 'I feel sorry for all these people; they have been with me now for three days and have nothing to eat. I do not want to send them away unfed; they might

33 turn faint on the way.' The disciples replied, 'Where in this lonely place can we find bread enough to

34 feed such a crowd?' 'How many loaves have you?' Jesus asked. 'Seven,' they replied; 'and there

35 are a few small fishes.' So he ordered the people to sit down on the

36 ground; then he took the seven loaves and the fishes, and after giving thanks to God he broke them and gave to the disciples, and the disciples gave to the people.

37 They all ate to their hearts' content; and the scraps left over, which they picked up, were enough

38 to fill seven baskets. Four thousand men shared in this meal, to say nothing of women and chil-

39 dren. He then dismissed the crowds, got into a boat, and went to the neighbourhood of Magadan.

16 The Pharisees and Sadducees came, and to test him they asked him to show them a sign from

2, 4 heaven. His answer was:[a] 'It is a wicked generation that asks for a sign; and the only sign that will be given it is the sign of Jonah.' So he went off and left them.

5 In crossing to the other side the disciples had forgotten to take

6 bread with them. So, when Jesus said to them, 'Beware, be on your guard against the leaven of the

7 Pharisees and Sadducees', they began to say among themselves, 'It is

because we have brought no bread!'
8 Knowing what was in their minds, Jesus said to them: 'Why do you talk about bringing no bread?
9 Where is your faith? Do you not understand even yet? Do you not remember the five loaves for the five thousand, and how many basketfuls you picked up? Or the 10 seven loaves for the four thousand, and how many basketfuls you picked up? How can you fail to see 11 that I was not speaking about bread? Be on your guard, I said, against the leaven of the Pharisees and Sadducees.' Then they under- 12 stood: they were to be on their guard, not against baker's leaven, but against the teaching of the Pharisees and Sadducees.

WHEN he came to the territory of 13 Caesarea Philippi, Jesus asked his disciples, 'Who do men say that the Son of Man is[b]?' They answer- 14 ed, 'Some say John the Baptist, others Elijah, others Jeremiah, or one of the prophets.' 'And you,' he 15 asked, 'who do you say I am?' Simon Peter answered: 'You are 16 the Messiah, the Son of the living God.' Then Jesus said: 'Simon son 17 of Jonah, you are favoured indeed! You did not learn that from mortal man; it was revealed to you by my heavenly Father. And I say this to 18 you: You are Peter, the Rock; and on this rock I will build my church, and the powers of death shall never conquer it.[c] I will give you the keys 19 of the kingdom of Heaven; what you forbid on earth shall be forbidden in heaven, and what you allow on earth shall be allowed in heaven.' He then gave his dis- 20 ciples strict orders not to tell anyone that he was the Messiah.

From that time Jesus began to 21

---

[a] *Some witnesses here insert* 'In the evening you say, "It will be fine weather, for the sky is red"; (3) and in the morning you say, "It will be stormy today; the sky is red and lowering." You know how to interpret the appearance of the sky; can you not interpret the signs of the times?'
[b] *Some witnesses read* that I, the Son of Man, am.
[c] *Or* the gates of death shall never close upon it.

make it clear to his disciples that he had to go to Jerusalem, and there to suffer much from the elders, chief priests, and doctors of the law; to be put to death and to 22 be raised again on the third day. At this Peter took him by the arm and began to rebuke him: 'Heaven forbid!' he said. 'No, Lord, this shall 23 never happen to you.' Then Jesus turned and said to Peter, 'Away with you, Satan; you are a stumbling block to me. You think as men think, not as God thinks.'

24   Jesus then said to his disciples, 'If anyone wishes to be a follower of mine, he must leave self behind; he must take up his cross and come 25 with me. Whoever cares for his own safety is lost; but if a man will let himself be lost for my sake, he 26 will find his true self. What a man gain by winning the whole world, at the cost of his true self? Or what can he give that will buy 27 that self back? For the Son of Man is to come in the glory of his Father with his angels, and then he will give each man the due reward for 28 what he has done. I tell you this: there are some of those standing here who will not taste death before they have seen the Son of Man coming in his kingdom.'

17 Six days later Jesus took Peter, James, and John the brother of James, and led them up a high mountain where they were alone; 2 and in their presence he was transfigured; his face shone like the sun, and his clothes became white as 3 the light. And they saw Moses and Elijah appear, conversing with 4 him. Then Peter spoke: 'Lord,' he said, 'how good it is that we are here! If you wish it, I will make three shelters here, one for you, one for Moses, and one for Elijah.' 5 While he was still speaking, a bright cloud suddenly overshadowed them, and a voice called from

the cloud: 'This is my Son, my Beloved,[a] on whom my favour rests; listen to him.' At the sound of the 6 voice the disciples fell on their faces in terror. Jesus then came up 7 to them, touched them, and said, 'Stand up; do not be afraid.' And 8 when they raised their eyes they saw no one, but only Jesus.

On their way down the moun- 9 tain, Jesus enjoined them not to tell anyone of the vision until the Son of Man had been raised from the dead. The disciples put a 10 question to him: 'Why then do our teachers say that Elijah must come first?' He replied, 'Yes, Elijah 11 will come and set everything right. But I tell you that Elijah has 12 already come, and they failed to recognize him, and worked their will upon him; and in the same way the Son of Man is to suffer at their hands.' Then the disciples under- 13 stood that he meant John the Baptist.

When they returned to the 14 crowd, a man came up to Jesus, fell on his knees before him, and said, 'Have pity, sir, on my son: he 15 is an epileptic and has bad fits, and he keeps falling about, often into the fire, often into water. I brought 16 him to your disciples, but they could not cure him.' Jesus answer- 17 ed, 'What an unbelieving and perverse generation! How long shall I be with you? How long must I endure you? Bring him here to me.' Jesus then spoke sternly to 18 the boy; the devil left him, and from that moment he was cured.

Afterwards the disciples came to 19 Jesus and asked him privately, 'Why could not we cast it out?' He 20 answered, 'Your faith is too small. I tell you this: if you have faith no bigger even than a mustard-seed, you will say to this mountain, "Move from here to there!", and it will move; nothing will prove impossible for you.'[b]

---

[a] *Or* This is my only Son.   [b] *Some witnesses add* (21) But there is no means of casting out this sort but prayer and fasting.

22 THEY were going about together in Galilee when Jesus said to them, 'The Son of Man is to be given up into the power of men, 23 and they will kill him; then on the third day he will be raised again.' And they were filled with grief.

24 On their arrival at Capernaum the collectors of the temple-tax came up to Peter and asked, 'Does your master not pay temple-tax?' 25 'He does', said Peter. When he went indoors Jesus forestalled him by asking, 'What do you think about this, Simon? From whom do earthly monarchs collect tax or toll? From their own people, or 26 from aliens?' 'From aliens', said Peter. 'Why then,' said Jesus, 27 'their own people are exempt! But as we do not want to cause offence, go and cast a line in the lake; take the first fish that comes to the hook, open its mouth, and you will find a silver coin; take that and pay it in; it will meet the tax for us both.'

18 At that time the disciples came to Jesus and asked, 'Who is the greatest in the kingdom of Hea- 2 ven?' He called a child, set him in 3 front of them, and said, 'I tell you this: unless you turn round and become like children, you will never enter the kingdom of Hea- 4 ven. Let a man humble himself till he is like this child, and he will be the greatest in the kingdom of 5 Heaven. Whoever receives one such child in my name receives 6 me. But if a man is a cause of stumbling to one of these little ones who have faith in me, it would be better for him to have a millstone hung round his neck and be drowned in the depths of the sea. 7 Alas for the world that such causes of stumbling arise! Come they must, but woe betide the man through whom they come! 8 'If your hand or your foot is your undoing, cut it off and fling it away; it is better for you to enter into life maimed or lame, than to keep two hands or two feet and be thrown into the eternal fire. If it is 9 your eye that is your undoing, tear it out and fling it away; it is better to enter into life with one eye than to keep both eyes and be thrown into the fires of hell.

'Never despise one of these little 10 ones; I tell you, they have their guardian angels in heaven, who look continually on the face of my heavenly Father.[a]

'What do you think? Suppose a 12 man has a hundred sheep. If one of them strays, does he not leave the other ninety-nine on the hillside and go in search of the one that strayed? And if he should find it, I 13 tell you this: he is more delighted over that sheep than over the ninety-nine that never strayed. In 14 the same way, it is not your heavenly Father's will that one of these little ones should be lost.

'If your brother commits a sin,[b] 15 go and take the matter up with him, strictly between yourselves, and if he listens to you, you have won your brother over. If he will 16 not listen, take one or two others with you, so that all facts may be duly established on the evidence of two or three witnesses. If he re- 17 fuses to listen to them, report the matter to the congregation; and if he will not listen even to the congregation, you must then treat him as you would a pagan or a tax-gatherer.

'I tell you this: whatever you 18 forbid on earth shall be forbidden in heaven, and whatever you allow on earth shall be allowed in heaven.

'Again I tell you this: if two of 19 you agree on earth about any request you have to make, that request will be granted by my heavenly Father. For where two 20 or three have met together in my name, I am there among them.'

---

[a] *Some witnesses add* (11) For the Son of Man came to save the lost.
[b] *Some witnesses insert* against you.

21 Then Peter came up and asked him, 'Lord, how often am I to forgive my brother if he goes on wronging me? As many as seven 22 times?' Jesus replied, 'I do not say seven times; I say seventy times seven.*a*

23 'The kingdom of Heaven, therefore, should be thought of in this way: There was once a king who decided to settle accounts with the 24 men who served him. At the outset there appeared before him a man whose debt ran into millions.*b* 25 Since he had no means of paying, his master ordered him to be sold to meet the debt, with his wife, his children, and everything he had. 26 The man fell prostrate at his master's feet. "Be patient with me," he said, "and I will pay in 27 full"; and the master was so moved with pity that he let the man go 28 and remitted the debt. But no sooner had the man gone out than he met a fellow-servant who owed him a few pounds;*c* and catching hold of him he gripped him by the throat and said, "Pay me what you 29 owe." The man fell at his fellow-servant's feet, and begged him, "Be patient with me, and I will 30 pay you"; but he refused, and had him jailed until he should pay the 31 debt. The other servants were deeply distressed when they saw what had happened, and they went to their master and told him 32 the whole story. He accordingly sent for the man. "You scoundrel!" he said to him; "I remitted the whole of your debt when you 33 appealed to me; were you not bound to show your fellow-servant the same pity as I showed you?" 34 And so angry was the master that he condemned the man to torture until he should pay the debt in full. 35 And that is how my heavenly Father will deal with you, unless you each forgive your brother from your hearts.'

WHEN Jesus had finished this 19 discourse he left Galilee and came into the region of Judaea across Jordan. Great crowds followed 2 him, and he healed them there.

Some Pharisees came and tested 3 him by asking, 'Is it lawful for a man to divorce his wife on any and every ground?'*d* He asked in re- 4 turn, 'Have you never read that the Creator made them from the beginning male and female?'; and 5 he added, 'For this reason a man shall leave his father and mother, and be made one with his wife; and the two shall become one flesh. It 6 follows that they are no longer two individuals: they are one flesh. What God has joined together, man must not separate.' 'Why 7 then', they objected, 'did Moses lay it down that a man might divorce his wife by note of dismissal?' He answered, 'It was because 8 your minds were closed that Moses gave you permission to divorce your wives; but it was not like that when all began. I tell you, if a 9 man divorces his wife for any cause other than unchastity, and marries another, he commits adultery.'*e*

The disciples said to him, 'If that 10 is the position with husband and wife, it is better not to marry.' To 11 this he replied, 'That is something which not everyone can accept, but only those for whom God has appointed it. For while some are 12 incapable of marriage because they were born so, or were made so by men, there are others who have themselves renounced marriage for the sake of the kingdom of Heaven. Let those accept it who can.'

They brought children for him to 13 lay his hands on them with prayer.

---

a Or seventy-seven times.
c Literally owed him 100 denarii.
lawful for a man to divorce his wife?
b Literally who owed 10,000 talents.
d Or Is there any ground on which it is
e Some witnesses add And the man
who marries a woman so divorced commits adultery.

14 The disciples rebuked them, but Jesus said to them, 'Let the children come to me; do not try to stop them; for the kingdom of Heaven 15 belongs to such as these.' And he laid his hands on the children, and went his way.

16 And now a man came up and asked him, 'Master, what good must I do to gain eternal life?' 17 'Good?' said Jesus. 'Why do you ask me about that? One alone is good. But if you wish to enter into life, keep the commandments.' 18 'Which commandments?' he asked. Jesus answered, 'Do not murder; do not commit adultery; do not steal; do not give false evi-19 dence; honour your father and mother; and love your neighbour 20 as yourself.' The young man answered, 'I have kept all these. 21 Where do I still fall short?' Jesus said to him, 'If you wish to go the whole way, go, sell your possessions, and give to the poor, and then you will have riches in hea-22 ven; and come, follow me.' When the young man heard this, he went away with a heavy heart; for he was a man of great wealth.

23 Jesus said to his disciples, 'I tell you this: a rich man will find it hard to enter the kingdom of 24 Heaven. I repeat, it is easier for a camel to pass through the eye of a needle than for a rich man to enter 25 the kingdom of God.' The disciples were amazed to hear this. 'Then who can be saved?' they 26 asked. Jesus looked at them, and said, 'For men this is impossible; but everything is possible for God.'

27 At this Peter said, 'We here have left everything to become your followers. What will there be for 28 us?' Jesus replied, 'I tell you this: in the world that is to be, when the Son of Man is seated on his throne in heavenly splendour, you my followers will have thrones of your own, where you will sit as judges of the twelve tribes of Israel. And 29 anyone who has left brothers or sisters, father, mother, or children, land or houses for the sake of my name will be repaid many times over, and gain eternal life. But 30 many who are first will be last, and the last first.

'The kingdom of Heaven is like 20 this. There was once a landowner who went out early one morning to hire labourers for his vineyard; and 2 after agreeing to pay them the usual day's wage*a* he sent them off to work. Going out three hours 3 later he saw some more men standing idle in the market-place. "Go 4 and join the others in the vineyard," he said, "and I will pay you a fair wage"; so off they went. At 5 midday he went out again, and at three in the afternoon, and made the same arrangement as before. An hour before sunset he went out 6 and found another group standing there; so he said to them, "Why are you standing about like this all day with nothing to do?" "Be-7 cause no one has hired us", they replied; so he told them, "Go and join the others in the vineyard." When evening fell, the owner of 8 the vineyard said to his steward, "Call the labourers and give them their pay, beginning with those who came last and ending with the first." Those who had started 9 work an hour before sunset came forward, and were paid the full day's wage.*b* When it was the turn 10 of the men who had come first, they expected something extra, but were paid the same amount as the others. As they took it, they 11 grumbled at their employer: "These 12 latecomers have done only one hour's work, yet you have put them on a level with us, who have sweated the whole day long in the blazing sun!" The owner turned to 13 one of them and said, "My friend, I am not being unfair to you. You agreed on the usual wage for the

---

a *Literally* one denarius for the day.　　*b* *Literally* one denarius each.

14 day,[a] did you not? Take your pay and go home. I choose to pay the
15 last man the same as you. Surely I am free to do what I like with my own money. Why be jealous be-
16 cause I am kind?" Thus will the last be first, and the first last.'

Challenge to Jerusalem

17 JESUS was journeying towards Jerusalem, and on the way he took the Twelve aside, and said to them,
18 'We are now going to Jerusalem, and the Son of Man will be given up to the chief priests and the doctors of the law; they will condemn him
19 to death and hand him over to the foreign power, to be mocked and flogged and crucified, and on the third day he will be raised to life again.'
20 The mother of Zebedee's sons then came before him, with her sons. She bowed low and begged a
21 favour. 'What is it you wish?' asked Jesus. 'I want you', she said, 'to give orders that in your kingdom my two sons here may sit next to you, one at your right, and the
22 other at your left.' Jesus turned to the brothers and said, 'You do not understand what you are asking. Can you drink the cup that I am to drink?' 'We can', they replied.
23 Then he said to them, 'You shall indeed share my cup; but to sit at my right or left is not for me to grant; it is for those to whom it has already been assigned by my Father.'
24 When the other ten heard this, they were indignant with the two
25 brothers. So Jesus called them to him and said, 'You know that in the world, rulers lord it over their subjects, and their great men make them feel the weight of authority;
26 but it shall not be so with you. Among you, whoever wants to be
27 great must be your servant, and whoever wants to be first must be

the willing slave of all – like the 28 Son of Man; he did not come to be served, but to serve, and to give up his life as a ransom for many.'

As they were leaving Jericho he 29 was followed by a great crowd of people. At the roadside sat two 30 blind men. When they heard it said that Jesus was passing they shouted, 'Have pity on us, Son of David.' The people told them 31 sharply to be quiet. But they shouted all the more, 'Sir, have pity on us; have pity on us, Son of David.' Jesus stopped and called 32 the men. 'What do you want me to do for you?' he asked. 'Sir,' they 33 answered, 'we want our sight.' Jesus was deeply moved, and 34 touched their eyes. At once their sight came back, and they followed him.

THEY were now nearing Jerusa- 21 lem; and when they reached Beth-phage at the Mount of Olives, Je-sus sent two disciples with these 2 instructions: 'Go to the village opposite, where you will at once find a donkey tethered with her foal beside her; untie them, and bring them to me. If anyone speaks 3 to you, say, "Our Master needs them"; and he will let you take them at once.'[b] This was to fulfil 4 the prophecy which says, 'Tell the 5 daughter of Zion, "Here is your king, who comes to you in gentle-ness, riding on an ass, riding on the foal of a beast of burden."'

The disciples went and did as 6 Jesus had directed, and brought 7 the donkey and her foal; they laid their cloaks on them and Jesus mounted. Crowds of people carpet- 8 ed the road with their cloaks, and some cut branches from the trees to spread in his path. Then the 9 crowd that went ahead and the others that came behind raised the shout: 'Hosanna to the Son of David! Blessings on him who

---

[a] *Literally* You agreed on a denarius.
[b] *Or* "Our Master needs them and will send them back straight away."

comes in the name of the Lord! Hosanna in the heavens!'

10 When he entered Jerusalem the whole city went wild with excitement. 'Who is this?' people asked, 11 and the crowd replied, 'This is the prophet Jesus, from Nazareth in Galilee.'

12 Jesus then went into the temple and drove out all who were buying and selling in the temple precincts; he upset the tables of the money-changers and the seats of the deal- 13 ers in pigeons; and said to them, 'Scripture says, "My house shall be called a house of prayer"; but you are making it a robbers' cave.'

14 In the temple blind men and cripples came to him, and he heal- 15 ed them. The chief priests and doctors of the law saw the wonderful things he did, and heard the boys in the temple shouting, 'Hosanna 16 to the Son of David!', and they asked him indignantly, 'Do you hear what they are saying?' Jesus answered, 'I do; have you never read that text, "Thou hast made children and babes at the breast 17 sound aloud thy praise"?' Then he left them and went out of the city to Bethany, where he spent the night.

18 Next morning on his way to the 19 city he felt hungry; and seeing a fig-tree at the roadside he went up to it, but found nothing on it but leaves. He said to the tree, 'You shall never bear fruit any more!'; and the tree withered away at 20 once. The disciples were amazed at the sight. 'How is it', they asked, 'that the tree has withered so 21 suddenly?' Jesus answered them, 'I tell you this: if only you have faith and have no doubts, you will do what has been done to the fig-tree; and more than that, you need only say to this mountain, "Be lifted from your place and hurled into the sea", and what you 22 say will be done. And whatever you pray for in faith you will receive.'

23 He entered the temple, and the chief priests and elders of the nation came to him with the question: 'By what authority are you acting like this? Who gave you this authority?' Jesus replied, 'I have a 24 question to ask you too; answer it, and I will tell you by what authority I act. The baptism of John: was 25 it from God, or from men?' This set them arguing among themselves: 'If we say, "from God", he will say, "Then why did you not believe him?" But if we say, "from 26 men", we are afraid of the people, for they all take John for a prophet.' So they answered, 'We do 27 not know.' And Jesus said: 'Then neither will I tell you by what authority I act.

'But what do you think about 28 this? A man had two sons. He went to the first, and said, "My boy, go and work today in the vineyard." "I will, sir", the boy 29 replied; but he never went. The 30 father came to the second and said the same. "I will not", he replied, but afterwards he changed his mind and went. Which of these 31 two did as his father wished?' 'The second', they said. Then Jesus answered, 'I tell you this: tax-gatherers and prostitutes are entering the kingdom of God ahead of you. For when John came to show 32 you the right way to live, you did not believe him, but the tax-gatherers and prostitutes did; and even when you had seen that, you did not change your minds and believe him.

'Listen to another parable. There 33 was a landowner who planted a vineyard: he put a wall round it, hewed out a winepress, and built a watch-tower; then he let it out to vine-growers and went abroad. When the vintage season approach- 34 ed, he sent his servants to the tenants to collect the produce due to him. But they took his servants 35 and thrashed one, killed another, and stoned a third. Again, he sent 36 other servants, this time a larger number; and they did the same to

37 them. At last he sent to them his son. "They will respect my son",
38 he said. But when they saw the son the tenants said to one another, "This is the heir; come on, let us kill him, and get his inheritance."
39 And they took him, flung him out of the vineyard, and killed him.
40 When the owner of the vineyard comes, how do you think he will
41 deal with those tenants?' 'He will bring those bad men to a bad end', they answered, 'and hand the vineyard over to other tenants, who will let him have his share of the
42 crop when the season comes.' Then Jesus said to them, 'Have you never read in the scriptures: "The stone which the builders rejected has become the main corner-stone. This is the Lord's doing, and it is
43 wonderful in our eyes"? Therefore, I tell you, the kingdom of God will be taken away from you, and given to a nation that yields the proper fruit.'[a]
45 When the chief priests and Pharisees heard his parables, they saw
46 that he was referring to them; they wanted to arrest him, but they were afraid of the people, who looked on Jesus as a prophet.

22 THEN Jesus spoke to them again
2 in parables: 'The kingdom of Heaven is like this. There was a king who prepared a feast for his son's
3 wedding; but when he sent his servants to summon the guests he had
4 invited, they would not come. He sent others again, telling them to say to the guests, "See now! I have prepared this feast for you. I have had my bullocks and fatted beasts slaughtered; everything is ready; come to the wedding at once."
5 But they took no notice; one went off to his farm, another to his
6 business, and the others seized the servants, attacked them brutally,
7 and killed them. The king was furious; he sent troops to kill those

murderers and set their town on fire. Then he said to his servants, 8 "The wedding-feast is ready; but the guests I invited did not deserve the honour. Go out to the 9 main thoroughfares, and invite everyone you can find to the wedding." The servants went out into 10 the streets, and collected all they could find, good and bad alike. So the hall was packed with guests.

'When the king came in to see 11 the company at table, he observed one man who was not dressed for a wedding. "My friend," said the 12 king, "how do you come to be here without your wedding clothes?" He had nothing to say. The king 13 then said to his attendants, "Bind him hand and foot; turn him out into the dark, the place of wailing and grinding of teeth." For though 14 many are invited, few are chosen.'

THEN the Pharisees went away 15 and agreed on a plan to trap him in his own words. Some of their fol- 16 lowers were sent to him in company with men of Herod's party. They said, 'Master, you are an honest man, we know; you teach in all honesty the way of life that God requires, truckling to no man, whoever he may be. Give us your 17 ruling on this: are we or are we not permitted to pay taxes to the Roman Emperor?' Jesus was a- 18 ware of their malicious intention and said to them, 'You hypocrites! Why are you trying to catch me out? Show me the money in which 19 the tax is paid.' They handed him a silver piece. Jesus asked, 'Whose 20 head is this, and whose inscription?' 'Caesar's', they replied. He 21 said to them, 'Then pay Caesar what is due to Caesar, and pay God what is due to God.' This 22 answer took them by surprise, and they went away and left him alone.

The same day Sadducees came 23 to him, maintaining that there is

---

[a] *Some witnesses add* (44) Any man who falls on this stone will be dashed to pieces; and if it falls on a man he will be crushed by it.

no resurrection. Their question was this: 'Master, Moses said, "If a 24 man should die childless, his brother shall marry the widow and carry on his brother's family." Now we knew of seven brothers. 25 The first married and died, and as he was without issue his wife was left to his brother. The same thing 26 happened with the second, and the third, and so on with all seven. Last of all the woman died. At the 7, 28 resurrection, then, whose wife will she be, for they had all married her?' Jesus answered: 'You are 29 mistaken, because you know neither the scriptures nor the power of God. At the resurrection men 30 and women do not marry; they are like angels in heaven.

'But about the resurrection of 31 the dead, have you never read what God himself said to you: "I 32 am the God of Abraham, the God of Isaac, and the God of Jacob"? He is not God of the dead but of the living.' The people heard what he 33 said, and were astounded at his teaching.

Hearing that he had silenced the 34 Sadducees, the Pharisees met together; and one of their number[a] 35 tested him with this question: 'Master, which is the greatest com- 36 mandment in the Law?' He an- 37 swered, '"Love the Lord your God with all your heart, with all your soul, with all your mind." That 38 is the greatest commandment. It comes first. The second is like it: 39 "Love your neighbour as yourself." Everything in the Law and 40 the prophets hangs on these two commandments.'

Turning to the assembled Phari- 41 sees Jesus asked them, 'What is 42 your opinion about the Messiah? Whose son is he?' 'The son of David', they replied. 'How then is 43 it', he asked, 'that David by inspiration calls him "Lord"? For he says, "The Lord said to my Lord, 44 'Sit at my right hand until I put your enemies under your feet.'" If David calls him "Lord", how 45 can he be David's son?' Not a man 46 could say a word in reply; and from that day forward no one dared ask him another question.

JESUS then addressed the people 23 and his disciples in these words: 2 'The doctors of the law and the Pharisees sit in the chair of Moses; therefore do what they tell you; 3 pay attention to their words. But do not follow their practice; for they say one thing and do another. They make up heavy packs and 4 pile them on men's shoulders, but will not raise a finger to lift the load themselves. Whatever they 5 do is done for show. They go about with broad phylacteries[b] and with large tassels on their robes; they 6 like to have places of honour at feasts and the chief seats in synagogues, to be greeted respectfully 7 in the street, and to be addressed as "rabbi".

'But you must not be called 8 "rabbi"; for you have one Rabbi, and you are all brothers. Do not 9 call any man on earth "father"; for you have one Father, and he is in heaven. Nor must you be called 10 "teacher"; you have one Teacher, the Messiah. The greatest among 11 you must be your servant. For 12 whoever exalts himself will be humbled; and whoever humbles himself will be exalted.

'Alas, alas for you, lawyers and 13 Pharisees, hypocrites that you are! You shut the door of the kingdom of Heaven in men's faces; you do not enter yourselves, and when others are entering, you stop them.[c]

'Alas for you, lawyers and Phari- 15 sees, hypocrites! You travel over

---

[a] *Some witnesses insert* a lawyer.   [b] *See Deuteronomy 6. 8–9 and Exodus 13.9.*
[c] *Some witnesses add* (14) Alas for you, lawyers and Pharisees, hypocrites! You eat up the property of widows, while you say long prayers for appearance' sake. You will receive the severest sentence.

sea and land to win one convert; and when you have won him you make him twice as fit for hell as you are yourselves.

16 'Alas for you, blind guides! You say, "If a man swears by the sanctuary, that is nothing; but if he swears by the gold in the sanctuary, he is bound by his oath."
17 Blind fools! Which is the more important, the gold, or the sanctuary which sanctifies the gold?
18 Or you say, "If a man swears by the altar, that is nothing; but if he swears by the offering that lies on the altar, he is bound by his oath."
19 What blindness! Which is the more important, the offering, or
20 the altar which sanctifies it? To swear by the altar, then, is to swear both by the altar and by what-
21 ever lies on it; to swear by the sanctuary is to swear both by the sanctuary and by him who dwells
22 there; and to swear by heaven is to swear both by the throne of God and by him who sits upon it.
23 'Alas for you, lawyers and Pharisees, hypocrites! You pay tithes of mint and dill and cummin; but you have overlooked the weightier demands of the Law, justice, mercy, and good faith. It is these you should have practised, without
24 neglecting the others. Blind guides! You strain off a midge, yet gulp down a camel!
25 'Alas for you, lawyers and Pharisees, hypocrites! You clean the outside of cup and dish, which you have filled inside by robbery and
26 self-indulgence! Blind Pharisee! Clean the inside of the cup first; then the outside will be clean also.
27 'Alas for you, lawyers and Pharisees, hypocrites! You are like tombs covered with whitewash; they look well from outside, but inside they are full of dead men's
28 bones and all kinds of filth. So it is with you: outside you look like honest men, but inside you are brim-full of hypocrisy and crime.

29 'Alas for you, lawyers and Pharisees, hypocrites! You build up the tombs of the prophets and embellish the monuments of the saints,
30 and you say, "If we had been alive in our fathers' time, we should never have taken part with them
31 in the murder of the prophets." So you acknowledge that you are the sons of the men who killed the
32 prophets. Go on then, finish off what your fathers began!*a*

33 'You snakes, you vipers' brood, how can you escape being con-
34 demned to hell? I send you therefore prophets, sages, and teachers; some of them you will kill and crucify, others you will flog in your synagogues and hound from
35 city to city. And so, on you will fall the guilt of all the innocent blood spilt on the ground, from innocent Abel to Zechariah son of Berachiah, whom you murdered between
36 the sanctuary and the altar. Believe me, this generation will bear the guilt of it all.

37 'O Jerusalem, Jerusalem, the city that murders the prophets and stones the messengers sent to her! How often have I longed to gather your children, as a hen gathers her brood under her wings; but you
38 would not let me. Look, look! there is your temple, forsaken by God.*b c*
39 And I tell you, you shall never see me until the time when you say, "Blessings on him who comes in the name of the Lord."'

Prophecies and warnings

24 JESUS was leaving the temple when his disciples came and point-
2 ed to the temple buildings. He answered, 'Yes, look at it all. I tell you this: not one stone will be left upon another; all will be thrown down.'
3 When he was sitting on the

---

a Or You too must come up to your fathers' standards.
b Or Look, your home is desolate.　　　*c Some witnesses add* and laid waste.

Mount of Olives the disciples came to speak to him privately. 'Tell us,' they said, 'when will this happen? And what will be the signal for your coming and the end of the age?'

4 Jesus replied: 'Take care that no 5 one misleads you. For many will come claiming my name and saying, "I am the Messiah"; and 6 many will be misled by them. The time is coming when you will hear the noise of battle near at hand and the news of battles far away; see that you are not alarmed. Such things are bound to happen; but 7 the end is still to come. For nation will make war upon nation, kingdom upon kingdom; there will be famines and earthquakes in many 8 places. With all these things the birth-pangs of the new age begin.

9 'You will then be handed over for punishment and execution; and men of all nations will hate you 10 for your allegiance to me. Many will fall from their faith; they will betray one another and hate one 11 another. Many false prophets will 12 arise, and will mislead many; and as lawlessness spreads, men's love 13 for one another will grow cold. But the man who holds out to the end 14 will be saved. And this gospel of the Kingdom will be proclaimed throughout the earth as a testimony to all nations; and then the end will come.

15 'So when you see "the abomination of desolation", of which the prophet Daniel spoke, standing in the holy place (let the reader un-16 derstand), then those who are in 17 Judaea must take to the hills. If a man is on the roof, he must not come down to fetch his goods from 18 the house; if in the field, he must 19 not turn back for his coat. Alas for women with child in those days, and for those who have children at 20 the breast. Pray that it may not be winter when you have to make 21 your escape, or Sabbath. It will be a time of great distress; there has

never been such a time from the beginning of the world until now, and will never be again. If that 22 time of troubles were not cut short, no living thing could survive; but for the sake of God's chosen it will be cut short.

'Then, if anyone says to you, 23 "Look, here is the Messiah", or, "There he is", do not believe it. Impostors will come claiming to be 24 messiahs or prophets, and they will produce great signs and wonders to mislead even God's chosen, if such a thing were possible. See, I 25 have forewarned you. If they tell 26 you, "He is there in the wilderness", do not go out; or if they say, "He is there in the inner room", do not believe it. Like lightning from 27 the east, flashing as far as the west, will be the coming of the Son of Man.

'Wherever the corpse is, there 28 the vultures will gather.

'As soon as the distress of those 29 days has passed, the sun will be darkened, the moon will not give her light, the stars will fall from the sky, the celestial powers will be shaken. Then will appear in hea-30 ven the sign that heralds the Son of Man. All the peoples of the world will make lamentation, and they will see the Son of Man coming on the clouds of heaven with great power and glory. With a trumpet 31 blast he will send out his angels, and they will gather his chosen from the four winds, from the farthest bounds of heaven on every side.

'Learn a lesson from the fig-tree. 32 When its tender shoots appear and are breaking into leaf, you know that summer is near. In the same 33 way, when you see all these things, you may know that the end is near,*a* at the very door. I tell you 34 this: the present generation will live to see it all. Heaven and earth 35 will pass away; my words will never pass away.

---

a Or *that he is near.*

36 'But about that day and hour no one knows, not even the angels in heaven, not even the Son; only the Father.

37 'As things were in Noah's days, so will they be when the Son of 38 Man comes. In the days before the flood they ate and drank and married, until the day that Noah went 39 into the ark, and they knew nothing until the flood came and swept them all away. That is how it will be when the Son of Man 40 comes. Then there will be two men in the field; one will be taken, the 41 other left; two women grinding at the mill; one will be taken, the other left.

42 'Keep awake, then; for you do not know on what day your Lord is 43 to come. Remember, if the householder had known at what time of night the burglar was coming, he would have kept awake and not have let his house be broken into. 44 Hold yourselves ready, therefore, because the Son of Man will come at the time you least expect him.

45 'Who is the trusty servant, the sensible man charged by his master to manage his household staff and issue their rations at the proper 46 time? Happy that servant who is found at his task when his master 47 comes! I tell you this: he will be put in charge of all his master's 48 property. But if he is a bad servant and says to himself, "The master is 49 a long time coming", and begins to bully the other servants and to eat and drink with his drunken friends, 50 then the master will arrive on a day that servant does not expect, 51 at a time he does not know, and will cut him in pieces. Thus he will find his place among the hypocrites, where there is wailing and grinding of teeth.

25 'When that day comes, the kingdom of Heaven will be like this. There were ten girls, who took their lamps and went out to meet the 2 bridegroom. Five of them were 3 foolish, and five prudent; when the foolish ones took their lamps, they took no oil with them, but the 4 others took flasks of oil with their lamps. As the bridegroom was late 5 in coming they all dozed off to sleep. But at midnight a cry was 6 heard: "Here is the bridegroom! Come out to meet him." With that 7 the girls all got up and trimmed their lamps. The foolish said to the 8 prudent, "Our lamps are going out; give us some of your oil." "No," 9 they said; "there will never be enough for all of us. You had better go to the shop and buy some for yourselves." While they were a- 10 way the bridegroom arrived; those who were ready went in with him to the wedding; and the door was shut. And then the other five came 11 back. "Sir, sir," they cried, "open the door for us." But he answered, 12 "I declare, I do not know you." Keep awake then; for you never 13 know the day or the hour.

'It is like a man going abroad, 14 who called his servants and put his capital in their hands; to one he 15 gave five bags of gold, to another two, to another one, each according to his capacity. Then he left the country. The man who had the five 16 bags went at once and employed them in business, and made a profit of five bags, and the man who had 17 the two bags made two. But the 18 man who had been given one bag of gold went off and dug a hole in the ground, and hid his master's money. A long time afterwards their 19 master returned, and proceeded to settle accounts with them. The 20 man who had been given the five bags of gold came and produced the five he had made: "Master," he said, "you left five bags with me; look, I have made five more." "Well done, my good and trusty 21 servant!" said the master. "You have proved trustworthy in a small way; I will now put you in charge of something big. Come and share your master's delight." The man 22 with the two bags then came and said, "Master, you left two bags with me; look, I have made two 23 more." "Well done, my good and trusty servant!" said the master. "You have proved trustworthy in a small way; I will now put you in charge of something big. Come and 24 share your master's delight." Then the man who had been given one bag came and said, "Master, I knew you to be a hard man: you reap where you have not sown, you gather where you have not scatter- 25 ed; so I was afraid, and I went and hid your gold in the ground. Here it is – you have what belongs to 26 you." "You lazy rascal!" said the master. "You knew that I reap where I have not sown, and gather 27 where I have not scattered? Then you ought to have put my money on deposit, and on my return I should have got it back with inter- 28 est. Take the bag of gold from him, and give it to the one with 29 the ten bags. For the man who has will always be given more, till he has enough and to spare; and the man who has not will forfeit even 30 what he has. Fling the useless servant out into the dark, the place of wailing and grinding of teeth!"

31 'When the Son of Man comes in his glory and all the angels with him, he will sit in state on his 32 throne, with all the nations gathered before him. He will separate men into two groups, as a shepherd separates the sheep from the 33 goats, and he will place the sheep on his right hand and the goats on 34 his left. Then the king will say to those on his right hand, "You have my Father's blessing; come, enter and possess the kingdom that has been ready for you since the world 35 was made. For when I was hungry, you gave me food; when thirsty, you gave me drink; when I was a stranger you took me into your 36 home, when naked you clothed me; when I was ill you came to my help, when in prison you visited

me." Then the righteous will reply, 37 "Lord, when was it that we saw you hungry and fed you, or thirsty and gave you drink, a stranger and 38 took you home, or naked and clothed you? When did we see you 39 ill or in prison, and come to visit you?" And the king will answer, "I 40 tell you this: anything you did for one of my brothers here, however humble, you did for me." Then he 41 will say to those on his left hand, "The curse is upon you; go from my sight to the eternal fire that is ready for the devil and his angels. For when I was hungry you gave 42 me nothing to eat, when thirsty nothing to drink; when I was a 43 stranger you gave me no home, when naked you did not clothe me; when I was ill and in prison you did not come to my help." And 44 they too will reply, "Lord, when was it that we saw you hungry or thirsty or a stranger or naked or ill or in prison, and did nothing for you?" And he will answer, "I tell 45 you this: anything you did not do for one of these, however humble, you did not do for me." And they 46 will go away to eternal punishment, but the righteous will enter eternal life.'

The final conflict

WHEN Jesus had finished this dis- 26 course he said to his disciples, 'You know that in two days' time 2 it will be Passover, and the Son of Man is to be handed over for crucifixion.'

Then the chief priests and the 3 elders of the nation met in the palace of the High Priest, Caiaphas; and there they conferred 4 together on a scheme to have Jesus arrested by some trick and put to death. 'It must not be during the 5 festival,' they said, 'or there may be rioting among the people.'

JESUS was at Bethany in the 6 house of Simon the leper, when a 7 woman came to him with a small bottle of fragrant oil, very costly; and as he sat at table she began to 8 pour it over his head. The disciples were indignant when they saw it. 9 'Why this waste?' they said; 'it could have been sold for a good sum and the money given to the 10 poor.' Jesus was aware of this, and said to them, 'Why must you make trouble for the woman? It is a fine 11 thing she has done for me. You have the poor among you always; but you will not always have me. 12 When she poured this oil on my body it was her way of preparing 13 me for burial. I tell you this: wherever in all the world this gospel is proclaimed, what she has done will be told as her memorial.'

14 THEN one of the Twelve, the man called Judas Iscariot, went to the 15 chief priests and said, 'What will you give me to betray him to you?' They weighed him out[a] thirty sil-16 ver pieces. From that moment he began to look out for an opportunity to betray him.

17 On the first day of Unleavened Bread the disciples came to ask Jesus, 'Where would you like us to prepare for your Passover supper?' 18 He answered, 'Go to a certain man in the city, and tell him, "The Master says, 'My appointed time is near; I am to keep Passover with 19 my disciples at your house.'"' The disciples did as Jesus directed them and prepared for Passover.

20 In the evening he sat down with 21 the twelve disciples; and during supper he said, 'I tell you this: one 22 of you will betray me.' In great distress they exclaimed one after the other, 'Can you mean me, 23 Lord?' He answered, 'One who has dipped his hand into this bowl 24 with me will betray me. The Son of Man is going the way appointed for him in the scriptures; but alas for that man by whom the Son of Man is betrayed! It would be better for that man if he had never been born.' Then Judas spoke, the one 25 who was to betray him: 'Rabbi, can you mean me?' Jesus replied, 'The words are yours.'[b]

During supper Jesus took bread, 26 and having said the blessing he broke it and gave it to the disciples with the words: 'Take this and eat; this is my body.' Then he took a 27 cup, and having offered thanks to God he gave it to them with the words: 'Drink from it, all of you. For this is my blood, the blood of 28 the covenant, shed for many for the forgiveness of sins. I tell you, 29 never again shall I drink from the fruit of the vine until that day when I drink it new with you in the kingdom of my Father.'

After singing the Passover Hymn, 30 they went out to the Mount of Olives. Then Jesus said to them, 31 'Tonight you will all fall from your faith on my account; for it stands written: "I will strike the shepherd down and the sheep of his flock will be scattered." But after I 32 am raised again, I will go on before you into Galilee.' Peter replied, 33 'Everyone else may fall away on your account, but I never will.' Jesus said to him, 'I tell you, to-34 night before the cock crows you will disown me three times.' Peter 35 said, 'Even if I must die with you, I will never disown you.' And all the disciples said the same.

JESUS then came with his dis-36 ciples to a place called Gethsemane. He said to them, 'Sit here while I go over there to pray.' He 37 took with him Peter and the two sons of Zebedee. Anguish and dismay came over him, and he said to 38 them, 'My heart is ready to break with grief. Stop here, and stay awake with me.' He went on a 39 little, fell on his face in prayer, and said, 'My Father, if it is possible, let this cup pass me by. Yet not as I will, but as thou wilt.'

---

[a] *Or* agreed to pay him...   [b] *Or* It is as you say.

40 He came to the disciples and found them asleep; and he said to Peter, 'What! Could none of you stay awake with me one hour? 41 Stay awake, and pray that you may be spared the test. The spirit is willing, but the flesh is weak.'

42 He went away a second time, and prayed: 'My Father, if it is not possible for this cup to pass me by without my drinking it, thy will be 43 done.' He came again and found them asleep, for their eyes were 44 heavy. So he left them and went away again; and he prayed the third time, using the same words as before.

45 Then he came to the disciples and said to them, 'Still sleeping? Still taking your ease? The hour has come! The Son of Man is 46 betrayed to sinful men. Up, let us go forward; the traitor is upon us.'

47 While he was still speaking, Judas, one of the Twelve, appeared; with him was a great crowd armed with swords and cudgels, sent by the chief priests and the 48 elders of the nation. The traitor gave them this sign: 'The one I 49 kiss is your man; seize him'; and stepping forward at once, he said, 50 'Hail, Rabbi!', and kissed him. Jesus replied, 'Friend, do what you are here to do.'[a] They then came forward, seized Jesus, and held him fast.

51 At that moment one of those with Jesus reached for his sword and drew it, and he struck at the High Priest's servant and cut off 52 his ear. But Jesus said to him, 'Put up your sword. All who take the 53 sword die by the sword. Do you suppose that I cannot appeal to my Father, who would at once send to my aid more than twelve legions of 54 angels? But how then could the scriptures be fulfilled, which say that this must be?'

55 At the same time Jesus spoke to the crowd: 'Do you take me for a bandit, that you have come out with swords and cudgels to arrest me? Day after day I sat teaching in the temple, and you did not lay hands on me. But this has all 56 happened to fulfil what the prophets wrote.'

Then the disciples all deserted him and ran away.

JESUS was led off under arrest to 57 the house of Caiaphas the High Priest, where the lawyers and elders were assembled. Peter followed 58 him at a distance till he came to the High Priest's courtyard, and going in he sat down there among the attendants, meaning to see the end of it all.

The chief priests and the whole 59 Council tried to find some allegation against Jesus on which a death-sentence could be based; but 60 they failed to find one, though many came forward with false evidence. Finally two men alleged 61 that he had said, 'I can pull down the temple of God, and rebuild it in three days.' At this the High 62 Priest rose and said to him, 'Have you no answer to the charge that these witnesses bring against you?' But Jesus kept silence. The High 63 Priest then said, 'By the living God I charge you to tell us: Are you the Messiah, the Son of God?' Jesus 64 replied, 'The words are yours.[b] But I tell you this: from now on, you will see the Son of Man seated at the right hand of God[c] and coming on the clouds of heaven.' At these words the High Priest 65 tore his robes and exclaimed, 'Blasphemy! Need we call further witnesses? You have heard the blasphemy. What is your opinion?' 66 'He is guilty,' they answered; 'he should die.'

Then they spat in his face and 67 struck him with their fists; and others said, as they beat him,

---

[a] *Or* Friend, what are you here for?
[b] *Or* It is as you say.　　[c] *Literally* of the Power.

68 'Now, Messiah, if you are a prophet, tell us who hit you.'
69 Meanwhile Peter was sitting
outside in the courtyard when a
serving-maid accosted him and
said, 'You were there too with
70 Jesus the Galilean.' Peter denied it
in face of them all. 'I do not know
71 what you mean', he said. He then
went out to the gateway, where
another girl, seeing him, said to the
people there, 'This fellow was with
72 Jesus of Nazareth.' Once again he
denied it, saying with an oath, 'I
73 do not know the man.' Shortly
afterwards the bystanders came up
and said to Peter, 'Surely you are
another of them; your accent gives
74 you away!' At this he broke into
curses and declared with an oath:
'I do not know the man.' At that
75 moment a cock crew; and Peter
remembered how Jesus had said,
'Before the cock crows you will
disown me three times.' He went
outside, and wept bitterly.

27 WHEN morning came, the chief
priests and the elders of the nation
met in conference to plan the death
2 of Jesus. They then put him in
chains and led him away, to hand
him over to Pilate, the Roman
Governor.
3 When Judas the traitor saw that
Jesus had been condemned, he
was seized with remorse, and returned the thirty silver pieces to
4 the chief priests and elders. 'I have
sinned,' he said; 'I have brought an
innocent man to his death.' But
they said, 'What is that to us? See
5 to that yourself.' So he threw the
money down in the temple and
left them, and went and hanged
himself.
6 Taking up the money, the chief
priests argued: 'This cannot be
put into the temple fund; it is
7 blood-money.' So after conferring
they used it to buy the Potter's
Field, as a burial-place for foreign-
8 ers. This explains the name 'Blood

Acre', by which that field has been
known ever since; and in this way 9
fulfilment was given to the prophetic utterance of Jeremiah:
'They took[a] the thirty silver pieces,
the price set on a man's head (for
that was his price among the Israelites), and gave the money for 10
the potter's field, as the Lord
directed me.'
Jesus was now brought before 11
the Governor; and as he stood
there the Governor asked him,
'Are you the king of the Jews?'
'The words are yours',[b] said Jesus;
and to the charges laid against him 12
by the chief priests and elders he
made no reply. Then Pilate said to 13
him, 'Do you not hear all this evidence that is brought against you?';
but he still refused to answer one 14
word, to the Governor's great
astonishment.
At the festival season it was the 15
Governor's custom to release one
prisoner chosen by the people.
There was then in custody a man 16
of some notoriety, called Jesus[c]
Bar-Abbas. When they were as- 17
sembled Pilate said to them,
'Which would you like me to release to you – Jesus[c] Bar-Abbas, or
Jesus called Messiah?' For he knew 18
that it was out of malice that they
had brought Jesus before him.
While Pilate was sitting in court 19
a message came to him from his
wife: 'Have nothing to do with
that innocent man; I was much
troubled on his account in my
dreams last night.'
Meanwhile the chief priests and 20
elders had persuaded the crowd to
ask for the release of Bar-Abbas
and to have Jesus put to death.
So when the Governor asked, 21
'Which of the two do you wish me
to release to you?', they said, 'Bar-
Abbas.' 'Then what am I to do 22
with Jesus called Messiah?' asked
Pilate; and with one voice they
answered, 'Crucify him!' 'Why, 23
what harm has he done?' Pilate

_____
[a] *Or* I took.   [b] *Or* It is as you say.   [c] *Some witnesses omit* Jesus.

asked; but they shouted all the louder, 'Crucify him!'

24 Pilate could see that nothing was being gained, and a riot was starting; so he took water and washed his hands in full view of the people, saying, 'My hands are clean of this man's blood; see to 25 that yourselves.' And with one voice the people cried, 'His blood 26 be on us, and on our children.' He then released Bar-Abbas to them; but he had Jesus flogged, and handed him over to be crucified.

27 PILATE'S soldiers then took Jesus into the Governor's headquarters, where they collected the whole 28 company round him. They stripped him and dressed him in a 29 scarlet mantle; and plaiting a crown of thorns they placed it on his head, with a cane in his right hand. Falling on their knees before him they jeered at him: 'Hail, 30 King of the Jews!' They spat on him, and used the cane to beat him 31 about the head. When they had finished their mockery, they took off the mantle and dressed him in his own clothes.

32 Then they led him away to be crucified. On their way out they met a man from Cyrene, Simon by name, and pressed him into service to carry his cross.

33 So they came to a place called Golgotha (which means 'Place of a 34 skull') and there he was offered a draught of wine mixed with gall; but when he had tasted it he would not drink.

35 After fastening him to the cross they divided his clothes among 36 them by casting lots, and then sat 37 down there to keep watch. Over his head was placed the inscription giving the charge: 'This is Jesus the king of the Jews.'

38 Two bandits were crucified with him, one on his right and the other on his left.

39 The passers-by hurled abuse at him: they wagged their heads and 40 cried, 'You would pull the temple down, would you, and build it in three days? Come down from the cross and save yourself, if you are indeed the Son of God.' So too the 41 chief priests with the lawyers and elders mocked at him: 'He saved 42 others,' they said, 'but he cannot save himself. King of Israel, indeed! Let him come down now from the cross, and then we will believe him. Did he trust in God? 43 Let God rescue him, if he wants him – for he said he was God's Son.' Even the bandits who were 44 crucified with him taunted him in the same way.

From midday a darkness fell 45 over the whole land, which lasted until three in the afternoon; and 46 about three Jesus cried aloud, '*Eli, Eli, lema sabachthani?*', which means, 'My God, my God, why hast thou forsaken me?' Some of 47 the bystanders, on hearing this, said, 'He is calling Elijah.' One of 48 them ran at once and fetched a sponge, which he soaked in sour wine, and held it to his lips on the end of a cane. But the others said, 49 'Let us see if Elijah will come to save him.'

Jesus again gave a loud cry, and 50 breathed his last. At that moment 51 the curtain of the temple was torn in two from top to bottom. There was an earthquake, the rocks split and the graves opened, and many 52 of God's saints were raised from sleep; and coming out of their 53 graves after his resurrection they entered the Holy City, where many saw them. And when the 54 centurion and his men who were keeping watch over Jesus saw the earthquake and all that was happening, they were filled with awe, and they said, 'Truly this man was a son of God.'[a]

A NUMBER of women were also 55 present, watching from a distance;

a Or the Son of God.

56 they had followed Jesus from Galilee and waited on him. Among them were Mary of Magdala, Mary the mother of James and Joseph, and the mother of the sons of Zebedee.

57 When evening fell, there came a man of Arimathaea, Joseph by name, who was a man of means, and had himself become a disciple 58 of Jesus. He approached Pilate, and asked for the body of Jesus; and Pilate gave orders that he 59 should have it. Joseph took the body, wrapped it in a clean linen 60 sheet, and laid it in his own unused tomb, which he had cut out of the rock; he then rolled a large stone against the entrance, and went 61 away. Mary of Magdala was there, and the other Mary, sitting opposite the grave.

62 Next day, the morning after that Friday, the chief priests and the Pharisees came in a body to 63 Pilate. 'Your Excellency,' they said, 'we recall how that impostor said while he was still alive, "I am to be raised again after three days." 64 So will you give orders for the grave to be made secure until the third day? Otherwise his disciples may come, steal the body, and then tell the people that he has been raised from the dead; and the final deception will be worse than 65 the first.' 'You may have your guard,' said Pilate; 'go and make 66 it secure as best you can.' So they went and made the grave secure; they sealed the stone, and left the guard in charge.

28 THE Sabbath was over, and it was about daybreak on Sunday, when Mary of Magdala and the other Mary came to look at the grave. 2 Suddenly there was a violent earthquake; an angel of the Lord descended from heaven; he came to the stone and rolled it away, 3 and sat himself down on it. His face shone like lightning; his gar- 4 ments were white as snow. At the sight of him the guards shook with fear and lay like the dead.

The angel then addressed the 5 women: 'You', he said, 'have nothing to fear. I know you are look- ing for Jesus who was crucified. He 6 is not here; he has been raised again, as he said he would be. Come and see the place where he was laid, and then go quickly and tell 7 his disciples: "He has been raised from the dead and is going on before you into Galilee; there you will see him." That is what I had to tell you.'

They hurried away from the 8 tomb in awe and great joy, and ran to tell the disciples. Suddenly 9 Jesus was there in their path. He gave them his greeting, and they came up and clasped his feet, fall- ing prostrate before him. Then 10 Jesus said to them, 'Do not be afraid. Go and take word to my brothers that they are to leave for Galilee. They will see me there.'

The women had started on their 11 way when some of the guard went into the city and reported to the chief priests everything that had happened. After meeting with the 12 elders and conferring together, the chief priests offered the soldiers a substantial bribe and told them to 13 say, 'His disciples came by night and stole the body while we were asleep.' They added, 'If this should 14 reach the Governor's ears, we will put matters right with him and see that you do not suffer.' So they 15 took the money and did as they were told. This story became widely known, and is current in Jewish circles to this day.

The eleven disciples made their 16 way to Galilee, to the mountain where Jesus had told them to meet him. When they saw him, they fell 17 prostrate before him, though some were doubtful. Jesus then came up 18 and spoke to them. He said: 'Full authority in heaven and on earth has been committed to me. Go 19 forth therefore and make all nations my disciples; baptize men everywhere in the name of the Father and the Son and the Holy Spirit, and teach them to observe 20 all that I have commanded you. And be assured, I am with you always, to the end of time.'

THE GOSPEL ACCORDING TO

MARK

The coming of Christ

1 HERE begins the Gospel of Jesus Christ the Son of God.[a]

2 In the prophet Isaiah it stands written: 'Here is my herald whom I send on ahead of you, and he will 3 prepare your way. A voice crying aloud in the wilderness, "Prepare a way for the Lord; clear a straight 4 path for him."' And so it was that John the Baptist appeared in the wilderness proclaiming a baptism in token of repentance, for the 5 forgiveness of sins; and they flocked to him from the whole Judaean country-side and the city of Jerusalem, and were baptized by him in the River Jordan, confessing their sins.

6 John was dressed in a rough coat of camel's hair, with a leather belt round his waist, and he fed on 7 locusts and wild honey. His proclamation ran: 'After me comes one who is mightier than I. I am 8 not fit to unfasten his shoes. I have baptized you with water; he will baptize you with the Holy Spirit.'

9 It happened at this time that Jesus came from Nazareth in Galilee and was baptized in the Jordan 10 by John. At the moment when he came up out of the water, he saw the heavens torn open and the Spirit, like a dove, descending 11 upon him. And a voice spoke from heaven: 'Thou art my Son, my Beloved;[b] on thee my favour rests.'

Thereupon the Spirit sent him 12 away into the wilderness, and 13 there he remained for forty days tempted by Satan. He was among the wild beasts; and the angels waited on him.

In Galilee: success and opposition

AFTER John had been arrested, 14 Jesus came into Galilee proclaiming the Gospel of God: 'The time 15 has come; the kingdom of God is upon you; repent, and believe the Gospel.'

Jesus was walking by the Sea of 16 Galilee when he saw Simon and his brother Andrew on the lake at work with a casting-net; for they were fishermen. Jesus said to 17 them, 'Come with me, and I will make you fishers of men.' And at 18 once they left their nets and followed him.

When he had gone a little fur- 19 ther he saw James son of Zebedee and his brother John, who were in the boat overhauling their nets. He 20 called them; and, leaving their father Zebedee in the boat with the hired men, they went off to follow him.

They came to Capernaum, and 21 on the Sabbath he went to synagogue and began to teach. The 22 people were astounded at his

---

[a] *Some witnesses omit* the Son of God.

[b] *Or* Thou art my only Son.

teaching, for, unlike the doctors of the law, he taught with a note of
23 authority. Now there was a man in the synagogue possessed by an
24 unclean spirit. He shrieked: 'What do you want with us, Jesus of Nazareth? Have you*a* come to destroy us? I know who you are – the
25 Holy One of God.' Jesus rebuked him: 'Be silent', he said, 'and come
26 out of him.' And the unclean spirit threw the man into convulsions
27 and with a loud cry left him. They were all dumbfounded and began to ask one another, 'What is this? A new kind of teaching! He speaks with authority. When he gives orders, even the unclean spirits
28 submit.' The news spread rapidly, and he was soon spoken of all over the district of Galilee.

29 On leaving the synagogue they went straight to the house of Simon and Andrew; and James and
30 John went with them. Simon's mother-in-law was ill in bed with fever. They told him about her at
31 once. He came forward, took her by the hand, and helped her to her feet. The fever left her and she waited upon them.

32 That evening after sunset they brought to him all who were ill or
33 possessed by devils; and the whole town was there, gathered at the
34 door. He healed many who suffered from various diseases, and drove out many devils. He would not let the devils speak, because they knew who he was.

35 Very early next morning he got up and went out. He went away to a lonely spot and remained there in
36 prayer. But Simon and his com-
37 panions searched him out, found him, and said, 'They are all looking
38 for you.' He answered, 'Let us move on to the country towns in the neighbourhood; I have to proclaim my message there also; that
39 is what I came out to do.' So all through Galilee he went, preaching

in the synagogues and casting out the devils.

40 Once he was approached by a leper, who knelt before him begging his help. 'If only you will,' said the man, 'you can cleanse me.'
41 In warm indignation Jesus stretched out his hand,*b* touched him, and said, 'Indeed I will; be clean again.'
42 The leprosy left him immediately,
43 and he was clean. Then he dismissed him with this stern warn-
44 ing: 'Be sure you say nothing to anybody. Go and show yourself to the priest, and make the offering laid down by Moses for your cleansing; that will certify the
45 cure.' But the man went out and made the whole story public; he spread it far and wide, until Jesus could no longer show himself in any town, but stayed outside in the open country. Even so, people kept coming to him from all quarters.

2 When after some days he returned to Capernaum, the news went round that he was at home;
2 and such a crowd collected that the space in front of the door was not big enough to hold them. And while he was proclaiming the mes-
3 sage to them, a man was brought who was paralysed. Four men
4 were carrying him, but because of the crowd they could not get him near. So they opened up the roof over the place where Jesus was, and when they had broken through they lowered the stretcher on which the paralysed man was
5 lying. When Jesus saw their faith, he said to the paralysed man, 'My son, your sins are forgiven.'

6 Now there were some lawyers sitting there and they thought to
7 themselves, 'Why does the fellow talk like that? This is blasphemy! Who but God alone can forgive
8 sins?' Jesus knew in his own mind that this was what they were thinking, and said to them: 'Why

a Or You have.   *b Some witnesses read* Jesus was sorry for him and stretched out his hand; *one witness has simply* He stretched out his hand.

do you harbour thoughts like 9 these? Is it easier to say to this paralysed man, "Your sins are forgiven", or to say, "Stand up, take 10 your bed, and walk"? But to convince you that the Son of Man has the right on earth to forgive sins' – he turned to the paralysed man – 11 'I say to you, stand up, take your 12 bed, and go home.' And he got up, and at once took his stretcher and went out in full view of them all, so that they were astounded and praised God. 'Never before', they said, 'have we seen the like.'

13   Once more he went away to the lake-side. All the crowd came to 14 him, and he taught them there. As he went along, he saw Levi son of Alphaeus at his seat in the custom-house, and said to him, 'Follow me'; and Levi rose and followed him.

15   When Jesus was at table in his house, many bad characters – tax-gatherers and others – were seated with him and his disciples; for there were many who followed 16 him. Some doctors of the law who were Pharisees noticed him eating in this bad company, and said to his disciples, 'He eats with tax-17 gatherers and sinners!' Jesus heard it and said to them, 'It is not the healthy that need a doctor, but the sick; I did not come to invite virtuous people, but sinners.'

18   Once, when John's disciples and the Pharisees were keeping a fast, some people came to him and said, 'Why is it that John's disciples and the disciples of the Pharisees are 19 fasting, but yours are not?' Jesus said to them, 'Can you expect the bridegroom's friends to fast while the bridegroom is with them? As long as they have the bridegroom with them, there can be no fasting. 20 But the time will come when the bridegroom will be taken away from them, and on that day they will fast.

21   'No one sews a patch of unshrunk cloth on to an old coat; if he does, the patch tears away from it, the new from the old, and leaves a bigger hole. No one puts new wine 22 into old wine-skins; if he does, the wine will burst the skins, and then wine and skins are both lost. Fresh skins for new wine!'

One Sabbath he was going 23 through the cornfields; and his disciples, as they went, began to pluck ears of corn. The Pharisees 24 said to him, 'Look, why are they doing what is forbidden on the Sabbath?' He answered, 'Have 25 you never read what David did when he and his men were hungry and had nothing to eat? He went 26 into the House of God, in the time of Abiathar the High Priest, and ate the sacred bread, though no one but a priest is allowed to eat it, and even gave it to his men.'

He also said to them, 'The Sab-27 bath was made for the sake of man and not man for the Sabbath: therefore the Son of Man is 28 sovereign even over the Sabbath.'

On another occasion when he 3 went to synagogue, there was a man in the congregation who had a withered arm; and they were 2 watching to see whether Jesus would cure him on the Sabbath, so that they could bring a charge against him. He said to the man 3 with the withered arm, 'Come and stand out here.' Then he turned to 4 them: 'Is it permitted to do good or to do evil on the Sabbath, to save life or to kill?' They had nothing to say; and, looking round at them 5 with anger and sorrow at their obstinate stupidity, he said to the man, 'Stretch out your arm.' He stretched it out and his arm was restored. But the Pharisees, on 6 leaving the synagogue, began plotting against him with the partisans of Herod to see how they could make away with him.

JESUS went away to the lake-side 7 with his disciples. Great numbers from Galilee, Judaea and Jerusa-8

lem, Idumaea and Transjordan, and the neighbourhood of Tyre and Sidon, heard what he was
9 doing and came to see him. So he told his disciples to have a boat ready for him, to save him from
10 being crushed by the crowd. For he cured so many that sick people of all kinds came crowding in upon
11 him to touch him. The unclean spirits too, when they saw him, would fall at his feet and cry aloud, 'You are the Son of God';
12 but he insisted that they should not make him known.

13   He then went up into the hill-country and called the men he wanted; and they went and joined
14 him. He appointed twelve as his companions, whom he would send
15 out to proclaim the Gospel, with a
16 commission to drive out devils. So he appointed the Twelve: to Simon
17 he gave the name Peter; then came the sons of Zebedee, James and his brother John, to whom he gave the name Boanerges, Sons of
18 Thunder; then Andrew and Philip and Bartholomew and Matthew and Thomas and James the son of Alphaeus and Thaddaeus and Simon, a member of the Zealot
19 party, and Judas Iscariot, the man who betrayed him.

20   He entered a house; and once more such a crowd collected round them that they had no chance to
21 eat. When his family heard of this, they set out to take charge of him; for people were saying that he was out of his mind.[a]

22   The doctors of the law, too, who had come down from Jerusalem, said, 'He is possessed by Beelzebub', and, 'He drives out devils by
23 the prince of devils.' So he called them to come forward, and spoke to them in parables: 'How can
24 Satan drive out Satan? If a kingdom is divided against itself, that
25 kingdom cannot stand; if a household is divided against itself, that
26 house will never stand; and if

Satan is in rebellion against himself, he is divided and cannot stand; and that is the end of him.

27   'On the other hand, no one can break into a strong man's house and make off with his goods unless he has first tied the strong man up; then he can ransack the house.

28   'I tell you this: no sin, no slander, is beyond forgiveness for men;
29 but whoever slanders the Holy Spirit can never be forgiven; he is
30 guilty of eternal sin.' He said this because they had declared that he was possessed by an unclean spirit.

31   Then his mother and his brothers arrived, and remaining outside sent in a message asking him
32 to come out to them. A crowd was sitting round and word was brought to him: 'Your mother and your brothers are outside asking for
33 you.' He replied, 'Who is my mo-
34 ther? Who are my brothers?' And looking round at those who were sitting in the circle about him he said, 'Here are my mother and my
35 brothers. Whoever does the will of God is my brother, my sister, my mother.'

4   ON another occasion he began to teach by the lake-side. The crowd that gathered round him was so large that he had to get into a boat on the lake, and there he sat, with the whole crowd on the beach right down to the water's edge.
2 And he taught them many things by parables.

3   As he taught he said:
'Listen! A sower went out to
4 sow. And it happened that as he sowed, some seed fell along the footpath; and the birds came and ate it up. Some seed fell on rocky
5 ground, where it had little soil, and it sprouted quickly because it had
6 no depth of earth; but when the sun rose the young corn was scorched, and as it had no root it withered
7 away. Some seed fell among thistles; and the thistles shot up

---

[a] Or of him. 'He is out of his mind', they said.

and choked the corn, and it yielded
8 no crop. And some of the seed fell into good soil, where it came up and grew, and bore fruit; and the yield was thirtyfold, sixtyfold,
9 even a hundredfold.' He added, 'If you have ears to hear, then hear.'
10 When he was alone, the Twelve and others who were round him questioned him about the par-
11 ables. He replied, 'To you the secret of the kingdom of God has been given; but to those who are outside everything comes by way
12 of parables, so that (as Scripture says) they may look and look, but see nothing; they may hear and hear, but understand nothing; otherwise they might turn to God and be forgiven.'
13 So he said, 'You do not understand this parable? How then are you to understand any parable?
14, 15 The sower sows the word. Those along the footpath are people in whom the word is sown, but no sooner have they heard it than Satan comes and carries off the word which has been sown in them.
16 It is the same with those who receive the seed on rocky ground; as soon as they hear the word, they
17 accept it with joy, but it strikes no root in them; they have no staying-power; then, when there is trouble or persecution on account of the word, they fall away at once.
18 Others again receive the seed a-mong thistles; they hear the word,
19 but worldly cares and the false glamour of wealth and all kinds of evil desire come in and choke the
20 word, and it proves barren. And there are those who receive the seed in good soil; they hear the word and welcome it; and they bear fruit thirtyfold, sixtyfold, or a hundredfold.'
21 He said to them, 'Do you bring in the lamp to put it under the meal-tub, or under the bed? Surely it is brought to be set on the lamp-
22 stand. For nothing is hidden unless it is to be disclosed, and nothing

put under cover unless it is to come into the open. If you have ears to 23 hear, then hear.'
He also said, 'Take note of what 24 you hear; the measure you give is the measure you will receive, with something more besides. For the 25 man who has will be given more, and the man who has not will forfeit even what he has.'
He said, 'The kingdom of God is 26 like this. A man scatters seed on the land; he goes to bed at night 27 and gets up in the morning, and the seed sprouts and grows – how, he does not know. The ground pro- 28 duces a crop by itself, first the blade, then the ear, then full-grown corn in the ear; but as soon 29 as the crop is ripe, he plies the sickle, because harvest-time has come.'
He said also, 'How shall we pic- 30 ture the kingdom of God, or by what parable shall we describe it? It is like the mustard-seed, which 31 is smaller than any seed in the ground at its sowing. But once 32 sown, it springs up and grows taller than any other plant, and forms branches so large that the birds can settle in its shade.'
With many such parables he 33 would give them his message, so far as they were able to receive it. He never spoke to them except in 34 parables; but privately to his disciples he explained everything.

Miracles of Christ

THAT day, in the evening, he said 35 to them, 'Let us cross over to the other side of the lake.' So they left 36 the crowd and took him with them in the boat where he had been sitting; and there were other boats accompanying him. A heavy squall 37 came on and the waves broke over the boat until it was all but swamped. Now he was in the stern 38 asleep on a cushion; they roused him and said, 'Master, we are sinking! Do you not care?' He awoke, 39 rebuked the wind, and said to the sea, 'Hush! Be still!' The wind dropped and there was a dead 40 calm. He said to them, 'Why are you such cowards? Have you no 41 faith even now?' They were awe-struck and said to one another, 'Who can this be? Even the wind and the sea obey him.'

5 So they came to the other side of the lake, into the country of the 2 Gerasenes. As he stepped ashore, a man possessed by an unclean spirit came up to him from among the 3 tombs where he had his dwelling. He could no longer be controlled; 4 even chains were useless; he had often been fettered and chained up, but he had snapped his chains and broken the fetters. No one was 5 strong enough to master him. And so, unceasingly, night and day, he would cry aloud among the tombs and on the hill-sides and cut him-6 self with stones. When he saw Jesus in the distance, he ran and flung himself down before him, 7 shouting loudly, 'What do you want with me, Jesus, son of the Most High God? In God's name do 8 not torment me.' (For Jesus was already saying to him, 'Out, un-clean spirit, come out of this man!') 9 Jesus asked him, 'What is your name?' 'My name is Legion,' he said, 'there are so many of us.' 10 And he begged so hard that Jesus would not send them out of the country. 11 Now there happened to be a large herd of pigs feeding on the 12 hill-side, and the spirits begged him, 'Send us among the pigs and 13 let us go into them.' He gave them leave; and the unclean spirits came out and went into the pigs; and the herd, of about two thou-sand, rushed over the edge into the lake and were drowned. 14 The men in charge of them took to their heels and carried the news to the town and country-side; and the people came out to see what

had happened. They came to Jesus 15 and saw the madman who had been possessed by the legion of devils, sitting there clothed and in his right mind; and they were afraid. The spectators told them 16 how the madman had been cured and what had happened to the pigs. Then they begged Jesus to 17 leave the district.

As he was stepping into the boat, 18 the man who had been possessed begged to go with him. Jesus 19 would not allow it, but said to him, 'Go home to your own folk and tell them what the Lord in his mercy has done for you.' The man went 20 off and spread the news in the Ten Towns[a] of all that Jesus had done for him; and they were all amazed.

As soon as Jesus had returned by 21 boat to the other shore, a great crowd once more gathered round him. While he was by the lake-side, the president of one of the 22 synagogues came up, Jairus by name, and, when he saw him, threw himself down at his feet and 23 pleaded with him. 'My little daugh-ter', he said, 'is at death's door. I beg you to come and lay your hands on her to cure her and save her life.' So Jesus went with him, 24 accompanied by a great crowd which pressed upon him.

Among them was a woman who 25 had suffered from haemorrhages for twelve years; and in spite of 26 long treatment by many doctors, on which she had spent all she had, there had been no improvement; on the contrary, she had grown worse. She had heard what people 27 were saying about Jesus, so she came up from behind in the crowd and touched his cloak; for she said 28 to herself, 'If I touch even his clothes, I shall be cured.' And 29 there and then the source of her haemorrhages dried up and she knew in herself that she was cured of her trouble. At the same time 30 Jesus, aware that power had gone

[a] Greek Decapolis.

44

out of him, turned round in the crowd and asked, 'Who touched
31 my clothes?' His disciples said to him, 'You see the crowd pressing upon you and yet you ask, "Who
32 touched me?"' Meanwhile he was looking round to see who had done
33 it. And the woman, trembling with fear when she grasped what had happened to her, came and fell at his feet and told him the
34 whole truth. He said to her, 'My daughter, your faith has cured you. Go in peace, free for ever from this trouble.'

35 While he was still speaking, a message came from the president's house, 'Your daughter is dead; why trouble the Rabbi further?'
36 But Jesus, overhearing the message as it was delivered, said to the president of the synagogue, 'Do not be afraid; only have faith.'
37 After this he allowed no one to accompany him except Peter and James and James's brother John.
38 They came to the president's house, where he found a great commotion, with loud crying and wail-
39 ing. So he went in and said to them, 'Why this crying and commotion? The child is not dead: she
40 is asleep'; and they only laughed at him. But after turning all the others out, he took the child's father and mother and his own companions and went in where the
41 child was lying. Then, taking hold of her hand, he said to her, '*Talitha cum*', which means, 'Get up, my
42 child.' Immediately the girl got up and walked about – she was twelve years old. At that they were beside
43 themselves with amazement. He gave them strict orders to let no one hear about it, and told them to give her something to eat.

6 He left that place and went to his home town accompanied by his
2 disciples. When the Sabbath came he began to teach in the synagogue; and the large congregation who heard him were amazed and said, 'Where does he get it from?', and, 'What wisdom is this that has been given him?', and, 'How does
3 he work such miracles? Is not this the carpenter, the son of Mary,[a] the brother of James and Joseph and Judas and Simon? And are not his sisters here with us?' So they fell foul of him. Jesus said to them,
4 'A prophet will always be held in honour except in his home town, and among his kinsmen and fami-
5 ly.' He could work no miracle there, except that he put his hands on a few sick people and healed
6 them; and he was taken aback by their want of faith.

ON one of his teaching journeys round the villages he summoned
7 the Twelve and sent them out in pairs on a mission. He gave them authority over unclean spirits, and
8 instructed them to take nothing for the journey beyond a stick: no bread, no pack, no money in their belts. They might wear sandals,
9 but not a second coat. 'When you
10 are admitted to a house', he added, 'stay there until you leave those parts. At any place where
11 they will not receive you or listen to you, shake the dust off your feet as you leave, as a warning to them.' So they set out and called
12 publicly for repentance. They
13 drove out many devils, and many sick people they anointed with oil and cured.

Now King Herod heard of it, for
14 the fame of Jesus had spread; and people were saying,[b] 'John the Baptist has been raised to life, and that is why these miraculous powers are at work in him.' Others
15 said, 'It is Elijah.' Others again, 'He is a prophet like one of the old prophets.' But Herod, when he
16 heard of it, said, 'This is John, whom I beheaded, raised from the dead.'

---

[a] *Some witnesses read* Is not this the son of the carpenter and Mary...
[b] *Some witnesses read* and he said...

17 For this same Herod had sent and arrested John and put him in prison on account of his brother Philip's wife, Herodias, whom he 18 had married. John had told Herod, 'You have no right to your brother's wife.' 19 Thus Herodias nursed a grudge against him and would willingly have killed him, but she 20 could not; for Herod went in awe of John, knowing him to be a good and holy man; so he kept him in custody. He liked to listen to him, although the listening left him greatly perplexed.

21 Herodias found her opportunity when Herod on his birthday gave a banquet to his chief officials and commanders and the leading men 22 of Galilee. Her daughter came in[a] and danced, and so delighted Herod and his guests that the king said to the girl, 'Ask what you like 23 and I will give it you.' And he swore an oath to her: 'Whatever you ask I will give you, up to half 24 my kingdom.' She went out and said to her mother, 'What shall I ask for?' She replied, 'The head of 25 John the Baptist.' The girl hastened back at once to the king with her request: 'I want you to give me here and now, on a dish, the head 26 of John the Baptist.' The king was greatly distressed, but out of regard for his oath and for his guests he could not bring himself to refuse 27 her. So the king sent a soldier of the guard with orders to bring John's head. The soldier went off and be- 28 headed him in the prison, brought the head on a dish, and gave it to the girl; and she gave it to her mother.

29 When John's disciples heard the news, they came and took his body away and laid it in a tomb.

30 The apostles now rejoined Jesus and reported to him all that they 31 had done and taught. He said to them, 'Come with me, by yourselves, to some lonely place where you can rest quietly.' (For they had no leisure even to eat, so many were coming and going.) Accord- 32 ingly, they set off privately by boat for a lonely place. But many saw 33 them leave and recognized them, and came round by land, hurrying from all the towns towards the place, and arrived there first. When 34 he came ashore, he saw a great crowd; and his heart went out to them, because they were like sheep without a shepherd; and he had much to teach them. As the day 35 wore on, his disciples came up to him and said, 'This is a lonely place and it is getting very late; send the people off to the farms 36 and villages round about, to buy themselves something to eat.' 'Give 37 them something to eat yourselves', he answered. They replied, 'Are we to go and spend twenty pounds[b] on bread to give them a meal?' 'How many loaves have you?' he 38 asked; 'go and see.' They found out and told him, 'Five, and two fishes also.' He ordered them to 39 make the people sit down in groups on the green grass, and they sat 40 down in rows, a hundred rows of fifty each. Then, taking the five 41 loaves and the two fishes, he looked up to heaven, said the blessing, broke the loaves, and gave them to the disciples to distribute. He also divided the two fishes among them. They all ate to their hearts' 42 content; and twelve great basket- 43 fuls of scraps were picked up, with what was left of the fish. Those 44 who ate the loaves numbered five thousand men.

As soon as it was over he made 45 his disciples embark and cross to Bethsaida ahead of him, while he himself sent the people away. After 46 taking leave of them, he went up the hill-side to pray. It grew late 47 and the boat was already well out on the water, while he was alone on the land. Somewhere between 48

---

[a] *Or* A festive occasion came when Herod on his birthday gave...of Galilee. The daughter of Herodias came in...   [b] *Literally* 200 denarii.

three and six in the morning, seeing them labouring at the oars against a head-wind, he came towards them, walking on the lake. He was 49 going to pass them by; but when they saw him walking on the lake, they thought it was a ghost and 50 cried out; for they all saw him and were terrified. But at once he spoke to them: 'Take heart! It is I; do 51 not be afraid.' Then he climbed into the boat beside them, and the wind dropped. At this they were 52 completely dumbfounded, for they had not understood the incident of the loaves; their minds were closed.

53   So they finished the crossing and came to land at Gennesaret, 54 where they made fast. When they came ashore, he was immediately 55 recognized; and the people scoured that whole country-side and brought the sick on stretchers to any place where he was reported 56 to be. Wherever he went, to farmsteads, villages, or towns, they laid out the sick in the marketplaces and begged him to let them simply touch the edge of his cloak; and all who touched him were cured.

Growing tension

7 A GROUP of Pharisees, with some doctors of the law who had come 2 from Jerusalem, met him and noticed that some of his disciples were eating their food with 'defiled' hands – in other words, without 3 washing them. (For the Pharisees and the Jews in general never eat without washing the hands,[a] in obedience to an old-established 4 tradition; and on coming from the market-place they never eat without first washing. And there are many other points on which they have a traditional rule to maintain, for example, washing of cups and jugs and copper bowls.) According- 5 ly, these Pharisees and the lawyers asked him, 'Why do your disciples not conform to the ancient tradition, but eat their food with defiled hands?' He answered, 'Isaiah 6 was right when he prophesied about you hypocrites in these words: "This people pays me lip-service, but their heart is far from me: their worship of me is in vain, 7 for they teach as doctrines the commandments of men." You neg- 8 lect the commandment of God, in order to maintain the tradition of men.'

He also said to them, 'How well 9 you set aside the commandment of God in order to maintain[b] your tradition! Moses said, "Honour 10 your father and your mother", and, "The man who curses his father or mother must suffer death." But you 11 hold that if a man says to his father or mother, "Anything of mine which might have been used for your benefit is Corban"' (meaning, set apart for God), 'he is no longer 12 permitted to do anything for his father or mother. Thus by your 13 own tradition, handed down among you, you make God's word null and void. And many other things that you do are just like that.'

On another occasion he called 14 the people and said to them, 'Listen to me, all of you, and understand this: nothing that goes 15 into a man from outside can defile him; no, it is the things that come out of him that defile a man.'[c]

When he had left the people and 17 gone indoors, his disciples questioned him about the parable. He said 18 to them, 'Are you as dull as the rest? Do you not see that nothing that goes from outside into a man can defile him, because it does not 19 enter into his heart but into his

---

[a] *Some witnesses insert* with the fist; *others insert* frequently, *or* thoroughly.
[b] *Some witnesses read* establish.
[c] *Some witnesses here add* (16) If you have ears to hear, then hear.

20 stomach, and so passes out into the drain?' Thus he declared all foods clean. He went on, 'It is what comes out of a man that defiles

21 him. For from inside, out of a man's heart, come evil thoughts, acts of

22 fornication, of theft, murder, adultery, ruthless greed, and malice; fraud, indecency, envy, slander,

23 arrogance, and folly; these evil things all come from inside, and they defile the man.'

24 Then he left that place and went away into the territory of Tyre. He found a house to stay in, and he would have liked to remain unrecognized, but this was impossible.

25 Almost at once a woman whose young daughter was possessed by an unclean spirit heard of him,

26 came in, and fell at his feet. (She was a Gentile, a Phoenician of Syria by nationality.) She begged him to drive the spirit out of her

27 daughter. He said to her, 'Let the children be satisfied first; it is not fair to take the children's bread

28 and throw it to the dogs.' 'Sir,' she answered, 'even the dogs under the table eat the children's scraps.'

29 He said to her, 'For saying that, you may go home content; the unclean spirit has gone out of your

30 daughter.' And when she returned home, she found the child lying in bed; the spirit had left her.

31 On his return journey from Tyrian territory he went by way of Sidon to the Sea of Galilee through the territory of the Ten Towns.[a]

32 They brought to him a man who was deaf and had an impediment in his speech, with the request that

33 he would lay his hand on him. He took the man aside, away from the crowd, put his fingers into his ears,

34 spat, and touched his tongue. Then, looking up to heaven, he sighed, and said to him, '*Ephphatha*',

35 which means 'Be opened.' With that his ears were opened, and at the same time the impediment was removed and he spoke plainly.

36 Jesus forbade them to tell anyone; but the more he forbade them, the

37 more they published it. Their astonishment knew no bounds: 'All that he does, he does well,' they said; 'he even makes the deaf hear and the dumb speak.'

8 THERE was another occasion about this time when a huge crowd had collected, and, as they had no food, Jesus called his disciples and

2 said to them, 'I feel sorry for all these people; they have been with me now for three days and have no-

3 thing to eat. If I send them home unfed, they will turn faint on the way; some of them have come from

4 a distance.' The disciples answered, 'How can anyone provide all these people with bread in this lonely

5 place?' 'How many loaves have you?' he asked; and they answered,

6 'Seven.' So he ordered the people to sit down on the ground; then he took the seven loaves, and, after giving thanks to God, he broke the bread and gave it to his disciples to distribute; and they served it

7 out to the people. They had also a few small fishes, which he blessed and ordered them to distribute.

8 They all ate to their hearts' content, and seven baskets were filled

9 with the scraps that were left. The people numbered about four thousand. Then he dismissed them;

10 and, without delay, got into the boat with his disciples and went to the district of Dalmanutha.[b]

11 Then the Pharisees came out and engaged him in discussion. To test him they asked him for a sign

12 from heaven. He sighed deeply to himself and said, 'Why does this generation ask for a sign? I tell you this: no sign shall be given to this

13 generation.' With that he left them, re-embarked, and went off to the other side of the lake.

14 Now they had forgotten to take bread with them; they had no more

15 than one loaf in the boat. He began

[a] Greek Decapolis.   [b] Some witnesses give Magedan; others give Magdala.

to warn them: 'Beware,' he said, 'be on your guard against the leaven of the Pharisees and the 16 leaven of Herod.' They said among themselves, 'It is because we have 17 no bread.' Knowing what was in their minds, he asked them, 'Why do you talk about having no bread? Have you no inkling yet? Do you still not understand? Are your 18 minds closed? You have eyes: can you not see? You have ears: can you not hear? Have you forgotten? 19 When I broke the five loaves among five thousand, how many basketfuls of scraps did you pick up?' 20 'Twelve', they said. 'And how many when I broke the seven loaves among four thousand?' They 21 answered, 'Seven.' He said, 'Do you still not understand?'

22   They arrived at Bethsaida. There the people brought a blind man to Jesus and begged him to touch 23 him. He took the blind man by the hand and led him away out of the village. Then he spat on his eyes, laid his hands upon him, and asked whether he could see anything. 24 The man's sight began to come back, and he said, 'I see men; they look like trees, but they are walk-25 ing about.' Jesus laid his hands on his eyes again; he looked hard, and now he was cured so that he 26 saw everything clearly. Then Jesus sent him home, saying, 'Do not tell anyone in the village.'*a*

27 JESUS and his disciples set out for the villages of Caesarea Philippi. On the way he asked his disciples, 28 'Who do men say I am?' They answered, 'Some say John the Baptist, others Elijah, others one 29 of the prophets.' 'And you,' he asked, 'who do you say I am?' Peter replied: 'You are the Messiah.' 30 Then he gave them strict orders 31 not to tell anyone about him; and he began to teach them that the Son of Man had to undergo great

sufferings, and to be rejected by the elders, chief priests, and doctors of the law; to be put to death, and to rise again three days afterwards. He spoke about it plainly. 32 At this Peter took him by the arm and began to rebuke him. But 33 Jesus turned round, and, looking at his disciples, rebuked Peter. 'Away with you, Satan,' he said; 'you think as men think, not as God thinks.'

Then he called the people to him, 34 as well as his disciples, and said to them, 'Anyone who wishes to be a follower of mine must leave self behind; he must take up his cross, and come with me. Whoever cares 35 for his own safety is lost; but if a man will let himself be lost for my sake and for the Gospel, that man is safe. What does a man gain by 36 winning the whole world at the cost of his true self? What can he 37 give to buy that self back? If any-38 one is ashamed of me and mine*b* in this wicked and godless age, the Son of Man will be ashamed of him, when he comes in the glory of his Father and of the holy angels.'*c*

He also said, 'I tell you this: 9 there are some of those standing here who will not taste death before they have seen the kingdom of God already come in power.'

Six days later Jesus took Peter, 2 James, and John with him and led them up a high mountain where they were alone; and in their presence he was transfigured; his 3 clothes became dazzling white, with a whiteness no bleacher on earth could equal. They saw Elijah 4 appear, and Moses with him, and there they were, conversing with Jesus. Then Peter spoke: 'Rabbi,' 5 he said, 'how good it is that we are here! Shall we make three shelters, one for you, one for Moses, and one for Elijah?' (For he did not 6 know what to say; they were so terrified.) Then a cloud appeared, 7

---

a Some witnesses read Do not go into the village.   *b* Some witnesses read me and my words.   *c* Some witnesses read Father with the holy angels.

casting its shadow over them, and out of the cloud came a voice: 'This is my Son, my Beloved;[a] listen to

8 him.' And now suddenly, when they looked around, there was nobody to be seen but Jesus alone with themselves.

9 On their way down the mountain, he enjoined them not to tell anyone what they had seen until the Son of Man had risen from the dead.

10 They seized upon those words, and discussed among themselves what this 'rising from the dead' could

11 mean. And they put a question to him: 'Why do our teachers say that

12 Elijah must come first?' He replied, 'Yes, Elijah does come first to set everything right. Yet how is it[b] that the scriptures say of the Son of Man that he is to endure great sufferings and to be treated

13 with contempt? However, I tell you, Elijah has already come, and they have worked their will upon him, as the scriptures say of him.'

14 When they came back to the disciples they saw a large crowd surrounding them and lawyers

15 arguing with them. As soon as they saw Jesus the whole crowd were overcome with awe, and they ran

16 forward to welcome him. He asked them, 'What is this argument

17 about?' A man in the crowd spoke up: 'Master, I brought my son to you. He is possessed by a spirit which makes him speechless.

18 Whenever it attacks him, it dashes him to the ground, and he foams at the mouth, grinds his teeth, and goes rigid. I asked your disciples to cast it out, but they failed.'

19 Jesus answered: 'What an unbelieving and perverse generation! How long shall I be with you? How long must I endure you? Bring him

20 to me.' So they brought the boy to him; and as soon as the spirit saw him it threw the boy into convulsions, and he fell on the ground and rolled about foaming at the mouth. Jesus asked his father, 21 'How long has he been like this?'

22 'From childhood,' he replied; 'often it has tried to make an end of him by throwing him into the fire or into water. But if it is at all possible for you, take pity upon us and help us.' 'If it is possible!' said 23 Jesus. 'Everything is possible to one who has faith.' 'I have faith,' 24 cried the boy's father; 'help me where faith falls short.' Jesus saw 25 then that the crowd was closing in upon them, so he rebuked the unclean spirit. 'Deaf and dumb spirit,' he said, 'I command you, come out of him and never go back!' After crying aloud and 26 racking him fiercely, it came out; and the boy looked like a corpse; in fact, many said, 'He is dead.' But Jesus took his hand and raised 27 him to his feet, and he stood up.

28 Then Jesus went indoors, and his disciples asked him privately, 'Why could not we cast it out?' He said, 'There is no means of 29 casting out this sort but prayer.'[c]

30 THEY now left that district and made a journey through Galilee. Jesus wished it to be kept secret; for he was teaching his disciples, 31 and telling them, 'The Son of Man is now to be given up into the power of men, and they will kill him, and three days after being killed, he will rise again.' But they 32 did not understand what he said, and were afraid to ask.

33 So they came to Capernaum; and when he was indoors, he asked them, 'What were you arguing about on the way?' They were 34 silent, because on the way they had been discussing who was the greatest. He sat down, called the 35 Twelve, and said to them, 'If anyone wants to be first, he must make himself last of all and servant of all.' Then he took a child, set him 36 in front of them, and put his arm

---

[a] Or This is my only Son.   [b] Or Elijah, you say, comes first to set everything right: then how is it...

[c] Some witnesses add and fasting.

37 round him. 'Whoever receives one of these children in my name', he said, 'receives me; and whoever receives me, receives not me but the One who sent me.'

38 John said to him, 'Master, we saw a man driving out devils in your name, and as he was not one 39 of us, we tried to stop him.' Jesus said, 'Do not stop him; no one who does a work of divine power in my name will be able the next moment 40 to speak evil of me. For he who is 41 not against us is on our side. I tell you this: if anyone gives you a cup of water to drink because you are followers of the Messiah, that man assuredly will not go unrewarded.

42 'As for the man who is a cause of stumbling to one of these little ones who have faith, it would be better for him to be thrown into the sea with a millstone round his 43 neck. If your hand is your undoing, cut it off; it is better for you to enter into life maimed than to keep both hands and go to hell and the 45 unquenchable fire.[a] And if your foot is your undoing, cut it off; it is better to enter into life a cripple than to keep both your feet and 47 be thrown into hell.[b] And if it is your eye, tear it out; it is better to enter into the kingdom of God with one eye than to keep both 48 eyes and be thrown into hell, where the devouring worm never dies and the fire is not quenched.

49 'For everyone will be salted with fire.

50 'Salt is a good thing; but if the salt loses its saltness, what will you season it with?

'Have salt in yourselves; and be[c] at peace with one another.'

10 ON leaving those parts he came into the regions of Judaea and Transjordan; and when a crowd gathered round him once again, he followed his usual practice and taught them. The question was 2 put to him:[d] 'Is it lawful for a man to divorce his wife?' This was to test him. He asked in return, 'What 3 did Moses command you?' They 4 answered, 'Moses permitted a man to divorce his wife by note of dismissal.' Jesus said to them, 'It 5 was because your minds were closed that he made this rule for you; but in the beginning, at 6 the creation, God made them male and female. For this reason 7 a man shall leave his father and mother, and be made one with his wife;[e] and the two shall become 8 one flesh. It follows that they are no longer two individuals: they are one flesh. What God has 9 joined together, man must not separate.'

When they were indoors again 10 the disciples questioned him about this matter; he said to them, 'Who- 11 ever divorces his wife and marries another commits adultery against her: so too, if she divorces her 12 husband and marries another, she commits adultery.'

They brought children for him 13 to touch. The disciples rebuked them, but when Jesus saw this he 14 was indignant, and said to them, 'Let the children come to me; do not try to stop them; for the kingdom of God belongs to such as these. I tell you, whoever does not 15 accept the kingdom of God like a child will never enter it.' And he 16 put his arms round them, laid his hands upon them, and blessed them.

As he was starting out on a 17 journey, a stranger ran up, and, kneeling before him, asked, 'Good

---

[a] *Some witnesses add* (44) *where the devouring worm never dies and the fire is not quenched.*　　[b] *Some witnesses add* (46) *where the devouring worm never dies and the fire is not quenched.*　　[c] *Or* Have the salt of fellowship and be. . . ; *or* You have the salt of fellowship between you; then be. . .　　[d] *Some witnesses read* The Pharisees came forward and asked him the question. . .
[e] *Some witnesses omit* and be made. . . wife.

Master, what must I do to win eternal life?' Jesus said to him, 'Why do you call me good? No one is good except God alone. You know the commandments: "Do not murder; do not commit adultery; do not steal; do not give false evidence; do not defraud; honour your father and mother."' 'But, Master,' he replied, 'I have kept all these since I was a boy.' Jesus looked straight at him; his heart warmed to him, and he said, 'One thing you lack: go, sell everything you have, and give to the poor, and you will have riches in heaven; and come, follow me.' At these words his face fell and he went away with a heavy heart; for he was a man of great wealth.

Jesus looked round at his disciples and said to them, 'How hard it will be for the wealthy to enter the kingdom of God!' They were amazed that he should say this, but Jesus insisted, 'Children, how hard it is[a] to enter the kingdom of God! It is easier for a camel to pass through the eye of a needle than for a rich man to enter the kingdom of God.' They were more astonished than ever, and said to one another, 'Then who can be saved?' Jesus looked at them and said, 'For men it is impossible, but not for God; everything is possible for God.'

At this Peter spoke. 'We here', he said, 'have left everything to become your followers.' Jesus said, 'I tell you this: there is no one who has given up home, brothers or sisters, mother, father or children, or land, for my sake and for the Gospel, who will not receive in this age a hundred times as much — houses, brothers and sisters, mothers and children, and land — and persecutions besides; and in the age to come eternal life. But many who are first will be last and the last first.'

Challenge to Jerusalem

THEY were on the road, going up to Jerusalem, Jesus leading the way; and the disciples were filled with awe, while those who followed behind were afraid. He took the Twelve aside and began to tell them what was to happen to him. 'We are now going to Jerusalem,' he said; 'and the Son of Man will be given up to the chief priests and the doctors of the law; they will condemn him to death and hand him over to the foreign power. He will be mocked and spat upon, flogged and killed; and three days afterwards, he will rise again.'

James and John, the sons of Zebedee, approached him and said, 'Master, we should like you to do us a favour.' 'What is it you want me to do?' he asked. They answered, 'Grant us the right to sit in state with you, one at your right and the other at your left.' Jesus said to them, 'You do not understand what you are asking. Can you drink the cup that I drink, or be baptized with the baptism I am baptized with?' 'We can', they answered. Jesus said, 'The cup that I drink you shall drink, and the baptism I am baptized with shall be your baptism; but to sit at my right or left is not for me to grant; it is for those to whom it has already been assigned.'[b]

When the other ten heard this, they were indignant with James and John. Jesus called them to him and said, 'You know that in the world the recognized rulers lord it over their subjects, and their great men make them feel the weight of authority. That is not the way with you; among you, whoever wants to be great must be your servant, and whoever wants to be first must be the willing slave of all. For even the Son of Man did not come to be served

---

[a] *Some witnesses insert* for those who trust in riches.
[b] *Some witnesses add* by my Father.

but to serve, and to give up his life as a ransom for many.'

46 They came to Jericho; and as he was leaving the town, with his disciples and a large crowd, Bartimaeus son of Timaeus, a blind beggar, was seated at the roadside.

47 Hearing that it was Jesus of Nazareth, he began to shout, 'Son of David, Jesus, have pity on me!'

48 Many of the people told him to hold his tongue; but he shouted all the more, 'Son of David, have

49 pity on me.' Jesus stopped and said, 'Call him'; so they called the blind man and said, 'Take heart;

50 stand up; he is calling you.' At that he threw off his cloak, sprang up,

51 and came to Jesus. Jesus said to him, 'What do you want me to do for you?' 'Master,' the blind man answered, 'I want my sight

52 back.' Jesus said to him, 'Go; your faith has cured you.' And at once he recovered his sight and followed him on the road.

11 THEY were now approaching Jerusalem, and when they reached Bethphage and Bethany, at the Mount of Olives, he sent two of his

2 disciples with these instructions: 'Go to the village opposite, and, just as you enter, you will find tethered there a colt which no one has yet ridden. Untie it and bring

3 it here. If anyone asks, "Why are you doing that?", say, "Our Master[a] needs it, and will send it back

4 here without delay."' So they went off, and found the colt tethered at a door outside in the street. They

5 were untying it when some of the bystanders asked, 'What are you

6 doing, untying that colt?' They answered as Jesus had told them, and were then allowed to take it.

7 So they brought the colt to Jesus and spread their cloaks on it, and

8 he mounted. And people carpeted the road with their cloaks, while others spread brushwood which

9 they had cut in the fields; and those

who went ahead and the others who came behind shouted, 'Hosanna! Blessings on him who comes in the name of the Lord! Blessings 10 on the coming kingdom of our father David! Hosanna in the heavens!'

He entered Jerusalem and went 11 into the temple, where he looked at the whole scene; but, as it was now late, he went out to Bethany with the Twelve.

On the following day, after they 12 had left Bethany, he felt hungry, and, noticing in the distance a fig- 13 tree in leaf, he went to see if he could find anything on it. But when he came there he found nothing but leaves; for it was not the season for figs. He said to the 14 tree, 'May no one ever again eat fruit from you!' And his disciples were listening.

So they came to Jerusalem, and 15 he went into the temple and began driving out those who bought and sold in the temple. He upset the tables of the money-changers and the seats of the dealers in pigeons; and he would not allow anyone to 16 use the temple court as a thorough-fare for carrying goods. Then he 17 began to teach them, and said, 'Does not Scripture say, "My house shall be called a house of prayer for all the nations"? But you have made it a robbers' cave.' The chief 18 priests and the doctors of the law heard of this and sought some means of making away with him; for they were afraid of him, because the whole crowd was spellbound by his teaching. And when 19 evening came he went out of the city.

Early next morning, as they 20 passed by, they saw that the fig-tree had withered from the roots up; and Peter, recalling what had 21 happened, said to him, 'Rabbi, look, the fig-tree which you cursed has withered.' Jesus answered 22 them, 'Have faith in God. I tell 23

a Or Its owner.

you this: if anyone says to this mountain, "Be lifted from your place and hurled into the sea", and has no inward doubts, but believes that what he says is happening, it 24 will be done for him. I tell you, then, whatever you ask for in prayer, believe that you have received it and it will be yours.

25   'And when you stand praying, if you have a grievance against anyone, forgive him, so that your Father in heaven may forgive you the wrongs you have done.'*a*

27 THEY came once more to Jerusalem. And as he was walking in the temple court the chief priests, law-28 yers, and elders came to him and said, 'By what authority are you acting like this? Who gave you 29 authority to act in this way?' Jesus said to them, 'I have a question to ask you too; and if you give me an answer, I will tell you by what 30 authority I act. The baptism of John: was it from God, or from 31 men? Answer me.' This set them arguing among themselves: 'What shall we say? If we say, "from God", he will say, "Then why did 32 you not believe him?" Shall we say, "from men"?' – but they were afraid of the people, for all held that John was in fact a prophet. 33 So they answered, 'We do not know.' And Jesus said to them, 'Then neither will I tell you by what authority I act.'

12   He went on to speak to them in parables: 'A man planted a vineyard and put a wall round it, hewed out a winepress, and built a watch-tower; then he let it out to vine-growers and went abroad. 2 When the season came, he sent a servant to the tenants to collect from them his share of the produce. 3 But they took him, thrashed him, and sent him away empty-handed. 4 Again, he sent them another servant, whom they beat about the head and treated outrageously. So 5 he sent another, and that one they killed; and many more besides, of whom they beat some, and killed others. He had now only one left 6 to send, his own dear son.*b* In the end he sent him. "They will respect my son", he said. But the tenants 7 said to one another, "This is the heir; come on, let us kill him, and the property will be ours." So they 8 seized him and killed him, and flung his body out of the vineyard. What will the owner of the vine- 9 yard do? He will come and put the tenants to death and give the vineyard to others.

'Can it be that you have never 10 read this text: "The stone which the builders rejected has become the main corner-stone. This is the 11 Lord's doing, and it is wonderful in our eyes"?'

Then they began to look for a 12 way to arrest him, for they saw that the parable was aimed at them; but they were afraid of the people, so they left him alone and went away.

A NUMBER of Pharisees and men 13 of Herod's party were sent to trap him with a question. They came 14 and said, 'Master, you are an honest man, we know, and truckle to no one, whoever he may be; you teach in all honesty the way of life that God requires. Are we or are we not permitted to pay taxes to the Roman Emperor? Shall we pay or not?' He saw how 15 crafty their question was, and said, 'Why are you trying to catch me out? Fetch me a silver piece, and let me look at it.' They brought 16 one, and he said to them, 'Whose head is this, and whose inscription?' 'Caesar's', they replied. Then Jesus 17 said, 'Pay Caesar what is due to Caesar, and pay God what is due to God.' And they heard him with astonishment.

a Some witnesses add (26) But if you do not forgive others, then the wrongs you have done will not be forgiven by your Father in heaven.   *b Or his only son.*

18 Next Sadducees came to him. (It is they who say that there is no resurrection.) Their question 19 was this: 'Master, Moses laid it down for us that if there are brothers, and one dies leaving a wife but no child, then the next should marry the widow and carry on his 20 brother's family. Now there were seven brothers. The first took a 21 wife and died without issue. Then the second married her, and he too died without issue. So did the third. 22 Eventually the seven of them died, all without issue. Finally the wo- 23 man died. At the resurrection, when they come back to life, whose wife will she be, since all seven had 24 married her?' Jesus said to them, 'You are mistaken, and surely this is the reason: you do not know either the scriptures or the power of 25 God. When they rise from the dead, men and women do not marry; they are like angels in heaven.

26 'But about the resurrection of the dead, have you never read in the Book of Moses, in the story of the burning bush, how God spoke to him and said, "I am the God of Abraham, the God of Isaac, and 27 the God of Jacob"? God is not God of the dead but of the living. You are greatly mistaken.'

28 Then one of the lawyers, who had been listening to these discussions and had noted how well he answered, came forward and asked him, 'Which commandment 29 is first of all?' Jesus answered, 'The first is, "Hear, O Israel: the Lord 30 our God is the only Lord; love the Lord your God with all your heart, with all your soul, with all your mind, and with all your strength." 31 The second is this: "Love your neighbour as yourself." There is no other commandment greater 32 than these.' The lawyer said to him, 'Well said, Master. You are right in saying that God is one

and beside him there is no other. And to love him with all your 33 heart, all your understanding, and all your strength, and to love your neighbour as yourself – that is far more than any burnt offerings or sacrifices.' When Jesus saw how 34 sensibly he answered, he said to him, 'You are not far from the kingdom of God.'

After that nobody ventured to put any more questions to him; and Jesus went on to say, as he 35 taught in the temple, 'How can the teachers of the law maintain that the Messiah is "Son of David"? David himself said, when inspired 36 by the Holy Spirit, "The Lord said to my Lord, 'Sit at my right hand until I put your enemies under your feet.'" David himself calls 37 him "Lord"; how can he also be David's son?'

There was a great crowd and they listened eagerly.[a] He said as 38 he taught them, 'Beware of the doctors of the law, who love to walk up and down in long robes, receiving respectful greetings in the street; and to have the chief 39 seats in synagogues, and places of honour at feasts. These are the men 40 who eat up the property of widows, while they say long prayers for appearance' sake, and they will receive the severest sentence.'[b]

Once he was standing opposite 41 the temple treasury, watching as people dropped their money into the chest. Many rich people were giving large sums. Presently there 42 came a poor widow who dropped in two tiny coins, together worth a farthing. He called his disciples 43 to him. 'I tell you this,' he said: 'this poor widow has given more than any of the others; for those 44 others who have given had more than enough, but she, with less than enough, has given all that she had to live on.'

[a] *Or* The mass of the people listened eagerly.   [b] *Or* As for those who eat up the property of widows, while they say long prayers for appearance' sake, they will have an even sterner judgement to face.

13 As he was leaving the temple, one of his disciples exclaimed, 'Look, Master, what huge stones! What 2 fine buildings!' Jesus said to him, 'You see these great buildings? Not one stone will be left upon another; all will be thrown down.' 3 When he was sitting on the Mount of Olives facing the temple he was questioned privately by Peter, James, John, and Andrew. 4 'Tell us,' they said, 'when will this happen? What will be the sign when the fulfilment of all this is at hand?'

5 Jesus began: 'Take care that no 6 one misleads you. Many will come claiming my name, and saying, "I am he"; and many will be misled by them.

7 'When you hear the noise of battle near at hand and the news of battles far away, do not be alarmed. Such things are bound to happen; but the end is still to 8 come. For nation will make war upon nation, kingdom upon kingdom; there will be earthquakes in many places; there will be famines. With these things the birth-pangs of the new age begin.

9 'As for you, be on your guard. You will be handed over to the courts. You will be flogged in synagogues. You will be summoned to appear before governors and kings on my account to testify in their 10 presence. But before the end the Gospel must be proclaimed to all 11 nations. So when you are arrested and taken away, do not worry beforehand about what you will say, but when the time comes say whatever is given you to say; for it is not you who will be speaking, 12 but the Holy Spirit. Brother will betray brother to death, and the father his child; children will turn against their parents and send them 13 to their death. All will hate you for your allegiance to me; but the man who holds out to the end will be saved.

'But when you see "the abomi- 14 nation of desolation" usurping a place which is not his (let the reader understand), then those who are in Judaea must take to the hills. If a man is on the roof, he 15 must not come down into the house to fetch anything out; if in the 16 field, he must not turn back for his coat. Alas for women with child 17 in those days, and for those who have children at the breast! Pray 18 that it may not come in winter. For those days will bring distress 19 such as never has been until now since the beginning of the world which God created – and will never be again. If the Lord had not cut 20 short that time of troubles, no living thing could survive. However, for the sake of his own, whom he has chosen, he has cut short the time.

'Then, if anyone says to you, 21 "Look, here is the Messiah", or, "Look, there he is", do not believe it. Impostors will come claiming 22 to be messiahs or prophets, and they will produce signs and wonders to mislead God's chosen, if such a thing were possible. But you be 23 on your guard; I have forewarned you of it all.

'But in those days, after that 24 distress, the sun will be darkened, the moon will not give her light; the stars will come falling from the 25 sky, the celestial powers will be shaken. Then they will see the 26 Son of Man coming in the clouds with great power and glory, and 27 he will send out the angels and gather his chosen from the four winds, from the farthest bounds of earth to the farthest bounds of heaven.

'Learn a lesson from the fig-tree. 28 When its tender shoots appear and are breaking into leaf, you know that summer is near. In the same 29 way, when you see all this happening, you may know that the end is near,[a] at the very door. I tell you 30

---

[a] *Or that he is near.*

this: the present generation will
31 live to see it all. Heaven and earth
will pass away; my words will
never pass away.

32 'But about that day or that hour
no one knows, not even the angels
in heaven, not even the Son; only
the Father.

33 'Be alert, be wakeful.ᵃ You do
not know when the moment comes.

34 It is like a man away from home:
he has left his house and put his
servants in charge, each with his
own work to do, and he has ordered
the door-keeper to stay awake.

35 Keep awake, then, for you do not
know when the master of the house
is coming. Evening or midnight,

36 cock-crow or early dawn – if he
comes suddenly, he must not find

37 you asleep. And what I say to you,
I say to everyone: Keep awake.'

The final conflict

14 Now the festival of Passover and
Unleavened Bread was only two
days off; and the chief priests and
the doctors of the law were trying
to devise some cunning plan to
seize him and put him to death.

2 'It must not be during the festival,'
they said, 'or we should have rioting
among the people.'

3 Jesus was at Bethany, in the
house of Simon the leper. As he
sat at table, a woman came in
carrying a small bottle of very
costly perfume, pure oil of nard.
She broke it open and poured the

4 oil over his head. Some of those
present said to one another angrily,

5 'Why this waste? The perfume
might have been sold for thirty
poundsᵇ and the money given to
the poor'; and they turned upon

6 her with fury. But Jesus said, 'Let
her alone. Why must you make
trouble for her? It is a fine thing

7 she has done for me. You have the
poor among you always, and you
can help them whenever you like;

but you will not always have me.
8 She has done what lay in her power;
she is beforehand with anointing
9 my body for burial. I tell you this:
wherever in all the world the Gospel is proclaimed, what she has
done will be told as her memorial.'

10 Then Judas Iscariot, one of the
Twelve, went to the chief priests
11 to betray him to them. When they
heard what he had come for, they
were greatly pleased, and promised
him money; and he began to look
for a good opportunity to betray
him.

12 Now on the first day of Unleavened Bread, when the Passover
lambs were being slaughtered, his
disciples said to him, 'Where would
you like us to go and prepare for
your Passover supper?' So he sent
13 out two of his disciples with these
instructions: 'Go into the city, and
a man will meet you carrying a jar
14 of water. Follow him, and when
he enters a house give this message
to the householder: "The Master
says, 'Where is the room reserved
for me to eat the Passover with
15 my disciples?'" He will show you
a large room upstairs, set out in
readiness. Make the preparations
16 for us there.' Then the disciples
went off, and when they came into
the city they found everything
just as he had told them. So they
prepared for Passover.

17 In the evening he came to the
18 house with the Twelve. As they
sat at supper Jesus said, 'I tell you
this: one of you will betray me –
19 one who is eating with me.' At this
they were dismayed; and one by
one they said to him, 'Not I, sure-
20 ly?' 'It is one of the Twelve', he
said, 'who is dipping into the same
21 bowl with me. The Son of Man is
going the way appointed for him
in the scriptures; but alas for that
man by whom the Son of Man is
betrayed! It would be better for

ᵃ Some witnesses add and pray.
ᵇ Literally 300 denarii; some witnesses read more than 300 denarii.

that man if he had never been born.'

22 During supper he took bread, and having said the blessing he broke it and gave it to them, with the words: 'Take this; this is my 23 body.' Then he took a cup, and having offered thanks to God he gave it to them; and they all drank 24 from it. And he said, 'This is my blood, the blood of the covenant, 25 shed for many. I tell you this: never again shall I drink from the fruit of the vine until that day when I drink it new in the kingdom of God.' 26 After singing the Passover Hymn, they went out to the Mount 27 of Olives. And Jesus said, 'You will all fall from your faith; for it stands written: "I will strike the shepherd down and the sheep will 28 be scattered." Nevertheless, after I am raised again I will go on 29 before you into Galilee.' Peter answered, 'Everyone else may fall 30 away, but I will not.' Jesus said, 'I tell you this: today, this very night, before the cock crows twice, you yourself will disown me three 31 times.' But he insisted and repeated: 'Even if I must die with you, I will never disown you.' And they all said the same.

32 WHEN they reached a place called Gethsemane, he said to his disciples, 33 'Sit here while I pray.' And he took Peter and James and John with him. Horror and dismay came over 34 him, and he said to them, 'My heart is ready to break with grief; stop 35 here, and stay awake.' Then he went forward a little, threw himself on the ground, and prayed that, if it were possible, this hour 36 might pass him by. 'Abba, Father,' he said, 'all things are possible to thee; take this cup away from me. Yet not what I will, but what thou wilt.' 37 He came back and found them asleep; and he said to Peter, 'Asleep, Simon? Were you not able to stay awake for one hour? Stay awake, 38 all of you; and pray that you may be spared the test. The spirit is willing, but the flesh is weak.' Once 39 more he went away and prayed.[a] On his return he found them asleep 40 again, for their eyes were heavy; and they did not know how to answer him.

The third time he came and said 41 to them, 'Still sleeping? Still taking your ease? Enough![b] The hour has come. The Son of Man is betrayed to sinful men. Up, let us go forward! 42 My betrayer is upon us.'

Suddenly, while he was still 43 speaking, Judas, one of the Twelve, appeared, and with him was a crowd armed with swords and cudgels, sent by the chief priests, lawyers, and elders. Now the trai- 44 tor had agreed with them upon a signal: 'The one I kiss is your man; seize him and get him safely away.' When he reached the spot, he 45 stepped forward at once and said to Jesus, 'Rabbi', and kissed him. Then they seized him and held 46 him fast.

One of the party[c] drew his sword, 47 and struck at the High Priest's servant, cutting off his ear. Then 48 Jesus spoke: 'Do you take me for a bandit, that you have come out with swords and cudgels to arrest me? Day after day I was within 49 your reach as I taught in the temple, and you did not lay hands on me. But let the scriptures be fulfilled.' Then the disciples all 50 deserted him and ran away.

Among those following was a 51 young man with nothing on but a linen cloth. They tried to seize him; but he slipped out of the 52 linen cloth and ran away naked.

THEN they led Jesus away to the 53 High Priest's house, where the

---

[a] *Some witnesses add* using the same words.   [b] *The Greek is obscure; a possible meaning is* 'The money has been paid', 'The account is settled.'
[c] *Or of the bystanders.*

chief priests, elders, and doctors of the law were all assembling.

54 Peter followed him at a distance right into the High Priest's courtyard; and there he remained, sitting among the attendants, warming himself at the fire.

55 The chief priests and the whole Council tried to find some evidence against Jesus to warrant a death-sentence, but failed to find any.

56 Many gave false evidence against him, but their statements did not

57 tally. Some stood up and gave false evidence against him to this effect:

58 'We heard him say, "I will pull down this temple, made with human hands, and in three days I will build another, not made with

59 hands."' But even on this point their evidence did not agree.

60 Then the High Priest stood up in his place and questioned Jesus: 'Have you no answer to the charges that these witnesses bring against

61 you?' But he kept silence; he made no reply.

Again the High Priest questioned him: 'Are you the Messiah, the

62 Son of the Blessed One?' Jesus said, 'I am; and you will see the Son of Man seated at the right hand of God[a] and coming with the clouds

63 of heaven.' Then the High Priest tore his robes and said, 'Need we

64 call further witnesses? You have heard the blasphemy. What is your opinion?' Their judgement was unanimous: that he was guilty and should be put to death.

65 Some began to spit on him, blindfolded him, and struck him with their fists, crying out, 'Prophesy!'[b] And the High Priest's men set upon him with blows.

66 Meanwhile Peter was still below in the courtyard. One of the High Priest's serving-maids came by

67 and saw him there warming himself. She looked into his face and said, 'You were there too, with

this man from Nazareth, this Jesus.' But he denied it: 'I know 68 nothing,' he said; 'I do not understand what you mean.' Then he went outside into the porch;[c] and 69 the maid saw him there again and began to say to the bystanders, 'He is one of them'; and again he 70 denied it.

Again, a little later, the bystanders said to Peter, 'Surely you are one of them. You must be; you are a Galilean.' At this he 71 broke out into curses, and with an oath he said, 'I do not know this man you speak of.' Then the cock 72 crew a second time; and Peter remembered how Jesus had said to him, 'Before the cock crows twice you will disown me three times.' And he burst into tears.

A s soon as morning came, the chief 15 priests, having made their plan with the elders and lawyers in full council, put Jesus in chains; then they led him away and handed him over to Pilate. Pilate asked him, 2 'Are you the king of the Jews?' He replied, 'The words are yours.'[d] And the chief priests brought many 3 charges against him. Pilate ques- 4 tioned him again: 'Have you nothing to say in your defence? You see how many charges they are bringing against you.' But, to 5 Pilate's astonishment, Jesus made no further reply.

At the festival season the Gov- 6 ernor used to release one prisoner at the people's request. As it hap- 7 pened, the man known as Barabbas was then in custody with the rebels who had committed murder in the rising. When the crowd appeared[e] 8 asking for the usual favour, Pilate 9 replied, 'Do you wish me to release for you the king of the Jews?' For 10 he knew it was out of malice that they had brought Jesus before him. But the chief priests incited the 11

---

[a] Literally of the Power.
[b] Some witnesses add Who hit you? as in Matthew and Luke.
[c] Some witnesses insert and a cock crew.
[d] Or It is as you say.
[e] Some witnesses read shouted.

12 crowd to ask him to release Barabbas rather than Jesus. Pilate spoke to them again: 'Then what shall I do with the man you call king of 13 the Jews?' They shouted back, 14 'Crucify him!' 'Why, what harm has he done?' Pilate asked; but they shouted all the louder, 'Cruci-15 fy him!' So Pilate, in his desire to satisfy the mob, released Barabbas to them; and he had Jesus flogged and handed him over to be crucified.

16 Then the soldiers took him inside the courtyard (the Governor's headquarters[a]) and called together 17 the whole company. They dressed him in purple, and plaiting a crown of thorns, placed it on his head. 18 Then they began to salute him with, 19 'Hail, King of the Jews!' They beat him about the head with a cane and spat upon him, and then knelt and 20 paid mock homage to him. When they had finished their mockery, they stripped him of the purple and dressed him in his own clothes.

21 THEN they took him out to crucify him. A man called Simon, from Cyrene, the father of Alexander and Rufus, was passing by on his way in from the country, and they pressed him into service to carry his cross.

22 They brought him to the place called Golgotha, which means 23 'Place of a skull'. He was offered drugged wine, but he would not 24 take it. Then they fastened him to the cross. They divided his clothes among them, casting lots to decide what each should have.

25 The hour of the crucifixion was 26 nine in the morning, and the inscription giving the charge against him read, 'The king of the Jews.' 27 Two bandits were crucified with him, one on his right and the other on his left.[b]

29 The passers-by hurled abuse at him: 'Aha!' they cried, wagging their heads, 'you would pull the temple down, would you, and build 30 it in three days? Come down from 31 the cross and save yourself!' So too the chief priests and lawyers jested with one another: 'He saved others,' they said, 'but he cannot 32 save himself. Let the Messiah, the king of Israel, come down now from the cross. If we see that, we shall believe.' Even those who were crucified with him taunted him.

33 At midday a darkness fell over the whole land, which lasted till three 34 in the afternoon; and at three Jesus cried aloud, '*Eli, Eli, lema sabachthani?*', which means, 'My God, my God, why hast thou forsaken me?'[c] Some of the bystanders, on 35 hearing this, said, 'Hark, he is calling Elijah.' A man ran and 36 soaked a sponge in sour wine and held it to his lips on the end of a cane. 'Let us see', he said, 'if Elijah will come to take him down.' 37 Then Jesus gave a loud cry and 38 died. And the curtain of the temple was torn in two from top to bottom. 39 And when the centurion who was standing opposite him saw how he died,[d] he said, 'Truly this man was a son of God.'[e]

40 A NUMBER of women were also present, watching from a distance. Among them were Mary of Magdala, Mary the mother of James the younger and of Joseph, and Salome, who had all followed him 41 and waited on him when he was in Galilee, and there were several others who had come up to Jerusalem with him.

42 By this time evening had come; and as it was Preparation-day (that is, the day before the Sabbath), Joseph of Arimathaea, a 43

---

[a] *Greek praetorium.*   [b] *Some witnesses add* (28) Thus that text of Scripture came true which says, 'He was reckoned among criminals.'
[c] *Some witnesses read* My God, my God, why hast thou shamed me?
[d] *Some witnesses read* saw that he died with a cry.   [e] *Or* the Son of God.

respected member of the Council, a man who looked forward to the kingdom of God, bravely went in to Pilate and asked for the body 44 of Jesus. Pilate was surprised to hear that he was already dead; so he sent for the centurion and asked him whether it was long since he 45 died. And when he heard the centurion's report, he gave Joseph 46 leave to take the dead body. So Joseph bought a linen sheet, took him down from the cross, and wrapped him in the sheet. Then he laid him in a tomb cut out of the rock, and rolled a stone against 47 the entrance. And Mary of Magdala and Mary the mother of Joseph were watching and saw where he was laid.

16 When the Sabbath was over, Mary of Magdala, Mary the mother of James, and Salome bought[a] aromatic oils intending to go and 2 anoint him; and very early on the Sunday morning, just after sun-3 rise, they came to the tomb. They were wondering among themselves who would roll away the stone for them from the entrance to the 4 tomb, when they looked up and saw that the stone, huge as it was, 5 had been rolled back already. They went into the tomb, where they saw a youth sitting on the right-hand side, wearing a white robe; 6 and they were dumbfounded. But he said to them, 'Fear nothing; you are looking for Jesus of Nazareth, who was crucified. He has been raised again; he is not here; look, there is the place where they laid 7 him. But go and give this message to his disciples and Peter: "He is going on before you into Galilee; there you will see him, as he told 8 you."' Then they went out and ran away from the tomb, beside

themselves with terror. They said nothing to anybody, for they were afraid.[b]

When he had risen from the dead 9 early on Sunday morning he appeared first to Mary of Magdala, from whom he had formerly cast out seven devils. She went and 10 carried the news to his mourning and sorrowful followers, but when 11 they were told that he was alive and that she had seen him they did not believe it.

Later he appeared in a different 12 guise to two of them as they were walking, on their way into the country. These also went and took 13 the news to the others, but again no one believed them.

Afterwards while the Eleven 14 were at table he appeared to them and reproached them for their incredulity and dullness, because they had not believed those who had seen him after he was raised from the dead. Then he said to 15 them: 'Go forth to every part of the world, and proclaim the Good News to the whole creation. Those 16 who believe it and receive baptism will find salvation; those who do not believe will be condemned. Faith will bring with it these 17 miracles: believers will cast out devils in my name and speak in strange tongues; if they handle 18 snakes or drink any deadly poison, they will come to no harm; and the sick on whom they lay their hands will recover.'

So after talking with them the 19 Lord Jesus was taken up into heaven, and he took his seat at the right hand of God; but they 20 went out to make their proclamation everywhere, and the Lord worked with them and confirmed

---

[a] Some witnesses omit When the Sabbath. . .Salome, reading And they went and bought. . .   [b] At this point some of the most ancient witnesses bring the book to a close; others continue with verses 9–20, as printed here, or in some cases expanded with additional matter; yet others insert here the paragraph And they delivered. . . eternal salvation (here printed below verse 20), and in one of them this is the conclusion of the book; in the remainder, verses 9–20 follow it.

their words by the miracles that followed.

And they delivered all these instructions briefly to Peter and his companions. Afterwards Jesus himself sent out by them from east to west the sacred and imperishable message of eternal salvation.[a]

THE GOSPEL ACCORDING TO

LUKE

1 THE author to Theophilus: Many writers have undertaken to draw up an account of the events that have happened 2 among us, following the traditions handed down to us by the original eyewitnesses and servants of the 3 Gospel. And so I in my turn, your Excellency, as one who has gone over the whole course of these events in detail, have decided to write a connected narrative for 4 you, so as to give you authentic knowledge about the matters of which you have been informed.

The coming of Christ

5 IN the days of Herod king of Judaea there was a priest named Zechariah, of the division of the priesthood called after Abijah. His wife also was of priestly descent; 6 her name was Elizabeth. Both of them were upright and devout, blamelessly observing all the commandments and ordinances of the 7 Lord. But they had no children, for Elizabeth was barren, and both were well on in years.

8 Once, when it was the turn of his division and he was there to take 9 part in divine service, it fell to his lot, by priestly custom, to enter the sanctuary of the Lord and offer 10 the incense; and the whole congregation was at prayer outside. It was the hour of the incense-offering. There appeared to him an angel 11 of the Lord, standing on the right of the altar of incense. At this sight, 12 Zechariah was startled, and fear overcame him. But the angel said 13 to him, 'Do not be afraid, Zechariah; your prayer has been heard: your wife Elizabeth will bear you a son, and you shall name him John. Your heart will thrill with 14 joy and many will be glad that he was born; for he will be great in 15 the eyes of the Lord. He shall never touch wine or strong drink. From his very birth he will be filled with the Holy Spirit; and he will bring 16 back many Israelites to the Lord their God. He will go before him 17 as forerunner,[b] possessed by the spirit and power of Elijah, to reconcile father and child, to convert the rebellious to the ways of the righteous, to prepare a people that shall be fit for the Lord.'

Zechariah said to the angel, 18 'How can I be sure of this? I am an old man and my wife is well on in years.'

The angel replied, 'I am Gabriel; 19 I stand in attendance upon God, and I have been sent to speak to you and bring you this good news. But now listen: you will lose your 20 power of speech, and remain silent until the day when these things happen to you, because you have

[a] See p. 61, note b.   [b] Or In his sight he will go forth.

not believed me, though at their proper time my words will be proved true.'

21 Meanwhile the people were waiting for Zechariah, surprised that he was staying so long inside.
22 When he did come out he could not speak to them, and they realized that he had had a vision in the sanctuary. He stood there making signs to them, and remained dumb.
23 When his period of duty was completed Zechariah returned home.
24 After this his wife Elizabeth conceived, and for five months she
25 lived in seclusion, thinking, 'This is the Lord's doing; now at last he has deigned to take away my reproach among men.'

26 In the sixth month the angel Gabriel was sent from God to a town in Galilee called Nazareth,
27 with a message for a girl betrothed to a man named Joseph, a descendant of David; the girl's name was
28 Mary. The angel went in and said to her, 'Greetings, most favoured
29 one! The Lord is with you.' But she was deeply troubled by what he said and wondered what this
30 greeting might mean. Then the angel said to her, 'Do not be afraid, Mary, for God has been gracious
31 to you; you shall conceive and bear a son, and you shall give him the
32 name Jesus. He will be great; he will bear the title "Son of the Most High"; the Lord God will give him the throne of his ancestor David,
33 and he will be king over Israel[a] for ever; his reign shall never end.'
34 'How can this be?' said Mary; 'I am
35 still a virgin.' The angel answered, 'The Holy Spirit will come upon you, and the power of the Most High will overshadow you; and for that reason the holy child to be born will be called "Son of
36 God".[b] Moreover your kinswoman Elizabeth has herself conceived a son in her old age; and she who is reputed barren is now in her sixth
37 month, for God's promises can never fail.'[c]
38 'Here am I,' said Mary; 'I am the Lord's servant; as you have spoken, so be it.' Then the angel left her.

39 About this time Mary set out and went straight to a town in the
40 uplands of Judah. She went into Zechariah's house and greeted
41 Elizabeth. And when Elizabeth heard Mary's greeting, the baby stirred in her womb. Then Elizabeth was filled with the Holy Spirit
42 and cried aloud, 'God's blessing is on you above all women, and his blessing is on the fruit of your
43 womb. Who am I, that the mother of my Lord should visit me? I tell
44 you, when your greeting sounded in my ears, the baby in my womb
45 leapt for joy. How happy is she who has had faith that the Lord's promise would be fulfilled!'

46 And Mary[d] said:

'Tell out, my soul, the greatness of the Lord,
47 rejoice, rejoice, my spirit, in God my saviour;
48 so tenderly has he looked upon his servant,
humble as she is.
For, from this day forth,
all generations will count me blessed,
49 so wonderfully has he dealt with me,
the Lord, the Mighty One.

His name is Holy;
50 his mercy sure from generation to generation
toward those who fear him;
51 the deeds his own right arm has done
disclose his might:
the arrogant of heart and mind he has put to rout,

---

[a] *Literally* the house of Jacob.　　[b] *Or* the child to be born will be called holy, "Son of God".　　[c] *Some witnesses read* for with God nothing will prove impossible.　　[d] *So the majority of witnesses; some read* Elizabeth; *the original may have had no name.*

52 he has brought down monarchs
   from their thrones,
   but the humble have been lifted
   high.
53 The hungry he has satisfied with
   good things,
   the rich sent empty away.

54 He has ranged himself at the side
   of Israel his servant;
55 firm in his promise to our forefathers,
   he has not forgotten to show mercy
   to Abraham
   and his children's children, for
   ever.'

56   Mary stayed with her about three
months and then returned home.

57 Now the time came for Elizabeth's
   child to be born, and she gave
58 birth to a son. When her neighbours and relatives heard what
   great favour the Lord had shown
   her, they were as delighted as she
59 was. Then on the eighth day they
   came to circumcise the child; and
   they were going to name him
60 Zechariah after his father. But his
   mother spoke up and said, 'No!
61 he is to be called John.' 'But', they
   said, 'there is nobody in your
62 family who has that name.' They
   inquired of his father by signs what
63 he would like him to be called. He
   asked for a writing-tablet and to
   the astonishment of all wrote
64 down, 'His name is John.' Immediately his lips and tongue were
   freed and he began to speak,
65 praising God. All the neighbours
   were struck with awe, and everywhere in the uplands of Judaea
   the whole story became common
66 talk. All who heard it were deeply
   impressed and said, 'What will this
   child become?' For indeed the
   hand of the Lord was upon him.[a]
67   And Zechariah his father was
filled with the Holy Spirit and
uttered this prophecy:

'Praise to the God of Israel!   68
For he has turned to his people,
   saved them and set them free,
and has raised up a deliverer of 69
   victorious power
from the house of his servant
   David.

So he promised: age after age he 70
   proclaimed
by the lips of his holy prophets,
that he would deliver us from our 71
   enemies,
out of the hands of all who hate
   us;
that he would deal mercifully with 72
   our fathers,
calling to mind his solemn covenant.

Such was the oath he swore to our 73
   father Abraham,
to rescue us from enemy hands,   74
and grant us, free from fear, to
   worship him
with a holy worship, with upright- 75
   ness of heart,
in his presence, our whole life long.

And you, my child, you shall be 76
   called Prophet of the Highest,
for you will be the Lord's forerunner, to prepare his way
and lead his people to salvation 77
   through knowledge of him,
by the foregiveness of their sins:
for in the tender compassion of 78
   our God
the morning sun from heaven will
   rise[b] upon us,
to shine on those who live in dark- 79
   ness, under the cloud of death,
and to guide our feet into the way
   of peace.'

   As the child grew up he became 80
strong in spirit; he lived out in the
wilds until the day when he appeared publicly before Israel.

IN those days a decree was issued 2
by the Emperor Augustus for a

---

[a] *Some witnesses read* 'What will this child become, for indeed the hand of the Lord
is upon him?'   [b] *Some witnesses read* has risen.

registration to be made throughout the Roman world. This was the first registration of its kind; it took place when Quirinius[a] was governor of Syria. For this purpose everyone made his way to his own town; and so Joseph went up to Judaea from the town of Nazareth in Galilee, to register at the city of David, called Bethlehem, because he was of the house of David by descent; and with him went Mary who was betrothed to him. She was expecting a child, and while they were there the time came for her baby to be born, and she gave birth to a son, her first-born. She wrapped him in his swaddling clothes, and laid him in a manger, because there was no room for them to lodge in the house.

Now in this same district there were shepherds out in the fields, keeping watch through the night over their flock, when suddenly there stood before them an angel of the Lord, and the splendour of the Lord shone round them. They were terror-stricken, but the angel said, 'Do not be afraid; I have good news for you: there is great joy coming to the whole people. Today in the city of David a deliverer has been born to you – the Messiah, the Lord.[b] And this is your sign: you will find a baby lying wrapped in his swaddling clothes, in a manger.' All at once there was with the angel a great company of the heavenly host, singing the praises of God:

'Glory to God in highest heaven,
and on earth his peace for men on
  whom his favour rests.'[c]

After the angels had left them and gone into heaven the shepherds said to one another, 'Come, we must go straight to Bethlehem and see this thing that has happened, which the Lord has made known to us.' So they went with all speed and found their way to Mary and Joseph; and the baby was lying in the manger. When they saw him, they recounted what they had been told about this child; and all who heard were astonished at what the shepherds said. But Mary treasured up all these things and pondered over them. Meanwhile the shepherds returned glorifying and praising God for what they had heard and seen; it had all happened as they had been told.

Eight days later the time came to circumcise him, and he was given the name Jesus, the name given by the angel before he was conceived.

Then, after their purification had been completed in accordance with the Law of Moses, they brought him up to Jerusalem to present him to the Lord (as prescribed in the law of the Lord: 'Every first-born male shall be deemed to belong to the Lord'), and also to make the offering as stated in the law: 'A pair of turtle doves or two young pigeons.'

There was at that time in Jerusalem a man called Simeon. This man was upright and devout, one who watched and waited for the restoration of Israel, and the Holy Spirit was upon him. It had been disclosed to him by the Holy Spirit that he would not see death until he had seen the Lord's Messiah. Guided by the Spirit he came into the temple; and when the parents brought in the child Jesus to do for him what was customary under the Law, he took him in his arms, praised God, and said:

'This day, Master, thou givest thy
  servant his discharge in peace;
now thy promise is fulfilled.'

---

[a] Or This was the first registration carried out while Quirinius...
[b] *Some witnesses read* to you – the Lord's Messiah.
[c] *Some witnesses read* and on earth his peace, his favour towards men.

30 For I have seen with my own eyes
31 the deliverance which thou hast made ready in full view of all the nations:
32 a light that will be a revelation to the heathen,
and glory to thy people Israel.'

33 The child's father and mother were full of wonder at what was
34 being said about him. Simeon blessed them and said to Mary his mother, 'This child is destined to
35 be a sign which men reject; and you too shall be pierced to the heart. Many in Israel will stand or fall[a] because of him, and thus the secret thoughts of many will be laid bare.'
36 There was also a prophetess, Anna the daughter of Phanuel, of the tribe of Asher. She was a very old woman, who had lived seven years with her husband after she
37 was first married, and then alone as a widow to the age of eighty-four.[b] She never left the temple, but worshipped day and night,
38 fasting and praying. Coming up at that very moment, she returned thanks to God; and she talked about the child to all who were looking for the liberation of Jerusalem.
39 When they had done everything prescribed in the law of the Lord, they returned to Galilee to their
40 own town of Nazareth. The child grew big and strong and full of wisdom; and God's favour was upon him.
41 Now it was the practice of his parents to go to Jerusalem every
42 year for the Passover festival; and when he was twelve, they made
43 the pilgrimage as usual. When the festive season was over and they started for home, the boy Jesus stayed behind in Jerusalem. His
44 parents did not know of this; but thinking that he was with the party they journeyed on for a whole day, and only then did they begin looking for him among their
45 friends and relations. As they could not find him they returned
46 to Jerusalem to look for him; and after three days they found him sitting in the temple surrounded by the teachers, listening to them
47 and putting questions; and all who heard him were amazed at his intelligence and the answers he gave.
48 His parents were astonished to see him there, and his mother said to him, 'My son, why have you treated us like this? Your father and I have been searching for you in
49 great anxiety.' 'What made you search?' he said. 'Did you not know that I was bound to be in my Father's house?' But they did
50 not understand what he meant.
51 Then he went back with them to Nazareth, and continued to be under their authority; his mother treasured up all these things in
52 her heart. As Jesus grew up he advanced in wisdom and in favour with God and men.

3 IN the fifteenth year of the Emperor Tiberius, when Pontius Pilate was governor of Judaea, when Herod was prince of Galilee, his brother Philip prince of Ituraea and Trachonitis, and Lysanias prince of Abilene, during the high-priest
2 hood of Annas and Caiaphas, the word of God came to John son of
3 Zechariah in the wilderness. And he went all over the Jordan valley proclaiming a baptism in token of repentance for the forgiveness
4 of sins, as it is written in the book of the prophecies of Isaiah:

'A voice crying aloud in the wilderness,
"Prepare a way for the Lord;
clear a straight path for him.
5 Every ravine shall be filled in,
and every mountain and hill levelled;

---

[a] *Or* Many in Israel will fall and rise again...
[b] *Or* widow for another eighty-four years.

the corners shall be straightened,
and the rugged ways made smooth;
6 and all mankind shall see God's
deliverance."'

7 Crowds of people came out to
be baptized by him, and he said
to them: 'You vipers' brood! Who
warned you to escape from the
8 coming retribution? Then prove
your repentance by the fruit it
bears; and do not begin saying to
yourselves, "We have Abraham
for our father." I tell you that God
can make children for Abraham
9 out of these stones here. Already
the axe is laid to the roots of the
trees; and every tree that fails to
produce good fruit is cut down
and thrown on the fire.'
10 The people asked him, 'Then
11 what are we to do?' He replied,
'The man with two shirts must
share with him who has none, and
anyone who has food must do the
12 same.' Among those who came to
be baptized were tax-gatherers,
and they said to him, 'Master, what
13 are we to do?' He told them, 'Exact
no more than the assessment.'
14 Soldiers on service also asked him,
'And what of us?' To them he said,
'No bullying; no blackmail; make
do with your pay!'
15 The people were on the tiptoe
of expectation, all wondering about
John, whether perhaps he was the
16 Messiah, but he spoke out and said
to them all: 'I baptize you with
water; but there is one to come
who is mightier than I. I am not
fit to unfasten his shoes. He will
baptize you with the Holy Spirit
17 and with fire. His shovel is ready
in his hand, to winnow his threshing-floor and gather the wheat into
his granary; but he will burn the
chaff on a fire that can never go out.'
18 In this and many other ways he
made his appeal to the people and
19 announced the good news. But

Prince Herod, when he was rebuked
by him over the affair of his brother's wife Herodias and for his
other misdeeds, crowned them all 20
by shutting John up in prison.

DURING a general baptism of the 21
people, when Jesus too had been
baptized and was praying, heaven
opened and the Holy Spirit de- 22
scended on him in bodily form like
a dove; and there came a voice
from heaven, 'Thou art my Son,
my Beloved;[a] on thee my favour
rests.'[b]

When Jesus began his work he 23
was about thirty years old, the son,
as people thought, of Joseph, son of
Heli, son of Matthat, son of Levi, 24
son of Melchi, son of Jannai, son
of Joseph, son of Mattathiah, son 25
of Amos, son of Nahum, son of
Esli, son of Naggai, son of Maath, 26
son of Mattathiah, son of Semein,
son of Josech, son of Joda, son of Jo- 27
hanan, son of Rhesa, son of Zerubbabel, son of Shealtiel, son of Neri,
son of Melchi, son of Addi, son of 28
Cosam, son of Elmadam, son of Er,
son of Joshua, son of Eliezer, son 29
of Jorim, son of Matthat, son of
Levi, son of Symeon, son of Judah, 30
son of Joseph, son of Jonam, son
of Eliakim, son of Melea, son of 31
Menna, son of Mattatha, son of
Nathan, son of David, son of Jesse, 32
son of Obed, son of Boaz, son of
Salmon, son of Nahshon, son of 33
Amminadab,[c] son of Arni,[d] son of
Hezron, son of Perez, son of Judah,
son of Jacob, son of Isaac, son of 34
Abraham, son of Terah, son of
Nahor, son of Serug, son of Reu, 35
son of Peleg, son of Eber, son
of Shelah, son of Cainan, son of 36
Arpachshad, son of Shem, son of
Noah, son of Lamech, son of 37
Methuselah, son of Enoch, son of
Jared, son of Mahalaleel, son of
Cainan, son of Enos, son of Seth, 38
son of Adam, son of God.

[a] Or Thou art my only Son.   [b] Some witnesses read My Son art thou; this day I have begotten thee.   [c] Some witnesses add son of Admin.
[d] Some witnesses read Aram; Ruth 4. 19 and 1 Chronicles 2. 9 have Ram.

4 Full of the Holy Spirit, Jesus
2 returned from the Jordan, and for
forty days was led by the Spirit
up and down the wilderness and
tempted by the devil.

All that time he had nothing to
eat, and at the end of it he was
3 famished. The devil said to him,
'If you are the Son of God, tell this
4 stone to become bread.' Jesus
answered, 'Scripture says, "Man
cannot live on bread alone."'

5 Next the devil led him up and
showed him in a flash all the king-
6 doms of the world. 'All this dominion will I give to you,' he said,
'and the glory that goes with it;
for it has been put in my hands
and I can give it to anyone I
7 choose. You have only to do
homage to me and it shall all be
8 yours.' Jesus answered him, 'Scripture says, "You shall do homage
to the Lord your God and worship
him alone."'

9 The devil took him to Jerusalem
and set him on the parapet of the
temple. 'If you are the Son of God,'
10 he said, 'throw yourself down; for
Scripture says, "He will give his
angels orders to take care of you",
11 and again, "They will support you
in their arms for fear you should
strike your foot against a stone."'
12 Jesus answered him, 'It has been
said, "You are not to put the Lord
your God to the test."'
13 So, having come to the end of
all his temptations, the devil departed, biding his time.

In Galilee: success and opposition

14 THEN Jesus, armed with the
power of the Spirit, returned to
Galilee; and reports about him
spread through the whole country-
15 side. He taught in their synagogues
and all men sang his praises.
16 So he came to Nazareth, where
he had been brought up, and went
to synagogue on the Sabbath day
as he regularly did. He stood up to
read the lesson and was handed 17
the scroll of the prophet Isaiah.
He opened the scroll and found
the passage which says,

'The spirit of the Lord is upon me 18
     because he has anointed me;
he has sent me to announce good
     news to the poor,
to proclaim release for prisoners
     and recovery of sight for the
     blind;
to let the broken victims go free,
to proclaim the year of the Lord's 19
     favour.'

He rolled up the scroll, gave it back 20
to the attendant, and sat down;
and all eyes in the synagogue were
fixed on him.

He began to speak: 'Today', he 21
said, 'in your very hearing this
text has come true.'[a] There was 22
a general stir of admiration; they
were surprised that words of such
grace should fall from his lips. 'Is
not this Joseph's son?' they asked.
Then Jesus said, 'No doubt you 23
will quote the proverb to me,
"Physician, heal yourself!", and
say, "We have heard of all your
doings at Capernaum; do the same
here in your own home town." I 24
tell you this,' he went on: 'no
prophet is recognized in his own
country. There were many widows 25
in Israel, you may be sure, in
Elijah's time, when for three years
and six months the skies never
opened, and famine lay hard over
the whole country; yet it was to 26
none of those that Elijah was sent,
but to a widow at Sarepta in the
territory of Sidon. Again, in the 27
time of the prophet Elisha there
were many lepers in Israel, and
not one of them was healed, but
only Naaman, the Syrian.' At 28
these words the whole congregation were infuriated. They leapt 29
up, threw him out of the town,
and took him to the brow of the
hill on which it was built, meaning

---

[a] Or 'Today', he said, 'this text which you have just heard has come true.'

30 to hurl him over the edge. But he walked straight through them all, and went away.

31 Coming down to Capernaum, a town in Galilee, he taught the 32 people on the Sabbath, and they were astounded at his teaching, for what he said had the note of 33 authority. Now there was a man in the synagogue possessed by a devil, an unclean spirit. He shrieked at the top of his voice, 34 'What do you want with us, Jesus of Nazareth? Have you*a* come to destroy us? I know who you are – 35 the Holy One of God.' Jesus rebuked him: 'Be silent', he said, 'and come out of him.' Then the devil, after throwing the man down in front of the people, left him without doing him any injury. 36 Amazement fell on them all and they said to one another: 'What is there in this man's words? He gives orders to the unclean spirits with authority and power, and out 37 they go.' So the news spread, and he was the talk of the whole district.

38 On leaving the synagogue he went to Simon's house. Simon's mother-in-law was in the grip of a high fever; and they asked him 39 to help her. He came and stood over her and rebuked the fever. It left her, and she got up at once and waited on them.

40 At sunset all who had friends suffering from one disease or another brought them to him; and he laid his hands on them one by 41 one and cured them. Devils also came out of many of them, shouting, 'You are the Son of God.' But he rebuked them and forbade them to speak, because they knew that he was the Messiah.

42 When day broke he went out and made his way to a lonely spot. But the people went in search of him, and when they came to where he was they pressed him not to leave them. But he said, 'I must 43 give the good news of the kingdom of God to the other towns also, for that is what I was sent to do.' So 44 he proclaimed the Gospel in the synagogues of Judaea.*b*

One day as he stood by the Lake 5 of Gennesaret, and the people crowded upon him to listen to the word of God, he noticed two boats 2 lying at the water's edge; the fishermen had come ashore and were washing their nets. He got 3 into one of the boats, which belonged to Simon, and asked him to put out a little way from the shore; then he went on teaching the crowds from his seat in the boat. When he had finished speaking, 4 he said to Simon, 'Put out into deep water and let down your nets for a catch.' Simon answered, 5 'Master, we were hard at work all night and caught nothing at all; but if you say so, I will let down the nets.' They did so and made 6 a big haul of fish; and their nets began to split. So they signalled 7 to their partners in the other boat to come and help them. This they did, and loaded both boats to the point of sinking. When Simon saw 8 what had happened he fell at Jesus's knees and said, 'Go, Lord, leave me, sinner that I am!' For 9 he and all his companions were amazed at the catch they had made; so too were his partners 10 James and John, Zebedee's sons. 'Do not be afraid,' said Jesus to Simon; 'from now on you will be catching men.' As soon as they had 11 brought the boats to land, they left everything and followed him.

He was once in a certain town 12 where there happened to be a man covered with leprosy; seeing Jesus, he bowed to the ground and begged his help. 'Sir,' he said, 'if only you will, you can cleanse me.' Jesus 13 stretched out his hand, touched him, and said, 'Indeed I will; be

---

a Or You have.
b Or the Jewish synagogues; *some witnesses read* the synagogues of Galilee.

clean again.' The leprosy left him
14 immediately. Jesus then ordered
him not to tell anybody. 'But go,'
he said, 'show yourself to the
priest, and make the offering laid
down by Moses for your cleansing;
15 that will certify the cure.' But the
talk about him spread all the more;
great crowds gathered to hear him
and to be cured of their ailments.
16 And from time to time he would
withdraw to lonely places for
prayer.
17 One day he was teaching, and
Pharisees and teachers of the law
were sitting round. People had
come from every village of Galilee
and from Judaea and Jerusalem,*a*
and the power of the Lord was
18 with him to heal the sick. Some
men appeared carrying a paralysed
man on a bed. They tried to bring
him in and set him down in front
19 of Jesus, but finding no way to
do so because of the crowd, they
went up on to the roof and let him
down through the tiling, bed and
all, into the middle of the company
20 in front of Jesus. When Jesus saw
their faith, he said, 'Man, your sins
are forgiven you.'
21 The lawyers and the Pharisees
began saying to themselves, 'Who
is this fellow with his blasphemous
talk? Who but God alone can for-
22 give sins?' But Jesus knew what
they were thinking and answered
them: 'Why do you harbour
23 thoughts like these? Is it easier to
say, "Your sins are forgiven you",
or to say, "Stand up and walk"?
24 But to convince you that the Son
of Man has the right on earth to
forgive sins' – he turned to the
paralysed man – 'I say to you,
stand up, take your bed, and go
25 home.' And at once he rose to his
feet before their eyes, took up the
bed he had been lying on, and went
26 home praising God. They were all
lost in amazement and praised
God; filled with awe they said,

'You would never believe the
things we have seen today.'
Later, when he went out, he saw 27
a tax-gatherer, Levi by name, at
his seat in the custom-house, and
said to him, 'Follow me'; and he 28
rose to his feet, left everything
behind, and followed him.
Afterwards Levi held a big re- 29
ception in his house for Jesus;
among the guests was a large party
of tax-gatherers and others. The 30
Pharisees and the lawyers of their
sect complained to his disciples:
'Why do you eat and drink', they
said, 'with tax-gatherers and sinners?' Jesus answered them: 'It is 31
not the healthy that need a doctor,
but the sick; I have not come to 32
invite virtuous people, but to call
sinners to repentance.'
Then they said to him, 'John's 33
disciples are much given to fasting
and the practice of prayer, and so
are the disciples of the Pharisees;
but yours eat and drink.' Jesus 34
replied, 'Can you make the bridegroom's friends fast while the
bridegroom is with them? But a 35
time will come: the bridegroom
will be taken away from them, and
that will be the time for them to
fast.'
He told them this parable also: 36
'No one tears a piece from a new
cloak to patch an old one; if he
does, he will have made a hole in
the new cloak, and the patch from
the new will not match the old.
Nor does anyone put new wine into 37
old wine-skins; if he does, the new
wine will burst the skins, the wine
will be wasted, and the skins ruined.
Fresh skins for new wine! And no 38, 39
one after drinking old wine wants
new; for he says, "The old wine is
good."'
One Sabbath he was going 6
through the cornfields, and his
disciples were plucking the ears of
corn, rubbing them in their hands,
and eating them. Some of the 2

---

a Some witnesses read and Pharisees and teachers of the law, who had come from
every village of Galilee and from Judaea and Jerusalem, *were sitting round.*

Pharisees said, 'Why are you doing what is forbidden on the Sabbath?'

3 Jesus answered, 'So you have not read what David did when he and 4 his men were hungry? He went into the House of God and took the sacred bread to eat and gave it to his men, though priests alone are allowed to eat it, and no one else.'

5 He also said, 'The Son of Man is sovereign even over the Sabbath.'

6 On another Sabbath he had gone to synagogue and was teaching. There happened to be a man in the congregation whose right arm was 7 withered; and the lawyers and the Pharisees were on the watch to see whether Jesus would cure him on the Sabbath, so that they could find a charge to bring against him.

8 But he knew what was in their minds and said to the man with the withered arm, 'Get up and stand out here.' So he got up and 9 stood there. Then Jesus said to them, 'I put the question to you: is it permitted to do good or to do evil on the Sabbath, to save life or 10 to destroy it?' He looked round at them all and then said to the man, 'Stretch out your arm.' He did so, 11 and his arm was restored. But they were beside themselves with anger, and began to discuss among themselves what they could do to Jesus.

12 During this time he went out one day into the hills to pray, and spent 13 the night in prayer to God. When day broke he called his disciples to him, and from among them he chose twelve and named them 14 Apostles: Simon, to whom he gave the name of Peter, and Andrew his brother, James and John, Philip 15 and Bartholomew, Matthew and Thomas, James son of Alphaeus, and Simon who was called the 16 Zealot, Judas son of James, and Judas Iscariot who turned traitor.

17 He came down the hill with them and took his stand on level ground. There was a large concourse of his disciples and great numbers of people from Jerusalem and Judaea and from the seaboard of Tyre and Sidon, who had come to listen to him, and to be cured of their diseases. Those who were troubled 18 with unclean spirits were cured; and everyone in the crowd was 19 trying to touch him, because power went out from him and cured them all.

THEN turning to his disciples he 20 began to speak:

'How blest are you who are in need; the kingdom of God is yours.

'How blest are you who now go 21 hungry; your hunger shall be satisfied.

'How blest are you who weep now; you shall laugh.

'How blest you are when men 22 hate you, when they outlaw you and insult you, and ban your very name as infamous, because of the Son of Man. On that day be glad 23 and dance for joy; for assuredly you have a rich reward in heaven; in just the same way did their fathers treat the prophets.

'But alas for you who are rich; 24 you have had your time of happiness.

'Alas for you who are well-fed 25 now; you shall go hungry.

'Alas for you who laugh now; you shall mourn and weep.

'Alas for you when all speak 26 well of you; just so did their fathers treat the false prophets.

'But to you who hear me I say: 27

'Love your enemies; do good to those who hate you; bless those 28 who curse you; pray for those who treat you spitefully. When a man 29 hits you on the cheek, offer him the other cheek too; when a man takes your coat, let him have your shirt as well. Give to everyone who 30 asks you; when a man takes what is yours, do not demand it back. Treat others as you would like 31 them to treat you.

'If you love only those who love 32 you, what credit is that to you? Even sinners love those who love

33 them. Again, if you do good only to those who do good to you, what credit is that to you? Even sinners 34 do as much. And if you lend only where you expect to be repaid, what credit is that to you? Even sinners lend to each other to be 35 repaid in full. But you must love your enemies and do good; and lend without expecting any return;[a] and you will have a rich reward: you will be sons of the Most High, because he himself is kind to the 36 ungrateful and wicked. Be compassionate as your Father is compassionate.

37 'Pass no judgement, and you will not be judged; do not condemn, and you will not be condemned; acquit, and you will be acquitted; 38 give, and gifts will be given you. Good measure, pressed down, shaken together, and running over, will be poured into your lap; for whatever measure you deal out to others will be dealt to you in return.'

39 He also offered them a parable: 'Can one blind man be guide to another? Will they not both fall 40 into the ditch? A pupil is not superior to his teacher; but everyone, when his training is complete, will reach his teacher's level.

41 'Why do you look at the speck of sawdust in your brother's eye, with never a thought for the great 42 plank in your own? How can you say to your brother, "My dear brother, let me take the speck out of your eye", when you are blind to the plank in your own? You hypocrite! First take the plank out of your own eye, and then you will see clearly to take the speck out of your brother's.

43 'There is no such thing as a good tree producing worthless fruit, nor yet a worthless tree producing 44 good fruit. For each tree is known by its own fruit: you do not gather figs from thistles, and you do not

pick grapes from brambles. A good 45 man produces good from the store of good within himself; and an evil man from evil within produces evil. For the words that the mouth utters come from the overflowing of the heart.

'Why do you keep calling me 46 "Lord, Lord" – and never do what I tell you? Everyone who comes 47 to me and hears what I say, and acts upon it – I will show you what he is like. He is like a man who, in 48 building his house, dug deep and laid the foundations on rock. When the flood came, the river burst upon that house, but could not shift it, because it had been soundly built. But he who hears and 49 does not act is like a man who built his house on the soil without foundations. As soon as the river burst upon it, the house collapsed, and fell with a great crash.'

WHEN he had finished addressing 7 the people, he went to Capernaum. A centurion there had a servant 2 whom he valued highly; this servant was ill and near to death. Hearing about Jesus, he sent some 3 Jewish elders with the request that he would come and save his servant's life. They approached Jesus 4 and pressed their petition earnestly: 'He deserves this favour from you,' they said, 'for he is a friend 5 of our nation and it is he who built us our synagogue.' Jesus went with 6 them; but when he was not far from the house, the centurion sent friends with this message: 'Do not trouble further, sir; it is not for me to have you under my roof, and that is why I did not presume 7 to approach you in person. But say the word and my servant will be cured. I know, for in my position 8 I am myself under orders, with soldiers under me. I say to one, "Go", and he goes; to another, "Come here", and he comes; and

[a] Or *without ever giving up hope; some witnesses read* without giving up hope of anyone.

to my servant, "Do this", and he
9 does it.' When Jesus heard this, he
admired the man, and, turning to
the crowd that was following him,
he said, 'I tell you, nowhere, even
in Israel, have I found faith like
10 this.' And the messengers returned
to the house and found the servant
in good health.

11   Afterwards[a] Jesus went to a
town called Nain, accompanied by
12 his disciples and a large crowd. As
he approached the gate of the town
he met a funeral. The dead man
was the only son of his widowed
mother; and many of the towns-
13 people were there with her. When
the Lord saw her his heart went
out to her, and he said, 'Weep no
14 more.' With that he stepped forward and laid his hand on the
bier; and the bearers halted. Then
he spoke: 'Young man, rise up!'
15 The dead man sat up and began
to speak; and Jesus gave him back
16 to his mother. Deep awe fell upon
them all, and they praised God.
'A great prophet has arisen among
us', they said, and again, 'God has
17 shown his care for his people.' The
story of what he had done ran
through all parts of Judaea and
the whole neighbourhood.

18   John too was informed of all this
19 by his disciples. Summoning two
of their number he sent them to
the Lord with this message: 'Are
you the one who is to come, or are
20 we to expect some other?' The
messengers made their way to
Jesus and said, 'John the Baptist
has sent us to you: he asks, "Are
you the one who is to come, or are
21 we to expect some other?"' There
and then he cured many sufferers
from diseases, plagues, and evil
spirits; and on many blind people
22 he bestowed sight. Then he gave
them his answer: 'Go', he said, 'and
tell John what you have seen and

heard: how the blind recover their
sight, the lame walk, the lepers
are made clean, the deaf hear, the
dead are raised to life, the poor
are hearing the good news – and 23
happy is the man who does not
find me a stumbling-block.'

After John's messengers had 24
left, Jesus began to speak about
him to the crowds: 'What was the
spectacle that drew you to the
wilderness? A reed-bed swept by
the wind? No? Then what did you 25
go out to see? A man dressed in
silks and satins? Surely you must
look in palaces for grand clothes
and luxury. But what did you go 26
out to see? A prophet? Yes indeed,
and far more than a prophet. He 27
is the man of whom Scripture says,

"Here is my herald, whom I send
    on ahead of you,
and he will prepare your way
    before you."

I tell you, there is not a mother's 28
son greater than John, and yet the
least in the kingdom of God is
greater than he.'

When they heard him, all the 29
people, including the tax-gatherers, praised God, for they had
accepted John's baptism; but the 30
Pharisees and lawyers, who refused
his baptism, had rejected[b] God's
purpose for themselves.

'How can I describe the people 31
of this generation? What are they
like? They are like children sitting 32
in the market-place and shouting
at each other,

"We piped for you and you would
    not dance."
"We wept and wailed, and you
    would not mourn."

For John the Baptist came neither 33
eating bread nor drinking wine,

---

[a] *Some witnesses read* On the next day.   [b] *Or* '...greater than he. And all the
people, including the tax-gatherers, when they heard him, accepted John's baptism
and acknowledged the righteous dealing of God; but the Pharisees and lawyers, by
refusing his baptism, rejected...'

34 and you say, "He is possessed." The Son of Man came eating and drinking, and you say, "Look at him! a glutton and a drinker, a friend of 35 tax-gatherers and sinners!" And yet God's wisdom is proved right by all who are her children.'

36   One of the Pharisees invited him to eat with him; he went to the Pharisee's house and took his 37 place at table. A woman who was living an immoral life in the town had learned that Jesus was at table in the Pharisee's house and had brought oil of myrrh in a small 38 flask. She took her place behind him, by his feet, weeping. His feet were wetted with her tears and she wiped them with her hair, kissing them and anointing them 39 with the myrrh. When his host the Pharisee saw this he said to himself, 'If this fellow were a real prophet, he would know who this woman is that touches him, and what sort of woman she is, a sinner.' 40 Jesus took him up and said, 'Simon, I have something to say to you.' 41 'Speak on, Master', said he. 'Two men were in debt to a moneylender: one owed him five hundred 42 silver pieces, the other fifty. As neither had anything to pay with he let them both off. Now, which 43 will love him most?' Simon replied, 'I should think the one that was let off most.' 'You are right', said 44 Jesus. Then turning to the woman, he said to Simon, 'You see this woman? I came to your house: you provided no water for my feet; but this woman has made my feet wet with her tears and wiped them 45 with her hair. You gave me no kiss; but she has been kissing my 46 feet ever since I came in. You did not anoint my head with oil; but she has anointed my feet with 47 myrrh. And so, I tell you, her great love proves that her many sins have been forgiven; where little has been forgiven, little love 48 is shown.' Then he said to her, 49 'Your sins are forgiven.' The other

guests began to ask themselves, 'Who is this, that he can forgive sins?' But he said to the woman, 50 'Your faith has saved you; go in peace.'

AFTER this he went journeying 8 from town to town and village to village, proclaiming the good news of the kingdom of God. With him were the Twelve and a number of 2 women who had been set free from evil spirits and infirmities: Mary, known as Mary of Magdala, from whom seven devils had come out, Joanna, the wife of Chuza a 3 steward of Herod's, Susanna, and many others. These women provided for them out of their own resources.

People were now gathering in 4 large numbers, and as they made their way to him from one town after another, he said in a parable: 'A sower went out to sow his seed. 5 And as he sowed, some seed fell along the footpath, where it was trampled on, and the birds ate it up. Some seed fell on rock and, 6 after coming up, withered for lack of moisture. Some seed fell in 7 among thistles, and the thistles grew up with it and choked it. And 8 some of the seed fell into good soil, and grew, and yielded a hundredfold.' As he said this he called out, 'If you have ears to hear, then hear.'

His disciples asked him what 9 this parable meant, and he said, 10 'It has been granted to you to know the secrets of the kingdom of God; but the others have only parables, so that they may look but see nothing, hear but understand nothing.

'This is what the parable means. 11 The seed is the word of God. Those 12 along the footpath are the men who hear it, and then the devil comes and carries off the word from their hearts for fear they should believe and be saved. The 13 seed sown on rock stands for those who receive the word with joy when they hear it, but have no root; they are believers for a while, but in the time of testing they

14 desert. That which fell among thistles represents those who hear, but their further growth is choked by cares and wealth and the pleasures of life, and they bring

15 nothing to maturity. But the seed in good soil represents those who bring a good and honest heart to the hearing of the word, hold it fast, and by their perseverance yield a harvest.

16 'Nobody lights a lamp and then covers it with a basin or puts it under the bed. On the contrary, he puts it on a lamp-stand so that those who come in may see the

17 light. For there is nothing hidden that will not become public, nothing under cover that will not be made known and brought into the open.

18 'Take care, then, how you listen; for the man who has will be given more, and the man who has not will forfeit even what he thinks he has.'

19 His mother and his brothers arrived but could not get to him

20 for the crowd. He was told, 'Your mother and brothers are standing outside, and they want to see you.'

21 He replied, 'My mother and my brothers – they are those who hear the word of God and act upon it.'

22 One day he got into a boat with his disciples and said to them, 'Let us cross over to the other side of

23 the lake.' So they put out; and as they sailed along he went to sleep. Then a heavy squall struck the lake; they began to ship water and

24 were in grave danger. They went to him, and roused him, crying, 'Master, Master, we are sinking!' He awoke, and rebuked the wind and the turbulent waters. The storm subsided and all was calm.

25 'Where is your faith?' he asked.

In fear and astonishment they said to one another, 'Who can this be? He gives his orders to wind and waves, and they obey him.'

26 So they landed in the country of the Gergesenes,[a] which is opposite Galilee. As he stepped ashore

27 he was met by a man from the town who was possessed by devils. For a long time he had neither worn clothes nor lived in a house, but stayed among the tombs.

28 When he saw Jesus he cried out, and fell at his feet shouting, 'What do you want with me, Jesus, son of the Most High God? I implore you, do not torment me.'

29 For Jesus was already ordering the unclean spirit to come out of the man. Many a time it had seized him, and then, for safety's sake, they would secure him with chains and fetters; but each time he broke loose, and with the devil in charge made off to the solitary places.

30 Jesus asked him, 'What is your name?' 'Legion', he replied. This was because so many devils had

31 taken possession of him. And they begged him not to banish them to the Abyss.

32 There happened to be a large herd of pigs nearby, feeding on the hill; and the spirits begged him to

33 let them go into these pigs. He gave them leave; the devils came out of the man and went into the pigs, and the herd rushed over the edge into the lake and were drowned.

34 The men in charge of them saw what had happened, and, taking to their heels, they carried the news

35 to the town and country-side; and the people came out to see for themselves. When they came to Jesus, and found the man from whom the devils had gone out sitting at his feet clothed and in his

36 right mind, they were afraid. The spectators told them how the madman had been cured. Then the

37 whole population of the Gergesene[b]

---

[a] *Some witnesses read* Gerasenes; *others read* Gadarenes.
[b] *Some witnesses read* Gerasene; *others read* Gadarene.

district asked him to go, for they were in the grip of a great fear. So he got into the boat and returned.

38 The man from whom the devils had gone out begged leave to go with him; but Jesus sent him away:

39 'Go back home,' he said, 'and tell them everything that God has done for you.' The man went all over the town spreading the news of what Jesus had done for him.

40 When Jesus returned, the people welcomed him, for they were all

41 expecting him. Then a man appeared – Jairus was his name and he was president of the synagogue. Throwing himself down at Jesus's feet he begged him to come to his

42 house, because he had an only daughter, about twelve years old, who was dying. And while Jesus was on his way he could hardly breathe for the crowds.

43 Among them was a woman who had suffered from haemorrhages for twelve years; and[a] nobody had

44 been able to cure her. She came up from behind and touched the edge of[b] his cloak, and at once her

45 haemorrhage stopped. Jesus said, 'Who was it that touched me?' All disclaimed it, and Peter and his companions said, 'Master, the crowds are hemming you in and

46 pressing upon you!' But Jesus said, 'Someone did touch me, for I felt that power had gone out from

47 me.' Then the woman, seeing that she was detected, came trembling and fell at his feet. Before all the people she explained why she had touched him and how she had been

48 instantly cured. He said to her, 'My daughter, your faith has cured you. Go in peace.'

49 While he was still speaking, a man came from the president's house with the message, 'Your daughter is dead; trouble the Rab-

50 bi no further.' But Jesus heard, and interposed. 'Do not be afraid,' he said; 'only show faith and she

will be well again.' On arrival at 51 the house he allowed no one to go in with him except Peter, John, and James, and the child's father and mother. And all were weeping 52 and lamenting for her. He said, 'Weep no more; she is not dead: she is asleep'; and they only laugh- 53 ed at him, well knowing that she was dead. But Jesus took hold of 54 her hand and called her: 'Get up, my child.' Her spirit returned, she 55 stood up immediately, and he told them to give her something to eat. Her parents were astounded; but 56 he forbade them to tell anyone what had happened.

HE now called the Twelve together 9 and gave them power and authority to overcome all the devils and to cure diseases, and sent them to 2 proclaim the kingdom of God and to heal. 'Take nothing for the 3 journey,' he told them, 'neither stick nor pack, neither bread nor money; nor are you each to have a second coat. When you are ad- 4 mitted to a house, stay there, and go on from there. As for those who 5 will not receive you, when you leave their town shake the dust off your feet as a warning to them.' So they set out and travelled from 6 village to village, and everywhere they told the good news and healed the sick.

Now Prince Herod heard of all 7 that was happening, and did not know what to make of it; for some were saying that John had been raised from the dead, others that 8 Elijah had appeared, others again that one of the old prophets had come back to life. Herod said, 9 'As for John, I beheaded him myself; but who is this I hear such talk about?' And he was anxious to see him.

On their return the apostles told 10 Jesus all they had done; and he took them with him and withdrew

---

[a] *Some witnesses add* though she had spent all she had on doctors.
[b] *Some witnesses omit* the edge of.

privately to a town called Beth-
11 saida. But the crowds found out
and followed him. He welcomed
them, and spoke to them about
the kingdom of God, and cured
those who were in need of healing.
12 When evening was drawing on, the
Twelve came up to him and said,
'Send these people away; then they
can go into the villages and farms
round about to find food and
lodging; for we are in a lonely place
13 here.' 'Give them something to eat
yourselves', he replied. But they
said, 'All we have is five loaves and
two fishes, nothing more – unless
perhaps we ourselves are to go and
buy provisions for all this com-
14 pany.' (There were about five
thousand men.) He said to his
disciples, 'Make them sit down in
15 groups of fifty or so.' They did so
16 and got them all seated. Then,
taking the five loaves and the two
fishes, he looked up to heaven, said
the blessing over them, broke them,
and gave them to the disciples to
17 distribute to the people. They all
ate to their hearts' content; and
when the scraps they left were
picked up, they filled twelve great
baskets.

18 One day when he was praying
alone in the presence of his disciples,
he asked them, 'Who do the people
19 say I am?' They answered, 'Some
say John the Baptist, others Elijah,
others that one of the old prophets
20 has come back to life.' 'And you,'
he said, 'who do you say I am?'
Peter answered, 'God's Messiah.'
21 Then he gave them strict orders
22 not to tell this to anyone. And he
said, 'The Son of Man has to undergo great sufferings, and to be rejected by the elders, chief priests,
and doctors of the law, to be put
to death and to be raised again on
the third day.'
23 And to all he said, 'If anyone
wishes to be a follower of mine, he
must leave self behind; day after
day he must take up his cross, and

come with me. Whoever cares for 24
his own safety is lost; but if a man
will let himself be lost for my sake,
that man is safe. What will a man 25
gain by winning the whole world,
at the cost of his true self? For 26
whoever is ashamed of me and
mine,[a] the Son of Man will be
ashamed of him, when he comes
in his glory and the glory of the
Father and the holy angels. And 27
I tell you this: there are some of
those standing here who will not
taste death before they have seen
the kingdom of God.'

About eight days after this con- 28
versation he took Peter, John, and
James with him and went up into
the hills to pray. And while he was 29
praying the appearance of his face
changed and his clothes became
dazzling white. Suddenly there 30
were two men talking with him;
these were Moses and Elijah, who 31
appeared in glory and spoke of his
departure, the destiny he was to
fulfil in Jerusalem. Meanwhile 32
Peter and his companions had been
in a deep sleep; but when they
awoke, they saw his glory and the
two men who stood beside him.
And as these were moving away 33
from Jesus, Peter said to him,
'Master, how good it is that we are
here! Shall we make three shelters,
one for you, one for Moses, and
one for Elijah?'; but he spoke
without knowing what he was saying. The words were still on his lips, 34
when there came a cloud which
cast a shadow over them; they
were afraid as they entered the
cloud, and from it came a voice: 35
'This is my Son, my Chosen; listen
to him.' When the voice had 36
spoken, Jesus was seen to be alone.
The disciples kept silence and at
that time told nobody anything of
what they had seen.

Next day when they came down 37
from the hills he was met by a
large crowd. All at once there was 38
a shout from a man in the crowd:

---

[a] *Some witnesses read* me and my words.

'Master, look at my son, I implore
39 you, my only child. From time to
time a spirit seizes him, gives a
sudden scream, and throws him
into convulsions with foaming at
the mouth, and it keeps on mauling
him and will hardly let him go.
40 I asked your disciples to cast it
41 out, but they could not.' Jesus
answered, 'What an unbelieving
and perverse generation! How long
shall I be with you and endure you
42 all? Bring your son here.' But
before the boy could reach him
the devil dashed him to the ground
and threw him into convulsions.
Jesus rebuked the unclean spirit,
cured the boy, and gave him back
43 to his father. And they were all
struck with awe at the majesty
of God.

Amid the general wonder and
admiration at all he was doing,
44 Jesus said to his disciples, 'What
I now say is for you: ponder my
words. The Son of Man is to be
given up into the power of men.'
45 But they did not understand this
saying; it had been hidden from
them, so that they should not[a]
grasp its meaning, and they were
afraid to ask him about it.
46 A dispute arose among them:
which of them was the greatest?
47 Jesus knew what was passing in
their minds, so he took a child by
the hand and stood him at his side,
48 and said, 'Whoever receives this
child in my name receives me; and
whoever receives me receives the
One who sent me. For the least
among you all – he is the greatest.'
49 'Master,' said John, 'we saw a
man driving out devils in your
name, but as he is not one of us
50 we tried to stop him.' Jesus said
to him, 'Do not stop him, for he
who is not against you is on your
side.'

Journeys and encounters

As the time approached when he 51
was to be taken up to heaven, he
set his face resolutely towards
Jerusalem, and sent messengers 52
ahead. They set out and went into
a Samaritan village to make arrangements for him; but the villag- 53
ers would not have him because
he was making for Jerusalem.
When the disciples James and 54
John saw this they said, 'Lord,
may we call down fire from heaven
to burn them up[b]?' But he turned 55
and rebuked them,[c] and they went 56
on to another village.

As they were going along the 57
road a man said to him, 'I will
follow you wherever you go.' Jesus 58
answered, 'Foxes have their holes,
the birds their roosts; but the Son
of Man has nowhere to lay his
head.' To another he said, 'Follow 59
me', but the man replied, 'Let me
go and bury my father first.' Jesus 60
said, 'Leave the dead to bury their
dead; you must go and announce
the kingdom of God.'

Yet another said, 'I will follow 61
you, sir; but let me first say good-
bye to my people at home.' To him 62
Jesus said, 'No one who sets his
hand to the plough and then keeps
looking back[d] is fit for the kingdom
of God.'

After this the Lord appointed a 10
further seventy-two[e] and sent
them on ahead in pairs to every
town and place he was going to
visit himself. He said to them: 2
'The crop is heavy, but labourers
are scarce; you must therefore beg
the owner to send labourers to
harvest his crop. Be on your way. 3
And look, I am sending you like
lambs among wolves. Carry no 4
purse or pack, and travel barefoot.
Exchange no greetings on the road.

---

[a] *Or it was so obscure to them that they could not* . . .   [b] *Some witnesses add*
as Elijah did.   [c] *Some witnesses insert* 'You do not know', he said, 'to what
spirit you belong; (56) for the Son of Man did not come to destroy men's lives but
to save them.'   [d] *Some witnesses read* No one who looks back as he sets
hand to the plough . . .   [e] *Some witnesses read* seventy.

5 When you go into a house, let your first words be, "Peace to this 6 house." If there is a man of peace there, your peace will rest upon him; if not, it will return and rest 7 upon you. Stay in that one house, sharing their food and drink; for the worker earns his pay. Do not 8 move from house to house. When you come into a town and they make you welcome, eat the food 9 provided for you; heal the sick there, and say, "The kingdom of 10 God has come close to you." When you enter a town and they do not make you welcome, go out into its 11 streets and say, "The very dust of your town that clings to our feet we wipe off to your shame. Only take note of this: the king-12 dom of God has come close." I tell you, it will be more bearable for Sodom on the great Day than for that town.

13   'Alas for you, Chorazin! Alas for you, Bethsaida! If the miracles that were performed in you had been performed in Tyre and Sidon, they would have repented long ago, sitting in sackcloth and ashes. 14 But it will be more bearable for Tyre and Sidon at the Judgement 15 than for you. And as for you, Capernaum, will you be exalted to the skies? No, brought down to the depths!

16   'Whoever listens to you listens to me; whoever rejects you rejects me. And whoever rejects me rejects the One who sent me.'

17   The seventy-two[a] came back jubilant. 'In your name, Lord,' they said, 'even the devils submit 18 to us.' He replied, 'I watched how Satan fell, like lightning, out of the 19 sky. And now you see that I have given you the power to tread under-foot snakes and scorpions and all the forces of the enemy, and no-20 thing will ever harm you.[b] Never-theless, what you should rejoice over is not that the spirits submit to you, but that your names are enrolled in heaven.'

At that moment Jesus exulted 21 in the Holy[c] Spirit and said, 'I thank thee, Father, Lord of heaven and earth, for hiding these things from the learned and wise, and revealing them to the simple. Yes, Father, such[d] was thy choice.' Then turning to his disciples he 22 said,[e] 'Everything is entrusted to me by my Father; and no one knows who the Son is but the Father, or who the Father is but the Son, and those to whom the Son may choose to reveal him.'

Turning to his disciples in pri-23 vate he said, 'Happy the eyes that see what you are seeing! I tell you, 24 many prophets and kings wished to see what you now see, yet never saw it; to hear what you hear, yet never heard it.'

ON one occasion a lawyer came 25 forward to put this test question to him: 'Master, what must I do to inherit eternal life?' Jesus said, 26 'What is written in the Law? What is your reading of it?' He replied, 27 'Love the Lord your God with all your heart, with all your soul, with all your strength, and with all your mind; and your neighbour as your-self.' 'That is the right answer,' said 28 Jesus; 'do that and you will live.'

But he wanted to vindicate him-29 self, so he said to Jesus, 'And who is my neighbour?' Jesus replied, 'A 30 man was on his way from Jerusa-lem down to Jericho when he fell in with robbers, who stripped him, beat him, and went off leaving him half dead. It so happened that a 31 priest was going down by the same road; but when he saw him, he went past on the other side. So too 32 a Levite came to the place, and when he saw him went past on the other side. But a Samaritan who 33

---

[a] *Some witnesses read* seventy.   [b] *Or* and he will have no way at all to harm you.
[c] *Some witnesses omit* Holy.   [d] *Or* Yes, I thank thee, Father, that such...
[e] *Some witnesses omit* Then...he said.

was making the journey came upon him, and when he saw him 34 was moved to pity. He went up and bandaged his wounds, bathing them with oil and wine. Then he lifted him on to his own beast, brought him to an inn, and looked 35 after him there. Next day he produced two silver pieces and gave them to the innkeeper, and said, "Look after him; and if you spend any more, I will repay you on my 36 way back." Which of these three do you think was neighbour to the man who fell into the hands of the 37 robbers?' He answered, 'The one who showed him kindness.' Jesus said, 'Go and do as he did.'

38   While they were on their way Jesus came to a village where a woman named Martha made him 39 welcome in her home. She had a sister, Mary, who seated herself at the Lord's feet and stayed there 40 listening to his words. Now Martha was distracted by her many tasks, so she came to him and said, 'Lord, do you not care that my sister has left me to get on with the work by myself? Tell her to come and lend 41 a hand.' But the Lord answered, 'Martha, Martha, you are fretting and fussing about so many things; 42 but one thing is necessary.[a] The part that Mary has chosen is best; and it shall not be taken away from her.'

11   Once, in a certain place, Jesus was at prayer. When he ceased, one of his disciples said, 'Lord, teach us to pray, as John taught 2 his disciples.' He answered, 'When you pray, say,

"Father,[b] thy name be hallowed; thy kingdom come.[c]
3 Give us each day our daily bread.[d]

And forgive us our sins,   4
for we too forgive all who have done us wrong.
And do not bring us to the test." '[e]

Then he said to them, 'Suppose 5 one of you has a friend who comes to him in the middle of the night and says, "My friend, lend me three loaves, for a friend of mine 6 on a journey has turned up at my house, and I have nothing to offer him"; and he replies from inside, 7 "Do not bother me. The door is shut for the night; my children and I have gone to bed; and I cannot get up and give you what you want." I tell you that even if he 8 will not provide for him out of friendship, the very shamelessness of the request will make him get up and give him all he needs. And 9 so I say to you, ask, and you will receive; seek, and you will find; knock, and the door will be opened. For everyone who asks receives, 10 he who seeks finds, and to him who knocks, the door will be opened.

'Is there a father among you 11 who will offer his son[f] a snake when he asks for fish, or a scorpion when 12 he asks for an egg? If you, then, 13 bad as you are, know how to give your children what is good for them, how much more will the heavenly Father give the Holy Spirit[g] to those who ask him!'

HE was driving out a devil which 14 was dumb; and when the devil had come out, the dumb man began to speak. The people were astonished, but some of them said, 'It 15 is by Beelzebub prince of devils that he drives the devils out.' Others, by way of a test, demanded 16 of him a sign from heaven. But he 17

---

[a] *Some witnesses read* but few things are necessary, or rather, one alone; *others omit* you are fretting…necessary.   [b] *Some witnesses read* Our Father in heaven.
[c] *One witness reads* thy kingdom come upon us; *some others have* thy Holy Spirit come upon us and cleanse us; *some insert* thy will be done, on earth as in heaven.
[d] *Or* our bread for the morrow.   [e] *Some witnesses add* but save us from the evil one (*or* from evil).   [f] *Some witnesses insert* a stone when he asks for bread, or…   [g] *Some witnesses read* a good gift; *some others read* good things.

knew what was in their minds, and said, 'Every kingdom divided against itself goes to ruin, and a 18 divided household falls. Equally if Satan is divided against himself, how can his kingdom stand? – since, as you would have it, I drive out 19 the devils by Beelzebub. If it is by Beelzebub that I cast out devils, by whom do your own people drive them out? If this is your argument, they themselves will refute you. 20 But if it is by the finger of God that I drive out the devils, then be sure the kingdom of God has already come upon you.

21 'When a strong man fully armed is on guard over his castle his pos-22 sessions are safe. But when someone stronger comes upon him and overpowers him, he carries off the arms and armour on which the man had relied and divides the plunder.

23 'He who is not with me is against me, and he who does not gather with me scatters.*a*

24 'When an unclean spirit comes out of a man it wanders over the deserts seeking a resting-place; and if it finds none, it says, "I will 25 go back to the home I left." So it returns and finds the house*b* swept 26 clean, and tidy. Off it goes and collects seven other spirits more wicked than itself, and they all come in and settle down; and in the end the man's plight is worse than before.'

27 While he was speaking thus, a woman in the crowd called out, 'Happy the womb that carried you and the breasts that suckled you!' 28 He rejoined, 'No, happy are those who hear the word of God and keep it.'

29 With the crowds swarming round him he went on to say: 'This is a wicked generation. It demands a sign, and the only sign that will be given it is the sign of Jonah. For just as Jonah was a sign to the 30 Ninevites, so will the Son of Man be to this generation. At the Judge-31 ment, when the men of this generation are on trial, the Queen of the South will appear against*c* them and ensure their condemnation, for she came from the ends of the earth to hear the wisdom of Solomon; and what is here is greater than Solomon. The men of Nineveh 32 will appear at the Judgement when this generation is on trial, and ensure*d* its condemnation, for they repented at the preaching of Jonah; and what is here is greater than Jonah.

33 'No one lights a lamp and puts it in a cellar,*e* but rather on the lamp-stand so that those who enter may see the light. The lamp of your 34 body is the eye. When your eyes are sound, you have light for your whole body; but when the eyes are bad, you are in darkness. See to it 35 then that the light you have is not darkness. If you have light for your 36 whole body with no trace of darkness, it will all be as bright as when a lamp flashes its rays upon you.'

WHEN he had finished speaking, a 37 Pharisee invited him to a meal. He came in and sat down. The Pharisee 38 noticed with surprise that he had not begun by washing before the meal. But the Lord said to him, 39 'You Pharisees! You clean the outside of cup and plate; but inside you there is nothing but greed and wickedness. You fools! Did not he 40 who made the outside make the inside too? But let what is in the 41 cup*f* be given in charity, and all is clean.

'Alas for you Pharisees! You pay 42 tithes of mint and rue and every garden-herb, but have no care for justice and the love of God. It is

---

a Some witnesses add me.　　　*b Some witnesses insert unoccupied.*
c Or will be raised to life together with...　　　*d Or At the Judgement the men of Nineveh will rise again together with this generation and will ensure...*
e Some witnesses insert or under the meal-tub.　　　*f Or what you can afford.*

these you should have practised, without neglecting the others.[a]

43 'Alas for you Pharisees! You love the seats of honour in synagogues, and salutations in the market-places.

44 'Alas, alas, you are like unmarked graves over which men may walk without knowing it.'

45 In reply to this one of the lawyers said, 'Master, when you say things like this you are insulting 46 us too.' Jesus rejoined: 'Yes, you lawyers, it is no better with you! For you load men with intolerable burdens, and will not put a single finger to the load.

47 'Alas, you build the tombs of the prophets whom your fathers 48 murdered, and so testify that you approve of the deeds your fathers did; they committed the murders and you provide the tombs.

49 'This is why the Wisdom of God said, "I will send them prophets and messengers; and some of these 50 they will persecute and kill"; so that this generation will have to answer for the blood of all the prophets shed since the foundation 51 of the world; from the blood of Abel to the blood of Zechariah who perished between the altar and the sanctuary. I tell you, this generation will have to answer for it all.

52 'Alas for you lawyers! You have taken away the key of knowledge. You did not go in yourselves, and those who were on their way in, you stopped.'

53 After he had left the house, the lawyers and Pharisees began to assail him fiercely and to ply him 54 with a host of questions, laying snares to catch him with his own words.

12 MEANWHILE, when a crowd of many thousands had gathered, packed so close that they were treading on one another, he began to speak first to his disciples: 'Beware of the leaven of the Pharisees;

I mean their hypocrisy. There is 2 nothing covered up that will not be uncovered, nothing hidden that will not be made known. You may take 3 it, then, that everything you have said in the dark will be heard in broad daylight, and what you have whispered behind closed doors will be shouted from the house-tops.

'To you who are my friends I 4 say: Do not fear those who kill the body and after that have nothing more they can do. I will warn you 5 whom to fear: fear him who, after he has killed, has authority to cast into hell. Believe me, he is the one to fear.

'Are not sparrows five for two- 6 pence? And yet not one of them is overlooked by God. More than 7 that, even the hairs of your head have all been counted. Have no fear; you are worth more than any number of sparrows.

'I tell you this: everyone who 8 acknowledges me before men, the Son of Man will acknowledge before the angels of God; but he who 9 disowns me before men will be disowned before the angels of God.

'Anyone who speaks a word a- 10 gainst the Son of Man will receive forgiveness; but for him who slanders the Holy Spirit there will be no forgiveness.

'When you are brought before 11 synagogues and state authorities, do not begin worrying about how you will conduct your defence or what you will say. For when the 12 time comes the Holy Spirit will instruct you what to say.'

A man in the crowd said to him, 13 'Master, tell my brother to divide the family property with me.' He 14 replied, 'My good man, who set me over you to judge or arbitrate?'[b] Then he said to the people, 'Be- 15 ware! Be on your guard against greed of every kind, for even when a man has more than enough, his wealth does not give him life.' And 16 he told them this parable: 'There

---

[a] *Some witnesses omit* It is...others.

[b] *Some witnesses omit* or arbitrate.

was a rich man whose land yielded
17 heavy crops. He debated with himself: "What am I to do? I have not the space to store my produce.
18 This is what I will do," said he: "I will pull down my storehouses and build them bigger. I will collect in them all my corn and other
19 goods, and then say to myself, 'Man, you have plenty of good things laid by, enough for many years: take life easy, eat, drink,
20 and enjoy yourself.'" But God said to him, "You fool, this very night you must surrender your life; you have made your money – who will
21 get it now?" That is how it is with the man who amasses wealth for himself and remains a pauper in the sight of God.[a]

22 'Therefore', he said to his disciples, 'I bid you put away anxious thoughts about food to keep you alive and clothes to cover your
23 body. Life is more than food, the
24 body more than clothes. Think of the ravens: they neither sow nor reap; they have no storehouse or barn; yet God feeds them. You are
25 worth far more than the birds! Is there a man among you who by anxious thought can add a foot to
26 his height[b]? If, then, you cannot do even a very little thing, why are you anxious about the rest?
27 'Think of the lilies: they neither spin nor weave;[c] yet I tell you, even Solomon in all his splendour was not attired like one of these.
28 But if that is how God clothes the grass, which is growing in the field today, and tomorrow is thrown on the stove, how much more will he clothe you! How little faith you
29 have! And so you are not to set your mind on food and drink; you
30 are not to worry. For all these are things for the heathen to run after; but you have a Father who knows
31 that you need them. No, set your mind upon his kingdom, and

all the rest will come to you as well.

'Have no fear, little flock; for 32 your Father has chosen to give you the Kingdom. Sell your possessions 33 and give in charity. Provide for yourselves purses that do not wear out, and never-failing treasure in heaven, where no thief can get near it, no moth destroy it. For 34 where your treasure is, there will your heart be also.

'Be ready for action, with belts 35 fastened and lamps alight. Be like 36 men who wait for their master's return from a wedding-party, ready to let him in the moment he arrives and knocks. Happy are those ser- 37 vants whom the master finds on the alert when he comes. I tell you this: he will fasten his belt, seat them at table, and come and wait on them. Even if it is the middle 38 of the night or before dawn when he comes, happy they if he finds them alert. And remember, if the 39 householder had known what time the burglar was coming he would not have let his house be broken into. Hold yourselves ready, then, 40 because the Son of Man will come at the time you least expect him.'

Peter said, 'Lord, do you intend 41 this parable specially for us or is it for everyone?' The Lord said, 'Well, 42 who is the trusty and sensible man whom his master will appoint as his steward, to manage his servants and issue their rations at the proper time? Happy that servant 43 who is found at his task when his master comes! I tell you this: he 44 will be put in charge of all his master's property. But if that 45 servant says to himself, "The master is a long time coming", and begins to bully the menservants and maids, and eat and drink and get drunk; then the master will 46 arrive on a day that servant does

---

[a] *Some witnesses omit* That . . . God; *others add at the end* When he said this he cried out, 'If you have ears to hear, then hear.'　　　　[b] *Or* a day to his life.
[c] *Some witnesses read* they grow, they do not toil or spin.

not expect, at a time he does not know, and will cut him in pieces. Thus he will find his place among the faithless.

47 'The servant who knew his master's wishes, yet made no attempt to carry them out, will be flogged

48 severely. But one who did not know them and earned a beating will be flogged less severely. Where a man has been given much, much will be expected of him; and the more a man has had entrusted to him the more he will be required to repay.

49 'I have come to set fire to the earth, and how I wish it were al-

50 ready kindled! I have a baptism to undergo, and what constraint I am under until the ordeal is over!

51 Do you suppose I came to establish peace on earth? No indeed, I have

52 come to bring division. For from now on, five members of a family will be divided, three against two

53 and two against three; father against son and son against father, mother against daughter and daughter against mother, mother against son's wife and son's wife against her mother-in-law.'

54 He also said to the people, 'When you see cloud banking up in the west, you say at once, "It is going

55 to rain", and rain it does. And when the wind is from the south, you say, "There will be a heat-

56 wave", and there is. What hypocrites you are! You know how to interpret the appearance of earth and sky; how is it you cannot interpret this fateful hour?

57 'And why can you not judge for yourselves what is the right course?

58 When you are going with your opponent to court, make an effort to settle with him while you are still on the way; otherwise he may drag you before the judge, and the judge hand you over to the constable, and the constable put you

59 in jail. I tell you, you will not come out till you have paid the last farthing.'

AT that very time there were some 13 people present who told him about the Galileans whose blood Pilate had mixed with their sacrifices. He 2 answered them: 'Do you imagine that, because these Galileans suffered this fate, they must have been greater sinners than anyone else in Galilee? I tell you they 3 were not; but unless you repent, you will all of you come to the same end. Or the eighteen people 4 who were killed when the tower fell on them at Siloam – do you imagine they were more guilty than all the other people living in Jerusalem? I tell you they were 5 not; but unless you repent, you will all of you come to the same end.'

He told them this parable: 'A 6 man had a fig-tree growing in his vineyard; and he came looking for fruit on it, but found none. So he 7 said to the vine-dresser, "Look here! For the last three years I have come looking for fruit on this fig-tree without finding any. Cut it down. Why should it go on using up the soil?" But he replied, 8 "Leave it, sir, this one year while I dig round it and manure it. And 9 if it bears next season, well and good; if not, you shall have it down."'

One Sabbath he was teaching 10 in a synagogue, and there was a 11 woman there possessed by a spirit that had crippled her for eighteen years. She was bent double and quite unable to stand up straight. When Jesus saw her he called her 12 and said, 'You are rid of your trouble.' Then he laid his hands on 13 her, and at once she straightened up and began to praise God. But 14 the president of the synagogue, indignant with Jesus for healing on the Sabbath, intervened and said to the congregation, 'There are six working-days: come and be cured on one of them, and not on the Sabbath.' The Lord gave 15 him his answer: 'What hypocrites you are!' he said. 'Is there a single one of you who does not loose his ox or his donkey from the manger and take it out to water on the 16 Sabbath? And here is this woman, a daughter of Abraham, who has been kept prisoner by Satan for eighteen long years: is it wrong for her to be freed from her bonds 17 on the Sabbath?' At these words all his opponents were covered with confusion, while the mass of the people were delighted at all the wonderful things he was doing.

18　'What is the kingdom of God like?' he continued. 'What shall 19 I compare it with? It is like a mustard-seed which a man took and sowed in his garden; and it grew to be a tree and the birds came to roost among its branches.'

20　Again he said, 'The kingdom of God, what shall I compare it with? 21 It is like yeast which a woman took and mixed with half a hundred-weight of flour till it was all leavened.'

22 HE continued his journey through towns and villages, teaching as he made his way towards Jerusalem. 23 Someone asked him, 'Sir, are only a few to be saved?' His answer 24 was: 'Struggle to get in through the narrow door; for I tell you that many will try to enter and not be able.

25　'When once the master of the house has got up and locked the door, you may stand outside and knock, and say, "Sir, let us in!", but he will only answer, "I do not 26 know where you come from." Then you will begin to say, "We sat at table with you and you taught in 27 our streets." But he will repeat, "I tell you, I do not know where you come from. Out of my sight, all of you, you and your wicked ways!" 28 There will be wailing and grinding of teeth there, when you see Abraham, Isaac, and Jacob, and all the prophets, in the kingdom of God,

and yourselves thrown out. From 29 east and west people will come, from north and south, for the feast in the kingdom of God. Yes, and 30 some who are now last will be first, and some who are first will be last.'

At that time a number of Phari- 31 sees came to him and said, 'You should leave this place and go on your way; Herod is out to kill you.' He replied, 'Go and tell that fox, 32 "Listen: today and tomorrow I shall be casting out devils and working cures; on the third day I reach my goal." However, I must 33 be on my way today and tomorrow and the next day, because it is unthinkable for a prophet to meet his death anywhere but in Jerusalem.

'O Jerusalem, Jerusalem, the city 34 that murders the prophets and stones the messengers sent to her! How often have I longed to gather your children, as a hen gathers her brood under her wings; but you would not let me. Look, look! there 35 is your temple, forsaken by God. And I tell you, you shall never see me until the time comes when you say, "Blessings on him who comes in the name of the Lord!"'

ONE Sabbath he went to have a 14 meal in the house of a leading Pharisee; and they were watching him closely. There, in front of 2 him, was a man suffering from dropsy. Jesus asked the lawyers 3 and the Pharisees: 'Is it permitted to cure people on the Sabbath or not?' They said nothing. So he took 4 the man, cured him, and sent him away. Then he turned to them and 5 said, 'If one of you has a donkey[a] or an ox and it falls into a well, will he hesitate to haul it up on the Sabbath day?' To this they could 6 find no reply.

When he noticed how the guests 7 were trying to secure the places of honour, he spoke to them in a parable: 'When you are asked by 8 someone to a wedding-feast, do

a Some witnesses read son.

not sit down in the place of honour. It may be that some person more distinguished than yourself has 9 been invited; and the host will come and say to you, "Give this man your seat." Then you will 10 look foolish as you begin to take the lowest place. No, when you receive an invitation, go and sit down in the lowest place, so that when your host comes he will say, "Come up higher, my friend." Then all your fellow-guests will 11 see the respect in which you are held. For everyone who exalts himself will be humbled; and whoever humbles himself will be exalted.'

12   Then he said to his host, 'When you are having a party for lunch or supper, do not invite your friends, your brothers or other relations, or your rich neighbours; they will only ask you back again and so 13 you will be repaid. But when you give a party, ask the poor, the crippled, the lame, and the blind; 14 and so find happiness. For they have no means of repaying you; but you will be repaid on the day when good men rise from the dead.'

15   One of the company, after hearing all this, said to him, 'Happy the man who shall sit at the feast in 16 the kingdom of God!' Jesus answered, 'A man was giving a big dinner party and had sent out 17 many invitations. At dinner-time he sent his servant with a message for his guests, "Please come, every-18 thing is now ready." They began one and all to excuse themselves. The first said, "I have bought a piece of land, and I must go and look over it; please accept my 19 apologies." The second said, "I have bought five yoke of oxen, and I am on my way to try them out; 20 please accept my apologies." The next said, "I have just got married and for that reason I cannot come." 21 When the servant came back he reported this to his master. The master of the house was angry and

said to him, "Go out quickly into the streets and alleys of the town, and bring me in the poor, the crippled, the blind, and the lame." The servant said, "Sir, your orders 22 have been carried out and there is still room." The master replied, 23 "Go out on to the highways and along the hedgerows and make them come in; I want my house to be full. I tell you that not one 24 of those who were invited shall taste my banquet."'

Once when great crowds were 25 accompanying him, he turned to them and said: 'If anyone comes 26 to me and does not hate his father and mother, wife and children, brothers and sisters, even his own life, he cannot be a disciple of mine. No one who does not carry his cross 27 and come with me can be a disciple of mine. Would any of you think 28 of building a tower without first sitting down and calculating the cost, to see whether he could afford to finish it? Otherwise, if he has 29 laid its foundation and then is not able to complete it, all the onlookers will laugh at him. "There is the 30 man", they will say, "who started to build and could not finish." Or 31 what king will march to battle against another king, without first sitting down to consider whether with ten thousand men he can face an enemy coming to meet him with twenty thousand? If he can-32 not, then, long before the enemy approaches, he sends envoys, and asks for terms. So also none of you 33 can be a disciple of mine without parting with all his possessions.

'Salt is a good thing; but if salt 34 itself becomes tasteless, what will you use to season it? It is useless 35 either on the land or on the dung-heap: it can only be thrown away. If you have ears to hear, then hear.'

ANOTHER time, the tax-gather-15 ers and other bad characters were all crowding in to listen to him; and the Pharisees and the doctors 2 of the law began grumbling among themselves: 'This fellow', they said, 'welcomes sinners and eats with 3 them.' He answered them with this 4 parable: 'If one of you has a hundred sheep and loses one of them, does he not leave the ninety-nine in the open pasture and go after the missing one until he has found 5 it? How delighted he is then! He 6 lifts it on to his shoulders, and home he goes to call his friends and neighbours together. "Rejoice with me!" he cries. "I have found 7 my lost sheep." In the same way, I tell you, there will be greater joy in heaven over one sinner who repents than over ninety-nine righteous people who do not need to repent.

8 'Or again, if a woman has ten silver pieces and loses one of them, does she not light the lamp, sweep out the house, and look in every 9 corner till she has found it? And when she has, she calls her friends and neighbours together, and says, "Rejoice with me! I have found 10 the piece that I lost." In the same way, I tell you, there is joy among the angels of God over one sinner who repents.'

11 Again he said: 'There was once 12 a man who had two sons; and the younger said to his father, "Father, give me my share of the property." So he divided his estate between 13 them. A few days later the younger son turned the whole of his share into cash and left home for a distant country, where he squan-14 dered it in reckless living. He had spent it all, when a severe famine fell upon that country and he 15 began to feel the pinch. So he went and attached himself to one of the local landowners, who sent him on to his farm to mind the pigs. 16 He would have been glad to fill his belly with[a] the pods that the pigs were eating; and no one gave 17 him anything. Then he came to his senses and said, "How many of my father's paid servants have more food than they can eat, and here am I, starving to death! I will 18 set off and go to my father, and say to him, 'Father, I have sinned, against God and against you; I am 19 no longer fit to be called your son; treat me as one of your paid servants.'" So he set out for his 20 father's house. But while he was still a long way off his father saw him, and his heart went out to him. He ran to meet him, flung his arms round him, and kissed him. The son said, "Father, I have sin-21 ned, against God and against you; I am no longer fit to be called your son."[b] But the father said to his 22 servants, "Quick! fetch a robe, my best one, and put it on him; put a ring on his finger and shoes on his feet. Bring the fatted calf and 23 kill it, and let us have a feast to celebrate the day. For this son of 24 mine was dead and has come back to life; he was lost and is found." And the festivities began.

'Now the elder son was out on 25 the farm; and on his way back, as he approached the house, he heard music and dancing. He called one 26 of the servants and asked what it meant. The servant told him, 27 "Your brother has come home, and your father has killed the fatted calf because he has him back safe and sound." But he was angry and 28 refused to go in. His father came out and pleaded with him; but he 29 retorted, "You know how I have slaved for you all these years; I never once disobeyed your orders; and you never gave me so much as a kid, for a feast with my friends. But now that this son of yours 30 turns up, after running through your money with his women, you kill the fatted calf for him." "My 31 boy," said the father, "you are always with me, and everything I have is yours. How could we help 32

---

[a] *Some witnesses read* to have his fill of . . .
[b] *Some witnesses add* treat me as one of your paid servants.

celebrating this happy day? Your brother here was dead and has come back to life, was lost and is found."'

16 He said to his disciples, 'There was a rich man who had a steward, and he received complaints that this man was squandering the pro-2 perty. So he sent for him, and said, "What is this that I hear? Produce your accounts, for you cannot be 3 manager here any longer." The steward said to himself, "What am I to do now that my employer is dismissing me? I am not strong enough to dig, and too proud to 4 beg. I know what I must do, to make sure that, when I have to leave, there will be people to give 5 me house and home." He summoned his master's debtors one by one. To the first he said, "How much 6 do you owe my master?" He replied, "A thousand gallons of olive oil." He said, "Here is your account. Sit down and make it five hundred; 7 and be quick about it." Then he said to another, "And you, how much do you owe?" He said, "A thousand bushels of wheat", and was told, "Take your account and 8 make it eight hundred." And the master applauded the dishonest steward for acting so astutely. For the worldly are more astute than the other-worldly in dealing with their own kind.

9 'So I say to you, use your world-ly wealth to win friends for your-selves, so that when money is a thing of the past you may be received into an eternal home.

10 'The man who can be trusted in little things can be trusted also in great; and the man who is dis-honest in little things is dishonest 11 also in great things. If, then, you have not proved trustworthy with the wealth of this world, who will trust you with the wealth that is 12 real? And if you have proved un-trustworthy with what belongs to another, who will give you what is your own?

'No servant can be the slave of 13 two masters; for either he will hate the first and love the second, or he will be devoted to the first and think nothing of the second. You cannot serve God and Money.'

The Pharisees, who loved money, 14 heard all this and scoffed at him. He said to them, 'You are the 15 people who impress your fellow-men with your righteousness; but God sees through you; for what sets itself up to be admired by men is detestable in the sight of God.

'Until John, it was the Law and 16 the prophets: since then, there is the good news of the kingdom of God, and everyone forces his way in.

'It is easier for heaven and earth 17 to come to an end than for one dot or stroke of the Law to lose its force.

'A man who divorces his wife 18 and marries another commits adul-tery; and anyone who marries a woman divorced from her husband commits adultery.

'There was once a rich man, who 19 dressed in purple and the finest linen, and feasted in great magnifi-cence every day. At his gate, cover- 20 ed with sores, lay a poor man named Lazarus, who would have 21 been glad to satisfy his hunger with the scraps from the rich man's table. Even the dogs used to come and lick his sores. One day the 22 poor man died and was carried away by the angels to be with Abraham. The rich man also died and was buried, and in Hades, 23 where he was in torment, he looked up; and there, far away, was Abraham with Lazarus close be-side him. "Abraham, my father," 24 he called out, "take pity on me! Send Lazarus to dip the tip of his finger in water, to cool my tongue, for I am in agony in this fire." But 25 Abraham said, "Remember, my child, that all the good things fell to you while you were alive, and all the bad to Lazarus; now he has

his consolation here and it is you
26 who are in agony. But that is not
all: there is a great chasm fixed
between us; no one from our side
who wants to reach you can cross
it, and none may pass from your
27 side to us." "Then, father," he
replied, "will you send him to my
28 father's house, where I have five
brothers, to warn them, so that
they too may not come to this place
29 of torment?" But Abraham said,
"They have Moses and the prophets; let them listen to them."
30 "No, father Abraham," he replied,
"but if someone from the dead
visits them, they will repent."
31 Abraham answered, "If they do
not listen to Moses and the prophets they will pay no heed even
if someone should rise from the
dead."'

17 HE said to his disciples, 'Causes of
stumbling are bound to arise; but
woe betide the man through whom
2 they come. It would be better for
him to be thrown into the sea with
a millstone round his neck than
to cause one of these little ones
3 to stumble. Keep watch on yourselves.

'If your brother wrongs you,
reprove him; and if he repents,
4 forgive him. Even if he wrongs you
seven times in a day and comes
back to you seven times saying,
"I am sorry", you are to forgive
him.'

5 The apostles said to the Lord,
6 'Increase our faith'; and the Lord
replied, 'If you had faith no bigger
even than a mustard-seed, you
could say to this mulberry-tree,
"Be rooted up and replanted in
the sea"; and it would at once obey
you.

7 'Suppose one of you has a servant
ploughing or minding sheep. When
he comes back from the fields, will
the master say, "Come along at
8 once and sit down"? Will he not

rather say, "Prepare my supper,
fasten your belt, and then wait
on me while I have my meal; you
can have yours afterwards"? Is he 9
grateful to the servant for carrying
out his orders? So with you: when 10
you have carried out all your
orders, you should say, "We are
servants and deserve no credit;
we have only done our duty."'

In the course of his journey 11
to Jerusalem he was travelling
through the borderlands of Samaria
and Galilee. As he was entering 12
a village he was met by ten men
with leprosy. They stood some way
off and called out to him, 'Jesus, 13
Master, take pity on us.' When 14
he saw them he said, 'Go and show
yourselves to the priests'; and
while they were on their way, they
were made clean. One of them, 15
finding himself cured, turned back
praising God aloud. He threw him- 16
self down at Jesus's feet and
thanked him. And he was a Samaritan. At this Jesus said: 'Were 17
not all ten cleansed? The other
nine, where are they? Could none 18
be found to come back and give
praise to God except this foreigner?'
And he said to the man, 'Stand up 19
and go on your way; your faith has
cured you.'

THE Pharisees asked him, 'When 20
will the kingdom of God come?'
He said, 'You cannot tell by observation when the kingdom of God
comes. There will be no saying, 21
"Look, here it is!" or "there it is!";
for in fact the kingdom of God is
among you.'[a]

He said to the disciples, 'The 22
time will come when you will long
to see one of the days of the Son
of Man, but you will not see it.
They will say to you, "Look! 23
There!" and "Look! Here!" Do
not go running off in pursuit. For 24
like the lightning-flash that lights
up the earth from end to end, will

[a] Or for in fact the kingdom of God is within you, or for in fact the kingdom of God
is within your grasp, or for suddenly the kingdom of God will be among you.

25 the Son of Man be when his day comes. But first he must endure much suffering and be repudiated by this generation.

26 'As things were in Noah's days, so will they be in the days of the

27 Son of Man. They ate and drank and married, until the day that Noah went into the ark and the flood came and made an end of

28 them all. As things were in Lot's days, also: they ate and drank; they bought and sold; they planted

29 and built; but the day that Lot went out from Sodom, it rained fire and sulphur from the sky and

30 made an end of them all – it will be like that on the day when the Son of Man is revealed.

31 'On that day the man who is on the roof and his belongings in the house must not come down to pick them up; he, too, who is in

32 the fields must not go back. Re-

33 member Lot's wife. Whoever seeks to save his life will lose it; and whoever loses it will save it, and live.

34 'I tell you, on that night there will be two men in one bed: one

35 will be taken, the other left. There will be two women together grinding corn: one will be taken, the

37 other left.'[a] When they heard this they asked, 'Where, Lord?' He said, 'Where the corpse is, there the vultures will gather.'

18 HE spoke to them in a parable to show that they should keep on praying and never lose heart:

2 'There was once a judge who cared

3 nothing for God or man, and in the same town there was a widow who constantly came before him demanding justice against her oppo-

4 nent. For a long time he refused; but in the end he said to himself, "True, I care nothing for God or

5 man; but this widow is so great a nuisance that I will see her righted before she wears me out with her persistence."' The Lord said, 'You 6 hear what the unjust judge says; and will not God vindicate his 7 chosen, who cry out to him day and night, while he listens patiently to them[b]? I tell you, he will vindicate 8 them soon enough. But when the Son of Man comes, will he find faith on earth?'

And here is another parable that 9 he told. It was aimed at those who were sure of their own goodness and looked down on everyone else. 'Two men went up to the temple 10 to pray, one a Pharisee and the other a tax-gatherer. The Pharisee 11 stood up and prayed thus:[c] "I thank thee, O God, that I am not like the rest of men, greedy, dishonest, adulterous; or, for that matter, like this tax-gatherer. I 12 fast twice a week; I pay tithes on all that I get." But the other kept 13 his distance and would not even raise his eyes to heaven, but beat upon his breast, saying, "O God, have mercy on me, sinner that I am." It was this man, I tell you, 14 and not the other, who went home acquitted of his sins. For everyone who exalts himself will be humbled; and whoever humbles himself will be exalted.'

They even brought babies for 15 him to touch. When the disciples saw them they rebuked them, but 16 Jesus called for the children and said, 'Let the little ones come to me; do not try to stop them; for the kingdom of God belongs to such as these. I tell you that who- 17 ever does not accept the kingdom of God like a child will never enter it.'

A man of the ruling class put 18 this question to him: 'Good Master, what must I do to win eternal life?' Jesus said to him, 'Why do you 19

[a] *Some witnesses add* (36) two men in the fields: one will be taken, the other left.
[b] *Or* delays to help them.
[c] *Some witnesses read* stood up by himself and prayed thus; *others read* stood up and prayed thus privately.

call me good? No one is good
20 except God alone. You know the
commandments: "Do not commit
adultery; do not murder; do not
steal; do not give false evidence;
honour your father and mother." '
21 The man answered, 'I have kept all
22 these since I was a boy.' On hearing
this Jesus said, 'There is still one
thing lacking: sell everything you
have and distribute to the poor, and
you will have riches in heaven; and
23 come, follow me.' At these words
his heart sank; for he was a very
24 rich man. When Jesus saw it he
said, 'How hard it is for the
wealthy to enter the kingdom of
25 God! It is easier for a camel to go
through the eye of a needle than
for a rich man to enter the kingdom
26 of God.' Those who heard asked,
27 'Then who can be saved?' He answered, 'What is impossible for
men is possible for God.'

28 Peter said, 'We here have left
our belongings to become your
29 followers.' Jesus said, 'I tell you
this: there is no one who has given
up home, or wife, brothers, parents,
or children, for the sake of the
30 kingdom of God, who will not be
repaid many times over in this
age, and in the age to come have
eternal life.'

Challenge to Jerusalem

31 H E took the Twelve aside and said,
'We are now going up to Jerusalem;
and all that was written by the
prophets will come true for the
32 Son of Man. He will be handed
over to the foreign power. He will
be mocked, maltreated, and spat
33 upon. They will flog him and kill
him. And on the third day he will
34 rise again.' But they understood
nothing of all this; they did not
grasp what he was talking about;
its meaning was concealed from
them.

35 As he approached Jericho a blind
man sat at the roadside begging.
36 Hearing a crowd going past, he
asked what was happening. They 37
told him, 'Jesus of Nazareth is
passing by.' Then he shouted out, 38
'Jesus, Son of David, have pity on
me.' The people in front told him 39
to hold his tongue; but he called
out all the more, 'Son of David,
have pity on me.' Jesus stopped 40
and ordered the man to be brought
to him. When he came up he asked
him, 'What do you want me to 41
do for you?' 'Sir, I want my sight
back', he answered. Jesus said to 42
him, 'Have back your sight; your
faith has cured you.' He recovered 43
his sight instantly; and he followed
Jesus, praising God. And all the
people gave praise to God for what
they had seen.

Entering Jericho he made his 19
way through the city. There was 2
a man there named Zacchaeus; he
was superintendent of taxes and
very rich. He was eager to see 3
what Jesus looked like; but, being
a little man, he could not see him
for the crowd. So he ran on ahead 4
and climbed a sycomore-tree in
order to see him, for he was to
pass that way. When Jesus came 5
to the place, he looked up and said,
'Zacchaeus, be quick and come
down; I must come and stay with
you today.' He climbed down as 6
fast as he could and welcomed him
gladly. At this there was a general 7
murmur of disapproval. 'He has
gone in', they said, 'to be the guest
of a sinner.' But Zacchaeus stood 8
there and said to the Lord, 'Here
and now, sir, I give half my possessions to charity; and if I have
cheated anyone, I am ready to
repay him four times over.' Jesus 9
said to him, 'Salvation has come
to this house today! – for this man
too is a son of Abraham, and the 10
Son of Man has come to seek and
save what is lost.'

While they were listening to 11
this, he went on to tell them a
parable, because he was now close
to Jerusalem and they thought
the reign of God might dawn at

12 any moment. He said, 'A man of noble birth went on a long journey abroad, to be appointed king and 13 then return. But first he called ten of his servants and gave them a pound each, saying, "Trade with 14 this while I am away." His fellow-citizens hated him, and they sent a delegation on his heels to say, "We do not want this man as our 15 king." However, back he came as king, and sent for the servants to whom he had given the money, to see what profit each had made. 16 The first came and said, "Your pound, sir, has made ten more." 17 "Well done," he replied; "you are a good servant. You have shown yourself trustworthy in a very small matter, and you shall have 18 charge of ten cities." The second came and said, "Your pound, sir, 19 has made five more"; and he also was told, "You too, take charge 20 of five cities." The third came and said, "Here is your pound, sir; I kept it put away in a handkerchief. 21 I was afraid of you, because you are a hard man: you draw out what you never put in and reap 22 what you did not sow." "You rascal!" he replied; "I will judge you by your own words. You knew, did you, that I am a hard man, that I draw out what I never put in, and 23 reap what I did not sow? Then why did you not put my money on deposit, and I could have claimed it with interest when I came back?" 24 Turning to his attendants he said, "Take the pound from him and 25 give it to the man with ten." "But, sir," they replied, "he has ten al-26 ready." "I tell you," he went on, "the man who has will always be given more; but the man who has not will forfeit even what he has. 27 But as for those enemies of mine who did not want me for their king, bring them here and slaughter them in my presence."'

28 WITH that Jesus went forward and began the ascent to Jerusalem.

As he approached Bethphage and 29 Bethany at the hill called Olivet, he sent two of the disciples with 30 these instructions: 'Go to the village opposite; as you enter it you will find tethered there a colt which no one has yet ridden. Untie it and bring it here. If anyone 31 asks why you are untying it, say, "Our Master needs it."' The two 32 went on their errand and found it as he had told them; and while 33 they were untying the colt, its owners asked, 'Why are you un-tying that colt?' They answered, 34 'Our Master needs it.' So they 35 brought the colt to Jesus.

Then they threw their cloaks on the colt, for Jesus to mount, and 36 they carpeted the road with them as he went on his way. And now, as 37 he approached the descent from the Mount of Olives, the whole company of his disciples in their joy began to sing aloud the praises of God for all the great things they had seen:

'Blessings on him who comes as 38 king in the name of the Lord! Peace in heaven, glory in highest heaven!'

Some Pharisees who were in the 39 crowd said to him, 'Master, repri-mand your disciples.' He answered, 40 'I tell you, if my disciples keep silence the stones will shout aloud.' When he came in sight of the 41 city, he wept over it and said, 'If 42 only you had known, on this great day, the way that leads to peace! But no; it is hidden from your sight. For a time will come upon you, 43 when your enemies will set up siege-works against you; they will encircle you and hem you in at every point; they will bring you to 44 the ground, you and your children within your walls, and not leave you one stone standing on another, because you did not recognize God's moment when it came.' Then he went into the temple 45

and began driving out the traders,
46 with these words: 'Scripture says,
"My house shall be a house of
prayer"; but you have made it a
robbers' cave.'
47   Day by day he taught in the
temple. And the chief priests and
lawyers were bent on making an
end of him, with the support of the
48 leading citizens, but found they
were helpless, because the people
all hung upon his words.

20 ONE day, as he was teaching the
people in the temple and telling
them the good news, the priests
and lawyers, and the elders with
2 them, came upon him and accosted
him. 'Tell us', they said, 'by what
authority you are acting like this;
3 who gave you this authority?' He
answered them, 'I have a question
4 to ask you too: tell me, was the
baptism of John from God or from
5 men?' This set them arguing a-
mong themselves: 'If we say,
"from God", he will say, "Why
6 did you not believe him?" And if
we say, "from men", the people
will all stone us, for they are convinced that John was a prophet.'
7 So they replied that they could
8 not tell. And Jesus said to them,
'Then neither will I tell you by
what authority I act.'
9   He went on to tell the people
this parable: 'A man planted a
vineyard, let it out to vine-
growers, and went abroad for a
10 long time. When the season came,
he sent a servant to the tenants to
collect from them his share of the
produce; but the tenants thrashed
him and sent him away empty-
11 handed. He tried again and sent a
second servant; but he also was
thrashed, outrageously treated,
12 and sent away empty-handed. He
tried once more with a third; this
one too they wounded and flung
13 out. Then the owner of the vineyard said, "What am I to do? I will
send my own dear son;ª perhaps

they will respect him." But when 14
the tenants saw him they talked it
over together. "This is the heir,"
they said; "let us kill him so that
the property may come to us." So 15
they flung him out of the vineyard
and killed him. What then will the
owner of the vineyard do to them?
He will come and put these tenants 16
to death and let the vineyard to
others.'
   When they heard this, they said,
'God forbid!' But he looked 17
straight at them and said, 'Then
what does this text of Scripture
mean: "The stone which the
builders rejected has become the
main corner-stone"? Any man 18
who falls on that stone will be
dashed to pieces; and if it falls on
a man he will be crushed by it.'
   The lawyers and chief priests 19
wanted to lay hands on him there
and then, for they saw that this
parable was aimed at them; but
they were afraid of the people. So 20
they watched their opportunity
and sent secret agents in the guise
of honest men, to seize upon some
word of his as a pretext for handing him over to the authority and
jurisdiction of the Governor. They 21
put a question to him: 'Master,'
they said, 'we know that what you
speak and teach is sound; you pay
deference to no one, but teach in
all honesty the way of life that God
requires. Are we or are we not per- 22
mitted to pay taxes to the Roman
Emperor?' He saw through their 23
trick and said, 'Show me a silver 24
piece. Whose head does it bear,
and whose inscription?' 'Caesar's',
they replied. 'Very well then,' he 25
said, 'pay Caesar what is due to
Caesar, and pay God what is due
to God.' Thus their attempt to 26
catch him out in public failed, and,
astonished by his reply, they fell
silent.
   Then some Sadducees came for- 27
ward. They are the people who
deny that there is a resurrection.

ª *Or my only son.*

28 Their question was this: 'Master, Moses laid it down for us that if there are brothers, and one dies leaving a wife but no child, then the next should marry the widow and carry on his brother's family.
29 Now, there were seven brothers: the first took a wife and died child-
30 less; then the second married her,
31 then the third. In this way the seven of them died leaving no
32 children. Afterwards the woman
33 also died. At the resurrection whose wife is she to be, since all seven had
34 married her?' Jesus said to them, 'The men and women of this world
35 marry; but those who have been judged worthy of a place in the other world and of the resurrection
36 from the dead, do not marry, for they are not subject to death any longer. They are like angels; they are sons of God, because they share
37 in the resurrection. That the dead are raised to life again is shown by Moses himself in the story of the burning bush, when he calls the Lord, "the God of Abraham, Isaac,
38 and Jacob". God is not God of the dead but of the living; for him all are^a alive.'

39   At this some of the lawyers said,
40 'Well spoken, Master.' For there was no further question that they ventured to put to him.

41   He said to them, 'How can they say that the Messiah is son of
42 David? For David himself says in the Book of Psalms: "The Lord said to my Lord, 'Sit at my right
43 hand until I make your enemies
44 your footstool.'" Thus David calls him "Lord"; how then can he be David's son?'

45   In the hearing of all the people
46 Jesus said to his disciples: 'Beware of the doctors of the law who love to walk up and down in long robes, and have a great liking for respectful greetings in the street, the chief seats in our synagogues, and places
47 of honour at feasts. These are the men who eat up the property of widows, while they say long prayers for appearance' sake; and they will receive the severest sentence.'

He looked up and saw the rich 21 people dropping their gifts into the chest of the temple treasury; and 2 he noticed a poor widow putting in two tiny coins. 'I tell you this,' he 3 said: 'this poor widow has given more than any of them; for those 4 others who have given had more than enough, but she, with less than enough, has given all she had to live on.'

SOME people were talking about 5 the temple and the fine stones and votive offerings with which it was adorned. He said, 'These things 6 which you are gazing at – the time will come when not one stone of them will be left upon another; all will be thrown down.' 'Master,' 7 they asked, 'when will it all come about? What will be the sign when it is due to happen?'

He said, 'Take care that you are 8 not misled. For many will come claiming my name and saying, "I am he", and, "The Day is upon us." Do not follow them. And when 9 you hear of wars and insurrections, do not fall into a panic. These things are bound to happen first; but the end does not follow immediately.' Then he added, 'Na- 10 tion will make war upon nation, kingdom upon kingdom; there will 11 be great earthquakes, and famines and plagues in many places; in the sky terrors and great portents.

'But before all this happens they 12 will set upon you and persecute you. You will be brought before synagogues and put in prison; you will be haled before kings and governors for your allegiance to me. This will be your opportunity 13 to testify; so make up your minds 14 not to prepare your defence beforehand, because I myself will give 15 you power of utterance and a

---

^{a} *Or they are all.*

wisdom which no opponent will be
16 able to resist or refute. Even your
parents and brothers, your relations and friends, will betray you.
Some of you will be put to death;
17 and all will hate you for your
18 allegiance to me. But not a hair of
19 your head shall be lost. By standing firm you will win true life for
yourselves.

20　　'But when you see Jerusalem encircled by armies, then you may be
sure that her destruction is near.
21 Then those who are in Judaea
must take to the hills; those who
are in the city itself must leave it,
and those who are out in the
22 country must not enter; because
this is the time of retribution, when
all that stands written is to be ful-
23 filled. Alas for women who are with
child in those days, or have children at the breast! For there will
be great distress in the land and a
terrible judgement upon this peo-
24 ple. They will fall at the sword's
point; they will be carried captive
into all countries; and Jerusalem
will be trampled down by foreigners
until their day has run its course.
25　　'Portents will appear in sun,
moon, and stars. On earth nations
will stand helpless, not knowing
which way to turn from the roar
26 and surge of the sea; men will faint
with terror at the thought of all
that is coming upon the world; for
the celestial powers will be shaken.
27 And then they will see the Son of
Man coming on a cloud with great
28 power and glory. When all this
begins to happen, stand upright
and hold your heads high, because
your liberation is near.'

29　　He told them this parable:
'Look at the fig-tree, or any other
30 tree. As soon as it buds, you can
see for yourselves that summer is
31 near. In the same way, when you
see all this happening, you may
know that the kingdom of God is
near.
32　　'I tell you this: the present

generation will live to see it all.
Heaven and earth will pass away; 33
my words will never pass away.

'Keep a watch on yourselves; do 34
not let your minds be dulled by
dissipation and drunkenness and
worldly cares so that the great
Day closes upon you suddenly
like a trap; for that day will come 35
on all men, wherever they are, the
whole world over. Be on the alert, 36
praying at all times for strength to
pass safely through all these immi-
nent troubles and to stand in the
presence of the Son of Man.'

His days were given to teaching 37
in the temple; and then he would
leave the city and spend the night
on the hill called Olivet. And in the 38
early morning the people flocked
to listen to him in the temple.[a]

The final conflict

Now the festival of Unleavened 22
Bread, known as Passover, was approaching, and the chief priests 2
and the doctors of the law were
trying to devise some means of
doing away with him; for they
were afraid of the people.

Then Satan entered into Judas 3
Iscariot, who was one of the
Twelve; and Judas went to the 4
chief priests and officers of the
temple police to discuss ways and
means of putting Jesus into their
power. They were greatly pleased 5
and undertook to pay him a sum
of money. He agreed, and began to 6
look out for an opportunity to betray him to them without collecting a crowd.

Then came the day of Unlea- 7
vened Bread, on which the Passover victim had to be slaughtered,
and Jesus sent Peter and John 8
with these instructions: 'Go and
prepare for our Passover supper.'
'Where would you like us to make 9
the preparations?' they asked. He 10
replied, 'As soon as you set foot in
the city a man will meet you carry-

---

[a] *Some witnesses here insert the passage printed on p. 131.*

ing a jar of water. Follow him into 11 the house that he enters and give this message to the householder: "The Master says, 'Where is the room in which I may eat the Passover with my disciples?'" He will 12 show you a large room upstairs all set out: make the preparations there.' They went and found every-13 thing as he had said. So they prepared for Passover.

When the time came he took his 14 place at table, and the apostles with him; and he said to them, 15 'How I have longed[a] to eat this Passover with you before my death! For I tell you, never again 16 shall I[b] eat it until the time when it finds its fulfilment in the kingdom of God.'

Then he took a cup, and after 17 giving thanks he said, 'Take this and share it among yourselves; for 18 I tell you, from this moment I shall drink from the fruit of the vine no more until the time when the kingdom of God comes.' And he 19 took bread, gave thanks, and broke it; and he gave it to them, with the words: "This is my body."[c]

'But mark this – my betrayer is 21 here, his hand with mine on the table. For the Son of Man is going 22 his appointed way; but alas for that man by whom he is betrayed!'

At this they began to ask among 23 themselves which of them it could possibly be who was to do this thing.

Then a jealous dispute broke 24 out: who among them should rank highest? But he said, 'In the world, 25 kings lord it over their subjects; and those in authority are called their country's "Benefactors". Not 26 so with you: on the contrary, the highest among you must bear himself like the youngest, the chief of

you like a servant. For who is 27 greater – the one who sits at table or the servant who waits on him? Surely the one who sits at table. Yet here am I among you like a servant.

'You are the men who have 28 stood firmly by me in my times of trial; and now I vest in you the 29 kingship which my Father vested in me; you shall eat and drink at 30 my table in my kingdom and sit[d] on thrones as judges of the twelve tribes of Israel.

'Simon, Simon, take heed: Satan 31 has been given leave to sift all of you like wheat; but for you I have 32 prayed that your faith may not fail; and when you have come to yourself, you must lend strength to your brothers.' 'Lord,' he re-33 plied, 'I am ready to go with you to prison and death.' Jesus said, 34 'I tell you, Peter, the cock will not crow tonight until you have three times over denied that you know me.'

He said to them, 'When I sent 35 you out barefoot without purse or pack, were you ever short of anything?' 'No', they answered. 'It is 36 different now,' he said; 'whoever has a purse had better take it with him, and his pack too; and if he has no sword, let him sell his cloak to buy one. For Scripture says, "And 37 he was counted among the outlaws", and these words, I tell you, must find fulfilment in me; indeed, all that is written of me is being fulfilled.' 'Look, Lord,' they 38 said, 'we have two swords here.' 'Enough, enough!' he replied.

THEN he went out and made his 39 way as usual to the Mount of Olives, accompanied by the disciples. When he reached the place 40

---

[a] Or said to them, 'I longed...'   [b] Some witnesses read For I tell you, I shall not...   [c] Some witnesses add, in whole or in part, and with various arrangements, the following: 'which is given for you; do this as a memorial of me.' (20) In the same way he took the cup after supper, and said, 'This cup, poured out for you, is the new covenant sealed by my blood.'   [d] Or trial; and as my Father gave me the right to reign, so I give you the right to eat and to drink...and to sit...

he said to them, 'Pray that you may be spared the hour of testing.'

41 He himself withdrew from them about a stone's throw, knelt down, 42 and began to pray: 'Father, if it be thy will, take this cup away from me. Yet not my will but thine be done.'

43 And now there appeared to him an angel from heaven bringing him 44 strength, and in anguish of spirit he prayed the more urgently; and his sweat was like clots of blood falling to the ground.[a]

45 When he rose from prayer and came to the disciples he found them asleep, worn out by grief. 46 'Why are you sleeping?' he said. 'Rise and pray that you may be spared the test.'

47 WHILE he was still speaking a crowd appeared with the man called Judas, one of the Twelve, at their head. He came up to Jesus to 48 kiss him; but Jesus said, 'Judas, would you betray the Son of Man with a kiss?' 49 When his followers saw what was coming, they said, 'Lord, shall 50 we use our swords?' And one of them struck at the High Priest's servant, cutting off his right ear. 51 But Jesus answered, 'Let them have their way.' Then he touched the man's ear and healed him.[b] 52 Turning to the chief priests, the officers of the temple police, and the elders, who had come to seize him, he said, 'Do you take me for a bandit, that you have come out with swords and cudgels to arrest 53 me? Day after day, when I was in the temple with you, you kept your hands off me. But this is your moment – the hour when darkness reigns.'

54 Then they arrested him and led him away. They brought him to the High Priest's house, and Peter followed at a distance. They lit a 55 fire in the middle of the courtyard and sat round it, and Peter sat among them. A serving-maid who 56 saw him sitting in the firelight stared at him and said, 'This man was with him too.' But he denied 57 it: 'Woman,' he said, 'I do not know him.' A little later someone 58 else noticed him and said, 'You also are one of them.' But Peter said to him, 'No, I am not.' About 59 an hour passed and another spoke more strongly still: 'Of course this fellow was with him. He must have been; he is a Galilean.' But Peter 60 said, 'Man, I do not know what you are talking about.' At that moment, while he was still speaking, a cock crew; and the Lord turned 61 and looked at Peter. And Peter remembered the Lord's words, 'Tonight before the cock crows you will disown me three times.'[c]

The men who were guarding 63 Jesus mocked at him. They beat him, they blindfolded him, and 64 they kept asking him, 'Now, prophet, who hit you? Tell us that.' And so they went on heaping in- 65 sults upon him.

WHEN day broke, the elders of 66 the nation, chief priests, and doctors of the law assembled, and he was brought before their Council. 'Tell us,' they said, 'are you the 67 Messiah?' 'If I tell you,' he replied, 'you will not believe me; and if I 68 ask questions, you will not answer. But from now on, the Son of Man 69 will be seated at the right hand of Almighty God.'[d] 'You are the Son 70 of God, then?' they all said, and he replied, 'It is you who say I am.'[e] They said, 'Need we call further 71 witnesses? We have heard it ourselves from his own lips.'

With that the whole assembly 23 rose, and they brought him before

---

[a] Some witnesses omit And now . . . ground.
[b] Or 'Let me do as much as this', and touching the man's ear, he healed him.
[c] Some witnesses add (62) He went outside, and wept bitterly, as in Matthew 26. 75.
[d] Literally of the Power of God.   [e] Or You are right, for I am.

2 Pilate. They opened the case against him by saying, 'We found this man subverting our nation, opposing the payment of taxes to Caesar, and claiming to be Mes-
3 siah, a king.'[a] Pilate asked him, 'Are you the king of the Jews?' He replied, 'The words are yours.'[b]
4 Pilate then said to the chief priests and the crowd, 'I find no case for
5 this man to answer.' But they insisted: 'His teaching is causing disaffection among the people all through Judaea. It started from Galilee and has spread as far as this city.'
6 When Pilate heard this, he asked
7 if the man was a Galilean, and on learning that he belonged to Herod's jurisdiction he remitted the case to him, for Herod was also
8 in Jerusalem at that time. When Herod saw Jesus he was greatly pleased; having heard about him, he had long been wanting to see him, and had been hoping to see some miracle performed by him.
9 He questioned him at some length
10 without getting any reply; but the chief priests and lawyers appeared and pressed the case against him
11 vigorously. Then Herod and his troops treated him with contempt and ridicule, and sent him back to Pilate dressed in a gorgeous robe.
12 That same day Herod and Pilate became friends; till then there had been a standing feud between them.
13 Pilate now called together the chief priests, councillors, and peo-
14 ple, and said to them, 'You brought this man before me on a charge of subversion. But, as you see, I have myself examined him in your presence and found nothing in him to
15 support your charges. No more did Herod, for he has referred him back to us. Clearly he has done nothing
16 to deserve death. I therefore propose to let him off with a flogging.'

18 But[c] there was a general outcry, 'Away with him! Give us Barab-
19 bas!' (This man had been put in prison for a rising that had taken place in the city, and for murder.)
20 Pilate addressed them again, in his desire to release Jesus, but they
21 shouted back, 'Crucify him, cruci-
22 fy him!' For the third time he spoke to them: 'Why, what wrong has he done? I have not found him guilty of any capital offence. I will therefore let him off with a flogging.'
23 But they insisted on their demand, shouting that Jesus should be crucified. Their shouts prevailed
24 and Pilate decided that they should
25 have their way. He released the man they asked for, the man who had been put in prison for insurrection and murder, and gave Jesus up to their will.

26 As they led him away to execution they seized upon a man called Simon, from Cyrene, on his way in from the country, put the cross on his back, and made him walk behind Jesus carrying it.
27 Great numbers of people followed, many women among them, who mourned and lamented over
28 him. Jesus turned to them and said, 'Daughters of Jerusalem, do not weep for me; no, weep for your-
29 selves and your children. For the days are surely coming when they will say, "Happy are the barren, the wombs that never bore a child, the breasts that never fed one."
30 Then they will start saying to the mountains, "Fall on us", and to
31 the hills, "Cover us." For if these things are done when the wood is green, what will happen when it is dry?'
32 There were two others with him, criminals who were being led away
33 to execution; and when they reached the place called The Skull, they crucified him there, and the

---

[a] *Or* to be an anointed king.   [b] *Or* It is as you say.
[c] *Some witnesses read* (17) At festival time he was obliged to release one person for them; (18) and now...

criminals with him, one on his right and the other on his left. 34 Jesus said, 'Father, forgive them; they do not know what they are doing.'ᵃ

They divided his clothes among 35 them by casting lots. The people stood looking on, and their rulers jeered at him: 'He saved others; now let him save himself, if this is 36 God's Messiah, his Chosen.' The soldiers joined in the mockery and came forward offering him their 37 sour wine. 'If you are the king of the Jews,' they said, 'save your- 38 self.' There was an inscription above his head which ran: 'This is the king of the Jews.'

39 One of the criminals who hung there with him taunted him: 'Are not you the Messiah? Save your- 40 self, and us.' But the other rebuked him: 'Have you no fear of God? You are under the same sentence 41 as he. For us it is plain justice; we are paying the price for our mis- deeds; but this man has done no- 42 thing wrong.' And he said, 'Jesus, remember me when you come to 43 your throne.'ᵇ He answered, 'I tell you this: today you shall be with me in Paradise.'

44 By now it was about midday and a darkness fell over the whole land, which lasted until three in the 45 afternoon; the sun's light failed. And the curtain of the temple was 46 torn in two. Then Jesus gave a loud cry and said, 'Father, into thy hands I commit my spirit'; and 47 with these words he died. The cen- turion saw it all, and gave praise to God. 'Beyond all doubt', he said, 'this man was innocent.'

48 The crowd who had assembled for the spectacle, when they saw what had happened, went home beating their breasts.

49 HIS friends had all been standing at a distance; the women who had accompanied him from Galilee stood with them and watched it all.

Now there was a man called Jo- 50 seph, a member of the Council, a good, upright man, who had dis- 51 sented from their policy and the action they had taken. He came from the Judaean town of Arima- thaea, and he was one who looked forward to the kingdom of God. This man now approached Pilate 52 and asked for the body of Jesus. Taking it down from the cross, he 53 wrapped it in a linen sheet, and laid it in a tomb cut out of the rock, in which no one had been laid be- fore. It was Friday, and the Sab- 54 bath was about to begin.

The women who had accom- 55 panied him from Galilee followed; they took note of the tomb and observed how his body was laid. Then they went home and pre- 56 pared spices and perfumes; and on the Sabbath they rested in obe- dience to the commandment. But 24 on the Sunday morning very early they came to the tomb bringing the spices they had prepared. Find- 2 ing that the stone had been rolled away from the tomb, they went 3 inside; but the body was not to be found. While they stood utterly at 4 a loss, all of a sudden two men in dazzling garments were at their side. They were terrified, and stood 5 with eyes cast down, but the men said, 'Why search among the dead for one who lives?ᶜ Remember 6 what he told you while he was still in Galilee, about the Son of Man: 7 how he must be given up into the power of sinful men and be cruci- fied, and must rise again on the third day.' Then they recalled his 8 words and, returning from the 9 tomb, they reported all this to the Eleven and all the others.

The women were Mary of Mag- 10 dala, Joanna, and Mary the mo- therᵈ of James, and they, with the

---

ᵃ *Some witnesses omit* Jesus said, 'Father...doing.'
ᵇ *Some witnesses read* come in royal power.
ᶜ *Some witnesses insert* He is not here: he has been raised.　　ᵈ *Or* wife, *or* daughter.

other women, told the apostles.
11 But the story appeared to them to
be nonsense, and they would not
believe them.ᵃ

13 THAT same day two of them were
on their way to a village called
Emmaus, which lay about seven
14 miles from Jerusalem, and they
were talking together about all
15 these happenings. As they talked
and discussed it with one another,
Jesus himself came up and walked
16 along with them; but something
kept them from seeing who it was.
17 He asked them, 'What is it you are
debating as you walk?' They halt-
18 ed, their faces full of gloom, and
one, called Cleopas, answered, 'Are
you the only person staying in
Jerusalem not to knowᵇ what has
happened there in the last few
19 days?' 'What do you mean?' he
said. 'All this about Jesus of
Nazareth,' they replied, 'a prophet powerful in speech and action
before God and the whole people;
20 how our chief priests and rulers
handed him over to be sentenced
21 to death, and crucified him. But we
had been hoping that he was the
man to liberate Israel. What is
more, this is the third day since it
22 happened, and now some women of
our company have astounded us:
23 they went early to the tomb, but
failed to find his body, and returned
with a story that they had seen a
vision of angels who told them he
24 was alive. So some of our people
went to the tomb and found things
just as the women had said; but
him they did not see.'
25   'How dull you are!' he answered.
'How slow to believe all that the
26 prophets said! Was the Messiah
not bound to suffer thus before
27 entering upon his glory?' Then
he began with Moses and all the

prophets, and explained to them
the passages which referred to himself in every part of the scriptures.
By this time they had reached 28
the village to which they were going, and he made as if to continue
his journey, but they pressed him: 29
'Stay with us, for evening draws on,
and the day is almost over.' So he
went in to stay with them. And 30
when he had sat down with them
at table, he took bread and said the
blessing; he broke the bread, and
offered it to them. Then their eyes 31
were opened, and they recognized
him; and he vanished from their
sight. They said to one another, 32
'Did we not feel our hearts on fire
as he talked with us on the road
and explained the scriptures to
us?'
Without a moment's delay they 33
set out and returned to Jerusalem.
There they found that the Eleven
and the rest of the company had
assembled, and were saying, 'It is 34
true: the Lord has risen; he has
appeared to Simon.' Then they 35
gave their account of the events of
their journey and told how he had
been recognized by them at the
breaking of the bread.
As they were talking about all 36
this, there he was, standing among
them.ᶜ Startled and terrified, they 37
thought they were seeing a ghost.
But he said, 'Why are you so per- 38
turbed? Why do questionings arise
in your minds? Look at my hands 39
and feet. It is I myself. Touch me
and see; no ghost has flesh and
bones as you can see that I have.'ᵈ
They were still unconvinced, still 41
wondering, for it seemed too good
to be true. So he asked them, 'Have
you anything here to eat?' They 42
offered him a piece of fish they had
cooked, which he took and ate 43
before their eyes.

ᵃ *Some witnesses add* (12) Peter, however, got up and ran to the tomb, and, peering
in, saw the wrappings and nothing more; and he went home amazed at what had
happened.   ᵇ *Or* Have you been staying by yourself in Jerusalem, that you do
not know...   ᶜ *Some witnesses insert* And he said to them, 'Peace be with you!'
ᵈ *Some witnesses insert* (40) After saying this he showed them his hands and feet.

44 And he said to them, 'This is what I meant by saying, while I was still with you, that everything written about me in the Law of Moses and in the prophets and psalms was bound to be fulfilled.'
45 Then he opened their minds to
46 understand the scriptures. 'This', he said, 'is what is written: that the Messiah is to suffer death and to rise from the dead on the third
47 day, and that in his name repentance bringing the forgiveness of sins is to be proclaimed to all na-
48 tions. Begin from Jerusalem; it is you who are the witnesses to it all.
49 And mark this: I am sending upon you my Father's promised gift; so stay here in this city until you are armed with the power from above.'

50 Then he led them out as far as Bethany, and blessed them with
51 uplifted hands; and in the act of blessing he parted from them.[a]
52 And they[b] returned to Jerusalem
53 with great joy, and spent all their time in the temple praising God.

THE GOSPEL ACCORDING TO

JOHN

The coming of Christ

1 WHEN all things began, the Word already was.[c] The Word dwelt with God, and what God was, the Word
2 was. The Word, then, was with
3 God at the beginning, and through him all things came to be; no single thing was created without him.
4 All that came to be was alive with his life,[d] and that life was the light
5 of men. The light shines on in the dark, and the darkness has never mastered it.

6 There appeared a man named
7 John, sent from God; he came as a witness to testify to the light, that all might become believers through
8 him. He was not himself the light; he came to bear witness to the light.
9 The real light which enlightens every man was even then coming into the world.[e]

10 He was in the world;[f] but the world, though it owed its being to
11 him, did not recognize him. He entered his own realm, and his own
12 would not receive him. But to all who did receive him, to those who have yielded him their allegiance, he gave the right to become chil-
13 dren of God, not born of any human stock, or by the fleshly desire of a human father, but the off-
14 spring of God himself. So the Word became flesh; he came to dwell among us, and we saw his glory, such glory as befits the Father's only Son, full of grace and truth.

15 Here is John's testimony to him: he cried aloud, 'This is the man I meant when I said, "He comes after me, but takes rank before me"; for before I was born, he already was.'

16 Out of his full store we have all
17 received grace upon grace; for

---

[a] *Some witnesses add* and was carried up into heaven.   [b] *Some witnesses insert* worshipped him and. . .   [c] *Or* The Word was at the creation.
[d] *Or* no single created thing came into being without him. There was life in him. . .
[e] *Or* The light was in being, light absolute, enlightening every man born into the world.   [f] *Or* The Word, then, was in the world.

while the Law was given through Moses, grace and truth came 18 through Jesus Christ. No one has ever seen God; but God's only Son, he who is nearest to the Father's heart, he has made him known.*[a]*

19 THIS is the testimony which John gave when the Jews of Jerusalem sent a deputation of priests and 20 Levites to ask him who he was. He confessed without reserve and avowed, 'I am not the Messiah.' 21 'What then? Are you Elijah?' 'No', he replied. 'Are you the prophet we await?' He answered, 'No.' 22 'Then who are you?' they asked. 'We must give an answer to those who sent us. What account do you 23 give of yourself?' He answered in the words of the prophet Isaiah: 'I am a voice crying aloud in the wilderness, "Make the Lord's highway straight."'

24 Some Pharisees who were in the 25 deputation asked him, 'If you are not the Messiah, nor Elijah, nor the prophet, why then are you bap- 26 tizing?' 'I baptize in water,' John replied, 'but among you, though you do not know him, stands the 27 one who is to come after me. I am not good enough to unfasten his 28 shoes.' This took place at Bethany beyond Jordan, where John was baptizing.

29 The next day he saw Jesus coming towards him. 'Look,' he said, 'there is the Lamb of God; it is he who takes away the sin of the 30 world. This is he of whom I spoke when I said, "After me a man is coming who takes rank before me"; for before I was born, he al- 31 ready was. I myself did not know who he was; but the very reason why I came, baptizing in water, was that he might be revealed to Israel.'

32 John testified further: 'I saw the Spirit coming down from heaven like a dove and resting upon him. I did not know him, but he who 33 sent me to baptize in water had told me, "When you see the Spirit coming down upon someone and resting upon him, you will know that this is he who is to baptize in Holy Spirit." I saw it myself, and 34 I have borne witness. This is God's Chosen One.'*[b]*

The next day again John was 35 standing with two of his disciples when Jesus passed by. John looked 36 towards him and said, 'There is the Lamb of God.' The two disciples 37 heard him say this, and followed Jesus. When he turned and saw 38 them following him, he asked, 'What are you looking for?' They said, 'Rabbi' (which means a teacher), 'where are you staying?' 'Come and see', he replied. So they 39 went and saw where he was staying, and spent the rest of the day with him. It was then about four in the afternoon.

One of the two who followed 40 Jesus after hearing what John said was Andrew, Simon Peter's brother. The first thing he did was to 41 find*[c]* his brother Simon. He said to him, 'We have found the Messiah' (which is the Hebrew for 'Christ'). He brought Simon to Jesus, who 42 looked at him and said, 'You are Simon son of John. You shall be called Cephas' (that is, Peter, the Rock).

The next day Jesus decided to 43 leave for Galilee. He met Philip, who, like Andrew and Peter, came 44 from Bethsaida, and said to him, 'Follow me.' Philip went to find 45 Nathanael, and told him, 'We have met the man spoken of by Moses in the Law, and by the prophets: it is Jesus son of Joseph, from Nazareth.' 'Nazareth!' Nathanael ex- 46 claimed; 'can anything good come

---

[a] Some witnesses read but the only one, the one nearest to the Father's heart, has made him known; *others read* but the only one, himself God, the nearest to the Father's heart, has made him known.   *[b] Some witnesses read* This is the Son of God.   *[c] Some witnesses read* In the morning he found...

from Nazareth?' Philip said, 'Come
47 and see.' When Jesus saw Nathanael coming, he said, 'Here is an
Israelite worthy of the name; there
48 is nothing false in him.' Nathanael
asked him, 'How do you come to
know me?' Jesus replied, 'I saw
you under the fig-tree before Philip
49 spoke to you.' 'Rabbi,' said Nathanael, 'you are the Son of God; you
50 are king of Israel.' Jesus answered,
'Is this the ground of your faith,
that I told you I saw you under the
fig-tree? You shall see greater
51 things than that.' Then he added,
'In truth, in very truth I tell you
all, you shall see heaven wide
open, and God's angels ascending
and descending upon the Son of
Man.'

Christ the giver of life

2 ON the third day there was a
wedding at Cana-in-Galilee. The
2 mother of Jesus was there, and
Jesus and his disciples were guests
3 also. The wine gave out, so Jesus's
mother said to him, 'They have no
4 wine left.' He answered, 'Your concern, mother, is not mine. My hour
5 has not yet come.' His mother said
to the servants, 'Do whatever
6 he tells you.' There were six stone
water-jars standing near, of the
kind used for Jewish rites of purification; each held from twenty to
7 thirty gallons. Jesus said to the
servants, 'Fill the jars with water',
and they filled them to the brim.
8 'Now draw some off', he ordered,
'and take it to the steward of the
9 feast'; and they did so. The steward tasted the water now turned
into wine, not knowing its source;
though the servants who had drawn
the water knew. He hailed the
10 bridegroom and said, 'Everyone
serves the best wine first, and waits
until the guests have drunk freely
before serving the poorer sort; but
you have kept the best wine till
now.'
11 This deed at Cana-in-Galilee is

the first of the signs by which Jesus
revealed his glory and led his disciples to believe in him.

AFTER this he went down to 12
Capernaum in company with his
mother, his brothers, and his disciples, but they did not stay there
long. As it was near the time of the 13
Jewish Passover, Jesus went up to
Jerusalem. There he found in the 14
temple the dealers in cattle, sheep,
and pigeons, and the money-
changers seated at their tables.
Jesus made a whip of cords and 15
drove them out of the temple,
sheep, cattle, and all. He upset the
tables of the money-changers,
scattering their coins. Then he 16
turned on the dealers in pigeons:
'Take them out,' he said; 'you must
not turn my Father's house into a
market.' His disciples recalled the 17
words of Scripture, 'Zeal for thy
house will destroy me.' The Jews 18
challenged Jesus: 'What sign', they
asked, 'can you show as authority
for your action?' 'Destroy this 19
temple,' Jesus replied, 'and in three
days I will raise it again.' They 20
said, 'It has taken forty-six years
to build this temple. Are you going
to raise it again in three days?'
But the temple he was speaking of 21
was his body. After his resurrec- 22
tion his disciples recalled what he
had said, and they believed the
Scripture and the words that Jesus
had spoken.

WHILE he was in Jerusalem for 23
Passover many gave their allegiance to him when they saw the
signs that he performed. But Jesus 24
for his part would not trust himself
to them. He knew men so well, all of
them, that he needed no evidence 25
from others about a man, for he
himself could tell what was in a
man.

THERE was one of the Pharisees 3
named Nicodemus, a member of

2 the Jewish Council, who came to Jesus by night. 'Rabbi,' he said, 'we know that you are a teacher sent by God; no one could perform these signs of yours unless God were with 3 him.' Jesus answered, 'In truth, in very truth I tell you, unless a man has been born over again he cannot 4 see the kingdom of God.' 'But how is it possible', said Nicodemus, 'for a man to be born when he is old? Can he enter his mother's womb a 5 second time and be born?' Jesus answered, 'In truth I tell you, no one can enter the kingdom of God without being born from water and 6 spirit. Flesh can give birth only to flesh; it is spirit that gives birth to 7 spirit. You ought not to be astonished, then, when I tell you that 8 you must be born over again. The wind[a] blows where it wills; you hear the sound of it, but you do not know where it comes from, or where it is going. So with everyone who is born from spirit[a].'

9 Nicodemus replied, 'How is this 10 possible?' 'What!' said Jesus. 'Is this famous teacher of Israel ignor- 11 ant of such things? In very truth I tell you, we speak of what we know, and testify to what we have seen, and yet you all reject our testi- 12 mony. If you disbelieve me when I talk to you about things on earth, how are you to believe if I should talk about the things of heaven?

13 'No one ever went up into heaven except the one who came down from heaven, the Son of Man whose 14 home is in heaven.[b] This Son of Man must be lifted up as the serpent was lifted up by Moses in the 15 wilderness, so that everyone who has faith in him may in him possess eternal life.

16 'God loved the world so much that he gave his only Son, that everyone who has faith in him may 17 not die but have eternal life. It was not to judge the world that God sent his Son into the world, but that through him the world might be saved.

18 'The man who puts his faith in him does not come under judgement; but the unbeliever has already been judged in that he has not given his allegiance to God's 19 only Son. Here lies the test: the light has come into the world, but men preferred darkness to light 20 because their deeds were evil. Bad men all hate the light and avoid it, for fear their practices should be 21 shown up. The honest man comes to the light so that it may be clearly seen that God is in all he does.'

22 AFTER this, Jesus went into Judaea with his disciples, stayed there with them, and baptized. 23 John too was baptizing at Aenon, near to Salim, because water was plentiful in that region; and people were constantly coming for bap- 24 tism. This was before John's imprisonment.

25 Some of John's disciples had fallen into a dispute with Jews about purification; so they came to 26 him and said, 'Rabbi, there was a man with you on the other side of the Jordan, to whom you bore your witness. Here he is, baptizing, and crowds are flocking to him.' John's 27 answer was: 'A man can have only what God gives him. You your- 28 selves can testify that I said, "I am not the Messiah; I have been sent as his forerunner." It is the 29 bridegroom to whom the bride belongs. The bridegroom's friend, who stands by and listens to him, is overjoyed at hearing the bridegroom's voice. This joy, this perfect joy, is now mine. As he grows 30 greater, I must grow less.'

31 He who comes from above is above all others; he who is from the earth belongs to the earth and uses earthly speech. He who comes

---

[a] wind *and* spirit *are translations of the same Greek word, which has both meanings.*
[b] *Some witnesses omit* whose home is in heaven.

32 from heaven[a] bears witness to what he has seen and heard, yet no one 33 accepts his witness. To accept his witness is to attest that God speaks 34 the truth; for he whom God sent utters the words of God, so measureless is God's gift of the Spirit. 35 The Father loves the Son and has entrusted him with all authority. 36 He who puts his faith in the Son has hold of eternal life, but he who disobeys the Son shall not see that life; God's wrath rests upon him.

4 A REPORT now reached the Pharisees: 'Jesus is winning and baptizing more disciples than John'; 2 although, in fact, it was only the disciples who were baptizing and not Jesus himself. When Jesus 3 learned this, he left Judaea and set 4 out once more for Galilee. He had 5 to pass through Samaria, and on his way came to a Samaritan town called Sychar, near the plot of ground which Jacob gave to his 6 son Joseph and the spring called Jacob's well. It was about noon, and Jesus, tired after his journey, sat down by the well.

8 The disciples had gone away to 7 the town to buy food. Meanwhile a Samaritan woman came to draw water. Jesus said to her, 'Give me 9 a drink.' The Samaritan woman said, 'What! You, a Jew, ask a drink of me, a Samaritan woman?' (Jews and Samaritans, it should be noted, do not use vessels in com- 10 mon.[b]) Jesus answered her, 'If only you knew what God gives, and who it is that is asking you for a drink, you would have asked him and he would have given you living water.' 11 'Sir,' the woman said, 'you have no bucket and this well is deep. How can you give me "living water"? 12 Are you a greater man than Jacob our ancestor, who gave us the well, and drank from it himself, he and 13 his sons, and his cattle too?' Jesus

said, 'Everyone who drinks this water will be thirsty again, but 14 whoever drinks the water that I shall give him will never suffer thirst any more. The water that I shall give him will be an inner spring always welling up for eternal life.' 'Sir,' said the woman, 'give 15 me that water, and then I shall not be thirsty, nor have to come all this way to draw.'

Jesus replied, 'Go home, call 16 your husband and come back.' She answered, 'I have no husband.' 17 'You are right', said Jesus, 'in saying that you have no husband, for, although you have had five 18 husbands, the man with whom you are now living is not your husband; you told me the truth there.' 'Sir,' 19 she replied, 'I can see that you are a prophet. Our fathers worshipped 20 on this mountain, but you Jews say that the temple where God should be worshipped is in Jerusalem.' 'Believe me,' said Jesus, 21 'the time is coming when you will worship the Father neither on this mountain, nor in Jerusalem. You 22 Samaritans worship without knowing what you worship, while we worship what we know. It is from the Jews that salvation comes. But 23 the time approaches, indeed it is already here, when those who are real worshippers will worship the Father in spirit and in truth. Such are the worshippers whom the Father wants. God is spirit, and 24 those who worship him must worship in spirit and in truth.' The 25 woman answered, 'I know that Messiah' (that is Christ) 'is coming. When he comes he will tell us everything.' Jesus said, 'I am he, 26 I who am speaking to you now.'

At that moment his disciples re- 27 turned, and were astonished to find him talking with a woman; but none of them said, 'What do you want?' or, 'Why are you talking

---

[a] *Some witnesses insert* is above all and...
[b] *Or* Jews, it should be noted, are not on familiar terms with Samaritans; *some witnesses omit these words.*

28 with her?' The woman put down her water-jar and went away to the town, where she said to the
29 people, 'Come and see a man who has told me everything I ever did.
30 Could this be the Messiah?' They came out of the town and made their way towards him.

31 Meanwhile the disciples were urging him, 'Rabbi, have some-
32 thing to eat.' But he said, 'I have food to eat of which you know no-
33 thing.' At this the disciples said to one another, 'Can someone have
34 brought him food?' But Jesus said, 'It is meat and drink for me to do the will of him who sent me until I have finished his work.

35 'Do you not say, "Four months more and then comes harvest"? But look, I tell you, look round on the fields; they are already white,
36 ripe for harvest. The reaper is drawing his pay and gathering a crop for eternal life, so that sower and reaper may rejoice together.
37 That is how the saying comes true: "One sows, and another reaps."
38 I sent you to reap a crop for which you have not toiled. Others toiled and you have come in for the harvest of their toil.'

39 Many Samaritans of that town came to believe in him because of the woman's testimony: 'He told
40 me everything I ever did.' So when these Samaritans had come to him they pressed him to stay with them; and he stayed there two
41 days. Many more became believers because of what they heard from
42 his own lips. They told the woman, 'It is no longer because of what you said that we believe, for we have heard that we ourselves; and we know that this is in truth the Saviour of the world.'

43 WHEN the two days were over he
44 set out for Galilee; for Jesus him-self declared that a prophet is with-out honour in his own country. On
45 his arrival in Galilee the Galileans gave him a welcome, because they had seen all that he did at the festival in Jerusalem; they had been at the festival themselves.

46 Once again he visited Cana-in-Galilee, where he had turned the water into wine. An officer in the royal service was there, whose son
47 was lying ill at Capernaum. When he heard that Jesus had come from Judaea into Galilee, he came to him and begged him to go down and cure his son, who was at the
48 point of death. Jesus said to him, 'Will none of you ever believe without seeing signs and portents?'
49 The officer pleaded with him, 'Sir, come down before my boy dies.'
50 Then Jesus said, 'Return home; your son will live.' The man be-lieved what Jesus said and started
51 for home. When he was on his way down his servants met him with the news, 'Your boy is going to live.'
52 So he asked them what time it was when he began to recover. They
53 said, 'Yesterday at one in the afternoon the fever left him.' The father noted that this was the exact time when Jesus had said to him, 'Your son will live', and he and all his household became believers.

54 This was now the second sign which Jesus performed after com-ing down from Judaea into Galilee.

5 LATER on Jesus went up to Jeru-salem for one of the Jewish festi-vals.[a] Now at the Sheep-Pool in
2 Jerusalem there is a place with five colonnades. Its name in the lan-guage of the Jews is Bethesda. In
3 these colonnades there lay a crowd of sick people, blind, lame, and paralysed.[b] Among them was a
5 man who had been crippled for
6 thirty-eight years. When Jesus

---

[a] *Some witnesses read* for the Jewish festival.   [b] *Some witnesses add* waiting for the disturbance of the water; *some further insert* (4) for from time to time an angel came down into the pool and stirred up the water. The first to plunge in after this disturbance recovered from whatever disease had afflicted him.

saw him lying there and was aware that he had been ill a long time, he asked him, 'Do you want to re- 7 cover?' 'Sir,' he replied, 'I have no one to put me in the pool when the water is disturbed, but while I am moving, someone else is in the pool 8 before me.' Jesus answered, 'Rise to your feet, take up your bed and 9 walk.' The man recovered instant- ly, took up his stretcher, and began to walk.

10 That day was a Sabbath. So the Jews said to the man who had been cured, 'It is the Sabbath. You are not allowed to carry your bed on 11 the Sabbath.' He answered, 'The man who cured me said, "Take up 12 your bed and walk."' They asked him, 'Who is the man who told you to take up your bed and walk?' 13 But the cripple who had been cured did not know; for the place was crowded and Jesus had slipped 14 away. A little later Jesus found him in the temple and said to him, 'Now that you are well again, leave your sinful ways, or you may suffer 15 something worse.' The man went away and told the Jews that it was Jesus who had cured him.

16 It was works of this kind done on the Sabbath that stirred the Jews 17 to persecute Jesus. He defended himself by saying, 'My Father has never yet ceased his work, and I am 18 working too.' This made the Jews still more determined to kill him, because he was not only breaking the Sabbath, but, by calling God his own Father, he claimed equality with God.

19 To this charge Jesus replied, 'In truth, in very truth I tell you, 'The Son can do nothing by himself; he does only what he sees the Father doing: what the Father does, the 20 Son does. For the Father loves the Son and shows him all his works, and will show greater yet, to fill 21 you with wonder. As the Father raises the dead and gives them life, so the Son gives life to men, as he 22 determines. And again, the Father

does not judge anyone, but has given full jurisdiction to the Son; it 23 is his will that all should pay the same honour to the Son as to the Father. To deny honour to the Son is to deny it to the Father who sent him.

24 'In very truth, anyone who gives heed to what I say and puts his trust in him who sent me has hold of eternal life, and does not come up for judgement, but has already passed from death to life. In truth, 25 in very truth I tell you, a time is coming, indeed it is already here, when the dead shall hear the voice of the Son of God, and all who hear shall come to life. For as the Father 26 has life-giving power in himself, so has the Son, by the Father's gift.

27 'As Son of Man, he has also been given the right to pass judgement. Do not wonder at this, because the 28 time is coming when all who are in the grave shall hear his voice and 29 come out: those who have done right will rise to life; those who have done wrong will rise to hear their doom. I cannot act by my- 30 self; I judge as I am bidden, and my sentence is just, because my aim is not my own will, but the will of him who sent me.

31 'If I testify on my own behalf, that testimony does not hold good. There is another who bears witness 32 for me, and I know that his testi- mony holds. Your messengers have 33 been to John; you have his testi- mony to the truth. Not that I rely 34 on human testimony, but I remind you of it for your own salvation. John was a lamp, burning brightly, 35 and for a time you were ready to exult in his light. But I rely on a 36 testimony higher than John's. There is enough to testify that the Father has sent me, in the works my Father gave me to do and to finish – the very works I have in hand. This testimony to me was 37 given by the Father who sent me, although you never heard his voice, or saw his form. But his 38

word has found no home in you, for you do not believe the one whom
39 he sent. You study the scriptures diligently, supposing that in having them you have eternal life; yet, although their testimony points to
40 me, you refuse to come to me for that life.

41 'I do not look to men for honour.
42 But with you it is different, as I know well, for you have no love for
43 God in you. I have come accredited by my Father, and you have no welcome for me; if another comes self-accredited you will welcome
44 him. How can you have faith so long as you receive honour from one another, and care nothing for the honour that comes from him
45 who alone is God? Do not imagine that I shall be your accuser at the Father's tribunal. Your accuser is Moses, the very Moses on whom
46 you have set your hope. If you believed Moses you would believe what I tell you, for it was about me
47 that he wrote. But if you do not believe what he wrote, how are you to believe what I say?'

6 SOME time later Jesus withdrew to the farther shore of the Sea of
2 Galilee (or Tiberias), and a large crowd of people followed who had seen the signs he performed in
3 healing the sick. Then Jesus went up the hill-side and sat down with
4 his disciples. It was near the time of Passover, the great Jewish festi-
5 val. Raising his eyes and seeing a large crowd coming towards him, Jesus said to Philip, 'Where are we to buy bread to feed these people?'
6 This he said to test him; Jesus himself knew what he meant to do.
7 Philip replied, 'Twenty pounds*a* would not buy enough bread for every one of them to have a little.'
8 One of his disciples, Andrew, the brother of Simon Peter, said to
9 him, 'There is a boy here who has five barley loaves and two fishes;

but what is that among so many?'
Jesus said, 'Make the people sit 10 down.' There was plenty of grass there, so the men sat down, about five thousand of them. Then Jesus 11 took the loaves, gave thanks, and distributed them to the people as they sat there. He did the same with the fishes, and they had as much as they wanted. When every- 12 one had had enough, he said to his disciples, 'Collect the pieces left over, so that nothing may be lost.'
This they did, and filled twelve 13 baskets with the pieces left uneaten of the five barley loaves.

When the people saw the sign 14 Jesus had performed, the word went round, 'Surely this must be the prophet that was to come into the world.' Jesus, aware that they 15 meant to come and seize him to proclaim him king, withdrew again to the hills by himself.

At nightfall his disciples went 16 down to the sea, got into their boat, 17 and pushed off to cross the water to Capernaum. Darkness had already fallen, and Jesus had not yet joined them. By now a strong wind 18 was blowing and the sea grew rough. When they had rowed about 19 three or four miles they saw Jesus walking on the sea and approaching the boat. They were terrified, but he called out, 'It is I; do not be 20 afraid.' Then they were ready to 21 take him aboard, and immediately the boat reached the land they were making for.

NEXT morning the crowd was 22 standing on the opposite shore. They had seen only one boat there, and Jesus, they knew, had not embarked with his disciples, who had gone away without him. Boats 23 from Tiberias, however, came ashore*b* near the place where the people had eaten the bread over which the Lord gave thanks.*c* When 24 the people saw that neither Jesus

---

a Literally 200 denarii.   *b* Some witnesses read Other boats from Tiberias came ashore...   *c* Some witnesses omit over which...thanks.

nor his disciples were any longer there, they themselves went aboard these boats and made for Caper- 25 naum in search of Jesus. They found him on the other side. 'Rabbi,' they said, 'when did you 26 come here?' Jesus replied, 'In very truth I know that you have not come looking for me because you saw signs, but because you ate the bread and your hunger was satis- 27 fied. You must work, not for this perishable food, but for the food that lasts, the food of eternal life.

'This food the Son of Man will give you, for he it is upon whom God the Father has set the seal of 28 his authority.' 'Then what must we do', they asked him, 'if we are to work as God would have us 29 work?' Jesus replied, 'This is the work that God requires: believe in the one whom he has sent.'

30 They said, 'What sign can you give us to see, so that we may believe you? What is the work you 31 do? Our ancestors had manna to eat in the desert; as Scripture says, "He gave them bread from heaven 32 to eat."' Jesus answered, 'I tell you this: the truth is, not that Moses gave you the bread from heaven, but that my Father gives you the 33 real bread from heaven. For the bread that God gives comes down[a] from heaven and brings life to the 34 world.' They said to him, 'Sir, give us this bread now and always.' 35 Jesus said to them, 'I am the bread of life. Whoever comes to me shall never be hungry, and whoever believes in me shall never be 36 thirsty. But you, as I said, do not believe although you have seen.[b] 37 All that the Father gives me will come to me, and the man who comes to me I will never turn 38 away. I have come down from heaven, not to do my own will, but 39 the will of him who sent me. It is his will that I should not lose even one of all that he has given me, but raise them all up on the last day.

For it is my Father's will that 40 everyone who looks upon the Son and puts his faith in him shall possess eternal life; and I will raise him up on the last day.'

At this the Jews began to mur- 41 mur disapprovingly because he said, 'I am the bread which came down from heaven.' They said, 42 'Surely this is Jesus son of Joseph; we know his father and mother. How can he now say, "I have come down from heaven"?' Jesus an- 43 swered, 'Stop murmuring among yourselves. No man can come to 44 me unless he is drawn by the Father who sent me; and I will raise him up on the last day. It is written in 45 the prophets: "And they shall all be taught by God." Everyone who has listened to the Father and learned from him comes to me.

'I do not mean that anyone has 46 seen the Father. He who has come from God has seen the Father, and he alone. In truth, in very truth I 47 tell you, the believer possesses eternal life. I am the bread of life. 48 Your forefathers ate the manna in 49 the desert and they are dead. I am 50 speaking of the bread that comes down from heaven, which a man may eat, and never die. I am that 51 living bread which has come down from heaven; if anyone eats this bread he shall live for ever. Moreover, the bread which I will give is my own flesh; I give it for the life of the world.'

This led to a fierce dispute a- 52 mong the Jews. 'How can this man give us his flesh to eat?' they said. Jesus replied, 'In truth, in very 53 truth I tell you, unless you eat the flesh of the Son of Man and drink his blood you can have no life in you. Whoever eats my flesh and 54 drinks my blood possesses eternal life, and I will raise him up on the last day. My flesh is real food; my 55 blood is real drink. Whoever eats 56 my flesh and drinks my blood dwells continually in me and I

---

[a] *Or is he who comes down...*

[b] *Some witnesses add* me.

57 dwell in him. As the living Father sent me, and I live because of the Father, so he who eats me shall 58 live because of me. This is the bread which came down from heaven; and it is not like the bread which our fathers ate: they are dead, but whoever eats this bread shall live for ever.'

59 THIS was spoken in synagogue when Jesus was teaching in Caper- 60 naum. Many of his disciples on hearing it exclaimed, 'This is more than we can stomach! Why listen 61 to such talk?' Jesus was aware that his disciples were murmuring a-bout it and asked them, 'Does this 62 shock you? What if you see the Son of Man ascending to the place 63 where he was before? The spirit alone gives life; the flesh is of no avail; the words which I have spoken to you are both spirit and 64 life. And yet there are some of you who have no faith.' For Jesus knew all along who were without faith 65 and who was to betray him. So he said, 'This is why I told you that no one can come to me unless it has been granted to him by the Father.' 66 From that time on, many of his disciples withdrew and no longer 67 went about with him. So Jesus asked the Twelve, 'Do you also 68 want to leave me?' Simon Peter an-swered him, 'Lord, to whom shall we go? Your words are words of 69 eternal life. We have faith, and we know that you are the Holy One 70 of God.' Jesus answered, 'Have I not chosen you, all twelve? Yet one 71 of you is a devil.' He meant Judas, son of Simon Iscariot. He it was who would betray him, and he was one of the Twelve.

The great controversy

7 AFTERWARDS Jesus went about in Galilee. He wished to avoid Judaea because the Jews were looking for a chance to kill him.

As the Jewish Feast of Taber- 2 nacles was close at hand, his bro- 3 thers said to him, 'You should leave this district and go into Judaea, so that your disciples there may see the great things you are doing. Surely no one can hope to be in the 4 public eye if he works in seclusion. If you really are doing such things as these, show yourself to the world.' For even his brothers had 5 no faith in him. Jesus said to them, 6 'The right time for me has not yet come, but any time is right for you. The world cannot hate you; but it 7 hates me for exposing the wicked-ness of its ways. Go to the festival 8 yourselves. I am not[a] going up to this festival because the right time for me has not yet come.' With this 9 answer he stayed behind in Galilee.

Later, when his brothers had 10 gone to the festival, he went up himself, not publicly, but almost in secret. The Jews were looking for 11 him at the festival and asking, 'Where is he?', and there was much 12 whispering about him in the crowds. 'He is a good man', said some. 'No,' said others, 'he is leading the people astray.' How- 13 ever, no one talked about him openly, for fear of the Jews.

WHEN the festival was already 14 half over, Jesus went up to the temple and began to teach. The 15 Jews were astonished: 'How is it', they said, 'that this untrained man has such learning?' Jesus replied, 16 'The teaching that I give is not my own; it is the teaching of him who sent me. Whoever has the will to 17 do the will of God shall know whether my teaching comes from him or is merely my own. Anyone 18 whose teaching is merely his own, aims at honour for himself. But if a man aims at the honour of him who sent me he is sincere, and there is nothing false in him.

'Did not Moses give you the 19 Law? Yet you all break it. Why

[a] *Some witnesses read* not yet.

20 are you trying to kill me?' The crowd answered, 'You are possess-
21 ed! Who wants to kill you?' Jesus replied, 'Once only have I done work on the Sabbath, and you are
22 all taken aback. But consider: Moses gave you the law of circumcision (not that it originated with Moses but with the patriarchs) and you circumcise on the Sabbath.
23 Well then, if a child is circumcised on the Sabbath to avoid breaking the Law of Moses, why are you indignant with me for giving health on the Sabbath to the whole of a
24 man's body? Do not judge superficially, but be just in your judgements.'
25 At this some of the people of Jerusalem began to say, 'Is not this the man they want to put to
26 death? And here he is, speaking openly, and they have not a word to say to him. Can it be that our rulers have actually decided that
27 this is the Messiah? And yet we know where this man comes from, but when the Messiah appears no one is to know where he comes
28 from.' Thereupon Jesus cried aloud as he taught in the temple, 'No doubt you know me; no doubt you know where I come from.^{a} Yet I have not come of my own accord. I was sent by the One who truly is,
29 and him you do not know. I know him because I come from him and
30 he it is who sent me.' At this they tried to seize him, but no one laid a hand on him because his ap-
31 pointed hour had not yet come. Yet among the people many believed in him. 'When the Messiah comes,' they said, 'is it likely that he will perform more signs than this man?'
32 The Pharisees overheard these mutterings of the people about him, so the chief priests and the Pharisees sent temple police to
33 arrest him. Then Jesus said, 'For a little longer I shall be with you; then I am going away to him who sent me. You will look for me, but 34 you will not find me. Where I am, you cannot come.' So the Jews said 35 to one another, 'Where does he intend to go, that we should not be able to find him? Will he go to the Dispersion among the Greeks, and teach the Greeks? What did he 36 mean by saying, "You will look for me, but you will not find me. Where I am, you cannot come"?'^{b}

ON the last and greatest day of the 37 festival Jesus stood and cried aloud, 'If anyone is thirsty let him come to me; whoever believes in 38 me, let him drink.' As Scripture says, 'Streams of living water shall flow out from within him.'^{c} He was 39 speaking of the Spirit which believers in him would receive later; for the Spirit had not yet been given, because Jesus had not yet been glorified.

On hearing this some of the 40 people said, 'This must certainly be the expected prophet.' Others said, 41 'This is the Messiah.' Others again, 'Surely the Messiah is not to come from Galilee? Does not Scripture 42 say that the Messiah is to be of the family of David, from David's village of Bethlehem?' Thus he 43 caused a split among the people. Some were for seizing him, but no 44 one laid hands on him.

The temple police came back to 45 the chief priests and Pharisees, who asked, 'Why have you not brought him?' 'No man,' they answered, 46 'ever spoke as this man speaks.' The Pharisees retorted, 'Have you 47 too been misled? Is there a single 48 one of our rulers who has believed in him, or of the Pharisees? As for 49 this rabble, which cares nothing for the Law, a curse is on them.' Then one of their number, Nico- 50

^{a} *Or* Do you know me? And do you know where I come from?
^{b} *Some witnesses here insert the passage printed on p. 131.*
^{c} *Or* 'If any man is thirsty let him come to me and drink. He who believes in me, as Scripture says, streams of living water shall flow out from within him.'

demus (the man who had once 51 visited Jesus), intervened. 'Does our law', he asked them, 'permit us to pass judgement on a man unless we have first given him a hearing 52 and learned the facts?' 'Are you a Galilean too?' they retorted. 'Study the scriptures and you will find that prophets do not come from Galilee.'[a]

8 12 ONCE again Jesus addressed the people: 'I am the light of the world. No follower of mine shall wander in the dark; he shall have the light 13 of life.' The Pharisees said to him, 'You are witness in your own cause; 14 your testimony is not valid.' Jesus replied, 'My testimony is valid, even though I do bear witness about myself; because I know where I come from, and where I am going. You do not know either where I come from or where I am going. 15 You judge by worldly standards. 16 I pass judgement on no man, but if I do judge, my judgement is valid because it is not I alone who judge, but I and he who sent me. 17 In your own law it is written that the testimony of two witnesses is 18 valid. Here am I, a witness in my own cause, and my other witness is 19 the Father who sent me.' They asked, 'Where is your father?' Jesus replied, 'You know neither me nor my Father; if you knew me you would know my Father as well.'

20 These words were spoken by Jesus in the treasury as he taught in the temple. Yet no one arrested him, because his hour had not yet come.

21 Again he said to them, 'I am going away. You will look for me, but you will die in your sin; where 22 I am going you cannot come.' The Jews then said, 'Perhaps he will kill himself: is that what he means when he says, "Where I am going 23 you cannot come"?' So Jesus con-

tinued, 'You belong to this world below, I to the world above. Your home is in this world, mine is not. That is why I told you that you 24 would die in your sins. If you do not believe that I am what I am, you will die in your sins.' They 25 asked him, 'Who are you?' Jesus answered, 'Why should I speak to you at all?[b] I have much to say 26 about you – and in judgement. But he who sent me speaks the truth, and what I heard from him I report to the world.'

They did not understand that he 27 was speaking to them about the Father. So Jesus said to them, 28 'When you have lifted up the Son of Man you will know that I am what I am. I do nothing on my own authority, but in all that I say, I have been taught by my Father. He 29 who sent me is present with me, and has not left me alone; for I always do what is acceptable to him.' As 30 he said this, many put their faith in him.

Turning to the Jews who had be- 31 lieved him, Jesus said, 'If you dwell within the revelation I have brought, you are indeed my disciples; you shall know the truth, 32 and the truth will set you free.' They replied, 'We are Abraham's 33 descendants; we have never been in slavery to any man. What do you mean by saying, "You will become free men"?' 'In very truth 34 I tell you', said Jesus, 'that everyone who commits sin is a slave. The slave has no permanent 35 standing in the household, but the son belongs to it for ever. If then 36 the Son sets you free, you will indeed be free.

'I know that you are descended 37 from Abraham, but you are bent on killing me because my teaching makes no headway with you. I am 38 revealing in words what I saw in my Father's presence; and you are revealing in action what you

[a] *Some witnesses here insert the passage* 7. 53 – 8. 11, *which is printed on p. 131.*
[b] *Or* What I have told you all along.

39 learned from your father.' They retorted, 'Abraham is our father.' 'If you were Abraham's children', Jesus replied, 'you would do as
40 Abraham did.*a* As it is, you are bent on killing me, a man who told you the truth, as I heard it from God. That is not how Abraham
41 acted. You are doing your own father's work.'

They said, 'We are not baseborn; God is our father, and God
42 alone.' Jesus said, 'If God were your father, you would love me, for God is the source of my being, and from him I come. I have not come of my own accord; he sent
43 me. Why do you not understand my language? It is because my revelation is beyond your grasp.
44 'Your father is the devil and you choose to carry out your father's desires. He was a murderer from the beginning, and is not rooted in the truth; there is no truth in him. When he tells a lie he is speaking his own language, for he is a liar
45 and the father of lies. But I speak the truth and therefore you do not
46 believe me. Which of you can prove me in the wrong?*b* If what I say is true, why do you not be-
47 lieve me? He who has God for his father listens to the words of God. You are not God's children; that is why you do not listen.'
48 The Jews answered, 'Are we not right in saying that you are a Samaritan, and that you are possess-
49 ed?' 'I am not possessed,' said Jesus; 'I am honouring my Father,
50 but you dishonour me. I do not care about my own glory; there is one who does care, and he is judge.
51 In very truth I tell you, if anyone obeys my teaching he shall never know what it is to die.'
52 The Jews said, 'Now we are certain that you are possessed. Abra-

ham is dead; the prophets are dead; and yet you say, "If anyone obeys my teaching he shall not know what it is to die." Are you 53 greater than our father Abraham, who is dead? The prophets are dead too. What do you claim to be?'

Jesus replied, 'If I glorify my- 54 self, that glory of mine is worthless. It is the Father who glorifies me, he of whom you say, "He is our God", though you do not know him. But 55 I know him; if I said that I did not know him I should be a liar like you. But in truth I know him and obey his word.

'Your father Abraham was over- 56 joyed to see my day; he saw it and was glad.' The Jews protested, 57 'You are not yet fifty years old. How can you have seen Abraham?'*c* Jesus said, 'In very truth I 58 tell you, before Abraham was born, I am.'

They picked up stones to throw 59 at him, but Jesus was not to be seen; and he left the temple.*d*

As he went on his way Jesus saw a 9 man blind from his birth. His dis- 2 ciples put the question, 'Rabbi, who sinned, this man or his parents? Why was he born blind?' 'It is not 3 that this man or his parents sinned,' Jesus answered; 'he was born blind so that God's power might be displayed in curing him. While daylight lasts we*e* must 4 carry on the work of him who sent me; night comes, when no one can work. While I am in the world I am 5 the light of the world.'

With these words he spat on the 6 ground and made a paste with the spittle; he spread it on the man's eyes, and said to him, 'Go and 7 wash in the pool of Siloam.' (The name means 'sent'.) The man went

---

a Some witnesses read 'If you are Abraham's children', Jesus replied, 'do as Abraham did.'   *b Or* Which of you convicts me of sin?
c Some witnesses read How can Abraham have seen you?   *d Or the division may be made after the words* was not to be seen; *the paragraph following would then begin* Then Jesus left the temple, and as he went...   *e Some witnesses read* I.

away and washed, and when he returned he could see.

8 His neighbours and those who were accustomed to see him begging said, 'Is not this the man
9 who used to sit and beg?' Others said, 'Yes, this is the man.' Others again said, 'No, but it is someone like him.' The man himself said,
10 'I am the man.' They asked him,
11 'How were your eyes opened?' He replied, 'The man called Jesus made a paste and smeared my eyes with it, and told me to go to Siloam and wash. I went and washed, and
12 gained my sight.' 'Where is he?' they asked. He answered, 'I do not know.'

13 THE man who had been blind was
14 brought before the Pharisees. As it was a Sabbath day when Jesus made the paste and opened his
15 eyes, the Pharisees now asked him by what means he had gained his sight. The man told them, 'He spread a paste on my eyes; then I
16 washed, and now I can see.' Some of the Pharisees said, 'This fellow is no man of God; he does not keep the Sabbath.' Others said, 'How could such signs come from a sinful man?' So they took different
17 sides. Then they continued to question him: 'What have you to say about him? It was your eyes he opened.' He answered, 'He is a prophet.'

18 The Jews would not believe that the man had been blind and had gained his sight, until they had
19 summoned his parents and questioned them: 'Is this man your son? Do you say that he was born blind? How is it that he can see
20 now?' The parents replied, 'We know that he is our son, and that
21 he was born blind. But how it is that he can now see, or who opened his eyes, we do not know. Ask him; he is of age; he will speak for him-
22 self.' His parents gave this answer because they were afraid of the Jews; for the Jewish authorities had already agreed that anyone who acknowledged Jesus as Messiah should be banned from the synagogue. That is why the parents 23 said, 'He is of age; ask him.'

24 So for the second time they summoned the man who had been blind, and said, 'Speak the truth before God. We know that this fellow is a sinner.' 'Whether or not 25 he is a sinner, I do not know', the man replied. 'All I know is this: once I was blind, now I can see.' 'What did he do to you?' they 26 asked. 'How did he open your eyes?' 'I have told you already,' he 27 retorted, 'but you took no notice. Why do you want to hear it again? Do you also want to become his disciples?' Then they became abu- 28 sive. 'You are that man's disciple,' they said, 'but we are disciples of Moses. We know that God spoke to 29 Moses, but as for this fellow, we do not know where he comes from.'

30 The man replied, 'What an extraordinary thing! Here is a man who has opened my eyes, yet you do not know where he comes from! It is common knowledge 31 that God does not listen to sinners; he listens to anyone who is devout and obeys his will. To open the eyes 32 of a man born blind – it is unheard of since time began. If that man 33 had not come from God he could have done nothing.' 'Who are you 34 to give us lessons,' they retorted, 'born and bred in sin as you are?' Then they expelled him from the synagogue.

35 Jesus heard that they had expelled him. When he found him he asked, 'Have you faith in the Son of Man[a]?' The man answered, 'Tell 36 me who he is, sir, that I should put my faith in him.' 'You have seen 37 him,' said Jesus; 'indeed, it is he who is speaking to you.' 'Lord, I 38 believe', he said, and bowed before him.

39 Jesus said, 'It is for judgement

---

[a] *Some witnesses read* Son of God.

that I have come into this world – to give sight to the sightless and to 40 make blind those who see.' Some Pharisees in his company asked, 'Do you mean that we are blind?' 41 'If you were blind,' said Jesus, 'you would not be guilty, but because you say "We see", your guilt remains.

10 'In truth I tell you, in very truth, the man who does not enter the sheepfold by the door, but climbs in some other way, is nothing but a 2 thief or a robber. The man who enters by the door is the shepherd 3 in charge of the sheep. The door-keeper admits him, and the sheep hear his voice; he calls his own sheep by name, and leads them out. 4 When he has brought them all out, he goes ahead and the sheep follow, 5 because they know his voice. They will not follow a stranger; they will run away from him, because they do not recognize the voice of strangers.'

6 This was a parable that Jesus told them, but they did not understand what he meant by it.

7 So Jesus spoke again: 'In truth, in very truth I tell you, I am the 8 door of the sheepfold. The sheep paid no heed to any who came before me, for these were all thieves 9 and robbers. I am the door; anyone who comes into the fold through me shall be safe. He shall go in and out and shall find pasturage.

10 'The thief comes only to steal, to kill, to destroy; I have come that men may have life, and may have it 11 in all its fullness. I am the good shepherd; the good shepherd lays 12 down his life for the sheep. The hireling, when he sees the wolf coming, abandons the sheep and runs away, because he is no shepherd and the sheep are not his. Then the wolf harries the flock and 13 scatters the sheep. The man runs

away because he is a hireling and cares nothing for the sheep.

'I am the good shepherd; I know 14 my own sheep and my sheep know 15 me – as the Father knows me and I know the Father – and I lay down my life for the sheep. But there are 16 other sheep of mine, not belonging to this fold, whom I must bring in; and they too will listen to my voice. There will then be one flock, one shepherd. The Father loves me 17 because I lay down my life, to receive it back again. No one has 18 robbed me of it; I am laying it down of my own free will. I have the right to lay it down, and I have the right to receive it back again; this charge I have received from my Father.'

These words once again caused a 19 split among the Jews. Many of 20 them said, 'He is possessed, he is raving. Why listen to him?' Others 21 said, 'No one possessed by an evil spirit could speak like this. Could an evil spirit open blind men's eyes?'

It was winter, and the festival of 22 the Dedication was being held in Jerusalem. Jesus was walking in 23 the temple precincts, in Solomon's Portico. The Jews gathered round 24 him and asked: 'How long must you keep us in suspense? If you are the Messiah say so plainly.' 'I have 25 told you,' said Jesus, 'but you do not believe. My deeds done in my Father's name are my credentials, but because you are not sheep of 26 my flock you do not believe. My 27 own sheep listen to my voice; I know them and they follow me. I 28 give them eternal life and they shall never perish; no one shall snatch them from my care. My 29 Father who has given them to me is greater than all, and no one can snatch them[a] out of the Father's care. My Father and I are one.' 30

---

[a] *Some witnesses read* My Father is greater than all, and that which he has given me no one can snatch. . . ; *others read* That which my Father has given me is greater than all, and no one can snatch it. . .

31 Once again the Jews picked up
32 stones to stone him. At this Jesus said to them, 'I have set before you many good deeds, done by my Father's power; for which of these
33 would you stone me?' The Jews replied, 'We are not going to stone you for any good deed, but for your blasphemy. You, a mere man,
34 claim to be a god.'[a] Jesus answered, 'Is it not written in your own
35 Law, "I said: You are gods"? Those are called gods to whom the word of God was delivered – and Scrip-
36 ture cannot be set aside. Then why do you charge me with blasphemy because I, consecrated and sent into the world by the Father, said, "I am God's son"?
37 'If I am not acting as my Father
38 would, do not believe me. But if I am, accept the evidence of my deeds, even if you do not believe me, so that you may recognize and know that the Father is in me, and I in the Father.'
39 This provoked them to one more attempt to seize him. But he escaped from their clutches.

Victory over death

40 JESUS withdrew again across the Jordan, to the place where John had been baptizing earlier. There
41 he stayed, while crowds came to him. They said, 'John gave us no miraculous sign, but all that he said about this man was true.'
42 Many came to believe in him there.
11 There was a man named Lazarus who had fallen ill. His home was at Bethany, the village of Mary and
2 her sister Martha. (This Mary, whose brother Lazarus had fallen ill, was the woman who anointed the Lord with ointment and wiped
3 his feet with her hair.) The sisters sent a message to him: 'Sir, you should know that your friend lies
4 ill.' When Jesus heard this he said, 'This illness will not end in death; it has come for the glory of God,

to bring glory to the Son of God.'
5 And therefore, though he loved Martha and her sister and Lazarus,
6 after hearing of his illness Jesus waited for two days in the place where he was.
7 After this, he said to his disciples, 'Let us go back to Judaea.'
8 'Rabbi,' his disciples said, 'it is not long since the Jews there were wanting to stone you. Are you
9 going there again?' Jesus replied, 'Are there not twelve hours of daylight? Anyone can walk in day-time without stumbling, because he sees
10 the light of this world. But if he walks after nightfall he stumbles, because the light fails him.'
11 After saying this he added, 'Our friend Lazarus has fallen asleep,
12 but I shall go and wake him.' The disciples said, 'Master, if he has
13 fallen asleep he will recover.' Jesus, however, had been speaking of his death, but they thought that he
14 meant natural sleep. Then Jesus spoke out plainly: 'Lazarus is dead.
15 I am glad not to have been there; it will be for your good and for the good of your faith. But let us go to
16 him.' Thomas, called 'the Twin', said to his fellow-disciples, 'Let us also go, that we may die with him.'

17 ON his arrival Jesus found that Lazarus had already been four
18 days in the tomb. Bethany was just under two miles from Jerusalem,
19 and many of the people had come from the city to Martha and Mary to condole with them on their bro-
20 ther's death. As soon as she heard that Jesus was on his way, Martha went to meet him, while Mary stayed at home.
21 Martha said to Jesus, 'If you had been here, sir, my brother
22 would not have died. Even now I know that whatever you ask of
23 God, God will grant you.' Jesus said, 'Your brother will rise again.'
24 'I know that he will rise again', said Martha, 'at the resurrection

---

[a] Or claim to be God.

25 on the last day.' Jesus said, 'I am the resurrection and I am life.[a] If a man has faith in me, even though
26 he die, he shall come to life; and no one who is alive and has faith shall ever die. Do you believe this?'
27 'Lord, I do,' she answered; 'I now believe that you are the Messiah, the Son of God who was to come into the world.'
28 With these words she went to call her sister Mary, and taking her aside, she said, 'The Master is here;
29 he is asking for you.' When Mary heard this she rose up quickly and
30 went to him. Jesus had not yet reached the village, but was still at the place where Martha had met
31 him. The Jews who were in the house condoling with Mary, when they saw her start up and leave the house, went after her, for they supposed that she was going to the tomb to weep there.
32 So Mary came to the place where Jesus was. As soon as she caught sight of him she fell at his feet and said, 'O sir, if you had only been here my brother would not have
33 died.' When Jesus saw her weeping and the Jews her companions weeping, he sighed heavily and
34 was deeply moved. 'Where have you laid him?' he asked. They re-
35 plied, 'Come and see, sir.' Jesus
36 wept. The Jews said, 'How dearly
37 he must have loved him!' But some of them said, 'Could not this man, who opened the blind man's eyes, have done something to keep Lazarus from dying?'
38 Jesus again sighed deeply; then he went over to the tomb. It was a cave, with a stone placed against
39 it. Jesus said, 'Take away the stone.' Martha, the dead man's sister, said to him, 'Sir, by now there will be a stench; he has been
40 there four days.' Jesus said, 'Did I not tell you that if you have faith
41 you will see the glory of God?' So they removed the stone.
Then Jesus looked upwards and

said, 'Father, I thank thee; thou hast heard me. I knew already that 42 thou always hearest me, but I spoke for the sake of the people standing round, that they might believe that thou didst send me.'
Then he raised his voice in a 43 great cry: 'Lazarus, come forth.' The dead man came out, his hands 44 and feet swathed in linen bands, his face wrapped in a cloth. Jesus said, 'Loose him; let him go.'

N o w many of the Jews who had 45 come to visit Mary and had seen what Jesus did, put their faith in him. But some of them went off to 46 the Pharisees and reported what he had done.
Thereupon the chief priests and 47 the Pharisees convened a meeting of the Council. 'What action are we taking?' they said. 'This man is performing many signs. If we leave 48 him alone like this the whole populace will believe in him. Then the Romans will come and sweep away our temple and our nation.' But 49 one of them, Caiaphas, who was High Priest that year, said, 'You know nothing whatever; you do 50 not use your judgement; it is more to your interest that one man should die for the people, than that the whole nation should be destroyed.' He did not say this of his 51 own accord, but as the High Priest in office that year, he was prophesying that Jesus would die for the nation – would die not for the 52 nation alone but to gather together the scattered children of God. So from that day on they 53 plotted his death.
Accordingly Jesus no longer 54 went about publicly in Judaea, but left that region for the country bordering on the desert, and came to a town called Ephraim, where he stayed with his disciples.

T H E Jewish Passover was now at 55 hand, and many people went up

[a] *Some witnesses omit* and I am life.

from the country to Jerusalem to purify themselves before the festi-
56 val. They looked out for Jesus, and as they stood in the temple they asked one another, 'What do you think? Perhaps he is not coming to
57 the festival.' Now the chief priests and the Pharisees had given orders that anyone who knew where he was should give information, so that they might arrest him.

12 Six days before the Passover festival Jesus came to Bethany, where Lazarus lived whom he had raised
2 from the dead. There a supper was given in his honour, at which Martha served, and Lazarus sat
3 among the guests with Jesus. Then Mary brought a pound of very costly perfume, pure oil of nard, and anointed the feet of Jesus and wiped them with her hair, till the house was filled with the fragrance.
4 At this, Judas Iscariot, a disciple of his – the one who was to betray
5 him – said, 'Why was this perfume not sold for thirty pounds[a] and
6 given to the poor?' He said this, not out of any care for the poor, but because he was a thief; he used to pilfer the money put into the common purse, which was in
7 his charge. 'Leave her alone' said Jesus. 'Let her keep it till the day when she prepares for my burial;
8 for you have the poor among you always, but you will not always have me.'[b]
9 A great number of the Jews heard that he was there, and came not only to see Jesus but also Lazarus whom he had raised from
10 the dead. The chief priests then resolved to do away with Lazarus
11 as well, since on his account many Jews were going over to Jesus and putting their faith in him.

12 The next day the great body of pilgrims who had come to the festival, hearing that Jesus was on the way to Jerusalem, took palm 13 branches and went out to meet him, shouting, 'Hosanna! Blessings on him who comes in the name of the Lord! God bless the king of Israel!' Jesus found a donkey and mounted 14 it, in accordance with the text of Scripture: 'Fear no more, daughter 15 of Zion; see, your king is coming, mounted on an ass's colt.'

At the time his disciples did not 16 understand this, but after Jesus had been glorified they remembered that this had been written about him, and that this had happened to him. The people who were present 17 when he called Lazarus out of the tomb and raised him from the dead told what they had seen and heard. That is why the crowd went to 18 meet him; they had heard of this sign that he had performed. The 19 Pharisees said to one another, 'You see you are doing no good at all; why, all the world has gone after him!'

Among those who went up to 20 worship at the festival were some Greeks. They came to Philip, who 21 was from Bethsaida in Galilee, and said to him, 'Sir, we should like to see Jesus.' So Philip went and told 22 Andrew, and the two of them went to tell Jesus. Then Jesus replied: 23 'The hour has come for the Son of Man to be glorified. In truth, in 24 very truth I tell you, a grain of wheat remains a solitary grain unless it falls into the ground and dies; but if it dies, it bears a rich harvest. The man who loves himself is lost, 25 but he who hates himself in this world will be kept safe for eternal life. If anyone serves me, he must 26 follow me; where I am, my servant will be. Whoever serves me will be honoured by my Father.

'Now my soul is in turmoil, and 27 what am I to say? Father, save me from this hour.[c] No, it was for this that I came to this hour. Father, 28

---
[a] *Literally* for 300 denarii.   [b] *Some witnesses omit* for you have...have me.
[c] *Or* ...turmoil. Shall I say, "Father, save me from this hour"?

118

glorify thy name.' A voice sounded from heaven: 'I have glorified it, 29 and I will glorify it again.' The crowd standing by said it was thunder, while others said, 'An 30 angel has spoken to him.' Jesus replied, 'This voice spoke for your 31 sake, not mine. Now is the hour of judgement for this world; now shall the Prince of this world be 32 driven out. And I shall draw all men to myself, when I am lifted up 33 from the earth.' This he said to indicate the kind of death he was to die.

34　　The people answered, 'Our Law teaches us that the Messiah continues for ever. What do you mean by saying that the Son of Man must be lifted up? What Son of Man is 35 this?' Jesus answered them: 'The light is among you still, but not for long. Go on your way while you have the light, so that darkness may not overtake you. He who journeys in the dark does not know 36 where he is going. While you have the light, trust to the light, so that you may become men of light.' After these words Jesus went away from them into hiding.

37　IN spite of the many signs which Jesus had performed in their presence they would not believe in 38 him, for the prophet Isaiah's utterance had to be fulfilled: 'Lord, who has believed what we reported, and to whom has the Lord's power 39 been revealed?' So it was that they could not believe, for there is an- 40 other saying of Isaiah's: 'He has blinded their eyes and dulled their minds, lest they should see with their eyes, and perceive with their minds, and turn to me to heal 41 them.' Isaiah said this because[a] he saw his glory and spoke about him.

42　　For all that, even among those in authority a number believed in him, but would not acknowledge him on account of the Pharisees, for fear of being banned from the synagogue. For they valued their 43 reputation with men rather than the honour which comes from God.

So Jesus cried aloud: 'When a man 44 believes in me, he believes in him who sent me rather than in me; seeing me, he sees him who sent me. 45 I have come into the world as 46 light, so that no one who has faith in me should remain in darkness. But if anyone hears my words and 47 pays no regard to them, I am not his judge; I have not come to judge the world, but to save the world. There is a judge for the man who 48 rejects me and does not accept my words; the word that I spoke will be his judge on the last day. I do 49 not speak on my own authority, but the Father who sent me has himself commanded me what to say and how to speak. I know that 50 his commands are eternal life. What the Father has said to me, therefore – that is what I speak.'

Farewell discourses

IT was before the Passover festi- 13 val. Jesus knew that his hour had come and he must leave this world and go to the Father. He had always loved his own who were in the world, and now he was to show the full extent of his love.

The devil had already put it into 2 the mind of Judas son of Simon Iscariot to betray him. During supper, Jesus, well aware that the 3 Father had entrusted everything to him, and that he had come from God and was going back to God, rose from table, laid aside his gar- 4 ments, and taking a towel, tied it round him. Then he poured water 5 into a basin, and began to wash his disciples' feet and to wipe them with the towel.

When it was Simon Peter's turn, 6 Peter said to him, 'You, Lord, washing my feet?' Jesus replied, 7 'You do not understand now what

[a] *Some witnesses read* when.

I am doing, but one day you will.'

8 Peter said, 'I will never let you wash my feet.' 'If I do not wash you,' Jesus replied, 'you are not in 9 fellowship with me.' 'Then, Lord,' said Simon Peter, 'not my feet only; wash my hands and head as well!'

10 Jesus said, 'A man who has bathed needs no further washing;[a] he is altogether clean; and you are clean, though not every one of you.'

11 He added the words 'not every one of you' because he knew who was going to betray him.

12 After washing their feet and taking his garments again, he sat down. 'Do you understand what I have done for you?' he asked.

13 'You call me "Master" and "Lord", and rightly so, for that is what I 14 am. Then if I, your Lord and Master, have washed your feet, you also ought to wash one an- 15 other's feet. I have set you an example: you are to do as I have 16 done for you. In very truth I tell you, a servant is not greater than his master, nor a messenger than 17 the one who sent him. If you know this, happy are you if you act upon it.

18 'I am not speaking about all of you; I know whom I have chosen. But there is a text of Scripture to be fulfilled: "He who eats bread with me has turned against me."[b] 19 I tell you this now, before the event, so that when it happens you may believe that I am what I am. 20 In very truth I tell you, he who receives any messenger of mine receives me; receiving me, he receives the One who sent me.'

21 After saying this, Jesus exclaimed in deep agitation of spirit, 'In truth, in very truth I tell you, one of you is going to betray me.' 22 The disciples looked at one another in bewilderment: whom could he 23 be speaking of? One of them, the disciple he loved, was reclining close beside Jesus. So Simon Peter 24 nodded to him and said, 'Ask who it is he means.' That disciple, as he 25 reclined, leaned back close to Jesus and asked, 'Lord, who is it?' Jesus 26 replied, 'It is the man to whom I give this piece of bread when I have dipped it in the dish.' Then, after dipping it in the dish, he took it out and gave it to Judas son of Simon Iscariot. As soon as Judas 27 had received it Satan entered him. Jesus said to him, 'Do quickly what you have to do.' No one at the 28 table understood what he meant by this. Some supposed that, as Judas 29 was in charge of the common purse, Jesus was telling him to buy what was needed for the festival, or to make some gift to the poor. As soon 30 as Judas had received the bread he went out. It was night.

WHEN he had gone out Jesus said, 31 'Now the Son of Man is glorified, and in him God is glorified. If God 32 is glorified in him,[c] God will also glorify him in himself; and he will glorify him now. My children, for a 33 little longer I am with you; then you will look for me, and, as I told the Jews, I tell you now, where I am going you cannot come. I give 34 you a new commandment: love one another; as I have loved you, so you are to love one another. If 35 there is this love among you, then all will know that you are my disciples.'

Simon Peter said to him, 'Lord, 36 where are you going?' Jesus replied, 'Where I am going you cannot follow me now, but one day you will.' Peter said, 'Lord, why 37 cannot I follow you now? I will lay down my life for you.' Jesus an- 38 swered, 'Will you indeed lay down your life for me? I tell you in very truth, before the cock crows you will have denied me three times.

'Set your troubled hearts at rest. 14 Trust in God always; trust also in

---

[a] *Some witnesses read* needs only to wash his feet.
[b] *Literally* has lifted his heel against me.   [c] *Some witnesses omit* If God . . . in him.

2 me. There are many dwelling-places in my Father's house; if it were not so I should have told you; for I am going there on purpose to 3 prepare a place for you.[a] And if I go and prepare a place for you, I shall come again and receive you to myself, so that where I am you 4 may be also; and my way there is 5 known to you.'[b] Thomas said, 'Lord, we do not know where you are going, so how can we know the 6 way?' Jesus replied, 'I am the way; I am the truth and I am life; no one comes to the Father except by me.

7 'If you knew me you would know my Father too.[c] From now on you do know him; you have seen him.' 8 Philip said to him, 'Lord, show us the Father and we ask no more.' 9 Jesus answered, 'Have I been all this time with you, Philip, and you still do not know me? Anyone who has seen me has seen the Father. Then how can you say, "Show us 10 the Father"? Do you not believe that I am in the Father, and the Father in me? I am not myself the source of the words I speak to you: it is the Father who dwells in me 11 doing his own work. Believe me when I say that I am in the Father and the Father in me; or else accept the evidence of the deeds 12 themselves. In truth, in very truth I tell you, he who has faith in me will do what I am doing; and he will do greater things still because 13 I am going to the Father. Indeed anything you ask in my name I will do, so that the Father may be 14 glorified in the Son. If you ask[d] anything in my name I will do it.

15 'If you love me you will obey my 16 commands; and I will ask the Father, and he will give you another to be your Advocate, who will be 17 with you for ever – the Spirit of truth. The world cannot receive him, because the world neither sees nor knows him; but you know him, because he dwells with you and is[e] 18 in you. I will not leave you bereft; 19 I am coming back to you. In a little while the world will see me no longer, but you will see me; because 20 I live, you too will live; then you will know that I am in my Father, 21 and you in me and I in you. The man who has received my commands and obeys them – he it is who loves me; and he who loves me will be loved by my Father; and I will love him and disclose myself to him.'

22 Judas asked him – the other Judas, not Iscariot – 'Lord, what can have happened, that you mean to disclose yourself to us alone and not to the world?' Jesus replied, 23 'Anyone who loves me will heed what I say; then my Father will love him, and we will come to him and make our dwelling with him; 24 but he who does not love me does not heed what I say. And the word you hear is not mine: it is the word 25 of the Father who sent me. I have told you all this while I am still 26 here with you; but your Advocate, the Holy Spirit whom the Father will send in my name, will teach you everything, and will call to mind all that I have told you.

27 'Peace is my parting gift to you, my own peace, such as the world cannot give. Set your troubled hearts at rest, and banish your 28 fears. You heard me say, "I am going away, and coming back to you." If you loved me you would have been glad to hear that I was going to the Father; for the Father is greater than I. I have told you 29 now, beforehand, so that when it happens you may have faith.

30 'I shall not talk much longer with you, for the Prince of this world approaches. He has no

---

[a] *Or if it were not so, should I have told you that I am going to prepare a place for you?* [b] *Some witnesses read also. You know where I am going and you know the way.* [c] *Some witnesses read If you know me you will know my Father too.* [d] *Some witnesses insert me.* [e] *Some witnesses read shall be.*

31 rights over me; but the world must be shown that I love the Father, and do exactly as he commands; so up, let us go forward![a]

15 'I AM the real vine, and my Father 2 is the gardener. Every barren branch of mine he cuts away; and every fruiting branch he cleans, to 3 make it more fruitful still. You have already been cleansed by the 4 word that I spoke to you. Dwell in me, as I in you. No branch can bear fruit by itself, but only if it remains united with the vine; no more can you bear fruit, unless you remain united with me.

5 'I am the vine, and you the branches. He who dwells in me, as I dwell in him, bears much fruit; for apart from me you can do no- 6 thing. He who does not dwell in me is thrown away like a withered branch. The withered branches are heaped together, thrown on the fire, and burnt.

7 'If you dwell in me, and my words dwell in you, ask what you 8 will, and you shall have it. This is my Father's glory, that you may bear fruit in plenty and so be my 9 disciples.[b] As the Father has loved me, so I have loved you. Dwell in 10 my love. If you heed my commands, you will dwell in my love, as I have heeded my Father's commands and dwell in his love.

11 'I have spoken thus to you, so that my joy may be in you, and 12 your joy complete.[c] This is my commandment: love one another, 13 as I have loved you. There is no greater love than this, that a man should lay down his life for his 14 friends. You are my friends, if you 15 do what I command you. I call you servants no longer; a servant does not know what his master is about. I have called you friends, because I have disclosed to you everything that I heard from my Father. You 16 did not choose me: I chose you. I appointed you to go on and bear fruit, fruit that shall last; so that the Father may give you all that you ask in my name. This is my 17 commandment to you: love one another.

'If the world hates you, it hated 18 me first, as you know well.[d] If you 19 belonged to the world, the world would love its own; but because you do not belong to the world, because I have chosen you out of the world, for that reason the world hates you. Remember what I said: 20 "A servant is not greater than his master." As they persecuted me, they will persecute you; they will follow your teaching as little as they have followed mine. It is on 21 my account that they will treat you thus, because they do not know the One who sent me.

'If I had not come and spoken to 22 them, they would not be guilty of sin; but now they have no excuse for their sin: he who hates me, 23 hates my Father. If I had not 24 worked among them and accomplished what no other man has done, they would not be guilty of sin; but now they have both seen and hated both me and my Father.[e] However, this text in their 25 Law had to come true:[f] "They hated me without reason."

'But when your Advocate has 26 come, whom I will send you from the Father – the Spirit of truth that issues from the Father – he will bear witness to me. And you 27 also are my witnesses, because you have been with me from the first.

---

[a] Or for the Prince of this world is coming, though he has nothing in common with me. But he is coming so that the world may recognize that I love the Father, and do exactly as he commands. Up, and let us go forward to meet him!
[b] Some witnesses read that you may bear fruit in plenty. Thus you will be my disciples.   [c] Or so that I may have joy in you and your joy may be complete.
[d] Or bear in mind that it hated me first.   [e] Or but now they have indeed seen my work and yet have hated both me and my Father.
[f] Or let this text in their Law come true.

16 'I have told you all this to guard you against the breakdown of your faith. They will ban you from the synagogue; indeed, the time is coming when anyone who kills you will suppose that he is performing a religious duty. They will do these things because they do not know either the Father or me. I have told you all this so that when the time comes for it to happen you may remember my warning. I did not tell you this at first, because then I was with you; but now I am going away to him who sent me. None of you asks me "Where are you going?" Yet you are plunged into grief because of what I have told you. Nevertheless I tell you the truth: it is for your good that I am leaving you. If I do not go, your Advocate will not come, whereas if I go, I will send him to you. When he comes, he will confute the world, and show where wrong and right and judgement lie. He will convict them of wrong, by their refusal to believe in me; he will convince them that right is on my side, by showing that I go to the Father when I pass from your sight; and he will convince them of divine judgement, by showing that the Prince of this world stands condemned.

'There is still much that I could say to you, but the burden would be too great for you now. However, when he comes who is the Spirit of truth, he will guide you into all the truth; for he will not speak on his own authority, but will tell only what he hears; and he will make known to you the things that are coming. He will glorify me, for everything that he makes known to you he will draw from what is mine. All that the Father has is mine, and that is why I said, "Everything that he makes known to you he will draw from what is mine."

'A LITTLE while, and you see me no more; again a little while, and you will see me.' Some of his disciples said to one another, 'What does he mean by this: "A little while, and you will not see me, and again a little while, and you will see me", and by this: "Because I am going to my Father"?' So they asked, 'What is this "little while" that he speaks of? We do not know what he means.'

Jesus knew that they were wanting to question him, and said, 'Are you discussing what I said: "A little while, and you will not see me, and again a little while, and you will see me"? In very truth I tell you, you will weep and mourn, but the world will be glad. But though you will be plunged in grief, your grief will be turned to joy. A woman in labour is in pain because her time has come; but when the child is born she forgets the anguish in her joy that a man has been born into the world. So it is with you: for the moment you are sad at heart; but I shall see you again, and then you will be joyful, and no one shall rob you of your joy. When that day comes you will ask nothing of me. In very truth I tell you, if you ask the Father for anything in my name, he will give it you.[a] So far you have asked nothing in my name. Ask and you will receive, that your joy may be complete.

'Till now I have been using figures of speech; a time is coming when I shall no longer use figures, but tell you of the Father in plain words. When that day comes you will make your request in my name, and I do not say that I shall pray to the Father for you, for the Father loves you himself, because you have loved me and believed that I came from God. I came from the Father and have come into the world. Now I am leaving the world

[a] *Some witnesses read* if you ask the Father for anything, he will give it you in my name.

29 again and going to the Father.' His disciples said, 'Why, this is plain speaking; this is no figure of speech. 30 We are certain now that you know everything, and do not need to be questioned; because of this we believe that you have come from God.'

31 Jesus answered, 'Do you now 32 believe? Look,[a] the hour is coming, has indeed already come, when you are all to be scattered, each to his home, leaving me alone. Yet I am not alone, because the Father is 33 with me. I have told you all this so that in me you may find peace. In the world you will have trouble. But courage! The victory is mine; I have conquered the world.'

17 AFTER these words Jesus looked up to heaven and said:

'Father, the hour has come. Glorify thy Son, that the Son may 2 glorify thee. For thou hast made him sovereign over all mankind, to give eternal life to all whom thou 3 hast given him. This is eternal life: to know thee who alone art truly God, and Jesus Christ whom thou hast sent.

4 'I have glorified thee on earth by completing the work which thou 5 gavest me to do; and now, Father, glorify me in thy own presence with the glory which I had with thee before the world began.

6 'I have made thy name known to the men whom thou didst give me out of the world. They were thine, thou gavest them to me, and they 7 have obeyed thy command. Now they know that all thy gifts have 8 come to me from thee; for I have taught them all that I learned from thee, and they have received it: they know with certainty that I came from thee; they have had faith to believe that thou didst send me.

'I pray for them; I am not pray- 9 ing for the world but for those whom thou hast given me, because they belong to thee. All that is 10 mine is thine, and what is thine is mine; and through them has my glory shone.

'I am to stay no longer in the 11 world, but they are still in the world, and I am on my way to thee. Holy Father, protect by the power of thy name those whom thou hast given me,[b] that they may be one, as we are one. When I was with 12 them, I protected by the power of thy name those whom thou hast given me,[c] and kept them safe. Not one of them is lost except the man who must be lost, for Scripture has to be fulfilled.

'And now I am coming to thee; 13 but while I am still in the world I speak these words, so that they may have my joy within them in full measure. I have delivered thy 14 word to them, and the world hates them because they are strangers in the world, as I am. I pray thee, not 15 to take them out of the world, but to keep them from the evil one. They are strangers in the world, as 16 I am. Consecrate them by the 17 truth;[d] thy word is truth. As thou 18 hast sent me into the world, I have sent them into the world, and for 19 their sake I now consecrate myself, that they too may be consecrated by the truth.[d]

'But it is not for these alone that 20 I pray, but for those also who through their words put their faith in me; may they all be one: as thou, 21 Father, art in me, and I in thee, so also may they be in us, that the world may believe that thou didst send me. The glory which thou 22 gavest me I have given to them, that they may be one, as we are one; I in them and thou in me, may 23

---

[a] Or At the moment you believe; but look... those whom thou hast given me; *some witnesses read* protect them by the power of thy name which thou hast given me.   [b] Or keep in loyalty to thee [c] Or kept in loyalty to thee those whom thou hast given me; *some witnesses read* protected them by the power of thy name which thou hast given me.   [d] Or in truth.

they be perfectly one. Then the world will learn that thou didst send me, that thou didst love them as thou didst me.

24 'Father, I desire that these men, who are thy gift to me, may be with me where I am, so that they may look upon my glory, which thou hast given me because thou didst love me before the world 25 began. O righteous Father, although the world does not know thee, I know thee, and these men know that thou didst send me. 26 I made thy name known to them, and will make it known, so that the love thou hadst for me may be in them, and I may be in them.'

The final conflict

18 AFTER these words, Jesus went out with his disciples, and crossed the Kedron ravine. There was a garden there, and he and his dis-2 ciples went into it. The place was known to Judas, his betrayer, because Jesus had often met there 3 with his disciples. So Judas took a detachment of soldiers, and police provided by the chief priests and the Pharisees, equipped with lanterns, torches, and weapons, and 4 made his way to the garden. Jesus, knowing all that was coming upon him, went out to them and asked, 5 'Who is it you want?' 'Jesus of Nazareth', they answered. Jesus said, 'I am he.' And there stood 6 Judas the traitor with them. When he said, 'I am he', they drew back 7 and fell to the ground. Again Jesus asked, 'Who is it you want?' 'Jesus 8 of Nazareth', they answered. Then Jesus said, 'I have told you that I am he. If I am the man you want, 9 let these others go.' (This was to make good his words, 'I have not lost one of those whom thou gavest 10 me.') Thereupon Simon Peter drew the sword he was wearing and struck at the High Priest's servant, cutting off his right ear.

(The servant's name was Malchus.) Jesus said to Peter, 'Sheathe your 11 sword. This is the cup the Father has given me; shall I not drink it?'

THE troops with their commander, 12 and the Jewish police, now arrested Jesus and secured him. They took 13 him first to Annas.[a] Annas was father-in-law of Caiaphas, the High Priest for that year[a] – the 14 same Caiaphas who had advised the Jews that it would be to their interest if one man died for the whole people. Jesus was followed 15 by Simon Peter and another disciple. This disciple, who was acquainted with the High Priest, went with Jesus into the High Priest's courtyard, but Peter 16 halted at the door outside. So the other disciple, the High Priest's acquaintance, went out again and spoke to the woman at the door, and brought Peter in. The maid on 17 duty at the door said to Peter, 'Are you another of this man's disciples?' 'I am not', he said. The 18 servants and the police had made a charcoal fire, because it was cold, and were standing round it warming themselves. And Peter too was standing with them, sharing the warmth.

The High Priest questioned 19 Jesus about his disciples and about what he taught. Jesus replied, 'I 20 have spoken openly to all the world; I have always taught in synagogue and in the temple, where all Jews congregate; I have said nothing in secret. Why ques-21 tion me? Ask my hearers what I told them; they know what I said.' When he said this, one of the 22 police who was standing next to him struck him on the face, exclaiming, 'Is that the way to answer the High Priest?' Jesus 23 replied, 'If I spoke amiss, state it in evidence; if I spoke well, why strike me?'

[a] *See note on verse 24.*

24   So Annas sent him bound to Caiaphas the High Priest.[a]

25   Meanwhile Simon Peter stood warming himself. The others asked, 'Are you another of his disciples?' But he denied it: 'I am not', he

26   said. One of the High Priest's servants, a relation of the man whose ear Peter had cut off, insisted, 'Did I not see you with him

27   in the garden?' Peter denied again; and just then a cock crew.

28   FROM Caiaphas Jesus was led into the Governor's headquarters. It was now early morning, and the Jews themselves stayed outside the headquarters to avoid defilement, so that they could eat the

29   Passover meal.[b] So Pilate went out to them and asked, 'What charge do you bring against this man?'

30   'If he were not a criminal,' they replied, 'we should not have

31   brought him before you.' Pilate said, 'Take him away and try him by your own law.' The Jews answered, 'We are not allowed to put

32   any man to death.' Thus they ensured the fulfilment of the words by which Jesus had indicated the manner of his death.

33   Pilate then went back into his headquarters and summoned Je-

34   sus. 'Are you the king of the Jews?' he asked.[c] Jesus said, 'Is that your own idea, or have others

35   suggested it to you?' 'What! am I a Jew?' said Pilate. 'Your own nation and their chief priests have brought you before me. What have

36   you done?' Jesus replied, 'My kingdom does not belong to this world. If it did, my followers would be fighting to save me from arrest by the Jews. My kingly authority

37   comes from elsewhere.' 'You are a king, then?' said Pilate. Jesus answered, '"King" is your word. My task is to bear witness to the truth. For this was I born; for this I came into the world, and all who are not deaf to truth listen to my voice.' Pilate said, 'What is truth?',

38   and with those words went out again to the Jews. 'For my part,' he said, 'I find no case against him.

39   But you have a custom that I release one prisoner for you at Passover. Would you like me to release the king of the Jews?' Again the

40   clamour rose: 'Not him; we want Barabbas!' (Barabbas was a bandit.)

19   Pilate now took Jesus and had

2   him flogged; and the soldiers plaited a crown of thorns and placed it on his head, and robed him in a purple cloak. Then time

3   after time they came up to him, crying, 'Hail, King of the Jews!', and struck him on the face.

4   Once more Pilate came out and said to the Jews, 'Here he is; I am bringing him out to let you know that I find no case against him';

5   and Jesus came out, wearing the crown of thorns and the purple cloak. 'Behold the Man!' said

6   Pilate. The chief priests and their henchmen saw him and shouted, 'Crucify! crucify!' 'Take him and crucify him yourselves,' said Pilate; 'for my part I find no case against him.' The Jews answered,

7   'We have a law; and by that law he ought to die, because he has claimed to be Son of God.'

8   When Pilate heard that, he was more afraid than ever, and going

9   back into his headquarters he asked Jesus, 'Where have you come from?' But Jesus gave him no answer. 'Do you refuse to

10   speak to me?' said Pilate. 'Surely you know that I have authority to release you, and I have authority to crucify you?' 'You would have

11   no authority at all over me', Jesus replied, 'if it had not been granted

---

[a] *Some witnesses give this verse after* first *to Annas in verse 13; others at the end of verse 13.*

[b] *Or* could share in the offerings of the Passover season.

[c] *Or* 'You are king of the Jews, I take it', *he said.*

you from above; and therefore the deeper guilt lies with the man who handed me over to you.'

12 From that moment Pilate tried hard to release him; but the Jews kept shouting, 'If you let this man go, you are no friend to Caesar; any man who claims to be a king is 13 defying Caesar.' When Pilate heard what they were saying, he brought Jesus out and took his seat on the tribunal at the place known as 'The Pavement' ('Gab-batha' in the language of the Jews). 14 It was the eve of Passover,[a] about noon. Pilate said to the Jews, 'Here 15 is your king.' They shouted, 'Away with him! Away with him! Crucify him!' 'Crucify your king?' said Pilate. 'We have no king but 16 Caesar', the Jews replied. Then at last, to satisfy them, he handed Jesus over to be crucified.

17 JESUS was now taken in charge and, carrying his own cross, went out to the Place of the Skull, as it is called (or, in the Jews' language, 18 'Golgotha'), where they crucified him, and with him two others, one on the right, one on the left, and Jesus between them.

19 And Pilate wrote an inscription to be fastened to the cross; it read, 'Jesus of Nazareth King of the 20 Jews.' This inscription was read by many Jews, because the place where Jesus was crucified was not far from the city, and the inscription was in Hebrew, Latin, and 21 Greek. Then the Jewish chief priests said to Pilate, 'You should not write "King of the Jews"; write, "He claimed to be king of 22 the Jews."' Pilate replied, 'What I have written, I have written.'

23 The soldiers, having crucified Jesus, took possession of his clothes, and divided them into four parts, one for each soldier, leaving out the tunic. The tunic was seamless, 24 woven in one piece throughout; so

they said to one another, 'We must not tear this; let us toss for it'; and thus the text of Scripture came true: 'They shared my garments among them, and cast lots for my clothing.'

That is what the soldiers did. But meanwhile near the cross 25 where Jesus hung stood his mother, with her sister, Mary wife of Clo-pas, and Mary of Magdala. Jesus 26 saw his mother, with the disciple whom he loved standing beside her. He said to her, 'Mother, there is your son'; and to the disciple, 27 'There is your mother'; and from that moment the disciple took her into his home.

After that, Jesus, aware that all 28 had now come to its appointed end, said in fulfilment of Scripture, 'I thirst.' A jar stood there full of 29 sour wine; so they soaked a sponge with the wine, fixed it on a javelin,[b] and held it up to his lips. Having received the wine, he said, 30 'It is accomplished!' He bowed his head and gave up his spirit.[c]

Because it was the eve of Pass-31 over,[d] the Jews were anxious that the bodies should not remain on the cross for the coming Sabbath, since that Sabbath was a day of great solemnity; so they requested Pilate to have the legs broken and the bodies taken down. The 32 soldiers accordingly came to the first of his fellow-victims and to the second, and broke their legs; but when they came to Jesus, they 33 found that he was already dead, so they did not break his legs. But one 34 of the soldiers stabbed his side with a lance, and at once there was a flow of blood and water. This is 35 vouched for by an eyewitness, whose evidence is to be trusted. He knows that he speaks the truth, so that you too may believe; for this happened in fulfilment of 36 the text of Scripture: 'No bone of his shall be broken.' And another 37

---

[a] *Or* It was Friday in Passover.　　[b] *So one witness; the others read* on marjoram.
[c] *Or* breathed out his life.　　[d] *Or* Because it was Friday in Passover...

text says, 'They shall look on him whom they pierced.'

38 AFTER that, Pilate was approached by Joseph of Arimathaea, a disciple of Jesus, but a secret disciple for fear of the Jews, who[a] asked to be allowed to remove the body of Jesus. Pilate gave the permission; so Joseph came and took 39 the body away. He was joined by Nicodemus (the man who had first visited Jesus by night), who brought with him a mixture of myrrh and aloes, more than half a 40 hundredweight. They took the body of Jesus and wrapped it, with the spices, in strips of linen cloth according to Jewish burial-cus- 41 toms. Now at the place where he had been crucified there was a garden, and in the garden a new tomb, not yet used for burial. 42 There, because the tomb was near at hand and it was the eve of the Jewish Sabbath, they laid Jesus.

20 EARLY on the Sunday morning, while it was still dark, Mary of Magdala came to the tomb. She saw that the stone had been moved away from the entrance, 2 and ran to Simon Peter and the other disciple, the one whom Jesus loved. 'They have taken the Lord out of his tomb,' she cried, 'and we do not know where they have laid 3 him.' So Peter and the other set out and made their way to the 4 tomb. They were running side by side, but the other disciple outran Peter and reached the tomb first. 5 He peered in and saw the linen wrappings lying there, but did not 6 enter. Then Simon Peter came up, following him, and he went into the tomb. He saw the linen wrappings 7 lying, and the napkin which had been over his head, not lying with the wrappings but rolled together 8 in a place by itself. Then the

disciple who had reached the tomb first went in too, and he saw and believed; until then they had not 9 understood the scriptures, which showed that he must rise from the dead.

So the disciples went home again; 10 but Mary stood at the tomb out- 11 side, weeping. As she wept, she peered into the tomb; and she saw 12 two angels in white sitting there, one at the head, and one at the feet, where the body of Jesus had lain. They said to her, 'Why are 13 you weeping?' She answered, 'They have taken my Lord away, and I do not know where they have laid him.' With these words she turned 14 round and saw Jesus standing there, but did not recognize him. Jesus said to her, 'Why are you 15 weeping? Who is it you are looking for?' Thinking it was the gardener, she said, 'If it is you, sir, who removed him, tell me where you have laid him, and I will take him away.' Jesus said, 'Mary!' She turned to 16 him and said, 'Rabbuni!' (which is Hebrew for 'My Master'). Jesus 17 said, 'Do not cling to me,[b] for I have not yet ascended to the Father. But go to my brothers, and tell them that I am now ascending[c] to my Father and your Father, my God and your God.' Mary of Mag- 18 dala went to the disciples with her news: 'I have seen the Lord!' she said, and gave them his message.

Late that Sunday evening, 19 when the disciples were together behind locked doors, for fear of the Jews, Jesus came and stood among them. 'Peace be with you!' he said, and then showed them his 20 hands and his side. So when the disciples saw the Lord, they were filled with joy. Jesus repeated, 21 'Peace be with you!', and said, 'As the Father sent me, so I send you.' Then he breathed on them, saying, 22 'Receive the Holy Spirit! If you 23

[a] Or of Arimathaea. He was a disciple of Jesus, but had gone into hiding for fear of the Jews. He now...
[b] Or Touch me no more.   [c] Or I am going to ascend...

forgive any man's sins, they stand forgiven; if you pronounce them unforgiven, unforgiven they remain.'

24 One of the Twelve, Thomas, that is 'the Twin', was not with the rest 25 when Jesus came. So the disciples told him, 'We have seen the Lord.' He said, 'Unless I see the mark of the nails on his hands, unless I put my finger into the place where the nails were, and my hand into his side, I will not believe it.'

26 A week later his disciples were again in the room, and Thomas was with them. Although the doors were locked, Jesus came and stood among them, saying, 'Peace be 27 with you!' Then he said to Thomas, 'Reach your finger here; see my hands. Reach your hand here and put it into my side. Be unbelieving 28 no longer, but believe.' Thomas 29 said, 'My Lord and my God!' Jesus said, 'Because you have seen me you have found faith. Happy are they who never saw me and yet have found faith.'

30 There were indeed many other signs that Jesus performed in the presence of his disciples, which are 31 not recorded in this book. Those here written have been recorded in order that you may hold the faith[a] that Jesus is the Christ, the Son of God, and that through this faith you may possess life by his name.

21 SOME time later, Jesus showed himself to his disciples once again, by the Sea of Tiberias; and in this 2 way. Simon Peter and Thomas 'the Twin' were together with Nathanael of Cana-in-Galilee. The sons of Zebedee and two other disciples 3 were also there. Simon Peter said, 'I am going out fishing.' 'We will go with you', said the others. So they started and got into the boat. But that night they caught nothing.

4 Morning came, and there stood Jesus on the beach, but the disciples did not know that it was Jesus. He 5 called out to them, 'Friends, have you caught anything?' They answered 'No.' He said, 'Shoot the 6 net to starboard, and you will make a catch.' They did so, and found they could not haul the net aboard, there were so many fish in it. Then the disciple whom Jesus 7 loved said to Peter, 'It is the Lord!' When Simon Peter heard that, he wrapped his coat about him (for he had stripped) and plunged into the sea. The rest of them came on in 8 the boat, towing the net full of fish; for they were not far from land, only about a hundred yards.

When they came ashore, they 9 saw a charcoal fire there, with fish laid on it, and some bread. Jesus 10 said, 'Bring some of your catch.' Simon Peter went aboard and 11 dragged the net to land, full of big fish, a hundred and fifty-three of them; and yet, many as they were, the net was not torn. Jesus said, 12 'Come and have breakfast.' None of the disciples dared to ask 'Who are you?' They knew it was the Lord. Jesus now came up, took the 13 bread, and gave it to them, and the fish in the same way.

This makes the third time that 14 Jesus appeared to his disciples after his resurrection from the dead.

After breakfast, Jesus said to 15 Simon Peter, 'Simon son of John, do you love me more than all else[b]?' 'Yes, Lord,' he answered, 'you know that I love you.'[c] 'Then feed my lambs', he said. A second 16 time he asked, 'Simon son of John, do you love me?' 'Yes, Lord, you know I love you.'[c] 'Then tend my sheep.' A third time he said, 17 'Simon son of John, do you love me[d]?' Peter was hurt that he asked him a third time, 'Do you love me?'[e] 'Lord,' he said, 'you know

---

[a] *Some witnesses read* that you may come to believe... [b] *Or* more than they do. [c] *Or* that I am your friend. [d] *Or* are you my friend. [e] *Or* that at the third asking he should have said, 'Are you my friend?'

everything; you know I love you.'[a] Jesus said, 'Feed my sheep.

18 'And further, I tell you this in very truth: when you were young you fastened your belt about you and walked where you chose; but when you are old you will stretch out your arms, and a stranger will bind you fast, and carry you where 19 you have no wish to go.' He said this to indicate the manner of death by which Peter was to glorify God. Then he added, 'Follow me.'

20 Peter looked round, and saw the disciple whom Jesus loved following – the one who at supper had leaned back close to him to ask the question, 'Lord, who is it that will 21 betray you?' When he caught sight of him, Peter asked, 'Lord, what will happen to him?' Jesus said, 'If 22 it should be my will that he wait until I come, what is it to you? Follow me.'

That saying of Jesus became 23 current in the brotherhood, and was taken to mean that that disciple would not die. But in fact Jesus did not say that he would not die; he only said, 'If it should be my will that he wait until I come, what is it to you?'

It is this same disciple who 24 attests what has here been written. It is in fact he who wrote it, and we know that his testimony is true.[b]

There is much else that Jesus 25 did. If it were all to be recorded in detail, I suppose the whole world could not hold the books that would be written.

---

[a] Or that I am your friend.
[b] *Some witnesses here insert the passage printed on p. 131.*

An incident in the temple*

53* AND they went each to his home, and Jesus to the Mount of Olives.
2 At daybreak he appeared again in the temple, and all the people gathered round him. He had taken his seat and was engaged in teach-
3 ing them when the doctors of the law and the Pharisees brought in a woman caught committing adultery. Making her stand out in the
4 middle they said to him, 'Master, this woman was caught in the very
5 act of adultery. In the Law Moses has laid down that such women are to be stoned. What do you say
6 about it?' They put the question as a test, hoping to frame a charge against him. Jesus bent down and wrote with his finger on the ground. When they continued to press 7 their question he sat up straight and said, 'That one of you who is faultless shall throw the first stone.' Then once again he bent 8 down and wrote on the ground. When they heard what he said, 9 one by one they went away,[a] the eldest first; and Jesus was left alone, with the woman still standing there. Jesus again sat up and[b] 10 said to the woman, 'Where are they? Has no one condemned you?' She answered, 'No one, sir.' Jesus 11 said, 'Nor do I condemn you. You may go; do not sin again.'

* This passage, which in the most widely received editions of the New Testament is printed in the text of John, 7. 53 – 8. 11, has no fixed place in our witnesses. Some of them do not contain it at all. Some place it after Luke 21. 38, others after John 7. 36, or 7. 52, or 21. 24.

[a] Some witnesses insert convicted by their conscience.
[b] Some witnesses insert seeing no one but the woman.

ACTS OF THE
APOSTLES

ACTS OF THE APOSTLES

The beginnings of the church

1 IN the first part of my work, Theophilus, I wrote of all that Jesus did and taught from the 2 beginning until the day when, after giving instructions through the Holy Spirit to the apostles whom he had chosen, he was taken up to 3 heaven. He showed himself to these men after his death, and gave ample proof that he was alive: over a period of forty days he appeared to them and taught them about the 4 kingdom of God. While he was in their company he told them not to leave Jerusalem. 'You must wait', he said, 'for the promise made by my Father, about which you have 5 heard me speak: John, as you know, baptized with water, but you will be baptized with the Holy Spirit, and within the next few days.'

6 So, when they were all together, they asked him, 'Lord, is this the time when you are to establish once again the sovereignty of 7 Israel?' He answered, 'It is not for you to know about dates or times, which the Father has set within 8 his own control. But you will receive power when the Holy Spirit comes upon you; and you will bear witness for me in Jerusalem, and all over Judaea and Samaria, and away to the ends of the earth.'

9 When he had said this, as they watched, he was lifted up, and a cloud removed him from their 10 sight. As he was going, and as they were gazing intently into the sky, all at once there stood beside them 11 two men in white who said, 'Men of Galilee, why stand there looking up into the sky? This Jesus, who has been taken away from you up to heaven, will come in the same way as you have seen him go.'

12 Then they returned to Jerusalem from the hill called Olivet, which is near Jerusalem, no farther than a Sabbath day's journey. Entering 13 the city they went to the room upstairs where they were lodging: Peter and John and James and Andrew, Philip and Thomas, Bartholomew and Matthew, James son of Alphaeus and Simon the Zealot, and Judas son of James. All these 14 were constantly at prayer together, and with them a group of women, including Mary the mother of Jesus, and his brothers.

15 It was during this time that Peter stood up before the assembled brotherhood, about one hundred and twenty in all, and said: 'My friends, the prophecy in 16 Scripture was bound to come true, which the Holy Spirit, through the mouth of David, uttered about Judas who acted as guide to those who arrested Jesus. For he was one 17 of our number and had his place in this ministry.' (This Judas, be it 18 noted, after buying a plot of land with the price of his villainy, fell forward on the ground, and burst open, so that his entrails poured out. This became known to every- 19 one in Jerusalem, and they named the property in their own language Akeldama, which means 'Blood Acre'.) 'The text I have in mind', 20 Peter continued, 'is in the Book of Psalms: "Let his homestead fall

desolate; let there be none to inhabit it"; and again, "Let another take over his charge."

21 Therefore one of those who bore us company all the while we had the Lord Jesus with us, coming and

22 going, from John's ministry of baptism until the day when he was taken up from us – one of those must now join us as a witness to his resurrection.'

23 Two names were put forward: Joseph, who was known as Barsabbas, and bore the added name

24 of Justus; and Matthias. Then they prayed and said, 'Thou, Lord, who knowest the hearts of all men, declare which of these two thou hast

25 chosen to receive this office of ministry and apostleship which Judas abandoned to go where he

26 belonged.' They drew lots and the lot fell on Matthias, who was then assigned a place among the twelve apostles.[a]

2 WHILE the day of Pentecost was running its course they were all to-

2 gether in one place, when suddenly there came from the sky a noise like that of a strong driving wind, which filled the whole house where

3 they were sitting. And there appeared to them tongues like flames of fire, dispersed among them and

4 resting on each one. And they were all filled with the Holy Spirit and began to talk in other tongues, as the Spirit gave them power of utterance.

5 Now there were living in Jerusalem devout Jews[b] drawn from

6 every nation under heaven; and at this sound the crowd gathered, all bewildered because each one heard

7 his own language spoken. They were amazed and in their astonishment exclaimed, 'Why, they are all Galileans, are they not, these men

8 who are speaking? How is it then that we hear them, each of us in his

9 own native language? Parthians,

Medes, Elamites; inhabitants of Mesopotamia, of Judaea and Cap-

10 padocia, of Pontus and Asia, of Phrygia and Pamphylia, of Egypt and the districts of Libya around Cyrene; visitors from Rome, both

11 Jews and proselytes, Cretans and Arabs, we hear them telling in our own tongues the great things God

12 has done.' And they were all amazed and perplexed, saying to one another, 'What can this mean?'

13 Others said contemptuously, 'They have been drinking!'

14 But Peter stood up with the Eleven, raised his voice, and addressed them: 'Fellow Jews, and all you who live in Jerusalem, mark this and give me a hearing.

15 These men are not drunk, as you imagine; for it is only nine in the

16 morning. No, this is what the

17 prophet spoke of: "God says, 'This will happen in the last days: I will pour out upon everyone a portion of my spirit; and your sons and daughters shall prophesy; your young men shall see visions, and your old men shall dream dreams.

18 Yes, I will endue even my slaves, both men and women, with a portion of my spirit, and they shall

19 prophesy. And I will show portents in the sky above, and signs on the earth below – blood and fire and

20 drifting smoke. The sun shall be turned to darkness, and the moon to blood, before that great, resplendent day, the day of the Lord,

21 shall come. And then, everyone who invokes the name of the Lord shall be saved.'"

22 'Men of Israel, listen to me: I speak of Jesus of Nazareth, a man singled out by God and made known to you through miracles, portents, and signs, which God worked among you through him,

23 as you well know. When he had been given up to you, by the deliberate will and plan of God, you used heathen men to crucify and

---

[a] *Some witnesses read* was then appointed a colleague of the eleven apostles.
[b] *Some witnesses read* devout men.

24 kill him. But God raised him to life again, setting him free from the pangs of death, because it could not be that death should keep him in its grip.

25 'For David says of him:

"I foresaw that the presence of the Lord would be with me always, for he is at my right hand so that I may not be shaken;

26 therefore my heart was glad and my tongue spoke my joy; moreover, my flesh shall dwell in hope,

27 for thou wilt not abandon my soul to death, nor let thy loyal servant suffer corruption.

28 Thou hast shown me the ways of life, thou wilt fill me with gladness by thy presence."

29 'Let me tell you plainly, my friends, that the patriarch David died and was buried, and his tomb

30 is here to this very day. It is clear therefore that he spoke as a prophet, who knew that God had sworn to him that one of his own direct descendants should sit on

31 his throne; and when he said he was not abandoned to death, and his flesh never suffered corruption, he spoke with foreknowledge of the

32 resurrection of the Messiah. The Jesus we speak of has been raised by God, as we can all bear witness.

33 Exalted thus with[a] God's right hand, he received the Holy Spirit from the Father, as was promised, and all that you now see and hear

34 flows from him. For it was not David who went up to heaven; his own words are: "The Lord said to my Lord, 'Sit at my right hand

35 until I make your enemies your

36 footstool.'" Let all Israel then accept as certain that God has made this Jesus, whom you crucified, both Lord and Messiah.'

37 When they heard this they were cut to the heart, and said to Peter and the apostles,[b] 'Friends, what are we to do?' 'Repent,' said Peter, 38 'repent and be baptized, every one of you, in the name of Jesus the Messiah for the forgiveness of your sins; and you will receive the gift of the Holy Spirit. For the promise 39 is to you, and to your children, and to all who are far away, everyone whom the Lord our God may call.'

In these and many other words 40 he pressed his case and pleaded with them: 'Save yourselves', he said, 'from this crooked age.' Then 41 those who accepted his word were baptized, and some three thousand were added to their number that day.

They met constantly to hear the 42 apostles teach, and to share the common life, to break bread, and to pray. A sense of awe was every- 43 where, and many marvels and signs were brought about through the apostles. All whose faith had 44 drawn them together held everything in common:[c] they would sell 45 their property and possessions and make a general distribution as the need of each required. With one 46 mind they kept up their daily attendance at the temple, and, breaking bread in private houses, shared their meals with unaffected joy, as they praised God and en- 47 joyed the favour of the whole people. And day by day the Lord added to their number those whom he was saving.

ONE day at three in the afternoon, 3 the hour of prayer, Peter and John were on their way up to the temple. Now a man who had been a cripple 2 from birth used to be carried there and laid every day by the gate of the temple called 'Beautiful Gate', to beg from people as they went in. When he saw Peter and John on 3 their way into the temple he asked for charity. But Peter fixed his eyes 4

---

[a] Or at.   [b] Some witnesses read the rest of the apostles.
[c] Or All who had become believers held everything together in common.

on him, as John did also, and said, 5 'Look at us.' Expecting a gift from them, the man was all attention. 6 And Peter said, 'I have no silver or gold; but what I have I give you: in the name of Jesus Christ of 7 Nazareth, walk.' Then he grasped him by the right hand and pulled him up; and at once his feet and 8 ankles grew strong; he sprang up, stood on his feet, and started to walk. He entered the temple with them, leaping and praising God as 9 he went. Everyone saw him walk-10 ing and praising God, and when they recognized him as the man who used to sit begging at Beauti-ful Gate, they were filled with wonder and amazement at what had happened to him.

11   And as he was clutching Peter and John all the people came running in astonishment towards them in Solomon's Portico, as it is 12 called. Peter saw them coming and met them with these words: 'Men of Israel, why be surprised at this? Why stare at us as if we had made this man walk by some power or 13 godliness of our own? The God of Abraham, Isaac, and Jacob, the God of our fathers, has given the highest honour to his servant Jesus, whom you committed for trial and 14 repudiated in Pilate's court – re-pudiated the one who was holy and righteous when Pilate had de-cided to release him. You begged as a favour the release of a mur-15 derer, and killed him who has led the way to life. But God raised him from the dead; of that we are 16 witnesses. And the name of Jesus, by awakening faith, has strength-ened this man, whom you see and know, and this faith has made him completely well, as you can all see for yourselves.

17   'And now, my friends, I know quite well that you acted in ig-norance, and so did your rulers; 18 but this is how God fulfilled what he had foretold in the utterances of all the prophets: that his Messiah should suffer. Repent then and 19 turn to God, so that your sins may be wiped out. Then the Lord may grant you a time of recovery and 20 send you the Messiah he has al-ready appointed, that is, Jesus. He 21 must be received into heaven until the time of universal restoration comes, of which God spoke by his holy prophets.[a] Moses said, "The 22 Lord God will raise up a prophet for you from among yourselves as he raised me;[b] you shall listen to everything he says to you, and any-23 one who refuses to listen to that prophet must be extirpated from Israel." And so said all the pro-24 phets, from Samuel onwards; with one voice they all predicted this present time.

'You are the heirs of the pro-25 phets; you are within the covenant which God made with your fathers, when he said to Abraham, "And in your offspring all the families on earth shall find blessing." When 26 God raised up his Servant, he sent him to you first, to bring you bless-ing by turning every one of you from your wicked ways.'

They were still addressing the 4 people when the chief[c] priests came upon them, together with the Con-troller of the Temple and the Sad-ducees, exasperated at their teach-2 ing the people and proclaiming the resurrection from the dead – the resurrection of Jesus. They were 3 arrested and put in prison for the night, as it was already evening. But many of those who had heard 4 the message became believers. The number of men now reached about five thousand.

Next day the Jewish rulers, 5 elders, and doctors of the law met in Jerusalem. There were present 6 Annas the High Priest, Caiaphas, Jonathan,[d] Alexander, and all who were of the high-priestly family.

---

[a] *Some witnesses add* from the beginning of the world.   [b] Or like me.
[c] *Some witnesses omit* chief.   [d] *Some witnesses read* John.

7 They brought the apostles before the court and began the examination. 'By what power', they asked, 'or by what name have such men as 8 you done this?' Then Peter, filled with the Holy Spirit, answered, 9 'Rulers of the people and elders, if the question put to us today is about help given to a sick man, and we are asked by what means he was 10 cured, here is the answer, for all of you and for all the people of Israel: it was by the name of Jesus Christ of Nazareth, whom you crucified, whom God raised from the dead; it is by his name[a] that this man stands 11 here before you fit and well. This Jesus is the stone rejected by the builders which has become the keystone – and you are the builders. 12 There is no salvation in anyone else at all,[b] for there is no other name under heaven granted to men, by which we may receive salvation.'

13 Now as they observed the boldness of Peter and John, and noted that they were untrained laymen, they began to wonder, then recognized them as former companions 14 of Jesus. And when they saw the man who had been cured standing with them, they had nothing to say 15 in reply. So they ordered them to leave the court, and then discussed the matter among themselves. 16 'What are we to do with these men?' they said; 'for it is common knowledge in Jerusalem that a notable miracle has come about through them; and we cannot deny 17 it. But to stop this from spreading further among the people, we had better caution them never again to 18 speak to anyone in this name.' They then called them in and ordered them to refrain from all public speaking and teaching in the name of Jesus.

19 But Peter and John said to them in reply: 'Is it right in God's eyes for us to obey you rather than 20 God? Judge for yourselves. We cannot possibly give up speaking of things we have seen and heard.'

21 The court repeated the caution and discharged them. They could not see how they were to punish them, because the people were all giving glory to God for what had happened. The man upon whom 22 this miracle of healing had been performed was over forty years old.

23 As soon as they were discharged they went back to their friends and told them everything that the chief priests and elders had said. When 24 they heard it, they raised their voices as one man and called upon God:

'Sovereign Lord, maker of heaven and earth and sea and of everything in them, who by the 25 Holy Spirit,[c] through the mouth of David thy servant, didst say,

"Why did the Gentiles rage and the peoples lay their plots in vain? The kings of the earth took their 26 stand and the rulers made common cause
against the Lord and against his Messiah."

They did indeed make common 27 cause in this very city against thy holy servant Jesus whom thou didst anoint as Messiah. Herod and Pontius Pilate conspired with the Gentiles and peoples of Israel to 28 do all the things which, under thy hand and by thy decree, were foreordained. And now, O Lord, mark 29 their threats, and enable thy servants to speak thy word with all boldness. Stretch out thy hand to 30 heal and cause signs and wonders to be done through the name of thy holy servant Jesus.'

When they had ended their 31 prayer, the building where they were assembled rocked, and all were filled with the Holy Spirit and spoke the word of God with boldness.

---

[a] *Some witnesses insert* and no other.   [b] *Some witnesses omit* There is no...at all.
[c] *Some witnesses omit* by the Holy Spirit.

32 THE whole body of believers was united in heart and soul. Not a man of them claimed any of his possessions as his own, but everything 33 was held in common, while the apostles bore witness with great power to the resurrection of the Lord Jesus. They were all held in 34 high esteem; for they had never a needy person among them, because all who had property in land or houses sold it, brought the pro-35 ceeds of the sale, and laid the money at the feet of the apostles; it was then distributed to any who stood in need.

36 For instance, Joseph, surnamed by the apostles Barnabas (which means 'Son of Exhortation'), a 37 Levite, by birth a Cypriot, owned an estate, which he sold; he brought the money, and laid it at the apostles' feet.

5 But there was another man, called Ananias, with his wife Sap-2 phira, who sold a property. With the full knowledge of his wife he kept back part of the purchase-money, and part he brought and 3 laid at the apostles' feet. But Peter said, 'Ananias, how was it that Satan so possessed your mind that you lied to the Holy Spirit, and kept back part of the price of the 4 land? While it remained, did it not remain yours? When it was turned into money, was it not still at your own disposal? What made you think of doing this thing? You have 5 lied not to men but to God.' When Ananias heard these words he dropped dead; and all the others 6 who heard were awestruck. The younger men rose and covered his body, then carried him out and buried him.

7 About three hours passed, and then his wife came in, unaware of 8 what had happened. Peter turned to her and said, 'Tell me, were you paid such and such a price for the land?' 'Yes,' she said, 'that was the price.' Then Peter said, 'Why did 9 you both conspire to put the Spirit of the Lord to the test? Hark! there at the door are the footsteps of those who buried your husband; and they will carry you away.' And 10 suddenly she dropped dead at his feet. When the young men came in, they found her dead; and they carried her out and buried her beside her husband. And a great awe 11 fell upon the whole church, and upon all who heard of these events; and many remarkable and wonder-12 ful things took place among the people at the hands of the apostles.

THEY used to meet by common consent in Solomon's Portico, no 13 one from outside their number venturing to join with them. But people in general spoke highly of them,[a] and more than that, num-14 bers of men and women were added to their ranks as believers in the Lord.[b] In the end the sick were 15 actually carried out into the streets and laid there on beds and stretchers, so that even the shadow of Peter might fall on one or another as he passed by; and the 16 people from the towns round Jerusalem flocked in, bringing those who were ill or harassed by unclean spirits, and all of them were cured.

Then the High Priest and his 17 colleagues, the Sadducean party as it then was, were goaded into action by jealousy. They proceeded 18 to arrest the apostles, and put them in official custody. But an angel of 19 the Lord opened the prison doors during the night, brought them out, and said, 'Go, take your place 20 in the temple and speak to the people, and tell them about this new life and all it means.' Ac-21 cordingly they entered the temple at daybreak and went on with their teaching.

---

[a] Or . . . Portico. Although others did not venture to join them, the common people spoke highly of them.   [b] Or and an ever-increasing number of believers, both men and women, were added to the Lord.

When the High Priest arrived with his colleagues they summoned the 'Sanhedrin', that is, the full senate of the Israelite nation, and sent to the jail to fetch the prisoners. 22 But the police who went to the prison failed to find them there, so they returned and reported, 23 'We found the jail securely locked at every point, with the warders at their posts by the doors, but when we opened them we found no one inside.' 24 When they heard this, the Controller of the Temple and the chief priests were wondering what could have become of them,[a] 25 and then a man arrived with the report, 'Look! the men you put in prison are there in the temple teaching the people.' 26 At that the Controller went off with the police and fetched them, but without using force for fear of being stoned by the people.

27 So they brought them and stood them before the Council; and the High Priest began his examination. 28 'We expressly ordered you', he said, 'to desist from teaching in that name; and what has happened? You have filled Jerusalem with your teaching, and you are trying to make us responsible for that 29 man's death.' Peter replied for himself and the apostles: 'We must 30 obey God rather than men. The God of our fathers raised up Jesus whom you had done to death[b] by hanging 31 him on a gibbet. He it is whom God has exalted with his own right hand[c] as leader and saviour, to grant Israel repentance and for-32 giveness of sins. And we are witnesses to all this, and so is the Holy Spirit given by God to those who are obedient to him.'

33 This touched them on the raw, and they wanted to put them to 34 death. But a member of the Council rose to his feet, a Pharisee called Gamaliel, a teacher of the law held in high regard by all the people. He moved that the men be put outside for a while. Then he said, 'Men of 35 Israel, be cautious in deciding what to do with these men. Some time 36 ago Theudas came forward, claiming to be somebody, and a number of men, about four hundred, joined him. But he was killed and his whole following was broken up and disappeared. After him came Judas 37 the Galilean at the time of the census; he induced some people to revolt under his leadership, but he too perished and his whole following was scattered. And so now: 38 keep clear of these men, I tell you; leave them alone. For if this idea of theirs or its execution is of human origin, it will collapse; but if it is 39 from God, you will never be able to put them down, and you risk finding yourselves at war with God.'

They took his advice. They sent 40 for the apostles and had them flogged; then they ordered them to give up speaking in the name of Jesus, and discharged them. So the 41 apostles went out from the Council rejoicing that they had been found worthy to suffer indignity for the sake of the Name. And every day 42 they went steadily on with their teaching in the temple and in private houses, telling the good news of Jesus the Messiah.[d]

The church moves outwards

6 DURING this period, when disciples were growing in number, there was disagreement between those of them who spoke Greek[e] and those who spoke the language of the Jews.[f] The former party complained that their widows were being overlooked in the daily distribution. So the Twelve called the 2 whole body of disciples together and said, 'It would be a grave

---

[a] *Or wondering about them, what this could possibly mean.*
[b] *Or . . . Jesus, and you did him to death. . .*
[c] *Or at his right hand.*
[d] *Or the good news that the Messiah was Jesus.*
[e] *Literally the Hellenists.*
[f] *Literally the Hebrews.*

mistake for us to neglect the word of God in order to wait at table. 3 Therefore, friends, look out seven men of good reputation from your number, men full of the Spirit and of wisdom, and we will appoint them to deal with these matters, 4 while we devote ourselves to prayer and to the ministry of the 5 Word.' This proposal proved acceptable to the whole body. They elected Stephen, a man full of faith and of the Holy Spirit, Philip, Prochorus, Nicanor, Timon, Parmenas, and Nicolas of Antioch, a former convert to 6 Judaism. These they presented to the apostles, who prayed and laid their hands on them.

7   The word of God now spread more and more widely; the number of disciples in Jerusalem went on increasing rapidly, and very many of the priests adhered to the Faith. 8   Stephen, who was full of grace and power, began to work great miracles and signs among the 9 people. But some members of the synagogue called the Synagogue of Freedmen, comprising Cyrenians and Alexandrians and people from Cilicia and Asia, came forward and 10 argued with Stephen, but could not hold their own against the inspired 11 wisdom with which he spoke. They then put up men who alleged that they had heard him make blasphemous statements against Moses 12 and against God. They stirred up the people and the elders and doctors of the law, set upon him and seized him, and brought him 13 before the Council. They produced false witnesses who said, 'This man is for ever saying things against this holy place and against the Law. 14 For we have heard him say that Jesus of Nazareth will destroy this place and alter the customs handed 15 down to us by Moses.' And all who were sitting in the Council fixed their eyes on him, and his face appeared to them like the face of an angel.

Then the High Priest asked, 'Is 7 this so?' And he said, 'My brothers, 2 fathers of this nation, listen to me. The God of glory appeared to Abraham our ancestor while he was in Mesopotamia, before he had settled in Harran, and said: "Leave 3 your country and your kinsfolk and come away to a land that I will show you." Thereupon he left the 4 land of the Chaldaeans and settled in Harran. From there, after his father's death, God led him to migrate to this land where you now live. He gave him nothing in it to 5 call his own, not one yard; but promised to give it in possession to him and his descendants after him, though he was then childless. God 6 spoke in these terms: "Abraham's descendants shall live as aliens in a foreign land, held in slavery and oppression for four hundred years. And I will pass judgement", said 7 God, "on the nation whose slaves they are; and after that they shall come out free, and worship me in this place." He then gave him the 8 covenant of circumcision, and so, after Isaac was born, he circumcised him on the eighth day; and Isaac begot Jacob, and Jacob the twelve patriarchs.

'The patriarchs out of jealousy 9 sold Joseph into slavery in Egypt, but God was with him and rescued 10 him from all his troubles. He also gave him a presence and powers of mind which so commended him to Pharaoh king of Egypt, that he appointed him chief administrator for Egypt and the whole of the royal household.

'But famine struck all Egypt 11 and Canaan, and caused great hardship; and our ancestors could find nothing to eat. But Jacob 12 heard that there was food in Egypt and sent our fathers there. This was their first visit. On the second 13 visit Joseph was recognized by his brothers, and his family connections were disclosed to Pharaoh. So Joseph sent an invitation to his 14

father Jacob and all his relatives, seventy-five persons altogether;
15 and Jacob went down into Egypt. There he ended his days, as also
16 our forefathers did. Their remains were later removed to Shechem and buried in the tomb which Abraham had bought and paid for from the clan of Emmor at Shechem.

17 'Now as the time approached for God to fulfil the promise he had made to Abraham, our nation in Egypt grew and increased in num-
18 bers. At length another king, who knew nothing of Joseph, ascended
19 the throne of Egypt. He made a crafty attack on our race, and cruelly forced our ancestors to expose their children so that they
20 should not survive. At this time Moses was born. He was a fine child, and pleasing to God. For three months he was nursed in his
21 father's house, and when he was exposed, Pharaoh's daughter herself adopted him and brought him
22 up as her own son. So Moses was trained in all the wisdom of the Egyptians, a powerful speaker and a man of action.

23 'He was approaching the age of forty, when it occurred to him to look into the conditions of his fellow-countrymen the Israelites.
24 He saw one of them being ill-treated, so he went to his aid, and avenged the victim by striking
25 down the Egyptian. He thought his fellow-countrymen would understand that God was offering them deliverance through him, but they
26 did not understand. The next day he came upon two of them fighting, and tried to bring them to make up their quarrel. "My men," he said, "you are brothers; why are you
27 ill-treating one another?" But the man who was at fault pushed him away. "Who set you up as a ruler
28 and judge over us?" he said. "Are you going to kill me as you killed
29 the Egyptian yesterday?" At this

Moses fled the country and settled in Midianite territory. There two sons were born to him.

'After forty years had passed, an 30 angel appeared to him in the flame of a burning bush in the desert near Mount Sinai. Moses was amazed at 31 the sight. But as he approached to look closely, the voice of the Lord was heard: "I am the God of your 32 fathers, the God of Abraham, Isaac, and Jacob." Moses was terrified and dared not look. Then 33 the Lord said to him, "Take off your shoes; the place where you are standing is holy ground. I have 34 indeed seen how my people are oppressed in Egypt and have heard their groans; and I have come down to rescue them. Up, then; let me send you to Egypt."

'This Moses, whom they had 35 rejected with the words, "Who made you ruler and judge?" – this very man was commissioned as ruler and liberator by God himself, speaking through the angel who appeared to him in the bush. It 36 was Moses who led them out, working miracles and signs in Egypt, at the Red Sea, and for forty years in the desert. It was he again who 37 said to the Israelites, "God will raise up a prophet for you from among yourselves as he raised me."[a] He it was who, when they 38 were assembled there in the desert, conversed with the angel who spoke to him on Mount Sinai, and with our forefathers; he received the living utterances of God, to pass on to us.

'But our forefathers would not 39 accept his leadership. They thrust him aside. They wished themselves back in Egypt, and said to Aaron, 40 "Make us gods to go before us. As for that Moses, who brought us out of Egypt, we do not know what has become of him." That was when 41 they made the bull-calf, and offered sacrifice to the idol, and held a feast in honour of the thing their

a Or like me.

42 hands had made. But God turned away from them and gave them over to the worship of the host of heaven, as it stands written in the book of the prophets: "Did you bring me victims and offerings those forty years in the desert, you 43 house of Israel? No, you carried aloft the shrine of Moloch and the star of the god Rephan, the images which you had made for your adoration. I will banish you beyond Babylon."

44 'Our forefathers had the Tent of the Testimony in the desert, as God commanded when he told Moses to make it after the pattern 45 which he had seen. Our fathers of the next generation, with Joshua, brought it with them when they dispossessed the nations whom God drove out before them, and there it was until the time of David. 46 David found favour with God and asked to be allowed to provide a dwelling-place for the God of 47 Jacob;[a] but it was Solomon who 48 built him a house. However, the Most High does not live in houses made by men: as the prophet says, 49 "Heaven is my throne and earth my footstool. What kind of house will you build for me, says the Lord; where is my resting-place? 50 Are not all these things of my own making?"

51 'How stubborn you are, heathen still at heart and deaf to the truth! You always fight against the Holy 52 Spirit. Like fathers, like sons. Was there ever a prophet whom your fathers did not persecute? They killed those who foretold the coming of the Righteous One; and now you have betrayed him and mur-53 dered him, you who received the Law as God's angels gave it to you, and yet have not kept it.'

54 This touched them on the raw and they ground their teeth with 55 fury. But Stephen, filled with the Holy Spirit, and gazing intently up to heaven, saw the glory of God, and Jesus standing at God's right hand. 'Look,' he said, 'there is a 56 rift in the sky; I can see the Son of Man standing at God's right hand!' At this they gave a great shout and 57 stopped their ears. Then they made one rush at him and, flinging 58 him out of the city, set about stoning him. The witnesses laid their coats at the feet of a young man named Saul. So they stoned 59 Stephen, and as they did so, he called out, 'Lord Jesus, receive my spirit.' Then he fell on his knees 60 and cried aloud, 'Lord, do not hold this sin against them', and with that he died. And Saul was among 8 those who approved of his murder.

THIS was the beginning of a time of violent persecution for the church in Jerusalem; and all except the apostles were scattered over the country districts of Judaea and Samaria. Stephen was 2 given burial by certain devout men, who made a great lamentation for him. Saul, meanwhile, 3 was harrying the church; he entered house after house, seizing men and women, and sending them to prison.

As for those who had been scat- 4 tered, they went through the country preaching the Word. Phil- 5 ip came down to a city in Samaria and began proclaiming the Messiah to them. The crowds, to a 6 man, listened eagerly to what Philip said, when they heard him and saw the miracles that he performed. For in many cases of pos- 7 session the unclean spirits came out with a loud cry; and many paralysed and crippled folk were cured; and there was great joy in 8 that city.

A man named Simon had been in 9 the city for some time, and had swept the Samaritans off their feet with his magical arts, claiming to be someone great. All of them, 10 high and low, listened eagerly to

---

[a] *Some witnesses read* for the house of Jacob.

him. 'This man', they said, 'is that power of God which is called "The 11 Great Power".' They listened because they had for so long been 12 carried away by his magic. But when they came to believe Philip with his good news about the kingdom of God and the name of Jesus Christ, they were baptized, men 13 and women alike. Even Simon himself believed, and was baptized, and thereupon was constantly in Philip's company. He was carried away when he saw the powerful signs and miracles that were taking place.

14   The apostles in Jerusalem now heard that Samaria had accepted the word of God. They sent off 15 Peter and John, who went down there and prayed for the converts, asking that they might receive the 16 Holy Spirit. For until then the Spirit had not come upon any of them. They had been baptized into the name of the Lord Jesus, that 17 and nothing more. So Peter and John laid their hands on them and they received the Holy Spirit.

18   When Simon saw that the Spirit was bestowed through the laying on of the apostles' hands, he offer-19 ed them money and said, 'Give me the same power too, so that when I lay my hands on anyone, he will 20 receive the Holy Spirit.' Peter replied, 'Your money go with you to damnation, because you thought 21 God's gift was for sale! You have no part nor lot in this, for you are 22 dishonest with God. Repent of this wickedness and pray the Lord to forgive you for imagining such a 23 thing. I can see that you are doomed to taste the bitter fruit and 24 wear the fetters of sin.'[a] Simon answered, 'Pray to the Lord for me yourselves and ask that none of the things you have spoken of may fall upon me.'

25   So, after giving their testimony and speaking the word of the Lord, they took the road back to Jerusalem, bringing the good news to many Samaritan villages on the way.

Then the angel of the Lord said 26 to Philip, 'Start out and go south to the road that leads down from Jerusalem to Gaza.' (This is the desert road.) So he set out and was 27 on his way when he caught sight of an Ethiopian. This man was a eunuch, a high official of the Kandake, or Queen, of Ethiopia, in charge of all her treasure. He had been to Jerusalem on a pilgrimage and was now on his way home, 28 sitting in his carriage and reading aloud the prophet Isaiah. The 29 Spirit said to Philip, 'Go and join the carriage.' When Philip ran up 30 he heard him reading the prophet Isaiah and said, 'Do you understand what you are reading?' He 31 said, 'How can I understand unless someone will give me the clue?' So he asked Philip to get in and sit beside him.

The passage he was reading was 32 this: 'He was led like a sheep to be slaughtered; and like a lamb that is dumb before the shearer, he does not open his mouth. He has been 33 humiliated and has no redress. Who will be able to speak of his posterity? For he is cut off from the world of living men.'

'Now', said the eunuch to Philip, 34 'tell me, please, who it is that the prophet is speaking about here: himself or someone else?' Then 35 Philip began. Starting from this passage, he told him the good news of Jesus. As they were going 36 along the road, they came to some water. 'Look,' said the eunuch, 'here is water: what is there to prevent my being baptized?';[b] and he 38 ordered the carriage to stop. Then they both went down into the water, Philip and the eunuch; and

---

[a] *Literally* you are for gall of bitterness and a fetter of unrighteousness.
[b] *Some witnesses insert* (37) Philip said, 'If you whole-heartedly believe, it is permitted.' He replied, 'I believe that Jesus Christ is the Son of God.'

39 he baptized him. When they came up out of the water the Spirit snatched Philip away, and the eunuch saw no more of him, but 40 went happily on his way. Philip appeared at Azotus, and toured the country, preaching in all the towns till he reached Caesarea.

9 MEANWHILE Saul was still breathing murderous threats against the disciples of the Lord. He 2 went to the High Priest and applied for letters to the synagogues at Damascus authorizing him to arrest anyone he found, men or women, who followed the new way, and bring them to Jerusalem. 3 While he was still on the road and nearing Damascus, suddenly a light flashed from the sky all around him. He fell to the ground 4 and heard a voice saying, 'Saul, Saul, why do you persecute me?' 5 'Tell me, Lord,' he said, 'who you are.' The voice answered, 'I am Jesus, whom you are persecuting. 6 But get up and go into the city, and you will be told what you have 7 to do.' Meanwhile the men who were travelling with him stood speechless; they heard the voice 8 but could see no one. Saul got up from the ground, but when he opened his eyes he could not see; so they led him by the hand and 9 brought him into Damascus. He was blind for three days, and took no food or drink.

10 There was a disciple in Damascus named Ananias. He had a vision in which he heard the voice of the Lord: 'Ananias!' 'Here I am, 11 Lord', he answered. The Lord said to him, 'Go at once to Straight Street, to the house of Judas, and ask for a man from Tarsus named Saul. You will find him at prayer; 12 he has had a vision of a man named Ananias coming in and laying his hands on him to restore his sight.' 13 Ananias answered, 'Lord, I have often heard about this man and all the harm he has done to thy

people in Jerusalem. And he is 14 here with authority from the chief priests to arrest all who invoke thy name.' But the Lord said to him, 15 'You must go, for this man is my chosen instrument to bring my name before the nations and their kings, and before the people of Israel. I myself will show him all 16 that he must go through for my name's sake.'

So Ananias went. He entered the 17 house, laid his hands on him and said, 'Saul, my brother, the Lord Jesus, who appeared to you on your way here, has sent me to you so that you may recover your sight, and be filled with the Holy Spirit.' And immediately it seemed 18 that scales fell from his eyes, and he regained his sight. Thereupon he was baptized, and afterwards he 19 took food and his strength returned.

He stayed some time with the disciples in Damascus. Soon he was 20 proclaiming Jesus publicly in the synagogues: 'This', he said, 'is the Son of God.' All who heard were 21 astounded. 'Is not this the man', they said, 'who was in Jerusalem trying to destroy those who invoke this name? Did he not come here for the sole purpose of arresting them and taking them to the chief priests?' But Saul grew more and 22 more forceful, and silenced the Jews of Damascus with his cogent proofs that Jesus was the Messiah.

As the days mounted up, the 23 Jews hatched a plot against his life; but their plans became known 24 to Saul. They kept watch on the city gates day and night so that they might murder him; but his 25 converts took him one night and let him down by the wall, lowering him in a basket.

When he reached Jerusalem he 26 tried to join the body of disciples there; but they were all afraid of him, because they did not believe that he was really a convert. Barnabas, however, took him by 27 the hand and introduced him to the apostles. He described to them how Saul had seen the Lord on his journey, and heard his voice, and how he had spoken out boldly in the name of Jesus at Damascus.

28 Saul now stayed with them, mov-
29 ing about freely in Jerusalem. He spoke out boldly and openly in the name of the Lord, talking and debating with the Greek-speaking Jews.[a] But they planned to mur-
30 der him, and when the brethren learned of this they escorted him to Caesarea and saw him off to Tarsus.

31 MEANWHILE the church, throughout Judaea, Galilee, and Samaria, was left in peace to build up its strength. In the fear of the Lord, upheld by the Holy Spirit, it held on its way and grew in numbers.

32 Peter was making a general tour, in the course of which he went down to visit God's people at
33 Lydda. There he found a man named Aeneas who had been bedridden with paralysis for eight
34 years. Peter said to him, 'Aeneas, Jesus Christ cures you; get up and make your bed', and immediately
35 he stood up. All who lived in Lydda and Sharon saw him; and they turned to the Lord.

36 In Joppa there was a disciple named Tabitha (in Greek, Dorcas, meaning a gazelle), who filled her days with acts of kindness and
37 charity. At that time she fell ill and died; and they washed her body
38 and laid it in a room upstairs. As Lydda was near Joppa, the disciples, who had heard that Peter was there, sent two men to him with the urgent request, 'Please come over to us without delay.'
39 Peter thereupon went off with them. When he arrived they took him upstairs to the room, where all the widows came and stood round him in tears, showing him the

shirts and coats that Dorcas used to make while she was with them. Peter sent them all outside, and 40 knelt down and prayed. Then, turning towards the body, he said, 'Get up, Tabitha.' She opened her eyes, saw Peter, and sat up. He 41 gave her his hand and helped her to her feet. Then he called the members of the congregation and the widows and showed her to them alive. The news spread all over 42 Joppa, and many came to believe in the Lord. Peter stayed on in 43 Joppa for some time with one Simon, a tanner.

At Caesarea there was a man 10 named Cornelius, a centurion in the Italian Cohort, as it was called. He was a religious man, and he and 2 his whole family joined in the worship of God. He gave generously to help the Jewish people, and was regular in his prayers to God. One 3 day about three in the afternoon he had a vision in which he clearly saw an angel of God, who came into his room and said, 'Cornelius!' He 4 stared at him in terror. 'What is it, my lord?' he asked. The angel said, 'Your prayers and acts of charity have gone up to heaven to speak for you before God. And now send 5 to Joppa for a man named Simon, also called Peter: he is lodging with 6 another Simon, a tanner, whose house is by the sea.' So when the 7 angel who was speaking to him had gone, he summoned two of his servants and a military orderly who was a religious man, told them 8 the whole story, and sent them to Joppa.

Next day, while they were still 9 on their way and approaching the city, about noon Peter went up on the roof to pray. He grew hungry 10 and wanted something to eat. While they were getting it ready, he fell into a trance. He saw a rift 11 in the sky, and a thing coming down that looked like a great sheet of sail-cloth. It was slung by the

---

[a] *Literally* the Hellenists.

four corners, and was being lower-
12 ed to the ground. In it he saw
creatures of every kind, whatever
13 walks or crawls or flies. Then
there was a voice which said to
14 him, 'Up, Peter, kill and eat.' But
Peter said, 'No, Lord, no: I have
never eaten anything profane or
15 unclean.' The voice came again a
second time: 'It is not for you to
call profane what God counts
16 clean.' This happened three times;
and then the thing was taken up
again into the sky.

17   While Peter was still puzzling
over the meaning of the vision he
had seen, the messengers of Cornelius had been asking the way to
Simon's house, and now arrived at
18 the entrance. They called out and
asked if Simon Peter was lodging
19 there. But Peter was thinking over
the vision, when the Spirit said to
him, 'Some*a* men are here looking
20 for you; make haste and go down-
stairs. You may go with them without any misgiving, for it was I who
21 sent them.' Peter came down to
the men and said, 'You are looking
for me? Here I am. What brings
22 you here?' 'We are from the centurion Cornelius,' they replied, 'a
good and religious man, acknowledged as such by the whole Jewish
nation. He was directed by a holy
angel to send for you to his house
and to listen to what you have to
23 say.' So Peter asked them in and
gave them a night's lodging. Next
day he set out with them, accompanied by some members of the
congregation at Joppa.

24   The day after that, he arrived at
Caesarea. Cornelius was expecting
them and had called together his
25 relatives and close friends. When
Peter arrived, Cornelius came to
meet him, and bowed to the ground
26 in deep reverence. But Peter raised
him to his feet and said, 'Stand up;
27 I am a man like anyone else.' Still
talking with him he went in and
28 found a large gathering. He said to

them, 'I need not tell you that a
Jew is forbidden by his religion to
visit or associate with a man of
another race; yet God has shown
me clearly that I must not call any
man profane or unclean. That is 29
why I came here without demur
when you sent for me. May I ask
what was your reason for sending?'

Cornelius said, 'Four days ago, 30
just about this time, I was in the
house here saying the afternoon
prayers, when suddenly a man in
shining robes stood before me. He 31
said: "Cornelius, your prayer has
been heard and your acts of charity
remembered before God. Send to 32
Joppa, then, to Simon Peter, and
ask him to come. He is lodging in
the house of Simon the tanner, by
the sea." So I sent to you there and 33
then; it was kind of you to come.
And now we are all met here before
God, to hear all that the Lord has
ordered you to say.'

Peter began: 'I now see how true 34
it is that God has no favourites, but 35
that in every nation the man who is
godfearing and does what is right is
acceptable to him. He sent his 36
word to the Israelites and gave the
good news of peace through Jesus
Christ, who is Lord of all. I need 37
not tell you what happened lately
all over the land of the Jews, starting from Galilee after the baptism
proclaimed by John. You know 38
about Jesus of Nazareth, how God
anointed him with the Holy Spirit
and with power. He went about
doing good and healing all who
were oppressed by the devil, for
God was with him. And we can 39
bear witness to all that he did in
the Jewish country-side and in
Jerusalem. He was put to death by
hanging on a gibbet; but God 40
raised him to life on the third day,
and allowed him to appear, not to 41
the whole people, but to witnesses
whom God had chosen in advance –
to us, who ate and drank with him
after he rose from the dead. He 42

---

a One witness reads Two; *others read* Three.

commanded us to proclaim him to the people, and affirm that he is the one who has been designated by God as judge of the living and the 43 dead. It is to him that all the prophets testify, declaring that everyone who trusts in him receives forgiveness of sins through his name.'

44 Peter was still speaking when the Holy Spirit came upon all who 45 were listening to the message. The believers who had come with Peter, men of Jewish birth, were astonished that the gift of the Holy Spirit should have been poured out even 46 on Gentiles. For they could hear them speaking in tongues of ecstasy and acclaiming the greatness 47 of God. Then Peter spoke: 'Is anyone prepared to withhold the water for baptism from these persons, who have received the Holy Spirit just as we did ourselves?' 48 Then he ordered them to be baptized in the name of Jesus Christ. After that they asked him to stay on with them for a time.

11 News came to the apostles and the members of the church in Judaea that Gentiles too had ac- 2 cepted the word of God; and when Peter came up to Jerusalem those who were of Jewish birth raised the 3 question with him. 'You have been visiting men who are uncircumcised,' they said, 'and sitting at 4 table with them!' Peter began by laying before them the facts as they had happened.

5 'I was in the city of Joppa', he said, 'at prayer; and while in a trance I had a vision: a thing was coming down that looked like a great sheet of sail-cloth, slung by the four corners and lowered from 6 the sky till it reached me. I looked intently to make out what was in it and I saw four-footed creatures of the earth, wild beasts, and 7 things that crawl or fly. Then I heard a voice saying to me, "Up,

Peter, kill and eat." But I said, 8 "No, Lord, no: nothing profane or unclean has ever entered my mouth." A voice from heaven an- 9 swered a second time, "It is not for you to call profane what God counts clean." This happened 10 three times, and then they were all drawn up again into the sky. At 11 that moment three men, who had been sent to me from Caesarea, arrived at the house where I was[a] staying; and the Spirit told me to 12 go with them.[b] My six companions here came with me and we went into the man's house. He told us 13 how he had seen an angel standing in his house who said, "Send to Joppa for Simon also called Peter. He will speak words that will bring 14 salvation to you and all your household." Hardly had I begun 15 speaking, when the Holy Spirit came upon them, just as upon us at the beginning. Then I recalled 16 what the Lord had said: "John baptized with water, but you will be baptized with the Holy Spirit." God gave them no less a gift than 17 he gave us when we put our trust in the Lord Jesus Christ; then how could I possibly stand in God's way?'

When they heard this their 18 doubts were silenced. They gave praise to God and said, 'This means that God has granted life-giving repentance to the Gentiles also.'

MEANWHILE those who had been 19 scattered after the persecution that arose over Stephen made their way to Phoenicia, Cyprus, and Antioch, bringing the message to Jews only and to no others. But there 20 were some natives of Cyprus and Cyrene among them, and these, when they arrived at Antioch, began to speak to Gentiles as well, telling them the good news of the Lord Jesus. The power of the Lord 21

---

[a] *Some witnesses read* we were.   [b] *Some witnesses add* making no distinctions; *others add* without any misgiving, *as in* 10. 20.

was with them, and a great many became believers, and turned to the Lord.

22 The news reached the ears of the church in Jerusalem; and they 23 sent Barnabas to Antioch. When he arrived and saw the divine grace at work, he rejoiced, and encouraged them all to hold fast to the 24 Lord with resolute hearts; for he was a good man, full of the Holy Spirit and of faith. And large numbers were won over to the Lord.

25 He then went off to Tarsus to 26 look for Saul; and when he had found him, he brought him to Antioch. For a whole year the two of them lived in fellowship with the congregation there, and gave instruction to large numbers. It was in Antioch that the disciples first got the name of Christians.

27 During this period some prophets came down from Jerusalem 28 to Antioch. One of them, Agabus by name, was inspired to stand up and predict a severe and worldwide famine, which in fact occur- 29 red in the reign of Claudius. So the disciples agreed to make a contribution, each according to his means, for the relief of their fellow- 30 Christians in Judaea. This they did, and sent it off to the elders, in the charge of Barnabas and Saul.

12 It was about this time that King Herod attacked certain members 2 of the church. He beheaded James, 3 the brother of John, and then, when he saw that the Jews approved, proceeded to arrest Peter also. This happened during the festival of Unleavened Bread. 4 Having secured him, he put him in prison under a military guard, four squads of four men each, meaning to produce him in public after 5 Passover. So Peter was kept in prison under constant watch, while the church kept praying fervently for him to God.

6 On the very night before Herod had planned to bring him forward, Peter was asleep between two soldiers, secured by two chains, while outside the doors sentries kept guard over the prison. All at once 7 an angel of the Lord stood there, and the cell was ablaze with light. He tapped Peter on the shoulder and woke him. 'Quick! Get up', he said, and the chains fell away from his wrists. The angel then said to 8 him, 'Do up your belt and put your sandals on.' He did so. 'Now wrap your cloak round you and follow me.' He followed him out, 9 with no idea that the angel's intervention was real: he thought it was just a vision. But they passed the 10 first guard-post, then the second, and reached the iron gate leading out into the city, which opened for them of its own accord. And so they came out and walked the length of one street; and the angel left him.

Then Peter came to himself. 11 'Now I know it is true,' he said; 'the Lord has sent his angel and rescued me from Herod's clutches and from all that the Jewish people were expecting.' When he realized 12 how things stood, he made for the house of Mary, the mother of John Mark, where a large company was at prayer. He knocked at the outer 13 door and a maid called Rhoda came to answer it. She recognized 14 Peter's voice and was so overjoyed that instead of opening the door she ran in and announced that Peter was standing outside. 'You 15 are crazy', they told her; but she insisted that it was so. Then they said, 'It must be his guardian angel.'

Meanwhile Peter went on knock- 16 ing, and when they opened the door and saw him, they were astounded. With a movement of 17 the hand he signed to them to keep quiet, and told them how the Lord had brought him out of prison. 'Report this to James and the members of the church', he said.

Then he left the house and went off elsewhere.

18 When morning came, there was consternation among the soldiers: what could have become of Peter?
19 Herod made close search, but failed to find him, so he interrogated the guards and ordered their execution.

Afterwards he left Judaea to
20 reside for a time at Caesarea. He had for some time been furiously angry with the people of Tyre and Sidon, who now by common agreement presented themselves at his court. There they won over Blastus the royal chamberlain, and sued for peace, because their country drew its supplies from the king's
21 territory. So, on an appointed day, attired in his royal robes and seated on the rostrum, Herod
22 harangued them; and the populace shouted back, 'It is a god speaking, not a man!' Instantly an angel
23 of the Lord struck him down, because he had usurped the honour due to God; he was eaten up with worms and died.
24 Meanwhile the word of God continued to grow and spread.
25 Barnabas and Saul, their task fulfilled, returned from Jerusalem,[a] taking John Mark with them.

The church breaks barriers

13 THERE were at Antioch, in the congregation there, certain prophets and teachers: Barnabas, Simeon called Niger, Lucius of Cyrene, Manaen, who had been at the court of Prince Herod, and Saul.
2 While they were keeping a fast and offering worship to the Lord, the Holy Spirit said, 'Set Barnabas and Saul apart for me, to do the work to which I have called them.'
3 Then, after further fasting and prayer, they laid their hands on them and let them go.
4 So these two, sent out on their

mission by the Holy Spirit, came down to Seleucia, and from there sailed to Cyprus. Arriving at Sala- 5 mis, they declared the word of God in the Jewish synagogues. They had John with them as their assist- ant. They went through the whole 6 island as far as Paphos, and there they came upon a sorcerer, a Jew who posed as a prophet, Bar-Jesus by name. He was in the retinue of 7 the Governor, Sergius Paulus, an intelligent man, who had sent for Barnabas and Saul and wanted to hear the word of God. This Elymas 8 the sorcerer (so his name may be translated) opposed them, trying to turn the Governor away from the Faith. But Saul, also known as 9 Paul, filled with the Holy Spirit, fixed his eyes on him and said, 10 'You swindler, you rascal, son of the devil and enemy of all goodness, will you never stop falsifying the straight ways of the Lord? Look now, the hand of the Lord 11 strikes: you shall be blind, and for a time you shall not see the sunlight.' Instantly mist and darkness came over him and he groped about for someone to lead him by the hand. When the Governor saw 12 what had happened he became a believer, deeply impressed by what he learned about the Lord.

Leaving Paphos, Paul and his 13 companions went by sea to Perga in Pamphylia; John, however, left them and returned to Jerusalem. From Perga they continued their 14 journey as far as Pisidian Antioch. On the Sabbath they went to synagogue and took their seats; and 15 after the readings from the Law and the prophets, the officials of the synagogue sent this message to them: 'Friends, if you have anything to say to the people by way of exhortation, let us hear it.' Paul 16 rose, made a gesture with his hand, and began:

'Men of Israel and you who

---

[a] *Some witnesses read* their task fulfilled, returned to Jerusalem; *or, as it might be rendered,* their task at Jerusalem fulfilled, returned.

17 worship our God, listen to me! The God of this people of Israel chose our fathers. When they were still living as aliens in Egypt he made them into a nation and brought them out of that country with arm
18 outstretched. For some forty years he bore with their conduct[a] in the
19 desert. Then in the Canaanite country he overthrew seven nations, whose lands he gave them to
20 be their heritage for some four hundred and fifty years, and afterwards appointed judges for them until the time of the prophet Samuel.
21 'Then they asked for a king and God gave them Saul the son of Kish, a man of the tribe of Benjamin, who reigned for forty years.
22 Then he removed him and set up David as their king, giving him his approval in these words: "I have found David son of Jesse to be a man after my own heart, who will
23 carry out all my purposes." This is the man from whose posterity God, as he promised, has brought Israel
24 a saviour, Jesus. John made ready for his coming by proclaiming baptism as a token of repentance to
25 the whole people of Israel. And when John was nearing the end of his course, he said, "I am not what you think I am. No, after me comes one whose shoes I am not fit to unfasten."
26 'My brothers, you who come of the stock of Abraham, and others among you who revere our God, we are the people to whom the message of this salvation has been
27 sent. The people of Jerusalem and their rulers did not recognize him, or understand the words of the prophets which are read Sabbath by Sabbath; indeed they fulfilled
28 them by condemning him. Though they failed to find grounds for the sentence of death, they asked
29 Pilate to have him executed. And when they had carried out all that

the scriptures said about him, they took him down from the gibbet and laid him in a tomb. But God 30 raised him from the dead; and 31 there was a period of many days during which he appeared to those who had come up with him from Galilee to Jerusalem.

'They are now his witnesses be- 32 fore our nation; and we are here to give you the good news that God, who made the promise to the fathers, has fulfilled it for the 33 children[b] by raising Jesus from the dead, as indeed it stands written, in the second[c] Psalm: "You are my son; this day I have begotten you." Again, that he raised him from the 34 dead, never again to revert to corruption, he declares in these words: "I will give you the blessings promised to David, holy and sure." This is borne out by another 35 passage: "Thou wilt not let thy loyal servant suffer corruption." As for David, when he had served 36 the purpose of God in his own generation, he died, and was gathered to his fathers, and suffered corruption; but the one whom God 37 raised up did not suffer corruption; and you must understand, my bro- 38 thers, that it is through him that forgiveness of sins is now being proclaimed to you. It is through 39 him that everyone who has faith is acquitted of everything for which there was no acquittal under the Law of Moses. Beware, then, lest 40 you bring down upon yourselves the doom proclaimed by the prophets: "See this, you scoffers, won- 41 der, and begone; for I am doing a deed in your days, a deed which you will never believe when you are told of it."'

As they were leaving the syna- 42 gogue they were asked to come again and speak on these subjects next Sabbath; and after the con- 43 gregation had dispersed, many Jews and gentile worshippers went

---

[a] *Some witnesses read* he sustained them. children; *others read* us their children.

[b] *Some witnesses read* our
[c] *Some witnesses read* first.

152

along with Paul and Barnabas, who spoke to them and urged them to hold fast to the grace of God.

44 On the following Sabbath almost the whole city gathered to 45 hear the word of God. When the Jews saw the crowds, they were filled with jealous resentment, and contradicted what Paul said, with 46 violent abuse. But Paul and Barnabas were outspoken in their reply. 'It was necessary', they said, 'that the word of God should be declared to you first. But since you reject it and thus condemn yourselves as unworthy of eternal life, we now 47 turn to the Gentiles. For these are our instructions from the Lord: "I have appointed you to be a light for the Gentiles, and a means of salvation to earth's farthest bounds."' 48 When the Gentiles heard this, they were overjoyed and thankfully acclaimed the word of the Lord, and those who were marked out for 49 eternal life became believers. So the word of the Lord spread far 50 and wide through the region. But the Jews stirred up feeling among the women of standing who were worshippers, and among the leading men of the city; a persecution was started against Paul and Barnabas, and they were expelled from 51 the district. So they shook the dust off their feet in protest against 52 them and went to Iconium. And the converts were filled with joy and with the Holy Spirit.

14 At Iconium similarly they went[a] into the Jewish synagogue and spoke to such purpose that a large body both of Jews and Gentiles 2 became believers. But the unconverted Jews stirred up the Gentiles and poisoned their minds 3 against the Christians. For some time Paul and Barnabas stayed on and spoke boldly and openly in reliance on the Lord; and he confirmed the message of his grace by causing signs and miracles to be worked at their hands. The mass of 4 the townspeople were divided, some siding with the Jews, others with the apostles. But when a 5 move was made by Gentiles and Jews together, with the connivance of the city authorities, to maltreat them and stone them, they got wind of it and made their 6 escape to the Lycaonian cities of Lystra and Derbe and the surrounding country, where they 7 continued to spread the good news.

At Lystra sat a crippled man, 8 lame from birth, who had never walked in his life. This man listen- 9 ed while Paul was speaking. Paul fixed his eyes on him and saw that he had the faith to be cured, so he 10 said to him in a loud voice, 'Stand up straight on your feet'; and he sprang up and started to walk. When the crowds saw what Paul 11 had done, they shouted, in their native Lycaonian, 'The gods have come down to us in human form.' And they called Barnabas Jupiter, 12 and Paul they called Mercury, because he was the spokesman. And 13 the priest of Jupiter, whose temple was just outside the city, brought oxen and garlands to the gates, and he and all the people were about to offer sacrifice.

But when the apostles Barnabas 14 and Paul heard of it, they tore their clothes and rushed into the crowd shouting, 'Men, what is this 15 that you are doing? We are only human beings, no less mortal than you. The good news we bring tells you to turn from these follies to the living God, who made heaven and earth and sea and everything in them. In past ages he allowed all 16 nations to go their own way; and 17 yet he has not left you without some clue to his nature, in the kindness he shows: he sends you rain from heaven and crops in their seasons, and gives you food and good cheer in plenty.'

---

a Or At Iconium they went together...

18 With these words they barely managed to prevent the crowd from offering sacrifice to them.

19 Then Jews from Antioch and Iconium came on the scene and won over the crowds. They stoned Paul, and dragged him out of the 20 city, thinking him dead. The converts formed a ring round him, and he got to his feet and went into the city. Next day he left with Barnabas for Derbe.

21 After bringing the good news to that town, where they gained many converts, they returned to Lystra, then to Iconium, and then 22 to Antioch, heartening the converts and encouraging them to be true to their religion. They warned them that to enter the kingdom of God we must pass through many 23 hardships. They also appointed elders for them in each congregation, and with prayer and fasting committed them to the Lord in whom they had put their faith.

24 Then they passed through Pisidia and came into Pamphylia. 25 When they had given the message at Perga, they went down to At-26 talia, and from there set sail for Antioch, where they had originally been commended to the grace of God for the task which they had 27 now completed. When they arrived and had called the congregation together, they reported all that God had done through them, and how he had thrown open the gates 28 of faith to the Gentiles. And they stayed for some time with the disciples there.

15 Now certain persons who had come down from Judaea began to teach the brotherhood that those who were not circumcised in accordance with Mosaic practice 2 could not be saved. That brought them into fierce dissension and controversy with Paul and Barnabas. And so it was arranged that these two and some others from Antioch should go up to Jerusalem to see the apostles and elders about this question.

They were sent on their way by 3 the congregation, and travelled through Phoenicia and Samaria, telling the full story of the conversion of the Gentiles. The news caused great rejoicing among all the Christians there.

When they reached Jerusalem 4 they were welcomed by the church and the apostles and elders, and reported all that God had done through them. Then some of the 5 Pharisaic party who had become believers came forward and said, 'They must be circumcised and told to keep the Law of Moses.'

The apostles and elders held a 6 meeting to look into this matter; and, after a long debate, Peter 7 rose and addressed them. 'My friends,' he said, 'in the early days, as you yourselves know, God made his choice among you and ordained that from my lips the Gentiles should hear and believe the message of the Gospel. And God, who 8 can read men's minds, showed his approval of them by giving the Holy Spirit to them, as he did to us. He made no difference between 9 them and us; for he purified their hearts by faith. Then why do you 10 now provoke God by laying on the shoulders of these converts a yoke which neither we nor our fathers were able to bear? No, we believe 11 that it is by the grace of the Lord Jesus that we are saved, and so are they.'

At that the whole company fell 12 silent and listened to Barnabas and Paul as they told of all the signs and miracles that God had worked among the Gentiles through them.

When they had finished speak- 13 ing, James summed up: 'My friends,' he said, 'listen to me. Simeon has told how it first hap- 14 pened that God took notice of the Gentiles, to choose from among them a people to bear his name;

15 and this agrees with the words of the prophets, as Scripture has it:

16 "Thereafter I will return and rebuild the fallen house of David; even from its ruins I will rebuild it, and set it up again,

17 that they may seek the Lord – all the rest of mankind, and the Gentiles, whom I have claimed for my own. Thus says the Lord, whose work it is,

18 made known long ago."

19 'My judgement therefore is that we should impose no irksome restrictions on those of the Gentiles

20 who are turning to God, but instruct them by letter to abstain from things polluted by contact with idols, from fornication, from anything that has been strangled,

21 and from blood.[a] Moses, after all, has never lacked spokesmen in every town for generations past; he is read in the synagogues Sabbath by Sabbath.'

22 Then the apostles and elders, with the agreement of the whole church, resolved to choose representatives and send them to Antioch with Paul and Barnabas. They chose two leading men in the community, Judas Barsabbas and

23 Silas, and gave them this letter to deliver:

'We, the apostles and elders, send greetings as brothers to our brothers of gentile origin in An-

24 tioch, Syria, and Cilicia. Forasmuch as we have heard that some of our number, without any instructions from us, have[b] disturbed you with their talk and unsettled

25 your minds, we have resolved unanimously to send to you our chosen representatives with our well-beloved Barnabas and Paul, who

26 have devoted themselves to the cause of our Lord Jesus Christ. We

27 are therefore sending Judas and Silas, who will themselves confirm this by word of mouth. It is the

28 decision of the Holy Spirit, and our decision, to lay no further burden upon you beyond these essentials:

29 you are to abstain from meat that has been offered to idols, from blood, from anything that has been strangled,[c] and from fornication.[d] If you keep yourselves free from these things you will be doing right. Farewell.'

30 So they were sent off on their journey and travelled down to Antioch, where they called the congregation together, and deliv-

31 ered the letter. When it was read, they all rejoiced at the encouragement it brought. Judas and Silas,

32 who were prophets themselves, said much to encourage and strengthen the members, and, after

33 spending some time there, were dismissed with the good wishes of the brethren, to return to those who had sent them.[e] But Paul and

35 Barnabas stayed on at Antioch, and there, along with many others, they taught and preached the word of the Lord.

Paul leads the advance

36 AFTER a while Paul said to Barnabas, 'Ought we not to go back now to see how our brothers are faring in the various towns where we proclaimed the word of the

37 Lord?' Barnabas wanted to take John Mark with them; but Paul

38 judged that the man who had deserted them in Pamphylia and had not gone on to share in their work was not the man to take with

---

[a] *Some witnesses omit* from fornication; *others omit* from anything that has been strangled; *some add* (*after* blood) and to refrain from doing to others what they would not like done to themselves.   [b] *Some witnesses read* have gone out and . . .   [c] *Some witnesses omit* from anything that has been strangled.   [d] *Some witnesses omit* and from fornication; *and some add* and refrain from doing to others what you would not like done to yourselves.   [e] *Some witnesses add* (34) But Silas decided to remain there.

39 them now. The dispute was so sharp that they parted company. Barnabas took Mark with him and
40 sailed for Cyprus, while Paul chose Silas. He started on his journey, commended by the brothers to the
41 grace of the Lord, and travelled through Syria and Cilicia bringing new strength to the congregations.

16 He went on to Derbe and to Lystra, and there he found a disciple named Timothy, the son of a Jewish Christian mother and a
2 Gentile father. He was well spoken of by the Christians at Lystra and
3 Iconium, and Paul wanted to have him in his company when he left the place. So he took him and circumcised him, out of consideration for the Jews who lived in those parts; for they all knew that his
4 father was a Gentile. As they made their way from town to town they handed on the decisions taken by the apostles and elders in Jerusalem and enjoined their observance.
5 And so, day by day, the congregations grew stronger in faith and increased in numbers.
6 They travelled through the Phrygian and Galatian region,[a] because they were prevented by the Holy Spirit from delivering the message
7 in the province of Asia; and when they approached the Mysian border they tried to enter Bithynia; but the Spirit of Jesus would not
8 allow them, so they skirted[b] Mysia and reached the coast at Troas.
9 During the night a vision came to Paul: a Macedonian stood there appealing to him and saying, 'Come across to Macedonia and
10 help us.' After he had seen this vision we at once set about getting a passage to Macedonia, concluding that God had called us to bring them the good news.
11 So we sailed from Troas and made a straight run to Samothrace,
12 the next day to Neapolis, and from there to Philippi, a city of the first rank in that district of Macedonia, and a Roman colony. Here
13 we stayed for some days, and on the Sabbath day we went outside the city gate by the riverside, where we thought there would be a place of prayer,[c] and sat down and talked to the women who had
14 gathered there. One of them named Lydia, a dealer in purple fabric from the city of Thyatira, who was a worshipper of God, was listening, and the Lord opened her heart to
15 respond to what Paul said. She was baptized, and her household with her, and then she said to us, 'If you have judged me to be a believer in the Lord, I beg you to come and stay in my house.' And she insisted on our going.
16 Once, when we were on our way to the place of prayer, we met a slave-girl who was possessed by an oracular spirit and brought large profits to her owners by telling
17 fortunes. She followed Paul and the rest of us, shouting, 'These men are servants of the Supreme God, and are declaring to you a
18 way of salvation.' She did this day after day, until Paul could bear it no longer. Rounding on the spirit he said, 'I command you in the name of Jesus Christ to come out of her', and it went out there and then.
19 When the girl's owners saw that their hope of gain had gone, they seized Paul and Silas and dragged them to the city authorities in the
20 main square; and bringing them before the magistrates, they said, 'These men are causing a disturbance in our city; they are Jews;
21 they are advocating customs which it is illegal for us Romans to adopt
22 and follow.' The mob joined in the attack; and the magistrates tore off the prisoners' clothes and order-
23 ed them to be flogged. After giving them a severe beating they flung them into prison and ordered the

---

[a] Or through Phrygia and the Galatian region.　　　[b] Possibly traversed.
[c] Some witnesses read where there was a recognized place of prayer.

24 jailer to keep them under close guard. In view of these orders, he put them in the inner prison and secured their feet in the stocks.

25 About midnight Paul and Silas, at their prayers, were singing praises to God, and the other 26 prisoners were listening, when suddenly there was such a violent earthquake that the foundations of the jail were shaken; all the doors burst open and all the prisoners 27 found their fetters unfastened. The jailer woke up to see the prison doors wide open, and assuming that the prisoners had escaped, drew his sword intending to kill 28 himself. But Paul shouted, 'Do yourself no harm; we are all here.' 29 The jailer called for lights, rushed in and threw himself down before Paul and Silas, trembling with fear. 30 He then escorted them out and said, 'Masters, what must I do to 31 be saved?' They said, 'Put your trust in the Lord Jesus, and you will be saved, you and your house- 32 hold.' Then they spoke the word of the Lord[a] to him and to everyone 33 in his house. At that late hour of the night he took them and washed their wounds; and immediately afterwards he and his whole family 34 were baptized. He brought them into his house, set out a meal, and rejoiced with his whole household in his new-found faith in God.

35 When daylight came the magistrates sent their officers with in- 36 structions to release the men. The jailer reported the message to Paul: 'The magistrates have sent word that you are to be released. So now you may go free, and blessings on 37 your journey.'[b] But Paul said to the officers: 'They gave us a public flogging, though we are Roman citizens and have not been found guilty; they threw us into prison, and are they now to smuggle us out privately? No indeed! Let them come in person and escort us out.'

38 The officers reported his words. The magistrates were alarmed to hear that they were Roman citi- 39 zens, and came and apologized to them. Then they escorted them out and requested them to go away 40 from the city. On leaving the prison, they went to Lydia's house, where they met their fellow-Christians, and spoke words of encouragement to them; then they departed.

17 THEY now travelled by way of Amphipolis and Apollonia and came to Thessalonica, where there was a Jewish synagogue. Following 2 his usual practice Paul went to their meetings; and for the next three Sabbaths he argued with them, quoting texts of Scripture which he expounded and applied 3 to show that the Messiah had to suffer and rise from the dead. 'And this Jesus,' he said, 'whom I am proclaiming to you, is the Messiah.' Some of them were convinced and 4 joined Paul and Silas; so did a great number of godfearing Gentiles and a good many influential women.[c]

5 But the Jews in their jealousy recruited some low fellows from the dregs of the populace, roused the rabble, and had the city in an uproar. They mobbed Jason's house, with the intention of bringing Paul and Silas before the town assembly. Failing to find them, 6 they dragged Jason himself and some members of the congregation before the magistrates, shouting, 'The men who have made trouble all over the world have now come here; and Jason has harboured 7 them. They all flout the Emperor's laws, and assert that there is a rival king, Jesus.' These words 8 caused a great commotion in the mob, which affected the magistrates also. They bound over Jason 9 and the others, and let them go.

[a] *Some witnesses read* of God.   [b] *Some witnesses read* . . . free and take your journey.   [c] *Some witnesses read* a good many wives of leading men.

10 As soon as darkness fell, the members of the congregation sent Paul and Silas off to Beroea. On arrival, they made their way to the 11 synagogue. The Jews here were more civil than those at Thessalonica: they received the message with great eagerness, studying the scriptures every day to see whether 12 it was as they said. Many of them therefore became believers, and so did a fair number of Gentiles, women of standing as well as men. 13 But when the Thessalonian Jews learned that the word of God had now been proclaimed by Paul in Beroea, they came on there to stir up trouble and rouse the rabble. 14 Thereupon the members of the congregation sent Paul off at once to go down to the coast, while Silas and Timothy both stayed 15 behind. Paul's escort brought him as far as Athens, and came away with instructions for Silas and Timothy to rejoin him with all speed.

16 Now while Paul was waiting for them at Athens he was exasperated to see how the city was full of 17 idols. So he argued in the synagogue with the Jews and gentile worshippers, and also in the city square every day with casual 18 passers-by. And some of the Epicurean and Stoic philosophers joined issue with him. Some said, 'What can this charlatan be trying to say?'; others, 'He would appear to be a propagandist for foreign deities' – this because he was preaching about Jesus and Resur-19 rection. So they took him and brought him before the Court of Areopagus[a] and said, 'May we know what this new doctrine is 20 that you propound? You are introducing ideas that sound strange to us, and we should like to know 21 what they mean.' (Now the Athenians in general and the foreigners there had no time for anything but talking or hearing about the latest novelty.)

22 Then Paul stood up before the Court of Areopagus[b] and said: 'Men of Athens, I see that in everything that concerns religion you are uncommonly scrupulous. For 23 as I was going round looking at the objects of your worship, I noticed among other things an altar bearing the inscription "To an Unknown God". What you worship but do not know – this is what I now proclaim.

24 'The God who created the world and everything in it, and who is Lord of heaven and earth, does not live in shrines made by men. It is 25 not because he lacks anything that he accepts service at men's hands, for he is himself the universal giver of life and breath and all else. He 26 created every race of men of one stock, to inhabit the whole earth's surface. He fixed the epochs of their history[c] and the limits of their territory. They were to seek 27 God, and, it might be, touch and find him; though indeed he is not far from each one of us, for in him 28 we live and move, in him we exist; as some of your own poets[d] have said, "We are also his offspring." As God's offspring, then, we ought 29 not to suppose that the deity is like an image in gold or silver or stone, shaped by human craftsmanship and design. As for the times of 30 ignorance, God has overlooked them; but now he commands mankind, all men everywhere, to repent, because he has fixed the day 31 on which he will have the world judged, and justly judged, by a man of his choosing; of this he has given assurance to all by raising him from the dead.'

32 When they heard about the raising of the dead, some scoffed; and others said, 'We will hear you on this subject some other time.' And so Paul left the assembly. 33

---

[a] Or brought him to Mars' Hill.
[c] Or fixed the ordered seasons...

[b] Or in the middle of Mars' Hill.
[d] Some witnesses read some among you.

34 However, some men joined him and became believers, including Dionysius, a member of the Court of Areopagus; also a woman named Damaris, and others besides.

18 After this he left Athens and 2 went to Corinth. There he fell in with a Jew named Aquila, a native of Pontus, and his wife Priscilla; he had recently arrived from Italy because Claudius had issued an edict that all Jews should leave 3 Rome. Paul approached them and, because he was of the same trade, he made his home with them, and they carried on business together; 4 they were tent-makers. He also held discussions in the synagogue Sabbath by Sabbath, trying to convince both Jews and Gentiles.

5 Then Silas and Timothy came down from Macedonia, and Paul devoted himself entirely to preaching, affirming before the Jews that 6 the Messiah was Jesus. But when they opposed him and resorted to abuse, he shook out the skirts of his cloak and said to them, 'Your blood be on your own heads! My conscience is clear; now I shall go 7 to the Gentiles.' With that he left, and went to the house of a worshipper of God named Titius Justus, who lived next door to the 8 synagogue. Crispus, who held office in the synagogue, now became a believer in the Lord, with all his household; and a number of Corinthians listened and believed, and 9 were baptized. One night in a vision the Lord said to Paul, 'Have no fear: go on with your preaching 10 and do not be silenced, for I am with you and no one shall attempt to do you harm;[a] and there are many in this city who are my 11 people.' So he settled down for eighteen months, teaching the word of God among them.

12 But when Gallio was proconsul of Achaia, the Jews set upon Paul in a body and brought him into court. 'This man', they said, 'is 13 inducing people to worship God in ways that are against the law.' Paul was just about to speak when 14 Gallio said to them, 'If it had been a question of crime or grave misdemeanour, I should, of course, have given you Jews a patient hearing, but if it is some bickering 15 about words and names and your Jewish law, you may see to it yourselves; I have no mind to be a judge of these matters.' And he 16 had them ejected from the court. Then there was a general attack on 17 Sosthenes, who held office in the synagogue, and they gave him a beating in full view of the bench. But all this left Gallio quite unconcerned.

Paul stayed on for some time, 18 and then took leave of the brotherhood and set sail for Syria, accompanied by Priscilla and Aquila. At Cenchreae he had his hair cut off, because he was under a vow. When 19 they reached Ephesus he parted from them and went himself into the synagogue, where he held a discussion with the Jews. He was asked 20 ed to stay longer, but declined and 21 set out from Ephesus, saying, as he took leave of them, 'I shall come back to you if it is God's will.' On 22 landing at Caesarea, he went up and paid his respects to the church, and then went down to Antioch. After spending some time 23 there, he set out again and made a journey through the Galatian country and on through Phrygia, bringing new strength to all the converts.

N ow there arrived at Ephesus a 24 Jew named Apollos, an Alexandrian by birth, an eloquent man,[b] powerful in his use of the scriptures. He had been instructed in 25 the way of the Lord and was full of spiritual fervour; and in his discourses he taught accurately the facts about Jesus,[c] though he knew

---

[a] Or and you will not be harmed by anyone's attacks.   [b] Or a learned man.
[c] *Some witnesses read* about the Lord.

26 only John's baptism. He now began to speak boldly in the synagogue, where Priscilla and Aquila heard him; they took him in hand and expounded the new way[a] to 27 him in greater detail. Finding that he wished to go across to Achaia, the brotherhood gave him their support, and wrote to the congregation there to make him welcome. From the time of his arrival, he was very helpful to those who had by God's grace become believers; 28 for he strenuously confuted the Jews, demonstrating publicly from the scriptures that the Messiah is Jesus.

19 While Apollos was at Corinth, Paul travelled through the inland regions till he came to Ephesus. There he found a number of con-2 verts, to whom he said, 'Did you receive the Holy Spirit when you became believers?' 'No,' they replied, 'we have not even heard that 3 there is a Holy Spirit.' He said, 'Then what baptism were you given?' 'John's baptism', they an-4 swered. Paul then said, 'The baptism that John gave was a baptism in token of repentance, and he told the people to put their trust in one who was to come after him, that is, 5 in Jesus.' On hearing this they were baptized into the name of the 6 Lord Jesus; and when Paul had laid his hands on them, the Holy Spirit came upon them and they spoke in tongues of ecstasy and 7 prophesied. Altogether they were about a dozen men.

8 During the next three months he attended the synagogue and, using argument and persuasion, spoke boldly and freely about the king-9 dom of God. But when some proved obdurate and would not believe, speaking evil of the new way before the whole congregation, he left them, withdrew his converts, and continued to hold discussions daily in the lecture-hall of Tyran-

nus. This went on for two years, 10 with the result that the whole population of the province of Asia, both Jews and Gentiles, heard the word of the Lord. And through 11 Paul God worked singular miracles: when handkerchiefs and 12 scarves which had been in contact with his skin were carried to the sick, they were rid of their diseases and the evil spirits came out of them.

But some strolling Jewish exor-13 cists tried their hand at using the name of the Lord Jesus on those possessed by evil spirits; they would say, 'I adjure you by Jesus whom Paul proclaims.' There were 14 seven sons of Sceva, a Jewish chief priest, who were using this method, when the evil spirit answered back 15 and said, 'Jesus I acknowledge, and I know about Paul, but who are you?' And the man with the 16 evil spirit flew at them, overpowered them all, and handled them with such violence that they ran out of the house stripped and battered. This became known to 17 everybody in Ephesus, whether Jew or Gentile; they were all awestruck, and the name of the Lord Jesus gained in honour. Moreover 18 many of those who had become believers came and openly confessed that they had been using magical spells. And a good many of 19 those who formerly practised magic collected their books and burnt them publicly. The total value was reckoned up and it came to fifty thousand pieces of silver. In such 20 ways the word of the Lord showed its power, spreading more and more widely and effectively.

When things had reached this 21 stage, Paul made up his mind[b] to visit Macedonia and Achaia and then go on to Jerusalem; and he said, 'After I have been there, I must see Rome also.' So he sent 22 two of his assistants, Timothy and

[a] *Some witnesses read* the way of God.
[b] *Or* Paul, led by the Spirit, resolved...

Erastus, to Macedonia, while he himself stayed some time longer in the province of Asia.

23 Now about that time, the Christian movement gave rise to a
24 serious disturbance. There was a man named Demetrius, a silversmith who made silver shrines of Diana and provided a great deal of
25 employment for the craftsmen. He called a meeting of these men and the workers in allied trades, and addressed them. 'Men,' he said, 'you know that our high standard of living depends on this industry.
26 And you see and hear how this fellow Paul with his propaganda has perverted crowds of people, not only at Ephesus but also in practically the whole of the province of Asia. He is telling them that gods made by human hands
27 are not gods at all. There is danger for us here; it is not only that our line of business will be discredited, but also that the sanctuary of the great goddess Diana will cease to command respect; and then it will not be long before she who is worshipped by all Asia and the civilized world is brought down from her divine pre-eminence.'
28 When they heard this they were roused to fury and shouted, 'Great
29 is Diana of the Ephesians!' The whole city was in confusion; they seized Paul's travelling-companions, the Macedonians Gaius and Aristarchus, and made a concerted rush with them into the theatre.
30 Paul wanted to appear before the assembly but the other Christians
31 would not let him. Even some of the dignitaries of the province, who were friendly towards him, sent and urged him not to venture
32 into the theatre. Meanwhile some were shouting one thing, some another; for the assembly was in confusion and most of them did not know what they had all come for.
33 But some of the crowd explained the trouble to Alexander, whom the Jews had pushed to the front,

and he, motioning for silence, attempted to make a defence before the assembly. But when they 34 recognized that he was a Jew, a single cry arose from them all: for about two hours they kept on shouting, 'Great is Diana of the Ephesians!'

The town clerk, however, quiet- 35 ed the crowd. 'Men of Ephesus,' he said, 'all the world knows that our city of Ephesus is temple-warden of the great Diana and of that symbol of her which fell from heaven. Since these facts are be- 36 yond dispute, your proper course is to keep quiet and do nothing rash. These men whom you have 37 brought here as culprits have committed no sacrilege and uttered no blasphemy against our goddess. If 38 therefore Demetrius and his craftsmen have a case against anyone, assizes are held and there are such people as proconsuls; let the parties bring their charges and countercharges. If, on the other hand, 39 you have some further question to raise, it will be dealt with in the statutory assembly. We certainly 40 run the risk of being charged with riot for this day's work. There is no justification for it, and if the issue is raised we shall be unable to give any explanation of this uproar.' With that he dismissed the as- 41 sembly.

WHEN the disturbance had ceased, 20 Paul sent for the disciples and, after encouraging them, said goodbye and set out on his journey to Macedonia. He travelled through 2 those parts of the country, often speaking words of encouragement to the Christians there, and so came into Greece. When he had 3 spent three months there and was on the point of embarking for Syria, a plot was laid against him by the Jews, so he decided to return by way of Macedonia. He 4 was accompanied by Sopater son of Pyrrhus, from Beroea, the

Thessalonians Aristarchus and Secundus, Gaius the Doberian[a] and Timothy, and the Asians Tychicus 5 and Trophimus. These went ahead 6 and waited for us at Troas; we ourselves set sail from Philippi after the Passover season,[b] and in five days reached them at Troas, where we spent a week.

7 On the Saturday night, in our assembly for the breaking of bread, Paul, who was to leave next day, addressed them, and went on 8 speaking until midnight. Now there were many lamps in the upper room where we were as-9 sembled; and a youth named Eutychus, who was sitting on the window-ledge, grew more and more sleepy as Paul went on talking. At last he was completely overcome by sleep, fell from the third storey to the ground, and was 10 picked up for dead. Paul went down, threw himself upon him, seizing him in his arms, and said to them, 'Stop this commotion; 11 there is still life in him.' He then went upstairs, broke bread and ate, and after much conversation, which lasted until dawn, he 12 departed. And they took the boy away alive and were immensely comforted.

13 We went ahead to the ship and sailed for Assos, where we were to take Paul aboard. He had made this arrangement, as he was 14 going to travel by road. When he met us at Assos, we took him aboard and went on to Mitylene. 15 Next day we sailed from there and arrived opposite Chios, and on the second day we made Samos. On the following day[c] we reached 16 Miletus. For Paul had decided to pass by Ephesus and so avoid having to spend time in the province of Asia; he was eager to be in Jerusalem, if he possibly could, on

the day of Pentecost. He did, how-17 ever, send from Miletus to Ephesus and summon the elders of the congregation; and when they joined 18 him, he spoke as follows:

'You know how, from the day that I first set foot in the province of Asia, for the whole time that I was with you, I served the Lord in 19 all humility amid the sorrows and trials that came upon me through the machinations of the Jews. You 20 know that I kept back nothing that was for your good: I delivered the message to you; I taught you, in public and in your homes; with 21 Jews and Gentiles alike I insisted on repentance before God and trust in our Lord Jesus. And now, 22 as you see, I am on my way to Jerusalem, under the constraint of the Spirit.[d] Of what will befall me there I know nothing, except that 23 in city after city the Holy Spirit assures me that imprisonment and hardships await me. For myself, I 24 set no store by life; I only want to finish the race, and complete the task which the Lord Jesus assigned to me, of bearing my testimony to the gospel of God's grace.

'One word more: I have gone 25 about among you proclaiming the Kingdom, but now I know that none of you will see my face again. That being so, I here and now 26 declare that no man's fate can be laid at my door; for I have kept 27 back nothing; I have disclosed to you the whole purpose of God. Keep watch over yourselves and 28 over all the flock of which the Holy Spirit has given you charge, as shepherds of the church of the Lord,[e] which he won for himself by his own blood.[f] I know that when I 29 am gone, savage wolves will come in among you and will not spare the flock. Even from your own 30 body there will be men coming for-

---

[a] *Some witnesses read* the Derbaean. [b] *Literally* after the days of Unleavened Bread. [c] *Some witnesses read* . . . Samos, and, after stopping at Trogyllium, on the following day . . . [d] *Or* under an inner compulsion. [e] *Some witnesses read* of God. [f] *Or, according to some witnesses,* by the blood of his Own.

ward who will distort the truth to induce the disciples to break away 31 and follow them. So be on the alert; remember how for three years, night and day, I never ceased to counsel each of you, and how I wept over you.

32 'And now I commend you to God and to his gracious word, which has power to build you up and give you your heritage among 33 all who are dedicated to him. I have not wanted anyone's money 34 or clothes for myself; you all know that these hands of mine earned enough for the needs of myself and 35 my companions. I showed you that it is our duty to help the weak in this way, by hard work, and that we should keep in mind the words of the Lord Jesus, who himself said, "Happiness lies more in giving than in receiving."'

36 As he finished speaking, he knelt down with them all and prayed. 37 Then there were loud cries of sorrow from them all, as they folded Paul in their arms and kissed him. 38 What distressed them most was his saying that they would never see his face again. So they escorted him to his ship.

21 When we had parted from them and set sail, we made a straight run and came to Cos; next day to Rhodes, and thence to Patara.[a] 2 There we found a ship bound for Phoenicia, so we went aboard and 3 sailed in her. We came in sight of Cyprus, and leaving it to port, we continued our voyage to Syria, and put in at Tyre, for there the ship 4 was to unload her cargo. We went and found the disciples and stayed there a week; and they, warned by the Spirit, urged Paul to abandon 5 his visit to Jerusalem. But when our time ashore was ended, we left and continued our journey; and they and their wives and children all escorted us out of the city. We knelt down on the beach and 6 prayed, then bade each other

good-bye; we went aboard, and they returned home.

We made the passage from Tyre 7 and reached Ptolemais, where we greeted the brotherhood and spent one day with them. Next day we 8 left and came to Caesarea. We went to the home of Philip the evangelist, who was one of the Seven, and stayed with him. He 9 had four unmarried daughters, who possessed the gift of prophecy. When we had been there several 10 days, a prophet named Agabus arrived from Judaea. He came to 11 us, took Paul's belt, bound his own feet and hands with it, and said, 'These are the words of the Holy Spirit: Thus will the Jews in Jerusalem bind the man to whom this belt belongs, and hand him over to the Gentiles.' When we heard this, 12 we and the local people begged and implored Paul to abandon his visit to Jerusalem. Then Paul gave his 13 answer: 'Why all these tears? Why are you trying to weaken my resolution? For my part I am ready not merely to be bound but even to die at Jerusalem for the name of the Lord Jesus.' So, as he would not be 14 persuaded, we gave up and said, 'The Lord's will be done.'

At the end of our stay we packed 15 our baggage and took the road up to Jerusalem. Some of the dis- 16 ciples from Caesarea came along with us, bringing a certain Mnason of Cyprus, a Christian from the early days, with whom we were to lodge. So we reached Jerusalem, 17 where the brotherhood welcomed us gladly.

Next day Paul paid a visit to 18 James; we were with him, and all the elders attended. He greeted 19 them, and then described in detail all that God had done among the Gentiles through his ministry. When they heard this, they gave 20 praise to God. Then they said to Paul: 'You see, brother, how many thousands of converts we have

[a] Some witnesses add and Myra.

163

among the Jews, all of them staunch
21 upholders of the Law. Now they
have been given certain information about you: it is said that you
teach all the Jews in the gentile
world to turn their backs on Moses,
telling them to give up circumcis-
ing their children and following
22 our way of life. What is the position, then? They are sure to hear
23 that you have arrived. You must
therefore do as we tell you. We
have four men here who are under
24 a vow; take them with you and go
through the ritual of purification
with them, paying their expenses,
after which they may shave their
heads. Then everyone will know
that there is nothing in the stories
they were told about you, but that
you are a practising Jew and keep
25 the Law yourself. As for the gentile
converts, we sent them our decision that they must abstain from
meat that has been offered to idols,
from blood, from anything that
has been strangled,[a] and from forni-
26 cation.' So Paul took the four
men, and next day, after going
through the ritual of purification
with them, he went into the temple
to give notice of the date when the
period of purification would end
and the offering be made for each
one of them.

From Jerusalem to Rome

27 BUT just before the seven days
were up, the Jews from the province of Asia saw him in the
temple. They stirred up the whole
28 crowd, and seized him, shouting,
'Men of Israel, help, help! This is
the fellow who spreads his doctrine
all over the world, attacking our
people, our law, and this sanctuary. On top of all this he has
brought Gentiles into the temple
and profaned this holy place.'
29 For they had previously seen
Trophimus the Ephesian with
him in the city, and assumed that

Paul had brought him into the
temple.

The whole city was in a turmoil, 30
and people came running from all
directions. They seized Paul and
dragged him out of the temple; and
at once the doors were shut. While 31
they were clamouring for his death,
a report reached the officer commanding the cohort, that all Jerusalem was in an uproar. He im- 32
mediately took a force of soldiers
with their centurions and came
down on the rioters at the double.
As soon as they saw the commandant and his troops, they stopped
beating Paul. The commandant 33
stepped forward, arrested him,
and ordered him to be shackled
with two chains; he then asked
who the man was and what he had
been doing. Some in the crowd 34
shouted one thing, some another.
As he could not get at the truth
because of the hubbub, he ordered
him to be taken into barracks.
When Paul reached the steps, he 35
had to be carried by the soldiers
because of the violence of the mob.
For the whole crowd were at their 36
heels yelling, 'Kill him!'

Just before Paul was taken into 37
the barracks he said to the commandant, 'May I have a word with
you?' The commandant said, 'So
you speak Greek, do you? Then you 38
are not the Egyptian who started
a revolt some time ago and led a
force of four thousand terrorists
out into the wilds?' Paul replied, 'I 39
am a Jew, a Tarsian from Cilicia, a
citizen of no mean city. I ask your
permission to speak to the people.'
When permission had been given, 40
Paul stood on the steps and with a
gesture called for the attention of
the people. As soon as quiet was
restored, he addressed them in the
Jewish language:

'Brothers and fathers, give me a 22
hearing while I make my defence
before you.' When they heard him 2
speaking to them in their own

---

[a] *Some witnesses omit* from anything that has been strangled.

language, they listened the more
3 quietly. 'I am a true-born Jew,' he
said, 'a native of Tarsus in Cilicia. I
was brought up in this city, and as
a pupil of Gamaliel I was thoroughly trained in every point of our
ancestral law. I have always been
ardent in God's service, as you all
4 are today. And so I began to persecute this movement to the death,
arresting its followers, men and
women alike, and putting them in
5 chains. For this I have as witnesses
the High Priest and the whole
Council of Elders. I was given
letters from them to our fellow-
Jews at Damascus, and had started out to bring the Christians there
to Jerusalem as prisoners for pun-
6 ishment; and this is what happened. I was on the road and nearing
Damascus, when suddenly about
midday a great light flashed from
7 the sky all around me, and I fell to
the ground. Then I heard a voice
saying to me, "Saul, Saul, why do
8 you persecute me?" I answered,
"Tell me, Lord, who you are." "I
am Jesus of Nazareth," he said,
9 "whom you are persecuting." My
companions saw the light, but did
not hear the voice that spoke to
10 me. "What shall I do, Lord?" I
said, and the Lord replied, "Get up
and continue your journey to
Damascus; there you will be told
of all the tasks that are laid upon
11 you." As I had been blinded by the
brilliance of that light, my companions led me by the hand, and so
I came to Damascus.
12 'There, a man called Ananias, a
devout observer of the Law and
well spoken of by all the Jews of
13 that place, came and stood beside
me and said, "Saul, my brother,
recover your sight." Instantly I
recovered my sight and saw him.
14 He went on: "The God of our
fathers appointed you to know his
will and to see the Righteous One
15 and to hear his very voice, because
you are to be his witness before the

world, and testify to what you
have seen and heard. And now why 16
delay? Be baptized at once, with
invocation of his name, and wash
away your sins."
'After my return to Jerusalem, I 17
was praying in the temple when I
fell into a trance and saw him there, 18
speaking to me. "Make haste", he
said, "and leave Jerusalem without
delay, for they will not accept your
testimony about me." "Lord," I 19
said, "they know that I imprisoned
those who believe in thee, and
flogged them in every synagogue;
and when the blood of Stephen thy 20
witness was shed I stood by,
approving, and I looked after the
clothes of those who killed him."
But he said to me, "Go, for I am 21
sending you far away to the Gentiles."'
Up to this point they had given 22
him a hearing; but now they began
shouting, 'Down with him! A
scoundrel like that is better dead!'
And as they were yelling and wav- 23
ing their cloaks and flinging dust
in the air, the commandant order- 24
ed him to be brought into the
barracks and gave instructions to
examine him by flogging, and find
out what reason there was for such
an outcry against him. But when 25
they tied him up for the lash,[a] Paul
said to the centurion who was
standing there, 'Can you legally
flog a man who is a Roman citizen,
and moreover has not been found
guilty?' When the centurion heard 26
this, he went and reported it to the
commandant. 'What do you mean
to do?' he said. 'This man is a
Roman citizen.' The commandant 27
came to Paul. 'Tell me, are you a
Roman citizen?' he asked. 'Yes',
said he. The commandant rejoin- 28
ed, 'It cost me a large sum to
acquire this citizenship.' Paul said,
'But it was mine by birth.' Then 29
those who were about to examine
him withdrew hastily, and the
commandant himself was alarmed

---

[a] Or tied him up with thongs.

when he realized that Paul was a Roman citizen and that he had put him in irons.

30 THE following day, wishing to be quite sure what charge the Jews were bringing against Paul, he released him and ordered the chief priests and the entire Council to assemble. He then took Paul down and stood him before them.

23 Paul fixed his eyes on the Council and said, 'My brothers, I have lived all my life, and still live to-day, with a perfectly clear con- 2 science before God.' At this the High Priest Ananias ordered his attendants to strike him on the 3 mouth. Paul retorted, 'God will strike you, you whitewashed wall! You sit there to judge me in accordance with the Law; and then in defiance of the Law you order 4 me to be struck!' The attendants said, 'Would you insult God's High 5 Priest?' 'My brothers,' said Paul, 'I had no idea that he was High Priest; Scripture, I know, says: "You must not abuse the ruler of your people."'

6 Now Paul was well aware that one section of them were Sadducees and the other Pharisees, so he called out in the Council, 'My brothers, I am a Pharisee, a Pharisee born and bred; and the true issue in this trial is our hope of the 7 resurrection of the dead.' At these words the Pharisees and Sadducees fell out among themselves, and the assembly was divided. 8 (The Sadducees deny that there is any resurrection, or angel, or spirit, but the Pharisees accept 9 them.) So a great uproar broke out; and some of the doctors of the law belonging to the Pharisaic party openly took sides and declared, 'We can find no fault with this man; perhaps an angel or 10 spirit has spoken to him.' The dissension was mounting, and the commandant was afraid that Paul would be torn in pieces, so he ordered the troops to go down, pull him out of the crowd, and bring him into the barracks.

The following night the Lord 11 appeared to him and said, 'Keep up your courage; you have affirmed the truth about me in Jerusalem, and you must do the same in Rome.'

When day broke, the Jews band- 12 ed together and took an oath not to eat or drink until they had killed Paul. There were more than forty 13 in this conspiracy. They came to 14 the chief priests and elders and said, 'We have bound ourselves by a solemn oath not to taste food until we have killed Paul. It is now 15 for you, acting with the Council, to apply to the commandant to bring him down to you, on the pretext of a closer investigation of his case; and we have arranged to do away with him before he arrives.'

But the son of Paul's sister heard 16 of the ambush; he went to the barracks, obtained entry, and report- ed it to Paul. Paul called one of the 17 centurions and said, 'Take this young man to the commandant; he has something to report.' The cen- 18 turion took him and brought him to the commandant. 'The prisoner Paul', he said, 'sent for me and asked me to bring this young man to you; he has something to tell you.' The commandant took him 19 by the arm, drew him aside, and asked him, 'What is it you have to report?' He said, 'The Jews have 20 made a plan among themselves and will request you to bring Paul down to the Council tomorrow, on the pretext of obtaining more precise information about him. Do not 21 listen to them; for a party more than forty strong are lying in wait for him. They have sworn not to eat or drink until they have done away with him; they are now ready, and wait only for your consent.' So the commandant dis- 22 missed the young man, with orders not to let anyone know that he had given him this information.

23 Then he called a couple of his centurions and issued these orders: 'Get ready two hundred infantry to proceed to Caesarea, together with seventy cavalrymen and two hundred light-armed troops;[a] parade three hours after sunset.
24 Provide also mounts for Paul so that he may ride through under safe
25 escort to Felix the Governor.' And he wrote a letter to this effect:
26 'Claudius Lysias to His Excellency the Governor Felix. Your
27 Excellency: This man was seized by the Jews and was on the point of being murdered when I intervened with the troops and removed him, because I discovered
28 that he was a Roman citizen. As I wished to ascertain the charge on which they were accusing him, I
29 took him down to their Council. I found that the accusation had to do with controversial matters in their law, but there was no charge against him meriting death or im-
30 prisonment. However, I have now been informed of an attempt to be made on the man's life, so I am sending him to you at once, and have also instructed his accusers to state their case against him before you.'[b]
31 Acting on their orders, the infantry took Paul and brought him
32 by night to Antipatris. Next day they returned to their barracks, leaving the cavalry to escort him
33 the rest of the way. The cavalry entered Caesarea, delivered the letter to the Governor, and handed
34 Paul over to him. He read the letter, asked him what province he was from, and learned that he was
35 from Cilicia. 'I will hear your case', he said, 'when your accusers arrive.' He then ordered him to be held in custody at his headquarters in Herod's palace.

FIVE days later the High Priest 24 Ananias came down, accompanied by some of the elders and an advocate named Tertullus, and they laid an information against Paul before the Governor. When the 2 prisoner was called, Tertullus opened the case.

'Your Excellency,' he said, 'we owe it to you that we enjoy unbroken peace. It is due to your provident care that, in all kinds of ways and in all sorts of places, improvements are being made for the good of this province. We welcome 3 this, sir, most gratefully. And 4 now, not to take up too much of your time, I crave your indulgence for a brief statement of our case. We have found this man to be a 5 perfect pest, a fomenter of discord among the Jews all over the world, a ringleader of the sect of the Nazarenes. He even made an attempt 6 to profane the temple; and then we arrested him.[c] If you will examine 8 him yourself you can ascertain from him the truth of all the charges we bring.' The Jews sup- 9 ported the attack, alleging that the facts were as he stated.

Then the Governor motioned to 10 Paul to speak, and he began his reply: 'Knowing as I do that for many years you have administered justice in this province, I make my defence with confidence. You 11 can ascertain the facts for yourself. It is not more than twelve days since I went up to Jerusalem on a pilgrimage. They did not find me 12 arguing with anyone, or collecting a crowd, either in the temple or in the synagogues or up and down the city; and they cannot make good 13 the charges they bring against me. But this much I will admit: I am a 14 follower of the new way (the "sect" they speak of), and it is in that

---

[a] Or two hundred spearmen (*the meaning of the Greek word is uncertain*).
[b] *Some witnesses read* '. . . before you. Farewell.'
[c] *Some witnesses insert* It was our intention to try him under our law; (7) but Lysias the commandant intervened and took him by force out of our hands, (8) ordering his accusers to come before you.

manner that I worship the God of our fathers; for I believe all that is written in the Law and the pro-
15 phets, and in reliance on God I hold the hope, which my accusers too accept, that there is to be a resurrection of good and wicked alike.
16 Accordingly I, no less than they, train myself to keep at all times a clear conscience before God and man.
17 'After an absence of several years I came to bring charitable gifts to my nation and to offer
18 sacrifices. They found me in the temple ritually purified and engaged in this service. I had no crowd with me, and there was no disturbance. But some Jews from the province of Asia were there,
19 and if they had any charge against me it is they who ought to have
20 been in court to state it. Failing that, it is for these persons here present to say what crime they
21 discovered when I was brought before the Council, apart from this one open assertion which I made as I stood there: "The true issue in my trial before you today is the resurrection of the dead." '
22 Then Felix, who happened to be well informed about the Christian movement, adjourned the hearing. 'When Lysias the commanding officer comes down', he said, 'I will
23 go into your case.' He gave orders to the centurion to keep Paul under open arrest and not to prevent any of his friends from making themselves useful to him.
24 Some days later Felix came with his wife Drusilla, who was a Jewess, and sending for Paul he let him talk to him about faith in
25 Christ Jesus. But when the discourse turned to questions of morals, self-control, and the coming judgement, Felix became alarmed and exclaimed, 'That will do for the present; when I find it convenient I will send for you
26 again.' At the same time he had hopes of a bribe from Paul; and for

this reason he sent for him very often and talked with him. When 27 two years had passed, Felix was succeeded by Porcius Festus. Wishing to curry favour with the Jews, Felix left Paul in custody.

THREE days after taking up his 25 appointment Festus went up from Caesarea to Jerusalem, where the 2 chief priests and the Jewish leaders brought before him the case against Paul. They asked Festus to 3 favour them against him, and pressed for him to be brought up to Jerusalem, for they were planning an ambush to kill him on the way. Festus, however, replied, 'Paul is 4 in safe custody at Caesarea, and I shall be leaving Jerusalem shortly myself; so let your leading men 5 come down with me, and if there is anything wrong, let them prosecute him.'

After spending eight or ten days 6 at most in Jerusalem, he went down to Caesarea, and next day he took his seat in court and ordered Paul to be brought up. When he 7 appeared, the Jews who had come down from Jerusalem stood round bringing many grave charges, which they were unable to prove. Paul's plea was: 'I have committed 8 no offence, either against the Jewish law, or against the temple, or against the Emperor.' Festus, anxious to ingratiate himself with the Jews, turned to Paul and asked, 'Are you willing to go up to Jerusalem and stand trial on these charges before me there?' But Paul 10 said, 'I am now standing before the Emperor's tribunal, and that is where I must be tried. Against the Jews I have committed no offence, as you very well know. If I am 11 guilty of any capital crime, I do not ask to escape the death penalty; but if there is no substance in the charges which these men bring against me, it is not open to anyone to hand me over as a sop to them. I appeal to Caesar!' Then 12

Festus, after conferring with his advisers, replied, 'You have appealed to Caesar: to Caesar you shall go.'

13　After an interval of some days King Agrippa and Bernice arrived at Caesarea on a courtesy visit to 14 Festus. They spent several days there, and during this time Festus laid Paul's case before the king. 'We have a man', he said, 'left in 15 custody by Felix; and when I was in Jerusalem the chief priests and elders of the Jews laid an information against him, demanding his 16 condemnation. I answered them, "It is not Roman practice to hand over any accused man before he is confronted with his accusers and given an opportunity of answering 17 the charge." So when they had come here with me I lost no time; the very next day I took my seat in court and ordered the man to be 18 brought up. But when his accusers rose to speak, they brought none of 19 the charges I was expecting; they merely had certain points of disagreement with him about their peculiar religion, and about someone called Jesus, a dead man whom Paul alleged to be alive. 20 Finding myself out of my depth in such discussions, I asked if he was willing to go to Jerusalem and stand his trial there on these 21 issues. But Paul appealed to be remanded in custody for His Imperial Majesty's decision, and I ordered him to be detained until I could send him to the Emperor.' 22 Agrippa said to Festus, 'I should rather like to hear the man myself.' 'Tomorrow', he answered, 'you shall hear him.'

23　So next day Agrippa and Bernice came in full state and entered the audience-chamber accompanied by high-ranking officers and prominent citizens; and on the orders of Festus Paul was brought 24 up. Then Festus said, 'King Agrippa, and all you gentlemen here present with us, you see this man: the whole body of the Jews approached me both in Jerusalem and here, loudly insisting that he had no right to remain alive. But 25 it was clear to me that he had committed no capital crime, and when he himself appealed to His Imperial Majesty, I decided to send him. But I have nothing 26 definite about him to put in writing for our Sovereign. Accordingly I have brought him up before you all and particularly before you, King Agrippa, so that as a result of this preliminary inquiry I may have something to report. There is no 27 sense, it seems to me, in sending on a prisoner without indicating the charges against him.'

Agrippa said to Paul, 'You have **26** our permission to speak for yourself.' Then Paul stretched out his hand and began his defence:

'I consider myself fortunate, 2 King Agrippa, that it is before you that I am to make my defence today upon all the charges brought against me by the Jews, particu- 3 larly as you are expert in all Jewish matters, both our customs and our disputes. And therefore I beg you to give me a patient hearing.

'My life from my youth up, the 4 life I led from the beginning among my people and in Jerusalem, is familiar to all Jews. Indeed they 5 have known me long enough and could testify, if they only would, that I belonged to the strictest group in our religion: I lived as a Pharisee. And it is for a hope 6 kindled by God's promise to our forefathers that I stand in the dock today. Our twelve tribes hope 7 to see the fulfilment of that promise, worshipping with intense devotion day and night; and for this very hope I am impeached, and impeached by Jews, Your Majesty. Why is it considered incredible 8 among you that God should raise dead men to life?

'I myself once thought it my 9 duty to work actively against the

10 name of Jesus of Nazareth; and I did so in Jerusalem. It was I who imprisoned many of God's people by authority obtained from the chief priests; and when they were condemned to death, my vote was 11 cast against them. In all the synagogues I tried by repeated punishment to make them renounce their faith; indeed my fury rose to such a pitch that I extended my persecution to foreign cities.

12 'On one such occasion I was travelling to Damascus with authority and commission from the 13 chief priests; and as I was on my way, Your Majesty, in the middle of the day I saw a light from the sky, more brilliant than the sun, shining all around me and my 14 travelling-companions. We all fell to the ground, and then I heard a voice saying to me in the Jewish language, "Saul, Saul, why do you persecute me? It is hard for you, 15 this kicking against the goad." I said, "Tell me, Lord, who you are"; and the Lord replied, "I am Jesus, 16 whom you are persecuting. But now, rise to your feet and stand upright. I have appeared to you for a purpose: to appoint you my servant and witness, to testify both to what you have seen and to what 17 you shall yet see of me. I will rescue you from this people and from the Gentiles to whom I am 18 sending you. I send you to open their eyes and turn them from darkness to light, from the dominion of Satan to God, so that, by trust in me, they may obtain forgiveness of sins, and a place among those whom God has made his own."

19 'And so, King Agrippa, I did not 20 disobey the heavenly vision. I turned first to the inhabitants of Damascus, and then to Jerusalem and all the country of Judaea, and to the Gentiles, and sounded the call to repent and turn to God, and to prove their repentance by deeds. 21 That is why the Jews seized me in the temple and tried to do away with me. But I had God's help, and 22 so to this very day I stand and testify to great and small alike. I assert nothing beyond what was foretold by the prophets and by Moses: that the Messiah must 23 suffer, and that he, the first to rise from the dead, would announce the dawn to Israel and to the Gentiles.'

24 While Paul was thus making his defence, Festus shouted at the top of his voice, 'Paul, you are raving; too much study is driving you mad.' 'I am not mad, Your Excel- 25 lency,' said Paul; 'what I am saying is sober truth. The king is well 26 versed in these matters, and to him I can speak freely. I do not believe that he can be unaware of any of these facts, for this has been no hole-and-corner business. King A- 27 grippa, do you believe the prophets? I know you do.' Agrippa 28 said to Paul, 'You think it will not take much to win me over and make a Christian of me.' 'Much or 29 little,' said Paul, 'I wish to God that not only you, but all those also who are listening to me today, might become what I am, apart from these chains.'

30 With that the king rose, and with him the Governor, Bernice, and the rest of the company, and 31 after they had withdrawn they talked it over. 'This man', they said, 'is doing nothing that deserves death or imprisonment.' Agrippa said to Festus, 'The fellow 32 could have been discharged, if he had not appealed to the Emperor.'

WHEN it was decided that we 27 should sail for Italy, Paul and some other prisoners were handed over to a centurion named Julius, of the Augustan Cohort. We em- 2 barked in a ship of Adramyttium, bound for ports in the province of Asia, and put out to sea. In our party was Aristarchus, a Macedonian from Thessalonica. Next day 3 we landed at Sidon; and Julius very considerately allowed Paul to go to his friends to be cared for.

4 Leaving Sidon we sailed under the lee of Cyprus because of the head-

5 winds, then across the open sea off the coast of Cilicia and Pamphylia, and so reached Myra in Lycia.

6 There the centurion found an Alexandrian vessel bound for Italy

7 and put us aboard. For a good many days we made little headway, and we were hard put to it to reach Cnidus. Then, as the wind continued against us, off Salmone we began to sail under the lee of

8 Crete, and, hugging the coast, struggled on to a place called Fair Havens, not far from the town of Lasea.

9 By now much time had been lost, the Fast was already over, and it was risky to go on with the voyage. Paul therefore gave them

10 this advice: 'I can see, gentlemen,' he said, 'that this voyage will be disastrous: it will mean grave loss, loss not only of ship and cargo but

11 also of life.' But the centurion paid more attention to the captain and to the owner of the ship than to

12 what Paul said; and as the harbour was unsuitable for wintering, the majority were in favour of putting out to sea, hoping, if they could get so far, to winter at Phoenix, a Cretan harbour exposed south-

13 west and north-west. So when a southerly breeze sprang up, they thought that their purpose was as good as achieved, and, weighing anchor, they sailed along the coast

14 of Crete hugging the land. But before very long a fierce wind, the 'North-easter' as they call it, tore

15 down from the landward side. It caught the ship and, as it was impossible to keep head to wind, we had to give way and run before it

16 We ran under the lee of a small island called Cauda, and with a struggle managed to get the ship's

17 boat under control. When they had hoisted it aboard, they made use of tackle and undergirded the ship. Then, because they were a-fraid of running on to the shallows of Syrtis, they lowered the main-sail and let her drive. Next day, as 18 we were making very heavy weather, they began to lighten the ship; and on the third day they 19 jettisoned the ship's gear with their own hands. For days on end 20 there was no sign of either sun or stars, a great storm was raging, and our last hopes of coming through alive began to fade.

When they had gone for a long 21 time without food, Paul stood up among them and said, 'You should have taken my advice, gentlemen, not to sail from Crete; then you would have avoided this damage and loss. But now I urge you not to 22 lose heart; not a single life will be lost, only the ship. For last night 23 there stood by me an angel of the God whose I am and whom I wor-ship. "Do not be afraid, Paul," he 24 said; "it is ordained that you shall appear before the Emperor; and, be assured, God has granted you the lives of all who are sailing with you." So keep up your courage: 25 I trust in God that it will turn out as I have been told; though 26 we have to be cast ashore on some island.'

The fourteenth night came and 27 we were still drifting in the Sea of Adria. In the middle of the night the sailors felt that land was get-ting nearer. They sounded and 28 found twenty fathoms. Sounding again after a short interval they found fifteen fathoms; and fearing 29 that we might be cast ashore on a rugged coast they dropped four anchors from the stern and prayed for daylight to come. The sailors 30 tried to abandon ship; they had already lowered the ship's boat, pretending they were going to lay out anchors from the bows, when 31 Paul said to the centurion and the soldiers, 'Unless these men stay on board you can none of you come off safely.' So the soldiers cut the 32 ropes of the boat and let her drop away.

33 Shortly before daybreak Paul urged them all to take some food. 'For the last fourteen days', he said, 'you have lived in suspense and gone hungry; you have eaten
34 nothing whatever. So I beg you to have something to eat; your lives depend on it. Remember, not a hair of your heads will be lost.'
35 With these words, he took bread, gave thanks to God in front of them all, broke it, and began eat-
36 ing. Then they all plucked up courage, and took food themselves.
37 There were on board two hundred
38 and seventy-six of us in all. When they had eaten as much as they wanted they lightened the ship by dumping the corn in the sea.

39 When day broke they could not recognize the land, but they noticed a bay with a sandy beach, on which they planned, if possible,
40 to run the ship ashore. So they slipped the anchors and let them go; at the same time they loosened the lashings of the steering-paddles, set the foresail to the wind, and let
41 her drive to the beach. But they found themselves caught between cross-currents and ran the ship aground, so that the bow stuck fast and remained immovable, while the stern was being pounded
42 to pieces by the breakers. The soldiers thought they had better kill the prisoners for fear that any
43 should swim away and escape; but the centurion wanted to bring Paul safely through and prevented them from carrying out their plan. He gave orders that those who could swim should jump overboard
44 first and get to land; the rest were to follow, some on planks, some on parts of the ship. And thus it was that all came safely to land.

28 Once we had made our way to safety we identified the island as
2 Malta. The rough islanders treated us with uncommon kindness: because it was cold and had started

to rain, they lit a bonfire and made us all welcome. Paul had got to- 3 gether an armful of sticks and put them on the fire, when a viper, driven out by the heat, fastened on his hand. The islanders, seeing the 4 snake hanging on to his hand, said to one another, 'The man must be a murderer; he may have escaped from the sea, but divine justice has not let him live.' Paul, however, 5 shook off the snake into the fire and was none the worse. They still 6 expected that any moment he would swell up or drop down dead, but after waiting a long time without seeing anything extra-ordinary happen to him, they changed their minds and now said, 'He is a god.'

In the neighbourhood of that 7 place there were lands belonging to the chief magistrate of the island, whose name was Publius. He took us in and entertained us hospitably for three days. It so 8 happened that this man's father was in bed suffering from recurrent bouts of fever and dysentery. Paul visited him and, after prayer, laid his hands upon him and healed him; whereupon the other sick 9 people on the island came also and were cured. They honoured 10 us with many marks of respect, and when we were leaving they put on board provision for our needs.

Three months had passed when 11 we set sail in a ship which had wintered in the island; she was the *Castor and Pollux* of Alexandria. We put in at Syracuse and spent 12 three days there; then we sailed 13 round and arrived at Rhegium. After one day a south wind sprang up and we reached Puteoli in two days. There we found fellow-Chris- 14 tians and were invited to stay a week with them. And so to Rome. The Christians there had had news 15 of us and came out to meet us as far as Appii Forum and Tres Tabernae, and when Paul saw them, he gave thanks to God and took courage.

16 WHEN we entered Rome Paul was allowed to lodge by himself with a soldier in charge of him. 17 Three days later he called together the local Jewish leaders; and when they were assembled, he said to them: 'My brothers, I, who never did anything against our people or the customs of our forefathers, am here as a prisoner; I was handed over to the Romans at 18 Jerusalem. They examined me and would have liked to release me because there was no capital charge 19 against me; but the Jews objected, and I had no option but to appeal to the Emperor; not that I had any accusation to bring against my 20 own people. That is why I have asked to see you and talk to you, because it is for the sake of the hope of Israel that I am in chains, 21 as you see.' They replied, 'We have had no communication from Judaea, nor has any countryman of ours arrived with any report or 22 gossip to your discredit. We should like to hear from you what your views are; all we know about this sect is that no one has a good word to say for it.'

23 So they fixed a day, and came in large numbers as his guests. He dealt at length with the whole matter; he spoke urgently of the kingdom of God and sought to convince them about Jesus by appealing to the Law of Moses and the prophets. This went on from dawn to dusk. Some were won over 24 by his arguments; others remained sceptical. Without reaching any 25 agreement among themselves they began to disperse, but not before Paul had said one thing more: 'How well the Holy Spirit spoke to your fathers through the prophet Isaiah when he said, "Go to this 26 people and say: You may hear and hear, but you will never understand; you may look and look, but you will never see. For this people's 27 mind has become gross; their ears are dulled, and their eyes are closed. Otherwise, their eyes might see, their ears hear, and their mind understand, and then they might turn again, and I would heal them." Therefore take notice that 28 this salvation of God has been sent to the Gentiles; the Gentiles will listen.'[a]

He stayed there two full years 30 at his own expense, with a welcome for all who came to him, proclaim- 31 ing the kingdom of God and teaching the facts about the Lord Jesus Christ quite openly and without hindrance.

[a] *Some witnesses add* (29) After he had spoken, the Jews went away, arguing vigorously among themselves.

LETTERS

THE LETTER OF PAUL

TO THE

ROMANS

The Gospel according to Paul

1 FROM Paul, servant of Christ Jesus, apostle by God's call, set apart for the service of the Gospel.

2 This gospel God announced beforehand in sacred scriptures

3 through his prophets. It is about his Son: on the human level he was

4 born of David's stock, but on the level of the spirit – the Holy Spirit – he was declared Son of God by a mighty act in that he rose from the dead:[a] it is about Jesus

5 Christ our Lord. Through him I received the privilege of a commission in his name to lead to faith and obedience men in all nations,

6 yourselves among them, you who have heard the call and belong to Jesus Christ.

7 I send greetings to all of you in Rome whom God loves and has called to be his dedicated people. Grace and peace to you from God our Father and the Lord Jesus Christ.

8 Let me begin by thanking my God, through Jesus Christ, for you all, because all over the world they are telling the story of your faith.

9 God is my witness, the God to whom I offer the humble service of my spirit by preaching the gospel of his Son: God knows how con-

10 tinually I make mention of you in my prayers, and am always asking that by his will I may, somehow or other, succeed at long last in

11 coming to visit you. For I long to see you; I want to bring you some spiritual gift to make you strong;

12 or rather, I want to be among you to be myself encouraged by your faith as well as you by mine.

13 But I should like you to know,[b] my brothers, that I have often planned to come, though so far without success, in the hope of achieving something among you, as I have in other parts of the

14 world. I am under obligation to Greek and non-Greek, to learned

15 and simple; hence my eagerness to declare the Gospel to you in

16 Rome as well as to others. For I am not ashamed of the Gospel. It is the saving power of God for everyone who has faith – the Jew first, but

17 the Greek also – because here is revealed God's way of righting wrong, a way that starts from faith and ends in faith;[c] as Scripture says, 'he shall gain life who is justified through faith'.

18 FOR we see divine retribution revealed from heaven and falling upon all the godless wickedness of men. In their wickedness they are stifling the truth. For all that may

19 be known of God by men lies plain before their eyes; indeed God him-

20 self has disclosed it to them. His invisible attributes, that is to say his everlasting power and deity, have been visible, ever since the world began, to the eye of reason, in the things he has made. There is therefore no possible defence for

21 their conduct; knowing God, they have refused to honour him as God, or to render him thanks.

---

[a] Or declared Son of God with full powers from the time when he rose from the dead.
[b] Some witnesses read I believe you know.
[c] Or . . . wrong. It is based on faith and addressed to faith.

Hence all their thinking has ended in futility, and their misguided minds are plunged in darkness. 22 They boast of their wisdom, but they have made fools of themselves, 23 exchanging the splendour of immortal God for an image shaped like mortal man, even for images like birds, beasts, and creeping things.

24 For this reason God has given them up to the vileness of their own desires, and the consequent degra- 25 dation of their bodies, because they have bartered away the true God for a false one,[a] and have offered reverence and worship to created things instead of to the Creator, who is blessed for ever; amen.

26 In consequence, I say, God has given them up to shameful passions. Their women have ex- changed natural intercourse for 27 unnatural, and their men in turn, giving up natural relations with women, burn with lust for one another; males behave indecently with males, and are paid in their own persons the fitting wage of such perversion.

28 Thus, because they have not seen fit to acknowledge God, he has given them up to their own de- praved reason. This leads them to 29 break all rules of conduct. They are filled with every kind of in- justice, mischief, rapacity, and malice; they are one mass of envy, murder, rivalry, treachery, 30 and malevolence; whisperers and scandal-mongers, hateful to God, insolent, arrogant, and boastful; they invent new kinds of mischief, 31 they show no loyalty to parents, no conscience, no fidelity to their plighted word; they are without natural affection and without pity. 32 They know well enough the just decree of God, that those who be- have like this deserve to die, and yet they do it; not only so, they actually applaud such practices.

2   You therefore have no defence –

you who sit in judgement, whoever you may be – for in judging your fellow-man you condemn yourself, since you, the judge, are equally guilty. It is admitted that God's 2 judgement is rightly passed upon all who commit such crimes as these; and do you imagine – you who pass 3 judgement on the guilty while committing the same crimes your- self – do you imagine that you, any more than they, will escape the judgement of God? Or do you 4 think lightly of his wealth of kind- ness, of tolerance, and of patience, without recognizing that God's kindness is meant to lead you to a change of heart? In the rigid 5 obstinacy of your heart you are laying up for yourself a store of retribution for the day of retribu- tion, when God's just judgement will be revealed, and he will pay every 6 man for what he has done. To those 7 who pursue glory, honour, and immortality by steady persistence in well-doing, he will give eternal life; but for those who are govern- 8 ed by selfish ambition, who refuse obedience to the truth and take the wrong for their guide, there will be the fury of retribution. There will 9 be trouble and distress for every human being who is an evil-doer, for the Jew first and for the Greek also; and for every well-doer there 10 will be glory, honour, and peace, for the Jew first and also for the Greek.

For God has no favourites: those 11, 12 who have sinned outside the pale of the Law of Moses will perish outside its pale, and all who have sinned under that law will be judged by the law. It is not by 13 hearing the law, but by doing it, that men will be justified before God. When Gentiles who do not 14 possess the law carry out its pre- cepts by the light of nature, then, although they have no law, they are their own law, for they display 15 the effect of the law inscribed on their hearts. Their conscience is

[a] Or the truth of God for the lie.

called as witness, and their own thoughts argue the case on either side, against them or even for 16 them, on the day when God judges the secrets of human hearts through Christ Jesus. So my gospel declares.

17 But as for you – you may bear the name of Jew; you rely upon the law and are proud of your God; 18 you know his will; instructed by the law, you know right from 19 wrong; you are confident that you are the one to guide the blind, to 20 enlighten the benighted, to train the stupid, and to teach the immature, because in the law you see the very shape of knowledge and 21 truth. You, then, who teach your fellow-man, do you fail to teach yourself? You proclaim, 'Do not steal'; but are you yourself a thief? 22 You say, 'Do not commit adultery'; but are you an adulterer? You abominate false gods; but do 23 you rob their shrines? While you take pride in the law, you dis-24 honour God by breaking it. For, as Scripture says, 'Because of you the name of God is dishonoured among the Gentiles.'

25 Circumcision has value, provided you keep the law; but if you break the law, then your circumcision is as if it had never been. 26 Equally, if an uncircumcised man keeps the precepts of the law, will 27 he not count as circumcised? He may be uncircumcised in his natural state, but by fulfilling the law he will pass judgement on you who break it, for all your written 28 code and your circumcision. The true Jew is not he who is such in externals, neither is the true circumcision the external mark in the 29 flesh. The true Jew is he who is such inwardly, and the true circumcision is of the heart, directed not by written precepts but by the Spirit; such a man receives his commendation not from men but from God.

Then what advantage has the 3 Jew? What is the value of circumcision? Great, in every way. In the 2 first place, the Jews were entrusted with the oracles of God. What if 3 some of them were unfaithful? Will their faithlessness cancel the faithfulness of God? Certainly not! God 4 must be true though every man living were a liar; for we read in Scripture, 'When thou speakest thou shalt be vindicated, and win the verdict when thou art on trial.'

Another question: if our in- 5 justice serves to bring out God's justice, what are we to say? Is it unjust of God (I speak of him in human terms) to bring retribution upon us? Certainly not! If God 6 were unjust, how could he judge the world?

Again, if the truth of God brings 7 him all the greater honour because of my falsehood, why should I any longer be condemned as a sinner? Why not indeed 'do evil that good 8 may come', as some libellously report me as saying? To condemn such men as these is surely no injustice.

What then? Are we Jews any 9 better off?[a] No, not at all![b] For we have already drawn up the accusation that Jews and Greeks alike are all under the power of sin. This has 10 scriptural warrant:

'There is no just man, not one;
no one who understands, no one 11
who seeks God.
All have swerved aside, all alike 12
have become debased;
there is no one to show kindness;
no, not one.

Their throat is an open grave, 13
they use their tongues for treachery,
adders' venom is on their lips,
and their mouth is full of bitter 14
curses.

---

[a] *Or* Are we Jews any worse off?
[b] *Or* Not in all respects.

15 Their feet hasten to shed blood,
16 ruin and misery lie along their paths,
17 they are strangers to the high-road of peace,
18 and reverence for God does not enter their thoughts.'

19　Now all the words of the law are addressed, as we know, to those who are within the pale of the law, so that no one may have anything to say in self-defence, but the whole world may be exposed to the
20 judgement of God. For (again from Scripture) 'no human being can be justified in the sight of God' for having kept the law: law brings only the consciousness of sin.

21 BUT now, quite independently of law, God's justice has been brought to light. The Law and the prophets
22 both bear witness to it: it is God's way of righting wrong, effective through faith in Christ for all who have such faith – all, without dis-
23 tinction. For all alike have sinned, and are deprived of the divine
24 splendour, and all are justified by God's free grace alone, through his act of liberation in the person of
25 Christ Jesus. For God designed him to be the means of expiating sin by his sacrificial death, effective through faith. God meant by this to demonstrate his justice, because in his forbearance he had
26 overlooked the sins of the past – to demonstrate his justice now in the present, showing that he is himself just and also justifies any man who puts his faith in Jesus.
27　What room then is left for human pride? It is excluded. And on what principle? The keeping of the law would not exclude it, but faith
28 does. For our argument is that a man is justified by faith quite apart from success in keeping the law.
29　Do you suppose God is the God of the Jews alone? Is he not the God of Gentiles also? Certainly, of Gentiles also, if it be true that God 30 is one. And he will therefore justify both the circumcised in virtue of their faith, and the uncircumcised through their faith. Does this mean 31 that we are using faith to undermine law? By no means: we are placing law itself on a firmer footing.

WHAT, then, are we to say about 4 Abraham, our ancestor in the natural line? If Abraham was justi- 2 fied by anything he had done, then he has a ground for pride. But he has no such ground before God; for 3 what does Scripture say? 'Abraham put his faith in God, and that faith was counted to him as righteousness.' Now if a man does 4 a piece of work, his wages are not 'counted' as a favour; they are paid as debt. But if without any 5 work to his credit he simply puts his faith in him who acquits the guilty, then his faith is indeed 'counted as righteousness'. In the 6 same sense David speaks of the happiness of the man whom God 'counts' as just, apart from any specific acts of justice: 'Happy are 7 they', he says, 'whose lawless deeds are forgiven, whose sins are buried away; happy is the man 8 whose sins the Lord does not count against him.' Is this happiness con- 9 fined to the circumcised, or is it for the uncircumcised also? Consider: we say, 'Abraham's faith was counted as righteousness'; in what 10 circumstances was it so counted? Was he circumcised at the time, or not? He was not yet circumcised, but uncircumcised; and he later 11 received the symbolic rite of circumcision as the hall-mark of the righteousness which faith had given him when he was still uncircumcised. Consequently, he is the father of all who have faith when uncircumcised, so that righteousness is 'counted' to them; and 12 at the same time he is the father of such of the circumcised as do not rely upon their circumcision alone, but also walk in the footprints of the faith which our father Abraham had while he was yet uncircumcised.

13 For it was not through law that Abraham, or his posterity, was given the promise that the world should be his inheritance, but through the righteousness that 14 came from faith. For if those who hold by the law, and they alone, are heirs, then faith is empty and 15 the promise goes for nothing, because law can bring only retribution; but where there is no law 16 there can be no breach of law. The promise was made on the ground of faith, in order that it might be a matter of sheer grace, and that it might be valid for all Abraham's posterity, not only for those who hold by the law, but for those also who have the faith of Abraham. 17 For he is the father of us all, as Scripture says: 'I have appointed you to be father of many nations.' This promise, then, was valid before God, the God in whom he put his faith, the God who makes the dead live and summons things that are not yet in existence as if they 18 already were. When hope seemed hopeless, his faith was such that he became 'father of many nations', in agreement with the words which had been spoken to him: 'Thus 19 shall your descendants be.' Without any weakening of faith he contemplated his own body, as good as dead (for he was about a hundred years old), and the deadness 20 of Sarah's womb, and never doubted God's promise in unbelief, but, strong in faith, gave honour to 21 God, in the firm conviction of his power to do what he had promised. 22 And that is why Abraham's faith was 'counted to him as righteousness'.

23 Those words were written, not 24 for Abraham's sake alone, but for our sake too: it is to be 'counted' in the same way to us who have faith in the God who raised Jesus our Lord from the dead; for he was 25 given up to death for our misdeeds, and raised to life to justify us.[a]

THEREFORE, now that we have 5 been justified through faith, let us continue at peace[b] with God through our Lord Jesus Christ, through whom we have been al- 2 lowed to enter the sphere of God's grace, where we now stand. Let us exult[c] in the hope of the divine splendour that is to be ours. More 3 than this: let us even exult[d] in our present sufferings, because we know that suffering trains us to endure, and endurance brings 4 proof that we have stood the test, and this proof is the ground of 5 hope. Such a hope is no mockery, because God's love has flooded our inmost heart through the Holy Spirit he has given us.

For at the very time when we 6 were still powerless, then Christ died for the wicked. Even for a just 7 man one of us would hardly die, though perhaps for a good man one might actually brave death; but 8 Christ died for us while we were yet sinners, and that is God's own proof of his love towards us. And 9 so, since we have now been justified by Christ's sacrificial death, we shall all the more certainly be saved through him from final retribution. For if, when we were 10 God's enemies, we were reconciled to him through the death of his Son, how much more, now that we are reconciled, shall we be saved by his life! But that is not all: we also 11 exult in God through our Lord Jesus, through whom we have now been granted reconciliation.

Mark what follows. It was 12 through one man that sin entered the world, and through sin death, and thus death pervaded the whole

---

[a] Or raised to life because we were now justified.
[b] Some witnesses read we are at peace.   [c] Or We exult.   [d] Or we even exult.

human race, inasmuch as all men 13 have sinned. For sin was already in the world before there was law, though in the absence of law no 14 reckoning is kept of sin. But death held sway from Adam to Moses, even over those who had not sinned as Adam did, by disobeying a direct command – and Adam foreshadows the Man who was to come.

15 But God's act of grace is out of all proportion to Adam's wrongdoing. For if the wrongdoing of that one man brought death upon so many, its effect is vastly exceeded by the grace of God and the gift that came to so many by the grace of the one man, Jesus Christ. 16 And again, the gift of God is not to be compared in its effect with that one man's sin; for the judicial action, following upon the one offence, issued in a verdict of condemnation, but the act of grace, following upon so many misdeeds, 17 issued in a verdict of acquittal. For if by the wrongdoing of that one man death established its reign, through a single sinner, much more shall those who receive in far greater measure God's grace, and his gift of righteousness, live and reign through the one man, Jesus Christ.

18 It follows, then, that as the issue of one misdeed was condemnation for all men, so the issue of one just act is acquittal and life 19 for all men. For as through the disobedience of the one man the many were made sinners, so through the obedience of the one man the many will be made righteous.

20 Law intruded into this process to multiply law-breaking. But where sin was thus multiplied, grace immeasurably exceeded it, 21 in order that, as sin established its reign by way of death, so God's grace might establish its reign in righteousness, and issue in eternal life through Jesus Christ our Lord.

6 What are we to say, then? Shall we persist in sin, so that there may be all the more grace? No, no! We 2 died to sin: how can we live in it any longer? Have you forgotten 3 that when we were baptized into union with Christ Jesus we were baptized into his death? By baptism we were buried with him, and 4 lay dead, in order that, as Christ was raised from the dead in the splendour of the Father, so also we might set our feet upon the new path of life.

For if we have become incorporate with him in a death like his, 5 we shall also be one with him in a resurrection like his. We know that 6 the man we once were has been crucified with Christ, for the destruction of the sinful self, so that we may no longer be the slaves of sin, since a dead man is no longer 7 answerable for his sin. But if we 8 thus died with Christ, we believe that we shall also come to life with him. We know that Christ, once 9 raised from the dead, is never to die again: he is no longer under the dominion of death. For in dying as 10 he died, he died to sin, once for all, and in living as he lives, he lives to God. In the same way you must 11 regard yourselves as dead to sin and alive to God, in union with Christ Jesus.

So sin must no longer reign in 12 your mortal body, exacting obedience to the body's desires. You 13 must no longer put its several parts at sin's disposal, as implements for doing wrong. No: put yourselves at the disposal of God, as dead men raised to life; yield your bodies to him as implements for doing right; for sin shall no longer be 14 your master, because you are no longer under law, but under the grace of God.

What then? Are we to sin, be- 15 cause we are not under law but under grace? Of course not. You 16 know well enough that if you put yourselves at the disposal of a master, to obey him, you are slaves of the master whom you obey; and this is true whether you serve sin, with death as its result; or obedience, with righteousness as its 17 result. But God be thanked, you, who once were slaves of sin, have yielded whole-hearted obedience to the pattern of teaching to which 18 you were made subject,[a] and, emancipated from sin, have become 19 slaves of righteousness (to use words that suit your human weakness) – I mean, as you once yielded your bodies to the service of impurity and lawlessness, making for moral anarchy, so now you must yield them to the service of righteousness, making for a holy life.

20 When you were slaves of sin, you were free from the control of 21 righteousness; and what was the gain? Nothing but what now makes you ashamed, for the end of 22 that is death. But now, freed from the commands of sin, and bound to the service of God, your gains are such as make for holiness, and the 23 end is eternal life. For sin pays a wage, and the wage is death, but God gives freely, and his gift is eternal life, in union with Christ Jesus our Lord.

7 You cannot be unaware, my friends – I am speaking to those who have some knowledge of law – that a person is subject to the law so long as he is alive, and no longer. 2 For example, a married woman is by law bound to her husband while he lives; but if her husband dies, she is discharged from the obliga- 3 tions of the marriage-law. If, therefore, in her husband's lifetime she consorts with another man, she will incur the charge of adultery; but if her husband dies she is free of the law, and she does not commit adultery by consorting with 4 another man. So you, my friends, have died to the law by becoming identified with the body of Christ, and accordingly you have found another husband in him who rose

from the dead, so that we may bear fruit for God. While we lived on the 5 level of our lower nature, the sinful passions evoked by the law worked in our bodies, to bear fruit for death. But now, having died to 6 that which held us bound, we are discharged from the law, to serve God in a new way, the way of the spirit, in contrast to the old way, the way of a written code.

What follows? Is the law identi- 7 cal with sin? Of course not. But except through law I should never have become acquainted with sin. For example, I should never have known what it was to covet, if the law had not said, 'Thou shalt not covet.' Through that command- 8 ment sin found its opportunity, and produced in me all kinds of wrong desires. In the absence of law, sin is a dead thing. There was 9 a time when, in the absence of law, I was fully alive; but when the commandment came, sin sprang to life and I died. The command- 10 ment which should have led to life proved in my experience to lead to death, because sin found its op- 11 portunity in the commandment, seduced me, and through the commandment killed me.

Therefore the law is in itself 12 holy, and the commandment is holy and just and good. Are we to 13 say then that this good thing was the death of me? By no means. It was sin that killed me, and thereby sin exposed its true character: it used a good thing to bring about my death, and so, through the commandment, sin became more sinful than ever.

We know that the law is spiri- 14 tual; but I am not: I am unspiritual, the purchased slave of sin. I 15 do not even acknowledge my own actions as mine, for what I do is not what I want to do, but what I detest. But if what I do is against 16 my will, it means that I agree with the law and hold it to be admirable.

---

[a] *Or* which was handed on to you.

17 But as things are, it is no longer I who perform the action, but sin
18 that lodges in me. For I know that nothing good lodges in me – in my unspiritual nature, I mean – for though the will to do good is
19 there, the deed is not. The good which I want to do, I fail to do; but what I do is the wrong which is
20 against my will; and if what I do is against my will, clearly it is no longer I who am the agent, but sin that has its lodging in me.
21 I discover this principle, then: that when I want to do the right, only the wrong is within my reach.
22 In my inmost self I delight in the
23 law of God, but I perceive that there is in my bodily members a different law, fighting against the law that my reason approves and making me a prisoner under the law*a* that is in my members, the
24 law of sin. Miserable creature that I am, who is there to rescue me out of this body doomed to death*b*?
25 God alone, through Jesus Christ our Lord! Thanks be to God! In a word then, I myself, subject to God's law as a rational being, am yet,*c* in my unspiritual nature, a slave to the law of sin.

8 The conclusion of the matter is this: there is no condemnation for those who are united with Christ
2 Jesus, because in Christ Jesus the life-giving law of the Spirit has set you free from the law of sin and
3 death. What the law could never do, because our lower nature robbed it of all potency, God has done: by sending his own Son in a form like that of our own sinful nature, and as a sacrifice for sin,*d* he has passed judgement against sin with-
4 in that very nature, so that the commandment of the law may find fulfilment in us, whose conduct, no longer under the control of our lower nature, is directed by the Spirit.

Those who live on the level of 5 our lower nature have their out- 6 look formed by it, and that spells death; but those who live on the level of the spirit have the spiritual outlook, and that is life and peace. For the outlook of the lower 7 nature is enmity with God; it is not subject to the law of God; indeed it cannot be: those who live on such 8 a level cannot possibly please God. But that is not how you live. 9 You are on the spiritual level, if only God's Spirit dwells within you; and if a man does not possess the Spirit of Christ, he is no Christian. But if Christ is dwelling with- 10 in you, then although the body is a dead thing because you sinned, yet the spirit is life itself because you have been justified.*e* Moreover, if 11 the Spirit of him who raised Jesus from the dead dwells within you, then the God who raised Christ Jesus from the dead will also give new life to your mortal bodies through his indwelling Spirit.

It follows, my friends, that our 12 lower nature has no claim upon us; we are not obliged to live on that level. If you do so, you must die. 13 But if by the Spirit you put to death all the base pursuits of the body, then you will live.

For all who are moved by the 14 Spirit of God are sons of God. The 15 Spirit you have received is not a spirit of slavery leading you back into a life of fear, but a Spirit that makes us sons, enabling us to cry 'Abba! Father!' In that cry the 16 Spirit of God joins with our spirit in testifying that we are God's children; and if children, then 17 heirs. We are God's heirs and Christ's fellow-heirs, if we share his sufferings now in order to share his splendour hereafter.

For I reckon that the sufferings 18 we now endure bear no comparison with the splendour, as yet un-

---

a Or *by means of the law.*   *b* Or *out of the body doomed to this death.*
c Or *Thus, left to myself, while subject . . . rational being, I am yet . . .*
d Or *and to deal with sin.*   *e* Or *so that you may live rightly.*

revealed, which is in store for us. 19 For the created universe waits with eager expectation for God's sons to 20 be revealed. It was made the victim of frustration, not by its own choice, but because of him who made it so;[a] yet always there was 21 hope, because[b] the universe itself is to be freed from the shackles of mortality and enter upon the liberty and splendour of the children of 22 God. Up to the present, we know, the whole created universe groans in all its parts as if in the pangs of 23 childbirth. Not only so, but even we, to whom the Spirit is given as firstfruits of the harvest to come, are groaning inwardly while we wait for God to make us his sons 24 and[e] set our whole body free. For we have been saved, though only in hope. Now to see is no longer to hope: why should a man endure and wait[d] for what he already sees? 25 But if we hope for something we do not yet see, then, in waiting for it, we show our endurance.

26   In the same way the Spirit comes to the aid of our weakness. We do not even know how we ought to pray,[e] but through our inarticulate groans the Spirit himself is plead-27 ing for us, and God who searches our inmost being knows what the Spirit means, because he pleads for God's people in God's own way; 28 and in everything, as we know, he co-operates for good with those who love God[f] and are called ac-29 cording to his purpose. For God knew his own before ever they were, and also ordained that they should be shaped to the likeness of his Son, that he might be the eldest among a large family of brothers; 30 and it is these, so fore-ordained,

whom he has also called. And those whom he called he has justified, and to those whom he justified he has also given his splendour.

With all this in mind, what are 31 we to say? If God is on our side, who is against us? He did not spare 32 his own Son, but gave him up for us all; and with this gift how can he fail to lavish upon us all he has to give? Who will be the accuser of 33 God's chosen ones? It is God who pronounces acquittal; then who 34 can condemn? It is Christ – Christ who died, and, more than that, was raised from the dead – who is at God's right hand, and indeed pleads our cause.[g] Then what can 35 separate us from the love of Christ? Can affliction or hardship? Can persecution, hunger, nakedness, peril, or the sword? 'We are being 36 done to death for thy sake all day long,' as Scripture says; 'we have been treated like sheep for slaughter' – and yet, in spite of all, over-37 whelming victory is ours through him who loved us. For I am con-38 vinced that there is nothing in death or life, in the realm of spirits or superhuman powers, in the world as it is or the world as it shall be, in the forces of the universe, in 39 heights or depths – nothing in all creation that can separate us from the love of God in Christ Jesus our Lord.

The purpose of God in history

I AM speaking the truth as a Chris-9 tian, and my own conscience, en-lightened by the Holy Spirit, assures me it is no lie: in my heart 2 there is great grief and unceasing sorrow. For I could even pray to be 3

---

[a] *Or* because God subjected it.   [b] *Or* with the hope that. . .   [e] *Some witnesses* omit make us his sons and.   [d] *Some witnesses read* why should a man hope. . . [e] *Or* what it is right to pray for.   [f] *Or* and, as we know, all things work together for good for those who love God; *some witnesses read* and we know God himself co-operates for good with those who love God.   [g] *Or* Who will be the accuser of God's chosen ones? Will it be God himself? No, he it is who pronounces acquittal. Who will be the judge to condemn? Will it be Christ – he who died, and, more than that, . . . right hand? No, he it is who pleads our cause.

outcast from Christ myself for the sake of my brothers, my natural 4 kinsfolk. They are Israelites: they were made God's sons; theirs is the splendour of the divine presence, theirs the covenants, the law, the temple worship, and the promises. 5 Theirs are the patriarchs, and from them, in natural descent, sprang the Messiah.[a] May God, supreme above all, be blessed for ever![b] Amen.

6 It is impossible that the word of God should have proved false. For not all descendants of Israel are 7 truly Israel, nor, because they are Abraham's offspring, are they all his true children;[c] but, in the words of Scripture, 'Through the line of Isaac your descendants shall be 8 traced.'[d] That is to say, it is not those born in the course of nature who are children of God; it is the children born through God's promise who are reckoned as Abra-9 ham's descendants. For the promise runs: 'At the time fixed I will come, and Sarah shall have a son.'

10 But that is not all, for Rebekah's children had one and the same 11 father, our ancestor Isaac; and yet, in order that God's selective purpose might stand, based not upon men's deeds but upon the 12 call of God, she was told, even before they were born, when they had as yet done nothing, good or ill, 'The elder shall be servant to 13 the younger'; and that accords with the text of Scripture, 'Jacob I loved and Esau I hated.'

14 What shall we say to that? Is God to be charged with injustice? 15 By no means. For he says to Moses, 'Where I show mercy, I will show mercy, and where I pity, I will 16 pity.' Thus it does not depend on man's will or effort, but on God's 17 mercy. For Scripture says to Pharaoh, 'I have raised you up for this very purpose, to exhibit my power in my dealings with you, and to spread my fame over all the world.' Thus he not only shows mercy as 18 he chooses, but also makes men stubborn as he chooses.

You will say, 'Then why does 19 God blame a man? For who can resist his will?' Who are you, sir, to 20 answer God back? Can the pot speak to the potter and say, 'Why did you make me like this?'? Surely 21 the potter can do what he likes with the clay. Is he not free to make out of the same lump two vessels, one to be treasured, the other for common use?

But what if God, desiring to 22 exhibit[e] his retribution at work and to make his power known, tolerated very patiently those vessels which were objects of retribution due for destruction, and did so 23 in order to make known the full wealth of his splendour upon vessels, which were objects of mercy, and which from the first had been prepared for this splendour?

Such vessels are we, whom he 24 has called from among Gentiles as well as Jews, as it says in the Book 25 of Hosea: 'Those who were not my people I will call My People, and the unloved nation I will call My Beloved. For in the very place 26 where they were told "you are no people of mine", they shall be called Sons of the living God.' But 27 Isaiah makes this proclamation about Israel: 'Though the Israelites be countless as the sands of the sea, only a remnant shall be saved; for the Lord's sentence on the land 28 will be summary and final'; as also 29 he said previously, 'If the Lord of Hosts had not left us the mere germ of a nation, we should have become like Sodom, and no better than Gomorrah.'

Then what are we to say? That 30

---

[a] *Greek* Christ.   [b] *Or* sprang the Messiah, supreme above all, God blessed for ever; *or* sprang the Messiah, who is supreme above all. Blessed be God for ever! [c] *Or* all children of God.   [d] *Or* God's call shall be for your descendants in the line of Isaac.   [e] *Or* although he had the will to exhibit . . .

Gentiles, who made no effort after righteousness, nevertheless achieved it, a righteousness based on 31 faith; whereas Israel made great efforts after a law of righteousness, 32 but never attained to it. Why was this? Because their efforts were not based on faith, but (as they supposed) on deeds. They fell over 33 the 'stone' mentioned in Scripture: 'Here I lay in Zion a stone to trip over, a rock to stumble against; but he who has faith in him will not be put to shame.'

10 BROTHERS, my deepest desire and my prayer to God is for their 2 salvation. To their zeal for God I can testify; but it is an ill-informed 3 zeal. For they ignore God's way of righteousness, and try to set up their own, and therefore they have not submitted themselves to God's 4 righteousness. For Christ ends the law and brings righteousness for everyone who has faith.*a*

5 Of legal righteousness Moses writes, 'The man who does this 6 shall gain life by it.' But the righteousness that comes by faith says, 'Do not say to yourself, "Who can go up to heaven?"' (that is to 7 bring Christ down), 'or, "Who can go down to the abyss?"' (to bring 8 Christ up from the dead). But what does it say? 'The word is near you: it is upon your lips and in your heart.' This means the word 9 of faith which we proclaim. If on your lips is the confession, 'Jesus is Lord', and in your heart the faith that God raised him from the dead, then you will find salvation. 10 For the faith that leads to righteousness is in the heart, and the confession that leads to salvation is upon the lips.

11 Scripture says, 'Everyone who has faith in him will be saved from 12 shame' – everyone: there is no distinction between Jew and Greek, because the same Lord is Lord of all, and is rich enough for the need of all who invoke him. For every- 13 one, as it says again –'everyone who invokes the name of the Lord will be saved'. How could they 14 invoke one in whom they had no faith? And how could they have faith in one they had never heard of? And how hear without someone to spread the news? And how 15 could anyone spread the news without a commission to do so? And that is what Scripture affirms: 'How welcome are the feet of the messengers of good news!'

But not all have responded to 16 the good news. For Isaiah says, 'Lord, who has believed our message?' We conclude that faith is 17 awakened by the message, and the message that awakens it comes through the word of Christ.

But, I ask, can it be that they 18 never heard it? Of course they did: 'Their voice has sounded all over the earth, and their words to the bounds of the inhabited world.' But, I ask again, can it be that 19 Israel failed to recognize the message? In reply, I first cite Moses, who says, 'I will use a nation that is no nation to stir your envy, and a foolish nation to rouse your anger.' But Isaiah is still more daring: 'I 20 was found', he says, 'by those who were not looking for me; I was clearly shown to those who never asked about me'; while to Israel he 21 says, 'All day long I have stretched out my hands to an unruly and defiant people.'

I ASK then, has God rejected his 11 people? I cannot believe it! I am an Israelite myself, of the stock of Abraham, of the tribe of Benjamin. No! God has not rejected the 2 people which he acknowledged of old as his own. You know (do you not?) what Scripture says in the story of Elijah – how Elijah pleads with God against Israel: 'Lord, 3

---

a Or Christ is the end of the law as a way to righteousness for everyone who has faith.

they have killed thy prophets, they have torn down thine altars, and I alone am left, and they are seeking 4 my life.' But what does the divine voice say to him? 'I have left myself seven thousand men who have 5 not knelt to Baal.' In just the same way at the present time a 'remnant' has come into being, selected 6 by the grace of God. But if it is by grace, then it does not rest on deeds done, or grace would cease to be grace.

7　　What follows? What Israel sought, Israel has not achieved, but the selected few have achieved it. The rest were made blind to the 8 truth, exactly as it stands written: 'God brought upon them a numbness of spirit; he gave them blind eyes and deaf ears, and so it is still.' 9 Similarly David says:

'May their table be a snare and a trap,
both stumbling-block and retribution!
10 May their eyes become so dim that they lose their sight!
Bow down their backs unceasingly!'

11　　I now ask, did their failure mean complete downfall? Far from it! Because they offended, salvation has come to the Gentiles, to stir 12 Israel to emulation. But if their offence means the enrichment of the world, and if their falling-off means the enrichment of the Gentiles, how much more their coming to full strength!

13　　But I have something to say to you Gentiles. I am a missionary to the Gentiles, and as such I give all 14 honour to that ministry when I try to stir emulation in the men of my own race, and so to save some of 15 them. For if their rejection has meant the reconciliation of the world, what will their acceptance mean? Nothing less than life from 16 the dead! If the first portion of dough is consecrated, so is the whole lump. If the root is conse-17 crated, so are the branches. But if some of the branches have been lopped off, and you, a wild olive, have been grafted in among them, and have come to share the same 18 root and sap as the olive, do not make yourself superior to the branches. If you do so, remember that it is not you who sustain the root: the root sustains you.

19　　You will say, 'Branches were lopped off so that I might be 20 grafted in.' Very well: they were lopped off for lack of faith, and by faith you hold your place. Put away your pride, and be on your 21 guard; for if God did not spare the native branches, no more will he 22 spare you. Observe the kindness and the severity of God – severity to those who fell away, divine kindness to you, if only you remain within its scope; otherwise 23 you too will be cut off, whereas they, if they do not continue faithless, will be grafted in; for it is in God's power to graft them in 24 again. For if you were cut from your native wild olive and against all nature grafted into the cultivated olive, how much more readily will they, the natural olive-branches, be grafted into their native stock!

25　　For there is a deep truth here, my brothers, of which I want you to take account, so that you may not be complacent about your own discernment: this partial blindness has come upon Israel only until the Gentiles have been admitted in full strength; when that has happened, 26 the whole of Israel will be saved, in agreement with the text of Scripture:

'From Zion shall come the Deliverer;
he shall remove wickedness from Jacob.
And this is the covenant I will 27 grant them,
when I take away their sins.'

28 In the spreading of the Gospel they are treated as God's enemies for your sake; but God's choice stands, and they are his friends for the 29 sake of the patriarchs. For the gracious gifts of God and his call- 30 ing are irrevocable. Just as former- ly you were disobedient to God, but now have received mercy in 31 the time of their disobedience, so now, when you receive mercy, they have proved disobedient, but only in order that they too may receive 32 mercy. For in making all mankind prisoners to disobedience, God's purpose was to show mercy to all mankind.

33 O depth of wealth, wisdom, and knowledge in God! How unsearch- able his judgements, how untrace- 34 able his ways! Who knows the mind of the Lord? Who has been 35 his counsellor? Who has ever made a gift to him, to receive a gift in 36 return? Source, Guide, and Goal of all that is – to him be glory for ever! Amen.

Christian behaviour

12 THEREFORE, my brothers, I im- plore you by God's mercy to offer your very selves to him: a living sacrifice, dedicated and fit for his acceptance, the worship offered by 2 mind and heart.[a] Adapt yourselves no longer to the pattern of this present world, but let your minds be remade and your whole nature thus transformed. Then you will be able to discern the will of God, and to know what is good, acceptable, and perfect.

3 In virtue of the gift that God in his grace has given me I say to everyone among you: do not be conceited or think too highly of yourself; but think your way to a sober estimate based on the mea- sure of faith that God has dealt to 4 each of you. For just as in a single human body there are many limbs

and organs, all with different func- tions, so all of us, united with 5 Christ, form one body, serving individually as limbs and organs to one another.

The gifts we possess differ as 6 they are allotted to us by God's grace, and must be exercised ac- cordingly: the gift of inspired ut- terance, for example, in proportion to a man's faith; or the gift of 7 administration, in administration. A teacher should employ his gift in teaching, and one who has the gift 8 of stirring speech should use it to stir his hearers. If you give to charity, give with all your heart; if you are a leader, exert yourself to lead; if you are helping others in distress, do it cheerfully.

Love in all sincerity, loathing 9 evil and clinging to the good. Let 10 love for our brotherhood breed warmth of mutual affection. Give pride of place to one another in esteem.

With unflagging energy, in ard- 11 our of spirit, serve the Lord.[b]

Let hope keep you joyful; in 12 trouble stand firm; persist in prayer.

Contribute to the needs of God's 13 people, and practise hospitality.

Call down blessings on your 14 persecutors -- blessings, not curses.

With the joyful be joyful, and 15 mourn with the mourners.

Care as much about each other 16 as about yourselves. Do not be haughty, but go about with humble folk. Do not keep thinking how wise you are.

Never pay back evil for evil. Let 17 your aims be such as all men count honourable. If possible, so far as it 18 lies with you, live at peace with all men. My dear friends, do not seek 19 revenge, but leave a place for divine retribution; for there is a text which reads, 'Justice is mine, says the Lord, I will repay.' But 20 there is another text: 'If your

---

[a] *Or* . . .acceptance, for such is the worship which you, as rational creatures, should offer. [b] *Some witnesses read* meet the demands of the hour.

enemy is hungry, feed him; if he is thirsty, give him a drink; by doing this you will heap live coals on his 21 head.' Do not let evil conquer you, but use good to defeat evil.

13 Every person must submit to the supreme authorities. There is no authority but by act of God, and the existing authorities are 2 instituted by him; consequently anyone who rebels against authority is resisting a divine institution, and those who so resist have themselves to thank for the punish-3 ment they will receive. For government, a terror to crime, has no terrors for good behaviour. You wish to have no fear of the authorities? Then continue to do right and you will have their approval, 4 for they are God's agents working for your good. But if you are doing wrong, then you will have cause to fear them; it is not for nothing that they hold the power of the sword, for they are God's agents of pun-5 ishment, for retribution on the offender. That is why you are obliged to submit. It is an obligation imposed not merely by fear of retribution but by conscience. 6 That is also why you pay taxes. The authorities are in God's service and to these duties they devote their energies.

7 Discharge your obligations to all men; pay tax and toll, reverence and respect, to those to whom 8 they are due. Leave no claim outstanding against you, except that of mutual love. He who loves his neighbour has satisfied every claim 9 of the law. For the commandments, 'Thou shalt not commit adultery, thou shalt not kill, thou shalt not steal, thou shalt not covet', and any other commandment there may be, are all summed up in the one rule, 'Love your 10 neighbour as yourself.' Love cannot wrong a neighbour; therefore the whole law is summed up in love.*a*

In all this, remember how criti- 11 cal the moment is. It is time for you to wake out of sleep, for deliverance is nearer to us now than it was when first we believed. It is 12 far on in the night; day is near. Let us therefore throw off the deeds of darkness and put on our armour as soldiers of the light. Let us 13 behave with decency as befits the day: no revelling or drunkenness, no debauchery or vice, no quarrels or jealousies! Let Christ Jesus 14 himself be the armour that you wear; give no more thought to satisfying the bodily appetites.

IF a man is weak in his faith you 14 must accept him without attempting to settle doubtful points. For 2 instance, one man will have faith enough to eat all kinds of food, while a weaker man eats only vegetables. The man who eats 3 must not hold in contempt the man who does not, and he who does not eat must not pass judgement on the one who does; for God has accepted him. Who are you to 4 pass judgement on someone else's servant? Whether he stands or falls is his own Master's business; and stand he will, because his Master has power to enable him to stand.

Again, this man regards one day 5 more highly than another, while that man regards all days alike. On such a point everyone should have reached conviction in his own mind. He who respects the day has 6 the Lord in mind in doing so, and he who eats meat has the Lord in mind when he eats, since he gives thanks to God; and he who abstains has the Lord in mind no less, since he too gives thanks to God.

For no one of us lives, and 7 equally no one of us dies, for himself alone. If we live, we live for the 8 Lord; and if we die, we die for the Lord. Whether therefore we live or die, we belong to the Lord. This is 9

a Or *the whole law is fulfilled by love.*

why Christ died and came to life again, to establish his lordship
10 over dead and living. You, sir, why do you pass judgement on your brother? And you, sir, why do you hold your brother in contempt? We shall all stand before God's
11 tribunal. For Scripture says, 'As I live, says the Lord, to me every knee shall bow and every tongue
12 acknowledge God.' So, you see, each of us will have to answer for himself.

13 Let us therefore cease judging one another, but rather make this simple judgement: that no obstacle or stumbling-block be placed
14 in a brother's way. I am absolutely convinced, as a Christian,[a] that nothing is impure in itself; only, if a man considers a particular thing
15 impure, then to him it is impure. If your brother is outraged by what you eat, then your conduct is no longer guided by love. Do not by your eating bring disaster to a
16 man for whom Christ died! What for you is a good thing must not become an occasion for slanderous
17 talk; for the kingdom of God is not eating and drinking, but justice, peace, and joy, inspired by the
18 Holy Spirit. He who thus shows himself a servant of Christ is acceptable to God and approved by men.

19 Let us then pursue the things that make for peace and build up
20 the common life. Do not ruin the work of God for the sake of food. Everything is pure in itself, but anything is bad for the man who by
21 his eating causes another to fall. It is a fine thing to abstain from eating meat or drinking wine, or doing anything which causes your bro-
22 ther's downfall. If you have a clear conviction, apply it to yourself in the sight of God. Happy is the man who can make his decision with a
23 clear conscience![b] But a man who

has doubts is guilty if he eats, because his action does not arise from his conviction, and anything which does not arise from conviction is sin.[c] Those of us who have a 15 robust conscience must accept as our own burden the tender scruples of weaker men, and not consider ourselves. Each of us must con- 2 sider his neighbour and think what is for his good and will build up the common life. For Christ too 3 did not consider himself, but might have said, in the words of Scripture, 'The reproaches of those who reproached thee fell upon me.' For 4 all the ancient scriptures were written for our own instruction, in order that through the encouragement they give us we may maintain our hope with fortitude. And 5 may God, the source of all fortitude and all encouragement, grant that you may agree with one another after the manner of Christ Jesus, so that with one mind and 6 one voice you may praise the God and Father of our Lord Jesus Christ.

In a word, accept one another as 7 Christ accepted us, to the glory of God. I mean that Christ became a 8 servant of the Jewish people to maintain the truth of God by making good his promises to the patriarchs, and at the same time to 9 give the Gentiles cause to glorify God for his mercy. As Scripture says, 'Therefore I will praise thee among the Gentiles and sing hymns to thy name'; and again, 'Gen- 10 tiles, make merry together with his own people'; and yet again, 11 'All Gentiles, praise the Lord; let all peoples praise him.' Once again, 12 Isaiah says, 'There shall be the Scion of Jesse, the one raised up to govern the Gentiles; on him the Gentiles shall set their hope.' And 13 may the God of hope fill you with all joy and peace by your faith in

---

[a] *Or* on the authority of the Lord Jesus.
[b] *Or* who does not bring judgement upon himself by what he approves!
[c] *See p. 193, note g.*

him, until, by the power of the Holy Spirit, you overflow with hope.

14 MY friends, I have no doubt in my own mind that you yourselves are quite full of goodness and equipped with knowledge of every kind, well able to give advice to one 15 another; nevertheless I have written to refresh your memory, and written somewhat boldly at times, in virtue of the gift I have from 16 God. His grace has made me a minister of Christ Jesus to the Gentiles; my priestly service is the preaching of the gospel of God, and it falls to me to offer the Gentiles to him as[a] an acceptable sacrifice, consecrated by the Holy Spirit.

17 Thus in the fellowship of Christ Jesus I have ground for pride in 18 the service of God. I will venture to speak of those things alone in which I have been Christ's instrument to bring the Gentiles into his 19 allegiance, by word and deed, by the force of miraculous signs and by the power of the Holy Spirit. As a result I have completed the preaching of the gospel of Christ from Jerusalem as far round as 20 Illyricum. It is my ambition to bring the Gospel to places where the very name of Christ has not been heard, for I do not want to build on another man's founda-21 tion; but, as Scripture says,

'They who had no news of him shall see,
and they who never heard of him shall understand.'

22 That is why I have been prevented all this time from coming to 23 you. But now I have no further scope in these parts, and I have been longing for many years to 24 visit you on my way to Spain; for I hope to see you as I travel through, and to be sent there with your support after having enjoyed your company for a while. But at the 25 moment I am on my way to Jerusalem, on an errand to God's people there. For Macedonia and 26 Achaia have resolved to raise a common fund for the benefit of the poor among God's people at Jerusalem. They have resolved to do so, 27 and indeed they are under an obligation to them. For if the Jewish Christians shared their spiritual treasures with the Gentiles, the Gentiles have a clear duty to contribute to their material needs. So 28 when I have finished this business and delivered the proceeds under my own seal, I shall set out for Spain by way of your city, and I 29 am sure that when I arrive I shall come to you with a full measure of the blessing of Christ.

I implore you by our Lord Jesus 30 Christ and by the love that the Spirit inspires, be my allies in the fight; pray to God for me that I 31 may be saved from unbelievers in Judaea and that my errand to Jerusalem may find acceptance with God's people, so that by his 32 will I may come to you in a happy frame of mind and enjoy a time of rest with you. The God of peace be 33 with you all. Amen.[b]

I COMMEND to you Phoebe, a 16 fellow-Christian who holds office in the congregation at Cenchreae. Give her, in the fellowship of the 2 Lord, a welcome worthy of God's people, and stand by her in any business in which she may need your help, for she has herself been a good friend to many, including myself.

Give my greetings to Prisca and 3 Aquila, my fellow-workers in Christ Jesus. They risked their necks to 4 save my life, and not I alone but all the gentile congregations are grateful to them. Greet also the congre-5 gation at their house.

___

[a] Or ...of God, so that the worship which the Gentiles offer may be...
[b] See p. 193, note g.

Give my greetings to my dear friend Epaenetus, the first convert 6 to Christ in Asia, and to Mary, 7 who toiled hard for you. Greet Andronicus and Junias[a] my fellow-countrymen and comrades in captivity. They are eminent among the apostles, and they were Christians before I was.

8 Greetings to Ampliatus, my dear friend in the fellowship of the 9 Lord, to Urban my comrade in Christ, and to my dear Stachys. 10 My greetings to Apelles, well proved in Christ's service, to the house- 11 hold of Aristobulus, and my countryman Herodion, and to those of the household of Narcissus who are 12 in the Lord's fellowship. Greet Tryphaena and Tryphosa, who toil in the Lord's service, and dear Persis who has toiled in his service 13 so long. Give my greetings to Rufus, an outstanding follower of the Lord, and to his mother, whom I 14 call mother too. Greet Asyncritus, Phlegon, Hermes, Patrobas, Hermas, and all friends in their com- 15 pany. Greet Philologus and Julia,[b] Nereus and his sister, and Olympas, and all God's people associated with them.

16 Greet one another with the kiss of peace. All Christ's congregations send you their greetings.

17 I implore you, my friends, keep your eye on those who stir up quarrels and lead others astray, contrary to the teaching you received. Avoid them, for such 18 people are servants not of Christ our Lord but of their own appetites, and they seduce the minds of innocent people with smooth and specious words. The fame of your 19 obedience has spread everywhere. This makes me happy about you; yet I should wish you to be experts in goodness but simpletons in evil; and the God of peace will soon 20 crush Satan beneath your feet. The grace of our Lord Jesus be with you![c]

Greetings to you from my col- 21 league Timothy, and from Lucius, Jason, and Sosipater my fellow-countrymen. (I Tertius, who took 22 this letter down, add my Christian greetings.) Greetings also from 23 Gaius, my host and host of the whole congregation, and from Erastus, treasurer of this city, and our brother Quartus.[d]

To him who has power to make 25 your standing sure, according to the Gospel I brought you and the proclamation of Jesus Christ, according to the revelation of that divine secret kept in silence for long ages but now disclosed, and 26 through prophetic scriptures by eternal God's command made known to all nations, to bring them to faith and obedience – to God 27 who alone is wise, through Jesus Christ,[e] be glory for endless ages! Amen.[f][g]

---

[a] Or Junia; *some witnesses read* Julia, *or* Julias.   [b] Or Julias; *some witnesses read* Junia, *or* Junias.   [c] *The words* The grace...with you *are omitted at this point in some witnesses; in some, these or similar words are given as verse 24, and in some others after verse 27 (see note on verse 23).*   [d] *Some witnesses add* (24) The grace of our Lord Jesus Christ be with you all! Amen.   [e] *Some witnesses insert* to whom.   [f] *Here some witnesses add* The grace of our Lord Jesus Christ be with you!   [g] *Some witnesses place verses 25–27 at the end of chapter 14, one other places them at the end of chapter 15, and others omit them altogether.*

THE FIRST LETTER OF PAUL

TO THE

CORINTHIANS

Unity and order in the church

1 FROM Paul, apostle of Jesus Christ at God's call and by God's will, together with our 2 colleague Sosthenes, to the congregation of God's people at Corinth, dedicated to him in Christ Jesus, claimed by him as his own, along with all men everywhere who invoke the name of our Lord Jesus Christ – their Lord as well as ours. 3 Grace and peace to you from God our Father and the Lord Jesus Christ.

4 I am always thanking God for you. I thank him for his grace 5 given to you in Christ Jesus. I thank him for all the enrichment that has come to you in Christ. You possess full knowledge and you can give full expression to it, 6 because in you the evidence for the truth of Christ has found confirm- 7 ation. There is indeed no single gift you lack, while you wait expectantly for our Lord Jesus Christ 8 to reveal himself. He will keep you firm to the end, without reproach 9 on the Day of our Lord Jesus. It is God himself who called you to share in the life of his Son Jesus Christ our Lord; and God keeps faith.

10 I appeal to you, my brothers, in the name of our Lord Jesus Christ: agree among yourselves, and avoid divisions; be firmly joined in unity 11 of mind and thought. I have been told, my brothers, by Chloe's people that there are quarrels 12 among you. What I mean is this: each of you is saying, 'I am Paul's man', or 'I am for Apollos'; 'I follow Cephas', or 'I am Christ's.'

Surely Christ has not been divided 13 among you! Was it Paul who was crucified for you? Was it in the name of Paul that you were baptized? Thank God, I never bap- 14 tized one of you – except Crispus and Gaius. So no one can say you 15 were baptized in my name. – Yes, 16 I did baptize the household of Stephanas; I cannot think of anyone else. Christ did not send me to 17 baptize, but to proclaim the Gospel; and to do it without relying on the language of worldly wisdom, so that the fact of Christ on his cross might have its full weight.

This doctrine of the cross is sheer 18 folly to those on their way to ruin, but to us who are on the way to salvation it is the power of God. Scripture says, 'I will destroy the 19 wisdom of the wise, and bring to nothing the cleverness of the clever.' Where is your wise man 20 now, your man of learning, or your subtle debater – limited, all of them, to this passing age? God has made the wisdom of this world look foolish. As God in his wisdom 21 ordained, the world failed to find him by its wisdom, and he chose to save those who have faith by the folly of the Gospel. Jews call for 22 miracles, Greeks look for wisdom; but we proclaim Christ – yes, 23 Christ nailed to the cross; and though this is a stumbling-block to Jews and folly to Greeks, yet to 24 those who have heard his call, Jews and Greeks alike, he is the power of God and the wisdom of God.

Divine folly is wiser than the 25 wisdom of man, and divine weakness stronger than man's strength.

26 My brothers, think what sort of people you are, whom God has called. Few of you are men of wisdom, by any human standard; few 27 are powerful or highly born. Yet, to shame the wise, God has chosen what the world counts folly, and to shame what is strong, God has chosen what the world counts 28 weakness. He has chosen things low and contemptible, mere nothings, to overthrow the existing 29 order. And so there is no place for human pride in the presence of 30 God. You are in Christ Jesus by God's act, for God has made him our wisdom; he is our righteousness; in him we are consecrated 31 and set free. And so (in the words of Scripture), 'If a man must boast, let him boast of the Lord.'

2 As for me, brothers, when I came to you, I declared the attested truth of God[a] without display of 2 fine words or wisdom. I resolved that while I was with you I would think of nothing but Jesus Christ – 3 Christ nailed to the cross. I came before you weak, nervous, and 4 shaking with fear. The word I spoke, the gospel I proclaimed, did not sway you with subtle arguments; it carried conviction by 5 spiritual power, so that your faith might be built not upon human wisdom but upon the power of God.

6 And yet I do speak words of wisdom to those who are ripe for it, not a wisdom belonging to this passing age, nor to any of its governing powers, which are declining to 7 their end; I speak God's hidden wisdom, his secret purpose framed from the very beginning to bring 8 us to our full glory. The powers that rule the world have never known it; if they had, they would not have crucified the Lord of 9 glory. But, in the words of Scripture, 'Things beyond our seeing, things beyond our hearing, things beyond our imagining, all prepared by God for those who love him', these it is that God has revealed to 10 us through the Spirit.

For the Spirit explores everything, even the depths of God's own nature. Among men, who 11 knows what a man is but the man's own spirit within him? In the same way, only the Spirit of God knows what God is. This is the Spirit that 12 we have received from God, and not the spirit of the world, so that we may know all that God of his own grace has given us; and, be- 13 cause we are interpreting spiritual truths to those who have the Spirit, we speak of these gifts of God in words found for us not by our human wisdom but by the Spirit. A man who is unspiritual refuses 14 what belongs to the Spirit of God; it is folly to him; he cannot grasp it, because it needs to be judged in the light of the Spirit. A man gifted 15 with the Spirit can judge the worth of everything, but is not himself subject to judgement by his fellowmen. For (in the words of Scrip- 16 ture) 'who knows the mind of the Lord? Who can advise him?' We, however, possess the mind of Christ.

3 FOR my part, my brothers, I could not speak to you as I should speak to people who have the Spirit. I had to deal with you on the merely natural plane, as infants in Christ. And so I gave you 2 milk to drink, instead of solid food, for which you were not yet ready. Indeed, you are still not ready for it, for you are still on the merely 3 natural plane. Can you not see that while there is jealousy and strife among you, you are living on the purely human level of your lower nature? When one says, 'I am 4 Paul's man', and another, 'I am for Apollos', are you not all too human?

After all, what is Apollos? What 5 is Paul? We are simply God's

[a] *Some witnesses read* I declared God's secret purpose...

agents in bringing you to the faith. Each of us performed the task which the Lord allotted to him: I planted the seed, and Apollos watered it; but God made it grow. Thus it is not the gardeners with their planting and watering who count, but God, who makes it grow. Whether they plant or water, they work as a team,[a] though each will get his own pay for his own labour. We are God's fellow-workers;[b] and you are God's garden.

Or again, you are God's building. I am like a skilled master-builder who by God's grace laid the foundation, and someone else is putting up the building. Let each take care how he builds. There can be no other foundation beyond that which is already laid; I mean Jesus Christ himself. If anyone builds on that foundation with gold, silver, and fine stone, or with wood, hay, and straw, the work that each man does will at last be brought to light; the day of judgement will expose it. For that day dawns in fire, and the fire will test the worth of each man's work. If a man's building stands, he will be rewarded; if it burns, he will have to bear the loss; and yet he will escape with his life, as one might from a fire. Surely you know that you are God's temple, where the Spirit of God dwells. Anyone who destroys God's temple will himself be destroyed[c] by God, because the temple of God is holy; and that temple you are.

Make no mistake about this: if there is anyone among you who fancies himself wise – wise, I mean, by the standards of this passing age – he must become a fool to gain true wisdom. For the wisdom of this world is folly in God's sight. Scripture says, 'He traps the wise in their own cunning', and again, 'The Lord knows that the argu-

ments of the wise are futile.' So never make mere men a cause for pride. For though everything belongs to you – Paul, Apollos, and Cephas, the world, life, and death, the present and the future, all of them belong to you – yet you belong to Christ, and Christ to God.

We must be regarded as Christ's subordinates and as stewards of the secrets of God. Well then, stewards are expected to show themselves trustworthy. For my part, if I am called to account by you or by any human court of judgement, it does not matter to me in the least. Why, I do not even pass judgement on myself, for I have nothing on my conscience; but that does not mean I stand acquitted. My judge is the Lord. So pass no premature judgement; wait until the Lord comes. For he will bring to light what darkness hides, and disclose men's inward motives; then will be the time for each to receive from God such praise as he deserves.

Into this general picture, my friends, I have brought Apollos and myself on your account, so that you may take our case as an example, and learn to 'keep within the rules', as they say, and may not be inflated with pride as you patronize one and flout the other. Who makes you, my friend, so important? What do you possess that was not given you? If then you really received it all as a gift, why take the credit to yourself?

All of you, no doubt, have everything you could desire. You have come into your fortune already. You have come into your kingdom – and left us out. How I wish you had indeed won your kingdom; then you might share it with us! For it seems to me God has made us apostles the most abject of mankind. We are like men condemned to death in the arena, a

---

[a] *Or* Whether they plant or water, it is all the same.   [b] *Or* We are fellow-workers in God's service.   [c] *Some witnesses read* is himself destroyed.

spectacle to the whole universe –
10 angels as well as men. We are fools
for Christ's sake, while you are
such sensible Christians. We are
weak; you are so powerful. We are
11 in disgrace; you are honoured. To
this day we go hungry and thirsty
and in rags; we are roughly
handled; we wander from place to
12 place; we wear ourselves out working with our own hands. They
curse us, and we bless; they per-
13 secute us, and we submit to it; they
slander us, and we humbly make
our appeal. We are treated as the
scum of the earth, the dregs of
humanity, to this very day.

14 I am not writing thus to shame
you, but to bring you to reason; for
15 you are my dear children. You may
have ten thousand tutors in Christ,
but you have only one father. For
in Christ Jesus you are my offspring, and mine alone, through
16 the preaching of the Gospel. I
appeal to you therefore to follow
17 my example. That is the very
reason why I have sent Timothy,
who is a dear son to me and a most
trustworthy Christian; he will remind you of the way of life in
Christ which I follow, and which I
teach everywhere in all our con-
18 gregations. There are certain persons who are filled with self-
importance because they think I
19 am not coming to Corinth. I shall
come very soon, if the Lord will;
and then I shall take the measure
of these self-important people, not
by what they say, but by what
20 power is in them. The kingdom of
God is not a matter of talk, but of
21 power. Choose, then: am I to come
to you with a rod in my hand, or in
love and a gentle spirit?

5 I ACTUALLY hear reports of sexual
immorality among you, immorality such as even pagans do not
tolerate: the union of a man with
2 his father's wife. And you can still
be proud of yourselves! You ought
to have gone into mourning; a

man who has done such a deed
should have been rooted out of
your company. For my part, 3
though I am absent in body, I am
present in spirit, and my judgement upon the man who did this
thing is already given, as if I were
indeed present: you all being as- 4
sembled in the name of our Lord
Jesus, and I with you in spirit,
with the power of our Lord Jesus
over us, this man is to be consigned 5
to Satan for the destruction of the
body, so that his spirit may be
saved on the Day of the Lord.

Your self-satisfaction ill be- 6
comes you. Have you never heard
the saying, 'A little leaven leavens
all the dough'? The old leaven of 7
corruption is working among you.
Purge it out, and then you will be
bread of a new baking. As Christians you are unleavened Passover
bread; for indeed our Passover has
begun; the sacrifice is offered –
Christ himself. So we who ob- 8
serve the festival must not use the
old leaven, the leaven of corruption and wickedness, but only
the unleavened bread which is
sincerity and truth.

In my letter I wrote that you 9
must have nothing to do with loose
livers. I was not, of course, refer- 10
ring to pagans who lead loose lives
or are grabbers and swindlers or
idolaters. To avoid them you
would have to get out of the world
altogether. I now write that you 11
must have nothing to do with any
so-called Christian who leads a
loose life, or is grasping, or idolatrous, a slanderer, a drunkard, or
a swindler. You should not even
eat with any such person. What 12
business of mine is it to judge
outsiders? God is their judge. You 13
are judges within the fellowship.
Root out the evil-doer from your
community.

IF one of your number has a dis- 6
pute with another, has he the face
to take it to pagan law-courts

instead of to the community of God's people? 2 It is God's people who are to judge the world; surely you know that. And if the world is to come before you for judgement, are you incompetent to deal with these 3 trifling cases? Are you not aware that we are to judge angels? How much more, mere matters of 4 business! If therefore you have such business disputes, how can you entrust jurisdiction to outsiders, men who count for nothing 5 in our community? I write this to shame you. Can it be that there is not a single wise man among you able to give a decision in a brother- 6 Christian's cause? Must brother go to law with brother – and before 7 unbelievers? Indeed, you already fall below your standard in going to law with one another at all. Why not rather suffer injury? Why not 8 rather let yourself be robbed? So far from this, you actually injure and rob – injure and rob your bro- 9 thers! Surely you know that the unjust will never come into possession of the kingdom of God. Make no mistake: no fornicator or idolater, none who are guilty either of adultery or of homosexual perver- 10 sion, no thieves or grabbers or drunkards or slanderers or swindlers, will possess the kingdom of 11 God. Such were some of you. But you have been through the purifying waters; you have been dedicated to God and justified through the name of the Lord Jesus and the Spirit of our God.

12 'I am free to do anything', you say. Yes, but not everything is for my good. No doubt I am free to do anything, but I for one will not let 13 anything make free with me. 'Food is for the belly and the belly for food', you say. True; and one day God will put an end to both. But it is not true that the body is for lust; it is for the Lord – and the Lord for 14 the body. God not only raised our Lord from the dead; he will also raise us by his power. Do you not 15 know that your bodies are limbs and organs of Christ? Shall I then take from Christ his bodily parts and make them over to a harlot? Never! You surely know that any- 16 one who links himself with a harlot becomes physically one with her (for Scripture says, 'The pair shall become one flesh'); but he who 17 links himself with Christ is one with him, spiritually. Shun forni- 18 cation. Every other sin that a man can commit is outside the body; but the fornicator sins against his own body. Do you not know that 19 your body is a shrine of the indwelling Holy Spirit, and the Spirit is God's gift to you? You do not belong to yourselves; you were 20 bought at a price. Then honour God in your body.

The Christian in a pagan society

AND now for the matters you 7 wrote about.

It is a good thing for a man to have nothing to do with women;[a] 2 but because there is so much immorality, let each man have his own wife and each woman her own husband. The husband must give 3 the wife what is due to her, and the wife equally must give the husband his due. The wife cannot 4 claim her body as her own; it is her husband's. Equally, the husband cannot claim his body as his own; it is his wife's. Do not deny your- 5 selves to one another, except when you agree upon a temporary abstinence in order to devote yourselves to prayer; afterwards you may come together again; otherwise, for lack of self-control, you may be tempted by Satan.

All this I say by way of con- 6 cession, not command. I should 7 like you all to be as I am myself; but everyone has the gift God has granted him, one this gift and another that.

---

[a] *Or* You say, 'It is a good thing...women';...

8   To the unmarried and to widows I say this: it is a good thing if they 9 stay as I am myself; but if they cannot control themselves, they should marry. Better be married than burn with vain desire.

10   To the married I give this ruling, which is not mine but the Lord's: a wife must not separate herself 11 from her husband; if she does, she must either remain unmarried or be reconciled to her husband; and the husband must not divorce his wife.

12   To the rest I say this, as my own word, not as the Lord's: if a Christian has a heathen wife, and she is willing to live with him, he must 13 not divorce her; and a woman who has a heathen husband willing to live with her must not divorce her 14 husband. For the heathen husband now belongs to God through his Christian wife, and the heathen wife through her Christian husband. Otherwise your children would not belong to God, whereas 15 in fact they do. If on the other hand the heathen partner wishes for a separation, let him have it. In such cases the Christian husband or wife is under no compulsion; but God's call is a call to live in peace. 16 Think of it: as a wife you may be your husband's salvation; as a husband you may be your wife's salvation.

17   However that may be, each one must order his life according to the gift the Lord has granted him and his condition when God called him. That is what I teach in all our 18 congregations. Was a man called with the marks of circumcision on him? Let him not remove them. Was he uncircumcised when he was called? Let him not be circum-19 cised. Circumcision or uncircumcision is neither here nor there; what matters is to keep God's 20 commands. Every man should remain in the condition in which he

was called. Were you a slave when 21 you were called? Do not let that trouble you; but if a chance of liberty should come, take it.[a] For 22 the man who as a slave received the call to be a Christian is the Lord's freedman, and, equally, the free man who received the call is a slave in the service of Christ. You 23 were bought at a price; do not become slaves of men. Thus each one, 24 my friends, is to remain before God in the condition in which he received his call.

On the question of celibacy, I 25 have no instructions from the Lord, but I give my judgement as one who by God's mercy is fit to be trusted.

It is my opinion, then, that in a 26 time of stress like the present this is the best way for a man to live – it is best for a man to be as he is. Are 27 you bound in marriage? Do not seek a dissolution. Has your marriage been dissolved? Do not seek a wife. If, however, you do marry, 28 there is nothing wrong in it; and if a virgin marries, she has done no wrong. But those who marry will have pain and grief in this bodily life, and my aim is to spare you.

What I mean, my friends, is this. 29 The time we live in will not last long. While it lasts, married men should be as if they had no wives; mourners should be as if they had 30 nothing to grieve them, the joyful as if they did not rejoice; buyers must not count on keeping what they buy, nor those who use the 31 world's wealth on using it to the full. For the whole frame of this world is passing away.

I want you to be free from 32 anxious care. The unmarried man cares for the Lord's business; his aim is to please the Lord. But the 33 married man cares for worldly things; his aim is to please his wife; and he has a divided mind. The 34

[a] *Or* but even if a chance of liberty should come, choose rather to make good use of your servitude.

unmarried or celibate woman cares[a] for the Lord's business; her aim is to be dedicated to him in body as in spirit; but the married woman cares for worldly things; her aim is to please her husband.

35 In saying this I have no wish to keep you on a tight rein. I am thinking simply of your own good, of what is seemly, and of your freedom to wait upon the Lord without distraction.

36 But if a man has a partner in celibacy[b] and feels that he is not behaving properly towards her, if, that is, his instincts are too strong for him,[c] and something must be done, he may do as he pleases; there is nothing wrong in it; let 37 them marry.[d] But if a man is steadfast in his purpose, being under no compulsion, and has complete control of his own choice; and if he has decided in his own mind to preserve his partner[e] in 38 her virginity, he will do well. Thus, he who marries his partner[f] does well, and he who does not will do better.

39 A wife is bound to her husband as long as he lives. But if the husband die, she is free to marry whom she will, provided the marriage is 40 within the Lord's fellowship. But she is better off as she is; that is my opinion, and I believe that I too have the Spirit of God.

8 Now about food consecrated to heathen deities.

Of course we all 'have knowledge', as you say. This 'knowledge' breeds conceit; it is love that 2 builds. If anyone fancies that he knows, he knows nothing yet, in 3 the true sense of knowing. But if a man loves,[g] he is acknowledged by God.[h]

Well then, about eating this 4 consecrated food: of course, as you say, 'a false god has no existence in the real world. There is no god but one.' For indeed, if there be so- 5 called gods, whether in heaven or on earth – as indeed there are many 'gods' and many 'lords' – yet for us there is one God, the 6 Father, from whom all being comes, towards whom we move; and there is one Lord, Jesus Christ, through whom all things came to be, and we through him.

But not everyone knows this. 7 There are some who have been so accustomed to idolatry[i] that even now they eat this food with a sense of its heathen consecration, and their conscience, being weak, is polluted by the eating. Certainly 8 food will not bring us into God's presence: if we do not eat, we are none the worse, and if we eat, we are none the better. But be careful 9 that this liberty of yours does not become a pitfall for the weak. If a 10 weak character sees you sitting down to a meal in a heathen temple – you, who 'have knowledge' – will not his conscience be emboldened to eat food consecrated to the heathen deity? This 11 'knowledge' of yours is utter disaster to the weak, the brother for whom Christ died. In thus sinning 12 against your brothers and wounding their conscience,[j] you sin against Christ. And therefore, if 13 food be the downfall of my brother, I will never eat meat any more, for I will not be the cause of my brother's downfall.

9 Am I not a free man? Am I not an apostle? Did I not see Jesus our Lord? Are not you my own handiwork, in the Lord? If others do not 2

---

[a] *Some witnesses read* . . . his wife. And there is a difference between the wife and the virgin. The unmarried woman cares . . .   [b] *Or a virgin daughter (or ward)*.
[c] *Or if she is ripe for marriage.*   [d] *Or let the girl and her lover marry.*
[e] *Or his daughter.*   [f] *Or gives his daughter in marriage.*
[g] *Some witnesses read* loves God.   [h] *Or he is recognized.*
[i] *Some witnesses read* in whom the consciousness of the false god is so persistent . . .
[j] *Some witnesses insert* weak as it is.

accept me as an apostle, you at least are bound to do so, for you are yourselves the very seal of my apostleship, in the Lord.

3 To those who put me in the dock 4 this is my answer: Have I no right 5 to eat and drink? Have I no right to take a Christian wife about with me, like the rest of the apostles and the Lord's brothers, and Cephas? 6 Or are Barnabas and I alone bound 7 to work for our living? Did you ever hear of a man serving in the army at his own expense? or planting a vineyard without eating the fruit of it? or tending a flock 8 without using its milk? Do not suppose I rely on these human analogies, for the law says the 9 same; in the Law of Moses we read, 'You shall not muzzle a threshing ox.' Do you suppose 10 God's concern is with oxen? Or is the reference clearly to ourselves? Of course it refers to us, in the sense that the ploughman should plough and the thresher thresh in the hope 11 of getting some of the produce. If we have sown a spiritual crop for you, is it too much to expect from 12 you a material harvest? If you allow others these rights, have not we a stronger claim?

But I have availed myself of no such right. On the contrary, I put up with all that comes my way rather than offer any hindrance to 13 the gospel of Christ. You know (do you not?) that those who perform the temple service eat the temple offerings, and those who wait upon the altar claim their share of the 14 sacrifice. In the same way the Lord gave instructions that those who preach the Gospel should earn 15 their living by the Gospel. But I have never taken advantage of any such right, nor do I intend to claim it in this letter. I had rather die! No one shall make my boast an empty 16 boast. Even if I preach the Gospel, I can claim no credit for it; I can-

not help myself; it would be misery to me not to preach. If I did it of 17 my own choice, I should be earning my pay; but since I do it apart from my own choice, I am simply discharging a trust.[a] Then what is 18 my pay? The satisfaction of preaching the Gospel without expense to anyone; in other words, of waiving the rights which my preaching gives me.

I am a free man and own no 19 master; but I have made myself every man's servant, to win over as many as possible. To Jews I be- 20 came like a Jew, to win Jews; as they are subject to the Law of Moses, I put myself under that law to win them, although I am not myself subject to it. To win Gen- 21 tiles, who are outside the Law, I made myself like one of them, although I am not in truth outside God's law, being under the law of Christ. To the weak I became weak, 22 to win the weak. Indeed, I have become everything in turn to men of every sort, so that in one way or another I may save some. All this 23 I do for the sake of the Gospel, to bear my part in proclaiming it.

You know (do you not?) that at 24 the sports all the runners run the race, though only one wins the prize. Like them, run to win! But 25 every athlete goes into strict training. They do it to win a fading wreath; we, a wreath that never fades. For my part, I run with a 26 clear goal before me; I am like a boxer who does not beat the air; I 27 bruise my own body and make it know its master, for fear that after preaching to others I should find myself rejected.

You should understand, my 10 brothers, that our ancestors were all under the pillar of cloud, and all of them passed through the Red Sea; and so they all received bap- 2 tism into the fellowship of Moses in cloud and sea. They all ate the 3

---

[a] *Or* If I do it willingly I am earning my pay; if I did it unwillingly I should still have a trust laid upon me.

4 same supernatural food, and all drank the same supernatural drink; I mean, they all drank from the supernatural rock that accompanied their travels – and that

5 rock was Christ. And yet, most of them were not accepted by God, for the desert was strewn with their corpses.

6 These events happened as symbols to warn us not to set our desires on evil things, as they did.

7 Do not be idolaters, like some of them; as Scripture has it, 'the people sat down to feast and rose

8 up to revel'. Let us not commit fornication, as some of them did – and twenty-three thousand died in

9 one day. Let us not put the power of the Lord[a] to the test, as some of them did – and were destroyed by

10 serpents. Do not grumble against God, as some of them did – and were destroyed by the Destroyer.

11 All these things that happened to them were symbolic, and were recorded for our benefit as a warning. For upon us the fulfilment of

12 the ages has come. If you feel sure that you are standing firm, be-

13 ware! You may fall. So far you have faced no trial beyond what man can bear. God keeps faith, and he will not allow you to be tested above your powers, but when the test comes he will at the same time provide a way out, by enabling you to sustain it.

14 So then, dear friends, shun idol-

15 atry. I speak to you as men of sense. Form your own judgement

16 on what I say. When we bless 'the cup of blessing', is it not a means of sharing in the blood of Christ? When we break the bread, is it not a means of sharing in the body of

17 Christ? Because there is one loaf, we, many as we are, are one body;[b] for it is one loaf of which we all partake.

18 Look at the Jewish people. Are not those who partake in the sacrificial meal sharers in the altar? What do I imply by this? that an 19 idol is anything but an idol? or food offered to it anything more than food? No; but the sacrifices 20 the heathen offer are offered (in the words of Scripture) 'to demons and to that which is not God'; and I will not have you become partners with demons. You cannot drink 21 the cup of the Lord and the cup of demons. You cannot partake of the Lord's table and the table of demons. Can we defy the Lord? Are 22 we stronger than he?

'We are free to do anything', you 23 say. Yes, but is everything good for us? 'We are free to do anything', but does everything help the building of the community? Each of you 24 must regard, not his own interests, but the other man's.

You may eat anything sold in the 25 meat-market without raising questions of conscience; for the earth is 26 the Lord's and everything in it.

If an unbeliever invites you to a 27 meal and you care to go, eat whatever is put before you, without raising questions of conscience. But if somebody says to you, 'This 28 food has been offered in sacrifice', then, out of consideration for him, and for conscience' sake, do not eat it – not your conscience, I mean, 29 but the other man's.

'What?' you say, 'is my freedom to be called in question by another man's conscience? If I partake 30 with thankfulness, why am I blamed for eating food over which I have said grace?' Well, whether you eat 31 or drink, or whatever you are doing, do all for the honour of God: give 32 no offence to Jews, or Greeks, or to the church of God. For my part 33 I always try to meet everyone halfway, regarding not my own good but the good of the many, so that they may be saved. Follow my ex- 11 ample as I follow Christ's.

---

[a] *Some witnesses read* of Christ.
[b] *Or* For we, many as we are, are one loaf, one body.

2 I COMMEND you for always keeping me in mind, and maintaining the tradition I handed on to you.
3 But I wish you to understand that, while every man has Christ for his Head, woman's head is man,[a] as
4 Christ's Head is God. A man who keeps his head covered when he prays or prophesies brings shame
5 on his head; a woman, on the contrary, brings shame on her head if she prays or prophesies bareheaded; it is as bad as if her head
6 were shaved. If a woman is not to wear a veil she might as well have her hair cut off; but if it is a disgrace for her to be cropped and shaved, then she should wear a
7 veil. A man has no need to cover his head, because man is the image of God, and the mirror of his glory, whereas woman reflects the glory
8 of man.[b] For man did not originally spring from woman, but woman
9 was made out of man; and man was not created for woman's sake, but woman for the sake of man;
10 and therefore it is woman's duty to have a sign of authority[c] on her head, out of regard for the angels.[d]
11 And yet, in Christ's fellowship woman is as essential to man as
12 man to woman. If woman was made out of man, it is through woman that man now comes to be; and God is the source of all.
13 Judge for yourselves: is it fitting for a woman to pray to God bare-
14 headed? Does not Nature herself teach you that while flowing locks
15 disgrace a man, they are a woman's glory? For her locks were given for covering.
16 However, if you insist on arguing, let me tell you, there is no such custom among us, or in any of the congregations of God's people.
17 In giving you these injunctions I must mention a practice which I cannot commend: your meetings tend to do more harm than good.

To begin with, I am told that when 18 you meet as a congregation you fall into sharply divided groups; and I believe there is some truth in it (for dissensions are necessary if 19 only to show which of your members are sound). The result is that 20 when you meet as a congregation, it is impossible for you to eat the Lord's Supper, because each of you 21 is in such a hurry to eat his own, and while one goes hungry another has too much to drink. Have 22 you no homes of your own to eat and drink in? Or are you so contemptuous of the church of God that you shame its poorer members? What am I to say? Can I commend you? On this point, certainly not!

For the tradition which I hand- 23 ed on to you came to me from the Lord himself: that the Lord Jesus, on the night of his arrest, took bread and, after giving thanks to 24 God, broke it and said: 'This is my body, which is for you; do this as a memorial of me.' In the same way, 25 he took the cup after supper, and said: 'This cup is the new covenant sealed by my blood. Whenever you drink it, do this as a memorial of me.' For every time you eat this 26 bread and drink the cup, you proclaim the death of the Lord, until he comes.

It follows that anyone who eats 27 the bread or drinks the cup of the Lord unworthily will be guilty of desecrating the body and blood of the Lord. A man must test himself 28 before eating his share of the bread and drinking from the cup. For he 29 who eats and drinks eats and drinks judgement on himself if he does not discern the Body. That is 30 why many of you are feeble and sick, and a number have died. But 31 if we examined ourselves, we should not thus fall under judgement. When, however, we do fall 32

---

[a] Or a woman's head is her husband. [b] Or a woman reflects her husband's glory. [c] Some witnesses read to have a veil. [d] Or and therefore a woman should keep her dignity on her head, for fear of the angels.

under the Lord's judgement, he is disciplining us, to save us from being condemned with the rest of the world.

33 Therefore, my brothers, when you meet for a meal, wait for one 34 another. If you are hungry, eat at home, so that in meeting together you may not fall under judgement. The other matters I will arrange when I come.

Spiritual gifts

12 ABOUT gifts of the Spirit, there are some things of which I do not wish you to remain ignorant.

2 You know how, in the days when you were still pagan, you were swept off to those dumb heathen gods, however you hap-3 pened to be led.[a] For this reason I must impress upon you that no one who says 'A curse on Jesus!' can be speaking under the influence of the Spirit of God. And no one can say 'Jesus is Lord!' except under the influence of the Holy Spirit.

4 There are varieties of gifts, but 5 the same Spirit. There are varieties of service, but the same Lord. 6 There are many forms of work, but all of them, in all men, are the 7 work of the same God. In each of us the Spirit is manifested in one particular way, for some useful pur-8 pose. One man, through the Spirit, has the gift of wise speech, while another, by the power of the same Spirit, can put the deepest know-9 ledge into words. Another, by the same Spirit, is granted faith; another, by the one Spirit, gifts of 10 healing, and another miraculous powers; another has the gift of prophecy, and another ability to distinguish true spirits from false; yet another has the gift of ecstatic utterance of different kinds, and another the ability to interpret it. 11 But all these gifts are the work of one and the same Spirit, distribut-ing them separately to each individual at will.

12 For Christ is like a single body with its many limbs and organs, which, many as they are, together make up one body. For indeed we 13 were all brought into one body by baptism, in the one Spirit, whether we are Jews or Greeks, whether slaves or free men, and that one Holy Spirit was poured out for all of us to drink.

14 A body is not one single organ, but many. Suppose the foot should 15 say, 'Because I am not a hand, I do not belong to the body', it does belong to the body none the less. Suppose the ear were to say, 'Be-16 cause I am not an eye, I do not belong to the body', it does still belong to the body. If the body were 17 all eye, how could it hear? If the body were all ear, how could it smell? But, in fact, God appointed 18 each limb and organ to its own place in the body, as he chose. If 19 the whole were one single organ, there would not be a body at all; in 20 fact, however, there are many different organs, but one body. The eye cannot say to the hand, 'I 21 do not need you'; nor the head to the feet, 'I do not need you.' Quite the contrary: those organs 22 of the body which seem to be more frail than others are indispensable, and those parts of the body which 23 we regard as less honourable are treated with special honour. To our unseemly parts is given a more than ordinary seemliness, whereas 24 our seemly parts need no adorning. But God has combined the various parts of the body, giving special honour to the humbler parts, so 25 that there might be no sense of division in the body, but that all its organs might feel the same concern for one another. If one organ 26 suffers, they all suffer together. If one flourishes, they all rejoice together.

[a] Or ...pagan, you would be seized by some power which drove you to those dumb heathen gods.

27 Now you are Christ's body, and each of you a limb or organ of it.
28 Within our community God has appointed, in the first place apostles, in the second place prophets, thirdly teachers; then miracle-workers, then those who have gifts of healing, or ability to help others or power to guide them, or the gift of ecstatic utterance of various kinds.
29 Are all apostles? all prophets? all teachers? Do all work
30 miracles? Have all gifts of healing? Do all speak in tongues of ecstasy?
31 Can all interpret them? The higher gifts are those you should aim at.
  And now I will show you the best way of all.

13 I may speak in tongues of men or of angels, but if I am without love, I am a sounding gong or a clanging
2 cymbal. I may have the gift of prophecy, and know every hidden truth; I may have faith strong enough to move mountains; but if
3 I have no love, I am nothing. I may dole out all I possess, or even give my body to be burnt,[a] but if I have no love, I am none the better.
4 Love is patient; love is kind and envies no one. Love is never boast-
5 ful, nor conceited, nor rude; never selfish, not quick to take offence.
6 Love keeps no score of wrongs; does not gloat over other men's sins, but
7 delights in the truth. There is nothing love cannot face; there is no limit to its faith, its hope, and its endurance.
8 Love will never come to an end. Are there prophets? their work will be over. Are there tongues of ecstasy? they will cease. Is there knowledge? it will vanish away;
9 for our knowledge and our pro-
10 phecy alike are partial, and the partial vanishes when wholeness
11 comes. When I was a child, my speech, my outlook, and my thoughts were all childish. When I grew up, I had finished with child-
12 ish things. Now we see only puzzling reflections in a mirror, but

then we shall see face to face. My knowledge now is partial; then it will be whole, like God's knowledge of me. In a word, there are 13 three things that last for ever: faith, hope, and love; but the greatest of them all is love.

  Put love first; but there are 14 other gifts of the Spirit at which you should aim also, and above all prophecy. When a man is using the 2 language of ecstasy he is talking with God, not with men, for no man understands him; he is no doubt inspired, but he speaks mysteries. On the other hand, 3 when a man prophesies, he is talking to men, and his words have power to build; they stimulate and they encourage. The language of 4 ecstasy is good for the speaker himself, but it is prophecy that builds up a Christian community. I 5 should be pleased for you all to use the tongues of ecstasy, but better pleased for you to prophesy. The prophet is worth more than the man of ecstatic speech – unless indeed he can explain its meaning, and so help to build up the community. Suppose, my friends, that 6 when I come to you I use ecstatic language: what good shall I do you, unless what I say contains something by way of revelation, or enlightenment, or prophecy, or instruction?

  Even with inanimate things 7 that produce sounds – a flute, say, or a lyre – unless their notes mark definite intervals, how can you tell what tune is being played? Or 8 again, if the trumpet-call is not clear, who will prepare for battle? In the same way if your ecstatic 9 utterance yields no precise meaning, how can anyone tell what you are saying? You will be talking into the air. How many different kinds 10 of sound there are, or may be, in the world! Nothing is altogether soundless. Well then, if I do not 11 know the meaning of the sound the

---

[a] *Some witnesses read* even seek glory by self-sacrifice.

speaker makes, his words will be gibberish to me, and mine to him.

12 You are, I know, eager for gifts of the Spirit; then aspire above all to excel in those which build up the church.

13 I say, then, that the man who falls into ecstatic utterance should

14 pray for the ability to interpret. If I use such language in my prayer, the Spirit in me prays, but my

15 intellect lies fallow. What then? I will pray as I am inspired to pray, but I will also pray intelligently. I will sing hymns as I am inspired to sing, but I will sing intelligently

16 too. Suppose you are praising God in the language of inspiration: how will the plain man who is present be able to say 'Amen' to your thanksgiving, when he does not

17 know what you are saying? Your prayer of thanksgiving may be all that could be desired, but it is no

18 help to the other man. Thank God, I am more gifted in ecstatic utter-

19 ance than any of you,[a] but in the congregation I would rather speak five intelligible words, for the benefit of others as well as myself, than thousands of words in the language of ecstasy.

20 Do not be childish, my friends. Be as innocent of evil as babes, but at least be grown-up in your think-

21 ing. We read in the Law: 'I will speak to this nation through men of strange tongues, and by the lips of foreigners; and even so they will

22 not heed me, says the Lord.' Clearly then these 'strange tongues' are not intended as a sign for believers, but for unbelievers, whereas prophecy is designed not for unbelievers but for those who hold

23 the faith. So if the whole congregation is assembled and all are using the 'strange tongues' of ecstasy, and some uninstructed persons or unbelievers should enter, will they

24 not think you are mad? But if all are uttering prophecies, the visitor, when he enters, hears from everyone something that searches his conscience and brings convic-

25 tion, and the secrets of his heart are laid bare. So he will fall down and worship God, crying, 'God is certainly among you!'

26 To sum up, my friends: when you meet for worship, each of you contributes a hymn, some instruction, a revelation, an ecstatic utterance, or the interpretation of such an utterance. All of these must aim at one thing: to build up the church. If it is a matter of

27 ecstatic utterance, only two should speak, or at most three, one at a time, and someone must interpret.

28 If there is no interpreter, the speaker had better not address the meeting at all, but speak to himself and to God. Of the prophets,

29 two or three may speak, while the rest exercise their judgement upon

30 what is said. If someone else, sitting in his place, receives a revela-

31 tion, let the first speaker stop. You can all prophesy, one at a time, so that the whole congregation may receive instruction and encourage-

32 ment. It is for prophets to control

33 prophetic inspiration, for the God who inspires them is not a God of disorder but of peace.

34 As in all congregations of God's people, women[b] should not address the meeting. They have no licence to speak, but should keep their

35 place as the law directs. If there is something they want to know, they can ask their own husbands at home. It is a shocking thing that a woman should address the congregation.

36 Did the word of God originate with you? Or are you the only

37 people to whom it came? If anyone claims to be inspired or a prophet, let him recognize that what I write

38 has the Lord's authority. If he

[a] *Or . . . man.* I say the thanksgiving; I use ecstatic speech more than any of you.

[b] *Or of peace, as in all communities of God's people.* Women . . .

does not acknowledge this, God does not acknowledge him.[a]

39 In short, my friends, be eager to prophesy; do not forbid ecstatic 40 utterance; but let all be done decently and in order.

Life after death

15 AND now, my brothers, I must remind you of the gospel that I preached to you; the gospel which you received, on which you have 2 taken your stand, and which is now bringing you salvation. Do you still hold fast the Gospel as I preached it to you? If not, your conversion was in vain.[b]

3 First and foremost, I handed on to you the facts which had been imparted to me: that Christ died for our sins, in accordance with the 4 scriptures; that he was buried; that he was raised to life on the third day, according to the scrip- 5 tures; and that he appeared to Cephas, and afterwards to the 6 Twelve. Then he appeared to over five hundred of our brothers at once, most of whom are still alive, 7 though some have died. Then he appeared to James, and afterwards to all the apostles.

8 In the end he appeared even to me. It was like an abnormal birth; 9 I had persecuted the church of God and am therefore inferior to all other apostles – indeed not fit 10 to be called an apostle. However, by God's grace I am what I am, nor has his grace been given to me in vain; on the contrary, in my labours I have outdone them all – not I, indeed, but the grace of God 11 working with me. But what matter, I or they? This is what we all proclaim, and this is what you believed.

12 Now if this is what we proclaim, that Christ was raised from the dead, how can some of you say there is no resurrection of the dead? If there be no resurrection, 13 then Christ was not raised; and if 14 Christ was not raised, then our gospel is null and void, and so is your faith; and we turn out to be 15 lying witnesses for God, because we bore witness that he raised Christ to life, whereas, if the dead are not raised, he did not raise him. For if the dead are not raised, it 16 follows that Christ was not raised; and if Christ was not raised, your 17 faith has nothing in it and you are still in your old state of sin. It 18 follows also that those who have died within Christ's fellowship are utterly lost. If it is for this life only 19 that Christ has given us hope,[c] we of all men are most to be pitied.

But the truth is, Christ was 20 raised to life – the firstfruits of the harvest of the dead. For since it 21 was a man who brought death into the world, a man also brought resurrection of the dead. As in 22 Adam all men die, so in Christ all will be brought to life; but each in 23 his own proper place: Christ the firstfruits, and afterwards, at his coming, those who belong to Christ. Then comes the end, when 24 he delivers up the kingdom to God the Father, after abolishing every kind of domination, authority, and power. For he is destined to reign 25 until God has put all enemies under his feet; and the last enemy to be 26 abolished is death.[d] Scripture says, 27 'He has put all things in subjection under his feet.' But in saying 'all things', it clearly means to exclude God who subordinates them; and when all things are thus sub- 28 ject to him, then the Son himself will also be made subordinate to God who made all things subject

---

[a] *Some witnesses read* If he refuses to recognize this, let him refuse!
[b] *Or* Do you remember the terms in which I preached the Gospel to you? – for I assume you did not accept it thoughtlessly.   [c] *Or* If it is only an uncertain hope that our life in Christ has given us...   [d] *Or* Then at the end, when...power (for he...feet), the last enemy, death, will be abolished.

to him, and thus God will be all in all.

29 Again, there are those who receive baptism on behalf of the dead. Why should they do this? If the dead are not raised to life at all, what do they mean by being baptized on their behalf?

30 And we ourselves – why do we face these dangers hour by hour?

31 Every day I die: I swear it by my pride in you, my brothers – for in Christ Jesus our Lord I am proud

32 of you. If, as the saying is, I 'fought wild beasts' at Ephesus, what have I gained by it?[a] If the dead are never raised to life, 'let us eat and drink, for tomorrow we die'.

33 Make no mistake: 'Bad company is the ruin of a good charac-

34 ter.' Come back to a sober and upright life and leave your sinful ways. There are some who know nothing of God; to your shame I say it.

35 But, you may ask, how are the dead raised? In what kind of body?

36 How foolish! The seed you sow does not come to life unless it has

37 first died; and what you sow is not the body that shall be, but a naked grain, perhaps of wheat, or of some

38 other kind; and God clothes it with the body of his choice, each seed with its own particular body.

39 All flesh is not the same flesh: there is flesh of men, flesh of beasts, of birds, and of fishes – all differ-

40 ent. There are heavenly bodies and earthly bodies; and the splendour of the heavenly bodies is one thing, the splendour of the earthly, an-

41 other. The sun has a splendour of its own, the moon another splendour, and the stars another, for star differs from star in brightness.

42 So it is with the resurrection of the dead. What is sown in the earth as a perishable thing is raised im-

43 perishable. Sown in humiliation, it is raised in glory; sown in weakness, it is raised in power; sown as 44 an animal body, it is raised as a spiritual body.

If there is such a thing as an animal body, there is also a spiritual body. It is in this sense that 45 Scripture says, 'The first man, Adam, became an animate being', whereas the last Adam has become a life-giving spirit. Observe, the 46 spiritual does not come first; the animal body comes first, and then the spiritual. The first man was 47 made 'of the dust of the earth': the second man is from heaven. The 48 man made of dust is the pattern of all men of dust, and the heavenly man is the pattern of all the heavenly. As we have worn the like- 49 ness of the man made of dust, so we shall wear the likeness of the heavenly man.

What I mean, my brothers, is 50 this: flesh and blood can never possess the kingdom of God, and the perishable cannot possess immortality. Listen! I will unfold a 51 mystery: we shall not all die, but we shall all be changed in a flash, in 52 the twinkling of an eye, at the last trumpet-call. For the trumpet will sound, and the dead will rise immortal, and we shall be changed. This perishable being must be 53 clothed with the imperishable, and what is mortal must be clothed with immortality. And when[b] our 54 mortality has been clothed with immortality, then the saying of Scripture will come true: 'Death is swallowed up; victory is won!' 'O 55 Death, where is your victory? O Death, where is your sting?' The 56 sting of death is sin, and sin gains its power from the law; but, God be 57 praised, he gives us the victory through our Lord Jesus Christ.

Therefore, my beloved brothers, 58 stand firm and immovable, and

---

[a] *Or* If, as men do, I had fought wild beasts at Ephesus, what good would it be to me? *or* If I had been in no better case than one fighting beasts in the arena at Ephesus, what good would it be to me?　　[b] *Some witnesses insert* our perishable nature has been clothed with the imperishable, and...

work for the Lord always, work without limit, since you know that in the Lord your labour cannot be lost.

Christian giving

16 AND now about the collection in aid of God's people: you should follow my directions to our congre-
2 gations in Galatia. Every Sunday each of you is to put aside and keep by him a sum in proportion to his gains, so that there may be no
3 collecting when I come. When I arrive, I will give letters of intro-duction to persons approved by you, and send them to carry your
4 gift to Jerusalem. If it should seem worth while for me to go as well, they shall go with me.
5 I shall come to Corinth after passing through Macedonia – for I am travelling by way of Mace-
6 donia – and I may stay with you, perhaps even for the whole winter, and then you can help me on my
7 way wherever I go next. I do not want this to be a flying visit; I hope to spend some time with you, if the
8 Lord permits. But I shall remain
9 at Ephesus until Whitsuntide, for a great opportunity has opened for effective work, and there is much opposition.
10 If Timothy comes, see that you put him at his ease; for it is the Lord's work that he is engaged
11 upon, as I am myself; so no one must slight him. Send him happily on his way to join me, since I am waiting for him with our friends.

As for our friend Apollos, I urged 12 him strongly to go to Corinth with the others, but he was quite deter-mined not to go[a] at present; he will go when opportunity offers.

Be alert; stand firm in the faith; 13 be valiant and strong. Let all you 14 do be done in love.

I have a request to make of you, 15 my brothers. You know that the Stephanas family were the first converts in Achaia, and have laid themselves out to serve God's people. I wish you to give their due 16 position to such persons, and in-deed to everyone who labours hard at our common task. It is a great 17 pleasure to me that Stephanas, Fortunatus, and Achaicus have arrived, because they have done what you had no chance to do; they have relieved my mind – and 18 no doubt yours too. Such men deserve recognition.

Greetings from the congrega- 19 tions in Asia. Many greetings in the Lord from Aquila and Prisca and the congregation at their house. Greetings from all the brothers. 20 Greet one another with the kiss of peace.

This greeting is in my own 21 hand – PAUL.

If anyone does not love the 22 Lord, let him be outcast. *Marana tha* – Come, O Lord! The grace of the Lord Jesus 23 Christ be with you. My love to you all in Christ 24 Jesus. Amen.

---

[a] Or but it was by no means the will of God that he should go...

THE SECOND LETTER OF PAUL
TO THE
CORINTHIANS

Personal religion and the ministry

1 FROM Paul, apostle of Christ Jesus by God's will, and our colleague Timothy, to the congregation of God's people at Corinth, together with all who are dedicated to him throughout the whole of Achaia.

2 Grace and peace to you from God our Father and the Lord Jesus Christ.

3 Praise be to the God and Father of our Lord Jesus Christ, the all-merciful Father, the God whose 4 consolation never fails us! He comforts us in all our troubles, so that we in turn may be able to comfort others in any trouble of theirs and to share with them the consolation 5 we ourselves receive from God. As Christ's cup of suffering overflows, and we suffer with him, so also through Christ our consolation 6 overflows. If distress be our lot, it is the price we pay for your consolation, for your salvation; if our lot be consolation, it is to help us to bring you comfort, and strength to face with fortitude the same 7 sufferings we now endure. And our hope for you is firmly grounded;[a] for we know that if you have part in the suffering, you have part also in the divine consolation.

8 In saying this, we should like you to know, dear friends, how serious was the trouble that came upon us in the province of Asia. The burden of it was far too heavy for us to bear, so heavy that we even despaired of life. Indeed, we 9 felt in our hearts that we had received a death-sentence. This was meant to teach us not to place reliance on ourselves, but on God who raises the dead. From such 10 mortal peril God delivered us; and he will deliver us again,[b] he on whom our hope is fixed. Yes, he will continue to deliver us, if you 11 will co-operate by praying for us. Then, with so many people praying for our deliverance, there will be many to give thanks on our behalf for the gracious favour God has shown towards us.

There is one thing we are proud 12 of: our conscience assures us that in our dealings with our fellow-men, and above all in our dealings with you, our conduct has been governed by a devout and godly sincerity,[c] by the grace of God and not by worldly wisdom. There is 13 nothing in our letters to you but what you can read for yourselves, and understand too. Partial as 14 your present knowledge of us is, you will I hope come to understand fully that you have as much reason to be proud of us, as we of you, on the Day of our Lord Jesus.

It was because I felt so confident 15 about all this that I had intended to come first of all to you[d] and give you the benefit of a double visit: I 16 meant to visit you on my way to Macedonia, and after leaving Macedonia, to return to you, and you would then send me on my way to Judaea. That was my intention; 17

---

[a] Some witnesses give these clauses If distress...firmly grounded in different sequence.
[b] Some witnesses read and he still delivers us.
[c] Some witnesses read by sincere and godly singleness of mind.
[d] Or had originally intended to come to you...

did I lightly change my mind?[a] Or do I, when I frame my plans, frame them as a worldly man might, so that it should rest with me to say 'yes' and 'yes', or 'no' 18 and 'no'? As God is true, the language in which we address you is not an ambiguous blend of Yes and 19 No. The Son of God, Christ Jesus, proclaimed among you by us (by Silvanus and Timothy, I mean, as well as myself), was never a blend of Yes and No. With him it was, 20 and is, Yes. He is the Yes pronounced upon God's promises, every one of them. That is why, when we give glory to God, it is through Christ Jesus that we say 21 'Amen'. And if you and we belong to Christ, guaranteed as his and 22 anointed, it is all God's doing; it is God also who has set his seal upon us, and as a pledge of what is to come has given the Spirit to dwell in our hearts.

23   I appeal to God to witness what I am going to say; I stake my life upon it: it was out of consideration for you that I did not after all come 24 to Corinth. Do not think we are dictating the terms of your faith; your hold on the faith is secure enough. We are working with you 2 for your own happiness. So I made up my mind that my next visit to you must not be another painful 2 one. If I cause pain to you, who is left to cheer me up, except you, 3 whom I have offended? This is precisely the point I made in my letter: I did not want, I said, to come and be made miserable by the very people who ought to have made me happy; and I had sufficient confidence in you all to know that for me to be happy is for all of 4 you to be happy. That letter I sent you came out of great distress and anxiety; how many tears I shed as I wrote it! But I never meant to cause you pain; I wanted you rather to know the love, the more

than ordinary love, that I have for you.

Any injury that has been done, 5 has not been done to me; to some extent, not to labour the point, it has been done to you all. The pen- 6 alty on which the general meeting has agreed has met the offence well enough. Something very different 7 is called for now: you must forgive the offender and put heart into him; the man's sorrow must not be made so severe as to overwhelm him. I urge you therefore to assure 8 him of your love for him by a formal act. I wrote, I may say, to see 9 how you stood the test, whether you fully accepted my authority. But anyone who has your forgive- 10 ness has mine too; and when I speak of forgiving (so far as there is anything for me to forgive), I mean that as the representative of Christ I have forgiven him for your sake.[b] For Satan must not be 11 allowed to get the better of us; we know his wiles all too well.

Then when I came to Troas, 12 where I was to preach the gospel of Christ, and where an opening a- waited me for the Lord's work, I 13 still found no relief of mind, for my colleague Titus was not there to meet me; so I took leave of the people there and went off to Mace- donia. But thanks be to God, who 14 continually leads us about, cap- tives in Christ's triumphal pro- cession, and everywhere uses us to reveal and spread abroad the fra- grance of the knowledge of himself! We are indeed the incense offered 15 by Christ to God, both for those who are on the way to salvation, and for those who are on the way to perdition: to the latter it is a 16 deadly fume that kills, to the for- mer a vital fragrance that brings life. Who is equal to such a calling? At least we do not go hawking the 17 word of God about, as so many do; when we declare the word we

---

[a] Or In forming this intention, did I act irresponsibly?
[b] Or that I have forgiven him for your sake, in the presence of Christ.

do it in sincerity, as from God and in God's sight, as members of Christ.

3 ARE we beginning all over again to produce our credentials? Do we, like some people, need letters of introduction to you, or from you? 2 No, you are all the letter we need, a letter written on our heart; any man can see it for what it is and 3 read it for himself. And as for you, it is plain that you are a letter that has come from Christ, given to us to deliver: a letter written not with ink but with the Spirit of the living God, written not on stone tablets but on the pages of the human heart.

4 It is in full reliance upon God, through Christ, that we make such 5 claims. There is no question of our being qualified in ourselves: we cannot claim anything as our own. The qualification we have comes 6 from God; it is he who has qualified us to dispense his new covenant – a covenant expressed not in a written document, but in a spiritual bond; for the written law condemns to death, but the Spirit gives life.

7 The law, then, engraved letter by letter upon stone, dispensed death, and yet it was inaugurated with divine splendour. That splendour, though it was soon to fade, made the face of Moses so bright that the Israelites could not gaze 8 steadily at him. But if so, must not even greater splendour rest upon the divine dispensation of the 9 Spirit? If splendour accompanied the dispensation under which we are condemned, how much richer in splendour must that one be 10 under which we are acquitted! Indeed, the splendour that once was is now no splendour at all; it is outshone by a splendour greater 11 still. For if that which was soon to fade had its moment of splendour,

how much greater is the splendour of that which endures!

With such a hope as this we 12 speak out boldly; it is not for us to 13 do as Moses did: he put a veil over his face to keep the Israelites from gazing on that fading splendour until it was gone. But in any case 14 their minds had been made insensitive, for that same veil is there to this very day when the lesson is read from the old covenant; and it is never lifted, because only in Christ is the old covenant abrogated.[a] But to this very day, 15 every time the Law of Moses is read, a veil lies over the minds of the hearers. However, as Scripture 16 says of Moses, 'whenever he turns to the Lord the veil is removed'.[b] Now the Lord of whom this pass- 17 age speaks is the Spirit; and where the Spirit of the Lord is, there is liberty. And because for us there is 18 no veil over the face, we all reflect as in a mirror the splendour of the Lord; thus we are transfigured into his likeness, from splendour to splendour; such is the influence of the Lord who is Spirit.

SEEING then that we have been 4 entrusted with this commission, which we owe entirely to God's mercy, we never lose heart. We 2 have renounced the deeds that men hid for very shame; we neither practise cunning nor distort the word of God; only by declaring the truth openly do we recommend ourselves, and then it is to the common conscience of our fellow-men and in the sight of God. And if 3 indeed our gospel be found veiled, the only people who find it so are those on the way to perdition. Their unbelieving minds are so 4 blinded by the god of this passing age, that the gospel of the glory of Christ, who is the very image of God, cannot dawn upon them and bring them light. It is not our- 5

---

[a] Or in Christ is it abolished.
[b] Or as Scripture says, when one turns to the Lord the veil is removed.

selves that we proclaim; we proclaim Christ Jesus as Lord, and ourselves as your servants, for 6 Jesus' sake. For the same God who said, 'Out of darkness let light shine', has caused his light to shine within us, to give the light of revelation – the revelation of the glory of God in the face of Jesus Christ.

7   We are no better than pots of earthenware to contain this treasure, and this proves that such transcendent power does not come 8 from us, but is God's alone. Hard-pressed on every side, we are never hemmed in; bewildered, we are 9 never at our wits' end; hunted, we are never abandoned to our fate; struck down, we are not left to die. 10 Wherever we go we carry death with us in our body, the death that Jesus died, that in this body also life may reveal itself, the life 11 that Jesus lives. For continually, while still alive, we are being surrendered into the hands of death, for Jesus' sake, so that the life of Jesus also may be revealed in this 12 mortal body of ours. Thus death is at work in us, and life in you.

13   But Scripture says, 'I believed, and therefore I spoke out', and we too, in the same spirit of faith, be-14 lieve and therefore speak out; for we know that he who raised the Lord Jesus to life will with Jesus raise us too, and bring us to his 15 presence, and you with us. Indeed, it is for your sake that all things are ordered, so that, as the abounding grace of God is shared by more and more, the greater may be the chorus of thanksgiving that ascends to the glory of God.

16   No wonder we do not lose heart! Though our outward humanity is in decay, yet day by day we are 17 inwardly renewed. Our troubles are slight and short-lived; and their outcome an eternal glory 18 which outweighs them far. Meanwhile our eyes are fixed, not on the things that are seen, but on the things that are unseen: for what is seen passes away; what is unseen is eternal. For we know that if the 5 earthly frame that houses us today should be demolished, we possess a building which God has provided – a house not made by human hands, eternal, and in heaven. In this 2 present body we do indeed groan; we yearn to have our heavenly habitation put on over this one – in the hope that, being thus cloth-3 ed, we shall not find ourselves naked. We groan indeed, we who 4 are enclosed within this earthly frame; we are oppressed because we do not want to have the old body stripped off. Rather our desire is to have the new body put on over it, so that our mortal part may be absorbed into life immortal. God himself has shaped us for 5 this very end; and as a pledge of it he has given us the Spirit.

Therefore we never cease to be 6 confident. We know that so long as we are at home in the body we are exiles from the Lord; faith is our 7 guide, we do not see him.[a] We are 8 confident, I repeat, and would rather leave our home in the body and go to live with the Lord. We 9 therefore make it our ambition, wherever we are, here or there, to be acceptable to him. For we must 10 all have our lives laid open before the tribunal of Christ, where each must receive what is due to him for his conduct in the body, good or bad.

WITH this fear of the Lord before 11 our eyes we address our appeal to men. To God our lives lie open, as I hope they also lie open to you in your heart of hearts. This is not 12 another attempt to recommend ourselves to you: we are rather giving you a chance to show yourselves proud of us; then you will have something to say to those whose pride is all in outward show

---

[a] *Or* faith is our guide and not the things we see.

13 and not in inward worth. It may be we are beside ourselves, but it is for God; if we are in our right mind, 14 it is for you. For the love of Christ leaves us no choice, when once we have reached the conclusion that one man died for all and therefore 15 all mankind has died. His purpose in dying for all was that men, while still in life, should cease to live for themselves, and should live for him who for their sake died and 16 was raised to life. With us therefore worldly standards have ceased to count in our estimate of any man; even if once they counted in our understanding of Christ, they 17 do so now no longer. When anyone is united to Christ, there is a new world;[a] the old order has gone, and a new order has already begun.[b]

18 From first to last this has been the work of God. He has reconciled us men to himself through Christ, and he has enlisted us in this ser-19 vice of reconciliation. What I mean is, that God was in Christ reconciling the world to himself,[c] no longer holding men's misdeeds against them, and that he has entrusted us with the message of 20 reconciliation. We come therefore as Christ's ambassadors. It is as if God were appealing to you through us: in Christ's name, we implore 21 you, be reconciled to God! Christ was innocent of sin, and yet for our sake God made him one with the sinfulness of men,[d] so that in him we might be made one with the 6 goodness of God himself. Sharing in God's work, we urge this appeal upon you: you have received the grace of God; do not let it go for 2 nothing. God's own words are:

'In the hour of my favour I gave heed to you;
on the day of deliverance I came to your aid.'

The hour of favour has now come; now, I say, has the day of deliverance dawned.

3 In order that our service may not be brought into discredit, we avoid giving offence in anything. 4 As God's servants, we try to recommend ourselves in all circumstances by our steadfast endurance: in distress, hardships, and 5 dire straits; flogged, imprisoned, mobbed; overworked, sleepless, 6 starving. We recommend ourselves by the innocence of our behaviour, our grasp of truth, our patience and kindliness; by gifts of the Holy 7 Spirit, by sincere love, by declaring the truth, by the power of God. We wield the weapons of righteousness 8 in right hand and left. Honour and dishonour, praise and blame, are alike our lot: we are the impostors 9 who speak the truth, the unknown men whom all men know; dying we still live on; disciplined by suffering, we are not done to death; 10 in our sorrows we have always cause for joy; poor ourselves, we bring wealth to many; penniless, we own the world.

11 Men of Corinth, we have spoken very frankly to you; we have open-12 ed our heart wide to you all. On our part there is no constraint; any constraint there may be is in your-13 selves. In fair exchange then (may a father speak so to his children?) open wide your hearts to us.

Problems of church life and discipline

14 Do not unite yourselves with unbelievers; they are no fit mates for you. What has righteousness to do with wickedness? Can light con-15 sort with darkness? Can Christ agree with Belial, or a believer join 16 hands with an unbeliever? Can there be a compact between the

---

[a] *Or* a new act of creation.   [b] *Or* When anyone is united to Christ
he is a new creature: his old life is over; a new life has already begun.
[c] *Or* God was reconciling the world to himself by Christ.
[d] *Or* and yet God made him a sin-offering for us.

temple of God and the idols of the heathen? And the temple of the living God is what we are. God's own words are: 'I will live and move about among them; I will be their God, and they shall be my 17 people.' And therefore, 'come away and leave them, separate yourselves, says the Lord; touch nothing unclean. Then I will 18 accept you, says the Lord, the Ruler of all being; I will be a father to you, and you shall be my sons 7 and daughters.' Such are the promises that have been made to us, dear friends. Let us therefore cleanse ourselves from all that can defile flesh or spirit, and in the fear of God complete our consecration.

2 Do make a place for us in your hearts! We have wronged no one, ruined no one, taken advantage of 3 no one. I do not want to blame you. Why, as I have told you before, the place you have in our heart is such that, come death, come life, we 4 meet it together. I am perfectly frank with you. I have great pride in you. In all our many troubles my cup is full of consolation, and overflows with joy.

5 Even when we reached Macedonia there was still no relief for this poor body of ours; instead, there was trouble at every turn, quarrels all round us, forebodings 6 in our heart. But God, who brings comfort to the downcast, has comforted us by the arrival of Titus, 7 and not merely by his arrival, but by his being so greatly comforted about you. He has told us how you long for me, how sorry you are, and how eager to take my side; and that has made me happier still.

8 Even if I did wound you by the letter I sent, I do not now regret it. I may have been sorry for it when I saw that the letter had caused you pain, even if only for a time; 9 but now I am happy, not that your feelings were wounded but that the wound led to a change of heart. You bore the smart as God would have you bear it, and so you are no losers by what we did. For the 10 wound which is borne in God's way brings a change of heart too salutary to regret; but the hurt which is borne in the world's way brings death. You bore your hurt in God's 11 way, and see what its results have been! It made you take the matter seriously and vindicate yourselves. How angered you were, how apprehensive! How your longing for me awoke, yes, and your devotion and your eagerness to see justice done! At every point you have cleared yourselves of blame in this trouble. And so, although I did send you 12 that letter, it was not the offender or his victim that most concerned me. My aim in writing was to help to make plain to you, in the sight of God, how truly you are devoted to us. That is why we have been so 13 encouraged.

But besides being encouraged ourselves we have also been delighted beyond everything by seeing how happy Titus is: you have all helped to set his mind completely at rest. Anything I may 14 have said to him to show my pride in you has been justified. Every word we ever addressed to you bore the mark of truth; and the same holds of the proud boast we made in the presence of Titus: that also has proved true. His heart 15 warms all the more to you as he recalls how ready you all were to do what he asked, meeting him as you did in fear and trembling. How 16 happy I am now to have complete confidence in you!

WE must tell you, friends, about 8 the grace of generosity which God has imparted to*a* our congregations in Macedonia. The troubles 2 they have been through have tried them hard, yet in all this they have been so exuberantly happy that

a Or how gracious God has been to...

from the depths of their poverty they have shown themselves lav-
3 ishly open-handed. Going to the limit of their resources, as I can testify, and even beyond that
4 limit, they begged us most insistently, and on their own initiative, to be allowed to share in this generous service to their fellow-Chris-
5 tians. And their giving surpassed our expectations; for they gave their very selves, offering them in the first instance to the Lord, but
6 also, under God, to us. The upshot is that we have asked Titus, who began it all, to visit you and bring this work of generosity also to com-
7 pletion. You are so rich in everything – in faith, speech, knowledge, and zeal of every kind, as well as in the loving regard you have for us[a] – surely you should show yourselves equally lavish in
8 this generous service! This is not meant as an order; by telling you how keen others are I am putting
9 your love to the test. For you know how generous our Lord Jesus Christ has been: he was rich, yet for your sake he became poor, so that through his poverty you might become rich.
10 Here is my considered opinion on the matter. What I ask you to do is in your own interests. You made a good beginning last year both in the work you did and in your willingness to undertake it.
11 Now I want you to go on and finish it: be as eager to complete the scheme as you were to adopt it, and give according to your means.
12 Provided there is an eager desire to give, God accepts what a man has; he does not ask for what he has not.
13 There is no question of relieving others at the cost of hardship to
14 yourselves; it is a question of equality. At the moment your surplus meets their need, but one day your need may be met from their surplus. The aim is equality;

15 as Scripture has it, 'The man who got much had no more than enough, and the man who got little did not go short.'
16 I thank God that he has made Titus as keen on your behalf as we
17 are! For Titus not only welcomed our request; he is so eager that by his own desire he is now leaving to
18 come to you. With him we are sending one of our company whose reputation is high among our congregations everywhere for his ser-
19 vices to the Gospel. Moreover they have duly appointed him to travel with us and help in this beneficent work, by which we do honour to the Lord himself and show our own
20 eagerness to serve. We want to guard against any criticism of our
21 handling of this generous gift; for our aims are entirely honourable, not only in the Lord's eyes, but also in the eyes of men.

22 With these men we are sending another of our company whose enthusiasm we have had many opportunities of testing, and who is now all the more earnest because of the great confidence he has in
23 you. If there is any question about Titus, he is my partner and my associate in dealings with you; as for the others, they are delegates of our congregations, an honour to Christ.[b] Then give them clear ex-
24 pression of your love and justify our pride in you; justify it to them, and through them to the congregations.

9 About the provision of aid for God's people, it is superfluous for
2 me to write to you. I know how eager you are to help; I speak of it with pride to the Macedonians: I tell them that Achaia had everything ready last year; and most of them
3 have been fired by your zeal. My purpose in sending these friends is to ensure that what we have said about you in this matter should not prove to be an empty boast. By

---

[a] *Some witnesses read* the love we have for you, *or* the love which we have kindled in your hearts.　　　[b] *Or* they are...congregations; they reflect Christ.

that I mean, I want you to be prepared, as I told them you were; for 4 if I bring with me men from Macedonia and they find you are not prepared, what a disgrace it will be to us, let alone to you, after all the confidence we have shown! I have 5 accordingly thought it necessary to ask these friends to go on ahead to Corinth, to see that your promised bounty is in order before I come; it will then be awaiting me as a bounty indeed, and not as an extortion.

6 Remember: sparse sowing, sparse reaping; sow bountifully, and you 7 will reap bountifully. Each person should give as he has decided for himself; there should be no reluctance, no sense of compulsion; God 8 loves a cheerful giver. And it is in God's power to provide you richly with every good gift; thus you will have ample means in yourselves to meet each and every situation, with enough and to spare for every 9 good cause. Scripture says of such a man: 'He has lavished his gifts on the needy, his benevolence stands 10 fast for ever.' Now he who provides seed for sowing and bread for food will provide the seed for you to sow; he will multiply it and swell the harvest of your benevolence; 11 and you will always be rich enough to be generous. Through our action such generosity will 12 issue in thanksgiving to God, for as a piece of willing service this is not only a contribution towards the needs of God's people; more than that, it overflows in a flood of 13 thanksgiving to God. For through the proof which this affords, many will give honour to God when they see how humbly you obey him and how faithfully you confess the gospel of Christ; and will thank him for your liberal contribution to their need and to the general good. 14 And as they join in prayer on your

behalf, their hearts will go out to you because of the richness of the grace which God has imparted to you. Thanks be to God for his gift 15 beyond words!

Trials of a Christian missionary

BUT I, Paul, appeal to you by the 10 gentleness and magnanimity of Christ – I, so feeble (you say) when I am face to face with you, so brave when I am away. Spare me, 2 I beg you, the necessity of such bravery when I come, for I reckon I could put on as bold a face as you please against those who charge us with moral weakness. Weak men 3 we may be, but it is not as such that we fight our battles. The 4 weapons we wield are not merely human,[a] but divinely potent to demolish strongholds; we demolish 5 sophistries and all that rears its proud head against the knowledge of God; we compel every human thought to surrender in obedience to Christ; and we are prepared to 6 punish all rebellion when once you have put yourselves in our hands.

Look facts in the face.[b] Someone 7 is convinced, is he, that he belongs to Christ? Let him think again, and reflect that we belong to Christ as much as he does. Indeed, if I am 8 somewhat over-boastful about our authority – an authority given by the Lord to build you up, not pull you down – I shall make my boast good. So you must not think of me 9 as one who scares you by the letters he writes. 'His letters', so it is said, 10 'are weighty and powerful; but when he appears he has no presence, and as a speaker he is beneath contempt.' People who talk 11 in that way should reckon with this: when I come, my actions will show the same man as my letters showed in my absence.

We should not dare to class our- 12

---

[a] *Or* charge us with worldly standards. We live, no doubt, in the world; but it is not on that level that we fight our battles. The weapons we wield are not those of the world...   [b] *Or* You are looking only at what catches the eye.

selves or compare ourselves with any of those who put forward their own claims. What fools they are to measure themselves by themselves, to find in themselves their own standard of comparison![a]

13 With us there will be no attempt to boast beyond our proper sphere; and our sphere is determined by the limit God laid down for us, which permitted us to come as far

14 as Corinth. We are not over-stretching our commission, as we should be if it did not extend to you, for we were the first to reach Corinth in preaching the gospel of

15 Christ. And we do not boast of work done where others have laboured, work beyond our proper sphere. Our hope is rather that, as your faith grows, we may attain a position among you greater than ever before, but still within the

16 limits of our sphere. Then we can carry the Gospel to lands that lie beyond you, never priding ourselves on work already done in

17 another man's sphere. If a man must boast, let him boast of the

18 Lord. Not the man who recommends himself, but the man whom the Lord recommends – he and he alone is to be accepted.

11 I wish you would bear with me in a little of my folly; please do bear

2 with me. I am jealous for you, with a divine jealousy; for I betrothed you to Christ, thinking to present you as a chaste virgin to her true

3 and only husband. But as the serpent in his cunning seduced Eve, I am afraid that your thoughts may be corrupted and you may lose your[b] single-hearted devotion

4 to Christ. For if someone comes who proclaims another Jesus, not the Jesus whom we proclaimed, or if you then receive a spirit different from the Spirit already given to you, or a gospel different from the

gospel you have already accepted, you manage to put up with that

5 well enough. Have I in any way come short of those superlative

6 apostles? I think not. I may be no speaker, but knowledge I have; at all times we have made known to you the full truth.

7 Or was this my offence, that I made no charge for preaching the gospel of God, lowering myself to

8 help in raising you? It is true that I took toll of other congregations, accepting[c] support from them to

9 serve you. Then, while I was with you, if I ran short I sponged on no one; anything I needed was fully met by our friends who came from Macedonia; I made it a rule, as I always shall, never to be a burden

10 to you. As surely as the truth of Christ is in me, I will preserve my pride in this matter throughout Achaia, and nothing shall stop me.

11 Why? Is it that I do not love you? God knows I do.

12 And I shall go on doing as I am doing now, to cut the ground from under those who would seize any chance to put their vaunted apostleship on the same level as ours.

13 Such men are sham-apostles, crooked in all their practices, masquer-

14 ading as apostles of Christ. There is nothing surprising about that; Satan himself masquerades as an

15 angel of light. It is therefore a simple thing for his agents to masquerade as agents of good. But they will meet the end their deeds deserve.

16 I repeat: let no one take me for a fool; but if you must, then give me the privilege of a fool, and let me have my little boast like others.

17 I am not speaking here as a Christian, but like a fool, if it comes to

18 bragging. So many people brag of their earthly distinctions that I

19 shall do so too. How gladly you

---

[a] *Some witnesses read* On the contrary we measure ourselves by ourselves, by our own standard of comparison.
[b] *Some witnesses insert* purity and...
[c] *Or* Did I take toll of other congregations by accepting...?

20 bear with fools, being yourselves so wise! If a man tyrannizes over you, exploits you, gets you in his clutches, puts on airs, and hits you 21 in the face, you put up with it. And we, you say, have been weak! I admit the reproach.

But if there is to be bravado (and here I speak as a fool), I can in- 22 dulge in it too. Are they Hebrews? So am I. Israelites? So am I. Abra- 23 ham's descendants? Are they servants of Christ? I am mad to speak like this, but I can outdo them. More overworked than they, scourged more severely, more often imprisoned, many a time face to 24 face with death. Five times the Jews have given me the thirty- 25 nine strokes; three times I have been beaten with rods; once I was stoned; three times I have been shipwrecked, and for twenty-four hours I was adrift on the open sea. 26 I have been constantly on the road; I have met dangers from rivers, dangers from robbers, dangers from my fellow-countrymen, dangers from foreigners, dangers in towns, dangers in the country, dangers at sea, dangers from false 27 friends. I have toiled and drudged, I have often gone without sleep; hungry and thirsty, I have often gone fasting; and I have suffered from cold and exposure.

28 Apart from these external things,[a] there is the responsibility that weighs on me every day, my anxious concern for all our congre- 29 gations. If anyone is weak, do I not share his weakness? If anyone is made to stumble, does my heart 30 not blaze with indignation? If boasting there must be, I will boast of the things that show up my 31 weakness. The God and Father of the Lord Jesus (blessed be his name for ever!) knows that what I 32 say is true. When I was in Damas-

cus, the commissioner of King Aretas kept the city under obser- vation so as to have me arrested; and I was let down in a basket, 33 through a window in the wall, and so escaped his clutches.

I AM obliged to boast. It does no 12 good; but I shall go on to tell of visions and revelations granted by the Lord. I know a Christian man 2 who fourteen years ago (whether in the body or out of it, I do not know – God knows) was caught up as far as the third heaven. And I 3 know that this same man (whether in the body or out of it, I do not know – God knows) was caught up 4 into paradise, and heard words so secret that human lips may not repeat them. About such a man as 5 that I am ready to boast; but I will not boast on my own account, ex- cept of my weaknesses. If I should 6 choose to boast, it would not be the boast of a fool, for I should be speaking the truth. But I refrain, because I should not like anyone to form an estimate of me which goes beyond the evidence of his own eyes and ears. And so, to keep 7 me from being unduly elated by the magnificence of such revela- tions, I was given[b] a sharp physical pain[c] which came as Satan's mes- senger to bruise me; this was to save me from being unduly elated. Three times I begged the Lord to 8 rid me of it, but his answer was: 9 'My grace is all you need; power comes to its full strength in weak- ness.' I shall therefore prefer to find my joy and pride in the very things that are my weakness; and then the power of Christ will come and rest upon me. Hence I am well 10 content, for Christ's sake, with weakness, contempt, persecution, hardship, and frustration; for when I am weak, then I am strong.

[a] Or Apart from things which I omit.
[b] Some witnesses read . . . ears, and because of the magnificence of the revelations themselves. Therefore to keep me from being unduly elated I was given . . .
[c] Or a painful wound to my pride (literally a stake, or thorn, for the flesh).

11 I AM being very foolish, but it was you who drove me to it; my credentials should have come from you. In no respect did I fall short of these superlative apostles, even if I
12 am a nobody. The marks of a true apostle were there, in the work I did among you, which called for such constant fortitude, and was attended by signs, marvels, and
13 miracles. Is there anything in which you were treated worse than the other congregations – except this, that I never sponged upon you? How unfair of me! I crave forgiveness.
14 Here am I preparing to pay you a third visit; and I am not going to sponge upon you. It is you I want, not your money; parents should make provision for their children,
15 not children for their parents. As for me, I will gladly spend what I have for you – yes, and spend myself to the limit. If I love you overmuch, am I to be loved the less?
16 But, granted that I did not prove a burden to you, still I was unscrupulous enough, you say, to use a
17 trick to catch you. Who, of the men I have sent to you, was
18 used by me to defraud you? I begged Titus to visit you, and I sent our friend with him. Did Titus defraud you? Have we not both been guided by the same Spirit, and followed the same course?
19 Perhaps you think that all this time we have been addressing our defence to you. No; we are speaking in God's sight, and as Christian men. Our whole aim, my own dear
20 people, is to build you up. I fear that when I come I may perhaps find you different from what I wish you to be, and that you may find me also different from what you wish. I fear I may find quarrelling and jealousy, angry tempers and personal rivalries, backbiting and gossip, arrogance and general dis-
21 order. I am afraid that, when I come again, my God may humili-

ate me in your presence, that I may have tears to shed over many of those who have sinned in the past and have not repented of their unclean lives, their fornication and sensuality.

This will be my third visit to 13 you; and all facts must be established by the evidence of two or three witnesses. To those who have 2 sinned in the past, and to everyone else, I repeat the warning I gave before; I gave it in person on my second visit, and I give it now in absence. It is that when I come this time, I will show no leniency. Then you will have the proof you 3 seek of the Christ who speaks through me, the Christ who, far from being weak with you, makes his power felt among you. True, he 4 died on the cross in weakness, but he lives by the power of God; and we who share his weakness shall by the power of God live with him in your service.

Examine yourselves: are you 5 living the life of faith? Put yourselves to the test. Surely you recognize that Jesus Christ is among you? – unless of course you prove unequal to the test. I hope you will 6 come to see that we are not unequal to it. Our prayer to God is that you 7 may do no wrong; we are not concerned to be vindicated ourselves; we want you to do what is right, even if we should seem to be discredited. For we have no power to 8 act against the truth, but only for it. We are well content to be weak 9 at any time if only you are strong. Indeed, my whole prayer is that all may be put right with you. My 10 purpose in writing this letter before I come, is to spare myself, when I come, any sharp exercise of authority – authority which the Lord gave me for building up and not for pulling down.

And now, my friends, farewell! 11 Mend your ways; take our appeal to heart; agree with one another; live in peace; and the God of love

12 and peace will be with you. Greet one another with the kiss of peace.
13 All God's people send you greetings.

The grace of the Lord Jesus 14 Christ, and the love of God, and fellowship in the Holy Spirit, be with you all.

THE LETTER OF PAUL
TO THE
GALATIANS

Faith and freedom

1 FROM Paul, an apostle, not by human appointment or human commission, but by commission from Jesus Christ and from God the Father who raised
2 him from the dead. I and the group of friends now with me send greetings to the Christian congregations of Galatia.
3 Grace and peace to you from God the Father and our Lord Jesus
4 Christ,[a] who sacrificed himself for our sins, to rescue us out of this present age of wickedness, as our
5 God and Father willed; to whom be glory for ever and ever. Amen.
6 I am astonished to find you turning so quickly away from him who called you by grace,[b] and fol-
7 lowing a different gospel. Not that it is in fact another gospel; only there are persons who unsettle your minds by trying to distort the
8 gospel of Christ. But if anyone, if we ourselves or an angel from heaven, should preach a gospel at variance with the gospel we preached to you, he shall be held
9 outcast. I now repeat what I have said before: if anyone preaches a gospel at variance with the gospel

which you received, let him be outcast!

Does my language now sound as 10 if I were canvassing for men's support? Whose support do I want but God's alone? Do you think I am currying favour with men? If I still sought men's favour, I should be no servant of Christ.

I must make it clear to you, my 11 friends, that the gospel you heard me preach is no human invention. I did not take it over from any 12 man; no man taught it me; I received it through a revelation of Jesus Christ.

You have heard what my man- 13 ner of life was when I was still a practising Jew: how savagely I persecuted the church of God, and tried to destroy it; and how in the 14 practice of our national religion I was outstripping many of my Jewish contemporaries in my boundless devotion to the traditions of my ancestors. But then in 15 his good pleasure God, who had set me apart from birth and called me through his grace, chose to re- 16 veal his Son to me and through me, in order that I might proclaim him among the Gentiles. When that happened, without consulting any

---

[a] *Some witnesses read* God our Father and the Lord Jesus Christ.
[b] *Some witnesses read* from Christ who called you by grace, *or* from him who called you by grace of Christ.

17 human being, without going up to Jerusalem to see those who were apostles before me, I went off at once to Arabia, and afterwards returned to Damascus.

18 Three years later I did go up to Jerusalem to get to know Cephas. I stayed with him for a fortnight, 19 without seeing any other of the apostles, except*a* James the Lord's 20 brother. What I write is plain truth; before God I am not lying.

21 Next I went to the regions of 22 Syria and Cilicia, and remained unknown by sight*b* to Christ's con- 23 gregations in Judaea. They only heard it said, 'Our former persecutor is preaching the good news of the faith which once he tried to des- 24 troy'; and they praised God for me.

2 Next, fourteen years later, I went again*c* to Jerusalem with 2 Barnabas, taking Titus with us. I went up because it had been revealed by God that I should do so. I laid before them – but at a private interview with the men of repute – the gospel which I am accustomed to preach to the Gentiles, to make sure that the race I had run, and was running, should 3 not be run in vain. Yet even my companion Titus, Greek though he is, was not compelled to be circum- 4 cised. That course was urged only as a concession to certain*d* sham-Christians, interlopers who had stolen in to spy upon the liberty we enjoy in the fellowship of Christ Jesus. These men wanted to bring 5 us into bondage, but not for one moment did I yield to their dictation; I was determined that the full truth of the Gospel should be maintained for you.*e*

6 But as for the men of high repu-
tation (not that their importance matters to me: God does not recognize these personal distinctions) – these men of repute, I say, did not prolong the consultation,*f* but on 7 the contrary acknowledged that I had been entrusted with the Gospel for Gentiles as surely as Peter had been entrusted with the Gospel for Jews. For God whose action 8 made Peter an apostle to the Jews, also made me an apostle to the Gentiles.

Recognizing, then, the favour 9 thus bestowed upon me, those reputed pillars of our society, James, Cephas, and John, accepted Barnabas and myself as partners, and shook hands upon it, agreeing that we should go to the Gentiles while they went to the Jews. All they 10 asked was that we should keep their poor in mind, which was the very thing I made*g* it my business to do.

But when Cephas came to An- 11 tioch, I opposed him to his face, because he was clearly in the wrong. For until certain persons*h* 12 came from James he was taking his meals with gentile Christians; but when they*i* came he drew back and began to hold aloof, because he was afraid of the advocates of circumcision. The other Jewish Chris- 13 tians showed the same lack of principle; even Barnabas was carried away and played false like the rest. But when I saw that their 14 conduct did not square with*j* the truth of the Gospel, I said to Cephas, before the whole congregation, 'If you, a Jew born and bred, live like a Gentile, and not like a Jew, how can you insist that Gentiles must live like Jews?'

---

a Or but only.   *b* Or unknown personally.   *c* Some witnesses omit again.
d Or The question was later raised because of certain...   *e* Or, following the reading of some witnesses, Yet even...is, was under no absolute compulsion to be circumcised, but for the sake of certain...of Christ Jesus, with the intention of bringing us into bondage, I yielded to their demand for the moment, to ensure that gospel truth should not be prevented from reaching you.
f Or gave me no further instructions.   *g* Or had made, or have made.
h Some witnesses read a certain person.   *i* Some witnesses read he.
j Or I saw that they were not making progress towards...

15 We ourselves are Jews by birth,
16 not Gentiles and sinners. But we know that no man is ever justified by doing what the law demands, but only through faith in Christ Jesus; so we too have put our faith in Jesus Christ, in order that we might be justified through this faith, and not through deeds dictated by law; for by such deeds, Scripture says, no mortal man shall be justified.

17 If now, in seeking to be justified in Christ, we ourselves no less than the Gentiles turn out to be sinners against the law,[a] does that mean that Christ is an abettor of sin? No,
18 never! No, if I start building up again a system which I have pulled down, then it is that I show myself up as a transgressor of the law.
19 For through the law I died to law –
20 to live for God. I have been crucified with Christ: the life I now live is not my life, but the life which Christ lives in me; and my present bodily life is lived by faith in the Son of God, who loved me and gave
21 himself up for me. I will not nullify the grace of God; if righteousness comes by law, then Christ died for nothing.

3 You stupid Galatians! You must have been bewitched – you before whose eyes Jesus Christ was openly
2 displayed upon his cross! Answer me one question: did you receive the Spirit by keeping the law or by
3 believing the gospel message[b]? Can it be that you are so stupid? You started with the spiritual; do you now look to the material to make
4 you perfect? Have all your great experiences been in vain – if vain
5 indeed they should be? I ask then: when God gives you the Spirit and works miracles among you, why is this? Is it because you keep the law, or is it because you have faith
6 in the gospel message? Look at Abraham: he put his faith in God,

and that faith was counted to him as righteousness.

You may take it, then, that it is 7 the men of faith who are Abraham's sons. And Scripture, fore- 8 seeing that God would justify the Gentiles through faith, declared the Gospel to Abraham beforehand: 'In you all nations shall find blessing.' Thus it is the men of 9 faith who share the blessing with faithful Abraham.

On the other hand those who 10 rely on obedience to the law are under a curse; for Scripture says, 'A curse is on all who do not persevere in doing everything that is written in the Book of the Law.' It 11 is evident that no one is ever justified before God in terms of law; because we read, 'he shall gain life who is justified through faith'. Now law is not at all a matter of 12 having faith: we read, 'he who does this shall gain life by what he does'.

Christ bought us freedom from 13 the curse of the law by becoming for our sake an accursed thing; for Scripture says, 'A curse is on everyone who is hanged on a gibbet.' And the purpose of it all was that 14 the blessing of Abraham should in Jesus Christ be extended to the Gentiles, so that we might receive the promised Spirit through faith.

My brothers, let me give you an 15 illustration. Even in ordinary life, when a man's will and testament has been duly executed, no one else can set it aside or add a codicil. Now the promises were pro- 16 nounced to Abraham and to his 'issue'. It does not say 'issues' in the plural, but in the singular, 'and to your issue'; and the 'issue' intended is Christ. What I am saying 17 is this: a testament, or covenant, had already been validated by God; it cannot be invalidated, and its promises rendered ineffective, by a law made four hundred and thirty years later. If the inheritance 18

---

[a] Or no less than the Gentiles have accepted the position of sinners against the law.
[b] Or or by the message of faith, *or* or by hearing and believing.

is by legal right, then it is not by promise; but it was by promise that God bestowed it as a free gift on Abraham.

19 Then what of the law? It was added to make wrongdoing a legal offence.[a] It was a temporary measure pending the arrival of the 'issue' to whom the promise was made. It was promulgated through angels, and there was an inter-

20 mediary; but an intermediary is not needed for one party acting alone, and God is one.

21 Does the law, then, contradict the promises? No, never! If a law had been given which had power to bestow life, then indeed righteousness would have come from keep-

22 ing the law. But Scripture has declared the whole world to be prisoners in subjection to sin, so that faith in Jesus Christ may be the ground on which the promised blessing is given, and given to those who have such faith.

23 Before this faith came, we were close prisoners in the custody of law, pending the revelation of

24 faith. Thus the law was a kind of tutor in charge of us until Christ should come,[b] when we should be

25 justified through faith; and now that faith has come, the tutor's charge is at an end.

26 For through faith you are all sons of God in union with Christ

27 Jesus. Baptized into union with him, you have all put on Christ as a

28 garment. There is no such thing as Jew and Greek, slave and freeman, male and female; for you are all

29 one person in Christ Jesus. But if you thus belong to Christ, you are the 'issue' of Abraham, and so heirs by promise.

4 This is what I mean: so long as the heir is a minor, he is no better off than a slave, even though the

whole estate is his; he is under 2 guardians and trustees until the date fixed by his father. And so it 3 was with us. During our minority we were slaves to the elemental spirits of the universe,[c] but when 4 the term was completed, God sent his own Son, born of a woman, born under the law, to purchase 5 freedom for the subjects of the law, in order that we might attain the status of sons.

To prove that you are sons, God 6 has sent into our hearts the Spirit of his Son, crying, 'Abba! Father!' You are therefore no longer a slave 7 but a son, and if a son, then also by God's own act an heir.

Formerly, when you did not 8 acknowledge God, you were the slaves of beings which in their nature are no gods.[d] But now 9 that you do acknowledge God – or rather, now that he has acknowledged you – how can you turn back to the mean and beggarly spirits of the elements?[e] Why do you propose to enter their service all over again? You keep special 10 days and months and seasons and years. You make me fear that all 11 the pains I spent on you may prove to be labour lost.

PUT yourselves in my place, my 12 brothers, I beg you, for I have put myself in yours. It is not that you did me any wrong. As you know, it 13 was bodily illness that originally[f] led to my bringing you the Gospel, and you resisted any temptation 14 to show scorn or disgust at the state of my poor body;[g] you welcomed me as if I were an angel of God, as you might have welcomed Christ Jesus himself. Have you 15 forgotten how happy you thought yourselves in having me with you? I can say this for you: you would

---

[a] *Or* added because of offences.   [b] *Or* a kind of tutor to conduct us to Christ.
[c] *Or* the elements of the natural world, *or* elementary ideas belonging to this world.
[d] *Or* were slaves to 'gods' which in reality do not exist.   [e] *See note on* 4. 3.
[f] *Or* formerly, *or* on the first of my two visits.
[g] *Or* you showed neither scorn nor disgust at the trial my poor body was enduring.

have torn out your very eyes, and given them to me, had that been 16 possible! And have I now made myself your enemy by being frank with you?

17 The persons I have referred to are envious of you, but not with an honest envy:[a] what they really want is to bar the door to you so that you may come to envy[b] them. 18 It is always a fine thing to deserve an honest envy[c] – always, and not only when I am present with you, 19 dear children. For my children you are, and I am in travail with you over again until you take the shape 20 of Christ. I wish I could be with you now; then I could modify my tone;[d] as it is, I am at my wits' end about you.

21 TELL me now, you who are so anxious to be under law, will you not listen to what the Law says? 22 It is written there that Abraham had two sons, one by his slave and the other by his free-born wife. 23 The slave-woman's son was born in the course of nature, the free woman's through God's promise. 24 This is an allegory. The two women stand for two covenants. The one bearing children into slavery is the covenant that comes from Mount 25 Sinai: that is Hagar. Sinai is a mountain in Arabia and it represents the Jerusalem of today, for she and her children are in slavery. 26 But the heavenly Jerusalem is the free woman; she is our mother. 27 For Scripture says, 'Rejoice, O barren woman who never bore child; break into a shout of joy, you who never knew a mother's pangs; for the deserted wife shall have more children than she who lives with the husband.' 28 And you, my brothers, like Isaac, are children of God's pro- 29 mise. But just as in those days the natural-born son persecuted the

spiritual son, so it is today. But 30 what does Scripture say? 'Drive out the slave-woman and her son, for the son of the slave shall not share the inheritance with the free woman's son.' You see, then, my 31 brothers, we are no slave-woman's children; our mother is the free woman. Christ set us free, to be 5 free men.[e] Stand firm, then, and refuse to be tied to the yoke of slavery again.

Mark my words: I, Paul, say to 2 you that if you receive circumcision Christ will do you no good at all. Once again, you can take 3 it from me that every man who receives circumcision is under obligation to keep the entire law. When you seek to be justified by 4 way of law, your relation with Christ is completely severed: you have fallen out of the domain of God's grace. For to us, our hope of 5 attaining that righteousness which we eagerly await is the work of the Spirit through faith. If we are 6 in union with Christ Jesus circumcision makes no difference at all, nor does the want of it; the only thing that counts is faith active in love.[f]

You were running well; who was 7 it hindered you from following the truth? Whatever persuasion he 8 used, it did not come from God who is calling you; 'a little leaven', 9 remember, 'leavens all the dough'. United with you in the Lord, I am 10 confident that you will not take the wrong view; but the man who is unsettling your minds, whoever he may be, must bear God's judgement. And I, my friends, if I 11 am still advocating circumcision, why is it I am still persecuted? In that case, my preaching of the cross is a stumbling-block no more. As for these agitators, they had 12 better go the whole way and make eunuchs of themselves!

---

[a] *Or* paying court to you, but not with honest intentions.   [b] *Or* pay court to.
[c] *Or* to be honourably wooed.   [d] *Or* now, and could exchange words with you.
[e] *Or* What Christ has done is to set us free.   [f] *Or* inspired by love.

13 YOU, my friends, were called to be free men; only do not turn your freedom into licence for your lower nature, but be servants to one 14 another in love. For the whole law can be summed up in a single commandment: 'Love your neighbour 15 as yourself.' But if you go on fighting one another, tooth and nail, all you can expect is mutual destruction.

16 I mean this: if you are guided by the Spirit you will not fulfil the 17 desires of your lower nature. That nature sets its desires against the Spirit, while the Spirit fights against it. They are in conflict with one another so that what you will 18 to do you cannot do. But if you are led by the Spirit, you are not under law.

19 Anyone can see the kind of behaviour that belongs to the lower nature: fornication, impurity, and 20 indecency; idolatry and sorcery; quarrels, a contentious temper, envy, fits of rage, selfish ambitions, 21 dissensions; party intrigues, and jealousies; drinking bouts, orgies, and the like. I warn you, as I warned you before, that those who behave in such ways will never inherit the kingdom of God.

22 But the harvest of the Spirit is love, joy, peace, patience, kind-23 ness, goodness, fidelity, gentleness, and self-control. There is no law dealing with such things as these.

24 And those who belong to Christ Jesus have crucified the lower nature with its passions and desires. 25 If the Spirit is the source of our life, let the Spirit also direct our course.

26 We must not be conceited, challenging one another to rivalry, 6 jealous of one another. If a man should do something wrong, my brothers, on a sudden impulse,[a] you who are endowed with the Spirit must set him right again very gently. Look to yourself, each one of you: you may be 2 tempted too. Help one another to carry these heavy loads, and in this way you will fulfil the law of Christ.

For if a man imagines himself to 3 be somebody, when he is nothing, he is deluding himself. Each man 4 should examine his own conduct for himself; then he can measure his achievement by comparing himself with himself and not with anyone else. For everyone has his 5 own proper burden to bear.

When anyone is under instruc-6 tion in the faith, he should give his teacher a share of all good things he has.

Make no mistake about this: 7 God is not to be fooled; a man reaps what he sows. If he sows seed in the 8 field of his lower nature, he will reap from it a harvest of corruption, but if he sows in the field of the Spirit, the Spirit will bring him a harvest of eternal life. So let us 9 never tire of doing good, for if we do not slacken our efforts we shall in due time reap our harvest. Therefore, as opportunity offers, 10 let us work for the good of all, especially members of the household of the faith.

YOU see these big letters? I am 11 now writing to you in my own hand. It is all those who want to 12 make a fair outward and bodily show who are trying to force circumcision upon you; their sole object is to escape persecution for the cross of Christ. For even those 13 who do receive circumcision are not thoroughgoing observers of the law; they only want you to be circumcised in order to boast of your having submitted to that outward rite. But God forbid that I should 14 boast of anything but the cross of our Lord Jesus Christ, through which[b] the world is crucified to me and I to the world! Circumcision is 15 nothing; uncircumcision is nothing; the only thing that counts is new creation! Whoever they are 16

---

[a] Or If a man is caught doing something wrong, my brothers,...   [b] Or whom.

who take this principle for their guide, peace and mercy be upon them, and upon the whole Israel of God!

17 In future let no one make trouble for me, for I bear the marks of Jesus branded on my body.

18 The grace of our Lord Jesus Christ be with your spirit, my brothers. Amen.

THE LETTER OF PAUL
TO THE
EPHESIANS

The glory of Christ in the church

1 FROM Paul, apostle of Christ Jesus, commissioned by the will of God, to God's people at Ephesus,[a] believers incorporate in Christ Jesus.

2 Grace to you and peace from God our Father and the Lord Jesus Christ.

3 Praise be to the God and Father of our Lord Jesus Christ, who has bestowed on us in Christ every spiritual blessing in the heavenly

4 realms. In Christ he chose us before the world was founded, to be dedicated, to be without blemish

5 in his sight, to be full of love; and he[b] destined us – such was his will and pleasure – to be accepted as

6 his sons through Jesus Christ, in order that the glory of his gracious gift, so graciously bestowed on us in his Beloved, might redound to

7 his praise. For in Christ our release is secured and our sins are forgiven through the shedding of his blood. Therein lies the richness of God's

8 free grace lavished upon us, imparting full wisdom and insight.

9 He has made known to us his hidden purpose – such was his will and pleasure determined before-

10 hand in Christ – to be put into effect when the time was ripe: namely, that the universe, all in heaven and on earth, might be brought into a unity in Christ.

11 In Christ indeed we have been given our share in the heritage, as was decreed in his design whose purpose is everywhere at work.

12 For it was his will that we, who were the first to set our hope on Christ,[c] should cause his glory to

13 be praised. And you too, when you had heard the message of the truth, the good news of your salvation, and had believed it, became incorporate in Christ and received the seal of the promised Holy

14 Spirit; and that Spirit is the pledge that we shall enter upon our heritage, when God has redeemed what is his own, to his praise and glory.

15 Because of all this, now that I have heard of the faith you have in the Lord Jesus and of the love you

16 bear towards all God's people, I never cease to give thanks for you when I mention you in my prayers.

17 I pray that the God of our Lord Jesus Christ, the all-glorious Father, may give you the spiritual powers of wisdom and vision, by which there comes the knowledge

---

[a] *Some witnesses omit* at Ephesus.
[b] *Or ...sight. In his love he...*
[c] *Or who already enjoyed the hope of Christ, or whose expectation and hope are in Christ.*

18 of him. I pray that your inward eyes may be illumined, so that you may know what is the hope to which he calls you, what the wealth and glory of the share he offers you among his people in 19 their heritage, and how vast the resources of his power open to us who trust in him. They are measured by his strength and the 20 might which he exerted in Christ when he raised him from the dead, when he enthroned him at his right 21 hand in the heavenly realms, far above all government and authority, all power and dominion, and any title of sovereignty that can be named, not only in this age but in 22 the age to come. He put everything in subjection beneath his feet, and appointed him as supreme head to the church, which is 23 his body and as such holds within it the fullness of him who himself receives the entire fullness of God.*

2 TIME was when you were dead in 2 your sins and wickedness, when you followed the evil ways of this present age, when you obeyed the commander of the spiritual powers of the air, the spirit now at work 3 among God's rebel subjects. We too were once of their number: we all lived our lives in sensuality, and obeyed the promptings of our own instincts and notions. In our natural condition we, like the rest, lay under the dreadful judgement of 4 God. But God, rich in mercy, for 5 the great love he bore us, brought us to life with Christ even when we were dead in our sins; it is by his 6 grace you are saved. And in union with Christ Jesus he raised us up and enthroned us with him in the 7 heavenly realms, so that he might display in the ages to come how immense are the resources of his

grace, and how great his kindness to us in Christ Jesus. For it is by 8 his grace you are saved, through trusting him; it is not your own doing. It is God's gift, not a re- 9 ward for work done. There is nothing for anyone to boast of. For 10 we are God's handiwork, created in Christ Jesus to devote ourselves to the good deeds for which God has designed us.

Remember then your former 11 condition: you, Gentiles as you are outwardly,* you, 'the uncircumcised' so called by those who are called 'the circumcised' (but only with reference to an outward rite) – you were at that time separ- 12 ate from Christ, strangers to the community of Israel, outside God's covenants and the promise that goes with them. Your world was a world without hope and without God. But now in union with Christ 13 Jesus you who once were far off have been brought near through the shedding of Christ's blood. For 14 he is himself our peace. Gentiles and Jews, he has made the two one, and in his own body of flesh and blood has broken down the enmity which stood like a dividing wall between them; for he annulled the 15 law with its rules and regulations, so as to create out of the two a single new humanity in himself, thereby making peace. This was his pur- 16 pose, to reconcile the two in a single body to God through the cross, on which he killed the enmity.*

So he came and proclaimed the 17 good news: peace to you who were far off, and peace to those who were near by; for through him we both 18 alike have access to the Father in the one Spirit. Thus you are no 19 longer aliens in a foreign land, but fellow-citizens with God's people,

---

a Or *as supreme head to the church, which is his body and as such holds within it the fullness of him who fills the universe in all its parts; or as supreme head to the church which is his body, and to be all that he himself is who fills the universe in all its parts.*   *b* Or *by birth.*
c Or *...cross. Thus in his own person he put the enmity to death.*

20 members of God's household. You are built upon the foundation laid by the apostles and prophets, and Christ Jesus himself is the founda-
21 tion-stone.[a] In him the whole building[b] is bonded together and grows into a holy temple in the
22 Lord. In him you too are being built with all the rest into a spiritual dwelling for God.

3 WITH this in mind I make my prayer, I, Paul, who in the cause of you Gentiles am now the prisoner
2 of Christ Jesus – for surely you have heard how God has assigned the gift of his grace to me for your
3 benefit. It was by a revelation that his secret was made known to me. I have already written a brief ac-
4 count of this, and by reading it you may perceive that I understand
5 the secret of Christ. In former generations this was not disclosed to the human race; but now it has been revealed by inspiration to his dedicated apostles and prophets,
6 that through the Gospel the Gentiles are joint heirs with the Jews, part of the same body, sharers together in the promise made in
7 Christ Jesus. Such is the gospel of which I was made a minister, by God's gift, bestowed unmerited on
8 me in the working of his power. To me, who am less than the least of all God's people, he has granted of his grace the privilege of proclaiming to the Gentiles the good news of the unfathomable riches of
9 Christ, and of bringing to light how this hidden purpose was to be put into effect. It was hidden for long ages in God the creator of the uni-
10 verse, in order that now, through the church, the wisdom of God in all its varied forms might be made known to the rulers and authorities
11 in the realms of heaven. This is in accord with his age-long purpose, which he achieved in Christ Jesus our Lord. In him we have access to
12 God with freedom, in the confidence born of trust in him. I beg
13 you, then, not to lose heart over my sufferings for you; indeed, they are your glory.

With this in mind, then, I kneel
14 in prayer to the Father, from whom
15 every family[c] in heaven and on earth takes its name, that out of
16 the treasures of his glory he may grant you strength and power through his Spirit in your inner being, that through faith Christ
17 may dwell in your hearts in love. With deep roots and firm foundations, may you be strong to
18 grasp, with all God's people, what is the breadth and length and height and depth of the love of
19 Christ, and to know it, though it is beyond knowledge. So may you attain to fullness of being, the fullness of God himself.[d]

Now to him who is able to do
20 immeasurably more than all we can ask or conceive, by the power which is at work among us, to him
21 be glory in the church and in Christ Jesus from generation to generation evermore! Amen.

I ENTREAT you, then – I, a pris-
4 oner for the Lord's sake: as God has called you, live up to your calling. Be humble always and
2 gentle, and patient too. Be forbearing with one another and charitable. Spare no effort to make
3 fast with bonds of peace the unity which the Spirit gives. There is one
4 body and one Spirit, as there is also one hope held out in God's call to you; one Lord, one faith, one
5 baptism; one God and Father of
6 all, who is over all and through all and in all.

[a] Or built upon the foundation of the apostles and prophets, and Christ Jesus himself is the keystone.
[b] Or every structure.
[c] Or his whole family.
[d] Or the fullness which God requires.

7 But each of us has been given his gift, his due portion of Christ's
8 bounty. Therefore Scripture says:

'He ascended into the heights
with captives in his train;
he gave gifts to men.'

9 Now, the word 'ascended' implies that he also descended to the lowest level, down to the very
10 earth.[a] He who descended is no other than he who ascended far above all heavens, so that he might
11 fill the universe. And these were his gifts: some to be apostles, some prophets, some evangelists, some
12 pastors and teachers, to equip God's people for work in his service, to the building up of the body
13 of Christ. So shall we all at last attain to the unity inherent in our faith and our knowledge of the Son of God – to mature manhood, measured by nothing less than the full
14 stature of Christ. We are no longer to be children, tossed by the waves and whirled about by every fresh gust of teaching, dupes of crafty rogues and their deceitful schemes.
15 No, let us speak the truth in love; so shall we fully grow up into
16 Christ. He is the head, and on him the whole body depends. Bonded and knit together by every constituent joint, the whole frame grows through the due activity of each part, and builds itself up in love.
17 This then is my word to you, and I urge it upon you in the Lord's name. Give up living like pagans with their good-for-nothing
18 notions. Their wits are beclouded, they are strangers to the life that is in God, because ignorance prevails among them and their minds
19 have grown hard as stone. Dead to all feeling, they have abandoned themselves to vice, and stop at nothing to satisfy their foul de-
20 sires. But that is not how you
21 learned Christ. For were you not

told of him, were you not as Christians taught the truth as it is in Jesus? – that, leaving your former 22 way of life, you must lay aside that old human nature which, deluded by its lusts, is sinking towards death. You must be made new in 23 mind and spirit, and put on the 24 new nature of God's creating, which shows itself in the just and devout life called for by the truth.
Then throw off falsehood; speak 25 the truth to each other, for all of us are the parts of one body.
If you are angry, do not let anger 26 lead you into sin; do not let sunset find you still nursing it; leave no 27 loop-hole for the devil.
The thief must give up stealing, 28 and instead work hard and honestly with his own hands, so that he may have something to share with the needy.
No bad language must pass your 29 lips, but only what is good and helpful to the occasion, so that it brings a blessing to those who hear it. And do not grieve the Holy 30 Spirit of God, for that Spirit is the seal with which you were marked for the day of our final liberation. Have done with spite and passion, 31 all angry shouting and cursing, and bad feeling of every kind.
Be generous to one another, 32 tender-hearted, forgiving one another as God in Christ forgave you.
In a word, as God's dear children, 5 try to be like him, and live in love 2 as Christ loved you, and gave himself up on your behalf as an offering and sacrifice whose fragrance is pleasing to God.
Fornication and indecency of 3 any kind, or ruthless greed, must not be so much as mentioned among you, as befits the people of God. No coarse, stupid, or flippant 4 talk; these things are out of place; you should rather be thanking God. For be very sure of this: no 5 one given to fornication or indecency, or the greed which makes

***

[a] Or descended to the regions beneath the earth.

an idol of gain, has any share in the kingdom of Christ and of God.

6 Let no one deceive you with shallow arguments; it is for all these things that God's dreadful judgement is coming upon his 7 rebel subjects. Have no part or lot 8 with them. For though you were once all darkness, now as Christians you are light. Live like men 9 who are at home in daylight, for where light is, there all goodness springs up, all justice and truth. 10 Try to find out what would please 11 the Lord; take no part in the barren deeds of darkness, but show 12 them up for what they are. The things they do in secret it would be 13 shameful even to mention. But everything, when once the light has shown it up, is illumined, and everything thus illumined is all 14 light. And so the hymn says:

'Awake, sleeper,
rise from the dead,
and Christ will shine upon you.'

15 Be most careful then how you conduct yourselves: like sensible 16 men, not like simpletons. Use the present opportunity to the full, for 17 these are evil days. So do not be fools, but try to understand what 18 the will of the Lord is. Do not give way to drunkenness and the dissipation that goes with it, but let 19 the Holy Spirit fill you: speak to one another in psalms, hymns, and[a] songs; sing and make music in 20 your hearts to the Lord; and in the name of our Lord Jesus Christ give thanks every day for everything to our God and Father.

21 Be subject to one another out of reverence for Christ.

22 Wives, be subject to your hus-
23 bands as to the Lord; for the man is the head of the woman, just as Christ also is the head of the church. Christ is, indeed, the 24 Saviour of the body; but just as the church is subject to Christ, so

must women be to their husbands in everything.

Husbands, love your wives, as 25 Christ also loved the church and gave himself up for it, to conse- 26 crate it, cleansing it by water and word, so that he might present the 27 church to himself all glorious, with no stain or wrinkle or anything of the sort, but holy and without blemish. In the same way men also 28 are bound to love their wives, as they love their own bodies. In loving his wife a man loves himself. For no one ever hated his own 29 body: on the contrary, he provides and cares for it; and that is how Christ treats the church, because it 30 is his body, of which we are living parts. Thus it is that (in the words 31 of Scripture) 'a man shall leave his father and mother and shall be joined to his wife, and the two shall become one flesh'. It is a great 32 truth that is hidden here. I for my part refer it to Christ and to the church, but it applies also indivi- 33 dually: each of you must love his wife as his very self; and the woman must see to it that she pays her husband all respect.

Children, obey your parents, for 6 it is right that you should. 'Honour 2 your father and mother' is the first commandment with a promise attached, in the words: 'that it may 3 be well with you and that you may live long in the land'.

You fathers, again, must not 4 goad your children to resentment, but give them the instruction, and the correction, which belong to a Christian upbringing.

Slaves, obey your earthly mas- 5 ters with fear and trembling, single-mindedly, as serving Christ. Do not offer merely the outward 6 show of service, to curry favour with men, but, as slaves of Christ, do whole-heartedly the will of God. Give the cheerful service of those 7 who serve the Lord, not men. For 8 you know that whatever good each

[a] *Some witnesses insert* spiritual, *as in Colossians 3. 16*

man may do, slave or free, will be repaid him by the Lord.

9 You masters, also, must do the same by them. Give up using threats; remember you both have the same Master in heaven, and he has no favourites.

10 Finally then, find your strength in the Lord, in his mighty power.

11 Put on all the armour which God provides, so that you may be able to stand firm against the devices

12 of the devil. For our fight is not against human foes, but against cosmic powers, against the authorities and potentates of this dark world, against the superhuman forces of evil in the heavens.

13 Therefore, take up God's armour; then you will be able to stand your ground when things are at their worst, to complete every task and

14 still to stand. Stand firm, I say. Fasten on the belt of truth; for

15 coat of mail put on integrity; let the shoes on your feet be the gospel of peace, to give you firm footing;

16 and, with all these, take up the great shield of faith, with which you will be able to quench all the flaming arrows of the evil one.

Take salvation for helmet; for 17 sword, take that which the Spirit gives you – the words that come from God. Give yourselves wholly 18 to prayer and entreaty; pray on every occasion in the power of the Spirit. To this end keep watch and persevere, always interceding for all God's people; and pray for me, 19 that I may be granted the right words when I open my mouth, and may boldly and freely make known his hidden purpose, for which I am 20 an ambassador – in chains. Pray that I may speak of it boldly, as it is my duty to speak.

You will want to know about my 21 affairs, and how I am; Tychicus will give you all the news. He is our dear brother and trustworthy helper in the Lord's work. I am 22 sending him to you on purpose to let you know all about us, and to put fresh heart into you.

Peace to the brotherhood and 23 love, with faith, from God the Father and the Lord Jesus Christ. God's grace be with all who love 24 our Lord Jesus Christ, grace and immortality.[a]

THE LETTER OF PAUL
TO THE
PHILIPPIANS

The apostle and his friends

1 FROM Paul and Timothy, servants of Christ Jesus, to all those of God's people, incorporate in Christ Jesus, who live at Philippi, including their bishops and deacons.

2 Grace to you and peace from

God our Father and the Lord Jesus Christ.

I thank my God whenever I 3 think of you; and when I pray for 4 you all, my prayers are always joyful, because of the part you 5 have taken in the work of the Gospel from the first day until now. Of one thing I am certain: the One 6

---

a *Or who love. . .Christ with love imperishable.*

who started the good work in you will bring it to completion by the
7 Day of Christ Jesus. It is indeed only right that I should feel like this about you all, because you hold me in such affection, and because, when I lie in prison or appear in the dock to vouch for the truth of the Gospel, you all share in the privilege that is mine.[a]
8 God knows how I long for you all, with the deep yearning of Christ
9 Jesus himself. And this is my prayer, that your love may grow ever richer and richer in knowledge
10 and insight of every kind, and may thus bring you the gift of true discrimination.[b] Then on the Day of Christ you will be flawless and
11 without blame, reaping the full harvest of righteousness that comes through Jesus Christ, to the glory and praise of God.
12 Friends, I want you to understand that the work of the Gospel has been helped on, rather than hindered, by this business of
13 mine. My imprisonment in Christ's cause has become common knowledge to all at headquarters[c] here, and indeed among the public at
14 large; and it has given confidence to most of our fellow-Christians to speak the word of God fearlessly and with extraordinary courage.
15 Some, indeed, proclaim Christ in a jealous and quarrelsome spirit; others proclaim him in true good-
16 will, and these are moved by love for me; they know that it is to defend the Gospel that I am where
17 I am. But the others, moved by personal rivalry, present Christ from mixed motives, meaning to stir up fresh trouble for me as I lie
18 in prison.[d] What does it matter? One way or another, in pretence or sincerity, Christ is set forth, and for that I rejoice.

Yes, and rejoice I will, knowing 19 well that the issue of it all will be my deliverance, because you are praying for me and the Spirit of Jesus Christ is given me for support.[e] For, as I passionately hope, 20 I shall have no cause to be ashamed, but shall speak so boldly that now as always the greatness of Christ will shine out clearly in my person, whether through my life or through my death. For to me life is Christ, 21 and death gain; but what if my 22 living on in the body may serve some good purpose? Which then am I to choose? I cannot tell. I am 23 torn two ways: what I should like is to depart and be with Christ; that is better by far; but for your 24 sake there is greater need for me to stay on in the body. This indeed 25 I know for certain: I shall stay, and stand by you all to help you forward and to add joy to your faith, so 26 that when I am with you again, your pride in me may be unbounded in Christ Jesus.

Only, let your conduct be worthy 27 of the gospel of Christ, so that whether I come and see you for myself or hear about you from a distance, I may know that you are standing firm, one in spirit, one in mind, contending as one man for the gospel faith, meeting your 28 opponents without so much as a tremor. This is a sure sign to them that their doom is sealed, but a sign of your salvation, and one afforded by God himself; for you 29 have been granted the privilege not only of believing in Christ but also of suffering for him. You and 30 I are engaged in the same contest; you saw me in it once, and, as you hear, I am in it still.

---

[a] *Or* I am justified in taking this view about you all, because I hold you in closest union, as those who, when I lie...of the Gospel, all share in the privilege that is mine.   [b] *Or* may teach you by experience what things are most worth while.
[c] *Or* to all the imperial guard, *or* to all at the Residency (*Greek* Praetorium).
[d] *Or* meaning to make use of my imprisonment to stir up fresh trouble.
[e] *Or* supplies me with all I need.

2 IF then our common life in Christ yields anything to stir the heart, any loving consolation, any sharing of the Spirit, any warmth of 2 affection or compassion, fill up my cup of happiness by thinking and feeling alike, with the same love for one another, the same turn of mind, and a common care for unity. 3 There must be no room for rivalry and personal vanity among you, but you must humbly reckon others 4 better than yourselves. Look to each other's interest and not merely to your own.

5 Let your bearing towards one another arise out of your life in 6 Christ Jesus.[a] For the divine nature was his from the first; yet he did not think to snatch at equality 7 with God,[b] but made himself nothing, assuming the nature of a slave. Bearing the human likeness, 8 revealed in human shape, he humbled himself, and in obedience accepted even death – death on a 9 cross. Therefore God raised him to the heights and bestowed on him the name above all names, 10 that at the name of Jesus every knee should bow – in heaven, on 11 earth, and in the depths – and every tongue confess, 'Jesus Christ is Lord', to the glory of God the Father.

12 So you too, my friends, must be obedient, as always; even more, now that I am away, than when I was with you. You must work out your own salvation in fear and 13 trembling; for it is God who works in you, inspiring both the will and the deed, for his own chosen purpose.

14 Do all you have to do without 15 complaint or wrangling. Show yourselves guileless and above reproach, faultless children of God in a warped and crooked generation, in which you shine[c] like stars in a dark world[d] and proffer the 16 word of life.[e] Thus you will be my pride on the Day of Christ, proof that I did not run my race in vain, or work in vain. But if my life- 17 blood is to crown that sacrifice which is the offering up of your faith, I am glad of it, and I share my gladness with you all. Rejoice, 18 you no less than I, and let us share our joy.

I HOPE (under the Lord Jesus) to 19 send Timothy to you soon; it will cheer me to hear news of you. There is no one else here who sees 20 things as I do, and takes[f] a genuine interest in your concerns; they are 21 all bent on their own ends, not on the cause of Christ Jesus. But 22 Timothy's record is known to you: you know that he has been at my side in the service of the Gospel like a son working under his father. Timothy, then, I hope to send as 23 soon as ever I can see how things are going with me; and I am con- 24 fident, under the Lord, that I shall myself be coming before long.

I feel also I must send our 25 brother Epaphroditus, my fellow-worker and comrade, whom you commissioned to minister to my needs. He has been missing all of 26 you sadly, and has been distressed that you heard he was ill. (He was 27 indeed dangerously ill, but God was merciful to him, and merciful no less to me, to spare me sorrow upon sorrow.) For this reason I am 28 all the more eager to send him, to give you the happiness of seeing him again, and to relieve my sorrow. Welcome him then in the 29 fellowship of the Lord with whole-hearted delight. You should honour men like him; in Christ's cause he 30 came near to death, risking his life to render me the service you could not give.

---

[a] Or Have that bearing towards one another which was also found in Christ Jesus. [b] Or yet he did not prize his equality with God. [c] Or ...generation. Shine out among them... [d] Or in the firmament. [e] Or as the very principle of its life. [f] Or no one else here like him, who takes...

3 And now, friends, farewell; I wish you joy in the Lord.

To repeat what I have written to you before is no trouble to me, and
2 it is a safeguard for you. Beware of those dogs and their malpractices. Beware of those who insist on mutilation – 'circumcision' I will
3 not call it; we are the circumcised, we whose worship is spiritual,[a] whose pride is in Christ Jesus, and who put no confidence in anything
4 external. Not that I am without grounds myself even for confidence of that kind. If anyone thinks to base his claims on externals, I could make a stronger case for
5 myself: circumcised on my eighth day, Israelite by race, of the tribe of Benjamin, a Hebrew born and bred;[b] in my attitude to the law,
6 a Pharisee; in pious zeal, a persecutor of the church; in legal recti-
7 tude, faultless. But all such assets I have written off because of
8 Christ. I would say more: I count everything sheer loss, because all is far outweighed by the gain of knowing Christ Jesus my Lord, for whose sake I did in fact lose everything. I count it so much garbage,[c] for the sake of gaining
9 Christ and finding myself incorporate in him, with no righteousness of my own, no legal rectitude, but the righteousness which comes[d] from faith in Christ, given by God
10 in response to faith. All I care for is to know Christ, to experience the power of his resurrection, and to share his sufferings, in growing
11 conformity with his death, if only I may finally arrive at the resurrection from the dead.
12 It is not to be thought that I have already achieved all this. I have not yet reached perfection, but I press on, hoping to take hold

of that for which Christ once took hold of me. My friends, I do not 13 reckon myself to have got hold of it yet. All I can say is this: forgetting what is behind me, and reaching out for that which lies ahead, I press towards the goal to win the 14 prize which is God's call to the life above, in Christ Jesus.

Let us then keep to this way of 15 thinking, those of us who are mature. If there is any point on which you think differently, this also God will make plain to you. Only let our conduct be consistent 16 with the level we have already reached.

Agree together, my friends, to 17 follow my example. You have us for a model; watch those whose way of life conforms to it. For, as 18 I have often told you, and now tell you with tears in my eyes, there are many whose way of life makes them enemies of the cross of Christ. They are heading for 19 destruction, appetite is their god, and they glory in their shame. Their minds are set on earthly things. We, by contrast, are citi- 20 zens of heaven, and from heaven we expect our deliverer to come, the Lord Jesus Christ. He will 21 transfigure the body belonging to our humble state, and give it a form like that of his own resplendent body, by the very power which enables him to make all things subject to himself. Therefore, my 4 friends, beloved friends whom I long for, my joy, my crown, stand thus firm in the Lord, my beloved!

I beg Euodia, and I beg Syn- 2 tyche, to agree together in the Lord's fellowship. Yes, and you 3 too, my loyal comrade, I ask you to help these women, who shared my struggles in the cause of the Gospel, with Clement and my other

---

[a] *Some witness read* who worship God in the spirit; *others read* who worship by the Spirit of God.
[b] *Or* a Hebrew-speaking Jew of a Hebrew-speaking family.　　　　[c] *Or* dung.
[d] *Or* and in him finding that, though I have no righteousness of my own, no legal rectitude, I have the righteousness which comes...

fellow-workers, whose[a] names are in the roll of the living.

4 Farewell; I wish you all joy in the Lord. I will say it again: all joy be yours.

5 Let your magnanimity be manifest to all.

6 The Lord is near; have no anxiety, but in everything make your requests known to God in prayer and petition with thanksgiving.

7 Then the peace of God, which is beyond our utmost understanding,[b] will keep guard over your hearts and your thoughts, in Christ Jesus.

8 And now, my friends, all that is true, all that is noble, all that is just and pure, all that is lovable and gracious,[c] whatever is excellent and admirable – fill all your thoughts with these things.

9 The lessons I taught you, the tradition I have passed on, all that you heard me say or saw me do, put into practice; and the God of peace will be with you.

10 IT is a great joy to me, in the Lord, that after so long your care for me has now blossomed afresh. You did care about me before for that matter; it was opportunity that you

11 lacked. Not that I am alluding to want, for I have learned to find resources in myself whatever my cir-

12 cumstances. I know what it is to be brought low, and I know what it is to have plenty. I have been very thoroughly initiated into the human lot with all its ups and downs – fullness and hunger, plenty and want. I have strength for anything 13 through him who gives me power. But it was kind of you to share 14 the burden of my troubles.

As you know yourselves, Philip- 15 pians, in the early days of my mission, when I set out from Macedonia, you alone of all our congregations were my partners in payments and receipts; for even 16 at Thessalonica you contributed to my needs, not once but twice over. Do not think I set my heart 17 upon the gift; all I care for is the profit accruing to you. However, 18 here I give you my receipt for everything – for more than everything; I am paid in full, now that I have received from Epaphroditus what you sent. It is a fragrant offering, an acceptable sacrifice, pleasing to God. And my God will 19 supply all your wants out of the magnificence of his riches in Christ Jesus. To our God and Father be 20 glory for endless ages! Amen.

Give my greetings, in the fellow- 21 ship of Christ Jesus, to each one of God's people. The brothers who are now with me send their greetings to you, and so do all God's 22 people here, particularly those who belong to the imperial establishment.

The grace of our Lord Jesus 23 Christ be with your spirit.

---

[a] *Some witnesses read* my fellow-workers, and the others whose...
[b] *Or* of far more worth than human reasoning.   [c] *Or* of good repute.

THE LETTER OF PAUL

TO THE

COLOSSIANS

The centre of Christian belief

1 FROM Paul, apostle of Christ Jesus commissioned by the will of God, and our colleague
2 Timothy, to God's people at Colossae, brothers in the faith, incorporate in Christ.

Grace to you and peace from God our Father.

3 In all our prayers to God, the Father of our Lord Jesus Christ, we
4 thank him for you, because we have heard of the faith you hold in Christ Jesus, and the love you bear towards all God's people.
5 Both spring from the hope stored up for you in heaven – that hope of which you learned when the
6 message of the true Gospel first came to you. In the same way it is coming to men the whole world over; everywhere it is growing and bearing fruit as it does among you, and has done since the day when you heard of the graciousness of God and recognized it for what in
7 truth it is. You were taught this by Epaphras, our dear fellow-servant, a trusted worker for
8 Christ on our[a] behalf, and it is he who has brought us the news of your God-given love.[b]

9 For this reason, ever since the day we heard of it, we have not ceased to pray for you. We ask God that you may receive from him all wisdom and spiritual understanding for full insight into his
10 will, so that your manner of life may be worthy of the Lord and entirely pleasing to him. We pray that you may bear fruit in active goodness of every kind, and grow in the knowledge of God. May he
11 strengthen you, in his glorious might, with ample power to meet whatever comes with fortitude, patience, and joy; and to give
12 thanks[c] to the Father who has made you fit to share the heritage of God's people in the realm of light.

13 He rescued us from the domain of darkness and brought us away into the kingdom of his dear Son, in whom our release is secured and
14 our sins forgiven. He is the image
15 of the invisible God; his is the primacy over[d] all created things. In him everything in heaven and
16 on earth was created, not only things visible but also the invisible orders of thrones, sovereignties, authorities, and powers: the whole universe has been created through
17 him and for him. And he exists before everything, and all things
18 are held together in him. He is, moreover, the head of the body, the church. He is its origin, the first to return from the dead, to be in all things alone supreme.
19 For in him the complete being of God, by God's own choice, came
20 to dwell. Through him God chose to reconcile the whole universe to himself, making peace through the shedding of his blood upon the cross – to reconcile all things, whether on earth or in heaven, through him alone.

21 Formerly you were yourselves estranged from God; you were his

---

[a] *Some witnesses read* your.   [b] *Or* your love within the fellowship of the Spirit.
[c] *Or* with fortitude and patience, and to give joyful thanks...
[d] *Or* image of the invisible God, born before...

enemies in heart and mind, and
22 your deeds were evil. But now by
Christ's death in his body of flesh
and blood God has reconciled you
to himself, so that he may present
you before himself as dedicated
men, without blemish and innocent
23 in his sight. Only you must continue in your faith, firm on your
foundations, never to be dislodged
from the hope offered in the gospel
which you heard. This is the gospel
which has been proclaimed in the
whole creation under heaven; and
I, Paul, have become its minister.
24 It is now my happiness to suffer
for you. This is my way of helping
to complete, in my poor human
flesh, the full tale of Christ's
afflictions still to be endured, for
the sake of his body which is the
25 church. I became its servant by
virtue of the task assigned to me
by God for your benefit: to deliver
26 his message in full; to announce
the secret hidden for long ages and
through many generations, but
27 now disclosed to God's people, to
whom it was his will to make it
known – to make known how rich
and glorious it is among all nations.
The secret is this: Christ in*a* you,
the hope of a glory to come.
28 He it is whom we proclaim. We
admonish everyone without distinction, we instruct everyone in all
the ways of wisdom, so as to present
each one of you as a mature mem-
29 ber of Christ's body. To this end I
am toiling strenuously with all the
energy and power of Christ at work
2 in me. For I want you to know
how strenuous are my exertions
for you and the Laodiceans and
all who have never set eyes on me.
2 I want them to continue in good
heart and in the unity of love, and
to come to the full wealth of
conviction which understanding
brings, and grasp God's secret.

That secret is Christ himself; in 3
him lie hidden all God's treasures
of wisdom and knowledge. I tell 4
you this to save you from being
talked*b* into error by specious
arguments. For though absent in 5
body, I am with you in spirit, and
rejoice to see your orderly array
and the firm front which your faith
in Christ presents.

THEREFORE, since Jesus was de- 6
livered to you as Christ and Lord,
live your lives in union with him.
Be rooted in him; be built in him; 7
be consolidated in the faith you
were taught;*c* let your hearts overflow with thankfulness. Be on your 8
guard; do not let your minds be
captured by hollow and delusive
speculations, based on traditions
of man-made teaching and centred
on the elemental spirits of the
universe*d* and not on Christ.
For it is in Christ that the com- 9
plete being of the Godhead dwells
embodied,*e* and in him you have 10
been brought to completion. Every
power and authority in the universe
is subject to him as Head. In him 11
also you were circumcised, not in
a physical sense, but by being
divested of the lower nature; this
is Christ's way of circumcision. For 12
in baptism*f* you were buried with
him, in baptism also you were
raised to life with him through
your faith in the active power of
God who raised him from the dead.
And although you were dead be- 13
cause of your sins and because you
were morally uncircumcised, he
has made you alive with Christ.
For he has forgiven us all our sins;
he has cancelled the bond which 14
pledged us to the decrees of the
law. It stood against us, but he has
set it aside, nailing it to the cross.
On that cross he discarded the 15
cosmic powers and authorities like

a Or among.   *b Or* What I mean is this: no one must talk you...
c Or by your faith, as you were taught.   *d Or* the elements of the natural
world, *or* elementary ideas belonging to this world.   *e Or* corporately.
f Or ...nature, in the very circumcision of Christ himself; for in baptism...

a garment; he made a public spectacle of them and led them[a] as captives in his triumphal procession.

16 ALLOW no one therefore to take you to task about what you eat or drink, or over the observance of festival, new moon, or sabbath.
17 These are no more than a shadow of what was to come; the solid
18 reality is Christ's. You are not to be disqualified by the decision of people who go in for self-mortification and angel-worship, and try to enter into some vision of their own. Such people, bursting with the futile conceit of worldly minds,
19 lose hold upon the Head; yet it is from the Head that the whole body, with all its joints and ligaments, receives its supplies, and thus knit together grows according to God's design.
20 Did you not die with Christ and pass beyond reach of the elemental spirits of the universe[b]? Then why behave as though you were still living the life of the world? Why
21 let people dictate to you: 'Do not handle this, do not taste that, do
22 not touch the other' – all of them things that must perish as soon as they are used? That is to follow merely human injunctions and
23 teaching. True, it has an air of wisdom, with its forced piety, its self-mortification, and its severity to the body; but it is of no use at all in combating sensuality.
3 Were you not raised to life with Christ? Then aspire to the realm above, where Christ is, seated at
2 the right hand of God, and let your thoughts dwell on that higher
3 realm, not on this earthly life. I repeat, you died; and now your life lies hidden with Christ in God.
4 When Christ, who is our life, is

manifested, then you too will be manifested with him in glory.
5 Then put to death those parts of you which belong to the earth – fornication, indecency, lust, foul cravings, and the ruthless greed which is nothing less than idolatry.
6 Because of these, God's dreadful judgement is impending; and in
7 the life you once lived these are the ways you yourselves followed.
8 But now you must yourselves lay aside all anger, passion, malice, cursing, filthy talk – have done with them! Stop lying to one
9 another, now that you have discarded the old nature with its
10 deeds and have put on the new nature, which is being constantly renewed in the image of its Creator
11 and brought to know God. There is no question here of Greek and Jew, circumcised and uncircumcised, barbarian, Scythian, slave and freeman; but Christ is all, and is in all.

12 Then put on the garments that suit God's chosen people, his own, his beloved: compassion, kindness,
13 humility, gentleness, patience. Be forbearing with one another, and forgiving, where any of you has cause for complaint: you must forgive as the Lord forgave you.
14 To crown all, there must be love, to bind all together and complete
15 the whole. Let Christ's peace be arbiter in your hearts; to this peace you were called as members of a single body. And be filled with
16 gratitude. Let the message of Christ dwell among you in all its richness. Instruct and admonish each other with the utmost wisdom. Sing thankfully in your hearts to God,[c] with psalms and
17 hymns and spiritual songs. Whatever you are doing, whether you speak or act, do everything in the

---

[a] *Or* he stripped himself of his physical body, and thereby boldly made a spectacle of the cosmic powers and authorities, and led them . . . ; *or* he despoiled the cosmic powers and authorities, and boldly made a spectacle of them, leading them . . .
[b] *Or* the elements of the natural world, *or* elementary ideas belonging to this world.
[c] *Some witnesses read* the Lord.

name of the Lord Jesus, giving thanks to God the Father through him.

18 WIVES, be subject to your husbands; that is your Christian duty.
19 Husbands, love your wives and
20 do not be harsh with them. Children, obey your parents in everything, for that is pleasing to God
21 and is the Christian way. Fathers, do not exasperate your children, for fear they grow disheartened.
22 Slaves, give entire obedience to your earthly masters, not merely with an outward show of service, to curry favour with men, but with single-mindedness, out of reverence
23 for the Lord. Whatever you are doing, put your whole heart into it, as if you were doing it for the
24 Lord and not for men, knowing that there is a Master who will give you your heritage as a reward for your service. Christ is the Master whose slaves you must be.
25 Dishonesty will be requited, and
4 he has no favourites. Masters, be just and fair to your slaves, knowing that you too have a Master in heaven.
2   Persevere in prayer, with mind
3 awake and thankful heart; and include a prayer for us, that God may give us an opening for preaching, to tell the secret of Christ; that indeed is why I am now in prison.
4 Pray that I may make the secret plain, as it is my duty to do.
5   Behave wisely towards those outside your own number; use the present opportunity to the full.
6 Let your conversation be always gracious, and never insipid; study how best to talk with each person you meet.

You will hear all about my affairs 7 from Tychicus, our dear brother and trustworthy helper and fellow-servant in the Lord's work. I am 8 sending him to you on purpose to let you know all about us and to put fresh heart into you. With him 9 comes Onesimus, our trustworthy and dear brother, who is one of yourselves. They will tell you all the news here.

Aristarchus, Christ's captive like 10 myself, sends his greetings; so does Mark, the cousin of Barnabas (you have had instructions about him; if he comes, make him welcome), and Jesus Justus. Of the Jewish 11 Christians, these are the only ones who work with me for the kingdom of God, and they have been a great comfort to me. Greetings from 12 Epaphras, servant of Christ, who is one of yourselves. He prays hard for you all the time, that you may stand fast, ripe in conviction[a] and wholly devoted to doing God's will. For I can vouch for him, that he 13 works tirelessly for you and the people at Laodicea and Hierapolis. Greetings to you from our dear 14 friend Luke, the doctor, and from Demas. Give our greetings to the 15 brothers at Laodicea, and Nympha and the congregation at her house.[b] And when this letter is read among 16 you, see that it is also read to the congregation at Laodicea, and that you in return read the one from Laodicea. This special word to 17 Archippus: 'Attend to the duty entrusted to you in the Lord's service, and discharge it to the full.'

This greeting is in my own 18 hand – PAUL. Remember I am in prison. God's grace be with you.

---

[a] *Or* stand fast, mature and complete...
[b] *Some witnesses read* Nymphas and the congregation at his house.

THE FIRST LETTER OF PAUL
TO THE
THESSALONIANS

Hope and discipline

1 FROM Paul, Silvanus, and Timothy to the congregation of Thessalonians who belong to God the Father and the Lord Jesus Christ.

Grace to you and peace.

2 We always thank God for you all, and mention you in our prayers 3 continually. We call to mind, before our God and Father, how your faith has shown itself in action, your love in labour, and your hope of our Lord Jesus Christ in forti- 4 tude. We are certain, brothers beloved by God, that he has cho- 5 sen you and that*a* when we brought you the Gospel, we brought it not in mere words but in the power of the Holy Spirit, and with strong conviction, as you know well. That is the kind of men we were at Thessalonica, and it was for your sake.

6 And you, in your turn, followed the example set by us and by the Lord; the welcome you gave the message meant grave suffering for you, yet you rejoiced in the Holy 7 Spirit; thus you have become a model for all believers in Mace- 8 donia and in Achaia. From Thessalonica the word of the Lord rang out; and not in Macedonia and Achaia alone, but everywhere your faith in God has reached men's ears. No words of ours are needed, 9 for they themselves spread the news of our visit to you and its effect: how you turned from idols, to be servants of the living and true 10 God, and to wait expectantly for the appearance from heaven of his

Son Jesus, whom he raised from the dead, Jesus our deliverer from the terrors of judgement to come.

You know for yourselves, bro- 2 thers, that our visit to you was not fruitless. Far from it; after all the 2 injury and outrage which to your knowledge we had suffered at Philippi, we declared the gospel of God to you frankly and fearlessly, by the help of our God. A hard struggle it was. Indeed, the appeal 3 we make never springs from error or base motive; there is no attempt to deceive; but God has approved 4 us as fit to be entrusted with the Gospel, and on those terms we speak. We do not curry favour with men; we seek only the favour of God, who is continually testing our hearts. Our words have never 5 been flattering words, as you have cause to know; nor, as God is our witness, have they ever been a cloak for greed. We have never 6 sought honour from men, from you or from anyone else, although as Christ's own envoys we might have made our weight felt; but we were 7 as gentle with you as a nurse caring fondly for her children. With such 8 yearning love we chose to impart to you not only the gospel of God but our very selves, so dear had you become to us. Remember, 9 brothers, how we toiled and drudged. We worked for a living night and day, rather than be a burden to anyone, while we proclaimed before you the good news of God.

We call you to witness, yes and 10 God himself, how devout and just and blameless was our behaviour

---

a Or ...chosen you, because...

11 towards you who are believers. As you well know, we dealt with you one by one, as a father deals with his children, appealing to you by encouragement, as well as by 12 solemn injunctions, to live lives worthy of the God who calls you into his kingdom and glory.

13 This is why we thank God continually, because when we handed on God's message, you received it, not as the word of men, but as what it truly is, the very word of God at[a] work in you who hold the 14 faith. You have fared like the congregations in Judaea, God's people in Christ Jesus. You have been treated by your countrymen as they are treated by the Jews, 15 who killed the Lord Jesus and the prophets[b] and drove us out, the Jews who are heedless of God's will and enemies of their fellow-16 men, hindering us from speaking to the Gentiles to lead them to salvation. All this time they have been making up the full measure of their guilt, and now retribution has overtaken them for good and all.[c]

17 MY friends, when for a short spell you were lost to sight, not to our hearts – we were exceedingly anxious to see you again. 18 So we did propose to come to Thessalonica – I, Paul, more than 19 once – but Satan thwarted us. For after all, what hope or joy or crown of pride is there for us, what indeed but you, when we stand before our 20 Lord Jesus at his coming? It is you who are indeed our glory and our joy.

3 So when we could bear it no longer, we decided to remain alone 2 at Athens, and sent Timothy, our brother and God's fellow-worker[d] in the service of the gospel of Christ, to encourage you to stand 3 firm for the faith and, under all

these hardships, not to be shaken;[e] for you know that this is our appointed lot. When we were with 4 you we warned you that we were bound to suffer hardship; and so it has turned out, as you know. And thus it was that when I could 5 bear it no longer, I sent to find out about your faith, fearing that the tempter might have tempted you and my labour might be lost.

But now Timothy has just ar- 6 rived from Thessalonica, bringing good news of your faith and love. He tells us that you always think kindly of us, and are as anxious to see us as we are to see you. And 7 so in all our difficulties and hardships your faith reassures us about you. It is the breath of life to us 8 that you stand firm in the Lord. What thanks can we return to 9 God for you? What thanks for all the joy you have brought us, making us rejoice before our God while we pray most earnestly night 10 and day to be allowed to see you again and to mend your faith where it falls short?

May our God and Father himself, 11 and our Lord Jesus, bring us direct to you; and may the Lord make 12 your love mount and overflow towards one another and towards all, as our love does towards you. May 13 he make your hearts firm, so that you may stand before our God and Father holy and faultless when our Lord Jesus comes with all those who are his own.

AND now, my friends, we have one 4 thing to beg and pray of you, by our fellowship with the Lord Jesus. We passed on to you the tradition of the way we must live to please God; you are indeed already following it, but we beg you to do so yet more thoroughly.

For you know what orders we 2 gave you, in the name of the Lord

---

[a] Or word of God who is at...   [b] Some witnesses read their own prophets.
[c] Or now at last retribution has overtaken them.   [d] Or and fellow-worker for God; one witness has simply and fellow-worker.   [e] Or beguiled away.

3 Jesus. This is the will of God, that you should be holy: you must
4 abstain from fornication; each one of you must learn to gain mastery over his body, to hallow and
5 honour it, not giving way to lust like the pagans who are ignorant
6 of God; and no man must do his brother wrong in this matter,[a] or invade his rights, because, as we told you before with all emphasis, the Lord punishes all such offences.
7 For God called us to holiness, not
8 to impurity. Anyone therefore who flouts these rules is flouting, not man, but God who bestows upon you his Holy Spirit.

9 About love for our brotherhood you need no words of mine, for you are yourselves taught by God to
10 love one another, and you are in fact practising this rule of love towards all your fellow-Christians throughout Macedonia. Yet we appeal to you, brothers, to do
11 better still. Let it be your ambition to keep calm and look after your own business, and to work with
12 your hands, as we ordered you, so that you may command the respect of those outside your own number, and at the same time may never be in want.

13 WE wish you not to remain in ignorance, brothers, about those who sleep in death; you should not grieve like the rest of men, who
14 have no hope. We believe that Jesus died and rose again; and so it will be for those who died as Christians; God will bring them to life with Jesus.[b]
15 For this we tell you as the Lord's word: we who are left alive until the Lord comes shall not forestall
16 those who have died; because at the word of command, at the sound of the archangel's voice and God's trumpet-call, the Lord himself will descend from heaven; first the
17 Christian dead will rise, then we who are left alive shall join them, caught up in clouds to meet the Lord in the air. Thus we shall always be with the Lord. Console 18 one another, then, with these words.

About dates and times, my 5 friends, we need not write to you, for you know perfectly well that 2 the Day of the Lord comes like a thief in the night. While they 3 are talking of peace and security, all at once calamity is upon them, sudden as the pangs that come upon a woman with child; and there will be no escape. But you, 4 my friends, are not in the dark, that the day should overtake you like a thief.[c] You are all children 5 of light, children of day. We do not belong to night or darkness, and 6 we must not sleep like the rest, but keep awake and sober. Sleepers 7 sleep at night, and drunkards are drunk at night, but we, who belong 8 to daylight, must keep sober, armed with faith and love for coat of mail, and the hope of salvation for helmet. For God has not destined 9 us to the terrors of judgement, but to the full attainment of salvation through our Lord Jesus Christ. He 10 died for us so that we, awake or asleep, might live in company with him. Therefore hearten one an- 11 other, fortify one another – as indeed you do.

WE beg you, brothers, to acknow- 12 ledge those who are working so hard among you, and in the Lord's fellowship are your leaders and counsellors. Hold them in the 13 highest possible esteem and affection for the work they do.

You must live at peace among yourselves. And we would urge 14 you, brothers, to admonish the careless, encourage the faint-hearted, support the weak, and to be very patient with them all.

See to it that no one pays back 15 wrong for wrong, but always aim

---

[a] Or *must overreach his brother in his business* (*or* in lawsuits).
[b] Or *will bring them in company with Jesus.*   [c] *Some witnesses read* thieves.

at doing the best you can for each other and for all men.

16, 17 Be always joyful; pray continually; give thanks whatever happens; for this is what God in Christ wills for you.

19, 20 Do not stifle inspiration, and do not despise prophetic utterances, 21 but bring them all to the test and 22 then keep what is good in them and avoid the bad of whatever kind.[a]

23 May God himself, the God of peace, make you holy in every part, and keep you sound in spirit, soul, and body, without fault when our Lord Jesus Christ comes. He 24 who calls you is to be trusted; he will do it.

Brothers, pray for us also. 25

Greet all our brothers with the 26 kiss of peace.

I adjure you by the Lord to have 27 this letter read to the whole brotherhood.

The grace of our Lord Jesus 28 Christ be with you!

THE SECOND LETTER OF PAUL
TO THE
THESSALONIANS

Hope and discipline

1 FROM Paul, Silvanus, and Timothy to the congregation of Thessalonians who belong to God our Father and the Lord Jesus Christ.

2 Grace to you and peace from God the Father and the Lord Jesus Christ.

3 Our thanks are always due to God for you, brothers. It is right that we should thank him, because your faith increases mightily, and the love you have, each for all and all for each, grows ever greater.

4 Indeed we boast about you ourselves among the congregations of God's people, because your faith remains so steadfast under all your persecutions, and all the troubles 5 you endure. See how this brings out the justice of God's judgement. It will prove you worthy of the kingdom of God, for which indeed you are suffering.

It is surely just that God should 6 balance the account by sending trouble to those who trouble you, and relief to you who are troubled, 7 and to us as well, when our Lord Jesus Christ is revealed from heaven with his mighty angels in 8 blazing fire. Then he will do justice upon those who refuse to acknowledge God and upon those who will not obey[b] the gospel of our Lord Jesus. They will suffer the punish- 9 ment of eternal ruin, cut off from the presence of the Lord and the splendour of his might, when on 10 that great Day he comes to be glorified among his own and adored among all believers; for you did indeed believe the testimony we brought you.

With this in mind we pray for 11 you always, that our God may

---

[a] Or ...utterances. Put everything to the test; keep hold of what is good and avoid every kind of evil.

[b] Or justice upon those who refuse...and will not obey...

count you worthy of his calling, and mightily bring to fulfilment every good purpose and every act 12 inspired by faith, so that the name of our Lord Jesus may be glorified in you, and you in him, according to the grace of our God and the Lord Jesus Christ.

2 AND now, brothers, about the coming of our Lord Jesus Christ and his gathering of us to himself: 2 I beg you, do not suddenly lose your heads or alarm yourselves, whether at some oracular utterance, or pronouncement, or some letter purporting to come from us, alleging that the Day of the Lord 3 is already here. Let no one deceive you in any way whatever. That day cannot come before the final rebellion against God, when wickedness will be revealed in human form, the man doomed to perdition. 4 He is the Enemy. He rises in his pride against every god, so called, every object of men's worship, and even takes his seat in the temple of God claiming to be a god himself.

5 You cannot but remember that I told you this while I was still 6 with you; you must now be aware of the restraining hand which ensures that he shall be revealed only 7 at the proper time. For already the secret power of wickedness is at work, secret only for the present until the Restrainer disappears 8 from the scene. And then he will be revealed, that wicked man whom the Lord Jesus will destroy with the breath of his mouth, and annihilate by the radiance of his 9 coming. But the coming of that wicked man is the work of Satan. It will be attended by all the powerful signs and miracles of the 10 Lie, and all the deception that sinfulness can impose on those doomed to destruction. Destroyed they shall be, because they did not open their minds to love of the

truth, so as to find salvation. Therefore God puts them under 11 a delusion, which works upon them to believe the lie, so that they may 12 all be brought to judgement, all who do not believe the truth but make sinfulness their deliberate choice.

BUT we are bound to thank God 13 always for you, brothers beloved by the Lord, because from the beginning of time God chose you*a* to find salvation in the Spirit that consecrates you, and in the truth that you believe. It was for this 14 that he called you through the gospel we brought, so that you might possess for your own the splendour of our Lord Jesus Christ.

Stand firm, then, brothers, and 15 hold fast to the traditions which you have learned from us by word or by letter. And may our Lord 16 Jesus Christ himself and God our Father, who has shown us such love, and in his grace has given us such unfailing encouragement and such bright hopes, still encourage 17 and fortify you in every good deed and word!

And now, brothers, pray for us, 3 that the word of the Lord may have everywhere the swift and glorious course that it has had among you, and that we may be 2 rescued from wrong-headed and wicked men; for it is not all who have faith. But the Lord is to be 3 trusted, and he will fortify you and guard you from the evil one. We 4 feel perfect confidence about you, in the Lord, that you are doing and will continue to do what we order. May the Lord direct your 5 hearts towards God's love and the steadfastness of Christ!

These are our orders to you, 6 brothers, in the name of our Lord Jesus Christ: hold aloof from every Christian brother who falls into idle habits, and does not follow the tradition you received from us.

a Some witnesses read because God chose you as his firstfruits...

7 You know yourselves how you ought to copy our example: we 8 were no idlers among you; we did not accept board and lodging from anyone without paying for it; we toiled and drudged, we worked for a living night and day, rather than 9 be a burden to any of you – not because we have not the right to maintenance, but to set an example 10 for you to imitate. For even during our stay with you we laid down the rule: the man who will not 11 work shall not eat. We mention this because we hear that some of your number are idling their time away, minding everybody's 12 business but their own. To all such we give these orders, and we appeal to them in the name of the Lord Jesus Christ to work quietly for their living.

13 But you, my friends, must never 14 tire of doing right. If anyone disobeys our instructions given by letter, mark him well, and have no dealings with him until he is 15 ashamed of himself. I do not mean treat him as an enemy, but give him friendly advice, as one of the 16 family. May the Lord of peace himself give you peace at all times and in all ways.[a] The Lord be with you all.

17 The greeting is in my own hand, signed with my name, PAUL; this authenticates all my letters; this is 18 how I write. The grace[b] of our Lord Jesus Christ be with you all.

THE FIRST LETTER OF PAUL
TO
TIMOTHY

Church order

1 FROM Paul, apostle of Christ Jesus by command of God our Saviour and Christ Jesus 2 our hope, to Timothy his true-born son in the faith.

Grace, mercy, and peace to you from God the Father and Christ Jesus our Lord.

3 When I was starting for Macedonia, I urged you to stay on at Ephesus. You were to command certain persons to give up teaching 4 erroneous doctrines and studying those interminable myths and genealogies, which issue in mere speculation and cannot make known God's plan for us, which works through faith.[c]

5 The aim and object of this command is the love which springs from a clean heart, from a good conscience, and from faith that is 6 genuine. Through falling short of these, some people have gone astray into a wilderness of words. 7 They set out to be teachers of the moral law, without understanding either the words they use or the subjects about which they are so dogmatic.

8 We all know that the law is an excellent thing, provided we treat 9 it as law, recognizing that it is not aimed at good citizens, but at the

---

[a] *Some witnesses read* at all times, wherever you may be.
[b] Or ...letters. My message is this: the grace...
[c] Or cannot promote the faithful discharge of God's stewardship.

lawless and unruly, the impious and sinful, the irreligious and worldly; at parricides and matricides, murderers and fornicators, perverts, kidnappers, liars, perjurers – in fact all whose behaviour flouts the wholesome teaching which conforms with the gospel entrusted to me, the gospel which tells of the glory of God in his eternal felicity.

I thank him who has made me equal to the task, Christ Jesus our Lord; I thank him for judging me worthy of this trust and appointing me to his service – although in the past I had met him with abuse and persecution and outrage. But because I acted ignorantly in unbelief I was dealt with mercifully; the grace of our Lord was lavished upon me, with the faith and love which are ours in Christ Jesus.

Here are words you may trust, words that merit full acceptance: 'Christ Jesus came into the world to save sinners'; and among them I stand first. But I was mercifully dealt with for this very purpose, that Jesus Christ might find in me the first occasion for displaying all his patience, and that I might be typical of all who were in future to have faith in him and gain eternal life. Now to the King of all worlds, immortal, invisible, the only God, be honour and glory for ever and ever! Amen.

This charge, son Timothy, I lay upon you, following that prophetic utterance which first pointed you out to me. So fight gallantly, armed with faith and a good conscience. It was through spurning conscience that certain persons made shipwreck of their faith, among them Hymenaeus and Alexander, whom I consigned to Satan, in the hope that through this discipline they might learn not to be blasphemous.

FIRST of all, then, I urge that petitions, prayers, intercessions, and thanksgivings be offered for all men; for sovereigns and all in high office, that we may lead a tranquil and quiet life in full observance of religion and high standards of morality. Such prayer is right, and approved by God our Saviour, whose will it is that all men should find salvation and come to know the truth. For there is one God, and also one mediator between God and men, Christ Jesus, himself man, who sacrificed himself to win freedom for all mankind, so providing, at the fitting time, proof of the divine purpose; of this I was appointed herald and apostle (this is no lie, but the truth), to instruct the nations in the true faith.

It is my desire, therefore, that everywhere prayers be said by the men of the congregation, who shall lift up their hands with a pure intention, excluding angry or quarrelsome thoughts. Women again must dress in becoming manner, modestly and soberly, not with elaborate hair-styles, not decked out with gold or pearls, or expensive clothes, but with good deeds, as befits women who claim to be religious. A woman must be a learner, listening quietly and with due submission. I do not permit a woman to be a teacher, nor must woman domineer over man; she should be quiet. For Adam was created first, and Eve afterwards; and it was not Adam who was deceived; it was the woman who, yielding to deception, fell into sin. Yet she will be saved through motherhood[a] – if only women continue in faith,[b] love, and holiness, with a sober mind.

There is a popular saying:[c] 'To aspire to leadership is an honour-

---

[a] Or *saved through the Birth of the Child, or* brought safely through childbirth.
[b] Or *if only husband and wife continue in mutual fidelity* . . .
[c] *Some witnesses read* Here are words you may trust, *which some interpreters attach to the end of the preceding paragraph.*

2 able ambition.' Our leader, therefore, or bishop, must be above reproach, faithful to his one wife,[a] sober, temperate, courteous, hos-
3 pitable, and a good teacher; he must not be given to drink, or a brawler, but of a forbearing disposition, avoiding quarrels, and no
4 lover of money. He must be one who manages his own household well and wins obedience from his children, and a man of the highest
5 principles. If a man does not know how to control his own family, how can he look after a congregation
6 of God's people? He must not be a convert newly baptized, for fear the sin of conceit should bring upon him a judgement contrived
7 by the devil.[b] He must moreover have a good reputation with the non-Christian public, so that he may not be exposed to scandal and get caught in the devil's snare.

8   Deacons, likewise, must be men of high principle, not indulging in double talk, given neither to excessive drinking nor to money-
9 grubbing. They must be men who combine a clear conscience with a firm hold on the deep truths of
10 our faith. No less than bishops, they must first undergo a scrutiny, and if there is no mark against
11 them, they may serve. Their wives,[c] equally, must be women of high principle, who will not talk scandal, sober and trustworthy in every
12 way. A deacon must be faithful to his one wife,[d] and good at managing his children and his own house-
13 hold. For deacons with a good record of service may claim a high standing and the right to speak openly on matters of the Christian faith.

14   I am hoping to come to you
15 before long, but I write this in case I am delayed, to let you know how men ought to conduct themselves in God's household, that is, the church of the living God, the pillar and bulwark of the truth. And 16 great beyond all question is the mystery of our religion:

'He who was manifested in the body,
vindicated in the spirit,
seen by angels;
who was proclaimed among the nations,
believed in throughout the world,
glorified in high heaven.'

THE Spirit says expressly that in 4 after times some will desert from the faith and give their minds to subversive doctrines inspired by devils, through the specious false- 2 hoods of men whose own conscience is branded with the devil's sign. They forbid marriage and incul- 3 cate abstinence from certain foods, though God created them to be enjoyed with thanksgiving by believers who have inward knowledge of the truth. For everything 4 that God created is good, and nothing is to be rejected when it is taken with thanksgiving, since 5 it is hallowed by God's own word and by prayer.

By offering such advice as this 6 to the brotherhood you will prove a good servant of Christ Jesus, bred in the precepts of our faith and of the sound instruction which you have followed. Have nothing 7 to do with those godless myths, fit only for old women. Keep yourself in training for the practice of religion. The training of the body 8 does bring limited benefit, but the benefits of religion are without limit, since it holds promise not only for this life but for the life to come. Here are words you may 9 trust, words that merit full acceptance: 'With this before us we 10

---

[a] Or married to one wife, *or* married only once.
[b] Or the judgement once passed on the devil.
[c] Or . . . serve. Deaconesses . . .
[d] Or married to one wife, *or* married only once.

labour and struggle,[a] because[b] we have set our hope on the living God, who is the Saviour of all men'—the Saviour, above all, of believers.

11, 12 Pass on these orders and these teachings. Let no one slight you because you are young, but make yourself an example to believers in speech and behaviour, in love, 13 fidelity, and purity. Until I arrive devote your attention to the public reading of the scriptures, to ex- 14 hortation, and to teaching. Do not neglect the spiritual endowment you possess, which was given you, under the guidance of prophecy, through the laying on of the hands of the elders as a body.[c]

15 Make these matters your business and your absorbing interest, so that your progress may be plain 16 to all. Persevere in them, keeping close watch on yourself and your teaching; by doing so you will further the salvation of yourself and your hearers.

5 Never be harsh with an elder; appeal to him as if he were your father. Treat the younger men as 2 brothers, the older women as mothers, and the younger as your sisters, in all purity.

3 The status of widow is to be granted only to widows who are 4 such in the full sense. But if a widow has children or grandchildren, then they should learn as their first duty to show loyalty to the family and to repay what they owe to their parents and grandparents; for this God ap- 5 proves. A widow, however, in the full sense, one who is alone in the world, has all her hope set on God, and regularly attends the meetings for prayer and worship night and 6 day. But a widow given over to self-indulgence is as good as dead.

Add these orders to the rest, so 7 that the widows may be above reproach. But if anyone does not 8 make provision for his relations, and especially for members of his own household, he has denied the faith and is worse than an unbeliever.

A widow should not be put on 9 the roll under sixty years of age. She must have been faithful in marriage to one man, and must 10 produce evidence of good deeds performed, showing whether she has had the care of children, or given hospitality, or washed the feet of God's people, or supported those in distress – in short, whether she has taken every opportunity of doing good.

Younger widows may not be 11 placed on the roll. For when their passions draw them away from Christ, they hanker after marriage and stand condemned for breaking 12 their troth with him. Moreover, in 13 going round from house to house they learn to be idle, and worse than idle, gossips and busybodies, speaking of things better left unspoken. It is my wish, therefore, 14 that young widows shall marry again, have children, and preside over a home; then they will give no opponent occasion for slander. For there have in fact been some 15 who have taken the wrong turning and gone to the devil.

If a Christian man or woman 16 has widows in the family, he must support them himself;[d] the congregation must be relieved of the burden, so that it may be free to support those who are widows in the full sense of the term.

Elders who do well as leaders 17 should be reckoned worthy of a double stipend, in particular those who labour at preaching and

---

[a] *Some witnesses read* suffer reproach. [b] *Or since* 'It holds promise...to come.' These are words...acceptance. For this is the aim of all our labour and struggle, since... [c] *Or through your ordination as an elder.* [d] *Some witnesses read* If a Christian woman has widows in her family, she must support them herself.

18 teaching. For Scripture says, 'You shall not muzzle a threshing ox'; and besides, 'the worker earns his pay'.

19 Do not entertain a charge against an elder unless it is supported by

20 two or three witnesses. Those who commit sins you must expose publicly, to put fear into the others.

21 Before God and Christ Jesus and the angels who are his chosen, I solemnly charge you, maintain these rules, and never pre-judge the issue, but act with strict im-

22 partiality. Do not be over-hasty in laying on hands in ordination,[a] or you may find yourself responsible for other people's misdeeds; keep your own hands clean.

23 Stop drinking nothing but water; take a little wine for your digestion, for your frequent ailments.

24 While there are people whose offences are so obvious that they run before them into court, there are others whose offences have not

25 yet overtaken them. Similarly, good deeds are obvious, or even if they are not, they cannot be concealed for ever.

6 All who wear the yoke of slavery must count their own masters worthy of all respect, so that the name of God and the Christian teaching are not brought into dis-

2 repute. If the masters are believers, the slaves must not respect them any less for being their Christian brothers. Quite the contrary; they must be all the better servants because those who receive the benefit of their service are one with them in faith and love.

3 THIS is what you are to teach and preach. If anyone is teaching otherwise, and will not give his mind to wholesome precepts – I mean those of our Lord Jesus Christ – and to good religious

4 teaching, I call him a pompous ignoramus. He is morbidly keen on mere verbal questions and quib-

bles, which give rise to jealousy, quarrelling, slander, base suspicions, and endless wrangles: all 5 typical of men who have let their reasoning powers become atrophied and have lost grip of the truth. They think religion should yield dividends; and of course religion 6 does yield high dividends, but only to the man whose resources are within him. We brought nothing 7 into the world; for that matter we cannot take anything with us when we leave, but if we have food and 8 covering we may rest content. Those who want to be rich fall 9 into temptations and snares and many foolish harmful desires which plunge men into ruin and perdition. The love of money is the root of all 10 evil things, and there are some who in reaching for it have wandered from the faith and spiked themselves on many thorny griefs.

But you, man of God, must 11 shun all this, and pursue justice, piety, fidelity, love, fortitude, and gentleness. Run the great race of 12 faith and take hold of eternal life. For to this you were called; and you confessed your faith nobly before many witnesses. Now in the 13 presence of God, who gives life to all things, and of Jesus Christ, who himself made the same noble confession and gave his testimony to it before Pontius Pilate, I charge you to obey your orders irreproachably 14 and without fault until our Lord Jesus Christ appears. That appear- 15 ance God will bring to pass in his own good time – God who in eternal felicity alone holds sway. He is King of kings and Lord of lords; he alone possesses immortal- 16 ity, dwelling in unapproachable light. No man has ever seen or ever can see him. To him be honour and might for ever! Amen.

Instruct those who are rich in 17 this world's goods not to be proud, and not to fix their hopes on so uncertain a thing as money, but

---

[a] *Or in restoring an offender by the laying on of hands.*

upon God, who endows us richly
18 with all things to enjoy. Tell them
to do good and to grow rich in
noble actions, to be ready to give
19 away and to share, and so acquire
a treasure which will form a good
foundation for the future. Thus
they will grasp the life which is
life indeed.

Timothy, keep safe that which 20
has been entrusted to you. Turn
a deaf ear to empty and worldly
chatter, and the contradictions of
so-called 'knowledge', for many 21
who lay claim to it have shot far
wide of the faith.

Grace be with you all!

THE SECOND LETTER OF PAUL
TO
TIMOTHY

Character of a Christian minister

1 FROM Paul, apostle of Jesus
Christ by the will of God,
whose promise of life is ful-
2 filled in Christ Jesus, to Timothy
his dear son.

Grace, mercy, and peace to you
from God the Father and our Lord
Jesus Christ.

3 I thank God – whom I, like my
forefathers, worship with a pure
intention – when I mention you
in my prayers; this I do constantly
4 night and day. And when I remember the tears you shed, I long
to see you again to make my
5 happiness complete. I am reminded of the sincerity of your faith, a
faith which was alive in Lois your
grandmother and Eunice your
mother before you, and which, I
am confident, lives in you also.

6 That is why I now remind you
to stir into flame the gift of God
which is within you through the
7 laying on of my hands. For the
spirit that God gave us is no craven
spirit, but one to inspire strength,

love, and self-discipline. So never 8
be ashamed of your testimony to
our Lord, nor of me his prisoner,
but take your share of suffering
for the sake of the Gospel, in the
strength that comes from God. It 9
is he who brought us salvation and
called us to a dedicated life, not
for any merit of ours but of his
own purpose and his own grace,
which was granted to us in Christ
Jesus from all eternity, but has now 10
at length been brought fully into
view by the appearance on earth
of our Saviour Jesus Christ. For he
has broken the power of death and
brought life and immortality to
light through the Gospel.

Of this Gospel I, by his appoint- 11
ment, am herald, apostle, and
teacher. That is the reason for my 12
present plight; but I am not
ashamed of it, because I know
who it is in whom[a] I have trusted,
and am confident of his power to
keep safe what he has put into my
charge,[b] until the great Day. Keep 13
before you an outline of the sound
teaching which[c] you heard from

[a] *Or* I know the one whom... [b] *Or* what I have put into his charge.
[c] *Or* Keep before you as a model of sound teaching that which...

me, living by the faith and love which are ours in Christ Jesus.

14 Guard the treasure put into our charge, with the help of the Holy Spirit dwelling within us.

15 As you know, everyone in the province of Asia deserted me, including Phygelus and Hermo-

16 genes. But may the Lord's mercy rest on the house of Onesiphorus! He has often relieved me in my

17 troubles. He was not ashamed to visit a prisoner, but took pains to search me out when he came

18 to Rome, and found me. I pray that the Lord may grant him to find mercy from the Lord on the great Day. The many services he rendered at Ephesus you know better than I could tell you.

2 Now therefore, my son, take strength from the grace of God

2 which is ours in Christ Jesus. You heard my teaching in the presence of many witnesses; put that teaching into the charge of men you can trust, such men as will be competent to teach others.

3 Take your share of hardship, like

4 a good soldier of Christ Jesus. A soldier on active service will not let himself be involved in civilian affairs; he must be wholly at his

5 commanding officer's disposal. A-gain, no athlete can win a prize

6 unless he has kept the rules. The farmer who gives his labour has

7 first claim on the crop. Reflect on what I say, for the Lord will help you to full understanding.

8 Remember Jesus Christ, risen from the dead, born of David's line. This is the theme of my gospel,

9 in whose service I am exposed to hardship, even to the point of being shut up like a common criminal; but the word of God is not shut

10 up. And I endure it all for the sake of God's chosen ones, with this end in view, that they too may attain the glorious and eternal salvation which is in Christ Jesus.

11 Here are words you may trust:

'If we died with him, we shall live with him;

if we endure, we shall reign with 12 him.

If we deny him, he will deny us.

If we are faithless, he keeps faith, 13 for he cannot deny himself.'

Go on reminding people of this, 14 and charge them solemnly before God to stop disputing about mere words; it does no good, and is the ruin of those who listen. Try hard 15 to show yourself worthy of God's approval, as a labourer who need not be ashamed; be straight-forward in your proclamation of the truth. Avoid empty and world- 16 ly chatter; those who indulge in it will stray further and further into godless courses, and the infection 17 of their teaching will spread like a gangrene. Such are Hymenaeus and Philetus; they have shot wide 18 of the truth in saying that our resurrection has already taken place, and are upsetting people's faith. But God has laid a founda- 19 tion, and it stands firm, with this inscription: 'The Lord knows his own', and, 'Everyone who takes the Lord's name upon his lips must forsake wickedness.' Now in any 20 great house there are not only utensils of gold and silver, but also others of wood or earthen-ware; the former are valued, the latter held cheap. To be among 21 those which are valued and dedi-cated, a thing of use to the Master of the house, a man must cleanse himself from all those evil things;[a] then he will be fit for any honour-able purpose.

Turn from the wayward im- 22 pulses of youth, and pursue justice, integrity, love, and peace with all who invoke the Lord in singleness of mind. Have nothing to do with 23 foolish and ignorant speculations. You know they breed quarrels, and 24 the servant of the Lord must not be quarrelsome, but kindly to-

___
[a] Or must separate himself from these persons.

wards all. He should be a good
25 teacher, tolerant, and gentle when
discipline is needed for the refractory. The Lord may grant
them a change of heart and show
26 them the truth, and thus they may
come to their senses and escape
from the devil's snare, in which
they have been caught and held
at his will.[a]

3 You must face the fact: the final
age of this world is to be a time of
2 troubles. Men will love nothing but
money and self; they will be arrogant, boastful, and abusive; with
no respect for parents, no gratitude,
3 no piety, no natural affection; they
will be implacable in their hatreds,
scandal-mongers, intemperate and
fierce, strangers to all goodness,
4 traitors, adventurers, swollen with
self-importance. They will be men
who put pleasure in the place of
5 God, men who preserve the outward form of religion, but are a
standing denial of its reality. Keep
6 clear of men like these. They are
the sort that insinuate themselves
into private houses and there get
miserable women into their clutches, women burdened with a sinful
past, and led on by all kinds of
7 desires, who are always wanting
to be taught, but are incapable of
reaching a knowledge of the truth.
8 As Jannes and Jambres defied
Moses, so these men defy the truth;
they have lost the power to reason,
and they cannot pass the tests of
9 faith. But their successes will be
short-lived, for, like those opponents of Moses, they will come to
be recognized by everyone for the
fools they are.
10 But you, my son, have followed,
step by step, my teaching and my
manner of life, my resolution, my
faith, patience, and spirit of love,
11 and my fortitude under persecutions and sufferings – all that I
went through at Antioch, at Iconium, at Lystra, all the persecutions I endured; and the Lord
rescued me out of them all. Yes, 12
persecution will come to all who
want to live a godly life as Christians, whereas wicked men and 13
charlatans will make progress from
bad to worse, deceiving and deceived. But for your part, stand 14
by the truths you have learned
and are assured of. Remember
from whom you learned them;
remember that from early child- 15
hood you have been familiar with
the sacred writings which have
power to make you wise and lead
you to salvation through faith in
Christ Jesus. Every inspired scrip- 16
ture has its use for teaching the
truth and refuting error, or for
reformation of manners and discipline in right living, so that the 17
man who belongs to God may be
efficient and equipped for good
work of every kind.

Before God, and before Christ 4
Jesus who is to judge men living
and dead, I charge you solemnly
by his coming appearance and his
reign, proclaim the message, press 2
it home on all occasions,[b] convenient or inconvenient, use argument, reproof, and appeal, with
all the patience that the work of
teaching requires. For the time 3
will come when they will not stand
wholesome teaching, but will follow
their own fancy and gather a crowd
of teachers to tickle their ears.
They will stop their ears to the 4
truth and turn to mythology. But 5
you yourself must keep calm and
sane at all times; face hardship,
work to spread the Gospel, and
do all the duties of your calling.

As for me, already my life is being 6
poured out on the altar, and the
hour for my departure is upon me.
I have run the great race, I have 7
finished the course, I have kept
faith. And now the prize awaits 8
me, the garland of righteousness

[a] *Or escape from the devil's snare, caught* now by God and made subject to his will.
[b] *Or be on duty at all times.*

which the Lord, the all-just Judge, will award me on that great Day; and it is not for me alone, but for all who have set their hearts on his coming appearance.

9 10   Do your best to join me soon; for Demas has deserted me because his heart was set on this world; he has gone to Thessalonica, Crescens to Galatia,[a] Titus to Dalmatia;

11 I have no one with me but Luke. Pick up Mark and bring him with you, for I find him a useful assistant.

12 Tychicus I have sent to Ephesus.

13 When you come, bring the cloak I left with Carpus at Troas, and the books, above all my notebooks.

14   Alexander the copper-smith did me a great deal of harm. Retribution will fall upon him from the

15 Lord. You had better be on your guard against him too, for he violently opposed everything I

16 said. At the first hearing of my case no one came into court to support me; they all left me in the lurch; I pray that it may not be held against them. But the Lord 17 stood by me and lent me strength, so that I might be his instrument in making the full proclamation of the Gospel for the whole pagan world to hear; and thus I was rescued out of the lion's jaws. And 18 the Lord will rescue me from every attempt to do me harm, and keep me safe until his heavenly reign begins.[b] Glory to him for ever and ever! Amen.

Greetings to Prisca and Aquila, 19 and the household of Onesiphorus.

Erastus stayed behind at Co- 20 rinth, and I left Trophimus ill at Miletus. Do try to get here before 21 winter.

Greetings from Eubulus, Pudens, Linus, and Claudia, and from all the brotherhood here.

The Lord be with your spirit. 22 Grace be with you all!

THE LETTER OF PAUL TO

TITUS

Training for the Christian life

1 FROM Paul, servant of God and apostle of Jesus Christ, marked as such by faith and knowledge and hope – the faith of God's chosen people, knowledge of

2 the truth as our religion has it, and the hope of eternal life.[c] Yes, it is eternal life that God, who cannot

3 lie, promised long ages ago, and now in his own good time he has openly declared himself in the proclamation which was entrusted to me by ordinance of God our Saviour.

To Titus, my true-born son in 4 the faith which we share, grace and peace from God our Father and Christ Jesus our Saviour.

My intention in leaving you be- 5 hind in Crete was that you should set in order what was left over, and in particular should institute elders in each town. In doing so, observe the tests I prescribed: is he a man 6 of unimpeachable character, faithful to his one wife,[d] the father of

---

[a] Or Gaul; *some witnesses read* Gallia. bring me safely into his heavenly kingdom. bring God's chosen people to faith and to a knowledge of the truth as our religion has it, with its hope for eternal life.

[b] Or from all that evil can do, and [c] Or apostle of Jesus Christ, to knowledge of the truth as our religion

[d] *See note on* 1 Timothy 3. 2.

children who are believers, who are under no imputation of loose living, and are not out of control? 7 For as God's steward a bishop must be a man of unimpeachable character. He must not be overbearing or short-tempered; he must be no drinker, no brawler, no money-8 grubber, but hospitable, right-minded, temperate, just, devout, 9 and self-controlled. He must adhere to the true doctrine, so that he may be well able both to move his hearers with wholesome teaching and to confute objectors.

10 There are all too many, especially among Jewish converts, who are out of all control; they talk wildly and lead men's minds astray. 11 Such men must be curbed, because they are ruining whole families by teaching things they should not, 12 and all for sordid gain. It was a Cretan prophet, one of their own countrymen, who said, 'Cretans were always liars, vicious brutes, 13 lazy gluttons' – and he told the truth! All the more reason why you should pull them up sharply, so that they may come to a sane 14 belief, instead of lending their ears to Jewish myths and commandments of merely human origin, the work of men who turn their backs upon the truth.

15 To the pure all things are pure; but nothing is pure to the tainted minds of disbelievers, tainted alike 16 in reason and conscience. They profess to acknowledge God, but deny him by their actions. Their detestable obstinacy disqualifies them for any good work.

2 For your own part, what you say must be in keeping with wholesome 2 doctrine. Let the older men know that they should be sober, high-principled, and temperate, sound in faith, in love, and in endurance. 3 The older women, similarly, should be reverent in their bearing, not scandal-mongers or slaves to strong drink; they must set a high

standard, and school the younger 4 women to be loving wives and mothers, temperate, chaste, and 5 kind, busy at home, respecting the authority of their own husbands. Thus the Gospel will not be brought into disrepute.

Urge the younger men, similar-6 ly, to be temperate in all things, 7 and set them a good example yourself. In your teaching, you must show integrity and high principle, and use wholesome speech to which 8 none can take exception. This will shame any opponent, when he finds not a word to say to our discredit.

Tell slaves to respect their mas-9 ters' authority in everything, and to comply with their demands without answering back; not to 10 pilfer, but to show themselves strictly honest and trustworthy; for in all such ways they will add lustre to the doctrine of God our Saviour.

For the grace of God has 11 dawned upon the world with healing for all mankind; and by it we 12 are disciplined to renounce godless ways and worldly desires, and to live a life of temperance, honesty, and godliness in the present age, looking forward to the happy ful-13 filment of our hope when the splendour of our great God and Saviour[a] Christ Jesus will appear. He it is who sacrificed himself for 14 us, to set us free from all wickedness and to make us a pure people marked out for his own, eager to do good.

These, then, are your themes; 15 urge them and argue them. And speak with authority: let no one slight you.

Remind them to be submissive 3 to the government and the authorities, to obey them, and to be ready for any honourable form of work;[b] to slander no one, not to 2 pick quarrels, to show forbearance and a consistently gentle disposition towards all men.

---

[a] *Or of the great God and our Saviour...*　　　[b] *Or ready always to do good.*

3 For at one time we ourselves in our folly and obstinacy were all astray. We were slaves to passions and pleasures of every kind. Our days were passed in malice and envy; we were odious ourselves 4 and we hated one another. But when the kindness and generosity of God our Saviour dawned upon 5 the world, then, not for any good deeds of our own, but because he was merciful, he saved us through the water of rebirth and the renewing power of[a] the Holy Spirit. 6 For he sent down the Spirit upon us plentifully through Jesus Christ 7 our Saviour, so that, justified by his grace, we might in hope become 8 heirs to eternal life. These are words you may trust.

Such are the points I should wish you to insist on. Those who have come to believe in God should see that they engage in honourable occupations, which are not only honourable in themselves, but also 9 useful to their fellow-men.[b] But steer clear of foolish speculations, genealogies, quarrels, and controversies over the Law; they are unprofitable and pointless.

A heretic should be warned 10 once, and once again; after that, have done with him, recognizing 11 that a man of that sort has a distorted mind and stands self-condemned in his sin.

When I send Artemas to you, 12 or Tychicus, make haste to join me at Nicopolis, for that is where I have determined to spend the winter. Do your utmost to help 13 Zenas the lawyer and Apollos on their travels, and see that they are not short of anything. And our 14 own people must be taught to engage in honest employment to produce the necessities of life; they must not be unproductive.

All who are with me send you 15 greetings. My greetings to those who are our friends in truth.[c] Grace be with you all!

[a] *Or* the water of rebirth and of renewal by...
[b] *Or* should make it their business to practise virtue. These precepts are good in themselves and useful to society.
[c] *Or* our friends in the faith.

THE LETTER OF PAUL TO

PHILEMON

A runaway slave

1 FROM Paul, a prisoner of Christ Jesus, and our colleague Timothy, to Philemon our dear friend and fellow-worker, 2 and Apphia our sister, and Archippus our comrade-in-arms, and the congregation at your house. 3 Grace to you and peace from God our Father and the Lord Jesus Christ.

4 I thank my God always when 5 I mention you in my prayers, for I hear of your love and faith towards the Lord Jesus and towards 6 all God's people. My prayer is that your fellowship with us in our common faith may deepen the understanding of all the blessings that our union with Christ brings 7 us.[a] For I am delighted and encouraged by your love; through you, my brother, God's people have been much refreshed.

8 Accordingly, although in Christ I might make bold to point out 9 your duty, yet, because of that same love, I would rather appeal to you. Yes, I, Paul, ambassador as I am of Christ Jesus – and now 10 his prisoner – appeal to you about my child, whose father I have become in this prison.

11 I mean Onesimus, once so little use to you, but now useful indeed, 12 both to you and to me. I am sending him back to you, and in doing so I am sending a part of myself. 13 I should have liked to keep him with me, to look after me as you would wish, here in prison for the Gospel. But I would rather do 14 nothing without your consent, so that your kindness may be a matter not of compulsion, but of your own free will. For perhaps this is 15 why you lost him for a time, that you might have him back for good, no longer as a slave, but as more 16 than a slave – as a dear brother, very dear indeed to me and how much dearer to you, both as man and as Christian.

If, then, you count me partner 17 in the faith, welcome him as you would welcome me. And if he has 18 done you any wrong or is in your debt, put that down to my account. Here is my signature, PAUL; I 19 undertake to repay – not to mention that you owe your very self to me as well. Now brother, as a 20 Christian, be generous with me, and relieve my anxiety; we are both in Christ!

I write to you confident that 21 you will meet my wishes; I know that you will in fact do better than I ask. And one thing more: have 22 a room ready for me, for I hope that, in answer to your prayers, God will grant me to you.

Epaphras, Christ's captive like 23 myself, sends you greetings. So do 24 Mark, Aristarchus, Demas, and Luke, my fellow-workers.

The grace of the Lord Jesus 25 Christ be with your spirit!

---

[a] *Or that bring us to Christ.*

A LETTER TO

HEBREWS

Christ divine and human

1 WHEN in former times God spoke to our fore-fathers, he spoke in fragmentary and varied fashion
2 through the prophets. But in this the final age he has spoken to us in the Son whom he has made heir to the whole universe, and through whom he created all orders of exis-
3 tence: the Son who is the effulgence of God's splendour and the stamp of God's very being, and sustains[a] the universe by his word of power. When he had brought about the purgation of sins, he took his seat at the right hand of Majesty on
4 high, raised as far above the angels, as the title he has inherited is superior to theirs.

5 For God never said to any angel, 'Thou art my Son; today I have begotten thee', or again, 'I will be father to him, and he shall be my
6 son.' Again, when he presents the first-born to the world, he says, 'Let all the angels of God pay him
7 homage.' Of the angels he says,

'He who makes his angels winds,
and his ministers a fiery flame';

8 but of the Son,

'Thy throne, O God, is for ever and ever,
and the sceptre[b] of justice is the sceptre of his kingdom.
9 Thou hast loved right and hated wrong;
therefore, O God, thy God[c] has set thee above thy fellows,
by anointing with the oil of exultation.'

And again,   10

'By thee, Lord, were earth's foundations laid of old,
and the heavens are the work of thy hands.
They shall pass away, but thou 11 endurest;
like clothes they shall all grow old;
thou shalt fold them up like a 12 cloak;
yes, they shall be changed like any garment.
But thou art the same, and thy years shall have no end.'

To which of the angels has he ever 13 said, 'Sit at my right hand until I make thy enemies thy footstool'? What are they all but ministrant 14 spirits, sent out to serve, for the sake of those who are to inherit salvation?

Thus we are bound to pay all 2 the more heed to what we have been told, for fear of drifting from our course. For if the word spoken 2 through angels had such force that any transgression or disobedience met with due retribution, what es- 3 cape can there be for us if we ignore a deliverance so great? For this deliverance was first announced through the lips of the Lord himself; those who heard him confirmed it to us, and God added his 4 testimony by signs, by miracles, by manifold works of power, and by distributing the gifts of the Holy Spirit at his own will.

For it is not to angels that he 5 has subjected the world to come, which is our theme. But there is 6 somewhere a solemn assurance which runs:

---

[a] Or bears along.   [b] Or God is thy throne for ever and ever, and thy sceptre...
[c] Or therefore God who is thy God...

'What is man, that thou rememberest him,
or the son of man, that thou hast
regard to him?
7 Thou didst make him for a short
while lower than the angels;
thou didst crown him with glory
and honour;
8 thou didst put all things in subjection beneath his feet.'

For in subjecting all things to him,
he left nothing that is not subject.
But in fact we do not yet see all
9 things in subjection to man. In
Jesus, however, we do see one who[a]
for a short while was made lower
than the angels, crowned now with
glory and honour because he
suffered death, so that, by God's
gracious will, in tasting death he
should stand[b] for us all.
10 It was clearly fitting that God
for whom and through whom all
things exist should, in bringing
many sons to glory, make the
leader who delivers them perfect
11 through sufferings. For a consecrating priest and those whom he
consecrates are all of one stock; and
that is why the Son does not shrink
from calling men his brothers,
12 when he says, 'I will proclaim thy
name to my brothers; in full as-
13 sembly I will sing thy praise'; and
again, 'I will keep my trust fixed
on him'; and again, 'Here am I,
and the children whom God has
14 given me.' The children of a family
share the same flesh and blood;
and so he too shared ours, so that
through death he might break
the power of him who had death
at his command, that is, the devil;
15 and might liberate those who,
through fear of death, had all their
16 lifetime been in servitude. It is not
angels, mark you, that he takes to
himself, but the sons of Abraham.
17 And therefore he had to be made

like these brothers of his in every
way, so that he might be merciful
and faithful as their high priest
before God, to expiate the sins of
the people. For since he himself 18
has passed through the test of
suffering, he is able to help those
who are meeting their test now.

Therefore, brothers in the family 3
of God, who share a heavenly calling, think of the Apostle and High
Priest of the religion we profess,[c]
who was faithful to God who ap- 2
pointed him. Moses also was faithful in God's household; and Jesus, 3
of whom I speak, has been deemed
worthy of greater honour than
Moses, as the founder of a house
enjoys more honour than his
household. For every house has its 4
founder; and the founder of all is
God. Moses, then, was faithful as 5
a servitor in God's whole household; his task was to bear witness
to the words that God would
speak; but Christ is faithful as a 6
son, set over his household. And
we are that household of his, if
only we are fearless and keep our
hope high.

'TODAY', therefore, as the Holy 7
Spirit says –

'Today if you hear his voice,
do not grow stubborn as in those 8
days of rebellion,
at that time of testing in the
desert,
where your forefathers tried me 9
and tested me,
and saw[d] the things I did for forty
years.
And so, I was indignant with that 10
generation
and I said, Their hearts are for
ever astray;
they would not discern my ways;
as I vowed in my anger, they shall 11
never enter my rest.'

---

[a] Or *in subjection to him. But we see Jesus, who...*
[b] *Some witnesses read* so that apart from God he should taste death...
[c] Or *of him whom we confess as God's Envoy and High Priest.*
[d] Or *though they saw...*

12 See to it, brothers, that no one among you has the wicked, faithless heart of a deserter from the 13 living God; but day by day, while that word 'Today' still sounds in your ears, encourage one another, so that no one of you is made 14 stubborn by the wiles of sin. For we have become Christ's partners[a] if only we keep our original confidence firm to the end.

15 When Scripture says, 'Today if you hear his voice, do not grow stubborn as in those days of rebel- 16 lion', who, I ask, were those who heard and rebelled? All those, surely, whom Moses had led out of 17 Egypt. And with whom was God indignant for forty years? With those, surely, who had sinned, whose bodies lay where they fell 18 in the desert. And to whom did he vow that they should not enter his rest, if not to those who had refused 19 to believe? We perceive that it was unbelief which prevented their entering.

4 Therefore we must have before us the fear that while the promise of entering his rest remains open, one or another among you should be found to have missed his chance. 2 For indeed we have heard the good news, as they did. But in them the message they heard did no good, because it met with no faith in those 3 who heard it. It is we, we who have become believers, who enter the rest referred to in the words, 'As I vowed in my anger, they shall never enter my rest.' Yet God's work has been finished ever since 4 the world was created; for does not Scripture somewhere speak thus of the seventh day: 'God rested from all his work on the 5 seventh day'? – and once again in the passage above we read, 'They 6 shall never enter my rest.' The fact remains that someone must enter it, and since those who first heard the good news failed to enter

through unbelief, God fixes an- 7 other day. Speaking through the lips of David after many long years, he uses the words already quoted: 'Today if you hear his voice, do not grow stubborn.' If 8 Joshua had given them rest, God would not thus have spoken of another day after that. Therefore, 9 a sabbath rest still awaits the people of God; for anyone who 10 enters God's rest, rests from his own work as God did from his. Let 11 us then make every effort to enter that rest, so that no one may fall by following this evil example of unbelief.

For the word of God is alive and 12 active. It cuts more keenly than any two-edged sword, piercing as far as the place where life and spirit, joints and marrow, divide. It sifts the purposes and thoughts of the heart. There is nothing in 13 creation that can hide from him; everything lies naked and exposed to the eyes of the One with whom we have to reckon.

Since therefore we have a great 14 high priest who has passed through the heavens, Jesus the Son of God, let us hold fast to the religion we profess. For ours is not a high 15 priest unable to sympathize with our weaknesses, but one who, because of his likeness to us, has been tested every way,[b] only without sin. Let us therefore boldly 16 approach the throne of our gracious God, where we may receive mercy and in his grace find timely help.

The shadow and the real

FOR every high priest is taken 5 from among men and appointed their representative before God, to offer gifts and sacrifices for sins. He is able to bear patiently with 2 the ignorant and erring, since he too is beset by weakness; and 3 because of this he is bound to make

---

,[a] Or have been given a share in Christ.
 [b] Or who has been tested every way, as we are.

sin-offerings for himself no less than for the people. And nobody 4 arrogates the honour to himself: he is called by God, as indeed 5 Aaron was. So it is with Christ: he did not confer upon himself the glory of becoming high priest; it was granted by God, who said to him, 'Thou art my Son; today I 6 have begotten thee'; as also in another place he says, 'Thou art a priest for ever, in the succession 7 of Melchizedek.' In the days of his earthly life he offered up prayers and petitions, with loud cries and tears, to God who was able to deliver him from the grave. Because of his humble submission 8 his prayer was heard: son though he was, he learned obedience in 9 the school of suffering, and, once perfected, became the source of eternal salvation for all who obey 10 him, named by God high priest in the succession of Melchizedek.

11 About Melchizedek we have much to say, much that is difficult to explain, now that you have 12 grown so dull of hearing. For indeed, though by this time you ought to be teachers, you need someone to teach you the ABC of God's oracles over again; it has come to this, that you need milk 13 instead of solid food. Anyone who lives on milk, being an infant, does 14 not know[a] what is right. But grown men can take solid food; their perceptions are trained by long use to discriminate between good and evil.

6 Let us then stop discussing the rudiments of Christianity. We ought not to be laying over again the foundations of faith in God and of repentance from the dead- 2 ness of our former ways, by instruction[b] about cleansing rites and the laying-on-of-hands, about the resurrection of the dead and

eternal judgement. Instead, let us advance towards maturity; and so 3 we shall, if God permits.

For when men have once been 4 enlightened, when they have had a taste of the heavenly gift and a share in the Holy Spirit, when 5 they have experienced the goodness of God's word and the spiritual energies of the age to come, and 6 after all this have fallen away, it is impossible to bring them again to repentance; for with their own hands they are crucifying[c] the Son of God and making mock of his death. When the earth drinks in 7 the rain that falls upon it from time to time, and yields a useful crop to those for whom it is cultivated, it is receiving its share of blessing from God; but if it bears 8 thorns and thistles, it is worthless and God's curse hangs over it; the end of that is burning. But although 9 we speak as we do, we are convinced that you, my friends, are in the better case, and this makes for your salvation. For God would 10 not be so unjust as to forget all that you did for love of his name, when you rendered service to his people, as you still do. But we 11 long for every one of you to show the same eager concern, until your hope is finally realized. We want 12 you not to become lazy, but to imitate those who, through faith and patience, are inheriting the promises.

When God made his promise to 13 Abraham, he swore by himself, because he had no one greater to swear by: 'I vow that I will bless 14 you abundantly and multiply your descendants.' Thus it was that 15 Abraham, after patient waiting, attained the promise. Men swear 16 by a greater than themselves, and the oath provides a confirmation to end all dispute; and so God, 17

---

[a] *Or* is incompetent to speak of...
[b] *Or, according to some witnesses,* laying the foundations over again: repentance from the deadness of our former ways and faith in God, instruction...
[c] *Or* crucifying again.

desiring to show even more clearly to the heirs of his promise how unchanging was his purpose, guaran- 18 teed it by oath. Here, then, are two irrevocable acts in which God could not possibly play us false, to give powerful encouragement to us, who have claimed his protection by grasping[a] the hope set before 19 us. That hope we hold. It is like an anchor for our lives, an anchor safe and sure. It enters in through 20 the veil, where Jesus has entered on our behalf as forerunner, having become a high priest for ever in the succession of Melchizedek.

7 THIS Melchizedek, king of Salem, priest of God Most High, met Abraham returning from the rout 2 of the kings and blessed him; and Abraham gave him a tithe of everything as his portion. His name, in the first place, means 'king of righteousness'; next he is king of Salem, that is, 'king of 3 peace'. He has no father, no mother, no lineage; his years have no beginning, his life no end. He is like the Son of God: he remains a priest for all time.

4   Consider now how great he must be for Abraham the patriarch to give him a tithe of the finest of 5 the spoil. The descendants of Levi who take the priestly office are commanded by the Law to tithe the people, that is, their kinsmen, although they too are descendants 6 of Abraham. But Melchizedek, though he does not trace his descent from them, has tithed Abraham himself, and given his blessing to the man who received 7 the promises; and beyond all dispute the lesser is always blessed 8 by the greater. Again, in the one instance tithes are received by men who must die; but in the other, by one whom Scripture affirms to 9 be alive. It might even be said that Levi, who receives tithes, has himself been tithed through Abra-

ham; for he was still in his ances- 10 tor's loins when Melchizedek met him.

Now if perfection had been at- 11 tainable through the Levitical priesthood (for it is on this basis that the people were given the Law), what further need would there have been to speak of another priest arising, in the succession of Melchizedek, instead of the succession of Aaron? For a change of 12 priesthood must mean a change of law. And the one here spoken 13 of belongs to a different tribe, no member of which has ever had anything to do with the altar. For 14 it is very evident that our Lord is sprung from Judah, a tribe to which Moses made no reference in speaking of priests.

The argument becomes still 15 clearer, if the new priest who arises is one like Melchizedek, owing his 16 priesthood not to a system of earth-bound rules but to the power of a life that cannot be destroyed. For here is the testi- 17 mony: 'Thou art a priest for ever, in the succession of Melchizedek.' The earlier rules are cancelled as 18 impotent and useless, since the 19 Law brought nothing to perfection; and a better hope is introduced, through which we draw near to God.

How great a difference it makes 20 that an oath was sworn! There was 21 no oath sworn when those others were made priests; but for this priest an oath was sworn, as Scripture says of him: 'The Lord has sworn and will not go back on his word, "Thou art a priest for ever."' How far superior must the 22 covenant also be of which Jesus is the guarantor! Those other 23 priests are appointed in numerous succession, because they are prevented by death from continuing in office; but the priesthood which 24 Jesus holds is perpetual, because he remains for ever. That is why 25

<hr>

[a] Or to give to us, who have claimed his protection, a powerful incentive to grasp...

he is also able to save absolutely those who approach God through him; he is always living to plead on their behalf.

26 Such a high priest does indeed fit our condition – devout, guileless, undefiled, separated from sinners, raised high above the heavens.

27 He has no need to offer sacrifices daily, as the high priests do, first for his own sins and then for those of the people; for this he did once and for all when he offered up

28 himself. The high priests made by the Law are men in all their frailty; but the priest appointed by the words of the oath which supersedes the Law is the Son, made perfect now for ever.

8 Now this is my main point: just such a high priest we have, and he has taken his seat at the right hand of the throne of Majesty in

2 the heavens, a ministrant in the real sanctuary, the tent pitched

3 by the Lord and not by man. Every high priest is appointed to offer gifts and sacrifices; hence, this one too must have[a] something to offer.

4 Now if he had been on earth, he would not even have been a priest, since there are already priests who offer the gifts which the Law pre-

5 scribes, though they minister in a sanctuary which is only a copy and shadow of the heavenly. This is implied when Moses, about to erect the tent, is instructed by God: 'See to it that you make everything according to the pattern shown you on the mountain.'

6 But in fact the ministry which has fallen to Jesus is as far superior to theirs as are the covenant he mediates and the promises upon which it is legally secured.

7 Had that first covenant been faultless, there would have been no need to look for a second in its

8 place. But God, finding fault with them, says, 'The days are coming, says the Lord, when I will conclude a new covenant with the house of Israel and the house of Judah. It

9 will not be like the covenant I made with their forefathers when I took them by the hand to lead them out of Egypt; because they did not abide by the terms of that covenant, and I abandoned them, says the Lord. For the covenant I will

10 make with the house of Israel after those days, says the Lord, is this: I will set my laws in their understanding and write them on their hearts; and I will be their God, and they shall be my people. And they

11 shall not teach one another, saying to brother and fellow-citizen,[b] "Know the Lord!" For all of them, high and low, shall know me; I will

12 be merciful to their wicked deeds, and I will remember their sins no more.' By speaking of a new

13 covenant, he has pronounced the first one old; and anything that is growing old and ageing will shortly disappear.

9 The first covenant indeed had its ordinances of divine service and its sanctuary, but a material

2 sanctuary. For a tent was prepared – the first tent – in which was the lamp-stand, and the table with the bread of the Presence; this is

3 called the Holy Place. Beyond the second curtain was the tent called

4 the Most Holy Place. Here was a golden altar of incense, and the ark of the covenant plated all over with gold, in which were a golden jar containing the manna, and Aaron's staff which once budded, and the tablets of the covenant;

5 and above it the cherubim of God's glory, overshadowing the place of expiation. On these we cannot now enlarge.

6 Under this arrangement, the priests are always entering the first tent in the discharge of their

7 duties; but the second is entered only once a year, and by the high priest alone, and even then he

---

[a] *Or* must have had.　　　[b] *Some witnesses read* brother and neighbour.

must take with him the blood which he offers on his own behalf and for the people's sins of ignor-

8 ance. By this the Holy Spirit signifies that so long as the earlier tent still stands, the way into the

9 sanctuary remains unrevealed. All this is symbolic, pointing to the present time. The offerings and sacrifices there prescribed cannot give the worshipper inward per-

10 fection. It is only a matter of food and drink and various rites of cleansing – outward ordinances in force until the time of reformation.

11 But now Christ has come, high priest of good things already in being.[a] The tent of his priesthood is a greater and more perfect one, not made by men's hands, that is, not belonging to this created world;

12 the blood of his sacrifice is his own blood, not the blood of goats and calves; and thus he has entered the sanctuary once and for all and

13 secured an eternal deliverance. For if the blood of goats and bulls and the sprinkled ashes of a heifer have power to hallow those who have been defiled and restore their ex-

14 ternal purity, how much greater is the power of the blood of Christ; he offered himself without blemish to God, a spiritual and eternal sacrifice; and his blood will cleanse our conscience from the deadness of our former ways and fit us for the service of the living God.

15 And therefore he is the mediator of a new covenant, or testament, under which, now that there has been a death to bring deliverance from sins committed under the former covenant, those whom God has called may receive the promise

16 of the eternal inheritance. For where there is a testament it is necessary for the death of the

17 testator to be established. A testament is operative only after a death: it cannot possibly have

force while the testator is alive.

18 Thus we find that the former covenant itself was not inaugurated

19 without blood. For when, as the Law directed, Moses had recited all the commandments to the people, he took the blood of the calves, with water, scarlet wool, and marjoram, and sprinkled the law-book itself and all the people,

20 saying, 'This is the blood of the covenant which God has enjoined

21 upon you.' In the same way he also sprinkled the tent and all the vessels of divine service with blood.

22 Indeed, according to the Law, it might almost be said, everything is cleansed by blood and without the shedding of blood there is no forgiveness.

23 If, then, these sacrifices cleanse the copies of heavenly things, those heavenly things themselves require better sacrifices to cleanse

24 them. For Christ has entered, not that sanctuary made by men's hands which is only a symbol of the reality, but heaven itself, to appear now before God on our

25 behalf. Nor is he there to offer himself again and again, as the high priest enters the sanctuary year by year with blood not his

26 own. If that were so, he would have had to suffer many times since the world was made. But as it is, he has appeared once and for all at the climax of history to abolish sin by the sacrifice of him-

27 self. And as it is the lot of men to die once, and after death comes

28 judgement, so Christ was offered once to bear the burden of men's sins,[b] and will appear a second time, sin done away, to bring salvation to those who are watching for him.

10 FOR the Law contains but a shadow, and no true image,[c] of the good things which were to come; it provides for the same sacrifices

[a] *Some witnesses read* good things which were (*or* are) to be.
[b] *Or* to remove men's sins.   [c] *One witness reads* a shadow and likeness...

year after year, and with these it can never bring the worshippers 2 to perfection for all time.[a] If it could, these sacrifices would surely have ceased to be offered, because the worshippers, cleansed once for all, would no longer have any sense 3 of sin. But instead, in these sacrifices year after year sins are brought 4 to mind, because sins can never be removed by the blood of bulls and goats.

5 That is why, at his coming into the world, he says:

'Sacrifice and offering thou didst not desire,
but thou hast prepared a body for me.
6 Whole-offerings and sin-offerings thou didst not delight in.
7 Then I said, "Here am I: as it is written of me in the scroll,
I have come, O God, to do thy will."'

8 First he says, 'Sacrifices and offerings, whole-offerings and sin-offerings, thou didst not desire nor delight in'—although the Law pre-9 scribes them—and then he says, 'I have come to do thy will.' He thus annuls the former to establish the 10 latter. And it is by the will of God that we have been consecrated, through the offering of the body of Jesus Christ once and for all.

11 Every priest stands performing his service daily and offering time after time the same sacrifices, 12 which can never remove sins. But Christ offered for all time one sacrifice for sins, and took his seat 13 at the right hand of God, where he waits henceforth until his ene-14 mies are made his footstool. For by one offering he has perfected for all time those who are thus 15 consecrated. Here we have also the testimony of the Holy Spirit: 16 he first says, 'This is the covenant which I will make with them after

those days, says the Lord: I will set my laws in their hearts and write them on their understanding'; then he adds, 'and their sins and 17 wicked deeds I will remember no more at all.' And where these have 18 been forgiven, there are offerings for sin no longer.

So now, my friends, the blood of 19 Jesus makes us free to enter boldly into the sanctuary by the new, 20 living way which he has opened for us through the curtain, the way of his flesh.[b] We have, more- 21 over, a great priest set over the household of God; so let us make 22 our approach in sincerity of heart and full assurance of faith, our guilty hearts sprinkled clean, our bodies washed with pure water. Let 23 us be firm and unswerving in the confession of our hope, for the Giver of the promise may be trusted. We ought to see how each 24 of us may best arouse others to love and active goodness, not stay- 25 ing away from our meetings, as some do, but rather encouraging one another, all the more because you see the Day drawing near.

For if we wilfully persist in sin 26 after receiving the knowledge of the truth, no sacrifice for sins re-mains: only a terrifying expecta- 27 tion of judgement and a fierce fire which will consume God's enemies. If a man disregards the Law of 28 Moses, he is put to death without pity on the evidence of two or three witnesses. Think how much more 29 severe a penalty that man will deserve who has trampled under foot the Son of God, profaned the blood of the covenant by which he was consecrated, and affronted God's gracious Spirit! For we know 30 who it is that has said, 'Justice is mine: I will repay'; and again, 'The Lord will judge his people.' It is a terrible thing to fall into 31 the hands of the living God.

[a] *Or* bring to perfection the worshippers who come continually.
[b] *Or* through the curtain of his flesh.

32 Remember the days gone by, when, newly enlightened, you met the challenge of great sufferings 33 and held firm. Some of you were abused and tormented to make a public show, while others stood loyally by those who were so 34 treated. For indeed you shared the sufferings of the prisoners, and you cheerfully accepted the seizure of your possessions, knowing that you possessed something better 35 and more lasting. Do not then throw away your confidence, for 36 it carries a great reward. You need endurance, if you are to do God's will and win what he has promised. 37 For 'soon, very soon' (in the words of Scripture), 'he who is to come 38 will come; he will not delay; and by faith my righteous servant shall find life; but if a man shrinks back, 39 I take no pleasure in him.' But we are not among those who shrink back and are lost; we have the faith to make life our own.

A call to faith

11 A N D what is faith? Faith gives substance[a] to our hopes, and makes us certain of realities we do not see.
2 It is for their faith that the men of old stand on record.
3 By faith we perceive that the universe was fashioned by the word of God, so that the visible came forth from the invisible.
4 By faith Abel offered a sacrifice greater than Cain's, and through faith his goodness was attested, for his offerings had God's approval; and through faith he continued to speak after his death.
5 By faith Enoch was carried away to another life without passing through death; he was not to be found, because God had taken him. For it is the testimony of Scripture that before he was taken
6 he had pleased God, and without faith it is impossible to please him; for anyone who comes to God must

believe that he exists and that he rewards those who search for him.
7 By faith Noah, divinely warned about the unseen future, took good heed and built an ark to save his household. Through his faith he put the whole world in the wrong, and made good his own claim to the righteousness which comes of faith.
8 By faith Abraham obeyed the call to go out to a land destined for himself and his heirs, and left home without knowing where he 9 was to go. By faith he settled as an alien in the land promised him, living in tents, as did Isaac and Jacob, who were heirs to the same 10 promise. For he was looking forward to the city with firm foundations, whose architect and builder is God.
11 By faith even Sarah herself received strength to conceive, though she was past the age, because she judged that he who had 12 promised would keep faith; and therefore from one man, and one as good as dead, there sprang descendants numerous as the stars or as the countless grains of sand on the sea-shore.
13 All these persons died in faith. They were not yet in possession of the things promised, but had seen them far ahead and hailed them, and confessed themselves no more than strangers or passing 14 travellers on earth. Those who use such language show plainly that they are looking for a country of 15 their own. If their hearts had been in the country they had left, they could have found opportunity to 16 return. Instead, we find them longing for a better country – I mean, the heavenly one. That is why God is not ashamed to be called their God; for he has a city ready for them.
17 By faith Abraham, when the test came, offered up Isaac: he had received the promises, and

---

[a] *Or* assurance.

yet he was on the point of offering
18 his only son, of whom he had been told, 'Through the line of Isaac your descendants shall be traced.'[a]
19 For he reckoned that God had power even to raise from the dead – and from the dead, he did, in a sense, receive him back.
20 By faith Isaac blessed Jacob and Esau and spoke of things to come.
21 By faith Jacob, as he was dying, blessed each of Joseph's sons, and worshipped God, leaning on the
22 top of his staff. By faith Joseph, at the end of his life, spoke of the departure of Israel from Egypt, and instructed them what to do with his bones.
23 By faith, when Moses was born, his parents hid him for three months, because they saw what a fine child he was; they were not
24 afraid of the king's edict. By faith Moses, when he grew up, refused to be called the son of Pharaoh's
25 daughter, preferring to suffer hardship with the people of God rather than enjoy the transient pleasures
26 of sin. He considered the stigma that rests on God's Anointed greater wealth than the treasures of Egypt, for his eyes were fixed upon the coming day of recom-
27 pense. By faith he left Egypt, and not because he feared the king's anger; for he was resolute, as one who saw the invisible God.
28 By faith he celebrated the Passover and sprinkled the blood, so that the destroying angel might not touch the first-born of Israel.
29 By faith they crossed the Red Sea as though it were dry land, whereas the Egyptians, when they attempted the crossing, were drowned.
30 By faith the walls of Jericho fell down after they had been encircled
31 on seven successive days. By faith the prostitute Rahab escaped the doom of the unbelievers, because

she had given the spies a kindly welcome.

Need I say more? Time is too 32 short for me to tell the stories of Gideon, Barak, Samson, and Jephthah, of David and Samuel and the prophets. Through faith they 33 overthrew kingdoms, established justice, saw God's promises fulfilled. They muzzled ravening lions, quenched the fury of fire, escaped 34 death by the sword. Their weakness was turned to strength, they grew powerful in war, they put foreign armies to rout. Women 35 received back their dead raised to life. Others were tortured to death, disdaining release, to win a better resurrection. Others, again, 36 had to face jeers and flogging, even fetters and prison bars. They were 37 stoned,[b] they were sawn in two, they were put to the sword, they went about dressed in skins of sheep or goats, in poverty, distress, and misery. They were too good 38 for a world like this. They were refugees in deserts and on the hills, hiding in caves and holes in the ground. These also, one and all, 39 are commemorated for their faith; and yet they did not enter upon the promised inheritance, because, 40 with us in mind, God had made a better plan, that only in company with us should they reach their perfection.

A N D what of ourselves? With all 12 these witnesses to faith around us like a cloud, we must throw off every encumbrance, every sin to which we cling,[c] and run with resolution the race for which we are entered, our eyes fixed on 2 Jesus, on whom faith depends from start to finish: Jesus who, for the sake of the joy that lay ahead of him,[d] endured the cross, making light of its disgrace, and has taken

[a] Or God's call shall be for your descendants in the line of Isaac.
[b] Some witnesses insert they were put to the question.
[c] Or every clinging sin; one witness reads the sin which all too readily distracts us.
[d] Or who, in place of the joy that was open to him, . . .

his seat at the right hand of the throne of God.

3 Think of him who submitted to such opposition from sinners: that will help you not to lose heart and 4 grow faint. In your struggle against sin, you have not yet resisted to the point of shedding your blood. 5 You have forgotten the text of Scripture which addresses you as sons and appeals to you in these words:

'My son, do not think lightly of the Lord's discipline,
nor lose heart when he corrects you;
6 for the Lord disciplines those whom he loves;
he lays the rod on every son whom he acknowledges.'

7 You must endure it as discipline: God is treating you as sons. Can anyone be a son, who is not disci-8 plined by his father? If you escape the discipline in which all sons share, you must be bastards and 9 no true sons. Again, we paid due respect to the earthly fathers who disciplined us; should we not submit even more readily to our spiritual Father, and so attain life? 10 They disciplined us for this short life according to their lights; but he does so for our true welfare, so that we may share his holiness. 11 Discipline, no doubt, is never pleasant; at the time it seems painful, but in the end it yields for those who have been trained by it the peaceful harvest of an honest 12 life. Come, then, stiffen your drooping arms and shaking knees, 13 and keep your steps from wavering. Then the disabled limb will not be put out of joint, but regain its former powers.

14 Aim at peace with all men, and a holy life, for without that no one 15 will see the Lord. Look to it that there is no one among you who forfeits the grace of God, no bitter, noxious weed growing up to poison

the whole, no immoral person, no 16 one worldly-minded like Esau. He sold his birthright for a single meal, and you know that although he 17 wanted afterwards to claim the blessing, he was rejected; though he begged for it to the point of tears, he found no way open for second thoughts.

REMEMBER where you stand: 18 not before the palpable, blazing fire of Sinai, with the darkness, gloom, and whirlwind, the trumpet-blast 19 and the oracular voice, which they heard, and begged to hear no more; for they could not bear the 20 command, 'If even an animal touches the mountain, it must be stoned.' So appalling was the sight, 21 that Moses said, 'I shudder with fear.'

No, you stand before Mount 22 Zion and the city of the living God, heavenly Jerusalem, before myriads of angels, the full con-23 course and assembly of the first-born citizens of heaven, and God the judge of all, and the spirits of good men made perfect, and Jesus 24 the mediator of a new covenant, whose sprinkled blood has better things to tell than the blood of Abel. See that you do not refuse 25 to hear the voice that speaks. Those who refused to hear the oracle speaking on earth found no escape; still less shall we escape if we refuse to hear the One who speaks from heaven. Then indeed 26 his voice shook the earth, but now he has promised, 'Yet once again I will shake not earth alone, but the heavens also.' The words 'once 27 again' – and only once – imply that the shaking of these created things means their removal, and then what is not shaken will remain. The kingdom we are given is un-28 shakable; let us therefore give thanks to God, and so worship him as he would be worshipped, with reverence and awe; for our God is 29 a devouring fire.

13 NEVER cease to love your fellow-Christians.

2 Remember to show hospitality. There are some who, by so doing, have entertained angels without knowing it.

3 Remember those in prison as if you were there with them; and those who are being maltreated, for you like them are still in the world.

4 Marriage is honourable; let us all keep it so, and the marriage-bond inviolate; for God's judgement will fall on fornicators and adulterers.

5 Do not live for money; be content with what you have; for God himself has said, 'I will never leave 6 you or desert you'; and so we can take courage and say, 'The Lord is my helper, I will not fear; what can man do to me?'

7 Remember your leaders, those who first spoke God's message to you; and reflecting upon the outcome of their life and work, follow the example of their faith.

8 Jesus Christ is the same yester-9 day, today, and for ever. So do not be swept off your course by all sorts of outlandish teachings; it is good that our souls should gain their strength from the grace of God, and not from scruples about what we eat, which have never done any good to those who were governed by them.

10 Our altar is one from which*a* the priests of the sacred tent have 11 no right to eat. As you know, those animals whose blood is brought as a sin-offering by the high priest into the sanctuary, have their bodies burnt outside the camp, 12 and therefore Jesus also suffered outside the gate, to consecrate the people by his own blood. Let us 13 then go to him outside the camp, bearing the stigma that he bore. For here we have no permanent 14 home, but we are seekers after the city which is to come. Through 15 Jesus, then, let us continually offer up to God the sacrifice of praise, that is, the tribute of lips which acknowledge his name, and never 16 forget to show kindness and to share what you have with others; for such are the sacrifices which God approves.

Obey your leaders and defer to 17 them; for they are tireless in their concern for you, as men who must render an account. Let it be a happy task for them, and not pain and grief, for that would bring you no advantage.

Pray for us; for we are convinced 18 that our conscience is clear; our one desire is always to do what is right. All the more earnestly I ask 19 for your prayers, that I may be restored to you the sooner.

May the God of peace, who 20 brought up from the dead our Lord Jesus, the great Shepherd of the sheep, by the blood of the eternal covenant, make you per- 21 fect in all goodness so that you may do his will; and may he make of us what he would have us be through Jesus Christ, to whom be glory for ever and ever! Amen.

I beg you, brothers, bear with 22 this exhortation; for it is after all a short letter. I have news for you: 23 our friend Timothy has been released; and if he comes in time he will be with me when I see you.

Greet all your leaders and all 24 God's people. Greetings to you from our Italian friends.

God's grace be with you all!   25

a Or one like that from which...

A LETTER OF

JAMES

Practical religion

1 FROM James, a servant of God and the Lord Jesus Christ.

Greetings to the Twelve Tribes dispersed throughout the world.

2 My brothers, whenever you have to face trials of many kinds, count 3 yourselves supremely happy, in the knowledge that such testing 4 of your faith breeds fortitude, and if you give fortitude full play you will go on to complete a balanced character that will fall short in 5 nothing. If any of you falls short in wisdom, he should ask God for it and it will be given him, for God is a generous giver who neither refuses nor reproaches anyone. 6 But he must ask in faith, without a doubt in his mind; for the doubter is like a heaving sea ruffled by 7 the wind. A man of that kind must not expect the Lord to give him 8 anything; he is double-minded, and never can keep[a] a steady course. 9 The brother in humble circumstances may well be proud that 10 God lifts him up; and the wealthy brother must find his pride in being brought low. For the rich man will disappear like the flower 11 of the field; once the sun is up with its scorching heat the flower withers, its petals fall, and what was lovely to look at is lost for ever. So shall the rich man wither away as he goes about his business. 12 Happy the man who remains steadfast under trial, for having passed that test he will receive for his prize the gift of life promised 13 to those who love God. No one under trial or temptation should say, 'I am being tempted by God'; for God is untouched by evil,[b] and does not himself tempt anyone. Temptation arises when a man is 14 enticed and lured away by his own lust; then lust conceives, and gives 15 birth to sin; and sin full-grown breeds death.

Make no mistake, my friends. 16 All good giving, every perfect gift, 17 comes[c] from above, from the Father of the lights of heaven. With him there is no variation, no play of passing shadows.[d] Of his 18 set purpose, by declaring the truth, he gave us birth to be a kind of firstfruits of his creatures.

Of that you may be certain, my 19 friends. But each of you must be quick to listen, slow to speak, and slow to be angry. For a man's anger 20 cannot promote the justice of God. Away then with all that is sordid, 21 and the malice that hurries to excess, and quietly accept the message planted in your hearts, which can bring you salvation.

Only be sure that you act on 22 the message and do not merely listen; for that would be to mislead yourselves. A man who listens to 23 the message but never acts upon it is like one who looks in a mirror at the face nature gave him. He 24 glances at himself and goes away, and at once forgets what he looked like. But the man who looks closely 25 into the perfect law, the law that makes us free, and who lives in its company, does not forget what he hears, but acts upon it; and that is the man who by acting will find happiness.

---

[a] Or anything; a double-minded man never keeps...   [b] Or God cannot be tempted by evil.   [c] Or All giving is good, and every perfect gift comes... [d] Some witnesses read no variation, or shadow caused by change.

26 A man may think he is religious, but if he has no control over his tongue, he is deceiving himself; 27 that man's religion is futile. The kind of religion which is without stain or fault in the sight of God our Father is this: to go to the help of orphans and widows in their distress and keep oneself untarnished by the world.

2 M Y brothers, believing as you do in our Lord Jesus Christ, who reigns in glory, you must never 2 show snobbery. For instance, two visitors may enter your place of worship, one a well-dressed man with gold rings, and the other a 3 poor man in shabby clothes. Suppose you pay special attention to the well-dressed man and say to him, 'Please take this seat', while to the poor man you say, 'You can stand; or you may sit here*a* on 4 the floor by my footstool', do you not see that you are inconsistent and judge by false standards? 5 Listen, my friends. Has not God chosen those who are poor in the eyes of the world to be rich in faith and to inherit the kingdom he has promised to those who love 6 him? And yet you have insulted the poor man. Moreover, are not the rich your oppressors? Is it not 7 they who drag you into court and pour contempt on the honoured name by which God has claimed you? 8 If, however, you are observing the sovereign law laid down in Scripture, 'Love your neighbour 9 as yourself', that is excellent. But if you show snobbery, you are committing a sin and you stand convicted by that law as trans- 10 gressors. For if a man keeps the whole law apart from one single point, he is guilty of breaking all 11 of it. For the One who said, 'Thou shalt not commit adultery', said also, 'Thou shalt not commit

murder.' You may not be an adulterer, but if you commit murder you are a law-breaker all the same. Always speak and act 12 as men who are to be judged under a law of freedom. In that judge- 13 ment there will be no mercy for the man who has shown no mercy. Mercy triumphs over judgement.

M Y brothers, what use is it for a 14 man to say he has faith when he does nothing to show it? Can that faith save him? Suppose a brother 15 or a sister is in rags with not enough food for the day, and one of you 16 says, 'Good luck to you, keep yourselves warm, and have plenty to eat', but does nothing to supply their bodily needs, what is the good of that? So with faith; if it 17 does not lead to action, it is in itself a lifeless thing.

But someone may object: 'Here 18 is one who claims to have faith and another who points to his deeds.' To which I reply: 'Prove to me that this faith you speak of is real though not accompanied by deeds, and by my deeds I will prove to you my faith.' You have faith 19 enough to believe that there is one God. Excellent! The devils have faith like that, and it makes them tremble. But can you not see, you 20 quibbler, that faith divorced from deeds is barren? Was it not by his 21 action, in offering his son Isaac upon the altar, that our father Abraham was justified? Surely you 22 can see that faith was at work in his actions, and that by these actions the integrity of his faith was fully proved. Here was fulfil- 23 ment of the words of Scripture: 'Abraham put his faith in God, and that faith was counted to him as righteousness'; and elsewhere he is called 'God's friend'. You see 24 then that a man is justified by deeds and not by faith in itself. The same is true of the prostitute 25

---

a Some witnesses read Stand where you are or sit here . . . ; *others read* Stand where you are or sit . . .

Rahab also. Was not she justified by her action in welcoming the messengers into her house and sending them away by a different 26 route? As the body is dead when there is no breath left in it, so faith divorced from deeds is lifeless as a corpse.

3 My brothers, not many of you should become teachers, for you may be certain that we who teach shall ourselves be judged with 2 greater strictness. All of us often go wrong; the man who never says a wrong thing is a perfect character, 3 able to bridle his whole being. If we put bits into horses' mouths to make them obey our will, we can 4 direct their whole body. Or think of ships: large they may be, yet even when driven by strong gales they can be directed by a tiny rudder on whatever course the 5 helmsman chooses. So with the tongue. It is a small member but it can make huge claims.[a]

What an immense stack of timber[b] can be set ablaze by the 6 tiniest spark! And the tongue is in effect a fire. It represents among our members the world with all its wickedness; it pollutes our whole being; it keeps the wheel of our existence red-hot, and its flames 7 are fed by hell. Beasts and birds of every kind, creatures that crawl on the ground or swim in the sea, can be subdued and have been sub-8 dued by mankind; but no man can subdue the tongue. It is an intractable evil, charged with 9 deadly venom. We use it to sing the praises of our Lord and Father, and we use it to invoke curses upon our fellow-men who are made 10 in God's likeness. Out of the same mouth come praises and curses. My brothers, this should not be 11 so. Does a fountain gush with both fresh and brackish water from the 12 same opening? Can a fig-tree, my brothers, yield olives, or a vine

figs? No more does salt water yield fresh.

Who among you is wise or clever? 13 Let his right conduct give practical proof of it, with the modesty that comes of wisdom. But if you are 14 harbouring bitter jealousy and selfish ambition in your hearts, consider whether your claims are not false, and a defiance of the truth. This is not the wisdom that 15 comes from above; it is earth-bound, sensual, demonic. For with 16 jealousy and ambition come dis-order and evil of every kind. But 17 the wisdom from above is in the first place pure; and then peace-loving, considerate, and open to reason; it is straightforward and sincere, rich in mercy and in the kindly deeds that are its fruit. True 18 justice is the harvest reaped by peacemakers from seeds sown in a spirit of peace.

What causes conflicts and quar- 4 rels among you? Do they not spring from the aggressiveness of your bodily desires? You want some- 2 thing which you cannot have, and so you are bent on murder; you are envious, and cannot attain your ambition, and so you quarrel and fight. You do not get what you want, because you do not pray for it. Or, if you do, your requests 3 are not granted because you pray from wrong motives, to spend what you get on your pleasures. You false, unfaithful creatures! 4 Have you never learned that love of the world is enmity to God? Whoever chooses to be the world's friend makes himself God's enemy. Or do you suppose that Scripture 5 has no meaning when it says that the spirit which God implanted in man turns towards envious desires? And yet the grace he gives is 6 stronger. Thus Scripture says, 'God opposes the arrogant and gives grace to the humble.' Be 7 submissive then to God. Stand up

---

[a] *Or* it is a great boaster.   [b] *Or* What a huge forest...

to the devil and he will turn and 8 run. Come close to God, and he will come close to you. Sinners, make your hands clean; you who are double-minded, see that your 9 motives are pure. Be sorrowful, mourn and weep. Turn your laughter into mourning and your gaiety 10 into gloom. Humble yourselves before God and he will lift you high.

11 Brothers, you must never disparage one another. He who disparages a brother or passes judgement on his brother disparages the law and judges the law. But if you judge the law, you are not keeping it but sitting in judgement upon 12 it. There is only one lawgiver and judge, the One who is able to save life and destroy it. So who are you to judge your neighbour?

13 A WORD with you, you who say, 'Today or tomorrow we will go off to such and such a town and spend a year there trading and making 14 money.' Yet you have no idea what tomorrow will bring. Your life, what is it? You are no more than a mist, seen for a little while and 15 then dispersing. What you ought to say is: 'If it be the Lord's will, we shall live to do this or that.' 16 But instead, you boast and brag, and all such boasting is wrong. 17 Well then, the man who knows the good he ought to do and does not do it is a sinner.

5 Next a word to you who have great possessions. Weep and wail over the miserable fate descending 2 on you. Your riches have rotted; your fine clothes are moth-eaten; 3 your silver and gold have rusted away, and their very rust will be evidence against you and consume your flesh like fire. You have piled up wealth in an age that is near its 4 close. The wages you never paid to the men who mowed your fields are loud against you, and the outcry of the reapers has reached the 5 ears of the Lord of Hosts. You

have lived on earth in wanton luxury, fattening yourselves like cattle – and the day for slaughter has come. You have condemned 6 the innocent and murdered him; he offers no resistance.

Be patient, my brothers, until 7 the Lord comes. The farmer looking for the precious crop his land may yield can only wait in patience, until the autumn and spring rains have fallen. You too must be 8 patient and stout-hearted, for the coming of the Lord is near. My 9 brothers, do not blame your troubles on one another, or you will fall under judgement; and there stands the Judge, at the door. If 10 you want a pattern of patience under ill-treatment, take the prophets who spoke in the name of the Lord; remember: 'We count 11 those happy who stood firm.' You have all heard how Job stood firm, and you have seen how the Lord treated him in the end. For the Lord is full of pity and compassion.

ABOVE all things, my brothers, do 12 not use oaths, whether 'by heaven' or 'by earth' or by anything else. When you say yes or no, let it be plain 'Yes' or 'No', for fear that you expose yourselves to judgement.

Is anyone among you in trouble? 13 He should turn to prayer. Is anyone in good heart? He should sing praises. Is one of you ill? He should 14 send for the elders of the congregation to pray over him and anoint him with oil in the name of the Lord. The prayer offered in faith 15 will save the sick man, the Lord will raise him from his bed, and any sins he may have committed will be forgiven. Therefore confess 16 your sins to one another, and pray for one another, and then you will be healed. A good man's prayer is powerful and effective. Elijah was 17 a man with human frailties like our own; and when he prayed earnestly that there should be no rain, not a drop fell on the land

18 for three years and a half; then he prayed again, and down came the rain and the land bore crops once more.

19 My brothers, if one of your number should stray from the truth and another succeed in bringing him back, be sure of this: any 20 man who brings a sinner back from his crooked ways will be rescuing his soul from death and cancelling innumerable sins.

THE FIRST LETTER OF

PETER

The calling of a Christian

1 FROM Peter, apostle of Jesus Christ, to those of God's scattered people who lodge for a while in Pontus, Galatia, Cappa-
2 docia, Asia, and Bithynia – chosen of old in the purpose of God the Father, hallowed to his service by the Spirit, and consecrated with the sprinkled blood of Jesus Christ. Grace and peace to you in fullest measure.

3 Praise be to the God and Father of our Lord Jesus Christ, who in his great mercy gave us new birth into a living hope by the resurrection of Jesus Christ from the
4 dead! The inheritance to which we are born is one that nothing can destroy or spoil or wither. It is
5 kept for you in heaven, and you, because you put your faith in God, are under the protection of his power until salvation comes – the salvation which is even now in readiness and will be revealed at the end of time.

6 This is cause for great joy, even though now you smart for a little while, if need be, under trials of
7 many kinds. Even gold passes through the assayer's fire, and more precious than perishable gold is faith which has stood the test. These trials come so that your faith may prove itself worthy of all praise, glory, and honour when Jesus Christ is revealed.

8 You have not seen him, yet you love him; and trusting in him now without seeing him, you are transported with a joy too great for words, while you reap the harvest 9 of your faith, that is, salvation for your souls. This salvation was the 10 theme which the prophets pondered and explored, those who prophesied about the grace of God awaiting you. They tried to find out 11 what was the time,[a] and what the circumstances, to which the spirit of Christ in them pointed, foretelling the sufferings in store for Christ and the splendours to follow; and it was disclosed to them that 12 the matter they treated of was not for their time but for yours. And now it has been openly announced to you through preachers who brought you the Gospel in the power of the Holy Spirit sent from heaven. These are things that angels long to see into.

You must therefore be mentally 13 stripped for action, perfectly self-controlled. Fix your hopes on the gift of grace which is to be yours when Jesus Christ is revealed. As 14 obedient children, do not let your characters be shaped any longer by the desires you cherished in

---

[a] *Or who was the person...*

15 your days of ignorance. The One who called you is holy; like him, be holy in all your behaviour,
16 because Scripture says, 'You shall be holy, for I am holy.'
17 If you say 'our Father' to the One who judges every man impartially on the record of his deeds, you must stand in awe of him while you live out your time on earth.
18 Well you know that it was no perishable stuff, like gold or silver, that bought your freedom from the empty folly of your traditional
19 ways. The price was paid in precious blood, as it were of a lamb without mark or blemish – the
20 blood of Christ. Predestined before the foundation of the world, he was made manifest in this last period
21 of time for your sake. Through him you have come to trust in God who raised him from the dead and gave him glory, and so your faith and hope are fixed on God.
22 Now that by obedience to the truth you have purified your souls until you feel sincere affection towards your brother Christians, love one another whole-heartedly
23 with all your strength. You have been born anew, not of mortal parentage but of immortal, through the living and enduring word of
24 God.[a] For (as Scripture says)

'All mortals are like grass;
all their splendour like the flower of the field;
the grass withers, the flower falls;
25 but the word of the Lord endures for evermore.'

And this 'word' is the word of the Gospel preached to you.
2 Then away with all malice and deceit, away with all pretence and jealousy and recrimination of every
2 kind! Like the new-born infants you are, you must crave for pure milk (spiritual milk, I mean), so that you may thrive upon it to

your souls' health. Surely you have 3 tasted that the Lord is good.
So come to him, our living Stone 4 – the stone rejected by men but choice and precious in the sight of God. Come, and let yourselves be 5 built, as living stones, into a spiritual temple; become a holy priesthood,[b] to offer spiritual sacrifices acceptable to God through Jesus Christ. For it stands written: 6

'I lay in Zion a choice corner-stone of great worth.
The man who has faith in it will not be put to shame.'

The great worth of which it speaks 7 is for you who have faith. For those who have no faith, the stone which the builders rejected has become not only the corner-stone,[c] but also 8 'a stone to trip over, a rock to stumble against'. They fall when they disbelieve the Word. Such was their appointed lot!
But you are a chosen race, a 9 royal priesthood, a dedicated nation, and a people claimed by God for his own, to proclaim the triumphs of him who has called you out of darkness into his marvellous light. You are now the 10 people of God, who once were not his people; outside his mercy once, you have now received his mercy.

DEAR friends, I beg you, as aliens 11 in a foreign land, to abstain from the lusts of the flesh which are at war with the soul. Let all your 12 behaviour be such as even pagans can recognize as good, and then, whereas they malign you as criminals now, they will come to see for themselves that you live good lives, and will give glory to God on the day when he comes to hold assize.
Submit yourselves to every hu- 13 man institution for the sake of the Lord, whether to the sovereign as

[a] *Or* through the word of the living and enduring God.   [b] *Or* a spiritual temple for the holy work of priesthood.   [c] *Or* the apex of the building.

14 supreme, or to the governor as his deputy for the punishment of criminals and the commendation
15 of those who do right. For it is the will of God that by your good conduct you should put ignorance and stupidity to silence.

16 Live as free men; not however as though your freedom were there to provide a screen for wrongdoing,
17 but as slaves in God's service. Give due honour to everyone: love to the brotherhood, reverence to God, honour to the sovereign.

18 Servants, accept the authority of your masters with all due submission, not only when they are kind and considerate, but even
19 when they are perverse. For it is a fine[a] thing if a man endure the pain of undeserved suffering be-
20 cause God is in his thoughts. What credit is there in fortitude when you have done wrong and are beaten for it? But when you have behaved well and suffer for it, your fortitude is a fine thing[b] in the
21 sight of God. To that you were called, because Christ suffered[c] on your behalf, and thereby left you an example; it is for you to follow
22 in his steps. He committed no sin, he was convicted of no falsehood;
23 when he was abused he did not retort with abuse, when he suffered he uttered no threats, but committed his cause to the One who judges
24 justly. In his own person he carried our sins to[d] the gibbet, so that we might cease to live for sin and begin to live for righteousness. By his wounds you have been healed.
25 You were straying like sheep, but now you have turned towards the Shepherd and Guardian of your souls.

3 In the same way you women must accept the authority of your husbands, so that if there are any of them who disbelieve the Gospel they may be won over, without a
2 word being said, by observing the chaste and reverent behaviour of their wives. Your beauty should 3 reside, not in outward adornment – the braiding of the hair, or jewellery, or dress – but in the inmost 4 centre of your being, with its imperishable ornament, a gentle, quiet spirit, which is of high value in the sight of God. Thus it was 5 among God's people in days of old: the women who fixed their hopes on him adorned themselves by submission to their husbands. Such 6 was Sarah, who obeyed Abraham and called him 'my master'. Her children you have now become, if you do good and show no fear.

In the same way, you husbands 7 must conduct your married life with understanding: pay honour to the woman's body, not only because it is weaker, but also because you share together in the grace of God which gives you life. Then your prayers will not be hindered.

To sum up: be one in thought 8 and feeling, all of you; be full of brotherly affection, kindly and humble-minded. Do not repay 9 wrong with wrong, or abuse with abuse; on the contrary, retaliate with blessing, for a blessing is the inheritance to which you yourselves have been called.

'Whoever loves life and would see 10 good days
must restrain his tongue from evil and his lips from deceit;
must turn from wrong and do 11 good,
seek peace and pursue it.
For the Lord's eyes are turned to- 12 wards the righteous,
his ears are open to their prayers;
but the Lord's face is set against wrong-doers.'

WHO is going to do you wrong if 13 you are devoted to what is good? And yet if you should suffer for 14 your virtues, you may count yourselves happy. Have no fear of

---

[a] *Or* creditable.   [b] *Or* is creditable.   [c] *Some witnesses read* died.   [d] *Or* on.

15 them:[a] do not be perturbed, but hold the Lord Christ in reverence in your hearts.[b] Be always ready with your defence whenever you are called to account for the hope that is in you, but make that defence with modesty and respect.
16 Keep your conscience clear, so that when you are abused, those who malign your Christian conduct
17 may be put to shame. It is better to suffer for well-doing, if such should be the will of God, than for
18 doing wrong. For Christ also died[c] for our sins[d] once and for all. He, the just, suffered for the unjust, to bring us to God.

In the body he was put to death; in the spirit he was brought to life.
19 And in the spirit he went and made his proclamation to the imprisoned
20 spirits. They had refused obedience long ago, while God waited patiently in the days of Noah and the building of the ark, and in the ark a few persons, eight in all, were brought to safety through the
21 water. This water prefigured the water of baptism through which you are now brought to safety. Baptism is not the washing away of bodily pollution, but the appeal made to God by a good conscience; and it brings salvation through the resurrection of Jesus Christ,
22 who entered heaven after receiving the submission of angelic authorities and powers, and is now at the right hand of God.

4 Remembering that Christ endured bodily suffering, you must arm yourselves with a temper of mind like his. When a man has thus endured bodily suffering he
2 has finished with sin, and for the rest of his days on earth he may live, not for the things that men desire, but for what God wills.
3 You had time enough in the past to do all the things that men want to do in the pagan world. Then

you lived in licence and debauchery, drunkenness, revelry, and tippling, and the forbidden worship of idols.
Now, when you no longer plunge 4 with them into all this reckless dissipation, they cannot understand it, and they vilify you accordingly; but they shall answer 5 for it to him who stands ready to pass judgement on the living and the dead. Why was the Gospel 6 preached to those who are dead? In order that, although in the body they received the sentence common to men, they might in the spirit be alive with the life of God.

The end of all things is upon us, 7 so you must lead an ordered and sober life, given to prayer. Above 8 all, keep your love for one another at full strength, because love cancels innumerable sins. Be hos- 9 pitable to one another without complaining. Whatever gift each 10 of you may have received, use it in service to one another, like good stewards dispensing the grace of God in its varied forms. Are you 11 a speaker? Speak as if you uttered oracles of God. Do you give service? Give it as in the strength which God supplies. In all things so act that the glory may be God's through Jesus Christ; to him belong glory and power for ever and ever. Amen.

My dear friends, do not be be- 12 wildered by the fiery ordeal that is upon you, as though it were something extraordinary. It gives you a 13 share in Christ's sufferings, and that is cause for joy; and when his glory is revealed, your joy will be triumphant. If Christ's name is 14 flung in your teeth as an insult, count yourselves happy, because then that glorious Spirit which is the Spirit of God is resting upon you. If you suffer, it must not be 15

---

[a] *Or* Do not fear what they fear.   [b] *Or* hold Christ in reverence in your hearts, as Lord.   [c] *Some witnesses read* suffered.
[d] *Some witnesses read* for sins; *others read* for sins on our behalf.

for murder, theft, or sorcery,[a] nor for infringing the rights of others.

16 But if anyone suffers as a Christian, he should feel it no disgrace, but confess that name to the honour of God.

17 The time has come for the judgement to begin; it is beginning with God's own household. And if it is starting with you, how will it end for those who refuse to obey the

18 gospel of God? It is hard enough for the righteous to be saved; what then will become of the impious

19 and sinful? So even those who suffer, if it be according to God's will, should commit their souls to him – by doing good; their Maker will not fail them.

5 And now I appeal to the elders of your community, as a fellow-elder and a witness of Christ's sufferings, and also a partaker in the splendour that is to be revealed.

2 Tend that flock of God whose shepherds you are, and do it, not under compulsion, but of your own free will, as God would have it; not for gain but out of sheer

3 devotion; not tyrannizing over those who are allotted to your care, but setting an example to the

4 flock. And then, when the Head Shepherd appears, you will receive for your own the unfading garland of glory.

5 In the same way you younger men must be subordinate to your elders. Indeed, all of you should wrap yourselves in the garment of humility towards each other, because God sets his face against the arrogant but favours the humble.

6 Humble yourselves then under God's mighty hand, and he will lift you up in due time. Cast all 7 your cares on him, for you are his charge.

8 Awake! be on the alert! Your enemy the devil, like a roaring lion, prowls round looking for someone to devour. Stand up to 9 him, firm in faith, and remember that your brother Christians are going through the same kinds of suffering while they are in the world. And the God of all grace, 10 who called you into his eternal glory in Christ, will himself, after your brief suffering, restore, establish, and strengthen you on a firm foundation. He holds dominion for 11 ever and ever. Amen.

12 I write you this brief appeal through Silvanus, our trusty brother as I hold him, adding my testimony that this is the true grace of God. In this stand fast.

13 Greetings from her who dwells in Babylon, chosen by God like you, and from my son Mark. Greet 14 one another with the kiss of love.

Peace to you all who belong to Christ!

[a] *Or* other crime.

THE SECOND LETTER OF

PETER

The remedy for doubt

1 FROM Simeon Peter, servant and apostle of Jesus Christ, to those who through the justice of our God and Saviour Jesus Christ share our faith and enjoy equal privilege with ourselves.

2 Grace and peace be yours in fullest measure, through the knowledge of God and Jesus our Lord.

3 His divine power has bestowed on us everything that makes for life and true religion, enabling us to know the One who called us by his own splendour and might.

4 Through this might and splendour he has given us his promises, great beyond all price, and through them you may escape the corruption with which lust has infected the world, and come to share in the very being of God.

5 With all this in view, you should try your hardest to supplement your faith with virtue, virtue with 6 knowledge, knowledge with self-control, self-control with fortitude, 7 fortitude with piety, piety with brotherly kindness, and brotherly kindness with love.

8 These are gifts which, if you possess and foster them, will keep you from being either useless or barren in the knowledge of our 9 Lord Jesus Christ. The man who lacks them is short-sighted and blind; he has forgotten how he was 10 cleansed from his former sins. All the more then, my friends, exert yourselves to clinch God's choice and calling of you. If you behave so, you will never come to grief. 11 Thus you will be afforded full and free admission into the eternal kingdom of our Lord and Saviour Jesus Christ.

And so I will not hesitate to 12 remind you of this again and again, although you know it and are well grounded in the truth that has already reached you. Yet I think 13 it right to keep refreshing your memory so long as I still lodge in this body. I know that very soon 14 I must leave it; indeed our Lord Jesus Christ has told me so.[a] But 15 I will see to it that after I am gone you will have means of remembering these things at all times.

It was not on tales artfully spun 16 that we relied when we told you of the power of our Lord Jesus Christ and his coming; we saw him with our own eyes in majesty, when at the hands of God the 17 Father he was invested with honour and glory, and there came to him from the sublime Presence a voice which said: 'This is my Son, my Beloved,[b] on whom my favour rests.' This voice from 18 heaven we ourselves heard; when it came, we were with him on the sacred mountain.

All this only confirms for us the 19 message of the prophets,[c] to which you will do well to attend, for it is like a lamp shining in a murky place, until the day breaks and the morning star rises to illuminate your minds.

BUT first note this: no one can 20 interpret any prophecy of Scripture by himself. For it was not 21 through any human whim that men prophesied of old; men they were, but, impelled by the Holy

---

[a] Or I must leave it, as our Lord Jesus Christ told me.   [b] Or This is my only Son.
[c] Or And in the message of the prophets we have something still more certain.

Spirit, they spoke the words of God.

2 But Israel had false prophets as well as true; and you likewise will have false teachers among you. They will import disastrous heresies, disowning the very Master who bought them, and bringing swift disaster on their own heads. 2 They will gain many adherents to their dissolute practices, through whom the true way will be brought 3 into disrepute. In their greed for money they will trade on your credulity with sheer fabrications.

But the judgement long decreed for them has not been idle; perdition waits for them with unsleeping 4 eyes. God did not spare the angels who sinned, but consigned them to the dark pits of hell,[a] where they 5 are reserved for judgement. He did not spare the world of old (except for Noah, preacher of righteousness, whom he preserved with seven others), but brought the deluge upon that world of godless 6 men. The cities of Sodom and Gomorrah God burned to ashes, and condemned them to total destruction, making them an object-lesson for godless men in future 7 days. But he rescued Lot, who was a good man, shocked by the dissolute habits of the lawless society 8 in which he lived; day after day every sight, every sound, of their evil courses tortured that good 9 man's heart. Thus the Lord is well able to rescue the godly out of trials, and to reserve the wicked under punishment until the day of judgement.

10 Above all he will punish those who follow their abominable lusts. They flout authority; reckless and headstrong, they are not afraid to 11 insult celestial beings, whereas angels, for all their superior strength and might, employ no insults in seeking judgement against them before the Lord.

These men are like brute beasts, 12 born in the course of nature to be caught and killed. They pour abuse upon things they do not understand; like the beasts they will perish, suffering hurt for the hurt 13 they have inflicted. To carouse in broad daylight is their idea of pleasure; while they sit with you at table they are an ugly blot on your company, because they revel in their own deceptions.[b]

They have eyes for nothing but 14 women, eyes never at rest from sin. They lure the unstable to their ruin; past masters in mercenary greed, God's curse is on them! They have abandoned the straight 15 road and lost their way. They have followed in the steps of Balaam son of Beor, who consented to take pay for doing wrong, but had his 16 offence brought home to him when the dumb beast spoke with a human voice and put a stop to the prophet's madness.

These men are springs that give 17 no water, mists driven by a storm; the place reserved for them is blackest darkness. They utter big, 18 empty words, and make of sensual lusts and debauchery a bait to catch those who have barely begun to escape from their heathen environment. They promise them 19 freedom, but are themselves slaves of corruption; for a man is the slave of whatever has mastered him. They had once escaped the world's 20 defilements through the knowledge of our Lord and Saviour Jesus Christ; yet if they have entangled themselves in these all over again, and are mastered by them, their plight in the end is worse than before. How much better never 21 to have known the right way, than, having known it, to turn back and abandon the sacred commandments delivered to them! For them 22 the proverb has proved true: 'The dog returns to its own vomit', and,

---

[a] *Some witnesses read* consigned them to darkness and chains in hell.
[b] *Some witnesses read* in their love-feasts.

'The sow after a wash rolls in the mud again.'

3 THIS is now my second letter to you, my friends. In both of them I have been recalling to you what you already know, to rouse you 2 to honest thought. Remember the predictions made by God's own prophets, and the commands given by the Lord and Saviour through your apostles.

3 Note this first: in the last days there will come men who scoff at religion and live self-indulgent 4 lives, and they will say: 'Where now is the promise of his coming? Our fathers have been laid to their rest, but still everything continues exactly as it has always been since the world began.'

5 In taking this view they lose sight of the fact[a] that there were heavens and earth long ago, created by God's word out of water 6 and with water; and by water that first world was destroyed, the 7 water of the deluge. And the present heavens and earth, again by God's word, have been kept in store for burning; they are being reserved until the day of judgement when the godless will be destroyed.

8 And here is one point, my friends, which you must not lose sight of: with the Lord one day is like a thousand years and a thou-9 sand years like one day. It is not that the Lord is slow in fulfilling his promise, as some suppose, but that he is very patient with you, because it is not his will for any to be lost, but for all to come to repentance.

But the Day of the Lord will 10 come; it will come, unexpected as a thief. On that day the heavens will disappear with a great rushing sound, the elements will disintegrate in flames, and the earth with all that is in it will be laid bare.[b]

Since the whole universe is to 11 break up in this way, think what sort of people you ought to be, what devout and dedicated lives you should live! Look eagerly for 12 the coming of the Day of God and work to hasten it on; that day will set the heavens ablaze until they fall apart, and will melt the elements in flames. But we have his 13 promise, and look forward to new heavens and a new earth, the home of justice.

With this to look forward to, do 14 your utmost to be found at peace with him, unblemished and above reproach in his sight. Bear in mind 15 that our Lord's patience with us is our salvation, as Paul, our friend and brother, said when he wrote to you with his inspired wisdom. And so he does in all his other 16 letters, wherever he speaks of this subject, though they contain some obscure passages, which the ignorant and unstable misinterpret to their own ruin, as they do the other scriptures.[c]

But you, my friends, are fore-17 warned. Take care, then, not to let these unprincipled men seduce you with their errors; do not lose your own safe foothold. But grow 18 in the grace and in the knowledge of our Lord and Saviour Jesus Christ.[d] To him be glory now and for all eternity!

---

[a] *Or* They choose to overlook the fact . . .
[b] *Some witnesses read* will be burnt up.
[c] *Or* his other writings.
[d] *Or* But grow up, by the grace of our Lord and Saviour Jesus Christ, and by knowing him.

THE FIRST LETTER OF

JOHN

Recall to fundamentals

1 IT was there from the beginning; we have heard it; we have seen it with our own eyes; we looked upon it, and felt it with our own hands; and it is of this we tell. 2 Our theme is the word of life. This life was made visible; we have seen it and bear our testimony; we here declare to you the eternal life which dwelt with the Father and 3 was made visible to us. What we have seen and heard we declare to you, so that you and we together may share in a common life, that life which we share with the Father and his Son Jesus 4 Christ. And we write this in order that the joy of us all may be complete.

5 Here is the message we heard from him and pass on to you: that God is light, and in him there is 6 no darkness at all. If we claim to be sharing in his life while we walk in the dark, our words and our 7 lives are a lie; but if we walk in the light as he himself is in the light, then we share together a common life, and we are being cleansed from every sin by the blood of Jesus his Son.

8 If we claim to be sinless, we are self-deceived and strangers to the 9 truth. If we confess our sins, he is just, and may be trusted to forgive our sins and cleanse us from every 10 kind of wrong; but if we say we have committed no sin, we make him out to be a liar, and then his word has no place in us.

2 My children, in writing thus to you my purpose is that you should not commit sin. But should anyone

commit a sin, we have one to plead our cause[a] with the Father, Jesus Christ, and he is just. He is himself 2 the remedy for the defilement of our sins, not our sins only but the sins of all the world.

Here is the test by which we 3 can make sure that we know him: do we keep his commands? The 4 man who says, 'I know him', while he disobeys his commands, is a liar and a stranger to the truth; but in the man who is obedient to 5 his word, the divine love has indeed come to its perfection.

Here is the test by which we can make sure that we are in him: whoever claims to be dwelling in 6 him, binds himself to live as Christ himself lived. Dear friends, I give 7 you no new command. It is the old command which you always had before you; the old command is the message which you heard at the beginning. And yet again it is 8 a new command that I am giving you – new in the sense that the darkness is passing and the real light already shines. Christ has made this true, and it is true in your own experience.

A man may say, 'I am in the 9 light'; but if he hates his brother, he is still in the dark. Only the 10 man who loves his brother dwells in light: there is nothing to make him stumble. But one who hates 11 his brother is in darkness; he walks in the dark and has no idea where he is going, because the darkness has made him blind.

I write to you, my children, be- 12 cause your sins have been forgiven for his sake.[b]

---

[a] Literally we have an advocate...
[b] Or forgiven, since you bear his name.

282

13 I write to you, fathers, because
you know him who is and has
been from the beginning.[a]
I write to you, young men, because
you have mastered the evil one.

To you, children, I have written
because you know the Father.
14 To you, fathers, I have written
because you know him who is and
has been from the beginning.[a]
To you, young men, I have written
because you are strong; God's
word remains in you, and you
have mastered the evil one.

15 Do not set your hearts on the
godless world or anything in it.
Anyone who loves the world is a
stranger to the Father's love.
16 Everything the world affords, all
that panders to the appetites or
entices the eyes, all the glamour
of its life, springs not from the
Father but from the godless world.
17 And that world is passing away
with all its allurements, but he who
does God's will stands for evermore.

18 MY children, this is the last hour!
You were told that Antichrist was
to come, and now many antichrists
have appeared; which proves to
us that this is indeed the last hour.
19 They went out from our company,
but never really belonged to us;
if they had, they would have stayed with us. They went out, so that
it might be clear that not all in
our company truly belong to it.[b]
20 You, no less than they, are
among the initiated;[c] this is the
gift of the Holy One, and by it
21 you all have knowledge.[d] It is not
because you are ignorant of the
truth that I have written to you,
but because you know it, and

because lies, one and all, are alien
to the truth.

Who is the liar? Who but he 22
that denies that Jesus is the Christ?
He is Antichrist, for he denies both
the Father and the Son: to deny 23
the Son is to be without the Father;
to acknowledge the Son is to have
the Father too. You therefore must 24
keep in your hearts that which you
heard at the beginning; if what
you heard then still dwells in you,
you will yourselves dwell in the
Son and also in the Father. And 25
this is the promise that he himself
gave us, the promise of eternal
life.

So much for those who would 26
mislead you. But as for you, the 27
initiation[e] which you received
from him stays with you; you need
no other teacher, but learn all you
need to know from his initiation,
which is real and no illusion. As he
taught you, then, dwell in him.

Even now, my children, dwell 28
in him, so that when he appears
we may be confident and un-
ashamed before him at his coming.
If you know that he is righteous, 29
you must recognize that every man
who does right is his child. How 3
great is the love that the Father
has shown to us! We were called
God's children, and such we are;[f]
and the reason why the godless
world does not recognize us is that
it has not known him. Here and 2
now, dear friends, we are God's
children; what we shall be has not
yet been disclosed, but we know
that when it is disclosed[g] we shall
be like him,[h] because we shall see
him as he is. Everyone who has this 3
hope before him purifies himself,
as Christ is pure.

To commit sin is to break God's 4
law: sin, in fact, is lawlessness.

---

[a] *Or* him whom we have known from the beginning.   [b] *Or* that none of
them truly belong to us.   [c] *Literally* have an anointing (*Greek* chrism).
[d] *Some witnesses read* you have all knowledge.   [e] *Literally* the anointing.
[f] *Or* We are called children of God! Not only called, we really are his children.
[g] *Or* when he appears.   [h] *Or* we are God's children, though he has not yet
appeared; what we shall be we know, for when he does appear we shall be like him.

5 Christ appeared, as you know, to do away with sins, and there is
6 no sin in him. No man therefore who dwells in him is a sinner; the sinner has not seen him and does not know him.

7 My children, do not be misled: it is the man who does right who is righteous, as God is righteous;
8 the man who sins is a child of the devil, for the devil has been a sinner from the first; and the Son of God appeared for the very purpose of undoing the devil's work.
9 A child of God does not commit sin, because the divine seed remains in him; he cannot be a sinner, because he is God's child.
10 That is the distinction between the children of God and the children of the devil: no one who does not do right is God's child, nor is anyone who does not love his
11 brother. For the message you have heard from the beginning is this: that we should love one another;
12 unlike Cain, who was a child of the evil one and murdered his brother. And why did he murder him? Because his own actions were wrong, and his brother's were right.

13 My brothers, do not be surprised
14 if the world hates you. We for our part have crossed over from death to life; this we know, because we love our brothers. The man who does not love is still in the realm
15 of death, for everyone who hates his brother is a murderer, and no murderer, as you know, has eternal
16 life dwelling within him. It is by this that we know what love is: that Christ laid down his life for us. And we in our turn are bound to lay down our lives for our brothers.
17 But if a man has enough to live on, and yet when he sees his brother

in need shuts up his heart against him, how can it be said that the divine love[a] dwells in him?

18 My children, love must not be a matter of words or talk; it must be genuine, and show itself in
19 action. This is how we may know that we belong to the realm of truth, and convince ourselves in
20 his sight that even if our conscience condemns us, God is greater than our conscience[b] and knows all.

21 Dear friends, if our conscience does not condemn us, then we can approach God with confidence,
22 and obtain from him whatever we ask, because we are keeping his commands and doing what he
23 approves. This is his command: to give our allegiance to his Son Jesus Christ and love one another as he
24 commanded. When we keep his commands we dwell in him and he dwells in us. And this is how we can make sure that he dwells within us: we know it from the Spirit he has given us.

4 BUT do not trust any and every spirit, my friends; test the spirits, to see whether they are from God, for among those who have gone out into the world there are many
2 prophets falsely inspired. This is how we may recognize the Spirit of God: every spirit which acknowledges that Jesus Christ has come in the flesh is from God, and every
3 spirit which does not thus acknowledge Jesus is not from God. This is what is meant by 'Antichrist';[c] you have been told that he was to come, and here he is, in the world already!
4 But you, my children, are of God's family, and you have the mastery over these false prophets, because he who inspires you is greater than he who inspires the

---

[a] *Or* that love for God...
[b] *Or* and reassure ourselves in his sight in matters where our conscience condemns us, because God is greater than our conscience...; *or* and yet we shall do well to convince ourselves that if even our own conscience condemns us, still more will God who is greater than conscience...   [c] *Or* This is the spirit of Antichrist.

5 godless world. They are of that world, and so therefore is their teaching; that is why the world
6 listens to them. But we belong to God, and a man who knows God listens to us, while he who does not belong to God refuses us a hearing. That is how we distinguish the spirit of truth from the spirit of error.

7 Dear friends, let us love one another, because love is from God. Everyone who loves is a child of
8 God and knows God, but the unloving know nothing of God. For
9 God is love; and his love was disclosed to us in this, that he sent his only Son into the world to
10 bring us life. The love I speak of is not our love for God, but the love he showed to us in sending his Son as the remedy for the defile-
11 ment of our sins. If God thus loved us, dear friends, we in turn are
12 bound to love one another. Though God has never been seen by any man, God himself dwells in us if we love one another; his love is brought to perfection within us.
13 Here is the proof that we dwell in him and he dwells in us: he has
14 imparted his Spirit to us. Moreover, we have seen for ourselves, and we attest, that the Father sent the Son to be the saviour of
15 the world, and if a man acknowledges that Jesus is the Son of God, God dwells in him and he dwells
16 in God. Thus we have come to know and believe the love which God has for us.

God is love; he who dwells in love is dwelling in God, and God
17 in him. This is for us the perfection of love, to have confidence on the day of judgement, and this we can have, because even in this
18 world we are as he is. There is no room for fear in love; perfect love banishes fear. For fear brings with it the pains of judgement, and anyone who is afraid has not at-
19 tained to love in its perfection. We
20 love because he loved us first. But if a man says, 'I love God', while hating his brother, he is a liar. If he does not love the brother whom he has seen, it cannot be that he loves God whom he has not seen. And indeed this command comes 21 to us from Christ himself: that he who loves God must also love his brother.

Everyone who believes that 5 Jesus is the Christ is a child of God, and to love the parent means to love his child; it follows that when 2 we love God and obey his commands we love his children too. For 3 to love God is to keep his commands; and they are not burdensome, because every child of God is 4 victor over the godless world. The victory that defeats the world is our faith, for who is victor over the 5 world but he who believes that Jesus is the Son of God?

This is he who came with water 6 and blood: Jesus Christ. He came, not by water alone, but by water and blood; and there is the Spirit to bear witness, because the Spirit is truth. For there are three wit- 7, 8 nesses, the Spirit, the water, and the blood, and these three are in agreement. We accept human 9 testimony, but surely divine testimony is stronger, and this threefold testimony is indeed that of God himself, the witness he has borne to his Son. He who believes 10 in the Son of God has this testimony in his own heart, but he who disbelieves God, makes him out to be a liar, by refusing to accept God's own witness to his Son. The 11 witness is this: that God has given us eternal life, and that this life is found in his Son. He who possesses 12 the Son has life indeed; he who does not possess the Son of God has not that life.

THIS letter is to assure you that 13 you have eternal life. It is addressed to those who give their allegiance to the Son of God. We can approach God with 14 confidence for this reason: if we make requests which accord with his will he listens to us; and if we ¹⁵ know that our requests are heard, we know also that the things we ask for are ours.

¹⁶ If a man sees his brother committing a sin which is not a deadly sin, he should pray to God for him, and he will grant him life – that is, when men are not guilty of deadly sin. There is such a thing as deadly sin, and I do not suggest that he should pray about that; ¹⁷ but although all wrongdoing is sin, not all sin is deadly sin.

We know that no child of God ¹⁸ is a sinner; it is the Son of God who keeps him safe, and the evil one cannot touch him.

We know that we are of God's ¹⁹ family, while the whole godless world lies in the power of the evil one.

We know that the Son of God ²⁰ has come and given us understanding to know him who is real; indeed we are in him who is real, since we are in his Son Jesus Christ. This is the true God, this is eternal life. My children, be on the watch ²¹ against false gods.

THE SECOND LETTER OF

JOHN

Truth and love

¹ THE ELDER to the Lady chosen by God, and her children, whom I love in truth – and not I alone but all who know ² the truth – for the sake of the truth that dwells among us and will be with us for ever.

³ Grace, mercy, and peace shall be with us from God the Father and from Jesus Christ the Son of the Father, in truth and love.

⁴ I was delighted to find that some of your children are living by the truth, as we were commanded by ⁵ the Father. And now I have a request to make of you. Do not think I am giving a new command; I am recalling the one we have had before us from the beginning: ⁶ let us love one another. And love means following the commands of God. This is the command which was given you from the beginning, to be your rule of life.

⁷ Many deceivers have gone out into the world, who do not acknowledge Jesus Christ as coming in the flesh. These are the persons described as the Antichrist, the arch-deceiver. Beware of them, so that ⁸ you may not lose all that we worked for, but receive your reward in full.

Anyone who runs ahead too far, ⁹ and does not stand by the doctrine of the Christ, is without God; he who stands by that doctrine possesses both the Father and the Son. If anyone comes to you who ¹⁰ does not bring this doctrine, do not welcome him into your house or give him a greeting; for anyone ¹¹ who gives him a greeting is an accomplice in his wicked deeds.

I have much to write to you, but ¹² I do not care to put it down in black and white. But I hope to visit you and talk with you face to face, so that our joy may be complete. The children of your ¹³ Sister, chosen by God, send their greetings.

THE THIRD LETTER OF

JOHN

Trouble in the church

1 THE ELDER to dear Gaius, whom I love in truth.
2 My dear Gaius, I pray that you may enjoy good health, and that all may go well with you, as I know it goes well with your
3 soul. I was delighted when friends came and told me how true you have been; indeed you are true in
4 your whole life. Nothing gives me greater joy than to hear that my children are living by the truth.

5 My dear friend, you show a fine loyalty in everything that you do for these our fellow-Christians, strangers though they are to you.
6 They have spoken of your kindness before the congregation here. Please help them on their journey in a manner worthy of the God we
7 serve. It was on Christ's work that they went out; and they would
8 accept nothing from pagans. We are bound to support such men, and so play our part in spreading the truth.

9 I sent a letter to the congregation, but Diotrephes, their would-be leader,[a] will have nothing to do
10 with us. If I come, I will bring up the things he is doing. He lays baseless and spiteful charges against us; not satisfied with that, he refuses to receive our friends, and he interferes with those who would do so, and tries to expel them from the congregation.

11 My dear friend, do not imitate bad examples, but good ones. The well-doer is a child of God; the evil-doer has never seen God.

12 Demetrius gets a good testimonial from everybody – yes, and from the truth itself. I add my testimony, and you know that my testimony is true.

13 I have much to write to you, but I do not care to set it down
14 with pen and ink. I hope to see you very soon, and we will talk face to face. Peace be with you. Our friends send their greetings. Greet our friends one by one.

[a] Or who enjoys being their leader.

A LETTER OF

JUDE

The danger of false belief

1 FROM Jude, servant of Jesus Christ and brother of James, to those whom God has called, who live in the love of God the Father and in the safe keeping of Jesus Christ.

2 Mercy, peace, and love be yours in fullest measure.

3 My friends, I was fully engaged in writing to you about our salvation – which is yours no less than ours – when it became urgently necessary to write at once and appeal to you to join the struggle in defence of the faith, the faith which God entrusted to his people 4 once and for all. It is in danger from certain persons who have wormed their way in, the very men whom Scripture long ago marked down for the doom they have incurred. They are the enemies of religion; they pervert the free favour of our God into licentiousness, disowning Jesus Christ, our only Master and Lord.[a]

5 You already know it all, but let me remind you how the Lord,[b] having once delivered the people of Israel out of Egypt, next time destroyed those who were guilty 6 of unbelief. Remember too the angels, how some of them were not content to keep the dominion given to them but abandoned their proper home; and God has reserved them for judgement on the great Day, bound beneath the darkness 7 in everlasting chains. Remember Sodom and Gomorrah and the neighbouring towns; like the angels, they committed fornication and followed unnatural lusts; and they paid the penalty in eternal fire, an example for all to see.

8 So too with these men today. Their dreams lead them to defile the body, to flout authority, and to insult celestial beings. In con- 9 trast, when the archangel Michael was in debate with the devil, disputing the possession of Moses's body, he did not presume to condemn him in insulting words,[c] but said, 'May the Lord rebuke you!'

10 But these men pour abuse upon things they do not understand; the things they do understand, by instinct like brute beasts, prove their undoing. Alas for them! They 11 have gone the way of Cain; they have plunged into Balaam's error for pay; they have rebelled like Korah, and they share his doom.

12 These men are a blot on your love-feasts, where they eat and drink without reverence. They are shepherds who take care only of themselves. They are clouds carried away by the wind without giving rain, trees that in season bear no fruit, dead twice over and pulled up by the roots. They are 13 fierce waves of the sea, foaming shameful deeds; they are stars that have wandered from their course, and the place for ever reserved for them is blackest darkness.

14 It was to them that Enoch, the seventh in descent from Adam, directed his prophecy when he said: 'I saw the Lord come with his myriads of angels, to bring all 15 men to judgement and to convict all the godless of all the godless deeds they had committed, and of

---

[a] Or disowning our one and only Master, and Jesus Christ our Lord.
[b] Some witnesses read Jesus (which might be understood as Joshua).
[c] Or to charge him with blasphemy.

all the defiant words which godless sinners had spoken against him.'

16 They are a set of grumblers and malcontents. They follow their lusts. Big words come rolling from their lips, and they court favour to gain their ends. 17 But you, my friends, should remember the predictions made by the apostles of 18 our Lord Jesus Christ. This was the warning they gave you: 'In the final age there will be men who pour scorn on religion, and follow their own godless lusts.'

19 These men draw a line between spiritual and unspiritual persons, although they are themselves[a] 20 wholly unspiritual. But you, my friends, must fortify yourselves in your most sacred faith. Continue to pray in the power of the Holy Spirit. Keep yourselves in the love 21 of God, and look forward to the day when our Lord Jesus Christ in his mercy will give eternal life.

There are some doubting souls 22 who need your pity;[b] snatch them 23 from the flames and save them.[c] There are others for whom your pity must be mixed with fear; hate the very clothing that is contaminated with sensuality.

Now to the One who can keep 24 you from falling and set you in the presence of his glory, jubilant and above reproach, to the only God 25 our Saviour, be glory and majesty, might and authority, through Jesus Christ our Lord, before all time, now, and for evermore. Amen.

[a] *Or* These men create divisions; they are...
[b] *Some witnesses read* There are some who raise disputes; these you should refute.
[c] *So one witness; the rest read* some you should snatch from the flames and save.

THE REVELATION
OF JOHN

THE REVELATION
OF JOHN

1 THIS is the revelation given by God to Jesus Christ. It was given to him so that he might show his servants what must shortly happen. He made it known by sending his angel to his 2 servant John, who, in telling all that he saw, has borne witness to the word of God and to the testimony of Jesus Christ.[a]

3 Happy is the man who reads, and happy those who listen to the words of this prophecy and heed what is written in it. For the hour of fulfilment is near.

A message from Christ to the churches

4 JOHN to the seven churches in the province of Asia.

Grace be to you and peace, from him who is and who was and who is to come, from the seven spirits 5 before his throne, and from Jesus Christ, the faithful witness, the first-born from the dead and ruler of the kings of the earth.

To him who loves us and freed us from our sins with his life's 6 blood, who made of us a royal house, to serve as the priests of his God and Father – to him be glory and dominion for ever and ever! Amen.

7 Behold, he is coming with the clouds! Every eye shall see him, and among them those who pierced him; and all the peoples of the world shall lament in remorse. So it shall be. Amen.

8 'I am the Alpha and the Omega', says the Lord God, who is and who was and who is to come, the sovereign Lord of all.

9 I, John, your brother, who share with you in the suffering and the sovereignty and the endurance which is ours in Jesus – I was on the island called Patmos because I had preached God's word and borne my testimony to Jesus. It 10 was on the Lord's day, and I was caught up by the Spirit; and behind me I heard a loud voice, like the sound of a trumpet, which said 11 to me, 'Write down what you see on a scroll and send it to the seven churches: to Ephesus, Smyrna, Pergamum, Thyatira, Sardis, Philadelphia, and Laodicea.' I turned 12 to see whose voice it was that spoke to me; and when I turned I saw seven standing lamps of gold, and among the lamps one 13 like a son of man, robed down to his feet, with a golden girdle round his breast. The hair of his head 14 was white as snow-white wool, and his eyes flamed like fire; his feet 15 gleamed like burnished brass refined in a furnace, and his voice was like the sound of rushing waters. In his right hand he held 16 seven stars, and out of his mouth came a sharp two-edged sword; and his face shone like the sun in full strength.

17 When I saw him, I fell at his feet as though dead. But he laid his right hand upon me and said, 'Do not be afraid. I am the first and the last, and I am the living 18 one; for I was dead and now I am

[a] Or has borne his testimony to the word of God and to Jesus Christ.

alive for evermore, and I hold the keys of Death and Death's domain. Write down therefore what you have seen, what is now, and what will be hereafter.

20 'Here is the secret meaning of the seven stars which you saw in my right hand, and of the seven lamps of gold: the seven stars are the angels of the seven churches, and the seven lamps are the seven churches.

2 'To the angel of the church at Ephesus write:
'"These are the words of the One who holds the seven stars in his right hand and walks among 2 the seven lamps of gold: I know all your ways, your toil and your fortitude. I know you cannot endure evil men; you have put to the proof those who claim to be apostles but are not, and have 3 found them false. Fortitude you have; you have borne up in my 4 cause and never flagged. But I have this against you: you have 5 lost your early love. Think from what a height you have fallen; repent, and do as you once did. Otherwise, if you do not repent, I shall come to you and remove 6 your lamp from its place. Yet you have this in your favour: you hate the practices of the Nicolaitans, as 7 I do. Hear, you who have ears to hear, what the Spirit says to the churches! To him who is victorious I will give the right to eat from the tree of life that stands in the Garden of God."

8 'To the angel of the church at Smyrna write:
'"These are the words of the First and the Last, who was dead 9 and came to life again: I know how hard pressed you are, and poor – and yet you are rich; I know how you are slandered by those who claim to be Jews but are not – they 10 are Satan's synagogue. Do not be afraid of the suffering to come. The Devil will throw some of you

into prison, to put you to the test; and for ten days you will suffer cruelly. Only be faithful till death, and I will give you the crown of life. Hear, you who have ears to 11 hear, what the Spirit says to the churches! He who is victorious cannot be harmed by the second death."

'To the angel of the church at 12 Pergamum write:
'"These are the words of the One who has the sharp two-edged sword: I know where you live; it 13 is the place where Satan has his throne. And yet you are holding fast to my cause. You did not deny your faith in me even at the time when Antipas, my faithful witness, was killed in your city, the home of Satan. But I have a few 14 matters to bring against you: you have in Pergamum some that hold to the teaching of Balaam, who taught Balak to put temptation in the way of the Israelites. He encouraged them to eat food sacrificed to idols and to commit fornication, and in the same way 15 you also have some who hold the doctrine of the Nicolaitans. So 16 repent! If you do not, I shall come to you soon and make war upon them with the sword that comes out of my mouth. Hear, you who 17 have ears to hear, what the Spirit says to the churches! To him who is victorious I will give some of the hidden manna; I will give him also a white stone, and on the stone will be written a new name, known to none but him that receives it."

'To the angel of the church at 18 Thyatira write:
'"These are the words of the Son of God, whose eyes flame like fire and whose feet gleam like burnished brass: I know all your 19 ways, your love and faithfulness, your good service and your fortitude; and of late you have done even better than at first. Yet I have 20 this against you: you tolerate that

Jezebel, the woman who claims to be a prophetess, who by her teaching lures my servants into fornication and into eating food sacri²¹ficed to idols. I have given her time to repent, but she refuses to ²²repent of her fornication. So I will throw her on to a bed of pain,ᵃ and plunge her lovers into terrible suffering, unless they forswear ²³what she is doing; and her children I will strike dead. This will teach all the churches that I am the searcher of men's hearts and thoughts, and that I will reward each one of you according to his ²⁴deeds. And now I speak to you others in Thyatira, who do not accept this teaching and have had no experience of what they like to call the deep secrets of Satan; on you I will impose no further ²⁵burden. Only hold fast to what ²⁶you have, until I come. To him who is victorious, to him who perseveres in doing my will to the end, I will give authority over the ²⁷nations – that same authority which I received from my Father – and he shall rule them with an iron rod, smashing them to bits like ²⁸earthenware; and I will give him ²⁹also the star of dawn. Hear, you who have ears to hear, what the Spirit says to the churches!"

3 'To the angel of the church at Sardis write:
'"These are the words of the One who holds the seven spirits of God, the seven stars: I know all your ways; that though you have a name for being alive, you are dead. ²Wake up, and put some strength into what is left, which must otherwise die! For I have not found any work of yours completed in the ³eyes of my God. So remember the teaching you received; observe it, and repent. If you do not wake up, I shall come upon you like a thief, and you will not know the ⁴moment of my coming. Yet you have a few persons in Sardis who

have not polluted their clothing. They shall walk with me in white, for so they deserve. He who is ⁵victorious shall thus be robed all in white; his name I will never strike off the roll of the living, for in the presence of my Father and his angels I will acknowledge him as mine. Hear, you who have ears ⁶to hear, what the Spirit says to the churches!"

'To the angel of the church at ⁷Philadelphia write:
'"These are the words of the holy one, the true one, who holds the key of David; when he opens none may shut, when he shuts none may open: I know all your ⁸ways; and look, I have set before you an open door, which no one can shut. Your strength, I know, is small, yet you have observed my commands and have not disowned my name. So this is what ⁹I will do: I will make those of Satan's synagogue, who claim to be Jews but are lying frauds, come and fall down at your feet; and they shall know that you are my beloved people. Because you have ¹⁰kept my command and stood fast, I will also keep you from the ordeal that is to fall upon the whole world and test its inhabitants. I am ¹¹coming soon; hold fast what you have, and let no one rob you of your crown. He who is victorious ¹² – I will make him a pillar in the temple of my God; he shall never leave it. And I will write the name of my God upon him, and the name of the city of my God, that new Jerusalem which is coming down out of heaven from my God, and my own new name. Hear, you ¹³who have ears to hear, what the Spirit says to the churches!"

'To the angel of the church at ¹⁴Laodicea write:
'"These are the words of the Amen, the faithful and true witness, the prime source of all God's creation: I know all your ways; ¹⁵

ᵃ *One witness reads* into a furnace.

you are neither hot nor cold. How I wish you were either hot or cold!
16 But because you are lukewarm, neither hot nor cold, I will spit
17 you out of my mouth. You say, 'How rich I am! And how well I have done! I have everything I want.' In fact, though you do not know it, you are the most pitiful wretch, poor, blind, and naked.
18 So I advise you to buy from me gold refined in the fire, to make you truly rich, and white clothes to put on to hide the shame of your nakedness, and ointment for
19 your eyes so that you may see. All whom I love I reprove and discipline. Be on your mettle therefore
20 and repent. Here I stand knocking at the door; if anyone hears my voice and opens the door, I will come in and sit down to supper
21 with him and he with me. To him who is victorious I will grant a place on my throne, as I myself was victorious and sat down with
22 my Father on his throne. Hear, you who have ears to hear, what the Spirit says to the churches!'''

The opening of the sealed book

4 AFTER this I looked, and there before my eyes was a door opened in heaven; and the voice that I had first heard speaking to me like a trumpet said, 'Come up here, and I will show you what must happen
2 hereafter.' At once I was caught up by the Spirit. There in heaven stood a throne, and on the throne
3 sat one whose appearance was like the gleam of jasper and cornelian; and round the throne was a rain-
4 bow, bright as an emerald. In a circle about this throne were twenty-four other thrones, and on them sat twenty-four elders, robed in white and wearing crowns of
5 gold. From the throne went out flashes of lightning and peals of thunder. Burning before the throne were seven flaming torches, the
6 seven spirits of God, and in front

of it stretched what seemed a sea of glass, like a sheet of ice.

In the centre, round the throne itself, were four living creatures, covered with eyes, in front and behind. The first creature was like 7 a lion, the second like an ox, the third had a human face, the fourth was like an eagle in flight. The four 8 living creatures, each of them with six wings, had eyes all over, inside and out; and by day and by night without a pause they sang:

'Holy, holy, holy is God the sovereign Lord of all, who was, and is, and is to come!'

As often as the living creatures 9 give glory and honour and thanks to the One who sits on the throne, who lives for ever and ever, the 10 twenty-four elders fall down before the One who sits on the throne and worship him who lives for ever and ever; and as they lay their crowns before the throne they cry:

'Thou art worthy, O Lord our God, 11 to receive glory and honour and power, because thou didst create all things; by thy will they were created, and have their being!'

Then I saw in the right hand of 5 the One who sat on the throne a scroll, with writing inside and out, and it was sealed up with seven seals. And I saw a mighty angel 2 proclaiming in a loud voice, 'Who is worthy to open the scroll and to break its seals?' There was no 3 one in heaven or on earth or under the earth able to open the scroll or to look inside it. I was in tears 4 because no one was found who was worthy to open the scroll or to look inside it. But one of the 5 elders said to me: 'Do not weep; for the Lion from the tribe of Judah, the Scion of David, has won the right to open the scroll and break its seven seals.'

6 Then I saw standing in the very middle of the throne, inside the circle of living creatures and the circle of elders,[a] a Lamb with the marks of slaughter upon him. He had seven horns and seven eyes, the eyes which are the seven spirits of God sent out over all the world. 7 And the Lamb went up and took the scroll from the right hand of the One who sat on the throne. 8 When he took it, the four living creatures and the twenty-four elders fell down before the Lamb. Each of the elders had a harp, and they held golden bowls full of incense, the prayers of God's 9 people, and they were singing a new song:

'Thou art worthy to take the scroll and to break its seals, for thou wast slain and by thy blood didst purchase for God men of every tribe and language, people and 10 nation; thou hast made of them a royal house, to serve our God as priests; and they shall reign upon earth.'

11 Then as I looked I heard the voices of countless angels. These were all round the throne and the living creatures and the elders. Myriads upon myriads there were, 12 thousands upon thousands, and they cried aloud:

'Worthy is the Lamb, the Lamb that was slain, to receive all power and wealth, wisdom and might, honour and glory and praise!'

13 Then I heard every created thing in heaven and on earth and under the earth and in the sea, all that is in them, crying:

'Praise and honour, glory and might, to him who sits on the throne and to the Lamb for ever and ever!'

And the four living creatures said, 14 'Amen', and the elders fell down and worshipped.

THEN I watched as the Lamb 6 broke the first of the seven seals; and I heard one of the four living creatures say in a voice like thunder, 'Come!' And there before 2 my eyes was a white horse, and its rider held a bow. He was given a crown, and he rode forth, conquering and to conquer.

When the Lamb broke the 3 second seal, I heard the second creature say, 'Come!' And out 4 came another horse, all red. To its rider was given power to take peace from the earth and make men slaughter one another; and he was given a great sword.

When he broke the third seal, 5 I heard the third creature say, 'Come!' And there, as I looked, was a black horse; and its rider held in his hand a pair of scales. And I heard what sounded like 6 a voice from the midst of the living creatures, which said, 'A whole day's wage for a quart of flour, a whole day's wage for three quarts of barley-meal! But spare the olive and the vine.'

When he broke the fourth seal, 7 I heard the voice of the fourth creature say, 'Come!' And there, 8 as I looked, was another horse, sickly pale; and its rider's name was Death, and Hades came close behind. To him was given power over a quarter of the earth, with the right to kill by sword and by famine, by pestilence and wild beasts.

When he broke the fifth seal, I 9 saw underneath[b] the altar the souls of those who had been slaughtered for God's word and for the testimony they bore. They gave a great 10 cry: 'How long, sovereign Lord, holy and true, must it be before thou wilt vindicate us and avenge

[a] Or standing between the throne, with the four living creatures, and the elders...
[b] Or at the foot of...

297

our blood on the inhabitants of the
11 earth?' Each of them was given
a white robe; and they were told
to rest a little while longer, until
the tally should be complete of all
their brothers in Christ's service
who were to be killed as they had
been.
12   Then I watched as he broke the
sixth seal. And there was a violent
earthquake; the sun turned black
as a funeral pall and the moon all
13 red as blood; the stars in the sky
fell to the earth, like figs shaken
14 down by a gale; the sky vanished,
as a scroll is rolled up, and every
mountain and island was moved
15 from its place. Then the kings of
the earth, magnates and marshals,
the rich and the powerful, and all
men, slave or free, hid themselves
16 in caves and mountain crags; and
they called out to the mountains
and the crags, 'Fall on us and hide
us from the face of the One who
sits on the throne and from the
17 vengeance of the Lamb.' For the
great day of their vengeance has
come, and who will be able to
stand?

7   After this I saw four angels
stationed at the four corners of
the earth, holding back the four
winds so that no wind should blow
on sea or land or on any tree.
2   Then I saw another angel rising
out of the east, carrying the seal
of the living God; and he called
aloud to the four angels who had
been given the power to ravage
3 land and sea: 'Do no damage to
sea or land or trees until we have
set the seal of our God upon the
4 foreheads of his servants.' And I
heard the number of those who
had received the seal. From all the
tribes of Israel there were a hundred and forty-four thousand:
5 twelve thousand from the tribe of
Judah, twelve thousand from the
tribe of Reuben, twelve thousand
6 from the tribe of Gad, twelve
thousand from the tribe of Asher,
twelve thousand from the tribe of

Naphtali, twelve thousand from
the tribe of Manasseh, twelve 7
thousand from the tribe of Simeon,
twelve thousand from the tribe of
Levi, twelve thousand from the
tribe of Issachar, twelve thousand 8
from the tribe of Zebulun, twelve
thousand from the tribe of Joseph,
and twelve thousand from the
tribe of Benjamin.

After this I looked and saw a 9
vast throng, which no one could
count, from every nation, of all
tribes, peoples, and languages,
standing in front of the throne and
before the Lamb. They were robed
in white and had palms in their
hands, and they shouted together: 10

'Victory to our God who sits on
the throne, and to the Lamb!'

And all the angels stood round the 11
throne and the elders and the four
living creatures, and they fell on
their faces before the throne and
worshipped God, crying: 12

'Amen! Praise and glory and wisdom, thanksgiving and honour,
power and might, be to our God
for ever and ever! Amen.'

Then one of the elders turned 13
to me and said, 'These men that
are robed in white – who are they
and from where do they come?'
But I answered, 'My lord, you 14
know, not I.' Then he said to me,
'These are the men who have passed through the great ordeal; they
have washed their robes and made
them white in the blood of the
Lamb. That is why they stand 15
before the throne of God and
minister to him day and night in
his temple; and he who sits on the
throne will dwell with them. They 16
shall never again feel hunger or
thirst, the sun shall not beat on
them nor any scorching heat, be- 17
cause the Lamb who is at the heart
of the throne will be their shepherd
and will guide them to the springs

of the water of life; and God will wipe all tears from their eyes.'

8 Now when the Lamb broke the seventh seal, there was silence in heaven for what seemed half an 2 hour. Then I looked, and the seven angels that stand in the presence of God were given seven trumpets. 3 Then another angel came and stood at the altar, holding a golden censer; and he was given a great quantity of incense to offer with the prayers of all God's people upon the golden altar in front of 4 the throne. And from the angel's hand the smoke of the incense went up before God with the prayers of 5 his people. Then the angel took the censer, filled it from the altar fire, and threw it down upon the earth; and there were peals of thunder, lightning, and an earthquake.

The powers of darkness conquered

6 THEN the seven angels that held the seven trumpets prepared to blow them.

7 The first blew his trumpet; and there came hail and fire mingled with blood, and this was hurled upon the earth. A third of the earth was burnt, a third of the trees were burnt, all the green grass was burnt.

8 The second angel blew his trumpet; and what looked like a great blazing mountain was hurled into the sea. A third of the sea was 9 turned to blood, a third of the living creatures in it died, and a third of the ships on it foundered.

10 The third angel blew his trumpet; and a great star shot from the sky, flaming like a torch; and it fell on a third of the rivers and springs.

11 The name of the star was Wormwood; and a third of the water turned to wormwood, and men in great numbers died of the water because it had been poisoned.

12 The fourth angel blew his trumpet; and a third part of the sun was struck, a third of the moon, and a third of the stars, so that the third part went dark and a third of the light of the day failed, and of the night.

13 Then I looked, and I heard an eagle calling with a loud cry as it flew in mid-heaven: 'Woe, woe, woe to the inhabitants of the earth when the trumpets sound which the three last angels must now blow!'

9 Then the fifth angel blew his trumpet; and I saw a star that had fallen from heaven to earth, and 2 the star was given the key of the shaft of the abyss. With this he opened the shaft of the abyss; and from the shaft smoke rose like smoke from a great furnace, and the sun and the air were darkened 3 by the smoke from the shaft. Then over the earth, out of the smoke, came locusts, and they were given the powers that earthly scorpions 4 have. They were told to do no injury to the grass or to any plant or tree, but only to those men who had not received the seal of God 5 on their foreheads. These they were allowed to torment for five months, with torment like a scorpion's sting; but they were not to kill 6 them. During that time these men will seek death, but they will not find it; they will long to die, but death will elude them.

7 In appearance the locusts were like horses equipped for battle. On their heads were what looked like golden crowns; their faces were 8 like human faces and their hair like women's hair; they had teeth 9 like lions' teeth, and wore breastplates like iron; the sound of their wings was like the noise of horses and chariots rushing to battle; 10 they had tails like scorpions, with stings in them, and in their tails lay their power to plague mankind 11 for five months. They had for their king the angel of the abyss, whose name, in Hebrew, is Abaddon, and in Greek, Apollyon, or the Destroyer.

12 The first woe has now passed. But there are still two more to come.

13 The sixth angel then blew his trumpet; and I heard a voice coming from between the horns of the golden altar that stood in

14 the presence of God. It said to the sixth angel, who held the trumpet: 'Release the four angels held bound

15 at the great river Euphrates!' So the four angels were let loose, to kill a third of mankind. They had been held ready for this moment, for this very year and month, day

16 and hour. And their squadrons of cavalry, whose count I heard, numbered two hundred million.

17 This was how I saw the horses and their riders in my vision: They wore breastplates, fiery red, blue, and sulphur-yellow; the horses had heads like lions' heads, and out of their mouths came fire, smoke, and

18 sulphur. By these three plagues, that is, by the fire, the smoke, and the sulphur that came from their mouths, a third of mankind was

19 killed. The power of the horses lay in their mouths, and in their tails also; for their tails were like snakes, with heads, and with them too they dealt injuries.

20 The rest of mankind who survived these plagues still did not abjure the gods their hands had fashioned, nor cease their worship of devils and of idols made from gold, silver, bronze, stone, and wood, which cannot see or hear or

21 walk. Nor did they repent of their murders, their sorcery, their fornication, or their robberies.

10 THEN I saw another mighty angel coming down from heaven. He was wrapped in cloud, with the rainbow round his head; his face shone like the sun and his legs were like

2 pillars of fire. In his hand he held a little scroll unrolled. His right foot he planted on the sea, and his

3 left on the land. Then he gave a great shout, like the roar of a lion;

and when he shouted, the seven thunders spoke. I was about to 4 write down what the seven thunders had said; but I heard a voice from heaven saying, 'Seal up what the seven thunders have said; do not write it down.' Then the angel 5 that I saw standing on the sea and the land raised his right hand to heaven and swore by him who lives 6 for ever and ever, who created heaven and earth and the sea and everything in them: 'There shall be no more delay; but when the 7 time comes for the seventh angel to sound his trumpet, the hidden purpose of God will have been fulfilled, as he promised to his servants the prophets.'

Then the voice which I heard 8 from heaven was speaking to me again, and it said, 'Go and take the open scroll in the hand of the angel that stands on the sea and the land.' So I went to the angel 9 and asked him to give me the little scroll. He said to me, 'Take it, and eat it. It will turn your stomach sour, although in your mouth it will taste sweet as honey.' So I took 10 the little scroll from the angel's hand and ate it, and in my mouth it did taste sweet as honey; but when I swallowed it my stomach turned sour.

Then they said to me, 'Once 11 again you must utter prophecies over peoples and nations and languages and many kings.'

I was given a long cane, a kind 11 of measuring-rod, and told: 'Now go and measure the temple of God, the altar, and the number of the worshippers. But have nothing to 2 do with the outer court of the temple; do not measure that; for it has been given over to the Gentiles, and they will trample the Holy City underfoot for forty-two months. And I have two witnesses, 3 whom I will appoint to prophesy, dressed in sackcloth, all through those twelve hundred and sixty days.' These are the two olive-trees 4 and the two lamps that stand in the presence of the Lord of the 5 earth. If anyone seeks to do them harm, fire pours from their mouths and consumes their enemies; and thus shall the man die who seeks 6 to do them harm. These two have the power to shut up the sky, so that no rain may fall during the time of their prophesying; and they have the power to turn water to blood and to strike the earth at will with every kind of plague. 7 But when they have completed their testimony, the beast that comes up from the abyss will wage war upon them and will defeat and 8 kill them. Their corpses will lie in the street of the great city, whose name in allegory is Sodom, or Egypt, where also their Lord was 9 crucified. For three days and a half men from every people and tribe, of every language and nation, gaze upon their corpses and refuse them 10 burial. All men on earth gloat over them, make merry, and exchange presents; for these two prophets were a torment to the whole earth. 11 But at the end of the three days and a half the breath of life from God came into them; and they stood up on their feet to the terror 12 of all who saw it. Then a loud voice was heard speaking to them from heaven, which said, 'Come up here!' And they went up to heaven in a cloud, in full view of their 13 enemies. At that same moment there was a violent earthquake, and a tenth of the city fell. Seven thousand people were killed in the earthquake; the rest in terror did homage to the God of heaven.

14   The second woe has now passed. But the third is soon to come.

15   Then the seventh angel blew his trumpet; and voices were heard in heaven shouting:

'The sovereignty of the world has passed to our Lord and his Christ, and he shall reign for ever and ever!'

And the twenty-four elders, seated 16 on their thrones before God, fell on their faces and worshipped God, saying: 17

'We give thee thanks, O Lord God, sovereign over all, who art and who wast, because thou hast taken thy great power into thy hands and entered upon thy reign. The nations 18 raged, but thy day of retribution has come. Now is the time for the dead to be judged; now is the time for recompense to thy servants the prophets, to thy dedicated people, and all who honour thy name, both great and small, the time to destroy those who destroy the earth.'

Then God's temple in heaven 19 was laid open, and within the temple was seen the ark of his covenant. There came flashes of lightning and peals of thunder, an earthquake, and a storm of hail.

NEXT appeared a great portent in 12 heaven, a woman robed with the sun, beneath her feet the moon, and on her head a crown of twelve stars. She was pregnant, and in 2 the anguish of her labour she cried out to be delivered. Then a second 3 portent appeared in heaven: a great red dragon with seven heads and ten horns; on his heads were seven diadems, and with his tail 4 he swept down a third of the stars in the sky and flung them to the earth. The dragon stood in front of the woman who was about to give birth, so that when her child was born he might devour it. She 5 gave birth to a male child, who is destined to rule all nations with an iron rod. But her child was snatched up to God and his throne; and the woman herself fled into 6 the wilds, where she had a place prepared for her by God, there to be sustained for twelve hundred and sixty days.

Then war broke out in heaven. 7

Michael and his angels waged war upon the dragon. The dragon and 8 his angels fought, but they had not the strength to win, and no foothold was left them in heaven. 9 So the great dragon was thrown down, that serpent of old that led the whole world astray, whose name is Satan, or the Devil – thrown down to the earth, and his angels with him.

10 Then I heard a voice in heaven proclaiming aloud: 'This is the hour of victory for our God, the hour of his sovereignty and power, when his Christ comes to his rightful rule! For the accuser of our brothers is overthrown, who day and night accused them before 11 our God. By the sacrifice of the Lamb they have conquered him, and by the testimony which they uttered;[a] for they did not hold their lives too dear to lay them down. 12 Rejoice then, you heavens and you that dwell in them! But woe to you, earth and sea, for the Devil has come down to you in great fury, knowing that his time is short!'

13 When the dragon found that he had been thrown down to the earth, he went in pursuit of the woman who had given birth to 14 the male child. But the woman was given two great eagle's wings, to fly to the place in the wilds where for three years and a half she was to be sustained, out of reach of the 15 serpent. From his mouth the serpent spewed a flood of water after the woman to sweep her away with 16 its spate. But the earth came to her rescue and opened its mouth and swallowed the river which the dragon spewed from his mouth. 17 At this the dragon grew furious with the woman, and went off to wage war on the rest of her offspring, that is, on those who keep God's commandments and maintain their testimony to Jesus. He 13 took his stand on the sea-shore.

Then[b] out of the sea I saw a beast rising. It had ten horns and seven heads. On its horns were ten diadems, and on each head a blasphemous name. The beast I 2 saw was like a leopard, but its feet were like a bear's and its mouth like a lion's mouth. The dragon conferred upon it his power and rule, and great authority. One of its 3 heads appeared to have received a death-blow; but the mortal wound was healed. The whole world went after the beast in wondering admiration. Men worshipped the 4 dragon because he had conferred his authority upon the beast; they worshipped the beast also, and chanted, 'Who is like the Beast? Who can fight against it?'

The beast was allowed to mouth 5 bombast and blasphemy, and was given the right to reign for forty-two months. It opened its mouth 6 in blasphemy against God, reviling his name and his heavenly dwelling.[c] It was also allowed to wage 7 war on God's people and to defeat them, and was granted[d] authority over every tribe and people, language and nation. All on earth 8 will worship it, except those whose names the Lamb that was slain keeps in his roll of the living, written there since the world was made.

Hear, you who have ears to 9 hear! Whoever is to be made 10 prisoner, a prisoner he shall be. Whoever takes the sword to kill, by the sword he is bound to be killed. This is where the fortitude and faithfulness of God's people have their place.

Then I saw another beast, which 11 came up out of the earth; it had two horns like a lamb's, but spoke

---

[a] Or the word of God to which they bore witness.   [b] Some witnesses read ...testimony to Jesus. Then I stood by the sea-shore and...   [c] Some witnesses read reviling his name and his dwelling-place, that is, those that live in heaven. [d] Some witnesses read It was granted... (omitting the words was also...them, and).

12 like a dragon. It wielded all the authority of the first beast in its presence, and made the earth and its inhabitants worship this first beast, whose mortal wound had 13 been healed. It worked great miracles, even making fire come down from heaven to earth before 14 men's eyes. By the miracles it was allowed to perform in the presence of the beast it deluded the inhabitants of the earth, and made them erect an image in honour of the beast that had been wounded by 15 the sword and yet lived. It was allowed to give breath to the image of the beast, so that it could speak, and could cause all who would not worship the image to be put to 16 death. Moreover, it caused everyone, great and small, rich and poor, slave and free, to be branded with a mark on his right hand or 17 forehead, and no one was allowed to buy or sell unless he bore this beast's mark, either name or 18 number. (Here is the key; and anyone who has intelligence may work out the number of the beast. The number represents a man's name, and the numerical value of its letters is six hundred and sixty-six.)

Visions of the end

14 THEN I looked, and on Mount Zion stood the Lamb, and with him were a hundred and forty-four thousand who had his name and the name of his Father written on 2 their foreheads. I heard a sound from heaven like the noise of rushing water and the deep roar of thunder; it was the sound of harpers playing on their harps. 3 There before the throne, and the four living creatures and the elders, they were singing a new song. That song no one could learn except the hundred and forty-four thousand,

who alone from the whole world had been ransomed. These are men 4 who did not defile themselves with women, for they have kept themselves chaste, and they follow the Lamb wherever he goes. They have been ransomed as the firstfruits of humanity for God and the Lamb. No lie was found in their lips; they 5 are faultless.

Then I saw an angel flying in 6 mid-heaven, with an eternal gospel to proclaim to those on earth, to every nation and tribe, language and people. He cried in a loud 7 voice, 'Fear God and pay him homage; for the hour of his judgement has come! Worship him who made heaven and earth, the sea and the water-springs!'

Then another angel, a second, 8 followed, and he cried, 'Fallen, fallen is Babylon the great, she who has made all nations drink the fierce wine of*[a]* her fornication!'

Yet a third angel followed, cry- 9 ing out loud, 'Whoever worships the beast and its image and receives its mark on his forehead or hand, he shall drink the wine of God's 10 wrath, poured undiluted into the cup of his vengeance. He shall be tormented in sulphurous flames before the holy angels and before the Lamb. The smoke of their 11 torment will rise for ever and ever, and there will be no respite day or night for those who worship the beast and its image or receive the mark of its name.' This is where 12 the fortitude of God's people has its place – in keeping God's commands and remaining loyal to Jesus.

Moreover, I heard a voice from 13 heaven, saying, 'Write this: "Happy are the dead who die in the faith of Christ! Henceforth",*[b]* says the Spirit,*[c]* "they may rest from their labours; for they take with them the record of their deeds."'

a Or drink the wine of God's wrath upon...   *b* Or Assuredly.
c *Some witnesses read* "...the dead who henceforth die in the faith of Christ!" "Yes," says the Spirit...

14 Then as I looked there appeared a white cloud, and on the cloud sat one like a son of man. He had on his head a crown of gold and in his 15 hand a sharp sickle. Another angel came out of the temple and called in a loud voice to him who sat on the cloud: 'Stretch out your sickle and reap; for harvest-time has come, and earth's crop is over-ripe.' 16 So he who sat on the cloud put his sickle to the earth and its harvest was reaped.

17 Then another angel came out of the heavenly temple, and he 18 also had a sharp sickle. Then from the altar came yet another, the angel who has authority over fire, and he shouted to the one with the sharp sickle: 'Stretch out your sickle, and gather in earth's grape-harvest, for its clusters are ripe.' 19 So the angel put his sickle to the earth and gathered in its grapes, and threw them into the great 20 winepress of God's wrath. The winepress was trodden outside the city, and for two hundred miles around blood flowed from the press to the height of the horses' bridles.

15 Then I saw another great and astonishing portent in heaven: seven angels with seven plagues, the last plagues of all, for with them the wrath of God is consummated.

2 I saw what seemed a sea of glass shot with fire, and beside the sea of glass, holding the harps which God had given them, were those who had won the victory over the beast and its image and the number of its name.

3 They were singing the song of Moses, the servant of God, and the song of the Lamb, as they chanted:

'Great and marvellous are thy deeds, O Lord God, sovereign over all; just and true are thy ways, thou king of the ages.[a] Who shall not revere thee, Lord, and do homage to thy name? For thou alone art holy. All nations shall come and worship in thy presence, for thy just dealings stand revealed.'

After this, as I looked, the 5 sanctuary of the heavenly Tent of Testimony was thrown open, and 6 out of it came the seven angels with the seven plagues. They were robed in fine linen, clean and shining, and had golden girdles round their breasts. Then one of the four 7 living creatures gave the seven angels seven golden bowls full of the wrath of God who lives for ever and ever; and the sanctuary 8 was filled with smoke from the glory of God and his power, so that no one could enter it until the seven plagues of the seven angels were completed.

Then from the sanctuary I heard 16 a loud voice, and it said to the seven angels, 'Go and pour out the seven bowls of God's wrath on the earth.'

So the first angel went and pour- 2 ed his bowl on the earth; and foul malignant sores appeared on those men that wore the mark of the beast and worshipped its image.

The second angel poured his 3 bowl on the sea, and it turned to blood like the blood from a corpse; and every living thing in the sea died.

The third angel poured his bowl 4 on the rivers and springs, and they turned to blood.

Then I heard the angel of the 5 waters say, 'Just art thou in these thy judgements, thou Holy One who art and wast; for they shed 6 the blood of thy people and of thy prophets, and thou hast given them blood to drink. They have their deserts!' And I heard the 7 altar cry, 'Yes, Lord God, sovereign over all, true and just are thy judgements!'

---

[a] *Some witnesses read* king of the nations.

8 The fourth angel poured his bowl on the sun; and it was allowed 9 to burn men with its flames. They were fearfully burned; but they only cursed the name of God who had the power to inflict such plagues, and they refused to repent or do him homage.

10 The fifth angel poured his bowl on the throne of the beast; and its kingdom was plunged in darkness. Men gnawed their tongues in 11 agony, but they only cursed the God of heaven for their sores and pains, and would not repent of what they had done.

12 The sixth angel poured his bowl on the great river Euphrates; and its water was dried up, to prepare the way for the kings from the east. 13 Then I saw coming from the mouth of the dragon, the mouth of the beast, and the mouth of the false prophet, three foul spirits 14 like frogs. These spirits were devils, with power to work miracles. They were sent out to muster all the kings of the world for the great day of battle of God the sovereign 15 Lord. ('That is the day when I come like a thief! Happy the man who stays awake and keeps on his clothes, so that he will not have to go naked and ashamed for all 16 to see!') So they assembled the kings at the place called in Hebrew Armageddon.

17 Then the seventh angel poured his bowl on the air; and out of the sanctuary came a loud voice from the throne, which said, 'It is over!' 18 And there followed flashes of lightning and peals of thunder, and a violent earthquake, like none before it in human history, so 19 violent it was. The great city was split in three; the cities of the world fell in ruin; and God did not forget Babylon the great, but made her drink the cup which was filled with the fierce wine of his 20 vengeance. Every island vanished; there was not a mountain to be seen. Huge hailstones, weighing 21 perhaps a hundredweight, fell on men from the sky; and they cursed God for the plague of hail, because that plague was so severe.

THEN one of the seven angels that 17 held the seven bowls came and spoke to me and said, 'Come, and I will show you the judgement on the great whore, enthroned above the ocean. The kings of the earth 2 have committed fornication with her, and on the wine of her fornication men all over the world have made themselves drunk.' In the 3 Spirit he carried me away into the wilds, and there I saw a woman mounted on a scarlet beast which was covered with blasphemous names and had seven heads and ten horns. The woman was clothed 4 in purple and scarlet and bedizened with gold and jewels and pearls. In her hand she held a gold cup, full of obscenities and the foulness of her fornication; and written on 5 her forehead was a name with a secret meaning: 'Babylon the great, the mother of whores and of every obscenity on earth.' The 6 woman, I saw, was drunk with the blood of God's people and with the blood of those who had borne their testimony to Jesus.

As I looked at her I was greatly astonished. But the angel said to 7 me, 'Why are you so astonished? I will tell you the secret of the woman and of the beast she rides, with the seven heads and the ten horns. The beast you have seen is 8 he who once was alive, and is alive no longer, but has yet to ascend out of the abyss before going to perdition. Those on earth whose names have not been inscribed in the roll of the living ever since the world was made will all be astonished to see the beast; for he once was alive, and is alive no longer, and has still to appear.

'But here is the clue for those 9 who can interpret it. The seven

heads are seven hills on which the
10 woman sits. They represent also
seven kings,[a] of whom five have
already fallen, one is now reigning,
and the other has yet to come; and
when he does come he is only to
11 last for a little while. As for the
beast that once was alive and is
alive no longer, he is an eighth –
and yet he is one of the seven, and
12 he is going to perdition. The ten
horns you saw are ten kings who
have not yet begun to reign, but
who for one hour are to share with
the beast the exercise of royal
13 authority; for they have but a
single purpose among them and
will confer their power and autho-
14 rity upon the beast. They will wage
war upon the Lamb, but the Lamb
will defeat them, for he is Lord of
lords and King of kings, and his
victory will be shared by his followers, called and chosen and
faithful.'[b]
15 Then he said to me, 'The ocean
you saw, where the great whore
sat, is an ocean of peoples and po-
pulations, nations and languages.
16 As for the ten horns you saw, they
together with the beast will come
to hate the whore; they will strip
her naked and leave her desolate,
they will batten on her flesh and
17 burn her to ashes. For God has put
it into their heads to carry out
his purpose, by making common
cause and conferring their sovereignty upon the beast until all
that God has spoken is fulfilled.
18 The woman you saw is the great
city that holds sway over the kings
of the earth.'

18   After this I saw another angel
coming down from heaven; he
came with great authority and the
earth was lit up with his splendour.
2 Then in a mighty voice he proclaimed, 'Fallen, fallen is Babylon
the great! She has become a dwelling for demons, a haunt for every

unclean spirit, for every vile and
loathsome bird. For all nations 3
have drunk deep of[c] the fierce wine
of her fornication; the kings of
the earth have committed fornication with her, and merchants
the world over have grown rich
on her bloated wealth.'
Then I heard another voice from 4
heaven that said: 'Come out of her,
my people, lest you take part in
her sins and share in her plagues.
For her sins are piled high as 5
heaven, and God has not forgotten
her crimes. Pay her back in her 6
own coin, repay her twice over
for her deeds! Double for her the
strength of the potion she mixed!
Mete out grief and torment to 7
match her voluptuous pomp! She
says in her heart, "I am a queen
on my throne! No mourning for
me, no widow's weeds!" Because 8
of this her plagues shall strike her
in a single day – pestilence, bereavement, famine, and burning –
for mighty is the Lord God who
has pronounced her doom!'
The kings of the earth who com- 9
mitted fornication with her and
wallowed in her luxury will weep
and wail over her, as they see the
smoke of her conflagration. They 10
will stand at a distance, for horror
at her torment, and will say, 'Alas,
alas for the great city, the mighty
city of Babylon! In a single hour
your doom has struck!'
The merchants of the earth also 11
will weep and mourn for her, because no one any longer buys their
cargoes, cargoes of gold and silver, 12
jewels and pearls, cloths of purple
and scarlet, silks and fine linens;
all kinds of scented woods, ivories,
and every sort of thing made of
costly woods, bronze, iron, or
marble; cinnamon and spice, in- 13
cense, perfumes and frankincense;
wine, oil, flour and wheat, sheep
and cattle, horses, chariots, slaves,

[a] *Or* emperors.
[b] . . . kings, and his followers are faithful men, called and selected for service.
[c] *witnesses read* have been ruined by . . .

14 and the lives of men. 'The fruit you longed for', they will say, 'is gone from you; all the glitter and the glamour are lost, never to be 15 yours again!' The traders in all these wares, who gained their wealth from her, will stand at a distance for horror at her torment, 16 weeping and mourning and saying, 'Alas, alas for the great city, that was clothed in fine linen and purple and scarlet, bedizened with 17 gold and jewels and pearls! Alas that in one hour so much wealth should be laid waste!'

Then all the sea-captains and voyagers, the sailors and those who traded by sea, stood at a 18 distance and cried out as they saw the smoke of her conflagration: 'Was there ever a city like the 19 great city?' They threw dust on their heads, weeping and mourning and saying, 'Alas, alas for the great city, where all who had ships at sea grew rich on her wealth! Alas that in a single hour she should be laid waste!'

20 But let heaven exult over her; exult, apostles and prophets and people of God; for in the judgement against her he has vindicated your cause!

21 Then a mighty angel took up a stone like a great millstone and hurled it into the sea and said, 'Thus shall Babylon, the great city, be sent hurtling down, never 22 to be seen again! No more shall the sound of harpers and minstrels, of flute-players and trumpeters, be heard in you; no more shall craftsmen of any trade be found in you; no more shall the sound 23 of the mill be heard in you; no more shall the light of the lamp be seen in you; no more shall the voice of the bride and bridegroom be heard in you! Your traders were once the merchant princes of the world, and with your sorcery you deceived all the nations.

24 For the blood of the prophets and of God's people was found in her, the blood of all who had been done to death on earth.

After this I heard what sounded 19 like the roar of a vast throng in heaven; and they were shouting:

'Alleluia! Victory and glory and power belong to our God, for true 2 and just are his judgements! He has condemned the great whore who corrupted the earth with her fornication, and has avenged upon her the blood of his servants.'

Then once more they shouted: 3

'Alleluia! The smoke goes up from her for ever and ever!'

And the twenty-four elders and 4 the four living creatures fell down and worshipped God as he sat on the throne, and they too cried:

'Amen! Alleluia!'

Then a voice came from the throne 5 which said: 'Praise our God, all you his servants, you that fear him, both great and small!'

Again I heard what sounded like 6 a vast crowd, like the noise of rushing water and deep roars of thunder, and they cried:

'Alleluia! The Lord our God, sovereign over all, has entered on his reign! Exult and shout for joy and 7 do him homage, for the wedding-day of the Lamb has come! His bride has made herself ready, and 8 for her dress she has been given fine linen, clean and shining.'

(Now the fine linen signifies the righteous deeds of God's people.)

Then the angel said to me, 'Write 9 this: "Happy are those who are invited to the wedding-supper of the Lamb!"' And he added, 'These are the very words of God.' At this 10 I fell at his feet to worship him. But he said to me, 'No, not that!

I am but a fellow-servant with you and your brothers who bear their testimony to Jesus. It is God you must worship. Those who bear testimony to Jesus are inspired like the prophets.'[a]

11 THEN I saw heaven wide open, and there before me was a white horse; and its rider's name was Faithful and True, for he is just in judge-
12 ment and just in war. His eyes flamed like fire, and on his head were many diadems. Written upon him was a name known to none
13 but himself, and he was robed in a garment drenched in blood.[b] He
14 was called the Word of God, and the armies of heaven followed him on white horses, clothed in fine
15 linen, clean and shining. From his mouth there went a sharp sword with which to smite the nations; for he it is who shall rule them with an iron rod, and tread the winepress of the wrath and retribution of God the sovereign Lord.
16 And on his robe and on his thigh there was written the name: 'King of kings and Lord of lords.'
17 Then I saw an angel standing in the sun, and he cried aloud to all the birds flying in mid-heaven: 'Come and gather for God's great
18 supper, to eat the flesh of kings and commanders and fighting men, the flesh of horses and their riders, the flesh of all men, slave
19 and free, great and small!' Then I saw the beast and the kings of the earth and their armies muster-ed to do battle with the Rider and
20 his army. The beast was taken prisoner, and so was the false prophet who had worked miracles in its presence and deluded those that had received the mark of the beast and worshipped its image. The two of them were thrown alive into the lake of fire with its
21 sulphurous flames. The rest were killed by the sword which went

out of the Rider's mouth; and all the birds gorged themselves on their flesh.

Then I saw an angel coming 20 down from heaven with the key of the abyss and a great chain in his hands. He seized the dragon, that 2 serpent of old, the Devil or Satan, and chained him up for a thousand years; he threw him into the abyss, 3 shutting and sealing it over him, so that he might seduce the nations no more till the thousand years were over. After that he must be let loose for a short while.

Then I saw thrones, and upon 4 them sat those to whom judgement was committed. I could see the souls of those who had been be-headed for the sake of God's word and their testimony to Jesus, those who had not worshipped the beast and its image or received its mark on forehead or hand. These came to life again and reigned with Christ for a thousand years, though 5 the rest of the dead did not come to life until the thousand years were over. This is the first resur-rection. Happy indeed, and one of 6 God's own people, is the man who shares in this first resurrection! Upon such the second death has no claim; but they shall be priests of God and of Christ, and shall reign with him for the thousand years.

When the thousand years are 7 over, Satan will be let loose from his dungeon; and he will come out 8 to seduce the nations in the four quarters of the earth and to muster them for battle, yes, the hosts of Gog and Magog, countless as the sands of the sea. So they marched 9 over the breadth of the land and laid siege to the camp of God's people and the city that he loves. But fire came down on them from heaven and consumed them; and 10 the Devil, their seducer, was flung into the lake of fire and sulphur,

---

[a] Or . . . worship. For testimony to Jesus is the spirit that inspires prophets.
[b] *Some witnesses read* spattered with blood.

where the beast and the false prophet had been flung, there to be tormented day and night for ever.

11 Then I saw a great white throne, and the One who sat upon it; from his presence earth and heaven vanished away, and no place was 12 left for them. I could see the dead, great and small, standing before the throne; and books were opened. Then another book was opened, the roll of the living. From what was written in these books the dead were judged upon the record 13 of their deeds. The sea gave up its dead, and Death and Hades gave up the dead in their keeping; they were judged, each man on the 14 record of his deeds. Then Death and Hades were flung into the lake of fire. This lake of fire is the second 15 death; and into it were flung any whose names were not to be found in the roll of the living.

21 THEN I saw a new heaven and a new earth, for the first heaven and the first earth had vanished, and there was no longer any sea. 2 I saw the holy city, new Jerusalem, coming down out of heaven from God, made ready like a bride 3 adorned for her husband. I heard a loud voice proclaiming from the throne: 'Now at last God has his dwelling among men! He will dwell among them and they shall be his people, and God himself will be 4 with them.*a* He will wipe every tear from their eyes; there shall be an end to death, and to mourning and crying and pain; for the old order has passed away!'

5 Then he who sat on the throne said, 'Behold! I am making all things new!' (And he said to me, 'Write this down; for these words 6 are trustworthy and true. Indeed they are already fulfilled.') 'I am the Alpha and the Omega, the beginning and the end. A draught

from the water-springs of life will be my free gift to the thirsty. All 7 this is the victor's heritage; and I will be his God and he shall be my son. But as for the cowardly, 8 the faithless, and the vile, murderers, fornicators, sorcerers, idolaters, and liars of every kind, their lot will be the second death, in the lake that burns with sulphurous flames.'

Then one of the seven angels 9 that held the seven bowls full of the seven last plagues came and spoke to me and said, 'Come, and I will show you the bride, the wife of the Lamb.' So in the Spirit he 10 carried me away to a great high mountain, and showed me the holy city of Jerusalem coming down out of heaven from God. It shone 11 with the glory of God; it had the radiance of some priceless jewel, like a jasper, clear as crystal. It had 12 a great high wall, with twelve gates, at which were twelve angels; and on the gates were inscribed the names of the twelve tribes of Israel. There were three gates to 13 the east, three to the north, three to the south, and three to the west. The city wall had twelve founda- 14 tion-stones, and on them were the names of the twelve apostles of the Lamb.

The angel who spoke with me 15 carried a gold measuring-rod, to measure the city, its wall, and its gates. The city was built as a 16 square, and was as wide as it was long. It measured by his rod twelve thousand furlongs, its length and breadth and height being equal. Its wall was one 17 hundred and forty-four cubits high, that is, by human measurements, which the angel was using. The wall was built of jasper, while 18 the city itself was of pure gold, bright as clear glass. The founda- 19 tions of the city wall were adorned with jewels of every kind, the first

---

a Some witnesses read God-with-them shall himself be their God *(see Isaiah 7. 14; 8. 8).*

of the foundation-stones being jasper, the second lapis lazuli, the third chalcedony, the fourth eme-
20 rald, the fifth sardonyx, the sixth cornelian, the seventh chrysolite, the eighth beryl, the ninth topaz, the tenth chrysoprase, the eleventh torquoise, and the twelfth ame-
21 thyst. The twelve gates were twelve pearls, each gate being made from a single pearl. The streets of the city were of pure gold, like translucent glass.
22   I saw no temple in the city; for its temple was the sovereign Lord
23 God and the Lamb. And the city had no need of sun or moon to shine upon it; for the glory of God gave it light, and its lamp was the
24 Lamb. By its light shall the nations walk, and the kings of the earth shall bring into it all their splen-
25 dour. The gates of the city shall never be shut by day – and there
26 will be no night. The wealth and splendour of the nations shall be
27 brought into it; but nothing unclean shall enter, nor anyone whose ways are false or foul, but only those who are inscribed in the Lamb's roll of the living.
22   Then he showed me the river of the water of life, sparkling like crystal, flowing from the throne
2 of God and of the Lamb down the middle of the city's street. On either side of the river stood a tree of life, which yields twelve crops of fruit, one for each month of the year; the leaves of the trees serve for the healing of the nations.
3 Every accursed thing shall disappear. The throne of God and of the Lamb will be there, and his
4 servants shall worship him; they shall see him face to face, and bear
5 his name on their foreheads. There shall be no more night, nor will they need the light of lamp or sun, for the Lord God will give them light; and they shall reign for evermore.

6 Then he said to me, 'These words are trustworthy and true. The Lord God who inspires the prophets has sent his angel to show his servants what must shortly happen. And, remember, I am 7 coming soon!'

Happy is the man who heeds the words of prophecy contained in this book! It is I, John, who 8 heard and saw these things. And when I had heard and seen them, I fell in worship at the feet of the angel who had shown them to me. But he said to me, 'No, not that! 9 I am but a fellow-servant with you and your brothers the prophets and those who heed the words of this book. It is God you must worship.' Then he told me, 'Do 10 not seal up the words of prophecy in this book, for the hour of fulfilment is near. Meanwhile, let the 11 evil-doer go on doing evil and the filthy-minded wallow in his filth, but let the good man persevere in his goodness and the dedicated man be true to his dedication.'

'Yes, I am coming soon, and 12 bringing my recompense with me, to requite everyone according to his deeds! I am the Alpha and the 13 Omega, the first and the last, the beginning and the end.'

Happy are those who wash their 14 robes clean! They will have the right to the tree of life and will enter by the gates of the city. Outside are dogs, sorcerers and 15 fornicators, murderers and idolaters, and all who love and practise deceit.

'I, Jesus, have sent my angel 16 to you with this testimony for the churches. I am the scion and offspring of David, the bright star of dawn.'

'Come!' say the Spirit and the 17 bride.

'Come!' let each hearer reply.

Come forward, you who are thirsty; accept the water of life, a free gift to all who desire it.

For my part, I give this warning 18 to everyone who is listening to the

words of prophecy in this book: should anyone add to them, God will add to him the plagues de-
19 scribed in this book; should anyone take away from the words in this book of prophecy, God will take away from him his share in the tree of life and the Holy City, described in this book.

He who gives this testimony 20 speaks: 'Yes, I am coming soon!'

Amen. Come, Lord Jesus!

The grace of the Lord Jesus be 21 with you all.[a]

[a] *Some witnesses read* with all; *others read* with all God's people; *others read* with God's people; *some add* Amen.

CONCISE
READER'S GUIDE

PREFACE

This Guide, based on the New English Bible, has been compiled to help the general reader. Information is given on those words, events and themes on which he is most likely to need guidance about meaning, background and setting within the framework of the whole Bible. Facts about the most significant people and places; about the books and their contents, the botany, animals and birds, arts and crafts, and customs are also included.

While every use has been made of up-to-date scholarship and recent archaeological discoveries, technical terms are avoided and the vocabulary has been kept as simple as possible. Where a biblical site has been definitely identified its modern name is given in italics.

Information which is directly obtainable from the text of the Bible itself is not normally repeated, but the carefully chosen references point to where the essential information necessary for a full appreciation of the Bible narrative, message and teaching can be found.

As in the translation itself, there is no bias in this Guide towards any particular school of interpretation, and it may be used with confidence by Christians of every church. It is hoped that this approach, fully in accord with modern educational practice, will stimulate the user to further study and to a greater understanding of the Bible, the life and times of its people and the religious practices of Jews and Christians.

CONCISE READER'S GUIDE

Aaron The elder brother of Moses who assisted him in the work of freeing the Israelites from slavery in Egypt, and whose family became hereditary priests. Ex. 4. 10 – 5. 13; 6. 20–27; 24. 1–15; 28. 1 – 29. 35; 32; Nu. 20. 22–29; Ac. 7. 40; Heb. 5. 4; 9. 4.

Abana A river of Damascus. 2 K. 5. 10–12. *Nahr Barada.*

abba An Aramaic term of affection for father. Mk. 14. 36; Rom. 8. 15; Gal. 4. 6.

Abed-nego A companion of Daniel cast into the fire for refusing to worship Nebuchadnezzar's image. Dan. 1. 7; 3. 8–30.

Abel The son of Adam, murdered by his brother Cain. Gen. 4. 1–16; Mt. 23. 35; Lk. 11. 51; Heb. 11. 4.

Abiathar The high priest, descended from Eli, in office during David's reign, who conspired against Solomon. 1 S. 22; 23. 6; 2 S. 15; 17. 15–16; 1 K. 1. 7 – 2. 27.

Abigail The widow of Nabal whom David married. 1 S. 25. 2–43; 30. 1–18.

Abijah or **Abijam** The successor to Jeroboam as king of Judah. 1 K. 15; 2 Ch. 13. Others of the same name. 1 S. 8; 1 K. 14; 1 Ch. 24; 2 Ch. 29; Neh. 12.

Abilene A district in the E mountain range, roughly parallel to the Lebanon in N Syria, under the rule of Lysanias. Its chief town was Abila. Lk. 3. 1. *Sûq Wâdi Baradā.*

Abimelech (1) The Philistine king of Gerar who made a covenant with Abraham. Gen. 20. (2) The son of Gideon. Judg. 9.

Abishai The nephew of David, and his devoted and loyal follower. 1 S. 26. 4–12; 2 S. 2. 17–24; 18. 1–13.

Abner Saul's cousin and commander-in-chief. 1 S. 14. 51; 17. 55–58; 2 S. 2. 8–9; 3. 6–34.

Abomination of Desolation Dan. 11. 31; 12. 11; Mk. 13. 14.

Abraham The son of Terah and the founder of the Hebrew nation. At God's call he emigrated, with his wife Sarah and nephew Lot, from Ur to Canaan (via Haran) where God made a covenant with him and promised that he would be the ancestor of a great nation. Gen. ch. 11–25; Mt. 3. 9; 8. 11; Mk. 12. 26; Lk. 13. 16; Jn. 8. 31–59; Rom. 4; Gal. ch. 3–4; Jas. 2. 21–24.

Absalom (1) David's third and favourite son who plotted against him. 2 S. ch. 13–18. (2) The father of Mattathias. 1 Mac. 11. 70.

acacia A tree, found in the Jordan valley, especially valued for its durability and much used in construction work. Ex. 25. 10; 26. 26–28; Is. 41. 19.

Accad A city in the land of Shinar or Babylonia which became the capital of Sargon I and gave its name to the whole of N Babylonia. Gen. 10. 10.

Acclamation, Day of Also known as the Feast of Trumpets, it marked the beginning of the Jewish civil new year and the month in which fell the Day of Atonement and the Feast of Tabernacles. It was set aside as a day of rest. Today it is known as Rosh Hashanah. Nu. 29. 1–6. *See also* Lev. 23. 24–25.

Achaia The Roman province, which included Greece, with its headquarters at Corinth. Ac. 18. 12; 19. 21; 1 Cor. 16. 15–16; 2 Cor. 9. 2.

Achan An Israelite who broke Joshua's ban on looting after the fall of Jericho. Jos. 7.

Achior An Ammonite leader who became a Jewish convert. Judith 14. 10.

Achish The Philistine king of Gath who protected David from Saul. 1 S. ch. 21; 27–29.

Acts of the Apostles Generally believed to have been written by Luke the physician as a sequel to his Gospel. It is an account of the spread of Christianity through the work of the apostles under the guidance and in the power of the Holy Spirit during the first thirty years of the church's life.

3

At first, Peter is prominent in the account of the growth of the church in Jerusalem; then Paul, whose missionary journeys to Asia Minor, Greece and Rome are described.

Adam The Hebrew for 'man' or 'mankind', and the name of the first creature made in the image and likeness of God. Gen. 1. 26 – 3. 24.

Adasa A place near Beth-horon where Judas defeated and killed Nicanor. 1 Mac. 7. 39–50. *Khirbet ʿAddâseh.*

Adida A place in the Shephelah fortified by Simon where he camped. 1 Mac. 12. 38; 13. 12–19.

Adonijah The fourth son of David who conspired to seize the throne in rivalry to Solomon. 1 K. 1. 5 – 2. 25.

adoption The act of taking officially the child of another as one's own. Ex. 2. 10; Est. 2. 7. In the Bible, sonship is not man's by nature but comes as the gift of God through Christ who is Son in his own right. Rom. 8. 14–21; 9. 4; Gal. 4. 4-7; Eph. 1. 5.

Adramyttium A seaport in Mysia in Asia Minor. Ac. 27. 2. *Edremit.*

Adullam An ancient Canaanite city in the low country SW of Jerusalem. Nearby was the limestone cave where David hid from Saul. 1 S. ch. 22–23. *Tell esh-Sheikh-Madhkûr.*

adultery In the O.T. unconditional faithfulness in marriage is demanded. Ex. 20. 14; Lev. 20. 10. In the N.T. Jesus goes beyond this in his teaching. Mt. 5. 27–32; 19. 9. 'Adultery' is also used metaphorically for the worship of false gods. Jer. 3. 8–9; Ezek. 23. 37; Hos. ch. 1–3.

Adummim A place on the road between Jericho and Jerusalem, and traditionally the site of the inn of the Good Samaritan. Jos. 15. 7; 18. 17. *See also* Lk. 10. 34. *Talʿat ed-Damm.*

Advocate Found only in the writings of John, and used of the Holy Spirit in the sense of one who not only consoles but who, with authority, strengthens. Jn. ch. 14–16.

Aeneas A paralytic healed by Peter at Lydda. Ac. 9. 32–35.

Agabus A Jerusalem prophet who foretold a famine and predicted Paul's imprisonment. Ac. 11. 27–28; 21. 8–14.

Agag The king of Amalek, captured by Saul and killed by Samuel. 1 S. 15.

agriculture The excavation of O.T. Jericho has shown that Palestine was one of the earliest agricultural countries with an irrigation culture existing around 7500 B.C. The principal crops were wheat and barley with a secondary crop of lentils, peas and beans. Vegetables, especially onions and garlic, were widely grown. The heavy winter rains gave the crops their major moisture, but the rains of March–April were needed to bring the grain to head. The cultivation of grapes, cucumbers and melons was made possible by the heavy summer dews in many parts of the country.

Agrippa (1) Herod Agrippa I who put James to death. Ac. 12. 1–23. (2) Herod Agrippa II before whom Paul made his defence. Ac. 25. 13 – 26. 1.

Ahab Son of Omri and seventh king of Israel. His foreign-born wife, Jezebel, introduced the worship of the Tyrian Baal and she was denounced by Elijah. 1 K. 16. 28–31; 18; 20. 34; 21; 22.

Ahasuerus Traditionally the Persian king Xerxes I. Ezr. 4. 6; Est. 1. 1; Tobit 14. 15.

Ahaz The king of Judah who, when attacked by Syria and Israel, appealed for help to Assyria against the advice of Isaiah. 2 K. 16. 1–20; Is. 7. 1–25; 14. 28.

Ahaziah (1) The king of Israel, denounced by Elijah for continuing idolatrous worship, who died from an accident after a brief reign. 1 K. 22. 51 – 2 K. 1. 18. (2) A king of Judah who followed the pagan religious policy of the house of Ahab. 2 K. 9. 16–28; 2 Ch. 22. 1–12.

Ahijah There are nine of this name in the O.T., the most important being (1) The great-grandson of Eli. 1 S. 14. 18. (2) The prophet of Shiloh who foretold the division of the kingdom. 1 K. 11. 29–39; 2 Ch. 9. 29.

Ahikam The son of Shaphan the scribe and one of the deputation sent by Josiah to the prophetess Huldah. Later, he was the protector of Jeremiah and the father of Gedaliah. 2 K. 22. 12–14; Jer. 26. 24.

Ahikar Tobit's nephew, appointed as head of his entire administration by Esarhaddon. Tobit 1. 19–22.

Ahimelech Saul's high priest who assisted David at the cost of his life. 1 S. ch. 21–22.

Ahithophel The politically skilled, but unprincipled, counsellor of David who committed suicide after the failure of Absalom's revolt. 2 S. ch. 15–17.

Ai A royal city of central Canaan, close to Bethel, which strongly resisted Joshua's assault. Jos. 7. 2–5; 8. 1–28. Excavations made at Et-Tell by Mme J. Marquet-Krause 1933–5.

Akeldama The piece of land bought with the money received by Judas for betraying Christ. Ac. 1. 18–19.

Alcimus A priest, descended from Aaron, who collaborated with the enemies of the Jews while attempting to get himself appointed high priest. 1 Mac. 7. 1–25; 9. 54–57; 2 Mac. 14. 3–27.

Alexander (1) Alexander the Great who defeated Darius and left valuable weapons in the temple of Elymais. 1 Mac. 1. 1–9; 6. 1–2. (2) Alexander Epiphanes who successfully revolted against Demetrius and appointed Jonathan high priest. Later he was attacked by his father-in-law, Ptolemy, and fled to Arabia where he was murdered. 1 Mac. 10. 1 – 11. 17. (3) The son of Simon of Cyrene. Mk. 15. 21. (4) A kinsman of Annas the high priest. Ac. 4. 6. (5) A copper-smith who opposed Paul. 2 Tim. 4. 14.

Alexandria The city founded on the N coast of Egypt by Alexander the Great which became famous as an intellectual centre and wealthy as a seaport. It attracted a large Jewish community, and the Septuagint was made here. It early became a strong centre of Christianity. Ac. 6. 9; 18. 24; 27. 6; 28. 11.

algum A tree which grows freely on the mountains of Lebanon and Gilead. Reaching up to 65 feet, it grows in pyramidal form. 2 Ch. 2. 8; 9. 10–11.

almond A tree, growing wild in Palestine, but also cultivated for its fruit from which oil is produced. It grows to over 15 feet. Gen. 43. 11; Nu. 17. 6–8; Eccles. 12. 5. Used figuratively Jer. 1. 11.

alms Something given freely to the needy; an act of charity. The Bible constantly insists that it is one of the duties of the religious man. See Deut. 15. 11; Mt. 6. 1–4; Ac. 20. 35; 1 Cor. 16. 1–4; 2 Cor. 9. 7.

almug A sweet-smelling and durable timber, like red sandalwood, used for building and making musical instruments. It grows to a height of about 20 feet. 1 K. 10. 11–12.

aloes A plant with thick, fleshy leaves from which hang bell-shaped flowers. A substance known as aloin, used in the making of spices, was taken from its leaves. Ps. 45. 8; Pr. 7. 17; Jn. 19. 38–40.

Alphaeus (1) The father of James the Less. Mt. 10. 3. (2) The father of Levi (Matthew). Mk. 2. 14.

altar Any raised structure on which sacrifices and incense were burnt and thus offered to God. The shape, size and material used varied widely. 1 S. 14. 33–35; 1 K. 18. 30–32. In the Tabernacle were two altars. Ex. ch. 27; 30. New altars were made in Solomon's Temple. 1 K. 8. 64; 2 Ch. 4. 1, 19.

Amalekites Nomadic wanderers of the Sinai peninsula and desert regions in S Palestine from the times of Abraham to Hezekiah. Descendants of Esau, they were fierce enemies of the Israelites. Ex. 17. 8–16; Nu. 14. 43–45; Dt. 25. 17–19; 1 S. ch. 15; 30.

Amasa Nephew of David and commander-in-chief of Absalom's troops during his revolt. 2 S. 17. 25 – 20. 12.

Amaziah A king of Judah who defeated the Edomites but was unsuccessful against the Israelites. After a long reign he was assassinated. 2 K. 14. 1–21.

amen A transliteration of a Hebrew word from a root meaning 'to be firm, steady, trustworthy'. It passes in meaning from an expression of solemn assent to an oath in the O.T. Nu. 5. 23. In the Gospels it often introduces a saying of Christ's to give it emphasis. See Jn. 1. 51; 14. 12. It is also used in the N.T. to express agreement with an act of praise or blessing. 1 Cor. 14. 16.

Ammonites Traditionally descended from Ben-ammi, they lived E of the Jordan and NE of the Dead Sea. Notorious for their cruelty, they worshipped the god Kemosh. Frequently at war with the Israelites, they were friendly for a time during the reign of Solomon. Gen. 19. 38; Judg. 3. 13; 1 S. 11; 2 S. 10; 1 K. 11. 7; Jer. 49; Am. 1. 13–15.

Amorites A Semitic people who migrated to Canaan before the Israelites and inhabited mainly the hilly regions. After fiercely resisting the Israelite invasion, they became menials and were gradually absorbed when the land was settled. Ex. 3. 8; Nu. 21; Jos. 12; Judg. 3; 1 K. 9. 20.

Amos A shepherd from Tekoa in Judah who prophesied at the northern shrine of Bethel in the time of Jeroboam. Am. 1. 1.

Amos, Book of The theme is that religion divorced from morality is no religion at all. No idea of geographical limits to God's power is accepted. Jehovah is the God of all nations 9. 7. Israel has been chosen by him and is therefore subjected to the greater judgement which goes with greater privilege and responsibility 3. 2; 4. 11–12. Since Jehovah is a God of justice, the Israelites cannot please him with sacrifices while continuing to practise injustice 5. 21–27. Hence the urgent call to repentance; and the promise of a brighter day if the call is heard and obeyed 9. 14.

Amphipolis An important town on a bend of the river Strymon in Macedonia. Ac. 17. 1.

Anakim A race of giants living in S Palestine, driven from the Hebron district by Caleb. Remnants were left in the Gaza area. Dt. 1. 28. *See also* Nu. 13. 22; Judg. 1. 20.

Ananias (1) A Jerusalem Christian who lied to the apostles. Ac. 5. 1–12. (2) The high priest presiding at Paul's trial before the Council. Ac. ch. 23–24. (3) A Christian Jew of Damascus who baptized Saul. Ac. 9. 1-19. (4) A relative of Tobit's with whose son the angel, Raphael, identified himself. Tobit 5. 12.

Anathoth Personal name and also the name of a city of Benjamin allocated to the priests. It was the birthplace of Jeremiah. Jos. 21. 18; 1 Ch. 6. 60; Jer. 1. 1; 32. 7–15. Excavations by A. Bergman

of the American Schools of Oriental Research 1936. *Râs el-Kharrûbeh.*

Andrew One of the twelve apostles and the brother of Peter. A fisherman from Bethsaida, he lived in Capernaum and was first a disciple of John the Baptist. Mt. 10. 2; Mk. 1. 16–18; Jn. 1. 35–42; 6. 8; 12. 22.

Andronicus (1) A Jewish believer, once a fellow-prisoner of Paul. Rom. 16. 7. (2) An officer of Antiochus who treacherously murdered Onias. 2 Mac. 4. 30–38.

angel A heavenly being, attendant on God. Belief in angels was widespread in O.T. times, and was accepted by Jesus in his teaching. Gen. 22. 15–18; 1 S. 29. 9; 2 S. 24. 16; Ps. 148. 2–5; Is. 63. 9; Dan. 3. 28; Mt. 18. 10; 22. 30; 26. 53; 28. 5–7; Lk. 1. 26–38; 12. 8; Ac. 5. 19; Col. 2. 18; Heb. 1. 4–7; 2 Pet. 2. 11.

angel of the LORD The messenger of God, sent by him to deal with men as his personal agent and spokesman. Ex. 3. 2; 1 K. 19. 5–8; 2 K. 19. 35; Ps. 35. 5; Zech. 1. 7 – 6. 8; Mt. 1. 20; Lk. 1. 11.

Anna (1) A widowed prophetess who, in the Temple, recognized the infant Jesus as the Messiah. Lk. 2. 36–38. (2) The wife of Tobit. Tobit 1. 9, 20.

Annas High priest at Jerusalem from A.D. 6 until deposed by the Romans in A.D. 15. His influence continued during the high-priesthood of his son-in-law, Caiaphas. Lk. 3. 2; Jn. 18. 12–24; Ac. 4. 6.

anoint Persons and places were anointed in both the O.T. and N.T. as a sign of holiness or setting apart for God. Ex. 28. 41; 30. 22–33; Judg. 9. 8; 1 S. 10. 1–7; 16. 13; 2 S. 2. 4; 1 K. 19. 16; Ac. 10. 38. *See also* 1 Jn. 2. 20, 27. In the N.T. anointing is also referred to as a sign of hospitality Lk. 7. 46; treatment for wounds 10. 34; in connection with burial Jn. 12. 3; and spiritual healing Mk. 6. 13; Jas. 5. 14.

ant This insect is referred to only twice in the Bible; as an example of industry and wisdom. The most likely species is the Harvester Ant. Pr. 6. 6; 30. 24–25.

Antichrist Used in the N.T. only by John, and then of false prophets. 1 Jn. 2. 18–22; 4. 3; 2 Jn. 7. However, the idea of a great power hostile to God appears elsewhere.

Ezek. 38; Dan. 11; 2 Th. 2; Rev. ch. 13; 17; 20.

Antioch (1) A Syrian city on the Orontes some 300 miles N of Jerusalem intimately connected with the spread of Christianity. Ac. 11. 19–30; 13; 14. 26; 15. 22–35; 18. 22; Gal. 2. 11. *Anṭâkiyeh.* (2) A Roman colony and the administrative centre of Galatia. It had a synagogue and was visited by Paul and Barnabas. Ac. 13. 14–52; 14. 19 – 15. 2; 2 Tim. 3. 11. *Yahaç.*

Antiochus Kings of the Seleucid dynasty who ruled over the more westerly regions of Alexander's eastern empire: (1) Antiochus I who was compelled to replace his wife, Laodice, by Ptolemy's daughter, Berenice. *See* Dan. 11. 6. (2) Antiochus III, the Great, who annexed Palestine in 198 B.C. 1 Mac. 8. 5–8. *See also* Dan. 11. 11–19. (3) Antiochus IV, Epiphanes, who robbed the Temple of its treasures and by other acts of sacrilege provoked the revolt of the Maccabees. 1 Mac. 1. 41 – 2. 48.

Antipas A martyr of the church at Pergamum. Rev. 2. 13.

Antipater The son of Jason, sent as a Jewish envoy to Rome and Sparta. 1 Mac. 12. 16–17; 14. 20–23.

Antipatris The town founded by Herod the Great on the road between Jerusalem and Caesarea on the site of the Canaanite city, Aphek. Ac. 23. 12–31. *Râs el-'Ain.*

Antonia, Tower of A castle connected with the Temple at Jerusalem, rebuilt by Herod the Great and named after Mark Antony. *See* Ac. 21. 30–40.

apes These are mentioned only among the animal imports made by Solomon, and the interpretation depends on the origin of the cargo. If it came from India these were probably langurs; if from Egypt, then baboons or vervet monkeys. 1 K. 10. 22.

Apherema A district added to Judaea from Samaria by Demetrius I. 1 Mac. 10. 29–35; 11. 30–37. *eṭ Ṭaiyibeh.*

Apocrypha Literally 'hidden', but now a technical term applied to the books included in the Greek (Septuagint) and Latin (Vulgate) Christian Old Testaments but excluded from the Hebrew Bible. For the most part they were written between 200 B.C. and A.D. 70, and the contents is very varied. They are important historically as bridging the gap of nearly 400 years between the writings of the O.T. and N.T.

Apollonia A town, standing between the rivers Strymon and Axino, through which Paul passed on his way from Philippi to Macedonia. Ac. 17. 1. *Pollina.*

Apollonius Governor of Coele-syria and Phoenicia at whose suggestion Seleucus sent Heliodorus to rob the Temple. 2 Mac. 3. 4–40; 5. 24–26.

Apollos A Christian Jew of Alexandria, famous for his oratory, who taught in Ephesus and Corinth. Ac. 18. 24–28; 1 Cor. 1. 10–17; 3. 1–9.

apostle A commissioned envoy. (1) The Twelve chosen by Jesus to be eyewitnesses of the events of his life and his resurrection, and hearers of his teaching. Mt. 10. 2–4; Mk. 3. 16–19; Lk. 6. 14–16; Jn. 20. 21–29; Ac. 1. (2) In a subordinate sense, Christian messengers accredited by a community. Ac. 14. 4, 14; Rom. 16. 7; 1 Cor. 12. 28; 2 Cor. 11. 13; Eph. 4. 11.

Appii Forum A town on the Appian Way 40 miles from Rome. Ac. 28. 15.

apple A difficult tree to grow in Palestine, and the fruit is usually of poor quality. It is seldom cultivated today. Joel 1. 12.

Aquila A Jew, banished from Rome, who settled with his wife Priscilla in Corinth, where Paul met them. Later they settled in Ephesus where their house became a Christian centre. Ac. 18. 1–4, 18, 24–26; Rom. 16. 3–5; 2 Tim. 4. 19.

Arabah The rift running, mostly below sea-level, from the Sea of Galilee to the Gulf of Aqabah. Much of it is desert but copper was mined in the south. Jos. 18. 18; 2 S. 2. 29; 2 K. 14. 25; Jer. 39. 4.

Arabia Originally the N part of the peninsula between the Red Sea and the Persian Gulf, but later the whole of it. 1 K. 10. 15; 2 Ch. 9. 14; Ezek. 27. 21.

Aram A person, a people and a region: (1) The son of Shem, ancestor of the Semitic Aramaeans. Gen. 10. 22. (2) The area, largely NNE of Palestine, extending from Haran (E of the Euphrates) to Hauran (E of Galilee). Gen. 24. 10; Nu. 23. 7; 2 S. 8. 5; 10. 16; 1 K. 15. 18.

Aram-naharaim *See* Mesopotamia.

Ararat The mountainous area in the northern part of modern Armenia; one source of the Euphrates. Gen. 8. 4; 2 K. 19. 37; Jer. 51. 27.

Araunah A Jebusite whose threshing-floor was bought by David. It became the site of Solomon's Temple. 2 S. 24. 18–25. *See also* 2 Ch. 3. 2.

Arbatta A Palestinian district from which Simon rescued some Jews. 1 Mac. 5. 21–23. *'Arrâbeh.*

arbour A simple shelter made of branches which featured especially in the Feast of Tabernacles. Lev. 23. 35–43; Neh. 8. 15. *See also* Job 27. 18; Is. 1. 8.

archaeology Biblical archaeology contributes enormously to our understanding of the Bible, and to our knowledge of the background against which it was written. It is detective work in the service of history which tries to fill up the gaps in our knowledge by reconstructing what happened from the clues which have been left behind. Archaeology gives us perspective and enables us to understand much more fully practices, circumstances and allusions in the Bible which were so familiar to the writer and his circle that there was no need to explain them.

Many of the interesting things which have been found in Palestine by archaeologists can be seen in museums. In the U.S.A., the Brooklyn Museum, the University of Chicago, the Oriental Institute and the Boston Museum of Fine Arts have especially good collections. For a full, but non-technical explanation which includes the most recent discoveries see *Understanding the Old Testament* in the Cambridge Bible Commentaries on the New English Bible.

The principal excavated sites are at Ai, Anathoth, Ashkelon, Bethel, Bethlehem, Beth-shan, Beth-shemesh, Beth-zur, Capernaum, Carmel, Debir, Dibon, Dothan, Eglon, Ezion-geber, Gaza, Gerasa, Gezer, Gibeah, Gibeon, Hazor, Jericho, Jerusalem, Lachish, Megiddo, Mizpah, Qumran, Rabbath-Ammon, Samaria, Sela, Shechem, Shiloh, Succoth, Taanach, Tirza.

Areopagus A rocky hill opposite the Acropolis, and the meeting-place of the supreme court of Athens. Ac. 17. 16–34.

Aretas The name of four Nabataean (Arab) rulers, of whom two are mentioned in the Bible: (1) Aretas I who was friendly to the Maccabeans. 2 Mac. 5. 8. (2) Aretas IV who tried to capture Paul. 2 Cor. 11. 32–33.

Ariel A name for Jerusalem, probably meaning 'altar-hearth'. It is found on the Moabite Stone. Is. 29. 1–8. *See also* Ezek. 43. 15.

Arimathaea The town NW of Jerusalem from which came the Joseph who buried the body of Jesus. Mt. 27. 57–60.

Aristarchus A Jew from Thessalonica who was a fellow-worker with Paul. Ac. 19. 29; 20. 4; 27. 2; Col. 4. 10; Philem. 24.

Aristobulus (1) The teacher of Ptolemy. 2 Mac. 1. 10. (2) A Roman Christian. Rom. 16. 10.

Arius A king of the Spartans to whom Onias had written. 1 Mac. 12. 7–23.

Ark The name of the sacred chest, dating from the wilderness period, containing the tables of the law. In early times it was regarded as a symbol of the presence of God. Ex. 25. 10–22; Nu. 10. 33–35; Dt. 10. 1-9; 2 S. 6; 1 K. 8.

Armageddon The final battleground between the forces of good and evil. Rev. 16. 16.

army Originally a tribal levy. Nu. 1; Dt. 20. 1–9; Judg. 6. 34–35; 1 S. 11. 7. When this failed to overcome the Philistines, Saul and David began to build up a professional standing army as well. 1 S. 14. 52; 22. 1–2; 2 S. 8. 18; 23. 8–39. Organization Ex. 18. 24–26; Nu. 31. 14; 2 K. 1. 9. In the earlier period an infantry force; Solomon introduced chariots and cavalry. 1 K. 4. 26; 10. 26.

Arnon A swift river flowing into the Dead Sea from the east, forming the boundaries of Moab and the Amorites. Nu. 21. 13; Judg. 11. 18.

Aroer A town on the N bank of the Arnon where David's census began. It is mentioned on the Moabite Stone. Jos. 12. 1–3; 2 S. 24. 1–5; Jer. 48. 16–19. *'Arâ'ir.*

Arphaxad King of the Medes. Judith 1. 1–16.

art Because of the commandment against representational art, Israel did little with painting and sculpture, but music was a familiar part of Hebrew life from early times. Ex. 20. 4.

Artaxerxes The Persian king who allowed the Jews to return to Jerusalem from exile and to rebuild the Temple. Ezr. 7; Neh. 2.

arts and crafts The Jews had a high regard for manual labour, and every boy had to learn a trade. The more skilled artisans lived in special quarters of the towns and formed guilds. Ezr. 2. 42. Artisans included boat-builders 2 Ch. 9. 21; brickmakers Gen. 11. 3; Ex. 5. 14; carpenters 2 S. 5. 11; Is. 44. 13–17; Mk. 6. 3; embroiderers Ex. 35. 35; fullers 2 K. 18. 17; masons 2 Ch. 24. 12; metal-workers Ex. 26. 37; 35. 32; 38. 3; Nu. 33. 52; 1 K. 7. 23; miners Job 28. 1–11; potters Is. 30. 14; Jer. 18. 6; smiths 1 S. 13. 19; Is. 44. 12; spinners Ex. 35. 25–26; stonemasons 1 K. 5. 17–18; 6. 36; tanners Ac. 9. 43; tentmakers Ac. 18. 3; timber-cutters 1 K. 5. 6, 18; weavers Ex. 35. 35.

Asa The third king of Judah, known for his piety and religious zeal. His long reign was a time of prosperity. 1 K. 15. 8–24; 2 Ch. ch. 14–16.

ascension The last post-resurrection appearance of Jesus to his disciples. Mk. 16. 19; Lk. 24. 50; Ac. 1. 1–11.

Ashdod A Philistine city commanding the entrance to Palestine from Egypt; the centre of Dagon worship to which the captured Ark was taken. Jos. 13. 3; 1 S. ch. 5–6; 2 Ch. 26. 6; Is. 20. 1; Neh. 4. 7; 13. 23. *Esdûd.*

Asherah A Canaanite fertility goddess sometimes worshipped in Israel. 1 K. 18. 19–40; 2 K. 23. 4–7.

Ashkelon A Philistine city on the coast between Joppa and Gaza, and the birthplace of Herod the Great. It is called Ashkalon and Ascalon in the Apocrypha. Jos. 13. 3; Judg. 14. 19; 1 S. 6. 17; Jer. 47. 7; Judith 2. 28; 1 Mac. 10. 86. Excavations 1920–2 by J. Garstang. *Khirbet 'Asqalân.*

Ashtaroth The general name for the goddesses of Canaan. Judg. 2. 13; 10. 6.

Ashtoreth The principal goddess of the Sidonians whose worship, which involved immoral practices, was forbidden to the Israelites. 1 S. 31. 10; 1 K. 11. 5, 33; 2 K. 23. 13.

Asia The rich and important Roman province which comprised Syria, Mysia, Lydia, Phrygia and Caria, with its capital at Ephesus. In the books of the Maccabees it is used for the Seleucid empire. 2 Mac. 3. 3; Ac. 19. 10, 22; 20. 18–19; 1 Cor. 16. 19; 2 Cor. 1. 8; 2 Tim. 1. 15.

Asmodaeus An evil demon who had slain each of the seven husbands of Sarah. Tobit 3. 7–17.

Asnapper The Assyrian king who the Samaritans claimed had brought men from Susa and Elam to their city. Ezr. 4. 9–10.

aspen A tall tree with crisp leaves which hang down and sway as if 'weeping'. 2 S. 5. 23; 1 Ch. 14. 14–15.

ass The donkey, or ass, is mentioned over one hundred times in the Bible. The secret of its success in Mediterranean countries is that it is both sure-footed and able to manage on poor forage. The Hebrews were one of the few people who rode asses. Ex. 21. 33; Is. 1. 3; 30. 24; Zech. 9. 9.

Assos A seaport of Mysia, where Paul embarked after going by land from Troas. Ac. 20. 13–14. *Berhamköy.*

assurance Heb. 10. 22. *See also* Is. 32. 17; Eph. 3. 12; Col. 2. 2; 1 Th. 1. 5; 2 Tim. 1. 12; Heb. 6. 11, 19; 1 Jn. 3. 14, 19.

Assyria, Assyrians The country E of the Tigris which took its name from its ancient capital, Asshur. Its rise and fall played an important part in international affairs in the O.T. period. At its greatest extent the empire, centred on Nineveh, stretched from the Persian Gulf to the Mediterranean. Prophets like Isaiah saw in Assyrian aggression an instrument used by God to punish national unfaithfulness. 2 K. 15. 17–20, 27–29; 16. 15–18; 17. 1–6, 24–29; Ezr. 4. 2; Is. 10. 5 – 12. 6; ch. 36–37.

astrologer(s) Wise men who interpreted the messages of the gods and dreams from astronomical observations. The usage broadens to include all who practised magic arts. Mt. 2. 1–12. *See also* Dan. 1. 20; 2. 27; 5. 15; Ac. 8. 9; 13. 6.

Astyages The last king of Media, conquered by Cyrus. Bel & Snake 1.

Atargatis A Syrian goddess who had a temple at Carnaim. 1 Mac. 5. 43–44; 2 Mac. 12. 26.

Athaliah Daughter of Ahab and Jezebel, and the only woman to occupy the throne of Judah. 2 K. 8. 18, 25–28; 11. 1–20; 2 Ch. 22. 1 – 23. 21; 24. 7.

Athenobius A friend of Antiochus sent to Simon. 1 Mac. 15. 26–35.

Athens The centre of Greek culture where Paul preached. Ac. 17. 14–34; 1 Th. 3. 1.

atonement God's appointed way of dealing with the problem posed by the sin of man and of bringing sinners into a right relationship with God. In the O.T. *see* Ex. 29. 36; 30. 10; Lev. 16. 17. In the N.T. *see* Jn. 1. 29; Rom. 5. 8–11; 2 Cor. 5. 18–19; Gal. 1. 4; 1 Tim. 2. 5–6; Heb. 2. 9–18; 9. 11 – 10. 25; 1 Pet. 2. 24; 1 Jn. 2. 2; 4. 10.

Atonement, Day of Celebrated annually on 10th Tishri (September–October), and known today as Yom Kippur, it was the most solemn holy day of Israel and a strict fast. No work was done and, in addition to the regular sacrifices, the blood of an animal was shed to expiate the sins of both priests and people. Lev. 23. 27–32. *See also* Ex. 30. 10; Lev. 16; Nu. 29. 7–11.

Attalia The seaport of Pamphylia from which Paul and Barnabas sailed during the first missionary journey. Ac. 14. 25–26. *Adalia.*

Attalus King of Pergamum to whom the consul wrote announcing the friendship of the Romans for the Jews. 1 Mac. 15. 22.

Augustus The first Roman emperor. He ruled from 31 B.C. to A.D. 14 and ordered the census of Lk. 2. 1.

Auranus The old man who led an attack on the Jews who rose against the sacrilege of Lysimachus. 2 Mac. 4. 39–42.

avenger of blood One who carried out on a murderer the law of a life for a life. *See* Nu. 35. 11–34; 2 K. 14. 5–7; Mt. 5. 38–48.

Azariah A common name among Hebrew families, especially among priests. Among the more important were: (1) The son of Ahimaaz. 1 Ch. 6. 9. (2) The king of Judah, also called Uzziah. 2 K. 14. 21. (3) The son of Oded, a prophet. 2 Ch. 15. 1.

Azarias The name assumed by the angel Raphael. Tobit 5. 4–15.

Azotus The Greek form of Ashdod found in the Apocrypha and N.T. It was sacked by the Maccabeans on several occasions. Judith 2. 28; 1 Mac. 5. 68; 10. 83–87; 16. 10; Ac. 8. 40.

Baal A Canaanite farm god, the son of Asherah and El, who controlled the weather and fertility of man, beast and crops. Each locality had its own Baal which was worshipped at a hill-shrine, but these were gradually amalgamated into a single divinity. The Baal cult affected and challenged the worship of Jehovah and was denounced by the prophets for three centuries. Judg. 2. 12; 6. 25–32; 1 K. 16. 31; 2 K. 10. 18–28; 23. 4–7; 2 Ch. 17. 3; Jer. 7. 1–13; 19. 5; Hos. 2. 8. It also occurs in place-names.

Baal-hamon (= Baal of abundance) The site of Solomon's vineyard. S. of S. 8. 11.

Baalis The king of Ammon who instigated the murder of Gedaliah. Jer. 40. 14.

Baal-zebub (Beelzebub) (= Lord of the flies) A Philistine god worshipped at Ekron. 2 K. 1. 1–16. *See also* Mt. 12. 22–28.

Baanah A Benjamite who killed Saul's son, Ishbosheth. 2 S. 4.

Baasha A usurper king of Israel. 1 K. 15. 16 – 16. 14.

Babel A city of Nimrod's kingdom where the tower was built. Gen. 10. 10; 11. 2–9.

Babylon, Babylonia The country, and capital city, of the area bounded by the Tigris and Euphrates (Mesopotamia) which reached its peak under Nebuchadnezzar. As the place of exile in the 6th century B.C., it strongly influenced later Jewish thought, business and worship. The Bible is filled with prophecies against it. Is. ch. 13; 14; 21; 46; 47; Jer. ch. 29; 50; 51. In the N.T. it refers to Rome in Rev. 14. 8; 16. 19; 17. 5; 18. 1–24.

Bacchides The friend of Demetrius who was sent to support Alcimus against Judas at the battle of Elasa; and later also fought against Jonathan. 1 Mac. 7. 8–20; 9. 1–73.

bags These were usually of leather, cloth or skin, sometimes fastened with a cord for carrying money or weights. Dt. 25. 13; 2 K. 5. 23; Mt. 25. 15–28.

baker, baking This was usually done by the housewife, but professionals existed in towns and were attached to royal households. Gen. 40. 2; Jer. 37. 21.

Balaam A heathen occultist hired by Balak, king of Moab, to curse the Israelites. Nu. ch. 22–24; Rev. 2. 14.

Balak A Moabite king. See Balaam.

balance A simple form was a cross-bar with two hooks on slings hanging down. The word is used of mental or moral attitudes Dan. 5. 27. The prophets frequently stressed the necessity for just balances and true weights. See Lev. 19. 36; Am. 8. 5; Mic. 6. 11.

balm An evergreen shrub, reaching a height of 12–14 feet with white blossom and apple-like fruit, growing freely today around the Dead Sea. Gum resin from its bark was used for medicinal purposes. Gen. 37. 25; Jer. 8. 22; 46. 11; 51. 8.

banner Signal, standard and banner are all used in the O.T. and, on the whole, seem interchangeable as rallying terms. Nu. 1. 52; 2. 2; 21. 8; Is. 11. 12; 13. 2.

banquet (feast) Because of the eastern belief that a common meal establishes a close bond, these were usually (though not invariably: Est. 1; Dan. 5) held on special occasions such as: weddings Gen. 29. 22; Jn. 2; birthdays Gen. 40. 20; Mk. 6. 21; sheep-shearing 1 S. 25. 4, 36; funerals 2 S. 3. 35; Jer. 16. 5; vintage Judg. 9. 27; laying of foundations Pr. 9. 1–5; weaning of a child Gen. 21. 8; offering a sacrifice Ex. 34. 15; Judg. 16. 23–25; the establishing of a covenant Gen. 26. 30. General arrangements Mt. 22. 2–14; Lk. 7. 36–45; 14. 17. Many Jews believed that there would be a great banquet when God delivered his people. Is. 25. 6; Mt. 8. 11.

baptism Ceremonial washing with water is often mentioned in the O.T. Ex. 29. 4; 30. 17–21; Lev. 11. 25; 15; and converts from paganism to Judaism underwent a ceremony which included a bath of purification. A fuller meaning was given to the baptism which was characteristic of John the Baptist's ministry. Mt. 3; Mk. 1.

1–13; Lk. 3. 15–17. Baptism by Jesus's disciples. Mt. 28. 19; Jn. 3. 22; 4. 2. Baptism in the early church. Ac. 2. 38–41; 8. 35–38; 9. 19; 10. 47–48; 19. 1–6; Rom. 6. 3–4; 1 Cor. 1. 14–17; 12. 13; Gal. 3. 27. See also Eph. 5. 26; Heb. 10. 22.

Bar An Aramaic word meaning 'son', often prefixed to proper names. Mt. 27. 16; Ac. 13. 7. See also Mt. 16. 17; Jn. 1. 42.

Barabbas A bandit arrested for political terrorism. Mt. 27. 15–26; Mk. 15. 6–15.

Barak The son of Abiram summoned by the prophetess, Deborah, to lead the Israelites against the confederate Canaanite forces under Sisera. Judg. ch. 4–5.

barbarian Originally one who did not speak Greek, and therefore a foreigner. Col. 3. 11. See also Ac. 28. 2–4; Rom. 1. 14; 1 Cor. 14. 11.

Bar-Jesus A charlatan at the court of Sergius Paulus who opposed Paul in Cyprus. Ac. 13. 4–12.

Bar-Jona See Mt. 16. 17; Jn. 1. 42.

barley A staple cereal cultivated universally from ancient times. Ex. 9. 31; Dt. 8. 8; Ru. 2. 15–17; 2 K. 7. 1; Jn. 6. 3–13.

Barnabas A Levite convert from Cyprus who commended Paul to the Jerusalem church and became his fellow-worker. Ac. 4. 36; 11. 19–30; ch. 13–15; 1 Cor. 9. 6; Gal. 2.

Barsabbas The surname of the Joseph who was nominated to succeed Judas Iscariot. Ac. 1. 23.

Bartholomew One of the twelve apostles. Mt. 10. 3; Mk. 3. 18; Lk. 6. 14; Ac. 1. 13. On the grounds that this is a family name he has been identified by some with Nathanael. Jn. 1. 44–50.

Bartimaeus A blind man of Jericho healed by Jesus. Mk. 10. 46–52.

Baruch The aristocratic friend and secretary of Jeremiah associated with his prophetic work for over 20 years. Jer. 36. 4–20; 43. 1–7.

Baruch, Book of A book of prophecy included in the Apocrypha, possibly written after the destruction of Jerusalem in A.D. 70, to which it refers in veiled language. Wisdom, which may be found in the law of Moses, is praised; and the exiles in Babylon are comforted by the promise that they will return home.

Barzillai A wealthy Gileadite who befriended David when he fled from Absalom. 2 S. 17. 27–29; 19. 31–40; 1 K. 2. 7.

Bashan A hilly, fertile region SE of the Sea of Galilee. Nu. 21. 33; Dt. 3. 1; 29. 7; Ps. 68. 15.

baskets Many kinds, shapes and sizes were used by the Israelites for a variety of purposes: domestic Dt. 26. 2; agricultural 2 K. 10. 7; Jer. 24. 1; trapping birds Jer. 5. 27; presenting bread in the sanctuary Gen. 40. 16; Ex. 29. 3. Two words are used in the N.T., both denoting hampers. Mt. 14. 20; 15. 37.

bat Several species of this animal, which thrives in hot climates, have been identified in Palestine. They were declared unclean in the law and not fit for food. Lev. 11. 19; Is. 2. 20.

bathe, bathing Generally used in the Bible in connection with the ceremonial washing of the body in water. Travellers and guests were always offered this facility. Jn. 13. 10. *See also* Gen. 18. 4; Ex. 30. 17–21; Mt. 6. 17; Mk. 7. 1–8. *See* washing.

Bathsheba The wife of Uriah the Hittite. David married her after causing the death of her husband. She was the mother of Solomon. 2 S. 11. 2 – 12. 25.

bear In biblical times the Syrian bear was found over most of the hilly, wooded parts of Palestine where the rock formation gave it good cover. It is now extinct. 1 S. 17. 34–36; Prov. 17. 12; 28. 15; Hos. 13. 8.

beard To the Jews it was a mark of manly dignity, and was shaved off as a sign of mourning. To mutilate another's beard was a great humiliation. 2 S. 10. 4; 19. 24; Ps. 133. 2; Is. 15. 2; Jer. 48. 37.

Beatitudes The word, meaning 'blessedness', is not scriptural, but is universally associated with Jesus's sayings in Mt. 5. 3–12; Lk. 6. 20–23.

Beautiful Gate A gate of the Temple, which was the scene of a healing by Peter and John, probably the bronze gate leading into the Court of Women. Ac. 3. 1–10.

bed In early times the poor slept on the ground using their outer garments as both mattress and cover; or sometimes a rug or straw-filled sack. Bedsteads were known quite early, and in elaborate form for the wealthy. 2 S. 4. 7; Am. 6. 4. *See also* Ex. 22. 26–27; Est. 1. 6.

bee The Palestinian bee is small and plentiful, and the honey has been cultivated from biblical times. The name 'Deborah' = bee. Dt. 1. 44; Judg. 14. 5–9; Is. 7. 18.

Beer (1) A stopping-place in the wilderness wanderings between the Arnon and Jordan. Nu. 21. 16. (2) The place to which Jotham fled. Judg. 9. 21.

Beer-lahai-roi A well where Hagar was met by an angel. Isaac also met Rebecca here. Gen. 16. 5–14; 24. 62–67.

Beersheba The most southerly town of Judah with many patriarchal associations; important because of its excellent water supply. Gen. 21. 14–20; 26. 23–25; 28. 10; Judg. 20. 1; 1 K. 19 3; Neh. 11. 25–30; Am. 8. 14. *Tell es-Seba'*.

Bel The Babylonian equivalent to Baal, used as both a proper name and a title. Is. 46. 1; Jer. 50. 2. *See* Daniel, Bel, and the Snake.

Belial Used by Paul as a synonym for Satan. 2 Cor. 6. 15.

bellows The Egyptians especially, but the Middle East in general, knew the use of these for stimulating fire. Jer. 6. 29. *See also* Is. 54. 16.

bells Small tinkling bells were worn as ornaments on women's ankles. They were also attached to the bottom of the high priest's robe, and to the harness of war-horses. Ex. 28. 33–34; Is. 3. 16–17; Zech. 14. 20.

Belshazzar According to the book of Daniel the last king of Babylon, at the time of its capture in 539 B.C. Dan. 5.

Belteshazzar The name given to Daniel in Babylon. Dan. 1. 7; 2. 26; 5. 12.

Benaiah The captain of David's bodyguard who succeeded Joab as commander-in-chief of the army. 2 S. 8. 18; 23. 20–22; 1 K. 1. 38; 2. 35.

Ben-hadad A religious title of the kings of Damascus. Three of this name are mentioned in the O.T. (1) 1 K. 15. 17–20. (2)

1 K. 20; 2 K. 8. 7–15. (3) 2 K. 13. 24; Jer. 49. 27; Am. 1. 4.

Ben-hinnom A valley SW of Jerusalem associated with the worship of Molech. It was desecrated by Josiah and used for burning refuse. 2 K. 23. 10; Jer. 7. 31; 32. 35.

Benjamin (1) The youngest son of Jacob and Rachel. Gen. 35. 16–18; ch. 42–44. (2) The tribe settled in Palestine between Ephraim and Judah. Jos. 18. 11–28; Judg. ch. 19–21; 1 S. 9. 1–2; Rom. 11. 1.

Berea A place, about 15 miles N of Jerusalem, to which Bacchides marched against Judas. 1 Mac. 9. 4. *Bîr ez-Zeit.*

Bernice The daughter of Herod Agrippa I who was present with her brother, Agrippa II, at Paul's defence before Festus. Ac. 25. 23 – 26. 32.

Beroea (1) A town in Macedonia where Paul preached. Ac. 17. 10–13; 20. 4. *Verria.* (2) The place where Menelaus was killed. 2 Mac. 13. 3–8. *Ḥaleb.*

Bethany A village less than 2 miles from Jerusalem on the road to Jericho, and the home of Lazarus and his family. Christ's ascension took place here. Mt. 26. 6–13; Mk. 11. 11; Lk. 19. 29; 24. 50; Jn. 11. 1–46. *el-ʿAzariyeh.*

Bethel The Canaanite town of Luz 12 miles N of Jerusalem, renamed Bethel by Jacob. When the kingdom was divided it became a royal shrine for the north and a centre of idolatry; and as such it was denounced by the prophets. Gen. 28. 10–19; 1 K. 12. 25 – 13. 32; 2 K. 10. 29; Am. 3. 14; 5. 5–6. Excavations by W. F. Albright and J. L. Kelso of the American Schools of Oriental Research 1935–8. *Tell Beitin.*

Bethesda A pool in Jerusalem where Jesus healed a cripple. Jn. 5. 1–7.

Beth-horon Here Judas defeated Seron and Nicanor, but it was occupied and fortified by Bacchides. Judith 4. 4–7; 1 Mac. 3. 13–24; 7. 39–45; 9. 50–51.

Bethlehem (= house of bread) A town 5 miles S of Jerusalem called Ephrath in Jacob's time, and the home of Naomi and Boaz. David was anointed here, and Micah's prophecy was fulfilled by the birth of Jesus. Ru. ch. 1–4; 1 S. 16. 1–13;

Mic. 5. 2; Mt. 2. 1–2; Lk. 2. 1–16. Excavations by E. W. Garner 1934–6 and H. Richmond 1935. *Beit Laḥm.*

Beth-peor One of Israel's last camp sites and the place where Moses was buried. Dt. 3. 29; 4. 46; 34. 6. *Khirbet esh-Sheikh-Jâyil.*

Bethphage A village close to Bethany on the Mt of Olives from which came the colt used for the triumphal entry into Jerusalem. Lk. 19. 28–36. *Kefr eṭ-Ṭûr.*

Bethsaida The village on the NE shore of the Sea of Galilee from which Philip, Andrew and Peter came. Mt. 11. 21; Lk. 9. 10–11; Jn. 1. 44; 12. 21. *Khirbet el-ʿAraj.*

Bethzacharia A place where Judas camped and was defeated. 1 Mac. 6. 32–47. *Khirbet Beit Skāriā.*

Beth-zur (= house of the rock) A city in the hill-country of Judah, fortified by Rehoboam. Jos. 15. 58; 2 Ch. 11. 7. It is frequently mentioned in 1 and 2 Maccabees. *Khirbet eṭ-Ṭubeiqah.* Excavations by the American Schools of Oriental Research 1931, 1957.

betrothal *See* bride, bridegroom.

Bible The work of many writers over a period of more than a thousand years. There are two collections of writings (Scriptures) in the Bible. In the O.T. (written almost entirely in Hebrew) are the remains of the literature of the Jewish people, the books of which took their final shape between the 8th and 2nd centuries B.C. In the N.T. are the writings of the Christian church during about the first half-century of its existence.

The central message of the Bible is the story of salvation in which three strands can be distinguished: the bringer of salvation, the way of salvation, and the heirs of salvation. God's message to man has been communicated by his chosen spokesmen, and finally by Jesus Christ. *See* Heb. 1. 1–2.

Bildad One of the three friends of Job. Job 2. 11; ch. 8; 18; 25; 42. 7–9.

Bilhah Rachel's slave-girl who became the mother of Dan and Naphtali. Gen. 29. 29; 30. 1–8; 46. 25.

birds Palestine is a land very rich in birds because of its wide range of climates varying from semi-tropical to true desert. Moreover, one of the main migration routes from Africa into Europe and W Asia runs from the northern point of the Red Sea through the whole length of the country, and there is some movement in progress almost every month.

birthright The special privilege and position belonging to the first-born son in the family who inherited the headship of the household and a double portion of his father's wealth. Gen. 25. 21–34. *See also* Dt. 21. 15–17; 25. 5–10.

Bithynia The Roman province in NW Asia Minor bordering on the Black Sea which early attracted the attention of Paul. Ac. 16. 6–10; 1 Pet. 1. 1.

bitter herbs Salads eaten at Passover time. Ex. 12. 8; Nu. 9. 11.

bitumen Mineral pitch with waterproofing properties found especially near the Dead Sea. Gen. 11. 3; 14. 10. *See also* Gen. 6. 14; Ex. 2. 3.

Black Obelisk A black limestone pillar, about 6½ feet high, found by a young English excavator, A. H. Layard, in 1846 at Nimrud, about 25 miles S of Nineveh where Shalmaneser III of Assyria had his palace. It is now in the British Museum. One of its carved panels in bas-relief shows Jehu offering Israel's tribute: the only known portrayal of an Israelite king.

blasphemy In the O.T. this was any attack on the majesty, honour or authority of God. Ex. 20. 7; Lev. 24. 10–16. The meaning is extended in the N.T. where God is blasphemed in his representatives. Ac. 6. 11.

bless, blessing In very early times this was a magical utterance or act, charged with power to bring about some desired good, often material, to a person. Only gradually was it understood in the fully religious sense as an act of God. Gen. 27. 7–40; 39. 5–6; 48. 12–20; Nu. 6. 22–27; Dt. 28. 1–8; 1 K. 8. 54–61; Pr. 10. 22. The N.T. takes up and develops the idea and practice. Lk. 6. 28; Rom. 12. 14; 1 Cor. 4. 13; 1 Pet. 3. 9.

blight A fungus disease caused by damp. Dt. 28. 22; 1 K. 8. 37; Am. 4. 9; Hag. 2. 17.

blind, blindness A common condition in the Middle East, but also the result of old age. The Mosaic law commanded kindness to the blind; and by healing the blind Jesus fulfilled messianic prophecies. Lev. 19. 14; 21. 18; Dt. 27. 18; Is. 29. 18; 35. 5; 42. 7; Mt. 20. 30; Mk. 8. 22–25. *See also* Gen. 27. 1; 1 S. 3. 2.

blood Its use for food was forbidden. Gen. 9. 3–6; Lev. 3. 17; Ac. 15. 19–29. In the O.T. ritual it played a significant part. Ex. 24. 3–8; Lev. 1. 5; 4. 6–7; 17. 10–14; Dt. 12. 15–28. In the N.T. it is also used as a sacrificial term. Mk. 14. 24; Col. 1. 20; Heb. 9. 11–28; 1 Pet. 1. 19; 1 Jn. 5. 6. *See also* Rom. 3. 25; 5. 9; Heb. 10. 5–14.

Boanerges The nickname (= sons of thunder) given to the brothers James and John. Mk. 3. 17.

boar The wild boar was plentiful in Palestine in biblical times, especially in the Jordan valley where it still survives. It is unclean to both Muslim and Jew. Ps. 80. 13.

boats The Israelites were not a seafaring people, and the Phoenicians held the best coastal harbours, but boats were used for inshore and lake fishing. Lk. 5. 1–11; Jn. 6. 16–24.

Boaz (1) A wealthy Benjamite who married Ruth. Ru. ch. 2–4; Mt. 1. 5. (2) The pillar on the N side of the entrance to Solomon's Temple. 1 K. 7. 21.

body of Christ Mt. 26. 26; Rom. 12. 5; 1 Cor. 12. 12–27; Eph. 1. 23; 4.1–16. *See also* Jn. 2. 21; Heb. 2. 14; 1 Jn. 4. 2–4.

boil A common term used in the O.T. to denote different kinds of local inflammation. Ex. 9. 9; Dt. 28. 27; 2 K. 20. 7. *See also* Lev. 13. 18–44; Job 2. 7; Rev. 16. 2.

book The first writings were inscriptions on plaster and stone; but later materials were leather and papyrus which were kept rolled. *See* Dt. 27. 2–3; Is. 30. 8; Jer. 36. 2; Ezek. 2. 9; 2 Tim. 4. 13; 2 Jn. 12.

bottles These were usually made from complete animals' skins, most often goat, softened and tanned and used to hold wine, water, milk and other liquids. *See* Gen. 21. 14; Jos. 9. 4, 13; Judg. 4. 19; Lk. 5. 37–38.

boundary A landmark between property, the removal of which was punishable by law. Dt. 19. 14; 27. 17; Job 24. 2; Pr. 22. 28; 23. 10; Hos. 5. 10.

bow A weapon used for hunting and war, bent by either hand or foot, and made of wood with ox or camel gut string, and using arrows tipped with stone, bronze or iron according to period. Gen. 27. 3; Job 6. 4; Is. 49. 2; Lam. 3. 13; Ezek. 39. 9. *See also* Gen. 21. 20.

bowls These were of various sizes but usually spherically shaped. Nu. 4. 14; 2 S. 17. 28; Is. 22. 24; Am. 6. 6. *See also* Ex. 12. 22.

box A bush-like tree which flourished in the Lebanon and Cyprus and provided durable timber. Is. 41. 19; 60. 13.

Bozrah (1) A city of Edom frequently mentioned in prophecy. Is. 34. 6; 63. 1; Jer. 49. 13, 22; Am. 1. 12. (2) A city of Moab. Jer. 48. 24.

bracelet Worn by both men and women on the wrist or upper arm. Gen. 24. 22; Ezek. 16. 11. *See also* 2 S. 1. 10; Is. 3. 20.

brazier Used for carrying hot charcoal. Jer. 36. 22. *See also* Ex. 27. 3; Lev. 10. 1; 1 K. 7. 50.

breast-piece (1) Part of the high priest's sacred vestments. Ex. 28. 3–30; 39. 8–21; Lev. 8. 8. (2) Part of a soldier's defensive armour, generally of leather for the ordinary soldier and of metal for officers. *See* 1 S. 17. 5. Used figuratively. *See* Is. 59. 17; Eph. 6. 14; 1 Th. 5. 8.

bribe, bribery Strictly forbidden by the law. Ex. 23. 8; 1 S. 8. 3; 2 Ch. 19. 7.

bricks These were usually made of mud and sun-dried. Gen. 11. 3; Ex. 1. 11–14; 5. 6–19; 2 S. 12. 31; Is. 9. 10; 65. 3.

bride, bridegroom Betrothal and marriage customs. Gen. 29. 27; Judg. 14. 12; Ps. 45. 15; Is. 61. 10; Ezek. 16. 8–12; Mt. 25. 1–12. Used metaphorically Mk. 2. 19; Jn. 3. 29; Rev. 19. 7–8; 21. 2. *See also* 2 Cor. 11. 2; Eph. 5. 22.

brimstone Volcanic deposits associated with destruction. Gen. 19. 24; Dt. 29. 23. Used figuratively of punishment. Ps. 11. 6; Is. 30. 33; 34. 9.

bronze Much use of this brown-coloured alloy of copper and tin, which was known to the patriarchs, was made in the Tabernacle. Ex. 38. Other uses included the making of armour, chains, cymbals and idols. Nu. 21. 9; 1 S. 17. 5; 2 K. 25. 7; 1 Ch. 15. 19; Ps. 107. 16; Rev. 9. 20.

brook A small stream or wadi which usually flows only in the rainy season. *See* 1 K. 17. 2–7; Job 6. 15; Ps. 42. 1; Is. 16. 6.

broom A flowering desert tree highly valued as fuel. Its flowers and fruit resemble that of a pea. 1 K. 19. 4; Job 30. 4.

burial It was customary for the Israelites to bury their dead. Gen. 23. 3–20; 25. 9–10; 35. 8; Dt. 21. 22; 1 S. 31. 11–13; 2 S. 3. 31; 1 K. 13. 22; Jer. 9. 22; 14. 16; Mk. 15. 46; Jn. 19. 40; Ac. 5. 6.

burning bush The scene of Moses' call. Ex. 3. 2; Dt. 33. 16; Mk. 12. 26.

burnt-offering *See* offerings.

butler An important official in royal households. Gen. 40. 1–5. *See also* Neh. 2. 1–8.

butter Thickened or hardened milk; curds obtained by long churning in a goatskin bag. Ps. 55. 21. *See also* Gen. 18. 8; Job 20. 17.

Caesar The official title of all Roman emperors. Those referred to in the Bible are: Augustus Lk. 2. 1; Tiberius Mk. 12. 14; Is. 3. 1; Claudius Ac. 17. 7; 18. 2; Nero Ac. 25. 11.

Caesarea The coastal city 60 miles NW of Jerusalem, built by Herod the Great and the residence of the Roman Governor of Palestine. Ac. 8. 40; 9. 30; 10; 18. 22; 21. 8–16; 23. 23 – 25. 14. *Qaisâriyeh.*

Caesarea Philippi A city at the southern tip of Mt Hermon where the Jordan rises, built by Philip the tetrarch. Previously known as Paneas, it was near here that Antiochus III defeated Egypt and brought Palestine under Seleucid rule. Mt. 16. 13; Mk. 8. 27. *Bâniyâs.*

Caiaphas The son-in-law of Annas and high priest A.D. 18–36. Mt. 26. 3, 57–66; Lk. 3. 2; Jn. 11. 49–53; 18. 24; Ac. 4. 5–6.

Cain The first son of Adam and Eve. Gen. 4. 1–25; Heb. 11. 4.

cakes Various kinds are mentioned in the Bible, some being used in the sanctuary as offerings. Gen. 18. 6; Lev. 2. 4–7; Nu. 11. 7–8; 2 S. 6. 19; Jer. 7. 18.

Calah A city of Assyria, on the banks of the Tigris, founded by Nimrod. Gen. 10.

11. Excavations by the British School. Giant alabaster slabs from the site are in the collections of Philadelphia, Boston and New York museums. *Nimrûd.*

Caleb One of the spies sent into Canaan by Joshua. Nu. ch. 13–14; Jos. 14. 6–14.

Calf, Golden The image made for the rebellious Israelites by Aaron during Moses' absence. Similar idols were set up by Jeroboam. Ex. 32; 1 K. 12. 25–33.

Callisthenes A Syrian captured and burnt to death by the Jews because he had set fire to the gates of the Temple. 2 Mac. 8. 33.

camel The Arabian, one-humped camel, mostly used in ancient Palestine, can carry 400 pounds at an average of 28 miles a day and go for three or four days without water. Although its meat was forbidden by Mosaic law, its rich but not very sweet milk could be drunk or made into butter or cheese. Gen. 37. 25; Judg. 6. 5; 1 K. 10. 2; 1 Ch. 27. 30; Is. 30. 6; 60. 6; Mt. 3. 4. Used figuratively Mt. 19. 24.

Cana A Galilean village near Capernaum. Jn. 2. 1–11; 4. 46–54; 21. 2. *Khirbet Qana.*

Canaan, Canaanites All the land between the Jordan and the Mediterranean from Egypt into Syria. Its inhabitants were Semites. Gen. 10. 15–19; 17. 8. *See also* Dt. 34. 1–4. Numerous excavations. *See* archaeology.

candle, candlestick *See* lamp.

caper A prickly bush growing freely in Palestine whose flower-buds were used as a digestive acid and a stimulant. Eccles. 12. 5.

Capernaum A Roman garrison town on the NW shore of the Sea of Galilee, used by Jesus as his headquarters. Mt. 4. 13; 8. 5–17; 11. 23; 17. 24; Mk. 1. 21 – 2. 12; 9. 33; Lk. 4. 31–37; 10. 15; Jn. 4. 46–53; 6. 59. *Tell Ḥûm.* Excavations 1905–14 by the Deutsche Orient-Gesellschaft.

Caphtor The land (probably Crete) from which the Philistines originally came. Jer. 47. 4; Am. 9. 7.

Cappadocia The Roman province in E Asia Minor known as good grain country. Ac. 2. 9; 1 Pet. 1. 1.

Captivity (1) Of the northern kingdom of Israel in 722 B.C. after a series of invasions by the Assyrians. 2 K. 15. 29; 17. 3–

6. (2) Of Judah in 586 B.C. by Nebuchadnezzar. 2 K. 24. 14–16; 25. 2–21; 2 Ch. 36. 2–7; Dan. 1. 1–4.

caravan A group of merchants travelling together for safety. Gen. 37. 25; Job 6. 18; Ezek. 27. 25.

Carchemish The capital of the Hittite empire, guarding the main ford of the Euphrates. 2 Ch. 35. 20; Is. 10. 9; Jer. 46. 2. *Jerablus.*

Carmel A range of well-wooded hills between Samaria and the Mediterranean some 30 miles long and rising to 1700 feet in the NW. It had rich pasture land and was renowned for its beauty. 1 S. 15. 12; 1 K. 18; 2 K. 4. 25; S. of S. 7. 5; Is. 35. 2; Am. 1. 2. *Jebel Mâr Elyâs.*

carpenter A skilled worker in wood capable of undertaking all the carpentry tasks required in building. 1 Ch. 22. 15; Mt. 13. 55; Mk. 6. 3. *See also* Is. 10. 15; 44. 13–17; Jer. 10. 3–4.

Carpus A man of Troas. 2 Tim. 4. 13.

cassia Similar to the cinnamon-tree, it had many uses. A substance made from the pods and leaves was an important article of commerce; its bark was used as a spice, and its buds as a food-seasoning. Ex. 30. 22–25; Ezek. 27. 19.

castanets These take their name from the two chestnuts which in ancient times were attached to the fingers and beaten together to make music. Later, they were made from small spoon-shaped cymbals of wood or bone. 2 S. 6. 4–5.

Castor and Pollux Two gods regarded as the special protectors of sailors in Greek mythology. Ac. 28. 11.

cat The domesticated form of the N African Wild Cat became popular in Egypt shortly after Joseph's time. Letter of Jer. 6. 22.

cattle Human wealth and the sacrificial worship of God in O.T. times centred round cattle which included oxen, bullocks, heifers, goats and sheep. Gen. 13. 2; Ex. 34. 19; Jn. 4. 12. *See also* 1 K. 1. 19.

Cauda A small island in the Mediterranean off Crete. Ac. 27. 16–17. *Gaudho.*

caves These were abundant in the soft limestone hills of Palestine and were sometimes enlarged for shelter and defence. Gen. 19. 30; 23; Jos. 10. 16–27; 1 S. 22. 1; 24; 1 K. 18. 4.

cedar A stately evergreen tree growing on the high mountains of the Lebanon and often reaching a height of 120 feet. It has a distinctive resinous smell, and its great durability made it a great favourite for use in furniture and boats. 1 K. 5. 6; 6. 2 – 7. 12; Ezek. 27. 5. It is a symbol of strength, beauty, nobility, goodness, and of the Messiah. Ezek. 17. 22–24.

Cenchreae The southern harbour of Corinth. Ac. 18. 18–21; Rom. 16. 1. *Kichries.*

censer An incense burner. 2 Ch. 26. 19; Ezek. 8. 11; Rev. 8. 3–5.

census The numbering of the population. Ac. 5. 37. See also Ex. 30. 11–15; Nu. 1. 1–45; 2 S. 24. 1–15; Lk. 2. 1–5.

centurion The commander of 100 soldiers in the Roman army. Mt. 8. 5–13; 27. 54; Lk. 7. 2–10; Ac. 22. 25; 23. 17; 27. 1–43.

Cephas The name given by Jesus to Peter. Jn. 1. 42.

Chabris A magistrate of Bethulia. Judith 6. 15; 8. 10; 10. 6.

Chaereas The commander of the fortress of Gazara taken by Judas. 2 Mac. 10. 32–38.

chain(s) Used as a mark of distinction Gen. 41. 41–43; Dan. 5. 7; for ornaments in the Tabernacle Ex. 28. 14; for fetters Ps. 149. 8; Is. 45. 14; Lam. 3. 7.

Chaldaea(ns), Chaldees Strictly S Babylonia and its semi-nomadic inhabitants, but later used for Babylonia as a whole. Gen. 11. 28–31; 2 K. 24. 2; 25; Jer. 37. 1–16; 39. 1–14.

chameleon A lizard-like reptile flourishing especially in the Jordan valley where its effective camouflage makes it hard to see. It is famous for its ability to change its colour to match its surroundings, and for its muscular tongue which can flick out to almost the length of its body when catching an insect. Lev. 11. 30.

chariot A two-wheeled vehicle used for war and state processions. In common use by their enemies, it only became a main arm of the Israelite army from the time of Solomon. Gen. 41. 43; 46. 29; Ex. ch. 14–15; 1 S. 8. 11; 2 S. 8. 4; 1 K. 7. 33; 9. 19; 10. 26.

chastity See Ex. 20. 14; 34. 28; Pr. 5. 3–6; 6. 25–26; 7; Mt. 5. 28; 1 Cor. 7. 1–9; Gal. 5. 19–21; Eph. 5. 3; 1 Th. 4. 2–8; Heb. 13. 4; Rev. 22. 14–15.

cherub, cherubim Heavenly beings represented as winged creatures having hands and feet. Ex. 25. 16–21; 1 K. 6. 21–35; Ezek. 10. See also Rev. 4. 6–8.

child, children See Ex. 20. 12; 21. 17; Nu. 3. 40–51; Pr. 13. 24; 20. 11; 22. 6; 23. 13; 29. 15; Mt. 11. 25; 18. 3; Mk. 9. 33–37; 10. 13–16; Eph. 6. 1–4; 2 Tim. 3. 15.

Chios An Aegean island in the Mediterranean. Ac. 20. 15.

Chloe A woman of Corinth. 1 Cor. 1. 11.

Chorazin A town near Capernaum which Jesus denounced. Mt. 11. 21; Lk. 10. 13. *Khirbet Kerâzeh.*

Christ The Greek equivalent of the Hebrew 'Messiah' (= the anointed one). Jn. 4. 21–25; 20. 30–31; Ac. 3. 12 – 4. 12. See also Mk. 8. 27–30; 14. 60–62; Lk. 2. 8–18, 22–32; Jn. 7. 40–42; Ac. 5. 42; 9. 22.

Christian The name for a follower of Jesus, first used at Antioch. Ac. 11. 25–26; 19. 23; 26. 28; Gal. 1. 2; 1 Pet. 4. 16.

Chronicles, Books of In the Hebrew Bible these formed one book. They were probably compiled during the Babylonian captivity and were intended to supplement existing records. The focal points are David, the Temple and its worship.

church The congregation of God realized or represented by Christians meeting in community as God's people, wherever they may be. Mt. 16. 18; Ac. 5. 11–16; 9. 31; 12. 17; 18. 22; 1 Cor. 14. 26; Eph. 1. 23; 5. 25–29; 1 Tim. 3. 15.

Chuza The steward of Herod. Lk. 8. 3.

Cilicia The territory in SE Asia Minor whose capital was Tarsus. Ac. 15. 23, 41; 21. 39; 22. 3; Gal. 1. 21.

cinnamon A spice obtained from the inner bark of the tree which grows in Arabia and Ceylon. Ex. 30. 22–25; Rev. 18. 13. Used as a figure of speech S. of S. 4. 14.

circumcision Commanded by God as the sign of his covenant with Abraham. Gen. 17. 9–14; Lev. 12. 3; Lk. 1. 59; 2. 21. Insistence on it as an essential condition for membership of the church caused serious dispute. Ac. 10. 28 – 11. 18; 15. 1–29. Used figuratively Dt. 10. 16; Jer. 6. 10; Rom. 2. 29; Gal. 5. 6.

cistern An underground tank dug in the rock or earth for collecting rain-water. Ex. 21. 33; Lev. 11. 36; Dt. 6. 11; 1 S. 19. 22; 2 K. 18. 31; Pr. 5. 15; Is. 36. 16.

city, cities These are distinguished as places surrounded by a wall rather than by size. Dt. 3. 5. *See also* Lev. 25. 29; Jos. 2. 15; Jer. 17. 19. The prophets denounced their corrupting influence. Is. 1. 21–23; Ezek. 9. 9; 24. 6. The heavenly city. Rev. ch. 21.

city of refuge A place of asylum set apart for those who had committed accidental manslaughter. Ex. 21. 12–14; Nu. 35. 9–34.

Claudius The Roman emperor who expelled the Jews from Rome. Ac. 11. 28; 18. 2.

Claudius Lysias The Roman officer who arrested Paul in the Temple. Ac. 21. 30 – 23. 30.

clay Found especially in the Jordan valley and widely used in Israel. Ex. 1. 14; Job 4. 19; 10. 9; Dan. 2. 33.

clean, uncleanness Much of the Mosaic law was directed to securing the ritual purity of Israel. Lev. 20. 25; Dt. 14.

Cleopas One of the two disciples met by the risen Jesus. Lk. 24. 13–35.

Cleopatra The daughter of Ptolemy who became the wife of Alexander, and then of Demetrius. 1 Mac. 10. 51–58; 11. 9–12.

clouds Often used figuratively by biblical writers. Gen. 9. 13; Job 3. 5; Is. 19. 1; 44. 22; Ezek. 30. 3. A symbol of God's presence. Ex. 13. 21; 19. 9; 33. 9; 40. 34; Mt. 17. 1–7.

Cnidus A coastal port in SW Asia Minor. Ac. 27. 7.

cobra A poisonous snake known for its ability to expand its upper neck into a disc-shaped hood. Ps. 91. 13; Pr. 23. 32.

cock By N.T. times it had become economically important and was regularly eaten by the Romans. It had long been used to indicate time and was carried on camel caravans as an 'alarm clock'. Pr. 30. 31; Mt. 26. 34; Mk. 13. 35.

cohort A subdivision of a Roman legion or the more lightly-armed auxiliary infantry. Ac. 10. 1; 21. 30–33; 27. 1.

colony An organized group of Roman citizen-soldiers with special privileges, settled at strategic points in conquered territory. Ac. 16. 12.

Colossae An ancient Phrygian city on the river Lycus, on the trade route from Ephesus to the Euphrates. Col. 1. 2. *See also* Col. 2. 1; 4. 12.

Colossians, Letter to the Written from prison in Rome, its immediate purpose was to warn the Colossians against false teaching and to strengthen their understanding of the true faith. In doing so, Paul develops the fullest conception of the nature and work of Christ to be found in the N.T.

Coming of Christ Mt. ch. 24–25; Lk. 21. 27; Ac. 1. 11; 1 Cor. 15. 23; Phil. 3. 20; 1 Th. 3. 13; 5. 2; 2 Th. 2. 1–12; Heb. 9. 28.

Commandments God's laws for his people given to Moses on Mt Sinai. Ex. 20. 1–17; 34. 28; Dt. ch. 5–6; Mt. 22. 34–40.

commerce Until the time of the monarchy, the Israelites farmed and left trade to the Canaanites. After the exile they became engaged more and more in commerce, and this had become an accepted way of life by N.T. times. *See* 1 K. 9. 26 – 10. 29; Pr. 31. 24; Is. 23; Ezek. 27; Hos. 12. 7; Jas. 4. 13.

communion *See* fellowship

compassion A divine as well as a human quality, and synonymous with pity and mercy. Zech. 7. 8–10. *See also* Dt. 14. 29; 24. 19; Ps. 146. 9; Pr. 19. 17; Jer. 22. 3; Mt. 9. 36; 11. 28; Lk. 7. 13; Jn. 11. 33; 2 Cor. 11. 29; Gal. 6. 2; 1 Pet. 3. 8–12; 1 Jn. 3. 17.

conduit A channel, usually cut through rock, to bring water from its source. 2 K. 20. 20; Is. 7. 3.

confess, confession Either an acknowledgement of sin before God. Lev. 5. 5; 26. 40; Nu. 5. 7; Mk. 1. 4–5; Ac. 19. 18; Jas. 5. 16. *See also* Ps. 51. Or a profession of faith before men. Rom. 10. 9; Phil. 2. 11. *See also* Ps. 48. 13; Jn. 9. 22; 1 Jn. 4. 3, 14.

congregation Ac. 13. 43. *See also* Ex. 12. 6; 35. 1; Lev. 4. 13; Nu. 10. 7; 16. 3; 1 K. 8. 14, 65; Heb. 2. 12.

Coniah *See* Jehoichin.

conquest of Canaan The biblical accounts show this to have been a complex operation, consisting partly of guerrilla warfare, well-planned campaigns and peaceful infiltration.

conscience The awareness of what God reveals as right. Ac. 23. 1; 24. 16; Rom. 9. 1; 1 Cor. 8. 7–13; 1 Tim. 1. 5, 19; Heb. 9. 14.

consecration The setting apart of men or things for the service of God. Ex. 28. 3, 41; 29. 36; Lev. 8. 11; Nu. 3. 13; 1 K. 9. 3. *See also* Ex. 13. 2.

contentment *See* Ps. 37. 16; 1 Tim. 6. 6–10; Heb. 13. 5–6.

conversion A turning or returning to God. Ac. 15. 3. *See also* Mt. 18. 3; Jn. 6. 44; Ac. 3. 19–20; 11. 21; 26. 20.

cook, cooking Boiling was the most usual method but sometimes meat was roasted. *See* Gen. 25. 29; Ex. 12. 8–10; 23. 19; 2 K. 4. 38. Professional cooks existed. 1 S. 8. 13; 9. 23.

copper The most important metal in O.T. times. It was mined in Palestine and put to a variety of uses. Nu. 16. 39; Dt. 8. 9; 1 K. 7. 15–22; Job 28. 2.

Corban An offering dedicated to God and therefore not free to be used for other purposes. Mk. 7. 11–13. *See also* Lev. 1. 2; Nu. 7. 3.

coriander A member of the carrot family, with leaves like parsley, which grows wild in Palestine. It has white or pinkish flowers and a round seed often used for flavouring bread and cakes. Ex. 16. 31; Nu. 11. 6–8.

Corinth The capital of the Roman province of Achaia, situated on the Isthmus. Ac. 18. 1–8; 19. 1.

Corinthians, Letters to the The first letter, written from Ephesus, deals with a number of practical issues all related to the general theme of Christian conduct. It is outstanding for its picture of life in a first-century church and for its practical application of gospel principles.

In the second letter, written about a year later, Paul faces a crisis and a wave of distrust. He defends his sincerity and his apostolic authority in a very personal and autobiographical letter.

cormorant A large fish-eating bird, regarded as unclean, commonly seen along the Jordan and the Sea of Galilee. Lev. 11. 19; Dt. 14. 18.

Cornelius A Roman centurion of Caesarea who was converted to Christianity. Ac. 10. 1–48.

Corner Gate A gate in the wall of Jerusalem. 2 K. 14. 13; 2 Ch. 26. 9; Jer. 31. 38.

corner-stone An important stone specially cut to hold together the sides of a building at the bottom, or the top. Ps. 118. 22; Is. 28. 16. Used figuratively Mt. 21. 42; 1 Pet. 2. 5–7. *See also* Eph. 2. 20.

Cos A small island in the Aegean. Ac. 21. 1.

cosmetics Beautifying applications were valued by all peoples in the Near and Middle East. *See* Ex. 30. 25; 1 S. 8. 13; 2 K. 9. 30; Neh. 3. 8; Est. 2. 3; Ps. 45. 8; Pr. 7. 17; Is. 3. 24; Jer. 4. 30; Ezek. 23. 40; Am. 6. 6; Rev. 18. 13.

Council This was the Sanhedrin, the highest court of justice of the Jewish people. Its origins are uncertain, but it was reorganized by Ezra after the exile. The number of members varied but its full size was seventy or seventy-one, and a quorum was twenty-three. Both Pharisees and Sadducees were members, and in N.T. times the influence of the former was strongest. The Council's president was the high priest, and when in session it sat in a semicircle. It had its own police force, authority to arrest and to inflict all penalties except the death sentence. Mk. 14. 55; Ac. 5. 21; 6. 8–15; 22. 5, 30.

covenant, new covenant An agreement between individuals, or between God and individuals or people, usually accompanied by symbolic actions. Gen. 9. 8–17; 17. 1–14; Ex. 34. 10–28; Dt. 29. 1. *See also* Gen. 31. 44–54. The new covenant. Jer. 31. 31–34; Ezek. 37. 21–28; Mt. 26. 26–29; 1 Cor. 11. 25.

creation In Scripture always the act of God. It is used specifically of the creation of the world and all that is in, on and around it. Gen. 1. 1 – 2. 4; 2. 5–25; Ps. 104.

Crescens A companion of Paul's sent to Galatia. 2 Tim. 4. 10.

Crete A large island S of Greece and once the centre of Minoan culture. Ac. 2. 11; 27. 6–15; Tit. 1. 5–14.

crime and punishment Actual crimes, civil and religious, were catalogued with their penalties in the several law codes. Ex. ch. 20–23; Lev. ch. 17–26; Dt. ch. 12–28.

Crispus The chief ruler of the Jewish synagogue in Corinth. Ac. 18. 8; 1 Cor. 1. 14.

crocodile In ancient times the only species around the E Mediterranean was the Nile crocodile. It is a carnivore, largely aquatic, coming ashore only to bask in the sun and lay its eggs. Job 40. 15 – 41. 34.

cross, crucify The Roman method of execution for slaves and rebels. Mt. 27. 32–54. The theological significance of the cross. Mk. 8. 34; Rom. 6. 5; 1 Cor. 1. 17–24; Gal. 2. 20; 5. 24–25; 6. 14; Eph. 2. 16; Phil. 2. 5–11; Col. 2. 13–15. *See also* 1 Pet. 4. 13.

crow The giant of the Perching Birds, and a carnivorous scavenger forbidden to the Israelites as food. Lev. 11. 15; Dt. 14. 14.

crown, crown of thorns A symbol of authority of one kind or another, worn on the head. 2 S. 1. 10; 12. 30; Ps. 21. 3; Zech. 6. 11; Mk. 15. 17. Used symbolically Pr. 12. 4; 16. 31. *See also* 1 Cor. 9. 25.

cucumber A common variety, smaller than the western species, is indigenous to NW India and spread to the Mediterranean area in quite early times. Nu. 11. 5; Is. 1. 8.

cummin A small, delicate plant whose fruit had medicinal uses and whose seed was used as a spice. Is. 28. 25–27; Mt. 23. 23.

cup(s) These were of many materials, shapes and sizes, and for both secular and religious use, but the commonest form was a bowl, wider and shallower than the modern coffee cup and made of pottery. 2 S. 12. 3; 1 K. 7. 26; 2 K. 12. 13; Mt. 26. 27. Used symbolically Mt. 23. 25; 26. 39; Rev. 17. 4.

cupbearer A palace official of high trust. 1 K. 10. 5; 2 Ch. 9. 4; Neh. 2. 1. *See also* Gen. 40. 1–23.

curds A substance made from milk by churning in a goatskin bag, similar to yoghurt. Gen. 18. 8; Job 20. 17.

curse On the human level to wish harm to someone; on the divine to impose judgement. Gen. 3; Nu. 22. 4–12; Dt. 11. 26–28; 27; Jos. 6. 26; Jer. 17. 5; Mt. 25. 41; Lk. 6. 28; Rom. 12. 14; Gal. 3. 10–14. *See also* Ex. 20. 7; 21. 17; 22. 28; Lev. 24. 11.

cymbals These were used especially in O.T. times at festivals and ceremonies. Some were concave plates of brass clanged together. Others were a neat conical shape with handles and were beaten together vertically. 2 S. 6. 5; 1 Ch. 15. 19; Ezr. 3. 10; Ps. 150. 5; 1 Cor. 13. 1.

Cyprus A large island in the Mediterranean. A contingent of troops from here were in the Seleucid army, and Nicanor was governor of the island. 2 Mac. 4. 29; 10. 13; 12. 2; Ac. 4. 36; 11. 19–20; 13. 4–12; 15. 39; 21. 16.

Cyrene A city of Libya in N Africa. Mt. 27. 32; Ac. 2. 10; 6. 9; 11. 20; 13. 1.

Cyrus 'The Mede' and founder of the Persian empire who permitted the Jews to return home to Palestine from exile to rebuild the Temple. 2 Ch. 36. 22–23; Ezr. 1. 1–11; Dan. 1. 21; 6. 28; 10. 1.

Cyrus Cylinder During extensive excavations in Babylon carried out by Hormuzd Rassam 1879–82 a clay, barrel-shaped inscription in cuneiform writing was found. It is now in the British Museum. It gives Cyrus the Mede's own account of his overthrow of the Babylonian empire in 539 B.C., and scholars date it about 536 B.C. It also records the release of the Jews and their return to Jerusalem. *See* 2 Ch. 36. 23; Ezr. 1. 1, 5; Ps. 137.

dagger A short weapon used for thrusting in hand-to-hand fighting. Jos. 8. 18; 1 S. 17. 6.

Dagon A Philistine god with a temple at Ashdod. Judg. 16. 23; 1 S. 5. 1–5; 1 Ch. 10. 10; 1 Mac. 10. 83–85.

Dalmanutha On the W coast of the Sea of Galilee. Mk. 8. 10.

Dalmatia A district on the E coast of the Adriatic. 2 Tim. 4. 10.

Damascus The capital of Syria, strategically placed at a road terminus some 130 miles NE of Jerusalem. Gen. 14. 15; 15. 2; 2 S. 8. 5; 1 K. 20. 34; 2 K. 16. 10–11; Is. 8. 4. In N.T. times it had a large colony of Jews. Ac. 9; 22. 5–16.

Dan (1) The territory occupied by this tribe. Jos. 19. 40–48; Judg. 1. 34. (2) The city, formerly Laish, occupied by the Danites. Judg. 18. 29; 20. 1; 1 K. 12. 25–30. *Tell el Qâḍi.* (3) The son of Jacob by Bilhah. Gen. 30. 1–6.

dancing There are occasional references to secular dancing in the Bible, but generally it had a religious or ritualistic function. Ex. 15. 20–21; 32. 19; Judg. 21. 21; 1 S. 18. 6; 2 S. 6. 13–16; 1 K. 18. 26; Eccles. 3. 4; Mk. 6. 22; Lk. 7. 32; 15. 25.

Daniel (1) A post-exilic priest. Ezr. 8. 2; Neh. 10. 6. (2) A son of David. 1 Ch. 3. 1. (3) The hero of the book of Daniel.

Daniel and Susanna A short book of the Apocrypha which tells the story of the beautiful and virtuous wife of a wealthy Jew in Babylon who was falsely accused and condemned for adultery. The young Daniel protests against this injustice, and in a re-trial the lie of the two accusing elders is uncovered.

Daniel, Bel, and the Snake A short book of the Apocrypha written to ridicule idolatry. Daniel shows that it is the priests of Bel and not the image of the god who consume the nightly food-offerings.

Daniel, Book of The theme is God's sovereignty over the kingdoms of this world, and the book falls into two parts. The first six chapters tell of the experiences of the young Jewish exile, Daniel, in Babylon. The rest consist of four visions predicting the course of world history.

Daphne A place, some 5 miles from Antioch, famous for its temple, its right of asylum, its fountain and its shameless morals. Onias took refuge here. 2 Mac. 4. 33–34. *Beit el-Mâ.*

Darius (1) The Great, who reorganized the Persian empire and assisted in the restoration of the Temple at Jerusalem after the exile. Ezr. 4. 5; 5. 6; Hag. 1. 1; 2. 10;

Zech. 1. 1, 7. (2) The Mede. Dan. 5. 31 – 6. 9. (3) Darius III, the Persian. Neh. 12. 22; Mac. 1. 1.

darnel A most destructive weed because it is indistinguishable from wheat in the early stages of growth. Separation is best done by sifting the lighter darnel seeds at the harvest. Mt. 13. 24–30, 36–43.

David The youngest son of Jesse and the second king of Israel. His conquest of Edom and Syria gave him splendid opportunities to develop profitable commercial activities, but these were not exploited until the time of his son, Solomon. 1 S. ch. 16–31; 2 S. ch. 1–24; 1 K. ch. 1–2.

David, City of (1) The former Jebusite stronghold and most ancient part of Jerusalem. 2 S. 5. 6–8. Excavations by the Palestine Exploration Fund 1924. (2) Bethlehem, his ancestral home. Lk. 2. 4, 11.

day The Israelites counted their day from one sunset to another. Ex. 12. 18; Lev. 23. 32.

Day of the Lord This was popularly regarded as the time when God would destroy Israel's enemies. Amos declared that it would involve the certainty of judgement for all peoples, including Israel. Am. 5. 18–20; Joel ch. 1–2. In the N.T. it is the second coming of Christ. 1 Cor. 1. 8; 5. 5; Phil. 1. 6–11; 1 Th. 5. 2; 2 Th. 2. 1–12; 2 Pet. 3. 2–14.

deacon Phil. 1. 1; 1 Tim. 3. 8–13. *See also* Ac. 6. 2–6.

Dead Sea The lowest stretch of water in the world, into which the Jordan flows. It has no outlet, and its waters are so salty that no fish can live in them. Gen. 14. 3; Nu. 34. 3; Dt. 3. 17.

Dead Sea Scrolls The popular name given to the collection of biblical manuscripts found at Qumran and other regions W of the Dead Sea in 1947 and following years. Fragments of every book in the O.T. except Esther have been found in the caves, and are now housed at the Hebrew University of Jerusalem. Many readings from the Scrolls, especially in the book of Isaiah, have been included in the translation of the New English Bible.

death The lot of all men and the result of sin, but conquered by Christ. 2 S. 14. 14;

Rom. 5. 12; 6. 23; 1 Cor. 15. 12–29; 2 Tim. 1. 10.

Debir (1) City in the hill-country of Judah. Jos. 11. 21; 15. 15. *Tell Beit Mirsim.* Excavations by Albright and Kyle of the American Schools of Oriental Research 1926–32. (2) The king of Eglon. Jos. 10. 1–10.

Deborah (1) The prophetess who inspired Barak to deliver Israel. Judg. ch. 4–5. (2) Tobit's grandmother, who taught him charity. Tobit 1. 8.

debt Regarded as a misfortune. Usury was forbidden by the Mosaic law, and the poor were protected. *See* Ex. 22. 25–27; Lev. 25. 25–55; Dt. 28. 12.

Decapolis *See* Ten Towns.

deceit 1 Pet. 2. 1; 3. 10. *See also* Ps. 5. 6; 36. 3; 38. 12; Pr. 24. 28; Is. 53. 9; Mk. 7. 22; Rom. 1. 28–32; 3. 13; 2 Cor. 4. 2; 1 Th. 2. 3–4; 1 Pet. 2. 21–22.

Decision, Valley of The place of God's judgement on the nations. Joel 3. 14.

Dedication, Feast of A festival kept on 25th Kislev (November–December) in honour of the purifying of the Temple by Judas Maccabaeus in 164 B.C. after its desecration by Antiochus Epiphanes. It was also known as the Feast of Lights since each evening for eight days the Temple and houses were specially lit with lamps. It is known today as Hanukkah. 1 Mac. 4. 41–58; Jn. 10. 22.

Delilah The Philistine woman who outwitted Samson. Judg. 16. 4–22.

Demas A companion of Paul in prison. Col. 4. 14; 2 Tim. 4. 10; Philem. 24.

Demetrius (1) A silversmith of Ephesus. Ac. 19. 23–41. (2) Demetrius I, Soter, king of Syria, who was a hostage in Rome when his father, Seleucus, was assassinated. He escaped and succeeded to the throne after the death of his uncle Antiochus. He was defeated and killed by Alexander. 1 Mac. 7. 1–4; 10. 1–50.

Demophon The Governor of Syria during the time of Judas. 2 Mac. 12. 2.

denarius A Roman silver coin reckoned as a day's wage. *See* Mt. 20. 9; Mk. 12. 13–17.

Derbe A city in the Roman province of Galatia. Ac. 14. 6–7; 16. 1. *Kerti Hüyük.*

Deuteronomy, Book of (= Repetition of the Law) It contains Moses' farewell discourses, and explains God's commandments and the exclusive obligations of the covenant relationship to the ordinary Israelite. It is quoted by Christ in the N.T. more than any other book.

Devil The personification of all evil and all that is against God. Mt. 4. 1–11; 13. 39; Jn. 8. 44; 13. 2; Eph. 6. 11; 1 Tim. 3. 6; Heb. 2. 14; 1 Jn. 3. 8; Rev. 2. 10; 12. 9; 20. 2, 10.

dew Plentiful in Palestine at certain seasons and a great help in growing fruit and vegetables. It is used figuratively of the word and power of God. Dt. 32. 2; Is. 26. 19.

Diana The Asiatic goddess of fertility, also known as Artemis. Ac. 19. 24.

Dibon A city E of the Dead Sea and N of the Arnon. The Moabite Stone was found here. Nu. 21. 29–30; Jos. 13. 8–9. Excavations by the American Schools of Oriental Research 1950–57 have shown occupation from the Early Bronze to Arab time with a gap from c. 1850 to 1300 B.C. *Dhibān.*

dill A flower, also grown in Europe, with grey-green foliage and upright yellow flowers whose leaves and seeds were used for flavouring and medicinal purposes. Is. 28. 25–27; Mt. 23. 23.

Dinah The daughter of Jacob by Leah. Gen. 30. 21; 34.

Dionysius (1) A member of the Areopagus. Ac. 17. 34. (2) A Thracian vegetation god, commonly called Bacchus, who became associated with the vine. In the time of Antiochus, Jews were compelled to share in the celebration of his festival. 2 Mac. 6. 7; 14. 33.

Diotrephes An unworthy member of the church. 3 Jn. 9–10.

disciples Literally 'learners': the followers of a religious leader. Is. 8. 16; Mt. 10. 1; Mk. 2. 18; Lk. 6. 17; Jn. 1. 35; 6. 66; Ac. 6. 1–7.

disease In biblical times this was regarded as closely connected with sin or some breach of the law. *See* Gen. 12. 17; Nu. 12. 9; 2 S. 12. 15; Mt. 9. 2, 35; Lk. 13. 16; Jn. 9. 1–3; 2 Cor. 12. 7.

disobedience See Gen. 3. 1–7; Is. 3. 8–9; Jer. 9. 12–16; 12. 17; 18. 8–10; Eph. 5. 6–17; Tit. 1. 16; 3. 3.

Dispersion Forecast as the penalty for the breaking of the law. See Lev. 26. 14–33; Dt. 28. 58–68. Many Jews did not return from the exile, and settlements outside Palestine continued to spread widely throughout the Graeco-Roman world. These communities, known as the Dispersion or Diaspora, retained their faith and worship, and provided the Christians with their first opportunities of preaching the gospel.

divination Attempts to foretell the future by abnormal means. Gen. 44. 5, 15; Lev. 19. 26; Ezek. 13. 6–7. See also 1 S. 28. 8; Is. 47. 13; Ezek. 21. 21; Ac. 16. 16.

divisions Condemned in the church as contrary to the mind of Christ. 1 Cor. 1. 10–13. See also Mt. 12. 25–27; Jn. 10. 16–17; 17. 20–23; Rom. 16. 17; 1 Cor. 3. 1–9; 11. 17–22.

divorce In the O.T. Dt. 24. 1–4. In the N.T. Mt. 5. 31–32; 19. 3–9; Mk. 10. 2–12; 1 Cor. 7. 10–16.

doctors of the law Mk. 7. 1; Ac. 6. 12. See lawyers.

Doeg An Edomite herdsman of Saul. 1 S. 21. 7; 22. 7–23.

dog Although highly valued in Egypt and Mesopotamia, in Palestine the dog was mainly a pariah and scavenger, and did in the larger towns what the hyenas helped to do outside the walls. Ex. 22. 31; 1 S. 17. 43; 2 S. 16. 9; 2 K. 8. 13; 9. 30–37; Job 30. 1; Ps. 59. 6; Is. 56. 10; Tobit 6. 1; 11. 4; Mt. 7. 6; Lk. 16. 21.

Dok A stronghold, about 4 miles NW of Jericho, where Simon was treacherously murdered. 1 Mac. 16. 15. *Jebel Qaranṭal*.

Dorcas A Christian woman of Joppa, also called Tabitha. Ac. 9. 36–41.

Dothan A city N of Shechem associated with Joseph, Elijah and Holophernes. Gen. 37. 12–35; 2 K. 6. 8–19; Judith 3. 9–10; 7. 18. *Tell Dôthā*. Excavations have revealed continuous occupation from the early Bronze Age to the time of the Assyrian invasion c. 725 B.C. Areas of the Iron Age town have been cleared to show the narrow streets and small houses of Elisha's day.

dove, turtle-dove The poetic name for pigeons of which there are several varieties in Palestine. It was used as a sacrifice by the poorer people. Lev. 1. 14; Ps. 55. 6; S. of S. 2. 12; Is. 38. 14; 60. 8; Jer. 48. 28; Lk. 2. 22–24. Christian artists have used it as a symbol for peace, hope and the Holy Spirit. Lk. 3. 21–22.

dreams One of the means by which God communicates with men. Gen. ch. 40–41; Nu. 12. 6; Job 33. 15–18; Dan. 2. 24–30; Mt. 1. 20; 2. 12–13; 27. 19.

dress Originally animal skins were worn. Gen. 3. 21; 2 K. 1. 8; Mt. 3. 4. Then came the use of wool or linen. Pr. 31. 13. Apart from the veil, women's dress differed little basically from men's, consisting of a long shirt or tunic reaching to the ankles and close-fitting at the neck, with a girdle. Ex. 28. 4; Job 30. 18; Jer. 13. 1. An outer garment or cloak was protection against cold. Ex. 22. 26. Workmen wore loin-cloths. Is. 3. 24.

dromedary A thoroughbred camel used for riding and racing, and longer in the leg than the freight camel. Is. 60. 6; 66. 20.

drunkenness Lk. 21. 34; Gal. 5. 16–21; Eph. 5. 15–18. See also Is. 5. 11; 28. 7; Hos. 4. 12.

Drusilla The wife of Felix. Ac. 24. 24.

dumb, dumbness This was sometimes regarded as the sign of God's judgement, and the healing of it as a sign of the coming of his kingdom. Is. 35. 6; Ezek. 3. 22–27; Mt. 9. 32–33; 12. 22; Mk. 7. 31–37; Lk. 1. 20; 11. 14–15.

dung Used in the Middle East today, as in biblical times, both for fuel and manure. Ezek. 4. 12, 15. See also Lk. 13. 8.

Dung Gate One of the eleven gates of Jerusalem. Neh. 3. 14.

Dura The plain where Nebuchadnezzar set up his image. Dan. 3. 1.

dust Used literally and in simile for multitude Gen. 13. 16; Is. 29. 5; smallness Dt. 9. 21; poverty 1 S. 2. 8; abasement Gen. 18. 27; sorrow Job 2. 12; Rev. 18. 19; contrition Jos. 7. 6; lowliness Gen. 2. 7; 3. 19; Job 4. 19; 42. 6; judgement Mt. 10. 14; Ac. 13. 51.

eagle There are several species of this bird in Palestine. Though not strictly a scavenger, its flesh was forbidden as food. It is often used as a figure of speech because of its graceful flight and skill in caring for its young. Dt. 32. 11; 2 S. 1. 23; Ps. 103. 5; Pr. 23. 5; Rev. 4. 7.

ear(s) Hearing, for the Hebrews, involved the whole personality. 'Ear' and 'to hear' signify attention resulting in obedience. Ex. 29. 20; Ps. 40. 6; Is. 6. 10; Jer. 6. 10; Mt. 11. 15.

earrings Worn more often by women. Ex. 32. 2. Rings were also worn in the nose. Gen. 24. 22; Is. 3. 20; Ezek. 16. 12.

earthquake In the biblical record, earthquakes are recorded at various periods. 1 S. 14. 15; 1 K. 19. 11; Ps. 18. 7; Mt. 27. 51–54; Ac. 16. 26. Used in prophetic imagery. Is. 29. 6; Mk. 13. 8; Rev. 6. 12; 8. 5; 11. 13.

Ebal The mountain near Shechem where Joshua erected a copy of the law on stones. Dt. 11. 29; 27. 4, 13; Jos. 8. 30–35. *Jebel Eslāmīyeh.*

Ebed-melech The Ethiopian or Cushite who rescued Jeremiah. Jer. 38. 7–13; 39. 15–18.

Eben-ezer (1) The scene of two battles with the Philistines and the loss of the Ark. 1 S. 4. 1–11; 5. 1. (2) A stone erected by Samuel. 1 S. 7. 12.

Ecbatana The capital of Media where the decree of Cyrus was found. Tobit married Sarah there. Ezr. 6. 2; Tobit 3. 7; 7; 14. 12–14; Judith 1. 1–4, 13–14; 2 Mac. 9. 3.

Ecclesiastes, Book of Largely autobiographical, it is the considered conclusion of a man who has tried everything and found that there is no meaning or satisfaction to be found in life apart from God.

Ecclesiasticus The name given in its Greek dress to the book of the Apocrypha known also as the Wisdom of Jesus son of Sirach, a Jew of Jerusalem who wrote about 180 B.C. Like the other Wisdom books it is a collection of sayings, short maxims and good advice for a successful life thought of in the widest sense. The fear of the Lord and the keeping of his law are joined in the author's teaching with 'practical' wisdom drawn from his own observation and his own life. It

represents the beginning of the ideal of the scribe which became the type of Jewish orthodoxy.

Eden The first home of Adam and Eve. Gen. 2. 8–17; 3. 24; Is. 51. 3; Ezek. 28. 13; 36. 35.

Edna The wife of Raguel and the mother of Sarah. Tobit 7.

Edom The hilly country S of the Dead Sea. Gen. 32. 3; Nu. 20. 14–21; 24. 18; 2 K. 3. 8.

Edomites Descendants of Esau but hostile to the Israelites. Nu. 20. 14–21; Dt. 23. 7; 1 S. 14. 47.

education This was pre-eminently religious and children were taught at home in early times. Dt. 6. 20–25; Pr. 1. 7. After the exile, the Book of the Law became the textbook and the synagogue the place of instruction. Neh. 8. 1–8.

Eglon A city destroyed by Joshua. Jos. 10. 3–10, 34; 12. 12; 15. 40. Excavations in 1890 by W. F. Petrie brought to light pottery and weapons.

Egypt The Nile basin from the Mediterranean to the first cataract. The Hebrew settlement there. Gen. ch. 42–50; Ex. ch. 1–2. Later relations between it and Israel and Judah. 1 K. 3. 1; 14. 25–26; 2 K. 23. 28–29; Is. 36. 4–6; Jer. 37. 3–8; Mt. 2. 13. After the death of Alexander the Great, Egypt came under the rule of the Ptolemies for more than a century until the time of Antiochus III. Alexander Balas married the daughter of Ptolemy VI. 1 Mac. 10. 51–58; 11. 1–18.

Egyptian The terrorist for whom Paul was mistaken in Jerusalem. Ac. 21. 38.

Ekron The northernmost of the five great Philistine cities. Jos. 13. 3; 1 S. 5. 1–12; 2 K. 1. 2–6; Am. 1. 8. Alexander Balas gave it (Accaron) to Jonathan. *See* 1 Mac. 10. 89.

Elam The country E of Babylonia whose capital was Susa. Gen. 14. 1–16; Neh. 1. 1; Is. 21. 2; Jer. 49. 34–39; Ezek. 32. 24; Dan. 8. 2. In the Apocrypha it is called Elymais. Tobit 2. 10; 1 Mac. 6. 1.

Eldad One of Moses' elders. Nu. 11. 26–29.

elder One of the older men of a community appointed to take decisions. Ex. 3. 16; 24. 1; Nu. 11. 25; Dt. 19. 12; 21. 2; 25. 7;

1 S. 8. 4; 2 S. 5. 3; 1 K. 8. 1; 2 K. 23. 1; Ezek. 8. 1; Mt. 27. 12; Ac. 14. 23; 20. 17; Jas. 5. 14; 1 Pet. 5. 1–5.

Eleazar (1) Aaron's third son who succeeded him as high priest. Nu. 20. 25–28. (2) One of David's heroes. 2 S. 23. 9. (3) The brother of Judas, surnamed Avaran. 1 Mac. 2. 5; 6. 43–46; 2 Mac. 8. 23.

elect, election These words occur rarely in English versions of the Bible but the thought expressed by 'choose' or 'chosen' is present everywhere in the Scriptures. In order to carry out his purposes God moves from less to more; taking a part and using it as his chosen instrument for bringing blessing to many. See Gen. 17. 1–21; Dt. 4. 37; 7. 7; Is. 42₁ 1; 45. 4; Jer. 1. 5; Mt. 5. 13–16; Lk. 9. 35; 10. 20; 17. 1–21; Ac. 9. 15; Rom. 8. 28–30; 9. 11–16; 11. 5; Eph. 1. 4–10; 1 Th. 1. 4; 2 Th. 2. 13; Tit. 1. 1; 1 Pet. 2. 9.

elephant The nearest elephants to Palestine in biblical times were in N Mesopotamia. These were the Indian variety which were trained for use in war as shock-troops. 1 Mac. 3. 34; 6. 32–37; 2 Mac. 13. 1–2, 15.

Elephantine Papyri These are Aramaic documents and letters, now in the Brooklyn Museum, U.S.A., which have gradually come to light since 1893, all dating from the 5th century B.C. when the Jewish colony on the island of Elephantine in the Nile opposite Aswan acted as a military garrison for the Persian conquerors of Egypt.

Eleutherus A river flowing from the Lebanon to the Mediterranean, and the boundary between Syria and Phoenicia. 1 Mac. 11. 7; 12. 30. *Nahr el-Kebîr.*

Eli The priest of Shiloh who judged Israel for forty years, and who brought up Samuel. 1 S. 1. 9 – 4. 18.

Eliakim The overseer of Hezekiah's household who was sent to negotiate with Sennacherib. 2 K. 18. 18; Is. 22. 20–25.

Eliezer (1) Abraham's servant. Gen. 15. 2. (2) The second son of Moses. Ex. 18. 4.

Elihu (1) An ancestor of Samuel. 1 S. 1. 1. (2) A friend and adviser of Job. Job ch. 32–37.

Elijah The prophet from Tishbe in Gilead who opposed the cult of the god Baal

during the reigns of Ahab and Ahaziah. 1 K. 17. 1 – 19. 21; 2 K. 1. 1 – 2. 11; Mt. 11. 14; 17. 11; Mk. 6. 14–15; 8. 27–28.

Elim A camp site in the wilderness wanderings. Ex. 15. 27; Nu. 33. 9.

Elimelech The husband of Naomi. Ru. 1. 1–3; 2. 1; 4. 1–10.

Eliphaz (1) The son of Esau. Gen. 36. 4. (2) One of Job's three friends. Job 2. 11; 4; 15; 22; 42. 7–9.

Elisha The prophet from Abel-meholah who succeeded Elijah. 1 K. 19. 16–21; 2 K. 2. 1 – 9. 10; 13. 14–20.

Elizabeth The wife of Zechariah and mother of John the Baptist. Lk. 1. 5–25, 57–66.

Elkanah The husband of Hannah and father of Samuel. 1 S. 1. 1; 2. 11, 20.

Elymas See Bar-Jesus.

embalming The Egyptian method of preserving dead bodies from decay. Gen. 50. 1–3.

Emmanuel See Immanuel.

Emmaus The village, some 7 miles from Jerusalem, where Jesus appeared after his resurrection. Lk. 24. 13–32.

En-dor A town, 6 miles SE of Nazareth, where a medium lived. Jos. 17. 11; 1 S. 28; Ps. 83. 10.

En-gedi A place in Judah on the W shore of the Dead Sea. 1 S. 23. 29 – 24. 2; 2 Ch. 20. 2. *Tell el-Jurn.*

Enoch (1) The son of Cain and father of Irad. Gen. 4. 17. (2) The father of Methuselah. Gen. 5. 18–24; Lk. 3. 37; Heb. 11. 5.

Epaenetus The first convert in the Roman province of Asia. Rom. 16. 5.

Epaphras A fellow-prisoner of Paul. Col. 1. 7; 4. 12; Philem. 23.

Epaphroditus A fellow-worker with Paul sent by him to Philippi. Phil. 2. 25–30; 4. 18.

Ephes-dammim The site of the battle in which Goliath was killed. 1 S. 17. 1.

Ephesians, Letter to the Written from prison in Rome and apparently addressed to no specific situation. Its central thought is the disunity and disharmony that exist in nature, man, time, eternity, and between man and God; and the conviction that all that disunity can only become unity when all men and all powers are united in Christ. The church is the body of Christ through which he can work to bring about God's plan, and the community within which that unity of discordant elements can be realized.

Ephesus The capital of the province of Asia on the left bank of the Cayster. Ac. 18. 24–28; 19. 1 – 20. 1; 20. 16; 1 Cor. 16. 8; 1 Tim. 1. 3; 2 Tim. 4. 12; Rev. 1. 11; 2. 1–7.

ephod A vestment worn by the high priest when ministering before the LORD. Ex. 28. 4–35; 39. 2–26.

Ephphatha The word of command used by Christ when healing a deaf and dumb man. Mk. 7. 31–35.

Ephraim (1) The son of Joseph. Gen. 41. 50–53; 48. 1–21. (2) The hill-country of W Palestine occupied by the tribe. Jos. 17. 14–18; 21. 20; 2 S. 18. 6.

Ephron The Hittite from whom Abraham bought the cave and plot of land for Sarah's burial. Gen. 23. 1–20.

Epicureans Greek philosophers who advocated the achievement of happiness by supreme detachment. Ac. 17. 16–33.

Erastus (1) The city treasurer of Corinth. Rom. 16. 23. (2) An assistant of Paul. Ac. 19. 22; 2 Tim. 4. 20.

Esarhaddon The successor of Sennacherib. 2 K. 19. 37; Ezr. 4. 2.

Esau The son of Isaac called Edom. Gen. 25. 25–34; 27; 33.

Esdras, First and Second Books of The first two books of the Apocrypha. Most of 1 Esdras recounts the same story that Ezra tells in the O.T., with excerpts from Nehemiah and 2 Chronicles. The Second Book of Esdras is chiefly a Jewish composition dating from about 100 A.D. It contains a series of visions in the form of a dialogue between the Seer and the Angel, and is the only apocalyptic book in the Apocrypha.

Esther The Jewish queen of Ahasuerus, also called Hadassah, who succeeded Vashti as his wife. Est. 2. 1–23; 3. 12 – 9. 32.

Esther, Book of Although this is the only book in the Bible in which the name of God does not appear, it shows very clearly the hand of God at work in the life of his people, the Jews. Through the courage of the beautiful Jewess, Esther, and her uncle, Mordecai, the scheme of Haman to persuade the Persian king, Ahasuerus, to authorize a pogrom of the Jews is frustrated. The book also makes clear the origin of the Feast of Purim.

Esther, The Rest of the Book of A short book of the Apocrypha containing Greek additions which are not found in the Hebrew or Syriac texts of the O.T. Book of Esther.

Ethiopia The region bordering on Egypt and the Red Sea, called Cush in Hebrew. Est. 1. 1; 8. 9; Ac. 8. 26–39. *See also* Is. 45. 14; Ezek. 30. 1 – 32. 32.

Eunice The mother of Timothy. Ac. 16. 1; 2 Tim. 1. 5.

Euodia A Christian woman of Philippi. Phil. 4. 2–3.

Euphrates The longest river in Asia, rising in Armenia and joined by the Tigris before reaching the Persian Gulf. Under the Persians, the country W of the Euphrates formed an administrative province, and under the Seleucid monarch, Antiochus IV, Lysias was left in charge of the same area. Gen. 2. 14; Ex. 23. 31; 1 K. 4. 24; Ezr. 4. 9–10; Judith 1. 6; 2. 24; Ecclus. 24. 26; 1 Mac. 3. 32–37; Rev. 9. 14; 16. 12.

Eupolemus An ambassador sent by Judas to Rome. 1 Mac. 8. 17–32; 2 Mac. 4. 11.

Eutychus A young man brought back to life by Paul. Ac. 20. 6–12.

evangelist One who proclaims the good news about Jesus Christ. Ac. 21. 8; Eph. 4. 11. *See also* 2 Tim. 4. 5.

Eve The first woman and the wife of Adam. Gen. 2. 18 – 3. 24; 2 Cor. 11. 3.

Evil-merodach The son and successor of Nebuchadnezzar who freed Jehoiachin. Jer. 52. 31–34.

evil spirits Called 'unclean' because they produced evil effects. Mt. 10. 1; 12. 43–45; Mk. 1. 23–27; 5. 8; 7. 25; Lk. 8. 26–39; 11. 24–26; Ac. 5. 16; 8. 7; Rev. 16. 13–14.

excommunication Disciplinary exclusion from church fellowship. *See* Mt. 18. 15–17; Lk. 6. 22; Jn. 9. 34; 1 Cor. 5. 13; 2 Cor. 2. 5–11; 1 Tim. 1. 20; Tit. 3. 10.

Exile The period, lasting until 538 B.C., when many of the people of Israel and Judah were in captivity in Babylonia. *See* Captivity.

exodus The journey of Israel from Egypt into Canaan. Ex. ch. 1–15; Nu. ch. 10–33. It was commemorated at the Feast of the Passover.

Exodus, Book of It describes the escape from Egypt of a group of Hebrew slaves and the process by which God moulded them into a full-grown theocratic nation, redeemed and set apart for his purposes. It describes Israel's covenant relationship with God and the law codes and form of worship to be adopted in consequence of this relationship.

exorcism The driving out of an evil spirit by the invocation of a holy name. Ac. 19. 13–20. Christ commanded on his own authority. Mt. 8. 16; 10. 1. The apostles commanded in Christ's name. Ac. 16. 18.

expiation *See* Atonement, Day of.

Ezekiel The son of the priest Buzi, he was taken into captivity in Babylon where he received his call as a prophet. Ezek. 1. 1–3. *See also* 2 K. 24. 8–17.

Ezekiel, Book of In language, often figurative, the prophet reveals to the Jews that their predicament is the result of their own sin but that God offers deliverance to the repentant. He foretells the day when Israel will worship the one true God again in the rebuilt Temple in Jerusalem. He outlines the plans for this rebuilding and the organization of the priesthood and cultus.

Ezion-geber A settlement at the NE end of the Gulf of Aqabah near Elath, and a terminal port for Solomon's Red Sea trading fleet. Nu. 33. 35; 1 K. 9. 26; 22. 48. *Tell el-Kheleifeh.* Excavations by N. Glueck of the American Schools of Oriental Research 1937–40 uncovered 5th and 4th century B.C. Aramaic ostraca and 7th century B.C. Edomite sealings.

Ezra The priest and scribe authorized by King Artaxerxes to lead a party of Jewish exiles back to Jerusalem. Ezr. 7. 10–27; Neh. 8. 1–8.

Ezra, Book of Tells the story of the return of the Jews from the captivity in Babylonia with special emphasis on the rebuilding of the Temple in Jerusalem.

face Used literally, figuratively and idiomatically. Gen. 4. 5; Ex. 3. 6; 33. 20; Nu. 6. 25; 12. 14; Ps. 13. 1; 27. 9; Pr. 21. 29; Jer. 21. 10; Lk. 9. 51; Rev. 22. 3.

Fair Havens A harbour on the S coast of Crete. Ac. 27. 8. *Kali Limenes.*

faith, faithful In the O.T. the idea is more frequently expressed by 'belief', 'trust', 'hope' and by example. It is man's response of trustful acceptance of the revelation and promise of God. Hab. 2. 4; Mk. 11. 22; Lk. 7. 50; Rom. 5. 1; Gal. 3. 6–26; 5. 6; Heb. 11. 8 – 12. 2; Jas. 2. 14–26. *See also* Eph. 2. 8.

falcon Palestine has a wide range of the smaller birds which catch their prey by sheer speed. Lev. 11. 14; Dt. 14. 13; Job 28. 7.

Fall, The Theological term applied to the story told in Gen. 3. 1–20. *See also* Rom. 5. 12–21; 1 Cor. 15. 21–26; 1 Tim. 2. 13.

falsehood Prov. 12. 13. *See also* Pr. 19. 1 and 'lie, lying'.

familiar spirit The spirit of a dead person allegedly consulted by mediums. 1 S. 28. 7; Is. 8. 19. *See also* Lev. 19. 31; 20. 6; Dt. 18. 11.

family *See* household.

famine Caused by lack of rain Gen. 41; Jer. 14. 1–9; by war and siege 2 K. 6. 25; Dt. 28. 45–57. Sometimes regarded as a judgement of God. Lev. 26. 19; 1 K. 17. 1; Am. 4. 6.

farming The chief occupation of the Israelites after the settlement in Canaan. *See* Gen. 26. 12; Ex. 23. 10–11; Lev. 27. 16; Dt. 8. 7–10; 19. 14; Ru. 2; Is. 28. 24–28. Used in parables. Mt. 3. 12; 13. 24–30; Mk. 4. 26–32.

fast, fasting This was practised mainly for religious reasons and was also associated with mourning. 1 S. 7. 6; 2 S. 1. 12; Zech. 8. 19; Mt. 4. 2; 6. 16–18; Mk. 2. 18–20; Lk. 2. 37; 18. 12; Ac. 13. 2; 14. 23.

father His authority over his children was almost complete in biblical times. *See* Gen. 24. 4; Ex. 21. 7; Heb. 12. 7–10. Used of God. Mal. 2. 10; Lk. 11. 1–13; Jn. 8. 41–47.

fathom A Roman measure of depth, about 6 feet. Ac. 27. 28.

fear The awe and reverence due to God. Dt. 10. 12; Ps. 34. 11; Pr. 1. 7. The fear which has to do with punishment as the result of sin. Rom. 8. 15; Heb. 2. 15; 1 Jn. 4. 18.

feast See festivals.

Felix, Antoninus The Roman Governor of Judaea. Ac. 23. 23 – 24. 27.

fellowship The sharing of something in common. 1 Cor. 15. 18; 2 Cor. 13. 14. See also Jn. 15. 4; Ac. 2. 42–47; 1 Cor. 1. 9; Gal. 2. 9; 3. 28; 6. 2; Phil. 2. 1–5, 14–15; 3. 10; 1 Jn. 1. 3.

Fertile Crescent A modern description of the well-watered territory reaching NW from the Persian Gulf through Mesopotamia, then W to the N of Syria and Palestine.

festivals There were three main pilgrimage festivals in the Jewish calendar. These were: the Passover, Pentecost or Weeks, and Tabernacles. Another important feast was Purim.

Festus, Porcius The successor of Felix as Governor of Judaea. Ac. 24. 27 – 26. 32.

fig The fig is referred to at least fifty times in the Bible; and the tree is a common sight in Palestine where its useful fruit is seen on the branches for about ten months of the year. Gen. 3. 7; Judg. 9. 7–15; 2 K. 20. 7; S. of S. 2. 13; Jer. 8. 13; Joel 2. 22; Mt. 7. 16; Mk. 11. 12–14; Jn. 1. 47–50.

fine(s) These were originally compensation paid to the injured party. See Ex. ch. 21–22; Lev. 6. 2–7.

fir A cone-bearing tree which can grow to a height of some 60 feet. In ancient times it was a symbol of nobility; and its timber was used in building. S. of S. 1. 17; Is. 41. 19; 60. 13.

fire Frequently used symbolically in the Bible record. Ex. 3. 2; 13. 21; 19. 16–18; 2 K. 6. 17; Is. 9. 18; 66. 15–16; Jer. 6. 29; Ezek. 1. 4, 13; Mt. 3. 11; Lk. 12. 49–50; Ac. 2. 3; 1 Cor. 3. 13; Heb. 12. 29.

first-born The Jews attached special value to the elder son. Ex. 13. 1; Dt. 15. 19–20; 21. 17. See also Gen. 25. 29–34. Used figuratively. Ex. 4. 22; Rom. 8. 29; Heb. 1. 6.

firstfruits These were to be offered to God on the three great annual festivals of Passover, Pentecost and Tabernacles. Ex. 22. 29; 23. 16; 34. 22; Dt. 18. 4. Used of Christ. 1 Cor. 15. 20–26.

fish, fishing Fish was plentiful, especially in the Sea of Galilee, and was eaten salted and dried, as well as fresh. Lev. 11. 9–12; Neh. 13. 16; Job 41. 7; Is. 19. 8; Mt. 4. 18–22; 13. 47; Jn. 21. 1–13.

Fish Gate One of the eleven gates of Jerusalem on the N side of the city. 2 Ch. 33. 14; Neh. 3. 3; 12. 39; Zeph. 1. 10.

flax An important plant in Palestine and Egypt from the inner stem of which linen was made. Ex. 9. 31; Jos. 2. 1–6; Pr. 31. 13.

flea The dry countries of the Middle East are notorious for the flea with its irritating bite which makes it a plague to both man and animal. 1 S. 24. 14; 26. 20.

fleece The shorn wool of a sheep. Dt. 18. 4; Judg. 6. 37–40.

flesh (1) The edible parts of an animal. Ex. 16. 8. (2) The frailty of human nature. Is. 31. 3. See also Is. 40. 6; Jn. 1. 14. (3) Used in opposition to mental and spiritual qualities. Mt. 26. 41. See also Rom. 8. 1–8; Gal. 5. 16–21.

flogging A recognized form of punishment, in which no more than 40 strokes were allowed. Dt. 25. 2–3; Mt. 10. 17; 20. 19; Jn. 19. 1; Ac. 5. 40; 16. 22; 22. 19–29.

Flood The deluge of water sent by God in Noah's time to destroy all but a selected few from the earth. Gen. ch. 6–8; 9. 11, 28; 10. 1, 32; Mt. 24. 38; Lk. 17. 27; 2 Pet. 2. 5. Clean water-laid clay has been found by archaeologists at various levels in the Tigris–Euphrates valley.

flour This was made by crushing wheat or barley. Gen. 18. 6; Lev. 6. 15; Dt. 32. 14; 1 K. 4. 22. See also Lev. 2. 14–16.

flute A wind instrument made of wood, bone or metal and constructed on similar basic principles to the modern instrument. Job 21. 12; Ps. 150. 4.

fly, flies In the Near and Middle East these are present in great numbers, and are carriers of eye and other diseases. Ex. 8. 21–25; Ps. 78. 45; 105. 31; Eccles. 10. 1.

food The basic food of the people was wheat and barley, beans and lentils eaten either as bread or stew. This was eked out by vegetables such as onions, cucumbers, melons, radishes, garlic and various herbs; possibly also various nuts and fruit. Eggs were a useful addition to the diet, as was the milk of the domestic cattle, goats and sheep, which was usually preserved by turning it into curds, a form of yoghurt. Meat, usually of goat, was a luxury; but small birds could be trapped at any time of the year. And by the Persian period, poultry and pigeons were kept for food. Fish was preserved by drying and salting. *See* Ex. 12. 8; Lev. 11. 1–45; Nu. 6. 3; 11. 5; Dt. 14. 4–21; 32. 13–14; Judg. 7. 13; Ru. 2. 14; 1 S. 17. 18; 25. 18; 2 Ch. 31. 5; Pr. 15. 17; Is. 10. 14; Ezek. 44. 30; Lk. 15. 29; Jn. 21. 9–13.

fool One in whom there is no wisdom or judgement. Pr. 12. 15; 13. 10; 18. 2; 20. 3; Eccles. 7. 6; Lk. 12. 20. *See also* Pr. 14. 16; 17. 24; 18. 6; 19. 3.

foot Often used figuratively in the Bible. Foot-washing was a sign of hospitality and humility. Gen. 18. 4; Jos. 10. 24; 1 S. 25. 24, 41; Ps. 73. 2; Jer. 18. 22; Ezek. 24. 17; Lk. 7. 36–38; Jn. 13. 3–9; Ac. 4. 35; 1 Cor. 15. 25. *See also* Ex. 3. 5.

footstool Used literally 2 Ch. 9. 18; Jas. 2. 3. Used figuratively 1 Ch. 28. 2; Ps. 99. 5; 132. 7; Is. 66. 1; Lam. 2. 1; Mt. 5. 35; Ac. 2. 35.

ford A shallow place for crossing a river or stream. Gen. 32. 22; Jos. 2. 7; Judg. 12. 5; Is. 16. 2.

foreigner (1) One passing through. *See* Gen. 31. 15; Dt. 23. 20; Job 31. 32. (2) A permanent refugee (alien). *See* Lev. 24. 22; Judg. 17. 8; 2 S. 1. 13; Jer. 7. 6.

forerunner A herald or courier. Heb. 6. 20. *See also* Is. 40. 3; Mt. 11. 10.

forest In O.T. times Palestine was extensively wooded. Jos. 17. 15; 2 S. 18. 6; Is. 10. 18.

forget, forgetfulness The Bible draws a contrast between God and man in this respect. 1 S. 12. 9; Ps. 78. 11; Is. 49. 14–16; Jer. 18. 15; Hos. 8. 14. *See also* Jer. 31. 34; Lk. 12. 6; Heb. 8. 12.

forgive, forgiveness This is not regarded in the O.T. as in the nature of things, but something to be received with gratitude and only because God is compassionate. Ex. 34. 6–7; Dt. 29. 20; 1 K. 8. 35–40; Neh. 9. 17; Ps. 86. 5; 130. 4; Jer. 5. 7; 31. 34; 36. 3; Dan. 9. 9. *See also* Gen. 45; Lev. 17. 11; 19. 18; Mic. 7. 18–20. It is an essential part of the teaching of the N.T. where a readiness to forgive others is an indication of true repentance. Mt. 6. 9–15; 18. 21–35; 26. 28; Mk. 1. 4; 2. 10; Lk. 23. 34; Ac. 2. 38; 5. 31; 13. 38; Eph. 1. 7; Col. 1. 14; 1 Jn. 1. 9. *See also* Rom. 3. 25.

Fortunatus A Christian of Corinth. 1 Cor. 16. 17.

Foundation Gate A gate of Jerusalem leading from the royal palace to the Temple. 2 Ch. 23. 5.

fountain A spring of fresh water. Used literally and figuratively. Ps. 36. 9; Pr. 13. 14; 14. 27; Hos. 13. 15. *See also* Ex. 15. 27; Pr. 25. 26; Jn. 4. 14.

fox Three species are found in Palestine and Egypt: the Red, the Desert and the Fennec fox. They are solitary hunters, living in the drier parts of the country and taking a wide range of prey. Neh. 4. 3; Mt. 8. 20; Lk. 13. 32.

frankincense This hardwood tree grows mainly in India and N Arabia. The juice or resin of the tree is used as incense. Ex. 30. 34; Lev. 5. 11; Nu. 5. 15; Is. 60. 6; Jer. 6. 20; Mt. 2. 11.

frog The commonest kind in Palestine is the edible frog which spends most of its time in the water. The tree-frog is also found in the Jordan valley. Ex. 8. 2–13; Ps. 78. 45; 105. 30; Rev. 16. 13.

fruit Those most often mentioned are grape, pomegranate, fig, olive, and apple. Used metaphorically Dt. 7. 13; Pr. 1. 31. *See also* Jn. 4. 36; Gal. 5. 22.

fuel This was usually dried grass, branches of bushes and trees, and dung. Ezek. 4. 12, 15; 15. 4–5; 21. 32. *See also* Mt. 6. 30.

fulfil This is most notably used in connection with the correspondence between the events of the Old and New Testaments. Mt. 1. 22; 2. 15; Jn. 19. 36; Ac. 13. 27. *See also* Jn. 19. 24; Ac. 1. 16.

fuller One who washed, bleached, and sometimes dyed cloth. Mal. 3. 2. *See also* Mk. 9. 3. The Fuller's Field was the name of a place outside the walls of Jerusalem. 2 K. 18. 17; Is. 7. 3; 36. 2.

furnace Used both literally and figuratively. Dt. 4. 20; 1 K. 8. 51; Dan. 3; Is. 31. 9; 48. 10; Jer. 11. 4; Mt. 13. 36–42; Rev. 9. 2.

furnishings, furniture Used principally of the articles used in the Tabernacle and the Temple. Ex. 31. 7–9; 39. 33–43; 1 K. 7. 48–50. *See also* Judg. 1. 7; 2 K. 4. 10.

Gabael (1) An ancestor of Tobit. Tobit 1. 1. (2) The friend in Rages with whom Tobit had left some money which Tobias was sent to collect. Tobit 1. 14; 4. 20 – 5. 12; 9. 2–6.

Gabbatha The place in Jerusalem where Jesus was tried by Pilate. Jn. 19. 13.

Gabriel The archangel and messenger of God. Dan. 8. 16–26; 9. 21–27; Lk. 1. 11–38.

Gad The son of Jacob and ancestor of the tribe. Gen. 30. 11; Nu. 32; 1 Ch. 5. 18–22.

Gadara, Gadarenes A city of the Decapolis some 6 miles SE of the Sea of Galilee. Lk. 8. 26–39. *Umm Qeis.*

Gaddi One of Joshua's twelve spies. Nu. 13. 11.

Gaius A common Roman name appearing frequently in the N.T. Ac. 19. 29; 20. 4; Rom. 16. 23; 1 Cor. 1. 14; 3 Jn. 1.

Galatia The Roman province in central Asia Minor. Ac. 16. 6; 18. 23; 1 Cor. 16. 1; Gal. 1. 2; 2 Tim. 4. 10; 1 Pet. 1. 1.

Galatians, Letter to the Written when both Paul himself and the gospel he was preaching were under an attack which, if it had succeeded, would have resulted in Christianity becoming just another Jewish sect. He defends the source of his apostleship by the unique qualification of his meeting the risen Christ on the Damascus road. Then he shows his Gentile converts that although the Jewish law is an essential stage on the Christian way, since it shows us what sin is and convinces us of our own helplessness, the only thing that can save us is the grace of God. So the great theme of this letter is the glory of the grace of God, and the necessity of realizing that by our own works we can never earn our own salvation.

Galilee Originally the fertile territory in N Palestine W of the Jordan, but in N.T. times a Roman province. In the Maccabean war, fighting took place in Galilee. 1 K. 9. 11; Is. 9. 1; Tobit 1. 2; Judith 1. 8; 15. 5; 1 Mac. 5. 14–23; 11. 63; 12. 47–52; Mt. 4. 12–16; 26. 69; Lk. 23. 5–7; Jn. 7. 52.

Galilee, Sea of A large fresh-water lake in N Palestine some 18 miles long by 8 miles wide; 650 feet below sea level, and subject to sudden and violent storms. Mt. 4. 18; Mk. 4. 35–41. *See also* Nu. 34. 11; Jos. 12. 3; Lk. 5. 2; Jn. 6. 1. *Bahr Tabarîyeh.*

gall (1) Possibly the juice of the opium poppy and a kind of narcotic which could render a person unconscious. Mt. 27. 34. (2) Fish-gall, used as a medicine. Tobit 11. 10–14.

Gallio The Roman proconsul of Achaia and the brother of the philosopher Seneca. Ac. 18. 12–17.

Gamaliel A great Jewish rabbi: a Pharisee, member of the Council and Paul's former tutor. Ac. 5. 34–40; 22. 3.

games Life left little time for physical recreation in biblical times for the ordinary Hebrew, whose chief form of relaxation was music and dancing.

garden The term is used of ground, usually enclosed and under cultivation of vegetables, fruit or flowers. Gen. 2. 10; 1 K. 21. 2; 2 K. 21. 26; Is. 1. 30; Jer. 31. 12; Jn. 19. 41. *See also* Pr. 24. 31.

garlic Many species are known in Palestine and, as today, it was used for flavouring. Nu. 11. 5.

gate(s) These were made of wood, bronze or iron. The city gates were the recognized places for meeting and conducting business. Dt. 21. 18–19; Ru. 4. 1; Neh. 2. 17; 3. 1–32; Est. 4. 1–2; Pr. 32. 31. Used figuratively Gen. 28. 17; Ps. 87. 2; Mt. 16. 18.

Gath This was the nearest Philistine city to Israelite territory. 1 S. 5. 8–9; 17. 4; 21. 10; 1 K. 2. 39; 2 K. 12. 17; 1 Ch. 18. 1.

Gaza A Philistine city and a great trade centre. Jos. 13. 3; Judg. 1. 18; 16. 1–3; 2 K. 18. 8; Am. 1. 6–7; Ac. 8. 26. Flinders Petrie excavated the site 1930–34, uncovering five occupation levels from the Middle Bronze to the Late Bronze Age.

gazelle A medium-sized antelope like the South African springbok. They are common and widespread in Palestine and there are several families of this graceful species. Both sexes have horns. Dt. 12. 22; 1 K. 4. 24; Pr. 6. 5; Ac. 9. 36.

gecko This strange little lizard is most frequently seen in the desert, where it lives among the rocky outcrops and is most active at night. Other species are closely connected with houses due to their amazing ability to cling to smooth surfaces. Lev. 11. 30.

Gedaliah The son of Ahikam, appointed Governor of the remnant left behind in Judah. 2 K. 25. 22–26; Jer. 40. 7 – 41. 3.

Gehazi The servant of the prophet Elisha. 2 K. 4. 8–37; 5; 8. 1–6.

Gehenna See Ben-hinnom.

Gemariah (1) The son of Shaphan. Jer. 36. 10–26. (2) A messenger of Zedekiah. Jer. 29. 3.

genealogy For details of ancestors, descendants, and other lists of people and tribes see Gen. 5; 10; 11. 10–32; 35. 23 – 36. 43; 46. 8–27; 1 Ch. ch. 1–9; Ezr. 2. 1–67; 8. 1–20; Neh. 7. 5–69; Mt. 1. 1–17; Lk. 3. 23–38.

Genesis The book of 'beginnings' which tells in religious language the origins of heaven and earth, man, sin, death, and the Jewish people. The theme is that of the Bible as a whole – the saving acts of God.

Gennesaret 1 Mac. 11. 67; Lk. 5. 1. See Galilee, Sea of.

Gentiles Originally any non-Israelite people, but after the exile exclusiveness, based solely on religion, developed. However, converts to Judaism were welcomed; and the Christian church admitted both Jewish and non-Jewish converts without distinction. Ac. 10; 15. 22–29; Gal. 3. 8. See also Is. 2. 2–3; 42. 6.

Gerasenes Inhabitants of Gerasa, a city of the Decapolis. Mk. 5. 1–20. Excavations by the American Schools of Oriental Research 1928–34.

Gerizim A mountain near Shechem facing Mt Ebal. Dt. 11. 29; Judg. 9. 7–21. See also Jn. 4. 19–22. Jebel eṭ-Ṭôr.

Gethsemane The place on the western slope of the Mt of Olives where Christ was betrayed. Mt. 26. 36–56; Mk. 14. 32–52. See also Lk. 22. 39–53; Jn. 18. 1–11.

Gezer A Canaanite city 18 miles NW of Jerusalem. It figures frequently in the Maccabean struggles. Jos. 10. 33; 1 K. 9. 15–16. Tell Jezer. Extensive excavations by R. A. S. Macalister, 1902–5, 1907–9, have been carried out here and important discoveries made, including the Gezer Calendar, a schoolboy's mnemonic rhyme describing the agricultural year.

giant When the Israelites entered Canaan they found it inhabited by tall, powerfully built peoples. See Gen. 6. 4; Nu. 13. 32–33; Dt. 2. 10–11; 1 S. 17. 4.

Gibeah A military stronghold 4 miles N of Jerusalem. Judg. 20. 5; 1 S. 10. 26 – 11. 4. Tell el-Fûl. Excavations by W. F. Albright 1922–3 show it to have been inhabited and fortified early in the Iron Age. There is good reason to identify its destruction with Judg. ch. 19–20. The second level dates from the time of Saul, and pottery and an iron plough-tip have been found in the rebuilt fortress. It lost its importance after David's reign and was deserted until about the 9th century B.C. when the fortress was rebuilt on a smaller scale.

Gibeon A hill town 5 miles NW of Jerusalem. Jos. 9. 3 – 11. 19; 2 S. 21. 1–9; 1 K. 3. 4–15. el Jîb. Excavations by the University Museum, Philadelphia, 1956 7 have revealed remains, including a pit and tunnel, of the Early and Middle II Bronze Age and of the Iron Age from its beginning to the Persian period. An extensive wine-making industry was centred here in the 7th century B.C.

Gideon One of the Judges, who delivered the Israelites from the Midianites. Judg. ch. 6–8; Heb. 11. 32.

gifts, giving In the O.T. these are recorded as having been given with many and mixed motives. Gen. 34. 12; 1 Ch. 29. 14; Ps. 45. 12; 72. 10; Pr. 18. 16; Dan. 2. 48; Mt. 5. 23; Phil. 4. 17. In the N.T. the word is used primarily of God's gift to men. Rom. 6. 23; 8. 32; 11. 35; Eph. 4. 7–13. See also Jn. 3. 16; 14. 16; 16. 7; Gal. 5. 22.

Gihon The place near Jerusalem, and the site of a spring, where Solomon was anointed king. 1 K. 1. 33–40; 2 Ch. 32. 30. '*Ain Sitti Maryam.*

Gilboa A ridge of hills W of the Jordan where Saul fought his last battle. 1 S. 28. 4; 31. 1–6. *Jebel Fuqqû'ah.*

Gilead Mountainous country E of the Jordan. Jos. 13. 24–25; Judg. ch. 10–11; 1 K. 17. 1; Jer. 8. 22.

Gilgal (1) A place some 5 miles N of where the Jordan enters the Dead Sea. Jos. 4. 19–24; 1 S. 11. 14; Hos. 4. 15; Am. 4. 4. *Khirbet el-Mefjer.* (2) A village of Bethel. 2 K. 2. 1–2; 4. 38.

girdle A sash or belt with various uses. Is. 3. 24; Rev. 1. 13; 15. 6. *See also* Ex. 12. 11; 28. 4; 2 S. 20. 8; Pr. 31. 24; Is. 22. 21; Ezek. 9. 2; Dan. 10. 5.

glass This was made at an early date by the Phoenicians, but it is used only figuratively in the N.T. Rev. 4. 6; 15. 2; 21. 18. *See also* 1 Cor. 13. 12.

glean The custom of allowing the poor to follow the harvesters and collect the remnants. Lev. 19. 9; Ru. 2; Is. 17. 6.

glory What is of real, as opposed to reputed, worth and its visible appearance. Ex. 16. 6–10; 24. 13–17; 33. 19–23; 40. 34; Lev. 9. 5–7; 1 K. 8. 11; 2 Ch. 7. 1–3; Is. 40. 5; 60. 1–3; Ezek. 1. 28; Mt. 16. 27; Jn. 1. 14; 2. 11; 17. 5; Rom. 2. 7–10; Rev. 21. 10 – 22. 5. *See also* Ex. 34. 29–35; Mt. 17. 2; Lk. 2. 9; 2 Cor. 3. 7–18; Phil. 3. 21.

goad A long spiked pole used for urging on cattle, and sometimes as a weapon. 1 S. 13. 21; Judg. 3. 31; Eccles. 12. 11; Ac. 26. 14.

goat The earliest accepted evidence for its domestication is from the New Stone Age pre-pottery levels of Jericho 6000–7000 B.C. Varieties were distinguished by their colour and horn-shapes, corkscrew and scimitar. At first they were kept as milk-producers, but the kid was very edible and was the standard meal prepared for strangers. Their skin was used especially to make containers for water and wine. Gen. 30. 32; Lev. 4. 27–28; 1 S. 25. 2; Pr. 27. 27; Ezek. 43. 22–25; Mt. 25. 31–33.

God The supreme power in the universe and the source of all existence Is. 40. 28; Mk. 13. 19; controller of history Is. 10. 5–6; Am. 9. 7; eternal Rev. 4. 8–11; immortal 1 Tim. 6. 16; omnipotent Gen. 17. 1; omnipresent Jer. 23. 23–24; omniscient Ps. 139. 1–18; Pr. 5. 21; unchanging Jas. 1. 17; invisible Jn. 5. 37; 1 Tim. 1. 17; spirit Jn. 4. 24; perfect Job 11. 7; one Dt. 6. 4; only wise Rom. 16. 27; holy Ps. 99. 9; Is. 6. 3; good Mt. 5. 48; faithful 1 Cor. 1. 9; just Rom. 3. 25; truthful Tit. 1. 2; gracious Rom. 5. 15; electing Eph. 1. 4; saving Ex. 14. 30; 1 Cor. 1. 18; patient Nu. 14. 18; compassionate Ex. 34. 6; Ps. 86. 5; Jas. 5. 11; father Mal. 2. 10; Jn. 8. 41–47; loving 1 Jn. 4. 9; known by his acts and fully revealed in Jesus Christ Jn. 1. 14, 18; Heb. 1. 1 – 2. 4.

Gog A prince of Meshech and Tubal, and the leader of the hosts of evil against God and his people. Ezek. 38. 1 – 39. 16. He is associated with Satan in Rev. 20. 8.

gold The precious metal which was found at Havilah, Sheba and Ophir and used in the furnishings of the Tabernacle. Gen. 2. 11–12; Ex. 37; 1 K. 10. 2; 22. 48. It serves as a symbol of worth and value. Ps. 12. 6; Lam. 4. 1–2; Rev. 21. 18–21.

Golgotha The place where Jesus was crucified. Mt. 27. 33; Mk. 15. 22; Jn. 19. 17–30.

Goliath The giant of Gath killed by David. 1 S. 17. 4, 23–58.

Gomorrah One of the cities of the Plain. Gen. 14. 2–11; 18. 20–21; Is. 1. 9; Jer. 50. 40; Mt. 10. 15; Rom. 9. 29; 2 Pet. 2. 6.

Gorgias One of the army commanders of Antiochus who fought against Judas. 1 Mac. 3. 38–41; 4. 1–18; 5. 55–60; 2 Mac. 8. 9; 10. 14; 12. 32–35.

Gortyna A city in Crete to which the Roman Consul wrote announcing the friendship of the Romans for the Jews. 1 Mac. 15. 23. *Gortyn.*

Goshen (1) The region of Egypt on the Nile delta where Jacob and his family settled. Gen. 45. 9–13; 46. 28 – 47. 11; Ex. 8, 22; 9. 26. (2) A place in the Judaean highlands. Jos. 15. 51.

Gospel The good news about Jesus Christ and the kingdom. Mt. 4. 23; Mk. 1. 1; Rom. 1. 1, 16; 15. 19; 2 Cor. 4. 4; 10. 14. *See also* Mt. 9. 35; 1 Th. 2. 2, 9.

Gospels, the Four The post-biblical name given to the writings of Matthew, Mark, Luke and John, each of which contains a record of the life of Jesus.

gourd A large bush, which could reach to a height of 10 feet, with bronze-coloured leaves and a grey-green fruit from which an oil was obtained. Jon. 4. 6–10.

grace That attitude of God towards sinful man which moves him to help rather than to condemn him. Jn. 1. 17; Ac. 15. 11; Rom. 3. 24; 5. 21; 11. 5; 1 Cor. 15. 10; 2 Cor. 12. 9; Gal. 1. 15; 5. 4; Eph. 2. 4–10; 6. 24; 2 Th. 2. 16; 2 Tim. 1. 9; Heb. 4. 16; 2 Pet. 3. 18. *See also* Dt. 7. 7–10; 9. 4–5; Jn. 3. 16; Rom. 5. 8; 2 Cor. 8. 9.

Greece The land in the SE corner of Europe known as Javan in the O.T. Is. 66. 19; Ezek. 27. 13; Zech. 9. 13. After its conquest by Rome in 146 B.C. it became the province of Achaia. Ac. 18. 12; 20. 2.

Greek language The language of the ancient Greeks which spread over the Mediterranean world in a simplified form, and in which the N.T. is written. The spread of Christianity was greatly helped by the existence of this common language. Ac. 21. 37.

Habakkuk, Book of Habakkuk Little is known of the prophet apart from what is in the book itself. Its theme is the moral problem of how a righteous God can use the wicked Chaldaeans to punish Judah's sin. *See* 2 K. ch. 21–22. In the Apocrypha there is a story that Habakkuk was carried to Babylon to feed Daniel. Bel & Snake 33.

Hadad (1) The supreme Syrian god. Zech. 12. 11. (2) The grandson of Abraham. Gen. 25. 14.

Hadadezer The king of Zobah. 2 S. 8. 3–12; 10. 16–19; 1 K. 11. 23.

Hadassah The Jewish name of Esther. Est. 2. 7.

Hades *See* 'hell' and 'Sheol'.

Hagar The Egyptian slave-girl of Sarah. Gen. 16; 21. 14–20.

Haggai, Book of Haggai The prophet, and contemporary of Zechariah, whose task it was to persuade and encourage the re-turned exiles to complete the rebuilding of the Temple. The book contains his five messages.

hair Usually worn long, though kept trimmed. Baldness was despised. Lev. 14. 8; 19. 27; 21. 5; Nu. 6. 5; Judg. 16. 13; 20. 16; 1 S. 14. 45; 2 S. 14. 26; Ps. 40. 12; Ezek. 44. 20; Mt. 10. 29. *See also* 2 K. 2. 23; 1 Cor. 11. 14.

Halicarnassus A town on the coast of Cassia, to which the Roman Consul wrote announcing friendship for the Jews. 1 Mac. 15. 23. *Bodrum*.

Ham The son of Noah. Gen. 6. 10; 9. 18–19; 10. 6.

Haman The chief official of Ahasuerus and a bitter enemy of the Jews. Est. ch. 3–7.

Hamath A city on the Orontes in Syria which gave its name to the region of which it was the capital. Jonathan marched there against Demetrius. 2 S. 8. 9–12; 2 K. 14. 28; 17. 24–33; 25. 21; 2 Ch. 8. 4; Jer. 39. 5; 52. 9, 27; Zech. 9. 2; 1 Mac. 12. 25. *Ḥamā*.

hamlet *See* village.

hammer The ordinary hammer Judg. 4. 21; 1 K. 6. 7; Is. 44. 12; Jer. 10. 4; and one used for breaking rocks Jer. 23. 29.

hand(s) Used in many figurative senses. For power Ex. 13. 3; Ps. 31. 15; 1 Pet. 5. 6; anger Nu. 24. 10; protection Ps. 63. 8; Is. 49. 2; punishment 1 S. 5. 6; supplication Ex. 9. 33; 17. 11; Ps. 28. 2; ratifying an agreement Gen. 14. 22; 24. 9; communicating authority or blessing Gen. 48. 14; Dt. 34. 9.

hands, laying on A symbolical act associated with (1) sacrifice Lev. 1. 4; 3. 2; 4. 4; (2) blessing Gen. 48. 14–20; Mt. 19. 13; (3) healing Mk. 6. 5; Lk. 4. 40; 13. 13; (4) appointment Nu. 27. 18–23; Ac. 6. 6; 1 Tim. 5. 22; (5) the gift of the Holy Spirit Ac. 8. 17; 9. 17; 19. 6; 1 Tim. 4. 14; 2 Tim. 1. 6.

hands, washing This was an action intended to convey innocence and also ceremonial cleanness. Dt. 21. 6; Ps. 26. 6; Mt. 15. 1–9; 27. 24; Mk. 7. 1–8.

Hannah The wife of Elkanah and the mother of Samuel. 1 S. 1. 1 – 2. 10.

Haran The brother of Abraham. Gen. 11. 27–30.

hare The hare of Palestine is a sub-species of the European variety and is smaller, paler and has shorter ears. It appears in the Bible only as an unclean animal, possibly because of its habit of 'refection'. Lev. 11. 6; Dt. 14. 7.

harp The first instrument mentioned in the Bible. Made of wood, usually cypress or almug, it was stringed, and played with the fingers or a plectrum; and small enough to be carried about. Gen. 4. 21; 1 S. 16. 16; 1 K. 10. 12; Ps. 71. 22; Neh. 12. 27.

Harran An important commercial city in N Mesopotamia, strategically placed on the main route from Nineveh to the river Euphrates and Aleppo. Gen. 11. 31 – 12. 6; 27. 43; Is. 37. 12; Ezek. 27. 23. Excavations since 1951 have shown that it was inhabited from at least as early as the third millennium B.C.

harvest There were three each year. First the barley reaping, followed by the wheat and vine. The main religious festivals (Passover, Pentecost and Tabernacles) fitted respectively into this agricultural economy. Ex. 23. 16–17; 34. 22.

hate, hatred Condemned in the O.T. between fellow-Israelites. Ex. 23. 5; Lev. 19. 17; Pr. 10. 12; 15. 17. In the N.T. it is shown to be utterly contrary to the teaching of Christ. Mt. 5. 43–48; 1 Jn. 2. 9–11; 3. 15; 4. 20. See also Gal. 5. 20; Col. 3. 8.

hawk A common bird of prey in Palestine whose flesh was forbidden by the law. Lev. 11. 16; Dt. 14. 15; Job 39. 26.

Hazael The Syrian who murdered Benhadad and usurped his throne. 1 K. 19. 15; 2 K. 8. 7–15; 12. 17.

Hazor A Canaanite city in N Palestine. Jos. 11. 1–13; Judg. 4. 2; 1 K. 9. 15; 2 K. 15. 29. *Tell el-Qebaḥ.* Excavations by J. Garstang 1926–8 and Y. Yadin 1955–8 have disclosed its size and importance, and its destruction in the period of the Israelite settlement. Among the discoveries in the lower city were a pottery jug with the earliest known inscription scratched on it, a Canaanite temple and a shrine. Evidence from the later Israelite period includes a city gate from the time of Solomon and a pillared public building of Ahab's time.

head Regarded by the Hebrews as the seat of life rather than of the intellect, and often used with a figurative meaning. Gen. 48. 14–19; Lev. 16. 21; Jos. 2. 19; Judg. 8. 28; 2 S. 1. 2; 15. 30; Job 20. 6; Ps. 27. 6; 83. 2; Mt. 5. 36; Rom. 12. 20; Eph. 1. 22; 5. 23; Col. 2. 19.

heart The physical organ, also regarded as the seat of the mind and the governing centre which makes a man what he is. Gen. 6. 6; Dt. 8. 5; 1 S. 2. 35; 2 K. 9. 24; Ps. 51. 10; Pr. 4. 23; 23. 7; Ezek. 36. 26; Mt. 5. 8; 13. 19; Lk. 8. 15; 24. 32; Rom. 5. 5; 2 Cor. 1. 22; Eph. 3. 17.

heathen In the O.T. the term is used of the pagan nations surrounding Israel. In the N.T. it refers to non-Jews or Gentiles. Lk. 2. 32. See also Gen. 22. 18; 49. 10; 2 K. 16. 3; Ezr. 6. 21; Ps. 2. 8; 72. 11; 135. 15; Is. 42. 6; 49. 6; 60. 3; Ac. 18. 6; Gal. 3. 8.

Heber The Kenite husband of Jael. Judg. 4. 11–24.

Hebrew(s) The word is used of Abraham and his descendants. Gen. 14. 13; 1 S. 13. 19; Phil. 3. 5. See also Israel, Israelite.

Hebrew language The NW branch of the Semitic language family in which almost all of the O.T. is written.

Hebrews, A Letter to Written to a group of persecuted Christian Jews tempted to deny their faith, it encourages them to continue to live the Christian life through all trials. To the writer, religion is access to God: it is that which removes all barriers and opens the way to his presence. And he shows his readers how Christianity is the final and absolute religion because Christ is the true high priest and mediator who, by what he was and did, has opened the door that had been shut. See 10. 19–23.

Hebron An ancient Canaanite city 20 miles SW of Jerusalem. Later, it was taken by Jonathan after being re-occupied by the Edomites. Gen. 13. 18; 23. 1–19; Nu. 13. 22; Jos. 10. 1–10; 14. 13–15; 20. 1–7; 2 S. 2. 1–4; 15. 7–12; 1 Mac. 5. 65. *el-Khalil.*

heifer A young, unmated cow, sometimes used for threshing or ploughing, but also for sacrificial purposes. Dt. 21. 3; Judg.

14. 18. Used figuratively Jer. 46. 20; Hos. 10. 11.

heir The principle of inheritance and the concept play a great part in the Bible story. Gen. 15. 3; Mk. 12. 7; Rom. 8. 16; Heb. 1. 2. *See also* Gen. 21. 10; Nu. 27. 1–11; Dt. 21. 17; Job 42. 15; Jn. 1. 12; Heb. 9. 15.

Heli The father of Joseph. Lk. 3. 23.

Heliodorus An officer of Seleucus sent to plunder the Temple. 2 Mac. 3. 7–40.

hell A common translation of the O.T. 'Sheol' and the N.T. 'Hades'. Originally the place of departed spirits, it came to be thought of as the place of punishment for the wicked. Mt. 18. 9; Mk. 9. 45; 2 Pet. 2. 4. *See also* 2 S. 22. 6; Job 26. 6; Ps. 16.10; 139. 8; Lk. 16. 23; Rev. 20. 14.

Heman The musician and grandson of Samuel. 1 Ch. 6. 33; 15. 16–21.

hen By Jesus's day eggs, as well as the bird, were established as a food in Palestine. Used figuratively of Jerusalem. Mt. 23. 37; Lk. 13. 34. *See also* Lk. 11. 12

henna A shrub originating in N India and widely used there and in the Middle East as a cosmetic and orange hair dye. It grows wild in Palestine and has spiny branches tipped with clusters of white flowers. S. of S. 1. 14.

Hercules The Graeco-Roman god, to whose temple in Tyre Jason sent an offering. 2 Mac. 4. 18–20.

Hermas A Christian of Rome. Rom. 16. 14.

Hermon The snow-clad mountain in Syria, over 9000 feet high, marking the limit of Israel's conquests. Dt. 3. 9; 4. 48; Jos. 12. 1–5; 13. 11; Ps. 133. 3. *Jebel esh-Sheikh.*

Herod Agrippa *See* Agrippa.

Herod Antipas The son of Herod the Great and the ruler of Galilee and Perea. Mt. 14. 1–11; Lk. 3. 1; 13. 31–32; 23. 7–12.

Herod the Great The ruler of Judaea at the time of Christ's birth. Mt. 2. 1–19.

Herodians An influential group of Jews supporting the dynasty of Herod and so, indirectly, Rome. It was largely through them that Greek influences entered the life of Israel. *See* Mt. 22. 16.

Herodias The half-sister of Herod Agrippa I. She married her uncle, Philip. Mt. 14. 3–11.

Heshbon A Moabite city 20 miles E of the Jordan with an excellent spring. Nu. 21. 26; Jos. 13. 26; 21. 39; Is. 15. 4; 16. 8; Jer. 48. 34. *Hesbân.*

Hezekiah The king of Judah who, in his long and prosperous reign, reformed religious worship. 2 K. ch. 18–20; 2 Ch. ch. 29–32; Is. ch. 36–39; Jer. 26. 17–19.

Hierapolis A city in the Lycus valley where Epaphras ministered. Col. 4. 13. *Pambuk Kalesi.*

Hieronymus A Syrian officer under Antiochus who harassed the Jews. 2 Mac. 12. 2.

high priest The man who spoke for the nation to God, and who reported God's will to the nation. Mk. 14. 53–65. *See also* Ex. ch. 28–29; Lev. 4; 16; 21. 16–23; Nu. 27. 21.

Hilkiah (1) The father of Eliakim. 2 K. 18. 18–37; Is. 22. 20–25. (2) The high priest under Josiah. 2 K. 22. 3 – 23. 4.

hill-country Generally applied to the uplands of Judaea in the N.T. (*see* Lk. 1. 39, 65); and in the O.T. to the southern part of Lebanon E of Sidon. Jos. 13. 6.

hill-shrine(s) Usually consisting of a level platform with an altar and standing stones, these were used for the sacrificial worship of pagan gods. They were bitterly denounced by the prophets, and destroyed by Hezekiah and Josiah. 1 S. 9. 12–14; 10. 5; 1 K. 3. 2–3; 11. 7; 14. 23; 2 K. 23. 1–8; 2 Ch. 33; Is. 36. 7. *See also* Nu. 22. 41; Dt. 12. 13; Jer. 19. 5.

hin *See* Appendix to the O.T. in the New English Bible.

hinge Used figuratively Pr. 26. 14.

Hinnom, Valley of *See* Ben-hinnom.

Hiram (1) King of Tyre. 2 S. 5. 11; 1 K. 5. 1–18; 9. 10–14. (2) A craftsman. 1 K. 7. 13.

Hittites An ethnic group living in Palestine from patriarchal times until after the Israelite settlement. Gen. 15. 20; 23. 1–20; 26. 34; Dt. 7. 1; Judg. 3. 5.

Hivites Early inhabitants of Syria and Palestine. Gen. 10. 17; Ex. 3. 8; Judg. 3. 3; 1 K. 9. 20.

Holophernes The general of Nebuchadnezzar whom Judith outwitted and killed. Judith ch. 2–13.

holy, holiness The root idea is separateness. It originates in the revealed character of God and is communicated to things, places, times and persons engaged in his service. Ex. 19. 6; 20. 8; Lev. 19. 2; Ps. 2. 6; 24. 3–4; 65. 4; Is. 41. 14; Mk. 1. 24; Ac. 4. 30; Heb. 12. 10; 1 Pet. 1. 15. *See also* Heb. 7. 26.

Holy Spirit In the O.T. the term is used twice Ps. 51. 11; Is. 63. 10; but the meaning is simply that God deals with men by his spirit which is holy because it is the spirit of God who is himself holy.

This tradition continues in the N.T. Mt. 3. 1–17; 4. 1; 12. 28; Lk. 4. 16–21; but it also develops a much deeper meaning. The turning-point in the usage is largely provided by the events of Pentecost when the prophecies of both Joel and Christ himself are fulfilled Ac. 2. 1–39. With the coming of Christ, and faith in him as saviour, there developed a fuller knowledge of the nature of God which remained with men even after Christ's ascension. Thus, the Holy Spirit is called the Spirit of Truth and regarded as a personal reality, 'God-with-man', because he would lead man to the Truth itself. In this work Father, Son and Spirit are each involved: a work which would not be possible unless each did his own part, though not working in the same way. *See* Jn. 14. 15–17; 16. 12–15; Rom. 5. 5; 8. 9; 14; 15. 16; 1 Cor. 3. 16; 6. 11. *See also* Spirit.

homicide *See* avenger of blood.

honey Prized as food and delicacy, and for sweetening since sugar was unknown. Gen. 43. 11; Ex. 3. 8; 16. 31; Lev. 2. 11; Dt. 32. 13; Judg. 14. 9; Ps. 19. 10; Mk. 1. 6.

hook Used for various purposes. Ex. 26. 32, 37; 27. 10, 17; Job 41. 2; Joel 3. 9; Mt. 17. 27.

hoopoe A bird, seen in Palestine in spring and summer, which has a long, curved beak and a crest in its head which it can spread out as a fan. Lev. 11. 19; Dt. 14. 18.

hope In the later O.T. books true hope is linked with faith in God. Ps. 39. 7; 71. 5; 119. 74; 146. 5. In the N.T. it is based on the resurrection. Rom. 4. 18; 5. 3–5; 15. 4, 13; 1 Cor. 13. 13; 15. 19; Eph. 2. 12; Col. 1.

27; 1 Th. 1. 3; 5. 8; 1 Tim. 1. 1; Tit. 1. 1; Heb. 6. 19; 11. 1; 1 Jn. 3. 3.

Hophni One of the wicked sons of Eli. 1 S. 1. 3; 2. 13 – 4. 18.

Hor The mountain, on the borders of Edom, where Aaron died. Nu. 20. 22–29; 33. 37–39.

Horeb The 'mountain of God' situated between Canaan and Egypt, also known as Sinai. Ex. 3. 1–6; 17. 5–7; 19. 1–21; 31. 18 – 32. 15; Dt. 1. 2–8; 4. 10–19; 9. 8–19.

horn A simple curved wind instrument, first made from a ram's horn but later also of metal. Jos. 6. 4–5; Ps. 98. 6; Dan. 3. 4–5.

horns The projections at the corners of altars. Ex. 29. 12; 1 K. 1. 50; Ps. 118. 27. Also used to signify strength. Ps. 75. 4; Jer. 48. 25; Rev. 17. 7–14.

horse A symbol of war because it was used for chariots; but it seems that they were not widely used by the Israelites until the times of David and Solomon when they became an integral part of Israel's armed forces. Dt. 17. 14–16; Jos. 11. 4–9; 2 S. 8. 4; 1 K. 10. 25, 28–29; Job 39. 19; Ps. 33. 16–17. Used symbolically Zech. 1. 8; 6. 1–7; Rev. 6. 2–8.

Horse Gate One of the eleven gates of Jerusalem. Neh. 3. 28; Jer. 31. 40.

hosanna The Greek transliteration of the Hebrew word meaning 'save now'. Mt. 21. 9. *See also* Ps. 118. 25.

Hosea (= salvation) The son of Beri, a prophet of Israel, contemporary with Isaiah, Amos and Micah.

Hosea, Book of The theme is the unfaithfulness of Israel set out in the terms of the familiar marriage relationship between God and his chosen people. Hosea uses his own personal experiences as an allegory of God's experience with Israel.

Hoshea (1) The last king of the northern kingdom of Israel. 2 K. 15. 30; 17. 1–6; 18. 1. (2) Joshua's early name. Nu. 13. 8.

hospitality A necessity among nomads, and counted a major virtue throughout the Bible. Rom. 12. 13; 1 Tim. 3. 2; Tit. 1. 8; 1 Pet. 4. 9. *See also* Gen. 18. 1–8; Ex. 2. 20; Dt. 23. 4; 1 K. 17. 10–16; 2 K. 4. 8–15; Ps. 41. 9; Mt. 10. 11; 25. 35–45; Lk. 7. 44–46; Col. 4. 10; 2 Jn. 10; 3 Jn. 5–8.

hour The Jews reckoned days from sunrise to sunset, dividing them into 12 lengths differing according to season. Mt. 20. 1–16; 24. 36; Mk. 14. 37; 15. 25; Jn. 11. 9; Ac. 5. 7; 19. 34; 23. 23; Rev. 17. 12. *See also* Jn. 4. 52.

house(s) Construction and design Ex. 12. 27; Dt. 6. 8; 20. 5; 22. 8; 2 S. 17. 18; 1 K. 6; 2 Ch. 8. 16; Ezr. 6. 16; Job 4. 19; Hos. 13. 3; Lk. 5. 19. Furnishings and utensils Gen. 24. 15; 2 S. 4. 7; 17. 28; 1 K. 17. 12; Job 37. 18; Jer. 36. 22; Am. 3. 12; Jn. 2. 6.

household Everyone who lived beneath the roof, including servants and slaves. Gen. 7. 1.

household gods *See* teraphim.

Huldah A prophetess in the time of Josiah. 2 K. 22. 14–20.

humility Praised in the O.T. *See* Nu. 12. 3; Pr. 15. 33; 18. 12; 22. 4. It is not defined in the N.T. but is taught and exemplified by Christ. *See* Mt. 11. 29; 18. 4; 23. 12; Lk. 14. 11; 18. 14; Jn. 13. 3–9; Ac. 20. 19; 1 Cor. 13. 4; 2 Cor. 8. 9; Phil. 2. 3; 1 Pet. 5. 5.

hunter, hunting A necessity rather than a pastime. Gen. 10. 8; 25. 27; 27. 3. *See also* Gen. 21. 20; Ex. 23. 29; Dt. 12. 15; 15. 22; Judg. 14. 5; 1 S. 17. 34.

Hur (1) An attendant on Moses at Rephidim. Ex. 17. 10–13; 24. 14. (2) A king of Midian. Nu. 31. 8.

hyena This is the striped hyena which ranges from India through SW Asia to E Africa. It has a body length of about 40 inches with a massive head and jaws. Its main food is carrion. Jer. 12. 9.

hypocrite One who pretends to be what he is not. Mt. 6. 1–6, 16–18; 7. 5; 23. 13–32; Mk. 7. 6; Lk. 12. 56; 13. 15. *See also* Rom. 2. 17–29.

hyssop Ps. 51. 7. *See* marjoram.

I AM The name by which God revealed himself to Moses showing that he is faithful and unchangeable. Ex. 3. 14.

Ibleam A Canaanite town SE of Megiddo. Judg. 1. 27; 2 K. 15. 10.

Ibzan The Judge who succeeded Jephthah. Judg. 12. 8–10.

Ichabod The grandson of Eli whose mother died in childbirth. 1 S. 4. 19–21.

Iconium An important centre of missionary activity in the Roman province of Galatia, situated on the trade route linking Ephesus and Syria. Ac. ch. 14; 2 Tim. 3. 11.

idleness The effects of idleness illustrated. Pr. 10. 4; 19. 15; 24. 30–34; 2 Th. 3. 11–12; 1 Tim. 5. 13. *See also* Pr. 12. 27; 13. 4; 18. 9; 20. 4, 13; 26. 14–16; Mt. 25. 14–30; Heb. 6. 12.

idol, idolatry Common in the ancient world where it was believed that the god represented lived in the idol. *See* Judg. 6. 25–32; 1 S. 5. 1–5. It was prohibited by Israelite laws and denounced by the prophets. Lev. 26. 1; Is. 10. 10–11; 44. 9–20. *See also* Ex. 20. 4; Is. 40. 18–20. The N.T. takes up and emphasizes this teaching. 1 Cor. 10. 19–21; Eph. 5. 5; Col. 3. 5; 1 Th. 1. 9. *See also* Rom. 1. 22; 1 Cor. 8. 4; 1 Jn. 5. 21.

ignorance In the O.T. inadvertence is regarded as a mitigating feature of sinful acts. *See* Nu. 15. 22–29; Lev. ch. 4–5. This is reflected in N.T. use. Ac. 17. 30; Eph. 4. 18; 1 Tim. 1. 13; 1 Pet. 1. 14; 2. 15.

illness For the Israelites, this was divine punishment caused by sin. *See* Ex. 4. 11; Dt. 7. 15; 28. 22; Job 2. 7; 7. 20; Jn. 5. 14; 9. 2. Specific illnesses mentioned. Lev. 13. 1–46; 26. 16; Nu. 5. 2; Dt. 28. 22, 27; 1 S. 25. 37; 1 K. 15. 23; Is. 32. 4; Mt. 9. 20; 17. 15; Mk. 7. 32; Lk. 5. 12; 6. 6; 8. 27; 13. 11; 14. 2; Jn. 5. 3; Ac. 12. 23.

Illyricum The Roman province on the E side of the Adriatic. Rom. 15. 19.

image The mental and moral attributes in which man resembles God. Blurred through sin, the image is restored in the redemption of Christ. Gen. 1. 26–27; Col. 1. 15; 3. 10. *See also* Gen. 5. 1; Rom. 8. 29; Eph. 4. 24; Heb. 1. 3; Jas. 3. 9. For manmade images *see* idol.

Imalcue An Arab to whom Alexander sent his son. 1 Mac. 11. 39.

Immanuel (Emmanuel) (= God is with us) The symbolic name given by Isaiah to the child whose birth he predicted. In the N.T. it is applied to Jesus. Is. 7. 14; Mt. 1. 21–24.

immortality There is no equivalent in the O.T. In the N.T. God alone is immortal; but death has been overcome through

Christ, and 'immortality' is given to man as a gift. Rom. 2. 7; 1 Cor. 15. 50–57; 1 Tim. 1. 17; 6. 16; 2 Tim. 1. 10.

incense (frankincense) Aromatic resins and spices burned in ceremonial worship and regarded as a symbol of prayer rising to God. Ex. 30. 1–9, 34; Ps. 141. 2; Is. 43. 23; Jer. 6. 20; Mt. 2. 11; Rev. 5. 8; 8. 3.

India That part of the country watered by the river Indus, and the E boundary of the empires of Ahasuerus, Artaxerxes and Darius. Est. 1. 1; 8. 9; 1 Esd. 3. 2; Rest of Est. 13. 1; 16. 1.

industry Commended in both O.T. and N.T. See Pr. 6. 6–11; 31. 10–28; Eph. 4. 28; 1 Th. 2. 9; 4. 11–12.

ingratitude A characteristic of the wicked. See Job 19. 13–16; Ps. 35. 12; 38. 20; Pr. 17. 13; Jer. 18. 20; 2 Cor. 12. 15; 2 Tim. 3. 2.

inheritance This is chiefly used in the O.T. in connection with the patrimony of Canaan. See Jos. 13. 33; Ps. 105. 8–45. Later the concept becomes broadened. Ps. 2. 8; 16. 5–11; 73. 26; Is. 19. 25. In the N.T. it is spiritualized and connected with the person and work of Christ. Heb. 6. 12; 1 Pet. 1. 4. See also Rom. 8. 14–17; Gal. 3. 29; 4. 7; Eph. 1. 13–14; Col. 1. 12; 3. 24; Heb. 1. 2; Rev. 21. 7. See heir.

ink This was made from smoke-black mixed with a gum solution to which water was added. Jer. 36. 18; 2 Cor. 3. 3; 3 Jn. 13. See also Nu. 5. 23.

inn A night resting-place, usually consisting of a number of small unfurnished rooms opening at one side on to a court and well. Lk. 10. 34. See also Jer. 9. 2; Lk. 2. 7.

innocent, innocence The word conveys the idea of being 'clean from guilt'. Job 4. 7; 9. 28; Ps. 19. 13; 26. 6; Jer. 2. 34; Mt. 10. 16; 27. 4.

inspire, inspiration The action of the Holy Spirit enabling men to give their witness to what God has revealed. 2 Tim. 3. 16. See also Mt. 16. 17; Jn. 16. 13; 2 Pet. 1. 21; 1 Jn. 1. 1–7.

intercession The duty of all Christians, and practised throughout the biblical record. See Gen. 18. 20–34; Ex. 32. 30–32; 1 S. 7.

7–9; Ps. 122. 6–9; Is. 53. 12; Lk. 23. 24; Jn. 17; 1 Tim. 2. 1–8; Jas. 5. 16.

interest See usury.

iron Most O.T. history falls within the Iron Age. Originally almost a Philistine monopoly, iron became available for ordinary purposes after David's conquests. Judg. 1. 19; 4. 13; 2 S. 23. 7; 2 K. 6. 6; Ps. 105. 18. See also 1 S. 13. 19–22.

irrigation This was not easy in Palestine because of the scarcity of wells. Dt. 11. 10. See also Is. 58. 11.

Isaac The only son of Abraham by Sarah and one of the three patriarchs who were the ancestors of the Hebrews. Gen. 17. 19; 21. 13; ch. 22; 24–27; 35. 28.

Isaiah The great evangelical prophet who received his call in the last year of Uzziah's reign and prophesied throughout those of Ahaz and Hezekiah. He applied certain basic principles to all problems. Judah was chosen by God and must therefore serve God. In this alone, and not in any political manoeuvrings, lay Judah's safety. Is. 1. 1; 6. 1; 7. 1–4; 8. 3; ch. 37–39.

Isaiah, Book of The themes are the righteousness of God and the necessity of faith; the coming of the Messiah and the deliverance he will bring; the need for a moral and religious reformation in Judah. It is quoted in the N.T. more than any other book.

Ishbosheth The son of Saul who succeeded him until he was murdered. 2 S. ch. 2–4.

Ishmael The son of Abraham by Hagar. Gen. 16. 15; 17. 23–27; 25. 17; 28. 9. See also Gen. 21. 14–21.

Ishmaelites A nomadic N Arabian people of mixed blood descended from Ishmael. Gen. 37. 25–28.

island(s) In the O.T. this usually means 'habitable land', or unknown territory at the end of the earth. Is. 41. 5; 66. 19; Jer. 31. 10; Ezek. 27. 15. It is used to emphasize God's rule. Ps. 97. 1; Is. 51. 5.

Israel, Israelite (1) The name given to Jacob. Gen. 32. 28. (2) The nation made up of his descendants Ex. 3. 16; and in a narrower sense the northern tribes 2 S. 19. 39–43; 1 K. 12; 2 K. 17; Ezr. 4. (3) Used in the N.T. of Christians as descendants of Abraham by faith. Rom. ch. 9–11; Gal. 6. 16. *See also* Gal. 3. 29.

Issachar The son of Jacob by Leah and the founder of the tribe. Gen. 30. 18; 35. 23; 49. 14; Jos. 19. 17.

Italy, Italian The country between the Alps and Messina of which Rome was the capital. Ac. 10. 1; 18. 2; 27. 1–2; Heb. 13 24. *See also* Ac. 28. 12–31.

Ittai The Gittite who supported David against Absalom. 2 S. 15. 18–23; 18. 2.

Ituraea The mountainous country NE of the Sea of Galilee. Lk. 3. 1.

ivory An imported source of wealth and a sign of luxury. 1 K. 10. 22; 22. 39; 2 Ch. 9. 17; Ps. 45. 8; S. of S. 5. 14; Ezek. 27. 15; Am. 6. 4; Rev. 18. 12.

Jabbok The river flowing into the Jordan 20 miles N of the Dead Sea. Gen. 32. 22–30; Judg. 11. 12–13. *Nahr ez-Zerqâ.*

Jabesh-gilead A town in the highlands E of the Jordan. Judg. 21. 8–14; 1 S. 11. 1–11; 31. 12; 2 S. 2. 4–7. *Tell Abū Kharâz.*

Jabin A Canaanite king defeated by Joshua. Jos. 11. 1–9; Judg. 4. 1–2, 23–24.

Jachin One of the two symbolic pillars in the porch of Solomon's Temple. 1 K. 7. 13–22. *See also* 2 K. 25. 13–17.

jackal Basically a night scavenger about the size of the fox, with a dirty-yellow coat, which goes about in packs. It is more typical of dry and desolate places than the fox, which likes some cover. Judg. 15. 3–5; Ps. 63. 10; S. of S. 2. 15; Lam 5. 18. Used figuratively Is. 13. 22.

Jacob The younger son of Isaac and Rebecca who received the promise of God that the covenant would continue in him and was given the name Israel. Gen. 25. 19 – 50. 13.

Jacob's Well A mile E of Shechem on the slope of Mt Ebal. Jn. 4. 3–15. *See also* Gen. 33. 18–20.

Jael The wife of Heber who murdered Sisera. Judg. 4. 15–22; 5. 24–27.

Jambrites The Arab tribe which kidnapped and killed John. 1 Mac. 9. 32–42.

James (1) The son of Zebedee. Mt. 4. 21; Mk. 5. 37; 9. 2; 10. 35–40; Lk. 9. 54; Ac. 12. 2. (2) The son of Alphaeus. Mt. 10. 3; Mk. 15. 40; Ac. 1. 13. (3) The brother of Jesus. Mt. 13. 55; Mk. 6. 3; Ac. 12. 17; Gal. 1. 19; 2. 9. *See also* Mk. 3. 21, 31; Jn. 7. 5.

James, Letter of A series of pithy, straightforward didactic sayings – and as such a good example of an ancient sermon – reflecting the style and teaching of the Sermon on the Mount, and laying stress on practical Christian living. It complements Paul's teaching on justification from this point of view.

Japheth One of the sons of Noah. Gen. 6. 10; 9. 18 – 10. 5.

Jashar, Book of Probably a collection of ballads. Jos. 10. 13; 2 S. 1. 18.

Jason (1) Paul's host at Thessalonica. Ac. 17. 5–9. (2) The brother of Onias whom he displaced as high priest only to be 'bought out' himself by Menelaus. 2 Mac. 4. 7–29. (3) An ambassador sent by Judas to Rome. 1 Mac. 8. 17–32.

jealousy Mainly used in the Bible to express zeal or intense devotion and linked to God's choice of Israel. Ex. 20. 5; Nu. 25. 10; Jos. 24. 19; 1 K. 14. 22; 2 Cor. 11. 2. *See also* Joel 2. 18.

Jebus The old name for the fortress of Jerusalem taken by David. Jos. 15. 63; 18. 28; Judg. 19. 10.

Jebusite(s) A Canaanite tribe. Gen. 10. 16; Jos. 18. 28; Judg. 19. 11; 2 S. 5. 6–8; 24. 16–24.

Jeconiah *See* Jehoiachin.

Jedidiah The name given to Solomon by Nathan. 2 S. 12. 24–25.

Jegar-sahadutha The cairn built by Laban in the N highlands of Gilead. Gen. 31. 45–48.

Jehoahaz (1) The son and successor of Jehu who had to face Syrian attacks on Israel. 2 K. 13. 1–9. (2) The son of Josiah, made king of Judah on his father's death but deposed by Pharaoh Necho and taken to Egypt. 2 K. 23. 30–34. Also called Shallum Jer. 22. 11; and Joachaz 1 Esd. 1. 34.

Jehoash The son and successor of Jehoahaz as king of Israel who stemmed the tide of Syrian aggression. 2 K. 13. 10 – 14. 17.

Jehoiachin The son and successor of Jehoiakim as king of Judah, taken prisoner to Babylon after a reign of only three months. 2 K. 24. 8–15; 25. 27–30. He is also called Jeconiah Est. 2. 6; Baruch 1. 3; and Coniah Jer. 22. 24–28.

Jehoiada A priest in Jerusalem at the time of Athaliah and Joash. 2 K. 11. 13–20; 12. 4–16; 2 Ch. 24. 15–22.

Jehoiakim (1) The son of Josiah and originally named Eliakim, he was placed on the throne by Pharaoh Necho. 2 K. 23. 34 – 24. 6; Jer. 22. 18–19; 26. 20–24; 36. 13–32. (2) The high priest to whom the exiles sent gifts for sacrifices. Baruch 1. 1–7.

Jehonadab The founder of the Rechabites and an ally of Jehu. 2 K. 10. 15–29.

Jehoram The son of Ahab who succeeded his brother, Ahaziah, as king of Israel, in whose reign there were hostilities with Edom and Syria. 2 K. 3. 1–25; 9. 14–26.

Jehoshaphat (1) The father of Jehu. 2 K. 9. 2, 14. (2) The son and successor of Asa as king of Judah who made an alliance with Israel. 1 K. 22. 2–50; 2 Ch. 19. 1 – 21. 1.

Jehovah The English rendering of the four Hebrew consonants YHWH, one of the names of God. Ex. 3. 15. Because of the commandment in Ex. 20. 7 the name was not pronounced on normal occasions but replaced in reading by Adonay (= my lord). The word Jehovah arose from the combination of the vowels of Adonay with the consonants YHWH.

Jehovah-jireh The name given by Abraham to the place where he prepared to sacrifice Isaac. Gen. 22. 14.

Jehu (1) One who prophesied against Baasha. 1 K. 16. 1–7; 2 Ch. 19. 1–3. (2) The founder of a dynasty of kings of Israel who seized the throne by violence. 2 K. 9. 1 – 10. 36.

Jephthah One of the most important Judges of Israel. Judg. 11. 1 – 12. 7; Heb. 11. 32.

jerboa One of the commonest of small mammals, familiarly known as the Desert Rat. It spends the day in burrows and comes out at night in search of seeds, fruits and roots. It seldom needs to drink. Lev. 11. 29. See also Is. 66. 17.

Jeremiah The young priest of Anathoth

called to prophesy in the reign of Josiah. A contemporary of Zephaniah and Habbakuk, he was a devoted patriot, but was persecuted for his unwelcome message about the impending captivity. After the fall of Jerusalem he chose, voluntarily, not to go to Babylon but to remain in Judah with the remnant. Against his will he was taken to Egypt after the murder of Gedaliah. Jer. ch. 1; 11; 25–26; 37–39; 43.

Jeremiah, Book of Of an intensely personal nature, the theme is that even if the Temple and its worship ceased to exist, personal religion could and must continue in the hearts of the Israelites.

Jeremiah, Letter of A short book of the Apocrypha which is a typical Hellenistic attack on idolatry in the guise of a letter written from Jeremiah to the exiles in Jerusalem. Idols are ridiculed and the evils and follies connected with them exposed.

Jericho An ancient city 17 miles ENE of Jerusalem and 6 miles from the Dead Sea, standing in a key position defending the Jordan valley. Its capture was essential for any further penetration into Canaan. Jos. 2. 1–21; 5. 10 – 6. 26; 1 K. 16. 34; 2 K. 2. 4–22; Mk. 10. 46–52; Lk. 10. 30–37; 19. 1–10. O.T. site Tell es-Sultân. N.T. site Tulûl Abû el-'Alayiq. Excavations by J. Garstang 1930–36 and K. Kenyon 1952–58 have uncovered remains which throw great light on Abraham's Canaanite and Amorite town-dwelling neighbours. Splendid pottery, wooden tables, stools and beds, trinket boxes with bone inlay, basketry, metal daggers and bracelets have been found. The remains of the Jericho of the 9th to 6th centuries B.C. are fragmentary but quite definite.

Jeroboam (1) Jeroboam I, the leader of the discontent against Solomon, crowned king over the ten northern tribes. He made the shrines of Bethel and Dan into royal sanctuaries. 1 K. 11. 26–40; 12. 20 – 13. 10; 13. 33 – 14. 20, 30. (2) Jeroboam II, the son of Joash, in whose reign Israel prospered but the accompanying social and religious evils were denounced by the prophets. 2 K. 14. 23–29; Hos. 1. 1; Am. 1. 1.

Jerusalem On a rocky plateau 2723 feet above sea level, 30 miles E of the Mediterranean and 14 miles W of the Dead Sea; access to the city on the E, S and W is hampered by deep ravines. The original site was called Ophel (Jebus) and occupied by the Jebusites. From the time of its occupation by David, it became the heart of the history and religion of the O.T. 2 S. 5. 6–12; 1 K. ch. 5–9; Ps. 122; 125; 128; 137; 147; Is. 52. 1–2; 62. 1–11; 65. 18–25; Mt. 5. 35; 23. 37–39; Lk. 21. 20–24; 24. 44–49; Ac. 1. 8; Rom. 15. 19; Gal. 4. 26; Rev. 21. 2. *See also* Ps. 48; 87.

Jeshua The son of Jozadak and high priest in Jerusalem after the exile. Ezr. 3. 1–13.

Jesse The father of David. Ru. 4. 17; 1 S. 16; Is. 11. 1–10; Rom. 15. 12.

Jesus The Greek form of the Hebrew 'Joshua' (= God saves). Mt. 1. 1–25; Lk. 1. 26–38; 2. 21–40; Jn. 20. 31.

Jesus ben Sirach *See* Ecclesiasticus.

Jethro The priest-shepherd of a Midianite tribe, and father-in-law of Moses. Ex. 3. 1; 18. 1–27. *See also* Ex. 2. 16–22.

Jew(s) A member of the Hebrew race. The word was used especially, during and after the exile, of those who had gone from and returned to Judaea. Jn. 4. 22; Rom. 1. 16; 1 Th. 2. 14.

jewel, jewellery This was used for personal adornment, especially in connection with marriage ceremonies and religious festivals. *See* Gen. 24. 22–23; Ex. 32. 3; Pr. 25. 11–12; Is. 3. 18–23; Ezek. 16. 11–13.

Jezebel The daughter of Ethbaal of Sidon who married Ahab and promoted Baal worship in Israel. 1 K. 16. 31; 18. 4; 19. 1–2; 21. 5–15, 23–25; 2 K. 9. 30–37; Rev. 2. 20.

Jezreel (1) A city on a spur of Mt Gilboa. 1 K. 18. 45; 21. 1; 2 K. 9. 15–26. (2) Hosea's eldest son. Hos. 1. 4.

Jezreel, Vale of The only break of any size in the range of hills running the length of Palestine to the W of the Jordan, and the key to the whole area. Also known as the Plain of Esdraelon. Jos. 17. 16.

Joab The son of Zeruiah and David's ruthless commander-in-chief who murdered Abner and had Absalom killed. 2 S.

2. 12–32; 3. 22–32; 8. 16; 11. 6–25; 12. 26–29; 18. 5 – 19. 3; 1 K. 2. 5, 28–34.

Joash The son and successor of Ahaziah as king of Judah who reigned for forty years. 2 K. 11. 1–3; 12. 1–21.

Job The central figure of the book of Job. A pious and prosperous man who was accused by Satan of being pious because it paid. He is put to incredible tests but bears them all with patience, denying the accusations of his three friends that he has brought his sufferings on himself. Job ch. 1; 2; 3–31; 32; 38; 42; Ezek. 14. 14, 20; Jas. 5. 11.

Job, Book of Largely a poem from Israel's Wisdom literature which grapples with the problem of why the good suffer. It teaches that, although the purposes and causes of suffering are not always clear, suffering can strengthen character and enrich personality. Man cannot always understand God's justice which will be perfected in eternity, but God does reveal enough to enable man to trust; and he also provides the strength to endure.

Joel, Book of The background is a vivid picture, largely in poetic form, of a plague of locusts, regarded by the prophet as a punishment for sin and a preview of the day of the LORD. This causes him to urge national repentance and to predict a more terrible judgement. Joel's greatest contribution to Christian thought is his teaching of the outpouring of the Spirit on all mankind. *See* Ac. 2. 14–21.

John (1) The son of Mattathias, surnamed Gaddis, who was murdered by the Jamnites. 1 Mac. 2. 2; 9. 35–42. (2) The son of Simon, who succeeded Jonathan as high priest of the Jews. He is known as John Hyrcanus. 1 Mac. 16. 2–24.

John, the Apostle The son of Zebedee and the brother of James. Mt. 4. 21; 17. 1; Mk. 3. 16–19; 14. 33; Lk. 8. 51; Ac. 3. 1 – 4. 31; 8. 14–25. *See also* Jn. 13. 23; 19. 26; 20. 1–9; 21. 1–24.

John the Baptist The cousin and forerunner of Jesus. Mt. 3. 1–15; 11. 2–19; 14. 1–12; Lk. 1. 5–25, 57–80; Jn. 1. 19–37; Ac. 18. 25; 19. 3.

John, First Letter of A family letter reassuring its readers that Jesus had truly come in the flesh and died for them, and that loving one another is the real test of true discipleship.

John, Second Letter of This echoes the teaching of the First Letter, warning against false teachers who endanger the Christian faith by preaching only certain aspects of it.

John, Third Letter of This gives a glimpse of an early church with its worthy members and a too ambitious official. It commends hospitality to travelling missionaries.

John, Gospel of The theme is given in 20. 31 which explains why the full sweep of Jesus's ministry is not covered. Intended primarily as a clarification and explanation of the other Gospels, it assumes a knowledge of what Jesus did. Its message is driven home by the great themes of light, life, love, truth, and the Father-relationship which are developed by means of signs 2. 1–11, and conversations 3. 1–21. New material is included ch. 13–17, and where Synoptic material is used 6. 3–58, a new and spiritual element is usually added.

Jonadab David's nephew. 2 S. 13. 1–5, 32–33.

Jonah (1) The prophet, son of Amittai, who was sent to Nineveh much against his will and, after being shipwrecked, converted the city. Jon. ch. 1–4. (2) The father of Simon Peter. Mt. 16. 17.

Jonah, Book of The outstanding missionary book of the O.T. Through a personal life story it foreshadows the subsequent history of the nation of Israel, and shows God's love even for the Gentiles. *See also* Mt. 12. 38–41.

Jonathan (1) The son of Saul who became a close friend of David. 1 S. 14. 1–15, 24–46; 18. 1–4; 19. 1–7; 20; 31. 2; 2 S. 1. 17–27. (2) The son of Mattathias, surnamed Apphus, who succeeded Judas in the leadership of the Jews. He became high priest, and by his skill in playing off the rivals for the Syrian throne he advanced the fortunes of the Jews. 1 Mac. 9. 29–49; 10. 3–21; 12. 39–52.

Joppa The chief harbour of SW Palestine. Jos. 19. 46; Jon. 1. 3; Ac. 9. 36–43; 10. 4 – 11. 17. *Jaffa.*

Joram The son and successor of Jehoshaphat as king of Judah who married Athaliah. 2 K. 8. 16–24; 2 Ch. 21. 12–20.

Jordan (= the descender) The longest river in Palestine. Rising 1200 feet above sea level near Caesarea Philippi, it flows through the Sea of Galilee to the Dead Sea, much of its course below sea level. Jos. 3. 9–17; Judg. 12. 5–6; 2 K. 2. 4–14; 5. 9–14; Jer. 12. 5; Mt. 3. 4–6; Lk. 4. 1.

Joseph (1) The eleventh son of Jacob and Rachel, through whom the whole of his father's clan came to settle in Egypt. Gen. 30. 22–24; ch. 37–50. (2) The husband of Mary. Mt. 1. 18 – 2. 22; Lk. 2. 1–16; 3. 23. *See also* Mt. 13. 55. (3) The brother of Jesus. Mt. 13. 55; Mk. 6. 3. (4) The son of Mary. Mt. 27. 56; Mk. 15. 40.

Joseph Barsabbas One of the two put forward to fill the place of Judas Iscariot. Ac. 1. 23–26.

Joseph of Arimathaea The secret disciple of Jesus who buried his body. Mt. 27. 57–60; Lk. 23. 50–53.

Josephus An officer under Judas who was defeated by Gorgias. 1 Mac. 5. 18, 55–62.

Joshua The successor to Moses who led the Israelites into the Promised Land. Ex. 17. 9; Nu. 27. 18–23; Jos. ch. 1–24.

Joshua, Book of It describes the conquest of Canaan under Moses' successor and its division between the 12 tribes. It shows clearly how God's promises were fulfilled and how he remains faithful to his covenant though his people may fail in complete obedience.

Josiah The son and successor of Amon as king of Judah whose reign was marked by religious reforms. 2 K. 21. 24; 22. 3 – 23. 30; 2 Ch. 33. 24 – 35. 27.

Jotham (1) The youngest son of Gideon (Jerubaal). Judg. 9. 5–21. (2) The regent in the reign of Uzziah and his successor as king of Judah. 2 K. 15. 5, 32–38; 2 Ch. 27 1–9.

Journey, Sabbath Day's *See* Sabbath Day's Journey.

joy In both the O.T. and the N.T. it is a quality grounded on and derived from God himself, and it is consistently the mark of both the individual believer and the corporate fellowship. Ps. 16. 11; 104.

42

34; 137. 6; Is. 35. 2; 51. 11; Zeph. 3. 17; Lk. 2. 10; 15. 10; Jn. 15. 11; Ac. 2. 42–47; Rom. 14. 17; Gal. 5. 22.

jubilee The fiftieth year, or the one after seven 'sabbaths of years'. It was a year of freedom and deliverance to the poor and rest for all Israel. Lev. 25. 8–55; 27. 17; Nu. 36. 4.

Judaea The Greek and Roman name for Judah. Used for the whole country but more commonly for the southern region of Palestine. Lk. 23. 5.

Judah (1) The fourth son of Leah and Joseph and founder of the tribe. Gen. 29. 35; 49. 8; 1 Ch. 5. 2. (2) The kingdom formed when the monarchy divided and to which the exiles returned. Though small, some fifty miles by fifty, its capital was Jerusalem and it was the scene of the most important events in Christ's ministry.

Judas (1) An apostle. Lk. 6. 16; Jn. 14. 22. (2) The brother of Jesus. Mt. 13. 55. (3) A Galilean rebel leader. Ac. 5. 37. (4) A Damascus Jew with whom Paul stayed. Ac. 9. 11. (5) Barsabbas. Ac. 15. 22–33. (6) The son of Mattathias, and surnamed Maccabaeus, who commanded the army against Antiochus. His battles and career are recorded in 1 Mac. 2. 4, 66; 3. 1 – 9. 22; 2 Mac. 8. 5 – 15. 36. (7) The son of Simon who was murdered by Ptolemy. 1 Mac. 16. 2–17.

Judas Iscariot The treasurer of the Twelve and the traitor who betrayed Jesus. Mt. 26. 14–25; 27. 3–10; Jn. 6. 71; 12. 4–8; 13. 21–30; 18. 1–6; Ac. 1. 15–20. See also Lk. 22. 21–23; Jn. 13. 10–11.

Jude, Letter of Written to condemn false teachers of a particularly dangerous and immoral type who were endangering the fellowship of a group of churches.

Judgement Day From the conviction that everything is subject to God's rule and control, the O.T. prophets were convinced that one day the whole world would show the perfection of God's rule. The judgement of God would mean the demonstration of God's might and glory; salvation for the faithful; and condemnation for the wicked. See Is. 2. 12–22; Dan. 12. 1–4; Joel 1. 15; 2. 1–14; Am. 5. 18–20; 9. 11. The N.T. says that it will come 'at the end

of time' and that Christ will be the judge. Mt. 13. 36–43; 25. 31–46; Mk. 13. 14–36; Jn. 5. 22; 2 Cor. 5. 10; Rev. 20. 11–15.

Judges Local hero-leaders who sprang into prominence in the early days of the settlement in Canaan because of their military skill and their ability to rally the Israelite forces when a crisis arose. The exploits of 13 of them are described in the book of Judges.

Judges, Book of This handles the historical material from the death of Joshua to the time of Samuel, showing the recurring cycle of rebellion, retribution, repentance and restoration; and how confusion exists when people follow their own whims instead of responsible leadership. See Judges.

Judith, Book of A book of the Apocrypha, written originally in Hebrew about 150 B.C. The heroine is a young Jewish widow who, by her guile, helped to save the city of Bethulia when it was attacked by Holophernes.

juniper A form of white broom which grows wild in Palestine in the form of a dense bush, sometimes reaching 12 feet. Jer. 17. 6.

Jupiter The chief god in the Roman mythology. Ac. 14. 8–18. See 2 Mac. 6. 2.

justice One aspect of the righteousness of God who is completely fair and impartial Gen. 18. 25; Is. 30. 18; Jas. 1. 17. As the source of all human justice Ex. 20. 1–17; Ps. 25. 8; 86. 11, he demands that man shall practise it in his dealings with his fellows Is. 1. 17, 27; Am. 5. 24; Mic. 6. 8. An even higher standard is demanded in the N.T., and this is made possible by the new relationship with God established for him by Christ. Mt. 5. 20–48; Jn. 1. 17.

justification, justify This relates to man's status as a sinner before God, and the relationship he may enter into with him through Christ. See Rom. ch. 3–5; Gal. ch. 2–3.

Kabzeel A town in S Judah and the birthplace of Benaiah. 2 S. 23. 20–21.

Kadesh, Kadesh-barnea An oasis in the wilderness of Zin 70 miles E of Hebron where Miriam died. Nu. 13. 26; 20. 1–22; 27. 14; Dt. 1. 19–24. 'Ain Qedeirât.

Kandake The title of the rulers of Ethiopia. Ac. 8. 26–27.

Karkor The place, in Ammonite territory, where Gideon defeated Zebah and Zalmunna. Judg. 8. 10–12.

Kebar A river in Babylonia where a colony of Jewish exiles lived, and the scene of Ezekiel's visions. Ezek. ch. 1; 3. 23; 10. 15–22; 43. 1–3.

Kedar (1) The son of Ishmael. Gen. 25. 13. (2) The Bedouin tribe descended from him. Ps. 120. 5; S. of S. 1. 5; Is. 42. 11; 60. 7; Ezek. 27. 21.

Kedesh A fortified Canaanite town. Jos. 20. 7; 21. 32; Judg. 4. 6–10; 2 K. 15. 29. *Tell Qades.*

Kedorlaomer The king of Elam defeated by Abraham. Gen. 14. 1–7.

Kedron A place fortified by Kendebaeus to which he fled. 1 Mac. 15. 39–41; 16. 9.

Keilah A town in the lowland of Judah. 1 S. 23. 1–13.

Kemosh The god of the Moabites whose worship was introduced into Jerusalem by Solomon. Nu. 21. 29; 1 K. 11. 7, 33; 2 K. 23. 13; Jer. 48. 13. *See also* 2 K. 3. 27.

Kendebaeus A commander under Antiochus who was sent against Simon and was defeated by him. 1 Mac. 15. 38 – 16. 10.

Kenites A Midianite tribe closely connected with Judah and the Rechabites. Judg. 1. 16; 4. 11; 1 Ch. 2. 55.

Kerethites Mercenaries who formed the core of David's standing army. 1 S. 30. 14; 2 S. 8. 18; 20. 7, 23.

Kerith The brook, E of the Jordan, where Elijah lived. 1 K. 17. 1–7. *Wâdi Yâbis.*

Keturah The wife Abraham married after Sarah's death. Gen. 25. 1–4.

key(s) In O.T. times a piece of wood with pins fixed along the side. Judg. 3. 25. Used figuratively as a symbol of authority. Is. 22. 22; Mt. 16. 19; Rev. 1. 18.

Keziah The daughter of Job. Job 42. 14.

Kibroth-hattaavah A stopping-place in the wilderness where the people were punished by a plague. Nu. 11. 31–34; Dt. 9. 22.

kid Gen. 27. 9; 1 S. 16. 20; Is. 11. 6. *See* goat.

kidnap The kidnapping of an Israelite was punishable by death. Ex. 21. 16; Dt. 24. 7.

kidney Regarded as the most precious part of the victim and, therefore, reserved for God in burnt-offerings. Ex. 29. 13; Lev. 3. 4; 4. 9; 7. 4.

Kidron The torrent valley running along the E side of Jerusalem and extending to the Dead Sea. 2 S. 15. 23; 1 K. 15. 13; 2 K. 23. 4–6. *See also* Jn. 18. 1. *Wâdis el-Jawz, Sitti Maryam, el-Qeini.*

kin, kinsman One who shares the same race or family and so has certain privileges and obligations. Lev. 25. 25–28; Nu. 35. 9–12; Ru. ch. 2–4; Jer. 32. 8–10.

kingdom of God, kingdom of Heaven That condition of human life in which the will of God as revealed in Jesus Christ is in complete control. It is the theme of Jesus's teaching and the subject of many parables. Mt. 13. 1–52; Mk. 1. 15. Entry is by the new birth, and men belong to it if they accept and obey him. Mt. 12. 28; Mk. 10. 15; Lk. 6. 20; 17. 20–37. Yet there is a sense in which it is still in the future. Mt. 8. 11; Mk. 14. 25; Lk. 18. 28–30.

kings The need for centralized government was felt only after the nomadic tribes settled in Canaan and had to withstand attacks. Saul was the first king. Besides being the chief general, the king was supreme judge, leader of worship, and was regarded as God's representative, though still subject to his laws. 1 S. 8. 4–22; 10. 1, 24; 11. 12–15; 2 S. 2. 1–4; 5. 1–5; 12. 1–12.

Kings, First Book of Originally one unit with 2 Kings, this book traces Israel's history from David to Ahab's death, and shows that most kings turned their back on God in spite of the covenant.

Kings, Second Book of This records the history of the Jewish people from the deaths of Ahab and Jehoshaphat until a few years after the Babylonian Captivity. The great theme of the O.T. that obedience to God and his covenant will bring blessing, and disobedience only punishment, is dramatically illustrated.

King's Garden An open space in Jerusalem close to the Pool of Siloam. 2 K. 25. 4; Neh. 3. 15; Jer. 39. 4; 52. 7.

King's Highway An ancient caravan route, marked by Early Bronze Age settlements and Roman milestones, running from the

Gulf of Aqaba to Syria, passing through the hill-country E of the Jordan valley. Nu. 20. 17; 21. 22; Dt. 2. 27.

Kinnereth A city in Naphtali which gave its name to the sea of Kinnereth (Galilee). Nu. 34. 10–12; Jos. 19. 35.

Kiriath-jearim (= city of forests) A Gibeonite frontier town. Jos. 9. 17; 15. 9; 18. 14; Judg. 18. 12; 1 S. 6. 21 – 7. 2; Neh. 7. 29; Jer. 26. 20–22.

Kish (1) The father of Saul. 1 S. 9. 1; 14. 51; Ac. 13. 21. (2) An ancestor of Mordecai. Est. 2. 5.

Kishon A seasonal river flowing through the plain of Esdraelon to enter the Mediterranean near Haifa. Judg. 4. 7, 13; 5. 21; 1 K. 18. 40. *Nahr el-Mukatta'.*

kiss The customary salutation of affection or respect given on the cheek or neck, or the feet as a mark of the greatest reverence. Gen. 27. 26; 29. 13; 48. 10; Ru. 1. 14; 2 S. 15. 5; Mt. 26. 49; Lk. 7. 38; Ac. 20. 37; Rom. 16. 16; 1 Pet. 5. 14.

kitchen In an Israelite house meals were prepared outside in the courtyard or in its single room. Kitchens are mentioned only in the Temple. Ezek. 46. 24.

kite Both black and red species of this bird are known in Palestine, and they are said to have remarkably keen vision. Lev. 11. 14; Dt. 14. 13; Is. 34. 15.

Kittim The son of Javan whose descendants settled in Cyprus and whose name came to apply to the islands and coastlands of the E Mediterranean. Gen. 10. 5; Nu. 24. 24; Is. 23. 1, 12; Jer. 2. 10; Ezek. 27. 6. It stands for Greece or Macedonia in 1 Mac. 1. 1.

kneading-trough A large shallow bowl of pottery or wood in which dough was prepared. Ex. 8. 3; 12. 34; Dt. 28. 5, 17.

knee, kneel An action expressing homage, worship or prayer. 1 K. 19. 18; 2 K. 1. 13; Dan. 6. 10; Mk. 1. 40; 10. 17; 15. 19; Ac. 7. 60; 9. 40; 21. 5; Rom. 11. 4; 14. 11; Eph. 3. 14; Phil. 2. 10.

knife Excavations have revealed many sharp-edged cutting-instruments made of flint and metal. Gen. 22. 6; Jos. 5. 2; Jer. 36. 23.

know, knowledge Conceived by the Hebrews as making demands on the will as well as on the understanding. Ps. 139; Jer. 1. 5; 8. 7; 24. 7; 31. 34; Hos. 13. 4; 1 Cor. 13. 12; 1 Tim. 2. 4; 2 Tim. 2. 19; 3. 7; Tit. 1. 1. See also Job 28. 20–28.

Kohath, Kohathites The son of Levi who gave his name to a section of the Levites. Gen. 46. 11; Ex. 6. 16–18; 2 Ch. 20. 19.

Korah (1) The son of Esau. Gen. 36. 4–5. (2) The leader of a revolt against Moses. Nu. 16. 1–33.

Laban Rebecca's brother. Gen. ch. 29–31.

labour Regarded as honourable in Hebrew society, and idleness was condemned. Gen. 3. 17; Ex. 20. 8; Ps. 104. 23; 128. 2; Pr. 10. 16. See also Dt. 24. 14; Pr. 6. 6; 1 Th. 4. 11.

Lachish A stronghold 30 miles SW of Jerusalem dominating the Palestine–Egypt route. 2 K. 14. 19; 18. 14–17; 2 Ch. 11. 9; Neh. 11. 30; Is. 36. 2; 37. 8. *Tell ed-Duweir.* Excavations by the Wellcome-Marston expedition (J. Starkey) 1932–38 showed that the site had been occupied from at least the Early Bronze Age and had become a military fortress by about 1650 B.C. Fortifications dating from the time of Rehoboam or earlier have been uncovered.

Lachish Letters In 1935 eighteen ostraca inscribed in Hebrew of the time of Jeremiah were found in a small guardroom under the gate-tower of Lachish. As well as being the earliest known copies of documents in classical Hebrew yet discovered, they throw light on the conditions prevailing during the Babylonian attack made at the time of the siege of Jerusalem 589–587 B.C.

Laish The original name of Dan. Judg. 18. 7–10. See also Jos. 19. 47.

lamb Frequently referred to from earliest times in connection with sacrifice. In fact, no Hebrew festival took place without the offering of a lamb. Ex. 12. 3–10; Dt. 32. 14; Am. 6. 4. See also Ex. 29. 38–42; Lev. 4. 32–35. Used of Christ in the N.T. Jn. 1. 29–36; Ac. 8. 32; Rev. 5. 6–12.

Lamb of God The title given to Jesus by John the Baptist. Jn. 1. 29-36. See also Is. 53. 7; 1 Cor. 5. 7; Rev. 5. 6; 12. 11; 17. 14.

Lamech (1) A descendant of Cain. Gen. 4. 19–24. (2) The father of Noah. Gen. 5. 25–31.

lameness A common affliction but a bar from the priesthood. Lev. 21. 17; 2 S. 4. 4; 9. 13. Jesus healed many cripples. Mt. 11. 5; 15. 30; Lk. 14. 13. Used figuratively Job 29. 15; Is. 35. 6; Mt. 18. 8.

Lamentations, Book of A supplement to the book of Jeremiah; and quite literally a lamenting over Judah's sins and the subsequent destruction she suffered as the judgement of God.

lamp Originally a clay saucer containing oil which fed a flax or rush wick, it developed into a closed bowl with a hole for the oil, a spout for the wick, and a handle. It was used both domestically and in worship. Ex. 27. 20; 30. 7; Lev. 24. 2–4; 2 K. 4. 10; Pr. 31. 18; Mt. 5. 15; Lk. 11. 33; 15. 8. Used figuratively Ps. 119. 105; Mt. 6. 22; Lk. 12. 35; Rev. 21. 23; 22. 5.

lamp-stand Ex. 25. 31–40; 1 K. 7. 49; 1 Ch. 28. 15; 2 Ch. 4. 20; Zech. 4. 2; Mt. 5. 15; Mk. 4. 21.

language(s) The family of Semitic languages spoken in O.T. Palestine were as numerous as the peoples. The Israelites originally spoke Hebrew which remained the literary language, but in everyday conversation Aramaic later replaced it. Gen. 11. 1–9; Ezr. 4. 7; Ac. 2. 5–11.

Laodicea An important commercial centre in the Lycus valley in Asia Minor. Col. 2. 1; 4. 13–16; Rev. 3. 14–22. *Eski Hisar.*

Lappidoth The husband of Deborah. Judg. 4. 4.

Lasea A town in Crete. Ac. 27. 8.

Latin The official language of Roman-occupied Palestine. Jn. 19. 20.

laugh Sometimes mentioned in a purely joyful sense. Ps. 126. 2; Eccles. 3. 4; Lk. 6. 21. More generally, however, it is associated with scorn or scepticism. Gen. 18. 11–15; Ps. 2. 4; 37. 13; Mk. 5 40.

law Specifically the Pentateuch containing the Mosaic codes. Ex. 20. 1–17; ch. 21–23; 25.1–31. 17; ch. 35–40; Lev. ch.17–26; Dt. ch. 12–26. For the N.T. teaching on the law Mt. 5. 17–48; 22. 35–40; Jn. 13. 34; Rom. 2. 14; 7. 22; 8. 3; 13. 7–10;

Gal. 2. 16 – 3. 25; 6. 2; Heb. 10. 1–18; Jas. 2. 8–13.

lawyers In pre-exilic times, primarily priests by profession, they served as secretaries handling correspondence and book-keeping for the king. *See* 2 K. 12. 10 Later, they began copying the law and various sacred writings. Ezr. 7. 11. Gradually they separated themselves from the priestly class and became official interpreters of both the written and oral law. They are also called 'doctors of the law' and 'scribes'. Mt. 23. 1–32; Lk. 7. 30; 10. 25; 11. 43–54. *See also* Ecclus. 39. 1–11.

laying on of hands A symbolic act of dedication transferring blessing, power or authority. Gen. 48. 14; Dt. 34. 9; Mt. 9. 18; Mk. 6. 5; 10. 16; 16. 18; Lk. 13. 13; Ac. 6. 6; 8. 17; 13. 3; 19. 6; 1 Tim. 4. 14; 2 Tim. 1. 6.

Lazarus (1) The brother of Martha and Mary. Jn. 11. 1–44. (2) The beggar in a parable. Lk. 16. 19–31.

lead The main sources of this metal were the Sinai peninsula, Egypt and Tarshish. Nu. 31. 22–23; Job 19. 24; Jer. 6. 29; Ezek. 27. 12; Zech. 5. 7. Used figuratively Ezek. 22. 18.

Leah The elder daughter of Laban. Gen. 29. 16 – 30. 21; 49. 31.

leather The skin of animals prepared for use as clothing. 2 K. 1. 8; Mt. 3. 4. Also used as a writing material. *See* Dead Sea Scrolls.

leaven A substance which causes fermentation when added to dough. Ex. 12. 14–20; 23. 18; Lev. 2. 11. Used figuratively Mt. 13. 33; Mk. 8. 15; 1 Cor. 5. 6.

Lebanon The mountain mass, 100 miles long and averaging 7000 feet in height, in N Palestine; famed for its snowy peaks and cedars, and the source of the Jordan. Jos. 13. 6; 1 K. 5. 9; 2 Ch. 2. 8; Ps. 92. 12; S. of S. 4. 8, 15; Jer. 18. 14.

Lebbaeus An apostle, also known as Thaddaeus and Judas. Mt. 10. 4; Mk. 3. 18; Lk. 6. 16; Ac. 1. 13.

leech This blood-sucking and tenacious worm, which fastens on to the skin, was abundant in Palestine before the swamps were drained. Pr. 30. 15.

leek A common and popular vegetable, resembling the onion, which is also used for medicinal purposes. Nu. 11. 5.

legion A division of the Roman army totalling 6000 men. It is used in the N.T. for any very large number. Mt. 26. 53; Mk. 5. 1–17.

Lemuel The king of Massa. Pr. 31. 1–9.

lentil A cereal which grows freely in Palestine, looking something like a pea. Gen. 25. 34; 2 S. 23. 11; Ezek. 4. 9.

leopard Well known over most of Palestine in biblical times, this large spotted carnivore can reach a body length of up to 5 feet. Its ability to hide in the scantiest cover has helped it to survive in the Fertile Crescent. S. of S. 4. 8; Jer. 5. 6; 13. 23; Hos. 13. 7. Used symbolically Is. 11. 6; Dan. 7. 6; Rev. 13. 2.

leper, leprosy Used in the Bible of skin diseases which are deep-seated, spreading or chronic and require isolation. 2 K. 5. 1–14; 7. 3; 2 Ch. 26. 19; Mt. 8. 2–4; Lk. 17. 11–19.

Levi (1) The son of Jacob and Leah, and ancestor of the priestly tribe. Gen. 29. 34; 49. 5; Ex. 6. 16; Dt. 33. 8–10. (2) An ancestor of Jesus. Lk. 3. 24. (3) Another name for Matthew. Mk. 2. 14.

Leviathan A transliteration of a Hebrew root (= gathering itself in folds). The context of its use in the O.T. suggests some form of sea monster. Ps. 74. 12–14; Is. 27. 1.

levirate marriage See Dt. 25. 5–10; Mt. 22. 23–30.

Levites Descendants of Levi who became the priestly tribe. Nu. 1. 47–53; Judg. 17. 7–13. After the exile, those not descended from Aaron became an inferior order. Ezek. 44. 10 – 45. 5.

Leviticus, Book of Written to make clear to the Israelites what it means to live a holy life, and that the proper way to come to God is through sacrifice. Laws designed for holy living are coupled with technical instructions to the priesthood.

liberty The essence of Christian liberty, found in Christ, lies in its freedom from the bondage of sin. 2 Cor. 3. 17; Gal. 2. 4. See also Lk. 4. 18; Jn. 8. 31–36; Rom. 6.

20–23; 8. 3–17; Gal. 5. 1, 13; 1 Pet. 2. 16; 2 Pet. 2. 19; Jas. 2. 12.

Libnah A Canaanite city near Lachish. Jos. 10. 29–31; 12. 14; 15. 42.

lie, lying God is, above all, a God of truth, and any attempts to veil or suppress the truth are unworthy of the people of God. Nu. 23. 19; Pr. 19. 22; 21. 28; 30. 8; Jer. 14. 14; Hos. 7. 13; Mic. 6. 12; Jn. 8. 44; Ac. 5. 3; Col. 3. 9. See also Lev. 19. 11; Dt. 19. 16–19; Jn. 17. 17.

life Thought of in the O.T. as the gift of God, and believed to be in the blood by the early Hebrews. Gen. 2. 7; Ps. 27. 1; 36. 9; 91. 16. In the N.T. it has a spiritual meaning and is shown to be the real life lived in fellowship with God now, and not interrupted by death; though its perfection is in the life to come. Mt. 6. 25; Jn. 1. 4; 3. 36; 5. 24–26; 14. 6; 17. 3; 20. 31; Rom. 2. 7; 8. 6; 2 Pet. 1. 3; 1 Jn. 3. 14; 5. 12.

light The O.T. associates it closely with God. Gen. 1. 3; Ps. 104. 2; Is. 2. 5; 10. 17. In the N.T. Jesus is called the 'light of the world', as are also his followers. Mt. 5. 14; Jn. 1. 4; 8. 12.

lightning Associated in the Bible as a symbol of God's power. Ex. 19. 16; 20. 18; Job 38. 35; Ps. 18. 14; 144. 6; Ezek. 1. 13; Dan. 10. 6; Nah. 2. 5; Zech. 9. 14; Mt. 28. 3; Lk. 10. 18; Rev. 4. 5; 8. 5; 16. 18.

Lights, Feast of See Dedication.

likeness Used by biblical writers as almost identical with 'image'. Gen. 1. 26; 2 Cor. 3. 18. See also Eph. 4. 24; Col. 3. 10.

lilies Bulbous plants abounding in Palestine in numerous varieties, but not specified in the Bible. They probably included the iris and lotus, and possibly the anemone. S. of S. 2. 1; Ecclus. 50. 8; Mt. 6. 28.

limestone Abundant in Palestine and burned to produce lime for plastering. See Dt. 27. 2; Dan. 5. 5; Am. 2. 1; Mt. 23. 27.

linen A material prepared from the fibre of flax, well known in the ancient world and a mark of quality. The dead were usually wrapped in it. Ex. 28. 4–8; 35. 25; 2 Ch. 3. 14; 5. 12; Mt. 27. 59; Mk. 14. 51; Lk. 16. 19; Jn. 20. 3–7; Rev. 19. 8, 14.

lintel The horizontal beam above a doorway. Ex. 12. 21–23.

Linus A Christian at Rome. 2 Tim. 4. 21.

lion Throughout O.T. times these were widespread in Palestine, and common enough to be some danger to both humans and their stock. They are mentioned over one hundred times. Judg. 14. 5–6; 1 S. 17. 34–36; 1 K. 13. 23–26; Job 38. 38–40; Dan. 6. 1–24; Heb. 11. 33. Used figuratively Ps. 7. 2; 10. 9; 22. 13, 21; Pr. 26. 13; 2 Tim. 4. 17; Rev. 5. 5.

lizard The most conspicuous vertebrates in Palestine, other than birds, numbering some 40 species and ranging in size from 2 feet down to about 2 inches. Lev. 11. 29–30; Pr. 30. 28.

loaf(ves) Mt. 15. 32–38; Mk. 8. 1–9; 1 Cor. 10. 17.

Lo-ammi The symbolic name given to Hosea's third child. Hos. 1. 9; 2. 23.

loan In early times these were made only for personal need. Interest was forbidden until trading methods changed in N.T. times. Lev. 25. 35–38; Dt. 24. 10–13. *See also* Ex. 22. 25; Dt. 28. 12; Ps. 15. 5; 37. 21; Mt. 25. 27; Lk. 19. 23.

locust One of the most important insects in the Bible with over fifty mentions. It breeds in the Middle East and swarms can form clouds large enough to obscure the sun and strip trees and crops of all their leaves. Some species were, and are, eaten as a great delicacy and source of protein. Ex. 10. 3–5; Lev. 11. 20–22; Is. 33. 4; Joel 1. 4; Mt. 3. 4.

Lo-debar A town in Gilead E of Jordan. 2 S. 9. 1–5; 17. 27.

Lois The grandmother of Timothy. 2 Tim. 1. 5.

longsuffering The loving patience of God to men which must also be theirs in dealing with their fellows. Nu. 14. 18. *See also* Ex. 34. 6; Rom. 2. 4; 3. 25; 9. 22; 2 Cor. 6. 6; Gal. 5. 22; 2 Pet. 3. 8–9.

LORD *See* Jehovah.

LORD of Hosts A title for God, used especially by the prophets, showing that he is at all times the saviour and protector of his people. 1 S. 1. 3; 17. 45; Ps. 24. 10; 46. 7, 11; Jas. 5. 4.

Lord's Day, the The occasion when the Christian community met together for worship. Rev. 1. 10. *See also* Ac. 20. 7; 1 Cor. 16. 2.

Lord's Prayer The pattern prayer taught to his disciples by Christ. Mt. 6. 7–13; Lk. 11. 1–4.

Lord's Supper The name used for the commemoration of the last supper of Christ. *See* Mt. 26. 26–29; Mk. 14. 22–24; 1 Cor. 11. 17–26. It is also referred to as the 'breaking of bread'. Ac. 20. 7; 1 Cor. 10. 16.

Lot The nephew of Abraham. Gen. 11. 31; 12. 4; 13. 1–13; 19. 1–30; Lk. 17. 28–30; 2 Pet. 2. 7.

lots, casting of A popular method of divination in the O.T., and used to make choices. Nu. 26. 55; Ps. 22. 18; Jon. 1. 7; Mt. 27. 35; Ac. 1. 26. *See also* Urim.

love Although in the O.T. Hebrew the word has as wide a range of meanings as in English, it comes to stand for the chief quality of the ideal character because it is the very nature of God himself. Lev. 19. 18; Dt. 6. 4; Hos. 3. 1; 11. 1. The N.T. is mainly concerned with the love of God as shown in Christ and the Christian love it awakens and commands in man. Mt. 5. 44–48; 22. 37–40; Jn. 13. 34–35; Rom. 5. 5; 1 Cor. 13. 4–13; 2 Cor. 5. 14–17; 1 Jn. 3. 13–24; 4. 7–21.

Lucifer *See* Is. 14. 12.

Lucius A Christian of Cyrene. Ac. 13. 1.

Luke The author of the third Gospel and of the Acts, a doctor and companion of Paul on some of his missionary journeys. Col. 4. 14; 2 Tim. 4. 11; Philem. 24. *See also* Ac. 20. 6 – 28. 31.

Luke, Gospel of The longest and most stylishly written of the Gospels. Addressed primarily to the Greeks, it shows how God's promises to Israel have now been extended to them also. It emphasizes the perfect humanity of Christ; draws attention to his care for the poor, despised and weak; his practice and teaching on prayer; and the importance of women in the kingdom.

lute A stringed instrument similar to the lyre or harp. Ps. 33. 2; 144. 9.

Luz A Canaanite town N of Jerusalem. Gen. 28. 19; 35. 6; Jos. 18. 13.

LXX The Roman form of the number 70, used for the Greek (Septuagint) translation of the O.T. and Apocrypha.

Lycia A fertile region in SW Asia Minor almost opposite Alexandria. Ac. 27. 5.

Lydda The Greek name for Lod, one of the cities ceded to Jonathan by Demetrius. 1 Mac. 11. 28–34.

Lydia (1) The region on the W coast of Asia Minor, with its capital at Sardis. Jer. 46. 9; Ezek. 30. 5; 1 Mac. 8. 8. (2) A woman convert of Paul. Ac. 16. 14–15, 40.

Lysanias The governor of a territory on the N side of Mt. Hermon. Lk. 3. 1.

Lysias A general of Antiochus who fought against Judas. 1 Mac. 3. 32–39; 4. 26–35; 6. 17; 7. 2.

Lysimachus The brother of Menelaus who committed many acts of sacrilege. 2 Mac. 4. 29–42.

Lystra A city some 25 miles SSW of Iconium on the 'imperial road' to Pisidian Antioch. Ac. 14. 5–20; 16. 1–3. *Zoldera.*

Maacah (1) The mother of Absalom. 2 S. 3. 3. (2) The favourite wife of Rehoboam. 2 Ch. 11. 20.

Maccabees The family, also known as the Hasmonaeans, who ruled Judaea from 166 to 37 B.C. Mattathias first raised the revolt against Antiochus which was successfully carried on by his sons, Judas, Jonathan, Simon, and John Hyrcanus.

Maccabees, First and Second Books of The last two books of the Apocrypha which deal with Jewish history between 175 and 134 B.C. They describe the Maccabean war of independence in which Jerusalem was liberated and the Temple restored, and other wars against the enemies of the Jews. The Second Book contains much the same subject matter as the First but does not go beyond the campaigns and defeat of Nicanor. There are a number of discrepancies in chronological and numerical matters between the two books; and it is customary to place more reliance on 1 Maccabees.

Macedonia The region in the Balkan peninsula where Paul first preached in Europe. 1 Mac. 1. 1; Ac. 16. 9 – 17. 14; 18. 5.

Machir (1) The grandson of Joseph. Nu. 27. 1. (2) A man who helped Mephibosheth. 2 S. 9. 1–6; 17. 27.

madness In early times disorders of the mind were thought to be caused by evil spirits. Later it was recognized that the Spirit of the Lord might cause a man to prophesy while showing some of the signs of 'madness'. See 1 S. 10. 5–7; 18. 10; 21. 12–15; 2 K. 9. 11; Ac. 26. 24; 1 Cor. 14. 20–25.

Magdala A town on the edge of the Sea of Galilee some 3 miles N of Tiberias. Mk. 15. 40; Lk. 8. 2; Jn. 20. 1.

magic All processes designed to tap and use supernatural powers to influence events, including divination, necromancy, sorcery, exorcism, soothsaying and witchcraft; all of which were forbidden to the Israelites. See Ex. 22. 18; Lev. 19. 26; 20. 27; Dt. 18. 10–11; 1 S. 28. 8; Is. 47. 9; Jer. 27. 9; Ezek. 21. 21; Ac. 8. 9; 13. 6–8; 19. 13–16.

magistrate The civil authority in a Roman colony. Ac. 16. 20–40.

Magog (1) The son of Japheth. Gen. 10. 2. (2) A land in the far north. Ezek. 38. 2; 39. 6. Used symbolically Rev. 20. 8.

Mahalath (1) The wife of Esau. Gen. 28. 9. (2) The first wife of Rehoboam. 2 Ch. 11. 18.

Mahanaim An important site E of the Jordan on the frontier of Gad and Manasseh. Gen. 32. 2; Jos. 13. 24–30; 21. 38–40; 2 S. 2. 8; 17. 24–27; 1 K. 4. 14.

Maher-shalal-hash-baz The symbolic name Isaiah gave to his second son. Is. 8. 1–4.

Mahli (= weak, sickly) The founder of a prominent levitical family. Nu. 3. 20, 33; Ezr. 8. 18.

Mahlon The first husband of Ruth. Ru. 1. 2–5; 4. 9–10.

Makkedah A Canaanite royal city in the Shephelah. Jos. 10. 10–30.

Malachi, Book of (= my messenger) Its aim was to make clear, in the form of a disputation, the sin and apostasy of both the priests and people of Israel; and to underline the sovereign judgement of God, although blessing awaited those who repented. The reappearance of Elijah was to herald the Day of the Lord.

Malchus The servant of the high priest, Caiaphas. Jn. 18. 10. *See also* Lk. 22. 50.

Malta The rocky Mediterranean island of about 100 square miles colonized by the Phoenicians and Greeks before its Roman conquest. Ac. 27. 39 – 28. 10.

Mamre A place in the Hebron district. Gen. 18. 1; 23. 17–19; 49. 29–31.

man The being who has a nature in which is both the promise of sonship to God and brotherhood with his fellows, but both are made impossible by a deep-seated evil that affects his true nature. Gen. 1. 26; 3; 6. 5; Rom. 1. 18–23, 28–32. The Bible tells of God's persistent purpose to win man from that evil and how he chooses Israel to be the instrument of his grace and love to all men. Rom. 5; 2 Cor. 5. 14–20; Eph. 2. 3–10; Heb. 9. 27–28.

Manaen A Christian at Antioch. Ac. 13. 1.

Manasseh (1) Joseph's son and the ancestor of the tribe. Gen. 41. 51; 48. 1–20. (2) The king of Judah after Hezekiah. 2 K. 20. 21 – 21. 18; 2 Ch. 33. 1–20.

Manasseh, Prayer of A short prayer in poetical form which claims to be the one made in 2 Ch. 33. 11–13. It is the shortest, and probably the finest, piece of writing in the Apocrypha.

mandrake A stemless perennial of the nightshade family which grows wild in Palestine, and has emetic, purgative and narcotic qualities. Gen. 30. 14–16; S. of S. 7. 13.

manger The feeding-trough for animals in a stall or stable which, in Palestine, would be attached to the owner's house. Lk. 2. 7–16; 13. 15.

manna The food miraculously supplied to the Israelites during their wanderings in the desert. Ex. 16. 11–36; Jos. 5. 12. Throughout the Bible it is regarded as an example of God's blessing to man. Ps. 78. 24; Jn. 6. 31; Rev. 2. 17.

Manoah The father of Samson. Judg. 13. 2–24; 16. 31.

mantle A loose cloak, usually of good quality. Jos. 7. 21; 2 K. 2. 13.

Maon A place in the hill-country of Judah, the home of Nabal. 1 S. 25. 2–42. *Tell Ma'in.*

Mara The name Naomi gave to herself. Ru. 1. 20.

Marah (= bitter) The first camp of the Israelites after crossing the Red Sea. Ex. 15. 22–26.

Marana tha An Aramaic expression used by Paul. Possibly a form of early Christian watchword. 1 Cor. 16. 22. *See also* Rev. 22. 20.

marble Recrystallized limestone which can be highly polished. 1 Ch. 29. 2; S. of S. 5. 15; Rev. 18. 12.

Marisa The place to which Gorgias escaped, later plundered by Judas. 1 Mac. 5. 66–67; 2 Mac. 12. 35.

marjoram A plant of the mint family bearing small leaves and bunches of yellow flowers on its hairy stems. Ex. 12. 21–23; Lev. 14. 4; 1 K. 4. 33. *See also* Ps. 51. 7.

Mark The Roman name for the cousin of Barnabas who finally became Paul's trusted helper in spite of an earlier disagreement. Ac. 12. 12, 25; 13. 5, 13; 15. 37–40; Col. 4. 10; 2 Tim. 4. 11; Philem. 24; 1 Pet. 5. 13.

Mark, Gospel of Its contents suggests that its purpose was to help Christians to know their Lord better and to understand what it means to follow him. Written principally for the Roman world, it explains Jewish customs and presents Christ as the Messiah of the Jews and the Servant of the Lord sent to accomplish a specific work of God. The emphasis is therefore more on deeds than words, with the miracles pointing to his power as Son of God. Although the shortest of the Gospels, it often gives the most vivid and detailed account of an incident.

market, market-place This was used also for recreation, public business, and for a court room. Mt. 11. 16; 20. 3; Mk. 7. 4; Lk. 11. 43. *See also* Ac. 16. 19; 17. 17.

marriage One wife was the ideal; and though polygamy was not expressly forbidden it is shown to be more likely to cause strife. *See* Gen. 2. 24; 16. 2–3; 1 S. 1. 1–7; 1 K. 11. 1–4; Ps. 128; Pr. 31. 10–31. Marriages were arranged and certain unions were forbidden or actively discouraged. Gen. 21. 21; 24. 45–58; 29. 17–19; 34. 1–12; Lev. 18. 6–8; Jos. 15. 16;

Judg. 14. 1–3; 1 Cor. 7. 39. Used symbolically of God and Israel, and of Christ and his church. Is. 54. 5–8; Hos. 2. 2–20; 2 Cor. 11. 2; Eph. 5. 25–32; Rev. 19. 7–8; 21. 2.

marriage ceremonies Special clothes were worn; there were bridesmaids and a 'best man'; a procession with music and dancing to the bride's house; and a wedding feast. Judg. 14. 20; Is. 61. 10; Jer. 2. 32; 7. 34; 1 Mac. 9. 39; Mt. 25. 1–13; Jn. 2. 1–10.

marriage customs Betrothal was almost as binding as marriage itself. Dt. 22. 23–24; Mt. 1. 18–19. Gifts were exchanged. Gen. 34. 12; Ex. 22. 16–17; 1 K. 9. 16; Tobit 8. 21. A public declaration of the relationship was followed by a written contract. Mal. 2. 14; Tobit 7. 14.

marrow The heart of the bone. Job 21. 24; Heb. 4. 12.

Mars' Hill *See* Areopagus.

Martha The sister of Lazarus and Mary. Lk. 10. 38–42; Jn. 11. 1–45.

Mary (1) The mother of Jesus. Lk. 1. 26–56; 2. 1–35; 8. 19–21; Jn. 19. 26–27; Ac. 1. 14. (2) The sister of Martha. Lk. 10. 38–42; Jn. 11. 1–45; 12. 1–7. (3) Mary of Magdala (Mary Magdalene). Mk. 15. 40; 16. 1–7; Lk. 8. 2; Jn. 20. 11–18. (4) The mother of James and Joseph. Mt. 27. 55–56. (5) The mother of John Mark. Ac. 12. 12.

mason The simple Palestinian house was built by craftsmen who were stoneshapers, masons and carpenters all at once. Masons proper were employed in specialized work on fortifications, palaces and the Temple. 2 S. 5. 11; 2 K. 12. 11; 22. 6.

Massah (= testing) The scene of the miraculous gift of water to the thirsty Israelites in the wilderness. Ex. 17. 1–7; Ps. 95. 8.

Mattaniah The original name of king Zedekiah. 2 K. 24. 17.

Mattathias A priest of Modin who refused to offer sacrifice on the pagan altar and, with his sons, began the Maccabean rising against Antiochus. 1 Mac. 2. 1–70.

Matthan The grandfather of Joseph. Mt. 1. 15.

Matthew (= gift of God) One of the Twelve, also known as Levi. Mt. 10. 3; Lk. 5. 27–29; 6. 15; Ac. 1. 13.

Matthew, Gospel of The author writes as a Jew for Jews to show that Jesus, the son of David, is the true Messiah and the fulfilment of O.T. prophecies. He emphasizes that the Christian church is continuous with the old Israel, but the Gentiles are now to be included. The Marcan outline is used but rearranged, and new material is added.

Matthias The disciple chosen to fill Judas's place. Ac. 1. 15–26.

mattock A more robust agricultural implement than the wooden Egyptian hoe. 1 S. 13. 20; Is. 2. 4; Joel 3. 9; Mic. 4. 3.

Media, Medes The ancient names for NW Iran and its steppe dwellers. Overrun by the Assyrians, they later founded the Persian empire in alliance with the Chaldaeans but were finally merged into it as a province. 2 K. 17. 6; 18. 11; Dan. 5. 28, 31; 6. 8.

mediator, mediation An intermediary who brings together two or more estranged people. Christ is the mediator of the new covenant between God and man. 1 Tim. 2. 5; Heb. 8. 6; 9. 15; 12. 24. *See also* 1 S. 2. 25; Job 9. 33; Rom. 8. 34.

medicine Doctors were known from earliest times, and although scientific medical knowledge was scanty, basic laws of hygiene existed. Lev. ch. 11–15; Dt. 23. 9–14. Forms of treatment. Is. 1. 6; 38. 21; Lk. 10. 34.

Megiddo An important fortress on the Carmel range 20 miles SSE of Haifa, guarding the crossing place of the great commercial and military highway between Egypt and Syria. Jos. 17. 11–13; Judg. 5. 19; 1 K. 9. 15; 2 K. 9. 27; 23. 29; Zech. 12. 11. *Tell el-Mutesillim.* A major excavation site which has shown the formidable civilization facing the Israelites when they invaded Canaan; and has yielded many treasures from its twenty main occupation levels, including examples of carved ivory of the Later Bronze Age now in the Oriental Institute of the University of Chicago.

Melchizedek The priest-king of Salem. Gen. 14. 18–20. And, in this dual role, regarded as the forerunner and type of Christ. Ps. 110. 4; Heb. 5. 6; 6. 20 – 7. 28.

Memphis The capital of ancient Egypt, a few miles S of Cairo. Hos. 9. 6. Given its Hebrew name 'Noph' in Is. 19. 13; Jer. 2. 16; 44. 1; 46. 14, 19; Ezek. 30. 13. *Mît Rahîneh.*

Menahem (= comforter) The son of Gadi who usurped the throne of Israel. 2 K. 15. 14–22.

Mene mene tekel u-pharsin The Aramaic inscription interpreted by Daniel during Belshazzar's feast. Dan. 5. 1–31.

Mephibosheth Jonathan's lame son. 2 S. 4. 4; 9. 1–13.

Merab Saul's eldest daughter. 1 S. 14. 49; 18. 17–20.

Merari The third and youngest son of Levi and ancestor of a division of the Levites. Nu. 3. 16–20, 33–37; Jos. 21. 34–40; 1 Ch. 15. 16–21.

Merathaim The region where the Tigris and Euphrates enter the sea. Used symbolically of Babylon. Jer. 50. 21.

Mercury The spokesman and messenger of the Roman gods. Ac. 14. 8–18.

mercy, merciful The basic idea is compassion to one in need or distress who has no claim to favourable treatment. Dt. 4. 31; Mt. 5. 7; Eph. 2. 4; 1 Tim. 1. 2; Tit. 3. 5; Jas. 2. 13. *See also* Ex. 34. 6; Ps. 103. 8; Lk. 6. 36.

Meribah The place where the Israelites rebelled against Moses. Ex. 17. 1–7; Ps. 106. 32.

Merodach-baladan The leader of the Chaldaeans who seized the throne of Babylon and tried to persuade Hezekiah to join an alliance against Assyria. 2 K. 20. 12–19.

Merom, Waters of The scene of Joshua's victory over his allies. Jos. 11. 1–9.

Mesha The king of Moab who rebelled against Israel and offered his son as a human sacrifice. 2 K. 3. 4–27.

Meshach The name given to Mishael, one of Daniel's three companions. Dan. 1. 6 – 3. 30.

Meshech The grandson of Noah and the ancestor of a warlike people inhabiting what is now E Anatolia. 1 Ch. 1. 5; Ps. 120. 5; Ezek. 27. 13; 39. 1–6.

Mesopotamia A rendering of the Hebrew Aram-naharaim. The whole area between the rivers Euphrates and Tigris, but often restricted to the western portion. The home of Abraham. Ac. 2. 9; 7. 2. *See also* Gen. 24. 10; Judg. 3. 8; 1 Ch. 19. 6.

Messiah The Hebrew for 'anointed one'. This Israelite way of making a king became specially applied to the line of David from where the prophets looked for a deliverer who would bring in a rule of universal peace and justice. *See* 2 S. 22. 51; Is. 9. 2–7; 11. 1–11; Jer. 23. 5–6; Ezek. 34. 23–24. The N.T. concept of the Messiah follows from that in the O.T. but includes more directly the concept of suffering for others. Is. ch. 53. Jesus claims to be the Messiah and is acknowledged as such by his disciples. Mt. 1. 18; Lk. 4. 14–21; 24. 26; Ac. 4. 27. *See* Christ.

Methuselah The grandfather of Noah who lived to a great age. Gen. 5. 21–27.

Micah (1) A prophet of Judah contemporary with Hosea and Isaiah. Jer. 26. 18. (2) An Ephraimite who set up a shrine in his house and persuaded a wandering Levite to be its priest. Judg. 17. 1 – 18. 26.

Micah, Book of The theme is the justice and morality which characterize the nature of God and must, therefore, be reflected in the social conditions of his people. Corrupt judges, hypocritical priests, and false prophets in both Judah and Israel are denounced; and the destruction of Jerusalem by God's instrument, the Assyrians, is foretold. Restoration, however, would be marked by a new, universalistic religion under the promised Messiah to be born in Bethlehem among the common people.

Micaiah The son Imlah, and the prophet who advised Ahab and Jehoshaphat on their proposed attack on Ramoth-gilead. 1 K. 22. 1–38.

Michael The guardian of the Jews. Dan. 10. 13; 11. 1; 12. 1. An archangel. Jude 9; Rev. 12. 7–9.

Michal Saul's youngest daughter, and the wife of David. 1 S. 18. 17–29; 19. 11–17; 25. 44; 2 S. 3. 12–15; 6. 20–23.

Michmash A city on the pass from Bethel to Jericho and 7 miles N of Jerusalem.

1 S. 13. 2 – 14. 31; Neh. 11. 31; 1 Mac. 9. 73. *Mukhmâs.*

midge A very small, irritating, blood-sucking insect like the sand-fly. Mt. 23. 24.

Midian, Midianites The son of Abraham and Keturah and ancestor of the Bedouin tribe living in N Arabia opposite the Sinai peninsula. Their relations with the Israelites varied from time to time. Gen. 25. 1–6; 37. 28; Ex. 2. 15–22; Nu. 31. 1–10; Judg. 6. 1 – 8. 28.

midwife These were practising as early as the time of Jacob. Gen. 35. 17; 38. 28; Ex. 1. 15–21. *See also* Ezek. 16. 4.

Milcah Rebecca's grandmother. Gen. 11. 29; 24. 15.

Milcom The national god of the Ammonites. 1 K. 11. 5; 2 K. 23. 13–14.

mile The Roman mile of about 1000 double paces or 1620 yards. Mt. 5. 41.

milk The staple diet of the Hebrews, obtained from sheep, goats, cows and camels and often churned into curds. Gen. 32. 15; Dt. 32. 14; Pr. 27. 27. Jewish dietary law forbade the eating of meat and milk at the same meal. Dt. 14. 21. Used as a symbol of prosperity and fertility. Ex. 3. 8; Joel 3. 18.

mill, millstones A combination of two stones, one resting on the other. The upper was moved, usually by hand, to grind the grain put between them. Dt. 24. 6; Job 41. 24; Jer. 25. 10; Mk. 9. 42. *See also* Judg. 16. 21.

millennium The Latin for a thousand years; the period given in Rev. 20. 1–15 for the reign of Christ and his resurrected saints. *See also* Ac. 3. 20; 1 Cor. 15. 3–28.

millet Used only as an ingredient of bread, and not as a substitute for flour. Ezek. 4. 9.

Millo An ancient fortification or bastion of Jerusalem. 2 S. 5. 9; 1 K. 11. 27; 2 Ch. 32. 5.

mines, mining Excavations for various mineral ores were known to have existed from an early date. Job 28. 1–11. *See also* Gen. 4. 22; Nu. 31. 22; Dt. 8. 9.

ministry The Greek word used, found mainly in the Acts and Letters of Paul, applies generally to work for Christ in the church. Ac. 6. 4. *See also* 1 Cor. 12. 27; 2 Cor. 4 1; Eph. 4. 11–12; Col. 4. 17.

minstrel A player on a stringed instrument who often sang to his own accompaniment. 2 K. 3. 15; Ps. 68. 25. *See also* 1 S. 16. 23.

mint There are three varieties in Palestine growing wild on banks and in ditches. It was commonly used medicinally, and as a perfume and flavouring. Mt. 23. 23; Lk. 11. 42.

miracle(s) A number of Greek and Hebrew words are used in the Bible to refer to the personal activity in nature and history of a loving God. These characterize it as distinctive, powerful and meaningful; and are variously translated as 'miracle', 'portent', 'sign'. Miracles in the Gospels:

Found only in Matthew

Two blind men cured	Mt. 9. 27–31
A dumb man cured	9. 32–33
The temple-tax money	17. 24–27

Found only in Mark

Deaf and dumb man cured	Mk. 7. 31–37
Blind man cured	8. 22–26

Found only in Luke

The big haul of fish	Lk. 5. 1–11
The widow of Nain's son raised	7. 11–17
A crippled woman cured	13. 11–17
Dropsy cured	14. 1–6
Ten lepers cured	17. 11–19
Malchus's ear healed	22. 50–51

Found only in John

Water made wine at Cana	Jn. 2. 1–11
Roman officer's son cured of fever	4. 46–54
A cripple healed at Jerusalem	5. 1–9
A man born blind cured	9. 1–7
Lazarus raised from the dead	11. 38–44
The catch of big fish	21. 1–14

Common to Matthew and Mark

Canaanite woman's daughter cured	Mt. 15. 28; Mk. 7. 24
Four thousand fed	Mt. 15. 32; Mk. 8. 1
Fig-tree cursed	Mt. 21. 19; Mk. 11. 13

Common to Matthew and Luke

Centurion's paralysed servant cured	Mt. 8. 5; Lk. 7. 1
Blind and dumb man cured	Mt. 12. 22; Lk. 11. 14

Common to Mark and Luke

Possessed man cured in synagogue	Mk. 1. 23; Lk. 4. 33

Common to Matthew, Mark, Luke

Leper cured	Mt. 8. 2; Mk. 1. 40; Lk. 5. 12
Peter's mother-in-law cured	Mt. 8. 14; Mk. 1. 30; Lk. 4. 38
Storm calmed	Mt. 8. 23; Mk. 4. 37; Lk. 8. 22
Possessed men cured	Mt. 8. 28; Mk. 5. 1; Lk. 8. 26
Paralysed man cured	Mt. 9. 2; Mk. 2. 3; Lk. 5. 18
Jairus's daughter raised	Mt. 9. 23; Mk. 5. 23; Lk. 8. 41
Woman with haemorrhages cured	Mt. 9. 20; Mk. 5. 25; Lk. 8. 43
Man's withered arm cured	Mt. 12. 10; Mk. 3. 1; Lk. 6. 6
Epileptic boy cured	Mt. 17. 14; Mk. 9. 17; Lk. 9. 37
Blind man cured	Mt. 20. 30; Mk. 10. 46; Lk. 18. 35

Common to Matthew, Mark, John

Christ walks on the lake	Mt. 14. 25; Mk. 6. 48; Jn. 6. 19

Common to All

Five thousand fed	Mt. 14. 15; Mk. 6. 34; Lk. 9. 10; Jn. 6. 3

Miriam The eldest sister of Moses and Aaron. Ex. 15. 20–21; Nu. 12. 1–15; 20. 1. *See also* Ex. 2. 4–8.

mirror(s) These consisted of round or oval polished metal surfaces, usually of bronze. Ex. 38. 8; Job 37. 18; 1 Cor. 13. 12; Jas. 1. 23.

Mithredath The treasurer of Cyrus of Persia. Ezr. 1. 7–8.

Mizpah(Mizpeh) (= watchtower) (1) Where Jacob and Laban made a covenant. Gen. 31. 44–54. (2) The home of Jephthah E of the Jordan. Judg. 11. 11, 29–39. (3) A town of Benjamin near Gibeon and Ramah. 1 S. 7. 11; 1 K. 15. 22; 2 K. 25. 23–25; Jer. 40. 6–15; 1 Mac. 3. 46.

Mnason A Christian from Cyprus. Ac. 21. 16.

Moab, Moabites The ancient people and kingdom in the highlands E of the Jordan opposite Bethlehem. Though probably kinsmen of the Israelites, they opposed their entry into Palestine and there was constant war between them. Judg. 3. 12–30; 11. 16–18; 2 S. 8. 2; Is. ch. 15–16; Ezek. 25. 8–11; Zeph. 2. 8–10.

Moabite Stone Slabs of black basalt discovered at *Dhibhan* in Transjordan in 1863, now in the Louvre. Dated about 830 B.C. the inscription, left by Mesha, king of Moab, commemorates his revolt against Israel and supplements the O.T. narrative of the events of the reigns of Omri and Ahab.

Modin The home of Mattathias where the revolt against Antiochus began. 1 Mac. 2. 1, 15–28, 70; 9. 19; 13. 25. *el-Midyeh.*

Molech (Moloch) An Amorite god whose worship was associated with the sacrifice of children in the fire. Lev. 20. 1–5; 1 K. 11. 6–8; 2 K. 23. 10; Ac. 7. 40–43. *See also* 2 K. 16. 2–3; Jer. 7. 30–31.

mole-rat Burrowers which have become modified to an underground life and are a common sight in areas with a rainfall of more than 4 inches and enough soil for them to work in. They can do serious damage to grain and crop roots with their large gnawing teeth. Lev. 11. 29.

money There was no coined money in Israel until after the exile. Before this, payment was made by barter. Later it took the form of paying out an agreed quantity of precious metal. *See* Gen. 13. 2; 23. 16. Until the Maccabean period the Jews used the coinage of their conquerors. The N.T. emphasizes the spiritual dangers that money can bring. Mk. 10. 23–25; 1 Tim. 6. 10, 17–19.

money-changers Since only Jewish money could be offered in the Temple, these dealers changed, at a commission, all currencies for the Jews of the Dispersion. Mt. 21. 12; Jn. 2. 15.

monkeys *See* apes.

month There were twelve months of 29 or 30 days running from one new moon to the next. In order to keep the lunar and solar year synchronized it was necessary from time to time to add a supplementary month. Names, of Canaanite origin, were given according to the season. Ex. 13. 4; 1 K. 6. 37–38; 8. 2. After the exile, numbers were used until the Babylonian calendar was adopted. Neh. 1. 1; 2. 1; Zech. 1. 7.

moon The object of pagan worship, forbidden to the Israelites. Dt. 4. 19; 17. 2–5; 2 K. 23. 5. It was associated with the coming of the Messiah and the Day of the Lord. Joel 2. 10, 31; Mk. 13. 24; Rev. 21. 23.

Mordecai A Jewish exile and the deliverer of his countrymen from Persian persecution. Est. 2. 5 – 10. 3.

Moriah The place where God tested Abraham, and the site of Solomon's Temple. Gen. 22. 2; 2 Ch. 3. 1.

Moses The great political and religious leader of the Israelites from slavery in Egypt to a developed nationhood. He was the instrument of God's revelation by which Israel was made the people of God. Ex. 2. 1 – 40. 38; Lev. ch. 1–27; Nu. ch. 1–36; Dt. ch. 1–34; Mt. 17. 1–5; Lk. 24. 44.

moth An insect common to all parts of the world which damages and destroys material of many kinds. Is. 50. 9; Mt. 6. 19–20.

mother Both the O.T. and N.T. refer to motherhood as a privilege and joy. Gen. 3. 20; Pr. 31. 1; Jn. 16. 21. She was to be honoured equally with the father. Ex. 20. 12. Also used of the earthly and heavenly Jerusalem. Is. 66. 7–13; Gal. 4. 26.

mount, mountain Like most ancient people, the Israelites thought of mountains as the dwelling-place of God. Dt. 33. 2; Ps. 74. 2. Their own worship became contaminated by the hill-shrines of the Canaanites. 2 K. 23. 13–20. Mountains also served as refuges, landmarks, look-outs, assembly-places and cemeteries. Jos. 8. 33; Judg. 6. 2; Is. 18. 3.

mountain-goat This is the Nubian Ibex or Rock Goat which stands about 34 inches at the shoulder with slender, clearly-ridged horns sweeping back in a wide curve. The general colour is grey, and the species is confined to the mountains E of the Nile. Dt. 14. 5; Job 39. 1; Ps. 104. 18.

mourning The Israelites had elaborate and varied ways of showing sorrow. Dt. 14. 1; 1 S. 31. 13; 2 S. 1. 2; 3. 31; 2 Ch. 35. 25; Jer. 16. 5–7; Mt. 9. 23. The period of mourning also varied. Gen. 50. 4; Nu. 20. 29; 1 S. 31. 13.

mulberry The tree was cultivated in biblical times for its fruit, though it is rather rare in Palestine today. Lk. 17. 6.

mule There was an implicit ban on breeding this cross between a donkey stallion and a horse mare, but they appear to have been imported for load-carrying (being sure-footed in hilly country). Their use for riding seems to have been confined to the nobility. 2 S. 13. 29; 1 K. 1. 33; 10. 25; Ps. 32. 9; Ezek. 27. 14. *See also* Lev. 19. 19.

murder, murderer Premeditated murder is punishable by death in all O.T. law codes, and an obligation was on the nearest relative to see that the death sentence was carried out. Ex. 21. 12–14; Nu. 35. 16–21; Dt. 19. 11–13. When the murderer could not be found, a special atonement service had to be offered. Dt. 21. 1–9.

music Both instrumental and vocal music were a familiar part of Israelite life from early times in ceremonial, military exercises and as recreation. The Levites provided a choir and orchestra for the Temple worship which kept together right through the exile. *See* Gen. 4. 21; 31. 27; 1 S. 10. 5; 16. 23; 1 Ch. 6. 31–32; 15. 16; 2 Ch. 5. 12–14; 7. 6; Neh. 12. 27, 45; Ps. 150; Eccles. 2. 8. Music played an important part in the Christian life. Eph. 5. 19; Col. 3. 16.

mustard Both the black and white varieties of this plant are known in Palestine. While the leaves were used as vegetables, the seeds provided powder for seasoning. In N.T. times the black mustard-seed was also cultivated for its oil. Mt. 13. 31–32; 17. 20.

muzzle The Mosaic law had specific and humane regulations about oxen. Dt. 25. 4.

Myra A town in Asia Minor. Ac. 27. 5. Dembre.

myrrh The resin or droppings of a thorny bush with a thin, papery bark which was used as a spice and in the making of cosmetics, in the preparation of the holy oil for anointing, and for embalming. It is a native of Arabia and Africa. Ex. 30. 23–25; S. of S. 1. 13; Mt. 2. 11; Jn. 19. 39–40.

myrtle An evergreen tree well known in Palestine and used for making the arbours used at the Feast of Tabernacles. Neh. 8. 15; Is. 41. 19; 55. 13; Zech. 1. 8–11. Esther's Hebrew name 'Hadassah' = 'myrtle'. Est. 2. 7.

Mysia A region in NW Asia Minor. Ac. 16. 6–8.

mystery In N.T. times it was widely used of the 'secret knowledge' given to initiates into certain pagan religions. N.T. writers contrast with it God's eternal purpose for the world which is made known through Christ. 1 Cor. 15. 51. See also 1 Cor. 2. 6–10; Eph. 1. 9; Col. 1. 26.

Naamah (1) Tubal-cain's sister. Gen. 4. 22. (2) Solomon's wife. 1 K. 14. 21.

Naaman The commander-in-chief of Ben-hadad, king of Damascus. 2 K. 5. 1–19; Lk. 4. 27.

Nabal A wealthy sheep-farmer who refused to pay tribute to David. 1 S. 25. 2–42.

Nabataea, Nabataeans The territory occupied by the Arab people who made their way from Arabia into Edom during the Persian and Hellenistic periods; and later controlled an area running E of the Jordan up to and including Damascus, with their capital at Petra. 1 Mac. 5. 25; 9. 35. See also 2 Mac. 5. 8; 2 Cor. 11. 32.

Naboth A citizen of Jezreel who refused to sell his vineyard to Ahab. 1 K. 21. 1–25. See also Lev. 25. 23; 2 K. 9. 30–37.

Nadab (1) The eldest son of Aaron. Ex. 6. 23; Lev. 10. 1–7. (2) The son and successor of Jeroham, king of Judah. 1 K. 15. 25–32. (3) The nephew and foster-son of Ahikar. Tobit 11. 18; 14. 10.

Nadabath A place E of the Jordan where Jonathan and Simon avenged their brother John's murder. 1 Mac. 9. 37.

Nahash An Ammonite king who tried to humiliate the Israelites. 1 S. 11. 1–11.

Nahor (1) The grandfather of Abraham. Gen. 11. 22–27. (2) The brother of Abraham who stayed in Harran, and was the ancestor of the Aramaean tribes. Gen. 22. 20–24.

Nahum (= full of comfort) A prophet of Elkosh, contemporary with Jeremiah.

Nahum, Book of A magnificent ode, written with feeling and vividness, which foretells the downfall of Nineveh; for the God of Israel, the nation whom Assyria had despised, controls the destinies of all nations.

nail The carpenter's nail as understood today. Is. 41. 7; Jn. 20. 25.

nails To leave the nails untrimmed was a sign of mourning. Dt. 21. 12.

Nain A town SE of Nazareth where Jesus performed a miracle. Lk. 7. 11–17.

name In the biblical record a person's name is important both to himself and to others. The choice of a name often has special significance. Gen. 25. 25–26; 35. 18; 1 S. 4. 21; Is. 8. 3; Hos. 1. 4. To give someone a new name is to give him a new character. Gen. 17. 5–8; 32. 24–30. Since the name was thought of as in a sense representing the person, knowing it gave one power over him. Mk. 5. 2–13.

Nanea A goddess whose temple Antiochus attempted to rob. 2 Mac. 1. 10–17.

Naomi The wife of Elimelech who emigrated to Moab. Ru. ch. 1–4.

Naphtali (1) The sixth son of Jacob and ancestor of the tribe. Gen. 30. 7–8; Nu. 1. 42–43; Jos. 19. 32–39; 2 K. 15. 29. (2) The territory which in N.T. times was included in Galilee, and so became the cradle of the Christian faith. Mt. 4. 13–16.

Narcissus A Roman whose family was greeted by Paul. Rom. 16. 11.

nard The fragrant oil of an Indian plant. Mk. 14. 3; Jn. 12. 3.

Nathan A notable prophet in the reigns of David and Solomon. 2 S. 7. 1–17; 12. 1–25; 1 K. 1. 5–45.

Nathanael One of Christ's disciples from Cana in Galilee. Jn. 1. 44–51; 21. 2.

nations Although used literally Job 12. 24, it also refers to the non-Israelite nations in the sense of 'outsiders' or 'heathen'. Is. 43. 9; Ezek. 5. 6. *See also* Lk. 12. 30.

Nazarene (= one from Nazareth) A term often applied to Christ, at first with some condescension. Mt. 2. 23. Later used as a popular name for the early Christians. Ac. 24. 5.

Nazareth A village in the hills of Galilee overlooking the caravan routes through Palestine, and the boyhood home of Jesus. Mt. 2. 23; Lk. 1. 26; 2. 4, 51; 4. 16–30. *En Nâṣirah.*

Nazirite One who put himself completely at the disposal of God by vow for a certain period, and undertook strict self-discipline. Nu. 6. 1–21; Am. 2. 11–12. *See also* Lk. 1. 15; Ac. 18. 18; 21. 23–24.

Neapolis The port of Philippi. Ac. 16. 11. *Kavalla.*

Nebo (1) The mountain in Moab where Moses died. Dt. 34. 1–5. *Jebel en-Nebâ.* (2) The Babylonian god of literature and science. Is. 46. 1.

Nebuchadnezzar (Nebuchadrezzar) The son of Nabopolassar, founder of the neo-Babylonian empire. He made Judah a vassal state, and on three occasions deported Jews to Babylon. He went out of his mind and died in 562 B.C. 2 K. 24. 1 – 25. 22; 2 Ch. 36. 5–13; Jer. 39. 1–12; 46. 2–28; Dan. ch. 2–4.

Nebuzaradan The chief of Nebuchadnezzar's bodyguard. 2 K. 25. 8–12; Jer. 39. 11–14; 52. 12–30.

Necho The Pharaoh of Egypt who supported Assyria against Babylon. He defeated the forces of Judah under Josiah at Megiddo and made it a vassal state. 2 Ch. 35. 20 – 36. 5.

needle Many have been found in Bible lands made of bone, bronze and iron. Mt. 19. 24. *See also* Gen. 3. 7; Job 16. 15.

Negeb An area of semi-desert country S of Judah, E of the coastal plain and W of the Dead Sea. Gen. 12. 9; Nu. 13. 17–29; Judg. 1. 9; 1 S. 27. 10–11; Zech. 7. 7.

Nehemiah A Jewish exile who reached high rank at the court of Artaxerxes of Persia, and obtained permission to return as governor of Judah to supervise the task of reconstruction. Neh. 1. 1 – 2. 18; 6. 15.

Nehemiah, Book of This tells the story of Nehemiah's deep concern for the people of Jerusalem and for the city itself, expressed in the rebuilding of its walls through prayer and tenacity in the face of strong opposition. Reforms were carried out which inspired a revival of the national life, but which tended to isolate the Israelites from communication with the surrounding peoples.

Nehushtan The bronze serpent made by Moses as a symbol of deliverance which became an object of idolatrous worship. 2 K. 18. 4.

neighbour Normally a fellow-Israelite, but foreigners taking up permanent residence came within the range of neighbourly conduct. In the N.T. the scope is widened to include any person whom one is able to help. Ex. 20. 16–17; Lev. 19. 18, 33–34; Lk. 10. 25–27.

Nereus A Roman Christian greeted by Paul. Rom. 16. 15.

Nergal A Babylonian deity worshipped as the god of storm, war, pestilence and hunting. 2 K. 17. 30.

Nergalsarezer The Babylonian general who released Jeremiah from prison. Jer. 39. 13–14.

Nero The Roman emperor to whom Paul appealed. *See* Ac. 25. 10–12.

net Used for catching birds and fish in O.T. times. Pr. 1. 17; Is. 19. 8. The N.T. mentions three methods of fishing with nets. Mt. 4. 18; 13. 47; Lk. 5. 4. Used metaphorically of the plots of the wicked. Ps. 10. 9; 141. 10.

new moon This marked the opening of a new month and was celebrated with sacrifices, social gatherings and recreation. 2 K. 4. 22–23; Is. 66. 23; Hos. 2. 11; Am. 8. 5. *See also* Nu. 10.10.

New Testament Only about one-third the size of the O.T., it contains twenty-seven short books, the Scriptures of the Christians and the record of a covenant made through Jesus Christ. Written over a period of some 75 years, it contains accounts of the life and works of Jesus Christ, the beginnings of the Christian church and the essentials of Christian teaching.

New Year Originally it was kept at the end of the harvest (September–October). *See* Ex. 23. 16. During the exile the Babylonian spring New Year was adopted (March–April). After the exile the emphasis came back to the original date. *See* Lev. 23. 23–25; Nu. 29. 1–6.

Nicanor (1) One of those chosen to distribute relief to the poor. Ac. 6. 1–6. (2) The Syrian general who fought against Judas and whose defeat was commemorated by an annual festival. 1 Mac. 3. 38–40; 7. 26–50.

Nicodemus A wealthy Pharisee who, from a cautious inquirer, became an open disciple of Christ. Jn. 3. 1–12; 7. 50–52; 19. 38–42.

Nicolaitans A sect which arose in the churches of Ephesus and Pergamum. Rev. 2. 6, 15–16. *See also* Ac. 15. 28–29.

Nicolas One of those chosen to distribute relief to the poor. Ac. 6. 1–6.

Nicopolis A city in Epirus where Paul invited Titus to spend the winter with him. Tit. 3. 12. *Paleoprevaza.*

Niger The surname of Simeon of Antioch. Ac. 13. 1.

Nile The great river of Egypt whose annual flooding renewed the fertility of the land. Gen. 41. 1; Ex. 1. 22 – 2. 3; 7. 17–21; Is. 18. 2; 19. 5–7; Jer. 46. 7; Am. 8. 8.

Nimrod The great-grandson of Noah who lived in Babylonia. Gen. 10. 8–12.

Nimshi The father of Jehu. 1 K. 19. 16.

Nineveh The capital of the Assyrian empire, on the E bank of the Tigris defended by a great wall and moat, which fell about 612 B.C. It figures in the stories of Tobit and Judith. 2 K. 19. 36; Jon. 1. 2; 3; 4. 11; Nah. 3. 7; Zeph. 2. 13–15; Tobit ch. 1; 11; 14; Judith 1. 1; 2. 21. *Tell Quyunjiq* and *Tell Nebi Yûnus.*

Nisroch An Assyrian god worshipped in Nineveh. 2 K. 19. 37.

No, No-amon Thebes, the chief city of Upper Egypt, built on both sides of the Nile. Jer. 46. 25; Ezek. 30. 14; Nah. 3. 8.

Noah The grandson of Methuselah who appears as the first cultivator, and the hero of the Flood. Gen. 5. 28–32; 6. 5 – 9. 17; Mt. 24. 37–38; Heb. 11. 7.

Nob A city of priests, near Anathoth, whose inhabitants were massacred by Saul after Ahimelech had assisted the fugitive David. 1 S. ch. 21–22.

Nod The land of Cain's exile. Gen. 4. 16.

Numbers, Book of This recounts the years of nomadic wanderings under the discipline, care and guidance of Jehovah, who remained faithful to his covenant in spite of rebellions; and prepared the new generation to live rightly under his rule in the promised land. Its name derives from the census of ch. 1–4; 26.

Nun The father of Joshua. Ex. 33. 11.

nurse Generally, Hebrew women suckled their own children, but wet nurses were employed and regarded as an important member of the household. Gen. 24. 59; Ex. 2. 7–9; 2 K. 11. 2. 'Nurse' in the sense of 'attendant' is used in 2 S. 4. 4; Ru. 4. 16.

Nympha The owner of a house in Laodicea where a church met. Col. 4. 15.

oak Many species of this tree grow in Palestine and it is frequently mentioned in the Bible. Gen. 35. 8; 2 S. 18. 9–10; Ezek. 27. 6; Zech. 11. 2. In some religions it was considered sacred. Is. 1. 29. Also used to symbolize power and strength. Is. 2. 13; Am. 2. 9.

oath A method of calling God to witness that one is telling the truth, and therefore absolutely binding. Gen. 21. 23; Nu. 5. 20–24; ch. 30; Dt. 6. 13; Ru. 1. 17; Mt. 5. 33–37; Heb. 6. 16; Jas. 5. 12. *See also* Ex. 22. 10; Ps. 63. 11; Zech. 5. 3.

Obadiah Ahab's minister who protected the prophets. 1 K. 18. 2–16.

Obadiah, Book of The shortest book in the O.T. marked by vigorous poetic language. It foretells the complete destruction of Edom for her treacherous behaviour towards Israel; and then deals in general terms with God's judgement of all the nations and the establishment of his kingdom.

Obed The grandfather of David and the ancestor of Jesus. Ru. 4. 17–21.

Obed-edom The man in whose house David left the Ark for safe keeping. 2 S. 6. 9–12.

obedience, obey The supreme test of faith in God, and the response which he looks for in men. Gen. 22. 18; Jn. 14. 15; Rom. 5. 19; 6. 17; Phil. 2. 8; Heb. 5. 8; 1 Pet. 1. 14; 1 Jn. 2. 3–5. Man must discharge his obligations to those in lawful authority over him. *See* Pr. 5. 12; Mt. 22. 21; Rom. 13. 1–7; Eph. 6. 1; Col. 3. 20; 1 Pet. 2. 18.

offerings Making offerings to God was a very ancient practice. Gen. 4. 3–4; 8. 20; Ex. 10. 25. The detailed form and order laid down in Lev. ch. 1–7 arose from the need for purification from sin and the desire to enter into fellowship with God. *See* sacrifice.

Og A giant king of the Amorites. Dt. 3. 1–11; 31. 4; Ps. 135. 10–11.

Oholah, Oholibah Symbolic names for Samaria and Jerusalem. Ezek. ch. 23.

Oholibamah The wife of Esau. Gen. 36. 2–25.

oil Obtained mainly from the olive-tree by crushing the berries. It was an important element in the economy of the people. Nu. 18. 12; Ezr. 3. 7; Neh. 5. 11. It was used for cooking 1 K. 17. 12–16; lighting Ex. 27. 20; Mt. 25. 1–4; anointing kings, priests, sacred objects, guests and the sick Ex. 30. 25–33; 1 S. 10. 1; Is. 1. 6; Mk. 6. 13; Lk. 7. 46; and for personal use 2 S. 12. 20; Dan. 10. 3.

ointment Used medicinally, for personal use and in embalming. The base was olive oil with various spices added. Rev. 3. 18. *See also* Est. 2. 8–12; Ps. 133. 2; Jer. 8. 22; Mt. 26. 6–13.

Old Testament This consists of those books in Hebrew (and Aramaic) which tell how God made a covenant with his chosen people, and how that special relationship was worked out in history. The Jews make a threefold division into Law, Prophets and Writings, the historical books being included under the Prophets.

It is more usual among Christians to class the books as Law, Histories, Prophets, Poetical Books and Wisdom Literature. *See* Mt. 5. 17; Lk. 24. 44–47.

olive A slow-growing, but long-lived tree which grows best in the dry, stony soil of the Middle East. It was greatly valued for its fruit, used as a food, and for the oil made from it which was used in cooking and as a fuel for lamps. Used as a common figure of speech in the Bible for prosperity and joy. Gen. 8. 10–11; Dt. 24. 20; 1 Ch. 27. 28; Ps. 52. 8; Jer. 11. 16; Hos. 14. 6; Mt. 26. 30; Rom. 11. 17–18.

Olives, Mount of (Olivet) A ridge of hills running for about a mile on the E of Jerusalem and separated from it by the Kidron gorge. It had deep religious associations. 2 S. 15. 30; Zech. 14. 4; Mt. 21. 1; 26. 30; Lk. 19. 37; 21. 37; 22. 39; Ac. 1. 12. *See also* Ezek. 11. 23. *Jebel et̲ T̲ûr*.

Olympas A Roman Christian. Rom. 16. 15.

omega The last letter of the Greek alphabet. Used with 'alpha', the first letter, as a symbol of the inclusiveness of God. Rev. 1. 8; 21. 6; 22. 13.

omer A measure of capacity. *See* Appendix to the O.T. in the New English Bible.

Omri One of the most important of Israel's kings, who seized the throne and established his dynasty by a military coup. He is the first to be mentioned in non-biblical records: the Moabite Stone. 1 K. 16. 8–28.

On An ancient city of Lower Egypt near Memphis. Associated with sun worship, it was called Heliopolis by the Greeks. Gen. 41. 45; Ezek. 30. 17.

Onesimus (= profitable) The slave of Philemon of Colossae who ran away from his master. *See* Philemon, Letter to.

Onesiphorus A Christian of Ephesus. 2 Tim. 1. 16–18; 4. 19.

Onias (1) Onias I, high priest and contemporary of Arius. 1 Mac. 12. 7–23. (2) Onias III, a man of piety who had a disagreement with Simon. 2 Mac. ch. 3–4.

Ophel Part of the E hill of Jerusalem. 2 Ch. 27. 3; Neh. 3. 27.

Ophir The country from which fine gold, precious stones and almug wood were imported into Judah. 1 K. 9. 26–28; 10. 11.

Ophrah The home of Gideon in Manasseh. Judg. 6. 11–24; 8. 27, 32.

oracle(s) Used for the entire O.T., or a specific part of it; and for God's final revelation through Jesus Christ. Rom. 3. 2; Heb. 5. 12; 1 Pet. 4. 11.

Oreb A Midianite chief who invaded Israel. Judg. 7. 24–25; Is. 10. 26.

Orion A group of fixed stars visible for the greater part of the year. Job 38. 31.

ornaments Many examples of personal ornaments have been found in excavations, perhaps the most outstanding being those at Ur. Although the wearing of ornaments at such special occasions as weddings was considered fit and proper, the excessive wearing of ornaments is condemned in both the O.T. and N.T. Details of ornaments commonly worn are given in Gen. 24. 22–23; Ex. 32. 3; 33. 5; Pr. 25. 11–12; Is. 3. 18–23; 61.10; Ezek. 16. 11–13; 1 Tim. 2. 9.

Orpah The sister-in-law of Ruth. Ru. 1. 4–14.

orphan(s) From earliest times their care was to be the concern of Israelites. Dt. 10. 18; 24. 17; 26. 12; 27. 19. See also Ex. 22. 22–24. However, there was a general failure to do this. Job 24. 3; Is. 1. 23; Jer. 5. 28.

osprey A rather large bird of prey sometimes known as the 'fishing eagle'. It has a hooked beak and a sizeable wing-spread. Lev. 11. 18; Dt. 14. 17.

ostrich A very large bird which can run at great speeds. It was much more common in Palestine in biblical times than it is today. Job 39. 13; Is. 43. 20; Lam. 4. 3.

Othniel The nephew of Caleb and the first of the Judges. Judg. 1. 13; 3. 8–11.

oven Originally a hole in the ground with the sides coated in clay; later made of stone or well-baked bricks. Ex. 8. 3. Used figuratively Hos. 7. 7.

owl Many species of this nocturnal bird live in Palestine, building their nests in areas near villages, preferably in olive-trees. It is listed among the unclean birds. Lev. 11. 16–18; Dt. 14. 15–17; Job 30. 29; Ps. 102. 6; Is. 13. 21; 34. 11; Jer. 50. 39; Mic. 1. 8; Zeph. 2. 14.

ox, oxen By the beginning of the Bronze Age, before the patriarchs settled in Palestine, the ox was part of the farming scene in the Nile valley. Several distinct types were known around 4500 B.C. in Mesopotamia; and biblical records show that cattle were widely kept. Nu. 7. 3; Dt. 22. 10; 1 K. 1. 9; Ezek. 1. 10; Lk. 14. 3–6.

Ozni The son of Gad and founder of a clan. Nu. 26. 16.

Paddan-aram The region in Mesopotamia where Laban lived. Gen. 28. 2–7; 46. 15.

paint Used with powder by Egyptian women as they are today, but the practice was frowned on by the Hebrews. 2 K. 9. 30. See also Jer. 4. 30.

palace The royal residence, often fortified. 1 K. 21. 1; 2 K. 20. 18; Dan. 4. 4. See also 1 K. 7. 1–12; 22. 39. Archaeological excavation has shown that those in Palestine differed little from palaces in neighbouring countries.

Palestine A form of the name 'Philistine', and at first restricted to the coastal plain. Ps. 60. 8. Later, it was used of the whole country which the Bible calls 'Canaan' Gen. 11. 31, or of the land of Israel 1 S. 3. 20; 13. 19. Only about 150 miles long and 75 miles wide, it has a great variety of altitude and temperature. Geographically, it consists of four zones running from north to south. The coastal plain with the foothills (Shephelah); the western highlands stretching from the Lebanon to Judah, broken only by the plain of Esdraelon; the Jordan valley, with the Dead Sea (deeper than the Grand Canyon) at its extremity; and the central plateau consisting of the highlands E of the Jordan. As the strategic highway between Egypt and Mesopotamia it was an area of military conflict throughout its history.

palm The only species of this tree which flourishes in Palestine is the date-palm. Its fruit is not directly mentioned but reference is made to the beauty of the tree and the use of its branches. Nu. 33. 9; 2 Ch. 28. 15; Jn. 12. 12–13; Rev. 7. 9.

Palti The man to whom Saul gave David's wife. 1 S. 25. 44.

Pamphylia The coastal region of Asia Minor between Cilicia and Lycia, walled in on the N by the Taurus mountains. Its chief town was Perga. Ac. 2. 10; 13. 13; 14. 24; 15. 37–38.

Paphos The name of two settlements in Cyprus. The old Phoenician one and the Roman. It was the latter at which Paul first presented the Christian faith before the Roman authorities. Ac. 13. 6–12. *Baffo.*

papyrus A plant-like reed common in the rivers of Egypt and Palestine from which a writing-paper was made. The outer layer of the stem was removed and the inner pith was thinly sliced lengthwise, shaped and squared, and laid edge to edge. Sheets were glued together into rolls. Papyrus, however, becomes brittle with age and decays easily in damp conditions. It was used for many of the Bible manuscripts.

parable(s) (= putting things side by side) A short descriptive story told with an interesting illustration which enables the reader to discover for himself a moral and religious truth. The form was known before the time of Christ, but examples in the O.T. are few. 2 S. 12. 1–6; Is. 5. 1–7. Only in his teaching was the parable used to its fullest and highest effect. Parables in the Gospels:

Found only in Matthew

The darnel	Mt. 13. 24–30
The buried treasure	13. 44
The pearl of great value	13. 45–46
The fishing-net	13. 47–48
The unmerciful servant	Mt. 18. 23–34
Labourers in the vineyard	20. 1–16
The man with two sons	21. 28–32
The wedding-feast	22. 1–14
The prudent and foolish girls	25. 1–13
The useless servant	25. 14–30
The sheep and the goats	25. 31–46

Found only in Mark

The seed growing in the ground	Mk. 4. 26–29
Keep awake!	13. 34–36

Found only in Luke

The two debtors	Lk. 7. 36–50
The good Samaritan	10. 25–37
The friend in the middle of the night	11. 5–8

The rich fool	12. 16–21
The alert servants	12. 35–40
The trusty steward	12. 42–48
The barren fig-tree	13. 6–9
The big dinner party	14. 16–24
The tower and its cost	14. 28–33
The lost sheep	15. 3–7
The lost piece of silver	15. 8–10
The son who came back	15. 11–32
The dishonest steward	16. 1–13
The rich man and Lazarus	16. 19–31
The master and the servant	17. 7–10
The persistent widow	18. 1–8
The Pharisee and the tax-gatherer	18. 9–14
The pounds	19. 12–27

Common to Matthew and Luke

The house with foundations on rock	Mt. 7. 24–27; Lk. 6. 48–49
The yeast	Mt. 13. 33; Lk. 13. 20–21
The lost sheep	Mt. 18. 12–14; Lk. 15. 3–7.

Common to Matthew, Mark, Luke

The lamp under the meal-tub	Mt. 5. 14–16; Mk. 4. 21–22; Lk. 8. 16–17
The new patch on the old coat	Mt. 9. 16; Mk. 2. 21; Lk. 5. 36
New wine and old wine-skins	Mt. 9. 17; Mk. 2. 22; Lk. 5. 37–38
The sower	Mt. 13. 24–30; Mk. 4. 3–20; Lk. 8. 4–15
The mustard-seed	Mt. 13. 31–32; Mk. 4. 31–32; Lk. 13. 18–19
The vineyard tenants	Mt. 21. 33–41; Mk. 12. 1–9; Lk. 20. 9–16
The buds on the fig-tree	Mt. 24. 32–35; Mk. 13. 28–31; Lk. 21. 29–33

paradise A word of Persian origin meaning a walled garden. Used by Jesus for the place where souls go immediately after death. Lk. 23. 43. *See also* Lk. 16. 19–31; 2 Cor. 12. 2–4; Rev. 2. 7.

Paran An area of wild country in the central part of the Sinai peninsula. Gen. 21. 21; Nu. 10. 12; 13. 1–3; 1 S. 25. 1; 1 K. 11. 18.

parched corn Roasted grain as in certain modern breakfast cereals. Lev. 23. 14.

parchment A specially prepared skin of animals (mainly sheep, pigs and goats) which came into use as a writing material in the later O.T. period.

Parmenas One of those chosen to distribute relief to the poor. Ac. 6. 5.

Parthians A warlike people, originally inhabiting a region SE of the Caspian Sea, who established a considerable empire under Mithradates out of the ruins of the Persian empire. They invaded Judaea and placed Antigonus on the throne. Ac. 2. 9.

partridge A common bird in the deserts of Palestine and round the Dead Sea. There are several species varying in size and colour. 1 S. 26. 20; Is. 34. 15; Jer. 17. 11.

Passover The most important of the Israelite festivals kept annually on 14th Nisan or Abib (March–April) to commemorate their deliverance from the last plague and slavery in Egypt. Also known as the Feast of Unleavened Bread. Ex. 12. 1–36; Lev. 23. 4–8; Nu. 9. 2–4; 28. 16–25; Dt. 16. 1–8. In N.T. times there were always big crowds in Jerusalem at Passover time. Mk. 14. 1–2; Lk. 2. 41.

Patara A seaport near the mouth of the Xanthus, convenient for ships sailing for Phoenicia and Egypt. Ac. 21. 1–2. *Gelemish.*

Pathros An area of Upper Egypt between Cairo and Aswan where papyri show a colony of Jews lived. Is. 11. 11; Jer. 44. 1–30; Ezek. 29. 14.

patience, patient A characteristic of God's nature and a quality which he prizes highly in men. Is. 48. 9; Rom. 2. 4; 1 Cor. 13. 4; Eph. 4. 2; Col. 1. 11; 3. 12; 2 Tim. 4. 2; Jas. 5. 7; 1 Pet. 3. 9.

Patmos A small island of the Dodecanese to which John was exiled. Rev. 1. 9.

patriarch(s) The word is usually applied to the male head of a long family line as in Gen. 5. 3–31; but especially to the three great ancestors of Israel, Abraham, Isaac, and Jacob, and Jacob's twelve sons. Ac. 7. 8; Rom. 9. 1–5.

Patrobas A Roman Christian. Rom. 16. 14.

Paul Formerly Saul, he was born in Tarsus with the full privileges of a Roman citizen, though educated in Jerusalem as a Pharisee. At first he was violently anti-Christian, but after his conversion he became a great missionary who took the faith to Europe. He was imprisoned and executed in Rome. A number of his letters are preserved in the N.T. Ac. 7. 58 – 8. 3; 9. 1–30; 11. 19–30; 12. 25 – 28. 31.

Paulus, Sergius The Roman Governor of Cyprus at the time of Paul's visit. Ac. 13. 4–12.

peace offering *See* offering.

pearl Highly prized gems known from the time of Solomon. Mt. 7. 6; 13. 45; 1 Tim. 2. 19; Rev. 21. 21.

Pekah A usurper who seized the throne of Israel and attempted to organize an anti-Assyrian faction. 2 K. 15. 25–31.

Pekahiah The son and successor of Menahem as king of Israel, assassinated by Pekah. 2 K. 15. 22–26.

Pekod An Aramaean tribe living near the mouth of the Tigris. Jer. 50. 21; Ezek. 23. 23.

Pelethites Members of David's bodyguard, of Philistine ancestry. 2 S. 15. 18; 20. 7.

pen These were specially cut with a penknife for writing on papyrus or parchment. Ps. 45. 1; Jer. 8. 8; 36. 23; 3 Jn. 13.

Peniel (Penuel) The place near the Jabbok where Jacob wrestled with the angel. Gen. 32. 24–32.

Pentateuch The Greek name for the first five books of the O.T., the traditional five books of Moses. They are also called the Books of the Law, and contain the early history of the Israelites and the Mosaic Law.

Pentecost Derived from the Greek word for 'fiftieth' since the festival was kept fifty days after the beginning of the Passover on 5th Sivan (May–June), and marked the end of the harvest. It was the second in importance of Jewish festivals and was also called the Feast of Weeks, the Feast of Harvest, and the Day of Firstfruits. Ex. 23.16; Nu. 28. 26; Dt. 16. 10. *See also* Lev. 23. 15–21. It was at this time that the Holy Spirit came upon the apostles. Ac. 1. 5; 2. 1–4. *See also* 1 Cor. 16. 8.

Peor A mountain N of the Dead Sea and opposite Jericho. Nu. 23. 25 – 24. 25. *Khirbet Faghûr.*

perfume(s) Used from early times in worship, on the person and in connection with burial. Ex. 30. 25, 34–38; Est. 2. 12; S. of S. 1. 3; 4. 10; Lk. 23. 56.

Perga The civil capital and centre of the worship of Diana in Pamphylia. Ac. 13. 13–14; 14. 24–25. *Murtana.*

Pergamum The administrative capital of the Roman province of Asia in what is now W Turkey; famous for its great library and as a centre of pagan worship. Rev. 1. 11; 2. 12–17. *Bergama.*

Perizzites One of the original Canaanite tribes who became merged with the Israelites. Gen. 15. 20; Judg. 3. 5.

persecute, persecution This persistent hostility, directed against sincere and godfearing people, was known in O.T. days. *See* 1 K. 19; Jer. 20. 1–2; Dan. 3. 8–30. In the N.T. Christ predicts it for his followers. Mt. 5. 10–12; 10. 17–23; Ac. 8. 1. *See also* Mt. 24. 9-14; Ac. 12. 1–2; 19. 23–40; 1 Pet. 4. 12–16; Rev. 2. 10.

Persia The Iranian plateau bounded on the W and S by the Tigris and Indus valleys and on the E and N by the Armenian ranges and the Caspian Sea, and inhabited by Indo-European peoples. It was the greatest empire in biblical times and, under a succession of very able leaders such as Cyrus and Darius, it dominated the Middle East for nearly 200 years. Its religion was Zoroastrianism. In the Hellenistic period it was claimed by the Seleucids, but their control was far from secure. Ezr. 1. 1–11; 4. 1 – 6. 15; 7. 1–26; 1 Mac. 3. 31; 6. 1–4; 14. 1–3.

Persis A Christian convert in Rome. Rom. 16. 12.

pestilence Usually mentioned in the O.T. as a general epidemic. 2 S. 24. 15. The prophets class it with sword and famine as punishments laid on a disobedient people. Jer. 14. 12; 21. 7; 24. 10; Ezek. 7. 15; 12. 16.

Peter One of the three disciples closest to Jesus, and the leader of the Twelve. He was the first to recognize him as the Messiah and to welcome Gentiles into the church. Mt. 4. 18–20; 16. 13–19; 17. 1–4; Mk. 14. 53–72; Jn. 20. 1–9; 21. 1–22; Ac. 1. 12–22; 2. 1–41; 9. 31 – 11. 18; 15. 1–12.

Peter, First Letter of The theme is suffering for the faith, and the Christian method of meeting it. This great pastoral letter was written to help the Gentile Christians of Asia Minor who were being persecuted, and upon whom worse things were still to come. The keynote is steady encouragement to endurance in conduct, and innocence in character.

Peter, Second Letter of A general pastoral letter written to combat the beliefs and actions of men who were undermining the Christian ethic and doctrine by living immoral lives themselves and encouraging others to do the same. They justified their actions by interpreting Scripture to please themselves.

Pethor A city in N Mesopotamia S of Carchemish. Nu. 22. 2 – 24. 25.

Phanuel The father of the prophetess Anna. Lk. 2. 36.

Pharaoh The Egyptian royal title. Several are mentioned in the O.T. but few by their individual names. Gen. 12. 10–20; 39. 1 – 41. 55; Ex. 1. 8 – 2. 10; 5. 1–21; 1 K. 3. 1; 9. 16; 11. 18; 14. 25 (Shishak); 2 K. 23. 29 (Necho); Jer. 44. 30 (Hophra). *See also* 2 K. 18. 21; 19. 9.

Pharisee(s) (= separated ones) A sect of Judaism which flourished for about two centuries before and after the birth of Christ; and had arisen in protest against laxity in keeping the law and the introduction of foreign customs into Palestine. Their emphasis on the exact observance of dietary and ritual rules led them ultimately to reverence the letter rather than the spirit of the law. Mt. 5. 17–20; 15. 1–9; 16. 5–12; 23. 1–32; Ac. 5. 34; 23. 1–9.

Pharpar One of the two rivers of Damascus. 2 K. 5. 1–14.

Philadelphia (= brotherly love) A commercial centre of Lydia in Asia Minor situated in a fertile but seismic area. Rev. 1. 11; 3. 7–13. *Alashehir.*

Philemon A convert of Paul who lived in Colossae. Philem. 1–2.

Philemon, Letter to The only private letter of Paul that has been preserved. It is a tactful plea for the forgiveness and reception as a Christian brother of a runaway slave, Onesimus. Paul believes that the true test of the sincerity of the conversion of both slave and master would be their reaction to this situation.

Philetus A teacher accused of undermining the true doctrine of the resurrection. 2 Tim. 2. 17. *See also* 1 Cor. ch. 15.

Philip (= lover of horses) (1) The apostle. Mt. 10. 3; Jn. 1. 43–50; 12. 20–22; 14. 7–9; Ac. 1. 13. (2) The evangelist. Ac. 6. 1–6; 8. 1–40; 21. 8–15. (3) The son of Herod the Great and ruler of Ituraea from 4 B.C. to A.D. 34. Lk. 3. 1.

Philippi An important city on the E border of Macedonia about 10 miles inland, where the gospel was first preached in Europe. Ac. 16. 11–40; 20. 6. *See also* 2 Cor. 2. 13–14; Phil. 4. 10–20.

Philippians, Letter to the Written from prison to the church which had closer ties of friendship with Paul than any other. It is a letter of thanks for a gift brought to him by Epaphroditus; encouragement in the testing they are going through; and an appeal to maintain the unity of the church in the face of false teachers. Joy is the main emphasis throughout the letter.

Philistines The people who invaded Canaan from the south about the same time as the Israelites crossed the Jordan, and who settled in the coastal plain. Although not Semites, they gave their name in a modified form to the whole country. When they tried to extend their power into central Palestine they soon came into conflict with the Israelites. In early clashes they were victorious; and although David finally defeated them, they continued to be a thorn in the side of Israel. Judg. ch. 13–16; 1 S. ch. 4–6; 13–14; 17. 1 – 18. 7; 28–29; 31; 2 S. 5. 17–25; 8. 1; Is. 9. 12; Am. 1. 6–8; Zech. 9. 5–6.

Phinehas (= mouth of brass) (1) The grandson of Aaron. Ex. 6. 25; Nu. 25. 1–13; Judg. 20. 28. (2) The younger of Eli's evil sons. 1 S. 1. 4; 2. 12–17; 4. 17.

Phoebe A woman who held office in the church at Cenchreae. Rom. 16. 1.

Phoenicia The narrow coastal strip along the E Mediterranean known as Canaan, which is the modern Lebanon. Its Semitic population were seafarers and merchants with their chief towns at Tyre and Sidon. 1 Esd. 2. 17, 24–29; 4. 48; 6. 3; 2 Mac. 3. 5, 8; 4. 4, 22; 8. 8; Ac. 11. 19; 15. 3; 21. 2–3. *See also* 1 K. 5. 1–14; 16. 31; 18. 19; Mt. 15. 21.

Phrygia An inland region in W Asia Minor forming part of the Roman province of Asia which was extensively evangelized by Paul. Ac. 2. 10; 16. 6; 18. 23. *See also* Ac. 13. 14 – 14. 24; 19. 1.

Phygelus One of the Asiatic Christians who deserted Paul. 2 Tim. 1. 15.

phylacteries (= safeguard) Small boxes or pouches fastened to leather straps and worn either on the forehead or the left arm by Jewish males over thirteen. They contained small pieces of parchment on which were written certain passages from the law (Ex. 13. 1–10, 11–16; Dt. 6. 4–9; 11. 13–21). Dt. 6. 8; Mt. 23. 5.

physician(s) Men skilled in the art of healing practised in Bible lands from an early date. Gen. 50. 2; 2 Ch. 16. 12; Jer. 8. 22; Lk. 4. 23. *See also* Ecclus. 38. 1; Mt. 9. 12; Mk. 5. 26; Col. 4. 14.

piety The spirit represented by this word is present everywhere in Scripture. The basic idea is the love and loyalty that are the duties required of a man by the relationships of family, society and God. *See* Gen. 47. 29; 2 S. 16. 17–19; Ps. 30. 4; 85. 8; 1 Tim. 5. 4.

pig One of the earliest domesticated animals, dated back to the neolithic period. An omnivorous eater and scavenger, all five O.T. references reflect its unclean character. Lev. 11. 7; Dt. 14. 8; Pr. 11. 22; Is. 66. 3, 17; Mk. 5. 1–13; Lk. 15. 11–24.

Pi-hahiroth A place in NE Egypt where the Israelites were overtaken by the pursuing Egyptians. Ex. 14. 1–20.

Pilate The fifth Roman Governor of Judaea from about A.D. 26 to 36, appointed by Tiberius Caesar. Mt. 27. 11–26; Lk. 13. 1; 23. 1–25; Jn. 18. 28 – 19. 16, 38; Ac. 3. 13; 4. 27; 13. 28; 1 Tim. 6. 13.

pilgrimage Special journeys to sacred places were a feature of the ancient world, and by N.T. times Jerusalem was well established as such a centre for the main festivals. Lk. 2. 41–50. *See also* Ps. 122. For the figurative sense *see* 1 Ch. 29. 15; Heb. 11. 13; 1 Pet. 2. 11.

pillar(s) The pillars of cloud and fire in the wilderness were regarded as signs of God's presence. Ex. 13. 21–22. Heaps of stones commemorated important and sacred happenings. Gen. 28. 18; 31. 45; 35. 14. Two great pillars stood at the entrance to Solomon's Temple. 1 K. 7. 15–22. In O.T. times pillars were associated with pagan worship. Dt. 12. 3; Hos. 10. 2. Used symbolically of the church and the apostles. Gal. 2. 9; 1 Tim. 3. 15.

pine A tall, cone-bearing tree found on the slopes of the Lebanon, and used in the building of the Temple. 1 K. 5. 8; 6. 15; 9. 11; Ezek. 27. 5. Used figuratively Hos. 14. 8.

pipe(s) Some were simple, straight tubes with holes, others had two parallel tubes to provide melody and a kind of accompaniment; some were more like the modern flute. Gen. 4. 21; Dan. 3. 5.

Pisgah A headland in the Abarim range of Moab W of the Jordan. Nu. 21. 20; 23. 13–14; Dt. 3. 27; 34. 1–5.

Pisidia A mountainous region at the W end of the Taurus range. Ac. 13. 14; 14. 24.

pit Although used literally Gen. 14. 10; 37. 22; it also refers to death, the grave, or to Sheol. Job 33. 18; Ps. 16. 10. *See also* Nu. 16. 30–33.

pitch A resinous product of the petroleum which is now widely exploited in the Middle East in the form of oil. Gen. 6. 14; Is. 34. 9. *See also* Gen. 14. 10; Ex. 2. 3.

Pithom A city in Egypt in the valley between the Nile and Lake Timsâh, dedicated to the sun-god Atum. Ex. 1. 11.

plague No indication is given of its exact nature, but the bubonic plague was endemic in Bible lands. Nu. 11. 33; 14. 37; 16. 46–47; 25. 8. *See also* 2 K. 19. 35.

Plagues, The Ten The means by which Pharaoh was persuaded to let the Israelites leave their slavery in Egypt. *See* Ex. 7. 14 – 12. 36; Ps. 78. 42–51.

plane-tree A tree, greatly valued for the shade of its vine-like leaves, which grows particularly well in Syria and along the Mediterranean coast. The bark peels annually. Gen. 30. 37; Ezek. 31. 8.

plants It is not possible always to identify these with absolute correctness, partly due to the fact that for the original writers present-day standards of accuracy in botanical matters were not primary considerations, and also because their terminology was not so precise and comprehensive as that of the modern botanist.

plaster The inner, and sometimes the outer, walls of buildings were coated with a covering mixture of clay, or clay and straw in the case of the poor. Dt. 27. 2; Dan. 5. 5.

pledge The taking of a pledge from a debtor as guarantee for the repayment of a debt was allowed by the law, but with certain humane provisos. Dt. 24. 6, 10–13, 17.

Pleiades A constellation of seven stars. Job 9. 9; 38. 31.

plough, ploughshare This was simple and light, made of wood with a coulter tipped with iron. It scratched the soil rather than turned it. Dt. 22. 10; 1 S. 13. 20; Lk. 9. 62.

plumb-line, plummet A simple instrument consisting of a cord, with a stone or other weight attached, for testing whether a wall was straight. 2 K. 21. 13; Am. 7. 7–8.

pods These could very well be the large black, bean-like pods of the carob-tree. Lk. 15. 11–16.

poetry Associated with music and dancing from the earliest times, the teaching of the wise and the oracles of the prophets were delivered in poetic form. The structure of Hebrew poetry, in general, consists of parallelism (lines are in pairs and the second resembles the first but is not exactly the same) and metre (the number of stressed or emphasized words in each line). Over 35 per cent of the O.T. consists of poetry.

Pollux *See* Castor and Pollux.

polygamy Under the earlier system of polygamy a secondary and inferior wife could be taken to ensure the continuation of the family. However, the practice was discouraged and monogamy advocated. *See*

Gen. 16. 1–16; Dt. 17. 17; Pr. 31. 10–31;
Eph. 5. 22–33.

pomegranate A shrub, with spreading
branches and dark-green, shiny leaves
which grows wild in Persia and Syria. Its
fruit, dark-red in colour and about the
size of an orange, has a juicy pulp and
many seeds. The blossoms were used in
treating dysentery. Ex. 28. 31–34; Nu. 13.
23; 1 S. 14. 2; S. of S. 7. 12.

Pontus The coastal strip in NE Asia Minor
bordering on the Black Sea administered
with Bithynia as a Roman province. Ac.
2. 9; 18. 2; 1 Pet. 1. 1.

pool A natural or artificial reservoir to
collect rainfall or water from springs. Neh.
3. 15; Eccles. 2. 6; Is. 22. 9; Jn. 9. 7.

poplar This tree, which grows to a height
of between 30 and 60 feet, is a native of
Syria and Palestine. Its green leaves are
white on the underside. Gen. 30. 37; Job
40. 22; Hos. 4. 13.

portico A covered walk, like cloisters. Jn.
10. 23.

Potiphar The captain of Pharaoh's guard.
Gen. 39. 1–20.

Potiphera An Egyptian priest of On. Gen.
41. 45; 46. 20.

potter The clay and water were trodden
into a mixture of the right consistency
and then moulded on a flat wheel turned
by hand. Is. 41. 25; Jer. 18. 1–6.

Potter's Field A piece of land in or near
Jerusalem used to bury strangers in. Mt.
27. 3–10. *See also* Ac. 1. 15–20.

prayer Met with in the lives of all the great
biblical figures, and at its greatest takes
the form of intimate conversation with
God. Among the most noteworthy prayers in the O.T. are: 1 K. 8. 15–53; Jer. 15.
15–18; 17. 14–18; 20. 7–18; Dan. 9. 3–19.
N.T. prayer differs from that in the O.T.
because of the teaching and example of
Christ. Mt. 6. 5–13; Jn. 17; 1 Cor. 14. 13–
15.

preaching The proclamation of the good
news of the coming of God's kingdom.
1 Cor. 9. 16; 1 Tim. 5. 17. *See also* Mt. 4.
17; 10. 7; Ac. 5. 42; 8. 35–36; 28. 31; Rom.
1. 15–17; Eph. 4. 11; 1 Tim. 4. 13.

precious stones There are four principal
lists of gem stones recorded in the Bible.

These are (1) The 12 precious stones of
Aaron's breast-piece, each stone representing a tribe of Israel. Ex. 28. 17–20;
39. 10–13. (2) The wisdom list of Job. Job
28. 16–19. (3) The gems of the king of
Tyre. Ezek. 28. 13. (4) The precious stones
of the holy city, Rev. 21. 18–21, with one
for each of the 12 foundations.

The stones named in these lists are:
agate, alabaster, amethyst, beryl, chalcedony, chrysolite, chrysoprase, coral
(red and black), cornelian, crystal, emerald, felspar (green), garnet, jade, jasper,
lapis lazuli, pearls, sardin, sardonyx, topaz, turquoise.

pride There is a constant condemnation of
human arrogance throughout the Bible.
Ps. 10. 2; Pr. 8. 13; 16. 18; Is. 14. 11;
1 Cor. 4. 6. *See also* Ex. 5. 2; 2 K. 5. 10–13;
Dan. 4. 28–32; Mt. 23. 1–12; Mk. 10. 45;
Lk. 18. 11–12; Jn. 13. 12–17; Jas. 4. 6;
1 Pet. 5. 5.

priest(s) In early Israel any man could
present an offering to God. Gen. 12. 8; but
at Sinai, Aaron and his descendants were
nominated as priests. Ex. 28. 1–2. They
had to meet very rigid requirements and
to wear special vestments when they performed the ritual in the sanctuary, which
became elaborate. Ex. 28. 40–43; 29. 36–
42; Lev. 21. 16–23; Nu. 18. 1–7; 1 Ch. 24.
1–19. Other functions Lev. 7. 29–36; ch.
13–14; Nu. 10. 1–10; 18. 8–20. In the N.T.
Christ is described as a high priest after
the order of Melchizedek and Christians
as sharing in his priestly activity. Heb. 4.
14–15; 5. 1–10; 1 Pet. 2. 9; Rev. 1. 6; 5.
10; 20. 6.

Prisca, Priscilla The wife of a Jewish
Christian tent-maker. Ac. 18. 24–26;
Rom. 16. 3; 1 Cor. 16. 19.

prison(s) These were usually sordid, often
consisting of natural pits or cave-like
dungeons. Gen. 37. 22–24; 39. 20–23;
Judg. 16. 21; Ps. 79. 11; Jer. 37. 15–16;
Mt. 14. 3; Ac. 12. 5–10; 16. 16–40.

Prochorus One of those chosen to see to
the needs of Christian widows. Ac. 6. 5.

proconsul The chief official of provinces
which were administered by the Roman
Senate. Ac. 18. 12. *See also* Ac. 13. 7.

prophecy, prophets This arose and developed in Israel against a background of

prophecy in the Near East; but in Israel it became something unique. 1 S. 9. 1–14; 19. 20–24; 1 K. 18. 17–29. The true prophet was the spokesman of God, and his messages to the people were consistent with the character of God as revealed in the law. The great prophets denounced every denial of the spirit of Israel's religion. Is. 1. 10–17; Hos. 6. 4–6; Am. 5. 21–24; Mic. 6. 6–8. They were not, however, pessimistic, but believed that there was a core of the nation which, as the Remnant, would inherit the promises of God, and that there would be a brighter age when the will of God would be perfectly done. Is. 1. 9; 2. 2–4; 9. 6–7; 11. 1–10; Jer. 23. 5–6; 38. 14–28; Ezek. 34. 22–31.

prophetess A woman called by God to the work of prophecy. Ex. 15. 20 (Miriam); Judg. 4. 4 (Deborah); 2 K. 22. 14 (Huldah); Neh. 6. 14 (Noadiah). *See also* Is. 8. 3; Rev. 2. 20.

prophets, false The O.T. mentions prophets of heathen gods 1 K. 18. 19; but there were also prophets in Israel who spoke falsely in the LORD's name. Various explanations for this are given, as are also the distinguishing marks of true prophecy. Dt. 18. 21–22; 1 K. 22. 1–28; Jer. 14. 14–15; 23. 12–22, 25–32; Ezek. 13. 1–10.

proverbs The name given by the Israelites to short, pithy sentences containing valuable truths in familiar language. Job 14. 19; Jer. 13. 23; Ezek. 16. 44; Jn. 4. 37.

Proverbs, Book of An intensely practical collection of pithy sayings in which, by comparison or contrast, some important truth is illustrated. Every area of life is treated. Moral and ethical implications are drawn, and positive instruction for everyday living is given with an incisiveness unmatched in the world's literature. 'Wisdom' (knowledge + the ability to use it meaningfully) is the key word of the book, and it is shown to begin with and to centre on God.

province An administrative unit of the Roman empire. Those presenting no special problems were ruled by a proconsul appointed by the Senate. Provinces on the frontier were under the control of a legate or procurator appointed by the emperor.

Psalms, Book of Derived from the Greek, the word means 'a poem sung to the accompaniment of musical instruments'. Written over a long period of time, they became the hymnbook of the Temple. They sum up and express the whole religious experiences of the Jews, and in them every mood and condition of life is brought before God in worship. Expressing complete trust in him, their praise is directed to God alone, making known his pure character and the need for his worshippers to obey the moral law. Although the book expresses every kind of feeling, the note of joy predominates.

Ptolemais The Greek name of Acco whose people were hostile to the Maccabees. 1 Mac. 5. 14–22; 10. 1–60; 12. 39–48.

Ptolemy The dynastic title of the Egyptian Pharaohs descended from Ptolemy Soter, one of Alexander's generals. Ptolemy VI, Philometer. 1 Mac. 1. 18; 10. 57–58; 11. 13–18.

Publius The chief magistrate of Malta at the time of Paul's shipwreck. Ac. 28. 1–10.

Pul Tiglath-pileser III of Assyria. 2 K. 15. 19; 1 Ch. 5. 26.

punishment(s) The two forms laid down in the O.T. for wrongdoing are retaliation Ex. 21. 23–25; Lev. 24. 14–22; and restitution Ex. 21. 19–22, 26–34; 22. 1–4, 5–15. The underlying principle was that the evil was punished rather than the wrongdoer. Dt. 17. 12–13. The N.T. goes further in stressing that the aim is for the offender to recognize his guilt and to repent. 1 Cor. 5. 5.

Pur, Purim A Jewish festival kept on 14th and 15th Adar (February–March) celebrating their deliverance from the pogrom planned by Haman. Gifts were exchanged and given to the poor. Est. 3. 7; 9. 1–32.

purification, purify The O.T. laws lay down rules for purifying persons and objects which have become 'ritually' unclean. Lev. ch. 12–15 (Lk. 2. 22–24); Nu. 19. In the N.T., although there is a movement from the outer to the inner, there is no relaxation in the basic requirement of purity itself. *See* Mt. 5. 8, 27; 19. 3–9;

Mk. 7. 14–23; Lk. 11. 37–41; 1 Cor. 5. 9–13; 6. 12–20.

purple A famous Tyrian dye obtained from a species of shellfish. Its use in clothing was a sign of rank and wealth. Ex. 28. 1–8; Judg. 8. 26; 2 Ch. 3. 14; Est. 1. 6; 2 Mac. 4. 38; Mk. 15. 17–20; Lk. 16. 19.

Puteoli An important harbour on the W coast of Italy. Ac. 28. 13. *Pozzuoli.*

quail One of the smallest game birds. They breed in many parts of Europe and go south in the winter to the Mediterranean areas, many reaching Africa. Ex. 16. 13; Nu. 11. 31–32; Ps. 105. 40.

Quartus A Corinthian Christian who sent greetings to the Roman church. Rom. 16. 23.

queen(s) The most influential in the biblical records were dowager queens or queen mothers. Jezebel 1 K. 16. 29 – 2 K. 9. 37; Athaliah 2 K. 11. 1–16; Bathsheba 1 K. 1. Among foreign queens are Vashti Est. 1; Esther Est. 2. 17; the Queen of Sheba 1 K. 10. 1–13; Bernice Ac. 25. 13–23; Drusilla Ac. 24. 24.

Queen of Heaven The female fertility goddess, possibly the Phoenician Ashtoreth. Jer. 7. 18; 44. 15–30.

Quirinius The Governor of Syria at the time of Jesus's birth. Lk. 2. 2.

quiver A case for carrying arrows, worn either on the back or at the side. Is. 49. 2; Lam. 3. 13.

Qumran The name of a wadi and an ancient ruin in its vicinity NW of the Dead Sea. Excavations by G. L. Harding and R. de Vaux 1948–58 have shown that the site was inhabited during the time of the Judaean monarchy, and that the complex of buildings uncovered formed the headquarters of the community (probably Essenes) to which the Qumran manuscripts belonged. 'Ain Feshka. See Scrolls, Dead Sea.

quotations There are some 250 direct citations of the O.T. in the N.T. If indirect or partial quotations and allusions are added, then the total exceeds a thousand. Quotations are sometimes taken from the Hebrew text, but more often from the Greek (Septuagint) translation. The minor verbal differences which occur show that the biblical writers' concern was with the meaning rather than with the words in themselves.

Raamah A region and its people in SW Arabia. Gen. 10. 7; Ezek. 27. 22.

Rabbah The capital city of Ammon 22 miles E of the Jordan. Dt. 3. 11; 2 S. 12. 26–30; Ezek. 21. 18–21; Am. 1. 14. *See also* Jer. 49. 1–3. In the Hellenistic period it was called Philadelphia and became one of the cities of the Decapolis. *'Ammân.*

Rabbi A title of respect (= my master) which became the name for the authorized Jewish teachers. Mt. 23. 1–12; Jn. 1. 35–39; 3. 1–2, 26.

Rabbuni An even more respectful title than Rabbi. Jn. 20. 16.

race This pastime seems to have been known to the Israelites, and Paul uses it to illustrate his teaching. Eccles. 9. 11; 1 Cor. 9. 24; 2 Tim. 4. 7.

Rachel The younger daughter of Laban. Gen. ch. 29–33; 35. 16–20.

Raguel The father of Sarah. Tobit 3. 7–17; 14. 12.

Rahab (1) The woman of Jericho who hid Joshua's spies. Jos. 2. 1–24; 6. 22–25; Mt. 1. 5; Heb. 11. 31; Jas. 2. 25. (2) A poetical name for the Egypt of the Exodus. Ps. 89. 10; Is. 51. 9–10.

rain There are two periods of rainfall in the Palestinian area, the light rains which fall about the end of October before the sowing, and the heavier rains about March. Annual rainfall varies considerably from zero in the Negeb desert to 60 inches in the Lebanon range. Jerusalem has an average of 25 inches.

rainbow The outward appearance of the glory of the Lord in the visions of Ezekiel and John. Ezek. 1. 28; Rev. 4. 3; 10. 1. *See also* Gen. 9. 13–15, where God's bow in the clouds is the sign of his covenant with Noah.

ram(s) The male sheep, sometimes used for sacrifice. Gen. 22. 13; Lev. 23. 13. Their skins were used in the Tabernacle and their heat-flattened horns as trumpets. Ex. 36. 19; Jos. 6. 6.

Rama, Ramah (1) A town near Bethel N of Gibeah, fortified by Baasha. Judg. 4. 5; 1 K. 15. 16–22; Jer. 40. 1–2; Mt. 2. 18. (2) The birthplace of Samuel in Ephraim. 1 S. 1. 19–20; 7. 15–17; 8. 4–22; 19. 18–24. It is called Ramathaim in 1 Mac. 11. 34.

Rameses A district and town in NE Egypt. Gen. 47. 1–12; Ex. 1. 11; 12. 37.

Ramoth-gilead A walled city in Gilead near the Syrian border. Dt. 4. 41–43; Jos. 21. 38; 1 K. 4. 7, 13; 22. 1–38; 2 K. 9. 1–6.

ransom The price paid for injury or damage. Lev. 19. 20. For other laws about restitution *see* Ex. 21. 26 – 22. 15; Lev. ch. 25; 27. As applied to Christ in the N.T. Mk. 10. 45. *See also* redeem, redemption.

Raphael The archangel who assumed the name of Azarias when sent to help Tobit and Tobias. Tobit 3. 17; 5. 4 – 12. 22.

Ras Shamra The modern name for the ancient city of Ugarit on the Syrian coast opposite Cyprus where clay tablets were found (1929–36) which throw great light on Canaanite culture and religion, and the world in which Israel developed.

rat These very small rodents are found in Palestine. The black rat, host to the flea which carries the bubonic plague, had made its way into Mesopotamia from the East well before Israel's entry into Canaan. 1 S. 5. 6 – 6. 5; Is. 66. 17.

raven Palestine has six species of this bird which shares the scavenging habits of many birds of prey. Gen. 8. 6–7; 1 K. 17. 2–6; Job 38. 41; Is. 34. 11; Lk. 12. 24.

razor The razor, or at least a knife used for shaving, was in common use in Israel from ancient times. Nu. 6. 5; Judg. 13. 5; 16. 17; 1 S. 1. 11. *See also* Nu. 8. 7. Used metaphorically Ps. 52. 2; Is. 7. 20; Ezek. 5. 1.

reaping In ancient times the grain was pulled up by the roots or cut with a sickle, and the stalks collected into bundles for threshing. Strict rules were laid down. Lev. 19. 9; 23. 10–11; 25. 11; 1 S. 8. 12. Used figuratively Pr. 22. 8; Hos. 8. 7; Gal. 6. 7–8.

Rebecca The sister of Laban and the wife of Isaac. Gen. 24; 25. 20 – 26. 11; 27. 1 – 28. 3.

Rechab, Rechabites (1) A Kenite who helped Jehu stamp out Baal worship. His descendants followed the nomadic life as in the wilderness period to show their loyalty to Jehovah and, in particular, took no intoxicating drink. 2 K. 10. 15–28; Jer. 35. 1–19. (2) One of the murderers of Ishbosheth. 2 S. 4. 5–12.

redeem, redemption The basic idea has two parts. Deliverance *from* the penalty of the law (including the price paid); and deliverance *to* a new freedom from sin, a new relationship with God and a new life in Christ. *See* Rom. 3. 21–26; 6. 1–4; 1 Cor. 6. 20; Gal. 3. 13–14; Eph. 1. 4–10; 1 Pet. 1. 18–19; 3. 18; Rev. 5. 9.

redemption of land Any land forfeited by economic distress could be bought back by the nearest relation. Lev. 25. 23–34. *See also* Lev. 27. 16–25.

Red Sea The thousand-mile stretch of water separating Africa from Arabia, part of the great Rift Valley. In the O.T. it refers to the Bitter Lakes region in the Egyptian Delta north of Suez Ex. 10. 19; 13. 17 – 15. 22; and also to the Gulfs of Suez and Aqabah 1 K. 9. 26.

reeds Several varieties of reed grow along the river banks and the lake edges in Palestine and Egypt. They were used for making pens, paper (papyrus) and boats. Job 40. 21; Is. 18. 2.

refiner, refining The process of separating metal from alloy and dross was known by the Canaanites and Philistines from early times. Is. 1. 25; Jer. 6. 29. Used figuratively of God purifying Israel in the furnace of suffering. *See* Pr. 17. 3; 27. 21; Is. 48. 10; Zech. 13. 9; Mal. 3. 2–3.

regeneration The new birth of the Christian. *See* Ezek. 36. 26–27; Jn. 1. 12–13; 3. 5; Rom. 6. 4; 12. 2; Eph. 2. 4–6; Tit. 3. 4–7; 1 Pet. 1. 23; 2 Pet. 1. 3–4; 1 Jn. 3. 9.

Rehob The northern limit to which Joshua's spies went. Nu. 13. 21.

Rehoboam The son of Solomon who succeeded only to the territory of Judah and Benjamin. 1 K. 12. 1–24; 14. 21–31.

Rehoboth A well dug by Isaac's servants. Gen. 26. 16–22.

Rehum The high commissioner of the Samaritans whose complaints to Artaxerxes delayed the rebuilding of Jerusalem's walls. Ezr. 4. 6–24. Rathymus in 1 Esd. 2. 16–25.

Rekem One of the kings of Midian killed by Moses. Nu. 31. 8; Jos. 13. 21.

Remaliah The father of king Pekah. 2 K. 15. 25.

remnant The spiritual kernel of Israel who would survive God's judgement and become the means through which he continues his work in the world. Is. 1. 9; 10. 20–23; 11. 11–12; Rom. 9. 27–29; 11. 5–7. See also Gen. 6. 7–8; 7. 1; Jer. 32. 36–40; Ezek. 36. 22–29; Zeph. 3. 11–13; Zech. 8. 7–13; Heb. 8. 8–12.

repent, repentance In the Bible this always means something much deeper than man's regret for sin or his resolution to do better. It is a complete turning to God, made possible only by him, which must be sincere and must show itself in appropriate action. Mt. 4. 17; Lk. 3. 3–9; Ac. 20. 20–21; 2 Pet. 3. 9.

Rephaim The name of a giant people who were in Canaan before Abraham's time. Gen. 14. 5; 15. 20; Dt. 2. 10–11; Jos. 12. 4.

Rephaim, Vale of A fertile plain between Jerusalem and Bethlehem. 1 Ch. 11. 15–19; 14. 8–17.

Rephan A pagan god worshipped by the Israelites in the wilderness. Ac. 7. 39–43.

Rephidim A camping site in the wilderness where the Amalekites were defeated. Ex. 17. 1–13.

resurrection Literally, the return to life of the dead: a belief which arose in later O.T. times but was not accepted by all Jews. The Christian hope is based on the resurrection of Christ. Mt. 22. 23–33; Lk. 20. 34–38; Jn. 11. 21–26; Ac. 23. 6–8; 24. 14–15; 1 Cor. 15. 20–27; Rev. 20. 4–15. See also Job 19. 25–27; Ps. 16. 9–11; Is. 26. 19; Dan. 12. 2; Jn. 5. 25–29; 2 Cor. 5. 1; Phil. 3. 20–21; 1 Th. 4. 13–17. The resurrection of Christ Mt. 27. 57 – 28. 20; Mk. 15. 42 – 16. 14; Lk. 23. 50 – 24. 49; Jn. 19. 38 – 21. 14.

Reuben, Reubenites The first child of Jacob and Leah whose descendants formed the tribe. Gen. 29. 15–32; 37. 12–30; 42. 18–38; 46. 9; 49. 1–4; Nu. 26. 5–11; 32. 1–38; Jos. 13. 15–23.

Reuel The priest of Midian and father-in-law of Moses. Ex. 2. 16–22. See Jethro.

revelation The various means by which God makes himself, his character and his will known to men. See Gen. 28. 10–16; Ps. 19. 1; Jer. 1. 4–10; Ezek. 37. 1–6; Am. 7. 7–8; Lk. 10. 22; Jn. 1. 1–18; 7. 15–17; 14. 9; 15. 15; 16. 13; 17. 6; 1 Cor. 12. 3; Heb. 1. 1–3.

Revelation of John, The The author is writing to persecuted Christians, whom he believes may have to face even greater danger in the near future, because he has a message of encouragement from Jesus Christ for the faithful and of warning for the complacent. He believes that God is about to intervene in human affairs in a way which would usher in a new age and be the triumph of Christ and his church and of good over evil. The writer uses a code to protect his readers because outright Christian literature and the spreading of the gospel were banned in the Roman empire.

revenge See avenger of blood.

reverence The respect that man should show in the presence of God, inspired by his goodness. Lev. 19. 30; Eph. 5. 21; Heb. 12. 28; 1 Pet. 3. 15. See also Ex. 3. 5; Ps. 95. 6; Is. 6. 5.

Rezin The last king of Samaria to reign in Damascus. 2 K. 15. 37; 16. 5–9; Is. 7. 1–9.

Rezon A guerrilla leader who made himself king of Damascus. 1 K. 11. 23–24.

Rhegium A safe and strategically important harbour in SW Italy opposite Messina. Ac. 28. 13. Reggio.

Rhoda The servant girl of John Mark's mother. Ac. 12. 6–17.

Rhodes An important Greek city on the island of the same name. Ezek. 27. 15; 1 Mac. 15. 23; Ac. 21. 1.

Rhodocus A Jewish traitor. 2 Mac. 13. 21.

Riblah An important town on the E bank of the river Orontes. 2 K. 25. 1–7; Jer. 39. 1–8; 52. 26–27. Ribleh.

riddle A form of hidden saying. Nu. 12. 3–8; Judg. 14. 5–19; Ps. 49. 4; Pr. 1. 5–6; Dan. 5. 12. See also Heb. 2. 6; Rev. 13. 18.

righteous, righteousness The O.T. teaches that behaviour which is just and good agrees with the will of God, and this teaching is continued and developed in the N.T. Ps. 103. 6; Is. 45. 8; Ezek. 18. 5–9; Mal. 4. 2. *See also* Ex. 20. 1–17; Dt. 6. 25; Mt. 5. 6–10; Jn. 16. 8–11; 1 Jn. 1. 6–10.

Rimmon A Syrian storm god worshipped at Damascus. 2 K. 5. 18–19.

ring A popular form of jewellery worn by both men and women. Ex. 35. 22. Rulers had signet-rings to seal official documents. Gen. 41. 42; Est. 3. 10; 8. 2.

river(s) With the exception of the Jordan, the rivers of Palestine are mostly small streams or wadis, often seasonal, and important only for irrigation. In the O.T. the word is used chiefly of foreign rivers. Gen. 2. 10; 15. 18; 2 K. 5. 12. Used symbolically Ps. 46. 4; Is. 43. 2; Rev. 22. 1–2.

roads As a buffer state between Egypt and the great empires of the north, Palestine was crossed by military and commercial highways serviceable for chariots. Secondary roads were mere tracks. Is. 40. 3; 62. 10; Jer. 31. 21. *See also* Nu. 20. 17; Is. 57. 14; Mt. 13. 4.

robbery Such illegal seizure of another's property, although forbidden by law, still persisted. Judg. 9. 25; Is. 10. 2; Ezek. 22. 29; Hos. 6. 9; Lk. 10. 30–37; Jn. 10. 1; 2 Cor. 11. 26.

rock A natural fortress. Judg. 20. 45–47. Used figuratively 2 S. 22. 2–3; Ps. 18. 2; 71. 3; Mt. 16. 18.

rock-badger A form of the Syrian Rock Hyrax. Round-backed and with no visible tail, it has short, sturdy legs and feet with flexible soles. The general colour is grey-brown and it is roughly rabbit-sized. Lev. 11. 5; Ps. 104. 18; Pr. 30. 26.

Rocks of the Wild Goats The place where David saved Saul's life. 1 S. 24. 1–22.

roebuck This is a small deer, standing only some 30 inches, with short upright antlers. It stays mostly in cover, coming out only to graze. Dt. 14. 5; 1 K. 4. 23.

Roman(s) (1) Inhabitants of Rome. Ac. 2. 10. (2) Officials representing the Roman authority. Jn. 11. 48; Ac. 25. 16. (3) Citizens of the empire who enjoyed important privileges. Ac. 16. 16–39; 22. 22–29.

Romans, Letter to the Written by Paul from prison to a church he had not founded, it provides (together with the letter to the Galatians) one of the most comprehensive sources of the central truths of Christianity. Its main theme is the righteousness of God and salvation through faith: a theme which is developed by a systematic and doctrinal argument (ch. 1–11), and then by an ethical or practical application (ch. 12–15). This is, however, essentially a letter from Paul to the church at Rome and the subject is why he is coming to visit them. He stresses that Christianity, a faith for all men, is the one and only means of salvation and he urges them to cultivate Christian ideals and to practise Christian actions.

Rome The capital of the ancient world, situated on the left bank of the Tiber some 15 miles from the sea. Although not mentioned in the O.T., it figures frequently in the Apocrypha. 1 Mac. 1. 10; 7. 1; 8. 17–32; 12. 1–4; 15. 15–21. Jews were expelled by Claudius, but the city soon became a centre of Christianity. Ac. 2. 10; 18. 2; 19. 21; 28. 14–16, 30–31; Rom. 1. 15; 2 Tim. 1. 15–18. In later days, like Babylon, it became a symbol of organized paganism and opposition to Christianity. *See* Rev. ch. 17–18.

rose At least four wild species now exist in Palestine as well as oleanders. 2 Esd. 2. 19; Wisd. 2. 8; Ecclus. 24. 14; 39. 13.

rudder In biblical times these were, in effect, steering paddles at the stern of the ship on the port or starboard side which could be lifted and fixed to the side of the ship in rough weather. *See* Ac. 27. 40. Used figuratively Jas. 3. 3–5.

rue A plant, growing up to 5 feet tall, with clusters of bright yellow flowers at the top of its stems. It was in great use medicinally as an antiseptic, and in cooking. Lk. 11. 42.

Rufus The son of the Simon who carried Christ's cross. Mk. 15. 21.

rush The soft, or bog, rush grows along the edges of Palestinian streams or rivers and its grasslike leaves are used for basket-making. Job 8. 11; Is. 19. 6; 35. 7.

Ruth A Moabitess, the widow of Mahlon, who married Boaz. Ru. ch. 1–4; Mt. 1. 5.

Ruth, Book of Its historical purpose is to trace the ancestry of king David back to Ruth the Moabitess; but its deeper purpose is to show that genuine religion is not confined to people of any one race or religion, and that God blesses all who truly serve him.

sabbath (= ceasing) Usually applied to the seventh day of the week, it lasted from sunset on Friday to the appearance of the first stars on Saturday. It was observed as a memorial of the creation, of the deliverance from Egypt, a humane provision of rest for man and beast, and a day to worship the LORD. Ex. 20. 8–11; Lev. 23. 3; Dt. 5. 15. During and after the exile its observance became an important mark distinguishing the Jews from their heathen neighbours, but this led to its being hedged around with many petty restrictions. Neh. 10. 31; Mk. 2. 3 – 3. 5; Lk. 4. 16–21; Jn. 7. 19–24. For other N.T. teaching *see* Ac. 15. 28–29; 20. 7; Rom. 14. 5; 1 Cor. 16. 1–2; Col. 2. 16–17; Rev. 1. 10.

Sabbath Day's Journey The distance that could be travelled on that day without breaking the law, worked out by the scribes on the basis of Ex. 16. 29; Jos. 3. 3–4. Ac. 1. 12.

Sabbatical Year Special legislation was provided in the O.T. governing every seventh year. Behind this lay an awareness that land, like people, needed rest and that human dignity is entitled to land, liberty and the pursuit of happiness. Ex. 21. 2–6; 23. 10–11; Lev. 25. 1–55; Dt. 15. 1–3.

sackcloth A coarse material, often made from goat hair, usually associated with mourning, humiliation and penitence. Gen. 37. 34; 2 S. 3. 31; 1 K. 20. 31–32; 21. 27; 2 K. 6. 30; Job 16. 15; Is. 3. 24; Mt. 11. 21; Rev. 11. 3.

sacrifice The O.T. writers saw sacrifice as a means which God had given men to enable them to have fellowship with him. The fundamental underlying belief was the idea of the covenant. At bottom, sacrifice was always a prayer to which was added the idea of giving, of real offering.

Later, other elements mingled with this. First, the search for a sure and exclusive relationship with God through blood. Then sacrifice became an accepted punishment, a sort of penance. Finally, there came the idea of at-one-ment effected by a restitution sacrifice.

The origin of sacrifice goes back further than Moses Jer. 7. 22; but food offerings were seldom involved before the settlement in Canaan, and even then they were considered of less value than sacrifices of domestic animals. During the early monarchy, sacrifices were first presented to God and then burnt; and they could be offered almost anywhere and even without the help of a priest, but the worshipper must be ritually pure. Gen. 35. 2; 1 S. 16. 5–6; 20. 26. All the circumstances of life could be the occasion of a sacrifice, but most were associated with gratitude for the harvests.

When worship became centralized at Jerusalem, regular sacrifices began to be made on behalf of the community rather than the individual, in which the priests became necessary intermediaries between the people and God. This led to a detailed organization of the sacrificial ritual; but it is noticeable that the evolution and development of the cult of sacrifice marked a time of spiritual cooling-off in Israel. After the return from the exile, these meticulous details were extended to concern the choice of offerings.

The N.T. speaks of the death of Christ in words that recall O.T. sacrifices. 1 Cor. 5. 7; Eph. 5. 1–2; Heb. 9. 11–28. The sacrifice which Christians offer is essentially that of themselves in God's service. Rom. 12. 1; Phil. 2. 17; Heb. 13. 15–16; 1 Pet. 2. 4–5. *See* offerings.

Sadducees A Jewish party which took its name from Zadok. 1 K. 1. 34. From about 200 B.C. it consisted chiefly of the aristocratic priestly and lay families. They were conservative in religion, rejecting the oral traditions of the elders as well as belief in the resurrection of the dead. Politically, they were concerned to maintain good relations with the Roman occupying power. Little is heard of them after the destruction of Jerusalem in A.D. 70. Mt. 3. 7–8; 22. 23–34; Ac. 5. 17; 23. 6–8.

saffron A substance, produced from the dried styles and stigmas of several species of crocus native to Greece and Asia Minor, which was used for dyeing and for colouring foodstuffs. S. of S. 4. 14.

saints (=holy ones) God's people, who are called to reflect his holiness in their own lives. 2 Chr. 6. 41. *See also* Rom. 1. 7; 8. 28; 1 Cor. 1. 2; 16. 1; 2 Cor. 3. 18; Phil. 1. 1.

Salamis An important city on the SE coast of Cyprus. Ac. 13. 4–5. *Famagusta.*

Salem The city of the priest-king Melchizedek, traditionally associated with Jerusalem. Gen. 14. 18–19; Ps. 76. 2; Heb. 7. 1–2.

Salim A place near Aenon on the Jordan. Jn. 3. 23.

Salome (1) The wife of Zebedee and the mother of James and John. Mt. 27. 56; Mk. 15. 40; 16. 1. (2) The daughter of Herodias who danced before Herod. *See* Mt. 14. 3–11.

salt There are two special uses in the Bible. It was an accompaniment of all sacrifices Lev. 2. 13; Ezek. 43. 23–24; and the word acquired a symbolic significance for permanence since salt preserves from decay. Nu. 18. 19; Mt. 5. 13; Mk. 9. 49–50. It also stands for barrenness because of the extreme sterility of the land surrounding the Dead (Salt) Sea. *See* Dt. 29. 23; Judg. 9. 45.

Salt, Valley of The scene of David's, and also Amaziah's, victories over the Edomites. 2 S. 8. 13; 2 K. 14. 7. *Wâdi el-Milḥ.*

saltwort Some twenty species are found in Palestine. It is a sturdy shrub related to the spinach, some varieties in the Dead Sea area reaching a height of 10 feet. Job 30. 4.

salutation(s) These played, and still do, an important function in the East, and were laid down in detail for observance at every kind of social occasion. They could be time-consuming. *See* Gen. 33. 3–4; 1 S. 20. 41–42; 25. 6; 2 K. 4. 29; Est. 3. 1–6; Mt. 5. 47; Lk. 10. 5–6; 15. 20; Rom. 16. 16; 1 Pet. 5. 14.

salvation, save Basically, it implies 'deliverance' from any kind of evil. From defeat in battle Ex. 15. 1–18; trouble Ps. 34. 6; violence 2 S. 22. 1–51; reproach Ps. 57. 1–3; exile Ps. 106. 47; death Ps. 6. 4;

sin Ezek. 36. 22–31. At first, the conception of salvation was primarily national, but the prophet's horizon gradually widened to include the Gentiles. Is. 49. 5–6; 55. 1–5. There is also increasing stress on the righteous remnant and the individual rather than the whole nation; and deliverance is from sin itself as well as from the consequences of it. *See* Ps. 51; Jer. 31. 31–34; Ezek. 36. 24–28.

In the O.T. the most important human conditions necessary for salvation are complete trust in God, obedience to his moral law, and repentance accompanied by the required ritual sacrifice. The central theme of the N.T. is the salvation brought by Christ. *See* Mt. 1. 18–21; Lk. 19. 9–10; Ac. 4. 12; 13. 26; Rom. 5. 6–11; Eph. 1. 11–14.

Samaria (1) Built by Omri as the capital of the northern kingdom of Israel on a hill 7 miles NW of Shechem which commanded the main trade routes through the plain of Esdraelon. Captured by the Assyrians about 721 B.C., many non-Jews were settled there. Hostile to the Maccabeans, it was conquered by John Hyrcanus and rebuilt by Herod the Great as Sebaste. 1 K. 16. 24, 29–32; 20. 1–34; 2 K. 3. 1–6; 6. 24 – 7. 16; 10. 1–7, 17–28; 17. 1–6, 24–33; Am. 4. 1; 1 Mac. 3. 10–12. *See also* 1 K. 22. 39. *Sebastiyeh.* Excavations by G. A. Reisner 1908–10 and J. W. Crowfoot 1931–5 have shown that the site was unoccupied from the Early Bronze Age until the Israelite kingdom. Fortifications and palaces dating from the time of Omri until its fall have been uncovered in the 16 levels of occupation. Particularly fine remains, including buildings, coins, stamped jar-handles, pottery and papyri, of the Hellenistic period have been found. (2) The administrative area and district in the centre of Palestine, and another name for the kingdom of Israel, which extended from Bethel to Dan and from the Mediterranean to Syria. 1 K. 18. 1–6; Jer. 31. 5; Hos. 8. 1–13; Am. 3. 1–12; Judith 4. 4; 1 Mac. 3. 10; 10. 38; 2 Mac. 15. 1; Lk. 17. 11; Jn. 4. 3–4; Ac. 1. 8; 8. 1; 9. 31; 15. 3.

Samaritans The people of the region of Samaria, between whom and the Jews of

Judaea hostility increasingly developed in post-exilic times. The breach was completed with the establishment of a rival Temple at Mt Gerizim. Some of their descendants still live at *Nablus*. Ezr. 4; Lk. 10. 30–37; Jn. 4. 3–26, 39–42; Ac. 8. 4–25.

Samos A rocky island in the Mediterranean, only about a mile off the mainland of Asia Minor. 1 Mac. 15. 23; Ac. 20. 15.

Samothrace A small Aegean island between Asia and Macedonia. Ac. 16. 11.

Samson An Israelite hero of the tribe of Dan famous for his one-man guerrilla war against the Philistines. Judg. ch. 13–16.

Samuel The last of the great Judges and the first of the prophets after Moses, who created the kingship in Israel by anointing Saul as the first king. He played a vital role in the transition of the Israelite tribes into a nation; and no other O.T. figure combined in himself so many different functions. 1 S. ch. 1–3; 7. 1–17; 8. 6–22; ch. 9–12; 13. 8–15; ch. 15–16; 19. 18–24; 25. 1.

Samuel, First and Second Books of These were one book in the Hebrew manuscripts but were divided when the Septuagint translation was made. 1 Samuel records Jewish history following the period of the Judges; and shows the origin of the monarchy, making clear the criteria of a good king. 2 Samuel covers the entire period of David's reign, recording the power of the monarchy during the greatest period in Israel's history.

Sanballat The Governor of Samaria in the time of Nehemiah, and his bitterest enemy. Neh. 2. 10, 19–20; 4. 1–9; 6. 1–9; 13. 28.

sanctuary A place set aside for worship; but in the Bible the place where Jehovah was worshipped. At first this was the Tabernacle, but after the occupation of Canaan, Solomon built the Temple in Jerusalem as a permanent sanctuary. 1 Ch. 22. 19; Ps. 114. 2; Ezek. 23. 39; 28. 18; Zeph. 3. 4. In the N.T. the earthly sanctuary is shown to be only a type of the true heavenly one. Heb. 8. 1–2; 9. 1–12; 10. 19.

sandal The normal outdoor footwear, consisting of a plain sole of leather or wood held to the foot by a leather thong, though the poor went barefoot. For various customs concerning sandals: Ex. 3. 5; Dt. 25. 7–10; Ru. 4. 7–8; 2 S. 15. 30.

Sanhedrin Ac. 5. 21. *See* Council.

Sarah (1) The wife of Abraham, first called Sarai. Gen. 11. 29; 12. 10–20; 16. 1–6; 17. 15–22; 20. 1 – 21. 13; 23. 1–2, 19. (2) The daughter of Raguel and wife of Tobias who was her eighth husband. Tobit 3. 7–17; 7. 8 – 8. 9.

Sardis A city in Asia Minor, capital of the kingdom of Sardis. Rev. 1. 11; 3. 1–6. *Sart.*

Sargon A usurper who succeeded to the throne of Assyria (772–705 B.C.) after the murder of Shalmaneser V. He completed the siege of Samaria and, after the conquest of Israel, settled the city with other peoples. Is. 20. 1.

Satan (= adversary) The evil power that stands in opposition to God, but which is always subject to his will in the end. 1 Ch. 21. 1; Job 1. 6–12; Zech. 3. 1–2; Mk. 1. 12; 3. 22–26; Lk. 10. 17–18; Ac. 26. 12–18; Rev. 20. 1–3.

Saul (1) The son of Kish and the first king of Israel, who set up his capital at Gibeah. He led Israel to victory against her enemies, especially the Philistines. In later life he became moody and suspicious, quarrelled with his advisers and drove his son-in-law, David, out of the kingdom. After his defeat at Mt Gilboa he committed suicide. 1 S. 8. 1 – 2 S. 1. 27. (2) Saul of Tarsus. *See* Paul.

saviour It is a basic O.T. concept that man cannot save himself and that God alone is the deliverer of his people. *See* Ps. 44. 1–3; Is. 43. 11; Jer. 14. 8–9. In the N.T. the term is used of God the Father, the author of salvation, and God the Son through whom it comes. Mt. 1. 18–21; Lk. 1. 47; 2 Tim. 1. 9–10; 2 Pet. 3. 2, 18.

saw(s) In prehistoric times these were made of flint. Later, small metal handsaws which, because of the set of the teeth, were pulled and not pushed against the wood, came into use. 2 S. 12. 31; 1 K. 7. 9; Is. 10. 15; Heb. 11. 37.

scales Instruments for weighing. Pr. 16. 11; 20. 23. *See* balance.

scarlet A bright red colour obtained from the eggs of the cochineal insect. As a material it was expensive and was used as a mark of distinction. Ex. 28. 3–6; 2 S. 1. 24; Mt. 27. 28. Its bright colour is sometimes associated with wickedness. Is. 1. 18; Rev. 17. 3–4.

sceptre A rod or staff held in the hand as a symbol of authority. Gen. 49. 10; Est. 4. 11; Ps. 45. 6; Am. 1. 5; Heb. 1. 8.

school In early times education was given at home and was mainly concerned with religion. *See* Gen. 18. 19; Dt. 6. 6–7; 2 Tim. 3. 14–15. After the exile, the synagogue acted as a school and the hazzan (verger) taught children to memorize the principal parts of the law in addition to simple reading and writing.

scorpion About 5 of the world's 500 or more known varieties of this carnivore are found in parts of Palestine. Although differing in size and colour, their outline – almost that of a lobster or crayfish – is unmistakable. Their sting is painful but seldom fatal. Dt. 8. 15; Ezek. 2. 6; Lk. 10. 19.

scribes Learned laymen who, after the exile, took over from the priests the task of applying the Mosaic law to the conditions of changing times. Their position and authority was similar to that of the Supreme Court of the U.S.A. Ezr. 7. 12. *See* 'lawyers' and 'doctors of the law'.

Scripture(s) (= writings) Used of the writings of the O.T. When the O.T. revelation is considered as a whole it is used in the singular Jn. 7. 42; Gal. 3. 22; and in the plural when the thought is of a number of separate passages, or of the O.T. as made up of a number of books Lk. 24. 27; Rom. 1. 2.

scroll Documents in biblical times were on papyrus or parchment, sewn into long strips and wound around sticks at both ends. Is. 34. 4; Jer. 36. 21–23; Ezek. 2. 9–10; Lk. 4. 16–20; Rev. 5. 1; 10. 1–10.

Scrolls, Dead Sea Manuscripts discovered in and around Qumran, NW of the Dead Sea, since 1947, which were probably written between 170 and 34 B.C. and between 4 B.C. and A.D. 70; and formed part of the library of a strict Jewish community. Among the 500 scrolls and frag-

ments found are about 100, representing all books of the O.T. in Hebrew except Esther, which are some 1000 years earlier than any other existing O.T. manuscripts.

Scythians A nomadic people living between the Danube and the Don whose name became a general term for barbarians. Col. 3. 11.

Scythopolis The Greek name for Bethshan. Judith 3. 10; 2 Mac. 12. 29–31. *Tell el-Husn.*

sea Although created and controlled by God, the Israelites disliked and feared it as the home of horrible monsters. Ex. 20. 11; Job 38. 8–11; Is. 27. 1; Rev. 21. 1. The word is used of the Red Sea Ex. 13. 18; the Mediterranean Nu. 34. 6; Ac. 10. 6; the Sea of Galilee Nu. 34. 11; Mt. 4. 18; the Dead Sea Nu. 34. 12; Dt. 3. 17.

Sea of Bronze The great basin in Solomon's Temple where the priests ceremonially washed their hands and feet. 1 Ch. 18. 8; 2 Ch. 4. 2–6.

seal, signet An implement, often made of a hard semi-precious stone, engraved with a recognizable design or name which could be used to stamp its impression on clay or wax as a mark of authority or authenticity. Among the Hebrews, these were usually oval and could be set in a ring or worn on a chain around the neck. Gen. 38. 18; 41. 42; 1 K. 21. 8; Is. 29. 11; Jer. 32. 10–14; Dan. 6. 17; Mt. 27. 66. Used figuratively Job 14. 17; Jn. 6. 27; Rom. 15. 28; 2 Cor. 1. 22; Eph. 1. 13; 4. 30. One of the greatest collections of cylinder seals in the world is in the Pierpont Morgan Library, New York.

sect (= choosing) In the N.T. the basic idea is of a party within the parent community. Ac. 24. 5. *See also* Ac. 5. 17; 15. 5; 1 Cor. 11. 19; Gal. 5. 20.

Seir A mountainous district S of the Dead Sea originally inhabited by Horites. Gen. 36. 9, 21; Dt. 2. 1–5.

Sela (= rock) The Edomite capital, 50 miles S of the Dead Sea, captured by Amaziah. 2 K. 14. 7; 2 Ch. 25. 11–14; Is. 42. 11. It has been identified as *Umm el-Bayâra* on the massive rocky plateau 1000 feet above Petra and 3700 above sea level. Excavations by N. Glueck 1933 and

W. H. Morton 1955 established the existence of an Iron Age Edomite settlement here.

Seleucus The general of Alexander who, on his death, established his rule over Syria and much of the eastern part of the conqueror's empire. The founder of the Seleucid dynasty. Seleucus IV, the son of Antiochus, sent Heliodorus to plunder the Temple. 2 Mac. 3. 1–7.

senate (1) The full assembly of Jewish elders. *See* Council. (2) The Roman Senate. 1 Mac. 8. 19.

Sennacherib The son of Sargon, whom he succeeded as king of Assyria in 705 B.C., and a contemporary of Hezekiah who rebelled against him. 2 K. 18. 7, 13 – 19. 37.

Septuagint The most important Greek translation of the Hebrew O.T., traditionally made by 70 (LXX) Jewish elders for the Greek-speaking colony of Jews around Alexandria. It became the Bible of the early church and most O.T. quotations in the N.T. come from it. Because the manuscripts are so ancient the LXX is a valuable companion to the Hebrew Bible.

seraphim (= burning ones) Heavenly beings described in the prophet Isaiah's vision. Is. 6. 1–8.

Sermon on the Mount, The The name commonly given to Christ's teaching about the character and conduct of the true believer in Mt. ch. 5–7. *See also* Lk. 6. 20–49.

serpent Used both literally and figuratively. Its character traits are thought of as those of the Devil: deceptive, crawling, poisonous and cunning. Gen. 3. 1–7; Ex. 7. 8–13.

Serpent, Bronze The image made by Moses to remind the Israelites that the LORD was able to heal and protect them. It later became an object of worship in Jerusalem. Nu. 21. 4–9; 2 K. 18. 1–4; Jn. 3. 14.

servant A general term used of anyone working for another, from slaves to trusted officials. It is also used of a man's relationship to God and his fellow men. Gen. 32. 16; Ex. 32. 13; 2 K. 5. 2; Ps. 31. 16; 105. 6; Jer. 25. 9; Lk. 15. 17; Jn. 13. 12–17; Ac. 16. 17.

Servant of the LORD The title is most notably used in Is. ch. 40–55, especially 42. 1–7 and 53. In these passages the Servant is at times to be understood as the people of Israel, at times as the faithful remnant; but, in the end, the Servant is that one individual, the Messiah, in whom the full destiny of Israel is summed up and achieved. Mt. 12. 15–21; Ac. 3. 26; 4. 23–30.

Seventy, The (1) Those appointed by Moses to assist him in taking care of the people. Nu. 11. 16–17, 24–26. (2) The seventy-two followers sent out by Jesus on an evangelistic tour. Lk. 10. 1–20.

shadow, shade Used as a metaphor referring to the protection of the weak by the strong, or of man by God, Job 7. 1–2; Ps. 63. 6–8; as a passing thing, like man's life compared with God, 1 Ch. 29. 15; Job 8. 8–9; Jas. 1. 16–17; as insubstantial compared with the real. Col. 2. 16–17; Heb. 8. 1–6; 10. 1–18.

Shadrach The Babylonian name given to Daniel's companion, Hananiah. Dan. 1. 7; 3. 8–30.

Shallum (1) The assassin of Zechariah who ruled Israel for one month. 2 K. 15. 13. (2) A king of Judah also called Jehoahaz. Jer. 22. 10–12.

Shalmaneser The name of several kings of Assyria. That Shalmaneser III fought Ahab and Jehu is recorded on the Black Obelisk of Nimrûd, a copy of which is in the Museum of the Oriental Institute, Chicago. It was Shalmaneser V (727–722 B.C.) who besieged Samaria, and to whom Hoshea became a vassal. 2 K. 17. 1–6.

shame Often used in the Bible of the human feeling of humiliation or self-condemnation. 2 S. 19. 1–5; Ezr. 9. 7; Ps. 97. 7; Jer. 6. 15; Joel 2. 27.

Shamgar An Israelite champion who killed 600 Philistines. Judg. 3. 31; 5. 6.

Shaphan The adjutant-general of King Josiah of Judah when the book of the law was found in the Temple. 2 K. 22. 3–20; 2 Ch. 34. 8–28.

shark This family, which includes the rays and skate, having no scales was barred as unclean. Ps. 74. 14.

Sharon The most fertile part of the coastal plain, stretching from Mt Carmel to Joppa, on the caravan route to Egypt. S. of S. 2. 1; Is. 35. 1–2.

Sheba, Queen of The ruler of a district in Arabia, corresponding roughly with the modern Yemen, which controlled the trade in precious spices. 1 K. 10. 1–13.

Shechem A town in the central hill-country of Palestine 41 miles N of Jerusalem between Mt Ebal and Mt Gerizim. Originally a Canaanite town, it was both a religious and political centre, and became the first capital of the northern kingdom of Israel. Gen. 12. 6; 33. 18; 35. 4; Jos. 20. 1–7; 24. 1–27, 32; Judg. 9. 1–49; 1 K. 12. 1, 25; Jer. 41. 2–10; Ecclus. 50. 26.

sheep Most commonly the fat-tailed variety which were kept for their meat, milk and wool. 1 S. 14. 32–34; 25. 2–8. *See also* Dt. 32. 14. They were used in sacrifice. Lev. 4. 32; 22. 21.

shekel The fundamental unit of both weight and money. Ex. 38. 25; 1 K. 10. 16. *See* Appendix to the O.T. in the New English Bible.

Shem The second son of Noah and the ancestor of the Semitic people. Gen. 5. 32; 9. 26; 10. 21–31.

Shemaiah (= Jah has heard) The prophet who checked Rehoboam from making war on the 10 tribes of Israel after their secession. 1 K. 12. 21–24; 2 Ch. 12. 2–10. (2) A false prophet during the exile. Jer. 29. 24–32.

Sheol The O.T. counterpart of the Greek and Roman gloomy underworld (Hades) of the departed spirits. Ps. 18. 5; 86. 13; Is. 14. 15.

Shephelah A geographical term for the low hill tract between the coastal plain of Palestine and the high central ranges. Jos. 9. 1; 11. 2; Judg. 1. 9; 1 K. 10. 27; 1 Mac. 12. 38.

shepherd Since the Palestinian shepherd leads, rather than drives, his sheep to water and pasture, the word is aptly applied to God and Christ. Ps. 23; Jn. 10. 2–17; 1 Pet. 5. 4.

Sheshbazzar The Persian name of the Jewish governor appointed by Cyrus to take back to Jerusalem the sacred vessels looted from the Temple by Nebuchadnezzar. Ezr. 1. 7–11; 5. 13–17.

shibboleth (= ears of corn) A word used by Jephthah to test whether or not fugitives belonged to his own people. Judg. 12. 4–6.

shield These were of two kinds: the smaller, round shield; and the heavy shield covering the whole body. 1 K. 10. 16–17; 14. 27; 1 Ch. 12. 8. Used metaphorically for God's protection. Ps. 5. 12; 18. 2; Eph. 6. 16.

Shiloh A town 12 miles N and E of Bethel where the Tent of the Presence was kept, and which became the central sanctuary. Jos. 18. 1; 1 S. 1. 1–4; 1 K. 11. 29–37; 14. 1–18; Ps. 78. 60; Jer. 7. 11–15; 26. 4–9. *Seilûn.* Excavations by Danish expeditions 1926–9 and 1932 suggest that it was destroyed about 1050 B.C. and not reoccupied until Hellenistic times.

Shimei (1) The grandfather of Mordecai. Est. 2. 5. (2) The Benjamite who opposed David and was executed by Solomon. 2 S. 16. 5–14; 19. 15–23; 1 K. 2. 36–46.

ship(s) Although the Israelites were not a seafaring people, there are a surprising number of detailed references to foreign ships in the Bible. Solomon's ships were manned by Phoenician crews. The Egyptians used papyrus boats; and the general design of ships in the O.T. would be similar to that of the modern dhow with square sails. 1 K. 9. 26–28; 2 Ch. 20. 35–37; Ps. 107. 23–27; Is. 18. 1–2; Ezek. 27. 1–9, 25–29. There is frequent mention of ships in the N.T. since several apostles were fishermen and Paul was a great traveller. Ac. 27. *See* boat.

Shishak An Egyptian king who invaded Judah in Jeroboam's reign. 1 K. 11. 40; 14. 25–26.

Shittim The last camp site of Israel, in the plains of Moab E of the NE end of the Dead Sea opposite Jericho, before they crossed the Jordan. Nu. ch. 25–36; Jos. 2. 1; 3. 1. *Tell el-Ḥammâm.*

Shunem, Shunammite A border town of Issachar near Mt Gilboa. 1 S. 28. 4; 1 K. 1. 1–4; 2 K. 4. 8–37. *Sôlem.*

Sidon A seaport of Phoenicia and its oldest city, 22 miles N of Tyre, whose inhabitants were skilled metal-workers and which provided timber for the Temple. Gen. 10. 19; 49. 13; Jos. 11. 8; 1 K. 17. 9; Is. 23. 1–4, 11–12; Ezek. 28. 20–23; Mk. 7. 31; Lk. 4. 26; Ac. 27. 3–4. Ṣaidā.

sign(s) Something visible and remarkable which serves as a witness to God or the will of God. The rainbow, the rite of circumcision, the plagues of Egypt were signs. Gen. 9. 12; 17. 11; Ex. 10. 1–2. Gideon and Saul were granted signs. Judg. 6. 11–24; 1 S. 10. 1–8. And the Jews demanded miracles from Jesus as signs. Mt. 16. 1–4. They are to precede the end of the age. Mt. 24. 29–31; 2 Th. 2. 9–10.

Sihon The king of the Amorites in Trans-jordan who refused to let the Israelites through his territory. Nu. 21. 21–30; 32. 33.

Silas A prophet of the Jerusalem church who went with Paul on his second missionary journey. Ac. 15. 22–41; 16. 19 – 17. 15; 18. 5. See Silvanus.

silk A fine cloth woven from the threads produced by the silkworm but little known in ancient Palestine. Rev. 18. 12.

Siloam A reservoir, still existing, constructed within the walls of Jerusalem by Hezekiah. 2 Ch. 32. 1–4, 30; Jn. 9. 1–8. In 1880 the tunnel, 1700 feet long, was found with a Hebrew inscription (now in Istanbul) describing the method of construction.

Silvanus Generally identified as the Latin form of Silas. 2 Cor. 1. 19; 1 Th. 1. 1; 2 Th. 1. 1; 1 Pet. 5. 12. See Silas.

silver, silversmith Used from very early times for vessels, ornaments, and, by weight, as a form of money. Nu. 7. 13; 10. 2; Judg. 17. 1–4; 1 K. 10. 27; Ac. 19. 23–27. It was mined in Middle East countries. 2 Ch. 9. 14; Jer. 10. 9. Used figuratively Ps. 12. 6.

Simeon (1) The second son of Jacob by Leah and ancestor of one of the tribes of Israel. Gen. 29. 32–33; 34. 25–31; 49. 5–7. (2) The devout old man who recognized the infant Jesus as the Messiah. Lk. 2. 25–35.

Simon (1) The high priest and son of Onias who is praised in Ecclus. 50. 1–21. (2) The son of Mattathias who succeeded

Jonathan in the leadership of the Jews until murdered by Ptolemy. 1 Mac. 13. 1–53; 14. 4–15; 16. 11–17. (3) One of the twelve apostles who had been a member of the extreme nationalist group, the Zealots. Mk. 3. 19. (4) A brother of Jesus. Mt. 13. 55; Mk. 6. 1–3. (5) Simon the Leper. Mk. 14. 3–9. (6) A Pharisee who entertained Jesus. Lk. 7. 36–47. (7) The father of Judas Iscariot. Jn. 13. 2. (8) A man from Cyrene who carried Christ's cross. Mk. 15. 21. (9) A magician of Samaria. Ac. 8. 9–24. (10) A tanner of Joppa. Ac. 9. 43. (11) See Peter.

simple The root meaning in the O.T. is 'openness', and it can be a virtue in one who is ignorant but sincere and willing to be taught. More often it denotes the man who is easily deceived by smooth words. See Ps. 19. 7; Pr. 1. 32; 7. 7; 9. 1–6.

sin The Bible recognizes the power of evil as everywhere present in the whole of human existence. It is a fact which has to be accepted and overcome in the power of God.

Three different Hebrew words are used. The first means 'rebellion': a wrong attitude taken up by man towards a personal God who is his father and creator. The second word means a deliberate turning towards what a man knows to be evil and contrary to the will of God. The third means 'missing the mark'; and it stands for that element of wickedness in man's nature which seems to drive him into sinful acts, even when he knows how disastrous the consequences will be.

Since sinful man cannot enter into the presence of the holy God, a great part of Israel's sacrificial system was directed to the means by which the impurity could be removed. But throughout, the emphasis is on man's inability to cleanse himself.

In later times, especially during the exile when no sacrifice could be offered, the sense of sin deepened in Israel. Ezek. 33. 10–20. Some realized that even sacrifice could not really meet the need of men; and there arose a growing, though confused, hope and faith in the forgiveness of God. Ps. 130.

The N.T. takes over the O.T. understanding of the nature of sin, but deepens both it and the meaning of forgiveness. In the teaching of Jesus, the emphasis is not so much on the action as on the motives behind the action. Mt. ch. 5. The social consequences of sin are emphasized, as is the fact that failure to act rightly may be as serious as committing wrong acts. Mt. 18. 5–7; 25. 31–46. Finally, it is the dishonesty or 'hypocrisy' involved in refusing to face the human situation which makes it impossible for man to be reconciled with God. Lk. 18. 9–14.

With this deepened sense of sin comes also a new emphasis on forgiveness, associated with the death of Christ who has broken the power of sin and reconciled man with God. Rom. ch. 7; Mt. 1. 21; Ac. 2. 37–38; 10. 38–43; Col. 2. 13–15.

Sinai The volcanic mountain in the south of the Sinai peninsula, also known as Horeb, where Jehovah gave the law to Moses. Ex. 19. 1–21; 31. 18. *See also* Dt. 5. 1–23.

sin-offering Like the guilt-offering, this kind of sacrifice was offered to cover faults committed in ignorance but, unlike the other which was rather for restitution, this was to expiate both moral and ritual offences. Lev. 4. 1 – 5. 13.

sins In general, the Bible distinguishes between 'sin', the state of alienation from God in which natural man lives, and 'sins', which are the outward expression of this condition. *See* Jn. 1. 29; Gal. 5. 19–21.

Sisera The commander-in-chief of the Canaanite king, Jabin, defeated by Deborah and killed by Jael. Judg. ch. 4–5.

slander Malicious gossip is condemned throughout the Bible. Lev. 19. 16; 1 Tim. 5. 13. *See also* Ex. 23. 1; Dt. 5. 20; Pr. 6. 16, 19; 2 Cor. 12. 20; 1 Tim. 3. 11; Jas. 4. 11.

slave, slavery In the O.T. slaves were in law the property of their master; and were obtained in war, from the slave-trade, as prisoners undergoing punishment, or native Israelites who had sold themselves owing to poverty or debt. Ex. 20. 17. However, they still had various rights and privileges and could rise to a position of responsibility in a household. Gen. 15. 3; Ex. 12. 44; 20. 10, 17; 21. 20–

21, 26–27; Lev. 25. 39–55; Dt. 15. 12–18; Pr. 17. 2.

sleep A gift of God who himself never sleeps. Ps. 121. 4. While men sleep God can speak to them in dreams. Gen. 28. 10–16; Mt. 1. 18–21; 2. 19–20.

sling The common form of the weapon was a narrow strip of leather with two strings attached, in which a stone was laid. When this was whirled round the head and one thong released, the stone could be flung with great force and accuracy. Judg. 20. 16; 1 S. 17. 40–50; 2 K. 3. 25. Flint slingstones have been excavated at Megiddo weighing about 2¼ pounds and about 4 inches in diameter.

smith(s) These seem to have been unknown in the pastoral period and emerged with the general use of metal about the 11th century B.C. 1 S. 13. 19–22; Is. 41. 7; 54. 16. *See also* 1 K. 6. 20; 2 Ch. 34. 3.

Smyrna An important city on the W coast of Asia Minor, a centre of worship of the Asian goddess Cybele, it became one of the seven churches of Asia. Rev. 1. 11; 2. 8–11. *Izmir.*

snakes These are used both literally and figuratively. One or two species are mentioned, but often they are referred to in general terms. Their characteristics are usually seen as deceptive, crawling, poisonous and cunning. Ex. 4. 1–5; Nu. 21. 6.

snow Not a common sight on the hills of Palestine even in winter, though the summit of Mt Hermon was always snow-capped. 2 S. 23. 20; Pr. 31. 21; Jer. 18. 14. Used symbolically for purity. Is. 1. 18; Dan. 7. 9; Mt. 28. 3; Rev. 1. 14.

soap A solution of potash and soda obtained from vegetable ash and sometimes mixed with oil. Job 9. 30; Jer. 2. 22; Mal. 3. 2.

Sodom One of the five cities of the plain of the Jordan in what is now the southern part of the Dead Sea, where Lot chose to settle. Its wickedness was proverbial, and it was destroyed by an earthquake. Gen. 13. 1–13; 18. 16 – 19. 29; Jer. 23. 14; Mt. 10. 15.

Solomon David's son by Bathsheba and his successor. Famous for his wisdom and wealth, he exploited to the full the trading and commercial possibilities of the territory won by David, built the Temple and a chain of defence cities. 1 K. ch. 1–11.

Solomon's Portico A covered walk or cloister on the E side of Herod's Temple where the scribes taught and money-changers had their tables. Jn. 10. 23; Ac. 3. 11; 5. 13. *See also* Lk. 2. 46; Jn. 2. 14–16.

son Used in a wider sense than today, and may refer to a grandson or even a more distant descendant. It may also mean that a person belongs to a particular group, or possesses certain qualities or characteristics in his life which 'relate' him. 2 K. 9. 20; Lam. 4. 2; Mal. 3. 6; Lk. 20. 36; 1 Tim. 1. 18.

Son of God In the O.T. the term is used of those who stand in any special relationship with God. Job 38. 7; Hos. 11. 1. In the N.T. it signifies the very special relationship between God and Jesus which the apostles placed centrally in their preaching. Mt. 3. 16–17; 11. 26–27; 17. 1–5; 26. 63–64; Jn. 1. 14–18; 10. 36; Ac. 9. 20; Rom. 1. 4; Heb. 1. 5–14.

Son of Man The title is used 78 times in the Gospels but only by Christ about himself in connection with both his earthly mission and his future glory. Mt. 8. 20; 9. 1–7; 12. 1–8; 16. 27–28; 25. 31–32. Elsewhere in the N.T. it occurs only once, used by Stephen. Ac. 7. 56.

Song of Songs, The An ancient oriental poem in dialogue form which celebrates pure marital love as ordained by God in creation, and vindicates it against both asceticism and lust. It has been interpreted as a parable of the intensity of God's love for his children which is the source of all human love.

Song of the Three, The A short book once included in the Greek version of the Hebrew scriptures but now in the Apocrypha. It consists mainly of a prayer and a hymn in praise of creation, sung by the three companions in the fiery furnace of Nebuchadnezzar.

Sosthenes The ruler of the synagogue at Corinth who was beaten up as a result of Paul's preaching. Ac. 18. 13–17.

Spain Unknown in O.T. times, it was regarded as the limit of the world to the west, which may explain Paul's great desire to take the gospel there. Rom. 15. 22–29.

sparrow Many varieties (House, Spanish, Dead Sea) of this bird are to be found in all parts of Palestine, and an even greater number of Palestinian birds are sparrow-like in their appearance and behaviour. Ps. 84. 3; Pr. 26. 2; Lk. 12. 6–7.

Sparta An important city in S Greece whose people were called Spartans or Lacedaemonians. Some Jews escaped the persecution of Jason and migrated there. 1 Mac. 12. 1–23; 14. 16–23. *Sparte*.

spear(s) Long, sharp-pointed instruments of varying shapes and sizes, but all designed for thrusting or throwing. 1 S. 17. 7; 18. 11; 26. 7. When stuck into the ground it indicated the king's headquarters. 1 S. 17. 7; 18. 11; 26. 7. *See also* Judg. 5. 8; Jer. 46. 4.

spelt A grain resembling wheat which grows in very poor soil. Ex. 9. 32; Is. 28. 25; Ezek. 4. 9.

spices Fragrant, vegetable substances used in making incense, preparing bodies for burial, and in flavouring food and wine. Ex. 30. 34–35; 2 Ch. 16. 13–14; S. of S. 4. 10; Jn. 19. 40.

spider Used figuratively and only in Job 8. 14.

spies The use of secret agents is age-old. Gen. 42. 5–17; Jos. 2. 1–23; 2 S. 10. 1–3.

spikenard This small plant from N India was the source of one of the costliest perfumes of biblical times. S. of S. 1. 12; 4. 14.

spirit In the O.T. it stands for a life-giving power belonging to God. Gen. 6. 17; Nu. 11. 25; 1 S. 10. 10; Eccles. 12. 7; Ezek. 37. 1–14. In the N.T. it more frequently refers to the non-material side of human personality and that part of a man which survives death. Ac. 7. 59; 2 Cor. 7. 1; Col. 2. 5; 1 Pet. 3. 18–19. The underlying Greek and Hebrew words also mean 'breath' or 'wind'.

star(s) Created by God and carefully ordered by him. Gen. 1. 16; Ps. 8. 3; Is. 13. 10; Jer. 31. 35. *See also* Am. 5. 8. Worship of them was forbidden. Dt. 4. 19.

Stephanas The first man to be baptized in Achaia (Greece) by Paul. 1 Cor. 1. 16.

Stephen One of the Greek-speaking section of the Jewish church appointed to assist the apostles by taking over responsibility for the worldly affairs of the Jerusalem Christians. His bold proclamation of the gospel led to his martyrdom which was a factor in Paul's conversion. Ac. ch. 6–7.

Stoics Philosophers who believed in the rule of reason to the exclusion of all emotional impulses; and that a man should do what he sees to be right without regard to the consequences. Ac. 17. 18.

stone(s) Extremely common in Palestine and used for many purposes: pillow Gen. 28. 18; seat Ex. 17. 12; cover or door Gen. 29. 2–3; Jos. 10. 18; Mt. 27. 60; building 1 K. 5. 17–18; Neh. 4. 2–3; Am. 5. 11; memorials Gen. 31. 45–48; weapons 1 S. 17. 40. Used metaphorically Ps. 118. 22; Mk. 12. 10.

stoning In earliest times a simple but violent expression of anger, it became the normal method of capital punishment in Israel. Ex. 17. 4; Nu. 15. 32–36; Dt. 17. 2–7; Ac. 7. 58.

stork Two kinds of stork, the white and slightly smaller black, pass through Palestine every year. They are mixed feeders but the large concentrations tend to settle in Upper Galilee. Lev. 11. 19; Dt. 14. 18; Ps. 104. 17; Jer. 8. 7; Zech. 5. 9.

stranger (1) An alien who put himself under the protection of Israel and Israel's God, and, submitting to many requirements of the law, was given in return certain privileges. See Ex. 20. 10; 22. 21; Nu. 15. 14–16; Dt. 24. 19. (2) Foreigners who did not have cultus-fellowship with Israel. See Ezek. 44. 7–9. (3) People different from and hostile to Israel. Is. 1. 7.

stumbling, stumbling-block Anything that trips up or is a hindrance materially or spiritually. Jer. 18. 15; Mt. 16. 23; Rom. 9. 33; 11. 9; 14. 13; 1 Pet. 2. 8. See also 1 Cor. 8. 7–13.

Succoth A town E of the Jordan and W of Penuel. Gen. 33. 17; Judg. 8. 4–17; 1 K. 7. 40–46. Excavations by H. Francken of the Nederlands Inst. 1961. Tell Deir'alla.

suffering A necessary part of man's life on earth and a sign of his mortality and im-perfection. It is represented in the Bible as the direct consequence of sin Dt. 28. 15–68; Judg. 2. 16–23; Hos. 8. 7; Gal. 6. 7–8; or as a divine testing Ps. 66. 10–12; Jas. 1. 12; 1 Pet. 1. 6–7; or as educative Pr. 3. 12; Rom. 5. 3–4. It may result from persecution, even undeserved as in Job's case. Dan. 7. 25; Job 1. 1 – 2. 10. Christ accepted his share of it and told his followers of the redemptive power of the way of the cross. Mk. 8. 30–31; Heb. 2. 14–18. Christians are to share in Christ's sufferings and endure them without resentment that they may live with him. Mt. 5. 11–12; Rom. 8. 17; 2 Cor. 1. 5–7; Phil. 3. 10–11; 2 Tim. 2. 3–13; 1 Pet. 3. 13–18; 4. 12–19.

sun Regarded as the greatest and most important of the heavenly bodies. Job 9. 7; Ps. 19. 4–6; 74. 16. The day was divided according to its light and heat. Gen. 43. 16; 1 S. 11. 9; Ps. 50. 1. See also 2 K. 20. 8–11. Eclipses were taken as a sign of God's judgement. Joel 2. 30–31; Rev. 6. 12. Sun-worship, though forbidden, was practised at Jerusalem at certain periods. Dt. 17. 2–5; 2 K. 23. 5, 11; Ezek. 8. 16. Used metaphorically Is. 30. 26; Mal. 4. 2; Mt. 13. 43; Rev. 21. 23.

Susa The capital of Elam in SW Persia. Ezr. 4. 8–10; Neh. 1. 1; Est. 1. 1–2; Dan. 8. 1–2.

swallow Several members of this family, which take their food in the air and nest in man-made situations, are found in Palestine. Ps. 84. 3; Pr. 26. 2; Is. 38. 14.

swear See oath.

sweet-cane Not a native of Palestine but was imported from India and Arabia. A strong-smelling oil was taken from its root. S. of S. 4. 14; Is. 43. 24; Ezek. 27. 19.

swift Although a different species from the swallow, this bird has developed on similar lines and lives in almost exactly the same way. The common swift has a habit of flying noisily in flocks. Jer. 8. 7.

swine Is. 65. 4. See pig.

sword Usually made of iron with a fairly short, straight blade, sometimes with two edges. It was worn sheathed, hanging from a girdle. Gen. 3. 24; Ex. 17. 13; Judg. 7. 20; 2 S. 20. 8; Ps. 149. 6. Used symbolically Dt. 32. 25; Mt. 10. 34; Rom. 13. 4; Heb. 4. 12.

Sychar A village of Samaria on the main road from Jerusalem to Galilee. Jn. 4. 3–6.

sycomore Unlike the sycamore of the west, this is a tree producing yellowish fig-like fruit, resembling the mulberry in its greenery, with branches growing close to the ground. 1 K. 10. 27; Is. 9. 10; Am. 7. 14; Lk. 19. 1–4.

Syene A fortress town on the border of Egypt and Ethiopia opposite the island of Elephantine. Ezek. 29. 10; 30. 6. Aramaic papyri found in 1903 show that a Jewish military colony existed there in the 5th century B.C. with its own Temple. *Aswân.*

Symeon The grandfather of Mattathias. 1 Mac. 2. 1.

synagogue (= gathering together) The centre for the form of worship which grew up during the exile when it was impossible to sacrifice at the Temple, consisting of readings from the scriptures, an address, prayers and psalms. *See* Neh. 8. 1–8. The building also served as a school and meeting-house. Lk. 4. 15–30; 13. 10–17; Jn. 12. 42–43; 16. 1–3; Ac. 13. 13–15; 14. 1; 15. 21; 17. 1–3.

synoptic The name usually given to the first three Gospels, because, by and large, they tell the same story in the same way; and although differing in details, each is complementary to the other since it was written for different readers. *See* Matthew, Mark, Luke, John, Gospel of.

Syracuse On the E coast of Sicily, it was the most important and prosperous Greek city on the island. Ac. 28. 12. *Siracusa.*

Syria (Aram) A continuation of Palestine with no well-defined frontier, it was more a political than a geographical unit. It was peopled by Aramaeans whose small kingdoms seem to have formed some sort of federation under the king of Damascus. They were great traders and carried their language (Aramaic) well beyond Asia Minor. Both Israel and Judah had close relations with Syria, and its influence was always strong until it was absorbed into the Assyrian empire in 732 B.C. *See*

2 S. 8. 3–6; 10. 16–19; 1 K. 11. 23–24; 15. 16–20; 2 K. 6. 8 – 7. 20; 9. 14–16; 10. 32–33. *See* 'Aram' and 'Damascus'.

Syrtis Treacherous sandbanks on the N coast of Africa between the headlands of Tunis and Barce. Ac. 27. 17.

Taanach A Canaanite royal city whose king was defeated by Joshua. Jos. 12. 21; 21. 25; Judg. 1. 27; 5. 19; 1 K. 4. 12. *Tell Ta'annak.* Excavations by E. Sellin of the Vienna Academy 1902–4 revealed a strong Late Bronze Age defensive system. Finds included 12 cuneiform tablets of about 1450 B.C. and an earthenware incense-altar of the Iron Age.

Tabernacle The sanctuary set up to shelter the Ark of the Covenant in the desert which served the Israelites as a place of worship and their appointed meeting-place with God. It was used long after the entry into Canaan. Under the Judges it was at Shiloh, in Saul's reign at Nob and later at Gibeon; and eventually Solomon placed it in the Temple. *See* Jos. 18. 1; 1 S. 21; 1 K. 8. 1–13; 1 Ch. 16. 39. The detailed instructions for its construction are in Ex. ch. 25–27; 30–31; 35–40. The whole ritual of the service and method of approach to God are laid down in Lev. ch. 1–10.

Tabernacles, Feast of The third most important of the great annual festivals. Kept from 15th to 22nd Tishri (September–October), it marked the completion of the fruit, wine and oil harvests and also commemorated the beginnings of the wilderness wanderings. Everyone born an Israelite had to live in an arbour made from branches during the feast. Lev. 23. 34–36, 39–44; Dt. 16. 13–15; 31. 10–13; Jn. 7. 2. *See also* Ex. 23. 16; 34. 22; Nu. 29. 12–39.

Tabor (1) The place where Gideon's brothers were killed. Judg. 8. 13–21. (2) An isolated mountain over 1800 feet high in the NE of the plain of Esdraelon and 7 miles E of Nazareth. Jos. 19. 17–22; Judg. 4. 4–7; Ps. 89. 12; Jer. 46. 18; Hos. 5. 1.

Tahpanhes A city in Egypt to which Jeremiah was taken, and where we get our last glimpse of him. Jer. 43. 1 – 44. 30. *Tel Defneh.*

Tahpenes The queen of Egypt whose sister married Hadad. 1 K. 11. 14–20.

Tamar (1) A Canaanite woman who married into the family of Judah. Gen. 38. 6–30. (2) Absalom's sister. 2 S. 13. 1–22. (3) A daughter of Absalom. 2 S. 14. 27. (4) A city in the wilderness built by Solomon. 1 K. 9. 18.

tamarisk Many varieties of this tree with its graceful, curved branches, small leaves and pink flowers grow in the Mediterranean area; some to a considerable size. It was regarded as sacred in O.T. times. 1 S. 22. 6; 31. 13; Is. 44. 4.

tambourine This resembled a tom-tom and consisted of a wooden hoop with skins pulled across the frame. Its use is particularly associated with merrymaking. Ex. 15. 20; Judg. 11. 34; Ps. 68. 25.

Tammuz A Mesopotamian fertility god, the counterpart of the Egyptian Osiris and the Greek Adonis, who gave his name to the fourth Jewish month (June–July). Ezek. 8. 14.

Tarshish Its occurrence in the O.T. in association with ships and ports suggests that it may have been a land in the W Mediterranean where deposits of minerals existed. Ps. 72. 10; Is. 23. 1–7; 66. 18–19; Jer. 10. 9; Ezek. 27. 12; 38. 13; Jon. 1. 1–3; 4. 1–2.

Tarsus The capital city of the Roman province of Cilicia on the river Cnidus and some 10 miles inland. The birthplace of Paul, it was a centre of Greek learning which revolted with Mallus against Antiochus Epiphanes. 2 Mac. 4. 30; Ac. 9. 11, 28–30; 21. 39; 22. 1–3. *Tersous.*

Tattenai The Governor of the province of Beyond-the-Euphrates under King Darius. Ezr. 5. 1 – 6. 14.

taxes Civil taxation, as opposed to money for the support of the Tabernacle, began under David to provide for administrative costs, and was in kind rather than cash. *See* Ex. 30. 13; 1 K. 4. 7–28 Special taxes were imposed to meet emergencies. 2 K. 23. 35. In the Persian empire each territory had its quota of tolls to meet. Neh. 5. 15. Under the Romans the system varied, but it was usual for them to be farmed out and the right to collect the taxes of a district sold to the highest bidder. After the exile, each Israelite over twenty had to pay an annual Temple tax. Mt. 17. 24–25; 22. 17–21.

Taylor Prism One of the hexagonal prisms found at Nineveh, and now in the British Museum, on which Sennacherib of Assyria gave his account of his invasion of Judah. It is dated about 691 B.C. Is. 37. 36–37.

teacher, teaching At the time of the settlement of Canaan there were no schools as such, and instruction, which concerned the traditions and faith of the nation, came through parents, prophets, priests and wise men. After the exile, the synagogue came to be used as a school for boys, and instruction was entirely in the hands of the scribes or official teachers of the law. Pr. 4. 2; 13. 14; Is. 8. 16; Lk. 5. 17. *See also* Pr. 1. 8; Mic. 3. 11; Mal. 2. 7. The Jews were amazed that Jesus should presume to teach. Mk. 1. 27; Jn. 7. 14–18. In the early church, teaching was a recognized occupation. Eph. 4. 11.

Tekoa A fortified town on the edge of the wilderness 12 miles S of Jerusalem and the same distance NE of Hebron. It was the home of Amos, and the place where Jonathan and Simon hid. 2 S. 14. 1–20; 2 Ch. 11. 6; Am. 1. 1; 1 Mac. 9. 33.

Tell An Arabic word for a flat-topped mound with steeply-sloping sides. It almost always indicates the site of an ancient city, and its distinctive shape results from using the same site for city after city.

Tell el-Amarna Tablets These were found accidentally in 1877 at a site about 200 miles S of Cairo. They consist of Egyptian (Foreign Office) State Department files dealing with correspondence between the kings of small city states in W Asia and the Pharaoh Akhen-aten and his father between 1400 and 1360 B.C. They tell us a great deal about the state of affairs in Canaan before the Exodus.

Teman A region of Edom and its people, descendants of Esau, who were famous for their wisdom. Gen. 36. 10–11; Job 2. 11; Jer. 49. 7; Ezek. 25. 12–13.

Temple The name given to the complex of buildings in Jerusalem on Mt Moriah which was the centre of the sacrificial worship of Israel. The first, built by Solomon, consisted of three parts and was the royal chapel as well as the central sanctuary of the people. *See* 1 K. 6. 1–38; 7. 13–51. A model is on display at the Agnes Scott College, Decatur, Georgia.

This Temple was burnt by the Babylonians, and a second was built by the returned exiles after 520 B.C. It was less elaborate in design and construction, but tended to keep the laity at an ever-increasing distance from the inner shrine. This Temple was pillaged and desecrated in 168 B.C. by Antiochus Epiphanes, but was recaptured and rededicated by Judas Maccabaeus. Ezr. 6; 1 Mac. 4. 36–59.

About 19 B.C. Herod the Great began to rebuild and enlarge it with a whole series of surrounding covered courts. This is the building referred to in the N.T. and which was destroyed by the Romans in A.D. 70. Only the 'Wailing Wall' now remains.

tempt, temptation (= 'testing', 'trial', 'prove') When God tests man it is to teach him something or to strengthen his character. Mt. 4. 1–11; 1 Th. 3. 4–5; Jas. 1. 12–15. *See also* Gen. 22. 1–18; Ex. 20. 18–20; Dt. 8. 16; Mt. 6. 13; Heb. 2. 18; 4. 14–15; 1 Pet. 1. 7.

Ten Commandments These were the laws given orally to Moses by God on Sinai and engraved on the two stones which were placed in the Ark. They set out plainly and briefly the way in which men ought to live together in society before God. In the Roman Catholic and Lutheran churches, the first and second commandment in the usual English numbering are treated as one, and the last is divided into two. Ex. 19. 17 – 20. 17; 24. 3; 1 K. 8. 9.

Ten Towns, The The territory at the mouth of the Jordan on the plain of Esdraelon occupied by Greek settlers, also known as Decapolis. Mt. 4. 25; Mk. 5. 20; 7. 31.

tent The normal dwelling of the desert nomad which differed little from those used today by the Bedouin of the Negeb. Although stone houses were built after the settlement, it seems that the poorer people continued to live in tents on the outskirts of towns throughout the O.T. period. Gen. 9. 27; Job 8. 22; Is. 54. 2.

Tent of the Presence Ex. 40. 1–2. *See* Tabernacle.

Terah The father of Abraham. Gen. 11. 26–32.

teraphim Idols in the form of small human statues, used as household gods and consulted for oracles. They fell into disuse after the exile. Judg. 17. 5; Ezek. 21. 21. *See also* Gen. 31. 19–35; 1 S. 15. 23; 19. 11–17; 2 K. 23. 24; Hos. 3. 4; Zech. 10. 2. Archaeology has shown that among some peoples possession of these by the woman's husband ensured for him the succession to the father-in-law's property.

terebinth A tall tree common in Palestine, also known as the holm oak, and similar in shape to the spreading chestnut. Its seed, which can be eaten, also produces turpentine. In early O.T. times it was considered sacred. Gen. 35. 4; Jos. 24. 26; Judg. 6. 11; 1 K. 13. 14; Is. 1. 30; 6. 13.

Teresh A eunuch of King Ahasuerus who plotted against him. Est. 2. 21–23.

Tertius The Christian who wrote down Paul's letter to the Romans. Rom. 16. 22.

Tertullus The attorney for the prosecution in Paul's trial before Felix. Ac. 24. 1–8.

Thaddaeus One of the twelve apostles. Mk. 3. 18. His name is replaced by 'Lebbaeus' in Mt. 10. 3, and by 'Judas the son of James' in Lk. 6. 16; Ac. 1. 13.

thanks, thanksgiving The mark of all true worship. Ps. 95. 2; 100. 4; 107. 8–31; Mt. 26. 27–29; Lk. 22. 17–19; 1 Cor. 1. 4–5; Eph. 5. 20; Phil. 1. 3–5.

theatre These were built in most parts of the ancient world where Greek civilization had penetrated, and were used for meetings as well as dramatic performances. They were usually in the open air: a semi-circular excavation in a hill-side, cut into steps for seats. Ac. 19. 29.

Theophilus The person to whom Luke dedicated both his Gospel and the Acts. Lk. 1. 1; Ac. 1. 1.

Thessalonians, Letters to the The two letters were written from Corinth within months or weeks of each other. Paul was worried whether his short stay of three weeks (Ac. 17. 1–10) had been long enough to plant Christianity securely, and he had sent Timothy back on a visit to report. The news was good but it was clear that Paul's preaching about the Second Coming had been misunderstood, and that the Thessalonians had got their ideas out of balance and proportion. They had been neglecting their work and their duty under the impression that the end of the world was at hand. At the same time they were worried in case Christians who had died would miss the glories of the kingdom. In these two loving pastoral letters, Paul gives them sound practical advice about keeping life running in a normal Christian course, waiting in patient hope and sobriety. Both these letters are a great help in showing the mind and problems of a first-century church.

Thessalonica An important city on the Gulf of Salonika, originally called Therme. Situated where the road from Italy to the east joined the sea route from the Aegean to the Danube, it was the key to the spread of Christianity both west and east and to its establishment as a world religion. Ac. 17. 1–10; 20. 4; 27. 2; Phil. 4. 16; 2 Tim. 4. 10. *Salonika.*

Theudas A Jewish nationalist leader who led a revolt against Rome. Ac. 5. 35–36.

thief Stealing is forbidden in the O.T. and special restitution had to be made. Ex. 20. 15; 22. 1–13; Pr. 6. 30–31; Jer. 2. 26; Jn. 10. 10; 12. 3–6; 1 Pet. 4. 15. *See also* Mt. 27. 38.

thistle A tall weed with mauve or yellow flowers and a spiny stem. Varieties known on the shore of the Sea of Galilee grow up to thirteen feet. Is. 17. 13; Hos. 10. 8; Mt. 7. 16.

Thomas One of the twelve apostles, known as 'the Twin'. Although devoted to Jesus, he was pessimistic and rather slow to believe. Mt. 10. 3; Jn. 11. 16; 14. 1–6; 20. 24–29; 21. 2.

thorn Several species are found in Palestine of which the buck-thorn and camel-thorn seem to have been the most common. It was used for hedging and fuel. Judg. 9. 14–15; Ps. 58. 9; Hos. 10. 8; Ecclus. 24. 15; Mk. 15. 16–18. It is

constantly referred to figuratively. Ezek. 28. 24; Hos. 2. 6.

Thrace A country E of Macedonia with a coastline on the Aegean, Sea of Marmora and the Black Sea. 2 Mac. 12. 32–35.

threshing The process of separating grain from chaff which was done with a stick on a windy day in ancient times. Later, an ox-drawn sledge with a heavy curved base was used on a specially prepared hard floor. 2 S. 24. 22; Is. 41. 15; Am. 1. 3.

throne(s) (1) The chair of state occupied by one in authority. 2 S. 3. 10; 1 K. 10. 18–20. (2) The throne of God or Christ. Ps. 93. 2; Is. 6. 1; Heb. 12. 2. (3) The unseen powers of good and evil which are finally brought under the authority of Christ. Col. 1. 16.

thunder This commonly occurs in storms at the beginning and end of the rainy season. In both the O.T. and N.T. it is associated with the presence and activity of God. Ex. 9. 22–23; 19. 14–16; 1 S. 7. 10; Ps. 104. 7; Jn. 12. 28–30; Rev. 4. 5; 10. 3.

Thyatira A city in the Roman province of Asia on the road from Pergamum to Laodicea. It was a centre for dyeing, cloth manufacture, pottery, brass-working and other trades. Ac. 16. 12–15; Rev. 1. 11; 2. 18–29. *Akhisar.*

Tiberias A town on the W shore of the Sea of Galilee built by Herod Antipas about A.D. 20 in honour of Tiberius. Jn. 6. 23. *Tabariyeh.* The name is also given to the Sea of Galilee Jn. 6. 1.

Tiberius The second Roman emperor A.D. 14–37 who followed Augustus. With the exception of Lk. 2. 1 he is the 'Caesar' of the Gospels. *See* Mt. 22. 17; Mk. 12. 14; Lk. 3. 1; Jn. 19. 12.

Tiglath-pileser The king of Assyria, also known as 'Pul', from about 745 to 727 B.C. who revitalized the empire. He made successful attacks on Israel, carrying off many captives from the northern cities, and made all the petty kingdoms of Palestine and Syria his vassals. *See* 2 K. 15. 17–20; 16. 5–18.

Tigris A river of Asia which joins the Euphrates 40 miles N of the Persian Gulf. Gen. 2. 14; Dan. 10. 4; Tobit 6. 1; Judith 1. 6; Ecclus. 24. 25.

time This was marked in the early biblical period by sunrise and sunset and by phases of the moon. Nu. 9. 3; Ps. 104. 19; Eccles. 3. 1–8. In particular, it refers to the times appointed by God and the opportunities given by him. Lk. 19. 41–44; Ac. 1. 6–7; Tit. 1. 2–3; 1 Pet. 1. 11. *See also* Dt. 11. 11–15; Ps. 145. 15; Is. 49. 8; Jer. 18. 23; Mk. 13. 29–32; Ac. 17. 26.

Timnath The place where Samson's first wife came from. Judg. 14. 1–18. *Khirbet Tibnah.*

Timothy The son of a Gentile father and Jewish mother who became Paul's trusted companion and official representative. Ac. 16. 1 – 17. 15; 18. 5 – 19. 22; Rom. 16. 21; 1 Cor. 4. 17; 16. 10–11; 2 Cor. 1. 1, 19; 1 Th. 1. 1; 2 Th. 1. 1; Philem. 1.

Timothy, First Letter to An ordinary personal letter written from Macedonia from a senior minister to a junior. It is very practical, giving advice on the responsibility of the ministry, matters of public worship, and the dangers of false teaching. Paul then moves on to suggest how to achieve good church organization and management, with some very worldly-wise observations on widows, especially young ones, and the tactful handling of elderly officials by a younger minister.

Timothy, Second Letter to This continues the good advice given in the first letter and repeats some of it. It is more personal, and particularly touching is the obvious concern of the old man facing death, for the young man facing life. Together with the letter to Titus, these two letters are known as the Pastoral Epistles because they were written to Paul's special envoys to meet the needs of the hour.

tin A metal essential to the making of bronze and well known to the Israelites. Nu. 31. 22; Ezek. 22. 18; 27. 12–13.

Tirhakah King of Ethiopia or Cush who became the ruler of Egypt. He is mentioned in connection with Sennacherib's campaign against Hezekiah. 2 K. 19. 8–13.

Tirzah A Canaanite city which Jeroboam I made the capital of the northern kingdom until Omri moved it to Samaria.

Jos. 12. 24; 1 K. 14. 17; 16. 6–24; S. of S. 6. 4. *Tell el-Fâr'ah.* Excavations by de Vaux of the Ecole Biblique, Jerusalem, 1946–7, 50– , have shown it to be a city which flourished in the 9th century B.C. but later sank to the status of an ordinary provincial town.

tithe The custom of giving to God one tenth of one's possessions in recognition of him as lord of the land and in thankfulness for his blessings. This was used for the support of the Levites. Lev. 27. 30–33; Nu. 18. 20–32; Dt. 14. 22–29. *See also* Gen. 28. 20–22.

titles and names of Christ *See* Mt. 1. 23; Mk. 1. 24; Lk. 1. 76; 9. 20; Jn. 1. 9, 29; 5. 27; 6. 35; 8. 12; 10. 14; 11. 25; 15. 1; Rom. 11. 26; 22. 16; 1 Cor. 10. 4; 15. 45; Eph. 2. 20; 5. 23; 1 Th. 1. 10; 1 Tim. 2. 5; Heb. 4. 14; 6. 20; Jas. 4. 12; 1 Pet. 5. 4; 2 Pet. 2. 20; 1 Jn. 1. 1; 5. 20; Rev. 1. 5; 13. 8.

Titus A Greek convert and one of Paul's most reliable companions and trusted helpers who is associated particularly with the Corinthian church. 2 Cor. 7. 5–7, 13–16; 8. 1–24; 12. 14–18; Gal. 2. 1; 2 Tim. 4. 10.

Titus, Letter to Written from somewhere in Asia near the end of Paul's life to Titus who was establishing a church in Crete. Paul tells him what his aim should be and how he should go about the job. He deals with the character of the good minister, the danger of counterfeit Christians, the selection of church officers, the personal characteristics needed to develop a thoroughly Christian church and the attitude of the Christian to the civil authority.

Tob A region S of Damascus where Jephthah lived when an outlaw. Judg. 11. 2–5.

Tobiah An Ammonite governor, partly Jewish, who, with Sanballat, opposed Nehemiah's efforts to rebuild the walls of Jerusalem after the exile. Neh. 2. 9–20; 4. 1–9; 6. 1–19; 13. 1–9.

Tobias The son of Tobit who went to Rages, accompanied by the angel Raphael disguised as Azarias, to collect a debt. Tobit ch. 1–14.

Tobit A pious Naphtalite Jew who was cured of his blindness by the angel Raphael. Tobit ch. 1–14.

Tobit, Book of One of the books of the Apocrypha, written in Egypt about 200 B.C. The text is based on eastern stories, and praises the giving of alms through the story of a pious Jew of the northern captivity who is persecuted for helping his fellow-Israelites under the tyranny of Esarhaddon.

tomb Any burial place, from a modest hole in the ground or cave to a beehive-vault or one cut from the rock itself. The stone door to the last could weigh up to three tons. 2 S. 2. 32; Lk. 23. 55 – 24. 2; Jn. 11. 38–41. *See also* Gen. 50. 12–13.

tongues of ecstasy A spiritual gift regarded by some early Christians, especially the Corinthians, as the highest of the gifts of the Spirit. Paul stresses that it is, in fact, a lesser gift than love or even prophecy. Its value is to be judged by the extent to which it results in the increase of Christian charity in those who claim the gift. Ac. 10. 44–46; 19. 1–7; 1 Cor. 13. 8; 14. 1–33, 39–40. *See also* Ac. 2. 1–4; 1 Cor. 13. 1.

Topheth A place near Jerusalem where Molech worship, which included human sacrifice, was practised in the times of Ahaz and Manasseh. 2 K. 23. 10; Jer. 19. 1–15.

tower(s) Cities were usually fortified; and towers built into the walls, especially near the gates, were an important part of the defence. Watch, or siege, towers were often built by attacking armies; and defence chains of towers or forts were built in desert areas. 2 Ch. 26. 9–10; Ezek. 21. 22.

town clerk An official of Graeco-Roman cities in the empire whose many duties included responsibility for law and order. Ac. 19. 35–41.

Trachonitis A region SE of Damascus governed by Herod Philip. Lk. 3. 1. *Lejā.*

tradition (1) The interpretation of the law handed down by word of mouth to the Jewish elders which the Pharisees tended to make of even greater authority than the scriptures. Mk. 7. 1–13; Gal. 1. 14. (2) The gospel truths and the behaviour

which those who accept them must show. 2 Th. 2. 15; 3. 6.

trance A condition of suspended animation, as practised by yogi, when a person becomes unaware of his material surroundings and his mind is left free to receive divine revelation. Ac. 11. 5–11; 22. 17–21.

Transfiguration The occasion in the life of Jesus (probably on Mt Hermon) when, in the presence of his three closest disciples, the spirit which possessed him became visible to others. Mt. 17. 1–13; Mk. 9. 2–13; Lk. 9. 28–36.

treasury A place where treasure is kept, generally attached to a sanctuary or belonging to a king. Jos. 6. 19, 24; Est. 3. 9. In the N.T. it refers to the thirteen trumpet-shaped boxes for money offerings in the Court of the Women. Lk. 21. 1.

tree In ancient times Palestine must have been extensively wooded. There are more than 300 references to over 20 varieties in the Bible. They were associated with heathen worship. Dt. 12. 2; 16. 21; 1 K. 14. 23.

Tres Tabernae A village on the Appian Way about 33 miles from Rome. Ac. 28. 15.

Trial of Jesus After his arrest Jesus was informally examined by the high priest. At dawn the Council condemned him for blasphemy. Since it had no power to inflict the death-sentence and the Roman authorities would not listen to a charge of blasphemy, Jesus was brought before Pilate charged with high treason. Unwilling to condemn an innocent man, Pilate tried to get Herod to try the prisoner. When this failed, Pilate tried to save Jesus at the expense of Barabbas but finally yielded and condemned him. Mt. 26. 57 – 27. 31; Mk. 14. 53 – 15. 20; Lk. 22. 54 – 23. 25; Jn. 18. 12 – 19. 16.

Tribes of Israel The twelve sons of Jacob and their households who settled in Egypt and became tribes by the end of the period of slavery. Gen. 49. 1–28; Nu. 1. 20–44; 26. 5–51; Jos. 13. 1 – 22. 8.

Tribes, the Ten Those who rebelled against Rehoboam on Solomon's death and formed the kingdom of Israel. Conquered by the Assyrians in 722 B.C., many of its inhabitants were deported. Those left behind formed the nucleus of the people later known as Samaritans. 1 K. 11. 29–39. *See also* 1 K. 12. 16–20; 2 K. 17. 4–6.

tribute Enforced contributions, either of money or labour, imposed on subject peoples. 2 K. 17. 1–6. *See also* Jos. 16. 10; 1 K. 20. 1–7; 2 K. 23. 33; Ezr. 4. 13; Lk. 20. 21–26.

triumph In Rome, victorious generals were granted 'triumphs' which were official celebrations of a victory. They included a procession in which foreign prisoners were shown to the people, and this thought lies behind 2 Cor. 2. 14; Col. 2. 15.

Troas A city in Asia Minor on the Aegean shore about 10 miles from ancient Troy. Ac. 16. 6–11; 20. 5–12; 2 Cor. 2. 12–13; 2 Tim. 4. 13. *Eskistanbul.*

Trophimus A Christian from Ephesus who went with Paul on missionary work to Asia and Jerusalem. Ac. 20. 3–4; 21. 18–29; 2 Tim. 4. 20.

trumpet(s) Those used for signals in war were usually made from rams' horns. Those used as musical instruments in worship were long and made of metal. Nu. 10. 1–10; Jos. 6. 4; Judg. 3. 27; 7. 15–22; 1 K. 1. 34; 2 K. 12. 13; Hos. 5. 8; 1 Th. 4. 16; Rev. 8. 2.

Trumpets, Feast of *See* Acclamation, Day of.

truth Basically the meaning as understood today, but especially God's will as made known to men in the gospel of Jesus Christ: God's reality as contrasted with what is false or merely seems to be true. Pr. 12. 17; Jn. 8. 40–47; 14. 6; Rom. 1. 18; 2 Cor. 4. 1–2; Gal. 2. 1–5; 5. 7.

Tubal A region of Asia Minor whose people, though traders, were warlike. Is: 66. 19; Ezek. 27. 13; 38. 1–9.

Tubal-cain The son of Lamech and a skilled metal-worker or tinker. His descendants were probably Kenites who worked the copper and iron mines SE of the Dead Sea. Gen. 4. 19–22.

Twelve, The Those disciples chosen by Jesus to be his constant companions and to proclaim the gospel. They were called apostles, and their number corresponded to that of the tribes of Israel. Mk. 3. 13–19; Lk. 6. 13–16. *See also* Ac. 1. 15–26.

Tychicus An Asian Christian who accompanied Paul to Jerusalem and, at various times, acted as his trusted messenger. Ac. 20. 4; Eph. 6. 21–22; Col. 4. 7–8; 2 Tim. 4. 12; Tit. 3. 12.

Tyrannus A Greek teacher in Ephesus in whose lecture-hall Paul held discussions. Ac. 19. 8–11.

Tyre An important and wealthy Phoenician city built on a rocky island 22 miles S of Sidon and 35 miles N of Carmel. It had good relations with Israel until the Maccabean period. 2 S. 5. 11; 1 K. 5. 1–18; Ezek. ch. 26–28; 29. 18; 1 Mac. 5. 15; 2 Mac. 4. 18, 32, 44–49; Mk. 7. 24–31; Ac. 12. 20–21; 21. 3–7. Ṣûr.

Ulai A river of Elam beside which Daniel saw a vision. Dan. 8. 1–2, 16.

unclean, uncleanness The eating of certain kinds of animals was forbidden to the Israelites. The only clean animals were cattle, sheep, goats and the deer family. All beasts of prey, carrion, bats; all insects except the locust; water creatures without both fins and scales; anything strangled or that had died of itself was unclean. Lev. 11. 1–47. The N.T. shows that God requires moral rather than outward distinctions, and that Christians should deal gently with other's scrupulous consciences. Mk. 7. 14–23; Ac. 10. 9–16; Rom. 14. 13–15; Col. 2. 16–22.

universe, Hebrew From scattered verses it is possible to reconstruct the view of the universe held in O.T. times. The foundations of the earth Ps. 18. 15 support it and stand in the springs of a great abyss Gen. 7. 11; 49. 25. The vault of heaven Gen. 1. 14; Ps. 104. 2; Job 37. 18 holds the sun, moon and stars Gen. 15. 5. The earth is surrounded by sea Gen. 1. 7; and Sheol, the abode of the dead, is like a great chasm Nu. 16. 30. When the windows of the sky Gen. 7. 11 are opened, the water above the vault pours through them and falls as rain on the earth Job 38. 37. The LORD's throne is in highest heaven Dt. 10. 14; Ps. 148. 4; above the earth Gen. 1. 14.

Unleavened Bread, Feast of A festival which was very closely connected with the Passover in time, lasting from 15th to 21st Nisan or Abib (March–April); and at some periods in Jewish history was kept simultaneously with it. Ex. 23. 14–15; Dt. 16. 3–8; Mk. 14. 1.

Ur of the Chaldees The city in S Iraq from which Abraham began his journey to Canaan via Haran. Gen. 11. 28–31; 15. 6–7; Neh. 9. 7. *el-Muqaiyar.* Spectacular discoveries of many remarkable and beautiful objects, now in the British Museum, were made on the site by C. L. Woolley 1922–34.

Urban A Roman Christian greeted by Paul. Rom. 16. 9.

Uriah (1) The Hittite husband of Bathsheba. 2 S. 11. 2 – 12. 14. (2) A prophet in the reign of Jehoiakim. Jer. 26. 20–24. (3) High priest in the reign of Ahaz. 2 K. 16. 10–16.

Urim and Thummim Sacred symbols kept in the breast-piece of the high priest's vestments. They were used to discover God's will on important matters. Ex. 28. 30; Nu. 27. 18–21; 1 S. 14. 36–42.

usury The Israelites were allowed to charge interest only on loans made to foreigners. This was because they were shepherds and farmers, not traders. In N.T. times when conditions were different, traders expected interest on loans but Jews were still bound not to have such dealings among themselves. *See* Ex. 22. 25; Lev. 25. 35–37; Dt. 23. 19–20; Mt. 25. 27; Lk. 19. 23.

Uz The homeland of Job which may have been in the area of Edom. Job 1. 1; Jer. 25. 20; Lam. 4. 21.

Uzza, Garden of The place, adjoining the palace of Manasseh, where both he and King Amon were buried. 2 K. 21. 18, 26.

Uzzah A driver of the cart which took the Ark from Abinadab's house to Obed-edom. 2 S. 5. 6. 1–11.

Uzziah The son and successor of Amaziah, also known as Azariah, who made Judah strong externally and prosperous at home. 2 K. 14. 21; 15. 1–7; 2 Ch. 26. 1–23.

vale, valley Fertile areas, common in Palestine, fed by water running into them in the rainy season. The former generally means a wide depression in a mountainous area, and the latter a narrower space between hills. Gen. 26. 17; 1 S. 6. 13; Ps. 65. 13.

Vashti The Persian queen of Ahasuerus (Xerxes I) whom he divorced. Est. 1. 1 – 2. 4.

veil (1) A covering for the face or head. Gen. 24. 62–65; Ex. 34. 34–35; Ezek. 13. 17–23. (2) The curtain separating the holy place from the holy of holies in the Tabernacle and Temple. Ex. 26. 31–35. *See also* Mt. 27. 50–51; Heb. 6. 19–20; 10. 19–20.

vengeance Any punishment inflicted for retribution. Dt. 32. 40–41; Is. 34. 8; Jer. 20. 12. *See also* Ex. 21. 23–25; Judg. 15. 7. In the N.T. Christ substitutes the law of forgiveness. *See* Mt. 6. 14; 18. 21; Mk. 11. 25; 1 Th. 5. 15; 1 Pet. 3. 9.

venison Properly the flesh of the deer, but is also used of any meat taken in hunting. Gen. 25. 28; 27. 1–34.

Versions of the Bible As the Christian church became more and more centred on Rome, the need was found for a translation into Latin as well as the existing Greek. The most widely used was that made by Jerome in the 4th century A.D., which was known as the Vulgate and was *the* Bible for a thousand years.

John Wycliffe and others made the first complete Bible into English (1380–4) from the Vulgate, but the real 'father' of our present English Bible is William Tyndale who worked direct from the *original* languages. Eighty per cent of the words in even the Revised Version of 1881 stand precisely as they did in Tyndale's N.T.

Coverdale produced the first English Bible entirely by one man (1535); and other versions such as the Great Bible (1539), the Geneva Bible (1560), the Bishop's Bible (1568) were based on Tyndale's and Coverdale's work.

The King James (or Authorized) Version of 1611 was an attempt to provide a Bible without any theological notes which would be acceptable to all shades of Protestant thought. It was not so much a new translation as the careful revision of the best existing versions.

The Revised Version of 1881 (American Standard Version 1901) was a conservative revision intended to introduce changes in the KJ Bible only where newly discovered knowledge and manuscripts showed the need for correction.

The Revised Standard Version 1937–57 was yet a further revision, aimed primarily at removing out-of-date usages. It has been said that the RSV kept what it could and changed what it must, and so lacks a certain unity.

During the past one hundred years many entirely new translations have been made, intended to supplement the KJ Bible by making the meaning clearer in modern idiom. The most accurate and authoritative of these is the New English Bible 1961–70 which is approved for use by all the major Christian bodies, and the Bible Societies, in the British Isles. It is ecumenical, completely free from any denominational or doctrinal bias; and is the work of the best available scholars in their respective fields. The aim of the translators has been to present the true meaning of the original, taking account of the most up-to-date scholarship.

vestments The garments worn by Aaron and the priests when officiating in the sanctuary. Ex. 28. 2–43.

village(s) These were usually grouped around a walled town into which the people could retreat in time of war. Nu. 21. 25; Neh. 11. 25. *See also* Lev. 25. 31.

vine, vineyard The soil and climate of Palestine are well suited to the grapevine and this was grown to make wine and provide raisins for food. 1 S. 25. 18; 1 K. 4. 25; Is. 5. 1–10; Mk. 12. 1. In the O.T. Israel is pictured as the vine of God. Ps. 80. 8–15; Ezek. 17. 5–10. And in the N.T. Jesus uses it in parables about the kingdom, and to show the relationship between himself and his church. Mt. 21. 33–43; Jn. 15. 1–8.

vinegar The name given to the light wine of Palestine after it has gone sour. Ps. 69. 21; Pr. 10. 26. *See also* Ru. 2. 14; Jn. 19. 28–30.

viper There are several species in the Palestinian area, all poisonous. Gen. 49. 17; Is. 11. 8; 30. 6; Ac. 28. 1–6. Used figuratively Mt. 12. 34–35.

virgin A woman who has not had sexual intercourse. Gen. 24. 16. Used figuratively of a country. 2 K. 19. 21; Is. 47. 1; Am. 5. 2.

vision An experience of special awareness of God shared by saintly men. In many cases what is heard is as important as what is seen. 1 S. 3. 1–18; Ps. 89. 19; Is. 1. 1; Ezek. 1. 1 – 3. 14; 12. 26–28; Dan. 2. 19–23; Ob. 1–4; Lk. 1. 5–22; Ac. 9. 10–16; 10. 9–23. *See also* Is. 6. 1–13; Jer. 1. 4–19; Ac. 9. 1–9.

vow A promise made either to give something to God, or to honour and thank him by worship and self-denial. Gen. 28. 20–22; Nu. 6. 2; Dt. 23. 21–23; 1 S. 1. 11; Ps. 66. 13–14; Jon. 1. 15–16.

vulture A large bird of prey, not unlike the eagle, of which several varieties were known in Palestine. Lev. 11. 13; Dt. 14. 12; 28. 49; Job 39. 27; Mic. 1. 16.

wafer A thin cake made of flour, sometimes mixed with honey. Ex. 16. 31.

wages In a subsistence agricultural community there was not much room for the hired hand. Wages, which were not high, had to be paid daily. Lev. 19. 13; Dt. 24. 14–15; Jer. 22. 13. Used figuratively Rom. 6. 23. *See also* Lk. 3. 14; 1 Tim. 5. 18.

wagon This had a low wooden body with one pair of wooden wheels with 6 or 8 spokes. It was drawn by a pair of oxen yoked to a pole which passed between them. Gen. 45. 19; Nu. 7. 3; 1 S. 6. 7.

wail In funeral processions wailing relatives, often accompanied by hired professional women mourners and musicians, preceded the body to the grave. Jer. 9. 17–21; Am. 5. 16. *See also* Mt. 9. 23.

wait Both the O.T. and N.T. teach that those who trust in God's character and promises must wait in hope and patience. Ps. 27. 14; Is. 30. 18; Lk. 2. 25; Ac. 1. 4; Rom. 8. 19; 1 Th. 1. 9–10.

wall(s) Those of houses were usually made of mud or rough brick; stone being kept for the fortifications of towns, which were often double and could be very formidable. Excavations at Gibeon (*Tell el-Fûl*) have shown walls 8–10 feet thick. Nu. 32. 17; Dt. 3. 5; Jos. 2. 15; Neh. 12. 37–39. *See also* Dt. 1. 28; 22. 8. Used symbolically Is. 26. 1; Jer. 15. 20; Zech. 2. 4–5; Eph. 2. 14; Rev. 21. 10–21.

Walls, Gate between the Two   The way by which Zedekiah escaped from Jerusalem. 2 K. 25. 4.

wanderings   The books of Exodus, Numbers and Deuteronomy tell of the wanderings of the tribes of Israel in the wilderness S of Judah, before they entered the promised land.

war, warfare   Palestine, situated in a position of great strategic importance, and the natural highway for trading caravans, was an area of constant conflict. Every department of Israel's existence, including war, was bound up with her God, and the rules governing it were meant not only to restrain savagery and self-enrichment but to keep Israel a holy nation. Nu. 21. 14; Joel 3. 9. *See also* Dt. 7. 1–6; 20. 2–9; Jos. 6. 17; 1 S. 23. 1–2.

Spring was the best season, and the usual methods and weapons were used. *See* Jos. 8; Judg. 7. 8–25; 11; 20; 1 S. 14; 17; 2 S. 11. 1; 1 K. 20; 2 K. 3. 25; 2 Ch. 14. 8–17; Ezek. 4. 2–3.

Originally people's wars; the concept of a standing army was introduced by David and extended by Solomon. 1 S. 11. 6–7. *See also* Dt. 20. 5–8; 1 K. 4. 26–27. Israel thus entered on a career as a nation involved in alliances and balances of power which was consistently denounced by the prophets.

In the N.T. the soldier is neither condemned nor commended. However, the teaching of Jesus brought an almost wholly new idea into the world. *See* Mt. 24. 6–7; 26. 51–52; Lk. 3. 14; Jn. 18. 36. Spiritual warfare is referred to in 2 Cor. 10. 3–6; Eph. 6. 11–18; Rev. 12. 7–9.

Wars of the Lord, Book of the   A lost book quoted in Numbers, and evidently a collection of poems about Israelite victories. Nu. 21. 14–15.

washing   Frequent washing is necessary in hot climates to preserve health, and the O.T. law contained rules which also covered ceremonial cleanness. Ex. 19. 10;

30. 17–21; Lev. 14. 8; 15. 1–31; Nu. 19. 11–22. Used symbolically Ps. 51. 2; Jer. 4. 14. In the N.T. Christ condemns the Pharisees for neglecting the inner cleanliness of which washing is supposed to be the outward sign. Mk. 7. 1–8, 14–23; Lk. 11. 37–42.

watch   A division into which the twelve hours of the night were made. The Jews, like the Babylonians, had three watches. Judg. 7. 19; 1 S. 11. 11; Lam. 2. 19.

watchman   A guard for a city who kept his lookout from the walls; or a night watchman. 2 S. 18. 24–27; S. of S. 5. 7; Is. 21. 11–12; Jer. 31. 6.

water   Because of its scarcity in the dry season (May–October) when springs failed, great efforts were made to store it in cisterns and reservoirs. 1 K. 17. 1–11; 18. 1–6; Jer. 38. 6. It is often used figuratively of the life-giving power of God. Jer. 2. 13; Jn. 4. 13–15.

Water Gate   On the E side of Jerusalem. Ezra read the law in the square in front of it. Neh. 3. 26; 8. 1–4; 12. 37.

way   In addition to its literal meaning of path, it is used in both O.T. and N.T. in a moral and religious sense: (1) A man's character or conduct. Pr. 2. 8; Jer. 18. 11. (2) The moral order which God has established in the world. Ps. 18. 30. (3) The earliest name for the Christian church. Ac. 9. 2; 18. 25; 19. 9. (4) Christ speaks of himself as 'the Way'. Jn. 14. 5–6; Heb. 10. 19–22.

weave, weaving   The ancient process of preparing sheeps' wool, camels' and goats' hair, flax and hemp into material for clothes, tents and curtains. The wooden loom on which the work was done could be either horizontal or upright. Judg. 16. 13–15; Is. 19. 9. *See also* Ex. 26. 1–13; Lev. 13. 47–49; 1 S. 17. 7; Ac. 18. 3.

week   A period of seven days, probably first used as a measurement of time because it is a quarter of the moon. *See* Gen. 29. 27.

Weeks, Feast of   One of the three great annual festivals. It marked the completion of the barley harvest, and it was named after the seven-week period from the offering of the barley sheaf at the beginning of the Passover to this festival. It was

also known as Pentecost. Ex. 34. 22;
Lev. 23. 9–21; Dt. 16. 16–17.

weights and measures *See* Appendix to the
O.T. in the New English Bible.

well A pit or hole dug down to the water
table and filled through seepage. Water
was hauled up by a bucket on a rope.
Gen. 21. 30–31; 29. 1–3; Ex. 21. 33;
Jn. 4. 3–15. Be'er = well is found in a
number of place-names. Gen. 21. 31.

Western Sea A name for the Mediterranean
as contrasted with the Eastern (Dead)
Sea. Dt. 11. 24; Zech. 14. 8.

whale The sperm whale is the only one of
this group which comes into the Mediterranean and is recorded from time to time
off the Palestine coast. The male can
grow to nearly 60 feet. Job 41. 1; Lam.
4. 3. *See also* Jon. 1. 17.

wheat A cereal grown in Palestine from
early times. Gen. 30. 14; Judg. 6. 11;
Ezek. 4. 9. Used in metaphor. Mt. 3. 12;
13. 29–30; Jn. 12. 24–25.

wheels These were probably at first just a
disc of wood cut from a log, but quite
early they developed into something resembling the modern device. Metal wheels
were being made in Solomon's time. Ex.
14. 24–25; 1 K. 7. 30–33. The word for
potter's wheel = 'two stones'. Jer. 18.
1–2.

whole-offering *See* offering.

wicked Although used in the general moral
or judicial sense of 'wrong' (Ps. 18. 21), it
more commonly means active mischief in
the Bible. Nu. 16. 26; Ps. 10. 1–11; 37. 35;
Pr. 21. 10. *See also* Gen. 6. 5; Mt. 13. 19;
Mk. 7. 21–23; Rom. 1. 28–32.

widow They wore distinctive dress, and
from early times it was laid down that
they should be treated with special consideration. Ex. 22. 22–24; Dt. 24. 17–22;
Ps. 68. 4–5; Pr. 15. 25; Is. 47. 8; Jer. 7. 6;
Ac. 6. 1–4; 1 Tim. 5. 3–6; Jas. 1. 27.

wife Legally a wife was owned by her
husband. *See* Gen. 3. 16; Ex. 20. 17. And
although polygamy was practised from
early times, both the O.T. and N.T. show
God intending husband and wife to be
equal partners. Gen. 2. 18–24; 30. 1–13;
Pr. 31. 10–31; Mk. 10. 2–9.

wilderness A wild, treeless area with little
vegetation other than thorn and tamarisk
bushes, except when the rains provided
temporary pasturage. In addition to the
wilderness of the wanderings in the Sinai
peninsula under Moses, others are
named in Gen. 21. 14; Dt. 2. 8; Jos. 18. 12;
Judg. 1. 16; 1 S. 23. 24; 1 K. 19. 15. It was
thought of as God's meeting-place with
man. Jer. 2. 2; Mt. 3. 1–3; 4. 1–11.

wild ox This is the Aurochs, and ancestor
of domestic cattle. The bulls were enor-
mous, over 6 feet at the shoulder and
long, forward-pointing horns. Remains
dating from the Pleistocene period have
been found in Palestine, but it had disappeared well before N.T. times. O.T.
references to it are in more or less figurative contexts. Nu. 23. 22; Dt. 33. 17; Job
39. 9; Ps. 29. 6; 92. 10; Is. 34. 6–7.

willow A tree common to almost every
country, growing near water and having a
long, narrow leaf, green on top and white
underneath. Lev. 23. 40; Ps. 137. 2;
Ezek. 17. 5.

wind The Hebrews thought of the wind as
an instrument of God and a sign of his
presence. Gen. 8. 1; Ex. 10. 13; Ps. 18. 10;
104. 3. In Palestine the winds affect climate and vegetation. During the dry
season, May–October, they blow mainly
from the N and temper the heat. From
September–October dry E winds blow
from across the desert, followed by hot S
winds. Then W winds bring the rain.
1 K. 18. 41–45; S. of S. 4. 16; Ezek. 17. 10;
Lk. 12. 55.

window(s) Only large dwellings had windows, usually upstairs and closed with
lattice work. In the ordinary house, light
came in through the door. Judg. 5. 28;
1 S. 19. 12; 2 K. 1. 2; 13. 17.

wine An everyday drink in Palestine,
though forbidden to priests on duty in the
sanctuary. Although in general it was
considered as a food, the dangers of excess
were recognized and some abstained completely. Gen. 49. 11; Lev. 10. 9; Nu. 6.
1–4; Ps. 104. 15; Jer. 35. 3–7; Jn. 2. 1–10;
Rom. 14. 20–22. *See also* Is. 5. 22; Mk.
14. 25; Eph. 5. 18; 1 Tim. 3. 8.

winepress This was in two parts: the press
vat where the grapes were trampled, and

the wine vat into which the juice ran and remained for the beginning of fermentation. Judg. 6. 11; Neh. 13. 15; Is. 63. 2–3; Mt. 21. 33. Used figuratively of the anger of God. Lam. 1. 15; Rev. 14. 19–20; 19. 15.

winnow After harvesting, the grain was threshed or beaten to strip the chaff from the ears of corn. It was then all tossed into the air with a fork for the wind to blow away the straw. Ru. 3. 3; Is. 30. 24. Used as a picture of God's judgement. Mt. 3. 12.

winter Usually short and mild in Palestine, but the hilly regions have hail and snow. Gen. 8. 22; Ps. 74. 17; Zech. 14. 8.

wisdom In the Bible it is both religious and practical. Stemming from the fear of the LORD who is the source of all wisdom, it branches out to touch all life, taking insights from the knowledge of God's ways and applying them to daily living. Only in humble trust in God and in obedience to his will can a man attain this wisdom. Job 28. 12–28; Ps. 111. 10; Pr. ch. 1–5; 8–9. The N.T. stands in the same tradition as the O.T., that all wisdom has ultimately to do with God. 1 Cor. 1. 30; 2. 6–15.

Wisdom Literature A literary form, common in the ancient Near East, in which instructions for successful living are given. The traditional form is a crisp, popular saying expressed in a short couplet. 1 K. 20. 11; Jer. 31. 29. The deposit of Israel's oral wisdom is recorded in the books of Proverbs, Job and Ecclesiastes in the O.T., and in the Wisdom of Solomon and Ecclesiasticus in the Apocrypha.

Wisdom of Jesus son of Sirach See Ecclesiasticus.

Wisdom of Solomon, The A book of the Apocrypha whose roots are in the same stream of Jewish wisdom writings as Proverbs, Job and Ecclesiastes. It was probably written within the last fifty years before the birth of Christ and has little to do with Solomon. It is an exhortation to seek wisdom, and an encouragement to Jews not to forsake their ancestral faith. It reviews O.T. history in illustration of the theme that wisdom has

helped her friends the Jews and brought punishment on her enemies.

witch, witchcraft The attempt by man to use supernatural powers through charms and spells to secure his ends. Though practised by Israel's neighbours, it was forbidden in the law and condemned by the prophets. Ex. 22. 18. See also Lev. 19. 26; Dt. 18. 9–11; 1 S. 28. 3–8; Jer. 27. 9.

witness One who can state the truth about a debatable matter because he was present. 1 S. 12. 1–6; Job 16. 19; Rom. 1. 9; 2 Cor. 1. 23. These were necessary in legal business. Nu. 35. 30; Dt. 19. 16–19; Jer. 32. 10. Even a material thing such as a stone may be described as a 'witness'. Gen. 31. 44; Jos. 24. 27. The word is especially used of those who tell what God has done. Is. 43. 10–12; Lk. 24. 45–48; Ac. 2. 32; 22. 14–15; Heb. 12. 1–2. See also Rev. 17. 6.

wolf A familiar beast of prey in biblical times but referred to figuratively in the Bible: often for someone in authority who is misusing his position. Gen. 49. 27; Is. 65. 25; Ezek. 22. 27; Mt. 7. 15; Jn. 10. 12; Ac. 20. 29.

woman Although the creation story shows woman created by God as an equal partner with man (Gen. 2. 18–24; 3. 16), in Hebrew society a woman 'belonged' to her father or husband. See Ex. 21. 7. However, some women reached positions of leadership. See Ex. 15. 20–21; Judg. 4. 4–10. In the N.T. Jesus treats women with respect and gives them a new freedom. Mt. 15. 21–28; Mk. 14. 3–9; 15. 40–41; Lk. 8. 1–3; 10. 38–42; Jn. 4. 7–30; Ac. 16. 12–15; 18. 26. See also Mk. 12. 41–44; Jn. 20. 11–18; Gal. 3. 28.

wood-offering Special arrangements were made for the provision of wood for burning on the altar of the Temple. Neh. 10. 34–35; 13. 31.

wool The soft hair of sheep or goats widely used in making clothes, though not to be woven together with linen. Lev. 13. 47; Dt. 22. 11. It was a valuable article of trade. 2 K. 3. 4; Ezek. 27. 21. Used as a symbol of purity. Is. 1. 18; Rev. 1. 14.

word Apart from its literal meaning, it contains and carries something of the speaker's own self, character and purpose in it. Thus, God created the world by his 'word' which stands for ever and must be fulfilled. Ps. 33. 6; Is. 9. 8; 40. 8; 55. 11. It comes to men through the prophets. Is. 8. 11; Jer. 17. 19; Ezek. 21. 18; Am. 3. 1. In the N.T. it is often applied to the Christian gospel. Lk. 8. 11; Ac. 8. 4. In Jn. 1. 1–18 the 'Word' means Jesus Christ, where the O.T. idea of the 'word of the LORD' has been developed to mean a unique Person who shares the very being of God.

work   Used of God's work in creation and in saving, guiding and correcting his people. Gen. 2. 2; Ps. 111. 7; Jn. 5. 17; Eph. 1. 11. Man was made to find satisfaction in his own daily work which is also his duty. Ps. 104. 23; Eccles. 3. 22; 2 Cor. 6. 1; 2 Th. 3. 10. *See also* Gen. 2. 15.

world   In the N.T. this usually means the universe which God has created, and more especially the earth where man lives. Mt. 25. 34; Mk. 8. 36. Sin has entered into it, but Christ has also entered to reconcile man with God. Rom. 5. 12; 2 Cor. 5. 13–21. The Gospel of John often speaks of 'the world' as hostile to God and under the power of evil, but God is working to win it back to himself. Jn. 3. 16–17; 7. 7; 12. 31.

wormwood   Several species of this tree grow in Palestine. Its leaves were used medicinally, and a bitter juice obtained from its roots. It is associated with pain and sorrow. Dt. 29. 18; Pr. 5. 4; Jer. 9. 15; Rev. 8. 11.

worship   Four elements seem to have been continuously present in Israel's worship: (1) The recitation of the way God had delivered his people and made them a nation. Jos. 24. 14–27. *See also* Ps. 105; 106. (2) Sacrifice and daily offerings, which were a perpetual reminder of God's covenant with his people. (3) The offering of praise to God for what he is, king and creator, as well as for what he does. (4) The annual festivals in which the early events of the farmer's year, brought into relationship with God's great acts, were made occasions for the renewed dedication of the people to God.
   Worship in the sanctuary at Jerusalem became very elaborate, but the prophets

seem to object less to the cult of sacrifice itself than to the magic-working ideas borrowed from the fertility cults which became associated with it, and to the fact that much worship was outward only.
   In the N.T. the church seems to have taken over much of its form of worship from the post-exilic synagogue, though everything assumed a new character since it was centred in Jesus Christ. Its unique feature, however, was the Lord's Supper. *See* Ac. 2. 42–47; 1 Cor. 11. 17–29; 14. 26–40.

writing   In early times inscriptions were made on stones; but later, clay tiles or tablets, pieces of pottery (shards or ostraca), wood with an inlaid wax surface, leather, papyrus and parchment were used.
   In the earliest forms of writing, evolved before 3000 B.C., each word or syllable was represented by a picture sign and later by a conventional, stylized form of it. Shortly before the Israelites entered Canaan there developed in the Palestinian–Phoenician–Syrian area a partly alphabetic form with only 22 letters, all consonants, which was adopted by them and in which the O.T. was written. The first complete alphabet (24 letters, including vowels) was perfected by the Greeks about 850 B.C. The N.T. is written in this.

Xerxes   A Greek form of the Hebrew name, Ahasuerus.

year   Although used of the natural division of time, it also refers to the time when God acts both to judge and save men. Is. 61. 1–2; Lk. 4. 18–19.

YHWH   The four consonants standing for the Hebrew name for God, usually referred to as 'Jehovah' or 'Yahweh'. YHWH was considered too sacred to be pronounced, so Adonay (= my lord) was substituted in reading.

yoke   A wooden frame fitted on the necks of two animals when ploughing. Nu. 19. 2. Used as a figure of the subjection of one person to another. Gen. 27. 40; 1 K. 12. 14; Mt. 11. 29–30.

Zacchaeus (1) A citizen of Jericho, and a superintendent of taxes, converted by Jesus. Lk. 19. 1–10. (2) A Jewish traitor killed by Judas. 2 Mac. 10. 18–22.

Zadok A descendant of Aaron and a priest in Jerusalem under David and Solomon. A guardian of the Ark during Absalom's rebellion, he became sole high priest; and the office remained in his family until the 2nd century B.C. 2 S. 8. 15–17; 15. 16–29; 1 K. 1. 5–8, 32–40; 2. 35.

Zalmunna *See* Zebah.

Zarephath A town belonging to Sidon where Elijah stayed during the famine. 1 K. 17. 8–24. *See also* Lk. 4. 25–26. *Sarafand.*

Zaretan A town in the Jordan val'ey near the spot where the Israelites crossed the river. Jos. 3. 15–16.

Zealot(s) A Jewish nationalist party formed in the time of Quirinius to resist Herod and the Romans. Simon the Zealot was one of the Twelve. Mk. 3. 13–18.

Zebah A Midianite king who, with Zalmunna, had oppressed Israel. Both were defeated and killed by Gideon. Judg. 8. 4–27.

Zeboyim One of the five cities in the Dead Sea area destroyed with Sodom and Gomorrah. Abraham rescued Lot from its king. Gen. 14. 1–16; Dt. 29. 22–23; Hos. 11. 8.

Zebulun The son of Jacob and Leah and ancestor of the tribe. Gen. 30. 20. It occupied the fertile area of southern and central Galilee. Dt. 33. 18–19; Jos. 19. 10–16; Judg. 4. 10. Many of its people were deported by the Assyrians in 721 B.C. *See* 2 K. 15. 29.

Zechariah (1) The father of John the Baptist. Lk. 1. 5–25, 57–79. (2) The son of Jehoida the priest who was stoned to death. 2 Ch. 24. 17–22; Lk. 11. 51. (3) The prophet who returned from Babylon in 537 B.C. with Haggai. Ezr. 5. 1; 6. 14.

Zechariah, Book of Zechariah began to prophesy in Jerusalem early in Darius's reign at a time when those who had returned from exile were few, poor and weak, and when there were signs of growing tension between them and those who had remained behind in Palestine. Like Haggai, his aim was to challenge the people to finish the rebuilding of the Temple, and he is concerned with the spiritual implications of the challenge as the symbol of their faith. He makes some of the most revealing and inspiring of Messianic declarations in prophetic literature, including that deliberately fulfilled by Jesus in his triumphal entry into Jerusalem. Zech. 9. 9–10; Mt. 21. 1–9.

Zedekiah The last of the kings of Judah, placed on the throne as a puppet king by Nebuchadnezzar in 597 B.C. His advisers plotted with Egypt against the advice of Jeremiah, and their rebellion led to the fall of Jerusalem in 586 B.C. 2 K. 24. 10 – 25. 7; Jer. 27; 38. 14–28.

Zelophehad A man of Manasseh who died in the wilderness wanderings leaving five daughters but no son. His daughters successfully made their claim to the inheritance, and the precedent of female succession was established provided that the heiress married within the tribe. Nu. 27. 1–11; 36. 1–12.

Zephaniah The great-grandson of Hezekiah, who lived and prophesied about the same time as Jeremiah.

Zephaniah, Book of Prophesying in the earlier years of Josiah, he warns Judah of its inevitable punishment if corruption and wickedness continue unchecked. Not even the fact that they are the chosen people will prevent the judgement, for God is just. The 'Day of the LORD' will prove his justice, but it will be tempered with mercy for the pure and good remnant who will be delivered.

Zerubbabel A grandson of Jehoiachin of Judah and a direct ancestor of Jesus. One of the leaders of the first groups returning from the Babylonian captivity, he became Governor of Judah and took a leading part, with Joshua the high priest, in rebuilding the Temple. Ezr. 2. 1–2; 5. 1–2; Neh. 7. 6–7; Hag. 1. 1–15; Zech. 4. 6–10.

Ziba A member of Saul's household staff, appointed by David to work for Mephibosheth who, by slandering his master, obtained his property. 2 S. 9. 1–13; 16. 1–4; 19. 24–30.

ziggurat An artificial brick platform built in terraces to give the effect of a stepped pyramid. Outer staircases led to a temple at the top. The tower of Babel may have been the ziggurat at Babylon. *See* Gen. 11. 2–4.

Ziklag A town in S Judah assigned to Simeon, which was taken by the Philistines and later given by them to David to use as his headquarters in his guerrilla warfare with Saul. Jos. 19. 5; 1 S. 27. 1–6; 30. 1–4; 2 S. 1. 1–16.

Zilpah The servant whom Laban gave to his daughter Leah, and later, through Jacob, the mother of Gad and Asher. Gen. 30. 9–13.

Zimri (1) An army officer who seized the throne of Israel after a military revolt and reigned for one week. 1 K. 16. 9–20; 2 K. 9. 31–34. (2) A Simeonite prince who defied Moses. Nu. 25. 6–15.

Zion The Jebusite hill fortress captured by David and made his royal city of Jerusalem. 2 S. 5. 6–7; 1 K. 8. 1. From early times it stands for the place of God's choice where he reigns. Ps. 2. 4–6; 48. 2; Is. 24. 23. In the N.T. it is the invisible city of God, the new Jerusalem. Heb. 12. 22–24.

Zipporah The daughter of Jethro, or Reuel, the priest of Midian, who became Moses' first wife. Ex. 2. 16–22; 18. 1–4.

Zoan A city in the NE delta of Egypt and a royal residence of the Pharaohs, Set I and Rameses II. It continued to be important in later times. Nu. 13. 23; Ps. 78. 12, 43; Is. 19. 11–18; Ezek. 30. 14. *Sân el-Ḥagar.*

Zoar One of the cities SE of the Dead Sea to which Lot escaped when Sodom and Gomorrah were destroyed. Gen. 19. 12–26.

Zobah An Aramaean kingdom whose king, Hadadezer, took a leading part in Syrian attacks on David, but was finally defeated. 2 S. 8. 3–12; 10. 6–19.

Zoheleth The place where Adonijah, David's fourth son, gathered his conspirators before his father's death. 1 K. 1. 9–10.

Zorah A city about 15 miles W of Jerusalem on the borders of Judah and Dan; Samson's family home near which he was buried. Judg. 13. 2; 16. 31.

---

1 Peter 3:1–7 Relationships of Husbands + Wives

Philippians 4:6–7 Anxiety → Peace

Isaiah 41:10 Fear not!

"Be Strong and of Good Courage; be not dismayed: for the Lord Thy God is with thee, whithersoever Thy goest" Joshua 1:9